INTERNATIONAL
LITERARY
MARKET PLACE
1984–85

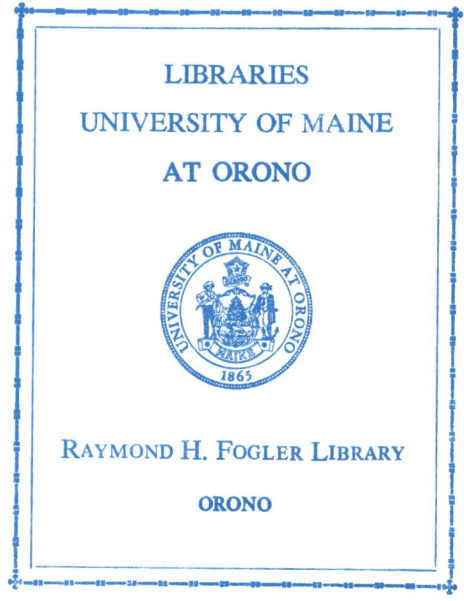

INTERNATIONAL LITERARY MARKET PLACE 1984–85

R. R. BOWKER COMPANY
New York & London, 1984

Published by R. R. Bowker Company (a Xerox Publishing Company)
205 East 42nd Street
New York, N.Y. 10017

Copyright © 1984 by Xerox Corporation

All rights reserved.
Reproduction of this work, in whole or in part,
without written permission of the publisher is prohibited.

International Standard Book Number 0-8352-1868-6
International Standard Serial Number 0074-6827
Library of Congress Catalog Card Number 77-70295

Printed and bound in the United States of America

The publishers do not assume and hereby
disclaim any liability to any party for
any loss or damage caused by errors or
omissions in *International Literary
Market Place*, whether such errors or
omissions result from negligence,
accident or any other cause.

Computer typeset by Millford Reprographics International Ltd, Luton, England

Contents

The material for each country or territory is grouped under a series of sub-headings which appear always in the same order, and the omission of any of them from a particular country or territory implies that no information is available. The headings are as follows:

General Information (language, population, currency, etc)
Book Trade Organizations
Book Trade Reference Books and Journals
Publishers
Remainder Dealers
Literary Agents
Book Clubs
Major Booksellers
Major Libraries
Library Associations
Library Reference Books and Journals
Literary Associations and Societies
Literary Periodicals
Literary Prizes
Translation Agencies and Associations

Preface	vii
Abbreviations	viii
Afghanistan	1
Albania	1
Algeria	2
Angola	2
Argentina	3
Australia	9
Austria	24
Bahamas	31
Bahrain	32
Bangladesh	32
Barbados	33
Belgium	33
Belize	45
Benin	45
Bermuda	46
Bolivia	46
Botswana	47
Brazil	47
Brunei	57
Bulgaria	58
Burma	59
Burundi	60
United Republic of Cameroun	61
Central African Republic	62
Chad	62
Channel Islands	62
Chile	62
People's Republic of China	64
Colombia	65
Popular Republic of Congo	68
Costa Rica	68
Cuba	69
Cyprus	70
Czechoslovakia	70
Denmark	74
Dominican Republic	81
Ecuador	82
Egypt	83
El Salvador	85
Ethiopia	85
Fiji	86
Finland	86
France	90
French Guiana	114
French Polynesia	114
Gabon	115
The Gambia	115
German Democratic Republic	115
Federal Republic of Germany	120
Ghana	171
Gibraltar	173
Greece	173
Guatemala	176
Guinea	177
Guyana	177
Haiti	178
Honduras	178
Hong Kong	178
Hungary	180
Iceland	183
India	185
Indonesia	204
Iran	207
Iraq	208
Republic of Ireland	208
Isle of Man	212
Israel	212
Italy	218
Ivory Coast	236
Jamaica	237
Japan	237
Jordan	247
Kampuchea	248
Kenya	248
Democratic People's Republic of Korea	249
Republic of Korea	250
Kuwait	253
Laos	253
Lebanon	253
Lesotho	255
Liberia	255
Libya	255
Liechtenstein	256
Grand Duchy of Luxembourg	256
Macau	257
Democratic Republic of Madagascar	257
Malawi	258
Malaysia	259
Mali	261
Malta	262
Martinique	262
Mauritania	263
Mauritius	263
Mexico	263
Monaco	270
Mongolian People's Republic	270
Montserrat	270
Morocco	270
Mozambique	271
Namibia	271
Nepal	272
Netherlands	272
Netherlands Antilles	286
New Caledonia	286
New Zealand	286
Nicaragua	292
Niger	292
Nigeria	292
Norway	297
Pakistan	301
Panama	304
Papua New Guinea	305
Paraguay	306
Peru	306
Philippines	308
Poland	310
Portugal	315
Puerto Rico	319
Qatar	320
Réunion	320
Romania	321
Rwanda	323
Saudi Arabia	323
Senegal	323
Seychelles	324
Sierra Leone	324
Republic of Singapore	325
Somalia	328
Republic of South Africa	328
Spain	336
Sri Lanka	349
Sudan	350
Suriname	350
Swaziland	351
Sweden	351
Switzerland	360
Syria	377
Taiwan	377
Tanzania	378
Thailand	380
Togo	382
Trinidad and Tobago	382
Tunisia	383
Turkey	384
Uganda	386
Union of Soviet Socialist Republics	386
United Arab Emirates	390
United Kingdom	390
Upper Volta	451
Uruguay	451
Vatican City State	452
Venezuela	453
Socialist Republic of Viet Nam	455
Western Samoa	455
People's Democratic Republic of the Yemen	455
Yemen Arab Republic	456
Yugoslavia	456
Zaire	461
Zambia	463
Zimbabwe	464
INTERNATIONAL SECTION	466
Copyright Conventions	466
International Organizations	466
International Bibliography	472
International Literary Prizes	474
The ISBN System	480
BOOK TRADE CALENDAR	484
INDEX	493

Preface

In common with each of the recent editions of *International Literary Market Place* (*ILMP*), the 1984-85 edition contains over 44% of updated and new material. Replies containing amendments were received in response to nearly 12,000 questionnaires despatched to 160 territories worldwide. In addition questionnaires were sent to over 800 potential entrants.

An important new feature in this edition of *ILMP* is the identification (by a following plus sign) of those publishers who have indicated their interest in buying or selling international rights or editions. We hope this new information will be of considerable service to users of *ILMP*.

In compiling *ILMP* we are fortunate in the excellent response received from existing entrants and are grateful for this continued cooperation in enabling the presentation of up-to-date information. It is unfortunate that troubled national and international situations continue to mean that recent contact with some countries has not been possible and therefore the information given for them must be treated with caution.

In *ILMP* are listed only territories outside Canada and the United States: North America is covered in detail by the companion volume *Literary Market Place* (*LMP*). Information in *ILMP* is set out by country, and within each country by activity. To facilitate the location of an entry for a known organization there is an entry index at the back of the book.

In a number of entries, particularly in the publishers sections, other organizations which feature elsewhere in *ILMP* may be mentioned. Thus 'qv' following the name of an organization indicates that fuller information may be found under the separate entry for that name. (In the case of book clubs listed within publishers entries no 'qv' is added since all such clubs appear in the separate book clubs sections.)

Grateful acknowledgement goes to Pat Brown, Dennis Corbyn, Rosemary Harley, newcomer Anne Marshall, and Martha Ross for their use of a variety of skills in efficiently dealing with information received in different languages and styles; thanks are also due to Brenda Lynch for her indispensable contribution in the office.

Comments and suggestions for improvements in *ILMP* are always welcome and should be sent to the Editorial Department, Bowker Publishing Co, Erasmus House, High Street, Epping, Essex, England CM16 4BU.

LINDA REDMAN
Editor

Abbreviations

+	Publishers' indication of interest in buying/selling international rights or editions
*	questionnaire not returned for this edition
AB	aktiebolag (= limited company)
AE	anõnumos 'etaireía
AG	Aktiengesellschaft (= public limited company)
al	aleja
Apdo	apartado (= post-box)
ApS	anpartsselskab (= private limited company)
A/S	(Norwegian) aksjeselskap, (Swedish) aktieselskab, (= limited company)
AŞ	anonim şirketi
ASBL	association sans but lucratif (= non-profit-making society)
Ave	(English, French) avenue, (Portuguese, Spanish) avenida
Bldg	building
Blvd	(Bulgarian, Romanian) bulevard, (English, French) boulevard
BP	boîte postale (= post-box)
BV	besloten vennootschap (= private limited company)
C	compagnía (= company)
CA	compañía anónima (= public limited company)
CEDEX	Courrier d'entreprise à distribution exceptionnelle
CFA	Communauté financière africaine
CFP	comptoirs français du Pacifique
Cia	companhia (= company)
Cía	compañía (= company)
Cie	compagnie (= company)
Co	(English) company, county, (German) Kompanie
c/o	care of
CP	(Italian) casetta postale, (Portuguese) caixa postal, (= post-box)
CV	commanditaire vennootschap (= limited partnership)
Dept	department
Dir	director
EE	'eterórruthmos 'etaireía
eV	eingetragener Verein (= registered society)
ext	extension
GmbH	Gesellschaft mit beschränkter Haftung (= private limited company)
Inc	incorporated
ISBN	international standard book number
Jl	jalan (= street)
KG	Kommanditgesellschaft (= partnership)
KK	kabushiki kaisha (= public limited company)
Lda	limitada (= limited)
Ltd	limited
Ltda	limitada (= limited)
Man Dir	managing director
Nachf	Nachfolger(s) (= successor(s))
nám	náměstí (= square)
NV	naamloze vennootschap (= public limited company)
OE	'omórruthmos 'etaireía
of	oficina (= office)
Off	office
Oy	osakeyhtiö (= limited company)
pA	per Adresse (= care of)
Pl	(Bulgarian) ploshtad, (English, French) place, (Polish) plac, (Russian) ploshchad', (Spanish) plaza
PL	postilokero (= post-box)
PLC	public limited company
PMB	private mail bag
PO	Post Office
Pty	proprietary
PVBA	personenvennootschap met beperkte aansprakelijkheid (= private limited company)
Pvt	private
qqv	quae vide (= which see)
qv	quod vide (= which see)
Rd	road
SA	(French) société anonyme, (Portuguese) sociedade anónima, (Spanish) sociedad anónima (= public limited company)
Sàrl	société à responsabilité limitée (= private limited company)
SAS	società in accomandita semplice (= limited partnership)
SCA	sociedad en comandita por acciones (= limited partnership)
S de RL	sociedad de responsabilidad limitada (= private limited company)
Sdn Bhd	sendirian berhad (= private limited company)
SL	sociedad de responsabilidad limitada (= private limited company)
SNC	società in nome collettivo (= partnership)
SpA	società per azioni (= public limited company)
SPRL	société de personnes à responsabilité limitée (= private limited company)
SRL	(Italian) società à responsabilità limitata, (Spanish) sociedad de responsabilidad limitada, (= private limited company)
St	Saint, street
STD	subscriber trunk dialling
Str	(Danish) straede, (Dutch) straat, (German) Strasse, (Icelandic) stræti, (Italian) strada, (Romanian) stradă (= street)
Sq	square
Tel	telephone number
u	utca (= street)
UCC	Universal Copyright Convention
ul	(Bulgarian) ulitsa, (Czech) ulice, (Polish) ulica, (Romanian) ulită, (Russian) ulitsa, (Serbocroatian, Slovak, Slovene) ulica (= street)
VEB	volkseigener Betrieb (= people's enterprise)
VZW	vereniging zonder winstoogmerk (= non-profit-making society)

A limited company is a corporation owned by shareholders (or stockholders) who may contribute capital to the company but are not otherwise generally liable for its debts.

A public company may invite anyone to become a shareholder, and its shares (or stock) are usually traded on a stock exchange. A private, or proprietary, company has a restricted number of shareholders and its shares are not traded on a stock exchange.

The owners of a partnership are generally liable for its debts, but a limited partnership has some owners who only contribute capital and are not otherwise liable for debts.

Afghanistan

General Information

Note: No replies were received to questionnaires sent to Afghanistan for this edition of *International Literary Market Place*. The information given in the 1983-84 edition has been repeated here but should be treated with caution.

Language: Pushtu and Persian
Religion: Sunni Muslim with approximately 1 million Shiite Muslim
Population: 15.1 million
Literacy rate (1975): 12.2% of population aged 6 or more (26.8% of urban population, 19.5% of rural)
Bank Hours: 0800-1200, 1300-1600 Saturday-Wednesday; 0800-1300 Thursday
Shop Hours: 0800-about 1800 Saturday-Thursday
Currency: 100 puls = 1 afghani
Copyright: Florence (see International section)

Publishers

Afghan Kitab*, Kabul
Subject: Translations

Book Publishing Institute*, Herat
Subjects: Fiction, History, Religion
Founded: 1970 (by cooperation of Government Press and citizens of Herat)

Franklin Book Programs Inc*, PO Box 332, Kabul

Government Press*, Kabul
Subjects: Afghan history & literature, Textbooks, Newspapers, Magazines, Journals
Founded: 1870
Miscellaneous: Under supervision of Ministry of Information and Culture

Historical Society of Afghanistan*, Kabul
Dir: M Yakub Wahidi
Founded: 1931
Subjects: Afghan History and Culture
Publications: Afghanistan (in English, French and German); *Aryana* (in Dari and Pushtu), both quarterly

Kabul University, Institute of Geography*, Kabul
Subject: Maps

Ministry of Culture and Information, Book Publishing Department*, Kabul

Ministry of Education, Department of Educational Publications*, Kabul
Subjects: Primary & Secondary Textbooks in Pushtu and Dari

Pushtu Toulana, Afghan Academy*, Kabul
Subjects: Pushtu Language

Major Booksellers

Behzad Bookshop*, Welayat Ave, Kabul

Behzad Bookstore*, Shop No 122, Chahrahi-Malikasghar, Kabul

Royal Afghanistan Press Department*, Kabul

University of Kabul Bookstores*, Ali-Abad, Kabul

Zuri Book Shop*, Charahi-Sadarat, Kabul

Major Libraries

Institute of Education Library, Kabul University*, Kabul

Ministry of Education Library*, Kabul

Library of the **National Bank***, Kabul

Library of the **Press Department***, Kabul

Public Library*, Kabul

Library of the **Royal Palace***, Kabul

University Library*, Kabul

Library Association

Anjuman Kitab-Khana-I-Afghanistan*, PO Box 3142, Kabul
Afghan Library Association
Publication: Afghan Library Association Bulletin

Library Reference Journal

Afghan Library Association Bulletin, Anjuman-Kitab-Khani-I-Afghanistan, PO Box 3142, Kabul

Albania

General Information

Note: No replies were received to questionnaires sent to Albania for this edition of *International Literary Market Place*. The information given in the 1983-84 edition has been repeated here but should be treated with caution.

Language: Albanian
Religion: Muslim, but religious observances are discouraged by the government
Population: 2.6 million
Currency: 100 qintars = 1 lek
Export/Import Information: Importation of books is through State Trading Organization, Nah Shperndarjes Të (or NST) Librit, Blvd e Pezës, Tirana. Correspondence should be in Italian or French. Copies of correspondence to Albanian Legation in Rome. Import licences and strict exchange controls

Book Trade Organizations

Drejtoria Quëndrore e Përhapjes dhe e Propagandimit të Librit*, Tirana
Central Administration for the Dissemination and Propagation of the Book

Union of Writers and Artists of Albania*, 37 Z Baboci St, Tirana
Chairman: Dritero Agolli
Publications: Nëndori, Drita

Book Trade Reference Journals

The Albanian Book, National Library, Tirana

Articles from Albanian Periodicals, National Library, Tirana

Bibliografia kombëtare e Republikës Popullore të Shqipërisë (Albanian National Bibliography), Botim i Bibliotekës Kombëtare, Tirana

Libri (The Book), Rruga Konferenca e Pezës, Tirana

Publishers

'8' Nentori Publishing House*, Tirana
Subjects: Books and journals on Albania; documents and publications of the Albanian Party of Work

N I S H Shtypshkronjave 'Mihal Duri'*, Tirana
Subjects: Government Publications, Education, Politics, Law

Naim Frasheri*, Tirana
Subject: Books in foreign languages

Ndërmarrja e Botimeve Ushtarake*, Tirana
Subjects: Military, Technology

Major Booksellers

Nah Shperndarjes Të Librit (NST)*, Blvd e Pezës, Tirana
State trading organization controlling importation of books

Ndërmarrja e Librit*, Konfercenca e Pezës, Tirana Tel: 3323 Cable Add: Ndlibri Tirana
Distributor of books, journals and newspapers published in Albania in Albanian and foreign languages

Major Libraries

Biblioteka Kombëtare*, Tirana Tel: 5887
National Library
Dir: Marika Vegli

Biblioteka **Shkencore e Universitetit Shtetëror të Tiranës***, Tirana
Scientific Library of the State University of Tirana

Shkodër Public Library*, Shkodër

Library Association

Council of Libraries*, Rruga 'Abdi Toptani', No 3, Tirana
President: M Domi

Literary Periodicals

Drita (The Light), Union of Writers and Artists of Albania, 37 Z Baboci St, Tirana

Nëndori (November), Union of Writers and Artists of Albania, 37 Z Baboci St, Tirana

Shejzat (Pleiades) (Albanian language and literature), Piazza della Balduina 59, I-00136 Rome, Italy

Algeria

General Information

Language: Arabic. French is the language of business and administration
Religion: Muslim
Population: 18.5 million
Literacy Rate (1971): 26.4%
Bank Hours: 0900-1500 or 1600 Saturday-Wednesday
Shop Hours: 0900-1200, 1500-1900 Monday-Saturday
Currency: 100 centimes = 1 Algerian dinar
Export/Import Information: Books may be imported or exported only by or with permission of SNED State Monopoly, 3 blvd Zirout Yousef, BP 49, Alger Strasbourg. There are also quota restrictions. Permission to import usually entitles holder to obtain necessary foreign exchange; strict controls are in effect. Documentation formalities are rigidly enforced
Copyright: UCC (see International section)

Publishers

Publishing in Algeria is carried out by the following State monopoly:

Enterprise nationale du Livre (ENAL)+, 3 blvd Zirout Youcef, BP 49, Algiers Tel: 639712 Cable Add: Sneda Alger Telex: 53845 Sneda Dz
Dir-General: Seghir Benamar; *Editorial:* D Khellas
Subjects: General Fiction, General Non-fiction, Belles Lettres, Poetry, Biography, History, Africana, Philosophy, Religion, Juveniles, Arabic language & literature, English language, Dictionaries, Paperbacks, General & Social Science, University & Secondary Textbooks, Scientific & Technical, Sport, Travel
Bookshops: At above address, also 32 others throughout Algeria
Founded: 1983

Société nationale d'Edition et de Diffusion (SNED), now Enterprise nationale du Livre (ENAL) (qv)

Major Booksellers

Librairie **'Maison des Livres'***, 12 rue Ali Boumendjel, Algiers Tel: 636768

Librairie **S N E D** (Société nationale d'Edition et de Diffusion), 3 blvd Zirout Youcef, Algiers Tel: 639643
Sole importer, exporter and distributor of books and periodicals

Librairie du **Tiers Monde***, Pl Emir Abdelkader, Algiers

Major Libraries

Archives nationales*, Palais du Gouvernement, Esplanade d'Afrique, Algiers

Bibliothèque centrale municipale*, 12 rue du Février, Algiers

Bibliothèque municipale de Constantine*, Hôtel de Ville, Constantine

Bibliothèque municipale d'Oran*, 24 rue Dorgham Adda, Oran

Bibliothèque nationale*, ave du Docteur Fanon, Algiers Tel: 630632
Dir: Mahmoud Agha Bouayed
Publication: Bibliographie de l'Algérie (in Arabic and French, twice a year)

Centre culturel français de Constantine, Bibliothèque, 1 blvd de l'Indépendance, Constantine Tel: 933563 Telex: 92745 Cefco Dz
Librarian: Louys Etienne
Publications include: L'Esthétique de Baudelaire, Antonin Artauol, Boris Vian et la chanson

Centre culturel français d'Oran, Bibliothèque, 112 rue Larbi Ben M'Hidi, Oran Tel: 392049/393568
Chief Librarian: Eric Besnier

Ecole nationale polytechnique, Bibliothèque*, ave Pasteur, El-Harrach, Algiers

Institut d'etudes politiques et de l'information, Bibliothèque*, 37 rue Larbi Ben M'Hidi, Algiers
Chief Librarian: Ms Z Lemkami

Institut national agronomique, Bibliothèque*, El-Harrach Tel: 765415
Chief Librarian: Jocelyne Amara

Institut Pasteur d'Algérie, Bibliothèque*, rue du Dr Laveran, Algiers Tel: 653496/8
Chief Librarian: Mrs F Rafat

Bibliothèque universitaire, **Université d'Alger***, 2 rue Didouche Mourad, Algiers Tel: 640215 Telex: 5385
Librarian: Zoulikha Bekadour

Bibliothèque de l'**Université de Constantine***, BP 325, Constantine (Located at: Route de Ain el Bey, Constantine) Tel: 931125
Chief Librarian: Sari Mahmoud

Université d'Oran, Bibliothèque*, BP 16, Es Sahia, Oran

Library Association

Institut de Bibliothéconomie et des Sciences documentaires, Université d'Alger, 2 rue Didouche Mourad, Algiers
Institute of Library Management and Documentary Science

Library Reference Journal

Bibliographie de l'Algérie (in Arabic and French, twice a year), Bibliothèque nationale, ave du Docteur Fanon, Algiers

Literary Associations and Societies

Union des Ecrivains algériens*, 12 rue Ali Boumendjel, Algiers
Union of Algerian Writers

Literary Prizes

Union des Ecrivains algériens*
Awards annual literary prize for fiction, 10,000 Algerian dinars. Enquiries to Union des Ecrivains algériens, 12 rue Ali Boumendjel, Algiers

Angola

General Information

Language: Portuguese, Bantu languages
Religion: Christian, Animist
Population: 6.7 million
Currency: 100 centavos = 1 kwanza
Export/Import Information: No tariff on books and advertising. Very restricted issuance of import licences. Advertising matter is currently given considerably lower priority. Exchange controls

Book Trade Organization

União dos Escritores Angolanos*, CP 2767, Luanda Tel: 22155
Union of Angolan Writers
Secretary-General: António Cardoso

Publishers

Nova Editorial **Angolana** SARL*, CP 1225, Luanda
Man Dir: Pombo Fernandes
Subjects: General Books, Educational Books
Founded: 1935

Lello & Cia Lda*, CP 1245, Luanda
Bookshop: See under Major Booksellers
Subjects: General Fiction & Non-fiction, Secondary & Primary Textbooks

Major Booksellers

Livraria **4 Fevereiro***, Largo D João IV, CP 1245, Luanda Tel: 32678

Argente, Sentos & Cia Lda*, CP 1314, Luanda

Industrias ABC*, CP 1245, Luanda

Lello & Cia Lda*, CP 1300, Luanda
Also Publisher (qv)

Livraria **Magalhães** Sarl, CP 70, Lobito Tel: 2241/2/3 Cable Add: Aljoma Telex: 8217 Aljoma

Major Libraries

Biblioteca Municipal*, CP 1227, Luanda
Librarian: Alberto Serra

Biblioteca Nacional Doutor Antonio Agustinho Neto*, CP 2915, Luanda Tel: 37317
Director: Edgar Selsan Batalha
Publication: Novas

Direcção dos Serviços de Geologia e Minas de Angola Biblioteca*, CP 3244, Luanda

Universidade de Luanda Biblioteca*, CP 815, Luanda Tel: 764
Librarian: A C Ferraz Correia

Library Reference Journal

Novas (News), National Library, CP 2915, Luanda

Argentina

General Information

Language: Spanish
Religion: Roman Catholic
Population: 26.1 million
Literacy Rate (1970): 92.6%
Bank Hours: 1000-1600 Monday-Friday
Shop Hours: 0900-1900 Monday-Saturday
Currency: 100 centavos = 1 peso
Export/Import Information: Import licences required, goods require prior deposit of 40%
Copyright: UCC, Berne, Buenos Aires (see International section)

Book Trade Organizations

Cámara Argentina de Editores de Libros*, Maipú 359 — 2° piso of 31, Buenos Aires Tel: 451322
Association of Argentine Book Publishers
President: Hector Oscar Tucci

Cámara Argentina de Editoriales Tecnicas*, Venezuela 668, Buenos Aires
Argentinian Association of Technical Publishers

Cámara Argentina de Publicaciones*, Montevideo 48 – 4° piso, Buenos Aires
Argentine Publications Association
President: Fernando Vidal Buzzi

Cámara Argentina del Libro*, Ave Belgrano 1580 – 6° piso, 1093 Buenos Aires Tel: 388383
Argentine Book Association
Secretary: A Sisco

Federación Argentina de Librerías, Papelerías y Actividades Afines*, España 848, Losario, Santa Fé
Federation of Bookstores, Stationers and Related Activities

S A D E (Sociedad Argentina de Escritores)*, Uruguay 1371, 1016 Buenos Aires Tel: 413520/420773
Association of Argentine Writers
Dir: Horatio E Tarri
Publication: Boletín de la SADE (bi-monthly)

Sociedad General de Autores de la Argentina*, Pacheco de Melo 1818-20, Buenos Aires Tel: 444518
Argentine Society of Authors
Publications: Boletín Social (quarterly), *Argentores* (monthly)

Standard Book Numbering Agency*, Cámara Argentina del Libro, Ave Belgrano 1580 – 6° piso, 1093 Buenos Aires Tel: 388383
ISBN Administrator: Isay Klasse

Publishers

A Z Editora SA*, Paraguay 1536, 1057 Buenos Aires Tel: 446832/410845
Man Dir: José Rodolfo Carozzo; *Production:* Aníbal Emrique Villalba
Subjects: Law, Economics, History, Psychology
Founded: 1976

Editorial **Abacacia** SRL, Lavalle 1282 – 2ᵇ 8, 1048 Buenos Aires Tel: 327505 Cable Add: Abacacia
Man Dir: Alfonso Barrio; *Editorial:* Rosa Linda Denari; *Sales:* Maria Magdalena Campañaro; *Production:* Julio Luis Pita; *Publicity:* Maria Teresa Barrio
Subjects: Law, Economics, Finance
1981-82: 2 titles *Founded:* 1979
ISBN Publisher's Prefix: 950-0148

Editorial **Abaco** de Rodolfo Depalma SRL*, Tucumán 1429 4°D, 1050 Buenos Aires Tel: 40165
Man Dir & Editorial: Rodolfo Depalma; *Sales:* James Farbinger; *Production:* Marcos José Azubel; *Psychology Section:* Daniel P Gómez Dupertuis
Branch Off: Centenera 461, Buenos Aires
Subjects: Law, Economics, Sociology, Philosophy, History, Psychology
Founded: 1975

Editorial **Abeledo** Perrot SAE e I+, Lavalle 1280-1328, 1048 Buenos Aires Tel: 352848
Man Dirs: Juan Carlos Abeledo, Emilio José Perrot; *Sales Dir:* Carlos Alberto Pazos
Subject: Law
Bookshop: At above address
Founded: 1901

Editorial **Abril** SA, Ave Belgrano 624 — 5°, 1092 Buenos Aires Tel: 307891/9 Telex: 17216 Jukor Ar
Man Dir and Editor: Salvador Sammaritano; *Sales, Publicity:* Juan Carlos Macia; *Rights & Permissions:* Teresa Vernengo
Editorial Huemul SA is the division of the company producing secondary & primary school textbooks
Subjects: Fiction, Non-fiction, Children's Books, Textbooks (Huemul)
1981: 50 titles *1982:* 28 titles *Founded:* 1961

Ediciones **Acervo** de Argentina SRL*, Casillas 81 y 82, Sucursal 2-B (Congreso), 1402 Buenos Aires (Located at: Virrey Cevallos 645, P Baja, 1077 Capital Federal) Tel: 374141 Telex: 18522 Cecba Ar 028
Editorial: José Gamarra Alcalde
Parent Company: Ediciones Acervo, Spain (qv)
Subjects: Politics, Religion, Crime, Science Fiction, Fiction, General

Editorial **Acme** SA, Santa Magdalena 633, 1277 Buenos Aires Tel: 282014
Man Dir: Emilio I González
Subjects: General Fiction, Belles Lettres, Biography, How-to, Juveniles, Paperbacks, Technical, University & Primary Textbooks
Founded: 1949

Aguilar Argentina SA de Ediciones, Balcarce 363, 1064 Buenos Aires Tel: 301197/309887
Man Dir: Manuel Rodríguez; *Sales Dir:* Domingo A Ongárato
Parent Company: Aguilar SA de Ediciones, Spain (qv)
Branch Off: 9 de Julio 231, Córdoba
Subjects: Philosophy, Literature, Art, Psychology, Economics, Technical, Juveniles, Maps and Cartographical Materials
Founded: 1946

Librería **Akadia** Editorial+, Paraguay 2078, 1121 Buenos Aires Tel: 8218664/8541345
Man Dir: José F Patlallan
Subject: Medicine
Bookshop: At above address
Founded: 1967

Editorial **Albatros** SRL*, Lavalle 3975, 1190 Buenos Aires Tel: 861215
Man Dir: Roberto R Canevaro
Subjects: Agriculture, Animal Care & Breeding, Technical, How-to, Social Sciences, Medicine, University Textbooks
Founded: 1967

Editorial **Alfa** Argentina SA*, Defensa 599 – 3er piso, 1065 Buenos Aires Tel: 331199/341473
Man Dir: Leonardo Milla; *Manager:* Héctor Allegrini
Subjects: General Fiction, Literature, Philosophy, Psychology, University Textbooks
Founded: 1971

Editorial Rodolfo **Alonso** SRL, Ricardo Gutiérrez 3337 esq Uzal, 1636 Olivos Tel: 7976312
Man Dir: Rodolfo Alonso; *Sales Manager:* Raquel Rebaudi Basavilbaso
Subjects: General Fiction & Non-fiction
Founded: 1968

Editorial **Américalee** SRL*, Andonaegui 1138, 1427 Buenos Aires Tel: 511491/522167
Man Dir: Héctor E Landolfi; *Sales Dir:* Josefa A S de Landolfi
Subjects: Technical Sciences, Sports, Cooking
Founded: 1939

Editorial **Americana***, Brasil 675, 1154 Buenos Aires Tel: 238862
Man Dir: Manuel Rey Tosar
Subjects: History, Politics, Social Sciences, Arts, Fiction

Amorrortu Editores SA*, Icalma 2001, Esq José A Salmún Feijóo, 1274 Buenos Aires Tel: 282630/282818
Man Dir: Horacio de Amorrortu
Subjects: Anthropology & Religion, Economy, Philosophy, Psychology, Sociology, Argentine current affairs
Founded: 1967

Ediciones **Andromeda***, Mexico 625 – 1° piso, 1097 Buenos Aires Tel: 308280
Man Dir, Rights & Permissions: Carlos Samonta; *Editorial:* Jorge A Sanchez
Subjects: General Fiction, Literature
Founded: 1975

Arbó SAC e I, Ave Martín García 653, 1268 Buenos Aires Tel: 3620643/3620747
Man Dir: Ariel Arbó; *Technical Dir:* J M Barcala; *Publicity:* Clotilde E H de Arbó
Subjects: Science & Technology, Electronics & Telecommunications
Founded: 1912

Asociación Bautista Argentina de Publicaciones*, Rivadavia 3464, 1203 Buenos Aires Tel: 888938/888924
Man Dir: Hans Iver Jorgensen; *Assistant Manager:* Emanuel Benavídez; *Editorial Dir:* Arnoldo Canclini
Branch Offs: San Martín 1572, 2000 Rosario, Santa Fe; Tucumán 351, 5000 Córdoba; San Martín 2242, 5500 Mendoza
Subject: Religion
Founded: 1906

Asociación Educacionista Argentina, see Editorial Stella

Editorial **Astrea** de Alfredo y Ricardo Depalma SRL, Lavalle 1208, 1048 Buenos Aires Tel: 351880
Man Dir: Alfredo Depalma; *Sales Dir:* Ricardo Depalma
Associate Company: Ediciones La Bastilla (qv)
Subjects: Law, Sociology, Politics, History, Philosophy, Economics
Bookshop: Librería Astrea (at above address)
Founded: 1968

Editorial El **Ateneo**, Pedro García SA, Patagones 2463, 1282 Buenos Aires Tel: 9429002/9429152/9429052 Cable Add: Ateneo
Dirs: Pedro García, Eustasio A García
Subjects: Medicine, Agronomy, Veterinary Science, Economics, Technical, Education, Business, University Textbooks
Bookshop: El Ateneo (qv under Major Booksellers)
Founded: 1912

ARGENTINA

Editorial **Atlántida** SA, Florida 643, 1005 Buenos Aires Tel: 3115416 Cable Add: Ediatlán Telex: 21163
Man Dir: Alfredo J Vercelli; *Sales Dir:* Fernando A Parodi
Subjects: Juveniles, Textbooks, Fiction
Bookshop: At above address
Founded: 1918

Asociación Ediciones La **Aurora***, Federico Lacroze 2985, 1426 Buenos Aires Tel: 5514204
Dir: Pablo A La Moglie; *Sales Dir:* Mario C Ale
Subjects: Literature, History, Philosophy, Religion, Theology, Sociology, Psychology, Linguistics
Bookshop: Librería La Aurora, Corrientes 728, 1043 Buenos Aires
Founded: 1923

B A E S A (Buenos Aires Edita SA)*, Cordoba 1249, Buenos Aires

Barry Editorial Com Ind SRL, Talcahuano 860, 1013 Buenos Aires Tel: 447075
Subject: Music

Ediciones la **Bastilla***, Lavalle 1208, 1048 Buenos Aires Tel: 351880
Man Dir: Alfredo Depalma; *Sales Dir:* Ricardo Depalma
Associate Company: Editorial Astrea de Alfredo y Ricardo Depalma SRL (qv)
Subjects: Politics, History
Founded: 1972

SA Editorial **Bell***, Otamendi 215-17, 1405 Buenos Aires Tel: 901076/77/78 Cable Add: Edibell
Man Dir: Hugo O Varela; *Sales Dir:* C E Lippold; *Publicity Dir:* S Frasso; *Advertising Dir:* Susana Tubal; *Rights & Permissions:* Mario Martínez
Subjects: How-to, General Science, Technical, Sports
Founded: 1927

Editorial **Beta** SRL, Ave Santa Fe 2669 – 2° D, 2669 Buenos Aires Tel: 389586
Man Dir: Miguel Angel Bini
Subjects: Medicine, Psychology, University Textbooks
Founded: 1948

Bias Editora, Lavalle 1294, 1048 Buenos Aires Tel: 354161 Cable Add: Biasedita
Man Dir: Ival Rocca; *Editorial:* Ignacio Javier Barrio; *Sales:* Gustavo Jorge Claret; *Production:* Francisco Spatafora; *Publicity:* Rodolfo Esteban Amigorena
Subjects: Law, Economics
Bookshop: Bias Editora (Libros Jurídicos) (qv under Major Booksellers)
Founded: 1966
ISBN Publisher's Prefix: 950-0013

Librería **Bonum** SACI*, Maipú 859, 1006 Buenos Aires Tel: 3929763 Cable Add: Bonum
Man Dir & Sales: Antonio Gremmelspacher
Subjects: Religion, Textbooks, Music, Philosophy, Psychology
Founded: 1960

Ediciones **Botella** al Mar*, Viamonte 2754-1° '5', 1213 Buenos Aires Tel: 898073

Editorial **Bruguera** Argentina SAFIC, Avalos 365, 1427 Buenos Aires Tel: 588122/580698
Man Dir: Jorge Merlini
Parent Company: Editorial Bruguera SA, Spain (qv)

Editorial **Calicanto***, Suipacha 831-3° 'C', 1008 Buenos Aires Tel: 317028
Man Dir: Eduardo Irazabal
Subjects: Literature & Criticism
Founded: 1975

Editorial **Cangallo** SACI, Ave Belgrano 609, 1092 Buenos Aires Tel: 338848/330204/332453
Man Dir: Norberto del Hoyo
Subjects: Law, Economics, Business, University Textbooks
Bookshop: At above address
1983: 62 titles *Founded:* 1968
ISBN Publisher's Prefix: 950-543

Editorial **Caymi**, 15 de Noviembre 1149, 1130 Buenos Aires Tel: 232474
Subjects: Popular Science & Medicine, Yoga, Judo & Karate, Magic & Fortune-Telling, Occultism, Sexology, Science Fiction, Spanish & South American Classics

Celcius — J J Vallory*, Dean Funes 472-476, 1214 Buenos Aires Tel: 932469/939414
Subject: Medicine

Centro Editor de America Latina SA*, Cangallo 1228 – 2° D, 1038 Buenos Aires Tel: 359449/350142 Cable Add: Centroedit
Man Dir: José Boris Spivacow; *Sales Dir:* Aldo Antonio Sangoi
Subjects: Literature, Biography, History, Art, Psychology, How-to, Juveniles, General Science, Social Science, Educational Materials
Founded: 1966

El **Cid** Editor SRL*, Alsina 500, 1087 Buenos Aires Tel: 330071/349267/83795
President: Dr Eduardo Varela-Cid; *General Manager:* Julio A Oliva; *Sales:* Carlos Hurs; *Production:* Nilda Montesi
Subsidiary Companies: El Cid Editor CA, Apdo 60010, Caracas 1060, Venezuela; El Cid Editor SAE, Spain (qv)
Bookshop: Librería Ciudad Educativa SA (Antigua Librería del Colegio) (qv under Major Booksellers)

Editorial **Científica Argentina***, Paraguay 1300, Buenos Aires Tel: 443562
Man Dir: Fernando Duelo Cavero
Subjects: Argentine history, Pedagogy, Various

Editorial **Ciordia** SRL*, Ave Belgrano 2271, 1094 Buenos Aires Tel: 481681
Man Dir: Eduardo B Ciordia; *Sales Dirs:* Manuel Ciordia, Carlos Danzini
Subjects: Literature, Philosophy, Psychology, University & Secondary Textbooks
Founded: 1938

Editorial **Claretiana**, Lima 1360, 1138 Buenos Aires Tel: 279250 Cable Add: Editorial Claretiana
Man Dir, Editorial, Rights & Permissions: P Andrés Berasain; *Editor:* Ricardo F Isaguirre; *Sales:* Eduardo Righetti; *Publicity:* José Luis Pérez
Subject: Religion
Founded: 1956

Editorial **Claridad** SA*, San José 1627, Buenos Aires Tel: 235573 Cable Add: Claridad Baires
Man Dir: Dr Elio M A Colle; *Sales Manager:* José Zamora
Subject: General Literature
Founded: 1922

Editora **Close Up** SA*, Thames 2450, 1425 Buenos Aires Tel: 7742961

Club de Lectores*, Ave de Mayo 624, 1084 Buenos Aires Tel: 343955
Man Dir: Juan Manuel Fontenla; *Sales:* Carlos A Alvano, María Mercedes Fontenla; *Publicity:* María Inés Fontenla
Subjects: History, Philosophy, Religion, Psychology, Social Science, University Textbooks
1981: 214 titles *Founded:* 1938

Librería del **Colegio** SA, Humberto 1° 545, 1103 Buenos Aires Tel: 3621222/3621332/3625995
Subjects: Educational Books, Textbooks

Colmegna SA, San Martín 2546, 3000 Santa Fe Tel: 23102
Man Dir, Editorial, Sales: Nestor Lammertyn
Subjects: Literature, History, Poetry
Bookshop: At above address
Founded: 1889
ISBN Publisher's Prefix: 950-535

Editorial **Columba** SA, Sarmiento 1889 – 5°, 1044 Buenos Aires Tel: 454297
Man Dir: Claudio A Columba
Subjects: Classics in translation, Twentieth century themes
Founded: 1953

Compañia Impresora Argentina SA*, Alsina 2049, 1090 Buenos Aires Tel: 472308

Editorial **Conjunta** SRL*, Fr J S M de Oro 2587, 1425 Buenos Aires Tel: 7741734

Ediciones **Contabilidad** Moderna SACIC, Dr Regimiento de Patricios 1837, 1225 Buenos Aires Tel: 217808/218448/281745
Man Dir: Juan Carlos García Stella; *Sales Manager:* Alberto D Lopez
Subjects: Business, Administration, Taxes, Law, Accounting
Founded: 1943

Editorial **Contempora** SRL, Sarmiento 643, of 522, 1382 Buenos Aires Tel: 451793/452575
Subjects: Architecture, Gardening

Ediciones **Corregidor** SAICI y E*, Hipolito Irigoyen 1287, 1086 Buenos Aires Tel: 468148
Dir: Manuel Pampín
Subject: General Literature
Founded: 1972

Cosmopolita SRL, Piedras 744, 1070 Buenos Aires Tel: 307049
Man Dir: Eva Ruth F de Rapp
Subjects: Technical, Agriculture
Founded: 1940

Editorial **Crea** SA, now Editorial Abril SA (qv)

Editorial **Crespillo** SA*, Defensa 485, 1065 Buenos Aires Tel: 347384
Subjects: History, Arts, Maps

Depalma SRL, Talcahuano 494, 1013 Buenos Aires Tel: 461815
Man Dir: Roque Depalma; *Sales Dir:* Alberto E Barón
Subjects: Law, History, Social Science, Business, University Texts
Bookshop: At above address
Founded: 1944

Editorial **Difusión** SA*, Sarandí 1065, Buenos Aires Tel: 9410118
Man Dir, Sales Dir: Domingo Palombella
Subjects: Literature, Philosophy, Religion, Juveniles, Education, Textbooks
Founded: 1936

Distasa*, Córdoba 2064, 1120 Buenos Aires Tel: 457609/469059
General Manager: Lorenzo Mario Lugo
Associate Companies: See under Alianza Editorial SA, Spain

E C A (Ediciones Culturales Argentinas)*, Ave Alvear 1690, 1014 Buenos Aires Tel: 444124
Man Dir: Juan Luis Gallardo
Subjects: Argentine Literature, Publications of the Ministry of Culture & Education
Founded: 1961

EUDEBA (Editorial Universitaria de Buenos Aires)*, Ave Rivadavia 1571-73, 1033 Buenos Aires
Tel: 372202/378025/385478
Executive Delegate: General Arturo A Corbetta; *General Manager:* Colonel Francisco Basaldua; *Editorial:* José Rodolfo Carozzo; *Sales:* Enrique Ossuni
Subjects: Literature, History, Logic, Philosophy, Theology, Art, Music, Dance, Drama, Geography, Topography, Architecture, Anthropology, Archaeology, Paleontology, Astronomy, Meteorology, Natural Sciences, Physics, Chemistry, Plastics, Agronomy, Medicine, Psychiatry, Psychology, Veterinary, Mathematics, Accountancy, Economics, Law, Education
Bookshop: Pasaje El Fundador-Local, 9 Obispo Trejo, 29 Cordoba, 5000 Codigo
Founded: 1958

Edicient SAIC+, Mario Bravo 465, Avellaneda, 1870 Buenos Aires Tel: 2087451
President: José S Coda; *Technical Dir:* Ing Mario Carlos Ginzburg; *Sales Dir:* Carlos Norberto Rojas; *Publicity:* Teresa de Hermosilla
Subjects: Technical, Electronics

Editorial Sudamericana SA, Humberto 1° 545, 1103 Buenos Aires Tel: 3621222/3621332/3621467 Cable Add: Librecol
President: Edith K de Lopez Llovet; *Man Dir:* Jaime Rodrigué; *Editorial:* Enrique Pezzoni; *Sales Dir:* Francisco La Falce; *Publicity Dir:* Maria Eugenia Ramos Mejía; *Rights & Permissions:* Gloria Lopez de Rodrigué
Associate Companies: EDHASA (Editora y Distribuidora Hispano-Americana SA), Spain (qv); Editorial Hermes SA, Mexico (qv)
Subjects: General Fiction & Non-fiction, Literature, Biography, History, Philosophy, Psychology
Founded: 1939

Editorial Universidad SRL*, Corrientes 1250 – 4° 'J', 1043 Buenos Aires Tel: 356490/6850
Subject: Textbooks

Editorial Universitaria de Buenos Aires, see EUDEBA

Emecé Editores SA, Carlos Pellegrini 1069 – 9° piso, 1009 Buenos Aires Tel: 3114710/3114906/3117327 Cable Add: Emece Baires Telex: 17736 Emece Ar
President: Dr Bonifacio del Carril; *Administration:* Marcos I Fantin; *Sales Dirs:* Oscar Guerrieri, Eduardo Fantin; *Publicity Dir:* José A Mateo; *Rights & Permissions:* Jorge O Naveiro, Bonifacio P del Carril; *Editorial:* Jorge O Naveiro, Carlos V Frias, Eduardo García Belsunce; *Production:* Francisco F Del Carril
Orders to: Emece Distribuidora SA, Alsina 2062, 1090 Buenos Aires
Subsidiary Companies: Emecé Distribuidora SA, Alsina 2062, 1090 Buenos Aires
Associate Company: Emecé Mexicana SA de CV, Madrid 4, Mexico 5 DF
Book Club: Club 'El Libro del Mes'
Subjects: General Fiction, Non-fiction, Biography, Essays, Mystery, History, Art, Poetry
1981: 100 titles *1982:* 94 titles *Founded:* 1939

Espacio Editora SA, Malabia 615 – 1° piso, 1414 Buenos Aires Tel: 8559082
President: Guillermo Raúl Kliczkowski; *Editorial:* Hugo Alberto Kliczkowski; *Sales:* Inés A de Gomez; *Production:* Silvia Leonor Wladimirski; *Publicity:* Mirta Adriana Kracoff; *Rights & Permissions:* Silvia Leonor Wladimirski

Associate Company: Sociedad Ambiente (at above address)
Subjects: Architecture, Design, History, Ecology, Urban Planning
Founded: 1977
ISBN Publisher's Prefix: 84-0116

Espasa-Calpe Argentina SA*, Tacuarí 328, Buenos Aires
Head Office: Editorial Espasa-Calpe SA, Spain (qv)

Angel **Estrada** y Cía SA*, Bolivar 462-66, 1066 Buenos Aires Tel: 336521/27
Man Dir: Angel M de Estrada
Subjects: How-to, Primary & Secondary Textbooks, Books for Infants, Teaching Guides, Atlas
Founded: 1869

Fabril Editora SA*, California 2098 – 3°, 1289 Buenos Aires Tel: 213601
Subjects: General Non-fiction, Textbooks, Reference Books, Arts, Humanities

Ediciones Librerías **Fausto***, Ave Corrientes 1316, 1043 Buenos Aires Tel: 453914/456266
Manager: Rafael Zorrilla
Bookshops: Librería Fausto, Librería Martín Fierro (qqv under Major Booksellers)

Ediciones de la **Flor** SRL, Anchoris 27, 1280 Buenos Aires Tel: 235529
Man Dir: Daniel Divinsky; *Sales Dir:* Ana M Miler; *Publicity & Advertising Dir and Rights & Permissions:* Yvonne G de Losada
Subjects: Fiction, Literature, History, Psychology, Juveniles, Humour
1981: 23 titles *1982:* 20 titles *Founded:* 1967
ISBN Publisher's Prefix: 950-515

Ediciones **Formentor** SRL*, Ave Belgrano 1462, 1093 Buenos Aires Tel: 371657/382769
Man Dir: Ruben Duran; *Sales Dir:* Enrique Celis
Parent Company: Editorial Seix Barral SA, Spain (qv)
Subjects: Literature, Philosophy, Religion, Social Sciences, Psychology, Engineering, University Textbooks
Founded: 1971

Editorial **Galerna** SA, Charcas 3741, 1425 Buenos Aires Tel: 711739 Cable Add: Galerna
Dirs: Julio Martín Alonso, Hugo B Levin
Subsidiary Company: Librería Piloto (foreign sales & bibliographic service)
Subjects: Literature, History, Social Sciences, Paperbacks, Patagonia
Bookshops: Librerías Galerna, Tucumán 1425, Buenos Aires
Founded: 1967

Fernando **García Cambeiro**, Cochabamba 244, 1150 Buenos Aires Tel: 361043
Man Dir: Fernando García Cambeiro
Subjects: Essays on Latin American Writers

Librería y Papelería Casa **García** SA*, C Pellegrini 41, 3500 Resistencia Chaco Tel: 25930
Man Dir: José García Pulido; *Sales Dir:* Luis Aguirre
Subjects: Fiction, Poetry, General Literature & Literary Criticism, History, Geography, Politics
Bookshop: At above address
Founded: 1939

Editorial **Géminis** SRL*, Barcena 2105 — 8° B, 1431 Buenos Aires Tel: 513491
Executive President: Leonor de Pirro de Baran; *Editorial:* Walter J Baran; *Sales:* Norma Richard; *Production:* Mario di Bartolo

Ediciones G **Gili** SA*, Cochabamba 156, 1064 Buenos Aires Tel: 3619998 Cable Add: Edig
Parent Company: Editorial Gustavo Gili SA, Spain (qv)

Editorial **Glem** SACIF*, Ave Caseros 2056, 1264 Buenos Aires Tel: 266641
President: José Alfredo Tucci; *Vice-President:* Héctor Oscar Tucci; *Dir:* Eduardo Anibal Tucci
Subjects: Technical, Psychology
Founded: 1933

Editorial y Librería **Goncourt***, Ave Callao 1519, 1024 Buenos Aires Tel: 449743
Man Dir: Jaime Fariña
Subjects: Fiction & Non-fiction
Bookshop: At above address
Founded: 1952

Goyanarte Editor SA*, Esmeralda 923 – 3° 'B', 1007 Buenos Aires Tel: 320023/8362
Man Dir: César Amadeo López; *Sales Dir:* Hugo Hanuel Vázquez
Subject: Fiction
Founded: 1969 (as Juan Goyanarte Editore)

Gram Editora*, Cochabamba 1652, 1148 Buenos Aires Tel: 268397
Dir: Manuel Herrero Montes
Subjects: Educational Books, Religion
Founded: 1925

Editorial Juan Carlos **Granda***, Corrientes 1243, 1043 Buenos Aires Tel: 356114

Librería y Editorial Alfa **Graziano** SACI*, Sarmiento 1343 – 1° piso, 1041 Buenos Aires Tel: 495349
Man Dir: Mauricio Domingo Graziano
Bookshop: Librería Alfa Graziano (qv under Major Booksellers)
Subjects: Medicine, Law, Social Sciences, Economics, General Culture

Grijalbo SA*, Belgrano 1256, 1093 Buenos Aires
Parent Company: Ediciones Grijalbo SA, Spain (qv)
Subjects: Fiction & Non-fiction

Editorial **Guadalupe**, Mansilla 3865, 1425 Buenos Aires Tel: 846066
Man Dir: José Gallinger; *Sales Dir:* Alberto Klein; *Publicity Dir:* Norberto Bossio; *Production, Rights & Permissions:* Manuel de Gracia
Subjects: Pedagogy, Social Sciences, Religion, Literature
Bookshops: Librería Guadalupe (at above address); Librería Verbo Divino, Deán Funes 165, Local 27, Córdoba
Founded: 1942

Librería **Hachette** SA, Rivadavia 739, 1002 Buenos Aires Tel: 348481 Cable Add: Aglibrairi Baires Telex: 17479 Hacba Ar
President: Juan A Musset; *Vice-President:* Carmen P de Picó; *Commercial Manager:* José Manuel Caneda
Subjects: History, Travel, Literature, Philosophy
Bookshop: See under Major Booksellers

Editorial **Hemisferio** Sur SA, Pasteur 743, 1028 Buenos Aires Tel:489825/488454
Man Dirs: Juan Angel Peri, Adolfo Luis Peña
Associate Companies: Editorial Agropecuaria Hemisferio Sur SRL, Alzaibar 1328, Montevideo, Uruguay; Librería Agropecuaria SA, Pasteur 743, 1028 Buenos Aires, Argentina
Subjects: Agriculture, Veterinary Science, Natural Science
Founded: 1966

Editorial **Hobby***, Constitución 2348, Buenos Aires Tel: 9414255
Man Dir: Marcelo Oscar Castroman; *Sales*

Manager: Norberto Luis Carca
Subjects: Technical
Founded: 1936

Editorial **Huemul** SA, Textbook division of Editorial Abril SA (qv)

Librería **Huemul** SA+, Ave Santa Fe 2237, 1123 Buenos Aires Tel: 831666
Man Dir, Editorial: Antonio Rego; *Sales, Publicity, Rights & Permissions:* Carlos L Sánchez
Subjects: University, Secondary & Primary Textbooks, Children's Books
Bookshop: See under Major Booksellers
Founded: 1941

Editorial **Humanitas***, Carlos Calvo 644, 1102 Buenos Aires Tel: 7821449
Dir: Sela Sierra de Villaverde; *Sales:* Osvaldo R Dubini; *Publicity:* Mauricio Faistman
Orders to: Tres Américas, Alsina 722, Buenos Aires
Subjects: Social Sciences, Psychology, Education, Psychological Textbooks
Founded: 1955

Instituto de Publicaciones Navales*, Córdoba 354, 1054 Buenos Aires Tel: 310042

Editorial **Inter-Médica** SAICI, Junín 917 — 1°, Casilla de Correo 4625, Buenos Aires Tel: 833234/833148/855572
President: Jorge Modyeievsky; *Vice-President:* Sonia M B de Modyeievsky; *General Manager:* Deborah Modyeievsky Bakenroth
Subjects: Medicine, Dentistry, General Science, University Textbooks
Founded: 1959

Intersea*, México 924, Buenos Aires

Biblioteca Popular **Judía**, Casilla de Correo 20, Suc 53, 1453 Buenos Aires (Located at: Larrea 744, 1030 Buenos Aires) Tel: 485028/474535 Cable Add: Worldgress Baires
Editorial: Roberto Brzostowski
Subjects: Jewish History & Biography, Jewish Latinamerican Conference publications

Ediciones y Librería **Jurídica***, Calle 45, No 532, 1900 La Plata Tel: 41427
Subject: Law

Editorial **Juventud** Argentina*, Defensa 355, 1065 Buenos Aires Tel: 333756
Parent Company: Editorial Juventud SA, Spain (qv)
Subjects: History, Juveniles, Fiction, Maps

Editorial **Kapelusz** SA, Moreno 372, 1091 Buenos Aires Tel:346451/3928905 Cable Add: Kapelusz Telex: 18342 Ekasa Ar
President: Ricardo R Pascual Robles; *Editorial, Rights & Permissions:* Fernando Lida García; *Marketing Manager:* Antonio S Gordiola; *Publicity:* Carlos Otero
Subsidiary Companies: Editorial Kapelusz Colombiana SA, Colombia (qv for further subsidiary companies); Editorial Cincel SA, Spain (qv)
Subjects: Primary, Secondary & University Textbooks, Psychology, Pedagogy, Juveniles
Bookshop: Corrientes 999, Buenos Aires
1981: 40 titles *1982:* 28 titles *Founded:* 1905
ISBN Publisher's Prefix: 950-13

Editorial **Kier** SACIFI, Ave Santa Fe 1260, 1059 Buenos Aires Tel: 410507/418243
President: Alfonso Florencio Pibernus; *Vice President:* José Grigna; *Man Dir:* Héctor Pibernus; *Sales Dir:* Alberto Pibernus
Subjects: Eastern Religions, Astrology, Tarots, Occultism, Rosicrucianism, Medicine
Bookshop: Librería Kier (qv under Major Booksellers)
1981: 126 titles *Founded:* 1907

Editorial **Labor** Argentina SA*, Venezuela 617, 1095 Buenos Aires Tel: 334135
Man Dir: Pedro Clotas Cierco
Parent Company: Editorial Labor, Spain (qv)

Ediciones **Larousse** Argentina SA*, Valentin Gómez 3530, 1191 Buenos Aires Tel: 876671 Telex: 0121783 Cable Add: Editlarousse
President: Georges Lucas
Subjects: Dictionaries, Encyclopaedias

Luis **Lasserre** y Cía, SACIFI*, Alsina 1666, 1088 Buenos Aires Tel: 405803/451693
Subjects: Textbooks, Public Health, Maps

Latina SA, Ave de Mayo 953 – 11°, 1084 Buenos Aires Tel: 389108/4631
Editorial: Juan Carlos Orgueira
Subjects: Pre-school books, Juveniles
Founded: 1971

Editorial Victor **Lerú** SA*, Don Bosco 3834, 1206 Buenos Aires (Located at: Casilla 2793, Correo central, 1000 Buenos Aires) Tel: 9816098/9816198/9818978
Man Dir: Victor Nep; *Sales Dir:* León Nep
Orders to: Editorial Victor Lerú SA, Casilla 2793, Correo central, 1000 Buenos Aires
Subjects: Art, Architecture, Technology, Primary, Secondary & University Textbooks, Music, Dictionaries, History
Founded: 1944
ISBN Publisher's Prefix: 950-8205

La **Ley** SA Editora e Impresora, Tucumán 1471, 1050 Buenos Aires Tel: 495481
President: Dr Carlos M Oliva Vélez; *Vice-President:* Carlos M Oliva-Vélez Jnr; *General Dir:* Enrique Algorta Gaona; *Commercial Manager:* Julio Blanco; *Production:* Ing Roberto Pedretti
Branch Offs: In all Argentinian provinces, in Asunción (Republic of Paraguay) and Madrid (Spain)
Subjects: Law, Economics, Philosophy, History
Founded: 1935

Carlos **Lohlé** SA, Tacuarí 1516, Casilla de Correo 3097, 1000 Buenos Aires Tel: 279969
President: Carlos F P Lohlé; *Man Dir:* Francisco M Lohlé
Subjects: Literature, Poetry, Philosophy, Religion, Psychology, Social Science
Founded: 1953

López Libreros Editores, Junín 863, 1113 Buenos Aires Tel: 837744
Man Dir: Dr Pablo A López; *Sales Manager:* R Enrique Lohrmann
Subject: Medicine
Bookshop: At above address
Founded: 1927

Editorial **Losada** SA, Morena 3362, 1209 Buenos Aires Tel: 387267/389902 Cable Add: Edilosada
President: Gonzalo Pedro Losada; *Man Dir:* Carlo Alberto Aramburu; *Sales Dir:* Manuel Taboada
Subjects: Fiction & Non-fiction, Classics, Poetry, Literary Studies, Philosophy, Psychology, Biography, History, Pedagogy, Secondary Textbooks
Founded: 1938

Ediciones **Macchi***, Alsina 1535 PB, 1088 Buenos Aires Tel: 460594
Man Dir: Raúl Luis Macchi; *Sales Dir:* Julio Ricardo Mora
Subjects: Economic Sciences
Bookshop: Córdoba 2015, 1120 Buenos Aires
Founded: 1947

Macondo Ediciones SRL*, Lavalle 1882 — 1° piso, 1051 Buenos Aires Tel: 458535
Man Dir: Dr Samuel Tarnopolsky; *Editorial, Publicity, Rights & Permissions:* Haydée M Jofre Barroso; *Sales, Production:* José Antonio Serrano
Subjects: Belles Lettres, Science, Economics, Politics, Fiction, Science Fiction, Poetry
Founded: 1976
ISBN Publisher's Prefix: 950-89000

Marymar Ediciones SA, Chile 1432, 1098 Buenos Aires Tel: 380391
President: Isay Klasse; *Man Dir, Production Dir:* Saúl Cherny
Subjects: Social, Political & General Science, Economics, Philosophy, Architecture, Technology, Music, Cinema, History, Teaching, Library Science, Ecology, Fiction & Classics, Psychology
Founded: 1960

Librería y Editorial La **Médica***, Córdoba 2901, 2000 Rosario Tel: 397858
Man Dir: Cataline C de Radeff; *Sales Dir:* Ruben T Radeff, Ricardo A Radeff, Roberto A Radeff
Subject: Medicine
Miscellaneous: Major Distributor of Schoolbooks and General literature

Editorial **Médica** Panamericana SA, Junin 831, 1113 Buenos Aires Tel: 838819
Man Dir, Editorial: Roberto Brik; *Sales:* Hector Brik; *Production:* Daniel Brik; *Publicity:* Hugo A Brik
Branch Offs: Santa Izabel 267, São Paulo, Brazil; Carrera 7a No 40-20, Bogotá, Colombia; Marcoleta 328, Santiago de Chile, Chile; Hilarión Eslava 55, Madrid 15, Spain; Herschel 153, Mexico 5, DF; Edificio Las Fundaciones 14, Ave Andrés Bello, Caracas, Venezuela
Subjects: Medicine, Dentistry, Rehabilitation, Nursing
1981: 550 titles *Founded:* 1953

Editorial Librería **Mitre** SRL*, Bartólome Mitre 2063, 1039 Buenos Aires Tel: 495856
Man Dir: Rodolfo Amura
Subject: Technical (especially Mechanics)
Founded: 1949

Editorial **Mundi** SAIC y F+, Casilla Correo 47, Suc 53, 1453 Capital Federal Tel: 839339/839663
Production, Publicity, Rights & Permissions: Elena Garcia Mila
Subject: Dentistry
1981: 6 titles *1982:* 4 titles *Founded:* 1939
ISBN Publisher's Prefix: 950-545

Editorial **Mundo** Técnico SRL, Guanahaní 176, 1274 Buenos Aires Cable Add: Muntex
Man Dir: Gustavo A Marini; *Sales Dir:* Juan C García Venturini
Subjects: Technical, Engineering, Atlases, How-to, School Dictionaries & Textbooks
Founded: 1972

Librería y Editorial **Nigar** SRL*, Humberto 1° 667, 1103 Buenos Aires Tel: 331794

Editorial **Norte** SAIC*, José Mármol 2131, 1255 Buenos Aires Tel: 9239507

Editorial **Nova** SACI*, Perú 858, 1068 Buenos Aires Tel: 348698
Man Dir: Horacio D Rolando; *Publicity & Sales Dir:* María del Pilar Lopez Soto de Rolando
Subjects: Literature, Biography, History, Art, Philosophy, Religion, Medicine, Psychology, Education, University & Secondary Textbooks
Founded: 1945

Ediciones **Nueva Visión** SAIC*, Tucumán 3748, 1189 Buenos Aires Tel: 895050
Man Dir: Jorge José Grisetti; *Sales Manager:* Anibal Victor Giacone
Subjects: Social Sciences, Psychology, Architecture, Art, Theatre
Founded: 1954

La **Obra***, Ave Santa Fe 3478 — 1°, 1425
Capital Federal Tel: 849146
Dir: Carlos G Salas; *Commercial Manager:*
Hugo Mario Botti
Subject: Primary Textbooks

Ediciones **Orion***, Ägüero 1412 5°, 1425
Buenos Aires Tel: 8214101
Subjects: General Fiction & Non-fiction

Editorial **Paidós***, Defensa 599 — 1°, 1065
Buenos Aires Tel: 332275
Man Dir, Rights & Permissions: Enrique
Butelman; *Sales Dir:* Renato Modai
Subsidiary Company: Ediciones Paidós
Ibérica SA, Spain (qv)
Subjects: Social Sciences, Psychology,
Medicine, Philosophy, Religion, History,
Biography, Literature, University Textbooks
Bookshop: Librería Paidós, Las Heras and
Canning, Buenos Aires
Founded: 1945

Ediciones **Pannedille***, Chacabuco 129,
Buenos Aires Tel: 354957
Man Dir: Oscar Buonano
Subjects: History, Law, Technical
Founded: 1970

Casa **Pardo** SAC*, Defensa 1170, 1065
Buenos Aires Tel: 346676 Cable Add:
Pardoroman
Dir: Roman José Pardo
Subjects: General Literature, Humanism
Founded: 1892

Editora **Patria Grande***, Rivadavia 6251,
1406 Buenos Aires Tel: 6324374/6323255
General Manager and Rights & Permissions:
Washington Uranga; *Editorial:* Carlos J
Durán; *Sales:* Elsa S de Férnández;
Production: Carlos D Arnedillo; *Publicity:*
Duilio López
Branch Off: Casila de Correo 5 — suc 8,
1408 Buenos Aires
Subjects: Religious, Poetry, Juvenile
Bookshops: Librería Patria Grande (at
above address); Librería Didajé, José Cubas
3543, Buenos Aires
1981: 8 titles *Founded:* 1974
ISBN Publisher's Prefix: 950-046

Ediciones **Paulinas**+, Nazca 4249, 1419
Buenos Aires Tel: 5723926/5724810
Cable Add: Paulinas
Man Dir: Ana Maria Killing; *Editorial,
Production, Rights & Permissions:* Teresa
Groselj; *Sales Dir:* Bianca de Toni; *Publicity:*
Ana Maria Martinez
Branch Offs: Buenos Aires 837, Rosario; San
Jerónimo 2136, Sante Fé; 24 de Setiembre
512, Tucumán; San Martín 980, Mendoza;
Antártida Argentina 178, Resistencia
Subjects: Education, Religion
Founded: 1940

A **Peña** Lillo SA*, H Yrigoyen 1394-1086,
Buenos Aires Tel: 370994
Man Dir: Arturo Peña Lillo; *Sales Dir:*
María Luisa Comellí; *Production &
Publicity:* Laura Peña
Orders to: Rivadavia 739, Buenos Aires
(Librería Hachette SA)
Subjects: History, Political Science,
Economics, Sociology, Literature
Founded: 1956
ISBN Publisher's Prefix: 950-8203

Ediciones **Periferia** SRL*, Cangallo 1730 —
6° of 68, 1037 Buenos Aires Tel: 450574
Subjects: Social Sciences, University
Textbooks
Founded: 1971

Editorial Argentina **Plaza y Janés** SA*,
Lambaré 893, Buenos Aires Tel:
866769/866785
Man Dir: Jorge Perez; *Sales Dir:* Ernesto
Pena
Subjects: General Fiction & Non-fiction

Editorial **Pleamar***, Corrientes 1994 — 1°,
Buenos Aires
Man Dir: Andrés Alfonso Bravo
Subjects: Political & Social Science
Founded: 1965

Editorial **Plus Ultra** SAI & C*, Viamonte
1755, 1055 Buenos Aires Tel:
446605/446694/446788 Cable Add:
Plusultra
Man Dirs: Rafael Román, Lorenzo
Marengo, Diego Mazzitelli; *Editorial:* Carlos
Alberto Loprete, José Isaacson; *Sales:*
Ricardo Errea; *Production:* Renato Gardoni;
Publicity: Lily Sosa de Newton
Subjects: Literature, History, Law,
Textbooks, Economics, Philosophy, Politics,
Sociology, Psychology, Pedagogy, Children's
Books
Bookshops: At above address; Suipacha 552,
1008 Buenos Aires
Founded: 1964

Editorial **Pomaire** SA, Espinosa 2365, 1416
Buenos Aires Tel: 590868
Man Dir: Andres Vergara P
Head Off: Editorial Pomaire SA, Spain (qv)
Subject: Fiction

Prolam SRL (Ediciones Economia y
Empresa)*, México 625, Buenos Aires
Tel: 308280
Man Dir: Beatriz E P de Lambruschini
Subjects: Economics, Business, Science &
Technology
Founded: 1958

Editorial **Proyección** SRL*, Yapeyú 321,
Buenos Aires Tel: 8115086
Man Dirs: Ernesto Portela, Noe Bursuck;
Sales Dir: Carlos Garcia Iribarren
Subject: Political Science
Founded: 1968

Ediciones **Quevedo** Sacif*, Hipólito
Vrigoyen 4245, 1212 Capital Federal Tel:
8112816
President: Oscar Luis Jorge Quevedo;
Editorial: Oscar del Carmen Quevedo; *Sales:*
Carlos Caballero; *Production:* Alejandro
Carlos Quevedo; *Rights & Permissions:*
Pablo Daniel Quevedo
Subjects: General Culture, Geography,
Atlases, Cooking, Juvenile, Teaching, Poetry
relating to Gauchos
Founded: 1965

Ricordi Americana SAEC, Cangallo 1558,
1037 Buenos Aires Tel: 409841/3 Cable
Add: Ricordamericana Telex: 122580
Man Dir: Renzo Valcarenghi; *Manager:*
Ernesto Larcade; *Marketing:* Claudio
Firmenich
Associate Companies: Ricordi Brasileira,
Sao Paulo, Brazil; G & C Ricordi, Italy (qv);
G & C Ricordi, Mexico
Subjects: Music, Musical Teaching Methods
Founded: 1924

Librería **Rodríguez***, Sarmiento 835, Buenos
Aires Tel: 358125
President: Ernesto J Rodríguez; *Dir:*
Ernesto J Rodríguez Gerino; *General
Manager:* Bautista L Tello
Subject: Children's books
Bookshop: See under Major Booksellers

Ruy Diaz SAEIC+, Irigoyen 453-455, 1407
Buenos Aires Tel: 697117 Cable Add:
Ediruy
Man Dir: Rafael Zuccotti
Branch Off: Casilla de Correo 46,
Sucursal 6, 1406 Buenos Aires
Subjects: Educational, Atlases, Dictionaries
Founded: 1966

Editorial **Santiago** Rueda SRL*, Sarmiento
680 - 1°, 1041 Buenos Aires Tel:
491874/497860
Man Dir: Enrique S Rueda

Subject: Literature
Founded: 1940

Schapire Editor SRL*, Uruguay 1249, 1016
Buenos Aires Tel: 440765
Man Dir: Miguel Schapire
Subjects: Literature, Biography, History,
Art, Psychology, Social Science, Juveniles
Founded: 1935

Selcon SAEC & I (Selección Contable)*,
Sarandí 1067, 1222 Buenos Aires
Tel: 9410118
Sales & Advertising Dir: Domingo
Palombella
Subjects: Business, Economics
Founded: 1942

Santiago **Sentis** Melendo*, Rivadavia 4076,
1205 Buenos Aires

Ediciones **Siglo XX** SAC & I*, Maza 177,
1206 Buenos Aires Tel: 882758 Cable Add:
Sigloveinte
Man Dir: Isidoro Wainer; *Sales Dir:* Carlos
Zorrilla
Subjects: General Fiction & Non-fiction
Bookshop: At above address
Founded: 1943

Editorial **Sigmar** SACI, Belgrano 1580 —
7°, 1093 Buenos Aires Tel: 373045/384474
Cable Add: Sigmar
Man Dir: Sigfrido Chwat
Subject: Juveniles, Children's Books
1981: 43 titles *1982:* 51 titles *Founded:* 1941

Ediciones del **Sol** SA*, Ave Roque Saénz
Peña 974, 8° piso B, Buenos Aires
Tel: 350473
Man Dir: Adolfo Colombres; *Sales Dir:*
Manuel Valiz
Subjects: Fiction, General Literature, Social
Sciences
Founded: 1973

Editorial **Sopena** Argentina SACI e I,
Moreno 970 - 1°, Buenos Aires Tel: 372938
Executive President: Daniel Carlos Olsen;
Dirs: Marta A J Sopena de Olsen, Leopoldo
Costa Urruty; *Manager:* Hipólito O Dhers
Subjects: Dictionaries, Language &
Linguistics, Literature & Criticism, Spanish
& Hispano-American classics, Chess, Health
& Beauty, Practical Guides, Contemporary
Politics, History, Children's Anthologies, all
mainly paperback

Editorial **Stella***, Viamonte 1984, 1056
Buenos Aires Tel: 460346
Asociación Educacionista Argentina
Subjects: Non-fiction, Textbooks

Studia Croatica*, Carlos Pelegrini 743.P.3,
Buenos Aires Tel: 3927254

Editorial **Sur** SA*, Independencia 802, 1099
Buenos Aires Tel: 231689

T E A (Tipográfica Editora Argentina)*,
Lavalle 1430, 1048 Buenos Aires
Tel: 405668
Man Dir: Pedro San Martín; *Sales Dir:*
María Teresa San Martín
Subjects: History, Social Science, Law,
Economics, Philosophy
Founded: 1946

Instituto Torcuato di **Tella**, 11 de
Septiembre 2139, 1428 Buenos Aires Tel:
7848264/7815013/7815015 Cable Add:
Instella Baires
President: Roberto Cortés Conde
Subjects: Social Sciences, Economics,
History, Political Science, Epistemology and
Methodology of the Social Sciences
1981: 2 titles *Founded:* 1958

Ediciones **Theoria** SRL*, Rivadavia 1255, 4°
piso of 407, Casilla de Correo 5096, 1033
Buenos Aires Tel: 380131
Man Dir: Jorge O Orús; *Sales Dir:* José Luis

Menéndez
Subjects: Literature, Biography, History, Religion
Founded: 1954

Editorial **Tiempo Contemporaneo***, Viamonte 1453, 10° piso of 66, 1055 Buenos Aires Tel: 459640
Man Dir: Alberto Mario Serebresky; *Sales Dir:* José Fuster
Subjects: General Fiction, History, Philosophy, Psychology, Technical, Medicine, Social Sciences, University Textbooks
Founded: 1969

Ediciones **Tres Tiempos** SRL, Ave Belgrano 225, 1092 Buenos Aires Tel: 342913/347184/338785
Man Dirs: José C Orríes e Ibars, Canio Carmelo Cillo; *Assistant Manager:* José Luis Tato; *Editor:* Susana Margulies; *Production Dir:* Ana Barkacs van Gyarmath; *Sales Dirs:* Lidia N de Guastavino, Raúl Villar; *Advertising & Promotion:* Florinda Mintz; *Rights & Permissions:* Teresa Cillo; *Imports/Exports:* Alejandro Luis Calegari
Branch Off: Moreno 3201, Buenos Aires Tel: 936498
Subjects: Anthropology, Architecture and Urbanism, Arts, Cinematography and Theatre, Demography, Ecology, Economics, Education, Philosophy, Psychology, Management, Technology, Sciences, Social & Political Sciences, Novels, Fiction & Poetry
Founded: 1975

Editorial **Troquel** SA, San José 157, 1076 Buenos Aires Tel: 380118/380349 Cable Add: Troquelsa
President: María A C de Ressia; *Sales Manager:* Oscar Gonzalez
Subjects: General Literature, Technology, Textbooks
Founded: 1954
ISBN Publisher's Prefix: 950-16

Turismo Editorial*, Corrientes 369, Buenos Aires

Turner Ediciones SRL*, Alsina 1535 — 8° piso of 803, 1088 Buenos Aires Tel: 466477
Man Dir: Mary C Turner
Subjects: Reference, Bibliography

Javier **Vergara** Editor SA, San Martin 969 6° piso, 1004 Buenos Aires Tel: 3112890/3117335/3113248 Telex: 18352 Trexa
President: Javier Vergara; *Rights:* Gabriela Cruz de Vergara
Branch Offs: Fernando Agulló 22, Bajos, Barcelona 21, Spain; Ave Cuauhtemoc 1100, México DF, Mexico; Aldunate 484, Santiago, Chile
Subjects: General Fiction, Non-fiction, Biography, Juveniles
1981: 70 titles *Founded:* 1975

Victor P de **Zavalía**, Editor, Alberti 835, 1223 Buenos Aires Tel: 9421274/9423046
Man Dir: Ricardo L de Zavalía; *Sales Dir:* Araceli L de Zavalía
Subject: Law
1981: 3 titles *1982:* 5 titles *Founded:* 1950
ISBN Publisher's Prefix: 950-572

Literary Agents

International Editors' Co*, Nicolás Costa, Cabildo 1156, Buenos Aires Tel: 7844613
Cable Add: Lifeplay
Also office in Spain (qv)

Lawrence **Smith**, Ave de los Incas 3110, 1426 Buenos Aires Tel: 5525012 Cable Add: Litagent Baires
President: Lawrence Smith

Specialize in Book, Serial and Performing Rights in Spanish and Portuguese languages worldwide

Book Clubs

Círculo de Lectores SA, Ave Belgrano 1370 — 1° y 2°, 1093 Buenos Aires Tel: 389091-5 Cable Add: Cilec Telex: 18212 Calar
Owned by: Verlagsgruppe Bertelsmann GmbH, Federal Republic of Germany (qv)
Founded: 1971

Club 'El **Libro** del Mes', Alsina 2041, 1090 Buenos Aires
Members: 25,000
Owned by: Emecé Editores SA (qv)
Founded: 1968

Major Booksellers

Librerías **A B C** SA*, Ave Córdoba 685, 1054 Buenos Aires
Also: Avda Libertador 13777, Martinez, 1646 Buenos Aires

American Books*, Tucumán 994 — 1°, Buenos Aires Tel: 353704

El **Ateneo**, Florida 340, 1005 Buenos Aires Tel: 466801
Manager: Ing Jorge Letemendia
Also Publisher (qv)

Bias Editora (Libros Jurídicos), Lavalle 1294, 1048 Buenos Aires Tel: 354161
Owned by: Bias Editora (qv)

Librería **Ciudad Educativa** SA (Antigua Librería del Colegio)*, Alsina 500, 1087 Buenos Aires
Owned by: Ed Cid Editor SRL (qv)

Distribuidora **Cuspide**, Suipacha 764, 1008 Buenos Aires Tel: 3921727/3928868/3927434
Manager: Joaquín Gil Paricio

Librería **Española** SCA, Florida 943, 1005 Buenos Aires Tel: 3123214/3125850

Librerías **Fausto**, Ave Corrientes 1311, 1043 Buenos Aires Tel: 401222
Manager: Rafael Pedro Zorrilla
Also: Ave Santa Fé 1715, 1060 Buenos Aires Tel: 412708
Owned by: Ediciones Librerías Fausto (qv)

Librería 'Martín **Fierro**'*, Ave Corrientes 1264, 1043 Buenos Aires Tel: 350444
Owned by: Ediciones Librerías Fausto (qv)

Ediciones **Garriga** Argentinas SA*, Talcahuano 897, Buenos Aires Tel: 443562

Librería Alfa **Graziano***, Sarmiento 1343, 1041 Buenos Aires Tel: 495349
Owned by: Librería y Editorial Alfa Graziano SACI (qv)

Librería **Hachette**, Rivadavia 739, 1002 Buenos Aires Tel: 348481 Cable Add: Aglibrairi Baires Telex: 17479 Hacba Ar
Also Publisher (qv)

Carlos **Hirsch** SRL, Florida 165, Galería Güemes — 4° piso, 1333 Buenos Aires Tel: 332391/331787/307122 Cable Add: Hirsch Baires
Managers: Leandro Moreiras, Mónica Bustos

Librería **Huemul** SA, Ave Santa Fe 2237, 1123 Buenos Aires Tel: 831666
Manager: Carlos L Sánchez
Also Publisher (qv)

Librería **Kier**, Ave Santa Fe 1260, 1059 Buenos Aires Tel: 410507/418243
Owned by: Editorial Kier SACIFI (qv)

Librerías **MacKern** SA*, Lavalle 1765, Buenos Aires Tel: 460737

H F **Martínez** de Murguía SAC y E*, Ave Córdoba 2270, Buenos Aires Tel: 486173
President: Agustín T Aparicio

Librería **Norte***, Las Heras 2225, Buenos Aires Tel: 843944

Nueva Visión*, Viamonte 500, Buenos Aires Tel: 326434

Librería General de Tomas **Pardo***, Maipú 618, Buenos Aires Tel: 3920496

Pigmalión*, Corrientes 515, Buenos Aires Tel: 494621

Librerías **Premier***, Corrientes 1583, Talcahuano 459, Callao 1180, Buenos Aires

Librería **Rodríguez***, Sarmiento 835, Buenos Aires Tel: 358125
Also Publisher (qv)

Librería **Ross***, Córdoba 1347, Rosario Tel: 65378

Librería **Santa Fe**, Santa Fe 2386, 1123 Buenos Aires Tel: 835746
Also: Santa Fe 2928, 1125 Buenos Aires Tel: 8219442
Importers

Librería **Sarmiento***, Libertad 1214-20, 1012 Buenos Aires Tel: 414792
Managers: Alejandro Orloff, Enrique Orloff

Tres Américas Libros, Alsina 722, 1087 Buenos Aires Tel: 339072/339082 Telex: 18593 Tresa Ar
President: Isay Klasse

Major Libraries

Biblioteca del **Banco** Central de la República Argentina*, Reconquista 266, Buenos Aires
Library of the Central Bank

Biblioteca **Nacional***, México 564, 1097 Buenos Aires Tel: 347370

Biblioteca **Nacional** de Maestros*, Pizzurno 935, Buenos Aires
National Teachers' Library

Biblioteca **Publico** Central*, Calle 47, No 510, La Plata

Biblioteca del **Congreso** de la Nación*, Rivadavia 1850, Buenos Aires
National Library of Congress

Biblioteca **Lincoln***, Florida 935, Buenos Aires

Biblioteca Pública Gratuita de 'La **Prensa**'*, Rivadavia 552, Buenos Aires

Instituto Bibliotecológico, **Universidad de Buenos Aires**, Casilla de Correo 901, 1000 Buenos Aires (Located at: Azcuénaga 280, Buenos Aires) Telex: 18694 Abuba AR

Biblioteca de la **Universidad del Salvador***, Callao 542, Buenos Aires

Biblioteca Mayor de la **Universidad Nacional de Córdoba**, Casilla de Correo 63, 5000 Córdoba (Located at: Calle Obispo Trejo y Sanabria 242, Córdoba) Tel: 46323 Telex: 51822 BUCOR-Ar
Principal Library of the National University of Córdoba
Dir: Professor Joaquín García
Publications: Informativo (irregular), Monographs

Biblioteca Pública de la **Universidad Nacional de La Plata**, Plaza Rocha 137, La Plata, 1900 Provincia de Buenos Aires
Tel: 214109 Telex: 31151 Bulapar
Dir: Dr Carlos J Tejo
Publications: Bulletin *Informaciones*

ARGENTINA — AUSTRALIA 9

Library Associations

A B G R A (Asociación de Bibliotecarios Graduados de la República Argentina)*, Casilla de Correo 68 — suc 1, 1401 Ciudad de Buenos Aires
Association of Graduate Librarians of Argentina
President: Iris Rossi; *Executive Secretary:* Nidia Chiesa
Publications: Documentos Ocasionales, Reuniones Nacionales de Bibliotecarios (Documentos de Base; Actas); Memoria annual, *Bibliotecologia y Documentacion, Boletín Informativo*

Asociación Argentina de Bibliotecas y Centros de Información Científicos y Tecnicos*, Santa Fe 1145, Buenos Aires
Tel: 411405
Executive Secretary: Olga E Veronelli

Asociación de Ex-Alumnos de la Escuela Nacional de Bibliotecarios*, c/o Biblioteca Nacional, México 564, Buenos Aires

Dirección de **Bibliotecas Públicas** Municipales, Talcahuano 1261, Buenos Aires

Centro De Documentación Bibliotecológica, Universidad Nacional del Sur, Ave Alem 1253, Bahía Blanca
Centre for Library Science Documentation
Dir: Atilio Peralta
Publications: Bibliografía Bibliotecológica Argentina, Quien es Quien en la Bibliotecología Argentina, Guía de las Bibliotecas Universitarias Argentinas, Documentacion Bibliotecologica, Indices de Revistas de Bibliotecología

Colegio de Bibliotecarios de la Provincia de Buenos Aires, Calle 48 — No 633 — piso 3 of 315, 1900 La Plata

Instituto de Bibliográfia del Ministerio de Educación de la Provincia de Buenos Aires*, Calle 47, No 510, 6 piso, 1900 La Plata
Dir: María del Carmen Crespi de Bustos
Publications: Bibliografía Argentina de Historia, Boletín de Información Bibliográfica

Library Reference Books and Journals

Books

Bibliografía Bibliotecológica Argentina (Argentine Library Science Bibliography), Centre for Library Science Documentation, Ave Alem 1253, Bahía Blanca

Guía de las Bibliotecas Universitarias Argentinas (Guide to Argentine University Libraries), Centre for Library Science Documentation, Ave Alem 1253, Bahía Blanca

Journal

Boletín Informativo (Information Bulletin), Association of Graduate Librarians of Argentina, Casilla de Correo 68 — suc 1, 1401 Ciudad de Buenos Aires

Literary Associations and Societies

Academia Argentina de Letras*, Sánchez de Bustamante 2663, Buenos Aires
Secretary: Juan Carlos Ghiano
Publications: Boletín de la Academia Argentina de Letras (quarterly)
Library Publications: Serie de Clásicos Argentinos, Serie de Estudios Académicos, Serie de Discursos Académicos, Serie de Acuerdos acerca del Idioma, Boletín, Serie Estudios Lingüísticos y Filológicos

Club de Poetas*, Casilla de Correo 881, 1000 Buenos Aires
Secretary: Carlos Paz
Publications include: Anuario de Poetas Contemporaneos

The **Dickens** Fellowship*, Basavilbaso 12A, Buenos Aires
Honarary Secretary: Miguel Alfredo Olivera

Instituto de Literatura, Calle 47, No 625, La Plata
Dir: Arturo Cambours
Publications: Investigaciones, Boletín

P E N Club International de Argentina, Diagonal R Sáenz Pena 570 – piso 10°, 1035-Buenos Aires
Secretaries: Norberto Silvetti Paz, Carlos Villafuerte
Publications: Boletín and books

Literary Periodicals

Boletín, Argentine Academy of Letters, Sánchez de Bustamante 2663, Buenos Aires

Boletín, Association of Argentine Writers, Uruguay 1371, 1016 Buenos Aires

Comentario, Tucuman 2137 y San Martin 663, Buenos Aires

Criterio, Alsina 840, Buenos Aires

Davar, Sociedad Hebraica Argentina, Sarmiento 2233, Buenos Aires

Histonium, Paraná 464, Buenos Aires

Igitur Revista Literaria, Republica de Israel 115, Córdoba

Sur, Viamonte 494, 8° piso, Buenos Aires

Literary Prizes

Argentine National Prize for Literature*
For best works of prose and poetry. Awarded every three years. Enquiries to Argentinian Ministry of Education and Culture, General Directorate of Culture, Ave Alvear 1630, Buenos Aires

Alfredo A **Bianchi** Essay Prize*
For the best scholarly essay on any subject. Awarded annually. Enquiries to Association of Argentine Writers, Uruguay 1371, 1016 Buenos Aires

Buenos Aires Literary Prizes*
For the best works written or published during the year in Buenos Aires. Awards are given for fiction; essay (including biography and literary criticism); poetry. Awarded annually. Enquiries to Buenos Aires Municipality, Secretariat of Culture and Social Activities, Ave de Mayo 525, Buenos Aires

Carlos **Casavalle** Prize*
Awarded in turn for the best book published in Argentina in the following categories: fiction; poetry and drama; essay, including scientific writing. Awarded annually. Enquiries to Argentine Book Association, Ave Belgrano 1580 - 6° piso, 1093 Buenos Aires

Premio **Emecé** Annual Prize
Established 1954. For the best novel or book of short stories in the Spanish language by an unpublished writer. 1982-83 award to Amalia M Raffo for *El angel verde*. Enquiries to Emecé Editores SA, Carlos Pellegrini 1069 - 9° piso, 1009 Buenos Aires

First Book Prize*
For the first literary work written by an author under 30. Awarded annually. Enquiries to Argentine Book Association, Ave Belgrano 1850 - 6° piso, 1093 Buenos Aires

Kraft Prize*
For the best unpublished novel, particularly by young and unknown authors. Awarded biennially. Enquiries to Guillermo Kraft Publishing Ltd, Moreno 872, Buenos Aires

Fernando **Moreno** Poetry Prize*
For outstanding work in Poetry. Enquiries to Association of Argentine Writers, Uruguay 1371, 1016 Buenos Aires

Premio de 'La **Nación**' Prize*
Given by the newspaper 'La Nación' for different types of literature. Enquiries to 'La Nación', Florida 343/San Martin, Buenos Aires CF

Pablo **Rojas** Paz Prize*
For the best unpublished biography. Enquiries to Association of Argentine Writers, Uruguay 1371, 1016 Buenos Aires

Ricardo **Rojas** Prize*
For prose work (imaginative writing, criticism, essay). Awarded biennially. Enquiries to Buenos Aires Municipality, Secretariat of Culture and Social Activities, Ave de Mayo 525, Buenos Aires

Medalla de Oro de la **S A D E** (Sociedad Argentina de Escritores)*
Annual prize for the total output of an author. Enquiries to Association of Argentine Writers, Uruguay 1371, 1016 Buenos Aires

Sarmiento Prize*
For the best book of prose written during the year. Awarded annually. Enquiries to Association of Argentine Writers, Uruguay 1371, 1016 Buenos Aires

Australia

General Information

Language: English
Religion: Predominantly Protestant
Population: 14.2 million
Bank Hours: 1000-1500 Monday-Thursday; 1000-1700 Friday
Shop Hours: 0900-1700 Monday-Friday; usually 0900-1200 Saturday
Currency: 100 cents = 1 Australian dollar
Export/Import Information: No tariffs on books. Most books, especially of literary or educational nature, free of sales tax. No import licences for books; no seditious literature permitted
Copyright: UCC, Berne (see International section)

Book Trade Organizations

Association of Australian University Presses, c/o New South Wales University Press, PO Box 1, Kensington, NSW 2033 Tel: (02) 6623503 Telex: AA 26054
President: Douglas S Howie
Incorporating Australian National University Press, Melbourne University Press, Sydney University Press, University of Queensland Press, University of Western Australia Press, University of New South

Wales Press (qqv under Publishers), Deakin University Press
Publication: Scholarly Books in Australia (annual bibliography)

Australian Book Publishers Association, 161 Clarence St, Sydney, NSW 2000 Tel: (02) 295422
Dir: Sandra Forbes
Publication: Directory of Members

Australian Booksellers Association, Correspondence Book House, 199 Cardigan St, Carlton, Victoria 3053 Tel: (03) 3478121
The ABA is a Federal Association with branches in every State
Federal Dir: Terry Cheshire

Australian Copyright Council, 22 Alfred St, Milsons Point, NSW 2061 Tel: (02) 921151
Chairman: G C O'Donnell; *Executive Officer:* Peter Banki

Australian Society of Indexers, GPO Box 1251L, Melbourne, Victoria 3001
Secretary: Mrs Jennifer Challis
Affiliated with The Society of Indexers, UK (qv)
Publication: Australian Society of Indexers' Newsletter (quarterly)

Australian Standard Book Numbering Agency, National Library of Australia, Parkes Pl, Canberra, ACT 2600 Tel: (062) 621431 Cable Add: Natlibaust Telex: 62100
Administrator: Mrs Cornel Platzer

Book Trade Group (Queensland)*, Barker, Conlan and Ferret Pty Ltd, Brisbane, Queensland 4000

Children's Book Council of Australia, PO Box 420, Dickson, ACT 2602
President: Stephen Williams
Branches in New South Wales, Queensland, South Australia, Tasmania, Victoria, Western Australia
Publication: Reading Time (quarterly)

Christian Bookselling Association of Australia, 47 Gawler Place, Adelaide, South Australia 5000
Secretary: Laurie Russell

Copyright Agency Ltd*, PO Box 440, Milsons Point, NSW 2061 (Located at: Suite 301, 30 Glen St, Milsons Point) Tel: 4362820

I B I S Information Services Ltd, PO Box 995, Sydney, NSW 2001 Tel: (02) 2902844 Telex: 27585
Secretary: Mark Melling

Literature Board of the Australia Council, PO Box 302, 168 Walker St, North Sydney, NSW 2060 Tel: 9233333 Telex: 26023
Director: Dr Michael Costigan

National Book Council, 199 Cardigan St, Carlton, Victoria 3053
Chairman: S Murray-Smith

New South Wales Booksellers' Association, PO Box Q87, Sydney, NSW 2000 (Located at: 66 King St, Sydney) Tel: 279471
Secretary: Robyn Quill

Public Lending Right Scheme, Department of Home Affairs and Environment, Box 812, PO North Sydney, NSW 2060 (Located at: 5th Fl, Northside Gdns, 168 Walker St, North Sydney) Tel: (02) 9233379 Cable Add: Ozart Sydney Telex: 26023
Administrator, PLR: A N Johnson

Society of Editors, c/o PO Box 176, Carlton South, Victoria 3053 Tel: (03) 3872650
Secretary: John Bangsund
Publications: The Society of Editors Newsletter (monthly), *Register of Freelance Publishing Services* (annual)

Society of Women Writers, PO Box 197, Greenacres, SA 5086
Hon Secretary: Helen Baker
The Society is served by a changing State Federal Committee which every two years is nominated by a State branch

Standard Book Numbering Agency, see Australian Standard Book Numbering Agency

Tasmanian Booksellers' Association*, GPO Box 170, Launceston, Tasmania 7250
President: R F Tilley
Secretary: Y G Tilley

United States Book Association, PO Box 300, North Ryde, NSW 2113
Secretary: F S Symes

Western Australian Booksellers' Association, c/o Dorringtons Bookshop, 308 Great Eastern Highway, Midland, WA 6056
President: J Dorrington

Book Trade Reference Books and Journals

Books

Australian and Pacific Book Prices Current, OP Books Pty Ltd, PO Box 591, Brookvale, NSW 2100

Australian Book Publishers' Association: Guide to Book Outlets in Australia, Meldrum, Johnston and Weston, 163 Clarence St, Sydney, NSW 2000

Australian Books in Print, D W Thorpe Pty Ltd, 384 Spencer St, Melbourne, Victoria 3003

Books Australia (annual catalogue), PO Box 41, Glebe, NSW 2037

Current Australian Serials; a select list, National Library of Australia, Parkes Pl, Canberra, ACT 2600

Directory of Australian Booksellers, Australian Book Trade Advisory Committee, 163 Clarence St, Sydney, NSW

Scholarly Books in Australia (annual bibliography), Association of Australian University Presses, c/o New South Wales University Press, PO Box 1, Kensington, NSW 2033

Journals

The Australian Author (quarterly), Australian Society of Authors Ltd, 22 Alfred St, Milsons Point, NSW 2061

Australian Book Review, 46 Porter St, Prahran, Victoria 3181

Australian Books, National Library of Australia, Parkes Pl, Canberra, ACT 2600

Australian Bookseller & Publisher, D W Thorpe Pty Ltd, 384 Spencer St, Melbourne, Victoria 3003

Australian Government Publications (quarterly), National Library of Australia, Parkes Pl, Canberra, ACT 2600

Australian National Bibliography (twice monthly with annual cumulation), National Library of Australia, Parkes Pl, Canberra, ACT 2600

Australian Society of Indexers Newsletter (quarterly), Australian Society of Indexers, GPO Box 1251L, Melbourne, Victoria 3001

The Indexer, c/o Hazel K Bell, 139 The Ryde, Hatfield, Herts AL9 5DP, UK (Journal of Australian, American and British Societies of Indexers)

Weekly Book Newsletter, D W Thorpe Pty Ltd, 384 Spencer St, Melbourne, Victoria 3003

Publishers

A D I S Health Science Press+, PO Box 132, Balgowlah, NSW 2093 (Located at: 404 Sydney Rd, Balgowlah)
Tel: (02) 9492022 Telex: Adis AA25868
Executive Chairman: W W Hughes; *Man Dir and Rights & Permissions:* Tom MacLennan; *Editorial Dir:* Pamela Petty
Parent Company: ADIS Press Australasia Pty Ltd (qv)
Subjects: Medical and Allied Health
ISBN Publisher's Prefix: 0-86792

A D I S Press Australasia Pty Ltd, PO Box 132, Balgowlah, NSW 2093 (Located at: 404 Sydney Road, Balgowlah) Tel: (02) 9492022 Cable Add: Adinfo Sydney Telex: Adis AA25868
Chief Editorial Office: ADIS Press Ltd, 15 Rawene Rd, PO Box 34-030, Birkenhead, Auckland 10, New Zealand Tel: 486125 Telex: Adis NZ21334
Man Dir: Graeme S Avery; *Editor-in-Chief:* Rennie C Heel
Subsidiary Company: ADIS Health Science Press (qv)
Associate Companies: ADIS Press Publications Ltd, Hong Kong (qv); ADIS Press International Inc, 401 South State St, Newtown, Pa 18940, USA
Subject: Medicine
1982: 15 titles *Founded:* 1960
ISBN Publisher's Prefixes: 0-9599827, 0-909337

A N Z, an imprint of Australia & New Zealand Book Co Pty Ltd (qv)

A P C O L, an imprint of Alternative Publishing Co-operative Ltd (qv)

Addison-Wesley Publishing Co, A1/6-8 Byfield St, North Ryde, NSW 2113 Tel: (02) 8882733 Cable Add: Adiwes Sydney Telex: 71919
General Manager, Editorial and Rights & Permissions: M S Dane; *Marketing and Sales:* John Munro (college, school, juveniles and general)
Parent Company: Addison-Wesley Publishing Company, Reading, Mass, USA
Associate Company: Addison-Wesley Publishers Ltd, UK (qv for other associates)
Subjects: Educational Books, Scientific and Technical Books, Juveniles
1981: 9 titles

Albatross Books, PO Box 320, Sutherland, NSW 2232 (Located at: Unit 3, 115 Bath Rd, Kirrawee, NSW 2232) Tel: (02) 5211515 Telex: AA 70808 Numcon
Chief Executive: John Waterhouse; *Sales:* Kevin Goddard
Subject: Religion: Illustrated children's books, Teenage and adult fiction, Bible reference books, General adult paperbacks
1981: 23 titles *1982:* 22 titles *Founded:* 1980
ISBN Publisher's Prefix: 0-86760

Algona Publications Pty Ltd, 16 Charles St, Northcote, Victoria 3070 Tel: 4813337
Chief Executives: John R Brownlie, Gloria E Harman
Subjects: Australian flora, fauna, history and landscape for travellers
Founded: 1970
ISBN Publisher's Prefix: 0-909594

Allara Publishing*, 47 Deakin St, East Bentleigh 3165
ISBN Publisher's Prefix: 0-85887

George Allen & Unwin Australia Pty Ltd,
PO Box 764, North Sydney, NSW 2065 Tel:
9226399 Cable Add: Deucalion Sydney
Telex: 24331 Gaua
Man Dir: P A Gallagher; *Editorial:* John
Iremonger; *Sales:* Roger Ward; *Production:*
Rhonda Black; *Publicity:* Maggie Hamilton
Parent Company: George Allen & Unwin
(Publishers) Ltd, UK (qv)
Associate Company: Allen & Unwin Inc, 9
Winchester Terrace, Winchester, Mass
01890, USA
Branch Off: 156 Collins St, Melbourne,
Victoria 3000
Subjects: Academic, Social Science, General
Non-fiction
Founded: 1976
ISBN Publisher's Prefix: 0-86861

Alpha Books*, c/o Library of Australian
History, 17 Mitchell St, North Sydney, NSW
2060 Tel: (02) 9295087
Parent Company: Library of Australian
History

Alternative Publishing Co-operative Ltd, 26
Atkinson St, Arncliffe, NSW 2205 Tel: (02)
2113837/591937
Chairman: Michael Law; *Editorial, Sales,
Production, Publicity, Rights & Permissions:*
D K Cleaver
Imprint: APCOL
Subjects: Reference, High-priced
Paperbacks, Psychology, University &
Secondary Textbooks, History, Political
Science, Sociology, Economics
1981: 12 titles *Founded:* 1975

And/or, an imprint of Wild & Woolley Pty
Ltd (qv)

Angus & Robertson/Bay Books, PO Box
290, North Ryde, NSW 2113 (Located at:
Unit 4, 31 Waterloo Rd, North Ryde Tel:
(02) 8872233 Cable Add: Fragment,
Sydney Telex: 26452
Chief Executive: Richard Walsh; *Publishing
Manager:* Jennifer Rowe; *Marketing
Manager:* Peter Ackroyd; *Production
Manager:* Barry Smith; *Publicity Manager:*
Phyllida FitzGerald; *Rights & Permissions:*
Gwenda Jarred
Subsidiary Company: Angus & Robertson
(UK) Ltd, UK (qv)
Subjects: General Fiction, Belles Lettres,
Poetry, Biography, History, How-to, Art,
Reference, Juveniles, Low- & High-Priced
Paperbacks, Medicine, Psychology, General
& Social Science, University
1981: 223 titles *1982:* 211 titles *Founded:*
1884
ISBN Publisher's Prefix: 0-207

Ansay Pty Ltd, PO Box 90, 2040 Leichardt,
NSW (Located at: 19-25 Beeson St,
Leichhardt 1) Tel: 5602044 Cable Add:
Cowboy Sydney
Man Dir: Philip Lindsay; *Editorial,
Production:* H E Lindsay; *Sales, Rights &
Permissions:* P S Lindsay; *Publicity:* C Rijks
Parent Companies: A L Lindsay & Co Pty
Ltd, Lindsays Leichardt Pty Ltd
Imprint: Dollar Books
Subjects: Fiction, Educational
Founded: 1972
ISBN Publisher's Prefix: 0-909245

Edward Arnold (Australia) Pty Ltd, PO Box
234, Caulfield East, Victoria 3145 (Located
at: 80 Waverley Rd, Caulfield East) Tel:
(03) 5722211 Cable Add: Edarnold Telex:
35974 AA
Man Dir: Robert J Blackmore; *Editorial and
Permissions:* Annette J Carter; *Sales:* Terry
M Coyle
Parent Company: Edward Arnold
(Publishers) Ltd, UK (qv)
Subjects: All categories, specializing in
University and Secondary Textbooks

Founded: 1966, changed name 1975
ISBN Publisher's Prefix: 0-7131

Ashton Scholastic, PO Box 579, Gosford,
NSW 2250 Tel: (043) 283555 Cable Add:
Tonash Sydney Telex: 24881
Shipping Add: Railway Crescent, Lisarow,
via Gosford
Man Dir: Ken A Jolly; *Publishing, Rights &
Permissions:* Ruth A Hamilton; *Marketing
Manager:* Leonie M Sweeney; *National Sales
Co-ordinator:* Gavin S Shepherd
Parent Company: Scholastic Inc, 730
Broadway, New York, NY 10003, USA
Imprints: Classroom Magazine, Four Winds
Press, Microzine, Scholastic, Twistaplot,
Vagabond, Wildfire, Windswept, Wizware
Branch Offs: 260 Auburn Road, Hawthorn,
Victoria 3122; 5th Floor, Teachers Bldg, 495
Boundary St, Spring Hill, Queensland 4000;
254 Halifax St, Adelaide, South Australia
5000; 2nd Floor, Teachers Union Bldg, 150-
152 Adelaide Terrace, Perth, WA 6000
Subjects: Juveniles, Paperbacks, Secondary
& Primary Textbooks, Educational
Materials
Book Clubs: Arrow; Lucky; Star; Teachers
Bookshelf; Teenage
Bookshop: Oldmeadow Booksellers
(Australia) Pty Ltd, 18 Helen St, West
Heidelberg, Victoria 3081
1981: 19 titles *Founded:* 1968
ISBN Publisher's Prefix: 0-86896

Associated Book Publishers (Aust) Ltd,
44-50 Waterloo Rd, North Ryde, NSW
2113 Tel: 8870177 Cable Add: Asbook
Sydney
Man Dir: W Mackarell; *Legal Division Dir:*
D S Lees; *Trade Division Manager:* K W
Shearman
Parent Company: Associated Book
Publishers PLC, UK (qv)
Subsidiary Companies: The Law Book Co
Ltd (qv); Methuen Australia Pty Ltd (qv);
Methuen LBC Ltd; Associated Book
Publishers (NZ) Ltd, New Zealand (qv)
Branch Offs: 15 Burwood Rd, Hawthorn,
Victoria; IOOF House, Cnr Allenby and
Leichhardt Sts, North Brisbane, Queensland
4000; 6 Sherwood Court, Perth, WA 6000
Subjects: See subsidiary companies

Aurora Press, an imprint of Chatto, Bodley
Head & Jonathan Cape Australia Pty Ltd
(qv)

Australasian Publishing Co Pty Ltd, Corner
Bridge Rd and Jersey St, Hornsby, NSW
2077 Tel: 4762000 Cable Add: Publishing
Hornsby Telex: AA23274
Chairman: A S M Harrap; *Man Dir:* G A
Rutherford; *Sales Dir:* J E Bullivant;
Publicity Dir and Rights & Permissions:
John Cody; *Distribution Dir:* K A Harrap
Subsidiary Company: Chatto, Bodley Head
& Jonathan Cape Australia Pty Ltd (qv)
Branch Offs: 83 Glen Eira Rd, Ripponlea,
Victoria 3183; 6 Nurran St, Mt Gravatt,
Queensland 3122; 33 Pirie St, Adelaide,
South Australia 5000
Subjects: General Fiction, Belles Lettres,
Juveniles, Education, General Science
ISBN Publisher's Prefix: 0-900882

Australia & New Zealand Book Co Pty
Ltd*, PO Box 459, Brookvale, NSW 2100
(Located at: 10 Aquatic Drive, Frenchs
Forest, NSW 2086) Tel: (02) 4524411 Cable
Add: Anzbook Sydney Telex: 70727 AA
Chairman: Geoffrey M King; *Man Dir,
Rights & Permissions:* G Ross King;
Publishing Dir: Peter Benjamin
Parent Company: G M King Investments
Pty Ltd
Subsidiary Company: Australian & New
Zealand Editions Ltd
Imprint: ANZ

Branch Offs: Brisbane and Melbourne,
Australia; Auckland, New Zealand (qv)
Subjects: Science, Technical, Medical,
General Non-fiction, Arts and Crafts, Sports
Founded: 1964
ISBN Publisher's Prefix: 0-85552

Australian Academy of Science, GPO Box
783, Canberra, ACT 2601 Tel: (062) 486011
Cable Add: Acscican Telex: 62406 Acsci
Executive Secretary: H A W Southon;
*Publications Officer, Sales and Rights &
Permissions:* C J Dixon
Branch Off: 191 Royal Parade, Parkville,
Melbourne, Victoria 3000
Subjects: High-quality educational, academic
and scholastic books on a wide range of
disciplines
Founded: 1956
ISBN Publisher's Prefix: 0-85847

The **Australian Council** for Educational
Research Ltd, PO Box 210, Hawthorn,
Victoria 3122 (Located at: Radford House,
Frederick St, Hawthorn) Tel: 8181271
Cable Add: Aceres
Man Dir: Dr J P Keeves; *Sales Dir:* E V
Ivan; *Publicity:* P Jeffery; *Editorial,
Production, Rights & Permissions:* Don
Maguire
Subjects: Education, Textbooks,
Educational materials
Bookshop: At above address
Founded: 1930
ISBN Publisher's Prefix: 0-85563

Australian Encyclopaedia Pty Ltd, see The
Grolier Society of Australia Pty Ltd

Australian Government Publishing Service,
GPO Box 84, Canberra, ACT 2601 (Located
at: 109 Canberra Ave, Griffith, ACT 2603)
Tel: (062) 954711 Telex: AA62013
Warehouse & Shipping Add: Wentworth
Ave, Kingston, ACT 2604
Chief Executive: J L Leonard; *Government
Printer:* C J Thompson; *Director,
Publishing, Rights & Permissions:* B P
Shurman; *Editorial:* M J Greenane;
Production: J A Wainwright; *Sales,
Publicity:* L J Gwyther
Parent Company: Branch of the Department
of Administrative Services
Subjects: Australian Government
Publications. Also sales agent for
publications of Canadian Government; New
Zealand Government Printer; HMSO (UK);
FAO, UNESCO, WHO (United Nations)
Bookshops: 12 Pirie Street, Adelaide; 294
Adelaide Street, Brisbane; 70 Alinga St,
Canberra; 162 Macquarie Street, Hobart;
347 Swanston Street, Melbourne; 200 St
George's Terrace, Perth; 309 Pitt Street,
Sydney
1981: approx 4029 *Founded:* 1970
ISBN Publisher's Prefix: 0-642

Australian Institute of Aboriginal Studies,
PO Box 553, Canberra City 2601 Tel: (062)
461111 Cable Add: Abinst
Warehouse: Acton House, Acton, ACT 2601
Principal: Eric Willmot; *Executive Officer,
Publications and Rights & Permissions:* Jill
Mendham
Subjects: Anthropology, Archaeology,
Ethnology, Ethnomusicology, Linguistics,
Human Biology, Prehistory, Material
culture, Aboriginal art, Education
ISBN Publisher's Prefix: 0-85575

Australian Institute of Criminology*, PO
Box 28, Woden, ACT 2606 (Located at:
10-18 Colbee Court, Phillip, ACT 2606) Tel:
822111 Cable Add: Austcrim
Dir: William Clifford; *Editorial:* Jack
Sandry
Subject: Criminology
Founded: 1976
ISBN Publisher's Prefix: 0-642

Australian National Gallery+, PO Box 1150, Canberra, ACT 2601 Tel: (062) 712411 Cable Add: ANG Canberra Telex: AA 61500
Head of Publications: Alan R Dodge; *Editorial*: Bruce Semler; *Sales*: Manfred Claasz; *Production*: Alistair Hay; *Publicity*: Inga Lidums; *Rights & Permissions*: Robyn Worsnop
Orders to: GPO Box 15, Canberra, ACT 2601
Subjects: Art (related to the collection of the Australian National Gallery)
Bookshops: The Gallery Shop (at above main address)
1982: 9 titles *Founded*: 1982
ISBN Publisher's Prefix: 0-642

Australian National University Press, GPO Box 4, Canberra, ACT 2601 Tel: (062) 492812 Cable Add: Natuniv Press, Canberra Tel: 62760 AA
Warehouse: Old Administration Area, Australian National University, Canberra, ACT
Dir and Sales, Publicity & Advertising: D Bradmore; *Editor and Rights & Permissions*: D Cox
Subjects: Belles Lettres, Poetry, Biography, Geography, History, Reference, Social Science, Earth Sciences, University Textbooks, High-priced Paperbacks
1981: 83 titles *Founded*: 1965
ISBN Publisher's Prefix: 0-7081

Australian Universities Press Pty Ltd*, Offset House, 169-171 Philip St, Waterloo, NSW 2017 Tel: (02) 695633/4
Man Dir: R G Hackett
Subjects: Cookery Books, Australiana, Children's Books
ISBN Publisher's Prefix: 0-7249

S John **Bacon** Pty Ltd, 13 Windsor Ave, PO Box 345, Mt Waverley, Victoria 3149 Tel: (03) 2773944 Cable Add: Interbac, Melbourne
Dirs: Mary Bacon, Joan Diemar, Neville Cuthbert; *Editorial*: Bert Eadon; *Sales & Marketing*: Joan Helmore
Subsidiary Company: Lantern House Pty Ltd
Subjects: Theology, Christian Education, Devotional Music, Primary and Secondary Educational Books and Aids, Children's Books
Founded: 1938
ISBN Publisher's Prefix: 0-85579

Bantam, an imprint of Transworld Publishers (Australia) Pty Ltd (qv)

Bay Books, see Angus & Robertson

Blackwell Scientific Publications (Australia) Pty Ltd, 99 Barry St, Carlton, Victoria 3053 Tel: (03) 3470019 Cable Add: Blackwell Melbourne
Chief Executive: M Robertson
Parent Company: Blackwell Scientific Publications Ltd, UK (qv)
Subsidiary Company: Blackwell Scientific Book Distributors Pty Ltd, 31 Advantage Rd, Highett, Victoria 3190
Subjects: Medicine; Life, Earth and Computer Sciences
1982: 2 titles *Founded*: 1981
ISBN Publisher's Prefix: 0-86793

Bookwise (Australia) Pty Ltd*, 101 Argus St, Cheltenham, Victoria 3192 Tel: (03) 5844109 Cable Add: Bookwise Melbourne Telex: 33626 AA Scholib
Man Dir: John Redrup; *Editorial, Sales, Production, Publicity and Rights & Permissions*: Graeme Venn
Branch Off: 104 Sussex St, Sydney, NSW 2000
Subjects: Oriental Arts, Social Sciences, Languages, Cooking and Quality Non-fiction generally, Travel Guides
Founded: 1957
Miscellaneous: Firm is also a wholesale distributor
ISBN Publisher's Prefix: 0-908054

Boolarong Publications, PO Box 106, Spring Hill, Queensland 4000 (Located at: 24 Little Edward St, Brisbane, Queensland 4000) Tel: 2214872 Cable Add: Pressetch
Man Dir, Sales, Publicity, Rights & Permissions: L T Padman; *Editorial*: Mrs E M Bagnall; *Production*: G A Peake
Parent Company: Artists Associated Pty Ltd
Subjects: Art, Historical, Biographies, Children's Books
1981: 12 titles *1982*: 12 titles *Founded*: 1977
ISBN Publisher's Prefix: 0-908175

David **Boyce** Publishing & Associates*, PO Box Q187, Queen Victoria Bldg, Sydney, NSW 2000 (Located at: 44 Regent St, Sydney) Tel: (02) 2111096/2111962 Telex: 020 7110101
Man & Sales Dir: David Boyce; *Production*: Jan Kenyon
Subjects: Automotive Technical
Founded: 1975
ISBN Publisher's Prefix: 0-909682

Butterworths Pty Ltd, 271-273 Lane Cove Rd, North Ryde, NSW 2113 Tel: (02) 8873444 Telex: 22033
Man Dir, Sales: D J Jackson; *Editorial*: J Broadfoot; *Rights & Permissions*: S Elkins; *Production*: B Coats
Parent Company: Butterworth & Co (Publishers) Ltd, UK (qv)
Branch Offs: 233 Macquarie St, Sydney NSW 2000; 343 Little Collins St, Melbourne, Victoria 3000; Commonwealth Bank Bldg, King George Sq, Brisbane, Queensland 4000; 45 St George's Terrace, Perth, WA 6000; 1st Floor, Rechabite Chambers, 195 Victoria Square, Adelaide, SA 5000; 3rd Floor Canberra House, Canberra, ACT 2600; 6 Balmoral St, Sandy Bay, Tasmania 7005
Subjects: Law, Business, Medicine, Science, Technology, Textbooks
Bookshops: At some Branch Office addresses
1981: 40 titles *1982*: 35 titles *Founded*: 1910
ISBN Publisher's Prefix: 0-409

C S I R O (Commonwealth Scientific and Industrial Research Organization), 314 Albert St, PO Box 89, East Melbourne, Victoria 3002 Tel: (03) 4187333 Telex: AA30236
Shipping Add: 19 Rokeby St, Collingwood, Victoria 3066
Publisher: B J Walby; *Sales and Publicity*: Ros McLeod; *Production*: Paul Lynch
Subjects: Engineering, Science & Technology
Founded: 1926
ISBN Publisher's Prefix: 0-643

Cambridge University Press, 296 Beaconsfield Parade, Middle Park, Victoria 3206 Tel: 5340697 Cable Add: Cantabaust
Dir: Brian Harris
Subjects: Education, University, Secondary & Primary Textbooks
Head Office: Cambridge University Press, UK (qv)
ISBN Publisher's Prefix: 0-521

Carroll's Horwitz Publications, see Horwitz Grahame Books Pty Ltd

Cavalier Press Pty Ltd*, PO Box 5, South Yarra, Victoria 3141 (Located at: 45 Richmond Terrace, Richmond 3121) Tel: (03) 4292280 Telex: 38225 AA
Joint Executive Dirs: Josef Vondra, Geoffrey M Gold
Subjects: Australian History, Ethnic History, Multiculturalism, Multilingual books on Australiana, International Affairs
Founded: 1979
ISBN Publisher's Prefix: 0-949743

Centre Publications, PO Box 114, Saint Kilda, Melbourne, Victoria 3182 (Located at: 25 Chapel St, Saint Kilda, Melbourne 3182) Tel: (03) 510631
Man Dir: Paul Sumner
Parent Company: Yoco Pty Ltd (at above address)
Associate Companies: The Helen Vale Foundation (qv); The Yoga Education Centre (at above address)
Subjects: Education, Health
Founded: 1974

Challenge, an imprint of Sapphire Books Pty Ltd (qv)

Chatto, Bodley Head & Jonathan Cape Australia Pty Ltd, c/o Australasian Publishing Co Pty Ltd, Cnr Bridge Rd and Jersey St, Hornsby, NSW 2077 Tel: 4762000 Telex: 23274
Man Dir: John Cody
Orders to: Australasian Publishing Co Pty Ltd (at above address)
Parent Company: Australasian Publishing Co Pty Ltd (qv)
Imprint: Aurora Press
Subjects: Fiction, Non-fiction, Reference, History, Children's, Australiana
Founded: 1977

Cheshire, an imprint of Longman Cheshire Pty Ltd (qv)

Chevalier Press, PO Box 13, Kensington, NSW 2033
Publicity: Bernard Carrick

Chi Rho, an imprint of Lutheran Publishing House (qv)

Childerset Pty Ltd*, 67 Katrina St, Blackburn North, 3130 Melbourne Tel: (03) 8775121 Telex: 33571
Man Dir: Haworth H Bartram; *Sales, Publicity, Rights & Permissions*: Denise Burt; *Production*: Veronica Capper
Subjects: Juveniles, Educational Materials, Children's Picture Books, Classroom Pictures
Founded: 1970
ISBN Publisher's Prefix: 0-909404

Churchill Livingstone, an imprint of Longman Cheshire Pty Ltd (qv)

Circus Books, now Schwartz Publishing Group (Victoria) Pty Ltd (qv)

Classroom Magazine, an imprint of Ashton Scholastic (qv)

Clearway, an imprint of Sapphire Books Pty Ltd (qv)

R J **Cleary**, PO Box 939, Darlinghurst, NSW 2010 (Located at: 86 Riley St, Sydney) Cable Add: Clearpub Sydney
Man Dir: R J Cleary
Subjects: Biography, History, How-to, Reference, Juveniles, High-priced Paperbacks, Australiana, Series Books, Part-Works, Primary and Secondary Textbooks, Educational Materials, Children's Activities, Audiovisual, video, computer software, Co-editions, Special Projects
1981: 71 titles *Founded*: 1969
ISBN Publisher's Prefix: 0-85567

The **Clifford** Press, PO Box 120, Hawthorn, Victoria 3122 Tel: 810231
Shipping Add: 597 Burwood Rd, Hawthorn
Business Manager: Alma M Widdicombe
Subjects: Religion, Juveniles, Educational Materials
Founded: 1956
ISBN Publisher's Prefix: 0-85044

Cole Publications, 3 Creswick St, Hawthorn, Victoria 3122 Tel: 8185640
Man Dir: Cole Turnley
Parent Company: Alterns Pty Ltd (at above address)
Subjects: Juveniles, Technical, Humour
Founded: 1868
ISBN Publisher's Prefix: 0-909900

William **Collins** Pty Ltd+, GPO Box 476, Sydney, NSW 2001 (Located at: 55 Clarence St, Sydney) Tel: (02) 2902066 Cable Add: Folio Sydney Telex: 26292 Folio
Warehouse & Shipping Add: Yarrawa Rd, Moss Vale, NSW 2577
Chairman: K W Wilder; *Paperback Sales Dir:* A R Jollye; *Special Projects Dir, Rights & Permissions:* A S Rein; *Publisher (hardback):* Richard Smart; *Senior Editor:* Elizabeth Bradhurst; *Children's Editor:* Anne Ingram; *Publicity & Advertising:* Mrs J Garvan; *Foreign Rights:* Margaret Jones (adult); *Marketing Dir:* I L Morton
Parent Company: William Collins Sons & Co Ltd, UK (qv)
Branch Offs: 389 Stanley St, South Brisbane, Queensland 4101; 25 Trent St, Burwood, Victoria 3125; 7-9 Maple Ave, Forestville, SA 5034; 26 Boag Pl, Morley, WA 6062
Subjects: General Fiction, Biography, History, How-to, Music, Art, Philosophy, Reference, Religion, Juveniles, Low- & High-priced Paperbacks, University, Secondary & Primary Textbooks
Founded: 1872

Commemorative Editions Pty Ltd*, PO Box 451, Hawthorn, Victoria 3122 (Located at: 3rd Floor, 316 Queen St, Melbourne, Victoria 3000) Tel: (03) 675747/828999 Telex: 38225 AA
Man Dir: Charles Wantrup; *Publisher:* Geoffrey M Gold
Subjects: Australian commemorative issues, History, Biography, Culture, Business
Founded: 1979
ISBN Publisher's Prefix: 0-949763

Corgi, an imprint of Transworld Publishers (Australia) Pty Ltd (qv)

Croft Press, see Gryphon Books Pty Ltd

Currawong Press Pty Ltd*, PO Box 233, Milson's Point, NSW 2061 Tel: 9698122
Chief Executive: Phillip Mathews
Subjects: Books of general appeal, mainly by Australian writers, and mainly Non-fiction
Founded: 1946
Miscellaneous: Publishers of *Australian Children's Dictionary*
ISBN Publisher's Prefix: 0-85041

Currency Press Pty Ltd, 330 Oxford St, Paddington, NSW 2021 Tel: (02) 3576401 Cable Add: Dramabooks, Sydney
Chief Executive: Katharine Brisbane Parsons; *Editorial and Rights & Permissions:* Ian Murdoch
Orders to: Cambridge University Press, 296 Beaconsfield Parade, Middle Park, Victoria
Subjects: Drama, Films, Theatre History
1981-82: 46 titles *Founded:* 1971
ISBN Publisher's Prefix: 0-86819

Currey O'Neil Ross Pty Ltd, 56 Claremont St, South Yarra, Victoria 3141 Tel: (03) 2419901 Telex: AA 36472
Dirs: Lloyd O'Neil, John Ross, Geoff Currey
Associate Companies: Lloyd O'Neil Pty Ltd (qv); George Philip and O'Neil Pty Ltd
Subjects: Australian History, Natural History, Art, Pictorial and General books relating to Australia
1982-83: 22 titles
ISBN Publisher's Prefix: 0-85902

Curriculum Development Centre, PO Box 52, Dickson, ACT 2602 Tel: (062) 433011 Telex: Education Canberra
Dir: David Francis; *Editorial, Rights & Permissions:* Pamela Hewitt
Subjects: Educational
ISBN Publisher's Prefix: 0-642

Cygnet Books, an imprint of University of Western Australia Press (qv)

Darling Downs Institute Press*, PO Darling Heights, Toowoomba, Queensland 4350 Tel: (076) 301300 Cable Add: Ddiae Toowoomba Telex: 40010
Dir: Walter G Spundy
Parent Company: The Darling Downs Institute of Advanced Education
Subjects: Scholarly, Regional History, Literature
Founded: 1975
ISBN Publisher's Prefix: 0-909306

J M **Dent** Pty Ltd+, PO Box 289, Ferntree Gully, Victoria 3156 (Located at: 34-36 Wadhurst Drive, Boronia, Victoria 3155) Tel: (03) 2217333 Cable Add: Malaby Melbourne Telex: 134858 AA Dentoz
Man Dir: I H Drakeford; *Publishing Manager, Publicity and Rights & Permissions:* Ms J L Day; *National Sales Manager, Marketing:* S P Walters
Parent Company: J M Dent & Sons Ltd, UK (qv)
Branch Off: Suite 24, 67 Christie St, St Leonards, NSW 2065
Subjects: Children's Books, General, Music, Fiction, Classics, Australiana
1981: 2 titles *1982:* 5 titles *Founded:* 1977
ISBN Publisher's Prefix: 0-86770

Dezsery Ethnic Publications+, GPO Box 1499, Adelaide, South Australia 5001 (Located at: 25 King William St, Adelaide, South Australia 5000) Tel: (08) 512910/2674536
Chief Executive: Dr Andrew Steven Dezsery
Parent Company: Dezsery Cleaning Pty Ltd
Subject: Immigrant writers in Australia, of different ethnic backgrounds, writing in English and other languages
1981: 2 titles *1982:* 1 title *Founded:* 1975
ISBN Publisher's Prefixes: 0-908287, 0-9597437

Dollar Books, an imprint of Ansay Pty Ltd (qv)

Doubleday Australia Pty Ltd, PO Box 184, Lane Cove, NSW 2066 (Located at: 14 Mars Rd, Lane Cove, NSW 2066) Tel: 4270377 Telex: 20901 Dubday
Publishing Division is at 2A Woodcock Pl, Lane Cove, NSW 2066
Man Dir: Peter B Madgwick; *Editorial, Rights & Permissions:* Lisa Highton; *Publishing Manager:* Jon Attenborough; *Book Club Editorial:* Suzanne Delmont; *Book Club Marketing:* John D Madgwick
Parent Company: Doubleday & Co Inc, New York, USA
Subsidiary Company: Doubleday New Zealand Ltd, New Zealand (qv)
Branch Offs: Unit 1, 57 Parkhurst Drive, Knoxfield, Victoria 3180; 8 Taylors Rd, Morningside, Auckland 3, New Zealand
Subjects: General and Biographical Australian Non-fiction
Book Clubs: Doubleday Australia Pty Ltd, Book Club Division, operates book clubs in Australia and New Zealand (see Book Clubs sections for individual clubs)
1981: 24 titles *1982:* 31 titles
ISBN Publisher's Prefix: 0-86824

Dove Communications Pty Ltd, PO Box 316, Blackburn, Victoria 3130 (Located at: Suite 1, 60-64 Railway Rd, Blackburn, Victoria) Tel: (03) 8771333 Cable Add: Dovcom
Man Dir: J Garry Eastman; *Editorial:* David C Lovell; *Sales:* Ken Tetley
Associated imprints: Drummond, Primary Education
Subjects: Catholic Theology, Religion, Moral Philosophy, Education, Teacher Reference, Politics
Founded: 1972
ISBN Publisher's Prefix: 0-85924

Drummond, an associated imprint of Dove Communications Pty Ltd (qv)

E A **Books**, 18 Chandos St, St Leonards, NSW 2065 Tel: (02) 4381533 Telex: AA 27640 Eameab
General Manager: Geof Murray
Parent Company: Institution of Engineers Australia, 11 National Ct, Barton, ACT 2600
Associate Companies: Engineers Australia Magazine, Chemical Engineering in Australia Magazine
Imprint: I E Aust Publications
Subjects: Civil, Electrical, Mechanical and Chemical Engineering
1982: 180 titles *Founded:* 1919 (I E Aust), 1976 (E A Books)
ISBN Publisher's Prefix: 0-85825

Educational Material Aid, 10 South St, Strathfield, NSW 2135 Tel: (02) 767962
Dir: Yvonne McBurney
Subjects: Australian History and Novels designed to improve reading skills, and other remedial material, Australian History for general reading
Bookshop: At above address
1981: 2 titles *1982:* 1 title *Founded:* 1976
ISBN Publisher's Prefix: 0-908053

Edwards & Shaw Pty Ltd*, 79-80 Buckingham St, Surry Hills, NSW 2010 Tel: (02) 6996758
Dirs: Eric Edwards, Roderick Malcolm Shaw; *Rights & Permissions:* Eric Edwards; *Publicity:* R M Shaw
Subjects: Poetry, Belles Lettres
ISBN Publisher's Prefix: 0-85551

David **Ell** Press Pty Ltd, PO Box 353, Darlinghurst, NSW 2010 (Located at: 226 Crown St, Darlinghurst) Tel: (02) 3561800 Cable Add: Ellsyd
Chief Executive, Sales, Production: David Ell; *Editorial, Publicity and Rights & Permissions:* K Lamberton
Subjects: Australiana (historical, art, mining, children's books)
1981: 8 titles *Founded:* 1978
ISBN Publisher's Prefix: 0-908197

Encyclopaedia Britannica (Australia) Inc, 22 Lambs Rd, Artarmon, NSW 2064 Tel: (02) 9224799 Telex: Enbrit AA 23044
President: R Grott; *Vice-President, Sales Administration:* N Bechler
Parent Company: Encyclopaedia Britannica Inc, USA
Associate Company: Encyclopaedia Britannica International Ltd, UK (qv for other associate companies)
Subjects: Educational Reference, Dictionaries, Geography, Biography, Art, Science, Suitable for levels from Kindergarten to Tertiary Education, Audio Visual material and teaching aids
ISBN Publisher's Prefix: 0-909263

Era Publications, 220 Grange Rd, Flinders Park, SA 5025 Tel: (08) 3524440 Telex: AA 88765 Telcom AD077
Chief Executives: Rodney David Martin, Sandra Dorothy Martin
Parent Company: R D Martin Pty Ltd (at above address)
Imprints: Play to Learn; Keystone Picture Books
Subjects: Children's Picture Books, Educational Aids Material, Educational Toys
1982: 4 titles *1983:* 4 titles *Founded:* 1972
ISBN Publisher's Prefix: 0-908507

14 AUSTRALIA

John Ferguson Pty Ltd, 133 Macquarie St, Sydney, NSW 2000 Tel: 272841
Man Dir: John R Ferguson; *Editorial:* Annette Robinson
Orders to: Angus & Robertson Pty Ltd, 4 Eden Park, 31 Waterloo Rd, North Ryde, NSW 2113
Subjects: Australian General & Historical
1981: 10 titles *1982:* 20 titles *Founded:* 1975
ISBN Publisher's Prefix: 0-909134

Fine Arts Press Pty Ltd, 34 Glenview St, Gordon, NSW 2072 Tel: 4984656/4987452 Cable Add: Imprint Sydney Telex: AA 74072 Artfap
Publisher: Sam Ure Smith
Subjects: Art and the Fine Arts, *Art and Australia* (quarterly)
Miscellaneous: Company also produces books for other publishers
ISBN Publisher's Prefix: 0-86917

Four Winds Press, an imprint of Ashton Scholastic (qv)

Georgian House Pty Ltd, 296 Beaconsfield Parade, Middle Park, Victoria 3206 Tel: 5340697
Man Dir: Brian Harris
Subjects: General Australian Literature
Founded: 1943
ISBN Publisher's Prefix: 0-85585

Golden Press Pty Ltd, 2-12 Tennyson Rd, Gladesville, NSW 2111 Tel: (02) 890421 Cable Add: Goldpress Telex: AA 26070
Man Dir: John Fink; *Publisher:* John Fenton-Smith; *Market Dir:* Peter McGill; *Publicity:* Marita Webb
Subsidiary Company: Shakespeare Head Press (qv)
Associated imprints include: Whitman, Australia Pty Ltd
Branch Offs: 16 Copsey Place, Avondale, Auckland, New Zealand, and all Australian States
Subjects: Biography, History, How-to, Juveniles, Secondary & Primary Textbooks, Australiana, Non-fiction
1982: 20 titles *1983:* 70 titles
ISBN Publisher's Prefix: 0-85558

Granada Publishing Australia Pty Ltd, PO Box Q164, Queen Victoria Bldgs, Sydney, NSW 2000 Tel: (02) 295239 Cable Add: Granada Telex: 27867 AA Grapub
Dirs: W M Blanshard, W Carr, A R H Birch, E G Grigor, G Wallis-Smith; *Sales:* E G Grigor
Parent Company: Granada Publishing Ltd, UK (qv)
Subjects: General Books, Science, Technical Books, Yachting, Education, Juveniles, Fiction, Paperbacks

Grass Roots, an imprint of Night Owl Publishers Pty Ltd (qv)

Greenhouse Publications, 385 Bridge Rd, Richmond, Victoria 3121 Tel: (03) 4292122 Telex: AA 33626
Dirs: Sally R Milner, Peter Steer
Subjects: Technical, Educational, Children's, Feminist, Historical, General Adult
Founded: 1975

The **Grolier** Society of Australia Pty Ltd*, PO Box 410, Crows Nest, NSW 2065 (Located at: 1 Campbell St, Artarmon, NSW 2064) Tel: (02) 4392355 Cable Add: Grolier Sydney Telex: 26584
Man Dir, Rights & Permissions: A G Fox; *Editorial, Production:* R Appleton
Parent Company: Grolier Inc, New York, USA
Associate Companies: Grolier Inc, Canada, Latin America, UK, Europe, Africa, Far East, New Zealand; Franklin Watts Inc, USA; Franklin Watts Ltd, UK (qv)
Subsidiary Company: Australian Encyclopaedia Pty Ltd, Sydney
Subjects: Reference, Educational, Children
Founded: 1960

Gryphon Books Pty Ltd*, 256 Albert Rd, South Melbourne, Victoria 3205 Tel: 6994541
Man Dir, Editorial, Rights & Permissions: Richard Griffin; *Sales, Publicity:* Lyn Bevan
Subsidiary Company: Pegasus Books (at above address)
Associate Company: Croft Press (at above address)
Subjects: Limited Editions of Illustrated Books
Founded: 1977

Harcourt Brace Jovanovich Group (Australia) Pty Ltd, PO Box 300, North Ryde, NSW 2113 (Located at: Unit E, Centrecourt, 25-27 Paul St, North Ryde, NSW 2113) Tel: 8883655 Cable Add: Jovan Telex: AA23394
Man Dir: Barry Dingley; *Editorial Dir:* Grant Walker; *Marketing Dir:* Don Conson; *Publicity:* Janet Taylor
Parent Company: Harcourt Brace Jovanovich Inc, 757 Third Ave, New York, NY 10017, USA
Associate Companies: Academic Press Inc (London) Ltd, UK (qv); Academic Press Inc, 111 Fifth Ave, New York, NY 10003, USA; Coronado Publishers Inc, 1250 Sixth Ave, San Diego, California 92101, USA; Grune & Stratton Inc, 111 Fifth Ave, New York, NY 10003, USA; Harcourt Brace Jovanovich Ltd, UK (qv); Instructor Publications Inc, Instructor Park, Dansville, NY 14437; Johnson Reprint Corporation, 111 Fifth Ave, New York, NY 10003, USA
Branch Off: 22 St Kilda Rd, Melbourne, Victoria 3004
Subjects: Educational, Science, Technical, Medicine, Reprints, Trade

Hargreen Publishing Co, PO Box 4710, Melbourne, Victoria 3001 (Located at: 144 Chetwynd St, North Melbourne, Victoria 3051) Tel: 3299714
Chief Executive: Michael Haratsis Snr; *Editorial, Production, Rights & Permissions:* Tim Morfesse; *Sales, Publicity:* Michael Haratsis Jnr
Parent Company: M and M A H Nominees Pty Ltd
Subjects: Educational, Reference, Non-fiction
1981: 6 titles *1982:* 6 titles *Founded:* 1972
ISBN Publisher's Prefix: 0-949905

Harper & Row (Australasia) Pty Ltd, PO Box 226, Artarmon, NSW 2064 (Located at: Frederick St, Artarmon) Tel: 4396155 Cable Add: Bookserv Telex: 72598 AA
Man Dir: B D Wilder; *Trade Sales:* Harry Howell; *College Sales:* Adrian McComb; *Publicity:* Kerstin Gova
Parent Company: Harper & Row Inc, New York, NY 10022, USA
Associate Companies: Editora Harper & Row do Brasil Ltda, Brazil (qv); Harper & Row Ltd, UK (qv); Harper & Row Latinoamericana-Harla SA de CV, Mexico (qv)

The **Hawthorn** Press Pty Ltd, Viewfield, Mt Macedon Rd, Mt Macedon, Victoria 3441 Tel: (054) 261516
Man Dir, Editorial, Production, Publicity: John Gartner; *Sales Dir:* Zelma Gartner
Subsidiary Company: The Hawthorn Publishing Co Pty Ltd (at above address)
Subject: Philately
Founded: 1945
ISBN Publisher's Prefix: 0-7256

William **Heinemann** Australia, an imprint of Heinemann Publishers Australia Pty Ltd (qv)

Heinemann Educational Australia, an imprint of Heinemann Publishers Australia Pty Ltd (qv)

Heinemann/Ginn, an imprint of Heinemann Publishers Australia Pty Ltd (qv)

Heinemann Publishers Australia Pty Ltd, 85 Abinger St, PO Box 133, Richmond, Victoria 3121 Tel: (03) 4293622 Cable Add: Hebooks Melb Telex: Heaust 35347
Man Dir: Nicholas J Hudson; *Editorial:* Anne Norton (Educational), John Kerr (General); *Sales Dir:* Jim Warburton (Educational), Terry Greenwood (General); *Production:* Roger Seddon; *Publicity:* Peter Lademann; *Rights & Permissions:* Marcelle Rerley
Parent Company: Heinemann Educational Books International Ltd, UK (qv)
Imprints: William Heinemann Australia (General); Heinemann Educational Australia (mainly Secondary School material); Heinemann/Ginn (mainly Primary School material)
Branch Offs: PO Box 218, Ryde, NSW 2112; PO Box 299, Spring Hill, Queensland 4000
Subjects: Educational (mainly Secondary, some Primary and Tertiary), General (Non-fiction, Drama)
Founded: 1967
ISBN Publisher's Prefix: 0-85859

Heritage, an imprint of Lansdowne Press (qv)

Hicks Smith & Sons Pty Ltd, now Methuen Australia Pty Ltd (qv)

Hill of Content Publishing Co Ltd, 86 Bourke St, Melbourne, Victoria 3000 Tel: (03) 6622711 Cable Add: Colbook
Man Dir, Rights & Permissions: M G Zifcak; *Editorial:* M Anderson, L Gregory; *Sales:* P Shaw
Orders to: 17-21 Drewery Lane, Melbourne, Victoria 3000
Associate Company: Collins Booksellers Pty Ltd (qv under Major Booksellers)
Subjects: Australiana, Archive series, Australian Literature, Educational, Politics, Health
Founded: 1965
ISBN Publisher's Prefix: 0-85572

Hodder & Stoughton (Australia) Pty Ltd, 2 Apollo Pl, Lane Cove, NSW 2066 Tel: (428) 1022 Cable Add: Expositor Telex: AA24858
Man Dir: Edward Coffey; *Publishing Director, Children's Editor:* Margaret Hamilton; *Sales & Marketing:* John Vermeer (Hardback), Stuart Smith (Paperback); *Publicity, Rights & Permissions:* Erica Graham Harding
Parent Company: Hodder & Stoughton Ltd, UK (qv)
Branch Offs: 9 Yertchuk Ave, Ashwood, Victoria 3147; Cnr Elizabeth & Albert Sts, Brisbane, Queensland 4000; 318 Walcott St, Mount Lawley, WA 6050; 32b Dew St, Thebarton, SA 5031
Subjects: General, Fiction, Children's Books, History, Education, Dictionaries, Religion, General Science, Travel
1981: 30 titles *1982:* 49 titles
ISBN Publisher's Prefix: 0-340

Holt-Saunders Pty Ltd, 9 Waltham St, PO Box 154, Artarmon, NSW 2064 Tel: (02) 4393633 Cable Add: Aytcholt, Sydney Telex: 21217
Man Dir: D McCamey; *Publishing Dir:* P Evans; *Production:* D Huffell
Associate Company: Holt-Saunders Ltd, UK (qv for other associates)
Subject: Education
Founded: 1967
ISBN Publisher's Prefix: 0-003

Horwitz Grahame Books Pty Ltd+, Horwitz Cammeray Centre, 506 Miller St, PO Box 306, Cammeray, NSW 2062 Tel: (02) 9296144 Cable Add: Horbooks Sydney Telex: Horwtz AA27833
Man Dir: L J Moore; *Rights & Permissions:* Miss B Benjamin
Orders to: c/o Frank Cridland Pty Ltd, 154 Sussex St, Sydney, NSW 2000 (exclusive of Grahame Book Company Orders)
Branch Off: c/o U Spalinger and Co Ltd, PO Box 765, General Post Office, Hong Kong
Subjects: General Fiction, Biography, History, How-to, Reference, Low- & High-priced Paperbacks, Secondary & Primary Textbooks, Educational Materials
Bookshops: Grahames Bookshop (qv under Major Booksellers)
Founded: 1921
Miscellaneous: The Horwitz Group includes Martin Educational, Carroll's Horwitz Publications, Scripts Publications, Grahame Book Co Pty Ltd (all at 506 Miller St, Cammeray, NSW 2062)
ISBN Publisher's Prefixes: 0-7252 (Scripts), 0-7253 (Martin Educational), 0-7255 (Horwitz)

Hutchinson Group (Australia) Ltd, PO Box 2031, Richmond South, Victoria 3121 (Located at: 30-32 Cremorne St, Richmond, Victoria 3121) Tel: (03) 4283511 Cable Add: Kahminyah Telex: AA37972
Man Dir: Otto Hofner; *Sales Dir:* Paul Jaboor; *Man Editor, Rights & Permissions:* Elizabeth Douglas; *Publicity Manager:* Susan Boundy
Associate Company: The Hutchinson Publishing Group Ltd, UK (qv)
Branch Offs: 330-370 Wattle St, Ultimo, NSW 2007 Tel: (02) 2113233 Cable Add: Kahminyah Sydney; PO Box 151 Broadway, NSW 2007; 236 Elizabeth St, Brisbane, Queensland 4000; 3 Norman Rd, Roleystone, Western Australia
Subjects: Biography, History, Reference, Juveniles, Fiction, Humour, Sporting, General Non-fiction
ISBN Publisher's Prefix: 0-09

Hyland House Publishing Pty Ltd*, 23 Bray St, South Yarra, Victoria 3000 Tel: 2416336
Editorial, Rights & Permissions: Anne Godden; *Sales, Production, Publicity:* Al Knight
Subjects: General Australian
1981: 8 titles *Founded:* 1977
ISBN Publisher's Prefix: 0-908090

I E Aust Publications, an imprint of E A Books (qv)

Inkata Press Pty Ltd+, 4 Longbourne Ave, North Clayton, Victoria 3168 Tel: 5600272 Cable Add: Inkata Melbourne Telex: AA 10104 Intmb Melbourne
Man Dir: C H Jerram; *Editorial Dir:* Patricia Sellar
Subjects: Science, Technology, Natural History, Agriculture
Founded: 1968
ISBN Publisher's Prefix: 0-909605

Island Press, PO Box R217, Royal Exchange, Sydney, NSW 2000
Man Dir: Philip Hammial
Subject: Poetry
1982: 14 titles *Founded:* 1973
ISBN Publisher's Prefix: 0-909771

Jacaranda Wiley Ltd*, GPO Box 859, Brisbane, Queensland 4001 (Located at: 65 Park Road, Milton, Queensland 4064) Tel: (07) 3699755 Cable Add: Japress Telex: AA 41845
Shipping Add: 172 Robinson Road, Geebung, Queensland 4034
Man Dir: John Collins; *Publishing Manager:* Colin Cunnington; *Marketing Managers:* John Braithwaite (school, general), John Collins (college); *Production:* Alan Robbie; *Business Manager:* Quentin Smith; *Advertising:* Tom Costin; *Rights & Permissions:* Eva Kupis
Orders to: 65 Park Rd, Milton, Queensland 4064
Parent Company: John Wiley & Sons Inc, Publishers, 605 Third Avenue, New York, NY 10158, USA
Associate Companies: Editorial Limusa SA, Mexico (qv); LTC-Livros Técnicos e Científicos Editora SA, Brazil (qv); Wiley Eastern Ltd, India (qv); John Wiley & Sons Ltd, UK (qv); John Wiley & Sons Canada Ltd
Subsidiary Companies: Jacaranda Wiley (Hong Kong) Ltd, 19D, 257 Gloucester Rd, Causeway Bay, Hong Kong; Niugini Press Pty Ltd, PO Box 15, Port Moresby, Papua New Guinea
Imprints: The Jacaranda Press, John Wiley, Niugini Press
Branch Offs: 9 Massey St, Gladesville, NSW 2111; 303 Wright Street, Adelaide, SA 5000; 90 Ormond Rd, Elwood, Victoria 3184 (all in Australia); 4 Kirk St, Grey Lynn, Auckland 2, New Zealand; PO Box 15, Port Moresby, Papua New Guinea
Subjects: Pre-school, Primary, Secondary and Tertiary Textbooks, Atlases, General
1981: 128 titles *Founded:* 1954
ISBN Publisher's Prefixes: 0-7016 (The Jacaranda Press, Niugini Press), 0-471 (John Wiley)

The **Joint Board** of Christian Education of Australia and New Zealand, 5th Floor, 177 Collins St, Melbourne, Victoria 3000 Tel: (03) 6544988
Chief Executive and Editorial: Dr D R Merritt; *Sales:* Mary Denton; *Production:* Howard Weedon; *Publicity:* Margaret Parry; *Rights & Permissions:* Mavis Grierson
Imprint: Uniting Church Press
Branch Off: 75 Taranaki St, Wellington 1, New Zealand
Subjects: Religious Education, Pastoral Care, Youth Work, Worship
Bookshop: Educational Resources Centre (at above Melbourne address)
1981: 31 titles *1982:* 66 titles *Founded:* 1914
ISBN Publisher's Prefix: 0-85819

Kangaroo Press, PO Box 75, Kenthurst, NSW 2154 (Located at: 3 Whitehall Rd, Kenthurst) Tel: (02) 6541502 Cable Add: Kangaroops
Partners: David and Priscilla Rosenberg
Orders to: c/o Doubleday Publishing, 2a Woodcock Pl, Lane Cove, NSW 2066
Subjects: Non-fiction, Natural History, History, Biography, Australiana, Crafts, Gardening
1981: 12 titles *1982:* 18 titles *Founded:* 1981
ISBN Publisher's Prefix: 0-949924

Kelly Books, PO Box 313, Prahran, Victoria (Located at: 763 Glenhuntly Rd, South Caulfield, Melbourne) Tel: (03) 679249/(02) 293911

Kestrel, an imprint of Penguin Books Australia Ltd (qv)

Keystone Picture Books, an imprint of Era Publications (qv)

Kookaburra Technical Publications Pty Ltd*, PO Box 648, Dandenong, Victoria 3175 Tel: 5600841
Man Dir, Production: Geoff Pentland; *Editorial:* Miss J Martin; *Sales:* Mr F Parks
Branch Offs: 214 Kenmark Rd, Newark, Delaware 19713, USA; 1204 Campbell St, Joliet, Illinois 60435, USA
Subject: Aviation history
Founded: 1964
ISBN Publisher's Prefix: 0-85880

L & S Publishing Co, 99 Argus Street, Cheltenham, Melbourne, Victoria 3192 Tel: (03) 5846311 Cable Add: Scholib Melbourne Telex: 38233 AA
A Division of L & S Educational Supplies (part of Syme Media Pty Ltd)
General Manager, Rights & Permissions: Lawrence Flight; *Editorial, Sales, Production:* Brian Barratt; *Publicity, Advertising:* Malcolm MacArthur
Imprint: Vantage House (General)
Branch Offs: Brisbane, Sydney, Orange, Canberra
Company Divisions: L & S Educational Equipment Pty Ltd; L & S School Library Service Pty Ltd; L & S Textbook & Stationery Co Pty Ltd; L & S Design Development & Export Co; L & S Education & Music Centre Pty Ltd
Subjects: General Secondary & Primary Textbooks, Children's Books, Educational Materials, Audiovisual Materials
Founded: 1963
ISBN Publisher's Prefix: 0-86898

Ladybird, an imprint of Penguin Books Australia Ltd (qv)

Allen **Lane**, an imprint of Penguin Books Australia Ltd (qv)

Lansdowne Editions, an imprint of Lansdowne Press (qv)

Lansdowne Press+, 176 South Creek Rd, Dee Why West, NSW 2099 Tel: (02) 9810444 Cable Add: Rigby Group Sydney Telex: AA21546
Chief Executive: Rod Davis; *Publishing, Production:* Warwick Jacobson; *Advertising:* Felicity Snell; *Export Sales:* Warwick Page; *Rights & Permissions:* Overseas branch offices (qv)
Parent Company: RPLA Pty Ltd (at above address)
Imprints: Heritage, Lansdowne Editions, Lansdowne Press, Summit Books, Universal Books, Ure Smith
Branch Offs (Australia): Hardie House, 594 St Kilda Rd, Melbourne, Victoria 3004; 10 Edmondstone St, South Brisbane, Queensland 4101; 30 North Terrace, Kent Town, SA 5067; 106 Howe St, Osborne Park, Perth, WA 6017
Branch Offs: (Overseas): Lansdowne Press Ltd, 3 Marken Pl, Glenfield, Auckland, New Zealand; Lansdowne Press Inc, 420 Madison Ave, New York, NY 10017, USA; Lansdowne International, 5 Great James St, London WC1, UK
Subjects: Most subjects, including Cooking, Gardening, General, Children's Books, Australiana, Art, Maps, Road Guides, Craft, Nature, Budget Books, Literature, Sport, Limited Editions
ISBN Publisher's Prefixes: 0-7018 (Lansdowne), 0-7271 (Summit)

The **Law** Book Co Ltd, 44-50 Waterloo Rd, North Ryde, NSW 2113 Tel: (02) 8870177 Cable Add: Asbook Telex: Asbook 27995
Man Dir, Rights & Permissions: D S Lees; *Sales:* C McMurray; *Marketing Manager:* J K Leonard; *Production:* P Finneran
Parent Company: Associated Book Publishers (Aust) Ltd (qv)
Branch Offs: 389 Lonsdale St, Melbourne, Victoria 3000; 6 Sherwood Court, Perth, WA 6000
Subjects: Law, Accountancy, Commerce
1982: 35 titles
ISBN Publisher's Prefix: 0-455

Libra Books Pty Ltd, GPO Box 10, Hobart, Tasmania 7001 Tel: (002) 251479
Chief Executive: B M Wicks
Subjects: Horse racing and breeding
Founded: 1972
ISBN Publisher's Prefix: 0-909619

Little Hills Press+, PO Box 90, Burwood, NSW 2134 (Located at: 2 Hornsey St, Burwood) Tel: (02) 7454884
Chief Executive and Sales: Charles C Burfitt; *Publicity:* Pam Saunderson
Associate Company: Dentsu (at above address)
Branch Offs: Kingfisher Books, Cnr Brixton and Wangard Rds, Cheltenham, Victoria; Colonial Book Agency, 13 Jacaranda Ave, Albany Creek, Queensland 4035
Subjects: Non-fiction
1981: 2 titles *1982:* 1 title *Founded:* 1980
ISBN Publisher's Prefix: 0-949773

Lonely Planet Publications Pty Ltd, PO Box 88, South Yarra, Victoria 3141 Tel: (03) 4295268 Cable Add: Loneplan Melbourne Telex: 30333 AA Loneplan
Man Dir: Tony Wheeler; *Editorial:* Maureen Wheeler; *Sales:* Andy Neilson; *Production:* Jim Hart
Branch Off: 15 Heatherway, Crowthorne, Berks RG11 6HG, UK
Subject: Travel guides
1982: 8 titles *1983:* 9 titles *Founded:* 1973
ISBN Publisher's Prefix: 0-908086

Longman Cheshire Pty Ltd*, Longman Cheshire House, 346 St Kilda Rd, Melbourne, Victoria 3004 Tel: 6991522 Cable Add: Miscellany Melbourne Telex: AA 33501
Man Dir: N J Ryan; *Deputy Man Dir:* B J Sprant; *Sales Manager:* F R Priatel; *Rights & Permissions:* Mrs E Moody, N J Ryan; *Production:* P H R Hylands; *Publicity:* R Everest
Orders to: Penguin Books Australia, 487 Maroondah Highway, Ringwood, Victoria 3134
Parent Company: Longman Group Ltd, UK (qv)
Associate Company: Penguin Books Australia Ltd (qv)
Imprints: Cheshire, Churchill Livingstone, Oliver & Boyd, Sorrett
Branch Offs: 33 Cooper St, Surry Hills, NSW 2010; 139 Merivale St, South Brisbane, Queensland 4101; 105 Gouger St, Adelaide, SA 5000; CWA House, 1174 Hay St, West Perth, WA 6005
Subjects: Educational (Primary, Secondary, Tertiary, Medical Textbooks)
1981: 93 titles *Founded:* 1976 (formed by merger of Longman Australia Pty Ltd and Cheshire Publishing Pty Ltd)
ISBN Publisher's Prefixes: 0-582, 0-7015

Lothian Publishing Co Pty Ltd, 4-12 Tattersalls Lane, Melbourne, Victoria 3000 Tel: (03) 6634976 Cable Add: Thorough Telex: 39476 AA Tcloth
Man Dir and Rights: Louis A Lothian; *Sales Director:* Peter H Lothian; *Publicity:* Marie Cameron
Associate Company: Thomas C Lothian Pty Ltd (at above address)
Branch Offs: Australia: Shop 192, 392 Jones St, Ultimo, NSW 2007; 170 Magill Rd, Norwood, SA 5067; 53 Spitfire Ave, Strathpine, Queensland 4500; c/o Graden Enterprises, Unit 9, 183-187 Bank St, East Victoria Park, WA 6101
New Zealand: 88 Nelson St, Auckland 1
Subjects: How-to, Juveniles, Horticulture, Local history, Non-fiction
1981: 5 titles *1982:* 5 titles *Founded:* 1910
ISBN Publisher's Prefix: 0-85091

Lowden Publishing Co*, Lowdens Rd, Kilmore, Victoria 3601 Tel: (057) 821118 Cable Add: Lowden, Kilmore
Man Dir: Jim Lowden
Subjects: Biography, History, Reference, Religion, Transport
1981: 3 titles *1982:* 4 titles *Founded:* 1969
ISBN Publisher's Prefix: 0-909706

Lutheran Publishing House+, GPO Box 1368, Adelaide, South Australia 5001 (Located at: 205 Halifax St, Adelaide, South Australia 5000) Tel: (618) 2235468
General Manager: Martin Hoopmann; *Editorial and Rights & Permissions:* Everard Leske; *Sales:* Warren Schirmer; *Production:* Eric Winter; *Publicity:* Irwin Traeger
Imprint: Chi Rho
Branch Off: 20 McDougall St, Milton, Queensland 4064
Subjects: Religion, Social Questions, Children, Religious Education
Bookshops: The Open Book, at 110 Gawler Pl, Adelaide 5000, 38 Murray St, Tanunda 5352 and 20 McDougall St, Milton, Queensland 4064; Australia Arcade, Ruthven St, Toowoomba, Queensland 4350; 198 Gray St, Hamilton, Victoria 3300; 538 David St, Albury, NSW 2640
Founded: 1913
ISBN Publisher's Prefix: 0-85910

McGraw-Hill Book Co Australia Pty Ltd, 4 Barcoo St, Roseville East, NSW 2069 Tel: (02) 4064288 Telex: 20849
Man Dir, Rights & Permissions: D J Pegrem; *General Manager Service:* J H Fowlstone; *Production:* M Bagnato
Parent Company: McGraw-Hill Inc, 1221 Ave of the Americas, New York, NY 10020, USA
Subsidiary Company: Computer Reporting Services Pty Ltd
Subjects: Technology, Management, Educational, Professional & Reference, General Interest, Secondary Textbooks, Training Programs
1981: 29 titles *1982:* 33 titles
ISBN Publisher's Prefix: 0-07

The **Macmillan Co** of Australia Pty Ltd*, Locked Bag 12, South Melbourne, Victoria 3205 (Located at: 107 Moray St, South Melbourne) Tel: (03) 6998922 Cable Add: Scriniaire Melbourne Telex: 34454 AA
Man Dir: Brian Stonier
Education Division: Man Dir: John Rolfe; *Marketing Dir:* Marek Palka; *School Publishing Dir:* Brian McCurdy; *Academic Publisher:* Celia Tikotin
General Division: Publishers: Bill Reed, Peter Phillips; *Associate Publisher:* Susan Haynes
Parent Company: Macmillan Publishers Ltd, UK (qv for associate companies)
Subsidiary Company: Sun Books Pty Ltd (qv)
Branch Offs: 6-8 Clarke St, Crows Nest, NSW; 115 Quay St, Brisbane, Queensland 4000; 9 Hackney Rd, Hackney, SA 5069; 44 Irvine Rd, Bayswater, WA 6053
Subjects: General Fiction, Biography, History, Music, Art, Religion, Juveniles, Paperbacks, Engineering, General & Social Sciences, University, Secondary & Primary Textbooks
Bookshops: Mary Martin Bookshop Pty Ltd at 68 Grenfell St, Adelaide, SA; Canberra Arcade, Alinga St, Canberra, ACT; 269 Swanston St, Melbourne, Victoria; 36 Toorak Rd, South Yarra, Victoria; 47 York St, Sydney, NSW; 256 Queen St, Brisbane, Queensland
Founded: 1896
ISBN Publisher's Prefix: 0-333

McNamara's Books, an imprint of Second Back Row Press Pty Ltd (qv)

McPhee Gribble Publishers Pty Ltd, 66 Cecil St, Fitzroy, Victoria 3065 Tel: (03) 4199010 Telex: 31494 AA Mt 45
Principals: H J McPhee, D M Gribble
Subject: Non-fiction Paperbacks, Children's Non-fiction, Australian Fiction
1982: 35 titles *Founded:* 1975
ISBN Publisher's Prefix: 0-86914

Martin Educational, see Horwitz Grahame Books Pty Ltd

Martindale Press Pty Ltd, associate company of A H & A W Reed Pty Ltd (qv)

Mead & Beckett Publishing, 139 Macquarie St, Sydney, NSW 2000 Tel: 277251 Cable Add: Meadbeck Sydney Telex: AA23406
Chief Executives: Barbara Beckett, Rod Mead
Parent Company: Mead & Beckett Pty Ltd (at above address)
Subjects: Illustrated General Books (mainly adult and about Australia)
1981: 11 titles *1982:* 13 titles *Founded:* 1978
Miscellaneous: Co-publishers and packagers

Megalong Books, an imprint of Second Back Row Press Pty Ltd (qv)

Melbourne University Press, PO Box 278, Carlton South, Victoria 3053 Tel: (03) 3473455 Cable Add: Mupress
Shipping Add: 138 Cardigan St, Carlton, Victoria 3053
Dir: P A Ryan; *Rights & Permissions:* Miss S A Hardiman; *Production:* P Jones
Branch Off: Library of Australian History, 17 Mitchell St, North Sydney, NSW 2060
Subjects: Belles Lettres, Poetry, Biography, History, Music, Art, Philosophy, Reference, Paperbacks, Medicine, Psychology, Engineering, General & Social Sciences, University & Secondary Textbooks
Bookshop: University Bookroom, University of Melbourne, PO Box 278, Carlton South, Victoria 3053
1981: 20 titles *1982:* 20 titles *Founded:* 1922
ISBN Publisher's Prefix: 0-522

Methuen Australia Pty Ltd, 44 Waterloo Rd, North Ryde, NSW 2113 Tel: (02) 8870177 Telex: 21206 Asbook
Man Dir: W J Mackarell; *Divisional Managers:* K W Shearman (Trade), A J Dwyer (Education)
Parent Company: Associated Book Publishers PLC, UK (qv)
Subjects: General, Academic, Educational
ISBN Publisher's Prefix: 0-454

Microzine, an imprint of Ashton Scholastic (qv)

Minerva's Express, PO Box 71, Beaconsfield, NSW 2014 Tel: 6988013
Man Dir: D Hunter; *Editorial, Production:* N Williams; *Sales, Publicity, Rights & Permissions:* P Henderson
Subject: Photographic Dictionary/Travel Aid in 12 languages, Australian Fiction
1981: 12 titles *Founded:* 1979

Modern Teaching Aids Pty Ltd*, 26-28 Chard Rd, PO Box 608, Brookvale 2100 Tel: 9392355 Telex: Teaid 27109
Branch Off: 14A Trent St, Moorabbin
Subject: Educational Books

Moving Into Maths Pty Ltd, 56 Claremont St, South Yarra, Victoria 3141 Tel: (03) 2419901 Cable Add: Windsorpub Telex: AA 36472
Chairman: Lloyd O'Neil; *Editorial, Sales and Production Dir:* Sue Donovan
Parent Company: Rigby Publishers Ltd (qv)
Associate Company: Lloyd O'Neil Pty Ltd (qv)
Subjects: Primary Mathematics, Primary Reading Scheme
1981: 30 titles *1982:* 30 titles *Founded:* 1980
ISBN Publisher's Prefix: 0-7270

National Library of Australia, Parkes Pl, Canberra, ACT 2600 Tel: (062) 621111 Cable Add: Natlibaust Canberra Telex: 62100
Dir: A T Bolton; *Editor:* Sally McCann; *Publications Officer:* David R Brown
Subjects: National bibliographical

publications, publications based on materials in the Library's collections
1981: 58 titles *1982:* 108 titles *Founded:* 1960
ISBN Publisher's Prefix: 0-642

Thomas **Nelson** Australia+, 480 La Trobe St, Melbourne, Victoria 3000 Tel: 3295199 Cable Add: Thonelson Melbourne Telex: 33088
A Division of Thomson Australian Holdings Pty Ltd
Man Dir: B Rivers; *General Manager, Trade Division:* T Paparella; *Editorial:* R Sessions (trade), R Andersen (educational); *Educational Sales:* B Clayton; *Production:* S Scannapiego; *Publicity:* S Roberts; *Rights & Permissions:* E McDonald
Parent Company: Thomas Nelson International, a Division of International Thomson Organization Ltd (Canada)
Associate Companies: Thomas Nelson & Sons (Canada) Ltd, Canada; Thomas Nelson & Sons Ltd, UK (qv)
Branch Offs: 7th Floor, Dunstan House, 236 Elizabeth St, Brisbane, Queensland 4000; 89-97 Jones St, Ultimo, NSW 2007; 145 Tynte St, North Adelaide, SA 5006
Subjects: Fiction, General Non-fiction, Juveniles, History, Gardening; Educational: Reading programmes, Primary and Secondary Texts
1981: 103 titles *1982:* 140 titles
ISBN Publisher's Prefix: 0-17

New Directions, an imprint of Wild & Woolley Pty Ltd (qv)

New South Wales University Press Ltd+, PO Box 1, Kensington, NSW 2033 Tel: (02) 6623503 Telex: AA 26054
General Manager: D S Howie
Imprint: Tafe Educational Books
Subjects: Biography, History, How-to, Philosophy, Reference, Engineering, General & Social Science, University and College Textbooks
Bookshop: College Shop, George St, Sydney
1981: 20 titles *1982:* 17 titles *Founded:* 1961
ISBN Publisher's Prefix: 0-86840

Night Owl Publishers Pty Ltd, PO Box 900, Shepparton, Victoria 3630 Tel: (057) 947256
Chief Executive and Rights & Permissions: David A Miller; *Production:* Meg Miller
Imprint: Grass Roots
Subjects: Homesteading, Self-sufficiency, Alternative Lifestyles
1981: 2 titles *1982:* 1 title *Founded:* 1973

Nimaroo Publishers, PO Box 2046, Wollongong 2500 Tel: (042) 292297
Manager & Publicity: Stephen Standish; *Editorial:* P Balnaves; *Sales:* T Balnaves; *Production:* M Standish; *Rights & Permissions:* N Standish
Branch Off: 11 Airds Rd, Lower Templestone, Victoria 3107
Subjects: Commercial, Scientific
Founded: 1978
ISBN Publisher's Prefix: 0-9596525

Niugini Press, an imprint of Jacaranda Wiley Ltd (qv)

Odana Editions Pty Ltd+, 65 Edward St, North Sydney, NSW 2060 Tel: (02) 9295546
Chief Executive: Lin Bloomfield
Associate Company: The Bloomfield Galleries, 118 Sutherland St, Paddington, NSW 2021
Subject: Art
Founded: 1978
ISBN Publisher's Prefix: 0-908154

Anne **O'Donovan** Pty Ltd, 40 Berkeley St, Hawthorn, Victoria 3122 Tel: (03) 8186849
Man Dir: Anne O'Donovan
Subject: Adult Non-fiction
1982: 4 titles *1983:* 3 titles *Founded:* 1978
ISBN Publisher's Prefix: 0-908476

Oliver & Boyd, an imprint of Longman Cheshire Pty Ltd (qv)

Omnibus Books+, 3 Hackney Rd, Hackney, SA 5069 Tel: (08) 424873 Telex: AA 88765 Ad 027
Chief Executive, Sales and Production Dir: Sue Williams; *Chief Executive and Publicity Dir:* Jane Covernton; *Rights & Permissions:* Rosemary Williams
Subject: Children's Picture Books and Fiction
1981: 3 titles *1982:* 11 titles *Founded:* 1980
ISBN Publisher's Prefix: 0-949641

Lloyd **O'Neil** Pty Ltd, 56 Claremont St, South Yarra, Victoria 3141 Tel: (03) 2419901 Cable Add: Windsorpub Telex: Hornby AA 36472
Chairman: Lloyd O'Neil; *Man Dir:* Sue Donovan; *Editorial Dir:* Celia Schmaler
Associate Companies: Currey O'Neil Ross Pty Ltd (qv); Moving Into Maths Pty Ltd (qv); George Philip and O'Neil Pty Ltd
Subjects: Educational, Primary & Secondary Atlases, Australiana, General
ISBN Publisher's Prefix: 0-85550

Outback Press Pty Ltd, now Schwartz Publishing Group (Victoria) Pty Ltd (qv)

Oxford University Press, GPO Box 2784Y, Melbourne, Victoria 3001 (Located at: 7 Bowen Crescent, Melbourne 3000, Victoria) Tel: (03) 2677466 Cable Add: Oxonian Melbourne Telex: 35330
Regional Manager: David Cunningham; *Academic & General Manager:* Jim Bebbington; *Educational Manager:* Chris Roering; *Academic & General Editorial:* Jim Hall; *Academic Marketing:* Geoff Dobbs; *Production Manager:* Anita Karl; *Publicity:* Julie Morgan
Head Office: Oxford University Press, UK (qv)
Subjects: Non-fiction, Juveniles
ISBN Publisher's Prefix: 0-19

Pacific Publications (Australia) Pty Ltd, GPO Box 3408, Sydney, NSW 2001 (Located at: 76 Clarence Street, Sydney, 2000) Tel: (02) 20231 Cable Add: Pacpub Telex: 21242
Manager: John Berry
Parent Company: The Herald and Weekly Times of Melbourne
Branch Off: Pacific Publications, Herald & Weekly Times Bldg, 61 Flinders Lane, Melbourne, Victoria
Subjects: Pacific Island Subjects — General & Reference, Australian Agricultural/Technical Handbooks, *Pacific Islands Yearbook, Papua New Guinea Handbook*
Founded: 1930
ISBN Publisher's Prefix: 0-85807

Pan Books (Australia) Pty Ltd*, 68 Moncur St, Woollahra, NSW 2025 Tel: (02) 320241 Telex: 70157
Chief Executive: Lyndsay Brown
Orders to: William Collins Book Distributors Pty Ltd, 55 Clarence St, Sydney, NSW 2000
Parent Company: Pan Books Ltd, UK (qv)
Imprints: Pan, Picador, Piccolo
Subjects: Fiction, General Literature, Children's Books, Reference, Technical, Educational
1981: 13 titles *Founded:* 1973
ISBN Publisher's Prefix: 0-330

Pegasus Books, see Gryphon Books Pty Ltd

Pelican, an imprint of Penguin Books Australia Ltd (qv)

Penguin Books Australia Ltd, 487 Maroondah Highway, PO Box 257, Ringwood, Victoria 3134 Tel: (03) 8703444 Cable Add: Penguinook Melbourne Telex: AA32458
Man Dir: T D Glover; *Publishing Dir:* B Johns; *Sales Dir:* P Field
Parent Company: Penguin Books Ltd, UK (qv)
Associate Companies: Longman Cheshire Pty Ltd Australia (qv); Penguin Books Canada Ltd, Canada; Penguin Books (NZ) Ltd, New Zealand (qv); Ladybird Books Ltd, Longman Group Ltd (UK — qqv); Viking-Penguin Inc, USA
Imprints: Kestrel, Ladybird, Allen Lane, Pelican, Penguin, Puffin
Subjects: Low & high-priced Paperbacks and Hardbacks, Juveniles, Fiction and Non-fiction
1981: 55 titles *1982:* 53 titles *Founded:* 1946
ISBN Publisher's Prefixes: 0-14 (Penguin), 0-670 (Viking) (see UK entries for other ISBNs)

Pergamon Press (Australia) Pty Ltd, 19A Boundary St, Rushcutters Bay, NSW 2011 Tel: (02) 3315211 Telex: Pergap AA27458
Chairman: I R Maxwell; *Man Dir and Rights & Permissions:* Jerry Mayer; *Marketing Dir:* Laurie Giles; *Publishing Manager:* Gillian Hewitt
Sales Offs: Melbourne, Sydney, Brisbane, Perth
Subjects: Reference, Medicine, Psychology, Engineering, General & Social Science, University, Secondary & Primary Textbooks, Educational Materials, General Literature
1981-82: 22 titles *Founded:* 1968
ISBN Publisher's Prefix: 0-80

Picador, an imprint of Pan Books (Australia) Pty Ltd (qv)

Piccolo, an imprint of Pan Books (Australia) Pty Ltd (qv)

Pinchgut Press, 6 Oaks Ave, Cremorne, NSW 2090 Tel: 905548
Chief Executives: Marjorie Pizer, Anne Spencer Parry
Subjects: Poetry, Fiction
Founded: 1947
ISBN Publisher's Prefix: 0-9598913

Pioneer Design Studio Pty Ltd+, North Rd, Lilydale, Victoria 3140 Tel: (03) 7355505
Man Dir: Derrick I Stone; *General Manager:* Carolyn R Stone
Subjects: History, Nature, Gardening
1981: 3 titles *1982:* 2 titles
ISBN Publisher's Prefix: 0-909674

Pitman Publishing Pty Ltd, 158 Bouverie St, Carlton, Victoria 3053 Tel: (03) 3473055 Cable Add: Fono Telex: 30107
Man Dir: Philip Harris; *Editorial & Rights & Permissions:* Tudor Day; *Marketing:* Sandy Grant; *Production:* Bernard Handley; *Publicity & Advertising:* Mariel Beros
Associate Company: Pitman Books Ltd, UK (qv)
Subjects: How-to, Music, Art, High-priced Paperbacks, Medicine, Engineering, Social Science, University, Secondary & Primary Textbooks, Educational Materials, General, Educational Computer Books and Software
1982-83: 60 titles *Founded:* 1913
ISBN Publisher's Prefix: 0-85896

Play to Learn, an imprint of Era Publications (qv)

Pluto, an imprint of Wild & Woolley Pty Ltd (qv)

The **Polding** Press*, 343 Elizabeth St, Melbourne, Victoria 3000 Tel: (03) 671740/675157
Chief Executive: John A Phillips SJ; *Sales Dir:* Robert Humphries
Subjects: Biography, History, Religion, High-

priced Paperbacks
Bookshop: Central Catholic Library Bookshop (at above address)
1981: 5 titles *Founded:* 1968

Prentice-Hall of Australia Pty Ltd+, 7 Grosvenor Place, Brookvale, NSW 2100 Tel: (02) 9391333 Cable Add: Prenhall Sydney Telex: AA 74010 Phasyd
Man Dir: Patrick F Gleeson; *Editorial and Rights & Permissions:* Charles Lucas; *Australian Marketing Manager:* James McGrath; *Publicity:* Caroline Leslie
Associate Company: Prentice Hall International, UK (qv for other associates)
Branch Off: 209 Glenhuntly Rd, Elsternwick, Victoria 3185
Subjects: Elementary, Secondary and University Textbooks, Trade, Professional Reference, Art, Technical, Management, Medicine, Business, Nursing
ISBN Publisher's Prefix: 0-7248

Primary Education, an associated imprint of Dove Communications Pty Ltd (qv)

Prism Books (Poetry Society of Australia)*, Box N110 Grosvenor Street PO, Sydney 2000, NSW Tel: (02) 9602304
Business Manager: Robert Adamson
Subjects: Art, Poetry (Commercial & Collector's Editions), Art, Music, Photography
1982: 18 titles *Founded:* 1952
ISBN Publisher's Prefix: 0-909081

Puffin, an imprint of Penguin Books Australia Ltd (qv)

Quartet Books Australia Pty Ltd*, 23 Bray St, South Yarra, Victoria 3000 Tel: 671816
Editorial, Rights & Permissions: Anne Godden; *Sales, Production, Publicity:* Al Knight
Parent Company: Quartet Books Ltd, UK (qv)
Subjects: General Australian
1981: 8 titles *Founded:* 1978
ISBN Publisher's Prefix: 0-908128

Reader's Digest Services Pty Ltd*, GPO Box 4353, Sydney, NSW 2001 (Located at: 26-32 Waterloo St, Surry Hills, NSW 2010) Tel: (02) 6990111 Cable Add: Readigest Sydney
Man Dir: M Maton; *Editorial:* Barbara Ker Wilson (Condensed Books), Nelson Kenny (Other Books); *Product Managers:* David Knibbs (Condensed Books), Sandra Step (Other Books)
Subjects: Condensed books, Reference, Educational, General
Book Club: Reader's Digest Condensed Book Services Pty Ltd
ISBN Publisher's Prefix: 0-909486

A H & A W Reed Pty Ltd*, 2 Aquatic Drive, Frenchs Forest, NSW 2086 Tel: (02) 4518122 Telex: AA 27212 Reedoz
Man Dir, Rights & Permissions: J M Reed; *Marketing Dir:* R Alexander; *Publisher & Editorial:* W Templeman; *Production:* L Somerville
Parent Company: Times Enterprises (Aust) Pty Ltd
Associate Company: Martindale Press Pty Ltd
Subjects: Books on Australia, General Non-fiction
1981: 60 titles *Founded:* 1964
ISBN Publisher's Prefix: 0-589

Review Publications Pty Ltd, 1 Sterling St, Dubbo, NSW 2830 Tel: (068) 823283
Man Dir: William Hornadge
Subjects: Philately, Australian history
1981: 2 titles *1982:* 3 titles *Founded:* 1947
ISBN Publisher's Prefix: 0-909895

Rigby Publishers Ltd+, PO Box 104, Norwood, South Australia 5067 Tel: (08) 2235566 Cable Add: Rigbylim Telex: 88090
Chief Executive: Rodney A Davis; *Publishing Manager* (General): F W Thompson; *General Manager* (Education): J D Gilder; *National Sales Manager* (General): Michael Gutzeit; *National Promotions Co-ordinator:* Pat Fedoguk
Orders to: 30 North Terrace, Kent Town, South Australia 5067
Parent Company: RPLA Pty Ltd, 176 Creek Rd South, Dee Why West, NSW 2099
Subsidiary Company: Moving Into Maths Pty Ltd (qv)
Branch Offs (Australia): 594 St Kilda Rd, Melbourne, Victoria 3004; 10 Edmonstone St, South Brisbane, Queensland 4101; 176 South Creek Rd, Dee Why West, NSW 2099; 106 Howe St, Osborne Park, Western Australia 6017
Branch Offs (Overseas): Merewether Press Inc, Suite 1202, 420 Madison Ave, New York, NY 10017, USA; Rigby International & Lansdowne International Pty Ltd, 5 Great James St, London WC1, UK
Subjects: General Fiction, Australiana, History, How-to, Art, Reference, Juveniles, Low- and High-priced Paperbacks, Secondary & Primary Textbooks, Educational Materials
Bookshop: Rigby Bookshop (qv under Major Booksellers)
1981: 181 titles *Founded:* 1859
ISBN Publisher's Prefixes: 0-85179, 0-7270

Robin Books*, PO Box 355, Wynyard, Tasmania 7321 Tel: (004) 422025
Man Dir, Editorial, Sales, Rights & Permissions: Barney Roberts; *Production, Publicity:* Bruce McM Roberts
Subjects: Poetry, Short Stories
Founded: 1976
ISBN Publisher's Prefix: 0-908030

Roebuck Books, 42 Araba St, Aranda, ACT 2614 Tel: 513284
Man Dir: Dr J S Cumpston
Subject: Australian History
Founded: 1970
ISBN Publisher's Prefixes: 0-9500858, 0-909434

Sapphire Books Pty Ltd+, PO Box 222, Strathfield, NSW 2135 (Located at: 22 Gould St, Enfield, NSW 2136) Tel: (02) 6428200
Man Dir: J Franklin
Imprints: Challenge, Clearway
Subjects: School textbooks, Study guides
1981: 54 titles *1982:* 72 titles *Founded:* 1971
ISBN Publisher's Prefixes: 0-909286, 0-85861

Scholastic, an imprint of Ashton Scholastic (qv)

Schwartz Publishing Group (Victoria) Pty Ltd*, 126 Wellington Parade, East Melbourne, Victoria 3002 Tel: (03) 4198644 Cable Add: Circus Melbourne Telex: Circus AA37222
Man Dir, Editor-in-Chief: Morry Schwartz; *Publicity Dir:* Margaret Gee
Imprint: Unicorn Books
Subjects: Fiction, Non-fiction
Founded: 1979
ISBN Publisher's Prefixes: 0-86753 (Schwartz), 0-86757 (Unicorn)

Science Research Associates Pty Ltd*, 82-84 Waterloo Rd, North Ryde, NSW 2113 Tel: (02) 8887833 Cable Add: Sciresant North Ryde Telex: AA70185
Man Dir, Rights & Permissions: R J Barton; *Editorial, Production:* A Wong; *Marketing:* C Trew
Associate Company: Science Research Associates Ltd, UK (qv for other associates)
Subjects: Primary, Secondary, Tertiary & Other Textbooks, Multimedia Learning Systems, Business tests, Computer Training Programs
ISBN Publisher's Prefix: 0-574

Scripts Publications, see Horwitz Grahame Books Pty Ltd

Second Back Row Press Pty Ltd+, PO Box 43, Leura, NSW 2060 Tel: (047) 823588
Man Dirs: Tom Whitton, Wendy Whitton
Imprints include: McNamara's Books (social & political reprints), Megalong Books (regional interest titles)
Subjects: Alternative Lifestyles, Technology, Politics, Feminism, Education, Juveniles
1981: 4 titles *Founded:* 1973
ISBN Publisher's Prefix: 0-909325

Shakespeare Head Press, 2-12 Tennyson Rd, Gladesville, NSW 2111 Tel: (02) 890421 Cable Add: Goldpress Telex: AA 26070
Man Dir: John Fink; *Publisher:* John Fenton-Smith; *Market Dir:* Peter McGill
Parent Company: Golden Press Pty Ltd (qv)
Subjects: Secondary & Primary Textbooks
1982: 6 titles *1983:* 20 titles
ISBN Publisher's Prefix: 0-85558

Sorrett, an imprint of Longman Cheshire Pty Ltd (qv)

South End Press, an imprint of Wild & Woolley Pty Ltd (qv)

South Head Press (Poetry Australia), Market Place, Berrima, NSW 2577 Tel: (048) 771384
Man Dir: Grace Perry; *Sales & Publicity:* John Millett
Subjects: Poetry & Criticism
Founded: 1964
ISBN Publisher's Prefix: 0-901760

Spectrum Publications Pty Ltd, PO Box 75, Richmond, Victoria 3121 (Located at: 127 Burnley Street, Richmond) Tel: 4291404
Man Dir: H Rohr; *Editorial:* Irene Aili; *Sales:* M Peters; *Publicity:* Henry Rohr
Subjects: Religion, Australiana, Art
1981: 10 titles
ISBN Publisher's Prefixes: 0-909837, 0-86786

Sugar and Snails Books, see Women's Movement Children's Literature Co-op Ltd

Summit Books, an imprint of Lansdowne Press (qv)

Sun Books Pty Ltd, 107 Moray St, South Melbourne, Victoria 3205 Tel: (03) 6998922 Cable Add: Sunbooks Telex: AA 34454
Man Dir: Brian Stonier
Parent Company: The Macmillan Co of Australia Pty Ltd (qv)
Imprint: Sun Papermac (Non-fiction Trade)
Subjects: General Fiction, Non-fiction, Biography, History, Music, Philosophy, Reference, Low- & High-priced Paperbacks
1981: 50 titles
ISBN Publisher's Prefix: 0-7251

Sun Papermac, an imprint of Sun Books Pty Ltd (qv)

Sydney University Press, Press Bldg, University of Sydney, NSW 2006 Tel: (02) 6604997 Cable Add: Sydpress
Dir: David New
Subjects: Scholarly Books, University Textbooks
1981: 12 titles *1982:* 10 titles *Founded:* 1964
ISBN Publisher's Prefix: 0-424

Tafe Educational Books, an imprint of New South Wales University Press Ltd (qv)

D W Thorpe Pty Ltd, 384 Spencer St, Melbourne, Victoria 3003 Tel: (03) 3295288 Cable Add: Bookstat Melbourne
Man Dir, Production, Rights & Permissions, Editorial: Michael Webster; *Sales & Advertising Manager:* Pat White

Subject: Reference
Founded: 1921
ISBN Publisher's Prefix: 0-909532

Transworld Publishers (Australia) Pty Ltd, 26 Harley Crescent, Condell Park, NSW 2200 Tel: (02) 7092022 Cable Add: Transcable Telex: 71471 AA Trapub
Man Dir: G S Rumpf; *Sales Manager:* J Crowe; *Publicity and Promotions Manager:* Miss J Curr
Associate Company: Transworld Publishers Ltd, UK (qv for other associates)
Imprints: Bantam, Corgi
Subjects: Paperbacks: General, Fiction, Educational, Juveniles; Hardbacks: Fiction, Non-fiction
Founded: 1981

Turton & Armstrong, 1 Carden Ave, Wahroonga, NSW 2076 Tel: 4872406
Publisher: Paul Armstrong
Subjects: Industrial Archaeology, Special Interest, Technical
1981: 6 titles *1982:* 6 titles *Founded:* 1977
ISBN Publisher's Prefix: 0-908031

Twistaplot, an imprint of Ashton Scholastic (qv)

Unicorn Books, an imprint of Schwartz Publishing Group (Victoria) Pty Ltd (qv)

Uniting Church Press, an imprint of The Joint Board of Christian Education of Australia and New Zealand (qv)

Universal Books, an imprint of Lansdowne Press (qv)

Universal Business Directories Pty Ltd, PO Box 155, North Ryde, NSW 2113 (Located at: 64 Talavera Rd, North Ryde) Tel: (02) 8881877 Cable Add: Directory Telex: AA 10101 Directory
General Manager: P J Coleman
Branch Offs: Melbourne, Brisbane, Adelaide, Perth
Subjects: Business Directories, Street Directories, Maps and Travel Guides
1981: 3 titles *1982:* 3 titles *Founded:* 1938
ISBN Publisher's Prefix: 0-7261

University of New South Wales, now New South Wales University Press Ltd (qv)

University of Queensland Press, PO Box 42, St Lucia, Queensland 4067 Tel: (072) 3772127 Telex: Uniqld Press AA40315
Editorial: D'Arcy Randall, Vivienne Dickson; *Sales (including Rights):* Malcolm J Beazley; *Publicity & Advertising:* Anne Barkl; *Permissions:* Sue Abbey; *Production:* Terry Farley
Subjects: Literature, Poetry, Biography, History, Music, Art, Philosophy, Reference, Religion, Low- & High-priced Paperbacks, Medicine, Psychology, Engineering, General & Social Science, University & Secondary Textbooks, Educational Materials
Bookshop: University Bookshop (at above address)
Founded: 1948
ISBN Publisher's Prefix: 0-7022

University of Western Australia Press, Nedlands, Western Australia 6009 Tel: (092) 3803182 Cable Add: Uniwest Perth
Manager, Editorial, Sales, Production, Promotion and Rights & Permissions: V S Greaves
Imprint: Cygnet Books
Subjects: Literary Criticism, Biological Sciences, Biography, History, Music, Art, Philosophy, Reference, Religion, Social Sciences, University & Secondary Textbooks, General Adult Non-fiction
1981: 23 titles *1982:* 11 titles *Founded:* 1954
ISBN Publisher's Prefix: 0-85564

Ure Smith, an imprint of Lansdowne Press (qv)

V C T A Publishing Pty Ltd, 68 Greville St, Prahran, Victoria 3181 Tel: 5293400
Dir: Mike Sherry; *Publishing Manager:* Garry Bell
Parent Company: Victorian Commercial Teachers' Association
Subjects: Educational textbooks and teacher guides in Accountancy, Economics, Legal Studies, Consumer Education, Secretarial Studies, General Business Education
1981: approx 100 titles *Founded:* 1953
ISBN Publisher's Prefix: 0-86859

Vagabond, an imprint of Ashton Scholastic (qv)

The Helen **Vale** Foundation, PO Box 359, Warwick, Queensland 4370 (Located at: Freestone Rd, Kingsford Heights, Warwick)
Executive Dir: Kenneth J Ingbritsen
Associate Company: Centre Publications (qv)
Branch Off: 25 Chapel St, East Saint Kilda, Melbourne, Victoria 3182
Subjects: Education, Health
1983: 7 titles *Founded:* 1970
ISBN Publisher's Prefix: 0-909698

Vantage House, an imprint of L & S Publishing Co (qv)

Visa Books, PO Box 186, Glen Iris, Victoria 3146 (Located at: 3rd Floor, 316 Queen St, Melbourne, Victoria 3000) Tel: (03) 675747/256456 Telex: 38225 AA
Man Dir: Charles Wantrup; *Publisher:* Geoffrey M Gold
Associate Company: General Magazine Co Pty Ltd
Subjects: Politics, Sports, History, Biography, Media & Communications, Economics, Culture
Founded: 1977
ISBN Publisher's Prefix: 0-949763

Wadsworth International Group, PO Box 278, Artarmon, NSW 2064 Cable Add: Wadspur Sydney Telex: AA 79010101 Intsy
Head Off: 10 Davis Dr, Belmont, California 94002, USA

Was Is Press*, PO Box 2, Moreland 3058 Tel: (03) 3863166
Proprietor: Yvonne Rousseau

Wentworth Books Pty Ltd, 26 Harriett St, Marrickville, NSW 2204 Tel: 5592223
Dirs: Walter P Stone, Peter E Stone
Associate Companies: Stone Printing Co Pty Ltd, Wentworth Press Pty Ltd
Subjects: Australian History, Literature, Biography, Educational, Bibliography
ISBN Publisher's Prefix: 0-85587

Westbooks Pty Ltd*, 127 Burswood Rd, Victoria Park, WA 6100 Tel: (09) 3618288
Dirs: Rayma and David Turton (Westbooks), Paul Armstrong (Turton & Armstrong)
Subjects: Educational, Technical, Juvenile, Industrial Archaeology
Bookshops (specialist children's): At above address; 4/29 Bayview Terrace, Claremont, WA 6010; Rapid Creek Shopping Centre, Rapid Creek, NT

Whitman, Australia Pty Ltd, an associated imprint of Golden Press Pty Ltd (qv)

Wild & Woolley Pty Ltd, PO Box 41, Glebe, NSW 2037 (Located at: 16 Darghan St, Glebe, NSW 2037) Tel: (02) 6920166
Man Dir: Pat Woolley
Associate Company: Allbooks Distribution
Imprints: And/or, New Directions, Pluto, South End Press, Writers & Readers
Branch Off: 13162 Highway 8 No 204, El Cajon, California 92021, USA

Subjects: Fiction, Cartoons, Art, Politics
1981: 5 titles *Founded:* 1974
ISBN Publisher's Prefix: 0-909331

Wildfire, an imprint of Ashton Scholastic (qv)

John **Wiley**, an imprint of Jacaranda Wiley Ltd (qv)

Windswept, an imprint of Ashton Scholastic (qv)

Wizware, an imprint of Ashton Scholastic (qv)

Wobbledagger*, 5/1 Parkview Rd, Manly, NSW 2095 Tel: 2901411
Man Dirs: Ian Hoyle, Sally Hoyle
Subjects: Children's Books
Founded: 1977

Women's Movement Children's Literature Co-op Ltd, PO Box 119, Mooroolbark, Victoria 3138 Tel: 7283291
Chief Executive: Jan Harper; *All other offices:* Noelle McCracken
Subsidiary Company: Sugar and Snails Books
Subjects: Counter-sexist children's books, Fiction and Non-fiction
1981: 4 titles *Founded:* 1974
ISBN Publisher's Prefix: 0-908092

Writers & Readers, an imprint of Wild & Woolley Pty Ltd (qv)

Remainder Dealers

Universal Books*, 176 South Creek Rd, Dee Why West, NSW 2099 Tel: (02) 9822344
Manager: Ken Beaton
Parent Company: Lansdowne Press (qv)

Literary Agents

Curtis Brown (Australia) Pty Ltd, 86 William St, Paddington, Sydney, NSW 2021 Tel: 3315301/336161 Cable Add: Browncurt Sydney
Man Dir: Tim Curnow; *Dir:* Barbara Mobbs

Book Clubs

Arrow, PO Box 579, Gosford, NSW 2250
Owned by: Ashton Scholastic (qv)

Book Australia, see Doubleday Australia Pty Ltd, Book Club Division

Book-of-the-Month Club, see Doubleday Australia Pty Ltd, Book Club Division

Doubleday Australia Pty Ltd, Book Club Division, 14 Mars Rd, Lane Cove, NSW 2066
Man Dir: Peter B Madgwick; *Editorial:* Suzanne Delmont; *Marketing:* John D Madgwick
Includes: Book-of-the-Month Club, Doubleday Book Club, The Literary Guild, Doubleday History Book Club, Book Australia, Military Book Club, Postmarket

Doubleday Book Club, see Doubleday Australia Pty Ltd, Book Club Division

Doubleday History Book Club, see Doubleday Australia Pty Ltd, Book Club Division

The **Literary Guild**, see Doubleday Australia Pty Ltd, Book Club Division

Lucky, PO Box 579, Gosford, NSW 2250
Owned by: Ashton Scholastic (qv)

Military Book Club, see Doubleday Australia Pty Ltd, Book Club Division

Postmarket, see Doubleday Australia Pty Ltd, Book Club Division

Reader's Digest Condensed Book Services Pty Ltd, GPO Box 4353, Sydney, NSW 2001
Editor: Barbara Ker Wilson
Owned by: Reader's Digest Services Pty Ltd (qv)

Star, PO Box 579, Gosford, NSW 2250
Owned by: Ashton Scholastic (qv)

Teachers Bookshelf, PO Box 579, Gosford, NSW 2250
Owned by: Ashton Scholastic (qv)

Teenage, PO Box 579, Gosford, NSW 2250
Owned by: Ashton Scholastic (qv)

Major Booksellers

Abbey's Bookshop, 66 King St, Sydney, NSW 2000 Tel: (02) 291093
Manager: Peter Milne

Angus & Robertson Bookshops, GPO Box 1516, Sydney, NSW 2000 (Located at: Imperial Arcade, Sydney) Tel: (02) 2351188 Telex: 25460 AA
This is the main shop; there are about 70 branches, including all states of NSW

Australian Government Publications*, Mt Newman House, 200 St George's Terrace, Perth, Western Australia 6000 Tel: (093) 224737

Birchalls*, 118-120 Brisbane St, PO Box 170, Launceston, Tasmania 7250 Tel: 313011 Telex: 58816
Man Dir: Raymond F Tilley
Parent Company: A W Birchall & Sons Pty Ltd (at above address)
Branches: Birchalls Hobart Bookshop, 152 Elizabeth St, Hobart, Tasmania; University Bookshop, University of Tasmania, Student Union Bldg, Churchill Ave, Sandy Bay, Hobart, Tasmania; The College Bookroom, Tasmania College of Advanced Education, Plumer St, Mowbray, Tasmania; The College Bookshop, Tasmania College of Advanced Education, Olinda Grove, Mt Nelson, Tasmania
Australia's oldest (founded 1844) and Tasmania's largest bookseller

Collins Booksellers Pty Ltd, 86 Bourke St, Melbourne, Victoria 3000 Tel: (03) 6622711
This is the head office; there are 29 branches
Man Dir: Michael Zifcak; *General Manager:* Peter Shaw
Associate Company: Hill of Content Publishing Co Ltd (qv)

Dymock's Pty Ltd, 428 George St, Sydney, NSW 2000 Tel: (02) 2334111 (several branches)
Man Dir: J P C Forsyth

Foreign Language Bookshop, 94 Elizabeth St, Melbourne, Victoria 3000 Tel: (03) 6542883
Manager: A Monester

Grahames Bookshop, Corner Pitt and Hunter Sts, Sydney, NSW 2000 Tel: (02) 2321966
Branches: Bankstown Shopping Square, Bankstown, NSW 2200; Mid-City Centre, 197 Pitt St, Sydney, NSW 2000; City Tatts, 200 Pitt St, Sydney, NSW 2000; MLC Building, 105 Miller St, North Sydney, NSW 2060; Imperial Centre, Mann St, Gosford, NSW 2250
Division of Horwitz Grahame Books Pty Ltd (qv)

Language Book Centre, 127 York St, Sydney 2000 Tel: 2671397
Manager: Hanni Bäaske

Queensland Book Depot, 61-63 Adelaide St, Brisbane, Queensland 4000 Tel: (072) 312331
This is the head office; there are 18 branches

Rigby Bookshop, School Centre, 30 North Terrace, Kent Town, SA 5067 Tel: (08) 2235566
Manager: Paul Wadham
Division of Rigby Publishers (qv)

University Co-operative Bookshop Ltd, 80 Bay St, Broadway, NSW 2007 Tel: (02) 2122211 Telex: AA21968
25 branches
General Manager: J McLoone

Major Libraries

Australian National University Library, GPO Box 4, Canberra, ACT 2601 Tel: (062) 495111 Cable Add: Natuniv Telex: AA 62760
Librarian: C R Steele

The **Barr Smith** Library*, The University of Adelaide, Adelaide, South Australia 5001 Tel: (08) 2285333 Telex: Univad AA89141
University Librarian: E J Wainwright

C S I R O (Commonwealth Scientific and Industrial Research Organization), Central Information, Library and Editorial Section, Bureau of Scientific Services, PO Box 89, East Melbourne, Victoria 3002 (Located at: 314 Albert St, East Melbourne) Tel: (03) 4187333 Telex: 30236
Officer-in-Charge: P J Judge; *Editor-in-Chief:* B J Walby; *Chief Librarian:* P H Dawe; *Manager, Information Service:* C Garrow
Publications include: CSIRO Index, Australian Science Index, Commonwealth Regional Renewable Energy Resources Index (microfiche), Scientific Serials in Australian Libraries (microfiche), Scientific and Technical Research Centres in Australia (microfiche), CSIRO-SDI User Manuals, CILES Biennial Report

High Court of Australia Library, Parkes Pl, Canberra, ACT 2600 Tel: 706922
Librarian: Mark Powell

The **Library Board of Western Australia**, Henley House, 102 Beaufort St, Perth, WA 6000 Tel: (09) 3287466 Telex: Wainf 92231
State Librarian: Robert Sharman
Publication: Bibla (monthly)

National Library of Australia, Parkes Pl, Canberra, ACT 2600 Tel: (062) 621111 Cable Add: Natlibaust Canberra Telex: 62100
Director of Publications: A T Bolton
Publications include: Australian National Bibliography (twice monthly with annual cumulation), APAIS (monthly with annual cumulation), Australian Government Publications (quarterly), SALSSAH (Serials in Australian Libraries Social Sciences and Humanities) (quarterly)

Patent, Trade Marks and Designs Office Library*, Scarborough House, Phillip, PO Box 200, Woden, ACT 2606 Tel: (062) 832304 Cable Add: Compat Telex: 61517

The **State Library of New South Wales**, Macquarie St, Sydney, NSW 2000 Tel: (02) 2211388 Telex: 21150
State Librarian: R F Doust
Publications include: Annual Report, New South Wales Official Publications Received in the State Library, Public Libraries Division: Newsletter

State Library of Queensland*, William St, Brisbane, Queensland 4000
Includes the Oxley Library
Librarian: S L Ryan
Publications include: Annual Statistical Bulletin of Queensland Public Libraries Services, 1968- ; Queensland Government Publications, 1977- (quarterly); Directory of State and Public Library Service in Queensland (annual); The Development of State Libraries and their effect on the Public Library Movement in Australia, 1809-1964; North Queensland Towns and Districts Bibliography, 1975

State Library of South Australia, GPO Box 419, Adelaide, SA 5001 (Located at: North Terrace, Adelaide, SA 5000) Tel: 2238911 Telex: 82074
Formerly Public Library of South Australia
Publications: South Australiana (twice yearly), Pinpointer (two-monthly), Annual Report

State Library of Tasmania, 91 Murray St, Hobart, Tasmania 7000 Tel: (002) 308033 Telex: 58222
State Librarian: W L Brown
Publication: Annual report

State Library of Victoria, 328 Swanston St, Melbourne, Victoria 3000 Tel: (03) 6699888 Telex: 38104
State Librarian: W M Horton
Publications include: Annual report, La Trobe Library Journal (two a year)

University of Melbourne Library, Parkville, Victoria 3052 Tel: (03) 3415378 Telex: 30815 AA
University Librarian: W D Richardson

University of New South Wales Library, PO Box 1, Kensington, NSW 2033 Tel: 6630351 Telex: 20467 AA Unitech
Librarian: A R Horton
Publications include: Annual Report, Staff Papers

University of Queensland Library, St Lucia, Queensland, Australia 4067 Tel: (07) 3772304 Cable Add: Brisbane University Telex: 40315 AA Univqld
University Librarian: F D O Fielding
Publications include: Annual Report, Know your University

University of Sydney Library, Sydney, NSW 2006 Tel: (02) 6922222 Telex: 20056
University Librarian: Dr Neil A Radford

University of Western Australia Library, Nedlands, Western Australia 6009 Tel: 3803838 Cable Add: Uniwest Telex: Uniwa 92992
Librarian: A Ellis

Library Associations

Australian Advisory Council on Bibliographical Services (AACOBS), National Library, Canberra, ACT 2600
Chairman: The Hon Sir Peter Crisp
Publications include: Library Services for Australia: The Work of AACOBS (annual); Current Australian Reference Books: a list for medium and small libraries; Joint-use Libraries in the Australian Community; 'Pinpointer' Popular Periodicals on Microfiche (annual); You name it! Helpful hints for editors and publishers of journals

Australian Archives, NSW Regional Office, PO Box C328, Clarence St, Sydney, NSW 2000 (Located at: Level 5, National Mutual Centre, 44 Market St, Sydney, NSW) Tel: (02) 296352
Regional Director: P J Scott
Publications: Inventories, Guides (irregular)

Australian Library Promotion Council, Executive Director, 328 Swanston St, Melbourne, Victoria 3000 Tel: (03) 635994
President: Dulcie Stretton, CBE; *Honorary Secretary:* Joyce Nicholson
Publications: Australian Library News (8 issues per year), *Bookmark* (Annual Directory/Diary), *Report to the Nation*

Australian School Library Association*, PO Box 122, Nunawading, Victoria 3131 Tel: (03) 8423741
Executive Secretary: Rosemary Flora
Publications include: School Libraries in Australia (official quarterly journal)

Australian Society of Archivists Inc, PO Box 83, O'Connor, ACT 2601
President: Ms B Berzins; *Secretary:* Ms A M Schwirtlich (at above address)

International Association of Music Libraries, Australian Branch (IAMLANZ), National Library of Australia, Canberra, ACT 2600
President: Prue Neidorf
Publication: Continuo

Lasie Australia Co Ltd, PO Box 602, Lane Cove, NSW 2066 Tel: (02) 4272181
The Library Automated Systems Information Exchange
President: Dorothy G Peake; *Executive Officer:* Arne L Pedersen
Publication: LASIE (Information Bulletin)

Library Association of Australia*, 473 Elizabeth St, Surry Hills, NSW 2010
Executive Director: Susan Acutt
Publications include: Australian Library Journal, Incite, Handbook, Directory of Special Libraries in Australia, Australian Academic and Research Libraries, Australian Special Libraries News, Orana, Cataloguing Australia, Conference Proceedings, Copyright Kit, Library Services in Distance Education, Periodicals for School Libraries, Teacher Librarians: the mid 80s and beyond

The **Library Automated Systems** Information Exchange, see Lasie

Medical Librarians' Group, Central Library, Australian Department of Health, PO Box 100, Woden, ACT 2606
Convener: Mrs P Ramsay (at above address)

Public Lending Right Scheme, The Administrator PLR, PO Box 812, North Sydney, NSW 2060 Tel: 9233379 Telex: 26013

State Librarians' Council, c/o State Library of Tasmania, 91 Murray St, Hobart, Tasmania 7000 Tel: (002) 302450 Telex: 58222 AA
Chairman: W L Brown

Library Reference Books and Journals

Books

Current Australian Reference Books: a list for medium and small libraries, Australian Advisory Council on Bibliographical Services (AACOBS), National Library, Canberra, ACT 2600

Directory of Special Libraries in Australia, Library Association of Australia, 473 Elizabeth St, Surry Hills, NSW 2010

Library Association of Australia: Handbook, Library Association of Australia, 473 Elizabeth St, Surry Hills, NSW 2010

Journals

Acquisitions Newsletter (five or six times yearly), Sales and Subscriptions Unit, National Library of Australia, Parkes Pl, Canberra, ACT 2600

Archives and Manuscripts, A Lemon (Editor), 704 Toorak Rd, Malvern, Victoria 3144

Australian Academic and Research Libraries, Library Association of Australia, 473 Elizabeth St, Surry Hills, NSW 2010

Australian Library Journal, Library Association of Australia, 473 Elizabeth St, Surry Hills, NSW 2010

Australian Library News, Australian Library Promotion Council, 328 Swanston St, Melbourne, Victoria 3000

Australian School Librarian (quarterly), PO Box 280, East Melbourne, Victoria 3001

Australian Special Libraries News, Library Association of Australia, Special Libraries Section, 32 Belvoir St, Surry Hills, NSW 2010

Biblia (monthly), The Library Board of Western Australia, Henley House, 102 Beaufort St, Perth, WA 6000

Cataloguing Australia (quarterly), c/o School of Librarianship, University of New South Wales, Kensington, NSW 2033

Incite (Library Association Newsletter), Library Association of Australia, 473 Elizabeth St, Surry Hills, NSW 2010

La Trobe Library Journal (two a year), State Library of Victoria, 328 Swanston St, Melbourne, Victoria 3000

Library Services for Australia: the Work of AACOBS (annual), Australian Advisory Council on Bibliographical Services (AACOBS), National Library, Canberra, ACT 2600

Orana (Children's Libraries Newsletter), Library Association of Australia, 473 Elizabeth St, Surry Hills, NSW 2010

'Pinpointer' Popular Periodicals on Microfiche (annual), Australian Advisory Council on Bibliographical Services (AACOBS), National Library, Canberra, ACT 2600

School Libraries in Australia (official quarterly journal), Australian School Library Association, PO Box 122, Nunawading, Victoria 3131

School Library Bulletin (quarterly), Education Department, Library Branch, 449 Swanston St, Melbourne, Victoria 3000

Teacher-Librarian (quarterly), PO Box 21, Waverley, NSW 2024

Literary Associations and Societies

Association for the Study of Australian Literature, c/o Department of English, University of Adelaide, GPO Box 498, Adelaide, SA 5001 Tel: (08) 2285333
Secretary: Robin Eaden
Founded: 1978

Australian Literature Society, incorporated in 1982 within Association for the Study of Australian Literature (qv)

Australian Society of Authors Ltd, 22 Alfred St, Milsons Point, NSW 2061 Tel: (02) 927235
Executive Officer: Margot Hilton
Publications: The Australian Author (quarterly), *Australian Book Contracts, The Australian and New Zealand Writers' Handbook, Guidelines in the acquisition of film rights in literary properties* and other publications of professional/industrial interest to those who write for publication

Australian Writers' Guild Ltd, Suite 505, Fifth Floor, 83 York St, Sydney, NSW 2000 Tel: (02) 291402
General Secretary: Angela Wales
Publications include: Copyright and Technology: a symposium; The Writers' Directory: writers for screen, stage, radio and television in Australia; Conference Proceedings

Bibliographical Society of Australia and New Zealand, c/o GPO Box 419, Adelaide, SA 5001
Secretary: Helen M Thomson
Publications include: Bulletin (quarterly); *Broadsheet* (three times a year)

Book Collectors' Society of Australia, 64 Young St, Cremorne, NSW 2090 Tel: 902184
President: John Fletcher (at above address)
Publication: Biblionews and Australian Notes and Queries (quarterly), plus *Index 1947-1979*

Bread and Cheese Club*, 51 Elizabeth St, Newport, Victoria 3015 Tel: 3913039
Secretary: Dr Cyril Goode

The **Dickens** Fellowship*, 29 Henley Beach Rd, Henley Beach, Adelaide, SA 5022
Honorary Secretary: G J Rowe
Also at:
Brisbane: Unit No 3, 12 Sydney St, New Farm, Queensland 4005
Honorary Secretary: Mrs G M Taylor
Melbourne: Flat 143, 200 Dorcas St, South Melbourne 3205, Victoria
Honorary Secretary: Mrs Barbara Barrett

Fellowship of Australian Writers (NSW), GPO Box 3448, Sydney, NSW 2001
Secretary: Shirley Goon
Membership: 700
Publication: Bulletin (bi-monthly)
Seventeen regional branches in suburbs of Sydney and country towns

Fellowship of Australian Writers, Victorian, see Victorian Fellowship of Australian Writers

Fellowship of Australian Writers (WA), Tom Collins House, 9 Servetus St, Swanbourne, WA 6010

International **P E N** (Melbourne Centre)*, President, 101 Edgevale Rd, Kew, Victoria 3101
President: Barbara Giles; *Secretary:* Anne Parratt

International **P E N** (Sydney Centre), President, 1 Sussex St, St Ives, Woollahra, NSW 2025 Tel: 325668
President: Stephen Kelen; *Secretary:* Susan Yorke
Publication: Newsletter (quarterly)

Poetry Society of Australia*, Box N110 Grosvenor Street PO, Sydney, NSW 2000
Joint Secretaries: Robert and Debra Adamson
Publication: New Poetry (quarterly). Publishes poems, articles, reviews, notes and comments, interviews

Society of Australian Writers, Australia House, Strand, London WC2, UK
Secretary: Alessandra Miach

Victorian Fellowship of Australian Writers, J Hamilton, 1/317 Barkers Rd, Kew, Victoria 3101
Membership: 1600

Literary Periodicals

A U M L A, a journal of literary criticism, philology and linguistics (text in English and French), Australasian Universities Language and Literature Association, James Cook University of North Queensland, Townsville, Queensland 4811

The Australian Author (quarterly), Australian Society of Authors, 22 Alfred St, Milsons Point, NSW 2061

Australian Literary Studies, Department of English, University of Queensland, Saint Lucia, Queensland 4067

Australian Writers and Their Work, Oxford University Press, 7 Bowen Crescent, Melbourne, Victoria 3000

Biblionews and Australian Notes and Queries (quarterly), Book Collectors' Society of Australia, 64 Young St, Cremorne, NSW 2090

Island Magazine (quarterly), PO Box 207, Sandy Bay, Tasmania 7005

Meanjin Quarterly, a magazine of literature, art and discussion, University of Melbourne, Parkville, Victoria 3052

New Poetry, Box 110, George St North PO, Sydney, NSW 2001

Overland, GPO Box 98a, Melbourne, Victoria 3001

Poetry Australia, 350 Lyons Rd, Five Dock, NSW 2046

Quadrant, Box C344, Clarence St Post Office, Sydney, NSW 2000

Reading Time, Children's Book Council of Australia, New South Wales Branch, PO Box 159, Curtin, ACT 2605

Southerly, a review of Australian literature (English Association, Sydney Branch), Department of English, University of Sydney, Sydney, NSW 2006

Westerly, English Department, University of Western Australia, Nedlands, Western Australia 6009

Literary Prizes

'The **Age**' Book of the Year
Prizes of $2,000 each will be awarded by 'The Age' to the two Australian books of outstanding literary merit which best express Australia's identity or character. One prize will be for a work of imaginative writing; the other for a non-fiction work. One will be named 'The Age' Book of the Year, the other the best work in its category. Enquiries to The Literary Editor, 'The Age', 250 Spencer St, Melbourne, Victoria 3000

The **Alice** Literary Award
Presented by The Society of Women Writers (Australia) biennially for a distinguished and long-term contribution to literature by an Australian woman. First presented in 1978. The 1982 award went to Dame Mary Durack-Miller. Enquiries to Ethel Shippen, Chief Executive, Society of Women Writers, PO Box 197, Greenacres, SA 5086

Angus & Robertson Writers' Fellowship
For a manuscript or book project of outstanding originality, preferably by a new author. Contract with advance of $2,000. Enquiries to The Publisher, Angus & Robertson Publishers, PO Box 290, North Ryde, NSW 2113

The Kitty **Archer-Burton** Award
Presented by the Society of Women Writers (Australia) biennially for verse by a youth of under 19 years of age. First presented in 1979. The 1981 award went to Susan Kennedy. Enquiries to Ethel Shippen, Chief Executive, Society of Women Writers, PO Box 197, Greenacres, SA 5086

Australian Awards for Young Writers
Awarded by BHP, Shell, the State of Victoria and the Victorian FAW for poetry, stories, essays, scripts and collections; for young writers 15-21 years. Varying conditions. It includes the BHP-FAW Young Poets Publishing Project. Administered by Victorian Fellowship of Australian Writers. Closing date 31 January. Enquiries to J Hamilton, 1/317 Barkers Rd, Kew, Victoria 3101

Australian Literature Society Gold Medal
Awarded for the best Australian literary work published each year, or, occasionally, for outstanding services to Australian literature. Originated by Colonel, the Honourable R A Crouch in 1899. Enquiries to Secretary, Association for the Study of Australian Literature, c/o Department of English, University of Adelaide, GPO Box 498, Adelaide, SA 5001

Australian Natives' Association Literature Award
Founded in 1978 as an award for a book on an Australian theme. Prize $300. Administered by Victorian Fellowship of Australian Writers. Closing date 31 December. Enquiries to J Hamilton, 1/317 Barkers Rd, Kew, Victoria 3101

Bookman of the Year Award*
Awarded by the National Book Council to a person who has made a substantial contribution to the promotion of books, but who might not necessarily be expected to be eligible for many of the other awards listed in this section. Enquiries to National Book Council. 199 Cardigan St, Carlton, Victoria 3053

Christopher **Brennan** Award, see FAW Christopher Brennan Award

Bronze Swagman Award
Awarded annually for Bush Verse. Bronze statuette of The Swagman, sculpted by Daphne Mayo, valued at $500, and a Winton opal, valued at $50. Closes May 31st. Enquiries to Winton Tourist Promotion Association, PO Box 44, Winton, Queensland 4735

The '**Canberra Times**' National Short Story of the Year Competition
$2,500 and $1,000 awarded annually for a short story. Enquiries to The 'Canberra Times', GPO Box 443, Canberra, ACT 2601

Ronald **Carson-Gold** Memorial Short Story Competition*
Awarded annually. Closes 23 April. Short story by Australian with Australian setting. 1st Prize $600, 2nd Prize $300, 3rd Prize $100. Administered by the Union Fidelity Trust. Enquiries to Carson-Gold Short Story Competition, PO Box 339, Toowong, Brisbane, Queensland 4066

Children's Book of the Year Awards
Awarded annually by the Children's Book Council of Australia. The awards now fall into three sections. (1) Book of the Year, established 1946. Primarily for literary merit but quality of production considered. The Literature Board makes $2,500 available, of which at least $1,500 must go to the winner, who also receives the Council's medal. Awarded in 1983 to Victor Kelleher for *Master of the Grove* (Penguin). (2) Picture Book of the Year, for younger children. The Visual Art Board award $2,500 to illustrators; a minor portion may be given to runner(s) up. Awarded in 1983 to Pamela Allen for *Who Sank the Boat?* (Nelson Australia). (3) Junior Book of the Year, established 1982. The Council's medal is awarded to the author, and also to the illustrator if the illustrations add significantly to the text. The award is for a book intended primarily for children with independent reading skills, but who have not yet the maturity to appreciate fully the Book of the Year. Awarded in 1983 to Robin Klein (author) and Alison Lester (illustrator) for *Thing* (Oxford University Press). Authors and illustrators entered for awards in the three sections must be Australian citizens, or resident in Australia for five of the last ten years, or provide evidence of intention to reside permanently in Australia. Closing date is 31 December, for books published during that year. Entries must be sent by publishers to the State Children's Book Council which is providing the executive for that particular year. Enquiries to The Secretary, Children's Book Council of Australia, PO Box 420, Dickson, ACT 2602 or Library Services, 35 Mitchell St, North Sydney, NSW 2060

Tom **Collins** Poetry Prize
Administered by Western Australia FAW. Prize of $250. First awarded in 1977. Annual closing date mid-January. Enquiries to Secretary, Fellowship of Australian Writers (WA), Tom Collins House, 9 Servetus St, Swanbourne, WA 6010

James **Cook** Australian Literary Studies Award
$1,500 from the Townsville Foundation for Australian Literary Studies at the James Cook University of North Queensland. The award is made to the author of the best book dealing with any aspect of Australian life. The book must have been published in Australia, even though printed elsewhere. The publication may be in any field of writing — fiction, poetry, drama, letters, biographical or historical. Closing date is 28 February. Enquiries to Executive Director, Foundation for Australian Literary Studies, English Department, James Cook University, Townsville, Queensland 4811

C J **Dennis** Award
$1,000, originally for a book about Australian flora and/or fauna, but not necessarily for that category in future. Award provided by Victorian Government and administered by Victorian Fellowship of Australian Writers. Closing date 31 December. Enquiries to J Hamilton, 1/317 Barkers Rd, Kew, Victoria 3101

Anne **Elder** Poetry Award
$900 for first books of poetry. Administered by Victorian Fellowship of Australian Writers. Closing date 31 December. Enquiries to J Hamilton, 1/317 Barkers Rd, Kew, Victoria 3101

F A W Barbara **Ramsden** Award
Awarded by the Victorian Fellowship of Australian Writers to both the author and to the editor of an outstanding work of quality writing and presentation published each year. It is the Fellowship's major national award for quality writing and was founded by public subscription to honour Barbara Ramsden, MBE, a publisher's editor of distinction. The winning author and editor are each presented with a plaquette specially designed by sculptor Andor Meszaros, depicting the origin of art. More than one work may be submitted by any publisher, author or publisher's editor in Australia. The

'editor' is to be that person the publisher regards as responsible for editing the work. Closing date 31 December. Enquiries to J Hamilton, 1/317 Barkers Rd, Kew, Victoria 3101

F A W Christopher Brennan Award
Formerly called the Robert Frost Award. A plaque designed by sculptor Michael Meszaros is awarded to a poet in Australia whose work, particularly if sustained, achieves distinction. Entries not required. The 1982 award was made to Bruce Beaver. Administered by the Victorian Fellowship of Australian Writers. Enquiries to J Hamilton, 1/317 Barkers Rd, Kew, Victoria 3101

F A W John Shaw Neilson Poetry Award
Awarded by the Victorian Fellowship of Australian Writers. Any kind of poem is acceptable with a minimum of 14 lines. Merit will be the criterion. First prize at least $150. In 1982 the first prize was awarded to Vera Urban. Closing date 31 December. Enquiries to J Hamilton, 1/317 Barkers Rd, Kew, Victoria 3101

F A W Local History Award
Formerly awarded by the Australian and New Zealand Bank for a book of Australian local or regional history published during the year. Administered by Victorian Fellowship of Australian Writers. Closing date 31 December. Enquiries to J Hamilton, 1/317 Barkers Rd, Kew, Victoria 3101

F A W Regional Branch Awards
Various FAW regional branches such as Parramatta, Ballarat, Eastwood, Geelong, Latrobe Valley and North Central hold occasional or regular awards, usually in the area of stories and poetry, for small cash prizes and sometimes publication. They are sometimes open within the State or the Nation

Miles **Franklin** Award
Awarded annually for a published novel portraying Australian life in any of its phases. Entrants must submit one copy of the published work to each of the five judges, and also one copy to the Permanent Trustee Co Ltd, within two months of its publication. Closing date is 31 January. For 1982 the award was $3,500. Enquiries to The Manager, Permanent Trustee Co Ltd, Box 4270, GPO Sydney, NSW 2001

Robert **Frost** Award, now called FAW Christopher Brennan Award (qv)

Grenfell 'Henry Lawson' Festival Prizes
Awarded annually in June with engraved bronze statuettes created by Sydney sculptor Alan Ingham, and cash. Awards are made for prose, verse, art and the words and music of an Australian popular song. Prose (a short story up to 4,000 words); Verse (up to 60 lines). Enquiries to Honorary Secretary, PO Box 77, Grenfell, NSW 2810

Lyndal **Hadow** Short Story Award
Prize of $200 for a short story not exceeding 3000 words. Annual closing date mid-June. Enquiries to Secretary, Fellowship of Australian Writers (WA), Tom Collins House, 9 Servetus St, Swanbourne, WA 6010

The Grace **Leven** Prize for Poetry
Instituted under the Will of William Baylebridge, the Australian poet, who died in 1942. This prize of $200 is offered annually for 'the best volume of poetry published during the twelve months immediately preceding the year in which the award is made'. Competitors must be either Australian born, and writing as Australians, or they must be naturalized in Australia and have lived in that country for at least ten years. The volume chosen may have been published in any country, but copies of it must be freely obtainable in Australia. Enquiries to Perpetual Trustee Co Ltd, 39 Hunter St, Sydney, NSW 2000

Jessie **Litchfield** Memorial Award*
A cash prize of $300 and a bronze plaque awarded annually by the Bread and Cheese Club, Melbourne, to encourage writers who, in the opinion of the Committee, may make a contribution to Australian literature. Entry forms available on request accompanied by return postage. Enquiries to Dr Cyril Goode, Bread and Cheese Club, 51 Elizabeth St, Newport, Victoria 3015

Literature Board of the Australia Council
The Literature Board supports the writing of all forms of creative literature, including novels, short stories, poetry and plays. Aid is also given to some non-fiction (especially biography, autobiography, history and the humanities). All individual applicants must use the Literature Board's application form. Enquiries to Secretary, Literature Board of the Australia Council, PO Box 302, North Sydney, NSW 2060

Local History Award, see FAW Local History Award

The Walter **McRae Russell** Award
To be awarded annually to a young writer for, for example, a work of literary history. Originated in 1983. Enquiries to Secretary, Association for the Study of Australian Literature, c/o Department of English, University of Adelaide, GPO Box 498, Adelaide, SA 5001

Alan **Marshall** Award
For the best unpublished manuscript that encourages literature and which contains a strong narrative element. Prize currently $500. Sponsored and administered by Victorian Fellowship of Australian Writers. Closing date 31 December. Enquiries to J Hamilton, 1/317 Barkers Rd, Kew, Victoria 3101

The Charles **Meeking** Award
Presented by the Society of Women Writers (Australia) biennially for verse by an Australian woman. First presented in 1979. The 1981 award went to Margaret Galbraith. Enquiries to Ethel Shippen, Chief Executive, Society of Women Writers, PO Box 197, Greenacres, SA 5086

National Book Council Awards*
Awarded by the National Book Council, first prize $3,000 ($600 to publisher) for book of highest literary merit, 2nd prize $2,000 ($400 to publisher) for book of highest literary merit in a category other than that of the book winning first prize. Enquiries to Executive Secretary, National Book Council, 199 Cardigan St, Carlton, Victoria 3053

John Shaw **Neilson** Poetry Award, see FAW John Shaw Neilson Poetry Award

Barbara **Ramsden** Award, see FAW Barbara Ramsden Award

Shell Book of the Year
A copy of the chosen book is distributed to the library of each post-primary school in Australia. Sponsored by Shell Oil Company (see also Australian Awards for Young Writers). Closing date 31 December. Enquiries to J Hamilton, 1/317 Barkers Rd, Kew, Victoria 3101

South Australian Government Biennial Literature Prize
Two awards for literature were given by the South Australian Government in 1982. Each award was of $3,000, the first for a South Australian regional history or biography, the second (for writers who have had no more than two books published) for a work of poetry, fiction or drama. Enquiries to Arts Development Division, Department for the Arts, PO Box 2308, Adelaide, SA 5001

State of Victoria Short Story Awards
(1) Awarded annually; prizes of $700, $250 and $200 to Australian writers for original short stories. There will also be other awards, e.g. of $50 each for unpublished writers. Stories should be unpublished and not exceed 4,000 words. More than one entry may be submitted in all sections.
(2) Awarded annually; prizes of $140, $40 and $20 to young writers 15-22 years. Sponsored by the Victorian Ministry for the Arts and administered by Victorian Fellowship of Australian Writers. Closing date 31 December. Enquiries to J Hamilton, 1/317 Barkers Rd, Kew, Victoria 3101

Walter **Stone** Memorial Award
For a monograph, biography or bibliography on some aspect of Australian literature. Biennial prize of $300 plus certificate. Enquiries to Walter Stone Memorial Award, Fellowship of Australian Writers, Box 3448 GPO, Sydney, NSW

Townsville Foundation for Australian Literary Studies Award
For the best book dealing with any aspect of Australian life. 1982 award was $1,500. Enquiries to Executive Director, Foundation for Australian Literary Studies, English Department, James Cook University, Townsville, Queensland 4811

Warana Writers' Awards*
Awarded annually by the Fellowship of Australian Writers (Queensland Branch) for poetry, feature article and short story. Closes 25 August. Enquiries to Mrs Jean Scott, PO Box 339, Toowong, Brisbane, Queensland 4066

Con **Weickhardt** Award
Awarded for a published work of biography, autobiography or a memoir. $500. Administered by the Victorian Fellowship of Australian Writers. Closing date 31 December. Enquiries to Secretariat, 1/317 Barkers Rd, Kew, Victoria 3101

Patricia **Weickhardt** Award
Cash prize to an aboriginal writer. Administered by Victorian Fellowship of Australian Writers. Closing date 31 December. Enquiries to J Hamilton, 1/317 Barkers Rd, Kew, Victoria 3101

Patrick **White** Award
Patrick White has applied his Nobel Prize money to establish a trust to make grants to Australian writers who have been inadequately recognized. Submissions are not required. Enquiries to J Allison, c/o Woollahra Municipal Library, Double Bay, NSW 2028

Wilke Literary Award
For a work of non-fiction, of literary merit, published and wholly manufactured in Australia. Administered by the Victorian Fellowship of Australian Writers. Closing date 31 December. Enquiries to J Hamilton, 1/317 Barkers Rd, Kew, Victoria 3101

Austria

General Information

Language: German. There are speakers of Slovene in Lower Carinthia, Hungarian and a Croatian dialect in Burgenland
Religion: Predominantly Roman Catholic
Population: 7.5 million
Bank Hours: 0800-1230, 1330-1530 Monday-Wednesday, Friday; 0800-1230, 1330-1730 Thursday
Shop Hours: 0800-1800 Monday-Friday; 0800-1200 or 1300 Saturday
Currency: 100 groschen = 1 schilling
Export/Import Information: Member of the European Free Trade Association. Import licences not required for books. No exchange controls.
Copyright: UCC, Berne, Florence (see International section)

Book Trade Organizations

Bundesgremium des Handels mit Büchern, Kunstblättern und Musikalien, Zeitungen und Zeitschriften, A-1011 Vienna, Bauernmarkt 13 Tel: (0222) 635763
Federal Group for Traders in Books, Prints and Sheet Music, Newspapers and Periodicals
Man Dir: Dr Karl Widhalm

Hauptverband der graphischen Unternehmungen Österreichs, A-1010 Vienna 1, Grünangergasse 4
Austrian Graphical Association

Hauptverband des österreichischen Buchhandels, A-1010 Vienna 1, Grünangergasse 4 Tel: (0222) 521535 Cable Add: Buchverein, Vienna
Austrian Publishers' and Booksellers' Association
Secretary: Dr Gerhard Prosser
Miscellaneous: A number of subsidiary organizations are administered from the same office: e.g. Verband der Antiquare Österreichs (qv); Verband der österr, Kommissionäre, Grossobuchhändler und Auslieferer Österreichischer Verlegerverband (qv); Standard Book Numbering Agency (qv)
Publications include: Anzeiger des österreichischen Buchhandels (bi-monthly); Adressbuch des österreichischen Buchhandels (directory); Das österreichische Buch (catalogue) (annual); Bücher: Das Lesemagazin für Sie (catalogue) (annual)

Landesgremium Kärnten des Handels mit Büchern, Kunstblättern, Musikalien, Zeitungen und Zeitschriften, A-9020 Klagenfurt, Bahnhofstr 40-42 Tel: 04222/80411
Carinthian Regional Group of Traders in Books, Prints, Sheet Music, Periodicals and Newspapers

Landesgremium Niederösterreich des Handels mit Büchern, Kunstblättern, Musikalien, Zeitungen und Zeitschriften, A-1014 Vienna, Herrengasse 10 Tel: 636691
Lower Austria Regional Group of Traders in Books, Prints, Sheet Music, Periodicals and Newspapers

Landesgremium Oberösterreich des Handels mit Büchern, Kunstblättern, Musikalien, Zeitungen und Zeitschriften, A-4010 Linz, Hessenpl 3 Tel: 2800/328
Upper Austria Regional Trade Association of Traders in Books, Prints, Sheet Music, Periodicals and Newspapers
General Secretary: Dr Helmut Hagenauer

Landesgremium Salzburg des Handels mit Büchern, Kunstblättern, Musikalien, Zeitungen und Zeitschriften, A-5027 Salzburg, Julius-Raab-Platz 1 Tel: 71571/251 Telex: 3633
Salzburg Regional Group of Traders in Books, Prints, Sheet Music, Periodicals and Newspapers
Secretary: Dr Helmut Maurer

Landesgremium Steiermark des Handels mit Büchern, Kunstblättern, Musikalien, Zeitungen und Zeitschriften, A-8021 Graz, Körblergasse 111-113 Tel: 601571
Styrian Regional Group of Traders in Books, Prints, Sheet Music, Periodicals and Newspapers

Landesgremium Tirol des Handels mit Büchern, Kunstblättern, Musikalien, Zeitungen und Zeitschriften, A-6020 Innsbruck, Meinhardstr 14/IV Tel: 35651/290
Tyrol Regional Group of Traders in Books, Prints, Sheet Music, Periodicals and Newspapers

Landesgremium Vorarlberg des Handels mit Büchern und Musikalien, A-6800 Feldkirch, Wichnergasse 9 Tel: (05522) 22511441 Telex: 22511 DW 441
Vorarlberg Regional Group of Traders in Books and Sheet Music
Man Dir: Heribert Eggler; *Secretary:* Dr Manfred Fiel

Landesgremium Wien des Handels mit Büchern, Kunstblättern, Musikalien, Zeitungen und Zeitschriften, A-1041 Vienna, Schwarzenbergpl 14 Tel: 652174
Vienna Regional Group of Traders in Books, Prints, Sheet Music, Periodicals and Newspapers

Literar-Mechana, Wahrnehmungsgesellschaft für Urheberrechte GmbH, A-1060 Vienna VI, Linke Wienzeile 18 Tel: (0222) 572161
Organization for Copyright Protection
Man Dir: Franz-Leo Popp

Musikverleger Union Österreich, A-1030 Vienna, Baumannstr 8-10
Union of Austrian Music Publishers

Österreichischer Buchhändlerverband, A-1010 Vienna 1, Grünangergasse 4 Tel: (0222) 521535
Austrian Booksellers' Association
Secretary: Dr Gerhard Prosser

Österreichischer Verlegerverband, A-1010 Vienna 1, Grünangergasse 4 Tel: (0222) 521535
Association of Austrian Publishers
President: Hans W Polak; *Secretary-General:* Dr Gerhard Prosser

Staatlich genehmigte Literarische Verwertungsgesellschaft (LVG) Gen mbH, A-1060 Vienna VI, Linke Wienzeile 18 Tel: (0222) 572161
National Licensing Society for Literary Exploitation
President: Milo Dor; *Man Dir:* Franz-Leo Popp

Standard Book Numbering Agency, c/o H Walter Ess, Hauptverband des Österreichischen Buchhandels, A-1010 Vienna 1, Grünangergasse 4 Tel: (0222) 521535

Verband der Antiquare Österreichs, A-1010 Vienna 1, Grünangergasse 4 Tel: (0222) 521535
Austrian Antiquarian Booksellers' Association
President: Dkfm Werner Taeuber; *Secretary-General:* Dr Gerhard Prosser

Verband österreichischer Kommissionäre, Grossobuchhändler und Auslieferer, A-1010 Vienna 1, Grünangergasse 4 Tel: (0222) 521535
Association of Austrian Book Wholesalers and Distributors
President: Dr Emmerich Selch; *Secretary-General:* Dr Gerhard Prosser

Book Trade Reference Books and Journals

Books

Adressbuch des österreichischen Buch-Kunst-Musikalien-und Zeitschriftenhandels (Directory of Austrian Book, Art, Music and Magazine Trade), Austrian Publishers' and Booksellers' Association, A-1010 Vienna 1, Grünangergasse 4

(See also reference books listed under Federal Republic of Germany)

Journals

Anzeiger des österreichischen Buchhandels (Austrian Book Trade Gazette), Austrian Publishers' and Booksellers' Association, A-1010 Vienna 1, Grünangergasse 4

Anzeiger des Verbandes der Antiquare Österreichs (Austrian Antiquarian Booksellers' Association Gazette), Austrian Publishers' and Booksellers' Association, A-1010 Vienna 1, Grünangergasse 4

Österreichische Bibliographie (Austrian Bibliography), Austrian Publishers' and Booksellers' Association, A-1010 Vienna 1, Grünangergasse 4

Wiener Bücherbriefe (Viennese Book Letters), Druck- und Verlagsanstalt Forum Verlag, A-1050 Vienna, Sonnenhofgasse 8

Zeit im Buch (Today in the Book), A-1010 Vienna, Stephans Platz 6

Publishers

Adyar-Verlag, A-8011 Graz, Wartingergasse 31, Postfach 655 Tel: (0316) 657055
Man Dir: Norbert Lauppert
Subjects: Specialist Publishing House for Theosophical Literature: The Occult, Mysticism, Yoga, Eastern Religions
1981: 3 titles 1982: 2 titles Founded: 1947
ISBN Publisher's Prefix: 3-85005

Age d'Homme-Karolinger Verlag GmbH & Co KG*, A-1070 Vienna, Neustiftgasse 85 Tel: (0222) 4302093
Man Dir, Sales: Jean-Jacques Langendorf; *Editorial:* Dr Peter Weiss; *Publicity:* Cornelia Langendorf; *Rights & Permissions:* Hans Hofinger
Subjects: German, French and Slav Literature and History, History of German Ideologies
1981: 10 titles Founded: 1980
ISBN Publisher's Prefix: 3-85418

Akademische Druck- und Verlagsanstalt, A-8011 Graz, Auersperggasse 12, Postfach 598 Tel: 31165 Cable Add: Adeva Graz Telex: 032234 Grade A
Owner: Else Strzl; *Manager:* Dr Manfred Kramer; *Editors:* Inge Schwarz, Dr Hans Biedermann, Dr Karl Gratzl
Subjects: Encyclopaedias, Philology, Linguistics, Dictionaries, Anthropology, Arms and Military History, Orientalistics, Numismatics, History of Art, Archaeology, Musicology, Facsimile Editions of Illuminated Manuscripts
Founded: 1949
ISBN Publisher's Prefix: 3-201

Amalthea-Verlag*, A-1030 Vienna 3, Am Heumarkt 19 Tel: (0222) 723560
Dir: Dr Herbert Fleissner
Subjects: Belles Lettres, Art, Music, Fiction
Founded: 1917
Miscellaneous: Firm is a member of Verlagsgruppe Langen-Müller/Herbig, Federal Republic of Germany (qv)

Jörn **Andreas** Verlag*, A-5023 Salzburg, Mayrwies 385 Tel: (06222) 71581
Subjects: Popular Scientific and other Non-fiction

Andreas und Andreas Verlagsbuchhandel, A-5023 Salzburg, Mayrwies 385 Tel: 71581 Cable Add: Andreasverlag Salzburg Telex: 06632022
Publishers: Wolf-Dietrich Andreas, Ingrid Andreas; *Dir:* Franz Pemwieser
Branch Offs: Oskar Andreas Nachfolger Herzog & Co, Reise- und Versandbuchhandel, A-1170 Vienna, Parhamerpl 9; Andreas und Andreas Verlagsbuchhandel Zweigniederlassing, D-8228 Freilassing, Federal Republic of Germany; Andreas und Andreas Verlagsanstalt, FL-9490 Vaduz, Liechtenstein
Subjects: General Fiction
Founded: 1956
ISBN Publisher's Prefix: 3-85012

Ferdinand **Berger** und Söhne, A-3580 Horn, Wiener Str 21-23, Postfach 14 Tel: (02982) 2318 Cable Add: Berger Horn Telex: 078/77123
Subjects: Folk History, Art History, Anthropology, Archaeology, Reference, Natural Sciences, Periodicals
Founded: 1868

Bergland Verlag, A-1051 Vienna, Spengergasse 39 Tel: 555641
Man Dir: Friedrich Geyer

Verlag 'Das **Bergland**-Buch' (R Kiesel GmbH)+, A-5021 Salzburg, Rainerstr 19, Postfach 175 Tel: (06222) 73587 Cable Add: Berglandbuch Salzburg Telex: 633588
Man Dir: Alfred Schulz
Orders to: A-1030 Vienna, ZG-Mohr (for Austria)
Subjects: General Fiction, History, General Science, *Tieck* books
1983: 15 titles *Founded:* 1929
ISBN Publisher's Prefix: 3-7023

Verlag Alexander **Bernhardt**, A-6134 Vomperberg, Tirol Tel: (5242) 2131
Associate Company: Verlag der Stiftung Gralsbotschaft GmbH, Federal Republic of Germany (qv)
Subject: Philosophy
Founded: 1945

Annette **Betz** Verlag, A-1095 Vienna, Postfach 60 (Located at: Alserstr 24, Vienna) Tel: (0222) 425684/481538 Telex: 114802
Man Dir: Dr Otto Mang
Parent Company: Verlag Carl Ueberreuter (qv)
Subjects: Juveniles, Picture Books
Founded: 1962
ISBN Publisher's Prefix: 3-219

Bibliographisches Institut GmbH, Vienna, see Bibliographisches Institut AG, Federal Republic of Germany

Josef Gotthard **Bläschke**-Verlag, A-9143 St Michael, Feistritz 31 Tel: (04235) 2152
Man Dir: J G Bläschke
Subjects: Literature, Poetry, Biography, Memoirs
ISBN Publisher's Prefix: 3-7053

Verlag Hermann **Böhlau** Nachf GmbH, A-1010 Vienna, Dr Karl Lueger-Ring 12 Tel: (0222) 638735
Man Dir: Dr Dietrich Rauch; *Editorial:* Dr Peter Rauch; *Production and Rights & Permissions:* Robert Paula; *Publicity:* Ellen Raunacher
Associate Company: Verlagsbuchhandlung Hermann Böhlau Nachfolger GmbH, A-8010 Graz, Kroisbach, Ob Plattenweg 39
Branch Off: Böhlau-Verlag GmbH & Cie, Federal Republic of Germany (qv)
Subjects: Theatre, Biography, History, Music, Art and the Arts generally, Philosophy, Religion, Psychology, General & Social Science, University Textbooks, Economics, Education, Law, Linguistics, Geography
Bookshop: Antiquariat Böhlau, A-1010 Vienna, Dr Karl Lueger-Ring 12
Founded: 1947
ISBN Publisher's Prefix: 3-205

Bohmann Druck und Verlag AG*, A-1010 Vienna 1, Canovagasse 5 Tel: 658685 Telex: 132312
Dir: Dr Rudolf Bohmann
Subjects: Trade, Technical, Industrial
Founded: 1936
ISBN Publisher's Prefix: 3-7002

Verlag Dr Gerda **Borotha-Schoeler**, A-1190 Vienna, Glatzgasse 4 Tel: 3494382/3490365
Orders to: Lechner & Sohn, A-1010 Vienna, Seilerstätte 5
Subject: General Knowledge

Wilhelm **Braumüller** Universitätsverlag GmbH, A-1092 Vienna, Servitengasse 5 Tel: 348124 Cable Add: Braumüller
Man Dir: Albert F Reiterer
Subjects: History, Philosophy, Psychology, General Non-fiction, Juveniles, Agriculture, Literature, Education, Social Science, Economics, Periodicals
Founded: 1783
ISBN Publisher's Prefix: 3-7003

Verlagsbuchhandlung Julius **Breitschopf**+, A-1170 Vienna, Bergsteiggasse 5 Tel: 437203 Cable Add: Breitschopfbuch Telex: 07114539
Associate Companies: Julius Breitschopf KG, Verlagsbuchhandlung, Federal Republic of Germany (qv); Moderne Jugend Heute GmbH (qv)
Subjects: Picture Books, Juveniles
Bookshops: A-1090 Vienna 9, Nussdorferstr 62; A-1170 Vienna 17, Kalvarienborgstr 30
Founded: 1913
ISBN Publisher's Prefix: 3-7004

Verlag **Carinthia**, A-9010 Klagenfurt, Völkermarkter Ring 25, Postfach 197 Tel: (04222) 57377 Telex: 042204
Publicity: Anton Kreuzer
Subjects: Fiction, Art, Religion

Codices Selecti+, A-8010 Graz, Auersperggasse 12, Postfach 598 Tel: (0316) 31165/31
Subject: Facsimile Editions

Compass Verlagsgesellschaft Rudolf Hanel und Sohn, A-1013 Vienna 1, Wipplingerstr 32, Postfach 29 Tel: 636616/17/18 Cable Add: Compass Vienna
Man Dir: Werner Futter
Subjects: Austrian Industrial, Financial & Commercial Directories, Economics, Reference, Business
1982-83: 5 titles *Founded:* 1867
ISBN Publisher's Prefix: 3-85041

Cura Verlag GmbH, A-1037 Vienna, Beatrixgasse 32, Postfach 49 Tel: 736480
Man Dir: G Plattner
Subjects: Belles Lettres, Educational, Religious, Reference, *Selbsthilfen* series
1982: 10 titles *1983:* approx 8 titles
ISBN Publisher's Prefix: 3-7027

Denzel Verlag Auto-und Wander Führer, A-6020 Innsbruck, Maximilianstr 9 Tel: (05222) 26880
Subjects: Geography, Atlases, Travel, Touring, Climbing
Founded: 1952
ISBN Publisher's Prefix: 3-85047

Franz **Deuticke** Verlagsges mbH, A-1011 Vienna 1, Helferstorferstr 4, Postfach 761 Tel: (0222) 634345/636429
Man Dir: Franz Scharetzer
Orders to: Österr Bundesverlag GmbH, A-2351 Wiener Neudorf, Postfach
Subjects: Non-fiction, Technical, Psychology, General Science, University & Secondary Textbooks, Earth Sciences (Geography, Cartography, Geology, Environmental Protection), Law
Bookshops: Buchhandlung Franz Deuticke, Antiquariat Franz Deuticke, A-1011 Vienna 1, Helferstorferstr 4
Founded: 1878
ISBN Publisher's Prefix: 3-7005

Ludwig **Doblinger** (Bernard Herzmansky) Musikverlag, A-1010 Vienna 1, Dorotheergasse 10, Postfach 882 Tel: 523504
Man Dir: Helmuth Pany
Subject: Music
Founded: 1876
ISBN Publisher's Prefix: 3-90035

Wilhelm **Ennsthaler**+, A-4400 Steyr, Stadtpl 26 Tel: (07252) 22053 Telex: 28309 Ennsb A
Subjects: Belles Lettres, Poetry, Natural Health, History
Bookshop: At above address
Founded: 1880
ISBN Publisher's Prefix: 3-85068

Europa Verlags-GmbH, A-1232 Vienna, Altmannsdorferstr 154-156 Tel: (0222) 672622 Cable Add: Europaverlag Telex: 131326
Dir: Erich Pogats; *Editorial:* Dr Peter Dempe; *Sales, Publicity:* Christian Lunzer; *Production:* Georg Prechtl; *Rights & Permissions:* Elfriede Nussgruber
Subjects: Philosophy, Natural, Social & Political Science, Current Events, Literature, Economics, Law, Psychology, Belles Lettres
1982: 50 titles *Founded:* 1946
ISBN Publisher's Prefix: 3-203

Evangelischer Pressverband in Österreich, A-1030 Vienna, Ungargasse 9 Tel: 725475/725461 Telex: 115551
Founded: 1925

Facultas Verlag, A-1090 Vienna, Berggasse 4 Tel: 315659/343685 Telex: 076529 lcpfa A
Associate Company: Literas-Verlag GmbH (qv)
Subject: Sciences
1981: 100 titles *1982:* 20 titles
ISBN Publisher's Prefix: 3-85076

Forum Verlag GmbH*, A-1050 Vienna 5, Sonnenhofgasse 8 Tel: 526411
Man Dir: N Schnabl; *Publicity Dir:* M Soukup
Subjects: General Fiction, General Science, Art, Juveniles
Founded: 1952
ISBN Publisher's Prefix: 3-7006

Freytag-Berndt und Artaria, Kartographische Anstalt, A-1071 Vienna 7, Schottenfeldgasse 62 Tel: (0222) 939501 Telex: 133526
Chairmen: Dr W R Petrowitz, Harald Hochenegg; *Sales Manager:* Wolfgang Kaiser
Bookshops: A-1010 Vienna, Kohlmarkt 9; A-6020 Innsbruck, Wilhelm-Greil Str 15
Subjects: Geography, Atlases, Road maps

Georg **Fromme** und Co, A-1051 Vienna 5, Arbeitergasse 1-7 Tel: 555641 Telex: 111969
Man Dir: Friedrich Geyer
Subjects: Textbooks, General Science, Technology
Founded: 1748
ISBN Publisher's Prefix: 3-85086

Dr Heinrich **Fuchs***, A-1180 Vienna, Thimiggasse 82

Gerold & Co*, A-1011 Vienna, Graben 31 Tel: (0222) 522235/525739 Cable Add: Geroldbuch Vienna Telex: 847136157 Gerol A
Man Dirs: Dr Heinrich Neider, Hans Neusser
Subjects: Philosophy, Linguistics
Bookshop: See under Major Booksellers
ISBN Publisher's Prefix: 3-900190

Verlag für **Geschichte und Politik**, A-1030 Vienna, Neulinggasse 26/12 Tel: 726258/753106
Man Dir: Dr Karl Cornides; *Sales Dir:* Gerda Adler; *Publicity & Advertising:* Dr Erika Rüdegger
Associate Company: Verlag Oldenbourg (qv)
Subjects: History, Sociology, Economics, Political Science
Founded: 1947
ISBN Publisher's Prefix: 3-7028

'**Globus**' Zeitungs-, Druck- und Verlagsanstalt GmbH, A-1206 Vienna 20, Höchstädtpl 3 Tel: 334501 Cable Add: Globusbuch Wien
General Manager: H Zaslawski
Subjects: Politics, Popular Sciences, Belles Lettres, Sports, Fiction, Newspapers
Founded: 1945
Miscellaneous: Firm are also general representatives and distributors

Alois **Göschl** & Co, A-1190 Vienna 19, Trummelhofgasse 12 Tel: 321180
Proprietor: Hiltraud Lechner
Subjects: Health, Veterinary, Domestic Science, Juveniles
Founded: 1949

Verlag **Herder** & Co, A-1011 Vienna 1, Wollzeile 33, Postfach 248 Tel: (0222) 521413 Cable Add: Herderbuch Wien Telex: 011046 (inland); 11046 (foreign)
Man Dir: Fritz Wieninger
Associate Companies: Verlag Herder GmbH & Co KG, Federal Republic of Germany (qv); Herder Editrice e Libreria, Italy (qv); Editorial Herder SA and Librería Herder, Spain (qqv); Herder AG, Switzerland (qv); Verlag A G Ploetz GmbH & Co KG, Federal Republic of Germany (qv)
Bookshop: See under Major Booksellers
Subjects: Religion, Reference, Psychology, Philosophy, Juveniles, History
Founded: 1886
ISBN Publisher's Prefix: 3-210

Herold Druck- und Verlagsgesellschaft mbH+, A-1081 Vienna 8, Strozzigasse 8, Postfach 321 Tel: (0222) 431551
Man Dir: Mag Fritz Müller
Associate Company: Herold Verlagsgesellschaft mbH, D-8000 Munich 95, Claude Lorrainstr 11, Federal Republic of Germany
Subjects: Art, History, Religion (Catholic)
Founded: 1893
ISBN Publisher's Prefix: 3-7008

Bernhard **Herzmansky**, see Ludwig Doblinger

Johannes **Heyn**, A-9020 Klagenfurt, Krassniggstr 42 Tel: (04222) 57012 Cable Add: Heyn Klagenfurt Telex: 042401
Man Dir: Gerd Zechner
Subjects: General Fiction, Belles Lettres, Poetry, Biography, History, How-to, Music, Art, Reference, Juveniles, Low- & High-priced Paperbacks, General Science, University, Secondary & Primary Textbooks
Bookshop: Buchhandlung Johannes Heyn (qv under Major Booksellers)
Founded: 1868
ISBN Publisher's Prefix: 3-85366

Edition E **Hilger**, A-1010 Vienna, Dorotheergasse 5 Tel: (0222) 525315
Man Dir & Production: Ernst Hilger; *Sales & Publicity:* Monica Zimmermann
Subjects: Collectors' Books, Art, Limited editions of original graphics
Founded: 1973

Ferdinand **Hirt** mbH & Co KG*, A-1094 Vienna, Postfach 39 (Located at: Vienna, Widerhofergasse 8) Tel: (0222) 343558 Telex: 115014
Managers: Götz Hirt-Reger, Herwig Seebauer, Sabine Hirt-Reger
Orders to: A-1232 Vienna, Allmannsolorferstr 154-156
Subjects: Science, Education, Academic, Geographical, Teachers' Training, Serials
Founded: 1965
ISBN Publisher's Prefix: 3-7019

Brüder **Hollinek** & Co GmbH, A-1130 Vienna, Gallgasse 40A Tel: (0222) 845346
Man Dir: Mag Ing R Hollinek; *Sales Dir:* Dr P Schübert; *Advertising Dir, Rights & Permissions:* E Hollinek
Subsidiary Company: Druckerei Brüder Hollinek, A-2384 Breitenfurt-Wien
Subjects: Reference, Medicine, Law
Bookshop: A-1130 Vienna, Gallgasse 40A
Founded: 1872

Inn-Verlag, A-6021 Innsbruck, Roseggerstr 30, Postfach 516 Tel: (05222) 43240 Cable Add: Innverlag Innsbruck Telex: 05-3617 Innvlg A
Publisher: Käte Glotz-Hagleitner; *Sales:* Günther Glotz; *Production:* Klaus Hagleitner
Subjects: Technical Books, History, Sport, School Books, Political Books
Bookshop: Kommissions-Reise- & Versandbuchhandlung (at above address)
1981: 20 titles *Founded:* 1947
ISBN Publisher's Prefix: 3-85123

Jasomirgott-Verlag*, A-3400 Klosterneuburg, Leopoldstr 19 Tel: (02243) 7570
Man Dir: Herbert Neumaerker

Jugend und Volk Verlagsgesellschaft mbH, A-1014 Vienna, Tiefer Graben 7-9, Postfach 123 Tel: 630771-0
Man Dir: Alfred Jelinek; *Marketing & Publicity:* Hans Otto Steidl; *Rights and Permissions:* Friedrich Themel
Subsidiary Company: Jugend und Volk Verlag GmbH, Federal Republic of Germany (qv)
Subjects: Belles Lettres, Music, Art, Picture Books, Juveniles, High-priced Paperbacks, Psychology, Social Science, Education, Viennese Memorabilia, Secondary & Primary Textbooks, Educational Materials, Austrian post-war literature, Periodicals, Reprints
Bookshop: Büchhandlüng Tiefer Graben (at above address)
1981: approx 270 titles *Founded:* 1921
ISBN Publisher's Prefix: 3-224

Verlag **Jungbrunnen**+, A-1011 Vienna 1, Rauhensteingasse 5, Postfach 583 Tel: (0222) 521299
Man Dir, Editorial, Rights and Permissions: Wolf Harranth
Subjects: Juveniles, Psychology, Education
Founded: 1923
ISBN Publisher's Prefix: 3-7026

Juridica-Verlag GmbH*, A-1070 Vienna, Wimbergergasse 33 Tel: 933292
Managers: Ing Werner Sopper, Karl Weidlich

Verlag A F **Koska***, A-1095 Vienna, Zimmermanngasse 1, Postfach 61 Tel: (0222) 424689, 432137
Manager: Prof Alfred F Koska

Verlag **Kremayr und Scheriau***, A-1120 Vienna, Niederhofstr 37 Tel: 834501 Telex: 131405
Man Dir: Heinz Siegert
Orders to (Trade Dept): Zentralgesellschaft Dr Berger, A-1010 Vienna, Singerstrasse 12
Parent Company: Verlagsgruppe Bertelsmann GmbH, Federal Republic of Germany (qv)
Subjects: General Fiction, History, How-to, Music, Art, Juveniles
Book Club: Buchgemeinschaft Donauland
Bookshop: Buchhandlung ünd Zeitschriftenvertrieb Kremayr und Scheriau, A-1121 Vienna, Niederhofstr 37
Founded: 1950
ISBN Publisher's Prefix: 3-218

Kümmerly und Frey Verlags GmbH*, Nikolsdorferstr 8, A-1050 Vienna
Associate Companies: J Fink-Kümmerly und Frey Verlag, Federal Republic of Germany (qv); Kümmerly und Frey (Geographischer Verlag), Switzerland (qv)
Subjects: Maps, Travel

Elisabeth **Lafite**, A-1010 Vienna 1, Hegelgasse 13 Tel: 526869
Subjects: Music books and periodicals
Founded: 1962
ISBN Publisher's Prefix: 3-85151

Langenscheidt-Verlag GmbH, A-1010 Vienna, Singerstr 12
Parent Company: Langenscheidt KG, Federal Republic of Germany (qv)
Subject: Foreign Languages

Leykam Buchverlagsges mbH*, A-8011 Graz, Stempfergasse 3, Postfach 424 Tel: (0316) 76676 Cable Add: Leykam Graz Telex: 032209
Man Dir: Dr Karl Schober
Subjects: Art, General Fiction, Textbooks
Bookshops: A-8605 Kapfenberg, Kol Wallischpl; A-8700 Leoben, Am Durchbruch 5; A-8940 Liezen, Hauptstr 29; A-8680 Mürzzuschlag, Toni Schruf-Str 12; A-8330 Feldbach, Grazerstr 9
1981: 16 titles *Founded:* 1585
ISBN Publisher's Prefix: 3-7011

Literas-Verlag GmbH, A-1090 Vienna, Berggasse 4 Tel: 315659/343685 Telex: 076529 Icpfa A
Associate Company: Facultas Verlag (qv)
Subjects: Psychology, Belles-Lettres
1981-82: 20 titles *Founded:* 1981
ISBN Publisher's Prefix: 3-85429

Löcker Verlag, A-1010 Vienna, Annagasse 3A Tel: 520282
General Manager: Erhard Löcker; *Publication projects:* Paul Stein; *Publicity, Rights & Permissions:* Dr Claudia Mazanek
Subjects: Modern Austrian History, Austrian Literature, Architecture, Design, Art, Photography
Associated Bookshops: Antiquariat Löcker und Wögenstein, A-1010 Vienna, Annagasse 5; Löcker GmbH, A-1010 Vienna, Gluckgasse 3
1981: 19 titles *1982:* 12 titles *Founded:* 1974
ISBN Publisher's Prefix: 3-85409

Paul **Mangold** Verlag, A-8042 Graz, Neue Welt Hohe 3 Tel: (0316) 52536 Cable Add: Mangoldverlag
Man Dir: Paul Mangold
Subject: Juveniles

1981: 5 titles *Founded:* 1977
ISBN Publisher's Prefix: 3-900301

Manz'sche Verlags- und Universitätsbuchhandlung, A-1014 Vienna, Kohlmarkt 16 Tel: (0222) 631781
Man Dirs: Dkfm Franz Stein, Dr Anton C Hilscher
Subjects: Law, Economics, University Textbooks, Educational Materials
Bookshops: Manz'sche Verlags- und Universitätsbuchhandlung (qv under Major Booksellers); FRIC, Technische Fachbuchhandlung, A-1040 Vienna, Wiedner Hauptstr 13
Founded: 1849
ISBN Publisher's Prefix: 3-214

Verlag Wilhelm **Maudrich**, A-1097 Vienna 9, Lazarettg 1, Postfach 21 Tel: 425241 Cable Add: Maudrich Verlag Wien
Man Dir: Gerhard Grois
Subjects: How-to, Medicine, Psychology, University Textbooks
Bookshop: Buchhandlung Wilhelm Maudrich (qv under Major Booksellers)
Founded: 1909
ISBN Publisher's Prefix: 3-85175

Progress-Verlag Dr **Micolini**'s Wtw, A-8010 Graz, Glacisstr 57 Tel: (03162) 79508 Cable Add: Micolini Graz
Founded: 1934

Moderne Jugende Heute GmbH+, A-1170 Vienna, Bergsteiggasse 5 Tel: 437203 Cable Add: Breitschopfbuch Telex: 07114539
Man Dir: Julius P Breitschopf
Associate Company: Verlagsbuchhandlung Julius Breitschopf (qv)
Subjects: Theme Books for Children and Young People, Painting Books
Founded: 1975

Modulverlag GmbH, Seilergasse 16, A-1010 Vienna Telex: 112816 Aplan A
Subjects: Architecture, Design

Verlag Fritz **Molden***, A-1190 Vienna Grinzing, Sandgasse 33 Tel: (0222) 323151 Cable Add: Moldenverlag Vienna Telex: 074306
Publisher: Fritz P Molden; *Man Dir, Rights & Permissions:* Dr Hans-Peter Übleis; *Sales:* Klaus P Frank (Federal Republic of Germany), Josef Lukes (Austria, Switzerland); *Publicity:* Dr Arnica-Verena Langenmaier (Munich), Renate Wunderer (Vienna); *Advertising:* Gerhart Langthaler
Subsidiary Company: Buch ins Haus GmbH, Munich, Federal Republic of Germany
Associate Companies: Molden Press AG, Glarus, Switzerland; Buch in's Haus GmbH, Vienna; Molden Edition Graphische Kunst, Vienna; Verlag Fritz Molden, A-6020 Innsbruck, Maria Theresienstr 10; Fritz Molden Publishing Inc, 350 Fifth Ave, Suite 6312, New York, NY 10001, USA
Subjects: General Fiction, Biography, History, How-to, Music, Art, Travel, Paperbacks, General & Social Science
Founded: 1965
ISBN Publisher's Prefix: 3-217

Morawa & Co*, A-1041 Vienna 14, Hackingerstr 52
Associate Companies: Bayerische Verlagsanstalt Bamberg (BVB) Federal Republic of Germany (qv); Adolf Zwimpfer, CH-8954 Geroldswil ZH, Switzerland (qv)
Book Club: Welt im Heim Morawa & Co

Otto **Müller** Verlag KG, A-5021 Salzburg, Ernst-Thunstr 11, Postfach 167 Tel: 72152 Cable Add: Müller Verlag
Man Dir, Sales & Publicity: Alexander Weiger
Subjects: Belles Lettres, Poetry, History, Religion, Psychology
Founded: 1937
ISBN Publisher's Prefix: 3-7013

Mundus, Österreichische Verlagsgesellschaft mbH, see Paul Zsolnay Verlag GmbH

Paul **Neff** Verlag KG, A-1060 Vienna 6, Gumpendorferstr 5 Tel: (0222) 574767 Cable Add: Neffverlag
Man Dir: Karl Andreas Edlinger
Subjects: General Fiction, Biography, Music, Art
Founded: 1829
ISBN Publisher's Prefix: 3-7014

Edition **Neue Mitte**, A-1033 Vienna, Postfach 12 (Located at: A-1030 Vienna, Landstrasser Hauptstrasse 13/43) Tel: (0222) 733703
Man Dir: Kurt Sattlberger
Subjects: Political/Social (especially, alternatives to Marxism, future political projections)
Founded: 1976
ISBN Publisher's Prefix: 3-85401

Neufeld-Verlag und Galerie, A-6890 Lustenau Tel: (05577) 4657 Cable Add: Neufeld Telex: 59162
Editorial, Rights & Permissions: Ivo Löpfe
Parent Company: Löpfe KG (at above address)
Associate Company: Neufeld-Verlag und Galerie, Switzerland (qv)
Founded: 1962

Wolfgang **Neugebauer***, A-5033 Salzburg, Alpenstr 12, Postfach 64 Tel: (06222) 23136
Man Dir: Wolfgang Neugebauer
Subjects: Natural Sciences, Theology, Philosophy, Psychology, History, German Literature
Bookshop: Buchhandlung W Neugebauer GmbH & Co KG (qv under Major Booksellers)
Founded: 1975
ISBN Publisher's Prefix: 3-85376

Verlag **Niederösterreichisches Pressehaus** mbH, A-3100 St Pölten, Gutenbergstr 12 Tel: 02742/51561 Telex: 015512
Man Dir, Sales & Editorial: Dr Ingeborg Ornazeder; *Publicity:* Franz Gloser
Orders to: R Lechner & Sohn, A-1232 Vienna, Heizwerkstr 10
Subjects: History, Literature, Architecture, Art
Bookshop: Hippolyt-Buchhandlung, A-3100 St Pölten, Linzerstr 4
Founded: 1889
ISBN Publisher's Prefix: 3-85326

Obelisk-Verlag, A-6020 Innsbruck, Falkstr 1 Tel: (05222) 20733
Proprietor: Helga Buchroithner
Subject: Children's Books

Oberösterreichischer Landesverlag, A-4010 Linz, Landstr 41 Tel: (0732) 78121
Man Dir: Hubert Lehner
Subjects: Biography, History, Art, Religion
Bookshops: At above address; A-4810 Gmunden, Rathauspl 1; A-4710 Grieskirchen, Stadtpl 42, Postfach 26; A-4910 Ried i Innkreis, Bahnhofstr 5-7, Postfach 116; A-4150 Rohrbach, Marktpl 28, Postfach 3; A-4690 Schwanenstadt, Stadtpl 45; A-4600 Wels, Bahnhofstr 16, Postfach 146; A-4820 Bad-Ischl, Pfarrgasse 11; A-4840 Vöcklabruck, Mühlbachgasse 4; A-4470 Enns, Hauptplatz 4 (all in Austria)
1982: 23 titles *Founded:* 1872
ISBN Publisher's Prefix: 3-85214

Octopus Verlag, A-1236 Vienna, Postfach 53 Tel: (0222) 527146
Man Dir: Erich Skrleta
Subjects: Buddhism & Oriental Philosophies, Vienna
Bookshop: A-1010 Vienna, Fleischmarkt 16
1981: 5 titles *1982:* 5 titles *Founded:* 1973
ISBN Publisher's Prefix: 3-900290

Verlag **Oldenbourg**, A-1030 Vienna, Neulinggasse 26/12 Tel: 726258/753106
Man Dir: Dr Karl Cornides; *Sales Dir:* Gerda Adler; *Publicity & Advertising:* Dr Erika Rüdegger
Parent Company: R Oldenbourg Verlag GmbH, Federal Republic of Germany (qv)
Associate Company: Verlag für Geschichte und Politik (qv)
Subjects: History, Philosophy, Engineering, General & Social Science, University & Secondary Textbooks
Founded: 1957
ISBN Publisher's Prefix: 3-7029

Verlag **Orac**, A-1014 Vienna, Graben 17, Postfach 56 Tel: 528552
Man Dir, Sales, Production, Rights & Permissions: Dkfm Helmut Hanusch; *Editorial, Publicity:* Gerhard Höller
Subjects: Economics, Jurisprudence, Management, Sport, General Non-fiction
Bookshop: At above address
Founded: 1946

Österreichische Verlagsanstalt GmbH, A-1051 Vienna, Spengergasse 39 Tel: 555641
Man Dir: Friedrich Geyer

Verlag der **österreichischen Akademie der Wissenschaften**, A-1010 Vienna, Dr Ignaz Seipelpl 2 Tel: (0222) 529681 Telex: 0112628
Publishing House of the Austrian Academy of Sciences
Man Dir: Brigitta Nowotny
Subjects: Archaeology, Architecture, Art, Belles Lettres, Biography, Byzantine and Oriental Studies, English Language and Literature, History, Jurisprudence, Maps, Music, Numismatics, Philology & Dialect Studies, Philosophy, Psychology, Reference, Social Science, Theatre, Urbanism, Paperbacks
1981: 73 titles *1982:* 68 titles *Founded:* 1973
ISBN Publisher's Prefix: 3-7001

Verlag des **österreichischen Gewerkschaftsbundes** GmbH, A-1232 Vienna 23, Altmannsdorfer Str 154-156 Tel: 672622
Man Dir: Erich Pogats
Founded: 1947

Österreichischer Agrarverlag, Druck- und Verlags- GmbH, A-1014 Vienna, Bankgasse 1-3, Postfach 136 Tel: 639676 Cable Add: Agrarverlag Telex: 074030
Man Dir: Dr Wolfgang Brandstetter
Orders to: A-1141 Vienna, Linzerstr 32
Subjects: Agriculture, Fiction, Periodicals
1981: 24 titles *1982:* 23 titles *Founded:* 1945
ISBN Publisher's Prefix: 3-7040

Österreichischer Bundesverlag GmbH, A-1010 Vienna 1, Schwarzenbergstr 5 Tel: 522561 Cable Add: Bundesverlag Vienna
Man Dir: Dkfm Kurt Biak
Orders to: Österreichischer Bundesverlag, A-2351 Wiener Neudorf, Postfach
Subjects: Belles Lettres, History, Juveniles, Textbooks, Reference, Educational Materials, Art, Music, General Fiction, General Science
Founded: 1772
ISBN Publisher's Prefixes: 3-215, 3-7037

Österreichisches Katholisches Bibelwerk, A-3400 Klosterneuburg, Stiftspl 8, Postfach 48 Tel: (02243) 2938
Man Dir, Editorial, Rights & Permissions: Dr Norbert Höslinger; *Sales:* Gerlinde Bieder
Subjects: Bibles, Pius Parsch Institute texts, Scriptural Studies
Bookshop: A-1010 Vienna, Singerstr 7
Founded: 1966
Miscellaneous: Company is a member of AMB (qv under Federal Republic of

Germany) and WCBFA (World Catholic Federation for the Biblical Apostolate)
ISBN Publisher's Prefix: 3-85396

Perlinger Verlag, A-6300 Worgl, Brixentaler Str 61, Postfach 42 Tel: (05332) 3341 Cable Add: Perlinger Verlag, Worgl Telex: 051205 Teltaz
Man Dir: Engelbert Perlinger
Subsidiary Company: Engelbert Perlinger GmbH, Bahnhofstr 27, D-8205 Kiefersfelden, Federal Republic of Germany
Subjects: Philosophy, Natural Medicine
Bookshops: Perlinger Verlags-Buchhandlung, A-6300 Worgl, Innsbrucker Str 104; Perlinger Verlags-Buchhandlung, A-6130 Schwaz, Munchener Str 31
1981: 8 titles *Founded:* 1977
ISBN Publisher's Prefix: 3-85399

Pinguin-Verlag, Pawlowski KG+, A-6021 Innsbruck, Lindenbühelweg 2 Tel: (05222) 81183/81587 Telex: 053173 Cable Add: Pinguinverlag Innsbruck
Man Dirs: Olaf Pawlowski, Hella Pflanzer
Subjects: Art, Juveniles, Non-fiction, Reference Books, Calendars
Founded: 1945
ISBN Publisher's Prefix: 3-7016

Georg **Prachner**, A-1010 Vienna, Kärntnerstr 30 Tel: 528549
Man Dir: O G Prachner
Subjects: Architecture, Art, Belles Lettres, History, Fiction
Bookshop: See under Major Booksellers

Prugg Verlag*, A-7000 Eisenstadt, Haydngasse 10 Tel: (02682) 2114
ISBN Publisher's Prefix: 3-85238

Universitätsverlag Anton **Pustet**, A-5021 Salzburg, Bergstrasse 12, Postfach 144 Tel: (06222) 73507/76392 Cable Add: Pustet Salzburg
Branch Off: Anton Pustet, Federal Republic of Germany (qv)
Subjects: Philosophy, Religion, Psychology, Education, Political Science, Law, Poetry and Iconographs of the University of Salzburg, Music
Founded: 1598
ISBN Publisher's Prefix: 3-7025

Verlag Dr Herta **Ranner**, A-1070 Vienna, Zeismannsbrunngasse 1 Tel: (0222) 935387
Subject: Books, Periodicals

Residenz Verlag, A-5020 Salzburg, Gaisbergstr 6 Tel: (06222) 25771
Man Dir: Wolfgang Schaffler; *Editorial:* Dr Jochen Jung, Renate Buchmann, Dr Gundl Hradil; *Sales Manager:* Christl Sennewald; *Production:* Friedel Schafleitner; *Publicity:* Dr Barbara Brunner; *Rights & Permissions:* Renate Buchmann
Subjects: Belles Lettres, Poetry, Music, Art, Architecture
Founded: 1956
ISBN Publisher's Prefix: 3-7017

E **Rötzer** Verlag*, A-7001 Eisenstadt, Postfach 25 (Burgenland) Tel: (02682) 2473
Proprietor: Elfriede Weber
Subjects: Periodicals, Reference, Guidebooks

S N-Verlag, Salzburger Nachrichten Verlags GmbH & Co KG*, A-5020 Salzburg, Bergstr 14, Postfach 154 Tel: (06222) 775910
Subjects: Regional (Salzburg), Architecture, History, Music, Theatre

Verlag der **Salzburger Druckerei**, A-5020 Salzburg, Bergstr 12, Postfach 144 Tel: (06222) 73507/76392
Subjects: Arts, Poetry, History and Chronicles of Salzburg
ISBN Publisher's Prefix: 3-85338

Verlag für **Sammler***, A-8011 Graz, Sankt Peter Hauptstr 35e, Postfach 54 Tel: 42230
Subjects: History of Art, Culture, Manners & Morals, Folklore, Early History

Verlag **Sankt Gabriel**, A-2340 Mödling Tel: (02236) 86351
Man Dir: Mag P Hubert Winkler
Parent Company: Missionshaus Sankt Gabriel (at above address)
Associate Company: Steyler Verlag, Federal Republic of Germany (qv)
Subjects: Books for Children and Young People, Religious Knowledge, Practical Theology, Belles Lettres, Travel, Education
Bookshops: At above address and A-1010 Vienna
Founded: 1905
ISBN Publisher's Prefix: 3-85264

Verlag **Sankt Peter**, A-5010 Salzburg, Postfach 113 Tel: (0662) 4216682 Telex: 063094
Man Dir: Dr R Rinnerthaler
Subjects: Austrian Church Art, Austrian Guidebooks, Religion
1981: 12 titles *Founded:* 1946
ISBN Publisher's Prefix: 3-900173

Paul **Sappl**, Schulbuch- und Lehrmittelverlag*, A-6332 Kufstein, Kaiserbach 43 Tel: (05372) 4300 Telex: 5119115
Branch Off: A-1050 Vienna, Stolberggasse 31-33
Subjects: School Books, Driving School Text Books
Founded: 1953

Dr A **Schendl** GmbH und Co KG, A-1041 Vienna, Karlsgasse 15, Postfach 29 Tel: (0222) 655593-96
Dirs: Dr Anna Schendl, Franz Ogg
Subjects: History, Ethnography, Geography, Folklore, Art, Literature, Music, Economy, Periodicals

Schönbrunn-Verlag GmbH*, A-1010 Vienna 1, Schulerstr 1-3 Tel: 526905
Subject: Art
Founded: 1946

Anton **Schroll** & Co+, Buch und Kunstverlag, A-1051 Vienna 5, Spengergasse 39 Tel: 555641 Cable Add: Schrollverlag Vienna
Man Dir: Friedrich Geyer
Branch Off: Anton Schroll & Co GmbH, Federal Republic of Germany (qv)
Subjects: Belles Lettres, History, Art
1981: 24 titles *Founded:* 1884
ISBN Publisher's Prefix: 3-7031

Severin Presse, A-2346 Suedstadt Vienna, Dobrastr 112, Postfach 15 Tel: (02236) 811744
Publisher: Peter Croy
Subject: Art (Original Engravings)

Verlag Josef Otto **Slezak**, A-1040 Vienna, Wiedner Hauptstr 42 Tel: (0222) 570259
Sales Managerial: Ilse Slezak
Subjects: Transport, especially historical accounts of railways and tramways in Austria and Europe generally
1981: 8 titles *1982:* 6 titles

Springer-Verlag KG*, A-1011 Vienna, Mölkerbastei 5, Postfach 367 Tel: (0222) 639614 Cable Add: Springerbuch Wien Telex: 074506
Man Dir: Dr Wilhelm Schwabl; *Sales Manager:* Rudolf Siegle; *Promotion, Rights & Permissions:* Dr Erna Ungersbaeck; *Production Dir:* Bruno Skuhra
Associate Companies: Springer-Verlag Berlin — Heidelberg — New York — Tokyo, Federal Republic of Germany (qv); Springer-Verlag Inc, 175 Fifth Ave, New York, NY 10010, USA

Subjects: Medicine, Natural Sciences, Engineering, General & Social Science, Economics, Law, Philosophy, University Textbooks, Reference
Bookshop: Minerva Wissenschaftliche Buchhandlung GmbH, A-1010 Vienna, Schottengasse 7
1981: 64 titles *Founded:* 1924
ISBN Publisher's Prefix: 3-211

Leopold **Stocker** Verlag*, A-8011 Graz, Bürgergasse 11, Postfach 438 Tel: (0316) 71636 Cable Add: Stockerverlag Graz
Publisher: Dr Ilse Dvorak-Stocker; *Editorial Sales, Publicity, Rights and Permissions:* Dr Peter Strallhofer
Subjects: Belles Lettres, Contemporary Literature, Hunting, Nature and Mountain Books, Specialist Books, Agricultural Textbooks and School Books
Founded: 1917

Verlag **Styria**, A-8010 Graz, Schönaugasse 64, Postfach 871 Tel: 775610 Cable Add: Styriaverlag Graz Telex: 031782 Kleine Zeitung
Man Dir, Editorial: Dr Gerhard Trenkler; *Sales:* Wolfgang Fath; *Production:* Hans Paar; *Publicity:* Peter Altenburg; *Rights & Permissions:* Margarethe Katholnig
Parent Company: Katholischer Pressverein
Branch Offs: Verlag Styria — Meloun & Co, D-5000 Cologne 51, Schillerstr 6, Postfach 511029, Federal Republic of Germany; Verlag Styria, Repräsentanz Wien, A-1010 Vienna, Lobkowitzpl 1
Subjects: Religion, History, Philosophy, Biography, Education, Belles Lettres, Reference Books, Current Affairs
Bookshops: Buchhandlung Styria (qv under Major Booksellers); Buchhandlung Ulrich Moser, A-8010 Graz, Herrengasse 23; Bücherbox, A-8010 Graz, Goethestr 42
Founded: 1869
ISBN Publisher's Prefix: 3-222

Rudolf **Trauner** Verlag, A-4020 Linz, Baumbachstr 4a Tel: (0732) 78241-5
Man Dir: Rudolf Trauner
Branch Off: A-4020 Linz, Köglstr 14
Subjects: Gastronomy, Cookery, Textbooks, Science, Books of Illustrations, Popular Medicine
1981-82: 20 titles *Founded:* 1946
ISBN Publisher's Prefix: 3-85320

Edition **Tusch**, A-1160 Vienna, Wilhelminenstr 80 Tel: (0222) 455334/462470 Cable Add: Editusch Wien Telex: 76262 Tusch A
Subject: Art

Verlagsanstalt **Tyrolia**, A-6020 Innsbruck, Exlgasse 20, Postfach 220 Tel: 81541 Cable Add: Tyrolia-Verlag Innsbruck Telex: 053620
Dir: Dr Schiemer
Subjects: Theology, School Books, Juveniles, Tour Guides, Illustrated Books, General Non-fiction
Bookshops: Tyrolia (qv under Major Booksellers)
Founded: 1888
ISBN Publisher's Prefix: 3-7022

Verlag Carl **Ueberreuter**, A-1095 Vienna, Alserstr 24, Postfach 60 Tel: (0222) 425684/481538 Cable Add: Ueberreuter Vienna Telex: 114802
Publishers: Michael Salzer, Andreas Salzer; *Man Dir:* Dr Otto Mang; *Editorial:* Dr Marion Pongracz, Ingrid Weixelbaumer; *Sales, Publicity:* Thomas C Sacken
Subsidiary Company: Annette Betz Verlag (qv)
Branch Offs: A-2100 Korneuburg, Industriestr 1; D-6900 Heidelberg/Schlierbach, In der Aue 32A, Federal Republic of Germany

Subjects: Juveniles, Children's Books (fiction and non-fiction), Books for Young Adults, Secondary & Primary Textbooks, Educational Materials
Founded: 1548
ISBN Publisher's Prefix: 3-8000

Universal Edition AG*, A-1015 Vienna, Bösendorfer Str 12, Postfach 3 Tel: 658695 Cable Add: Musikedition Wien Telex: 11397
Dirs: Dr J Juranek, S Harpner, A Schlee, M Kalmus
Subsidiary Company (jointly owned with B Schott's Söhne, Federal Republic of Germany, qv): Wiener Urtext Edition-Musikverlag GmbH & Co KG (qv)
Subjects: Music, Musicology
Founded: 1901

Urban und **Schwarzenberg***, A-1096 Vienna 9, Frankgasse 4, Postfach 102 Tel: (0222) 422731/2
Man Dir: Gunter Royer
Head Office: Verlag Urban und Schwarzenberg, Federal Republic of Germany (qv)
Subjects: Medicine, Psychology, Physics
Bookshop: See under Major Booksellers
Founded: 1866
ISBN Publisher's Prefix: 3-85327

V W G Ö, see Verband der wissenschaftlichen Gesellschaften Österreichs

Verband der wissenschaftlichen Gesellschaften Österreichs (VWGÖ), A-1070 Vienna, Lindengasse 37 Tel: (0222) 932166/934756 Telex: 134981 Vwgoe A
Man Dir: Dr Rainer Zitta
1981: 42 titles *Founded:* 1954
ISBN Publisher's Prefix: 3-85369

Veritas-Verlag, A-4010 Linz, Harrachstr 5, Postfach 403 Tel: (0732) 276451
Man Dir: Werner Höffinger
Branch Offs: Veritas, A-1010 Vienna, Singerstr 26; Veritas-Neuefeind, D-8390 Passau, Rindermarkt 4
Subjects: Religion, Health, School Books, Music
Bookshop: At above Linz address
1983: 35 titles *Founded:* 1945
ISBN Publisher's Prefix: 3-85329

Vorarlberger Verlagsanstalt GmbH*, A-6850 Dornbirn, Schwefel 81 Tel: (05572) 646970
Subject: Literature

Universitätsverlag Wagner GmbH*, A-6010 Innsbruck, Andreas-Hoferstr 13/1, Postfach 165 Tel: (05222) 27721 Cable Add: Universitätsverlag Wagner, A-6010 Innsbruck
Man Dir: Gottfried Grasl
Subjects: Scientific Works, Maps, Illustrated Motoring Guides, Literature, Colloquial Poetry
1981: 13 titles *Founded:* 1554
ISBN Publisher's Prefix: 3-7030

Weilburg-Verlag*, A-2500 Baden bei Wien, Am Fischertor 5 Tel: 02252/2906 Cable Add: Weilburg Verlag 2500 Baden
Subjects: Art Books, Lyrical Poetry, Numbered and Autographed Bibliophile Editions

Verlag Galerie **Welz** Salzburg, A-5010 Salzburg, Sigmund-Haffner-Gasse 16, Postfach 123 Tel: 41771
Publisher: Franz Eder; *Sales:* Hannes Lüftenegger
Subject: Art, Art Books and Prints

Wiener Dom-Verlag*, A-1080 Vienna, Strozzigasse 8
General Manager: Mag Fritz Müller
Subject: Religion
Founded: 1946
ISBN Publisher's Prefix: 3-85351

Wiener Urtext Edition-Musikverlag GmbH & Co KG*, A-1010 Vienna, Bösendorferstr 12 Tel: (publication) 658695, (sales) 657651 Cable Add: Musikedition Telex: 1397
Man Dir: Stefan G Harpner; *Sales Dir:* Vladimir Prusa
Parent Companies: B Schott's Söhne, Federal Republic of Germany (qv) and Universal Edition AG, Austria (qv)
Subject: Music, especially *original scores* of Bach, Beethoven, Brahms, Chopin, Haydn, Mozart, Schubert, Schumann. All accompanying texts are in German and English
1981: 69 titles *Founded:* 1972

Kunstverlag **Wolfrum***, A-1010 Vienna 1, Augustinerstr 10 Tel: 525398/524178 Cable Add: Witwolf Vienna
Man Dir: Hubert Wolfrum
Subjects: Art, Art Reproductions
Bookshop: See under Major Booksellers
Founded: 1919
ISBN Publisher's Prefix: 3-900178

Wort und Welt Verlag+, A-6020 Innsbruck, Heiliggeiststr 21 Tel: (05222) 25923 Cable Add: Wortwelt Innsbruck
Publisher: Professor Dr Walter Miess; *Editorial:* Günther Schick; *Publicity:* Ingrid Formentini
Orders to: Thaurdruck, A-6065 Thaur bei Innsbruck
Branch Off: D-8039 Puchheim, Munich, Postfach 1516, Federal Republic of Germany
Subjects: Humour, Textbooks, Art, Belles Lettres, Factbooks
1982: 12 titles *1983:* 12 titles *Founded:* 1972
ISBN Publisher's Prefix: 3-85373

Paul **Zsolnay** Verlag GmbH, A-1041 Vienna, Prinz-Eugen-Str 30 Tel: (0222) 657661/651816 Cable Add: Zsolnayverlag Wien Telex: 131515
Dirs: Hans W Polak, August Langer; *Sales Manager:* Wolfgang Dechant; *Editor:* Maria Gridling; *Production:* Peter Baumgartner; *Public Relations:* Elisabeth Roth; *Rights & Permissions:* Olga Kaindl
Parent Company: Heinemann & Zsolnay Ltd (see William Heinemann International Ltd, UK)
Associate Companies: Mundus, Österreichische Verlagsgesellschaft mbH (at above address); Paul Zsolnay Verlag GmbH, Federal Republic of Germany (qv)
Subjects: General Fiction, Non-fiction, Belles Lettres, Poetry, Biography, History, How-to, Music, Juveniles, Social & Political Science, Art, Medicine, Sports
1982: 34 titles *1983:* 37 titles *Founded:* 1923
ISBN Publisher's Prefix: 3-552

Book Clubs

Deutsche Buch-Gemeinschaft C A Koch's Verlag Nachfolger, Zweigniederlassung Wien, A-1210 Vienna, Berlagasse 7-11 Tel: (0222) 392635 Telex: 114971 Dbgw
Owned by: Deutsche Buch-Gemeinschaft C A Koch's Verlag Nachfolger, Federal Republic of Germany (qv)

Buchgemeinschaft **Donauland***, A-1120 Vienna, Niederhofstr 37 Tel: 834501 Telex: 131405
Owned by: Verlag Kremayr und Scheriau (qv)

Jos A **Kienreich***, A-8011 Graz, Sackstr 6, Postfach 828

Osterreichischer Buchklub der Jugend, A-1041 Vienna, Mayerhofgasse 6 Tel: (0222) 651754
Members: 600,000
Founded: 1947

Elisabeth **Reiter***, A-6600 Reutte, Attlmayrstr 10

Welt im Heim Morawa & Co, A-1041 Vienna 14, Hackingerstr 52, Postfach 54 Tel: (0222) 947641
Owned by: Morawa & Co (qv)

Major Booksellers

Hans **Fürstelberger***, A-4010 Linz, Landstr 49 Tel: (0732) 73177

Gerold & Co*, A-1011 Vienna, Graben 31 Tel: (0222) 522235/525739 Telex: 847136157 Gerol A
Subscription agents and library jobber for European books and periodicals
Man Dirs: Dr Heinrich Neider, Hans Neusser
Also Publisher (qv)

Anna **Hadwiger** GmbH*, A-1060 Vienna, Hornbostelgasse 3 Tel: (0222) 577554 Telex: 133386 (wholesaler)
Import Sales Managers: Oskar A Wuthe (German publications), Erika Mayer (English publications)

A L **Hasbach**, A-1010 Vienna, Wollzeile 9 Tel: 528876/528932
Manager: Dr Herbert Borufka

Leopold **Heidrich**, A-1011 Vienna, Plankengasse 7 Tel: 523701

Gebhard **Heinzle's** Erben, A-6700 Bludenz, Josef-Wolf-Platz 2 Tel: (05552) 2066 (export and library supplier)

Herder & Co, A-1011 Vienna, Wollzeile 33 Tel: (0222) 521413
Manager: Rainer Lendl
Also Publisher (qv)

Buchhandlung Johannes **Heyn**, A-9010 Klagenfurt, Kramergasse 2-4 Tel: (04222) 54249/57012 (export and library supplier)
Man Dir: Volkmar Zechner
Owned by: Johannes Heyn (qv)

Buchhandlung Karl **Hofbauer**, A-8430 Leibnitz, Hauptpl 31, Postfach 68 Tel: (03452) 2793 and 2177
Also: A-8430 Leibnitz, Grazerg 73 Tel: (03452) 3166
Managers: Karl & Jutta Hofbauer

Eduard **Höllrigl**, A-5020 Salzburg, Sigmund-Haffner-Gasse 10 Tel: (0662) 41146/42651 (export and library supplier)
Manager: H Stierle

Jos A **Kienreich**, A-8011 Graz, Sackstrasse 6 (export and library supplier)
Manager: Peter Schmelzer

Walter **Krieg***, A-1010 Vienna, Kärntnerstr 4 Tel: (0222) 521193 (export and library supplier)

Franz **Leo** & Co KG*, Universitätsbuchhandlung, A-1010 Vienna, Lichtensteg 1 Tel: (0222) 631451 (export and library supplier)

Manz'sche Verlags- und Universitätsbuchhandlung, A-1014 Vienna, Kohlmarkt 16 Tel: (0222) 631781 (export and library supplier)
Also Publisher (qv)

Wilhelm **Maudrich**, Buchhandlung und Verlag für medizinische Wissenschaften, A-1097 Vienna, Spitalg 21a Tel: (0222) 424712 (export and library supplier)
Manager: Gerhard Grois
Owned by: Verlag Wilhelm Maudrich (qv)

Robert **Mohr**, A-1010 Vienna, Singerstr 12 Tel: (0222) 525711 (wholesaler)

30 AUSTRIA

Buchhandlung W **Neugebauer** GmbH und Co KG*, A-5033 Salzburg, Alpenstr 12 Tel: (06222) 23136 (export and library supplier)
Owned by: Wolfgang Neugebauer

Max **Pock**, Universitätsbuchhandlung*, A-8010 Graz, Hauptplatz 1 Tel: (03122) 75254/79042 Telex: 03-1873 (export and library supplier)

Georg **Prachner** KG, A-1010 Vienna, Kärntnerstr 30 Tel: 528549
Manager: O G Prachner
Also Publisher (qv)

Schottentor*, A-1014 Vienna, Schottengasse 9

Buchhandlung **Styria**, A-8010 Graz, Albrechtgasse 5 Tel: 0316/79355
Branches: A-1010 Vienna, Opernring 15; A-8750 Judenburg, Hauptplatz 15; A-8720 Knittelfeld, Kapuzinerplatz 3, Postfach 72
Owned by: Verlag Styria (qv)

Tyrolia, A-6010 Innsbruck, Maria Theresienstr 15 Tel: (05222) 24944
Branches: Ehrwald, Fulpmes, Imst, Landeck, Lienz, Mayrhofen, St Johann, Schwaz, Vienna, Wattens
Owned by: Verlagsanstalt Tyrolia (qv)

Urban und Schwarzenberg GmbH*, A-1096 Vienna 9, Frankgasse 4, Postfach 102 Tel: (0222) 422731/2
Manager: Gunter Royer
Also Publisher (qv)

Wagner'sche Universitätsbuchhandlung, A-6021 Innsbruck, Museumstr 4 Tel: (05222) 22316 Telex: 053793 (export and library supplier)
Dir: Ernst Angerer

Rupertusbuchhandlung Augustin **Weis** und Söhne KG, A-5024 Salzburg, Dreifaltigkeitsg 12, Linzer Gasse 29 Tel: (06222) 71661 (export and library supplier)

Fachbuchhandlung für **Wirtschaft und Recht**, A-1181 Vienna, Währinger Str 122 Tel: (0222) 348391 (export and library supplier)
Proprietor: Eleonore Stropek

Kunstverlag **Wolfrum***, A-1010 Vienna, Augustinerstr 10 Tel: (0222) 524178/525398
Cable Add: Witwolf Wien (export and library supplier of art books)
Manager: Erich Pospisil
Also Publisher (qv)

Zentralgesellschaft für buchgewerbliche und graphische Betriebe, A-1010 Vienna, Singerstr 12 Tel: (0222) 526136 (wholesaler)
Proprietor: Dr Gottfried Berger

Major Libraries

Archiv der Universität Wien*, A-1010 Vienna, Dr Karl Luger Ring 1

Bibliothek des **Benediktinerklosters** Melk in Niederösterreich*, A-3390 Melk Tel: (02752) 2312342
Library of the Melk Benedictine Monastery in Lower Austria
Librarian: P Gottfried Glassner

Administrative Bibliothek und Österreichische Rechtsdokumentation im **Bundeskanzeramt***, A-1010 Vienna, Herrengasse 23
Administrative Library and Law Documentation of the Chancellery

Bibliothek des **Kriegsarchivs** Wien, A-1070 Vienna, Stiftgasse 2
Library of the War Archives Dept of the Austrian State Archives
Librarian: Dr Edith Wohlgemuth

Bibliothek der **Österreichischen Akademie der Wissenschaften**, A-1010 Vienna, Dr Ignaz Seipelpl 2 Tel: 529681 Telex: 12628
Library of the Austrian Academy of Science
Dir: Mrs B Amstädter

Österreichische Nationalbibliothek, A-1015 Vienna, Josefspl 1 Tel: (0222) 525255
Telex: 112624 Oenb
Austrian National Library
Publications include: Handbüch österreichischer Bibliotheken, Biblos

Bibliothek des **Österreichischen Patentamtes**, A-1014 Vienna, Kohlmarkt 8-10
Library of the Austrian Patent Office
Librarian: Dr Ingrid Weidinger
Publications: Österreichisches Patentblatt, Österreichischer Markenanzeiger, Patentschriften

Österreichisches Staatsarchiv, A-1010 Vienna 1, Minoritenpl 1
Austrian State Archives
Publication: Mitteilungen des Österreichischen Staatsarchivs

Universitätsbibliothek Graz, Universitätspl 3, Graz Tel: (0316) 31581/2 Telex: 031662
Librarian: Dr Franz Kroller
Publications: Jahresbericht; Fachliche Benützungsanleitungen für die Bibliotheken der Universität Graz, Heft 1 (1973); Bibliographische Informationen, 1 (1974); Schriftenreihe EDV-Projekt, 1 (1978); Grazer Zeitschriften-Verzeichnis, 1 (1974)

Universitätsbibliothek Innsbruck, A-6010 Innsbruck, Innrain 50 Tel: (05222) 7240 Telex: 53708

Universitätsbibliothek Wien, A-1010 Vienna, Dr-Karl-Lueger-Ring 1 Tel: (0222) 43002376/43002371

Wiener Stadt- und Landesarchiv, A-1082 Vienna, Magistratsabteilung 8, 1 Rathaus
Vienna Municipal Archives

Wiener Stadt- und Landesbibliothek, A-1082 Vienna, Rathaus Tel: (0222) 42800/42771
Vienna Municipal and County Library
Dir: Hofrat Mag Dr Franz Patzer

Library Associations

Dokumentationsstelle für neuere österreichische Literatur, A-1060 Vienna, Gumpendorferstr 15/1/13 Tel: (0222) 561249
Documentation Centre for Modern Austrian Literature
General Secretary: Dr Heinz Lunzer
Publication: Zirkular

Österreichische Gesellschaft für Dokumentation und Information, c/o Austrian Standards Institute, A-1021 Vienna, Leopoldsgasse 4, Postfach 130
Austrian Society for Documentation and Information
Executive Secretary: B Hofer
Publication: Fakten Daten Zitate

Österreichisches Institut für Bibliotheksforschung, Dokumentations- und Informationswesen*, A-1014 Vienna, Josefsplatz 1
Austrian Institute for Library Research, Documentation and Information
President: Prof Dr Josef Mayerhöfer; *Secretary-General:* Dr Gottfried Loibl
Publication: Biblos

Verband österreichischer Archivare, c/o A-1010 Vienna, Minoritenpl 1
Association of Austrian Archivists
Publication: Scrinium (twice yearly)

Verband österreichischer Volksbüchereien und Volksbibliothekare, A-1080 Vienna, Lange Gasse 37 Tel: (0222) 439722
Association of Austrian Public Libraries
Managing Chairman: Dr F Pascher

Vereinigung österreichischer Bibliothekare, A-1015 Vienna, Josefspl 1 (Österreichische National-Bibliothek) Tel: 521684
Association of Austrian Librarians
President: Ferdinand Baumgartner; *Secretary:* Ronald Zwanziger
Publication: Mitteilungen (quarterly)

Library Reference Books and Journals

Books

Dokumentation und Information in Österreich (Documentation and Information in Austria), Brüder Hollinek & Co GmbH, A-1130 Vienna, Gallgasse 40A

Handbuch österreichischer Bibliotheken (Handbook of Austrian Libraries), Austrian National Library, A-1015 Vienna, Josefspl 1

Journals

Biblos, Austrian journal for book and library personnel, documentation, bibliography and bibliophily (text in English and German), c/o Austrian National Library, A-1015 Vienna, Josefspl 1

Mitteilungen der Vereinigung österreichischer Bibliothekare (Bulletin of the Association of Austrian Librarians), Vereinigung österreichischer Bibliothekare, A-1015 Vienna, Josefspl 1

Scrinium, Association of Austrian Archivists, c/o A-1010 Vienna, Minoritenpl 1

Literary Associations and Societies

Österreichische Exlibris-Gesellschaft, A-1040 Vienna, Johann Strauss-Gasse 28-18
Austrian Bookplate-collectors' Society
Secretary: Oj Shattner, A-1021 Vienna, Postfach 74
Publications: Jahrbuch, Mitteilungen, books on the art of the bookplate and on bookplate-collecting

Österreichische Gesellschaft für Literatur, A-1010 Vienna, Herrengasse 5
Austrian Literary Society
President: Dr W Kraus

Österreichischer Schriftstellerverband, A-1050 Vienna V, Kettenbrückeng 11 Tel: (0222) 564151
Austrian Writers' Association
General Secretary: Wilhelm Meissel

Österreichischer P E N-Club, Concordia Haus, A-1010 Vienna 1, Bankgasse 8
Secretary: Franz Richter

Wiener Goethe-Verein*, A-1010 Vienna, Reitschulgasse 2
President: Dr Conrad H Lester; *Vice-President:* Dr Herbert Zeman
Publication: Jahrbuch (yearbook)

Literary Periodicals

Blätter für Volksliteratur (Popular Literature Magazine), Verein der Freunde der Volksliteratur, Graz, Naglergasse 22

Eröffnungen (Communications), magazine for literature and pictorial art (text mainly in German, occasionally in English or Slovene),

Hubert Fabian Kulterer, A-1120 Vienna, Unter-Meidlinger Str 16-18

Eselsohr (Dog's Ear), G Pilz, A-4320 Perg, Stifterstr 4a

Literatur und Kritik (Literature and Criticism), Otto Müller Verlag KG, A-5021 Salzburg, Ernst-Thunstr 11

Literaturspiegel (Mirror to Literature), Vienna 4, Schleifmühlgasse 23-29

Manuskripte (Manuscripts); journal for literature, art, criticism, A-8010 Graz, Forum Stadtpark 1 Tel: (03122) 77734

Modern Austrian Literature (text and summaries in English and German), Arthur Schnitzler International Research Association, c/o Donald G Daviau, Editor, Department of German, University of California, Riverside, California 92502, USA

Moderne Literatur (Modern Literature), Zeitschriftenverlag, Vienna, Favoritenstr 235/26

Das Pult (The Desk); literature, art, criticism, Klaus Sandler, A-3100 St Pölten, Schiessfach 12

Schrifttumsspiegel (Mirror to Literature), Gesellschaft für Ganzhehsforschung, A-1191 Vienna, Franz Klein Gasse 1

Sprachkunst (Art of Language) (text in English, French, German and Russian); contributions to the study of literature, Verlag der österreichischen Akademie der Wissenschaften, A-1010 Vienna, Dr Ignaz Seipelpl 2

Literary Prizes

Austrian literary prizes are generally not associated with a single work, and are not often awarded in a lump sum, because of the high taxes authors have to pay. In addition to those cited below, each province has its own prize

Austrian Children's and Young People's Book Prizes
There are six categories: for books for children up to seven years, up to 10 years, up to 13 years; an 'Austrian Young People's Book Prize', an 'Austrian Children's and Young People's Non-fiction Book Prize', an 'Austrian Children's and Young People's Translation Prize', for Book Illustration. The total prize money available for distribution in 1982 was 165,000 Schillings. Prizewinning books are purchased by the Ministry of Education and Art to an overall value of 125,000 Schillings. Enquiries to Bundesministerium für Unterricht und Kunst, A-1014 Vienna, Minoritenplatz 5, Postfach 65

Austrian State Prize for Literature for Children and Young People
Conferred on an author in appreciation of his life's work. Presented in 1980 for the first time in a three-yearly cycle. Enquiries to Bundesministerium für Unterricht und Kunst, A-1014 Vienna, Postfach 65, Sektion V/Abteilung 3A

'Encouragement Prize'
40,000 Schillings, awarded by jury. Submissions accepted. Enquiries to Bundesministerium für Unterricht und Kunst, A-1014 Vienna, Postfach 65, Sektion IV/Abteilung 3

Great Austrian State Prize
200,000 Schillings, for life's work. Awarded by Österreichischer Kunstsenat. No applications. Enquiries to Bundesministerium für Unterricht und Kunst, A-1014 Vienna, Postfach 65, Sektion V/Abteilung 3A

Literature Prize of the Province of Steiermark
Annual prize of 50,000 Schillings for a writer's entire literary output. Enquiries to Amt der Steiermärkischen Landesregierung, A-8011 Graz, Rechtsabteilung 6, Karmeliterplatz 2

New Writers Stipendium for Literature
Four given each year. 6,000 Schillings each month for twelve months, awarded by jury. Submissions accepted. Enquiries to Bundesministerium för Unterricht und Kunst, A-1014 Vienna, Postfach 65, Sektion IV/Abteilung 3

Rauriser Encouragement Award
Annual literary award sponsored by the Salzburg provincial government and the village of Rauris. 30,000 Schillings awarded for a specific topic, as decided by jury. Enquiries to Salzburger Landesregierung, A-5010 Salzburg, Kulturabteilung, Chiemseehof

Rauriser Literature Prize
Annual award sponsored by the Salzburg provincial government. 75,000 Schillings awarded for an outstanding first publication in prose, as decided by jury. Enquiries to Salzburger Landesregierung, Kulturabteilung, A-5010 Salzburg, Chiemseehof

'Recognition Prize'
75,000 Schillings. Awarded by jury. No applications. Enquiries to Bundesministerium für Unterricht und Kunst, A-1014 Vienna, Postfach 65, Sektion IV/Abteilung 3

State Stipendium for Literature
Eight given each year. 6,000 Schillings each month for twelve months, awarded by jury. Submissions accepted. Enquiries to Bundesministerium für Unterricht und Kunst, A-1014 Vienna, Postfach 65, Sektion IV/Abteilung 3

Georg Trakl Prize
An irregular award to a writer of lyric poetry for his/her complete poetical works. 75,000 Schillings. Last awarded in 1982 to Christoph Meckel. Enquiries to Salzburger Landesregierung, Kulturabteilung, A-5010 Salzburg, Chiemseehof

City of Vienna Prize*
Originally founded in 1924. An annual award of 40,000 Schillings is made to an author for total literary output. Enquiries to Magistratsabteilung 7, A-1082 Vienna, Friedrich Schmidtpl 5

City of Vienna Prize for Books for Children and Young People
Awarded annually by the City of Vienna for distinguished books for children and young people, including illustration. Enquiries to Kulturamt der Stadt Wien, A-1082 Vienna, MA 7 Friedrich Schmidtpl 5

Anton Wildgans Prize of Austrian Industry
Awarded annually, at the beginning of the autumn, to an Austrian lyric poet, dramatist, novelist or essayist, young or middle aged. The author must be an Austrian citizen, writing in German, who lives either in Austria or abroad. Maximum prize 100,000 Schillings. Awarded by a committee. No applications. 1982 prize went to Ernst Jandl. Enquiries to Vereinigung österreichischer Industrieller, A-1031 Vienna

Bahamas

General Information

Language: English
Religion: Largest of 12 denominations are Baptist, Roman Catholic and Anglican
Population: 225,000
Bank Hours: 0930-1500 Monday-Thursday; 0930-1700 Friday
Shop Hours: 0900-1700 Monday-Thursday and Saturday; 0900-1200 Friday
Currency: 100 cents = 1 Bahamian dollar
Export/Import Information: No tariffs on books and advertising matter. No import licences required
Copyright: Berne, UCC (see International section)

Publishers

Brice Advertising and Publishing Ltd*, PO Box N4181, Nassau

Etienne Dupuch Jr Publications Ltd*, PO Box N7513, Nassau
Subjects: Maps, Educational Colouring Books, Periodicals

Major Booksellers

Bahamas Anglo American Book Store*, PO Box N9046, 9 Nassau Arcade, Hoffer Bldg, Bay St, Nassau Tel: 50388

Bahamas Book & Bible House*, PO Box N356, Nassau Tel: 23032

Calypso Distributors Ltd*, PO Box ES 6220, Chesapeake Rd, Nassau Tel: 28986 (wholesaler)

Christian Book Shop, PO Box N4924, Rosetta St, Palmdale, Nassau Tel: (809) 3258744/3221306
Manager: Marilyn Johnson

The **Island** Shop*, PO Box N3947, Bay St, Nassau Tel: 24183/21588

Lee's Book Centre*, Bank Lane, PO Box N-8196, Nassau Tel: 22128
Manager: Maria Lee

Tryma Book Shop*, PO Box N1243, Independence Shopping Centre, Nassau Tel: 57478

United Bookshop & Stationers Ltd, PO Box SS6220, Nassau Tel: (809) 3228770/3237315 Cable Add: Fantasia
The above is the office and wholesale department; retail stores are at Madeira St Shopping Centre Tel: (809) 3228597 and Oakes Field Shopping Centre Tel: (809) 3250316
President: Sigmund A Pritchard

Major Libraries

Department of **Archives**, Public Records Office, Ministry of Education and Culture, PO Box SS6341, Nassau Tel: (809) 3223045
Chief Archivist: D Gail Saunders

College of the Bahamas Library*, PO Box N4912, Nassau Tel: 36456/7
Librarian: Vanrea Thomas Rolle
Publication: Bahamas Reference Collection: a Bibliography (1980, with annual supplements)

John Harvard Lending Library*, PO Box F40, Freeport, Grand Bahama

32 BAHAMAS — BANGLADESH

Nassau Public Library*, PO Box N3210, Nassau Tel: (809) 3224907
Librarian: Anthony J Kriz

Bahrain

General Information

Language: Arabic (English used commercially)
Religion: Muslim, officially
Population: 345,000
Literacy Rate (1971): 40.2%
Bank Hours: 0730-1200 Saturday-Wednesday; 0730-1100 Thursday
Bazaar Hours: 0800-1200, 1530-1800 Saturday-Thursday (few shops open Friday morning)
Currency: 1000 fils = 1 Bahrain dinar
Export/Import Information: Generally books dutied at 10%, most schoolbooks free of duty; none on advertising matter. No import licence required but no obscene literature permitted and for books (not for advertising) a Chamber of Commerce certificate is mandatory. No exchange controls

Major Booksellers

Al-**Aadab** Bookshop*, PO Box 384, Manama

Bahrain Bookshop*, PO Box 443, Manama Tel: 54415

Family Bookshop (Bahrain) WLL, PO Box 1, Manama (Main branch located at: 129 Essa Al Kabeer Ave, Manama) Tel: 254288/256059 Cable Add: Synodical Telex: 8444 Fambah Bn
Manager: Hugh Cade
Parent Company: Family Bookshop Group

Islamic Cultural Bookshop*, PO Box 873, Manama

National Bookshop and Branches*, PO Box 594, Manama

Literary Associations and Societies

Bahrain Writers and Literators Association, PO Box 1010, Manama
Secretary: Abdul Qadir Aqeel

Bangladesh

General Information

Language: Bengali (English widely used commercially)
Religion: Muslim
Population: 84.7 million
Bank Hours: 0930-1330 Monday-Thursday; 0900-1100 Friday and Saturday
Shop Hours: 1000-2030 Monday-Friday; 1000-1400 Saturday
Currency: 100 paise = 1 taka
Export/Import Information: No tariff on books and advertising matter. Import licences required for all imports
Copyright: UCC

Book Trade Organizations

Bangladesh Pustak Prokashak o Bikreta Samity*, c/o Rahman Brothers, 5/1 Gopinath Datta, Kabiraj St (Babu Bazar), Dacca Tel: 282633 Bangladesh Publishers' & Booksellers' Association
Secretary: Azhirul Islam Khan

National Book Centre of Bangladesh*, 67a Purana Paltan, Dacca 2
Publication: Boi

Book Trade Reference Journal

Boi (Text in Bengali), National Book Centre of Bangladesh, 67a Purana Paltan, Dacca 2

Publishers

Adeylebros & Co*, 60 Patuatuly, Dacca 1
Bookshop: Adeyle Brothers (qv under Major Booksellers)

Anwari Publications*, 5/1 Simson Rd, Dacca 1

Banga Sahitya Bhavan*, 144 Government New Market, Dacca

Bangladesh Books International Ltd*, GPO Box 377, Dacca 3 (Located at: 1 Hefaq Bhaban, 1 RK Mission Rd, Dacca) Tel: 256071-5 ext 19 Cable Add: Bhabooks Dacca
Chairman: Moinul Hosein; *Man Dir:* Anower Hossain; *Dir:* Abdul Hafiz
Subjects: Educational, Academic, Reference, Children
Bookshop: See under Major Booksellers
Founded: 1975

Biswakosh*, 316 Government New Market, Dacca

Boighar*, 149 Government New Market, Dacca

Chalantika*, 177 Government New Market, Dacca

Crescent Publishers*, 77 Patuatuly, Dacca 1

Lekha Prokashani*, 18 Pyaridas Rd, Dacca 1

Mullick Bros*, 3/1 Bangla Bazar, Dacca
Subjects: Education, Secondary & Primary Textbooks
Bookshop: See under Major Booksellers

Pak Kitab Ghar*, 39 Patuatuly, Dacca

Paramount Book Corporation*, Ashraf Chamber, 66 Bangladesh Ave, Dacca
Administrator: D H Khondker
Subject: Literature

Rahman Brothers*, Educational Publishers, 5/1 Gopinath Datta, Kabiraj St (Babu Bazar), Dacca Tel: 282633

University Press Ltd*, PO Box 88, Dacca 2 (Located at: Red Cross Bldg, 114 Motijheel CA, Dacca) Tel: 242467/232950/255789 Cable Add: Dunipress
Man Dir, Chief Executive: Mohiuddin Ahmed; *Sales:* M A Halim; *Production:* G A Chowdhury
Subjects: Academic and Scholarly, Art and Architecture, Educational and Textbooks (Primary, Secondary, Tertiary), Supplementary Books for Schools, Reference, Scientific and Technical, Journals
Founded: 1975

Major Booksellers

Adeyle Brothers*, 60 Patuatuly, Dacca
Also Publisher (qv)

Ali Publications*, 77 Patuatuly, Dacca

Bangladesh Books International Ltd*, GPO Box 377, Dacca (Located at: Sales Centre, 1 Hefaq Bhaban, 1 RK Mission Rd, Dacca)
Manager: Abdul Hafiz
Also Publisher (qv)

Dacca Book Mart*, 38 Banglabazar, Dacca

Golden Book House*, 38 Banglabazar, Dacca

Green Book House Limited*, 85 Motighlel, Dacca

Hakkim's Bookshop*, 33 Banglabazar, Dacca

Hamidia Library*, 65 Chawk Circular Rd, Dacca

Islamia Library*, 41/42 Islampur Rd, Dacca

Mohammadi Library*, Chawk Circular Rd, Dacca

Mullick Bros*, 3/1 Bangla Bazar, Dacca
Also Publisher (qv)

Provincial Book Depot*, Dacca Stadium, Dacca

Provincial Library*, 109-A Sarat Gupta Rd, Narinda, Dacca

Puthigar Limited*, 74 Farashgunj, Dacca

Major Libraries

Bangladesh Institute of Development Studies Library*, Adamjee Ct, Motij Heel Commercial Area, Dacca 2 Tel: 257360

British Council Library*, GPO Box 161, Dacca 2 (Located at: 5 Fuller Rd, Dacca)
Librarian: N Lack

Dacca University Library*, Dacca 2

Central **Public Library**, Dacca*, Shahbagh, Dacca 2

University of Rajshahi Library*, Rajshahi

Library Associations

Bangladesh Granthagar Samity*, c/o Library, Bangladesh University of Engineering and Technology, Dacca 2
Library Association of Bangladesh
Secretary: Abu Bakr Siddique
Publication: Eastern Librarian (three times a year)

Directorate of Archives and Libraries, 106 Central Rd, Dacca 5
Director: Dr K M Karim
Publications: Bangladesh National Bibliography (annually), Article index published in the daily newspapers, *Bulletin of the Dissertations on Social Science*

Library Reference Journals

Bangladesh National Bibliography, Directorate of Archives and Libraries, 106 Central Rd, Dacca 5

Eastern Librarian (text in English), Library Association of Bangladesh, c/o Library, Bangladesh University of Engineering and Technology, Dacca 2

Literary Associations and Societies

Dacca Centre for International P E N Madhura, 62 Purana Paltan, Haroon Enterprises Bldg, 1st Floor, Dacca 2
Secretary: Fazal Shabuddin

Society of Arts, Literature and Welfare*, Society Park, K C Dey Rd, Chittagong
General Secretary: Md Abdul Hakim

Literary Prizes

Bengali Academy Literary Awards*
For an overall contribution to Bengali literature in the following categories: novel, short story, children's literature, poetry, essay, drama, literary research. Awarded annually. Enquiries to Bengali Academy, Burdwan House, Dacca

Barbados

General Information

Language: English
Religion: Anglican
Population: 265,000
Literacy Rate (1946): 89.8%
Bank Hours: 0800-1300 Monday-Thursday; 0800-1300, 1500-1750 Friday
Shop Hours: 0800-1600 Monday-Friday; 0800-1200 Saturday
Currency: 100 cents = 1 Barbados dollar
Export/Import Information: No tariff on books. Import licence covering exchange required; no obscene literature permitted

Publishers

The C E D A R Press*, Publishing House of the Caribbean Conference of Churches, PO Box 616, Bridgetown Tel: 72681 Cable Add: Christos Telex: 335
Editor: Dr David Mitchell; *Acting Publisher:* Mrs Muriel Forde
Subjects: Religion, Sociology, Education, Music, Agriculture, Communication, Politics, Caribbean History, Identity and Culture

P P C Ltd*, Eldino, Gills Rd, St Michael Tel: 75505

Yoruba* Publishing and Typesetting, Mottley Ho, Coleridge St, Bridgetown Tel: 63927

Major Booksellers

Christian Literature Crusade, PO Box 239, Bridgetown (Located at: St Michael Plaza, St Michael's Row, Bridgetown) Tel: 95630
Manager: Philip Bacon

Cloister Book Store Ltd, Hincks St, Bridgetown Tel: 62662
Dir: A Musgrave

Roberts Stationery Ltd*, PO Box 224, Bridgetown (Located at: 9 High St, Bridgetown) Tel: 65500/97268 Cable Add: Robertsco Telex: 2213 Pubtlx
Manager: T A L Roberts

Sandy Beach Book Store*, Worthing Plaza and Shopping Centre, Bridgetown Tel: 89432

Wayfarer Book Store Ltd, Sunset Crest, St James (4 other branches)
Man Dir: Nigel Deane

Major Libraries

Public Library*, Coleridge St, Bridgetown
Publications: National Bibliography of Barbados, West Indian Collection

University of the West Indies*, Main Library, Cave Hill Campus, PO Box 64, Bridgetown Tel: 51100 Cable Add: Univados Barbados Telex: 257 Univados WB
Librarian: Michael Gill

Library Association

Library Association of Barbados, PO Box 827E, Bridgetown Tel: 60512
Secretary: Hazel Gibbs
Publication: Bulletin (irregular)

Library Reference Journal

Bulletin of the Library Association of Barbados, PO Box 827E, Bridgetown

Belgium

General Information

Language: Dutch in the north, French in the south. Brussels is officially bilingual. German in eastern Belgium
Religion: Predominantly Roman Catholic
Population: 9.8 million
Literacy Rate (1947): 96.7%
Bank Hours: Variable locally. Brussels: 0900-1300 Monday-Friday; 1400-1630 Monday and Friday; 1430-1530 Tuesday-Thursday. Antwerp: 0930-1500 Monday-Friday; 1630-1800 Friday
Shop Hours: Variable. Department stores: 0915-1800 Monday-Saturday; open until 2100 Friday
Currency: 100 centimes = 1 Belgian franc
Export/Import Information: Member of the European Economic Community. No import licence required, just Model A form of notice of declaration of payment. No exchange controls
Copyright: UCC, Berne, Florence

Book Trade Organizations

Algemene Vlaamse Boekverkopersbond, Frankrijklei 93, B-2000 Antwerp
Flemish Booksellers' Association

Association des Editeurs belges, 111 ave du Parc, B-1060 Brussels Tel: (02) 5382167
Belgian Publishers' Association
Dir: Julien de Raeymaeker
Publications: Annuaire des Editeurs belges; L'edition en Belgique; Livres belges

Bond Alleenverkopers van Nederlandstalige Boeken (BANB), Dr Desmethlaan 4, B-1980 Tervuren
Association of Wholesalers of Dutch Books in Belgium
Secretary: M Kluwer

Cercle Belge de la Librairie, 5 rue du Luxembourg, BP 1, B-1040 Brussels Tel: (02) 5112158
Belgian Booksellers' Association
President: R Krings; *Secretary General:* M Wislet; *Administration:* N Mertens
Publications: Journal de la Librairie (6 a year), *Annuaire du CBL, Annuaire 1983 du Centenaire*

Standard Book Numbering Agency: for publications in Dutch see under Netherlands Book Trade Organizations, for publications in French see under French Book Trade Organizations

Syndicat belge de la Librairie ancienne et moderne*, 112 rue de Trèves, B-1040 Brussels
Belgian Association of Antiquarian and Modern Booksellers

Union des Editeurs de Langue française (UELF), 111 ave du Parc, B-1060 Brussels
International Union of Publishers of French Language Books
Dir: J de Raeymaeker

Union des Industries graphiques et du Livre (UNIGRA)*, 76 rue Renkin, B-1030 Brussels
Book & Graphics Industries Union

Vereniging ter Bevordering van het Vlaamse Boekwezen, Frankrijklei 93, Bus 3, B-2000 Antwerp Tel: (03) 2324684
Association for the Promotion of Flemish Books
Publication: Iijdingen

Vereniging van Uitgevers van Nederlandstalige Boeken, Frankrijklei 93, Bus 3, B-2000 Antwerp Tel: (03) 2324684
Association of Publishers of Dutch Language Books
Secretary: A Wouters
Publications: Lijstenbook; Tijdingen

Book Trade Reference Books and Journals

Books

Annuaire des Editeurs belges (Belgian Publishers' Annual), Belgian Publishers' Association, 111 ave du Parc, B-1060 Brussels

Annuaire du CBL (Annual), Belgian Booksellers' Association, 5 rue du Luxembourg, BP 1, B-1040 Brussels

L'Edition en Belgique (Publishing in Belgium), Belgian Publishers' Association, 111 ave du Parc, B-1060 Brussels

Lijstenbook (List of Booksellers), Association of Publishers of Dutch Language Books, Frankrijklei 93, Bus 3, B-2000 Antwerp

Liste des Sociétés savantes et littéraires de Belgique (List of Belgian Learned and Literary Societies), Service belge des Echanges Internationaux, 80-84 rue des Tanneurs, B-1000 Brussels

Livres belges (Books from Belgium), Belgian Publishers' Association, 111 ave du Parc, B-1060 Brussels

Journals

Belgica Selecta, Belgian Institute of Information, Montoyerstr 3, B-1040 Brussels (lists new Belgian books)

Belgische Bibliografie (Bibliography of Belgium), Koninklijke Bibliotheek Albert I, Keizerslaan 4, B-1000 Brussels

Bibliographie de Belgique see *Belgische Bibliografie*

34 BELGIUM

Boekengids (Guide to Books), Katholiek Centrum voor Lectuurinformatie en Bibliotheekvoorziening, Raapstr 4, Antwerp

Bulletin, Belgian Commission of Bibliography, 80-84 rue des Tanneurs, B-1000 Brussels

Journal de la Librairie (Book Trade Journal) (6 a year), Belgian Booksellers' Association, 5 rue du Luxembourg, BP 1, B-1040 Brussels

Livre et l'Estampe (The Book and the Print) (text in French), Royal Society of Bibliophiles and Iconophiles of Belgium, 4 blvd de l'Empereur, B-1000 Brussels

Répertoire annuel des principaux Travaux bibliographiques récents (Annual Catalogue of the Principal Recent Bibliographical Works), Belgian Commission of Bibliography, 80-84 rue des Tanneurs, B-1000 Brussels

Tijdingen (News), Association of Publishers of Dutch Language Books, Frankrijklei 93, Bus 3, B-2000 Antwerp

Publishers

3 Arches, see Trois Arches

Editions **A B C** Jeunesse SARL*, 160 ave Gabriel E Lebon, B-1150 Brussels Tel: (02) 7346601
Publisher: Emile D Probst
Subject: Juveniles

Acco SV+, Tiensestr 134-136, B-3000 Louvain Tel: (016) 233520 Telex: 62547
Dir: H Van Slambrouck
Orders to: Acco-Uitgeverij, at above address
Subjects: Classic Languages and Culture, Linguistics, Economics, Law, Social Sciences, Education, Pedagogy, Mathematics, General Science, History, Physiotherapy, Psychology, Medicine, Religion, Philosophy, Criminology, Ethics
1981: 168 titles *1982:* 143 titles *Founded:* 1960
ISBN Publisher's Prefix: 90-334

Acta Medica Belgica ASBL, 43 rue des Champs Elysées, B-1050 Brussels Tel: (02) 6480468
Subject: Medicine
Founded: 1945

Actuaquarto, 20 allée des Bouleaux, B-6280 Gerpinnes Tel: (071) 216153
Man Dir and Sales, Production, Publicity, Rights & Permissions: Michel Paunet; *Editorial:* Jean Delahaut
Subject: Education
1981: approx 50 titles *1982:* approx 50 titles
Founded: 1970

Agence belge des grandes Editions SA*, 146 Blvd Adolphe Max, B-1000 Brussels Tel: (02) 2191872 Cable Add: Belgeditions
Man Dir: Monique de Smet
Subjects: Medicine, Educational Materials, Encyclopaedias, Games, Sports
Founded: 1978

Bibliotheca **Alphonsiana** VZW*, Dekenstr 28, B-3000 Louvain Tel: (016) 23470
Subjects: Religion, Juveniles, Textbooks
Founded: 1927

Altiora NV, Abdijstr 1, B-3281 Averbode Tel: (013) 771751/4 Telex: 39104
Dirs: F Nauwelaerts, T Secuianu; *Editor:* N C Vranckx; *Production:* I Willems
Subjects: Education, Juveniles, Religion, Periodicals
ISBN Publisher's Prefix: 90-317

Angelet*, Potterie Rei 69, B-8000 Bruges Tel: (050) 335186
Dir: P Angelet

Subjects: Juveniles, Music
Founded: 1969

Editions Jacques **Antoine** SPRL+, 55-57 rue des Éperonniers, B-1000 Brussels Tel: (02) 5124337
Dir: J Antoine
Subjects: Literature, Arts, Theatre
1981: 7 titles *1982:* 8 titles *Founded:* 1968

Antwerpse Lloyd NV, see Lloyd Anversois SA

Editions **Arcade-Fonds** Mercator, Meir 85, B-2000 Antwerp Tel: 2313840 Telex: 71876
Man Dir: J Martens
Associate Company: Fonds Mercator SA (qv)
Subject: Art
Founded: 1952
ISBN Publisher's Prefix: 2-8005

Editions **Arscia** SA*, 60 rue de l'Etuve, B-1000 Brussels Tel: (02) 5114272
Dir: C Pirson
Subject: Belles Lettres
Founded: 1957

SC **Artis-Historia**+, 19 rue Général Gratry, B-1040 Brussels Tel: (02) 7362000 Telex: 64996
Director-General: C Kremer
Subjects: Geography, History, Ethnography, Nature, Art, Travel
Bookshops: 75 throughout Belgium
Founded: 1949, companies merged to form Artis-Historia in 1976

Editions **Arts et Voyages***, 88 ave de Tervueren, B-1040 Brussels Tel: (02) 7343560/7343582
Man Dir: Lucien de Meyer; *Rights & Permissions:* Dominique Schoofs
Associate Company: Editions d'Art Lucien de Meyer (qv)
Subjects: Art, Literature, History, Juveniles, Management, Sports
Founded: 1954
ISBN Publisher's Prefix: 2-8016

Assimil, Uitgaven Nelis PVBA, Steenstr 5-7, B-1000 Brussels Tel: (02) 5114502
Man Dir: R Nelis; *Commercial Dir:* A Van Damme
Subject: Languages (Home Studying)
ISBN Publisher's Prefix: 90-70077

Association des Sociétés scientifiques médicales belges (ASBL)*, 43 rue des Champs Elysées, B-1050 Brussels Tel: (02) 6480468
Vereniging van de belgische medische Wetenschappelijke Genootschappen VZW
Subjects: Medicine, Journals
Founded: 1945

Audivox*, Rubenslei 23, B-2000 Antwerp Tel: (031) 328465
Dir: W Gonnissen
Founded: 1953
Subjects: School Text Books
Bookshop: See under Major Booksellers

Aurelia Books PVBA*, Museumlaan 17, B-9831 Sint-Martens-Latem Tel: (091) 825582
Dir: A d'Oosterlynck; *Sales, Publicity:* L Bullaert
Subjects: Training of Nurses, School Books, Flemish Folklore, Popular Devotion
Founded: 1972

De **Backer** Publishers PVBA*, Penitentenstr 14, B-9000 Ghent Tel: (091) 231013
Dir: Chr de Backer
Subjects: Bibliography, Languages, History of Pharmacy, History, Travel, Medicine, Literature, Music
Founded: 1972

Maison d'Editions **Baha'ies** ASBL, rue du Trône 205, 1050 Brussels Tel: (02) 6470749
Subject: Bahai
Founded: 1970

Barbiaux (Drukkerij G — Uitgeverij de Garve) PVBA*, Groene Poortdreef 27, B-8200 St-Michiels, Bruges Tel: (050) 318283
Dir: W Barbiaux
Subjects: Law, Political, Administrative & Social Sciences, Mathematics, General Science, Music
Founded: 1909

Beckers SA Editions*, Antwerp Tower, de Keyserlei 5 B 14, B-2000 Antwerp Tel: (031) 317605
Parent Company: Geeris Holding BV, Netherlands

Belgisch Instituut voor Voorlichting en Documentatie (INBEL), see Institut belge d'Information et de Documentation

Uitgeverij van **Belle** PVBA*, Steenweg op Ninove 116, B-1080 Brussels Tel: (02) 5213417/5210221
Dir: R van Belle
Subjects: Geography, History, Ethnography, Travel, Juveniles, Sports
Founded: 1938

Editions Gérard **Blanchart** & Cie SA, 15 ave Ernest Masoin, B-1090 Brussels Tel: (02) 4783706 Telex: 25985 c/o Halbart
Administrator, Editorial and Sales: Charles Blanchart; *Production:* Thérèse Chantrenne; *Rights & Permissions:* Charles Blanchart, Thérèse Chantrenne
Subjects: Religion, Art, Photography, Children's and Teenagers' Books
1981: 10 titles *1982:* 15 titles *Founded:* 1958
ISBN Publisher's Prefix: 2-0121

Maison d'Edition A de **Boeck** SA+, ave Louise 203, BP 1, B-1050 Brussels Tel: (02) 6407272 Telex: 65701 Sipemb
Man Dir and Editorial, Production, Rights & Permissions: Christian de Boeck; *Sales:* Alain van Langhendonck; *Publicity:* Evelyne Stubbe
Subsidiary Company: Afrique-Editions, BP 20097, Kinshasa/Lemba, Zaire
Subjects: Textbooks for primary and secondary schools, Higher education
1981: 40 titles *1982:* 45 titles *Founded:* 1883
ISBN Publisher's Prefix: 2-8037

Société **Bordas-Dunod** Bruxelles SA, 44 rue Otlet, B-1070 Brussels Tel: (02) 5238133 Telex: 24899 Bordun
Parent Company: Editions Bordas, France (qv for associate companies)
Subject: Textbooks
Bookshop: Librairie Beranger, 48 rue Cathédrale, B-4000 Liège
Founded: 1969
Miscellaneous: Company's main function is as a distributor of French-language books

Bourdeaux-Capelle SA*, 69 rue Sax, B-5500 Dinant Tel: (082) 222283/222277
Dir: E Bourdeaux
Subjects: Bibliography, Languages, Journals
Founded: 1913

De **Branding** NV, Korte Winkelstr 13-15, B-2000 Antwerp Tel: (03) 2332739
Dir: L Ruys
Subjects: Nautical
Bookshop: Belgisch Maritiem Centrum
Founded: 1956

Brepols IGP Publishers, Baron F du Fourstr 8, B-2300 Turnhout Tel: (014) 415466/7 Telex: 34182
Chairman: Baron de Cartier de Marchienne; *Man Dir:* M Rolin
Head Off: Editions Brepols SA, France (qv)
Subjects: Religion (Patristics, Bibles, Prayerbooks), History

Vanden Broele PVBA, Magdalenastr 41, B-8200 Bruges Tel: (050) 315074
Dir: E de Jonghe
Subjects: Law, Political, Administrative & Social Sciences, Popular Medicine
1981: 17 titles *1982:* 17 titles
ISBN Publisher's Prefix: 90-6267

A W **Bruna** & Zoon NV, Antwerpsesteenweg 29a, B-2630 Aartselaar Tel: (03) 8874018/9
Telex: 73159
Dir: J Raedschelders
Head Office: A W Bruna en Zoon's Uitgeversmaatschappij BV, Netherlands (qv)
Subjects: Juveniles, Literature, Paperbacks
Founded: 1966

Etablissements Emile **Bruylant** SA, 67 rue de la Régence, B-1000 Brussels Tel: (02) 5129845
Man Dirs: Angèle Van Sprengel, Jean Vandeveld
Subjects: Law, High-priced Paperbacks, General & Social Science, University Textbooks
Bookshop: At above address
1981: 30 titles *1982:* 18 titles *Founded:* 1838
ISBN Publisher's Prefix: 2-8027

J E **Buschmann** PVBA*, Italiëlei 26, B-2000 Antwerp Tel: (031) 323130/325235
Dir: J Buschmann
Subjects: Arts, Geography, History, Ethnography, Travel, Journals

Erven J **Byleveld**, an imprint of Elsevier Librico NV (qv)

C E D-Samsom, Louizalaan 485, B-1050 Brussels Tel: (02) 7207180
Dir: O Chrispeels
Parent Company: Wolters-Samsom België NV (qv)
Subjects: General & Social Science, Documentation, Textbooks, Law
Founded: 1964

Editions **C E F A** (Centre d'Education à la Famille et à l'Amour), 58 rue de la Prévoyance, B-1000 Brussels Tel: (02) 5131749
Man Dir: Pierre de Locht; *Sales:* Josette Maufroy
Orders to: Above address or Librairie Novissima, 33 rue de la Concorde, B-1050 Brussels
Subjects: The Family, Sexual Education, Religion
Bookshops: Librairie Novissima, 33 rue de la Concorde, B-1050 Brussels
1981: 10 titles *Founded:* 1961

C F E Belgique*, 1033a chaussée d'Alsemberg (Boîte 28b), B-1180 Brussels Tel: (02) 3761167 Telex: 64797 Foblex
Parent Company: Les Cahiers Fiscaux Européens Sàrl, France (qv)
Associate Company: JURIF Belgique (qv)
Subjects: European Taxation, Fiscal Law

Cabay, Agora 11, B-1348 Louvain-la-Neuve Tel: (010) 419016 Cable Add: Cabaylln Telex: 59324 Cablln
Man Dir: Michel Jezierski
Imprint: Presses universitaires de Louvain-la-Neuve
Subjects: Sciences, Human Sciences, Philosophy
1981: 52 titles *1982:* 53 titles *Founded:* 1977
ISBN Publisher's Prefixes: 2-87077 (Cabay), 2-87078 (Presses universitaires)

Editions **Calozet** SPRL*, 40 rue des Chartreux, B-1000 Brussels Tel: (02) 5116026
Dir: J de Groef
Subjects: Mathematics, Cuisenaire Materials (educational)
Founded: 1874

Carmelitana VZW ('De Karmelieten')*, Burgstr 46, B-9000 Ghent Tel: (091) 255787
Dir: A Dupon
Subject: Religious books
ISBN Publisher's Prefix: 90-70092

Carto PVBA*, Gaucheretstr 139, B-1000 Brussels Tel: (02) 2161545 Cable Add: Cartopress
Man Dir: Wijnand Plaizier
Subsidiary Companies: Carpress, International Press Agency; European Cartographic Institute; Cremers Cartographic Institute (school maps)
Subjects: Geography, History, Secondary & Primary Textbooks, Educational Materials (Transparencies), Maps, Travel
Founded: 1950

Editions **Casterman**, rue des Soeurs noires 28, B-7500 Tournai Tel: (069) 224141 Cable Add: Casteredim Tournai Telex: 57328
Man Dir: Louis-Robert Casterman; *Sales Dir:* Jean-Jacques Dursin; *Rights & Permissions:* Pierre Servais, Ivan Noerdinger
Subsidiary Company: Editions Casterman, France (qv)
Branch Offs: 44 ave de Roodebeek, B-1040 Brussels; De Morinel 25-29, NL-8251 HT Dronten, Netherlands
Subjects: General Fiction, Belles Lettres, Poetry, Biography, History, Music, Art, Philosophy, Reference, Religion, Juveniles, High-priced Paperbacks, Psychology, General & Social Science, University & Secondary Textbooks, Languages, Law, Geography, Sports, Travel, Medicine
1981: 232 titles *1982:* 240 titles *Founded:* 1780
ISBN Publisher's Prefixes: 2-203 (French), 90-303 (Dutch)

Centre d'Education à la Famille et à l'Amour, see Editions CEFA

Centre international d'Etudes de la Formation religieuse Lumen Vitae ASBL, see Editions Lumen Vitae ASBL

Centre national d'Etudes et de Recherches socio-économiques (CERSE) ASBL*, 9 rue Vilain XIIII 9, B-1050 Brussels Tel: (02) 6495817
President: R Gubbels
Subjects: Law, Political, Administrative & Social Sciences
Founded: 1963

Centre national de Recherches 'Primitifs Flamands' ASBL, 1 parc du Cinquantenaire, B-1040 Brussels Tel: (02) 7354160
Dir and Rights & Permissions: R Sneyers; *Scientific Editor and Sales:* M Comblen
Subjects: Arts
Founded: 1950
ISBN Publisher's Prefix: 2-87033

Ceres*, Nukerkeplein 9, B-9681 Maarkedal Tel: (055) 211404
Dir: P de Riemaecker
Subjects: Geography, History, Ethnography, Travel
Founded: 1947

Chanlis*, 17 B rue de Lennery, B-6430 Walcourt Tel: (071) 326394/611770
Man Dir: Pierre Magain; *Sales:* M Nowak
Subsidiary Company: Chanlis, Route de Mons 25A, B-6000 Charleroi
Subjects: Numismatics, Archaeology, Arts
Bookshop: Route de Mons 25A, B-6000 Charleroi
1981: 18 titles *Founded:* 1968
ISBN Publisher's Prefix: 2-87039

Editions **Chantecler**, Cleydaellaan 8, B-2630 Aartselaar, Antwerp Tel: (03) 8878300 Telex: 31739 Zuidb
Man Dir: Joris Schaltin; *Editorial:* Emmanuel de Vocht; *Sales:* Jan Vande Velden; *Production:* Eric Feyten; *Rights & Permissions:* Wilfried Wuyts
Parent Company: Zuidnederlandse Uitgeverij NV (qv)
Imprint: Pre-Ecole
Subjects: Children's Fiction & Non-fiction
Founded: 1947
ISBN Publisher's Prefix: 2-8034

La **Charte** NV*, Oude Gentweg 108, B-8000 Bruges Tel: (050) 331235
Dir: H Bogaerts
Subjects: Bibliography, Languages, Textbooks, Law, Political, Administrative & Social Sciences, Primary & Secondary Textbooks
Founded: 1948

De **Clauwaert***, Koning Albertlaan 17, B-3040 Korbeek-Lo, Louvain Tel: (016) 462229
Man Dir: W Vanden Eynde; *Sales Dir:* J Raymaekers
Subjects: General Fiction, Belles Lettres, Secondary Textbooks
Book Club: Boekengilde de Clauwaert
Founded: 1948

Cogedi SA, galerie des Princes 2-4, B-1000 Brussels Tel: (02) 5132038
Dir: Pierre Mardaga; *Rights & Permissions:* Pierre Mardaga, Gigi Dony
Subjects: Education, Pedagogy, Psychology, Architecture
Founded: 1938

Colibrant, an imprint of Orbis en Orion Uitgevers NV (qv)

Editions **Complexe** SPRL+, 24 rue de Bosnie, B-1060 Brussels Tel: (02) 5388846 Telex: 64507 Batioa
Man Dir, Publicity: Danielle Vincken; *Man Dir, Editorial:* André Versaille
Associate Company: Nouvelle Diffusion (at above address)
Subjects: History, Human Sciences
1981: 19 titles *1982:* 23 titles *Founded:* 1971
ISBN Publisher's Prefix: 2-87027

Contact NV*, Elsbos 33, B-2520 Edegem Tel: (031) 572024/573486
Dir: A J H Binneweg
Subjects: Arts, Textbooks, Education, Pedagogy, Sports, Games, Literature, Paperbacks
Founded: 1946
ISBN Publisher's Prefix: 90-254

Creadif, 52 ave de Tervueren, B-1040 Brussels Tel: (02) 7360630
Dir: M Servais
Subjects: Geography, History, Ethnography, Travel, Economy, Commerce, Law
Founded: 1974

Crédit Communal de Belgique – Service Culturel, 44 blvd Pacheco, B-1000 Brussels Tel: (02) 2144111 Cable Add: Crédit Communal Brussels Cregem B 26354
Head of Cultural Dept: J-M Duvosquel
Subjects: History, Politics, Law, Music, Fine Arts
Founded: 1960
Miscellaneous: Incorporates Pro Civitate

Cremers (Schoollandkaarten) PVBA*, Gaucheretstr 139, B-1000 Brussels Tel: (02) 2161545 Cable Add: Cartopress
Dir: Wijnand Plaizier
Parent Company: Carto PVBA (qv)
Subjects: Textbooks, Geography, History, Ethnography, Travel, Journals
Founded: 1950

Crisp, 35 rue du Congrès, B-1000 Brussels Tel: (02) 2183226
Man Dir: J Gerard-Libois; *Editorial:* Xavier Mabille; *Management:* M Julin
Subjects: Political Science, Industry, Finance
Founded: 1958

36 BELGIUM

Editions **Culture et Civilisation**, 115 ave Gabriel Lebon, B-1160 Brussels Tel: (02) 7345005 Cable Add: Jadam
Man Dir: Jos Adam
Subsidiary Company: Imprimerie Jos Adam (at above address)
Subjects: Biography, History, Geography, Ethnography, Travel, Music, Art, Philosophy, Reference, Religion, Medicine, Psychology, University Textbooks, Bibliography, Languages, Law, Social & General Sciences, Literature
Founded: 1960

De **Dageraad** PVBA*, Perenstr 13-15, B-2000 Antwerp Tel: (031) 356866
Dir: R van Hevel
Founded: 1971

Le **Daily-Bul**, 29 rue Daily-Bul, B-7100 La Louvière Tel: (064) 222973
Man Dir: André Balthazar
Subjects: Literature, Poetry, Arts
1981: 6 titles *1982:* 6 titles *Founded:* 1957

Uitgeverij **Dap-Reinart** SV*, Industriepark B4, B-9140 Zele Tel: (052) 445171
Dir: A van Acker
Subjects: Juveniles, Literature, Education, Law, Religion
Book Club: Dap-Reinart Uitgeven
Founded: 1946

Editions **Daphne**, Mageleinstr 50, B-9000 Ghent Tel: (091) 253645
Man Dir: Albert Dubrulle
Subjects: Belles Lettres, Poetry, Music, Art, Education, Juveniles
Founded: 1945
ISBN Publisher's Prefix: 90-70090

Daphne Diffusion SPRL*, Poortakkerstr 29, B-9820 Gent Tel: (091) 214591
Telex: 11659
General Manager: F Dubrulle

Davidsfonds VZW+, Blijde Inkomststr 79, B-3000 Louvain Tel: (016) 221801
Dir: N D'Hulst; *Editorial:* L Peeraer
Subjects: Arts, Law, Political, Administrative & Social Sciences, Education, Pedagogy, Sports, Games, Juveniles, Religion, Philosophy, Literature, Journals
Founded: 1875
ISBN Publisher's Prefix: 90-6152

Maison d'Editions Cl **Dejaie***, 1208 chaussée de Dinant, B-5150 Wepion Namur Tel: (081) 460266
Dir: M Cl M Dejaie
Subjects: Bibliography, Languages, Law, Political, Administrative & Social Sciences, Religion, Philosophy, Literature
Founded: 1972
ISBN Publisher's Prefix: 2-1491

Editions **Delta**+, 92-94 sq Plasky, B-1040 Brussels Tel: (02) 7369060 Telex: 65968 Delta
Man Dir: Georges-Francis Seingry
Associate Company: Delta Périodiques SPRL (at above address)
Subjects: Reference books (Directories, Yearbooks, Guides) regarding EEC and other European Organizations; Belgian Restaurant Guides, General Literature, Art Books
1981: 7 titles *1982:* 7 titles *Founded:* 1976
ISBN Publisher's Prefix: 2-8029

Deltas, an imprint of Zuidnederlandse Uitgeverij NV (qv)

Denis & Co PVBA, Sterckshoflei 28-30, B-2100 Deurne Tel: (03) 3213299/3220804
Subjects: Art, Law, Education, History, Juveniles, Philosophy

Desclée, Editeurs, 13 rue Barthélemy Frison, B-7500 Tournai Tel: (069) 226101 Cable Add: Desclée-Tournai Telex: Gedit 57251
Dir: F Parys; *Literary Dir:* A Paul
Parent Company: Gedit SA (qv)
Associate Companies: Editions Desclée et Cie, France (qv); Editions Gamma (qv); Nouvelles Editions Mame, France (qv)
Subjects: Religion, Philosophy, Missals, Theology, Literature
Bookshop: At above address
Founded: 1872

Desmet-Huysmans PVBA*, Dam 67, B-8500 Kortrijk Tel: (056) 217242
Man Dir: G Desmet

H **Dessain** NV*, Regenboog 5-9, B-2800 Mechelen Tel: (015) 416986
Man Dir: Patrick Dessain
Subjects: Juveniles, Medicine, Music, Religion, Reference, Geography, History, Ethnography, Travel
Founded: 1854

F **Dessain** SPRL*, 7 rue Trappé, B-4000 Liège Tel: (041) 237882/3
Man Dir: Maximilien Dessain
Subjects: Religion, Mathematics, Textbooks, Education, Pedagogy, Sports, Games, General Science, Geography, History, Ethnography, Travel
Founded: 1719

A **Dewallens***, 60 Brusselse steenweg, B-3020 Herent Tel: (016) 225857
Dir: A Dewallens
Subjects: Bibliography, Philology, Languages, Education, Pedagogy, Sports, Games, Journals
Founded: 1946

Diligentia-Uitgeverij, Sint-Jozefstr 7, B-9040 Oostakker Tel: (091) 511281
Dir: Frank Vermeiren
Subject: Textbooks
Founded: 1908
ISBN Publisher's Prefix: 90-70021

Edition **Doepgen** Verlag*, PO Box 140, B-4700 Eupen (Located at: Gospertstr 7, Eupen) Tel: (87) 556042/556264
Chief Executive, Editorial, Publicity, Rights & Permissions: Wolfgang Trees; *Sales, Production:* Heinz Doepgen
Subjects: War and History (Aachen, Liège and Maastricht regions)
Bookshops: At above address; Malmedyerstr 19, B-4780 Sint Vith
Founded: 1978
Miscellaneous: Publishes in German language for German-speaking part of Belgium

Editions et Imprimerie J **Duculot** SA+, rue de la Posterie, Parc industriel, B-5800 Gembloux Tel: (081) 610061 Telex: 59309 Duculo B
Administrator: Jean Verougstraete; *Publishing Dir, Sales, Publicity:* Georges David; *Editorial, Rights & Permissions:* Christiane Lapp, Emmanuel Brutsaert; *Production:* Jean Flament
Orders to: Presses de Belgique, rue du Sceptre 25, B-1040 Brussels
Subsidiary Company: Editions J Duculot, 16 rue Séguier, F-75006, Paris, France
Subjects: Belles Lettres, General Literature, Art, Religion, Juveniles, Linguistics, General Science, University, Secondary & Primary Textbooks, Guides, Regional Literature
Founded: 1919
ISBN Publisher's Prefix: 2-8011

Editions Jean **Dupuis** SA, 39 rue Destrée, B-6001 Marcinelle-Charleroi Tel: (071) 364080 Telex: 51370
Dirs: Charles Dupuis, Michel Dupuis, Pierre Matthews
Branch Off: 13-14 Oberrue des Arts, B-1040 Brussels
Subjects: Art, How-to, Cinema, Paperbacks, Juveniles, Comics
Bookshop: 39 rue Destrée, B-6001 Marcinelle-Charleroi
Founded: 1898
ISBN Publisher's Prefix: 2-8001

E P O*, Lange Pastoorstr 25, B-2600 Berchem Tel: (031) 396874
Man Dir: Marie-Paule Doumen; *Editorial:* Dirk Cantillon; *Sales:* Patrick van Buyten
Subject: Politics
1981: 23 titles *Founded:* 1974
ISBN Publisher's Prefix: 90-6445

Edi-Art*, 340 blvd de Lambermont, B-1030 Brussels Tel: (02) 4269873
Man Dir: J Freydiger
Founded: 1975

Editeurs de Litterature Biblique*, ch de Tubize 479, B-1420 Braine-L'Alleud Tel: (02) 3845402
Man Dir: M Cl Kroeker
Subjects: Education, Juveniles, Philosophy, Religion, Music, Pocketbooks
Founded: 1959

Editions interuniversitaires, 52 ave de Tervueren, B-1040 Brussels Tel: (02) 7360630
Dir: M Servais
Subjects: Geography, History, Ethnography, Travel
Founded: 1974

Editions techniques et scientifiques SPRL*, 35-43 rue Borrens, B-1050 Brussels Tel: (02) 6401040
Man Dir: G Louis
Subjects: General Technology, Law, Mathematics, Science, Geography, History, Ethnography, Travel, General
Founded: 1919

Editions universitaires SA*, 25 rue du Sceptre, B-1040 Brussels Tel: (02) 6488026
Dir: L Honhon
Subjects: Textbooks, Law Political, Administrative & Social Sciences, Education, Pedagogy, Sports, Games, Mathematics, General Science, Geography, History, Ethnography, Travel, Religion, Philosophy, Literature, Languages, Journals
Founded: 1944

Elsevier Librico NV, Leuvensesteenweg 325, B-1940 Woluwe Tel: (02) 7209090 Cable Add: Elsbook Bruxelles Telex: 21831 Elsbru B
Man Dir, Rights & Permissions: Elie Berwaerts; *Sales:* Jacqy Vandenberghe; *Production:* Piet van Roemburg; *Publicity & Advertising:* Lieven Struye; *Editorial:* Ingrid Symons
Parent Company: Elsevier NDU nv, Netherlands (qv)
Associate Company: Uitgeversmaatschappij A Manteau NV (qv)
Imprint: Erven J Byleveld
Subjects: Biography, History, Literature, Reference, Juveniles, Art, Practical Guides, Nature, Documentaries, Children's Books, Travel
1981: 50 titles *Founded:* 1960
ISBN Publisher's Prefix: 90-10

Emmaus, an imprint of Orbis en Orion Uitgevers NV (qv)

Editions **Erasme** (Scriptoria NV), Belgiëlei 147a, BP 212, B-2000 Antwerp Tel: (03) 2395900 Telex: B Edista 31421
Man Dir: A Sap
Parent Company: Standaard Uitgeverij en Distributie BV, Netherlands (qv)
Associate Company: Standaard Uitgeverij

(Scriptoria NV) (qv)
Subjects: Medicine, Science, Reference, Encyclopaedias, Arts, Textbooks, Juveniles, Comic Books
Founded: 1924
ISBN Publisher's Prefix: 90-02

Erel PVBA*, St-Sebastiaanstr 16, B-8400 Ostend Tel: (059) 701308
Dir: R Lanoye; *Publicity:* Monique Lanoye
Subjects: Arts, Bibliography, Languages, Education, Pedagogy, Sports, Games, Geography, History, Ethnography, Travel, Literature, Journals
Bookshop: At above address
1981: 6 titles *Founded:* 1946

Editions **Est-Ouest***, 66 rue St Bernard, B-1060 Brussels Tel: (02) 5386177
Dir: C André
Subjects: Art, Travel, Belles Lettres, Bibliography, Languages
Founded: 1939

Etablissements Généraux d'Imprimerie SA, 14 blvd de l'Empereur, B-1000 Brussels
Tel: (02) 5118026
Man Dir: F Jacobs
Subject: Reference
Founded: 1831

Europa*, Botermarkt 10, B-3290 Diest
Tel: (013) 331187
Dir: R Peeters
Subjects: Arts, Geography, History, Numismatics, Folklore
ISBN Publisher's Prefix: 90-6188

European Press Scientific Publisher*, Kortrijksesteenweg 154, B-9000 Ghent Tel: (091) 213000/10/08 Telex: Eupress 11008
Man Dir: R Desmet; *Editorial, International Books Department:* M Guy
Branch Off: Citadellaan 36, B-9000 Ghent; Borluutstraat, B-9000 Ghent; Postbus Amsterdam, NL-3802 Amsterdam, Netherlands
Subjects: Science (especially Medicine and Pharmacology), Medical Periodicals, Scientific Translations

Familia et Patria PVBA*, Kortemarkstr 26, B-8120 Handzame Tel: (051) 567336
Dir: M Mispelon
Subjects: Bibliography, Languages, Law, Political, Administrative & Social Sciences, Geography, History, Ethnography, Travel, Literature
Founded: 1966

Les '**Feuilles Familiales**' ASBL*, 27 rue du Congrès, B-1000 Brussels Tel: (02) 2183482
Associate Companies: NFF (Nouvelles Feuilles Familiales) (qv); Mouvement pour le Couple et la Famille (qv)
Subjects: Marriage & Family Relations, Psychology, Educational, Religion
Founded: 1937

Fonds Mercator SA+, Meir 85, B-2000 Antwerp Tel: (03) 2313840 Telex: 71876 Mfnv
Publisher: Dr Jan Martens
Associate Company: Editions Arcade-Fonds Mercator (qv)
Subjects: Arts, Geography, History, Ethnography, Travel, Literature, Music
1983: 4 titles *Founded:* 1965

S A **Fonteyn** Medical Books NV, Fochplein 13, B-3000 Louvain Tel: (016) 202944
Telex: 26334
Man Dir: B Osaer
Subject: Medicine
Bookshop (specialist medical): at above address
Founded: 1836

Editions de la **Francité** (Imprimeries Havaux)*, 37c rue A Levêque, B-1400 Nivelles Tel: (067) 226131
Dir: LL Havaux
Branch Off: 20 rue du Pouvre, 75001 Paris, France
Subjects: Arts, Bibliography, Languages, Textbooks, Education, Pedagogy, Sports, Games, Geography, History, Ethnography, Travel, Medicine, Literature, Religion, Philosophy, Journals, Paperbacks

G I A SA*, 321 ave des Volontaires, B-1150 Brussels Tel: (02) 7620662
Art Director: J Carion; *Export:* M David
Subjects: Art, Medicine (*Savoir interpréter*)
Miscellaneous: Exporter of Belgian books

Editions **Gamma**, 11 rue Barthélemy Frison, B-7500 Tournai Tel: (069) 226105 Cable Add: Editions Gamma-Tournai
Telex: Gedit 57251
Dir: F Parys; *Production Manager:* R Selke
Parent Company: Gedit SA (qv)
Associate Companies: Desclée, Editeurs (qv); Desclée et Cie, France (qv); Editions Gamma, France (qv); Nouvelles Editions Mame, France (qv)
Subjects: Education, How-to, Science & Technology, Textbooks, Sports, Games, Mathematics, Juveniles
Founded: 1962

De **Garve** PVBA*, Groene Poortdreef 27, B-8200 St-Michiels, Bruges Tel: (050) 318283/320707
Dir: W Barbiaux
Subjects: Bibliography, Languages, Textbooks, Law, Politics, Social Science, Mathematics, Physics, Technical, Music
Founded: 1909

Gedit SA*, 13 rue Barthélemy Frison, B-7500 Tournai Tel: (069) 226105 Cable Add: Gedit Tournai Telex: Gedit 57251
Dir: J Desclée
Subsidiary Companies: Desclée, Editeurs (qv); Editions Desclée et Cie, France (qv); Editions Gamma (qv); Editions Gamma, France (qv); Nouvelles Editions Mame, France (qv)
Subjects: General (also printers)
Founded: 1872

Editions **Gérard** et Cie SPRL, see Les Nouvelles Editions Marabout SA

Girault **Gilbert** SPRL, 50 rue de l'Association, B-1000 Brussels Tel: (02) 2171430
Subjects: Cartography
Founded: 1928, Reconstituted: 1956

Uitgeverij het **Gouden** Spoor*, Grotenhof 38, B-2510 Mortsel Tel: (03) 498415
Dir: M Saldien
Subjects: Juveniles, How-to, Medicine
Founded: 1951

Hachette International*, 715 chaussée de Waterloo, B-1180 Brussels Tel: (02) 3435600 Telex: 25028 Hachette Bru B
Man Dir: J Andrieu-Delille
Subject: General

Imprimeries **Havaux**, a division of Editions de la Francité (qv)

Imprimerie **Hayez** SPRL, 4 rue Fin, B-1080 Brussels Tel: (02) 4287112
Man Dir: Serge Hayez; *Sales Dir:* Frédéric Hayez
Subjects: Belles Lettres, Poetry, Philosophy, Religion, Medicine, General Science, Sport
Founded: 1780

Heibrand*, Hoevebosstr 1, B-2460 Kasterlee Tel: (014) 557328
Dir: R Lievens

Heideland NV (Heideland PVBA), Grote Markt 1, B-3500 Hasselt Tel: (011) 224505
Dirs: L Nagels, Dr Johan Ducheyne
Subjects: Arts, Bibliography, Languages, Textbooks, Education, Sport & Games, Juveniles, Philosophy, Literature, Linguistics, General, Religion, Paperbacks, Periodicals
Bookshop: Boekhandel Heideland (qv under Major Booksellers)
Founded: 1945
ISBN Publisher's Prefix: 90-6440

Heideland-Orbis (M & I NV), Torenplein 6, Bus 13, B-3500 Hasselt Tel: (011) 212112
Telex: 39920
Dir: Theo van Erp; *Editorial Manager:* R Fransen; *Production:* J Cuyckens; *Publicity:* Mia Voordeckers
Subject: Reference Books
1981: 25 titles *1982:* 24 titles *Founded:* 1969
Miscellaneous: Firm is a member of the Kluwer Group, Netherlands (qv)
ISBN Publisher's Prefix: 90-291

Uitgeverij **Helios***, Kapelsestr 222, B-2080 Kapellen Tel: (03) 6645320 Telex: 32242 Anvers Dnb B
Man Dirs: J Pelckmans, R Pelckmans
Associate Companies: Uitgeverij De Nederlandsche Boekhandel (qv); Uitgeverij Patmos (qv)
Subjects: General
Bookshop: Sint Jacobsmarkt 7, Antwerp
Founded: 1893
ISBN Publisher's Prefix: 90-333

Editions **Hemma**+, 53 rue du Centre, BP 25, B-4081 Stoumont-Chevron Tel: (086) 433636 Cable Add: Hemma Telex: 41507
Dir: Albert Hemmerlin
Subsidiary Companies: Diffusion Hemma, 8 rue Florian, F-93500 Pantin, France; Hemma Holland, Savannahweg 63a, 3542 AW Utrecht, Netherlands; Hemma Verlag, Rotter-Bruch 26a, Postfach 1758, D-5100 Aachen, Federal Republic of Germany
Subjects: Juveniles, Educational Books and Materials
1983: approx 160 titles *Founded:* 1952
ISBN Publisher's Prefix: 2-8006

Hernieuwen-Uitgaven PVBA*, Noordstr 100, B-8800 Roeselare Tel: (051) 201541
Subjects: Juveniles, Religion, Philosophy

Drukkerij-Uitgeverij **Hertoghs***, Turnhoutsebaan 319, B-2110 Wijnegem
Tel: (031) 536040
Dir: J Hertoghs
Subject: Textbooks
Founded: 1945

M van **Hove** DPN*, Dorpstr 11, B-2080 Kapellen, Antwerp Tel: (031) 642407
Dir: M van Hove
Subjects: Religion, Philosophy, General
Founded: 1966

Van **Hyfte**-De Coninck*, Lindenlaan 28A-30, B-9068 Ertvelde Tel: (091) 447200
Dir: M van Hyfte

I N B E L, see Institut belge d'Information et de Documentation

Uitgeverij J van **In**, Grote Markt 39, B-2500 Lier Tel: (03) 4805511 Telex: 72343 Inboek B
Man Dir and Rights & Permissions: Dr Laurent Woestenburg; *Editorial:* Ludo Camps; *Sales:* Jacques Van Hellemont; *Production:* Luc van Baarle; *Publicity:* Fred Caluwé
Parent Company: VNU – Verenigde Nederlandse Uitgeversbedrijven, Netherlands (qv)
Subjects: Juveniles, University, Secondary & Primary Textbooks, Educational Materials, Law, Periodical
Bookshop: At above address
Founded: 1833
ISBN Publisher's Prefix: 90-306

38 BELGIUM

Infoboek*, Roosterputstr 34, B-3990 Meerhout Tel: (014) 300477
Dir: W Verhaert
Subjects: Textbooks, Education, Sport & Games, Juveniles, Religion, Philosophy, Literature, Linguistics, Music
Founded: 1971

Institut belge d'Information et de Documentation (INBEL)*, Montoyerstr 3, B-1200 Brussels Tel: (02) 5126688 Telex: Inbel Bru 21716
Belgisch Institut voor Voorlichting en Documentatie
Dir: F Coppieters
Subjects: Art, Bibliography, Law, Social Sciences, Literature, Periodicals
Founded: 1962

Institut national de Sténodactylographie*, 23 rue de l'Union, B-1030 Brussels Tel: (02) 2176859
Dir: H Pringels
Subject: Textbooks relating to study of typing and shorthand-typing
Founded: 1897

Institut royal des Relations internationales*, 88 av de la Couronne, B-1050 Brussels Tel: (02) 6482000
Koninklijk Instituut voor Internationale Betrekkingen
Man Dir: Dr E Coppieters
Subjects: Political Science, Law, Economics, International Relations, Periodical
Founded: 1947

Uitgaven van **Interbankendienst** NV*, Keizerslaan 14, B-1000 Brussels Tel: (02) 5132553
Dir: L Dewincklear
Subjects: Law, Political & Social Science, Periodicals
Founded: 1968

Interbooks, Holle Weg 70, B-2550 Kontich Tel: (03) 4570816/4571395 Telex: 35521 Inbook B
Chief Executive: F Vermeulen; *Production:* H de Schrÿver
Founded: 1950

De **Internationale Pers***, Karel Govaertsstr 56-58, B-2100 Deurne Tel: (031) 213873
La Presse Internationale
Dir, Editorial, Publicity, Rights & Permissions: A J Walvisch; *Sales:* C J van Wolferen; *Production:* A Schödl
Subjects: Medicine, Juveniles, Periodicals
Founded: 1947

J U R I F Belgique*, 1033a chaussée d'Alsemberg (Boîte 28b), B-1180 Brussels Tel: (02) 3761167 Telex: 64797 Foblex
Belgian Branch of the Société d'Etudes Juridiques Internationales et Fiscales (JURIF)
Parent Company: Les Cahiers Fiscaux Européens Sàrl, France (qv)
Associate Company: CFE Belgique (qv)
Subject: European Tax Laws

J **Janssens** PVBA*, Kruikstr 14, B-2000 Antwerp Tel: (031) 391220
Dir: J Janssens
Subjects: Arts, Education, Plays
Founded: 1876

Keesing — Internationale Drukkerij en Uitgeverij NV*, Keesinglaan 2-20, B-2100 Deurne Tel: (031) 243890 Cable Add: Systeka Telex: 32507
Dir: Mr Gillieron; *Publications Manager:* A Edwards
Subjects: Education, Sport & Games, Medicine, Juveniles, Periodicals
Founded: 1911

Die **Keure** NV*, Oude Gentweg 108, B-8000 Bruges Tel: (050) 331236
Dir: H Bogaerts
Subjects: Textbooks, Law, Political, Administrative & Social Sciences, Primary & Secondary Textbooks
Founded: 1948

NV Uitgeverij **Kluwer***, Santvoortbeeklaan 21-23, B-2100 Deurne Tel: (031) 247890/1/2
Dirs: R Roziers, J Wijnen
Subjects: Technical books and periodicals
Founded: 1954
Miscellaneous: Firm is part of Kluwer Group, Netherlands (qv)

Maarten **Kluwer's** Internationale Uitgeversonderneming NV*, Somersstraat 13-15, B-2000 Antwerp Tel: (031) 312900
Dirs: M Kluwer, E Boerwinkel
Subjects: Textbooks, Law, Political & Social Science, Education, Technical, Periodicals
1981: 65 titles *1982:* 96 titles *Founded:* 1972
Miscellaneous: Wholesaler (Dutch books)

Koninklijk Instituut voor Internationale Betrekkingen, see Institut royal des Relations internationales

Kritak uitgeverij, Andreas Vesaliusstraat 1, B-3000 Leuven Tel: (016) 230131
Man Dirs: Rik Coolsaet, André Van Halewijck
Subjects: Politics, Social affairs, Literature, Comics
Bookshops: At above address; Wÿngaardstraat 12, B-2000 Antwerp
1981: 17 titles *Founded:* 1976
ISBN Publisher's Prefix: 90-6303

Editions **Labor**, 342 rue Royale, B-1030 Brussels Tel: (02) 2168150
Man Dir: Alexandre André; *all other offices:* J Fauconnier
Orders to: 156-158 chaussée de Haecht, B-1030 Brussels
Subjects: Belles Lettres, Poetry, Biography, History, Philosophy, Reference, Psychology, General & Social Science, Primary, Secondary & University Textbooks, Pedagogy, Economics
Founded: 1927
ISBN Publisher's Prefix: 2-8259

Editions **Lampe** d'Or ASBL, 23 ave Giele, B-1090 Brussels Tel: (02) 4279277
Man Dir: F M Van Dÿk
Subjects: Religion, Juveniles
Founded: 1955
ISBN Publisher's Prefix: 2-87001

Lannoo, Kasteelstr 97, B-8880 Tielt Tel: (051) 402551 Telex: 81555
Man Dirs: Godfried Lannoo, Luc Demeester
Subjects: Art, Philosophy, Religion, Juveniles, Paperbacks, Psychology, Education, Sports, Games, Travel, Poetry
Founded: 1909
ISBN Publisher's Prefix: 90-209

Maison Ferdinand **Larcier** SA, 39 rue des Minimes, B-1000 Brussels Tel: (02) 5129679/5124712
Man Dir: Jean-Marie Ryckmans
Subjects: Law (Belgian and International/European), Social Science, Science & Technology, Periodicals
Founded: 1839

Latomus ASBL, 18 ave Van Cutsem, B-7500 Tournai
Editorial: L Herrmann, M Renard; *Sales, Production, Publicity, Rights & Permissions:* Mme J Dumortier-Bibauw
Subjects: Bibliography, Philology, Roman Literature and History, Archaeology
Founded: 1937
ISBN Publisher's Prefix: 2-87031

Edition **Le Cri**+, 118 rue Elise, B-1050 Brussels Tel: (02) 6473120
Man Dir, Sales, Rights & Permissions: Christian Lutz; *Editorial:* Arnaud de la Croix; *Production:* Francis Jacoby; *Publicity:* Nathalie Delattre
Parent Company: Edition Le Cri ASBL (at above address)
Subsidiary Company: Atelier de Composition, 82 rue Tenbosch, B-1050 Brussels
Subjects: Fiction, Theatre, Monographs
1981: 25 titles *1982:* 25 titles *Founded:* 1981
ISBN Publisher's Prefix: 2-87106

Editions **Legrand***, rue Champs de Tignee, B-4511 Barchon Tel: (041) 628152 Telex: 41193 Apal B
Deputy Administrator: Ch Legrand, 42 Rue des Chateaux, B-4510 Saive
Subjects: Children's activities

Uiteverij Leon **Lesoil** VZW*, Geuzenstr 20, B-2000 Antwerp Tel: (03) 2375372
Man Dir: Monique Laenen
Subject: Politics
1981: 6 titles *Founded:* 1973

Leuven University Press, Krakenstr 3, B-3000 Leuven
Dir: Prof H Van der Wee
Orders to: Peeters, Bondgenotenlaan 153, B-3000 Leuven
Subjects: Theology, Psychology, Pedagogy, Economics, Sociology, Political Studies, Music, Mathematics, Medicine, Philosophy, etc
1981: 13 titles *1982:* 17 titles *Founded:* 1971
ISBN Publisher's Prefix: 90-6186

Editions de la **Librairie encyclopédique***, 1593 chaussée de Waterloo, B-1180 Brussels Tel: (02) 5132467
Man Dir: A C Leyenberger
Subjects: History, Reference, Law, Economics, Political & Social Science
Bookshop: Librairie encyclopédique Exportation-Antiquariat (at above address)
Founded: 1939

Editeurs de **Littérature** biblique*, 479 chaussée de Tubize, B-1420 Braine-l'Alleud Tel: (02) 3845402
Biblical Publications
Dir: M Cl Kroeker
Subjects: Education, Pedagogy, Sport, Games, Juveniles, Religion, Philosophy, Music, Journals, Paperbacks
Founded: 1959

Lloyd Anversois SA (Antwerpse Lloyd NV), Eiermarkt 23, B-2000 Antwerp Tel: (03) 2340550 Telex: 31446
Man Dir: M R Jaumotte
Subjects: Transport, Law, Maritime, Languages
Founded: 1904

Lombard SA*, ave Paul-Henri Spaak 1-11, B-1070 Brussels Tel: (02) 5225600 Cable Add: Lombarbel-Brussels Telex: 23097
Dir: G Leblanc; *Rights & Permissions:* Viviane Rousie
Subjects: Juveniles, Sports, Games, Education, Geography, History, Ethnography, Travel
Founded: 1946

Uitgeverij **Lotus**/Editions Lotus*, Leopoldstr 43, B-2000 Antwerp Tel: (031) 327010/327001
Man Dir: Jean-Pierre Zinje
Orders to: (French language books) Garnier Frères, BP 168, 19 rue des plantes, F-75665 Paris; (Dutch language books, Belgium) Denis, Sterckshoflei 28-30, B-2100 Deurne; (Dutch language books, Netherlands) Centraal Boekhuis, Postbus 125, Erasmusweg 10, Culemborg
Subjects: Novels, Documentary Works, Juveniles
Founded: 1977
ISBN Publisher's Prefixes: 90-6290 (Dutch language books); 2-87053 (French language books)

Editions **Lumen** Vitae ASBL*, 184 rue Washington, B-1050 Brussels Tel: (02) 3441882
International Centre for Religious Education
Man Dir: Jean Bouvy; *Sales Dir:* Albert Drèze
Subjects: Religion, High-priced Paperbacks, Psychology, Secondary & Primary Textbooks, Educational Materials, Pastoral Studies
1981: 10 titles *Founded:* 1936

M I M, see Moderne Instructie Methoden

Magic-Strip SPRL+, 46 blvd Maurice Lemonnier, B-1000 Brussels Tel: (02) 5111831
Dirs: Daniel Pasamonik, Didier Pasamonik; *Rights & Permissions:* Daniel Pasamonik
Subjects: Juveniles, Comic Books, Art Books
Founded: 1979
ISBN Publisher's Prefix: 2-8035

Uitgeversmaatschappij A **Manteau** NV, Beeldhouwersstraat 12, B-2000 Antwerp Tel: (03) 2371792 Telex: 21831
Man Dir: J Weverbergh; *Sales Dir:* E Berwaerts
Parent Company: Elsevier-NDU nv, Netherlands (qv)
Subsidiary Company: A Manteau NV
Subjects: General Fiction, Belles Lettres, Poetry, Biography, Secondary Textbooks
1981: 80 titles *1982:* 83 titles *Founded:* 1932
ISBN Publisher's Prefix: 90-223

Les Nouvelles Editions **Marabout** SA, 65 rue de Limbourg, B-4800 Verviers Tel: (087) 313321
Man Dir: Jean-Etienne Cohen-Seat; *Sales Dir:* Jacques Closset
Branch Offs: 81 ave de Tervueren, B-1040 Brussels; 8 rue de Neslé, F-75006 Paris, France
Subject: Paperbacks
Founded: 1977
Miscellaneous: Formerly Editions Gérard et Cie SPRL

Pierre **Mardaga** SA, 2-4 galerie des Princes, B-1000 Brussels Tel: (02) 5132038
Man Dir: Pierre Mardaga; *Rights & Permissions:* Pierre Mardaga, Gigi Dony
Associate Company: Soledi (Imprimeur-Editeur) SA (qv)
Subjects: Psychology, Social Science, Architecture
Founded: 1938
ISBN Publisher's Prefix: 2-87009

Maredsous ASBL*, 8 rue de Maredsous, B-5642 Denee Tel: (082) 699155
Dir: Père Léon-Nicolas Dayez
Subjects: Geography, History, Religion, Philosophy, General, Ethnography, Travel
Bookshop: At above address
Founded: 1924

Editions **Marie-Médiatrice** ASBL, 172 ave Gevaert, B-1320 Genval Tel: (02) 6537613
Director-General: André Martin
Subjects: Juveniles, Religion, Paperbacks
Founded: 1941

Les Ateliers d'Art graphique **Meddens** SA*, 141-143 ave de Scheut, B-1070 Brussels Tel: (02) 5227925
Dir: F Van Den Bremt
Subjects: Fine Arts, Geography, History, Music, Theology

Mercatorfonds SA, see Fonds Mercator SA

Mercatorfonds Arcade, see Editions Arcade-Fonds Mercator

Editeur Paul F **Merckx***, 145a ave des Statuaires, B-1180 Brussels Tel: (02) 3744156/3745158
Subjects: Art, Geography, History, Touring in Belgium
Founded: 1958

Mercurius PVBA*, Rodestr 44, B-2000 Antwerp Tel: (031) 333708/333762
Dir: K Schenck
Subjects: Geography, History, Ethnography, Travel
Founded: 1894

Editions d'Art Lucien de **Meyer** ASBL*, 88 ave de Tervueren, B-1040 Brussels Tel: (02) 7343560/7343582
Executives: As for Editions Arts et Voyages (qv)
Subject: Art
Founded: 1977

Meysmans*, 23 rue de l'Union, B-1030 Brussels Tel: (02) 2176859
Dir: H Pringels
Subject: Textbooks
Founded: 1897

Michelin (Département Cartes & Guides) SA*, 33 quai de Willebroek, B-1020 Brussels Tel: (02) 2186100 ext 238 Cable Add: Pneumiclin
Dir: R Cammaerts
Subjects: Travel Guides, Maps
Founded: 1913

Moderne Instructie Methoden (MIM) PVBA*, Jules Moretuslei 760, B-2610 Wilrijk Tel: (031) 496271
Dir: M Callebaut
Subjects: Textbooks, Education, Sport & Games
Founded: 1971

Mouvement pour le Couple et la Famille*, 27 rue du Congrès, B-1000 Brussels Tel: (02) 2183482
Dir: J Hinnekens
Associate Companies: Les 'Feuilles Familiales' ASBL (qv); NFF (Nouvelles Feuilles Familiales) (qv)
Subject: Marriage and the Family
Founded: 1947

Louis **Musin** Editeur*, 99 ave de la Brabançonne, B-1040 Brussels Tel: (02) 7363727/7341276
Dir: L Musin
Subjects: Textbooks, Juveniles, Literature, Linguistics, History
Founded: 1960

N F F (Nouvelles Feuilles Familiales)*, 27 rue du Congrès, B-1000 Brussels Tel: (02) 2183482
Dir: Jean Hinnekens
Associate Companies: Mouvement pour le Couple et la Famille (qv); Les 'Feuilles Familiales' ASBL (qv)
Subjects: Marriage and Family Relations, Psychology, Educational, Religion, Pedagogy
Founded: 1937

NV Uitgeverij **Nauwelaerts** Edition SA, Mechelsestr 148, B-3000 Louvain Tel: (016) 229096
Man Dir: W Vandermeulen
Associate Company: Vander Publishing (qv)
Subjects: History, Philosophy, Theology, Medicine, Psychology, Social Science, Economics, University Textbooks, Educational Materials, Literature
Founded: 1938

Uitgeverij De **Nederlandsche Boekhandel***, Kapelsestr 222, B-2080 Kapellen Tel: (03) 6645320 Telex: 32272 Anvers Dnb B
Man Dirs: J Pelckmans, R Pelckmans
Associate Companies: Uitgeverij Helios (qv); Uitgeverij Patmos (qv); (Uitgeverij Opdebeek is now wholly incorporated in Uitgeverij De Nederlandsche Boekhandel)
Subjects: History, Philosophy, Religion, Juveniles, Social Science, University, Secondary & Primary Textbooks
Bookshop: Sint Jacobsmarkt 7, B-2000 Antwerp
Founded: 1892
ISBN Publisher's Prefix: 90-289

Nici*, Lousbergkaai 32, B-900 Ghent Tel: (031) 252897
Dir: G Vander Rol

Het **Noordnederlands** Boekbedrijf NV*, Paleisstr 23-25, B-2000 Antwerp Tel: (031) 374605/385506
Dir: F Doumh
Subjects: Bibliography, Philology, Languages, Textbooks, Law, Political & Social Sciences, Education, Sport & Games, Mathematics, Physics, Technical, Medicine, Juveniles, Religion, Philosophy, Literature, Linguistics, Music, Periodicals, General, Geography, History, Ethnography, Travel
Founded: 1951
ISBN Publisher's Prefix: 90-6154

Norma PVBA*, St Baafsplein 30, B-9000 Ghent Tel: (091) 252815
Subject: Textbooks
Founded: 1938

Nouvelle Diffusion, see Editions Complexe

Les **Nouvelles Editions Marabout** SA, see Marabout

Nouvelles Editions Vokaer SA, see Vokaer

Nouvelles Feuilles Familiales, see NFF

Uitgeverij S V **Ontwikkeling***, Leeuwerikstr 41, B-2000 Antwerp Tel: (031) 338659
Dir: R Binnemans
Subjects: Novels, Poetry, History, Textbooks
Bookshops: Boekhandel Ontwikkeling: Ommeganckstr 35-37, Antwerp; Dés Boucherystr 18-20, Mechelen; J Brochhovenstr 28, Deurne, Antwerp
Founded: 1923

Uitgeverij **Opdebeek**, now part of Uitgeverij De Nederlandsche Boekhandel (qv)

Orbis en Orion Uitgevers NV, Zwaluwbeek 3, B-2740 Beveren Tel: (03) 2526464 Telex: 33693
Administrative Delegate: A Goyvaerts
Imprints: Colibrant, Emmaus, Orion
Subjects: Encyclopaedias, Non-fiction, Belles-Lettres, School Textbooks, Religion, Philosophy, Journals, Paperbacks
1981: 73 titles *Founded:* 1979
ISBN Publisher's Prefix: 90-264

Ordina Editions*, 5 rue Forgeur, B-4000 Liège Tel: (041) 323472
Man Dir: Georges Derouaux
Subject: Problems of population
Founded: 1974
ISBN Publisher's Prefix: 2-87040

Uitgeverij **Orientaliste** PVBA*, Klein Dalenstr 42, B-3009 Winksele-Louvain Tel: (016) 488102
Man Dir: E Peeters
Subjects: History, Philosophy, Religion, Psychology, University Textbooks
Miscellaneous: Publish Oriental and foreign language books

Orion, an imprint of Orbis en Orion Uitgevers NV (qv)

De **Oude** Linden NV*, Abdijstr 40, B-3180 Tongerlo-Westerlo Tel: (014) 544206
Dir: C van Heijst o praem
Subjects: Juveniles, Religion, Philosophy
Founded: 1962

Parsifal Publishing Co*, Lange Elzenstr 59, B-2000 Antwerp Tel: (031) 323378
Chief Executive and Rights & Permissions: Christian Vandekerkhove; *Production:* Erna Droesbeke

Associate Company: Editions Verrycken (qv)
Subjects: Occult, Mystic, Parapsychology, Philosophy
Bookshops (jointly owned with Editions Verrycken, qv): Librairie Verrycken, Wiegstr 30, B-2000 Antwerp; Occult Bookshop, Hoogstr 68, B-2000 Antwerp
Founded: 1979
ISBN Publisher's Prefix: 90-6458

Uitgeverij **Patmos***, Kapelsestr 222, B-2080 Kapellen Tel: (03) 6645320 Telex: 32242 Anvers Dnb B
Dirs: J Pelckmans, R Pelckmans
Associate Companies: Uitgeverij Helios (qv); Uitgeverij De Nederlandsche Boekhandel (qv)
Subjects: Education, Juveniles, Religion
Bookshop: Sint Jacobsmarkt 7, Antwerp
ISBN Publisher's Prefix: 90-292

Editions **Peeters** SPRL*, Bondgenotenlaan 153, B-3000 Louvain Tel: (016) 235170
Dir: Mme Peeters
Subjects: Periodicals, General
Founded: 1970

Uitgeverij **Plantyn** SA NV, Santvoortbeeklaan 21-23, B-2100 Deurne, Antwerp Tel: (031) 247897
Dirs: J Vrints, F van Hoof
Subjects: Education, all levels
Founded: 1950
Miscellaneous: Firm is a member of the Kluwer Group, Netherlands (qv)

Pre-Ecole, an imprint of Editions Chantecler (qv)

Preschool, an imprint of Zuidnederlandse Uitgeverij NV (qv)

La **Presse** Internationale, see De Internationale Pers

Presses agronomiques de Gembloux ASBL, 22 ave de la Faculté d'Agronomie, B-5800 Gembloux Tel: (081) 611955
Dir: Mrs C Dagnelie
Subjects: Agriculture, Botany, Chemistry, Mathematics, Physics, Technical, Periodicals
Founded: 1965
ISBN Publisher's Prefix: 2-87016

Presses universitaires de Bruxelles ASBL, 42 ave Paul Heger, B-1050 Brussels Tel: (02) 6499780
President: Henry A Roba; *Man Dir:* Marc Oostens; *Sales:* Henri de Smet
Subjects: University Textbooks, especially Philosophy, Medicine, Engineering, Economics, General Science, Architecture
Bookshop: Librairie des Presses universitaires de Bruxelles (qv under Major Booksellers)
1981: approx 50 titles *Founded:* 1958
ISBN Publisher's Prefix: 2-500

Presses universitaires de Liège ASBL*, 7 pl du 20 Août, B-4000 Liège 1 Tel: (041) 420080
Dir: P Froidcoeur
Subjects: Law, Political & Social Sciences, Medicine, General
Founded: 1920

Presses universitaires de Louvain-la-Neuve, an imprint of Cabay (qv)

Presses universitaires de Namur, 8 Rempart de la Vierge, B-5000 Namur Tel: (081) 229061 Telex: 59222 Facna B
Dir: P Pellemans; *Commercial:* P Rummens
Subjects: History, Literature, Philosophy, Religion, Geography, Medicine, General Scientific, Social Sciences, University Textbooks, Quality Paperbacks
Founded: 1977
ISBN Publisher's Prefix: 2-87037

Het **Prisma** NV*, Corverstr 13, B-3700 Tongeren Tel: (012) 231325
Dir: G Michiels
Subject: Textbooks

Pro Civitate, now Crédit Communal de Belgique – Service Culturel (qv)

La **Procure***, 161 rue des Tanneurs, B-1000 Brussels Tel: (021) 5122672
Man Dir: J O Neukermans
Subjects: Travel, General & Political Science, Educational Materials
Founded: 1881

Prodim SPRL*, 184 blvd Général Jacques, B-1050 Brussels Tel: (02) 6405970
Production et Diffusion medico-techniques
Dir: P Nile
Subjects: Textbooks, Medicine, Science
Bookshop & Warehouse: At above address
Founded: 1968

Production et Diffusion medico-techniques SPRL, see Prodim SPRL

Henri **Proost** & Cie*, Everdongenlaan 23, B-2300 Turnhout Tel: (014) 416911 Telex: 33185
Man Dir: Jef Proost; *Sales Dir:* Frans Peeters
Subsidiary Company: Salamander Books Ltd, UK
Subjects: Religion, Juveniles, Cookery, Gardening, Travel, History

André De **Rache**, Editeur, 127 rue du Château d'Eau, B-1180 Brussels Tel: (02) 3743950
Man Dir: A De Rache
Subjects: Belles Lettres, Poetry, Biography, Art
Founded: 1954

Reader's Digest SA*, 12a Grande Place, B-1000 Brussels Tel: (02) 4287100 Telex: 21876
Man Dir: P Kittel
Subjects: Education, Sport & Games, Geography, History, Travel
Founded: 1967

Reinart Uitgaven, now Uitgeverij Dap-Reinart SV (qv)

La **Renaissance** du Livre SA, 12 pl du Petit-Sablon, B-1000 Brussels Tel: (02) 5119914/5134751
Man Dir: H Roland Bousson
Subjects: Belles Lettres, History, Art, Juveniles, Law, Business, Reference, Educational Materials
Founded: 1923

Fondation André **Renard***, 9-11 pl St Paul, B-4000 Liège Tel: (041) 237940
Dirs: R Gillon, G Vandersmissen, M Hockers

La **Revue** nouvelle ASBL*, 3-5 rue des Moucherons, B-1000 Brussels Tel: (02) 5119862
Dir: Michel Molitor
Subjects: Languages, Law, Economics, Political & Social Sciences, Education, Religion, Philosophy, Literature, Linguistics, Bibliography
Founded: 1945

De **Riemaecker** Uitgeverij*, Kerkewijk 2, B-9681 Nukerke Tel: (055) 211404
Dir: P de Riemaecker
Founded: 1947

Roeland Kamer Fonds VZW*, Groenendaalsesteenweg 135, B-1990 Hoeilaart Tel: (02) 6572602
Man Dir: Rienk H Kamer

De **Roerdomp***, Vandereydtlaan 46, B-2160 Brecht Tel: (031) 138401
Dir: J Lombaerts
Subjects: Law, Political & Social Sciences, Literature, Linguistics
Founded: 1967

Rossel Edition SA*, 134 rue Royale, B-1000 Brussels Tel: (02) 2177750 Telex: 24298
Manager: J Gerlache; *Rights & Permissions:* André-Paul Duchâteau
Associate Company: Rossel Edition, 73 rue d'Anjou, F-75008 Paris, France
Subjects: Education, Sports and Games, Documentary Reports, Period History, Juveniles; Periodicals
Founded: 1972

Publications de **Saint-André***, 1 allée de Clerlande, B-1340 Ottignies Tel: (010) 417463
Subjects: Pastoral, Liturgical, Anthropology, Contemporary Architecture (all periodicals)

Publications des Facultés universitaires **Saint Louis**, 43 blvd du Jardin Botanique, B-1000 Brussels Tel: (02) 2177653
Man Dir: M van de Kerchove; *Sales, Publicity:* Mella Thoua
Subjects: Humanities, Philosophy, Psychology, Theology, History, Law, Economics
1981: 6 titles *1982:* 5 titles *Founded:* 1973
ISBN Publisher's Prefix: 2-8028

Samsom (CED), see CED-Samsom

Sanderus PVBA*, Rempardenstr 36, B-9700 Oudenaarde Tel: (055) 311130
Dir: M van den Abeele
Subject: Textbooks
Founded: 1959

Schaubroeck PVBA*, Drapstr 23, B-9730 Nazareth Tel: (091) 854227
Dir: J Schaubroeck
Subjects: Law, Political & Social Sciences
Founded: 1911

Schott Frères SPRL (Éditeurs de Musique), 30 rue St-Jean, B-1000 Brussels Tel: (02) 5123980
Man Dir: Jean-Jacques Junne
Subject: Music
Founded: 1823

Editions **Sciences et Lettres**, see Imprimerie Georges Thone SA

Scribae-Uitgevers VZW*, Weilandstr 31, B-2000 Antwerp 6 Tel: (031) 328483
Chief Executive, Rights & Permissions: Magda Heeffer; *Editorial:* George Leemans; *Publicity:* John Fennell
Subjects: Fiction, Short Stories, Plays, Poetry
Founded: 1978
ISBN Publisher's Prefix: 90-6387

De **Seizoenen** PVBA*, Prins Leopoldlei 60, B-2510 Mortsel Tel: (031) 496034
Dir: P Vanhout
Subject: Juveniles
Founded: 1958

Service SPRL, 232 blvd Em Bockstael, B-1020 Brussels Tel: (02) 4282627/4280520
Dirs: G Vanden Avyle, M Geets
Subjects: Law, Technical, Periodicals
Founded: 1949

Services interbancaires SA, 52 ave de Tervueren, B-1040 Brussels Tel: (02) 7360507
Dir: L Dewincklear
Subjects: Law, Political & Social Sciences, Periodicals
Founded: 1968

Uitgeverij De **Sikkel** NV, Nijverheidsstr 8, B-2150 Malle
Man Dir: Karel de Bock
Subjects: Educational Books, Sports, Music, Materials and Periodicals; Technical Periodicals
Founded: 1919
ISBN Publisher's Prefix: 90-260

Editions Le **Sillon** d'Or*, Grotenhof 38, B-2510 Mortsel Tel: (031) 498415
Dir: M Saldien
Subject: General
Founded: 1951

Simon Stevin NV, Zennestr 37, B-1000 Brussels Tel: (02) 5121085/5138295 Telex: 23602 Boetis
Dirs: J Van Hoorick, M Strens-Van Hoorick
Parent Company: N V Drukkerij De Bouwkroniek
Subjects: Building, Wood Science, Technical, Surveying, Architecture, Engineering Science, Periodicals
Founded: 1930

Sinite Parvulos VBVB, B-3590 Hamont-Achel Tel: (011) 641078
Dir: L van Gassel
Subjects: Devotional Literature and Miscellaneous

Sintal, Dekenstr 28, B-3000 Louvain Tel: (016) 223470
Dir: J Devos
Subjects: Geography, History, Ethnography, Travel
Founded: 1928

Snoeck-Ducaju en Zoon NV*, Begijnhoflaan 464, B-9000 Ghent Tel: (091) 234897
Dir: S Snoeck
Subjects: Snoeck's Literary Yearbook, Snoeck's almanakken
Founded: 1782

Société Biblique belge ASBL*, 160 rue du Trône, B-1050 Brussels Tel: (02) 6401112/6401575
General Secretary: Rev R Catinus
Subject: Editions of the Bible in many languages

Walter **Soethoudt***, Perenstr 15, B-2000 Antwerp Tel: (031) 367055
Dir: W Soethoudt
Subjects: Literature, Poetry, Paperbacks, General
Founded: 1964

Soledi (Imprimeur-Editeur) SA, 37 rue de la Province, B-4020 Liège
Dir: P Mardaga; *Rights & Permissions:* P Mardaga, Gigi Dony
Associate Company: Pierre Mardaga SA (qv)
Subjects: Arts, Languages, Education, Philosophy, Architecture, Linguistics, General
Founded: 1919

Sonneville Press (Uitgeversmij) PVBA*, Orchideeënlaan 3, B-8200 St-Andries, Bruges Tel: (050) 321112
Dir: J Sonneville
Subjects: Arts, Law, Political & Social Sciences, Education, Sport & Games, Geography, History, Ethnography, Travel, Religion, Philosophy, Literature, Linguistics, Music, Periodicals, Paperbacks
Founded: 1966

Het **Spectrum** (IUM NV), Bijkhoevelaan 12, B-2110 Wijnegem Tel: (03) 3539800 Telex: 33545 Spant B
Dir: M Cornu
Parent Companies: Jointly owned by Uitgeverij Het Spectrum BV, Netherlands (qv) and Internationale Uitgevers Maatschappij NV, Van Schoonbekestr 34-38, B-2000 Antwerp
Subjects: Arts, Bibliography, Philology, Languages, Law, Political & Social Sciences, Education, Sport & Games, Mathematics, Physics, Technical, Geography, History, Ethnography, Travel, Medicine, Religion, Philosophy, Literature, Linguistics, Music, Periodicals, General, Comics
Founded: 1946

Le **Sphinx** SA*, 5 rue de Danemark, B-1060 Brussels Tel: (02) 5370437/5381044
Publisher: Marcel Leempoel
Subjects: General Fiction, Belles Lettres, General
Founded: 1951

Splichal SA, Apostoliekenstr 103, B-2300 Turnhout Tel: (014) 422441
Man Dir: L Verwaest Snr; *Dir:* L Verwaest Jnr
Subject: Religion
Founded: 1856

Standaard Uitgeverij (Scriptoria NV), Belgiëlei 147a, Postbus 212, B-2018 Antwerp Tel: (03) 2395900 Telex: Edista 31421
Man Dir: A Sap
Associate Companies: Editions Erasme (Scriptoria NV) (qv); Standaard Uitgeverij en Distributie BV, Netherlands (qv)
Subjects: General Fiction, How-to, Politics, Economics, Law, Reference, General Science, Textbooks, Encyclopaedias, Juveniles
Bookshops: Standaard Hoofdstadboekhandel (qv under Major Booksellers) and chain of 21 other bookshops throughout Belgium
Founded: 1924
ISBN Publisher's Prefix: 90-02

NV Uitgeverij **Stappaerts**, Letterkundestraat 138A, B-2610 Wilrijk (Antwerp) Tel: (031) 288531 Telex: 71288
Man Dir: Jozef Stappaerts
Subject: Juveniles
1981: approx 50 titles *Founded:* 1976

Steppe*, Aalstersesteenweg 99-101, B-9400 Ninove Tel: (054) 332591 Cable Add: Steppe-Ninove
Subjects: Textbooks, Mathematics, Physics, Technical

De **Ster** PVBA*, Lange Brilstr 9, B-2000 Antwerp Tel: (031) 322036
Dir: R De Smedt

E **Story-Scientia** NV M & I, Eekhout 2, B-9000 Ghent Tel: (091) 259413
Dir: A M Mys
Subjects: Science, Humanities, History, Business, Agriculture, Medicine, Law, Education, Economics, Psychology
Founded: 1960

De **Techniek***, J De Bomstr 61, B-2000 Antwerp Tel: (031) 378567
Dir: J Roggen
Subjects: Textbooks, Mathematics, Physics, Technical
Founded: 1926

Uitgeverij De **Tempel**, Tempelhof 41, B-8000 Bruges Tel: (050) 315505
Man Dir: Mrs M H Monseu
Subjects: Philosophy, Social Science (especially European unification), Archaeology
1981: 2 titles *1982:* 1 title *Founded:* 1905

Imprimerie Georges **Thone** SA, 11-19 rue de la Commune, B-4020 Liège Tel: (041) 426154
Man Dir: Louis Maraval; *Editorial, Sales, Production, Publicity, Rights & Permissions:* Irene Severyns
Subsidiary Company: Editions Sciences et Lettres (at above address)
Subject: School and University Textbooks
1981: 28 titles *1982:* 22 titles *Founded:* 1898

Toulon*, Sportstr 35, B-8400 Ostend Tel: (059) 800927
Dir: P A Toulon
Subjects: Educational, Technical, Juveniles

Trois Arches+, 496 ave Molière, B-1060 Brussels Tel: (02) 3447333
Also known as 3 Arches
Man Dir, Rights & Permissions: Hugues Boucher
Subjects: Literature, Fine Art, Architecture, Photography, Children's Books, Bibliography
1981: 2 titles *1982:* 5 titles *Founded:* 1978

Editions **U G A** (Uitgeverij)*, Stijn Streuvelslaan 73, B-8710 Kortrijk-Heule Tel: (056) 355881 Telex: 85579
Dir: L Deschildre
Branch Offs: 5 ave de Stassart, B-5000 Namur; 19 rue Guimard, Bte 2, B-1040 Brussels
Subjects: Administration, History, Social Science, Law, Language, Journals
Founded: 1948

U O P C, see Union et Orientation de Presse et de Culture

Union et Orientation de Presse et de Culture (UOPC) SA*, 216 chaussée de Wavre, B-1040 Brussels Tel: (02) 6489689
Dir: Mrs Lefebvre
Subjects: Religion, Philosophy
Bookshop: UOPC (qv under Major Booksellers)
Founded: 1923

Universa PVBA, Hoenderstr 24, B-9200 Wetteren Tel: (091) 691563
Man Dir: A De Meester
Subjects: Textbooks, Geography, History, Ethnography, Travel
Founded: 1958

Universitaire Pers Leuven, see Leuven University Press

Editions **universitaires** SA, see under Editions

Presses **universitaires** de Bruxelles, de Liège, de Namur, see under Presses

Publications des Facultés **universitaires** Saint Louis, see under Saint Louis

Editions de l'**Université** de Bruxelles, 26 ave Paul Héger, B-1050 Brussels Tel: (02) 6490030 Telex: 23069 Unilib B
Man Dir: Mrs S Unger
Subjects: Humanities, Social Sciences, Science, Medicine; Periodicals
1982: 41 titles *Founded:* 1950
ISBN Publisher's Prefix: 2-8004

Vademecum de Pharmacie, 3 pl Rotenberg, B-4700 Eupen Tel: (087) 553271
Man Dir: Paul Schiltz
Subjects: Reference, Medicine, Pharmacy
Founded: 1963
ISBN Publisher's Prefix: 2-87058

Imprimerie H **Vaillant Carmanne** SA, rue Fond St-Servais 4, B-4000 Liège Tel: (041) 529616
Man Dir: G Dengis
Subjects: Science, Education, Political Science, Belles Lettres, Religion, Medicine, Law, History, Science, Technical
Founded: 1838

Vander Publishing*, 321 ave des Volontaires, B-1150 Brussels Tel: (322) 7620662
Man Dir: Willy Vandermeulen
Associate Company: NV Uitgeverij Nauwelaerts Edition SA (qv)
Subjects: Psychology, General & Social Science, Law, Economics, Politics, Languages
Founded: 1880
ISBN Publisher's Prefix: 2-8008

Librairie **Vanderlinden** SA*, 17 rue des Grands-Carmes, B-1000 Brussels Tel: (02) 5116140

Man Dir: J Vanderlinden
Subjects: Art, General Fiction, Juveniles, Textbooks, Paperbacks, Science, Mathematics
Bookshop: See under Major Booksellers
Founded: 1897

L **Vanmelle** (Drukkerij) NV*, Lt Willemotlaan 80, B-9910 Mariakerke (Ghent) Tel: (091) 233586 Telex: 11850
Dir: L Vanmelle
Subjects: Textbooks, Juveniles

Vereniging van de belgische medische Wetenschappelijke Genootschappen VZW, see Association des Sociétés scientifiques médicales belges (ASBL)

Editions **Verrycken***, Wiegstr 30, B-2000 Antwerp Tel: (031) 323378
Man Dir, Editorial, Rights & Permissions: Christian Vandekerkhove; *Production:* E Droesbeke; *Sales, Publicity:* E Vandekerkhove
Orders to: Verrycken Booksellers (at above address)
Associate Company: Parsifal Publishing Co (qv)
Subjects: Philosophy, Medicine, Parapsychology, Occult
Bookshops (jointly owned with Parsifal Publishing Co, qv): Librarie Verrycken (at above address); Occult Bookshop, Hoogstr 68, B-2000 Antwerp
Founded: 1976
ISBN Publisher's Prefix: 90-70181

Les Editions **Vie** ouvrière ASBL*, 4 rue d'Anderlecht, B-1000 Brussels Tel: (02) 5125090
Chief Executive: André Samain
Subjects: Religion, Juveniles, Psychology, Social Science, University & Secondary Textbooks, History, Economics, Photography
Founded: 1958
ISBN Publisher's Prefix: 2-87003

Albert de **Visscher** Editeur, Ave du Golf 31, B-1640 Rhode-St-Genèse Tel: (02) 3587423
Man Dir: Albert de Visscher
Subjects: Music, Art, Medicine, General Science
Founded: 1944

Vlaams Ekonomisch Verbond VZW, Brouwersvliet 15, Postbus 7, B-2000 Antwerp Tel: (031) 311660
Man Dir: R de Feyter; *Publicity:* M Paeleman
Subjects: Economics, Statistics
Founded: 1926

Vlaamse Bijbelstichting*, St Michielsstr 2, B-3000 Louvain Tel: 337468
Subjects: Religious Literature connected with Catholic Bible production in Belgium, the Netherlands, Austria, Switzerland and Federal Germany
Miscellaneous: Company is a member of AMB (qv under Federal Republic of Germany)

Vlaamse Toeristenbond VZW, Sint-Jacobsmarkt 45, B-2000 Antwerp Tel: (03) 2343434
Dir: G Cooreman

De **Vlijt** NV*, Nationalestr 46, B-2000 Antwerp Tel: (031) 312880
Dir: J Huybrechts
Subjects: Arts, Educational, History, Geography

Nouvelles Editions **Vokaer** SA*, 131 rue de Birmingham, B-1070 Brussels Tel: (02) 5240070 Telex: 24326
Subjects: Arts, Geography, History, Tourism, Travel, General
Founded: 1969
ISBN Publisher's Prefix: 2-87012

Drukkerij Het **Volk** NV*, Forelstr 22, B-9000 Ghent Tel: (091) 255701 Telex: 11228
Man Dir: J van Haverbeke
Subject: Juveniles
Bookshop: Boekhandel Het Volk (qv under Major Booksellers)

C De **Vries** Brouwers PVBA, Haantjeslei 80, B-2000 Antwerp Tel: (03) 2374180
Dir: I de Vries
Subjects: Juveniles, History
Founded: 1946

De **Vroente**, Bosakkersstr 14, B-2460 Kasterlee Tel: (014) 556160
Dir: S Debroey
Subjects: Arts, Textbooks, Education

PVBA Imprimerie-Editions **Vyncke***, Savaanstr 92, B-9000 Ghent Tel: (091) 253960
Dirs: H Vyncke, D Vyncke, Frans Pauwels
Subjects: Textbooks (for technical schools), Periodicals
Founded: 1922

Eugène **Wahle***, 14A rue du Méry, B-4000 Liège Tel: (041) 322113
Manager: E Wahle
Subjects: History, Art, Archaeology, Geography, History of Glass
1981: 5 titles
ISBN Publisher's Prefix: 2-87011

Wereldbibliotheek NV*, Leeuwerikstr 23, B-2000 Antwerp Tel: (031) 323642
Dir: L Reinalda
Subjects: Education, Sport & Games, Juveniles, General
Founded: 1947
ISBN Publisher's Prefix: 90-284

Maison d'Editions Ad **Wesmael-Charlier** SA*, 69 rue de Fer, B-5000 Namur Tel: (081) 220148
Subjects: Secondary & Primary Textbooks
Bookshops: At above address and 62 rue de la Loi, Brussels
Founded: 1790

J B **Wolters Leuven** NV*, Blijde Inkomststr 50, B-3000 Louvain Tel: (016) 233488 Telex: 24525
Man Dir: W Vanden Eynde
Parent Company: Wolters Samsom België NV (qv)
Subjects: Instruction and Education, Secondary & Primary Textbooks, Educational Materials
Founded: 1959
ISBN Publisher's Prefix: 90-309

Wolters Samsom België NV, Louizalaan 485, B-1050 Brussels Tel: (02) 6499026 Telex: 62067 Icubel
Parent Company: Wolters Samsom Groep NV, Netherlands (qv)
Subsidiary Companies: CED-Samsom (qv); J B Wolters Leuven NV (qv)
Subjects: Publishing, literature distribution, social and fiscal information

Zuidnederlandse Uitgeverij NV+, Cleydaellaan 8, B-2630 Aartselaar, Antwerp Tel: (03) 8878300 Telex: 31739 Zuidb
Man Dir: Joris Schaltin; *Publisher:* Emmanuel de Vocht; *Sales:* Jan Vande Velden; *Production:* Eric Feyten; *Rights & Permissions:* Wilfried Wuyts
Subsidiary Companies: Editions Chantecler, Belgium (qv); Editions Chantecler, France; Centrale Uitgeverij, Netherlands
Imprints: Deltas, Preschool
Subjects: General Fiction and Non-fiction, Children's Books
Founded: 1946
ISBN Publisher's Prefix: 90-243

Literary Agents

Agence belge des grandes Editions SA*, 146 Blvd Adolphe Max, B-1000 Brussels Tel: (02) 2191872 Cable Add: Belgeditions

Firma **Denis** & Co PVBA, Sterckshoflei 28-30, B-2100 Deurne

A van **Hageland**, Blutsdelle 10, B-1641 Alsemberg (Beersel) Tel: (2) 3802219
General Manager: Albert van Hageland. Represents authors, publishers and agencies in and for the Dutch and French territories.
Specialization: Fantasy and Science Fiction; Anthologies. Only printed works (no manuscripts)

Book Clubs

Boekengilde de **Clauwaert***, Koning Albertlaan 17, B-3040 Korbeek-Lo, Louvain
Owned by: De Clauwaert (qv)

Dap-Reinart Uitgeven*, Industriepark B4, B-9140 Zele
Owned by: Uitgeverij Dap-Reinart SV (qv)

Nederlandse Boekenclub (Boek en Plaat), Apollostr 150, B-2600 Antwerp-Berchen
Manager: W Patroons
Owned by: Succes BV, Netherlands (qv)
Branch Office of Nederlandse Boekenclub, Netherlands (qv)

Major Booksellers

Audivox*, Rubenslei 23, B-2000 Antwerp Tel: (031) 328465
Wholesalers of imported educational books
Also Publisher (qv)

Boekhandel **Belis-Vinck**, Lange Leemstr 41, B-2018 Antwerp Tel: (03) 2327448

Librairie **Bellens***, 13 rue de la Wache, B-4000 Liège Tel: (041) 237860

Librairie **Castaigne** SPRL, 34 rue du Fosse-aux-Loups, B-1000 Brussels Tel: (02) 2170424
Manager: Alain Lonnoy

Boekhandel **Heideland**, Grote Markt 1, B-3500 Hasselt Tel: (011) 224505
Owned by: Heideland NV (Heideland PVBA) (qv)

Office international de Librairie*, 30 ave Marnix, B-1050 Brussels Tel: (02) 5136675

P C A-**Halbart** SA*, 7-9-9a rue des Carmes, B-4000 Liège Tel: (041) 232125/235428

Librairie des **Presses universitaires de Bruxelles**, 42 ave Paul Heger, B-1050 Brussels Tel: (02) 6499780
Scientific books
Owned by: Presses universitaires de Bruxelles ASBL

Standaard Hoofdstadboekhandel, Adolf Maxlaan 146, B-1000 Brussels Tel: (02) 2175642
Member of chain of 22 shops throughout Belgium
Manager: G Cramer
Owned by: Standaard Uitgeverij (Scriptoria NV) (qv)

J **Story-Scientia** PVBA*, Van Duyseplein 8, B-9000 Ghent Tel: (091) 255757
Manager: J Story
Also Importers

Libris **Toison** d'Or SA*, 29 ave de la Toison d'Or, B-1060 Brussels Tel: (02) 5116400 Telex: 24084

U O P C*, 216 chaussée de Wavre, B-1040 Brussels Tel: (02) 6489689
Owned by: Union et Orientation de Presse et de Culture

Librairie **Vanderlinden***, 17 rue des Grands-Carmes, B-1000 Brussels Tel: (02) 5116140
Also Publisher (qv)

Boekhandel Het **Volk**, Forelstr 22, B-9000 Ghent
Owned by: Drukkerij Het Volk NV (qv)

Major Libraries

Koninklijke Bibliotheek **Albert I**, Keizerslaan 4, B-1000 Brussels Tel: (02) 5136180
Bibliothèque royale Albert Ier
Publications include: Belgische Bibligrafie (Bibliographie de Belgique)

Archives générales du Royaume*, 2-6 rue de Ruysbroeck, B-1000 Brussels
National Archives

Bibliothèque centrale de la Ville de Bruxelles*, rue des Riches Claires 24, B-1000 Brussels Tel: 5129569 Telex: 26224

Bibliothèque **Fonds** Quetelet*, 6 rue de l'Industrie, B-1040 Brussels Tel: (02) 5127950
Library of the Ministry of Economic Affairs
Librarian: J de Buck
Publications: Accroissements de la Bibliothèque centrale (Fonds Quetelet), monthly

Goethe-Institut – Deutsche Bibliothek, 58 rue Belliard, B-1040 Brussels

Institut royal des Sciences naturelles de Belgique, Bibliothèque, 29 rue Vautier, B-1040 Brussels

Katholieke Universiteit Leuven, Universiteitsbibliotheek, Mgr Ladeuzeplein 21, B-3000 Leuven Tel: (016) 238678 Telex: Kulbib 25715
University Library of Louvain
Librarian: J Roegiers

Bibliothèque centrale du **Ministère de l'Education** nationale, 27 rue de Louvain, B-1000 Brussels

Bibliothèque Universitaire **Moretus Plantin***, 19 rue Grandgagnage, B-5000 Namur Tel: (081) 229061 Telex: 59222 Facnam 3
Librarian: R P J Denis

Bibliothèque du **Musée royal de Mariemont**, 100 chaussée de Mariemont, B-6510 Morlanwelz-Mariemont Tel: (064) 221243/226563/212193
Librarian: M-B Delattre

Bibliothèque du **Parlement***, 2 Palais de la Nation, pl de la Nation, Brussels

Museum **Plantin-Moretus**, Vrijdagmarkt 22, B-2000 Antwerp Tel: (03) 2322455/2330294
Librarian: Liliane Peeters-Demaeyer
Publications on sale include: The Plantin Press (1555-1589): A Bibliography of Works printed and published by Christopher Plantin at Antwerp and Leiden, 6 vols (Publisher: Van Hoeve, Amsterdam, 1981-1983)

Bibliotheek van de **Rijksuniversiteit te Gent**, Rozier 9, B-9000 Ghent Tel: (091) 257571 Telex: 11793 Ubgent B

Bibliotheek der Universitaire Faculteiten **Sint-Ignatius**, Prinsstr 13, B-2000 Antwerp
Librarian: J van Brabant, SJ

Stadsbibliotheek, Hendrik Conscienceplein 4, B-2000 Antwerp Tel: (03) 2323073 Telex: 33610 Stbianb
Municipal Library
Dir: L Simons; *Librarian:* A Pallemans

Bibliothèque centrale de l'**Université Catholique de Leuven**, see Katholieke Universiteit Leuven

Bibliothèque générale de l'**Université de Liège**, Place Cockerill 1, B-4000 Liège Tel: (041) 420080 Telex: 41456
Head Librarian: Paul Goret

Bibliothèques de l'**Université libre de Bruxelles**, 50 ave Franklin D Roosevelt, B-1050 Brussels Tel: (02) 6490030 Telex: 23654 Ulbipe B
Librarian: André Uyttebrouck

Library Associations

Archief- en Bibliotheekwezen in België, Koninklijke Bibliotheek Albert I, Keizerslaan 4, B-1000 Brussels
Belgian Association of Archivists and Librarians (Archives et Bibliothèques de Belgique)
General Secretary: Tony Verschaffel
Publication: Archives et Bibliothèques de Belgique

Association belge de Documentation, BP 110, B-1040 Brussels 26
Belgian Association for Documentation
President: R De Backer; *Secretary:* J C Smeets
Publication: Cahiers de la Documentation

Association des Bibliothécaires-Documentalistes de l'Institut d'Etudes sociales de l'Etat*, 24 rue de l'Abbaye, B-1050 Brussels Tel: 6493443
Association of Librarians and Documentalists of the State Institute of Social Studies
Secretary: Claire Gerard
Publication: Flash

Association des Bibliothécaires et du Personnel des Bibliothèques des Ministères de Belgique*, 22 rue des petits Carmes, B-1000 Brussels
Association of Librarians and Library Personnel in Belgian Government Departments
President: G Braive

Association nationale des Bibliothécaires d'Expression française*, 56 rue de la Station, B-5370 Havelange
National Association of French-speaking Librarians
Executive Secretary: J Peraux
Publications: Le Bibliothécaire: Revue d'Information culturelle et bibliographique

Association professionnelle des Bibliothécaires et Documentalistes, BP 31, B-1070 Brussels Tel: (02) 5216208 & (081) 229014

Centre national de Documentation scientifique et technique, 4 blvd de l'Empereur, B-1000 Brussels Tel: (02) 5136780 ext 570 Telex: 221157
National Centre for Scientific and Technical Documentation
Dir: Dr A Cockx
Publications: Catalogue collectif belge et luxembourgeois des Périodiques étrangers en cours de publication; Inventaire des Centres belges de Recherche disposant d'une Bibliothèque ou d'un Service de Documentation; Key to Belgian Science (KBS); Belgian Environmental Research Index; Translation Services and Translators' Index (CBT)

Institut belge d'Information et de Documentation (INBEL)*, Montoyerstr 3, B-1040 Brussels Tel: (02) 5126688 Telex: Inbel Bru 21716
Belgian Institute of Information

Dir: F Coppieters
Publication: Belgica Selecta

Vereniging van Religieus-Wetenschappelijke Bibliothecarissen, Minderbroederstr 5, B-3800 St Truiden
Association of Theological Librarians
Secretary: K Van de Casteele, Spoorweglaan 237, B-2610 Wilrijk Tel: (03) 4494886
Publication: VRB-Informatie (quarterly)

Vlaamse Vereniging van Bibliotheek-, Archief en Documentatie-Personeel*, Frans van Heymbeecklaan 4-6, Postbus 59, B-2100 Deurne Tel: (031) 252470
Flemish Association of Librarians, Archivists and Documentalists
General Secretary: J Bogaert
Publications: Bibliotheekgids (three monthly)

Library Reference Books and Journals

Books

Inventaire des Centres belges de Recherche disposant d'une Bibliothèque ou d'un Service de Documentation (Directory of Belgian Research Centres and Documentation Services), National Centre for Scientific and Technical Documentation, 4 blvd de l'Empereur, B-1000 Brussels

Journals

Archives et Bibliothèques de Belgique (Archief- en Bibliotheekwezen in België) (Archives and Libraries of Belgium), (text in Dutch, English, French German, Italian, Latin and Spanish), Belgian Association of Archivists and Librarians, Koninklijke Bibliotheek Albert I, Keizerslaan 4, B-1000 Brussels

Le Bibliothécaire (The Librarian), National Association of French-speaking Librarians, 56 rue de la Station, B-5370 Havelange

Bibliotheekgids (Library Guide), Flemish Association of Librarians, Archivists and Documentalists, Postbus 59, B-2100 Deurne

Bulletin de Documentation (Verkeersdocumentatie Bulletin) (Bulletin of Documentation), (text in Dutch, English, French and German), Ministère des Communications et des PTT, 62 rue de la Roi, B-1040 Brussels

Cahiers de la Documentation (Bladen voor de Documentatie) (Journal of Documentation), (text in Dutch, English, French), Belgian Association for Documentation, BP 110, B-1040 Brussels 26

Literary Associations and Societies

Académie royale de Langue et de Littérature françaises*, Palais des Académies, 1 rue Ducale, B-1000 Brussels
Royal Academy of French Language and Literature
Permanent Secretary: Georges Sion
Publications: Bulletin, Annuaire, Mémoires

Académie royale des Sciences, des Lettres et des Beaux-Arts de Belgique, Palais des Académies, 1 rue Ducale, B-1000 Brussels
Belgian Royal Academy of Sciences, Letters and Fine Arts
Permanent Secretary: Maurice Leroy
Publications: Monthly Bulletin, Memoirs, Year Book

Antwerp Bibliophile Society*, c/o Museum Plantin-Moretus, Vrijdagmarkt 22, B-2000 Antwerp
Publication: De Gulden Passer

Association des Ecrivains belges de langue française*, Maison Camille Lemonnier Maison des Ecrivains, 150 chaussée de Wavre, B-1050 Brussels Tel: (02) 5122968/5122863
Association of Belgian Writers in the French Language
President: Roger Foulon; *Secretary-General:* Philippe Delaby
Publications: Nos Lettres Informations (ten a year)

Commission belge de Bibliographie*, 80-84 rue des Tanneurs, B-1000 Brussels
Belgian Commission of Bibliography
Secretary: E Cosyns-Verhaegen
Publications: Bulletin (quarterly), *Bibliographia Belgica, Coll, Répertoire annuelles des principaux Travaux bibliographiques récents*

Icon*, Lobergenbos 27, B-3200 Louvain
Association on marginal literature and art
Secretary: Jozef Peeters
Publication: Cahier Jean Ray (annual) in Dutch, English & French

Koninklijke Academie voor Nederlandse Taal- en Letterkunde, Koningstr 18, B-9000 Ghent Tel: (091) 252774
Royal Academy of Dutch Language and Literature
Permanent Secretary: M Hoebeke

Koninklijke Academie voor Wetenschappen, Letteren en Schone Kunsten van België, Paleis der Academiën Hertogsstr 1, B-1000 Brussels Tel: (02) 5112623
Belgian Royal Academy of Science, Letters and Fine Arts
Permanent Secretary: G Verbeke
Publications: Proceedings (Academiae Analecta), Memoirs, National Biography, Letters of Justus Lipsius, Year Book, Reports and Proposals, Special Editions

International **P E N Club, Belgian French Centre***, ave du 11 novembre 76, BP 7, B-1040 Brussels Tel: (02) 7360214
President: Baron de Radzitzky
General Secretary: Raymond Quinot

International **P E N Club, Flemish Centre**, Albert Heyrbautlaan 48, B-1710 Dilbeek
General Secretary: Willem M Roggeman
Publication: PEN-Club Tijdingen

Société belge des Auteurs, Compositeurs et Editeurs (SABAM), 75-77 rue d'Arlon, B-1040 Brussels Tel: 2302660
Belgian Society of Authors, Composers and Publishers
President: Vic Legley; *Man Dirs:* Joseph Dethier, Ernest van der Eyken
Publication: Bulletin (quarterly)

Société de Langue et de Littérature wallones ASBL, Université de Liège, 7 pl du XX août, B-4000 Liège Tel: (041) 231960
Secretary: Victor George
Publications: Bulletin de la Société de Langue et de Littérature wallonnes, Dialectes de Wallonie (both periodically), Literary & Philological collections

Société royale des Bibliophiles et Iconophiles de Belgique, blvd de l'Empereur 4, B-1000 Brussels
Director: Eugène Rouir
Publication: Le Livre et l'Estampe (twice yearly)

Vereeniging der Antwerpsche Bibliophielen, Museum Plantin-Moretus, Vrijdagmarkt 22, B-2000 Antwerp Tel: (03) 2322455/2330294
Editorial Secretary: Dr L Voet
Publications: De Gulden Passer (annual)

Literary Periodicals

Dietsche Warande en Belfort, journal for literature, art and spiritual life, Standaard Uitgeverij (Scriptoria NV), Belgiëlei 147a, B-2018 Antwerp

Flambeau (Torch), Belgian review of political and literary questions, 75 ave Emile de Beco, Brussels 5

De Gulden Passer, Antwerp Bibliophile Society, c/o Museum Plantin-Moretus, Vrijdagmarkt 22, B-2000 Antwerp

Livres et Disques (Books and Records), Centre d'Action culturelle de la Communauté d'Expression française, 12 rue Saintraint, B-5000 Namur

Mandragora, journal for literature and art, (text in Dutch), Acacalaan 58, B-9620 Zottegem

Marginales (Marginalia), review of ideas and letters, Albert Ayguesparse, 118 rue Marconi, B-1180 Brussels

Nieuw Vlaams Tijdschrift (New Flemish Journal), Leeuwerikstr 41, Antwerp

Revue générale belge (General Belgian Review), 21 rue de la Limité, B-1030 Brussels

Revue nouvelle (New Review), 305 ave van Volxem, B-1190 Brussels

Ruimten (text in Dutch and German), Antwerpsesteenweg 488, Hoboken, Antwerp

Scarabée, Centre européen de Diffusion de la Culture, 137 rue de Livourne, Brussels

Streven, Sanderusstr 5, B-2000 Antwerp

Trefpunt (Meeting-point), Blankenbergs Literair Archief Trefpunt, Kerkstr 41, Te Blankenberge

Literary Prizes

Goblet d'Alviella Prize
For the best work of a strictly scientific and objective character relating to the history of religions, published by a Belgian author. 50,000 francs. Awarded every five years. Enquiries to Académie royale de Belgique, Palais des Académies, 1 rue Ducale, B-1000 Brussels

Lode Baekelmans Prize
For the best literary work in Dutch — novel, poetry, play, radio play, essay, etc — dealing with the sea, sailors, navigation, the harbour, inland navigation or related topics. A prize of 40,000 francs is awarded every three years: the recipients must be Belgian nationals. Enquiries to the Koninklijke Academie voor Nederlandse Taal- en Letterkunde, Koningstr 18, B-9000 Ghent

Beernaert Prize*
For the most outstanding work of a Belgian author written in French language. Awarded annually. Enquiries to Académie royale de Langue et de Littérature françaises, Palais des Académies, 1 rue Ducale, B-1000 Brussels

Belgian Government Prizes for Literature (Ministry of Flemish Culture)*
Triennial State Prizes for prose, poetry, drama, essay and youth and children's literature. A triennial Great State Prize for a Literary Career. A triennial State Prize for the best translation of a Flemish literary work. Each year two, and every three years three, of these prizes may be awarded. The ordinary prizes amount to 200,000 francs and the Great State Prize to 400,000 francs. Enquiries to Ministerie van de Vlaamse Gemeenschap, Koloniënstr 29-31, B-1000 Brussels

Belgian Government Prizes for Literature (Ministry of French Culture)*
An annual State Prize for Literature, in turn awarded for prose, drama and poetry. A quinquennial State Prize for Critique and Essay and a quinquennial State Prize for a Literary Career are also awarded. The annual State Prize amounts to 175,000 francs, the Prize for Critique and Essay to 225,000 francs, and the State Prize for a Literary Career to 300,000 francs. Enquiries to Ministère de la Communauté Française, 158 ave de Cortenbergh, B-1040 Brussels

Ernest Bouvier-Parviliez Prize*
For the entire work of a Belgian author written in French. Awarded every four years. Enquiries to Académie royale de Langue et de Littérature françaises, Palais des Académies, 1 rue Ducale, B-1000 Brussels

Felix Denayer Prize*
For a single work or the entire literary work of a Belgian written in French. Awarded annually. Enquiries to Académie royale de Langue et de Littérature françaises, Palais des Académies, 1 rue Ducale, B-1000 Brussels

Jules Duculot Prize
For a work in print or manuscript form, written in French, dealing with the history of philosophy. Awarded only to Belgians, or to foreigners holding an academic grade granted by a Belgian university. Printed work must have been published in the five years prior to the end of the relevant period. The prize is awarded for what appears the most deserving work, irrespective of whether it has been submitted for entry or not. 90,000 francs. Awarded every five years. Winner for third period (1976-1980), Guy Haarscher. Enquiries to Académie royale de Belgique, Palais des Académies, 1 rue Ducale, B-1000 Brussels

Charles Duvivier Prize
For the Belgian author of the best work on the history of Belgian or foreign law, or on the history of Belgian political, judicial or administrative institutions. 50,000 francs. Awarded every three years. Winner for twenty-fifth period (1979-1981), J Gilissen. Enquiries to Académie royale de Belgique, Palais des Académies, 1 rue Ducale, B-1000 Brussels

Joseph Gantrelle Prize
For a work in classical philology. 60,000 francs. Awarded biennially to Belgian authors. Winner for forty-fourth period (1980-1981), Robert Halleux. Enquiries to Académie royale de Belgique, Palais des Académies, 1 rue Ducale, B-1000 Brussels

Grand Franco-Belgian Literary Prize, see French Literary Prizes

Tobie Jonckheere Prize
For a work, in published or manuscript form, devoted to the educational sciences. 50,000 francs. Awarded every three years. Winner for eighth period (1977-1979), Mrs M Lohle-Tart-Esser. Enquiries to Académie royale de Belgique, Palais des Académies, 1 rue Ducale, B-1000 Brussels

Hubert Krains Prize
Awarded biennially (alternately prose and poetry) for the unpublished work of a writer below the age of 40. 20,000 francs. Founded by the Association of Belgian Writers in the French Language in memory of one of its presidents. Enquiries to Association des Ecrivains belges de langue française, Maison des Ecrivains, 150 chaussée de Wavre, B-1050 Brussels

Malpertuis Prize*
For an outstanding contribution to Belgian literature in the field of drama, poetry, short story or essay written in French. Awarded biennially. Enquiries to the Académie royale de Langue et de Littérature françaises, Palais des Académies, 1 rue Ducale, B-1000 Brussels

Joseph-Edmond **Marchal** Prize
For the Belgian author of the best work, in print or in manuscript form, on national antiques or archaeology. 50,000 francs. Awarded every five years. Winner for thirteenth period (1978-1982), Raymond Brulet. Enquiries to Académie royale de Belgique, Palais des Académies, 1 rue Ducale, B-1000 Brussels

Albert **Mockel** Grand Prize for Poetry*
For the best Belgian poet writing in French. Awarded every five years. Enquiries to Académie royale de Langue et de Littérature françaises, Palais des Académies, 1 rue Ducale, B-1000 Brussels

Emil **Polak** Prize*
For a distinguished literary work written in French, preferably by a poet. Awarded biennially. Enquiries to Académie royale de Langue et de Littérature françaises, Palais des Académies, 1 rue Ducale, B-1000 Brussels

Victor **Rossel** Prize*
For the best novel, or collection of short stories, of the year written in French by a Belgian author. 125,000 francs. Awarded annually. Enquiries to 'Le Soir', 112 rue Royale, Brussels

Saint-Genois Prize
For the author of the best historical or literary work written in Dutch. 50,000 francs. Awarded every five years. Winner for eighteenth period (1975-1980), Jan Art. Enquiries to Académie royale de Belgique, Palais des Académies, 1 rue Ducale, B-1000 Brussels

Suzanne **Tassier** Prize
For a Belgian woman who, following study at a Belgian university, has obtained at least a doctorate. The prize is awarded for a major scientific work, dealing with a subject from history, law, philology or the social sciences: failing a meritorious work from one of these branches, then for a subject from the natural sciences, medicine or mathematics. Preference will be given to a work of an historical nature, in its widest sense. 60,000 francs. Awarded every two years. Winner for the thirteenth period (1981-1982), M Th Isaac. Enquiries to Académie royale de Belgique, Palais des Académies, 1 rue Ducale, B-1000 Brussels

Auguste **Teirlinck** Prize
For a contribution to Flemish literature. 50,000 francs. Awarded every five years. Winner for seventeenth period (1975-1980), Jan De Roek. Enquiries to Académie royale de Belgique, Palais des Académies, 1 rue Ducale, B-1000 Brussels

Carton de **Wiart** Prize*
For a book in the field of literary history or on subjects which relate to Belgian life. Alternately awarded for a work in French and in Flemish. 10,000 francs. Awarded every five years. Enquiries to Belgian Ministry of National Education, 67 rue Royale, B-1000 Brussels

Translation Agencies and Associations

Centre belge de Traduction, 4 blvd de l'Empereur, B-1000 Brussels Tel: (02) 5136180 Ext 561 Telex: 21157
Dir: Mme I Clemens

Belize

General Information

Language: English (and Spanish)
Religion: Catholic and various Protestant denominations
Population: 153,000
Bank Hours: 0900-1500 Monday, Tuesday, Thursday, Friday; 0900-1130 Wednesday and Saturday
Shop Hours: 0730-1130, 1300-1600 Monday-Saturday (some open 1900-2100 evenings); generally early closing Wednesday
Currency: 100 cents = 1 Belize dollar
Export/Import Information: No tariff on books. General licence. Nominal exchange controls
Copyright: Berne, UCC (see International section)

Major Booksellers

Belize Book Shop (Anglican Diocese), PO Box 147, Belize City (Located at: Corner Regent St/Rectory Lane, Belize City) Tel: (02) 2054 Cable Add: Literary Belize
Manager: Shirley Smiling

Beuhler's Shoppe*, Fort George Hotel Lobby Tel: 3491

Cathedral Book Centre*, 144 North Front St, PO Box 426 Tel: 2757
Manager: Thomas Donovan

Christian Literature*, Christian Literature Centre, PO Box 76 (Located at: 14 New Rd) Tel: 2993

The **Emporium***, 2 Bishop St Tel: 2566

Major Libraries

National Library Service, The Central Library, PO Box 287, Bliss Institute, Belize City Tel: 7267
Chief Librarian: L G Vernon

Library Association

Belize Library Association*, Central Library, PO Box 287, Bliss Institute, Belize City Tel: 7267
Secretary: Robert Hulse
Publication: Belize Library Association Bulletin

Benin

General Information

Language: French
Religion: About 15% Christian (mostly Roman Catholic), 13% Muslim, rest follow traditional beliefs
Population: 3.4 million
Bank Hours: 0800-1130, 1430-1530 Monday-Friday
Shop Hours: 0800-1200, 1430-1730 Monday-Saturday. Larger ones close Monday, some open for a few hours Sunday morning
Currency: franc CFA
Export/Import Information: Import licence required but issued automatically for imports from EEC countries. Exchange controls for non-franc zone.
Copyright: Berne (see International section)

Publishers

Government Printer (Office nationale d'edition de presse et d'imprimerie)*, BP 1210, Porto Novo Tel: 314061

Maison d'Edition **A B M**, BP 889, Cotonou Tel: 330690
Bookshops: Librairie-Papeterie ABM (qv under Major Booksellers)

Major Booksellers

Librairie-Papeterie **A B M**, BP 9086, Cotonou Tel: 312819
Also: Porto Novo
Owned by: Maison d'Edition ABM (qv)

Centre de **Littérature** Chrétienne*, BP 34, Cotonou

Librairie **Drouot** (Ets Robert Drouot)*, BP 33, Cotonou Tel: 3451

La **Maison** du Livre*, BP 341, Cotonou

Librairie **Nationale** (Ministère Education National)*, Porto Novo

Librairie SA Gaston **Nègre***, BP 52, Cotonou

Librairie **Notre Dame**, Ave Clozel, BP 714, Cotonou Tel: 314094

Librairie **Protestante***, Ave Proche, BP 34, Cotonou

Sonapal*, BP 1389, Cotonou

Major Libraries

Archives nationales de la République Populaire du Benin*, BP 6, Porto Novo
Director: A S Tidjari

Bibliotheque nationale du Benin*, BP 526, Cotonou Tel: 360074/360126 Cable Add: Biblionationale
Chief Librarian: Valentine Quenum
Publication: Bibliographie nationale (in preparation)

Bibliothèque du **Centre National** de la recherche scientifique et technique*, BP 6, Porto Novo
Director: G Metinhoue
Publication: Courrier de la Recherche au Bénin

Institut national pour la formation et la recherche en éducation (Centre de documentation et d'information pédagogique)*, BP 6, Porto Novo Tel: 213486
Chief Librarian: Bernard Bondil

Bibliothèque de l'**Université du Benin**, see Bibliothèque nationale du Benin

Bermuda

General Information

Language: English
Religion: Anglican
Population: 58,000
Literacy Rate (1960): 97.6%
Bank Hours: 0930-1500 Monday-Thursday; 0930-1500, 1630-1800 Friday
Shop Hours: 0900-1700 Monday-Saturday
Currency: 100 cents = 1 Bermuda dollar. US currency circulates
Export/Import Information: No tariff on books and advertising matter. No import licence. Exchange controls on imports valued over $100
Copyright: Berne, UCC (see International section)

Publishers

Bermuda Press Ltd*, Reid St, Hamilton
Subject: Literature

Bermudian Publishing Co, PO Box 283, Hamilton 5
Editor: Dinah Darby
Subjects: Social, General Affairs, Sport

Royal Gazette Ltd, PO Box 1025, Hamilton Tel: (80929) 55881
General Manager and Rights & Permissions: K R Jensen; *Editorial:* D L White; *Sales:* R E Osborne
Subject: Literature

Major Booksellers

Baxters Ltd*, PO Box 1009, Hamilton 5 (Located at: Burnaby St, Hamilton) Tel: (80929) 23292 Telex: 3246 Cwt Xagy Ba
Manager: Jonathan Baxter

Bermuda Book Store Ltd*, Queen St, Hamilton Tel: (80929) 53698

The **Bookmart***, In the Annex on Reid St, Hamilton 5 Tel: (80929) 51647
Manager: E Linda Young

Major Libraries

Bermuda Archives, Government Administration Building, Hamilton 5-24
Archivist: Helen E Rowe
Publications include: A guide to the records of Bermuda (1980)

Bermuda Library, Par-la-Ville, Hamilton 5-31 Tel: (80929) 52905
Librarian: Mary Skiffington

Bolivia

General Information

Language: Spanish
Religion: Roman Catholic
Population: 5.3 million
Literacy Rate (1976): 62.7% (84% of urban population, 47% rural)
Bank Hours: 0900-1200, 1400-1630 Monday-Friday
Shop Hours: 0900-1200, 1400-1800 Monday-Friday; 0900-1200 Saturday
Currency: 100 centavos = 1 peso Boliviano
Export/Import Information: Member of the Latin American Free Trade Association. No tariffs on books, except for 10% on luxury bindings. No import licences, except for textbooks, but no pornography allowed. No advertising that includes imitation money, stamps, etc allowed. No exchange controls
Copyright: Buenos Aires (see International section)

Book Trade Organization

Cámara Boliviana del Libro*, Casilla 682, La Paz (Located at: Ave 20 de Octubre 2005, Edf Las Palmas Planta Baja of 5, La Paz) Tel: 327039
Bolivian Booksellers' Association
President: Javier Gisbert

Book Trade Reference Books and Journals

Books

Informativo Amigol literario ('Literary Friend'), Editorial los Amigos del Libro, Casilla 450, Cochabamba

Journals

Bibliografía Boliviana, Editorial los Amigos del Libro, Casilla 450, Cochabamba

Boletin Bibliografico Boliviano (text in Spanish, summaries in English and Spanish), Ediciones ISLA, Casilla N4311, La Paz

Publishers

Ediciones los **Amigos del Libro***, Calle Mercado 1315, Casilla 4415, La Paz Tel: 22794 Cable Add: Amigol
Dir: Werner Guttentag; *Manager:* Peter Lewy
Parent Company: Editorial los Amigos del Libro (qv)
Bookshop: Librería los Amigos del Libro (qv under Major Booksellers)
Founded: 1977

Editorial los **Amigos del Libro***, Casilla 450, Cochabamba Tel: 2920 Cable Add: Amigol
Man Dir: Werner Guttentag; *Sales Dir:* Peter Lewy; *Foreign Sales Manager:* Eva Guttentag; *Production:* Rene Hohenstein, Jaime Flores
Subsidiary Company: Ediciones los Amigos del Libro (qv)
Associate Company: Grijalbo Boliviana Ltda (qv)
Subjects: Bolivia, South America
Bookshops: Librería Universal Bookstore, Casilla 4415, La Paz; Calle 25 de Mayo N-0165, Cochabamba
1981: 40 titles *Founded:* 1945

Editorial **Difusión***, Casilla 1510, La Paz (Located at: Ave 16 de Julio 1601, La Paz) Tel: 328126

Man Dir: Jorge F Catalano; *Publicity & Advertising:* Carmelo Andrade
Subjects: Bolivian literature & history, Politics, Social Studies
Bookshop: qv under Major Booksellers
Founded: 1960

Universidad Boliviana Tomás **Frías**, Div de Extensión Universitaria*, Casilla 36, Potosí
Subjects: Literature, History

Gisbert y Cia SA*, Calle Comercio 1270, Casilla 195, La Paz Tel: 356806 Cable Add: Gisbercia
President: José Gisbert; *Managers:* Javier Gisbert, Armando Pagano
Subjects: Belles Lettres, History, Law, Textbooks, Accounting, Fiction
Bookshop: See under Major Booksellers
1981: 13 titles *Founded:* 1907

Grijalbo Boliviana Ltda*, Apdo 4415, La Paz
Manager: Peter Lewy
Parent Company: Ediciones Grijalbo SA, Spain (qv)
Associate Company: Editorial los Amigos del Libro (qv)

Librería y Editorial **Juventud**, Plaza Murillo 519, Casilla 1489, La Paz Tel: 341694 Cable Add: Juventud
Man Dir: Rafael Urquizo; *Assistant Dir, Publicity:* Gustavo Urquizo; *Production:* Rafael Urquizo Mendoza
Orders to: Casilla 1489, La Paz
Subsidiary Company: Empresa Editora Urquizo SA
Branch Off: Calle Puerto Rico 1135, La Paz
Subjects: Literature, History, Social Science, University, Secondary & Primary Textbooks; General Cultural Subjects
Bookshop: Librería Juventud (qv under Major Booksellers)
Founded: 1946

Universidad Mayor de San Andres*, Editorial Universitaria, Casilla 6548, La Paz

Major Booksellers

Librería los **Amigos del Libro***, Calle Mercado 1315, Casilla 4415, La Paz Tel: 22794
Managers: Peter Lewy, Werner Guttentag
7 other branches
Owned by: Ediciones los Amigos del Libro (qv)

Librería **Difusión***, Casilla 1510, La Paz (Located at: Ave 16 de Julio 1601, La Paz) Tel: 28126
Also Publisher (qv)

Gisbert y Cía SA*, Calle Comercio 1270, Casilla 195, La Paz Tel: 356806
Managers: Javier Gisbert, Armando Pagano
Also Publisher (qv)

Librería **Icthus***, Ave 16 de Julio 1800, Casilla 8353, La Paz Tel: 54007
Manager: Salvador de la Serna
Owned by: Methodist Evangelical Church in Bolivia

Librería **Juventud**, Plaza Murillo 519, Casilla 1489, La Paz Tel: 341694
Manager: Rafael Urquizo
Owned by: Librería y Editorial Juventud (qv)

Librería **La Paz***, Ingavi esq Yanacocha, Casilla 539, La Paz Tel: 53323

Librería **Selecciones** SRL, Casilla 972, La Paz (Located at: Ave 6 de Agosto 2105, La Paz) Tel: 324159/329480 Cable Add: Selecciones La Paz

Alfonso **Tejerina** Ltda*, Comercio 1073, Casilla 834, La Paz

Major Libraries

Biblioteca y Archivo Nacional de Bolivia*, Calle Bolívar, Sucre

Biblioteca del **Congreso** Nacional*, Palacio Legislativo, La Paz

Biblioteca de la **Dirección de Cultura***, Alcaldía Municipal, Casilla 1856, La Paz
Library of Cultural Affairs Administration

Biblioteca Universitaria, Departamento de Bibliotecas **Universidad Boliviana** Tomás Frías*, CP 54, Potosí
Dir: Adolfo Vera del Carpio
Publications: Boletin de la Biblioteca Universitaria and occasional papers

Biblioteca Central de la **Universidad Mayor de San Andrés***, Ave Villazón 1995, Casilla 6548, La Paz

Biblioteca Central de la **Universidad Mayor de San Francisco Xavier***, Plaza 25 de Mayo, Apdo 212, Sucre

Biblioteca Central de la **Universidad Mayor de San Simón***, Oquendo esq Sucre, Casilla correo 992, Cochabamba Tel: 25506
Dir: Mario Estenssoro
Publication: Boletin Bibliografico

Library Associations

Asociación Boliviana de Bibliotecarios (ABB)*, Casilla 992, Cochabamba
Bolivian Library Association
President: Dr Efraín Virreira Sánchez

Centro Nacional de Documentación Científica y Tecnológica, Casilla correo 3283, La Paz
National Scientific and Technological Documentation Centre
Dir: Hugo Loaiza-Terán
Publications include: Serie Bibliografica (3-5 a year); *Actualidades* (quarterly)

Centro Nacional de Documentación e Información Educativa*, c/o Ministerio de Educación y Cultura, La Paz
National Centre of Documentation and Education Information
Dir: Rosa Melgar de Ipiña

Literary Associations and Societies

P E N Club de Bolivia (Centro Internacional de Escritores)*, Calle Goitia 17, Casilla 149, La Paz
Secretary: Yolanda Bedregal de Cónitzer

Literary Periodicals

Cultura Boliviana, Universidad Tecnica de Oruro, Departamento de Extension Cultural, Oruro

Presencia Literaria, Casilla 1913, La Paz

Literary Prizes

Bolivian Grand Prize for Literature*
For an outstanding achievement in the field of literature. Enquiries to the Bolivian Government, La Paz

Premio Nacional de **Cultura***
Enquiries to Ministerio de Educación, La Paz

Premio de Novela 'Erich **Guttentag'***
'Erich Guttentag' annual prize for a previously unpublished novel. First prize 50,000 Bolivian pesos, second prize 20,000 Bolivian pesos. Enquiries to Editorial los Amigos del Libro, Casilla 450, Cochabamba

Franz **Tamayo** Prize*
For outstanding literary work. 25,000 Bolivian pesos, 15,000 pesos and 5,000 pesos. Awarded annually. Enquiries to La Paz Municipal Mayor's Office, La Paz

Botswana

General Information

Language: Setswana and English
Religion: Traditional
Population: 726,000
Bank Hours: 0830-1300 Monday-Friday; 0830-1100 Saturday
Shop Hours: 0800-1300, 1400-1700 or 1800 Monday-Saturday
Currency: 100 thebe = 1 pula
Export/Import Information: No tariffs on books or advertising matter. No import licence required; no obscene literature. Exchange controls

Book Trade Reference Journal

The National Bibliography of Botswana, Botswana National Library Service, Private Bag 0036, Gaborone

Publishers

Government Printer, Private Bag 0081, Gaborone

Longman Botswana (Pty) Ltd, PO Box 1083, Gaborone
Associate Company: Longman Group Ltd, UK (qv)

Major Booksellers

Botswana Book Centre, PO Box 91, Gaborone (Located at: The Mall) Tel: 52931/2 Cable Add: Books
Manager: J D Jones

Via Afrika Botswana Ltd*, PO Box 332, Gaborone
Owned by: Nasionale Boekhandel Ltd, Republic of South Africa (qv)

Major Libraries

Botswana National Archives*, PO Box 239, Gaborone Tel: 55227 Cable Add: Homes
Dir: Mrs T M Lekaukau

Botswana National Library Service*, Private Bag 0036, Gaborone Tel: 52397/52288 Cable Add: Bonalibs
Director of Library Services: Grace B Seame

Geological Survey Department Library*, Private Bag 14, Lobatse Tel: 327 Cable Add: Rocks Lobatse Telex: 2293 Geo Bd
Technical Information Specialist: G McEwen

Government Teacher Training College Library*, PO Box 96, Lobatse

The **National Institute** of Research Library, University of Botswana, Private Bag 0022, Gaborone
Librarian: Andrew Khutsoane

University of Botswana Library, Private Bag 0022, Gaborone Tel: 51155 Telex: 2429 Bd
Librarian: Mrs H K Raseroka
Publications: Annual Report, Accessions List

Library Association

Botswana Library Association, PO Box 1310, Gaborone
Secretary: Amos P N Thapisa
Publication: Botswana Library Association Journal

Library Reference Journal

Botswana Library Association Journal, Botswana Library Association, PO Box 1310, Gaborone

Literary Periodical

Marang, Department of English, University of Botswana, PO Box 0022, Gaborone

Brazil

General Information

Language: Portuguese (some English spoken)
Religion: Roman Catholic
Population: 115.4 million
Literacy Rate (1970): 66.2%
Bank Hours: Generally 1000-1600 Monday-Friday
Shop Hours: 0900-1700 Monday-Friday (many open much later); 0900-1230 or 1300 Saturday
Currency: 100 centavos = 1 cruzeiro
Export/Import Information: Member of the Latin American Free Trade Association. No tariffs on books and advertising, but luxury bindings and children's picture books are dutied. Import licences and deposits required; exchange controls operate.
Copyright: UCC, Berne, Buenos Aires, Florence (see International section)

Book Trade Organizations

Agência Brasileira do ISBN*, Seção de Contribuição Legal, Biblioteca Nacional, Ave Rio Branco 219/39 — 3° andar, 20042 Rio de Janeiro RJ Telex: 02122941 Bn Rj Br

Associação Brasileira de Livreiros Antiquarios, Rua do Rosario 137, 20000 Rio de Janeiro RJ
Brazilian Association of Antiquarian Booksellers

Associação Brasileira do Livro*, Ave 13 de Mayo 23 — 16° andar, Rio de Janeiro RJ Tel: 2327173
Brazilian Booksellers' Association
Dir: Alberjano Torres

Câmara Brasileira do Livro, Ave Ipiranga 1267 — 10° andar, 01039 São Paulo 2 SP Tel: 2297855/2295258
Brazilian Book Association
Superintendent: José Gorayeb

Instituto Nacional do Livro*, Edifício Venâncio V, Setor de Diversões Sul, 70000 Brasília DF Tel: 235628
National Book Institute
Dir: María Alice Barroso
Publications include: Bibliografia Brasileira

Sindicato Nacional dos Editores de Livros, Ave Rio Branco 37 — 15° andar — salas 1503-6 e 1510-12, 20097 Rio de Janeiro RJ Tel: 2336481/2335484 Cable Add: Sindelivros
Brazilian Publishers' Association
Man Dir: Berta Ribeiro
Publications: Boletim Informativo (bi-monthly bulletin); *Guia das Editoras Brasileiras; Guia das Livrarias Brasileiras*

Standard Book Numbering Agency, see Agência Brasileira do ISBN

Book Trade Reference Books and Journals

Books

O Mundo do Edição Luso-Brasileira (The World of Publishing, Portugal and Brazil), Publicações Europa-America Lda, Apdo 8, Estrada Lisbon-Sintra Km 14, Mem Martins, Portugal

Journals

Bibliografia Brasileira (Brazilian Bibliography), National Book Institute, Edifício Venâncio V, Setor de Diversões Sul, 70000 Brasília DF

Bibliografia Classificada (Classified Bibliography), Centre of Investigation and Documentation, CP 23, Petropolis, Rio de Janeiro

Boletim Bibliográfico, National Library, Ave Rio Branco 219-239, 20042 Rio de Janeiro RJ

Boletim Bibliográfico Brasileiro (Brazilian Bibliographical Bulletin), Estante Publicações, Ave Rio Branco 138, 11° andar, Rio de Janeiro RJ

O Editor do Livros, Revistas e Jornais (The Publisher of Books, Reviews and Journals), Editora Métodos Ltda, Rua da Lapa 180, sala 607, CP 15085, Rio de Janeiro GB

El Libro (The Book), Equilar Editores, Castillan 5, São Paulo 17

Guia das Editoras Brasileiras, Brazilian Publishers' Association, Ave Rio Branco 37 — 15° andar — salas 1503-6 e 1510-12, 20097 Rio de Janeiro RJ

Guia das Livrarias Brasileiras, Brazilian Publishers' Association, Ave Rio Branco 37 — 15° andar — salas 1503-6 e 1510-12, 20097 Rio de Janeiro RJ

Livros Novos (New Books) (text in English and Portuguese), Atlantis Livros Ltda, CP 3752, 01000 São Paulo SP

Pregão de Livros ('Pawnbroker of Books'), J C Amaral Guimarães, Rua Conde de Sarzedas 246, 01512 São Paulo SP

Resumo Bibliográfico (Bibliographical Résumé), Brazilian Publishers' Association, Centro de Bibliotécnia, Ave Rio Branco 37 — 15° andar — salas 1503-6 e 1510-12, 20097 Rio de Janeiro RJ

Revisto do Livro (Review of Books), (text in Portuguese and Spanish), Ministerio da Educação e Cultura, of 3068, Brasília DF

Publishers

A G I R (Artes Graficas Industrias Reunidas SA)*, CP 3291 ZC-00, Rio de Janeiro RJ (Located at: Rua dos Invalidos 198, Rio de Janeiro) Tel: 2528261 Cable Add: Agirsa
Man Dir: Affonso D Faveret; *Editorial:* Ernst Fromm
Branch Offs: São Paulo, Belo Horizonte
Subjects: Literature, Juveniles, Social Science, Religion
Bookshop: Livraria Agir (qv under Major Booksellers)
Founded: 1944

Abril SA Cultural e Industrial, Rua Paes Leme 524 - 10° andar, São Paulo SP Tel: (011) 8154677 Telex: 112209 Absa
Vice-President: João Gomez; *Man Dirs:* José Eduardo P Martins (Books), Anselmo Pecci (Education), Roberto Silveira (Partworks); *Rights:* Vicente Roig, Renê C X Santos (Book Club)
Branch Offs: 380 Lexington Ave, 17th Floor, New York, NY 10168, USA Tel: (212) 8838825; 44a Gloucester Ave, London NW1, UK Tel: (01) 586 5074
Subjects: Reference, General Encyclopedias, Literature, Music, Science, Illustrated Trade Books; School & Textbooks
Book Club: Círculo do Livro SA (owned jointly with Verlagsgruppe Bertelsmann GmbH, Federal Republic of Germany (qv))
Founded: 1950

Agents Editores Ltda*, Rua Almirante Baltazar 349, São Cristovão, 20941 Rio de Janeiro RJ Tel: (021) 2845988/2640687/2649988 Cable Add: Agentsrio
Superintendent-Director: Francisco da Gama Lima Netto; *Editorial:* João Sergio Rao, Gabriel de Almeida
Subjects: Security in Technical and Scientific fields (including Security, Counter-surveillance, Criminal investigation, Intelligence)
Founded: 1977

Editora Nova **Aguilar** SA+, Rua Maria Angélica 168, Lagoa, 22461 Rio de Janeiro RJ Tel: 2867822 Cable Add: Aguilar
President: Wellington Moreira Franco; *Vice-President:* Sergio Lacerda; *Dir:* Sebastião Lacerda
Branch Off: Ave Pedro Bueno 1509-1511, Jabaquara, 04342 São Paulo
Subject: General Literature
Founded: 1958

Livraria Francisco **Alves** Editora SA+, Rua Sete de Setembro 177, Centro, 20050 Rio de Janeiro RJ Tel: 2322009/2324064/2327188
Man Dir: Léo Magarinos de Souza Leão; *Editorial:* Rosemary Alves; *Sales:* Arthur Orlando Álvares dos Prazeres
Parent Companies: Companhia de Navegação Marítima Netumar, Ave Presidente Vargas 482-3 18, 23 e 27 andar, 20071 Rio de Janeiro RJ; Netumar International Inc, 26 Broadway, 6th floor, New York, NY 10004, USA
Branch Offs: Rua Pires de Mota 399, 01529 São Paulo SP; Rua da Bahia 1060, 30000 Belo Horizonte MG
Subjects: University, High School and Primary Textbooks, Science, Astronomy, Non-fiction, General Fiction, Crime, Science Fiction, Occultism, Literature
Bookshops: Rua Farme de Amoedo 57, Ipanema; Rua Sete de Setembro 177, Centro, Rio de Janeiro; Rua Vruguaiana 98, Rio de Janeiro; Rua da Bahia 1060, Belo Horizonte
Founded: 1854

Editora Das **Americas** SA Edameris*, Rua Santa Isabel 152, V Buarque, 01221 São Paulo SP Tel: 2217573/2218482
Man Dir: Mário Fittipaldi
Subjects: Poetry, Fiction, Biography, Crime & Adventure

Organização **Andrei** Editora Ltda+, Rua Conselheiro Nebias 1071, São Paulo SP Tel: 2207246 Cable Add: Carolandre
Dir: Edmondo L Andrei; *Sales Dir:* Alberto Mayer
Subjects: Medicine, Pharmacy, Veterinary Medicine
Founded: 1956

Antenna Edições Técnicas Ltda, Ave Mal Floriano 143, 20080 Rio de Janeiro RJ Tel: (021) 2232442 Cable Add: Antenna
Man Dir: Gilberto A Penna; *Publicity:* Helio N Santos
Associate Company: Seleções Eletrônicas Editora Ltda (qv)
Branch Off: Rua Vitoria 195, São Paulo
Subjects: Electronics, Telecommunications
Bookshops: Lojas do Livro Eletrônico, Ave Mal Floriano 148, Rio de Janeiro; Rua Vitória 383, São Paulo
1981: 4 titles *1982:* 4 titles *Founded:* 1926
ISBN Publisher's Prefix: 85-7036

Ao Livro Técnico SA Industria a Comércio*, CP 3655, 20930 Rio de Janeiro RJ (Located at: Rua Sá Freire 36-40, São Christovão, Rio de Janeiro) Tel: 2843112 Cable Add: Litecnico Telex: 2130472 Alte
Man Dir: Reynaldo Max Paul Bluhm; *Editorial, Production:* Sebastião Feital; *Sales:* Reynaldo Bluhm; *Publicity:* Gisela B Bluhm; *Rights & Permissions:* Paulo E Bluhm
Subsidiary Companies: DISAL (Distribuidores Associados de Livros Ltda); LTC (Livros Tecnicos e Cientificos Editora SA)
Subjects: Technical, Scientific, Children's books, Art, Language Textbooks, English Language Teaching, Schoolbooks
Bookshops: See under Major Booksellers; A Nossa Livraria de Brasília Ltda, CIS Quadra 104 — bloco C — lojas 18/19, 70342 Brasília DF; Livraria de Belo Horizonte Ltda, Rua Tupis 262, 30000 Belo Horizonte MG
1982: 156 titles *Founded:* 1946

Aquarius Editora e Distribuidora de Livros Ltda*, Rua Olavo Egidio 242, Santana, 02037 São Paulo SP Tel: 2902911/2994639
Man Dir: Alfredo Prata Ginja; *Sales:* Manuel Fonesca
Founded: 1976

Editora **Artenova** Ltda, Rua Prefeito Olimpio de Mello 1774, Benfica, 20000 Rio de Janeiro RJ Tel: 2649198/2340965 Cable Add: Artnova
Man Dir: Alvaro Pacheco; *Editorial, Rights & Permissions:* Luzia Regina Alves; *Sales, Publicity:* Luzia Regina Alves
Associate Companies: Artenova Filmes Ltda; Studio Artenova de Publicidade Ltda
Branch Off: Ave Augusto Pinto 122, Perdizes, São Paulo SP
Subjects: Literature, Sociology, Psychology, Occultism, Health, Cinema, History
Founded: 1971

Livraria Editora **Artes** Medicas Ltda, Rua Dr Cesario Motta Jr 63, Vila Buorque, 01221 São Paulo SP Tel: 2219033 Cable Add: Leam
Man Dir: Henrique Hecht; *Editorial, Rights & Permissions:* M Hecht; *Sales:* C dos Santos; *Production:* W Steinhoff; *Publicity:*

J Hecht
Subsidiary Companies: Editora Artes Medicas Sul Ltda, Rua General Vitorino 277, 90000 Pôrto Alegre; Livraria Artes Medicas Norte Ltda, Recifé
Subjects: Medicine, Dentistry
Founded: 1964

Livraria **Atheneu** Ltda, Rua Bambina 74 — lojas A/B, Botafogo, 22251 Rio de Janeiro RJ Tel: 2661295/2264793 Cable Add: Zigadag
Man Dir: Simão Rzezinski; *Editorial Dir, Rights & Permissions:* Paulo da Costa Rzezinski; *Sales Dir:* Carlos Silva; *Production Dir:* Eduardo Veiga
Branch Offs: Rua Senador Dantas 56B, Rio de Janeiro RJ; Rua Jesuino Pascoal 30, Santa Cecilia, São Paulo
Subjects: Medicine, Nursing, Psychology, Psychoanalysis, Psychiatry
Bookshops: 25 outlets
Founded: 1928

Editora **Atica** SA, CP 8656, 01507 São Paulo SP (Located at: Rua Barão de Iguape 110, Liberdade, São Paulo) Tel: 2789322 Cable Add: Bomlivro Telex: 32969 Edat
President: Anderson Fernandes Dias; *Marketing Dir:* Wander Soares
Branch Off: Rua Barão de Ubá 173, Estácio, 20260 Rio de Janeiro
Subjects: University, Secondary & Primary Textbooks, Pre-school Books, Children's Books, Brazilian and African Literature

Editora **Atlas** SA, CP 7186, São Paulo SP (Located at: Rua Helvétia 574-578, 01215 São Paulo) Tel: 2219144 Cable Add: Atlasedita
Man Dir: Luiz Herrmann; *Editorial, Rights & Permissions:* J P Rossetti; *Sales, Publicity:* A B Brandão; *Production:* P Gerencer
Branch Offs: Rio de Janeiro, Brazília, Amazonas, Ceará, Goiás, Paraná, Minas Gerais, Rio Grande do Sul, Santa Catarina
Subjects: Administration, Economics, Financial, Social Sciences
Founded: 1944

Atual Editora Ltda*, Rua José Antonio Coelho 785, V Mariana, 04011 São Paulo SP Tel: 717795/5491720
Man Dirs: Gelson Iezzi, Osvaldo Dolce; *Editorial:* Gelson Iezzi; *Sales:* Osvaldo Dolce; *Production:* Iorge Fuzii; *Publicity, Rights & Permissions:* José Roberto Brauner
Associate Companies: Livraria Capixaba Ltda, Rua Duque de Caxias 115, Vitoria ES; Cobra-Coord Bras Livro Ltda, Rua Rui Barbosa 465, Presidente Prudente SP; Livraria e Distribuidora Curitiba Ltda, Rua Voluntários da Pátria 205, Curitiba PR; Livraria Didática Ltda, Ave Laurício P Rasmussen 55, Goiania GO; Dontel Comercial Ltda, Rua 13 de Maio 2595, Campo Grande MS; Dontel Comercial Ltda, Ave Weimar G Torres 1973, Dourados MS; Fimac, Distribuidora de Livros Ltda, Ave Cipriano del Fávero 93, Uberlândia MG; Lunardelli Representações Ltda, Rua Vitor Meirelles 28, Florianópolis SC; J O Martins Alves, Rua Gal Glicério 325A, São José do Rio Preto SP; Editora e Distribuidora Pré Universitária Ltda, Trav José Gomes de Moura 67, Fortaleza CE; Reembolso Comercial Ltda, Rua Floriano Peixoto 4/29, Bauru SP; Papelaria Ritz Comércio e Industria Ltda, Corso 512 — bloco A 59, Brasília DF; Distribuidora de Livros Salvador Ltda, Trav da Ajuda 2 — salas 501-2, Salvador BA; Tecnolivro Com de Livros Ltda, Ave Saudade 584, Ribeirão Preto SP; Distribuidora União de Livros e Revistas Ltda, Rua Machado de Assis 222, Pôrto Alegre RS
Subject: Didactics

Bookshop: Atual Editora Ltda, Rua Barão de Mesquita 28, Rio de Janeiro RJ
Founded: 1973

Gráfica Editora **Aurora** Ltda*, CP 7041, 20211 Rio de Janeiro RJ (Located at: Rua Frei Caneca 19, Centro, Rio de Janeiro) Tel: 2220654
Man Dir: Francesco Molinaro; *Sales Dir:* Natale A Molinaro; *Publicity Dir:* Solange de Paula; *Advertising Dir:* Socrates de Paula
Subjects: Secondary & Primary Textbooks, Literature, Pedagogy, How-to, Law, Business, Masonic themes
Founded: 1945
ISBN Publisher's Prefix: 85-30

Editora **Beta** Ltda*, Estrada do Gabinal 1521, Jacarepaguá, Rio de Janeiro RJ Tel: 3421818
Man Dir: Jacob Horowicz
Subjects: Literature, Children's Books

Bloch Editores SA*, Rua do Russel 804, 22214 Rio de Janeiro RJ Tel: 2652012 Telex: 02121525
Publicity: Paulo Maia Poucinha, Expedito Jośe Chaves Grossi
Subject: Textbooks

Editora Edgard **Blücher** Ltda*, Rua Pedrosa Alvarenga 1245 — 2° andar — conj 22, 01000 São Paulo SP Tel: 648114/815613 Cable Add: Blucherlivro
Man Dir: Edgard Blücher
Subjects: Engineering, Science, Business, University Textbooks
Founded: 1966

Editora do **Brasil** SA*, CP 4986, 01203 São Paulo SP (Located at: Rua Conselheiro Nébias 887-889, Campos Elíseos, São Paulo) Tel: 2211663/2220211/2220818 Cable Add: Editabras
Branch Off: Rua do Resende 89, Centro, 20231 Rio de Janeiro RJ
Subjects: Education, Reference, Juveniles, History, Psychology, Sociology

Editora **Brasil-América** (EBAL) SA, Rua General Almério de Moura 302/320, São Cristóvão, 20921 Rio de Janeiro RJ Tel: 5800303 Cable Add: Ebalitada
Man Dir: Adolfo Aizen; *Editorial:* Naumin Aizen; *Production:* Fernando Albagli
Subject: Children's Books
Founded: 1945

Brasilia Editora Ltda*, Rua Cinco 15, Jardim da Penha, 29000 Vitória ES Tel: 2271962 Cable Add: Brasilivros
Subjects: Textbooks, Home Economics, Mathematics

Editora **Brasiliense** SA*, CP 30644, 01042 São Paulo SP (Located at: Rua General Jardim 160, 01223 São Paulo) Tel: 2311422 Cable Add: Edibrasa
Man Dir, Editorial, Rights & Permissions: C G Prado; *Sales:* C C Guerrato; *Production:* A Orzari
Subjects: Social Sciences, Humanities, Literature, Education, Juveniles
Bookshop: At above address
Founded: 1943

Editora **Bruguera** do Brasil Ltda, Rua Mato Grosso 456, Consolação, 01239 São Paulo SP
Parent Co: Editorial Bruguera SA, Spain (qv)

Livraria e Editora Juridica José **Bushatsky** Ltda, CP 2826, 01007 São Paulo SP (Located at: Riachuelo 195, São Paulo) Tel: 344148/344149 Cable Add: Bushatsky
Man Dir and Production: Anna Bushatsky
Subject: Law
Bookshop: At above address
Founded: 1953

C E P A — Centro Editor de Psicologia Aplicada Ltda*, CP 15131, 20031 Rio de Janeiro RJ (Located at: Rua Senador Dantas 118 — 9° andar, Centro, Rio de Janeiro) Tel: 2205545/2207195 Cable Add: Edicepa
Man Dir: Antonio Rodrigues
Subject: Psychology Textbooks and Tests
1981: 6 titles *Founded:* 1952

Editora **Campus** Ltda, Rua Japeri 35, Rio Comprido, 20261 Rio de Janeiro RJ Tel: 2848443
Man Dir, Editorial: Claudio M Rothmuller; *Sales, Publicity Dir:* Juarez Nery; *Production Dir:* Carlos Hamilton Rocha; *Rights & Permissions:* Emilia Fernandez
Parent Company: Elsevier-NDU nv, Netherlands (qv)
Subject: Textbooks (all fields, except Law and Medicine, particularly Computers and Electronics)
1982: 85 titles *1983:* 125 titles *Founded:* 1976

Livraria Editora **Cátedra** Ltda*, Rua Senador Dantas 20 — salas 806-7, Centro, 20031 Rio de Janeiro RJ Tel: 2227593
Subjects: Cookery, History, Children's Books, Reference Books, Sociology

Cedibra Editora Brasileira Ltda, Rua Leonidia 2, Olaria, 20000 Rio de Janeiro RJ Tel: 2807272 Cable Add: Edibras
Man Dir: Jan Rais; *Editorial:* Paulo Schvinger
Parent Company: BPCC PLC, UK (qv)
Subjects: Juveniles, Fiction, Paperbacks
Founded: 1952

Centro Editor de Psicologia Aplicada Ltda, see CEPA

Centro Editorial Latino Americano Ltda*, CP 45329, 04012 São Paulo SP (Located at: Rua Amâncio de Carvalho 82, V Mariana, São Paulo) Tel: 5442917
Man Dir: Ignácio de Loyola Gomes Bueno; *Editorial, Production, Publicity and Rights & Permissions:* José Carlos Rolo Venâncio; *Sales:* Luis Alves Jnr
Orders to: Rua Franca Pinto 836, 040016 São Paulo SP
Parent Company: Global Editora e Distribuidora Ltda (qv)
Associate Companies: Edart São Paulo Livreria Editora Ltda (qv); Editora Ground Ltda (qv)
Branch Off: Global Nordeste Representacões, Ave Dantas Barreto 564 — 11° andar — salas 1104-5, Recife PE
Subjects: History, Politics, Health
Bookshop: Livraria Ground, Rua Siqueira Campos 143 — sobreloja 56, São Paulo
Founded: 1979

Cidade Nova Editora*, Rua Cel Paulinos Carlos 29, 04006 São Paulo SP Tel: 2892608
Man Dir: Celso Frioli; *Editorial:* João Manoel Motta; *Publicity:* Joaci J de Oliveira
Parent Company: Città Nuova Editrice, Italy (qv for associate companies)
Branch Offices: Rua Mal Deodoro 311, Encruzilhada, Recife PE; Trav Sta Lucia 4, S Braz, 66000 Belém PA; Rua Sta Terezinha 395/31, 90000 Pôrto Alegre RS
Subjects: Religion, Family, Juveniles
Founded: 1960

Editora **Civilização** Brasileira SA*, Rua Muniz Barreto 715-721, 22251 Rio de Janeiro RJ Tel: 2860797 Cable Add: Civilização Rio
Man Dir: Enio Silveira; *Administrative Dir:* Joaquim Ignacio Baptista Cardoso; *Editorial Dir:* Enio Silveira
Branch Offs: Rua das Palmeiras 260-262,

São Paulo; Quadra 309, lojas 3 e 4, 70000 Brasília DF
Subjects: General Fiction, Belles Lettres, Poetry, Social Science
Founded: 1932

Editora **Codecri** Ltda*, Rua Saint Roman 142, Copacabana, 22071 Rio de Janeiro RJ Tel: 2875799
Man Dir: Sergio de Magalhães Gomes Jacuarire; *Editorial:* Alfredo Gonçalves Manso Filho; *Production:* Glauco Alexandre de Oliveira; *Publicity:* Douné Spínola
Subsidiary Company: Jornal Pasquim (at above address)
Subjects: Belles Lettres, Fiction, Dictionaries
Bookshop: Livraria do Pasquim, Ave Ataulfo de Paiva — loja 108, Leblon
Founded: 1976

Concordia Editora Ltda+, CP 3230, 90000 Pôrto Alegre RS (Located at: Ave São Pedro 639, Pôrto Alegre) Tel: 422859/429628 Cable Add: Concordia
Man Dir: Johanes Gedradt; *Sales, Publicity:* Luiz Ricardo Böttcher
Parent Company: Igreja Evangèlica Luterana do Brasil
Subjects: Religion, Music
1981: 45 titles *1982:* 53 titles *Founded:* 1923
Miscellaneous: Company previously known as Concordia SA-Artes Gráficas e Embalagens

Confraria dos Amigos do Livro Ltda+, Rua Maria Angélica 168, Lagoa, 22461 Rio de Janeiro RJ Tel: 2867822 Cable Add: Neofront Telex: 2122319 Enof Br
Man Dir, Sales & Publicity: Elson Mancen; *Editorial:* Sebastião Lacerda
Parent Company: Editora Nova Fronteira SA (qv)
Subject: Art books in special editions
Founded: 1976

Conquista, Empresa de Publicações Ltda, Ave 28 de Setembro 174, Vila Isabel, 20551 Rio de Janeiro RJ Tel: 2285709/2286752
Man Dir: Nilde Hersen da Costa
Subjects: Children's Books, Textbooks
1982: 80 titles *Founded:* 1951

Editora e Gráfica Miguel **Couto** SA, Rua Capitão Carlos 68, Bonsucesso, 21040 Rio de Janeiro RJ Tel: 2807699
Man Dir: Paulo Kobler Pinto Lopes Sampaio; *Editorial:* Octacilio Ribeiro Lessa; *Sales:* José Geraldo Verginelli; *Production:* Victor Mauricio Notrica; *Publicity:* Alcides Lourenco Gomes; *Rights & Permissions:* Antenor Romanholo
Associate Companies: Curso Miguel Couto SA, Somatório Administração SA, Curso MCB
Subject: Textbooks
Founded: 1969

Editora **Cultrix**+, Rua Mario Vicente 360, Ipiranga, 04270 São Paulo SP Tel: 2784811
Man Dir: Diaulas Riedel
Associate Company: Editora Pensamento (qv)
Subjects: General Literature, Social & General Science, Economics, Education, Philosophy, History, Children's Books, Psychology, Sociology
Founded: 1956

Editora **Cultura Médica** Ltda*, CP 24052, 20550 Rio de Janeiroiro RJ (Located at: Rua São Francisco Xavier 111, Rio de Janeiro) Tel: 2349798/2484888
Man Dir, Editorial, Rights & Permissions: Ezequiel Feldman; *Sales, Publicity Dir:* Ivo Feldman; *Production:* João Emanuel Paes de Andrade
Orders to: Ave Heitor Beltão 61, Apto 801, Rio de Janeiro
Subject: Medicine
Founded: 1966

D I F E L, see Difusão Editorial SA

Difusão Editorial SA (DIFEL), Ave Vieira de Carvalho 40 — 5° andar, 01210 São Paulo SP Tel: 2236923/2234619 Telex: 32294 Dfel Br
Man Dir: Fernando Baptista da Silva; *Sales Dir:* Lédio D Pinto; *Rights & Permissions:* Elvia Orlandini
Subjects: Sociology, History, Geography, General Fiction, Physical Fitness, Arts, Economics, Philosophy, Psychology, Religion
1982: 21 titles *Founded:* 1951

Livraria **Duas Cidades** Ltda*, CP 433, 01220 São Paulo SP (Located at: Rua Bento Freitas 158, Vila Buarque, São Paulo) Tel: 375257
Man Dir: José Petronillo de Santa Cruz; *Sales Dir:* Mitsuro Nagata; *Publicity Dir:* Mara Valles
Branch Off: Ave Rio Branco 9, Sala 116, Centro, 20090 Rio de Janeiro RJ
Subjects: Literature, Philosophy, Religion, Psychology, Social Science, University Textbooks
Bookshop: See under Major Booksellers
Founded: 1956

E B A L, see Editora Brasil-América (EBAL) SA

E P U, see Editora Pedagogica e Universitaria Ltda

E T A (Editora Técnica de Aviação Ltda)*, Rua Real Grandeza 193 — lojas 15-16, Botafogo, 22281 Rio de Janeiro RJ Tel: 2468633
Man Dir: João Dutra de Medeiros
Subject: Aviation
Founded: 1969

Ebraesp Editorial Ltda*, Rua Marechal Floriano Peixoto 16 — sobreloja 207, Santos, 11100 São Paulo Tel: 2884904/2848164 Cable Add: Ebraesp
Man Dir, Editorial: Fernando Santos Burguete; *Production:* Antonio Baeza; *Publicity:* Heliodoro Teixeira Bastos; *Rights & Permissions:* Yolanda Lhullier Santos
Subjects: Philosophy, Anthropology, Communications
Founded: 1971

Edameris, see Editora Das Americas SA Edameris

Edart São Paulo Livraria Editora Ltda*, CP 4108, 01224 São Paulo SP (Located at: Rua França Pinto 840, Vilamaliana, 04011 São Paulo) Tel: 5442418
Man Dirs: José Carlos Rolo Venâncio, Luis Alves Jnr; *Dir of Editions:* José Carlos Rolo Venâncio; *Sales Dir:* Luis Alves Jnr; *Publicity Dir:* Inácio Bueno
Associate Company: Global Editora e Distribuidora Ltda (qv)
Subjects: Medicine, Science, Technology, Psychology, History, Law, Mathematics, How-to, Primary, Secondary & University Textbooks
Founded: 1964

Editora Interamericana Ltda, Rua Coronel Cabrita 8, São Cristovão, 20920 Rio de Janeiro RJ Tel: 5800033 Cable Add: Edinter Telex: 2123036
Man Dir: T H Hughes; *Editorial, Sales and Publicity:* G M Sousa; *Production:* J Belmonte
Associate Company: CBS International Publishing (CIP), USA
Subjects: Medicine and Related Sciences, Psychology, Business, Chemistry, Physical Education, Biology
1981: 51 titles *Founded:* 1972

Editora Moderna Ltda+, CP 45364, 04511 São Paulo SP (Located at: Rua Afonso Brás 431, 04511 São Paulo) Tel: 5315099
Man Dir: Prof Ricardo Feltre
Branch Off: Rua Sen Furtado 31, 20270 Rio de Janeiro RJ
Subjects: Textbooks, Social Science, Literature
Founded: 1968

Cía **Editora Nacional***, CP 5312, 03016 São Paulo SP (Located at: Rua Joli 294, Brás, São Paulo) Tel: (291) 2355 Cable Add: Editora
Man Dir, Rights & Permissions: Jorge Antonio Miguel Yunls; *Editorial:* Paulo Marti
Branch Offs: Edifício Venãncio VI — DS bloco 0 — lojas 13 e 17, Brasília Tel: (224) 3472; Ave Lôbo Júnior 1011, Bairro Penha, Rio de Janeiro Tel: (270) 0547
Also: Bauru, Belém, Belo Horizonte, Campo Grande, Caruaru, Cuiabá, Curitiba, Fortaleza, Goiânia, Manaus, Natal, Pôrto Alegre, Recife, Ribeirão Preto, Salvador, São José do Rio Preto, São Luis, Teresina
Subjects: Pedagogy, History, Philosophy, Psychology, Technical, General & Social Science, Textbooks, Business, Fiction
Founded: 1925

Editora Pedagogica e Universitaria Ltda (EPU), CP 7509, 01047 São Paulo SP (Located at: Praça Dom José Gaspar 106 — 3° andar — sobrelcja 15, São Paulo)
Man Dir: Wolfgang Knapp; *Production:* Paulo Hiss
Subjects: Scientific, Technical, Didactics
1981: 53 titles *1982:* 35 titles *Founded:* 1952

Seleções **Eletrônicas Editora** Ltda, CP 771, 20001 Rio de Janeiro RJ (Located at: R Costa Ferreira 128, 20221 Rio de Janeiro) Tel: (021) 2832685
Man Dir: Maria B A Penna; *Editorial:* José F Kempner; *Publicity:* Helio N Santos
Associate Company: Antenna Edições Técnicas Ltda (qv)
Subjects: Electronics, Radio and TV Technology, Electricity
1981: 7 titles *1982:* 11 titles *Founded:* 1960
ISBN Publisher's Prefix: 85-7037

Editora **Espiritualista***, CP 7041, 20211 Rio de Janeiro RJ (Located at: Rua Frei Caneca 19, Centro, Rio de Janeiro) Tel: 2220654
Man Dir: Francesco Molinaro; *Sales Dir:* Natale A Molinaro; *Publicity & Advertising Dir:* Socrates de Paula
Subjects: Philosophy, Religion
Founded: 1945
ISBN Publisher's Prefix: 85-94

Exped-Expansaõ Editorial Ltda, Ave President Wilson 165 — sala 1/111, Castelo, Rio de Janeiro RJ Tel: 2406426/2406592 Telex: (021) 23186
Dir & Editor: Ferdinando Bastos de Souza; *Publisher:* Gilberto Huber; *Editorial Manager:* Ricardo Augusto Pamplona Vaz
Subjects: General Literature, Didactics, Reference Books
Founded: 1968

F E N A M E — Fundação Nacional de Material Escolar*, Rua Miguel Angelo 96, Maria da Graça, Rio de Janeiro RJ Tel: 2617750/2614140
Man Dir: Milton Durço Pereira; *Editorial Dir:* Tania Jatobá de Matos Menezes; *Sales Dir:* Murilo Alves Nunes; *Production Dir:* Antonio José de Britto; *Publicity Dir:* Ivan Estelita Campos; *Rights & Permissions:* José Ribeiro de Castro Neto
Subject: Textbooks
Bookshops: About 250 outlets throughout Brazil
Founded: 1967

Editora **F T D** SA*, CP 30402, 01519 São Paulo SP (Located at: Rua do Lavapés 1023, Cambuci, São Paulo) Tel: 2788264
President: João Tissi; *Man Dir:* Paulo Alves Ferraz
Branch Offs: Rua Agenor Meira 4/67, Bauru, São Paulo; Rua Lavras 235, Carmo Sion, Belo Horizonte MG; Rua Mal Deodoro 887, Curitiba PR; Ave Goiás 1146, Goiânia GO; Ave Rio Branco 185, Londrina PR; Ave Tiradentes 963, Maringa; Ave Joana Angélica 963, Salvador BA; Rua Prof Baltazar 12, Vitória ES; Rua André Cavalcanti 78, Rio de Janeiro GB; Rua Martins Junior 39, Recife PE; Ave do Imperador 1203, Fortaleza CE (all in Brazil)
Subject: Textbooks
Founded: 1897

Editora **Forense**—Universitaria Ltda*, CP 2284, 20020 Rio de Janeiro RJ (Located at: Ave Erasmo Braga 227 — 3° andar — grupo 309, Rio de Janeiro) Tel: 2526244/2225106-7

Editora e Encadernadora **Formar** Ltda*, CP 13250, 03168 São Paulo SP (Located at: Rua dos Trilhos 1126, Mooca, São Paulo) Tel: 935133 Cable Add: Formar
Subjects: Education, Scientific & Technical, Cookery, History, Geography, Children's Books, Reference Books

Livraria **Freitas** Bastos SA, Rua 7 de Setembro 127-129, 20050 Rio de Janeiro RJ Tel: 2220250/2228858/2228973 Cable Add: Etiel
Branch Off: Rua 15 de Novembro 62-66, São Paulo SP
Subject: Law
Bookshop: See under Major Booksellers

Fundação Instituto Brasileiro de Geografia e Estatística, Ave Brasil, 15671 Rio de Janeiro RJ Tel: 3917788/2808535/2806045
Dir: Aluísio Brandão de Albuquerque Mello
Subjects: Statistics, Geography, Maps
Founded: 1936

Fundação Nacional de Material Escolar, see FENAME

Editora Gustavo **Gili** do Brasil SA*, Rua Araripe Júnior 45, Andaraí, 20540 Rio de Janeiro RJ Tel: 2880881 Cable Add: Gustobras
Parent Company: Editorial Gustavo Gili SA, Spain (qv)
Subjects: Architecture, Engineering

Global Editora e Distribuidora Ltda, CP 45329, 04011 São Paulo SP (Located at: Rua França Pinto 836, São Paulo) Tel: 5493137/5442917/5499640
Man Dir, Sales: Luis Alves Jnr; *Editorial, Production, Publicity, Rights & Permissions:* José Carlos Rolo Venancio
Subsidiary Company: Centro Editorial Latino Americano Ltda (qv)
Associate Companies: Edart São Paulo Livraria Editora Ltda (qv); Editora Ground Ltda (qv)
Imprint: Parma
Subjects: Linguistics, Romance, Humour, UFOs, Politics, Economics, Poetry, History, Theatre, Health, Children
1982: 146 titles *Founded:* 1973

Editora **Globo** SA, CP 1520, 90000 Pôrto Alegre RS (Located at: Ave Getúlio Vargas 1271, Pôrto Alegre) Tel: 331300 Cable Add: Dicionario
Editorial Dir, Rights & Permissions: José O Bertaso; *Sales Dir:* Antonio C Leite
Parent Company: Livraria do Globo SA (qv under Major Booksellers)
Subsidiary Company: Instituto Áudio-Visual e de Idiomas SA
Branch Off: Rua Sargento Silvio Hollenbach 350, 21510 Rio de Janeiro RJ

Subjects: Education, Engineering, Dictionaries, Literature
1983: 32 titles *Founded:* 1954

Edições **Graal** Ltda, Rua Hermenegildo de Barros 31A, Glória, 20241 Rio de Janeiro RJ Tel: 2528582
Man, Editorial & Publicity Dir, and Rights & Permissions: Paul Joseph Christoph Jnr; *Sales Dir:* Jaime Fenneira da Silva; *Production Dir:* Orlando Fennandes
Subjects: Social Sciences, Philosophy, Psychology, Social Medicine, Economics, History, Sociology
1981: 24 titles *1982:* 25 titles *Founded:* 1977

Ordem do **Graal** na Terra, CP 128, Embu, 06800 São Paulo SP (Located at: Ave 7 de Setembro 29200, Embu, São Paulo)
Man Dir: Harry von Sass
Subjects: Religion, Philosophy, History
Founded: 1947

Editorial **Grijalbo** Ltda*, Rua 7 de Abril 264 — loja B-2, 01044 São Paulo SP Tel: 369544
Man Dir: José Monfort
Parent Company: Editorial Grijalbo SA, Spain (qv)
Subjects: Law, Technical
Founded: 1958

Editora **Ground** Ltda, Rua França Pinto 844, São Paulo SP Tel: 5499640
Man Dir: Armandina Venâncio
Associate Company: Global Editora e Distribuidora Ltda (qv)
Subjects: Natural Foods and Medicines, Alternative Living, Acupuncture, Ecology, Oriental Philosophy
Bookshop: At above address
Founded: 1973

Editora **Guanabara** Koogan SA, Travessa do Ouvidor 11, 20040 Rio de Janeiro RJ Tel: 2245877 Cable Add: Edigua
Man Dir: Joao Pedro Lorch; *Editorial:* R Berardinelli Filho; *Sales:* C A Barifouse; *Production:* M P Costa; *Rights & Permissions:* Christina Norén
Subjects: Medicine, Dentistry, Life Sciences
Bookshop: Livraria Triangulo SA (qv under Major Booksellers)

Livraria Pioneira Editora/Enio Matheus **Guazzelli** e Cia Ltd*, Praça Dirceu de Lima 313, Casa Verde, 02515 São Paulo SP Tel: 2660926/2666507
Dir: Enio M Guazzelli; *Marketing:* Renato Guazzelli; *Rights & Permissions:* Ricardo Guazzelli
Orders to: DISAL, Distribuidores Associados de Livros Ltda, Rua Vitória 302/304, São Paulo
Subjects: Social Sciences, Business and Management, Linguistics, Brazilian Studies, Architecture and Urbanism; General Subjects, Children's Books
Bookshop: At above address
1981: 25 titles *Founded:* 1960

H U C I T E C Ltda — Editora de Humanismo, Ciência e Tecnologia*, Rua Simão Alvares 687, Pinheiros, São Paulo SP Tel: (011) 8138219
Man Dirs: Adalgisa Pereira da Silva, Flávio George Aderaldo; *Editorial, Sales, Production, Publicity and Rights & Permissions:* Flávio George Aderaldo
Subjects: Textbooks, Education
Founded: 1971

Harbra, an imprint of Editora Harper & Row do Brasil Ltda (qv)

Editora **Harper & Row** do Brasil Ltda+, CP 45312, 01000 Vila Mariana, São Paulo SP Tel: 5703572/5704891 Cable Add: Habra Sao Telex: (11) 25631 Ehrb
Man Dir, Editorial, Rights & Permissions:

Julio E Emöd; *Sales:* Jose A Burgos; *Production:* Maria Pia Castiglia
Parent Company: Harper & Row Inc, New York, NY 10022, USA
Associate Companies: Basic Books Inc, New York, USA; T Y Crowell, New York, USA; J B Lippincott, Philadelphia, USA; Harper & Row (Australasia) Pty Ltd, Australia (qv); Harper & Row Ltd, UK (qv); Harper & Row Latinoamericana-Harla SA de CV, Mexico (qv)
Imprint: Harbra
Subjects: University and High School Text Books in Science, Mathematics, Engineering, Social Science, Business, Medicine, General Interest Books
1982: 63 titles *1983:* 71 titles *Founded:* 1976

Hemus Editora Ltda*, CP 9686, 01510 São Paulo SP (Located at: Rua da Glória 312, São Paulo) Tel: 2799911 Cable Add: Hetec Telex: 32005 Edil
President: Eli Behar; *Man Dir:* Maxim Behar
Subjects: Technical & Engineering, Textbooks, Juveniles, Philosophy, Science Fiction, General Literature
1981: 57 titles *Founded:* 1965

Editora de **Humanismo**, Ciência e Tecnologia, see HUCITEC Ltda

I B A M, see Instituto Brasileiro de Administraçao Municipal

I B E P, see Instituto Brasileiro de Edições Pedagógicas

I B I C T, see Instituto Brasileiro de Informação em Ciência e Tecnologia

I B R A S A (Instituçāo Brasileira de Difusão Cultural SA), CP 30927, 03047 São Paulo SP (Located at: Rua 21 de Abril 97, Brás, São Paulo) Tel: 939524
Man Dir: Jorge Leite
Orders to: IBREX Ltda, Rua 21 de Abril 101, CP 30927, São Paulo
Subjects: IBRASA Encyclopaedia, General Medical, Health & Sexuality, Parapsychology, Social Sciences, Psychology & Education, Philosophy, Politics, Economics, History, Exploration & Discovery, Modern Literature & Science
Founded: 1958

I P E A (Instituto de Planejamento Econômico e Social) Servicio Editorial*, CP 2672, Rio de Janeiro RJ (Located at: Ave President Antonio Carlos 51 — 13° andar, Centro, Rio de Janeiro) Tel: 2428098 Cable Add: Planipea Telex: 963
Man Dir, Editorial, Production: A F Vilar de Queiro; *Sales, Publicity:* Gilberto V de Carvalho
Subject: Economics
Founded: 1971

Livro **Ibero-Americano** Ltda, CP 816, 20241 Rio de Janeiro RJ (Located at: Rua Hermenegildo de Barros 40, Rio de Janeiro) Tel: 2325248/2528814/2329048 Cable Add: Nebrija
Man Dir: Ramón Martín González
Branch Offs: Rua Conselheiro Crispiniano 29, 1° pav, São Paulo SP
Bookshop: See under Major Booksellers
Subjects: History, Philosophy, Reference, Religion, Medicine, Psychology, Textbooks (all levels), Photography
Founded: 1946

Instituição Brasileira de Difusão Cultural SA, see IBRASA

Instituto Brasileiro de Administraçao Municipal (IBAM), Largo IBAM 1, 22282 Rio de Janeiro RJ Tel: 2666622 Cable Add: Ibambras
Superintendent-General: Diogo Lordello de Mello; *Editor:* Lilian Mary Gabriel Lopes da

Silva
Subjects: Law, Municipal Administration, Planning, O & M, Systems Analysis, Public Finance, Periodicals
Bookshop: At above address
Founded: 1952

Instituto Brasileiro de Edições Pedagógicas (IBEP)*, CP 5312, 03016 São Paulo SP (Located at: Rua Joli 294, Brás, São Paulo) Tel: 2912355
Branch Off: Ave Lóbo Júnior 1011, Penha, 21020 Rio de Janeiro RJ
Subjects: Textbooks, Reference Books

Fundação **Instituto Brasileiro de Geografia** e Estatística, see under Fundação

Instituto Brasileiro de Informação em Ciência e Tecnologia (IBICT), SCRN 708-709 — bloco 2 — lotes 2/10, 70740 Brasília DF
Brazilian Institute for Information in Science and Technology
Dir: Yone Sepulveda Chastinet
Subjects: Social, Natural and General Sciences, Technology, Bibliographies, Periodical *Ciencia da Informação*

Instituto Campineiro de Ensino Agrícola, CP 1148, 13100 Campinas SP (Located at: Rua Antonio Lapa 78, Campinas) Tel: (0192) 519499 Cable Add: Icampi
Man Dir: Gervásio Souza Cavalcanti; *Sales Dir:* Esmeralda B Cavalcanti
Subject: Agriculture
Founded: 1955

Instituto de Planejamento Econômico e Social, see IPEA Servicio Editorial

Livraria **Interciencia** Ltda, CP 1825, 20071 Rio de Janeiro RJ (Located at: Ave Pres Vargas 435 — 5° andar — sala 504, Centro, Rio de Janeiro) Tel: 2216850/2210993
Man Dir: Edson do Nascimento Pereira; *Rights & Permissions:* Joel José Gomes
Subject: Science in general
Bookshop: At above address
Founded: 1969 (1975 as publisher)

Junta de Educação Religiosa e Publicações da Convenção Batista Brasileira (JUERP), CP 320, 20001 Rio de Janeiro RJ Tel: 2690772 Cable Add: Batistas
General-Superintendent: Prof Joaquim de Paula Rosa; *Editorial and Rights & Permissions:* Prof Josemar de Souza Pinto; *Marketing:* Prof Napolião José Vieira; *Production:* Elias Borges de Athayde
Subject: Religion
Bookshops: Rua do Rosário 141 — s/loja 201, Centro, 20041 Rio de Janeiro RJ; Rua Mariz e Barros 39 — loja B, Praça da Bandeira, 20270 Rio de Janeiro RJ; Ave Nilo Pessanha 411, 25000 Duque de Caxias RJ; Rua Otávio Tarquínio 178, 26000 Nova Iguaçu RJ; Rua XV de Novembro 49, 24020 Niterói RJ; Ave Visconde de São Lourenço 6, 40000 Salvador BA; Ave São João 816-820, 01036 São Paulo SP; SDS B1 G - loja 17 - conj Baracat, 70302 Brasília DF; Rua Barão de Itapemirim 208, 29000 Vitória ES; Trav Padre Prudêncio 61 — loja 3, 66000 Belém PA; Rua do Hospício 187 – 1° andar, 50000 Recife PE; Rua Bahia 360, 30000 Belo Horizonte MG; Rua Cel Vicente 614, 90000 Pôrto Alegre RS
1981: 54 titles *1982:* 44 titles *Founded:* 1907

Livraria **Kosmos** Editora, CP 3481, 20041 Rio de Janeiro RJ (Located at: Rua do Rosario 137, Centro, Rio de Janeiro) Tel: 2529534/2529552
Man Dirs: Walter and Stefan Geyerhahn, Luiz C Poppi
Subjects: Engineering, History, Linguistics, Music, Reference Books, Tourism
Bookshop: See under Major Booksellers
Founded: 1935

L I S A (Livros Irradiantes SA)*, Rua Castro Alves 139, Aclimação, São Paulo Tel: 2788900/2797011/2797169 Cable Add: Lisalivros
Man Dir: Leonídio Balbino da Silva; *Sales Dir:* Francisco de Paula Oliveira Filho
Branch Off: Ave Presidente Vargas 446, Sala 1802, Centro, 20071 Rio de Janeiro RJ
Subjects: Textbooks, Reference, Education
Founded: 1965

L I T E C, see Livraria Editora Tecnica Ltda

L T C-Livros Técnicos e Científicos Editora SA, Ave Venezuela 163, 20220 Rio de Janeiro RJ Tel: 2831747 Cable Add: Litece
Superintendent: Propício Machado Alves; *Editorial:* P M Alves; *Production:* Antonio Carlos de Oliveira; *Sales and Rights & Permissions:* Severino Félix da Silva; *Publicity, Promotion:* Sergio Martins de Oliveira
Associate Company: John Wiley & Sons Inc Publishers, 605 Third Avenue, New York, NY 10158, USA
Branch Off: Rua Vitória 486 — sala 204, 01210 São Paulo
Subjects: Scientific and Technical
1981: 36 titles *Founded:* 1968
ISBN Publisher's Prefix: 85-216

L T r Editora Ltda*, Rua Jaguaribe 571-585, Vila Buarque, 01224 São Paulo SP Tel: 660458
Man Dir: Armando C Costa; *Sales:* Armando C Costa Jr; *Production:* Arnaldo C Costa
Branch Off: Rua Anfilófio de Carvalho 29, Salas 607/8, Castelo, 20030 Rio de Janeiro RJ
Subject: Law
Founded: 1937

Editorial **Labor** do Brasil SA*, CP 1519, Rio de Janeiro RJ (Located at: Rua do Senado 267 — sobrado, Rio de Janeiro) Tel: 2326698/2529323 Cable Add: Edilabor
Dirs: Paulo F de Carvalho, Osmar Nestor Gomes
Branch Offs: Mal Floriano 13 — 7 andar - conj 71/73, Pôrto Alegre; Rua Aurora 858 — 2 conj 23, São Paulo
Subjects: Art, Medicine, Science, Engineering, Technology

Editora **Laudes** SA*, Ave Almirante Barroso 90 — 3° andar, Castelo, 20031 Rio de Janeiro RJ Tel: 2682796/2689981
Subjects: Textbooks, Brazilian Literature

Lex Editora SA, CP 12888, 04106 São Paulo SP (Located at: Rua Machado de Assis 57, São Paulo) Tel: 5490122
Man Dir: Affonso Vitale Sobrinho; *Editorial:* Dra Dulce Eugênia de Oliveira; *Sales:* Oswaldo Messina Jnr
Branch Off: Rua Ubaldino do Amaral 40 — loja C, 20231 Rio de Janeiro
Subjects: Law, Jurisprudence
1981: 11 titles *1982:* 11 titles *Founded:* 1937

Editora **Liber Juris** Ltda, Rua da Assembléia 36 — 2° andar, Rio de Janeiro RJ Tel: (021) 2228742/2216664/2216954
Man Dir, Editorial, Production: Djalma de Magalhães; *Sales, Publicity:* André Luis Braga de Oliveira; *Rights & Permissions:* Djalma de Magalhães, Joao Manuel de Almeida
Parent Company: Livraria Cultural da Guanabara Ltda, Rua da Assembléia 38 — loja, Rio de Janeiro
Subject: Law
Bookshop: Livraria Cultural da Guanabara Ltda, Rua da Assembléia 38 — loja, Rio de Janeiro
1981: 23 titles *1982:* 17 titles *Founded:* 1972

Editora **Lidador** Ltda, Rua Paulino Fernándes 58, Botafogo, 20000 Rio de Janeiro RJ Tel: 2667179/2664105/2867593
Publicity Manager: Ruy Carvalho
Subjects: Economics, Music, Occultism, Sociology, Dramatic Art

Waldyr **Lima** Editora, Rua Dr Bulhões 947, 20730 Rio de Janeiro RJ Tel: (021) 2691332/2893995
Director-General, Rights & Permissions: Waldyr Lima; *Editorial (Research & Planning Dir):* Lilian Moreira Neves; *Sales, Production, Publicity Dir:* Richard Noel Taylor
Subjects: Didactics, English as a foreign language, Portuguese
1982: 77 titles *1983:* 82 titles *Founded:* 1967

Editora Max **Limonad** Ltda+, Rua Quintino Bocaiuva 191 — 4° andar — sala 41, 01004 São Paulo SP Tel: 357393
Man Dir, Editorial: Sara Limonad; *Commercial Dir:* Moisés Limonad
Subjects: Law, Literature
Founded: 1944

Livraria Editora Técnica Ltda (LITEC)*, CP 30869, São Paulo SP (Located at: Rua dos Timbiras 257, São Paulo) Tel: (011) 2208983
Man Dir: Adalbert Walter Miehe; *Sales Dir:* José Lopes
Subjects: Electronics, Technical
Bookshop: LITEC (qv under Major Booksellers)
Founded: 1971

Livros Irradiantes SA, see LISA

Editora **Logosófica**, Rua Coronel Oscar Porto 818, 04003 São Paulo SP Tel: 701476/706574
Man Dir, Editorial: José Antonio Antonini; *Sales:* José Maria Martins da Cunha; *Production:* Alvaro Puga Paz
Orders to: Rua Luiz Machado Pedrosa 96, 01431 São Paulo SP
Subject: Logosophy
Bookshops: SHCG — Norte, Area de Escolas Q704, 70000 Brasília DF; Rua Piauí 742, 30000 Belo Horizonte MG; Rua Barão de Rio Branco 63 — sala 1902, 80000 Curitiba PR; Rua Nunes Machado 14 — sala 25, 88000 Florianópolis SC; Rua 17A, 959 Setor Aeroporto, 74000 Goiânia GO; Rua General Polidoro 36, 22280 Rio de Janeiro RJ; Rua Capitão Domingos 72, 38100 Uberaba MG; and others in Argentina, Mexico, Paraguay and Uruguay
Founded: 1964

Edições **Loyola** SA*, CP 42335, 04216 São Paulo SP (Located at: Rua 1822 No 347, Ipiranga, São Paulo) Tel: 639695/2746028
Subjects: Law, Education, Literature, Cinema, Economics, Philosophy, Psychology, Religion, Textbooks

Edições '**Lumen Christi**', CP 2666, 20001 Rio de Janeiro RJ (Located at: Rua Dom Gerardo 40, Rio de Janeiro) Tel: 2917122 Cable Add: Mosteiro Sanbento
Man Dir, Production, Publicity: D Hildebrando P Martins OSB; *Sales:* Nicolau Mueller OSB
Subjects: Liturgy, Theology, Spiritualism, Art
Bookshop: At above address
Founded: 1935

Editora **McGraw-Hill** do Brasil Ltda, CP 20689, Itaim Bibi, 04533 São Paulo SP (Located at: Rua Tabapuá 1105, Itaim Bibi)
Man Dir: João Rodrigues Martins
Parent Company: McGraw-Hill Inc, 1221 Ave of the Americas, New York, NY 10020, USA
Associate Company: McGraw-Hill Book Co (UK) Ltd (qv for other associates)

Branch Offs: Rio de Janeiro, Belo Horizonte, Recife, Pôrto Alegre, Fortaleza, Curitiba
Subjects: Science & Technology
Founded: 1970

Editora **Mandarino** Ltda+, CP 11000, Rio de Janeiro RJ (Located at: Rua Marquês de Pombal 172, Rio de Janeiro) Tel: 2215016
Man Dir: Ernesto Emanuele Mandarino; *Editorial:* Elisa Maria Bruno, Mauricio Peixoto Mandarino; *Sales:* José Gabrielesco; *Production:* Ivan Giovanni Malgeri; *Publicity:* Niltom Mendes Mendonca
Associate Company: Publieco Promoçoes Ltda, Rua Marquês de Pombal 171, CP 11030, Rio de Janeiro
Subjects: Spiritualism, Magic, Afro-Brazilian Cults, Freemasonry
Founded: 1970

Editora **Manole** Ltda, CP 1489, 01327 São Paulo SP (Located at: Rua 13 de Maio 1026, São Paulo) Tel: 2870746
Man Dir, Editorial, Production, Rights & Permissions: Dinu Octau Manole; *Sales:* Glória Yasuda; *Publicity:* Ilma Manole
Subjects: Physiotherapy, Medicine, Psychology
Founded: 1969

Mapa Fiscal Editora Ltda*, CP 30027, 01540 São Paulo SP (Located at: Rua Miguel Telles Jr 394, Cambucí, São Paulo) Tel: 2784011 Cable Add: Mapa Fiscal Telex: 1130323 Mfel Br
Man Dir: Jayro Gonçalves; *Editorial, Sales, Production, Publicity Dir:* Roberto Mateus Ordine
Branch Off: Rua do Russel 680 terreo, Praia do Russel, Rio de Janeiro
Subject: Tax laws
Bookshop: Rua Barão de Paranapiacaba 93 6° of 63, Rio de Janeiro
Founded: 1952

Livraria **Martins** Editora SA*, Rua Rocha 274, Bela Vista, 01330 São Paulo SP Tel: 2880667
Branch Off: Rua Evaristo da Veiga 47, Rio de Janeiro GB
Subjects: Literature, Juveniles, Art, Social Sciences, Law, Economics, Geography, History

Editora **Masson** do Brasil Ltda*, Rua da Quitanda 20 — sala 301, 20011 Rio de Janeiro RJ Tel: 2218641
Associate Companies: Masson Editeur, France (qv); Masson Editores, Mexico (qv); Masson SA, Spain (qv); Masson Publishing USA Inc, 133 East 58th St, New York, NY 10022, USA
Branch Off: Rua D José de Barros 17 — conj 71, 01038 São Paulo SP
Subjects: Medicine, Nursing, Biological Sciences
Founded: 1978
ISBN Publisher's Prefix: 85-85005

Editora **Meca** Ltda*, Rua Araújo 81, Vila Buarque, São Paulo SP Tel: 2599049/2599034/2575346
Man Dir, Editorial, Production: Cosmo Juvela; *Sales:* Anna Maria Santos Brasil; *Publicity:* Eduardo Leonel; *Rights & Permissions:* Guarany Gallo
Subjects: General
Founded: 1970

Companhia **Melhoramentos** de São Paulo, CP 8120, 01000 São Paulo SP (Located at: Rua Tito 479, 05051 São Paulo)
Tel: 2626866 Cable Add: Melhoraluz Telex: 1123151 Melp Br
General Manager: Dr Alfried Ploeger; *Editorial & Production Manager:* Alfredo Weiszflog
Branch Off: Rua Pinto Guedes 24, Tijuca, 20511 Rio de Janeiro RJ
Subjects: Children's Books, Dictionaries, Reference, General Literature
Bookshop: Livroluz, Largo do Arouche 167, São Paulo SP
1981: 210 titles *1982:* 274 titles *Founded:* 1915

Mestre Jou SA, CP 24090, 05089 São Paulo SP (Located at: Rua Guaipá 518, Vila Leopoldina, São Paulo) Tel: 2602498/2611920 Cable Add: Mestrejou
Man Dir: Juan Ramón Mestre-Jou; *Dir:* Blanca Alcorta Berasategui
Subjects: Literature, History, Philosophy, Psychology, Medicine, Technical & Engineering, Social Sciences
Bookshops: See under Major Booksellers; Rua Senador Dantas 19, S/206, Rio de Janeiro
Founded: 1946
Miscellaneous: Firm is also an importer and distributor for all Brazil

Editora **Monterrey** Ltda*, Rua Visconde de Pirajá 550 — 14° andar — sala 1401, Ipanema, 22410 Rio de Janeiro RJ Tel: 2272795/2272602
Man Dir, Editorial: J Gueiros; *Sales:* J Fernandez; *Production:* W Teixeira; *Publicity:* C Marquez
Subject: Fiction
Founded: 1963

Editora **Moraes** Ltda+, Rua Ministro Godoy 1002, 05015 São Paulo SP Tel: (011) 8647849/628987/8641298
Man Dir: Orozimbo José de Moraes
Subjects: Education, Philosophy, Psychology, Social Service, Literature, Communications
Bookshop: Rua Curt Nimuendajú 19, 05015 São Paulo
Founded: 1969

Livraria **Nobel** SA Editora, CP 2373, 02910 São Paulo SP (Located at: Rua da Balsa 559, São Paulo) Tel: 8579444
Publicity: Ary Kuflik Benclowicz
Subjects: Textbooks, Agronomy, Mathematics, Statistics, Science, Engineering, Management & Economics, Public Relations, Dictionaries, Veterinary, Husbandry, Gardening, Literature
Bookshops: See under Major Booksellers
Founded: 1943
Miscellaneous: Also distributor

Noblet Indústria Gráfica e Editora Ltda*, CP 15181, 01530 São Paulo SP (Located at: Rua Almeida Torres 119/163, São Paulo) Tel: 2786152 Cable Add: Altesse
Man Dir: Joseph Bekhor Abourbih; *Editorial:* Yasukazu Hamazaki; *Production:* Fausto Taoka; *Publicity:* Josette A H Savatovsky
Subjects: Fiction, Periodicals
1981: 10 titles *Founded:* 1968

Editorial **Nórdica** Ltda, Ave NS Copacabana 1189, 22070 Rio de Janeiro RJ Tel: (021) 2872169 Cable Add: Nórdica Telex: (021) 31810 Noca Br
Chief Executive: Jaime Bernardes
Subjects: General Books, Juveniles, Humour, Politics, Cinema, Cookery, Economics, Sports, Occultism, Fiction

Editora **Nova Aguilar** SA*, Rua Maria Angélica 168, 22461 Rio de Janeiro RJ Tel: 2667474 Cable Add: Aguilar
President: Sérgio Lacerda; *Editorial Dir:* Pedro Paulo de Sena Madureira; *Sales:* Elson M F da Rocha
Parent Company: Editora Nova Fronteira SA (qv)
Branch Off: Ave Jurema 767, 04079 São Paulo
Subjects: Complete works of important Brazilian, Portuguese and International writers and poets in luxury editions
Founded: 1958

Nova Epoca Editorial Ltda*, Ave Angélica 55, Santa Cecilia, 01228 São Paulo SP Tel: 679505
Man Dir: Maria Dorell; *Sales Dir:* Dr Mark A Dorell; *Publicity Dir:* Poala Bassano; *Advertising Dir:* Roberto Zaccola; *Rights & Permissions:* Allan Delan
Subjects: General Fiction, Biography, History, Philosophy, Reference Books, Occultism
Founded: 1971

Editora **Nova Fronteira** SA+, Rua Maria Angélica 168, 22461 Rio de Janeiro RJ Tel: 2867822 Cable Add: Neofront
President: Sergio C A Lacerda; *Vice-President:* Sebastião Lacerda; *Editorial Dir:* Pedro Paulo de Sena Madureira; *Sales:* Elson M F da Rocha; *Production:* Beatriz de Affonseca; *Publicity:* Orlando Codá; *Rights & Permissions:* Angela Maria Ribeiro de Souza
Subsidiary Companies: Editora Nova Aguilar SA (qv); Confraria dos Amigos do Livro Ltda (qv)
Branch Off: Ave Pedro Bueno 1509-1511, Jabaquara, 04342 São Paulo
Subjects: Fiction, Literature, Biography, Psychology, History, Brazilian Problems, Dictionaries
1981: 92 titles *Founded:* 1965

Livraria José **Olympio** Editora SA*, CP 9018, 22251 Rio de Janeiro RJ (Located at: Rua Marquês de Olinda 12, Botafogo, Rio de Janeiro) Tel: 2660662/2665032 Cable Add: Jolympio
Dir: Hênio Rodrigues de Souza; *Sales Dirs:* Lidelmo Lima Terra, Harry de Almeida Costa; *Foreign Rights:* Gilda O Cruz Lehner
Branch Offs: Rua dos Gusmões 100-104, Santa Ifigênia, 01212 São Paulo SP; Rua Januária 258, Belo Horizonte MG; Comércio local da S Q Sul 108, Bloco D, Loja 5, Brasília DF; Rua dos Andradas 717, Pôrto Alegre RS; (all in Brazil)
Subjects: Juveniles, General Science, General Fiction, Textbooks, Sports, Philosophy, History, Humour, Music, Reference Books, Psychology, Religion, Sociology
Founded: 1931

Pallas SA*, Editora e Distribuidora, CP 7001, 21050 Rio de Janeiro RJ (Located at: Rua Frederico de Albuquerque 44, Higienopolis, Rio de Janeiro) Tel: 2700186
Man Dir: Martha Bozôti; *Editorial, Rights & Permissions:* D Marques; *Sales:* A C Fernandes
Subjects: Fiction, Social Sciences, National Literature, Economics, Law, Psychology, Occultism
Founded: 1975

Parma, an imprint of Global Editora e Distribuidora Ltda (qv)

Edições **Paulinas**, CP 12899, 04117 São Paulo SP (Located at: Rua Dr Pinto Ferraz 183, São Paulo) Tel: 5722362 Cable Add: Paulinos Telex: 1130791 Ramc Br
Man Dir and Publicity: W P Bosio; *Editorial:* Abramo Parmeggiani; *Sales:* H L Canella; *Production:* Arno Brustolin; *Rights & Permissions:* Abramo Parmeggiani, J B Alves
Subjects: Religion, Philosophy, Biography, Juveniles, Primary & Secondary Textbooks, Theological, Biblical, Liturgical, Sociology, Community Health
Bookshops: Praça da Sé 180, and three more in São Paulo; Rua México 111-B and one more in Rio de Janeiro; one each in Belo Horizonte, Brasília, Caxias do Sul, Curitiba, Fortaleza, Goiânia, Maringá, Niterói,

Cuiabá, Pôrto Alegre, Recife, Salvador, São Luís, Campo Grande, Juiz de Fora
1981: 200 titles *1982:* 190 titles *Founded:* 1930

Editora **Paz e Terra**, Rua São José 90 – 18° andar, Centro, 20010 Rio de Janeiro RJ Tel: 2213996
General Manager, Sales & Editorial: Fernando Gasparian; *Production:* Miriam Goldfeder; *Publicity and Rights & Permissions:* Helena Gasparian
Subjects: Brazilian Studies, Latin-American Studies, Social Sciences, Philosophy, Cinema, Theatre, Political Science, Literature & Literary Theory
Bookshops: Livraria Argumento, Rua Oscar Freire 608, São Paulo; Rua Dias Ferreira 199, Rio de Janeiro
Founded: 1966

Editora **Pensamento**+, Rua Mário Vicente 360, Ipiranga, 04270 São Paulo SP Tel: 2741733
Man Dir: Diaulas Riedel
Associate Company: Editora Cultrix (qv)
Subjects: Occult, Astrology, Psychology, Esotericism, Philosophy, Parapsychology, Orientalism, Theosophy
Founded: 1907

Editora **Perspectiva***, Ave Brigadeiro Luís Antônio 3025, Jardim Paulista, 01401 São Paulo SP Tel: 2888388/2886878
Man Dir: J Guinsburg
Subjects: Social Science, Humanities, Cinema, Economics, Education, History, Philosophy, Music, Psychology, Religion

Pink and Blue Editora Ltda*, Rua Jandaia 180, Bela Vista, 01320 São Paulo SP Tel: 325886/350036
Man Dir: Maria Cecília de sá Quartim Barbosa; *Editorial Dir:* Francisco Quartim Barbosa; *Sales Dir:* Lucia Barbosa Lemos; *Production Dirs:* Genny M Ramalho, Maria Eugenia C Obniski; *Publicity Dir:* Lucilia Ribas Chaves; *Rights & Permissions:* Ana Maria Quartim Barbosa Tartuce
Subject: English as a foreign language, primary & secondary stage
Founded: 1972

Pool Editorial Ltda*, CP 650, 50000 Recife PE (Located at: Rua Manoel Caetano 135, Derby, Recife) Tel: 2215096/2215179 Cable Add: Poolne Telex: 2273 Alpp Br
Man Dir, Editorial: Marco Aurèlio de Alcântara; *Sales:* Wilobaldo R Santos; *Production:* Manoel Alberto de Freitas; *Publicity:* Maristela da Rocha Oliveira
Parent Company: Alcântara Promoções e Publicidade Ltda (at above address)
Subsidiary Company: ANI — Agencia Nordestina de Informações (at above address)
Branch Off: Rua do Riachuelo 247 — apt 906, Fátima, Rio de Janeiro
Subjects: Politics, Economics, Poetry, Belles Lettres
Bookshop: Livraria do Estacionamento Periférico da Ilha Joana Bezerra, Recife

Casa Editora **Presbiteriana***, Rua Comendador Norberto Jorge 40, Brooklin Paulista, 04602 São Paulo SP Tel: 5431061/2236479
Man Dir: Rev Atael Fernando Costa
Subjects: History, Religion
Bookshop: Ave São João 439 — lojas 201-3, São Paulo
Founded: 1942

Editora **Primor** Ltda+, Ave Almirante Barroso 63 — sala 2716, 20031 Rio de Janeiro RJ Tel: (021) 2404425/3711385 Cable Add: Primor Telex: (021) 22150
Subsidiary Company: Gráfica Editora Primor SA (qv)
Subjects: Children's Books, Humour, Tourism, Illustrated Fiction and Non-fiction; International Co-Productions

Gráfica Editora **Primor** Ltda+, Ave Almirante Barroso 63 — sala 2716, 20031 Rio de Janeiro RJ Tel: (5521) 3716622 Telex: (021) 22150
Man Dirs: Sergio Jacques Waissman, Simão Waissman; *Editorial and Rights & Permissions:* Sergio Jacques Waissman; *Sales, Publicity:* Miguel Paixão; *Production:* Paulo Duante
Parent Company: Editora Primor Ltda (qv)
Subjects: Didactics, Pre-school & Juvenile Literature, Reference, Art, General Interest, Notebooks, Illustrated books
Founded: 1969

Proton Editora Ltda*, Ave Rebouças 3819, 05401 São Paulo SP Tel: 2103616/8147922/8159708
President: Norberto R Keppe; *Man Dir:* Cláudia S Pacheco
Branch Off: Ave Rebouças 3115, São Paulo Tel: 8535551
Subjects: Psychoanalysis, Psychology, Medicine, General Science
Founded: 1976

Editora de **Publicações Científicas** Ltda, CP 1555, 20911 Rio de Janeiro RJ (Located at: Rua Major Suckow 30-36, Rocha, Rio de Janeiro) Tel: 2013722/2612893
Man Dir: José Maria de Sousa e Melo; *Editorial:* Dr Ismar Chavés da Silveira; *Sales, Publicity:* Luiz Carlos Ávila de Souza; *Production:* Edson de Oliveira Vilar
Associate Companies: Editora de Publicações Médicas Ltda (EPUME) (at above address); Intersistemas SA de CV, Mexico (qv)
Branch Off: Rua Borges Lagoa 426, São Paulo
Subject: General Medicine
Book Club: Estante do Livro Científico
Founded: 1959

Distribuidora **Record** de Serviços de Imprensa SA, CP 884, 20291 Rio de Janeiro RJ (Located at: Rua Argentina 171, São Cristóvão, Rio de Janeiro) Tel: 5803668 Cable Add: Recordist Telex: (21) 30501 Book Br
President & General Manager: Alfredo C Machado; *Vice-President:* Sergio C Machado
Branch Offs: Ave Erasmo Braga 255 — sala 304, Rio de Janeiro; Rua José Antônio Coelho 801, São Paulo SP; Ave Augusto de Lima 233, Belo Horizonte MG
Subjects: General Fiction & Non-fiction, Biography, History, Philosophy, Juveniles, Primary Textbooks
1981: 562 titles *1982:* 590 titles *Founded:* 1942

Editora **Resenha** Tributaria Ltda, Rua Cel Xavier de Toledo 210 — cj 74 — 7° andar, Centro, 01048 São Paulo SP Tel: 354445
Man Dir: Vaner Bícego; *Editorial Dir:* Valdyr Rezende Xavier; *Commercial Dir:* José Figueira da Cruz
Subjects: Law, Education

Editora **Reverté** Ltda*, CP 23001, 20910 Rio de Janeiro RJ (Located at: Ave do Exército 49, São Cristóvão, Rio de Janeiro) Tel: 2845244
Man Dir: E Rosel Albero
Associate Companies: See under Editorial Reverté SA, Spain (qv)

Editora **Revista** dos Tribunais Ltda*, CP 8153, 01501 São Paulo SP (Located at: Rua Conde do Pinhai 78, Centro, São Paulo) Tel: 378689/379772
Man Dir: Nelson Palma Travassos; *Sales Dir:* Alvaro Malheiros
Subjects: Law, Economics, Philosophy, History, Reference Books, Sociology
Founded: 1955

Editora **Rideel** Ltda+, CP 12152, 02450 São Paulo SP (Located at: Alameda Afonso Schmidt 877, Santa Terezinha, São Paulo) Tel: 2678344
Man Dir, Editorial, Publicity and Rights & Permissions: Italo Amadio; *Sales and Production:* Regina Maria Azevedo
Subjects: Reference, Medicine, Philology, History, Cooking, Infant/Juvenile Books, Sexual Education, Religion
Founded: 1971

Rio Grafica e Editora SA*, Rua Itapiru 1209 — 5° andar, Rio Comprido, 20000 Rio de Janeiro RJ Tel: (021) 2735522 Telex: 23365
Subjects: Comic Books, Sports and Games; Activity Books

Editora Ana **Rosa***, Rua Aurora 858 — 6° andar, São Paulo SP Tel: 2212211
Subjects: Fashion & Design

Saraiva SA, Livreiros Editores, CP 2362, 01139 São Paulo SP (Located at: Ave Marquês de São Vicente 1697, Barra Funda, São Paulo) Tel: 8268422 Cable Add: Academica
President: Paulino Saraiva; *Vice-President:* Jorge Eduardo Saraiva; *Man Dir:* Ruy Mendes Gonçalves; *Editorial Dirs:* Antonio Alexandre Faccioli (Education), Juarez de Oliveira (Law); *Sales Dirs:* Nilson Lepera (Education), Antonio Luiz de Toledo Pinto (Universities); *Production Dir:* Antonio Xavier Cardoso
Branch Offs: Ave Marechal Rondon 2231, Rio de Janeiro; Rua Célia de Souza 571, Belo Horizonte; Ave Chicago 307, Pôrto Alegre; Ave Princesa Isabel 1555, Curitiba
Subjects: Law, Education, Business Administration, Economics, Primary, Secondary School and University Textbooks
Bookshops: 21 branches throughout Brazil
Founded: 1914

Sarvier — Editora de Livros Medicos Ltda, CP 12927, 04012 São Paulo SP (Located at: Rua Dr Amancio de Carvalho 459, Vila Mariana, São Paulo) Tel: 713439
Man Dir: Cid A Balieiro
Subjects: Medicine, Dentistry
Founded: 1965

Scipione Autores Editores Ltda, Rua Princesa Leopoldina 395-419, Alto da Lapa, 05081 São Paulo SP Tel: 2605878/2612902
Man Dir, Editorial, Sales and Publicity: Prof Dr Scipione di Pierro Netto; *Production:* José Augusto del Bianco; *Rights & Permissions:* Prof Dr Scipione di Pierro Netto, Luis Fernando di Pierro
Subsidiary Company: Módulus Orientação Pedagógica, Edição e Comercialização de Obras Didáticas Ltda (at above address)
Subject: Didactics
Founded: 1974

Seleções Eletrônicas Editora Ltda, see Eletrônicas Editora Ltda

Edições **Símbolo***, Rua General Flores 518, 01129 São Paulo SP Tel: 2200267/2215833 Cable Add: Simbolgraf
Man Dir: Moysés Baumstein; *Editorial Dir:* Alberto Baumstein; *Sales Dir:* Lina Araujo Ferreira
Parent Company: Simbolo SA: Industrias Gráficas
Subjects: Literature, Social Literature, University Textbooks, Sociology, History, Politics, Jungian Psychology, Education, Communications, Art Books (Photography)
Founded: 1976

Livraria **Sulina** Editora, CP 357, 90000 Pôrto Alegre RS (Located at: Ave Borges de Medeiros 1030-36, Pôrto Alegre) Tel: 254765   Cable Add: Zipasul
President: Leopoldo Bernardo Boeck Jr;
Vice-President: Vilson Nailor Noer
Parent Company: Organização Sulina de Representações SA, Rua Cel Genuino 290, Pôrto Alegre (Distributor)
Subjects: Science, Technical, Law, Textbooks, Psychology
Bookshops: See under Major Booksellers; Rua Julio de Castilhos 1657, Caxias do Sul; Ave 7 de Setembro 1169, L 12 Bagé; Rua Marechal Floriano 1000, c 63 Sta Maria, and 5 other bookshops in Pôrto Alegre
Founded: 1946

Edições **Tabajara***, CP 1918, 90000 Pôrto Alegre RS (Located at: Rua dos Andradas 1774, Pôrto Alegre)   Tel: 241073/247724
Assistant Manager: Maria Azambuja
Branch Off: Rua Santa Ifigênia 72, São Paulo
Subjects: Linguistics, Social & General Science, Mathematics, Sociology, Dramatic Art, Education, Textbooks

Livros **Técnicos e Científicos** Editora SA, see LTC

Editora **Tecnoprint** Ltda*, CP 1880, 21040 Rio de Janeiro RJ (Located at: Rua Nova Jerusalém 345, Bonsucesso, Rio de Janeiro) Tel: 2606122/2804090   Cable Add: Ediouro
Subjects: Cookery, Textbooks, Sports, Children's Books, Reference Books, Paperbacks
Founded: 1939

Editora da **U F R G S** (Universidade Federal do Rio Grande do Sul)*, Rua Ramiro Barcelos 2.600 — 1° andar, 90000 Pôrto Alegre RS   Tel: 328391
Manager: Antonio Dallazen; *Production:* Geraldo Huff; *Sales, Publicity:* José Francisco Schuster
Subjects: General & Academic
ISBN Publisher's Prefix: 85-7025

Editora **Universidade de Brasília**+, CP 153001, 70910 Brasília DF (Located at: Campus Universitário, Asa Norte, Brasília) Tel: (061) 2743182 (Editorial, Rights, Production), 2731055 (Sales), 2731055 ext 2221 (Advertising)   Cable Add: Univerbrasilia Editora   Telex: 611083 Unbs Br
Chairman: Carlos Henrique Cardim;
Editorial Dir: Octaciano Nogueira; *Sales Dir:* Sergio Sampaio; *Advertising Dir:* Amaro Senna; *Production:* Elmano Rodrigues Pinheiro, José Reis da Silva; *Rights & Permissions:* Manuel Montenegro da Cruz
Branch Offs: Escritório de Representação da Universidade de Brasília, Ave Presidente Vargas 542 — grupo 1309, 20210 Rio de Janeiro RJ   Tel: (021) 2636959; Rua João Adolfo 118 — 6° andar — sala 608, 01050 São Paulo SP   Tel: (011) 321413
Subjects: Social, Political and Physical Sciences, Humanities
Book Club: Clube do Livro da Universidade de Brasília
1981: 101 titles *1982:* approx 200 titles

Editora da **Universidade de São Paulo***, CP 11465, 05508 São Paulo SP (Located at: Edificio da Antiga Reitoria — 6° andar, Cidade Universitária 'Armando de Salles Oliveira', Butantã, São Paulo) Tel: 2116988   Cable Add: Ruspaulo
President: Mario Guimarães Ferri
Subjects: Scholarly, General Non-fiction
Founded: 1964

Universidade Federal do Rio Grande do Sul, see Editora da UFRGS

Livraria e Editora **Universitária de Direito** Ltda*, Rua Benjamin Constant 171 — 1° andar — salas 1-5, 01005 São Paulo SP   Tel: 356374/340314
Man Dir, Production: Armando Luiz Almeida Martins; *Editorial Dir:* Pedro Gellindo Sommavilla; *Sales Dir:* Armando des Santos Mesquita Martins
Subject: Legal works
Founded: 1968

Fundação Getúlio **Vargas**, CP 9052, 22250 Rio de Janeiro RJ (Located at: Praia de Botafogo 188, Rio de Janeiro)   Tel: 5510698
Cable Add: Fugevar
Man Dir: Mauro Gama; *Sales Dir:* Jorge Rangel da Matta
Subjects: Administration, Economics, Business, Sociology, Psychology, Education, Marketing, Accounting

Editora **Vecchi** SA*, Rua do Resende 144, Centro, 20231 Rio de Janeiro RJ   Tel: 2210822   Cable Add: Vekieditora   Telex: 32756
Dir Superintendent: Delman Bonatto
Subjects: Biography, Cookery, Philosophy, Reference Books, Occultism, Religion, Juveniles, Magazines
Founded: 1913

Editora **Verbo** Ltda*, CP 8811, 01526 São Paulo SP (Located at: Rua Bueno de Andrade 480-484, Liberdade, São Paulo) Tel: 2792776   Cable Add: Verbo
Subjects: Art, Social Science, Reference, Juveniles, Cinema, Education, Geography, History, Psychology, Religion

Vertente Editora Ltda*, Rua General Jardim 570, 01223 São Paulo SP   Tel: 2555194
Man Dir: Wladyr Nader; *Production Dir:* Paulo Douglas Barsotti
Subjects: Literature, The Humanities, Periodicals *Escrita* and *Escrita/Ensaio*
Bookshop: Escrita (at above address)
Founded: 1968

Editora **Vigília** Ltda, CP 2468, 30000 Belo Horizonte MG (Located at: Rua Felipe dos Santos 508, Bairro de Lourdes, Belo Horizonte)   Tel: 3372744/3372363/3372834
Branch Off: Rua Pareto 23, Tijuca, 20550 Rio de Janeiro RJ
Subjects: Textbooks, Linguistics, Brazilian Literature, Religion

Editora **Visão** Ltda, Rua Alfonso Celso 243, Vila Mariana, 04119 São Paulo SP   Tel: 5494344   Cable Add: Revista Visão   Telex: (011) 23552/30665 Sevl Br
Man Dir: Henry Maksoud; *Publisher:* Isaac Jardanovski; *Sales Dir and Rights & Permissions:* Ayrton Pedro de Oliveira; *Production Manager:* Antonio Lopes Colhado; *Publicity Manager:* Antonio Carlos Moreira
Associate Company: Visão SA Editorial (at above address)
Branch Off: Conjunto Baracat — sala 301, Brasília DF
Subjects: Humanities, Economics, Finance, Agriculture, Cattle Breeding, Diet, Commerce, Hobbies, Tourism, Politics, Science, Technology
Founded: 1952

Vozes Editora Ltda*, CP 90023, 25600 Petrópolis RJ (Located at: Rua Frei Luís 100, Petrópolis, Rio de Janeiro)   Tel: 435112   Cable Add: Vozes
Man Dir: Miguel Mourão de Castro
Branch Offs: Rua Senador Dantas 118, Rio de Janeiro; Rua Senador Feijó 168, São Paulo; Rua Tupis 85, Loja 10, Belo Horizonte; Rua Riachuelo 1280, Pôrto Alegre; CRL/Norte, Q704 Bloco A 15, Brasília DF; Rua Conselheiro Portela 354, Recife PE; Rua Alferes Poli 52, Curitiba PR

Subjects: Belles Lettres, Linguistics, Communications, Philosophy, Religion, Administration, Psychology, Sociology
Founded: 1901

Zahar Editores+, CP 207, ZC-00, Rio de Janeiro RJ (Located at: Rua México 31, Rio de Janeiro)   Tel: 2400226
General Manager: Jorge Zahar; *Editorial:* Ana Cristina Zahar; *Sales Dir:* Jorge Zahar Jr
Subjects: Social Science, Psychology, Business & Economics
Founded: 1957

Zip Editora Ltda*, Rua Filomena Nunes 162, Olaria, Rio de Janeiro   Tel: 2306470
Man Dir: Jan Rais; *Editorial:* Rubens Lucchetti; *Sales:* Francisco Nigro; *Production:* Nildo Vicente
Subjects: Juveniles, Fiction, Paperbacks
Founded: 1978

Literary Agents

Carmen **Balcells** Agencia Literaria, CP 33113, Rua Joaô Lira 97 — sala 202, Leblon, 22430 Rio de Janeiro RJ   Tel: 2943248   Cable Add: Copyright Rio
Manager: Ana Maria Santeiro
Head Office: Spain (qv)

Rômulo **Paes Barreto***, CP 16083, Largo do Machado, 22221 Rio de Janeiro RJ   Tel: 2659478

Mrs Karin **Schindler** — Dr J E Bloch Literary Agency, CP 19051, 04599 São Paulo SP   Tel: 2419077/2419177   Cable Add: Copyright Sãopaulo

Book Clubs

Círculo do Livro SA, CP 7413, São Paulo SP (Located at: Al Ministro Rocha Azevedo 346, São Paulo)   Tel: 8818644   Cable Add: Cirlivro   Telex: 1132900/1131747
Man Dir: Renê Cesar Xavier dos Santos; *Editorial Dir:* Flávio Barros Pinto
Owned by: Verlagsgruppe Bertelsmann GmbH, Federal Republic of Germany (qv); Abril SA Cultural e Industrial (qv)

Estante do **Livro Científico**, Rua Major Suckow 30-36, Rocha, 20911 Rio de Janeiro RJ
Owned by: Editora de Publicações Científicas Ltda (qv)

Clube do Livro da **Universidade de Brasília**, CP 153001, 70910 Brasília DF (Located at: Campus Universitário, Asa Norte, Brasília) Tel: (061) 2720000 ext 2186/2128   Cable Add: Univerbrasilia Editora   Telex: 611083 Unbs
Owned by: Editora Universidade de Brasília (qv)

Major Booksellers

Livraria **Agir**, Rua México 98 B, Rio de Janeiro RJ   Tel: 2401978
Manager: Jorge Eduardo d'Almeida Castro Faveret
Also Publisher (qv)

Ao Livro Técnico*, CP 3655, 20000 Rio de Janeiro RJ (Located at: Rua Miguel Couto 35 — loja C, Rio de Janeiro)   Tel: 2243177/2420275/2422636
Manager: Fernando Jorge da Silva
Branches in Brasília, Belo Horizonte, Rio de Janeiro, São Paulo, Curitiba, Belém, Recife, Salvador, Pôrto Alegre
Also Publisher (qv) and widespread wholesaler and distributors

Livraria **Brasiliense** Editora SA*, Rua Barão de Itapetininga 93-99, 01042 São Paulo SP Tel: 2311344

Livraria **Canuto** Ltda, Rua da Consolação 348 — 2° andar, São Paulo SP Tel: 2564564/2568990

Livraria **Científica Técnica***, Rua Riachuelo 453 — loja 4, 50000 Recife PE Tel: 24933

Livraria **Duas Cidades***, CP 433, 01220 São Paulo SP (Located at: Rua Bento Freitas 158, Vila Buarque, São Paulo) Tel: 2204702
Also Publisher (qv)

A Casa do Livro **Eldorado** Ltda*, Ave Copacabana 1189, 22070 Rio de Janeiro RJ Tel: 2872147
Manager: Decio de Abreu

Livraria **Freitas** Bastos, Rua 7 de Setembro 127-129, Rio de Janeiro RJ Tel: 2220250/2228858
Also Publisher (qv)

Livraria do **Globo**, Rua dos Andradas 1416, Pôrto Alegre RS Tel: 24811
Subsidiary Company: Editora Globo SA (qv)

I B R E X — Distribuidora de Livros e Material de Escritório Ltda, Rua 21 de Abril 101, São Paulo SP Tel: 929639

Livro **Ibero-Americano** Ltda, Rua do Rosario 99 — 3-4° andares, Rio de Janeiro RJ Tel: 2212026
Also Publisher (qv)

Livraria **Kosmos**, CP 3481, 20041 Rio de Janeiro RJ (Located at: Rua do Rosario 137, Centro, Rio de Janeiro) Tel: 2529552
Also Publisher (qv)

Livraria **L E R***, Rua México 31 — sobreloja, 20031 Rio de Janeiro RJ Tel: 2215073/74/75/76 Cable Add: Livreril
Also at Praça Olavo Bilac 28, Rio de Janeiro; Praça da República 71, 01045 São Paulo
Importer, Exporter & Distributor

L I T E C — Livraria Editora Técnica Ltda*, CP 30869, São Paulo SP (Located at: Rua dos Timbiras 257, São Paulo) Tel: (011) 2208983
Manager: A W Miehe
Also Publisher (qv)

Livraria D **Landy**, Rua 7 de Abril 252 — 5° andar, São Paulo SP Tel: 2551953/2553272
Manager: Desiderio Landy

Nova Livraria **Leonardo da Vinci** Ltda*, Ave Rio Branco 185 — lojas 2 3 e 9, 20040 Rio de Janeiro RJ Tel: 2527192/2241329
Manager: Vanna Piraccini

Mestre Jou SA, CP 24090, 05089 São Paulo SP (Located at: Rua Guaipá 518, Vila Leopoldina, São Paulo) Tel: 2602498/2611920
Manager: Juan Ramón Mestre-Jou
Also Publisher (qv) and an importer and distributor for all Brazil

Livraria **Nobel**, CP 2373, São Paulo SP (Located at: Rua de Consolação 49 and Rua Maria Antonia 108, São Paulo) Tel: 2572144
Dir: Ary Kuflik Benclowicz
Also Publisher (qv) and distributor

Livraria **Parthenón***, Rua Barão de Itapetininga 140 — 1° andar — sala 14, 01042 São Paulo SP Tel: 372623

Livraria Científica Ernesto **Reichmann** Ltda, CP 3935, 01051 São Paulo SP (Located at: Rua Dom José de Barros 168 — 6° andar — conj 61-62, 01038 São Paulo) Tel: 2557501/2551342
Manager: Ernesto Reichmann

Livraria **Sulina**, CP 357, 90000 Pôrto Alegre RS (Located at: Ave Borges de Medeiros 1030-36, Pôrto Alegre) Tel: 254755
Also Publisher (qv)

Livraria **Triangulo** SA, CP 30317, 01000 São Paulo SP (Located at: Rua Barão de Itapetininga 255 — loja 23-24, São Paulo) Tel: 2310922/2553384
Manager: Peter Paul Richard Scholzel
Owned by: Editora Guanabara Koogan SA (qv)

Major Libraries

Arquivo Nacional, Praça da República 26, 20211 Rio de Janeiro RJ Tel: 2522338 Telex: 2134103 Anmj
Librarian: Maria de la Encarnacion de España Santos

Biblioteca Estadual*, Ave Presidente Vargas 1261, Rio de Janeiro RJ
State Library

Biblioteca Múnicipal Mário de Andrade, CP 8170, 01302 São Paulo SP (Located at: Rua da Consolação 94, São Paulo) Tel: 2394384/2565777
Dir: Maria da Guia de Oliveira Santiago
Publication: Boletim Bibliográfico Biblioteca Mário de Andrade (quarterly)

Biblioteca Nacional*, Ave Rio Branco 219-239, 20042 Rio de Janeiro RJ Tel: 2408629/2408579 Telex: 02122941 Bn Rj Br
Dir: Celia Ribeiro Zaher
Publications include: Anais; Boletim Bibliográfico; Coleção Rodolfo Garcia

Biblioteca Publica do Estado do Rio de Janeiro*, Praça da República, Niterói, Rio de Janeiro RJ

Centro de Documentação e Informaçao da Camara dos Deputados*, Coordenaçao de Publiçacoẽs, Praça dos Tres Poderes, Brasília DF
House of Representatives' Centre of Documentation & Information

Biblioteca do **Ministerio das Relações Exteriores***, Esplanada dos Ministérios, 70170 Brasília DF Tel: 2264305
Dir: Lilian Thome Andrade (Librarian)
Publications: Aquisiçoẽs (bi-monthly), *Aquisiçoẽs Bibliograficas* (annual), *Referência de Periodicos* (monthly)

Biblioteca da **Sociedade Brasileira** de Cultura Inglesa, Rua Raul Pompéia 231 — 7° andar, Rio de Janeiro RJ
Librarian: Ilka Beauchamp

Universidade de Brasília, Biblioteca Central, Ag Postal UnB, CP 152951, 70910 Brasília DF Tel: (061) 2720000 Telex: 1083 Ramal 2400
Dir: Cybele Villares Coelho

Sistema de Bibliotecas da **Universidade de São Paulo** (SIBI), CP 8191, 05508 São Paulo SP (Located at: Cidade Universitária, Butantan, São Paulo) Tel: 2117448 Telex: 22092
University of São Paulo Library System
Dir: Dinah Aguiar Población
Publications include: Recentes Publicações da USP

Centro de Ciências da Saude da **Universidade Federal do Rio de Janeiro***, Biblioteca Central — bloco L, Cidade Universitária, Ilha do Fundão, 20000 Rio de Janeiro RJ
Medical School Library of the University of Rio de Janeiro

Universidade Federal do Rio Grande do Sul, Biblioteca Central, Edificio da Reitoría-térreo, Ave Paulo Gama, 90000 Pôrto Alegre RS Tel: (0512) 242431 Telex: 0511055
Librarian: H B Schreiner

Library Associations

Associação Brasileira de Bibliotecários, now Associação Profissional de Bibliotecários do Estado do Rio de Janeiro (qv)

Associação dos Arquivistas Brasileiros, Praia de Botafoga 186 — sala B-217, 22253 Rio de Janeiro RJ Tel: 5510748
Association of Brazilian Archivists
President: Afonso Carlos Marques dos Santos; *Secretary:* Maria Lúcia Gonçalves
Publication: Arquivo e Administração (4-monthly)

Associação Paulista de Bibliotecários*, CP 343, 01327 São Paulo SP (Located at: Rua 13 de Maio 1100 — 3° andar, São Paulo)
Library Asociation of São Paulo
Executive Secretary: Marcia Rosetto
Publications: Boletim Informativo, Jornal

Associação Profissional de Bibliotecários do Estado do Rio de Janeiro (APBERJ)*, Rua Martins Torres 99, Santa Rosa, Niterói, 24000 Rio de Janeiro RJ
Brazilian Library Association
Previously known as Associação Brasileira de Bibliotecários
Publication: Guia de Bibliografia Especializada

Associação Rio-Grandense de Bibliotecários, CP 2344, Pôrto Alegre, 90000 Rio Grande do Sul RS (Located at: Rua Dr Flores 245 — 7° andar — conj 902, Pôrto Alegre)
Library Association of the State of Rio Grande do Sul
President: Carlos Luiz da Silva

Centro de Investigação e Documentação*, CP 23, Petropolis, Rio de Janeiro RJ

Comissão Brasileira de Documentação Agricola (CBDA)*, c/o Museu Paraense 'Emilio Goeldi', CP 399, Belém, Pará PA
Headquarters of Brazilian Commission for Agricultural Documentation
Secretary: Cely Farias Raphael
Publication: Agricolas

Conselho Federal de Biblioteconomia (CFB)*, SCLRN 712-713 — bloco A — entr 31 sobreloja — sala 02, 70760 Brasília DF
Federal Council of Librarianship
President: Nancy Westphalen Corrêa

Federação Brasileira de Associações de Bibliotecários (FEBAB), Rua Avanhandava 40 — conj 110, 01306 São Paulo SP Tel: 2579979
Brazilian Federation of Library Associations
President: Antonio Gabriel; *Secretary-General:* Francisca Pimenta Evrard; *Editor:* Carminda Nogueira de Castro Ferreira
Publication: Revista Brasileira de Biblioteconomia e Documentação

Federação Brasileira de Associações de Bibliotecários — Comissão Brasileira de Documentação Jurídica (FEBAB/CBDJ)*, Rua Prof Antônio Maria Teixeira 120 — apt 802, Leblon, 22430 Rio de Janeiro RJ Tel: 2592763
Brazilian Federation of Library Associations — Brazilian Committee of Legal Documentation
President: Nylma Thereza de Salles Velloso Amarante; *Executive Secretaries:* Tania Cordeiro Alvarez, Sérgio da Costa Velho
Publications: Many publications dealing with legal and related matters

Instituto Brasileiro de Informação em Ciência e Tecnologia (IBICT), SCRN 708-709 - bloco 2 - lotes 2/10, 70740 Brasília DF Tel: 2738077
Brazilian Institute for Information in Science and Technology
Dir: Yone Sepulveda Chastinet
Publication: Ciência da Informação (bi-annual)

Library Reference Books and Journals

Books

Guia de Bibliografia Especializada (Guide to Specialist Libraries), Brazilian Library Association, Rua Martins Torres 99, Santa Rosa, Niterói, 24000 Rio de Janeiro (covers all Latin America)

Journals

Boletim Informativo (Information Bulletin), Library Association of São Paulo, Rua 13 de Maio 1100 - 3° andar, São Paulo SP

Jornal, Library Association of São Paulo SP, Rua 13 de Maio 1100 - 3° andar, São Paulo

Notícias (News), Brazilian Federation of Library Associations, Brazilian Committee of Legal Documentation, Rua Prof Antônio Maria Teixeira 120 — apt 802, Leblon, 22430 Rio de Janeiro RJ

Revista Brasileira de Bibliteconomia e Documentação (Brazilian Review of Librarianship and Documentation), Brazilian Federation of Library Associations, Rua Avanhandava 40 - conj 110, 01306 São Paulo SP

Literary Associations and Societies

Academia Amazonense de Letras*, Rua Ramos Ferreira 1009, Manaus, 69000 Amazonas AM
President: Dr Mario Y Monteiro; *Secretary:* Tânia Regina Mesquita
Publication: Revista

Academia Cachoeirense de Letras*, Praça Jerônimo Monteiro 105 — 2° andar, Cachoeiro de Itapemerim, Espírito Santo ES

Academia Catarinense de Letras, Rua Vidal Ramos, Edifício José Daux — 5° andar, Florianópolis, 88000 Santa Catarina SC
Secretary-General: Sylvia Amélia Carneiro da Cunha
Publication: Revista

Academia Cearense de Letras, Palácio Senador Alencar, Rua São Paulo 51, 60000 Fortaleza CE
Secretary-General: Cândida Maria Santiago Galeno
Publications: Revista da Academia Cearense de Letras, Coléção Dolor Barreira, Coléção Antonio Sales

Academia de Letras*, João Pessôa, Paraíba PB

Academia de Letras da Bahia*, CP 662, Bahia BA (Located at: Ave 7 de Setembro 283, Salvador, Bahia)
Secretary: Edith Mendes de Gama e Abreu
Publication: Revista (every 6 months)

Academia de Letras de Piauí*, Teresina, Piauí PI
Publication: Revista

Academia Feminina Espírito Santense de Letras*, Rua Bernardo Horta 30 — apdo 1, Jucutuara, Vitoria, Espírito Santo ES
Women's Academy of Letters

Academia Matogrossense de Letras*, Rua 13 de Junho 173, Cuiabá, Mato Grosso MT
President: José de Merquita
Publication: Revista

Academia Mineira de Letras*, Rua Carijos 150 — 6° andar, Belo Horizonte, Minas Gerais MG

Academia Paranaense de Letras*, CP 8610, Curitiba, 80000 Paraná PR
President: Vasco José Taborda
Publications: Revista, and books

Academia Paulista de Letras*, Largo do Arouche 312, 01219 São Paulo SP Tel: 2212660/2239725
President: Francisco Marins
Publications: Revista da Academia Paulista de Letras, Biblioteca Academia Paulista de Letras

Academia Pernambucana de Letras*, CP 50000, Recife, Pernambuco PE (Located at: Ave Rui Barbosa 1596, Graças, Recife, Pernambuco)
President: Dr Mauro Mota; *Secretary:* Dr Andrade Lima Filho
Publication: Revista

Academia Riograndense de Letras*, Rua Candido Silveira 43, Pôrto Alegre, Rio Grande do Sul RS
Publication: Revista

P E N Clube do Brasil (Associação Universal de Escritores)*, Praia do Flamengo 172 — 11° andar, Rio de Janeiro RJ
President: Professor Marcos Almir Madeira
Publications: Boletim, novels, poetry
Also: PEN Centre de São Paulo, c/o Instituto Historico e Geografico, Rua Benjamin Constant 157 - 7° andar, São Paulo, SP
President: Dr João de Scantimburgo

Literary Periodicals

Escrita (Writing), Vertente Editora Ltda, Rua General Jardim 570, 01223 São Paulo SP

Jornal de Letras (Journal of Letters), Rua Barata Ribeiro 774 s/1-101, Copacabana-Rio, Estado da Guanabara

Opinião (Opinion), Ramos 78, Jardim Botanico, Rio de Janeiro

Verbum (The Word), Universidade Catolica, Rua Marques de São Vicente 209, Rio de Janeiro

Veritas (The Truth), Pontificia Universidade Catolica do Rio Grande do Sul, Ave Iparanga 6681, Pôrto Alegre

Literary Prizes

Graca Aranha Prize*
For the best Brazilian novel. Enquiries to PEN Clube do Brasil, Praia do Flamengo 172 — 10° andar, Rio de Janeiro RJ

Afonso Arinos Prize*
For the best work of fiction published or written during the two years preceding the year of award. Awarded annually. Enquiries to the Brazilian Academy, Ave Presidente Wilson 203, Rio de Janeiro

Olavo Bilac Prize*
For the best book of poetry. Awarded annually. Enquiries to the Brazilian Academy, Ave Presidente Wilson 203, Rio de Janeiro

Viriato Correa Prize*
To the author of the best unpublished book for children. Enquiries to Instituto Nacional do Livro, Edifício Venâncio V, Setor de Diversões Sul, 70000 Brasília DF

Monteiro Lobato Prize*
For children's literature. Awarded annually. Enquiries to Brazilian Academy, Ave Presidente Wilson 203, Rio de Janeiro

Julia Lopes de Ameida Prize*
For the best unpublished or published literary work written by a woman, preferably for a novel or collection of short stories. Awarded annually. Enquiries to Brazilian Academy, Ave Presidente Wilson 203, Rio de Janeiro

Machado de Assis Prize*
Founded in 1943, this award is to an outstanding Brazilian writer for the sum of his work. Awarded annually. One of Brazil's highest literary honours. Enquiries to Brazilian Academy, Ave Presidente Wilson 203, Rio de Janeiro

Odorico Mendes Prize*
For the best translation from foreign literature into the Portuguese language. Awarded annually. Enquiries to Brazilian Academy, Ave Presidente Wilson 203, Rio de Janeiro

National Book Institute Prizes*
For outstanding unpublished literary works of fiction, poetry, history and essays. In addition, one prize is awarded for the best unpublished work of children's literature and another for illustrations of books for children. Awarded annually. Enquiries to Instituto Nacional do Livro, Edifício Venâncio V, Setor de Diversões Sul, 70000 Brasília DF

Silvio Romero Prize*
For best works in literary criticism and history of literature. Awarded annually. Enquiries to the Brazilian Academy, Ave Presidente Wilson 203, Rio de Janeiro

Luisa Claudio de Sousa Prize*
For the best book published in the previous year. Novels, plays, literary history and criticism works are considered. Awarded annually. Enquiries to PEN Clube do Brasil, Praia do Flamengo 172 — 10° andar, Rio de Janeiro RJ

José Verissimo Prize*
For the best essay and a work of scholarship. Awarded annually. Enquiries to Brazilian Academy, Ave Presidente Wilson 203, Rio de Janeiro

Brunei

General Information

Language: Malay and Chinese
Religion: Predominantly Muslim
Population: 201,000
Literacy Rate (1971): 63.9%
Bank Hours: 0900-1200, 1400-1500 Monday-Friday; 0900-1100 Saturday
Shop Hours: 0730-1930 or 2000 Monday-Saturday in Bandar Seri Begawan, Tuesday-Sunday in Seria, Wednesday-Monday in Kuala Belait
Currency: 100 cents = 1 Brunei dollar

58 BRUNEI — BULGARIA

Export/Import Information: No tariff on books. No obscene literature allowed. Import licences not required. No exchange controls

Publishers

Leong Brothers*, 52 Jalan Bunga Kuning, PO Box 164, Seria Tel: Seria 22381 Cable Add: Leong

The **Star** Press*, Bandar Seri Begawan
Manager: F W Zimmermann
Founded: 1963

Major Booksellers

The **Brunei** Press*, Jalan Sungai, Kuala Belait
Stockists and dealers for books handled by the Strait Times Press, Singapore

Sharikat Toko Buku **Kwang Hwa***, PO Box 1211, Brunei (Located at: 308A Kiaw Lian Bldg, B S Begawan, Brunei) Tel: 24075
Manager: Frederick Yong

Rex Bookstore*, PO Box 500, Brunei Hotel, Jalan Chevalier Tel: 2060

Major Libraries

Language and Literature Bureau Library*, Jalan Elizabeth II, Bandar Seri Begawan
Librarian: Thelma T Salazar

Bulgaria

General Information

Language: Bulgarian (English becoming common foreign language. Russian widely used)
Religion: About 27% Eastern Orthodox, about 7% Muslim
Population: 8.8 million
Literacy Rate (1965): 90.2% (94.8% Urban, 86.2% Rural)
Bank Hours: 0830-1145 Monday-Friday; 0800-1100 Saturday
Shop Hours: 0800-1300, 1600-1900 Monday-Saturday
Currency: 100 stotinki = 1 lev
Export/Import Information: Foreign trade is a state monopoly and tariffs are paid by enterprise involved. Books imported by the foreign trade organization 'Hemus', pl Slavejkov 11, Sofia. Exchange controls
Copyright: UCC, Berne (see International section)

Book Trade Organizations

Obedinenie **'Bulgarska Kniga'***, pl Slavejkov 11, Sofia Tel: 879111 Telex: 22927 Kpms
'Bulgarian Book' Corporation

Suyuz Knigoizdatelite i Knizharite*, vu Solum 4, Sofia
Union of Publishers and Booksellers

Book Trade Reference Books and Journals

Books

Bulgarian Academic Books, Catalogue of the Books and Periodicals of the Bulgarian Academy of Sciences and the Academy of Agricultural Sciences in Bulgaria, Bulgarian Academy of Sciences, blvd Vitosha 39, Sofia C

Búlgarski Knigi (Bulgarian Books), Jusautor, pl Slavejkov 11, Sofia

Publishers

Knigoizdatelstvo 'Georgi **Bakalov**'*, blvd Hristo Botev 3, Varna Tel: 25077
Subjects: Maritime, Economics

Izdatelstvo na **Bulgarskata Akademia** na Naukite*, ul Academician G Bonchev 1113, Sofia Tel: 724643
Publishing House of the Bulgarian Academy of Sciences
Subject: Science

Izdatelstvo na **Bulgarskata Komunisticheska Partiya***, blvd Lenin 47, 1507 Sofia Tel: 4631
Publishing House of the Bulgarian Communist Party
Subjects: Geodesy, Philosophy, Politics, Popular Sciences, Sociology, Political Economy

Bulgarski Houdozhnik*, ul Moskovska 37, Sofia Tel: 884480/884275
Dir: Prof Petr Tchuchovski
Subjects: Art, Archaeology, Juveniles
Founded: 1952

Bulgarski Pissatel*, ul 6 Septemvri 35, Sofia Tel: 884734
Publishing House of the Union of Bulgarian Writers
Dir: Simeon Sultanov
Subjects: General Fiction, Belles Lettres

Izdatelstvo na **Bulgarskiya Zemedelski Naroden Suyuz***, ul Yanko Zabounov 1, Sofia Tel: 881951
Subjects: Social & Popular Politics, Agriculture, Fiction

Darzhavno Izdatelstov 'Christo G **Danov**'*, ul Petko Karavelov 17, 4000 Plovdiv Tel: 25232
Dir: Peter Anastassov: *Editorial:* Atanas Mossengov
Parent Company: TPO 'Bulgarcka Kniga', pl Slavejkov 11, Sofia 1000
Subjects: Agriculture, University Textbooks, Poetry, Fiction translations, Bulgarian Fiction
Founded: 1855

Meditsina i Fizkultura*, pl Slavejkov 11, Sofia 1000 Tel: 879111
Subjects: Biology, Geography, Hygiene, Medicine, Sports

Darzhavno Izdatelstvo '**Muzica**'*, blvd Georgi Traykov 2a, Sofia Tel: 662031
Subjects: Music, Theory of Music

Narodna Kultura, ul Gavril Genov 4, 1000 Sofia Tel: 878063
Subject: Belles Lettres

Narodna Mladezh*, ul Kaloyan 10, Sofia Tel: 8681
People's Youth Publishing House
Manager: Marko Nedyalkov
Subjects: Juveniles, Philosophy, Mathematics, General, Political & Social Science, Original and Translated Fiction

Darzhavno Izdatelstvo '**Narodna Prosveta**'*, ul Vasil Drumev 37, Sofia Tel: 442211
Dir: Paunka Gocheva
Subject: Educational

Izdatelstvo na **Natsionalniya Savet** na Otetchestveniya Front*, blvd Dandukov 32, Sofia Tel: 878481/882991
Publishing House of the National Council of the Fatherland Front
Subjects: History, Politics, Popular Sciences, Belles Lettres

Darzhavno Izdatelstvo '**Nauka** i Izkustvo'*, blvd Rouski 6, 1080 Sofia Tel: 875701
State Publishing House 'Science & Art'
Dir: Ganka Slavctheva
Subjects: History, Art, Law, Philosophy, General & Social Science, Technology, Business, Languages, Mathematics, Physics and Natural Sciences
Founded: 1949

Izdatelstvo **Profizdat***, blvd Dondukov 82, Sofia Tel: 872501
Publishing House of the Central Council of Bulgarian Trade Unions
Manager: Ivan Daskalov
Subjects: General Fiction, Belles Lettres, Political Science, Philosophy, General & Social Science

Sinodalno Izdatelstvo*, ul Sveta Sofia 2, Sofia Tel: 883313
Synodal Publishing House
Subject: Liturgical Books

Sofia Press Agency*, ul Levski 1, Sofia Tel: 885831/885832 Cable Add: Sofia Press Telex: 22622
General Dir: Kristo Santov
Subjects: General Fiction, Belles Lettres, Poetry, Biography, History, Political Science, Music, Art, Philosophy, Reference, Guides
Bookshop: At above address
Founded: 1967

Technica*, blvd Rouski 6, Sofia Tel: 875701
Subjects: Encyclopaedias and Dictionaries, Textbooks

Voenno Izdatelstvo*, ul Ivan Vazov 12, Sofia Tel: 878116
Subjects: History, Social Sciences, Military

Darzhavno Izdatelstvo **Zemizdat***, blvd Lenin 47, 1504 Sofia, PB 422 Tel: 4631
State Agricultural Publishing House
Dir: Yosif Grigorov
Subjects: General Science, Agriculture, Textbooks, Hobbies, Non-fiction
Founded: 1949

Literary Agents

Jusautor*, pl Slavejkov 11, Sofia Tel: 884817 Cable Add: Jusautor Sofia
Dir General: Trayan Ivanov
Copyright Agency
The agency is the exclusive representative of Bulgarian authors of literary, scientific and art works, and also acts as an intermediary between foreign authors, publishers and agencies and Bulgarian users of their works

Major Booksellers

'**Hemus**' Foreign Trade Organization, blvd Roussky 6, Sofia Tel: 870365 Telex: 22267 Hemkik

Major Libraries

Central Historical **Archives***, ul Zhdanov 5, Sofia

Central **Archives** of the People's Republic of Bulgaria*, ul Slavanjska 4, Sofia

Central Library, **Bulgarian Academy of Sciences**, 7 Noemvri 1, 1040 Sofia Tel: 878966
Library Dir: Prof Elena Savova
Publications: Bulgarian Academic Books, Collected Papers (irregular)

Central Institute for Scientific and Technical Information (of the State Committee for Science, Technical Progress and Higher Education)*, Chapaev 56, Sofia

Central Medical Library*, blvd G Sofiiski 1, Sofia 1431
Dir: Mrs N Kudreva

Central Scientific Technical Library*, blvd G A Nasser 50, 1040 Sofia

Centre for Pedagogical Information and Documentation*, Lenin 125, Sofia

Cyril and Methodius National Library*, blvd Tolbuhin 11, 1504 Sofia Tel: 882811 Telex: 22432 Natlib
Dir: Mrs K Kalajozieva
Publications include: Biblioteki Bolgarii; Bibliotekoznanie, Bibliografiya, Knigoznanie Nauchna Informatsiya; Bŭlgarski Knigopis; Statisticheski Danni za Bibliotekite v Bŭlgariya

Central Agricultural Library of the 'G **Dimitrov**' Academy of Agricultural Sciences*, Dr Cankov 6, Sofia

Municipal Library*, ul Gurko 1, Sofia

National Library 'Ivan Vazov'*, Nikola Vaptzarov 17, 4000 Plovdiv Tel: 22915
Dir: Johan Lautliev

Sofia City and District State Archives*, ul Vitosha 2, Sofia
There are 26 District State Archives

Sofiiski Universitet 'Kliment Ohridsky' Biblioteka*, blvd Rouski 15, Sofia
University of Sofia Library

Central Library of the Higher **Technical Institutes***, Dr Cankov 2, Sofia

University of Sofia Library, see Sofiiski Universitet 'Kliment Ohridsky' Biblioteka

Library Associations

Bulgarian Union of Public Libraries*, ul Alabin 31, Sofia

Sekciya na Bibliotechnite Rabotnitsi pri Centralniya Komitet na Profesionalniya Sŭyuz na Rabotnitsite ot **Poligraficheskata Promishlenost i Kulturnite Instituti***, c/o Cyril and Methodius National Library, blvd Tolbuhin 11, 1504 Sofia Tel: 882811
Section of the Librarians at the Professional Organization of the Workers in Polygraphics and Culture
President: Stefan Káncev
Publications: Issues annual reports, and occasional publications jointly with the National Library, eg on IBY

Library Reference Books and Journals

Books

Biblioteki Bolgarii (Bulgarian Libraries), Cyril and Methodius National Library, blvd Tolbuhin 11, 1504 Sofia

Bibliotekoznanie, Bibliografiya, Knigoznanie Nauchna Informatsiya (Library Science, Bibliography, Scientific Information), Cyril and Methodius National Library, blvd Tolbuhin 11, 1504 Sofia

Journals

Bibliotekar (The Librarian), periodical for library work (Contents page in Bulgarian, English and Russian), Committee for Culture and Art and the Cyril and Methodius National Library, blvd Tolbuhin 11, 1504 Sofia

Bŭlgarski Knigopis (National Bibliography), Cyril and Methodius National Library, blvd Tolbuhin 11, 1504 Sofia

Statisticheski Danni za Bibliotekite v Bŭlgariya (Statistical Data on Libraries in Bulgaria), Cyril and Methodius National Library, blvd Tolbuhin 11, 1504 Sofia

Literary Associations and Societies

Bulgarian Academy of Sciences, Institute of Literature*, blvd Vitosha 39, Sofia C
Publication: Literatourna Missul

Bulgarian **P E N** Centre, angel Kanchev 5, 1000 Sofia
President: Liliana Stefanova

Bulgarian Writers' Union*, angel Kanchev 5, 1000 Sofia
President: M Lyubomir Levchev
Publications: Literaturen Front (weekly), *Septemvri* (monthly), *Plamak* (monthly), *Slaveiche* (monthly, for children), *Savremennik* (quarterly), *Obzor* (quarterly)

Komitet za Izkoustvo i Koultoura*, blvd Stambolissky 18, Sofia
Committee for Arts and Culture

Society of Aesthetes, Art and Literary Critics*, pl Evtimij 48, Sofia
Secretary: Dr K Goranov

Literary Periodicals

Literaturen Front (weekly), Bulgarian Writers' Union, angel Kanchev 5, 1000 Sofia

Literatourna Missul (Literary Thought), (text in Bulgarian, contents page in English and French), Bulgarian Academy of Sciences, Institute of Literature, blvd Vitosha 39, Sofia C

Obzor (Survey), Bulgarian quarterly review of literature and the arts (text in English, Spanish and French), Bulgarian Writers' Union, Committee for Friendship and Cultural Relations with Foreign Countries, angel Kanchev 5, 1000 Sofia

Plamak (The Flame), literature, art, publicity, Bulgarian Writers' Union, angel Kanchev 5, 1000 Sofia

Savremennik (quarterly), Bulgarian Writers' Union, angel Kanchev 5, 1000 Sofia

Literary Prizes

A competition for the best Bulgarian book published abroad is held at the annual Sofia International Book Fair

Bulgarian Publishing Award*
For the best artistic and technical achievements in the art of book publishing. Awarded annually. Enquiries to 'Bulgarian Book' Corporation and the Union of Bulgarian Artists, pl Slavejkov 11, Sofia

Burma

General Information

Language: Burmese (English used for foreign correspondence)
Religion: Buddhism
Population: 32.2 million
Literacy Rate (1953): 69.1%
Bank Hours: 1000-1400 Monday-Friday; 1000-1200 Saturday
Shop Hours: Generally 0800-1700 Monday-Saturday
Currency: 100 pyas = 1 kyat
Export/Import Information: Burma has own complex tariff system, but duties are paid by State Trading Corporation No 9, 550-552 Merchant St, Rangoon, and Printing and Publishing Corporation, 228 Theinbyu St, Rangoon, principally. No tariffs on advertising. Books exempt from sales tax. Import licence required. Exchange controls; priorities apply
Copyright: No copyright conventions signed

Book Trade Organization

Burmese Publishers' Union*, 146 Bogyoke Market, Rangoon

Publishers

Hanthawaddy Book House*, 157 Bo Aung Gyaw St, Rangoon
Subjects: Textbooks, Multilingual Dictionaries
Bookshop: Hanthawaddy Bookshop (qv under Major Booksellers)

Knowledge Printing & Publishing House*, 130 Bo Gyoke Aung San St, Yegyaw, Rangoon
Subjects: Art, Education, Politics, Religion, Sociology
Bookshop: Knowledge Book House (qv under Major Booksellers)

Kyi-Pwar-Ye Book House*, 84th St, Letsegan Mandalay
Subjects: Travel, Arts, Religion, Juveniles

Sarpay Beikman Board, 529 Merchant St, Rangoon Tel: 83611 Cable Add: Sarbeikman
Chairman: Aung Htay; *Secretary:* Lt-Col Mg MgLay; *Sales, Publicity & Advertising:* U Tin Gyi; *Editorial:* Myo Thant
Subjects: Encyclopaedia, General Information, Culture, History, Applied Science, Agriculture, Law, Literature, Biography, Children's Journal
Bookshop: Sarpay Beikman Bookshop (qv under Major Booksellers)
Book Club: Sarpay Beikman Book Club
Founded: 1947

Shumawa Publishing House*, 146 Bogyoke Aung San Market, Rangoon
Bookshop: Shumawa Book House (qv under Major Booksellers)
Subjects: Mechanical Engineering, Technical

Shwepyidan Printing & Publishing House*, 12(A) Hninban St, Yegwaw Quarter, Rangoon
Subjects: Politics, Law, Religion

Smart & Mookerdum*, 221 Sule Pagoda Rd, Rangoon
Subjects: Arts, Juveniles, Cookery, Popular Sciences

Than Myit Baho Publishing House*, 230 Anawyatha Rd, Rangoon
Subjects: Scientific, Technical

Thudhammawaddy Press*, 55-56 Moung Khine St, Rangoon
Subject: Religion

Universities Administration Office*, Prome Rd, University Post Office, Rangoon
Chief Editor, Translations and Publications Department: U Wun

Book Club

Sarpay Beikman Book Club, 529 Merchant St, Rangoon
Owned by: Sarpay Beikman Board (qv)

Major Booksellers

Chindwin Book Distributors*, 180 47th St, Rangoon

Gondu*, 209 33rd St, Rangoon

Hanthawaddy Bookshop*, 357 Bo Aung Gyaw St, Rangoon
Also Publisher (qv)

Hna Lon Hla*, 5 100th St, PO Box 87, Kandawlay PO, Rangoon

Knowledge Book House*, 130 Bo Gyoke Aung San St, Rangoon
Also Publisher (qv)

Pagan Publishing House*, 123 Myamagonyi St, Kandawlay, Rangoon

Sabe U*, 148-150 33rd St, Rangoon

Sarpay Beikman Bookshop, 529 Merchant St, Rangoon
Manager: U Tin Gyi
Owned by: Sarpay Beikman Board (qv)

Sarpay Lawka*, 173 33rd St, Rangoon

Shumawa Book House*, 1 Sandwith Rd, Rangoon
Also Publisher (qv)

Thwe Thauk*, 341 Bo Aung Gyaw St, Rangoon

Major Libraries

Arts & Science University Library*, University Estate, Mandalay

Institute of Economics Library*, University Estate, Rangoon

Institute of Education Library*, University Estate, Rangoon

Rangoon Institute of Technology Library, Gyogon, Insein PO, Rangoon
Librarian: Daw Myint Myint Khyn

International Institute of Advanced Buddhistic Studies Library*, Kaba-aye Pagoda Compound, Rangoon

Magwe College Library*, Magwe

National Library*, Town Hall, Rangoon

State Library*, Moulmein

Universities' Central Library*, University Estate, Rangoon

Library Associations

Burma Library Association*, c/o International Institute of Advanced Buddhistic Studies, Kaba Aya, Rangoon

Jubilee Library Association*, c/o Steel Road, Toungoo

Literary Associations and Societies

Department of Ancient Literature and Culture, **Ministry of Culture***, 1 Church Rd, Rangoon

Literary Prizes

National Literary Awards
When the Burma Translation Society (now renamed Sarpay Beikman Board) was founded in 1947 it established the Best-Published-Novel-of-the-Year Prize. Min Aung won the prize for 1948 with his book *Mo Auk Mye Byin* (Land under the Sky). The prize money was K1000 (one thousand kyats).
The awards were gradually increased and in 1962 Sarpay Beikman was offering nine awards. They were for the best published novel of the year, the best collection of short stories, the best belles lettres, the best book of knowledge, the best book of poems, the best translation of a world classic, and the best published play of the year. In the absence of any official literary awards, the Sarpay Beikman literary awards were then virtually honoured as national literary awards.
When Sarpay Beikman was taken over by the Revolutionary Government in August 1963 the Sarpay Beikman Literary Awards were transformed into National Literary Awards. More literary awards were gradually added and there are now 13 awards. The awards are for the best published novel of the year, the best collection of short stories, the best belles lettres, the best book of knowledge (arts), the best book of knowledge (science), the best book of poems, the best translation of a world classic, the best translation in the general knowledge field, the best published play, the best book for children, the best book for youth, the best book on Burmese culture and the best book on political affairs. A panel of literary specialists is formed every two years by the State to adjudicate the published works.
Each national literary award now draws prize money of K6000. The awards are presented at a ceremony on Sarsodaw Day (Literary Day), which usually falls in December. Enquiries to The Secretary, Sarpay Beikman Board, 529 Merchant St, Rangoon

Sarpay Beikman Best Manuscripts Awards
In order to discover new writers and to enable promising manuscripts to be published, Sarpay Beikman Board has established a competition for the Best-Manuscripts-of-the-Year-Awards since 1969. There are 11 prizes for the best manuscripts of the year: for novels, short stories, belles lettres, general knowledge (arts), general knowledge (science), plays, children's literature, literature for youth, Burmese cultural affairs, political affairs and translations of a prescribed literary material. There are first, second and third prizes for each award and prize moneys are K5000, K3000 and K2000 respectively.
All prize-winning manuscripts (except translations) are published by Sarpay Beikman. Only the manuscript which wins the first prize in translation is published by Sarpay Beikman. The right to print and publish prize-winning manuscript for the first time is solely reserved with Sarpay Beikman. No payment is needed to pay for the first printing; for second printing, payments are made on royalty basis.
Enquiries to The Secretary, Sarpay Beikman Board, 529 Merchant St, Rangoon

Burundi

General Information

Language: French and Kirundi (a Bantu language)
Religion: About half Roman Catholic; others follow traditional beliefs
Population: 4.3 million
Bank Hours: Normally closed for cash transactions in afternoon but open for all other business morning and afternoon
Shop Hours: 0800-1200, 1400-1630 Monday-Friday; 0800-1200 Saturday
Currency: Burundi franc
Export/Import Information: Import licence required over value of 20,000 Burundi francs

Publishers

Government Printer*, BP 1400, Bujumbura

Les Presses **Lavigerie**, 5 ave de l'Uprona, BP 1640, Bujumbura

Major Booksellers

Burundi Literature Center*, BP 18, Gitega Tel: 2266

Imparudi (Imprimerie et Papeterie du Burundi)*, BP 509, Bujumbura Tel: 3125

Librairie Evangélique du Burundi*, BP 630, Bujumbura

Librairie **Saint Paul***, BP 1360, Bujumbura

Major Libraries

Bibliothèque publique*, BP 960, Bujumbura

Bibliothèque publique de Kitega*, Kitega

Ecole normale supérieure, Bibliothèque*, BP 1065, Bujumbura Tel: 3544
Librarian: Deogratias Ndayizeye
Publication: Pédagogie

Institut Murundi d'Information et de Documentation (IMIDOC)*, 7 ave Malfeyt, BP 902, Bujumbura

Bibliothèque de l'**Université du Burundi***, BP 1320, Bujumbura Tel: 5196/5446 Cable Add: Univarwa
Librarian: H Mununi

Literary Associations and Societies

Centre culturel du Burundi*, BP 1582, Bujumbura

United Republic of Cameroun

General Information

Language: French and English (officially bilingual)
Religion: Predominantly traditional in west and south, Muslim in centre and north
Population: 8.06 million
Bank Hours: East: 0800-1130, 1430-1530 Monday-Friday; West: 0800-1330 Monday-Friday
Shop Hours: 0800-1200, 1430-1730 (earlier closing in West) Monday-Friday; 0800-1200 Saturday
Currency: CFA franc
Export/Import Information: Member of Customs and Economic Union of Central Africa. Import licence, entitling holder to provision for necessary foreign exchange, required if value of import is over 500,000 CFA francs
Copyright: UCC Berne, Florence (see International section)

Book Trade Reference Book

Cameroon Imprints, BP 338, Douala

Publishers

Editions **Buma Kor***, BP 727, Yaoundé Tel: 221556 Telex: 8231 Kn
Man Dir and Rights & Permissions: B D Buma Kor; *Sales:* Arrey Martin Ebot
Parent Company: Buma Kor & Co (Sàrl)
Imprint: Chemin Facile
Subjects: General, Children's and Christian Literature; Educational
Bookshop: Librairie Bilingue (qv under Major Booksellers)
Founded: 1977

Editions **C L E**, BP 1501, Yaoundé Tel: 223554 Cable/Telex: Cle Yaoundé
General Manager: Jean Dihang; *Sales Manager:* Sindjui Etienne
Subjects: General Fiction & Non-fiction, Belles Lettres, Poetry, Biography, History/Africana, How-to, Study Guides, Philosophy, Religion, Juveniles, Paperbacks, Medicine, General & Social Science, University & Secondary Textbooks
Founded: 1963
ISBN Publisher's Prefix: 2-7235

Centre d'Edition et de Production pour l'Enseignement et la Recherche (CEPER)*, Elig-Essono, BP 808, Yaoundé Tel: 221323 Cable Add: Cepmae Yaoundé Telex: 8338
Dir General: Michel Dzukou Tahouo; *Sales Manager:* Wilfred W Banmbuh; *Production Manager:* John Matute Ewoma-Esunge
Subjects: General Non-fiction, History/Africana, Paperbacks, Science & Technology, General & Social Science, University & Secondary Textbooks
Founded: 1967

Centre d'Edition et de Production de Manuels scolaires de l'UNESCO*, Yaoundé

Chemin Facile, an imprint of Editions Buma Kor (qv)

Editions Le **Flambeau***, BP 113, Yaoundé Tel: 223672
Man Dir: Joseph Ndzie; *Sales:* Thomas Etoundi; *Production:* Raphael Nkonda
Subjects: General
Bookshop: At above address
Founded: 1977

Government Printer*, BP 1091, Yaoundé

Librairie/Imprimerie **Saint Paul***, Ave Monseigneur Vogt, BP 763, Yaoundé
Subjects: Religion, Christian tracts, Paperbacks, Secondary & Primary Textbooks
Bookshop: See under Major Booksellers

Editions **Semences** Africaines+, BP 2180, Yaoundé-Messa
Man Dir, Production: Philippe-Louis Ombede; *Editorial, Rights & Permissions:* Martin King Mbida; *Sales:* Lea Ombede
Orders to: BP 5329, Yaoundé-Nlongkak
Subjects: General Fiction, History, Africana, Religion, Paperbacks, Secondary & Primary Textbooks (in French and English only), Poetry, Theatre
Bookshop: BP 5329, Yaoundé-Nlongkak
Founded: 1974

Société Kenkoson d'Etudes Africaines*, BP 4064, Yaoundé
Chief Executive: Marie Salomé
Subjects: Academic, Law
Founded: 1975

Book Club

Academic Book Club*, BP 345, Kumba, South West Province
Manager: M P Napong

Major Booksellers

Librairie '**Aux Frères Réunis**'*, BP 5346, Douala

Cameroun Book Centre*, 2C Nambeke St, BP 123, Victoria Tel: 332255

Centre de Diffusion du Livre Camerounais, BP 611, Douala Tel: 422044
Manager: Lalande Isnard

Ebibi Book Centre, BP 89, Mankon-Bamenda, North West Province Tel: 361123

Librairie Bilingue/The Bilingual Bookshop, BP 727, Mvog-Ada, Yaoundé Tel: 221556 Telex: 8231
Owned by: Editions Buma Kor (qv)

Librairie-Papeterie Moderne*, BP 495, Yaoundé

Librairie-Papeterie Protestante CEBEC*, BP 225, Douala

Librairie Populaire*, BP 322, Baffoussam Tel: 441105

Presbyterian Book Depot and Printing Press Ltd (PRESBOOK)*, BP 13, Victoria Tel: Victoria 337214/335246 Telex: 5613 Kw
Manager: J Andoseh
Branches: Presbook Mankon, BP 39, Bamenda; Presbook Kumba, BP 4; Presbook Buea, BP 19; Presbook Kumba, BP 87; Presbook Douala (Akwa), BP 5419

Librairie **Saint Paul**, BP 763, Yaoundé Tel: 223404
Also Publisher (qv)

Major Libraries

Archives nationales du Cameroun*, BP 1053, Yaoundé Tel: 220078

Bibliothèque nationale du Cameroun*, BP 1053, Yaoundé Tel: 220078

British Council Library, BP 818, Yaoundé (Located at: Les Galeries, rue J F Kennedy, Yaoundé) Tel: 221696/223172

Centre culturel américain, Bibliothèque de Prêt*, American Embassy, BP 817, Yaoundé
This is a lending library
Librarian: Emile Mongo-Bebey
Publications include: Selected bibliographies

Centre culturel français, Bibliothèque*, BP 513, Yaoundé Tel: 220533
Chief Librarian: Anne-Marie Bot

Collège camerounais des Arts, des Sciences et de la Technologie, Bibliothèque*, Bamili, BP Bamenda

Ecole normale supérieure, Bibliothèque*, BP 47, Yaoundé Tel: 221215

Pan African Institute for Development, The Library, BP 133, Buea, South-West Province Tel: 328216
Librarian: Eugene O Nwanosike

Université de Yaoundé, Bibliothèque*, BP 1312, Yaoundé Tel: 220744
Librarian: Peter Nkangafaok Chateh
Publications: Discours de la Rentrée Solennelle de l'Université (annual)

Victoria Public Library*, BP 13, Victoria Tel: 336211
Chief Librarian: Albert Kalle

Library Association

Association des Bibliothécaires, Archivistes, Documentalistes et Muséographes du Cameroun (ABADCAM)*, c/o P N Chateh, President, ABADCAM, Bibliothèque Universitaire, BP 1312, Yaoundé Tel: 220744
Association of Librarians, Archivists, Documentalists and Museum Curators of Cameroon
Secretary General: Th Eno Belinga
Publications: Newsletter

Library Reference Journal

Newsletter, Association of Librarians, Archivists, Documentalists and Museum Curators of Cameroun, c/o P N Chateh, President, ABADCAM, Bibliothèque Universitaire, BP 1312, Yaoundé

Literary Associations and Societies

Association nationale des Poètes et Ecrivains camerounais (APEC)*, BP 2180, Yaoundé-Messa
National Association of Cameroun Poets and Writers
Secretary-General: R Philombe
Publication: Cameroun littéraire

Forum littéraire camerounais*, BP 73, Yaoundé
Cameroun Literary Workshop
Publication: Ozila

Literary Periodicals

Abbia, BP 879, Yaoundé
Literary and cultural magazine edited by Bernard Fonlon, articles in English and French

Cameroun littéraire (Literary Cameroun) (text in English and French), National Association of Cameroun Poets and Writers, BP 2180, Yaoundé-Messa

Ozila, Cameroun Literary Workshop, BP 73, Yaoundé
A 'little magazine' edited by Jean-Pierre Togolo

Central African Republic

General Information

Language: French, Sangho
Religion: About half Christian, half traditional
Population: No reliable figures available; perhaps about 2 million
Bank Hours: 0700-1200 Monday-Saturday
Shop Hours: 0700 or 0800-1200 or 1230, 1430 or 1500-1830 or 1900 Tuesday-Saturday, mostly
Currency: CFA franc
Export/Import Information: Member of Customs and Economic Union of Central Africa. Import licence required but granted automatically for imports from EEC countries. Imports subject to quotas. Exchange controls outside franc zone
Copyright: Berne (see International Section)

Publishers

Government Printer (Imprimerie Centrale d'Afrique)*, BP 329, Bangui

Major Booksellers

Au Messager*, BP 823, Bangui

Librairie centrafricaine*, BP 823, Bangui (Located at: Ave de l'Independance) Tel: 611466

Librairie évangélique*, BP 240, Bangui

Papeterie Centrale*, BP 1442, Bangui

'Papyrus'*, BP 920, Bangui

Major Libraries

Centre culturel français, Bibliothèqueque*, BP 971, Bangui Tel: 2927

Ecole normale primaire et supérieure, Bibliothèque*, BP 858, Bangui

Bibliothèque de l'Université Jean-Bédel Bokassa*, BP 1450, Bangui Tel: 2424
National Library

Chad

General Information

Note: No replies were received to questionnaires sent to Chad for this edition of *International Literary Market Place*. The information given in the 1983-84 edition has been repeated here but should be treated with caution.

Language: French
Religion: Muslim in north, traditional and some Christian in south
Population: 4.3 million
Bank Hours: 0700-1200 Monday-Saturday
Shop Hours: 0700 or 0800-1200 or 1230, 1600-1900 Monday-Saturday; some close Monday
Currency: CFA franc
Export/Import Information: No tariff on books. Consumption tax on children's picture books and advertising. Import licences required except for imports from the EEC and the Franc Zone.
Copyright: Berne (see International section)

Publishers

Government Printer*, BP 453, N'Djamena

Major Booksellers

Georges **Abtour** SA, Librairie-Papeterie*, BP 103, N'Djamena

Bielmas Librairie-Papeterie*, BP 71, N'Djamena

Librairie **Billeret***, BP 463, N'Djamena

Librairie évangélique*, BP 127, N'Djamena

Librairie **Notre Dame***, BP 7, N'Djamena Tel: 3330

Major Libraries

Bibliothèque paroissiale*, Cathédrale Notre-Dame, BP 456, N'Djamena Tel: 3350
Parochial Library

Centre culturel américain, Bibliothèque*, BP 3, N'Djamena Tel: 2846

Centre culturel français, Bibliothèque*, BP 901, N'Djamena Tel: 2920

Centre de Documentation Pédagogique, Bibliothèque*, BP 731, N'Djamena Tel: 2327

Bibliothèque de l'**Université du Tchad***, BP 1117, N'Djamena Tel: 2176
Chief Librarian: Ngaoudandi Djaokamla

Channel Islands

General Information

Language: English. French widely known. Norman-French now spoken by only a few
Religion: Predominantly Protestant (Church of England)
Population: 130,000
Bank Hours: 0930-1530 Monday-Friday
Shop Hours: 0900-1730 Monday-Wednesday, Friday and Saturday; 0900-1300 Thursday
Currency: Guernsey: 100 pence = 1 Guernsey pound. Jersey: 100 pence = 1 Jersey pound. 1 Guernsey pound = 1 Jersey pound = £1 sterling. British currency circulates and Bank of England notes are legal tender. Guernsey currency circulates in Jersey and vice versa

Publishers

Ashton & Denton Publishing Co (CI) Ltd, 5 Burlington House, St Saviour's Rd, St Helier, Jersey Tel: 35461/75805
Man Dir & Sales: A D W Mackenzie; *Editorial, Publicity:* Mrs Y E Aston; *Production:* M Mackenzie
Subjects: Local History, Holiday Guides
Founded: 1957

Neville **Spearman** (Jersey) Ltd*, Normandy House, PO Box 75, St Helier, Jersey
Dirs: Neville Armstrong, M J Armstrong
Subjects: Occult, Metaphysical and Unorthodox
ISBN Publisher's Prefix: 0-85978

Toucan Press, Mount Durand, St Peter Port, Guernsey Tel: 45091
Man Dir: G Stevens Cox; *Editorial:* G and J Stevens Cox; *Sales:* J Stevens Cox
Subjects: Archaeology, History, Thomas Hardy, Somerset, Dorset, Hairdressing, Wigmaking, Channel Islands, Folklore
Bookshops: Coleridge Bookshop, Rue des Monts, St Sampson, Guernsey; Old Curiosity Shop, Commercial Rd, St Sampson, Guernsey
Founded: 1850
ISBN Publisher's Prefix: 0-85694

Vallancey International Ltd*, PO Box 280, St Peter Port, Guernsey Tel: 21673 (STD code 0481)
Man Dir: Mrs J M Bishop
Subjects: Economic & Financial Reference
1981: 2 titles *Founded:* 1912

Chile

General Information

Language: Spanish
Religion: Roman Catholic
Population: 10.9 million
Literacy Rate (1970): 88.1% (92.4% Urban, 72.8% Rural)
Bank Hours: 0900-1400 Monday-Friday
Shop Hours (Santiago): 1000-1900 Monday-Friday; 0900-1300 Saturday
Currency: 100 centavos = 1 peso
Export/Import Information: Member of Latin American Free Trade Association
Copyright: UCC, Berne, Buenos Aires (see International section)

Book Trade Organization

Cámara Chilena del Libro AG, Ahumada 312, DF 806, 13526 Santiago Tel: 89519
Chilean Publishers' and Booksellers' Association
President: Manuel Melero Abaroa; *Secretary:* Jorge Barros Torrealba

Book Trade Reference Journal

Bibliografía chilena (Chilean Bibliography), National Library of the Office of Libraries, Archives & Museums, Ave Bernardo O'Higgins 651, Santiago

Publishers

Aguilar Chilena de Ediciones SA, Gálvez 176-180, Casilla 10133, Santiago
Parent Company: Aguilar SA de Ediciones, Spain (qv)

Editorial Andrés **Bello**/Editorial Juridíca de Chile+, Ave Ricardo Lyon 946, Casilla 4256, Providencia, Santiago Tel: 2253600/2234565 Cable Add: Edibel
General Manager: William Thayer Arteaga; *Editorial:* Mercedes Gaju
Subjects: Medicine, History, Social Science, Literature, Law, Arts
Bookshop: Librería Andrés Bello (qv under Major Booksellers)
Book Club: Clubs de Lectores 'Andrés Bello'
1981: 151 titles *1982:* 65 titles *Founded:* 1947

Centro Latinoamericano de Demografía (CELADE)*, Edificio Naciones Unidas, Ave Dag Hammarskjöld, Casilla 91, Santiago Tel: 283206
Dir: Oscar Julián Bardeci
Branch Off: Apdo 5249, San José, Costa Rica
Subjects: Demography, Statistics, Sociology, Periodicals

Editorial Gustavo **Gili** Ltda*, Santa Victoria 151, Santiago Tel: 2224567 Cable Add: Gusto
Parent Company: Editorial Gustavo Gili SA, Spain (qv)

Grijalbo y Cía Ltda*, Almirante Barroso 27, Santiago Tel: 723027 Cable Add: Grijalbo Telex: 340260 Pbvtr Ck Grijalbo
Parent Company: Ediciones Grijalbo SA, Spain (qv)

Editorial **Jurídica** de Chile, see Editorial Andrés Bello

Editora Nacional Gabriela **Mistral** Ltda*, Ave Santa María 076, Santiago Tel: 779522
Man Dir: José Harrison de la Barra; *Sales & Publicity Dir:* Jorge Sims Sn Roman
Subjects: Literature, Biography, History, Philosophy, Reference, Religion, How-to, Art, Juveniles, Secondary & Primary Textbooks
Miscellaneous: Government-owned

Editorial **Nascimento** SA, Casilla 2298, Santiago Tel: 50254 Cable Add: Nascimento
Man Dir: Carlos George-Nascimento Marquez
Subjects: General Fiction & Non-fiction, Scholarly Books
Bookshop: Librería Nascimento, San Antonio 390, Santiago Tel: 32062
Founded: 1898

Editorial del **Pacifico** SA*, Alonso Ovalle 766, Casilla 3547, Santiago Tel: 397805/395317
General Manager: Arturo Valdes Phillips; *Editorial:* Lidio Ramirez Rivera; *Sales:* Jose de Gregorio Aroca; *Production:* Emilio Pot Von; *Publicity:* Mrs Magali Zamorano Castro; *Rights & Permission:* Raul Zamora Messina
Associate Company: Ediciones Mar del Sur, Casilla 13844, Santiago
Subsidiary Company: Distribuidora Alonso Ovalle Ltda

Subjects: History, Politics, Economics, Literature, Educations, Primary, Secondary and University Textbooks
Founded: 1946

Ediciones **Paulinas**, Vicuña Mackenna 10777, Casilla 3746, Santiago Tel: 2212883/2216065
Orders to: Libreria San Pablo, Casilla 3746, Santiago Tel: 89145
Branches and associated companies in 20 countries
Subjects: Catholic texts, Books for Youth and Mass-Media series
Bookshops: Librería San Pablo (qv under Major Booksellers)
1981-82: 120 titles

Pineda Libros*, Bandera 101, Casilla 13556, Santiago Tel: 721807
Man Dir: A Gonzalo Pineda
Subjects: Literature, History, Juveniles, Paperbacks
Bookshops: Pergola del Libro: Merced 838; Bandera 101 (both in Santiago)
Founded: 1944

Editorial **Pomaire** Ltda*, Casilla 10460, Santiago (Located at: Ave Manuel Montt 2534, Santiago) Tel: 43330
Manager: Jorge Barros T
Head Off: Editorial Pomaire SA, Spain (qv for other branches)

Editorial El **Sembrador***, Casilla 2037, Santiago (Located at: Sargento Aldea 1041, Santiago) Tel: 569454
Dir, Editorial: Isaías Gutiérrez V
Bookshop: Librería El Sembrador (qv under Major Booksellers)

Editorial **Universitaria***, Maria Luisa Santander 0447, Casilla 10220, Santiago Tel: 234555 Cable Add: Edunsa
Man Dir: Gabriela Matte Alessandri
Subjects: General Literature, General & Social Science, Technical, Textbooks
Founded: 1947

Ediciones **Universitarias** de la Universidad Católica de Valparaíso, Casilla 1415, Valparaíso (Located at: Dr Montt, Saavedra 44, Valparaíso) Tel: 52900 Telex: 230389 Ucval
General Manager: Karlheinz Laage Hidalgo; *Production:* Luis A Briones Solís; *Art Dir:* Allan Browne Escobar; *Sales:* Julio George-Nascimento Failla
Branch Off: Moneda 673, 8° piso, Santiago Tel: 32230
Subjects: General Literature, Social Sciences, Engineering, Education, Music, Arts, Textbooks, Children's Books
Founded: 1970

Empressa Editora **Zig-Zag** SA*, Casilla 84-D, Santiago (Located at: Amapolas 2075, Santiago) Tel: 235766 Telex: 94455 Zig Zag Ku
General Manager: Rodrigo Castro Cuevas

Book Clubs

Clubs de Lectores 'Andrés **Bello**', Lyon 946, Casilla 4256, Santiago
Owned by: Editorial Andrés Bello (qv)
There are two clubs: one for children (membership 20,000); the other for adults (membership 37,000)
Founded: 1979

Studio Book Club*, Casilla 1227, Santiago (Located at: Andres de Fuenzalida 36, Santiago) Tel: 2259432/2250452 Cable Add: Studio Telex: 40084 Studi Cl
Members: 200
Owned by: Elise Friedler Weiss (Librería Studio – qv under Major Booksellers)

Major Booksellers

Librería Andrés **Bello**, Huérfanos 1158, Santiago Tel: 722116
Manager: Francisco Hoyl Sotomayor
Also Publisher (qv)

Librería y Editorial **Cultura***, Huérfanos 1179, Santiago Tel: 88830

Feria Chilena del Libro*, Huérfanos 1112, Santiago Tel: 721420

Librería **Universitaria***, Alameda 1050, Santiago Tel: 84135

Librería **Orellana**, Esmeralda 1148, Casilla 280, Valparaíso Tel: 51281

Librería **Parera***, Condell 1202-1206, Valparaíso Tel: 57162

Librería y Editorial **Pax-Chile** Ltda, Casilla 1499, Santiago (Located at: Almirante Barroso 337, Santiago) Tel: 727841
Manager: Rene Ramirez Ramirez
Also: Huérfanos 786 y 973, Santiago

Librería **San Pablo**, Ave Bernardo O'Higgins 1626, Casilla 3746, Santiago Tel: 89145/716884
Manager: Hermano Pablo Uriarte
Branches: Calle Manuel Matta 2588, Casilla 232, Antofagasta; Calle Barros Arana 540, Casilla 1921, Concepcion; Calle Pedro Montt, Casilla 1892, Valparaíso; Centro Catequistico, Calle Cienfuegos 60, Casilla 3429, Santiago; Hijas de San Pablo, Ave Vicuña Mackenna 6299, Casilla 3429, Santiago
Owned by: Ediciones Paulinas (qv)

Librería El **Sembrador***, Pasaje Matte 342-344, Casilla 2037, Santiago Tel: 396675/35295
Branches: two in Santiago, and one in Africa
Owned by: Editorial El Sembrador (qv)

Librería **Studio***, Andrés de Fuenzalida 36, Santiago Tel: 2259432/2250452 Cable Add: Studio Telex: 40084 Studi Cl
Manager: Elise Friedler Weiss
Branch in Valparaíso (Viña de Mar)

Major Libraries

Biblioteca Nacional de Chile de la Dirección de Bibliotecas, Archivos y Museos, Ave Bernardo O'Higgins 651, Santiago Tel: 383206
National Library of the Office of Libraries, Archives & Museums
Dir: Enrique Campos Menendez
Publications: Bibliografía chilena (formerly *Anvario de la Prensa*), *Referencias Críticas de Autores Chilenos, Mapocho*

Biblioteca del **Congreso** Nacional, Compañia 1175 – 2° piso, Clasificador 1199, Santiago
Library of Congress
Dir: Jorge Ivan Hübner Gallo; *Chief Librarian:* Jose Miguel Vicuña Lagarrigue
Publications include: *Boletín bibliográfico; Efimeros; Indice de artículos de Prensa Extranjera referentes a Chile* (Index of foreign press articles referring to Chile) (1977-); *Bibliografías especializadas* (periodical series)

Biblioteca del **Instituto** Chileno-Británico de Cultura*, Casilla 3900, Santiago Tel: 382156

Biblioteca Central de la Pontificia **Universidad Católica de Chile***, Vicuña Mackenna 4860, Santiago Tel: 515871 Telex: 40395
Dir: Soledad Ferreiro
Publications: Bibliografía Eclesiástica Chilena; Presentación del trabajo escrito

Biblioteca de la **Universidad Católica de Valparaíso***, Casilla 4059, Valparaíso (Located at: Ave Brasil 2950, Valparaíso) Tel: 51024

Biblioteca Central de la **Universidad de Chile***, Calle Arturo Prat 23, Santiago

Biblioteca Central de la **Universidad de Concepción***, Casilla 1807, Concepción

Library Associations

Centro Nacional de Información y Documentación (CENID), Casilla 297-V, Correo 21, Santiago (Located at: Canada 308, Santiago)
National Centre of Information and Documentation
Publication: Guía de Bibliotecas y Centros de Documentacion de Chile

Colegio de Bibliotecarios de Chile, Diagonal Paraguay 383, Torre II, Departamento 122, Casilla 3741, Santiago
Chilean Library Association
President: Ursula Schadlich Schonhals
Publications: Noticias del Colegio, Indices de Publicaciones Periodicas en Bibliotecología

Library Reference Books and Journals

Books

Guía de Bibliotecas y Centros de Documentación de Chile (Guide to Chilean Libraries and Centres of Documentation), National Centre of Information and Documentation, Casilla 297-V, Correo 21, Santiago

Journals

Indices de Publicaciones Periodicas en Bibliotecología (Catalogue of Periodical Publications on Librarianship), Chilean Library Association, Diagonal Paraguay 383, Torre II, Departamento 122, Casilla 3741, Santiago

Literary Associations and Societies

Chilean **P E N** Centre, Tomas Guevara 2985, Santiago
Secretary: Eliana Cerda de Jarnholt

Sociedad de Bibliófilos Chilenos*, Casilla 895, Santiago
Society of Chilean Bibliophiles
Secretary: Ramón Eyzaguirre
Publication: El Bibliófilo Chileno (annual)

Literary Periodicals

El Bibliófilo Chileno (The Chilean Bibliophile), Society of Chilean Bibliophiles, Casilla 895, Santiago

Efimeros, Biblioteca del Congreso Nacional, Compãnia 1175 — 2° piso, Clasificador 1199, Santiago

Mapocho, Editorial Universitaria, Maria Luisa Santander 0447, Casilla 10220, Santiago

Revista Chilena de Literatura (Chilean Review of Literature), Editorial Universitaria, Maria Luisa Santander 0447, Casilla 10220, Santiago

Taller de Letras (Workshop of Letters), Editorial Universidad Católica, Diagonal Oriente 3300, Santiago

Literary Prizes

Andrés **Bello** Prize*
Founded to encourage Chilean authors. A prize of $US7,500, and publication of the novel, awarded every two years. Most recent winner was José Luis Rosasco for *Donde estás, Constanza*.... Enquiries to Editorial Andrés Bello, Ave Ricardo Lyon 946, Casilla 4256, Santiago

National Prize for Literature
Founded in 1942 in recognition of an author's sum of work. A monetary prize is awarded biennially. Enquiries to Ministerio de Educación de Chile, Dirección de Bibliotecas, Archivos y Museos, Ave Bernardo O'Higgins 651, Santiago

People's Republic of China

General Information

Language: Chinese: a single written language is used by speakers of several diverse spoken dialects. The most important spoken form is Mandarin, known in the People's Republic as *Putonghua* (= generally understood speech), which has been adopted as the national language of China. Other important spoken forms are Wu, Fukienese, Cantonese, Hakka and Amoy-Swatow
Religion: Confucian, Buddhist, Taoist
Population: 933 million
Shop Hours: Generally 0900-1900 every day
Currency: 10 fen = 1 jiao; 10 jiao = 1 yuan
Export/Import Information: Foreign trade is a state monopoly. The foreign distributor for Chinese publications is Guoji Shudian, PO Box 399, Beijing. The importing organization is Waiwen Shudian, PO Box 88, Beijing

Book Trade Reference Journal

Quan guo xin shu mu bian ji bu (Chinese National Bibliography), Bei Zong Bu Hu Tong 33 Hao, Beijing

Publishers

China National Publishing Industry Trading Corp, PO Box 614, Beijing Tel: 555005 Cable Add: Cnpitc Telex: 22497 Npapc
Subjects: All

China Youth Publishing House*, Beijing
Subjects: Literature, Journals
Founded: 1953

Chinese Philatelic Magazine Press*, 27 Dong Chang An St, Beijing
Editor-in-Chief: Wang Yongsheng
Subject: Philatelic magazines and books

Commercial Press*, 36 Wang Fu Jing St, Beijing
Subject: Foreign translations

Foreign Languages Press+, 24 Baiwanzhuang Rd, Beijing 37 Tel: 893238 Cable Add: Folapress Telex: 22496
Dir: Fan Yuan
Subjects: Chinese Language study books, Translations of Chinese authors, Books about China
1981: 54 titles *1982:* 80 titles *Founded:* 1952

National Minorities Publishing House*, Beijing
Subject: Books in languages spoken by minorities in China

People's Literature Publishing House*, Beijing
Also: Shanghai

People's Sports Publishing House, Beijing
Chief Executive: Liu Xiuzheng
Subjects: Sport books (including Chinese boxing, Wushu), Periodicals

Publishing Department*, Beijing
Special agency of the State Council; undertakes the major part of book publishing in China

'Sanlian Shudian' Publishing House*, Beijing
A state publishing house; general, political and literary

Workers' Press*, Beijing
Publishing house of All China Federation of Trade Unions

Writers' Publishing House*, Beijing
A state enterprise publishing reprints of Chinese literature

Youth Publishing House*, Beijing

Zhong Hua Book Co, Beijing
Subject: Chinese Classics

Major Booksellers

China Publications Centre (Guoji Shudian)*, PO Box 399, Beijing (Located at: Chegongzhuang Xilu 21) Tel: 891203 Cable Add: Guozi Beijing Telex: 22496 Guoji Cn
Man Dir: Cao Jianfei
Distributor abroad for Chinese publications

Guoji Shudian, see China Publications Centre

Waiwen Shudian*, PO Box 88, 38 Suchou Hutong, Beijing
Importer for foreign publications

Major Libraries

Beijing daxue tushuguan, Beijing
Peking University Library
Director: Zihuang Shoujing

Beijing tushuguan, now incorporated in Zhong-guo guo jia tushuguan (qv)

Chongqing Library*, Chongqing

Liaoning Library*, Shenyang (Mukden)

Nanjing tushuguan*, Nanjing, Jiangsu
Nanking Library

Qinghua daxue tushuguan*, Beijing
Qinghua University Library (formerly Tsing Hua University)

Shanghai tushuguan*, 325 Nanjing Rd, Shanghai
Shanghai Library
Director: Ku Ting-lung

Yunnan Provincial Library*, Kunming
Director: Mo Tien-chuang

Zhejiang tushuguan*, Hangzhou
Chekiang Library, Hangchow

Zhong-guo guo jia tushuguan, Beijing 7
National Library of China
Deputy Director: Ding Zhigang

Zhong-guo ke xue yuan tushuguan*, 271
Wanfu Dajie, Beijing
Library of Academic Science
Director: Fan Xinsan

Zhongshan Library of Guangdong
Province*, 62 Wende Rd, Guangzhou
(Canton) Tel: 33306
Director: Mrs Wang Zhi-Hua

Literary Associations and Societies

China P E N Centre, 2 Shatan Beijie, Beijing
Secretary: Bi Shuowang

Guangzhou Chinese P E N Centre, 1/69
Wende Lu, Guangzhou
Secretary: Miss Huang Qingyun

Literary Periodicals

China Books (English edition), organ of the
China Publications Centre (Guoji Shudian),
PO Box 399, Beijing

Chinese Literature (English and French
editions), Foreign Languages Press, 24
Baiwanzhuang, Beijing 37. Subscriptions to
China Publications Centre (Guoji Shudian),
PO Box 399, Beijing

Colombia

General Information

Language: Spanish (English widely used in
business)
Religion: Roman Catholic
Population: 25 million
Literacy Rate (1973): 80.8% (88.8% of urban
population, 65.3% rural)
Bank Hours: 0900-1500 Monday-Friday
Shop Hours: 0900-1230, 1430-1830 Monday-
Saturday
Currency: 100 centavos = 1 peso
Export/Import Information: Member of
Latin American Free Trade Association.
Value added taxes on all imports; no sales
tax on books. Ad valorem: none generally
on books except on books bound in leather
or similar materials, on photonovels of
thrillers, detective stories etc, on horoscopes,
on children's picture books, on atlases and
on advertising catalogues. No import licence
for books. Exchange licence from Banco de
la Republica required
Copyright: UCC, Buenos Aires (see
International section)

Book Trade Organizations

Asociación Nacional de Autores de Obras
Didacticas (AUCOLDI)*, Calle 14 No 12-15
of 508, Bogotá Tel: 349845
National Association of Authors of
Textbooks and Teaching Materials

Cámara Colombiana de la Industria
Editorial*, Carrera 7a, No 17-51 of 409 y
410, Apdo 8998, Bogotá Tel: 821117/428403
Colombian Publishers' Association
Executive Secretary: Hipólito Hincapié
Publication: Libros Colombianos

Cámara Colombiana del Libro*, Carrera 50,
52-126 of 411, Medellín Tel: 425714;
Carrera 54, 52-15P3 Tel: 457778
Colombian Book Association

Standard Book Numbering Agency*, Centro
Regional para el Fomento del Libro en
América Latina y el Caribe, Apdo Aéreo
17438, Bogotá (Located at: Calle 70 No 9-52)

Book Trade Reference Books and Journals

Books

*Guia de Editoriales, Distribuidores y
Librerias de Bogotá*, CERLAL, Calle 70 No
9-52, Apdo 17438, Bogotá

Journals

*Anuario Bibliográfico Colombiano 'Rubén
Pérez Ortiz'* (Colombian Bibliographical
Annual), Instituto Caro y Cuervo, Apdo
Aéreo 51502, Bogotá

Bibliografia Oficial Colombiana (Official
Colombian Bibliography), Escuela
Interamericana de Bibliotecología,
Universidad de Antioquia, Apdo Aéreo
1226, Medellín

Libros Colombianos (Colombian Books),
Colombian Publishers' Association, Apdo
8998, Bogotá

Publishers

A C P O, see Accion Cultural Popular –
Editorial Andes

Accion Cultural Popular ACPO – Editorial
Andes*, Apdo Aéreo 20037, Bogotá
(Located at: Carrera 39A No 15-81, Bogotá)
Tel: 2682741/2684800 ext 240 Cable Add:
Radiofonicas Bogota Telex: 45623 Accpo
Co
Man Dir: Hernán Jaramillo Mejia; *Editorial:*
Diego Llano Echeverri; *Sales and Rights &
Permissions:* Jaime Ramirez Palmar,
Manuel Escobar Escobar
Subjects: Art, Colombia, Social Sciences,
Literature
Founded: 1947 (ACPO-Editôra Dosmil
1964)
Miscellaneous: Formerly Accion Cultural
Popular ACPO – Editora Dosmil
ISBN Publisher's Prefix: 84-8275

Aguilar Colombiana de Ediciones*, Calle 13
7-40, Bogotá Tel: 2432046
Man Dir: Gustavo de Florza; *Sales:* José
Montenegro García
Parent Company: Aguilar SA de Ediciones,
Spain (qv)

Editorial Andes, see Accion Cultural
Popular ACPO

Editorial Bedout SA, Apdo Aéreo 760,
Medellín (Located at: Calle 61 No 51-04,
Medellín) Tel: 316900 Cable Add: Bedout
President: Dr Elías Vélez; *Manager:* Dr
Libardo Statizábal C; *Publicity:* Dr Gustavo
Velásquez A
Branch Offs: Calle 10 No 5-23, of 404, Cali;
Plaza Fernández Madrid No 7-26 of 301,
Apdo Aéreo 524, Cartagena; Apdo Aéreo
283, Ibagué; Calle 29 No 6-42, Montería;
Calle 24 No 6-49, Apdo Aéreo 1957, Pereira
Subjects: Literature, Social Science,
Didactics, Textbooks, Juveniles
1982: 210 titles *Founded:* 1889

Editorial Bruguera Colombiana Ltda*, Calle
20 No 42-C-43, Bogotá Tel: 2682563
Man Dir: Antonio Mourin
Parent Company: Editorial Bruguera SA,
Spain (qv)

C E D E (Centro de Estudios sobre
Desarollo Economico), Universidad de los
Andes, Faculdad de Economia, Carrera 1°E
No 18A-10, Apdo Aéreo 4976, Bogotá Tel:
2824066 ext 189/2430295 ext 68
Dir: Dr Nobora Rey de Marutanda
Subjects: Economics, Social Sciences
1981: 12 titles *1982:* 5 titles *Founded:* 1958

Instituto Caro y Cuervo*, Apdo Aéreo
51502, Bogotá Tel: 557753
Man Dir: José Manuel Rivas Sacconi
Subjects: Belles Lettres, Linguistics,
Philology, Reference
Bookshops: Librería Yerbabuena, Carrera 11
No 64-37, Bogotá; Librería Cuervo, Calle 10
No 4-77, Bogotá
Founded: 1942

Carvajal SA, Apdo Aéreo 46, Cali
Tel: 681111 Cable Add: Carvajales Cali
Telex: 055555/055650
Subsidiary Company: Edinorma Ltda y Cía
SCA (qv)
Subjects: Children's Pop-ups, Juveniles,
Textbooks, Magazines, Atlases

Fundación Centro de Investigación y
Educación Popular (CINEP), Carrera 5
No 33 A 08, Apdo Aéreo 25916, Bogotá
Tel: 2324440/2871284
Man Dir and Rights & Permissions: Manuel
Uribe; *Sales Manager:* Bernardo Botero;
*Production, Publicity and Publications
Manager:* Alejandro Angulo
Subjects: Colombian Politics & Economics,
Sociology
Founded: 1959

Editorial La Chispa Ltda*, Calle 26 No 25-
61, Bogotá Tel: 2694362
Man Dir, Editorial: Jacobo Naidorf; *Sales:*
Guillermo Marin; *Production:* Gerardo
Rivas; *Rights & Permissions:* Ana Arango,
Jorge Osorio
Associate Company: Ediciones Tiempo
Presento, Apdo 10717, Bogotá
Imprint: Lachispa
Subjects: Literature, Sciences
Founded: 1979

Colombiana de Ediciones SA Colediciones*,
Carrera 22 No 36-63 – 1° piso, Bogotá Tel:
2690670/2854312 Cable Add: Colediciones
Man Dir, Editorial, Rights & Permissions:
Carlos Senior Pava; *Sales:* Harold Valencia
Salinas; *Production:* Guillermo Cajale
Santacoloma
Subsidiary Companies: Arte Libros Editores
(at above address); Servicio de
Documentacion (SD), Ave 22 No 37-90,
Apdo 101, Bogotá
Associate Company: Librerías Unidas Ltda,
Ave 22 No 37-90 – Apdo 101, Bogotá
Branch Off: Colediciones Medellin, Calle 48
No 67-152, Bogotá
Subjects: The Family, Spiritualism,
Sociology
Bookshop: Librería Ancora, Ave 22 No 37-
90, Apdo 101, Bogotá
Founded: 1978

Cultural Colombiana Ltda*, Calle 72
No 16-15/21, Apdo Aéreo 6307, Nacional
2169, Bogotá Tel:
2355494/2483311/2483236 Cable Add:
Culbiana
Man Dir: José Porto; *Editorial:* José Porto
Vazquez; *Sales Dirs:* Hernando Salazar;
Production: Maximilian Nicolás
Subjects: Primary & Secondary Textbooks
Bookshop: Librería Cultural Colombiana
(qv under Major Booksellers)

Founded: 1951
ISBN Publisher's Prefix: 84-8273

Edinorma Ltda y Cía SCA*, Calle 37 No 13-08, Apdo Aéreo 53550, Bogotá Tel: 2851600/853297 Cable Add: Edinorma
President: Alberto José Carvajal: *General Manager:* Humberto Serna Gómez; *Editorial Dir:* Daniel Ordóñez
Parent Company: Carvajal SA (qv)
Subjects: Textbooks, Children's Books, Juveniles, General Interest, Magazines

Fondo Educativo Interamericano SA, Apdo Aéreo 29696, Bogotá (Located at: Calle 36 No 22-33, Bogotá) Tel: 2459279/2852773/2852542 Cable Add: Adiwes Bogota Telex: 45581
Man Dir: Luis Felipe Martínez
Associate Company: Addison-Wesley Publishers Ltd, UK (qv for other associates)
Subjects: University Textbooks, School Texts, Trade Books
Founded: 1970
Miscellaneous: This is the editorial department of Fondo Educativo Interamericano, Ave Federico Boyd y Calle 51, Edificio Eastern — 6° piso, Panamá, Panama

Inversiones Editoriales La Carreta*, Apdo 9026, Bogotá (Located at: Calle 17 No 4-95 — of 205, Bogotá) Tel: 2431249
Man Dir and *Editorial:* Mario Arrubla; *Sales:* Catalina Arrubla; *Production:* César Hurtado
Subsidiary Company: Distribuidora Letras, Carrera 50 No 52-8 — of 407, Medellín
Subjects: History, Economics, Politics (generally on Colombia)
Bookshop: Librería Letras, Carrera 5A No 8-12, Cali
Founded: 1975

Editorial **Ipler** Ltda*, Carrera 11 No 71-75, Bogotá Tel: 559916
Man Dir: C Abel Barahona Castro; *Editorial:* Olga Flor Barahona Castro; *Sales, Production:* Carmento Paipillo; *Publicity:* Maria Cecilia de Morales
Subject: Scientific Works
Founded: 1978

Editorial **Juventud** Ltda*, Calle 58 No 19-41, Bogotá 2 Tel: 481634
Man Dir: Santiago Preckler
Parent Company: Editorial Juventud SA, Spain (qv)

Editorial **Kapelusz** Colombiana SA, Apdo Aéreo 54926, Bogotá (Located at: Calle 57 No 13-49, Bogotá) Tel: 2353340/2117649 Cable Add: Kapelusz
Man Dir: Eduardo Gonzalez Casas; *Sales:* Carlos Trogolo Mattea; *Rights & *Permissions:* Elsa Mantilla
Parent Company: Editorial Kapelusz SA, Argentina (qv)
Subsidiary Companies: Kapelusz Mexicana SA, Morelos 64, Apdo 32-491, México 1, DF, México; Editorial Kapelusz SA, Ave Uruguay 1331, Montevideo, Uruguay; Kapelusz Venezolana SA, Venezuela (qv)
Subjects: Pre-school, Primary, Secondary & University Textbooks, Pedagogy, Psychology, Physics
Bookshop: At above address
Founded: 1964

Editorial **Labor** Colombiana Ltda*, Carrera 16 No 30-25, Bogotá Tel: 698301
Man Dir: Enrique Fajardo
Parent Company: Editorial Labor, Spain (qv)

Lachispa, an imprint of Editorial La Chispa Ltda (qv)

Legislación Económica Ltda+, Apdo Aéreo 98888, Bogotá (Located at: Ave Eldorado 8110, Bogotá) Tel: 2634100 Cable Add: Legislación Telex: 43300 Legis
Man Dir: Tito Livio Caldas
Subsidiary Company: Legislación Económica Srl, URB Industrial la Urbina, Calle 8, Edifico Lec, Caracas, Venezuela
Subjects: Economics, Law, Commerce
Founded: 1952

Ediciones **Lerner** Ltda*, Ave Jiménez 4-35, Bogotá Tel: 430567 Cable Add: Edilerner Telex: 43195
Man Dir: Salomon Lerner Mutzmajer; *Editorial:* Jack A Grimberg; *Sales:* A Londono
Subjects: Literature, History, Medicine
Bookshop: Librería Lerner (qv under Major Booksellers)
Founded: 1959

Editorial **McGraw-Hill** Latinoamericana SA*, Calle 60 No 15-99, Apdo Aéreo 11255, Bogotá Tel: 2351952/2357741 Telex: 43306
Man Dir, Editorial: Dubier Alvarez; *Sales:* Hernán Muñoz; *Production:* Carlos Schneerson; *Promotion:* Hermencia Morales
Orders to: Apdo Postal 2036, Colon, Panamá
Parent Company: McGraw-Hill de España SA, Spain (qv)
Associate Company: McGraw-Hill Book Co (UK) Ltd, UK (qv for other associates)
Subjects: Engineering, Technology, Biology, Physics, Chemistry, Mathematics, Psychology, Sociology, Textbooks, Business Administration, Economics, Accounting
Founded: 1969
ISBN Publisher's Prefix: 958-451

Editorial **Marca** Ltda*, Calle 39A No 22-43 — 1° piso, Bogotá Tel: 2445116
Man Dir: Constanza Galvis; *Sales:* Ana Maria de Galvis; *Production:* Maria Teresa de Leal
Subjects: Scholarly, Cultural, Periodicals
Founded: 1977

Ediciones **Monserrate** Ltda, Apdo Aéreo 100127, Bogotá (Located at: Calle 117 No 11A-65, Bogotá) Tel: 2139398/2132041/2142417
Man Dir and Editorial: P Enrique Fajardo Villarraga; *Sales:* Maria Gladys de Diaz
Subjects: Technical, Scientific, Law, Dictionaries, Encyclopedias
Founded: 1977

Editorial **Norma** y Cia SCA*, Calle 37 No 13-08, Apdo Aéreo 53550, Bogotá Tel: 453152/2851600 Cable Add: Edinorma Telex: 44855
Man Dir: Humberto Serna G; *Editorial:* D Ordonez, J Camacho; *Sales:* G Mateus C; *Production:* A Martinez (Infants and Juveniles), J Bonfante (School Textbooks)
Parent Company: Carvajal SA (qv)
Subsidiary Company: Publicar Ltda
Branch Offs: Bogotá, Cali, Medellín, Barranquilla, Cartagena, Manizales, Ibaqué, Neiva, Bucaramanga, Cúcuta
Subjects: General, Juveniles, Primary & Secondary Textbooks, Education
Founded: 1964

Editorial La **Oveja** Negra Ltda, Apdo Aéreo 23940, Bogotá DE (Located at: Carrera 14 No 79-17, Bogotá) Tel: 2181301/2569111/2368198 Telex: 45369 Oveja Co
Man Dir, Editorial and Rights & Permissions: José Vicente Kataraín Velez; *Sales Dir:* Ricardo Arango Dávila; *Production Dir:* Hernando Vargas; *Publicity Dir:* Iván Gutiérrez
Branch Offs: Transversal 93 No 62-46 Interior 16, Bogotá; also in Caracas, Lima, Quito, La Paz

Subjects: Works of Gabriel Garcia Marquez, Latin-American Literature, Social Sciences, Politics, History, Education, Children's Books
Bookshops: At above address and at Calle 18 No 6-08, Bogotá
1981: 90 titles *1982:* 126 titles *Founded:* 1977

Papusa Ltda*, Calle 26 No 13A-23 — 7° piso, Bogotá Tel: 2825692 Telex: 0441302
Man Dir: Jaime Muñoz Polit; *Editorial:* Amanda Quijano, Ignacio Montealegre
Parent Company: Ediciones Libra SA, Matias Romero 1221, Mexico 12, DF
Subsidiary Companies: Dinalpusa; Janibi Editores: each at Matias Romero 1221, Mexico 12, DF
Associate Companies: Munoz Hnos SA, General Aguirre 166 y 10 de Agosto, Quito, Ecuador; Distribuidora Inca SA, Emilio Altahus, Lima, Peru
Subjects: Teaching of Music (Books, Periodicals)
Book Club: Guitarra Facil
Founded: 1977

Editorial **Pluma** Ltda, Apdo Aéreo 345, Bogotá (Located at: Carrera 20 No 39B-50, Bogotá) Tel: 2871412/2871432 Telex: 45101 Ntctv
Man Dir: Ernesto Gamboa Morales; *Sales:* Federico Rivas Franco; *Production:* Pilar Mahecha; *Publicity:* Carlos José Herrera; *Rights & Permissions:* Deborah Dixon
Associate Company: Indice Ltda (at above address)
Subjects: Psychology, Sexology, Economics, Politics, Literature
Founded: 1976

Editorial **Pomaire** SA*, Calle 54A No 9-29, Apdo Aéreo 51042, Bogotá Tel: 488454/558551
Manager: Manuel Edwards
Head Off: Editorial Pomaire SA, Spain (qv)

Editorial **Presencia** Ltda, Calle 23 No 24-50, Bogotá Tel: 2681634/2681817/2682241
Man Dir, Publicity: Alberto Umaña Carrizosa; *Editorial:* M C Jimero; *Sales:* José Antonio Umaña; *Production:* Carla Marularda; *Rights & Permissions:* Alberto Umaña
Subsidiary Companies: Ediciones Contemporanea, Carrera 4A No 25B-12, Bogotá; El Mural, Carrera 4A No 25B-12, Bogotá

Siglo XXI Editores de Colombia Ltda, Apdo Aéreo 19434, Bogotá
Man Dir: Santiago Pombo Vejarano
Parent Company: Siglo XXI Editores de España SA, Spain (qv)
Associate Company: Siglo XXI Editores SA, Mexico (qv)
Subjects: Anthropology, Sociology, Psychology, History, Fiction, Linguistics, Art, Architecture, Politics, Philosophy
Founded: 1976

Editorial **Temis** Ltda, Calle 13 No 6-45, Apdos 5941 y 12008, Bogotá 1 Tel: 2694721/2699235/2445297 Cable Add: Editemis
Man Dir: Jorge Guerrero; *Sales Dir:* Erwin Guerrero Pinzon
Subject: Law
Bookshop: Librería Temis Ltda (qv under Major Booksellers)
Founded: 1951
ISBN Publisher's Prefix: 84-8272

Ediciones **Tercer** Mundo Ltda*, Carrera 30 No 42-32, Apdo Aéreo 4817, Bogotá Tel: 695129/695149 Cable Add: Tercer Mundo
Man Dir: Luis Carlos Ibáñez
Subjects: General Literature, Social Science
Bookshop: Librería Tercer Mundo (qv under

Major Booksellers)
Founded: 1961

Carlos Valencia Editores SA, Calle 71 No 1-50, Apdo Aéreo 22197, Bogotá Tel: 2114928/2491825
Man Dir: Carlos Valencia Goelkel; *Editorial:* Juan Fernando Esguerra; *Sales:* Ester Wasserman; *Production, Publicity:* Jesus Anibal Suarez; *Rights & Permissions:* Armando Santoyo
Subjects: Art, Children's Literature, Economics, Politics, Sociology, Colombian subjects and authors
1981: 12 titles *1982:* 12 titles *Founded:* 1976
ISBN Publisher's Prefix: 84-8277

Vértice Ltda*, Apdo Aéreo 41137, Bogotá DE1 (Located at: Calle 110 No 15-15, Bogotá) Tel: 2143521
General Manager: Jesús Antonio Villa Posse
Subjects: History, Literature, Law, Agriculture, Art, Economics & Finance
Founded: 1980

Voluntad Editores Ltda y Cía SCA, Calle 37 No 7-43 — 2° piso, Apdo Aéreo 4692, Bogotá Tel: 2858711 Cable Add: Voluntad
Man Dir: Samuel de Bedout Tamayo; *Editorial Dir and Rights & Permissions:* Gastón de Bedout Arbeláez; *Sales and Publicity Dir:* Gabriel Gil
Branch Offs: Barranquilla, Bogotá, Bucaramanga, Cali, Cartagena, Cúcuta, Ibague, Medellín, Montería, Pereira, Santa Marta
Subjects: Kindergarten, Primary and Secondary Textbooks
Bookshop: Ave 19 No 3-16 — 2° piso, Bogotá
1981: 57 titles *1982:* 63 titles *Founded:* 1930
ISBN Publisher's Prefix: 84-8270

Book Clubs

Círculo de Lectores SA, Apdo Aéreo 52111, Bogotá (Located at: Calle 57 No 6-35 - 6° piso, Bogotá) Tel: 2123211/2118525 Telex: 41255
Members: 860,000
Owned by: Verlagsgruppe Bertelsmann GmbH, Federal Republic of Germany (qv)
Founded: 1971

Guitarra Facil*, Calle 26 No 13A-23 - 7° piso, Bogotá Tel: 2825692
Owned by: Papusa Ltda (qv)

Major Booksellers

Librería **Aguirre**, Calle 53 No 49-123, Medellín Tel: 424268 Cable Add: Laguirre
Manager: Aura López Posada

Librería **América**, Calle 51 No 49-58, apdo 11-92, Medellín Tel: 412878

Librería **Buchholz***, Ave Jiménez 8-40, Bogotá Tel: 341309/415896/426350

Librería **Casa del Libro***, Calle 18 No 6-43, Bogotá Tel: 432668

Círculo de Lectores SA, Apdo Aéreo 52111, Bogotá (Located at: Calle 57 No 6-35 - 6° piso, Bogotá)
Branches: Barranquilla, Bogotá (4), Cali (3), Cartagena, Manizales, Medellín, Pereira, Tunja

Librería **Cultural** Colombiana, Calle 72 No 16-15, Bogotá Tel: 2483236/2483306
Manager: José Porto
Also at Carrera 9a No 16-72, Bogotá

El Dorado Ltda*, Apdo Aéreo 80048, Bogotá (Located at: Ave de las Américas 34-49, Bogotá) Tel: 2691272/2691532

Librería La **Gran Colombia***, Calle 18 No 6-30, Bogotá Tel: 421359/411755

Librería del **Ingeniero**, Ave Jiménez 7-45, Apdo Aéreo 14825, Bogotá Tel: 2412507/2823610/2343260

Librería **Lerner**, Ave Jiménez 4-35, Bogotá Tel: 347826/430567
Manager: Luis A Burgos H
Also Publisher (qv)

Librería **Central**, Calle 16 No 6-34, Bogotá Tel: 426767

Librería **Continental**, Carrera 50 No 52-06, Medellín Tel: 414948

Librería **Nacional***, Carrera 5a No 11-50, Cali Tel: 731250 Telex: 55472
Manager: Hernando Ordoñez

Librería **San Pablo***, Carrera 9 No 15-01, Bogotá Tel: 2433653/2345036
Also at Calle 57 No 13-71, Bogotá Tel: 494167

Librería del **Seminario**, Apdo Aéreo 4567, Medellín, Antioquia (Located at: Calle 57 No 49-44, loc 110 y 314, Centro Comercial Villanueva) Tel: 518142/513622
Director: Lucila Hoyos Gómez
Distributors

Librería **Temis** Ltda, Calle 13 No 6-45, Bogotá Tel: 423035/413325
Also Publisher (qv)

Librería **Tercer** Mundo*, Carrera 7a No 16-91, Bogotá Tel: 695129/695149
Owned by: Ediciones Tercer Mundo Ltda (qv)

Major Libraries

Biblioteca Luis-Angel **Arango***, Banco de la República, Apdo Aéreo 12362, Bogotá (Located at: Calle 11 No 4-14, Bogotá) Tel: 2439100/2420605 Cable Add: Redesbanco-Biblioteca
Dir: Jaime Duarte French
Publication: Boletín Cultural y Bibliográfico

Archivo Nacional de Colombia, Biblioteca Nacional, Calle 24 No 5-60 — 4° piso, Bogotá
Dir: Pilar Moreno de Angel

Biblioteca Nacional de Colombia, Calle 24 No 5-60, Apdo Aéreo 27600, Bogotá Tel: 414029

Biblioteca y Centro Nacional de Documentación Pedagógica, Sección de Servicios Bibliotecarios*, Apdo Nacional 8475, Bogotá
National Centre of Educational Documentation

British Council Library, Apdo Aéreo 4682, Bogotá (Located at: Carrera 9 No 86-54, Bogotá) Tel: 2363811/2369839 Telex: 45715 Britco

Universidad de los Andes, Centro de Estudios sobre Desarollo Economico (CEDE), Carrera 1-E No 18A-10, Bogotá Tel: 2430295 ext 68, 2824066 ext 189
Centre for Studies on Economic Development

Universidad Nacional de Colombia, Biblioteca Central, c/o Hugo Parra Acq Libr, Apdo Aéreo 14490, Bogotá DE

Library Associations

Asociación Colombiana de Bibliotecarios*, Calle 10 No 3-16, Apdo Aéreo 30883, Bogotá Tel: 825798
Colombian Library Association
Executive Secretary: Beatriz de Tabares
Publication: Boletín

Bibliotecarios Agricolas Colombianos, c/o Biblioteca de Tibaitata, Apdo Aéreo 7984, Bogotá DE
Agricultural Librarians of Colombia
Dir: Francisco Salazar Alonso

Departamento de Bibliotecas*, Universidad de Antioquia, Apdo Aéreo 1226, Medellín

Library Reference Books and Journals

Books

Bibliografía Bibliotecológica, Bibliográfica y de Obras de Referencia Colombianas (Bibliography of Library Science, Bibliography and Colombian Works of Reference), Universidad de Antioquia, Apdo Aéreo 1226, Medellín

Journals

Boletín (Bulletin), Colombian Library Association, Calle 10 No 3-16, Apdo Aéreo 30883, Bogotá

Boletin Cultural y Bibliografico (Cultural and Bibliographical Bulletin), Biblioteca Luis-Angel Arango, Banco de la República, Calle 11 No 4-14, Bogotá

Boletin Informativo y Bibliografico (Informative and Bibliographical Bulletin), Universidad de Narino, Biblioteca Central, Apdo Aéreo 505, Nacional 75, Narino

Literary Associations and Societies

Centro Filosófico-Literario*, Apdo Nacional 298, Manizales

P E N Internacional de Escritores de Colombia, Apdo Aéreo S1748, Bogotá
PEN International of Colombian Writers
President: David Mejía Velilla; *Secretary:* Maruja Vieira

Literary Periodicals

Letras Nacionales (National Letters), Calle 17, 7-71, Of 401, Bogotá

Razón y Fábula (Reason and Fiction), Universidad de los Andes, Apdo Aéreo 4976, Bogotá

Literary Prizes

'Revista Vivencias' and the Instituto Colombiano de Cultura have annual prizes

Colombian Novel Contest Awards*
For stimulating Colombian writers. 100,000 Colombian pesos. Awarded annually. Enquiries to Universidad del Valle, Apdo Aéreo 2188, Cali

Cordoba Stories Prizes*
For stimulating and developing literary tastes. Diploma plus three prizes of 5,000, 3,000 and 2,000 Colombian pesos. Awarded annually. Enquiries to Cordoba Department, Secretary of Education, Montaria

Pamplona and its Culture Prize*
For stimulating a liking for reading in children. Awarded annually. Enquiries to Pedro de Orsua Public Library, Pamplona

José Ma **Vergara** y Vergara Prize*
For Colombian authors, to promote literary development. Diploma plus 10,000 Colombian pesos. Awarded annually. Enquiries to Colombian Ministry of National Education, Centro Administrativo Nacional (CAN), Bogotá

Popular Republic of Congo

General Information

Language: French
Religion: Traditional animist religions, Roman Catholicism
Population: 1.46 million
Bank Hours: 0630-1100 Monday-Saturday
Shop Hours: 0700 or 0800-1200 or 1300, 1500-1700 or 1730 Tuesday-Friday; 0700 or 0800-1200 or 1300 Saturday
Currency: CFA franc
Export/Import Information: Member of Customs and Economic Union of Central Africa. Goods for schools, the army, the police and health authorities are exempt from VAT. Import licences required for all goods. Favourable terms for imports from EEC countries
Copyright: Berne (see International section)

Publishers

Government Printer*, BP 58, Brazzaville

Société congolaise **Hachette***, BP 919, Brazzaville
Subjects: General Fiction, Belles Lettres, Education, Juveniles, Textbooks

Major Booksellers

Librairie **Hachette***, BP 2150, Brazzaville Tel: 2302

Librairie **Populaire***, BP 2212, Brazzaville

Maison de la Presse, Société congolaise Hachette*, BP 2150, Brazzaville

Office national des Librairies Populaires (ONLP), BP 577, Brazzaville Tel: 811582
Cable Add: Lipolaire Brazzaville
Director-General: Jean-Marie Niabia

Major Libraries

Bibliothèque nationale populaire*, BP 114, Brazzaville Tel: 811287
Librarian: Francis Abaraka

Centre culturel français, Bibliothèque*, BP 2141, Brazzaville Tel: 3852

Centre Orstom de Brazzaville, Bibliothèque*, BP 165, Brazzaville Tel: 812680
Librarian: B Boccas

Ecole normale supérieure de l'Afrique centrale, Bibliothèque*, BP 237, Brazzaville Tel: 4454

Institut supérieure des sciences de l'éducation, Bibliothèque*, BP 1090, Brazzaville Tel: 813950
Librarian: Hildebert Banda

Bibliothèque universitaire, **Université Marien Ngouabi***, BP 2025, Brazzaville Tel: 8430
Dir: François Wellot-Samba
Publications: Dimi; Annales; Repertoire d'auteurs congolais; Revue d'histoire anthropologie. Also other lists and catalogues

Library Association

Direction générale des **Services** de Bibliothèques, Archives et Documentation*, BP 114, Brazzaville
General Management of Library, Archives and Documentation Services

Literary Periodical

Les cahiers du cercle littéraire de Brazzaville, Centre culturel français, BP 2141, Brazzaville

Costa Rica

General Information

Language: Spanish
Religion: Roman Catholic
Population: 2.11 million
Literacy Rate (1973): 88.4%
Bank Hours: 0900-1500 Monday-Friday
Shop Hours: 0800-1200, 1400-1800 Monday-Saturday (some close Saturday afternoon)
Currency: 100 centimos = 1 colon
Export/Import Information: No import licences, but statistical recording prior to importation necessary. Imports over a certain value must be registered with Banco Central to be eligible for foreign exchange allocation
Copyright: Berne, UCC, Buenos Aires (see International section)

Book Trade Reference Journal

Anuario bibliográfico costarricense (Costa Rican Annual Bibliography), Costa Rican Association of Librarians, Apdo 3308, San José

Publishers

Editorial **Costa Rica***, Apdo 10010, San José Tel: 234875/239303
Subject: Literature of Costa Rica
Founded: 1959

Dirección de Publicaciones*, Apdo 10227, San José Tel: 230797
Dir: Roberto Corella Furntes; *Editor:* Juan Frutos Verdesia
Subject: Literature in general

Editorial Universitaria Centroamericana (EDUCA), Apdo 64, Ciudad Universitaria 'Rodrigo Facio', San José (Located at San Pedro de Montes de Oca, San José) Tel: 258740/243727 Cable Add: Cosuca Telex: 3011 Cosuca
Dir: Sebastián Vaquerano L; *Sales:* Joaquín Matarrita; *Production:* Alfredo Aguilar
Subjects: Science, Art, Philosophy
Founded: 1969
ISBN Publisher's Prefix: 84-8360

Instituto Centro Americano de Administración Pública (ICAP), Dpto de Publicaciones, Apdo 10025, San José
Dir: Carlos Cordero d'Aubuisson
Subject: Technical
Founded: 1954

Instituto Interamericano de Cooperación para la Agricultura (IICA)*, CIDIA, Apdo 55, San José (Located: Coronado 2200, San José) Tel: 290222 Cable Add: Iicasanjose Telex: 214411

Librería Imprenta y Litografía **Lehmann** SA*, Ave Central, Apdo 10011, San José Tel: 231212 Telex: 2540 Lill Eh
Man Dir: Antonio Lehmann Struve; *Publicity:* Orlando Mora
Subjects: General Fiction & Non-fiction
Bookshop: See under Major Booksellers
Founded: 1894

Editorial **Pomaire** SA*, Apdo 26, Escazu Tel: 281479/282664
Manager: Cristián Santa María
Head Off: Editorial Pomaire SA, Spain (qv)

Universal Librería, Imprenta y Fotolitografia (Carlos Federspiel & Co) SA*, Ave Fernández Guell 42-E, Apdo 1532, San José Tel: 222222
Subject: Textbooks

Editorial **Universidad** de Costa Rica, Apdo 75, Ciudad Universitaria 'Rodrigo Facio', San José Tel: 247957
President (Editorial Commission): Dr José M Jimínez Sáenz; *Editorial Dir:* Jaime Guzmán S
Subjects: Textbooks, Technical, Social Science, Music, Poetry, Local interest

Major Booksellers

Librería Universal Carlos **Federspiel***, Ave Fernández Guell 42-E, Apdo 1532, San José Tel: 222222

Librería Imprenta y Litografía **Lehmann** SA*, Ave Central, Apdo 10011, San José Tel: 231212
Also Publisher (qv)

Librería **Trejos**, Calle 11-13, Ave Fernández Guell, Apdo 1313, San José Tel: 217055 Telex: 2858 Ltsa Cr

Major Libraries

Biblioteca Nacional, Apdo 10008, San José (Located at: Calle 15 y 17, Ave 3 y 3 Bis, San José)
Director-General: Lic Efraín Picado Azofeifa

Biblioteca del **Centro** Cultural Costarricense-Norteamericano*, Apdo 1489, San José
International Communication Agency Library

Biblioteca de la **Universidad de Costa Rica**, Ciudad Universitaria Rodrigo Facio, San José Tel: 257372
Publications include: San Pedro de Montes de Oca

Library Associations

Asociación Costarricense de Bibliotecarios*, Apdo 3308, San José
Costa Rican Association of Librarians
Secretary-General: Nelly Kopper
Publication: Boletín

Colegio de Bibliotecarios de Costa Rica*, c/o Lupita Rodriguez Mendez, Encargada de Biblioteca, Instituto de Fomento Asesoria Municipal, San José
Library Association of Costa Rica

Library Reference Journal

Boletín (Bulletin), Costa Rican Association of Librarians, Apdo 3308, San José

Literary Prize

Aquileo T **Echeverria** Prize*
For Costa Rican citizens who have excelled in the fields of literature (novel, short story, poetry, essay, scientific literature); history; theatre; music; fine arts. 40,000 colones divided between the selected works. Total sum of awards cannot exceed 8,000,000 colones. Awarded annually. Enquiries to Costa Rican Ministry of Culture, Youth and Sport, General Directorate of Arts and Letters, San José

Cuba

General Information

Language: Spanish
Religion: Roman Catholic predominantly
Population: 9.7 million
Literacy Rate (1953): 75.8%
Bank Hours: 0800-1200, 1415-1615 Monday-Friday; 0800-1200 Saturday
Currency: 100 centavos = 1 peso
Export/Import Information: Control of all import and export by Ministry of Foreign Trade; books imported and exported by Ediciones Cubanas, Apdo 605, Havana. No commercial advertising permitted in Cuba; brochures etc must be sent to the appropriate foreign trade organization. Exchange controlled by National Bank of Cuba
Copyright: UCC, Florence (see International section)

Book Trade Organization

Unión de Escritores y Artistas de Cuba*, Calle 17 No 351, Vedado, Havana Tel: 324551
Union of Writers and Artists of Cuba
Administrative Secretary: William Mafud
Publications include: Union, La Nueva Gaceta

Book Trade Reference Journal

Revolutionary Cuba, a bibliographical guide, University of Miami Press, Coral Gables, Florida, USA (annual)

Publishers

Editorial **Arte** y Literatura*, Calle G No 505, Plaza de la Revolución, Havana
Dir: Abel E Prieto
Subjects: Art, Literature
Founded: 1967

Ediciones **C O R***, Revolutionary Orientation Commission of the Communist Party, Havana
Subject: Politics

Casa de las Américas, Tercera y G, Vedado 3, Havana
Dir: Roberto Fernández Retamar
Subject: Latin American Literature
Founded: 1960

Editorial de **Ciencias Sociales**, Calle 14 No 4104e 41 y 43, Playa, Havana Tel: 24801/23959
Dir: Ricardo Garcia Pampin
Subject: Social Sciences

Editorial **Científico** Técnica*, Calle 2 No 58e 3 y 5, Vedado, Havana
Dir: Jorge Luis Victorero Gonta
Subjects: Science, Engineering

Editorial **Gente Nueva**, Palacio del Segundo Cabo, Calle O'Reilly No 4 esq a Tacón, Havana
Dir: Elenia Rodríguez Oliva
Subject: Juvenile Literature

Instituto Cubano del Libro*, Belascoaín 864, Apdo 6540, Havana
Dir: Rolando Rodríguez
Subject: Government Publications
Founded: 1967

Editorial **Letras Cubanas***, Calle G No 505e 21 y 23, Vedado, Havana
Dir: Pablo Pacheco López; *Editorial:* Rosario Esteva; *Production:* Francisco Fernández; *Publicity:* Zenaida Brene
Subject: Literature
Founded: 1977

Editorial **Orbe***, Calle 17 No 1057e 12 y 14, Vedado, Havana
Dir: Osvaldo Navarro

Editorial **Oriente***, José Antonio Saco 356, Santiago
Dir: Reinaldo Cuesta Reina

Editorial **Pueblo** y Educación*, Calle 15 No 604e B y C, Vedado, Havana
Dir: Ana María Santana Romero
Subject: Education

Ediciones **Unión**, Calle 17 No 351, Vedado, Havana Tel: 328114
Dir: Joaquín G Santana; *Production:* Juan Coury Giat; *Publicity:* Adolfo Martí Fuentes; *Rights & Permissions:* Centro Nacional de Derechos de Autor, Línea y G, Vedado
Subjects: Literature, Art

Universidad Central de la Villas, Carretera de Camajuani*, Km 10, Santa Clara
Subjects: Academic

Universidad de la Habana*, Apdo 3060, Havana 3 Tel: 325238/328815
Subjects: Academic
Founded: 1934

Major Booksellers

Ediciones **Cubanas***, Apdo 605, Havana (Located at: Obispo 461, Havana)
This is part of Empresa de Comercio Exterior de Publicaciones
Manager: José Manuel Castro
Wholesale importers and exporters of books, periodicals and printing material

Major Libraries

Academia de Ciencias de la República de Cuba*, Biblioteca Central, Capitolio Nacional, Havana

Archivo Histórico Municipal de la Habana*, Plaza de Catedral, Havana

Biblioteca Histórica Cubana y Americana*, Municipio de la Habana, Oficina del Historiador de la Ciudad, Havana

Biblioteca Nacional José Martí, Plaza de la Revolución, Apdo Oficial 3, Havana
Tel: 73613
National Library
Publications include: Revista de la Biblioteca Nacional José Martí; Bibliografía Cubana; Indice General de Publicaciones Periódicas Cubanas; Boletín Referativos e Información Señal; Bibliografías Especializadas; Ediciones Especializadas sobre la Cultura y el Arte; Documentos Extranjeros Adquiridos

Biblioteca del **Colegio de Belén***, Apdo 221, Marianao, Havana

Biblioteca 'José Antonio **Echevarría**'*, Casa de las Americas, Tercera y G, Vedado, Havana
Specialize in Latin-American Literature, History and Sociology

Biblioteca del **Instituto de Literatura** y Linguistica*, Salvador Allende 710, Havana

Biblioteca del **Instituto Pre-universitario** de la Habana*, Zulueta y San José, Havana
Library of the Pre-University Institute of Education

Biblioteca del **Museo de Zoologia***, 42 No 3307, Marianao 13, Havana

Biblioteca 'Manuel **Sanguily**'*, Ministerio de Relaciones Exteriores, Calzada y G, Vedado, Havana

Biblioteca General de la **Universidad Central** de las Villas*, Santa Clara, Las Villas

Biblioteca Central 'Rubén Martínez Villena' de la **Universidad de la Habana***, Havana

Biblioteca Central de la **Universidad de Oriente**, Apdo 5015, Santiago (Located at: Ave Patricio Lumumba s/n, Santiago

Library Reference Books and Journals

Book

Guía de Bibliotecas y Centros de Documentación de la República de Cuba (Guide to Libraries and Centres of Documentation of Cuba), National Library, Plaza de la Revolución, Apdo Oficial 3, Havana

Journals

Bibliotecas (Libraries), National Library, Plaza de la Revolución, Apdo Oficial 3, Havana

Revista de la Biblioteca Nacional José Martí (Review of the National Library), National Library, Plaza de la Revolución, Apdo Oficial 3, Havana

Literary Periodicals

Taller Literario (Literary Workshop), Universidad de Oriente, Escuela de Letras, Apdo 5015, Santiago

Union, Union of Writers and Artists of Cuba, Calle 17 No 351, Vedado, Havana

Literary Prizes

David Prize*
An annual award of $500 is made to a writer whose work has not previously been published. Enquiries to Unión de Escritores y Artistas de Cuba, Calle 17 No 351, Vedado, Havana

U N E A C Prize*
An annual award of $1,000 is made to a professional writer. Enquiries to Unión de Escritores y Artistas de Cuba, Calle 17 No 351, Vedado, Havana

Cyprus

General Information

Language: Greek and Turkish (English widely spoken)
Religion: Greek Orthodox and Muslim (among Turks)
Population: 616,000
Literacy Rate (1960): 74.5%
Bank Hours: 0830-1200 Monday-Saturday
Shop Hours: Winter: 0800-1300, 1430-1730 Monday-Wednesday and Friday; 0800-1300 Thursday and Saturday. Summer 0730-1300, 1600-1900 Monday-Wednesday and Friday; 0730-1300 Thursday and Saturday
Currency: 1000 mils = 1 Cyprus pound. 50 mils is known as a shilling. Turkish currency circulates in area under Turkish control
Export/Import Information: No tariffs on books or advertising matter. No import licence specially required. Exchange control administered by Central Bank of Cyprus
Copyright: Berne, Florence (see International section)

Book Trade Organizations

Cyprus Booksellers Association*, Hatzisavva Bldg, Evagora Ave, Box 1455, Nicosia Tel: 49500/62312
Secretary: Panikos Michaelides

Standard Book Numbering Agency, c/o Cyprus Centre for Registration of Books & Serials, Ministry of Education Cultural Service, Office of the Inspector of Libraries, Nicosia Tel: (021) 403331 Cable Add: Mined
ISBN Administrator: Savvas L Petrides

Book Trade Reference Journal

O Kosmos Tou Kypriakou Vivliou (The World of Cypriot Books), (text in Greek), MAM, PO Box 1722, Nicosia

Publishers

M A M (The House of the Cyprus Book)*, PO Box 1722, Nicosia Tel: (21) 72744
Subjects: Various, specializing in publications about Cyprus and works by Cypriot authors
Bookshop: See under Major Booksellers
Miscellaneous: Authorized distributors of Cyprus Government publications and works about Cyprus, and of publications by United Nations agencies and major international organizations

Major Booksellers

Arcane Bookshop, 15 Saripolou St, PO Box 373, Limassol Tel: (051) 63541
Manager: A Stylianou

Hellenic Distribution Agency (Cyprus) Ltd*, Chr Sozou 2E, Nicosia Tel: (021) 44488/73664 Telex: 2616

A **Joannides** & Co, 30-32 Athens St, PO Box 141, Limassol Tel: (051) 62204
Manager: A Joannides
Also: Archbishop Makarios III Ave 147, Limassol

K P **Kyriakou** (Books — Stationery) Ltd, PO Box 159, Limassol (Located at: 3 Grivas Digenis Ave, Panagides Bldg, Limassol)
Tel: 68508 Cable Add: Cybooks Telex: 3392 Prc Cy
Man Dir: Kyriakos P Kyriakou

M A M (The House of the Cyprus Book)*, PO Box 1722, Nicosia Tel: (21) 72744
Specializes in publications about Cyprus and works by Cypriot authors. Authorized distributors of Cyprus Government publications and of publications of international organizations. Also Publisher (qv)

K **Rustem** & Bro*, 24 Kyrenia St, Nicosia Tel: (021) 2681 Cable Add: Rustem Br 4

Iakovou **Yiannakis***, 22 Greg Xenopoulous St, Nicosia Tel: (021) 52197 Cable Add: Vivliopolis

Major Libraries

Library of the **Archbishopric***, PO Box 1130, Nicosia
Librarian: Christodoulos Theodoton

British Council Library, PO Box 1995, Nicosia (Located at: 3 Museum St, Nicosia) Tel: 42152/3

Library of the **Cyprus Museum**, PO Box 2024, Nicosia

Ministry of Education Library*, Didaskalikon Megaron, Archbishop Makarios III Ave, Nicosia

Municipal Library*, PO Box 41, Famagusta

Municipal Library*, Limassol

Library of the **Paedagogiki Academia**, Nicosia
Librarian: Costas D Stephanou

Library of **Phaneromeni***, PO Box 1637, Nicosia

Sultan's Library*, Evcaf, Nicosia

Turkish Public Library*, 49 Mecediye St, Nicosia

Library Association

Cyprus Library Association*, PO Box 1039, Nicosia Tel: 402310
Secretary: Paris G Rossos

Library Reference Journal

Deltion Vivliothikarion (Library Bulletin), Cyprus Library Association, PO Box 1039, Nicosia

Literary Associations and Societies

Cyprus **P E N**, PO Box 3836, Nicosia
President: Panos Ioannides; *Secretary:* Dr Klitos Ioannides

Czechoslovakia

General Information

Language: Czech in Bohemia and Moravia, Slovak and Hungarian in Slovakia. Russian is common second language
Religion: Roman Catholic and Protestant
Population: 15 million
Bank Hours: 0800-1400 Monday-Friday
Shop Hours: 0900-1200, 1400-1800 Monday-Friday; most open half day Saturdays
Currency: 100 haler = 1 koruna
Export/Import Information: Import policy administered by Federal Ministry of Foreign Trade. Appropriate corporations for book importation are Artia, 11127 Prague 1, Ve Smečkách 30, or Slovart, Bratislava, Gorkého 17. Exchange control administered by State Bank
Copyright: UCC, Berne (see International section)

Book Trade Organizations

Výtvarná služba Českého fondu výtvarných umělcu, sekce krásné knihy a grafiky*, Prague 1, Nové Město, třída Politických vězňu 7
Creative service of the Czech Fund for Creative Artists, Section for the Well-designed book and Prints

Ministerstvo kultury CSR, Odbor knižní kultury*, Prague 1, Staré Město, Na Perštýně 1
Czechoslovak Ministry of Culture, Department for Publishing and Book Trade

Slovenské ústredie knižnej kultúry*, Bratislava, nám SNP 12
Slovak Centre for Publishing and Book Trade

Spoločnost pro krásné písmo a typografii*, Prague 1, Malá Strana, Riční 5
Association of Design and Typography

Zväz československých spisovatelu, 11147 Prague 1, Národní trída 11
Union of Czechoslovak Writers
Chairman: Jan Kozák

Zväz českych spisovatelu, 11147 Prague 1, Národní trída 11
Union of Czech Writers
Chairman: Ivan Skábe
Publication: Literární městčnik (literary monthly)

Zväz slovenských spisovateľov, 81508 Bratislava, Obrancov mieru 14
Union of Slovak Writers
Secretary-General: Ján Solovič
Publication: Meridians 12-23

Book Trade Reference Books and Journals

Book

Books in Czechoslovakia, a survey of Czech and Slovak publishers, book-museums and important libraries, Czechoslovak Ministry of Culture, Prague 1, Staré Město, Na Perštýně 1

Journals

Bibliografický katalog ČSSR (Czech National Bibliography), consisting of:
České knihy (Czech Books), State Library of the Czech Socialist Republic, 11001 Prague 1, Klementinum 190 (weekly); *Slovenská národná bibliografia* (Slovak National Bibliography), Slovak National Library, 03652 Martin, Mudroňova 13 (monthly); *České hudebniny* (Czech Music), State Library of the Czech Socialist Republic, 11001 Prague 1, Klementinum 190 (quarterly); *Slovenské hudebniny* (Slovak Music), State Library of the Czech Socialist Republic, 11001 Prague 1, Klementinum 190 (annual)

Czech Books in Print, Artia, 11127 Prague 1, Ve Smečkách 30, PO Box 790

Nové knihy (New Books), Prague 1, Vězeňská 5

Slovak Books in Print, Slovart Ltd, Foreign Trade Company, Bratislava, Gorkého 17

Věda a knihy (Science and Books), Academia, 11229 Prague 1, Vodičkova 40

Publishers

Academia, 11229 Prague 1, Vodičkova 40 Tel: 246241/8 Cable Add: Academybooks Prague
Publishing House of the Slovak Academy of Sciences
Man Dir: Dr Radoslav Švec; *Export Manager:* Mrs Z Záková; *Publicity & Advertising:* J Vinkler; *Rights & Permissions:* Dr K Cerný
Subjects: History, Philosophy, Psychology, Economy, Archaeology, Linguistics, Mathematics, Physics, Chemistry, Engineering, Geology; Monographs and University Textbooks
Bookshop: At above address
Founded: 1953

Albatros, Prague 1, Na Perštýně 1 Tel: 263850 Telex: 121605 Alba C
Man Dir: Václav Mikeš; *Sales, Publicity & Advertising:* Jiří Lapáček
Subject: Books for Children and Young People
Book Club: KMC (Young Readers' Club)
Founded: 1949

Alfa — Vydavateľstvo technickej a ekonomickej literatúry, 89331 Bratislava, Hurbanovo nám 3 Tel: 331441/5 Cable Add: Alfa Bratislava
Publishers of technical and economic literature
Dir: Rudolf Schallerz; *Sales Dir:* Jozef Bednárik
Subjects: Engineering, General, Special Dictionaries, University & Secondary Textbooks
Bookshop: Bratislava, Palackého ul 1
Founded: 1952
Miscellaneous: Sole importers of scientific and technical books from Western countries in Slovakia

Artia, 11127 Prague 1, Ve Smečkách 30, PO Box 790 Tel: 246041 Cable Add: Artiapublish Telex: 121065/122775
Foreign language publishers
Man Dir: Dr V Šilar; *Sales Dir:* Peter Lančarič
Subjects: Art Books, Books on Nature, Children's Books
Bookshop: See under Major Booksellers
Founded: 1953

Avicenum, zdravotnické nakladatelství, 11802 Prague 1, Malostranské nám 28 Tel: 536601
Czechoslovak Medical Press
Subject: Medicine
Founded: 1953

Nakladatelství **Blok**, 60000 Brno, Rooseveltova 4
Dir: Ivo Odehnal
Subjects: Belles Lettres, Fiction, Regional Literature

Československý spisovatel, 11147 Prague 1, Národní 9 Tel: 266941 Cable Add: Spisovatel Prague
Dir: Dr Jan Pilař
Subjects: General Fiction, Belles Lettres, Poetry, Biography, Philosophy, Juveniles
Book Club: Klub přátel poezie (Club of the Friends of Poetry)
Bookshops: At above address; Brno, Česká 7
Founded: 1949

Nakladatelství **Dopravy** a spojů*, 11578 Prague 1, Hybernská ul 5, Nové Město
Publishing House of the Ministry of Transport and Communications
Dir: Bohumil Klail
Subjects: Science & Technology, Transport

Geodetický a kartografický podnik v Praze NP, 17030 Prague 7, Kostelní 42 Cable Add: Geokart
Geodetic and Cartographic Enterprise in Prague
Man Dir: Dimitris Gebauer; *Editor-in-Chief:* Dipl Ing Aleš Hašek
Orders to: Artia, Foreign Trade Corporation, 11127 Prague 1, Ve Smečkách 30
Subject: Cartography
Founded: 1971

Kruh*, 50021 Hradec Králové, Klicperova 197 Tel: 22076/225458
Eastern Bohemian Regional Publishing House
Dir: Dr Josef Kubíček
Subjects: General Fiction, Biography, History, Music, Art, Low- & High-priced Paperbacks, Regional Literature
Founded: 1966

Landwirtschaftlicher Staatsverlag (Agricultural Publishing House), see Státní zemědělské nakladatelství

Lidové nakladatelství*, 11565 Prague 1, Václavské nám 36 Tel: 226383/5 Cable Add: Lidové Nakladatelství Praha
Publishing House of the Union of Czechoslovak-Soviet Friendship
Dir: F J Kolár
Subjects: General Fiction, Belles Lettres, Poetry, Biography, History, Philosophy, Juveniles, Low-priced Paperbacks, Social Science
Founded: 1968 (formerly Svět Sovětu)

Madáh*, Bratislava, Martarovicova 10
Publishing House for Books and Journals in the Hungarian Language
Subject: Books in Hungarian

Matica slovenská, 03652 Martin, Mudroňova 1
Publicity Manager: Dr Oudrej Kučera
Subjects: Bibliography, Museum Science, Information Sciences, Biography, History of Slovak Emigration

Melantrich*, 11212 Prague 1, Václavské nám 36 Tel: 260341 Cable Add: Melantrich Telex: 121422
Publishing House of the Czechoslovak Socialist Party
Man Dir: Ing Jiří Krátký; *Sales Dir:* K Voleský; *Editorial:* Ph Dr K Houba; *Production:* M Nevole
Subjects: Belles Lettres, Poetry, Biography, Philosophy, High-priced Paperbacks, Textbooks
Bookshop: Prague 1, Na příkopě 3
1981: 37 titles *1982:* 37 titles *Founded:* 1898

Mladá fronta, 11222 Prague 1, Panská 8 Tel: 224141 Telex: 00245
Publishing House of the Czechoslovak Union of Youth
Dir: Dr Kornel Vavrinčík
Subjects: General Fiction, Belles Lettres, Poetry, Biography, History, Handbooks, Art, Philosophy, Juveniles, Low-priced Paperbacks
Founded: 1945

Mladé letá*, 81519 Bratislava, nám SNP 12 Tel: 50475 Telex: 93421
Young Years: Slovak Publishing House of Children's Literature
Man Dir: Rudo Moric; *Editorial:* Dr Juraj Klaučo; *Sales Dir:* Vlasta Strnadová; *Production:* Jan Columby; *Publicity:* Eva Hornišová
Subjects: Juveniles, Reference
Book Club: Club of Young Readers
Bookshop: Detská Kniha (The Child's Book), Bratislava, Hurbanovo nám 7
Founded: 1950

Nakladatelství a distribuce knih **Naše Vojsko***, 12812 Prague 2, Na Děkance 3 Tel: 547241/8
Publishing and Distribution House of Czechoslovak Army
Dir: Dr Lubomír Baroš
Subjects: General Fiction, Medicine, Technical, Paperbacks, Juveniles, Military Science, Psychology, History, Aviation, Book Industry
Founded: 1945

Nakladatelství **Obelisk***, Prague 1, Mikulandská 10
Publishing House of Czechoslovak Artists
Man Dir: Jiří Dvořák
Subject: Art

Obzor, vydavateľstvo kníh a časopisov NP*, 81585 Bratislava, ul Československej armády 29a Tel: 57251 Cable Add: Vydavateľstvo Obzor Bratislava
Horizon: Slovak Book & Periodical Publishing House for People's Education
Dir: Ján Mojžiš (acting)
Subjects: General Fiction, Non-fiction, Encyclopaedias, Law, General Science, Textbooks, Paperbacks, Educational, Maps
Founded: 1953

Odeon, nakladatelství krásné literatury a umění, 11587 Prague 1, Národní 36 Tel: 247141 Cable Add: Odeon Praha Telex: 023086 Odeo
Publishing House of Literature and Art
Dir: Josef Kuliček; *Assistant Dir:* Dr Edvard Vonka; *Editorial:* Karel Boušek; *Sales:* Dr M Burkon; *Production:* M Filipová; *Publicity:* J Janovský; *Rights & Permissions:* Dr V Vocetková
Subjects: General Fiction, Belles Lettres, Poetry, Biography, Art, Reproductions
Book Club: Odeon Book Club (Klub čtenářů)
Bookshop: 11586 Prague 1, Knihkupectví Odeon Na Florenci 3
1981: 135 titles *Founded:* 1953

CZECHOSLOVAKIA

Nakladatelství **Olympia**, 11588 Prague 1, Klimentská 1 Tel: 2312493 Cable Add: Olympia Prague
Publishing House of Sports and Tourism
Man Dir: Ludvík Uhlíř; *Sales Dir:* M Karas; *Publicity & Advertising:* M Urbanová
Subjects: Sports, Travel, Juveniles, Albums
Bookshop: Prague 1, Hybernská 34
Founded: 1954
Miscellaneous: Formerly Sportovní a turistické nakladatelství

Opus Records and Publishing House, 81504 Bratislava, Dunajská 18 Tel: 53241/50783/52665 Telex: 92219
Man Dir: Dr Ivan Stanislav; *Commercial Dir:* Dr Alexius Aust; *Editorial:* Marian Jurík; *Publicity:* Pavol Fellegi; *Rights & Permissions:* Dr Zlatica Môciková
Subject: Music
1981: 40 titles *1982:* 36 titles (each including sheet music) *Founded:* 1971

Nakladatelství **Orbis**, dissolved in 1977, part of activity taken over by Nakladatelství a vydavatelství Panorama (qv); name Orbis now attached to Press Agency

Osveta, 03654 Martin, Osloboditelov 21
Dir: Ján Krajč
Subjects: Education, Popular Sciences, Tourism, Medicine

Vydavateľstvo SFVU **Pallas***, 88209 Bratislava, Štúrova 1/b
Publishing House of the Slovak Fund of Fine Arts
Subjects: Art, Literature, Biography

Nakladatelství a vydavatelství **Panorama**, PO Box 75, 12072 Prague 2, Hálkova 1 Tel: 245449 Cable Add: Panorama Prague 2
Telex: 122657
Man Dir: Dr František Hanzlík
Subjects: Popular Science, Local History, Picture Books, Art, Law, Concise Encyclopedias, Travels, Juveniles, Periodicals, Postcards, Applied Arts, Publicity Materials
Founded: 1978
Miscellaneous: Formerly Nakladatelství Orbis

Panton, 11839 Prague 1, Říční 12 Tel: 538151/5 Cable Add: Panton
Publishers of the Czech Music Fund — Prague
Man Dir: Miloš Konvalinka
Subjects: Music (Instruction, Works, Biography, General), Juveniles, Educational Materials
Bookshops: Prague 1, Jungmanova 30; Brno, Česká 14; Bratislava, Sedlářská 10
Founded: 1958

Peace and Socialism International Publishers, 16616 Prague 6, Thakurova 3 Tel: 325731/325132 Cable Add: Cssr Prag Srozt Telex: 123542 Wmr
Subjects: International Communist and Working-Class Movement (in English, French, German, Russian, Spanish), Periodicals, including *World Marxist Review* (in 40 languages), *Information Bulletin* (in English, French, German, Spanish, Italian, Arabic, Portuguese)

Vydavateľstvo ROH '**Práca**'*, 81271 Bratislava, Obrancov mieru 19 Tel: 330838/333779/332347 Telex: 93329/93383
Publishing House of the Revolutionary Trade Union Movement
Dir: Ján Duži
Subjects: Trade Unions (history and contemporary studies), Labour Problems, Social Security, Economics, Ergonomics, Labour Law, Work Safety, Needlework Handbooks
Bookshop: Knižná predajňa PRACA, 81271 Bratislava, nám SNP 20
1981: 63 titles *Founded:* 1946

Práce*, 11258 Prague 1, Václavské nám 17, Nové Město
Publishing House of the Czech Trade Union Movement
Dir: Vilém Kún
Subjects: Belles Lettres, How-to, General, Social & Political Science, Juveniles, Law, Engineering, Fiction, Non-fiction
Book Club: ERB
Founded: 1945

Pragopress*, Prague Tel: 224651 Cable Add: Pragobublish Praha
Subjects: Reprints, Facsimilies

Nakladatelstvo **Pravda***, CS-81306 Bratislava, Gunduličova ul 12 Tel: 335574
Dir: Viliam Kačer
Subjects: Fiction, Biography, History, Political Science, Philosophy, Social Science, Law, Economics
Book Club: ČKP (Členská knižnica Pravdy)
Miscellaneous: Firm is the publishing house of the Central Committee of the Communist Party of Slovakia

Príroda, vydavateľstvo kníh a časopisov*, 81534 Bratislava, Krížkova 9 Tel: 47241
Dir: Vincent Šugár; *Editorial:* Ján Braun
Subjects: Agriculture, Veterinary Science, Biology, Husbandry, Forestry, Nature Protection, Phytopathology, Beekeeping, Mechanisation of Agriculture, Horticulture, Specialized Multilingual Dictionaries, Encyclopedias
Founded: 1949

Nakladatelství **Profil***, 70100 Ostrava 1, Cihlářská 51 Tel: 53559/55129
Northern Moravian Publishing House
Dir: František Cečetka
Subjects: General Fiction, Belles Lettres, Poetry, Biography, History, Music, Art, Reference, Juveniles, Social Science, Psychology
Founded: 1957

Nakladatelství **ruže***, 37196 České Budějovice, Zižkovo nám 5
Tel: 2250/5620/7693
Southern Bohemian Publishing House
Dir: František Podlaha
Subjects: General Fiction, Belles Lettres, History, Juveniles, Low-priced Paperbacks, Regional Literature
Founded: 1960

S N T L-Nakladatelství technické literatury+, 11302 Prague 1, Spálená 51 Tel: 203774
Man Dir: Ing Jindřich Sucharda; *Editorial:* Dr V Šesták; *Rights & Permissions:* Dr A Vacek
Subjects: Engineering and Applied Technology, Science, Economics, Dictionaries, Reference, Periodicals
Book Club: Klub čtenářů technické literatury (Club for Readers of Technical Literature)
Bookshop: Středisko technické literatury (Centre of Technical Literature), at above address
Founded: 1895

Severočeské nakladatelství, 40021 Ústí nad Labem, Velká Hradební 33 Tel: 28581
North Bohemian Publishing House
Dir: Jan Suchl; *Editor-in-Chief:* Dr Václav Houžvička; *Sales:* Karel Sebesta
Subjects: General Fiction, Belles Lettres, Poetry, Biography, History, Music, Art, Philosophy, Juveniles, General Science, Low-priced Paperbacks, Regional Literature
Founded: 1971

Slovenská kartografia NP, 83407 Bratislava-Krasňany, Pekná cesta 17 Tel: 282001/282020
Slovak Cartographic Publishing House
Dir: P Kmeťko; *Editorial:* Zd Matula

Orders to: Slovart AG, 81764 Bratislava, Gottwaldovo nám 6
Founded: 1957

Slovenské pedagogické nakladateľstvo, Bratislava, Sasinkova 5 Tel: 64551/3 Cable Add: Spn Bratislava
Slovak Publishing House for Educational Literature
Man Dir: František Mráz
Subjects: History, Music, Art, Psychology, General Science, University, Secondary & Primary Textbooks, Education, Reference
Founded: 1920

Vydavateľstvo **Slovenskej akadémie vied**, see VEDA

Slovenský spisovateľ*, 81367 Bratislava, Leningradská 2 Tel: 333922
Publishing House of the Slovak Literary Fund
Man Dir: Vojtech Mihálik; *Editorial:* Vladimír Dudáš; *Sales, Production:* Rudolf Pernica; *Publicity:* Anna Sigmundová; *Rights & Permissions:* Oľga Peťková
Subjects: General Fiction, Belles Lettres, Poetry, Literary Theory and Criticism
Book Clubs: SPKK — Spoločnosť priateľov krásnych kníh; KMP — Kruh milovníkov poézie; NST — Nová sovietska tvorba; Vavrín
Bookshop: Dom knihy (at above address)
Founded: 1950

Smena, 81284 Bratislava, Pražská 11
Tel: 48539/48541 Cable Add: Bratislava Smena Telex: 09341
Publishing House of Slovak Central Committee of Socialist Youth Union
Dir: Rudolf Belan
Subjects: General Fiction, Belles Lettres, Poetry, Biography, History, Philosophy, Low- & High-priced Paperbacks, Psychology, Social Science, Juveniles, Hobbies
Book Club: Máj
Founded: 1949

Sport*, 83258 Bratislava, Vajnorská 100
Dir: Ing František Mikloš
Subject: Sport
Miscellaneous: Firm is the publishing house of the Slovak Central Committee of the Czechoslovak Physical Culture Organization

Statisticke a evidencni vydavatelství tiskopisu*, 11000 Prague 1, Malá strana, Trziste 9
Publishing House of Statistics and Data
Subject: Reference

Státní pedagogické nakladatelství, 11301 Prague 1, Nové Město, Ostrovní 30 Tel: 203787 Cable Add: Stapena Prague
State Publishing House for Educational Literature
Man Dir: Ing Josef Papež
Subjects: History, Juveniles, Medicine, Psychology, Engineering, Social Science, Primary, Secondary & University Textbooks, Pedagogical Journals, Reference
Founded: 1775

Státní zemědělské nakladatelství*, 11311 Prague 1, Nové Město, Václavské náměstí 47 Tel: 226641
Agricultural Publishing House
Man Dir: Karel Koukal
Subjects: Agriculture, Forestry, Veterinary Science, Agronomy, Hobbies

Středočeské nakladatelství knihkupectví*, 11000 Prague 1, U Prašné brány 3
Central Bohemian Publishing House & Bookshop
Dir: František Pěkný
Subjects: Regional Literature, Fiction, General, Belles Lettres

CZECHOSLOVAKIA

Supraphon, Prague 1, Palackého ul 1 Tel: 268141 Cable Add: Supraphon Praha Telex: 121218 Sunp
Publishing House of Music, Recordings, Sheet Music and Musicological Literature. Rental library of orchestral materials
Man Dir: Jan Kvídera; *Foreign Connections, Rights & Permissions:* Dr Pavel Smola; *Editorial:* Karel Vacek; *Commercial Director:* Karel Arbes
Subject: Music
Bookshops: 150 branches
Founded: 1946

Svepomoc*, 11000 Prague 1, Gorkého nám 10, Nové Město
Publishing House of the Central Cooperative Council

Svoboda, 11303 Prague 1, Revoluční 15 Tel: 2317051
Dir: Evžen Paloncy
Subjects: History, Philosophy, Politics, Belles-Lettres
Book Clubs: Friends of Antiquity, Readers Club, Svoboda Book Club
Miscellaneous: Firm is the publishing house of the Central Committee of the Communist Party of Czechoslovakia

Tatran*, 89134 Bratislava, Michalská 9 Tel: 30141/3
Slovak Publishing House of Belles Lettres
Man Dir: Dr Anton Markuš; *Sales, Publicity & Advertising:* Kamil Pecho; *Rights & Permissions:* LITA, Slovak Literary Agency, Bratislava, ul Ceskoslovenskej armády 31/III
Subjects: Belles Lettres, Poetry, Art, Low-priced Paperbacks
Book Club: Hviezdoslavova knižnica
Bookshop: At above address
Founded: 1947

V E D A, vydavatel'stvo Slovenskej akadémie vied*, 89530 Bratislava, Klemensova 19 Tel: 50355 Cable Add: Veda Bratislava
Publishing House of the Slovak Academy of Sciences
Man Dir: Ing Miroslav Murín; *Editorial:* Dr Ján Jankovič; *Publicity Manager:* Terézia Zelenáková
Subjects: Technical Sciences, Natural Sciences, Linguistics, History, Archaeology, Philosophy, Psychology, Encyclopedias, Dictionaries
Bookshop: Kníhkupectvo SAV, 89530 Bratislava, Dunajská 5
Founded: 1953

Východoslovenské vydavatel'stvo NP*, 04011 Košice 1, Alejová 3 Tel: 66436/65205/65206
Slovak Publishing House
Man Dir: Mikuláš Jáger
Subjects: Belles Lettres, History, Political Science, Juveniles, Regional Literature
1981: 40 titles *Founded:* 1960

Vyšehrad, Prague 2, Karlovo náměstí 5
Publishing House of the Czechoslovak People's Party
Subjects: Works of Contemporary Czech and World Writers, Popular Science, Contemporary Politics

Západočeské nakladatelství*, 30100 Plzeň, Moskevská 36
Western Bohemian Regional Publishing House
Dir: Václav Brašna
Subjects: General Fiction, Belles Lettres, History, Regional Literature, Juveniles

Literary Agents

D I L I A, 12824 Prague 2, Vyšehradská 28, Post Box 34 Tel: 296651/5 Cable Add: Dilia Prag Telex: 121367 Dili C
Theatrical and Literary Agency
Contact: Robert Jurák

L I T A, 81530 Bratislava, ul Cs Armády 37 Tel: 328223 Cable Add: Lita Bratislava
Slovak Literary Agency: the exclusive copyright organization representing Slovak authors in foreign transactions and foreign authors on the territory of Slovakia
Contact: Judr Matej Andráš

Book Clubs

Č K P (Členská knižnica Pravdy)*, CS-88205 Bratislava, Gunduličová ul 12
Members: 43,500
Owned by: Nakladatelstvo Pravda (qv)
Founded: 1958

Club of Young Readers*, 81519 Bratislava, nám SNP 12
Owned by: Mladé letá (qv)

E R B*, 11258 Prague 1, Václavské nám 17, Nové Město
Owned by: Práce (qv)

Friends of Antiquity, 11303 Prague 1, Revoluční 15
Owned by: Svoboda (qv)

Hviezdoslavova knižnica*, 89134 Bratislava, Michalská 9
Owned by: Tatran (qv)

K M C, Prague 1, Na Perštýně 1
Young Readers' Club
Owned by: Albatros (qv)

K M P (Kruh milovníkov poézie), 81367 Bratislava, Leningradská 2
Club for Poetry Lovers
Owned by: Slovenský spisovatel' (qv)

Klub čtenářů technické literatury, 11302 Prague 1, Spálená 51
Club for Readers of Technical Literature
Members: 45,000
Supervised by: SNTL-Nakladatelství technické literatury (qv)
Subjects: Engineering and Applied Technology, Science, Dictionaries, Applied Economics
Founded: 1958

Klub přátel poezie, 11147 Prague 1, Národní 9
Club of the Friends of Poetry
Owned by: Československý spisovatel (qv)

Máj, 81284 Bratislava, Pražská 11
Owned by: Smena (qv)

N S T (Nová sovietska tvorba), 81367 Bratislava, Leningradská 2
Owned by: Slovenský spisovatel' (qv)

Odeon Book Club (Klub čtenářů), 11697 Prague 1, Celetna 11
Members: 200,000
Owned by: Odeon (qv)
Subject: Fiction

Readers Club, 11303 Prague 1, Revoluční 15 Tel: 2317051
Owned by: Svoboda (qv)

S P K K (Spoločnost' priatel'ov' krásnych kníh), 81367 Bratislava, Leningradská 2
Society of Friends of Beautiful Books
Owned by: Slovenský spisovatel' (qv)

Svoboda Book Club, 11303 Prague 1, Revoluční 15 Tel: 2317051
Owned by: Svoboda (qv)
Subjects: History, Philosophy, Politics, Belles Lettres

Vavrín, 81367 Bratislava, Leningradská 2
Owned by: Slovenský spisovatel' (qv)

Major Booksellers

Artia, 11127 Prague 1, Ve Smečkách 30, PO Box 790 Tel: 246041
Import/export organization
Also Publisher (qv)

Kniha (The Book)*, Prague 2, Nové Město, 8 Zitna
Dir: Miloslav Jeřábek
The central purchasing place for single bookselling businesses in Prague

Slovart Co Ltd, 81764 Bratislava, Gottwaldovo nám 6
Import/export organization

Major Libraries

Státní knihovna **České socialistické republiky**, 11001 Prague 1, Klementinum 190 Tel: (Main switchboard) 266541/267241; (Dir) 225192
State Library of the Czech Socialist Republic

Knihovna Národniho muzea, 11579 Prague 1, trh Vítězného února 74 Tel: 269451/9
National Museum Library
Dir: Dr Jaroslav Vrchotka CSc
Publication: Sborník Národniho muzea v Praze, řada C-literární historie (quarterly)

Matica slovenská*, 03692 Martin, Mudroňova 13 Tel: 31371-2/31792/31795
Telex: 75331
Slovak National Library

Městská knihovna v Praze, 11572 Prague 1, nám primátora Dr V Vacka 1
The City Library in Prague

Památník národního písemnictví, Strahovská knihovna*, 11838 Prague 1, Strahovské nádvoří 132 Tel: 538841
Museum of National Literature, Strahov Library

Slovenská technická knižnica*, 81223 Bratislava, Gottwaldovo nám 19
Slovak Technical Library

Ustredná knižnica **Slovenskej akadémie** vied, 81467 Bratislava, Klemensova 19 Tel: 56321/51733 Telex: 93464 Uksav
Central Library of the Slovak Academy of Sciences

Státní technická knihovna*, 11307 Prague 1, nám primátora Dr V Vacka 5
State Technical Library
Dir: Dr Eva Sošková
Periodicals include: Technická Knihovna (Technical Library); Czechoslovak scientific and technical periodicals contents

Státní vědecká knihovna, 60187 Brno, Leninova 5-7 Tel: 58321 Telex: 62299
State Research Library
Chief Librarian: Dr Jiřina Sýkorová CSc

Státní vědecká knihovna, 77177 Olomouc, Bezručova 2
State Scientific Library

Státní vědecká knihovna odbor technické literatury*, 66231 Brno, Veveří 95
State Technical Library in Brno

Universitná knižnica*, Bratislava, Michalská 1 Tel: 333247 Telex: 09255 Uknz C
University Library
Dir: Ing Vincent Kútik

Knihovny fakult a ústavu **University Karlovy***, Prague
Libraries of Faculties and Institutes of Charles University

Library Associations

Slovenská knižničná RADA*, Ministerstvo kultúry SSR, 81331 Bratislava, Suvorovová 12
Slovak Library Council
Chairman: Dr S Pasiar

Ústřední knihovnická rada ČSSR*, Prague 1, Valdštejnká 30
Central Library Council of the Czechoslovak Socialist Republic
President: Dr Jiří Kábrt
Publication: Knihovnik

Zväz slovenských knihovníkov a informatikov, 81417 Bratislava, Michalská 1 Tel: 330557 Telex: 093255
Association of Slovak Librarians and Information Scientists
Executive Secretary: Ing Štefan Kimlička
Publication: Zväzový bulletin

Library Reference Journals

Journals

Československá akademie věd. Ustřední archiv. Archivní zpravy (Czechoslovak Academy of Sciences. Central Archives. Archival Reports), Academia, 11229 Prague 1, Vodičkova 40

Čitatel (The Reader) (text in Slovak, summaries in German and Russian), Slovak National Library, 03652 Martin, Mudroňova 13

Informačný bulletin (Information Bulletin), Association of Slovak Librarians and Information Scientists, 81417 Bratislava, Michalská 1

Literary Associations and Societies

Institute of Slovak Literature*, Bratislava, Klemensová 27

Kruh priatelov detskej knihy*, 89426 Bratislava, nám SNP12
Association of Friends of Children's Books in Slovakia

Matice moravská, Brno, Gorkého 14
Moravian Society of History and Literature
Secretary: Dr Jiří Malíř
Publication: Časopis Matice moravské (quarterly)

Czechoslovakian **P E N** Centre, 1180 Prague 1, Hradčanské nam 11
Secretary: Marta Kadlečikova

Společnost přátel knihy pro mládež, 11000 Prague 1, Na Perštýně 1
Association of Friends of Children's Books
Publication: Bulletin (irregular)

Index-**Společnost pro Československou literaturu** v zahraničí*, Postfach 410511, D-5000 Cologne 41, Federal Republic of Germany
Society for the Promotion of Czechoslovak Literature Abroad

Spolek Českých bibliofilu*, Prague, Nové Město, Václavské nám 39
Association of Czech Bibliophiles

Literary Periodicals

Červený Květ (The Red Flower), literature and art, Ostrava 1, Tyrsová 9

Česká literatura (Czech Literature) (text in Czech, summaries in English, French, German and Russian), Academia, Publishing House of the Czechoslovak Academy of Sciences, 11229 Prague 1, Vodičkova 40

Literarní měsíčnik (Literary Monthly), Union of Czech Writers, 11147 Prague 1, Národní trída 11

Meridians 12-23, Union of Slovak Writers, 81508 Bratislava, ul Obrancov mieru 14

Novinky literatury (Literary News), State Library of the Czech Socialist Republic, 11001 Prague 1, Klementinum 190

Sborník narodního muzea v Praže rada C: literarni historie (Magazine of the National Museum, Prague. Series 3: Literary History) (title also in Latin, summaries in English, French, German and Russian), National Museum, 11579 Prague 1, trh Vítězného února 74

Slovenská literatúra (Slovak Literature) (contents page and summaries in German and Russian), Slovak Academy of Sciences, Institute of Slovak Literature, Bratislava, Klemensová 27

Slovenské pohlady na literatúru a umĕnie (Slovak View on Literature and Art), Slovenský spisovatel', 81367 Bratislava, Leningradská 2

Slowakei (Slovakia), literary, scientific and political review, Matus-Cernak-Institut, Kulturelles Zentrum der Slowaken in Deutschland, D-5000 Cologne 1, Postfach 100924, Federal Republic of Germany

Svědectví (Czech literary journal published abroad), 6 rue du Pont de Lodi, Paris 6e, and Vienna V, Margaretenpl 7

Svetova literatura, review of foreign literature, Odeon, 11587 Prague 1, Národní 36

Literary Prizes

Bratislava Town Prize
Awarded annually for outstanding work in fields including literature relating to the town of Bratislava. In 1982 a literary prize was awarded to Mária Ďuríčková for her trilogy of tales for children about the town of Bratislava. Enquiries to Zväz slovenských spisovatel'ov, 81508 Bratislava, Obrancov mieru 14

Brno Literary Prize*
For the best book written and published in Brno. Awarded annually. Enquiries to Zväz slovenských spisovatel'ov, 81508 Bratislava, Obrancov mieru 14

Jan **Holly** Prize
Awarded annually by the Slovak Literary Fund for the best literary translations. Awarded in 1983 to Ružena Dúbravová, Hana Ferková and Jana Kantorová-Báliková. Enquiries to Zväz slovenských spisovatel'ov, 81508 Bratislava, Obrancov mieru 14

Fraňo **Kráľ** Prize
For existing works or for outstanding achievements in the field of juvenile literature. The executive body of Fraňo Král Prize is the Slovak Literary Fund, the Circle of Friends of Juvenile Literature and publishing house Mladé letá. The prize is awarded annually. Enquiries to Zväz slovenských spisovatel'ov, 81508 Bratislava, Obrancov mieru 14

Marie **Majerove** Prize
The highest award for a life's work in the fields of Czech literature and art for children and young people. Awarded every other year. Enquiries to Zväz slovenských spisovatel'ov, 81508 Bratislava, Obrancov mieru 14

Mladá fronta Award
Awarded annually by the publishing house Mladá fronta (Young Front) for literary works of prose, poetry, journalism, popular science, also translations, published by them during the preceding year. Enquiries to Zväz slovenských spisovatel'ov, 81508 Bratislava, Obrancov mieru 14

Mladé letá Prize
Awarded annually by the publishing house Mladé letá (Young Years) for outstanding books by Slovak writers published by them during the preceding year. Awarded in 1983 to Vladimír Ferko for *Čertovo rebro* (children's). Enquiries to Zväz slovenských spisovatel'ov, 81508 Bratislava, Obrancov mieru 14

Naše vojsko Prizes*
For a political book, a book on military theory and a book of fiction. Monetary prize is divided between the winners in each category. Enquiries to Zväz slovenských spisovatel'ov, 81508 Bratislava, Obrancov mieru 14

Prague Literary Prize*
For the best creative work which has enriched human knowledge, contributed to the construction of socialism and furthered the development of culture in the City of Prague. Awarded annually. Enquiries to Zväz slovenských spisovatel'ov, 81508 Bratislava, Obrancov mieru 14

Slovenský spisovatel' Prize
Awarded annually by the publishing house Slovak Writer for outstanding books by Slovak writers published by them during the preceding year. Awarded in 1983 to Ján Beňo for *Vyberanie hniezda* (novel), Dezider Banga for *Horiaca višňa* (poetry), Vincent Šabík for *Čitajúci Titus* (theoretical). Enquiries to Zväz slovenských spisovatel'ov, 81508 Bratislava, Obrancov mieru 14

Smena Prize
Awarded annually by the publishing house Smena for outstanding books by Slovak writers published by them during the preceding year. Awarded in 1983 to Lýdia Vadkertiová for *Víno* (poetry). Enquiries to Zväz slovenských spisovatel'ov, 81508 Bratislava, Obrancov mieru 14

Zväz slovenských spisovatel'ov Prize
Awarded annually by the Union of Slovak Writers for outstanding works of original Slovak poetry, prose, literary science and literature for children. Awarded in 1983 to Ján Turan for *Nežne* (poetry), Oliver Rácz for *Rogožanova krčma* (prose), Vladimír Mináč for *Texty a kontexty* and František Miko for *Hodnoty a literárny proces* (both literary science), Tomáš Janovic for *Jeleňvízor* (children's). Enquiries to Zväz slovenských spisovatel'ov, 81508 Bratislava, Obrancov mieru 14

Denmark

General Information

Language: Danish (English and German widely spoken). Faeroese in the Faeroes. Greenlandic in Greenland
Religion: Lutheran
Population: 5.1 million
Bank Hours: 0930-1600 Monday-Friday; open until 1800 Thursday
Shop Hours: 0800 or 0900-1700 or 1730

DENMARK 75

Monday-Thursday; open until 1900 or 2000 Friday; open until 1400 Saturday
Currency: 100 øre = 1 krone
Export/Import Information: Member of European Economic Community. No tariff on books except children's picture books from non-EEC. No import licences required. Importers must use longest of alternative credit terms in contract, otherwise no exchange controls
Copyright: UCC, Berne, Florence (see International section)

Book Trade Organizations

Bog- og Papirbranchens Kreditor-Udvalg*, Kompagnistr 11, DK-1208 Copenhagen K
Committee of Inspection for the Book and Paper Trade

Dansk Boghandlermedhjaelperforening*, Boghandlernes Hus, Siljangade 6, DK-2300 Copenhagen S
Danish Book Trade Employees' Association
Publication: Bogormen

Dansk Bogtjeneste*, Rostrup Bogmarked, Østergade 20, DK-7400 Copenhagen
Danish Collective Book Advertising Organization
Chairman: Frits Rostrup

Dansk Forfatterforening*, Forfatternes Hus, Nyhavn 21, DK-1051 Copenhagen K
Danish Authors' Society (also represents interests of Danish book illustrators)
Chairman: Peter Seeberg; *General Secretary:* Svend Erichsen
Publication: Forfatteren (8 a year)

Danske Antikvarboghandlerforening, Postboks 2184, DK-1017 Copenhagen K
Danish Antiquarian Booksellers' Association

Danske Boghandleres Importørforening (DANBIF), Blegdamsvej 28, DK-2200 Copenhagen N   Tel: (01) 356287
Danish Booksellers' Import Association
Chairman: Hans Jespersen

Danske Boghandleres Kommissionsanstalt (DBK)*, Siljangade 6, DK-2300 Copenhagen
Danish Booksellers Clearing House
Man Dir: Jorgen G Hensen

Den **Danske Boghandlerforening**, Boghandlernes Hus, Siljangade 6, DK-2300 Copenhagen S
Danish Booksellers' Association
Secretary: Elisabeth Brodersen
Publication: Det Danske Bogmarked (with Danske Forlaeggerforening)

Den **Danske Forlaeggerforening***, Købmagergade 11, DK-1150 Copenhagen K   Tel: (01) 156688
Danish Publishers' Association
Dir: Erik V Krustrup
Publication: Det Danske Bogmarked (with Danske Boghandlerforening)

Fællesekspeditionen*, Njalsgade 19, DK-2300 Copenhagen S
Joint Trade Counter

Forening for Boghaandvaerk, Nørregade 26, DK-1165 Copenhagen K
Danish Book-craft Association
Publication: Bogvennen (yearbook)

Forening for Forlagsfolk, Kommunetryk, Erik Langkjaer, Sommerstedgade 7, DK-1718 Copenhagen V   Tel: (451) 229725
Association of Young Publishers

Standard Book Numbering Agency, Dansk Bogfortegnelse, Bibliotekscentralen, Telegrafvej 5, DK-2750 Ballerup   Tel: (02) 975555   Cable Add: Danliber   Telex: 27249
Administrator: Morten Garde

Book Trade Reference Books and Journals

Book

Fortegnelse over Samhandels-Berettigede Boghandlere MV (Register of Licensed Booksellers etc), Danish Publishers' Association, Købmagergade 11, DK-1150 Copenhagen K

Journals

Bogormen (The Bookworm), journal for book trade employees, Danish Book Trade Employees' Association, Boghandlernes Hus, Siljangade 6, DK-2300 Copenhagen S

Bogvennen (The Book Lover), Brolaeggerstr 4, DK-1211 Copenhagen K or Danish Book-craft Association, Nørregade 26, DK-1165 Copenhagen K

Dansk Bogfortegnelse (Danish National Bibliography), Bibliotekscentralen, Telegrafvej 5, DK-2750 Ballerup

Dansk Periodicafortegnelse (Danish National Bibliography, Serials), Bibliotekscentralen, Telegrafvej 5, DK-2750 Ballerup

Den Danske Bogmarked (The Danish Book Market), Danish Booksellers' Association, Boghandlernes Hus, Siljangade 6, DK-2300 Copenhagen S

Publishers

Akademisk Forlag, Store Kannikestr 6-8, DK-1169 Copenhagen K   Tel: (01) 119826
Man Dir: Per Holm Rasmussen
Subjects: History, Philosophy, High-priced Paperbacks, Psychology, Engineering, General Science, University Textbooks, Educational Materials
1981: 100 titles   *Founded:* 1962
ISBN Publisher's Prefix: 87-500

Arnkrone Forlaget A/S*, Fuglebækvej 4, DK-2770 Kastrup   Tel: (01) 507000
Man Dir: J Juul Rasmussen
Subjects: Art, Cultural History, Popular Medicine
Founded: 1941
ISBN Publisher's Prefix: 87-87007

Aschehoug Dansk Forlag A/S+, Klosterrisvej 7, DK-2100 Copenhagen Ø   Tel: (01) 294422   Cable Add: Asdanfo   Telex: 16987 Boggra
Man Dir: Erik Ipsen; *Marketing Manager:* Jan B Thomsen; *Rights & Permissions:* Kaj Påskesen
Subsidiary Companies: J Fr Clausens Forlag (qv); Grafisk Forlag (qv); H Hagerups Forlag (qv); H Hirschsprungs Forlag (qv)
Subjects: School Books, Textbooks
1981: 60 titles   *Founded:* 1914
ISBN Publisher's Prefix: 87-11

H M **Bergs** Forlag ApS, Peder Skrams Gade 5, DK-1054 Copenhagen K   Tel: (01) 135480
Man Dir: H M Berg
Subjects: General Non-fiction, Juveniles, Art
1981: 2 titles   *1982:* 3 titles   *Founded:* 1965
ISBN Publisher's Prefix: 87-7228

Berlingske Forlag A/S*, Antonigade 7, DK-1147 Copenhagen K   Tel: (01) 157575   Cable Add: Berlingske   Telex: 27094
Publisher: Henrik Fonss
Subjects: Berlingske Encyclopaedic Series, Dictionaries, Reference Books, Study Books
Founded: 1733
ISBN Publisher's Prefix: 87-19

Bibliotekscentralens Forlag, Telegrafvej 5, DK-2750 Ballerup   Tel: (02) 975555   Cable Add: Danliber   Telex: 35370
Man Dir: Asger Hansen; *Editorial, Sales:* Jørgen Rishøj
Subjects: Bibliographies, Catalogues, Classification and cataloguing rules. Publish Danish National Bibliography
1982: 20 titles   *Founded:* 1939
ISBN Publisher's Prefix: 87-552

Bierman og Fothergill – Bierman og Bierman ApS, Vestergade 120, DK-7200 Grindsted   Tel: (05) 320288/320481   Cable Add: Bierbook Grindsted
Also: Helleskraenten 33, DK-2860 Soborg   Tel: (01) 695635
Man Dirs: H A Bierman, Ailsa Fothergill
Holding Company: Bierman Invest A/S
Subsidiary Company: Helle Samuels & Co Ltd, 32 Bodmin Road, Luton, Beds, UK
Subjects: Children's Books, Culture
Bookshops: See under Major Booksellers
Founded: 1968

Bogans Forlag A/S, Kastaniebakken 8, DK-3540 Lynge   Tel: (02) 188055
Owner: Evan Bogan
Subjects: Quality Paperbacks (factual, general), Popular Science, Occult

Borgens Forlag A/S+, Valbygard, Valbygardsvej 33, DK-2500 Valby   Tel: (01) 462100   Cable Add: Borgenbooks
Man Dir and Editorial: Jarl Borgen; *Sales:* Else-Marie Hyldekrog; *Production:* Erik Crillesen; *Publicity:* Egon Dinesen; *Rights & Permissions:* Mette Nymark
Orders to: Faellesekspeditionen, Njalsgade 19, DK-2300 Copenhagen S
Subjects: General Fiction and Non-fiction, Art, Children's Books, Educational Books, Religion, Craft and Leisure, Practical Handbooks, Health & Social Science, Textbooks
Book Club: Lyrikbogklubben Borgen-Gyldendal (jointly owned)
1981: 185 titles   *1982:* 300 titles   *Founded:* 1948
ISBN Publisher's Prefix: 87-418

Børsen Forlaget A/S*, Postboks 2103, DK-1014 Copenhagen K (Located at: Moentergade 19, DK-1014 Copenhagen)   Tel: (01) 157250
Publishing Manager: Ib Topholm; *Editorial:* Jan Erik Olsen; *Sales Manager:* Rehné Erik Jensen; *Production:* Gitte Mortensen
Subject: Management
ISBN Publisher's Prefix: 87-7553

Branner og Korch's Forlag A/S*, H C Oerstedsvej 7B, DK-1879 Kastrup V   Tel: (01) 224511   Cable Add: Bookbranner
Man Dir: Torbar Schur
Subjects: General Fiction & Non-fiction, Technical, Juveniles, Reference, Textbooks, Politics
Founded: 1949
ISBN Publisher's Prefix: 87-411

Nyt Nordisk Forlag Arnold **Busck** A/S, Købmagergade 49, DK-1150 Copenhagen K   Tel: (01) 111103   Cable Add: Bookbusck
Man Dirs: Helge Arnold Busck, Ole Arnold Busck
Subsidiary Company: Det Schoenbergske Forlag A/S (qv)
Subjects: General Fiction, Biography, History, How-to, Music, Art, Philosophy, Reference, Religion, High-priced Paperbacks, Medicine, Psychology, General & Social Science, University, Secondary & Primary Textbooks
Bookshops: Arnold Busck International Boghandel A/S, Nordisk Boghandel (qqv under Major Booksellers); Birkerød Boghandel, Arnold Busck A/S, Hovedgaden 37, DK-3460 Birkerød; Arnold Busck Antiquarians, Fiolstr 24, DK-1171 Copenhagen K
1981: 300 titles   *Founded:* 1896
ISBN Publisher's Prefix: 87-17

76 DENMARK

Carit Andersens Forlag A/S, Malmøgade 3, DK-2100 Copenhagen Ø Tel: (01) 16121
Parent Company: Paul Klinge A/S
Subjects: Travel, Limited Editions, Illustrated books

Carlsen if International Publishers A/S*, Postboks 6, Købmagergade 9, DK-1001 Copenhagen K Tel: (01) 143596 Cable Add: Carlsenif Telex: 22426 Carl DK
Man Dir: Per Hjald Carlsen
Parent Company: SEMIC, Sweden (qv)
Subsidiary Company: Carlsen/if AB, Sweden (qv)
Subject: Children's Picture Books

J Fr Clausens Forlag+, Klosterrisvej 7, DK-2100 Copenhagen Ø Tel: (01) 294422 Cable Add: Asdanfo Telex: 16987 Boggra
Man Dir: Erik Ipsen; *Marketing Manager:* Jan B Thomsen; *Rights & Permissions:* Kaj Påskesen
Parent Company: Aschehoug Dansk Forlag A/S (qv)
Subject: Practical Handbooks
1981: 37 titles
ISBN Publisher's Prefix: 87-11

Forlaget **Danmark** A/S, now incorporated in Lademann Ltd, Publishers (qv)

Dansk Historisk Haandbogsforlag Ltd+, Klintevej 25, DK-2800 Lyngby Tel: (02) 988500
Owner, Man Dir: Henning Jensen
Subjects: Genealogy, Heraldry, Culture, Local History
1981: 29 titles *Founded:* 1976
ISBN Publisher's Prefix: 87-85207

Christian **Ejlers'** Forlag A/S, Brolaeggerstr 4, DK-1211 Copenhagen K Tel: (01) 122114
Man Dir: Christian Ejlers
Subjects: Educational & Academic, Art, Bibliography
Founded: 1967
ISBN Publisher's Prefix: 87-7241

Chr **Erichsens** Forlag A/S, Kronprinsensgade 1, DK-1114 Copenhagen K Tel: (01) 159595 Cable Add: Bogerich
Man Dir: Mr Kay Holkenfeldt
Subjects: Fiction, Mysteries, How-to, Juveniles, Handbooks
Founded: 1902
ISBN Publisher's Prefix: 87-555

Forlaget **Europa**, Kompagnistr 33, DK-1208 Copenhagen K Tel: (01) 156273 Telex: 19280 Euroin dk
Editorial: Lars Kvistskov Larsen
Subjects: Secondary and Grammar School Textbooks
1982: 7 titles

F A D L's Forlag A/S (Foreningen af danske Laegestuderendes Forlag), Blegdamsvej 28, DK-2200 Copenhagen N Tel: (01) 356200 Telex: 16698 Unbog Dk
Man Dirs: Hans Jespersen, Steen Brynitz
Subjects: Medicine, Biology
Founded: 1964
ISBN Publisher's Prefix: 87-7437

Forlaget for **Faglitteratur** A/S, Vandkunsten 6, DK-1467 Copenhagen K Tel: (01) 137900
Subjects: Medicine, Technology
ISBN Publisher's Prefix: 87-573

Fogtdals Blade A/S*, Nørre Farimagsgade 49, DK-1364 Copenhagen K Tel: (01) 126612 Telex: 15712 Fogtdl Dk
Chief Man Dir: Erik Skipper Larsen
Subsidiary Company: Norsk Fogtdal A/S, Lille Frogner Allé 5a, Elisenberg, Oslo, Norway
Branch Off: Fogtdals Förlag, Ängelholmsgatan 1-3, S-214 22 Malmö, Sweden
Subjects: Home Decoration, DIY, Cooking, Gardening, Motoring, Boating, Fashion, Needlework
Founded: 1959

Forlaget **Forum** A/S, Snaregade 4, DK-1205 Copenhagen K Tel: (01) 147714 Cable Add: Forumbooks
Man Dir: Claus Brøndsted
Parent Company: Gyldendalske Boghandel — Nordisk Forlag A/S (qv)
Subjects: Fiction, General, Juveniles, Mysteries, High-priced Paperbacks
1982: 85 titles *Founded:* 1940
ISBN Publisher's Prefix: 87-553

Fremad, Nørrebrogade 54, DK-2200 Copenhagen N Tel: (01) 394040 Cable Add: Bogfremad
Man Dir: Mogens Bang; *Editorial:* Per Kofod
Subjects: General Fiction, Juveniles, Textbooks, Periodicals
Bookshop: Boghandelen Fremad (at above address)
1981: 50 titles *Founded:* 1912
ISBN Publisher's Prefix: 87-557

J Frimodts Forlag, Korskaervej 25, DK-7000 Fredericia Tel: (05) 926100
Man Dir: Bent Hansen
Associate Company: Lohses Forlag (qv)
Subjects: Religion, Fiction
ISBN Publisher's Prefix: 87-7446

Forlaget **G M T**+, Meilgaard, DK-8584 Tranehuse Tel: (06) 317511
Publishers: Hans Jørn Christensen, Erik Bjørn Olsen
Subjects: History, Aesthetics, Politics, Philosophy, Psychology, Sociology, General Fiction, Textbooks, Educational Materials
1981: 14 titles *1982:* 6 titles *Founded:* 1971
ISBN Publisher's Prefix: 87-7330

Hans **Gades** Harbour Pilots Succ A/S, Malmøgade 3, DK-2100 Copenhagen Ø Tel: (1) 260621 Cable Add: Gadepilot Telex: 16121
Chief Executive, Sales, Publicity and Rights & Permissions: Erik Albrechtsen; *Editorial Manager:* Helge Nagel; *Production Manager:* Lisbet Albrechtsen
Parent Company: Paul Klinge A/S (at above address)
Subject: Harbour Pilots (guides to ports)
1981: 1 title *1982:* 1 title *Founded:* 1980
ISBN Publisher's Prefix: 87-980203

G E C **Gads** Forlag, Vimmelskaftet 32, DK-1161 Copenhagen K Tel: (01) 150558 Cable Add: Boggad
Man Dir: Kaj Lynnerup
Subjects: Religion, Psychology, General Science, Education, Textbooks, Art, Reference, Law, Management
Bookshop: G E C Gad Dansk og Udenlandsk Boghandel A/S (qv under Major Booksellers)
Founded: 1855
ISBN Publisher's Prefix: 87-12

Jul **Gjellerup** Forlagsaktieselskab, Rømersgade 11, DK-1362 Copenhagen K Tel: (451) 137801 Telex: 19110 Gjbook Dk
Man Dir: Arne Møller; *Editorial Dir:* Harald Bertelsen; *Marketing Dir, Foreign Rights:* Ulf Thomsen
Orders to: Njalsgade 17-19, DK-2300 Copenhagen S Tel: (451) 548151
Subjects: Reference, Primary, Secondary & Tertiary Textbooks, Educational Materials
Bookshop: Jul Gjellerups Boghandel ApS (qv under Major Booksellers)
1983: approx 60 titles *Founded:* 1884
ISBN Publisher's Prefix: 87-13

Grafisk Forlag, Klosterrisvej 7, DK-2100 Copenhagen Ø Tel: (01) 294422 Cable Add: Asdanfo Telex: 16987 Boggra
Man Dir: Ove Mølbeck; *Deputy Manager:* Birger Schmith
Parent Company: Aschehoug Dansk Forlag A/S
Subjects: School Books, Textbooks, Easy Readers
Founded: 1941
ISBN Publisher's Prefix: 87-429

Grevas Forlag*, Skovfaldet 2 K, DK-8200 Århus N Tel: (06) 168387 Cable Add: Grevas Arhus
Man Dir: Eva Hemmer Hansen; *Sales Dir:* Luise Pihl
Subjects: General Fiction, Belles Lettres, Poetry, Biography, Art, Juveniles
Founded: 1966
ISBN Publisher's Prefix: 87-7235

Det **Grønlandske** Forlag, Postboks 1009, DK-3900 Godthåb, Greenland (Located at: Hans Egedesvej 21, DK-3900 Godthåb) Tel: 22122 Cable Add: Groefobo Telex: 90638
The Greenlandic Publishing House
Man Dir: Hans Mortensen
Subjects: Children's Books, Fiction
Bookshop: Atuagkat Bookstore (at above address)
Founded: 1956
ISBN Publisher's Prefix: 87-558

Guinness, an imprint under licence of Forlaget Komma A/S (qv)

Gutenberghus Publishing Service A/S, Vognmagergade 11, DK-1148 Copenhagen K Tel: (01) 151925 Cable Add: Gpspubl Telex: 16705
Dir: Johs Vilsøe; *Editorial:* Jorgen Hendel, Per Då
Parent Company: Gutenberghus Group, Copenhagen
Associate Companies: Oy Kirjalito, Finland; Ehapa-Verlag GmbH, Federal Republic of Germany; Hjemmet A/S and Hjemmets Bokforlag A/S, Norway (qqv); Hemmets Journal AB (qv) and Forlaget Kärnan AB, Sweden
Subjects: Juveniles, Albums
Book Club: Walt Disney Wonderful World of Reading

Gyldendalske Boghandel — Nordisk Forlag A/S, Klareboderne 3, DK-1001 Copenhagen K Tel: (01) 110775 Cable Add: Gyldendals Copenhagen Telex: 15887 Gyldaldk
Dirs: Kurt Fromberg, Ole Werner Thomsen, Niels Agner; *Editorial:* Mogens Knudsen (Literary Dir), Finn Donsbaek (Textbooks), Vagn Grosen (General Trade), Karen Margrethe Henriksen (Juveniles), Peter Holst (Non-fiction reference books), Ole Norling-Christensen (Dictionaries), Egon Schmidt (Audiovisual); *Sales Manager:* Poul Ringhof; *Rights & Permissions:* Kirsten Franke, Per Finn Jacobsen; *Co-productions Manager:* Eyvind Thorsen
Subsidiary Companies: Forlaget Forum A/S (qv); Forlaget Vindrose ApS (qv)
Subjects: General Fiction, Belles Lettres, Poetry, Biography, History, How-to, Music, Art, Philosophy, Reference, Juveniles, Low- & High-priced Paperbacks, Medicine, Psychology, General & Social Science, University, Secondary & Primary Textbooks, Educational Materials
Book Clubs: Gyldendals Bogklub, Gyldendals Børnebogklub, Lyrikbogklubben Borgen-Gyldendal (jointly owned), Samlerens Bogklub, Bogklubben Spaendende Bøger
Founded: 1770
ISBN Publisher's Prefix: 87-01

P **Haase** & Søns Forlag A/S, Løvstr 8, DK-1152 Copenhagen K Tel: (01) 115999 Cable Add: Boghaase
Man Dir: Niels Jørgen Haase; *Secretary:* Nina Jensen; *Treasurer:* Manne Andersen; *Product Manager:* Preben Bentzen; *Editorial Manager:* Knud Anderson; *Sales &*

Marketing: May Hasager
Subsidiary Companies: N J Haases Bookimport ApS; Rasmus Navers Forlag (qv)
Subjects: Juveniles, University, Secondary & Primary Textbooks, Educational Materials
Bookshop: P Haase & Søns Boghandel A/S (at above address)
1981: 89 titles *1982:* 103 titles *Founded:* 1877
ISBN Publisher's Prefix: 87-559

H **Hagerups** Forlag, Klosterrisvej 7, DK-2100 Copenhagen Ø Tel: (01) 294422 Cable Add: Asdanfo Telex: 16987 Boggra
Man Dir: Erik Ipsen; *Marketing Manager:* Jan B Thomsen; *Rights & Permissions:* Kaj Påskesen
Parent Company: Aschehoug Dansk Forlag A/S (qv)
Subjects: Juveniles, Secondary & Primary Textbooks
ISBN Publisher's Prefix: 87-11

Forlaget **Hamlet***, Frederiksborggade 26, DK-1360 Copenhagen K Tel: (01) 134421 Cable Add: Boglademann Telex: 19149 Ladpub Dk
Chief Executive: Herluf Stokholm; *Editorial:* Ib Askholm
Orders to: Lademann Ltd, Linnesgade 25, DK-1361 Copenhagen K
Parent Company: Lademann Ltd, Publishers (qv)
Subjects: Art, Handbooks on variety of subjects
Founded: 1974
ISBN Publisher's Prefix: 87-7321

Edition Wilhelm **Hansen**, Gothersgade 9-11, DK-1123 Copenhagen K Tel: (01) 117888 Cable Add: Musikhansen Telex: 19912 Musik Dk
Owners: Hanne and Lone Wilhelm Hansen
Subsidiary Company: AB Nordiska Musikförlaget (Edition Wilhelm Hansen, Stockholm), Sweden (qv)
Subjects: Music, Musicology, Art, Educational Materials
Founded: 1857
Miscellaneous: Also Literary Agent (Nordiska Teaterforlaget Edition Wilhelm Hansen)
ISBN Publisher's Prefix: 87-7455

Hekla Forlag ApS, Postboks 1109, DK-1009 Copenhagen K (Located at: Store Kongensgade 61a-b, D-1264 Copenhagen K) Tel: (01) 110911 Cable Add: Heklapress
Joint Owner & Man Dir, Editorial and Publicity: Helga W Lindhardt; *Joint Owner & Man Dir, Sales and Production:* Søren Melgaard; *Rights & Permissions:* Trine Licht
Orders to: Faellesekspeditionen, Njalsgade 19, DK-2300 Copenhagen S
Imprint: Vulkan
Subjects: General Trade, Fiction and Non-fiction
1981: 23 titles *1982:* 24 titles *Founded:* 1979
ISBN Publisher's Prefix: 87-7474

Hernovs Forlag, Bredgade 14-16, DK-1260 Copenhagen K Tel: (01) 156284/156209/113930
Man Dir: Johs G Hernov; *Publicity Dir:* P Leslie Holst
Subsidiary Company: Johs G Hernov, Vinimport ApS
Subjects: General Fiction, Juveniles
Book Club: Hernovs Book Club
Founded: 1941
ISBN Publisher's Prefix: 87-7215

H **Hirschsprungs** Forlag, Klosterrisvej 7, DK-2100 Copenhagen Ø Tel: (01) 294422 Cable Add: Asdanfo Telex: 16987 Boggra
Man Dir: Erik Ipsen; *Marketing Manager:* Jan B Thomsen; *Rights & Permissions:* Kaj Påskesen
Parent Company: Aschehoug Dansk Forlag A/S (qv)
Subjects: School Books, Textbooks
ISBN Publisher's Prefix: 87-11

Forlaget **Hönsetryk***, Godthåbsvej 15b, DK-3060 Espergaerde Tel: (03) 231074
Owner: Kirsten Hofstätter

Høst og Søns Forlag, Bredgade 35, DK-1260 Copenhagen K Tel: (01) 155051/153031 Cable Add: Bookhøst
Man Dir: Mogens C Lind; *Editorial:* Kirsten Skaarup
Subjects: Hobbies & Crafts, Languages, Books on Denmark, Juveniles, Reference
Founded: 1836
ISBN Publisher's Prefix: 87-14

Birgitte **Høvring's** Icelandic World Literature, Postboks 53, DK-3050 Humlebaek (Located at: Teglgårdsvej 531, DK-3050 Humlebaek) Tel: (02) 190926
Owner: Thorsteinn Stefánsson

Ibis, Skindergade 3B, DK-1159 Copenhagen K Tel: (1) 114255
Editorial Dir: Virginia Allen Jensen; *Rights & Permissions:* Karen Kjelstrup
Parent Company: International Children's Book Service (qv under Literary Agents)
Subjects: Books for Handicapped Children, Slides and filmstrips based on children's literature, supplementary enrichment materials

Informations Forlag ApS+, St Kongensgade 40, DK-1264 Copenhagen K Tel: (01) 141426 Telex: 22658
Parent Company: 'Information' Daily Newspaper
Subjects: Non-fiction informative books on current issues, Politics, Fiction
Founded: 1975
ISBN Publisher's Prefix: 87-7514

A/S **Interpresse***, PO Box 11, DK-2880 Bagsvaerd (Located at: 32 Krogshoejvej, Bagsvaerd) Tel: 02985227 Cable Add: Stonepress Telex: 37416 Stenby Dk
Man Dir: Arne Stenby
Associate Company: SEMIC, Sweden (qv)
Subjects: Juveniles, Comics
Founded: 1954
ISBN Publisher's Prefix: 87-7529

Jespersen og Pios Forlag, Valkendorfsgade 22, DK-1151 Copenhagen K Tel: (01) 129642 Cable Add: Jespio
Man Dir: Iver Jespersen; *Rights & Permissions:* Elly Sandal
Subjects: General Fiction & Non-fiction, Juveniles, Paperbacks
Founded: 1865
ISBN Publisher's Prefix: 87-419

Forlaget **Komma** A/S+, Frederiksborggade 26, DK-1360 Copenhagen K Tel: (01) 145583 Telex: 19149 ladpub
Man Dir, Rights & Permissions: Ludvig E Bramsen; *Production:* Jørn Ekstrøm; *Publicity:* Bente Reinvaldt
Parent Company: Lademann Ltd, Publishers (qv)
Imprints: Guinness, Komma Maritim, Kommas Dyrebøger, Piccolo-Bøger
Subjects: Popular Reference, Cookery, Maritime, How-to
1981: 28 titles *1982:* 32 titles *Founded:* 1977
ISBN Publisher's Prefix: 87-7512

Kraks Legat, Nytorv 17, DK-1450 Copenhagen K Tel: (451) 120308
Chief Executive: Finn Hilsted; *Editorial:* Mogens Handest; *Sales, Publicity:* Arne Nielsen; *Production and Rights & Permissions:* Mogens Handest, Arne Nielsen
Subjects: Trade and Export Directories — The Danish 'Who is Who', Mapbooks of Danish towns
1981: 13 titles *Founded:* 1770
ISBN Publisher's Prefix: 87-7225

Lademann Ltd, Publishers, Linnesgade 25, DK-1361 Copenhagen K Tel: (01) 131650 Cable Add: Boglademann Telex: 19149
Publisher: J Lademann; *Dir:* Jorgen Lundo; *Rights & Permissions:* Kirsten Jacobsen
Subsidiary Companies: Albatros Ltd; Forlaget Hamlet (qv); Kolon Ltd; Forlaget Komma A/S (qv); Sesam Ltd; Vintens Forlag Ltd (qv). Forlaget Denmark A/S is now incorporated in Lademann Ltd
Subjects: General
Book Clubs: Union Book Club, Union Crime Club, Union Novel Library, Danmark Book Club, Union Classics Library
1983: 160 titles *Founded:* 1954
ISBN Publisher's Prefix: 87-15

Lindhardt og Ringhof+, Studiestr 14, DK-1455 Copenhagen Tel: (01) 111955 Cable Add: Eleteredit
Owners: Otto B Lindhardt, Gert Ringhof
Subjects: General Fiction and Non-fiction, Paperbacks
1981: 46 titles *1982:* 63 titles *Founded:* 1971
ISBN Publisher's Prefix: 87-7560

Lohses Forlag, Korskaervej 25, DK-7000 Fredericia Tel: (05) 926100
Man Dir: Bent Hansen
Associate Company: J Frimodts Forlag (qv)
Subjects: Religion, Juveniles
Founded: 1868
ISBN Publisher's Prefix: 87-564

Mallings ApS, Gammel Kongevej 3-5, DK-1610 Copenhagen V Tel: (01) 243555 Cable Add: Mallingbook Telex: 15817 Jmco Dk
Man Dir, Editorial, Rights & Permissions: Joachim Malling; *Sales:* Hannah Malling; *Production:* Michael Malling; *Publicity:* Dorthe Malling
Subjects: Juveniles, Educational, Picture Books
Founded: 1975
ISBN Publisher's Prefix: 87-7333

Martins Forlag*, Kompagnistrade 34 4 sal, DK-1208 Copenhagen K Tel: (01) 146665
Owner: Erik Halkier
Subjects: General Fiction, Non-fiction, Juveniles
ISBN Publisher's Prefix: 87-566

Medicinsk Forlag ApS*, Tranevej 2, DK-3650 Ölstykke Tel: (02) 176592
Man Dir: Anni Lindelöv
Subjects: Medical, Scientific, Literature

Forlaget **Modtryk** AMBA+, Anholtsgade 4-6, DK-8000 Aarhus C Tel: (0045) 6127912/6137674 Telex: 4556785 Mod
Man Dir: Hans-Jørgen Schanz; *Editorial:* Jan Knus and Carsten Vengsgaard (Book Club); Knud Mahler and Ilse Noer (School Books); *Sales:* Niels Jørgen Jensen; *Production:* Jørgen Eie Christensen; *Publicity:* Jan Knus; *Rights & Permissions:* Preben Bach
Parent Company: Værtshuset Aesken, Anholtsgade 8, DK-8000 Aarhus C
Subjects: Political Writings and Essays (especially in the field of the 'New Left' movement), Children's Books, School Books, Fiction, Thrillers
Book Club: Socialistisk Bogklub ApS
1982: 34 titles *Founded:* 1972
ISBN Publisher's Prefixes: 87-458, 87-620, 87-817, 87-881

Munksgaard, International Booksellers & Publishers Ltd, Nørresøgade 35, DK-1370 Copenhagen K Tel: (01) 127030 Cable Add: Bogotto
Chairman of the Board: Per Saugman; *Man Dir:* Oluf V Møller; *Editorial:* Peter Hartmann, Sven Erik Olsen

78 DENMARK

Subjects: Medicine, Nursing, Dentistry, Social Sciences, Psychology, Schoolbooks, Children's Books, Scientific Journals
Bookshop: Munksgaard Export & Subscription Service (qv under Major Booksellers)
Founded: 1917
ISBN Publisher's Prefix: 87-16

Rasmus **Navers** Forlag, Løvstr 8, DK-1152 Copenhagen K Tel: (01) 115999
Man Dir: Niels Jørgen Haase
Parent Company: P Haase & Søns Forlag A/S (qv)
Subjects: Humour, Fiction, Poetry

New Era Publications ApS, Store Kongensgade 55, DK-1264 Copenhagen K Tel: (01) 145128 Telex: 16828 Pubsell Dk
Man Dir: Lena Moatty; *Sales Manager and Rights & Permissions:* Michel Moatty; *Manufacturing Dir:* Peter Maslin; *Publicity Dir:* Christian Fouché
Branch Off: Pubs UK, St Mary's College, Falmer Rd, Rottingdean, Sussex, UK
Subjects: Philosophy, Religion, Management, Education, Self Help, Self Improvement
Founded: 1967
Miscellaneous: Formerly Scientology Publications Organization ApS
ISBN Publisher's Prefix: 87-87347

Odense University Press, 36 Pjentedamsgade, DK-5000 Odense C Tel: (09) 141611
Man Dir: Lars Mikkelsen
Subjects: History, Literature, Philosophy, Medicine, Technology, Periodicals
1981: 33 titles *1982:* 40 titles *Founded:* 1970
ISBN Publisher's Prefix: 87-7492

Jörgen **Paludans** Forlag A/S*, Fiolstr 16, DK-1171 Copenhagen K Tel: (01) 15075, ext 45 & (01) 118203
Man Dir: Jörgen Paludan
Subjects: Non-fiction, Psychology, Sociology, History, Political Science, Economics, High-priced Paperbacks
ISBN Publisher's Prefix: 87-7230

Piccolo-Bøger, an imprint of Forlaget Komma A/S (qv)

Politikens Forlag A/S, Vestergade 26, DK-1456 Copenhagen K Tel: (01) 112122
Cable Add: Polbooks
Man Dir: Johannes Ravn; *Sales Dir:* Sören Seedorff; *Marketing Manager:* Morten Holm Madsen
Subjects: General Non-fiction: Nature Study, History and Documentary, Sports, Games, Hobbies, Children's Folklore, Art, Literature, Music, Maps and Atlases, Travel, How-to
Founded: 1946
ISBN Publisher's Prefix: 87-567

C A **Reitzel** A/S, Nørregade 20, DK-1165 Copenhagen K Tel: (01) 122400
Man Dir: Svend Olufsen
Subjects: General Science, Humanities, Non-fiction, Textbooks
Bookshop: See under Major Booksellers
1982: 60 titles *1983:* 125 titles *Founded:* 1819
ISBN Publisher's Prefix: 87-7421

Hans **Reitzels** Forlag A/S, Snaregade 4, DK-1205 Copenhagen K Tel: (01) 140451
Cable Add: Reitzelbooks
Man Dir: Hans Reitzel; *Editorial, Rights & Permissions:* Beate Nellemann
Subjects: Psychology, General & Social Science, University Textbooks, Philosophy, Reference, High-priced Paperbacks
1981: 35 titles *1982:* 73 titles *Founded:* 1949
ISBN Publisher's Prefix: 87-412

Rhodos, International Science and Art Publishers*, Niels Brocks Gård, Strandgade 36, DK-1401 Copenhagen K Tel: (01) 543020 Cable Add: Sciencebooks
Man Dir: Niels Blaedel
Subjects: Art, Nature, Fiction, High-priced Paperbacks, General & Social Science, Handbooks, Encyclopedias
Founded: 1959
ISBN Publisher's Prefix: 87-7496

Rosenkilde og Bagger, Postboks 2184, DK-1017 Copenhagen K (Located at: Kron-Prinsens-Gade 3, Copenhagen) Tel: (01) 157044 Cable Add: Bogkunst
Man Dir: Finn Jacobsen
Subjects: Reprints, Facsimile Editions, High-priced Paperbacks, General Science
Bookshop (and rare book department): At above address
1981: 18 titles *1982:* 20 titles *Founded:* 1941
ISBN Publisher's Prefix: 87-423

Samlerens Forlag A/S+, Christian den Niendesgade 2, DK-1111 Copenhagen K Tel: (01) 131023
Man Dir: Børge Priskorn
Subjects: Topical subjects, Contemporary History, Politics, Social Science, Biographies, Puzzle Books, Humour
1981: 50 titles
ISBN Publisher's Prefix: 87-568

Scandinavia Publishing House+, Nørregade 32, DK-1165 Copenhagen K Tel: (01) 140091 Cable Add: Scandico Telex: 19449 Scanco
Man Dir: Jørgen Vium Olesen; *Production Manager:* Per Hansen
Subjects: Juveniles, Educational, Religious (Christian) (all in Danish and other languages), Periodical
Book Club: Den Kristne Bogklub
1981: 11 titles *1982:* 14 titles *Founded:* 1979
ISBN Publisher's Prefix: 87-732

Det **Schoenbergske** Forlag A/S (Nyt Nordisk Forlag Arnold Busck A/S), Landemaerket 5, DK-1119 Copenhagen K Tel: (01) 113066 Cable Add: Schoenbook
Dir: Paul Monrad; *Sales Manager:* Max-Erik Reinhold; *Production:* Ole Stender
Parent Company: Nyt Nordisk Forlag Arnold Busch A/S (qv)
Subjects: General Fiction, Belles Lettres, Poetry, Biography, History, Art, Philosophy, Reference, Travel, Low- & High-priced Paperbacks, Psychology, Trade Books, University, Commercial School, Secondary & Primary Textbooks
1981: 61 titles *Founded:* 1857
ISBN Publisher's Prefix: 87-570

A/S J H **Schultz** Forlag, Møntergården, Møntergade 21, DK-1116 Copenhagen K Tel: (01) 121195 Cable Add: Bogschultz Telex: 19893
Manager: Poul Bay
Associate Company: Schultz Medical Information (qv)
Subjects: Non-fiction, Law, EEC publications
Founded: 1661
ISBN Publisher's Prefix: 87-569

Schultz Medical Information+, Møntergården, Møntergade 21, DK-1116 Copenhagen K Tel: (01) 121195 Cable Add: Bogschultz Telex: 19893
Manager: Henrik Borberg
Associate Company: A/S J H Schultz Forlag (qv)
Subjects: Medical

Scientology Publications Organization ApS, now New Era Publications ApS (qv)

Skarv – Nature Publications ApS+, Kongevejen 45B, DK-2840 Holte Tel: (02) 424745

Man Dir: Soren Koustrup
Subjects: Nature & Wildlife Books, Angling, Modern Biology, Geography, Animal Behaviour, Ecology, Ornithology
Founded: 1976
ISBN Publisher's Prefixes: 87-87581, 87-7545

A/S **Skattekartoteket**, Palaegade 4, DK-1261 Copenhagen K Tel: (01) 117874
Man Dir: Peter Taarnhøj
Subject: Taxation (national and international)

Sommer og Sörensen Forlag ApS, Mynstersvej 19, DK-1827 Copenhagen V Tel: (01) 232555
Dirs: Erik Sommer, Aage Börglum Sörensen

A/S **Sparevirke***, Köbmagergade 62-64, DK-1150 Copenhagen K Tel: (01) 151811
Man Dir: T G Söndergaard
Subjects: Handbooks, School Books
Founded: 1979
ISBN Publisher's Prefix: 87-7538

Strandbergs Forlag, Topstykket 17, DK-3460 Birkeröd Tel: (02) 816397
Owner: Hans Jörgen Strandberg
Subject: Cultural History

Strubes Forlag og Boghandel A/S, Söndergade 1, DK-4130 Gl Viby/Sjaelland Tel: (02) 394250 Cable Add: Strubebooks
Man Dirs: Jonna and Povl Strube
Subjects: Psychic & Occult, Philosophy, Art, Bibliophilic, Naval
Bookshop: Lille Triangel, DK-2100 Copenhagen OE

Finn **Suenson** Forlag, Rosernörns Alle 18, DK-1970 Copenhagen V Tel: (01) 359888
Man Dir: Finn Suenson
Subjects: Handbooks, Reference, Politics, History
Founded: 1971
ISBN Publisher's Prefix: 87-201

Teknisk Forlag A/S, Skelbaekgade 4, DK-1717 Copenhagen V Tel: (01) 216801 Cable Add: Technipress Telex: 16368 Tefko Dk
Man Dir: Peter Müller; *Editor-in-Chief:* Henrik Reinvaldt
Subjects: Engineering, Manuals, Directories, Guides
Founded: 1948
ISBN Publisher's Prefix: 87-571

Teknologisk Instituts Forlag, Postboks 141, DK-2630 Tåstrup Tel: (02) 996611
Subjects: Technical, Special Literature and Handbooks for Crafts and Industries
1981-83: 150 titles
ISBN Publisher's Prefix: 87-7511

Thaning og Appels Forlag*, H C Oerstedsvej 7b, DK-1879 Kastrup V Tel: (01) 224511
Man Dir: Absel Pedersen
Subjects: General Fiction, Belles Lettres, Art, History, Philosophy, Science & Technical Education, Psychology, How-to; Paperbacks
Founded: 1866
ISBN Publisher's Prefix: 87-413

Tiderne Skifter*, Sankt Pedersstr 28 B2, DK-1453 Copenhagen K Tel: (01) 124284
Chief Executive, Editorial and Production: Claus Clausen; *Sales, Publicity and Rights & Permissions:* Henning Lund
Orders to: Faelleseksspeditionen, Njalsgade 19, DK-2300 Copenhagen S
Subjects: Fiction, Sexual and Cultural Politics, Criticism
1981: 24 titles *Founded:* 1979
ISBN Publisher's Prefix: 87-7445

Ungdommens Forlag og Aamodts Forlag A/S*, Grundtvigsvej 37, DK-1864 Copenhagen K Tel: (01) 241500

Subjects: Special Literature, Juveniles
ISBN Publisher's Prefix: 87-7516

De Unges Forlag, Unitas Forlag, Amaliegade 24, DK-1256 Copenhagen K Tel: (01) 159363
Manager: Lorens Hedelund
Subjects: Religion, Fiction
1981: 9 titles *1982:* 6 titles *Founded:* 1914
ISBN Publisher's Prefix: 87-7517

Forlaget **Vindrose** ApS, Nybrogade 14, DK-1203 Copenhagen K Tel: (01) 135000
Man Dir: Erik Vagn Jensen; *Editorial:* Line Schmidt-Madsen; *Production:* Susanne Hejlesen; *Rights & Permissions:* Kirsten Franke
Parent Company: Gyldendalske Boghandel — Nordisk Forlag A/S (qv)
Subjects: General Fiction, Belles Lettres, Poetry, Science, Social Science, High-priced paperbacks
Founded: 1980
ISBN Publisher's Prefix: 87-7456

Vintens Forlag Ltd, Frederiksborggade 26, DK-1360 Copenhagen K Tel: (01) 122121 Cable Add: Boglademann Telex: 19149
Publisher: Ludvig E Bramsen
Parent Company: Lademann Ltd, Publishers (qv)
Subjects: General Fiction, Belles Lettres, Philosophy, Low- & High-priced Paperbacks
Founded: 1950
ISBN Publisher's Prefix: 87-414

Vulkan, an imprint of Hekla Forlag ApS (qv)

Wangels Forlag A/S, Postboks 1061, DK-1008 Copenhagen K (Located at: Gammeltorv 8, Copenhagen) Tel: (01) 156111
Man Dir: Benny Frederiksen
Associate Company: Hjemmets Bokforlag A/S, Norway (qv)
Subject: General Fiction
Book Club: Danske Bogsamleres Klub
Founded: 1946
ISBN Publisher's Prefix: 87-7220

Wilkenschildts Forlag*, Gedevasevej 3, DK-3520 Farum Tel: (02) 951828
Owner: Ebbe Wilkenschildt
Subjects: Handbooks, Non-fiction

Winthers Forlag ApS, Naverland 1A, DK-2600 Glostrup Tel: (02) 960666 Cable Add: Winnpub
Man Dir: Per Andreassen; *Rights & Permissions:* Anni Groth
Subsidiary Companies: Wennerberg, Finland; Wennerbergs Förlags AB, Sweden
Subjects: General Fiction, Low-priced Paperbacks, Comics
Founded: 1945
ISBN Publisher's Prefix: 87-18

Forlaget **Wøldike** K/S, Sankt Nikolajvej 4, DK-1955 Copenhagen V Tel: (01) 375009
Co-owner & Man Dir: Solveig Gervin
Subjects: Fiction & Non-fiction (all types of books for the general trade market)

Literary Agents

A/S **Bookman**, Fiolstr 12, DK-1171 Copenhagen K Tel: (01) 145720 Cable Add: Bookman
Miscellaneous: This company also acts as a Literary Agent in Sweden, Norway, Finland and Iceland for foreign authors

International Children's Book Service, Skindergade 3B, DK-1159 Copenhagen K Tel: (1) 114255 Cable Add: Bookchild
Contacts: Virginia Allen Jensen, Karen Kjelstrup
Subsidiary Company: Ibis (qv under Publishers)

Preben **Klein**, Postboks 16, DK-3200 Skaevinge (Located at: Borupvej 16, Skaevinge) Tel: (02) 288011
Also publishers' representative

Leonhardt Literary Agency ApS, Studiestraede 35, DK-1455 Copenhagen K Tel: (01) 132523 Cable Add: Leolitag

Michaels og Licht, Osterbrogade 84, DK-2100 Copenhagen Tel: (01) 424608 Cable Add: Literagent
Chief executives: Ole Licht, Agnes Licht

Svend **Mondrup** International Literary Agency*, Grenågade 12-14 — kldr, DK-1021 Copenhagen O Tel: (01) 267103/4 Telex: 16600 Fotex Dk (attn Interlitagent Copenhagen)
Chief Executive: Svend Mondrup

Nordiska Teaterforlaget Edition Wilhelm Hansen, Gothersgade 9-11, DK-1123 Copenhagen K Tel: (01) 117888
Owned by: Edition Wilhelm Hansen (qv)

Carl **Strakosch** og Olaf Nordgreen*, Nyhavn 5, DK-1051 Copenhagen K

Book Clubs

Danmark Book Club, Linnesgade 25, DK-1361 Copenhagen K
Owned by: Lademann Ltd, Publishers (qv)

Danske Bogsamleres Klub, Postboks 1061, DK-1008 Copenhagen K (Located at: Gammeltorv 8, Copenhagen)
Owned by: Wangels Forlag A/S (qv)

Gyldendals Bogklub, 51 Pilestraede, DK-1001 Copenhagen K
Owned by: Gyldendalske Boghandel — Nordisk Forlag A/S (qv)
Subjects: Fiction and General Non-fiction

Gyldendals Børnebogklub, Pilestraede 51, DK-1001 Copenhagen K
Owned by: Gyldendalske Boghandel — Nordisk Forlag A/S (qv)

Hernovs Book Club, Bredgade 14-16, DK-1260 Copenhagen K
Owned by: Hernovs Forlag (qv)

Den Kristne Bogklub, Nørregade 32, DK-1165 Copenhagen K Tel: (01) 140091 Cable Add: Scandico Telex: 19449 Scanco
Members: 400
Owned by: Scandinavia Publishing House (qv)
Founded: 1980

Lyrikbogklubben Borgen-Gyldendal, Postboks 62, Klareboderne 3, DK-1002 Copenhagen K Tel: (01) 152331
Owned by: Borgens Forlag A/S (qv) and Gyldendalske Boghandel — Nordisk Forlag A/S (qv)
Subject: Poetry
Founded: 1981

Samlerens Bogklub, Pilestraede 51, DK-1001 Copenhagen K
Owned by: Gyldendalske Boghandel — Nordisk Forlag A/S (qv)
Subjects: Fiction, Non-fiction, Political

Socialistisk Bogklub ApS, Anholtsgade 4-6, DK-8000 Aarhus C
Members: 4,000
Owned by: Forlaget Modtryk AMBA (qv)
Founded: 1977

Bogklubben **Spaendende** Bøger, Postboks 87, Klareboderne 3, DK-1003 Copenhagen K Tel: (01) 147782
Owned by: Gyldendalske Boghandel — Nordisk Forlag A/S (qv)
Founded: 1978

Union Book Club, Linnesgade 25, DK-1361 Copenhagen K Tel: (01) 131650 Cable Add: Boglademann Telex: 19149
Owned by: Lademann Ltd, Publishers (qv)
Subjects: Fiction, Illustrated Non-fiction
Founded: 1959

Union Classics Library, Linnesgade 25, DK-1361 Copenhagen K
Owned by: Lademann Ltd, Publishers (qv)

Union Crime Club, Linnesgade 25, DK-1361 Copenhagen K
Owned by: Lademann Ltd, Publishers (qv)

Union Novel Library, Linnesgade 25, DK-1361 Copenhagen K
Owned by: Lademann Ltd, Publishers (qv)

Walt Disney Wonderful World of Reading, Vognmagergade 11, DK-1148 Copenhagen K
Owned by: Gutenberghus Publishing Service A/S (qv)

Major Booksellers

Akademisk Boghandel, Universitetsparken, DK-8000 Århus C Tel: (06) 128844
Manager: Erling Sieverts

Biblioteksboghandelen ApS, Kultorvet 2, DK-1175 Copenhagen K
Manager: Nina E Jakobsen

Bierman og Fothergill – Bierman og Bierman ApS, Book Import and Sales, Vestergade 120, DK-7200 Grindsted Tel: (05) 320288/320481 Cable Add: Bierbook Grindsted
Also: Helleskraenten 33, DK-2860 Soborg Tel: (01) 695635
Man Dirs: H A Bierman, Ailsa Fothergill
Also Publisher (qv)

Clemens **Bøger** og Papir I/S*, Skt Clemens Torv 17, DK-8000 Århus C

Boghallen*, Rådhuspladsen 37, DK-1585 Copenhagen V Tel: (01) 118511

Arnold **Busck** International Boghandel A/S, Købmagergade 49, DK-1150 Copenhagen K Tel: (01) 122453
Export Division is at above address
Associate Company: Nordisk Boghandel (qv)
Owned by: Nyt Nordisk Forlag Arnold Busck A/S (qv)

Dansk Central-Boghandel*, Nørregade 49, DK-1165 Copenhagen K

G E C **Gad** Dansk og Udenlandsk Boghandel A/S, Vimmelskaftet 32, DK-1161 Copenhagen K Tel: (01) 150558
Owned by: G E C Gads Forlag (qv)

Jul **Gjellerups** Boghandel ApS, Sølvgade 87-89, DK-1307 Copenhagen K Tel: (01) 137233 Telex: 19110 Gj Book Dk
Manager: Joergen F Lauridsen
Owned by: Jul Gjellerup Forlagsaktieselskab (qv)

Magasin du Nord A/S, Book Department, The English Bookshop, Kongens Nytorv 13, DK-1095 Copenhagen K Tel: (451) 114433 Cable Add: Magdunord Telex 15975

Munksgaard Export & Subscription Service, Nørresøgade 35, DK-1370 Copenhagen K Tel: (01) 128570 Telex: 19431 Munks Dk
Also Publisher (qv)

Nordisk Boghandel, Østergade 16, DK-1100 Copenhagen K Tel: (01) 147007 (Mogens Staffeldt)
Associate Company: Arnold Busck International Boghandel A/S (qv)
Owned by: Nyt Nordisk Forlag Arnold Busck A/S (qv)

80 DENMARK

Erik **Paludans** Boghandel*, Fiolstr 10, DK-1171 Copenhagen K Tel: (01) 150675

Polyteknisk Boghandel og Forlag, Anker Engelundsvej 1, DK-2800 Lyngby Tel: (02) 881488
Manager: Ove Dela

C A **Reitzel** A/S, Nørregade 20, DK-1165 Copenhagen K Tel: (01) 122400
Man Dir: Svend Olufsen
Importers and exporters. Supply Universities, Scientific Libraries and Institutions worldwide
Also Publisher (qv)

Universitetsbogladen (Panumbogladen/Naturfagsbogladen), Blegdamsvej 3, DK-2200 Copenhagen N Tel: (01) 351643 Telex: 16698 Unbog Dk
Manager: Hans Jespersen
Branches: Panumbogladen (Medical bookshop), Blegdamsvej 3, DK-2200 Copenhagen N; Naturfagsbogladen (Natural Science bookshop), Universitetsparken 13, DK-2100 Copenhagen O

Major Libraries

Århus Kommunes Biblioteker, Mølleparken, DK-8000 Århus C Tel: (06) 136622 Telex: 64580 Arhubi
Århus Public Library

Bibliotekernes Oplysningskontor, Amaliegade 13B, DK-1256 Copenhagen K Tel: (01) 134633
The National Lending Centre
Librarian: Ane Marie Bonde

Danmarks Tekniske Bibliotek, Anker Engelunds Vej 1, DK-2800 Lyngby Tel: (02) 883088 Telex: 37148
National Technological Library of Denmark

Erhvervsarkivet-Statens Erhvervshistoriske Arkiv, Vester Allé 12, DK-8000 Århus C Tel: 128533
Danish National Business History Archives

Gentofte Kommunebibliotek*, Öregaards Allé 7, Hellerup, DK-2900 Copenhagen Tel: 45162/7500
Gentofte Municipal Library
Chief Librarian: Helge Stenkilde

Københavns Kommunes Biblioteker, Kultorvet 2, DK-1175 Copenhagen K Tel: (01) 136070 Telex: 16648 Kkbhb Dk
Copenhagen Municipal Libraries
Librarian: Brita Olsson

Københavns Stadsarkiv, Rådhuset, DK-1599 Copenhagen V
Copenhagen City Archives
Head Archivist: Helle Linde
Publication: Historiske Meddelelser om København (Historical Year-book)

Det **Kongelige Bibliotek**, Christians Brygge 8, DK-1219 Copenhagen K Tel: (01) 150111 Telex: 15009
Royal Library
National Librarian: Torkil Olsen
Publications: Contribution to the H C Andersen Bibliography; Bibliography of Old Norse-Icelandic Studies; Catalogue and Oriental Manuscripts, Xylographs, etc in Danish Collections; Discovery and Research in the Collections in the Royal Library

Det **Nordjyske Landsbibliotek**, Postboks 839, Nytorv 26, DK-9100 Ålborg Tel: (08) 162544 Telex: 69605 Aalbib Dk
Central Library for the County of North Jutland
Librarian: Birger Knudsen

Odense Centralbibliotek*, Ørbaekvej 95, DK-5220 Odense
Odense County Library

Odense Universitetsbibliotek, Campusvej 55, DK-5230 Odense M Tel: (09) 158600
Odense University Library

Rigsarkivet, Rigsdagsgården 9, DK-1218 Copenhagen K
National Record Office
Dir: Vagn Dybdahl

Statsbiblioteket, Universitetsparken, DK-8000 Århus C Tel: (06) 122022 Telex: 64515
State and University Library

Odense **Universitetsbibliotek**, see Odense

Universitetsbiblioteket, 1 afd, Fiolstraede 1, DK-1171 Copenhagen K Tel: (01) 130875
University Library: Humanities Department
Librarian: Torben Nielsen

Universitetsbiblioteket, 2 afd, Nørre allé 49, DK-2200 Copenhagen N Tel: (01) 396523 Telex: 15097 Ubisk Dk
University Library: Scientific and Medical Department
Chief Librarian: Kell Prehn
Publications include: Acta historica scientiarum naturalium et medicinalium

Library Associations

Arkivforeningen, Rigsarkivet, Rigsdagsgården 9, DK-1218 Copenhagen K Tel: (01) 123878
Archives Society
Secretary: Erik Gøbel

Bibliotekarforbundet, Jagtvej 111, DK-2200 Copenhagen N Tel: (01) 852822
Union of Librarians
Secretary: Steen Stegeager Hansen
Publication: Bibliotek 70

Bibliotekscentralen, Telegrafvej 5, DK-2750 Ballerup Tel: (02) 975555 Cable Add: Danliber Telex: 35370
Danish Library Bureau
Man Dir: Asger Hansen; *Editor:* Jørgen Rishøj
Subjects: Literature about Libraries, Bibliographical Manuals and Material
Publications: Dansk Artikelindeks, Aviser og Tidsskrifter (Danish Index of Articles, Periodicals and Newspapers), *Dansk Bogfortegnelse* (The Danish National Bibliography, Books), *Dansk Periodicafortegnelse* (The Danish National Bibliography, Serials)

Danmarks Biblioteksforening, Trekronergade 15, DK-2500 Copenhagen Valby Tel: (01) 308682
Danish Library Association
Dir: F Ettrup
Publications: Bogens Verden (Danish Library Journal); *Biblioteksvejviser* (Danish Library Guide); *Biblioteksårbog* (Danish Library Yearbook)

Danmarks Forskningsbiblioteksforening, Roskilde University Library, Postboks 258, DK-4000 Roskilde Tel: (02) 757711
Danish Research Library Association: Section 1 Research Libraries; Section 2 Staff members of Danish Research Libraries
President: Morten Laursen Vig; *Secretary:* Karl V Thomsen
Publication: DF-Revy

Danmarks Skolebibliotekarforening, Kildebakken 18, Blovstrød, DK-3450 Allerød Tel: (02) 271467
Association of Danish School Librarians
Publication: Skole Biblioteket (The School Librarian), Kongshvilebakken 10-12, DK-2800 Lyngby

Danmarks Skolebiblioteksforening, Frankrigsgade 4, DK-2300 Copenhagen S Tel: (01) 555095
Association of Danish School Libraries
Chief Executive: Ib Juul; *Manager:* Niels Jacobsen
Publication: Børn og Bøger; also books dealing with school libraries, youth culture, English summary

Dansk Musikbiblioteksforening, The Secretary, The Royal Library, Music Department, Christians Brygge 8, DK-1219 Copenhagen K
Association of Danish Music Libraries (Danish section of AIBM/IAML)

Dansk Teknisk Litteraturselskab — DTL, Danmarks Tekniske Bibliotek, Anker Engelunds Vej 1, DK-2800 Lyngby Tel: (02) 883088
Danish Society for scientific and technological information and documentation

Foreningen af Medarbejdere ved Danmarks Forskningsbiblioteker, Det Kongelige Bibliotek, Christians Brygge 8, DK-1219 Copenhagen K Tel: (01) 150111
Association of Staff Members of Danish Research Libraries (section 2 of the Danish Research Library Association)
President: Ulla Jensen; *Secretary:* Jytte Aunsbjerg Jensen

Sammenslutningem af Danmarks Forskningsbiblioteker, Roskilde University Library, Postboks 258, DK-4000 Roskilde Tel: (02) 757711
Association of Danish Research Libraries (section 1 of the Danish Research Library Association)
President: Morten Laursen Vig; *Secretary:* Jørgen Bro Glistrup

Library Reference Books and Journals

Books

Biblioteksårbog (Library Yearbook), Danish Library Association, Trekronergade 15, DK-2500 Copenhagen Valby

Biblioteksvejviser (Library Guide), Danish Library Association, Trekronergade 15, DK-2500 Copenhagen Valby

Public Libraries in Denmark, Det Danske Selskab, Kultorvet 2, DK-1175 Copenhagen K

Udenlandsk Bibliotekslitteratur i Danske Biblioteker (Foreign Library Literature in Danish Libraries), Bibliotekscentralen, Telegrafvej 5, DK-2750 Ballerup

Journals

Bibliotek 70 (Library 70), Union of Librarians, Jagtvej 111, DK-2200 Copenhagen N

Biblioteken (The Library), Biblioteksskole, Birketinget 6, DK-2300 Copenhagen S

Bogens Verden (Library Journal), magazine for Danish library employees, Danish Library Association, Trekronergade 15, DK-2500 Copenhagen Valby

DF-Revy, Danmarks Forskningsbiblioteksforening, Roskilde University Library, Postboks 258, DK-4000 Roskilde

Information for Forskningsbiblioteker (Information for Research Librarians), The Royal Library, Christians Brygge 8, DK-1219 Copenhagen K

Meddelelser frä Rigsbibliotekaren (Communications from the State Librarians), The Royal Library, Christians Brygge 8, DK-1219 Copenhagen K

Restaurator, International journal for the preservation of library and archival material (text in English, French, German and Russian), Restaurator Press, PO Box 96, DK-1004 Copenhagen K

Skole Biblioteket (The School Librarian), Kongshvilebakken 10-12, DK-2800 Lyngby

Literary Associations and Societies

Bogvennerne*, Madvigs Allé 2, DK-1829 Copenhagen
Friends of the Book

Dansk Exlibris Selskab*, PO Box 1519, DK-2700 Copenhagen Brh
Danish Bookplate Society
Publication: Exlibris-Nyt

Nyt **Dansk Litteraturselskab**, Bibliotekscentralen, Telegrafvej 5, DK-2750 Ballerup
New Danish Society for Literature
Manager: Jørgen Rishøj
Aims: Publication/Republication of books in short supply in libraries
Special activity: Magnaprint (large print books for partially-sighted)
Members: Public libraries only

Danske Sprog-og Litterurselskab, Frederiksholms Kanal 18A, DK-1220 Copenhagen Tel: (01) 130660
Danish Society of Language and Literature
Administrator: Dr Erik Dal

Kongelige Danske Videnskabernes Selskab, H C Andersens Boulevard 35, DK-1553 Copenhagen V Tel: (01) 113240
Royal Danish Academy of Sciences and Letters
President: Jens Lindhard; *Secretary:* Christian Crone; *Editor:* Erik Dal
Publications: Oversigt (annual); four-monograph series: Historisk-filosofiske Meddelelser, Historisk-filosofiske Skrifter, Biologiske Skrifter, Matematisk-fysiske Meddelelser; and occasional publications

Danish **P E N** Centre, Christian Ejlers' Forlag A/S, Brolaeggerstr 4, DK-1211 Copenhagen K
Secretary: Christian Ejlers

Samfund til Udgivelse af Gammel Nordisk Litteratur, Kjaerstrupvej 33, DK-2500 Copenhagen Valby
Society for the Publication of Old Norse Literature
Secretary: Agnete Loth

Literary Periodicals

Bog-anmelderen (The Book Review), Bog-Anmelderens Tidsskrifter, Gammel Torv 16, DK-1457 Copenhagen

Børn og Bøger (Children and Books), Association of Danish School Libraries, Frankrigsgade 4, DK-2300 Copenhagen 5

Exlibris-Nyt (Bookplate News), Danish Bookplate Society, PO Box 1519, DK-2700 Copenhagen Brh

Hvedekorn (Wheat Grain), Borgens Forlag A/S, Valbygard, Valbygardsvej 33, DK-2500 Valby

Language and Literature (text in English), Copenhagen University, English Institute, Lille Kirkestr 1, DK-1072 Copenhagen K

Orbis Litterarum, international review of literary studies (text mainly in English, occasionally in French and German), Munksgaard, Nørresøgade 35, DK-1370 Copenhagen K

Literary Prizes

Emil **Aarestrup** Prize*
For a poet. DKr 2,500 and a medal. Awarded annually. Enquiries to Danish Ministry of Cultural Affairs, Nybrogade 2, Copenhagen K

Hans Christian **Andersen** Prize
For the best Danish book for children. Established in 1955 to commemorate the 150th anniversary of the birth of Andersen. Awarded annually. Enquiries to Nyt Nordisk Forlag Arnold Busck A/S, Købmagergade 49, DK-1150 Copenhagen K

Danish Academy Prize for Literature
For an outstanding work of literature. DKr 100,000. Awarded bi-annually. Enquiries to The Danish Academy, Rungstedlund, 109 Rungsted Strandvej, DK-2960 Rungsted Kyst

Danish Authors' Colleagues Prize*
To a colleague who has published an interesting work. DKr 5,000. Awarded annually. Enquiries to Dansk Forfatterforening, Forfatternes Hus, Nyhavn 21, DK-1051 Copenhagen K

Danish Authors' Lyric Prize*
For poetry. DKr 5,000. Awarded annually. Enquiries to Dansk Forfatterforening, Forfatternes Hus, Nyhavn 21, DK-1051 Copenhagen K

Danish Critics Literary Prize, now known as Literaturkritikernes Laug (qv)

Danish Prize for Children's Literature*
For the best Danish books for children and teenagers. Established 1953. DKr 10,000. Awarded annually. Enquiries to Danish Ministry of Cultural Affairs, Nybrogade 2, Copenhagen K

Johannes **Ewald** Prize*
For prose, poetry and dramatic works. DKr 2,000. Awarded annually. Enquiries to Dansk Forfatterforening, Forfatternes Hus, Nyhavn 21, DK-1051 Copenhagen K

Adam Gottlob **Oehlenschläger** Prize*
For outstanding Danish writers. DKr 2,000. Awarded annually. Enquiries to Danish Ministry of Cultural Affairs, Nybrogade 2, Copenhagen K

Søren **Gyldendal** Prize
For authors from any field whose work is of great literary value. DKr 30,000. Awarded annually. Enquiries to Gyldendalske Boghandel - Nordisk Forlag A/S, Klareboderne 3, DK-1001 Copenhagen K

Holberg Medal*
For outstanding contributions to Danish literature. DKr 5,000 and a medal. Awarded annually. Enquiries to Dansk Forfatterforening, Forfatternes Hus, Nyhavn 21, DK-1051 Copenhagen K

Literaturkritikernes Laug (Critics Literary Prize)
For literary and art criticism. DKr 5,000. Awarded annually. Enquiries to Literaturkritikernes Laug, c/o Hans Andersen, Jyllands-Posten, DK-8260 Viby Jylland

Translation Agencies and Associations

Association of Translators*, Ribegade 8, Copenhagen

Danish Translations Centre (DTC), Risø Libry, Risø National Laboratory, DK-4000 Roskilde Tel: (02) 371212 Telex: 43116 A Risoe

Translatørforeningen*, Bornholmsgade 1, DK-1266 Copenhagen K Tel: (01) 126044
Association of Danish Sworn Translators

Dominican Republic

General Information

Language: Spanish
Religion: Roman Catholic
Population: 5.12 million
Literacy Rate (1970): 68.5%
Bank Hours: 0830-1230 Monday-Friday; some open 0830-1130 Saturday
Shop Hours: 0800-1200, 1400 or 1500-1800 Monday-Friday; some open Saturday
Currency: 100 centavos = 1 peso oro (= $US1). US currency is widely used
Export/Import Information: No import licences required for books. Exchange licence and approval from Central Bank required
Copyright: Buenos Aires (see International section)

Publishers

Publicaciones **Ahora** C por A*, Ave San Martin 236, Apdo 1402, Santo Domingo Tel: 5655581 Cable Add: Ahora Dr Telex: 326438
Editorial: R Molina Morillo; *Sales:* Luis R Cordero; *Production:* José R Grau; *Publicity:* Manuel Fco Santana

Juan Max **Alemany***, E Henriquez 12, Santo Domingo

Editora **Alfa y Omega***, M Cabral 11, Santo Domingo

Blas de la Rosa, Yolanda Guzmán 105, Santo Domingo
President: Mariano A Martinez Guzman

Editora El **Caribe***, Autop Duarte Km 7 1/2, Santo Domingo

Editora **Colonial***, Moca 27-B, Santo Domingo Tel: (809) 5657841/5671773

Rafael **Corporan** de los Santos*, S. Valverde 44, Santo Domingo

Editora **Cosmos***, Calle N No. 13, Feria, Santo Domingo

Dominican Books — Distribution Inc, Apdo 559, Santo Domingo Tel: 5322690 Cable Add: Domini Books
President: Luis Franco
Subjects: History, Social Science, Law, Philosophy
Founded: 1964

Ediciones Pedagógicas Dominicanas C por A*, Padre Billini 103, Apdo 1320, Santo Domingo Tel: 6889711

Man Dir: Miguel González Cano
Imprint: Escobo
Subjects: School Books and Educational Materials
Subsidiary Company: Editora Cultural Dominicana SA
Founded: 1962

Editora Cultural Dominicana*, San Martín 236, Santo Domingo

Editora Educativa Dominicana*, Mercedes 45, Santo Domingo

Editora Internacional*, Moca 31, Santo Domingo

Editorama SA*, Ave Tiradentes 56, Santo Domingo
Dir: Juan R Quiñones
Subjects: Large-print books (Literature and Art)

Editorial Librería Dominicana*, Mercedes 45-49, Santo Domingo Tel: 96293/23893 Cable Add: Sirviendo
Dir: Julio Postigo
Subjects: General Literature, Religion, Law, Textbooks
Founded: 1937

Editora **Enriquillo***, I la Catolica 41, Santo Domingo

Escobo, an imprint of Ediciones Pedagógicas Dominicanas C por A (qv)

P A **Gómez***, E Tejera 15, Santo Domingo

Editora **Horizontes** de América*, A Fleming 2, Santo Domingo

La **Información***, M Gómez 16, Santiago

Editora **Listín** Diario, Paseo de los Periodistas 52, Santo Domingo

Editorial Padilla*, San Fco Macorís 14, Santo Domingo
Bookshops: See under Major Booksellers

Editora Colegial **Quisqueyana** SA*, Ave Tiradentes, Centro Comercial Naco, Santo Domingo Tel: 5661808/5654277/5671818
Subjects: Pre-school, Primary & Secondary Textbooks and Educational Materials
Bookshop: See under Major Booksellers

Editora La **Razon***, J Verne 14, Santo Domingo

Editorial **Stella***, Guayacanes 7, Santo Domingo

Ultima Hora, Paseo de los Periodistas 12, Santo Domingo

Universidad Autónoma de Santo Domingo, Ciudad Universitaria, Apdo 1355, Santo Domingo Tel: 5332011 Cable Add: 3460182 Uniausd
Subjects: Academic

Universidad Católica Madre y Maestra*, Departamento de Publicaciones, Autopista Duarte, Santiago de los Caballeros Tel: 5825105 Cable Add: Ucmm
Man Dir, Editorial: Danilo de los Santos
Subjects: General
Founded: 1967

Major Booksellers

Caribe Grolier Inc*, L de Castro 203, Santo Domingo Tel: 6897373
Also: Hostos 208, Santo Domingo Tel: 6888544

Ediciones **Coquito***, E Tejera 19, Santo Domingo Tel: 6883021

Casa **Cuello***, El Conde 33, Santo Domingo Tel: 6896226/6874242

Disesa*, Hostos 202, Santo Domingo Tel: 6897644/6823533
Also: S Larga, Santo Domingo Tel: 6882163

Distribuidora Escolar SA (DISESA), Ave Abraham Lincoln-Pedro H Ureña, Santo Domingo Tel: 5654554
Also: Sabana Larga, Santo Domingo Tel: 5941780; El Sol, Santiago Tel: 5826006

Encyclopaedia Britannica de Venezuela SA*, El Conde 35, Santo Domingo Tel: 6829260

Papeleria **Fersobe** Hnos, Ave Duarte 16-A, Santo Domingo Tel: 6894744
Also: Ave Mella 156, Santo Domingo Tel: 6881848

Casa **Herrera***, Mercedes 125, Santo Domingo Tel: 97568

Febio **Herrera***, Bolivar 40, Santo Domingo Tel: 6878677
Importer

Librería y Papeleria **Lope de Vega***, L de Vega 55, Santo Domingo Tel: 5658066

Mella*, Ave Duarte 27, Santo Domingo Tel: 6886539

Niove*, 16 de Agosto 47, Santo Domingo Tel: 6894088

Editorial **Padilla***, El Conde 511, Santo Domingo Tel: 6820111/6880303
Branches: San Fco Macoris 14, Santo Domingo Tel: 6823101; El Conde 109, Santo Domingo Tel: 6880303
Also Publisher (qv)

Editora Colegial **Quisqueyana** SA*, Ave Tiradentes, Centro Comercial Naco, Santo Domingo Tel: 5654277/5661808
Also Publisher (qv)

Major Libraries

Archivo General de la Nación, Calle M E Diaz, Santo Domingo Tel: 5331608
National Archives

Biblioteca Dominicana*, Santo Domingo

Biblioteca Nacional*, César Nicolás Penson 91, Plaza de la Cultura, Santo Domingo
National Library

Biblioteca de la **Cámara** Oficial de Comercio, Agricultura e Industria del Distrito Nacional*, Apdo 815, Santo Domingo (Located at: Arzobispo Nouel 206, Altos, Santo Domingo)
Library of the Chamber of Commerce, Agriculture and Industry

Biblioteca Municipal de **Santo Domingo***, Padre Billini 18, Santo Domingo

Biblioteca de la **Secretaría de Estado de Relaciones Exteriores***, Estancia Ramfis, Santo Domingo
Library of the Secretariat of Foreign Affairs

Biblioteca de la **Universidad Autónoma** de Santo Domingo*, Ciudad Universitaria, Apdo 1355, Santo Domingo

Library Associations

Asociación Dominicana de Bibliotecarios (ASODOBI), c/o Biblioteca Nacional, Santo Domingo Tel: 6884086
Dominican Association of Librarians
President: Prospero J Mella-Chavier;
Secretary-General: Isabel Bethé del Rosario
Publication: El Papiro

Grupo Bibliografico Nacional de la Republica Dominicana*, c/o Emilio Rodriguez de Morizi, Director, Archivo General de la Nacion, Calle Chiclana de la Frontera, Santo Domingo

Servicio de Documentación y Biblioteca*, Palacio de Educación, Santo Domingo
Library and Documentation Service

Ecuador

General Information

Language: Spanish
Religion: Predominantly Roman Catholic
Population: 7.8 million
Literacy Rate (1962): 67.5% (88.1% Urban, 55.5% Rural)
Bank Hours: 0900-1300 Monday-Friday
Shop Hours: 0830-1230, 1430-1830 Monday-Friday; 0830-1230 Saturday
Currency: 100 centavos = 1 sucre
Export/Import Information: Member of the Latin American Free Trade Association. Books and most advertising catalogues not dutiable. No import licences or exchange controls for books
Copyright: UCC, Buenos Aires (see International section)

Book Trade Organization

Sociedad de Libreros del Ecuador*, Calle Bolivar 268 y Venezuela of 501, Quito
Booksellers' Society of Ecuador
Secretary: Eduardo Ruiz

Publishers

Editorial **Bruguera** Ecuatoriana SA*, Casilla 9001, Agencia 7, Ave de la República 17-25 y Azuay, Quito
Parent Company: Editorial Bruguera SA, Spain (qv)

Fondo Editorial de **C I E S P A L** (Centro Internacional de Estudios Superiores de Comunicación para América Latina)*, Departamento de Publicaciones, CP 584, Quito (Located at: Ave Diego de Almagro 2155 y Andrade Marín, Quito) Tel: 544624/545831 Cable Add: Ciespal Telex: 2474 Ciespl Ed
Dirs: Dr Luis E Proaño; Jorge Mantilla Jarrín (Orders)
Subjects: Social Communication, Development Planning, Research and Documentation; Periodicals
Founded: 1960

Cromograf SA*, Coronel 2207, PPB 4285, Guayaquil Tel: 346400 Cable Add: Cromograf Telex: 3387 Ariel Ed
Subjects: Juvenile/Children's Books; Paperbacks; Art Productions

Casa de la **Cultura** Ecuatoriana*, Ave 6 de Diciembre 332, Apdo 67, Quito Tel: 230260 Cable Add: Casacultura
Branch Offs: Núcleo del Azuay, Apdo 4907, Cuenca; Núcleo del Guayas, Guayaquil
Subjects: General Fiction & Non-fiction, General Science (Ecuadorian authors only)
Founded: 1944

Editorial **Interamericana** del Ecuador CA*, Ave America 542, Quito
Manager: Manuel de Castillo
Associate Company: Holt-Saunders Ltd, UK (qv for other associates)

Grijalbo Ecuatoriana Ltda*, Casilla 9139 — suc 7, General Salazar 1116 y José Luís Tamayo, Quito
Parent Company: Ediciones Grijalbo SA, Spain (qv)

Editorial **Labor** del Ecuador SA*, Portoviejo 105 y 10 de Agosto, Edificio Carrera, CP-710A, Quito
Parent Company: Editorial Labor, Spain (qv)

Editorial **Pomaire** SA*, Apdo 8424 — suc 8, Quito Tel: 243492
Manager: René Durney
Head Off: Editorial Pomaire SA, Spain (qv)

Pontificia **Universidad Católica** de Ecuador*, 12 de Octobre 1076 y Carrion, Apdo 2184, Quito Tel: 529240
Subjects: Literature, Art, Natural Sciences, Law, Anthropology, Sociology, Politics, Economics, Theology, Philosophy, History, Archaeology

Universidad Central del Ecuador, Dpto de Publicaciones*, Servicio de Almacén Universitario, Ciudad Universitaria, Quito

Universidad de Guayaquil, Dpto de Publicaciones*, Biblioteca Gral, Apdo 3834, Guayaquil Tel: 392430
Man Dir: Constantino Vinueza M
Subjects: General Literature, History, Philosophy, Fiction
Bookshop: Librería Universitaria (at above address)
Founded: 1930

Major Booksellers

Librería **Cervantes***, Vélez 416, Guayaquil Tel: 15573

Librería **Cima** Cia Ltda*, Ave 10 de Agosto 285, Quito Tel: 233066/544150 Cable Add: Cimale
Manager: Luis A Carrera
Also exporters

Librería **Científica** SA*, Venezuela y Pasaje Drouet Pérez, Quito Tel: 12556
Also: Luque 223, Guayaquil (Tel: 14555) and two other branches

Librería **Española***, Venezuela 961 y Mejía, Casilla 356, Quito Tel: 212060
Also: Librería Española Cía Ltda, Ave 10 de Agosto 1233, Casilla 356, Quito Tel: 543460

Librería **Universitaria***, García Moreno 739, Apdo 2982, Quito Tel: 212521
Dir: Ing Carlos E Wong Flores
Importer/Exporter

Una **Pequeña** Librería*, Ave 10 de Agosto 563, Quito Tel: 234296

Librería **Selecciones***, 9 de Octubre 735, Guayaquil; Calle Benalcázar 543, Quito

Su Librería*, Apdo 2556, Quito Tel: 210225
Manager: Carlos G Liebmann

Major Libraries

Archivo Nacional de Historia*, Ave 6 de Diciembre 332, Apdo 67, Quito
National Historical Archives

Biblioteca Ecuatoriana 'Aurelio Espinosa Pólit'*, Apdo 160, Quito Tel: 530420
Librarian: Julián G Bravo

Biblioteca Nacional del Ecuador*, García Moreno y Sucre, Quito
National Library

Biblioteca de la **Casa de la Cultura Ecuatoriana***, Ave 6 de Diciembre 332, Apdo 67, Quito Tel: 230260
Library of Ecuadorian Culture

Museo y Biblioteca Municipal*, Ave 10 de Agosto y Calle Pedro Carbo, Guayaquil

Biblioteca de la **Universidad Central de Ecuador***, Ciudad Universitaria, Quito

Biblioteca General, **Universidad de Guayaquil***, Apdo 3834, Guayaquil

Library Association

Asociación Ecuatoriana de Bibliotecarios (AEB)*, Casa de la Cultura Ecuatoriana, Casilla 87, Quito Tel: 528840 Headquarters: 263474
Ecuadorian Library Association
Executive Secretary: Elizabeth Carrion
Publications: Unidad Bibliotecaria

Library Reference Journal

Unidad Bibliotecaria, Ecuadorian Library Association, Casa de la Cultura Ecuatoriana, Casilla 87, Quito

Egypt

General Information

Language: Arabic (English and French widely used)
Religion: Muslim
Population: 39.6 million
Literacy rate (1976): 43.5% of population aged 10 or more
Bank Hours: Generally 0830-1230 Monday-Thursday; 1000-1200 Saturday
Shop Hours: 0830-1330, 1630-1900 Monday-Saturday
Currency: 100 piastres (1000 milliemes) = 1 Egyptian pound
Export/Import Information: No tariff on books. No import licences. Exchange control by Supreme Committee set up by Ministry of Finance, Economy and Foreign Trade. Banks authorized to execute foreign-exchange transactions. No longer government monopoly but some book importing done by Foreign Trade Company, Misr Import & Export Co, 6 Adly St, Cairo
Copyright: Berne, Florence (see International section)

Book Trade Organizations

Permanent Bureau of **Afro-Asian Writers***, 104 Kasr el-Aini St, Cairo

General Egyptian Book Organization, Corniche el Nil, Boulac, Cairo Tel: 775000/775109 Cable Add: Gebo Telex: 93932 Book Un
Chairman: Dr Ezz El Dine Ismail
See also entry under Publishers

The **Public Organization** for Books and Scientific Appliances*, Cairo University, Orman, Ghiza, Cairo
Chairman: Kamil Seddik

Standard Book Numbering Agency, c/o Dr Ezz El Dine Ismail, General Egyptian Book Organization, Corniche el Nil, Boulac, Cairo Tel: 775371/775649 Telex: 93932 Book Un

Publishers

Al **Ahram** Establishment, Al-Galaa St, Cairo Tel: 758333/745666/755500 Cable Add: Al Ahram Cairo Telex: 92001 Un
Chairman, Man Dir: Abdalla Abdel Bari; *Editor-in-Chief:* Ibrahim Nafei; *Sales:* Hany Tolba; *Production:* Fathi Al Charkawi; *Rights & Permissions:* Mrs Nawal El Mahallawi
Subsidiary Companies: Al Ahram Center for Strategic & Political Studies, Al Ahram Center for Scientific Translation, Al Ahram Center for Microfilm & Organization, Al Ahram Center for Computer & Management
Associate Companies: Al Ahram Commercial Press, Al Ahram Agency for Distribution
Branch Offs: In all main cities in Egypt
Subjects: Sciences and Humanities
Book Club: Al Ahram Book Club
Bookshops: 20 in major locations throughout Egypt
1981: 20 titles *1982:* 25 titles *Founded:* 1875
Miscellaneous: Also translation agency, printer, distributor, importer, exporter

American University in Cairo Press+, 113 Sharia Qasr el Aini, PO Box 2511, Cairo Tel: 29781 Cable Add: Victorious Telex: 92224 Aucai Un
Dir: John Rodenbeck
Subjects: Literature, Art, History, Egyptology, Africana, Anthropology, Arabic Language, Architecture, Coptology, Social Science, Textbooks, Guidebooks, Egypt and the Arab World, Religion, Natural Sciences, Reference Works, Periodicals
Bookshop: AUC Press Bookshop (at above address)
1982: 12 titles *Founded:* 1960
ISBN Publisher's Prefix: 977-424

Al **Arab Publishing** House, 23 Faggalah St, Cairo Tel: 908025 Cable Add: Arabukshop Cairo
Man Dir: Prof Dr Saladin Boustany; *Sales Manager:* George G Eddé
Subjects: General Fiction, Belles Lettres, Poetry, Biography, History, Africana, Philosophy, Reference, Religion, Arabic Language & Literature, Arabic Manuscripts, Paperbacks, Social Science, University & Secondary Textbooks
Bookshop: Al Arab Bookshop (qv under Major Booksellers)
Founded: 1900

Cairo University Press*, Guiza-Orman, Giza, Cairo Tel: 846144
Subject: University Textbooks

E S D U C K, see The Egyptian Society for the Dissemination of Universal Culture and Knowledge

Les **Editions universitaires** d'Egypte*, 41 Sharia Sherif Pasha, Cairo
Subject: University Textbooks

The **Egyptian Society** for the Dissemination of Universal Culture and Knowledge (ESDUCK), PO Box 21, Cairo (Located at: 1081 Corniche el Nil St, Garden City, Cairo) Tel: 20295/25079 Cable Add: Esduck
Executive Manager: Dr Sayed R Haddara; *Editorial:* Inas Effat; *Production:* Faiza Hakim; *Rights & Permissions:* Khadiga Safwat
Subjects: Trade Books, Textbooks, Children's Books, Reference
Founded: 1953
Miscellaneous: Co-publisher with local and American firms. Translation agency

General Egyptian Book Organization, Corniche el Nil, Boulac, Cairo Tel: 775000/775109 Cable Add: Gebo Telex:

93932 Book Un
Chairman: Dr Ezz El Dine Ismail
Foreign Distribution Centre: Samady & Salha Bldg, Syria St, Beyrouth, Lebanon
Subjects: Arab classic and modern books in all fields
Bookshops: International Book Centre, Cairo, 13 branches throughout Egypt
Founded: 1961
ISBN Publisher's Prefix: 977-201

The **General Organization** for Government Press Affairs*, 22 Al Nil St, Imbaba, Guiza, Cairo
Government Printer

Government Printer, see The General Organization for Government Press Affairs

Dar Al **Hilal** Publishing Institution, 16 Sharia Mohammed Ezz El Arab, Cairo Tel: 20610 Cable Add: Al Mussawar Cairo Telex: 92703 Hilal Un
Chief Executive: Makram Mohamed Ahmed
Subjects: Fiction, Non-fiction, Periodicals

Dar Al **Maaref***, 1119 Corniche el Nil St, Cairo Tel: 777077-87 Cable Add: Damaref Telex: 92199 Maaref Un
Chairman & Man Dir: Anis Mansour
Subsidiary Company: Dar el-Maaref, Lebanon
Subjects: Academic, Scientific, General Islamic, Schoolbooks, Children's (in Arabic), University Textbooks (in English)
Bookshops: Cairo, Alexandria, Assiut, Qena, Tanta, Shebin, El-Kom, Asswan, Esmaillia, Mansora, El Arish, Sohage
Founded: 1890
ISBN Publisher's Prefix: 977-247

Dar Al-Kitab Al-**Masri***, PO Box 156, Cairo Tel: 742168/744657/754301 Cable Add: Kitamisr Telex: 92336 attn 134 Ktm Cairo
President, Man Dir: El-Zein Hassan
Parent Company: Dar Al-Kitab Allubnani, Lebanon (qv)
Branch Offs: Paris, Geneva, Madrid, Casablanca
Subjects: Islamic, Turath, School and General Educational Textbooks (in Arabic, English, French)
1981: 283 titles *Founded:* 1929
Miscellaneous: Also distributor and printer

Middle East Book Centre*, 45 Sharia Kasr el-Nil, Cairo Tel: 910980
Man Dir: Dr A M Mosharrafa; *Sales Manager:* A Ismail
Subjects: General Fiction, Belles Lettres, Poetry, Biography, History, Africana, Philosophy, Religion, Arabic Language & Literature, Paperbacks, General & Social Science, University & Secondary Textbooks
Founded: 1954

Maktabet **Misr***, 3 Kamel Sidki St, PO Box 16, Cairo Tel: 908920
Misr Bookshop
Man Dir: Amir Said Gouda El Sahhar
Subjects: General Fiction, Belles Lettres, Poetry, Biography, History, Books in Arabic language, University & School Textbooks
Bookshop: Misr Bookshop (qv under Major Booksellers)
Founded: 1932

Dar al-**Nahda** al Arabia*, 32 Sharia Abdel-Khalek Sharwat St, Cairo
Subjects: Arabic Language & Literature
Bookshop: At above address

Editions le **Progrès***, 6 Sharia Sherif Pasha, Cairo
Man Dir: Wedi Choukri

The **Public Organization** for Books and Scientific Appliances*, Cairo University, Orman, Ghiza, Cairo
Chairman: Kamil Seddik

Subject: University Textbooks
Founded: 1965

Senouhy Publishers*, 54 Sharia Abdel-Khalek, Sarwat, Cairo
Man Dir: Leila A Fadel
Subjects: General Non-fiction, Belles Lettres, Poetry, History, Africana, Religion
Founded: 1956

The **Sphinx***, Bookshop and Publishing House, 3 Shawarby St (Kasr El Nil) — 3rd Floor — Apartment 305, Cairo Tel: 744616 Cable Add: Bulhall Cairo Telex: 93927 Sfinx Un
Man Dir: Abd-el-Salam Hassan Sharara
Subjects: Educational and Academic Books
Founded: 1958

Literary Agents

The **Egyptian Society** for the Dissemination of Universal Culture and Knowledge (ESDUCK), PO Box 21, Cairo (Located at: 1081 Corniche el Nil St, Garden City, Cairo) Tel: 20295/25079 Cable Add: Esduck
Executive Manager: Dr Sayed R Haddara

Book Club

Al **Ahram** Book Club, Galaa St, Cairo Tel: 748080/755500/758203 Telex: 92001 Un
Owned by: Al Ahram Establishment (qv under Publishers)

Major Booksellers

Al **Ahd** Al Gadeed Bookstore*, Farouk Zaky & Co, 4-5 Kamel Sidky St, Cairo Tel: 900290/905296

Al **Ahram** Bookshops, Galaa St, Cairo Tel: 748080/755500/758203 Telex: 92001 Un 20 bookshops throughout Egypt
Owned by: Al Ahram Establishment (qv)

The **Anglo American** Bookshop*, 55 Algomhouria St, Cairo Tel: 905262

The **Anglo Egyptian** Bookshop*, 165 Mohamed Farid St, Cairo Tel: 914337
Proprietor: Sobhy Grais

Al **Arab** Bookshop, 28 Faggalah St, Cairo Tel: 908025 Cable Add: Arabukshop Cairo
Manager: Saladin Boustany
Agent of the Library of Congress PL 480
Also Publisher (qv)

Librairie **Hachette***, 45 bis rue Champolion, Cairo

Al **Ittihad** Bookstore*, Mohamed Abdel Mouty Ismail, 3 Kamel Sidky St, Al Ezbekia, Cairo Tel: 916403

Dar Al **Kutub** Al Hadeetha*, Tewfik Afeefi Amer & Co, 14 Al Goumhouria St, Abdeen, Cairo Tel: 916107

Lehnert & Landrock*, 44 Sherif St, PO Box 1013, Cairo

Livres de France*, Immeuble Immobilia, rue Kasr el Nil, Cairo Tel: 51512

Misr Bookshop*, 3 Kamel Sidki St, Faggalah, Cairo Tel: 908920 Cable Add: Dameltibaa Cairo
Manager: Amir Saïd El-Sahhar
Also Publisher (qv)

Misr Import & Export Co*, 6 Adly St, Cairo
Importer/Exporter

Modern Cairo Bookshop*, 169 Tahreer St, Cairo

Saladdine Publications & Distributors Inc, 28 Talaat Harb St, Abu Regela Building, Cairo Tel: 758542

Ahmed **Shaker** Al Ansary*, Midan Birkit Al Ratly, Sikit Al Ratly No 3, Bab Al Sharea, Cairo Tel: 932895

Major Libraries

Ain Shams University Library*, Kasr-el-Zaafran, Abbasiyah, Cairo

Alexandria Municipal Library*, 18 Sharia Menasce Moharrem Bey, Alexandria

American University in Cairo Library*, 113 Sharia Kasr El-Aini, Cairo Tel: 22969
Librarian: Jesse E Duggan

Al-**Azhar** University Library*, Al-Azhar St, Cairo Tel: 904051

Dar-ul-Kutub*, Kurnish Al-Nil St, Cairo
Egyptian National Library

Institute of Arab Research & Studies Library*, 1 Tolombat St, Cairo

Ministry of Education Library*, 16 Sharia El-Falaki, Cairo

Ministry of Justice Library*, Midan Lazoghli, Abassia, Cairo Tel: 831546
Librarian: Fekry Abou-El-Kheir

National Archives*, Citadel, nr Military Museum, Cairo Tel: 921534

National Assembly Library*, Palace of the National Assembly, Cairo

National Information and Documentation Centre*, Sh Al-Tahrir, Dokki, Cairo

University of Ain Shams Library, see Ain Shams

University of Alexandria Library*, 22 Al-Gueish Ave, Shatby, Alexandria Tel: 71675/8

University of Cairo Library*, Orman, Ghiza, Cairo Tel: 845186

Library Associations

Algamiia Almasriia Lilmaktabat Almadrasiia*, 35 Algalaa St, Cairo
Egyptian School Library Association
Publication: Sahifat al-Maktabát (Egyptian Library Journal)

Egyptian Association for Archives and Librarianship*, c/o Library of Fine Arts, 24 El Matbâa Al-Ahlia, Boulac, Cairo
Executive Secretary: Ahmed M Mansour
Publication: Alam al-Maktabát

National Information and Documentation Centre*, Al-Tahrir St, Dokki, Cairo

Library Reference Books and Journals

Book

Directory of Scientific and Technical Libraries, National Information and Documentation Centre, Al-Tahrir St, Dokki, Cairo

Journals

Alam al-Maktabát (Library World), Egyptian Association for Archives and Librarianship, c/o Library of Fine Arts, 24 El Matbâa Al-Ahlia, Boulac, Cairo

Sahifat al-Maktabát (Egyptian Library Journal), Egyptian School Library Association, 35 Algalaa St, Cairo

Literary Associations and Societies

Atelier*, 1 Sharia St, Saba, Alexandria
Society of Artists and Writers
Secretary-General: L Hergenstein

High Council of Arts & Literature*, 9 Sharia Hassan Sabri, Zamalek, Cairo
Secretary: Youssef Al Sibai

Egyptian **P E N** Centre, 34 Baghat Aly St, Zamalek, Cairo
Secretary: Dr Mursi Saad el Din

Literary Periodical

Lotus; Afro-Asian Writings, 104 Kasr el-Aini St, Cairo
Important quarterly review published for the Permanent Bureau of Afro-Asian Writers

Translation Agencies and Associations

Al **Ahram***, Al-Galaa St, Cairo Tel: 755500/745666/758333 Cable Add: Pyramidad Telex: 92001/92544 Ahram Un

The **Egyptian Society** for the Dissemination of Universal Culture and Knowledge (ESDUCK), PO Box 21, Cairo (Located at: 1081 Corniche el Nil St, Cairo) Tel: 20295/25079

El Salvador

General Information

Language: Spanish
Religion: Roman Catholic
Population: 4.35 million
Literacy Rate (1975): 62.1% of population aged 10 or more
Bank Hours: 0900-1200, 1500-1700 Monday-Friday
Shop Hours: 0800-1200, 1400-1800 Monday-Friday; 0800-1200 Saturday
Currency: 100 centavos = 1 colon
Export/Import Information: Member of the Central American Common Market. No import licences but exchange licence from Exchange Control Department of Central Reserve Bank required, if goods coming from outside Central America. Commercial banks authorize certain import payments
Copyright: UCC, Buenos Aires, Florence (see International section)

Publishers

Editorial Universitaria de la Universidad de El Salvador*, Apdo Postal 1703, San Salvador (Located at: Ciudad Universitaria, San Salvador) Tel: 256604
Dir: Armando Herrara
Subjects: Scholarly Books, Textbooks, General Literature
Founded: 1923

Ministerio de Educación del Gobierno de El Salvador*, Dirección General de Publicaciones, Pasaje Contreras 145, San Salvador Tel: 254605/259092
Man Dir, Rights & Permissions: Rafael Ruiz Blanco; *Editorial:* Mirna Priscila Gámez Sol; *Sales:* Raúl Vicente Parada; *Production:* Elmer Aristides Machuca; *Publicity:* Jorge Ortíz Espinosa
Orders to: Gerencia de Distribución, 9a Calle Oriente 104 y Ave España, San Salvador
Subjects: Literature, Art, Sociology, History, General Textbooks
Bookshop: 9a Calle Oriente 104 y Ave España, San Salvador
1982: 214 titles *Founded:* 1953

U C A Editores*, Apdo Postal 668, San Salvador (Located at: Universidad Centroamericana José Simeón Cañas, Autopista Sur, Jardines de Guadalupe, San Salvador) Tel: 234491
Dir: Italo López Vallecillos; *Editorial:* Armando Oliva, Francisco Miguel Estrada, Jon Sobrino, Eduardo Stein; *Sales:* José Alvarado Menjívar; *Production:* Salvador Ramírez
Subjects: Social Science, Religion, Theology, Economy and Scholarly Books
Founded: 1975

Major Booksellers

Librería Claudio **Bernard***, Calle Los Cedros 53, 100 metros al sur del IVU, San Salvador Tel: 256719

Clasicos Roxsil, 6a Ave Sur 1-6, Santa Tecla Tel: 281212
Manager: Rosa Victoria Serrano de López

Librería **Cultural** Salvadoreña SA de CV, Apdo Postal 2296, San Salvador (Located at: Calle Arce 423, San Salvador) Tel: 217206/221307

Dissal SA Le CU*, 9a Ave Norte 422, San Salvador Tel: 226983
Distribuidora Salvadorena Le Revistas y Libros SA Le CU
Manager: Ernesto Quijano

Librería e Importadora **Neruda**, PO Box 1764, San Salvador (Located at: 29 Calle Poniente 222, Local No 6, San Salvador) Tel: 251566
Manager: José Reynaldo Echeverría O

Librería **Renacimiento** SA de CV*, Apdo Postal 852, San Salvador (Located at: Final Pasaje 5 No 126 y 2a diagonal, Urbanización La Esperanza, San Salvador) Tel: 254541/263198

Distribuidora **Salvadoreña**, see Dissal SA Le CU

Librería **Universitaria** de la Universidad de El Salvador*, Apdo Postal 2028, San Salvador (Located at: Ciudad Universitaria, San Salvador) Tel: 258607/258022 ext 132

Librería **Universitaria** UCA*, Apdo Postal (06) 668, San Salvador (Located at: Universidad Centroamericana José Simeón Cañas, San Salvador) Tel: 240011 ext 193, 234491

Major Libraries

Biblioteca Nacional*, 8a Ave Norte y Calle Delgado, San Salvador Tel: 213249

Biblioteca de la **Universidad Centroamericana** José Simeón Cañas*, Apdo Postal (01) 168, San Salvador (Located at: Autopista Sur, Jardines de Guadalupe, San Salvador) Tel: 240011
Dir: Mélida Arteaga

Biblioteca Central de la **Universidad de El Salvador***, Apdo Postal 143, San Salvador (Located at: Ciudad Universitaria, San Salvador) Tel: 258022 ext 115
Dir: Ana Aurora de Kapsalis
Publications: Boletín (monthly); *Lista de Adquisiciones Recientes* (monthly)

Library Associations

Asociación de Bibliotecarios de El Salvador*, Urbanización Gerardo Barrios Polígono, 'B' No 5, San Salvador Tel: 220409/253471
El Salvador Library Association
Secretary-General: Edgar Antonio Pérez Borja
Publication: Informa (Newsletter) (monthly)

Asociación General de Archivistas de El Salvador*, Apdo Postal No 664, Edificio Sede 8, Calle Oriente 314, San Salvador
Association of Archivists of El Salvador

Library Reference Journal

Informa (Newsletter), El Salvador Library Association, Urbanización Gerardo Barrios Polígono, 'B' No 5, San Salvador

Literary Periodical

Guion Literario (Literary Summary), Ministerio de Educación del Gobierno de El Salvador, Dirección General de Publicaciones, Pasaje Contreras 145, San Salvador

Ethiopia

General Information

Language: Amharic (English, French and Italian spoken)
Religion: Ethiopian Orthodox (allied to Coptic Church)
Population: 29 million
Bank Hours: 0830-1230, 1430-1730 Monday-Friday; 0830-1230 Saturday
Shop Hours: Addis Ababa: 0900-1300, 1500-2000 Monday-Saturday. Asmara: 0800-1300, 1600-2000 Monday-Friday
Currency: 100 cents = 1 birr
Export/Import Information: No tariff on books, but additional taxes. Advertising subject to customs and same taxes. No import licence required but Exchange Payment Licence necessary
Copyright: No copyright conventions signed

Book Trade Reference Books and Journals

Book

List of Ethiopian Authors, Addis Ababa University Library, PO Box 1176, Addis Ababa

Journal

Ethiopian Publications (Ethiopian National Bibliography), Institute of Ethiopian Studies, Addis Ababa University, PO Box 1176, Addis Ababa

Publishers

Addis Ababa University Press*, PO Box 1176, Addis Ababa Tel: 119148 Cable Add: University Addis
Editor: Innes Marshall
Subjects: Public Health, Hydrology, Climatology, Botany, Ornithology, Conservation, Geology, Philosophy; University Textbooks, Reference; works in English language
Founded: 1968

The **Bible** Churchmen's Missionary Society*, PO Box 864, Asmara, Eritrea Tel: 114267
Dir: John Coracher
Subjects: General Fiction, Belles Lettres, Poetry, Biography, History, Africana, Religion, Juveniles, Amharic Language & Literature
Bookshop: PO Box 864, Asmara, Eritrea

Government Printer*, Government Printing Press, PO Box 1241, Addis Ababa

Major Booksellers

Asmara Bookshop*, 92 Victory St, Asmara Tel: 110511

Berhan Bookshop and Stationery*, PO Box 302, Addis Ababa

The **City** Bookshop*, PO Box 864, Asmara

E C A Bookshop Co-op Society*, PO Box 60100, Addis Ababa

Major Libraries

Addis Ababa University Library*, PO Box 1176, Addis Ababa Tel: 115673
Librarian: Getachew Birru

Agricultural Institute Library*, PO Box 307, Jimma
Librarian: Teshome Negero

Asmara Public Library*, PO Box 259, Asmara Tel: 117044

Asmara University Library, PO Box 1220, Asmara Tel: 113600
Librarian: M N Ramakrishnan

British Council Library, PO Box 1043, Addis Ababa (Located at: Artistic Bldg, Adua Ave, Addis Ababa) Tel: 110022/4 Cable Add: Britcoun
Librarian: A M Hunde

College of Agriculture Library*, Addis Ababa University, PO Box 138, Dire Dawa
Assistant Librarian: Asheber Haile

Ethiopian Manuscript Microfilm Library*, PO Box 30274, Addis Ababa
Publication: Bulletin (quarterly)

Institute of Ethiopian Studies Library*, Addis Ababa University, PO Box 1176, Addis Ababa Tel: 119904 Cable Add: AA Univ
Librarian: Degife Gabre-Tsadik

National Library and Archives of Ethiopia*, PO Box 717, Addis Ababa Tel: 442241
Librarian: T Solomon

Organization for African Unity Library*, PO Box 3243, Addis Ababa Tel: 157700 Cable Add: Oau Telex: 21046
Librarian: Mekonnen Tashu

Science and Engineering Library*, Faculty of Science, College of Technology, PO Box 1176, Addis Ababa

United Nations Economic Commission for Africa Library, PO Box 3001, Addis Ababa Tel: 447200 Cable Add: Eca Addis Ababa
Telex: 21029
Librarian: Abdel-Rahman M Tahir
Publications include: *Africa Index: Selected articles on socio-economic development* (quarterly); *ECA Index: Bibliography of selected ECA documents* (annual)

Library Association

Ethiopian Library Association*, PO Box 30530, Addis Ababa Tel: 110844 ext 353
Publications: Ethiopian Library Association Bulletin; Directory of Ethiopian Libraries

Library Reference Books and Journals

Book

Directory of Ethiopian Libraries, Ethiopian Library Association, PO Box 30530, Addis Ababa

Journals

Bulletin, Ethiopian Library Association, PO Box 30530, Addis Ababa

Bulletin, Ethiopian Manuscript Microfilm Library, PO Box 30274, Addis Ababa

Fiji

General Information

Language: English, Fijian, Hindi and Cantonese
Religion: Predominantly Protestant, with large minority of Hindus
Population: 607,000
Bank Hours: 1000-1500 Monday-Thursday; 1000-1600 Friday
Shop Hours: 0800-1630 or later Monday-Friday; early closing Wednesday or Saturday
Currency: 100 cents = 1 Fiji dollar
Export/Import Information: No tariffs on books and advertising. No import licences. Exchange control by central monetary authority; no specific exchange licence required and authorized banks perform transaction upon application
Copyright: Berne, UCC (see International section)

Book Trade Reference Journal

Publications Bulletin, Government Printing and Stationery Department, Suva

Publishers

Indian Printing and Publishing Co*, PO Box 151, Suva
Man Dir: S M Bidesi Jr
Subjects: Law, Administration, Business Management

Lotu Pasifika Productions, PO Box 208, Suva Tel: 24314 Cable Add: Lotupak
Manager: Seru L Verebalavu
Subjects: Education, Religion, Poetry, Cookery
1982: 10 titles

Oceania Printers Ltd*, PO Box 597, Suva Tel: 313044/313224
Subject: Literature

Sangam Sarada Printing Press*, PO Box 9, Nadi
Subjects: Literature, History, Geography

Tara Press*, Kings Rd, PO Box 923, Nasinu, Suva
Subjects: Literature, Music

Trans-Pacific Publishers*, PO Box 3083, Lami, Suva (Located at: Queens Rd, Lami, Suva) Tel: 361727

Major Booksellers

Desai Bookshops*, PO Box 160, Suva (Located at: Head Office: Rajobhai Patel Rd, Suva) Tel: 313477 Cable Add: Desai Suva Telex: 2319 Nldc Fj
14 branches throughout Fiji
General Manager: W Michael Jarema
Parent Company: Native Land Development Corp, PO Box 2110, Government Buildings, Suva

Suva Book Shop*, Greig St, PO Box 153, Suva Tel: 311355
Manager: Harinivas Singh

Major Libraries

Library Service of Fiji, Chief Librarian, PO Box 3244, Lami Tel: 60091/61866

National Archives of Fiji, PO Box 2125, Government Buildings, Suva Tel: 24031 Cable Add: Archivist

Suva City Library*, Victoria Arcade, Suva

Library Association

Fiji Library Association (FLA), c/o Secretary, PO Box 2292, Government Bldgs, Suva
Publication: Fiji Library Association Newsletter; Fiji Library Association Journal

Library Reference Journal

Journal and *Newsletter*, Fiji Library Association, c/o Honorary Secretary, PO Box 2292, Government Bldgs, Suva

Finland

General Information

Language: Finnish and Swedish (officially bilingual); English and German spoken widely
Religion: Lutheran
Population: 4.8 million
Bank Hours: 0915-1615 Monday-Friday
Shop Hours: 0900-1700 or later Monday-Friday; 0900-1600 (1400 in summer) Saturday
Currency: 100 pennia = 1 markka
Export/Import Information: Associate member of European Free Trade Association. Free trade agreed with European Economic Community. No tariff on books or advertising. No import licences required
Copyright: UCC, Berne, Florence (see International section)

Book Trade Organizations

Kirja-ja Paperikauppiasliitto*, Pieni Roobertinkatu 13-B26, SF-00130 Helsinki 13 Tel: (90) 603479
Finnish Booksellers' Association
Chief Executive: Pentti Kuopio

Standard Book Numbering Agency, Bibliographic Dept, Helsinki University Library, PL 312, SF-00170 Helsinki 17 Tel: (358) 410566/410359 Telex: 122785 Tsk Sf
This Agency is also a national ISDS Centre
Administrator: Dr Thea Aulo

Suomen Antikvariaattiyhdistys-Finska Antikvariatföreningen*, P Makasiininkatu 6, Magasinsgatan 6, SF-00130 Helsinki 13 Tel: 626352
Finnish Antiquarian Booksellers' Association

Suomen Kirjailijaliitto, Runeberginkatu 32 C 28, SF-00100 Helsinki 10 Tel: (90) 445392/492278
Association of Finnish Authors
Executive Secretary: Päivi Liedes
Publications: Suomen Runotar, Suomalaisetkertojat

Suomen Kustannusyhdistys, Merimiehenkatu 12 A 6, SF-00150 Helsinki 15 Tel: (90) 179185
The Finnish Book Publishers' Association
Secretary-General: U Lappi

Suomen Nuortenkirjaneuvosto ry*, Uudenkaupungintie 7 A 9, SF-00350 Helsinki 35
Finnish Section of the International Board on Books for Young People (IBBY)
President: Kaija Salonen, Haapaniemenkatu 16C, SF-00530 Helsinki 53
Secretary: Lilian Hakkarainen

Book Trade Reference Books and Journals

Book

Suomessa Ilmestyneen Kirjallisuuden Luettelo (Katalog över i Finland Utkommen Litteratur) (List of Books Published in Finland), The Finnish Book Publishers' Association, Merimiehenkatu 12 A 6, SF-00150, Helsinki 15

Journals

Books from Finland (quarterly, containing articles mostly in English, but also in French and German), Helsinki University Library, Unioninkatu 36, PO Box 312, SF-00171 Helsinki 17

Kirja Ja Paperi (Book and Paper), The Finnish Book Publishers' Association, Merimiehenkatu 12 A 6, SF-00150 Helsinki 15

Kirjakauppalehti (Book Trade Journal), The Finnish Book Publishers' Association, Merimiehenkatu 12 A 6, SF-00150 Helsinki 15

Libristi (Journal for Booksellers' Assistants), PO Box 10242, Helsinki 10

Suomen Kirjallisuus (Finlands Litteratur) (The Finnish National Bibliography), Helsinki University Library, Unioninkatu 36, PO Box 312, SF-00171 Helsinki 17

Publishers

Akateeminen Kustannusliike Oy*, Mikonk 20 B 12, SF-00100 Helsinki 10 Tel: (90) 174002
Manager: M O Mattila; *Sales:* Riitta Mattila
Subjects: Matriculation books, Religion, Fiction
Founded: 1927
ISBN Publisher's Prefix: 951-9023

Ekenäs Tryckeri AB*, PO Box 36, SF-10600 Ekenäs (Located at: Stationsvägen 1, Ekenäs) Tel: (911) 12800 Telex: 13150 Vne Sf
Man Dir: Sven Sundström
Subjects: History, Politics
Bookshop: Ekenäs Bokhandel — Boktjänst AB (at above address)
Founded: 1881
ISBN Publisher's Prefix: 951-9000

Etelä-Suomen Kustannus Oy*, PO Box 15, Huoltomiehentie 1, SF-21420 Lieto Tel: (921) 777502
Subjects: War, Reference, Science Fiction Paperbacks, Comics
ISBN Publisher's Prefix: 951-9064

Edition **Fazer**+, PO Box 260, SF-00101 Helsinki 10 (Located at: Takomotie 3, SF-00380 Helsinki 38) Tel: (90) 56011 Cable Add: Musikfazer Telex: 121738 Mufa Sf
Man Dir (of Parent Company): John-Eric Westö; *Publishing Manager:* Ilkka Kuusisto; *Rights & Permissions:* Mirjam Saksa
Parent Company: Oy Musiikki Fazer Musik AB, PO Box 260, SF-00101 Helsinki 10
Subjects: Music, Music Education
Bookshop: Aleksanterink 11, SF-00100 Helsinki 10
1982: 60 titles *Founded:* 1897
ISBN Publisher's Prefix: 951-757

Forsamlingsforbundets Forlags AB, PO Box 285, SF-00121 Helsinki 12 (Located at: Bangatan 29 A 1, SF-00120 Helsinki 12) Tel: 170221
Man Dir and Production: Bjarne Boije; *Sales:* Aili Hellström
Associate Company: Ab Fram (printing house), Vasaesplanaden 24, SF-65100 Vasa 10
Subject: Religion
Bookshops: Ab Gamlakarleby Bokhandel, Strandgatan 13, SF-67100 Karleby 10; Gros Bokhandels Ab, Hovrättsesplanaden 9, SF-65100 Vasa 10
1981: 22 titles *1982:* 18 titles *Founded:* 1920
ISBN Publisher's Prefix: 951-550

Government Printing Centre*, PO Box 516, SF-00101 Helsinki 10 (Located at: Annankatu 44, Helsinki) Tel: (90) 539011
Bookshop: At above address

K J Gummerus Oy, PO Box 130, SF-40101 Jyväskylä 10 (Located at: Asemakatu 4, Jyväskylä) Tel: (941) 218522 Cable Add: Gummerus Telex: 28351
Man Dir: Pekka Salojärvi; *Publishing Dir:* Raili Mäkinen; *Literary Dir:* Risto Lehmusoksa; *Editorial:* Jussi Sorjonen; *Sales Manager:* Mikko Meronen; *Rights & Permissions:* Anna Thorwall
Subjects: Fiction, Juveniles, Reference Books
Book Clubs: Koko Kansan Kirjakerho Oy, Uusi Kirjakerho Oy (jointly owned)
Bookshops: Helsinki, Jyväskylä, Mänttä, Seinäjoki, Tampere, Turku
1981: 220 titles *1982:* 200 titles *Founded:* 1872
ISBN Publisher's Prefix: 951-20

Karas-Sana Oy, PO Box 48, Vivamo, SF-08101 Lohja 10 Tel: (912) 87755
Man Dir: Matti Valtonen; *Editorial and Rights & Permissions:* Eva Mesiäinen
Parent Company: Kansan Raamattuseuran Säätio (at above address)
Subject: Christian Religion
1981: 22 titles *Founded:* 1974
ISBN Publisher's Prefix: 951-655

Arvi A Karisto Oy, PO Box 102, SF-13101 Hämeenlinna 10 (Located at: Paroistentie 2, Hämeenlinna) Tel: (917) 23551 Cable Add: Arvikaristo
Man Dir: Jaakko Karisto; *Literary Dir:* Ilmari Lehmusvaara; *Editorial and Foreign Rights:* Pirkko Mikkola; *Sales, Advertising:* Leo Räiha; *Production:* Onni Helin
Branch Off: Keskusk 3, Helsinki 10
Subjects: General Fiction and Non-fiction, Juvenile Fiction
Book Club: Uusi Kirjakerho Oy (jointly owned)
Founded: 1900
ISBN Publisher's Prefix: 951-23

Kustannusliike **Kirjaneliö**, Töölönkatu 55, SF-00250 Helsinki 25 Tel: (90) 440561
Orders to: Raamattutalo, PO Box 21, SF-76101 Pieksämäki 10
Subjects: Religion, Fiction, Juveniles
1981: 33 titles *1982:* 28 titles *Founded:* 1905
ISBN Publisher's Prefix: 951-600

Kirjayhtymä Oy, Eerikinkatu 28, SF-00180 Helsinki 18 Tel: 6944522 Cable Add: Kirjayhtymä
Man Dir: Pentti Nurmio; *Publishing Dir:* Keijo Immonen; *Marketing Dir:* Viljo Salin; *Publicity Manager:* Heikki Rönnqvist; *Rights & Permissions:* Ritva Mäkelä, Aila Järvenpää (Geography & Biology)
Subjects: Fiction, Non-fiction, Textbooks
Book Club: Uusi Kirjakerho Oy (jointly owned)
Founded: 1958
ISBN Publisher's Prefix: 951-26

Lasten Keskus Oy+, Särkinigmende 7, SF-00210 Helsinki 2 Tel: (90) 6926344 Cable Add: Lasten Keskus
643203 Cable Add: Lasten Keskus
Man Dir: Pertti Rosenholm; *Publishing Manager, Production, Rights & Permissions:* Juhani Järvelä; *Head Salesman, Publicity:* Anna-Maija Kurvinen
Associate Company: Yhteiskirjat, Merimiehenkatu 36 O 522, SF-00750 Helsinki 15
Subjects: Juveniles, Books for Parents and Teachers, Religion (Lutheran)
Bookshop: Lasten Kirjakauppa (Children's Bookshop), Fredrikinkatu 61, SF-00100 Helsinki 10
1982: 44 titles *Founded:* 1974
ISBN Publisher's Prefix: 951-626

Otava Kustannusosakeyhtiö, PO Box 134, SF-00121 Helsinki 12 (Located at: Uudenmaankatu 8-12, Helsinki) Tel: (90) 647022 Cable Add: Otava Helsinki Telex: 124560
Chairman: Heikki A Reenpää; *Man Dir:* Olli Reenpää; *Literary Dirs:* Paavo Haavikko (Fiction), Pentti Huovinen (Non-fiction & Encyclopaedias), Manu Renko (Textbooks, Educational Materials); *Export Manager:* Matti Käki
Subjects: General Fiction, Belles Lettres, Biography, History, How-to, Music, Art, Philosophy, Reference, Religion, Juveniles, Low- & High-priced Paperbacks, Textbooks, Educational Materials
Book Club: Suuri Suomalainen Kirjakerho Oy (jointly owned)
Bookshops: Kuopion Kirja-Otava (qv under Major Booksellers) and 6 branches throughout Finland
1981: 767 titles *1982:* 860 titles *Founded:* 1890
ISBN Publisher's Prefix: 951-1

FINLAND

Rakennuskirja Oy*, Bulevardi 3B, SF-00120 Helsinki 12 Tel: 645615
Building Book Ltd
Man Dir: Timo Olkkonen; *Marketing Manager:* Tuula Lätti
Parent Company: Rakennustietosäätio (Building Information Institute), Lonnrotinkatu 20B, SF-00120 Helsinki 12
Subject: Building
1981: 8 titles *Founded:* 1974
ISBN Publisher's Prefix: 951-682

Ristin Voitto ry+, PO Box 75, SF-01301 Vantaa 30 Tel: (90) 826377
Man Dir: Valtter Luoto; *Publishing Manager:* Tytti Träff; *Editorial:* Eero J Anttur
Book Clubs: Kristillinen Kirjarengas (Christian Book Club), Nuorten Kirjakerho (Youth Book Club)
Subjects: Religion, Periodicals
1981: 62 titles *1982:* 47 titles *Founded:* 1926
ISBN Publisher's Prefix: 951-605

Holger **Schildts** Förlagsaktiebolag, Annegatan 16, SF-00120 Helsinki 12
Tel: (90) 604892 Cable Add: Bokschildt
Man Dir: J af Hällström; *Rights & Permissions:* Helen Svensson
Subjects: General Fiction, Belles Lettres, Poetry, Biography, History, Music, Art, Philosophy, University Textbooks, Reference, Juveniles, High-priced Paperbacks
1981: 119 titles *Founded:* 1913
ISBN Publisher's Prefix: 951-50

Söderström et Co Förlagsaktiebolag*, Murbacksgatan 6, SF-00210 Helsinki 21
Tel: 6923681 Cable Add: Söderströms
Man Dir: Göran Appelberg
Subjects: General Fiction, Belles Lettres, Poetry, Biography, History, How-to, Music, Art, Philosophy, Reference, Religion, Juveniles, Medicine, Psychology, General Science, University, Secondary & Primary Textbooks
1981: 294 titles *Founded:* 1891
ISBN Publisher's Prefix: 951-52

Suomalaisen Kirjallisuuden Seura, PO Box 259, SF-00171 Helsinki 17 (Located at: Hallituskatu 1, SF-00171 Helsinki 17) Tel: (90) 171229
Finnish Literature Society
Secretary-General/Director: Urpo Vento
Subjects: Folklore, Ethnology, Literary History, Linguistics
Founded: 1831
ISBN Publisher's Prefix: 951-717

Tammi Kustannusosakeyhtiö, Hämeentie 15, SF-00500 Helsinki 50 Tel: (0) 716522 Cable Add: Tammi Telex: 125482 Tammi
Man Dir: Olli Arrakoski; *Marketing Dir:* Sakari Lahtinen; *Rights & Permissions:* Martina Sunell
Subjects: General Fiction, Belles Lettres, Poetry, Biography, History, How-to, Music, Art, Philosophy, Reference, Juveniles, Paperbacks, Psychology, Engineering, Social Science, University Textbooks, Easy Readers
Book Clubs: Kansan Kirjarengas, Suuri Suomalainen Kirjakerho Oy (jointly owned), Uudet Kirjat (associate partner)
1982: approx 350 titles *Founded:* 1943
ISBN Publisher's Prefix: 951-30

Tietoteos Publishing Co, PO Box 40, SF-02211 Espoo 21 (Located at: Yläportti 1 A, SF-02211 Espoo 21) Tel: (90) 881133
Man Dir: Jyrki K Talvitie
Associate Company: Multilibro Ltd, Ilmarinkatu 8, SF-00101 Helsinki 10
Subjects: Technical Dictionaries, Travel Guides, Finnish Air Force History series, Stock Market Manual, General Technical
1982: 10 titles *Founded:* 1948
ISBN Publisher's Prefix: 951-9035

Kustannus Oy **Uusi Tie**, PO Box 54, SF-00601 Helsinki 60 (Located at: Oulunkyläntie 5, SF-00600 Helsinki 60) Tel: (90) 799244
Man Dir: Eino J Honkanen; *Sales:* Olavi Maijala
Subjects: Christian Religion, Theology, Children
1981: 10 titles *Founded:* 1964
ISBN Publisher's Prefix: 951-619

Amer-yhtymä Oy **Weilin ja Göös**, Ahertajantie 5, SF-02100 Espoo 10 Tel: 461322 Cable Add: Weilingöös Telex: 122597 Weigs Sf
Man Dir: Seppo Saario; *Publishing Dir:* Ville Repo; *Dirs:* Jaakko Manninen (Non-fiction & Encyclopaedias), Eero Syrjänen (Education); *Rights & Permissions:* Tuula Kuusi
Subjects: General Fiction & Non-fiction, Belles Lettres, Poetry, Biography, History, Business, Reference, Juveniles, Economics, Textbooks, Educational Materials
Book Club: Uusi Kirjakerho Oy (jointly owned)
Bookshop: Kirjakievari, Mannerheimintie 40, Helsinki 10
Founded: 1872
ISBN Publisher's Prefix: 951-35

Werner Söderström Osakeyhtiö (WSOY), PO Box 222, SF-00121 Helsinki 12 (Located at: Bulevardi 12, Helsinki) Tel: (90) 61681 Cable Add: Wsoy Helsinki Telex: 122644 Wsoy Sf
Man Dir: Hannu Tarmio; *Publishing Dir:* Keijo Ahti (Non-fiction, Encyclopaedias, Educational); *Assistant Literary Dir:* Matti Snell (Foreign Relations, Fiction and Non-fiction); *Managers:* Simo Mäenpää (Foreign Fiction and Non-fiction), Helena Ahti (How-to and Reference Books); *Assistant Dirs:* Petri Arpo (Educational), Asko Rysa (Juveniles); *Rights & Permissions:* Satu Suomala
Subjects: General Fiction, Non-fiction, Juveniles, Textbooks, Encyclopaedias, Audio-Visual Materials, Educational Materials
Book Clubs: Suuri Suomalainen Kirjakerho Oy (jointly owned), Uudet Kirjat
1982: 1371 titles *Founded:* 1878
ISBN Publisher's Prefix: 951-0

Yritystieto Oy — Foretagsdata AB, PO Box 148, SF-00181 Helsinki 18 (Located at: Kalevankatu 45 A 1, Helsinki) Tel: (90) 648292/648293 Cable Add: Hibernia Telex: 121394 Tltx Sf for Hibernia
Publisher: Börje Thilman
Subjects: Business, Directories, Reference
1983: 5 titles *Founded:* 1972
ISBN Publisher's Prefix: 951-9102

Literary Agents

Werner Söderström Osakeyhtiö (WSOY), PO Box 222, SF-00121 Helsinki 12 (Located at: Bulevardi 12, Helsinki)
Also Publisher (qv)

Book Clubs

Kansan Kirjarengas, Hämeentie 15, SF-00500 Helsinki 50 Tel: (0) 716522 Cable Add: Tammi Telex: 125482 Tammi
Owned by: Tammi Kustannusosakeyhtiö (qv)

Koko Kansan Kirjakerho Oy, PO Box 130, SF-40101 Jyväskylä 10 (Located at: Asemakatu 4, Jyväskylä) Tel: (941) 218522 Cable Add: Gummerus Telex: 28351
Owned by: K J Gummerus Oy (qv)

Kristillinen Kirjarengas, PO Box 75, SF-01301 Vantaa 30 Tel: (90) 826377
Christian Book Club
Members: 6500
Owned by: Ristin Voitto ry (qv)
Founded: 1969

Nuorten Kirjakerho, PO Box 75, SF-01301, Vantaa 30
Youth Book Club
Members: 1900
Owned by: Ristin Voitto ry (qv)
Founded: 1974

Suuri Suomalainen Kirjakerho Oy, Hietalahdenranta 17, SF-00180 Helsinki 18
Tel: 601466 Telex: 121394 Tltx Sf Kirjakerho
The Great Finnish Book Club Ltd
Man Dir: Pauli Leimio
Owned by: Werner Söderström Osakeyhtiö, Otava Kustannusosakeyhtiö, Tammi Kustannusosakeyhtiö (qqv)

Bokklubben **Tre Böcker***, SF-02510 Oitbacka
Subjects: Classics, Current Affairs, Dictionaries, Encyclopaedias, Detective fiction, Periodicals

Uudet Kirjat, PO Box 222, SF-00121 Helsinki 12 (Located at: Bulevardi 12, Helsinki) Tel: (90) 61681 Telex: 122644 Wsoy
The New Books
Members: 100,000
Contact: Kyösti Nuotio
Owned by: Werner Söderström Osakeyhtiö (WSOY), Tammi Kustannusosakeyhtiö (associate partner) (qqv)

Uusi Kirjakerho Oy, PO Box 29, SF-00381 Helsinki 38
Owned by: Kirjayhtymä Oy, K J Gummerus Oy, Amer-yhtymä Oy Weilin ja Göös, Arvi A Karisto Oy (qqv)
Subjects: Bestselling Novels, General Non-fiction, Encyclopaedias

Major Booksellers

Akateeminen Kirjakauppa, Keskuskatu 1, SF-00100 Helsinki 10 Tel: (90) 651122 Cable Add: Akateeminen Telex: 125080
Chief Executive: Jorma Kaimio
Branch Offs: Jyväskylä, Lahti, Lappeenranta, Oulu, Tampere, Turku

Gummeruksen Kirjakauppa*, Kauppakatu 16, SF-40100 Jyväskylä 10 Tel: (941) 10760
Telex: 28289 Kjgoy Sf
Manager: Paavo Harju

Kuopion **Kirja-Otava**, Tulliportinkatu 33, SF-70100 Kuopio 10 Tel: (971) 116611
Overseas Marketing Manager: Heikki Pykäläinen
Owned by: Otava Kustannusosakeyhtiö (qv)
Four other bookstores are run by group under the Kirja-Otava name in Iisalmi, Joensuu, Jyväskylä, Tampere

Lappeenrannan Kirjakauppa Oy*, Valtakatu 36, SF-53100 Lappeenranta 10 Tel: (953) 15117

Pohjalainen Kirjakauppa Oy*, Kirkkokatu 17, SF-90100 Oulu 10 Tel: (981) 227133

Suomalainen Kirjakauppa Oy, Koivuvaarankuja 2, SF-01640 Vantaa 64
Manager: Antti Remes
Seven other branches in Helsinki, and branches in Espoo, Hämeenlinna, Joensuu, Jyväskylä, Kouvola, Kuopio, Lahti, Mikkeli, Oulu, Tampere, Vaasa, Vantaa

Tampereen Kirjakauppa Oy, Hämeenkatu 27, SF-33200 Tampere 20 Tel: (931) 28380
Telex: 22521 Tamki Sf
Manager: Martti Helminen

Turun Kansallinen Kirjakauppa Oy*, PO Box 135, SF-20101 Turku 10 Tel: (921) 29451
Manager: Eero O Korte

Yliopistokirjakauppa Oy*, Fredrikinkatu 30A, SF-00120 Helsinki 12 Tel: (90) 640109

Major Libraries

Library of the **Central Statistical** Office of Finland, PO Box 504, SF-00101 Helsinki 10 (Located at: Annankatu 44 — 2nd floor, Helsinki) Telex: 122656 Tikes
Chief Librarian: Hellevi Yrjölä

Eduskunnan Kirjasto, SF-00102 Eduskunta Tel: (90) 4321 Telex: 121464 Ekirj Sf
Library of Parliament
Chief Librarian: Eeva-Maija Tammekann
Publications include: Valtion virallisjulkaisut (Government publications in Finland; annual bibliography); *Eduskunnan kirjaston julkaisuja* (Library of Parliament publications)

Helsingin Kaupunginkirjasto – Valtakunnallinen yleisten kirjastojen keskuskirjasto, Rikhardinkatu 3, SF-00130 Helsinki 13 Tel: 35801661 (central), 1662814 (information) Telex: 124794 Hkk
Helsinki City Library – National Central Library for Public Libraries
Chief Librarian: Prof Sven Hirn

Helsingin Yliopiston Kirjasto, Unioninkatu 36, PO Box 312, SF-00171 Helsinki 17 Tel: (1911) 1912740 Telex: 121538 Hyk Sf
Helsinki University Library (National Library of Finland)
Librarian: Prof Esko Häkli
Branches: Slavonic Library, Neitsytpolku 1B, PO Box 313, SF-00171 Helsinki 17 Tel: 661791; Science Library, Tukholmankatu 2, SF-00250 Helsinki 25 Tel: 410566 Telex: 122785 Tsk Sf; Undergraduate Library, Leppäsuonkatu 7-9, SF-00100 Helsinki 10 Tel: 440171
Publications: Books from Finland (quarterly); *The Finnish National Bibliography; Publications of the University Library at Helsinki*

Jyväskylän Yliopiston Kirjasto*, Seminaarinkatu 15, SF-40100 Jyväskylä 10 Tel: (941) 291500 Telex: 28219
Jyväskylä University Library

Lääketieteellinen Keskuskirjasto, Haartmanink 4, SF-00290 Helsinki 29 Telex: 121498 Lkk Sf
Central Medical Library
Librarian: Ritva Sievänen-Allen

Oulun Yliopiston Kirjasto*, PO Box 186, SF-90101 Oulu 10 (Located at: Kasarmintie 7, SF-90100 Oulu 10) Tel: (981) 223455 Telex: 32256 Oyk Sf
Oulu University Library

Sibelius-Akatemian Kirjasto*, Pohj Rautatiek 9, Helsinki
Sibelius Academy Library

Statistics Library, see under Library of the Central Statistical Office of Finland

Tampereen Yliopiston Kirjasto, PL 617, SF-33100 Tampere 10 (Located at: Tammelan Puistokatu 38, Tampere) Tel: (931) 156111 Telex: 22263 Tayk Sf
Library of the University of Tampere

Teknillisen Korkeakoulun Kirjasto, Otaniementie 9, SF-02150 Espoo 15
Helsinki University of Technology Library (National Library for Technology in Finland)

Turun Yliopiston Kirjasto, SF-20500 Turku 50 Telex: 62123 Tyk
Turku University Library
Librarian: H Eskelinen

University Libraries, see under town names

Valtionarkisto, PO Box 258, SF-00171 Helsinki 17
National Archives of Finland

Library Associations

Arkistoyhdistys ry, Rauhankatu 17, SF-00170 Helsinki 17 Tel: (90) 176911
Archival Association
Secretary-Treasurer: Lisa Salasmaa

Kirjastonhoitajaliitto — Bibliotekarieförbundet ry, Temppelikatu 1 A 12, SF-00100 Helsinki 10
Finnish Librarians' Association
Executive Secretary: Anna-Maija Hintikka

Kirjastonhoitajien Keskusliitto-Bibliotekariernas Centralforbund ry, Temppelikatu 1 A, SF-00100 Helsinki 10
Central Federation of Librarians
Executive Secretary: Anna-Maija Hintikka

Kirjastovirkailijat-Biblioteksanstallda ry*, c/o Helsinki University Library, PO Box 312, SF-00171 Helsinki 17 (Located at: Unioninkatu 36, Helsinki) Tel: (90) 1912737
Association for Non-Professional Staff of Public and Research Libraries
Headquarters: Vipusentie 8, Helsinki Tel: (90) 794276
Executive Secretary: Kirsti Tuominen
Publication: Volyymi

Suomen Kirjallisuuspalvelun Seura*, c/o Helsinki University of Technology Library, Otaniementie 9, SF-02150 Espoo 15
Finnish Association for Documentation

Suomen Kirjastoseura, Museokatu 18 A 15, SF-00100 Helsinki 10 Tel: 492632
Finnish Library Association
Secretary General: Hilkka M Kauppi
Publication: Kirjastolehti (Library Journal)

Suomen Tieteellinen Kirjastoseura, c/o Library of Parliament, SF-00102 Helsinki 10 Tel: 4323463 Telex: 121764 Ckirj Sf
Finnish Research Library Association
Secretary: Marjo Tolvanen

Tieteellisen Informoinnin Neuvosto, c/o Central Statistical Office of Finland, PO Box 504, SF-00101 Helsinki 10 Telex: 122656
Finnish Council for Scientific Information and Research Libraries
General Secretary: Hellevi Yrjölä

Tieteellisten Kirjastojen Virkailijat — Vetenskapliga Bibliotekens Tjänstemannaförening ry*, c/o Library of the Soviet Institute, Armfeltintie 10, SF-00150 Helsinki 15
Association of Research and University Librarians
Executive Secretary: Anneli Virtanen
Publications: Issues newsletter to members

Library Reference Books and Journals

Book

Suomen Erikoiskirjastojen Luettelo (Directory of Special Libraries in Finland), Finnish Association for Documentation, c/o Helsinki University of Technology Library, Otaniementie 9, SF-02150 Espoo 15

Journals

The Finnish National Bibliography, Helsinki University Library, Unioninkatu 36, PO Box 312, SF-00171 Helsinki 17

Kirjastokalenteri (Library Calendar), Finnish Library Association, Museokatu 18 A 15, SF-00100 Helsinki 10

Kirjastolehti (Library Journal), Finnish Library Association, Museokatu 18 A 15, SF-00100 Helsinki 10 (jointly with Central Federation of Librarians)

Signum (text in Finnish and Swedish; summaries in English), Finnish Research Library Association, c/o Library of Parliament, SF-00102 Helsinki 10

Volyymi (The Volume), Association for Non-Professional Staff of Public and Research Libraries, c/o Helsinki University Library, Unioninkatu 36, PO Box 312, SF-00171 Helsinki 17

Literary Associations and Societies

Bibliofiilien Seura*, Lauttasaarentie 5 C 29, SF-00200 Helsinki 20
President: Onni M Turtiainen
Society of Bibliophiles

Finlands Svenska Författareförening, Runebergsgatan 32 C 27, SF-00100 Helsinki 10 Tel: (90) 446266
Association of Swedish Authors in Finland
Secretary: Mette Jensen Sundholm

Kirjallisuudentutkijain Seura, Marjaniementie 34, SF-00930 Helsinki 93
The Literary Research Society
Secretary: Touko Siltala
Publication: Kirjallisuudentutkijain Seuran Vuosikirja (The Yearbook of the Literary Research Society)

Finnish **P E N** Club, c/o Otra Publishing Co Ltd, Undenmaankatu 8-12, SF-00120, Helsinki 12
Secretary: Ann-Christine Salonen

Suomalainen Tiedeakatemia, Snellmaninkatu 9-11, SF-00170 Helsinki 17 Tel: (90) 636800
Finnish Academy of Science and Letters
Secretary-General: Lauri A Vuorela
Publications: Annales Academiae Scientiarum Fennicae; F F Communications; Documenta Historica; Vuosikirja (Yearbook)

Suomalaisen Kirjallisuuden Seura, PO Box 259, SF-00171 Helsinki 17 (Located at: Hallituskatu 1, SF-00171 Helsinki 17) Tel: (90) 171229
Finnish Literature Society
Secretary-General/Director, Publications Dept: Urpo Vento; *Librarian:* Rauni Puranen; *Director, Folklore Archive:* Pekka Laaksonen; *Director, Literature Archive:* Kaarina Sala; *Secretary-General, Finnish Literature Information Centre:* Marja-Leena Rautalin
Publications: Studia Fennica; Suomi; Tietolipas; Toimituksia; (irregular)

Suomen Arvostelijain Liitto, Bulevardi 3 B 19, SF-00120 Helsinki 12 Tel: (90) 644463
Union of Finnish Critics
General-Secretary: Riitta Kaipainen

Svenska Litteratursällskapet i Finland, Snellmaninkatu 9-11, SF-00170 Helsinki 17 Tel: (90) 636738
Swedish Literary Society in Finland
Publication: Skrifter

Svenska Österbottens Litteraturförening, Auroravägen 10, SF-65610 Smedsby
Swedish Österbottens Literary Association
Secretary: Yvonne Hoffman
Publications: +21 (anthology of Österbotnian prose, 1975); *Österbottnisk dikt — Runo Pohjanmaalla* (anthology of Swedish and Finnish poetry, 1977); *Horisont* (literary magazine)

Literary Periodicals

Horisont, Swedish Österbottens Literary Association, Auroravägen 10, SF-65610 Smedsby

Katsaus (Review) (text mainly in Finnish, occasionally in Swedish), Kulttuurikeskus Kriittisen Korkeakoulun Kannatusyhdistys ry, Lehtikuusentie 6, SF-00270 Helsinki 27

Parnasso, Hietalahdenranta 13, SF-00180 Helsinki 18

Skrifter (Writings), Swedish Literary Society in Finland, Snellmaninkatu 9-11, SF-00170 Helsinki 17

Virittäjä (The Kindler) (Summaries in English, French, or German), Society for the Study of the Mother Tongue, Fabianink 33, SF-00170 Helsinki 17

Literary Prizes

Helsinki Prize
Awarded annually by the City of Helsinki to the Helsinki artist of the year (in the widest sense, authors included). Enquiries to Helsingin Kaupungin Kulttuuriasiainkeskus, Annankatu 30, SF-00100 Helsinki 10

Tauno Karilas Prize*
For the writer of the year's best Finnish book for children. Awarded annually. Enquiries to Finnish Section of the International Board on Books for Young People, Suomen Nuortenkirjaneuvosto ry, Laiduntie 8, SF-02300 Espoo 30

Rudolf Koivu Prize*
For the best illustrated children's book. Awarded annually. Enquiries to Rudolf Koivu Foundation, c/o State Committee for Literature, Ministry of Education, Rauhankatu 4, SF-00170 Helsinki

Arvid Lydecken Prize*
For the writer of the year's best Finnish book for children. Awarded annually. Enquiries to Finnish Section of the International Board on Books for Young People, Suomen Nuortenkirjaneuvosto ry, Laiduntie 8, SF-02300 Espoo 30

State Prizes for Literature*
Prizes for the best literary works. Awarded annually. Enquiries to State Committee for Literature, Ministry of Education, Rauhankatu 4, SF-00170 Helsinki

Anni Swan Prize*
For the best children's and/or young adults' book of the previous three years. Awarded every three years. Enquiries to Finnish Section of the International Board on Books for Young People, Suomen Nuortenkirjaneuvosto ry, Laiduntie 8, SF-02300 Espoo 30

Tampere Prize*
For the best authors connected with the city of Tampere. Awarded annually. Enquiries to Tampere City Government, Tampere

Topelius Prize*
For the writer of the year's best Finnish book for young adults. Awarded annually. Enquiries to Finnish Section of the International Board on Books for Young People, Suomen Nuortenkirjaneuvosto ry, Laiduntie 8, SF-02300 Espoo 30

Translation Agencies and Associations

Suomen Kääntäjäin Yhdists*, Urheilukatu 14 A 10, SF-00250 Helsinki 25 Tel: (90) 440025
Finnish Translators' Association

France

General Information

Language: French. Basque in the Basque country of the southwest, Breton in Brittany, Catalan in Roussillon, Corsican in Corsica, Dutch along parts of border with Belgium, German in Alsace, Occitan in south; most people in these minority linguistic groups also speak French
Religion: Roman Catholic predominantly
Population: 53.3 million
Bank Hours: 0900-1600 Monday-Friday
Shop Hours: 0900-1200, 1400-1800 Tuesday-Saturday
Department Stores: 0930-1830 Tuesday-Saturday; open Monday in Paris
Currency: 100 centimes = 1 franc
Export/Import Information: Member of the European Economic Community. No tariff on books, except children's picture books from non-EEC. Import licences not required. Nominal exchange controls over a certain value. For imports over 50,000 francs, documents must be 'domiciliated' before any other transaction occurs. There is control of the book trade based on a number of legal and regulating provisions applying to the import of pirated publications, articles and writings that offend against morality, publications harmful to youth, writings forbidden by the Minister for the Interior; the customs official must submit articles subject to control for examination by the General Information Service of the Ministry of the Interior
Copyright: UCC, Berne, Buenos Aires, Florence (see International section)

Book Trade Organizations

Agence francophone pour la Numération internationale du Livre (AFNIL-ISBN), 35 rue Grégoire de Tours, F-75279 Paris cedex 06

Cercle de la Librairie (Syndicat des Industries et Commerces du Livre), 35 rue Grégoire de Tours, F-75279 Paris cedex 06 Tel: 3292101
Booksellers' Circle (Association of Book Trades and Industries)
Man Dir: Pierre Fredet; *Commercial Dir:* Michel Bony
Publications include: Bibliographie de la France; Notices établies par le Dépôt Légal (Copyright Depositions); *Les Livres Disponibles* (French Books in Print); *Le Répertoire International des Éditeurs et Diffuseurs de Langue Française* (International List of French Language Publishers and Distributors); *Répertoire des Livres au Format de Poche* (List of Paperback (or Pocket Edition) Books); *Études et Statistiques sur le Livre français* (Statistics and Research on French Books); *Catalogue général des ouvrages parus en langue française* (General Catalogue of Works which have appeared in the French Language)

Chambre syndicale des Editeurs d'Annuaires et de Publications similaires, Permanent Secretariat, Cercle de la Librairie, 35 rue Grégoire de Tours, F-75279 Paris cedex 06 Tel: (01) 3292101
Association of Publishers of Directories and Similar Publications
President: Jean Verdier

Fédération française des Syndicats de Libraires, 259 rue St-Honoré, F-75001 Paris
The French Booksellers' Association
President: Jacques Plaine
Publications: Lettre du Libraire; Libraires de France — L'Officiel de la Librairie

Office de Promotion de L'Edition Française, 35 rue Grégoire de Tours, F-75279 Paris cedex 06 Tel: 3266166
French Publishing Promotion Bureau
Dir: Pierre-Dominique Parent; *Secretary:* Marc Franconie
Miscellaneous: Function of the office is to organize the national stands of all French publishing companies at international book fairs as well as specific exhibitions throughout the world. It represents all French publishing houses

S L A M, see Syndicat national de la Librarie Ancienne et Moderne

Standard Book Numbering Agency, see Agence francophone pour la Numération internationale du Livre

Syndicat des Réprésentants littéraires français*, 6 rue Jean Carriès, F-75007 Paris Tel: (01) 7348241
Association of French Literary Agents
Secretary: Michele Lapautre

Syndicat national de la Librairie Ancienne et Moderne (SLAM), 47 rue St-André des Arts, F-75006 Paris Tel: (01) 3265075 Telex: Jjm 202351 F Att: Slam
National Association of Antiquarian and Modern Booksellers
President: Jeanne Laffitte

Syndicat national de l'Edition*, 35 rue Grégoire de Tours, F-75279 Paris cedex 06 Tel: (01) 3292101
National Union of Publishers. Member of the Cercle de la Librairie (qv)
Secretary: Pierre Fredet

Syndicat national des Annuaires et Supports divers de Publicité, 40 blvd Malesherbes, F-75008 Paris Tel: 7421248
National Federation of Yearbooks and Sundry Publicity Aids

Syndicat national des Importateurs et Exportateurs de Livres, 35 rue Grégoire de Tours, F-75279 Paris cedex 06 Tel: 3292101 ext 468
National Federation of Book Importers and Exporters

U D E F Export, 96 rue Mazarine, F-75006 Paris Tel: (01) 3546746
Dir: P Monnet
This is the Union of French Publishers, with the aim of international promotion of books in the French language. It has five associated Groups: Groupe des Editeurs d'Art, Groupe des Editeurs de Poésie, Groupe des Editeurs d'Erudition, Groupe des Editeurs de Religion, Groupe des Editeurs de Sport (Groups associated with Art, Poetry, Learning, Religion and Sport respectively)
Founded: 1963

Union d'Editeurs Français, see U D E F

Book Trade Reference Books and Journals

Books

Catalogue de l'Edition française (Catalogue of French Language Publishing), 22 rue de Condé, F-75006 Paris

Etudes et Statistiques sur le Livre français (Studies and Statistics on the French Book), Cercle de la Librairie, 35 rue Grégoire de Tours, F-75279 Paris cedex 06

Guide du Livre Ancien et du Livre d'Occasion (Antiquarian and second-hand book guide), Cercle de la Librairie, 35 rue Grégoire de Tours, F-75279 Paris cedex 06

Répertoire des Livres au Format de Poche (Catalogue of Paperback Books), 35 rue Grégoire de Tours, F-75279 Paris cedex 06

Répertoire international des Editeurs et Diffuseurs de Langue française (International List of French Language Publishers and Distributors), Cercle de la Librairie, 35 rue Grégoire de Tours, F-75279 Paris cedex 06

Répertoire international des Librairies de Langue française (International List of French Language Bookshops), Cercle de la Librairie, 117 blvd Saint-Germain, F-75279 Paris cedex 06

Journals

Art et Métiers du Livre (Art and Crafts of the Book), Cercle de la Librairie, 35 rue Grégoire de Tours, F-75279 Paris cedex 06

La Bibliographie de la France — Biblio (French National Bibliography), Cercle de la Librairie, 35 rue Grégoire de Tours, F-75279 Paris cedex 06

Book Promotion News (French edition), Unesco, 7 pl de Fontenoy, F-75700 Paris

Bulletin, Association of Antiquarian and Modern Booksellers, 35 rue Grégoire de Tours, F-75279 Paris cedex 06

Bulletin critique du Livre français (Critical Report on French Books) (text in English and Spanish), Association pour la Diffusion de la Pensée française, 21 bis rue la Perouse, F-75116 Paris

Bulletin du Livre (Book Report), 18 rue Dauphine, F-75006 Paris

Connaissance et Formation (Knowledge and Training), France Expansion, 336-340 rue St-Honoré, F-75001 Paris (trade journal for the educational market)

La Documentation française; 'Bibliographie sélective' des Publications officielles françaises (French Documentation; 'Selective Bibliography' of French Official Publications), Secrétariat général du Gouvernement, Paris

Documentation — technique, scientifique et commerciale (Documentation — Technical, Scientific and Commercial) (text and summaries in English, French and German), Librairie Lavoisier, 11 rue Lavoisier, F-75008 Paris

Francophonie-Edition; revue bibliographique de l'Edition de Langue française dans le Monde (Bibliographical review of French publishing world-wide), France Expansion, 336-340 rue St-Honoré, F-75001 Paris

Lettre du Libraire (The Bookseller's Letter), Fédération française des Syndicats de Libraires, 259 rue St-Honoré, F-75001 Paris

Libraires de France — l'Officiel de la Librairie (Official Gazette of the Book Trade), Fédération française des Syndicats de Libraires, 259 rue St-Honoré, F-75001 Paris

Liens (Links), Editions du Cap, Palais de la Scala, Monte Carlo, Monaco

Livres (Books), Institut national de Recherches et de la Documentation pédagogique, 29 rue d'Ulm, F-75230 Paris

Livres-Actualité (Books of Today), Information Promotion et Culture Sàrl, 17 rue de la Félicité, Paris 17e

Livres de France, 18 rue Dauphine, F-75006 Paris

Les Livres Disponibles (French Books in Print), Cercle de la Librairie, 35 rue Grégoire de Tours, F-75279 Paris cedex 06

New French Books (English extracts from *Bulletin Critique du Livre français*), Association pour la Diffusion de la Pensée française, 21 bis rue la Perouse, F-75116 Paris

Publishers

Edition No 1, 4 rue de Galliera, F-75116 Paris Tel: (01) 7230026
Man Dir: Bernard Fixot; *Rights & Permissions:* Antoine Audouard
Parent Company: Librairie Hachette (qv)
Subjects: Fiction, Children's, Sport
1982: 20 titles *Founded:* 1977
ISBN Publisher's Prefix: 2-86391

A R E D I P (Agence de Recherches Droits Internationaux et Promotion)*, 10 rue des Pyramides, F-75001 Paris Tel: 2603633
Telex: 240620
President/Man Dir: André Limansky
Subject: Juveniles

Academy Editions, 5 rue d'Artois, F-75008 Paris
Publisher: Dr Andreas Papadakis
Orders to: Diffedit, 96 blvd du Montparnasse, F-75680 Paris cedex 14 Tel: 3260877
Parent Company: Academy Editions, UK (qv)
Subjects: Art, Architecture
1983: 16 titles *Founded:* 1978

Editions **Acropole**+, 4 ave Elisée Reclus, F-75007 Paris Tel: (01) 5512688 Telex: 260717 Orem 309
The above is the Editorial office, the Administrative office is at 216 blvd St-Germain, F-75007 Paris Tel: (01) 5443823 Telex: 260717 Orem 309
Chairman: Franca Belfond; *General Manager, Editorial:* Hortense Chabrier; *Rights & Permissions:* Véronique Garrigues; *Sales:* J P Naddeo
Parent Company: Editions Pierre Belfond (qv)
Associate Companies: Nouvel Office d'Edition (qv), Presses de la Renaissance (qv), Editions du Pré-au-Clerc
Subjects: General Fiction and Non-fiction, Belles Lettres
1982: 18 titles *1983:* 52 titles
ISBN Publisher's Prefixes: 2-7144, 2-7357

Editions **Albatros**, an imprint of Copernic (qv)

Editions **Albin** Michel*, 22 rue Huyghens, F-75680 Paris cedex 14 Tel: (01) 3201220
Telex: 203379 Amichel f
President: Robert Esménard; *Man Dir:* Francis Esménard; *Assistant Man Dir, Publicity:* Richard Ducousset; *Sales Dir:* Jean-Yves Bry; *Dir Foreign Department:* Ivan Nabokov; *Public Relations:* Raymonde Leroux, M C Elsen; *Children's Books:* H Lauriott-Prevost; *Rights & Permissions:* Marie-France Fontaine
Subjects: General Fiction, Science Fiction, Fine Arts, History, Philosophy, Reference, Religion, How-to, General & Social Science, Popular Music, The Occult, Juvenile, Adult/Juvenile Comic Strips
Founded: 1902
ISBN Publisher's Prefix: 2-226

Editions **Alpina**, 60 rue Mazarine, F-75006 Paris Tel: (01) 3298740
Man Dir: Alain Gründ; *Assistant Manager:* Marie Troubnikoff
Associate Company: Librairie Gründ (qv)
Subjects: Guide Books
Founded: 1928
ISBN Publisher's Prefix: 2-7000

Alsatia SA*, 31 rue de la Semm, BP 121, F-68003, Colmar cedex Tel: (89) 245321
Telex: Alco 88200 F 508
Man Dir: André Clemessy; *Sales, Publicity, Advertising, Rights & Permissions:* Auguste Rimelé
Subjects: Belles Lettres, Poetry, Biography, History, How-to, Religion, Low-priced Paperbacks, Medicine, Primary Textbooks, Educational Materials
Bookshops: Librairie Alsatia, 31 pl de la Cathédrale, F-67000 Strasbourg; Librairie Union, 4 pl de la Réunion, F-68100 Mulhouse; Librairie Union, 28 rue des Têtes, F-68000 Colmar; Librairie Union, 26 rue Charles de Gaulle, F-68130 Altkirch; Librairie Alsatia, 114 rue de la République, F-68500 Guebwiller
Founded: 1896
ISBN Publisher's Prefix: 2-7032

Editions d'**Amérique et d'Orient**, see Adrien Maisonneuve

Les **Amis de Milosz**, 6 rue José-Maria-de-Heredia, F-75007 Paris 7
Associate Company: Editions André Silvaire SA (qv)

Editions de l'**Amitié**, G-T Rageot, 21 rue Cassette, F-75006 Paris Tel: (01) 5480731
Man Dir: Jean Vilnet; *All other offices:* Mrs C Scob
Orders to: Librairie Hatier SA, 8 rue d'Assas, F-75006 Paris
Subjects: Juveniles, Picture Books
1981: 24 titles *1982:* 26 titles *Founded:* 1941
Miscellaneous: Editions de l'Amitié is an imprint of Librairie Hatier (qv)
ISBN Publisher's Prefix: 2-7002

L'Amitié par le Livre*, F-25160 Labergement
Dir General: Henri Frossard
Subjects: Prose fiction, Poetry, Philosophy, Belles Lettres
Book Club: L'Amitié par le Livre
1981: 12 titles *Founded:* 1930
ISBN Publisher's Prefix: 2-7121

Editions **Amphora** SA+, 14 rue de l'Odéon, F-75006 Paris Tel: (01) 3261087
Administration and Accounts: 51 blvd Saint-Michel, F-75005 Paris Tel: (01) 3253461
Man Dir: Roland Antoine; *Editorial, Publicity:* Françoise Antoine; *Sales, Production:* Michel Vaultier
Subjects: Sports and Leisure Activities
Founded: 1954
ISBN Publisher's Prefix: 2-85180

Editions **Anthropos** SA+, 15 rue Lacèpède, F-75005 Paris Tel: (01) 5352247
Man Dir: Serge Jonas
Subjects: History, Philosophy, Social Sciences, Anthropology, Economy

Bookshop: Librairie des Sciences de l'Homme (at above address)
1981: 40 titles *1982:* 40 titles *Founded:* 1965
ISBN Publisher's Prefix: 2-7157

L'**Arbalète***, Marc Barbezat, F-69150 Décines-Charpieu Tel: 495101
Subjects: Literature, Art

Publications **Aredit**+, 357 blvd Gambetta, F-59200 Tourcoing Tel: 267981 Telex: 130372F
Publicity: Emile Keirsbilk
Subjects: Picture-Strip Books in instalments on War, Adventure, Westerns, Romance, Schoolgirl interests

Arted (Editions d'Art), 6 ave du Coq, F-75009 Paris Tel: (01) 8747184
Subjects: Fine Arts (especially Sculpture, Modern Painting)
Imprints: Editions d'Art, Septimus Editions
ISBN Publisher's Prefix: 2-85067

Editions **Arthaud** SA, 20 rue Monsieur le Prince, F-75006 Paris Tel: (01) 3291220 Telex: Flamedi 204034 F
President: Henri Flammarion; *Dir:* R de Ayala; *Rights & Permissions:* as for Flammarion (qv)
Parent Company: Flammarion et Cie (qv)
Subjects: Literature, Arts, History, Travel Books, Sailing, Mountaineering, Sports
Founded: 1890
ISBN Publisher's Prefix: 2-7003

Editions d'**Artrey** now CILF (qv)

Arts et Métiers Graphiques, 26 rue Racine, F-75006 Paris 6 Tel: (01) 3291220
Man Dir: Adam Bizo
Parent Company: Flammarion et Cie (qv)
Subject: Art
Founded: 1927
ISBN Publisher's Prefix: 2-7004

Compagnie Française des **Arts Graphiques** SA*, 3 rue Duguay-Trouin, F-75006 Paris Tel: (01) 5487285
President: V P Victor-Michel
Subject: Art
Founded: 1939
ISBN Publisher's Prefix: 2-85001

L'**Asiathèque***, 6 rue Christine, F-75006 Paris Tel: (01) 3253457
Editorial, Production: Alain Thiollier; *Sales, Publicity:* Oscar Ferreyros
Subjects: Far East (language, literature, etc)
Bookshop: At above address
Founded: 1973

Editions **Assimil** SA, 13 rue Gay-Lussac, PO Box 25, F-94430 Chennevières sur Marne Tel: 5768737 Telex: 210311F Assimil Code 777
Dirs: J L Cherel, J le Gal; *Editorial:* J L Cherel; *Sales, Production, Publicity:* J le Gal
Subjects: Self-instruction in Languages (textbooks, cassettes, records)
Bookshop: 11 rue des Pyramides, F-75001 Paris
Founded: 1929
ISBN Publisher's Prefix: 2-7005

L'**Astrolabe**, La Librairie du Voyageur, 46 rue de Provence, F-75009 Paris Tel: 2854295
Man Dir: Jacques P Nobecourt; *Editorial:* Raymond M Chabaud; *Sales:* Odile Nobecourt
Subsidiary Company: Blondel La Rougery (qv)
Subjects: Travel, Geography, Cartography
1981: 3 titles *1982:* 3 titles *Founded:* 1974
ISBN Publisher's Prefix: 2-86230

Aubanel SA+, 7 pl Saint-Pierre, F-84028 Avignon cedex Tel: (90) 824626
Man Dir: Laurent Theodore-Aubanel
Subjects: General Fiction, Psychology, Secondary Textbooks, Latin, Regional History, Tourist Guides, Provençal interest
Founded: 1744
ISBN Publisher's Prefix: 2-7006

Editions **Aubier-Montaigne** SA*, 13 quai Conti, F-75006 Paris Tel: (01) 3265559
Man Dir: Mrs M Aubier-Gabail; *Sales Manager, Rights & Permissions:* Patrice Mentha
Parent Company: Flammarion et Cie (qv)
Subjects: Belles Lettres, Poetry, History, Philosophy, Reference, Religion, Psychology, University Textbooks, Pedagogy, Sociology, Languages
Founded: 1924

Etudes **Augustiniennes**, see under Etudes

Editions d'**Aujourd'hui**, F-83120 Plan de La Tour Tel: (94) 437079
Man Dir: Odette Charrière
Subjects: Literature, Music, Drama, Cinema, Poetry, Fiction, Human Sciences, Folklore, Esoteric
1981: 38 titles *Founded:* 1974
ISBN Publisher's Prefix: 2-7307

Editions Philippe **Auzou**, see Editions Michel de Lile

Editions l'**Avant-Scène***, 27 rue Saint-André-des-Arts, F-75006 Paris Tel: (01) 3255229
Man Dir: C Dupeynon
Subjects: Theatre, Cinema, Opera, Ballet, Dance, Periodicals
Founded: 1949

Editions **B P I** (Bureau de Presse et d'Informations), 5 rue Duc, F-75018 Paris
Man Dir: J Milinaire
Subjects: Science & Technical, Hotels and Restaurants, Surface Treatments

Editions **B R G M**, see Bureau de Recherches Géologiques et Minières

Editions J-B **Baillière**, 10 rue Thénard, F-75005 Paris Tel: 6342110 Telex: Livrcom 201326 F
Man Dir: M Roux Dessarps
Subjects: Medicine, Dentistry, Surgery, Agriculture and Horticulture, Technology and Industry
Founded: 1819
ISBN Publisher's Prefix: 2-7008

André **Balland**+, 33 rue St-André-des-Arts, F-75006 Paris Tel: 3257440
Publisher: André Balland; *Sales:* Sabine Balland; *Rights & Permissions:* Françoise Adelstain
Subjects: Fiction, Documentaries, Humour, Sexology
1981: 65 titles *1982:* 58 titles *Founded:* 1966
ISBN Publisher's Prefix: 2-7158

Baschet et Cie, Editeurs, an imprint of Editions de l'Illustration (qv)

Bayard-Presse SA, Editions du Centurion*, 17 rue de Babylone, F-75007 Paris Tel: (01) 2229315
President: Jean Gelamur
Associate Company: Editions du Centurion (qv)
Subjects: Juveniles, Religion, Literature
Founded: 1873
ISBN Publisher's Prefix: 2-7009

Editions **Beauchesne***, 72 rue des Saints-Pères, F-75007 Paris
Tel: (01) 5488028
Dir: Miss M Cadic
Subjects: Religion and Theology, Social and Political Science, Humanities, Reference, Current Affairs, Spirituality, The Church Today, Holy Scripture, Biography, History, Literature, Essays
Founded: 1851
ISBN Publisher's Prefix: 2-7010

Editions Pierre **Belfond**, 216 blvd St-Germain, F-75007 Paris Tel: (01) 5443823 Telex: 260717F
Chairmen: Pierre Belfond, Franca Belfond; *Rights & Permissions:* Véronique Garrigues
Subsidiary Companies: Presses de la Renaissance (qv); Editions Acropole (qv); Editions du Pré aux Clercs
Subjects: General Fiction, Belles Lettres, Bibliophily, Poetry, Biography, History, Music, Art
Founded: 1963

Editions **Belin**, 8 rue Férou, F-75278 Paris cedex 06 Tel: (01) 6342142 Telex: Libelin 202978F
Man Dir & Chairman: Max Brossollet; *Editorial:* Marie-Claude Brossollet; *Documentation:* Soraya Eghbal-Dupouey; *Marketing:* Henri Gibelin; *Production, Rights & Permissions:* Françoise Fougeron
Subjects: Secondary & Primary Textbooks, Educational Material, Literary & Scientific Magazines, Juveniles, General Science
Founded: 1777
ISBN Publisher's Prefix: 2-7011

Société d'Edition 'Les **Belles Lettres**', 95 blvd Raspail, F-75006 Paris Tel: (01) 5487055/5445189 Telex: 641155 elita E 55
President, Man Dir: Pierre de Mijolla; *Commercial Dir, Editorial, Production:* Jean Malye
Subjects: Poetry, History, Philosophy, Literature, Religion, Scholarly, University Textbooks, Ancient History, Classical Philology
Bookshop: Librairie Guillaume Budé, 95 blvd Raspail, F-75006 Paris
1982: 80 titles *Founded:* 1919
Miscellaneous: This Société now incorporates the formerly independent firm Cathasia
ISBN Publisher's Prefix: 2-251

Berg International Editeurs*, 129 blvd St-Michel, F-75005 Paris Tel: (01) 3267273 Cable Add: Bergedit Paris
Man Dir: Monique Gougaud
Subjects: Art, History, General & Social Science, Reference, Religion
ISBN Publisher's Prefix: 2-900269

Berger-Levrault SA*, 229 blvd St-Germain, F-75007 Paris Tel: (01) 7055614 Telex: 270797 F
Above address is the Publishing Department of Company. The Trade Offices in Paris are at 5 rue Auguste-Comte
Man Dir: Marc Friedel; *Editorial:* Jean-Jacques Brisebarre, Françoise Juhel, Hubert Cuny; *Sales:* Daniele Boespflug; *Production:* Louise Champion; *Press, Promotion:* Catherine Riand; *Public Relations:* Didier Bonnet; *Rights & Permissions:* Anne Benoist-Khayat
Parent Company: Berger-Levrault Imprimerie, 18 rue des Glacis, F-54000 Nancy (Head Office and Printing Works)
Branch Off: 23 pl Broglie, F-67000 Strasbourg
Subjects: Co-editions in: Architecture (world and French regional), Ethnology, History, Juvenile, Human Sciences, Art, Third World and Administration, Paperbacks
Bookshop: Librairie Berger-Levrault, 23 pl Broglie, F-67000 Strasbourg
1981: 55 titles *Founded:* 1676
ISBN Publisher's Prefix: 2-7013

Société Internationale des Ecoles **Berlitz** SA*, 31 blvd des Italiens, F-75002 Paris Tel: (01) 7420509 Cable Add: Berliscool Paris
Subjects: Education, Textbooks
Founded: 1907
ISBN Publisher's Prefix: 2-7014

Bias (Société Nouvelle des Editions) SA*, 26 rue Vauquelin, F-75005 Paris Tel: (01) 3376590
Man Dir: Georges Lauvaux; *Editorial, Production:* G Lauvaux; *Publicity, Advertising, Rights & Permissions:* Jean Lauvaux
Subjects: Stories, How-to and Information Books for all age juveniles; Travel, Hobbies, Popular Science & Technology
Founded: 1941
ISBN Publisher's Prefix: 2-7015

Société **Biblique** Française, 30 ave Lénine, BP 31, F-93380 Pierrefitte Tel: (01) 8223896 Telex: ubssbf 610948 F
Man Dir: Jean-P Boyer; *Editorial:* Sylvia Barbu; *Sales, Production:* Dominique Donzelot; *Publicity:* Philippe Cirier
Subject: Bibles
ISBN Publisher's Prefix: 2-85300

Blondel La Rougery SA, 7 rue St-Lazare, F-75009 Paris Tel: (01) 8789554
Chairman: J Barbotte
Parent Company: L'Astrolabe (qv)
Subjects: Maps & Charts, Science & Technical
Founded: 1902
ISBN Publisher's Prefix: 2-7016

Editions E de **Boccard**, 11 rue de Médicis, F-75006 Paris Tel: (01) 3260037
Subjects: Archaeology, History, Ancient History, Religion
ISBN Publisher's Prefix: 2-7018

Boosey & Hawkes Sagem, 7 rue Boutard, F-92200 Neuilly-sur-Seine Tel: 7478992
Cable Add: Sonorous, Neuilly-sur-Seine
Subject: Music

Editions **Bordas**+, 17 rue Rémy-Dumoncel, F-75661 Paris Tel: (01) 3201550 Telex: 260776
President, General Manager: Jean-Manuel Bourgois; *Man Dir:* Jean-François Grollemund; *Editorial:* Michel Legrain (Trade), Jean Lissarrague (Scientific/Technical), Dominique Desgranges (School); *Sales:* Dominique Desmottes (Bookshops), Fernand Joffre (Personal), Luc Tiberghien (Export); *Production:* Jacques Patry; *Publicity:* Philippe Fournier-Bourdier (Trade Books), Dominique de Romanet (Scientific/Technical), Etienne Gotschaux (School); *Rights & Permissions:* Mireille Debenne (Trade/School), Maryvonne Guérin (Scientific/Technical)
Orders to: 11 rue Gossin, F-92543 Montrouge cedex Tel: (01) 6565266
Subsidiary Companies: Société Générale de Diffusion (SGED), 11 rue Gossin, as above; Société Gauthier-Villars (qv); Société Bordas-Dunod Bruxelles SA, Belgium (qv)
Imprints: Bordas, Dunod, Gauthier-Villars (qv), Pédagogie Moderne, Technique et Vulgarisation (qv)
Subjects: Educational (from Elementary to Higher Levels), General Non-fiction, Scientific, Technical, Reference (especially Dictionaries and Encyclopaedias)
Bookshops: Librairie Dunod, 30 rue Saint-Sulpice, F-75006 Paris; Librairie Beranger, Liège, Belgium
1981: 270 titles *Founded:* 1946
ISBN Publisher's Prefix: 2-04 (Bordas), 2-7294 (Pédagogie Moderne)

Pierre **Bordas et Fils***, BP 7, F-77630 Barbizon
Branch Off: 7 rue Princesse, F-75006 Paris Tel: (01) 3250451
Man Dir: Nicole Bordas; *Editorial, Rights & Permissions:* Pierre Bordas
Subjects: Leisure Pursuits, Tourism, Gastronomy, Guide Books, Photo Books, Juvenile, Educational, Literature, Poetry

1981: 12 titles *Founded:* 1978
ISBN Publisher's Prefix: 2-86311

Editions **Bornemann**, 15 rue de Tournon, F-75006 Paris Tel: (01) 3260588
Manager: Maurice Bornemann
Subjects: Art, How-to, Sports, Nature, Easy Readers
Founded: 1829
ISBN Publisher's Prefix: 2-85182

Société Nouvelle Editions N **Boubée**, 11 Place St-Michel, F-75006 Paris Tel: (01) 6330030
Subjects: Biology, Archaeology, Entomology
Founded: 1941
ISBN Publisher's Prefix: 2-85004

Editorial **Bouret**, Imprint of Dessain et Tolra (qv)

Christian **Bourgois**, Editeur, 8 rue Garancière, F-75006 Paris Tel: (01) 6341280 Telex: Precite 204807F
Subject: Literature, University and Political series
Miscellaneous: Member of the Presses de la Cité group (qv)
ISBN Publisher's Prefix: 2-267

Editions Colin **Bourrelier**, see Armand Colin

Bréa Éditions, 24 ave Ledru-Rollin, F-75012 Paris Tel: 3452090
Man Dir: Eric Brébant; *Commercial Manager:* Jean Arcache
Orders to: Inter-Forum, 13 rue de la Glacière, F-75013 Paris Tel: 5701180
Subjects: Tourist Guides, Show Business series, Practical Information books, Car/Camping Guides
1981: 11 titles *1982:* 24 titles *Founded:* 1978

Editions **Brepols** SA, 23 rue des Grands Augustins, F-75006 Paris Tel: (01) 6342188
Head Off: Brepols IGP Publishers, Belgium (qv)
Subjects: Religion, General Literature
ISBN Publisher's Prefix: 2-85006

Michèle **Broutta** Oeuvres Graphiques Contemporaines, 31 rue des Bergers, F-75015 Paris Tel: (01) 5779371/5779379
Man Dir: Michèle Broutta
Subject: Art
Founded: 1970
ISBN Publisher's Prefix: 2-900332

Editions **Buchet/Chastel***, 18 rue de Condé, F-75006 Paris Tel: (01) 3260620; (Sales) (01) 3269200 Cable Add: Buchet/Chastel Paris
Man Dir: Guy Buchet; *Editorial Dir:* Edmond Buchet; *Sales Dir:* René Charbonnier; *Publicity & Advertising:* Guy Buchet; *Rights & Permissions:* Anne Buchet
Subjects: General Fiction, Belles Lettres, Biography, History, Philosophy, Music, Religion, Social Science, Medicine
Founded: 1930
ISBN Publisher's Prefix: 2-7020

Bureau de Presse et d'Informations, see B P I

Bureau de Recherches Géologiques et Minières (BRGM), BP 6009, F-45060 Orléans cedex (Located at: ave de Concyr, Orléans) Tel: (38) 638001 ext 3028 Telex: brgm a 780258 F
The above is the address of the Editorial and Sales offices. Administrative offices are at 191 rue de Vaugirard, F-75737 Paris cedex 15
BRGM is the Office of Geological and Mineral Research in France (National Geological Department)
Subjects: Earth Sciences: texts connected with mineralogical and geological research (principally in France and Francophone areas of world); Specialized Maps and Charts
ISBN Publisher's Prefix: 2-7159

C D U, see Centre de Documentation Universitaire

C E D S, see Centre d'Etudes et de Documentation Scientifiques

C E F A G, see Centre d'Etudes et Fabrication Arts Graphiques

C E L, see Coopérative de L'Enseignement Laïc

CELSE (Compagnie d'Editions Libres, Sociales et Economiques SA)*, 68 rue Cardinet, F-75017 Paris Tel: (01) 2674123
Subjects: Road Transport (Vocational Training, Economics, Administration, Management, Social Science, Vocabulary of International Transport), Railway Systems world-wide
ISBN Publisher's Prefix: 2-85009

C E P Edition, 17 rue d'Uzès, F-75002 Paris Tel: 2961550 Telex: 680876 Upress
Man Dir: Marc Noel Vigier; *Editorial:* Guy de Dampierre, Jean-Marc Pilpoul; *Sales:* Yves Louis Walle; *Rights & Permissions:* Guy de Dampierre
Associate Company: Editions du Moniteur et Editions de l'Usine Nouvelle
Subjects: Architecture, Building
Bookshops: Librairie du Moniteur, 7 Place de l'Odéon, F-75006 Paris; Librairie du Moniteur, 15 rue d'Uzès, F-75002 Paris
1981: 100 titles *1982:* 85 titles *Founded:* 1980
ISBN Publisher's Prefix: 2-281

C E P A D, see Cepadues Editions SA

C E P L (Centre d'Etude et de Promotion de la Lecture)*, 2 rue du Roule, F-75001 Paris Tel: (01) 233 8962
Subjects: Education, Popular Reference Works

C I L F*, 103 rue de Lille, F-75007 Paris Tel: (01) 7050793
Subjects: French Language
Formerly Editions d'Artrey

C L D, BP 203, 42 ave des Platanes, F-37172 Chambray-Les-Tours cedex Tel: (47) 282068
Man Dir, Editorial: Jean-Pierre Normand; *Sales and Rights & Permissions:* Jack Normand; *Production:* Pierre Proust; *Publicity:* Michel Magat
Subjects: Regional Interest, Folklore, History, Architecture, Religion, Tourism, Hunting
1981: 30 titles *Founded:* 1960

Editions du **C N R S** (Centre national de la recherche scientifique), 15 quai Anatole France, F-75700 Paris Tel: (01) 5559225 Telex: 260034
Man Dir: Gérard Lilamand; *Publicity & Advertising:* Denis Cotard
Parent Company: Centre national de la recherche scientifique
Associate Company: CNRS Laboratoire Intergeo (qv)
Bookshop: Librairie des Editions du CNRS, 15 quai Anatole France, F-75700 Paris
Subjects: History, Geography, Literature, Linguistics, Music, Art, Philosophy, Reference, Religion, Psychology, Social Sciences, Education, Science & Technology, Law, Economics, Mathematics, Information Sciences, Electronics, Mechanics, Energy, Chemistry and Physics, Geology, Biology, Astronomy, Archaeology, Ecology, Ethnology
1981: 146 titles *1982:* 160 titles *Founded:* 1939
ISBN Publisher's Prefix: 2-222

C N R S, Laboratoire Intergeo, see Intergeo

C R E R, see Coopérative Régionale de l'Enseignement Religieux

Editions **Cahiers d'Art**, 14 rue du Dragon, F-75006 Paris Tel: (01) 5487673
Man Dir: Yves de Fontbrune
Subject: Art
Founded: 1926
ISBN Publisher's Prefix: 2-85117

Les **Cahiers Fiscaux** Européens Sàrl*, 51 ave Reine Victoria, F-06000 Nice Tel: (93) 810326
Man Dir: Simone Branca
Parent Company: Société d'Etudes Juridiques Internationales et Fiscales (JURIF) (at above address)
Subsidiary Companies: CFE Belgique, JURIF Belgique (both Belgium — qqv)
Subjects: European Taxation Systems, Fiscal Law, Economics, Social Science (embraced in 3 separate series and 1 periodical)
Founded: 1968

Editions **Calmann-Lévy** Sàrl, 3 rue Auber, F-75009 Paris Tel: (01) 7423833 Cable Add: Caledit
Man Dirs: Alain Dulman, François Propper; *Publicity & Advertising:* Michèle Truchan-Saporta; *Sales Dir:* Richard le Cocq; *Rights & Permissions:* Thérèse Scaroni, Suzanne Lescoat
Subjects: General Fiction, Science Fiction, History, Biography, Philosophy, Psychology, Social Sciences, Economics, Practical, Memoirs, Humour, Sport
Founded: 1836
ISBN Publisher's Prefix: 2-7021

Editions **Capendu***, 3 rue des Haudriettes, F-75003 Paris Tel: (01) 2721319
Man Dir: J F Capendu
Subject: Juveniles
ISBN Publisher's Prefix: 2-85124

Carré-Chapron*, 10 rue du Docteur-Robin, 22600 Loudéac Tel: (96) 280127
Publishers/Authors: J Chapron, Mrs M J Carré-Chapron
Subjects: Educational, Juvenile; the 'Boscher' Method of Infant Teaching

Editions André **Casteilla**, see Nouveautés de l'Enseignement

Editions **Casterman**, 66 rue Bonaparte, F-75006 Paris Tel: (01) 3252005 Telex: 200001 F Edicast
President: Louis-Robert Casterman; *Dir:* Gabriel Chamozzi; *Sales Dir:* Daniel Robinshon; *Publicity & Advertising:* Louis Gérard; *Rights & Permissions:* Pierre Servais, Ivan Noerdinger
Parent Company: Editions Casterman, Belgium (qv)
Branch Off: De Morinel 25-29, NL-8251 HT Dronten, Netherlands
Subjects: Children's Books and Albums, Picture Strips, Religion, Economics, Politics, Practical Living, Urban questions, Architecture, Painting, Photography, Cinema, Music, Poetry, Fiction, Records, Diaries
Founded: Tournai, 1780; Paris, 1857
ISBN Publisher's Prefix: 2-203

Catalogue de l'Edition Française, see Compagnie Européene

Cathasia, see Société d'Edition 'Les Belles Lettres'

Editions **Cedic**, 32 blvd Saint-Germain, F-75005 Paris Tel: (01) 3264271
Man & Sales Dir: François Robineau; *Publicity, Advertising, Rights & Permissions:* Daniele Azoulai
Subjects: Low-priced Paperbacks, Biology, Biochemistry, Computer Science, Education, Mathematics, Physics, Secondary Textbooks, Languages
Founded: 1971
ISBN Publisher's Prefix: 2-7124

Centre d'Etude et de Promotion de la Lecture, see C E P L

Editions du **Centre d'Etudes et de Documentation** Scientifiques (CEDS Editions), 144 rue Gustave Brindeau, F-76600 Le Havre Tel: (35) 240405 Telex: 190406F
Dir: Ms S Mallol; *Literary Dir:* Dr G Mathieu
Subjects: Science & Technology, Nature & Health, Humour, Practical guides
ISBN Publisher's Prefix: 2-85256

Centre de Documentation Universitaire et Société d'Edition d'Enseignement Supérieur Réunis (CDU & SEDES), 88 blvd St-Germain, F-75005 Paris Tel: (01) 3252323
Manager: Pierre Constans
Subjects: History, Philosophy, Social Science, Science & Technology, Economics, Education, School Books, Fiction, Literature, Psychology, Maps
Founded: 1933
ISBN Publisher's Prefix: 2-202

Centre national d'Art et de Culture Georges Pompidou, F-75191 Paris cedex 04 Tel: 2771223 Telex: cnac gp 212276
President, Production: Jean Maheu; *Sales:* Marcel Lefranc
Orders to: Service Commercial (at above address)
Subjects: Art (Modern Art, Contemporary Painting, Sculpture, Drawings, Photography); Industrial Design (Architecture, Environment, Urbanism); Musical and Acoustic Research (Modern Music, Music Composition); Various
1982: 25 titles
ISBN Publisher's Prefix: 2-85850

Centre National de la Recherche Scientifique, see CNRS

Editions du **Centurion***, 17 rue de Babylone, F-75007 Paris Tel: (01) 2229315
Man Dir, Editorial, Production: Charles Ehlinger; *Publicity, Advertising:* Daniele Guilbert; *Rights & Permissions:* Magdeleine Leblanc
Orders to: Sofedis, 29 rue Saint Sulpice, F-75006 Paris
Associate Company: Bayard-Presse (qv)
Subjects: Religion, Juveniles, Social Sciences, General & Social Science, Paperbacks, How-to, Education
1981: 120 titles *Founded:* 1870
ISBN Publisher's Prefix: 2-227

Cepadues Editions (CEPAD) SA+, 111 rue Nicolas Vauquelin, F-31100 Toulouse Tel: (61) 405736 Telex: message 520987F
Man Dir: Guy Collin
Subjects: Scientific, Advanced Technology, Data Processing, Teaching, Aviation, Space Research
1981-82: 10 titles *Founded:* 1969
ISBN Publisher's Prefix: 2-85428

Editions **Cercle d'Art** SA*, 90 rue du Bac, F-75006 Paris Tel: (01) 5442890
Man Dir: Charles Feld
Subjects: Art
Founded: 1950
ISBN Publisher's Prefix: 2-7022

Editions du **Cerf**, 29 blvd La Tour Maubourg, F-75007 Paris cedex 07 Tel: (01) 5503407 Cable Add: Edicerf
General Dir: M Houssin; *Man Dir:* G Eschbach; *Editorial Dir:* M Joulin; *Sales Dir:* J Mignon; *Publicity & Advertising:* Mrs L Rossi; *Rights & Permissions:* Mrs F de Chassey
Subjects: Religion, History, Philosophy, Juveniles, Social Science, Paperbacks, Reference, Textbooks, Crafts, Psychology, Economics
Founded: 1929
ISBN Publisher's Prefix: 2-204

Editions R **Chaix***, 1 rue de Fleurus, F-75006 Paris Tel: 5444111/5485124
Man Dir, Rights & Permissions: J-Y Vincent; *Editorial:* R Chaix; *Sales:* J Farge
Subjects: Leisure pursuits, Practical
Founded: 1977

Editions du **Chalet**, 77 rue de Vaugirard, F-75006 Paris Tel: (01) 5487860 Telex: 202036 F
Subjects: Roman Catholic Devotional, Liturgical, Catechisms
Orders to: (France) Begedis, 77 rue de Vaugirard, F-75006 Paris Tel: (01) 5487860 Telex: 202036 F; (Foreign) Arc-en-Ciel International, 11 rue Barthélemy Frison, B-7500 Tournai, Belgium
Associate Company: Editions Desclée et Cie (qv for other Associate Companies)
1983: 15 titles *Founded:* 1946
ISBN Publisher's Prefix: 2-7023

Editions **Champ Libre**, 13 rue de Béarn, F-75003 Paris Tel: (01) 2722700/2723480
Subjects: Classics, History, Social Science, Literature, Modern Theory
Founded: 1970
ISBN Publisher's Prefix: 2-85184

Librairie des **Champs-Elysées** SA, 79 blvd St-Germain, F-75006 Paris Tel: (01) 3291224
Man Dir: Michel Averlant
Imprints: Le Masque, Club des Masques
Subjects: Several fiction series dealing exclusively with one theme, viz: Crime and Police (Editions Le Masque, Club des Masques)
Founded: 1927
ISBN Publisher's Prefix: 2-7024

Chancerel Editions SA, 4 rue Aumont Thiéville, F-75017 Paris Tel: (01) 7660302 Telex: 640093 Chanced F
Chairman: Philippe Chancerel
Associate Company: Chancerel Publishers Ltd, UK (qv)
Subjects: Educational strip cartoons, Sport, Hobbies, Homecraft (in French and other European languages)
Founded: 1960
ISBN Publishers' Prefix: 2-85429

Editions **Charles-Lavauzelle** SA, BP 8, F-87350 Panazol Tel: (55) 341515
Man Dir: Jean Claude Mazaud; *Sales:* Guy Devautour; *Publicity:* Geneviève Giry; *Production:* Henri Chabrier
Branch Off: 20 rue de Léningrad, F-75008 Paris cedex Tel: 3874230
Subjects: Military History, Law, Equestrian
1982: 45 titles *Founded:* 1831
ISBN Publisher's Prefix: 2-7025

Editions du **Chat** Perché, an imprint of Flammarion et Cie (qv)

Editions du **Chêne**+, 79 blvd St-Germain, F-75288 Paris cedex 06 Tel: (01) 3291224 Telex: 250302 Publ bti Paris
Man Dir, Editorial, Rights & Permissions: Hervé de La Martinière; *Editorial Assistant:* Françoise Bonnefoy
Orders to: Groupe International Hachette (at above address)
Parent Company: Librairie Hachette (qv)
Subjects: Ancient, Graphic and Contemporary Art, Architecture, Photography, Cinema, Documentaries
Founded: 1939
ISBN Publisher's Prefix: 2-85108

Le **Cherche-Midi**, Éditeur+, 110 rue du Cherche-Midi, F-75006 Paris Tel: (01) 2227120
Dirs: Jean Breton, Michel Breton, Jean Orizet; *Publicity:* Philippe Héraclès
Subjects: Belles Lettres, Poetry, Paperbacks
Founded: 1978
Miscellaneous: Managing company responsible for Editions Saint-Germain-des-Prés SA (qv)

Editions du **Chiendent** Sàrl*, Marcevol Vinça F-66320 (Eastern Pyrenees) Tel: (68) 962185
Man Dir: Xavier d'Arthuys; *Production:* Dominique Poilpré
Orders to: Distique, 1 rue de Fossés, Saint Jacques, F-75005 Paris
Subjects: Four series deal generally with (1) people in conflict with events; (2) man's conflict with his apparent destiny; (3) Eastern Pyrenees regional; (4) writings by children
Founded: 1977
ISBN Publisher's Prefix: 2-85999001

Editions de **Chiré**, Chiré-en-Montreuil, F-86190 Vouillé Tel: (049) 518304
Man Dir: Jean Auguy; *Publicity Dir:* Jean Sechet
Branch Off: Duquesne Diffusion, 27 ave Duquesne, F-75007 Paris
Subjects: History, Social Science, Counter-revolution, Religion
1981: 1 title *1982:* 1 title *Founded:* 1966

Editions **Chiron**, 40 rue de Seine, F-75006 Paris Tel: (01) 6331893
Chairman: Denys Ferrando-Dufort; *Promotion & Marketing:* Liliane Bertrand
Subjects: Education, Juveniles, Sports, Scientific, Technical, Leisure Pursuits, Health
Founded: 1906
ISBN Publisher's Prefix: 2-7027

Chotard et Associés, Editeurs, 68 rue Jean-Jacques Rousseau, F-75001 Paris Tel: (01) 2338065 Telex: 680126 Chotar
Man Dir: Yvon Chotard; *Sales Dir:* Jacques Chapellon; *Rights & Permissions:* Anne Chotard
Orders to: Sofemis, 29 rue St Sulpice, F-75006 Paris
Parent Company: Editions France Empire (qv)
Subjects: Psychology, Engineering, Technical, Economics, Marketing, Management, Social Science, University Textbooks, Educational Material
1981: 14 titles *1982:* 12 titles *Founded:* 1969
ISBN Publisher's Prefix: 2-7127

Editions de la **Chronique** des Lettres Françaises*, 33 rue de Verneuil, F-75007 Paris Tel: (01) 6477641
Editorial: Jean Michel Place; *Sales:* Mrs P Place
Orders to: 12 rue Pierre et Marie Curie, F-75005 Paris
Parent Company: Chronique des Lettres Françaises
Associate Company: Editions Jean-Michel Place (qv)
Subjects: Academic (Ancient and Modern), Bibliographies
Founded: 1922
ISBN Publisher's Prefix: 2-85185

Clé International, 88 blvd Arago, F-75014 Paris Tel: 3376112 Telex: 201466f
Man Dir: Pierre Coupry; *Editorial, Production:* Michel Gudimard; *Sales, Rights & Permissions:* Jean-Claude Richard
Orders to: (outside France): as company address; (in France): Ed Fernand Nathan, 9 rue Méchain, F-75676 Paris cedex 14
Subjects: Books for the Foreign Market, especially connected with teaching French as a foreign language; also teaching French as a second language
1982: 120 titles *Founded:* 1973

Club des Masques, an imprint of Librairie des Champs-Elysées SA (qv)

Armand **Colin**, Editeur, 103 blvd St-Michel, F-75005 Paris Tel: (01) 6341219 Telex: Acolin 201269 F
Man Dir: Jean-Max Leclerc; *Sales Dir:*
Rémy Bourrelier; *Publicity & Advertising:* Yvette Dardenne; *Rights & Permissions:* Anne Nesteroff
Orders to: Armand Colin, F-75300 Paris-Brune cedex 66
Subjects: History, Philosophy, Psychology, Pedagogy, Geography, General Literature, General & Social Science, University, Secondary & Primary Textbooks, Educational Materials
Founded: 1870
Miscellaneous: Incorporates publications of former separate Company, Editions Colin Bourrelier
ISBN Publisher's Prefix: 2-200

Editions **Comindus***, 1 rue Descombes, F-75017 Paris Tel: (01) 3807916
Subject: Trade Annuals connected with agricultural and foodstuffs industries

Compagnie d'Editions Libres, Sociales et Economiques, see C E L S E

Compagnie Européenne de Fournitures et de Services Informatiques*, 9-13 rue Séguier, F-75006 Paris Tel: (01) 3256170
European Company for Data Processing Supplies and Services
Man Dir: Serge Ciregna
Subject: Bibliography of current titles of Data Processing Companies

Le **Concours** Médical*, 37 rue de Bellefond, F-75009 Paris Tel: (01) 2850536
Subject: Medicine

Coopérative de l'Enseignement Laïc (CEL) SA, BP 109, F-06322 Cannes La Bocca cedex (Located at: 189 ave Francis-Tonner, Cannes La Bocca) Tel: (93) 479611
Man Dir: Daniel le Blay; *Editorial:* Michel Barré
Subjects: Educational, Pedagogic, Periodicals
Book Club: Publications de l'Ecole Moderne Française (PEMF)
Bookshop: Librairie CEL, Alpha du Marais, 13 rue du Temple, Paris 4ème
Founded: 1928
ISBN Publisher's Prefix: 2-85311

Coopérative Regionale de l'Enseignement Religieux (CRER)*, 7 rue du Parvis St-Maurice, BP 2307, F-49023 Angers cedex Tel: (41) 884695
Man Dir: Michel P Pourrias
Subject: Religion

Copernic, 14 rue de l'Armorique, F-75015 Paris Tel: (01) 3207670
Man Dir: Bertrand Sorlot; *Sales, Production, Rights & Permissions, Publicity:* Jeanne Bordeau
Associate Companies: Editions Albatross, Publeditec
Subjects: History, Documentary, Modern Thought, Philosophy/Religion, Myth and Fantasy
Founded: 1976
ISBN Publisher's Prefix: 2-85984

Verlagshaus **Corsica**, see Auberge du Sambucco

Courrier du Livre Sàrl, 21 rue de Seine, F-75006 Paris Tel: (01) 3541891
Subjects: Philosophy, Religion, Ecology, Health and Nutrition, Organic Gardening, Yoga
ISBN Publisher's Prefix: 2-7029

Editeurs **Crépin-Leblond** et Cie SA*, 12 rue Duguay-Trouin, F-75006 Paris Tel: (01) 5489350
Man Dir: Mrs A R Henry; *Publicity:* E-G Souquet
Subjects: Hunting, Shooting, Arms, Dogs, Horse-Riding, Nature
1981: 4 titles *Founded:* 1952
ISBN Publisher's Prefix: 2-7030

Editions **Cujas***, 4, 6 & 8 rue de la Maison Blanche, F-75013 Paris Tel: (01) 5889657/5888436
Man Dir: Pierre Joly; *Publicity Dir:* Jacqueline Joly
Subjects: Politics, Economics, Education, mainly in France and Francophone countries, Social Sciences
Bookshops: Librairie J Joly, 19 rue Cujas, F-75005 Paris; Cujas Librairie, 2 rue de Rouen, F-92000 Nanterre
Founded: 1946
ISBN Publisher's Prefix: 2-254

D A F S A (Société de Documentation et d'Analyses Financières), 125 rue Montmartre, F-75002 Paris Tel: (01) 2332123 Telex: 640472 Daf Doc
Man Dir: Michel Vieillard
Subjects: Economics, Finance

Les Editions Roger **Dacosta**, 19 blvd Raspail, F-75007 Paris Tel: (01) 5441491
Man Dir: Jean Dacosta; *Sales Dir:* Carole Dacosta
Subjects: Medicine, Medical History, Dentistry
1981: 16 titles
ISBN Publisher's Prefix: 2-85128

Jurisprudence Générale **Dalloz**, 11 rue Soufflot, F-75240 Paris Cedex 05 Tel: (01) 3295080 Telex: 210023 Ogtel Ref 703
President, General Manager: Patrice Vergé; *Man Dir, Rights & Permissions:* G de Nussac; *Editorial, Production:* M Dunes; *Sales:* M Hapiot; *Publicity Dir:* A Stein
Bookshop: Dalloz, 14 rue Soufflot, F-75240 Paris cedex 05
Subjects: Law, Political Science, Reference, Business, Economics, Philosophy
Founded: 1845
ISBN Publisher's Prefix: 2-247

Editions **Dangles** SA, 18 rue Lavoisier, BP 36, F-45802 St Jean-de-Braye cedex Tel: (01) 38864180
Man Dir, Editorial, Production, Publicity, Rights & Permissions: J-Y Anstet Dangles; *Sales:* Alain Queant
Subjects: Naturopathy, Esotericism and Spirit Life, Psychology, Physical Culture, Ecology
1981: 15 titles *1982:* 16 titles *Founded:* 1926
ISBN Publisher's Prefix: 2-7033

Editions **Dardelet** SA, 22 rue René-Thomas, F-38000 Grenoble Tel: 961681
Subjects: Regional topics

Dargaud Editeur*, 12 Blaise Pascal, BP 155, F-92201 Neuilly-sur-Seine Tel: 7471133
Cable Add: Editfranc Neuilly Telex: 620631
Editorial: Guy Vidal, Claude Moliterni; *Publisher:* Georges Dargaud; *Rights & Permissions:* Anthéa Shackleton, Michel Lieuré
Subjects: Juveniles, Strip Cartoons, Magazines
ISBN Publisher's Prefix: 2-205

Editions du **Dauphin**, 43-45 rue de la Tombe-Issoire, F-75014 Paris Tel: (01) 3277900
Publishing Manager: Anne Tromelin
Subjects: General Fiction, Poetry, Social Science, How-to, Dictionaries, Documentaries, Regional Studies
Founded: 1936
ISBN Publisher's Prefix: 2-7163

Editions **De Vecchi** SA*, 32 rue Troyon, F-75008 Paris Tel: 6217376
Man Dir: Robert Pinto; *Editorial:* Evelyne Level
Subjects: Practical Guides on Legal Questions, Animals, Games, Leisure, Gardening, Health, Mystery, Cookery, History
Founded: 1971
ISBN Publisher's Prefix: 2-85177

Nouvelles Editions Debresse, 17 rue Duguay-Trouin, F-75006 Paris cedex 6 Tel: (01) 5481047
Man Dir: Pierre Moulin; *Editorial:* Paul Poncelet; *Sales:* Vincent Moulin; *Production, Publicity:* Josiane Muller
Subjects: General Fiction, Poetry, History, Social Science
Founded: 1933

Librairie Générale de l'Enseignement Mme **Decombe**, 4 rue Dante, Paris 5 Tel: 3540698
Man Dir and Other Offices: Mrs Decomble
Subject: Botany, Apiculture
Founded: 1903
ISBN Publisher's Prefix: 2-85022

La Découverte/Maspero, 1 pl Paul-Painlevé, F-75005 Paris Tel: (01) 6334116
Man Dir: François Geze
Subjects: Belles Lettres, Poetry, History, Philosophy, Sociology, Political Economy, Low- & High-priced Paperbacks
1982-83: 200 titles *Founded:* 1959
ISBN Publisher's Prefix: 2-7071

Editions **Delachaux et Niestlé Spes**, 32 rue de Grenelle, F-75007 Paris Tel: (01) 5483842
Orders to: 6 rue du Mail, F-75002 Paris (for French publications); 79 route d'Oron, CH-1000 Lausanne 21, Switzerland (for international publications)
Parent Company: Editions Delachaux et Niestlé, Switzerland (qv)
Subjects: Medicine, Psychology, Education, Social & Natural History, Science, Juveniles, Technical, Mathematics, Architecture, Sports
Founded: 1860
ISBN Publisher's Prefix: 2-603

Librairie **Delagrave** Sàrl, 15 rue Soufflot, F-75240 Paris cedex 05 Tel: (01) 3258866 Cable Add: Delagrave Paris Telex: 210311F Code 690
Manager: Fabrice Delagrave; *Sales Dir:* J Roustan; *Publicity:* L Leiglon; *Rights & Permissions:* Y Blaise
Subjects: Juveniles, General Science, University, Technical, Secondary & Primary Textbooks, Educational Materials, Languages
Founded: 1865
ISBN Publisher's Prefix: 2-206

Jean-Pierre **Delarge** SA, 10 rue Mayet, F-75006, Paris Tel: 7837070
Man Dir: François Chagneau; *Rights & Permissions:* Chantal Galtier Roussel
Subjects: General Non-fiction; especially Popular Reference Works, Juveniles, Reportage, Literature, History, Biography, Philosophy, Education, Religion, Sociology; Paperbacks (Astrology)
Founded: 1942
ISBN Publisher's Prefix: 2-7113

Editions **Delarue**, see Editions Guy Le Prat

Editions J **Delmas** et Cie*, 13 rue de l'Odéon, F-75006 Paris Tel: (01) 3250832
Man Dir: Jacques Delmas; *Sales, Rights & Permissions:* Jacques Delmas; *Publicity:* Evelyne Alaux
Subjects: Accountancy, Law, Finance, Management, Insurance, Data Processing, Social and Factory Legislation, Dictionaries
Founded: 1947
ISBN Publisher's Prefix: 7034

Editions **Denoël** SA+, 19 rue de l'Université, F-75007 Paris Tel: (01) 2615085 Cable Add: Edepege
Man Dir: Gérard Bourgadier; *Rights & Permissions:* Thérèse Mairesse
Parent Company: Editions Gallimard (qv)
Associate Company: Mercure de France (qv)
Imprint: Société Nouvelle des Editions Gonthier Sàrl

Subjects: General and Science Fiction, Art, Reference, Sports, Documents, Political Science, Economics, De Luxe Editions
ISBN Publisher's Prefix: 2-207

Desclée de Brouwer SA, 76 bis rue des Saints-Pères, F-75007 Paris Tel: (01) 5440763 Telex: 202098
Man Dir, Publicity: André Bourgeois; *Editorial:* Jacques Deschanel; *Sales:* Anna-Marie Coquier; *Production:* Yves-Noël Lelouvier; *Rights & Permissions:* Yvonne Tomazi
Subjects: Religion and Theology, Juvenile and Educational, Music, Art, Psychiatry
1981: 45 titles *Founded:* 1875
ISBN Publisher's Prefix: 2-220

Editions **Desclée et Cie**, 77 rue de Vaugirard, F-75006 Paris Tel: (01) 5487860 Telex: 202036 F
Man Dir: Marcel Vervaet
Orders to: Begedis, 77 rue de Vaugirard, F-75006 Paris Tel: (01) 5487860 Telex: 202036
Parent Company: Gedit SA, Tournai, Belgium (qv)
Associate Companies: Desclée, Editeurs; Editions Gamma (both in Belgium, qqv); Editions Gamma (qv); Nouvelles Editions Mame (qv); Editions du Chalet (qv)
Subjects: History, Philosophy, Religion, Social Science
1983: 30 titles *Founded:* 1872
ISBN Publisher's Prefix: 2-7189

Librairie **Desforges**, 29 quai des Grands-Augustins, F-75006 Paris Tel: (01) 3546054
Subjects: Technology, Building, Electrotechnology, Esoteric, Naturopathy, Craft work, Technical Textbooks

Dessain et Tolra SA*, 10 rue Cassette, F-75006 Paris Tel: (01) 2229020 Telex: elita 641155 ref d 32
Man Dir: Pierre Zech; *General Manager:* Jean Varney; *Publicity:* Marie-Claude Charbonnier; *Editorial:* (Sénevé): Françoise Desgrandchamps; *Rights & Permissions:* Françoise Houssin, Jean-Pierre Grongnet
Imprints: Editorial Bouret, P Lethielleux, Les Editions du Sénevé (qv)
Subjects: Children's and Young Adults' books, Handicrafts and Do-it-yourself, Art, Pastoral works and Catechisms
1981: 73 titles *Founded:* 1964
ISBN Publisher's Prefix: 2-249

Librairie André **Desvigne***, 53-54 Quai Pierre Scize, F-69321 Lyon cedex 1 Tel: (7) 82863/286374
President: André Desvigne
Subject: School Books, Higher Grade Education
ISBN Publisher's Prefix: 2-7037

Les Editions des **Deux Coqs d'Or**, 28 rue de la Boëtie, F-75008 Paris Tel: (01) 5621052 Cable Add: Deucodo Paris Telex: 650780
Man Dirs: Philip A Jarvis, François Martineau; *Publicity & Advertising:* Claude Gille; *Rights & Permissions:* Suzanna MacMahon
Subjects: Art, How-to, Juveniles, Reference, Paperbacks
Book Clubs: Education et Culture; Presses d'Or
Founded: 1948
ISBN Publisher's Prefix: 2-7192

La Maison du **Dictionnaire**, see Maison

John **Didier Editions***, 1 rue des Chailles, F-92500 Rueil Malmaison Tel: 7514545 Telex: 250303 Service Didier 7084545 Cable Add: Didier 92500 Rueil-Malmaison
Man Dir & Editor: John Didier; *Assistant Editor:* Barbara Lyon; *Sales Dir:* C Perrin; *Advertising Dir:* R Mercier; *Publicity Dir:* L Meynier; *Rights & Permissions:* Miss R Camus
Subjects: Fiction, Non-fiction, General Trade, Belles Lettres, Biography, History, Theses, How-to, Art, Philosophy, Religion, Juveniles
Bookshop: The American Bookshop (at above address)
Founded: 1962

Société **Didot-Bottin** SA, 28 rue du Docteur Finlay, F-75738 Paris cedex 15 Tel: (01) 5786166 Telex: 204286F
Subjects: Encyclopaedias and Annuals concerning Business, Trades, International Commerce and Touring, French Administration, Transport, Motor Cycling
Bookshop: At above address
Founded: 1796
ISBN Publisher's Prefix: 2-7039

Société de **Documentation et d'Analyses** Financières, see D A F S A

La Documentation Française, 29-31 quai Voltaire, F-75340 Paris cedex 07 Tel: (01) 2615010 Telex: 204826 Docfran Paris
Publications of the General Secretary's Office of the French Government
Man Dir: Françoise Gallouedec-Genuys; *Sales, Promotion:* Jean Paitel, Alain-Marie Bassy; *Publicity:* Laura Esterházy; *Production, Foreign Rights:* Celina Kader
Mail Order and Documentation requests to: 124 rue Henri Barbusse, F-93308 Aubervilliers cedex
Subjects: French and Foreign Politics, Economics, Regional Administration, Environment, Social Problems, Science and Technology, Law, the Arts, Audio visual; 50 Periodicals
Bookshops: 29-31 quai Voltaire, F-75007 Paris; 165 rue Garibaldi, F-69401 Lyon cedex 03; 124 rue Henri Barbusse, F-93308 Aubervilliers cedex
Founded: 1945
Miscellaneous: Responsible for sales and distribution for the National Archives Administration, for *Editeur officiel du Quebec* and for Cooperation-Development Ministry publications; also comprises a library, three bookshops, a photograph and slide library and an information service (all at main address)
ISBN Publisher's Prefix: 2-11001

Doin Editeurs, 8 pl de l'Odéon, F-75006 Paris Tel: (01) 3253402
Man Dir: M Abadie
Subjects: Medicine, Psychology, General & Social Science, University Textbooks, Periodicals
Founded: 1874
ISBN Publisher's Prefix: 2-7040

Doubleday-France, 9 rue du Pré-Aux-Clercs, Paris 7 Tel: 2611898/2611899 Cable Add: Doubday Paris
Business Manager: Véronique Poderzay; *Editorial:* Beverly Gordey; *Rights & Permissions:* Susan Sevray
Parent Company: Doubleday & Co, Inc, 245 Park Ave, New York, NY 10017, USA
Associate Company: Doubleday & Co, Inc, UK (qv)
Founded: 1959 (Doubleday-France)

Draeger Editeur*, 46 rue de Bagneux, F-92120 Montrouge Tel: 6571154 Telex: 270294F
Man Dir: Claude Draeger
Subjects: Art, Architecture, Documents, Biography, De Luxe Editions
ISBN Publisher's Prefix: 2-85119

Droguet et Ardant, 41 rue Henri Giffard, BP 1010, F-87004 Limoges 57 cedex Tel: (055) 374306 Telex: 580934
Man Dir: Robert Ardant; *Publicity Dir:* Suzanne Ardant

Subjects: Roman Catholic Devotional
1982: 10 titles
ISBN Publisher's Prefix: 2-7041

Librairie Générale de Droit et de Jurisprudence, 20 rue Soufflot, F-75005 Paris Tel: (01) 3540719 Telex: 210023 Ogtel 741
Man Dirs: Françoise Marty, Jacqueline Hebert; *Sales Manager, Rights & Permissions:* Vincent Marty
Subjects: Social Science, Law, University Textbooks, Jurisprudence
Bookshop: LGDJ, 20 rue Soufflot, Paris
Founded: 1836
ISBN Publisher's Prefix: 2-275

Dunod, an imprint of Editions Bordas (qv)

Maison d'Editions J Dupuis Fils et Cie SA, 8 rue Bellini, F-75782 Paris cedex 16 Tel: (01) 7277280
Subjects: Juveniles, Literature

E A C, an imprint of Editions des Archives Contemporaines (qv)

E D H I S, see Histoire Sociale

E P A SA, 83 rue de Rennes, F-75006 Paris Tel: (01) 6090005 Telex: 202891F
Man Dir, Editorial, Rights & Permissions: Arnauld de Fouchier; *Managing Editor:* Antoine Prunet; *Sales:* Thierry Quentin; *Production:* Gilles Blanchet; *Publicity and Mail Order:* Rosine Bertrand; *Press Agents:* Rosine Bertrand, Guta Chabasson
Orders to: E P A, 18 rue d'Issy, F-92100 Boulogne Billancourt
Subjects: Aviation, Automobile, Railways, Military, Marine Interest, Photographic, Historical
Bookshops: 83 rue de Rennes, 75006 Paris; 92 rue Saint Lazare, 75009 Paris; 192 ave Victor Hugo, F-75116 Paris; 18 rue de l'Ancienne Préfecture, 69002 Lyon; 6 rue du Sec Arembault, 59800 Lille
1981: 100 titles *1982:* 100 titles *Founded:* 1953
ISBN Publisher's Prefix: 2-85120

Editions E S F (Editions Sociales Françaises), 17 rue Viète, F-75854 Paris cedex 17 Tel: (01) 7636876
President: Gérard Didier; *Man Dir:* Claude Chichet
Subsidiary Company: Entreprise Moderne d'Edition (qv)
Subjects: Education, Re-education, Pedagogy, Problems of Handicapped Children, Psychology, Social Problems and Legislation, Health and Nutrition
1981: 25 titles *Founded:* 1928
ISBN Publisher's Prefix: 2-7101

E T S F, see Editions Techniques et Scientifiques Françaises

L'Ecole/L'Ecole des Loisirs Sàrl+, 11 rue de Sèvres, F-75006 Paris Tel: (01) 2229410
Cable Add: Librecole
Man Dir: Jean Fabre; *Export Sales Manager:* H Doulmet; *Rights & Permissions, Publicity and Advertising:* Jean Delas
Subjects: Juveniles, High-priced Paperbacks, University, Secondary & Primary Textbooks, Educational Materials
ISBN Publisher's Prefix: 2-211

Ediscience, see McGraw-Hill Inc

Edisud, La Calade, RN 7, F-13090 Aix-en-Provence Tel: (42) 216144/216437
Man Dir, Sales, Production: Charles-Yves Chaudoreille; *Publicity, Rights & Permissions:* Anne-Marie Lapillonne
Subjects: Ecology, Energy, Agriculture, History, Geography, Music, Regional Interest (Provence), General Topics
1981: 25 titles *1982:* 25 titles *Founded:* 1971
ISBN Publisher's Prefix: 2-85744

Société **Editart** Quatre Chemins, 3 pl St-Sulpice, F-75006 Paris Tel: (01) 3544073
Dir: François Heim
Bookshop: Librairie des Quatre Chemins Editart (at above address)
Subject: Art
Founded: 1924

Les Editeurs Réunis, 11 rue de la Montagne-Ste-Geneviève, F-75005 Paris Tel: (01) 3547446/3544381
Subjects: The company acts as sole agent for YMCA Press (qv), Bradda Books and Prideaux Press in publishing a very comprehensive list of Russian books in the original Russian
Founded: 1932

Edition No 1, see No 1

Editions des Archives Contemporaines, 58 rue Lhomond, F-75005 Paris Tel: (01) 3362404 Telex: 201307 Sienpub F
Man Dir: Françoise Chantrel-Riols
Orders to: Offilib, 48 rue Gay Lussac, F-75005 Paris
Imprint: EAC
Subjects: History, Anthropology, Philosophy, Music, Social and Political Sciences, Reprints
1982: 4 titles *Founded:* 1981
ISBN Publisher's Prefix: 2-903928

Editions Juridiques et Techniques, see Lamy SA

Editions Maritimes et d'Outre-Mer SA, 17 rue Jacob, F-75006 Paris Tel: (01) 6340310 Telex: 270461 emom
Managing Editor: Pierre Gutelle; *Rights & Permissions:* Ursula Veit
Subjects: Sailing, Maritime History, Navigation, Reference
Bookshops: Librairie EMOM (at above address)
Founded: 1839
ISBN Publisher's Prefix: 2-7070

Editions Modernes Média*, 21 rue du Cardinal-Lemoine, F-75005 Paris Tel: (01) 3268384
Subjects: Philosophy, Linguistics, School Books, Pedagogy, Literature
ISBN Publisher's Prefix: 2-83398

Les Editions Sociales-Messidor*, 146 rue du Faubourg-Poissonnière, F-75010 Paris Tel: (01) 2819103 Telex: 226 Sogedil
Man Dir: Lucien Seve; *Editorial:* Richard Lagache, Nicole Chiaverini; *Publicity:* Katia Favard; *Rights & Permissions:* Gisèle Jachimiak
Orders to: Odéon Diffusion (at above address)
Imprint: Messidor
Subjects: Philosophy, Social Science, Politics, Literature, Education, Languages, Economics
Book Club: Livre Club Diderot
Bookshop: Les Librairies de la Renaissance; Librairie Racine, 24 rue Racine, F-75006 Paris
Founded: 1920
Miscellaneous: see also Editions La Farandole/Messidor
ISBN Publisher's Prefix: 2-209

Editions Sociales Françaises, see E S F

Editions Techniques SA*, 123 rue d'Alésia, F-75678 Paris cedex 14 Tel: (01) 5392291 Telex: Editec 270737F; 18 rue Séguier, F-75006 Paris Tel: (01) 3292130
Man Dir: Philippe Durieux; *Assistant Dir:* Robert Turberg; *Export Sales Dir:* J P Chamoux
Subjects: Law, Medicine, Engineering, University Textbooks, Encyclopaedias
Founded: 1907
ISBN Publisher's Prefix: 2-7110

Editions Techniques et Scientifiques Françaises, 2-12 rue de Bellevue, F-75940 Paris cedex 19 Tel: 2003305 Telex: PGV 230472F
Man Dir: Jean-Pierre Ventillard; *Editorial, Sales, Production, Publicity:* Christian Cheneau
Subjects: Technical (radio, television, electronics, information science and associated themes), Periodicals

Editions Universitaires-Editions du Jour SA, now Éditions Jean Pierre Delarge SA (qv)

Editions Elsevier Séquoia Sàrl*, 1 rue du 29 Juillet, F-75001 Paris Tel: (01) 2601556
Man Dir: Georges Merlin
Subjects: History, Reference, Juveniles, Medicine and Health, Nature, Psychology, Travel, Family, Sports and Hobbies, Management, Education, Cookery
Founded: 1960
ISBN Publisher's Prefix: 2-8003

Editions Encre*, 9 rue Duphot, F-75001 Paris Tel: 2969002
Man Dir: Michel Coquart; *Dir:* Gérard Sakon; *Sales:* Serge Beltz; *Production:* Jacques Lacogue; *Rights & Permissions:* Antonella Ortoli
Parent Company: Société IMC
Subsidiary Company: Encre-Dif, at above address
Subjects: General Literature, Fiction, Documentary and Reportage, How-to
Founded: 1978

Encyclopaedia Universalis France SA+, 10 rue Vercingétorix, F-750014 Paris Tel: 5394539/5396114 Cable Add: Encyversal Telex: 220064F Code 3121
President, Man Dir: Mr Baumberger; *Editorial:* Mr Bersani; *Production:* Mr Schweizer; *Rights & Permissions:* Mr Alba
Subjects: Encyclopaedias, Atlases
Founded: 1967
ISBN Publisher's Prefix: 2-85229

Coopérative de l'**Enseignement laïc**, see Coopérative

Librairie Générale de l'**Enseignement Sàrl**, see Decomble

Editions Entente*, 12 rue Honoré-Chevalier, F-75006 Paris Tel: (01) 2228070
Man Dir: Edouard Esmerian
Subjects: Ecology, Economics, Third World, Essays, Monographs on Minorities, Documentary Accounts, Novels
Bookshop: Librairie Entente (at above address)
1981: 54 titles *1982:* 62 titles *Founded:* 1975
ISBN Publisher's Prefix: 2-7266

Entreprise Moderne d'Edition, 17 rue Viète, F-75854 Paris cedex 17 Tel: 9246876
President: Gérard Didier; *Man Dir:* Claude Chichet
Parent Company: Editions E S F (qv)
Subjects: Business Management, Personnel Training and Management, Data Processing, Technology, Periodicals
1981: 20 titles *Founded:* 1953
ISBN Publisher's Prefix: 2-7043

Les Editions de l'Epargne, 174 blvd St-Germain, F-75297 Paris cedex 06 Tel: (01) 5482452
Man Dir: Dominique Therond
Subjects: Investment, Savings Banks, Economy and Finance, Family Budgets, aspects of Law, Penal Codes
ISBN Publisher's Prefix: 2-85015

Epi SA Editeurs, 76 bis rue des Saints-Pères, F-75007 Paris Tel: (01) 5440763 Telex: 202098
Editorial: Yves Le Gall; *Rights & Permissions:* Yvonne Tomazi
Subjects: Social Sciences, Education, Group

Therapy, Psychology, Yoga, Juvenile
Founded: 1947
ISBN Publisher's Prefix: 2-7045

Publications **Estoup et Roy** Sàrl*, 47 rue du Château-des-Rentiers, F-75013 Paris
Tel: (01) 5838550
Subject: Education
ISBN Publisher's Prefix: 2-85016

Etudes Augustiniennes, 3 rue de l'Abbaye, F-75006 Paris Tel: (01) 3548025
Man Dir: Georges Folliet
Subjects: Theology and Church History, especially in relation to Saint Augustine; the Works of Saint Augustine
Founded: 1954
ISBN Publisher's Prefix: 2-85121

Eurédif (Société Européenne d'Edition et de Diffusion)*, Tour Atlas, 10 Villa d'Este, F-75648 Paris cedex 13 Tel: 5838040
Man Dir: A L Fiore; *Commercial Dir:* Eric Prevost
Subjects: General Fiction, Low-priced Paperbacks
Founded: 1969
ISBN Publisher's Prefix: 2-7167

L'**Expansion** Scientifique Française, 15 rue St-Benoît, F-75278 Paris cedex 06 Tel: (01) 5484260
Man Dir: Pierre Bergeaud
Subject: Medicine
Bookshop: Librairie des Facultés de Médecine et de Pharmacie, 174 blvd St-Germain, F-75297 Paris cedex 06
Founded: 1925
ISBN Publisher's Prefix: 2-7046

Éditions **Eyrolles**, 61 blvd St-Germain, F-75240 Paris cedex 05 Tel: (01) 6342199
Telex: eyrotp 203385f
Man Dir: Claude Schoedler; *Editorial:* Jean Pierre Tissier
Subsidiary Company: Les Editions d'Organisation (qv)
Subjects: Physical Sciences, Earth Sciences, Electricity, Mechanics, Data Processing, Electronics, Building and Architecture, Agriculture, Hobbies
Bookshop: Librairie Eyrolles (at above address)
Founded: 1918
ISBN Publisher's Prefix: 2-212

Editions La **Farandole**/Messidor, 146 rue du Faubourg Poissonnière, F-75010 Paris Tel: (01) 2819103
Man Dir: Ghilaine Povinha; *Editorial:* Michèle Courtois; *Sales:* Christian Boudeau; *Promotion:* Alain Leroy; *Publicity:* Katia Favard
Subject: Juveniles
Founded: 1955
Miscellaneous: See also Les Editions Sociales/Messidor
ISBN Publisher's Prefix: 2-7047

Librairie Arthème **Fayard**, 75 rue des Sts-Pères, F-75006 Paris Tel: (01) 5443845
Telex: 250302 Publi 11189132
Man Dir: Claude Durand; *Publicity:* Sylvaine Pasquet; *Advertising Dir:* Claude Danis; *Rights & Permissions:* Josette Wittorski
Subsidiary Company: Editions Le Sarment (qv)
Subjects: General Fiction, Biography, History, Religion, Music, Spirituality, Human and Social Science
Founded: 1854
ISBN Publisher's Prefix: 2-213

Des **Femmes**, 6 rue de Mézières, F-75006 Paris Tel: (01) 2226074
Subjects: General Fiction, Essays, Documents, History, Poetry, Biography, Art, Photography, Theatre, Juveniles, Low-priced Paperbacks
Bookshops: Librairie 'Des Femmes', 2 pl des Célestins, Lyon 2; Librairie 'Des Femmes', 35 rue Pavillon, F-13001 Marseille; Librairie 'Des Femmes', 74 rue de Seine, F-75006 Paris
1983: 250 titles *Founded:* 1974
ISBN Publisher's Prefix: 2-7210

Groupe **Femmes d'aujourd'hui**, 20-22 rue de Clichy, F-75009 Paris Tel: (01) 2806465
Cable Add: Parisgraph Telex: 643433 Fer-Sen
Subjects: Domestic Crafts, Medicine, Bible
ISBN Publisher's Prefix: 2-87024

Editions du **Feu** Nouveau, 8 ave César-Caire, F-75008 Paris Tel: (01) 5224638
The above address is the Editorial Management office. Administration is at 5 rue Bayard, F-75393 Paris cedex 08 Tel: (01) 5625151 (ext 374)
Man Dir: Odile Gaudin
Subjects: Religion, Literature
Founded: 1946
ISBN Publisher's Prefix: 2-85017

Editions **Filipacchi***, 63 Champs Elysées, F-75008 Paris Tel: (01) 2567272 Cable Add: JazMag Telex: UEM 290294
Manager: Didier Guerin; *Editorial, Publicity, Rights & Permissions:* Anne-Marie Périer
Subjects: Modern Art, Photo-books and Photo-journalism, Sex, Jazz, Monographs of Star Personalities
Founded: 1970
ISBN Publisher's Prefix: 2-85018

Librairie **Fischbacher**, International Art Book Distribution (import-export)*, 33 rue de Seine, F-75006 Paris Tel: (01) 3268487
Man Dir, Production, Publicity, Rights and Permissions: H Earle-Fischbacher; *Editorial:* M C Galand; *Sales:* P Diani
Parent Company: Librairie Fischbacher SA
Subsidiary Companies: International Art Books Distribution; Office de Documentation Bibliographique et de Diffusion
Subjects: Art, Primitive Art, Architecture, Belles Lettres, Musicology, Philosophy, History, Education, Religion, Juveniles
Bookshop: At above address
Founded: 1850
ISBN Publisher's Prefix: 2-7179

Flammarion et Cie*, 26 rue Racine, F-75278 Paris cedex 06 Tel: (01) 3291220 Cable Add: Flamedit Telex: flamedi 204034F
Chairman: Henri Flammarion; *Man Dir:* Charles-Henri Flammarion; *Sales Manager:* Alain Flammarion; *Publicity:* Anne de Cazanove, Charles Rubinsztein, Micheline Amar; *Advertising:* Catherine Bachelez; *Rights & Permissions:* Koukla Bonnier, Catherine Cullaz
Orders to: Flammarion, 106-110 rue du Petit Leroy, BP 403, F-94152 Rungis cedex
Subsidiary Companies: Editions Arthaud SA, Editions Aubier-Montaigne SA, La Maison Rustique SA, J'ai Lu, Arts et Métiers Graphiques (qqv); Editions d'Art Albert Skira SA, Switzerland (qv)
Imprints: Garnier-Flammarion, Père Castor, Editions du Chat Perché
Subjects: General Fiction, Belles Lettres, Poetry, History, How-to, Photography, Art, Philosophy, Reference, Juveniles, Low- & High-priced Paperbacks, Economics, General & Social Science, University Textbooks, Education, Medicine
Bookshops: Librairies Flammarion — 5 in Paris, 3 in Lyons, 1 in Bordeaux, 2 in Grenoble, 1 in Marseilles, 1 in Dijon. Also 6 in Montreal, Canada
Founded: 1875
ISBN Publisher's Prefix: 2-08

Editions **Fleurus** SA*, 31 rue de Fleurus, F-75296 Paris cedex 06 Tel: (01) 5443834
Telex: 201650
Man Dir: Jacques Anfray; *Editorial:* Ms M C Maine, Yves Jolly; *Sales Dir:* Jean Li Sen Lie; *Production:* Gérard Piassale; *Publicity:* Marie Fr Daru; *Rights & Permissions:* R J Pintigny
Parent Company: Fleurus-Presse (at above address)
Subjects: Religion, Psycho-Sociological, Illustrated Children's Albums, Picture strip stories, Technical Manuals
Bookshop: Librairie du Soleil, 45 rue de Vaugirard, Paris 75006
Founded: 1944
ISBN Publisher's Prefix: 2-215

Editions **Fleuve** Noir*, 6 rue Garancière, F-75278 Paris cedex 06 Tel: 3292161
Telex: Flenoir 204870 F
Man Dir: Armand de Caro; *Editorial Dir:* Patrick Siry; *Sales Dir:* André de Caro; *Publicity Dir:* Jacques Dartus; *Rights & Permissions:* Jean-Marie Carpentier
Orders to: 35 rue Jean-Jacques Rousseau, F-94200 Ivry
Subjects: General Fiction (especially Crime and Science Fiction), Low-priced Paperbacks
Founded: 1949
Miscellaneous: Firm is a member of the Presses de La Cité group (qv)
ISBN Publisher's Prefix: 2-265

Les Editions **Foucher**, 128 rue de Rivoli, F-75001 Paris Tel: (01) 2363890
Founder-President: Ms Burgod-Foucher; *General Manager:* Bernard Foulon; *Publishing Manager:* A Tavard
Subjects: Education, Medicine, Economics, General & Social Science
Founded: 1934
ISBN Publisher's Prefix: 2-216

France-Caraïbes, an imprint of Editions Louis Soulanges 'Le Livre Ouvert' (qv)

Editions **France Empire**, 68 rue Jean-Jacques Rousseau, F-75001 Paris 1
Tel: (01) 2332519 Telex: 680126
President, Man Dir: Yvon Chotard; *Editorial:* Herve le Boterf; *Sales Dir:* Jacques Chapellon; *Production:* Pierre Pousset; *Publicity:* Christine Colinet; *Rights & Permissions:* Anne Chotard, Dominique de Saint-Ours
Orders to: Messageries du Livre, 8 rue Garancière, F-75006 Paris
Subsidiary Company: Chotard et Associés, Editeurs (qv)
Branch Off: 13 rue des Lombards, F-27000 Evreux
Subjects: Biography, History, Documentary, Religion, Reference, Novels, Aviation, Marine Interest, How-to, General Literature, Cinema, Theatre
1981: 80 titles *1982:* 85 titles *Founded:* 1945

France Expansion, 15 square de Vergennes, F-75015 Paris Tel: (01) 8281013 Telex: Pubfran 202003 F
President: Jacques Dodeman; *Man Dir:* Pascal Paradis; *Foreign Rights:* Annie Weber
Imprint: Editions Vitamine
Subjects: Bibliography, Reference, Humanities, Linguistics, Management, Teaching French as Foreign Language, Microfiche and Facsimile Editions
Founded: 1970
ISBN Publisher's Prefix: 2-229

France-Loisirs, 123 blvd de Grenelle, F-75015 Paris Tel: (01) 5673565
Publicity: A Cinar
Subjects: Juveniles, Literature, Art

Les Editions **Franciscaines** SA*, 9 rue Marie-Rose, F-75014 Paris 14e Tel: (01) 5407351
Imprint: Editions Franciscaines La Cordelle
Subjects: Saint Francis and the Franciscans (history and spirituality)
ISBN Publisher's Prefix: 2-85020

Henri **Frossard**, see L'Amitié par le Livre

La Société **G 3** (Groupement d'Intérêt Economique), Zone Industrielle des Paluds, Voie 2, Lot 10 bis, F-13400 Aubagne Tel: (42) 703975
Man Dir and other offices: Jean-Claude Brouillet
Parent Company: This is a publishing group administered by Les Editions Magnard Sàrl (qv)
Associate Companies: Société Pédagogie et Information, 91 blvd St-Germain, F-75279 Paris cedex 06; Librairie Saint Martin Jeune, 11 Grande Rue, F-23002 Guéret; Editions Magnard (qv)
Subjects: Educational and Popular Educational, School Books
1983: 1 title *Founded:* 1979
ISBN Publisher's Prefix: 2-903352

J **Gabalda** et Cie (Librairie Lecoffre) SA, 90 rue Bonaparte, F-75006 Paris Tel: (01) 3265355
Proprietor: J Gabalda
Subject: Religion, especially Biblical Studies and Archaeology
Founded: 1845
ISBN Publisher's Prefix: 2-85021

Editions **Galilée***, 9 rue Linné, F-75005 Paris Tel: (01) 3312384
Man Dir: Michel Delorme
Subjects: History, Philosophy, Art, Social Science, Economics, Belles Lettres, Poetry, How-to, University Textbooks
Founded: 1971
ISBN Publisher's Prefix: 2-7186

Editions **Gallimard***, 5 rue Sébastien-Bottin, F-75007 Paris Tel: (01) 5443919 Cable Add: Enerefene Paris 044 Telex: 204121 Gallim
Man Dir: Claude Gallimard; *Editorial:* François Erval, Pierre Marchand; *Rights & Permissions:* Ania Chevallier, Hedwige Pasquet
Subsidiary Companies: Editions Denoël (qv); Mercure de France (qv)
Subjects: General Fiction, Belles Lettres, Poetry, Biography, History, Music, Art, Philosophy, Juveniles
Bookshop: Librairie Gallimard, 15 blvd Raspail, F-75007 Paris
Founded: 1911
ISBN Publisher's Prefix: 2-07

Editions **Gamma**, 77 rue de Vaugirard, F-75006 Paris Tel: (01) 5487860 Telex: 202036
Man Dir: Marcel Vervaet
Orders to: Begedis (at above address)
Parent Company: Gedit SA Tournai, Belgium (qv)
Associate Companies: Editions Desclée et Cie, Editions du Chalet, Nouvelles Editions Mame (all in France — qqv); Desclée Editeurs, Editions Gamma (both in Belgium — qqv)
Subjects: Science & Technology, Reference, Social Science, Juveniles, School Books
1983: 80 titles *Founded:* 1963
ISBN Publisher's Prefix: 2-7130

Imprimerie Librairie **Gardet**, 16 rue du Pâquier, F-74000 Annecy Tel: (50) 454437 Telex: 310543 Gardet
Man Dir: Clément Gardet
Subjects: Arts, Crafts, Hobbies, Educational
1981: 4 titles *Founded:* 1836
ISBN Publisher's Prefix: 2-7049

Garnier-Flammarion, an imprint of Flammarion et Cie (qv)

Editions **Garnier** Frères, BP 168, F-75665 Paris cedex 14 (Located at: 19 rue des Plantes, F-75014 Paris) Tel: (01) 5409815 Telex: 270105F Txfra/Ref 665
Man Dir: Bernard Vereano
Subjects: Literary Classics, Juvenile, Strip Cartoons, Art, Travel Pictorial, History, Dictionaries
Founded: 1833

Société **Gauthier-Villars***, 70 rue de Saint-Mandé, F-93100 Montreuil
Parent Company: Editions Bordas (qv)

Les Editions **Gautier-Languereau** Sàrl, 18 rue Jacob, F-75006 Paris 6 Tel: (01) 3250751 Cable Add: Editlangue Telex: 641155 Elita G31
Man Dir & Sales: Bernard Moreau
Subjects: General Fiction, How-to, Juveniles
Founded: 1885
ISBN Publisher's Prefix: 2-217

Editions M Th **Genin**, see LITEC

Librairie Orientaliste Paul **Geuthner** SA*, 12 rue Vavin, F-75006 Paris Tel: (01) 6347130 Cable Add: Liborient Paris
Man Dirs: Marie Schiffer, Marc Seidl-Geuthner
Subjects: Archaeology, Assyriology, Islam, Near & Far East, General Orientalia, Linguistics, Numismatics, Religion
1981: 6 titles *Founded:* 1902
ISBN Publisher's Prefix: 2-7053

Gibert Jeune SNC, 27 quai St-Michel, F-75005 Paris Tel: (01) 3545732
Subject: Education
ISBN Publisher's Prefix: 2-900002

Editions De **Gigord***, 15 rue Cassette, F-75006 Paris Tel: (01) 5485521
Subjects: General Fiction, Belles Lettres, Education, Religion, University & Secondary Textbooks
Founded: 1830
ISBN Publisher's Prefix: 2-7054

Editions J **Glenat** SA, 6 rue Lieutenant Chanaron, BP 285, F-38009 Grenoble cedex Tel: (076) 873758 Telex: 320030 F
President/Man Dir: Jacques Glénat; *Editorial:* Henri Filippini; *Sales:* Yves Lafont; *Production:* Hubert Odier; *Publicity:* Eric Barrachet; *Rights & Permissions:* Marie Thérèse Priser
Branch Off: 5 rue Cochin, F-75005 Paris
Subsidiary Company: Glénat-Images, 15 ter route d'Avignon, F-84300 Cavaillon
Subjects: Humour, Adventure, Thrillers, Science Fiction, Erotica, Children's (all in strip cartoon form); Travel, Sport
1981: 70 titles *Founded:* 1974
ISBN Publisher's Prefix: 2-27234

Société Nouvelle des Editions **Gonthier** Sàrl, an imprint of Editions Denoël Sàrl (qv)

Jacques **Grancher**, Editeur, 98 rue de Vaugirard, F-75006 Paris Tel: 2226480 Cable Add: Sce de Vente/Librairies 5480317, 14 rue Littre, F-75006 Paris
Man Dir: Jacques Grancher
Subjects: Military Series (Uniforms, Arms), Memoirs (Art World), Health, Diet, Cookery Series
Founded: 1952
ISBN Publisher's Prefix: 2-7146

Société des Editions **Grasset et Fasquelle**, 61 rue des Saints-Pères, F-75006 Paris Tel: (01) 5443814
Chairman: Jean-Claude Fasquelle; *Man Dirs:* Yves Berger, Bernard-Henri Lévy; *Sales:* Gérard Porra; *Publicity and Advertising:* Monique Mayaud; *Production:* Jean Fournier; *Administrative Dir:* Philippe Méry; *Rights and Permissions:* Marie-Hélène d'Ovidio; *Public Relations:* Claude Dalla-Torre, Claudine Lemaire
Subjects: General Fiction and Non-fiction, Belles Lettres, Philosophy, Juveniles
Founded: 1908
ISBN Publisher's Prefix: 2-246

Jean **Grassin** Editeur, 50 rue Rodier, F-75009 Paris Tel: (01) 5269040
Man Dir: Jean Grassin
Orders to: BP 75, F-56340 Carnac-Plage
Subjects: Literature, Poetry, History, Bibliophily
Book Club: Poètes Présents
Bookshop (and Gallery): Pl de Port-en-Dro, ave de l'Atlantique, F-56340 Carnac-Plage Tel: (97) 529363
1983: approx 10 titles *Founded:* 1957
ISBN Publisher's Prefix: 2-7055

Groupe Expansion, 67 ave de Wagram, BP 570, F-75017 Paris cedex 17 Tel: (01) 7631211 Telex: 650242 manxpan
President and Man Dir: Jean-Louis Servan-Schreiber; *General Manager:* Hubert Zieseniss; *Publicity:* Jacques Louvet; *International Advertising Dir:* Jacques Louvet
Subjects: Economics, Politics, Social Sciences, Education, Literature, Law, Architecture, Scientific and Technical

Librairie **Grund**, 60 rue Mazarine, F-75006 Paris 6 Tel: (01) 3298740 Cable Add: Gründ Paris Telex: 270105 F Txfra/ref 888
President: Michel Gründ; *Man Dir:* Alain Gründ; *Assistant Manager:* Marie Troubnikoff; *Rights & Permissions, Advertising:* P A Touttain
Associate Company: Editions Alpina (qv)
Subjects: Nature, Animals, Travel, Arts, How-to, Juvenile, 10-vol Benezit Biographical Dictionary of International Artists, Sculptors and Designers; Gift Books
Founded: 1880
ISBN Publisher's Prefix: 2-7000

Librairie **Guénégaud** Sàrl, 10 rue de l'Odéon, F-75006 Paris Tel: 3260791
Man Dir: Mr Huret
Subjects: History, Topography (France)
1982: 70 titles *Founded:* 1947
ISBN Publisher's Prefix: 2-85023

Editions d'Art Albert **Guillot***, 4 rue de Sèze, F-69006 Lyon Tel: (078) 521026
Subject: Art
ISBN Publisher's Prefix: 2-85096

Librairie **Hachette***, 79 blvd St-Germain, F-75006 Paris Tel: (01) 3291224 Cable Add: Hachechi Paris 25 Telex: Hacsieg Paris 204434
Branch Off: Hachette Inc, 2 Park Ave, New York, NY 10016
Subsidiary Companies: Hachette/Enseignment (qv); Hachette Guides Bleus (qv); Hachette-Jeunesse (qv); Hachette Littérature (qv); Hachette Pratique (qv); Hachette Réalités (qv); Hachette-Sciences Humaines; Editions du Chêne (qv); Editions Stock (qv); Edition No 1 (qv)
Subjects: General Fiction, Non-fiction, History, How-to, Philosophy, Art, Travel, Reference, Education, Juveniles, Science, Paperbacks, Textbooks, Architecture, Bibliography, Engineering, Music, Politics, Social Science, Games, Sport, Languages, Economics
Bookshops: Bookshops throughout the world
Founded: 1826
ISBN Publisher's Prefix: 2-01

Hachette/Enseignement (Hachette Educational)*, 79 blvd St-Germain, F-75288 Paris cedex 6 Tel: 3291224 Cable Add:

Hacheci-Paris 25 Telex: 204145 Haclass
Dirs: Marc Moingeon, Jacques Berthelot, Mireille Maurin
Parent Company: Librairie Hachette (qv)
Subjects: Pedagogic and para-pedagogic books on every subject and for every level from Nursery School to University

Hachette Guides Bleus*, 284 blvd St-Germain, F-75007 Paris Tel: (01) 5556001
Publisher: Gérald Gassiot-Talabot; *Sales:* Patrick Panthou
Parent Company: Librairie Hachette (qv)
Subjects: Guides, Art

Hachette International*, 254 blvd St-Germain, F-75340 Paris cedex 07 Tel: (01) 3201322 Telex: Hacoliv 203822 F
Subjects: General Fiction, Art Books, Classics, Juveniles, History, Educational Materials

Hachette-Jeunesse, 79 blvd St-Germain, BP 1506, F-75006 Paris Tel: 3291224 Cable Add: Hacheci-Paris 25 Telex: Hacsieg-Paris 204434
Executive: Jean-Claude Dubost; *Rights & Permissions:* Françoise Laurent
Parent Company: Librairie Hachette (qv)
Subjects: Illustrated Children's Books, Reference and educational series, How-to, Novels for the Young

Hachette-Littérature Générale*, 6 ave Pierre 1er de Serbie, F-75116 Paris Tel: 7236163
Parent Company: Librairie Hachette (qv)
Subjects: Reference Works, Science, Historical, Essays, Biographical, Documentation, Fine Editions, Practical Works, Fiction
Founded: 1970

Hachette Pratique*, 4 rue de Gallière, F-75116 Paris Tel: (01) 7236138
Parent Company: Librairie Hachette (qv)
Subjects: How-to, Games, Sport, Cookery, Illustrated Books, Handicraft Manuals

Hachette-Réalités*, 284 blvd St-Germain, F-75007 Paris Tel: (01) 5556001 Telex: 26624 Hachepr-Paris
Publisher: Gérald Gassiot-Talabot
Parent Company: Librairie Hachette (qv)
Subjects: Art, History, Reference
Founded: 1956

Le **Hameau**, Editeur+, 15 rue Servandoni, F-75005 Paris Tel: (01) 3290550
Man Dir, Rights & Permissions: Paule Truchaud; *Sales:* C Navelet; *Production:* C Noualhier; *Publicity:* A R L, 17 rue St-Séverin, F-75006 Paris
Orders to: Le Hameau Diffusion (at above address)
Subjects: Psychology, Psychoanalysis, Social Science, Medicine, Parapsychology, Fiction, Essays, Poetry
Bookshop: At above address
Founded: 1973
ISBN Publisher's Prefix: 2-7203

Harwood Academic Publishers*, 58 rue Lhomond, F-75005 Paris Tel: (01) 3362404 Telex: 201307 f
Parent Company: Harwood Academic Publishers GmbH, Switzerland (qv)

Librairie **Hatier** SA, 8 rue d'Assas, F-75006 Paris Tel: (01) 5443838 Cable Add: Libhatier Paris Telex: 202732 F
Man Dir: Michel Foulon; *Sales Dirs:* André Cazaux, Alain Jauson; *Rights & Permissions:* Marie-Blanche D'Ussel
Imprint: Editions de l'Amitié (qv)
Subjects: Children's Fiction, Nature, Tour Guides, Chess, Sport, Educational, Language Teaching, Illustrated books, Computer Software
Bookshop: 59 blvd Raspail, F-75006 Paris

Founded: 1880
ISBN Publisher's Prefix: 2-218

Pierre **Hautot** SA*, 36 rue du Bac, F-75007 Paris Tel: (01) 2611015
Subject: Art
Founded: 1952

Fernand **Hazan** Editeur SA, 35-37 rue de Seine, F-75006 Paris Tel: (01) 3546872
Chairman: Blanche Hazan; *Man Dir:* Eric Hazan
Subjects: Art, Reference, Juveniles, Paperbacks
Founded: 1945
Bookshop: Editions Fernand Hazan (at above address)

Hermann (Editeurs des Sciences et des Arts) SA, 293 rue Lecourbe, F-75015 Paris Tel: (01) 5574540 Cable Add: Piby Paris Telex: Hermann Paris 200595
Man Dir: Pierre Berès
Subjects: Science, Art, Medical and Technical, Textbooks, Reference, Paperbacks
Bookshop: 6 rue de la Sorbonne, F-75005, Paris
Founded: 1870
ISBN Publisher's Prefix: 2-7056

Editions de l'**Herne**, 41 rue de Verneuil, F-75007 Paris Tel: (01) 2612506
Chairman, Man Dir, Rights & Permissions: Constantin Tacou; *Editorial, Press Agent:* Miss Laurence Mauriac; *Sales:* Sodis
Subjects: Belles Lettres, Poetry, Philosophy, Social Science, Politics, Art, Novels, Strategy, Monograph Series (Cahiers) on major literary figures/movements
Founded: 1964
ISBN Publisher's Prefix: 2-85197

Editions d'Art Les **Heures Claires** SA*, 19 rue Bonaparte, F-75006 Paris Tel: (01) 3293750
Owner: Jean Estrade
Subject: Art
Founded: 1945
ISBN Publisher's Prefix: 2-85026

Editions d'**Histoire Sociale** (EDHIS), 23 rue de Valois, F-75001 Paris Tel: (01) 2614778
Man Dir: Léon Centner
Subjects: Social History, Revolutions in France, Historical Documents
Bookshops: 23 rue de Valois, Paris; 144 Galerie de Valois, Paris 1er
1983: 152 titles *Founded:* 1967

Editions **Hommes et Techniques**+, Tour Chenonceaux, 204 R-P du Pont de Sèvres, F-92516 Boulogne-Billancourt cedex Tel: 6206021 Telex: 201536 idecgos
Man Dir: Martine Basset
Subjects: Business Management, Organizational Development
1981: 17 titles *1982:* 10 titles *Founded:* 1945
ISBN Publisher's Prefix: 2-7057

Pierre **Horay** Editeur*, 22 bis passage Dauphine, F-75006 Paris Tel: (01) 3545390
Man Dir: Sophie Horay; *Editorial:* Jean-Jacques Lévêque; *Production:* Jean Paoli; *Rights & Permissions:* Colette Haro
Orders to: Editions Garnier, 19 rue des Plantes, F-75014 Paris
Subjects: General Fiction, Belles Lettres, Poetry, Biography, History, How-to, Music, Art, Juveniles, High-priced Paperbacks
1981: 16 titles *Founded:* 1946
ISBN Publisher's Prefix: 2-7058

Les **Humanoïdes** Associés, see SENHA

I G N (Institut Géographique National), 107 rue La Boëtie, F-75008 Paris Tel: 2258790 Telex: Ign lb 660320 F
Man Dir: J A Winghart; *Editorial:* M Osché; *Sales:* D Wintrebert; *Production:* L Massiani; *Publicity:* J Monteil; *Rights &*

Permissions: Fr Chemouilli
Subject: Maps
Bookshop: At above address
1981: 10 titles *Founded:* 1940

Editions de l'**Illustration**, 13 rue St-Georges, F-75009 Paris 9 Tel: (01) 2806118
Man Dir: Roger Allegret
Imprint: Baschet et Cie, Editeurs
Subjects: History, Art, How-to, Encyclopaedias, Travel, Science, Geography
Founded: 1843
ISBN Publisher's Prefix: 2-7059

Institut Géographique National, see IGN

InterEditions Paris, 87 ave du Maine, F-75014 Tel: 3277450 Telex: 210311 Publi 147
Man Dir: Geoffrey M Staines; *Production, Publicity:* Monika Neumann; *Rights & Permissions:* Véronique Buret
Orders to: Bordas SA, 11 rue Gossin, F-92543 Montrouge cedex
Parent Company: Inter-European Editions, Amsterdam, Netherlands
Subjects: Biology, Chemistry, Physics, Mathematics, Computer Science, Business and Professional Subjects, Psychology
1981: 8 titles *1982:* 10 titles *Founded:* 1976
ISBN Publisher's Prefix: 2-7296

CNRS Laboratoire **Intergéo**, 191 rue Saint-Jacques, F-75005 Paris Tel: 6337431
Man Dir: Michel Drain
Parent Company: Centre National de la Recherche Scientifique (CNRS)
Subjects: Geography, Documentation, Periodicals
1981: 3 titles *1982:* 1 title *Founded:* 1947
ISBN Publisher's Prefix: 2-901560

International Book Promotion, 6 ave Pierre 1er de Serbie, F-75116 Paris
Man Dir: Gérald Gauthier; *Rights & Permissions:* Colette Veron
Subjects: Fiction, Non-fiction, Medicine, Social Sciences, Practical

Editions **J'ai Lu***, 31 rue de Tournon, F-75006 Paris Tel: (01) 3267759 Telex: Jailu 202765
Parent Company: Flammarion et Cie (qv)
Subjects: General Fiction, Belles Lettres, Low-priced Paperbacks
Founded: 1958

Editions **Jeune Afrique***, 3 rue Roquépine, F-75008 Paris Tel: (01) 2656930/2656931 Cable Add: Edijia Paris Telex: Edijia 641654F
President: Bechir Ben Yahmed; *General Manager, Foreign Rights:* Danielle Ben Yahmed; *Literary Manager:* Michel Weber; *Commercial Manager:* R Chabrier ; *Press/Publicity:* C Eyquem
Subjects: History, Biography, Geography and Travel, Politics, Reference Works, Natural Sciences, Fine Arts, Periodicals
Founded: 1968
ISBN Publisher's Prefix: 2-85258

Journal des Notaires et des Avocats SA*, 6 rue de Mézières, F-75006 Paris Tel: (01) 5481210
Subject: Law
ISBN Publisher's Prefix: 2-85028

Editions René **Julliard***, 8 rue Garancière, F-75008 Paris Tel: (01) 6341280 Cable Add: Edijulliard Paris 110
Man Dir: Bernard de Fallois; *Rights & Permissions:* Josiane Bontron
Subjects: General Fiction, Belles Lettres, History, Political Science, Biography
Founded: 1931
Miscellaneous: Firm is a member of the Presses de la Cité group (qv)
ISBN Publisher's Prefix: 2-260

Editions **Jupiter** Sàrl, 21-23 rue du Mont-Thabor, F-75001 Paris Tel: (01) 2607465/2607778
Man Dir: Pierre Legrand
Subjects: Law, Politics, Encyclopaedias
ISBN Publisher's Prefix: 2-7060

Editions **Juridiques et Techniques**, see Lamy SA

Jurif (Société d'Etudes Juridiques Internationales et Fiscales), see Cahiers Fiscaux Européens Sàrl

Editions **Klincksieck**, 11 rue de Lille, F-75007 Paris Tel: (01) 2603825
Man Dir: Andrée Laurent-Klincksieck; *Publicity, Rights & Permissions:* Sylvette Gassan
Subjects: Social Sciences, Philology, Linguistics, Archaeology, History, Belles Lettres, Aesthetics, Reference, General & Social Science
Founded: 1842
ISBN Publisher's Prefixes: 2-252, 2-86563

L I C E T, see Librairie Commerciale et Technique Sàrl

L I T E C, Libraries Techniques SA, 27 pl Dauphine, F-75001 Paris Tel: (01) 3266090/3290771
Management and Production offices are at 6 rue Victor-Cousin, F-75005 Paris Tel: (01) 6332237
Dir: Mrs Argenson
Parent Company: Editions Techniques, 18 rue Séguier, F-75006 Paris
Branch Off: 26 rue Soufflot, F-75005 Paris
Subjects: Politics, Law, Commerce
1981: 60 titles *1982:* 76 titles
Miscellaneous: Firm incorporates Editions M Th Genin
ISBN Publisher's Prefix: 2-7111

L T Editions, see J Lanore

Editions Robert **Laffont**, 6 pl St-Sulpice, F-75279 Paris cedex 06 Tel: (01) 3291233 Cable Add: Edilaf Paris 110 Telex: 270607
Man Dir: Robert Laffont; *Rights & Permissions:* Olga Begin, Béatrix Vernet
Associate Company: Les Editions Seghers (qv)
Subjects: General Fiction and Non-fiction, especially History, Documentary, Philosophy, Religion, Art, Music, Biography, Juveniles, Medicine, General & Social Science, Psychology, High-priced Paperbacks, Textbooks, Translations
Founded: 1941
ISBN Publisher's Prefix: 2-221

Librairie Léonce **Laget***, 75 rue de Rennes, F-75006 Paris Tel: (01) 5489018 Cable Add: Liblaget Paris 110
Man Dir: Léonce Laget
Subjects: Art, History, Trades and Crafts
Founded: 1955
ISBN Publisher's Prefix: 2-85204

Editions **Lahumière**, 88 blvd de Courcelles, F-75017 Paris Tel: (01) 7630395/6224367
Publisher: Anne Margarete Lahumière
Subject: Art

Editions **Lamarre-Poinat** SA, 47 rue Saint André-des-Arts, F-75006 Paris Tel: (01) 3265838
Publicity: Marie-Claude Chouzy
Subject: Medicine
ISBN Publisher's Prefix: 2-85030

Lamy SA, Editions Juridiques et Techniques, 155 rue Legendre, F-75850 Paris cedex 17 Tel: (01) 6272890 Telex: 650790
President: Gérard Lamy; *Sales:* Mr Chareton, Mr Desmouceaux; *Publicity:* Mr Pagnard
Subjects: Law (Social, Fiscal, Company, Commercial, Transport and Transport Methods)
Founded: 1949

Librairie Fernand **Lanore** Sàrl*, 1 rue Palatine, F-75006 Paris Tel: (01) 3256661
Dir: François Sorlot
Subjects: Belles Lettres, History, Philosophy, Secondary Textbooks, Education, Religion, Languages, Touring, Mountaineering
Founded: 1920

LT Editions-J **Lanore**-H Laurens+, 131 rue P V Couturier, F-92240 Malakoff Tel: 6542707 Telex: Ianata 202 330
Associate Companies: Librairie-Editions J Lanore, 12 rue Oudinot, F-75007 Paris (Tel: 7340288); Librairie LT, 4 rue de Tournon, F-75006 Paris (Tel: 3294350)
Subjects: Pedagogy and Teaching Texts on Cookery and Catering, Dressmaking, Home Economy, Law, Technology, Careers, Art, Tourism, Architecture
1981: 100 titles

Librairie **Larousse**, 17 rue du Montparnasse, F-75298 Paris cedex 06 Tel: (01) 5443817 Cable Add: Liblarous 43 Paris Telex: 250828
Man Dirs: Georges Lucas, Claude Moreau, Claude Labouret; *Foreign Trade Dir:* Francis Trébinjac; *Rights & Permissions:* J L Chifflet, Agence SEU, 2 rue de Cicé, F-75006 Paris Tel: (01) 5481994 Telex: 202594
Subsidiary & Affiliated Companies: Ediciones Larousse Argentina SA, Valentin Gomez 3530, Buenos Aires 1191, Argentina; Larousse-Belgique, 25-27 rue Godefroid Kurth, B-1140 Brussels, Belgium; Editora Larousse do Brasil, Av Almte Barrosa, 63s/2609, Rio de Janeiro, Brazil; Editions Françaises Inc, 1411 rue Ampère, Boucherville, QC J4B 5B0, Canada; Ediciones Larousse SA, Marsella 53, Col Juarez, Delegacion cuautemoc, 06600 Mexico City, Mexico; Larousse (Suisse) SA, Switzerland (qv); Ediciones Larousse SA, Marsella 53, Esq Nápoles, Mexico City 6, Mexico; Larousse (Suisse) SA, Switzerland (qv); Larousse & Co Inc, 572 Fifth Ave, New York, NY, USA
Subjects: Dictionaries, Encyclopaedias, Reference, Textbooks, Juveniles, Paperbacks, Technical, General & Social Science, Linguistics
Founded: 1852
ISBN Publisher's Prefix: 2-03

Editions Jean-Claude **Lattès**, 17 rue Jacob, F-75006 Paris Tel: (01) 6340310 Telex: 270461 emom
Man Dir: Nicole Lattès; *Rights & Permissions:* Ursula Veit
Subjects: General Fiction & Non-fiction, Biography, Documents, Low-priced Paperbacks, Music
Founded: 1968

Editions Henri **Laurens** Successeurs Sàrl, see Editions J Lanore

Editions Charles-**Lavauzelle** SA, see Charles

Editions Guy **Le Prat**, 5 rue des Grands-Augustins, F-75006 Paris Tel: (01) 3265782
Man Dir: Guy Le Prat
Subjects: Reference, Leisure, Sports, Oriental and Occult, Natural Medicine, Environment, Ecology, Juvenile, Management, Investment, Glues/Adhesives, Fine Arts, Limited Editions; General Literature, Reprints, Paperbacks
Founded: 1825
Miscellaneous: Formerly Editions Delarue
ISBN Publisher's Prefix: 2-85205

Editions **Lechevalier** Sàrl*, 19 rue Augereau, F-75007 Paris Tel: (01) 5554369/5555510
Man Dir: Jacques Lechevalier
Subjects: Natural Sciences, Natural History, Biology, Entomology, Mycology, Ornithology, Silviculture, Botany, Zoology, Periodicals
Founded: 1875
ISBN Publisher's Prefix: 2-7205

Librairie **Lecoffre**, see J Gabalda et Cie

Francis **Lefebvre***, 5 rue Jacques Bingen, F-75854 Paris cedex 17 Tel: 7531260
Dir: Francis Lefebvre
Subjects: Commercial Law, Fiscal Law
Bookshop: At above address
ISBN Publisher's Prefix: 2-85115

Editions Dominique **Leroy**+, 68-70 rue du Cherche-Midi, F-75006 Paris Tel: (01) 5490248 Telex: Edl 202987 F
Man Dir: Dominique Leroy
Subjects: Adult Strip Cartoons, Erotic Fiction, Paperbacks
Imprints: Scarabée d'Or, Septième Rayon, Vertige
Bookshop: At above address
1981: 30 titles *Founded:* 1970
ISBN Publisher's Prefix: 2-86688

Lethielleux, an imprint of Dessain et Tolray (qv)

Société Nouvelle des Editions **Letouzey** et Ané Sàrl*, 87 blvd Raspail, F-75006 Paris Tel: (01) 5488014
Dir: J Letouzey
Subjects: Dictionaries, Religion, History
Founded: 1885
ISBN Publisher's Prefix: 2-7063

Lettres Modernes Minard, see Minard

Librairie Commerciale et Technique (Licet) Sàrl, 110 rue de Rivoli, F-75001 Paris Tel: (01) 2332261
Man Dir: Gérard Lambret; *All other offices:* J P Le Gall
Subjects: Accountancy, Typewriting, Business Techniques, Economics, Law, English, Statistics, Data Processing
Founded: 1963
ISBN Publisher's Prefix: 2-85232

Librairie **Générale de Droit** et de Jurisprudence, see Droit et Jurisprudence

Librairie **Générale** Française SA*, 14 rue de l'Ancienne-Comédie, F-75006 Paris Tel: (01) 3265393
The above is the Head Office. Editorial and Production are run from Le Livre de Poche (qv)

Librairies Techniques SA, see LITEC

Licet, see Librairie Commerciale et Technique

Editions **Lidis** SA*, 37 rue du Four, F-75006 Paris Tel: (01) 5490950 Cable Add: Elidis Paris Telex: Elidis 270900 F
Man Dir, Rights & Permissions: Noël Schumann; *Editorial, Production:* Claire de la Pradelle; *Sales:* J Souci; *Publicity:* Laurence Santantonios
Subsidiary Company: La Diffusion (at above address)
Subjects: Encyclopaedias, Art
1981: 2 titles *Founded:* 1955
ISBN Publisher's Prefix: 2-85032

Editions **Ligel***, 77 rue de Vaugirard, F-75006 Paris Tel: (01) 5487860
Man Dir: Henri Creff; *Deputy Director:* Jules Desmyetter
Subject: School Textbooks
Bookshop: At above address
Founded: 1909
ISBN Publisher's Prefix: 2-7064

Editions Michel de **Lile** et Philippe Auzou*, 1 rue du Dahomey, F-75014 Paris Tel: (01) 5421877 Telex: Lile-Auzou Sofadif 220686 F
Man Dir: Michel de Lile
Subjects: Art Editions, Facsimile

Reproductions
Founded: 1978

Office Central de **Lisieux** SA, see under Office Central

Editions **Lito**, 41 rue de Verdun, F-94500 Champigny-sur-Marne Tel: 8821538 Telex: Edlit 680284
Man Dir, Rights & Permissions: Lennart Rosdahl; *Editorial, Publicity:* Janine Ancelet
Parent Company: Lito Interco (at above address)
Subsidiary Companies: Jesco, 35 rue H Barbusse, F-91380 Chilly Mazarin, France; Lito Editrice, Via Passo di Brizio 8, I-20148 Milan, Italy
Subjects: Children's Books, Puzzles, Teaching Aids, Paperbacks
Founded: 1958
ISBN Publisher's Prefix: 2-244

Le **Livre de Paris** Hachette*, 3-5 ave de Garlande, F-92221 Bagneux Tel: (01) 6571140 Telex: Livpari 250026
Subjects: Dictionaries, Encyclopaedias, Art, How-to, Juveniles
ISBN Publisher's Prefix: 2-245

Le **Livre de Poche***, 79 blvd St-Germain, F-75006 Paris Tel: (01) 3291224
Man Dir, Rights & Permissions: G Deleau
Parent Company: Librairie Générale Française (qv)
Subjects: Pocket-size paperbacks only: especially Fiction, Drama, Poetry, Classics (all both French and translated Foreign); also History, Biography, Current Affairs, Reference, Nature, Puzzles
Founded: 1953

Lumiere Biblique, an imprint of Les Editions de la Source Sàrl (qv)

Editions **M D I** (La Maison des Instituteurs), Parc des 10 Arpents, Dept 113, PO Box 69, F-78630 Orgeval Tel: 9756381 Telex: MDI Edit 698094F
Man Dir: Alexandre Schajer; *Export Dir:* Philippe Notté
Subjects: Juveniles, History, Geography, General Science, Secondary and Primary Textbooks, Educational Materials, Wall Maps, Audiovisual
Founded: 1954
ISBN Publisher's Prefix: 2-223

M E D S I (Médecine et Sciences Internationales), 6 ave Daniel Lesueur, F-75007 Paris Tel: (01) 2732990 Telex: 205795
Man Dir: Marie-Hélène Rambaux; *Editorial:* Mariette Guéna; *Production:* Jean-Jacques Weber; *Publicity:* Liliane Le Gargasson
Subjects: Medical and Scientific
1981: 20 titles *1982:* 18 titles *Founded:* 1979
ISBN Publisher's Prefix: 2-86439

McGraw-Hill Inc*, 28 rue Beaunier, F-75014 Paris Tel: (01) 5409438 Telex: 250304
Man Dir and other offices: Lidy Arslan
Parent Company: McGraw-Hill International, 1221 Ave of the Americas, New York, NY 10020, USA
Associate Companies: See McGraw-Hill, UK
Subjects: General Science, Technology, Economics, Finance, Humanities, Current Affairs
1981: 14 titles *Founded:* 1967
ISBN Publisher's Prefix: 2-7042

Maeght Editeur*, 13 rue de Téhéran, F-75008 Paris Tel: (01) 5631319 Cable Add: Galmaeght Paris 037 Telex: 28660
Dir: Jean Frémon; *Sales Manager:* François Bruller
Subject: Art
ISBN Publisher's Prefix: 2-85087

Les Editions **Magnard** Sàrl*, 122 blvd St-Germain, F-75279 Paris cedex 06 Tel: (01) 3296420
Man Dir, Sales Dir: Louis Magnard; *Literary Dir:* Thérèse Roche-Magnard; *Export Manager:* Jean-Claude Brouillet, Rés Les Crêtes, Bat Géranium, Ave Marcel-Camusso, F-13600 La Ciotat
Subsidiary Company: La Société G3 (qv)
Subjects: Juveniles, University, Secondary & Primary Textbooks, Educational Materials, Pedagogy, Holiday Exercise books, International Series of Works in Basic French
Bookshop: Librairie de France (at above Paris address)
1981: over 1,200 titles *Founded:* 1934
ISBN Publisher's Prefix: 2-210

La **Maison des Instituteurs**, see M D I

La **Maison du Dictionnaire**, 95 bis rue Legendre, F-75017 Paris Tel: 2294836 Telex: 270105 ref 355 txfra b rungi
Man Dirs: Michel Feutry
Subjects: Technical, Specialized and General Dictionaries in many languages
Founded: 1976
ISBN Publisher's Prefix: 2-85608

La **Maison** Rustique SA*, Librairie Agricole et Horticole, 26 rue Jacob, F-75006 Paris 6 Tel: (01) 3256700
Parent Company: Flammarion et Cie (qv)
Subjects: Natural Science, Horticulture, Agriculture, Forestry
Founded: 1836
ISBN Publisher's Prefix: 2-7066

Adrien **Maisonneuve-Editions d'Amérique** et d'Orient*, 11 rue St-Sulpice, F-75006 Paris Tel: (01) 3268635
Man Dir: Jean Maisonneuve
Subjects: Orientalia (History, Philosophy, Religion, Art, Social Science, Economics)
Founded: 1926
ISBN Publisher's Prefix: 2-7200

Editions G P **Maisonneuve et Larose***, 15 rue Victor-Cousin, F-75005 Paris Tel: (02) 3543270
Man Dir: J-P Pinardon
Subjects: Scholarly, Social Science, Agriculture, Oriental & African Studies, Folklore
Founded: 1961
Miscellaneous: Firms merged in 1961. Founded 1853 and 1860, respectively
ISBN Publisher's Prefix: 2-7068

Maisonneuve SA, Editeur, 386 route de Verdun, BP 39, F-57160 Moulins les Metz Tel: 7601180
Man Dir: André-G Maisonneuve
Subjects: Principally Acupuncture and Auriculotherapy, also French and European Pharmacopoeia, Homoeopathy, Therapeutics
Founded: 1959
ISBN Publisher's Prefix: 2-7160

Librairie **Maloine**, 27 rue de l'École-de-Médecine, F-75006 Paris Tel: (01) 3256045 Telex: 203215F
President, Man Dir, Rights & Permissions: Antonin Philippart; *Editorial:* Dr A Blacque Belair; *Sales:* Dominique Frison-Roche, Nathalie Moury; *Production:* Jean Philippart; *Publicity & Advertising:* François Guérin
Subjects: Medicine, Veterinary, Reference
1981: 137 titles *1982:* 125 titles *Founded:* 1881
ISBN Publisher's Prefix: 2-224

Nouvelles Editions **Mame**, 77 rue de Vaugirard, F-75006 Paris Tel: 5487860 Telex: 202036 F
Man Dir: Marcel Vervaet; *Editorial, Production:* Suzel Vervaet

Orders to: Begedis (at above address)
Parent Company: Gedit SA, Tournai, Belgium (qv)
Associate Companies: Desclée, Editeurs; Editions Gamma (both in Belgium, qqv); Editions Gamma (qv); Editions Desclée et Cie (qv)
Subjects: The Bible, Religious Literature, Catechism, Liturgy, Juveniles
1983: 40 titles
ISBN Publisher's Prefix: 2-7289

Editions **Maritimes et d'Outre-Mer** SA, see Editions

François **Maspero** Editeur, now La Découverte/Maspero (qv)

Le **Masque**, an imprint of Librairie des Champs-Elysées SA (qv)

Editions Charles **Massin** et Cie*, 2 rue de l'Echelle, F-75039 Paris cedex 01 Tel: (01) 2603005 Telex: 240918 Trace
Subjects: Architecture, Interior Decoration, Arts
Founded: 1910
ISBN Publisher's Prefix: 2-7072

Masson Editeur, 120 blvd St-Germain, F-75280 Paris cedex 06 Tel: (01) 6342160 Cable Add: Gemas Paris 025 Telex: Massoned 260946
Dir: Dr Jérôme Talamon; *Man Dirs:* P Lahaye, D de Costigliole; *Sales Dir:* S Kebabtchieff; *Rights & Permissions:* Françoise Han
Orders to: CCLS, 69 rue Barrault, F-75013 Paris
Associate Companies: Masson SA, Spain (qv); Masson Publishing USA Inc, 133 West 58th St, New York, NY 10022, USA; Editora Masson do Brasil, Ltda, Brazil (qv); Masson Editores, Mexico (qv); Masson Italia Editori, via Giovanni Pascoli 55, 20133 Milan, Italy
Subjects: Medicine, Scientific, Technical, Social Science, Law, Economics
Founded: 1804
ISBN Publisher's Prefix: 2-225

Editions **Mayer**, 224 ave du Maine, F-75014 Paris Tel: 5407162
Man Dir: F van Wilder
Subsidiary Company: Editions Publisol, 235 East 85th St, (PO Box 39), New York, NY 10028, USA
Subjects: The Arts
Founded: 1962

Editions **Mazarine**, 8 rue de Nesle, F-75006 Paris Tel: (01) 3295640
President, Man Dir: J-E Cohen-Seat; *Editorial, Rights & Permissions:* Ronald Blunden
Subjects: General Literature, History, Current Affairs, Art, Science Reports
1981: 27 titles *Founded:* 1979
ISBN Publisher's Prefix: 2-86374

Editions d'Art Lucien **Mazenod***, 33 rue de Naples, F-75008 Paris Tel: (01) 5222366 Cable Add: Mazeditio Telex: 270105 f txfra
Man Dir: Lucien Mazenod
Subjects: History, Art, Architecture
ISBN Publisher's Prefix: 2-85088

Médecines et Sciences Internationales, see MEDSI

Editions **Mengès***, 13 Passage Landrieu, F-75007 Paris Tel: 5552667
Man Dirs: Bernard Blazin, Jean Paul Mengès; *Editorial, Production:* J P Mengès; *Sales, Publicity:* B Blazin; *Rights & Permissions:* M P Paillard
Subjects: Humour, Documentaries, Historical Novels, How-to, Illustrated Books
Founded: 1975
ISBN Publisher's Prefix: 2-85620

Mercure de France SA, 26 rue de Condé, F-75006 Paris Tel: (01) 3292113
Man Dir: Simone Gallimard; *Production Dir:* Gilbert Minazzoli; *Rights & Permissions:* Nicole Boyer
Parent Company: Editions Gallimard (qv)
Associate Company: Editions Denoël Sàrl (qv)
Subjects: General Fiction, Belles Lettres, Poetry, History, Philosophy, Social Science, Psychology
Founded: 1891
ISBN Publisher's Prefix: 2-7152

Messageries Centrales du Livre*, 8 rue Garancière, F-75005 Paris
Subjects: Cartoon strips, Juveniles
Miscellaneous: Firm is a member of the Presses de la Cité group (qv)

Messidor, an imprint of Les Editions Sociales-Messidor (qv)

Sylvie **Messinger**, Editrice+, 31 rue de l'Abbé Grégoire, F-75006 Paris Tel: (01) 2227667
Man Dir and other Offices: Sylvie Messinger
Orders to: Inter Forum, 13 rue de la Glacière, F-75624 Paris cedex 13
Subjects: General Literature
1983: 27 titles *Founded:* 1981
ISBN Publisher's Prefix: 2-86583

Editions Albin **Michel**, see under Albin

Michelin et Cie (Services de Tourisme)*, 46 ave de Breteuil, F-75341 Paris cedex 07
Tel: (01) 5392500
Associate Company: Michelin Tyre Company Ltd, UK (qv)
Subjects: Travel and Tourist Guides in several languages, Maps

Lettres Modernes **Minard***, 73 rue du Cardinal Lemoine, F-75005 Paris Tel: (01) 3544609
Man Dir, Production: J Michel Minard; *Sales:* Librairie Minard Diffusion; *Rights & Permissions:* Danièle Morgat
Associate Company: Librairie Minard (qv)
Subjects: General Literature, University Studies and Theses, Critical Studies
Founded: 1954
ISBN Publisher's Prefix: 2-256

Librairie **Minard***, 73 rue du Cardinal Lemoine, F-75005 Paris Tel: (01) 3544609
Man Dir: Michel Minard; *Sales:* Librairie Minard Diffusion
Associate Company: Lettres Modernes Minard (qv)
Subjects: University Studies and Theses
ISBN Publisher's Prefix: 2-85210

Les Editions de **Minuit** SA, 7 rue Bernard-Palissy, F-75006 Paris Tel: (01) 2223794
Man Dir: Jérôme Lindon
Orders to: Le Seuil, 27 rue Jacob, F-75006 Paris
Subjects: General Fiction, Philosophy, Social Science, History, Literary Works
Bookshop: Librairie Autrement Dit, 73 blvd St-Michel, F-75005 Paris
1981: 20 titles *Founded:* 1942
ISBN Publisher's Prefix: 2-7073

Miroir Sprint Publications, see Les Editions Vaillant

Gérard **Monfort**, Saint-Pierre de Salerne, F-27800 Brionne Tel: (32) 448741
Man Dir: Gérard Monfort
Subjects: Literature, History, Art, Law, Archaeology, Ethnology
1983: 115 titles *Founded:* 1960

Editions du **Moniteur** et Editions de l'Usine Nouvelle, 17 rue d'Uzès, F-75002 Paris Tel: (01) 2961550 Telex: 680876F
President: Marc N Vigier; *Man Dir:* Guy de Dampierre; *Editorial:* Jean-Marc Pilpoul; *Sales:* Y-L Walle

Associate Company: C E P Edition (qv)
Subjects: Architecture, Building Construction, Public Works, Home Economics, Laws and Regulations, International Trade
Bookshops: Librarie du Moniteur, 15 rue d'Uzès, F-75002 Paris; 7 pl de l'Odéon, F-75006 Paris
1982: 85 titles *1983:* 60 titles
ISBN Publisher's Prefix: 2-281

Editions **Montchrestien** Sàrl*, 158-160 rue St-Jacques, F-75005 Paris Tel: (01) 3262686
Man Dir: Yves Poussier
Subjects: Law, Economic and Political Science, Current Events
ISBN Publisher's Prefix: 2-7076

Publications Photo-Cinema Paul **Montel**, 189 rue St-Jacques, F-75005 Paris 5ème Tel: (01) 3294090
Man Dir: Boris Troyan; *Editorial:* Guy Mandery, Bernard Perrine; *Sales:* Mr Sainsson; *Production:* Daniel Just; *Publicity:* Xavier Bernard
Subjects: Photography and ciné-photography, Periodicals
Founded: 1920
ISBN Publisher's Prefix: 2-7075

Editions de **Montsouris** SA*, 9 rue d'Alexandrie, F-75002 Paris Tel: (01) 5080190
Branch Off: 176 rue de Paris, F-91300 Massy
Subjects: Science and Technical
ISBN Publisher's Prefix: 2-85035

Editions Albert **Morancé**, 1 rue Palatine, F-75006 Paris Tel: 6332455
Dir: F Sorlot
Subjects: Fine Arts, Architecture
Book Club: Club du Livre d'Art
Founded: 1781
ISBN Publisher's Prefix: 2-85307

Editions Alain **Moreau***, 5 rue Eginhard, F-75004 Paris Tel: (01) 2725151
Editorial, Rights & Permissions, Sales: Alain Moreau
Orders to: Diffédit, 96 blvd Montparnasse, F-75014 Paris
Subjects: Social, Economic & Political Sciences, Social History
Founded: 1972
ISBN Publisher's Prefix: 2-85209

Morel Editeurs, Les Imberts, F-84220 Gordes Tel: (90) 719175/718180
Dir: Robert Morel
Associate Companies: Editions 'R' (qv); Editions 'Pratique'; Le 'A' (Periodical); Minimos
Subjects: Belles Lettres, Poetry, Music, Art, Religion, Paperbacks, Architecture, Gastronomy, Folklore, Juvenile, Humour
Bookshops: La Fête (at above address); Alternative Diffusion, 36 rue des Bourdonnais, Paris 1; Payot Diffusion, Lausanne, Switzerland (qv under Major Booksellers); Nord-Sud, 74 rue Lesbroussart, B-1050 Brussels, Belgium
Founded: 1961

Editions de la Réunion des **Musées Nationaux**, 10 rue de l'Abbaye, F-75006 Paris Tel: (01) 3292145
Subjects: Art, Guides, Science & Technology, Architecture
Founded: 1931
ISBN Publisher's Prefix: 2-7118

Editions du **Muséum National** d'Histoire naturelle, 38 rue Geoffroy-Saint-Hilaire, F-75005 Paris Tel: (01) 3317124
Subjects: Natural History, especially Museum Archives, Monographs/Memoirs of Naturalists, Specialized Studies
1982: 1 title

N O E, see Nouvel Office d'Edition

Fernand **Nathan** Editeur*, 9 rue Méchain, F-75014 Paris Tel: (01) 5898949 Cable Add: Nathaned Paris Telex: Nataned 24525 F
Subjects: Reference, Dictionaries, Art, Philosophy, Textbooks, Psychology, General & Social Science, Guides, Nature, History, Education, Juvenile paperbacks
Founded: 1881
ISBN Publisher's Prefix: 2-09

Librairie A-G **Nizet** Sàrl, 3 bis pl de la Sorbonne, F-75005 Paris Tel: (01) 3547976
Man Dir: A G Nizet
Subjects: Belles Lettres, University Textbooks, Literary
Founded: 1922
ISBN Publisher's Prefix: 2-7078

F De **Nobèle***, 35 rue Bonaparte, F-75006 Paris Tel: (01) 3260862 Cable Add: Denobelef Paris 110
Man Dir: F de Nobèle
Subjects: History of Art, Bibliography
Founded: 1885
ISBN Publisher's Prefix: 2-85189

Nouveautés de l'Enseignement-éditions andré casteilla, 25 rue Monge, F-75005 Paris Tel: (01) 3542691
Commercial Manager: Mrs Casteilla
Subjects: Textbooks for Technical, Commercial and Secondary Education; Economy, Legislation, Technical Drawing
ISBN Publisher's Prefix: 2-7135

Nouvel Office d'Edition, 216 blvd St-Germain, F-75007 Paris Tel: (01) 5443823
Associate Companies: Editions Acropole (qv), Presses de la Renaissance (qv)
Subjects: Novels, History, How-to, Social Science, Belles Lettres
Founded: 1969
ISBN Publisher's Prefix: 2-7144

Nouvelle Cité+, 131 rue Castagnary, F-75015 Paris Tel: (01) 8281894
Man Dir, Rights & Permissions: Jean-Michel Merlin; *Editorial, Production, Publicity:* Jean-Pierre Rosa; *Sales:* Michel Visart
Parent Company: Città Nuova Editrice, Italy (qv for associate companies)
Subjects: Spiritual themes, Testimonies, Essays
1981: 9 titles *1982:* 12 titles *Founded:* 1963
ISBN Publisher's Prefix: 2-85313

Nouvelles Editions Françaises, 13 rue St-Georges, F-75009 Paris Tel: (01) 8785319
Dir: Denis Baschet; *Man Dir:* Elaine Allegret; *Sales Dir:* Roger Allegret
Subject: Art
Founded: 1946
ISBN Publisher's Prefix: 2-7079

Nouvelles Editions Latines, 1 rue Palatine, F-75006 Paris Tel: (01) 3547742
Man Dir: Jean Sorlot
Subjects: General Fiction, Belles Lettres, Poetry, History, Travel and Tourism, Religion
Founded: 1928
ISBN Publisher's Prefix: 2-7233

Nouvelles Editions Rationalistes SA*, 16 rue de l'Ecole-Polytechnique, F-75005 Paris
Tel: (01) 6330350
Subjects: Philosophy, Religion, History of Ideas, Rationalist Themes
Book Club: L'Oeil Ouvert

O R S T O M, see Office de la Recherche Scientifique

Office Central de Lisieux SA*, 51 rue du Carmel, F-14100 Lisieux Tel: (31) 620188
Subject: Religion

104 FRANCE

Office de Documentation Bibliographique et de Diffusion, subsidiary of Librairie Fischbacher (qv)

Office de la Recherche Scientifique et Technique Outre Mer (ORSTOM), 24 rue Bayard, F-75008 Paris Tel: (01) 7233829 Cable Add: Orstom Paris Telex: 640295 F
Man Dir: Alain Ruellan
Publishing Department and Orders to: Service des Editions, 70-74 route d'Alnay, F-93140, Bondy Tel: (847) 3195 Telex: 215203 F
Subjects: Scientific and Technical Texts, Social Sciences connected with the Tropical and Mediterranean Areas of the World
1981: 30 titles *1982:* 47 titles *Founded:* 1943
ISBN Publisher's Prefix: 2-7099

Editions **Ophrys***, 6 ave J Jaurès, F-05002 Gap Tel: (92) 513523
Man Dir, Publicity & Advertising: Mrs B Monnier
Subjects: Linguistics, Belles Lettres, History, Philosophy, Education, Economics, Sociology
Bookshops: Librairie Ophrys, 61 rue Monsieur le Prince, F-70006 Paris; Editions Ophrys, succursale de Paris, 10 rue de Nesle, F-75006 Paris
Founded: 1934
ISBN Publisher's Prefix: 2-7080

Editions de l'**Orante***, 6 rue du Général-Bertrand, F-75007 Paris Tel: (01) 5660016
Man Dir: Simone Lafarge
Subjects: Belles Lettres, Poetry, History, Philosophy, Religion
Founded: 1940
ISBN Publisher's Prefix: 2-7031

Editions Olivier **Orban**, 14 rue Duphot, F-75001 Paris Tel: 2603696
Man Dir: Olivier Orban; *Editorial:* Françoise Roth; *Rights & Permissions:* Hélène Obolensky
Subjects: General Fiction and Non-fiction
Founded: 1974
ISBN Publisher's Prefix: 2-85565

Les Editions d'**Organisation**, 5 rue Rousselet, F-75007 Paris 7 Tel: (01) 5671840
Dir: Dominique Bidart
Parent Company: Editions Eyrolles (qv)
Subjects: Business Management & Organization generally (especially Data Processing, Personnel Training, Sociology, Industrial Law)
Bookshop: 7 rue de la Bourse, F-75002 Paris Tel: 2974409
Founded: 1953
ISBN Publisher's Prefix: 2-7081

Librairie **Orientaliste**, see Paul Geuthner SA

Michel de l'**Ormeraie**, 4 rue Labrouste, F-75725 Paris cedex 15 Tel: 8284070
Man Dir, Editorial: Michel de l'Ormeraie; *Sales:* Jean Claude Pelos; *Publicity:* Frédéric Mercier
Subjects: Exact Facsimiles (text and binding), of famous illustrated editions of French and other Literary Classics
Bookshop: Galerie Michel de l'Ormeraie, 17 rue Castagnary, F-75015 Paris
Founded: 1970
ISBN Publisher's Prefix: 2-85135

Editions Pierre Jean **Oswald***, 7 rue de l'Ecole Polytechnique, F-75005 Paris Tel: (01) 0339007
Subjects: General Fiction, Poetry, Belles Lettres, Paperbacks, Music, Third World, Creative Literature
Founded: 1964
ISBN Publisher's Prefix: 2-7172

Les Editions **Ouvrières** SA*, 12 ave Soeur-Rosalie, F-75013 Paris Tel: (01) 3379385
Subjects: History, Religion, How-to, Education, Juveniles, Political & Social Science, Economics
Founded: 1939
ISBN Publisher's Prefix: 2-7082

Editions **P A C** (Presse-Auto-Conseil)*, 3 rue Saint Roch, F-75001 Paris Tel: 2615017
Subjects: Sport, Cinema, Crime Novels, Commentaries and Documentaries, Adventure Reports
Founded: 1975
ISBN Publisher's Prefix: 2-85336

P O F, see Publications Orientalistes de France

P U F, see Presses Universitaires de France

P U L, see Presses Universitaires de Lille

P Y C Edition+, 254 rue de Vaugirard, F-75740 Paris cedex 15 Tel: (01) 5322719
Man Dir: Pierre Benichou
Subjects: Mechanical Engineering, Heating, Air Conditioning, Solar Energy, Refrigeration, Metallurgy, Welding
1981-82: 17 titles *Founded:* 1934
ISBN Publisher's Prefix: 2-85330

Les Editions du **Pacifique**, see Société Nouvelle des Editions du Pacifique, French Polynesia

Paris-Caraïbes*, 34 rue Scheffer, F-75116 Paris Tel: 5240609
Man Dir, Editorial: Louis Drout Soulanges
Associate Company: Editions Louis Soulanges (qv)
Subjects: Current literary, tourist, artistic, economic and social affairs in the Antilles

Jean-Jacques **Pauvert** Editeur, 19 rue des Plantes, F-75014 Paris Tel: (01) 6335640
Dir: Jean-Jacques Pauvert
Orders to: Distribution Sodis, 128 ave de Mal de Lattre, F-77400 Lagny
Subjects: Fiction, Belles Lettres, Art, History, Reference, Social Science, Paperbacks, Poetry, Philosophy, Juveniles
Founded: 1945
ISBN Publisher's Prefix: 2-85092

Editions **Payot**, 106 blvd St-Germain, F-75006 Paris 6 Tel: (01) 3297410
Man Dir: Jean-Luc Pidoux-Payot
Associate Company: Librairie Payot SA, Switzerland (qv)
Subjects: Biography, History, Philosophy, Reference, Religion, Ethnology, Anthropology, Low-priced Paperbacks, Education, General Science, Humanities, Psychology and Psychoanalysis, Linguistics
Founded: 1912
ISBN Publisher's Prefix: 2-228

Pédagogie Moderne, an imprint of Editions Bordas (qv)

Editions **Pédone**, 13 rue Soufflot, F-75005 Paris Tel: (01) 3540597
Man Dir: Denis Pédone
Subjects: Law, Engineering, Agriculture, Mining, Management, Economics, Book Industry
1981: 35 titles *Founded:* 1837
ISBN Publisher's Prefix: 2-233

Pensée Moderne Jacques Grancher, see Jacques Grancher

Père Castor, an imprint of Flammarion et Cie (qv)

Librairie Académique **Perrin**, 8 rue Garancière, F-75006 Paris Tel: (01) 6341280
Chairman: Claude Nielsen; *Publicity Manager:* Nadia Leser; *Foreign Rights:* Josiane Bontron
Subjects: Belles Lettres, History, Reference, Scholarly, Bibliography, Fiction, Arts, Religion
Founded: 1827
Miscellaneous: Member of Presses de la Cité group (qv)
ISBN Publisher's Prefix: 2-262

Editions **Phébus**, 17 rue Pierre Lescot, F-75001 Paris Tel: 2602394
Man Dir: Jean-Pierre Sicre
Orders to: Inter-Forum, 13 rue de la Glacière, F-75013 Paris
Subjects: General Literature, Oriental (Eastern) Literature, Literary Criticism, Fine Arts

Editions A et J **Picard** SA, 82 rue Bonaparte, F-75006 Paris 6 Tel: (01) 3269673/3294489
Man Dirs: Jacques Picard, Chantal Pasini
Subjects: General, Art, Religious, Literary and Local History; Archaeology, Architecture, Reference, Education, Bibliography, Folklore, Philology, Textbooks, Musicology, Antiquarian Books
Founded: 1869
ISBN Publisher's Prefix: 2-7084

Editions **Pierron**+, Terrain Industriel, 4 rue Gutenberg, F-57206 Sarreguemines Tel: (8) 7951431/7951848 Telex: 860495 F
Dir: Jeannie Jung
Branch Off: Pierron Entreprise SA, 4 rue Gutenberg, F-57206 Sarreguemines
Subjects: Education, Audio Visual Media, History

Editions Jean-Michel **Place***, 12 rue Pierre et Marie Curie, F-75005 Paris Tel: 6330511
Man Dir and other offices: Jean-Michel Place; *Publicity:* Leah Poller
Associate Company: Éditions de la Chronique des Lettres Françaises (qv)
Subjects: Literature and Literary Research, Bibliographies, Reference, Poetry, Fiction
Bookshop: At above address
Founded: 1973
ISBN Publisher's Prefix: 2-85893

Librairie **Plon** SA*, 8 rue Garancière, F-75006 Paris Tel: (01) 3291280 Cable Add: Ploédit Paris 110 Telex: 204807
Chairman: Claude Nielsen; *Foreign Rights:* Josiane Bontron
Subjects: General Fiction, History, Belles Lettres, Philosophy, How-to, Religion, Reference, Economics, Social Science, Scholarly, Arts, Maps, Travel, Anthropology, Trade Books
Founded: 1844
Miscellaneous: Member of Presses de la Cité group (qv)
ISBN Publisher's Prefix: 2-259

Presses **Pocket***, 8 rue Garancière, F-75006, Paris Tel: 6341280 Telex: Precite 204807 F
Subjects: Novels, Memoirs, War, Documentary, Science Fiction (all paperback)
Miscellaneous: Member of Presses de la Cité group (qv)

Centre Georges **Pompidou** Edition, see Centre national d'art et de Culture Georges Pompidou

Julien **Prélat** Sàrl*, 17 rue du Petit-Pont, F-75005 Paris Tel: (01) 3547763
Management, Rights & Permissions: M Dargent, S Kolf; *Publicity & Advertising:* Mr Lizeux
Subjects: Odontology, Stomatology, (textbooks and special interest books), General Dentistry, Medicine, Periodicals
Bookshops: Librairie Odonto Stomatologie (at above address); Librairie Psychologie, 2 rue du Cardinal Lemoine, Paris 5e
Founded: 1946
ISBN Publisher's Prefix: 2-85039

Société Nouvelle **Présence Africaine**, 25 bis rue des Ecoles, F-75005 Paris Tel: (01) 3541374 Cable Add: Presafric Paris
Man Dir: Mrs Alioune Diop; *Publicity,*

Rights & Permissions: Geoffrey Jones
Subjects: General Fiction, Belles Lettres, Poetry, History, Philosophy, Reference, Religion, Low-priced Paperbacks, Primary Textbooks, Politics (all subjects pertain to Africa)
Bookshop: At above address
1982: 26 titles *Founded:* 1947
ISBN Publisher's Prefix: 2-7087

Presse-Auto-Conseil, see P A C

Les **Presses d'Ile-de-France** Sàrl, 23 rue de Ligner, F-75980 Paris cedex 20 Tel: (01) 3679821
Man Dir: Gilles Le Grontec; *Manager:* François Ardonceau
Orders to: Sofedis, 29 rue St-Sulpice, F-75007 Paris
Subject: Juveniles
ISBN Publisher's Prefix: 2-7088

Les **Presses de la Cité***, 8 rue Garancière, F-75006 Paris Tel: (01) 3291280 Cable Add: Svennil Paris
President and Distribution Dir: Claude Nielsen; *Publicity and Advertising:* Nadia Leser; *Rights & Permissions:* Josiane Bontron
Subjects: General Fiction, History, How-to, Low- & High-priced Paperbacks
Founded: 1947
Presses de la Cité group: Librairie Plon (qv); G P Rouge et Or (qv); Solar (qv); Librairie Académique Perrin (qv); Editions René Julliard (qv); Presses Pocket (qv); Editions Fleuve Noir (qv); Messageries Centrales du Livre (qv); Christian Bourgois (qv); le Rocher; UGE 10/18 (qv)
ISBN Publisher's Prefix: 2-258

Presses de la Fondation Nationale des Sciences Politiques, 27 rue St-Guillaume, F-75341 Paris cedex 07 Tel: (01) 2603960/2220985
Man Dir, Sales, Publicity, Rights & Permissions: Louis Bodin; *Editorial:* Mireille Perche; *Production:* Josée Cabillon
Subjects: Social Sciences, especially Political, Historical, Sociological, Economics
Founded: 1975
ISBN Publisher's Prefix: 2-7246

Presses de la Renaissance+, 198 blvd St-Germain, F-75007 Paris Tel: 5485982 Telex: 260717 orem 158
Man Dir, Sales: Fabienne Delmote; *Editorial:* Tony Cartano; *Rights & Permissions:* Françoise Triffaux
Parent Company: Pierre Belfond (qv)
Associate Companies: Nouvel Office d'Edition (qv); Editions Acropole (qv)
Subjects: General Fiction, Biography, Documentary, Folklore, Animals; French Classics, Foreign Literature in Translation, History
Founded: 1971
ISBN Publisher's Prefix: 2-85616

Les **Presses Monastiques**, see Zodiaque

Presses Universitaires de France (PUF), 108 blvd St-Germain, F-75279 Paris cedex 6 Tel: (01) 6341201
The above is the address of the Administration and Editorial offices; Public Relations and Publicity departments are at 90 blvd St-Germain, F-75005 Paris
President: Pierre Angoulvent; *Dirs:* Robert Ruelle, Pierre Wittmann; *Sales Dir:* Jean-Pierre Giband; *Editorial:* Michel Prigent; *Publicity, Advertising:* Gabrielle Gelber; *Rights & Permissions:* Françoise Laye, Arlette Monsallier
Orders to: 14 ave du Bois de L'Epine, BP 90, F-91003 Evry ccdcx Tel: 0778205 Telex: PUF 600474 F
Subjects: Belles Lettres, Poetry, Biography, History, Music, Art, Philosophy, Reference, Religion, Engineering, Low- & High-priced Paperbacks, Psychology, Medicine, General, Social & Political Science, University Textbooks
Book Club: 49 blvd, St-Michel, F-75005 Paris
Bookshops: Librairie générale des PUF (qv under Major Booksellers); La Pochotheque, 17 rue Soufflot, F-75005 Paris
Founded: 1921

Presses Universitaires de Grenoble+, Domaine Universitaire, BP 47X, F-38040 St Martin d'Hères Tel: (76) 444378 Telex: Unisog 980910
Manager: Olivier Gadet; *Commercial Managers:* Christian Auguste, Pierre Croce
Orders to: Sodis, 128 ave Maréchal de Lattre de Tassigny, F-77400 Lagny
Subjects: Architecture, Anthropology, Sociology, Law, Economics, Management, History, Statistics, Literature, Medicine, Data Processing, Physics, Politics
1981: 15 titles *1982:* 15 titles
ISBN Publisher's Prefix: 2-7061

Presses Universitaires de Lille (PUL), 9 rue Auguste Angellier, F-59000 Lille Tel: (20) 308585
Man Dir: University President; *Editorial, Production:* Ph Bonnefis; *Sales, Publicity, Rights & Permissions:* D Rosselle
Subjects: Social Sciences and Humanities, French and Foreign Literature, History, Philosophy, Law, Philology, Psychology
1981: 36 titles *Founded:* 1972
ISBN Publisher's Prefix: 2-85939

Presses Universitaires de Lyon+, 86 rue Pasteur, F-69007 Lyon Tel: (7) 8692048
Man Dir: Joël Saugnieux
Subjects: History, Economics, University Textbooks, Linguistics, Lyons Regional Interest, Literature, Law
1981: 25 titles *Founded:* 1976
ISBN Publisher's Prefix: 2-7297

Presses Universitaires de Nancy+, 25 rue Baron Louis, BP 454, F-54001 Nancy cedex Tel: (8) 3373765/3371297
Man Dir, Editorial: Jean-Marie Bonnet; *Sales, Production:* Christiane Richard; *Publicity, Rights & Permissions:* Agnès Pery, Thérèse Rambaut
Subjects: History, Geography, Literature and Linguistics, Philosophy, Psychology, Sociology, Jurisprudence, Economic and Political Bibliography Teaching, Works and Theses of the Nancy II University, the European University Centre, European Conferences, Periodicals
1981: 12 titles *1982:* 20 titles *Founded:* 1976
ISBN Publisher's Prefix: 2-86480

Editions Edouard **Privat** SA, 14 rue des Arts, F-31000 Toulouse 61 Tel: (61) 230926 Telex: 521 001 f
Man Dir: Pierre Privat; *Literary, Production:* Dominique Autié; *Sales Dir, Publicity:* Yves Suaudeau; *Press Relations:* Jacqueline Thomas; *Rights & Permissions:* Noëlle Lever
Subjects: French regional history and culture; Education, Psychology, Sociology, Philosophy, Pedagogy
Founded: 1834
ISBN Publisher's Prefix: 2-7089

Publi-Union*, 1 rue Théodule Ribot, F-75017 Paris Tel: (01) 2278920
Man Dir: Michel Weulersse
Subjects: Law, Economics, Social Science, Education, Science & Technical
ISBN Publisher's Prefix: 2-85200

Publications Filmées d'Art et d'Histoire, 9-15 rue Carvès, F-92120 Montrouge Tel: 6571413 (ext 78)
Man Dir: Marcel Hamelle; *Sales:* Viviane Mella
Subjects: Books illustrated by slides on Art, History, Space Exploration, World Events
ISBN Publisher's Prefix: 2-85228

Publications Orientalistes de France (POF), 2 rue de Lille, F-75007 Paris Tel: (01) 2606705
Dir: Simone Maviel
Orders to: Editions Ophrys (qv)
Subjects: Eastern Europe and the Middle and Far East (all aspects, especially literature, bibliographies, vocabularies)
1982-83: 30 titles
ISBN Publisher's Prefix: 2-7169

Editions **Pygmalion** — Gérard Watelet+, 70 Ave de Breteuil, F-75007 Paris Tel: (01) 5674077
Man Dir, Editorial: Gérard Watelet; *Sales, Rights & Permissions:* Luce Watelet
Subjects: General Literature, History, Biographies, Archaeology, Art, Fiction
Founded: 1977
ISBN Publisher's Prefix: 2-85704

Société **Quatre Chemins**, see Editart

Librairie Aristide **Quillet** SA*, 278 blvd St-Germain, F-75006 Paris Tel: (01) 5514810 Cable Add: Ariquillet Paris 44
Man Dir: Claude Bellenand; *Rights & Permissions:* Philippe Leturc
Subjects: Science & Technology, Dictionaries, Encyclopaedias
Founded: 1898
ISBN Publisher's Prefix: 2-85041

Editions '**R**', Société Civile Typo, Graphique et Littéraire, Les Imberts, F-84220 Gordes Tel: (90) 718180
Man Dir, Editorial, Rights & Permissions: Robert Morel; *Production, Publicity:* François Morel
Orders to: Morel, 5 rue du Mail, Paris 2 Tel: (01) 2600738
Associate Company: Morel Editeurs (qv)
Subjects: Rites, Myths and Symbols, Sorcery, Encylopaedia of Tarot, Alternative Medicine, Fiction, Practical Living, Vocabulary Traditions and Images, Popular Literature, Tourism
Founded: 1977

R E C T A Foldex, BP 94, F-92303 Levallois-Perret (Located at: 27 rue Trebois, Levallois-Perret) Tel: 2701203 Telex: 270105 f txfra 691
Man Dir: Mrs Costard
Subject: Maps, Charts
Miscellaneous: RECTA = Réalisations, Études Cartographiques Touristiques et Administratives (Cartographic design and production in the touring and administrative fields)

R E M I, see Réalisations pour l'Enseignement Multilingue International

Société des Editions **Radio**, see SECF — Editions Radio

Editions **Ramsay**, 9 rue du Cherche-Midi, F-75006 Paris Tel: 5445505
Man Dir: Alain de Sedouy; *Editorial:* Paul Fournel; *Production:* Dominique Muller; *Publicity:* Elisabeth Cailloux; *Rights & Permissions:* Sabine Delattre
Subjects: Novels, Documentary Books, Fine Editions, Essays, Science, History
Bookshop: At above address
1981: 48 titles *1982:* 59 titles *Founded:* 1976
ISBN Publisher's Prefix: 2-85956

Sélection du **Reader's Digest** SA*, 212 blvd St-Germain, F-75007 Paris Tel: 5480426 Cable Add: Readigest Paris
The above is the address of the Head Office; General Management is at 1-7 ave Louis Pasteur, BP 101, F-92223 Bagneux Tel: 6641616 Telex: Selread 200882 f

Man Dir: Claude Pothier; *Marketing Dir:* Henri Capdeville; *Editorial* (Books): Claude Janicot (General), Françoise Pitt-Rivers (Condensed)
Subjects: General Fiction, History, How-to, Juveniles, Medicine, Science & Technology, Reference, Art, Architecture, Social Science, Economics, Travel, Nature, Tourism, Atlases

Réalisations pour l'Enseignement Multilingue International (REMI)*, 39 rue de l'Abbé-Grégoire, F-75006 Paris Tel: (01) 2227090
Man Dir: Mrs D Holtzer
Subjects: Foreign language courses for Primary schools (French, German, English), Elementary French readers
Founded: 1966
ISBN Publisher's Prefix: 2-85134

Franco Maria **Ricci**, Galerie 12, 12 Rue des Beaux-Arts, F-75006 Paris Tel: 6339631
Man Dir, Editorial, Production, Rights & Permissions: Franco Maria Ricci; *Sales:* Yves Dantoing
Orders to: Weber Diffusion, 24 rue du Moulinet, F-75013 Paris
Parent Company: Franco Maria Ricci, Milan, Italy
Subjects: Art Books, Bodoni Editions, Diderot Encyclopaedia, Bibliophile Editions, Graphic Design (Deco Press)
Book Club: Les Amis de Franco Maria Ricci
Bookshop: 12 rue des Beaux Arts, F-75006 Paris
Founded: 1974

Yves **Rivière**, Editeur, 117 rue Vieille-du-Temple, F-75003 Paris Tel: (01) 2747784
Publisher, Man Dir: Yves Rivière
Subjects: Complete Lists of Artists' Works (Oeuvres Catalogues), Artist-illustrated books, Prints
Founded: 1971
ISBN Publisher's Prefix: 2-85666

Editions E **Robert**, L'Ecole et la Famille, BP 4384, F-69241 Lyons cedex 04 (Located at: 28 rue du Bon-Pasteur, F-69001 Lyons) Tel: (7) 8284889
Man Dir: Paul Chirat
Subjects: Primary Textbooks, Educational Materials, Periodical
1981: 4 titles *1982:* 3 titles *Founded:* 1873
ISBN Publisher's Prefix: 2-7093

Dictionnaire Le **Robert**, see Société du Nouveau Littré (SNL)

Editions **Rombaldi** SA, 15-17 rue de Rome, F-75008 Paris Tel: (01) 2618401/2618425 Telex: rombald 641854 F
President: Michel Leroux; *Commercial Dirs:* Henri Kaufman, Hervé le Henaff; *Production Manager:* Henri Kaufman
Subjects: Cartoon Comics, General Books, Cards (Cookery, Knitting, DIY, Beauty)
Founded: 1920
ISBN Publisher's Prefix: 2-231

Guide **Rosenwald***, 17 rue Tronchet, F-75008 Paris Tel: (01) 7423462
Subject: Annuals

Editions **Roudil***, 53 rue St-Jacques, F-75005 Paris Tel: (01) 0334797
Man Dir: Henry Roudil
Subjects: History, Philosophy, University & Secondary Textbooks, Fiction
Founded: 1954
ISBN Publisher's Prefix: 2-85044

Editions **Rouff** SA*, 36 rue du Vieux-Pont-de-Sèvres, F-92100 Boulogne-Billancourt Tel: 6090140
Subjects: Humour, Shooting, Periodicals
ISBN Publisher's Prefix: 2-85045

G P **Rouge et Or***, 8 rue Garancière, F-75006 Paris Tel: 6341280 Telex: Precite 204807 F
Subjects: Children's Literature
Miscellaneous: Firm is a member of the Presses de la Cité group (qv)

La **Rougery**, see Blondel La Rougery SA

Publications **Roy**, now incorporated in Publications Estoup et Roy (qv)

Ruedo Ibérico*, 6 rue de Latran, F-75005 Paris Tel: (01) 3255649
Man Dir: Mr Martínez
Bookshop: At above address
Subjects: Studies of Recent and Contemporary Spanish History, Spanish Politics, Social Science etc, General Fiction (many titles in Castilian)
Founded: 1962
ISBN Publisher's Prefix: 2-7153

S E C A Codes Rousseau, Ziat les Plesses, Chateau d' Olonne, F-85100 Les Sables d'Olonne Tel: 327731
Subjects: Education, Juveniles, Audio Visual & Electronic Media
ISBN Publisher's Prefix: 2-7095

S E C F — Editions Radio*, 9 rue Jacob, F-75006 Paris Tel: (01) 3296370
Subjects: Engineering, Mass Media
Founded: 1934
ISBN Publisher's Prefix: 2-7091

S E D E S, see Centre de Documentation Universitaire

S E N H A, Société d'Exploitation des Nouveaux Humanoïdes Associés+, 17 rue Monsigny, F-75002 Paris Tel: (01) 7424610 Telex: 213913
Also known as Les Humanoïdes Associés
Man Dir: Pascal Bourguigon; *Publishing Dir:* Jean-Pierre Dionnet
Subjects: Adult adventure and strip cartoons
1981: 55 titles *1982:* 65 titles *Founded:* 1975
ISBN Publisher's Prefix: 2-7316

S I M E P SA*, 38/46 rue de Bruxelles, BP 1214, F-69611 Villeurbanne cedex Tel: 7/8899710
Name denotes Société d'Information medicale et d'Enseignement post-universitaire (Medical Information and Post-University Teaching Association)
Chairman: Bernard Duportet; *Man Dir:* Micheline Duportet
Subject: Medicine, Periodicals
Founded: 1965
ISBN Publisher's Prefix: 2-85334

S N L, see Société du Nouveau Littré

Editions **S O S** (Editions du Secours Catholique), 106 rue de Bac, F-75007 Paris Tel: (01) 5486066
Man Dir: Maurice Herr; *Publicity & Advertising:* Georges Fanucchi
Subjects: History, Philosophy, Religion, Social Science
Founded: 1949
ISBN Publisher's Prefix: 2-7185

S P E L D, 6 rue Victor-Cousin, F-75005 Paris Tel: 6336910
A group of French publishers specializing in Law, Economics, Politics

S U D E L (Société Universitaire d'Editions et de Librairie)*, 20 rue Corvisart, F-75640 Paris cedex 13 Tel: (01) 5354846
Subject: Education
ISBN Publisher's Prefix: 2-7162

Les Editions du **Sagittaire***, 61 rue des Sts-Pères, F-75006 Paris Tel: (01) 2229976
Dirs: Jean-Claude Fasquelle
Subjects: Fiction, Biography, History, General Literature
Founded: 1929

Editions **Saint-Germain-des-Prés** SA+, 110 rue du Cherche-Midi, F-75006 Paris Tel: (01) 2227120
Publicity: Philippe Héraclès
Holding Company: Le Cherche-Midi, Editeur (qv)
Founded: 1969

Editions **Saint-Paul** SA*, 6 rue Cassette, F-75006 Paris Tel: (01) 2221783 (Paris); 6422980 (Issy-les-Moulineaux)
Man Dir: M Dumas
Subsidiary Company: Editions Saint-Paul SA, Dept des Classiques Africains (qv)
Branch Off: 184 ave de Verdun, F-92130 Issy-les-Moulineaux
Subjects: Religion, Religious History, Biography, Africana
Bookshop: Librairie Saint-Paul, 6 rue Cassette, F-75006 Paris
Founded: 1873
ISBN Publisher's Prefix: 2-85049

Editions **Saint-Paul, Département des Classiques Africains**+, 184 ave de Verdun, F-92130 Issy-les-Moulineaux Tel: 6422980
Parent Company: Editions Saint Paul SA (qv)
Subjects: Black Africa Literature, Daily Life, Tropical Medicine, School Books
Bookshop: Librairie Saint-Paul, 6 rue Cassette, F-75006 Paris

Editions **Salvator** Sàrl, BP 1175, F-68053 Mulhouse cedex (Located at: 9 Pont d'Altkirch) Tel: (89) 451430
Subject: Religion
Founded: 1924
ISBN Publisher's Prefix: 2-7067

Auberge du **Sambucco***, F-20242 Vezzani, Corsica Tel: (95) 440106
Man Dir, Sales, Rights & Permissions: Otto Königsdorff
Subjects: Paperbacks
1981: 6 titles *Founded:* 1981
Miscellaneous: Also known as Verlagshaus Corsica (Otto Königsdorff)

Editions **Sand et Tchou** Sàrl, 6 rue du Mail, F-75002 Paris Tel: 2961693 Telex: 213612 F
Man Dir: Carl van Eiszner; *Rights & Permissions:* Agnes de Gorter
Subjects: General Fiction, Belles Lettres, Poetry, Biography, History, How-to, Music, Art, Juveniles, Reference, Paperbacks, Social Science, Geography, Psychology
Founded: 1964
ISBN Publisher's Prefix: 2-7107

Editions Le **Sarment**, 75 rue des Sts-Pères, F-75006 Paris Tel: 5443845
Man Dir: Jean-Claude Didelot
Parent Company: Librairie Arthème Fayard (qv)
Subjects: Religious Works
1981: 15 titles *Founded:* 1980

K G **Saur** Editeur Sarl*, Agence centrale du livre, F-75017 Paris Tel: (01) 2260186 Telex: Iso bur 630144
Parent Company: K G Saur Verlag KG, Federal Republic of Germany (qv)

Scarabée & Co, éditeurs, 15 rue Ballu, F-75009 Paris Tel: 2813398
Man Dir: Eugène Simion
Subjects: Social Sciences, General Literature, History, Documents, Religion, Biography
Founded: 1982
ISBN Publisher's Prefix: 2-86722

Scarabée d'Or, an imprint of Editions Dominique Leroy (qv)

Schott Frères Sàrl, 35 rue Jean Moulin, F-94300 Vincennes Tel: 3743095
Subject: Music

Scolavox, 203 rue de Gençay, BP 429, F-86011 Poitiers Tel: (49) 462766
Man Dir: Claude Moreau; *Sales Dir:* Albert

Combe
Subjects: Poetry, Primary Textbooks, Educational Materials
1982: 21 titles *1983:* 12 titles *Founded:* 1959
ISBN Publisher's Prefix: 2-85052

Editions du **Secours** Catholique, see S O S

La Société **Sécuritas** SA, 2 rue de Châteaudun, F-75009 Paris Tel: (01) 8787206
Subjects: Science & Technical, Law, Economics, Social Science, Audio Visual & Electronic Media
ISBN Publisher's Prefix: 2-7097

Seditas (Société d'Editions et de Diffusion Tambourinaire-Sofradel)*, 186 rue du Faubourg-St-Honoré, F-75008 Paris Tel: (01) 5619600
Orders to: 41 rue Washington, F-75008 Paris
Subjects: Management, Scientific, Technical, Electronics
ISBN Publisher's Prefix: 2-85179

Les Editions **Seghers** SA, 6 pl St-Sulpice F-75006 Paris Tel: 3291233 Telex: Edilaf 270607
President, Man Dir: Robert Laffont; *Literary Manager:* Bernard Delvaille; *Rights & Permissions:* Béatrix Vernet
Orders to: Inter Forum, 13 rue de la Glacière, F-75013 Paris Telex: 250055
Associate Company: Les Editions Robert Laffont (qv)
Subjects: Belles Lettres, Poetry, Biography, Science & Technical, Fantasy, Art, Paperbacks
Founded: 1939
ISBN Publisher's Prefix: 2-22

Editions **Sélection** J Jacobs SA+, 66 rue Falguière, F-75015 Paris Tel: (01) 3203188
Subjects: Technology, Fine Arts, How-to series
ISBN Publisher's Prefix: 2-7174

Les Editions du **Sénevé**, 10 rue Cassette, F-75006 Paris Tel: (01) 2229020
Editorial: Françoise Desgrandchamps
Subjects: Catechisms, Juveniles, Religion, Religious Educational Materials
Founded: 1947
Miscellaneous: An imprint of Dessain et Tolra (qv)

Septieme Rayon, an imprint of Editions Dominique Leroy (qv)

Septimus Editions, an imprint of Arted (Editions d'Art) (qv)

Service Technique pour l'Education, 19 blvd Poissonnière, F-75002 Paris Tel: (01) 5084756
Man Dir: Mrs Gradvohl
Subjects: General Fiction, Belles Lettres, Poetry, Biography, History, Music, Art, Philosophy, Reference, Religion, Juveniles, Educational Materials, Judaica
Bookshop: At above address
Founded: 1962

Editions du **Seuil**, 27 rue Jacob, F-75261 Paris cedex 06 Tel: (01) 3291215 Cable Add: Ediseuil Telex: 600605 F
President, Man Dir: Michel Chodkiewicz; *General Manager:* Edouard de Andréis; *Editorial:* Anne Fréyer, Denis Roche, François Wahl, Bruno Flamand, Jean-Claude Guillebaud, Jean-Marie Borzeix; *Production:* Anne Poulain; *Press and Advertising:* Françoise Peyrot; *Rights & Permissions:* Prune Berge
Subsidiary Companies: Société d'Editions Scientifiques, Dimedia, (Montreal) Seuil-Diffusion
Subjects: General Fiction, Literature, Poetry, Biography, History, How-to, Music, Art, Philosophy, Reference, Religion, Low- & High-priced Paperbacks, Psychology, General & Social Science, University Textbooks, Politics
Founded: 1935
ISBN Publisher's Prefix: 2-02

Editions **Siloé** Sàrl*, 8 pl St-Sulpice, F-75006 Paris Tel: (01) 3260057
Subject: Religion, Art books
ISBN Publisher's Prefix: 2-85054

Editions André **Silvaire** SA+, 20 rue Domat, F-75005 Paris Tel: (01) 3267234
Associate Company: Les Amis de Milosz (qv)
Subjects: General Fiction, Belles Lettres, Poetry, Theatre, Philosophy, Social Sciences, Paperbacks, School Books
Founded: 1944
ISBN Publisher's Prefix: 2-85055

Sindbad+, 1 et 3 rue Feutrier, F-75018 Paris Tel: (01) 2553523
Man Dir: Pierre Bernard; *Publicity, Advertising:* Fattouma Haniche; *Rights & Permissions:* Claudine Rulleau
Subjects: General Fiction, Belles Lettres, Poetry, History, Art, Philosophy, Reference, Religion, Social and Political Science connected with the Arabic, Persian and general Muslim worlds
1982: 80 titles *Founded:* 1972
ISBN Publisher's Prefix: 2-7274

Editions **Sirey**, Diffusion Dalloz, 11 rue Soufflot, F-75240 Paris cedex 05 Tel: (01) 3295080 Telex: 210023 ogtel Ref 703
Dir: Patrice Vergé; *Dir:* Gérard de Nussac; *Sales:* Alain Hapiot; *Publicity:* Mrs A Stein
Subjects: History, Philosophy, Social Science, Law, Business, University & Secondary Textbooks, Economics
Founded: 1791
ISBN Publisher's Prefix: 2-248

Société de Recherche appliquée à l'Education, see S R A

Société d'Edition d'Enseignement Supérieur, see Centre de Documentation Universitaire

Société d'Editions Scientifiques, Dimedia, subsidiary company of Editions du Seuil (qv)

Société d'Etudes Juridiques Internationales et Fiscales, see Cahiers Fiscaux Européens Sàrl

Société d'Exploitation des Nouveaux Humanoïdes Associés, see S E N H A

Société d'Exploitation et de Diffusion des Codes Rousseau, see S E C A

Société d'Information médicale et d'enseignement post-universitaire, see S I M E P

Société du Nouveau Littré (SNL) Dictionnaire 'Le Robert', 107 ave Parmentier, F-75011 Paris Tel: (01) 3577313 Telex: Dicorob 240763 F
President, Man Dir: Charles-Albert de Waziers; *Commercial Manager & Publicity:* Jacques Fauchère; *Technical Manager:* Jacques Pierre; *Export Manager:* Michel Terrier
Subject: Dictionaries
1983: 33 titles *Founded:* 1951
ISBN Publisher's Prefix: 2-85036

Société Française des Imprimeries Administratives Centrales, see Sofiac

Société Universitaire d'Editions et de Librairie, see S U D E L

Sodel (Editeur) SA*, 336-340 rue St-Honoré, F-75001 Paris Tel: (01) 2603180
Subjects: Science & Technical
ISBN Publisher's Prefix: 2-7102

Sofiac (Société Française des Imprimeries Administratives Centrales), 8 rue de Furstenberg, F-75006 Paris Tel: (01) 6342020
General Manager: Pierre de Clerck
Subjects: Economics, Social Science, Business Administration, Legal and Judicial, Accountancy
1982: 25 titles

Sofradel-Seditas, see Seditas

Sofradif Editions Philippe Auzou+, 74 rue Stendhal, F-75020 Paris Tel: (01) 7972709
Publisher: Philippe Auzou; *Sales Manager:* Fred Frangeul
Subjects: Medicine, Law, Scientific and Technical Encyclopaedia in comic strip form

Solar*, 8 rue Garancière, F-75006 Paris Tel: 329180 Telex: Precite 204807
Subjects: Practical Books, Cookery, Sport, Nature
Miscellaneous: Firm is a member of the Presses de la Cité group (qv)

Editions **Soleil Noir***, 2 rue Fléchier, F-75009 Paris Tel: (01) 2804702
Man Dir: François di Dio
Subjects: Poetry, Art, Social Science, General Fiction and Non-fiction, Bibliophily
Founded: 1948
ISBN Publisher's Prefix: 2-85131

Editions d'Art Aimery **Somogy**+, 91 rue de Seine, F-75006 Paris Tel: (01) 3268981 Telex: 204473
Man Dir: Aimery Somogy
Subject: Art
Founded: 1937
ISBN Publisher's Prefix: 2-85056

Soprep (Editions de l'Instant Durable), 2 cours Sablon, F-63000 Clermont-Ferrand Tel: (073) 923278
General Manager: Alain de Bussac
ISBN Publisher's Prefix: 2-86404

Editions Louis **Soulanges** 'Le Livre Ouvert'*, 34 rue Scheffer, F-75116 Paris Tel: (01) 5538499
Man Dir, Sales Dir, Publicity: Louis Drouot Soulanges
Associate Company: Paris-Caraïbes
Imprint: France-Caraïbes
Branch Off: 5-7 rue Abel Ferry, F-75016 Paris Tel: 5240609
Subjects: General Fiction, Philosophy, Reference, Religion, Juveniles
Founded: 1960

Les Editions de la **Source** Sàrl, 5 rue de la Source, F-75016 Paris Tel: (01) 5253007
Man Dir: Rev Father Dom André Gozier; *All Other Offices:* Rev Father Dom Norbert Balladur
Orders to: Office Général du Livre, 14 bis rue Jean-Ferrandi F-75006, Paris (Tel: (01) 5483828)
Imprints: Lumière Biblique series
Subjects: Religion; Doctrine, Theology, Spirituality, Holy Scripture, Monasticism and Benedictine History
Bookshop: Librairie Sainte Marie, 5 rue de la Source, F-75016 Paris
Founded: 1927
ISBN Publisher's Prefix: 2-900005

Les Editions Internationales Alain **Stanké***, 30 rue de l'Université, F-75007 Paris Tel: 2615052 Telex: 05561358
Man Dir, Editorial: Alain Stanké
Subjects: Current Affairs, Biography, Fiction, How-to, Cookery, Art, Pocket Editions
Founded: 1975
ISBN Publisher's Prefix: 2-7604

Editions **Stock***, 14 rue de l'Ancienne Comédie, F-75006 Paris Tel: (01) 6342125
President, Man Dir: Jean Rosenthal;

General Manager: Bernard Barrault; *Production:* Jacques Menard; *Publicity & Advertising:* Pauline de Margerie; *Rights & Permissions:* Janine Noël
Parent Company: Librairie Hachette (qv)
Subjects: French and Foreign Literature, Human Sciences, Medicine, Juveniles, Cinema, Paperbacks
Founded: 1780
ISBN Publisher's Prefix: 2-234

Editions **Studia** SA, 40 bis rue Maurice-Arnoux, F-92120 Montrouge Tel: 2533811
Subject: Education
ISBN Publisher's Prefix: 2-7104

Les Editions de la **Table** Ronde*, 40 rue du Bac, F-75007 Paris Tel: (01) 2222891
President, Dir-General: Gwenn-Aël Bollore; *Man Dir:* Roland Laudenbach; *Editorial and Publicity:* Christian Poninski; *Press Dir:* Danièle Levêque; *Literary Dir:* Philippe de la Roche; *Rights & Permissions:* Mahaut Pascalis
Subjects: General Fiction, Belles Lettres,, Biography, History, Religion, Medicine, Psychology, Social Science
Founded: 1944
ISBN Publisher's Prefix: 2-7103

Les Presses de **Taizé**, Taizé-Communauté, F-71250 Cluny Tel: (85) 501414 Telex: Cotaize 800753F
Orders to: Editions du Seuil, 27 rue Jacob, F-75261 Paris cedex 06
Subject: Religious works
Founded: 1959

Librairie Jules **Tallandier***, 17 rue Rémy-Dumoncel, F-75677 Paris cedex 14 Tel: (01) 3277770
President, Director-General: Jacques Jourquin
Subjects: General Fiction (especially Romantic), Art, Belles Lettres, Reference, History, Geography, Paperbacks
Founded: 1865
ISBN Publisher's Prefix: 2-235

Editions **Tardy** SA, 22 rue Joyeuse, BP 56, F-18002 Bourges Tel: (24) 242986 Telex: 760909
Also: 89 rue de Seine, F-75006 Paris Tel: (01) 3260058
Man Dir, Rights & Permissions: Pierre Penet
Subjects: Religion, Catechisms, Parish Manuals, Religious Pedagogy
Founded: 1938
ISBN Publisher's Prefix: 2-7105

Editions **Taride** Sàrl, 2 bis pl du Puits de l'Ermite, F-75005 Paris Tel: (01) 3364040
Cable Add: Cartaride Paris
Subjects: Geography, Travel
Founded: 1852
ISBN Publisher's Prefix: 2-7106

Société d'Exploitation de **Tchou** Editeur Sàrl, now Sand et Tchou (qv)

Société des Éditions **Technip**, 27 rue Ginoux, F-75737 Paris cedex 15 Tel: (01) 5771108
Dir: Jacques Ledésert; *Man Dir:* Anna Beraud
Subjects: Petroleum Science & Technology
Founded: 1956
ISBN Publisher's Prefix: 2-7108

Technique et Documentation (Librairie Lavoisier)+, 11 rue Lavoisier, F-75384 Paris cedex 08 Tel: (01) 2653995
Publishers: Alain Deubel, Pierre Fenouil; *Publicity:* Cécile Prat
Subjects: Engineering, Industrial Safety, Environment, Metallurgy, Hydraulics, Chemistry, Electro-Technology, Biology, Food Industry, Civil Engineering, Oceanography, Reference
ISBN Publisher's Prefix: 2-85206

Technique et Vulgarisation SA*, 21 rue Claude Bernard, F-75005 Paris Tel: (01) 5811131
Dirs: Laurent Heilmann, Charles Miguet
Subjects: Industrial, General Technology, Educational Materials, Engineering, Secondary & Primary Textbooks
Founded: 1946
Miscellaneous: an imprint of Editions Bordas (qv)
ISBN Publisher's Prefix: 2-7109

Techniques de l'Ingénieur Sàrl, 21 rue Cassette, F-75006 Paris Tel: (01) 2223550
The above is the address of the Editorial office, the Commercial office is at 123 rue d'Alésia, F-75678 Paris cedex 14 Tel: (01) 5392291
Man Dir: Jacques Debaene; *Editorial Manager:* Jean-Jacques Baron; *Publicity Manager:* Gérard Delepoulle (at Commercial Office address)
Subjects: Scientific, Technical
ISBN Publisher's Prefix: 2-85059

Editions **Techniques Professionels**, see ETP

Librairie Pierre **Tequi** et Editions Tequi, 82 rue Bonaparte, F-75006 Paris Tel: (01) 3260458
Head Office: Le Roc St Michel, F-53150 St-Ceneve Tel: (43) 010181
General Manager: Pierre Lemaire; *Literary Manager:* G Cerbelaud Salagnac; *Commercial Manager:* Mrs Pascal
Subjects: Education, Literature, Religion, Juveniles
ISBN Publisher's Prefix: 2-85244

Editions **Tests***, 41 rue de la Grange-aux-Belles, F-75483 Paris cedex 10 Tel: (01) 2022910
Subjects: Science & Technical, Audio Visual & Electronic Media

Editions de **Trévise***, 34 rue de Trévise, F-75009 Paris Tel: (01) 8246713/7703604
Man Dir: Gérald Gauthier; *Literary Dir:* Alexis Ovtchinnikoff
Subjects: History, Encyclopaedias, Art, Reference, Languages, Novels & Short Stories, General Non-fiction
Founded: 1956
ISBN Publisher's Prefix: 2-7112

U G E 10/18, 8 rue Garancière, F-75006 Paris Tel: 6341280 Telex: Precite 204807 F
Subjects: University and Political series, Literature
Miscellaneous: Member of the Presses de la Cité group (qv)
ISBN Publisher's Prefix: 2-264

Presses **Universitaires** de France, de Grenoble, de Lille, de Lyon, de Nancy, see Presses

Editions de l'**Usine Nouvelle**, see Editions du Moniteur

Les Editions **Vaillant**/Miroir Sprint Publications, 126 rue Lafayette, F-75461 Paris Tel: (01) 2469225 Telex: Edipif 64067
Subject: Juveniles

Editions **Van de Velde***, La Petite Plaine, BP 22, Fondettes, F-37230 Luynes Tel: (47) 510623; Sales Office at 12 rue Jacob, F-75006 Paris Tel: 3259343
Man Dir, Sales: Jean-Michel Cocoual; *Editorial, Production:* Francis Van de Velde; *Publicity:* Ms Claude Jacquin; *Rights & Permissions:* Edith Airault
Subject: Music and Musical Instruction
Founded: 1898
ISBN Publisher's Prefix: 2-85868

Editions Francis **Van de Velde***, 12 rue Jacob, F-75006 Paris Tel: (01) 3259343
Man Dir, Editorial: Francis Van de Velde; *Sales, Rights and Permissions:* Ms Claude Jacquin
Subjects: Musicology, Music and Education

Editions de **Vecchi**, see De Vecchi

Editions de **Vergeures***, 23 ave Villemain, F-75014 Paris Tel: (01) 5456704 Telex: Vergenn 250894 F
President: Jacques Dodeman; *Man Dir, Rights & Permissions:* Paul Griffon
Subjects: Popular Encyclopaedias, Practical and How-to, Art Series
1981: 36 titles *Founded:* 1979
ISBN Publisher's Prefix: 2-7309

Vertige, an imprint of Editions Dominique Leroy (qv)

Veyrier, 12 rue de Nesle, F-75006 Paris Tel: 6332018
Man Dir: Henri Veyrier; *Editorial:* Jean-Claude Hache; *Sales:* Jean Gouezec
Orders to: Anagramme (at above address)
Parent Company: Anagramme (at above address)
Subjects: Illustrated Books on Art, Cinema, Paris, Fiction
Bookshops: 17 ter ave de Clichy, F-75018 Paris; 20 rue J H Fabre, Saint Ouen
Founded: 1973

Editions **Vigot** Frères, 23 rue de l'Ecole-de-Médecine, F-75006 Paris Tel: (01) 3295450 Telex: 201708 F
Man Dir: Daniel Vigot
Subjects: Medicine, General Science, Sports, Veterinary
Bookshop: Librairie Vigot (at above address)
Founded: 1890
ISBN Publisher's Prefix: 2-7114

Editions **Vilo** SA, 25 rue Ginoux, F-75015 Paris Tel: (01) 5770805 Cable Add: Edivilo Paris Telex: 200305 F
Man Dir: M Larfillon
Subjects: Art, History, Religion, Architecture, Reference, Maps, Literature, Aviation, Non-fiction, Sports, Languages, Tourism, Automobiles
ISBN Publisher's Prefix: 2-7191

Editions **Vitamine**, an imprint of France Expansion (qv)

Librairie Philosophique J **Vrin**, 6 pl de la Sorbonne, F-75005 Paris 5 Tel: (01) 3540347
Man Dir: Gérard Paulhac
Subjects: Philosophy, Reference, Religion, Psychology, University Textbooks, History
Bookshops (new and second hand books): Philosophy, Law, Religion at 6 Pl de la Sorbonne, Paris; Literature, Art, History at 71 rue St Jacques, Paris
1982: 50 titles *Founded:* 1920
ISBN Publisher's Prefix: 2-7116

Librairie **Vuibert** SA, 63 blvd St-Germain, F-75005 Paris Tel: (01) 3256100 Cable Add: Vuibert Paris Telex: 201005 F Vuibpar
President: Jean Adam; *Editorial:* Monique Griboval; *Sales:* Guy Lambin; *Export:* Sylvie Lua, Jacques Pieprzovnik; *Publicity:* Marie-Françoise Riou; *Rights & Permissions:* Evelyne Mur
Subjects: Mathematics, Physics, Chemistry, Biology, Earth Sciences, Schoolbooks, Children's Literature, Economics, Law
Founded: 1877
ISBN Publisher's Prefix: 2-7117

Gerard **Watelet**, see Editions Pygmalion

Weber*, 90 rue de Rennes, F-75006 Paris Tel: (01) 5481251 Cable Add: Webart-Paris
Subjects: Art, Architecture, Social Science, Juveniles, Reference
Founded: 1967
ISBN Publisher's Prefix: 2-7190

Galerie Lucie **Weill***, Au Pont des Arts, 6 rue Bonaparte, F-75006 Paris Tel: 3547195
President: Lucie Weill
Subjects: Books with illustrations by famous artists
Book Club: Nouveau Cercle Parisien du Livre (qv)
Founded: 1930

Editions **Weka**, 12 cour St Eloi, F-75012 Paris Tel: (01) 3076050 Telex: 210504
General Manager: M von Oertzen; *Editorial:* Philippe Chabaud, Laurence Martin, Laurence Regnault; *Production:* Olivier Dasson Ville, Marie-Françoise Zeitouni
Parent Company: Weka-Verlag, Postfach 1180, D-8901 Kissing, Federal Republic of Germany
Subjects: Law, Economics, Tax Law, Social Sciences, Management
1983: 13 titles *Founded:* 1979
ISBN Publisher's Prefix: 2-7337

Y M C A-Press*, 11 rue de la Montagne Ste-Geneviève, F-75005 Paris Tel: (01) 3547446
Imprint: Les Editeurs Réunis (qv) in association with Bredda Books and Prideaux Press
Subjects: Religion, Literature, Russian books (in Russian)
ISBN Publisher's Prefix: 2-85065

Editions Philateliques **Yvert et Tellier***, 35 bis rue de Provence, F-75009 Paris
Tel: 7706298
Subjects: General, Encyclopaedias, Sports

Zodiaque, la Pierre-qui-Vire, F-89830 St-Léger-Vauban Tel: (86) 322123 Cable Add: Zodiaque-89830 St Léger
Man Dir: José Surchamp
Distribution in France: Weber Diffusion, 24-28 rue du Moulinet, F-75013 Paris
Distribution outside France: Marcel Weber, 13 rue de Monthoux, CH-1211 Geneva 2, Switzerland
Subjects: Ancient and Modern Art, Music
1981: 4 titles *1982:* 4 titles *Founded:* 1951

Literary Agents

Jean-Pierre **Boscq***, 65 rue du Faubourg St-Honoré, F-75008 Paris

Mrs W A **Bradley**, 18 quai de Béthune, F-75004 Paris Tel: (01) 3547514

D M F D, 16 rue du Regard, F-75006 Paris
Tel: 5484503/2224233
Formerly McKee et Mouche
Dirs: Donine Mouche, Robert Fouques Duparc

Françoise **Germain**, 8 rue de la Paix, F-75002 Paris Tel: (01) 2616814

Agence **Hoffman**, 77 blvd St-Michel, F-75005 Paris Tel: (01) 3265694 Cable Add: Aghoff Paris Telex: 203605F
Contacts: Boris or Georges Hoffman
There is a branch of this Agency in Munich, Federal Republic of Germany (qv)

Michelle **Lapautre**, 6 rue Jean Carriès, F-75007 Paris Tel: (01) 7348241/7346450
Cable Add: Milalit Paris Telex: 205247

Anne **Lenclud**, Pierre Lenclud, Agence Renault-Lenclud, 18 rue Blanche, F-75009 Paris Tel: (01) 5262679

McKee et Mouche, see DMFD

Matthias-Estienne, 27 rue du Dragon, F-75006 Paris Tel: 2222912

La **Nouvelle Agence**, 7 rue Corneille, F-75006 Paris Tel: (01) 3258560 Telex: 270105 F Txfra/ref 124
Contact: Mary Kling

Promotion Littéraire, 26 rue Chalgrin, F-75116 Paris Tel: (01) 5004210 Cable Add: Promolit Paris
Dir: Mariella Giannetti

Bureau littéraire international Marguerite **Scialtiel**, 14 rue Chanoinesse, F-75004 Paris
Tel: (01) 3547116
Contact: Geneviève Ulmann

Greta **Strassova**, 4 rue Gît-Le-Coeur, F-75006 Paris Tel: (01) 6333457
Formerly Héléna Strassova

Le **Téléscope***, 10 rue Mayet, F-75006 Paris
Tel: (01) 7837070
Dir: Chantal Galtier Roussel

Ellen **Wright**, 20 rue Jacob, F-75006 Paris 6
Tel: (01) 3542378

Book Clubs

Les **Amis** de Franco Maria Ricci, Galerie 12, 12 rue des Beaux-Arts, F-75006 Paris
Also associated with Club dei Bibliofili, Italy (qv)
Owned by: Franco Maria Ricci (qv)

L'**Amitié par le Livre***, Henri Frossard, F-25160 Labergement
First Book Club founded in France (in 1930, by teaching profession), it is non-profitmaking and run by voluntary effort
Owned by: L'Amitié par le Livre (qv)

Club du Livre d'Art, 1 rue Palatine, F-75006 Paris
Owned by: Editions Albert Morancé (qv)

Club du Livre SA, 28 rue Fortuny, F-75017 Paris Tel: 7638055
Man Dir: Philippe Lebaud
Subjects: Art, De Luxe Editions

Club Français du Livre*, 6 rue Galilée, F-75116 Paris

Livre Club **Diderot***, 13 blvd Bourdon, F-75004 Paris Tel: (01) 8876519
Subjects: Political and Economic Science, History, Poetry, Literature
Owned by: Les Editions Sociales-Messidor (qv)

Education et Culture, 28 rue de la Boétie, F-75008 Paris
Owned by: Les Editions des Deux Coqs d'Or (qv)

Nouveau Cercle Parisien du Livre*, 6 rue Bonaparte, F-75006 Paris
President: Daniel S Sickles
Subjects: Illustrated Books
Club is associated with publisher Galerie Lucie Weill (qv)

L'**Oeil** Ouvert*, 16 rue de l'Ecole-Polytechnique, F-75005 Paris
Owned by: Nouvelles Editions Rationalistes SA (qv)
Subject: Historical texts expressing rationalist thought

Poètes Présents, BP75, F-56340 Carnac-Plage
Owned by: Jean Grassin Editeur (qv)
Subject: Poetry

Presses d'Or, 28 rue de la Boétie, F-75008 Paris
Owned by: Les Editions des Deux Coqs d'Or (qv)

Publications de L'Ecole Moderne Française (PEMF), 189 blvd F Tonner, BP 109, F-06322 Cannes la Bocca cedex Tel: (093) 479611 Cable Add: Pemf
This company runs five Book Clubs supplying series of books for children: aged 8-12 (BTJ), aged 10-15 (BT), aged over 15 (BT2); for teachers (L'Educateur), and for audiovisual supplies (BT Son)
Owned by: Coopérative de l'Enseignement Laïc (qv)

Société des Bibliophiles, associated with Book Club Les Amis de Franco Maria Ricci (qv)

Major Booksellers

Brentano's, 37 ave de l'Opéra, F-75002 Paris
Tel: (01) 2615250

F N A C*, 136 rue de Rennes, F-75006 Paris Tel: (01) 5443912
Manager: Simone Hussard

Flammarion, 19 pl Bellecour, F-69002 Lyon
Tel: (07) 8380157 Telex: Flamlyo 300460 F;
54 La Canebière, F-13231 Marseille cedex 1
Tel: (091) 542520 (for other bookshops see under entry in Publishers)
Manager: Lionel Cortès

Librairie Joseph **Gibert***, 26 blvd St-Michel, F-75006 Paris Tel: (01) 3292141 Telex: gibliv 270162 f

Librairie La **Hune**, 170 blvd St-Germain, F-75006 Paris Tel: (01) 5483585

Librairie **Mollat**, 11-15 rue Vital-Carles, F-33080 Bordeaux cedex Tel: (056) 448487
Telex: 541542 F
Also: 83-91 rue Porte-Dijeaux, F-33080 Bordeaux cedex

Librairie générale des **P U F**, 49 blvd St-Michel, F-75005 Paris Tel: (01) 3258340
Owned by: Presses Universitaires de France (qv)

Librairie de **Provence**, 31 cours Mirabeau, F-13100 Aix en Provence

Librairie **Sauramps**, Le Triangle, pl de la Comédie, BP 9551, F-34045 Montpellier cedex Tel: (067) 588515 Telex: 480728
Manager: P Torreilles

Sodexport, 35 rue Grégoire de Tours, F-75006 Paris Tel: (01) 3259130 Telex: Lifran 270838 F
Association française pour la Diffusion du Livre Scientifique, Technique et Medical (French Society for the Distribution of scientific, technical and medical books)
President: Mr Jean Adam

Librairie de l'**Université**, 17 rue de la Liberté, F-21025 Dijon cedex Tel: (80) 305117
Manager: Jacques Bazin

Major Libraries

Archives nationales, 60 rue des Francs-Bourgeois, F-75141 Paris cedex 03
Publications: National Archive documents, which are sold and distributed by La Documentation Française (qv under Publishers)

Bibliothèque de l'Arsenal, 1 rue de Sully, F-75004 Paris Tel: (01) 2774421
Chief Librarian: Jean-Claude Garreta

Bibliothèque d'Art et d'Archéologie (Fondation Jacques Doucet), 3 rue Michelet, F-75272 Paris 6 Tel: 3543527
Dir: Denise Gazier
This is a Paris University library

Bibliothèque mazarine, 23 Quai Conti, F-75006 Paris Tel: (01) 3548948
Chief Curator: Pierre Gasnault

Bibliothèque municipale de Besançon*, 1 rue de la Bibliothèque, F-25000 Besançon Tel: (081) 812089
Librarian: Jacques Mironneau

Bibliothèque municipale de Grenoble, blvd Maréchal Lyautey, BP 1095, RP, F-38021 Grenoble cedex Tel: 460156
Librarian: Sylvie Truc

Bibliothèque municipale de la Ville de Lyon, 30 blvd Vivier-Merle, F-69431 Lyon cedex 3 Tel: (078) 628520
Librarian: Jean-Louis Rocher

Bibliothèque nationale, 58 rue de Richelieu, F-75084 Paris cedex 2 Tel: (01) 2618283
National Library
Publication: Revue de la Bibliothèque Nationale

Bibliothèque nationale et universitaire de Strasbourg, 5 rue du Maréchal Joffre, BP 1029/F, F-67070 Strasbourg cedex Tel: (088) 360068 (main address and Management and Legal Section); 6 place de la République, BP 1029/F, F-67070 Strasbourg cedex Tel: (088) 360068 (Literature and Human Sciences Section); 3 bis rue du Maréchal Joffre, BP 1029/F, F-67070 Strasbourg cedex Tel: (088) 360068 (Section dealing with Alsace region affairs); 6 rue Kirschleger, F-67085 Strasbourg cedex Tel: (088) 362323 (Medical Section); 72 route du Rhin, F-67400 Illkirch-Graffenstaden Tel: (088) 669077 (Pharmaceutical Annex); 34 blvd de la Victoire, BP 1037/F, F-67070 Strasbourg cedex Tel: (088) 613323 (Scientific and Technical Section)
Dir: Lily Greiner
Publications include: Bibliographie alsacienne; Catalogue critique des manuscrits persans; Papyrus grecs de la BNUS

Bibliothèque de Documentation Internationale Contemporaine, Campus Universitaire, F-92001 Nanterre cedex Tel: 7214022
Librarian: Véronique Blum
This is a Paris University library

Bibliothèque littéraire Jacques **Doucet**, 10 pl du Panthéon, F-75005 Paris Tel: (01) 3296100 (ext 22, 56, 72)
Librarian: François Chapon

Bibliothèque de l'**Ecole** des Langues orientales, 4 rue de Lille, F-75007 Paris Tel: (01) 2613790/2616203
Dir: Mrs M Debout

Bibliothèque de **Géographie***, 191 rue St-Jacques, F-75005 Paris Tel: (01) 3290147
This is a Paris University library

Bibliothèque de l'**Institut de France**, 23 Quai Conti, F-75006 Paris Tel: (01) 3268540
Librarian: Françoise Dumas

Bibliothèque Interuniversitaire de **Médecine**, 12 rue de l'Ecole de Médecine, F-75270 Paris cedex 6 Tel: (01) 3541675/3292177
Dir and Chief Curator: Ms Y Gueniot
Publications: Catalogue des Périodiques de la Bibliothèque (1976-1981), Catalogue des Congrès (1968)
This is a Paris University library

Bibliothèque du **Musée de l'Homme**, Palais de Chaillot, pl du Trocadéro, F-75116 Paris Tel: (01) 7045394
Librarian: Françoise Weil
Publication: Liste des Périodiques reçus regulièrement par la Bibliothèque du Musée de l'homme (Not on sale)

Bibliothèque centrale du **Muséum national** d'Histoire naturelle*, 38 rue Geoffroy St-Hilaire, F-75005 Paris 5 Tel: (01) 3317124/3319560

Bibliothèque Interuniversitaire de **Pharmacie**, 4 ave de l'Observatoire, F-75270 Paris cedex 6 Tel: (01) 3291208 ext 238, 311, 241 Telex: 200707 f
Librarian: Marie-Edmée Michel
This is a Paris University library

Bibliothèque **Sainte-Geneviève**, 10 pl du Panthéon, F-75005 Paris Tel: (01) 3296100
Librarian: Paul Roux-Fouillet
This is a Paris University library

Bibliothèque de la **Sorbonne**, 47 rue des Ecoles, F-75230 Paris cedex 5 Tel: (01) 3291213 (DAN 2194)
Chief Librarian: André Tuilier; *Librarian:* Jacquette Reboul
This is a Paris University library

Bibliothèque de l'**Université de Strasbourg**, see Bibliothèque nationale et universitaire de Strasbourg

Bibliothèques des **Universités de Paris**
The following are Paris University Libraries (for further details please see individual listings in alphabetical order in this section):
Bibliothèque d'Art et d'Archéologie (Fondation Jacques Doucet)
Bibliothèque de Documentation Internationale Contemporaine
Bibliothèque de Géographie
Bibliothèque Interuniversitaire de Médecine
Bibliothèque Interuniversitaire de Pharmacie
Bibliothèque Sainte-Geneviève
Bibliothèque de la Sorbonne

Service des Travaux Historiques de la **Ville de Paris** et Bibliothèque historique de la Ville de Paris, 24 rue Pavée, F-75004 Paris Tel: (01) 2744444
Librarian: Hélène Verlet

Library Associations

A B E F, see Association des Bibliothèques ecclésiastiques de France

A M P, see Association pour la Médiathèque Publique

Association de l'Ecole nationale supérieure de Bibliothécaires*, 17-21 blvd du 11 Novembre 1918, F-69100 Villeurbanne Tel: (07) 8896445
Association of the National School of Librarianship
General Secretary: P J Lamblin
Founded: 1967
Publication: Annuaire de l'Association de l'Ecole nationale supérieure de Bibliothécaires

Association des Archivistes français, 60 rue des Francs-Bourgeois, F-75141 Paris cedex 3 Tel: 2771130
Association of French Archivists
President: Mr G Ermisse; *Secretaries:* Michele Bimbenet, Elisabeth Rabut
Publication: La Gazette des Archives (quarterly)

Association des Bibliothécaires français, 65 rue de Richelieu, F-75002 Paris Tel: (01) 2975767
Association of French Librarians
President: Jean-Claude Garreta; *Executive Secretary:* Marie-Thérèse Varlamoff
Founded: 1906
Publication: Bulletin d'Information

Association des Bibliothèques ecclésiastiques de France (ABEF), 6 rue du Regard, F-75006 Paris
Executive Secretary: Paul-Marie Guillaume
Publication: Bulletin de Liaison de l'ABEF

Association des Diplômés de l'Ecole de Bibliothécaires-Documentalistes, Bibliothèque du Saulchoir, 43 bis rue la Glacière, F-75013 Paris Tel: (01) 5870533
Association of Graduates of the School of Librarians and Documentalists
Executive Secretary: Miss A Debert
Publication: Bulletin d'Information

Association française des Documentalistes et Bibliothécaires spécialisés, 5 ave Franco-Russe, F-75007 Paris Tel: (01) 5555516
French Association of Information Scientists and Special Librarians
Publication: Documentaliste

Association nationale des Bibliothécaires Municipaux*, c/o Ms Pintaparis, Cité Administrative, 17 blvd Morland, F-75004 Paris
National Association of Municipal Librarians

Association pour la Médiathèque Publique (AMP), Bibliothèque municipale, 37 rue St-Georges, F-59400 Cambrai Tel: (027) 813520
Publication: Médiathèques Publiques (Quarterly Review)

Centre d'Archives et de Documentation politiques et sociales*, 86 blvd Haussmann, F-75008 Paris
Centre for Political and Social Archives and Documentation
Publications: Informations politiques et sociales; Est et Ouest

Direction des Bibliothèques des Musées et de l'Information Scientifique et Technique, 3-5 blvd Pasteur, F-75015 Paris Tel: 5392575
A library administration department of the Ministère de l'Education Nationale
Librarian: Andrée Ponderoux
Publication: Bulletin des Bibliothèques de France

Fédération des Amicales de Documentalistes et Bibliothécaires de l'Education nationale*, 29 rue d'Ulm, F-75007 Paris
Amalgamated Friendly Societies of National Educational Record Clerks and Librarians

Library Reference Books and Journals

Books

Les Bibliothèques (The Libraries), Presses Universitaires de France, 108 blvd St-Germain, F-75279 Paris cedex 6

Les Bibliothèques de France au Service du Public (Public Libraries in France), Ministère de l'Education nationale, Direction de Bibliothèque et de Lecture publique, 1 rue du Périgord, F-31000 Toulouse

Les Bibliothèques publiques en France, ENSB-Presses, 17-21 blvd du 11 novembre 1918, F-69100 Villeurbanne

Répertoire des Bibliothèques et Organismes de Documentation (Directory of Documentary Libraries and Systems), Bibliothèque nationale, 58 rue de Richelieu, F-75084 Paris cedex 2

Libraries in France, Clive Bingley Ltd, 7 Ridgmount St, London WC1E 7AE

Journals

Bulletin de Liaison de l'ABEF, Association des Bibliothèques ecclésiastiques de France, 6 rue du Regard, F-75006 Paris

Bulletin d'Information (Information Bulletin), Association des Bibliothécaires français, 65 rue de Richelieu, F-75002 Paris

Bulletin de la Bibliothèque (Library Report), Institut national de la Statistique et des Etudes économiques, 29 quai Branly, F-75000 Paris

Bulletin des Bibliothèques de France (French Libraries' Report), Direction des Bibliothèques des Musées et de l'Information Scientifique et Technique, 3-5 blvd Pasteur, F-75015 Paris

Documentaliste (Custodian of Records); review of documentary information and techniques, French Association of Information Scientists and Special Librarians, 5 ave Franco-Russe F-75007 Paris

La Gazette des Archives (Archives Gazette), Association des Archivistes français, 60 rue des Francs-Bourgeois, F-75003 Paris

Informatique (ata Processing), Editions d'Informatique, 82 rue Lauriston, F-75116 Paris

Revue Bitrimestrielle (bi-quarterly journal for specialist librarians), Inter-CDI, 7 Résidence de Guinette, F-91150 Etampes

Revue de la Bibliothèque nationale, Bibliothèque nationale, 58 rue Richelieu, F-75084 Paris

Literary Associations and Societies

Académie des Lettres et des Arts, see Société du Vieux Montmartre

Académie Goncourt*, Salons Drouant, pl Gaillon, Paris
President: Hervé Bazin

Association des Ecrivains combattants*, 8 rue Roquépine, F-75008 Paris
Armed Services Writers' Association
Secretary: Maurice Ch Renard
Publication: Bulletin

Centre national des Lettres*, 6 rue Dufrénoy, F-75116 Paris
National Literary Centre
Secretary-General: Jacques Charpillon

The **Dickens** Fellowship, 29 blvd Mariette, F-62200 Boulogne sur Mer
Honorary Secretary: Madeleine Petit

La **Joie** par les Livres, 8 rue Saint-Bon, F-75004 Paris
Joy through Books — an experimental library and a documentation centre on children's literature
Publications: La Revue des Livres pour Enfants and other special selections

P E N Club français, 6 rue François Miron, F-75004 Paris Tel: (01) 2773787
President: René Tavernier; *General Secretary:* Danielle Dordet
Publication: News Bulletins to members (monthly)

Société d'Etudes dantesques*, Centre universitaire méditerranéen, 65 promenade des Anglais, F-06100 Nice Tel: (093) 868156
President: Louis Gautier-Vignal (of The Society for Dantesque Studies)

Société d'Histoire littéraire de la France, 14 rue de l'Industrie, F-75013 Paris
French Literary History Association
President: R Pomeau
Publications: Revue d'Histoire littéraire de la France (alternate months)

Société des anciens Textes français*, 19 rue de la Sorbonne, F-75005 Paris
Antiquarian French Texts Society
Publications obtainable from Editions A et J Picard Sàrl (qv)
General Secretary: Professor J Monfrin

Société des Gens de Lettres, Hôtel de Massa, 38 rue du Faubourg St Jacques, F-75014 Paris
Society of Men and Women of Letters
General Secretary: Michèle Kahn
Publications: Revue des Lettres et de l'Audiovisual; Journal des Lettres et de l'Audiovisual

Société des Poètes Français, Hôtel de Massa, 38 rue du Faubourg St Jacques, F-75014 Paris
Vice-President: Roland le Cordier, 23 blvd Gl de Gaulle, F-92500 Rueil-Malmaison
Secretary-General: Brigitte Level, 217 rue du Faubourg St Honoré, F-75008 Paris
Publication: Bulletin Trimestriel

Société du Vieux Montmartre, c/o Musée de Montmartre, 12 rue Cortot, F-75018 Paris
Tel: (01) 6066111
Formerly known as Académie des Lettres et des Arts
President: Claude Charpentier

Syndicat des Critiques littéraires, 58 rue Claude Bernard, F-75005 Paris
Society of Literary Critics
Secretary: R André
Publication: Bulletin du Syndicat (quarterly)

Literary Periodicals

Bulletin critique du livre français, Association pour la Diffusion de la Pensée Française, 9 rue Anatole de la Forge, F-75017 Paris

Bulletin des Lettres (Literary Report); review of criticism and of literary and bibliophilic information, Librairie Lardanchet, 10 rue du Président-Carnot, F-69002 Lyon

Critique (Criticism); general review of publications in France and abroad, Editions de Minuit, 7 rue Bernard Palissy, F-75006 Paris

Figaro littéraire (Literary Figaro), 14 Rond-Point des Champs-Elysées, Paris 8e

Information littéraire (Literary News), Editions J-B Baillière, 10 rue Thénard, F-75005 Paris

Lecture et Tradition (Reading and Tradition), Association pour la Diffusion de la Pensée Française, 9 rue Anatole de la Forge, F-75017 Paris

Lettres françaises (French Literature), 5 rue du Faubourg Poissonnière, Paris 9e

Lettres nouvelles (New Literature); literary review, 19 rue Aurélie, F-75007 Paris

Littérature (Literature), Larousse, 17 rue du Montparnasse, F-75298 Paris cedex 6

Magazine littéraire (Literary Magazine), Magazine-Expansion, 40 rue des Sts-Pères, Paris 7e

Nouvelles littéraires, Arts, Sciences, Spectacles (News of Literature, the Arts, Sciences, Entertainments), 146 rue Montmartre, Paris 2e

Parler (To Speak); literary review, Galerie 'Parti-Pris', 4 rue Alexandre 1er du Yougoslavie, Grenoble

Passerelle (Footbridge); literary review, Pierre Béarn, 60 rue Monsieur le Prince, F-75006 Paris

Quinzaine littéraire (Literary Fortnightly), 43 rue du Temple, F-75004 Paris 4

Revue de Littérature comparée (Review of Comparative Literature) (text in English, French, German, Italian and Spanish), Librairie Marcel Didier SA, 15 rue Cujas, F-75005 Paris

La Revue des Livres pour Enfants, La Joie par les Livres, 8 rue St-Bon, F-75004 Paris

Strophes (Stanzas), literary review, Jean Fremon, 9 rue de Belfort, F-9200 Asnières

Trousse-livres (Review of books for Juveniles), ten issues per year, Ligue de l'Enseignement, 3 rue Récamier, F-75341 Paris cedex 7

Literary Prizes

Academy of Thirteen Prize*
Known as 'Prix le Boisson' and given for a work of prose or poetry. Sixteen bottles of famous wine. Awarded annually. Enquiries to Academy of Thirteen, 166 rue de la Burgonce, Niort, Deux-Sèvres

L'**Amitié par le Livre** Prize*
Awarded annually for a Novel. Value of prize in 1982 was 1,500 francs. The prize is allocated on result of votes cast by members of the Book Club L'Amitié par le Livre for one of four nominated titles. Enquiries to Henri Frossard, L'Amitié par le Livre, F-25160 Labergement

François-Joseph **Audiffred** Prize
For a published work best qualified to inspire love of the virtues, and to discourage egoism and envy; or to instil patriotism. Awarded annually. Enquiries to Academy of Moral and Political Sciences, Institut de France, 23 quai de Conti, F-75006 Paris

Aujourd'hui Prize*
For a historical or contemporary work on politics. 5,000 francs awarded annually. Enquiries to Secrétariat, 12 rue du Quatre Septembre, F-75002 Paris

Joseph **Autran** Prize
Awarded annually to a poet for the whole of his work. Enquiries to Société des Poètes Français, 38 rue du Faubourg St Jacques, F-75014 Paris

René **Bardet** Prize
For a poetic work. Awarded every two years. Enquiries to Académie Française, Institut de France, 23 quai de Conti, F-75006 Paris

André **Barre** Prize
For a work of the most original thought and clearest style by a non-cleric. Enquiries to Académie Française, Institut de France, 23 quai de Conti, F-75006 Paris

Alice Louis **Barthou** Prize
To a woman of letters. For one work or all of her work. Awarded annually. Enquiries to Académie Française, Institut de France, 23 quai de Conti, F-75006 Paris

Louis **Barthou** Prize
To a writer whose work or life has served the best interests of France. Awarded annually. Enquiries to Académie Française, Institut de France, 23 quai de Conti, F-75006 Paris

Max **Barthou** Prize
To a writer under 30 years of age whose talent has been proven or who has shown great promise. Awarded annually. Enquiries to Académie Française, Institut de France, 23 quai de Conti, F-75006 Paris

Charles **Blanc** Prize
For a written work, preferably treating issues in art. Awarded annually. Enquiries to Académie Française, Institut de France, 23 quai de Conti, F-75006 Paris

Pascal **Bonetti** Grand Prize
Annual award of 1,000 francs for the entire work of a poet. Enquiries to Société des Poètes Français, 38 rue du Faubourg St Jacques, F-75014 Paris

Bordin Prize
To encourage high quality literature. Awarded annually. Enquiries to Académie Française, Institut de France, 23 quai de Conti, F-75006 Paris

Jean Bouscatel Foundation Prize
Awarded every three years for a book of verse; failing this, for a book on poetry or on a poet or poets. Next award in 1984. Enquiries to Académie Française, Institut de France, 23 quai de Conti, F-75006 Paris

Broquette-Gonin Grand Prize
To the author of a philosophical, political or literary work, inspiring the love of truth, beauty and goodness. Awarded annually. Enquiries to Académie Française, Institut de France, 23 quai de Conti, F-75006 Paris

Louis Castex Prize
For a literary work celebrating a major voyage of exploration or archaeological or ethnological discovery. Fictional romance excluded. Awarded annually. Enquiries to Académie Française, Institut de France, 23 quai de Conti, F-75006 Paris

Hercule Catenacci Prize
To encourage the publication of de luxe illustrated books of poetry, literature, history, archaeology or music. Awarded annually. Enquiries to Académie Française, Institut de France, 23 quai de Conti, F-75006 Paris

Chateauneuf-du-Pape Grand Prize
Instituted by the town of Chateauneuf-du-Pape and other cities in the same area. Awarded every two years for a poetic work (unpublished, or published in previous five years) which, irrespective of subject, appears most deserving for its formal purity and lofty sentiments. 1,000 francs. Awarded preferably to a young poet. Enquiries to Société des Poètes Français, 38 rue du Faubourg St Jacques, F-75014 Paris

Honoré Chavée Prize
To encourage work in linguistics and in particular research on romance languages. Awarded biennially. Enquiries to Académie des Inscriptions et Belles-Lettres, Institut de France, 23 quai de Conti, F-75006 Paris

François Coppée Prize
For the work of a poet, preferably just beginning his career. Awarded every two years. Enquiries to Académie Française, Institut de France, 23 quai de Conti, F-75006 Paris

Albert Dauzat Prize
Awarded annually for a poetic work in praise of animals. Enquiries to Société des Poètes Français, 38 rue du Faubourg St Jacques, F-75014 Paris

Eve Delacroix Prize
For a literary work, essay or novel combining literary quality, a sense of human dignity and the responsibilities of authorship. 5,000 francs. Awarded annually. Enquiries to Académie Française, Institut de France, 23 quai de Conti, F-75006 Paris

Deldebat de Gonzalva Foundation Prize
Founded in 1941, a medal is awarded every two years for a small body of poems classical in form and noble in inspiration. Enquiries to Société des Poètes Français, 38 rue du Faubourg St Jacques, F-75014 Paris

Marceline Desbordes-Valmore Prize
Founded 1937. Awarded annually to a female member of the Poetry Society, with a recognized talent at the height of its development. Enquiries to Société des Poètes Français, 38 rue du Faubourg St Jacques, F-75014 Paris

Deux Magots Prize*
Founded in 1933. For an avant-garde book by a young writer. Awarded annually. Enquiries to Café des Deux Magots, pl St-Germain-des-Prés, Paris

Dumas-Millier Prize
To a French writer over 45 whose work will be a credit to the French language and to the dissemination of French thought. Enquiries to Académie Française, Institut de France, 23 quai de Conti, F-75006 Paris

Alfred Dutens Prize
For the most useful work on linguistics. Awarded every ten years. Enquiries to Académie des Inscriptions et Belles Lettres, Institut de France, 23 quai de Conti, F-75270 Paris

Erlanger Foundation Prize
Founded in 1921, a medal awarded every five years for a poem, 150 lines maximum, written by someone who has served in front line of combat. Next award in 1985. Enquiries to Société des Poètes Français, 38 rue du Faubourg St Jacques, F-75014 Paris

Fabien Prize
To the author who has made the best suggestions for improving the moral and material position of the largest class. Awarded annually. Enquiries to Académie Française, Institut de France, 23 quai de Conti, F-75006 Paris

Fantasia Prize, see Jeune France Prize

Jules Favre Prize
For a literary work by a woman, poetry or prose, dealing with moral, educational, philological or historical questions. Awarded every two years. Enquiries to Académie Française, Institut de France, 23 quai de Conti, F-75006 Paris

Fémina Prize*
Founded in 1904 by review 'Femina' to encourage writing and draw women of letters closer together. A jury of women of letters meets in Paris each December to select a literary work of imagination written in French, by man or woman, prose or poetry. 5,000 francs. Awarded annually. Enquiries to Secretary-General, 79 blvd St-Germain, F-75006 Paris

Jean Finot Prize
For a work of a humanitarian social trend. Awarded every two years. Enquiries to Academy of Moral and Political Sciences, Institut de France, 23 quai de Conti, F-75006 Paris

Paul Flat Prize
For the best critical work and the best novel published by a young writer (between 30 and 40 years of age). Awarded annually. Enquiries to Académie Française, Institut de France, 23 quai de Conti, F-75006 Paris

Ernest Fleury Prize
Instituted by Marthe-Claire Fleury in memory of her father, the poet Ernest Fleury. It is awarded annually for the whole of a poet's work (classical poetry, published or not). Enquiries to Société des Poètes Français, 38 rue du Faubourg St Jacques, F-75014 Paris

Marshal Foch Prize
For a book on the future of the nation's defence by a French officer, engineer, scholar or philosopher. Awarded every two years. Enquiries to Académie Française, Institut de France, 23 quai de Conti, F-75006 Paris

Pascal Fortuny Prize
To the author of a poem of 200 lines or less, preferably written in the classical form. Awarded annually. Enquiries to Académie Française, Institut de France, 23 quai de Conti, F-75006 Paris

Fouraignan Foundation Prize
Founded in 1914, a medal awarded every five years for a collection of poems in 18th century French style, inspired by current events. Next award in 1986. Enquiries to Société des Poètes Français, 38 rue du Faubourg St Jacques, F-75014 Paris

Gegner Prize
To a philosopher-writer whose works contribute to the science of philosophy. Awarded annually. Enquiries to Academy of Moral and Political Sciences, Institut de France, 23 quai de Conti, F-75006 Paris

Giles Prize
For a work on China, Japan or the Far East. Awarded every two years to a French national only. Enquiries to Académie des Inscriptions et Belles Lettres, Institut de France, 23 quai de Conti, F-75270 Paris

Goncourt Prize*
Founded by J and E de Goncourt, 21 December 1903, the annual prize honours a prose work by a younger writer with originality of spirit and form. The novel is the preferred medium. The award is the same as when the prize was originated, 50 francs. Enquiries to Académie Goncourt, to Académie Goncourt, Armand Lanoux, 7 route de Malnoue, F-77420 Champs sur Marne

Grand Franco-Belgian Literary Prize*
Established 1956. For the sum of work of a Belgian author written in the French language, free from any political, religious or philosophical bias. Monetary prize of 2,000 French francs. Awarded annually. Enquiries to Association des Ecrivains de Langue française (Mer et Outre-Mer), 38 rue du Faubourg St Jacques, F-75014 Paris, France

Grand Prize for Literature
To a prose-writer or poet for one or more works noteworthy in form and inspiration 10,000 francs. Awarded every two years. Enquiries to Académie Française, Institut de France, 23 quai de Conti, F-75006 Paris

Grand Prize for Poetry Criticism
Awarded every two years for a work or body of work of poetic criticism or exegesis. Enquiries to Société des Poètes Français, 38 rue du Faubourg St Jacques, F-75014 Paris

Grand Prize of French Poets
Awarded annually since 1936, for the whole body of a poet's work, as decided by the Committee of the Société des Poètes (no applications allowed). Enquiries to Société des Poètes Français, 38 rue du Faubourg St Jacques, F-75014 Paris

Cardinal Grente Foundation Prize
Awarded biennially for the entire works of a regular or secular member of the Roman Catholic clergy. Enquiries to Académie Française, Institut de France, 23 quai de Conti, F-75006 Paris

Edmond Haraucourt Prize
Replaces the J-M Renaitour Prize. Awarded annually to a member of the Société des Poètes for the whole body of his work (no applications allowed). Enquiries to Société des Poètes Français, 38 rue du Faubourg St Jacques, F-75014 Paris

Marie Havez-Planque Prize
One year for a collection of stories or for a psychological novel, in fine prose; the following year for a collection of classical poetry. Preferably to a previously unpublished author. Awarded annually. Enquiries to Académie Française, Institut de France, 23 quai de Conti, F-75006 Paris

Emile Hinzelin Foundation Prize
For a volume of verse or a play in verse following the rules of French prosody, and showing the author's love for France. Awarded every five years: next award in

1985. Enquiries to Société des Poètes Français, 38 rue du Faubourg St Jacques, F-75014 Paris

Clovis Hugues Prize
Awarded annually to a poet whose work is inspired by the same sentiments of social brotherhood as moved Clovis Hugues. Enquiries to Société des Poètes Français, 38 rue du Faubourg St Jacques, F-75014 Paris

Interallié Prize
Awarded since 1930 for a high quality novel, preferably written by a journalist. Awarded annually. The winner for 1982 was Eric Ollivier for *Orphelin Demer* (Editions Denoël). Enquiries to Roger Giron (General Secretary), 72 blvd de La Tour-Maubourg, F-75007 Paris

Jules Janin Prize
Awarded every three years for the best translation of a Greek or Latin work published during the period. Next award in 1986. Enquiries to Académie Française, Institut de France, 23 quai de Conti, F-75006 Paris

Jean-Christophe Prizes
Offered by Mrs Alice Cluchier in memory of the young tragedian, her son. These prizes are awarded every two years to two young poets for a manuscript each of minimum ten poems, one in classical form, the other in free verse. Enquiries to Société des Poètes Français, 38 rue du Faubourg St Jacques F-75014 Paris

Jeune France Prize*
For the best unpublished book for young people. The book can cover any field. Awarded every two years. Enquiries to Les Editions Magnard Sàrl, 122 blvd St-Germain, F-75279 Paris cedex 6

Jeunesse et Poésie Prize*
Awarded annually to a young poet. Enquiries to Henri Frossard, L'Amitié par le Livre, F-25160 Labergement

Jouy Prize
Awarded biennially for a work published during the period designed as a study of modern-day behaviour, from an imaginative, critical or observationary viewpoint. Enquiries to Académie Française, Institut de France, 23 quai de Conti, F-75006 Paris

Labbé-Vauquelin Foundation Prize
Founded in 1924, a medal awarded every five years for a collection of reflective poetry regionally inspired. Next award in 1984. Enquiries to Société des Poètes Français, 38 rue du Faubourg St Jacques, F-75014 Paris

Georges Lafenestre Foundation Prize
Founded in 1938 by the family of Georges Lafenestre on the occasion of the poet's centenary, a medal is given for an unpublished poem of high inspiration and classical form, 150 lines maximum. Awarded every five years: next award in 1986. Enquiries to Société des Poètes Français, 38 rue du Faubourg St Jacques, F-75014 Paris

Lafontaine Prize
Awarded biennially for a work of popular morality. Enquiries to Académie Française, Institut de France, 23 quai de Conti, F-75006 Paris

Lambert Prize
To men of letters (or their widows) deserving of public recognition. Awarded annually. Enquiries to Académie Française, Institut de France, 23 quai de Conti, F-75006 Paris

Langlois Prize
For the best translation in verse or prose of a Greek, Latin or other foreign work into the French language. Awarded annually. Enquiries to Académie Française, Institut de France, 23 quai de Conti, F-75006 Paris

Eugène Le Mouël Foundation Prize
Founded in 1936, this is a medal awarded every five years for a poem in any genre, but preferably inspired by Eugène Le Mouël. Next award in 1985. Enquiries to Société des Poètes Français, 38 rue de Faubourg St Jacques, F-75014 Paris

Sébastien-Charles Leconte Foundation Prize
Founded in 1935, and awarded biennially in honour of a volume of classical poetry published in the preceding two years. Enquiries to Société des Poètes Français, 38 rue du Faubourg St Jacques, F-75014 Paris

Literary Critics' Grand Prize
For the best work of literary criticism or literary history. Established 1959. 3,000 francs, awarded annually. Last awarded to René Etiemble for *Quelques Essais de Littérature Universelle* (Gallimard). Enquiries to Syndicat des Critiques littéraires, 58 rue Claude Bernard, F-75005 Paris

Literary Prize of the Resistance*
For a work contributing to the history and spirit of the Resistance. 10,000 francs. Awarded annually by the Resistance Action Committee. Enquiries to Secrétariat, 10 rue de Charenton, F-75012 Paris

Paul Lofler Foundation Prize
Awarded every two years for the best sonnet submitted for competition to the Société des Poètes. Enquiries to Société des Poètes Français, 38 rue du Faubourg St Jacques, F-75014 Paris

Jean Mace Prize*
For works of fiction or non-fiction either as published books or as manuscripts for readers aged 15-18. Awarded annually. Enquiries to General Secretary Georges Daverac, Ligue Française de l'Enseignement et de l'Education Permanente, Service Culture, 3 rue Récamier, F-75341 Paris cedex 7

Maille-Latour-Landry Prize
To a young, talented writer deserving encouragement to follow a literary career. Awarded biennially. Enquiries to Académie Française, Institut de France, 23 quai de Conti, F-75006 Paris

Maisondieu Prize
To the author or founder of a work contributing to the betterment of the working classes. Awarded every two years. Enquiries to Academy of Moral and Political Sciences, Institut de France, 23 quai de Conti, F-75006 Paris

Médicis Prize
Awarded to an avant-garde novel, story or collection whose publication has not been accompanied by the celebrity or fame the author's talent deserves. Founded in 1958. In 1981 awarded to François-Olivier Rousseau for *L'Enfant d'Edouard* (Mercure de France). Enquiries to 20 rue Cortot, F-75108 Paris

Narcisse Michaut Prize
For the best work of French literature. Awarded every two years. Enquiries to Académie Française, Institut de France, 23 quai de Conti, F-75006 Paris

Louis P Miller Prize
For works furthering the love of moral virtue, in particular remembrance and gratitude. Awarded annually. Enquiries to Académie Française, Institut de France, 23 quai de Conti, F-75006 Paris

Marcelle Millier Prize
To a female writer aged 45 or more, the entirety of whose work will do honour to French literature. Enquiries to Académie Française, Institut de France, 23 quai de Conti, F-75006 Paris

Montyon Prize
For any work published by a French author showing qualities of practical idealism. Awarded annually. Enquiries to Académie Française, Institut de France, 23 quai de Conti, F-75006 Paris

National Grand Prize for Literature*
To the French writer who has contributed most to French literature. 20,000 francs. Awarded annually. Enquiries to French Ministry of Cultural Affairs, Centre National des Lettres, 6 rue Dufrénoy, F-75116 Paris

National Grand Prize for Poetry*
To the French poet who has contributed most to French poetry. 20,000 francs. Awarded annually. Enquiries to French Ministry of Cultural Affairs, Centre National des Lettres, 6 rue Dufrénoy, F-75116 Paris

Alfred Née Prize
For a work showing originality of thought and style. Awarded annually. Enquiries to Académie Française, Institut de France, 23 quai de Conti, F-75006 Paris

Novel Prize
To a young prose-writer for a fictional work of high imaginative power. 20,000 francs. Awarded annually. Enquiries to Académie Française, Institut de France, 23 quai de Conti, F-75006 Paris

Paris Grand Prize for Literature*
For different forms of literature such as novel, poetry, criticism, essay, history, philosophy. Awarded annually (each year for a different form). Enquiries to Directeur des Affaires Culturelles, 17 Blvd Roland, F-75004 Paris

Paris Prize
For a novel. Awarded annually. Enquiries to Academy of Letters and Arts, c/o Musée de Montmartre, 12 rue Cortot, F-75018 Paris

De Pimodan Foundation Prize
Founded in 1926, a medal is awarded every five years to a regional poet celebrating his land. Next award in 1987. Enquiries to Société des Poètes Français, 38 rue du Faubourg St Jacques, F-75014 Paris

Charles Pitou Foundation Prize
Founded 1928, a medal is awarded every five years for a poem in strictly classical form celebrating a French province, preferably Normandy. Next award in 1987. Enquiries to Société des Poètes Français, 38 rue du Faubourg St Jacques, F-75014 Paris

Raymond Poincaré Prize*
For a literary work which promotes a favourable view of the defence forces. Awarded to French citizens, or to foreigners who have served in a French military unit. 2,000 francs. Awarded annually. Enquiries to National Union of Reserve Officers, 17 ave de l'Opéra, F-75001 Paris

Hélène Porgès Prize
Awarded every four years for a nature book which will encourage in schoolchildren a love of their country. Enquiries to Académie Française, Institut de France, 23 quai de Conti, F-75006 Paris

Prose Poétique Prize
Awarded periodically at discretion of Committee of Société des Poètes for a work of poetry which ignores classical prosody but is essentially poetic in spirit. Enquiries to Société des Poètes Français, 38 rue du Faubourg St Jacques, F-75014 Paris

R T L (Radio Télé Luxembourg)/Poésie 1 Prize
Given annually, this award aims to focus public attention on a poet of merit. It was won in 1982 by Alain Bosquet for *Sonnets pour une Fin de Siècle* (Gallimard). Enquiries to Secrétariat du Grand Prix RTL/Poésie 1, 110 rue du Cherche-Midi, F-75006 Paris

J-M **Renaitour** Prize, replaced by Edmond Haraucourt Prize (qv)

Jean **Reynaud** Prize
Awarded every five years for the most meritorious work produced in the period (the work always to be of an original, innovative and imaginative character). Next award due in 1984, but if no work considered worthy, money is otherwise disposed of. Enquiries to Académie Française, Institut de France, 23 quai de Conti, F-75006 Paris

Roberge Prizes
One year to a young poet who has published no more than two volumes of verse. The following year to a young author who has published no more than two novels. Enquiries to Académie Française, Institut de France, 23 quai de Conti, F-75006 Paris

Albéric **Rocheron** Foundation Prize
Awarded for the critical, literary or historical study which best illustrates the relationship between the character of a period and its literature. Enquiries to Académie Française, Institut de France, 23 quai de Conti, F-75006 Paris

Duchess of **Rohan** Foundation Prize
Medal awarded every five years to a poet, preferably young, who submits work of maximum 200 lines in competition. Next award in 1988. Enquiries to Société des Poètes Français, 38 rue du Faubourg St Jacques, F-75014 Paris

Roucoules Foundation Grand Prize for Poetry
10,000 francs. Awarded annually. Enquiries to Académie Française, Institut de France, 23 quai de Conti, F-75006 Paris

Saint-Cricq-Theis Prize
Awarded every three years for a poetic work of a spiritualistic, ethical, dramatic, patriotic nature. Enquiries to Académie Française, Institut de France, 23 quai de Conti, F-75006 Paris

Saintour Prize
For works (lexicons, grammars, critical studies, commentaries, etc) on the study of the French language, in particular from the 16th century to the present. Awarded annually. Enquiries to Académie Française, Institut de France, 23 quai de Conti, F-75006 Paris

Short Story Prize
Awarded annually for a collection of short stories. Enquiries to Académie Française, Institut de France, 23 quai de Conti, F-75006 Paris

Sobrier-Arnould Prize
To the authors of the two best works which are both ethical and instructive to youth. Awarded annually. Enquiries to Académie Française, Institut de France, 23 quai de Conti, F-75006 Paris

Paul **Teissonnière** Prize
For the best published work of a liberal tendency on moral or religious philosophy. Enquiries to Académie Française, Institut de France, 23 quai de Conti, F-75006 Paris

Thiers Prize
For the encouragement of literature and historical research. Awarded every three years for the best historical work published since the previous prize. Next award in 1985. Enquiries to Académie Française, Institut de France, 23 quai de Conti, F-75006 Paris

Lucien **Tisserand** Prize
To a French novelist, aged between 40 and 50, with proven talent and an expected long future. Awarded annually. Enquiries to Académie Française, Institut de France, 23 quai de Conti, F-75006 Paris

Maurice **Trubert** Prize
For a prose or verse work of any kind, but which respects classical traditions and a Catholic moral outlook. Author must be French-born and under 30. Awarded biennially. Enquiries to Académie Française, Institut de France, 23 quai de Conti, F-75006 Paris

Antony **Valabrègue** Prize
To encourage a young poet who has published one volume of verse. Awarded biennially. Enquiries to Académie Française, Institut de France, 23 quai de Conti, F-75006 Paris

Valentine Abraham **Verlain** Prize
To a woman of letters or for a needy female artist. Awarded annually. Enquiries to Académie Française, Institut de France, 23 quai de Conti, F-75006 Paris

Verlaine Prize
Contest for all types of poetry except dramatic. Awarded every three years: next award in 1984. Enquiries to Académie Française, Institut de France, 23 quai de Conti, F-75006 Paris

Claire **Virenque** Prize
To young authors. One year for a collection of poems, the next for a novel or biography showing Christian or high ethical inspiration. Enquiries to Académie Française, Institut de France, 23 quai de Conti, F-75006 Paris

Volney Prize
For a work in comparative philology. Enquiries to Académie des Inscriptions et Belles-Lettres, Institut de France, 23 quai de Conti, F-75006 Paris

J J **Weiss** Prize
For a prose work in the purest classic style on travel, literature, literary or dramatic criticism or politics. Awarded every two years. Enquiries to Académie Française, Institut de France, 23 quai de Conti, F-75006 Paris

Valentine de **Wolmar** Prize
For the finest novel or collection of poetry published during the year. Awarded annually. Enquiries to Académie Française, Institut de France, 23 quai de Conti, F-75006 Paris

Translation Agencies and Associations

Société française des Traducteurs*, 1 rue de Courcelles, F-75008 Paris
French Union of Translators

French Guiana

General Information

Language: French
Religion: Roman Catholic
Population: 66,000
Literacy Rate (1967): 73.9%
Bank Hours: 0700-1130, 1400-1600 Monday-Friday
Shop Hours: 0800-1300, 1500-1800 Monday-Friday
Currency: French currency
Export/Import Information: Overseas department of France, which is a member of the European Economic Community. Tariff as for France. See France for domiciliation of documents. No import licences required. Same exchange restrictions as France.
Copyright: Berne, UCC (see International Section

Major Booksellers

Mme **Beaufort***, 16 rue du Lieutenant-Brassé, BP 505, Cayenne Tel: 98

La **Boutique** Bleue*, ave Pasteur, BP 243, Cayenne

Emilio **Gratien***, 25 ave du Général de Gaulle, Cayenne Tel: 280

Librairie-Papeterie Universelle*, 26 rue Lallouette, Cayenne Tel: 240

Major Libraries

Bibliothèque Franconie, Préfecture de la Guyane, BP 303, 97300 Cayenne

Office de la Recherche Scientifique et Technique Outre-Mer*, Centre ORSTOM de Cayenne, Bibliothèque, BP 165, Cayenne
Office of Scientific and Technical Research Overseas

Literary Associations and Societies

Association des Amis du Livre, Préfecture de la Guyane, BP 303, 97300 Cayenne
Association of Book Lovers

French Polynesia

General Information

Language: French, Tahitian, English
Religion: Roman Catholic
Population: 146,000
Literacy Rate (1962): 94.5%
Bank Hours: 0730-1530 Monday-Friday; some 0730-1130 Saturday
Shop Hours: 0730-1100, 1400-1700 Monday-Friday; 0730-1130 Saturday
Currency: 100 centimes = 1 franc CFP
Export/Import Information: No tariff on books other than children's picture books; advertising matter subject to customs duty, import duty, although catalogues generally considered printed books. Advertising

subject to Statistical Tax. Miscellaneous tax of 2% of customs value on books and advertising. No import licence required. Exchange controls

Publishers

Société Nouvelle des Editions du **Pacifique**, BP 1722, Papeete, Tahiti Tel: 26643 Telex: 293 fp tahiti
Man Dir: Didier Millet; *Marketing Dir:* Olivier Canaveso
Orders to: Hachette Pacifique, BP 334, Papeete, Tahiti
Subjects: Travel Books, Natural Science (tropical environment), History, Non-fiction, Gift Books
ISBN Publisher's Prefix: 2-85700

Major Booksellers

Librairie **Au Ping-Pong***, 6 rue du Commandant-Destremeau, Papeete, Tahiti Tel: 133

Librairie **Hachette Pacifique** SA*, 10 ave Bruat, BP 334, Papeete, Tahiti Tel: 25610 Telex: Hachpac 293 FP
General Manager: Maurice Vasseur
Parent Company: Librairie Hachette, France (qv)
The following bookshops in French Polynesia are now under the management of Librairie Hachette Pacifique SA: Hachette Pacifique Bruat, Quartier-Latin, Hachette Vaïma, Kiosque Vaïma

Librairie R **Klima**, La Boutique, BP 31, pl Notre-Dame, Papeete, Tahiti Tel: 20063
Manager: Manuella Luciani

Librairie **Quartier-Latin**
Now under the Management of Libraririe Hachette Pacifique SA (qv)

Gabon

General Information

Language: French
Religion: About half Roman Catholic and half animist
Population: 538,000
Literacy Rate (1960-61): 14.8%
Bank Hours: 0700-1115, 1430-1615 Monday-Friday
Shop Hours: 0700 or 0800-1200 or 1230, 1430 or 1500-1830 or 1900 Monday-Saturday. Some close Monday
Currency: CFA franc
Export/Import Information: Member of the Customs and Economic Union of Central Africa. No tariff on books. Import licence required for all imports valued above a certain amount
Copyright: Berne (see International Section)

Publishers

Government Printer (Imprimerie Centrale d'Afrique)*, BP 154, Libreville

Saint-Joseph*, BP 58, Libreville

Major Booksellers

Centre de **Littérature** Evangélique*, BP 206, Oyem

Librairie **Hachette***, BP 121, Libreville Tel: 733131 Telex: 5418 go

Librairie **Nouvelle***, BP 612, Libreville Tel: 721616

Librairie **Sogalivre***, BP 50, Port-Gentil Tel: 52319

Major Libraries

Archives et bibliothèque nationale*, BP 1188, Libreville Tel: 732543
Librarian: Gaston Rapontchombo

Centre **Bibliothèque** d'Information*, BP 3127, Libreville Tel: 21115

Centre culturel **américain**, Bibliothèque, BP 2237, Libreville Tel: 721558/722161
Librarian: Carolle M'Vie

Centre culturel **français** St-Exupéry Bibliothèque*, BP 2103, Libreville Tel: 721120

Collège Jésus Marie Bibliothèque*, BP 120, Bitam Tel: 277

Ecole normale supérieure Bibliothèque*, BP 16030, Libreville
Teachers' Training College Library
Librarian: Miss M E Bouscarle

Institut polytechnique de l'Afrique centrale Bibliothèque*, BP 1158, Libreville

Bibliothèque de l'**Université nationale** du Gabon*, BP 11132, Libreville Tel: 32506
Librarian: J G Aboghe Obyan

Bibliothèque Centrale de l'**Université Omar Bongo***, BP 13131, Libreville Tel: 732956, 732979 Telex: 32506
Central Library of the Omar Bongo University, under the direction of the Ministry for Higher Teaching of Scientific Environmental Research and Nature Protection
Dir: Jean Grégoire Aboghe-Obyan
Publications: Liste des nouvelles acquisitions (six-monthly); *Liste des périodiques en cours* (annual); *Inventaire du fonds documentaire, par discipline* (annual)

The Gambia

General Information

Language: English
Religion: Muslim
Population: 569,000
Bank Hours: 0800-1300 Monday-Thursday; 0800-1100 Friday and Saturday
Shop Hours: 0800 or 0900-1200, 1400-1700 Monday-Thursday; 0800 or 0900-1200, 1500-1700 Friday; 0800 or 0900-1200 Saturday
Currency: 100 butut = 1 dalasi
Export/Import Information: No tariff on books. Import Tax on all. No import licence required. National Trading Corporation has no monopoly. Exchange controls

Book Trade Reference Books

National Bibliography of the Gambia, Gambia National Library, Banjul

Publishers

The **Government Press***, Banjul Tel: 399 Telex: 2204

Major Booksellers

The **Gambia** Methodist Bookshop Ltd*, PO Box 203, Banjul Tel: 8179

Jeng's Bookshop*, PO Box 234, Banjul

Major Libraries

Gambia College Library*, Gambia College, Yundum Campus, Yundum Tel: Yundum 811
Librarian: Rosanna A Ndaw

Gambia National Library, Ministry of Education, Youth, Sports and Culture, PMB 552, Banjul Tel: 8312
Chief Librarian: Sally P C N'Jie
Publications include: National Bibliography of the Gambia

Yundum College Library, see Gambia College Library

German Democratic Republic

General Information

Language: German. About 70,000 in Lusatia speak Serb but also speak German
Religion: About 60% Protestant, 8% Roman Catholic
Population: 17 million
Bank Hours: Generally 0800-1600 Monday-Friday; open Saturday morning
Shop Hours: Vary. Generally 0900 or 1000-1800 or 1900 Monday-Friday; open part day Saturday
Currency: 100 Pfennige = 1 Mark der DDR
Export/Import Information: Foreign trade is a state monopoly; books imported and exported by Buchexport, Leninstr 16, Postfach 160, DDR-7010 Leipzig. Import licences required and Foreign Trade Bank handles all payments. No advertising materials to be sent to private individuals; for preparation of advertising, contact Interwerbung GmbH, Berlin
Copyright: UCC, Berne (see International section)

Book Trade Organizations

Börsenverein der Deutschen Buchhändler zu Leipzig, Gerichtsweg 26, DDR-7010 Leipzig Tel: 293851 Cable Add: Buchbörse
Association of German Democratic Republic Booksellers in Leipzig
Publications: Börsenblatt für den Deutschen Buchhandel

Buchexport — Volkseigener Aussenhandelsbetrieb der Deutschen Demokratischen Republik, Leninstr 16, Postfach 160, DDR-7010 Leipzig Tel: 71370 Telex: 051678

GERMAN DEMOCRATIC REPUBLIC

GDR Foreign Trade Enterprise
Publications: Nova, Wissen und Können, Buch der Zeit, Land und Leute, DDR-Gesamtkatalog, DDR-Periodical.
The state organization for foreign trade. These catalogues contain particulars of the entire range of GDR publications

Ministerrat der Deutschen Demokratischen Republik, Ministerium für Kultur, Hauptverwaltung Verlage und Buchhandel*, DDR-1080 Berlin, Clara-Zetkin-Str 90
Council of Ministers of the German Democratic Republic, Ministry of Culture, Main Department — Publishing and Bookselling

Book Trade Reference Books and Journals

Books

Adressbuch des Volksbuchhandels der Deutschen Demokratischen Republik (Directory of the People's Book Trade of the GDR), Volksbuchhandel der DDR, Zentrale Zeitung, DDR-7010 Leipzig, Friedrich-Ebert-Str 25

Die Deutsche Demokratische Republik, ein Land des Buches (The German Democratic Republic, A Country for Books), Börsenverein der Deutschen Buchhändler zu Leipzig, Gerichtsweg 26, DDR-7010 Leipzig

Deutsches Bücherverzeichnis (5-yearly German Book List), Deutsche Bücherei, Deutscher Platz, DDR-7010 Leipzig

Schriftenreihen aus den Verlagen der Deutschen Demokratischen Republik (Series from the Publishers of the GDR), Buchexport, Leninstr 16, DDR-7010 Leipzig

Titel-Information (Title-Information), Leipziger Komissions- und Grossbuchhandel, Leninstr 16, DDR-7010 Leipzig

Verlage der Deutschen Demokratischen Republik (Publishers of the GDR), Börsenverein der Deutschen Buchhändler zu Leipzig, Gerichtsweg 26, DDR-7010 Leipzig

Journals

Beiträge zur Literaturkunde (Contributions to Literary Knowledge); bibliography of selected newspaper and periodical contributions, VEB, Bibliographisches Institut, Gerichtsweg 26, DDR-7010 Leipzig

Bibliographie der Bibliographien (Bibliography of Bibliographies), Deutsche Bücherei, Deutscher Platz, DDR-7010 Leipzig

Bibliographie der Übersetzungen deutschsprachiger Werke (Bibliography of Translations of German Language Works), Deutsche Bücherei, Deutscher Platz, DDR-7010 Leipzig

Bibliographie fremdsprachiger Germanica (Bibliography of Germanics in Foreign Languages), Deutsche Bücherei, Deutscher Platz, DDR-7010 Leipzig

Börsenblatt für den deutschen Buchhandel (German Book Trade Journal), Börsenverein der Deutschen Buchhändler zu Leipzig, Gerichtsweg 26, DDR-7010 Leipzig

Buch der Zeit (Books of the Day), (text in English and German), Buchexport, Leninstr 16, DDR-7010 Leipzig

Bücher aus der DDR (Books from the German Democratic Republic) Lists of new books and reprint editions on German Language and Literature, German history and culture etc published every 3 months by Buchexport, Leninstr 16, DDR-7010 Leipzig

DDR Gesamtkatalog (German Democratic Republic Complete Catalogue), Buchexport, Leninstr 16, DDR-7010 Leipzig
Annual catalogue in two volumes covering all titles published in preceding year

Deutsche National-Bibliographie (German National Bibliography), Deutsche Bücherei, Deutscher Platz, DDR-7010 Leipzig

Jahresverzeichnis der Verlagsschriften (Annual List of Publications), Deutsche Bücherei, Deutscher Platz, DDR-7010 Leipzig

Nova; forthcoming books (table of contents and subtitles in English, German and Russian), Buchexport, Leninstr 16, DDR-7010 Leipzig. Two issues per month

Selecta; titles immediately available from the publishers of the DDR, Buchexport, Leninstr 16, DDR-7010 Leipzig

Wissen und Können (To Know and Be Able), Buchexport, Leninstr 16, DDR-7010 Leipzig. A series of 26 Catalogues covering every branch of knowledge under the headings: I — Social Sciences; II — Art and Literature; III — Natural Sciences; IV — Technical Science/Engineering; V — Agriculture and Forestry, Veterinary Science; VI — Medicine. The Catalogues list all books under the particular subject selected which are available for sale, in print or in course of preparation.
Publication of each list is annual.

Publishers

Akademie-Verlag*, Leipziger Str 3-4, Postfach 1233, DDR-1080 Berlin Tel: 22360 Cable Add: Akademie-Verlag Berlin Telex: 114420 averl dd
Publicity: A Leister
Subjects: History, Philosophy, Literature, History of Art, Archaeology, Ethnography, Oriental, Biology, Geology, Mathematics, Physics, Chemistry, Medicine, Languages, Economics; Periodicals
Founded: 1946

Altberliner Verlag, Neue Schoenhauser Str 8, Postfach 44, DDR-1020 Berlin Tel: 2826749
Dir: Dr Gerhard Dahne; *Editorial:* Alfred Könner
Subject: Children's Books
1982: 58 titles *Founded:* 1945

Aufbau-Verlag Berlin und Weimar*, Französische Str 32, Postfach 1217, DDR-1080 Berlin Tel: 2202421 Cable Add: Aufbau Verlag Berlin Telex: Berlin 112527
Associate Company: Verlag Rütten und Loening, German Democratic Republic
Subjects: General Fiction, Library of World Literature, Belles Lettres, Literary Criticism, Paperbacks, Periodicals
Founded: 1945

Johann Ambrosius **Barth** Verlagsbuchhandlung, Salomonstr 18b, Postfach 109, DDR-7010 Leipzig Tel: 70131 Cable Add: Barth Leipzig
Man Dir: Klaus Wiecke
Orders to; Buchexport, Postfach 160, DDR-7010 Leipzig
Subjects: Medicine, Dentistry, Stomatology, Psychology, Natural Science, Chemistry, Astronomy, Physics; Periodicals, Publications of the German Academy of Naturalists
Founded: 1780

VEB Verlag für **Bauwesen***, Französische Str 13-14, Postfach 1232, DDR-1086 Berlin Tel: 20410 Cable Add: Bauwesenverlag Telex: 112229 Trave
Man Dir: Siegfried Seeliger; *Editorial:* Siegfried Schikora; *Sales, Publicity:* Franz Rautenstrauch; *Production:* Günter Langer
The Building Industry Publishing House
Subjects: Civil Engineering, Architecture and Building Construction, Materials and Mechanics, Periodicals
Founded: 1960

VEB **Bibliographisches Institut**, Leipzig, Gerichtsweg 26, Postfach 130, DDR-7010 Leipzig Tel: 7801 Cable Add: Biblio Leipzig Telex: 512773
Man Dir: HelmuT Bähring
Associate Companies: VEB Max Niemeyer Verlag (qv); VEB Verlag Enzyklopädie Leipzig (qv)
Subjects: General Dictionaries, Reference, Biography, Bibliographies, German Language, Library Science, Documentation, Literature, Languages, Periodicals
Miscellaneous: This organization has now taken over the titles of the former VEB Verlag für Buch- und Bibliothekswesen (dissolved)
Founded: 1826

Hermann **Böhlaus** Nachfolger, Meyerstr 50a, DDR-5300 Weimar Tel: 2071 Cable Add: Böhlauverlag DDR-5300 Weimar
Man Dir: Dr Leiva Petersen
Subjects: History of Law, Literature & Art, Critical Editions & Yearbooks, Mediaeval History
Founded: 1624

VEB **Breitkopf und Härtel** Musikverlag, Karlstr 10, Postfach 147, DDR-7010 Leipzig Tel: 7351 Cable Add: Breitkopfs
Man Dir: Dr Gunter Hempel; *Sales Dir:* Werner Hennig
Subjects: Music: Vocal and Instrumental Music, Biographies, Reference, Musicology
Founded: 1719

VEB F A **Brockhaus** Verlag, Leipzig, Salomonstr 17, DDR-7010 Leipzig Tel: 7846
Subjects: Picture and Travel books (relating to the German Democratic Republic and other countries), Popular Scientific History and Reportage, Reference

VEB **Deutscher Landwirtschaftsverlag**, Reinhardtstr 14, DDR-1040 Berlin Tel: 28930 Cable Add: Bauernbuch Berlin
Subject: Agriculture, Horticulture, Forestry

VEB **Deutscher Verlag der Wissenschaften**, Johannes-Dieckmann-Str 10, Postfach 1216, DDR-1080 Berlin Tel: 22900 Cable Add: Devauwe Berlin Telex: 114390 dvw dd
Subjects: History, Philosophy, Psychology; General, Natural & Social Sciences; Physics, Chemistry, Mathematics
Founded: 1954

VEB **Deutscher Verlag für Grundstoffindustrie**, Karl-Heine-Str 27, DDR-7031 Leipzig Tel: 44441 Cable Add: Grundstoffverlag Leipzig Telex: 051451 Grundstoffverlag
Subjects: Geological Sciences, Coal, Energy, Mining of Ores, Metallurgy, Potash, Chemistry and Chemical Process Technology; also Popular Scientific Literature, Periodicals

VEB **Deutscher Verlag für Musik**+, Karlstr 10, Postfach 147, DDR-7010 Leipzig Tel: 7351 Cable Add: Demusica Leipzig
Man Dir: Dr Gunter Hempel; *Sales Dir:* Werner Hennig
Subjects: Music: Vocal and Instrumental Music, Reference, Biographies, Children's

and Young Peoples' Books on Music, Musicology, Facsimilies, Musical Belles Lettres
Founded: 1954

Dieterich'sche Verlagsbuchhandlung, Mottelerstr 8, Postfach 88, DDR-7022 Leipzig Tel: 592356/52857/51868
Associate Companies: Insel-Verlag (qv); Gustav Kiepenhauer Verlag (qv); Paul List Verlag (qv)
Subjects: World literature in translation
Founded: 1766

Dietz Verlag*, Wallstr 76-79, Postfach 273, DDR-1020 Berlin Tel: 27030 Cable Add: Dietzverlag Berlin Telex: 0114741
Subjects: Social Science, Economics, Philosophy, Politics, History, Memoirs, Periodicals
Founded: 1945

VEB **Domowina** Verlag, Tischmacherstr 27, DDR-8600 Bautzen Tel: 511316 Telex: 287220
Man Dir: Martin Benad; *Editorial:* Dr Pivölkel
Subjects: Serbian — Literature, Popular Sciences, Textbooks, Periodicals
1981: 92 titles *1982:* 90 titles *Founded:* 1958

VEB Verlag **Enzyklopädie** Leipzig, Gerichtsweg 26, Postfach 130, DDR-7010 Leipzig Tel: 7801 Cable Add: Enzy Leipzig Telex: 512773
Man Dir: Helmut Bähring
Associate Companies: VEB Bibliographisches Institut (qv); VEB Max Niemeyer Verlag (qv)
Subjects: Languages, Dictionaries, Foreign Language Textbooks, Handbook on the German Democratic Republic
Founded: 1956

Eulenspiegel Verlag für Satir und Humor*, Kronenstr 73-74, Postfach 1239, DDR-1080 Berlin Tel: 2202126 Cable Add: Eulenspiegelverlag Berlin
Associate Company: Verlag Das Neue Berlin (qv)
Subjects: Humorous Publications generally: Satire, Caricature, Cartoons
Founded: 1954

Evangelische Verlagsanstalt GmbH, Krautstr 52, Postfach 114, DDR-1017 Berlin Tel: 2700131 Cable Add: Evaverlag Berlin
Dirs: Dr Forck, Dr Petzold
Subjects: Christian History, Devotional, Biblical Exegesis, Christian Fiction and Poetry, Biography, Art Books, Music, Periodicals
1981: 118 titles *1982:* 123 titles *Founded:* 1946

VEB **Fachbuchverlag**, Karl-Heine-Str 16, Postfach 67, DDR-7031 Leipzig Tel: 49500 Cable Add: Fachbuch Leipzig Telex: 51451 fachb d d
Man Dir: Dr Erhard Walter
Subjects: General Knowledge, Popular Science, Basic Technologies, Industries (various), Periodicals
1983: approx 140 titles *Founded:* 1949

VEB Gustav **Fischer** Verlag, Jena, Villengang 2, Postfach 176, DDR-6900 Jena Tel: Jena 27332 Cable Add: Fischerbuch Telex: 05886176
Parent Companies: Volkseigene Verlage für Medizin und Biologie, Berlin, Jena, Leipzig
Associate Companies: VEB Georg Thieme (qv); VEB Verlag Volk und Gesundheit (qv)
Subjects: Medicine, Veterinary, Biology, Periodicals
Founded: 1878

VEB **Fotokinoverlag**, Karl-Heine-Str 16, Postfach 67, DDR-7031 Leipzig Tel: 49500 Cable Add: Fachbuch Leipzig Telex: 51451 fachb d d
Man Dir: Dr Erhard Walter
Subjects: Photography, Film, Periodicals
1983: approx 20 titles *Founded:* 1957

Verlag für die **Frau***, Friedrich-Ebert-Str 76-78, Postfach 1005/1025, DDR-7010 Leipzig Tel: 71790 Telex: 51773
Subjects: Fashion, Family, Domestic Science, Periodicals
Founded: 1946

Akademische Verlagsgesellschaft **Geest und Portig** KG, Sternwarten Str 8, Postfach 106, DDR-7010 Leipzig Tel: 293158/59/297535 Cable Add: Akabuch Leipzig
Man Dir: Ing Heinz Kratz
Associate Company: BSB B G Teubner Verlagsgesellschaft (qv)
Subjects: Chemistry, Physics, Mathematics, History of Science, Electro-Technology, Periodicals
Founded: 1906

VEB Hermann **Haack**, Justus-Perthes-Str 3/9, Postfach 274, DDR-5800 Gotha Tel: 3872 Cable Add: Geokart Gotha Telex: 6185333 hago dd
Imprint: Haack Gotha
Subjects: Maps, Atlases, Geographic and Cartographic Publications, Periodicals
Founded: 1785

Henschelverlag Kunst und Gesellschaft, Oranienburger Str 67-68, Postfach 220, DDR-1040 Berlin Tel: 28790 Cable Add: Henschelverlag Berlin
Dir: K Mittelstädt
Subjects: General Fiction, Film, Theatre, Music, Art, Architecture, Periodicals
Founded: 1945

VEB **Hinstorff** Verlag+, Kröpeliner Str 25, Postfach 11, DDR-2500 Rostock Tel: 34441 Cable Add: Hinstorff Verlag Rostock
Subjects: Contemporary Literature of the DDR, German Language Literature in Series, Scandinavian Literature in Translation, Literature in Low German, Homeland Literature and Studies, Maritime Literature
1982: 30-40 titles *Founded:* 1831

VEB Friedrich **Hofmeister** Musikverlag, Karlstr 10, Postfach 147, DDR-7010 Leipzig Tel: 7351 Cable Add: Hofmeister Leipzig
Man Dir: Dr Gunter Hempel; *Sales Dir:* Werner Hennig
Subjects: Vocal and Instrumental Music, Song Books, Bibliographies, Yearbooks
Founded: 1807

Insel-Verlag Anton Kippenberg, Mottelerstr 8, Postfach 88, DDR-7022 Leipzig Tel: 592356/52857/51868
Associate Companies: Insel-Verlag issues a common catalogue with: Gustav Kiepenheuer Verlag (qv); Dieterich'sche Verlagsbuchhandlung (qv); Paul List Verlag (qv)
Subjects: Literature, Art, Facsimile Editions, Classics of World Literature in Translation
Founded: 1899

Verlag **Junge Welt***, Postfach 1026 Berlin Nr 43, DDR-1080 Berlin (Located at: Mauerstr 39-40, DDR-1080 Berlin) Tel: 22330 Telex: 114483
Man Dir: Manfred Rucht
Subjects: Juvenile, Education, Science, Technical, Periodicals
Founded: 1952

Gustav **Kiepenheuer** Verlag, Mottelerstr 8, Postfach 88, DDR-7022 Leipzig Tel: 592356/52857/51868
Associate Companies: Dieterich'sche Verlagsbuchhandlung (qv); Insel-Verlag (qv); Paul List Verlag (qv)
Subjects: Foreign Classics in Translation, Foreign Folklore, Far Eastern Studies, Quality German Literature
Founded: 1909

Der **Kinderbuchverlag** Berlin, Behrenstr 40-41, Postfach 1225, DDR-1080 Berlin Tel: 2030 Cable Add: Kinderbuch Berlin
Subject: Children's Books
Founded: 1949

Koehler und Amelang (VOB), Hainstr 2, DDR-7010 Leipzig Tel: 282379
Dir: Prof Dr Hubert Faensen
Associate Company: Union Verlag Berlin (VOB) (qv)
Branch Off: Talstr 3, DDR-7010 Leipzig Tel: 209519
Subjects: Cultural History, Art History, Biographical
Founded: 1925

VEB Verlag der **Kunst**, Spenerstr 21, DDR-8019 Dresden Tel: 34486 Cable Add: Kunstverlag Dresden
Subjects: Fine Arts, Reproductions
Founded: 1952

VEB Edition **Leipzig**+, Verlag für Kunst und Wissenschaft, Karl-Liebknecht-Str 77, Postfach 340, DDR-7010 Leipzig Tel: 312412 Cable Add: Edileip
Man Dir: Dr Dieter Nadolski; *Sales Dir:* Fritz Becker
Subjects: Art, History of Civilization, Nature Study, Hobbies, Scientific & Bibliophile Reprints (Publications are in numerous languages)
Founded: 1960

VEB **Lied** der Zeit Musikverlag, Rosa-Luxembourg-Str 41, Postfach 10, DDR-1020 Berlin Tel: 2825081
Subject: Music

Paul **List** Verlag, Mottelerstr 8, Postfach 88, DDR-7022 Leipzig Tel: 592356/52857/51868
Associate Companies: Dieterich'sche Verlagsbuchhandlung (qv); Insel-Verlag (qv); Gustav Kiepenheuer Verlag (qv)
Subjects: Foreign Literature in translation
Founded: 1894

Militärverlag der DDR (VEB), Storkower Str 158, Postfach 46551, DDR-1055 Berlin Tel: 4300618 Telex: 112673 mv
Man Dir: Dr Butter
Subjects: Military, Popular Science, Fiction, Periodicals
Founded: 1956

Mitteldeutscher Verlag Halle-Leipzig, Thälmannplatz 2, Postfach 295, DDR-4020 Halle/Saale Tel: 8730
Man Dir: Dr Eberhard Günther; *Publishing Manager:* Karin Röntsch
Subjects: General Fiction & Non-fiction, Collected Works, Poetry, Essays, Literary Criticism, Belles Lettres, Biography, Novels
1981: 146 titles *Founded:* 1946

Buchverlag Der **Morgen***, Seelenbinderstr 152, DDR-1170 Berlin Tel: 6572914 Cable Add: Buchmorgen Berlin Telex: 0112704
Man Dir: Dr Wolfgang Tenzler
Subjects: General Fiction, Belles Lettres, Poetry, Biography, Political Monographs
Founded: 1958

Verlag der **Nation**, Friedrichstr 113, Postfach 74, DDR-1040 Berlin Tel: 2825826
Dir: Hans-Otto Lecht
Subjects: Publications of the National Democratic Party of Germany, Current Politics, Biographical, Illustrated Texts, Historical Fiction, Belles Lettres, Cultural; Paperback Series
Founded: 1948

118 GERMAN DEMOCRATIC REPUBLIC

Verlag das **Neue Berlin***, Kronenstr 73/74, Postfach 1239, DDR-1080 Berlin Tel: 2202126 Cable Add: Neuesberlinbuch Berlin
Associate Company: Eulenspiegel Verlag (qv)
Subjects: Crime, Adventure, Science Fiction
Founded: 1946

Verlag **Neues Leben**, Behrenstr 40-41, Postfach 1223, DDR-1080 Berlin Tel: 2032765 Cable Add: Neuesleben Berlin
Man Dir: Rudolf Chowanetz
Subjects: General Fiction and Non-fiction; Juveniles, Science Fiction: Paperbacks
1983: 252 titles *Founded:* 1946

VEB Max **Niemeyer** Verlag, Gerichtsweg 26, Postfach 130, DDR-7010 Leipzig Tel: 7801 Telex: 51773
Man Dir: Helmut Bähring
Associate Companies: VEB Verlag Enzyklopädie Leipzig (qv); VEB Bibliographisches Institut (qv)
Subjects: Philology, University Textbooks, Protestant Theology, Literature, Languages; Periodicals
Founded: 1869

Prisma-Verlag Zenner und Gürchott, Leibnizstr 10, Postfach 1461, DDR-7010 Leipzig Tel: 281411
Man Dir: Klaus Zenner; *Publicity Dir:* Fritz Gürchott
Subjects: Archaeology, Art and Cultural History, Fine Illustrated Editions, Historical Novels: many Non-fiction books have texts in German, English and Russian
1981: 9 titles *1982:* 9 titles *Founded:* 1957

Verlag Philipp **Reclam** jun, Nonnenstr 38, DDR-7031 Leipzig Tel: 44501 Cable Add: Reclam Leipzig
Man Dir: Hans Marquardt; *Sales Dir:* Gottfried Berthold; *Publicity:* Sylvia Bösger; *Advertising Dir:* Peter Thieme
Branch Office: Margaretenstr 6, DDR-7050 Leipzig Tel: 64151
Subjects: Reclam's Universal Library (a paperback series covering Belles Lettres, Philosophy, History, Aesthetics, Music, Biography), Literature, Original Graphics (woodcuts, etchings, lithographs)
1981: 129 titles *Founded:* 1828

Verlag **Rütten und Loening** Berlin, see Aufbau Verlag

Sankt-Benno Verlag GmbH, Verlag für katholisches Schrifttum, Thüringer Str 1-3, Postfach 98 and 112, DDR-7033 Leipzig Tel: 44161 Cable Add: Bennoverlag Leipzig
Catholic Literature Publishing House
General Managers: Christoph Bockisch, Franz J Cordier
Subjects: Religion, Philosophy, Music, Catholic Literature in German and Latin Languages, Periodicals
Founded: 1951

VEB E A **Seemann** Buch- und Kunstverlag, Jacobstr 6, Postfach 846, DDR-7010 Leipzig Tel: 7736 Cable Add: Kunstsemann
Subjects: Art, Reference, Encyclopaedias
Founded: 1858

Seven Seas Publishers, Glinkastr 13-15, DDR-1086 Berlin Tel: 2202851 Cable Add: Sevenseasberlin
Subjects: General Fiction, Poetry, Biography, History, High-quality Paperbacks (in English), Secondary Textbooks
Founded: 1957

Sportverlag+, Neustädtische Kirchstr 15, Postfach 1218, DDR-1086 Berlin Tel: 22120 Cable Add: Sportverlag Berlin-DDR Telex: 112853 spov dd
Subjects: Physical Education, Sport, How-to, Chess, Angling
1981-82: 108 titles *Founded:* 1947

Staatsverlag der Deutschen Demokratischen Republik, Otto Grotewohl Str 17, DDR-1080 Berlin Tel: 2372502 (export); 2372516 (publicity); 2372498 (sales) Cable Add: Staatsverlag Berlin
The official State Publishing Company of the German Democratic Republic
Subjects: History, Social & Political Theory, Economics, Law, International Relations, Government Publications; Periodicals
Founded: 1963

VEB Verlag **Technik**, Oranienburger Str 13-14, Postfach 201, DDR-1020 Berlin Tel: 28700 Cable Add: Technikverlag Berlin Telex: Berlin 0112228 techn dd
Subjects: Science, Mechanical, Electrical and Electronics Engineering, Control Engineering and Automation, Cybernetics, Technical Dictionaries in numerous languages, Reference, University Textbooks, Periodicals
1981: 59 titles *1982:* 66 titles *Founded:* 1946

BSB B G **Teubner** Verlagsgesellschaft, Sternwartenstr 8, DDR-7010 Leipzig Postfach 930 Tel: 293158/59 Cable Add: Teubnerianum Leipzig
Man Dir: Ing Heinz Kratz
Associate Company: Akademische Verlagsgesellschaft Geest und Portig KG (qv)
Subjects: Mathematics, Physics, Electronics, Optics, History of Science, Geo-sciences, General Technology, Data Processing, Architecture and Building, Classics
Founded: 1811

VEB Georg **Thieme**, Leipzig, Verlag für Medizin und Naturwissenschaften, Hainstr 17-19, DDR-7010 Leipzig Tel: 291656 Cable Add: Buchthieme Telex: 051533
Trade Department: Villengang 2, DDR-6900 Jena
Associate Companies: VEB Gustav Fischer Verlag (qv); VEB Verlag Volk und Gesundheit (qv)
Subjects: Medicine, Bio-Science, Periodicals
1981: 24 titles *Founded:* 1886

VEB **Tourist** Verlag, Neue Grünster 17, DDR-1020 Berlin Tel: 2071018 Telex: 114488 über Volk und Gesundheit
Man Dir: Dr Reginald Pustkowski;
Editorial: Dr Seeler; *Sales:* Mr Kaiser; *Production:* Mr Graf, Mr Till; *Publicity:* Mr Jakubeit
Orders to: VEB Tourist Verlag, Grosse Hamburgerstr 32, DDR-1020 Berlin
Subject: Tourism (books, maps, guides)
1981: 17 titles *1982:* 11 titles *Founded:* 1953

Transpress, VEB Verlag für Verkehrswesen, Französische Str 13-14, Postfach 1235, DDR-1086 Berlin Tel: 20410 Cable Add: transpress Berlin Telex: 112229 travedd
Man Dir: Dr Harald Böttcher
Subjects: Transport and Traffic (Railways, Shipping, Motor Traffic, Aviation), Post and Telecommunications, Philately, Numismatics, Popular Science; Periodicals
1981: 94 titles *1982:* 96 titles *Founded:* 1960

Tribüne Verlag und Druckereien des FDGB, Am Treptower Park 28-30, DDR-1193 Berlin Tel: 27100 Cable Add: Bundesverlag Berlin Telex: Tribüne 0112611
Subjects: Trade Unionism, Belles Lettres
Founded: 1945

Union Verlag Berlin VOB, Charlottenstr 79, DDR-1080 Berlin Tel: 2202711 Cable Add: Unionverlag Berlin
Dir: Klaus-Peter Gerhardt
Associate Company: Koehler und Amelang (VOB) (qv)
Branch Off: Talstr 3, DDR-7010 Leipzig
Subjects: Political Science, Christian Literature, Belles Lettres, Christian Art, History of Philosophy and Religion
Founded: 1951

Urania-Verlag (für populärwissenschaftliche Literatur)+, Salomonstr 26-28, Postfach 969, DDR-7010 Leipzig Tel: 7426 Cable Add: Urania Leipzig
Publicity Manager: Claudius Markov
Subsidiary Companies: Neumann Verlag, Salomonstr 26-28, Postfach 969, DDR-7010 Leipzig; A Ziemsen Verlag, Lucas-Cranach-Str 21, Postfach 22, DDR-4600 Wittenberg Lutherstadt
Branch Offs: Jena and Berlin
Subjects: Popular Science, Non-fiction, Cultural History, Hobbies; Periodicals
1982: 150 titles *1983:* 170 titles *Founded:* 1924

VEB Verlag **Volk und Gesundheit**, Neue Grünstr 18, Postfach 53, DDR-1020 Berlin Tel: 2000621 Cable Add: Volksgesundheit Telex: 0114488
Trade Department: Villengang 2, DDR-6900 Jena
Parent Company: Volkseigene Verlag für Medizin und Biologie, Berlin, Jena, Leipzig
Associate Companies: VEB Gustav Fischer Verlag (qv); VEB Georg Thieme (qv)
Subjects: Scholarship, Medicine
Founded: 1952

Verlag **Volk und Welt** (Verlag für internationale Literatur), Glinkastr 13-15, DDR-1086 Berlin Tel: 2202851 Cable Add: Volkwelt Berlin
Man Dir: Jürgen Gruner
Subjects: General Fiction and Non-fiction (international) in German translation; Poetry, Reportage, Periodicals
Book Club: Buchklub 65
Founded: 1947

Volk und Wissen Volkseigener Verlag Berlin, Krausenstr 50, Am Spittelmarkt, DDR-1086 Berlin Tel: 20430 Cable Add: Volkwissen Berlin Telex: 112181 vowiv dd
Subjects: Schoolbooks, Pedagogy, Illustrated Instructional Material, Literary History, Sports Training
Founded: 1945

Verlag Die **Wirtschaft**, Am Friedrichshain 22, DDR-1055 Berlin Tel: 43870 Cable Add: wirtschaftsplan Berlin Telex: Berlin 114566
Subjects: Management, Economics, Mathematics, Statistics, Electronic Data Processing, Periodicals
Founded: 1946

Z A Reprints, see Zentralantiquariat der DDR

Verlag **Zeit** im Bild*, Julian-Grimau-Allee 10, DDR-8010 Dresden Tel: 48640 Telex: 2291
Manager: H Zumpe
Subjects: Politics, Foreign Languages, Economics, Periodicals
Founded: 1946

Zentralantiquariat der DDR — Reprintabteilung (ZA Reprints), Talstr 29, Postfach 1080, DDR-7010 Leipzig 1 Tel: 293641-43, 295808 Cable Add: Zentralanti Leipzig
The Reprint Department of the Central Antiquariat and Second Hand Book Dealers' Office of the German Democratic Republic
Subjects: Special Editions, Reprints of specialized texts, especially of History, Sociology, History of Civilization, Medicine, Natural Sciences, Philosophy and Religion, Law, Economics, the Arts, Linguistics, German Literature, Ancient History (Classical, Oriental, African); Periodicals
Founded: 1964

A **Ziemsen** Verlag, Postfach 22, DDR-4600
Wittenberg Lutherstadt Tel: 2528
Subjects: Natural Sciences, Biology,
Zoology, Botany, Palaeontology
Book Club: Die Neue Brehm-Bücherei
1981: 29 titles *1982:* 28 titles *Founded:* 1902

Literary Agents

Büro für Urheberrechte*, Clara-Zetkin-Str
105, DDR-1080 Berlin
Copyright Office, Authors' manuscripts and
publishing rights are submitted in the DDR
without agents, however agreements with
individuals and firms outside the DDR must
be sanctioned and handled by the above
Büro

Book Clubs

Buchclub 65, Glinkastr 13-15, DDR-1080
Berlin Tel: 2202851
Owned by: Verlag Volk und Welt (qv)
Founded: 1965

Buchklub der Schüler*, Clara-Zetkin-Str 90,
DDR-1080 Berlin
Schoolchildren's Book Club

Die **Neue Brehm-Bücherei**, Postfach 22,
DDR-4600 Wittenberg Lutherstadt Tel:
2528
Owned by: A Ziemsen Verlag (qv)

Major Booksellers

Volksbuchhandlung **Haus** des Buches*,
Ernst-Thälmann-Str 29, DDR-8010 Dresden

Volksbuchhandlung Edwin **Hoernle***, Ernst-
Thälmann-Str 13, DDR-2000
Neubrandenburg

Volksbuchhandlung Alexander von
Humboldt, Am Platz der Einheit,
DDR-1500 Potsdam Tel: 22539/23574
Manager: Friedrich Richter

Humboldt-Buchhandlung*, Bahnhofstr 1,
DDR-9001 Karl-Marx-Stadt

Ulrich v **Hutten** Volksbuchhandlung*, Karl-
Marx Str 184, DDR-12 Frankfurt an der
Oder

Keysersche Buchhandlung*, Anger 11,
DDR-5000 Erfurt

Volksbuchhandlung Robert **Koch***,
Universitätsring 7 und 10, DDR-4000 Halle

L K G, see Leipziger Kommissions- und
Grossbuchhandel

Leibniz-Volksbuchhandlung*, Otto-
Grotewohl-Str 3, DDR-2700 Schwerin

**Leipziger Kommissions- und
Grossbuchhandel** (LKG)*, Leninstr 16,
DDR-7010 Leipzig Tel: 70251
Leipzig Wholesale Booksellers and
Distributors
Dir: H Köhler

Volksbuchhandlung Thomas **Mann***,
Kollegiengasse, DDR-6900 Jena

Buchhandlung für **Medizin***, Friedrichstr
128, DDR-1040 Berlin

Universitätsbuchhandlung*, Str der
Freundschaft 77, DDR-2200 Greifswald

Universitätsbuchhandlung*, Grimmaische
Str 30, DDR-7010 Leipzig

Universitätsbuchhandlung*, Kröpeliner Str
15, DDR-2500 Rostock

Erich-**Weinert**-Buchhandlung*, Wilhelm-
Pieck-Allee 23-27, DDR-3010 Magdeburg
Tel: 3086416

Major Libraries

Ernst-Moritz-**Arndt** Universität
Universitätsbibliothek, Rubenowstr 4,
DDR-2200 Greifswald

Berliner Stadtbibliothek*, Breitestr 37,
Berlin C2

Deutsche Bücherei, Deutscher Platz, DDR-
7010 Leipzig Tel: 88120 Telex: 051562
dbuech dd
The German Library
Dir: Prof Dr Helmut Rötzsch
*Publications: Deutsche
Nationalbibliographie und Bibliographie des
im Ausland erschienenen deutschsprachigen
Schrifttums, Reihe A, B, C* (German
National Bibliography and Bibliography of
German Language Literature appearing
abroad, Series A, B, C); *Jahresverzeichnis
der Verlagsschriften* (Annual List of
Publications); *Deutsches Bücherverzeichnis*
(5-Year German Book List); *Bibliographie
der Übersetzungen deutschsprachiger Werke*
(quarterly: Bibliography of Translations of
German Language Works); *Bibliographie
fremdsprachiger Germanica* (quarterly:
Bibliography of Germanica in foreign
languages); *Bibliographie der Bibliographien*
(monthly: Bibliography of Bibliographies);
*Jahresverzeichnis der Hochschulschriften der
DDR, der BRD und Westberlins* (Annual
List of Academy Texts appearing in the
GDR, the FRG, and in West Berlin);
Deutsche Musikbibliographie (monthly:
German Bibliography of Music);
*Jahresverzeichnis der Musikalien und
Musikschriften* (Annual List of Musical
Scores and Texts); *Bibliographie der
Kunstblätter* (Bibliography of Art Prints);
Jahrbuch der Deutschen Bücherei (German
Library Yearbook); *Die Deutsche Bücherei
im Bild* (The German Library in Pictures);
Wissenwertes über die Deutsche Bücherei
(Facts about the German Library); also
other regularly-appearing Bibliographies and
Directories

Deutsche Staatsbibliothek, Unter den
Linden 8, Postfach 1312, DDR-1086 Berlin
Tel: 20780 Cable Add: Stabi Berlin Telex:
0112757
German State Library
Man Dir: Prof Dr Friedhilde Krause
*Publications include: Berliner Titeldrucke,
Jahreskatalog* (Annual List of Berlin Title
Impressions); *Zentralkatalog der DDR,
Zeitschriften und Serien des Auslandes*
(GDR Central Catalogue of Foreign Series
and Periodicals); *Bibliographische
Mitteilungen* (Bibliographical News);
Handschriften-Inventare (Inventory of
Manuscripts); *Kartographische
Bestandsverzeichnisse* (Cartographical Stock
Lists); *Preisgekrönte Kinder- und
Jugendbücher der Deutschen
Demokratischen Republik 1950-1979*
(Prizewinning Books for Children and
Young People in the GDR, 1950-1979);
Gesamtkatalog der Wiegendrucke (Global
Catalogue of Incunabula); *Bibliothek
seltener Bücher* (Library of Rare Books)

Humboldt Universität zu Berlin,
Universitätsbibliothek, Clara-Zetkin-Str 27,
DDR-1086 Berlin Tel: 2078356
Librarian: Prof Dr Waltraud Irmscher

Karl-Marx-Universität,
Universitätsbibliothek, Beethovenstr 6,
DDR-7010 Leipzig Tel: 3913310

Landwirtschaftliche Zentralbibliothek,
Krausenstr 38-39, Postfach 1295, DDR-1086
Berlin
Central Agricultural Library

Nationale Forschungs- und Gedenkstätten
der klassischen deutschen Literatur —
Zentralbibliothek der deutschen Klassik,
Platz der Demokratie 1, DDR-5300 Weimar
Tel: 3552 Telex: 618975 nfg dd
National Research and Memorial
Foundation of Classical German Literature
— Central Library of German Classicism

Wilhelm-Pieck-Universität **Rostock**
Universitätsbibliothek, Universitätsplatz 5,
DDR-2500 Rostock
Dir: Karl-Heinz Jügelt

Sächsische Landesbibliothek, Marienallee
12, Postfach 467/468, DDR-8060 Dresden
Tel: 52677/576097 Telex: 2368
Dir: Prof Dr sc Burghard Burgemeister
Publications: Sächsische Bibliographie
(Saxony Bibliography); *Bibliographie
Bildende Kunst* (Bibliography of Fine Arts);
Bibliographie Illustrierter Bücher der DDR
(Bibliography of Illustrated Books in the
GDR); *Bibliographie Geschichte der Technik*
(Bibliography of the History of Technology
— in German language literature world-
wide); *Bibliographie Musik* (Musical
Bibliography — covering both DDR
publications on Music and foreign
publications concerning the music of the
German Democratic Republic);
*Sozialistisches Musikschaffen in der
Deutschen Demokratischen Republik*
(Socialist Musical Production in the GDR)
— all annual

Zentrales Staatsarchiv, Berliner Str 98-101,
DDR-1500 Potsdam
The National Archives of the German
Democratic Republic

Stadt- und Bezirksbibliothek Leipzig,
Mozartstr 1, DDR-7010 Leipzig Tel:
3913712
Dir: Reinhard Stridde

Universitäts- und Landesbibliothek Sachsen-
Anhalt, August-Bebel-Str 13, DDR-4010
Halle/Saale Tel: 8950 Telex: 4252 ulb hal
dd

Universitätsbibliothek, Goetheallee 6,
DDR-6900 Jena Tel: 8222239
Telex: 0588634
Dir: Prof Dr Lothar Bohmüller
Subjects: Various bibliographical works
relating to Jena and the German Democratic
Republic, and also to international themes;
History, Medicine, Biology, Chemistry,
Physics, Philosophy

**Universitätsbibliothek der Technischen
Universität***, Mommsenstr 13, DDR-8027
Dresden

Zentralbibliothek der deutschen Klassik, see
Nationale Forschungs- und Gedenkstätten
der klassischen deutschen Literatur

Library Associations

Bibliotheksverband der Deutschen
Demokratischen Republik, Hermann-
Matern-Str 57, DDR-1040 Berlin Tel:
2362845 Telex: 113247 zib dd
The Library Association of the German
Democratic Republic
President: Gotthard Rückl; *Executive Dir:*
Klaus Plötz
*Publications include: Bibliotheksverband
aktuell* (Conference Reports, Publications
relating to Librarianship — 6 times per
year), *Das Bibliothekswesen der DDR*
(Librarianship in the DDR); *Kinder, Bücher,*

Bibliotheken: Informationen zur Bibliotheksarbeit mit Kindern in der DDR (Children, Books and Libraries: Information on Library work with children in the GDR)
Founded: 1964

Zentralinstitut für Bibliothekswesen, Hermann-Matern Str 57, DDR-1040 Berlin
The Central Institute for Library Science
Publications: Bibliothekar; Mitteilungen und Materialien; Bibliothekswesen in der Deutschen Demokratischen Republik (Annual Report); *Berichte und Informationen zum Bibliothekswesen; Informationsdienst Bibliothekswesen; Beiträge zu Theorie und Praxis der Bibliotheksarbeit*

Zentralinstitut für Information und Dokumentation der Deutschen Demokratischen Republik, Köpenicker Str 80-82, DDR-1020 Berlin Tel: 2391280 Telex: 114690 ZIID dd Cable Add: Zeniid Berlin
Central Institute for Information and Documentation of the German Democratic Republic
Director: Mr Och
Publications include: Informatik (periodical on information science and technology)

Library Reference Books and Journals

Books

Die Deutsche Bücherei im Bild (The German Library in Pictures), Deutsche Bücherei, Deutscher Platz, DDR-7010 Leipzig

Die Entwicklung des Bibliothekswesens in der Deutschen Demokratischen Republik (The Development of Library Science in the DDR) (annual), Zentralinstitut für Bibliothekswesen, Hermann-Matern Str 57, DDR-1040 Berlin

Jahrbuch der Bibliotheken, Archive und Informationsstellen der Deutschen Demokratischen Republik (Yearbook of the Libraries, Archives and Information Offices of the DDR), VEB Bibliographisches Institut, Gerichtsweg 26, Postfach 130, DDR-7010 Leipzig

Sigel Liste der Bibliotheken der Deutschen Demokratischen Republik (Classification List of Libraries of the DDR), Deutsche Staatsbibliothek, Unter den Linden 8, DDR-1080 Berlin

Wissenwertes über die Deutsche Bücherei (Facts About the German Library), Deutsche Bücherei, Deutscher Platz, DDR-7010 Leipzig

Journals

Bibliothekar (Librarian) (text in German; contents page in English, French, German and Russian), Zentralinstitut für Bibliothekswesen, Hermann-Matern Str 57, DDR-1040 Berlin

Informationsblatt (Information Sheet), Bibliotheksverband der Deutschen Demokratischen Republik, Hermann-Matern-Str 57, DDR-1040 Berlin

Informationsdienst Bibliothekswesen und Bibliographie der Literatur zum Bibliothekswesen (Information Service on Library Science and Bibliography of the Literature on Library Science), Zentralinstitut für Bibliothekswesen, Hermann-Matern Str 57, DDR-1040 Berlin

Literatur zum Bibliothekswesen (Literature on Library Science), Zentralinstitut für Bibliothekswesen, Hermann-Matern Str 57, DDR-1040 Berlin

Mitteilungen und Materialien (Communications and Materials), Zentralinstitut für Bibliothekswesen, Hermann-Matern Str 57, DDR-1040 Berlin

Zentralblatt für Das Bibliothekswesen (Central Journal for Library Science) (text in German; contents page in English, French, German and Russian), VEB Bibliographisches Institut, Gerichtsweg 26, Postfach 130, DDR-7010 Leipzig

Literary Associations and Societies

Institut für Literatur Johannes R **Becher**, Karl-Tauchnitzstr 8, Leipzig CI
Dir: Professor Max Walter Schulz

P E N Zentrum Deutsche Demokratische Republik, Friedrichstr 194-199, DDR-1080 Berlin
Secretary: Henryk Keisch

Literary Periodicals

Bücherkarren (Book-Cart), Verlag Volk und Welt, Glinkastr 13-15, DDR-1086 Berlin

Deutsche Literaturzeitung (German Literature Newspaper), Akademie-Verlag, Leipziger Str 3-4, DDR-1080 Berlin

Fontane-Blätter (Fontane Folios), Deutsche Staatsbibliothek, Unter den Linden 8, DDR-1086 Berlin

Ich Schreibe (I Write), VEB Friedrich Hofmeister Musikverlag, Karlstr 10, Postfach 147, DDR-7010 Leipzig

Kunst und Literatur (Art and Literature), Buchexport, Leninstr 16, Postfach 160, DDR-7010 Leipzig

Literatur und Gesellschaft (Literature and Society), Buchexport, Leninstr 16, Postfach 160, DDR-7010 Leipzig

Marginalien (Marginal Notes); journal for the art of the book and bibliophily, Aufbau-Verlag Berlin und Weimar, Französische Str 32, Postfach 1217, DDR-1080 Berlin

Neue deutsche Literatur (New German Literature), Aufbau-Verlag Berlin und Weimar, Französische Str 32, Postfach 1217, DDR-1080 Berlin

Sinn und Form (Sense and Form); contributions to literature, Deutsche Akademie der Künste, Rütten und Loening, Französische Str 32, Postfach 1217, DDR-1080 Berlin

Weimarer Beträge (Weimar Contributions); journal for literature, aesthetics and culture, Aufbau-Verlag Berlin und Weimar, Französische Str 32, Postfach 1217, DDR-1080 Berlin

Literary Prizes

Johannes R **Becher** Prize
For lyrical poetry, awarded every other year. Enquiries to Minister für Kultur der Deutschen Demokratischen Republik, Molkenmarkt 1-3, DDR-1102 Berlin

Beginners' Prize
Founded 1966. Awarded annually to beginners ('Debutanten') in the fields of prose, lyrical poetry and essay writing by the Institut für Literatur Johannes R Becher and the Mitteldeutscher Verlag. Enquiries to Institut für Literatur Johannes R Becher, Karl Tauchnitzstr 8, DDR-7010 Leipzig

Debutantenpreis, see Beginners' Prize

Federal Republic of Germany

General Information

Language: German. Danish in South Schleswig, North Frisian in North Frisian Islands
Religion: Protestant and Roman Catholic
Population: 62 million
Bank Hours: Vary. 0800 or 0830 or 0900-1400, or 0900-1200, 1400-1530 Monday-Friday; open until 1800 Thursday
Shop Hours: 0800 or 0900-1830 Monday-Friday; 0800 or 0900-1400 Saturday (but 1800 on first Saturday of each month)
Currency: 100 Pfennige = 1 Deutsche Mark
Export/Import Information: Member of the European Economic Community. No tariff on books except children's picture books from non-EEC. None on advertising to be distributed free, if exporter's country grants reciprocal treatment, otherwise charged. Import Turnover Tax on books and advertising. No import licence required. No exchange controls
Copyright: UCC, Berne, Florence (see International section)

Book Trade Organizations

Adressbuchausschuss der Deutschen Wirtschaft, Adenauerallee 148, D-5300 Bonn 1 Tel: (0228) 104502 Telex: 886805 diht d
German Trade Directory Committee

Arbeitsgemeinschaft Buchgemeinschaften und verwandte Unternehmen im Börsenverein des Deutschen Buchhandels eV, Grosser Hirschgraben 17/21, D-6000 Frankfurt am Main 1 Tel: (0611) 1306324
Alliance of Book Clubs/Societies and related concerns in the German Publishers' and Booksellers' Association

Arbeitsgemeinschaft der Vertriebsfachverbände*, pA Verband Deutscher Buch- Zeitungs- und Zeitschriften-Grossisten eV, Theodor-Heuss-Ring 32, D-5000 Cologne 1 Tel: (0221) 123803
Alliance of the Distributive Trades Associations

Arbeitsgemeinschaft literarische und Sachbuchverlage*, Charlottenstr 21c, D-7000 Stuttgart 1 Tel: (0711) 245272
Dir: Professor Dr Ferdinand Sieger
Joint Association of Literary and Non-fiction Publishers

Arbeitsgemeinschaft rechts- und staatswissenschaftlicher Verleger, Unter den Ulmen 96-98, D-5000 Cologne 51 Tel: (0221) 373021 Telex: 8883381
Jurisprudence and Political Science Publishers' Alliance

Arbeitsgemeinschaft von Jugendbuchverlegern in der Bundesrepublik Deutschland eV, Verlag Heinrich Ellermann, Romanstr 16, D-8000 Munich 19 Tel: (089) 133737 Cable Add: Ellerbuch
The Alliance of Publishers of Children's Books in the Federal Republic of Germany
Chairman: Berthold Spangenberg

Arbeitsgemeinschaft wissenschaftliche Literatur eV*, Postfach 21086, D-6000 Frankfurt am Main
Joint Association for Scientific Literature
Director: Peter Czerwonka

Arbeitskreis für Jugendliteratur eV, Elisabethstr 15, D-8000, Munich 40
Youth Literature Committee (Section of IBBY)
Man Dir: F Meyer

Aussenhandels-Ausschuss, Foreign Trade Committee of Börsenverein des deutschen Buchhandels eV (qv)

B A G Buchhändler-Abrechnungs-Gesellschaft mbH, Grosser Hirschgraben 17-21, Postfach 2422, D-6000 Frankfurt 1 Tel: (0611) 285535
Booksellers' Clearing-House Company
Manager: Heinz Günter Schmitz

Berliner Verleger- und Buchhändlervereinigung eV*, Lützowstr 105, D-1000 Berlin 30 Tel: (030) 2621040/2621049
Berlin Publishers' and Booksellers' Association

Börsenverein des deutschen Buchhandels eV, Grosser Hirschgraben 17-21, Postfach 2404, D-6000 Frankfurt am Main 1 Tel: (0611) 13061 Cable Add: Börsenblatt Telex: 413573 buchv d
German Publishers' and Booksellers' Association (Press and Information Dept); also has a Foreign Trade Committee (Aussenhandels-Ausschuss)
General Secretary: Dr Hans-Karl von Kupsch
Publications include: Börsenblatt für den deutschen Buchhandel (German Book Trade Journal); *Adressbuch für den deutschsprachigen Buchhandel* (German-Speaking Book Trade Directory); *Deutsche Bibliographie* (German Bibliography); *Neuerscheinungen-Sofortdienst (CIP)* (New Titles Express Service (CIP)); *Archiv für Geschichte des Buchwesens* (Book History Archives); *Buch und Buchhandel in Zahlen* (Books and the Book Trade in Figures); *Die schönsten deutschen Bücher* (The Finest German Books); *Verzeichnis lieferbarer Bücher* (Catalogue of Available Books); *LIT* (a general magazine for those connected with the Book Trade); *How to obtain German books and periodicals*

Buchhändler-Abrechnungs — Gesellschaft mbH, see BAG

Buchhändler-Vereinigung GmbH, Abteilung Dokumentation und Datenverarbeitung, Grosser Hirschgraben 17-21, Postfach 2404, D-6000 Frankfurt am Main 1 Tel: (0611) 1306282 Telex: 413573 buchvd
The Booksellers' Association, Documentation and Data Processing Department (Standard Book Numbering Agency)
Dir: Wilfried H Schinzel

Bundesverband der deutschen Versandbuchhändler eV*, An der Ringkirche 6, D-6200 Wiesbaden Tel: (06121) 449091
National Federation of German Mail-order Booksellers
Managers: Dr Stefan Rutkowsky, Kornelia Wahl

Bundesverband des werbenden Buch- und Zeitschriftenhandels eV*, Brusseler Str 96, D-5000 Cologne 1 Tel: 514774
National Federation of the Promotional Book and Periodical Trade
Publication: Der werbende Buch- und Zeitschriften Handel

Deutsches Jugendschriftenwerk eV, Lauterenstr 37, D-6500 Mainz 1 Tel: (06131) 232821/228609
German Young People's Writing

O **Gracklauer** Verlag und Bibliographische Agentur, Rheinstr 29, D-8000 Munich 40 Tel: (089) 392087
Book trade information agency
Proprietor: Ulfa von den Steinen

Hessischer Verleger- und Buchhändler-Verband eV*, Großer Hirschgraben 17-19, D-6000 Frankfurt am Main 1 Tel: (0611) 282643
Hessen Publishers' and Booksellers' Federation
Chairman: Dr Heribert Marré; *Manager:* Lisabeth Schubert

I M H V, see Interessengemeinschaft Musikwissenschaftlicher

Informations-Zentrum Buch, Book Information Centre: an Association of prominent publishers who share information about their varied publishing programmes. Information can be obtained from any of the participating companies:
Artemis/Winkler, Bouvier, Carl, Deutscher Taschenbuch Verlag, Duncker und Humblot, Ehrenwirth, W Fink, Frommann/Holzboog, Hanser, Herder, Hiersemann, Kiepenheuer und Witsch, Kindler, Klett, Klinkhardt, W Kohlhammer, Kösel, Metzler, M Niemeyer, Nymphenburger, Piper, Quelle und Meyer, Reclam, E Schmidt (qqv)

Interessengemeinschaft Musikwissenschaftlicher Herausgeber und Verleger (IMHV), Heinrich-Schütz-Allee 33, D-3500 Kassel-Wilhelmshöhe Tel: 30011/16
Association of Musicology Editors and Publishers

Landesverband der Buchhändler und Verleger in Niedersachsen eV, Hausmannstr 2, D-3000 Hanover 1 Tel: (0511) 14745
Provincial Federation of Booksellers and Publishers in Lower Saxony
Man Dir: Wolfgang Grimpe

Landesverband der Verleger und Buchhändler Bremen-Unterweser eV, Contrescarpe 17, D-2800 Bremen 1 Tel: 326949
Bremen (Lower Weser) Provincial Federation of Publishers and Booksellers

Landesverband der Verleger und Buchhändler Rheinland-Pfalz eV, Schönbornstr 3, D-6500 Mainz 1 Tel: (06131) 234035
Rhineland-Palatinate Provincial Federation of Publishers and Booksellers

Landesverband der Verleger und Buchhändler Saar eV (LVBS), Eisenbahnstr 68, D-6600 Saarbrücken Tel: (0681) 55050
Saar Provincial Federation of Publishers and Booksellers

Landesverband des werbenden Buch- und Zeitschriftenhandels von Südwestdeutschland eV*, Strohberg 38, D-7000 Stuttgart 1 Tel: (0711) 602088/604056
Provincial Federation of the Book and Periodical Trade of South-west Germany

Munchner Arbeitsgemeinschaft der Verlagshersteller*, Scharnitzer Str 58, D-8032 Gräfelfing Tel: 852238
Munich Association of Publishers' Production Assistants

Norddeutscher Verleger- und Buchhändler-Verband eV, Brahmsallee 24, D-2000 Hamburg 13 Tel: (040) 4103161
North German Publishers' and Booksellers' Federation

Presse-Grosso, see Verband deutscher Buch-, Zeitungs- und Zeitschriften-Grossisten eV

Standard Book Numbering Agency, see Buchhändler-Vereinigung GmbH

Verband bayerischer Buch- und Zeitschriftenhändler eV*, Enzenspergerstr 9, D-8000 Munich 80 Tel: (089) 488533
Bavarian Booksellers' and Newsagents' Federation

Verband bayerischer Verlage und Buchhandlungen eV*, Enzenspergerstr 9, Postfach 800949, D-8000 Munich 80 Tel: (089) 484141
Bavarian Publishers' and Booksellers' Federation

Verband der Schulbuchverlage eV, Zeppelinallee 33, Postfach 900540, D-6000 Frankfurt am Main 1 Tel: (0611) 703075 Telex: vsib 416213
Association of Publishers of Schoolbooks
Chief Executive: Dipl-Volkswirt H P Vonhoff

Verband der Verlage und Buchhandlungen in Baden-Württemberg eV, Paulinenstr 53, D-7000 Stuttgart 1 Tel: 625085 Telex: 721529 Vvb
Federation of Publishers and Booksellers in Baden-Württemberg

Verband der Verlage und Buchhandlungen in Nordrhein-Westfalen eV, Marienstr 41, D-4000 Düsseldorf 1 Tel: (0211) 320951
Federation of Publishers and Booksellers in North Rhine-Westphalia

Verband des werbenden Buch- und Zeitschriftenhandels Gross-Berlin eV*, Leydenallee 70, D-1000 Berlin 41 Tel: (030) 720461
Greater Berlin Federation of the Promotional Book and Periodical Trade

Verband deutscher Adressbuchverleger eV, Ritterstr 17-19, D-4000 Düsseldorf Tel: (0211) 320909 Telex: 8587075
Association of German Directory Publishers

Verband deutscher Antiquare eV, Unterer Anger 15, D-8000 Munich 2 Tel: (089) 263855
German Antiquarian Booksellers' Association
President: Friedrich Zisska

Verband deutscher Bahnhofsbuchhändler, Grosser Hirschgraben 19H, D-6000 Frankfurt am Main 1
Federation of German Railway Station Booksellers

Verband deutscher Buch- Zeitungs- und Zeitschriften-Grossisten eV, Classen-Kappelmann-Str 24, D-5000 Cologne 41 Tel: (0221) 401081/2 Telex: 08-885 203
Federation of German Wholesalers of Books, Newspapers and Periodicals (also known as Presse-Grosso)
Chairman: Dr Eberhard Nolte; *Manager:* Dr Hans Ziebolz

Verband deutscher Bühnenverleger eV, Bismarckstr 17, D-1000 Berlin 12 Tel: (030) 3416086
Federation of German Play Agencies and Stage Publishers

Verband deutscher Schriftsteller*, Geschäftsstelle in Bayern, Schwanthalerstr 64, D-8000 Munich 2
Association of German Writers, Bavarian office

Verband deutscher Schulbuchhändler eV, Marienstr 41, D-4000 Düsseldorf Tel: (0211) 320951
Federation of German School Book Dealers

Verband katholischer Verleger und Buchhändler eV, Lehenstr 31, D-7000 Stuttgart 1 Tel: 642061
Federation of Catholic Publishers and

122 FEDERAL REPUBLIC OF GERMANY

Booksellers
Manager: Wolfgang Grossmann

Verband norddeutscher Buch- und Zeitschriftenhändler eV*, An Der Rehbocksweide 22-24, D-3150 Hannoversch-Münden Tel: 4084/4089
Federation of North German Booksellers and Newsagents

Verein für Verkehrsordnung im Buchhandel eV, Postfach 2404, D-6000 Frankfurt am Main 1
Association for the Regulation of Dealing in the Book Trade

Vereinigung evangelischer Buchhändler*, Lehenstr 31, D-7000 Stuttgart 1
Association of Protestant Booksellers
Chairman: Dr Arndt Ruprecht

Vereinigung selbständiger Verlagsvertreter*, Schatten 6 Gewand, D-7000 Stuttgart (Büsnau) 80 Tel: (0711) 681457
Association of Independent Publishers' Representatives

Verlegervereinigung Rechtsinformatik eV*, Verlag Neue Wirtschafts-Briefe GmbH, Eschstr 16-22, D-4690 Herne Tel: 02323/54071 Telex: 8229870
Association of Publishers of Legal Documentation
Chairman: Dr Karl-Friedrich Peter

Book Trade Reference Books and Journals

Books

Adressbuch für den deutschsprachigen Buchhandel (Directory of German-speaking Book Trade) (including Austria, Switzerland, and German-speaking publishers and booksellers in other countries), Börsenverein des deutschen Buchhandels eV, Großer Hirschgraben 17-21, D-6000 Frankfurt am Main 1

Anschriften deutscher Buchhandlungen (Addresses of German Booksellers), Verlag der Schillerbuchhandlung Hans Banger, Mainzer Str 24, D-7142 Marbach 9

Anschriften deutscher Verlage und ausländischer Verlage mit deutschen Auslieferungen (Addresses of German Publishers and Foreign Publishers with German Distribution), Verlag der Schillerbuchhandlung Hans Banger, Mainzer Str 24, D-7142 Marbach

Die Begegnung (The Meeting); authors, publishers, booksellers, Elwert und Meurer, Hauptstr 101, D-1000 Berlin 62

Bibliographie des Buchhandels (Bibliography of the Book Trade), K G Saur KG, Pössenbacherstr 2, D-8000 Munich 71

Buch und Buchhandel in Zahlen (Books and the Book Trade in Figures), Börsenverein des deutschen Buchhandels eV, Großer Hirschgraben 17-21, D-6000 Frankfurt am Main 1

Buchhändler Kalender (Booksellers' Calendar), Bibliographisches Institut AG, Dudenstr 6, Postfach 311, D-6800 Mannheim

Deutsches Verlagsregister (German Publishers' List), Stamm-Verlag GmbH, Goldammerweg 16, D-4300 Essen 1

Freude mit Büchern (Joy with Books); the German book catalogue, Verlag Bücherschiff Walter Reutin, Rheinstr 122, Postfach 210947, D-7500 Karlsruhe

Handbuch des Buchhandels (Handbook of the Book Trade), Verlag für Buchmarktforschung, Beim Strohhause 34, D-2000 Hamburg 2

How to Obtain German Books and Periodicals, Börsenverein des deutschen Buchhandels eV, Postfach 2404, D-6000 Frankfurt am Main 1

Was erscheint wo. Verlage, Titel, Redaktionen (What Appears Where. Publishers, Titles, Editorials), Team Verlag, Helmut Müller GmbH & Co KG, Rossertstr 9, Postfach 2661, D-6000 Frankfurt am Main

Journals

AGB-Titeldienst (AGB-Title Service); recently published German-language books, Amerika-Gedenk-Bibliothek, Arbeitsstelle für das Bibliothekswesen, Fehrbelliner Platz 3, D-1000 Berlin 31

Antiquariat (Antiquarian Bookshop), Dr Lothar Rossipaul, Verlagsgesellschaft mbH, Finkenweg 6, D-7261 Stammheim/Calw, (monthly)

Börsenblatt für den deutschen Buchhandel (German Book Trade Journal) published by Buchhändler-Vereinigung GmbH, at the following address: Börsenverein des deutschen Buchhandels eV, Großer Hirschgraben 17-21, D-6000 Frankfurt am Main 1

Buch Aktuell (Contemporary Books), Westfalendamm 57, Postfach 1305, D-4600 Dortmund

Buch und Leser (Book and Reader), Börsenverein des deutschen Buchhandels eV Grosser Hirschgraben 17-21, Postfach 2404, D-6000 Frankfurt am Main 1

Buchhändler Heute (The Bookseller Today), Verlag Buchhändler Heute, Jahnstr 36, Düsseldorf (monthly)

Buchmarkt (Book Market), the largest independent journal for the book trade in German-speaking areas, Rochusstr 34, Postfach 320545, D-4000 Düsseldorf

Buchreport (Book Report), Westfalendamm 57, Postfach 1305, D-4600 Dortmund

Deutsche Bibliographie (German National Bibliography). Börsenverein des deutschen Buchhandels eV, Großer Hirschgraben 17-21, D-6000 Frankfurt am Main 1

Dokumentation deutschsprachiger Verlage (Documentation of German-speaking Publishers), Günter Olzog Verlag, Thierschstr 11, D-8000 Munich 22

Goldmann's Mitteilungen für den Buchhandel (Goldmann's Communications for the Book Trade), Wilhelm Goldmann Verlag GmbH, Neumarkterstr 18, Postfach 800709, D-8000 Munich 80

LIT (bi-monthly general magazine for patrons of the Book Trade), Börsenverein des Deutschen Buchhandels eV, Grosser Hirschgraben 17-21, Postfach 2404, D-6000 Frankfurt am Main 1

Mitteilungsblatt für Dolmetscher und Übersetzer (Interpreters' and Translators' News Sheet), Bundesverband der Dolmetscher und Übersetzer eV (BDÜ), Schlossallee 9, D-5300 Bonn 2 (twice monthly)

Die Neuen Bücher (New Books), Dr Lothar Rossipaul, Verlagsgesellschaft mbH, Finkenweg 6, D-7261 Stammheim/Calw

Philobiblon; quarterly journal for books and graphic art, Dr Ernst Hauswedell und Co Verlag, Magdalenenstr 8, D-2000 Hamburg 13

Taschenbücher, Halbjähriges Verzeichnis (Paperbacks, Half-yearly List), Verlag der Schillerbuchhandlung Hans Banger, Mainzer Str 24, D-7142 Marbach

Der Übersetzer (The Translator), Verband deutschsprachiger Übersetzer literarischer und wissenschaftlicher Werke eV (VDU), Kuhstr 11, D-4172 Straelen

Verzeichnis lieferbarer Bücher (German Books in Print), Börsenverein des deutschen Buchhandels eV, Großer Hirschgraben 17-21, D-6000 Frankfurt am Main 1

Welt der Bücher (World of Books), *Der werbende Buch- und Zeitschriftenhandel* (The Promotional Book and Periodical Trade), Bundesverband des werbenden Buch- und Zeitschriftenhandels eV, Brusseler Str 96, D-5000 Cologne 1

Publishers

A D A C Verlag GmbH, Am Westpark 8, Postfach 700126, D-8000 Munich 70 Tel: (089) 76760 Cable Add: Adacverlag Telex: 528404
Man Dir, Rights & Permissions:, Manfred M Angele; *Editorial:* Dr Bodo Bleinagel, Michael Dultz; *Sales, Promotion:* Helmut Engerer; *Production:* Uto Rogner; *Advertising:* Horst Nitschke
Subjects: Motoring (touring, holiday guides, car buying, repairs, insurance, driving instruction)
Publishers of magazines *ADAC-Motorwelt* and *Deutsches Autorecht*
1982: 56 titles *1983:* 70 titles *Founded:* 1958
ISBN Publisher's Prefix: 3-87003

A D L A F, see Arbeitsgemeinschaft Deutsche Lateinamerika-Forschung

A M B (Arbeitsgemeinschaft mitteleuropäischer Bibelwerke)
Association of Mid-European Biblical Presses, comprising Verlag Schweizerisches katholisches Bibelwerk, Switzerland (qv), Vlaamse Bijbelstichting, Belgium (qv), Österreichisches Katholisches Bibelwerk, Austria (qv), and Verlag Katholisches Bibelwerk GmbH, Federal Republic of Germany (qv)

Aar-Verlag*, Volkerstr 33, D-6200 Wiesbaden Tel: (06121) 88218
Proprietor: Iolanda Debus
Subject: General Literature
ISBN Publisher's Prefix: 3-87945

Abakon Verlagsgesellschaft mbH*, Luetzowstr 105, D-1000 Berlin 30 Tel: (030) 2611067 Telex: 184412
Man Dir, Rights & Permissions: Dr Achim Schneider
Orders to: Archibook, Westendallee 97F, D-1000 Berlin 19
Imprints: Abakon; Edition Lichterfelde; Life Sciences Research Reports
Subjects: Science (in English language), Architecture, Art
1982: 12 titles *Founded:* 1975
ISBN Publisher's Prefix: 3-8200

Abakus Schallplatten Barbara Fietz*, Haversbach 1, D-6349 Greifenstein 2, OT Allendorf Tel: (06478) 2250
Man Dirs: B and S Fietz; *Editorial, Sales, Publicity:* B Fietz; *Production:* S Fietz
Associate Companies: Ulmtal Musikverlags GmbH Ulmtal; Melos Musikverlag, Munich
Subjects: Song Books, Musical Scores, Musical Instructional Books (all with Christian religious emphasis)
Founded: 1974

FEDERAL REPUBLIC OF GERMANY 123

Accidentia und Zester Druck- und Verlagsgesellschaft mbH, Aachener Str 71, D-4000 Düsseldorf 1 Tel: (0211) 347042 Telex: 8584284
Man Dir: Horst W Zester
Subjects: Photography, Travel Calendar
Founded: 1959
ISBN Publisher's Prefix: 3-920005

F A **Ackermanns** Kunstverlag*, Wienerplatz 7-8, D-8000 Munich 80 Tel: (089) 488046 Cable Add: Kunstackermann Munich
Man Dir: Hubertus Weinert
Subjects: Art, Photographic
Founded: 1874
ISBN Publisher's Prefix: 3-87002

Agis Verlag GmbH, Eberbachstr 7, Postfach 3, D-7570 Baden Baden 19 Tel: (07221) 66810, (07222) 8321 Cable Add: Agis Baden Baden
Man Dirs: Karl G Fischer, Karin Grochowiak
Subjects: Aesthetics, Cybernetics, Information Theory, Human and Natural Sciences, Philosophy
ISBN Publisher's Prefix: 3-87007

Agora-Verlag*, Hanseatenweg 10, Postfach 210533, D-1000 Berlin 21 Tel: (030) 3913775/3931387 Cable Add: Agora
Man Dir, Production: Manfred Schlösser; *Sales & Publicity:* Monika Schlösser-Fischer
Subsidiary Company: Erato-Presse
Branch Off: Lucasweg 17, D-6100 Darmstadt
Subjects: Literary Criticism, Belles Lettres, Poetry, Juveniles, Music, Theatre, Literature by exiles
Founded: 1960
ISBN Publisher's Prefix: 3-87008

L B **Ahnert**-Verlag*, Markt 9, Postfach 14, D-6360 Friedberg 3 Tel: (06031) 3131/60 Cable Add: Ahnert-Verlag Echzell Telex: 415961 pvlg d
Subjects: Sports, Horse Breeding, Non-fiction, Periodicals, Reproductions
ISBN Publisher's Prefix: 3-921142

Akademische Verlagsgesellschaft, Bahnhofstr 39, Postfach 1107, D-6200 Wiesbaden Tel: (06121) 39794 Cable Add: AKA Wiesbaden Telex: 4186451 avg d
Man Dir: Dr Claus Steiner; *Sales:* Gerhard Stahl
Subsidiary Company: Akademische Verlagsgesellschaft Athenaion (qv)
Subjects: Educational, Data Processing, Life Science, Chemistry, Physics, Maths, Electro-technology, Sociology, Periodicals
Founded: 1906
ISBN Publisher's Prefix: 3-400

Akademische Verlagsgesellschaft Athenaion, Bahnhofstr 39, Postfach 1107, D-6200 Wiesbaden Tel: (06121) 39794 Telex: 4186451 avg d
Parent Company: Akademische Verlagsgesellschaft, (qv)
Subjects: Literary Science, Linguistics (with special reference to English, German, Romance Languages), History of Culture, of Germany, of World Literature, of Music; Periodicals
Founded: 1912
ISBN Publisher's Prefix: 3-7997

Michael **Akselrad**, see Kübler Verlag

Alba Buchverlag GmbH und Co KG*, Römerstr 9, Postfach 320108, D-4000 Düsseldorf 30 Tel: (0211) 482068
Man Dir, Rights & Permissions: Alf Teloeken; *Sales:* D Wiesent; *Production:* K Hartung; *Publicity:* Werner Thelen
Associate Company: Alba Publikation Alf Teloeken GmbH und Co KG (qv)
Subjects: Railways (Over- and Underground), Tunnelling, Buses, Modelmaking
Founded: 1951
ISBN Publisher's Prefix: 3-87094

Alba Publikation Alf Teloeken GmbH und Co KG*, Römerstr 9, Postfach 320109, D-4000 Düsseldorf Tel: (0211) 482069
Man Dir, Rights & Permissions: Alf Teloeken; *Sales:* D Wiesent; *Production:* K Hartung; *Publicity:* Werner Thelen
Associate Company: Alba Buchverlag GmbH und Co KG (qv)
Subjects: Model Railways, Public Transport, Modelling, Periodicals

Verlag Karl **Albér** GmbH*, Hermann-Herder-Str 4, D-7800 Freiburg im Breisgau Tel: (0761) 273495 Telex: 07721440 vh d
Man Dir: Dr Meinolf Wewel
Orders to: Auslieferungsgemeinschaft Herder, Postfach, D-7800 Freiburg im Breisgau Tel: (0761) 27171
Parent Company: Verlag Herder (qv)
Subjects: Logic, History & Theory of Science, Philosophy, Psychology, Pedagogy, History, Law, Sociology, Political Science
Founded: 1939
ISBN Publisher's Prefix: 3-495

Alpha 9 GmbH*, Eschborn, Postfach 3029, Königsbergerstr 9, D-6236 Eschborn II Tel: (06173) 62268/62368 Cable Add: alpha verlag eschborn
Subjects: Informative Books of Plates and Wall Calendars: speciality — book/calendar combinations

Alpha Literatur Verlag*, August-Siebert-Str 9, D-6000 Frankfurt am Main 1 Tel: (0611) 555325 Telex: 414890
Man Dir: Dr G Philipps
Subjects: Poetry, Belles Lettres, Theatre

Alternative Verlag GmbH*, Postfach 150230, D-1000 Berlin 15 (Located at: Konstanzer Str 11, D-1000 Berlin 31) Tel: (030) 8811970/8815550
Man Dir: H Brenner; *Sales & Advertising Dir:* Till Sauer
Subjects: Literature, Social and Political Sciences, Philosophy, Theatre, Art
Founded: 1958

Anneliese **Althoff**, see Asso Verlag

Amazonen Frauenverlag GmbH, Knesebeckstr 86-87, D-1000 Berlin 12
Managers: M Emmerich, M H Myers
Subjects: Women's Cultural and Historical, Female Homosexual Themes, Lesbians in the Women's Movement

Ambro Lacus, Buch- und Bildverlag W Kremnitz, see Lacus

Anabas-Verlag Günter Kämpf KG, Am unteren Hardthof, D-6300 Giessen an der Lahn 1 Tel: 0641/72455
Man Dir: Günter Kämpf
Orders to: Sova Verlagsauslieferung, 44 Franziusstraße, D-6000 Frankfurt am Main; West Berlin: Zirk und Ellenrieder, Lützowstr 105/106, D-1000 Berlin 30
Subjects: Belles Lettres, Poetry, History, Art, High-priced Paperbacks, Educational Materials
1981: 10 titles *Founded:* 1966
ISBN Publisher's Prefix: 3-87038

Verlag Roland **Angst**, Achleitnerstrasse 1, D-8000 Munich 90 Tel: 640532
Publisher: Roland Angst
Subject: Modern Art

Anrich Verlag GmbH, Neunkirchen 5, D-6101 Modautal 3 Tel: (06254) 7229
Man Dir: Gerold Anrich
Subjects: Juvenile and Children's
1981: 9 titles *Founded:* 1970
ISBN Publisher's Prefix: 3-920110

Arani-Verlag GmbH, Kurfürstendamm 126, D-1000 Berlin 31, Postfach 310829 Tel: (030) 8911008
Publisher: Horst Meyer; *Rights & Permissions:* Katharina Janike
Orders to: Libri VA, Postfach 3584, D-6000 Frankfurt am Main 3
Subjects: Belles Lettres, Poetry, History, books on Berlin
1982: 12 titles *1983:* 10 titles *Founded:* 1947
ISBN Publisher's Prefix: 3-7605

Ararat Verlag GmbH, Bergmannstr 99a, D-1000 Berlin 61 Tel: 6935080 Berlin 61
Man Dir: Dr A I Dogan; *Marketing Manager:* Peter T Kampmann
Subjects: Turkish Literature in German translation; German-Turkish Twin-Language books, Turkish Literature Information Periodical
1981: 19 titles *1982:* 27 titles *Founded:* 1977
ISBN Publisher's Prefix: 3-921889

Verlag **Arbeiterbewegung und Gesellschaftswissenschaft**, Rosenstr 12-13, Postfach 510, D-3550 Marburg an der Lahn Tel: (06421) 63666
Workers' Movement and Sociology Publishing Co
Man Dir: Karl-Heinz Flessenkemper; *Editors:* Wolfgang Abendroth, Frank Deppe, Georg Fülberth, Gerd Hardach
Subjects: Workers' Rights, Trade Unions, Social History
1982: 30 titles *1983:* 40 titles *Founded:* 1976
ISBN Publisher's Prefix: 3-921630

Arbeitsgemeinschaft Deutsche Lateinamerika-Forschung (ADLAF), pA Forschungsgruppe Lateinamerika FB22, Universität Fliednerstr 21, D-4400 Münster Tel: (0251) 839438 Telex: 892529 Unims D
German Association for Research on Latin America
Subjects: Embracing the work of more than 20 Member Institutes and more than 100 individual members in research areas of Archaeology, Ethnology, History, Literature, the Geo-Sciences, Economic and Social Sciences, Librarianship; also publish Periodicals and Bibliographies

Arbeitsgemeinschaft mitteleuropäischer Bibelwerke, see AMB

Arbeitsgemeinschaft sozialistischer und demokratischer Verleger und Buchhändler
Co-operative of Socialist and Democratic publishing houses and bookshops, comprising following 16 publishers: Brücken-Verlag GmbH, Düsseldorf (qv); Damnitz-Verlag, Munich (qv); Institut für Marxistische Studien und Forschungen (IMSF), Frankfurt am Main (qv); Verlag Marxistische Blätter GmbH, Frankfurt am Main (qv); Monitor-Verlag, Düsseldorf; Nachrichten-Verlags-GmbH, Frankfurt am Main (qv); Neue Kommentare, Frankfurt am Main; Pahl-Rugenstein Verlag, Cologne (qv); Plambeck und Co Druck und Verlag GmbH, Neuss (qv); Rochus-Verlag, Düsseldorf; Röderberg-Verlag GmbH, Frankfurt am Main (qv); W Runge-Verlag, Hamburg; Stimme-Verlag GmbH, Mainz; Weltkreis-Verlags-GmbH, Dortmund (qv)
Miscellaneous: The central marketing agency for this group is the Brücken-Verlag GmbH, Düsseldorf (qv)

Verlag Die **Arbeitswelt** GmbH*, Grimmstr 27, D-1000 Berlin 61 Tel: (030) 6933069
Dirs: Dr Ulrich Laube
Subject: Politics (especially trade union studies), Social Science

Verlag für **Architektur**, Martiusstr 8, Postfach 440254, D-8000 Munich 44 Tel: (089) 348074 Telex: 5215517
Branch Off: Limmatquai 18, CH-8024

Zurich, Switzerland
Associate Companies: Artemis und Winkler Verlag (qv); Druckenmüller Verlag, (qv); Artemis Verlags AG, Switzerland (qv)
Subjects: Collected Works of Leading World Architects, Studio Paperback Series, Works on Town Planning, Pre-Fabrication etc

Arena-Verlag Georg Popp GmbH & Co, Textorstr 24-26, Postfach 5169, D-8700 Würzburg 1 Tel: (0931) 50688 Telex: 068833
Man Dir, Publicity, Rights & Permissions: Hans-Georg Noack; *Sales Dir:* August Bartels; *Production:* Winfried Popp
Parent Company: Georg Westermann Verlags- und Druckerei-Verwaltungsgesellschaft mbH, Brunswick
Associate Companies: Verlag Heinz Vogel, Brunswick; Westermann Verlag GmbH (qv)
Subjects: General Non-fiction, Juvenile, Young Adults, Paperbacks, Art Books, Books for the Bibliophile
Founded: 1949
ISBN Publisher's Prefix: 3-401

Argos Press*, Oberbuschweg, Postfach 1940, D-5000 Cologne 50 Tel: 02236/64071 Telex: 888 3508
Man Dir: Robert Pütz; *Production and other offices:* Brigitte Klatt
Associate Companies: Druckerei Robert Pütz, Werbeagentur Robert Pütz, Fotostudio Robinson
Subjects: Illustrated books, Humour
Founded: 1978
ISBN Publisher's Prefix: 3-88420

Arkana-Verlag*, Fritz-Frey Str 21, Postfach 105767, D-6900 Heidelberg 1 Tel: (06221) 49974 Cable Add: arkanaverlag Telex: 46183 hvvfmd
Man Dir: Dr Ewald Fischer
Associate Companies: Karl F Haug Verlag GmbH & Co (qv); Verlag für Medizin Dr E Fischer GmbH (qv)
Subjects: Fringe Medicine, Occult, the Arts
ISBN Publisher's Prefix: 3-920042

Ars Edition GmbH, Friedrichstr 9, Postfach 430360, D-8000 Munich 43 Tel: (089) 393045 Telex: 5213554
Man Dir: Marcel Nauer; *Sales:* Rudolf Sommer; *Production:* Gregor Schulze
Subsidiary Company: Ars Edition Inc, 70 Air Park Drive, Ronkonkona, Seaford, New York, NY 11779, USA Tel: (516467) 2300
Branch Office: Ars Edition, Postfach 48, CH-6301 Zug, Switzerland
Subjects: Gift Books, Children's
1981: 25 titles *Founded:* 1896
Miscellaneous: Formerly Ars Sacra Josef Müller
ISBN Publisher's Prefix: 3-7607

Das **Arsenal**, Verlag für Kultur und Politik GmbH, Tegeler Weg 5, D-1000 Berlin 10 Tel: (030) 3441827
The above is the editorial office; administration is c/o Buchvertrieb Grimmstrasse, Grimmstr 27, D-1000 Berlin 61 Tel: (030) 6933069
Man Dir: Dr Peter Moses-Krause
Subjects: Politics (theory & general), Biography, Oral History, Publicity, Art, Film, Linguistics, Ethnology
Founded: 1977
ISBN Publisher's Prefix: 3-921810

Art Address Verlag Müller GmbH und Co KG, Grosse Eschenheimer Str 16, D-6000 Frankfurt am Main 1 Tel: (0611) 284486 Telex: 0411699 omf D
Publishers: Joachim Müller, Erwin Kohl; *Man Dir:* Michael Zils
Subject: Art
Founded: 1949

Artbook International, an imprint of Berghaus Verlag (qv)

Artemis und Winkler Verlag, Martiusstr 8, D-8000 Munich 40 Tel: (089) 348074 Cable Add: arte d Telex: 5215517
Man Dir: Hans-Jürgen Schmidt; *Publicity Dir:* Anita Donat; *Advertising Dir:* Sunhild Pacheco; *Rights & Permissions:* Birgit Endres
Associate Companies: Verlag für Architektur, Alfred Druckenmüller Verlag, (qqv, Federal Republic of Germany); Artemis Verlags AG, Verlag für Architektur (qqv, Switzerland)
Subsidiary Company: Winkler-Verlag (qv)
Subjects: (Artemis Verlag) Belles Lettres, The Humanities, Children's, Illustrated Books, History of Antiquity, Collected Works, Classics, Goethe, Oriental Studies; (Winkler Verlag) India Paper Editions and Special Editions of World Literature, Special series of Classics, Works of Zola, Germanistics
ISBN Publisher's Prefix: 3-7608

Aschendorffsche Verlagsbuchhandlung, Soesterstr 13, Postfach 1124, D-4400 Münster Tel: (0251) 6901 Cable Add: Verlag Aschendorff Münster Telex: 0892830
Man Dirs: Anton Wilhelm Hueffer, Maxfritz Hueffer
Subjects: History, Philosophy, Religion, Psychology, Education, Law, Folklore, Philology, Textbooks, Foreign Languages, Periodicals
Founded: 1720
Miscellaneous: Part of vgs — Verlagsgesellschaft Schulfernsehen mbH & Co KG (qv)
ISBN Publisher's Prefix: 3-402

Assimil-Verlag KG, now incorporated in Pädagogischer Verlag Schwann/Bagel (qv)

Asso Verlag Anneliese Althoff+, Josefplatz 3, D-4200 Oberhausen Tel: (0208) 802356
Orders to: VVA (Vereinigte Verlagsauslieferung GmbH), Postfach 7777, D-4830 Gütersloh 1; West Berlin: Zirk und Ellenrieder, Lützowstr 105-106, D-1000 Berlin 30
Subjects: Contemporary Political Literature in prose, poetry, songs, graphics; Miners' Solidarity

Ästhetik und Kommunikation Verlags-GmbH, Bogotastr 27, D-1000 Berlin 37 Tel: (030) 8028789
Man Dir, Editorial: Eberhard Knödler-Bunte; *Sales:* Bianca Bon; *Production:* Dr Walter Süss; *Publicity:* Gisela Kayser
Subjects: Contemporary Issues, Political Culture, Aesthetics, Art, Literature, Periodicals
1982: 62 titles *Founded:* 1969

Verlag **Atelier im Bauernhaus**, in der Bredenau 5, D-2802 Fischerhude Tel: (04293) 671
Subjects: Regional Books, Prose and Poetry in Bibliophile Editions, Novels, Graphics, Songbooks, Art Books

Atelier Verlag Andernach (AVA), Antel 74, D-547 Andernach Tel: 44432
Man Dir & Rights & Permissions: Rosa Werf; *Publicity Dir:* Frederik Marhofen
Subjects: Belles Lettres, Poetry, Art
Founded: 1967
ISBN Publisher's Prefix: 3-921042

Athenaion, see Akademische Verlagsgesellschaft

Athenäum Verlag GmbH, Adelheidstr 2, Postfach 1220, D-6240 Königstein/TS Tel: (06174) 3021 Telex: 0410664
Publisher: Axel Rütters; *Editorial:* Dr Beate Pinkerneil; *Sales, Publicity:* Daniel Herrmann; *Rights & Permissions:* Hildegard Willhöft
Subsidiary Companies: Peter Hanstein Verlag GmbH (qv), Jüdischer Verlag, Verlag Anton Hain Meisenheim GmbH (qv) is a subsidiary of this group of companies. All companies are located at above address
Subjects: Philosophy, History, Textbooks, Paperbacks, Linguistics, Pedagogy, Politics, Psychology, Social Science, Literary Criticism, Languages, Economics, General Non-fiction
Founded: 1973
ISBN Publisher's Prefix: 3-7610

Atlantis-Verlag GmbH & Co Kg*, Erwinstr 58-60, Postfach 127, D-7800 Freiburg im Breisgau Tel: (0761) 71570
Dir: Peter G Isler
Head Off: Atlantis Verlag AG, Switzerland (qv)
Subjects: Art, Literature, History, Pictorial Geography, Travel
Founded: 1930
ISBN Publisher's Prefix: 3-7611

Verlag Ludwig **Auer**, Heilig-Kreuz-Str 12, Postfach 1152, D-8850 Donauwörth Tel: (0906) 731 Cable Add: Auer Donauwörth Telex: 05-1845
Subjects: History, Religion, Education, Textbooks, Juveniles
Founded: 1875
Miscellaneous: Firm is member of TR-Verlagsunion GmbH (qv)
ISBN Publisher's Prefix: 3-403

Aulis Verlag Deubner & Co KG, Antwerpener Str 6/12, D-5000 Cologne 1 Tel: (0221) 518051 Telex: 8883068 avd d
Publishers: Karl-August Deubner, Wolfgang Deubner
Subjects: Non-fiction, (Natural Sciences), especially Biology, Chemistry, Mathematics, Physics, Geography
ISBN Publisher's Prefix: 3-7614

Aurum Verlag GmbH & Co KG, Franziskanerstr 9, Postfach 5204, D-7800 Freiburg im Breisgau Tel: (0761) 36409
Publisher: Günther Berkau; *Editorial:* Dr Elisabeth Sicard
Orders to: Walter-Verlag GmbH, Grissheimer Weg 36, Postfach 1147, D-7843 Heitersheim Tel: (07634) 948 Telex: 772961
Subjects: Psychology, Mysticism, Religion, Yoga, Meditation, Para-Medicine
1981: 22 titles *1982:* 13 titles
ISBN Publisher's Prefix: 3-591

Aussaat-und-Schriftenmissions-Verlag GmbH, Humboldstr 15, Postfach 548, D-4390 Gladbeck Tel: (02043) 28028
Dirs: Thomas S von Puskás, Volker Stork; *Sales, Advertising:* Michael Lippkau; *Production:* Liesel Rennscheidt
Subjects: Evangelical and Scriptural Texts, Religion, Education, Juveniles, Paperbacks
Bookshop: Humboldstr 15, D-4390 Gladbeck
1982: 41 titles *Founded:* 1978
ISBN Publisher's Prefixes: 3-7615 (Aussaat, Wuppertal); 3-7958 (Schriftenmissions, Gladbeck)

Verlag der **Autoren** GmbH & Co KG, Staufenstr 46, Postfach 174091, D-6000 Frankfurt am Main Tel: (0611) 726744/45
Dirs: Dr Karlheinz Braun, Michael Töteberg
Subjects: Texts for Theatre series *Theaterbibliothek*

Syndikat **Autoren-und Verlagsgesellschaft**, Savignystr 61-63, Postfach 174003, D-6000 Frankfurt am Main Tel: (0611) 742567 Telex: 4185532
Author/Publisher Syndicate Company
Man Dir: Axel Rütters
Orders to: VVA (Vereinigte

FEDERAL REPUBLIC OF GERMANY 125

Verlagsauslieferung GmbH), Postfach 7777, D-4830 Gütersloh 1; (West Berlin): Hans Schultz, Lützowstr 105-106, D-1000 Berlin 30
Subjects: Literary Criticism, Art Theory, Psychology, Psycho-analysis, Ethnology, Social Theory and Social History, Political Economy
Founded: 1976
ISBN Publisher's Prefix: 3-8108

Axel-Juncker Verlag Jacobi KG, see Juncker

B K V-Brasilienkunde Verlag GmbH, Postfach 1220, D-4532 Mettingen (Located at: Sunderstr 15, Mettingen)
Man Dir: Dr Hubertus Rescher
Subjects: Brazil and Latin America (Problems, Documentary)
1981: 6 titles *Founded:* 1979
ISBN Publisher's Prefix: 3-88559

B L V Verlagsgesellschaft mbH, Lothstr 29, Postfach 400320, D-8000 Munich 40 Tel: (089) 127050 Cable Add: BLV Verlag Telex: 5215087/5212630
Man Dir: Dr A Egger; *Publishing Dir:* Dr Rudolf Schneider; *Editorial:* Wilhelm Eisenreich, Jürgen Kemmler; *International Relations Dir:* Curt Ablaßmayer; *Rights & Permissions:* Ursula Holkko, Hannelore König
Subjects: General Non-fiction: especially Nature, Sports, Field and Travel Guides, Horses, Hunting, Household and Garden, Technical books on Agriculture, Forestry, Environment, Biology, Nutrition; Education, School Textbooks
Founded: 1946
Miscellaneous: Firm is member of TR-Verlagsunion GmbH (qv)
ISBN Publisher's Prefix: 3-405

b m p, an imprint of Gustav Bosse Verlag GmbH & Co KG (qv)

B S-Verlag Manfred Kerler*, Marbacher Str 8, Postfach 450, D-7057 Winnenden-Stuttgart Tel: (07195) 8012
Subject: Transport

B V B, see Bayerische Verlagsanstalt Bamberg

J P **Bachem** Verlag GmbH, Ursulaplatz 1, D-5000 Cologne 1 Tel: (0221) 135041 Cable Add: Bachemhaus Cologne
Dirs: Dr Peter Bachem, Gerd Horbach
Subjects: Books on Cologne and the Rhenish lands, Economics, Social Science, Religion
Founded: 1818
ISBN Publisher's Prefix: 3-7616

Karl **Baedeker** GmbH, Rosastr 7, D-7800 Freiburg im Breisgau Tel: (0761) 32915 Cable Add: Baedeker Freiburg
Man Dir, Editorial, Production: Eva Baedeker
Subjects: Guide Books (in English and French), Facsimile early guidebooks
Founded: 1827
ISBN Publisher's Prefix: 3-87954

Baedekers Autoführer-Verlag GmbH, Marco-Polo-Str 1, Postfach, D-7302 Ostfildern 4 (Kemnat) bei Stuttgart Tel: (0711) 4502262 Cable Add: Baedeker Stuttgart Telex: 721796 mair d
Man Dir: Dr Volkmar Mair; *Editorial:* Dr Peter Baumgarten
Subject: Travel Guides, Motoring Guides
1983-84: 10 titles *Founded:* 1951 (Stuttgart: originally 1827 Koblenz)
ISBN Publisher's Prefix: 3-87036

Hans A **Baensch**, see Mergus Verlag

Baha'i Verlag GmbH, Eppsteiner Str 89, D-6238 Hofheim-Langenhain Tel: (06192) 22921
Subject: The Baha'i Religion

1982: 15 titles *1981:* 8 titles
ISBN Publisher's Prefix: 3-87037

Friedrich **Bahn** Verlag GmbH, Zasiusstr 8, Postfach 1186, D-7550 Konstanz Tel: (07531) 23054/5
Man Dir: Herbert Denecke; *Manager, Rights & Permissions:* Herbert Denecke
Parent Company: Christliche Verlagsanstalt GmbH (qv)
Associate Company: Sonnenweg-Verlag (qv)
Subjects: Children's Books, Christian Instruction, Christianity
Founded: 1891
ISBN Publisher's Prefix: 3-7621

Bärenreiter-Verlag*, Heinrich-Schütz-Allee 29-37, D-3500 Kassel-Wilhelmshöhe Tel: (0561) 3001117 Cable Add: Bärenreiter, Kassel Telex: 0992376
Management: Wolfgang Matthei, Dr Wolfgang Rehm, Barbara Scheuch-Vötterle
Imprints include: Edition Nagel
Branch Offs: London, UK; Basle, Switzerland
Subjects: Music, Reproductions of Ancient Topographical Maps, Periodicals
Founded: 1924
ISBN Publisher's Prefix: 3-7618

Verlag **Bartels und Wernitz** KG*, Reinickendorfer Str 113, Postfach 650380, D-1000 Berlin 65 Tel: (030) 4611011 Cable Add: Bartelswernitz Westberlin Telex: 181331 bawer d
Man Dir: Harry Bartels; *Editorial:* Hans-Jürgen Ehrlich; *Sales & Advertising Dir:* Monika Schuchardt-Bartels
Orders to: Georg Lingenbrink, Postfach 3584, D-6000 Frankfurt am Main
Subjects: Sport (including training and history)
Founded: 1926
ISBN Publisher's Prefix: 3-87039

Otto Wilhelm **Barth**-Verlag KG, Stievestr 9, D-8000 Munich 19 Tel: (089) 172237 Telex: 5215282 d
Man Dir: Rudolf Streit-Scherz; *Editor:* Stephan Schuhmacher; *Sales:* Wolfgang Radaj, Alfred Vallotton; *Rights & Permissions:* Ursula Griessel
Parent Company: Scherz Verlag AG, Switzerland (qv)
Associate Company: Scherz Verlag GmbH, Munich (qv)
Subjects: Philosophy and Religions of the East, Mysticism
1982: 20 titles *Founded:* 1924
ISBN Publisher's Prefix: 3-87041

Barudio und Hess Verlag, Cornelius Str 19, D-6000 Frankfurt am Main Tel: (0611) 745324
Man Dirs, Editorial: Dr Gunter Barudio, Dr Stephan Hess; *Sales, Production, Publicity, Rights & Permissions:* Stephan Hess
Subjects: Literature, Politics, Art, History, Economics
Founded: 1978
ISBN Publisher's Prefix: 3-922182

Basis-Verlag, Postfach 645, D-1000 Berlin 15 (Located at: Mariannenplatz 23, D-1000 Berlin 36) Tel: (030) 6118016
Subjects: Juveniles, Comics, Education, Documentary
ISBN Publisher's Prefix: 3-88025

Friedrich **Bassermann'sche** Verlagsbuchhandlung im Falken-Verlag GmbH, Schöne Aussicht 21, Postfach 1120, D-6272 Niedernhausen/Ts Tel: (06127) 3011 Telex: 4186585 fves d
Parent Company: Falken-Verlag GmbH (qv)
Subjects: Wilhelm-Busch-Edition
ISBN Publisher's Prefix: 3-87043

Bastei-Verlag Gustav H Lübbe*, Scheidtbachstr 23-31, Postfach 200180, D-5070 Bergisch Gladbach 3 Tel: (02202) 1210 Cable Add: Scheidtbachstr 23-31 Telex: 887922
Man Dir: Gustav Lübbe; *Editorial:* Rolf Schmitz; *Sales:* H-J Karl; *Production:* D Deichmann (Fiction); J Dippmann (Juveniles and Paperbacks); *Publicity:* L Becker-Voss, I Sellmann
Associate Company: Gustav Lübbe Verlag (qv)
Subjects: Paperbacks
Founded: 1953
ISBN Publisher's Prefix: 3-404

Ernst **Battenberg** Verlag*, Prinzregentenstr 79, Postfach 800349, D-8000 Munich 80 Tel: (089) 4702066/67
Man Dir, Editorial, Sales, Rights & Permissions: Ernst Battenberg
Subjects: Art and Antiques, Numismatics, Heraldry, Orders and Decorations, Old Maps, Facsimile Editions
Founded: 1956
ISBN Publisher's Prefix: 3-87045

Hermann **Bauer** Verlag KG+, Kronenstr 2-4, Postfach 167, D-7800 Freiburg Tel: (0761) 70820 Telex: 0772821
Man Dir: Friedrich Kirner; *Editorial, Publicity, Rights & Permissions:* Gabriele Kirner; *Sales Manager:* Waltraud Kirner
Subjects: Astrology, Philosophy, Parapsychology, Yoga, Esoterica
1981: 10 titles
ISBN Publisher's Prefix: 3-7626

Bauverlag GmbH, Wittelsbacherstr 10, Postfach 1460, D-6200 Wiesbaden 1 Tel: (06121) 1390 Cable Add: Bauverlag Wiesbaden Telex: 4186792 bvwd
Dirs: Michael Schirmer, Eberhard Blottner; *Rights & Permissions:* Reinhart Knapp; *Sales:* Karlheinz Gross; *Publicity & Advertising:* Hans-Joachim Kopp
Subsidiary Companies: Verlag für Aufbereitung Schirmer und Zeh GmbH; Mauritius-Verlags-Messe- & Werbegesellschaft GmbH (both in Wiesbaden, Federal Republic of Germany)
Branch Off: Nikolsburger Str 11, D-1000 Berlin 31
Subjects: Civil Engineering, Architecture, Surveying, Town Planning, Building Materials, Draughtsmanship, Dictionaries, Books and Periodicals in both German and English languages
1981: 95 titles *Founded:* 1929
ISBN Publisher's Prefix: 3-7625

Bayerische Verlagsanstalt Bamberg (B V B), Lange Str 22/24, D-8600 Bamberg Tel: (0951) 25252 Telex: 06 62860 otvl
Man Dir: Kurt Kiening; *Other Offices:* Norbert Goebel
Associate Companies: Morawa & Co, Austria (qv); Adolf Zwimpfer, Switzerland (qv)
Subsidiary Company: Sankt Otto-Verlag GmbH (qv)
Subjects: Classics, World Literature Series, Poetry, Juveniles, Regional Literature
Bookshop: Goerres Buchhandlung (at above address)
1982: 45 titles *Founded:* 1949
ISBN Publisher's Prefix: 3-87052

Bayerischer Schulbuch-Verlag, Hubertusstr 4, Postfach 87, D-8000 Munich 19 Tel: (089) 174067/69
Dir: Heinz Klüter; *Sales Manager:* Hartmut Köppelmann
Orders to: BSV, Ohmstr 10, D-8047 Karlsfeld Tel: (08131) 95091
Branch Offs: Ohmstr 10, D-8047 Karlsfeld; Friedrichstr 26, D-4000 Düsseldorf
Subjects: School textbooks, Educational

Materials
ISBN Publisher's Prefix: 3-7627

Bechtle, Hubertusstr 4, D-8000 Munich 19 Tel: (089) 177041 Cable Add: Langenmüller Telex: 05215045
Dirs: Dr Herbert Fleissner, Otto Wolfgang Bechtle, Dr Friedrich Bechtle; *Man Dir:* Dr Konrad Dietzfelbinger
Orders to: VVA (Vereinigte Verlagsauslieferung GmbH), Postfach 7777, D-4830 Gütersloh 1 Tel: (05241) 801; West Berlin: BS Buch-Service GmbH Berlin, Kurfürstenstr 72-74, D-1000 Berlin 30 Tel: (030) 2695 232
Subjects: Poetry, Biography, History, Politics, High-priced Paperbacks, Series Bechtle Anekdoten
Founded: 1868 (Book Department, 1949)
Miscellaneous: Firm is a member of Verlagsgruppe Langen Müller-Herbig (qv)
ISBN Publisher's Prefix: 3-7623

Verlag C H **Beck***, Wilhelmstr 9, Postfach 400340, D-8000 Munich 40 Tel: 381891 Telex: 05215085 beckd
Dirs: Dr Hans D Beck, Wolfgang Beck; *Editorial:* E Wieckenberg, Ursula Pietsch, Günther Schiwy, B Rüster; *Sales Dirs:* G Elze, E Hoppe; *Publicity Dir:* P Schunemann; *Rights & Permissions:* Eva von Freeden
Associate Companies: Franz Vahlen (qv); Biederstein Verlag (qv)
Branch Off: Palmengartenstr 14, D-6000 Frankfurt am Main
Subjects: Ancient and Modern History, Archaeology, Literary History, Linguistics, Social Sciences, Anthropology, Economics, Law, Popular Non-fiction, Art, Illustrated Books, Textbooks, Classics, Periodicals
Founded: 1763
Miscellaneous: Firm is member of TR-Verlagsunion GmbH (qv)
ISBN Publisher's Prefixes: 3-406 (Beck), 3-8006 (Vahlen), 3-7642 (Biederstein)

Edition Monika **Beck**, Schwedenhof, D-6650 Homburg-Schwarzenacker/Saar Tel: (06848) 554
Man Dir/Proprietor: Monika Beck; *Publicity Dir:* B O Beck
Branch Off: Kaiserslauten
Subjects: Bibliophile portfolios, First editions, Monograph portfolios
Book Club: Kunstkreis für Bibliophile Mappen
Founded: 1967

M P **Belaieff**, see C F Peters Musikverlag Gmbh und Co KG

Chr **Belser** AG für Verlagsgeschäfte und Co KG, Falkertstr 73, Postfach 1002, D-7000 Stuttgart 1 Tel: (0711) 221359/221350 Cable Add: Belserverlag Telex: 0722334 belag d
Publishers: Hans Weitpert, Hilde Weitpert-Vogt; *General Manager:* Bernd Friedrich; *Sales Manager:* Herbert Lindauer; *Rights & Permissions:* Hubertus Wolf
Subjects: Art, Quality Reproductions, Architecture, Music, History, Natural History, Non-fiction, Travel, Book/Record combinations, Periodicals
1981: 22 titles *Founded:* 1835
ISBN Publisher's Prefix: 3-7630

Beltz Verlag, Am Hauptbahnhof 10a Werderstr, Postfach 1120, D-6940 Weinheim Tel: (06201) 63071 Telex: 465500
Man Dir: Dr Manfred Beltz-Ruebelmann; *Sales:* Anni Wetzel; *Publicity:* Gunter Holm
Subjects: Juveniles, Psychology, Social Science, Primary & University Textbooks
Founded: 1841
Miscellaneous: Part of vgs — Verlagsgesellschaft Schulfernsehen mbH & Co KG (qv)
ISBN Publisher's Prefix: 3-407

Benziger Verlag, Kölnerstr 248, D-5000 Cologne 90 Tel: (02203) 81081 Telex: 8874591
Marketing Dir: Robert F Oehler; *Sales & Publicity:* Klaus Opitz
Head Off: Benziger AG, Switzerland (qv)
Subjects: General Fiction, Juveniles, Education, Religion
ISBN Publisher's Prefix: 3-545

Johannes **Berchmans** Verlag GmbH, Münchhausenstr 4, D-8000 Munich 60 Tel: (089) 8114535
General Manager: Dr Erich Lampey
Subjects: Philosophy, Contemporary History
ISBN Publisher's Prefix: 3-87056

Verlag Schumann KG **Berg/Bodman**, see Hohenstaufen

Edition Sven Erik **Bergh**, formerly of Tübingen, see Edition Sven Erik Bergh im Europabuch AG, Switzerland

Berghaus Verlag, Ramerding 18, D-8347 Kirchdorf/Inn Tel: (08571) 2042/2043
Man Dir: Ursel Bader
Imprints: Artbook International, Berghaus International
Subject: Art
1982: 10 titles *Founded:* 1973
ISBN Publisher's Prefix: 3-7635

J F **Bergmann**, Agnes-Bernauer-Platz 8, D-8000 Munich 21 Tel: (089) 563532/5803023 Cable Add: Bergmannverlag Munich Telex: 529029
General Managers: Dr Heinz Goetze, Dr Konrad F Springer, Claus Michaletz
Parent Company: Springer-Verlag Berlin — Heidelberg — New York — Tokyo GmbH & Co KG (qv)
Subject: Medicine
Founded: 1878
ISBN Publisher's Prefix: 3-8070

Bergverlag Rudolf Rother GmbH, Landshuter Allee 49, Postfach 67, D-8000 Munich 19 Tel: (089) 160081
Publisher: Rudolf Rother
Subjects: Mountaineering and Ski-ing
1981: 200 titles *Founded:* 1920
ISBN Publisher's Prefix: 3-7633

Berlin Verlag Arno Spitz, Pacelli Allee 5, D-1000 Berlin 33 Tel: (030) 8326232
Proprietor, Publicity Manager: Arno Spitz
Subjects: International and Comparative Law, Politics, Bibliographic Guides to Literature on Scientific Studies and on Berlin, East European Studies
1982: approx 25 titles *Founded:* 1963
ISBN Publisher's Prefix: 3-87061

Berliner Handpresse Wolfgang Joerg und Erich Schoenig, Kohlfurter Str 35, D-1000 Berlin 36 Tel: (030) 6148728/6142605
Publisher: Wolfgang Joerg
Subjects: General Fiction, Arts, First Editions, Children's Books
Founded: 1961

Berliner Union GmbH, now absorbed by Verlag W Kohlhammer (qv)

Bernard und Graefe Verlag, Carl-Mand-Str 2, D-5400 Koblenz Tel: (0261) 803071
Branch Off: Waldweg 11, D-8028 Taufkirchen bei Munich Tel: (089) 6121003
Subjects: Military, History, Politics, Textbooks
Founded: 1918
ISBN Publisher's Prefix: 3-7637

C **Bertelsmann** Verlag GmbH, Neumarkterstr 18, Postfach 800360, D-8000 Munich 80 Tel: (089) 43189 Cable Add: Bertelsmann München Telex: 523259
Dir: Peter Gutmann
Parent Company: Verlagsgruppe Bertelsmann GmbH (qv)
Associate Companies: See Verlagsgruppe Bertelsmann GmbH
Subjects: General Fiction & Non-fiction, Juveniles, Arts, Biography, Current Events, Foreign Works in Translation
Founded: 1835
Miscellaneous: Firm is member of TR-Verlagsunion GmbH (qv)
ISBN Publisher's Prefix: 3-570

Verlagsgruppe **Bertelsmann** GmbH, Carl-Bertelsmann-Str 270, D-4830 Gütersloh 1 Tel: (05241) 801 Cable Add: Bertelsmann Gütersloh Telex: 933646
The Bertelsmann Publishing Group
Chairmen: Dr Ulrich Wechsler, Dr Horst Benzing, Olaf Paeschke, Franz Freiberg, Klaus Porada
Member Companies: Verlagsgruppe Bertelsmann International GmbH (qv); C Bertelsmann Verlag GmbH (qv); Bertelsmann Fachzeitschiften GmbH; Blanvalet Verlag GmbH (qv); Verlag für Buchmarkt- und Medien-Forschung (qv); Betriebswirt Verlag Dr Theodor Gabler GmbH (qv); Wilhelm Goldmann Verlag GmbH (qv); ILS Institut für Lernsysteme GmbH; Kartographisches Institut Bertelsmann (qv); Albrecht Knaus Verlag (qv); Lexikothek Verlag GmbH (qv); MMW — Medizin Verlag GmbH; Mosaik Verlag GmbH (qv); Prisma Verlag GmbH (qv); Proschule Verlag GmbH; RV Reise- und Verkehrsverlag (qv); Schulverlag Vieweg GmbH (qv); Friedr Vieweg und Sohn GmbH (qv); Verlag Heinrich Vogel Fachverlag GmbH; Westdeutscher Verlag GmbH (qv) (all Federal Republic of Germany); Verlag Kremayr und Scheriau, Austria (qv); Transworld Publishers Ltd, UK (qv); Bertelsmann Publishing Group, USA; Bantam Books, USA
Branch Offs: Neumarkter Str 18, D-8000 Munich 80 Tel: (089) 41730 Cable Add: Bertelsmann München Telex: 523259; Lützowstr 105-106, Berlin Tel: (030) 2621021; Verlag für Buchmarkt- und Medien-Forschung, Faulbrunnstr 13, D-6200 Wiesbaden Tel: (06121) 534
Book Clubs: Bertelsmann Lesering, Europaring der Buch- und Schallplattenfreunde (both owned by Bertelsmann Club GmbH), Europäische Bildungsgemeinschaft Verlag GmbH (all in Federal Republic of Germany); The Leisure Circle, UK; Círculo de Lectores SA, Argentina; Círculo do Livro SA, Brazil (owned jointly with Abril SA Cultural e Industrial, Brazil (qv); Círculo de Lectores SA, Colombia; Circulo de Leitores SA, Portugal; Círculo de Lectores SA, Spain
Founded: 1835
ISBN Publisher's Prefix: 3-570

Verlagsgruppe **Bertelsmann International** GmbH, Carl-Bertelsmann-Str 270, D-4830 Gütersloh 1 Tel: (05241) 801 Telex: 933646
Dirs: Peter Gutmann, Dr Jürgen Krämer, Jürgen Kreuzhage
Parent Company: Verlagsgruppe Bertelsmann GmbH (qv)
Branch Off: Neumarkter Str 18, D-8000 Munich 80 Tel: (089) 41730 Telex: 523259
Subjects: International Co-Productions
Founded: 1977

Verlag Das **Besondere**, Maxhöhe 12, D-8137 Berg 3 Tel: (08151) 51717
Man Dir and other offices: Peter Erd
Subjects: Parapsychology, Aids to Living
Founded: 1975
ISBN Publisher's Prefix: 3-8138

Verlag Das **Beste** GmbH, Augustenstr 1, Postfach 178, D-7000 Stuttgart 1 Tel: (0711) 66020 Cable Add: Readigest Stuttgart Telex: 0723539

Man Dir: Werner Weidmann
Parent Company: The Reader's Digest Association, Inc, PO Box 235, Pleasantville, NY 10570, USA
Subsidiary Companies: Pegasus Buch- und Zeischriften-Vertriebs-GmbH, Plieninger Str 100, D-7000 Stuttgart 80; Medit Verlag GmbH, Werinherstr 71, D-8000 Munich 90
Subjects: General
Founded: 1952

Beton-Verlag GmbH, Düsseldorfer Str 8, Postfach 110134, D-4000 Düsseldorf 11 Tel: (0211) 571068
General Manager: Emil Fuchs; *Editorial:* Dieter Bausch; *Publicity and Marketing:* Peter Fischer
Orders to: Abteilung Fachbuch (at above address)
Subjects: Structural Engineering, Technology and Architecture
Founded: 1958
ISBN Publisher's Prefix: 3-7640

Annette **Betz** Verlag, formerly of Munich, removed to Austria (qv)

Elke **Betzel** Verlag*, Bertha von Suttner Ring 5a, D-6000 Frankfurt am Main 78 Tel: (0611) 682600
Subjects: Artistic Philosophy, Author/Artist Co-operation, Poetry, Drama
Miscellaneous: Formerly Gruppe Hinterhaus

Beuroner Kunstverlag GmbH, D-7792 Beuron 1 Tel: (07466) 264 Cable Add: Beuroner Kunstverlag
Dir: Gabriel Gawletta; *Publicity Manager:* Siegfried Studer
Subjects: Arts, Religion, Periodicals
Founded: 1898
ISBN Publisher's Prefix: 3-87071

Beuth Verlag GmbH, Burggrafenstr 4-10, D-1000 Berlin 30 Tel: (030) 26011 Telex: 183622 bvb d
Man Dirs: Hans Hermann Plischke, Dr-Ing Helmut Reihlen; *Sales Dir:* Werner Schmitz; *Publicity Dir:* Albrecht Geuther; *Advertising Dir:* Christoph Trautmann
Branch Off: Kamekestr 2-8, D-5000 Cologne 1 Tel: (0221) 57131 Telex: 8881332 bvk d
Subjects: Science, Technical
1983: 2,000 titles *Founded:* 1924
ISBN Publisher's Prefix: 3-410

Bibellesebund eV, Höfel Nr 6, Postfach 1129, D-5277 Marienheide 1 Tel: (02264) 7575
Scripture Union of Germany
Man Dir: Karl Schäfer; *General Manager:* Helmut Klein
Head Office: Scripture Union, UK (qv for other branches)
Associate Company: Verlag Bibellesebund, Switzerland (qv)
Subjects: Christian Literature for Juveniles and Adults
Founded: 1950
ISBN Publisher's Prefix: 3-87982

Bibliographisches Institut AG+, Dudenstr 6, Postfach 311, D-6800 Mannheim 1 Tel: (0621) 39010 Cable Add: Biblio Telex: 04-62107 duden d
Man Dirs: Karl Felder, Claus Greuner, Dr Michael Wegner; *Sales:* Rosita Throm; *Sales Dir, Rights & Permissions:* Claus Greuner
Subsidiary Companies: Bibliographisches Institut AG, Switzerland (qv); Bibliographisches Institut GmbH, Vienna, Austria (qv); Südbuch Vertriebgesellschaft mbH, Mannheim, Federal Republic of Germany
Subjects: Technology, Arts and Sciences, German Language, General Knowledge, Juveniles, Low-priced Paperbacks, General Science, University Textbooks, Encyclopaedias, Geography

Founded: 1826
Miscellaneous: Publishers of the Duden series of Dictionaries and Meyer series of Lexicons
ISBN Publisher's Prefix: 3-411

Bibliomed — Medizinische Verlagsgesellschaft mbH, Stadtwald 6-7, Postfach 150, D-3508 Melsungen Tel: (05661) 6001
Man Dirs: Hans Kiefer, Hans-Martin Horn; *Editorial:* Margit Sbresny; *Sales, Production, Publicity, Rights & Permissions:* Dr Claus Wagner
Subjects: Medicine, Nursing
1981: 8 titles *Founded:* 1976
ISBN Publisher's Prefix: 3-921958

Biederstein Verlag*, Wilhelmstr 9, D-8000 Munich 40 Tel: (089) 381891 Telex: 05-215085 beck d
Man Dir: Wolfgang Beck; *Sales:* Günter Elze; *Rights & Permissions:* Eva von Freeden
Associate Companies: Verlag C H Beck (qv); Franz Vahlen (qv)
Subjects: General Fiction, Poetry, Biography, History, Natural Science
Founded: 1945
ISBN Publisher's Prefix: 3-7642

Birkhäuser Verlag, Olgastr 53, D-7000 Stuttgart 1
Parent Company: Birkhäuser Verlag AG, Switzerland (qv)

Georg **Bitter** Verlag+, Herner Str 62, Postfach 100265, D-4350 Recklinghausen Tel: (02361) 25888/21400
Man & Sales Dir: Dr Georg Bitter; *Editorial:* Hans-Sigismund von Buch; *Publicity, Advertising:* Walter Stolzenberg; *Rights & Permissions:* Dr Georg Bitter, Marion R Liebchen
Subjects: Literature for Juveniles, Young Adults
Founded: 1968
ISBN Publisher's Prefix: 3-7903

Blanvalet Verlag*, Neumarkterstr 18, Postfach 800360, D-8000 Munich 80 Tel: (089) 41730 Cable Add: Bertelsmann München Telex: 523259
Parent Company: Verlagsgruppe Bertelsmann GmbH (qv for associate companies)
Subjects: Belle Lettres, Juveniles, Biographies
Founded: 1935
ISBN Publisher's Prefix: 3-7645

Blaukreuz-Verlag Wuppertal*, Freiligrathstr 27, Postfach 201610 D-5600 Wuppertal 2 Tel: (0202) 621098
Publisher: Hans-Jürgen Weidtke
Parent Company: Blaues Kreuz in Deutschland eV, Wuppertal
Subjects: Alcoholism, Christian Books and Texts
1981: 20 titles
Miscellaneous: Firm is a contributor to the Telos (qv) series of evangelical paperbacks. See also Blaukreuz-Verlag Berne, Switzerland
ISBN Publisher's Prefix: 3-920106

Bleicher Verlag*, Holderäcker Str 14, Postfach 100123, D-7016 Gerlingen Tel: (07156) 21033 Cable Add: Bleicherverlag
Publisher, Editorial, Rights & Permissions: Heinz M Bleicher; *Sales, Publicity:* Thomas Bleicher; *Production:* Rainer Abel
Subjects: General Fiction, Picture Books, Poster Books, Comic Verse, Periodicals
Founded: 1968
ISBN Publisher's Prefixes: 3-921097, 3-88350

Deutsche **Blindenstudienanstalt** eV, see under Deutsche

Bock und Herchen Verlag, Reichenbergstr 11e, Postfach 1145, D-5340 Bad Honnef 1 Tel: (02224) 5443
Man Dirs: Karl Heinrich Bock, Hans-Alfred Herchen
Branch Off: Fichardstr 30, D-6000 Frankfurt am Main 1 Telex: 414838 huh d
Subjects: Scientific Papers, Librarianship
1982: 120 titles *Founded:* 1977
ISBN Publisher's Prefix: 3-88347

Böhlau-Verlag GmbH & Cie, Niehler Str 272-274, Postfach 600180, D-5000 Cologne 60 Tel: (0221) 765368 Cable Add: Böhlau, Cologne 60
Man Dir: Dr Günter J Henz
Head Off: Verlag Hermann Böhlau Nachf GmbH, Austria (qv)
Subjects: History, Music, Art, Philosophy, Modern Philology, Theology, General & Social Science
Founded: 1951

Boje-Verlag, Holzstrasse 19, Postfach 1278, D-7000 Stuttgart 1 Tel: (0711) 247305/07 Cable Add: Bojeverlag
Proprietor: Hanns-Jörg Fischer; *Editorial:* Dr Doris Stephan; *Sales:* Michael Fischer; *Production:* Hildegard Fischer-Schwartz; *Publicity:* Ursula Pfaffinger
Subject: Juveniles
1982: 28 titles *Founded:* 1947
ISBN Publisher's Prefix: 3-414

Harald **Boldt** Verlag GmbH, Postfach 110, D-5407 Boppard am Rhein Tel: (06742) 2511
Man Dir, Publicity: Harald Boldt; *Sales Dir:* Heidrun Tschentke; *Production:* Peter Boldt; *Rights & Permissions:* Edith Boldt
Associate Company: Boldt Druck Boppard GmbH
Subjects: Social, Political and Military History of Germany
Founded: 1951
ISBN Publisher's Prefix: 3-7646

Bollmann-Bildkarten-Verlag GmbH & Co KG, Lilienthalplatz 1, Postfach 1526, D-3300 Braunschweig Tel: (0531) 332069 Telex: 952546
Dir: Friedrich Bollmann
Subject: Maps

Dr **Bolte** KG, see Polyglott-Verlag

Verlag Aurel **Bongers** KG, Dortmunder Str 67, Postfach 100264, D-4350 Recklinghausen Tel: (02361) 41001 Cable Add: Bongers Recklinghausen
Proprietor, Publishing Dir, Rights & Permissions: Aurel Bongers Sr, Aurel Bongers Jr; *Sales Dir:* Renate Drygalla
Subjects: Art (Modern and Classical Painting and Sculpture, Eastern Church Art), Archaeology
1981: 6 titles *1982:* 6 titles *Founded:* 1931
ISBN Publisher's Prefix: 3-7647

Bonn Aktuell GmbH, Pforzheimer Str 377, Postfach 310807, D-7000 Stuttgart 31 Tel: (0711) 881149
Publisher: Horst Poller
Subjects: Politics, Current Affairs
ISBN Publisher's Prefix: 3-87959

Gebrüder **Borntraeger** Verlagsbuchhandlung, Johannesstr 3A, D-7000 Stuttgart 1 Tel: (0711) 623541/3
Man Dirs: Dr Erhard Naegele (Production), Klaus Obermiller (Sales)
Associate Company: E Schweizerbart'sche Verlagsbuchhandlung (qv)
Subjects: Geology, Geomorphology, Geography, Geophysics, Meteorology, Metallography, Botany, Biology, Oceanography, General Science
Founded: 1790
ISBN Publisher's Prefix: 3-443

C **Bösendahl**, Klosterstr 32-33, Postfach 1240, D-3260 Rinteln 1 Tel: (05751) 4551
Also: Obernstr 28, D-3060 Stadthagen Tel: (05721) 75700
Man Dir: C W Niemeyer
Subjects: Light Fiction, Local Interest
1982: approx 12 titles *Founded:* 1621
ISBN Publisher's Prefix: 3-87085

Gustav **Bosse** Verlag GmbH & Co KG, Vonder-Tann-Str 38, D-8400 Regensburg 1 Tel: (0941) 55455 Cable Add: Bosse Regensburg
Imprint: bmp (bosse musik paperback)
Subjects: New Religious Songs, Musicology, Musical Pedagogy, Periodicals, Music Paperbacks
1981: 20 titles *1982:* 20 titles

Oscar **Brandstetter** Verlag GmbH & Co KG, Stiftstr 30, Postfach 1708, D-6200 Wiesbaden Tel: (06121) 521002/3 Telex: 4186486 obra d
Man Dir: Martin Arndt; *Editorial:* Dr Antonin Kucera; *Rights & Permissions:* Doris Fürbeth
Subjects: Language & Technical Dictionaries
Founded: 1862
ISBN Publisher's Prefix: 3-87097

Brasilienkunde Verlag GmbH, see BKV

Bratt Institut für Neues Lernen GmbH+, Hervorsterstr 267, D-4180 Goch 5 Tel: (02823) 29094 Cable Add: Bratt Institut
Man Dir: Bertil Bratt; *Editorial, Rights & Permissions, Sales, Production, Publicity:* Joachim C Duderstadt
Orders to: Hervorsterstr 267, D-4180 Goch 5
Parent Company: Studentlitteratur AB, Sweden (qv)
Associate Company: Chartwell-Bratt Ltd, UK (qv)
Subjects: Psychology, Textbooks, Science, Computer Studies
Founded: 1979
ISBN Publisher's Prefix: 3-88598

Verlag G **Braun** GmbH*, Karl-Friedrich-Str 14-18, Postfach 1709, D-7500 Karlsruhe Tel: (0721) 1651 Cable Add: Braunverlag Telex: 07826904
Man Dir: Dr Eberhard Knittel; *Dirs:* Karl Breh, Rolf Feez
Subjects: General Science, Medicine, Secondary Textbooks, Music, Paperbacks, Periodicals
ISBN Publisher's Prefix: 3-7650

Verlag **Braun und Schneider***, Maximiliansplatz 9, D-8000 Munich 2 Tel: (089) 555580
Dirs: Dr Julius Schneider, Friedrich Schneider
Subjects: Juveniles, Paperbacks, Illustrated Books
Founded: 1843
ISBN Publisher's Prefix: 3-87099

Verlag die **Braunkohle**, see Droste Verlag

Umschau Verlag **Breidenstein** GmbH, see Umschau

Breitkopf und Härtel, Walkmühl-Str 52, Postfach 1707, D-6200 Wiesbaden 1 Tel: (06121) 402031 Cable Add: Breitkopfs Wiesbaden
Man Dirs: Lieselotte Sievers, Gottfried Möckel
Subjects: Music, Books, Education
Founded: 1719
ISBN Publisher's Prefix: 3-7651

Julius **Breitschopf** KG*, Verlagsbuchhandlung, Schleissheimerstr 37B, D-8000 Munich 45 Tel: (089) 3514747
Associate Company: Verlagsbuchhandlung Julius Breitschopf, Austria (qv)
Subjects: Juveniles, Television Tie-in Books
ISBN Publishers' Prefix: 3-87254

Breklumer Verlag*, Bundesstr 5/Kirchenstr, Postfach Bredstedt 1220, D-2257 Breklum Tel: (04671) 2028 Cable Add: Breklumer Verlag Breklum
Publisher: Manfred Siegel
Subject: Religion
ISBN Publisher's Prefix: 3-7793

Brendow-Verlag, Gutenbergstr 1, Postfach 1280, D-4130 Moers 1 Tel: (02841) 41036 Telex: 8121162
Dir: Hans Steinacker
Subjects: Evangelical Religious Literature; firm is a member of the Telos (qv) group of evangelical paperback publishers

Brigg Verlag GmbH (formerly Verlag die Brigg), Hermanstr 33, Postfach 101304, D-8900 Augsburg 1 Tel: (0821) 30008
Man Dir: Franz-Josef Büchler
Subjects: Fiction, Illustrated and Bibliophile Books, Travel, Children's Regional Books, Belles Lettres, Poetry, Music, Art, Juvenile, University Textbooks, Sport and Physical Fitness
Founded: 1950
ISBN Publisher's Prefix: 3-87101

F A **Brockhaus**+, Leberberg 25, Postfach 1709, D-6200 Wiesbaden 1 Tel: (06121) 5380 Cable Add: Brockhausverlag Telex: 04186699
Dirs: Ulrich Porak, Hubertus Brockhaus-Weyers; *Sales:* Theresia Möller; *Publicity:* Adelheid Schmitz-Valckenberg
Orders to: (Federal Republic of Germany) above address; (Berlin) Helga Hartwich, Lützowstr 105-106, D-1000 Berlin; (Austria) Zentralgesellschaft, Singerstr 12, A-1010 Vienna 1; (Switzerland) Schweizer Buchzentrum, POB, CH-4601 Olten
Subjects: Encyclopaedias, Language and other Dictionaries, Biography, History, General Science, Travel, Music, Schopenhauer, Nature, Animals, Fiction
1981: 10 titles *1982:* 10 titles *Founded:* 1805
ISBN Publisher's Prefix: 3-7653

R **Brockhaus** Verlag, Postfach 110152, D-5600 Wuppertal (Located at: Champagne 7, D-5657 Haan 2) Tel: (02104) 6311
Publisher: Dr Ulrich Brockhaus; *Editorial:* Elisabeth Wetter, Günter Balders; *Sales:* Karl-Heinz Eisner, Raimond Schmidt
Associate Company: Theologischer Verlag Rolf Brockhaus
Subjects: Popular Christian Literature, Biographies, Fiction, Juveniles, Song Books, Bibles and Bible Study
Bookshop: Evangelische Buchhandlung Brockhaus, Karlstr 50, D-5600 Wuppertal-Elberfeld
Founded: 1853
ISBN Publisher's Prefix: 3-417

Brönner Verlag Breidenstein GmbH, Stuttgarter Str 18-24, D-6000 Frankfurt am Main 1 Tel: (0611) 26001 Cable Add: Busda Frankfurtmain Telex: 0411964
Dirs: Klaus Breidenstein, Hans-Jürgen Breidenstein, Klaus-Jürgen Schlotte; *Editorial:* Eberhard Urban; *Sales Manager:* Hans-J Lesch
Associate Company: Umschau Verlag Breidenstein GmbH (qv for other Associate Companies)
Subject: Art
ISBN Publisher's Prefix: 3-599

Broschek Druck GmbH & Co KG*, Bargkoppelweg 61, D-2000 Hamburg 73
Publisher: Dr A Schneckenburger-Broschek
Subjects: Juveniles, Art History, Illustrated books
Founded: 1913
ISBN Publisher's Prefix: 3-87102

Broschek Verlag*, Bargkoppelweg 61, D-2000 Hamburg 73 Tel: (040) 67961 Cable Add: Christians Druck
Orders to: Hans Christians Druckerei & Verlag (qv)
Associate Company: Hans Christians Druckerei & Verlag (qv)
Subjects: Hamburg regional literature

Brücken-Verlag GmbH Literaturvertrieb Import-Export*, Ackerstr 3, Postfach 1928, D-4000 Düsseldorf 1 Tel: (0211) 350473-78 Cable Add: Brücken-Verlag Telex: 8588674 brve
Dir: Hans Walter von Oppenkowski; *Sales Managers:* Alfons Clemens, Gerd Fiegweil
Subjects: Textbooks, Literary Criticism, Reprints, Periodicals
Miscellaneous: This firm is the central marketing agency for the Arbeitsgemeinschaft sozialistischer und demokratischer Verleger und Buchhändler (qv for other members of organization)
ISBN Publisher's Prefix: 3-87106

Verlag F **Bruckmann** KG, Nymphenburger Str 86, Postfach 27, D-8000 Munich 20 Tel: (089) 125701 Cable Add: Bruckmannkoge Munich Telex: 523739
Editor: Erhardt D Stiebner; *Publishing Manager:* Dr J Stiebner; *Editorial Manager:* Dr K Beth; *Sales:* P Rossnagl; *Publicity:* Fritz Scheuer; *Production:* K Liese
Associate Company: Studio Bruckmann Kunst im Druck (qv)
Subjects: Art, Illustrated Books, Handbooks, Reference, History, Mountaineering, Bavaria
Founded: 1858
Miscellaneous: Firm is member of TR-Verlagsunion GmbH (qv)
ISBN Publisher's Prefix: 3-7654

Studio **Bruckmann Kunst** im Druck Fine Art GmbH, Nymphenburger Str 84, Postfach 27, D-8000 Munich 20 Tel: (089) 125701 Cable Add: Bruckmannkoge Telex: 523739
Editor: E D Stiebner; *Sales:* P Rossnagl; *Publicity:* Fritz Scheuer; *Production:* K Liese
Associate Company: Verlag F Bruckmann KG (qv)
Subjects: Art, Special Editions
Founded: 1972
ISBN Publisher's Prefix: 3-7854

Brunnen-Verlag GmbH, Gottlieb-Daimlerstr 22, Postfach 5205, D-6300 Giessen Tel: (0641) 12088
Man Dir: Wilfried Jerke; *Editorial:* Helmut Jablonski; *Rights & Permissions:* Rudolf Horn; *Sales Manager:* Andreas Walter
Branch Off: Brunnen-Verlag, Switzerland (qv)
Subjects: Religion, Juveniles
1981: 35 titles *1982:* 37 titles *Founded:* 1919
ISBN Publisher's Prefix: 3-7655

Brunner Verlagsgellschaft*, Hauptstr 4, D-8500 Nuremberg Tel: (0911) 831614
Man Dir: Monika Popp
Subjects: Children's Books
Founded: 1976
ISBN Publisher's Prefix: 3-88194

Brunnquell-Verlag der Bibel-und Missions-Stiftung Metzingen, Karlstr 4, Postfach 1155, D-7430 Metzingen Tel: (07123) 2280
Man Dir: Thomas Weber
Subject: Religion
Founded: 1945
ISBN Publisher's Prefix: 3-7656

Buch und Werbung — Helmut Krüger GmbH, see Krüger

Verlag C J **Bucher** GmbH, Ortlerstr 8, D-8000 Munich 70 Tel: (089) 769920 Telex: 522720 rin d

Publishing Dir, Editorial, Rights & Permissions: Axel Schenck; *Sales, Publicity:* Eduard Gogel; *Production:* Johannes Eikel
Subjects: Natural History, Animals, Cities and Countries, Art, Cultural History, Photography, Reference, Film Book series, General Non-fiction
1983: 31 titles *Founded:* 1870
ISBN Publisher's Prefix: 3-7658

Buchholz Verlag für Spiele und Freizeit*, Bütehorn KG, Am Boksberg 2, D-3203 SArstedt Tel: (05066) 5675 Telex: 0927142 kadis d
Production Manager: Mrs Buch
Subjects: Juveniles, How-to, Educational

Verlag für **Buchmarkt- und Medien-Forschung**, Carl-Bertelsmann-Str 270, Postfach 5555, D-4830 Gütersloh Tel: (05241) 802580 Telex: 933868/933646
Dir: Manfred Harnischfeger
Parent Company: Verlagsgruppe Bertelsmann GmbH (qv for associate companies)
Subjects: Book Trade, Bibliographies, Periodicals
Founded: 1962

Verlag **Büchse** der Pandora GmbH*, Postfach 2820, D-6330 Wetzlar (Located at: Alte Chaussee 4, D-6334 Asslar-Werdorf) Tel: (6443) 3361 Cable Add: 6334 Asslar-Werdorf
Man Dir: Peter Grosshaus, Stefan Blankertz
Subjects: 20th century Literature, Pedagogy, Philosophy, Art, Architecture, Anarchy
Bookshop (Associated): Buchladen Galerie/Werkstatt, Obertorstr 22-24, D-6330 Wetzler
Founded: 1977
ISBN Publisher's Prefix: 3-88178

Bund-Verlag GmbH, Hansestr 63a, Postfach 900840, D-5000 Cologne 90 Tel: (02203) 30030 Telex: 08873362
Man Dir: Tomas Kosta; *Sales:* Karl-Heinz Antoni; *Production:* Heinz Biermann; *Publicity:* Waldemar Block; *Rights & Permissions:* Gunther Heyder, Inge Stalker
Subjects: Trade Union Policy, Industrial Law, Social Law and Studies, Legal Texts and Commentaries, Economics, Politics, Taxation and Finance, WSI Studies (Industrial Series), Periodicals connected with Social Services and Workers' Rights, Fiction, Poetry, Juvenile
Bookshops: Bund-Verlag GmbH Buchhandlung (at above address); Bund-Verlag Buchhandlung, Wilhelm-Leuschner Str 64, D-6000 Frankfurt am Main; Bund-Verlag GmbH Buchhandlung, Schwanthalerstr 64, D-8000 Munich 2
1981: 70 titles *1982:* 55 titles *Founded:* 1947
ISBN Publisher's Prefix: 3-7663

Bundes-Verlag eG+, Bodenborn 43, Postfach 1240, D-5810 Witten Tel: (02302) 3457
Man Dir, Rights & Permissions: Erich Brenner; *Editorial, Production, Publicity:* Wilfrid Haubeck; *Sales:* Arno Buchholz
Orders to: R Brockhaus Verlag, Postfach 110152, D-5600 Wuppertal 11
Subjects: Current Christian topics, Aids to Everyday Living, Scriptural
Bookshop: Bundes-Verlag Buchhandlung, at Company address
1981: 13 titles *1982:* 13 titles *Founded:* 1887
ISBN Publisher's Prefix: 3-8137

Burckhardthaus-Laetare Verlag GmbH+, Herzbachweg 2, Postfach 1440, D-6460 Gelnhausen Tel: (06051) 891 Cable Add: Burckhardthaus
Dirs: Heinz van Rissenbeck, Hermann Schulz
Orders to: Postfach 1140, D-6460 Gelnhausen
Subjects: Humanities, Arts, Textbooks, Multimedia, Music, Education, Pedagogy, Psychology, Religion, Social Science, Games
Bookshops: Burckhardthaus-Buchhandlung, Langgasse 2, D-6460 Gelnhausen; Burckhardthaus-Buchhandlung, Teltower Damm 9, D-1000 Berlin 37; Burckhardthaus-Buchhandlung Hackhauser Hof, D-5650 Solingen 11
1981: 60 titles *1982:* 48 titles
ISBN Publisher's Prefix: 3-7664

Verlag Aenne **Burda**, Am Kestendamm 2, Postfach 1160, D-7600 Offenburg Tel: (0781) 8402 Cable Add: burdamoden offenburg Telex: 752804
Subjects: Hobbies, Cookery, Handicrafts, Periodicals
ISBN Publisher's Prefix: 3-920158

Kartographischer Verlag **Busche** GmbH, Kaiserstr 129, Postfach 114, D-4600 Dortmund 1 Tel: (0231) 597088/89 Telex: 0822270
Man Dir: Günter Schiffmann; *Editorial:* Alfred Heinemann; *Publicity & Advertising Dir:* Herr Klaffka; *Rights & Permissions:* Herr Schiffmann
Subjects: Street Maps, Atlases
Founded: 1972
ISBN Publisher's Prefixes: 3-921143, 3-88584

Helmut **Buske** Verlag, Schlüterstr 14, Postfach 132255, D-2000 Hamburg 13 Tel: (040) 452522
Man Dir: Helmut Buske
Subjects: Linguistics, Phonetics, Slav, Romance, Germanic and Oriental Studies, Philosophy, History, Minor Languages
Bookshop: At above address (academic and antiquarian)
1982: 40 titles *Founded:* 1959
ISBN Publisher's Prefix: 3-87118

Busse Kunstdokumentation GmbH*, Parkstr 23, Postfach 1803, D-6200 Wiesbaden Tel: (0611) 553292/557022
Managing Partner: Joachim Busse
Subject: Art Reference Books
Founded: 1976

Bussesche Verlagshandlung GmbH, Brüderstr 30, Postfach 1344, D-4900 Herford Tel: (05221) 775 Cable Add: Westverlag Herford Telex: 934717
Publishing Dir: Dr H C Lindner; *Commercial Manager, Rights & Permissions:* Heinz Zimmermann
Associate Companies: Westdeutsche Verlagsanstalt GmbH, Postfach 1344, D-4900 Herford; Buchdruckerei und Verlag Busse, Postfach 1344, D-4900 Herford
Subjects: Leisure, Sport, Travel, Boating, Games and Hobbies, Orientalia
Founded: 1947
ISBN Publisher's Prefix: 3-87120

Verlag **Butzon und Bercker** GmbH, Postfach 215, D-4178 Kevelaer 1 (Located at: Hoogeweg 71, Kevelaer 1) Tel: (02832) 2908 (Administration); (02832) 2909 (Publishing, Editorial, etc); (02832) 2906 (Sales, Despatch) Telex: 812207 bbkev Cable Add: Butzonbercker
Dirs: Edmund Bercker, Dr Edmund Bercker Jr, Klaus Bercker; *Editorial:* Josef Heckens; *Sales:* Heiner Janssen; *Production:* Otto Paustian; *Publicity:* Elisabeth Hübbecker; *Rights & Permissions:* Anne Moore
Subjects: Catholic Religion and Theology, Prayer and Meditation, Liturgy, Religious Teaching Books for Children
1981: 40 titles *Founded:* 1870
ISBN Publisher's Prefix: 3-7666

C V K und Schroedel GmbH & Co Geographische Verlagsgesellschaft KG, Mecklenburgische Str 53, Postfach 330109, D-1000 Berlin 33 Tel: (030) 829960
Man Dirs: Otto Berger, Anton Kemper, Manfred Lösing
Parent Companies: Cornelsen-Velhagen und Klasing GmbH & Co Verlag für Lehrmedien KG (qv), Schroedel Schulbuchverlag GmbH (qv)
Subjects: Secondary & Primary Textbooks on Geography, Atlases
1981: 8 titles *1982:* 4 titles *Founded:* 1963
ISBN Publisher's Prefix: 3-7680

Caann Verlag GmbH, von-Kleist-Weg 11, D-8037 Olching Tel: (08142) 14154
Man Dir: Klaus Wagner
Subjects: Christian Interest, Fiction, Non-fiction
Founded: 1969
ISBN Publisher's Prefix: 3-87121

Verlag Georg D W **Callwey**+, Streitfeldstr 35, Postfach 800409, D-8000 Munich 80 Tel: (089) 433096 Cable Add: Callweyverlag Telex: 5216752 cal v
Man Dir: Helmuth Baur-Callwey; *Editorial:* Roland Thomas, Dr Paulhans Peters; *Sales:* Traute Geier; *Production:* Christian Pfeiffer-Belli; *Publicity:* Ludger Marquardt
Subjects: Biography, History, Architecture, History of Art, Handicrafts, Landscape Architecture, Painting and Restoration, Stonemasonry, Periodicals
1982: 26 titles *1983:* 25 titles *Founded:* 1884
ISBN Publisher's Prefix: 3-7667

Calwer Verlag, Scharnhauser Str 44, D-7000 Stuttgart 70 Tel: (0711) 452019
Dir: Christof Munz; *Sales, Publicity, Rights & Permissions:* Sibylle Fritz
Subjects: Reference, Encyclopaedias, Dictionaries, Education, Audiovisual/Visual Media, Religion, Periodicals
Founded: 1836
ISBN Publisher's Prefix: 3-7668

Campus Verlag GmbH, Myliusstr 15, D-6000 Frankfurt am Main Tel: (0611) 725955
Man Dir, Rights & Permissions: Frank Schwoerer; *Editors:* Klaus Gabbert, Adalbert Hepp; *Advertising Dir:* Jochen Woerner; *Production:* Klaus Schoeffner
Subjects: Social Sciences, Psychology, Pedagogics, Economics, Politics, History, University Textbooks
1981: 157 titles *1982:* 180 titles *Founded:* 1975
ISBN Publisher's Prefix: 3-593

Editio **Cantor***, Verlag für Medizin und Naturwissenschaften KG, Zollenreuterstr 11, Postfach 1310, D-7960 Aulendorf Tel: (07525) 431/432/433 Cable Add: Cantor Aulendorfwürtt Telex: 0732225 vebu d
Subjects: Medicine, Pharmacy, Periodicals
Founded: 1947
ISBN Publisher's Prefix: 3-87193

Verlag Hans **Carl** GmbH & Co KG, Postfach 9110, D-8500 Nuremberg 11 (Located at: Breite Gasse 58-60, Nuremberg 1) Tel: (0911) 203831 Cable Add: Carlverlag Telex: 0623081
Man Dir, Editorial: Günter Schmiedel; *Sales, Production:* Raimund Schmitt; *Advertising Dir:* Rudolf Weidinger; *Publicity Dir:* Günter Schmiedel
Subjects: General Fiction, Belles Lettres, Poetry, History (especially of Nuremberg), Art, Philosophy, General Science, Biochemistry, University Textbooks, Literature for Brewers
1981: 10 titles *Founded:* 1861
Bookshop: Fachbuchhandlung Hans Carl (at above address)
ISBN Publisher's Prefix: 3-418

Carlsen Verlag GmbH, Postfach 1169, D-2057 Reinbek bei Hamburg (Located at: Dieselstr 6, D-2057 Reinbek bei Hamburg)

Tel: (040) 7224051   Telex: 217879 carl d
President: Per Hjald Carlsen; *Joint Man Dirs:* Carl-Johan Bonnier, Herbert Voss; *Rights & Permissions:* Per Hjald Carlsen, Carl-Johan Bonnier
Parent Company: SEMIC Förlags AB, Sweden (qv)
Subjects: Juveniles, Comics
Founded: 1953
ISBN Publisher's Prefix: 3-551

Ceres-Verlag Rudolf-August Oetker KG, Oldentruper Str 131, Postfach Bielefeld 85, D-4800 Bielefeld 1   Tel: (0521) 2993126
Cable Add: Ceres   Telex: 0932324
Man Dirs: Ernst A Kobusch, Peter Ruhl; *Editorial:* Gisela Knutzen; *Sales:* Konstantin Knust
Parent Company: August Oetker, Bielefeld
Subjects: Cookery, Wines, Bakery
1983: 70 titles   *Founded:* 1951
ISBN Publisher's Prefix: 3-7670

Verlag **Chemie** GmbH, Pappelallee 3, Postfach 1260/1280, D-6940 Weinheim/Bergstr   Tel: (06201) 6020   Cable Add: Chemieverlag Weinheimbergstr   Telex: 465516vchwh d
Man Dirs: Prof Dr Helmut Gruenewald, Hans Dirk Köhler; *Editorial:* Dr Hans Friedrich Ebel, Dr Gerd Giesler, Sylvia Osteen; *Production:* Maximilian Montkowski; *Sales, Publicity & Advertising:* Helmut Schmitzer; *Rights & Permissions:* Kornelia Herbig
Subsidiary Companies: Physik-Verlag GmbH (qv); W und P Buchversand für Wissenschaft und Praxis, Boschstr 12, Postfach 1808, D-6940 Weinheim; Verlag Chemie International Inc, Plaza Centre, Suite E, 1020 NW 6th St, Deerfield Beach, Florida 33441, USA; VC Verlag Chemie AG, Basle, Switzerland (qv)
Subjects: Life Sciences, Physical Sciences with emphasis on Chemistry & Chemical Engineering, University Textbooks, Periodicals
1982: 80 titles   *Founded:* 1921
ISBN Publisher's Prefix: 3-527

China Studien- und Verlagsgesellschaft mbH, Hungener Str 6-12, D-6000 Frankfurt am Main 60   Tel: (0611) 590461   Telex: 4189805 csv d
Man Dir, Sales, Publicity, Rights & Permissions: Ursula Menzel-Fischer
Subject: People's Republic of China: Language Courses, Dictionaries, Western Translations of Fiction, Art, Archaeology, Travel Guides, Cookery, History, Politics, Medicine
1981: 20 titles   *Founded:* 1979
ISBN Publisher's Prefixes: 3-922373, 3-88728

Christian-Verlag GmbH, Akademiestr 7, D-8000 Munich 40   Tel: (089) 398095
Joint Man Dirs: Michael von Oertzen, Christian Strasser
Subjects: Reference: Cultural History, Nature, Photography, Fine Arts, Music, Sports, Cooking, Illustrated Non-fiction
Founded: 1949
ISBN Publisher's Prefix: 3-88472

Hans **Christians** Druckerei und Verlag*, Kleine Theaterstr 9-10, Postfach 301021, D-2000 Hamburg 36   Tel: (040) 341456
Cable Add: Christians Druck
General Manager: Jens Christians
Associate Company: Broschek Verlag (qv)
Imprint: Glogau Verlag
Subjects: Art, Social History of Hamburg area, North German Topography and Dialect ('Op Platt'), Judaica, Folklore
Founded: 1740
ISBN Publisher's Prefix: 3-7672

Christliche Verlagsanstalt GmbH, Zasiusstr 8, Postfach 1186, D-7750 Konstanz
Tel: (07531) 23054/5
Man Dir, Manager, Rights & Permissions: Herbert Denecke
Subsidiary Companies: Friedrich Bahn Verlag (qv), Sonnenweg-Verlag, (qv)
Subjects: Novels, Biography, Religion, Juveniles, Low- & High-priced Paperbacks, Educational Materials
Bookshop: Buchhandlung der Christlichen Verlagsanstalt (at above address)
1981: 22 titles   *Founded:* 1892
ISBN Publisher's Prefix: 3-7673

Christliche Verlagsgesellschaft mbH, Moltekestr 1, Postfach 168, D-6340 Dillenburg 1   Tel: (02771) 34021/34022
Cable Add: Christlicher Verlag Dillenburg
Man Dirs; Dieter Boddenberg, Günther Kausemann; *Editorial, Publicity, Production:* Dieter Boddenberg; *Sales:* Dieter Braas; *Rights & Permissions:* Günther Kausemann
Subsidiary Company: Christliche Bücherstuben (at above address)
Associate Company: Emmaus-Fernbibelschule Deutschland (at above address)
Subjects: Working Texts for Scriptural Instruction, Evangelical Non-fiction
Bookshops: At above address, and Marburger Tor 32, D-5900 Siegen 1; Alte Linner Str 124, D-4150 Krefeld 1; Lindauerstr 8, D-8940 Memmingen; Harschbacherstr 12, D-5419 Ramubach; Bahnhofstr 10, D-5372 Schleiden-Gemünd; Poststr 24, D-4780 Lippstadt; Am Königshof 43, D-4020 Mettmann; Neustadtstr 12, D-5980 Werdohl
1981: 5 titles   *1982:* 7 titles   *Founded:* 1957
ISBN Publisher's Prefix: 3-921292

Christliches Verlagshaus GmbH, Senefelderstr 109, D-7000 Stuttgart 1
Tel: (0711) 221301
Man Dir: Heinz Schäfer
Subjects: Religion (Juvenile & Young Adult); Paperbacks, Periodicals
Founded: 1872
ISBN Publisher's Prefix: 3-7675

Christophorus-Verlag GmbH, Hermann-Herder-Str 4, D-7800 Freiburg im Breisgau
Tel: (0761) 27171   Telex: 07721440
Man Dir: Benno Baldes
Parent Company: Verlag Herder KG (qv)
Subjects: Christian Religious for all ages, Leisure Crafts, Sheet Music
1981: 95 titles   *1982:* 89 titles   *Founded:* 1935
ISBN Publisher's Prefix: 3-419

Verlag Ernst **Chur***, Dedersberg 3, Postfach 2114, D-5372 Schleiden   Tel: (02445) 7112
Cable Add: Dedersberg 3 D 5372 Schleiden
Man Dirs: Ernst & Gisela Chur
Subjects: Juveniles, Art, Periodicals
Founded: 1969
ISBN Publisher's Prefix: 3-87995

Cicero International Art GmbH*, Tierbergstr 6, D-7000 Stuttgart 30
Tel: (0711) 850829   Telex: 7252147 ciro d
Man Dir, Editorial, Sales, Rights & Permissions: F K Rothenbacher; *Production, Publicity:* Rolf Marxen, Waltraud Broghammer
Subject: Art
Founded: 1970
ISBN Publisher's Prefix: 3-921165

Claassen-Verlag GmbH, Grupellostr 28, Postfach 9229, D-4000 Düsseldorf 1
Tel: (0211) 360516   Cable Add: Claassen-Verlag   Telex: 8587327
Publisher: Ivo Frenzel; *Sales Manager:* Herbert Borgartz; *Publicity Manager:* Michael Tochtermann
Subjects: General Fiction, Literary Criticism, Linguistics, Languages, Biography
Miscellaneous: Firm is member of Econ Verlagsgruppe (qv)
ISBN Publisher's Prefix: 3-546

Claudius Verlag GmbH, Birkerstr 22, D-8000 Munich 19   Tel: (089) 184031
Telex: 523718 epdm d
Dirs: Paul Rieger; *Publicity:* Karl-Eberhard Beck
Parent Company: Evangelischer Pressverband für Bayern eV (qv)
Associate Company: Verlag J Pfeiffer GmbH & Co (qv)
Subjects: Religion, Paperbacks, University Textbooks, Educational Materials
Founded: 1954
ISBN Publisher's Prefix: 3-532

Colloquium Verlag Otto H Hess+, Unter den Eichen 93, D-1000 Berlin 45   Tel: (030) 8328085
Proprietors: Anja Hess, Otto H Hess; *Man Dir:* Otto H Hess; *Sales Dir:* Manfred Köppen; *Public Relations, Rights & Permissions:* Stefan Hess
Subsidiary Company: Zeitgeschichtlicher Buchversand GmbH, Unter den Eichen 93, D-1000 Berlin 45, (Mail-order Store)
Orders to: Koch, Neff, Oetinger & Co, Abt Verlagsauslieferung, Am Wallgraben 110, D-7000 Stuttgart-Vaihingen
Subjects: Current Affairs, Latin-American Studies, History, Pedagogy, Biography, School TV, Research and General Knowledge, Politics
1981: 29 titles   *1982:* 31 titles   *Founded:* 1948
ISBN Publisher's Prefix: 3-7678

Columbus Verlag Paul Oestergaard GmbH*, Columbus Haus, Postfach 1180, D-7056 Weinstadt-Beutelsbach   Tel: (07151) 68011
Cable Add: Columbus-verlag
Telex: 0724382
Publishers: Peter Oestergaard, Rudi Heubach; *Sales:* Gerhard Reuschle
Subjects: Cartography, Reference
Founded: 1909
ISBN Publisher's Prefix: 3-87129

Concert Verlag G Kowalski, see Kowalski

Verlag F **Coppenrath**, Martinstr 2, Postfach 3820, D-4400 Münster   Tel: (0251) 42225
Cable Add: Martinstr 2   Telex: 891566 hoeco d
Man Dir: Wolfgang Hölker; *Sales:* Manfred Goldschmidt; *Production:* Joerg Rinow; *Publicity:* Gertrud Posch
Subsidiary Company: Verlag Wolfgang Hölker (qv)
Subjects: Arts and Design, General Non-fiction, Juvenile
1983: 60 titles   *Founded:* 1768
ISBN Publisher's Prefix: 3-88547

Copress-Verlag, Schellingstr 39-43, Postfach 401280, D-8000 Munich 40   Tel: (089) 282423   Cable Add: Copress München
Telex: 524368
Man Dir: Klaus Britting
Subject: Sport
ISBN Publisher's Prefix: 3-7679

Cornelsen und Oxford University Press GmbH, Mecklenburgische Str 53, D-1000 Berlin 33   Tel: (030) 82996   Telex: 184968 cvk b
Man Dirs: Peter Collier, Goetz Manth
Orders to: Cornelsen-Velhagen und Klasing VG, Kammerratsheide 66, D-4800 Bielefeld 1
Parent Companies: Cornelsen-Velhagen und Klasing Verlag für Lehrmedien KG (qv); Oxford University Press, UK (qv)
Associate Companies: Cornelsen-Velhagen und Klasing VG (qv)
Subjects: Secondary & Primary Textbooks in English Language Teaching

1982: 52 titles and 13 textbook series
Founded: 1971
ISBN Publisher's Prefix: 3-8109

**Cornelsen-Velhagen und Klasing GmbH &
Co Verlag für Lehrmedien KG,**
Mecklenburgische Str 53, D-1000 Berlin 33
Tel: (030) 82996 Cable Add:
Cevaukamedien Telex: 184968
Man Dirs: Franz Cornelsen, Hans-H
Kannegiesser, Manfred Lösing, Goetz
Manth
Associate Company: Cornelsen-Velhagen
und Klasing VG (qv)
Subsidiary Companies: Cornelsen und
Oxford University Press GmbH (qv); CVK
und Schroedel GmbH & Co Geographische
Verlagsgesellschaft KG (qv); CVK und
Schroedel GmbH, Geographisch-
Kartographische Anstalt, Düppelstr 21,
D-4800 Bielefeld
Subjects: Textbooks, Audiovisual aids for all
student levels and adults
Founded: 1968
Miscellaneous: Part of vgs —
Verlagsgesellschaft Schulfernsehen mbH &
Co KG (qv)
ISBN Publisher's Prefix: 3-464

**Cornelsen-Velhagen und Klasing
Verlagsgesellschaft** mbH & Co KG,
Kammerratsheide 66, Postfach 8729, D-4800
Bielefeld 1 Tel: (0521) 70071 Cable Add:
Cevauka Bielefeld Telex: 932909 cvkbi d
Associate Companies: Cornelsen und Oxford
University Press GmbH (qv); Cornelsen-
Velhagen und Klasing GmbH & Co Verlag
fur Lehrmedien KG (qv)
Subjects: Mainly Teaching Aids in Natural
Sciences, Languages, History, Geography,
Social Studies, Sex Education

Corona Verlag KG, see Dipa-Verlag und
Druck

Corvus Verlag*, Kurfürstendamm 157,
Postfach 311120, D-1000 Berlin Tel: (030)
8854041 Telex: 0184212
Subjects: Popular Non-fiction, Lexicons,
Handbook to divining-rod practice, Special
commissions in Book Production

Verlag J G **Cotta'sche Buchhandlung,** now
incorporated in Ernst Klett Verlag (qv)

J **Cramer,** in den Springäckern 2, D-3300
Brunswick Tel: (0531) 65951
Associate Company: Strauss und Cramer
GmbH, D-6945 Hirschberg (Printers)
Subject: Botany (Specialized Technical,
Reprints, Texts in English, Latin, French),
Natural History
1983: 150 titles *Founded:* 1811
ISBN Publisher's Prefix: 3-7682

D E B Verlag (das europäische Buch
Literaturvertrieb GmbH), Thielallee 34,
D-1000 Berlin 33 Tel: (030) 8324051
Orders to: VVA (Vereinigte
Verlagsauslieferung GmbH), Postfach 7777,
D-4830 Gütersloh 1
Dir: Tell Schwandt
Subjects: History, Philosophy, Politics,
Economics, Marxism, Literature on
Germanistics
ISBN Publisher's Prefixes: 3-920303, 3-88436

D J I, see Deutsches Jugendinstitut

D R W-Verlag Weinbrenner-KG*, Postfach
104, D-7000 Stuttgart 1 (Located at:
Fasanenweg 18, D-7022 Leinfelden-
Echterdingen 1) Tel: (0711) 79891 Telex:
7255609 drw
Subsidiary Company: Verlagsanstalt
Alexander Koch GmbH (qv)
Subjects: Forestry, Timber, Woodworking,
Periodicals
ISBN Publisher's Prefix: 3-87181

D T V, see Deutscher Taschenbuch Verlag

D V A, see Deutsche Verlags-Anstalt GmbH

Damnitz Verlag GmbH*, Hohenzollernstr
144, D-8000 Munich 40 Tel: (089)
301015/301016
Man Dir: Otto Schmidl; *Sales Dir:* Rita
Grünauer; *Publicity Dir:* Liesl Neumann;
Advertising Dir, Rights & Permissions: Otto
Schmidl
Subjects: General Fiction, Belles Lettres,
Poetry, Biography, How-to, Music, Art,
Low-priced Paperbacks, Social Science
Founded: 1965
Miscellaneous: Member of
Arbeitsgemeinschaft sozialistischer und
demokratischer Verleger und Buchhändler
(qv for other members)

Verlag **Darmstädter Blätter** Schwarz und
Co, Haubachweg 5, D-6100 Darmstadt
Tel: (06151) 48196
Man Dir: Dr Günther Schwarz
Subjects: Semantics, Languages,
Dictionaries, Philosophy, Reference,
Psychology, Social Science, University,
Secondary & Primary Textbooks, Judaica
1981: 41 titles *Founded:* 1967
ISBN Publisher's Prefix: 3-87139

Verlag **Das Beste,** see Beste

Werner **Dausien,** Postfach 1355, D-6450
Hanau am Main (Located at: Frankfurter
Landstr 32, Hanau) Tel:
(06181)259052/82353 Telex: 4184879
Man Dir: Werner Dausien; *Editorial:* Eva
Lobin
Orders to: Burgallee 67, D-6450 Hanau am
Main Tel: (06181) 259052
Subsidiary Company: Verlag Müller und
Kiepenheuer (qv)
Subjects: How-to, Music, Art, Reference,
Juveniles, University Textbooks
Founded: 1949
Bookshop: Werner Dausien, Salzstr 18,
D-6450 Hanau am Main
ISBN Publisher's Prefix: 3-7684

R v **Decker's** Verlag G Schenck GmbH, im
Weiher 10, Postfach 102640, D-6900
Heidelberg Tel: (06221) 489250
Telex: 0461727 huehd
Dir: Dr Hans Windsheimer
Associate Companies: Kriminalistik Verlag
(qv); C F Müller Juristischer Verlag
GmbH (qv)
Subjects: Law, Economy, Administration,
Post and Telecommunications, Defence,
Automation, Data Processing, Periodicals

Delius, Klasing und Co, Siekerwall 21,
Postfach 4809, D-4800 Bielefeld 1,
Tel: (0521) 5590 Cable Add: Buchklasing
Telex: 0932934
Dirs: Konrad-Wilhelm Delius, Kurt Delius;
Production: Leo Siebzehnrübl; *Publicity:*
Wilhelm Meyerhenke; *Rights & Permissions:*
Ilsemarie Steinbrinker
Subsidiary Company: Klasing und Co
GmbH (qv)
Subjects: Yachting, Motor Boats, Seafaring
and Navigation, Model Boat Building,
Motor Cars, Surfing
Founded: 1911
ISBN Publisher's Prefix: 3-7688

Delphin Verlag GmbH, Reichenbachstr 3,
D-8000 Munich 5 Tel: (089) 557641/4
Cable Add: Delphinverlag Telex: 522522
Man Dir: Martin Greil
Parent Company: BPCC PLC, UK (qv)
Subsidiary Company: Delphin Verlag AG,
Switzerland (qv)
Founded: 1963
ISBN Publisher's Prefix: 3-7735

Delp'sche Verlagsbuchhandlung, St
Blasienstr 5, D-8000 Munich 13 Tel: (089)
358498 Telex: 61524
Man Dir: Heinrich Delp

Orders to: Delp, Kegetstr 11, D-8532 Bad
Windesheim
Subjects: Poetry, Art
1982: 12 titles *Founded:* 1961
ISBN Publisher's Prefix: 3-7689

Desire und Gegenrealismus*, Verlag für
Gegenrealismus, Lilienthalstr 8a, D-8460
Schwandorf 1 Tel: (09431) 60564/41561
Man Dir, Rights & Permissions: Günther
Dienelt; *Editorial:* Günther Dienelt,
Christian Hellmann; *Sales:* Günther Dienelt,
Christian Hellmann, Andreas Möckler;
Production: Günther Dienelt, Christian
Hellmann, Christian Kastner; *Publicity:*
Günther Dienelt, Christian Hellmann
Branch Off: Solaris-Edition, c/o Christian
Hellmann, Nünningweg 131, D-4400
Münster-Gievenbeck
Subjects: Surrealism, Anti-Surrealism,
Dadaism, Expressionism, Science-Fiction,
Fantasy Fiction, Stylistic Prose, Essays,
Poetry, Strip Cartoons, Graphics
Bookshop: Versandbuchhandlung edition
Balzac, c/o Karlheinz König, Glätzlstr 4a,
D-8460 Schwandorf 1
1981: 40 titles *Founded:* 1977
ISBN Publisher's Prefix: 3-88397

Engelbert **Dessart** Verlag KG, see Siebert
und Engelbert Dessart Verlag GmbH

Dr Peter **Deubner** Verlag GmbH, Fürst-
Pückler-Str 30, Postfach 410268, D-5000
Cologne 41 Tel: (0221) 403028
Publisher: Dr Peter Deubner; *Dir:* Manfred
Hufnagel
Associate Companies: Deubner und Lange
Verlag GmbH, Deubner und Wagner
GmbH, Gieseking Wirtschaftsverlag GmbH
(qv) (all at above address), Verlag Ernst und
Werner Gieseking, Bielefeld (qv)
Subject: Jurisprudence (especially Fiscal
Law)
Founded: 1974

Verlag für **Deutsch,** Schillerstr 5, D-8000
Munich 2 Tel: (089) 557825 Telex: 5213212
vfdf d
Man Dir: Dr Roland Schäpers; *Editorial:*
Renate Luscher; *Production:* Dieter
Rauschmayer
Associate Company: Verlag für
Fremdsprachen (at above address)
Subjects: Textbooks, Education
1983: 70 titles *Founded:* 1979
ISBN Publisher's Prefix: 3-88532

Verlag Harri **Deutsch**+, Gräfstr 47, D-6000
Frankfurt am Main 90 Tel: (0611) 775021
Telex: 4189561 deut d
Publisher: Harri Deutsch; *Man Dir:* Dr
Anton Reiter
Subsidiary Company: Verlag Harri Deutsch,
Switzerland (qv)
Subjects: Natural Sciences, Technical,
Textbooks, Reference, Mathematics,
Economics, Foreign Languages, Agriculture,
Paperbacks
Bookshop: Naturwissenschaftliche
Fachbuchhandlung Harri Deutsch (at above
address)
Founded: 1960
ISBN Publisher's Prefix: 3-87144

Deutsche Bibelgesellschaft, Balinger Str 31,
D-7000 Stuttgart 80 Tel: (0711) 720030
Cable Add: Bibelhaus Stuttgart Telex:
7255299 Bibl d
The German Bible Society
Dirs: Dr Gernot Winter, Rev Dr Siegfried
Meurer
Subjects: Bibles and New Testaments
(readings, scholarly editions)
Founded: 1812 (as Deutsche Bibelstiftung,
1981 as above)
ISBN Publisher's Prefix: 3-4380

132 FEDERAL REPUBLIC OF GERMANY

Deutsche Blindenstudienanstalt eV, Postfach 1160, D-3550 Marburg an der Lahn (Located at: Am Schlag 8, Marburg) Tel: (06421) 67053 Telex: 4821106
German Institute for the Blind
Man Dir: Jürgen Hertlein; *Deputy Dir and Publishing Manager:* Rainer F V Witte
Subjects: Braille Production, Library Services for the Blind

Deutsche Buch-Gemeinschaft C A Koch's Verlag Nachfolger*, Berliner Allee 6, Postfach 4131, D-6100 Darmstadt Tel: (06151) 8661 Cable Add: Lesestunde
Man Dir: Ernst Leonhard; *Rights & Permissions:* Gerald Trageiser
Subjects: General Fiction, Belles Lettres, Poetry, Biography, History, How-to, Music, Art, Philosophy, Reference, Juveniles
Book Clubs: Deutsche Buch-Gemeinschaft C A Koch's Nachfolger (Federal Republic of Germany and Austria)
Founded: 1924

Deutsche Jugend-Presse-Agentur KG, see Dipa-Verlag und Druck

Deutsche Philips GmbH, see Philips GmbH

Deutsche Verlags-Anstalt GmbH (DVA)+, Neckarstr 121, Postfach 209, D-7000 Stuttgart, 1 Tel: (0711) 26310 Cable Add: deva Stuttgart Telex: 0722503
Publisher: Ulrich Frank-Planitz; *Editorial Dir:* Dr Reinhard Lebe; *Editorial (Fiction), Publicity:* Renate Federhen-Roske; *Sales:* Isolde Kuhn; *Marketing:* Carol Bührle; *Subsidiary Rights:* Ingrid Zacke; *Foreign Rights:* Petra Bachstein
Subsidiary Company: Manesse Verlag, Switzerland (qv)
Subjects: Belles Lettres, Poetry, Biography, Politics, History, Philosophy, Psychology, General Science, Architecture, Music
Bookshop: Buchversand Herbert Krebs GmbH (at above address)
1981: 65 titles *Founded:* 1831
ISBN Publisher's Prefix: 3-421

Deutscher Adressbuch-Verlag für Wirtschaft und Verkehr GmbH, Holzhofallee 38, Postfach 110320, D-6100 Darmstadt Tel: (06151) 33661 Cable Add: Teladress Darmstadt Telex: 4 19548 dav d
The German Directory Publishing Company for Industry and Commerce
Man Dirs: Günter M Hulwa, Max Bach; *Editorial:* Claus Wonneberger; *Production:* Gerhard Poness; *Publicity:* Rudolf Diehl
Subjects: Business Reference Works
1981-2: 5 titles (revised annually) *Founded:* 1923
ISBN Publisher's Prefix: 3-87148

Deutscher Apotheker Verlag Dr Roland Schmiedel GmbH und Co, Birkenwaldstr 44, Postfach 40, D-7000 Stuttgart 1 Tel: (0711) 25820 Telex: 723636 dazd
Man Dirs: Hans Rotta, Dr W Wessinger; *Managers:* R Hack, K Hübler, B Schreck
Associate Companies: S Hirzel Verlag GmbH & Co (qv); Franz Steiner Verlag GmbH (qv); Wissenschaftliche Verlagsgesellschaft mbH (qv)
Subjects: Pharmacy, Periodicals
Bookshop: Deutscher Apotheker Verlag, Sortiments-Abteilung (at above address)
Founded: 1861
ISBN Publisher's Prefix: 3-7692

Deutscher Betriebswirte-Verlag GmbH, Bleichstr 20-22, Postfach 1332, D-7562 Gernsbach 1 Tel: (07224) 3091 Cable Add: dbv Gernsbach Telex: 78915 dbv-d
Man Dirs: Dr Casimir Katz, Christel Katz
Subjects: Business Administration, Management, Marketing, Company Organization, Accounting, Personnel, Forestry and Timber Industries
1981: 10 titles *Founded:* 1926
ISBN Publisher's Prefixes: 3-921099, 3-88640

Deutscher Eichverlag, Hopfengarten 21, Postfach 2903, D-3300 Brunswick Tel: (0531) 796030
Parent Company: Friedr Vieweg und Sohn GmbH (qv)

Deutscher Fachschriften-Verlag Braun GmbH & Co KG, Felsenstr 23, Postfach 2120, D-6200 Wiesbaden-Dotzheim 1 Tel: (06121) 42785
Publisher: Dr Herbert Braun; *Publicity Manager, Rights & Permissions:* Friedrich Vohl
Subjects: Public Health, Law, Official Reports
ISBN Publisher's Prefix: 3-8078

Deutscher Gemeindeverlag GmbH*, Luxemburger Str 72, Postfach 100448, D-5000 Cologne 1 Tel: (0221) 426761 Telex: dgv köln 08882662
The German Municipality Publishing Company
Parent Company: Verlag W Kohlhammer GmbH (qv)
Branch Offs (each responsible for own region): Hessbrühlstr 69, Postfach 800430, D-7000 Stuttgart 80; Alexanderstr 3, Postfach 1465, D-3000 Hanover Tel: (0511) 328721 Jägersberg 17, Postfach 1865, D-2300 Kiel 1 Tel: (0431) 554857; Philipp-Reis-Str 3, Postfach 421049, D-6500 Mainz 42 Tel: (06131) 59031/32; Theresienstr 124/1, Postfach 200625, D-8000 Munich 2 Tel: (089) 521359; Postfach 2125, D-6200 Wiesbaden 1 Tel: (06131) 59031/32
Subjects: Local Government – legislation, environmental protection, social services etc (texts and associated computer tape and microfilm services), Periodicals
ISBN Publisher's Prefix: 3-555

Deutscher Instituts-Verlag GmbH, Gustav-Heinemann Ufer 84-88, Postfach 510670, D-5000 Cologne 51 Tel: (0221) 37041 Cable Add: Deutstitut Telex: 8882768
Man Dir, Rights & Permissions: Horst Schlechter; *Sales:* Norbert Anselm; *Production:* Wilhelm Fischer; *Publicity:* Dr Monika Diesing-Fiebig
Parent Company: Institut der Deutschen Wirtschaft, Cologne (German Economics Institute)
Subsidiary Companies: Librex – Buchvertrieb der Deutschen Wirtschaft GmbH; Edition Agrippa GmbH
Subjects: Economic, Company and Educational Policy; Literature
Founded: 1951
ISBN Publisher's Prefix: 3-602

Deutscher Kunstverlag GmbH, Vohburger Str 1, D-8000 Munich 21 Tel: (089) 564722
Man Dirs: Dr Michael Meier, Helmut Kaufmann
Orders to: Koch, Neff, Oetinger & Co, Postfach 800620, Schockenriedstr 39, D-7000 Stuttgart 80
Subjects: Art, History, Pictorial Guidebooks, Regional Art Books, Guides to Artistic Monuments, Egypotology, Catalogues, Yearbooks, Periodicals
1981: 20 titles *1982:* 18 titles *Founded:* 1921
ISBN Publisher's Prefix: 3-422

Deutscher Literatur-Verlag, Mühlenstr 16-22, Postfach 701009, D-2000 Hamburg 70 Tel: 682476 Telex: 213126
Man Dirs: Gerhard Melchert, Otto Melchert
Associate Companies: Martin Kelter Verlag GmbH & Co, Mero-Druck GmbH & Co KG
Subjects: Light literature, Humour
1982: 40 titles *1983:* 40 titles *Founded:* 1905
ISBN Publisher's Prefix: 3-87152

D T V-Deutscher Taschenbuch Verlag GmbH & Co KG, Postfach 400422, D-8000 Munich 40 (Located at: Friedrichstr 1a, D-8000 Munich 40) Tel: (089) 340911 Telex: 05215396
Man Dir: Heinz Friedrich; *Assistant Man Dir:* Dr Wolfram Goebel; *Editorial:* Ulrike Bürgel-Goodwin, Maria Friedrich, Dr Lutz-Werner Wolff, Winfried Groth, Dr Walter Kumpmann, Maria Schedl-Jokl; *Sales Dir:* Wolfgang Josephi, Ole Schultheis; *Advertising:* Klaus Bäulke; *Rights & Permissions:* Lore Cortis
Subjects: General Fiction, Belles Lettres, Poetry, Biography, History, Music, Art, Philosophy, Reference, Religion, Juveniles, Medicine, Psychology, General and Social Science, Secondary & Primary Textbooks, Classical Literature, Travel Guides, Maps, Two-language editions (all in paperback format)
1982: 275 titles *Founded:* 1961
Miscellaneous: Part-owned by Carl Hanser Verlag (qv)
ISBN Publisher's Prefix: 3-423

Deutscher Verlag für Kunstwissenschaft GmbH, Lindenstr 76, D-1000 Berlin 61 Tel: (030) 25913864 Cable Add: Kunstbrief Berlin Telex: 183723
Man Dirs: Professors Dr Heinz Peters, Dr Peter Bloch, Dr Henning Bock
Associate Company: Gebr Mann Verlag (qv)
Subject: Art in Germany, Periodicals
Founded: 1964
ISBN Publisher's Prefix: 3-87157

Deutscher Wirtschaftsdienst John von Freyend GmbH, Fachverlag für Wirtschaft und Aussenhandel, Marienburger Str 22, D-5000 Cologne 51 Tel: (0221) 388011/388012 Telex: Cryo 8883406 Cable Add: DWD
Sales, Rights & Permissions Dir: Peter John von Freyend; *Editorial, Production:* Edelgard Reiche; *Publicity:* Karl Ludwig Ostermann
Subjects: Loose-leaf systems covering current international economic questions; Chamber of Commerce publications; Finance, Commercial Law
1981-82: 8 titles
ISBN Publisher's Prefix: 3-87156

Deutsches Jugendinstitut (DJI), Saarstr 7, Postfach 400425, D-8000 Munich 40 Tel: 381831
Man Dir: Dr Lothar Böhnisch; *Editorial, Publicity, Rights & Permissions:* Hans-Hermann Schwarzer; *Sales:* Christel Schwietering; *Production:* Hans-Hermann Schwarzer, Christel Schwietering
Subjects: Sociology, Social pedagogy
1981: 31 titles *Founded:* 1975
ISBN Publisher's Prefix: 3-87966

Dianus-Trikont Buchverlag GmbH+, Agnes Str 10, D-8000 Munich 40 Tel: (089) 2714400
Publisher, Rights & Permissions: Herbert Röttgen; *Editorial:* Christiane Thurn
Subjects: General Fiction, History, Public Health, Medicine, Politics, Non-fiction, Social Science, Economics, Biography
ISBN Publisher's Prefixes: 3-920385, 3-88167

Eugen **Diederichs** Verlag GmbH & Co KG, Bremer Str 5, Postfach 100526, D-5000 Cologne 1 Tel: (0221) 137011
Man Dir: Ulf Diederichs; *Editorial:* Dr Claudia Henn-Schmölders, Arnd Kösling; *Sales Dir:* Horst Biedermann; *Production:* Antje Ketteler, Roland Poferl; *Advertising & Publicity Dirs:* Anne Gripp, Eberhart May; *Rights & Permissions:* Christa Hinze
Orders to: Koch, Neff und Oetinger & Co, Schockenriedstr 39, D-7000 Stuttgart 80; (West Berlin) B A Claudius, Schillerstr 13,

D-1000 Berlin 12
Subjects: Belles Lettres, Biography, History, Philosophy, Eastern Religion and Literature, Sociology, Illustrated collections of Folk and Fairy Tales from all countries
Founded: 1896
ISBN Publisher's Prefix: 3-424

Verlag Moritz **Diesterweg**/Otto Salle Verlag, Hochstr 29-31, Postfach 110651, D-6000 Frankfurt am Main 1 Tel: (0611) 13011 Telex: 413234 md d
Orders to: Koch, Neff und Oetinger & Co, Postfach 800620, D-7000 Stuttgart 80
Man Dir: Dietrich Herbst; *Rights & Permissions:* Waltraud Soehnel
Subjects: Educational; Psychology, Social Science, University, Secondary & Primary Textbooks, Educational Materials
Founded: 1860
ISBN Publisher's Prefixes: 3-425 (Diesterweg), 3-7935 (Salle)

Verlag J H W **Dietz** Nachf GmbH, Godesberger Allee 143, Postfach 200189, D-5300 Bonn 2 Tel: (0228) 378021-378025
Orders to: Verlagsauslieferung Georg Lingenbrink, Postfach 3584, D-6000 Frankfurt am Main 1; (for Berlin) Zirk und Ellenrieder, Lützowstr 105 (bbz), D-1000 Berlin 30
Associate Company: Verlag Neue Gesellschaft GmbH (qv)
Subjects: History, Politics, Sociology, Economics, Legal, Reprints
ISBN Publisher's Prefix: 3-8012

Dipa-Verlag und Druck GmbH & Co, Deutsche Jugend-Presse-Agentur KG, Weberstr 69-71, D-6000 Frankfurt am Main 1 Tel: (0611) 556188
Man Dir: K-W Hesse (Am Röckerkopf 26, D-6238 Hofheim-Lorsbach Tel: (06192) 8210)
Subsidiary Company: Corona Verlag KG
Subjects: Biography, History, How-to, Psychology, Social Science, University Textbooks and Studies, Third World Problems
Founded: 1948
ISBN Publisher's Prefix: 3-7638

Verlag **Dokumentation** Saur KG, subsidiary of K G Saur Verlag KG (qv)

Domini sumus Verlag GmbH*, Postfach 100553, Rosenbergstr 16, D-4630 Bochum 1 Tel: (0234) 85511
Man Dir, Publicity, Rights & Permissions: Dieter Kohl; *Editorial:* Ulrike Kohl; *Sales:* Birgit Schwermer; *Production:* Friedel Steinmann
Subjects: Leisure Activities, Biblical Picture Strips
Bookshop: ds-versandbuchhandlung (at above address)
1981: 3 titles *Founded:* 1977
ISBN Publisher's Prefix: 3-88310

Don Bosco Verlag der Gesellschaft der Salesianer, Sieboldstr 11, D-8000 Munich 80 Tel: (089) 4138349
Dir: August Brecheisen; *Man Dir:* Johann Ernstberger; *Editorial:* Reinhold Storkenmaier; *Sales:* Johann Windmayer
Associate Company: Editorial Don Bosco SA, Mexico (qv)
Subjects: Education, How-to, Religion, Textbooks
Bookshop: Sieboldstr 11, D-8000 Munich 80
Founded: 1948
ISBN Publisher's Prefix: 3-7698

Dreisam-Verlag+, Schwaighofstr 6, D-7800 Freiburg im Breisgau Tel: (0761) 77037
Subjects: Campaign literature to combat nuclear plants, military drafting; Civil Rights and student advice on dealing with authorities; Ecology, Socio-political, Literary Works (Prose and Poetry)
1981: 13 titles *1982:* 15 titles *Founded:* 1975
ISBN Publisher's Prefix: 3-921472

Galerie **Dreiseitel**, Richmodstr 25, D-5000 Cologne 1 Tel: (0221) 244165
Man Dir: H Dreiseitel
Subjects: Art, Illustrated Books (with original illustrations)
1981: 3 titles *1982:* 5 titles *Founded:* 1971

Cecilie **Dressler** Verlag, Poppenbütteler Chaussee 55, Postfach 230, D-2000 Hamburg 65 Tel: (040) 6070484 Telex: 02174230
Man Dirs: Thomas Huggle, Uwe Weitendorf; *Editorial:* Angelika Kutsch; *Sales:* Thomas Huggle; *Publicity:* Anke Lüdtke; *Rights & Permissions:* Uwe Weitendorf
Associate Company: Verlag Friedrich Oetinger (qv)
Subjects: Fiction, Juveniles, Paperbacks
Founded: 1928

Droemersche Verlagsanstalt Th Knaur Nachf, Rauchstr 9-11, Postfach 800480, D-8000 Munich 80 Tel: (089) 92710 Cable Add: Droemerverlag Telex: 522707
Man Dirs: Dr Karl Blessing, Rüdiger Hildebrandt; *Editorial:* Dr Rolf Cyriax, Franz Mehling, Dr Herbert Neumaier; *Sales Manager:* Richard Schmeisser; *Production:* Werner Grabinger; *Publicity Manager:* Ulrike Netenjakob; *Foreign Rights:* Britta Lucas, Alice Meyer
Parent Company: Verlagsgruppe Georg V, Holtzbrinck GmbH, Gänsheidestr 26, Stuttgart
Branch Offs: Verlag Schoeller & Co, Via Borgo 10, Palazzo Centro, CH-6612 Ascona, Switzerland; Droemersche Verlagsanstalt AG, Switzerland (qv)
Subjects: General Fiction, Non-fiction, Dictionaries, Reference, Art, Architecture, Current Events, Popular Science, How-to, Self-Help, Juvenile, Maps, Paperbacks
1981: 200 titles *Founded:* 1901
Miscellaneous: Also known as Droemer Knaur Verlag
ISBN Publisher's Prefix: 3-426

Droste Verlag GmbH*, Pressehaus am Martin-Luther-Platz, Postfach 1122, D-4000 Düsseldorf 1 Tel: 8851 Cable Add: Drosteverlag Düsseldorf
Man Dir: Dr Joseph Schaffrath; *Publishing Dir:* Dr Manfred Lotsch; *Editorial:* Heidemarie Alertz; *Sales:* Klaus Ehrke; *Production, Publicity:* Helmut Schwanen
Subsidiary Companies: Verlag Die Braunkohle (at above address); Wilhelm Knapp Verlag (qv)
Subjects: History, Current Affairs, Politics, Economics, Social Sciences, Art, Belles Lettres, Humour and Satire, Picture Books, Düsseldorf local interest books
Bookshop: Buchhandlung Droste (at above address)
Founded: 1711
ISBN Publisher's Prefix: 3-7700

Druckenmüller Verlag, Martiusstr 8, Postfach 440254, D-8000 Munich 44 Tel: (089) 348074 Telex: 5215517
Associate Companies: Artemis und Winkler Verlag, Munich (qv); Verlag für Architektur, Munich (qv); Artemis Verlags AG, Verlag für Architektur (both in Switzerland, qqv)
Subjects: Encyclopaedia of Classical Antiquity, Classical Works, European Ancient History

Druffel-Verlag*, Assenbucherstr 28, D-8137 Leoni am Starnbergersee Tel: (08151) 5326
Dir: Dr Gert Sudholt; *Publisher:* Ursula Sündermann;
Subjects: Popular German History (especially relative to World War II), German Politics, Controversial Reportage
ISBN Publisher's Prefix: 3-8061

Monika **Dülk** Verlag, Kirchhainer Damm 11, Postfach 490132, D-1000 Berlin 49 Tel: (030) 7444040
Subjects: City maps, Travel Guides

Horst-Werner **Dumjahn** Verlag+, Immenhof 12, Postfach 1746, D-6500 Mainz 1 Tel: 06131/35600
Man Dir and Other Offices: Horst-Werner Dumjahn
Orders to: VVA (Vereinigte Verlagsauslieferung GmbH), Postfach 7777, D-4830 Gütersloh 1
Subjects: Railways and Railway History (Federal German and other countries)
Bookshop: Versandbuchhandlung und Antiquariat Horst-Werner Dumjahn (at above address), Antiquarian Bookshop and Despatch Office
1982: 25 titles *Founded:* 1974
ISBN Publisher's Prefixes: 3-921426, 3-88992

Wolfgang **Dummer** und Co, see Verlag Moderne Industrie

Ferd **Dümmlers** Verlag, Kaiserstr 31-37, Postfach 1480, D-5300 Bonn 1 Tel: (0228) 223031 Cable Add: Dümmlerbuch
Man Dir: Helmut Lehmann
Subjects: Textbooks and Pedagogic books in Natural Sciences, Arts, Linguistics for Schools of all levels; Sports, Hobbies, History, Politics, Periodicals
1982: 58 titles *Founded:* 1808
Miscellaneous: Part of vgs — Verlagsgesellschaft Schulfernsehen mbH & Co KG (qv)
ISBN Publisher's Prefix: 3-427

DuMont Buchverlag GmbH & Co KG, Mittelstr 12-14, Postfach 100468, D-5000 Cologne 1 Tel: (0221) 20531 Telex: 8882 975 dbe b d
Publisher: Ernst Brücher
Subjects: Archaeology, Art History, Art, Art Calendars, Travel, Games, Illustrated Books, Pocket Books
Founded: 1956
ISBN Publisher's Prefix: 3-7701

Duncker und Humblot, Dietrich-Schäfer-Weg 9, Postfach 410329, D-1000 Berlin 41 Tel: (030) 7912026
Subjects: History, Philosophy, General & Social Science, Law, University Textbooks
1981: 222 titles *1982:* 213 titles *Founded:* 1798
ISBN Publisher's Prefix: 3-428

Dustri-Verlag Dr Karl Feistle, Bahnhofstrasse 9, Postfach 49, D-8024 Deisenhofen-Munich Tel: (089) 6135041
Dirs: Dr Karl Feistle, Hans-Peter Eckardt
Subjects: Medicine, Reference, Paperbacks, Periodicals

E O S Verlag, Erzabtei Sankt Ottilien, D-8917 Sankt Ottilien Tel: 08193/71261
Man Dir: Dr P Bernhard Sirch
Subjects: Religious, especially Roman Catholic connected with the Benedictine Order, Biblical and Doctrinal Studies
Bookshop: Klosterladen (at above address)
1982: approx 30 titles *1983:* approx 20 titles
Founded: 1904
ISBN Publisher's Prefixes: 3-88096, 3-920289

Ebeling Verlag GmbH*, Langgasse 35, Postfach 2368, D-6200 Wiesbaden 1 Tel: (06121) 39081 Telex: 4186318
Subject: Art

Echter Würzburg Fränkische Gesellschafts-Druckerei, see Würzburg

Econ-Verlag GmbH, Grupellostr 28, Postfach 9229, D-4000 Düsseldorf 1 Tel: (0211) 360516 Cable Add: Econ-Verlag

134 FEDERAL REPUBLIC OF GERMANY

Telex: 8587327
Publisher: Ivo Frenzel; *Sales & Marketing:* Herbert Borgartz; *Advertising & Promotion:* Michael Tochtermann
Subjects: Biography, History, Politics, Music, Art, Travel, Reference, Religion, Archaeology, Medicine, Psychology, General & Social Science, Audio-visual Teaching Aids, General Fiction
Miscellaneous: Firm is member of Econ Verlagsgruppe (qv)
ISBN Publisher's Prefix: 3-430

Econ Verlagsgruppe, Grupellostr 28, Postfach 9229, D-4000 Düsseldorf 1 Tel: (0211) 360516 Telex: 8587327
Publishing group comprising Claassen Verlag GmbH, Econ Verlag GmbH, Marion von Schroeder Verlag GmbH (qqv). The group forms part of the newspaper publishing concern Rheinisch-Westfälische Verlagsgesellschaft mbH, Pressehaus NRZ, Sachsenstr 30, D-4300 Essen

Ehrenwirth Verlag GmbH, Postfach 860348, D-8000 Munich 86 (Located at: Vilshofenerstr 8) Tel: (089) 989025 Telex: 0529667
Publisher: Martin Ehrenwirth; *Man Dir, Rights & Permissions:* Frank Auerbach; *Sales, Publicity & Advertising Dir:* Gebhard von Doering; *Editorial:* Perdita Pasche, Inge Jauss, Reinhard Stachwitz
Distribution: Verlegerdienst München, Postfach 1280, D-8031 Gilching
Subjects: General Fiction, Poetry, History, Biography, How-to, Natural Healing, Beekeeping, Fishing, Reference, High-priced Paperbacks, Psychology, Social Science, University, Secondary and Primary Textbooks, Educational Materials, Periodicals
Founded: 1945
Miscellaneous: Firm is member of TR-Verlagsunion GmbH (qv)
ISBN Publisher's Prefix: 3-431

Eichborn Verlag+, Sachsenhäuser Landwehrweg 293, D-6000 Frankfurt am Main 70 Tel: (0611) 681079/681070
Man Dir, Editorial, Rights & Permissions: Vito von Eichborn; *Sales:* Peter Lugert; *Publicity:* Bodo Horn; *Production:* Uwe Gruhle
Associate Company: Fuldaer Verlagsanstalt, Rangstr 3-7, D-6400 Fulda
Subjects: Literature, Photography, Politics, Cartoons, Periodical
1981: 36 titles *1982:* 33 titles *Founded:* 1980
ISBN Publisher's Prefix: 3-8218

Eisenbahn-Kurier Verlag, Postfach 5560, D-7800 Freiburg-im-Breisgau Tel: (0761) 42058 Telex: 7721698 ekvd
Man Dir: Rudolf Wesemann; *Editorial:* Bernd von Mitzlaff; *Sales:* Karin Klemm; *Production:* Wolfgang Schumacher; *Publicity:* Peter Mihailescu; *Rights & Permissions:* Hansjürgen Wenzel
Subjects: Railways worldwide
1981: 28 titles *Founded:* 1966
ISBN Publisher's Prefix: 3-88255

Ellenberg Verlag GmbH, Postfach 100705, D-5000 Cologne 1 (Located at: Am Urbacher Wall 35, D-5000 Cologne 90) Tel: (02203) 22675 Telex: 887115 ell d
Man Dir: Dr Eduard Ellenberg; *Publicity:* Gisela Ellenberg
Subsidiary Company: Theaterverlag Ellenberg
Subjects: Belles Lettres, Anthologies, Documentaries, Politics, Theology, History, Philosophy, Economics, Art, Science, Poetry, Novels, Theatre, Literature, other areas of Scholarship; Periodicals
1981: 28 titles *Founded:* 1974
ISBN Publisher's Prefixes: 3-921369, 3-88577

Verlag Heinrich **Ellermann** GmbH & Co KG+, Romanstr 16, D-8000 Munich 19 Tel: (089) 133737 Cable Add: Ellerbuch, Munich
Man Dirs: Berthold and Christa Spangenberg; *Editorial, Sales, Production, Publicity, Rights & Permissions:* Christa Spangenberg
Orders to: Koch, Neff und Oetinger, Schockenriedstr 39, D-7000 Stuttgart 80 Tel: (0711) 78601
Imprints: Edition Spangenberg
Subjects: Belles Lettres, Juveniles
Founded: 1934
ISBN Publisher's Prefix: 3-7707

Elpis Verlag GmbH, Rohrbacherstr 20, D-6900 Heidelberg Tel: (06221) 15789
Man Dirs and other offices: Julian Köpke, Dr Manfred Thiel
Subjects: Philosophy, Encyclopaedias, Music, Poetry
1981: 1 title *1982:* 3 titles *Founded:* 1977

Elwert und Meurer GmbH*, Hauptstr 101, D-1000 Berlin 62 Tel: (030) 784001
Associate Company: Karl Ohm Verlag (qv)
Subjects: Psychology, Philosophy, Law, Sociology, Politics
ISBN Publisher's Prefix: 3-7669

N G **Elwert** Verlag, Postfach 1128, D-3550 Marburg an der Lahn (Offices at Reitgasse 7-9 and Pilgrimstein 30) Tel: (06421) 25024 Cable Add: Elwert Marburg
Man Dir: Dr W Braun-Elwert
Subjects: History, Religion, Law, German Language & Literary History, Social Science
Founded: 1726
ISBN Publisher's Prefix: 3-7708

Encyclopaedia Britannica, Berliner Allee 47, Postfach 200209, D-4000 Düsseldorf Tel: (0211) 324945
Manager: Rolf J Ellmers
Miscellaneous: Firm is an associate company of Encyclopaedia Britannica International Ltd, USA (see UK entry for other associates)

Friedemann von **Engel** Verlag*, Friedbergstr 5, D-1000 Berlin 19 Tel: (030) 3233145
Man Dir: F V Engel
Subsidiary Company: Globetrotter-Verlag (at above address)
Imprint: Tips für Trips
Subject: Travel Handbooks

Engelbert-Verlag GmbH, Widukindplatz 2, Postfach 360, D-5893 Balve/Sauerland Tel: (02375) 3089 Cable Add: Ever Balve Telex: 827755 gezi d
Publishers: Helmut Levermann, Heinz-Dirk Zimmermann; *Reader:* Alfons Schumacher; *Production:* Heinz Droste; *Sales Manager:* Helmut Levermann
Subjects: Juveniles, Popular Science, Information Books, General Fiction and Non-fiction
Founded: 1930
ISBN Publisher's Prefix: 3-536

Carl **Engels** Musikverlag, see P J Tonger

F **Englisch** Verlag GmbH+, Webergasse 12, Postfach 2309, D-6200 Wiesbaden Tel: (06121) 39478/9 Telex: 4186741
Man Dir: F-I Englisch
Orders to: VVA (Vereinigte Verlagsauslieferung GmbH), Postfach 7777, D-4830 Gütersloh 1
Subjects: General Non-fiction
1981: 25 titles *Founded:* 1973
ISBN Publisher's Prefix: 3-88140

Ferdinand **Enke** Verlag+, Postfach 1304, D-7000 Stuttgart 1 (Located at: Rüdigerstr 14, D-7000 Stuttgart 3U) Tel: (0711) 89310 Cable Add: Enkebuch Telex: 721942
Man Dirs: Dr Günther Hauff, Dr Jur Albrecht Greuner, Frau Dr M Kuhlmann; *Sales Dir, Rights & Permissions:* Joachim Niendorf; *Publicity:* Hans Kindt
Associate Company: Georg Thieme Verlag (qv)
Subjects: Medicine, Psychology, Social Science, Veterinary, Geology, Chemistry, University Textbooks, Scientific Journals
Founded: 1837
ISBN Publisher's Prefix: 3-432

Ensslin Jugendbuchverlag, see Ensslin und Laiblin

Ensslin und Laiblin Verlag GmbH & Co KG, Harretstr 6, Postfach 754, D-7412 Eningen Tel: (07121) 8471/2/3 Cable Add: Buchhaus Reutlingen Telex: 0729733
Man Dir: Joachim Ulrich Hebsaker; *Editorial:* Grit Hebsaker, Elke Schäle; *Sales:* Ariane Hebsaker-Schräpler; *Production:* Gerda Bailer; *Rights & Permissions:* Joachim Ulrich Hebsaker, Grit Hebsaker
Subjects: Children's Books, Non-fiction, Science Fiction, Education
1983: 25 titles *Founded:* 1818
ISBN Publisher's Prefix: 3-7709

Hans P **Eppinger***, Brenzstr 16, D-7170 Schwäbisch Hall Tel: (0791) 53061 Cable Add: Eppinger-Verlag Schwäbisch Hall
Man Dir: Hans Paul Eppinger
Subjects: Belles Lettres, Picture Books, History, Anthropology, Juveniles
Founded: 1970
ISBN Publisher's Prefix: 3-87176

Edition **Erdmann**, an imprint of K Thienemanns Verlag (qv)

Horst **Erdmann** Verlag für Internationalen Kulturaustausch*, Hartmayerstr 117, Postfach 1380, D-7400 Tübingen 1 Tel: (07071) 62061/2 Cable Add: Erdmannverlag Tübingen Telex: 7262741 erdm
Publicity & Sales Department: Milanweg 1, D-7400 Tübingen Tel: (07071) 64409
Man Dir: Horst J Erdmann; *Editorial and Production:* Dr Gernot Giertz; *Sales and Publicity:* Rosemarie Erdmann; *Rights & Permissions:* Margarete Graf
Orders to: VA Koch, Neff und Oetinger, Postfach 800620, D-7000 Stuttgart 80
Branch Off: Horst Erdmann Verlag & Co, Bachofenstr 10, CH-4000 Basle, Switzerland
Subjects: General Fiction, Belles Lettres, Poetry, Biography, History, How-to, Reference, Educational Materials
Founded: 1956
ISBN Publisher's Prefix: 3-7711

Eremiten-Presse und Verlag GmbH, Fortunastr 11, Postfach 170143, D-4000 Düsseldorf 1 Tel: (0211) 660590
Joint Man Dirs: Friedolin Reske, Jens D Olsson
Subjects: General Fiction, Belles Lettres, Poetry, Art, High- & Low-priced Paperbacks
Founded: 1949
ISBN Publisher's Prefix: 3-87365

Edition **Eres** Horst Schubert Musikverlag, Hauptstr 35, Postfach 1220, D-2804 Lilienthal-Bremen Tel: (04298) 1676
Man Dir: Horst Schubert
Subjects: Music, Art, High-priced Paperbacks, University, Secondary & Primary Textbooks, Educational Materials
Founded: 1946
ISBN Publisher's Prefix: 3-87204

Wilhelm **Ernst** und Sohn*, Hohenzollerndamm 170, D-1000 Berlin 31 Tel: (030) 860376/7/8 Telex: 0184143 Cable Add: Ernstsohn Berlin
Dir: Karlheinz Grassmann; *Editorial, Rights & Permissions:* Rudi Groll; *Sales:* Wilhelm Schreiber, H-J Winterstein; *Production:* Wilhelm Schreiber; *Publicity:* Bärbel

Schneider
Branch Off: Flüggenstr 13, D-8000 Munich 19
Subjects: Technical, Architecture
Bookshops: Gropius, Technische Fachbuchhandlung, Hohenzollerndamm 170, D-1000 Berlin 31; Flüggenstr 13, D-8000 Munich 19
Founded: 1851
ISBN Publisher's Prefix: 3-433

Erota-Press, see Odörfer-Verlags GmbH

Eulenhof-Verlag Ehrhardt Heinold, D-2351 Hardebek Post Brokstedt Tel: (04324) 502
Man Dir: Ehrhardt Heinold
Associate Company: Heinold Verlagsbüro (at above address)
Subject: Information Media on the Book Market
1981: 12 titles *1982:* 10 titles *Founded:* 1980
ISBN Publisher's Prefix: 3-88710

Euphorion Verlag Hans Imhoff*, Wilhelm-Busch-Str 41, D-6000 Frankfurt am Main 50 Tel: (0611) 523357 Cable Add: Euphorion Frankfurt
Man Dir: H Imhoff; *Sales Manager:* Klaus Nazarenus; *Publicity Dir:* Benja Bardé; *Rights & Permissions:* Ulrich Raschke
Subjects: Belles Lettres, Poetry, Philosophy
Book Club: Freundeskreis des Euphorion Verlages
Founded: 1963

Verlag **Europa-Lehrmittel**, Nourney, Vollmer GmbH & Co, Postfach 201815, D-5600 Wuppertal 2 (Located at: Kleiner Werth 50) Tel: (0202) 593970
General Manager: Joachim Nourney
Subjects: Textbooks for School and Professional use: in Metallurgy, Automobile, Electrical, Electronics, Physics, Building, Timber, Economics
Founded: 1947
ISBN Publisher's Prefix: 3-8085

Das **Europäische Buch**, see D E B Verlag

Europäische Gemeinschaften (European Communities), Zitelmannstr 22, D-5300 Bonn Tel: 238041 Telex: 886648
Subjects: Monographs, Documents, Periodicals on European integration, Official and Business Reports, Studies of Competition, Industry and Agriculture, European Instructional and Information Literature

Europäische Verlagsanstalt GmbH, Savignystr 61-63, Postfach 174003, D-6000 Frankfurt am Main 1 Tel: (0611) 742567
Man Dir: Axel Rütters; *Rights & Permissions:* Irmela Rütters
Subjects: History, Philosophy, Psychology, Social Science, Judaica, Political Science, Economics, Trade Unions
Founded: 1946
ISBN Publisher's Prefix: 3-434

Europrisma-Verlag*, Auf dem Gelling 7, D-5800 Hagen Tel: (02331) 46655
Dir: Stephan Ramrath

Verlag der **Evangelisch Lutherischen Mission***, Schenkstr 69, D-8520 Erlangen Tel: (09131) 33064
Publisher: Christoph Jahn; *Sales Manager:* Eva Mueller
Subjects: Juveniles, Religion, Social Science, Paperbacks
ISBN Publisher's Prefix: 3-87214

Verlag und Schriftenmission der **Evangelischen Gesellschaft** für Deutschland GmbH, Kaiserstr 78, D-5600 Wuppertal 11 Tel: (0202) 784018
Publishing House and Scriptural Mission of the German Evangelical Society
Man Dir: Ulrich Affeld; *Sales, Production, Publicity:* Herbert Becker

Subjects: Religious Literature; Telos and Junior Telos texts (see Miscellaneous)
1981: 6 titles *1982:* 6 titles *Founded:* 1954
Miscellaneous: Firm is a member of the Telos group (qv) publishing evangelical paperbacks
ISBN Publisher's Prefix: 3-87857

Evangelischer Missionsverlag*, Postfach 1380, D-7015 Korntal-Münchingen 1 Tel: (0711) 831083
Man Dir: Erwin Scherer
Subjects: Religion, Juveniles, Educational Materials
Bookshop: Buchhandlung des Evangelischen Missionsverlag (at above address)
Founded: 1920
ISBN Publisher's Prefix: 3-7714

Evangelischer Presseverband für Bayern eV, Birkerstr 22, D-8000 Munich 19 Tel: (089) 184031 Telex: 0523718
Bavarian Evangelical Press Union
Dir: Paul Rieger; *Publicity Manager:* Karl-Eberhard Beck
Subsidiary Company: Claudius Verlag GmbH (qv)
Subjects: Evangelical Press Service, School Books, Song Books, Christian weekly periodical
Founded: 1932
ISBN Publisher's Prefix: 3-583

Evangelisches Verlagswerk GmbH, Leerbachstr 42, D-6000 Frankfurt am Main 1 Tel: (06171) 53708
Man Dir: Helga Müller-Römheld
Subject: Religion
Founded: 1947
ISBN Publisher's Prefix: 3-7715

Expert Verlag GmbH+, Postfach 2, D-7031 Grafenau 1 Tel: (07033) 4783
Man Dir: Dipl-Ing FH Elmar Wippler; *Editorial, Sales, Publicity, Rights & Permissions:* Dipl-BW Thomas von Breitenbach; *Production:* Alfred Burghardt
Subjects: Occupational/Professional Instruction Manuals (Technologies, Commerce, Business Law, Management, Energy), Technical
1981: 80 titles *1982:* 100 titles *Founded:* 1979
ISBN Publisher's Prefix: 3-88508

Express Edition GmbH, Kottbusser Damm 79, D-1000 Berlin 61 Tel: (030) 6932064-5
Man Dir: Horst Herkner, Gisela Aglaster; *Editorial:* Dietrich Klitzke; *Sales:* Gisela Aglaster; *Rights & Permissions:* Horst Herkner
Subjects: Immigration themes, Migrant Homelands, Third World and South-East Asia, Social History
Bookshop: At above address
1982: 25 titles *1983:* 150 titles *Founded:* 1979
ISBN Publisher's Prefix: 3-88548

Extrabuch Verlag in der pädex-Verlags-GmbH, Rotlintstr 45H, D-6000 Frankfurt am Main Tel: (0611) 430124
Man Dir, Editorial, Production: Volkhard Brandes; *Publicity, Sales:* Michael Rittendorf
Parent Company: Pädex Verlags GmbH (at above address)
Subjects: Pedagogy, Social Sciences, Literature
Founded: 1976
ISBN Publisher's Prefixes: 3-921450, 3-88704

Fackelträger-Verlag GmbH, Goseriede 10-12, D-3000 Hanover 1 Tel: (0511) 14648
Man Dir: Hans Rauschning; *Sales:* Siegfried Liebrecht
Subjects: General Fiction, History, How-to, Art
Founded: 1949
ISBN Publisher's Prefix: 3-7716

Fackelverlag G Bowitz GmbH*, Herdweg 29-31, Postfach 442, D-7000 Stuttgart 1 Tel: (0711) 20171 Cable Add: Fackelverlag Stuttgart Telex: 0722875
Despatch Off: Schockenriedstr 46, D-7000 Stuttgart 80
Branch Off: A-6971 Hard-Bei-Bregenz, Ankergasse 18a, Austria
Subjects: General Fiction, History, How-to, Reference, Dictionaries, Low-priced Paperbacks
Book Club: Fackel-Buchklub
Founded: 1919
ISBN Publisher's Prefix: 3-87220

Falk-Verlag für Landkarten und Stadtpläne Gerhard Falk GmbH, Burchardstr 8, Postfach 102122, D-2000 Hamburg 1 Tel: (040) 331981 Cable Add: falkverlag Telex: 02162175
Man Dir: Dr Helge Lintzhöft, Handelsregister AG Hamburg HRB 23204
Subjects: Maps, Guidebooks, Phrasebooks
1981: 8 titles *1982:* 6 titles *Founded:* 1945
ISBN Publisher's Prefixes: 3-920317, 3-88445

Falken-Verlag GmbH+, Schöne Aussicht 21, Postfach 1120, D-6272 Niedernhausen/Ts Tel: (06127) 3011-3015 Telex: 4186585 fves d
Man Dirs: Frank Sicker, Dietrich John; *Editorial:* Dr Werner Jopp; *Publishing Manager:* Ulrich Watschounek; *Sales:* Manfred Abrahamsberg; *Production:* Horst Gemmerich; *Publicity:* Barbara Aschenberner; *Rights & Permissions:* Cordula Schlag
Subsidiary Company: Friedrich Bassermann'sche Verlagsbuchhandlung (qv)
Subjects: Natural foods and cookery, Herbalism, Popular Health, Natural History, Gardening, How-to, Sports and Pastimes, Motorcycling, Photography, Humour, Further Education
1983: 76 titles *Founded:* 1923
ISBN Publisher's Prefix: 3-8068

Dr Martin **Faltermaier**, see Juventa Verlag

Favorit-Verlag Huntemann & Co+, Stettiner Str 16, Postfach 1549, D-7550 Rastatt Tel: (07222) 22254/5 Cable Add: favoritverlag Telex: 786630
Subject: Children's Books

Willy F P **Fehling** GmbH*, Spichernstr 22-26, Postfach 1960, D-3000 Hanover Tel: (0511) 33921 Cable Add: Fehlingwerk Hannover Telex: 0922758
Publisher: Werner von Holtzendorff-Fehling; *Man Dir, Editorial:* Günther Ostermeier; *Production:* Gerd Gehrold
Orders to: B L V, Lothstr 29, D-8000 Munich 40
Subject: Horticulture
Founded: 1912
ISBN Publisher's Prefix: 3-921144

Dr Karl **Feistle**, see Dustri-Verlag

Feuervogel-Verlag GmbH, Gerh-Hauptmann Ring 107-109, Postfach 550122, D-6000 Frankfurt am Main Tel: (0611) 574257
Man Dir: Georg Treguboff
Subjects: Historical novels and documentation concerning post-1917 Russia
1983: 9 titles *Founded:* 1971
ISBN Publisher's Prefix: 3-921148

Wolfgang **Fietkau** Verlag*, Potsdamer Chaussee 16, D-1000 Berlin 37 Tel: (030) 8025493
Publisher: Wolfgang Fietkau
Founded: 1959
Subject: Poetry, Belles Lettres
ISBN Publisher's Prefix: 3-87352

Barbara **Fietz**, see Abakus Schallplatten

Fikentscher und Co, see Technik Tabellen Verlag

Wilhelm **Fink GmbH** & Co Verlags KG, Ohmstr 5, D-8000 Munich 40 Tel: (089) 348017 Cable Add: Fink München
Subjects: History, Literature, Law Study, Art, Criticism, Philosophy, Linguistics, Languages, Music, Classical Archaeology, Sociology, Psychology
ISBN Publisher's Prefix: 3-7705

J **Fink — Kümmerly und Frey** Verlag GmbH, Zeppelinstr 29-31, D-7302 Ostfildern 4 Tel: (0711) 45060 Cable Add: Buch-Fink Telex: 723737 fkfd
Dir and Public Relations: Bodo Neiss
Subjects: Touring and walking guides to regions of Germany and Europe and related Non-fiction
Miscellaneous: Firm has developed from an association between the German company J Fink (founded 1894) and the Swiss cartographic company Kümmerly und Frey (founded 1852). The latter firm also continues as an independent company in Switzerland (qv)
ISBN Publisher's Prefix: 3-7718

Emil **Fink Verlag**, Heidehofstr 15, D-7000 Stuttgart 1 Tel: (0711) 465330
Publisher: Richard Scheibel
Subjects: Arts, Maps
ISBN Publisher's Prefix: 3-7717

Finken-Verlag, Zimmersmühlenweg 40, Postfach 1420, D-6370 Oberursel/Ts Tel: 53073 Cable Add: Finkenverlag Oberursel
Dir: Manfred Krick
Subjects: Children's Books, Juveniles, Textbooks, Education, Games
1981: 15 titles
ISBN Publisher's Prefix: 3-8084

Verlag für Medizin Dr Ewald **Fischer**, see Medizin

Fischer Taschenbuch Verlag GmbH*, Geleitsstr 25, Postfach 700480, D-6000 Frankfurt am Main 70 Tel: (0611) 60621 Cable Add: Buchfischer Telex: 0412410
Man Dirs: Monika Schoeller, Karl-Michael Mehnert; *Sales, Publicity:* Ulrich Fritz, Frank Scheffter; *Production:* Wilfried Meiner
Parent Company: S Fischer Verlag GmbH (qv)
Subjects: General Fiction & Non-fiction, Paperbacks
Founded: 1952
ISBN Publisher's Prefix: 3-596

Gustav **Fischer Verlag** GmbH & Co KG, Wollgrasweg 49, Postfach 720143, D-7000 Stuttgart 70 (Hohenheim) Tel: (0711) 455038 Cable Add: Fischerbuch
Man Dirs: Bernd von Breitenbuch, Dr W D von Lucius; *Sales, Advertising & Publicity Dir:* Gerhard Weber; *Rights & Permissions:* Dr W D von Lucius
Subjects: Medicine, Biology, Anthropology, Psychology, Social Sciences, Economics, Paperbacks, University Textbooks, Scientific Journals
1981: 150 titles *1982:* 135 titles *Founded:* 1878
ISBN Publisher's Prefix: 3-437

Rita G **Fischer Verlag**, Alt Fechenheim 73, D-6000 Frankfurt 61 Tel: (0611) 422069/416061 Telex: 4189936 fivg d
Man Dir: Rita G Fischer
Subjects: Medicine, Politics, Psychology, Engineering, General and Social Science, How-to, University Textbooks, High-priced Paperbacks
1982: 350 titles *1983:* 420 titles *Founded:* 1977
ISBN Publisher's Prefix: 3-88323

S **Fischer Verlag** GmbH*, Geleitsstr 25, Postfach 700480, D-6000 Frankfurt am Main 70 Tel: (0611) 60621 Cable Add: Buchfischer Telex: 0412410
Dirs: Monika Schoeller, Karl-Michael Mehnert; *Sales:* Ulrich Fritz; *Production:* Wilfried Meiner; *Publicity:* Frank Scheffter
Subsidiary Companies: Fischer Taschenbuch Verlag GmbH (qv); Wolfgang Krüger Verlag GmbH (qv); Goverts im S Fischer Verlag
Subjects: General Fiction and Non-fiction, Belles Lettres, Poetry, Biography, History, Philosophy, Low- & High-priced Paperbacks, Psychology, Social Science, Music, Art, Reference Books for the layman
Founded: 1886
ISBN Publisher's Prefix: 3-10

W **Fischer Verlag**, Stresemannstr 30, Postfach 1864, D-3400 Göttingen Tel: (0551) 62038/9 Telex: 96746
Dir: Wilhelm Fischer; *Sales Manager:* Albert Köneke
Subject: Juvenile Fiction and Non-fiction
Founded: 1948
ISBN Publisher's Prefix: 3-439

Verlag Johannes **Fix***, Sonnenscheinstr 4, Postfach 1221, D-7060 Schorndorf Tel: (07181) 3236 Cable Add: Fix-Verlag Schorndorf
Man Dir: Johannes Fix
Subjects: Religion, Juveniles
ISBN Publisher's Prefix: 3-87228

Fleischhauer und Spohn Verlag*, Maybachstr 18, Postfach 301160, D-7000 Stuttgart 30 Tel: (0711) 89340 Telex: 723113 umco d
Owned by: Dr Max Bez, Thomas Bez, Ursula Roth
Associate Company: Barsortiment G Umbreit GmbH und Co, Maybachstr 18, D-7000 Stuttgart 30 (Book Wholesaler)
Subjects: Belles Lettres, Travel Literature, Regional Literature, History
Founded: 1830
ISBN Publisher's Prefix: 3-87230

Focus-Verlag*, Grünbergerstr 16, Postfach 110328, D-6300 Giessen Tel: (0641) 34760
Man Dirs: Mr Mende, Mr Schmid; *Sales Dir, Rights & Permissions:* Mr Linke; *Publicity & Advertising Dir:* Mr Schmid
Subjects: History, Reference, High-priced Paperbacks, Psychology, Social Science, University Textbooks
Founded: 1970
ISBN Publisher's Prefixes: 3-920352, 3-88349

Alfred **Förg** GmbH & Co KG, see Rosenheimer Verlagshaus

Forkel-Verlag GmbH, Felsenstr 23, Postfach 2120, D-6200 Wiesbaden-Dotzheim Tel: (06121) 42785
Man Dir: Dr Herbert Braun; *Sales & Advertising Dir, Publicity, Rights & Permissions:* Friedrich Vohl
Subjects: Business Administration, Business Law, Promotion & Marketing, Data Processing
Bookshop: Forkel-Kundendienst (at above address)
1982: 14 titles
ISBN Publisher's Prefix: 3-7719

Rat für **Formgebung**, Eugen-Bracht-Weg 6, D-6100 Darmstadt Tel: (06151) 44051 Design Council of the Federal Republic of Germany (Publishing Department)
Design Dir: Dipl-Ing Herbert Ohl; *Manager:* Ernst Jörg Kruttschnitt
Subjects: Industrial, Graphic and Environmental Design, Ergonomics

Fortschritt für alle-Verlag, Schlossweg 2, D-8501 Feucht Tel: (09128) 3126 Cable Add: Fortschrit
Man Dir: Erika Herbst
Orders to: Auslieferung-Lebenskunde Vertrieb, Jägerstr 4, D-4000 Düsseldorf 1
Subjects: Popular Explanation of Scientific Advances
Founded: 1974
ISBN Publisher's Prefix: 3-920304

A **Francke** GmbH, Dachauer Str 42, Postfach 200909, D-8000 Munich Tel: (089) 594713
Dir: C L Lang
Branch Off: Francke Verlag, Switzerland (qv)
Subjects: Linguistics, Literature, Sociology, Politics, History, Philosophy, Music, Periodicals
Founded: 1959

Verlag der **Francke Buchhandlung** GmbH, Am Schwanhof 19, Postfach 640, D-3550 Marburg an der Lahn Tel: (06421) 25036/37
Man Dir, Editorial, Production, Publicity: Gerhard Kuhlmann; *Sales:* Liselotte Kerste
Subjects: Evangelical Theology, Biblical Studies, Christian Books for Children
Bookshops: Marburg, Hebronberg, Gunzenhausen, Velbert, Lemförde, Oberursel
Founded: 1950
Miscellaneous: Firm is contributor to the Telos series of evangelical paperbacks (qv)
ISBN Publisher's Prefix: 3-88224

Franckh'sche Verlagshandlung W Keller & Co, Pfizerstr 5-7, Postfach 640, D-7000 Stuttgart 1 Tel: (0711) 21910 Cable Add: Kosmosverlag Stuttgart Telex: 721669 kosm d
Dirs: Rolf Keller, Claus Keller, Euchar Nehmann; *Editorial:* Rolf Keller; *Sales Dir:* Dieter Naveau; *Production:* Hansjörg-Staelin; *Publicity Dir:* Dr Juan-Hartwig Wulff; *Advertising Manager:* Jürgen Ritter; *Rights & Permissions:* Brigitta Ehrler
Subsidiary Companies: Franz Mittelbach-Verlag, Verlag Der Neue Schulmann (both at above address); W Spemann Verlag (qv)
Subjects: Natural Sciences, Technology, Sports and Hobbies, Young People's books, Reference
Book Club: Kosmos-Gesellschaft der Naturfreunde
Bookshop: Richard Bucholz, Alexanderstr 27, D-7000 Stuttgart 1
1981: 76 titles *Founded:* 1822
ISBN Publisher's Prefix: 3-440

Verlag **Frankfurter Bücher**, an imprint of Societäts-Verlag (qv)

Frankfurter Fachverlag Michael Kohl GmbH & Co KG, Emil Sulzbach Str 12, Postfach 970115, D-6000 Frankfurt am Main 97 Tel: (0611) 778410 and 776513
Associate Company: Kohl's Technischer Verlag Erwin Kohl GmbH & Co KG (qv)
Subjects: Electrical Engineering, Electronics, Industries, Crafts, Textbooks
ISBN Publisher's Prefix: 3-87234

Verlag **Frankfurter Kinderbücher** GmbH*, Forsthausstrasse 9, D-6246 Glashuetten 1 Tel: (06174) 61116
Publisher: Gerhard Hirschfeld
Parent Company: Verlag Gerhard Hirschfeld GmbH
Imprint: Verlag Frankfurter Kinderbücher, Glashuetten/Taunus
Subjects: Picture Books and Textbooks for Children
Founded: 1976
ISBN Publisher's Prefix: 3-88162

Fränkische Gesellschafts-Druckerei Würzburg/Echter Verlag, see under Würzburg

Frankonius Verlag GmbH*, Wiesbadener Str 1, Postfach 140, D-6250 Limburg 1 Tel: (06431) 401211 Telex: 0484764 palan d

Man Dir: Engelbert Tauscher; *Publicity:* Klemens Holdener; *Editorial:* Ursula Mock
Subjects: Textbooks for modern teaching methods, covering: History, Languages, Social Sciences, Physical Sciences, Pedagogy and Training, Sports
Founded: 1976
ISBN Publisher's Prefix: 3-87962

Ernst **Franz** und Sternberg-Verlag, Max-Planck-Str 25, Postfach 1262, D-7430 Metzingen/Württemberg Tel: (07123) 6237 Telex: 07245334
Publisher: Gerhard Heinzelmann
Subjects: Christian comment and exegesis; Swabian devotions
ISBN Publisher's Prefix: 3-7722

Franzis-Verlag GmbH, Postfach 370120, D-8000 Munich 37 (Located at: Karlstr 37-41, D-8000 Munich 2) Tel: (089) 5117/1 Telex: 522301
Dir: Peter G E Mayer; *Sales & Publicity Manager:* Georg Geschke; *Rights & Permissions:* Siegfried Pruskil
Founded: 1924
ISBN Publisher's Prefix: 3-7723

Frauenbuchverlag+, Gabelsberger Str 56, D-8000 Munich 2 Tel: (089) 521717
Parent Company: Weismann Verlag – Frauenbuchverlag GmbH (qv)
Subjects: Political Texts on Women's Emancipation, Reportage, Novels, Cartoons, Illustrated Books

Verlag **Frauenoffensive**, Kellerstr 39, D-8000 Munich 80 Tel: (089) 485102
Dirs: R Guckert, J Jakob, S Kahn-Ackermann, S Kohlstadt, G Kowitzke; *Editorial:* S Kahn-Ackermann, G Kowitzke; *Sales:* S Kohlstadt; *Production:* R Guckert; *Publicity:* S Kahn-Ackermann
Subjects: Feminist
1983: 100 titles *Founded:* 1976
ISBN Publisher's Prefix: 3-88104

Frauenpresse, renamed Sub Rosa Frauenverlag (qv)

Frech-Verlag GmbH und Co Druck KG, Turbinenstr 7, Postfach 310902, D-7000 Stuttgart 31 (Weilimdorf) Tel: (0711) 832061 Telex: 7252156 fr d
Man & Sales Dir: E A Krauss; *Publicity Dir, Rights & Permissions:* Mrs I Euler; *Advertising Dir:* W Krauss
Subjects: Topp series of books on crafts, hobbies and popular electronics
1983: 600 titles *Founded:* 1954
ISBN Publisher's Prefix: 3-7724

Verlag **freies Geistesleben**, Haussmann Str 76, D-7000 Stuttgart Tel: (0711) 283255
Man Dir: Dr W Niehaus; *Sales:* Heinrich Didwiszus
Subjects: Biography, History, How-to, Music, Art, Philosophy, Juveniles, High-priced Paperbacks, Medicine, Psychology, General & Social Science, Educational Materials
Bookshop: Buchhandlung freies Geistesleben, Alexanderstr 11, D-7000 Stuttgart
Founded: 1947

Verlag für **Fremdsprachen**, see Verlag für Deutsch

Verlag Dieter **Fricke** GmbH+, Gr Bockenheimer Str 32, D-6000 Frankfurt am Main 1 Tel: (0611) 285139
Man Dir: Dieter Fricke
Subjects: Photography, Fine Arts, Architecture, Design
1983: 49 titles *Founded:* 1976
ISBN Publisher's Prefix: 3-88184

Erhard **Friedrich** Verlag, Im Brande 15, D-3016 Seelze 6 Tel: (0511) 483051-54 Cable Add: Friedrich Telex: 0922923

Subjects: Theatre, Opera, Education, Arts
Founded: 1960
ISBN Publisher's Prefix: 3-7727

Frisia-Verlag GmbH, Mainzlarer Str 11, D-6301 Staufenberg 1 Tel: (06406) 3319
General Manager: Werner Struep; *Partner:* Gisela Struep
Subjects: North Sea Literature, Island Guides, Travel Guides, Maps
1981: 18 titles *1982:* 30 titles *Founded:* 1975
ISBN Publisher's Prefix: 3-88111

Verlag A **Fromm** GmbH & Co, Postfach 1948, D-4500 Osnabrück (Located at: Breiter Gang 11-14) Tel: (0541) 3100 Telex: 94916 fromm d
Publisher: Leo V Fromm; *Vice-President:* Annette Harms-Hunold; *Sales Manager:* Annegret Busch; *Public Relations:* Ursula Malzahn
Associate Companies: Edition Interfrom AG, Switzerland (qv); Fromm International Publishing Corp, 560 Lexington Ave at 50th Street, New York, NY 10022, USA
Subjects: Scientific texts by German-Speaking Authors on Politics, Economics, Society, Culture and Education, Nature, the Environment; Periodicals
ISBN Publisher's Prefix: 3-7729

Friedrich **Frommann** Verlag, Günther Holzboog GmbH & Co, König-Karl-Str 27, Postfach 500460, D-7000 Stuttgart 50 Tel: (0711) 569039 Telex: 7254754 frho d
Man Dir & Editorial: Günther Holzboog, Eva-Maria Holzboog; *Sales Dir:* H Gündert; *Publicity & Advertising Dir:* H Kruschwitz; *Rights & Permissions:* Dr R Pietsch
Subjects: History, Philosophy, Political Science, Reference, Religion, Psychology, Psychoanalysis, Social Science, Pedagogy, History of Science, University Textbooks, Philosophical Journal
Founded: 1727
ISBN Publisher's Prefix: 3-7728

G D Bücherei, an imprint of Jan Tholenaar Verlag GmbH (qv)

Franz-J **Gaber**, see Verlagsbuchhandlung Megapress

Betriebswirtschaftlicher Verlag Dr Theodor **Gabler** GmbH*, Taunusstr 54, Postfach 1546, D-6200 Wiesbaden 1 Tel: (06121) 5341 Cable Add: Gablerverlag Telex: 04186567
Man Dir: Dr Frank Lube; *Sales, Publicity:* H Stalter
Parent Company: Verlagsgruppe Bertelsmann GmbH (qv)
Subjects: Business Administration, Personnel Management, Accounting, Insurance, Banking, Periodicals
1981: 101 titles
ISBN Publisher's Prefix: 3-409

Verlag für **Gegenrealismus**, see Desire und Gegenrealismus

GeoCenter Verlagsvertrieb GmbH, Neumarkter Str 18, D-8000, Munich 80 Tel: (089) 431890 Telex: 523259
Man Dir: Wolfgang Kunth; *Sales Manager:* Wolfgang Völcker
Subjects: Maps, Travel
ISBN Publisher's Prefix: 3-921435

Kunstverlag Dr Rudolf **Georgi**, Woldemar Klein, Theaterstr 77, Postfach 407, D-5100 Aachen Tel: (0241) 26141 Telex: 832337
Man Dirs: Werner and Manfred Georgi
Subjects: History, How-to, Music, Art, General Science
Bookshops: Fachbuchhandlung Dr Rudolf Georgi, Theaterstr 77, Aachen
Founded: 1928
ISBN Publisher's Prefix: 3-87248

Carl **Gerber** Verlag, see Schwaneberger Verlag GmbH

Gerhardt Verlag, Jenaer Str 7, D-1000 Berlin 31 Tel: (030) 8543009
Man Dir: Renate Gerhardt
Subjects: Belles Lettres, Poetry, Art, High-priced Paperbacks, Educational Materials
Founded: 1962
ISBN Publisher's Prefix: 3-920372

Gerstenberg Verlag, Postfach 390, D-3200 Hildesheim (Located at: Rathausstr 20) Tel: (05121) 1060 Telex: 927108 gberg
Man Dir, Editorial: Dr Viktor Christen; *Sales, Publicity:* W J Dietrich; *Production:* Reinhard Fabian; *Rights & Permissions:* Elisabeth Franke
Subjects: Art, Music, Mathematics, Physics, Psychology, Religion, Literature, Historical Reprints, Nature, Culture, Humour, Children's Books
Founded: 1969
ISBN Publisher's Prefix: 3-8067

Musikverlag Klaus **Gerth**, see Turmberg

Verlag Ernst und Werner **Gieseking***, Deckertstr 30, Postfach 130120, D-4800 Bielefeld 13 Tel: (0521) 14674 Telex: 932240
Publisher: Werner Gieseking
Associate Companies: Dr Peter Deubner Verlag GmbH (qv), Deubner und Lange Verlag GmbH
Subjects: Law, Music
ISBN Publisher's Prefix: 3-7694

Gieseking Wirtschaftsverlag GmbH, Fürst-Pückler Str 30, Postfach 410268, D-5000 Cologne 41 Tel: (0221) 403028
Dir: Dr Peter Deubner
Associate Companies: Dr Peter Deubner Verlag GmbH (qv), Deubner und Lange Verlag GmbH
Subject: Economics
Founded: 1977

Gilles und Francke Verlag, Blumenstr 67-69, Postfach 100764, D-4100 Duisburg 1
Publisher, Proprietor: Werner Francke; *Editorial:* Dr K Körper; *Sales:* Barbara Francke; *Publicity:* Ralf Gruna
Subsidiary Company: G & F Book and Periodical Sales
Subjects: Leisure Activities, Poetry, Anthologies, Music, Fiction, Essays, Periodicals
Bookshop: G & F Buch und Zeitschriftenhandlung
Founded: 1900
ISBN Publisher's Prefix: 3-12251

Verlag W **Girardet**, Girardetstr 2-38, Postfach 101365, D-4300 Essen 1 Tel: (0201) 79960 Cable Add: Girardet Essen Telex: 0857888
Publisher: Dr Paul Girardet; *Editorial:* Ulrich Melzer
Subjects: Texts and Teachers' Texts for Technical Training Colleges, Universities and Institutions: Electro-Technology, Engineering, Basic Sciences, Business Administration, Languages
Founded: 1865
ISBN Publisher's Prefix: 3-7736

Glashuetten/Taunus, an imprint of Verlag Frankfurter Kinderbücher GmbH (qv)

Globetrotter-Verlag, see Friedemann von Engel Verlag

Glock und Lutz Verlag Heroldsberg, Hans-Sachs-Str no 2, D-8501 Heroldsberg bei Nuremberg Tel: (0911) 560738
Subjects: Religion, Regional Guides, Biography, History, Art, Periodicals
1983: 8 titles *Founded:* 1923
ISBN Prefix: 3-7738

FEDERAL REPUBLIC OF GERMANY

Glogau Verlag, an imprint of Hans Christians Druckerei und Verlag (qv)

PR Verlag Kurt **Glombig**, see Pinx-Verlag

Verlagsgesellschaft R **Glöss** und Co, Mörkenstr 7, Postfach 500344, D-2000 Hamburg 50   Tel: (040) 388573   Telex: 215667 vlg d
Publisher: Wolfgang Glöss
Subjects: Periodicals, Politics, Biography, Belles Lettres
ISBN Publisher's Prefix: 3-87261

Verlag **Glückauf** GmbH, Postfach 103945, D-4300 Essen 1   Tel: (0201) 1059545   Telex: 8579545 gauf d
Man Dir, Editorial: Dr-Ing R H Bachstroem; *Sales, Publicity:* K Thewissen; *Production:* W Amthor; *Rights & Permissions:* W Amthor, R H Bachstroem
Parent Company: Verein für die bergbaulichen Interessen, Friedrichstr 1, D-4300 Essen 1 (The Society for Mining Interests)
Subjects: Technical Literature, Periodicals connected with mining
Bookshop: At above address
1981: 32 titles   *1982:* 31 titles   *Founded:* 1912
ISBN Publisher's Prefix: 3-7739

Wilhelm **Goldmann** Verlag GmbH, Neumarkter Str 18, Postfach 800709, D-8000 Munich 80   Tel: (089) 41740   Cable Add: Goldmannverlag Munich
Man Dir: Gert Frederking; *Editorial:* Klaus Eck; *Sales:* Volker Neumann; *Publicity:* Günter Stöberlein
Parent Company: Verlagsgruppe Bertelsmann GmbH (qv for associate companies)
Subjects: General Fiction, Crime, Science Fiction, Poetry, Biography, History, How-to, Art, Classics, Religion, Law, Medicine, Psychology & Education, General & Social Science, Cinema, Astrology
ISBN Publisher's Prefix: 3-442

Goldstadtverlag, see Karl A Schäfer Buch- und Offsetdruckerei Goldstadtverlag

Gondrom Verlag GmbH & Co Kg*, Bahnhofstr 15, Postfach 2606, D-8580 Bayreuth   Tel: (0921) 21031   Telex: 642771
Man Dir: Volker Gondrom; *Editorial, Production, Rights & Permissions:* Jürgen Bergs
Subjects: Art, History, Juveniles, Literature
Founded: 1974
ISBN Publisher's Prefix: 3-8112

V **Gorachek** KG, see Possev-Verlag

Grabert-Verlag+, Am Apfelberg 18-20, Postfach 1629, D-7400 Tübingen 1   Tel: (07071) 61206   Cable Add: Grabert-Tübingen   Telex: 07262863 grav-d
Man Dir and Owner: Wigbert Grabert
Subjects: Belles Lettres, Biography, History (also pre-History and Contemporary History), High-priced Paperbacks
Book Club: Deutscher Buchkreis (qv)
1982: 8 titles   *1983:* 7 titles   *Founded:* 1953
ISBN Publisher's Prefix: 3-87847

Gräfe und Unzer GmbH, Isabellastr 32, Postfach 400709, D-8000 Munich 40   Tel: (089) 23710   Telex: 5216929 gu d
Man Dir: Kurt Prelinger; *Editorial:* Hans Scherz; *Sales:* Fritz Petermuller; *Marketing:* Dieter Banzhaf; *Rights & Permissions:* Ursula Feuerbacher
Orders to: Verlegerdienst München, Gutenbergstr, 8031 Gilching
Subjects: Cookery, Health, How-to, Nature, Animals, Reference
Founded: 1722
ISBN Publisher's Prefix: 3-7742

Verlag der Stiftung **Gralsbotschaft** GmbH, Lenzhalde 15, D-7000 Stuttgart 1   Tel: (0711) 294355
Associate Company: Verlag Alexander Bernhardt, Austria (qv)
Subjects: Philosophy, Religion

Greven Verlag Köln GmbH, Neue Weyerstr 1-3, D-5000 Cologne 1   Tel: (0221) 233333   Cable Add: Grevenverlag Köln   Telex: 8882249
Man Dir: Irene Greven
Subjects: Cologne and Region (Fine Art editions)
1981: 10 titles   *1982:* 7 titles   *Founded:* 1827
ISBN Publisher's Prefix: 3-7743

Julius **Groos** Verlag KG, Hertzstr 6, Postfach 102423, D-6900 Heidelberg 1   Tel: (06221) 33621   Cable Add: Groos Heidelberg
Man Dir: Dieter Wolff; *Sales Dir:* Renate Wolff
Subjects: Linguistics, Textbooks on Modern Languages, Educational Materials, Periodicals
1981: 29 titles   *1982:* 19 titles   *Founded:* 1804
ISBN Publisher's Prefix: 3-87276

Grote'sche Verlagsbuch-handlung KG*, Max-Planck-Str 12, Postfach 100448, D-5000 Cologne   Tel: (02234) 106   Cable Add: Groteverlag   Telex: dgv Köln 08882662
Dir: Friedrich Plagge
Parent Company: Unternehmensgruppe Verlag W Kohlhammer GmbH (qv)
Branch Off: Luxemburger Str 72, Postfach 100448, D-5000 Cologne 1
Subjects: History, Law, Literature, Economics, Administration, Social & Political Science, Periodicals
Founded: 1661
ISBN Publisher's Prefix: 3-7745

Verlag **Grundlagen** und Praxis GmbH & Co, Wissenschaftlicher Autorenverlag KG, Bergmannstr 40, Postfach 1507, D-2950 Leer   Tel: (0491) 61886
Man Dir: Mrs M Harms
Subjects: Homoeopathy, Graphology, Philology
Founded: 1972

Matthias-**Grünewald**-Verlag, Max Hufschmidt-Str 4a, Postfach 3080, D-6500 Mainz   Tel: (06131) 89055
Publisher: Dr Jakob Laubach; *Editorial:* Dr Schmidt; *Sales Dir:* Ludwig Hahn; *Production:* Mr Wagner; *Publicity:* Ulrike Bettermann
Subjects: Religion, Biography, History, Juveniles
Founded: 1918
ISBN Publisher's Prefix: 3-7867

Walter de **Gruyter** & Co, Mouton Publishers, Genthiner Str 13, D-1000 Berlin 30   Tel: (030) 260050   Cable Add: Wissenschaft Berlin 0184027   Telex: 184027
Man Dirs: Dr Kurt-Georg Cram, Dr Kurt Lubasch; *Sales:* Dietrich Rackow; *Publicity:* Joachim Oest
Associate Company: J Schweitzer Verlag (qv)
Subsidiary Companies: Aldine Publishing Company, Mouton Publishers, Walter de Gruyter Inc, all at 200 Saw Mill River Road, Hawthorne, NY 10532, USA
Branch Offs: Mouton Publishers, Amsterdam, Berlin, Paris
Subjects: Law, History, Linguistics, Philosophy, Theology, Classical Studies, Anthropology, Natural Sciences, Literary Criticism, Commerce, Technology, Social Sciences, Medicine; Works in German, English, French
ISBN Publisher's Prefixes: 3-11 (de Gruyter), 90-279 (Mouton), 0-202 (Aldine)

Verlag Klaus **Guhl**, Königin-Elizabethstr 8, D-1000 Berlin 19   Tel: 3213062
Man Dir: Dr Klaus-Dieter Guhl; *Editorial:* Fabian Carlos Guhl; *Sales:* Florian Robert Guhl; *Production:* Hans Paul Guhl; *Publicity:* Dr Kurt Kreiler; *Rights & Permissions:* Dr Thomas Bark
Orders to: Knobelsdorffstr 8, D-1000 Berlin 19
Subsidiary Companies: Fanel GmbH; Buchladen Bunter Bär GmbH
Branch Off: Knobelsdorffstr 8, D-1000 Berlin 19
Subjects: Politics, Literature, Art, Erotica
Bookshop: Bunter Bär-Guhl, Knobelsdorffstr 8, D-1000 Berlin 19
1981: 19 titles   *Founded:* 1974
ISBN Publisher's Prefix: 3-88220

D **Gundert** Verlag*, Wildstr 7, Postfach 1240, D-8202 Bad Aibling   Tel: (08061) 4046
Subjects: Juveniles, Young Adult
Founded: 1878
ISBN Publisher's Prefix: 3-87279

Verlag August **Güse** GmbH*, Hauptstr 103, D-6367 Karben 3   Tel: (06039) 2990/2991   Telex: 415505 Guese
Subjects: Horticulture, Floriculture
1981: 5 titles   *Founded:* 1954
ISBN Publisher's Prefix: 3-87278

Gutenberg-Gesellschaft, Liebfrauenpl 5, D-6500 Mainz   Tel: 06131/226420
President: J Fuchs; *Secretary:* Heinz Gehrmann; *Editorial:* Prof Kopitz
Subjects: Library Science, the Gutenberg Yearbook
Founded: 1901

Büchergilde **Gutenberg Verlagsgesellschaft** mbH*, Untermainkai 66, Postfach 16220, D-6000 Frankfurt am Main 16   Tel: (0611) 230115   Telex: 412063 buegi d
Man Dir: Erhard Schumacher; *Editorial, Rights & Permissions:* Edgar Pässler; *Sales:* Rolf Backhaus; *Production:* Juergen Suess, Grit Fischer; *Publicity:* Karin Hirschfeld
Parent Company: B G A G, Theaterplatz 2, D-6000 Frankfurt am Main 1
Subjects: Literary Works, Light Reading, Politics, History, Art, Children's, Juvenile
Book Clubs: Büchergilde Gutenberg (Federal Republic of Germany and Switzerland)
1981: approx 5 titles   *Founded:* 1924
Miscellaneous: Primarily a Book Club, but also a publisher
ISBN Publisher's Prefix: 3-7632

Gütersloher Verlagshaus Gerd Mohn, Königsstr 23, Postfach 1343, D-4830 Gütersloh 1   Tel: (05241) 1831   Cable Add: Gütersloher Verlagshaus   Telex: 0933868
Man Dir: Gerd Mohn; *Sales Dir, Publicity:* Otfrid Seippel; *Rights & Permissions:* Hansjürgen Meurer
Subjects: Religion, Philosophy, Politics, Juveniles, Paperbacks
Imprints: Gütersloher Taschenbücher Siebenstern (paperback series)
1981: 110 titles   *1982:* 90 titles   *Founded:* 1959
ISBN Publisher's Prefix: 3-579

H A D U – Hagemann Lehrmittel- und Verlagsgesellschaft mbH, Karlstr 20, Postfach 5129, D-4000 Düsseldorf   Tel: (211) 353811   Cable Add: Hagemannverlag   Telex: 8587623 hage d
Man Dir: Maria Schütte-Hagemann; *Editorial, Production:* Hans Peisker, Heinz W Schmidt; *Sales, Export, Finance:* W Kils-Hütten; *Publicity:* Heinz W Schmidt; *Rights & Permissions:* W Kils-Hütten, Hans Peisker, Heinz W Schmidt
Parent Company: Lehrmittelverlag Wilhelm Hagemann (qv)
Subjects: Teaching Aids and Pedagogy
1981: 188 titles   *1982:* 190 titles   *Founded:*

1929
Miscellaneous: Part of vgs —
Verlagsgesellschaft Schulfernsehen mbH &
Co KG (qv)
ISBN Publisher's Prefix: 3-544

Haag und Herchen Verlag, Fichardstr 30,
D-6000 Frankfurt am Main 1 Tel: (0611)
550911/12/13 Telex: 414838 huh d
Man Dir: Hans-Alfred Herchen
Subjects: How-to, High-priced Paperbacks,
Medicine, Politics, Psychology, Engineering,
General & Social Science, University
Textbooks
1981: 505 titles *1982:* 628 titles *Founded:*
1975
ISBN Publisher's Prefix: 3-88129

Dr Rudolf **Habelt** GmbH, Abt Verlag, Am
Buchenhang 1, Postfach 150104, D-5300
Bonn 1 Tel: (0228) 232015 Cable Add:
Buchhabelt Bonn
Man Dirs: Dr Rudolf Habelt, Wolfgang
Habelt; *Editorial, Production:* Renate
Schreiber
Subjects: Pre-History, Archaeology, Ancient
History, Regional, Folklore
Bookshop: (Antiquarian) at above address

Chris **Hablitzel**, see Lexika-Verlag

Walter **Hädecke** Verlag*, Postfach 1203,
D-7252 Weil der Stadt Tel: (07033) 2264
Man Dir: Hilde Graff-Hädecke; *Sales &
Advertising Dir, Rights & Permissions:*
Joachim Graff
Subjects: Reference, High-priced
Paperbacks, Cook Books, Public Health,
Natural Medicine
Founded: 1919
ISBN Publisher's Prefix: 3-7750

Lehrmittelverlag Wilhelm **Hagemann**,
Karlstr 20, Postfach 5129, D-4000
Düsseldorf Tel: (0211) 353811 Cable Add:
Hagemannverlag Telex: 8587623 hage d
Sales: Walter Kils-Hütten; *Production,
Rights & Permissions:* Hans Peisker,
Heinz W Schmidt
Subsidiary Company: HADU — Hagemann
Lehrmittel- und Verlagsgesellschaft
mbH (qv)
Subjects: Textbooks, especially on Biology,
Chemistry, Electrical Engineering,
Electronics, Public Health, Mathematics,
Education, Physics, Politics
Miscellaneous: Part of vgs —
Verlagsgesellschaft Schulfernsehen mbH &
Co KG (qv)
ISBN Publisher's Prefix: 3-544

Buchvertrieb **Hager** GmbH*, Mainzer
Landstr 147, Postfach 111162, D-6000
Frankfurt am Main 11 Tel: (0611) 730234
Telex: 04-13080 kuehl d
Managing & Sales Dir: Margrit Meyer
Subjects: History, Literature, Politics,
Philosophy, Juveniles, Low-priced
Paperbacks, Books from the People's
Republic of China, Social Science
Founded: 1974
ISBN Publisher's Prefix: 3-88145

Mary **Hahn's** Kochbuchverlag, Hubertusstr
4, D-8000 Munich 19 Tel: (089) 177041
Telex: 05215045
Subjects: Cookery, Home Economics
Miscellaneous: Firm is a member of
Verlagsgruppe Langen-Müller/Herbig (qv)
ISBN Publisher's Prefix: 3-87287

Verlag Anton **Hain**, see Meisenheim

Hallwag Verlagsgesellschaft mbH*, Marco-
Polo-Str 1, D-7302 Ostfildern 4 bei
Stuttgart Tel: (0711) 4502266 Cable Add:
Hallwagverlag Telex: 721796 mair d
Dir: Ulrich Mailänder
Subjects: Maps, Town Plans, Travel and
Touring Guides and Books; Pocket
Information series on General Knowledge;
Reference, Music
Head Office: Hallwag Verlag AG, Berne,
Switzerland (qv)
ISBN Publisher's Prefix: 3-444

Hamburger Lesehefte Verlag Iselt & Co Nfl
mbH, Nordbahnhofstr 2, Postfach 1480,
D-2250 Husum Tel: (04841) 6081 Telex:
28567 husum v d
Man Dir, Editorial, Rights & Permissions:
Ingwert Paulsen Jr; *Sales:* Alfred Lorenzen;
Production: Ingwert Paulsen Sr
Parent Company: Husum Druck- und
Verlagsgesellschaft mbH & Co KG (qv)
Associate Companies: Hansa Verlag Ingwert
Paulsen Jr (qv); Matthiesen Verlag Ingwert
Paulsen Jr (qv)
Subjects: Textbooks
Founded: 1953
ISBN Publisher's Prefix: 3-87291

Peter **Hammer** Verlag GmbH*, Foehrenstr
33-35, Postfach 200415, D-5600
Wuppertal 2 Tel: (0202) 505066
Dir: Hermann Schulz
Associate Companies: Jugenddienst Verlag
(qv); Burckhardthaus-Verlag
Subjects: Latin America, African Literature,
The Third World, Literature, Current
Affairs, Meditation, Christian Action
ISBN Publisher's Prefix: 3-87294

Hansa Verlag Ingwert Paulsen Jr,
Nordbahnhofstr 2, Postfach 1480, D-2250
Husum Tel: (04841) 6081 Telex: 28567
husumv d
Associate Companies: Hamburger Lesehefte
Verlag Iselt & Co Nfl mbH (qv); Husum
Druck- und Verlagsgesellschaft mbH & Co
KG (qv); Matthiesen Verlag Ingwert Paulsen
Jr (qv)
Subjects: Belles Lettres, Literary Criticism
ISBN Publisher's Prefix: 3-920421

Carl **Hanser** Verlag, Kolbergerstr 22,
Postfach 860420, D-8000 Munich 86
Tel: (089) 982511 Telex: 05/22837
Managing Partners: Joachim Spencker,
Christoph Schlotterer, Franz-Joachim
Klock; *Editorial:* Christoph Buchwald,
Stephan Sattler, Michael Krüger, Hans
Joachim Simm, Günther Fetzer, Hans
Joachim Niclas; *Sales Dirs:* Felicitas
Feilhauer, Christoph Sickel; *Advertising Dir:*
Günther Steidl; *Publicity Manager:* Günther
Fetzer
Subsidiary Companies: Part-owner of
Deutscher Taschenbuch Verlag (qv) and of
Verlegerdienst München, Gutenbergstr,
Gilching
Subjects: General Fiction, Belles Lettres,
Poetry, Biography, History, Philosophy,
High-priced Paperbacks, Engineering,
General Science, Macromolecular
Chemistry, Plastics, Business &
Management, Dentistry, Periodicals
1981: 160 titles *Founded:* 1928
ISBN Publisher's Prefix: 3-446

Hänssler-Verlag, Friedrich Hänssler KG,
Bismarckstr 4, Postfach 1220, D-7303
Neuhausen-Stuttgart Tel: (07158) 177
Man Dir: Friedrich Hänssler; *Rights &
Permissions:* Dieter Allgöwer
Subjects: Music, Art, Religion, Low-priced
Paperbacks
Bookshop: Laudate GmbH,
Versandbuchhandlung Friedrich Hänssler (at
above address)
Founded: 1920
Miscellanous: Firm is a member of the Telos
(qv) series publishing group; it also publishes
all publications of the American Institute of
Musicology
ISBN Publisher's Prefix: 3-7751

Peter **Hanstein** Verlag GmbH, Adelheidstr 2,
Postfach 1220, D-6240 Königstein/Ts Tel:
(06174) 3021
Publisher: Axel Rütters; *Sales, Publicity:*
Daniel Herrmann; *Rights & Permissions:*
Hildegard Willhöft
Parent Company: Athenäum Verlag GmbH
(qv)
Associate Companies: Jüdischer Verlag;
Verlag Anton Hain Meisenheim GmbH (qv)
is a subsidiary company of this Group
Subject: Theology
Founded: 1878
ISBN Publisher's Prefix: 3-7756

Harlekin-Presse, see Hertenstein

Harrach und Sabrow*, Wöllsteiner Str 8,
Postfach 745, D-6550 Bad Kreuznach
Tel: (0671) 67073 Telex: 042815
Associate Company: Inter-Kunst und Buch
GmbH (qv)
Subjects: Children's Books, Poetry

Verlag Otto **Harrassowitz**, Taunusstr 14,
Postfach 2929, D-6200 Wiesbaden 1
Tel: (06121) 521046 Cable Add: Otto
Harrassowitz Wiesbaden Telex: 04186135
Man Dir: Dr Helmut Petzolt; *Sales &
Publicity Dir:* Albrecht Weddigen
Subjects: History, Book Trade and Library
Science, Bibliographies, Orientalia and
associated Eastern linguistic and religious
studies, East European History and
associated Slavic Language and Educational
Studies, Classical Philology, Ethnology,
Middle East studies
Bookshop: Otto Harrassowitz, Taunusstr 5,
Postfach 2929, D-6200 Wiesbaden 1
1983: approx 30 titles *Founded:* 1872
ISBN Publisher's Prefix: 3-447

Verlag Karlheinz **Hartmann**, Rodheimer
Str 17, D-6382 Friedrichsdorf im Taunus
Tel: (06007) 7622
Man Dir: Karlheinz Hartmann; *Editorial:*
Monica Herber
Branch Off: Verlängerte Hedderichstr o Nv
(Südgüterbahnhof), D-6000 Frankfurt am
Main 70 Tel: (0611) 632345
Subjects: Contemporary Literature,
Reprints, Literary Criticism, Scenarios and
Film Scripts, Modern Poetry, Horror
Founded: 1976
ISBN Publisher's Prefix: 3-87293

Verlag Gerd **Hatje**, Wildunger Str 83,
Postfach 468, D-7000 Stuttgart 50
Tel: (0711) 561109 Cable Add: Hatjeverlag
Stuttgart
Man Dir: Gerd Hatje
Subjects: Architecture, Interior Decoration,
Art (especially Modern Art)
Founded: 1945
ISBN Publisher's Prefix: 3-7757

Haude und Spener Verlag, Postfach 620767,
D-1000 Berlin 62 (Located at:
Grossgörschenstr 6) Tel: (030)
7813514/7812004
General Manager: Volker Spiess
Associate Company: Verlag Volker Spiess
(qv)
Subjects: Literary History, Bibliographies,
Collected Works, History, Cultural History,
Reminiscences of Berlin
Founded: 1614
ISBN Publisher's Prefix: 3-7759

Rudolf **Haufe** Verlag GmbH & Co KG,
Hindenburgstr 64, Postfach 740, D-7800
Freiburg im Breisgau Tel: (0761) 31560
Cable Add: Haufeverlag Telex: 772442
haufe d
Man Dirs: Dr G Friedrich, Dr M
Jahrmarkt, G Osswald, F J Ruebsam;
Editorial: Dr G Friedrich, Dr M Jahrmarkt;
Sales, Production: F J Ruebsam; *Rights &
Permisions:* Dr G Friedrich

140 FEDERAL REPUBLIC OF GERMANY

Subsidiary Companies: WRS-Verlag (Wirtschaft, Recht, Steuern) (qv); Information Verlags-GmbH & Co KG, Hindenburgstr 64, Postfach 740, D-7800 Freiburg im Breisgau
Subjects: Business and Law, Financial, Management, Social Science, University Textbooks
Founded: 1934
ISBN Publisher's Prefix: 3-448

Karl F **Haug** Verlag GmbH & Co KG*, Postfach 102840, D-6900 Heidelberg 1 (Located at: Fritz-Frey Str 21) Tel: (06221) 49974-7 Cable Add: haugverlag
Man Dir: Dr E Fischer; *Production:* Dietmar Sieber; *Advertising, Public Relations:* Krisztina Fruh; *Sales:* Alfred Fuchs
Associate Companies: Arkana Verlag (qv); Verlag für Medizin Dr Ewald Fischer GmbH (qv); Fischer & Pflaum Verlag GmbH
Branch Off: Bergheimer Str 102, D-6900 Heidelberg
Subjects: Naturopathic, Homoeopathic, Fringe and Auxiliary Medical, Acupuncture, Health and Preventive Medicine, Periodicals
Bookshop: Haug & Cie Nachf GmbH, Med Wiss Buchhandlung und Antiquariat (Medical science books, new and second-hand/antiquarian)
Founded: 1903
ISBN Publisher's Prefix: 3-7760

Verlag H M **Hauschild** GmbH, Rigaer Str 3, D-2800 Bremen Tel: (0421) 392039 Telex: 244333 hwb d
Dirs: Friedrich Steimeyer, Andreas Nagel
Parent Company: Werbedruck Bremen Grafischer Betrieb GmbH
Subjects: Art, Reference, Bremen Regional
Founded: 1854
ISBN Publisher's Prefix: 3-920699

Dr Ernst **Hauswedell** und Co Verlag, Rosenbergstr 113, Postfach 723, D-7000 Stuttgart 1 Tel: (0711) 638264
Joint Man Dirs: Gerd Hiersemann, Dr Reimar W Fuchs; *All other offices:* Reinhold Busch
Subjects: Reference Works for Book and Print Collectors, Bibliographies, Illustrated Books
Founded: 1927
ISBN Publisher's Prefix: 3-7762

Heckners Verlag*, Postfach 1260, D-3340 Wolfenbüttel Tel: (05331) 5166
Subjects: Vocational (Business), Economics
Founded: 1895
Miscellaneous: Part of vgs — Verlagsgesellschaft Schulfernsehen mbH & Co KG (qv)

H **Heenemann** Verlagsgesellschaft mbH, Bessemerstr 83–91, Postfach 420342, D-1000 Berlin 42 Tel: (030) 7537051 Telex: 183 796 hekg d
Associate Company: Wilhelm Pansegrau Verlag (qv)
Subjects: Fishery and Fishing, Sociology and Popular Science, Enamels and Coatings
ISBN Publisher's Prefix: 3-87903

Heering-Verlag GmbH, see Ringier/Heering-Verlag

Heidmük-Verlag Günther U Müller*, C Fr Gauss-Str 59, D-2800 Bremen 33 Tel: (0421) 256454
Man Dir: Günther U Müller
Subjects: Juveniles, Games

Verlag Egon **Heinemann***, Kösliner Weg 16, D-2000 Norderstedt 3 Tel: (040) 5232368/5239023/5239024
Publisher: Egon Heinemann
Subjects: Sailing, Sailing Ships, Nautical Literature, Yachting Charts
ISBN Publisher's Prefix: 3-87321

Ehrhardt **Heinold**, see Eulenhof-Verlag

Heinrichshofen's Verlag+, Liebigstr 16, Postfach 620, D-2940 Wilhelmshaven Tel: (04421) 202004 Cable Add: Heinrichshofen Wilhelmshaven
Man Dir: Otto Heinrich Noetzel; *Editorial:* Dr Viktor Kreiner, Florian Noetzel; *Production:* Johann Reiners
Associate Companies: Otto Heinrich Noetzel Verlag; Arthur Türk KG; Heinrichshofen Edition New York
Subjects: Music & Musicology, Ballet, Opera, Song Books, Paperbacks
Founded: 1797
ISBN Publisher's Prefix: 3-7959

Verlag Georg **Heintz**, Wasserturmstr 7, D-6520 Worms Cable Add: Heintz
Subjects: Bibliography, German Exile Literature (from 1933), History and Documentation of Anti-Semitism, Fiction and Drama on related themes

G **Henle** Verlag, Postfach 710466, D-8000 Munich 71 (Located at: Forstenrieder Allee 122) Tel: (089) 754096/7/8 Telex: 05216392
Subsidiary Company: G Henle USA Inc, 10370 Page Industrial Blvd, St Louis, Mo 63132 (Tel: (314) 4275725)
Subject: Music, Original and Facsimile Editions, Reference Books (Music)
ISBN Publisher's Prefix: 3-87328

Henssel Verlag, Glienicker Str 12, D-1000 Berlin 39 Tel: (030) 8051493 Cable Add: Hensselverlag Berlin
Man Dir: Karl-Heinz Henssel; *Editorial:* Asta-Maria Henssel
Subjects: General Fiction, Humour, Travel, Literary Theory, Poetry, Biography, Quality Paperbacks
Founded: 1938
ISBN Publisher's Prefix: 3-87329

F A **Herbig** Verlagsbuchhandlung, Hubertusstr 4, D-8000 Munich 19 Tel: (089) 177041 Cable Add: Langenmüller Telex: 05215045
Man Dir: Dr Herbert Fleissner; *Editorial:* Dr Bernhard Strückmeyer; *Sales Manager:* Gisela Weichert; *Publicity Manager:* Dr Brigitte Sinhuber-Erbacher; *Rights & Permissions:* Renate Werner
Orders to: VVA (Vereinigte Verlagsauslieferung GmbH), Postfach 7777, D-4830 Gütersloh 1
Subjects: Novels, Belles Lettres, Poetry, History, Art, Hobbies, Gift Books
Founded: 1821
Miscellaneous: Firm is a member of Verlagsgruppe Langen-Müller/Herbig (qv)
ISBN Publisher's Prefix: 3-7766

Herchen, see Bock und Herchen

Verlag **Herder** GmbH & Co, KG, Hermann-Herder-Str 4, Postfach, D-7800 Freiburg im Breisgau Tel: (0761) 27171 Cable Add: Herder Freiburgbreisgau Telex: 07721440 vhd
Man Dir: Dr Hermann Herder; *Sales Dir:* Franz Grossmann; *Publicity Manager:* Dr Ludwig Muth; *Rights & Permissions:* Alfred Zimmermann
Subsidiary Companies: Verlag Karl Alber GmbH, Christophorus-Verlag Herder GmbH, Verlag F H Kerle, Verlag A G Ploetz GmbH & Co KG (qqv)
Associate Companies: Verlag Herder & Co, Austria (qv); Herder Editrice e Libreria, Italy (qv); Editorial Herder SA, Libreria Herder (both in Spain, qqv); Herder AG, Switzerland (qv); Herder und Herder GmbH, Federal Republic of Germany (qv)
Subjects: General Fiction, Belles Lettres, Poetry, Biography, History, Art, Philosophy, Reference, Religion, Juveniles, Low- and High-priced Paperbacks, Psychology, Social Science, University, Secondary & Primary Textbooks, Educational Materials, Atlases, Encyclopaedias
Book Club: Herder Buchgemeinde
Bookshops: Located in major cities throughout Federal Republic of Germany
Founded: 1801
ISBN Publisher's Prefix: 3-451

Herder und Herder GmbH*, Verlag für Wirtschaft und Gesellschaft, Rathenauplatz 14, D-6000 Frankfurt am Main 1
Associate Companies: Verlag Herder GmbH & Co KG, Verlag A G Ploetz GmbH & Co KG (both in Federal Republic of Germany, qqv); Herder AG, Switzerland (qv)
Subjects: Politics, Social Sciences, Economics
ISBN Publisher's Prefix: 3-585

Herold Verlag Brück KG*, Friedrichstr 16-20, Postfach 1940, D-7012 Fellbach 4 Tel: (0711) 513004
Dirs: Peter Schwend; *Editorial:* Ulrich Höfker
Subjects: Juveniles
Founded: 1871
ISBN Publisher's Prefix: 3-7767

Hertenstein-Presse, Mathystr 36, D-7530 Pforzheim Tel: (07231) 27084
Publicity Manager: Ulrike Strauss
Subject: Verse and other texts, with original illustrations
Miscellaneous: Formerly known as Harlekin-Presse

Hestia-Verlag GmbH, Egerländer Str 28, D-8580 Bayreuth Tel: (0921) 21007 Telex: 642103
Dirs: Heinz G Konsalik, Dagmar Stecher-Konsalik
Subjects: General Fiction and Non-fiction, History, Biography
1982-83: 113 titles *Founded:* 1954
ISBN Publisher's Prefix: 3-7770

Carl **Heymanns** Verlag KG, Gereonstr 18-32, D-5000 Cologne 1 Tel: (0221) 134022; Bonn (0228) 234550; Berlin (030) 3914081; Munich (089) 224811 Cable Add: Köln Rechtsverlag; also Bonn/Munich/Berlin Rechtsverlag; Telex: Cologne 8881888; Munich 0524058; Berlin 0181811
Man Dir: Hans-Jörg Gallus; *Editorial:* H E Wohlfarth, K W Frohn, K Pompe; *Production:* C Free; *Publicity:* K Brachvogel; *Sales:* N Becker, Gerhard Werthmüller
Subsidiary Companies: Gallus Druckerei KG, Berlin; Albert Nauck & Co, Cologne and Berlin; Gallus Verlag, Hans O Gallus KG, Munich; Euroliber Verlags- und Vertriebs-GmbH, Cologne; Gallus Verlag KG, Vienna, Austria; Scientia AG, Zug, Switzerland
Branch Offs: Adalbert-Stifter-Str 15, D-5300 Bonn; Steinsdorfstr 10, D-8000 Munich 22; Gutenbergstr 3-4, D-1000 Berlin 10
Subjects: Law, Political Science
Founded: 1815
ISBN Publisher's Prefix: 3-452

Wilhelm **Heyne** Verlag, Türkenstr 5-7, Postfach 201204, D-8000 Munich 2 Tel: (089) 288211/16 Cable Add: Heyneverlag München Telex: 0524218
Publisher: Rolf Heyne; *Administrative Dir:* Hans Joachim Brede; *Editorial Dirs:* Lothar Menne, Dr Hans-Peter Übleis; *Editorial:* Roswitha Heyne, Manfred Kluge, Wolfgang Jeschke, Bernhard Matt; *Sales Manager:* Friedhelm Koch; *Advertising Manager:* Horst Mikkat; *Rights & Permissions:* Traudel Eckardt
Subjects: (Paperbacks) General Fiction, Poetry, Biography, History, How-to,

Cookery, Mystery, Romances, Occult, Films, Psychology, Science Fiction and Westerns, Cartoons
Founded: 1934
ISBN Publisher's Prefix: 3-453

Anton **Hiersemann** Verlag+, Rosenbergstr 113, Postfach 723, D-7000 Stuttgart 1 Tel: (0711) 638264/5
Man Dir, Rights & Permissions: Karl G Hiersemann; *Editorial:* Dr Reimar W Fuchs
Subjects: Bibliography, Reference, History, Art, Bibliophilism, Germanic Literature, Theatre, Classical Studies, Religion, Theology
1981: 50 titles *Founded:* 1884
ISBN Publisher's Prefix: 3-7772

Verlag **Hinder und Deelmann**, Postfach 1206, D-3554 Gladenbach (Hessen) Tel: (06462) 1301
Publishers: Johannes Deelmann, Rolf Hinder
Subjects: Philosophy, Religion, Social Science
ISBN Publisher's Prefix: 3-87348

Hippokrates-Verlag GmbH, Postfach 593, D-7000 Stuttgart 1 (Located at: Rüdigerstr 14, D-7000 Stuttgart 30) Tel: (0711) 89310 Cable Add: Hippokratesverlag
Dirs: Ehrenfried Klotz, Albrecht Hauff; *Publicity:* H-G Zimnik; *Sales:* Dietrich Geyer
Orders to: Koch, Neff und Oetinger & Co, Verlagsauslieferung Hippokrates, Postfach 210, D-7000 Stuttgart 1
Parent Company: Georg Thieme Verlag KG (qv)
Subjects: Medicine, Natural Sciences, Psychology, University and Secondary Textbooks
1981: 50 titles *Founded:* 1925
ISBN Publisher's Prefix: 3-7773

Hirmer Verlag+, Maréesstrasse 15, D-8000 Munich 19 Tel: (089) 1781011
Man Dirs: Aenne Hirmer, Albert Hirmer; *Editorial:* Margret Haase
Subjects: Quality illustrated Works on Archaeology, History of Art from earliest civilizations, German and other Art and Picture Galleries
Founded: 1948
ISBN Publisher's Prefix: 3-7774

Ferdinand **Hirt***, Schauenburgerstr 36, Postfach 2580, D-2300 Kiel 1 Tel: (0431) 561066 Telex: 299873
Subjects: Science, Education, Academic, Geographical, Teacher Training
Founded: 1832
Miscellaneous: Part of vgs — Verlagsgesellschaft Schulfernsehen mbH & Co KG (qv)
ISBN Publisher's Prefix: 3-554

S **Hirzel** Verlag GmbH und Co, Birkenwaldstr 44, Postfach 347, D-7000 Stuttgart 1 Tel: (0711) 25820 Cable Add: Hirzelverlag, Stuttgart Telex: 723636 daz d
Man Dirs: Hans Rotta, Dr W Wessinger; *Managers:* R Hack, K Hübler, B Schreck
Associate Companies: Deutscher Apotheker Verlag Dr Roland Schmiedel (qv); Franz Steiner Verlag GmbH (qv); Wissenschaftliche Verlagsgesellschaft mbH (qv)
Subjects: Philosophy, Psychology, Engineering, General Science
Founded: 1853
ISBN Publisher's Prefix: 3-7776

Hobbit Presse, an imprint of Klett-Cotta Verlag (qv)

Hoch-Verlag, Kronprinzenstr 27, D-4000 Düsseldorf 1 Tel: (0211) 307001 Cable Add: Hochverlag
Man Dirs: Joachim Hoch, Eric Zinth de Kentzingen, Ursula Schareina; *Sales, Publicity and Advertising Dir:* Joachim Hoch; *Rights & Permissions:* Eric Zinth de Kenzingen
Subject: Juveniles
Founded: 1949
ISBN Publisher's Prefix: 3-7779

Ing W **Hofacker** GmbH Verlag, Tegernseerstr 18, D-8150 Holzkirchen/Obb Tel: 08024/7331
Man Dir, Rights & Permissions: Winfried Hofacker; *Editorial, Publicity:* J Maier; *Production:* A Gruenwald
Subjects: Electronics, Micro-Computers, Micro-Processing
Founded: 1968
ISBN Publisher's Prefix: 3-921682

Dieter **Hoffmann** Verlag*, Senefelderstr 75, D-6500 Mainz 41 Tel: (06136) 7016 Telex: 4187213
Dir: Dieter Hoffman
Subjects: History of German Aviation (in German and English texts), Aircraft Modelling, Hunting and Shooting Handbooks
Founded: 1960
ISBN Publisher's Prefix: 3-87341

Julius **Hoffmann** Verlag, Pfizerstr 5-7, Postfach 788, D-7000 Stuttgart 1 Tel: (0711) 2191320
Man Dir: Kurt Hoffmann
Subjects: Building and Architecture, History of Art (many texts in English and French)
Founded: 1827
ISBN Publisher's Prefix: 3-87346

Hoffmann und Campe Verlag, Harvestehuder Weg 45, D-2000 Hamburg 13 Tel: (040) 441881 Cable Add: Hoca Telex: 0214259
Man Dirs: Thomas Ganske, Hans Helmut Roehring, Karl-Udo Wrede; *Editorial:* Dr Hans-Jürgen Schmitt, Wolfgang Schuler, Dr Jutta Siegmund-Schultze; *Sales Dir:* Bruno Laudien; *Production:* Harmut Zierau; *Publicity and Advertising Dir:* Ulrich Meier; *Rights & Permissions:* Helga Eberhard (German), Ulla Thomsen (Foreign)
Subjects: General Fiction and Non-fiction, Belles Lettres, Poetry, Biography, History, Music, Art, Philosophy, Psychology, General & Social Science, Marine History, Illustrated Books
1981: 72 titles *Founded:* 1781
ISBN Publisher's Prefix: 3-455

Verlag Karl **Hofmann**, Steinwasenstr 6-8, Postfach 1360, D-7060 Schorndorf bei Stuttgart Tel: (07181) 7811 Cable Add: Hofmannverlag Schorndorf
Man Dir: Ottmar Hecht; *Sales, Publicity:* Thomas Hecht
Subjects: Sports, Technical Literature on glass utilization; Periodicals
1982: 50 titles *1983:* 40 titles
ISBN Publisher's Prefix: 3-7780

Hohenloher Druck- und Verlagshaus, Verlag Hohenloher Tagblatt, Blaufelderstr 44, Postfach 80, D-7182 Gerabronn Tel: (07952) 5126 Cable Add: HDV-Gerabronn Telex: 74334
Publisher: Rolf Wankmüller
Subjects: Fiction, Poetry, Biography, Juveniles
ISBN Publisher's Prefix: 3-87354

Hohenstaufen Verlag Schumann KG Berg/Bodman*, Postfach, D-8137 Berg 3/Starnbergersee
The above is the address of the Administration Office; the Publishing Office is at Im Gries 17, Postfach 29, D-7762 Bodman-Ludwigshafen
Administrative Dir: Dr Gert Sudholt; *Sales:* Elisabeth Steinhaus; *Publishing Dir:* Gerhard Schumann
Subjects: Belles Lettres, Memoirs, Contemporary History

Verlag Wolfgang **Hölker**, Martinistr 2, Postfach 3820, D-4400 Munster Tel: (0251) 42225 Cable Add: Martinistrasse 2 Telex: 891566 hoeco d
Man Dir: Wolfgang Hölker; *Sales:* Manfred Goldschmidt; *Production:* Joerg Rinow; *Publicity:* Gertrud Posch
Parent Company: F Coppenrath Verlag (qv)
Subject: Cookery
1983: 150 titles *Founded:* 1973
ISBN Publisher's Prefix: 3-88117

Holle Verlag GmbH, Friedhofstr 25, Postfach 320, D-7570 Baden Baden Tel: (07221) 23591 Telex: 0781108
Man Dir: G Du Ry van Beest Holle; *Sales & Advertising Dir:* F Litten
Subjects: History, Art, Encyclopaedias
Founded: 1933
ISBN Publisher's Prefix: 3-87355

Holsten Verlag Wolf Schenke KG*, Geschwister-Scholl-str 142, D-2000 Hamburg 20 Tel: (040) 470934
Man Dir: Wolf E Schenke
Subjects: History, Political Science
Founded: 1955

Verlag Gebr **Holzapfel**, Kienhorststr 61, D-1000 Berlin 51 Tel: (030) 4133098
Publisher: Klaus-J Holzapfel
Subject: Politics
ISBN Publisher's Prefix: 3-921226

Gunther **Holzboog** GmbH & Co, see Friedrich Frommann Verlag

Hans **Holzmann** Verlag GmbH und Co KG, Gewerbestr 2, Postfach F 1342, D-8939 Bad Wörishofen Tel: (08247) 1031/8 Cable Add: Holzmann Verlag Telex: 539331
Man Dir: Peter Holzmann; *Sales Dir:* Alfred Stempfle
Subjects: Business and Legal Advisory, Inventions and Patenting, Butchery and Meat Trade
Bookshop: Versandbuchhandlung Hans Holzmann, Postfach F 1342, D-8939 Bad Wörishofen
Founded: 1936
ISBN Publisher's Prefix: 3-7783

Horatio-verlag und Agentur+, Dirnitzweg 5, D-8491 Zandt Tel: (09944) 815
Dir: Genoveva Seydlitz; *Marketing Manager, Rights & Permissions:* Kurt Seydlitz; *Publicity:* Genoveva Seydlitz, Kurt Seydlitz
Subjects: Humour, Jokes, Games

Werner **Hörnemann** Verlag*, In der Wehrhecke 17, Postfach 130109, D-5300 Bonn 1 Tel: (0228) 251376
Subjects: Hobbies, Cookery, Pottery and Ceramics
1981: 72 titles
ISBN Publisher's Prefix: 3-87384

Horst-Werner Dumjahn Verlag, see Dumjahn

Max **Hueber** Verlag*, Max-Hueber-Str 4, D-8045 Ismaning bei Munich Tel: (089) 96021 Telex: 05-23613 Cable Add: Hubook
Man Dir: Armin Jetter; *Editorial Dir:* Heinrich Schrand; *Marketing Dir:* Bert Rech
Subsidiary Company: Hueber-Holzmann Pädagogischer Verlag (qv)
Subjects: Reference, Dictionaries, Foreign Languages, German for Foreigners, Linguistics, Adult Education, Periodicals
Bookshop: Universitätsbuchhandlung Max Hueber, Amalienstr 77-79, D-8000 Munich 40
Founded: 1921
ISBN Publisher's Prefix: 3-19

142 FEDERAL REPUBLIC OF GERMANY

Hueber-Holzmann Pädagoscher Verlag*, Max-Hueber-Str 4, D-8045 Ismaning bei Munich Tel: (089) 96021 Cable Add: Hubook Telex: 0523613
Man Dir: Armin Jetter; *Editorial Dir:* Heinrich Schrand; *Marketing Dir:* Bert Rech
Parent Company: Max Hueber Verlag (qv)
Subjects: Electrical Engineering, Electronics, Informatics, Data Processing, Textbooks, Mathematics, Social Sciences
ISBN Publisher's Prefix: 3-8096

Humboldt-Taschenbuchverlag Jacobi KG, Neusser Str 3, Postfach 401120, D-8000 Munich 40 Tel: (089) 3830 Cable Add: Langenscheidt Munich Telex: 5215379 lkgm d
Man Dir: Karl Ernst Tielebier-Langenscheidt; *Editorial, Rights & Permissions:* Manfred Überall; *Sales Dir:* Peter Haering; *Advertising Dir:* Dieter Krause; *Sales, Promotion:* through Langenscheidt KG (qv)
Subjects: Non-fiction Paperbacks, Practical Guides
1981: 24 titles *1982:* 24 titles *Founded:* 1953
Miscellaneous: Firm is a member of the Langenscheidt Group (qv)
ISBN Publisher's Prefix: 3-581

Edition **Hundertmark**, Reinoldstr 6, D-5000 Cologne 1 Tel: (0221) 231603
Man Dir: Armin Hundertmark
Subjects: Contemporary Art Books, Literature, Periodicals
Founded: 1970

Husum Druck- und Verlagsgesellschaft mbH & Co KG, Nordbahnhofstr 2, Postfach 1480, D-2250 Husum Tel: (04841) 6081/3 Telex: 28567 husum v d
Man Dir, Editorial, Rights & Permissions: Ingwert Paulsen Jr; *Sales:* Alfred Lorenzen; *Production:* Ingwert Paulsen Sr
Subsidiary Company: Hamburger Lesehefte Verlag Iselt & Co Nfl mbH (qv)
Associate Companies: Hansa Verlag Ingwert Paulsen Jr (qv); Matthiesen Verlag Ingwert Paulssen Jr (qv)
Subjects: Belles Lettres, Regional Interest
Founded: 1973
ISBN Publisher's Prefix: 3-88042

Dr Alfred **Hüthig** Verlag GmbH, Postfach 102869, D-6900 Heidelberg (Located at: Im Weiher 10) Tel: (06221) 4891 Cable Add: Hüthigverlag Heidelberg Telex: 0461727
Production: Willi Mayer; *Publicity:* Ulrich Stiehl
Associate Companies: Hüthig und Pflaum Verlag GmbH (qv); Hüthig und Wepf Verlag, Switzerland (qv)
Subjects: Chemistry, Chemical Engineering, Medicine, Dentistry, Cosmetics, Electronics, Periodicals
1981: 30 titles *1982:* 30 titles *Founded:* 1925
ISBN Publisher's Prefix: 3-7785

Hüthig und Pflaum Verlag GmbH & Co KG, Postfach 201920, D-8000 Munich 2 (Located at: Lazarettstr 4, D-8000 Munich 19) Tel: (089) 126070 Telex: 0529408
Branch Off: Im Weiher 10, D-6900 Heidelberg 1
Subjects: Electrical Engineering, Electronics
Associate Company: Dr Alfred Hüthig Verlag (qv)
ISBN Publisher's Prefix: 3-8101

I d W-Verlag GmbH, Cecilienallee 36, Postfach 320580, D-4000 Düsseldorf 30 Tel: (0211) 434391 Cable Add: ideweverlag Telex: 8584270
Subject: Business Administration, Tax Law, Finance, Auditing
1982: 13 titles
ISBN Publisher's Prefix: 3-8021

I L S (Institut für Lernsysteme) GmbH, member of Verlagsgruppe Bertelsmann GmbH (qv)

I M S F, see Institut für Marxistische Studien und Forschungen eV

I S P-Verlag (Internationale Sozialistische Publikationen)*, Kölnerstrasse 68, Postfach 111017, D-6000 Frankfurt am Main 2 Tel: (0611) 736797
Subject: Politics

Idea Verlag GmbH+, Krautgartenweg 6, Postfach 1361, D-8039 Puchheim bei Munich Tel: (089) 803265
Man Dir, Editorial, Production, Rights & Permissions: Dr Uwe K Paschke; *Sales, Publicity:* Hariet Paschke
Branch Off: Brucker Str 8, D-8031 Gilching Tel: (08105) 9124
Subjects: Technical and Scientific Texts, History, Hobbies, Games, Recreation
1981: 5 titles *1982:* 11 titles *Founded:* 1980
ISBN Publisher's Prefix: 3-88793

Hans **Imhoff**, see Euphorion-Verlag

Index eV*, Überlinger Str 13, Postfach 410511, D-5000 Cologne 41 Tel: (0221) 436939/372043
Publisher: Adolf Müller
Subjects: Belles Lettres, Poetry, Politics, Czech and Slovak Literature

Insel Verlag, Postfach 3325, D-6000 Frankfurt am Main (Located at: Suhrkamp House, Lindenstr 29-35) Tel: (0611) 75601 Cable Add: Inselverlag Telex: 413972
Publisher: Dr Siegfried Unseld; *Man Dir:* Dr Heribert Marré; *Sales:* Dr Joachim Unseld; *Publicity:* Dr Christoph Groffy; *Rights & Permissions:* Helene Ritzerfeld
Associate Companies: Suhrkamp Publishers Boston, Inc, 380 Green St, Cambridge, Mass 02139, USA; Nomos Verlagsgesellschaft mbH & Co KG, Suhrkamp Verlag KG (both in Federal Republic of Germany, qqv); Suhrkamp Verlag AG, Zeltweg 25, CH-8032, Switzerland
Subjects: Classic German Literature (especially Goethe), Classic foreign authors in translation, Modern Classics, Cultural History, Bibliophilia, Books on Great Artists
Founded: 1899
ISBN Publisher's Prefix: 3-458

Institut für Lernsysteme (ILS), member of Verlagsgruppe Bertelsmann GmbH (qv)

Institut für Marxistische Studien und Forschungen eV (IMSF), Liebigstr 6, D-6000 Frankfurt am Main Tel: 724914
Man Dir: Dr Heinz Jung; *All other offices:* Dr Schmidt
Subjects: Publication of results of studies, research etc, commentary on current political and social questions; Periodicals
Founded: 1968
Miscellaneous: Member of Arbeitsgemeinschaft sozialistischer und demokratischer Verleger und Buchhändler (qv for other members)

Inter-Kunst und Buch GmbH*, Wöllsteinerstr 8, D-6550 Bad Kreuznach Tel: (0671) 67073 Telex: 042815
Associate Company: Harrach und Sabrow (qv)
Subjects: Art Books, Graphics, Bibliophile Editions

Verlag **Internationale Solidarität** Verlagsgesellschaft mbH*, Zugweg 10, D-5000 Cologne Tel: (0221) 327817 Cable Add: Zugweg 10
Sales, Production: Ole Callsen
Subject: Politics

Internationales Landkartenhaus GmbH, Honigwiesenstr 25, D-7000 Stuttgart 80 Tel: (0711) 7827 Telex: 7255455
Man Dir: Wolfgang Kunth; *Sales Manager:* Herbert Leuser
Subject: Maps, Guide-books

Irisiana Druck und Verlag*, Wengenerstr 8, D-8961 Haldenwang Tel: (08374) 1574
Subjects: Holistic Medicine, Natural Food Cookery, Home Birth
Founded: 1973

Iselt und Co Nfl mbH, see Hamburger Lesehefte Verlag

J R O-Kartografische Verlagsgesellschaft mbH, Leopoldstrasse 175, Postfach 400940, D-8000 Munich 40 Tel: (089) 381031 Telex: 524123
General Manager: Dr Bernd Kobarg
Parent Company: Süddeutscher Verlag GmbH, Sendlonger Str 80, Postfach 202220, D-8000 Munich 2
Subjects: Maps, Cartography, Organizational charts
Founded: 1922
ISBN Publisher's Prefix: 3-87378

Verlag **Jacobi** KG, see Axel Juncker

Jaeger und Waldmann, see Telex-Verlag

Jahreszeitenverlag+, Poßmoorweg 5, Postfach 601220, D-2000 Hamburg 60 Tel: (040) 27170/2024 Cable Add: Jalag Telex: 0213214
Subject: Belles Lettres

Verlag Eduard **Jakobsohn***, Glogauer Str 22, D-1000 Berlin 36 Tel: 6181258
Orders to: Pro Media Literaturvertrieb GmbH, Werner Voss Damm 54, D-1000 Berlin 42
Subjects: Alternative Living, Communes, Spanish Civil War, Witch-hunting, Red Indians, Literature

Stern-Verlag **Janssen** und Co, see Stern-Verlag

Wolfgang **Joerg** und Erich Schoenig, see Berliner Handpresse

Jüdischer Verlag, subsidiary of Athenäum Verlag GmbH (qv)

Jugend und Volk Verlag GmbH*, Claude-Lorrainstr, D-8000 Munich 40 Tel: (089) 374560
Parent Company: Jugend und Volk Verlagsgesellschaft mbH, Austria (qv)
Subject: Juveniles
ISBN Publisher's Prefix: 3-8113

Jugenddienst-Verlag*, Foehrenstr 33-35, Postfach 200415, D-5600 Wuppertal 2 Tel: (0202) 551888
Dir: Hermann Schulz
Associate Company: Peter Hammer Verlag (qv)
Subjects: Playgroups, Learning, Sex Education, Meditation, Christian Action
ISBN Publisher's Prefix: 3-7795

Axel **Juncker**-Verlag Jacobi KG, Neusserstr 3, D-8000 Munich 40 Tel: (089) 3830
Man Dir: Karl Ernst Tielebier-Langenscheidt; *Sales Dir:* Peter Haering; *Publicity & Advertising:* Dieter Krause; *Sales, Promotion:* through Langenscheidt KG (qv); *Rights & Permissions:* Manfred Überall
Subjects: Reference, Dictionaries
Founded: 1902
Miscellaneous: Firm is a member of the Langenscheidt Group (qv)
ISBN Publisher's Prefix: 3-558

Junior International*, Postfach 285, D-7300 Esslingen (Located at: Liebigstr 1-11, D-7301 Deizisau) Tel: (07153) 22011 Cable Add:

FEDERAL REPUBLIC OF GERMANY 143

Verlag Schreiber Telex: 7266880 jfs d
Associate Company: Verlag J F Schreiber GmbH (qv)

Verlag **Jungjohann**, Postfach 1252, D-7107 Neckarsulm Tel: (07132) 2586
Man Dir, Sales, Production, Rights & Permissions: Dr med Harmut Jungjohann; *Publicity:* Mrs Scholz
Orders to: Lingenbrink, August-Schanz-Str, D-6000 Frankfurt am Main
Subjects: Basic Medical Studies, Intelligence/Psychology Tests for Medical Students, Natural Healing Practices
1981: 78 titles *1982:* 63 titles *Founded:* 1965
ISBN Publisher's Prefixes: 3-88454, 3-921689

Junius Verlag GmbH, von-Hutten-Str 18, D-2000 Hamburg 50 Tel: (040) 892599
Man Dirs: Rolf Wichmann, Jürgen Baumgarten
Subsidiary Company: Junius Verlag GmbH, Reindorfgasse 29, A-1150 Vienna, Austria
Subjects: German and International Politics, History, Social Sciences, the Workers' Movement, Trade Unions, East Europe and the USSR, Periodical
1981: 9 titles *Founded:* 1979
ISBN Publisher's Prefix: 3-88506

Juventa Verlag, Dr Martin Faltermaier, Böcklinstr 34, D-8000 Munich 19 Tel: (089) 155420
Man Dir: Dr Martin Faltermaier; *Publicity:* Katharina Spoerl
Subjects: Mainly connected with young people's training, education, psychology
1983: 5 titles *Founded:* 1953
ISBN Publisher's Prefix: 3-7799

Ernst **Kabel** Verlag GmbH, Hütten 86, D-2000 Hamburg 36 Tel: (040) 343528
Man Dirs: Jürgen P Hellfritz, Joachim Jessen, Detlef Lerch; *Editorial:* Joachim Jessen, Detlef Lerch; *Sales:* Karin Wenzel; *Production:* Jürgen P Hellfritz; *Publicity:* Detlef Lerch; *Rights & Permissions:* Joachim Jessen
Subsidiary Company: Ernst Kabel Druck GmbH (at above address)
Subjects: Non-fiction History, Current Events, Documentary, Historical Novels
1981: 11 titles *Founded:* 1977
ISBN Publisher's Prefix: 3-921909

Verlag Gerhard **Kaffke** GmbH & Co KG*, Domplatz 7, Postfach 110535, D-8400 Regensburg am Main 60 Tel: (0941) 55072
Man Dir: Manfred Kern
Subjects: Theology, Religion, Paperbacks
Founded: 1955
ISBN Publisher's Prefix: 3-87391

Chr **Kaiser** Verlag*, Postfach 509, D-8000 Munich 43 (Located at: Isabellastr 20, D-8000 Munich 40) Tel: (089) 2712097/2718786
Dir: Manfred Weber; *Sales Dir:* Erika Lampp
Subjects: Christian apologetics and exegesis, Theology, Religion and Society, Christian-Jewish Encounter
Founded: 1845
ISBN Publisher's Prefix: 3-459

Verlag Ferdinand **Kamp** GmbH & Co KG, Postfach 101309, D-4630 Bochum 1 (Located at: Widumestr 6, Bochum) Tel: (0234) 15071
Subjects: Textbooks, Reference, Dictionaries, Education, Non-fiction, Paperbacks, Periodicals
Miscellaneous: Part of vgs — Verlagsgesellschaft Schulfernsehen mbH & Co KG (qv)
ISBN Publisher's Prefix: 3-592

S **Karger** GmbH Verlag für Medizin und Naturwissenschaften*, Angerhofstr 9, Postfach 2, D-8034 Germering, Munich
Tel: (089) 844021 Cable Add: Kargermedbooks Telex: 524865
Man Dir: W Kunz
Parent Company: S Karger AG, Switzerland (qv)
Subjects: Medicine, Psychology, Natural Science
Bookshop: Karger-Buchhandlung Ausstellung und Vertrieb internationaler medizinischer Fachliteratur (at above address)

Karl-May-Verlag, Joachim Schmid & Co*, Karl-May-Str 8, D-8600 Bamberg Tel: (0951) 54051
Main Publicity Dir: Joachim Schmid; *Sales Dir:* Lothar Schmid; *Production Dir:* Roland Schmid; *Rights & Permissions:* Joachim, Lothar and Roland Schmid
Subject: Children's Fiction
Founded: 1913
ISBN Publisher's Prefix: 3-7802

Karo-Bücher, an imprint of A Weichert Verlag (qv)

Kartograpischer Verlag Wagner & Co KG, see Wagner

Kartographisches Institut Bertelsmann, Postfach 5555, D-4830 Gütersloh 1 (Located at Carl Bertelsmannstr 161, Gütersloh) Tel: (05241) 801 Telex: 933832
Dir: Karlheinz Thieme
Parent Company: Verlagsgruppe Bertelsmann GmbH (qv for associate companies)
Subjects: Atlases

Verlag **Katholisches Bibelwerk** GmbH, Silberburgstr 121A, D-7000 Stuttgart
Tel: (0711) 626003
Dir: Martin Günther
Subject: Religious literature on practical aspects of Catholic Bible work in Belgium, Federal Republic of Germany, Netherlands, Austria and Switzerland
Miscellaneous: Company is a member of AMB (qv)
ISBN Publisher's Prefix: 3-460

Katzmann-Verlag KG, Postfach 1827, D-7400 Tübingen 1 (Located at: Hausteigstr 26, D-7408 Kusterdingen) Tel: (07071) 34858 Cable Add: Katzmann Verlag
Man Dir, Publicity, Rights & Permissions: Dr Volker Katzmann; *Sales Dir:* Sibylle Katzmann; *Production:* Margarete Knöpfle
Associate Company: Heliopolis-Verlag Ewald Katzmann (at above address)
Subjects: Social Pedagogics, Social Work, Youth Work, Adult Education, Marriage and Family Counselling, Theology, Art, Religion, Periodical
Founded: 1945
ISBN Publisher's Prefix: 3-7805

Verlag Ernst **Kaufmann**, Alleestr 2, Postfach 1780, D-7630 Lahr/Schwarzwald
Tel: (07821) 26083 Cable Add: Ernstkauf Telex: 0754973
Man Dir: Heinz Kaufmann; *Chief Editor:* R Dessecker-Kaufmann; *Public Relations, Distribution:* Michael Jacob
Associate Company: Verlag J Pfeiffer GmbH & Co (qv)
Subjects: Religious Education (books, materials), Children's
Founded: 1816
Miscellaneous: Member of Verlagsring Religionsunterricht (VRU = Religious Instruction Publishing Ring)
ISBN Publisher's Prefix: 3-7806

Kaynar Buchhandlung, Hansastr 86, D-4100 Duisburg 1 Tel: (0203) 331795
Man Dir, Publicity, Rights & Permissions: Yasar Kaynar; *Editorial:* Serap Sekercioğlu; *Sales:* Reyhan Kaynar; *Production:* Bayram Özdemir
Subsidiary Company: Kaynar Kitabevi, K Liman Cad, 211 Kücükayasofya, Istanbul, Turkey
Subjects: Belles Lettres, Children's Books, Encyclopaedias, School Books
Bookshop: Hansastr 86, D-4100 Duisburg 1
1981: 8 titles *1982:* 6 titles *Founded:* 1973
ISBN Publisher's Prefix: 3-88689

Keip KG Antiquariat, Hainer Weg 46-48, D-6000 Frankfurt am Main 70 Tel: (0611) 614011 Cable Add: Antikeip Frankfurtmain Telex: D 689857 Keip
Publisher: Ulrich Keip; *Manager and Office Chief:* Johann Holler
Subjects: Law, Economics, Social Sciences, History
Founded: 1967
Miscellaneous: Also antiquarian bookseller

Franckh'sche Verlagshandlung, W **Keller** & Co, see Franckh'sche

Verlag F H **Kerle**, Tennenbacher Str 4, D-7800 Freiburg im Breisgau Tel: (0761) 2717512 Telex: 07721440
Man Dirs: Dr Hermann Herder, Harald Gläser; *Sales:* Dr Jürgen Bach; *Publicity:* Maria Schwaer
Parent Company: Verlag Herder GmbH & Co KG (qv)
Subjects: Belles Lettres
ISBN Publisher's Prefix: 3-600

Keysersche Verlagsbuchhandlung GmbH, Widenmayerstr 41, Postfach 243, D-8000 Munich 22 Tel: (089) 225055
Publishers: Christian Neumann, Hans Joachim Neumann; *Public Relations, Advertising;* Hanna Hutschenreiter
Subjects: Art, Reference
Founded: 1777
ISBN Publisher's Prefix: 3-87405

Kibu-Verlag GmbH, Gerhart-Hauptmann-Str 12a, D-5750 Menden 2 Tel: 02373 84588 Telex: 8202855
Dirs: Kunibert Birnkraut, Erhard Tamm
Subjects: Children's, Juveniles, Special Editions

Johannes **Kiefel** Verlag, Linderhauser Str 60, D-5600 Wuppertal 2 Tel: (0202) 642084/5 Cable Add: Kiefel, Wuppertal-2
Dir: Ingeborg Kiefel
Subjects: Religion, Juveniles, Textbooks
Founded: 1920
ISBN Publisher's Prefix: 3-7811

Friedrich **Kiehl** Verlag GmbH, Pfaustr 13, Postfach 210747, D-6700 Ludwigshafen
Tel: (0621) 695041/2 Telex: 0464810
Dir: Ernst-Otto Kleyboldt; *Sales Manager:* Regina König
Parent Company: Verlag Neue Wirtschafts-Briefe GmbH (qv)
Subjects: Law, Economics, Commerce, Banking
ISBN Publisher's Prefix: 3-470

Verlag **Kiepenheuer und Witsch**, Rondorfer Str 5, D-5000 Cologne-Marienburg
Tel: (0221) 380004 Cable Add: Kiepenbücher Cologne Telex: 8881142 kiwi
Man Dir: Dr Reinhold Neven Du Mont; *Editorial:* Bärbel Flad, Erika Stegmann, Renate Matthaei; *Sales:* Heinz Biehn; *Foreign Rights & Permissions:* Traudel Jansen
Subjects: General Fiction, Belles Lettres, Biography, History, Social Science
1981: 50 titles *Founded:* 1948
ISBN Publisher's Prefix: 3-462

Kilda Verlag*, Münsterstr 71, D-4402 Greven/Westfalen Tel: (0251) 36229 Cable Add: Kildagreven
Man Dir: Mr Pölking

Kindler Verlag GmbH*, Leopoldstr 54, Postfach 401043, D-8000 Munich 40 Tel: (089) 394041 Cable Add: Kindlerverlag Telex: 05215678
Editorial and Foreign Rights: Traut Felgentreff; *Sales:* Elke Gerhart
Orders to: VVA (Vereinigte Verlagsauslieferung GmbH), Postfach 7777, D-4830 Gütersloh 1
Associate Company: Lichtenberg Verlag GmbH (qv)
Subjects: General Fiction, Belles Lettres, Biography, History, How-to, Reference, Religion, Low- & High-priced Paperbacks, Medicine, Psychology, General & Social Science, Encyclopaedias, Educational Materials
Founded: 1951
ISBN Publisher's Prefix: 3-463

Klasing und Co GmbH, Siekerwall 21, Postfach 4809, D-4800 Bielefeld 1 Tel: (0521) 5590 Cable Add: Buchklasing Bielefeld Telex: 932934 Dekla
Publishers: Konrad-Wilhelm Delius, Kurt Delius; *Sales & Publicity Manager:* Wilhelm Meyerhenke; *Rights & Permissions:* Ilsemarie Steinbrinker
Parent Company: Delius, Klasing & Co (qv)
Subjects: Yachting, Motor Boats
Bookshop: At above address
ISBN Publisher's Prefix: 3-87412

Kunstverlag Dr Rudolf Georgi, Waldemar **Klein**, see Georgi

Klens-Verlag GmbH, Prinz-Georg-Str 44, Postfach 320620, D-4000 Düsseldorf 32 Tel: (0211) 480023
Publisher: Viktor Nolden
Subjects: Popular Christian Aids, Juveniles, and Youth Training
1981: 6 titles *1982:* 5 titles
ISBN Publisher's Prefix: 3-87309

Ernst **Klett** Verlag, Rotebühlstr 77, Postfach 809, D-7000 Stuttgart 1 Tel: (0711) 66720 Telex: 721715 klet d
Publisher: Michael Klett; *Publicity Manager:* Egon Schramm; *Foreign Relations:* Martin Veit; *Rights and Export Sales:* Joachim Lange
Associate Companies: Klett-Cotta Verlag (qv), Stuttgarter Verlagskontor, both in Federal Republic of Germany; ÖBV — Klett-Cotta Verlagsgesellschaft mbH, Austria; Verlag Klett und Balmer & Co, Switzerland (qv), Editôra Pedagogica é Universitaria Ltda, Praça D José Gaspar 106, 3ª sobreloja no 15, BR-01047 São Paulo SP, Brazil
Subjects: Textbooks and Educational Materials for all school subjects from Primary to College level, German as a foreign language, Pedagogics, Didactics
Miscellaneous: Company now also incorporates Verlag Helmut Küpper and Verlag J G Cotta'sche Buchhandlung works, which are published under the Klett-Cotta (qv) imprint. Klett is a member of TR-Verlagsunion GmbH (qv)
ISBN Publisher's Prefix: 3-12

Klett-Cotta Verlag, Rotebühlstr 77, Postfach 809, D-7000 Stuttgart 1 Tel: (0711) 66720 Telex: 721715 klet d
Man Dir: Michael Klett; *Editorial:* Dr Arbogast; *Foreign Relations:* Martin Veit; *Rights and Export Sales:* Joachim Lange
Associate Companies: Verlag Klett und Balmer & Co, Switzerland (qv); Ernst Klett (qv), Stuttgarter Verlags Kontor, both in Federal Republic of Germany; ÖBV — Klett-Cotta Verlagsgesellschaft mbH, Austria
Imprints: Hobbit Presse, Konzepte der Humanwissenschaften; see also Ernst Klett Verlag (Miscellaneous)
Subjects: Literature, Linguistics, Psychoanalysis, Psychotherapy, Psychology, Education, Philosophy, Mythology, Ecology, History, Politics, Sociology, the Arts
Founded: 1977
ISBN Publisher's Prefix: 3-12

Klinkhardt und Biermann Verlagsbuchhandlung GmbH+, Rosenheimer Str 12, D-8000 Munich 80 Tel: (089) 4487748
Manager: Heinz Friedrich Bläsing; *Trade Manager:* Norbert Jennen
Subjects: Art, Antiques, Numismatics
Founded: 1907
ISBN Publisher's Prefix: 3-7814

Erika **Klopp** Verlag GmbH, Kurfürstendamm 126, Postfach 310829, D-1000 Berlin 31 Tel: (030) 8911008
Publisher: Horst Meyer; *Rights & Permissions:* Katharina Janike
Subject: Juveniles
1982: 20 titles *1983:* 11 titles *Founded:* 1925
ISBN Publisher's Prefix: 3-7817

Vittorio **Klostermann** GmbH, Frauenlobstr 22, Postfach 900601, D-6000 Frankfurt am Main 90 Tel: (0611) 774011
Man Dirs: Michael Klostermann, Eckard Klostermann
Subjects: Philosophy, Bibliography, Romanistics, University Textbooks, General Science, History, Art, High-priced Paperbacks
Founded: 1930
ISBN Publisher's Prefix: 3-465

Ehrenfried **Klotz** Verlag, Theaterstr 13, Postfach 3753, D-3400 Göttingen Tel: (0551) 54031/3
Man Dir: Dr Arndt Ruprecht; *Sales:* Robert-Bosch-Breite
Subject: Religion
Parent Company: Vandenhoeck und Ruprecht (qv)
Founded: 1949
ISBN Publisher's Prefix: 3-525

Fritz **Knapp** Verlag GmbH*, Neue Mainzer Str 60, Postfach 111151, D-6000 Frankfurt am Main 11 Tel: (0611) 280151 Cable Add: Schauinsland Telex: 411397
Man Dirs: Alfons Binz, Peter Muthesius; *Editorial:* Peter Muthesius; *Sales, Publicity:* Werner Scholz; *Production, Rights & Permissions:* Alfons Binz
Associate Company: Verlag Helmut Richardi GmbH
Subjects: Money, Banking, Stock Exchange, Economics, Economic Science, Reference, High-priced Paperbacks, Specialist Dictionaries, German Law in English/French Translation
Founded: 1935
ISBN Publisher's Prefix: 3-7819

Wilhelm **Knapp** Verlag*, Pressehaus am Martin-Luther-Platz, Postfach 1122, D-4000 Düsseldorf 1 Tel: (0211) 885608
Man Dirs: Dr Max Nitsche, Dr Joseph Schaffrath, Werner Gutzki; *Publishing Dir:* Dr Manfred Lotsch; *Production, Promotion:* Helmut Schwanen
Parent Company: Droste Verlag GmbH (qv)
Subjects: Photography, Cinematography
Founded: 1838
ISBN Publisher's Prefix: 3-87420

Droemer **Knaur** Verlag, see Droemersche Verlagsanstalt

Albrecht **Knaus** Verlag, Postfach 520455, D-2000 Hamburg 52 (Located at: Beselerstr 2) Tel: (040) 897401 Cable Add: knausbooks Hamburg
Man Dir: Dr Albrecht Knaus; *Production:* Wolfgang Mudrak; *Sales:* Verlagsgruppe Bertelsmann GmbH (qv)
Orders to: VVA (Vereinigte Verlagsauslieferung GmbH), Postfach 7777, D-4830 Gütersloh 1
Parent Company: Verlagsgruppe Bertelsmann GmbH (qv)
Subjects: Fiction and Non-fiction: Memoirs, History, Politics
Founded: 1978
ISBN Publisher's Prefix: 3-8135

Verlag Josef **Knecht**-Carolusdruckerei GmbH, Liebfrauenberg 37, D-6000 Frankfurt am Main 1 Tel: (0611) 281767
Dir: Dr H Herder; *Editorial:* Dr Marianne Regnier
Subjects: General Fiction, Paperbacks, Religion, Social Science, Philosophy, Non-fiction
Founded: 1946
ISBN Publisher's Prefix: 3-7820

Knorr und Hirth Verlag GmbH, D-3167 Ahrbeck vor Hanover Tel: (05136) 5501 Cable Add: Knorrhirth Ahrbeck
Man Dir: Berthold Fricke
Subjects: Art, Geography, Travel Guides, Almanacs; Editions also in English, French, Dutch, Italian, Spanish and Japanese; Several Bilingual Editions
Founded: 1894
ISBN Publisher's Prefix: 3-7821

Verlagsanstalt Alexander **Koch** GmbH*, Postfach 3081, D-7000 Stuttgart 1 (Located at: Fasanenweg 18, D-7022 Leinfelden-Echterdingen 1) Tel: (0711) 79891 Telex: 7-255609 drw d
Man Dirs: Karl-Heinz Weinbrenner, L Drabarczyk; *Manager, Rights & Permissions:* Dr Erwin Schmid; *Editorial:* Max Fengler, Eberhard Höhn, Werner Rosskopf, Rolf Sellin
Parent Company: DRW-Verlag Weinbrenner KG (qv)
Subjects: Architecture, Interior Decoration, Building Technology; Periodicals
Founded: 1890
ISBN Publisher's Prefix: 3-87422

C A **Koch's** Verlag Nachfolger, see Deutsche Buch-Gemeinschaft

K F **Koehler** Verlag, Postfach 210, D-7000 Stuttgart 80 (Located at: Schockenriedstr 37) Tel: (0711) 78601 Telex: 7255684 knov d
Dir: Till Grupp
Subjects: Humanities, History, Politics, Law, Social Science, Geography
Founded: 1789
ISBN Publisher's Prefix: 3-87425

Koehlers Verlagsgesellschaft+, Steintorwall 17, Postfach 2352, D-4900 Herford Tel: (05221) 50001 Cable Add: Koehlers Vlg Herford/Westf Telex: 0934801 maxvg d
Publishers: Dr Kurt Schober, Gerhard Bollmann, Hans-Focko Koehler; *Sales:* Hans-Focko Koehler; *Publicity:* Gerhard Mindt
Associate Companies: Maximilian-Verlag, E S Mittler und Sohn GmbH, Verlag Offene Worte (all members of Maximilian-Verlagsgruppe — qv)
Subjects: Fiction and Non-fiction, Shipping, Shipbuilding, Maritime and Offshore interest, Contemporary maritime history, Periodicals
ISBN Publisher's Prefix: 3-7822

Verlag Valentin **Koerner** GmbH, Hermann-Sielcken-Str 36, Postfach 304, D-7570 Baden Baden Tel: (07221) 22423
Publisher: Valentin Koerner
1981: 48 titles
ISBN Publisher's Prefix: 3-87320

Unternehmensgruppe Verlag W **Kohlhammer** GmbH+, Hessbrühlstr 69, Postfach 800430, D-7000 Stuttgart 80 Tel: (0711) 78631 Cable Add: Kohlhammer Stuttgart Telex: 07255820

FEDERAL REPUBLIC OF GERMANY 145

Man Dirs: Dr Jürgen Gutbrod, Günter Haberland, Hans-Joachim Nagel; *Sales Dir:* Gerd W Ludwig; *Rights & Permissions:* Dr Alexander Schweickert
Subsidiary Companies: Deutscher Gemeindeverlag GmbH (qv); Grote'sche Verlagsbuch-handlung KG (qv); Kohlhammer und Wallishauser GmbH, Hechingen; W Kohlhammer Druckerei GmbH & Co, Stuttgart
Branch Offs: Berlin, Cologne, Mainz
Subjects: History, Art, Philosophy, Humanities, Religion, Law, Public Administration, Linguistics, Literary History, Economics, Natural Sciences, Medicine, Engineering, Electronics, Architecture, Travel
1981: 400 titles *1982:* approx 400 titles
Founded: 1866
ISBN Publisher's Prefix: 3-17

Kohl's Technischer Verlag Erwin Kohl GmbH & Co KG, Emil-Sulzbach-Str 12, Postfach 970115, D-6000 Frankfurt am Main 97 Tel: (0611) 778410 and 776513
Associate Company: Frankfurter Fachverlag Michael Kohl GmbH & Co KG (qv)
Subjects: Civil & Mechanical Engineering
ISBN Publisher's Prefix: 3-87430

Kolibri-Verlag, Else-Lasker-Schüler-Str 47-49, D-5600 Wuppertal 1 Tel: (0202) 443143
Dir: Maria Pfriem; *Sales:* Karin Bambek
Associate Company: Engelbert Pfrim Verlag (at above address)
Subjects: Children's Fiction and Non-fiction
Founded: 1950
ISBN Publisher's Prefix: 3-87434

Komar*, Oberaustr 1, Postfach 1132, D-8200 Rosenheim Tel: (08031) 17011 Telex: 0525793
Subjects: Juveniles, Psychology, Sports

Verlag **Kommentator**, Zeppelinallee 43, Postfach 970148, D-6000 Frankfurt am Main Tel: (0611) 774055
Man Dir: Dr Clemens J B Sandmann; *Editorial:* Gunter Herz; *Sales, Publicity:* Ernst F Grundl
Associate Company: Alfred Metzner (qv)
Subject: Law, Taxation
Miscellaneous: Firm is a member of the Kluwer Group, Netherlands (qv)
ISBN Publisher's Prefix: 3-7824

Verlag **Königshausen und Neumann**, Leistenstr 3, Postfach 6007, D-8700 Würzburg Tel: (0931) 76401
Man Dirs: Dr Johannes Königshausen, Dr Thomas Neumann
Subjects: Philosophy, Literary Science, Pedagogy, Sociology, Psychology, Economics, Archaeology, Law
1981: 18 titles *1982:* 25 titles *Founded:* 1979
ISBN Publisher's Prefix: 3-88479

Konkordia GmbH für Druck und Verlag, Eisenbahnstr 31-33, Postfach 1240, D-7580 Bühl/Baden Tel: (07223) 23201 Telex: 78733
Subject: Textbooks
ISBN Publisher's Prefix: 3-7826

Anton H **Konrad** Verlag*, Schulstr 5, Postfach 1206, D-7912 Weissenhorn Tel: (07309) 2657
Subjects: Arts, History
ISBN Publisher's Prefix: 3-87437

Konzepte der Humanwissenschaften, an imprint of Klett-Cotta Verlag (qv)

Konzert Verlag, see G Kowalski

Kösel-Verlag GmbH & Co, Flüggenstr 2, D-8000 Munich 19 Tel: (089) 175077 Cable Add: Köselverlag Munich Telex: 5215492 kvmud
Man Dir: Dr Christoph Wild; *Production:* Friedhelm Jochems; *Sales:* Dieter Amman; *Rights & Permissions:* Ingrid Fink; *Advertising & Public Relations:* Gudrun Loesel
Orders to: Flugplatzstr 1, D-8031 Gilching Tel: (08105) 9014 Telex: 524199 kvgid
Subjects: Pedagogy, Philosophy, Religion, Educational Materials, Psychology, Textbooks, Social Science
1981: 104 titles *Founded:* 1593
Miscellaneous: Firm is member of TR-Verlagsunion GmbH (qv)
ISBN Publisher's Prefix: 3-466

G **Kowalski** Konzert Verlag, Ringstr 105, D-1000 Berlin 45 Tel: (030) 8333337
Man Dir, Rights & Permissions: Gerhard Kowalski
Subjects: Music, Leisure Activities, Jazz, Theatre, Biography
Founded: 1974
Miscellaneous: Company also runs a Literary Agency (qv under Kowalski)
ISBN Publisher's Prefix: 3-921793

Karin **Kramer Verlag**, Postfach 440106, D-1000 Berlin-Neukölln 44 (Located at: Braunschweiger Str 26) Tel: (030) 6845055/6842598
Editorial and Publicity: Bernd Kramer
Subjects: Politics, Art, Literature, Education, Psychology, Anarchist Literature
Founded: 1970
ISBN Publisher's Prefix: 3-87956

Karl **Krämer Verlag GmbH** und Co, Schulze-Delitzsch-Str 15, Postfach 800650, D-7000 Stuttgart 80 Tel: (0711) 610700 Cable Add: Fachbuchkraemer Stuttgart
Man Dir, Rights & Permissions: Karl H Krämer; *Sales Dir:* Bernhard Prokop; *Production:* Horst Luckhaupt; *Publicity:* Gudrun Zimmerle
Orders to: Rotebühlstr 40, Postfach 808, D-7000 Stuttgart 1
Associate Company: Verlag Karl Krämer & Co, Switzerland (qv)
Subjects: Town Planning, Architecture, Building Construction, Sociology
Bookshop: Fachbuchhandlung Karl Krämer, Rotebühlstr 40, Postfach 808, D-7000 Stuttgart 1
1981: 13 titles *Founded:* 1930
ISBN Publisher's Prefix: 3-7828

Dr Waldemar **Kramer Verlagsbuchhandlung**+, Bornheimer Landwehr 57a, Postfach 600445, D-6000 Frankfurt am Main Tel: (0611) 449045
Publishers: Waldemar Kramer, Henriette Kramer
Subjects: Science and Natural History, Biology, History, Art Education, Psychology, Geography, Nature Study, Environment; Publications of the Senckenberg Nature Study Association; Periodicals
1981: 24 titles *1982:* 15 titles *Founded:* 1939
ISBN Publisher's Prefix: 3-7829

Vereinigte Fachverlage **Krausskopf** Ingenieur Digest GmbH*, Lessingstr 12, Postfach 2760, D-6500 Mainz Tel: (06131) 674041 Cable Add: Krausskopfverlag
Dirs: Hans Hauck, Peter M Fock
Parent Company: Elsevier-NDU nv, Netherlands (qv)
Subjects: Technical Books, Periodicals
Founded: 1937
ISBN Publisher's Prefix: 3-7830

Buch- und Bildverlag W **Kremnitz**, see Lacus

Kreuz Verlag, Breitwiesenstr 30, Postfach 800669, D-7000 Stuttgart 80 Tel: (0711) 7800281
Man Dir: Dieter Breitsohl; *Editor:* Helmut Weigel, Hildegunde Wöller; *Rights & Permissions:* Barbara Dressler; *Production:* Brigitte Gnieser; *Publicity:* Christa Altmann
Subsidiary Company: Feuerseebuchhandlung (at above address)
Subjects: Reference, Religion, Education, Juveniles, Psychology, Social Science, Periodicals
1982: 33 titles *1983:* 30 titles *Founded:* 1945
ISBN Publisher's Prefix: 3-7831

Kriminalistik Verlag GmbH, Postfach 102640, D-6900 Heidelberg (Located at: im Weiher 10) Tel: (06621) 498250 Telex: 04-61727 huedh
Associate Companies: R V Decker's Verlag G Schenck GmbH (qv); C F Müller Jüristischer Verlag GmbH (qv)
Subject: Criminology

Alfred **Kröner** Verlag, Reinsburgstr 56, Postfach 1109, D-7000 Stuttgart 1 Tel: (0711) 620221
Man Dirs: Arno Klemm, Walter Kohrs
Subjects: Philosophy, Religion, Culture, Psychology, Pedagogy, Sociology, Economics, Law, Politics, History, Literature, Art, Music, Theatre, Reference (especially Dictionaries, Lexicons)
Founded: 1904
ISBN Publisher's Prefix: 3-520

Buch und Werbung-Helmut **Krüger** GmbH*, Kurfürstendamm 65, D-1000 Berlin 15 Tel: (030) 8827058 Telex: 182993 agent d
Man Dir: Helmut Krüger
Subjects: Art, Photography
Founded: 1974

Wolfgang **Kruger** Verlag*, Geleitsstrasse 25, Postfach 700480, D-6000 Frankfurt am Main 70 Tel: (0611) 60621 Cable Add: buchfischer Telex: 0412410
Man Dirs: Monika Schoeller, Karl-Michael Mehnert; *Sales, Publicity:* Ulrich Fritz, Frank Schiffter; *Production:* Wilfried Meiner
Parent Company: S Fischer Verlag GmbH (qv)
Subjects: General Fiction and Non-fiction
ISBN Publisher's Prefix: 3-8105

Kübler Verlag Michael Akselrad, Hauptstr 156, D-6900 Heidelberg Tel: (06221) 29874
Dir: Michael Akselrad
Orders to: VVA (Vereinigte Verlagsauslieferung GmbH), Postfach 7777, D-4830 Gütersloh 1
Subjects: Social Studies, Politics, Literature
1982: 3 titles *1983:* 5 titles *Founded:* 1972
ISBN Publisher's Prefix: 3-921265

Kubon und Sagner, see Verlag Otto Sagner

Wilhelm **Kumm** Verlag, Tulpenhofstr 45, D-6050 Offenbach am Main Tel: (0611) 884349 Cable Add: Kummverlag
Proprietor, Man Dir: Wilhelm Kumm
Subjects: Belles Lettres, Poetry
Founded: 1967
ISBN Publisher's Prefix: 3-7836

Kümmerley und Frey, see J Fink — Kummerley und Frey

Kunst und Wissen Erich Bieber OHG, Wilhelmstr 4, Postfach 46, D-7000 Stuttgart 1, Tel: (0711) 241152 Cable Add: Kunstwissen Telex: 721929
Publishers: Erich, Jürgen and Wolfgang Bieber
Subjects: Technical Textbooks
ISBN Publisher's Prefix: 3-87953

Kunst und Wohnen Verlag, see Dr Wolfgang Schwarze Verlag

Deutscher Verlag für **Kunstwissenschaft**, see Deutscher Verlag

Florian **Kupferberg** Verlag, Postfach 2680, D-6500 Mainz Tel: (06131) 224977
Owner: Christian A Kupferberg
Subjects: Art, Architecture, Cultural &

Literary History, Mass Media
Founded: 1797/1938
ISBN Publisher's Prefix: 3-7837

Verlag Helmut **Küpper**, now incorporated in Ernst Klett Verlag (qv)

Kyrios-Verlag GmbH, Luckengasse 8, Postfach 1740, D-8050 Freising Tel: (08161) 5527
Dir: Ursula Blum; *Sales Manager:* Eveline Kamm
Subjects: Religion, Social Work, Periodicals
Founded: 1916
ISBN Publisher's Prefix: 3-7838

L N-Verlag Lübeck, Lübecker Nachrichten GmbH+, Königstr 53-57, Postfach 2238, D-2400 Lübeck 1 Tel: (0451) 1441 Telex: 026801
Man Dir: Charles Coleman; *Sales Dir:* Elmar Bruns
Subjects: Series of guidebooks and illustrated volumes on various countries world-wide, and areas of Germany
1982: 5 titles *1983:* 5 titles
ISBN Publisher's Prefix: 3-87498

Ambro **Lacus**, Buch- und Bildverlag W Kremnitz*, Frieding-Hurten-Str 25, D-8138 Andechs Tel: (08152) 1332 Cable Add: Kremnitz-Frieding
Man Dir: Ing Walter Kremnitz
Subjects: Illustrated foreign travel books, Folk Stories and Legends, Legal and Historical Reference, Botany
Founded: 1974
ISBN Publisher's Prefix: 3-921445

Laetare, see Burckhardthaus-Laetare Verlag GmbH

Lahn-Verlag*, Wiesbadener Str 1, Postfach 140, D-6250 Limburg an der Lahn 1 Tel: (06431) 401211 Telex: 0484764 palan d
Publisher: Engelbert Tauscher; *Editorial:* Ursula Mock; *Publicity Manager:* Raimund Zoellner
Subjects: Religion, Philosophy, Education
Founded: 1900
ISBN Publisher's Prefix: 3-7840

Lambertus Verlag GmbH, Wölflinstr 4, Postfach 1026, D-7800 Freiburg im Breisgau Tel: (0761) 31566
Man Dirs: Dr Lioba Knöbber, Gerhild Neugart
Subjects: Social Work (Community and Case Work etc, with youth, the old and disabled), Social Security
Bookshop: Freiburger Bücherdienst (at above address)
1981: 20 titles *1982:* 20 titles *Founded:* 1898
ISBN Publisher's Prefix: 3-7841

Lamuv Verlag GmbH, Martin Str 7, D-5303 Bornheim 3 Tel: (02227) 2111
Man Dir, Rights & Permissions: René Böll; *Editorial:* Karl-Klaus Rabe; *Sales:* Peter Flier; *Publicity:* Michael Lücher Bach
Subjects: Literature, Third World, Near East, Politics
1981: 13 titles *1982:* 18 titles *Founded:* 1976
ISBN Publisher's Prefixes: 3-921521, 3-88977

Landbuch-Verlag GmbH, Kabelkamp 6, Postfach 160, D-3000 Hanover Tel: (0511) 632006 Cable Add: Landbuch Hanover Telex: 921169
Man Dir, Production, Rights & Permissions: Friedrich Butenholz; *Sales, Publicity:* Willi Ludwig Kröck
Subjects: Arts, Agriculture, Animal Breeding, Forestry, Sports, Nature, Hunting, Wildlife; Periodicals
Founded: 1945
ISBN Publisher's Prefix: 3-7842

Landsberger Verlagsanstalt Martin Neumeyer*, Museumstr 14, Postfach 104, D-8910 Landsberg Tel: (08191) 4055
Subjects: History, Hobbies, Mass Media, the Art of Living, How-To, Regional Interest
ISBN Publisher's Prefix: 3-920216

Verlag Peter **Lang** GmbH*, Hinter den Ulmen 19, D-6000 Frankfurt am Main Tel: (0611) 520088 Telex: 4189343 lang d
Man Dir: Rainer Jurischka
Parent Company: Verlag Peter Lang AG, Switzerland (qv)
Subjects: Arts, Sciences
ISBN Publisher's Prefix: 3-8204

Albert **Langen**-Georg Müller Verlag, Hubertusstr 4, D-8000 Munich 19 Tel: (089) 177041 Telex: 05215045
Man Dir: Dr Herbert Fleissner; *Editorial:* Dr Bernhard Struckmeyer; *Sales:* Gisela Weichert; *Publicity:* Dr Brigitte Sinhuber; *Rights & Permissions:* Renate Werner
Subjects: General Fiction, Theatre, Reportage, Humour, Current Controversy
Founded: 1897
Miscellaneous: Firm is a member of the Verlagsgruppe Langen-Müller/Herbig (qv)
ISBN Publisher's Prefix: 3-7844

Verlagsgruppe **Langen-Müller**/Herbig, Hubertusstr 4, D-8000 Munich 19 Tel: (089) 177041 Telex: 05215045
Man Dir: Dr Herbert Fleissner
Members of the Group: Bechtle Verlag (qv); Mary Hahn's Kochbuchverlag (qv); F A Herbig Verlagsbuchhandlung (qv); Albert Langen-Georg Müller Verlag (qv); Georg Lentz Verlag (qv); Limes Verlag (qv); Nymphenburger Verlagshandlung (qv); Universitas Verlag (qv); Wirtschaftsverlag (qv) (all in Federal Republic of Germany); Amalthea-Verlag, Austria (qv)

Langenscheidt KG, Neusser Str 3, Postfach 401120, D-8000 Munich 40 Tel: (089) 3830 Cable Add: Langenscheidt Munich Telex: Munich 5215379 lkgm d (also at An der Langenscheidtbrücke, D-1000 Berlin 62)
Man Dirs: Karl Ernst Tielebier-Langenscheidt; *Editorial:* Dr Knut Mohr, Dr Walter Voigt, Dr Wolfgang Wieter, Dr Heinz F Wendt; *Production:* Helmut Wahl; *Sales Dir:* Peter Haering; *Advertising Dir:* Dieter Krause; *Export Dir:* Uwe Cordts; *Rights & Permissions:* Manfred Überall
Subsidiary Companies: Langenscheidt-Verlag GmbH, Austria (qv); Langenscheidt AG, Switzerland (qv); Langenscheidt Publishers Inc, New York, NY 11378, USA
Subjects: Foreign Languages, German for Foreigners; Dictionaries, Textbooks, Audio-Visual Materials
1981: 50 titles *1982:* 43 titles *Founded:* 1856
Miscellaneous: Firm is a member of the Langenscheidt Group and a member of TR- Verlagsunion GmbH (qqv for associate companies)
ISBN Publisher's Prefix: 3-468

The **Langenscheidt Group**, Neusser Str 3, Postfach 401120, D-8000 Munich 40 Tel: (089) 3830
The Group consists of: Langenscheidt KG (qv); Langenscheidt-Longman GmbH (qv); Langenscheidt-Hachette GmbH (qv); Polyglott-Verlag Dr Bolte KG (qv); Humboldt-Taschenbuchverlag Jacobi KG (qv); Mentor-Verlag Dr Ramdohr KG (qv); Axel Juncker-Verlag Jacobi KG (qv)

Langenscheidt-Hachette GmbH, Neusser Str 3, Postfach 401120, D-8000 Munich 40 Tel: (089) 3830 Cable Add: Langenscheidt Munich Telex: 5215379 lkgm d
Man Dirs: Karl Ernst Tielebier-Langenscheidt, Marc Moingeon; *Editorial:* Brigitte Peters; *Sales & Promotion:* Through Langenscheidt KG (qv)

Associate Companies: See entry for The Langenscheidt Group, also for Hachette SA, France
Subjects: French (Language Teaching) for German-speaking people
1981: 40 titles *1982:* approx 30 titles
Founded: 1977
Miscellaneous: Firm is a member of the Langenscheidt Group (qv)
ISBN Publisher's Prefix: 3-595

Langenscheidt-Longman GmbH, Neusser Str 3, Postfach 401120, D-8000 Munich 40 Tel: (089) 3830 Cable Add: Langenscheidt Munich Telex: 5215379 lkgm d
Man Dirs: Karl Ernst Tielebier-Langenscheidt, Paula Kahn; *Publishing Executive:* Uwe Mäder; *Sales & Promotion:* through Langenscheidt KG (qv)
Associate Companies: See entry for The Langenscheidt Group, also for the Longman Group, UK
Subjects: English Language Teaching
1981: 50 titles *1982:* 50 titles *Founded:* 1972
Miscellaneous: Firm is a member of the Langenscheidt Group (qv)
ISBN Publisher's Prefix: 3-526

Karl Robert **Langewiesche** Nachfolger Hans Koester KG, Grüner Weg 6, Postfach 1327, D-6240 Königstein 1 Tel: (06174) 7333 Cable Add: Langewiesche Königsteintaunus
Man Dir, Production, Sales and Publicity, Rights & Permissions: Hans-Curt Koester; *Editorial:* Hans Koester, Hans-Curt Koester
Subjects: Art, History, How-to, Music, University Textbooks, Architecture
1982: 16 titles *Founded:* 1902
ISBN Publisher's Prefix: 03-7845

Verlag **Langewiesche-Brandt** KG*, Lechnerstr 27, D-8026 Ebenhausen bei Munich Tel: (08178) 4857
Man Dir: Kristof Wachinger
Subjects: Belles Lettres, Art Books, Autobiographical, Poetry, Quality Paperbacks, Posters
Founded: 1906
ISBN Publisher's Prefix: 3-7846

Verlag **Laterna Magica** Joachim F Richter*, Stridbeckstr 48, D-8000 Munich 71 Tel: (089) 797091/4 Telex: 05-22425 color d
Publisher: Joachim F Richter; *Sales, Publicity, Production:* W Panckow
Subjects: Photography, Periodicals
Founded: 1966
ISBN Publisher's Prefix: 3-87467

August **Lax**, Postfach, Weinberg 56, D-3200 Hildesheim Tel: (05121) 38013/38014
Man Dir, Editorial, Rights & Permissions: Lorenz Lax; *Sales:* D Lax
Associate Company: Filmsatz Gesellschaft (at above address)
Subjects: Archaeology, History, Pre-history, Folklore, Art History, Literature (Prose, Poetry, Dialect), Lower Saxony Historical
Bookshop: Buchhandlung August Lax, Annenstr 36, D-3200 Hildesheim
Founded: 1849
ISBN Publisher's Prefix: 3-7848

Verlag Hermann **Leins**, see Rainer Wunderlich Verlag Hermann Leins

Leitfadenverlag Dieter Sudholt*, D-8131 Berg 3 (Assenhausen) Tel: (08151) 5342
Publisher: Volker Sudholt
Subjects: Tax Directories, Business, Law, Economics
ISBN Publisher's Prefix: 3-543

Verlag Otto **Lembeck**, Leerbachstr 42, D-6000 Frankfurt am Main 1 Tel: (06171) 53708 Cable Add: Lembeckdruck Frankfurtmain
Subject: Religion, Ecumenical Studies, Africa
Founded: 1945
ISBN Publisher's Prefix: 3-87476

FEDERAL REPUBLIC OF GERMANY 147

Verlag Lambert **Lensing** GmbH,
Kampstr 42, Postfach 875, D-4600
Dortmund 1 Tel: (0231) 147008 Cable
Add: Lensingbuch Telex: 0822106
Man Dir: F C Lorson; *Editorial:* Dr Werner
Jaeger; *Sales and Publicity:* R Rewald;
Production: G Marx
Subjects: Modern Languages, Modern
Language Teaching, Educational Materials
Bookshop: Westenhellweg 86-88, Postfach
875, D-4600 Dortmund 1
Founded: 1870
ISBN Publisher's Prefix: 3-559

Georg **Lentz** Verlag, Romanstr 16, D-8000
Munich 19 Tel: (089) 162051
Man Dir, Sales: Ingeborg Castell
Subjects: Fiction and Non-fiction for
Juveniles
Miscellaneous: Firm is a member of
Verlagsgruppe Langen-Müller/Herbig (qv)
ISBN Publisher's Prefix: 3-88010

Leske Verlag und Budrich GmbH*,
Fürstenbergstr 23, Postfach 300406, D-5090
Leverkusen 3 Tel: (02171) 45525
Man Dir: Edmund Budrich
Subjects: Social Science, Sexology, Middle
East, University, Secondary and Primary
Textbooks, Educational Materials
Founded: 1974
ISBN Publisher's Prefix: 3-8100

Leuchter-Verlag EG*, Industriestr 6-8,
Postfach 1161, D-6106 Erzhausen
Tel: (06150) 7565
Man & Sales Dir: Karl-Heinz Neumann
Subjects: Religion, Low-priced Paperbacks
Founded: 1946

Lexika-Verlag*, Chris Hablitzel,
Forchenrain 11, D-7252 Weil der Stadt 5
Tel: (07033) 41077 Cable Add: fhwd Telex:
7265883 fhw d
Publisher, Man Dir: Chris Hablitzel
Subjects: Study and Career Guidance,
Further and Adult Education, New learning
techniques, Bookselling aids
ISBN Publisher's Prefix: 3-920353

Lexikothek Verlag GmbH+, Carl-
Bertelsmann-Str 270 D-4830 Gütersloh 1
Tel: (05241) 801 Telex: 933646
Dirs: Dr Günter Hadding, Werner Lenz
Parent Company: Verlagsgruppe
Bertelsmann GmbH (qv for associate
companies)
Subjects: Encyclopaedias, Dictionaries and
other Reference Works

Liber Verlag GmbH, Hegelstr 45, Postfach
2946, D-6500 Mainz 1
Man Dir, Editorial: Tomo Matasić;
Production, Publicity: Renate Ammersbach
Subjects: Literature, Literary Criticism,
Linguistics, Foreign Language Teaching,
Theses on Slavistics, History, Politics
1982: 6 titles *1983:* 6 titles *Founded:* 1977
ISBN Publisher's Prefix: 3-83111

Lichtenberg Verlag GmbH*, Leopoldstr 54,
Postfach 401043, D-8000 Munich 40
Tel: (089) 394041 Cable Add:
Lichtenbergverlag Telex: 05215678
Dirs: Peter Nikel, Klaus Jost; *Publicity:*
Ingrid Ulrich
Orders to: VVA (Vereinigte
Verlagsauslieferung GmbH), Postfach 7777,
D-4830 Gütersloh 1
Associate Company: Kindler Verlag GmbH
(qv)
Subjects: General Fiction and Non-fiction,
Belles Lettres, Practical Guides, Humour
Founded: 1962
ISBN Publisher's Prefix: 3-7852

Edition **Lichterfelde**, an imprint of Abakon
Verlagsgesellschaft mbH (qv)

Verlag der **Liebenzeller** Mission,
Liobastr 21, Postfach 1265, D-7263 Bad
Liebenzell 1 Tel: (07052) 17131
Publisher: Arthur Klenk
Subjects: Mission Reports, Theology,
Methodology, also Fiction, Biographies and
Devotional
Founded: 1906
Miscellaneous: Member of the Telos (qv)
paperback series publishing group
ISBN Publisher's Prefix: 3-88002

Rudolf **Liebing**, see Physica-Verlag

Edition/Galerie **Lietzow**, Knesebeckstr 32,
D-1000 Berlin 12 Tel: (030) 8812895
Man Dir: Karl-Horst Hartmann
Subjects: Biography, Art, Reference
1982: 5 titles *Founded:* 1970

Life Sciences Research Reports, an imprint
of Abakon Verlagsgesellschaft mbH (qv)

Limes Verlag, Romanstr 16, D-8000
Munich 19 Tel: (089) 162051
Man Dir: Marguerite Schlüter; *Sales:*
Ingeborg Castell
Subjects: General Fiction, Belles Lettres,
Poetry, History, Music, Art
Founded: 1945
Miscellaneous: Firm is a member of
Verlagsgruppe Langen-Müller/Herbig (qv)
ISBN Publisher's Prefix: 3-8090

Limpert Verlag, Ferdinandstr 18,
Postfach 1951, D-6380 Bad Homburg
vdH 1 Tel: (06172) 6038 Telex: 0418135
limp
Man Dir, Rights & Permissions: Hermann
Farnung; *Sales, Publicity:* Ruprecht Sickel
Subject: Sport and Recreation
Founded: 1921

Lingen Verlag*, Marienburger Str 17,
Postfach 510729, D-5000 Cologne
Tel: (0221) 380066 Telex: 8882138
Man Dir: Helmut Lingen
Subjects: Atlases, Language, Cookery,
Popular Non-fiction

Paul **List** Verlag KG, Goethestr 43, D-8000
Munich 2 Tel: (089) 51480 Telex: 0522405
Man Dir, Rights & Permissions: Dr Dieter
Lutz; *Editorial:* Dr Hansjörg Graf; *Sales:*
Rose Bakes; *Publicity:* Ulrike Ramsauer;
Advertising: Michael Schindler
Associate Companies: Südwest Verlag
GmbH & Co KG (qv); Süddeutscher Verlag
Buchverlag (qv)
Subjects: General Fiction, Belles Lettres,
Poetry, Biography, History, Music, Art,
Philosophy, Reference, Religion,
Psychology, General & Social Science,
Secondary & Primary Textbooks
1982: 23 titles *Founded:* 1894
Miscellaneous: Firm is member of TR-
Verlagsunion GmbH (qv)
ISBN Publisher's Prefix: 3-471

Henry **Litolff's** Verlag, an imprint of
C F Peters Musikverlag GmbH & Co KG
(qv)

von **Loeper** Verlag GmbH, Kiefernweg 13,
Postfach 311205, D-7500 Karlsruhe 31 Tel:
(0721) 374043
Man Dir, Editorial, Rights & Permissions:
Dankwart von Loeper; *Sales:* Birgit Mall;
Publicity: Barbara Lippik
Subjects: Modern Literature, Gift Books,
Poetry, Indian Foreign Language Texts
Bookshops: Buchhandlung von Loeper,
Bärenweg 35, D-7500 Karlsruhe 31;
Universitätsbuchhandlung von Loeper,
Kaiserstr 69, D-7500 Karlsruhe 1
1981: 12 titles *Founded:* 1979
ISBN Publisher's Prefix: 3-88652

Loewes Verlag KG, Bahnhofstr 15, Postfach
2606, D-8580 Bayreuth Tel: (0921) 21031
Cable Add: Loewesverlag Bayreuth

Telex: 642771
Man Dir: Volker Gondrom; *Editorial:* Ingrid
Hammerstädt; *Publicity, Sales Dir, Rights &
Permissions:* Werner Skambraks
Subject: Juveniles
Founded: 1863
ISBN Publisher's Prefix: 3-7855

Lorber-Verlag, Hindenburgstr 3, Postfach
229, D-7120 Bietigheim Tel: (07142) 41081
Cable Add: Lorber, Bietigheim
Associate Company: Turm-Verlag (qv)
Subject: Religion
ISBN Publisher's Prefix: 3-87495

Lorch-Verlag GmbH, Schumannstr 27,
Postfach 2625, D-6000 Frankfurt am Main
Tel: (0611) 7433448/9 Telex: 0411862
Man Dirs: Eva Lorch, Klaus Kottmeier,
Peter Russ; *Publishing Manager:* Frank
Sellien
Parent Company: Deutscher Fachverlag (at
above address)
Associate Companies: Spohr-Verlag, Eder-
Verlag
Subjects: Handbooks, Trade Books (textiles,
meat processing), Management, Specialized
Law
Founded: 1950
ISBN Publisher's Prefix: 3-87496

R **Löwit** GmbH, see Vollmer/Löwit
Verlagsgruppe

Gustav **Lübbe** Verlag GmbH*,
Scheidtbachstr 29-31, Postfach 200127,
D-5060 Bergisch Gladbach 2 Tel: (02202)
1211 Telex: 887922
Man Dir: Dr G Deschner; *Manager, Rights
& Permissions:* Dr J Köhler; *Editorial:* A
Kleinlein; *Sales:* Hans-Jochen Mundt;
Advertising Dir: Lotte Becker-Voss; *Press
and Publicity:* Irmgard Sellmann
Associate Company: Bastei-Verlag Gustav
Lübbe (qv)
Subjects: General Fiction and Non-fiction,
Biographies, Illustrated books on
Archaeology, History, Current Affairs
1981: 25 titles *Founded:* 1964
ISBN Publisher's Prefix: 3-7857

Hermann **Luchterhand** Verlag GmbH & Co
KG, Neuwied und Darmstadt+,
Zweigniederlassung Darmstadt,
Donnersbergring 18a, Postfach 4250, D-6100
Darmstadt Tel: (06151) 33521 Telex:
0419310 Dvg
Man Dir: Dr Hans Altenhein; *Rights &
Permissions:* Hannelore Kirchem
Orders to: Hermann Luchterhand Verlag,
Postfach 1780, D-5450 Neuwied 1
Parent Company: Hermann Luchterhand
Verlag, Heddesdorfer Str 31, Postfach 1780,
D-5450 Neuwied
Imprint: Sammlung Luchterhand
Subjects: Fiction, Non-fiction
1981: 65 titles *Founded:* 1924
ISBN Publisher's Prefix: 3-472

W **Ludwig** Verlag*, Türltorstr 14, Postfach
86, D-8068 Pfaffenhofen/Ilm 1 Tel: (08441)
5051/5052 Telex: 55540
Man Dir: Wilhelm Ludwig; *Editorial, Rights
& Permissions:* Ernst Krammer-Keck; *Sales:*
Elfriede Bauer; *Production:* Siegfried Rist;
Publicity: Angelika Ludwig
Subsidiary Company: Afrika Verlag
Subjects: Popular Science, Current Affairs,
Belles Lettres, Poetry, History
1981: 27 titles *Founded:* 1950
ISBN Publisher's Prefix: 3-7787

Luther-Verlag GmbH*, Postfach 5660,
D-4800 Bielefeld 1 Tel: (0521) 44861 Telex:
0937325 epdbid
Dir: Dr Gerhard E Stoll
Subject: Religion
Founded: 1911
ISBN Publisher's Prefix: 3-7858

Lutherisches Verlagshaus GmbH, Knochenhauerstr 38-40, D-3000 Hanover 1 Tel: (0511) 1941739
Man Dir, Production, Publicity, Rights & Permissions: Klaus Wöhleke; *Editorial:* Dr Hans Weissgerber; *Sales:* Rainer Torren
Parent Company: Lutherhaus Verlag GmbH (at above address)
Subjects: Theology, Liturgical works and practical aids, the Church today, General Religious Literature

Verlag Waldemar **Lutz**, Basler Str 130, D-7850 Lörrach Tel: (07621) 88812
Man Dir: Waldemar Lutz
Subjects: Regional Literature, Children's, School Books
1981: 6 titles *Founded:* 1978
ISBN Publisher's Prefix: 3-922107

M F B (Phono- und Schriftenmission des Missionstrupps Frohe Botschaft eV)*, Nordstr 15, Postfach 1180, D-3432 Grossalmerode bei Kassel Tel: (05604) 361 and 5120
The Record and Text Mission of the 'Good News' Mission Team
Man Dir, Rights & Permissions: W Heiner
Subjects: Christian Evangelical, Juvenile Interest, How-to, Paperbacks, Texts in English, Periodicals
1981: 22 titles

M V G, see Moderne Verlags GmbH

Mäander Verlag GmbH, Hundingstr 9, D-8000 Munich 19 Tel: (089) 1781881
Man Dir: Prof Dr Friedrich Piel
Orders to: Herold Verlags-Auslieferungen, Claude-Lorrainstr 11, D-8000 Munich 95
Subjects: Art, Archaeology, Aesthetics, Philosophy
1981: 7 titles *1982:* 19 titles *Founded:* 1977
ISBN Publisher's Prefix: 3-88219

McGraw-Hill Book Co GmbH, Lademannbogen 136, D-2000 Hamburg 63 Tel: (040) 5382081-6 Telex: 2164048
Man Dir: Rolf Pakendorf; *Sales:* Hank Troemel
Imprint: Schaum
Subjects: Medicine, Psychology, Engineering, General & Social Science, University & Secondary Textbooks, Educational Materials
Founded: 1969
Miscellaneous: Firm is an associate company of McGraw-Hill International Book Co New York (see UK entry for other Associate Companies). The Hamburg branch is the one from which all McGraw-Hill publications in English may be ordered from any point in Europe except Spain and Portugal
ISBN Publisher's Prefix: 0-07

Magnus Verlag*, im Teelbruch 60-62, Postfach 185528, 4300 Essen 18 Tel: (02054) 7077/7078
Man Dir: Walter Stender
Subjects: Reference Books, Dictionaries

Otto **Maier** Verlag*, Marktstr 22-26 und Robert Bosch Str 1, Postfach 1860, D-7980 Ravensburg Tel: (0751) 861 Cable Add: Maierverlag Telex: 0732926/0732921
Presidents: Otto J Maier, Dorothee Hess-Maier; *Man Dir:* Claus Runge; *Editorial:* Walter Diem, Peter Hille, Christian Stottele; *Rights & Permissions:* Frank Jacoby-Nelson
Subsidiary Companies: Ravensburger Spiele GmbH, Vienna, Austria; Editions Ravensburger SA, Attenschwiller, France; Fritz Löhmann GmbH, Ravensburger Graphische Betriebe Otto Maier GmbH, Ravensburger Verlag GmbH, Union Verlag mbH (qv), all Federal Republic of Germany; Otto Maier Benelux BV, Netherlands (qv); Carlit und Ravensburger AG, Switzerland
Subjects: Juvenile Fiction and Non-fiction, Adult Craft and Hobby, Art, Educational (Pedagogics, Art, Pre- and Elementary School Materials), Paperbacks
Founded: 1883
ISBN Publisher's Prefix: 3-473

Mairs Geographischer Verlag*, Marco-Polo-Str 1, D-7302 Ostfildern 4 (Kemnat) Tel: (0711) 454055 Cable Add: Mairverlag Telex: 721796
Man Dir: Dr Volkmar Mair; *Sales Dir:* Claus Benath
Subjects: Road Maps, Atlases
Founded: 1948
ISBN Publisher's Prefix: 3-87504

Mai's Reiseführer Verlag+, Unterlindau 80, D-6000 Frankfurt am Main 1 Tel: (0611) 723783
Man & Sales Dir: Ingo and Marie-Luise Schmidt di Simoni
Subjects: Travel Guides, especially to non-European countries
1983: 45 titles *Founded:* 1951
ISBN Publisher's Prefix: 3-87936

Gebr **Mann** Verlag GmbH & Co, Lindenstr 76, Postfach 110303, D-1000 Berlin 61 Tel: (030) 25913864 Cable Add: Kunstbrief Berlin Telex: 183723
Man Dir: Professor Dr Heinz Peters
Associate Company: Deutscher Verlag für Kunstwissenschaft (qv)
Subjects: Archaeology, History of Art
Founded: 1917
ISBN Publisher's Prefix: 3-7861

Manz Verlag, Anzinger Str 1, D-8000 Munich 80 Tel: (089) 403031 Cable Add: Manzverlag Telex: 522504
Publisher: Eduard Niedernhuber; *Sales:* Erna Schmidt; *Publicity:* Starkmuth Eschrich
Subsidiary Company: Erich Wewel Verlag (qv)
Subjects: Educational Materials
Founded: 1830
ISBN Publisher's Prefix: 3-7863

Tibor **Marczell**, Nederlinger Str 93, D-8000 Munich 19 Tel: (089) 155985
Man Dir: Tibor Marczell
Subjects: Medical (including history, herbal, fringe)
Founded: 1964
ISBN Publisher's Prefix: 3-88015

Carl **Marhold** Verlagsbuchhandlung, Hessenallee 12, Postfach 191409, D-1000 Berlin 19 Tel: 3043732/3049032 Cable Add: Marholdverlag Berlin
Man Dir: Wolfgang Jaeh; *Other offices:* Thomas Jaeh
Subjects: Special Healing Pedagogy, Nursing Technologies, Teaching of Handicapped Children
Founded: 1891
ISBN Publisher's Prefix: 3-7864

Edition **Maritim**+, Schwanenwik 27, D-2000 Hamburg 76 Tel: (040) 2296656
Dirs: Frank Grube, Gerhard Richter
Subjects: Yachting, Nautical
ISBN Publisher's Prefix: 3-922117

Maro Verlag, Riedingerstr 24-6F, D-8900 Augsburg 1 Tel: (0821) 577131
Dir: B Kaesmayr
Subjects: Modern Poetry and Fiction
Founded: 1969
ISBN Publisher's Prefix: 3-87512

Verlag **Marxistische Blätter** GmbH, Heddernheimer Landstr 78a, D-6000 Frankfurt am Main 50 Tel: (0611) 571051
Publisher: Albert Maag; *Dir:* Jan Wienecke
Subjects: Politics, Marxist Literature; *Marxistische Blätter*
1981: 30 titles *1982:* 16 titles *Founded:* 1969
Miscellaneous: Member of Arbeitsgemeinschaft sozialistischer und demokratischer Verleger und Buchhändler (qv for other members)
ISBN Publisher's Prefix: 3-88012

Hugo **Matthaes** Druckerei und Verlag GmbH & Co KG*, Olgastr 87, Postfach 622, D-7000 Stuttgart 1 Tel: (0711) 21331 Cable Add: Matthaesverlag Telex: 721802
Subjects: Food Trade, Gastronomy

Matthes und Seitz Verlag GmbH*, Postfach 401324, D-8000 Munich 40 (Located at: Dietlindenstr 14) Tel: (089) 333170
Editorial, Rights & Permissions, Publicity: Axel Matthes; *Sales, Production, Publicity:* Claus Seitz
Subjects: Literature, Art and the Arts generally, Fiction, Memoirs
Founded: 1977
ISBN Publisher's Prefix: 3-88221

Matthias-Grünewald-Verlag, see Grünewald

Matthiesen Verlag Ingwert Paulsen Jr, Nordbahnhofstr 2, Postfach 1480, D-2250 Husum Tel: (04841) 6081/3 Telex: 28567 husumv d
Man Dir, Editorial, Rights & Permissions: Ingwert Paulsen Jr; *Sales:* Alfred Lorenzen
Associate Companies: Hamburger Lesehefte Verlag Iselt & Co Nfl mbH (qv); Hansa Verlag Ingwert Paulsen Jr (qv); Husum Druck- und Verlagsgesellschaft mbH & Co KG (qv)
Subjects: Textbooks, Science, Reference
Founded: 1892
ISBN Publisher's Prefix: 3-7868

Maximilian-Verlag, Steintorwall 17, Postfach 2352, D-4900 Herford Tel: (05221) 50001 Cable Add: Maximilian, Herford/Westf Telex: 0934801 maxvg d
Publishers: Dr Kurt Schober, Gerhard Bollmann; *Sales:* Hans-Focko Koehler; *Publicity:* Gerhard Mindt
Associate Companies: Koehlers Verlagsgesellschaft, E S Mittler und Sohn GmbH, Verlag Offene Worte; all members of Maximilian-Verlagsgruppe (qv)
Subjects: Philosophy, Law, Administration, History, Social Sciences; Periodicals
ISBN Publisher's Prefix: 3-7869

Maximilian-Verlagsgruppe, Postfach 2352, D-4900 Herford (Located at: Steintorwall 17) Tel: (05221) 50001 Telex: 0934801 maxgv d
Publishing Group comprising: Verlag E S Mittler und Sohn GmbH (qv), Maximilian-Verlag (qv), Koehlers Verlagsgesellschaft mbH (qv), Verlag Offene Worte (qv)
See individual Company entries for details
Branch Off (for all members of group): Bonngasse 3, Postfach 2009, D-5300 Bonn Tel: (0228) 631253

Karl-**May**-Verlag, see Karl

Edition Hansjörg **Mayer***, Engelhornweg 11, D-7000 Stuttgart 1 Tel: (0711) 282036
Man Dir: Hansjörg Mayer
Branch Off: London
Subjects: Belles Lettres, Poetry, Music, Art, Ethnology, High-priced Paperbacks
Founded: 1964

J A **Mayer'sche** Buchhandlung*, Ursulinerstr 17-19, Postfach 467, D-5100 Aachen Tel: (0241) 48142 Cable Add: Mayer Aachen Telex: 832768
Man Dir, Publicity: Helmut Falter
Branch Off: Templergraben 44, D-5100 Aachen
Bookshops: At company and branch office addresses
Founded: 1817
ISBN Publisher's Prefix: 3-87519

Medea Frauenverlag, Schopenhauerstr 11, D-6000 Frankfurt am Main 1 Tel: (0611) 442363
Man Dirs: Eve Cronberger, Angelika Eberlein; *Editorial:* Marockh Lautenschlag; *Publicity:* Gitta Mohrdieck; *Rights & Permissions:* A Eberlein
Orders to: Frauenliteraturvertrieb (FLV), Schloßstr 94, D-6000 Frankfurt am Main 90
Subjects: Women's Literature, Science Fiction Fantasy
1981: 4 titles *Founded:* 1980
ISBN Publisher's Prefix: 3-922764

Verlag für **Medizin** Dr Ewald Fischer GmbH, Fritz-Frey-Str 21, Postfach 105767, D-6900 Heidelberg 1 Tel: (06221) 49974 Cable Add: Verlagfürmedizin Telex: 461683 hvvfm d
Man Dir: Dr E Fischer; *Production:* Dietmar Sieber; *Advertising:* Krisztina Fruh
Associate Companies: Arkana Verlag (qv); Karl F Haug Verlag GmbH & Co (qv)
Branch Off: Bergheimer Str 102, D-6900 Heidelberg
Subjects: Neglected/little-recognized Medical fields, Chinese diagnosis, Periodicals
Bookshop: As for Karl F Haug Verlag & Co KG (qv)
Founded: 1967
ISBN Publisher's Prefixes: 3-921003, 3-88463

Medizinisch-Literarische Verlagsgesellschaft mbH, Postfach 120/140, D-3110 Uelzen Tel: (0581) 808-0 Cable Add: ML-Verlag 3110 Uelzen 1 Telex: 091326
Man Dir, Rights & Permissions: E J Wenske; *Sales:* B Pianka; *Production:* G Grätz; *Publicity:* M Jess
Parent Company: C Beckers Buchdruckerei, 3110 Uelzen 1
Subjects: Medical, Acupuncture, Orthopaedics, Electro-Acupuncture texts in English; Periodicals
Founded: 1957
ISBN Publisher's Prefix: 3-88136

Verlagsbuchhandlung **Megapress**, Franz-J Gaber und W Poth GbR, Frankfurter Str 39, D-6078 Neu Isenburg Tel: (06102) 25951/23817
Publisher: F J Gaber
Subjects: Politics, Periodical
ISBN Publisher's Prefix: 3-87979

Felix **Meiner** Verlag GmbH, Richardstr 47, D-2000 Hamburg 76 Tel: (040) 294870 Telex: 212120 hihe
Man Dirs: Richard Meiner, Manfred Meiner
Subject: Philosophy, Periodicals
Founded: 1911
ISBN Publisher's Prefix: 3-7873

Verlag Anton Hain **Meisenheim** GmbH, Adelheidstr 2, Postfach 1220, D-6240 Königstein/TS Tel: (06174) 3021 Telex: 410664
Man Dirs, Rights & Permissions: Axel Rütters, Dieter Hain; *Editorial:* Beate Pinkerneil; *Sales, Publicity:* Daniel Herrmann; *Production:* Edzard Storck
Parent Company: Publishing group Athenäum/Hanstein/Jüdischer (qv under Athenäum Verlag GmbH)
Subjects: Academic, Science
Founded: 1946
ISBN Publisher's Prefix: 3-445

Otto **Meissner** Verlag, Binger Str 29, D-1000 Berlin 33 Tel: (030) 8237007
Dir: Dieter Beuermann
Subjects: General Non-fiction, Hobbies, Humanities, Periodicals
Founded: 1848
ISBN Publisher's Prefix: 3-87527

J Ch **Mellinger** Verlag GmbH, Wolfgang Militz und Co KG, 55 Büssenstr, Postfach 131164, D-7000 Stuttgart 1 Tel: (0711) 463565/246401
Proprietors & Man Dirs: Wolfgang Militz, Elisabeth Militz
Subjects: Anthroposophy, Education, Literature, Juveniles, Games
Founded: 1926
ISBN Publisher's Prefix: 3-88069

Verlag Abi **Melzer** GmbH*, Wildscheuerweg 1, Postfach 301117, D-6072 Dreieich-Buchschlag Tel: (06103) 63061 Telex: 4185381 amp
General Manager: Abraham Melzer
Orders to: VVA (Vereinigte Verlagsauslieferung GmbH), Postfach 7777, D-4830 Gütersloh 1
Subjects: Picture Strips, Graphics, Comics, Children's Books, General Literature
Founded: 1975
ISBN Publisher's Prefix: 3-8201

Melzer Verlag KG*, Gutenbergstr, D-6101 Weiterstadt Tel: (06151) 86056 Telex: 419249
Man Dir: Horst Göhde; *Sales Dir:* Horst Beitlich
Subjects: Comics, Art, Juveniles
Founded: 1972
ISBN Publisher's Prefix: 3-7874

Verlag **Mensch und Arbeit** Robert Pfützner GmbH, Sandstr 3, D-8000 Munich 2 Tel: (089) 554861 Cable Add: Pronto Munich
Man Dir: Robert Pfützner; *Rights & Permissions:* Wilhelm Höfelmaier
Subjects: How-to, Art, Social Science, Professional, Technical
Founded: 1957

Mentor-Verlag Dr Ramdohr KG, Neusser Str 3, Postfach 401120, D-8000 Munich 40 Tel: (089) 3830 Cable Add: Langenscheidt Munich Telex: 5215379 lkgm d
Man Dir: Karl Ernst Tielebier-Langenscheidt; *Editorial:* Katharina Baudach; *Sales Dir:* Peter Haering; *Advertising Dir:* Dieter Krause; *Sales, Promotion:* through Langenscheidt KG (qv); *Rights & Permissions:* Manfred Überall
Subjects: Reference, Low-priced Paperbacks, Textbooks
1981: 8 titles *1982:* 23 titles *Founded:* 1904
Miscellaneous: Firm is a member of the Langenscheidt Group (qv)
ISBN Publisher's Prefix: 3-580

Mergus Verlag Hans A Baensch, Postfach 86, D-4520 Melle 1 Tel: (05422) 3636 Cable Add: Mergus Melle
Man Dir: Hans A Baensch
Subjects: Natural History, Care of Pets
1982: 6 titles *Founded:* 1977
ISBN Publisher's Prefix: 3-88244

Merlin Verlag Andreas Meyer Verlags GmbH und Co KG, Gifkendorf 3, D-2121 Vastorf Tel: (04137) 7207
Publisher: Andreas J Meyer; *Sales Manager:* Ilse Meyer
Subjects: Arts, Literature, History
ISBN Publisher's Prefix: 3-87536

Merve Verlag*, Crelle Str 22, D-1000 Berlin 62 Tel: (030) 7848433
Man Dirs: Hans-Peter Gente, Heidi Paris
1982: 10 titles

Verlag für **Messepublikationen**, see Thomas Neureuter KG

J B **Metzlersche** Verlagsbuchhandlung, Kernerstr 43, Postfach 529, D-7000 Stuttgart 1 Tel: (0711) 220367/68/69 Cable Add: Metzlerverlag Stuttgart
Man Dir: Günther Schweizer; *Sales Dir:* Horst Cziszinsky; *Advertising Dir:* Ulrich Gensicke; *Rights & Permissions:* Dr Bernd Lutz
Orders to: (Book Trade): Goethestrasse 6, D-7400 Tübingen; (in Berlin) A Muschal & Sohn, Lützowstr 105-6, D-1000 Berlin 30
Associate Company: C E Poeschel Verlag (qv)
Subjects: Philology, Human Sciences, Geodesy, Pedagogics, School Books
Founded: 1682
Miscellaneous: Firm is member of TR-Verlagsunion GmbH (qv)
ISBN Publisher's Prefix: 3-476

Alfred **Metzner** Verlag, Zeppelinallee 43, Postfach 970148, D-6000 Frankfurt am Main Tel: (0611) 774055 Telex: 4189621 kome d
Dir: Dr Clemens J B Sandmann; *Editorial:* Marigret Maeyer-Tabellion; *Publicity and Sales:* Ernst F Grundl
Associate Company: Verlag Kommentator (qv)
Subjects: Law, University Textbooks, International Finance Management
Founded: 1909
Miscellaneous: Alfred Metzner Verlag is a member of the Kluwer Group, Deventer, Netherlands (qv)
ISBN Publisher's Prefix: 3-7875

Meyster Verlag, Prinzenstr 43, D-8000 Munich 19 Tel: (089) 174051 Telex: 522569 meyst d
Man Dir, Rights & Permissions: Diether Curths
Subjects: Popular Science, Historical Novels, Gift Books, Illustrated Books
1981: 12 titles *1982:* 12 titles *Founded:* 1978
ISBN Publisher's Prefix: 3-8131

Gertraud **Middelhauve** Verlag, Wiener Platz 2, D-5000 Cologne 80 (Mülheim) Tel: (0221) 614982
Man Dir, Editorial, Rights & Permissions: Gertraud Middelhauve; *Publicity:* Claudia Sproedt
Orders to: VVA (Vereinigte Verlagsauslieferung GmbH), Postfach 7777, D-4830 Gütersloh 1
Subject: Juveniles
Founded: 1947
ISBN Publisher's Prefix: 3-7678

Wolfgang **Militz** und Co KG, see J Ch Mellinger Verlag

Minerva Publikation, Pössenbacherstr 2b, Postfach 711009, D-8000 Munich 71 Tel: (089) 798901/7915753 Cable Add: saur d Telex: 05212067 saur d
Man Dirs: Klaus G Saur, Rüdiger Hildebrandt; *Editorial, Production, Publicity:* Elisabeth Gruber; *Sales:* Paul Fertl
Parent Company: K G Saur Verlag KG (qv)
Subjects: Economics, Sociology, Jurisprudence, Political Science, Liberal Arts, Pedagogy, Psychology, Technology, Physical Sciences, Medicine, Art, Theology
1981: 73 titles *Founded:* 1977
ISBN Publisher's Prefix: 3-597

Missio aktuell Verlag GmbH, Bergdriesch 27, Postfach 1170, D-5100 Aachen Tel: (0241) 30556 Telex: 832719 mira d
Man Dir: Ludwig Hahn
Subject: Missionary Work
1981: 13 titles *1982:* 14 titles *Founded:* 1970
ISBN Publisher's Prefix: 3-921626

Missionstrupp Frohe Botschaft, see M F B

E S **Mittler** und Sohn GmbH+, Steintorwall 17, Postfach 2352, D-4900 Herford Tel: (05221) 50001 Cable Add: Mittler & Sohn, Herford/Westf Telex: 0934801 maxvg d
Publishers: Dr Kurt Schober, Gerhard Bollmann; *Sales:* Hans-Focko Koehler; *Publicity:* Gerhard Mindt; *Production:*

150 FEDERAL REPUBLIC OF GERMANY

Heinz Kameier
Associate Companies: Koehlers Verlagsgesellschaft, Maximilian-Verlag, Verlag Offene Worte (all members of Maximilian-Verlagsgruppe, qv)
Subjects: Military, Aviation, Maritime, Political, NATO Affairs, Periodicals
Founded: 1789
ISBN Publisher's Prefixes: 3-87547, 3-8132

Verlag **Moderne Industrie**, Wolfgang Dummer & Co, Justus-von-Liebig-Str 1, Postfach 334, D-8910 Landsberg am Lech Tel: (08191) 125 Telex: 527114
Man Dir, Rights & Permissions: Dr Reinhard Möstl; *Sales:* Ingrid Spitz
Associate Companies: Moderne Verlags GmbH (qv); Leviathan House Ltd, UK (qv)
Subjects: Management (Personnel, Sales), Advertising, Data Processing, Marketing, Textbooks
1982: 60 titles *Founded:* 1952
ISBN Publisher's Prefix: 3-478

Moderne Verlags GmbH (MVG), Wolfgang Dummer & Co*, Justus-von-Liebig-Str 1, Postfach 334, D-8910 Landsberg am Lech Tel: (08191) 125 Telex: 527114
Man Dir: Dr Reinhard Möstl; *Publicity:* Ulrich Eder; *Rights & Permissions:* Dr Anton Kovac
Associate Company: Verlag Moderne Industrie (qv)
Subjects: How-to, Cookery, Hobbies, Popular Science
ISBN Publisher's Prefix: 3-478

Gütersloher Verlagshaus Gerd **Mohn**, see Gütersloher

J C B **Mohr** (Paul Siebeck), Wilhelmstr 18, Postfach 2040, D-7400 Tübingen Tel: (07071) 26064 Cable Add: Siebeck Tübingen Telex: 7262872 mohr d
Man Dir: Georg Siebeck; *Sales, Publicity:* Johannes Krämer; *Production:* Rudolf Pflug; *Rights & Permissions:* Heinz-Jörg Staffend
Subjects: History, Philosophy, Religion, General & Social Science, Economics, Law, University Textbooks
1981: 95 titles *1982:* 110 titles *Founded:* 1801
ISBN Publisher's Prefix: 3-16

Verlag **Molden** — S Seewald GmbH, Stievestr 9, D-8000 Munich 19 Tel: (089) 176071 Telex: 529993
Publishers, Man Dirs: Sixt A Seewald, Dr Hansgeorg Kanno; *Editorial:* Sixt A Seewald; *Sales:* Dr Hansgeorg Kanno
Subjects: Non-fiction
Founded: 1982

Mönch-Verlag GmbH & Co*, Heilsbachstr 26, D-5300 Bonn 1 Tel: (02221) 643066-68 Telex: 8869429 mvkb d
Man Dir: Manfred Sadlowski; *Sales Dir:* Joachim Latka; *Publicity Dir:* Heinz-Jürgen Witzke; *Advertising Dir:* Peter Konietschke; *Rights & Permissions:* Herr Latka
Branch Off: Mönch-Verlag, D-5401 Waldesch, Hübingerweg 33
Subjects: History, How-to, Engineering, General Science, High-priced Paperbacks

Monitor Verlag, see Arbeitsgemeinschaft sozialistischer und demokratischer Verleger und Buchhändler

Heinz **Moos** Verlag GmbH & Co KG, Rottenbucher Str 30, D-8032 Gräfelfing vor Munich Tel: (089) 851311 Cable Add: Moosverlag
Man Dir: Heinz Moos
Subjects: Town Planning, History of Architecture, Preservation of Monuments, Fringe Areas of Science and Art, Book Production and Printing, Monographs, Current Affairs, German-American Dual Language (International Relations) Texts
Founded: 1959
ISBN Publisher's Prefix: 3-7879

Morsak Verlag, Kröllstr 5, Postfach 5, D-8352 Grafenau Tel: (08552) 1015/6 Telex: 57431
Man Dir, Production, Rights & Permissions: Erich Stecher; *Sales:* Rosa Zarham
Subjects: Bavaria, School books, Textbooks
Founded: 1884
ISBN Publisher's Prefix: 3-87553

Morus-Verlag, Grunewaldstr 24, D-1000 Berlin 41 Tel: (030) 8210101/8213443
Dirs: Erich Klausener, Elisabeth Jagdt
Subject: Religion
Founded: 1945
ISBN Publisher's Prefix: 3-87554

Mosaik Verlag, Neumarkter Str 18, Postfach 800360, D-8000 Munich 80 Tel: (089) 43189 Cable Add: Bertelsmann München Telex: 523259
Dir and Rights & Permissions: Peter Gutmann; *Publicity:* Lionel von dem Knesebeck
Parent Company: Verlagsgruppe Bertelsmann GmbH (qv for associate companies)
Subjects: Family and Household Interest books, especially How-to, Cookery, Health & Medicine, Gardening, Furnishing, Crafts, Hobbies, Reference
ISBN Publisher's Prefix: 3-570

Motorbuch-Verlag, Böblinger Str 18, Postfach 1370, D-7000 Stuttgart 1 Tel: (0711) 642031 Cable Add: pico d Telex: 0722662
Man Dir: Wolfgang Schilling; *Sales:* Thomas Günther, Kurt Wölfle; *Rights & Permissions:* Brigitte Weller
Subjects: How-to, Reference, Engineering
Founded: 1962
Miscellaneous: Firm is a division of Buch- & Verlagshaus Paul Pietsch GmbH & Co KG (at above address)
ISBN Publisher's Prefix: 3-87943

Mouton Publishers, Genthiner Str 13, D-1000 Berlin 30 Tel: (030) 26005235/26005185/26005236 Telex: 0184027
Man Dir: S Grunwald
Parent Company: (since 1977) Walter de Gruyter und Co (qv)
Branch Offs: Editions Mouton & Cie, 7 rue Dupuytren, F-75006 Paris, France; Mouton Publishers, Walter de Gruyter Inc, 200 Saw Mill River Rd, Hawthorne, NY 10532, USA; Mouton Publishers, Rivierstaete, Amsteldijk 166, 1079 LH Amsterdam, Netherlands
Subjects: Anthropology, Art, Economics, Education, Geography, History, Law, Linguistics, Belles Lettres, Mathematics, Philosophy, Psychology, Religion, Social Science
Founded: 1954
ISBN Publisher's Prefix: 3-11

Emil **Müller**, an imprint of Neukirchener Verlag (qv)

Verlag Ars Sacra Josef **Müller**, see Ars Edition GmbH

Verlag C F **Müller**, Amalienstr 29, Postfach 4320, D-7500 Karlsruhe 1 Tel: (0721) 20909 Telex: 7825909
Man Dir: Dr Christof Müller-Wirth; *Sales, Publicity:* Winfried Ammon; *Production, Rights & Permissions:* Bernhard Harzer
Subjects: Technical Specialist Books on Cold, Heat, Climate, Air, Environment, Energy and Solar Technology
Founded: 1797
ISBN Publisher's Prefix: 3-7880

Verlagsgesellschaft Rudolf **Müller** GmbH, Stolberger Str 84, Postfach 410949, D-5000 Cologne 41 Tel: (0221) 54971 Telex: 8881256
Publisher: Dr Walther Müller; *Dir:* Helmut Evers; *Sales Manager:* Peter von Klaudy; *Publicity Manager:* Peter Groth
Branch Off: Johnsallee 53, D-2000 Hamburg 13
Subjects: Architecture, Construction, Engineering, Data Processing, Education, Do-it-yourself, Pets
Miscellaneous: Part of vgs — Verlagsgesellschaft Schulfernsehen mbH & Co KG (qv)
ISBN Publisher's Prefix: 3-481

Verlagsgruppe Langen-**Müller**/Herbig, see Langen

C F **Müller** Jüristischer Verlag GmbH, Postfach 102640, D-6900 Heidelberg (Located at: im Weiher 10) Tel: (06221) 489250 Telex: 0461727 huehd
Associate Companies: Kriminalistik Verlag GmbH (qv); R v Decker's Verlag G Schenck GmbH (qv)
Subjects: Jurisprudence Textbooks; Commentaries and Law Practice; Academic Series

Verlag **Müller** und Kiepenheuer, Frankfurter Landstr 32, Postfach 1355, D-6450 Hanau am Main Tel: (06181) 259052/82353 Telex: 4184879
Publisher: Werner Dausien
Parent Company: Werner Dausien (qv)
Subjects: General Fiction, Arts, Maps
ISBN Publisher's Prefix: 3-7833

Müller und Steinicke Verlag, Lindwurmstr 21, D-8000 Munich 2 Tel: (089) 265881
Publisher: Werner Gissler
Subjects: Medicine and associated fields

Albert Langen-Georg **Müller** Verlag, see Langen

Munin Verlag GmbH*, Postfach 3023, D-4500 Osnabrück Tel: (0541) 572278
Subject: War Histories of Waffen SS units
1981: 2 titles *1982:* 6 titles *Founded:* 1955
ISBN Publisher's Prefix: 3-921242

Münster Verlag*, Hildastr 25, D-7800 Freiburg im Breisgau Tel: (0761) 35190
Subjects: Reference Works, Popular Fact-Books, Religious

Muster-Schmidt Verlag, Grünberger Weg 6, Postfach 421, D-3400 Göttingen Tel: (0551) 71741 Cable Add: Musterschmidt Telex: 96704 gofafi
Dirs: Hans Hansen-Schmidt, Eva Maria Gerhardy-Löcken
Branch Off: Waldmannstr 10a, Zurich, Switzerland
Subjects: Biography, History, Anthropology
Founded: 1905
ISBN Publisher's Prefix: 3-7881

N D V (Neue Darmstädter Verlagsanstalt), Postfach 1544, D-5340 Bad Honnef 1 (Located at: Hauptstr 72, D-5342 Rheinbreitbach) Tel: (02224) 3232/4353
Publisher: Klaus-J Holzapfel
Subject: Politics
ISBN Publisher's Prefix: 3-87576

Nachrichten-Verlags-GmbH, Glauburgstr 66, Postfach 180372, D-6000 Frankfurt am Main 1 Tel: (0611) 599791
Man Dir: Dr Werner Petschick; *Sales Dir:* Elfriede Krüger; *Publicity and Advertising Dirs:* Renate Bastian, Gisela Mayer; *Rights & Permissions:* Ruth Malkomes
Subjects: Political aspects of Trade Unionism, Economics, Social Sciences
Founded: 1969
Miscellaneous: Member of

FEDERAL REPUBLIC OF GERMANY 151

Arbeitsgemeinschaft sozialistischer und demokratischer Verleger und Buchhändler (qv for other members)
ISBN Publisher's Prefix: 3-88367

Edition **Nagel**, an imprint of Bärenreiter-Verlag (qv)

Gunter **Narr** Verlag, Postfach 2567, D-7400 Tübingen 1 (Located at: Stauffenbergstr 42) Tel: (07071) 24156
Manager, Sales Dir and Rights & Permissions: Gunter Narr; *Publicity Dir:* Brigitte Narr; *Advertising Dir:* Horst Schmid
Subjects: Linguistic studies (especially German, English and French); Literary Criticism; Romanesque Studies
Founded: 1969
Miscellaneous: Also incorporates TBL (Tübinger Beiträge zur Linguistik Verlag)
ISBN Publisher's Prefix: 3-87808

Paul **Neff** Verlag KG*, Herwarthstr 3, D-1000 Berlin 45 Tel: (030) 7725246
Man Dir: Fritz Pfenningstorff
Subjects: Novels, Belles Lettres, Poetry, Music, Art, Biography, History, Textbooks, Geography
Founded: 1829

Verlag Günther **Neske***, Kloster, Postfach 7240, D-7417 Pfullingen Tel: (07121) 71339 Cable Add: Neske-Verlag Pfullingen Telex: neflu d 0729790
Publisher: Günther Neske; *Editorial, Publicity:* Brigitte Neske
Subjects: General Fiction, Humanities, Literary Criticism, Philosophy, Politics, Poetry, Psychiatry, Theology, Swiridoff Picture Books
Founded: 1951
ISBN Publisher's Prefix: 3-7885

Neue Darmstädter Verlagsanstalt, see N D V

Verlag **Neue Gesellschaft** GmbH, Godesberger Allee 143, D-5300 Bonn 2 Tel: (0228) 378021/378025
Dir: Dr Heiner Lindner; *Editorial:* Charles Schüddekopf; *Sales:* Peter Marold
Orders to: Verlagsauslieferung Georg Lingenbrink, Postfach 3584, D-6000 Frankfurt am Main 1; For Berlin: Zirk und Ellenrieder, Lützowstr 105 (bbz), D-1000 Berlin 30
Associate Company: Verlag J H W Dietz Nachf GmbH (qv)
Subjects: Politics, Legal, History, Sociology, Economics, Periodicals
ISBN Publisher's Prefix: 3-87831

Neue Kommentare, see Arbeitsgemeinschaft sozialistischer und demokratischer Verleger und Buchhändler

Verlag **Neue Kritik** KG*, Myliusstr 58, D-6000 Frankfurt am Main Tel: (0611) 727576
Orders to: Sozialistische Verlagsauslieferung GmbH, Franziusstr 44, D-6000 Frankfurt am Main
Subjects: Mainly Socialist-orientated
Founded: 1965
ISBN Publisher's Prefix: 3-8015

Verlag der **Neue Schulmann**, see Franckh'sche Verlagshandlung

Verlag **Neue Stadt** GmbH+, Gleissner Str 87, D-8000 Munich 83 Tel: (089) 405081 Cable Add: Neue Stadt
Man Dir: Wolfgang Bader; *Sales, Publicity and Advertising:* Konrad Heil; *Rights:* Wolfgang Bader
Parent Company: Città Nuova Editrice, Italy (qv for associate companies)
Branch Offs: Trostr 116, A-1100 Vienna, Austria; Seestr 426, Postfach 435, CH-8032 Zurich, Switzerland
Subjects: Music, Religion, Juveniles, Periodicals

1982: 14 titles *Founded:* 1965
ISBN Publisher's Prefix: 3-87996

Verlag **Neue Wirtschafts-Briefe** GmbH, Eschstr 22, D-4690 Herne 1 Tel: (02323) 54071 Telex: 08229870 Cable Add: Steuerbriefe Herne
Man Dir: E-O Kleyboldt; *Sales and Advertising Dir:* J Müller-Grote
Subsidiary Company: Friedrich Kiehl Verlag GmbH (qv)
Subjects: Tax and Company Law, Accountancy, Industrial Management, Political Economics, Vocational Training, Periodicals
Founded: 1947
ISBN Publisher's Prefix: 3-482

Neuer Jugendschriften-Verlag, see A Weichert Verlag

Verlag **Neuer Weg** GmbH, Heusteigstr 88a, D-7000 Stuttgart 1, Postfach 3080 Tel: (0711) 6405894
Subjects: Marxist Politics, Communism, Novels, Song Books
Founded: 1971
ISBN Publisher's Prefix: 3-88021

Neukirchener Verlag des Erziehungvereins GmbH*, Andreas-Braem-Str 18-20, Postfach 216, D-4133 Neukirchen-Vluyn 2 Tel: (02845) 392222 Cable Add: Verlagshaus neukirchenvluyn
Man Dirs: Dr Rudolf Weth, Hans-Martin Dahlmann; *Editors:* Dr Christian Bartsch; *Sales Dir:* Margot Seidensticker; *Rights & Permissions:* Ursula Lisken
Subsidiary Company: Kalendar-Verlag des Erziehungs-Vereins (at above address)
Imprint: Emil Müller
Branch Off: Evangelische Schriften-Zentrale (esz), Barsortiment, Postfach 216, D-4133 Neukirchen-Vluyn 2
Subjects: Evangelical Christianity, Catholic and Reformed; Biblical Studies, Bible Archaeology, Belles Lettres
Bookshop: Neukirchener Buchhandlung, Andreas-Braem-Str 20, D-4133 Neukirchen-Vluyn 2
Founded: 1888
ISBN Publisher's Prefix: 3-7887

Verlag Dr Thomas **Neumann**, see Königshausen & Neumann

Verlag J **Neumann-Neudamm** KG*, Muhlenstr 9, Postfach 320, D-3508 Melsungen Tel: (05661) 2374/6374
Dir: Walter Schwartz
Subjects: Agriculture, Horticulture, Forestry, Hunting, Fishing, Natural Science, Aquarian Science
ISBN Publisher's Prefix: 3-7888

Martin **Neumeyer**, see Landsberger Verlagsanstalt

Verlag für Messepublikationen Thomas **Neureuter** KG*, Pettenkoferstr 7, Postfach 482, D-8000 Munich 2 Tel: (089) 597186
Publisher: Thomas Neureuter
Founded: 1948

Nicolaische Verlagsbuchhandlung Beuermann GmbH, Binger Str 29, D-1000 Berlin 33 Tel: (030) 8237007
General Manager: Dieter Beuermann
Subjects: Berlin, Politics, European Art and Photography
1981: 10 titles
ISBN Publisher's Prefix: 3-87584

Verlag C W **Niemeyer**, Osterstr 19, Postfach 447, D-3250 Hameln 1 Tel: (05151) 200310 Cable Add: Dewezet Telex: 92859
Dir: Dr Martin Oesch
Orders to: VVA (Vereinigte Verlagsauslieferung GmbH), Postfach 7777, D-4830 Gütersloh 1
Associate Company: Adolf Sponholtz Verlag

(qv)
Subjects: Scenic Picture Books (Germany), Quality Illustrated Books, Art and Architecture, Humour
Founded: 1797
ISBN Publisher's Prefix: 3-87585

Max **Niemeyer** Verlag, Pfrondorfer Str 4, Postfach 2140, D-7400 Tübingen Tel: (07071) 81104 Cable Add: Niemeyer Tübingen
Man Dir: Robert Harsch-Niemeyer; *Publicity and Marketing:* Manfred Korn-Weller
Subjects: General Literary Criticism; German, English & Romance Philology; Linguistics, Philosophy, History
1982: 81 titles *Founded:* 1870
ISBN Publisher's Prefix: 3-484

Nomos Verlagsgesellschaft mbH und Co KG, Waldseestr 3-5, Postfach 610, D-7570 Baden Baden Tel: (07221) 3441 Telex: 0781201
Man Dir: Volker Schwarz; *Publicity:* Annette Saeger
Associate Companies: Insel Verlag (qv); Suhrkamp Verlag (qv)
Subjects: Jurisprudence, Economics, European Economy, Business Sciences, International Co-operation, Periodicals
Founded: 1936
ISBN Publisher's Prefix: 3-7890

Verlag Wissenschaft und Politik, Berend von **Nottbeck**+, Salierring 14-16, D-5000 Cologne 1 Tel: (0221) 312878/315787 Cable Add: Politikbuch 5 Köln 1
Man Dir: Berend von Nottbeck; *Sales & Advertising Dir:* Siegmund Mindt; *Publicity Dir:* C P von Nottbeck
Branch Off: Redaktion 'Deutschland Archiv', Goltsteinstr 185, D-5000 Cologne 51
Subjects: Political Science (especially in context of East-West relations), International Law and Problems, Dialogue with the German Democratic Republic
Founded: 1960
ISBN Publisher's Prefix: 3-8046

Verlag Monika **Nüchtern***, Breisacherstr 14, D-8000 Munich 80 Tel: (089) 481230
Man Dir: Monika Nüchtern
Subject: Films
Founded: 1976

Numismatischer Verlag P N Schulten*, Bornwiesenweg 34, D-6000 Frankfurt am Main 1 Tel: (0611) 550286 Telex: 4189154
Publisher: Peter N Schulten
Subjects: Coins, Medals, Reprints
Founded: 1974
ISBN Publisher's Prefix: 3-921302

Nusser Verlag, Kaufbeurerstr 3, Postfach 500411, D-8000 Munich 50 Tel: (089) 146788
Man Dir: Dr Horst Nusser; *Sales:* Katharina Mühlberger
Subjects: History, Geography, Popular Science, Art, Culture, Asiatic Topics, Audiovisual, Educational
1982: 32 titles *1983:* 85 titles *Founded:* 1972
ISBN Publisher's Prefix: 3-88091

Nymphenburger Verlagshandlung GmbH, Romanstr 16, D-8000 Munich 19 Tel: (089) 162051 Cable Add: Nymphenbuch Munich
Man Dir: Dr Herbert Fleissmer; *Editorial:* Dr Konrad Dietzfelbingen; *Sales, Publicity:* Ingeborg Castell; *Rights & Permissions:* Renate Werner
Subjects: General Fiction, Belles Lettres, Biography, History, How-to, Philosophy, Sports, Hobbies, Mountaineering, General and Social Science
Founded: 1946
Miscellaneous: Firm is a member of Verlagsgruppe Langen-Müller/Herbig (qv)
ISBN Publisher's Prefix: 3-485

152 FEDERAL REPUBLIC OF GERMANY

Oberbaumverlag*, Stromstr 38, Postfach 127, D-1000 Berlin 21 Tel: (030) 3953099
Man Dir: Manfried Hammer; *Publicity & Advertising Dir:* Edelgard Abenstein
Subjects: Left Wing Political, German History, German and International Literature, General Culture
Founded: 1966

Odörfer-Verlags GmbH*, Mohrengasse 10, D-8500 Nuremberg Tel: (0911) 203611
Dir: Kurt Odörfer
Subjects: Sexual Literature, Pornography

Oekumenischer Verlag Dr R-F Edel, Annabergstr 46, D-5880 Lüdenscheid
Publicity Manager: Dr Reiner-Friedemann Edel
Orders to: Verlag M Claren, Werdohlerstr 11, D-5880 Lüdenscheid
Subject: Christian Evangelical and Devotional; Cultural, Philosophical, Art

Paul **Oestergaard** GmbH, see Columbus Verlag

Verlag Friedrich **Oetinger**, Poppenbütteler Chaussee 55, Postfach 220, D-2000 Hamburg 65 Tel: (040) 6070055 Cable Add: Oetingerbuch Telex: 02174230
Editorial: Else Marie Bonnet; *Sales:* Thomas Huggle; *Publicity:* Anke Lüdtke; *Rights & Permissions:* Uwe Weitendorf
Associate Company: Cecilie Dressler Verlag (qv)
Subjects: Juveniles, Illustrated Books
ISBN Publisher's Prefix: 3-7891

August **Oetker**, see Ceres-Verlag

Verlag **Offene Worte**, Steintorwall 17, Postfach 2352, D-4900 Herford Tel: (05221) 50001 Cable Add: Vlg Offene Worte, Herford/W Telex: 0934801 maxvg d
Publishers: Dr Kurt Schober, Gerhard Bollmann; *Sales:* Hans-Focko Koehler; *Publicity:* Gerhard Mindt
Associate Companies: Koehlers Verlagsgesellschaft, Maximilian-Verlag, E S Mittler und Sohn GmbH (all members of Maximilian-Verlagsgruppe, qv)
Subjects: Military, Politics, Periodicals
ISBN Publisher's Prefix: 3-87599

Karl **Ohm** Verlag*, Hauptstr 101, D-1000 Berlin 62 Tel: (030) 784001
Publisher: Kurt Meurer
Associate Company: Elwert und Meurer GmbH (qv)
Subject: Law
ISBN Publisher's Prefix: 3-87600

R **Oldenbourg** Verlag GmbH, Rosenheimer Str 145, Postfach 801360, D-8000 Munich 80 Tel: (089) 41121 Cable Add: Rograph München Telex: 0529296
Dirs: Dr Thomas von Cornides, Götz Ohmeyer, Johannes Oldenbourg
Orders to: Verlegerdienst München, Auslieferung R Oldenbourg Verlag, Gutenbergstr 1, Postfach 1280, D-8031 Gilching Tel: (08105) 21101
Subsidiary Companies: Verlag Oldenbourg, Austria (qv); Michael Prögel Verlag, Postfach 1663, D-8800 Ansbach; VaW Verlag für angewandte Wissenschaften, Munich
Subjects: Modern Science and Technology (Data Processing, Statistics etc); History and the Liberal Arts (Politics, Current Affairs, Philosophy, Art History, and especially Austrian and European History); Social Sciences, Psychology, Pedagogics and School Text Books, Reference Works and Library Editions, Periodicals
Founded: 1858
Miscellaneous: Firm is member of TR-Verlagsunion GmbH (qv)
ISBN Publisher's Prefix: 3-486 (Munich)

Verlag **Olle und Wolter**, Postfach 4310, D-1000 Berlin 30 (Located at: Paul Lincke Ufer 44a, D-1000 Berlin 36) Tel: (030) 6125060
General Manager, Editorial: Ulf Wolter; *Sales and Publicity:* Maria Sata; *Rights & Permissions:* Simon J David
Subjects: History of the Workers' Movement, Politics, Economics, Philosophy, Literature, Scientific and Science Fiction, Ecology, Biography, Crime Fiction, Periodical
Founded: 1972
ISBN Publisher's Prefixes: 3-921241, 3-88395

Georg **Olms** Verlag, Hagentorwall 7, D-3200 Hildesheim Tel: (05121) 37007 Cable Add: Bookolms Hildesheim Telex: 927358 hidvg d/Att: Olms
Publisher: W Georg Olms, Dr E Mertens; *Sales:* Edith Olms; *Production:* J-P Pracht; *Rights & Permissions:* Miss K Gottschalk
Subsidiary Company: Editions Olms AG, Switzerland (qv)
Branch Off: Georg Olms Verlag, c/o 110 West 67 St, New York, NY 10019, USA
Bookshop: Georg Olms, Verlagsbuchhandlung, Hagentorwall 7, D-3200 Hildesheim
Subjects: Languages and Language History (especially Slavic, Germanic, Romance), Books in foreign languages (especially English, French), History, Geography, Travel, Literature, Arts, Judaica, Science, Technology, Orientalia, Folklore, Theology, Law, Politics, Economics, Sociology, Psychology, Pedagogy, Philosophy, Paperbacks
Founded: 1945
Miscellaneous: The firm commenced production in 1976 of The *Bibliothek der Deutschen Sprache*, a complete library of significant writing in German from the earliest times till c.1900 in microfiche form
ISBN Publisher's Prefix: 3-487

Verlag **Ölschläger** GmbH, Georgenstr 112, D-8000 Munich 40
Man Dir: Christina Ölschläger
Subjects; Communications, Journalism
Founded: 1977
ISBN Publisher's Prefix: 3-88295

Verlag für Wirtschaftsskripten, Dipl Kfm C **Ölschläger** GmbH, see Wirtschaftsskripten

Günter **Olzog** Verlag GmbH, Thierschstr 11, D-8000 Munich 22 Tel: (089) 293272
Man Dir, Rights & Permissions: Dr Günter Olzog; *Sales, Publicity & Advertising Dir:* Johann Hacker
Subjects: History, Social Science, Educational Materials, Politics, East European Economics
1982: 27 titles *Founded:* 1949
Miscellaneous: Firm is member of TR-Verlagsunion GmbH (qv)
ISBN Publisher's Prefix: 3-7892

Oncken Verlag KG, Postfach 110152, D-5600 Wuppertal 11 Tel: (02104) 6311
Subject: Popular Religion
ISBN Publisher's Prefix: 3-7893

Orangerie Galerie und Verlag, Gerhard F Reinz*, Helenenstr 2, D-5000 Cologne 1 Tel: (0221) 234684 Cable Add: Orangerie Telex: 8882939
Subject: Art

Orion-Heimreiter Verlag GmbH*, Friedrich-Ebert-Str 5-7, Postfach 1324, D-6056 Heusenstamm Tel: (06104) 5013 Cable Add: Orionheimreiter
Publisher: Erich W Rüskamp; *Editorial:* Dr Ludwig Blanck-Conrady; *Sales, Production, Publicity:* Heidemarie Schaffer; *Rights & Permissions:* through Hodemacher-Poldner, 8 Munich 19
Subjects: Biography, Documentary, Local History, Art, History, Fiction
Founded: 1961
ISBN Publisher's Prefix: 3-87588

Verlag **Osterrieth**, an imprint of Societäts-Verlag (qv)

P I A G, see Verlag Presse Information Agentur GmbH

P R Verlag Wiesbaden, H G Schwieger*, Glückstr 12, D-6200 Wiesbaden Tel: (06121) 520030 Cable Add: PR Verlag, Wiesbaden
Man Dir: H G Schwieger
Subjects: Belles Lettres, Poetry, Educational Materials
Founded: 1974
ISBN Publisher's Prefix: 3-921261

Päd extra buchverlag in der pädex Verlags GmbH, now extrabuch Verlag in der pädex Verlags GmbH (qv)

Pädagogischer Verlag Schwann/Bagel GmbH, Am Wehrhahn 100, Postfach 7640, D-4000 Düsseldorf 1 Tel: (0211) 360301 Cable Add: Schwannverlag Düsseldorf Telex: paed d 858 1345
Dirs: Dr Hans Weymar, Wilhelm Biswanger; *Publicity Manager:* Christoph Berten
Associate Company: Patmos Verlag GmbH (qv)
Subjects: University, Secondary and Primary Textbooks, Educational Materials, History, Arts, Linguistics, Children's Books, Records
Founded: 1821
Miscellaneous: Now incorporates Assimil-Verlag KG
ISBN Publisher's Prefixes: 3-589, 3-590

Pahl-Rugenstein Verlag*, Gottesweg 54, D-5000 Cologne 51 Tel: (0221) 364051
Dir: Paul Neuhöffer; *Editorial:* Jürgen Hartmann, Dr Jürgen Harrer, Dr Christa Thoma-Herterich; *Sales Manager:* Hajo Leib
Subjects: History, Literary Criticism, Education, Philosophy, Politics, Psychology, Social Science, Paperbacks, Economics, Periodicals, Sports
Miscellaneous: Member of Arbeitsgemeinschaft sozialistischer und demokratischer Verleger und Buchhändler (qv for other members)
ISBN Publisher's Prefix: 3-7609

Wilhelm **Pansegrau** Verlag, Bessemerstr 83-91, Postfach 420342, D-1000 Berlin 42 Tel: 7537051
Associate Company: H Heenemann Verlagsgesellschaft mbH (qv)
Subjects: Corrosion Protection, Plastics, Lacquer and Coatings

Parabel Verlag GmbH und Co KG+, Pschorrstr 3, D-8133 Feldafing Tel: (08157) 8476 Telex: 0526474
Publisher: Nadine Lange-Siemens; *Sales:* Bärbel Kistner; *Rights & Permissions:* Wolfgang Heinzel
Subjects: Picture Books, Modern Children's Literature
ISBN Publisher's Prefix: 3-7898

Paracelsus Verlag GmbH, see Hippokrates Verlag GmbH

Verlag Paul **Parey**+, Spitalerstr 12, Postfach 106340, D-2000 Hamburg 1 Tel: (040) 321511 Cable Add: Pareyverlag Hamburg Telex: 2161391 parv d
Also: Lindenstr 44-47, D-1000 Berlin 61 Tel: (030) 2516011 Cable Add: Pareyverlag Berlin Telex: 184777 parv d
Man Dirs: Dr Friedrich Georgi, Dr Rudolf Georgi (Berlin); *Publicity:* Karlheinz Römer; *Rights & Permissions:* Gerhard Reichwald
Subjects: Biology, Veterinary Medicine, Foodstuffs, Agriculture, Starch Research and Application, Brewery and Distillery,

Forestry, Horticulture, Plant Medicine and Protection; Environment Protection, Hydro- and Cultural Technologies, Hunting, Sporting and Professional Fishing, Riding and Horses, Technical and Scientific Journals
1982: 100 titles *Founded:* 1848
ISBN Publisher's Prefixes: 3-490 (Hamburg), 3-489 (Berlin)

Parkland Verlag GmbH, Schwabstr 189, Postfach 229, D-7000 Stuttgart 1 Tel: (0711) 298805 Telex: 721907
Man Dirs: Gerd Seibert, Dr Erhard Wendelberger; *Sales Dir:* Martina Deissner
Subjects: Non-fiction, especially Belles Lettres, Art etc
Founded: 1974

Verlag **Passavia**, Postfach 2147, D-8390 Passau 1 Tel: (0851) 51081/82/83 and 56947 Cable Add: Passavia Telex: 57837
Publishing Dir, Rights & Permissions: M Teschendorff; *Sales:* Katharina Moritz
Subjects: Bavarian Topics, Folklore, Humour, Homecare, Belles Lettres, Fiction
1981: 10 titles *1982:* 12 titles *Founded:* 1888
ISBN Publisher's Prefix: 3-87616

Passavia Universitätsverlag und -Druck GmbH, Postfach 2147, D-8390 Passau 1 Tel: (0851) 56957
Publishing Dir, Rights & Permissions: Martin Teschendorff
Subjects: Sciences
1983: 26 titles
ISBN Publisher's Prefix: 3-922016

Galerie **Patio** Verlag, Waldstrasse 115, D-6078 Neu-Isenburg
Man Dir: Walter Zimbrich; *Editorial:* Volker Müller; *Sales:* Franz Gaber, Renate Kafitz-Pfeuffer; *Production:* Manfred Linke, Yves Daniel Zimbrich; *Publicity:* Klaus Münschschwander; *Rights & Permissions:* David Ward, Regine Behrends
Subjects: Young Authors, New Editions of Older Texts, Handmade Books, the *Parabü* series of new, experimental texts (Patio's Book Rarity Library)
1982: 3 titles *1983:* 5 titles *Founded:* 1964

Patmos Verlag GmbH, Am Wehrhahn 100, Postfach 6213, D-4000 Düsseldorf 1 Tel: (0211) 360301 Cable Add: Patmos Verlag Telex: paed d 8581345
Dir: Dr P Böhringer; *Sales:* Wilhelm Biswanger; *Publicity:* Christoph Berten
Associate Company: Pädagogischer Verlag Schwann/Bagel GmbH (qv)
Subjects: Roman Catholic Theology, Religion, Education, Juveniles, Textbooks
Founded: 1910
ISBN Publisher's Prefix: 3-491

Paul **Pattloch** Verlag GmbH & Co KG, Goldbacherstr IX, D-8750 Aschaffenburg Tel: (06021) 21277 Cable Add: Pattloch Aschaffenburg Telex: 4188517
Man & Sales Dir: Clemens Pattloch
Subjects: Religion, Bibles
Founded: 1947
ISBN Publisher's Prefix: 3-557

Paulinus Verlag, Fleischstr 62-65, Postfach 3040, D-5500 Trier Tel: (0651) 46040 Telex: 04-727315
Publisher: Dr Eberhard Schützinger; *Dir:* Erika Schwarzenberg
Parent Company: Paulinus Druckerei GmbH (at above address)
Associate Company: Spee Buchverlag GmbH (qv)
Subjects: Religion, Theology
ISBN Publisher's Prefix: 3-7902

Ingwert **Paulsen** Jr, see Hansa Verlag and Matthieson Verlag

Pawel Pan Presse*, Kennedystr 25, D-6072 Dreieich 4 Tel: (06103) 81347
Man Dir, Production: Sascha Juritz; *Editorial:* Hanne F Juritz
Branch Off: Zum Seemenbach 1, Büdingen 2 Tel: (06042) 5821
Subjects: Contemporary Literature, Educative Art, Poetry, First Publications in Bibliophile Editions
1982: 36 titles *Founded:* 1972
ISBN Publisher's Prefix: 3-921454

Manfred **Pawlak** Grossantiquariat und Verlagsgesellschaft mbH*, Postfach 1149, D-8036 Herrsching (Located at: Gachenau Str 13) Tel: (08152) 1067-69 Telex: 0527724 mph d
Proprietor, Man Dir: Manfred Pawlak
Subjects: Biography, History, Art
Founded: 1949
Miscellaneous: The Company is a wholesale antiquarian and second-hand book dealer as well as a Publishing House

Agentur für wissenschaftliche Literatur Ulf **Pedersen** GmbH, Steinweg 5, D-3300 Brunswick Tel: (0531) 40294
Man Dir: Ulf Pedersen
Orders to: Cornelsen-Velhagen und Klasing Verlagsauslieferung, Postfach 8729, D-4800 Bielefeld 1
Subject: Social Sciences
1981: 8 titles *Founded:* 1979
ISBN Publisher's Prefix: 3-88657

Perimed Fachbuch-Verlagsgesellschaft mbH, Vogelherd 35, Postfach 3740, D-8520 Erlangen Tel: (09131) 6091 Telex: 629851
Man Dir: Dr med Dietmar Straube; *Editorial Reader:* Dr Hans Muth; *Sales:* Hartmut Fandrey; *Production:* Norbert Wohlers; *Publicity:* Ilse Rottner; *Rights & Permissions:* Dr Hans Muth, Ilse Rottner
Subject: Medicine
1981: 54 titles *Founded:* 1969
ISBN Publisher's Prefixes: 3-88429, 3-921222

Pestalozzi-Verlag graphische Gesellschaft mbH, Am Pestalozziring 14, Postfach 2829, D-8520 Erlangen Tel: (09131) 6116 Cable Add: Pestalozzi Erlangen Telex: 629766 Pevau
Man Dirs: Dr Reinhold Weigand, Norbert Franke; *Editorial:* Wolfgang Kaiser
Subjects: Children's Books
Founded: 1844
ISBN Publisher's Prefix: 3-87624

Verlag J P **Peter**, Gebr Holstein*, Herrngasse 1, Postfach 19, D-8803 Rothenburg Tel: (09861) 3001 Cable Add: Peterverlag
Man Dir, Sales, Publicity: Dr Gerhard Prinz
Subjects: Belles Lettres, Poetry, History, Religion, Travel, Educational Materials, Fiction, Periodicals
Founded: 1825
ISBN Publisher's Prefix: 3-87625

C F **Peters** Musikverlag GmbH & Co KG, Kennedyallee 101, Postfach 700906, D-6000 Frankfurt am Main 70 Tel: (0611) 6313066 Cable Add: Petersedit Telex: 411686 edpe d
Managing Partner: Dr Johannes Petschull
Associate Companies: Hinrichsen Edition Ltd, London, UK; C F Peters Corporation, New York, USA
Imprints: Edition Peters, Henry Litolff's Verlag, Edition Schwann, MP Belaieff
Subjects: Musical scores, Books on Music (all areas of Classical and Contemporary Music)
Founded: 1800
ISBN Publisher's Prefix: 3-87626

Dr Hans **Peters** Verlag+, Salisweg 56, Postfach 2012, D-6450 Hanau 1 Tel: (06181) 21632 *Man Dir:* Wolfgang A Nagel; *Editorial:* Rainer G Tripp; *Sales:* Christa Buschbeck; *Production:* Barbara Nagel
Subjects: Art Books, Pictorial Books, Picture Books for Children
Founded: 1952
ISBN Publisher's Prefix: 3-87627

Fachbuchverlag Dr **Pfanneberg** & Co+, Postfach 110910, D-6300 Giessen 11 (Located at: Schanzenstr 18) Tel: (0641) 74034
Man Dirs, Rights & Permissions: Dr Günther Pfanneberg, Gero Pfanneberg; *Editorial:* Gero Pfanneberg; *Sales:* Christa Horn; *Production:* Gerhard Duske
Subjects: Hotels and Catering Trade Textbooks, Bakery and Confectionery, Technologies, Commerce, Trade Schools Textbooks
Founded: 1949
ISBN Publisher's Prefix: 3-8057

Verlag J **Pfeiffer** GmbH & Co+, Herzogspitalstr 5, D-8000 Munich 2 Tel: (089) 2603036
Man Dir, Rights & Permissions: Elizabeth Zuber; *Editorial:* A Arnold; *Sales, Publicity:* C Zynamon; *Production:* G Bitterauf
Associate Companies: Claudius Verlag GmbH (qv); Verlag Ernst Kaufmann (qv); Vandenhoeck und Ruprecht (qv)
Subjects: How-to, Philosophy, Psychology, Religion, Juveniles, High-priced Paperbacks, Social Science, Educational Materials
Bookshop: Buchhandlung J Pfeiffer GmbH & Co (at above address)
Founded: 1882
ISBN Publisher's Prefix: 3-7904

E **Pfister** GmbH*, Postfach 6485, Hussenstr 6, D-7750 Konstanz Tel: (07531) 23598
Associate Companies: Verlag der Arche, Switzerland (qv); Dr Franz Hain, Austria (qv); Sanssouci Verlag AG, Switzerland (qv)

Richard **Pflaum** Verlag KG*, Postfach 201920, D-8000 Munich 2 (Located at: Lazarettstr 4, D-8000 Munich 19) Tel: (089) 126070 Cable Add: Pflaumverlag Telex: 529408
Dir: Günther Heck
Subjects: Electrical Engineering, Electronics, Hobbies, Medicine, Periodicals
ISBN Publisher's Prefix: 3-7905

Udo **Pfriemer** Verlag GmbH, Landwehrstr 68, Postfach 201940, D-8000 Munich 2 Tel: 531604 Telex: 0523398
Subjects: Energy, Alternative Energies, Maintenance Technology in Water, Gas, Helio systems; Sanitary, Health, Heating, Sewage Technology, History of Culture and Technology

Robert **Pfützner** GmbH, see Verlag Mensch und Arbeit

Philips GmbH, Fachbuch-Verlag*, Mönckebergstr 7, Postfach 101420, D-2000 Hamburg 1 Tel: (040) 32971 Cable Add: Phihag Telex: 2161587 a dpu d
Man Dir: Wilfried von Hacht
Subjects: Electronics, Electrical Engineering, Radio & Television
1981: approx 100 titles
ISBN Publisher's Prefix: 3-87145

Philosophia Verlag GmbH, Widenmayerstr 34, Postfach 466, D-8000 Munich 22 Tel: (089) 221391 Telex: 0529070 iuskmd
Man Dir: Ulrich Staudinger; *Editorial Dirs:* Hans Burkhardt, Kurt Leube, Albert H Zlabinger, Barry Smith; *Sales, Production, Rights & Permissions:* Hilla Hueber
Subjects: Philosophy, Natiol Economy
Bookshop: Philosophia Book Service, Josephsburgstr 85, D-8000 Munich 80 Tel: (089) 434824
1982: 6 titles *1983:* approx 11 titles

154 FEDERAL REPUBLIC OF GERMANY

Founded: 1978 (originally 1966)
ISBN Publisher's Prefix: 3-88405

Physica-Verlag Rudolf Liebing GmbH und Co, Werner-von-Siemens-Str 5, Postfach 5840, D-8700 Würzburg 1 Tel: (0931) 22821 Telex: 68472 liewue-d
Man Dir: Arnulf Liebing
Branch Off: A-1010 Vienna, Seilerstätte 18, Austria
Subjects: Statistics, Economics, Business Administration, University Textbooks, Scientific Journals
1981: 25 titles *1982:* 20 titles *Founded:* 1952
ISBN Publisher's Prefix: 3-7908

Physik-Verlag GmbH, Pappelallee 3, Postfach 1260-80, D-6940 Weinheim/Bergstr Tel: (06201) 6020 Telex: 465516 vchw d
Man Dir: Prof Dr Helmut Grünewald, Hans Dirk Köhler; *Editorial:* Dr Hans-Friedrich Ebel, Dr Gerd Giesler; *Sales, Publicity and Advertising Dir:* Helmut Schmitzer; *Production:* Maximilian Montkowski; *Rights & Permissions:* Kornelia Herbig
Parent Company: Verlag Chemie, GmbH (qv)
Subjects: Science & Technology (especially Physics), University Textbooks
1982: 11 titles *Founded:* 1947
ISBN Publisher's Prefix: 3-87664

Pinx-Verlag Kurt Glombig*, Hartmann-Ibach-Str 68, D-6000 Frankfurt am Main 60 Tel: (0611) 454807
Publisher: Kurt Glombig
Subjects: Public Relations Texts in Popular editions, Pharmaceuticals, Travel Sketches, Series of Primers, Animals

R **Piper** & Co Verlag, Georgenstr 4, Postfach 430120, D-8000 Munich 40 Tel: (089) 397071 Cable Add: Piperverlag Munich Telex: 5215385
Orders to: Koch, Neff & Oetinger & Co, Am Wallgraben 110, D-7000 Stuttgart 80
Proprietor and President: Klaus Piper; *Man Dir:* Dr Ernst Reinhard Piper; *Editorial:* Dr Rainer Weiss, Dr Klaus Stadler, Jochen Rahe; *Sales Dir:* Michael Lechler; *Rights & Permissions:* Dorothee Grisebach
Branch Off: R Piper & Co Verlag GmbH, Switzerland (qv)
Subjects: Novels, Poetry, Biography, Sociology, Natural Sciences, Philosophy, Psychology, Arts, Education
1981: 113 titles *Founded:* 1904
ISBN Publisher's Prefix: 3-492

Plambeck & Co, Druck und Verlag GmbH, Xantener Str 7, Postfach 920, D-4040 Neuss Tel: (02101) 57081 Telex: 8517506 and 8517530 plad d
Subjects: Paperbacks, Pocket Books; Periodicals
Miscellaneous: Member of Arbeitsgemeinschaft sozialistischer und demokratischer Verleger und Buchhändler (qv for other members)

Verlag A G **Ploetz** GmbH & Co KG, Habsburgerstr 116, D-7800 Freiburg im Breisgau Tel: (0761) 2717387
Man Dir: Harald Glaeser; *Editorial:* Falk Redecker; *Advertising/Public Relations:* Hans-Georg von Weitzel
Orders to: Verlag Herder, Hermann-Herder-Str 4, D-7800 Freiburg im Breisgau
Parent Company: Verlag Herder GmbH & Co KG (qv)
Associate Companies: Herder AG, Switzerland (qv); Verlag Herder & Co, Austria (qv); Herder und Herder GmbH (qv)
Subjects: Illustrated Popular Reference Works on Historical, Biographical, Geographical Themes; School Books, Sociology, Linguistics
Founded: 1880
ISBN Publisher's Prefix: 3-87640

Podzun-Pallas Verlag GmbH*, Markt 9, Postfach 314, D-6360 Friedberg 3-Dorheim Tel: (06031) 3131 Cable Add: Podzun, Friedberg Telex: 415961
Man Dir, Production, Rights & Permissions: Rainer Ahnert; *Editorial:* Mrs Neisel; *Sales:* Mrs Hergesell
Subjects: Modern History, Illustrated Books, Periodicals
ISBN Publisher's Prefix: 3-7909

C E **Poeschel** Verlag*, Kernerstr 43, Postfach 529, D-7000 Stuttgart 1 Tel: (0711) 225074-6
Man Dir: Mr Schweizer; *Sales Dir:* Mr Cziszinsky; *Advertising Dir:* Mr Kegler; *Rights & Permissions:* Mrs Kästing
Orders to: (Federal Republic of Germany): Goethestrasse 6, D-7400 Tübingen; (in Berlin) A Muschal & Sohn, Lützowerstr 105-6, D-1000 Berlin 30
Associate Company: J B Metzlersche Verlagsbuchhandlung (qv)
Subject: Economics
Founded: 1902
ISBN Publisher's Prefix: 3-7910

Pohl Druckerei und Verlagsanstalt Otto Pohl, Herzog-Ernst-Ring 1, Postfach 103, D-3100 Celle Tel: (05141) 27081 Cable Add: Pohl, Celle
Dir: Manfred Senftleben
Subjects: Physical Education, Games, Sports, Gymnastics, Keep Fit
ISBN Publisher's Prefix: 3-7911

Verlag für **polizeiliches Fachschrifttum**, see Georg Schmidt-Römhild

Polyglott-Verlag Dr Bolte KG, Neusser Str 3, Postfach 401120, D-8000 Munich 40 Tel: (089) 3830 Cable Add: Langenscheidt Munich Telex: 5215379 lkgm d
Man Dir: Karl Ernst Tielebier-Langenscheidt; *Editor:* Dr Wilhelm Trappl; *Sales Dir:* Peter Haering; *Export Dir:* Uwe Cordts; *Advertising Dir:* Dieter Krause; *Rights & Permissions:* Manfred Überall
Subjects: Travel Guides, Phrasebooks, Dictionaries
1981: 8 titles *1982:* 5 titles *Founded:* 1902
Miscellaneous: Firm is a member of the Langenscheidt Group (qv)
ISBN Publisher's Prefix: 3-493

Polyglotte Buch- und Schallplatten-Verlag und Vertrieb*, Postfach 230147, D-4000 Düsseldorf Tel: 683191
Man Dir: F W Kreft
Subject: Educational Materials
ISBN Publisher's Prefix: 3-920754

Polygraph Verlag GmbH, Schaumainkai 85, Postfach 700940, D-6000 Frankfurt am Main 70 Tel: 639066 Cable Add: Polygraphverlag Frankfurt Main Telex: 0413562
Man Dir: H J Teichmann; *Sales Dir:* Peter Rüster; *Publicity Dir:* R Kreis; *Rights & Permissions:* Ulrike Schulz, H Sidoruk
Subjects: Textbooks and Reference Works for the Printing Industry and Allied Trades
Founded: 1947

Edition Georg **Popp** GmbH & Co, see Arena-Verlag Georg Popp GmbH & Co

Possev-Verlag V Gorachek KG, Flurscheideweg 15, D-6230 Frankfurt am Main 80 Tel: (0611) 341265
All Offices: N B Jdanoff
Subjects: Contemporary Russian authors in the original Russian, Periodicals in Russian
Founded: 1945
Miscellaneous: The Company also runs a translation agency (qv under Gorachek)

W **Poth** GbR, see Verlagsbuchhandlung Megapress

Praesentverlag Heinz Peter, Kleiststr 15, Postfach 2657, D-4830 Gütersloh Tel: (05241) 3188/9 Telex: 933831
Publisher: Heinz Peter
Subjects: General Fiction, Hobbies, Reference Books, Travel, Cookery
ISBN Publisher's Prefix: 3-87644

Präsenz-Verlag der Jesus-Bruderschaft, Gnadenthal, D-6257 Hünfelden Tel: (06438) 2003
Dir: Brother Samuel Ulmer
Subject: Religion
1981-82: 19 titles *Founded:* 1962
ISBN Publisher's Prefix: 3-87630

Verlag **Presse** Informations Agentur GmbH (PIAG)*, Stefanienstr 4, D-7570 Baden Baden Tel: (07221) 28994/25348 Cable Add: PIAG Baden Baden Telex: 781217 piag-d
Man Dir: Dieter Brinzer; *Publicity & Advertising Dir:* Thea Gutzeit; *Sales Dir:* Klaus Pittner
Subject: Photography
Founded: 1963

Guido **Pressler** Verlag, Auf dem Strifft, D-5165 Hürtgenwald Tel: (0249) 1385
Subjects: Art, History, Literature, Bibliographies, History of Sciences
ISBN Publisher's Prefix: 3-87646

Prestel Verlag, Mandlstr 26, D-8000 Munich 40 Tel: (089) 333055 Cable Add: Prestelverlag Telex: 5216366
Man Dir: Jürgen Tesch; *Sales Dir:* Gerda Behmenburg; *Advertising & Publicity Dir:* Grete Momsen; *Rights & Permissions:* Miss Aasta Fischer
Subjects: General Non-fiction, Art, Reference, History
1982: 40 titles *Founded:* 1924
ISBN Publisher's Prefix: 3-7913

Helmut **Preussler** Verlag*, Rothenburger Str 25, D-8500 Nuremberg 70 Tel: (0911) 262323/267124 Cable Add: Preussler-Verlag
Man Dir, Editorial: Helmut Preussler; *Sales, Publicity:* Wolfram Krause, Maria Pfann; *Production:* Werner Eckstein
Bookshop: Ernst Gebhard, Rothenburger Str 23-25, D-8500 Nuremberg
Founded: 1973
ISBN Publisher's Prefix: 3-921332

Prisma Verlag GmbH, Ringstr 16, D-4840 Rheda Tel: (05242) 4152695 Telex: 931149
Dir: Aloys Hellmold
Parent Company: Verlagsgruppe Bertelsmann GmbH (qv for associate companies)
Subjects: Reprints, Special Editions, Encyclopaedias, Mail Order Series

Albert **Pröpster***, Schillerstr 46, Postfach 2149, D-8960 Kempten Tel: 22797
Subjects: Cookery Books, Specialist Gastronomy Books, Picture Books, Roman Catholic Interest Books

Propyläen Verlag, Lindenstr 76, D-1000 Berlin 61 Tel: (030) 25911 Cable Add: Ullsteinbuch Berlin Telex: vlgul d 183723
Dir: Viktor Niemann; *Publicity:* Helmut Krüger; *Press:* Wolfgang Mönninghof
Parent Company: Verlag Ullstein GmbH (qv)
Subjects: Arts, History, Literature
ISBN Publisher's Prefix: 3-549

Verlag für **Psychologie**, Dr C J Hogrefe, Rohnsweg 25, Postfach 3751, D-3400 Göttingen Tel: (0551) 54044
Proprietor: Dr C J Hogrefe; *Man Dir:* Dr H Lundberg; *Sales & Publicity Dir:* O Kohl; *Advertising, Production, Rights & Permissions Dir:* B Otto
Branch Offs: C J Hogrefe Inc, 525 Eglinton Ave East, Toronto, Ontario M4P 1N5,

Canada; Verlag für Psychologie, Dr C J Hogrefe, Switzerland (qv)
Subjects: Psychology, Textbooks, Handbooks, Conference Reports, Yearbooks
Founded: 1949
ISBN Publisher's Prefix: 3-8017

Anton **Pustet**, Postfach 1921, D-8228 Freilassing
Man Dir: Dr F G Kuhn
Head Office: Universitätsverlag Anton Pustet, Austria (qv)
Subjects: Philosophy, Religion, Psychology, Social Science, Music
Founded: 1958
ISBN Publisher's Prefix: 3-7916

Verlag Friedrich **Pustet**, Gutenbergstr 8, Postfach 110441, D-8400 Regensburg 11 Tel: (0941) 96044 Cable Add: Pustet Telex: 65672
Man Dir: Dr Friedrich Pustet; *Editorial:* Dr Gerd J Maurer; *Sales & Advertising Dir, Rights & Permissions, Production:* Karl Wittman
Subjects: Christian Religion, Art, Monographs, Biography, Folklore, Bavaria
Bookshops: Buchhandlung Friedrich Pustet, Regensburg, Gesandtstr 6; Kleiner Exerzierplatz 4, Passau; Grottenau 4, Augsburg
Founded: 1826
ISBN Publisher's Prefix: 3-7917

Quell-Verlag, Furtbachstr 12A, Postfach 897, D-7000 Stuttgart 1 Tel: (0711) 605746/8
Dirs: Dr Wolfgang Reister, Walter Waldbauer; *Editorial, Rights & Permissions:* Dr Wolfgang Reister
Subjects: General Fiction, Biography, History, Philosophy, Religion
Bookshop: Buchhandlung der Evangelischen Gesellschaft, Stuttgart
1982: 25 titles *Founded:* 1830
ISBN Publisher's Prefix: 3-7918

Quelle und Meyer Verlag GmbH & Co, Schloss-Wolfsbrunnen-Weg 29, Postfach 104840, D-6900 Heidelberg 1 Tel: (06221) 22443 Cable Add: Quellmeyer Heidelberg
Man Dir: Dr Walter Kissling; *Sales, Advertising & Publicity Dir:* Hermann Klippel; *Foreign Rights Dir:* Hildegard Müller
Orders to: Koch, Neff und Oetinger & Co, Abt VA, Postfach 800620, D-7000 Stuttgart
Subjects: Philosophy, Religion, Psychology, Chemistry, Biology, Science, Social Science, Education, Languages, Literature, History, Geography, University, Secondary & Primary Textbooks
Founded: 1906
ISBN Publisher's Prefix: 3-494

R K W, see Rationalisierungs-Kuratorium

R V, see Reise- und Verkehrsverlag

Radius-Verlag GmbH+, Kniebisstr 29, D-7000 Stuttgart 1 Tel: (0711) 283091
Man Dir: Wolfgang Erk; *Sales, Publicity & Advertising Dir:* Gerhard Schroeder
Subjects: General Fiction, Philosophy, Religion, Paperbacks, Psychology, Periodical *Radius*
1982: 23 titles *1983:* 24 titles *Founded:* 1963
ISBN Publisher's Prefix: 3-87173

Rainer Verlag GmbH, Koertestr 10, D-1000 Berlin 61 Tel: (030) 6916536
Man Dir and Advertising: Rainer Pretzell; *Sales Dir:* Agnes Pretzell
Subjects: Belles Lettres, Poetry, Art, Quality Paperbacks
Founded: 1966

Dr **Ramdohr** KG, see Mentor-Verlag

Dokument und Analyse Verlag Bogislaw von **Randow***, Barer Str 43, D-8000 Munich 40 Tel: (089) 2720100
Publisher: Bogislaw von Randow; *General Manager:* Gerhard Fassmann; *Marketing Manager:* Angelika Meister; *Marketing Publicity:* Thomas Lingenthal
Subjects: Politics, Economics, Law, Sociology, Periodical
Founded: 1972

Rationalisierungs-Kuratorium der Deutschen Wirtschaft eV (RKW)*, Düsseldorfer Str 40, Postfach 5867, D-6236 Eschborn Tel: (06196) 4951 Cable Add: Erkawe Telex: 0418362 rkw d
Registered Society of the German Industrial Rationalization Board
Managers: Dr H W Büttner, Dr H Müller; *Publicity Manager:* Dipl-Kfm H Degenhard
Branch Offs: In all areas of the Federal Republic of Germany
Subjects: Business Operation and Management, Labour and Social Economics, Engineering/Technology Interchange, Construction, Packaging, Consultancy, Further Training
Founded: 1921

Walter **Rau** Verlag, Benderstr 168a, Postfach 120407, D-4000 Düsseldorf 12 Tel: (0211) 283095 Telex: 08586682
Dir: Gisela Rau
Subjects: Arts, Education, Non-fiction, Social Science, Literature, Translations, Chess
ISBN Publisher's Prefix: 3-7919

Karl **Rauch** Verlag KG*, Am Wehrhahn 100, Postfach 6520, D-4000 Düsseldorf 1
Man Dir: Harald Ebner
Subjects: Documentation, History, Fiction, Book Industry, Translations
Founded: 1923
ISBN Publisher's Prefix: 3-7920

Agentur des **Rauhen Hauses** Verlag GmbH*, Papenhuder Str 2, D-2000 Hamburg 76 Tel: (040) 2201291
Dirs: Max Lenz, Dieter Gätjens
Subjects: Religion, Belles Lettres, Fiction, Juveniles, Art, Paperbacks
Founded: 1842
ISBN Publisher's Prefix: 3-7600

Gerhard **Rautenberg** Druckerei und Verlag GmbH & Co KG+, Blinke 8, Postfach 1909, D-2950 Leer/Ostfriesland Tel: (0491) 4288 Cable Add: Rautenberg Leer
Dirs: Gerhard Rautenberg, Carl-Ludwig Rautenberg; *Editorial:* Gerhard Rautenberg
Branch Off: Druckerei und Verlag Gerhard Rautenberg GmbH & Co KG, Königstr 41, D-2208 Glückstadt
Subjects: Regional Guides within Germany, Humour, Popular Historical, General Fiction, Show Business
Bookshop: Rautenbergsche Buchhandlung, Postfach 1909, D-2950 Leer
Founded: 1825
ISBN Publisher's Prefix: 3-7921

Ravensburger Graphische Betriebe Otto Maier GmbH, see Otto Maier Verlag

Ravensburger Verlag GmbH, see Otto Maier Verlag

Ravenstein Verlag GmbH, Wielandstr 31-35, D-6000 Frankfurt am Main Tel: (0611) 590722/23/24 Cable Add: Ravensteinverlag
Man Dirs: Helga Ravenstein, Rüdiger Bosse
Subjects: Country and Regional Touring and Walking Maps, Town Maps and Guides, Pictorial Guides
Founded: 1830
ISBN Publisher's Prefix: 3-87660

Verlagsgesellschaft **Recht und Wirtschaft** mbH, Häusserstr 14, Postfach 105960, D-6900 Heidelberg Tel: (06221) 25661 Cable Add: Rechtwirtschaft Heidelberg Telex: 461665
Associate Company: I H Sauer Verlag, Heidelberg (qv)
Subjects: Law and Economics, Tax, Social and Industrial Questions, Periodicals

Philipp **Reclam** Jun Verlag GmbH, Postfach 1149, D-7257 Ditzingen 1 (Located at: Siemensstr 32, Ditzingen) Tel: (07156) 5021 Cable Add: Reclam Ditzingen Telex: 7266704 recl d
Publishers: Dr Heinrich Reclam, Dr Dietrich Bode; *Publicity Dir:* Christoph Wilhelmi; *Rights & Permissions:* Marianne Diehl
Subjects: General Fiction, Belles Lettres, Poetry, Music, Art, Philosophy, Reference, Religion, Low-priced Paperbacks, University, Secondary & Primary Textbooks
1982: approx 100 titles *Founded:* 1828
ISBN Publisher's Prefix: 3-15

Dr Ludwig **Reichert** Verlag+, Reissstr 10, D-6200 Wiesbaden-Dotzheim Tel: (06121) 465686
Publisher: Ludwig Reichert
Subjects: Facsimile Reprints, Art, Books and Libraries, Orientalia, Linguistics
Founded: 1970
ISBN Publisher's Prefixes: 3-920153, 3-88226

Otto **Reichl** Verlag, 'Der Leuchter', Haus Herresberg, D-5480 Remagen Tel: 02642/22271
Man Dir: Herwart von Guilleaume
Subjects: Philosophy, Religion, Parapsychology, Mysticism, Supernatural
1981: 2 titles *1982:* 2 titles *Founded:* 1957
ISBN Publisher's Prefix: 3-87667

Verlag Knut **Reim***, Dammtorstr 30, Postfach 302824, D-2000 Hamburg 36 Tel: (040) 342641
General Managers: Jens Christians, Knut Reim
Subjects: Juvenilia, Jurisprudence, Economics
Founded: 1958

Ernst **Reinhardt** GmbH & Co Verlag+, Kemnatenstr 46, D-8000 Munich 19 Tel: (089) 170266
Man Dir, Production: Karl Münster
Orders to: Postfach 380280, D-8000 Munich 38
Subjects: Psychology, Psychotherapy, Philosophy, Pedagogy
Founded: 1899
ISBN Publisher's Prefix: 3-497

Verlag Wilhelm G **Reinheimer**, see Edition Venceremos

Reise- und Verkehrsverlag GmbH (RV)*, Schockenriedstr 40a, Postfach 800863, D-7000 Stuttgart 80 Tel: (0711) 7803053 Cable Add: Verkehrsverlag
Man Dir: Olaf Paeschke; *Editorial:* Helmut Schaub; *Sales Manager, Publicity:* Wolfgang Kunth
Parent Company: Verlagsgruppe Bertelsmann GmbH (qv for associate companies)
Subjects: Maps, Atlases, Guides
Founded: 1927

Rembrandt Verlag GmbH, Schaperstr 35, D-1000 Berlin 15 Tel: (030) 2135003
Man Dir: Dr Klaus J Lemmer
Subjects: Biography, History, Music, Art
Founded: 1923
ISBN Publisher's Prefix: 3-7925

Verlag Klaus G **Renner**, Adelheidstr 26, D-8000 Munich 40 Tel: (089) 2715495
Man Dir: Klaus Renner; *Editorial:* Thomas Milch

Subjects: Belles Lettres, Poetry, Limited Editions
Founded: 1973
ISBN Publisher's Prefix: 3-921499

Verlag Norman **Rentrop**+, Theodor Heuss Str 4, D-5300 Bonn 2 Tel: (0228) 364055 Telex: 17228309 ttx d
Man Dir: Norman Rentrop; *Editorial, Rights & Permissions:* Reinhard Fey; *Sales:* Michael Sänger; *Production:* Monika Graf; *Publicity:* Michael Rieck
Subject: Business Management
1981: 6 titles *1982:* 8 titles *Founded:* 1975
ISBN Publisher's Prefix: 3-8125

Rheingauer Verlagsgesellschaft mbH, Postfach 90, D-6228 Eltville am Rhein (Located at: Walluferstr 5a) Tel: (06123) 2312 Telex: 04182921 rvg d
Man Dir, Rights & Permissions: Bernd Ley, Peter Halfar; *Sales:* Mr Mätzel, Mr Hülzer, Mr Stärk; *Production:* Bernd Ley; *Publicity:* Monika Ley, Ingrid Bader
Orders to: Unipart-Verlag GmbH, Hofener Weg 33a, D-7148 Remseck-Aldingen
Subjects: Quality Illustrated Works, Low-priced Foreign Classics in Translation, Saga and Legend, Juvenile, General Non-fiction
Founded: 1975
ISBN Publisher's Prefix: 3-17319

Rheinland-Verlag GmbH*, Landeshaus, Kennedy-Ufer 2, Postfach 210720, D-5000 Cologne 21 Tel: 82832687
Orders to: Dr Rudolf Habelt GmbH, Abt Verlag (qv)
Branch Off: Postfach 150104, D-5300 Bonn
Subjects: Rhineland excavations, Regional Knowledge, Folklore, Care of Art and Monuments

Dr **Riederer** Verlag GmbH, Gutbrodstr 9, Postfach 447, D-7000 Stuttgart 1 Tel: (0711) 639797
Man Dirs: M Groitzsch, H Schneider
Subjects: Science, Engineering, Metallography
Founded: 1945
ISBN Publisher's Prefix: 3-87675

Ringier/Heering-Verlag GmbH, Ortlerstr 8, Postfach 700840, D-8000 Munich 70 Tel: (089) 769920 Telex: 0522720
Man Dir: Wolf Prüter
Subjects: Photography, Cinematography, Mountaineering, Nature Study, Sports Periodicals
Founded: 1932
ISBN Publisher's Prefix: 3-7763

Ritzau KG Verlag Zeit und Eisenbahn, Landsberger Str 24, D-8911 Pürgen Tel: (08196) 252
Subjects: History of German Railways; old Timetables and General History of Transport in Germany from late 19th Century
1981: 20 titles *1982:* 24 titles *Founded:* 1968
ISBN Publisher's Prefix: 3-921304

Rochus-Verlag, Düsseldorf, see Arbeitsgemeinschaft sozialistischer und demokratischer Verleger und Buchhändler

Röderberg-Verlag GmbH, Schumannstr 56, Postfach 4129, D-6000 Frankfurt am Main 1 Tel: (0611) 751046 Telex: 414721
Manager: Johannes Bär; *Editorial, Production:* Peter Altmann; *Sales:* Hoerst Foerster
Subject: Politics
Miscellaneous: Member of Arbeitsgemeinschaft sozialistischer und demokratischer Verleger und Buchhändler (qv for other members)
ISBN Publisher's Prefix: 3-87682

Rogner und Bernhard GmbH & Co Verlags KG, Reichenbachstr 33, Postfach 140480, D-8000 Munich 5 Tel: (089) 2014336 Telex: 05215482 buch d
Dirs: Antje Ellermann, Thomas Landshoff, W H Schünemann
Subjects: General Fiction, Belles Lettres, Art, Photography
1982: 18 titles
ISBN Publisher's Prefix: 3-8077

Lev **Roitman** Verlag, Marienburgerstr 81, D-8000 Munich 81 Tel: (089) 933574/938358/2102622
Publisher: Lev Roitman; *Rights & Permissions:* Sharon Roitman
Orders to: Buchhandel-service, Schleissheimerstr 401, D-8000 Munich 45
Subjects: Fiction, Non-fiction
1983: 6 titles *Founded:* 1982
ISBN Publisher's Prefix: 3-923510

Rombach und Co GmbH, Verlag & Druckhaus*, Lörracher Str 3, Postfach 1349, D-7800 Freiburg im Breisgau Tel: (0761) 42323 Telex: 772820
Man Dir: Dr Hodeige
Subjects: History, Art, Social & Political Science, University Textbooks
Bookshop: Rombach-Center, Bertoldstr 10, D-7800 Freiburg
Founded: 1936
ISBN Publisher's Prefix: 3-7930

Rose-Verlag und Edition Rose-Verlag*, Seestr 12, D-8221 Seebruck Chiemsee Tel: (08667) 420 Cable Add: Rose-Verlag 8221 Seebruck Telex: 0526144 M Piepenstock
Man Dir, Rights & Permissions: Marianne Piepenstock; *Editorial, Sales, Production:* Michael Piepenstock
Subjects: Education and Upbringing, Health, Food, Religion
Founded: 1955
ISBN Publisher's Prefix: 3-920803

Rosenheimer Verlagshaus Alfred Förg GmbH & Co KG+, Am Stocket 12, D-8200 Rosenheim 2 Tel: (08031) 83181 Cable Add: Rosenheimer Verlagshaus Rosenheim Telex: 525732 rosen d
Man Dir: Alfred Förg; *Sales:* Klaus Bovers; *Rights & Permissions:* Hansjörg Decker
Subjects: General Fiction, Belles Lettres, Poetry, Biography, History, Music, Art, Needlecraft, Bavarica
1981: 200 titles *Founded:* 1968
ISBN Publisher's Prefix: 3-475

Rotbuch Verlag GmbH, Potsdamer Str 98, D-1000 Berlin 30 Tel: (030) 2611196
Man Dirs: Eberhard Delius, Angelika Spiekermann; *Editorial:* Gabriele Dietze, Marie-Luise Knott; *Sales, Advertising:* Walter Hellmann, Sigrid Ruschmeier, Angelika Spiekermann; *Publicity, Rights & Permissions:* Holger Behm, Ingrid Karsunke
Subjects: Belles Lettres, Poetry, History, Social Science
ISBN Publisher's Prefix: 3-88022

Verlag **Roter Morgen**, Wellinghoferstr 103, Postfach 300526, D-4600 Dortmund-Hörde (30) Tel: (0231) 433691/92
Subjects: Speeches and Writings of Stalin and Enver Hoxha, Communism, Publications of the Communist Party of Germany (Marxist-Leninist), Periodical
Founded: 1977
ISBN Publisher's Prefix: 3-88196

Verlag **Roter Stern**, Holzhausenstr 4, Postfach 180147, D-6000 Frankfurt am Main Tel: (0611) 599999
Publisher: K D Wolff
Associate Company: Stroemfeld Verlag AG, Switzerland (qv)
Subjects: Textbooks, Philosophy, Periodicals
ISBN Publisher's Prefix: 3-87877

Erich **Röth**-Verlag, Kassel, Korbacher Str 235, D-3500 Kassel-Nordshausen Tel: (0561) 401206 Cable Add: Röthverlag
Subjects: Folk tales and Folklore, Hungary, Translations from Hungarian, Music, Art
Founded: 1921
ISBN Publisher's Prefix: 3-87680

Bergverlag Rudolf **Rother**, see Bergverlag

Rowohlt Taschenbuch Verlag GmbH, Hamburger Str 17, Postfach 1349, D-2057 Reinbek bei Hamburg Tel: (040) 72721 Cable Add: Rowohltverlag Reinbek Telex: 0217854
Dirs: Dr Matthias Wegner, Horst Varrelmann, Götz Reese, Erwin Steen; *Editorial:* Dr Matthias Wegner; *Sales:* Horst Varrelmann; *Production:* Erwin Steen; *Publicity:* Michael Berent; *Rights & Permissions:* Marianne Sparr
Parent Company: Rowohlt Verlag GmbH (at above address)
Subsidiary Company: Hamburger Druckerei Betriebs Gesellschaft (at above address)
Imprint: Spiegel-Bücher
Subjects: Fiction and Non-fiction Paperbacks, especially, popular works on Life Sciences, History and Archaeology, Art, Politics, Psychology, Education, Philosophy, Religion, Social Sciences, Sports and Games, Juvenile, Foreign Literature in Translation
1981: 401 titles *Founded:* 1953
ISBN Publisher's Prefix: 3-499

Verlag Wilhelm C **Rübsamen**, Reinsburgstr 102, D-7000 Stuttgart 1

Ruhland Verlag, Goethestr 27, D-6000 Frankfurt am Main 1 Tel: (0611) 285604
Publisher: Erich Ruhland; *Publicity, Rights & Permissions:* Dietrich Luhrs
Subject: Instruction courses and texts on Secretarial Work, Commerce, Business Management
1982: 16 titles *1983:* 2 titles *Founded:* 1968
ISBN Publisher's Prefixes: 3-88509, 3-920793

W **Runge** Verlag, see Arbeitsgemeinschaft sozialistischer und demokratischer Verleger und Buchhändler

VWK **Ryborsch** GmbH, see VWK

S A S S-Verlagsgesellschaft mbH und Co KG, Postfach 249, D-6440 Bebra (Located at: Nürnberger Str) Tel: 06622/2005 Telex: 493412

S D V Saarbrücker Druckerei und Verlag GmbH, Halbergstr 3, Postfach 442, D-6600 Saarbrücken Tel: (0681) 64941
Man Dir, Editorial: Peter Neumann; *Publicity:* Josef Bronder
Parent Company: Paulinus-Druckerei GmbH, D-5500 Trier
Subjects: Folk Lore, Regional Lore, History, Art, Architecture, Language and Literature (especially of the Saar region)
1981: 9 titles *1982:* 15 titles *Founded:* 1884
ISBN Publisher's Prefix: 3-921646

Verlag Otto **Sagner**, Heßstr 39-41, Postfach 340110, D-8000 Munich 34 Tel: (0811) 522027 Cable Add: buchsagner München
Publisher: Otto Sagner; *Editorial:* Dr Peter Rehder
Orders to: Kubon und Sagner (at above address)
Parent Company: Kubon und Sagner (at above address)
Subject: Slavistics (Language and History)
Founded: 1959
ISBN Publisher's Prefix: 3-87690

Otto **Salle** Verlag, see Verlag Moritz Diesterweg/Otto Salle Verlag

Salvator Verlag GmbH*, Hermann-Josef-Str 4, Postfach 220, D-5370 Kall Tel: (02441) 5047
Dir: Andreas Münck
Subject: Religion

Eugen **Salzer** Verlag*, Titotstr 5, Postfach 3048, D-7100 Heilbronn 1 Tel: (07131) 68294 Cable Add: Salzerverlag
Man Dir: Hartmut Salzer; *Sales Dir:* J Glage
Subjects: Fiction, Belles Lettres, How-to, Reference, Juveniles
Founded: 1891
ISBN Publisher's Prefix: 3-7936

Sammlung Luchterhand, an imprint of Hermann Luchterhand Verlag GmbH & Co KG (qv)

Dr Martin **Sändig** GmbH, see Sändig Reprint Verlag, Liechtenstein

Verlag der **Sankt-Johannis-Druckerei** C Schweickhardt, Heiligenstr 24, Postfach 5, D-7630 Lahr 12 Tel: (07821) 581 Cable Add: Veritas Lahrschwarzwäld
Man Dir: Walter Guthmann; *Editorial, Publicity, Rights & Permissions:* Karl-Heinz Kern; *Sales:* Johannes Walter; *Production:* Helmut Schlegel
Subjects: Christian Devotional: stories, commentaries, travel books for young people and adults
1981: 27 titles *1982:* 27 titles *Founded:* 1896
Miscellaneous: Member of the Telos (qv) group publishing evangelical paperbacks
ISBN Publisher's Prefix: 3-501

Sankt Otto Verlag GmbH, Lange Str 22-24, Abholfach, D-8600 Bamberg Tel: (0951) 25252 Telex: 0662860 etvl
Joint Man Dirs: Kurt Kiening, Helmut Treml; *Other Offices:* Norbert Göbel
Parent Company: Bayerische Verlagsanstalt Bamberg (qv)
Associate Companies: Morawa und Co, Austria (qv); Adolf Zwimpfer, Switzerland (qv)
Subjects: Roman Catholic Religious Literature; Guides for Pilgrims, Bamberg Diocesan interest, Hymn Books, Devotional
Bookshop: Goerres Buchhandlung (at above address)
1982: 4 titles *Founded:* 1922
ISBN Publisher's Prefix: 3-87693

Sassafras Verlag*, Bismarckplatz 43, D-4150 Krefeld Tel: (02151) 599555
Subject: Contemporary Writing
ISBN Publisher's Prefix: 3-922690

Satire Verlag GmbH*, Auerstr 1, D-5000 Cologne 60 Tel: (0221) 735929
Man Dir: Saskia E Wollschon; *Editorial:* Reinhard Hippen, Gerd Wollschon
Subject: Satire
Founded: 1977
ISBN Publisher's Prefix: 3-88268

I H **Sauer** Verlag GmbH+, Häusserstr 14, Postfach 105960, D-6900 Heidelberg Tel: (06221) 25661 Cable Add: Rechtwirtschaft Heidelberg Telex: 461665
Associate Company: Verlagsgesellschaft Recht und Wirtschaft (qv)
Subjects: Industrial Management, Economics, Organization, Data Processing, Personnel Management, Rhetoric, Publicity, Series of Paperbacks for Industry

Verlag **Sauerländer**, Meisengasse 15, D-6000 Frankfurt am Main 1 Tel: (0611) 284953
Publisher: Hans C Sauerländer
Parent Company: Sauerländer AG, Switzerland (qv)
Associate Company: Verlag Sauerländer, Austria
Subjects: Juveniles, Fiction, Sciences
Founded: 1964
ISBN Publisher's Prefix: 3-7941

J D **Sauerländer's** Verlag, Finkenhofstr 21, D-6000 Frankfurt am Main 1 Tel: (0611) 555217
Publisher: Helmut A Baetz
Subjects: Forestry and Agricultural Sciences, Classical Philology
1982: 10 titles *Founded:* 1613/1816
ISBN Publisher's Prefix: 3-7939

K G **Saur** Verlag KG, Pössenbacherstr 2b, Postfach 711009, D-8000 Munich 70 Tel: (089) 798901/2/3 Cable Add: saur Telex: 5212067
Man Dirs: Klaus G Saur, Rudiger Hildebrandt; *Manager:* Manfred Westram; *Editorial:* Willi Gorzny, Dr Helga Lengenfelder; *Sales:* Paul Ferti; *Promotion:* Thyra Hoffmann-Heyden; *Production:* Manfred Link; *Rights & Permissions:* Dr Helga Lengenfelder, Barbara Verrel
Subsidiary Companies: Minerva Publikation (qv), Verlag Dokumentation Saur GmbH (both at above address); Uni-Taschenbücher GmbH (qv); K G Saur Publishing Inc, 1995 Broadway, New York, NY 10023, USA; K G Saur Editeur Sàrl, France (qv); K G Saur Ltd, Hans Zell Publishers, both UK (qqv)
Branch Off: PO Box 56, 14a St Giles, Oxford OX1 3EL, UK
Subjects: Reference, Social Science, Library Management, Documentation and Information Science, Data Processing
1981: approx 190 titles *Founded:* 1948
Miscellaneous: Formerly known as Verlag Dokumentation Saur KG, Munich. Firm is member of TR- Verlagsunion GmbH (qv)
ISBN Publisher's Prefix: 3-598

Karl A **Schäfer** Buch-und Offsetdruckerei-Goldstadtverlag*, Finkensteinstr 6, D-7530 Pforzheim Tel: (07231) 42095 Cable Add: Goldstadtverlag
Publisher: Günter Schäfer
Orders to: Geo-Center, Neumarkter Str 18, D-8000 Munich 80
Subject: Travel Guides
Founded: 1956
ISBN Publisher's Prefix: 3-87269

Hermann **Schaffstein** Verlag*, Postfach 1283, D-4600 Dortmund 1
Sales: Paul Lazar
Parent Company: Schroedel Schulbuchverlag GmbH (qv)
Orders to: Schroedel-Verlagsauslieferung, Postfach 810620, D-3000 Hanover
Subjects: Juveniles, High-priced Paperbacks
ISBN Publisher's Prefix: 3-588

F K **Schattauer** Verlag GmbH, Lenzhalde 3, Postfach 2945, D-7000 Stuttgart 1 Tel: (0711) 221733-7 Telex: 721886
Publishers: Prof Dr Paul Matis, Harald Schwer; *Sales Manager:* Jochen Hintermeier
Subject: Medicine (all aspects) and related sciences
ISBN Publisher's Prefix: 3-7945

Moritz **Schauenburg** Verlag GmbH und Co KG, Schillerstr 13, Postfach 2120, D-7630 Lahr 1 Tel: (07821) 23091 Cable Add: Schauenburg Lahrschwarzwald Telex: 0754943
Dir: Jörg Schauenburg
Subjects: General Fiction, Dialect texts, Music, Literature
Founded: 1794
ISBN Publisher's Prefix: 3-7946

Schaum, an imprint of McGraw-Hill Book Co GmbH (qv)

Verlag Heinrich **Scheffler**, an imprint of Societäts-Verlag (qv)

G **Schenck**, see R v Decker's Verlag GmbH

Scherpe Verlag*, Glockenspitz 140, Postfach 2630, D-4150 Krefeld Tel: (02151) 59211 Telex: 0853892
Subjects: General Fiction, Juveniles, Arts, Education, Illustrated Books, Belles Lettres, Politics
ISBN Publisher's Prefix: 3-7948

Scherz Verlag GmbH, Stievestr 9, D-8000 Munich 19 Tel: (089) 172237/38 Telex: 5215282 sherz d
Man Dir: Rudolf Streit-Scherz; *Editorial Dir:* Gert Woerner; *Sales Dir:* Wolfgang Radaj; *Crime/Suspense Pocket Books:* Ingeborg Ebel; *O W Barth-Verlag:* Stephan Schuhmacher
Associate Company: Otto Wilhelm Barth-Verlag KG (qv)
Head Off: Scherz Verlag AG, Switzerland (qv)
Subjects: General Fiction, History, Politics, Belles Lettres, Documentary Works
Founded: 1957
ISBN Publisher's Prefix: 3-502

Gertrud E **Scheuerer** Verlag, Hartmannsreit 44, D-8351 Schönberg Tel: (08554) 697
Man Dir: Gertrud Scheuerer; *Production:* Otto Scheuerer
Subject: Art
Founded: 1975

Fachverlag **Schiele und Schön** GmbH, Markgrafenstr 11, D-1000 Berlin 61 Tel: (030) 2516029 Cable Add: Schieleschön Berlin Telex: 181470 sunds d
Man Dir: Peter Schön
Subjects: Engineering, Electronics, Industry, Reference, Medicine, Hobbies, Periodicals
Founded: 1946

Kurt **Schilling**, see Scientia Verlag

Verlag Karl **Schillinger** KG, Wallstr 14, Postfach 1502, D-7800 Freiburg im Breisgau Tel: (0761) 33233/22891
Man Dir: Wolfgang Schillinger
Subjects: Nature Studies, Regional Literature
1981: 18 titles *Founded:* 1899
ISBN Publisher's Prefix: 3-921340

G **Schindele** Verlag GmbH, Hugo-Stotz-Str 14, D-6900 Heidelberg Tel: (06221) 73001
Man Dir: Eilert Erfling
Subjects: Pedagogy, Psychology, Sociology, Rehabilitation, Special Teaching, Social Instruction
1982: 14 titles *Founded:* 1969

Schirmer/Mosel Verlag GmbH, Franz-Joseph-Str 9, Postfach 401723, D-8000 Munich 40 Tel: (089) 393037 Telex: 5213687
Man Dirs: Lothar Schirmer, Erik Mosel; *Sales, Publicity, Rights & Permissions:* Lothar Schirmer; *Production:* Wulf Dietrich
Subjects: Art Books, Art History, Photo-Art
1981: 12 titles *Founded:* 1975
ISBN Publisher's Prefix: 3-88814

Verlag Bert **Schlender***, Auf der Wessel 53, D-3400 Göttingen Tel: (0551) 792651
Man Dirs: Bert Schlender, Aleke Thuja
Subjects: General Fiction, Belles Lettres, Poetry, Art, Low- & High-priced Paperbacks
Bookshop: Versandbuchhandlung Bert Schlender (at above address)
Founded: 1973

Joachim **Schmid** & Co, see Karl-May-Verlag

Erich **Schmidt** Verlag GmbH*, Genthiner Str 30G, D-1000 Berlin 30 Tel: (030) 2611741 Telex: 183 671 esbve d Cable Add: ESVerlag Berlin
Publicity: Karl-Heinz Rüttimann
Branch Offs: Viktoriastr 44a, Postfach 7330, D-4800 Bielefeld Tel: (0521) 66061; Paosostr 7, D-8000 Munich 60
Subjects: Pocket Reference, Law (Business, Agrarian), Foreign Trade, Journalism;

Economic, Social, Transport, Environmental Studies; Water and Waste Management, Building Technology, Linguistics, Folklore, History, Japan Studies, University and Secondary Textbooks, Paperbacks, Periodicals
1981: 115 titles *Founded:* 1924
ISBN Publisher's Prefix: 3-503

Verlag Dr Otto **Schmidt** KG, Unter den Ulmen 96-98, D-5000 Cologne 51 Tel: (0221) 373021 Telex: 8883381
Man Dir: Dr H M Schmidt; *Editorial:* Lopau Mechthild, Dr Katherine Knauth; *Sales, Publicity & Advertising Dir:* Edmund Arand
Subjects: University Textbooks, Jurisprudence, Tax Law
Bookshops: Buchhandlung Hermann Sack, Bahnstr 61, D-4000 Düsseldorf 1; Merlostr 4 and Luxemburgerstr, D-5000 Cologne 1; Buchhandlung Hermann Sack, Mercatorstr 27, D-6000 Frankfurt am Main
Founded: 1905
ISBN Publisher's Prefix: 3-504

Verlag für polizeiliches Fachschrifttum Georg **Schmidt-Römhild***, Mengstr 16, Postfach 2051, D-2400 Lübeck 1 Tel: 75001
Publisher: Norbert Beleke
Associate Company: Max Schmidt-Römhild Verlag (qv)
Subjects: Psychology, Criminology, Reference books for police officials, lawyers, public authorities
Founded: 1892
ISBN Publisher's Prefix: 3-8016

Max **Schmidt-Römhild**, Verlag+, Mengstr 16, Postfach 2051, D-2400 Lübeck 1 Tel: (0451) 75001 Telex: 26296 hvkl d
Publisher: Norbert Beleke
Associate Company: Verlag für polizeiliches Fachschrifttum Georg Schmidt-Römhild (qv)
Subjects: History, Medicine, General & Social Science, Reference (criminology, forensic, legal, medical and for public authorities)
1983: 20 titles *Founded:* 1579
ISBN Publisher's Prefix: 3-7950

Dr Roland **Schmiedel**, see Deutscher Apotheker-Verlag

Wilhelm **Schmitz** Verlag, Auf der Heide 5, D-6301 Wettenberg 2 (Wissmar) Tel: (06406) 2324
Dir: S Schmitz
Subjects: Art, Languages, German Studies, Slav Studies, East European Studies, Folklore
Founded: 1847

Galerie **Schmücking** Verlag*, Lessingplatz 12, D-3300 Brunswick Tel: (0531) 44960
Branch Offs: D-2286 Archsum/Sylt, Bobtäärp, Federal Republic of Germany; Galerie Schmücking, Sattelgasse 2, CH-4000 Basle, Switzerland
Subject: Art

Franz **Schneekluth** Verlag, Postfach 466, D-8000 Munich 22 (Located at: Widenmayer Str 34) Tel: (089) 221391 Telex: 0529070
Man Dir: Ulrich Staudinger; *Editorial:* Dr Michael Schmidt; *Sales:* Peter Zebold; *Production:* Ellen Reuter; *Publicity and Public Relations:* Sybille Götz; *Rights & Permissions:* Renate Abrasch
Orders to: VVA Verlegerdienst Munich GmbH & Co KG, Postfach 1280, D-8130 Gilching
Subject: Belles Lettres
1981: 38 titles *Founded:* 1949
ISBN Publisher's Prefix: 3-7951

Verlag Lambert **Schneider** GmbH+, Hausackerweg 16, Postfach 105802, D-6900 Heidelberg 1 Tel: (06221) 21354
Publisher: Lothar Stiehm
Subsidiary Company: Lothar Stiehm Verlag (qv)
Subjects: Belles Lettres, Poetry, Biography, Literature, Humanities, History, Music, Art, Judaica, Philosophy, Reference, Religion, University & Secondary Textbooks
Founded: 1925
ISBN Publisher's Prefix: 3-7953

Rudolf **Schneider** Verlag+, Freseniusstr 59, D-8000 Munich 60 Tel: (089) 8113466 Cable Add: Schneider Verlag Munich 60
Publisher and Man Dir: Karl-Heinz Biebl
Subjects: Gift volumes, Artist-illustrated books, Children's
1981: 7 titles *Founded:* 1980
ISBN Publisher's Prefix: 3-7955

Franz **Schneider** Verlag GmbH & Co KG, Frankfurter Ring 150, D-8000 Munich 46 Tel: (089) 381911 Telex: 05215804
Publisher: Franz Schneider; *Editorial:* Monika Raeithel-Thaler; *Sales:* Kurt Gerber; *Production:* Josef Loher; *Publicity:* Ursula Jacob; *Foreign Rights:* Gisela Essig
Subject: Juveniles
Founded: 1913
ISBN Publisher's Prefix: 3-505

Verlag **Schnell und Steiner** GmbH und Co, Postfach 112, D-8000 Munich 65 (Located at: Paganinistr 92, Munich 60) Tel: (089) 8112015 Cable Add: Schnellsteiner München
Man Dir, Rights and Permissions: Karl A Stich; *Editorial:* Dr P Mai; *Sales:* N Dinkel; *Production:* J A Fink, N Dinkel
Branch Off: Schnell und Steiner, CH-8260 Stein am Rhein, Switzerland
Subjects: Biography, History of Art, Art Guides, Religion, Travel Literature
Founded: 1934
ISBN Publisher's Prefix: 3-7954

Verlag die **Schönen Bücher**, see Dr Wolf Strache

Ferdinand **Schöningh** Verlag, Jühenplatz am Rathaus, Postfach 2540, D-4790 Paderborn Tel: (05251) 21322 Cable Add: Schönbuch Paderborn Telex: 936929 fspb
Subjects: Educational Publishers for Schools and Colleges, Earth Sciences, History, Literary Criticism, Mathematics, Education, Philosophy, Physics, Politics, Psychology, Law, Religion, Social Science, Linguistics, Languages, Paperbacks; UTB Library of mini-paperbacks
1982: 251 titles
ISBN Publisher's Prefix: 3-506

B **Schott's** Söhne, Musikverlag, Weihergarten, Postfach 3640, D-6500 Mainz 1 Tel: (06131) 246 Cable Add: Scotson Mainz Telex: 4187821 scot d
Man Dirs: Ludolf Frhr von Canstein, Jürgen M Luczak, Dr Peter Hanser-Strecker; *Sales, Export Dir:* Jürgen M Luczak; *Editorial:* Brigitte Franken, Friedrich Zehm, Friedrich Wanek, Lothar Friedrich, Hilger Schallehn; *Sales:* Helmut Fischer; *Production, Publicity:* Dr Hanser-Strecker; *Rights & Permissions:* Heinz Wolf, Volker Landtag
Orders to: Carl-Zeiss Str 1, PO Box 3640, D-6500 Mainz-Hechtsheim Tel: (06131) 59035
Associate Companies: Wega Verlag GmbH, Mainz; Ars-Viva-Verlag GmbH, Mainz; Eulenburg AG, Zurich, Switzerland
Subsidiary Company (jointly owned with Universal Edition AG, Austria — qv): Wiener Urtext Edition-Musikverlag GmbH & Co KG, Austria (qv)
Branch Offs: Schott Music Corp, New York, USA; Schott Japan Co Ltd, Tokyo, Japan; Schott & Co Ltd, 48 Great Marlborough St, London W1V 2BN, UK
Subjects: Music and Music Reference, High-priced Paperbacks, Journals, University, Secondary & Primary Textbooks, Educational Materials, Sheet Music
Founded: 1770
ISBN Publisher's Prefix: 3-7957

Verlag J F **Schreiber** GmbH+, Postfach 285, D-7300 Esslingen (Located at: Liebigstr 1-11, D-7301 Deizisau) Tel: (07153) 22011 Telex: 7266880 jfs d
Man Dirs: Heinz Stühmer, Gerhard Schreiber; *Editorial:* Gerhard Schreiber; *Sales:* Heidi Neubauer; *Production:* Rolf Bianchi; *Publicity:* Martin Ludwig; *Rights & Permissions:* Jutta Hinkelbein
Orders to: Koch, Neff und Oetinger & Co, Postfach 800620, D-7000 Stuttgart 80
Associate Company: Junior International (qv)
Branch Off: Möhlstr 34, D-8000 Munich 80
Subjects: Children's and Juvenile, Painting Books, Nature Guides
1982: 20 titles *1983:* 23 titles *Founded:* 1831
ISBN Publisher's Prefix: 3-480

Verlag und **Schriftenmission** der Ev Ges für Deutschland GmbH, see Evangelischen Gesellschaft

Schroedel Schulbuchverlag GmbH*, Hildesheimer Str 202-206, Postfach 810760, D-3000 Hanover 81 Tel: (0511) 33881 Telex: 923527 hsvha d
Man Dirs: Dipl-Kfm Anton Kemper, Dr Werner Kugel
Orders to: Breslauer Str 60, D-3203 Sarstedt; Deggingstr 93, D-4600 Dortmund 1
Subsidiary Companies: CVK und Schroedel GmbH & Co Geographische Verlagsgesellschaft KG (qv); Hermann Schaffstein Verlag (qv)
Branch Offs: Lützowstr 105-106, Berlin; Deggingstr 93, Dortmund; Graf-Adolf-Platz 6, Düsseldorf; Marsstr 4, Munich; Gustav-Stresemann-Ring 12-16, Wiesbaden; Wolframstr 36, Stuttgart; Hardstr 95, Basle, Switzerland
Subject: School textbooks
Founded: 1982
Miscellaneous: Formerly Hermann-Schroedel Verlag KG
ISBN Publisher's Prefix: 3-507

Kurt **Schroeder** Verlag, Am weissen Stein 48, D-5653 Leichlingen 1 Tel: (02175) 3355
Man Dir: Hannsgeorg Schroeder
Subject: Travel Guides to foreign countries world-wide; Plant Guides
1981: 4 titles *1982:* 2 titles *Founded:* 1919
ISBN Publisher's Prefix: 3-87722

Marion von **Schroeder** Verlag GmbH, Postfach 9229, D-4000 Düsseldorf (Located at: Grupellostr 28) Tel: (0211) 360516 Telex: 8587327
Publisher: Ivo Frenzel; *Sales Manager:* Herbert Borgartz; *Publicity Manager:* Michael Tochtermann
Subjects: Belles Lettres, Fiction, Foreign Literature, Biography, Fantastica
Founded: 1935
Miscellaneous: Firm is a member of Econ Verlagsgruppe (qv)
ISBN Publisher's Prefix: 3-547

Anton **Schroll** & Co GmbH, Boosstr 15, D-8000 Munich 95 Tel: (089) 653590
Man Dir: Friedrich Geyer
Head Off: Anton Schroll & Co, Austria (qv)
Subjects: Art, Travel
Founded: 1953

Ferdinand **Schroll**, see Titania-Verlag

FEDERAL REPUBLIC OF GERMANY 159

Verlag **Schule und Elternhaus***, Wilhelmshöher Allee 254-256, Postfach 410160, D-3500 Kassel Tel: (0561) 30076 Cable Add: Schule und Elternhaus Kassel-Wilhelmshöhe Telex: 0992450
Editorial: Hans-J Pfalzgraf
Associate Company: Druck- und Verlagshaus Thiele und Schwarz (qv)
Subjects: Education, Vocabularies, Series by Young Writers
ISBN Publisher's Prefix: 3-88056

Schuler Verlagsgesellschaft mbH, Schloss Mühlfeld, D-8036 Herrsching Tel: (08152) 1087 Telex: 526493
Dirs: Anton Bolza, Rudolf Blanckenstein
Subjects: Art, Juveniles, Reference
Founded: 1946
ISBN Publisher's Prefix: 3-7796

v g s — Verlagsgesellschaft **Schulfernsehen** mbH & Co KG, Postfach 180269, D-5000 Cologne 1 (Located at: Breite Str 118/120, Cologne) Tel: (0221) 219641
School Television Publishing Company
Man Dir: Dr Heinz Gollhardt
v g s comprises the following companies: Verlag Aschendorff (qv); Beltz Verlag (qv); C C Buchners Verlag, Bamberg; Cornelsen-Velhagen und Klasing GmbH & Co Verlag für Lehrmedien KG (qv); Ferd Dümmlers Verlag (qv); HADU — Hagemann Lehrmittel- und Verlagsgesellschaft mbH (qv); Lehrmittelverlag Wilhelm Hagemann (qv); Verlag Handwerk und Technik, Hamburg; Heckners Verlag (qv); Hirschgraben Verlag GmbH, Frankfurt am Main; Verlag Ferdinand Hirt (qv); Verlag Ferdinand Kamp (qv); Verlagsgesellschaft Rudolf Müller GmbH (qv); Verlag Eugen Ulmer GmbH & Co (qv); Westermann Verlag GmbH (qv)
Subjects: Books for TV programmes (educational, juvenile, hobby, natural sciences), Periodicals, Audiovisual Materials
Founded: 1970
ISBN Publisher's Prefix: 3-8025

Verlag **Schulte** und Gerth GmbH & Co KG*, Postfach 1148, D-6334 Asslar Tel: (06441) 8461 Telex: 483794
Publisher: Klaus Gerth
Subsidiary Company: Turmberg Verlag (Musikverlag Klaus Gerth) (qv)
Subjects: Music, Religion, Biography, Juveniles, General Non-fiction

P N **Schulten** see Numismatischer Verlag

Schulverlag Vieweg GmbH*, Corneliussstr 9-11, D-4000 Düsseldorf Tel: (0211) 370266
Dir: Benno Hasselsweiler
Parent Company: Verlagsgruppe Bertelsmann GmbH (qv for associate companies)
Subjects: Instructional Works in German Language, Evangelical Religion, Mathematics, Natural Sciences

Verlag R S **Schulz***, Berger Str 8-10, Seehang 4, D-8136 Percha-Kempfenhausen Tel: (08151) 13041 Telex: 0526427
Publisher: Rolf Simon Schulz
Subjects: Fiction, Architecture, Public Health, Law, Social Science, Veterinary Science, Periodicals
ISBN Publisher's Prefix: 3-7962

Hohenstaufen Verlag **Schumann** KG, see Hohenstaufen

Carl Ed **Schünemann** KG, Zweite Schlachtpforte 7, Postfach 106067, D-2800 Bremen 1 Tel: (0421) 36351 Cable Add: Schünemanns Bremen
Man Dir: Klaus Kirchner; *Sales & Publicity Dir:* Herbert Kuhangel
Subjects: Belles Lettres, Art
Founded: 1810
ISBN Publisher's Prefix: 3-7961

Verlag K W **Schütz** KG, Mindener Str 34, Postfach 1180, D-4994 Preußisch Oldendorf Tel: (05742) 2073/4
Man Dir: Erwin Höke
Subjects: History, Juveniles
Bookshop: Versandbuchdienst Göttingen (at above address)
Founded: 1948
ISBN Publisher's Prefix: 3-87725

Schwabenverlag AG, Senefelderstr 12, Postfach 4280, D-7302 Ostfildern 1 Tel: (0711) 47060 Telex: 0723556
Man Dir: Dieter Hirsmüller
Subsidiary Company: Süddeutsche Verlagsgesellschaft mbH (qv)
Subjects: Popular Christian Devotional, Swabian Regional Interest, Large Print Books
Bookshops: Schwabenverlag Buchhandlung, Bahnhofstr 21, D-7080 Aalen; Spitalstr 17, D-7030 Ellwangen
Founded: 1848
ISBN Publisher's Prefix: 3-7966

Verlag Haus **Schwalbach***, Bethelstr 35, D-6200 Wiesbaden Tel: (06121) 429288
Subjects: Textbooks, Education, Periodicals
ISBN Publisher's Prefix: 3-920427

Schwaneberger Verlag GmbH, Muthmannstr 4, D-8000 Munich 45 Tel: 381931 Cable Add: Schwanverlag München Telex: 5215342 gerb d
Man Dir, Rights & Permissions: Hans Hohenester; *Editorial:* Gerhard Webersinke; *Sales:* Karl-Heinz Nuss; *Publicity:* Horst Rogg
Associate Company: Carl Gerber Verlag GmbH
Subject: Philately
Founded: 1910
ISBN Publisher's Prefix: 3-87858

Edition **Schwann**, an imprint of C F Peters Musikverlag GmbH und Co KG (qv)

Pädagogischer Verlag **Schwann**/Bagel GmbH, see Pädagogischer

Otto **Schwartz** & Co, Verlag und Buchdruckerei, Annastr 7, D-3400 Göttingen Tel: (0551) 31051/2
Man Dir: Dr Herbert Weisser, Konrad Weisser
Subjects: Social Science, University Textbooks, Educational Materials
Bookshop: Fachbuchhandlung Otto Schwartz & Co (at above address)
Founded: 1871
ISBN Publisher's Prefix: 3-509

Verlag **Schwarz** GmbH*, Am Altenberg 7, D-7570 Baden Baden 23 Tel: (07223) 6923
Man Dir: Elke Schwarz-Fritz
Subjects: Belles Lettres, Poetry
Founded: 1980 (as GmbH)
ISBN Publisher's Prefix: 3-15859

Schwarz Bildbücher, an imprint of Verlag Wolfgang Zimmer (qv)

Dr Wolfgang **Schwarze** Verlag+, Heckinghauser Str 65, Postfach 202015, D-5600 Wuppertal 2 Tel: (0202) 622005/6
Man Dir, Rights & Permissions: Dr Wolfgang Schwarze; *Sales, Office Chief:* Ursula Rumker-Schulze
Subsidiary Company: Kunst und Wohnen Verlag GmbH (at above address)
Subjects: Art books on Antiquities, Illustrated books on the Home and Interior Architecture, Facsimile Engravings
Founded: 1968
ISBN Publisher's Prefix: 3-87741

Verlag der Sankt-Johannis-Druckerei C **Schweickhardt**, see Sankt-Johannis

J **Schweitzer** Verlag*, Geibelstr 8, D-8000 Munich 80 Tel: (089) 476047
Man Dir: Dr Arthur L Sellier
Associate Company: Walter de Gruyter & Co, Mouton Publishers (qv)
Subjects: Jurisprudence, Legal Information

E **Schweizerbart'sche** Verlagsbuchhandlung, Johannesstr 3A, D-7000 Stuttgart 1 Tel: (0711) 623541/3 Cable Add: Schweizerbartverlag Stuttgart
Man Dirs: Dr Erhard Naegele (Production), Klaus Obermiller (Sales)
Associate Company: Gebrüder Borntraeger Verlagsbuchhandlung (qv)
Subjects: Geology, Palaeontology, Mineralogy, Limnology, Botany, Fishery, Hydrobiology, Zoology, Anthropology, Periodicals
Founded: 1826
ISBN Publisher's Prefix: 3-510

H G **Schwieger**, see P R Verlag

Verlag Junge Gemeinde E **Schwinghammer** KG*, Fangelsbachstr 11, Postfach 979, D-7000 Stuttgart 1 Tel: (0711) 643015/16 Cable Add: Jungegemeindeverlag
Dir: Siegfried Krumrey
Subjects: Religion, Juveniles, Educational Materials, Periodicals
1981: 6 titles *1982:* 5 titles *Founded:* 1928
ISBN Publisher's Prefix: 3-7797

Scientia Verlag und Antiquariat Kurt Schilling, Adlerstr 65, Postfach 1660, D-7080 Aalen 1 Tel: (07361) 41700 Cable Add: Scientia Aalenwuertt
Man Dir: Kurt Schilling; *Other Offices:* Günter Schilling
Subjects: Reprints in History, Education, Philosophy, Law, Social Science, Economics
Founded: 1953
ISBN Publisher's Prefix: 3-511

Scriptor Verlag, c/o Hirschgraben Verlag, Fürstenbergerstr 223, D-6000 Frankfurt am Main 1 Tel: (06174) 3021
Publishers: Dr Franz Löffelholz/Michael A Schillo
Parent Company: Hirschgraben Verlag
Subjects: Linguistics, Communications, Literature, Sociology, Education, Reprints
Founded: 1973
ISBN Publisher's Prefix: 3-589

E A **Seemann** Verlag, Nassestr 14, D-5000 Cologne 41 Tel: (0221) 461915
Man Dir: Elert A Seemann
Subjects: Art Books and Colour Reproductions, 43-volume Thieme-Becker Artistlexicon
Founded: 1858

S **Seewald**, see Verlag Molden

Seewald Verlag GmbH & Co+, Postfach 700464, D-7000 Stuttgart 70 (Located at: Obere Weinsteige 44, Stuttgart) Tel: (0711) 765085 Telex: 7255361
Man Dirs: Dr Heinrich Seewald, Sixt A Seewald; *Sales, Publicity:* York Seewald; *Rights & Permissions:* Annegret Broschk
Subjects: History, Politics, Economics, Social Science, High-priced Paperbacks, Books on Wine, Biographies and Memoirs, Education, Philosophy
Founded: 1956
ISBN Publisher's Prefix: 3-512

Seibt Verlag GmbH*, Bavariaring 24, D-8000 Munich 2 Tel: (089) 5309005 Telex: 05-216 933 seib d
Man Dir: Otto Wirsching
Subjects: Directories (Export, Trade etc) in several languages
ISBN Publisher's Prefix: 3-922948

Sellier Verlag GmbH, Erfurter Str 4, D-8057 Eching bei München Tel: (089) 3192048
Man Dir: Kurt Sellier; *Editorial:* Marieta

Hegewisch; *Sales Dir:* Friedrich Otto
Subjects: Juveniles, Secondary & Primary Textbooks, Educational Materials
Founded: 1702
ISBN Publisher's Prefix: 3-87137

Paul **Siebeck**, see J C B Mohr

Siebert Verlag GmbH, see Siebert und Engelbert Dessart Verlag GmbH

Siebert und Engelbert Dessart Verlag GmbH*, Wildstr 7, Postfach 1240, D-8202 Bad Aibling Tel: (08061) 4045 Telex: 525957
Subjects: Children's Books, Puzzles and Games
Founded: 1967
ISBN Publisher's Prefixes: 3-8089 (Siebert), 3-920215 (Dessart)

J **Siegler**, see Symposium Verlag

Siemens AG — ZVW 5 Verlag, Postfach 3240, D-8520 Erlangen Tel: (09131) 76566 Cable Add: Siemens erlangen Telex: 62921-320
Publicity: Mr Fröhling
Subjects: Electronics, Electro-technology (especially Textbooks, Instructional Material), Technical Periodicals
Founded: 1963
ISBN Publisher's Prefix: 3-8009

Signal-Verlag Hans Frevert, Balger Hauptstr 8, Postfach 813, D-7570 Baden Baden Tel: (07221) 61817 Cable Add: Signal-Verlag Baden Baden
Publisher: Hans-Jürgen Frevert
Subjects: Juveniles, Reference, Encyclopaedias, Dictionaries, Politics
ISBN Publisher's Prefix: 3-7971

Verlag Ludwig **Simon**, Mozartstr 15, Postfach 247, D-8023 Munich-Pullach Tel: (089) 7930332
Subject: Illustrated Works
ISBN Publisher's Prefix: 3-7972

Skypress International, D-1000 Berlin 41, Grillparzerstr 10-11 Tel: (411) 694044 Telex: 58623 drzh

Societäts-Verlag*, Frankenallee 71-81, Postfach 2929, D-6000 Frankfurt am Main 1 Tel: (0611) 75011 Cable Add: Zeitung Frankfurtmain Telex: 0411655
Publisher: Marianne Menzel; *Sales Manager:* Jörg Emich
Imprints: Verlag Frankfurter Bücher, Verlag Heinrich Scheffler, Verlag Osterrieth
Subjects: History, Business, Literature, Art, Economics
Founded: 1921
ISBN Publisher's Prefix: 3-7973

Sonnenweg-Verlag, Raitenaugasse 11, Postfach 1186, D-7750 Konstanz Tel: (07531) 23054/5
Man Dir, Rights & Permissions: Herbert Denecke
Parent Company: Christliche Verlagsanstalt GmbH (qv)
Associate Company: Friedrich Bahn Verlag (qv)
Subjects: General Fiction, Religious Guides, Introductory Readers
Founded: 1922
ISBN Publisher's Prefix: 3-7975

Spangenberg, an imprint of Verlag Heinrich Ellermann (qv)

Spectrum Verlag Stuttgart GmbH*, Friedrichstr 16-20, Postfach 1940, D-7012 Fellbach 4 Tel: (0711) 513004 Cable Add: Spectrumverlag Telex: 07254675
Man Dir: Peter Schwend; *Sales, Publicity, Advertising Dir, Rights & Permissions:* Ulrich Höfker
Subjects: How-to, Reference, Juveniles, Natural Science, Textbooks

Founded: 1963
ISBN Publisher's Prefix: 3-7976

Spee Buchverlag GmbH, Fleischstr 62-65, Postfach 3040, D-5500 Trier Tel: (0651) 46040 Telex: 04-72735
Publisher: Dr Eberhard Schützinger; *Dir:* Erika Schwarzenberg
Parent Company: Paulinus Druckerei GmbH (at above address)
Associate Company: Paulinus Verlag (qv)
Subjects: History, Politics, Religion, Picture books
ISBN Publisher's Prefix: 3-87760

W **Spemann** Verlag, Pfizerstr 5-7, Postfach 640, D-7000 Stuttgart 1 Tel: (0711) 21910 Cable Add: Kosmosverlag Stuttgart Telex: 721669 kosm d
Dirs: Claus Keller, R Keller, E Nehmann
Parent Company: Franckh'sche Verlagshandlung W Keller & Co (qv)
Subjects: History, Culture, Art
Founded: 1873
ISBN Publisher's Prefix: 3-810305

Spiegel-Bucher, an imprint of Rowohlt Taschenbuch Verlag GmbH (qv)

Verlag Volker **Spiess**, Grossgörschenstr 6, Postfach 620767, D-1000 Berlin 62 Tel: (030) 7813514/7812004
Publisher, Editorial: Volker Spiess; *Production:* Brigitte Mietz, Yvonne Goetz
Associate Company: Haude & Spener (qv)
Subjects: Library Science, Publishing, Literary Criticism, Mass Media, Education, Social Science, Linguistics, Languages, Periodicals
Founded: 1967
ISBN Publisher's Prefixes: 3-920889, 3-88435

Arno **Spitz**, see Berlin Verlag

Adolf **Sponholtz** Verlag, Osterstr 19, Postfach 447, D-3250 Hameln 1 Tel: (05151) 200310 Cable Add: Dewezet Telex: 92859
Dir: Dr Martin Oesch
Associate Company: Verlag C W Niemeyer (qv)
Orders to: VVA (Vereinigte Verlagsauslieferung GmbH), Postfach 7777, D-4830 Gütersloh 1
Subjects: General Fiction and Non-fiction, Juveniles, Literature, Animal stories, Hunting, Environment, Energy
Founded: 1894
ISBN Publisher's Prefix: 3-87766

Verlag für **Sprachmethodik**, Kantering 51-55, D-5330 Königswinter am Rhein Tel: (02223) 22771
Man Dir: H-Willi Wolter
Subjects: University, Secondary & Primary Textbooks, Educational Materials
Founded: 1953
ISBN Publisher's Prefix: 3-8018

Springer-Verlag Berlin — Heidelberg — New York — Tokyo GmbH & Co KG, Tiergartenstr 17, D-6900 Heidelberg Tel: (06221) 4870 Telex: 461723
Managing Partners: Dr Heinz Götze, Dr Konrad Springer, Claus Michaletz; *Editorial Dir:* Karl Hauck; *Production Dir:* Heinz Sarkowski; *Sales, Marketing Dir:* Jolanda L von Hagen; *Advertising Dir:* Lothar Siegel; *Distribution Dir:* Horst Drescher; *Personnel Dir:* Manfred Gast
Parent Company: Springer Verwaltungs GmbH, Berlin
Associate Companies: Springer-Verlag New York — Berlin — Heidelberg — Tokyo, 175 Fifth Ave, New York, NY 10010, United States; Springer-Verlag KG, Austria (qv); J F Bergmann, Federal Republic of Germany (qv); Springer Books (India) Pte Ltd, India (qv); Eastern Book Service Inc, Tokyo, Japan; Springer-Verlag, Tokyo Inc,

Tokyo, Japan
Subsidiary Company: Dr Dietrich Steinkopff Verlag (qv)
Branch Offs: Heidelberger Pl 3, D-1000 Berlin 33; Tiergartenstr 17, D-6900 Heidelberg 1
Subjects: Scientific and Technical: especially Medicine, Psychology, Biology; Earth Sciences, Maths, Physics, Chemistry, Computers; Engineering, Economics, Philosophy, Law; Reference Books, Paperbacks, Technical Journals, Technical Journals in English (especially Medical)
Bookshops: Bookselling group comprises: Lange und Springer Antiquariat, Berlin; Lange und Springer Wissenschaftliche Buchhandlung, Berlin; Freihofer AG, Zürich, Switzerland; Minerva Wissenschaftliche Buchhandlung GmbH, Vienna, Austria
Founded: 1842
Miscellaneous: Firm is member of TR-Verlagsunion GmbH (qv)
ISBN Publisher's Prefix: 3-540

L **Staackmann** Verlag KG, Leopoldstr 116, D-8000 Munich 40 Tel: (08027) 337 and (089) 342248
Man Dir: Dr Friedrich Vogel
Subjects: General Fiction, Historical Novels, Folk Stories, Illustrated Primers on Curiosities and Folklore Objects
1983: 7 titles *Founded:* 1869

Städte-Verlag, E v Wagner und J Mitterhuber, Daimlerstr 60, Postfach 501169, D-7000 Stuttgart-Bad Cannstatt Tel: (0711) 561496 Cable Add: staedteverlag
Man Dir: J Mitterhuber; *Publicity Dir:* U H Moeller
Subjects: Maps, District and Town plans (especially for touring and sightseeing); Federal Republic of Germany Town Directories
Annually 400 new titles
Founded: 1951

Stähle und **Friedel** Verlagsgesellschaft mbH und Co*, Neue Weinsteige 36, Postfach 492, D-7000 Stuttgart 1 Tel: (0711) 604464/5 Cable Add: Stählefriedel
Man Dir: Willy Klahm
Subject: Travel
ISBN Publisher's Prefix: 3-8116

Verlag **Stahleisen** mbH, Breitestr 27, D-4000 Düsseldorf 1 Tel: (0211) 88941 Cable Add: Stahleisen Düsseldorf 8587086
Man Dirs: Dr Dirk Springorum, Dietrich Schnell, Reinhold Welina; *Sales Manager:* Günter Hecker
Associate Company: Giesserei-Verlag GmbH (Foundry Press)
Subjects: Iron and steel
1981: 11 titles *Founded:* 1908
ISBN Publisher's Prefix: 3-514

Stalling Verlag GmbH, Druck und Verlagshaus*, Ammergaustr 72-78, Postfach 2580, D-2900 Oldenburg Tel: (0441) 34011 Cable Add: Stallingdruck Oldenburgoldb
Man Dir: Joachim Wisotzki; *Editorial:* Hans Jürgen Hansen, Christa Cordes, Rene Rilz; *Sales Dir:* Harry Sticklorat; *Rights & Permissions:* Barbara Zollickhofer
Editorial Offices: Boschstr 8, D-8031 Puchheim-Bahnhof
Subjects: General Non-fiction, Contemporary History, Art, Marine History, Humour, Juveniles
Founded: 1789
ISBN Publisher's Prefix: 3-7979

Stapp Verlag Wolfgang Stapp, Ehrenbergstr 29, D-1000 Berlin 33 Tel: (030) 8313445
Publishers: Wolfgang Stapp
Subjects: Illustrated Books, Books on areas of the German Democratic Republic,

FEDERAL REPUBLIC OF GERMANY 161

Monographs on Artists
ISBN Publisher's Prefix: 3-87776

Hanns-Joachim **Starczewski**
Verlag/Künstlerhof-Galerie*, Kirchstr 15,
Postfach 137, D-5410 Hohr-Grenzhausen
Tel: (02624) 2052
Man Dir, Editorial: H-J Starczewski
Subjects: Painting, Sculpture
Founded: 1964
ISBN Publisher's Prefix: 3-7981

Johannes **Stauda** Verlag*, Heinrich-Schütz-
Allee 33, D-3500 Kassel Tel: 30013 Cable
Add: Stauda Kassel Telex: 992376
Subjects: Theology, Religious Instruction,
Wall Charts for Religious Instruction

Franz **Steiner** Verlag GmbH, Friedrichstr 24,
Postfach 5529, D-6200 Wiesbaden
Tel: (06121) 372011 Cable Add:
Steinerverlag Wiesbaden
Man Dirs: Hans Rotta, Vincent Sieveking;
Production: Gregor Hoppen; *Publicity:*
Barbara Gans
Orders to: Birkenwaldstr 44, Postfach 347,
D-7000 Stuttgart 1 Tel: (0711) 25820 Telex:
0723636 daz d
Associate Companies: Wissenschaftliche
Verlagsgesellschaft mbH (qv); S Hirzel
Verlag GmbH & Co (qv); Deutscher
Apotheker-Verlag Dr Roland Schmiedel
GmbH & Co (qv)
Subjects: Literary Criticism, Archaeology,
Art, Music, History, Religion, Classical and
Modern Philology, Oriental Studies,
Ethnology, Philosophy, Geography, History
of Medicine and Science, Sciences,
Periodicals
1981: 150 titles *Founded:* 1949
ISBN Publisher's Prefix: 3-515

J F **Steinkopf** Verlag GmbH,
Gutenbergstr 18, Postfach 849, D-7000
Stuttgart 1 Tel: (0711) 626303 Cable Add:
Steinkopf Stuttgart
Man Dir: Ulrich Weitbrecht
Subjects: General Fiction & Non-fiction,
Paperbacks, How-to, Religion, Social
Science, Swabian Literature
1982: 25 titles *1983:* 26 titles *Founded:* 1792
ISBN Publisher's Prefix: 3-7984

Dr Dietrich **Steinkopff** Verlag,
Saalbaustr 12, Postfach 111008, D-6100
Darmstadt 11 Tel: 26538/9 Cable Add:
Steinkopff
*Man Dir, Sales, Publicity, Rights &
Permissions:* Bernhard Lewerich;
Advertising: Springer-Verlag, Berlin —
Heidelberg — New York — Tokyo
Parent Company: Springer-Verlag Berlin —
Heidelberg — New York — Tokyo GmbH &
Co KG (qv)
Subjects: Reference, Low- & High-priced
Paperbacks, Medicine, Psychology,
Chemistry, Nutritional Science, University &
Secondary Textbooks, Periodicals
1982: 30 titles *Founded:* 1948
ISBN Publisher's Prefix: 3-7985

Steintor Verlag, Rudolf Jüdes*, Postfach 41,
D-3167 Burgdorf (Located at: Markstr 36)
Tel: (05136) 2110
Subject: Art
Bookshops: Gallerie Steintor Verlag, D-3167
Burgdorf; Gallerie Meiborssen, D-3451
Meiborssen
Founded: 1969

Stephanus Edition Verlags GmbH, Tüfinger
Str 3-5, Postfach 1160, D-7772 Uhldingen 1
Tel: (07556) 6509
Man Dir: Ursula Braun; *Editorial:* Hans
Braun
Parent Company: Stephanus Edition Verlags
AG, Switzerland (qv)
Subject: Christian persecution in Communist
countries

1981: 9 titles *Founded:* 1978
ISBN Publisher's Prefix: 3-921213

Carl **Stephenson** Verlag GmbH & Co*,
Gutenbergstr 12, Postfach 291, D-2390
Flensburg Tel: (0461) 8090 Telex: 022710
Sales Manager: Klaus Uhse
Subjects: Popular and Erotic Literature,
Belles Lettres

Stern-Verlag Janssen und Co, Friedrichstr
24-26, Postfach 7820, D-4000 Düsseldorf 1
Tel: (0211) 373033
Managing Partners: Horst and Klaus
Janssen; *Production and Sales:* Oswald
Sckaer
Subjects: Philosophy, Philology (especially
of English)
Bookshop: At above address
Founded: 1900
ISBN Publisher's Prefix: 3-87784

Sternberg-Verlag, see Verlag Ernst Franz

Steyler Verlag, Arnold-Janssen-Str 20-22,
D-5205 St Augustin 1 Tel: (02241) 197304
Associate Company: Verlag Sankt Gabriel,
Austria (qv)
Subjects: Roman Catholic Theology, Novels,
Juvenile, Meditations, Scientific Series,
Hierarchicus Atlas and Bible

Lothar **Stiehm** Verlag GmbH+,
Hausackerweg 16, Postfach 105802, D-6900
Heidelberg 1 Tel: (06221) 21354
Publisher: Lothar Stiehm
Parent Company: Lambert Schneider Verlag
GmbH (qv)
Subjects: Classical Philology, German
Language & Literature, Bibliography,
Literary Criticism
ISBN Publisher's Prefix: 3-7988

Stimme-Verlag GmbH, an
Arbeitsgemeinschaft sozialistischer und
demokratischer Verleger und Buchhändler

Stollfuss Verlag Bonn GmbH & Co KG*,
Dechenstr 7-11, Postfach 2428, D-5300
Bonn 1 Tel: (0228) 631171-76 Cable Add:
Stollfussverlag Telex: 8869477 stvd
Man Dir: Wolfgang Stollfuss; *Editorial:* Dr
Joachim Lieser; *Sales:* Herbert Rolfsmeyer;
Production: Werner Hartmann; *Publicity:*
Ernst-Wolfgang Buecken
Subjects: Official Publications of German
Finance Ministry, Reference Works, Fiscal
Law, Administration, Economics,
Investment, Taxes, Legal Studies
1981: 40 titles
ISBN Publisher's Prefix: 3-08

Verlag Dr Wolf **Strache** GmbH & Co KG*,
Friedhofstr 11, Postfach 1124, D-7000
Stuttgart Tel: (0711) 256010 Cable Add:
Schönbücher Telex: dbv c 723240
Subjects: Arts, Mass Media, Education
Miscellaneous: Formerly Verläg die Schönen
Bücher
ISBN Publisher's Prefix: 3-7956

Verlag für das **Studium** der
Arbeiterbewegung GmbH, see VSA

Stürtz Verlag, Beethovenstr 5, D-8700
Würzburg Tel: (0931) 385235 Telex: 068798
Publisher: Walter Thierfelder
Subjects: Art, Wine, History of Travel,
Guidebooks, Scenic photo books, Hobbies,
Sports

Sub Rosa Frauenverlag, Gustav-Müller-
Platz 4, D-1000 Berlin 62 Tel: (030) 7849129
Publicity: R Burgard, Dr Schultz
Subjects: Literature by and about women
(Pedagogy, Psychology, Medicine, History,
Poetry, Sexuality, Belles Lettres)

Südbuch Vertriebsgesellschaft mbH, see
Bibliographisches Institut AG (qv)

Süddeutsche Verlagsgesellschaft Ulm,
Sedelhofgasse 19-21, D-7900 Ulm Tel:
(0731) 62047
Man Dir: Robert Abt
Parent Company: Schwabenverlag AG (qv)
Subjects: Christian Devotion and
Meditation, Theology, Preparation for
Sacraments, Juvenile, Religious, Liturgical,
Pedagogy, Psychology, Social Problems,
Current Affairs
Founded: 1898
ISBN Publisher's Prefix: 3-88294

Süddeutscher Verlag Buchverlag, Goethestr
43, Postfach 780, D-8000 Munich Tel: (089)
51480 Telex: 05/22405
Man Dir, Rights & Permissions: Dr Dieter
Lutz; *Editorial:* Dr H-P Rasp; *Sales:* Rose
Backes; *Publicity:* Ulrike Ramsauer;
Advertising: Michael Schindler
Associate Companies: Paul List Verlag
KG (qv); Südwest Verlag GmbH &
Co KG (qv)
Subjects: History, How-to, Music, Art,
Fiction, Reference, Religion, Non-fiction
Founded: 1945
ISBN Publisher's Prefix: 3-7991

Südwest Verlag GmbH und Co KG,
Goethestr 43, D-8000 Munich 2 Tel: (089)
51480 Telex: 05/22405
Man Dir, Rights & Permissions: Dr Dieter
Lutz; *Sales:* Rose Bakes; *Production:* Roger
Seitz; *Publicity:* Ulrike Ramsauer;
Advertising: Michael Schindler
Associate Companies: Paul List Verlag
KG (qv); Süddeutscher Verlag
Buchverlag (qv)
Subjects: History, How-to, Music, Art
1982: 21 titles *Founded:* 1950
ISBN Publisher's Prefix: 3-517

Suhrkamp Verlag KG, Lindenstr 29-35,
Postfach 4229, D-6000 Frankfurt am Main
Tel: (0611) 740231 Cable Add:
Suhrkampverlag Telex: 413972
Publisher: Dr Siegfried Unseld; *Man Dir:* Dr
Heribert Marré; *Sales:* Dr Joachim Unseld;
Advertising, Publicity: Claus Carlé,
Christoph Groffy; *Rights & Permissions:*
Helene Ritzerfeld
Associate Companies: Insel Verlag (qv);
Nomos Verlagsgesellschaft mbH & Co KG
(qv)
Imprints: Suhrkamp Taschenbuchverlag,
Suhrkamp Verlag Wissenschaft
Subjects: General Fiction, Belles Lettres,
Poetry, Biography, Philosophy, German-
Jewish Writing in general, General Science,
High- & Low-priced Paperbacks, Juveniles,
Education, Psychology
Founded: 1950
ISBN Publisher's Prefix: 3-518

Sybex Verlag GmbH, Heyestr 22, D-4000
Düsseldorf 12, Postfach 120513 Tel: (0211)
287066 Telex: 8588163 sybx d
Man Dir: Alexander Schleber, Rodney Zaks;
Sales: Harald Kreuzberger
Associate Companies: Sybex Inc, 2344 Sixth
St, Berkeley, California 94710 USA Tel:
(415) 8488233; Sybex-Europe, 4 Pl Félix-
Eboue, F-75583 Paris cedex 12 Tel: (01)
3473020
Subjects: Micro-computer technology and
programming
1981: 11 titles *Founded:* 1981
ISBN Publisher's Prefix: 3-88745

Symposion-Verlag, J Siegler, Neckarstr 86,
Postfach 33, D-7300 Esslingen/N
Tel: (0711) 311141 Cable Add: Symposion,
Esslingen
General Manager: H A Siegler
Subjects: Equestrian Interest, International
Model Railways Guide; Periodicals
Founded: 1964 in Stuttgart
ISBN Publisher's Prefix: 3-920877

162 FEDERAL REPUBLIC OF GERMANY

Syndikat Autoren- und Verlagsgesellschaft, see Autoren- und Verlagsgesellschaft

T B L (Tübinger Beiträge zur Linguistik) Verlag, see Gunter Narr Verlag

T R- Verlagsunion GmbH, Thierschstr 11, Postfach 260202, D-8000 Munich 26
Man Dir: Dr Günter Olzog; *Editorial:* Ingeborg Ellwein, Gertrud Schwärzler; *Publicity:* Cornelia Kölbel; *Sales:* Rüdiger Dorbandt
Subjects: Educational Study Material for State examinations, Professional, Technical, Language Courses; Leisure Pursuit Study Companions. The Union publishes and distributes books, sets of lessons etc, to link up with educational TV and radio programmes
Founded: 1968
Miscellaneous: The T R (Television and Radio) Publishing Union comprises two broadcasting companies (Bayerischer Rundfunk and Südwestfunk) and 15 publishing companies: Verlag Ludwig Auer, B L V Verlagsgesellschaft GmbH, Verlag C H Beck, C Bertelsmann Verlag GmbH, Verlag F Bruckmann KG, Ehrenwirth Verlag GmbH, Ernst Klett Verlag, Kösel-Verlag GmbH & Co, Langenscheidt KG, Paul List Verlag KG, J B Metzlersche Verlagsbuchhandlung, R Oldenbourg Verlag GmbH, Günter Olzog Verlag GmbH, K G Saur Verlag KG, Springer-Verlag (qqv) and is also associated with publishers Gräfe und Unzer, Max Heuber Verlag, Franz Schneider, B Schott's Söhne (qqv)
ISBN Publisher's Prefix: 3-8058

Verlag **T Ü V** Rheinland GmbH, Sicherheitstechnik, Energie und Umweltschutz, Am Grauen Stein, Postfach 101750, D-5000 Cologne 91 Tel: (0221) 8393 2852 Telex: 8873659
Man Dir: Franz Dietrich; *Editorial:* J Fahrbach, M Peiffer; *Sales, Publicity:* Wolfgang Kierdorf; *Production:* Mr Braatz; *Rights & Permissions:* M Peiffer
Subjects: Safety Technology, Energy, Environmental Protection
1981: 29 titles *Founded:* 1972
ISBN Publisher's Prefix: 3-88585

Taylorix Fachverlag Stiegler und Co*, Mönchstr 29, Postfach 829, D-7000 Stuttgart 1 Tel: (0711) 2503202 Telex: 0723810
Dirs: Dr Werner Kresse, Dipl-Volkswirt Walter Alt; *Sales Manager:* Dipl-Kfm Dieter Salat
Subjects: Economics, Business, Law
ISBN Publisher's Prefix: 3-7992

Technik Tabellen Verlag Fikentscher und Co*, Eschollbrücker Str 39, Postfach 4135, D-6100 Darmstadt Tel: (06151) 61025 Cable Add: Fikentscher Telex: 419460
Publisher: Christoph Kässner; *Editorial:* Dr Thomas Krist
Subjects: Civil & Mechanical Engineering, Textbooks
ISBN Publisher's Prefix: 3-87807

Telex-Verlag Jaeger und Waldmann*, Holzhofallee 38, Postfach 111060, D-6100 Darmstadt 11 Tel: (06151) 33331 Cable Add: Telexverlag Telex: (Home) 419389 tlx d; (Foreign) 419253 telex d
Man Dir: Heinz Waldmann; *Sales Dir:* Wolfgang Lich; *Editor:* Willi Lucius; *Advertising Dir:* Ludwig Nicolay
Subjects: International Telex Directories
Founded: 1953
ISBN Publisher's Prefix: 3-87810

Alf **Teloeken** Verlag KG, see Alba Publikation

Telos series of Paperbacks. This is a series of Bible-based evangelical paperbacks (including works for children), each contributed by one of the following publishers:
Blaukreuz-Verlag Wuppertal (qv), Brendow-Verlag (qv), Verlag der Evangelischer Gesellschaft (qv), Verlag der Francke-Buchhandlung (qv), Hänssler-Verlag (qv), Verlag der Liebenzeller Mission (qv), Verlag der Sankt-Johannis-Druckerei C Schweickhardt (qv) (all in Federal Republic of Germany); Verlag der Schweizerischen Schallplattenmission (Swiss gramophone record mission), Schwengeler-Verlag (qv), Trachsel-Verlag (all in Switzerland)

Tende Verlag GmbH, Hammer Str 152, D-4400 Münster Tel: (0251) 793758
Man Dir: Annette Viktoria Uhlending; *Editorial:* J Monika Walther; *Production:* P Gorbach; *Publicity:* Alwine Uhlending; *Rights & Permissions:* A Uhlending
Orders to: Sova, Franziusstr 44, D-6000 Frankfurt am Main 1
Subjects: Belles Lettres, Art, Film, Women's Interests
1982: 10 titles *1983:* 10 titles *Founded:* 1980
ISBN Publisher's Prefix: 3-88633

B G Teubner GmbH, Industriestr 15, Postfach 801069, D-7000 Stuttgart 80 Tel: (0711) 7803076
Man Dir: Heinrich Krämer; *Sales, Publicity & Advertising Dir:* Walter Hirtz; *Rights & Permissions:* Sophie Penner
Subjects: History, Classical Philology, Reference, High-priced Paperbacks, Mathematics, Physics, Biology, Geography, Engineering, General & Social Science, Secondary & University Textbooks
Founded: 1811
ISBN Publisher's Prefix: 3-519

Edition **Text und Kritik** GmbH, Levelingstr 6a, Postfach 800529, D-8000 Munich 80 Tel: (089) 432929
Man Dir: Dr Berndt Oesterhelt
Subjects: Contemporary Literature and Criticism, Reference Works, Musical Studies
ISBN Publisher's Prefixes: 3-921402, 3-88377

Konrad **Theiss** Verlag GmbH*, Villastr 11, Postfach 730, D-7000 Stuttgart 1 Tel: (0711) 432981 Cable Add: Theissverlag Stuttgart
Dir: Hans Schleuning; *Publicity, Sales:* Bernhard Driehaus; *Production:* Rolf Bisterfeld
Subjects: History, Arts, Non-fiction
1981: 21 titles
ISBN Publisher's Prefix: 3-8062

Thesen Verlag Vowinckel und Co*, Kittlerstr 34, D-6100 Darmstadt Tel: (06151) 713326
Man Dirs: Heinrich Schirmer, Dr Ilse Vowinckel
Subjects: Literary Criticism, Linguistics, Social Science, University Textbooks, Educational Materials
1981: 4 titles *Founded:* 1970
ISBN Publisher's Prefix: 3-7677

Druck- und Verlagshaus **Thiele und Schwarz***, Wilhelmshöher Allee 254-256, Postfach 410160, D-3500 Kassel Tel: (0561) 30076 Cable Add: Thiele & Schwarz Kassel-Wilhelmshöhe Telex: 0992450
Proprietor: Rolf Schwarz; *Editorial:* Claus Reineke
Associate Company: Verlag Schule und Elternhaus (qv)
Subjects: General Fiction, Juveniles, Reprints
ISBN Publisher's Prefix: 3-87816

Georg **Thieme** Verlag+, PO Box 732, D-7000 Stuttgart 1 (Located at: Rüdigerstr 14, Stuttgart 30) Tel: (0711) 89310 Cable Add: Thiemebuch Telex: 7252275
Publishers: Dr Günther Hauff, Dr Albrecht Greuner; *Man Dir:* Achim Menge; *Sales:* Joachim Hillig; *Publicity:* Ursula Polaczek; *Foreign Rights:* Märit Schütt
Subsidiary Companies: Hippokrates Verlag GmbH (qv); Thieme-Stratton Inc, New York, USA
Associate Company: Ferdinand Enke Verlag (qv)
Subjects: Medicine, Dentistry, Bioscience, Pharmacy, Chemistry, Reference, Periodicals. Many works in English language.
1982: 285 titles *Founded:* 1886
ISBN Publisher's Prefix: 3-13

Karl **Thiemig** AG München, Pilgersheimer Str 38, Postfach 900740, D-8000 Munich 90 Tel: (089) 62480 Cable Add: Thiemigdruck
Man Dir: Klaus Zinn; *Advertising Dir:* Peter Schläus
Subjects: Art, Travel, Natural Science, Technical
Founded: 1950
ISBN Publisher's Prefix: 3-521

K **Thienemanns** Verlag, Blumenstr 36, D-7000 Stuttgart 1 Tel: 240641 Telex: 723933 thie d
Dirs: Hansjoerg Weitbrecht, Richard Weitbrecht, Gunter Ehni
Imprints: Edition Erdmann, Edition Weitbrecht
Subjects: Fiction, Non-fiction, Juveniles, Children's Picture Books, Dietetics
Founded: 1849
ISBN Publisher's Prefix: 3-522

Jan **Tholenaar** Verlag GmbH, G D Bücherei, Solseifen Nr 5, D-5222 Morsbach Tel: (02294) 6336
Man Dirs: Jan Tholenaar, Lilly Tholenaar; *all Other Offices:* Uwe Nersberg
Imprint: G D Bücherei (Large Print Library)
Subjects: Large Print: General Fiction (including English in translation), some Non-fiction
1982: 8 titles *1983:* 6 titles *Founded:* 1979
ISBN Publisher's Prefix: 3-88621

Jan **Thorbecke** Verlag GmbH & Co+, Karlstr 10, Postfach 546, D-7480 Sigmaringen Tel: (07571) 3016 Cable Add: Thorbecke Telex: 732534
Dir, Editorial, Rights & Permissions: Georg Bensch; *Production:* Ulrich Ulrichs; *Publishing, Publicity and Sales Dir:* Dr Lothar Johannes
Subjects: Historical, Geographical, Cultural Accounts of various European Regions, especially in Germany and Switzerland; Art History, Literature, Children's Books, European History
Founded: 1946
ISBN Publisher's Prefix: 3-7995

Tips für Trips, an imprint of Friedemann von Engel Verlag (qv)

Titania-Verlag Ferdinand Schroll, Oberer Hoppenlauweg 26, Postfach 1352, D-7000 Stuttgart 1 Tel: (0711) 293551 Cable Add: Titaniaverlag Stuttgart
Publishers: Wolfgang Schroll, Gerdi Schroll
Subjects: General Fiction; Children's Story Books for all ages
ISBN Publisher's Prefix: 3-7996

S **Toeche-Mittler** Verlag*, Hindenburgstr 33, D-6100 Darmstadt Tel: (06151) 311551
Subjects: Non-fiction, Law, Sports, Economics
Miscellaneous: Firm was formerly Mittler & Sohn, Berlin
Founded: 1789
ISBN Publisher's Prefix: 3-87820

Tomus Verlag GmbH+, Prinzenstr 7, D-8000 Munich 19 Tel: (089) 132001 Telex: 5215528
General Manager: Claus-Jürgen Frank; *Assistant General Manager:* Oliver A Frank; *Rights & Permissions:* Susanne Trieb
Associate Companies: Telelit Verlag AG
Branch Off: Dr Wernerstr 5, D-8031 Gröbenzell
Subjects: Nature, Science, Animals, Hobbies, Travel, Cookery, Exclusive Art Editions
Founded: 1962
ISBN Publisher's Prefix: 3-920954

P J **Tonger** Musikverlag GmbH & Co, Auf dem Brand 3, D-5000 Cologne 50 Tel: (0221) 392998
Man Dir: P J Tonger; *Sales Dir:* Hans Paul Zimmer; *Publicity Dir:* Hildegard Tonger; *Advertising Dir:* Peter Tonger
Subsidiary Company: Carl Engels Musikverlag
Subjects: Music, Art
Founded: 1822

Touropa-Urlaubsberater, Sandstr 3, D-8000 Munich 2 Tel: (089) 554861
Subject: Travel

Trautvetter und Fischer Nachf, Gladenbacher Weg 57, Postfach 546, D-3550 Marburg Tel: (06421) 23309
Owned by: Dr Wilhelm A Eckhardt
Subjects: Local History and Guidebooks, Church Histories (Protestant), Lyrical Poetry
1981: 8 titles *1982:* 4 titles *Founded:* 1941
ISBN Publisher's Prefix: 3-87822

Editions **Trèves**+, Postfach 1401, D-5500 Trier 1 Tel: (06501) 3183
Man Dirs: Rainer Breuer, Uschi Dahm; *Chief Reader:* Bernhard Hoffmann
Branch Offs: Editions Trèves Mainz, Postfach 1843, D-6500 Mainz; Editions Trèves Luxembourg, BP 57, L-6701 Grevenmacher, Luxembourg
Subjects: Music Books, Belles Lettres, Young Literature, Lyrical Poetry, Theatre, Art, Literary Periodicals, Politics, Satire
Founded: 1976
Miscellaneous: Publishing company for a society for the promotion of artistic activities run by its own (largely young) authors from throughout Europe
ISBN Publisher's Prefix: 3-88081

Trikont-Dianus, see Dianus Trikont

Editions **Trobisch** GmbH, Postfach 2048, D-7640 Kehl am Rhein 1 Tel: (07851) 4551
Man Dir: Volker Gscheidle
Subjects: Christian practice and devotions, sex and marriage counselling etc, in German, French and English
1982: 20 titles *Founded:* 1972
ISBN Publisher's Prefix: 3-87827

Tübinger Vereinigung für Volkskunde eV, Schloss, D-7400 Tübingen Tel: (07071) 292374
Man Dir: Wolfgang Alber; *Editorial, Production, Sales:* Prof H Bausinger, U Jeggle, M Scharfe, B J Warneken
Orders to: Chr Krämer, Postfach 1851, D-7400 Tübingen 1
Subjects: Paperbacks, Reference (Humanities), History, Social Science, University Textbooks
Founded: 1963

Tuduv Verlagsgesellschaft mbH, Postfach 340163, D-8000 Munich 34 (Located at: Gabelsbergstr 15, Munich 2) Tel: (089) 2809095
Subjects: Political Texts, Textbooks, Series connected with Political Science, Economics, Sociology, Jurisprudence, Philology, Literary Criticism, Cultural Arts
1982: 100 titles

Turm-Verlag, Hindenburgstr 3, Postfach 229, D-7120 Bietigheim Tel: (07142) 41081 Cable Add: Turm, Bietigheim
Associate Company: Lorber-Verlag (qv)
Subjects: Health, Religion
ISBN Publisher's Prefix: 3-7999

Turmberg-Verlag (Musikverlag Klaus Gerth)*, Emmeliusstr 31, Postfach 1148, D-6334 Asslar Tel: (06441) 8461 Telex: 483794
Parent Company: Verlag Schulte und Gerth (qv)
Subjects: Music

Verlag **Tüv Rheinland** GmbH, see T U V

U T B, see Uni-Taschenbücher GmbH

Verlag Dr Alfons **Uhl**, Mittlere Gerbergasse 1, D-8860 Nördlingen
Subjects: Architectural and Art History, Graphics and Book Illustration, Art Portfolios, Old Topographical Books

Verlag **Ullstein** GmbH, PO Box 110303, D-1000 Berlin 11 (Located at: Lindenstr 76, D-1000 Berlin 61) Tel: (030) 25911 Cable Add: Ullsteinbuch berlin Telex: vlgul d 183723
Man Dirs: Ernst Cramer, H Joachim Maître (Editorial), Viktor Niemann; *Marketing and Sales Dir:* Viktor Niemann; *Publicity:* Wolfgang Mönninghoff
Subsidiary Companies: Propyläen Verlag (qv), Ullstein Taschenbuchverlag
Subjects: Belles Lettres, Poetry, Biography, History, How-to, Music, Art, Travel, Geography, Ethnology, Popular Science, Social Sciences, Low- & High-priced Paperbacks, Educational Materials, Fiction, Military, Politics
Founded: 1903
ISBN Publisher's Prefix: 3-550

Verlag Eugen **Ulmer** GmbH & Co, Wollgrasweg 41, Postfach 700561, D-7000 Stuttgart 70 (Hohenheim) Tel: (0711) 45070 Telex: 723634
Man Dir: Roland Ulmer; *Deputy Dir:* Alexander Hunn; *Production:* Dieter Kleinschrot; *Reader:* Dr Steffen Volk; *Sales Dir:* Gerhard Rentschler; *Publicity Dir:* Siegfried Hauptfleisch
Subjects: How-to, Reference, General Science, University Textbooks, Agriculture, Horticulture, Veterinary Science, Gardening, Animals, Periodicals, Paperbacks
Founded: 1868
Miscellaneous: Part of vgs — Verlagsgesellschaft Schulfernsehen mbH & Co KG (qv)
ISBN Publisher's Prefix: 3-8001

Umschau Verlag Breidenstein GmbH, Stuttgarter Str 18-24, D-6000 Frankfurt am Main 1 Tel: (0611) 26001 Cable Add: Umschau Frankfurtmain Telex: 0411964
Man Dir: Hans-Jürgen Breidenstein; *Sales:* Peter Schumacher
Associate Companies: Brönner Verlag Breidenstein GmbH (qv), Brönners Druckerei Breidenstein GmbH, Sigma Studio Klaus Schlotte GmbH, Dateam Vertriebsgesellschaft mbH & Co KG (all at above address); Andres Kalender und Buch Verlag GmbH, Lenoustr 2, Hamburg; Report Verlag GmbH, Hengsbachstr 91, Siegen
Subjects: Non-fiction, especially Photographic Travel Books, Art, General Science, Low- & High-priced Paperbacks, Periodicals
Founded: 1850
ISBN Publisher's Prefix: 3-524

Ungarischer Kultureller und Sozialer Fonds eV in der BRD*, Zweibrückenstr 2/IV, D-8000 Munich 2 Tel: (089) 294376 Hungarian Social and Cultural Foundation in the Federal Republic of Germany
Man Dir: András Piffkó; *Editorial:* János Röczey; *Rights & Permissions:* János Popovits
Parent Company: Zentralverband Ungarischer Organisationen in der BRD eV, at above address (Central Association of Hungarian Organisations in the Federal Republic of Germany)
Subjects: Works by Hungarian authors
Bookshops: Ungarischer Kultureller und Sozialer Fond in der BRD eV at above address
Founded: 1971

Uni-Taschenbücher (UTB) GmbH, Breitwiesenstr 9, Postfach 801124, D-7000 Stuttgart 80 Tel: (0711) 7801826
Dir: Volkmar Kalki
Orders to: Brockhaus Commission, Am Wallgraben 127-129, Postfach 800205, D-7000 Stuttgart 80
Parent Company: K G Saur Verlag KG (qv)
Subjects: Library Science, Biology, Chemistry, Electrical Engineering, Electronics, Humanities, History, Public Health, Business, Informatics, Data Processing, Engineering, Agriculture, Literary Criticism, Mathematics, Medicine, Education, Philosophy, Physics, Politics, Psychology, Religion, Social Science, Linguistics, Languages, Veterinary Science, Economics (all in paperback)
Miscellaneous: The company represents a group of 17 publishers producing paperbacks of a general academic/technical/scientific nature

Union Verlag Stuttgart*, Alexanderstr 51, Postfach 326, D-7000 Stuttgart 1 Tel: (0711) 240996 Cable Add: Unionverlag
Man Dirs: Dr Heinz Winners, Ulrich Commerell
Parent Company: Otto Maier Verlag (qv)
Subject: Juveniles
Founded: 1890
ISBN Publisher's Prefix: 3-8002

Universitas Verlag, Hubertusstr 4, D-8000 Munich Tel: (089) 177041
Subjects: General Fiction, Biography, History, Low-priced Paperbacks, Cookbooks, Juveniles, Non-fiction
Founded: 1922
Miscellaneous: Firm is a member of Verlagsgruppe Langen-Müller/Herbig (qv)
ISBN Publisher's Prefix: 3-8004

Verlag **Urachhaus** Johannes M Mayer GmbH und Co KG, Urachstr 41, Postfach 131053, D-7000 Stuttgart 1 Tel: (0711) 260589/265939
Dir: Johannes Mayer; *Readers:* Inge Thöns, Dr Wolfgang Huber, Roswitha von dem Borne; *Publicity & Marketing:* Winfried Altmann
Orders to: Koch, Neff und Oetinger & Co, Verlagsauslieferung, Schockenried Str 39, D-7000 Stuttgart 80
Subjects: History, Literary Criticism, Philosophy, Religion, Anthroposophy, Occultism, Children's Books, Art Books, History of Art
1981: 40 titles *1982:* 40 titles *Founded:* 1924
ISBN Publisher's Prefix: 3-87838

Verlag **Urban und Schwarzenberg** (Medical Publishers), Pettenkoferstr 18, Postfach 202440, D-8000 Munich 2 Tel: (089) 530181 Telex: 523864
Man Dir: Michael Urban; *Marketing, Sales:* Lieselotte Meyer; *Rights & Permissions:* Gritta von Fircks; *Promotion:* Sven Soik
Associate Company: Urban & Schwarzenberg Inc, 7 East Redwood St, Baltimore, Md 21202, USA
Branch Off: Urban & Schwarzenberg, Austria (qv)

164 FEDERAL REPUBLIC OF GERMANY

Subjects: Medicine, Psychology, University Textbooks, Periodicals
Bookshop: Oscar Rothacker Buchhandlung, Pettenkoferstr 18, D-8000 Munich 2
1981: 130 titles *Founded:* 1866
ISBN Publisher's Prefix: 3-541

V D E-Verlag GmbH (Verband Deutscher Elektrotechniker)+, Bismarckstr 33, D-1000 Berlin 12 Tel: (030) 3413041
Telex: 0181683 vde d
Manager: F U Strobel; *Editorial:* Dr-Ing A Grütz, Merianstr 29, D-6050 Offenbach; *Sales:* Klaus Hitzschke
Subjects: Electrical Engineering, Electronics, Technical Specifications (many specifications may be bought in English), Communications Technology
Founded: 1929
ISBN Publisher's Prefix: 3-8007

V D I-Verlag GmbH (Verlag des Vereins Deutscher Ingenieure), Graf-Recke-Str 84, Postfach 1139, D-4000 Düsseldorf 1
Tel: (0211) 62141 Cable Add: Ingenieurverlag Düsseldorf Telex: 08586525
Man Dir: Dr Harald Wiebking; *Editorial:* Dr Gerhard Scheuch; *Rights & Permissions:* Susann E Neusen; *Sales:* Gunther Bicker
Subjects: Engineering, Technology, Scientific Reports, Proceedings, VDI Guidelines, Paperbacks, Serial Publications
1982: approx 50 titles, 130 Guidelines
Founded: 1923
ISBN Publisher's Prefix: 3-18

V-Dia-Verlag GmbH*, Heinrich-Fuchs-Str 95-97, Postfach 105980, D-6900 Heidelberg 1 Tel: (06221) 37041 Cable Add: Vaudia Heidelberg Telex: 04 61781
Subjects: Audiovisual Aids, Geography, Astronomy, Biology, Medicine, History
Founded: 1953

V F M, see Verlag für Medizin Dr Ewald Fischer GmbH

V G S, see Verlagsgesellschaft Schulfernsehen mbH & Co KG

V M B, see Verlag Marxistische Blätter

V S A (Verlag für das Studium der Arbeiterbewegung GmbH), Stresemannstr 384a, D-2000 Hamburg 50 Tel: (040) 8992561
Manager, Rights & Permissions: Gerd Siebecke; *Sales:* Brigitte Dudek
Orders to: VVA (Vereinigte Verlagsauslieferung GmbH), Postfach 7777, D-4830 Gütersloh 1
Subjects: Political and Social Science, Political and Social Movements, Periodical
ISBN Publisher's Prefix: 3-87975

V W K (Verlag für Wirtschafts-und-Kartographie Publikationen) Ryborsch GmbH+, Laubenstr 3, Postfach 2105, D-6053 Obertshausen 2 bei Frankfurt Tel: (06104) 7839
Dirs: Mrs H Ryborsch-Tschinkel, Reinhard Ryborsch
Subjects: Economics, Aviation, Geography, Travel, City and Road Maps, Aeronautical Charts and Maps
1981: 7 titles *1982:* 11 titles *Founded:* 1975
ISBN Publisher's Prefix: 3-920339

Franz **Vahlen** GmbH*, Wilhelmstr 9, D-8000 Munich 40 Tel: (089) 381891
Sales Dir: Günter Elze; *Publicity Dir:* Erhard Hoppe
Associate Companies: Verlag C H Beck (qv), Biederstein Verlag (qv)
Subjects: Law, Social Science, University Textbooks
Founded: 1870
ISBN Publisher's Prefix: 3-8006

Vandenhoeck und Ruprecht, Theaterstr 13, Postfach 3753, D-3400 Göttingen Tel: (0551) 54031/3 Telex: 965226 van d
Dirs: Dr Arndt Ruprecht, Dr Dietrich Ruprecht; *Editorial:* Dr Winfried Hellmann, Jörg Ohlemacher; *Sales and Publicity:* Ursula Nahrgang
Subsidiary Companies: Druckerei Hubert & Co, Robert-Bosch-Breite 6, D-3400 Göttingen; Ehrenfried Klotz Verlag (qv)
Associate Company: Verlag J Pfeiffer GmbH & Co (qv)
Branch Off: Vandenhoeck und Ruprecht, Badener Str 69, CH-8026 Zürich, Switzerland
Subjects: University Textbooks, Research Monographs and Handbooks, Religion, Philology, History, Economics, Mathematics, Medical Psychology, Periodicals
Bookshop: Deuerlich'sche Buchhandlung, D-3400 Göttingen, Weender Str 33
1981: 239 titles *1982:* 259 titles *Founded:* 1735
ISBN Publisher's Prefix: 3-525

Velhagen und Klasing GmbH & Co, Mecklenburgische Str 54, D-1000 Berlin 33
Man Dir: Franz Cornelsen
Subjects: Textbooks, Educational, Cartography
Miscellaneous: Part of Cornelsen-Velhagen und Klasing GmbH group (qv)
Founded: 1835

Edition **Venceremos**+, Verlag W G Reinheimer, Postfach 1212, D-6090 Rüsselsheim (Located at: Heinrichstr 15)
Tel: (06142) 65280/42855
Man Dir, Sales, Production, Publicity: Wilhelm G Reinheimer; *Editorial, Rights & Permissions:* Heinz Mees
Subjects: German and International Folklore, Songs, Cabaret, Periodical
Founded: 1974
ISBN Publisher's Prefix: 3-88541

Verlag für Deutsch, see Deutsch

Verlag für Fremdsprachen, see Verlag für Deutsch

Klaus Dieter **Vervuert** Buchhandel und Verlag, Wielandstr 40, D-6000 Frankfurt am Main 1 Tel: (0611) 599615
Subjects: Specialist in books about Latin America, Spain and Portugal
1981: 10 titles *1982:* 20 titles
ISBN Publisher's Prefix: 3-921600

Schulverlag **Vieweg**, see Schulverlag

Friedr **Vieweg & Sohn** Verlagsgesellschaft mbH, Faulbrunnenstr 13, Postfach 5829, D-6200 Wiesbaden 1 Tel: (06121) 5341
Telex: 4186928 vw v d
Orders to: VVA (Vereinigte Verlagsauslieferung GmbH), Postfach 7777, D-4830 Gütersloh 1
Man Dir: Dr Frank Lube; *Editorial:* Michael Langfeld; *Sales Manager:* Heinz Detering; *Rights & Permissions:* Angelika Bolisega
Parent Company: Verlagsgruppe Bertelsmann GmbH (qv for associate companies)
Subsidiary Company: Deutscher Eichverlag (qv)
Subjects: Textbooks in Mathematics, Natural Sciences, Technology, Architecture, Monographs, School Books, Teaching Programmes, Periodicals
1982: 90 titles *Founded:* 1786
ISBN Publisher's Prefix: 3-528

Curt R **Vincentz** Verlag, Schiffgraben 41-43, Postfach 6247, D-3000 Hanover 1
Tel: (0511) 3499944 Telex: 923846
Man Dir: Dr L Vincentz; *Sales:* Dr F Vincentz
Subjects: General Science, Paint Technology, Business, Nursing
Founded: 1893
ISBN Publisher's Prefix: 3-87870

Vogel-Verlag KG*, Max-Planck-Str 7-9, Postfach 6740, D-8700 Würzburg 1
Tel: (0931) 41021 Cable Add: Vogelverlag Würzburg Telex: 068883
Man Dirs: Dr Kurt Eckernkamp, Wolfgang Lüdicke
Subjects: Agricultural, Automotive, Consulting, Electrical, Mechanical and Textile Engineering, Electronics, Metalworking, Management, Scientific and Technical Text Books, Foreign Language Publications (in 14 languages), Periodicals
Founded: 1891
ISBN Publisher's Prefix: 3-8023

Emil **Vollmer** Verlag, see Vollmer/Löwit Verlagsgruppe

Vollmer/Löwit Verlagsgruppe*, Gustav-Stresemann-Ring 12-16, Postfach 4060, D-6200 Wiesbaden Tel: (06121) 39331
Telex: 4186294
Dir: Sylvia Vollmer
Subjects: Art and Artists, Collectors' Books, Mythology, Natural History, Religions, History, Fiction, Belles Lettres, Juveniles, Popular Editions of Classics
Miscellaneous: This is a merger of R Löwit GmbH, Wiesbaden and Emil Vollmer Verlag GmbH, Wiesbaden

Thesen Verlag **Vowinckel** und Co, see Thesen

Kurt **Vowinckel** Verlag, Kreuzanger 8, D-8137 Berg am See Tel: (08151) 51675
Dir: Dr Gert Sudholt
Subjects: Current Affairs, Politics
ISBN Publisher's Prefix: 3-87879

W R S-Verlag (Wirtschaft, Recht und Steuern), Irmgardstr 1, Postfach 711069, D-8000 Munich 71 Tel: (089) 792077
Dirs: Dr Guenther Friedrich, Dr Manfred Jahrmarkt
Parent Company: Rudolf Haufe Verlag (qv)
Subjects: Economics, Law, Taxation

Karl **Wachholtz** Verlag, Gänsemarkt 1-3, Postfach 2769, D-2350 Neumünster
Tel: (04321) 4091 Cable Add: courier
Telex: 299618
Dir: Walter Kardel
Subjects: Humanities, History, Arts, Reference, Encyclopaedias, Dictionaries, Literature, Reprints, Linguistics, Languages, Periodicals
ISBN Publisher's Prefix: 3-529

Verlag Klaus **Wagenbach**, Bamberger Str 6, Postfach 1409, D-1000 Berlin 30 Tel: (030) 2115060/69
Man Dir, Editorial: Dr Klaus Wagenbach; *Sales:* Galina Rave; *Production:* Gabriele Kronenberg; *Publicity, Rights & Permissions:* Barbara Herzbruch
Subjects: General Fiction, Belles Lettres, Poetry, Low- and High-priced Paperbacks, Political and Social Science, Periodical
Founded: 1964
ISBN Publisher's Prefix: 3-8031

Kartographischer Verlag **Wagner** & Co KG*, Georg-Wilhelm-Str 1, D-1000 Berlin 31 Tel: (030) 8914622
Man Dir: Heinz-Peter Wagner; *Sales, Publicity:* Norbert Schaepe
Parent Company: Kartographische Anstalt Dr K H Wagner
Subjects: Maps, Cartography
1982: 2 titles *Founded:* 1981
ISBN Publisher's Prefix: 3-88825

Walter-Verlag GmbH Freiburg, Grissheimer Weg 36, D-7843 Heitersheim Tel: (07634) 940/948 Telex: 772961
Dirs: Hermann Maschkowitz, Hanspeter

Keller; *Sales:* Richard Urbahn; *Publicity:* Karin Wagner
Parent Company: Walter Verlag AG, Switzerland (qv)
Subjects: Religion, Psychology, Travel Guides, Literature, Cultural History
Founded: 1924
ISBN Publisher's Prefix: 3-530

Ernst **Wasmuth** Verlagsbuchhandlung KG, Fürststr 133, Postfach 2728, D-7400 Tübingen Tel: (07071) 33658
Man Dir: Dr Gerhild Huebner; *Sales Dir:* Karl-Heinz Schattner; *Production:* Manfred Heinrich
Subjects: Architecture, Archaeology, History of Art, Applied Art
Bookshop: Wasmuth Buchhandlung & Antiquariat, Hardenbergstr 9A, D-1000 Berlin 12
Founded: 1872
ISBN Publisher's Prefix: 3-8030

Wehr und Wissen Verlagsgesellschaft mbH*, Heilsbachstr 26, D-5300 Bonn 1 (Duisdorf) Tel: (02221) 643066-68 Telex: 8869429 mvkb d
Man Dir: Manfred Sadlowski; *Sales Dir, Rights & Permissions:* Joachim Latka; *Publicity Dir:* Heinz-Jürgen Witzke; *Advertising Dir:* Peter Konietschke
Subjects: History, How-to, Quality Paperbacks, Military Manuals, Yearbooks

A **Weichert** Verlag*, Tieststr 14, D-3000 Hanover Tel: (0511) 813068 Cable Add: Buchweichert Telex: 0923872 awv
Man Dir: Alfred Trippo; *Sales:* Hans H Droste
Associate Company: Neuer Jugendschriften-Verlag (at above address)
Imprint: Karo-Bücher
Branch Off: Hans Feulner, Lindenallee 25, D-1000 Berlin 19
Subject: Juveniles (story books for all ages)
Founded: 1872
ISBN Publisher's Prefix: 3-483

Wolfgang **Weidlich** Verlag*, Savignystr 61, D-6000 Frankfurt am Main Tel: (0611) 746215
Publisher: Wolfgang H Weidlich; *Editorial:* Brigitte Weidlich; *Sales:* Burkhard Pape; *Production:* Wilfred Sindt; *Publicity:* Ingrid Schweinhardt; *Rights & Permissions:* Doris Böhler
Subjects: Architecture, General Fiction, History, Maps, Non-fiction
ISBN Publisher's Prefix: 3-8035

Verlag **Weinmann**, Beckerstr 7, D-1000 Berlin 41 Tel: (030) 8554895
Man Dir: Dr Weinmann
Subject: Sport (especially the martial arts), Instruction books for all ages, Yoga, Gymnastics, Fencing, Fitness Training, Sports Humour
Founded: 1961
ISBN Publisher's Prefix: 3-87892

Weismann Verlag-Frauenbuchverlag GmbH+, Gabelsberger Str 56, D-8000 Munich 2 Tel: (089) 521717
Man Dir: Peter Weismann; *Editorial:* Antje Kunstmann, Peter Weismann
Orders to: Verlagsauslieferung: mi, Justus-von-Liebigstr 1, D-8910 Landsberg
Subsidiary Company: Frauenbuchverlag (qv)
Subjects: Literature and Non-fiction for young people, Theatrical texts for juveniles, Politics
Founded: 1970
ISBN Publisher's Prefix: 3-921040

Gebrüder **Weiss** Verlag*, Hewaldstr 9, D-1000 Berlin 62 Tel: (030) 7817725
Owner: Richard Weiss
Subjects: General Fiction, Juveniles, Popular Science, Non-fiction, Paperbacks
Founded: 1945
ISBN Publisher's Prefix: 3-8036

Edition **Weitbrecht**, an imprint of K Thienemanns Verlag (qv)

Verlag **Welsermühl**, Kufsteiner Str 8, D-8000 Munich 80 Tel: (089) 982031 Cable Add: welsermuhldruck Telex: 5216349
Dir, Editorial, Rights & Permissions: Karl Prämendorfer; *Sales:* Friederike Weiss-Füreder; *Production:* Friedrich Spendou; *Publicity:* K Füreder
Subsidiary Company: Zweimühlen Verlag GmbH (at above address)
Branch Off: Verlag 'Welsermühl' Fritsch und Dusl KG, Austria (qv)
Subjects: General Non-fiction, Travel, Illustrated Books, Current Events
Founded: 1928
ISBN Publisher's Prefix: 3-85339

Weltforum Verlag GmbH, Kriemhildenstr 38/II, D-8000 Munich 19
Also Marienburgerstr 22, D-5000 Cologne 51
Dir: Sales, Rights & Permissions: Peter John von Freyend; *Editorial, Production:* Frau Barleben-Bohn; *Publicity:* Karl Ludwig Ostermann
Subjects: Political, Economic and Technological aspects of the Developing Nations
ISBN Publisher's Prefix: 3-8039

Weltkreis-Verlags-GmbH, Postfach 789, D-4600 Dortmund 1 Tel: (0231) 528581 Telex: 8227284 wkv el
Man Dir: Ulrich Scheibner; *Editorial:* Jürgen Starbatty; *Publicity & Advertising Dir:* Elke Steiner; *Sales Manager, Rights & Permissions:* Martin Strubelt
Orders to: (Federal Republic of Germany): Brücken Verlag, Postfach 1928, D-4000 Düsseldorf; (West Berlin): Zirk und Ellenrieder, Postfach 3147, D-1000 Berlin 30
Subjects: Belles Lettres, Poetry, Biography, How-to, Juveniles, Low-priced Paperbacks
Founded: 1958
Miscellaneous: Member of Arbeitsgemeinschaft sozialistischer und demokratischer Verleger und Buchhändler (qv for other members)
ISBN Publisher's Prefix: 3-88142

Karl **Wenschow** GmbH, Munich, see JRO – Verlagsgesellschaft, the subsidiary company which now handles all marketing and distribution

Werner Verlag GmbH, Berliner Allee 11a, Postfach 8529, D-4000 Düsseldorf 1 Tel: (0211) 320988 Cable Add: Wernerverlag Telex: 8587828
Man Dir: Klaus Werner; *Publicity Dir:* E Dickert
Subjects: University Textbooks, Reference, Engineering, Educational Materials, Law, Social Science, Economics
1981: 60 titles *Founded:* 1945
ISBN Publisher's Prefix: 3-8041

Westdeutscher Verlag GmbH, Faulbrunnenstr 13, Postfach 5829, D-6200 Wiesbaden Tel: (06121) 5341 Telex: 4186928 vwvd
Man Dir: Dr Frank Lube; *Editorial:* Manfred Müller; *Sales, Publicity:* Heinz Detering; *Rights & Permissions:* Angelika Bolisega
Orders to: VVA (Vereinigte Verlagsauslieferung GmbH), Postfach 7777, D-4830 Gütersloh 1
Parent Company: Verlagsgruppe Bertelsmann GmbH (qv for associate companies)
Branch Off: Reuschenberger Str 55, D-5090 Leverkusen 3
Subjects: History, Literature, Social Science, University Textbooks
1982: 45 titles *Founded:* 1947
ISBN Publisher's Prefix: 3-531

Westermann Verlag GmbH, Georg-Westermann-Allee 66, Postfach 3320, D-3300 Brunswick Tel: (0531) 708 Cable Add: Gewebuch Telex: 0952841 wbuch d
Man Dir: Dr Jürgen Mackensen; *Editorial, Production, Rights & Permissions:* Dr Carl-August Schröder, Mr von Bernuth; *Sales:* Mr Dick, Mr von Bernuth; *Publicity:* Mr Dick
Parent Company: Georg Westermann Verlag, Druckerei und Kartographische Anstalt GmbH & Co (Printing and Publishing Management Company), Brunswick
Associate Companies: Verlag Heinz Vogel, Brunswick; Arena-Verlag Georg Popp GmbH & Co (qv)
Subjects: History, Education, Paperbacks, University, Secondary & Primary Textbooks, Educational Materials, Atlases, Maps, Periodicals
Founded: 1838
Miscellaneous: Part of vgs — Verlagsgesellschaft Schulfernsehen mbH & Co KG (qv)
ISBN Publisher's Prefix: 3-14

Erich **Wewel** Verlag, Anzinger Str 1, D-8000 Munich 80 Tel: (089) 403031 Telex: 522504
Sales: Erna Schmidt; *Publicity:* Starkmuth Eschrich
Parent Company: Manz Verlag (qv)
Subjects: Philosophy, Religion
ISBN Publisher's Prefix: 3-87904

Who's Who — the International Red Series Verlag GmbH, Hauptstr 1, Postfach 1150, D-8031 Wörthsee bei München Tel: (08153) 8033 Telex: 0526496 whos d
President: H F Sutter; *Man Dir, Rights & Permissions:* Dr W T Knödel; *Editorial:* Monika Hirsch; *Sales:* Karl Freundlich; *Production:* Jürgen Schmalenbach; *Publicity:* Michael Stengl
Parent Company: A Sutter GmbH, Brunnenstr 61-65, D-4300 Essen 1
Subsidiary Company: Who's Who in Italy SRL, CP 61, Via Roma 16, I-20091 Bresso Milano, Italy
Subjects: English Language Encyclopaedias (comprising Biographies of prominent living personalities in Arts, Literature, Medicine, Technology, Fashion), *International Red Series* of 'Who's Who' in Europe and European Organizations
1982: 4 titles *1983:* 9 titles *Founded:* 1972
ISBN Publisher's Prefix: 3-921220

Herbert **Wichmann** Verlag GmbH, Amalienstr 29, Postfach 4320, D-7500 Karlsruhe 1 Tel: (0721) 20909 Telex: 7825909
Man Dir: Dr Christof Müller-Wirth; *Sales, Publicity:* Winfried Ammon; *Production, Rights & Permissions:* Bernhard Harzer
Subjects: Geodesy, Photogrammetry, Land Registration, Cartography, Estate Evaluation
Founded: 1889
ISBN Publisher's Prefix: 3-87907

Winkler-Verlag, Martiusstr 8, Postfach 440254, D-8000 Munich 44 Tel: (089) 348074 Telex: 5215517
Man Dir: Hans Jürgen Schmidt; *Publicity:* Anita Donat
Parent Company: Artemis Verlag, see Artemis und Winkler
Associate Companies: Verlag für Architektur, Artemis Verlags AG (both in Switzerland, qqv)
Subjects: Belles Lettres, Reference, General Science, University Textbooks, Reprints
Founded: 1945
ISBN Publisher's Prefix: 3-538

Carl **Winter** Universitätsverlag GmbH, Lutherstr 59, Postfach 106140, D-6900 Heidelberg 1 Tel: (06221) 49111 Telex: 0461660
Publisher: Dr Carl Winter; *Sales:* Ruth Wutke
Subject: University Books
1981: 72 titles *1982:* 53 titles *Founded:* 1822
ISBN Publisher's Prefix: 3-533

Wirtschaft, Recht, Steuern, see WRS-Verlag

Verlag für **Wirtschafts- und Kartographie-**Publikationen, Ryborsch, see V W K

Verlag für **Wirtschaftsskripten**, Dipl-Kfm C Ölschläger GmbH, Friedrichstr 1, D-8000 Munich 40 Tel: (089) 331057
Man Dir: Claus Ölschläger
Subjects: Economics, Business, Management, Law
Founded: 1974
ISBN Publisher's Prefix: 3-921636

Wirtschaftsverlag, Hubertusstr 4, D-8000 Munich 19 Tel: (089) 177041 Telex: 215045
Publicity Manager: Gerhard Koralus
Subjects: Business Economics, Work Study and Allied Subjects
Miscellaneous: Firm is a member of Verlagsgruppe Langen-Müller/Herbig (qv)

Wison Verlag GmbH*, Weyertal 59, Postfach 410948, D-5000 Cologne 41 Tel: 443031
Publicity: Michael Wienand
Subjects: Economic Sciences, Data Processing, Research Reports

Wissen Verlag GmbH, Schloss Mühlfeld, D-8036 Herrsching Tel: (08152) 1087 Telex: 526493
Dirs: Anton Bolza, Rudolf Blanckenstein
Subjects: Reference, Encyclopaedias, Dictionaries
ISBN Publisher's Prefix: 3-8075

Verlag **Wissenschaft und Politik**, see von Nottbeck

Verlag für **Wissenschaft, Wirtschaft und Technik** GmbH und Co KG, Amsbergstr 22, D-3388 Bad Harzburg Tel: (05322) 73333 Telex: 957623 DVG
Man Dir: Brigitte Barvencik; *Dirs:* Gisela Böhme, Reinhard Höhn
Subjects: Management, Sociology, Social Science, Primary and Secondary Textbooks, Economics, Rhetoric
Founded: 1960
ISBN Publisher's Prefix: 3-8020

Wissenschaftliche Buchgesellschaft, Hindenburgstr 40, Postfach 111129, D-6100 Darmstadt 11 Tel: (06151) 33141
Man Dir: Andreas Keiser; *Chief Reader:* Dr Ingold Dutz; *Rights & Permissions:* Christa Pantos
Subjects: History, Music, Art, Philosophy, Religion, Medicine, Psychology, General & Social Science, Classics, Literature, Language, Education, Mathematics, Archaeology, Jurisprudence, Economics
Book Club: Wissenschaftliche Buchgesellschaft
1981: 100 titles *Founded:* 1949
ISBN Publisher's Prefix: 3-534

Wissenschaftliche Verlagsgesellschaft mbH, Birkenwaldstr 44, Postfach 40, D-7000 Stuttgart 1 Tel: (0711) 25820 Telex: 723636 daz d
Man Dirs: Hans Rotta, Dr W Wessinger; *Managers:* R Hack, K Hübler, B Schreck
Associate Companies: Deutscher Apotheker Verlag Dr Roland Schmiedel GmbH & Co (qv); S Hirzel Verlag GmbH & Co (qv); Franz Steiner Verlag GmbH (qv)
Subjects: Medicine, Pharmacy, Biology, Chemistry, Physics
Founded: 1921
ISBN Publisher's Prefix: 3-8047

Wissenschaftlicher Autoren Verlag, see Verlag Grundlagen und Praxis GmbH & Co

Friedrich **Wittig** Verlag, Papenhuder Str 2, D-2000 Hamburg 76 Tel: (040) 221059 Cable Add: Wittigverlag
Man Dir, Sales: Friedrich B Holst; *Editorial:* Friedrich Wittig, Henning Wendland; *Production:* Henning Wendland
Subjects: Religion, Arts, History, Bibliophily
Founded: 1946
ISBN Publisher's Prefix: 3-8048

Verlag Konrad **Wittwer** KG+, Nordbahnhofstr 16, Postfach 147, D-7000 Stuttgart-N Tel: 25070 Telex: 723751
Man Dir: Konrad Wittwer; *Editorial, Sales, Publicity:* Mr Hasler
Subjects: Mathematics, Geodesy, Building Technology, General Literature, School Textbooks
Bookshop: Königstr 30, D-7000 Stuttgart 1
1981: 7 titles *1982:* 8 titles *Founded:* 1867
ISBN Publisher's Prefix: 3-87919

Gerhard **Witzstrock** GmbH*, Bismarckstr 9, Postfach 509, D-7570 Baden Baden Tel: (07221) 2047 Telex: 781162 gewi d
Man Dir, General Manager: Dr Harald Karja; *General Manager:* Lotte Witzstrock
Subsidiary Company: Gerhard Witzstrock Publishing House Inc, New York, 30 East 40th St, Suite 703, New York, NY 10016, USA
Subjects: Medicine, Electron Scanning Microscopy
Founded: 1969
ISBN Publisher's Prefix: 3-87921

The **World of Books** Ltd, Friedrich-Ebert-Str 80, D-6520 Worms Tel: (06241) 51425
Man Dirs: W P Smith, J M Ortez, R Becker
Head Office: 788-789 Finchley Rd, London, UK
Subjects: Current Events, Belles Lettres, Juvenile, Specialist Computer Operating Literature
1982: 30 titles *Founded:* 1976
ISBN Publisher's Prefix: 3-88325

Rainer **Wunderlich** Verlag Hermann Leins, Eduard-Haber-Str 15, Postfach 2740, D-7400 Tübingen Tel: (0711) 223067 Cable Add: Wunderlichverlag Telex: 7262891 mepo d
Man Dir: Günther Schweizer; *Sales & Publicity Manager:* Michael Hennig; *Rights & Permissions:* Kurt Neff
Subjects: Belles Lettres, Poetry, Biography, History, Music, Art, Politics
Founded: 1926
ISBN Publisher's Prefix: 3-8052

Echter **Würzburg**, Fränkische Gesellschaftsdruckerei und Verlag GmbH, Juliuspromenade 64, Postfach 5560, D-8700 Würzburg Tel: (0931) 50258 Telex: 068862 Cable Add: Echterverlag
Dirs: Elmar Wegner, Hans Kufner
Subjects: Religion, Art, Fiction, Youth, Periodicals
Founded: 1900
ISBN Publisher's Prefix: 3-429

Xenos Verlagsgesellschaft mbH+, Am Hehsel 42, D-2000 Hamburg 63 Tel: (040) 5381909 Telex: 2174727 bix d
Man Dir: Erwin Heimberger; *Sales Manager:* Rene Kellner; *Publicity:* Klaus-Dietrich Petersen; *Rights & Permissions:* Uwe Kehrhahn
Associate Company: Frankfurter Allgemeine Zeitung, Frankfurt am Main
Subjects: Juveniles, Non-fiction, Belles Lettres; Paperbacks
1981: 41 titles *1982:* 81 titles *Founded:* 1975

Z V W 5, see Siemens AG

Verlag Philipp von **Zabern**, Welschnonnengasse 13A, Postfach 4065, D-6500 Mainz Tel: (06131) 232214 Telex: 04187463 dwk
Man Dir: Franz Rutzen; *Sales:* Hermann Conrad
Subjects: Egyptology, Archaeology, Pre-history, Monographs, Periodicals
1981: 25 titles *Founded:* 1802
ISBN Publisher's Prefix: 3-8053

Dr **Zambon***, Leipziger Str 24, D-6000 Frankfurt am Main 90 Tel: (0611) 779223
Publisher: Giuseppe Zambon; *Sales:* Angela Biscotti
Subjects: Juveniles, Foreign-language Teaching, Reprints

Zechner und Hüthig Verlag GmbH, Daimlerstr 9, Postfach 2080, D-6720 Speyer am Rhein Tel: (06232) 33076 Cable Add: Zechner Verlag Speyer Telex: 465167
Publisher: Rudolf Zechner
Subject: General Science
ISBN Publisher's Prefix: 3-87927

Zero Verlag und Vertrieb, Vierbaumer Heide 82A, D-4134 Rheinberg 4 Tel: (02843) 2769
Man Dir, Production, Rights & Permissions: Carl-Heinz Urselmann; *Editorial, Publicity:* Benjamin Last; *Sales:* Frauke Urselmann
Subjects: Philosophy and Literature (avantegarde)
Bookshop: Zero Barsortiment (at above address)
1981: 4 titles *Founded:* 1978
ISBN Publisher's Prefix: 3-922253

Zester Druck- und Verlagsgesellschaft mbH, see Accidentia

Verlag Andreas **Zettner** KG*, Hofweg 12, Postfach 13, D-8702 Würzburg-Veitshöchheim Tel: (0931) 91970 Cable Add: Zettner Würzburg
Man Dir: Andreas Zettner
Subject: General Fiction
Book Club: Buchclub 69
Bookshops: Dr Müllers Buchboutique, D-8000 Munich 13, Citta 2000 & D-8500 Nuremberg, Breite Gasse 62; D-8100 Augsburg, Neuburger Str 67; D-854 Schwabach, Neutorstr 1
Founded: 1955

Verlag Wolfgang **Zeunert** GmbH & Co KG, Hindenburgstr 15, D-3170 Gifhorn Tel: (05371) 3542
Man Dir, Editorial, Production, Publicity, Rights & Permissions: Wolfgang Zeunert; *Sales:* Ingrid Zeunert
Parent Company: Zeunert GmbH (at above address)
Subjects: Railways, Model Railways, Trams, Maritime, Equestrianism
1981: 4 titles *1982:* 6 titles *Founded:* 1963
ISBN Publisher's Prefix: 3-921237

Verlag Wolfgang **Zimmer**, Haunstetter Str 18, D-8900 Augsburg 1 Tel: (0821) 554135
Publisher: Wolfgang Zimmer
Imprint: Schwarz Bildbücher
Subjects: Hobbies, Transport
ISBN Publisher's Prefixes: 3-87987, 3-87679

Paul **Zsolnay** Verlag GmbH*, Hohe Bleichen 7/Libri Haus, D-2000 Hamburg Tel: (040) 345156 Cable Add: Hakobuch Hamburg Telex: 214900
Dirs: Kurt Lingenbrink, Hans Polak
Parent Company: William Heinemann International Ltd, UK (qv)
Associate Companies: Paul Zsolnay Verlag GmbH, Austria (qv); see also the Heinemann Group, UK
Subjects: General Fiction, Poetry, Non-fiction
Founded: 1948
ISBN Publisher's Prefix: 3-552

Zweipunkt Verlag KG*, Wilhelm-Leuschner-Str 1, D-6078 Neu Isenburg Tel: (06102) 27247
Subjects: Picture Books, Activity Books, Puzzles

Literary Agents

Babylon Übersetzungen*, Düsseldorferstr 38, D-1000 Berlin 15 Tel: (03) 8838296
Man Dir: Walter Bengs
Literary, Copyright and Translation Agency

Balkan-Press, Schmied-Kochel-Str 20, D-8000 Munich 70 Tel: (089) 3204450

Mo **Cohen**, Wentzelstr 15, D-2000 Hamburg 60 Tel: (040) 273814 Telex: 2173453 Iwsd
Specializes in rights between publishers in Federal Republic of Germany, UK and USA

Dr rer pol Dr Julius **Démuth***, Krautgartenweg 22, D-6000 Frankfurt am Main 50 Tel: (0611) 571970

Fralit-F K Albrecht, Brahmsallee 29/1, D-2000 Hamburg 13 Tel: (040) 456073
Cable Add: Fralitagentur
Specializations: Tipposcripts and Photographs for Publishers, Press, Broadcasting, Film and Theatre besides those which are strictly specialized for Medicine, Technology, Economics and related subjects
Also acts as Translation and Photograph Supply Agency

Geisenheyner und Crone, Gymnasiumstr 31B, D-7000 Stuttgart 1 Tel: (0711) 293738
Cable Add: Gecelit Telex: 722664
Proprietor: Ernst W Geisenheyner
An international agency

Hans Hermann **Hagedorn**, Erikastr 142, D-2000 Hamburg 20 Tel: (040) 4603232

Münchner Verlagsbüro Horst **Hodemacher** — Axel Poldner GmbH & Co KG, see Münchner

Agence **Hoffman**, D-8000 Munich 40, Seestr 6 Tel: (089) 396402 Cable Add: Aghoff München
Contact: Frau Dagmar Henne
There is a branch of this Agency in Paris, France (qv)

Gerhard **Kowalski**, Ringstr 105, Postfach 450328, D-1000 Berlin 45 Tel: (030) 8333337 Telex: 0184560
Specialization: Memoirs, Biographies, Reference, Fiction, Theatre
Owned by: G Kowalski Konzert Verlag (qv)

Karl Ludwig **Leonhardt**, Mittelweg 22, D-2000 Hamburg 13

Rose M **Meerwein**, Literary Scout, Reuterpfad 6-8, D-1000 Berlin 33 Tel: (030) 8262039
No authors' representation

Münchner Verlagsbüro, Horst Hodemacher-Axel Poldner, Allacher Str 130b, D-8000 Munich 19 Tel: (089) 1491611

Gerd **Plessl** Agency, Seidlstr 18, D-8000 Munich 2 Tel: (089) 554084
Specialization: Selling rights to South and East European publishers

Axel **Poldner**, see Münchner Verlagsbüro

Quelle Press*, Postfach 1314, D-7800 Freiburg im Breisgau Tel: (0761) 7016
Cable Add: Quellepress Freiburg
Specializations: Romance, Gothic, Science Fiction, Fantasy, Western

Thomas **Schlueck**, Hinter der Worth 12, D-3008 Garbsen 9 Tel: (05131) 93053
Telex: 923419 litag d

Specialization: Full representation to Anglo-American authors, agents and publishers in German language areas

SCI **Singer** Communications Inc*, Postfach 1314, D-7800 Freiburg im Breisgau Tel: (0761) 7016
US Office: 3164 Tyler Ave, Anaheim, California 92801 USA
Specializations: Romance, Gothic and Science Fiction, Fantasy, Cartoons, Health/Diet, Public Affairs, Personality Profiles, International Co-productions

Skandinavia Verlag, Ithweg 31, D-1000 Berlin 37 Tel: (030) 8137006/8616074
Contacts: Marianne Weno, Michael Günther
Specialization: Scandinavian Stage, Radio and TV plays

Herta **Weber-Stumfohl***, Waldpromenade 32, D-8035 Gauting Tel: (089) 8501241
Specialization: Translations from Swedish; Reviews

Book Clubs

A G A V ev, Postfach 656, D-7000 Stuttgart 1
Owned by: Edition Leu, Switzerland (qv)

Bertelsmann Lesering, Carl-Bertelsmannstr 270, Postfach 555, D-4830 Gütersloh
Members: 3 million
Owned by: Bertelsmann Club GmbH, Gütersloh
Founded: 1950

Verlag **Bibliotheca** Christiana*, Endenicher Str 125, Postfach 1246, D-5300 Bonn

Bonner Buchgemeinde (BBG)*, Endenicherstr 125, Postfach 1246, D-5300 Bonn

Buchclub 69 GmbH*, Hofweg 12, Postfach 13, D-8702 Würzburg-Veitshöchheim
Owned by: Verlag Andreas Zettner KG (qv)

Christlicher Bildungskreis Verlags GmbH*, Lindenspürstr 32, Postfach 285, D-7000 Stuttgart 1

Deutsche Buch-Gemeinschaft C A Koch's Verlag Nachfolger*, Berliner Allee 6, Postfach 4131, D-6100 Darmstadt
Owned by: Deutsche Buch-Gemeinschaft C A Koch's Verlag Nachfolger (qv)

Deutscher Bücherbund GmbH & Co, Wolframstr 36, D-7000 Stuttgart 1 Tel: (0711) 25800 Telex: 0723829
Owned by: Georg von Holtzbrinck (at above address)

Deutscher Buchkreis, Postfach 1629, D-7400 Tübingen Tel: (07071) 61206 Telex: 07262863 grav-d
Owned by: Grabert-Verlag (qv)

Freundeskreis des **Euphorion** Verlags, Neumannstr 13, D-6000 Frankfurt am Main 50
Owned by: Euphorion Verlag (qv)
Founded: 1976

Europäische Bildungsgemeinschaft Verlags GmbH, Lindenspürstr 32, Postfach 1069, D-7000 Stuttgart 1 Tel: (0711) 66831 Telex: 722820 ebege d
European Educational Fellowship Publishers
Members: 1,700,000
Owned by: Verlagsgruppe Bertelsmann GmbH (qv)
Founded: 1950

Europaring der Buch- und Schallplattenfreunde, Carl-Bertelsmann-Str 270, D-4830 Gütersloh
Owned by: Bertelsmann Club GmbH, Gütersloh

Fackel-Buchklub, Verlags- und Vertriebs GmbH*, Herdweg 29-31, Postfach 442, D-7000 Stuttgart 1
Owned by: Fackelverlag G Bowitz GmbH (qv)

Büchergilde **Gutenberg***, Untermainkai 66, Postfach 16220, D-6000 Frankfurt am Main 16
Owned by: Büchergilde Gutenberg Verlagsgesellschaft mbH (qv)

Herder-Buchgemeinde, Hermann-Herder-Str 4, D-7800 Freiburg im Breisgau
Owned by: Verlag Herder GmbH & Co KG (qv)
Founded: 1952

Kosmos Gesellschaft, Pfizerstr 5-7, Postfach 640, D-7000 Stuttgart 1
Owned by: Franckh'sche Verlagshandlung W Keller & Co (qv)

Kunstkreis für Bibliophile Mappen, Schwedenhof, D-6650 Homburg-Schwarzenacker/Saar
Bibliophile Portfolios Art Circle
Owned by: Edition Monika Beck (qv)

Volksverband der Bücherfreunde Verlag GmbH & Co*, Heidberg 7, D-2000 Hamburg 60

Wissenschaftliche Buchgesellschaft, Hindenburgstr 40, Postfach 111129, D-6100 Darmstadt 11
Scientific Book Society
Owned by: Wissenschaftliche Buchgesellschaft (qv)

Major Booksellers

Artibus et Literis, Friedrichstr 26, D-4000 Düsseldorf 1
Worldwide export and import of books and journals
Managing Partners: Horst and Klaus Janssen

Buchhandlung G D **Baedeker**, Kettwiger Str 33-35, Postfach 100345, D-4300 Essen 1 Tel: (02141) 221381

Blazek und Bergmann, Inhaber Dr Hans Bergmann, Universitätsbuchhandlung, Goethestr 1, D-6000 Frankfurt am Main 1 Tel: (0611) 288648

Universitätsbuchhandlung **Bouvier** GmbH, Am Hof 32, D-5300 Bonn 1 Tel: (0228) 654445

Buchhandlung **Elwert und Meurer** GmbH*, Hauptstr 101, D-1000 Berlin 62 Tel: (030) 784001

F B V Frauenbuchvertrieb GmbH, Mehringdamm 32-34, D-1000 Berlin 61 Tel: (030) 2511666
Books written by women for women and published by women; subjects relating to women's movements
Managers: M Emmerich, R Krause, E Schoenkerl

Buchhandlung Heinrich **Gonski***, Neumarkt 24, D-5000 Cologne 1 Tel: (0221) 210528

Grossohaus Wegner und Co, Postfach 102540, D-2000 Hamburg 1 (Located at: Conventstr 12-14, D-2000 Hamburg 76) Tel: (040) 25760 Telex: (02) 15096 Cable Add: Grossohaus Hamburg
Wholesaler and Exporter of German books, including those in the English language published in German-speaking countries

Otto **Harrassowitz***, Taunusstr 5, Postfach 2929, D-6200 Wiesbaden Tel: (06121) 521046
Dirs: Dr Knut Dorn, Detlef Dorn

168 FEDERAL REPUBLIC OF GERMANY

Heinrich **Hugendubel**, Salvatorplatz 2, D-8000 Munich 2 Tel: (089) 23891 Cable Add: Hugendubel Munich Telex: 0529651

Internationale Presse, Import- und Export GmbH, Borsigallee 17, D-6000 Frankfurt am Main 60 Tel: (0611) 419198 Cable Add: Airedition Frankfurt Telex: 4189645 ip d
Man Dir and Associate: Gustav Stückrath
Book and periodical wholesaler representing companies in France, Italy, Portugal, Spain, United Kingdom, United States

Buchhandlung Chr **Kaiser**, Marienplatz 8, D-8000 Munich 2 Tel: (089) 223441
Owned by: Fritz Lempp
Branch Off: Theologie und französische Literatur, Schellingstr 3, D-8000 Munich 40 Tel: (089) 2809078

Koch, Neff und Oetinger & Co*, Schockenriedstr 39, Postfach 800620, D-7000 Stuttgart 80 Tel: (0711) 78603325 Telex: 07255684 knov d stgt
Wholesaler

Barsortiment Georg **Lingenbrink** (Wholesale Bookseller)*, Stresemannstr 300, Postfach 500925, D-2000 Hamburg 50 Tel: (040) 85431 Telex: 0214900 and 0214673
Also: D-6000 Frankfurt-Preungesheim; D-5000 Cologne; D-8047 Munich-Karlsfeld; Nüremberg; Stuttgart

J A **Mayersche** Buchhandlung, Ursulinerstr 17-19, D-5100 Aachen Tel: (0241) 48142 Cable Add: Mayer Aachen Telex: 832768
Manager: Helmut Falter

Vereinigte Verlagsauslieferung R **Mohn** HG, see VVA

Buchhandlung Wendelin **Niedlich** KG, Schmale Str 9, D-7000 Stuttgart 1 Tel: (0711) 223287
Manager: W Niedlich

Hans Heinrich **Petersen** Buchimport GmbH*, Rugenbarg 250, Postfach 530230, D-2000 Hamburg 53 Tel: (040) 83330 Cable Add: buchpetersen hamburg Telex: 211401 hhp d
Man Dir: Egon Schormann
Importer of books, journals, audiovisual material from throughout world (but especially UK, USA, Netherlands)

Pro Media Literaturvertrieb GmbH*, Werner Voss Damm 54, D-1000 Berlin 42 Tel: (030) 7855971
This is a wholesale marketing organization representing small publishing houses dealing with the alternative society
Manager: Ruth Westerwelle

Martin **Sandkühler***, Verlagsauslieferungen, Paracelsusstr 26, Postfach 720308, D-7000 Stuttgart 72 Tel: (0711) 454723

Stern-Verlag Janssen und Co, Friedrichstr 24-26, Postfach 7820, D-4000 Düsseldorf 1 Tel: (0211) 373033
Bookseller dealing with new and antiquarian/second-hand books; worldwide export and import of books and journals
Managing Partners: Horst and Klaus Janssen

V V A (Vereinigte Verlagsauslieferung GmbH), An der Autobahn, Postfach 7777, D-4830 Gütersloh 1 Tel: (05241) 80 Telex: 933827
Wholesale book supplier and publishers' delivery service
Man Dirs: Detthold Aden, Dr Hans Zopp

Buchandlung Konrad **Wittwer** KG, Königstr 30, PO Box 147, D-7000 Stuttgart 1 Tel: (0711) 25070 Telex: 723751

Major Libraries

Bayerische Staatsbibliothek, Ludwigstr 16, Postfach 340150, D-8000 Munich 34 Tel: (089) 21981
Librarian: Dr F G Kaltwasser

Bibliothek für Zeitgeschichte, Konrad-Adenauer-Str 8, Postfach 769, D-7000 Stuttgart 1 Tel: (0711) 244117
Library for contemporary history. This library is housed in same building as the Württembergische Landesbibliothek (qv) but has separate administration
Dir: Professor Dr Jürgen Rohwer
Publications: Jahresbibliographie, Schriften der Bibliothek für Zeitgeschichte, Dokumentationen der B fZ, Wehrtechnik im Bild

Bundesarchiv, Am Wöllershof 12, D-5400 Koblenz Tel: (0261) 3991 Telex: 0862 619
Federal Archives. Publishing is undertaken by Harald Boldt Verlag (qv) and R Oldenbourg Verlag (qv)

Deutsche Bibliothek (National Library)*, Zeppelinallee 4-8, D-6000 Frankfurt am Main 1 Tel: (0611) 75661 Telex: 416643 deubi

Herzog August Bibliothek, Lessingplatz 1, Postfach 1227, D-3340 Wolfenbüttel Tel: (05331) 5081
Dir: Prof Dr Paul Raabe

Hessische Landes- und Hoch-schulbibliothek Darmstadt, Schloss, D-6100 Darmstadt Tel: (06151) 125420
The Hesse Regional and University Library

Ibero-Amerikanisches Institut, Preussischer Kulturbesitz, Potsdamer Str 37, D-1000 Berlin 30 Tel: (030) 2662500
Dir: Dr Wilhelm Stegmann

Bibliothek des Instituts für Weltwirtschaft — Zentralbibliothek der Wirtschaftswissenschaften, Postfach 4309, D-2300 Kiel 1 (Located at: Düsternbrooker Weg 120, D-2300 Kiel 1) Tel: (0431) 8841 Telex: 0292479
Library of the Institute for World Economics — National Library of Economics

Niedersächsische Staats- und Universitätsbibliothek*, Prinzenstr 1, Postfach 2932-2934, D-3400 Göttingen Tel: (0551) 395212 (Secretariat) Telex: 96678 nsub
Librarian: Dir Helmut Vogt

Staats- und Universitätsbibliothek, Von-Melle Park 3, D-2000 Hamburg 13 Tel: (040) 41232213
Dir: Professor Dr Horst Gronemeyer

Staatsbibliothek Bamberg, Neue Residenz, Domplatz 8, D-8600 Bamberg Tel: (0951) 54014

Staatsbibliothek Preussischer Kulturbesitz, Potsdamer Str 33, Postfach 1407, D-1000 Berlin 30 Tel: (030) 2661 Telex 183160 staab d
State Library of the Prussian Cultural Foundation
Director: Dr Ekkehart Vesper
Publications: Jahresbericht (annual); *Mitteilungen* (three times a year); *Zeitschriften-Datenbank* (semi-annual), produced in association with das Deutsche Bibliotheksinstitut and Publisher Otto Harrassowitz (qv)
ISBN Publisher's Prefix: 3-88053

Stadt- und Universitätsbibliothek, Bockenheimer Landstr 134-138, D-6000 Frankfurt am Main 1 Tel: (0611) 79071 Telex: 414024 stub d
Director: Mr Lehmann

Universitäts- und Stadtbibliothek*, Universitätsstr 33, D-5000 Cologne 41 Tel: (0221) 4702260/4702214

Universitätsbibliothek, Werthmannpl 2, Postfach 1629, D-7800 Freiburg im Breisgau Tel: (0761) 2033901 (management); 2034000 (enquiries); 2033940 (main reading room) Telex: 772740/50 uf d

Universitätsbibliothek der Eberhard-Karls-Universität*, Wilhelmstr 32, Postfach 2620, D-7400 Tübingen 1 Tel: (07071) 292577

Universitätsbibliothek Erlangen-Nürnberg, Universitätsstr 4/Schuhstr 1a, D-8520 Erlangen Tel: (09131) 852151

Universitätsbibliothek Heidelberg, Plöck 107-109, Postfach 105749, D-6900 Heidelberg 1 Tel: (06221) 542380
Library Dir: Dr E Mittler
Publications: Neuerwerbungslisten der Sondersammelgebiete Ägyptologie, Klassische Archäologie, Mittlere und Neuere Kunstgeschichte, Heidelberger Zeitschriftenverzeichnis, Theke-Informationsblatt der Mitarbeiter im Bibliothekssystem der Universität Heidelberg, Heidelberger Bibliotheken, Heidelberger Bibliotheksschriften, Bibliothek-Forschung und Praxis, Bibliothek und Wissenschaft

Württembergische Landesbibliothek, Konrad-Adenauer-Str 8, Postfach 769, D-7000 Stuttgart 1 Tel: (0711) 2125424
Württemberg State Library
Director: Dr Hans-Peter Geh
Miscellaneous: The Bibliothek für Zeitgeschichte is housed in same building, but has separate administration

Library Associations

A Sp B, see Arbeitsgemeinschaft der Spezialbibliotheken eV

Arbeitsgemeinschaft der Archive und Bibliotheken in der evangelischen Kirche, Veilhofstr 28, D-8500 Nuremberg 20
Joint Association of Archives and Libraries in the Evangelical Church
President: Dr Helmut Baier
Publications: Mitteilungen der AABevK (AABevK News Bulletin); *Veröffentlichungen der AABevK* (Publications of the AABevK)

Arbeitsgemeinschaft der kirchlichen Büchereiverbände Deutschlands, Wittelsbacherring 9, D-5300 Bonn Tel: (0228) 631055
Joint Association of Library Associations of the Churches in Germany
Executive Secretary: Erich Hodick

Arbeitsgemeinschaft der Kunstbibliotheken, pA Zentralinstitut für Kunstgeschichte Bibliothek, Meiserstr 10, D-8000 Munich 1
Joint Association of Art Libraries

Arbeitsgemeinschaft der Parlaments- und Behördenbibliotheken, Bibliothek des Deutschen Bundestages, Bundeshaus, D-5300 Bonn
Joint Association of Parliamentary and Administration Libraries
Chairman: Wolfgang Dietz; *Executive Secretary:* Heinz-Ottmar Schmidt
Publications: Arbeitshefte (Work Programmes) and *Mitteilungen* (News Sheets)

Arbeitsgemeinschaft der Regionalbibliotheken, Staats- und Stadtbibliothek, Schaezlerstr 25, D-8900 Augsburg
Joint Association of Regional Libraries
President: Josef Bellot

Arbeitsgemeinschaft der Spezialbibliotheken eV (ASpB), Kekulé-Bibliothek, Bayer AG, D-5090 Leverkusen-Bayerwerk
Association of Special Libraries
Chairman: Dr Walter Manz; *Secretariat Dir:* Dr Marianne Schwarzer
Publication: Bericht über die Tagung (Conference Report; every 2 years)

Arbeitsgemeinschaft für juristisches Bibliotheks- und Dokumentationswesen, (Teilbibliothek Recht der Universitätsbibliothek), Eichleitnerstr 30, D-8900 Augsburg
Joint Association for Law Libraries and Legal Documentation
Chairman: Dietrich Pannier; *Editor:* Dr Hans-Burkard Meyer
Publications: Mitteilungen der Arbeitsgemeinschaft für juristisches Bibliotheks- und Dokumentationswesen (3 times yearly) and *Arbeitshefte* (irregularly)

Arbeitsgemeinschaft für medizinisches Bibliothekswesen, pA Fachbibliothek Medizin, Hufelandstr 55, D-4300 Essen 1 Tel: (0201) 79913330 Telex: 8579573 klies d
Joint Association for Medical Libraries

Arbeitsgemeinschaft katholischtheologischer Bibliotheken, c/o Bibliothek des Priesterseminars, Postfach 1330, D-5500 Trier Tel: (0651) 75011
Joint Association of Catholic Theological Libraries
Dir: Dr Franz Rudolf Reichert
Publications: Mitteilungsblatt (News Letter), *Veröffentlichungen der Arbeitsgemeinschaft katholischtheologischer Bibliotheken* (Publications of the Association — Nos 1-3 available), *Handbuch der kirchlichen katholisch-theologischen Bibliotheken in der Bundesrepublik Deutschland und in West-Berlin*

Bundesarbeitsgemeinschaft der katholisch-kirchlichen Büchereiarbeit, Wittelsbacherring 9, D-5300 Bonn Tel: (0228) 631055
National Joint Association of Library work in the Catholic Church
Executive Secretary: Erich Hodick

Deutsche Gesellschaft für Dokumentation eV, Westendstr 19, D-6000 Frankfurt am Main 1
German Society for Documentation
President: Prof P Canisius
Publications include: Nachrichten für Dokumentation (Documentation News — 5 per year); *Mitteilungen und Berichte* (Newsletter)

Deutscher Leihbuchhändler-Verband eV*
Martener Str 317, D-4600 Dortmund-Marten Tel: 614089
German Circulating Libraries Federation

Deutscher Verband evangelischer Büchereien eV, Bürgerstr 2, D-3400 Göttingen Tel: (0551) 74917
German Association of Evangelical (Protestant) Libraries
Chairman: Dr Hans Wulf; *Manager:* Christine Razum
Publications: Rezensionszeitschrift der eV Buchberater (quarterly), *Handwörterbuch der evangelischen Büchereiarbeit 1980*

Deutsches Bibliotheksinstitut, Bundesallee 184-185, D-1000 Berlin 31 Tel: (030) 85050 Telex: 184166 dbi d
German Library Institute
Dir: Prof Günter Beyersdorff
Publications: Bibliotheksdienst (monthly), *Forum Musikbibliothek* (quarterly), *Schulbibliothek Aktuell* (quarterly), also several reference books, monographs, bibliographical and statistical services

Gesellschaft für Bibliothekswesen und Dokumentation des Landbaues (GBDL), Paracelsusstr 2, D-7000 Stuttgart 70 Tel: (0711) 4501-2111
Society for Librarianship and Documentation in Agriculture
Publication: Mitteilungen der Gesellschaft für Bibliothekswesen und Dokumentation des Landbaues

Gesellschaft für Information und Dokumentation mbH (GID), GID-Informationszentrum (GID-IZ), Lyoner Str 44-48, Postfach 710370, D-6000 Frankfurt am Main 71 Tel: (0611) 66871 Telex: 414351
Documentation and Information Society
Dir: Dr Peter Budinger
Publications: Verzeichnis Deutscher Informations- und Dokumentationsstellen Bundesrepublik Deutschland und Berlin (West), Verzeichnis Informationswissenschaftlicher Zeitschriften, Bestandsverzeichnis Thesauri, Forschung- und Entwicklungsprojekte in Informationswissenschaft und -Praxis, Internationale IuD-Gremien mit Beteiligung aus der Bundesrepublik Deutschland und Berlin (West)

Institut für Jugendbuchforschung der J W Goethe-Universität*, Georg Voigt-Str 10, D-6000 Frankfurt am Main
Institute for Research into Books for the Young

Internationale Vereinigung der Musikbibliotheken, pA Musikarchive und Musikdokumentationszentren, Gruppe Bundesrepublik Deutschland, Fachhochschule für öffentliche Verwaltung, Postfach 769, D-7000 Stuttgart 1
German Section of the International Association of Music Libraries
Secretary-General: Barbara Delcker, Stadtbibliothek Nuremburg, Abteilung Musikbibliothek, Königstorgraben 3, D-8500 Nuremburg Tel: (0911) 163105

V D D, see Verein Deutscher Dokumentare eV

Verband der Bibliotheken des Landes Nordrhein-Westfalen eV, Maischützenstr 57, D-4630 Bochum 1 Tel: (0234) 234582
Association of Libraries of North Rhine-Westphalia
President: B J Schultheis; *Secretary:* R Baumhoff
Secretariat: At above address; *Editorial:* Universitätsbibliothek, D-5300 Bonn
Publication: Mitteilungsblatt (News Sheet)

Verband deutscher Werkbüchereien eV*, c/o BASF Aktiengesellschaft, Werkbücherei, Carl-Bosch Str, D-6700 Ludwigshafen Tel: (0621) 603689
Association of Industrial Libraries of the Federal Republic of Germany
President: Christiane Lüderssen

Verein Angehörige des mittleren und nichtdiplomierten Bibliotheksdienstes eV*, Klattenweg 59, Bremen
Association of Non-professional Librarians
Secretary: Melitta Thomas

Verein der Bibliothekare an öffentlichen Bibliotheken eV*, Roonstr 57, D-2800 Bremen
Association of Public Librarians
President: Dipl-Bibl Karl-Heinz Pröve
Publication: Buch und Bibliothek (from: Postfach 327, D-7410 Reutlingen)

Verein der Diplom-Bibliothekare an wissenschaftlichen Bibliotheken eV, pA Deutsches Bibliotheksinstitut, Bundesallee 184-185, D-1000 Berlin 31 Tel: (030) 8505145
Association of Certified Librarians at Academic Libraries
Chairman: Ulla Usemann-Keller
Publication: Rundschreiben

Verein Deutscher Archivare (VdA), Hessisches Staatsarchiv, Schloss, D-6100 Darmstadt
Association of German Archivists
Chairman: Dr Eckhart G Franz
Publication: Archive und Archivare (Register of Archives and Archivists) — at irregular intervals of several years

Verein Deutscher Bibliothekare eV, Universitätsbibliothek Stuttgart, Holzgartenstr 16, D-7000 Stuttgart 1 Tel: (0711) 2073/2222 Telex: 0722450
Secretary: Robert K Jopp
Association of German Librarians
President: Juergen Hering
Publications: Zeitschrift für Bibliothekswesen und Bibliographie; Jahrbuch der deutschen Bibliotheken

Verein Deutscher Dokumentare eV (VDD), Postfach 2509, D-5300 Bonn 1
Association of German Documentalists
Chairman: Dr Schmitz-Esser, Hamburg; *Vice-Chairman:* Dr Bernd Habel Königswinter
Publications: Nachrichten für Dokumentation, Westendstr 19, D-6000 Frankfurt am Main 1; *VDD Schriftenreihe* (irregular)

Württembergische Bibliotheksgesellschaft*, Postfach 769, D-7000 Stuttgart 1 (Located at: Konrad-Adenauer Str 8)
Society of Friends of the Württemberg State Library
Secretary: Dr Ursula Degenhard

Zentralstelle für maschinelle Dokumentation, see Gesellschaft für Information und Dokumentation

Library Reference Books and Journals

Books

Bibliothekswesen in Deutschland (Library Science in Germany), Börsenverein des deutschen Buchhandels eV, Großer Hirschgraben 17-21, D-6000 Frankfurt 1

Handbuch des Büchereiwesens (Handbook of Library Science), Verlag Otto Harrassowitz, Taunusstr 14, Postfach 2929, D-6200 Wiesbaden

Jahrbuch der Deutschen Bibliotheken (Yearbook of German Libraries), Verlag Otto Harrassowitz, Taunusstr 14, Postfach 2929, D-6300 Wiesbaden 1

Libraries in the Federal Republic of Germany, Verlag Otto Harrassowitz, Taunusstr 14, Postfach 2929, D-6200 Wiesbaden 1

Sigelverzeichnis für die Bibliotheken der Bundesrepublik Deutschland und West-Berlins (Classification List for the Libraries of the Federal Republic of Germany and West Berlin), Staatsbibliothek Preussicher Kulturbesitz, Potsdamer Str 33, Postfach 1407, D-1000 Berlin 30

Verzeichnis der Archivare (Register of Archivists), Verein deutscher Archivare, Hessisches Staatsarchiv, Schloss, D-6100 Darmstadt

Verzeichnis der Spezialbibliotheken in der Bundesrepublik Deutschland einschl West Berlin (List of Special Libraries in the BRD including West Berlin), Friedr Vieweg & Sohn Verlagsgesellschaft mbH,

Faulbrunnenstr 13, Postfach 5829, D-6200 Wiesbaden

Journals

Bibliotheksdienst (Library Service), Deutsches Bibliotheksinstitut, Bundesallee 184-185, D-1000 Berlin 31

Buch und Bibliothek (Book and Library), K G Saur KG, Pössenbacherstr 2, D-8000 Munich 71

Dokumentation, Fachbibliothek, Werksbücherei (DFW) Zeitschrift für Allgemein- und Spezial-bibliotheken, Büchereien und Dokumentationsstellen (Documentation, Technical Libraries' and Works Libraries' Journal for General and Special Libraries and Documentation Centres), Nordwestverlag Stephanie Schräpel, Güntherstr 21, D-3000 Hanover-Waldhausen

Musikbibliothek aktuell (Music Library Today), Deutsches Bibliotheksinstitut, Bundesallee 184-185, D-1000 Berlin 31

Nachrichten für Dokumentation (Documentation News), Deutsche Gesellschaft für Dokumentation eV, Westendstr 19, D-6000 Frankfurt am Main 1

Das Neue Buch; book profile for Catholic library work, Borromäusverein, Wittelsbacherring 9, D-5300 Bonn; St Michaelsbund, Herzog-Wilhelmstr 5, D-8000 Munich 2

Schulbibliothek Aktuell (School Library Today), Deutsches Bibliotheksinstitut, Bundesallee 184-185, D-1000 Berlin 31

Zeitschrift für Bibliothekswesen und Bibliographie (Journal of Library Science and Bibliography), Prof Dr Günther Pflug, Deutsche Bibliothek, Zeppelinallee 4-8, D-6000 Frankfurt am Main

Zentralblatt für Bibliothekswesen (Central Journal for Library Science), Verlag Otto Harrassowitz, Taunusstr 14, Postfach 2929, D-6200 Wiesbaden

Literary Associations and Societies

Arbeitskreis für Jugendliteratur eV, Elisabethstr 15, D-8000 Munich 40
Youth Literature Committee — Section of the International Board on Books for Young People
Man Dir: Franz Meyer

Deutsche Akademie für Sprache und Dichtung, Glückert-Haus, Alexandraweg 23, D-6100 Darmstadt Tel: 44823
German Academy of Language and Poetry
Secretary-General: Dr Gerhard Dette

Deutsche Shakespeare-Gesellschaft West eV, Rathaus, D-4630 Bochum
West German Shakespeare Society
President: Professor Dr Habicht
Publications: Shakespeare Jahrbuch

Free German Authors' Association, Brahmsallee 29/1, D-2000 Hamburg 13 Tel: (040) 456073
President: Dr Hubertus Prinz zu Löwenstein

Gutenberg-Gesellschaft, Liebfrauenplatz 5, D-6500 Mainz Tel: (06131) 226420
Gutenberg Society
President: J Fuchs
Publications: Gutenberg-Jahrbuch, Kleine Drucke, Veröffentlichungen

Verein für **Hamburgische Geschichte**, ABC-Strasse 19A, D-2000 Hamburg 36 Tel: (040) 344848
The Hamburg Historical Society

Literarischer Verein in Stuttgart eV, Rosenbergstr 113, Postfach 723, D-7000 Stuttgart 1 Tel: (0711) 638264/5
Stuttgart Literary Society
President: Karl G Hiersemann
Publication: Bibliothek des Literarischen Vereins in Stuttgart Vol 1 (1842) — Vol 308 (1983)
The aim of the Society (founded in 1839) is to publish the texts of valuable unpublished manuscripts and old printed texts in a new form — especially with regard to old German literature

P E N Zentrum Bundesrepublik Deutschland*, Sandstr 10, D-6100 Darmstadt
Secretary-General: Hanns Werner Schwarze

Literary Periodicals

Akzente (Accents); Carl Hanser Verlag, Kolberger Str 22, Postfach 860420, D-8000 Munich 80

Bücherkommentare (Book Commentaries); Verlag Rombach, Lörracher Str 3, Postfach 1349, D-7800 Freiburg im Breisgau

Bücherschiff (Book Galley); the German book journal. Verlag Bücherschiff Walter Reutin, Rheinstr 122, Postfach 210947, D-7500 Karlsruhe 21

Bulletin Jugend und Literatur (Youth and Literature Bulletin), Lesen Verlag GmbH, Eulenhof, D-2351 Hardebek

Deutschheft (German Copy), Verlag Pohl und Mayer, Postfach 24, Kaufbeuren

Epitaph, Belgradstr 24, D-8000 Munich 40

Formation, Zur Halle 5, D-6751 Sulybachtal 1, Kaiserlauten-Land

Imprint; the literary journal for German-language literature. Lesen Verlag GmbH, Eulenhof, D-2351 Hardebek

Kritikon Litterarum, Thesen Verlag Vowinckel und Co, Kittlerstr 34, D-6100 Darmstadt

Lektüre (Reading Matter), Lektüre Verlagsgesellschaft mbH, Friedrichstr 13, D-8000 Munich 40

Literarische Hefte (Literary Notes), Raith Verlag, Herzog Heinrich Str 21, D-8000 Munich 2

Literarische Umschau (Literary Review), Verlag Marie Hemmerle, Pullacherstr 1, D-8000 Munich 70

Literat (Man of Letters); journal for literature and art. Verband deutscher Schriftsteller Hessen, Goethestr 29, D-6000 Frankfurt am Main

Literature, Music, Fine Arts; a review of German-language research contributions on literature, music, and fine arts (text in English). Institut für Wissenschaftliche Zusammenarbeit (Institute for Scientific Co-operation), Landhusstr 18, D-7400 Tübingen

Litfass, Ostpreussendamm 159, D-1000 Berlin 45

Neue Rundschau (New Review), Fischer Verlag, Mainzer Landstr 10-12, D-6000 Frankfurt am Main

Text und Kritik (Text and Criticism); Edition Text und Kritik, Levelingstr 6a, D-8000 Munich 70

Universitas; journal for science, art and literature (editions in German, English and Spanish). Wissenschaftliche Verlagsgesellschaft mbH, Birkenwaldstr 44, Postfach 40, D-7000 Stuttgart 1

Viergroschenbogen ('Four Groschen Sheets'); journal for contemporary literature and art. Relief-Verlag-Eilers, Martin Greif Str 3, D-8000 Munich 2

Wissenschaft-Literaturanzeiger (Scientific Literature Advertiser), Verlag Rombach, Lörracher Str 3, Postfach 1349, D-7800 Freiburg im Breisgau

Wolfenbütteler Notizen zur Buchgeschichte (Wolfenbütteler Notes on the History of the Book), Pöseldorfer Weg 1, D-2000 Hamburg 13

Literary Prizes

Georg Büchner Prize
Founded in 1923 by Volksstaat Hessen, it has been given since 1951 by the Academy to writers who have been especially noteworthy through their work and have contributed to the current cultural scene in Germany. 30,000 DM. Awarded annually. Enquiries to Deutsche Akademie für Sprache und Dichtung, Glückert-Haus, Alexandraweg 23, D-6100 Darmstadt

Deutscher Jugendbuchpreis, see International Literary Prizes (The German Youth Book Award)

Alfred-Döblin Institution Prize
Inaugurated in 1983, this award will generally be made every one or two years for unpublished work of an epic nature (including poetry). The amount awarded will be up to DM 20,000. Enquiries to Akademie der Künste, Abteilung Literatur, Hanseatenweg 10, D-1000 Berlin 21

Konrad Duden Prize
For special achievement in the German language (co-sponsored by the Bibliographical Institute). 10,000 DM. Awarded every two years. Applications are not invited. Enquiries to Stadt Mannheim, Oberbürgermeister Abt Repräsentation, Rathaus E5, Postfach 2203, D-6800 Mannheim 1

Theodor Fontane Prize
Founded in 1948, this is the name for the major literary award given, either for a single work or for a body of work, by the Akademie der Künste (Academy of Arts). The award is 30,000 DM and is made once every six years (a similar award being made in other disciplines in the intervening five years). In addition, 'encouragement' prizes of 10,000 DM are given annually by the Akademie in each of the six disciplines — this includes one for literature and one for film/TV/radio work (which may be for writing). Enquiries to Akademie der Künste, Hanseatenweg 10, D-1000 Berlin 21

Sigmund Freud Prize
For a scientific presentation in prose. 10,000 DM. Awarded annually. Enquiries to Deutsche Akademie für Sprache und Dichtung, Glückert-Haus, Alexandraweg 23, D-6100 Darmstadt

German Youth Book Award, see International Literary Prizes

Goethe Prize
Founded in 1927 for work showing the value of, or respect for Goethe's ideals and thoughts. 50,000 DM awarded every three years. Prize for 1982 awarded to Ernst Jünger. Enquiries to Amt für Wissenschaft und Kunst, Brückenstr 3-7, D-6000 Frankfurt am Main 70

Friedrich Gundolf Prize for Germanistics abroad
For essays in German. 10,000 DM. Awarded annually. Enquiries to Deutsche Akademie

für Sprache und Dichtung, Glückert-Haus, Alexandraweg 23, D-6100 Darmstadt

The Alfred Kerr Prize for Literary Criticism*
Founded in 1976/77 by the Börsenblatt für den deutschen Buchhandel (German Book Trade Gazette). 5,000 DM plus a Certificate and the reimbursement of expenses incurred by the Presentation Ceremony. Awarded annually. For outstanding continuing literary criticism in a German newspaper, magazine, or TV or radio programme. Enquiries to Redaktion Börsenblatt, Chefredakteur Hanns Lothar Schütz, Grosser Hirschgraben 17-21, D-6000 Frankfurt am Main

Konsalik Novel Prize
Founded in 1982 jointly by Publishers Bastei-Verlag Gustav H Lübbe (qv), Wilhelm Goldmann Verlag GmbH, Munich (qv), and Wilhelm Heyne Verlag, Munich (qv). 20,000 DM, to be awarded annually, for a novel of contemporary life by a German author which also demonstrates national trends for an international readership. Enquiries to Fralit F K Albrecht Literary Agency, Brahmsallee 29/1, D-2000 Hamburg 13

Lessing Prize der Freien und Hansestadt Hamburg
To poets, writers, scholars in German cultural fields who are able to meet the challenge represented by the name of Lessing. 30,000 DM (less 10,000 DM for foundation fees). Awarded every four years. Last awarded in 1981 to Agnes Heller and Rolf Hochhüth. Enquiries to Kulturbehörde der Freien und Hansestadt Hamburg, Hamburgerstr 45, D-2000 Hamburg 76

Literature Prize
To a poet or writer for his whole work. A monetary prize awarded annually. Enquiries to Bayerische Akademie der Schönen Künste, Max Joseph Platz 3, D-8000 Munich 22

Thomas Mann Prize
Founded in 1975 in honour of Thomas Mann, to celebrate the 100th anniversary of his birth. The prize will be awarded to personalities who have, through their literary work, shown the humanitarian spirit set out in the work of Thomas Mann. 15,000 DM. Awarded every three years. Enquiries to Der Senat der Hansestadt Lübeck, Amt für Kultur, Rathaushof, Postfach, D-2400 Lübeck 1

Johann Heinrich Merck Prize
For literary criticism. 10,000 DM. Awarded annually. Enquiries to Deutsche Akademie für Sprache und Dichtung, Glückert-Haus, Alexandraweg 23, D-6100 Darmstadt

Rheinland-Palatinate Prize*
Founded in 1956 for a single work or body of work in literature (as well as fine art and music). Winner should be closely related to the area. 10,000 DM. Enquiries to Rheinland-Palatinate Ministry of Culture, Mittlere Bleiche 61, D-6500 Mainz 1

Nelly Sachs Prize
The cultural prize of Dortmund City, instituted by the Dortmund City Council in 1961. Awarded every two years to personalities who have produced outstanding creative work in the art or cultural field. Current value 20,000 DM. Last awarded to Horst Bienek. Enquiries to Kulturamt der Stadt Dortmund, Karl-Marx-Strasse 24, D-4600 Dortmund 1

Schiller Prize
For outstanding achievements in the cultural field. 25,000 DM. Awarded every four years;

applications are not invited. Enquiries to Stadt Mannheim, Oberbürgermeister Abt Repräsentation, Rathaus E5, Postfach 2203, D-6800 Mannheim 1

Johann Heinrich Voss Translation Prize
For a single work or life's work in translation. 10,000 DM. Awarded annually. Enquiries to Deutsche Akademie für Sprache und Dichtung, Glückert-Haus, Alexandraweg 23, D-6100 Darmstadt

Carl Zuckmayer Medal*
Instituted 1978 by the Minister President of Rheinland-Pfalz (Rhineland Palatinate). First award was made in 1979 to Günther Fleckenstein. The award is for those whose services to the German language make them worthy of honour in memory of Carl Zuckmayer, the noted German dramatist and poet. Enquiries to Rheinland-Pfalz Kulturministerium, Mittlere Bleiche 61, D-6500 Mainz 1

Translation Agencies and Associations

Babylon Übersetzungen*, Düsseldorfer Str 38, D-1000 Berlin 15 Tel: (030) 8838296
Man Dir: Walter Bengs

Bundesverband der Dolmetscher und Übersetzer eV (BDÜ), Rüdigerstr 79a, D-5300 Bonn 2 Tel: (0228) 345000
Federal German Association of Interpreters and Translators
President: Hans Thomas Schwarz; *Secretary-General:* Georg Frantz
Publication: Mitteilungsblatt für Dolmetscher und Übersetzer (Interpreters' and Translators' News Sheet), six times per year

V Gorachek KG, Flurscheideweg 15, D-6230 Frankfurt am Main 80 Tel: (0611) 341265
German-Russian-German Technical Translation Bureau
Owned by: Possev-Verlag V Gorachek KG (qv)
Chief Executive: N B Jdanoff

Verband deutschsprachiger Übersetzer literarischer und wissenschaftlicher Werke eV (VDU), Kuhstr 11, D-4172 Straelen Tel: (02834) 191151
Association of German-speaking translators of Literary and Scientific Works
Dir: Ursula Brackmann
Publication: Der Übersetzer (The Translator — monthly)

Ghana

General Information

Language: English
Religion: About 40 per cent Christian, remainder follow traditional beliefs
Population: 11 million
Literacy rate (1970): 30.2%
Bank Hours: 0830-1400 Monday-Thursday; 0830-1500 Friday
Shop Hours: 0830-1230, 1330-1730 Monday, Tuesday, Thursday, Friday; 0830-1330 Wednesday and Saturday
Currency: 100 pesawas = 1 cedi
Export/Import Information: No tariffs on books; advertising matter over 1 kg gross weight 50%. Import licence required, but single copies of books under Open General

Licence. Levy charged on import licences required. Credit terms not permitted
Copyright: UCC, Florence (see International section)

Book Trade Organizations

Ghana Association of Writers*, PO Box 2738, Accra
Publications: Okyeame, Takra

Ghana Book Development Council*, PO Box M430, Ministry Branch PO, Accra Tel: 29178 Cable Add: Ghanabook
An agency of the Ministry of Education, GBDC co-ordinates and promotes creation, production and distribution of books, but does not itself publish
Senior Book Development Officer: A P K Adzaho; *Assistant Development Officer:* Miss V S Ahiekpor
Publications: Ghana Book World

Ghana Book Publishers' Association*, c/o Sedco Publishing Ltd, PO Box 2051, Accra

Ghana Booksellers' Association*, PO Box 7869, Accra Tel: 21551 Cable Add: Book supply
Secretary: F J Reimmer

Standard Book Numbering Agency*, Ghana Library Board, Research Library on African Affairs, PO Box 2970, Accra
Administrator: A N de Heer

Book Trade Reference Journals

Ghana Book World (bi-annual), Ghana Book Development Council, Education Loop, PO Box M430, Accra

Ghana National Bibliography, c/o Research Library on African Affairs, PO Box 2970, Accra

Publishers

Advance Publishing Co Ltd*, New Town Rd, PO Box 2317, Accra New Town Tel: 21577
Man Dir: A O Mills
Subjects: General Non-fiction, Paperbacks

Adwinsa Publications (Ghana) Ltd*, PO Box 92, Legon (via Accra) Tel: Accra 63666
Man Dir, Rights & Permissions: Kwabena Amponsah; *Editorial, Production:* Eric Kyereme-Amponsah; *Sales, Publicity:* Kofi Kyere-Amponsah
Orders to: Adwinsa Distribution Agency Ltd (at above address)
Subsidiary Company: Adwinsa Distribution Agency (at above address)
Branch Off: Adwinsa Bookstand (Eredec Hotel), PO Box 845, Koforidua
Subjects: General Subjects, Educational from Primary to University Level
Bookshops: Adwinsa Distribution Agency Ltd, Adwinsa House, A/Mdn/947, Madina-Accra; PO Box 92, Legon
1981: 4 titles *Founded:* 1977
ISBN Publisher's Prefix: 9964-955

Afram Publications (Ghana) Ltd*, 29 Ring Road East, PO Box M18, Accra Tel: 74248 Cable Add: Aframbooks Telex: 2171 SIC Accra
Man Dir, Rights & Permissions: Kwesi Sam-Woode; *Editorial:* Emmanuel A Manful; *Marketing Manager:* George Braye; *Production:* Eric Ofei
Subjects: General Fiction, Belles Lettres, Poetry, Biography, History, Africana, How-to Study Guides, Religion, General and

Social Science, Paperbacks, Secondary and Primary Schools Textbooks
1981: 12 titles *Founded:* 1974
Miscellaneous: The Company is partly owned by the State Insurance Corporation of Ghana
ISBN Publisher's Prefix: 9964-70

Africa Christian Press*, PO Box 30, Achimota Tel: 25554
General Secretary: Donald Banks; *Sales Manager:* P Addo
Subjects: Christian Fiction & Non-fiction, Biography, Paperbacks and Booklets (priority is given to African writers)
Founded: 1964
ISBN Publisher's Prefixes: 9964-85352

Anowuo Educational Publications*, 2R McCarthy Hill, PO Box 3918, Accra Tel: 24910
Publisher: S A Konadu; *Sales Manager:* Samuel Tetteh
Subjects: Africana, How-to, Study Guides, Reference, Juveniles, Books in Ghanaian Languages, Paperbacks, General Science, Secondary Textbooks, General Fiction, Belles Lettres, Poetry, History
Founded: 1966

Asempa Publishers*, PO Box 919, Accra Tel: 21706
Man Dir: Rev Peter Barker; *Editorial, Production:* Rev Emmanuel Bortey; *Sales:* Alfred Hanson
Parent Company: Christian Council of Ghana (at above address)
Imprints: Asempa, IBRA (Ghana)
Subjects: Religion, Social Questions, African Music, Fiction
Founded: 1973
ISBN Publisher's Prefix: 9964-78

Benibengor Book Agency*, PO Box 40, Aboso
Man Dir: J Benibengor Blay
Subjects: General Fiction, Belles Lettres, Poetry, Biography, Juveniles, Paperbacks

Black Mask Ltd*, PO Box 252, FNT Kamasi Tel: 6454 Cable Add: BML
Branch Offs: Accra, Ghana; Freetown, Sierra Leone
Subjects: Educational Textbooks, Plays, Novels
1981: 1 title *Founded:* 1979
ISBN Publisher's Prefix: 9964-960

Bureau of Ghana Languages*, PO Box 1851, Accra Tel: 64130/65194/65461 ext 513 Cable Add: Velbo, Accra, Ghana
Dir, Rights & Permissions: F S Konu; *Deputy Dir:* J K Brantuo; *Sales Manager:* W K Adi
Branch Off: PO Box 177, Tamale, Northern Region, Ghana
Subjects: Fiction, Drama, Poetry, Biography, Science, School Text Books, Dictionaries, Bibliographies, Material for New Literates. Books are published in 11 Ghanaian languages
Founded: 1951
Miscellaneous: Also acts as a Translation Agency/Association

Editorial and Publishing Services*, PO Box 5743, Accra
Man Dir: M Danquah
Subjects: General, Reference

Emmanuel Publishing Services*, PO Box 5282, Accra Tel: 25238 Cable Add: Emmapus Accra
Dir: Emmanuel K Nsiah
Subjects: Educational, Children's
Bookshops: Mayan Book Centre, PO Box 6173, Accra
Founded: 1978
Miscellaneous: Company has reprint arrangements in Ghana for Oxford University Press publications
ISBN Publisher's Prefix: 9964-73

Encyclopaedia Africana Project*, PO Box 2797, Accra Tel: 76939 Cable Add: Enafsec
Man Dir: L H Ofosu-Appiah
Subject: Reference
Founded: 1962
ISBN Publisher's Prefix: 0-917256

Frank Publishing Ltd*, PO Box M414, Ministry Branch Post Office, Accra Tel: 29510 Cable Add: Knowledge
Man Dir, Editorial, Production: Francis K Dzokoto; *Sales, Public Relations:* Moses K Dzokoto
Subjects: Secondary School Textbooks
Founded: 1976

Ghana Publishing Corporation*, Publishing Division, PMB, Tema Tel: 4166/2521 (Tema); 66349 (Accra) Cable Add/Telex: Publishing Tema
Man Dir: M W Ofori; *General Manager (Publishing Division):* F K Nyarko; *Deputy General Manager (Editorial):* Isaac Dankyi Mensah; *Rights & Permissions:* Fauchie-Sobreh; *Sales Manager:* J K Adom; *Production:* K B Arkorful; *Publicity:* Fidelis D Adzakey
Parent Company: Ghana Publishing Corporation, Head Office, PO Box 4348, Accra
Printing Division: see Government Printer
Sales & Distribution Division: PO Box 3632 Accra
Branch Offs: Accra, Cape Coast, Ho, Tamale, Koforidua, Hohoe, Sunyani, Bolgatanga, Kumasi, Wa, Swedru
Subjects: General Fiction & Non-fiction, Belles Lettres, Poetry, Biography, History, Africana, Languages, Reference, Juveniles, Books in Various Ghanaian languages, Paperbacks, Science & Technology, General & Social Science; University, Secondary and Primary Textbooks
Bookshops: Throughout Ghana
Founded: 1965
ISBN Publisher's Prefix: 9964-1

Ghana Universities Press*, PO Box 4219, Accra Tel: 25032 Cable Add/Telex: Univpress Accra
Dir: A S K Atsu
Subjects: General Non-fiction, Belles Lettres, Poetry, Biography, History, Africana, Philosophy, Religion, Law, Medicine, Psychology, Science & Technology, General & Social Science, University Textbooks
1981: 5 titles *Founded:* 1962
ISBN Publisher's Prefix: 9964-3

The **Government Printer** (Ghana Publishing Corporation, Printing Division)*, PO Box 124, Accra

I B R A, an imprint of Asempa Publishers (qv)

Moxon Paperbacks*, Barnes Rd, PO Box M 160, Accra Tel: 65397
Man Dir: Chief James Moxon
Subjects: General Fiction & Non-fiction, Belles Lettres, Poetry, History, Africana, Reference, Juveniles, Guidebooks, Paperbacks
Bookshop: The Atlas Bookshop (qv)
Founded: 1967
ISBN Publisher's Prefix: 9964-954

Presbyterian Book Depot Ltd, see main entry under Major Booksellers and range of publications under Waterville Publishing House below

Sedco Publishing Ltd*, PO Box 2051 Accra Tel: 21332 Cable Add: Sedco
Man Dir: Courage Kwami Segbawu; *Editorial, Publicity, Rights & Permissions:* Ellicot Kwashie Seade (Publishing Manager); *Sales, Production:* Adams Ahima (General Manager)
Subjects: Science, Law, History, Poetry, Archaeology
Bookshop: At above address
1981: 3 titles *Founded:* 1977
ISBN Publisher's Prefix: 9964-72

Unilit Publishing Co*, PO Box 4432, Accra Tel: 22689
Publisher: Ronald Mensah
Subsidiary Company: Ghana Bible Research Centre (at above address)
Associate Company: Romans Book Company (at above address)
Subjects: Religion, Politics, Economics, Science, Fiction
Bookshops: Romans Book Shop (at above address)
Founded: 1970

Waterville Publishing House*, PO Box 195, Accra Tel: 63124/62415 Cable Add: Books Accra
Man Dir: C A Aboagye; *Publications Manager:* E K Asante
Parent Company: Presbyterian Book Depot Ltd (qv under Major Booksellers)
Subjects: General Fiction & Non-fiction, Belles Lettres, Poetry, Biography, History, Africana, Religion, Juveniles, Paperbacks, General & Social Science, Secondary & Primary Textbooks (in local languages and English)
1982: approx 10 titles *Founded:* 1963

Book Club

Academic Book Club*, GPO Box 441, Takoradi
Manager: Muhammed Kamal

Major Booksellers

Astab Books Ltd*, Osu R E, PO Box 346, Accra Tel: 76766

The **Atlas** Bookshop*, Ambassador Hotel Gardens, PO Box M 160, Accra Tel: 65397
Manager: James Moxon
Parent Company: Moxon Paperbacks (qv)

Cape Coast University Bookshop*, PMB, Cape Coast Tel: 24409

E P Book Depot*, PO Box 42, Ho

Ghana Publishing Corporation, Distribution and Sales Division*, PO Box 124, Accra

Kingsway Stores, Books and Periodicals Department*, PO Box 1638, Accra

Methodist Book Depot Ltd*, Atlantis House, Commercial St, PO Box 100, Cape Coast Tel: 2133/4, 2326
Man Dir: Samuel Markin Yankah
Branches: Accra, Berekum, Kumasi, Swedru, Takoradi, Tarkwa, Tema

Presbyterian Book Depot Ltd*, Thorpe Rd, PO Box 195, Accra Tel: 63124/62415 Cable Add: Books Accra
Man Dir: C A Aboagye
Branches: Accra, Tudu, Koforidua, Kumasi, Nkawkaw, Tamale, Akim Oda, Odumase, Ada
Founded: 1910
Miscellaneous: The organization comprises bookselling, stationery supply, printing and publishing activities (see Waterville Publishing House)

Queensway Bookshop and Stores Ltd*, Bank Lane, PO Box 4276, Accra Tel: 62707 (Accra) Cable Add: Success Accra
Branch Off: Bank St, PO Box 20, Kumasi Tel: 4047 Cable Add: Success Kumasi
Manager: Kwaku Mensah

Suppliers of Educational, Library and HMSO Publicications
University Bookshop*, University of Science and Technology, University Post Office, Kumasi Tel: 5351 ext 398/308 Cable Add: Kumasitech Kumasi
Manager: Joseph A Clifford-Wirrom

University Bookshop*, University of Ghana, PO Box 1, Legon, Accra Tel: 75381 ext 8227/8827
Manager: S O Cofie

Major Libraries

Armed Forces Library Service*, Ministry of Defence, Burma Camp, Accra Tel: 76111 ext 2769
Librarian: Daniel Mensah-Adrah
Publication: Armed Forces Library Bulletin

Balme Library, see University of Ghana

British Council Library*, Liberia Road, PO Box 771, Accra Tel: 21766
Also at PO Box 1996, Kumasi

C S I R Central Reference and Research Library*, PO Box M 32, Accra Tel: 77651, extensions 32, 58
Council for Scientific and Industrial Research Library
Librarian: J A Villars
Publications include: Ghana Science Abstracts, Directory of Special and Research Libraries in Ghana; Medical Research Centres in Ghana; Union List of Scientific Serials in Ghanaian Libraries (1976), C S I R Recorder; Directory of Research Projects (Science & Technology) in Ghana (1978)

Central Bureau of Statistics, Economic Library*, PO Box 1098, Accra Tel: 66512 Cable Add: Ghanastats
Librarian: Francis K Dzokoto

Geological Survey Department Reference Library*, PO Box M80, Accra Tel: 28093
Librarian: E Hammond

Ghana Institute of Management and Public Administration, Library and Documentation Centre*, Greenhill, PO Box 50, Achimota Tel: 77625

Ghana Library Board*, Thorpe Rd, PO Box 663, Accra Tel: 62795, 65083, 66337 Cable Add: Ghanlib Accra
Publications include: Ghana National Bibliography, A Guide to Creative Writing by Africans in English, Annual Reports

Institute of African Studies Library*, University of Ghana, PO Box 73, Legon Tel: 75381 ext 9348
Librarian: N D Mintah

Research Library on African Affairs*, PO Box 2970, Accra Tel: 23526, 28402
Librarian: A N deHeer
Publications: Ghana National Bibliography (annual), *Current Ghana Bibliography*

School of Administration Library*, University of Ghana, PO Box 78, Legon
Librarian: G Lamptey

University of Cape Coast Library*, PMB, Cape Coast Tel: 24409 ext 370
Librarian: E K Koranteng
Publication: Bulletin

University of Ghana Library*, Balme Library, PO Box 24, Legon Tel: 75381 ext 410
Librarian: J Michael Walpole
Publications: Annual Report, Bulletin

University of Science and Technology Library*, Private Bag, Kumasi Tel: 5351 ext 235
Librarian: G M Pitcher

Library Association

Ghana Library Association*, PO Box 4105, Accra
Secretary: Francis K Dzokoto
Publication: Ghana Library Journal (bi-annual)

Library Reference Books and Journals

Books

Directory of Libraries in Ghana, Department of Library and Archival Studies, University of Ghana, Legon

Directory of Special and Research Libraries in Ghana, CSIR Library, PO Box M 32, Accra

Journals

Ghana Library Journal, (bi-annual) Ghana Library Association, PO Box 4105, Accra

Literary Periodicals

Asemka, c/o French Department, University of Cape Coast, Cape Coast

Okyeame, Ghana Association of Writers, PO Box 2738, Accra (This journal has been defunct for some time now, but there are plans to recommence publication shortly. The Association also publishes a newsletter entitled *Takra*)

Translation Agencies and Associations

Bureau of Ghana Languages*, PO Box 1851, Accra
Also entry under Publishers

Gibraltar

General Information

Language: English (both English and Spanish used commercially)
Religion: Christian (mainly Catholic) and Jewish predominantly
Population: 30,000
Bank Hours: 0900-1530 Monday-Friday, plus 1630-1800 Friday
Shop Hours: 0900-1300, 1500-1930 Monday-Friday; 0900-1300 Saturday (Jewish shops closed Saturday)
Currency: 100 pence = 1 Gibraltar pound = £1 sterling. British coins are legal tender and Bank of England notes are widely used
Export/Import Information: No tariff on books or advertising matter. No import licence. Exchange controls except for transactions with the UK
Copyright: Berne, UCC see International section

Major Booksellers

The **Book Centre***, Church Lane
Junior fiction and non-fiction

Francis **Caruana***, 249 Main St

Gibraltar Bookshop*, 300 Main St Tel: 71894 Cable Add: Tito Gibraltar
Manager: A Benady

Gibraltar Junior Bookshop, 1 Governor's Parade Tel: 75554
Manager: Anne Benady
Junior literature

Imperial News Agency and Bookshop*, 291/293 Main St Tel: 4823
Junior and adult literature, especially paperbacks

Major Libraries

Gibraltar Garrison Library, Library Gardens, Governor's Parade Tel: 77418
Librarian: Mrs L M Huart
Secretary: J M Searle
Local and military history. Lending service for subscribing members

Gibraltar Library Service, see John Mackintosh Hall Library

John **Mackintosh Hall** Library, John Mackintosh Hall, Main St Tel: 78000
Free lending library set up under will of late John Mackintosh, mainly adult fiction. Now incorporating the Gibraltar Library Service

Greece

General Information

Language: Greek
Religion: Greek Orthodox
Population: 9.4 million
Literacy Rate (1971): 84.4%
Bank Hours: 0800-1300, 1730-1930 Monday-Saturday. Some open 0800-2200 daily
Shop Hours: Vary. Generally 0800-1500 Monday, Wednesday, Saturday; 0800-1330 Tuesday, Thursday, Friday; 1630-2000 Monday-Saturday
Currency: 100 lepta = 1 drachma
Export/Import Information: Member of the European Economic Community. No tariff on non-Greek books except children's picture books (free from EEC). Foreign-language advertising catalogues and other advertising matter free from EEC. Children's picture books and advertising matter subject to stamp duty, and books and advertising subject to small additional taxes, University Tax and Bank Fee, Contribution for Farmer's Social Assistance. Only books printed in Greek need import licence; all advertising matter other than price lists require licence. No special exchange controls
Copyright: UCC, Berne, Florence (see International section)

Book Trade Organizations

Association des Editeurs et des Libraires d'Athènes*, Solonos 71, Athens 143 Tel: 3629684/3625476
Association of Athens' Publishers and Booksellers
General Secretary: Michel Grigoris

The Circle of Greek Children's Books*, Zalongou 7, Athens 142 Tel: 3602990
Greek National Section of the International Board on Books for Young People (IBBY)
Founded: 1969

Etairia Ellinon Logotechnon, Gennadiou 6, Athens 126
Society of Greek Writers
Secretary: Phaedra Zambatha-Pagoulatou

Fédération panhellénique des Editeurs et Libraires, see Panhellenic Federation

Panhellenic Federation of Publishers and Booksellers (PFPB), Arahovis 61, Athens 145 Tel: 3625458
President: S Halkiadakis
General Secretary: Th Kastaniotis
Publications: Emis Ke To Vivlio (quarterly); *Bibliographical Bulletin* (quarterly)

Syllogos Ekdoton Bibliopolon, Themistocleus 54, Athens 145 Tel: 3630029
Greek Publishers' and Booksellers' Association
President: M Vouzakis
Secretary: M Panteleskos

Book Trade Reference Books and Journals

Book

Greek Bibliography, Ministry to the Prime Minister's Office, General Direction of Press, Research and Cultural Relations Division, Athens

Journals

Bulletin analytique de Bibliographie hellénique (Analytical Bulletin of Hellenic Bibliography), Institut Français d'Athènes, 29-31 Odos Sina, Athens 144

Emis Ke To Vivlio, Panhellenic Federation of Publishers and Booksellers (PFPB), Arahovis 61, Athens 145

New Books, bibliographic quarterly bulletin, I D Kollaros & Co Corporation, Solonos 60, Athens 135

Publishers

Alkaios-Tropaiatis*, Aristidou 5, Athens
Subjects: Literature, Children's Books

Anglohellenic, Kriezotou 3, Athens 134 Tel: 3607307/3609345/3606807 Telex: 8008
Man Dir: Tassos Psaropoulos; *Editorial:* Thalia Iacovidis; *Sales:* K Kessissoglou; *Production:* N Kastrinakis; *Publicity:* P Pissanos; *Rights & Permissions:* M Psaropoulos
Subsidiary Company: Anglohellenic Printing, Tatoiou 118, Varybobi, Attiki
Subjects: Medical, Fiction, Children's Books
1982: 10 titles *Founded:* 1962

Angyra Publishing House, D A Papadimitriou SA*, Pireaus 18, Athens 101 Tel: (021) 5223694
Man Dir: Dimitrios Papadimitriou
Subsidiary Company: Harmi-Press Publications, Haroula Papadimitriou (qv)
Subjects: General Fiction, Belles Lettres, Poetry, History, Religion, Juveniles, Low-priced Paperbacks, Psychology
Bookshops: Bookstore Angyra, Pireaus 18, Athens 101 Tel: 5223694
Founded: 1932 (as Angyra Ekdotikos Oikos)

John Arsenides Ekdotis*, Akadimias 57, Athens 143 Tel: (021) 618707/629538
Man Dir: John Arsenides
Subjects: Biography, History, Philosophy, Social Science

Aspioti-Elka SA*, Vouliagmenis 276, Athens 459 Tel: (021) 9711021/2/3 Cable Add: Elkasp Telex: 215519 Gon gr
Subjects: History, Archaeology, Folklore

Assimakopouli*, 45 Harilaou Trikoupi St, Athens Tel: 611720

Astir*, Papadimitriou, Alexandros, Lycourgou 10, Athens
Subjects: Religion, especially referring to Greek Orthodox Church; Children's and Juveniles

Ekdotike **Athenon** SA+, Vissarionos 1, Athens 135 Tel: (01) 3608911
Man Dirs: George A Christopoulos, John C Bastias
Associate Company: Ekdotike Hellados SA, Philadelphias 8, Athens (Printer)
Subjects: History, Archaeology, Art, High-priced Paperbacks
Bookshop: Ekdotike Athenon, Omirou 11, Athens 135
1982: 87 titles *Founded:* 1961

Atlantis M Pechlivanides & Co SA*, Korai 8, Athens 132 Tel: 3222846/3231624
Subjects: General Fiction, Non-fiction, Education, Art, Children's

Atlas-Diagoras*, Ch Trikoupi 13, Athens 142 Tel: (021) 627342

Bergadi Editions*, Michel Bergadis, Mavromichali 4, Athens TT 143 Tel: 3614263
Also Doryleou 22, Athens 602 Tel: 3614263
Subjects: History, Sociology, Belles Lettres, Juveniles

Boukoumanis' Editions*, Elias Boukoumanis, Mavromichali 1, Athens 143 Tel: 3606313 Cable Add: 214422 RC GR
Man Dir: Elias Boukoumanis; *Rights & Permissions:* Mrs Roee Scaras
Subjects: History, Sociology, Belles Lettres, Children's, Psychology, Education, Politics
Founded: 1968

Chrissi Penna — Les Editions de la Plume d'Or, Argentinis Dimokratias Sq 6, Athens 708 Tel: (01) 3618503/8071150/8071704
Man Dir: K Papachrysanthou
Orders to: Chrissi Penna, Skoufa 27, Athens 136
Parent Company: Papachrysanthou Chryss SA (qv)
Associate Company: Oscar Press (qv)
Subjects: Juvenile, Educational, Non-fiction
1981: 14 titles *1982:* 8 titles *Founded:* 1964

Chryssos Typos*, Harilaou Trikoupi 28, Athens Tel: 637945

G **Dardanos** — H Karakatsanis & Co Ltd — Gutenberg, Solonos 103, Athens Tel: 3600127/3626684/3624606
Also: Didotou 55-57, Athens
Man Dir, Editorial, Publicity, Rights & Permissions: George Dardanos; *Sales:* Christos Dardanos; *Production:* Haralambos Karakatsanis
Orders to: Didotou 55-57, Athens
Subjects: Art, Education, Literature, Sociology, History, Politics, Economics, Children's Books
Bookshop: Solonos 103, Athens
Founded: 1963

Difros*, Giannis Goudelis, Akademias 57, Athens
Subjects: Modern Greek Literature

Dodoni*, Asklipiou 3, Athens 143
Subjects: Fiction, Non-fiction, Juveniles, Encyclopaedias, History, Maps

Ekdoseis **Domi** AE*, Navarinou 20, Athens 144
Subjects: History, Encyclopaedias

Dorikos Makridis*, Zoodochou Pigis 4, Athens
Subjects: General Literary

P **Efstathiadis** & Sons SA*, Valtetsiou 14, Athens TT 144 Tel: 3600495/3615011 Cable Add: Efbook Athens Telex: 216176
Branch Off: Olympou-Diikitiriou 34, Salonika Tel: 511781
Subjects: English language teaching books and courses for Greek students; miscellaneous books connected with English (and some other languages)

G C **Eleftheroudakis** SA, Constitution Square, Nikis 4, Athens 126 Tel: (00301) 3222255 Cable Add: Elefbooks Telex: 0219410 Elef GR
Man Dir: Mrs V Eleftheroudakis-Gregos
Branch Off: Sinopis 2, Tower of Athens
Subjects: Greece, Dictionaries, Fiction, Juvenile, Texts in Greek, English
Bookshop: Nikis 4, Athens 126 (qv)
Founded: 1915

Eteria Ellinikon Ekdoseon*, Akadimias 84, Athens 142 Tel: 3630282/3631724/3607343
Man Dir: Stavros Tavoularis; *Editorial:* by Committee; *Sales:* Dr Caounis; *Production:* Rodakis Pericles; *Publicity:* Karayannis Nicolaos
Subjects: General Fiction, Belles Lettres, Poetry, History, Philosophy, Primary Textbooks, Educational Materials
Bookshop: Etairia Ellinikon Ekdoseon, Ermou 44, Salonika
Founded: 1958

Ekdoseis **Filon**, Panepistimiou 10, Athens 135 Tel: (01) 3618705
Subjects: Literature, Philosophy, Juveniles

Giovanis*, Zoodochou Pigis 7, Athens 142 Tel: (021) 638572
Subjects: General Science, Reference, Maps, Miscellaneous

Grigoris Publications*, Solonos 71, Athens 143
Man Dir: Michel Grigoris Tel: 629684
Associate Companies: Thessaloniki University Editions, Ioannina University Editions, Athens College Editions, Imha (qv), Athanassios Karavias (qv), Nikolaos Karavias (qv)
Subjects: Theology, Philosophy, Classical Literature, Literature in Translation, Linguistics, Archaeology, Bibliography, History, Humour, School Texts
Bookshop: Librairie Kassandra M Grigori, Solonos 71 and 73, Athens 143
Founded: 1967

Dardanos **Gutenberg**, see Dardanos

Harmi-Press Publications, Haroula Papadimitriou*, 85 Kifisou Ave, Egaleo, Athens Tel: 3455276/3471503 Telex: 210804 aste gr
Man Dir: Haroula Papadimitriou; *Editorial Dir:* Anastasia Papadimitriou
Parent Company: Angyra Publishing House (qv)
Subjects: Children's, Periodicals

Denise **Harvey** & Company*, Lambrou Fotiadi 6, Mets, Athens 407 Tel: 9233547
Man Dir: Denise Harvey; *General Manager:* Mary Frangaki; *Editorial:* Philip Sherrard
Subjects: In English: all aspects of Greek Life and Culture, Creative Writing, General Interest. In Greek: Original Works and Translations. Specialist in production of academic books with Greek texts, Classical or Modern, for other publishers

Ikaros Ekdotiki*, Voulis 4, Athens Tel: 3225152/3235262
Subject: Literature

Imha*, Solonos 71, Athens 143 Tel: 629684
Associate Companies: See Grigoris Publications
Subjects: Scientific Texts on Mediaeval and Modern Greek History

Athanassios **Karavias***, Solonos 71, Athens 143 Tel: 629684
Associate Companies: See Grigoris Publications
Subjects: Science, History

Nikolaos **Karavias***, Solonos 71, Athens 143 Tel: 629684
Associate Companies: See Grigoris Publications
Subjects: Catalogues, Bibliographies, Memoirs, Modern and Medieval Greek History

Kastaniotis Editions+, Zoodochou Pigis 3, TT 132 Athens Tel: 3603234/3601331/3638967
Man Dir, Editorial: Athanasios Kastaniotis; *Editorial:* Anna Stamatopoulou; *Sales:* Kostas Lambakis; *Production:* Alkis Tsakopiakos; *Publicity, Rights & Permissions:* George Papakyriakis
Subsidiary Company: Chronos Editions, Panepistimiou 39, Athens
Subjects: Psychology, Psychoanalysis, Philosophy, Pedagogy, Greek and Foreign Literature, Cinema, Essays, Juvenile
Founded: 1969

Kedros, G Gennadiou 6, Athens 142 Tel: (01) 3615783/3603572
Subjects: Literature, Philosophy, Juveniles
Founded: 1954

I D **Kollaros** & Co Corporation, Solonos 60, Athens 135 Tel: (021) 3635970
Publicity Manager: Evangelos Daskalou
Subjects: Fiction, History, Geography, Juveniles, Literature
Bookshop: Hestia Bookstore, 60 Solonos St, Athens

Koymantereas*, Mavromihali 83, Athens Tel: 3246188

Leon Editions, an imprint of Costas Spanos (qv)

Melissa Publishing House*, Nayarinou 10, Athens 144 Tel: (01) 3611692
Man Dir: George Rayas; *Sales Dir:* Chrys Rayas
Branch Off: Tsimiski 41, Salonika
Subjects: History, Art
Book Club: Athens Union
Founded: 1954

Minoas*, Androu 6, Athens 801 Tel: (01) 8231669
Man Dir: Elias Konstantazopoulos
Subjects: General Fiction, Belles Lettres, Poetry, Biography, History, Music, Art, Reference, Juveniles, High-priced Paperbacks
Bookshop: Patission 126, Athens
Founded: 1948

Editions **Moressopoulos***, Vass Georgiou Ave 21, PO Box 710, Salonika Tel: (031) 819624/819625 Telex: 412631 Syta Gr
Man Dir, Editorial: Stavros Moressopoulos; *Sales:* Yiannis Kokinides; *Production:* Lefteris Douranides; *Publicity:* Anna Vafiadou; *Rights & Permissions:* Voula Moressoloulos
Subsidiary Companies: Editions Fotografia, Editions Canal, Fotografia (all at above address)
Associate Company: S Moressopoulos & Cooperatives-Graphic Arts Ltd (at above address)
Branch Off: Mavromichali 9, Athens
Subjects: Photography, Cinematography, Video, Crafts & Hobbies, Sports, Literature, Juveniles, Non-fiction, Current Affairs
1981: 10 titles *Founded:* 1977

Multieditions Ltd*, Ippokratous St 88, Athens Tel: (01) 3609553/3606071 Telex: 219245 Aps Gr
Man Dir: Seraphim Tsakanikas; *Editorial:* Tilemachos Kanakis
Subjects: Fiction, Non-fiction, Comics
Founded: 1976

Nikas*, Solonos 102 and Mavromihali 16, Athens Tel: 634686

Oscar Press, Skoufa 27, Athens 136 Tel: (01) 3618503
Man Dir: Kir Papachrysanthou; *Production:* Konst Mastrantonis
Parent Company: Papachrysanthou Chryss SA (qv)
Associate Company: Chrissi Penna SA (qv)
Subjects: Paperbacks, Juvenile
1981: 134 titles *1982:* 128 titles *Founded:* 1979

Papachrysanthou Chryss SA, Graphic Arts, Skoufa 27, Athens 136 Tel: 3618503/8071704/8071150
Man Dir: K Papachrysanthou
Subsidiary Companies: Chrissi Penna (qv), Oscar Press (qv)
Subjects: General Books, Juvenile, Tourist Guides, Comic Magazines, Paperbacks
1982: 118 titles *Founded:* 1888

D A **Papadimitriou**, see Angyra Publishing House

Haroula **Papadimitriou**, see Harmi-Press

Kyr I **Papadopoulos** E E+, G Papandreou 118, Metamorfosi-Attikis Tel: (01) 2817127-8
Man Dir: Kyr Papadopoulos; *Sales:* P Hatjibodojis; *Production:* S T Giafalias; *Rights & Permissions:* R Papadopoulou
Subjects: Various, for children aged 2-14
Founded: 1953

Papaioannou*, Venizelou 34, Athens Tel: 618139
Associate Company: Educational Company

Papazissis Publishers SA*, Nikitara 2, Athens TT 142, Greece
Tel: 3622496/3609150/3638020 Telex: 219139 Hapsgr
Man Dir: Victor Papazissis; *Sales, Advertising:* Marios Haritopoulos; *Rights & Permissions:* Costas Sophoulis
Parent Company: Corais Ltd, Nikitara 2, Athens TT 142
Subjects: Economics, Sociology, Philosophy, Politics, Law, Education, Environment, Greek Recent History, University Handbooks (especially on Economics), School Books
Bookshop: Papazissis Bookshop, Nikitara 2, Athens TT 142
Founded: 1929

Papyros Press*, Voulis 17, Athens Tel: 3220013

Grigorios **Parissianos** 'Epistemonikai Ekdoseis'*, Solonos 69, Athens 701 Tel: (021) 610519
Subjects: Science, Medicine

Pergamini Editions, an imprint of Costas Spanos (qv)

G **Rayas***, Nayarinou 10, Athens Tel: 3611692

Siamandas*, Akadimias 61, Athens Tel: (021) 615777/627164
Subjects: General Fiction & Non-fiction, History, Juveniles

J **Sideris** OE Ekdoseis*, Stadiou 44, Athens Tel: (021) 3229638
Subjects: Literature, Science, Linguistics, Juvenile

Costas **Spanos***, Mavromihali 7, Athens 143 Tel: 3614332 Cable Add: Bibliospan
Man Dir, Editorial: C Spanos; *Sales:* John Papadakis; *Publicity:* Christiya Christacopoulou
Imprints: Leon, Pergamini
Subjects: Rare Books, Limited Editions, Byzantine and Post-Byzantine
Bookshop: At above address

Technical Chamber of Greece*, Kar Servias 4, Athens 125 Tel: (021) 3222466
General Director: Ath Iatrou
Subjects: Science, Technology, Periodicals
Founded: 1923
Miscellaneous: The Technical Chamber of Greece (TEE) is a corporate body, under public law, supervised by the Ministry of Public Works

Tegopoulos*, Panepistimiou 57, Athens

Travintal Ltd, PO Box 3392, Kolonaki, Athens Tel: 6717505 Cable Add: Travintal Athens Telex: 21 4716 elbr for travintal
Man Dir, Rights & Permissions: Nina Moselund; *Editorial:* Nina Casimaty; *Sales:* Nicolas Stavridis; *Production:* George Mansolas; *Publicity:* Niels G Moselund
Parent Company: Travintal Ltd, PO Box 12377, GPO Hong Kong
Subjects: Travel and Business Handbooks
Founded: 1975

Typos*, Londou 8, Athens Tel: 619084

D & J **Vardikos***, A Metaxa 2, TT 145 Exarchia, Athens Tel: 3631146/3602150
Man Dir & All Other Offices: Dimitrios Vardikos
Parent Company: Vivliotechnica Hellas (at above address)
Subsidiary Company: Bookbinding Industry (at above address)
Branch Off: Davaki 34, Kallithea, Athens
Subjects: Aviation Encyclopaedia and Dictionary, Attika Juvenile Books and Children's Encyclopaedia (all cassette-assisted)
Bookshops: Inter-Attica, Davaki 34, Kallithea, Athens
Founded: 1978

J **Vasiliou** Bibliopoleion*, Ippocratous 15, Athens 143 Tel: (021) 3623382/3623480
Subjects: Fiction, History, Philosophy

Frères **Vlasis***, Londou 2, Athens Tel: (021) 639128
Subjects: History, Reference, General Science

Word and Vision Ltd*, Trivonianou 42, Mets, Athens Tel: (021) 9216590 Telex: 215910
Subjects: English Language General and Travel Books, English and Greek Language Teaching Books

Z O E*, Karytsi 14, Athens 124 Tel: (021) 3223560
Man Dir: G Karadzas
Subject: Religion
Bookshops: At above address and St Sophia 41, Salonika; also in three other Greek cities
Founded: 1907

Har **Zolindakis***, Panepistimiou 65, Athens Tel: (021) 314546/316504
Subject: History

Literary Agents

Anglo-Hellenic Agency*, Kriezotou 3, Syntagma, Athens 134 Tel: 3606808/3606807
Specializations: Translations, Medical, Cartoons, Comics, Periodicals

Book Clubs

Athens Union*, c/o Melissa Publishing House, Nayarinou 10, Athens 144 Tel: (01) 3611692
Owned by: Melissa Publishing House (qv)

Vivliofilia*, Mavromichali 7, Athens 114

Major Booksellers

American Bookstore*, Amerikis 23, Athens Tel: (021) 3624151
See also A Samouhos Bookstore

Librairie **Cacoulides** (T Cacoulides & Co), blvd Panepistimiou 25-29, Athens 133 Tel: 3229560
Manager: Thomas Cacoulides

P **Efstathiadis** & Sons SA*, Valtetsiou 14, Athens TT 144 Tel: (021) 615011/3600495
Importers and exporters

G C **Eleftheroudakis** Co Ltd, International Bookstore, Constitution Sq, Nikis 4, Athens 126 Tel: (01) 3222255
Man Dir: Virginia Eleftheroudakis-Gregou

Librairie Kassandra M **Grigori***, Solonos 71 and 73, Athens 143
Owned by: Grigoris Publications (qv)

Hestia Bookstore, Solonos 60, Athens 135 Tel: (021) 3635970
Owned by: I D Kollaros & Co Corporation (qv under Publishers)
Manager: Marina Karaitidis

C **Kakoulides**, now Librairie Cacoulides (qv)

Gr **Kaloudis***, Filonos 31, Piraeus Tel: (021) 479027

Kaufmann*, Stadiou 28, Athens Tel: (021) 3222160

John **Mihalopoulos** & Son SA, Hermou 75, Salonika Tel: 279695/263786 Telex: 418562
Manager: C Mihalopoulos

Minoas*, Patission 126, Athens Tel: (021) 815664

Molho's International Bookshop, Tsimiski 10, Salonika Tel: 275271 Telex: 412885 limo gr

Pantelides*, Amerikis 11, Athens Tel: (01) 3623673

A **Samouhos** Bookstore*, Aghias Sofias 28, Salonika Tel: 229936
Also: Kassaveti 4, Kifisia, Athens
Both under same management as American Bookstore (qv)

Major Libraries

Athens Academy Library, 28 Odos Venizelou, Athens

Athens College Library*, Athens College, PO Box 5, Psychico, Athens Tel: 6714621

British Council Library, PO Box 488, Athens 138 Tel: 3633211/5
Librarian: Julie Carpenter

Eugenides Foundation Technical Library, Syngrou Ave, Amfithea, Athens
Librarian: Roxani Fessas

Gennadius Library, American School of Classical Studies at Athens, Souidias 61, Athens 140 Tel: (021) 7210536
Librarian: S Papageorgiou

National Library of Greece, Panepistemiou 32, Athens Tel: (021) 3614413 (Secretary)/3608495 (Director)
Dir: Dr Panayotis G Nicolopoulos

Library of the **National Technological University** of Athens*, Odos 28, Octovriou 42, Athens

Pan Library ('Circle of the Friends of Progress')*, Odos Giorgios 43, Tripolis, Arcadia

Parliament Library, Palaia Anactora, Athens Tel: (021) 3235030
Librarian: Maria Anastassopoulou
Publications include: Incunabula and Editions of the 15th and 16th Centuries

Library of the **Technical Chamber** of Greece*, Odos Karageorgi Servias 4, Athens Tel: (021) 3226001

Library of the **Three Hierarchs***, Odos Demetriados-Ogl, Volos

Library of the **University of Salonika**, Salonika Tel: 991618
Librarian: D Dimitriou

Library Association

Enossis Ellenon Bibliothakarion*, Skouleniou 4, Athens TT 124 Tel: 3226625
Greek Library Association
Secretary: Sofia Palamiotou
Publication: Bulletin

Library Reference Books and Journals

Book

Guide to Greek Libraries and Cultural Organizations, National Printing Office, Athens

Journal

Greek Library Association Bulletin, Skouleniou 4, Athens TT 124

Literary Associations and Societies

Association of Arts and Letters*, c/o Mitropoleos 38, Athens Tel: (021) 3233033
General Secretary: S Xefloudas

Kentron Ekdoseos Ellinon Syngrafeon*, Academy of Athens, Anaguostopoulou 14, Athens 136
Centre for the Publication of Ancient Greek Authors
Dir: Ch Floratos

P E N Centre*, Skoufa 60a, Athens 144
Secretary: Yannis Manglis

Vivliografiki Etaireia tis Ellados*, Stournara 51, Athens
Bibliographical Society of Greece
General Secretary: J A Thomopoulos

Women's Literary Society*, Evrou 4, Athens 611

Literary Periodicals

Aiolika Grammatia (Aeolian Letters), Hodos Nircos 41, Palaion Phaliron, Athens

Diaghonios (Diagonal), Dinos Christianopoulous, Franklin Roosevelt, Salonika 4

Nea Hestia (text in Greek), G C Eleftheroudakis AE, Nikis 4, Athens 126

Literary Prizes

Circle of the Greek Children's Book IBBY (Greek Section) Prizes*
The Circle awards annual prizes for the following works: Greek tales for children; stories taken from nature; poems taken from nature; plays for children; illustration of children's books; a novel for young people; a book for pre-school ages; the chronicle of a Greek city; humorous stories for children. Awards only made when standard is high enough. Enquiries to General Secretary, Circle of the Greek Children's Book IBBY (Greek Section), Zalongou 7, Athens 142

King Paul National Foundation Prize*
For an essay on community development written by an adolescent. Awarded annually. Enquiries to King Paul National Foundation, Philellinon 9, Athens 118

Tsakalos Prize*
For prose work, poetry and criticism, published by the members of the Society. 50,000 drachmas. Awarded annually. Enquiries to Society of Greek Writers, Mitropoleos 38, Athens 126

Women's Literary Society Prizes*
Each year the Society awards prizes for the following works for children: historical novel on a subject from Greek history; poems for very young children; poems for older children; a book of short stories; a theatrical play for older children; journeys and excursions within Greece. Enquiries to Women's Literary Society, Evrou 4, Athens 611

Guatemala

General Information

Language: Spanish
Religion: Roman Catholic
Population: 6.6 million
Literacy Rate: (1973): 46.1% (71.8% of urban population, 31.4% rural)
Bank Hours: 0900-1500 Monday-Friday
Shop Hours: 0800-1200, 1400-1800 Monday-Friday; 0800-1200 Saturday
Currency: 100 centavos = 1 quetzal
Export/Import Information: Member of the Central American Common Market. Duty on catalogues is Q 0.03 per gross kilo. No import licences, no exchange control
Copyright: UCC, Buenos Aires, Florence (see International section)

Book Trade Organization

Gremial de Libreros de Guatemala, Ave Reforma 13-70, Zona 9, Edificio Real Reforma Interior 13N, Guatemala City Tel: 313326/27505/26478
Association of Booksellers of Guatemala
President: Victor Hugo Granados Gonzalez

Publishers

Editorial del **Ministerio de Educacion** 'Jose de Pineda Ibarra'*, 15° Ave 3-22, Zona 1, Guatemala City

Piedra Santa*, 7a Ave 4-45, Zona 1, Guatemala City Tel: 21867/510231/28603
Man Dir: Oralia Díaz de Piedra Santa;

GUATEMALA — GUYANA 177

Sales: Nery Cuéllar; *Production:* Irene Piedra Santa
Subjects: Pre-Primary, Primary & Secondary Schoolbooks, University Textbooks, Further Education, Literature, Science & Technology, Social Sciences, Tourism, Pedagogy, Psychology, Philosophy, Belles Lettres, Accountancy, Engineering, Sports, Health
Bookshops: At above address and 6a Calle 9-68, Zona 1; 11 Calle 6-50, Zona 1; 9a Calle 3-64, Zona 4; 12 Calle 1-25, Zona 10 (Edificio Geminis 10); Ave Las Américas 15-89, Zona 13 (Edificio Obelisco) (all Guatemala City)

Seminario de Integración Social Guatemalteca, 11 Calle No 4-31, Zona 1, Guatemala City Tel: 29754
Subjects: Sociological, Ecological, Educational, Anthropological texts connected with Guatemala
Founded: 1956

Universidad de San Carlos de Guatemala, Editorial Universitaria*, Ciudad Universitaria, Zona 12, Guatemala City
Printing House: 10 Calle 9-59, Guatemala City 1
Subjects: Technical & Scientific University Textbooks

Book Club

Libroclub de Guatemala, Ave Elena 'B' 2-25 Zona 2, El Sauce, Guatemala City Tel: 313326
Man Dir: Victor Hugo Granados Gonzalez
See also Librería Cervantes (Bookseller)

Major Booksellers

Librería **'13 Calle** El Tecolote' *, 13 Calle 8-61, Zona 1, Guatemala City Tel: 81055
Manager: Mrs Consuelo Martínez

Librería **Acrópolis***, 9 Ave 13-20, Zona 1, Guatemala City Tel: 80819

Librería **C E E S***, Apdo postal 652, Guatemala City

Librería **Cervantes** — Libroclub de Guatemala*, Ave Reforma 13-70, Zona 9, Edificio Real Reforma Interior 13N, Guatemala City Tel: 313326
Direct Importers and Distributors of books in Spanish, English, German and French

Distribuidora de Libros*, Rodrigo Galindo, 11 Calle 4-15, Zona 1, Guatemala City Tel: 28746

Edelcid Libros Científicos*, 11 Calle 8-66, Zona 1, Guatemala City Tel: 20934

Ediciones **Hispanas***, 13 Calle 6-77, 408, Zona 1, Guatemala City

Distribuidora Cultural **I G A***, Ruta 1 Via 4, Zona 4, Guatemala City

Librería **Universal***, 13 Calle 4-16, Zona 1, Guatemala City
Manager: Olga A de Manrique
Owned by: Distribuidora General Universal

Piedra Santa*, 7a Ave 4-45, Zona 1, Guatemala City Tel: 510231/21867/23051
Owned by: Piedra Santa, Publisher (qv for full list of all bookshops under this proprietorship)

El **Tecolote**, see 13 Calle

Librería **Tuncho** Granados G*, 10 Calle 6-56, Zona 1, Apdo Postal 13, Guatemala City, CA Tel: 24736 and 27269
Also: La Plaza del Sol, Calle Montúfar y 2 Ave, Zona 9, Guatemala City CA

Major Libraries

Archivo General de Centro*, América, 4a Ave, 7a-8a Calles, Zona 1, Guatemala City

Biblioteca Nacional de Guatemala (National Library)*, 5a Ave 7-26, Zona 1, Guatemala City
Librarian: Eva Evans

Biblioteca Central de la **Universidad de San Carlos***, Ciudad Universitaria, Zona 12, Guatemala City
Publications: Boletín Bibliográfico, Boletín Contenidos

Library Association

Asociación Bibliotecologica Guatemalteca*, c/o The Director, Biblioteca Nacional de Guatemala, 5a Avenida 7-26, Zona 1, Guatemala, CA
Library Association of Guatemala

Literary Periodical

Alero (Eaves), Universidad de San Carlos, Confederacions Universitaria Centroamericana, Guatemala City

Guinea

General Information

Note: No replies were received to questionnaires sent to Guinea for this edition of *International Literary Market Place*. The information given in the 1983-84 edition has been repeated here but should be treated with caution.
Language: French
Religion: Muslim predominantly
Population: 4.8 million
Bank Hours: 0800-1300 Monday-Saturday
Shop Hours: 0730-1230, 1430-1830 Monday-Saturday
Currency: 100 cauris = 1 syli
Copyright: Berne (see International section)
Export/Import Information: Books imported by State Trading Corporation: Libraport, BP 270, Conakry. Tariffs listed as free for books except children's picture books. Import licences

Publishers

Editions du **Ministère de l'Education** Nationale*, Secrétariat à la Recherche Scientifique, BP 561, Conakry
Subjects: General, Educational

Major Booksellers

Libraport*, BP 270, Conakry
State Trading Corporation

Major Libraries

Bibliothèque nationale*, BP 561, Conakry
Librarian: M K Keita

Institut national de recherches et documentation, Bibliothèque*, BP 561, Conakry Tel: 41420
Librarian: S Bounama Sy

Institut polytechnique de Conakry Bibliothèque*, BP 1147, Conakry

International Communication Agency Library*, c/o American Embassy, BP 711, Conakry

Library Association

Institut national de Recherches et Documentation (National Research and Documentation Institute)*, BP 561, Conakry
Dir: S Bounama Sy

Guyana

General Information

Language: English
Religion: Hindu, Muslim, Christian
Population: 820,000
Bank Hours: 0800-1200 Monday-Friday; 0800-1100 Saturday
Shop Hours: 0800-1130, 1300-1600 Monday-Friday; 0800-1130 Saturday
Currency: 100 cents = 1 Guyana dollar
Export/Import Information: No tariff on books. Only advertising of commercial value, subject to duty. Guyana National Trading Corporation, 45-47 Water St, Georgetown is sole importer of books. Import licence required. Nominal exchange controls

Book Trade Reference Book

Guyanese National Bibliography, National Library, PO Box 10240, Georgetown

Publishers

Guyana National Printers Ltd*, 1 Public Rd, La Pénitence, Georgetown

Major Booksellers

Guyana National Trading Corporation (GNTC)*, 45-47 Water St, Georgetown Tel: 71543-5/72039
Manager: L F Austin
Sole importer of books

Major Libraries

Guyana Medical Science Library*, Georgetown Hospital Compound, Georgetown

National Library*, PO Box 10240, Georgetown Tel: (02) 62690/62699
Chief Librarian: Joan L Christiani
Publication: Guyanese National Bibliography

Library Association

Guyana Library Association, 76-77 Main St, PO Box 10240, Georgetown
Tel: 62690/62699
Secretary: Wenda Stephenson
Publication: Bulletin

Library Reference Journal

Bulletin, Guyana Library Association, 76-77 Main St, PO Box 110, Georgetown

Literary Periodical

University of Guyana Language Forum; review of literary, linguistic and educational studies (text in English), University of Guyana, PO Box 841, Georgetown

Haiti

General Information

Language: French and Creole
Religion: Roman Catholic
Population: 4.8 million
Literacy Rate (1971): 23.3%
Bank Hours: 0900-1300 Monday-Friday
Business Hours: Winter: 0800-1700; Summer: 0700-1600
Currency: 100 centimes = 1 gourde = $US 0.20. US currency is widely used
Export/Import Information: Books charged ad valorem, children's picture books per kilo net. Advertising matter under 1 kilo gross weight duty-free. No import licences or exchange controls, other than occasional exchange rationing, leading to delays
Copyright: UCC (see International section)

Publishers

Editions **Caraïbes***, Lalve, PO Box 2013, Port-au-Prince Tel: 2-3179 Telex: ITT 2030198

Deschamps*, Imprimerie, Grand' Rue, PO Box 164, Port-au-Prince
Subjects: History, Religion, Literature, Education, Fiction

Theodor*, Imprimerie, rue Dantes Destouches, Port-au-Prince
Subjects: History, Literature, Fiction

Major Libraries

Bibliothèque du petit Séminaire*, Port-au-Prince

Bibliothèque nationale d'Haiti (National Library)*, rue Hammerton Killick, Port-au-Prince

Centre de Documentation*, Port-au-Prince

Bibliothèque **Saint Louis de Gonzague**, Port-au-Prince
Librarian: Frère Constant

Literary Associations and Societies

Le **Bibliophile** (The Book Lover)*, Cap Haïtien
Secretary: Louis Toussaint
Publications: La Citadelle (weekly), *Stella* (monthly)

Literary Periodicals

La Citadelle, Le Bibliophile, Cap Haïtien
Stella, Le Bibliophile, Cap Haïtien

Honduras

General Information

Language: Spanish (English on northern coast)
Religion: Roman Catholic
Population: 3.4 million
Literacy Rate (1974): 56.9% (78.9% of urban population, 45.6% rural)
Bank Hours: 0830-1200, 1400-1630 Monday-Friday
Shop Hours: Tegucigalpa: 0800-1200, 1330-1800 Monday-Friday; 0800-1200 Saturday; San Pedro Sula: 0730-1100, 1330-1800 Monday-Friday; 0800-1200 Saturday
Currency: 100 centavos = 1 lempira = $US 0.50
Export/Import Information: Member of the Central American Common Market but has applied tariffs to imports from other CACM countries since December 1970. No tariff on books. Duty on catalogues is per kilo. No import licences. No exchange controls
Copyright: Buenos Aires (see International section)

Book Trade Reference Journal

Bibliografía hondureña (Honduras Bibliography), Banco Central de Honduras, PO Box C-58, 1A Calle, Tegucigalpa

Publishers

Editorial Universitaria*, Universidad de Honduras, Tegucigalpa

Industria Editorial **Lypsa**, Apdo Postal 167-C, Tegucigalpa Tel: 229775
Manager: José Bennaton
Bookshop: At above address

Editorial **Nuevo** Continente*, Ave Cervantes, Tegucigalpa Tel: 225073

Major Booksellers

Librería **Lypsa**, Apdo Postal 167 C, Tegucigalpa Tel: 226824
Manager: J A Bennaton
Owned by: Industria Editorial Lypsa (qv)

Ney's Libros and Revistas*, Apdo 609, Tegucigalpa Tel: 23865

Librería Universitaria Jose T **Reyes***, Universidad Nacional Autónoma de Honduras, Tegucigaipa DC

University Library, see Reyes

Major Libraries

Biblioteca Nacional de Honduras*, 6a Ave Salvador Mendieta, Tegucigalpa

Sistema Bibliotecario, Ciudad Universitaria, Carretera Suyapa, Tegucigalpa Tel: 322208/322189/322203 ext 212/122/124

Dir: Orfylia Pinel S
Publication: Boletín del Sistema Bibliotecario

Library Association

Asociación de Bibliotecarios y Archiveros de Honduras*, 3 Avenidas, 4 y 5 Calles, No 416 Comayagüela, DC, Tegucigalpa
Association of Librarians and Archivists of Honduras
Secretary-General: Juan Angel Ayes R

Library Reference Journal

Cátálogo de Préstamo, Asociación de Bibliotecarios y Archiveros de Honduras, 3 Avenidas, 4 y 5 Calles, No 416, Comayagüela, DC, Tegucigalpa

Hong Kong

General Information

Language: English and Cantonese
Religion: Traditional Chinese beliefs, especially Buddhism
Population: 4.6 million
Literacy Rate (1971): 77.3%
Bank Hours: 0930-1600 Monday-Friday; 0930-1200 Saturday
Department stores: 0900-1830 Monday-Friday; 0900-1730 Saturday
Currency: 100 cents = 1 Hong Kong dollar
Export/Import Information: No tariffs on books and advertising. No import licences required. No exchange controls
Copyright: Berne, UCC (see International Section)

Book Trade Organizations

Anglo-Chinese Textbook Publishers Organization Ltd, c/o Longman House, Tong Chong St, Quarry Bay Tel: (05) 648475
Chairman: William Shen; *Secretary:* Lawrence Pang

Books Registration Unit, Room 2201 Park-In Commercial Centre, 56 Dundas St, Mongkok, Kowloon Tel: (03) 316660
ISBN Administrator: Assistant Librarian

Hong Kong Booksellers' & Stationers' Association*, Man Wah House, Kowloon Tel: (03) 3882356

Hong Kong Educational Publishers Association Ltd*, 1105 Yau Yue Bldg, 127-131 Des Voeux Rd, C
President: Au Bak Ling

Hong Kong Publishers' & Distributors' Association*, National Bldg, 4th Floor, 240-246 Nathan Rd, Kowloon

Standard Book Numbering Agency, see Books Registration Unit

Publishers

A D I S Press Publications Ltd*, 1802-3 Tung Sun Commercial Centre, 194-200 Lockhart Rd, Wanchai
Publicity Manager: Mrs Lina Cheung
Associate Company: ADIS Press Australasia Ltd (qv)

The **Art** Publisher*, 166 Java Rd, 2/F, North Point
Subjects: Art, Textbooks

Asia Press Ltd*, 88 Yee Wo St, PO Box 20919, Causeway Bay
President: Chang Kuo-Sin
Subjects: General Fiction, Belles Lettres, General Science, Periodicals
Founded: 1952

Book Marketing Ltd, North Point Industrial Building, Flat A, 17F, 499 King's Rd Tel: (05) 5620121 Cable Add: Marketbook Telex: bmark 72216 hx
Man Dir: Bernard Chiu King Sum
Associate Companies: Swindon Book Co, Hong Kong Book Centre Ltd, Kelly and Walsh Ltd
Subjects: Educational books and periodicals
Founded: 1973
ISBN Publisher's Prefix: 0-962211

Books for Asia*, 30 Tat Chee St, Yau Yat Chuen, Kowloon
Subsidiary Companies: Books for Asia (M) Sdn Bhd, Malaysia; Books for Asia, Philippines; Books for Asia (S) Pte Ltd, Singapore (qv under Major Booksellers); Books for Asia, Thailand
Subject: Textbooks

C F W Publications Ltd+, 1602 Alliance Bldg, 130 Connaught Rd Central, Hong Kong Tel: (05) 430004 Cable Add: Amseltd Telex: 75645 bowen hx
Man Dir: Allan Amsel
Imprint: C F W Guidebooks
Subjects: Travel and Travel Guides, Oriental Cookery and General Themes
1981: 13 titles *Founded:* 1979
ISBN Publisher's Prefix: 962-7031

China Cultural Corporation, 345 Des Voeux Rd West, 5th Fl, Hong Kong Cable Add: Chinacult Hong Kong
Manager: Richard L C Wong
Associate Company: Shanghai Book Co Ltd (qv)
Subjects: Business Reference, Chinese Culture, Periodicals (in English and Chinese)

The **Chinese University Press**, The Chinese University of Hong Kong, Shatin, New Territories, Hong Kong Tel: (012) 633111 ext 461 Cable Add: sinoversity Telex: 50301 cuhk hx
Man Dir: Richard M Lai; *Editorial:* William C Ho, Y C Wei; *Sales:* Patrick Kwong; *Production:* Pansy Wong
Subjects: Chinese and South-East Asian Studies, Books on Hong Kong, Dictionaries, Books in Chinese and English on Business, the Arts, Sciences, Literature, Linguistics, History, Geography, Philosophy, Psychology, Journalism, Reprints of Rare Books, Periodicals
1981: 26 titles *1982:* 26 titles *Founded:* 1977
ISBN Publisher's Prefix: 962-201

Chopsticks Publications Ltd+, Kowloon Central PO Box 73515, Kowloon (Located at: 166D Waterloo Rd, Ground Floor, Kowloon) Tel: (03) 7115989/7115911 Cable Add: Chopcuisin, Hong Kong
Dir, Rights & Permissions: Cecilia J Au-Yeung; *Editor:* Caroline Au-Yeung; *Sales, Production, Publicity:* Wilson Au-Yeung
Subjects: Chinese Cuisine, Gourmet Trips in Hong Kong and China
1981: 2 titles *1982:* 2 titles *Founded:* 1975
ISBN Publisher's Prefix: 962-7018

The **Educational** Publishing House Ltd*, 14th Floor, Tsuen Wan Industrial Centre, T W T L, 24 Texaco Rd, Tsuen Wan, New Territories, Hong Kong Tel: (012) 289081-6/289932 Telex: 35330 eph hx
Associate Companies: Fook Hing Offset Printing Co Ltd, The World Publishing Co, Kam Pui Enterprises Ltd, The Seashore Publishing Co, Harris Book Co Ltd, Hong Kong Housing Projects Corp Ltd, Pan-Lloyds (HK) Ltd

Edutec International Ltd, subsidiary of Kingsway International Publications Ltd (qv)

F E P International (HK) Ltd*, 1204 Odell House, 32 Laichikok Rd, Mongkok, Kowloon
Subject: Textbooks

Federal Publications (HK) Ltd*, 5A Evergreen Industrial Mansion, Wong Chuk Hang Rd, Hong Kong
General Manager: Tom Ng
Associate Companies: Federal Publications Sdn Bhd, Malaysia (qv); Federal Publications (S) Pte Ltd, Singapore (qv)
Subjects: Textbooks, General Subjects, Periodicals

Good Earth Publishing Co*, c/o Everyman Book Co Ltd, 71A Prince Edward Rd, Chit King Industrial Bldg, 10th Floor, San Po Kong, Kowloon
Subject: Textbooks

Greenwood Press*, 47 Pokfulam Road, G/F
Subject: Textbooks

H K Health Knowledge Publication*, Flat A, 1st floor, 7 Gough St
Subject: Textbooks

Heinemann Educational Books (Asia) Ltd, KPO Box 96086, Tsimshatsui PO, Kowloon (Located at: Yik Yin Bldg, 1st Floor, 321-323 To Kwa Wan Rd, Kowloon) Tel: (03) 649221-4 Cable Add: Heinebooks Hong Kong Telex: HK 84463 (answerback — 84463 hebhk hx)
Man Dir: Leon Comber; *Editorial:* Geoffrey Bonsall; *Sales:* William Tsang
Branch Offs: 41 Jalan Pemimpin, Singapore 2057, Republic of Singapore; 2 Jalan 20/16A, Paramount Garden, Petaling Jaya, Selangor, Malaysia
Subjects: Belles Lettres, Poetry, Biography, History, Music, Art, Philosophy, Reference, Religion, Medicine, Engineering, General & Social Science, University & Secondary Textbooks, Educational Materials, Asiatic Studies, Management, Accountancy, English as Second Language, Writing in Asia
Founded: 1962

Hong Kong Cultural Press Ltd*, 8/F Lee Sum Factory Bldg, 23 Sze Mei St, San Po Kong, Kowloon
Subject: Textbooks

Hong Kong Publishing Co Ltd, 307 Yu Yuet Lai Bldg, 43-55 Wyndham St, Central, Hong Kong Tel: 5259053 Cable Add: Hkpublish Telex: 60904 sevex hx
Man Dir: Dean Barrett; *Sales Dir:* Rohini Delilkhan
Subjects: Guidebooks, Photo-books and Fiction about Asia, especially Thailand
1981: 3 titles *1982:* 4 titles *Founded:* 1975
ISBN Publisher's Prefix: 962-7035

Hong Kong University Press+, University of Hong Kong, 'Bethanie', 139 Pokfulam Rd Tel: (05) 502703 (Sales)/502791 (Editorial)/507871 (Publishing) Cable Add: University Telex: 71919 cereb hx
Publisher, Rights & Permissions: Ken Toogood; *Editor:* Y K Fung; *Sales:* Peter Ho; *Production:* W K Lau
Subjects: Archaeology, History, Life Sciences, Physical Sciences, Social Sciences, Economics, Languages (especially Chinese), Literature, Anatomy, Fine Arts, Geography, Law, Medicine, Philosophy, Seamanship, General Non-fiction, Paperbacks, Microprints
1981: 12 titles *1982:* 16 titles *Founded:* 1956
ISBN Publisher's Prefix: 962-209

Hong Kong Witman Publishing Co, 774E King's Rd, Ground Floor, North Point Tel: (05) 626279/631973
Subject: Textbooks

Hung Fung Book Co*, 18 Tsat Tse Mui Rd, G/F
Subject: Textbooks

Jing Kung Educational Press*, 53 Hollywood Rd
Subject: Textbooks

King Shing Publishing Co*, 89 Sai Yee St, G/F, Kowloon
Subject: Textbooks

Kingsway International Publications Ltd*, PO Box 3897, Kowloon (Located at: 20/F Ritz Bldg, 625 Nathan Rd, Kowloon Tel: (03) 308381 (10 lines) Cable Add: Kintpubs Telex: 34210 kinpu hx
Man Dir: Laurent Lee; *Chief Editor:* Fang Chun-le; *Sales Dir:* Jaffi Yee; *Production Dir:* Johnny Koo; *Publicity:* Paul Li; *Rights & Permissions:* Stephen Pang, Paul Li
Subsidiary Companies: Kingsway Advertising & Promotion Centre Ltd (at above address); Kingsway International Enterprises, PO Box 3897, KCPO Hong Kong; Edutec International Ltd, 18/F Gee Chang Hong Centre, 65 Wong Chuk Hang Rd, Aberdeen, Hong Kong
Subjects: Educational Material, Directories, Periodicals
Book Club: MIT International
1981: 4 titles *Founded:* 1977
ISBN Publisher's Prefix: 962-7051

T H Lee & Co Ltd*, 1-15 Electric St, Upper Ground Floor, Wanchai
Subject: Textbooks

The **Ling Kee Group**ABOVE*, c/o Ling Kee Publishing Co Ltd, Zung Fu Industrial Bldg, 1067 King's Rd, Quarry Bay
The group comprises: Ling Kee Publishing Co Ltd (qv), Lingwood Publications Ltd, Ling Kee Book Store Ltd (all Hong Kong); Ling Kee Publishing Co Ltd, Taiwan; Ward Lock Educational Co Ltd, UK (qv); BLA Publishing Ltd, Surrey, UK

Ling Kee Publishing Co Ltd*, Zung Fu Industrial Bldg, 1067 King's Rd, Quarry Bay Tel: (05) 616151/2 Cable Add: Bookland Telex: 62733 lkpc hx
Chairman, Chief Executive: B L Au; *Sales Dir:* Albert Au
Subjects: Reference, University, Secondary & Primary Textbooks, Educational Materials
Bookshops: Ling Kee Book Store Ltd, Yau Yue Building, 127-1Des Voeux Rd Central, Hong Kong; 678 Nathan Rd, Mongkok, Kowloon
Founded: 1949
Miscellaneous: Firm is a division of Ling Kee Group Ltd (qv)

Longman Group (Far East) Ltd*, Longman House, Tong Chong St, Quarry Bay, PO Box 223 Tel: (05) 618171/5
Man Dir: William Shen
Subjects: General Fiction, Belles Lettres, Art, History, General Science, Textbooks, Educational Materials, Juveniles, Languages
Miscellaneous: Firm is a member of the Longman Group Ltd, UK (qv)

Macmillan Publishers (HK) Ltd*, 19th Floor, Warwick House, Taikoo Trading Estate, 28 Tong Chong St, Quarry Bay Tel: (05) 636206-9/620101-2/643115 Cable Add: Macpublish, Hong Kong Telex: 85969 Penhk Hx
Man Dir: Nigel Carr
Parent Company: Macmillan Publishers, UK

(qv)
Subject: Secondary Textbooks
Founded: 1969

Oxford University Press, 18th Floor, Warwick House, Taikoo Trading Estate, 28 Tong Chong St, Quarry Bay Tel: (05) 610221-4/610138-9 Cable Add: Oxonian Hong Kong Telex: 65522 Hx
Manager: A F D Scott; *Editorial, Rights & Permissions:* R G Scriven; *Marketing:* P Tam; *Production:* P Ling; *Publicity:* B Ho
Parent Company: Oxford University Press, UK (qv)
Subjects: School textbooks/supplementary books in English, Chinese; Bi-Lingual Reference; Academic and General Works relating to Hong Kong and China
1981: 77 titles *1982:* 78 titles *Founded:* 1961
ISBN Publisher's Prefix: 0-19 (OUP UK)

Perfecting Press*, 233 Lockhart Rd, 20th Floor, Flat A
Publicity Manager: Fung Pui Ming
Subject: Textbooks

Shanghai Book Co Ltd, 179 Connaught Rd West, 5th Floor, Flat A Tel: (05) 498178/489889 Cable Add: Shoobook, Hong Kong
Man Dir: Richard L C Wong
Associate Companies: Shanghai Book Co (Pte) Ltd, Singapore (qv); Shanghai Book Co, (KL) Sdn Bhd, Malaysia; China Cultural Corporation, Hong Kong (qv)
Subjects: Textbooks and various, in Chinese and English

South China Morning Post Ltd+, Publications Division, PO Box 47, Morning Post Bldg, Tong Chong St, Hong Kong Tel: (05) 622271 Cable Add: Postscript Hong Kong Telex: hx 86008
General Manager, Rights & Permissions: Peter Carton; *Editorial:* Howard Coats; *Sales:* Paulette Martin; *Production, Publicity:* Winnie Zee
Subsidiary Company: Yee Tin Tong Printing Press Ltd (at above address)
Subjects: General, China, Hong Kong
Bookshops: SCM Post Family Bookshops in Star Ferry, Furama Hotel, Ocean Centre — on Hong Kong Island and Kowloon
1981: 50 titles *Founded:* 1976

Times Educational Co Ltd*, A 7/F Melbourne Industrial Bldg, 16 Westlands Road, Quarry Bay
Subsidiary Company: Times Educational Co Sdn Bhd, Malaysia (qv)
Subjects: Educational, General Works, Trade Books

Union Press Ltd*, 9 College Rd, Kowloon
Subject: Textbooks

Book Club

M I T International*, PO Box 3897, Kowloon (Located at: 20/F Ritz Bldg, 625 Nathan Rd, Kowloon) Tel: (03) 808381
Owned by: Kingsway International Publications Ltd (qv)

Major Booksellers

Asia Press Bookstore Ltd*, 88 Yee Wo St, Causeway Bay, PO Box 2919

East Asia Book Co*, 39 Shu Kuk St, North Point

Eastern Book Service Ltd, 11-C Majestic Bldg, 80 Nathan Rd, Kowloon Tel: (03) 685645 Cable Add: Bookseast H K Telex: 41255 ebs hx
Man Dir: Jack R Sherman
Publishers' Agents and Stockists. Associated with Eastern Book Service offices in Singapore, the Philippines and Malaysia (qqv)

Far East Publications Ltd*, Unit D, 2nd Floor, Freder Centre, 68 Sung Wong Toi Rd, Tokwawan, Kowloon Tel: (03) 656234/658862
General Manager: Tom Ng
Miscellaneous: Also major distributor of books, from Mok Chong St, Kowloon City Rd

Hong Kong Book Centre Ltd, On Lok Yuen Bldg, 25 Des Voeux Rd, C

Howard Book Co*, 74 Argyle St, Kowloon

Jing Kung Book Store*, 53 Hollywood Rd

Kwong Hin Bookstore*, 75 Hollywood Rd

Swindon Book Co*, 13-15 Lock Rd, Kowloon Cable Add: Swindon
Managers: Rupert S C Li, Daisy K Y Chang
Associate Companies: Hong Kong Book Centre Ltd, 25 Des Vouex Rd, Central Hong Kong; Kelly and Walsh Ltd, GPO Box 96, Hong Kong

Tai Kuen Book Co*, 323 Queen's Rd West

Times Book Centre, L/G 23 Houston Centre, 63 Mody Rd, Tsim Sha Tsui East, Kowloon Tel: (03) 7226583
Manager: Daisy Chan
Also G31 Hutchison House, 10 Harcourt Rd, Hong Kong

University Book Store*, University of Hong Kong, Pokfulam Rd

Major Libraries

British Council Library, Easey Commercial Bldg 1/F, 255 Hennessy Rd, Wanchai Tel: (05) 756501 Telex: 74141 bcoun hx

Chinese University of Hong Kong Library System, Shatin, New Territories
University Librarian: Dr Lai-bing Kan
Publications include: University Library Bibliographical Series: no 1 — *Union Catalogue of Serials;* no 2 — *Union Catalogue of Audio-Visual Materials;* no 3 — *An Annotated Guide to Serial Publications of Hong Kong Government;* no 4 — *Serials of Hong Kong 1845-1979;* no 5 — *Newspapers of Hong Kong 1841–1979*

Hong Kong Junior Chamber of Commerce Libraries*, 272 Queen's Rd Central, 15/F, Flat C Tel: (05) 543 8913
Contact: Alfred S W Tso (Chamber of Commerce National Secretary-General)

Hong Kong Polytechnic Library, Hung Hom, Kowloon Tel: (03) 638344 Cable Add: Polyteched Telex: 38964 polyx hx
Librarian: Barry L Burton
Publication: Hongkongiana (an index to selected Hong Kong periodicals)

Sun Yat-Sen Library*, 172-174 Boundary St, Kowloon

University of Hong Kong Libraries, University of Hong Kong, Pokfulam Rd Tel: (05) 468161 ext 219

Urban Council Public Libraries, 6th Floor, High Block, City Hall, Edinburgh Pl, Hong Kong Tel: (05) 233688 Telex: 60645 ucusd hx
Chief Librarian: Barbara Luk

Library Association

Hong Kong Library Association*, c/o The Chinese University Library, The Chinese University of Hong Kong, Shatin, New Territories Tel: (012) 633111 ext 300
Chairman: Dr L B Kan; *Honorary Secretary:* Meliza Ng
Publication: Journal of the Hong Kong Library Association (irregular)

Library Reference Journal

Journal of the Hong Kong Library Association (text in English and Chinese), Hong Kong Library Association, The Chinese University Library, The Chinese University of Hong Kong, Shatin, New Territories

Literary Associations and Societies

Chinese Language and Literature Association*, Block A1, Fa Po Villa, 1st Floor, Fa Po St, Yau Yat Chuen, Kowloon
Secretary: Leung Nga Mei

Hong Kong Chinese P E N Centre, Victoria Park Mansion, 15th Floor, Flat A, Paterson St
Secretary: William Hsu
Publication: PEN News (weekly in Chinese)

Hong Kong English P E N Centre*, c/o Catholic Chinese Weekly, Room 111 Catholic Diocese Centre, 16 Caine Rd
Secretary: Miss Lee Wai-ling

Literary Periodicals

Eastern Horizon (text in English), Lee Tsung-ying, 472 Hennessy Rd, 3rd Floor

PEN News (text in Chinese), Hong Kong Chinese PEN Centre, Victoria Park Mansion, 15th Floor, Flat A, Paterson St

Shui Hsing Cha Chi (Mercury Magazine) (text in Chinese, title in Chinese and English), Louise Bao, GPO Box 13154

Wu Hsia Shih Chieh, 7-13 Hsin Chieh, 2nd Floor

Hungary

General Information

Language: Hungarian (German widely known)
Religion: Predominantly Roman Catholic
Population: 10.7 million
Literacy Rate (1971): 98%
Bank Hours: 0830-1700 Monday-Friday; 0830-1330 Saturday
Shop Hours: 1000-1800 Monday-Friday; 1000-1500 Saturday
Currency: 100 fillér = 1 forint
Export/Import Information: Importation is a state monopoly so licences and tariff not of concern to exporter. Exchange controls. Book importing done through Kultura, H-1389 Budapest, Postafiók 149; atlases through Cartographia, H-1443 Budapest, Postafiók 132. Exporting is through the Hungarian Foreign Trade Organization,

H-1389 Budapest 62, Postafiók 149. Magyar Hirdeto, Budapest, is a full service advertising agency
Copyright: UCC, Berne (see International section)

Book Trade Organizations

Magyar Írók Szövetsége, Budapest VI, Bajza u 18
Union of Hungarian Writers
President: Miklós Hubay; *General Secretary:* Miklós Jovánovics

Magyar Könyvkiadók és Könyvterjesztők Egyesülése, H-1367 Budapest, Postafiók 130 (Located at: H-1051 Budapest V, Vörösmarty tér 1 X) Tel: 184758
Association of Hungarian Publishers and Booksellers
President: György Bernát; *Secretary General:* Ferenc Zöld
Founded: 1878
Publication: Könyvvilag; also 3 quarterly journals published in German, English and French on Hungarian books, viz: *Bücher aus Ungarn, Hungarian Book Review, Le Livre Hongrois*

Országos Széchényi Könyvtár Magyar ISBN Iroda, H-1827 Budapest Pollack Mihálytér 10 Telex: biblnathung 224226
ISBN Administrator: Dr Susánszky Zoltánné

Standard Book Numbering Agency, see Országos Széchényi Könyvtar Magyar ISBN Iroda

Book Trade Reference Journals

Hungarian Book Review (text in English, French and German), Kultura, H-1389 Budapest, Postafiók 149

Könyv és nevelés (Book and Education), Orszagos pedagógiai könyvtár és múzeum, Budapest V, Honvéd u 19, Postafiók 49

Könyvvilag (Book World), Magyar Könyvkiadók és Könyvterjesztők Egyesülése, H-1367 Budapest, Postafiók 130

Magyar könyvszemle (Hungarian Bibliographical Journal); review of Book history, Bibliography and Documentation (summaries in English, French, German or Russian), Magyar Tudományos Akadémiai Kiadó, Publishing House of the Hungarian Academy of Sciences, H-1363 Budapest, Postafiók 24

Magyar nemzeti bibliográfia (Hungarian National Bibliography), Országos Széchényi Könyvtár, H-1827 Budapest, Múzeum körút 14-16

Uj könyvek (New Books), Centre for Library Science and Methodology, H-1827 Budapest, Múzeum u 3

Publishers

Cartographia, H-1443 Budapest XIV, Bosnyák tér 5, Postafiók 132 Tel: 634639 Cable Add: Cartographia Telex: 226218
Subjects: Maps, Atlases

Corvina Press*, H-1364 Budapest 4, Vörösmarty tér 1, Postafiók 108 Tel: 176222 Cable Add: Corvina Budapest
Dir: József Szabó; *Asst Dir:* Dr Miklós Tóth; *Production Manager:* István Murányi; *Sales, Advertising & Publicity Dir:* Gábor Ila; *Editorial Dir:* Karoly Uéber
Orders to: Kultura, H-1389 Budapest 62, Postafiók 149
Subjects: Books in Hungarian & foreign languages, Art, Music, Fiction, Juveniles, Tourist Guides, General Information, Cookery Books, Sport
Founded: 1955
ISBN Publisher's Prefix: 963-13

Európa Könyvkiadó, H-1363 Budapest V, Kossuth Lajos tér 13-15, Postafiók 65 Tel: 312700 Cable Add: Euroliber Telex: 225645
Man Dir: János Domokos; *Editorial:* L Antal; *Sales, Rights & Permissions:* Dr L Sármány; *Production:* K Szegleth; *Publicity:* L Horváth
Subjects: General Fiction, Belles Lettres, Poetry, Biography, Philosophy, Bibliophile interest
Founded: 1945
ISBN Publisher's Prefixes: 963-07, 963-207

Gondolat Könyvkiadó, H-1088 Budapest, Bródy Sándor u 16 Tel: 343380
Man Dir: Dr Margit Siklós
Subjects: Reference, Art, General & Social Science
Founded: 1957
ISBN Publisher's Prefix: 963-281

Helikon Kiadó, H-1053 Budapest, Eötvös L u 8 Tel: 174765 Telex: 227100
Man Dir: Magda Molnár
Subjects: Belles Lettres, Art, History
Bookshop: Helikon Bookshop, H-1052 Budapest, Sütö u 2
1982: 19 titles *Founded:* 1982
ISBN Publisher's Prefix: 963-207

Képzömüvészeti Alap Kiadóvállalata*, H-1051 Budapest V, Vörösmarty tér 1, Postafiók 110 Tel: 176222
Manager: Dr László Seres; *Editorial:* Teréz Horváth; *Sales:* László Csajka; *Production:* György Szedlák; *Publicity:* Tibor Geröly
Publishing House of the Art Foundation
Subject: Fine Art
Bookshop: Képesbolt, Budapest VI, Deák tér 6
Founded: 1954

Kossuth Könyvkiadó, H-1366 Budapest, Steindl u 6, Postafiók 127 Tel: 117440
Publishing House of Political Literature
Man Dir: György Nonn; *Deputy Man Dir:* József Nyirö; *Sales Dir:* Sándor Méth; *Rights & Permissions:* Artisjus, Vörösmarty tér 1
Subjects: History, Philosophy, Belles Lettres, Social and Political Science, Psychology, Business; Periodicals
1981: 176 titles *Founded:* 1944
ISBN Publisher's Prefix: 963-09

Közgazdasági és Jogi Könyvkiadó, H-1374 Budapest V, Nagy Sándor u 6, Postafiók 578 Tel: 126430/312327 Telex: 226511
Man Dir: V Dalos; *Editorial, Publicity:* Dr K Cotel; *Sales:* L Szigeti; *Rights & Permissions:* Artisjus (qv under Literary Agents)
Imprint: Editor Minerva
Distribution: Artisjus, Budapest
Subjects: Economics, Law, Sociology, Education, Children's Literature
Founded: 1955
ISBN Publisher's Prefixes: 963-220, 963-221 (Közgazdasági és Jogi Könyvkiadó), 963-223 (Minerva)

Magvetö Könyvkiadó, H-1806 Budapest V, Vörösmarty tér 1 Tel: 176222
Man Dir: G Kardos, *Sales, Publicity:* I Matolcsy; *Managing Editors:* M Hegedös, A Bor; *Rights & Permissions:* Artisjus (qv under Literary Agents)
Subjects: General Fiction, Belles Lettres, Poetry, History, Music, Art, Aesthetics, Philosophy, Low-priced Paperbacks
1981: 202 titles *1982:* 205 titles *Founded:* 1955
ISBN Publisher's Prefix: 963-271

Magyar Tudományos Akadémiai Kiadó, H-1363 Budapest, Postafiók 24 Tel: 111010 Cable Add: Akadémaiai Kiadó Budapest Telex: 226228 Ak Nyo H
Publishing House of the Hungarian Academy of Sciences
Man Dir: György Bernat; *Sales & Advertising Dir:* József Tóth; *Publicity Dir:* György Kürti; *Rights & Permissions:* Géza Takács
Subjects: Belles Lettres, General & Social Science, Medicine, Biology, Earth Sciences, Engineering, University Textbooks, Archaeology, Book Industry, History, Arts, Reference, Literature, Music, Philosophy, Psychology, Politics, Law, Languages, Veterinary Science, Economics
Bookshop: Akadémiai Könyvesbolt, H-1052 Budapest V, Váci u 22
1981: 670 titles *Founded:* 1828
ISBN Publisher's Prefix: 963-05

Medicina Könyvkiadó, H-1361 Budapest, Postafiók 9 (Located at: H-1054 Budapest, Beloiannisz u 8)
Publishing House of Medical Literature
Man Dir: Dr István Árky; *Editors:* Dr János Brencsán, Dr Mihály Berend, Dr Bulcsu Buda; *Production:* Ferenc Fraunhoffer; *Rights & Permissions:* Artisjus (qv under Literary Agents)
Orders to: H-1361 Budapest, Póstafiók 9
Subjects: Medicine, Travel, Sports
Founded: 1957
ISBN Publisher's Prefixes: 963-240 (Medical), 963-243 (Travel), 963-253 (Sports)

Mezögazdasági Könyvkiadó Vállalat*, Budapest V, Báthory u 10 Tel: 116650/318397
Agricultural Publishing House
Manager: Dr Pál Sárkány
Subjects: Agriculture, Reference, General Science, Textbooks
Book Club: Club for Bibliophiles
Bookshop: Agricultural Bookstore, Budapest V, Vécsei u 5
1981: 96 titles *Founded:* 1950
ISBN Publisher's Prefixes: 963-230, 963-231

Editor **Minerva**, publishing imprint of Közgazdasági és Jogi Könyvkiadó (qv)

Móra Ferenc Ifjúsagi Könyvkiadó, H-1146 Budapest XIV, Május 1 út 57-59 Tel: 212390
Man Dir: János Sziládi
Subjects: Juveniles, Science Fiction
Founded: 1950
ISBN Publisher's Prefix: 963-11

Editio **Musica Budapest**, H-1370 Budapest, Postafiók 322 (Located at: Budapest V, Vörösmarty tér 1) Tel: 184228 Cable Add: Editiomusica Telex: 225500 embh
Man Dir: László Sarlós
Exports: via Kultura (qv under Major Booksellers)
Subject: Sheet Music, Books on Music
Founded: 1950

Müszaki Könyvkiadó, H-1014 Budapest I, Hess András tér 5 Tel: 160860 Cable Add: Editechn Telex: 226490 mkh
Publishing House of Technical Literature
Man Dir: Herbert Fischer; *Editorial:* András Kelen
Subjects: Science, Technical, Textbooks, Yearbooks, Catalogues
Book Club: Müszaki Könyvklub
Bookshops: 100 in Budapest, 154 elsewhere throughout country
Founded: 1949
ISBN Publisher's Prefix: 963-10

HUNGARY

Statisztikai Kiadó Vállalat+, H-1300 Budapest, Postafiók 99 (Located at: H-1033 Budapest 3, Kaszás Str 10-12) Tel: 688635/688460 Telex: 226699-skv-h
Statistical Publishing House
Despatch Add: Budapest III, Kaszás u 10-12
Man Dir: József Kecskés; *Sales Dir:* Géza Pánezél; *Publicity and Advertising Dir:* Piroska Gerely; *Rights & Permissions:* Artisjus (qv under Literary Agents)
Parent Company: Central Statistical Office, H-1024 Budapest, Keleti Károly u 5-7
Subjects: Statistics, Computing, Economics, Social Science
Bookshop: Statistical and Computing Bookshop, Budapest II, Keleti Károly u 10 Tel: 158018
Founded: 1954
ISBN Publisher's Prefix: 963-340

Szépirodalmi Kiadó*, H-1073 Budapest, Lenin Körút 9-11, Postafiók 58 Tel: 221285
Man Dir: Endre Illés; *Rights & Permissions:* Ministry of Culture
Subjects: General Fiction, Belles Lettres, Poetry, Low- & High-priced Paperbacks, Educational Materials
Founded: 1950
ISBN Publisher's Prefix: 963-15

Táncsics Szakszervezeti Kiadó*, H-1139 Budapest, Váci u 69-79 Tel: 141479/335790
Manager: István Kádár
Subjects: Technical, Non-fiction, Reference, Periodicals

Tankönyvkiadó Vállalat*, H-1055 Budapest V, Szalay u 10-14, Póstafiók 20 Tel: 324915
Textbook Publishing House
Man Dir: András Petró; *Editorial:* Sándor Hinora; *Sales:* Hugó Dobos; *Production:* Lajos Lojd; *Rights & Permissions:* Artisjus (qv under Literary Agents)
Subjects: Textbooks, Educational Literature, Language Books, Periodicals
Founded: 1949
ISBN Publisher's Prefix: 96317

Zrinyi Katonai Kiadó*, H-1440 Budapest, Kerepesi u 29/b
Publishing House of the Hungarian Army
Manager: László Bedö
Subjects: Military & Popular Science

Literary Agents

Artisjus*, H-1364 Budapest, Vörösmarty tér 1, Postafiók 67, Tel: 184704 Cable Add: Artisjus Telex: 226527 Arjus H
Agency for Literature, Theatre and Music of the Hungarian Bureau for Copyright Protection
Contact: Vera Acs

Book Clubs

Club for Bibliophiles*, Budapest V, Báthory u 10; Tel: 110025
Owned by: Mezögazdasagi Könyvkiadó Vállalat (qv)

Müszaki Könyvklub, H-1051 Budapest V, Bajczy-Zs út 20
Owned by: Müszaki Könyvkiadó (qv)

Major Booksellers

Állami könyvterjesztö vállalat, Budapest V, Deák Ferenc u 15
Hungarian State Book-Distributing Enterprise. It distributes books to its 112 bookshops

Állami könyvterjesztö vállalat országos antikvár*, Budapest V, Múzeum körút 21
Hungarian State Book-Distributing Enterprise, Department for Antiquarian Books

Hungarian Foreign Trade Organization*, H-1389 Budapest 62, Postafiók 149
The state exporting organization

Könyvértékesítö vállalat*, H-1052 Budapest, Petöfi Sandor u 3
Hungarian Wholesale Book Trading Enterprise
This organization holds stocks and despatches all editions from Hungarian publishers, and handles imported books for the retail trade. It also sells books directly for bookshops owned by co-operatives, and has a Library Service department which supplies the entire Hungarian Library network

Kultura*, H-1389 Budapest 62, Postafiók 149 Tel: 388511 Cable Add: Kulturpress Telex: 22-4441
Man Dir: A Goenyei
This company is the Hungarian export-import organization, representing the publications of different Hungarian publishers

Müvelt Nép Könyvterjesztö Vállalat, H-1370 Budapest V, Postafiók 370 (Located at: Budapest VI, Népköztársaság u 21) Tel: 429760/315175 Telex: 224914
Dir: Sándor Preszter
Firms has shops throughout Hungary; also importer of foreign language books

Major Libraries

Budapesti Müszaki Egyetem Központi Könyvtára*, Budapest XI, Budafoki u 4-6
Budapest Technical University Central Library

Eötvös Loránd Tudományegyetem Egyetemi Könyvtár, H-1372 Budapest, Károlyi Mihály u 10, Postafiók 483 Tel: 185866
Central Library of Loránd Eötvös University

Föapátsági Könyvtár*, H-9090 Pannonhalma Tel: Pannonhalma 7022
Library of the Archabbacy (Benedictine)
Librarian: Szabo Floris

Föszékesegyházi Könyvtár*, H-2500 Esztergom, Bajcsy Zsilinszky u 28 Tel: Esztergom 527
Cathedral Library
Dir: Dr Margit Beke

József Attila Tudományegyetem Központi Könyvtára, H-6701 Szeged, Dugonics tér 13
Central Library of the Attila József University
Chief Librarian: Dr Béla Karácsonyi
Publications: Dissertationes ex Bibliotheca Universitatis de Attila József Nominatae; Acta Universitatis Szegediensis de Attila József Nominatae: Acta Bibliothecaria (all irregular)

Kossuth Lajos Tudományegyetem Egyetemi Könyvtár*, H-4010 Debrecen
Lajos Kossuth University Library
Chief Librarian: Olga Gomba

Könyvtártudományi és módszertani központ, H-1827 Budapest, Múzeum u 3
Centre for Library Science and Methodology
Dir: Ferenc Szente
Publications: Uj könyvek, Könyvtári figyelö, Magyar könyvtári szakrodalom bibliográfiája, Hungarian Library and Information Science Abstracts; Könyvtári és Dokumentációs Szakirodalom, Referálo Lap

Központi statisztikai hivatal könyvtár és dokumentációs szolgálat, H-1525 Budapest II, Keleti Károly u 5, Postafiók 10
Library and Documentation Service of the Central Statistical Office
Librarian: Dr István Csahók
Publications include: Statisztikai módszerek (Statistical Methods Surveys); *Történeti statisztikai tanulmányok* (Studies in Historical Statistics); *Történeti statisztikai füzetek* (Papers in Historical Statistics)

Uj **Magyar Központi Levéltár***, H-1014 Budapest, Hess András tér 4
New Central Archives of Hungary

Magyar Országos Levéltár, H-1250 Budapest I, Bécsikapu tér 4, Postafiók 3 Tel: 160656
National Archives of Hungary

Magyar Tudományos Akadémia Könyvtára, H-1361 Budapest V, Akadémia u 2, Póstafiók 7 Tel: 126779/113400 Telex: 224132 aktar h
Library of the Hungarian Academy of Sciences
Librarian: Dr György Rózsa
Publications: Publicationes Bibliothecae Academiae Scientiarium Hungaricae; Catalogi Collectionis Manuscriptorum Bibliothecae Academiae Scientiarium Hungaricae; Oriental Studies; Budapest Oriental Reprints; Informatics and Scientometrics

Országos Müszaki, Információs Központ és Könyvtár*, H-1428 Budapest, Reviczky u 6, Postafiók 12 Tel: 336309 Telex: Omikk-h 224944
National Technical Information Centre and Library
Director-General: Mihály Ágoston;
Librarian: Tibor Futala
Publications: Many journals, abstracts, conference reports on technological subjects, often in translation
Miscellaneous: Technoinform, the Library's Foreign Trade Department, offers translation from Hungarian and other languages

Országos Széchényi Könyvtár, H-1827 Budapest, Póstafiók 486 (Located at: Budapest VIII, Múzeum körút 14/16) Tel: 131019 Telex: biblnathung 224226 (Information Dept: Tel: 341684)
National Széchényi Library
Dir: Dr Ferenc Molnár
Publications: Magyar Nemzeti Bibliográfia (Konyvek bibliográfiája; Zenemüvek bibliográfiája; Idöszaki kiadványok repertóriuma); Az Országos Széchényi Könyvtár Evkönyue; Magyar Irodalomtudományi Bibliográfia; Hungarica Irodalmi Szemle; Kurrens Külföldi Idöszaki Kiadványok a Magyar Könyvtárakban
Also a National Centre for Library Science and Methodology and a Hungarian national ISDS centre

Fövárosi Szabó Ervin Könyvtár*, H-1371 Budapest, Szabó Ervin tér 1, Postafiók 487 Tel: 330580 (Information Service: 343581)
Ervin Szabó Municipal Library
Chief Librarian: Jenö Kiss

Tiszáninneni Református Egyházkerület Nagykönyvtára, H-3950 Sárospatak, Rákóczy út 1 Tel: Sárospatak 11057
Library of the Cistibiscan Reformed Church District

University of Loránd Eötvös Central Library, see Eötvös Loránd Tudományegyetem Egyetemi Könyvtár

Library Associations

Müvelödési Minisztérium **Levéltári Osztály***,
H-1014 Budapest, Uri u 54-56
National Board of Archives

Magyar Könyvtárosok Egyesülete*, H-1368
Budapest, Postafiók 244 (Located at: H-1056
Budapest V, Molnár u 11)
Association of Hungarian Librarians
Secretary: Dezsö Kovács

Tájekoztatási tudományos társaság*,
Budapest VI, Anker köz 1
Information Science Society
Deputy General Secretary: Miklós Philip

Library Reference Journals

Hungarian Library and Information Science Abstracts (text in English and Russian), Centre for Library Science and Methodology, H-1827 Budapest, Múzeum u 3

Könyvtári figyelo (Library Review); (summaries in English, German and Russian), Centre for Library Science and Methodology, H-1827 Budapest, Múzeum u 3

Magyar könyvtári szakirodalom bibliográfiája (Hungarian Library Literature), (text in Hungarian, titles and summaries in English), Centre for Library Science and Methodology, H-1827 Budapest, Múzeum u 3

Literary Associations and Societies

Magyar Bibliofil társaság*, Budapest VIII, Brody Sándor u 16
Hungarian Society of Bibliophiles

Magyar Irodalomtörténeti Társaság,
Budapest 1052, Pesti Barnabás u 1
Society of Hungarian Literary History
President: Gabor Tolnai
Publications: Irodalomtörténet

Magyar Tudományos Akadémia
Irodalomtudományi Intézete, H-1118
Budapest XI, Ménesi u 11-13
Institute of Literary Studies of the Hungarian Academy of Sciences
Dir: Professor István Sötér
Publications: Irodalomtörténeti Közlemények (quarterly); *Helikon* (quarterly), *Literatura* (quarterly), *Irodalomtörténeti Könyvtár* (monographs), *Irodalomtörténeti Füzetek* (papers); *Neo-Helikon* (quarterly)

Magyar **P E N** Club, H-1051 Budapest V, Vörösmarty tér 1
General Secretary: István Bart
Publications: The Hungarian PEN, Le PEN hongrois (yearly bulletin)

Literary Periodicals

Kortárs (Contemporary), Kultura, H-1389 Budapest, Postafiók 149

Kritica (Critic) (summaries in French, German and Russian), Kultura, H-1389 Budapest, Postafiók 149

Literatura, Magyar Tudományos Akadémia Irodalomtudományi Intézete, H-1118 Budapest XI, Ménesi u 11-13

Magyar muhely (Hungarian Workshop); literary and artistic review (text in Hungarian), Paul Nagy, 139 ave Jean-Jaurès, F-92120 Montrouge, France

New Hungarian Quarterly (text in English), H-1088 Budapest 8, Rákóczi u 17

Literary Prizes

Jozsef **Attila** Prize*
For highly significant work in prose or poetry. Given to writers, poets and critics. Awarded annually. Enquiries to Ministry of Culture of the Hungarian People's Republic, Budapest

S Z O T Prizes*
Awarded annually. Established in 1958 by the Central Council of Hungarian Trade Unions, prizes are awarded to artists, scientists, educators, as well as for literary works. Nominees are people who excel in improving worker-artist contacts and in disseminating knowledge. Selection is by public opinion poll. SZOT is the Central Council of Hungarian Trade Unions. Enquiries to Szakszervezetek Országos Tanácsa DIJ, H-1415 Budapest 6, Dózsa György ut 84/B

Translation Agencies and Associations

Magyar Írok Szövetsége, Budapest VI, Bajza u 18 Tel: 228840
Hungarian Writers' Union
Has a section of Literary Translators

Iceland

General Information

Language: Icelandic (widespread knowledge of Danish and English)
Religion: Lutheran
Population: 230,000
Bank Hours: 0930-1530 Monday-Friday
Shop Hours: 0900-1800 Monday-Friday; open until 2200 Thursday or Friday, open until noon Saturday
Currency: 100 aurar (singular: eyrir) = 1 króna (plural: krónur)
Export/Import Information: Member of the European Free Trade Association. No tariff on books. Sales Tax. No import licences required. No exchange controls for books but they may not be imported on credit
Copyright: UCC, Berne, Florence (see International section)

Book Trade Organizations

Félag Islenzkra Bókaútgefenda, Laufásvegi 12, 101 Reykjavik Tel: (091) 27820
Icelandic Publishers' Association
Chairman: Oliver Steinn Jóhannesson;
General Manager: B Gíslason
Publication: Íslensk bókatídindi

Félag Islenzkra Bókaverzlana*,
Skólavödustig 2, Reykjavik
Icelandic Booksellers' Association
Publication: Bóksalafélag Islands Sjötíu Og Fimm Ára

Innkaupasamband Bóksala HF*,
Sundaborg 9, Reykjavik Tel: 85088 Telex: 2210 heild is
Booksellers' Import Association
Man Dir: Haukur H Gröndal

Rithöfundasamband Islands, PO Box 949, 121 Reykjavik Tel: 91-13190
Writers' Union of Iceland
Chairman: Njördur P Njardvík; *Secretary:* Rannveig G Ágústsdóttir

Book Trade Reference Books and Journals

Book

Bóksalafélag Islands Sjötíu og Fimm Ára (75 years of the Icelandic Booksellers' Association), Félag Islenzkra Bókaverzlana, Skólavödustig 2, Reykjavik; contains addresses of publishers and booksellers

Journals

Bókalisti (Booklist), Borgarbókasafn, Thingholtsstr 29A, Reykjavik

Bokaskara Boksalafelags Islands, Félag Islenskra Bókaútgefenda, Laufasvegi 12, 101 Reykjavik

Bókatídindi, Félag Islenzkra Bókaútgefenda, Laufasvegi 12, 101 Reykjavik (annual list of books published in Iceland)

Islenzk Bókaskrá (The Icelandic National Bibliography), Landsbókasafn Islands, Reykjavik (appears in *Íslensk Bókatídindi*)

Íslensk Bókatídindi (Icelandic Book News), Félag Islenzkra Bókaútgefenda, Laufasvegi 12, 101 Reykjavik

Landsbókasafn Islands Arbok (Year Book), Landsbókasafn Islands, Reykjavik; contains an annual list of Icelandic publications

Publishers

Bókaútgáfa Æskunnar, Laugavegi 56, 101 Reykjavik

Almenna Bókafélagid, Austurstr 18, PO Box 9, 101 Reykjavik Tel: 25544 Cable Add: Bókafélagid Telex: 2046
Man Dir: Brynjólfur Bjarnason; *Editorial:* Eirikur H Finnbogason; *Sales Dir:* Anton Örn Kaernested; *Production:* Kristinn Dagsson; *Rights & Permissions:* Stefania Pétursdóttir
Subjects: General Fiction, Non-fiction, Belles Lettres, Poetry, Biography, History, Secondary Textbooks, Juvenile, Children's
Bookshop: Bókaverzlun Sigfúsar Eymundssonar (BSE), Reykjavik
Book Club: The AB Book Club (BAB)
1981: 47 titles *1982:* 51 titles *Founded:* 1955

Bókaútgáfa Thórhalls **Bjarnarsonar***, Skemmuvegi 4, 200 Kopavogi

Bókaútgáfan **Björk***, Háholti 7, 300 Akranes

Bokaforlag Odds **Björnssonar**, Tryggvabraut 18-20, PO Box 558, 600 Akureyri Tel: 22500 Cable Add: Prentverk
Man Dir: Geir S Björnsson; *Advertising Dir:* Kirstjan Kristjansson
Subjects: General Fiction, Belles Lettres, Poetry, Biography, History, How-to, Music, Art, Philosophy, Reference, Religion, Juveniles, Educational Materials
Book Club: Heima er Bezt Book Club
1981: 12 titles *1982:* 12 titles *Founded:* 1897

Bokas hf*, Adalstr 35, 400 Isafirdi

Bókaútgáfan **Bragi***, Austurstr 17, 101 Reykjavik

Bókaverslun Sigfusar **Eymundssonar***, Austurstr 18, 101 Reykjavik
Subject: Educational Books
Bookshop: At above address

Bókaútgáfa Gudjóns Ó **Gudjónssonar***, Thverholti 13, Reykjavik Tel: 27233

Heimskringla, Laugavegi 18, Reykjavik Tel: 15199
Publications Editor: Thurídur Baxter; *General Manager:* Ólafur Ólafsson

Bókaútgáfan **Helgafell***, Veghúsastíg 7, 101 Reykjavik Tel: 16837

Bókaútgáfan **Hildur***, Skemmuvegi 36, 200 Kópavogi Tel: 76700

Hladbúd hf, subsidiary of Idunn (qv)

Bókaútgáfan **Hlidskjálf***, Ingólfsstr 22, 101 Reykjavik Tel: 17520

Iceland Review, PO Box 93, 121 Reykjavik (Located at: Höfdabakki 9 Tel: 84966 Telex: 2121
Man Dir: Haraldur J Hamar
Associate Company: Saga Publishing Co (qv)
Subjects: The *Iceland Review Series* (all in English) gives an overall picture of the country of Iceland, its culture and developing society; also History, Folklore, Industry (in English); Icelandic Literature in Foreign Translation
1983: 27 titles *Founded:* 1962

Iceland Travel Books, subsidiary of Örn og Örlygur (qv)

Icelandic Cultural Fund, Publishing Department, Menningarsgódur, Skalholtsstig 7, Reykjavik 101 PO Box 1398 Tel: 13652
Man Dir: Hrólfur Halldórsson
Parent Organization: Icelandic Cultural Ministry, Hverfisgata 6, Reykjavik 101
Subjects: Icelandic History and Literature, also selected Classics in translation
Bookshop: Skalholsstig 7, Reykjavik
1981: 20 titles *Founded:* 1928

Idunn, Braedraborgarstíg 16, PO Box 294, 121 Reykjavik Tel: 19156 Cable Add: Publishers, Reykjavik Telex: 2308 publis is
Owner: Valdimar Jóhannsson; *Man Dir:* J P Valdimarsson; *Production:* S Ragnarsson
Subsidiary Company: Hladbud (University Textbooks)
Subjects: General Fiction, Juveniles, Educational, Poetry, Law, Psychology, Philology, History, Natural Sciences, Philosophy, Management, Social Sciences, Art
1982: 130 titles *Founded:* 1945

Ísafoldarprentsmidja hf, Thingholtsstr 5, 101 Reykjavik Tel: 17165

Hid Íslenzka Bókmenntafélag, Thingholtsstr 3, Reykjavik Tel: 21960
President: Sigurdur Líndal; *Chief Executive:* Sverrir Kristinsson
Subjects: History, Art History, Law, Linguistics, Literature, Philosophy, Politics, Psychology, Social Science, Natural Science
Founded: 1816

Snaebjörn **Jonsson** & Co hf (The English Bookshop), Hafnarstr 4 & 9, PO Box 1131, 101 Reykjavik Tel: 11936/13133 Cable Add: Books Reyjavik
Man Dir: Benedikt Kristjánsson
Subjects: All Subjects
Bookshops: The English Bookshop (qv); Bókaverzlun Snaebjarnar, Hafnarstr 4, Reykjavik
Founded: 1927

Bókaútgáfa Thorsteins M **Jónssonar***, Eskihlíd 21, 105 Reykjavik

Kynning Ltd*, PO Box 1238, Reykjavik Tel: 38456, 74153
Subjects: Books on Iceland in general and on special subjects such as volcanoes, geology, geography, history, literature

Leiftur hf*, Höfdatúní 12, 105 Reykjavik Tel: 17554

Bókagerdin **Lilja***, Amtmannsstíg 2b, 101 Reykjavik

Mál og menning, Laugavegi 18, PO Box 392, 121 Reykjavik Tel: 15199
Man Dir: Ólafur Ólafsson; *Editorial:* Thuridur Baxter, Silja Adalsteinsdottir
Subsidiary Company: Heimskringla
Book Club: Mál og menning
Bookshop: At above address
Founded: 1937

Bókaútgáfa **Menningarsjóds og Pjódvinafélagsins**, Skálholtsstígur 7, 101 Reykjavik Tel: 13652
Manager: Hrólfur Halldórsson

Námsgagnastofnun, Tjarnargötu 10, PO Box 5192, 125 Reykjavik Tel: 28088
National Centre for Educational Materials, incorporating Ríkisútgáfa námsbóka (State Educational Publishing Department) and Froeoslumyndasafn ríkisins (State Educational Film Library)
Dir: Ásgeir Gudmundsson; *Sales:* Bragi Gudjónsson; *Production:* Bogi Indridason; *Rights & Permissions:* Eiríkur Grímsson; *Distribution:* Ragnar Gíslason
Subjects: School Textbooks, Educational Materials
Bookshop: At above address
1981: 129 titles *1982:* 146 titles *Founded:* 1937

Bókaútgáfan **Örn og Örlygur** hf+, Sídumúli 11, 170 Reykjavik Tel: 84866 Cable Add: Örn og Örlygur Telex: 2197 Ornice
Owner and Man Dir: Örlygur Hálfdanarson; *Editorial (Book Club):* S J Lúovíksson
Subjects: General Fiction, Belles Lettres, Poetry, Biography, History, How-to, Dictionaries, Reference, Religion, Juveniles, Low- & High-priced Paperbacks, Social Science
Book Club: Bókaklúbbur Arnar og Örlygs (qv)
1981: 50 titles *1982:* 60 titles *Founded:* 1966

Ríkisútgáfa Námsbóka, see Námsgagnastofnun

Rökkur, bókaútgáfan*, Flókagötu 15, Reykjavik Tel: 18768

Saga Publishing Co, PO Box 93, 121 Reykjavik (Located at: Höfdabakki 9) Tel: 84966 Telex: 2121
Man Dir: Haraldur J Hamar
Associate Company: Iceland Review (qv)
Subjects: General (Adults and Juveniles)
Founded: 1971

Setberg*, Freyjugötu 14, 101 Reykjavik Tel: 17667 Cable Add: Setbergpublish
Subjects: History, Juveniles, General Non-fiction, Fiction, Illustrated Juvenile

Bókaútgáfan **Skjaldborg** sf*, Hafnarstr 67, 600 Akureyri Tel: 11024

Skuggsja bókaforlag*, Strandgötu 31, 220 Hafnarfirdi Tel: 50045
Subject: General Fiction

Bókaútgáfan **Snaefell***, Alfaskeidi 58, 220 Hafnarfirdi

Bókaútgáfan **Sudri***, PO Box 1214, Kleppsvegi 2, 105 Reykjavik Tel: 36384

Bókaútgáfan **Thjódsaga**, Thingholtsstr 27, 101 Reykjavik Tel: 13510
Subjects: Icelandic Folklore, General Fiction, Travel, General Science, Juveniles

Bókaútgáfan **Valafell***, Thykkvabae 16, 110 Reykjavik Tel: 84179
Subject: General Fiction

Literary Agents

A/S **Bookman***, Fiolstr 12, DK-1171 Copenhagen K Tel: (01) 145720 Cable Add: Bookman, Copenhagen
This Danish-based company handles rights in Iceland, Denmark, Finland, Norway and Sweden for foreign authors

Sveinbjörn **Jonsson***, Gardastr 21, PO Box 438, Reykjavik Tel: (91) 28110/13206

Book Clubs

The **A B** Book Club (BAB), Austurstr 18, PO Box 9, Reykjavik
Members: 15,500
Owned by: Almenna Bókafélagid (qv)
Founded: 1974

Bókaklúbbur **Arnar og Örlygs**, Sídumúli 11, 105 Reykjavik Tel: 84866 Telex: 2197
Man Dir: Örlygur Hálfdanarson
Owned by: Örn og Örlygur hf (qv)
Miscellaneous: Incorporates activities of former Hraundragni Club

B A B, see AB Book Club

Heima er Bezt Book Club, Tryggvabraut 18-20, PO Box 558, 600 Akureyri
Owned by: Bokaforlag Odds Björnssonar

Hraundragni Book Club, see Arnar og Örlygs

The **Icelandic Libertarians'** Book Club, PO Box 1334, 121 Reykjavik (Located at: Haga v/Hofsvallagoetu, 107 Reykjavik) Tel: (91) 27866
Members: 395
Owned by: The Freedom Association (see also the Icelandic Libertarians' Bookshop, under Major Booksellers)
Specialization: Economics, History, Philosophy, Political Science, Libertarianism
Founded: 1979

Mal og menning, Laugavegi 18, Reykjavik Tel: 15199
Owned by: Mal og menning (qv)

Major Booksellers

The **English Bookshop**, Hafnarstr 4 & 9, PO Box 1131, Reykjavik Tel: (91) 13133, 14281, 11936 Cable Add: Books Reyjavik
Manager: Benedikt Kristjansson
Owned by: Snaebjörn Jónsson & Co hf (qv)

Bókábudin **Helgafell***, Laugavegur 100, Reykjavik
also Njalsgata 64, Reykjavik

The **Icelandic Libertarians'** Bookshop, PO Box 1334, 121 Reykjavik (Located at: Haga v/Hofsvallagoetu, 107 Reykjavik) Tel: (91) 27866 Telex: 2231 toggur is
Specializing in History, Politics, Economics, Philosophy, with special emphasis on the ideology of Libertarianism
Manager: Skafti Hardarson
Owned by: The Freedom Association (see also the Icelandic Libertarians' Book Club)

The **International Bookshop***, Bókaverzlun Sigfúsar Eymundssonar, Austurstr 18, Reykjavik Tel: 19707/16997/32620

Bókaverzlun **Ísafoldar***, Austurstr 10, Reykjavik

Bókabúd **Máls og menningar**, Laugavegi 18, 101 Reykjavik Tel: (91) 24242 Telex: 2265 istrav att MM
Manager: Jónsteinn Haraldsson
Importers and Exporters

Major Libraries

Borgarbókasafn, Thingholtsstr 27 & 29A, Reykjavik
City Library of Reykjavik
City Librarian: Elfa-Björk Gunnarsdóttir

Háskólabókasafn, 101 Reykjavik Tel: 25088 Telex: 2307 isinfo
University Library
Head Librarian: Einar Sigurdsson
Publication: Annual Report

Landsbókasafn Islands, Reykjavik Tel: 13375 (Director); 16864 (Staff)
National Library of Iceland
Librarian: Dr Finnbogi Gudmundsson
Publications: Landsbókasafn Islands Arbók (Yearbook); *Islenzk Bókaskrá* (Icelandic National Bibliography); *Handritasafn Landsbókasafns* (Catalogue of Manuscripts)

Thjodskjalasafn (National Archives)*, Safnahús, Reykjavik

University Library, see Háskólabókasafn

Library Associations

Bókavardafélag Islands*, Box 7050, 127 Reykjavik
Icelandic Library Association
President: Sigrun K Hannesdóttir
Secretary: Margrét Loftsdóttir
Publications: Fregnir (Newsletter) and *Bókasafnid* (The Library)

Felag bokavarda i islenskum rannsoknarbokasofnum, Kennarahaskoli Islands, v/Stakkahlid, 105 Reykjavik Tel: 32290
Society of Librarians in Icelandic Research Libraries
Executive Secretary Reference: Thorhildur Sigurdardottir

Library Reference Journal

Fregnir (Newsletter), Bókavardafélag Islands, Box 7050, 127 Reykjavik

Literary Associations and Societies

Íslenzka bókmenntafélag, Thingholtsstr 3, Reykjavik
Icelandic Literary Society
President: Sigurdur Lindal
Publication: Annual Journal, Skirnir

International P E N Centre, Hagamel 17, PO Box 7103, R-7 Reykjavik
Secretary: Hrafn Gunnlaugssson

Literary Periodical

Skirnir, Íslenszka bókmenntafélag, Thingholtsstr 3, Reykjavik

India

General Information

Language: Hindi and English are used for official purposes. Fourteen other languages are accorded recognition by the constitution, including Sanskrit which is not now spoken. Generally each administrative state includes speakers of a particular major language. In all, over 1500 languages and dialects are spoken in India
Religion: Predominantly Hindu
Population: 638 million
Literacy Rate (1971): 33.4% (59.9% of urban population, 26.4% rural)
Bank Hours: 1000-1400 (1100-1500 Bombay) Monday-Friday; 1000-1200 Saturday (1100-1300 Bombay)
Shop Hours: Delhi: 0930-1930; Calcutta and Bombay: 1000-1830; Madras: 0900-1930. All effective Monday-Saturday, some open Sunday. Many close 2 hours for lunch
Currency: 100 paise = 1 rupee
Export/Import Information: No tariff on books but advertising matter is dutied. Import licences required. Educational books may be imported by booksellers under open general licence. Exchange transactions restricted.
Copyright: UCC, Berne, Buenos Aires (see International section)

Book Trade Organizations

Ahmedabad Publishers' & Booksellers' Association, 47 Gandhi Rd, Ahmedabad 380001 Tel: 366917
President: C J Modi

Akhil Bhartiya Hindi Prakashak Sangh*, A2/1 Krishan Nagar, Delhi 110051
President: Dayanand Varma; *General Secretary:* Mishrilal Sharma

All India Booksellers' & Publishers' Association*, 17-L Connaught Circus, PO Box 328, New Delhi 110001 Tel: 42166
President: A N Varma

Assam Publishers' & Booksellers' Association*, Lawyers Book Stall, Gauhati

Authors' Guild of India*, C-44 Gulmohar Park, New Delhi 110049
Secretary: D R Mankekar
Publication: The Indian Author

Bihar Pustak Vyayasayi Sangh*, Bharati Bhawan, Govind Mitra Rd, Patna 4
Secretary: A Pandey

Bombay Booksellers' and Publishers' Association, 25 6th Floor Building No 3, Navjivan Co-op Housing Society Ltd, Dr Bhadkamkar Marg, Bombay 400008 Tel: 398691
Honorary Secretary: C P Gupta; *Executive Secretary:* U S Manikeri

Booksellers' and Publishers' Association of South India, c/o Higginbothams Ltd, 814 Anna Salai, Madras 600002 Tel: 86556/7

Chandigarh Booksellers' Association*, SCO No 3 Sector 17-E, Chandigarh Tel: 23594
President: V S Puri

Delhi State Booksellers' and Publishers' Association, c/o The Students' Stores, Kashmere Gate, PO Box 1511, Delhi 110006 Tel: 227088/225716
President: Devendra Sharma; *Honorary Secretary:* Bhupinder Chowdhri

Educational Publishers' Association*, 2607 Amir Chand Marg, New Delhi 110006

Federation of Indian Publishers, Federation House, 18/1-C Institutional Area, JNU Rd, New Delhi 110067 Tel: 654847
President: Narendra Kumar; *Executive Secretary:* R K Dhingra; *Honorary General Secretary:* S K Bhatia

Federation of Booksellers and Publishers Association in Gujarat*, PO Box 334 GPO, Ahmedabad 380001
Honorary Secretary: P D Shevade

Federation of Publishers and Booksellers Associations in India, 1st Floor, 4833/24 Govind Lane, Ansari Rd, New Delhi 110002 Tel: 272845
President: Sunil Sachdev; *Honorary Secretary:* Devendra Sharma
Publications include: Recent Indian Books; FPBA Newsletter; Directory of Members; Book Industry in India Problems & Prospects (1980); *Publishing as a Medium of Communication with the Third World* by Tarzie Vittachie (UNICEF) (1982)

Gujarat State English Language Booksellers' Association, Academic Book Centre, 10 Walkeshwar, Ambawadi, Ahmedabad 380015 Tel: 837883
President: R N Shah

The **Gujarat Textbook** Publishers' Association*, Balgovind Kuberdas & Co, Gandhi Rd, Ahmedabad

Himachal Publishers' & Booksellers' Association*, Goel Book Depot, Palampur Tel: 43151
President: H K S Goel

The **Hyderabad** & Secunderabad Publishers' & Booksellers' Association*, c/o Sri Satyanarayana Book House, Gowligudachaman, Hyderabad (AP)
Secretary: K Satya Narayana

Karnataka Publishers' and Booksellers' Association*, 504 Avenue Rd, Bangalore 560002

Kerala Publishers & Booksellers Association*, Paico Buildings, Jew St, Cochin 682011 Tel: 34068
President: D C Kizhakemuri, D C Books, Kottayam 686001 Tel: 3114/8214/3226; *Secretary:* E K Sekhar, Venus Press, Konni 689691

Lanka Booksellers' Association*, Kohinoor Bldgs, University Rd, Varanasi Tel: 62771
President: Lalchand Mankhand

Meerut Publishers' Association*, c/o Rastogi Publications, Shivaji Rd, Meerut 250002, Uttar Pradesh

Poona Booksellers' & Publishers' Association*, Hindustan Sahitya, 309 Shaniwar Peth, Poona 30

Publishers' & Booksellers' Association of Andhra Pradesh*, Sree Venkateswara Book Depot, Main Rd, Guntur 522003
Secretary: P Narasimha Rao

Publishers' and Booksellers' Association of Bengal*, 93 Mahatma Gandhi Rd, Calcutta 700007
Publication: Granthajagat

Publishers' and Booksellers' Guild*, 5-A Bhawani Dutta Lane, PO Box 12341, Calcutta 700073 Tel: 311541
President: N D Mehra; *Dir:* B K Dhur

Publishers' Association of South India*, 1 Sunkurama Chetty St, Madras 600001 Tel: 29402
President: T V S Mani

Punjabi Publishers' Association*, 354 Purani Kutchery, Jullundur City

Rajasthan Pustak Vyavasayee Sangh*, SMS Highway, Jaipur 3
President: J L Jasoria

Standard Book Numbering Agency, Ministry of Education & Culture (Department of Education), Raja Rammohun Roy National Educational Resources Centre, 1 W-3 C R Barracks, Kasturba Gandhi Marg, New Delhi 110001 Tel: 381739
ISBN Administrator: Mrs S Narasimhan

Book Trade Reference Books and Journals

Books

American Book Trade in India; a directory of wholesale and retail booksellers, Asian Bookmarket Information Service, 73-47-255th St, Glen Oaks, New York 11004, USA

Bookdealers in India; a directory of antiquarian booksellers in Bangladesh, Bhutan, India, Nepal, Pakistan and Sri Lanka, Sheppard Press Ltd, PO Box 42, Russell Chambers, Covent Garden, London WC2E 8AX, UK

Directory of Book Trade in India, National Guide Books Syndicate, 5c/54 Rohtak Rd, New Delhi 110005

Directory of Foreign Book Trade in India, Lord International, 19 Netaji Subhash Marg, Daryaganj, New Delhi 110002

Indian Books, Indian Bibliographic Centre, 236 Kot Kishan Chand, Jullundur 4, Punjab (books in English only) (annual)

Indian Books; an annual bibliography, Researchco Publications, 1865 Trinagar, Delhi 35 (books in English only) (annual)

Indian Books in Print, Indian Bibliographies Bureau, 2153/2 Fountain, Delhi 6

Indian Publishers' Directory, Mukherjee & Co Pvt Ltd, 2 Bankim Chatterjee St, Calcutta 700012

Journals

American and British Book News, Kunnuparampil P Punnoose, 6/77 WEA Karol Bagh, New Delhi 110005

Asian Literary Market Review, Kunnuparampil Bldgs, Kurichy 686549, Kottayam District, Kerala (English, bi-monthly)

BEPI; an annual bibliography of English publications in India, DKF Trust, 74-D Anand Nagar, Delhi 110035

Book Review Supplement, Delhi Library Association, PO Box 1270, c/o Hardayal (Hardinge) Public Library, Queen's Garden, Delhi 110006

Book Reviews in Public Administration, Indian Institute of Public Administration, Indraprastha Estate, Ring Rd, New Delhi 110001

Current Bulletin, Current Books, PO Box 212, Kottayam 686001

Directory of Members, Federation of Publishers and Booksellers Associations in India, 1st Floor, 4833/24 Govind Lane, Ansari Rd, New Delhi 110002

FPBA Newsletter, Federation of Publishers and Booksellers Associations in India, 1st Floor, 4833/24 Govind Lane, Ansari Rd, New Delhi 110002

Granthajagat, Publishers' and Booksellers' Association of Bengal, 93 Mahatma Gandhi Rd, Calcutta 700007

Indian Book Chronicle, Vivek Trust, G-11 Hauz Khas Market, New Delhi 110016. Book news and reviews (fortnightly)

Indian Book Industry, Sterling Publishers Pvt Ltd, AB-9 Safdarjang Enclave, New Delhi 110029

Indian Books; an information leaflet, Mukherjee Library, 1 Gopi Mohan Dutta Lane, Calcutta 700003

Indian National Bibliography, Central Reference Library, c/o National Library, Belvedere, Calcutta 27

Indian Publisher and Bookseller, Popular Book Depot, Dr Bhadkamkar Rd, Bombay 400007

Kerala Publisher, Kunnuparampil Bldgs, Kurichy 686549, Kottayam District, Kerala (bilingual, bi-monthly)

Paperbound Books, 6/77 WEA Karol Bagh, New Delhi 110005 (quarterly)

Publishing News, D K Agencies, 74-D Inderlok, Old Rohtak Rd, Delhi 110035

Pustak Parichaya (text in Hindi), 2/35 Ansari Rd, Daryaganj, Delhi 6

Recent Indian Books, Federation of Publishers and Booksellers Associations in India, 1st Floor, 4833/24 Govind Lane, Ansari Rd, New Delhi 110002

Publishers

A U Press & Publications+, Andhra University, Visakhapatnam 530003 Tel: 64871 ext 227
Registrar, Rights & Permissions: A U Waltair
Subjects: Languages, Literature, Humanities, Sciences
1981: 8 titles *1982:* 10 titles *Founded:* 1926

Aadiesh Book Depot, 7A-29 WEA Karol Bagh, New Delhi 110005 Tel: 564103/275365
Chief Executive: Aadiesh Kumar Jain
Imprint: Nalanda Books
Subject: Dictionaries
Bookshop: 4123 Nai Sarak, Delhi 110006

Abhinav Publications, E-37 Hauz Khas, New Delhi 110016
Dir: Shakti Malik
Subjects: Indian Art & Archaeology, Indology, Humanities, Literature, Social Sciences, Criminology, Politics
Founded: 1970

Abhishek Publications, SCO 57-58-59, Sector 17-C, Chandigarh 160017
Chief Executive, Production, Publicity: S L M Prachand; *Editorial:* Mrs Geeta Mehndiratta; *Sales, Rights & Permissions:* Bharat Bhushan
Associate Company: Nirjhar Prakashan, 3625 Sector 23-D, Chandigarh 160023
Subjects: History, Politics, Philosophy, General
1981: 2 titles *Founded:* 1977

The **Academic Press**, Old Subzi Mandi, Gurgaon, Haryana 122001 Tel: 2205
Editorial: Satya Prakash; *Sales:* Kapil Jain; *Publicity:* Pankaj Jain; *Production, Rights & Permissions:* Sanjeev Jain
Subjects: Social Sciences, Humanities
1981: 5 titles *1982:* 6 titles *Founded:* 1968

Academic Publishers, 5-A Bhawani Dutta Lane, PO Box 12341, Calcutta 700073 Tel: 340936/324697 Cable Add: Acabooks
Man Dir: Bimal Kumar Dhur; *Sales Dir:* Anit Talukdar; *Rights & Permissions:* L K Ghosh
Branch Off: Shantimohun House, I-1/16 Ansari Rd, New Delhi 110002
Subjects: Accountancy, Commerce, Management, Medicine, Research, University Textbooks
Founded: 1958

Academy of Comparative Philosophy & Religion*, Guruder Mandir, Hindwadi, Belgaum 590011 Tel: 22231
Chief Executive, Production, Publicity: J V Parulekar; *Editorial:* K D Tangol; *Sales:* G V Dharwadkar
Subjects: Philosophy, Religion, Mysticism, Morals
1981: 1 title *Founded:* 1966

Academy of Islamic Research and Publications, PO Box 119, Lucknow 226007 (Located at: Tagore Marg, Nadwa, Lucknow) Tel: 42948 Cable Add: Nadwi
President, Rights & Permissions: S Abdul Hasan Ali Nadwi; *Chief Executive, Editorial:* S Mohammad Rabey Nadwi; *Manager, Production:* Mohammad Ghiyathuddin Nadwi; *Sales:* Zakiuddin Nadwi; *Publicity:* S M Ghuran Nadwi
Branch Off: Karachi, Pakistan
Subjects: Islamic Literature, History, Current Affairs, Hadith and Quran
1981: 23 titles *1982:* 23 titles *Founded:* 1959

Directorate of **Adult** Education*, 34 Community Centre, Basant Lok, Vasant Vihar, New Delhi 110057 Tel: 671890/674860 Cable Add: Adultedu
Chief Executive: Miss H K Singh
Subject: Adult Education
Founded: 1978

Advaita Ashrama, 5 Dehi Entally Rd, Calcutta 700014 Tel: 44-2898 Cable Add: Vedanta
Subjects: Religion, Philosophy, Yoga, Vedanta, Indian Culture, Education
1982: 20 titles

Affiliated East-West Press Pvt Ltd*, 92 Montieth Rd, Madras 600008 Tel: 812258 Cable Add: Knowledge
Man Dir: K S Padmanabhan; *Editorial Dir:* Kamal Malik
Subjects: Science, Engineering, Technology, Humanities, Social Sciences, Low-priced Reprints of US and British Textbooks
Founded: 1962

Agam Kala Prakashan*, 34 Community Centre, Ashok Vihar, Delhi 110052 Tel: 713395
Editorial, Sales, Publicity, Rights & Permissions: Agam Prasad; *Production:* A K Bhargava
Associate Company: Agam Prakashan
Subjects: Indian Art, Archaeology, Culture
Founded: 1977

Agricole Publishing Academy+, D-76 Panchsheel Enclave, New Delhi 110017
Partners: Mrs L Jain, S C Jain; *Chief Development Officer:* T C Jain
Subjects: Agricultural Sciences, Technology, Behavioural Sciences, Economics, Industry, Rural Development, Sociology
Bookshop: 208 Shopping Complex, Defence Colony Flyover, New Delhi 110024
1982: 28 titles *1983:* 30 titles *Founded:* 1978

Ahlvwalia Book Depot*, PO Box 2507, New Delhi 110005 (Located at: 9953-4 New Rohtak Rd, New Delhi)
Partners: J N Ahlvwalia, R K Ahlvwalia
Subject: Urdu Literature (Fiction and Non-fiction)
Founded: 1954

Ajanta Books International, 1 UB Jawahar Nagar, Bungalow Rd, Delhi 110007
Man Dir, Editorial, Sales, Production: S Balwant
Associate Company: Ajanta Publications

(India) (qv)
Subjects: Social Sciences, Ancient Indian History, Art, Archaeology, Sanskrit Language and Literature, Philosophy, Politics, Management, English and Indian Literature, Linguistics, Yoga, Marxism, Aesthetics
Bookshop: Ajanta Books International
1981-82: 40 titles *Founded:* 1975
Miscellaneous: Also Literary Agent (qv)

Ajanta Publications (India)*, PO Box 2194, Malkaganj, Delhi 110007
Chief Executives: Jasbir Kaur, Jagdish Singh; *Editorial, Production, Publicity, Rights & Permissions:* S Balwant (Literary Agents)
Orders to: Ajanta Books International, 1-UB Jawahar Nagar, Bungalow Rd, Delhi 110007
Subsidiary Company: Thakshila Hard Bound (at above address)
Associate Company: Ajanta Books International (qv)
Subjects: Indology, Indian Literature, Philosophy, Hinduism, Archaeology, Art, Religion, Management, Public Administration, Sociology, Political Science, Anthropology, Linguistics, English Language and Literature
Bookshop: Ajanta Books International (at above address)
Founded: 1975

Akhila Bharaliya Sanskrit Parishad*, Mahatma Gandhi Marg, Hazratganj, Lucknow 226001 Tel: 43962
Subjects: Sanskrit and Indology, based on Sanskrit, Pali and Psakrita
Founded: 1951

Alekh Prakashan*, V-8 Navin Shahdara, Delhi 110032 Tel: 204331
Chief Executive: Umesh Chand
Subjects: Literature, Journalism, Linguistics (all in Hindi & English), General Science, Psychology, Social Science, Botany, Wildlife, Yoga
Founded: 1976

Allied Publishers Private Ltd*, 15 J N Heredia Marg, Ballard Estate, Bombay 400038 Tel: 261959 Cable Add: Folio
Man Dir: R N Sachdev; *Editorial, Rights & Permissions:* A Shukla; *Production:* Ravi Sachdev; *Publicity:* S Banerjee
Branch Offs: 13-14 Asaf Ali Rd, New Delhi 110002; 17 Chittaranjan Ave, Calcutta 700072; 150 B-6 Mount Rd, Madras 600002; Jayadeva Hostel Bldg, 5th Main Rd, Gandhinagar, Bangalore 500009
Subjects: General Fiction, Belles Lettres, Art, History, Philosophy, Education, How-to, Psychology, Law, Social, Political & General Science & Technology
Founded: 1934

Alpha-Beta Publications Ltd*, 55-1 College St, 2nd Floor, Calcutta 700012

Amar Prakashan+, A1-139B Lawrence Rd, Delhi 110035 Tel: 7113182 Cable Add: Amarpra
Chief Executive: H S Juneja; *Editorial:* Surjeet Anand; *Sales:* Hardeep Singh; *Publicity:* Sutinder Kaur; *Production:* Maheep Singh; *Rights & Permissions:* Miss Sukhwinder
Subjects: Sociology, History, Political Science, Indology
1982: 12 titles *Founded:* 1977

Amarko Book Agency*, B-42 Amar Colony, Lajpat Nagar, New Delhi 110024
Man Dir, Production, Publicity, Rights & Permissions: V N Bhardwaj; *Sales:* Ashok Bhardwaj
Subjects: History, Philosophy, Religion
Founded: 1973

Ambika Publications*, B-1/598 Janak Puri, New Delhi 110058 Tel: 591072 Cable Add: Ambika
Man Dir, Editorial, Rights & Permissions: P P Anand; *Sales:* Ms Manmeet Maini; *Production:* Suhas Nimbalkar; *Publicity:* Ms Nirdosh Anand
Associate Companies: Arpan International (at above address); Tagore Trading Co, ED 54 Tagore Gardens, New Delhi 110027
Branch Off: The Mall, Solan 173212, Western Himalayas
Subjects: Sociology, Politics, Anthropology, Ancient and Medieval History, Art, Religion, Buddhism, Tibetan Studies, Management
Bookshop: Himachal Book House, Mayur Complex, The Mall, Solan 173212, Western Himalayas Tel: 736
Founded: 1977

Amerind Publishing Co (P) Ltd, subsidiary of Oxford & IBH Publishing Co (qv)

Amina Book Stall*, Post Office Rd, Trichur 680001 Tel: 23387/23254
Chief Executive: Haji K B Aboobacker
Associate Company: Amina Printers (at above address)
Subjects: Humanities, Social Science, Fiction, Islamic Literature in Malayalam
Founded: 1948

Amudha Nilayam Ltd*, PO Box 674, Madras 600014 (Located at: 46 Royapettah High Rd, Madras) Tel: 841343
Man Dir: K V Jagannathan
Subjects: Tamil Classics, Literature, Fiction, Criticism
1981: 5 titles *Founded:* 1949

Anand Paperbacks, an imprint of Orient Paperbacks (qv)

Ananda Ashram, see Satya Press

Ankur Publishing House*, Uphaar Cinema Bldg, Green Park Extension, New Delhi 110016 Tel: 664611
Man Dir: Mrs Seema Mukerjee
Associate Company: Sanjay Composers and Printers (at above address)
Subjects: Politics, Science, Literature
Founded: 1976

Antiquarian Book House*, 7 Malka Ganj, Delhi 110007 Tel: 236080
Proprietor, Man Dir: Gajendra Singh
Parent Company: Bharatiya Publishing House (qv)
Subjects: Antiquarian, Indian History, Art, Architecture, Archaeology, Religion and Philosophy, Travel, Linguistics, Reference, Social Sciences
Founded: 1982

Archaeological Survey of India*, Janpath, New Delhi 110001 Tel: 382121 Cable Add: Archaeology
Editorial: H Sarkar; *Sales:* S R Varma
Subjects: Archaeology, Epigraphy, etc

Arnold-Heinemann Publishers (India) Pvt Ltd, AB-9 Safdarjang Enclave, New Delhi 110029 Tel: 667886 Cable Add: Heinemann
Man Dir: G A Vazirani; *Editorial, Rights & Permissions:* Ms Rashmi Bhushan; *Accounts:* Bhagwan Singh; *Production:* Mukesh Vazirani; *Publicity:* Ms Rani Roy; *Sales:* R K Rana
Associate Companies: Edward Arnold (Publishers) Ltd, UK (qv); Heinemann Educational Books Ltd, UK (qv)
Imprints: Mayfair Paperbacks, Sanskriti, Zebra Books for Children
Subjects: Art, General Fiction, Belles Lettres, Poetry, Philosophy, Religion, Reference, Literary Criticism, Medicine, Engineering, Social Science, Political Science, University, Secondary & Primary Textbooks, Low-priced Paperbacks
Founded: 1969

Ashish Publishing House*, 8/81 Punjabi Bagh, New Delhi 110026 Tel: 500581
Editorial: S B Nangia; *Sales:* Gopal Sharma
Subjects: History, Political Science, Economics, Education, Biography, Public Administration, Sociology, Rural Development

Asia Publishing Co*, A-132 College St Market, Calcutta 700007 Tel: 342386
Editorial: Gita Dutta; *Sales:* Ashim Mukherjee
Subject: Fiction
Founded: 1954

Asia Publishing House (P) Ltd*, Calicut St, Ballard Estate, Bombay 400038
Tel: 262631/3 Cable Add: Booklore
Chairman, Man Dir: Ananda Jaisingh; *Editorial Consultant:* Homi Vakeel
Branch Offs in India: 67 Ganesh Chandra Ave, Calcutta 700013; Indra Palace, Connaught Circus, New Delhi 110001; 199 Mount Rd, Madras 600002; 18 Purana Quilla, Lucknow 226001
Branch Off outside India: 141 East 44th St, New York, NY 10017, USA
Subjects: General Fiction, Belles Lettres, Poetry, Biography, History, Music, Art, Philosophy, Reference, Religion, Low- & High-priced Paperbacks, Medicine, Psychology, Engineering, General & Social Science, University Textbooks, Educational Materials, Business Studies
Founded: 1961
Miscellaneous: Firm is an imprint of Jaisingh & Mehta Publishers Pvt Ltd (qv)

Asian Educational Services, C-2/15 SDA, PO Box 4534, New Delhi 110016
Tel: 633325 Cable Add: Asia-Books New Delhi 110016
Chief Executive: Jagdish Jetley; *Production:* Mrs S Jetley; *Editorial, Rights & Permissions, Publicity:* A N Arora
Subjects: Ancient Indian History and Culture, South Indian History and Culture, Religion, Philosophy, Sociology, Literature, Linguistics, Current Affairs, Indian Language Dictionaries and Grammars
1981: 20 titles *1982:* 30 titles *Founded:* 1973

Asian Literary Market Review, Kunnuparampil Bldgs, Kurichy 686549, Kottayam District, Kerala Tel: (04826) 470
Man Dir, Editorial, Sales, Production, Rights & Permissions: K P Punnoose; *Publicity:* Jaffe Punnoose
Parent Company: K P Punnoose Communications Co (qv under Literary Agents)
Subject: Book Trade
1981: 3 titles *Founded:* 1975

Asian Publishers, an imprint of Sterling Publishers Pvt Ltd (qv)

Asian Publishers, PO Box 205, 85-C New Mandi, Muzaffarnagar, Uttar Pradesh 251001 Tel: 3775
Man Dir, Publicity: Mittal Ved Prakash; *Sales:* Mittal Satya Prakash; *Production:* Mittal Dinesh Prakash
Subsidiary Company: Kalanidhi Printing Press (at above address)
Subjects: Technical, Scientific, Agricultural
Bookshop: Mittal & Company (at above address)
Founded: 1971

Asian Trading Corporation, PO Box 2587, Bangalore 560025 (Located at: St Thomas Building, 150 Brigade Rd, Bangalore) Tel: 51807 Cable Add: Paspin
Chief Executive: F M Pais; *Sales:* P Travers
Associate Company: Jyothi Book House, 156 Brigade Rd, Bangalore 560025
Subjects: Religion, Theology, Philosophy, Counselling, Sociology, Psychology, Mass

Media Communication, Indology
Founded: 1946

Associated Publishing House, New Market, Karol Bagh, New Delhi 110005 Tel: 563069
Man Dir, Sales: Ravinder K Paul; *Editorial, Production Dir:* Ashok K Paul; *Publicity Dir, Rights & Permissions:* Sharda Paul
Subjects: General, Philosophy, Religion, Belles Lettres, Poetry, History, Art, Reference, Social Science, Business, Public Administration, Economics, Planning, Reprints
Founded: 1966

Atma Ram & Sons+, Kashmere Gate, PO Box 1429, Delhi 110006
Tel: 223092/228159 Cable Add: Books Delhi 6
Man Dir, Publicity, Rights & Permissions: Ish Kumar Puri; *Editorial, Production:* Sushil Kumar Puri; *Sales:* Ashutosh Pury
Branch Off: 17 Ashok Marg, Lucknow
Subjects: Belles Lettres, Art, History, Philosophy, Religion, Education, Reference, How-to, Juveniles, Medicine, Engineering, Social Science, Science & Technology, Paperbacks, Textbooks
Bookshop: See under Major Booksellers
1981: 49 titles *1982:* 48 titles *Founded:* 1909

Sri **Aurobindo** Books Distribution Agency (SABDA), Sri Aurobindo Ashram, Pondicherry 605002 Tel: 4980 Cable Add: Sabda
Man Dir: B Poddar; *Sales:* Mrs Sunanda Poddar; *Rights & Permissions:* Sri Harikant Patel
Branch Off: 'Sahakar' B Rd, Bombay 400020
Subjects: Yoga, Philosophy, Religion, Education, History, Social & Political Science (English, French, German, Sanskrit etc)
Bookshops: 9B rue de la Marine; 2 rue de la Caserne (both in Pondicherry)
1981: 50 titles *1982:* 64 titles *Founded:* 1952

Avinash Reference Publications*, 50 Ruikar Colony, Kolhapur, Maharashtra 416005 Tel: 3350
Chief Editor: Dr J A Naik; *Manager:* Mrs Sunanda Naik
Associate Company: Avinash Publications (at above address)
Subjects: Research Documents and Directories on Foreign Policy, Foreign Trade, International Defence, Indian Economics, Sociology and Agriculture
Founded: 1978

B R Publishing Corporation*, 461 Vivekananda Nagar, Delhi 110035 Tel: 278368 Cable Add: Deekay Pub
Chief Executive, Editorial, Production: I C Mittal; *Sales, Rights & Permissions:* S K Bhatia; *Publicity:* Praveen Mitaal
Orders to: D K Publishers' Distributors, 1 Ansari Rd, New Delhi 110002
Parent Company: D K Publishers' Distributors (qv under Major Booksellers)
Associate Companies: D K Publications (qv); Neeraj Publishing House (qv)
Subjects: Art, Archaeology, History, Social Sciences, Anthropology
1981: 10 titles *Founded:* 1974

K P **Bagchi** & Co+, 286 B B Ganguli St, Calcutta 700012, West Bengal Tel: 267474
Editorial, Chief Executive, Publicity, Rights & Permissions: P K Bagchi; *Editorial, Sales, Production:* K K Bagchi
Branch Off: I-1698 C R Park, New Delhi 110019 Tel: 644025
Subjects: Anthropology, History, Economics, Political Science, Indology, Sociology, Language and Literature
1982: 25 titles *1983:* 14 titles *Founded:* 1972

Baha'i Publishing Trust, PO Box 19, New Delhi 110001 (Located at: Baha'i House, 6 Canning Rd, New Delhi 110001) Tel: 389326/387004 Cable Add: Bahaifaith Telex: 0314881 Nsa In
Man Dir, Production, Rights & Permissions: D Vahedi; *Editorial, Sales, Publicity:* A Baram
Parent Company: National Spiritual Assembly of the Baha'is of India (at the above address)
Subject: The Baha'i Religion
1983: 90 titles *Founded:* 1954

The **Bangalore** Printing & Publishing Co Ltd, 88 Mysore Rd, PO Box 1807, Bangalore 560018, Karnataka Tel: 601638/601027 Cable Add: Mudrashala
Man Dir: H C Ramanna
Branch Off: The Bangalore Press, Statue Sq, Mysore
Subjects: Biography, Philosophy, Religion, Psychology, Social Science, University, Secondary & Primary Textbooks, Agriculture, Nutrition, Fiction (in English and Kannada languages)
Bookshop: Bangalore Press Agencies, Avenue Rd, Bangalore 2
1981: 25 titles *Founded:* 1916

Bani Mandir*, New Market, Dibrugarh, Assam 786001 Tel: 1255 Cable Add: Bani Mandir
Chief Executive: Chandra Kanta Hazarika; *Editorial, Rights & Permissions:* Surjya Kanta Hazarika; *Sales:* Ujjal Kumar Hazarika; *Publicity:* Utpal Kumar Hazarika
Subjects: Fiction, Criticism, School and College Textbooks, Reference Books
Founded: 1949

Bani Publications, 30 Pataldanga St, Calcutta 700009 Tel: 352901
Chief Executive: Sakti Sadan Bhattacharyya; *Editorial:* Sivasadhan Bhattacharyya; *Sales:* S R Mukherjee
Subject: Oriental & Indological Studies

Bansal & Co, K-16 Naveen Shahdara, Delhi 110032 Tel: 204292
Chief Executive: R S Bansal; *Editorial, Sales, Production, Publicity, Rights & Permissions:* Arun Bansal
Subjects: Bibliography, Indology, Hindi Literature in English (Series of 15 volumes, *Contours and Landmarks in Hindi Literature*)
Founded: 1959

Better Yourself Books, 28-B Chatham Lines, Allahabad 211002, Uttar Pradesh Tel: 53728
Man Dir: Fr Abraham Nedumpuram; *Publicity:* Arnold K
Parent Company: Saint Paul Publications (qv)
Subjects: Home Life, Self-improvement, Biography, Moral Science, Indology, Fiction, Practical Psychology, Sex Education, Media Education
1981: 46 titles *Founded:* 1954

Bhaimi Prakashan*, 537 Lajpat Rai Market, Delhi 110006 Tel: 269032
Editorial: P K Bhatia; *Sales:* Bhimsen Shastri
Subject: Sanskrit Language and Literature

Bhaktivedanta Book Trust*, Hare Krishna Land, Juhu, Bombay 400049 Tel: 566860 Cable Add: Iskcon Telex: 114964 Iskn In
Chief Executive: Poornabrahma Das; *Editorial:* Gopal Krishna Das; *Sales:* N Narayan
Subject: Religion

Bharat-Bharati*, B-28/15 Durgakund, Varanasi 5
Owner: Suresh Pandey; *Man Dir:* Ganga Nath Pandey
Subjects: Poetry, History, Music, Art, Philosophy, Religion, Oriental & Indian Studies
Founded: 1968

Bharat Law House, 15 Mahatma Gandhi Marg, Allahabad 211001 Tel: 3797
Chief Executive, Production: D C Puliani; *Sales:* Ashok Puliani; *Editorial:* Ravi Puliani; *Publicity:* Mahesh Puliani
Subject: Law
1981: 8 titles *1982:* 5 titles *Founded:* 1957

Bharati Sahitya Sadan Sales*, 30-90 Connaught Circus, New Delhi 110001 Tel: 343557
Editorial: Padmesh Datt; *Sales:* Yogendra Datt
Subject: Hindi Literature
Founded: 1946

Bharatiya Jnanpith*, B-45/47 Connaught Pl, New Delhi 110001 Tel: 322294 Cable Add: Jnanpith
Dir, Rights & Permissions: Lakshmi Chandra Jain; *Sales, Production, Publicity:* Dr Gulab Chandra Jain
Branch Off: Durgakunda, Varanasi 221001
Subjects: Rare and unpublished texts of Indology (in Sanskrit, Pali, Prakrit, Apbhramsha, Kannada and Tamil, with their translations), Hindi Literature (in original, as well as translations from Indian languages)
Founded: 1944

Bharatiya Publishing House, 42-43 UB Jawaharnagar, Delhi 110007 Tel: 236080/220274
Chief Executive, Production, Publicity: Gajendra Singh; *Sales:* Digvijay Singh
Subsidiary Company: Antiquarian Book House (qv)
Branch Off: B-9/45, Pilkhana, Sonarpura, Varanasi
Subjects: Ancient Indian History, Art, Architecture, Archaeology, Religion, Philosophy, Jainism, Yoga, Sanskrit
Founded: 1960

Bharatiya Vidya Bhavan, PO Box 4057, Munshi Sadan, Kulapati K M Munshi Marg, Bombay 400007 Tel: 351461 Cable Add: Bhavidya
Executive Secretary, Editorial, Rights & Permissions: S Ramakrishnan; *Sales:* V A Madhavan; *Production:* C K Venkataraman
Branch Offs: Ahmedabad, Amritsar, Bangalore, Baroda, Bhopal, Bhubaneswar, Calcutta, Chandigarh, Coimbatore, Dakor, Delhi, Ernakulam, Guntur, Hyderabad, Jammu, Jamnagar, Kakinada, Kanpur, Kodaikanal, Kurkunda, Madras, Madurai, Mangalore, Mukundgarh, Nagpur, New Delhi, Patna, Rajmundry, Shillong, Trichur, Varanasi, Visakhapatnam (all in India); 4a Castle Town Rd, London W14 9HQ, UK; 65-09 Queens Blvd, Woodside, NY 11377, USA
Subjects: History, Philosophy, Religion, Art, Literature, Culture, Biography, Gita, Vedas, Upanishads, Gandhiana, Mythology, Fiction, Sociology
Founded: 1938

Bihar Hindi Granth Akademi*, Sammelan Bhawan, Kadamkuan, Patna 800003 Tel: 50390
Chairman: Prof Devendra Nath Sharma; *Dir, Rights & Permissions:* Prof Damodar Thakur; *Editorial:* Dr Ramdeo Tripathy; *Sales, Production, Publicity:* Thakur Y N Singh
Subjects: Science and Humanities at University level (in Hindi)
Founded: 1970

The **Bihar State** Textbook Publishing Corporation Ltd*, Budh Marg, Patna 800001 Tel: 21975

Chief Executive: D P Chaudhary; *Editorial:* D N Jha; *Production:* Devabrat Sarkar
Subject: Academic
Founded: 1966

Book Field Centre, an imprint of Era Book Enterprises (qv)

Book Mark*, 6 Bankim Chatterjee St, Calcutta 700073
Chief Executive: Pradip Bose
Subject: Literature
Founded: 1974

Booklinks Corporation*, 3-4-423/5 & 6 Narayanaguda, Hyderabad 500029 Tel: 65021/62282/65550 Cable Add: Booklinks
Chief Executive, Editorial: K B Satyanarayana; *Sales, Production, Publicity:* T Jagannatham
Subject: Social Sciences
Bookshop: At above address
Founded: 1965

Bookventure*, 14 Thaninabhalam Chetty Rd, Madras 600017 Tel: 441970
Proprietor: Lakshmi Krushnamurti
Subjects: General Fiction, Belles Lettres, Poetry, Biography, History, Music, Art, Philosophy, General Science
Founded: 1965

Bright Careers Institute*, 1525 Nai Sarak, Delhi 110006 Tel: 269227
Chief Executive, Sales: S P S Phull; *Editorial:* D Sarna; *Production, Publicity:* P S Bright
Associate Company: Bright Careers Publications (at above address)
Branch Off: Bright Careers Publications, 17 Thambu Chetty St, Madras
Subjects: General Knowledge, English Language, Essays, Competition Books, History, Science, Mathematics, Management, Business, Humour
1981: 178 titles *Founded:* 1968

Business Promotion Bureau+, 376 Old Lajpat Rai Market, Delhi 110006 Tel: 224666/237147/269548 Cable Add: Radiocraft
President: G C Jain
Branch Offs: 4-3-269 Giriraj Lane, Bank St, Hyderabad 500001; 8/1 Ritchie St, Mount Rd, Madras 600002
Subjects: Electronics and Computers (in English)
Bookshop: Radio & Crafts Publications, 4794 Bharat Ram Rd, 23 Daryaganj, New Delhi 110002
1982: 125 titles *Founded:* 1958

Capital Book House*, 26 U B Jawahar Nagar, Delhi 110007 Tel: 220226
Chief Executive: R S Verma; *Editorial:* S Verma; *Sales:* Ajay Dev; *Production:* Rajiv
Subjects: Economics, History, Commerce
Founded: 1964

Central Book Depot (Publishers)*, 44 Johnstonganj, Allahabad Tel: 2408/2130/53727
Man Dirs: K L Bhargava, M L Bhargava; *Sales Dir:* H S Banerji
Subsidiary Company: Indian University Press, 18-C Queens Rd, Allahabad
Branch Off: 13 University Rd, Allahabad
Subjects: History, Philosophy, Medicine, Psychology, Engineering, General & Social Science, University & Secondary Textbooks
Founded: 1880

Central Hindi Directorate*, Ministry of Education, Government of India, West Block VII, RK Puram, New Delhi 110066 Tel: 699511 CabLe Add: Rajbhasha
Dir: Dr R C Rangra; *Deputy Dir (Publishing):* R M Jain; *Sales:* Dr B L Srivastava
Subjects: Scientific and Technical, Dictionaries and Reference in Hindi
Founded: 1960

Central Institute of Indian Languages, Manasagangotri, Mysore 570006 Tel: 24862/23558 Cable Add: Bharati
Chief Executive: D P Pattanayak
Subjects: Linguistics, Language Teaching
Founded: 1969

Chanakya Publications+, F10/14 Model Town, Delhi 110009 Tel: 711976 Cable Add: Chanakya
Man Dir, Editorial: Akhileshwar Jha; *Sales, Production:* R P Maurya; *Publicity, Rights & Permissions:* R Jha
Subjects: Indian Studies, Humanities, Social Sciences
1981: 6 titles *1982:* 7 titles *Founded:* 1980

S Chand & Co Ltd, Ravindra Mansion, PO Box 5733, Ram Nagar, New Delhi 110055 Tel: 517531 Cable Add: Eschand, New Delhi Telex: 0312185
Man Dir: S L Gupta; *Editorial, Publicity:* S D Sharma; *Sales:* R K Seth; *Rights & Permissions:* R K Gupta
Subsidiary Company: Eurasia Publishing House Pvt Ltd (qv)
Associate Companies: Bharati Sahitya Mandir; Bharati Vishwa Prakashan; Blackie & Son (Calcutta) Pvt Ltd; Rajendra Ravindra Printers Pvt Ltd, New Delhi; Shyamlal Charitable Trust (Publications), New Delhi
Branch Offs: Bombay, Calcutta, Patna, Lucknow, Jalandhar, Hyderabad, Madras, Bangalore, Nagpur, Cochin
Subjects: Arts, Philosophy, Economics, Commerce, Social & Political Science, Science and Technology, English and Hindi Literature
Bookshop: 4/16-B Asaf Ali Rd, New Delhi 110002
1981: 160 titles *1982:* 152 titles *Founded:* 1917

Charotar Publishing House, opp Amul Dairy, Civil Court Rd, Anand 388001 Tel: 3582
Chief Executive, Editorial, Production, Publicity, Rights & Permissions: Ramanbhai C Patel; *Sales:* Bhavin R Patel
Subsidiary Company: Charotar Books Distributors (at above address)
Branch Offs: Near Post Office, Vallabh Vidyanagar, Via Anand; Amul Dairy Rd, Anand
Subject: Engineering Textbooks
Founded: 1944

Chaukhambha Orientalia, PO Box 32, Varanasi 221001 (UP) (Located at: Gokul Bhawan K-37/109, Gopal Mandir Lane, Varanasi) Tel: 63354/65889 Cable Add: Gokulotsav
Managing Partner: Braj Bhavan Das Gupta
Branch Off: Bungalow Rd, 9 U B Jawahar Nagar, Delhi 110007
Subjects: Indian Classical Literature, Oriental Art, Science, Ayurved (Indian Medicine) (in Sanskrit, Hindi, English)
Founded: 1974

Chetana Pvt Ltd*, 34 Rampart Row, Bombay 400023
Man Dir: Sudhakar S Dikshit; *Publicity:* K K Govindan
Subjects: Philosophy, Religion
Founded: 1946

Children Book House*, South Extension Part I, New Delhi 110049 Tel: 692003/4
Sales: Zakarias Joseph; *Production:* R S Gupta
Subject: Children's Books

Children's Book Trust, Nehru House, 4 Bahadur Shah Zafar Marg, New Delhi 110002 Tel: 271921/5 Cable Add: Childtrust
Chief Executive: K Shankar Pillai; *General Manager, Rights & Permissions:* S P Chatterjea; *Editorial:* G Govindan; *Sales, Publicity:* H R Khurana; *Production:* Ravi Shankar
Subjects: Children's Books, *Children's World* (periodical in English)
1981: 23 titles *1982:* 19 titles *Founded:* 1957

Chinmaya Mission*, E-27 Defence Colony, Ring Rd, New Delhi 110024 Tel: 617257
Chief Executive, Sales: Brahmachari Radhakrishnan; *Production:* Swami Chinmayananda
Subject: Vedantic Literature

Chowkhamba Sanskrit Series Office*, PO Box 8, Varanasi 221001 (UP) (Located at: K-37/99 Gopal Mandir Lane, Varanasi) Tel: 63145 Cable Add: Chowkhamba Series, Varanasi
Man Dir, Publicity, Rights & Permissions: Bithal Das Gupta; *Editorial:* Pandit Ramchandra Jha; *Sales, Production:* Brij Mohan Das Gupta
Associate Company: Krishnadas Academy, K-37/118, Gopal Mandir Lane, Varanasi 221001
Subjects: Juveniles, Educational Materials, Primary, Secondary & University Textbooks, Poetry, Biography, History, Music, Art, Philosophy, Reference, Religion, Oriental, Indology
Bookshops: At above address; Chowk, Chitma Cinema Building, Varanasi 221001
Founded: 1892

The **Christian** Literature Society, PO Box 501, Park Town, Madras 600003 Tel: 39296/7 Cable Add: Vedic
General Secretary, Editorial, Rights & Permissions: Dr T Dayanandan Francis
Branch Offs: The Diocesan Press, PO Box 455, Madras 600007; The Wesley Press, PO Box 37, Mysore City 570001
Subjects: Religion, Textbooks, General, Children's Books
Bookshops: CLS in Hyderabad, Madras, Bangalore, Mysore City, Cochin, Tiruvalla, Coimbatore, Madurai
Founded: 1857

Chugh Publications, PO Box 101, Allahabad (Located at: 2 Strachey Rd, Allahabad) Tel: 3177
Chief Executive, Production, Publicity, Rights & Permissions: Ramesh Chugh; *Sales:* Suman Chugh
Associate Company: R S Publishing House, 20 Mahatma Gandhi Marg, Allahabad
Subjects: Humanities, Social Sciences
Bookshop: Universal Book Shop (qv under Major Booksellers)
1981: 12 titles *Founded:* 1975

College Book House+, PO Box 103, Trivandrum 695001 (Located at: Industrial Estate, Pappanamcode, Trivandrum) Tel: 2214
Man Dir, Editorial, Production, Rights & Permissions: M Easwaran; *Sales:* M Girija; *Publicity:* M Easwaran
Subjects: Indian Studies, Religion, Philosophy, Education, Economics, Sociology, History, Kerala (South India)
Bookshop: College Book House, Library Division (at above address)
1982: 5 titles *1983:* 12 titles *Founded:* 1973

Concept Publishing Co, H-13 Bali Nagar, New Delhi 110015 Tel: 503967
Chief Executive: Naurang Rai; *Editorial:* Suhasini Ramaswamy; *Sales, Publicity:* Ashok Kumar
Parent Company: D K Agencies (qv under

Major Booksellers)
Subjects: Indology, Anthropology, Art, Sociology, Philosophy, Economics, Public Administration, Geography, Bibliography, History, Political Science, Management, Agricultural Sciences
1981: 40 titles *1982:* approx 40 titles
Founded: 1975

Crescent Publishing Co*, 4 Abdul Qadir Market, Jail Rd, Aligarh 202001 Tel: 3711 Cable Add: Milestone
Man Dir, Publicity, Rights & Permissions: Firoz Ahmad; *Editorial:* M Rafat; *Sales:* Anwar Hussain; *Production:* N R Farooqui
Subjects: Religion, Academic
Founded: 1976

Current Books*, PO Box 212, Kottayam 686001 (Located at: VIII/493 Railway Station Rd, Kottayam) Tel: 3114/3226/5018 Cable Add: Current Books
Chief Executive: D C Kizhakemuri; *Editorial:* M S Chandrasekhara Warrier; *Sales:* P K Jayapalan; *Production, Publicity:* V R Radhakrishnan Nair; *Rights & Permissions:* Ponnamma Deecee
Associate Company: D C Books (qv)
Branch Offs and Bookshops: Alleppey (Tel: 4197), Ernakulam (Tel: 31590), Kottayam (Tel: 5342), Kozhikode (Tel: 76362), Tellicherry (Tel: 668), Trichur (Tel: 20660), Trivandrum (Tel: 61793)
Subjects: Fiction, Non-fiction
Founded: 1952

D C Books+, PO Box 214, Kottayam 686001 (Located at: Good Shepherd St, Kottayam) Tel: 3114/3226/8214 Cable Add: Deecibooks
Chief Executive, Rights & Permissions: D C Kizhakemuri; *Editorial:* M S Chandrasekhara Warrier; *Sales:* T K Murukesan; *Production, Publicity:* Muttambalam Sathyan
Associate Company: Current Books (qv)
Subjects: Fiction, Poetry, Literature, Children's Books, Reference Books
Book Clubs: Classics Club, D C Book Club
1981: 80 titles *1982:* 130 titles *Founded:* 1974

D K Publications, 29/10 Shakti Nagar, Delhi 110007 Tel: 710169 Cable Add: Deekaypub
Proprietor, Publicity: Praveen Mittal; *Editorial, Production:* I C Mittal; *Sales, Rights & Permissions:* S K Bhatia
Associate Companies: BR Publishing Corporation (qv); D K Publishers' Distributors (qv under Major Booksellers); Neeraj Publishing House (qv)
Branch Off: T C 789 Devivilas Compound, Chenthittal, Trivanorum 23
Subjects: Humanities and Social Sciences
Founded: 1974

D K F Trust, 74-D Anandnagar, Delhi 110035 Tel: 504418 Cable Add: Dikaybook
Chief Executive: Sh Khazan Chand; *Editorial, Sales, Production, Publicity, Rights & Permissions:* Naurang Rai
Subject: Directories
Founded: 1977

Dastane Ramchandra & Co+, 456 Raviwar Peth, Phadke Houd, PO Box 535, Poona 411002 Tel: 448193/54681
Man Dir: R D Dastane; *Editorial, Production:* S R Dastane; *Sales, Publicity, Rights & Permissions:* V R Dastane
Associate Company: Abhang Stores, Printers & Stationers (address as above)
Subjects: Chemistry, Geology, Geography, Botany, Sociology, Economics, Literature, Archaeology
Founded: 1960

Daystar Publications, B-2/48A Lawrence Rd, New Delhi 110035 Tel: 503928
Chief Executive: Mrs Indu Lekha; *Editorial, Sales, Production, Publicity, Rights & Permissions:* Dr G R Garg, Dr V P Garg
Subject: Book Trade
Bookshop: See under Major Booksellers
Founded: 1978

Debooks*, 9 Creek Row, Calcutta 700014
Publicity, Rights & Permissions: Mrs R De; *Marketing, Sales:* Ajoy De; *Accounts:* Asok De
Founded: 1975

Deep & Deep Publications*, D-1/24 Rajouri Garden, New Delhi 110027 Tel: 504498
Chief Executive, Rights & Permissions: K D Singh; *General Manager, Sales, Publicity:* G D Singh; *Editorial:* H S Bhatia; *Production:* G S Bhatia
Subjects: Politics, Military Affairs, Law
Founded: 1974
Miscellaneous: Also booksellers and exporters

Dey Sahitya Kutir (P) Ltd*, 21 Jhamapukur Lane, Calcutta 700009 Tel: 354294/5
Editorial: S C Mazumdar; *Sales:* Barun Chandra Mazumdar; *Production:* R Chatterjee
Subject: Children's Books

Dhanpat Rai & Sons*, 1683 Nai Sarak, Delhi 110006 Tel: 265367
Partners: O P Kapur, J C Kapur, K K Kapur
Branch Offs: Delhi, Jullundur
Subjects: Engineering, Education, Commerce
1982: 300 titles *Founded:* 1929

Diamond Comics (P) Ltd, 2715 Daryaganj, New Delhi 110002 Tel: 266317/273493
Man Dir: Narender Kumar Verma; *Editorial:* Gulshan Rai Verma
Associate Companies: Diamond Books International, Diamond Pocket Books (both at above address); Punjabi Pustak Bhandar (qv)
Subject: Juveniles (in Hindi and English)

Dini Book Depot*, 4160 Urdu Bazar, Jamamasjid, Delhi 110006 Tel: 268632/274855 Cable Add: Dini Book
Managing Partner, Sales, Production: Arshad Saeed; *Editorial:* Rashid Saeed; *Publicity:* Shahid Saeed
Subsidiary Company: Saeed International (Regd), 2112 Nahar Khan St, Daryaganj, New Delhi 2
Subjects: Islamic Studies, Textbooks
Founded: 1945
Miscellaneous: Also importers, exporters and suppliers

Doaba House*, 1688 Nai Sarak, Delhi 110006 Tel: 274669
Chief Executive, Editorial, Sales, Rights & Permissions: S N Malhotra; *Production, Publicity:* A C Seth
Bookshop: At above address
Subjects: Books in English, Literature, Education
Founded: 1924

Eastern Book Co+, 34 Lalbagh, Lucknow 226001 Tel: 43171/34316/46517 Cable Add: Lawbook
Chief Executive: C L Malik; *Editorial:* Surendra Malik; *Sales, Rights & Permissions:* P L Malik; *Production:* Kamal Malik; *Publicity:* Vijay Malik
Associate Companies: Law Times Press, 56-C Singarnagar, Lucknow 226005; Manav Law House, 2-A Strachey Rd, Civil Lines, Allahabad; Eastern Book Co (Sales), Kashmere Gate, Delhi 110006; Eastern Book Publishing Co, 34-A Lalbagh, Lucknow 226001

Subject: Law
1981: 150 titles *1982:* 165 titles *Founded:* 1947

Eastern Law House Pvt Ltd*, 54 Ganesh Chunder Ave, Calcutta 700013 Tel: 274989 Cable Add: Lauriports, Calcutta
Man Dir, Editorial, Production, Publicity, Rights & Permissions: A K De
Editorial Off: 11 Raja Subodh Mullick Sq, Calcutta 700013
Branch Off: 36 Netaji Subhas Marg, Daryaganj, New Delhi 110002
Subjects: Law, Accounting, Political & Social Science
Bookshops: 54 Ganesh Chunder Ave, Calcutta 700013; 36 Netaji Subhas Marg, Daryaganj, New Delhi 110002
Founded: 1918

Educational Enterprises, 5/1 Ramnath Mazumdar St, Calcutta 700009 Tel: 340101/424880
Chief Executive: S Ghosh; *Editorial:* Dr Arun Ghosh
Subjects: Education, Psychology

Era Book Enterprises*, PO Box 16622, Bombay 400019 (Located at: 14 Mohan Nivas, Chandavarkar Rd, Bombay 400019) Tel: 8828293 Cable Add: Goldenhill
Chief Executive, Rights & Permissions: Eranna R Jinde; *Editorial:* C V Bhimasankaram; *Sales:* V R Jinde; *Production:* B Ramakumar; *Publicity:* J E Rao
Subsidiary Company: Book Field Centre, 316/3 Sir Balchandra Rd, Bombay 400019
Imprint: Book Field Centre
Branch Off: 2/30 Khariboudi St, Adoni 518301
Subjects: Mathematics, Education
1981: 2 titles *Founded:* 1979

Ess Ess Publications*, 4837/24 Daryaganj, Ansari Rd, New Delhi 110002 Tel: 269667 Cable Add: Ess Ess Publications
Man Dir, Publicity, Rights & Permissions: Mrs Sheel Sethi; *Editorial, Sales, Production:* S K Sethi
Orders to: Ess Ess Publishers' Distributors, KD-6A Ashok Vihar, Delhi 110052
Parent Company: Ess Ess Publishers' Distributors, KD-6A Ashok Vihar, Delhi 110052
Subsidiary Company: Sumit Publications, KD-6A Ashok Vihar, Delhi 110052
Subjects: Humanities, Social Sciences
1982: 90 titles *Founded:* 1974

Eurasia Publishing House Pvt Ltd, Ravindra Mansion, Ram Nagar, New Delhi 110055 Tel: 517531 Cable Add: Eschand Telex: 0312185
Man Dir: S L Gupta; *Editorial, Publicity:* S D Sharma; *Sales Dir, Rights & Permissions:* R K Gupta
Parent Company: S Chand & Co Ltd (qv)
Subjects: Low-priced Reprints of American Educational Books, Psychology, Engineering, General & Social Sciences, University Textbooks
Founded: 1960

Firma KLM Private Ltd (Incorporating Firma KL Mukhopadhyay)*, 257B BB Ganguly St, Calcutta 700012 Tel: 274391 Cable Add: Indology (Calcutta)
Man Dir, Rights & Permissions: K L Mukhopadhyay; *Editorial, Production:* S P Ghosh; *Sales, Publicity:* R N Mukherji
Associate Company: Firma Mukhopadhyay, 2/1 Dr Aksay Pal Rd, Calcutta 700034
Subjects: Humanities, Social Sciences
Founded: 1950

Frank Bros & Co (Publishers) Pvt Ltd, 4675-A Ansari Rd, 21 Daryaganj, New Delhi 110002 Tel: 263393/279936
Man Dir: Suresh C Govil

G D K Publications*, 3623 Chawri Bazar, Delhi 110006 Tel: 266901/2 Cable Add: Gursons Delhi
Chief Executive: D P Chopra
Subjects: Indology, Social Sciences, History, Philosophy, Politics
1981: 15 titles *Founded:* 1978

Galgotia Booksource, PO Box 688, New Delhi 110001 (Located at: 17-B Connaught Place, New Delhi) Tel: 321844 Telex: 312879 Star In
Dir: Neeraj Galgotia
Bookshop: E D Galgotia & Sons (qv under Major Booksellers)
1982: 12 titles *Founded:* 1982
Miscellaneous: Mainly reprint publishers

Galgotia Publications*, 3B-12 Uttri Marg, Rajinder Nagar, New Delhi 110060 Tel: 589334
Chief Executive, Editorial: Suneel Galgotia; *Sales:* S K Nair; *Production:* P D Galgotia; *Publicity:* Rajinder Singh Bisht
Associate Company: E D Galgotia & Sons, 17-B Connaught Place, PO Box 688, New Delhi
Subjects: Technical, Management, General Paperbacks
Bookshop: E D Galgotia & Sons, 17-B Connaught Place, New Delhi
Founded: 1972

Ganesh & Co*, 41 Pondy Bazar, Madras 600017 Tel: 444938
Partners: S Ganesh Prasad, S Ranganathan
Subjects: Philosophy, Religion, Nutrition
1981: 3 titles *Founded:* 1910

Geetha Book House*, K R Circle, Mysore 570001 Tel: 21589 Cable Add: Books
General Manager: M Gopalakrishna; *Sales Manager:* M Gururaja Rao; *Rights & Permissions:* M Sathyanarayana Rao
Subjects: Belles Lettres, Poetry, Biography, History, Philosophy, Reference, Religion, Low- & High-priced Paperbacks, General & Social Science, University Textbooks
Bookshop: At above address

Geological Survey of India*, 27 Jawaharlal Nehru Rd, Calcutta 700016 Tel: 232314 Cable Add: Geosurvey
Director-General: S K Mukherjee
Subject: Geology

Gitanjali Prakashan*, Lajpat Nagar 4, New Delhi 110024 Tel: 621991
Subjects: Economics, Social Science, History, Politics, Humanities
Bookshop: Indian Book Service, Lajpat Nagar 4, New Delhi 110024
Founded: 1974

Goel Publishing House*, Subhash Bazar, Meerut 250002 Tel: 72843/76189
Man Dir, Editorial: B D Rastogi; *Sales:* Atul Krishna; *Production:* K Krishna; *Publicity & Advertising Dir:* Kamalni Rastogi
Subsidiary Company: Krishna Prakashan Mandir, 119 Krishna Vihar, Shivaji Road, Meerut 250001
Bookshop: Goel Publishing, Krishna Prakashan Mandir, Subhash Bazar, Meerut 250002 UP
Subjects: Mathematics, Chemistry, History, Art, Political Science, Economics, University & College textbooks
Founded: 1948

Good Companions*, Ushakirai Building, Raopura, Baroda Tel: 55433
Chief Executive: N K Kate; *Editorial, Sales, Production, Publicity:* Girish N Kate
Subjects: Economics, Social Science, Technical, General
Founded: 1945

Directorate of **Government** Publications*, Netaji Subhash Marg, Bombay 400004 Tel: 355181 Cable Add: Diprintery
Chief Executive: V K Vispute
Subject: General

Gyan Bharati*, 4-14 Roop Nagar, Delhi 7
An imprint of National Publishing House (qv)

Hans Prakashan*, 18 Nyaya Marg, Allahabad Tel: 3077
Chief Executive: Mahendra Pal Jha; *Production:* Amrit Rai
Subject: Fiction
Founded: 1949

Hans Publishers*, Kamani Chambers, Ballard Estate, Bombay 400038 Tel: 263516 Cable Add: Bukmel
Chief Executive: Miss M Pereira
Parent Company: Myna Press (qv)
Subjects: Great works of the present century and reprints of outstanding books
Founded: 1963

Harjeet & Co, PO Box 5752, New Delhi 110055 (Located at: 1920 Street 10th, Chuna Mandi, New Delhi) Tel: 518445/660391 Cable Add: Book Centre ND Telex: 0313176 ND
Chief Executive, Production: Dr P N Jain; *Editorial, Rights & Permissions:* Ashok Jain; *Sales, Publicity:* Kuldeep Jain
Associate Companies: B Jain Publishers; Jain Publishing Co; World Homoeopathic Links (qqv)
Subjects: Homoeopathy, Biochemistry, Magnetotherapy, Acupuncture, Allied Medical Topics
1982: 490 titles *Founded:* 1972

Hemkunt Publishers Pvt Ltd*, 1/E-15 Patel Rd, New Delhi 110008 Tel: 584174 Cable Add: Hembooks
Man Dir: Bhagat Singh; *Sales, Publicity, Advertising, Rights & Permissions:* G P Singh
Subjects: Religion, Juveniles, Low-priced Paperbacks, University, Secondary & Primary Textbooks
Founded: 1948

Heritage Publishers+, 4348 Madan Mohan St, 4C Ansari Rd, Daryaganj, New Delhi 110002 Tel: 266258 Cable Add: Heripub
Man Dir, Publicity: B R Chawla
Subsidiary Company: Intellectuals' Rendezvous, Aggarwal Bhawan, 4C Ansari Rd, New Delhi 110002
Subjects: Biography, History, Bibliography, Literature, Reference, Religion, Economics, Language, Social Science, Philosophy
Founded: 1973

Himalaya Prakashan*, 16 Resthouse Crescent, Bangalore 560001 Tel: 65207
Man Dir: Anand Kundaji
Associate Company: Artha Niti Publications, D390 Defence Colony, New Delhi 110024
Subjects: History, Philosophy, Religion, Mysticism
Founded: 1973

Himalaya Publishing House, 4A-16 Sangeeta, 71 Juhu Rd, Santa Cruz West, Bombay 400054 Tel: 351186, 355798
Chief Executive, Editorial, Sales, Publicity: D P Pandey; *Production:* Kooverjibhai; *Rights & Permissions:* Mrs Meena Pandey
Show Room: 'Ramdoot', Dr Bhalerao Marg (Kelewadi), Girgaum, Bombay 400004 Tel: 360170/355798
Subjects: Arts, Commerce, Science, Management, Law
Founded: 1976

Himalayan Books, 17-L Connaught Place, New Delhi 110001 Tel: 352126/351731 Cable Add: Himalayan Books
Man Dir, Editorial: Ms Pawan Chowdhri; *Sales, Production, Publicity, Rights & Permissions:* Ms V Chowdhri
Associate Company: English Book Store (qv under Major Booksellers)
Subjects: Architecture, Himalayas, Tourism, Religion, Culture, Nursing, Military Science, Aviation
1981: 5 titles *1982:* 6 titles *Founded:* 1981

Hind Pocket Books Private Ltd*, GT Rd, Shahdara, Delhi 110032
Tel: 202046/202332 Cable Add: Pocketbook Delhi
Man Dir: Dina N Malhotra; *Marketing, Rights & Permissions:* Shekhar Malhotra
Associate Companies: Indian Book Company, Clarion Books, Saraswati Vihar (all at above address)
Subjects: General, Fiction, Non-fiction, Self Improvement, Do-It-Yourself, Biography
Book Clubs: Gharelu Library Yojna, Clarion Book Club
Founded: 1958

Hindi Pracharak Sansthan, PO Box 106, Pishachmochan, Varanasi 221001 Tel: 62867/62114/52965 Cable Add: Prakashak
Editorial: K C Beri, V P Beri, R P Beri, A K Beri; *Sales:* Vivek Beri
Branch Offs: 23 Kabir Rd, Calcutta 700026; Adhyapak Prakashan Sansthan, 19 Garbarjhala Park, Lucknow 226001 (Tel: 46323); Sahitya Bharti, 263 Rabindra Sarani, Calcutta 700007
Subject: Hindi Literature, Periodical
Book Club: Pracharak Book Club
Founded: 1905

Hindustan Publishing Corporation (India), 6 U B Jawahar Nagar, Delhi 110007 Tel: 225059
Man Dir: S K Jain; *Editorial, Rights & Permissions:* J K Jain; *Sales:* P C Kumar; *Production:* B B Jain
Subsidiary Company: Hindustan Book Agency, 17 U B, Jawahar Nagar, Delhi 110007
Subjects: Archaeology, Bibliography and Information Science, Mathematics, Statistics, Physics, Chemistry, Earth Sciences, Life Sciences, Social Sciences
Founded: 1960

I B H Publishing Co, 412-415 Tulsiani Chambers, 212 Backbay Reclamation, Nariman Point, Bombay 400021 Tel: 240626/240779
Dirs: G L Mirchandani, Deepak G Mirchandani; *Managing Editor:* P C Manaktala
Associate Companies: India Book House, India Book House Educational Trust (both at Mahalaxmi Chambers, 22 Bhulabhai Desai Rd, Bombay 400026); India Book House Pvt Ltd (at above address); IBH Magazine Company, IBH Subscription Agency, IBH Export Division (all at Eruchshaw Bldg, 249 Dr D N Rd, Bombay 400001)
Subjects: Management, Health, Cookery, Humour, Biography, Indian Culture and Tradition, Children's
Bookshop: India Book House (qv under Major Booksellers)

I B I, an imprint of Sterling Publishers Pvt Ltd (qv)

I S P C K, see Indian Society for Promoting Christian Knowledge

Idarah-I-Adabiyat-I-Delli*, 2009 Qasimjan St, Delhi 110006 Tel: 513550
Editorial: Muhammad Ahmed; *Sales:* Lachhman Das

Subjects: Islamic Studies
Founded: 1972

Inba Nilayam*, 95 Kutchery Rd, Mylapore, Madras 600004 Tel: 72547
Chief Executive: Soma Swaminathan; *All other offices:* Ramanathan S
Associate Company: Vellayan Pathippagam (at above address)
Subjects: Politics, Philosophy, History, Novels, Juveniles
Founded: 1947

India Book House, see IBH Publishing Co

Indian Council for Cultural Relations, Azad Bhavan, Indraprastha Estate, New Delhi 110002 Tel: 272114/262052/262053 Cable Add: Culture Telex: 0314904
Subjects: Literature, Culture, Cultural Relations, Performing and Fine Arts

Indian Council of Agricultural Research*, Krishi Bhavan, Dr Rajendra Prasad Rd, New Delhi 110001
Dir: Dr V S Bhatt; *Chief Editor:* P L Jaiswal; *Advertising:* M M Chawla; *Publicity:* S K Sharma
Subjects: Agriculture, Animal Husbandry, Textbooks, Periodicals, Handbooks

Indian Council of Medical Research, PO Box 4508, New Delhi 110029 (Located at: Ansari Nagar, New Delhi) Tel: 660707/667136 Cable Add: Scientific Telex: 031-3807
Chief Executive: V Ramalingaswami; *Editorial, Sales, Publicity, Rights & Permissions:* G V Satyavati; *Production:* K Satyanarayana
Subject: Biomedical Research
Founded: 1911

Indian Council of Social Science Research (ICSSR), 35 Ferozshah Rd, New Delhi 110001 Tel: 385959 Cable Add: Icsores
Chief Executive, Editorial, Production, Rights & Permissions: D D Narula; *Sales, Publicity:* S P Agrawal
Subject: Social Sciences, Abstracts and reviews of research, Periodicals
Founded: 1969

Indian Documentation Service, Gurgaon, Haryana 122001 Tel: 2205
Editorial, Production, Rights & Permissions: Satyaprakash; *Sales:* Pankaj Kumar, Sanjeev Kumar; *Publicity:* Pankaj Kumar
Subject: Bibliography
1981: 5 titles *1982:* 1 title *Founded:* 1970

Indian Folklore Society*, 3 Abdul Hamid (British Indian) St, Calcutta 700069 Tel: 236334
President: Madame Sophia Wadia; *Honorary Dir of Research, General Secretary, Editorial, Rights & Permissions, Publicity:* Sankar Sen Gupta
Orders to: Indian Publications, 3 Abdul Hamid (British Indian) St, Calcutta 700069
Subjects: Folklore, Anthropology, Archaeology, Ethno-Musicology, Ethno-Botany, Psychology, Tribal Studies, Geography, Folk Performing Arts, Periodical *Folklore*
Founded: 1957

Indian Institute of Advanced Study*, Rashtrapathi Nivas, Simla 171005 Tel: 2227 Cable Add: Institute
Publication Officer: S K Sharma; *Sales:* B B Lal
Subject: Scholarly

Indian Institute of World Culture, PO Box 402, Basavangudi, Bangalore 560004 (Located at: 6 Shri B P Wadia Rd, Basavangudi, Bangalore) Tel: 602581
Honorary Secretary: Anand R Kundaji
Subject: East-West Culture

Indian Museum*, 27 Jawaharlal Nehru Rd, Calcutta 700016, West Bengal Tel: 239855, 234584, 230742 Cable Add: Imbot
Dir: Dr S C Ray
Subjects: Arts, Archaeology, Anthropology, Botany, Geology, Zoology
Founded: 1814

Indian Press (Publications) Pvt Ltd*, 36 Pannalal Rd, Allahabad, Uttar Pradesh Tel: 53190 Cable Add: Publikason
Man Dir: D P Ghosh; *Sales, Production, Publicity, Rights & Permissions:* N G Bagchi
Branch Off: Indian Publishing House, 22/1 Bidhan Sarani, Calcutta 6
Subject: Textbooks in Hindi, Bengali & English (also publishes in Gurmukhi, Urdu, Marathi & Nepali languages)
Founded: 1884

Indian Publications*, 3 Abdul Hamid (British Indian) St, Calcutta 700069 Tel: 236334/344733
Man Dir, Sales: C R Sen; *Editorial, Production, Rights & Permissions:* Sankar Sen Gupta; *Publicity:* Miss Putul Das
Subsidiary Company: Kalyani Prakashani (at above address)
Subjects: Social Science, Humanities, with special reference to Folklore, Anthropology, Archaeology, Ancient History, Bengali Literature, Mass Communication and Traditional Culture (in English and Bengali only)
Founded: 1956

Indian Publishing House*, 22/1 Bidhan Saranee, Calcutta 700006 Tel: 347398
Manager, Sales: D K Bose; *Editorial:* S P Ghosh; *Production:* D P Ghosh
Subjects: Political Science, Philosophy, History, Economics, Science, Engineering
Founded: 1908

Indian Society for Promoting Christian Knowledge (ISPCK), PO Box 1585, Kashmere Gate, Delhi 110006 Tel: 227363 Cable Add: Lithouse Delhi
General Secretary: V H Devadas; *Publications Secretary:* Rev James Massey; *Editorial:* Jane Caleb
Parent Company: SPCK (The Society for Promoting Christian Knowledge), UK (qv)
Subjects: Biblical, Biography, Church and Church History, Christian Life and Education, Comparative Religions, Devotional, Liturgy, Theology, Social, Political
Bookshops: 51 Chowringhee Rd, Calcutta 700016; opp Liberty Cinema, Residency Rd, Nagpur 440001
Founded: 1711 (as autonomous body 1958)

Institute for Christian Publishing & Communications Research, Kunnuparampil Bldgs, Kurichy 686549, Kottayam, Kerala State Tel: (04826) 470
Man Dir: K P Punnoose; *Editorial, Publicity:* Santhamma Punnoose
Parent Company: K P Punnoose Communications Co (qv under Literary Agents)
Subject: Christian Literature
Founded: 1980

Intellectual Publishing House, 23 Daryaganj, Pratap Gali, New Delhi 2 Tel: 279911
Associate Company: Intellectual Book Corner
Subjects: History, Politics, Sociology, Philosophy, Religion, Art, Archaeology
Founded: 1974

Inter-India Publications, WZ-1086 Basai Darapur, Bali Nagar, New Delhi 110015 Tel: 504418
Chief Executive, Editorial, Rights & Permissions: M C Mittal; *Sales:* Praveen Mittal
Parent Company: DK Publishers' Distributors (qv under Major Booksellers)
Subjects: Indology, Geography, Art, Anthropology, Sociology, Archaeology, Philosophy, Religion, Economics, History
1981: 3 titles *1982:* 11 titles *Founded:* 1977

Interprint, Mehta House, 16-A Naraina II, New Delhi 110028 Tel: 564234/589760/584387 Cable Add: Calmakers Telex: 2157 ND
Man Dir, Rights & Permissions: S N Mehta; *Production:* Dalip Tuli; *Publicity:* V V R Murty
Parent Company: Calendar Makers Corporation (at above address)
Subjects: Medicine, Life Sciences, Indian Art
1982: 8 titles *1983:* 15 titles *Founded:* 1976

Intertrade Publications (India) Pvt Ltd, subsidiary of KK Roy (Pvt) Ltd (qv)

Jaico Publishing House*, 125 Mahatma Gandhi Rd, Bombay 400023 Tel: 270621, 270746, 270760 Cable Add: Jaicobooks
Man Dir: Jaman H Shah; *Editorial, Production, Sales, Publicity, Rights & Permissions:* Ashwin J Shah
Subsidiary Company: Jaico Press Pvt Ltd
Branch Offs: Jaico Book House, 14-1 1st Main Rd, 6th Cross, Gandhi Nagar, Bangalore 560009; Jaico Book Distributors, G-2, 16 Ansari Rd, Daryaganj, New Delhi 110002
Subjects: Oriental and Western Classics, Indian and Western Fiction, Palmistry, Astrology, Philosophy, Religion, Biography, Autobiography, Reference, Language, Sex, Marriage, Love, Health, Yoga, Management, Economics, Humour, History, Politics, Cookery, Law, Crime, Psychology, Self-improvement
Bookshop: Jaico's Book Shop, 125 Mahatma Gandhi Rd, Bombay 400023
Founded: 1947

B Jain Publishers, 55-I Arjun Nagar, New Delhi 110029 Tel: 660391
Chief Executive, Sales, Production, Publicity: Kuldeep Jain; *Editorial, Rights & Permissions:* Ashok Jain
Orders to: PO Box 5752, New Delhi 110055
Associate Company: Harjeet & Co (qv)
Subjects: Homoeopathy, Magnetotherapy, Acupuncture, Nature Cure
1982: 250 titles *Founded:* 1967

Jain Publishing Co, 2798 Rajguru Rd, New Delhi 110055 Tel: 518445
Chief Executive, Production: Dr P N Jain; *Editorial, Sales, Publicity, Rights & Permissions:* Ashok Jain
Orders to: PO Box 5752, New Delhi 110055
Associate Company: Harjeet & Co (qv)
Subjects: Homoeopathy, Allied Medical Books
Founded: 1972

Jaipur Publishing House*, Chaura Rasta, Jaipur 302003 Tel: 62257
Manager: Rajesh Agarwal; *Production:* R C Agarwal; *Sales:* Dhoop Chand Jain
Subject: Academic
Founded: 1960

Jaisingh & Mehta Publishers Pvt Ltd, 18/20 K Dubash Marg, Bombay 400023 Tel: 225353/225425
Man Dir, Rights & Permissions: Ananda Jaisingh; *Editorial:* H J Vakeel; *Sales:* B N Chatterjee; *Production:* Mrs K Tandon; *Publicity:* C K Muraleedharan
Imprint: Asia Publishing House (qv)
Branch Off: New Delhi
Subjects: General, Art, Indology, Archaeology, University Textbooks
1981: 5 titles *1982:* 6 titles *Founded:* 1942
ISBN Publisher's Prefix: 0-210

Jaypee Brothers+, PO Box 7193, New Delhi 110002 (Located at: G-16 EMCA House, 23B Ansari Rd, New Delhi)
Editorial: Jitendar Vij; *Sales:* P Paul
Subject: Medical Sciences

Jnanada Prakashan+, Govind Mitra Rd, Patna 800004 Tel: 50331
Editorial: T Chowdhary; *Sales:* R Chowdhary; *Production, Publicity, Rights & Permissions:* S B Chowdhary
Subsidiary Company: Hastamalak Prakashan (at above address)
Branch Offs: Gurudwara Rd, Bhagalpur Tel: 898; Ashok Market, Motijhil, Muzaffarpur; 24 Daryaganj, New Delhi Tel: 272047; S N Gangully Rd, Ranchi Tel: 20769
Subjects: Accountancy, Commerce, Management, Secretarial, Vocational, Hobbies, Physics, Chemistry, Botany, Zoology, Mathematics, Statistics, Economics, Political Science, Philosophy, Psychology, Logic, Sociology, History, Languages
Founded: 1949

Kairali Mudralayam*, Moolepparambil Buildings, opp R M S Office, Kottayam 686001
Managing Partner: D C Kizhakemuri; *Editorial:* M S Chandrasekhara Warrier; *Sales:* D C Ponnamma; *Production, Publicity, Rights & Permissions:* Mary John
Subjects: Fiction, Biography, Humour, Crime Thrillers (especially Sherlock Holmes)
1981: approx 20 titles *Founded:* 1978

Kalyani Publishers+, 1/1 Rajinder Nagar, Ludhiana (Punjab)
Man Dir: Raj Kumar
Branch Off: 4863/2 Bharat Ram Rd, 24 Daryaganj, New Delhi 110002
Subject: Educational
Bookshop: Lyall Book Depot, Chaura Bazar, Ludhiana
1981-82: 125 titles

Karnataka Cooperative Publishing House Ltd*, 164 1st Main Rd, Chamarajpet, Bangalore 560018

B D **Kataria** & Sons*, opp Clock Tower, Ludhiana Tel: 21107
Chief Executive: Verinder Kataria
Subjects: Engineering, Technology

Kendriya Hindi Sansthan, Agra 282005 Tel: 76758/72352 Cable Add: Shikshan Agra
Chief Executive, Editorial, Rights & Permissions: Prof Dr Bal Govind Mishra; *Sales, Production, Publicity:* Dr Devendra Kumar Sharma
Branch Offs: Delhi, Gauhati, Hyderabad
Subjects: Linguistics, Language, Language Teaching
1982: 65 titles *Founded:* 1961
Miscellaneous: Autonomous body fully financed by Ministry of Education, Government of India

Kerala Sahitya Akademi, PO Box 6, Trichur 680020 (Located at: Town Hall Rd, Trichur) Tel: 23569
Secretary: Pavanan; *Publications Officer:* C K Anandan Pillai
Subject: Literary
1981: 18 titles *1982:* 15 titles *Founded:* 1956

Kerala University, Department of Publications, Trivandrum 695034 Tel: 60692
Chief Executive: Chemmanam Chacko; *Production, Sales:* S Krishna Iyer
Subject: Scholarly
Founded: 1939

Khanna Publishers, 2-B Nath Market, Nai Sarak, Delhi 110006 Tel: 262380
Subject: Engineering

Kitab Ghar*, Main Bazar, Gandhi Nagar, New Delhi 110031 Tel: 213206
Chief Executive, Rights & Permissions: Satya Brat Sharma; *Editorial, Production:* Jagat Ram Sharma; *Sales, Publicity:* Dev Datt
Subjects: Social and General Sciences, Novels, Poetry, Drama, Biography (in Hindi)
Founded: 1970

Kitab Mahal (W D) Pvt Ltd, 56 A Zero Rd, Allahabad, Uttar Pradesh Tel: 50540/2927 Cable Add: Kitab Mahal Allahabad
Man Dir: I K Agarwal; *Sales, Publicity Dir:* Naresh Agarwal
Branch Offs: Kitab Mahal Agencies, Ramdas Peth, Nagpur; Kitab Mahal Agencies, Ashokrajpath, Patna 4 (Bihar); Kitab Mahal Distributors, 28 Netaji Subhash Marg, Daryaganj, New Delhi 2
Founded: 1936

Kitabastan*, 30 Chak, Allahabad 211003 Tel: 51885 Cable Add: Kitabastan
Chief Executive: Anwar Ullah Khan
Subjects: General (in English, Urdu, Persian, Arabic)
Founded: 1932

Konkani Bhasha Mandal*, 49-B Erasmo Carvalho St, Margao, Goa 403601 Tel: 2331
Editorial: Udai L Bhmbro; *Sales:* M R Borkar
Subject: Konkani Literature

Kosi Books, an imprint of Vidyarthi Mithram Press & Book Depot (qv)

Kothari Publications+, Jute House, 12 India Exchange Pl, Calcutta 700001
Tel: 229563/226572 Cable Add: Zeitgeist
Man Dir: H Kothari
Parent Company: Kothari Organisation (at above address)
Associate Company: India-International News Service (at above address)
Subjects: Technical, Reference
Founded: 1961
Miscellaneous: Publisher of *Who's Who* series in India

Krishna Brothers*, Mahatma Gandhi Marg, Ajmer 305001 Tel: 20935
Editorial: J K Agarwal; *Sales:* C K Agarwal
Subject: Hindi literature
Founded: 1939

Krishna Prakashan Mandir, subsidiary of Goel Publishing House (qv)

Kundalini Research and Publication Trust, D-291 Sarvodaya Enclave, New Delhi Tel: 653864 Cable Add: Innerlight
Subjects: Yoga, Philosophy, Religion
Founded: 1977

Kunnuparampil Books*, 14 Station Rd, Dewas
Chief Executive: K A Abraham; *Sales:* K A Raju
Subjects: General, Scientific, Technical
Founded: 1980

Kutub Khana Ishayat-ul-Islam*, 3755 Churiwalan, Delhi 110006 Tel: 263567/265854 Cable Add: Kutubiexpo
Editorial, Sales: V K Sachdeva
Subject: Islamic Books

Lakshmi Narain Agarwal*, Hospital Rd, Agra 3 Tel: 73160
Man Dir: P N Agarwal
Subjects: Education, Textbooks
Founded: 1916

Lalit Kala Akademi (National Academy of Art), Rabindra Bhavan, Ferozeshah Rd, New Delhi 110001 Tel: 387241 Cable Add: Artakademi
Chairman: Dr K K Hebbar; *Secretary:* R L Bartholomew
Subject: Art (Journals, Books, Monographs, Brochures, Portfolios and Multicolour Reproductions)
Publications: Lalit Kala (Ancient Art), Lalit Kala Contemporary

Lalvani Brothers, PO Box 545, Taj Bldg, 210 Dr Dadabhai Naoroji Rd, Bombay 400001 Tel: 266811/2 Cable Add: Lalbrother Bombay Telex: 0116529 Nrvo In
Man Dirs, Editorial, Sales, Production, Publicity, Rights & Permissions: S P Lalvani, Mrs P K Sitlani
Associate Companies: Indian Lead, Rampart House, Rampart Row, Bombay; Lalvani Publishing House, 210 Dr DN Rd, Bombay 400001
Branch Offs: 4 Daryaganj, Ansari Rd, Delhi 110006; 8 State Bank Lane, Mount Rd, Madras 2; Globe Bldg, 7-E Lindsey St, Calcutta 16
Subjects: Juvenile, Art, Technical, Educational
Founded: 1924
ISBN Publisher's Prefix: 81-112

Law Books in Hindi Publishers*, Vidhi Sahitya Prakashan, Ministry of Law, Justice and Company Affairs, Indian Law Institute Building, Bhagwan Das Rd, New Delhi 110001 Tel: 389001 Cable Add: Patrika
Sales Manager: C B Deogam
Subjects: Law (publications include *Uchchatama Nyayalaya Nirnaya Patrika* and *Uchcha Nyayalaya Nirnaya Patrika*)

Law Publishers*, PO Box 77, Allahabad 1 (Located at: Sardar Patel Marg, Allahabad)
Tel: 2835/3716 Cable Add: Publishers Allahabad
Chief Executive: V Sagar
Associate Company: Delhi Law House, 77 Gokhale Market, Delhi 6
Subject: Law
1982: 100 titles *Founded:* 1961

Light & Life Publishers*, 2428 Tilak St, Paharganj, New Delhi 110055 Tel: 522455
Managing Partner: N Gopinath; *Sales & Publicity:* P N Nair; *Rights & Permissions:* Kartar Singh
Branch Offs: Residency Rd, Jammu Tawi (J & K); Mele Thampanoor, Trivandrum 695001, Kerala
Subjects: Philosophy, Political Science, Indology, Low-priced student editions of textbooks, Religion, History, Geography
Founded: 1971

Lipi Prakashan*, 1 Ansari Rd, Daryaganj, New Delhi 110002 Tel: 273729
Editorial, Production, Publicity, Rights & Permissions: J S Vyas; *Sales:* M L Sharma
Subjects: Novels, Short Stories, Biographies, Literary Criticism, Linguistics, Philology, Education, Politics, Political Science, Dictionaries, Children's Literature (in Hindi and English)
1982: 200 titles *Founded:* 1970

The **Little Flower** Co, 43 Ranganathan St, T Nagar, Madras 600017 Tel: 441538 Cable Add: Lifco
Senior Partner: T N C Varadan
Branch Off: Lifco Sales Dept, 17/1 Nandi Koil St, Teppakulam, Tiruchirapalli 620002
Subjects: General Fiction, History, How-to, Music, Art, Philosophy, Reference, Religion, Low-priced Paperbacks, Medicine, General Science, University, Secondary & Primary Textbooks
Founded: 1929

Little Swan, an imprint of Orient Longman Ltd (qv)

Lok Vangmaya Griha (Pvt) Ltd*, 85 Sayani Rd, Prabhadevi, Bombay 400025 Tel: 351324 Cable Add: Loksahitya
Man Dir: B D Gujarathi; *Sales:* S K

Kulkarni
Parent Company: People's Publishing House (P) Ltd (qv)
Branch Offs: Red Flag Building, Bindu Chowk, Kolhpur; 5-22-32 Tilak Path, Aurangabad; 562 Sadashive Peth, Pune 400030
Subjects: General, Humanities
Bookshops: PPH Book Stall, S V P Rd, Bombay 400004; People's Book House, Fort, Bombay 400001
Founded: 1973

Lord International, 19 Netaji Subhash Marg, Daryaganj, New Delhi 110002 Tel: 272375
Chief Executive, Editorial, Sales, Rights & Permissions: Sunil Chaudhry; *Production:* Ramesh Chaudhry; *Publicity:* Rajesh Chaudhry
Subjects: Book Trade, Mailing Lists
Founded: 1971
Miscellaneous: Also Distributors and Publishers' Representatives

M P Text Book Corporation*, M S Mandal Campus, Bhopal Tel: 62135/63059
Publisher: Raghunath Prasad
Subject: Academic
Founded: 1968

Macmillan India Ltd, 2/10 Ansari Rd, Daryaganj, New Delhi 110002 Tel: 273814/273624 Cable Add: Macind Telex: Nd 3741
Shipping Add: 40 Peters Rd, Royapettah, Madras 600014
Man Dir: S G Wasani; *Rights & Permissions:* Ravi Vyas
Branch Offs: 12-A Mahatma Gandhi Rd, Bangalore 560001; Mercantile House, Magazine St, Reay Rd (East), Bombay 400010; 294 Bepin Behari Ganguly St, Calcutta 700012; 3-4-424 Narayanaguda, Hyderabad 500029; Kala Bhawan, 6 Naval Kishore Rd, Hazratganj, Lucknow 226001; 4 Peters Rd, Royapettah, Madras 600014; Gandhari Bldg, Gandhari Amman Koil St, Trivandrum 695001
Subjects: Biography, History, Philosophy, Reference, Religion, Medicine, Psychology, Engineering, General & Social Science, University, Secondary & Primary Textbooks, Economics, Management, Political Science, Reference, Fiction, Dictionaries
1982: 30 titles *Founded:* 1903
Miscellaneous: Firm is 40 per cent owned by Macmillan Publishers Ltd, UK (qv)
ISBN Publisher's Prefix: 81-3390

Madhyo Pradesh Hindi Granth Academy*, Shivajj Nagar, Bhopal 462011 Tel: 62084 Cable Add: Academy
Director: Prof S D Misra; *Editorial:* Navin Sagar; *Sales:* Ram Prakash; *Production, Publicity:* Dr Shiv Kumar, Brij Bihari Dixit
Subjects: University Textbooks, Humanities, Science, Agriculture, Engineering, Medical Sciences
1981: 284 titles *1982:* 314 titles

Mahajan Brothers, Super Market Basement, Ashram Rd, nr Natraj Cinema, Ahmedabad 380009 Tel: 78547 Cable Add: Periodical
Man Dir: Dinker Mahajan
Subject: Textiles
Founded: 1953

Manohar Publications, 1 Ansari Rd, Daryaganj, New Delhi 110002 Tel: 262796/275162
Man Dir, Rights & Permissions: Ramesh Jain; *Editorial:* K K Saxema; *Sales, Production, Publicity:* Sanjay Banerjee
Subjects: History, Sociology, Politics, Indology
Founded: 1969

Munshiram **Manoharlal** Publishers Pvt Ltd*, PO Box 5715, New Delhi 110055 (Located at: 54 Rani Jhansi Rd, New Delhi) Tel: 513841/513600/512745 Cable Add: Literature New Delhi
Chief Executive: Manoharlal Jain; *Editorial:* Devendra Jain; *Sales:* Ashok Jain
Associate Companies: Indian Book Import Co, 11-B Court Rd, Delhi 110054; Oriental Books Reprint Corporation, PO Box 5715, 54 Rani Jhansi Rd, New Delhi 110055
Subjects: Art, Architecture, Religion, Philosophy, History, Politics, Linguistics, Languages, Encyclopaedias, Music, Dance, Drama, Theatre, Anthropology, Sociology
Bookshop: 4416 Nai Sarak (Amir Chand Marg), Delhi 110006
1981: 38 titles *Founded:* 1952

Manosabdam Books, an imprint of Vidyarthi Mithram Press & Book Depot (qv)

Marg Publications, 3rd floor, Army and Navy Bldg, 148 Mahatma Gandhi Rd, Bombay 400023 Tel: 242520
Chief Executive: J J Bhabha; *Editorial:* Dr Saryu Doshi; *Sales, Publicity:* A D Katrak; *Production:* B J Bilimoria; *Rights & Permissions:* Mrs R S Sabavala
Parent Company: Tata Sons Ltd
Subject: Art
Founded: 1947

Markazi Maktaba Islami, 1353 Chitli Qabar, Delhi 110006 Tel: 262862 Cable Add: Markaz
Sales: Firasat Ali
Subject: Islamic Literature

Marwah Publications+, H-39 Green Park Extension, New Delhi 110016 Tel: 664296
Proprietor: Jaspal Singh; *Editorial:* Anees Chishti; *Sales:* Aman Preet Singh
Subjects: Humanities, Social Sciences
Founded: 1975

Mayfair Paperbacks, an imprint of Arnold-Heinemann Publishers (India) Pvt Ltd (qv)

Mayoor Paperbacks, an imprint of National Publishing House (qv)

Meenakshi Prakashan*, Begum Bridge, Meerut 250002 Tel: 74133, 75062, 72001
Chief Executive: Shri Chandra Prakash; *Editorial:* Ashok Gupta; *Sales:* S Sudhakar; *Production:* Ashok Kumar; *Publicity:* M C Gupta; *Rights & Permissions:* T C Sharma
Branch Off: 4 Ansari Rd, Daryaganj, New Delhi 110002
Subjects: Economics, Education, Commerce, Psychology, Hindi Literature, Physical and Biological Sciences, History, Management, Political Science, Sociology
Founded: 1964

Milind Publications Pvt Ltd, 6-E Rani Jhansi Rd, New Delhi 110055 Tel: 520838
Man Dir, Sales, Rights & Permissions: Rajiv K Aggarwal; *Editorial, Production:* K R Seshagiri Rao
Subjects: Belles Lettres, Fiction, History, Law, Philosophy, Psychology, Politics, Social and General Science
1982: 8 titles *Founded:* 1980

Minerva Associates (Publications) Pvt Ltd, 7-B Lake Pl, Calcutta 700029 Tel: 42-3783
Chairman, Man Dir, Production, Publicity, Rights & Permissions: Sushil Mukherjea; *Editorial Dir:* O K Ghosh; *Sales:* T K Mukherjee
Associate Company: Minerva Sales and Distribution (at above address)
Subjects: Political Science, History, Social Science, Economics, Psychology, Education, Belles Lettres, Literary Criticism, Philosophy
1981-82: 10 titles *Founded:* 1973

The **Minerva** Publishing House*, 32 Halls Rd, Egmore, Madras 8

Ministry of Information & Broadcasting, Publications Division, Government of India, Patiala House, New Delhi 110001 Tel: 386942 Cable Add: Sooch Parkash
Dirs: P B Barthakur, P B Ray; *Business Managers:* S L Jaiswal, Jai Kishore, Ishwar Chandra, M N Chatterjee, R B Singh, S C Jain, C B Gupta
Branch Offs: Super Bazar (2nd Floor), Connaught Circus, New Delhi; Commerce House, Currimbhoy Rd, Ballard Pier, Bombay; 8 Esplanade East, Calcutta; LL Auditorium, Anna Salai, Madras; 10-B Station Rd, Lucknow; Bihar State Co-operative Bank Bldg, Ashoka Rajpath, Patna
Subjects: Art & Culture, History, Speeches & Writings, Land & People, Flora & Fauna, Biographies, Reference, Juveniles, General & Social Science

Mitra & Ghosh Publishers Pvt Ltd, 10 Shyama Charan De St, Calcutta 73 Tel: 343492/348791 Cable Add: Mitra & Ghosh, Calcutta
Chief Executive, Production: Sabitendra Nath Roy; *Editorial:* G K Mitra, S N Ghosh; *Sales:* M C Chakravarty; *Publicity:* P K Bose; *Rights & Permissions:* P K Pal
Branch Off: 86/1 Mahatma Gandhi Rd, Calcutta 700009
Subjects: Novels, Fiction, Travel, Essays, Juvenile, Periodical *Katha-Sahitya*
Bookshops: At both above addresses
1982: 550 titles *1983:* 610 titles *Founded:* 1934

Modern Book Agency Private Ltd*, 10 Bankim Chatterjee St, Calcutta 700073 Tel: 34-6888/34-6889 Cable Add: Bibliophil
Man Dir, Rights & Permissions: Rabindranarayan Bhattacharya; *Sales:* Nisith Kumar Bose; *Production:* Debnarayan Bhattacharya
Associate Company: B B Brothers & Co, 16/1 Shyamacharandey St, Calcutta 700073
Subjects: School and College Textbooks, Reference, Children's Literature (in English and Bengali)
Bookshop: At above address
1982: 158 titles *Founded:* 1928

Motilal Banarsidass+, Bungalow Rd, Jawahar Nagar, Delhi 110007
Tel: 228355/221985 Cable Add: Gloryindia
Man Dir: Shantilal Jain; *Publication Dir:* Narendra Prakash Jain; *Sales Dir:* R P Jain; *Advertising Dir:* Jainendra Prakash Jain
Branch Offs: Ashok Rajpath, Opp Patna College, Patna 800004 (Bihar) Tel: 51442; PO Box 75, Chowk, Varanasi 221001 (UP) Tel: 62898
Subjects: Religion, Philosophy, History, Linguistics, Sanskrit, Arts, Literature, Medicine
Bookshop: 41 U A Bungalow Rd, Jawahar Nagar, Delhi 110007 (qv under Major Booksellers)
1982: 90 titles *Founded:* 1903

Mouj Prakashan Griha*, Khatau Wadi Girgaum, Bombay 400004, Maharashtra

A **Mukherjee** & Co Pvt Ltd*, 2 Bankim Chatterjee St, Calcutta 700012
Tel: 341606/341499
Dir: B K Chatterjee
Subject: Educational Materials
Founded: 1940

Mukherji Book House*, 1 Gopi Mohan Dutta Lane, Calcutta 700003
Subjects: Reference, Bibliography
Founded: 1963

Myna Press*, PO Box 1526, Bombay 400038
(Located at: 32 R Kamani Marg, Bombay)
Tel: 261347   Cable Add: Bukmel
Chief Executive: Mohan Panjabi
Subsidiary Company: Hans Publishers (qv)
Subject: Juveniles
Founded: 1970

Nalanda Books, an imprint of Aadiesh Book Depot (qv)

Narosa Publishing House*, 2/35 Ansari Rd, Daryaganj, New Delhi 110002   Tel: 263829
Cable Add: Narosa New Delhi
Man Dir: N K Mehra
Associate Companies: Narosa Book Distributors, Springer Books (India) Pvt Ltd (qv) (both at above address)
Subjects: Pure and Applied Science, Medicine
1981: 8 titles   *Founded:* 1977

National Book Agency (P) Ltd*, 12 Bankim Chatterjee St, Calcutta 700073   Tel: 341677/348506   Cable Add: Marxislit
Man Dir: Sunil Kumar Basu
Subject: Marxist-Leninist Literature
Founded: 1939

National Book Trust India, A-5 Green Park, New Delhi 110016   Tel: 664667/664540
Cable Add: Nabotrust
Chairman: Krishna Kripalani; *Dir:* Dr Lokenath Bhattacharya; *Joint Dir (Development):* C N Rao; *Joint Dir (Administration, Finance):* H L Luthra; *Joint Dir (Publishing):* Dr Syed Asad Ali; *Deputy Dir (Sales):* M A Krishnamachari; *Deputy Dir (Information, Publicity):* D Das Gupta; *Deputy Dir (Production):* Dhruv Bhargava; *Deputy Dir (Arts):* Jyotish Datta Gupta
Book Centres: A-4 Green Park, New Delhi; City Central Library, Ashok Nagar, Hyderabad; 67/2 Mahatma Gandhi Rd, Calcutta; Government Higher Secondary School, Town Hall, Amritsar; University of Jabalpur, Jabalpur
Subjects: Covering all aspects of human endeavour with particular reference to India; meant for a general readership
Founded: 1957

National Council of Applied Economic Research, Publications Division, Parisila Bhavan, 11 Indraprastha Estate, New Delhi 110002   Tel: 273791/273798   Cable Add: Arthsandan   Telex: 313380 Ncar In
Director-General: I Z Bhatty
Subject: Economics and allied subjects
1982-83: 1 title   *Founded:* 1956

National Council of Educational Research & Training, Publication Department*, Sri Aurobindo Marg, New Delhi 110016   Tel: 663983/662707-8   Cable Add: Eduprint
Secretary: V K Pandit; *Business Manager:* U N Jha; *Chief Editor:* Jaipal Nangia; *Production Officer:* U P Rao; *Rights & Permissions:* Head, Publication Department
Subjects: Secondary & Primary Textbooks, Educational Materials
1981: 196 titles   *Founded:* 1962

National Museum*, Janpath, New Delhi 110011   Tel: 383459/389368
Editorial: C B Pandey; *Sales:* V P Dwivedi; *Production:* N R Banerjee
Subjects: Indian Art and Museology

National Publishing House*, 23 Daryaganj, New Delhi 110006   Tel: 274161/275267
Man Dir: K L Malik; *Editorial, Production, Rights & Permissions:* S K Malik; *Sales:* M K Malik
Parent Company: K L Malik & Sons Pvt Ltd (at above address)
Imprints: Mayoor Paperbacks, Gyan Bharati
Branch Offs: K L Malik & Sons Pvt Ltd, 34 Netaji Subhash Marg, Allahabad 3; Malik &

Co, Chaura Rasta, Jaipur 302003
Subjects: Humanities, Social Science, Hindi Literature
Bookshops: At company and branch office addresses
Founded: 1950

Navajivan Trust, Post Navajivan, Ahmedabad 380014   Tel: 447329
Man Dir, Rights & Permissions: Jitendra T Desai; *Editorial:* Balmukund Dave; *Sales, Publicity:* Ratilal Naik
Branch Off: 130 Princess St, Bombay 2
Subjects: Biography, History, Philosophy, Reference, Religion, Books on and by Mahatma Gandhi
1981: 6 titles   *Founded:* 1919

Navyug Publishers*, 9-B Pleasure Garden Market, Chandni Chowk, Delhi 110006   Tel: 278370
Editorial: Pritam Singh; *Sales:* Gurbachan Singh
Subject: Bengali Literature
Founded: 1949

Naya Prokash*, 206 Bidhan Sarani, Calcutta 700006   Tel: 349566
Man Dir, Production, Rights & Permissions: B Mitra; *Editorial:* R Ghosh; *Sales, Publicity:* P S Basu
Subsidiary Companies: Darbari Udjog; India Book Exchange
Subjects: Indology, Yoga, Social Science, Management, History, Economics, Politics, Military Studies, Linguistics, Botany, Medical Science
Bookshop: 206 Bidhan Sarani, Calcutta 700006
1981: 10 titles   *1982:* 12 titles   *Founded:* 1962

Neeraj Publishing House*, B-3/94, Ashok Vihar, Phase II, Delhi 110052
Chief Executive, Publicity: Praveen Mittal; *Editorial, Production:* I C Mittal; *Sales, Rights & Permissions:* S K Bhatia
Orders to: DK Publishers' Distributors, 1 Ansari Rd, New Delhi 110002
Parent Company: DK Publishers' Distributors (qv under Major Booksellers)
Associate Companies: BR Publishing Corporation (qv); DK Publications (qv)
Subjects: Art, Archaeology, History
1981: 10 titles   *Founded:* 1981

Nem Chand & Brothers*, Civil Lines, Roorkee 247667   Tel: 2258/2752   Cable Add: Enginjour
Warehouse: Opp Dy S P Office, Roorkee 247667
Man Dir, Rights & Permissions: N C Jain; *Editorial Dir:* Dr Ashok K Jain; *Sales Dir:* Anil Jain; *Production Dir:* P K Jain; *Publicity, Advertising Dir:* T K Jain
Subsidiary Company: Roorkee Press, Roorkee
Subject: Engineering (publish *International Journal of Structures*)
Founded: 1951

New Book Centre*, PO Box 10815, Calcutta 700009 (Located at: 14 Ramanath Majumdar St, Calcutta)
Manager, Sales: A K Das; *Editorial:* K Sen; *Production:* Suren Dutt
Subject: Reference

New Light Publishers, B-9 Rattan Jyoti, 18 Rajendra Pl, New Delhi 110008   Tel: 572137
Managing Partner: A S Chowdhry; *Editorial:* Prof R P Chopra; *Publicity, Advertising:* R D Chowdhry
Subjects: Self-Improvement, General Knowledge, Books for Competitive Examinations
Founded: 1964

The **New Order** Book Co, Ellis Bridge, Ahmedabad 380006   Tel: 79065/445409
Cable Add: Nyuorder

Proprietor: D V Trivedi
Subjects: Humanities, Indology, Antiquarian, Arts, Reprints
Founded: 1939

Nirmal Book Agency*, 89 Mahatma Gandhi Rd, Calcutta 700007   Tel: 348405
Editorial: Biswanath De; *Sales:* Nirmal Kumar Saha
Subject: Children's Books

Orient Longman Ltd, 5-9-41/1 Basheer Bagh, Hyderabad 500029   Tel: 220343/37936
Chairman: J Rameshwar Rao; *Editorial:* Sujit Mukherjee; *Sales:* E Raghavan; *Rights & Permissions:* N R Arur
Subsidiary Company: Sangam Books Ltd, UK (qv)
Imprints: Sangam Books, Swan, Little Swan
Branch Offs: Kamani Marg, Ballard Estate, Bombay 400038; 17 Chittaranjan Ave, Calcutta 700072; 160 Anna Salai, Madras 600002; 1/24 Asaf Ali Rd, New Delhi 110002; 80/1 Mahatma Gandhi Rd, Bangalore 560001; SP Verma Rd, Patna 800001
Subjects: General Non-fiction, Biography, History, Philosophy, Reference, Juveniles, Low- & High-priced Paperbacks, Medicine, Psychology, Engineering, General & Social Science, Technology, University, Secondary & Primary Textbooks, Educational Materials
Bookshop: The Bookpoint, Kamari Marg, Ballard Estate, Bombay 700038
Founded: 1948

Orient Paperbacks+, 36-C Connaught Place, New Delhi 110001   Tel: 352081/312978
Cable Add: Visionbook
A division of Vision Books
Man Dir: Vishwanath; *Editorial, Production:* Kapil Malhotra; *Sales, Publicity, Rights & Permissions:* Sudhir Malhotra
Orders to: Sales Office, Madrassa Rd, Kashmere Gate, Delhi 110006
Tel: 227011/2512267
Parent Company: Vision Books Pvt Ltd (qv)
Associate Companies: Rajpal & Sons (qv); Shiksha Bharati (qv); Shiksha Bharati Press, G T Rd, Shadara, Delhi 32
Imprints: Anand Paperbacks, Vision Books
Branch Off: Vasant, Ground Floor, 3-B Pedder Rd, Bombay 400026
Book Club: Orient Book Club
Subjects: International Bestseller Reprints, General Non-fiction, Self-Tuition Series, Indo Anglian Fiction, Indian Culture and Thought, Poetry, Drama, Occult, Palmistry, Astrology, Sports, Adventure, Yoga, Health, Alternative Medicine, Reference
1981: 45 titles   *1982:* 50 titles   *Founded:* 1967

Oxford & I B H Publishing Co, 66 Janpath, New Delhi 110001   Tel: 321035/320518
Cable Add: Indamer
Dirs: Gulab Primlani, Mohan Primlani; *Editorial:* Mrs I V Ramchandani; *Sales, Publicity:* Raju Primlani; *Production Manager:* A P Gopalakrishnan
Subsidiary Companies: Amerind Publishing Co (P) Ltd, 66 Janpath, New Delhi 110001; Oxonian Press (P) Ltd (qv)
Branch Off: 17 Park St, Calcutta 700016
Subjects: Reference, Medicine, Psychology, Engineering, University Textbooks
Bookshops: Oxford Book & Stationery Co, Scindia House, New Delhi 110001; 17 Park St, Calcutta 700016 (qv under Major Booksellers)
1981: 78 titles   *Founded:* 1962

Oxford University Press+, 2/11 Ansari Rd, PO Box 7035, Daryaganj, New Delhi 110002   Tel: 273841/2, 277812   Cable Add: Oxonian Delhi
General Manager: R Dayal; *Publicity:* Mrs

A F Dhalla
Parent Company: Oxford University Press, UK (qv)
Branch Offs: Faraday House, P17 Mission Row Extension, GPO Box 530, Calcutta 700013; Oxford House, Mount Rd, PO Box 1079, Madras 600006; Oxford House, Apollo Bunder, PO Box 31, Bombay 400039
Subjects: Academic & General books for all levels (school, college, University and research), Languages (Arabic, Assamese, Bengali, English, French, Garo, Gujarati, Hindi, Kannada, Khasi, Malayalam, Marathi, Oriya, Punjabi, Sanskrit, Tamil, Telugu, Urdu)
1981: 92 titles *1982:* 110 titles *Founded:* 1912
ISBN Publisher's Prefix: 19

Oxonian Press (P) Ltd, N-56 Connaught Circus, New Delhi 110001 Tel: 44957 Cable Add: Indamer
Dir, Rights & Permissions: Gulab Primlani; *Sales Dir:* Dr A M Primlani
Parent Company: Oxford & IBH Publishing Co (qv)
Branch Offs: 17 Park St, Calcutta 700016; 29 Wodehouse Rd, Bombay; 165 Golf Links, New Delhi 110003
Subjects: Reference, Medicine, Engineering, General Science, University Textbooks
Bookshop: See Oxford & IBH Publishing Co

Paico Publishing House*, M G Rd, Ernakulam, Cochin 11 Tel: 35835 Cable Add: Paico
Man Dir: Kenchana V Pai
Subjects: General Fiction, History, General Science, University, Secondary & Primary Textbooks, Childrens Books
Bookshop: Paico Books & Arts, M G Road, Cochin 682011
Founded: 1955

Panchasheel Prakashan*, Film Colony, Chaura Rasta, Jaipur 302003 Tel: 65072
Editorial: M C Gupta; *Sales:* M P Gupta
Subjects: Academic, Fiction
Founded: 1968

Panjab University Publication Bureau*, Chandigarh Tel: 22782
Secretary: R K Malhotra
Subjects: Belles Lettres, Poetry, Biography, History, Philosophy, Reference, Religion, Social Science, University Textbooks
Bookshop: Panjab University Publication Bureau, Chandigarh 160014
Founded: 1948

Parag Prakashan*, 3/114 Karan Gali, Vishwas Nagar, Delhi 110032 Tel: 203850
Partner: Krishan
Subjects: Fiction, Poetry
Founded: 1972

Parimal Prakashan+, 'Parimal', Khadkeshwar, Aurangabad 431001 Tel: 4556
Man Dir, Production: A B Dashrathe; *Sales:* K D Danekar
Branch Offs: 4th floor Shivganga Chambers, Bajirao Rd, Pune; 31-A Saifee Manzil, Kennedy Bridge, Bombay
Subjects: Social Sciences, Humanities, Marathi Literature, Archaeology, Medical Science, English Literature
Bookshop: Marathwada Book Distributors (at above address)
1981: 4 titles *1982:* 4 titles *Founded:* 1974

Parkash Brothers, 546 Books Market, Ludhiana 141008 Tel: 37258 Cable Add: Parkash Books
Chief Executive, Editorial: R P Tondon; *Sales, Production, Publicity:* K L Tondon; *Rights & Permissions:* R P Tondon, K L Tondon

Associate Company: Vijaya Publications (at above address)
Branch Off: Mai Hiran Gate, Jullundur
Subjects: Education, Physics, Engineering
Bookshop: At above address
Founded: 1948-9

Path Publishers*, 305A Hans Bhavan, Bahadur Shah Zafar Marg, New Delhi 110902 Tel: 272539/622120
Chief Executive, Editorial, Publicity, Rights & Permissions: P J Koshy; *Sales:* Mohan Eapen; *Production:* S K Bhatnagar
Subjects: Law, Commerce
Founded: 1979

Pearl Publishers*, 206 Bidhan Saranee, Calcutta 700006
Proprietor: M Bhattacharjee; *Editorial:* S Roy; *Sales:* T Roy
Subjects: Political Science, Economics
Founded: 1977

People's Publishing House (P) Ltd*, 5 Rani Jhansi Rd, New Delhi 110055 Tel: 529365/523349/521041 Cable Add: Quamikitab
Chairman: Dr G Adhikari; *General Manager:* Shri Jiten Sen; *Sales Manager:* Shri P N Gopinadhan
Subsidiary Company: Lok Vangmaya Griha (Pvt) Ltd (qv)
Subjects: Belles Lettres, Poetry, Biography, History, Philosophy, Juveniles, Low- & High-priced Paperbacks, Engineering, Social Science, University Textbooks
Bookshop: 2 Marina Arcade, Connaught Pl, New Delhi 110001
Founded: 1942

Pilgrim Publishers*, 56 Jatin Das Rd, Calcutta 700029, West Bengal Tel: 464323
Man Dir: S De; *Editorial:* Mrs R Mukherjee; *Sales:* F C Dutta; *Production, Publicity:* T K Mukherjee
Parent Company: Traco, India
Subjects: Literature, History, Art, Archaeology
Bookshop: 18B/1B Tamer Lane, Calcutta 700009
Founded: 1966

Pitambar Publishing Co, 888 East Park Rd, Karol Bagh, New Delhi 110005 Tel: 519433/562919/512041 Cable Add: Pitambar New Delhi
Man Dirs: Ved Bhushan, Anand Bhushan, Sushil Bhushan; *Sales:* P C Bhandari; *Publicity:* Anand Bhushan; *Editorial:* B N Ahuja; *Production, Rights & Permissions:* Sushil Bhushan
Parent Company: Pitambar Book Depot (at above address)
Associate Companies: Bharat Enterprises, Delhi; Ambar Prakashan; Parijat Enterprises, New Delhi; Pitambar Printing Press
Subjects: General Fiction, Reference, University, Secondary & Primary Textbooks
Bookshop: Pitambar Book Depot (at above address)
1981: 70 titles *1982:* 80 titles *Founded:* 1947

Popular Prakashan Pvt Ltd, 35-C Tardco Rd, Bombay 400034 Tel: 376294/376295/370656
Man Dir: Ramdas Ganesh Bhatkal; *Joint Dir:* Sadanand Ganesh Bhatkal
Subjects: Anthropology, Sociology, Arts, Crafts, Music, Biography, Economics, Education, History, Literature, Law, Philosophy, Religion, Politics, Administration, Physics, Mathematics, Chemistry, Medicine
1982: 60 titles

Prabhat Prakashan, 205 Chawri Bazar, Delhi 110006 Tel: 264676
Chief Executive: Shyam Sunder; *Editorial:*

Shyam Bahadur Verma; *Sales:* Raghuvir Verma; *Production:* Dharam Vir
Branch Off: Mathura
Subjects: Miscellaneous
1981: 75 titles *1982:* 79 titles *Founded:* 1952

Prachi Prakashan*, PO Box 3537, New Delhi 110024 (Located at: L-3 Lajpatnagar III, New Delhi) Tel: 693331
Proprietor: A K Dash
Subject: Anthropology
Founded: 1976

Pragati Prakashan, PO Box 62, Meerut 250001 (Located at: Lajpat Rai Market, Begum Bridge, Meerut) Tel: Meerut 73022/75246 Cable Add: Publication
Man & Sales Dir: K K Mittal; *Publicity, Advertising Dir:* A K Mittal
Subjects: Physics, Chemistry, Mathematics, General & Social Sciences, University Textbooks, Commerce, Management
Bookshop: At above address
1981: 8 titles *1982:* 10 titles *Founded:* 1955

Prakash Prakashan*, 8 Ram Nagar Colony, Agra 2, Uttar Pradesh

Prakasham Publications*, Alleppey 688003, Kerala State Tel: 2771/2181
Chief Executive: Vithuvattickal Lucas; *Editorial:* Hormice C Perumali; *Sales:* J Chirayail
Subjects: General, Fiction
Founded: 1967

Prayer Books*, 43–B Nandaram Sen St, Calcutta 700005 Tel: 54-2306
Chief Executive, Sales, Production: Subrata Saha; *Editorial:* Subhas Saha; *Publicity, Rights & Permissions:* Mrs Papiya Saha
Subject: Literature (in Bengali and English)
Founded: 1978

Prentice-Hall of India Pvt Ltd, M-97 Connaught Circus, New Delhi 110001 Tel: 352590/351779 Cable Add: Prenhall New Delhi
Chairman, Man Dir: Asoke K Ghosh
Associate Company: Prentice-Hall Inc, Englewood Cliffs, NJ 07632, USA
Subject: Textbooks
Founded: 1963

Printox*, E-210 Pragati Vihar, Lodhi Rd, New Delhi 110003 Tel: 693097
Proprietor: S G Nene
Branch Off: 1557 Sadashiv Peth, Pune 411030 Tel: 442960; K-15/7 Bibihatia, Varanasi 211001
Subjects: Politics, Social Science, Literary Criticism, Philosophy, Ancient Indian Literature, Art

Progressive Corporation Pvt Ltd*, 3rd floor, Jehangir Wadia Building, 51 Mahatma Gandhi Rd, Flora Fountain, Fort Bombay 400023 Tel: 251634/254813 Cable Add: Progcorp
Man Dir: Dr K D P Madon; *Sales Dirs:* Dr Rustom S Davar, Nanabhoy S Davar
Branch Off: 1 Velders St, Mount Rd, Madras 600002
Subjects: Management & Commerce, Accountancy, Business Law, Banking, Economics, Statistics, Marketing, Salesmanship, Advertising
Founded: 1932

Publication Board*, Assam, Bamunimaidan, Gauhati 781021

Publications & Information Directorate*, Hillside Rd, New Delhi 110012 Tel: 586301 Cable Add: Publiform
Editorial: Y R Chadha; *Sales:* Kishan Singh
Subject: Scientific

Punjab State University Textbook Board*, S C O 2935-36, Sector 22-C, Chandigarh 160022 Tel: 28983

Editorial: Prithipal Singh Kapur; *Production, Sales:* M Singh Rattan
Subject: Academic

Punjabi Pustak Bhandar*, Dariba, Delhi 110006 Tel: 266232
Managing Partner: Gulshan Rai Verma
Associate Companies: Diamond Books International, Diamond Pocket Books, Diamond Comics (P) Ltd (qv) (all at 2715 Daryaganj, New Delhi 11002)

Radha Krishna Prakashan*, 2 Ansari Rd, Daryaganj, New Delhi 110002 Tel: 275851 Cable Add: Lokpriya Delhi
Man Dir: Om Prakash
Subjects: General Fiction, Belles Lettres, Poetry, Biography, Juveniles, High-priced Paperbacks, University Textbooks
Founded: 1965

Radha Soami Satsang Beas, PO Dera Baba Jaimal Singh, Distt Amritsar 143204 Tel: Rayya 50, Dhilwan 40 Cable Add: Radhasoami Satsang Beas
Man Dir, Production, Publicity: K S Narang; *Secretary, Rights & Permissions:* S L Sondhi; *Sales:* J C Moorgai (Home), Krishin Babani (Abroad)
Parent Company: Charitable & Religious Society, Radhasoami Satsang Beas
Subjects: Religion, Philosophy
1981: 133 titles *1982:* 107 titles *Founded:* 1957

Radiant Publishers+, E-155 Kalkaji, New Delhi 110019 Tel: 635477
Man Dir, Sales, Rights & Permissions, Production, Publicity: V K Jain; *Editorial:* R Jain
Subjects: Politics, International Affairs, Economics, Sociology, History
1982: 6 titles *1983:* 12 titles *Founded:* 1973

Rajasthan Hindi Granth Academy*, A–26/2 Vidyalaya Marg, Tilak Nagar, Jaipur 302004 Tel: 61410
Chief Executive: Dr Ram Bali Upadhyaya; *Editorial:* Dr M P Dadhich; *Sales, Publicity:* S N Sharma; *Production:* Y D Shalaya
Subjects: Social Science, Science, Humanities
Founded: 1969

Rajesh Publications*, 1 Ansari Rd, Daryaganj, New Delhi 110002 Tel: 274550
Man Dir: Gupta Mohan Lal
Subjects: History, Geography, Religion, Philosophy, Economics, General
1981: 10 titles *Founded:* 1970

Rajhans Prakashan Mandir*, Dharma Alok, Ram Nagar, Meerut, Uttar Pradesh

Rajkamal Prakashan Pvt Ltd*, 8 Netaji Subhash Marg, New Delhi 110002
Subjects: Juveniles, Education, Paperbacks

Rajneesh Foundation*, Shree Rajneesh Ashram, 17 Koregaon Park, Poona 411001 Tel: 28127/20981/20982 Cable Add: Tathata Telex: 0145421 Tao
Man Dir, Sales, Rights & Permissions: Ma Yoga Laxmi; *Publicity:* Swami Krishna Prem
Subjects: Religion, Philosophy, Psychology; the teachings of Bhagwan Shree Rajneesh (English and Hindi)
Bookshop: At above address
Founded: 1969

Rajpal & Sons*, Kashmere Gate, PO Box 1064, Delhi 110006 Tel: 229174, 223904 Cable Add: Rajpalsons Delhi
Man Dir: Mr Vishwanath; *Sales:* Ishwar Chandra; *Editorial:* Mahendra Kulshreshtna; *Production:* Prakash Pandit; *Publicity, Rights & Permissions:* Kapil Malhotra
Associate Companies: Orient Paperbacks (qv); Shiksha Bharati (qv); Vision Books Pvt Ltd (qv)

Subjects: General Fiction, Literary Criticism, Humanities, Science, Juveniles
Bookshop: At above address
Founded: 1891

Ram Prasad & Sons*, Hospital Rd, Agra 282003 Tel: 72935 Cable Add: Modern
Man Dir: H N Agarwala; *Sales Dir:* R N Agarwala; *Publicity & Advertising:* B N Agarwala
Subsidiary Companies: Modern Printers, 1153 Bagh Muzaffar Khan, Agra 2; Sanchi Prakashan, Bhopal 1
Subjects: Agriculture & Veterinary Science, Commerce & Economics, Education & Psychology, Engineering & Technology, Geography, Mathematics & Statistics, Physics, Political Science, Sociology, Social Work, Criminology, University, Secondary & Primary Textbooks
Bookshops: Modern Book Depot, Hospital Rd, Agra 3; Bal Vihar, Hamidia Rd, Bhopal 1
Founded: 1905

Sri **Ramakrishna** Math, PO Box 635, Mylapore, Madras 600004 (Located at: 16 Sri Ramakrishna Math Rd, Mylapore, Madras) Tel: 71231
President: Sri Ramakrishna Math
Subjects: Religion, Culture, Philosophy
Bookshops: 16 Ramakrishna Math Rd, Mylapore, Madras 4; South Mada St, Mylapore Madras 4
1982: 350 titles *Founded:* 1897

Rastogi Publications*, Shivaji Rd, Meerut 250002 Tel: 73698, 73132 Cable Add: Rastogico
Editorial: Mrs Prakash Wati; *Sales, Publicity:* H K Rastogi; *Production, Rights & Permissions:* R K Rastogi
Associate Company: Rastogi Associates (at above address)
Subsidiary Companies: Pioneer Printers, Rastogi & Co (both at above address)
Subjects: University Textbooks in Botany, Political Science, Zoology and Education
Founded: 1966

Ratnabharati*, Ilaco House, Sir Pherozeshah Mehta Rd, PO Box 486, Bombay 400001 Tel: 297739 Cable Add: Pustaken
Editorial, Production: Punit Batra; *Sales, Publicity, Rights & Permissions:* Ranjit Batra
Subject: Illustrated children's books on Indian subjects
Founded: 1965

Rekha Prakashan, 16 Daryaganj, New Delhi 110002 Tel: 279907
Chief Executive, Rights & Permissions: K C Aryan; *Editorial:* S Aryan; *Sales:* B N Aryan; *Production, Publicity:* G D Aryan
Subjects: Art, Indology
1981: 2 titles *Founded:* 1973

Researchco, 1865 Trinagar, Delhi 110035 Tel: 7128547 Cable Add: Searchbook
Manager: O P Vaish; *Sales:* Anand Jain
Subsidiary Company: Researchco Reprints (at above address)
Associate Company: A J Reprints Agency, 24 B–5 Desh Bandhu Gupta Rd, Karol Bagh, New Delhi 110005
Branch Off: 2217 HAL, 3rd Stage, 10th Cross, Bangalore 560075
Subjects: Scientific, Technical
1981: 5 titles *Founded:* 1969

Roli Books International, 4378/4 Ansari Rd, Daryaganj, New Delhi 110002 Tel: 276325 Cable Add: Rolipub
Chief Executive, Rights & Permissions: Pramod Kapoor; *Editorial:* B N Varma; *Sales, Publicity:* Sanjeev Ohri
Subjects: Illustrated Books of General Interest
Founded: 1979

Roorkee Press, see Nem Chand & Brothers (qv)

K K Roy (Pvt) Ltd, PO Box 10210, Calcutta 700019 (Located at: 55 Gariahat Rd, Calcutta) Tel: 474872 Cable Add: Helbell
Man Dir: Dr K K Roy; *Sales Dir:* S Paul; *Publicity Dir:* Renu Roy; *Advertising Dir:* G Govindan; *Rights & Permissions:* Dr K K Roy
Subsidiary Company: Intertrade Publications (India) Pvt Ltd (at above address)
Subjects: Belles Lettres, Poetry, Biography, History, Philosophy, Reference, Religion, Medicine, University Textbooks
Founded: 1954

Rupa & Co, PO Box 12333, Calcutta 700073 (Located at: 15 Bankim Chatterjee St, Calcutta) Tel: 344821/346305 Cable Add: Rupanco
Man Dir, Editorial, Rights & Permissions: D Mehra; *Sales:* R N Barman; *Production:* N D Mehra, R K Mehra; *Publicity:* S K Mehra, C K Mehra
Branch Offs: 94 South Malaka, Allahabad 211001; 102 Prasad Chambers, Swadeshi Mills Compound, Opera House, Bombay 400004; 3831 Pataudi House Rd, Daryaganj, New Delhi 110002
Subjects: Art, Education, History, Literature, Fiction, Philosophy, Religion, Sport, Pastimes
Bookshop: At above address (qv under Major Booksellers)
Founded: 1936

Sahitya Bhawan Pvt Ltd*, 93 KP Kakkar Rd, Allahabad 211003 Tel: 51077
Man Dir, Rights & Permissions: Girish Tandon; *Editorial:* Onkar Sharad; *Sales:* Ram Chandra Sharma; *Production:* P K Singh; *Publicity:* Ram Nath
Associate Company: Vivek Prakishthan (at above address)
Subjects: Hindi Literature and University Textbooks
Bookshop: At above address
Founded: 1917

Sahitya Pravarthaka Co-operative Society Ltd, PO Box 94, Kottayam 686001, Kerala Tel: 4111/4112/4114 Cable Add: Sahithyam
Secretary: M K Madhavan Nayar; *Sales:* K S Pillai; *Production:* P Gopinath
Orders to: Sales Manager, National Book Stall, Kottayam
Subjects: Literature, Art, Science
Bookshops: National Book Stall, PO Box 40, Kottayam 686001 (and branches throughout Kerala)
Founded: 1945

Sahitya Samsad, an imprint of Shishu Sahitya Samsad Pvt Ltd (qv)

Saint Paul Publications, 28-B Chatham Lines, Allahabad 211002 Tel: 53728
Chief Executive: Fr Anselm Poovathanikunnel; *Editorial, Rights & Permissions:* Fr Joe Narivelil; *Sales:* Br Ignatius T; *Production:* Br Vincent C; *Publicity:* Fr George Chathanatt
Imprint: Better Yourself Books (qv)
Branch Offs: Bangalore 73; Bombay 50; Cochin 11; New Delhi 1; Madras 1
Subjects: Practical Psychology, Self-improvement, Fiction, Biography, Spiritual
Bookshops: Examiner Press Bookshop, 35 Dalal St, Bombay 400023; St Paul Book Centre, Broadway, Cochin 31, Kerala; Good Pastor International Book Centre, 63 Armenian St, Madras 600001; Saint Paul International Book Centre, H-30 Connaught Circus, New Delhi 110001
1981: 48 titles *1982:* 46 titles *Founded:* 1952

Sanchi Prakashan, subsidiary of Ram Prasad & Sons (qv)

Sangam Books, an imprint of Orient Longman Ltd (qv)

Sanskrit Pustak Bhandar, 38 Bidhan Sarani, Calcutta 700006 Tel: 34-1208
Chief Executive: Shyama Pada Bhattacharya
Subject: Indology, Reference
Founded: 1932
Miscellaneous: Also book dealers

Sanskriti, an imprint of Arnold-Heinemann Publishers (India) Pvt Ltd (qv)

Rashtriya Sanskrit **Sansthan**, 2-A Ramkishor Rd, Civil Lines, Delhi 54 Tel: 222545/6 Cable Add: Sansthan
Chief Executive: Dr R K Sharma; *Editorial, Sales, Production, Publicity:* A Sampathnarayanan
1981: 17 titles *1982:* 21 titles *Founded:* 1970

Saraswat Library*, 206 Bidhan Sarani, Calcutta 700006 Tel: 345492
Managing Partner: B Bhattacharyya
Subjects: Poetry, History, Music, Art, Philosophy, Reference, Religion, Juveniles, General & Social Science, University, Secondary Textbooks
Bookshop: At above address
Founded: 1914

Sarita Prakashan+, 175 Nauchandi Grounds, Meerut City Tel: 73515/75075 Cable Add: Prabhatpress Telex: 0594-215
Man Dir, Publicity, Rights & Permissions: K A Rastogi; *Editorial:* Rahul Rastogi; *Sales:* Atul Rastogi; *Production:* Abhay Rastogi
Subsidiary Companies: Prabhat Offset Printers Pvt Ltd; Prabhat Press
Branch Off: Netaji Subhash Marg, Daryaganj, New Delhi Tel: 276292
Subjects: Engineering, Botany, Literature, Reference
Founded: 1963

M C **Sarkar** & Sons (P) Ltd*, 14 Bankim Chatterjee St, Calcutta 700073

Sasta Sahitya Mandal*, N-77 Connaught Circus, New Delhi 110001 Tel: 40505 Cable Add: Satsahitya
Secretary: Shri Yashpal Jain
Branch Off: Zero Rd, Allahabad
Subjects: History, Agriculture, Textbooks, Literature, Education, Philosophy, Psychology, Languages, Paperbacks, Economics
1981: 43 titles *1982:* 44 titles *Founded:* 1925

Satya Press, c/o Ananda Ashram, Thattanchavady, Pondicherry 605009 Tel: 2403 Cable Add: Yoga Life
Chief Executive: Dr Swami Gitananda; *Editorial:* Meenakshi Devi
Imprint: Yoga Life
Subjects: Yoga, Indian Philosophy (in English only)
Bookshop: Ananda Book Shop (at above address)
1981: 22 titles *1982:* 30 titles *Founded:* 1969

Sawan Kirpal Publications, 2 Canal Rd, Vijay Nagar, Delhi 110009 Tel: 7110757
Man Dir: S Darshan Singh; *Editorial:* Dr Vinod Sena; *Sales:* Rajesh Seth; *Production:* Jay Linksman; *Publicity:* Chris McCluney
Parent Company: Sawan Kirpal Publications Spiritual Society, H-11 Vijay Nagar, Delhi 110009
Branch Off: Rt 1, PO Box 24, Bowling Green, Virginia 22427, USA
Subject: Religion
Founded: 1977

Scientific Book Agency*, 22 Raja Woodmunt St, PO Box 239, Calcutta 700001 Tel: 221500/229405 Cable Add: Argosy Telex: Argosy 0212846
Man Dir: J Sinha; *Editorial:* P Sinha; *Science Editors:* Atish Sinha, Soumendra Sinha; *Sales Dir:* S P Sinha; *Production:* S Sinha; *Publicity & Advertising:* Snehamoy Sinha; *Rights & Permissions:* Swapan Mitra
Branch Off: 79/2 Mahatma Ghandi Rd, Calcutta 700009; 56-D Mirza Ghalib St, Calcutta 700016
Subjects: History, Medicine, Economics, Politics, Physics, Chemistry, Biological Sciences, Veterinary, Engineering
1981: 19 titles *Founded:* 1954

Seemant Prakashan*, 922 Kucha Rohella Khan, Daryaganj, New Delhi 110002
Chief Executive: Narinder Nath Soz; *Sales:* Rajesh Didden; *Production:* Ajay Didden
Subjects: General (Hindi and Urdu)
1981: 9 titles *1982:* 9 titles *Founded:* 1976

Selina Publishers, 4725/21A Dayanand Marg, Daryaganj, New Delhi 110002 Tel: 277230/277375
Man Dir, Editorial, Production: H L Gupta; *Sales:* P C Gupta; *Publicity:* H S Ghoshal; *Rights & Permissions:* Mrs S L Gupta
Subsidiary Company: Sanket Paperbacks
Associate Company: Granth Bharati (Printing Press)
Branch Off: 4858/24A Daryaganj, New Delhi 110002
Subjects: Primary textbooks, Juveniles
Book Club: Sanket Library Yojna
Founded: 1975

Sharda Prakashan*, Mehrauli, New Delhi 110030 Tel: 653982
Chief Executive, Production, Rights & Permissions: Vijay Dev Jhari; *Editorial, Publicity:* Ravinder Jhari; *Sales:* R D Jhari
Subsidiary Company: Nalanda Prakashan, 33/1 Mehrauli, New Delhi 110030
Associate Company: Itihas Shodh Sansthan, 33/1 Mehrauli, New Delhi 110030
Subjects: Literary Criticism, Fiction, Drama, Memoirs, Children's Literature, General
Bookshop: 16–F3 Ansari Rd, Daryaganj, New Delhi 110002
1981: 40 titles *Founded:* 1971

R R **Sheth** & Co, PO Box 2517, Bombay 400002 (Located at: 110/112 S Gandhi Marg, Bombay) Tel: 313441 Cable Add: Literature Bombay 2
Man Dir: Bhagatbhai Bhuralal Sheth; *Other Offices:* Dhirajlal Chunilal Mody
Associate Company: Lokpriya Prakashan, 110 S Gandhi Marg, Bombay 400002
Branch Off: Opp Phuvara, Gandhi Rd, Ahmedabad 380001 Tel: 380573
Subjects: Gujarati books on all subjects for all ages and tastes
Bookshops: See under Major Booksellers
Founded: 1926

Shiksha Bharati, Madarsa Rd, Kashmere Gate, Delhi 110006 Tel: 223904
Man Dir, Rights & Permissions: Sudhir Malhotra; *Editorial:* Meera Johri; *Sales, Publicity:* Mrs Parveen Malhotra; *Production:* Indu Malhotra
Associate Companies: Orient Paperbacks (qv); Rajpal & Sons (qv); Vision Books Pvt Ltd (qv)
Subsidiary Company: Shiksha Bharati Press, 18 G T Rd, Shahdara, Delhi 110032
Subjects: Juveniles, Educational
Founded: 1959

Shishu Sahitya Samsad Pvt Ltd*, 32-A Acharya Prafulla Chandra Rd, Calcutta 700009 Tel: 35-7669
Man Dir: Mohendranath Dutt; *Editorial Manager, Publicity Manager:* Golokendu Ghosh; *Sales, Production, Rights & Permissions Dir:* Debajyoti Dutt
Imprint: Sahitya Samsad
Subjects: Juvenile Literature, Lexicons, Classics, Art
Founded: 1951

Shree Mahavir Book Depot (Publishers)*, 2603 Nai Sarak, Delhi 110006 Tel: 262993/710823
Chief Executive: Ram Kanwar; *Editorial:* Prem Chandra; *Sales, Rights & Permissions:* Hem Chandra; *Production:* Ram Chandra; *Publicity:* Harish Chandra
Subjects: Commerce, Accountancy, Economics, Political Science, History, Geography, Physics, Chemistry, Music, Domestic Science
Founded: 1948

Shree Saraswati Sadan*, A-I/32 Safdarjang Enclave, New Delhi 110029 Tel: 661539
Chief Executive, Sales, Production, Rights & Permissions: Amitabh Ranjan; *Editorial, Publicity:* Mrs Abha Ranjan
Branch Off: Mussoorie (UP)
Subjects: History, Politics, Sociology, Historical Fiction (in English and Hindi)
Founded: 1972

Shri Ram Centre for Industrial Relations and Human Resources, 5 Sadhu Vaswani Marg, New Delhi 110005 Tel: 568261 Cable Add: Sricir
Man Dir, Editorial, Rights & Permissions: Arun Joshi; *Sales, Production, Publicity:* K K Bhargava
Subject: Indian Journal of Industrial Relations
Founded: 1963

Skyline Publishing House*, 28/2 St No 3, Friends Colony, Shahdara, Delhi 110032 Tel: 203346
Chief Executive: Surjeet Gupta; *Editorial, Rights & Permissions:* S N Sarkar; *Sales:* Nawab Singh; *Production, Publicity:* Chandrasekhar
Subjects: Current Affairs, Economics, Self-improvement, Yoga, Cookery, Beauty Culture
Founded: 1979

Smriti Prakashan*, 124 Shah Rara Bagh, Allahabad 211003 Tel: 54589
Chief Executive, Editorial, Production: Bal Krishna Tripathi; *Sales:* Niraj Kumar Tripathi; *Publicity:* Deepak
Subjects: General
Bookshop: At above address
Founded: 1969

Somaiya Publications Pvt Ltd+, 172 Mumbai Marathi Grantha Sangrahalaya Marg, Dadar, Bombay 400014 Tel: 8820230 Cable Add: Bookmark, Bombay
Chief Editor, Rights & Permissions: S G Nene; *Educational Manager:* P S Warty
Parent Company: The Godavari Sugar Mills Ltd, Fazalbhoy Building, Mahatma Gandhi Rd, Bombay 400001
Associate Companies: The Book Centre Ltd (Book Sales Division), Ranade Rd, Dadar, Bombay 400028; The Book Centre Ltd (Printing Press Division), Plot No 103, 6th Rd, Sion, Bombay 400022
Branch Off: F-6 Bank of Baroda Bldg, Parliament St, New Delhi 110001
Subjects: Architecture, Commerce, Education, Engineering, History, Political Science, Religion and Philosophy, Language, Literature, Management, Mathematics, Physics, Chemistry
Founded: 1967

South Asian Publishers Pvt Ltd, 36 Netaji Subhash Marg, Daryaganj, New Delhi 110002 Tel: 276292
Chief Executive, Editorial, Rights & Permissions: Vinod Kumar; *Sales:* K Srinivasa Murthy; *Production, Publicity:* K A Rastogi
Branch Off: 177 Avvai Shanmugham Salai,

Madras 600086
Subjects: Academic Works in Science, Technology, Social Sciences
Founded: 1980

Spectrum Publications*, PO Box 45, Pan Bazar, Gauhati 781001, Assam Tel: 24791 Cable Add: Spectrum, Gauhati
Publisher: Krishan Kumar; *Editorial:* Alex P Joseph; *Sales:* R K Das; *Publicity:* Miss Rama Brahma
Subjects: Tourism, Reference, Anthropology, Sociology, Annual Yearbooks and Directories, Children's Books, Journals
Founded: 1976

Springer Books (India) Pvt Ltd*, 6 Community Centre, Panchsheel Park, New Delhi 110017 Tel: 654995 Cable Add: Spriverlag
Man Dir: N K Mehra
Associate Companies: Springer-Verlag Berlin — Heidelberg — New York — Tokyo GmbH & Co KG, Federal Republic of Germany (qv); Narosa Publishing House, Narosa Book Distributors (both at above New Delhi address)
Subjects: Pure and Applied Science, Medicine
Founded: 1980

Sree Rama Publishers*, 4000 Market St, Secunderabad 500025 Tel: 73128 Cable Add: Books, Secunderabad
Man Dir: Shiva Ramaiah Pabba; *Editorial:* Sreenivas Prabhu Pabba; *Sales:* Subash Chandra Sekhar Pabba; *Production:* Shivaramaiah Pabba; *Publicity, Rights & Permissions:* Shivarajaiah Pabba
Orders to: 113 Sarojini Devi Rd, Secunderabad 500003
Parent Company: Sree Rama Book Depot, Market St, Secunderabad
Associate Companies: Popular Book House, Pan Bazaar, Secunderabad; Sree Sita Rama Book Depot, Siddiamber Bazar, Hyderabad
Subjects: Primary & Secondary Textbooks, Theology in local language and English
Bookshops: Sree Rama Book Depot, Gunfoundry, Hyderabad 500001; Sree Rama Book Depot, Siddiamber Bazar, Hyderabad
Founded: 1916

The **Standard** Book Depot*, Avenue Rd, Bangalore 560002 Tel: 26535/72625 Cable Add: Stanbook
Man Dir, Rights & Permissions: B Rajashekar; *Editorial:* B Gurunath; *Sales:* B Ananth; *Production:* R L Narasimhiah; *Publicity:* S Sudhindra
Subjects: Fiction, General Literature, Popular Science, Juveniles
Bookshop: At above address
Founded: 1935

Star Publications (Pvt) Ltd*, 4/5B Asaf Ali Rd, New Delhi 110002 Tel: 273335/274874/265135 Cable Add: Starpublis Telex: 31-5328 Star In
Man Dir, Sales, Production, Publicity: Amar Nath
Associate Company: Star Book Centre, Delhi 110006
Subsidiary Company: Publications India, New Delhi 110001, also London W1, UK
Subjects: Paperbacks in Urdu and Hindi
Book Club: Star Book Bank
Founded: 1969
Miscellaneous: One of the largest exporters of Indian books to world libraries and booksellers

State Institute of Languages*, Kerala, 'Nalanda', Trivandrum 695003 Tel: 61306
Dir, Production, Publicity, Rights & Permissions: Dr A N P Ummerkutty; *Assistant Dirs:* Dr K Velayudhan Nair, N Ramesan; *Editorial:* N Vigayan (Social Sciences), Dr C G Kartha (Physical Sciences), K N Sreenivasan (Natural Sciences), K K Krishna Kumar (Technical Sciences), P Balan (Languages); *Sales:* N Velappan Nair
Subjects: University Level Textbooks in Regional Languages, Malayalam
Founded: 1968

Sterling Publishers Pvt Ltd, L-10 Green Park Extension, New Delhi 110016 Tel: 669560 Cable Add: Paperbacks
Man Dir: O P Ghai; *Editorial:* Minnie Sahai; *Publicity:* Cynthia Stephen; *Sales, Production, Rights & Permissions:* S K Ghai
Subsidiary Companies: Indian Book Industry, AB-9 Safdarjang Enclave, New Delhi 110029; Sterling Printers (at above address)
Imprints: Asian Publishers; IBI; Sterling Paperbacks
Branch Off: Sri Maruthi Complex, 325 5th Main Rd, Gandhinagar, Bangalore 560009
Subjects: History, Philosophy, Economics, Reference, Low-priced Paperbacks, Social Science, University Textbooks, Political Science, Agriculture, Art, Autobiography, Education, Fiction, International Relations, Library Science, Management and Administration, Religion, Sociology
Book Club: Sterling Book Club
Bookshop: At above address
1981: 85 titles *1982:* 96 titles *Founded:* 1965

The **Students'** Book Co*, SMS Highway, Jaipur 302003 Tel: 72455 (shop), 74087 (res)
Proprietor, Rights & Permissions: Tara Chand Verma; *Man Dir:* J D Verma; *Editorial, Sales, Production:* Subhash Chandra Verma; *Publicity:* Satish Chandra Verma
Subsidiary Company: United Printers, Radha Damoderji Ki Gali, Chaura Rasta, Jaipur 302003
Subjects: Science, Commerce, Arts, Sanskrit, Hindi, English, Rajasthani
Bookshops: Chinmaya Prakashan, Chaura Rasta, Jaipur 302003; Vaner Prakashan, Chaura Rasta, Jaipur 302003
Founded: 1939

Subodh Pocket Books*, 2/4240A Ansari Rd, New Delhi 110002 Tel: 274513/278858
Chief Executive, Rights & Permissions: Vijay Kumar; *Sales, Production:* Anil Kumar Arya
Subsidiary Companies: Govindram Hasanand, 4408 Nai Sarak, Delhi 110006; Subodh Publications, 2/3B Ansari Rd, New Delhi 110002
Subjects: Fiction, Non-fiction, Vedic literature
Founded: 1965

Sudha Publications Pvt Ltd*, 604 Prabhat Kiran, Rajendra Pl, New Delhi 110008 Tel: 582898
Man Dir: S K Sachdeva; *Sales Dir:* Amar Nath; *Publicity & Advertising Dir:* Vijay Lakshmi; *Rights & Permissions:* C G Advani
Founded: 1960

Sultan Chand and Sons+, 4792-23 Daryaganj, New Delhi 110002 Tel: 278659/277843/279080
Man Dir: Prakash Chand; *Editorial, Production:* S Chand; *Sales, Publicity, Rights & Permissions:* Manohar Pant
Associate Companies: Sultan Chand & Sons Pvt Ltd, 24 Daryaganj, New Delhi 110002; Sultan Chand Publishing House Pvt Ltd, 23 Daryaganj, New Delhi 110002
Subjects: Management, Business, Accounting, Law, Commerce, Economics, Chemistry, Physics, Maths, Statistics, Public Administration
Bookshop: Premier Book Co, 4792-23 Daryaganj, New Delhi 110002
1981: 25 titles *1982:* 30 titles *Founded:* 1950

Suman Prakashan (P) Ltd*, 16/1022 Arya Samaj Rd, 18 Hari Singh Nalwa, New Delhi 110005

Surjeet Book Depot (Regd)+, PO Box 1425, Delhi 110006 (Located at: 4074-75 Nai Sarak, Delhi) Tel: 263080/265987
Man Dir: Harnam Singh
Subjects: Literature, Social Science
1981: 160 titles *1982:* 190 titles *Founded:* 1950
Miscellaneous: Also booksellers, distributors and remainder dealers (qv)

Swan, an imprint of Orient Longman Ltd (qv)

Tamil Puthakalayam*, 58 T P Koil St, Triplicane, Madras 600005 Tel: 843226
Chief Executive: K N Muthiah; *All offices:* K N Muthiah, A Kannan
Subjects: Fiction, Drama, Literary Criticism, Religion, Medicine, General
Founded: 1946

Taraporevala (DB) Sons & Co Pvt Ltd, 210 Dr Dadabhai Naoroji Rd, Bombay 400001 Tel: 261433/269782 Cable Add: Bookshop, Bombay
Chief Executive: Professor Russi J Taraporevala; *Dirs:* Mrs Manekbai J Taraporevala, Miss Sooni J Taraporevala
Subjects: Indian Art, Culture, History, Sociology, Secondary & University Textbooks, Reprints of scientific and technical titles
Founded: 1864

Taraporevala Publishing Industries Pvt Ltd, 'Woodlands', 67 Dr D Deshmukh Marg, Bombay 400026 Tel: 393361 Cable Add: Tarabook, Bombay
Subjects: Management, Computer Technology, Social Science, Chemical Engineering, Natural Sciences, Technology, Reprints

Tata McGraw-Hill Publishing Co Ltd, 12/4 Asaf Ali Rd (3rd Floor), New Delhi 110002 Tel: 273105/271303 Cable Add: Corinthian Telex: 2257 Tmhd
Dir: Balan Subramanian; *General Manager:* Ish C Dawar; *Sales:* Dr N Subrahmanyam; *Publicity:* N S Nagan
Parent Company: McGraw-Hill International Book Co, 1221 Ave of the Americas, New York, NY 10020, USA
Subjects: Philosophy, Low- & High-priced Paperbacks, Medicine, Psychology, Engineering, General & Social Science, University Textbooks, Educational Materials, Agriculture, Biological Sciences, Management and Economics, Mathematics, Technology
1981: 56 titles *1982:* 48 titles *Founded:* 1970

Thacker & Co Ltd*, 18-20 Kaikhushroo Dubash Marg, Bombay 400023 Tel: 242745/242683/242667 Cable Add: Booknotes
Dir: J M Chudasama; *Chief Executive:* Anil Laud
Subjects: History, Political & Social Science, Law, Business, University Textbooks
Bookshop: At above address

The **Theosophical Publishing** House, Adyar, Madras 600020 Tel: 412904 Cable Add: Theotheca
Sales, Operations Manager: K Ramanathan; *Editorial, Publicity, Rights & Permissions:* C R N Swamy
Associate Companies: The Indian Bookshop, The Theosophical Society, Kamachha, Varanasi 221001; The Theosophical Publishing House, PO Box 270, Wheaton, Ill 60187, USA; The Theosophical Publishing House Ltd, 68 Great Russell St, London WC1B 3BU, UK
Subjects: Philosophy, Religion, Universal

Brotherhood, Occultism, Theosophy
1981: 18 titles *Founded:* 1913
ISBN Publisher's Prefix: 0-8356

Joseph **Thomasons** & Co*, 7 Anand Bazar, Ernakulam, Kerala State Tel: 35235 Cable Add: Jetco
Chief Executive: Andrew Nettikadan
Subjects: General
Founded: 1958

Thomson Press (India) Ltd*, PO Box 314, New Delhi 110001 (Located at: K Block Connaught Circus, New Delhi) Tel: 353808/350225/352724 Cable Add: Thompress Telex: ND 2651
Man Dir: Aroon Purie; *Sales:* S Srinivasan; *Marketing Manager:* Anup Roy
Associate Company: Living Media India Ltd (at above address)
Branch Off: 28 A&B Jolly Maker Chambers II, Nariman Point, Bombay 400021
Subject: Children's Books

Central **Tibetan** Secretariat, Information Office of His Holiness The Dalai Lama, Gangchen Kyishong, Dharamsala 176215, Himachal Pradesh Tel: 457
General Secretary: Sonam Topgyal; *Sales Manager:* Sonam Tenzin; *Production, Publicity, Rights & Permissions:* Samphel
Subsidiary Company: Tibetan Freedom Press, Toon Soong, Tenzin Sherpa Rd, Darjeeling, West Bengal
Subjects: Tibetan History, Religion, Culture, Current Events
Founded: 1961

Today & Tomorrow's Printers & Publishers*, 24-B/5 Desh Bandhu Gupta Rd, New Delhi 110005 Tel: 561928
Man Dir, Editorial, Rights & Permissions: Rajendra Kumar Jain; *Sales, Publicity:* R P Tiwari; *Production:* Mohindar Kumar
Subjects: Indian Studies, Agriculture, Natural History, Science, Textbooks, Reference
Bookshop: At above address
Founded: 1967

Travancore Law House*, M G Rd, Cochin 682001 Tel: 33766
Chief Executive: S Joseph
Subjects: Law, Commerce, Management
Founded: 1934

Trimurti Publications Pvt Ltd+, W-152 Greater Kailash-I, New Delhi 110048 Tel: 646317
Man Dir, Sales, Rights & Permissions: S P Kumria; *Publicity Dir:* Sudarshan Kumria
Branch Off: D-24 Odeon Bldg, Connaught Pl, New Delhi 11001
Subjects: History, Political Science, Economics, Religion, Philosophy, Reference, Social Science, University Textbooks
Founded: 1972

N M **Tripathi** Pvt Ltd, 164 Shamaldas Gandhi Marg, Bombay 400002
Man Dir: Arvind S Pandya; *Executive Manager:* Virendra Majmudar
Subjects: Law, Commerce, Gujarati
1981: 22 titles *1982:* 19 titles *Founded:* 1888

University Publishers*, Railway Rd, Jullundur City 144001 Tel: 2645 Cable Add: Best Books
Dirs: A N Chopra, R K Chopra; *Sales Dir:* O P Sharma; *Publicity Dir:* Rajinder Pal; *Advertising Dir:* Budh Ram
Subjects: Fiction, History, Political Science, Technology, Educational Materials
Founded: 1947

Upkar Prakashan*, 2/11A Swadeshi Bima Nagar, Agra 282002 Tel: 65110/66796 Cable Add: Competion
Chief Executive, Publicity, Rights & Permissions: M S Jain; *Sales, Production:*
N S Jain
Associate Company: Pratiyogita Darpan (at above address)
Subjects: General Knowledge, Competition Books, General
Bookshop: Vijaysing Jain, Bookseller, Hospital Rd, Agra
Founded: 1973

The **Upper India** Publishing House Pvt Ltd, Aminabad, Lucknow UP 226018 Tel: 42711 Cable Add: Balance
Man Dir: S Bhargava
Subjects: History, Reference, General & Social Science, Secondary & University Textbooks (in Hindi & English)
Founded: 1921

Vakils Feffer & Simons Ltd*, 9 Sprott Rd, Ballard Estate, Bombay 38 Tel: 261221 Cable Add: Fleetbooks
Man Dir: Mrs A F Shaikh
Subjects: Educational, College Textbooks, Cookery, Art

Vani Prakashan, 61-F Kamla Nagar, Delhi 110007 Tel: 225151
Chief Executive: Smt Shiramani Devi; *Editorial, Production, Publicity:* Ashok Kumar Maheshwari; *Sales:* Arun Kumar Maheshwari
Associate Companies: Konarka Prakashan (at above address); Ankur Prakashan, Maheshwari Publications, both at 1/3017 Ramnagar, Mandali Rd, Shadhara, Delhi 32
Subjects: Hindi Fiction, Poetry, Criticism
1981: 47 titles *1982:* 70 titles *Founded:* 1968

Venus Press & Book Depot*, Konni, Kerala Tel: 16
Editorial: E K Sekhar; *Sales:* P Viswaswaran Pillay
Subjects: Novels, Short Stories, Humour
Bookshop: Venus Book Depot (at above address)
Founded: 1946

Vidhi Sahitva Prakashan, see Law Books in Hindi Publishers

Vidyapuri*, Balubazar, Cuttack 753002, Orissa Tel: 23637 Cable Add: Vidyapuri
Chief Executive, Editorial, Production, Publicity, Rights & Permissions: Pitamber Mishra; *Sales:* S K Sarangi
Associate Companies: Goswami Press, Cuttack 753002; Graftek Pvt Ltd, Bhubaneswar 751002
Subjects: College Textbooks, General Literature, Children's Literature
Bookshop: At above address
Founded: 1961

Vidyarthi Mithram Press & Book Depot*, PO Box 81, Baker Rd, Kottayam 686001, Kerala State Tel: 2313/2316/4713 (after office hours 2616) Cable Add: Vidyarthi
Man Dir: Koshy P John
Associate Companies: Auroville Publishers, Kottayam; John Samuel Bros, Main Rd, Trivandrum
Imprints: Kosi Books, Manosabdam Books
Subjects: Fiction, Textbooks, Children's Books
Book Club: Vidyarthi Mithram Novel Club
Bookshop: Vidyarthi Mithram Book Depot (at above address, and ten other branches)
Founded: 1928

Vikas Publishing House Pvt Ltd+, 20/4 Industrial Area, Sahibabad 201010, Ghaziabad (UP) Tel: 205290/200536 Cable Add: Vikasbooks
Man Dir: Narendra Kumar
Subjects: Adventure, Mountaineering, Agriculture, Animal Husbandry, Art, Architecture, Travel, Biography, Memoirs, Botany, Chemistry, Cookery, Demography, Economics, Education, Engineering, Fiction, Futurology, Geography, Geology, History,
Culture, Library Science, Literature, Management, Commerce, Mass Media, Mathematics, Medicine, Military Affairs, Philosophy, Religion, Physics, Politics, Current Affairs, Psychology, Public Administration, Science, Sociology, Anthropology, Sports, Games, Zoology, Children's Books
Founded: 1969

Vishal Publications*, Adda Hoshiarpur, Jullundur City 144001 Tel: 5177/5388
Man Dir: Pardeep Jain; *Sales Dir:* Rajinder K Jain; *Publicity & Advertising:* Sunil Jain
Branch Offs: Vishal Publications, 6 U B Bungalow Rd, Delhi 110007
Founded: 1973

Vision Books Pvt Ltd+, Madarsa Rd, Kashmere Gate, Delhi 110006 Tel: 227011/2512267/352081 Cable Add: Vision Book
Chairman: Vishwa Nath; *Man Dir, Rights & Permissions, Publicity, Sales:* Sudhir Malhotra; *Publishing Dir:* Kapil Malhotra; *Editor:* Mahendra Kulshreshta
Subsidiary Company: Anand Paperbacks; Orient Paperbacks (qv)
Associate Companies: Rajpal & Sons (qv); Ravindra Printing Press; Shiksha Bharati (qv)
Branch Off: 3-B Peddar Rd, 'Vasant' Ground Floor, Bombay
Subjects: General Fiction, Military Science and History, Sciences, Current Affairs, Indology, Management, Religion, Anthropology, Education, International Relations, Medicine, Mountaineering, Travel, Health, Do-it-Yourself
Book Clubs: Anand Book Club, Orient Book Club
1981: 95 titles *1982:* 100 titles *Founded:* 1975

Voluntary Health Association of India, C-14 Community Centre, Safdarjung Development Area, New Delhi 110016 Tel: 668071/2 Cable Add: Volhealth
Editorial, Rights & Permissions: A L D'Souza; *Sales, Production, Publicity:* Augustine J Veliath
Subjects: Health, Nutrition, Management
Founded: 1974

Vora & Co Publishers Pvt Ltd*, 3 Round Bldg, Kalbadevi Rd, Bombay 400002
Man Dir: Manherlal K Vora; *Publicity:* K K Vora
Subjects: Education, Textbooks, Law, Economics, Banking, Literature, History, Science

A H **Wheeler** & Co (P) Ltd, 23 Lal Bahadur Marg, Allahabad 211001

Wilco Publishing House, 33 Ropewalk Lane, Rampart Row, Fort Bombay 400001 Tel: 242574 Cable Add: Wilbook
Man Dir: Jaisukh H Shah
Subjects: Fiction, Reference, Philosophy, Psychology, Business, Management, Inspirational, Self-help
Founded: 1958

Wiley Eastern Ltd*, 4835/24 Ansari Rd, Daryaganj, New Delhi 110002 Tel: 276802/267996 Cable Add: Wileyeast
Dir: Anand R Kundaji; *Chief Executive:* Asanga Machwe; *Sales Manager:* K K Gulati; *Editorial:* H S Poplai; *Production:* M S Sejwal
Associate Company: John Wiley & Sons Ltd, UK (qv for other associates)
Subjects: Psychology, Engineering, Social Science, University Textbooks, Indian Art, Science, Humanities
Bookshop: The Wiley Eastern Book Shop, 4654/21 Daryaganj, New Delhi 110002; Abid House, Dr Bhadkamkar Marg, Bombay

400007; Wiley Eastern Bookshop, 40/8 Ballygunje Circular Rd, Calcutta 700019; The Wiley Bookshop, 6 Shri BP Wadia Rd, Basavangudi, Bangalore 560004
1981: 70 titles *Founded:* 1966

World Homoeopathic Links, PO Box 5775, New Delhi 110055 (Located at: 1910 St 11, Chuna Mandi, New Delhi) Tel: 518445
Chief Executive: Dr P N Jain; *Editorial, Publicity, Rights & Permissions:* Ashok Jain; *Sales, Production:* Pradeep Jain
Associate Company: Harjeet & Co (qv)
Subjects: Homoeopathy, Medical Reference
1982: 79 titles *Founded:* 1979

The **World Press** Pvt Ltd*, 37-A College St, Calcutta 700073 Tel: 341444/343591/342426
Chairman: J Sinha; *Man Dir, Production:* P C Bhattacharji; *Sales, Editorial:* S Bhattacharyya; *Publicity, Advertising, Rights & Permissions:* L Bhattacharjee
Subjects: Economics, History, Political & Social Science, Business, Law, Mathematics, Geology, Botany, Statistics, Library Science, Reference
Bookshop: At above address
Founded: 1947

Writers Workshop*, 162/92 Lake Gardens, Calcutta 700045 Tel: 468325
Man Dir, Publicity: P Lal
Subjects: General Fiction, Belles Lettres, Poetry, Philosophy, Reference, Religion, Low- & High-priced Paperbacks
Founded: 1958

Yoga Life, an imprint of Satya Press (qv)

Zebra Books for Children, an imprint of Arnold-Heinemann Publishers (India) Pvt Ltd (qv)

Remainder Dealers

Books Bargain, 4-C Ansari Rd, Daryaganj, New Delhi 110002 Tel: 266258
Man Dir: Mrs L V Kalra
Also wholesalers

Gangarams Book Bureau*, 72 Mahatma Gandhi Rd, Bangalore 560001 Tel: (0812) 50277/565189
Manager: N Gangaram
All subjects. Main enterprise is as retail booksellers

Jaffe Books*, Aymanathuparampil House, Kurichy 686549, Kerala State
Proprietor: Santhamma Punnoose
Academic, scientific and technical

Koshal Book Depot*, 3611/5 Nowrang Colony, Trinagar, Delhi 110035
Partner: Rishi Pal Sharma
All subjects

Surjeet Book Depot, PO Box 1425, Delhi 110006 (Located at: 4074-75 Nai Sarak, Delhi) Tel: 263080/265987
Man Dir: Harnam Singh
Specialization: Literature, Social Science

Literary Agents

Ajanta Books International, 1 U B Jawahar Nagar, Bungalow Rd, Delhi 110007 Tel: 227425
Contact: S Balwant (proprietor)
Specialization: Social sciences

K P Punnoose Communications Co, Kunnuparampil Bldgs, Kurichy 686549, Kottayam District, Kerala State Tel: (04826) 470
Man Dir: K P Punnoose
Specialization: Original and reprint rights in academic books and general adult trade books. Sheet deals. Translation rights in Christian literature
Subsidiary Companies: Asian Literary Market Review (qv); Institute for Christian Publishing & Communications Research (qv)

Book Clubs

Anand Book Club, Madarsa Rd, Kashmere Gate, Delhi 110006
Owned by: Vision Books Pvt Ltd (qv)

Clarion Book Club*, G T Rd, Shahdara, Delhi 110032
Owned by: Hind Pocket Books Private Ltd (qv)

Classics Club, D C Books, PO Box 214, Kottayam 686001
Members: 4,500
Owned by: D C Books (qv)
Founded: 1982

D C Book Club, DC Books, PO Box 214, Kottayam 686001
Members: 2,500
Owned by: D C Books (qv)
Founded: 1975

E M E S C O Book Club*, 3237 R P Rd, Secunderabad 500003
Members: 3,700
Owned by: Andhra Pradesh Book Distributors
Founded: 1977

Gharelu Library Yojna*, G T Rd, Shahdara, Delhi 110032
Owned by: Hind Pocket Books Private Ltd (qv)

Home Library Plan*, 3237 R P Rd, Secunderabad 500003
Members: 3,000
Owned by: Andhra Pradesh Book Distributors
Founded: 1960

Orient Book Club, Madarsa Rd, Kashmere Gate, Delhi 110006
Members: 35,000
Owned by: Vision Books Pvt Ltd (qv)

Pracharak Book Club, PO Box 106, Pishachmochan, Varanasi 221001
Members: 3,978
Owned by: Hindi Pracharak Sansthan (qv)
Founded: 1976

Radical Book Club*, 6 Bankim Chatterjee St, Calcutta 12

Sanket Library Yojna, 4725/21A Dayanand Marg, Daryaganj, New Delhi 110002
Owned by: Selina Publishers (qv)

Star Book Bank, 4/5B Asaf Ali Rd, New Delhi 110002
Members: 10,000
Owned by: Star Publications (Pvt) Ltd (qv)
Subject: Books in Hindi

Sterling Book Club, L-10 Green Park Extension, New Delhi 110016
Owned by: Sterling Publishers Pvt Ltd (qv)

Vidyarthi Mithram Novel Club*, PO Box 81, Baker Rd, Kottayam 686001, Kerala State
Owned by: Vidyarthi Mithram Press & Book Depot (qv)

Major Booksellers

Al Book Co (Pvt) Ltd*, 210 D N Rd, Bombay 400001 Tel: 260019 Cable Add: Arabian Telex: 116683 Arabian
Man Dir: J K Kapur
Importers of children's books

Atma Ram & Sons, Kashmere Gate, Delhi 110006 Tel: 223092/228159 Cable Add: Books
Manager: Ish Kumar Puri
Importers — all subjects

Bangalore Book Bureau, PO Box 9928, Subedar Chatram Rd, Bangalore 560009 Tel: (0812) 77433/74558
Manager: G C Bhuj
Importers — all subjects

Current Technical Literature Co (Pvt) Ltd, Malhotra House, PO Box 1374, Bombay 400001 Tel: 261045 Cable Add: Cutelico
Man Dir: R K Murti
Scientific, technical and medical books

D K Agencies, H-12 Bali Nagar, New Delhi 110015 Tel: 504418/532702 Cable Add: Dikaybook
Exporters of books published in English, Tibetan and all regional languages of India. Specialize in blanket-order supply of English books

D K Publishers' Distributors*, 1 Ansari Rd, Daryaganj, New Delhi 110002 Tel: 278368 Cable Add: Deekaypub
Partners: I C Mittal, Praveen Mittal, Pramil Mittal; *Sales Manager:* S K Bhatia
The largest wholesale house for Indian books, stockists of the publications of more than 600 Indian publishers

Daystar Publications, B-2/48A Lawrence Rd, New Delhi 110035 Tel: 503928
Manager: Mrs Indu Lekha Garg
Importers and exporters of books and journals; also publisher (qv)

English Book Store, 17-L Connaught Circus, New Delhi 110001 Tel: 352126/351731
Partners: S D Chowdhri, Bhupinder Chowdhri
Associate Company: Himalayan Books (qv)
Importers — military science, aviation, nursing, foreign languages, travel, religion

E D Galgotia & Sons, PO Box 688, New Delhi 110001 (Located at: 17-B Connaught Pl, New Delhi) Tel: 321844 Telex: 312879 Star In
Dirs: Suneel Galgotia, Neeraj Galgotia; *Manager:* R S Bisht
Owned by: Galgotia Booksource (qv)
Importer, wholesaler and retail bookseller of technical, scientific, medical and management books

Higginbothams Ltd, 814 Anna Salai, Madras 600002 Tel: 86556 Cable Add: Booklover
Man Dir: V Balaraman
Importers — all subjects

Hindi Book Centre*, 4/5-B Asaf Ali Rd, New Delhi 110002 Tel: 274874/273335
Specialization: General books in Hindi

India Book House, Mahalaxmi Chambers, 22 Bhulabhai Desai Rd, Bombay 400026 Tel: 367049/388088
Import, Sales Dir: Deepak G Mirchandani; *Manager:* Lal Vasvani
Owned by: IBH Publishing Co (qv)
Publishers representatives and wholesale distributors

International Book House (Pvt) Ltd, Indian Mercantile Mansion (Extn), Madame Cama Rd, Bombay 400039 Tel: 231634 Cable Add: Interbook
General Manager: R Gopalan
Importers — adult trade books

International Book Traders, G3/46 Model Town, Delhi 110009 Tel: 741817
Manager: D S Chaudhary
Importers — scientific and technical books

J K Export House, 2944 Kucha Mai Das, Bazar Sita Ram, Delhi 110006
Proprietor: K Jitendra
Exporters of any books published in India

Jaico Book Shop, 121 Mahatma Gandhi Rd, Bombay 400023 Tel: 274099 Cable Add: Jaicobooks
Manager: Rafique Baghdadi
Importers

Motilal Banarsidass, 41 U A Bungalow Rd, Jawahar Nagar, Delhi 110007 Tel: 221985/228355 Cable Add: Gloryindia
Managing Partner: N P Jain
Owned by: Motilal Banarsidass, Publisher (qv)
Importers and exporters of Indological books

Oxford Book and Stationery Co, Scindia House, New Delhi 110001; 17 Park St, Calcutta 700016 Tel: 44957 Cable Add: Indamer
Manager: Gulab Primlani
Owned by: Oxford & IBH Publishing Co (qv)
Importers

Popular Book Depot*, Dr Bhadkamkar Rd, Bombay 400007 Tel: 359401 Cable Add: Quixote
Importers

Rupa & Co, 15 Bankim Chatterjee St, Calcutta 700073 Tel: 344821
Dir: D Mehra
Owned by: Rupa & Co, Publisher (qv)
Importers — all subjects

R R Sheth & Co, Princess St, Keshavbag, Bombay 400002 Tel: 313441 Cable Add: Literature Bombay 2
Manager: D C Mody
Also: PO Box 2517, 110-112 S Gandhi Marg, Bombay 400002; opp Phuvara, Gandhi Marg, Ahmedabad 380001
Owned by: R R Sheth & Co, Publisher (qv)
Largest wholesaler of Gujarati and Hindi Books

Star Publications (P) Ltd*, 4/5B Asaf Ali Rd, New Delhi 110002 Tel: 273335/274874/265135 Cable Add: Starpublis Telex: (081) 31-5328
Exporter of Indian books to world libraries and booksellers

N M Tripathi Pvt Ltd, 164 Shamaldas Gandhi Marg, Bombay 400002 Tel: 313651/294048
Manager: A S Pandya
Importers of law books

U B S Publishers' Distributors Ltd*, 5 Ansari Rd, PO Box 7015, New Delhi 110002 Tel: 273601 Cable Add: Allbooks Telex: ND 3916
Importers

United Publishers*, PO Box 82, Pan Bazar Main Rd, Gauhati 781001 Assam Tel: 26381 Cable Add: Unipub Gauhati
Manager: Krishan Kumar
Wholesaler and exporter

Universal Book Distributors*, 117/H-1/294-B Model Town, Pandu Nagar, Kanpur 208025 Tel: 81300 Cable Add: Worldmags
Managing Partner: A K Chawla
Importers and subscription agents

Universal Book Shop, 20 Mahatma Gandhi Marg, Allahabad Tel: 3177
Partner: Ramesh Chugh
Owned by: Chugh Publications (qv)

Vidyarthi Mithram Book Depot*, Baker Rd, Kottayam 686001, Kerala Tel: 2313/2316/2616 Cable Add: Vidyarthi
Branches: Calicut, Palghat, Ernakulam, Round North Trichur, Kottayam, Thiruvalla, Quinlon, Trivandrum

Major Libraries

American Center Library, 24 Kasturba Gandhi Marg, New Delhi 110001
Branches: 4 New Marine Lines, Bombay 400020; 7 Jawaharlal Nehru Rd, Calcutta 700013; 1 Bidhan Sarani, Calcutta 700073; Gemini Circle, Madras 600006

Asiatic Society Library*, Town Hall, Bombay 400023, Maharashtra

Bombay University Library, Bombay University, Karmaveer Bhaurao Patil Marg, Fort, Bombay 32 Tel: 273621

British Council Library*, AIFACS Bldg, Rafi Marg, New Delhi 110001 Tel: 381401 Cable Add: Britcoun Telex: 0314370
Southern India: 737 Anna Salai, Madras 600002 Tel: 86151 Cable Add: Britcoun;
Eastern India: 5 Shakespeare Sarani, Calcutta 700071 Tel: 445370 Cable Add: Britcoun Telex: 0213131; *Western and Central India:* C Wing, Mittal Tower, Nariman Point, Bombay 400021 Tel: 223560/223480/223484 Cable Add: Britcoun Telex: 0116991

The **British Library**, Lal Darwaja, Ahmedabad 380001
Librarian: V W Karnick
Branches: 29 St Mark's Rd, Bangalore 560001; New Shopping Centre, Roshanpura Naka, Bhopal 462003; 5-9-20/A Secretariat Rd, Hyderabad 500004; Mayfair Building, Hazratganj, Lucknow 226001; Bank Rd, Patna 800001; 917/1 Fergusson College Rd, Shivaji Nagar, Pune 411004; Club Rd, Ranchi; YMCA Bldg, Trivandrum 695001

Central Library*, Nr Mandvi Bank Rd, PO Box 15, Baroda Tel: 2932
Librarian: P V Mehta

Central Library*, Town Hall, Bombay 400023, Maharashtra

Central Secretariat Library*, G Block, Shastri Bhavan, New Delhi 110001

Connemara (State Central) Public Library*, Egmore, Madras 600008

Delhi Public Library*, S P Mukerji Marg, Delhi 110006 Tel: 252682 (Director)
Director: J C Mehta

Delhi University Library System*, University of Delhi, Delhi 110007 Tel: 229888

Gujarat Vidyapith Granthalaya, Ahmedabad 380014 Tel: 446148
(Combined university, state central and public library)
Librarian: K L Shah
Publications: Tapas Nibandh Suchi (Gujarati) (Bibliography of Dissertations); *Gujarati Samayik Lekh Suchi* (Gujarati) (Indexing of Articles from Selected Gujarati Journals), 1976

Indian Council of World Affairs Library*, Sapru House, Barakhamba Rd, New Delhi 110001
Librarian: Ashok Jambhekar
Publication: Documentation on Asia (annually)

Indian Institute of Technology Central Library*, Madras 600036 Tel: 415342 ext 207 Telex: 417362 Iitm In

Madras Literary Society Library*, College Rd, Madras 600006

National Archives of India*, Janpath, New Delhi 110001
Librarian: J C Srivastava

The **National Library**, Government of India*, Belvedere, Calcutta 700027 Tel: 455381 Cable Add: Librarian Telex: Ca 7935

National Museum Library*, Janpath, New Delhi 110001

Nehru Memorial Museum and Library, Teen Murti House, New Delhi 110011
Dir: Professor Ravinder Kumar

Sahitya Akademi Library*, 35 Ferozeshah Rd, New Delhi 110001

State Central Library, Hyderabad 12, Andhra Pradesh

Library Associations

Delhi Library Association, PO Box 1270, c/o Hardayal (Hardinge) Public Library, Queen's Garden, Delhi 110006
Publication: Book Review Supplement (quarterly), *Library Herald* (quarterly), *Indian Press Index* (monthly)

Documentation Research and Training Centre, Indian Statistical Institute, 31 Church St, Bangalore 560001 Tel: 579656 Cable Add: Statistica
Head: Dr G Bhattacharyya
Publications: Annual Seminar, DRTC (annual), *Refresher Seminar, DRTC* (annual)

Federation of Indian Library Associations*, Misri Bazar, Patiala, Punjab
President: Professor P N Kaula

Government of India Librarians Association, c/o Ministry of Home Affairs Library, Room 26, North Block, New Delhi 110001 Tel: 561701/372951
Secretary: O S Sachdeva
Publications include: GILA Bulletin (quarterly)

Indian Association of Academic Librarians, c/o Jawaharlal Nehru University Library, New Mehrauli Rd, New Delhi 110067 Tel: 650005/632360
Secretary: M M Kashyap
Publication: Newsletter

Indian Association of Special Libraries and Information Centres*, P 291 CIT Scheme No 6M, PO Kankurgachi, Calcutta 700054 Tel: 359651
General Secretary: S M Ganguly
Publications include: Bulletin (4 a year), *Newsletter* (12 a year), *Indian Library Science Abstracts* (4 a year)

Indian College Library Association, 66 Ranjan Colony, Hyderabad 500253 Tel: 45282/42659
President: A P Jain

Indian Library Association, A/40-41, Flat 201, Ansal Bldgs, Dr Mukerjee Nagar, Delhi 110009
President: Prof P B Mangla; *Secretary:* O P Trikha
Publication: Bulletin

Library Reference Books and Journals

Books

University Libraries in India: A guide for direct mail promotion, Asian Bookmarket Information Service, 73-47-255th St, Glen Oaks, New York 11004, USA

Journals

Annals of Library Science and Documentation, Indian National Scientific Documentation Centre, Hillside Rd, New Delhi 110012

Bulletin, Indian Association of Special Libraries and Information Centres, P 291 CIT Scheme No 6M, PO Kankurgachi, Calcutta 700054

Bulletin, Indian Library Association, A/40-41, Flat 201, Ansal Bldgs, Dr Mukerjee Nagar, Delhi 110009

GILA Bulletin (quarterly), Government of India Librarians Association, c/o Ministry of Home Affairs Library, Room 26, North Block, New Delhi 110001

Herald of Library Science, Banaras Hindu University, c/o Editor P N Kaula, C-1, Varanasi 221005

Indian Librarian, 233 Model Town, Jullundur 3, Punjab

Indian Library Movement, 148 Allenby Lines, Ambala Cantt

Indian Library Science Abstracts, Indian Association of Special Libraries and Information Centres, Albert Hall, 15 Bankim Chatterjee St, Calcutta (W Bengal)

Journal of Indexing and Reference Work, Mukherjee Library, 1 Gopi Mohan Dutta Lane, Calcutta 3

Journal of Library and Information Science, Department of Library Science, University of Delhi, Delhi 110007

Journal of Library Science, Nagpur University, Nagpur, Maharashtra

Journal of Library Service, Ravikrupa Trust, 1760 Gandhi Rd, Ahmedabad 1

Karnatak Granthalaya (text in Kannada, contents page in English and Kannada), S R Gunjal, Granthalaya Vijnana Prakashana, Saptapur, Dharwar, Karnatak State

Liblit, Library Literacy Circle, Kurukshetra, Haryana

Library Herald, Delhi Library Association, PO Box 1270, c/o Hardayal (Hardinge) Public Library, Queen's Garden, Delhi 110006

Pustakalaya (text in Gujurati), Gujarat Pustakalaya Sahayak Sahkari Mandal Ltd, PO Box 10, Raopura, Baroda

Literary Associations and Societies

Indian Folklore Society*, 3 Abdul Hamid (British Indian) St, Calcutta 700069 Tel: 236334
General Secretary: Sankar Sen Gupta
Publication: Folklore (monthly)

Madras Literary Society and Auxiliary of the Royal Asiatic Society*, College Rd, Madras 600006
Honorary Secretary: U Ramesh Rao

National Academy of Letters, see Sahitya Akademi

P E N All-India Centre, Theosophy Hall, 40 New Marine Lines, Bombay 400020 Tel: 292175 Cable Add: Aryasangha, Bombay
Founder-Organizer: Sophia Wadia
Secretary-Treasurer: Nissim Ezekiel
Publications: The Indian PEN (bimonthly), PEN series on Indian literatures, *PEN Conference Proceedings*

Sahitya Akademi*, Rabindra Bhavan, 35 Ferozeshah Rd, New Delhi 110001 Tel: 388667 Cable Add: Sahityakar
Secretary: Dr R S Kelkar
Publications: Indian Literature (bi-monthly), *Samskrita Pratibha* (twice yearly)

Literary Periodicals

Art & Poetry Today, Samkaleen Prakashan, 2762 Rajguru Marg, New Delhi 110055

Bengali Literature, 53 Bidhan Palli, Jadavpur, Calcutta 32

Contemporary Indian Literature (text in English), H-328 Narayana, New Delhi 28

Cultural News from India, Indian Council for Cultural Relations, I P Estate, New Delhi 110002

Dhara; a monthly review of Indian literature, Dhara Publications, 37 D Gupta Colony, Delhi 110009

Indian Author, C-44 Gulmohar Park, New Delhi 110049

Indian Horizons, Indian Council for Cultural Relations, Azad Bhavan, I P Estate, New Delhi 110002

Indian Literary Review, Chetna Publications, 4837/24 Ansari Rd, New Delhi 110002

Indian Literature, National Academy of Letters, Rabindra Bhavan, 35 Ferozeshah Rd, New Delhi 110001

The Indian PEN (text in English), PEN All-India Centre, Theosophy Hall, 40 New Marine Lines, Bombay 400020

Indian Writing Today, Nirmala-Sadanand Publishers, 35c Tardeo Rd, Bombay 400034

Katha-Sahitya (monthly), Mitra & Ghosh Publishers Pvt Ltd, 10 Shyama Charan De St, Calcutta 73

Lalit Kala, Lalit Kala Akademi, 35 Ferozeshah Rd, New Delhi 110001

Language Forum, Bahri Publications (Pvt) Ltd, 57 Sant Nagar, New Delhi 110065

Literary Criterion, Popular Prakashan, 35-C Tardeo Rd, Bombay 400034 WB

Literary Half-Yearly, Literary Press, H H A Gowda, Mysore 9

Literary Studies; a quarterly review of literature and criticism from the Panjab, Razdan House, Sirhindi Darwaza, Patiala, Panjab

Marg, Army & Navy Bldg, M G Rd, Bombay 400001

Miscellany, Writers Workshop, 162-92 Lake Gardens, Calcutta 700045

Opinion Literary Quarterly, 40-C Ridge Rd, Bombay 400006

Poet, 3 Venkatesan St, Madras 600017

Samskrita Pratibha; a six-monthly journal in Sanskrit devoted to contemporary writing of creative quality in Sanskrit, National Academy of Letters, Rabindra Bhavan, 35 Ferozeshah Rd, New Delhi 1

Triveni, Machilipatnam 521001

Vagartha; critical quarterly of Indian literature, Joshi Foundation, N-3 Panchsheel Park, New Delhi 110017

Literary Prizes

Andhra Pradesh Sahitya Akademi Awards
For best literary works in Telugu. Two prizes of 3,500 Indian rupees each and seven prizes of 2,500 Indian rupees each. Awarded annually. Enquiries to The Secretary, A P Sahitya Akademi, Saifabad, Hyderabad 500004

Bhai Santokh Singh Prize
Awarded annually to an Indian national domiciled in Haryana State for substantial contribution towards Punjabi literature. 2,100 Indian rupees. Enquiries to The Director, Haryana Sahitya Akademi, Chandigarh 160018

Books for Neoliterates Prizes
For manuscripts in Indian languages by Indian nationals. 1,000 Indian rupees for each book. Awarded annually. Enquiries to Director, Directorate of Adult Education, 34 Community Centre, Vasant Vihar, New Delhi

Central Hindi Directorate Awards
There are two schemes of literary awards. (1) For non-Hindi speaking authors, 16 prizes of 2,500 Indian rupees each, awarded annually. (2) Prizes for Indian authors writing in Indian languages other than Hindi, Sanskrit and the author's mother tongue: original writing and translated works are awarded prizes of 2,000 Indian rupees and 1,000 Indian rupees respectively. Enquiries to the Director, Central Hindi Directorate, West Block VII, RK Puram, New Delhi 110066

Certificate of Honour*
To Arabic, Persian and Sanskrit scholars who have made outstanding contributions to Arabic, Persian and Sanskrit study. 3,000 Indian rupees. Awarded annually by the President. Enquiries to Office of the President, Government of India, New Delhi

I C Chacko Award*
For the best book published in Malayalam during the preceding three years in the fields of science and linguistics. 1,000 Indian rupees awarded annually. Enquiries to Kerala Sahitya Akademi, PO Box 6, Town Hall Rd, Trichur, Kerala State

Escorts Book Award*
Instituted by Escorts Ltd in 1965 and administered by Delhi Management Association. For original books on management principles and practices by Indian writers. 5,000 and 3,000 Indian rupees each. Awarded annually. Enquiries to Secretary, Delhi Management Association, 1/21 Asaf Ali Rd, New Delhi 110002

Geeta Prize
Awarded annually to an Indian national domiciled in Haryana State for substantial contribution towards Sanskrit literature. 2,100 Indian rupees. Enquiries to The Director, Haryana Sahitya Akademi, Chandigarh 160018

Hali Prize
Awarded annually to an Indian national domiciled in Haryana State for substantial contribution towards Urdu literature. 2,100 Indian rupees. Enquiries to The Director, Haryana Sahitya Akademi, Chandigarh 160018

Haryana Sahitya Prize
Awarded annually to an Indian national for outstanding work on literature, art, history and culture of Haryana, 2,100 Indian rupees. Enquiries to The Director, Haryana Sahitya Akademi, Chandigarh 160018

Indian National Academy of Letters Awards, see Sahitya Akademi Awards

Jnanpith Literary Award*
For the best literary work in any Indian language by an Indian national. 100,000 Indian rupees awarded annually. Enquiries to Bharatiya Jnanpith, B/45-47 2nd Floor, Connaught Pl, New Delhi 110001

Sumnesh **Joshi** Award
For an outstanding first literary publication in Hindi. 750 Indian rupees awarded annually. The 1982-83 winner was Sanjeev Bhanawat for *Acharya Hazari Prasad Diwedi Ke Upanyason main Sanskritik Bodh* (Panchsheel Prakashan). Enquiries to The Secretary, Rajasthan Sahitya Akademi, Udaipur, Rajasthan

Kerala Sahitya Akademi Awards*
For literary works in Malayalam published during the preceding three years, in the following categories: fiction; drama; poetry; short stories; criticism; biography. 3,000 Indian rupees each awarded annually. Enquiries to The Secretary, Kerala Sahitya Akademi, PO Box 6, Town Hall Rd, Trichur 680001, Kerala State

Kesari Award
Best unpublished novel in Malayalam, 3,000 Indian rupees. Awarded annually. Enquiries to The Manager, D C Books, Kottayam 1, Kerala State

C B **Kumar** Award*
For best collection of essays in Malayalam. 1,500 Indian rupees awarded annually. Enquiries to The Secretary, Kerala Sahitya Akademi, PO Box 6, Town Hall Rd, Trichur 680001, Kerala State

Kunkumam Award*
For best unpublished novel in Malayalam. 11,111 and 3,000 Indian rupees awarded for first and second prize respectively. Enquiries to The Editor, Kunkumam Weekly, Quilon, Kerala State

Kuttippuzha Award*
For the best book of criticism published in Malayalam during the preceding three years. 2,000 Indian rupees awarded once every two years. Enquiries to Kerala Sahitya Akademi, PO Box 6, Town Hall Rd, Trichur, Kerala State

Law Books in Hindi Prize*
Awarded annually for law books/manuscripts in Hindi. 10,000 Indian rupees. Enquiries to Vidhi Sahitya Prakashan, Ministry of Law, Justice and Company Affairs, Govt of India, Indian Law Institute Bldgs, Bhagwandas Rd, New Delhi 110001

Meera Memorial Award
Founded 1959. For best literary work in Hindi. 9,000 Indian rupees awarded annually. The 1982-83 winner was Yadvendra Sharma Chandra for a novel, *Hazar Ghorhon Ka Sawar* (Sanmarg Prakashan). Enquiries to The Secretary, Rajasthan Sahitya Akademi, Udaipur, Rajasthan

K R **Namboodiri** Award*
For best work on Vedic literature in Malayalam. 1,000 Indian rupees awarded annually. Enquiries to The Secretary, Kerala Sahitya Akademi, PO Box 6, Town Hall Rd, Trichur 680001, Kerala State

Orissa Sahitya Akademi Award*
Founded in 1960 for best literary works in regional language published during a particular period of three years in six different categories of books: (1) novel and short stories; (2) poetry and Kavya; (3) drama, including one-act plays; (4) essay and literary criticism; (5) travelogue, biography, scientific literature; (6) children's literature. 1,000 Indian rupees awarded annually. Enquiries to Orissa Sahitya Akademi, Museum Buildings, Bhubaneswar 751014, Orissa

M P **Paul** Award
For best unpublished fiction in Malayalam. 3,000 Indian rupees awarded annually. Enquiries to The Manager, D C Books, Kottayam 1, Kerala State

M P **Paul** Prize*
For best published fiction in Malayalam. 1,000 Indian rupees awarded annually. Enquiries to The Secretary, Sahitya Pravarthaka Cooperative Society Ltd, PO Box No 94, Kottayam 1, Kerala State

Prithviraj Memorial Award*
For the best literary work in Rajasthani. 7,000 Indian rupees awarded annually. Enquiries to The Secretary, Rajasthan Sahitya Akademi, Udaipur, Rajasthan

Ranghey Raghav Award
For Hindi fiction. 2,000 Indian rupees awarded annually. The 1982-83 winner was Habib Kaifee for *Anayak* (Amit Prakashan). Enquiries to The Secretary, Rajasthan Sahitya Akademi, Udaipur, Rajasthan

Rajasthan Sahitya Akademi Awards*
For the best literary works in Hindi, Rajasthani and Sanskrit. Eight prizes of 2,000 Indian rupees each awarded annually. Enquiries to The Secretary, Rajasthan Sahitya Akademi, Udaipur, Rajasthan

Kanhaiyalal **Sahal** Award
For best work of Hindi prose. 2,000 Indian rupees awarded annually. The 1982-83 winner was Ratanlal Mishra for *Rajasthan Ke Durg* (Sahitya Sansthan). Enquiries to The Secretary, Rajasthan Sahitya Akademi, Udaipur, Rajasthan

Sahitya Akademi Awards*
For outstanding literary works written in each of the 22 regional languages of India recognized by the Indian National Academy of Letters (Sahitya Akademi). 5,000 Indian rupees each. Awarded annually to Indian nationals only, by the Executive Board of the Academy. Enquiries to The Secretary, Sahitya Akademi, Rabindra Bhavan, 35 Ferozeshah Rd, New Delhi 110001

Sahitya Pravarthaka Benefit Fund Awards*
For best works in Malayalam. Five prizes of 2,000 Indian rupees each awarded annually. Enquiries to The Secretary, Sahitya Pravarthaka Co-operative Society Ltd, PO Box 94, Kottayam 1, Kerala State

Sidhawat Award
For children's literature in Hindi. 1,100 rupees awarded annually. The 1982-83 winner was Manohar Verma for *Shareer Ke Nau Ratna* (Parag Prakashan). Enquiries to The Secretary, Rajasthan Sahitya Akademi, Udaipur, Rajasthan

Soviet Land Nehru Awards
For Indian nationals. For literary works, journalistic works in Indian languages and in English and meritorious work done in creative, cultural and public fields for promoting Indo-Soviet friendship, world peace and international amity.
Three prizes of 15,000 Indian rupees with a fortnight's trip to USSR and three prizes of 7,500 Indian rupees with a fortnight's trip to USSR. Ten prizes of 3,000 Indian rupees each. Five awards for children 10-13 age group for painting competition — a month's holiday at the Artek Young Pioneers Camp, Black Sea Coast, Crimea. Awarded annually. Enquiries to Soviet Land, Embassy of the USSR in India, 25 Barakhamba Rd, New Delhi 1

Sudhindra Award
For Hindi poetry. 2,000 Indian rupees awarded annually. The 1982-83 winner was Bhagwatilal Vyas for *Footpath Par Chiriya Nachti hai*. Enquiries to The Secretary, Rajasthan Sahitya Akademi, Udaipur, Rajasthan

Sur Prize
Awarded annually to an Indian national domiciled in Haryana State for outstanding contribution towards Hindi literature. 2,100 Indian rupees. Enquiries to Director, Haryana Sahitya Akademi, Chandigarh 160018

Sree Padmanabha **Swami** Prize*
For the best children's literature published in Malayalam during the preceding three years. 1,000 Indian rupees awarded annually. Enquiries to Kerala Sahitya Akademi, PO Box 6, Town Hall Rd, Trichur, Kerala State

Tagore Award
For the best unpublished novel in Malayalam, 7,500 Indian rupees awarded annually. Enquiries to The Manager, D C Books, Kottayam 686001, Kerala State

Urdu Akademy Awards*
Awarded annually to Indian nationals for Urdu literature. Enquiries to U P Urdu Akademy, 11 Hazratganj, Lucknow

Major Tek Singh **Virdi** Literary Prizes
Awarded annually to children under 15 years for short stories, essays and dramas in Punjabi. Three prizes of 100, 75 and 50 Indian rupees. Enquiries to Modern Sahit Academy, 'Gulfashan', East Mohan Nagar, Link Rd, Amritsar

Translation Agencies and Associations

Amerind Publishing Co (P) Ltd, N-56 Connaught Circus, New Delhi 110001 Tel: 44957 Cable: Indamer
Dir: Gulab Primlani
Translating Russian, German, Japanese, Hindi

Indian National Scientific Documentation Centre, 14 Satsang Vihar Marg, off SJS Sansanwal Marg, Special Institutional Area, New Delhi 110067 Tel: 665837 Cable Add: Insdoc Telex: 2499
Translating European languages into English

Social Science Documentation Centre*, 35 Ferozshah Rd, New Delhi 110001 Tel: 385959
Translation facility for European languages into English is available on request

Indonesia

General Information

Language: Bahasa Indonesia (a form of Malay) is official language. English is common second language. About 250 other languages are spoken in Indonesia
Religion: About 85% Muslim, 5% Hindu (principally on Bali), 5% Christian
Population: 145 million
Literacy Rate (1971): 59.6% (79.1% Urban, 55.3% Rural)
Bank Hours: Generally 0800-1400 Monday-Thursday; 0800-1100 Friday; 0800-1300 Saturday
Currency: Rupiah
Export/Import Information: Books subject to tariff and import sales tax, but on recommendation of Minister of Basic Education and Culture, partial or total exemption may be granted. Advertising duties and taxed. All imports subject to

margin of Profit Tax. Exchange control. Books and printed matter using Indonesian languages prohibited. Imports require no licence but are categorized into four groups for credit arrangement controls
Copyright: No copyright conventions signed

Book Trade Organization

Ikatan Penerbit Indonesia (IKAPI), Jl Kalipasir 32, Jakarta Pusat Tel: 351907
Association of Indonesian Book Publishers
President: Rozali Usman
Publication: Bulletin

Book Trade Reference Journals

Berita Bibliografi; Indonesian book news (text in Indonesian), Yayasan Idayu, Jl Dr Abdulrachman Salch 26, Jakarta

Bibliografi Nasional Indonesia Kumulasi (Cumulative Bibliography of Indonesia), National Scientific Documentation Centre, Jl Jendral Gatot-Subroto, PO Box 3065/JKT, Jakarta

Bulletin, Association of Indonesian Book Publishers, Jl Pengarengan 32, Jakarta Pusat III/4

Publishers

Akadoma*, Jl Proklamasi No 61, Jakarta Tel: 882328

B P **Alda***, Jl Ir H Juanda II No 44, Jakarta

Alma'Arif, Jl Tamblong No 48-50, Bandung Tel: 50708

Alumni Press, Jl Geusanulun 17, PO Box 272, Bandung Tel: (022) 50675/58290 Telex: 28460 Alumni Bd
Man Dir, Rights & Permissions: Eddy Damian; *Editorial:* I Wayan Parthiana, Yayat Ruchiyat; *Sales:* Iyan Rusmana; *Production Manager:* Philips
Branch Off: Wisma Sawah Besar, 8th Floor, Jl Sukarjo Wiryopranoto 30, Jakarta Tel: 372730 Telex: 46810 Alumni Ia
Subjects: Law, Economics, Social Sciences, Medicine, Psychology
Bookshop: H Juanda St 54, Bandung Tel: 58290
Founded: 1966

Angkasa*, Jl Merdeka No 6, Bandung Tel: 58330

Pustaka **Antara***, Jl Majapahit No 28, Jakarta Tel: 341321
Man Dir: H M Joesoef Ahmad
Founded: 1952
Subjects: School Textbooks, Children's books, Politics, Religion, General

Aries Lima, see PT New Aqua Press

Asia Afrika*, Jl Paneleh No 18, Surabaya Tel: 278175

PN **Balai** Pustaka, Jl Dokter Wahidin No 1, Jakarta Tel: 361701/365994/341714 Cable Add: PN Balai Pustaka
Chief Executive, Sales, Publicity, Rights & Permissions: Drs Soetojo Gondo; *Editorial, Production:* Mrs Dra Astuti Hendrato
Founded: 1917

Bale Bandung — Sumur Bandung*, Jl Asia Afrika 82, Bandung Tel: 59137/52156
Manager: H Moh Koerdi
Subject: Textbooks

P T **Bhakti** Centra Baru, Jl Jend Akhmad Yani No 15, Ujung Pandang Tel: 5192 Cable Add: Bhakti Baru Telex: 71156 Hakalla UP
Man Dir: Drs H M Jusuf Kalla; *Publicity Manager:* Alwi Hamu
Branch Off: Jl Lembang 9, Jakarta Tel: 356374
Subjects: Religion, General, Textbooks
Founded: 1972

Bhratara Karya Aksara*, Jl Rawabali II/5, Kawasan Industri Pulogadung, Jakarta Tel: 480280
Man Dir: Ahmad Jayusman; *Editorial Dir:* Moh O Masdoeki
Subjects: History, Public Health, Industry, Agriculture, Textbooks, Reference, Education, Philosophy, Politics, Law, Social Sciences, Economics
Bookshop: Toku Buku Bhratara, Jl Otista III/29, Jakarta Timur Tel: 811858
1981: 19 titles *Founded:* 1958

Bina Ilmu*, Jl Tunjungan No 53E, Surabaya Tel: 472214

Binacipta*, Jl Ganesya 4, Bandung Tel: 84319
Director: O Bardin

Bulan Bintang, Penerbit & Pustake NV*, Jl Kramat Kwitang I/8, Jakarta Tel: 342883/346247
Manager: Fauzi Amelz
Subjects: Art, Sociology, Science, Religion
Founded: 1954

Bumi Restu*, Jl Letjen Haryono M T Persil 23, PO Box 404, Jakarta Tel: 882746

Cemerlang*, Jl Kesatrian VIII No 30, Jakarta Tel: 591431

Cerdas*, Jl Palasari No 125, Bandung

Dian Rakyat*, Jl Rawa Gelam I No 4, PO Box 51, Jakarta Tel: 481809/584845

C V **Diponegoro**, Publisher, 44-46 Mohd Toha Bandung Tel: 50395 Cable Add: C V Diponegoro Bandung
Man Dir: A A Dahlan; *Editorial, Sales, Production, Publicity:* Dr M D Dahlan
Subjects: Religion, University Textbooks
1982: 60 titles *Founded:* 1962

P T **Djambatan** Penerbit NV*, Tromolpos 116, Jakarta Tel: 345131/341678
Manager: Roswitha Pamoentjak
Subjects: Art, Literature, Juveniles, Textbooks, Religion, Philosophy, Sociology, Maps
Founded: 1958

P T **Dunia** Pustaka Jaya*, Jl Kramat II/31A, Jakarta Tel: 366245/367479 Cable Add: Depeje
Dir: Rachmat M A S; *Editorial:* Sugiarta Sriwibawa; *Production:* Yus Rusamsi
Branch Off: Jl Banteng 37, Bandung Tel: 59597
Subjects: General Fiction, Poetry, Art, Essays, Drama, Culture, Islam, Children's Books
Founded: 1971

Eresco PT, Jl Hasanudin No 9, Bandung Tel: (022) 82311 Cable Add: Erescopete Bandung
Man Dir: Mrs H P Rochmat Soemitro; *Editorial:* Prof Dr H Rochmat Soemitro; *Sales:* Mr Amun, Mr Harsono
Branch Off: Jl Perapatan 22 Pav Jakarta Tel: (021) 361782
Subjects: Law, Economics, Philosophy, Psychology, Taxation
Book Club: Himpunan Masyarakat Pencinta Buku (HMPB)
Bookshops: Jl Hasanudin 9 Bandung; Jl Perapatan 22 Pav Jakarta Tel: (021) 361782
Founded: 1956

Erlangga*, Jl Kramat IV (Kernolong) No 11, Jakarta Tel: 356593
Dir: M Hutauruk S H

P T **Gaya** Favorit Press, Book Division+, Jl Rasuna Said, Blok B, Kav 32-33, Jakarta Selatan Tel: 513816 Telex: 45734 Fega IA
Man Dir: Sofjan Alisjahbana; *Editorial:* Christine Pangemanan, Soekanto SA; *Sales:* Irwan SLT; *Production, Publicity, Rights & Permissions:* Christine Pangemanan
Parent Company: P T Gaya Favorit Press (at above address)
Subjects: Juvenile Fiction, Adult Fiction, Homecraft, other Non-fiction
1982: 165 titles *Founded:* 1975

PT **Gramedia***, PO Box 615, Dak Jakarta Pusat (Located at: Palmerah Selatan 22 lantai 4) Tel: 543008 Cable Add: Kompas Jakarta Telex: Kompas JKT 46327
General Manager: J Adisubrata; *Editorial:* A Haryono (Fiction), G Sugijanto (General, Non-fiction); *Sales:* A M Sutartono; *Production:* A Harijadi; *Publicity:* G Aris Buntarman; *Rights & Permissions:* Nora Sutadi
Subjects: Children's, General, Fiction and Non-fiction
Bookshops: Jl Merdeka 43, Bandung; Jl Gajah Mada 109, Jakarta; Jl Pintu Air 72, Jakarta; Jl Melawai IV/13, Jakarta; Jl Basuki Rachmat 95, Surabaya; Jl Jendral Sudirman 56, Yogyakarta
Founded: 1973

PT **Grip***, Jl Kawung No 2, PO Box 129, Surabaya Tel: 22564
Man Dir, Editorial: Suripto; *Sales:* F D Praseno; *Production:* S Sawitri; *Publicity:* Satriyo Purwanto
Branch Off: Jl Kembung 22, Jakarta
Subjects: Textbooks, Politics, Social Science
Founded: 1957

Gunung Agung, PT*, Jl Kwitang 8, PO Box 145, Jakarta Tel: 362909 Cable Add: Gunungagung Telex: 01144359 Jkt
President: Mr Masagung; *Manager:* Ali Amran
Subsidiary Company: Gunung Agung (S) Pte Ltd, Singapore (qv)
Subjects: Librarianship, Juveniles, Textbooks, Science, Biography, Language, Literature
Bookshops: PT Gunung Agung; Toko Buku Sari Agung (qqv under Major Booksellers)
Founded: 1953

BPK **Gunung Mulia***, Jl Kwitang 22, Jakarta Tel: 343476
Dir: A Simandjuntak
Bookshop: At above address

Firma **Harris***, Jl Veteran Gedung Olahraga No 6, Medan Tel: 22272

Hidakarya Agung*, Jl Kebon Kosong F-74, Jakarta Tel: 351074

Ichtiar Baru*, Jl Mojopahit 6, Jakarta Tel: 341226/41551
Subjects: Textbooks, Reference, Law, Social Sciences, Economics

PD & I **Ikhwan***, Jl Bujana Dalam No 10, Blok G, Kebayoran Baru, Jakarta Tel: 772679

P T **Indira***, Jl Borobudur No 20, Jakarta Pusat Tel: 882754/882250/881018 Cable Add: Indira Jakarta
Man Dir: Wahyudi D
Bookshops: See under Major Booksellers
Subjects: Education, Technical, General
Founded: 1950

Indrajaya*, Jl Jatibaru No 20, Jakarta Tel: 364372

Institut Dagang Muchtar*, Jl Embong Wungu 8, Surabaya Tel: 42973

206 INDONESIA

Islamiyah*, Jl Sutomo P 328-329, Kotakpos 11, Medan Tel: 25421

Yayasan **Jaya Baya**, PO Box 250, Surabaya (Located at: Jl Penghela 2 (atas), Surabaya) Tel: 41169

Yayasan **Kanisius***, Jl Pangeran Senopati 24, Jogjakarta Tel: 2309
Subjects: Textbooks, Religion, Engineering, Juveniles, Arts, Education, Economics

Karunia*, Jl Paneleh 18-A, Surabaya Tel: 44120

Yayasan **Kawanku***, Jl Setia Budi Raya, Gg Sumbangsih 11/3A, Jakarta Tel: 583100

Kinta*, Jl Chik Di Tiro No 54-A, Jakarta Tel: 351394

Kurnia Esa*, Jl Jend Sudirman Kav 36A, Blok B4, Bendungan Hilir, Jakarta Tel: 350043/5/6 Telex: 44328

L P3 E S (Lembaga Penelitian, Pendidikan Dan Penerangan Ekonomi Dan Social), Jl Letjen S Parman 81, Slipi, PO Box 493 Jkt, Jakarta Tel: 597211
The Institute for Economics and Social Research, Education and Information
Chief Executive, Dir: M Dawan Rahardjo; *Deputy Dir, Editorial Manager:* Aswab Mahasin; *Sales Manager:* Maruto
Subjects: Academic, Popular Science
1981-82: 30 titles *Founded:* 1971

Madju*, Jl Sutomo No P 341-342, Medan Tel: 25428

Marfiah*, Jl Kalibutuh No 131, Surabaya

Masa Baru*, Jl Gereja 3, Bandung Tel: 52045

Mutiara*, Jl Rawagelam I, Blok N, No 15 Kawasan Industri P Gadung, Jakarta Tel: 882441
Subjects: Juveniles, Maps, Mathematics, Music, Education, Physics, Religion, Economics

P T **New Aqua** Press/Aries Lima*, Jl Rawa Gelam II/4, Jakarta Timur Tel: 482163

Nusa Indah*, Jl Katedral 5, Ende, Flores Tel: 198

P A T C O, Jl Sawahan Sarimulyo 14, Surabaya Tel: 310021
Man Dir: Adolf Pattyranie
Subjects: Local Interest, Maps and Guides
Bookshop: TB Puncak Agung, Pasar Tambahrejo Blok A 21A, Jl Kapas Krampung, Surabaya
1981: 2 titles *1982:* 1 title *Founded:* 1972

Pelajar*, Jl Palasari 83-85, Bandung Tel: 57559

Pelita Masa*, Jl Lodaya No 25, Bandung Tel: 50823

Pembangunan*, Jl Grinting I/15, Blok A, Kebayoran Baru, Jakarta Tel: 342469
Managers: Mr Sumantri, Mr Soewando
Branch Offs: Bandung, Jogjakarta, Madiun and Surabaya
Subjects: Textbooks, Juveniles, Sciences
Founded: 1953

Pembimbing Masa*, Pusat Perdagangan Senen, Blok I, Lantai IV/2, PO Box 3281, Jakarta Tel: 367645

Pradnya Paramita*, PO Box 146/Jkt, Jl Kebon Sirih 46, Jakarta Pusat Tel: (021) 360411 Cable Add: Pradnya/Jkt
Man Dir, Rights & Permissions: Sadono Dibyowiroyo SH *Editorial, Publicity:* Thaufik Arifin; *Sales:* A F Julianto; *Production:* Waslan Suriapranata
Subjects: General, Primary, Secondary & University Textbooks
Bookshops: Jl Kebon Sirih 46 pav, Jakarta Pusat; Jl Kiai Maja 2A, Kebayoran Baru, Jakarta Selatan
Founded: 1963

Remaja Karya*, Jl Ciateul No 34-36, kotakpos 284, Bandung Tel: 58226

Rosda*, Jl Raya Cimahi, Padalarang Km 12.5 No 858, Bandung Tel: 56627; Jl Kramat Kwitang II No 4, Jakarta Tel: 354920

Sastra Hudaya*, Jl Proklamasi No 61, Jakarta Tel: 882328

A B **Sitti** Syamsiyah*, Jl Secoyudan No 28, Sala/Surakarta Tel: 4721

Soeroengan*, Jl Pecenongan No 58, Jakarta Tel: 344460

Pustaka **Star***, Jl Moh Toha No 58, Bandung Tel: 58710

Sumatera*, Jl R Dewi Sartika I No 1, Bandung

Sumur Bandung*, Jl Asia Afrika 82, Bandung Tel: 59137

Tarate*, Jl Sumatera No 26-30, kotakpos 243, Bandung Tel: 51067

Tintamas Indonesia PT*, Jl Kramat Raya 60, Jakarta Pusat Tel: 346186
Dir: Ali Audah
Subjects: Biography, History, Philosophy, Reference, Religion, Law, High-priced Paperbacks
Bookshop: Jl Kramat Raya 60, Jakarta Pusat
Founded: 1947

Toko **Messir***, Jl Gudang No 135, Cirebon Tel: 57151

U P Indonesia*, Jl Jend A Yani No 19, Jogjakarta

Warga*, Jl Karangmenjangan 61, Surabaya Tel: 472160/472872

Widjaja*, Jl Pecenongan No 48-C, Jakarta Tel: 363446

C V **Yasaguna***, Jl Dr Saharjo 50, Jakarta Selatan Tel: 824528
Manager: Hilman Madewa
Subjects: Agriculture, Popular Manuals for Professional Vocations

Book Clubs

Himpunan Masyarakat Pencinta Buku, Jl Tebet Raya 69, PO Box 354 KBY, Jakarta, Selatan Tel: (021) 821573
The Association of Bibliophiles
Members: 14,300
Owned by: Eresco PT (qv)
Founded: 1979

Major Booksellers

Effendi Harahap Bookstore*, Jl Abimanyu Raya 17, Semarang

Gramedia Bookshop*, 109 Jl Gajahmada, Jakarta Tel: 627809
General Manager: Indra Gunawan

PT **Gunung Agung***, Jl Irian 5, Jayapura
Also: Kwitang 8, Jakarta
Owned by: Gunung Agung PT (qv)

Toko Buku BPK **Gunung Mulia***, Jl Kwitang 22, Jakarta Tel: 41768

P T **Indira***, Jl Braga No 10, Bandung
Also: Jl Braga No 10, Bandung; Jl Jendral Sudirman 62, Jogjakarta; Jl Sam Ratulangi 37, Jakarta Pusat; Jl Gajah Mada 3-5, Duta Merlin Shopping Arcade, Jakarta Pusat; Pusat Perdagangan Senen Blok I Lantai IV 32-34, Jakarta Pusat; Jl Melawai V No 6, Jakarta Selatan; Jl Braga 111, Bandung; Jl Tunjungan 71, Surabaya; Jl Veteran 3394A, Palembang; Jl Sumatera 37, Den Pasar, Bali
Miscellaneous: Importers of General/Trade books and Educational/Scientific/Technical books and textbooks. Library suppliers to foreign libraries of Indonesian printed books

Toko Buku **Malabar***, 347 Oto Iskandarinata Bandung

Toko Buku **Melawai***, Jakarta

Toko Buku **Merbabu***, Semarang

Toko Buku Pustaka **Mimbar***, Medan

P T **Pembimbing** Masa*, Pusat Perdagangan Senen, Blok 1, Lantai IV No 2, PO Box 3281 Jkt, Jakarta Pusat Tel: 367645
Importer, bookshop, subscription agency

Pradnya Paramita*, Jl Kebon Sirih 46, Jakarta Pusat Tel: (021) 360411
Manager: Sadono Dibyowiroyo

Toko Buku **Sari Agung***, Tunjungan 5, Surabaya
Manager: J I Adipradja
Owned by: Gunung Agung PT (qv)

CV Toko Buku **Tropen***, Tromolpos 3604/JKT, 113 Jl Pasar Baru, Jakarta Pusat Tel: 362695/363543 Cable Add: Tokobuku Tropen
Manager: Jani Dipokusumo

Major Libraries

Arsip Nasional Republik Indonesia*, Jl Ampera Raya, Cilandak III, Jakarta Selatan Tel: 781851
National Archives

Bidang Bibliografi dan Deposit, Pusat Pembinaan Perpustakaan*, Departemen P dan K, Jl Medan Merdeka Selatan 11, Jakarta Tel: 360136
National Bibliographic and Deposit Centre, Centre for Library Development
Librarian: Paul Permadi
Publication: Bibliografi Nasional Indonesia (quarterly)

Perpustakaan **Biro** Pusat Statistik, Jl Dr Sutomo 8, Jakarta
Library of Central Bureau of Statistics

Perpustakaan **Dewan** Perwakilan Rakjat Gotong Rojong*, Senajan Pintu 8, Jakarta
Library of Indonesian Parliament

Pusat **Dokumentasi Ilmiah Nasional**, Jl Jenderal Gatot Subroto, PO Box 3065/JKT, Jakarta Selatan Tel: 583465/7, 510719, 511063 Telex: 45875 IA
National Scientific Documentation Centre
Publications: Direktori Perpustakaan Khusus dan Sumber Informasi di Indonesia (Directory of Special Libraries and Information Sources in Indonesia) (irregular); *Indeks Majalah Ilmiah Indonesia* (Index of Indonesian Learned Periodicals) (semi-annual); *Baca* (Read) (bi-monthly); *Bibliografi Khusus* (Special Bibliography) (irregular); *Indeks Laporan Penelitian dan Survai* (Index of Research and Survey Report) (annual); and lists of acquisitions (books and microfiches)

Library of **Hasanuddin** University*, Perpustakaan Pusat, Universitas Hasanuddin, Kampus Baraya, Ujung Pandang Tel: 3029 Telex: 7179

Perpustakaan Jajasan **Hatta***, Malioboro 85, Jogjakarta
Hatta Foundation Library

Perpustakaan Pusat **Institut** Teknologi Bandung, Jl Ganesya 10, Bandung Tel: 83814 Telex: ITB BD 28324
Central Library, Bandung Institute of Technology
Chief Librarian: Dr Ai Andaniah Setiadi
Publications include: Proceedings Institut Teknologi Bandung

Perpustakaan **Islam**, Jl P Mangkubumi 38, Jogjakarta Tel: 2078
Islamic Library

Perpustakaan **Museum** Nasional, Departemen Pendidikan dan Kebudayaan*, Merdeka Barat 12, Jakarta Tel: 360551
Library of the National Museum, Ministry of Education and Culture
Librarian: Miss M H Prakoso
Publications: Library Guide, Newspaper catalogue and other subject catalogues

National Library for Agricultural Sciences*, Jl Ir Haji Juanda 20, Bogor Tel: (0251) 21746 Cable Add: Bibliotheca

Perpustakaan **Negara***, Malioboro 175, Jogjakarta
State Library

Pusat **Pembinaan** Perpustakaan, Departemen P dan K Bidang. Bibliografi dan Deposit*, Medan Merdeka Selatan 11, Tromolpos 274 Jakarta-Pusat Tel: 360136
Centre for Library Development, Department of Education and Culture, Deposit Library
Publication: Berita Bulanan, checklist of Serials in the Libraries of Indonesia

Library of **Political and Social History***, Medan Merdeka Selatan 11, Jakarta Tel: 360136
Librarian: Mrs Sayangbati-Dengah, WW
Publications: Press index; Index Artikel Tentang Negara (Index of Official Publications); *Index Pemilu* (Index of General Elections)

Library Associations

Ikatan Pustakawan Indonesia*, c/o Centre for Library Development, Medan Merdeka Selatan 11, Belakang, Jakarta Tel: 360136
Indonesian Library Association
President: Sukarman Kartosedono
Secretary-General: J P Rompas
Publication: Majalah Ikatan Pustakawan Indonesia

Library Reference Books and Journals

Books

Direktori Perpustakaan Khusus dan Sumber Informasi di Indonesia (Directory of Special Libraries and Information Sources in Indonesia), National Scientific Documentation Centre, Jl Jendral Gatot-Subroto, PO Box 3065/JKT, Jakarta

Journals

Baca (Read) (quarterly), PO Box 3065, Jakarta

Berita Bulanan (Bulletin), Centre for Library Development, Department of Education and Culture, Deposit Library, Medan Merdeka Selatan 11, Jakarta

Berita Idayu (Idayu News), Yayasan Idayu, Jl Dr Abdulrachman Saleh 26, Jakarta

Checklist of Serials in the Libraries of Indonesia, Centre for Library Development, Department of Education and Culture, Deposit Library, Medan Merdeka, Selatan 11, Jakarta

Diurnal Perpustakaan (Library Journal) (text in Indonesian or English), Perpustakaan Umum Makassar, Jl Kajaolalidjo 16, PO Box 16, Ujung Pandang

Index Artikel Tentang Negara (Index of Official Publications), Library of Political and Social History, Medan Merdeka Selatan 11, Jakarta

Majalah Ikatan Pustakawan Indonesia (Indonesian Library Association Journal), Indonesian Library Association, c/o Centre for Library Development, Medan Merdeka Selatan 11, Jakarta

Literary Associations and Societies

P E N Centre, c/o Jl Cemara 6, Jakarta Pusat
Secretary: Dr Toeti Heraty Noerhadi

Iran

General Information

Language: Persian (Farsi), Turkish and Armenian in Northwest, Arabic in Southwest, Kurdish in Kurdistan (English or French also)
Religion: Muslim (Shi'a sect)
Population: 35.2 million
Literacy Rate (1971): 36.9% of population aged 6 or over (58.6% of urban population, 20.4% rural)
Bank Hours: Generally Winter: 0800-1300 Saturday-Thursday; 1600-1800 Saturday-Wednesday; Summer: 0730-1300, 1700-1900 Saturday-Wednesday, 0730-1130 Thursday
Shop Hours: Generally Winter: 0800-2000 Saturday-Thursday; 0800-1200 Friday; Summer: 0800-1300, 1700-2100 Saturday-Thursday, 0800-1200 Friday
Currency: rial
Export/Import Information: No tariff on books and advertising but catalogues subject to VAT. Import licences required. Publications offending public order, official religion or morality prohibited. Exchange controls, with new regulations issued each March
Copyright: No copyright conventions signed

Book Trade Organization

Tehran Book Processing Centre (TEBROC)*, PO Box 51-1126, Tehran (Located at: 1188 Enqelab Ave, Tehran) Tel: 662940
Dir: Miss Z Shadman
Publications include: Books Catalogued by TEBROC; Iranian National Union Catalogue; School Libraries; Directory of Iranian Periodicals; Directory of National and International Organizations of Library and Documentation

Book Trade Reference Journals

Bibliography of Persia, Book Society of Islamic Republic of Iran, PO Box 1936, Tehran (annual)

Books Catalogued by Tehran Book Processing Centre, Tehran Book Processing Centre, 46 Shahreza Ave, PO Box 11-1126, Tehran

Iranian National Union Catalogue, Tehran Book Processing Centre, 46 Shahreza Ave, PO Box 11-1126, Tehran

National Bibliography, Iranian Publications, National Library, Si-Ye Tir St, Tehran 11

Publishers

Amir Kabir Publishing & Distributing Corporation*, Shahabd St, Tehran
Dir: Abdulrahim Ja'fari
Parent Company: Amir Kabir, 28 Vessal Shirazi St
Subjects: Textbooks, General
Founded: 1950

Eghbal Co*, Shahabad Ave, Tehran
Dir: Djavad Eghbal
Subject: Juveniles, Fiction

Majlis Press*, Baharistan Ave, Tehran
Subjects: Juveniles, Fiction

Shahrokh **Sabzerou***, 549 Mosadegh Ave, Tehran 15 Tel: 662692 Cable Add: Sabzerou Telex: 215574 Sbru
Man Dir: Shahrokh Sabzerou
Subjects: Children's Books, Painting and Colouring Books
Founded: 1972

Scientific and Cultural Publications Center, Ministry of Culture and Higher Education, PO Box 1936, Tehran Tel: 686320
President: F A Larijani
Subjects: Science, Culture

Tehran University Press*, Kargar shomali Ave 16, Tehran Tel: 632062/3, 630060/9
Man Dir: Dr Firuz Harirchi; *Sales, Publicity:* Hassan Sanaie; *Rights & Permissions:* J Qajarieh
Subjects: University Textbooks
Bookshops: Ave 16 Azar, Tehran; Enqelab Ave, Tehran; Kargar shomali Ave 16, Tehran
Founded: 1944

Major Booksellers

Daneshdjou Bookstore*, 222 Shah Reza St, Tehran Tel: 48365

Mebso Bookshop*, 466 Naderi St, Tehran Tel: 46822/64091

Major Libraries

Astan Qods Central Library, Mashhad

Iranian Documentation Centre (IRANDOC)*, Ad 1188, Enqelab Ave, Tehran Tel: 662223/662140 Cable Add: Asnad Telex: 212889 TN
Dir: Mohammad Naghi Mahdavi; *Librarian:* Mrs Masoudeh Tofigh

National Library, Si-Ye Tir St, Tehran 11 Tel: 673315/673564
Librarian: Mohammad Kazeme Zarkeshan
Publication: Kétab-Shinasi-Yé Méli-Yé Iran (Iran National Bibliography)

Parliament Library (Ketab-khaneh Majles-e Shoraye Melli)*, Tehran

Parliament Library, No 2 (Ketab-khaneh Majles-e Shoraye Eslami, no 2)*, Felestine Ave, Tehran

T E B R O C (Tehran Book Processing Centre)*, PO Box 51-1126 Tehran (Located at: 1188 Enqelab, Tehran) Tel: 662940 Telex: 212889 irdc ir

Central Library and Documentation Centre of **Tehran** University*, Shahreza Ave, Tehran

University of Ferdowsi Library*, PO Box 331, Mashhad Tel: 33075
Librarian: A J Darbandi

University of Isfahan Library*, Isfahan

Central Library, **University of Tabriz**, Tabriz
Dir: Mrs F Ghoreishy

Library Associations

Anjoman-e Ketabdaren-e Iran*, PO Box 11-1391, Tehran Tel: 622768
Iranian Library Association
Secretary: M Nikham Vazifeh
Publications: Nameh, Monthly News

Association of Registered Archivists of Iran Secretariat*, Lalezar Ave, Passage Afrashteh, 1st floor, Tehran

Library Reference Books and Journals

Books

Directory of National and International Organizations of Library and Documentation, Tebroc, PO Box 51-1126, Tehran

Journals

Monthly News, Iranian Library Association, PO Box 11-1391, Tehran

Nameh (Bulletin) (text in Persian, summaries in English), Iranian Library Association, PO Box 11-1391, Tehran

Literary Associations and Societies

Book Society of Islamic Republic of Iran*, PO Box 1936, Tehran Tel: 220326
Secretary: Fazel A Larijani
Publication: Bibliography of Persia

Iraq

General Information

Language: Arabic, Kurdish (English is the principal foreign language in Baghdad)
Religion: Muslim
Population: 12.3 million
Literacy Rate (1957): 11%
Bank Hours: Winter: 0900-1300 Saturday-Wednesday; 0900-1200 Thursday; Summer: 0800-1200 Saturday-Wednesday, 0800-1100 Thursday
Shop Hours: Winter: 0830-1430, 1700-1900 Saturday-Wednesday, 0830-1330 Thursday; Summer: 0800-1400, 1700-1900 Saturday-Wednesday, 0800-1300 Thursday
Currency: 1,000 fils = 1 Iraqi dinar
Export/Import Information: No tariffs on books and advertising. Import licences required. Exchange control, influenced by annual foreign exchange budget. Importation by state trading company or established importer. The state trading company is the National House for Publishing, Distributing and Advertising, Aljamhuria St, PO Box 624, Baghdad
Copyright: No copyright conventions signed

Book Trade Reference Journal

Iraqi Bulletin for Publications, National Library, al-Jumhuriya St, Baghdad

Publishers

Al Ma'arif Ltd*, Mutanabi St, Baghdad
Subjects: Books in several Middle-Eastern languages, French and English, Fiction, Politics
Founded: 1929

National House for Publishing, Distributing and Advertising*, Aljamhuria St, PO Box 624, Baghdad Tel: 68391 Cable Add: Donta Telex: 2392
Subjects: Politics, Economics, Education, Agriculture, Sociology, Commerce, General Science, Books in Arabic and other Middle-Eastern languages (also distributor)
Founded: 1972
Miscellaneous: Firm is attached to the Ministry of Information and is the sole importer and distributor of newspapers, magazines, periodicals and books

Major Booksellers

The export of Iraqi books is handled by the National House for Publishing, Distributing and Advertising (qv under Publishers)

Major Libraries

Al-Awqaf, PO Box 14146, Baghdad Tel: 66104/65650
Library of Waqfs
Librarian: Jassim Al-Juboori
Branches at: Al-Qazzaza Library, Baghdad; Munier Al-Qadhi Library, Baghdad; Adhamiya, Mosul; Main Mosque, Anbar, Amarah; Nasiriyah; Sulaymaniyah; Kerkuk; Diala

College of Agriculture Library, University of Baghdad*, Abu Ghraib

The **Diwan** Library, Ministry of Education*, Baghdad

Library of the **Iraq Museum***, Baghdad

Library of the **Iraq Natural History** Research Centre and Museum, University of Baghdad, Bab Al-Muadham, Baghdad Tel: 68361/65790
Publications include: Bulletin, Publication

Library of the **Mosul Museum***, Mosul

Mosul Public Library*, Mosul

National Centre of Archives*, Waziriah, Amr bin Kalthoom St 15/10/9, Baghdad Cable Add: Centarchiv
Director-General: Salim Al-Alousi

National Library*, al-Jumhuriya St, Baghdad
Dir: Fouad Y M Qazanchi
Publications: Iraqi National Bibliography (3 times yearly); *Accumulation List* (annual); *al-Maktaba al-Arabia Journal*

Scientific Documentation Centre, Council of Ministers, Council for Scientific Research, PO Box 2441, Jadiriyah, Baghdad Tel: 7760023/7764689 Telex: 2187 Bathilmi IK

Central Library of the **University of Baghdad**, Safi El-Din Ali-Hilli St, PO Box 12, Baghdad Tel: 64742

Library Associations

Arab Archivists Institute*, c/o National Centre of Archives, Waziriah, Amr bin Kalthoom St 15/10/9, Baghdad

Iraq Library Association*, PO Box 4081, Baghdad-Adhamya Tel: 27077
Secretary: N Kamalal-Deen

Library Reference Journals

Arab Archives Journal, National Centre of Archives, Waziriah, Amr bin Kalthoom St 15/10/9, Baghdad

Deposit Bulletin, National Library, Baghdad

The Library, Al-Muthanna Library, Al-Mutanabbi St, Baghdad

Republic of Ireland

General Information

Language: English and Irish
Religion: Roman Catholic
Population: 3.3 million
Bank Hours; 1000-1230, 1330-1500 Monday-Friday. Most open until 1700 one evening
Shop Hours: 0900 or 0930-1730 Monday-Saturday
Currency: 100 pence = 1 Irish pound
Export/Import Information: Member of the European Economic Community. No tariff on books except on prayer and similar books from non-UK and children's picture books from non-EEC. Pamphlets dutied from non-EEC. VAT is charged. No import licences. Exchange controls
Copyright: UCC, Berne (see International section)

Book Trade Organizations

Book Association of Ireland*, 21 Shaw St, Dublin 2
Honorary Secretary: Eoin O'Keeffe
Association is inactive at present time

Booksellers Association of Great Britain and Ireland, 154 Buckingham Palace Rd, London SW1W 9TZ

Cumann Leabharfhoilsitheoirí Éireann (CLÉ), Book House Ireland, 65 Middle Abbey St, Dublin 1 Tel: (01) 730477
Irish Book Publishers' Association
Contact: Sheila Crowley

Irish Book Publishers' Association, see Cumann Leabharfhoilsitheoirí Éireann

Irish Educational Publishers' Association, c/o C J Fallon Ltd, Lucan Rd, Palmerston, Dublin 20 Tel: (01) 265777
Honorary Secretary: M A Ledwidge

National Federation of Retail Newsagents*, Republic of Ireland District Council, 63 Middle Abbey St, Dublin 1 Tel: (01) 745347/787902

Book Trade Reference Journals

Books Ireland, Goslingstown, Kilkenny Tel: (0409) 5964 Telex: 8727 Kdw Ei (Attn Addis)
The trade journal and review medium of the Irish publishing industry. Published 10 times a year

Irish Publishing Record, School of Librarianship, University College, Belfield, Dublin 4

Leabharagan An Aosa Oig (Primary Bookshelf) (text in English and Gaelic), Nessa Ni Mhurchu, 45 St Brendan's Ave, Malahide Rd, Dublin 5

Publishers

A P C K*, Dawson St, Dublin 2

Academy Microfilms (Dublin), see The University Press of Ireland

The **Academy** Press, now part of The University Press of Ireland (qv)

Acorn Books, an imprint of The Children's Press Ltd (qv)

Anvil Books Ltd, 90 Lower Baggot St, Dublin 2 Tel: (01) 762359 Cable Add: Anvil, Dublin
Man Dir, Sales, Production, Publicity, Rights & Permissions: Rena Dardis; *Editorial:* Dan Nolan
Associate Company: The Children's Press Ltd (qv)
Imprint: The Geraldine Press
Subjects: Biography, Irish History, Folklore, Sociology, Children
1981: 2 titles *1982:* 2 titles *Founded:* 1964
ISBN Publisher's Prefix: 0-900068

Arlen House Ltd+, 69 Jones Rd, Dublin 3 Tel: (01) 786913
Chief Executive: Catherine Rose
Associate Company: Turoe Press Ltd (qv)
Imprint: The Women's Press
Subjects: Women's Studies, Feminist Literature, History, Biography, Poetry
1983: 17 titles *Founded:* 1975
ISBN Publisher's Prefix: 0-905223

The **Blackwater** Press, c/o Folens & Co Ltd, Airton Rd, Tallaght, Co Dublin Tel: 515311
Editor: Anne Senior
Subjects: Non-fiction books of Irish interest, Local History, History, Biography
ISBN Publisher's Prefix: 0-905471

Bluett & Co Ltd+, 95 Lower Baggot St, Dublin 2 Tel: (01) 762639
Chief Executive and all other offices: Syd Bluett
Subjects: Literature, Art, Humour
1982: 3 titles *Founded:* 1980
ISBN Publisher's Prefix: 0-907899

Boole Press Ltd*, PO Box 5, 51 Sandycove Rd, Dun Laoghaire, Co Dublin Tel: 808025 Cable Add: Boolepress Dublin Telex: 92240 Sotr Ei
Man Dir: M O'Reilly; *General Manager:* M J Mullarkey
Subjects: Scientific, Technical, Medical, Scholarly
1981: 2 titles *Founded:* 1979
ISBN Publisher's Prefix: 0-906783

Capel, an imprint of Co-op Books (Publishing) Ltd (qv)

The **Children's** Press Ltd+, 90 Lower Baggot St, Dublin 2 Tel: (01) 762359 Cable Add: Children's Press Dublin
Man Dir, Sales, Production, Publicity, Rights & Permissions: Rena Dardis; *Editorial:* Tony Hickey
Associate Company: Anvil Books Ltd (qv)
Imprint: Acorn Books
Subject: Children's
1981: 1 title *1982:* 3 titles *Founded:* 1981
ISBN Publisher's Prefix: 0-900068

An Clócomhar TTA*, 13 Gleann Carraig, Dublin 13 Tel: (01) 324906
Subjects: Books in Irish language
1981: 10 titles

Clódhanna Teo*, c/o 6 Harcourt St, Dublin 2 Tel: (01) 757401
Publicity Manager: Donnchadh Ó Laodha

Co-op Books (Publishing) Ltd*, 16 Lower Liffey St, Dublin 1 Tel: 726329/726688
Dirs: Leland Bardwell, Anthony Cronin
Imprints: Capel, Focus Ireland
Subjects: Fiction, Drama, General Non-fiction
1982: 40 titles *Founded:* 1976
ISBN Publisher's Prefix: 0-905441

Cork University Press*, University College, Cork Tel: (021) 26871 ext 2347
Sales Dir, Executive Secretary: D J Counihan
Subjects: Biography, History, Music, Art, Philosophy, Literature, Reference, Religion, Medicine, Psychology, Engineering, General & Social Science, University Textbooks
Bookshop: Cork University Press (Retail Sales), University College, Cork
1981: 1 title *Founded:* 1925
ISBN Publisher's Prefix: 0-902561

Cuala Press, Avalon, Leslie Ave, Dalkey, County Dublin Tel: Dublin 850406
Dirs: M B Yeats, Anne Yeats, Thomas Kinsella, Liam Miller, Patrick O'Carroll, Gráinne Yeats, Síle Yeats
Subjects: Books formerly selected by W B Yeats. The press continues the tradition of Irish hand-printing & publishing, and issues first editions of Irish writers, booklets, ballad sheets & hand-coloured prints
Founded: 1908

Gilbert **Dalton** Ltd*, 4 Dublin Rd, Stillorgan, Blackrock, Co Dublin Tel: (01) 889231/885268
Chief Executive, Production, Publicity, Rights & Permissions, Editorial: Jim McGowan; *Sales:* Mary Goldrick
Subjects: Irish Tradition, Folklore, Folk Music, Science Fiction, Gaelic Books
Bookshop: McGowan's Bookshop (at above address)
1981: 2 titles *Founded:* 1975
ISBN Publisher's Prefix: 0-86233

The **Dolmen** Press Ltd, The Lodge, Mountrath, Portlaoise Tel: Abbeyleix (0502) 32213
Man Dir: Liam Miller; *Sales, Publicity & Advertising Dir:* Josephine Miller
Orders to: Irish Bookhandling, North Richmond Industrial Estate, Dublin 1 Tel: (01) 740325
Subsidiary Company: The Five Lamps Press (at above address)
Subjects: Belles Lettres, Poetry, Biography, High-priced Paperbacks
1981: 6 titles *Founded:* 1951
ISBN Publisher's Prefix: 0-85105

Dominican Publications, Saint Saviour's, Granby Lane, Dublin 1 Tel: (01) 744144
Chief Executive, Editorial: Austin Flannery; *Sales, Production:* Bernard Treacy

Branch Off: 69 Upper O'Connell St, Dublin 1 Tel: (01) 788059
Subject: Religion
Book Clubs: Doctrine and Life Book Club, Religious Life Review Book Club, Scripture in Church Book Club
Bookshops: At above addresses
1981: 9 titles *1982:* 10 titles *Founded:* 1897
ISBN Publisher's Prefixes: 0-9504797, 0-907271

Dublin Institute for Advanced Studies, 10 Burlington Rd, Dublin 4 Tel: (01) 680748
Subjects: Celtic Studies, Physics

Eason & Son Ltd, 65 Middle Abbey St, Dublin 1 Tel: (01) 733811 Telex: 4286
Man Dir: S D Carpenter; *Editorial, Production, Publicity, Rights & Permissions:* W H Clarke; *Sales:* M Hoban
Associate Companies: Eason & Son (NI) Ltd, Boucher Rd, Belfast; Irish Representation, 52 Corporation St, Dublin 1
Imprint: Irish Heritage Series
Subject: Irish interest
Bookshops: See under Major Booksellers
1981: 5 titles *1982:* 6 titles *Founded:* 1886
ISBN Publisher's Prefix: 0-900346

Ecclesia Press, an imprint of Irish Academic Press (qv)

The **Educational** Company of Ireland Ltd, PO Box 43A, Ballymount Rd, Walkinstown, Dublin 12 Tel: (01) 500611 Telex: 5864
Dirs: F Maguire, J M Davin, S O'Neill, R J McBride
Branch Off: 20-1 Talbot St, Dublin 1
Subjects: History, Religion, Irish, English, Geography, French, Technical, Domestic Science, Computer Studies, Career Guidance
Subsidiary Company: Talbot Press Ltd (qv)
Founded: 1877
ISBN Publisher's Prefix: 0-901802

C J **Fallon** Ltd, Lucan Rd, Palmerstown, Dublin 20 Tel: (01) 265777
Chairman: E White; *Man Dir:* H McNicholas; *Editorial:* N White; *Secretary:* P Tolan
Subjects: Secondary & Primary Textbooks, Business
Bookshops: Fallon's Book Shop, 77 Marlboro St, Dublin 1
Founded: 1927
ISBN Publisher's Prefix: 0-7144

Allen **Figgis** & Co Ltd, 56 Dawson St, Dublin 2 Tel: (01) 778510
Man Dir: Allen Figgis
Subjects: General Fiction & Non-fiction
ISBN Publisher's Prefix: 0-900372

The **Five Lamps** Press, a subsidiary of The Dolmen Press Ltd (qv)

Focus Ireland, an imprint of Co-op Books (Publishing) Ltd (qv)

Foilseacháin Náisiúnta Tta*, 29 Sraid Ui Chonaill Iocht, Ath Cliath 1 Tel: Ath Cliath 745314

Folens and Co Ltd, Airton Rd, Tallaght, Co Dublin Tel: 515311
Man Dir: D Folens
Subject: Educational
ISBN Publisher's Prefix: 0-86121

An **Foras** Forbartha, St Martin's House, Waterloo Rd, Ballsbridge, Dublin 4 Tel: (01) 764211 Cable Add: Foras, Dublin Telex: 30846
National Institute for Physical Planning and Construction Research
Chief Executive Officer: W McCumiskey; *Rights & Permissions:* E Mulkeen
Subject: Environmental Research
Founded: 1964
ISBN Publisher's Prefix: 0-906120

REPUBLIC OF IRELAND

Four Courts Press Ltd+, Kill Lane, Blackrock, Co Dublin Tel: (01) 850922
Man Dir: Michael Adams
Associate Companies: Irish Academic Press (qv); The Round Hall Press (at above address)
Subjects: Philosophy, Theology
1981: 3 titles *1982:* 5 titles *Founded:* 1969
ISBN Publisher's Prefix: 0-906127

The **Gallery** Press, 19 Oakdown Rd, Dublin 14 Tel: (01) 985161
Chief Executive, Editorial: Peter Fallon
Associate Company: The Deerfield Press, Deerfield, Mass 01342, USA
Subjects: Poetry, Plays, Prose, Drawings
1981: 8 titles *1982:* 8 titles *Founded:* 1970
ISBN Publisher's Prefixes: 0-902996, 0-904011

The **Geraldine** Press, an imprint of Anvil Books Ltd (qv)

Gifford & Craven*, 50 Merrion Square, Dublin 2

Gill & Macmillan Ltd, Goldenbridge, Inchicore, Dublin 8 Tel: (01) 783288 Cable Add: Gillmac Dublin Telex: 92197
Man Dir: M H Gill; *Editorial Director:* H Mahoney; *Sales Dir:* Peter Thew; *Publicity, Rights & Permissions:* Eveleen Coyle; *Production Manager:* Eamonn O'Rouke
Associate Company: Macmillan Publishers Ltd, UK (qv)
Subjects: Belles Lettres, Biography, History, Philosophy, Religion, Paperbacks, University, Secondary & Primary Textbooks
1981: 45 titles *Founded:* 1968 (formerly Gill & Son)
ISBN Publisher's Prefix: 0-7171

Golden Eagle Books Ltd, subsidiary of The Mercier Press Ltd (qv)

The **Goldsmith** Press Ltd, Newbridge, Co Kildare Tel: (045) 33613
Publicity Manager: Vera Browne; *Business Manager:* V M Abbott
Subjects: Literature, Fiction, Poetry, Art, Children's, Cookery
1982: 5 titles *1983:* 8 titles
ISBN Publisher's Prefix: 0-904984

Institute of Public Administration, 59 Lansdowne Rd, Dublin 4 Tel: (01) 697011 Cable Add: Admin Dublin
Dir (Publications): James D O'Donnell; *Manager:* Tony Farmar; *Sales:* James Moraghan
Subjects: Irish Government, Economics, Law, Social Policy and Administrative History, *Administration Yearbook & Diary, Administration* (journal), *Young Citizen*
1981: 4 titles *1982:* 6 titles *Founded:* 1957
ISBN Publisher's Prefixes: 0-902173, 0-906980

Irish Academic Press+, Kill Lane, Blackrock, Co Dublin Tel: (01) 850922
Man Dir: Michael Adams
Associate Companies: Four Courts Press Ltd (qv); The Round Hall Press (at above address)
Imprints: Irish University Press, Ecclesia Press
Subjects: History, Government Documents, Irish Studies
1981: 3 titles *1982:* 5 titles *Founded:* 1974
ISBN Publisher's Prefix: 0-7165

Irish Heritage Series, an imprint of Eason & Son Ltd (qv)

Irish Humanities Centre (Publishing), Terrybaun, Bofeenaun, Ballina Tel: (01) 603565
General Manager, Editorial: Grattan Freyer
Subjects: Irish Literary, Political, Historical
1981: 1 title *1982:* 1 title *Founded:* 1979
ISBN Publisher's Prefix: 0-906462

Irish Management Institute+, Sandyford Rd, Dublin 14 Tel: (01) 983911 Telex: 30325
Chief Executive: Brian Patterson; *Editorial, Rights & Permissions, Sales, Publicity, Advertising Dir:* Alex Miller
Subjects: Management Practice, Economics, Research Reports
1981: 7 titles *1982:* 7 titles *Founded:* 1952
ISBN Publisher's Prefix: 0-903352

The **Irish Times** Ltd, General Services, 16 D'Olier St, Dublin 2 Tel: (01) 722022 Telex: 25167
Subjects: Reprints, Political, Satirical, Educational, Microfilm (1859 to present of *The Irish Times*)

Irish University Press, an imprint of Irish Academic Press (qv)

Albertine **Kennedy** Publishing, Woodhouse, Captain's Hill, Leixlip, Co Kildare Tel: 280236
Man Dir: Thomas Kennedy
Subjects: Irish Interest, Travel, Literature, Photography
1981: 4 titles *1982:* 3 titles *Founded:* 1975
ISBN Publisher's Prefix: 0-906002

The **Mercier** Press Ltd+, 4 Bridge St, Cork Tel: 504022 Telex: 75463
Man Dir: Captain J M Feehan; *Editorial:* M Feehan; *Rights & Permissions:* J F Spillane
Subsidiary Companies: Mercier Distributors Ltd; Golden Eagle Books Ltd (both at above address)
Branch Off: 24 Lower Abbey St, Dublin Tel: (01) 744141
Subjects: Irish Literature, History, Politics, Biography, Folklore, Travel, Humour, Theology, Philosophy, Religion, Music, Art, Reference, High-priced Paperbacks
Bookshops: The Mercier Bookshop Ltd (qv under Major Booksellers)
1981: 24 titles *Founded:* 1946
ISBN Publisher's Prefix: 0-85342

New Writers' Press*, 61 Clarence Mangan Rd, Dublin 8
Man Dir: Michael Smith
Subjects: Poetry, Criticism, Hardbacks and Paperbacks
Founded: 1967

O'Brien Educational, 20 Victoria Rd, Rathgar, Dublin 6 Tel: (01) 979598
Editorial, Rights & Permissions: Seamus Cashman; *Sales, Production:* Michael O'Brien; *Publicity:* Catherine Boland
Associate Companies: The O'Brien Press (qv); Wolfhound Press (qv)
Subjects: Science, Art, Humanities, English, History, Celtic Studies, Contrast Studies, Teachers' Handbooks and Aids, Career Guidance, Business Studies, Environmental Studies, Urban Studies
1983: 30 titles
Miscellaneous: Publishers to the Curriculum Development Unit, Trinity College, Dublin 2, and to other educational institutions in Ireland and the EEC
ISBN Publisher's Prefixes: 0-905140, 0-86278

The **O'Brien** Press, 20 Victoria Rd, Rathgar, Dublin 6 Tel: (01) 979598
Man Dir, Rights & Permissions: Michael O'Brien; *Production, Publicity:* Catherine Boland
Orders to: Irish Bookhandling Ltd, Nth Richmond Industrial Est, Dublin 1 Tel: (01) 740324
Associate Company: O'Brien Educational (qv)
Subjects: General Fiction, Belles Lettres, Biography, History, Architecture/Planning, Anthropology, Quality Paperbacks, Natural History, Illustrated Books, Folklore, Children's Books, Food and Drink, Language, Medicine, Music, Politics, Sociology, Topography, Sport
1983: 83 titles *Founded:* 1974
ISBN Publisher's Prefixes: 0-905140, 0-86278

Poolbeg Press Ltd, Knocksedan House, Forrest Great, Swords, Co Dublin Tel: (01) 401133 Telex: 24639
Man Dirs: Philip MacDermott, David Marcus; *Editorial:* David Marcus, Sean McMahon; *Sales:* Philip MacDermott Ltd; *Publicity:* Margaret Daly
Parent Company: Ward River Press (qv)
Subject: Fiction
1983: 60 titles *Founded:* 1976

Runa Press, 2 Belgrave Terrace, Monkstown, Dublin 1 Tel: (01) 801869
Subjects: Poetry, Philosophy, Sociology, Fiction, Psychology

Stationery Office (Oifig an tSolathair), St Martin's House, Waterloo Rd, Dublin 4 Tel: (01) 789644 Cable Add: Enactments
Sales, Publicity: Leo Ginnetty
Bookshop: Government Publications Sales Office, Sun Alliance House, Molesworth St, Dublin 2
1981: approx 700 titles *Founded:* 1922

Talbot Press Ltd, PO Box 43A, Ballymount Rd, Walkinstown, Dublin 12 Tel: (01) 500611
Dirs: J M Davin, S O'Neill, F Maguire
Parent Company: The Educational Company of Ireland Ltd (qv)
Subjects: General Fiction, History, Music, Religion, Juveniles, Political Science, Folklore, Religious & Liturgical
Founded: 1913
ISBN Publisher's Prefix: 0-85452

Tansy Books*, Knocktree Cottage, Enniskerry, Co Wicklow Tel: 868514
Dir: John Feeney
Subjects: Fiction, Psychology, Essays, History
Founded: 1976

Turoe Press Ltd+, 69 Jones Rd, Dublin 3 Tel: (01) 786913
Chief Executive: Michael F Roberts
Associate Company: Arlen House Ltd (qv)
Subjects: Social Questions, Sociology, Social History, Reference, Practical
1983: 10 titles *Founded:* 1980
ISBN Publisher's Prefix: 0-905223

Tycooly International Publishing Ltd, 6 Crofton Terrace, Dun Laoghaire, Co Dublin Tel: 800245/800246/807221 Telex: 90635 Tyco Ei
Chairman: Dr Tom Walsh; *Publisher, Chief Executive:* Francis O'Kelly; *Editorial Manager:* Carole Devaney; *Marketing Dir:* Kelvin Smith; *Promotion Manager:* Gillian Conan
Associate Company: Africascience International Publishing Ltd, PO Box 40047, Nairobi, Kenya
Subjects: Environment, Energy, Water Resources, Development
1981: 5 titles *1982:* 13 titles *Founded:* 1981
ISBN Publisher's Prefixes: 0-907567, 0-86346

The **University Press** of Ireland, 17 Brighton Square, Rathgar, Dublin 6 Tel: (01) 962946
Publisher: Sean I Browne; *Editorial:* Catherine Osborn
Associate Company: Academy Microfilms (Dublin) (at above address)
Subjects: History, Biography, Scholarly Monographs, Literature, Literary Criticism, Photography
Founded: 1976
ISBN Publisher's Prefix: 0-906187

Veritas Publications+, Veritas House, 7-8 Lower Abbey St, Dublin 1 Tel: (01) 788177 Telex: 32238 Vert EI

Dir: Séan O'Boyle; *Editorial:* Máire Quinn; *Sales:* Tom Griffin; *Production:* J McCurrie
Parent Company: The Catholic Communications Institute of Ireland
Subjects: Religion, Low- & High-priced Paperbacks, University, Secondary & Primary Textbooks, Educational Materials
Bookshops: Veritas, Bridge St, Cork; McGowan's, 4 Dublin Rd, Stillorgan, Co Dublin; Veritas, 7-8 Lower Abbey St, Dublin 1; Veritas, John St, Sligo
1983: 152 titles *Founded:* 1900
Miscellaneous: Veritas Publications is the publishing division of the Catholic Communications Institute of Ireland Inc
ISBN Publisher's Prefixes: 0-905092, 0-86217

Villa Books Ltd*, 55 Dame St, Dublin 2 Tel: (01) 775138
Man Dir: Anthony Dwyer; *Editorial:* Susan Dwyer
Subjects: General Non-fiction, Religion
Founded: 1978
ISBN Publisher's Prefix: 0-906408

Ward River Press, Knocksedan House, Forrest Great, Swords, Co Dublin Tel: 401133 Telex: 24639
Man Dirs: Philip MacDermott, Bernadette MacDermott, David Marcus; *Editorial, Rights & Permissions:* Cormac O'Cuilleanain; *Sales:* Philip MacDermott Ltd; *Publicity:* Margaret Daly
Subsidiary Company: Poolbeg Press Ltd (qv)
Subjects: General Interest
1983: 70 titles *Founded:* 1980

Wolfhound Press, 68 Mountjoy Square, Dublin 1 Tel: (01) 740354
Publisher: Seamus Cashman; *Publicity:* Mary Paul Keane
Orders to: Irish Bookhandling Ltd, North Richmond Industrial Estate, North Richmond St, Dublin 1 Tel: (01) 740324
Associate Company: O'Brien Educational (qv)
Subjects: Belles Lettres, Biography, History, Juveniles, Fiction, Literary Studies, Law
1981: 12 titles *1982:* 14 titles *Founded:* 1974
ISBN Publisher's Prefixes: 0-9503454, 0-905473, 0-86327

The **Women's** Press, an imprint of Arlen House Ltd (qv)

Book Clubs

Doctrine and Life Book Club, Saint Saviour's, Granby Lane, Dublin 1 Tel: (01) 744144
Members: 4,000
Owned by: Dominican Publications (qv)

Religious Life Review Book Club, Saint Saviour's, Granby Lane, Dublin 1 Tel: (01) 744144
Members: 4,000
Owned by: Dominican Publications (qv)

Scripture in Church Book Club, Saint Saviour's, Granby Lane, Dublin 1 Tel: (01) 744144
Members: 6,000
Owned by: Dominican Publications (qv)

Major Booksellers

Eason & Son Ltd, Patrick St, Cork; 40 Lower O'Connel St, Dublin 1
Tel: (01) 803005; Middle Abbey St, Dublin 1 Tel: (01) 741161
Also: Antrim, Belfast, Coleraine, Craigavon, Dun Laoghaire, Limerick, Lisburn, Newtownards
Also Publisher (qv)

The **Eblana** Bookshop*, Eblana House, 50 Middle Abbey St, Dublin Tel: (01) 787633

Wm **Egan** & Sons*, Patrick St, Cork, Co Cork

Greene & Co, 16 Clare St, Dublin 2 Tel: (01) 762554
Manager: E J Pembrey

Fred **Hanna** Ltd*, 27-29 Nassau St, Dublin 2 Tel: (01) 771255/720797

Hodges Figgis & Co Ltd, 56 Dawson St, Dublin 2 Tel: (01) 774754
Owned by: Pentos Bookselling Group Ltd

The **Kilkenny** Bookshop Ltd*, High St, Kilkenny Tel: (056) 22974 (New retail books); Kieran St, Kilkenny Tel: (056) 22974 (Secondhand and antiquarian books)
Proprietors: Don and Mary Roberts

The **Library** Shop*, Trinity College, College St, Dublin 2 Tel: (01) 772941
Manager: J G Duffy

The **Mercier** Bookshop Ltd, 4 Bridge St, Cork Tel: (021) 504022 Telex: 75463 Mrcr Ei
Also: The Mercier University Bookshop, Boole Library, University College, Cork Tel: (021) 504022; Mercier Library Suppliers, 24 Lower Abbey St, Dublin 1 Tel: (01) 788259
Owned by: The Mercier Press Ltd (qv)

O'Mahony & Co Ltd, 120 O'Connell St, Limerick Tel: (061) 48155
School Booksellers Department at 40 Thomas St, Limerick Tel: (061) 49322
Manager: Arthur O'Leary
Also: Unit 10, Dunnes Shopping Centre, Honan's Quay, Limerick

Paperback Centre*, 20 Suffolk St, Dublin 2 Tel: (01) 774210; Stillorgan Shopping Centre, Co Dublin Tel: (01) 886341

Willis Bookshops*, 31 South Anne St, Dublin 2 Tel: (01) 719273
Manager: Miss G Wratt
Also: 37 Cook St, Cork Tel: (021) 20937
Manager: Miss B Russell

Major Libraries

The Chester **Beatty** Library and Gallery of Oriental Art, 20 Shrewsbury Rd, Dublin 4 Tel: (01) 692386
Among items on display at the Library is material showing the development of the written word from 2700 BC (the date of the Library's earliest clay tablet) down to modern times
Librarian: W Lockwood

Central **Catholic** Library*, 74 Merrion Sq, Dublin 2

Dublin Public Libraries, Cumberland House, Fenian St, Dublin 2 Tel: (01) 687333
City and County Librarian: Mairin O'Byrne

James **Hardiman** Library, see University College Galway

National Library of Ireland, Kildare St, Dublin 2 Tel: (01) 765521

Oireachtas Library*, Leinster House, Dublin 2
(Selective works of parliamentary interest)

Public Record Office of Ireland, Four Courts, Dublin 7 Tel: (01) 725275

Representative Church Body Library, Braemor Park, Rathgar, Dublin 14 Tel: (01) 979979
Librarian: Miss G Willis

Royal College of Surgeons in Ireland Library, St Stephen's Green, Dublin 2
Tel: (01) 780200 Ex 248 Telex: 30795 Rcsi Ei
Librarian: Professor J B Lyons FRCPI; *Executive Librarian:* Mrs K M Bishop
Publication: Journal of the Irish Colleges of Physicians and Surgeons

Royal Dublin Society Library, Ballsbridge, Dublin 4 Tel: (01) 680645 Cable Add: Society, Dublin Telex: 90352 Rds Ei
Librarian: A R Eager

Trinity College Library*, College St, Dublin 2 Tel: (01) 772941 Telex: 25442
Librarian: Peter Brown

University College Cork Library*, University College, Cork Tel: (021) 26871 Telex: 6050

University College Dublin Library, Belfield, Dublin 4 Tel: (01) 693244 Telex: 4114
Librarian: S Phillips
Publication: Irish Publishing Record

University College Galway, James Hardiman Library, Galway
Librarian: Alf MacLochlainn

Library Associations

Central **Catholic** Library Association Inc, 74 Merrion Sq, Dublin 2

An **Chomhairle** Leabharlanna, 53/54 Upper Mount St, Dublin 2 Tel: (01) 761167/761963 Telex: 25733 Icls Ei
Library Council. This is the development agency for public libraries in Ireland
Dir: T Armitage
Publications: Annual Report; Irish Library News; Serial Holdings in Irish Libraries

Cumann Leabharlann na h-Éireann*, Crofton Mansions, 22 Crofton Rd, Dun Laoghaire, Co Dublin
Library Association of Ireland
Honorary Secretary: J R Steele
Publication: An Leabharlann (The Irish Library) (published jointly with the Northern Ireland Branch, The Library Association) (4 per year)

Cumann Leabharlannaithe Scoile (CLS)*, Irish Schools Library Association, Loreto College, Foxrock, Co Dublin
Irish Association of School Librarians
Executive Secretary: Sister Monaghan

Irish Society for Archives, 82 Saint Stephen's Green, Dublin 2 Tel: (01) 757255
Secretary: Mary E Clark
Publication: Irish Archives Bulletin

National Library of Ireland Society, Kildare St, Dublin 2

Library Reference Journals

An Leabharlann (The Irish Library), Library Association of Ireland, Crofton Mansions, 22 Crofton Rd, Dun Laoghaire, Co Dublin (published jointly with Northern Ireland Branch)

Irish Library News, An Chomhairle Leabharlanna, 53/54 Upper Mount St, Dublin 2 (monthly newsheet issued free to libraries)

Long Room, Trinity College, Friends of the Library, College St, Dublin 2

Serial Holdings in Irish Libraries, An Chomhairle Leabharlanna, 53/54 Upper Mount St, Dublin 2

Literary Associations and Societies

Irish Academy of Letters*, 4 Ailesbury Grove, Dundrum, Dublin 14
Secretary: Evan Boland

Irish P E N, 26 Rosslyn, Killarney Rd, Bray, Co Wicklow
Secretary: Arthur Flynn

Literary Periodicals

Comhar (Cooperation) (text in Irish), 37 Sraid na Bhfinini, Dublin

Dublin Magazine, Irish Academy of Letters, 4 Ailesbury Grove, Dundrum, Dublin 14

Journal of Irish Literature, Proscenium Press, PO Box 361, Newark, DE 19711, USA

Studies; an Irish quarterly review of letters, philosophy and science, Talbot Press Ltd, PO Box 43A, Ballymount Rd, Walkinstown Rd, Dublin 12

Literary Prizes

Allied Irish Banks' Awards for Literature*
An annual literary award of IR £500, made on the advice of the Irish Academy of Letters. The award, first made in 1972, is given in each of two categories: (1) established writers and (2) new writers. Enquiries to Allied Irish Banks Ltd, Development Division, Bankcentre, Ballsbridge, Dublin 4

Denis **Devlin** Memorial Award for Poetry
Given for the finest collection of poetry in the English language by an Irish citizen. Value IR £600. Awarded next in 1985. Enquiries to The Arts Council/An Chomhairle Ealaíon, 70 Merrion Sq, Dublin 2

Gregory Medal*
For distinction in letters or outstanding literary work in Irish. Awarded periodically, Enquiries to Irish Academy of Letters, 4 Ailesbury Grove, Dundrum, Dublin 14

Patrick **Kavanagh** Award
Annual award of IR £100 and 500 copies of printed manuscript to an Irish poet. Enquiries to Mr Heather, Patrick Kavanagh Society, c/o Irish Distillers Ltd, Bow St Distillery, Smithfield, Dublin 7

Macaulay Fellowship
Awarded in literature every three years to young Irish writers, usually under 30 years of age. Value IR £3,000. Next awarded 1984. Enquiries to The Arts Council/An Chomhairle Ealaíon, 70 Merrion Sq, Dublin 2

National Poetry Competition, see under UK Literary Prizes

Novel Prize*
For the best novel written in Irish. Awarded annually. Enquiries to Irish Academy of Letters, 4 Ailesbury Grove, Dundrum, Dublin 14

Rooney Prize
Annual prize of IR £1,000 awarded to an Irish writer between the ages of 20 and 40 years. Enquiries to Jim Sherwin, RTE, Donnybrook, Dublin 4

George **Russell** (AE) Memorial Awards
Awards are made periodically from the Fund in recognition of published or unpublished work, creative or scholarly, which, in the opinion of the Advisory Committee is of a high standard of merit. Awards may also be made for similar work planned, although not yet completed. The Award consists of a cash payment of IR £100. Candidates must be of Irish birth and ordinarily resident in any part of Ireland, and must not have attained 35 years of age on the 1st day of January of the year in which the Award is made. Enquiries to George Russell (AE) Memorial Fund, Bank of Ireland, Trustee Department, Lower Baggot St, Dublin 2

Marten **Toonder** Award
Awarded in literature every three years. Value IR £3,000. Enquiries to Literature Officer, The Arts Council/An Chomhairle Ealaíon, 70 Merrion Sq, Dublin 2

Isle of Man

General Information

Language: English. Manx is spoken as a second language by about 500 people
Religion: Predominantly Protestant
Population: 63,000
Bank Hours: 0930-1530 Monday to Friday
Shop Hours: 0900-1730
Currency: 100 pence = 1 Isle of Man pound = £1 sterling. British coins and banknotes are legal tender
Export/Import Information: In customs union with UK. No tariff or VAT on books
Copyright: Berne, UCC (see International section)

Publishers

The **Mansk** Svenska Publishing Co Ltd, 17 North View, Peel Tel: Peel 2855 (STD code 062484)
Man Dir: G V C Young, OBE
Branch Off: Sjustansvagen 3, S-254 84 Helsingborg, Sweden
Subjects: History, Historical Novels, Children's
1982: 12 titles *Founded:* 1980

Norris Press*, Victoria St, Douglas

Shearwater Press Ltd, East Field, Sulby, Ramsey Tel: Ramsey 812944 (STD code 0624)
Man Dir, Editorial: Clare Crellin
Subjects: History, Local History, Topography, Fine Art, Fiction, Isle of Man
Founded: 1973
ISBN Publisher's Prefix: 0-904980

Remainder Dealers

Mannin Dealer Agencies*, 32 Finch Rd, Douglas

Major Booksellers

Bridge Bookshop Ltd, Shore Rd, Port Erin

The **Lexicon** Bookshop, Strand St, Douglas
Proprietor: M H Castle

St Paul's Bookshop*, Church Walk, St Paul's Sq, Ramsey

Major Libraries

The **Douglas** Public Library, Ridgeway St, Douglas Tel: Douglas 23021 (STD code 0624)
Librarian: J R Bowring

Ramsey Library, The Town Hall, Parliament Sq, Ramsey Tel: Ramsey 812228 (STD code 0624)
Librarian: Miss A V McGeagh

The **Rural** Library*, Lord St, Douglas

Israel

General Information

Language: Hebrew and Arabic (English and German widely known)
Religion: Predominantly Jewish
Population: 3.7 million
Literacy Rate (1971): 87.9% (89.4% of urban population, 78.6% rural)
Bank Hours: 0830-1230 Sunday-Thursday; also 1600-1700 Sunday-Tuesday and Thursday
Shop Hours: Usually Sunday 0800-1300, 1600-1800; weekdays 0800-1300, 1600-1900; many close Friday afternoon
Currency: 100 agorot (singular: agora) = 1 Israeli shekel
Export/Import Information: Books (except for children's picture books) and advertising duty-free. Books exempt from most additional taxes. No import licence required for books but must apply for importing number; exchange granted automatically
Copyright: UCC, Berne, Florence (see International section)

Book Trade Organizations

Acum Ltd (Society of Authors, Composers and Music Publishers in Israel), 118-120 Rothschild Blvd, PO Box 14220, Tel Aviv 61140 Tel: (03) 240115 Telex: 35770 Coin Il/35771 Coin Il att Acum Ltd
Dir-General: R Kedar

Association of Hebrew Writers, PO Box 7111, Tel Aviv
Secretary General: Mordechy Ot-Yakar
Publication: Moznayim (monthly)

Book and Printing Center — Israel Export Institute, 29 Hamered St, PO Box 50084, Tel Aviv Tel: (03) 630830 Cable Add: Memex Telex: 35613
Dir: Baruch Schaefer
Division of the Israel Export Institute
Publications: Israel Book News (quarterly); *Israel Book Trade Directory* (biennially); (biennially); *Books from Israel Export Catalog* (annually); *Israeli Publishers and Authors and Their Books on the World Publishing Scene*

Book Publishers' Association of Israel, 29 Carlebach St, PO Box 20123, Tel Aviv 67132 Tel: (03) 284191 Telex: 341118 Bxtvil ext 5089
The Association administers two subsidiary co-operative associations and two joint publishing companies — Ma'alot and Yachdav (qqv)
Executive Dir: Benjamin Sella
Publication: Katalog Sefarim Kelali

The **Institute** for the Translation of Hebrew Literature Ltd, PO Box 11210, Tel Aviv 61111 (Located at: 66 Shlomo Hamelech St, Tel Aviv) Tel: (03) 244879
Man Dir: Mrs Nilli Cohen
Publications: Modern Hebrew Literature (quarterly, incorporating *Hebrew Book Review*); *Bibliography of Modern Hebrew Literature in Translation* (biannually); *Jewish Imaginative Writing* (biannually)
Activities of the Institute include promotion of modern Hebrew literature in translation and co-publishing projects, subsidies to authors and publishers for translations of Hebrew literary works and their publication abroad

Israel Book Importers' Association*, c/o Emanuel Brown, 35 Allenby Rd, Tel Aviv

Israel ISBN Group Agency*, c/o Centre for Public Libraries, PO Box 242, Jerusalem 91002 Tel: (02) 247392

Standard Book Numbering Agency, see Israel ISBN Group Agency

Book Trade Reference Books and Journals

Books

Israel Book Trade Directory (biennially), Book and Printing Center — Israel Export Institute, 29 Hamered St, PO Box 29732, Tel Aviv

Israeli Publishers and Authors and Their Books on the World Scene, Book and Printing Center — Israel Export Institute, 29 Hamered St, PO Box 29732, Tel Aviv

Publishers and Printers of Israel, Book and Printing Center — Israel Export Institute, 29 Hamered St, PO Box 29732, Tel Aviv

Journals

Annual Index to Hebrew Periodicals, University of Haifa Library, Mount Carmel, Haifa 31999

Bibliography of Modern Hebrew Literature in Translation (biannually), The Institute for the Translation of Hebrew Literature Ltd, 66 Shlomo Hamelech St, Tel Aviv

Books from Israel Export Catalog (annually), Book and Printing Center — Israel Export Institute, 29 Hamered St, PO Box 50084, Tel Aviv

Hadashot al Pirsuma Ha-memshala (News about Government Publications), Israel Government Printer, Jerusalem

Israel Book News (quarterly), Book and Printing Center — Israel Export Institute, 29 Hamered St, PO Box 50084, Tel Aviv

Katalog Sefarim Kelali (Israel Books In Print), Book Publishers' Association of Israel, 29 Carlebach St, PO Box 20123, Tel Aviv 67132

Kirjath Sepher (City of the Book); bibliographical quarterly (text in Hebrew), Jewish National and University Library, PO Box 503, Jerusalem

Publishers

'A' Publishing Institute*, PO Box 894, Jersualem
Manager: A Chitov
Subjects: Orthodox Textbooks, Religion

Academon (The Hebrew University Students' Printing and Publishing House), The Hebrew University Campus, PO Box 41, Jerusalem Tel: (02) 636253/817312
Man Dir: Yitzhak Tzur; *Sales Manager:* Haim Hazan; *Bookshop Manager:* Richard Sherman
Bookshop: Academon, The Hebrew University Campus, Jerusalem
Subjects: Academic
Founded: 1952

Academy of the Hebrew Language+, Giv'at Ram, PO Box 3449, Jerusalem 91034 Tel: (02) 632242
President: Prof Joshua Blair; *Man Dir:* Nathan Efrati
Subjects: Hebrew: Linguistics, Dictionaries, Terminology, Periodicals, Concordances

Achiasaf Publishing House Ltd*, 13 Yosef Hanassi St, PO Box 4810, Tel Aviv Tel: (03) 283339
Man Dir: Schachna Achiasaf
Subjects: General Non-fiction, Reference, Juveniles, Popular Science, Textbooks, Fiction, Dictionaries
Founded: 1933

Achiever, 22 Hahistadrut St, Jerusalem Tel: (02) 225740
Managers: D Kessler, S Atzmon
Subject: General

Adam Publishers*, PO Box 3329, Jerusalem (Located at: 18 Yehoshua Ben-Nun, Jerusalem) Tel: (02) 664893
Man Dirs: Yehuda Melzer, Aryeh Mor; *Editorial:* Muli Melzer; *Sales, Rights & Permissions:* Janee Hahn
Subjects: Belles Lettres, Juveniles, University Textbooks, Biography, Politics, Philosophy, General
Founded: 1978

Agudat Harashash*, 7 Bezalei St, Jerusalem Tel: (02) 226904
Manager: I Hasid
Subjects: Orthodox Textbooks, Religion

Alef Publishers Ltd*, 49 Nachmani St, Tel Aviv Tel: (03) 612003
Man Dir: B Feldenkreis
Subjects: Art, Science, History of Israel, Textbooks, Belles Lettres, Poetry, Juveniles, Reference
Founded: 1962

Am Hasefer*, 9 Bialik St, PO Box 4055, Tel Aviv Tel: (03) 53040
Man Dir: D Lipetz
Subjects: Belles Lettres, Biography, History, Art, Political Science, Periodicals, Numismatics
Founded: 1955

Am Oved Publishers Ltd, 22 Mazeh St, PO Box 470, Tel Aviv Tel: (03) 291526 Cable Add: Amoved, Telaviv
Man Dir: Dov Gorfung
Orders to: Distributor's Centre for Israeli Books Ltd, 22 Nachmani St, PO Box 2811, Tel Aviv
Subjects: General Fiction, Belles Lettres, Poetry, Biography, History, Philosophy, Reference, Juveniles, Low-priced Paperbacks, Psychology, Social Science, University, Secondary & Primary Textbooks
Founded: 1942

Amichai Publishing House Ltd*, 5 Josef Ha-Nassi St, Tel Aviv Tel: (03) 284990
Man Dir: Yehuda Orlinsky
Subjects: Reference, General Fiction, Juveniles, Popular Science, Textbooks, Languages
Founded: 1948

Amikam*, 33 Frishman St, Tel Aviv Tel: 228957

Amir Publishing Co Ltd, 5 Engel St, Tel Aviv Tel: (03) 615943
Man Dir: Avraham Amir; *Editorial:* Immanuel Blauschild
Subjects: Cartography, Guide Books, Historical and Biblical Subjects, Judaica
Founded: 1965

Ariel Publishing House, PO Box 3328, Jerusalem 91033 (Located at: 23 Hechalutz St, Jerusalem) Tel: (02) 524414
Chief Executive: Schiller Ely
Subjects: History, Religion, Historical Geography, Old photographs and art, concerning Jerusalem and the Holy Land
Founded: 1976

Armon Publishing House Ltd*, 36 Beit Vegan St, Jerusalem Tel: (02) 533991
Subjects: General Fiction, Languages
Founded: 1965

Arrow Co*, 6 Wedgwood St, PO Box 8022, Jerusalem Tel: 633830

Arsan Publishing House Ltd, see Kirvunim

Bar Ilan University, Book Publishing Committee*, Bar Ilan University, Ramat Gan Tel: 718111
Chairman: Professor Daniel Sperber
Subjects: Judaica, Philosophy, Psychology, Law, Literature, Linguistics, Education
1981: 13 titles *Founded:* 1958

Bar Urian Publishing House, Bar Ilan University, Ramat Gan Tel: 756012
Man Dir: M Wiesel
Subject: University Textbooks
Bookshop: Bar Ilan University
Founded: 1965

Barlevi*, PO Box 21557, Tel Aviv Tel: (03) 822030
Manager: Mr Barlevi
Subjects: Juveniles, Hobbies, Games, Sports

Beit Lochamei Hagetha'ot, Kibbutz Lochamei Hagetha'ot Tel: (04) 920412
Manager: B Anolik
Branch Off: 102 Arlosoroff St, Tel Aviv
Subjects: Holocaust, World War II, Jewish Resistance against Nazism
Founded: 1950

Ben-Zvi Institute, PO Box 7504, Jerusalem 91074 Tel: (02) 639204; Yad Ben-Zvi Tel: (02) 639201
Dir: Prof Nehemiah Levtzion; *Editorial Secretary:* Michael Glatzer
Subject: History and culture of Jewish Communities in the East

The **Bialik** Institute, 3 Ibn Gabirol St, PO Box 92, Jerusalem Tel: (02) 246977
Man Dir: Y J Taub
Subjects: Philosophy, Hebrew and Yiddish Literature, Belles Lettres, Poetry, Palestinology, Biblical Encyclopaedia, Archaeology, Jewish Studies, History, Arts
Founded: 1935

Biblos*, 54 Sokolov St, Holon
Miscellaneous: Also an exporter to Latin America

Bitan*, 8 Mordechai St, Ramat-Hasharon Tel: 484565
Manager: A Bitan
Associate Company: Zmora, Bitan-Publishers (qv)
Subjects: General

Boostan Publishing House*, 22 Nachmani St, Tel Aviv Tel: (03) 298883/5 Cable Add: Boostanmod Telaviv
Man Dir: Mordechai Sheingarten; *Sales Dir:* Roni Birkenfield; *Publicity Dir:* Riva Almagor; *Advertising Dir:* Sara Wohlfeiler; *Rights & Permissions:* Dalia Sheingarten
Subsidiary Company: Distributors' Centre for Israeli Books Ltd (address as above)
Subjects: General Fiction, Belles Lettres, Poetry, Biography, History, How-to, Juveniles, High-priced Paperbacks, Medicine, Psychology, Educational

ISRAEL

Materials
Founded: 1969

Bronfman's Agency Ltd, 2 Zlenov St, PO Box 1109, Tel Aviv 61010 Tel: (03) 611243
Manager: I Bronfman; *Deputy Manager:* C Aronson
Subject: Textbooks
Bookshop: See under Major Booksellers

Carta, The Israel Map and Publishing Co Ltd*, Yad Harutzim St, PO Box 2500, Jerusalem Tel: (02) 713536/7 Cable Add: Carmap
President: Emanuel Hausman; *Man Dir:* Shay Hausman; *Editorial:* Lorraine Kessel, Sara Potavski, Pirchia Cohen; *Art Dir:* Eli Kellerman
Subjects: Cartography, Juveniles, Educational Materials, General, History, Reference (publishes in Hebrew and English)
Bookshop: Carta Bookshop, Beit Hadar, Rechov Elias 5, Jerusalem
Founded: 1958
ISBN Publisher's Prefix: 965-220

Chatam Sofer Institute*, PO Box 836, Jerusalem Tel: (02) 38175
Manager: Mr Leible
Subject: Religion

Gaalyah **Cornfeld***, 185 Hayarkon St, Tel Aviv 63453 Tel: (03) 221737 Cable Add: Cornfeld Hayarkon 185
Chief Executive, Editorial: G Cornfeld
Subjects: Bibles, Archaeology, Palestine, Jewish History, Early Christianity, General
1982: 3 titles *Founded:* 1957

Davar*, 45 Sheinkin St, Tel Aviv
Tel: (03) 286141
Manager: I Shoham

The **Dvir** Publishing Co Ltd, 58 Mazeh St, PO Box 149, Tel Aviv 61001
Tel: (03) 622991
Man Dir: E Hausman
Associate Company: Reshafim Publishers
Subsidiary Companies: Amud Ltd; Karni Publishers Ltd (qv); Megiddo Publishing Co Ltd
Subjects: Belles Lettres, Poetry, Biography, History, Art, Philosophy, Reference, Juveniles, Low & High-priced Paperbacks, Psychology, General & Social Science, University, Secondary & Primary Textbooks, Educational Materials
1981: 37 titles *1982:* 43 titles *Founded:* 1924

E S H (English for Speakers of Hebrew), an imprint of University Publishing Co (qv)

Edanim Publishers, 24 Agron St, PO Box 7705, Jerusalem Tel: (02) 224486 Cable Add: Weilpub Jerusalem Telex: Tel Aviv 33847
Man Dir: Asher Weill
Parent Companies: Weill Publishers Ltd (qv) and Yedioth Ahronoth Newspaper
Subjects: Contemporary Events, Fiction, Biography, History, Reference
1982-83: 15 titles *Founded:* 1975

Eked Publishing House*, 29 Bar-Kochba St, Tel Aviv Tel: (03) 283648
Man Dir: Maritza Rosman
Subjects: Belles Lettres, Poetry, Fiction
Founded: 1959

El-Am Publishing (Israel) Ltd*, PO Box 16495, Tel Aviv Tel: (03) 228964/442918 Cable Add: Elampub, Telaviv
Man Dirs: Eliyahu Amiqam, Moshe Segalovitz; *Editorial:* Rabbi Dr A Zvi Ehrman
Subject: Judaica
Founded: 1966

Encyclopaedia Judaica*, Givat Shaul B, PO Box 7145, Jerusalem Tel: (02) 523261/521201 Telex: 25-275
Man Dir: Eliav Cohen; *Sales Dir:* Jorge Zafran
Parent Company: Keter Publishing House Jerusalem Ltd (qv)
Subject: Reference

Eshkol-Jerusalem*, PO Box 5202, Jerusalem Tel: (02) 285351
Manager: Mr Weinfeld
Subject: Judaica

Feldheim Publishers Ltd, PO Box 6525, Jerusalem Tel: (02) 533947/8/9
Man Dir: Yaakov Feldheim; *Sales Dir:* Yossie Katzberg
Branch Off: P Feldheim, 96 East Broadway, New York, NY
Subjects: Biography, History, Philosophy, Reference, Religion, Juveniles
1982: 18 titles *Founded:* 1939
ISBN Publisher's Prefix: 0-87306

H **Fisher***, PO Box 1951, Tel Aviv Tel: (03) 744892
Manager: H Fisher
Subject: Juveniles

Franciscan Printing Press, PO Box 14064, Jerusalem Tel: (02) 286594 Cable Add: Terrasanta Jerusalem
Man Dir: Fausto Celli (Father Beniamino)
Subjects: Religion, Theology, Archaeology, Guide Books, Periodicals
1981: 9 titles *1982:* 12 titles *Founded:* 1847

Freund Publishing House Ltd*, 61 Nachmani St, PO Box 35010, Tel Aviv
Tel: (03) 615335
Man Dir: Chaim Freund
Subjects: Scientific, Juveniles, Educational Games

S **Friedman***, 27 Gruzenberg St, Tel Aviv
Tel: (03) 656091/659756
General Manager: Shmuel Friedman
Subjects: General

Gazit*, 8 Zvi Brook St, Tel Aviv
Tel: (03) 53730
Manager: G Talpir
Subject: Art

Ghetto Fighters' House Publishers, see Beit Lochamei Hagetha'ot

Hadar*, PO Box 17061, Tel Aviv (Located at: 50 Reiness Street, Tel Aviv) Tel: (03) 237082/417971
Manager: I Amrami
Subjects: General
Founded: 1950

Hakibbutz Hameuchad Publishing House Ltd*, PO Box 16040, Tel Aviv Tel: (03) 220402
Man Dir: A Avishai; *Sales Manager:* Moshe Ne'eman
Subjects: General Fiction, Belles Lettres, Poetry, Biography, History, How-to, Music, Art, Philosophy, Reference, Religion, General & Social Science, University, Secondary & Primary Textbooks, Educational Materials, Agriculture, Psychology
Founded: 1940

Heritage*, 2 Kfar Yona St, Ramat Aviv

Holy Land Map Co Ltd, now Terra Sancta Arts (qv)

Institute for Publishing Hebrew Books*, PO Box 18, Zichron Yaakov (Located at: 9 Hazayit St, Zichron Yaakov) Tel: (063) 99540 Telex: 35770 Coin Il
Chief Executive: Rabbi S M Jungerman
Subject: The Talmud
Founded: 1973

Institute for the Talmudic Encyclopaedia and Complete Israeli Talmud*, Bait-Vagan, PO Box 16066, Jerusalem Tel: (02) 423242
Manager: Rab i Y Hotner

The **Institute for the Translation** of Hebrew Literature Ltd, PO Box 11210, Tel Aviv 61111 (Located at: 66 Shlomo Hamelech St, Tel Aviv 64511) Tel: (03) 244879
Dir: Mrs Nilli Cohen
Subject: Modern Hebrew Literature in Translation
1982: 7 titles *Founded:* 1962
ISBN Publisher's Prefix: 965-255

International Science Services*, PO Box 2039, Rehovot 76303 Tel: (054) 76216 Telex: 35770 Coin Il
Dir: Miriam Balaban
Branch Offs: 2242 Mount Carmel Ave, Glenside, PA 19038; Boston University, Center for Philosophy and History of Science, Boston, Ma 02115 (both USA); Couwenhoven 62-49, 3703 HN Zeist, Netherlands
Subjects: Science, Technology, Medicine, Education, Philosophy, Communications
Founded: 1968
ISBN Publisher's Prefix: 0-86689

The **Israel Academy** of Sciences & Humanities, 43 Jabotinsky Rd, PO Box 4040, Jerusalem 91040 Tel: (02) 636211
Man Dir: Dr Shimeon Amir
Bookshop: Direct sales at the Academy
Subjects: Archaeology, History, Philosophy, Religion, Scholarly Publications in Sciences, Humanities, Judaica
1981-82: 16 titles *Founded:* 1969
ISBN Publisher's Prefix: 965-208

Israel Exploration Society, 3 Shmuel Hanagid St, PO Box 7041, Jerusalem
Tel: (02) 227991
Man Dir: J Aviram
Subjects: Archaeology, Ancient History, Geography
Founded: 1913

Israel Program for Scientific Translations, subsidiary of Keter Publishing House Jerusalem Ltd (qv)

Israel Universities Press*, Givat Shaul B, PO Box 7145, Jerusalem Tel: (02) 523261/521201 Telex: 25-275
Man Dir: Eliav Cohen
Parent Company: Keter Publishing House Jerusalem Ltd (qv)
Subjects: General & Social Science, Reference, Middle East Studies, University Textbooks, Politics

Israel Yearbook Publications*, 21 Hasharon St, PO Box 1199, Tel Aviv

Israeli Music Publications Ltd, PO Box 7681, Jerusalem 91076 (Located at: 25 Keren Hayesod St, Jerusalem 94188) Tel: (02) 241377
Man Dir: R Kleiman
Subject: Music
Founded: 1949

Izrael Publishing House Ltd*, 76 Dizengoff St, Tel Aviv Tel: (03) 285350
Man Dir: Alexander Izrael
Subjects: General Fiction, Belles Lettres, Poetry, Biography, History, Reference, Psychology, Juveniles, University, Secondary & Primary Textbooks, Educational Materials
Founded: 1933

Jerusalem Publishing House Ltd, 39 Tchernechovski St, PO Box 7147, Jerusalem Tel: (02) 667744/636511 Cable Add: Pubjer Telex: 26144 ext 7065
Man Dir: Shlomo S Gafni; *Editorial Manager:* Rachel Gilon
Subjects: Illustrated Encyclopaedias, History, Archaeology, Reference, Literature, Politics, Art, The Bible, Cookbooks
1983: 18 titles *Founded:* 1967

The **Jewish Agency***, Publishing Department, 27 Hillel St, PO Box 7044, Jerusalem Tel: (02) 233271
Man Dir: Asher Bukshpan
Founded: 1945
Subjects: Hebrew and Zionist political thought and education

Karni Publishers Ltd, 58 Mazeh St, PO Box 149, Tel Aviv 61001 Tel: (03) 622991
Man Dir: E Hausman
Parent Company: The Dvir Publishing Co Ltd (qv)
Subsidiary Company: Megiddo Publishing Co (at above address)
Subjects: General Fiction, Belles Lettres, Poetry, Biography, How-to, Juveniles, Secondary & Primary Textbooks, Reference
1981: 5 titles *Founded:* 1951

Kernerman Publishing+, 27 Reading St, Ramat Aviv, Tel Aviv 69024 Tel: (03) 410046 Telex: 342184/5 Cosmi Il
Chief Executive: Ari Kernerman
Orders to: Lonnie Kahn Ltd, 5 Nachalat Binyamin St, Tel Aviv
Associate Company: Public Health Reviews, an international quarterly (at above address)
Subjects: English Language and Literature Textbooks, Medical Books
1981: 4 titles *1982:* 12 titles *Founded:* 1965

Keter Publishing House Jerusalem Ltd, PO Box 7145, Jerusalem 91071 (Located at: Givat Shaul B, Jerusalem) Tel: (02) 523261/521201 Telex: 25275
Man Dir: Eliav Cohen; *Production Manager:* Yaacov Zoreff; *International Division:* Beth Elon; *Translations Coordinator:* Hannah Ben-David
Subsidiary Companies: Encyclopaedia Judaica (qv); Israel Program for Scientific Translations; Israel Universities Press (qv); Keter Inc, New York, USA; Keter Marketing Services Ltd; Keterpress Enterprises
Subjects: Judaica, Religion, Philosophy, Reference, Juveniles, Medicine, Psychology, Engineering, Social Sciences
Founded: 1959

Kiryat Sefer Ltd, PO Box 370, Jerusalem (Located at: 15 Arlosorof St, Jerusalem) Tel: (02) 521141
Man Dir: Avraham Sivan
Subjects: Poetry, Juveniles, Atlases, Dictionaries, Secondary & Primary Textbooks, Fiction, Religion
Founded: 1933

Kivunim — Arsan Publishing House Ltd, PO Box 37517, Tel Aviv 61374 Tel: (054) 55132/56234
Man Dir: Arieh Sandler
Branch Off: 3 Achim Trebes St, Rehovot 76488
Subjects: Politics, Management, Administration, Sport, Humour, General
Founded: 1980

Koren Publishers, PO Box 4044, Jerusalem 91040 (Located at: 33 Herzog St, Jerusalem) Tel: (02) 660188
Man Dirs: Eliahu Koren, Eli Kahn; *Publicity:* Eli Kahn
Subjects: Bibles, Religion
Founded: 1962

Ledori*, 19 Geula St, Tel Aviv
Tel: (03) 58662
Manager: B Gefner
Subjects: General Books

Lewin-Epstein Ltd*, Rechov Harikma 7, PO Box 1020, Jerusalem Tel: (02) 531929
Dirs: J Gerlitz, M Weksler, A Friedman
Subjects: Judaica

A **Lewin-Epstein-Modan** Ltd*, Perelz Hayot 29, Tel Aviv Cable Add: Offset
Man Dir: C Modan; *Sales Dir:* Eliezer Ben-Ami
Subjects: General Fiction, Belles Lettres, Poetry, History, How-to, Music, Art, Reference, Juveniles, High-priced Paperbacks, Education, Science
Founded: 1930

Ma'alot, 29 Carlebach St, Tel Aviv
Tel: (03) 284191
Dir: Elazar Goor
Subjects: Secondary & Primary Textbooks
Founded: 1969
Miscellaneous: Established by the Book Publishers' Association of Israel as a jointly-owned publishing house in which most of the members of the Association are shareholders

Ma'arachot, imprint of Ministry of Defence Publishing House (qv)

Ma'ariv Book Guild (Sifriat Ma'ariv), 72A Dereh Petah Tikva Rd, PO Box 20208, Tel Aviv Tel: (03) 287211, (03) 338386 Cable Add: Ma'ariv Telaviv Telex: 033735
Publisher and Editor-in-Chief: Naftali Arbel; *Man Dir:* Yzack Yachin
Subjects: Biography, Reference, Education, History, Juveniles, Travel, Politics, Religion, Popular Science, Geography, Children, Encyclopaedias
Book Club: Ma'ariv Book Club
Founded: 1954

Machbarot Lesifrut*, PO Box 411, Tel Aviv (Located at: 32 Schocken St, Tel Aviv)
Manager: Ohad Zmora
Associate Company: Zmora, Bitan-Publishers (qv)
Subjects: Fiction, History, Juveniles, Literature (especially of Middle Ages), Politics, Linguistics

The **Magnes** Press*, Hebrew University, Jerusalem Tel: (02) 660341
Man Dir: B Yehoshua
Subjects: Biography, History, Music, Art, Philosophy, Psychology, Archaeology, Oriental Studies, Law, Sciences, Bibliography, University Textbooks
Founded: 1929

Makor Publishing Ltd*, 14 Nili St, Jerusalem Tel: (02) 717257
Man Dir: I Ravitzki; *Sales Manager:* E Fisher
Subjects: Judaica, Reprints
Founded: 1969

S J **Mansour***, 1 Meyouhas St, Mahane Yehuda, Jerusalem Tel: (02) 221650
Manager: S J Mansour
Subject: Judaica

Y **Marcus** & Co Ltd+, PO Box 10354, Jerusalem (Located at: 59 Beth Lehem St, Jerusalem) Tel: (02) 716084
Manager: Y Marcus
Subjects: General
Bookshop: 6 Ben Yehuda St, Jerusalem Tel: (02) 228281

Rubin **Mass** Ltd*, 11 David Marcus St, PO Box 990, Jerusalem 91000 Tel: (02) 632565 Cable Add: Rubin Mass Jerusalem
Man Dir: Oren Mass; *Sales:* Aharon Bier
Subjects: Religion, Medicine, Secondary Textbooks, Jewish Studies, Educational Materials, Politics, Philosophy, Psychology, Meteorology, Science
1981: 1,110 titles *Founded:* 1927

Massada Press Ltd*, 46 Beth Lehem Rd, Jerusalem Tel: (02) 719441/719444 Cable Add: Encyclomas Telex: 26144 Bxjm Il Ext 7067
Board Chairman, Chief Executive: Alexander Peli; *Sales, Production:* Nathan Regev; *Rights & Permissions:* David Peli; *Projects Manager:* I Hess
Branch Off: 21 Jabotinsky Rd, Ramat Gan 52511 Tel: (03) 734202/3
Subjects: Belles Lettres, Poetry, Biography, History, How-to, Cookery, Music, Art, Philosophy, Encyclopaedias, Judaica, Reference, Religion, Juveniles, High-priced Paperbacks, Psychology, General and Social Science, Educational Materials
Book Club: Massada Press Ltd, 46 Beth Lehem Rd, Jerusalem
Bookshop: Ruth Ltd, 2 Herzl Street, Tel Aviv
Founded: 1932

Massada Publishers Ltd, PO Box 842, Givatayim 53583 (Located at: 13 Tfutsot Israel St, Givatayim) Tel: (03) 740811 Cable Add: Peliprint Telex: 361211 Mape Il
Man Dir: Yoav Barash; *Marketing Dir:* Nissan Balaban
Associate Companies: Peli Printing Works Ltd; Reprocolor Ltd
Subjects: History, Art, Juveniles, Cookery, General Fiction, Reference, Travel, How-to, Textbooks
Founded: 1932
ISBN Publisher's Prefix: 965-10

Megiddo Publishing Co, subsidiary of Karni Publishers Ltd (qv)

Merkaz Le-Chinuch Torani*, PO Box 18, Zichron Yaakov Tel: (063) 99540 Telex: 35770 Coin Il
Man Dir: Rabbi Shalom Meir Jungerman
Subject: Orthodox Textbooks

Michaelmark Books Ltd, PO Box 45089, Tel Aviv 61450 (Located at: 12 Stand St, Tel Aviv) Tel: (03) 234805 Telex: 341667 Att MIC
Publisher: Myrna Pollak
Subjects: Fiction, Popular Non-fiction
Founded: 1976

Microshur Ltd*, PO Box 6838, Jerusalem 91067 Tel: (02) 232713 Telex: 26244 Raveh Il Microshur
Manager: Menachem Shalev; *Editorial:* Dr Gabriella Shalev
Subsidiary Company: Shure Publications Ltd
Subject: Legal
1981: 9 titles *Founded:* 1978
ISBN Publisher's Prefix: 965-215

Mifalei Tarbut Vehinuch*, 53 Weizmann St, Tel Aviv Tel: (03) 254867
Manager: Y Silver
Subjects: Music, Textbooks, Pedagogy

Ministry of Defence Publishing House*, 27 David Elazar St, Hakiriya, Tel Aviv
Tel: (03) 259165/212605
Dir: Shalom Seri; *Deputy Dir:* Moshe Oren; *Production:* Izack Kempler
Subjects: Military Science & History, Israeli Geography & History
Founded: 1939
Miscellaneous: Firm also publishes under Ma'arachot imprint

M **Mizrachi** Publishers*, 67 Lewinsky St, Tel Aviv Tel: (03) 625652 Cable Add: Mizedition, Telaviv
Man Dir: Meir Mizrachi
Subjects: Engineering, History, Medicine, Science, Juveniles, Encyclopaedias, Fiction
Founded: 1960

M C **Mor-Carmi** Ltd, 8 Ben-Avigdor St, Tel Aviv 67218 Tel: (03) 339774/5/6
Man Dir, Sales, Rights & Permissions: Uri Mor; *Editorial, Production, Publicity:* Yoram Shavit
Subsidiary Companies: Elrad Engineering Planning Ltd; M C Electronics Ltd; T P Technical Publications Ltd
Subjects: Technical, Scientific
Founded: 1968

216 ISRAEL

Moreshet*, 166 Ibn Gavirol St, Tel Aviv

Mossad Harav Kook, see Rav Kook Institute

Nateev-Printing and Publishing Enterprises Ltd*, by Reading Bridge, PO Box 6048, Tel Aviv Tel: (03) 454135 Cable Add: Nateevpub, Telaviv Telex: 03-2470 Att Nateev
Man Dir: Mordecai Ra'anan
Subjects: Religion, Juveniles, General
Founded: 1971
Miscellaneous: Associated imprints include Otpaz

Netzach*, PO Box 164, Bnei Brak Tel: 796413
Manager: Mr Rootenberg
Subject: Judaica

M Newman, 12 Hasharon St, Tel Aviv Tel: (03) 30621
Manager: M Newman
Subjects: Judaica, Bible Studies, Fiction, Juveniles, Education

Nitzanim, an imprint of Zur & Zur Ltd (qv)

Ofer Publishing House*, 7 Tabenkin St, Petah Tiqva Tel: 625483
Manager: S Aluf
Subject: Juveniles
Founded: 1958

Olamenu*, 7 Frishman St, Tel Aviv

Olive Books of Israel*, Reka-Or Production and Publishing Ltd, 22 Shlom-Zion Hamalka St, PO Box 22305, Tel Aviv Tel: (03) 448676/455199
Publishers: Yoad Avissar, Yosseph Zetouni
Associate Company: Omanei Offset, Printing House, Tel Aviv
Subsidiary Companies: Madim, Limud both publishing and distribution
Subjects: Israeli history, Judaica, Educational
Founded: 1974
Miscellaneous: Publishers of *Who's Who in World Jewry*

Otpaz, an imprint of Nateev-Printing and Publishing Enterprises Ltd (qv)

Otzar Hamoreh*, Israel Teachers' Union, 8 Ben Saruk St, PO Box 303, Tel Aviv Tel: (03) 260211
Subjects: Education, Pedagogy, Textbooks, Mathematics, Psychology, Didactic Games
1981: 3 titles *Founded:* 1951

Alexander Peli Ltd*, 46 Beth Lehem Rd, Jerusalem
Chairman: Alexander Peli; *Man Dir:* Nathan Regev; *Publicity Manager:* David Peli
Subsidiary Companies: Alumoth Company Ltd; Encyclopedia Publishing Company; Jewish History Publications 1961 Ltd; Ruth Ltd
Subjects: General, Judaica, Encyclopaedias, Belle Lettres, Poetry, Biography, History, How-to, Music, Art, Philosophy, Reference, Religion, Juveniles, High-priced Paperbacks, Psychology, General and Social Science, Secondary and Primary Textbooks, Educational Materials

Y L Peretz Publishing Co*, 14 Brener St, Tel Aviv 65246 Tel: (03) 281751
Man Dir: Moshe Gershonowitz
Subjects: Books (Poetry, Essays, History, Judaica, Belles Lettres, Philosophy, Sociology, Art) in Yiddish, also some in Hebrew
Founded: 1956

Ramdor Publishing Co Ltd*, 23 Levanda St, Tel Aviv Tel: (03) 32332
Man Dir: Uri Shalgi
Founded: 1960
Subject: Mass-market paperbacks

Rav Kook Institute, PO Box 642, Jerusalem Tel: (02) 526231
Dir: Rabbi M Katzenelenbogen
Subjects: Jewish Studies, History, Philosophy, Midrashic & Halachic Law, Theology
1981: 18 titles *Founded:* 1937
Miscellaneous: A non-profit-making public corporation supported by the Jewish Agency, Ministry of Education & Culture and Ministry of Religious Affairs. Also provides financial support for works in above subjects

Reka-Or Production and Publishing Ltd, see Olive Books of Israel

E Rubinstein*, 1 King David St, Jerusalem Tel: (02) 225785
Manager: E Rubinstein
Subject: Textbooks

Sadan Publishing House Ltd+, 1 David Hamelech Blvd, PO Box 16096, Tel Aviv 64953 Tel: (03) 267543 Cable Add: Sadanbooks Telex: 35770 Coin Il Sadan
President, Publicity: David Sadan; *Managing Editor:* Ronny Stein
Subsidiary Company: Sadan Publication International Inc, New York, NY, USA
Subjects: Reference, Geography, Natural History, Archaeology, Guides, Folklore, How-to, Bible Studies, Religion, Law
1981: 52 titles *Founded:* 1962
Miscellaneous: Firm is also an international co-publisher and packager
ISBN Publisher's Prefix: 965-234

Schocken Publishing House Ltd*, 8 Rothschild Blvd, PO Box 2316, Tel Aviv 61022 Tel: (03) 650961
Publisher: Racheli Edelman
Subjects: General Fiction and Non-fiction, Literature, Judaism, Poetry, Philosophy, Social Sciences, Politics, Law, Children's, Juvenile
Founded: 1938

Shikmona Publishing Co Ltd, PO Box 4044, Jerusalem 91040 (Located at: 33 Herzog St, Jerusalem) Tel: (02) 660188
Man Dirs: Eli Kahn, Eliyahu Korén
Subjects: History, Archaeology, Art, Politics, Zionism, Textbooks
Founded: 1965

Joseph Shimoni*, 13 Rambam St, Tel Aviv Tel: (03) 611732
Manager: J Shimoni
Subjects: General

Shmulik*, 18 Shivtei Yisrael St, Ramat Hasharon

Sifriat Poalim Ltd*, 66 Ahad Ha'am St, PO Box 37068, Tel Aviv Tel: (03) 291535
Dir: Zvi Raanan; *Editorial:* Nathan Yonathan; *Sales:* Israela Yalon; *Production:* Efraim Ben-Dor; *Rights & Permissions:* Levavi Bracha
Subjects: General Fiction, Belles Lettres, Art, Juveniles, History, Philosophy, Social Science, Paperbacks
Founded: 1939
Bookshop: See under Major Booksellers
Miscellaneous: Publishing House of the Labour Zionist Movement

Samuel Simson Ltd*, 100 Yehuda Halevi St, PO Box 14227, Tel Aviv Tel: (03) 280456
Man Dir: Samuel Simson
Subject: Juveniles
Founded: 1954

Siman Krai, an imprint of University Publishing Co (qv)

Sinai Publishing Co*, 72 Allenby St, Tel Aviv Tel: (03) 623622
Man Dir: Akiva Schlesinger; *Editorial, Rights & Permissions:* Moshe Schlesinger
Subsidiary Company: Sinai Export Co Ltd, 15 Balfour St, Tel Aviv
Subject: Judaica
Bookshop: Sinai Bookstore, 72 Allenby St, Tel Aviv
Founded: 1853

J Sreberk+, 16 Balfour St, Tel Aviv Tel: (03) 293343
Manager: Z Namir
Subjects: Textbooks, Juveniles, Literature

Steimatzky Ltd, PO Box 628, Tel Aviv 61006 (Located at: Citrus House, 22 Harakevet St, Tel Aviv) Tel: (03) 622536 Cable Add: Steimatzky Beithadar Telaviv Telex: 361430 Steim Il
Man Dirs: Ezekiel Steimatzky, Eri M Steimatzky
Subjects: General Fiction, Music, Art, Juveniles, Reference, Social Science, University, Secondary & Primary Textbooks, Low-priced Paperbacks
Bookshops: See under Major Booksellers
Founded: 1925

Talmudic Encyclopaedia Publications*, Yad Harav Herzog, Beit Vegan, Jerusalem Tel: 423242

Tarbut Vehinuch*, 53 Weizmann St, Tel Aviv Tel: 254867

Tcherikover Publishers Ltd, 12 Hasharon St, Tel Aviv 66185 Tel: (03) 330621
Manager, Editorial: B Tcherikover
Subjects: Textbooks, Pedagogy, Education, Handbooks, Psychology, Economics, Literature, History, Art, Languages, Geography, Criminology, Management
1981: 20 titles *1982:* 15 titles

Teachers' Union, see Otzar Hamoreh

Tel Aviv University, Publications Sales Division, Admin Hill, Bldg H, Tel Aviv 69978 Tel: (03) 411193/420897
Manager: Ya'akov Yariv
Subjects: Jewish Studies, History, Archaeology, Art, Musicology, Oriental Studies, African Studies, Law

Terra Sancta Arts, PO Box 10009, Zahala, Tel Aviv 61100 (Located at: 31 Ehud St) Tel: (03) 473597 Telex: 35770 Coin Il
Man Dir: Nachman Ran
Branch Off: Disengof Center, Tel Aviv Tel: (03) 289630
Subjects: Maps, Books on the Holy Land, the Bible
Founded: 1972
Miscellaneous: Formerly Holy Land Map Co Ltd

Tor, an imprint of Turtledove Publishing Ltd (qv)

Turtledove Publishing Ltd*, PO Box 1337, Ramat Gan (Located at: 15 Kinneret St, Bnei Brak) Tel: (03) 707125
Man Dir: Louis Williams
Orders to: Eurospan, 3 Henrietta St, London WC2E 8LY, UK or ISBS, PO Box 555, Forest Grove, Oregon 97116, USA
Imprints include: Tor
Subjects: Academic-Interdisciplinary: Political Science, Middle East Affairs, International Law, Medicine & Law, Federal Studies
Founded: 1978
ISBN Publisher's Prefix: 965-20

University Publishing Co*, 28 Hanatziv St, Tel Aviv Tel: (03) 259057
Dirs: Mordechai Mass, Natan Tzipkis
Imprints: ESH (English for Speakers of Hebrew), Siman Kria
Subjects: School Texts, Belles Lettres, Academic
Founded: 1971

Vaad Hayeshivot Be'eretz Israel*, 4 Havatzelet St, Jerusalem Tel: (02) 225042
Man Dir: A Halevi Sher
Subject: Judaica

The **Van Leer** Jerusalem Foundation, 43 Jabotinsky St, PO Box 4070, Jerusalem Tel: (02) 667141
Executive Editor: Esther Shashar
Subjects: Philosophy, History and Philosophy of Science, Sociology, Arab-Israel Relations
1981: 2 titles *1982:* 2 titles
ISBN Publisher's Prefix: 965-271

Weill Publishers Ltd, PO Box 7705, Jerusalem (Located at: 24 Agron St, Jerusalem) Tel: (02) 224486 Cable Add: Weilpub Jerusalem
Man Dir: Asher Weill
Subsidiary Company: Edanim Publishers (qv)
Subjects: Children's Books, Educational, Illustrated Books in English and Hebrew
Founded: 1975
Miscellaneous: Firm also offers publishers' editorial and production services

The **Weizmann** Science Press of Israel, Horkania 8a, PO Box 801, Jerusalem 91007 Tel: (02) 663203 Telex: 26144 Bx Jm attn Wspi ext 7086
Man Dir: Rami Michaeli; *Publicity Manager:* Mrs Hava Aspler
Subjects: General Science, General Technology, Periodicals
Founded: 1951

Yachdav, United Publishers Co Ltd, 29 Carlebach St, PO Box 20123, Tel Aviv Tel: (03) 284191
Man Dir: Benjamin Sella
Subjects: Philosophy, Psychology, Social Science, Administration
Founded: 1960
Miscellaneous: Established by the Book Publishers' Association of Israel as a jointly-owned publishing house in which most of the members of the Association are shareholders

Yad Eliahu Chitov*, PO Box 894, Jerusalem Tel: (02) 285617
Man Dir: H Ben-Arza
Subject: Orthodox Textbooks

Yad Vashem — Martyrs' and Heroes' Remembrance Authority*, PO Box 3477, Jerusalem 91034 Tel: (02) 531202 Cable Add: YadVashem Jerusalem
Chairman: Dr Yitzhak Arad; *Editorial:* Dr Livia Rothkirchen, Prof Yisrael Gutman; *Sales:* Josef Ohana; *Production:* Prof Y Gutman; *Secretary-General:* Shimshon Eden
Branch Off: Heychal Wolyn, 10 Korazin St, PO Box 803, Givatayim, near Tel Aviv
Subject: Holocaust
1981: 6 titles *1982:* 2 titles *Founded:* 1953

Yavneh Ltd, 4 Mazeh St, Tel Aviv Tel: (03) 297856
Man Dir: Avshalom Orenstein
Subjects: General Fiction, Reference, Music, Religion, General Science, Juveniles, Textbooks, Atlases
Founded: 1932

Yedioth Ahronoth Enterprises (Book Dept), 12 Mikveh Yisrael St, PO Box 37744, Tel Aviv 61376 Tel: (03) 621065 Telex: 33847
Manager: Moshe Bamberger
Parent Company: Yedioth Ahronoth (The Evening Newspaper of Israel)
Subjects: Non-fiction, Judaica, Health, Songs and Lyrics
1981: 9 titles *1982:* 12 titles *Founded:* 1952

Yeshurun*, Merkaz Le-Sifrut Chareidit, PO Box 511, Jerusalem Tel: (02) 534211
Dir: Mr Pardes
Subject: Orthodox Textbooks

Yesod*, 16 Mazeh St, Tel Aviv Tel: (03) 291180
Manager: Y Wachtel
Subject: Textbooks

Yuval*, 13a Yeffe Nof St, Haifa Tel: (04) 521564
Manager: I Blachman
Subject: Textbooks

S **Zak** & Co*, 2 King George St, Jerusalem Tel: (02) 227819
Man Dirs: D Zak, M Zak
Subjects: Science, Fiction, Philosophy, Reference, Religion, Juveniles, University, Secondary & Primary Textbooks, Educational Materials
Bookshop: 2 King George St, Jerusalem
Founded: 1930

Zelkowitz*, 6 Mazeh St, Tel Aviv Tel: (03) 296648
Manager: A Zelkowitz
Subject: Juveniles

Zmora, Bitan-Publishers, 32 Schocken St, Tel Aviv Tel: (03) 827510
Publishers: Ohad Zmora, Asher Bitan; *Sales:* Eran Zmora
Associate Companies: Bitan (qv); Machbarot lesifrut (qv)
Subsidiary Companies: Erez Books (at above address); Metziuth Books (at above address)
Subjects: Fiction, Politics, Middle East Studies, Juveniles, Military, History, Textbooks, Cookery, Nature
Founded: 1973

Zur & Zur Ltd*, 103 Shlomo Hamelech St, Tel Aviv 64586 Tel: (03) 223764 Cable Add: Zunil Telaviv
Man Dir: Shmuel Zur
Imprint: Nitzanim
Subjects: Pocket guides on Cookery, How-to, Children's Books
Founded: 1972

Literary Agents

Bar-David Literary Agency*, 1 Hashahar St, PO Box 1104, Tel Aviv Tel: (03) 656814/5/6 Cable Add: Davidbarco Telex: 33721 Brvid Il
Contact: Mrs Varda Mor

The **Book Publishers'** Association of Israel, International Promotion and Literary Rights Department, 29 Carlebach St, PO Box 20123, Tel Aviv 67132 Tel: (03) 284191 Telex: 341118 Bxtvil ext 5089
Contact: Lorna Soifer

Peter **Halban** Literary Agency*, PO Box 7474, Jerusalem 91073 (Located at: 38 Hatatsim St, Jerusalem) Tel: (02) 660868 Telex: 26144 Bxsm Il ext 7389
Contact: Peter Halban

Moadim*, 144 Hayarkon St, 63451 Tel Aviv Tel: (03) 444829
Play Publishers and Literary Agents
Contact: Maya Tavi

Barbara **Rogan** Literary Agency, PO Box 4006, 12 George Eliot St, Tel Aviv 61040 Tel: (03) 285589 Cable Add: Overworked Tel Aviv
Dir: Barbara Rogan

Shalom **Sella***, PO Box 1154, 9 Heleni Hamalka St, Jerusalem Tel: (02) 242881/242882/243962 Cable Add: Scitrans Telex: 26140

Book Clubs

Ma'ariv Book Club, 72A Dereh Petah Tikva Rd, Tel Aviv Tel: (03) 287211
Owned by: Ma'ariv Book Guild (qv)
Founded: 1979

Massada Press Ltd*, 46 Beth Lehem Rd, Jerusalem
Owned by: Massada Press Ltd, Publisher (qv)

Major Booksellers

Librairie Française **Alcheh***, 55 Nachlat Benyamin St, Tel Aviv Tel: (03) 614173
Largest Importer of French, Spanish and English books in Israel

Bronfman's Agency Ltd, 2 Zlenov St, PO Box 1109, Tel Aviv 61010 Tel: (03) 611243
Manager: I Bronfman
Also exporter, and Publisher (qv)

Emanuel **Brown**, 214 Dizengoff Rd, PO Box 10217, Tel Aviv 61101 Tel: (03) 225728
Specializes in general books, remainders and wholesaling

Distributors' Centre for Israeli Books Ltd*, 22 Nachmani St, PO Box 2811, Tel Aviv

Educational Book Centre*, PO Box 202, Ramallah Tel: 952122/954574/954570 Telex: 25281
Managers: G Soudah, J Soudah

Mifal **Hashichpul**, PO Box 39287, Ramat-Aviv, Tel-Aviv

Heiliger & Co Ltd, 3 Nathan Strauss St, Jerusalem 94227 Tel: (02) 225036 Telex: 26144 Bxjmil 7154
Also: 19 Balfour St, Tel Aviv 65211 Tel: (03) 285397; 25 Nordau St, Haifa 33122 Tel: (04) 664165
Managers: Ruth Ratzkowski, Hugo H Mendelsohn
Exporter, Importer and Distributor, Subscription Centre, specializing in Scientific and Medical books

Israbook*, PO Box 17130, Tel Aviv 61171 (Located at: 13 Blum St, Ramat Aviv) Tel: (03) 416881
Man Dir: Menachem Kna'an
Exporters and suppliers of books and journals in all languages originating with all publishers and learned institutions in Israel

Lonnie **Kahn** and Co Ltd, PO Box 4489, Tel Aviv 61044 (Located at: 5 Nachlat Benyamin St, Tel Aviv) Tel: (03) 623693/624138
Also importer

Ludwig **Mayer** Ltd, 4 Shlomzion Hamalka St, PO Box 1174, Jerusalem 91000 Tel: (02) 222628 Telex: 26144 Bxjm Il 7014

J **Robinson** & Co*, 31 Nachlat Benjamin St, PO Box 4308, Tel Aviv 61040 Tel: (03) 615461
Also exporter and antiquarian bookseller

Sharbain's Bookshop, Salah Eddin St, Jerusalem Tel: (02) 286775
Manager: Jiryes I Sharbain

Sifriat Poalim Ltd*, 73 Allenby St, PO Box 526, Tel Aviv Tel: (03) 291431
Owned by: Sifriat Poalim Ltd, Publisher (qv)

Steimatzky Ltd, PO Box 628, Tel Aviv 61006 (Located at: Citrus House, 22 Harakevet St, Tel Aviv) Tel: (03) 622536 Cable Add: Steimatzky Beithadar Tel Aviv Telex: 361430 Steim Il
Owned by: Steimatzky Ltd, Publisher (qv)
30 bookshops in Israel, plus 25 franchises. Importers, exporters, wholesalers and publishers' representatives

ISRAEL — ITALY

Universal Library*, Salah-e-Din St, East Jerusalem Tel: (02) 82624
Specializes in books on the Middle East and religious books

Major Libraries

Central Library of **Agricultural Science***, PO Box 12, Rehovot 76100

The Central **Archives** for the History of the Jewish People (formerly Jewish Historical General Archives), Jerusalem University Campus, Sprinzak Bldg, PO Box 1149, Jerusalem Tel: (02) 635716
Director: Dr Daniel J Cohen

Bar Ilan University Library*, Ramat Gan

Ben-Gurion University of the Negev Library*, PO Box 653, Beersheva 84105 Tel: (057) 64422

'Dvir Bialik' Municipal Central Public Library, Hibat-Zion St 14, Ramat Gan
Librarian: Ora Nebenzahl

Elisas Sourasky Central Library, Tel Aviv University*, PO Box 39038, Ramat Aviv, Tel Aviv Tel: (03) 420745/420883

Israel State Archives, Prime Minister's Office, Jerusalem 91919 Tel: (02) 639231
Publications: Documents on the Foreign Policy of Israel (series); *Israel Government Publications* (annual)

Jerusalem City (Public) Library, Betzalel St 11, PO Box 1409, Jerusalem Tel: (02) 224156/224126

Jewish National and University Library, PO Box 503, Jerusalem 91004 Tel: (02) 585039 Telex: 25367
Dir: Prof M Beit-Arié

Knesset Library, Hakirya, Jerusalem 91999 Tel: (02) 554245
Librarian: Dr Camillo Dresner

Municipal Library*, 25 King Saul Blvd, PO Box 32, Tel Aviv

Pevsner Public Library, 54 Pevsner St, PO Box 5345, Haifa 31053 Tel: (04) 667766

Tel Aviv University Library*, PO Box 39038, Ramat Aviv, Tel Aviv

University of Haifa Library*, Mount Carmel, Haifa 31999 Tel: (04) 240289/246650/240497 Telex: 04660
Dir: Prof Shmuel Sever
Publication: Annual Index to Hebrew Periodicals

Weizmann Institute of Science Libraries, Rehovot 76100 Tel: (054) 83298 (Central Library)/(054) 82111 (Weizmann Institute) Cable Add: Weizinst Telex: 361934
Chief Librarian: Alma Rosenheck

Library Associations

Centre for Public Libraries*, PO Box 242, Jerusalem 91000
Publications: Leket (reviews of books); *Yad-la-Koré* (The Reader's Aid) (library quarterly), and library monographs

Information Processing Association of Israel*, PO Box 13009, Jerusalem
Secretary: Tuvia Saks
Publication: Ma'ase Cho-shev (6 a year)

Israel Library Association*, PO Box 303, Tel Aviv Tel: 261111
Executive Secretary: Ruth Porath

Israel Society of Special Libraries and Information Centres (ISLIC), PO Box 20125, Tel Aviv 61200 Tel: (03) 297781

Executive Secretary: I Steinberg
Publications: Bulletin (2 times a year), *Contributions to Information Science* (irregular)

Library Reference Journals

Annual Index to Hebrew Periodicals, University of Haifa Library, Mount Carmel, Haifa 31999

Bibliography of Modern Hebrew Literature in Translation (bi-annually), The Institute for the Translation of Hebrew Literature Ltd, 66 Shlomo Hamelech St, Tel Aviv

Bulletin, Israel Society of Special Libraries and Information Centres, PO Box 20125, Tel Aviv 61200

Kethavim Benossey Med'a (Contributions to Information Science), Israel Society of Special Libraries and Information Centres, PO Box 20125, Tel Aviv 61200

Leket (Gleaning), Centre for Public Libraries, PO Box 242, Jerusalem 91000

Ma'ase Cho-shev (Action and Thought), Information Processing Association of Israel, PO Box 13009, Jerusalem

Yad-la-Koré (The Reader's Aid), Centre for Public Libraries, PO Box 242, Jerusalem 91000

Literary Associations and Societies

Mekise Nirdamin Society*, PO Box 4344, Jerusalem
Secretary: Dr I Ta-Shma
Publishes Hebrew works of the older classical Jewish literature

Israeli P E N Centre, 19 Shmaryahu Lewine St, Jerusalem 96664
Secretary: Haim Toren

Literary Periodicals

Caiet Pentru Literatura Si Istoriografie (Journal of Literature and Historiography) (text in Hebrew, Romanian and Yiddish), Cenaclul Literar 'Menora', PO Box 763, Jerusalem

HSL (Hebrew University Studies in Literature) (text in English and French), The Hebrew University of Jerusalem, Institute of Languages and Literatures, Jerusalem

Ha-Sifrut (Literature); theory, poetics, Hebrew and comparative literature (text in Hebrew, summaries in English), Tel Aviv University, Ramat Aviv, Tel Aviv

Image; English literary magazine, The Hebrew University of Jerusalem, Jerusalem

Modern Hebrew Literature (quarterly, incorporating Hebrew Book Review), Institute for the Translation of Hebrew Literature, 66 Shlomo Hamelech St, Tel Aviv

Siidemot (English Edition); literary digest of the kibbutz movement, Ichud Hakvutzot and Hakibbutzim, Youth Division, 10 Dubnov St, Tel Aviv

Literary Prizes

Bialik Prize for Literature
The highest literary award of the Tel-Aviv-Yafo Municipality, awarded in two categories: belles-lettres and Jewish studies. 80,000 shekels. Awarded annually. Enquiries to Tel-Aviv-Yafo Municipality, Tel Aviv

Brenner Prize
In recognition of outstanding literary works. 12,000 shekels. Awarded annually. Enquiries to Hebrew Writers' Association, PO Box 7111, Tel Aviv

Holon Literary Prize
To encourage literary talent in Israel. 10,000 shekels. Awarded every year. Enquiries to Holon Municipality, Holon

Israeli Prize in Humanities and Social Sciences*
For the most original, outstanding contribution to the humanities and social sciences. 50,000 shekels. Awarded annually in each one of the following areas: (1) Judaica, Modern Hebrew Literature and Education; (2) the Humanities and the Social Sciences; (3) the Arts; (4) Science and Technology; (5) outstanding life-long service to the welfare of Israeli society. Enquiries to Dr Moshe Gilbon, Israeli Ministry of Education and Culture, 15 Keren Hayesod St, Jerusalem 94188

Israeli Prize in Jewish Studies, Hebrew Literature and Education, see Israeli Prize in Humanities and Social Sciences

Israeli Prize in the Arts, see Israeli Prize in Humanities and Social Sciences

Shazar Prize
Awarded to immigrant writers, young authors and writers dealing with the Holocaust. 5,000-12,000 shekels to each author. Awarded annually. Enquiries to Israeli Ministry of Education and Culture, 34 Shivtei Israel St, Jerusalem 95105

Tchernichowsky Prize
For outstanding translations into Hebrew. 60,000 shekels divided between two translators: one of belles-lettres and one of scientific material. Awarded biennially. Enquiries to Tel-Aviv-Yafo Municipality, Tel Aviv

Translation Agencies and Associations

The **Institute** for the Translation of Hebrew Literature Ltd, PO Box 11210, Tel Aviv 61111 (Located at: 66 Shlomo Hamelech St, Tel Aviv) Tel: (03) 244879

Scientific Translations International Ltd, 9 Heleni Hamalka St, PO Box 1154, Jerusalem Tel: (02) 242881/242882/243962 Cable Add: Scitrans Telex: 26140

Italy

General Information

Language: Italian. German and Ladin are officially recognized in Trentino-Alto Adige; Slovene in Trieste
Religion: Roman Catholic
Population: 56.7 million
Literacy Rate (1971): 93.9%

Bank Hours: 0830-1330 Monday-Friday
Shop Hours: 0900-1230, 1500-1900 Monday-Saturday; many close Monday morning
Currency: Lira
Export/Import Information: Member of the European Economic Community. No tariff on books except children's picture books from non-EEC; advertising matter other than single copies is dutied. VAT on books and advertising matter. No import licence required.
Copyright: UCC, Berne, Florence (see International section)

Book Trade Organizations

Agenzia per l'Area di Lingua Italiana ISBN, Associazione Italiana Editori, Via delle Erbe 2, I-20121 Milan Tel: (02) 8059244
ISBN Administrator: Gianni Merlini

Associazione Italiana Editori*, Via delle Erbe 2, I-20121 Milan Tel: (02) 8059244
Rome office: Via Pietro della Valle 13, I-00193 Rome Tel: (06) 6540298
Italian Publishers' Association
Secretary-General: A Ormezzano
Publications: Catalogo dei Libri Italiani in Commèrcio; Giornale della Libreria

Associazione Librai Antiquari d'Italia, Via Jacopo Nardi 6, I-50132 Florence
Antiquarian Booksellers' Association of Italy
President: Dr Renzo Rizzi, Via Cernaia 4, I-20121 Milan

Associazione Librai Italiani, Piazza G G Belli 2, I-00153 Rome Tel: 5803844
Italian Booksellers' Association
Publication: Libreria

Associazione Italiana degli **Editori** di Musica (AIDEM), Piazza del Liberty 2, I-20121 Milan Tel: 796473
Italian Association of Music Publishers

I P L (Istituto Propaganda Libraria)*, Via Mercalli 23, Milan
Institute of Bookshop Advertising

Standard Book Numbering Agency, see Agenzia per l'Area di Lingua Italiana ISBN

Unione Editori di Musica Italiani (UNEMI)*, Via F Sforza 1, I-20122 Milan
Publishing Union of Italian Music

Book Trade Reference Books and Journals

Books

Gli Editori Italiani (over 2,000 Italian publishers listed), Editrice Bibliografica SRL, Viale Veneto 24, I-20124 Milan

Le Librerie Italiane (Italian Booksellers), Editrice Bibliografica SRL, Viale Veneto 24, I-20124 Milan

Journals

Bibliografia Nazionale Italiana (Italian National Bibliography), Central Institute of the Union Catalogue of Italian Libraries and Bibliographical Information, Viale Castro Pretorio 105, Rome

Bollettino (Bulletin), Ufficio della Proprietà Letteraria, Artistica e Scientifica, Rome (monthly)

Bollettino bibliografico, Libreria Seeber, Via dei Tornabuoni 70 r, I-50123 Florence

Catalogo dei Libri Italiani in Commèrcio (Italian Books in Print), Italian Publishers' Association, Via del Erbe 2, I-20121 Milan

Il Compratore (The Buyer), Editoriale A-Z, Via P Kolbe 8, I-20317 Milan

Gazzettino Librario (Book Trade Gazette), Piazza Lotario 6, Rome (advertises book wants and offers)

Giornale della Libreria (Book Trade Journal), Italian Publishers' Association, Via del Erbe 2, I-20121 Milan

Libreria (The Book Trade), Italian Booksellers' Association, Piazza G G Belli 2, I-00153 Rome

Libri e Riviste d'Italia (Italian Books and Periodicals) (available in Italian edition and international edition in English, French, German and Spanish), Via Boncompagni 15, I-00187 Rome

Libro Cattòlico (The Catholic Book), Union of Italian Catholic Publishers, Via Domenico Silveri 9, I-00165 Rome

Mundus, CP 2236, Rome

Ragguaglio Librario (Book Report), Institute of Bookshop Advertising, Via Mercalli 23, Milan

Publishers

A M Z Editrice SpA, Corso di Porta Romana 63, I-20122 Milan Tel: (02) 581071 Cable Add: Editamz Telex: 310607 Amzed I
Man Dir, Editorial: Mario Abriani; *Marketing:* Gianni Macchia; *Rights & Permissions:* Lucia Calza
Subjects: Juveniles, How-to
Founded: 1955

A P E, Bologna, see Ape

Edizioni **A P E** SpA, Via Abbondio Sangiorgio 12, I-20145 Milan Tel: (02) 315118/341807
Man Dir: Dr Piero Bajetta
Parent Company: Ugo Mursia Editore SpA (qv)
Subjects: Textbooks
Founded: 1974

Edizioni **A R E S**, Via Stradivari 7, I-20131 Milan Tel: (02) 209202
Dir: Dr Cesare Cavalleri
Subjects: Philosophy, Theology, Architecture, Psychology
Founded: 1957

Edizioni **Abete***, Via Prenestina 685, I-00155 Rome Tel: (06) 221841
Chief Executive: Dr Giancarlo Abete; *Editorial:* Dr Francesco Matassi; *Sales:* Franco Morbiducci
Parent Company: A Be T E SpA — Azienda Beneventana Tipografica Editoriale
Imprints: Il Melograno, L'Evento Teatrale, Studi Contemporanei
Subjects: Literature, Theatre, Philosophy, Economics, Law
Founded: 1946

Edizioni **Accordo**, Galleria del Corso 4, I-20122 Milan Tel: (02) 794746 Cable Add: Curcimusic Telex: 332683 Curci I
Chief Executive: Dr Giuseppe Gramitto Ricci
Subject: Music
1981: 10 titles *1982:* 1 title *Founded:* 1948

Adelphi Edizioni SpA, Via G Brentano 2, I-20121 Milan Tel: (02) 871266/866177
Man Dir: Luciano Foà; *Editorial Dir:* Roberto Calasso; *Publicity, Production:* Piero Bertolucci
Orders to: Edizioni Adelphi, Servizio Vendita Libri, c/o Fratelli Fabbri Editori, Via Mecenate 91, I-20138 Milan Tel: (02) 50951
Subjects: General Fiction, Belles Lettres, Biography, Music, Art, Philosophy, Religion, Psychology, General Science
1981: 37 titles *1982:* 37 titles *Founded:* 1962

Giacomo **Agnelli** Editore, see Giunti Publishing Group

Ermanno **Albertelli** Editore, CP 395, I-43100 Parma (Located at: Via dell'Assistenza 4, Parma) Tel: (0521) 21012/21289/94702 Cable Add: Albertelli Parma
Chief Executive, Production: Ermanno Albertelli; *Sales:* Viviana De Luca
Subsidiary Company: Tuttostoria (Azienda di distribuzione), Via La Spezia 97, I-43100 Parma
Subject: Military Modelling, Military History
Bookshop: Futurino e C, Via Bruno Longhi 10, I-43100 Parma
Founded: 1968

Alfa Edizioni e Rappresentanze Editoriali, Via Santo Stefano 13, I-40125 Bologna Tel: (051) 262805
Man Dir: Elio Castagnetti
Subjects: Belles Lettres, Poetry, History, Music, Art, Philosophy
Founded: 1954

Libreria **Alfani** Editrice Srl*, Via degli Alfani 88, I-50121 Florence Tel: 284397/298800
Chief Executive: Umberto Panerai
Subjects: University Publications
Bookshops: Libreria Alfani, Via degli Alfani 84/86 R, I-50121 Florence; Libreria Ateneo, Piazza San Marco 3/R, Florence
Founded: 1968

Alfieri Edizioni d'Arte, Cannaregio 6099, I-30124 Venice Tel: (041) 23323
Dirs: Giorgio Fantoni, Massimo Vitta Zelman; *Editorial:* Carlo Pirovano; *Rights & Permissions:* Marisa Inzaghi
Parent Company: Electa Editrice (qv)
Subjects: Modern Art, Venetian Art, Architecture, Periodicals, Numbered Editions
Founded: 1939

Alinari Fratelli SpA Istituto di Edizioni Artistiche*, Via Nazionale 6, I-50123 Florence Tel: (055) 212105 Cable Add: Idea
Man Dir: Filippo Zevi
Bookshops: Fratelli Alinari, Via Strozzi 19r, Florence; Fratelli Alinari, Via del Babuino 98, Rome
Subjects: Art, Educational Materials, Photography
Founded: 1854

Edizioni **All'Insegna** del Veltro, Viale Osacca 13, I-43100 Parma Tel: (0521) 31587
Chief Executive: Claudio Mutti
Subjects: Esoterica, History of Religion, Medieval Studies, Oriental Studies, Islamic Studies, Greek Philosophy
Founded: 1977

Editrice **Ancora** Milano, Via GB Niccolini 8, I-20154 Milan Tel: (02) 3189941
Man Dir: Medici Severino; *Editorial Dir:* Zini Vigilio; *Sales Dir:* Giordani Saverio
Subjects: Religion, Juveniles, Social Science
Founded: 1934

Franco **Angeli** Editore*, CP 17130, I-20127 Milan (Located at: Viale Monza 106, Milan) Tel: 2827651/2/3
Man Dir: Dr Franco Angeli; *Editorial:* L Gambi, E Becchi, M Cesa-Bianchi; *Sales:* Dr Stefano Angeli; *Production:* Marilena Aliata
Subjects: Anthropology, Architecture, Law of Employment and Labour Relations, Economics, Teaching and Education, Geography, History, Politics, Psychology, Finance, Sociology, Urban and Regional Studies, Physics, Electrical Engineering, Electronics, Data Processing, Mathematics, Science, Management, Marketing, Publicity, Public Relations, Essays
Founded: 1955

220 ITALY

Organizzazione Didattica Editoriale **Ape**+, Via Augusto Murri 56, I-40137 Bologna Tel: (051) 392670 Cable Add: Ape Murri 56 Bologna
Chief Executive, Editorial, Production, Rights & Permissions: Giorgio Ognibene; *Sales:* Gina Cesari
Subjects: Civics Textbooks for Children, Fiction, Local History
Founded: 1964

Ape, Milan, see A P E

Ruggero **Aprile***, Via Vittime di Bologna 14, I-10156 Turin Tel: (011) 240124 Telex: 213211
Man Dir: Ruggero Aprile; *Sales:* Valerio Aprile
Subjects: Fiction, History, Juveniles, Art
Founded: 1973
Miscellaneous: Also known as PEA — Produzioni Editoriale Aprile

Arcana Editrice Srl*, Via Giulia 167, I-00186, Rome Tel: (06) 6542409
Publicity: Raimondo Biffi
Subjects: Youth Questions, Pop Music, Oriental Thought

Edizioni L'**Arciere** Srl+, Corso IV Novembre 29, I-12100 Cuneo Tel: (0171) 3174 Cable Add: Arciere Edizioni Cuneo
Chief Executive, Sales, Rights & Permissions: Aldo Sacchetti; *Editorial, Production, Publicity:* Mario Donadei
Subjects: Local History, Art and Culture, History of the Resistance, Essays, Poetry, Fiction
1981: 12 titles *1982:* 15 titles *Founded:* 1973

Argalia Editore delle Arti Grafiche Editoriali Srl, CP 150, I-61029 Urbino (Located at: Via S Donato 148C, Urbino) Tel: (0722) 2774
Subjects: Philosophy, History, Literature, Criticism, Education, Science, Fiction, Poetry, Classical Drama, Economics
1982: 7 titles *Founded:* 1942

Editore Armando **Armando**, Via della Gensola 60-61, I-00153 Rome Tel: (06) 588441/5894525
Man Dir: Prof Armando Armando
Subjects: Psychology, Philosophy, Social Sciences, Politics, Textbooks, Education, Linguistics, Languages, Children's books, Sociology
1981: 72 titles *1982:* 52 titles *Founded:* 1963

Armenia Editore Srl, Viale Cà Granda 2, I-20162 Milan Tel: (02) 6438766
Chief Executive: Dr Giovanni Armenia
Associate Company: SIAD Edizioni SRL (qv)
Subjects: Paranormal, Astrology, Alternative Medicine
Founded: 1972

Casa Editrice **Arnaud***, Via XXVII Aprile 13, I-50129 Florence Tel: (055) 496333
Chief Executive: Ebe Laffi Arnaud
Subject: Art
Founded: 1944

Editrice **Arte** e Pensiero SRL+, Via Piana 10, I-50124 Florence Tel: (055) 222088/2299930
Man Dir: Dr Aleksandar V Stefanovic
Subjects: General Fiction, Belles Lettres, Art, Reference, Guides, Manuals, Miscellaneous
1982: 10 titles *Founded:* 1981

Casa Editrice **Astrolabio-Ubaldini** Editore, Via Guido d'Arezzo 16, I-00198 Rome Tel: (06) 862131
Chief Executive: Mario Ubaldini; *Editorial:* Francesco Gana; *Sales, Production:* Fiorenzo Bertillo; *Publicity:* Francesco Cardelli
Subjects: Psychoanalysis, Psychology, Psychiatry, Oriental Philosophy, Epistemology, Parapsychology, Sociology
Founded: 1946

Edizioni Dell'**Ateneo** SpA*, Via Boezio 6, CP 7216, I-00192 Rome Tel: (06) 7578853/7593456
Man Dir: Franco Volta; *Sales:* G Santo Geraci; *Production:* Sergio Petrelli
Orders to: Via Ruggero Bonghi 11/B, I-00184 Rome
Subjects: Belles Lettres, Poetry, Biography, History, Music, Art, Philosophy, Classical Philology, Cinema, Reference, Religion, High-priced Paperbacks, Psychology, Engineering, General & Social Science, Secondary and University Textbooks, Economics, Medicine, Aeronautics, Navy, Army
Founded: 1946

Verlagsanstalt **Athesia**+, Lauben 41, Postfach 417, I-39100 Bolzano-Bozen Tel: (0471) 932000 Cable Add: Athesia Verlag, Bozen Telex: 400161
Man Dir, Production: Peter Plattner; *Sales Manager:* Richard Fieg; *Publicity Manager:* Gustav Theiner
Subjects: Art, Travel, Guidebooks, Periodicals, History, Maps, Textbooks, Poetry, Mountaineering (in German and Italian)
Bookshops: in Bozen, Meran, Brixen, Bruneck, Sterzing, Schlanders
1981: 30 titles *Founded:* 1907
ISBN Publisher's Prefix: 88-7014

Atlantica Editrice SRL*, CP 34, I-71100 Foggia (Located at: Via Marchianò 22, Foggia)
Branch Off: CP 38, I-71043 Manfredonia
Subjects: Languages, General Science, Regional Culture
1981: 50 titles *Founded:* 1974

M d'**Auria** Editore della 'EST — Editoriale Studi e Testi — SNC'+, Calata Trinità Maggiore 52, I-80134 Naples Tel: (081) 328963
Dir: Gianni Macchiavelli; *Publicity:* Damiano Bianco; *Bookshop Dir:* Carlo Boccadamo
Subjects: Religion, History, Classical Literature
Bookshop: Libreria Internazionale—International Book Center M d'Auria, Calata Trinità Maggiore 53, I-80134 Naples
1981: 18 titles *1982:* 32 titles *Founded:* 1887

Edizioni delle **Autonomie** Srl, Via Cesare Balbo 35, I-00184 Rome Tel: (06) 4751307/4751906
Chief Executive, Sales, Production: Stelvio Minelli; *Editorial:* Bruno Puglielli; *Publicity:* Roberto Laviola
Parent Company: Lega per le Autonomie e i Poteri Locali, Via Cesare Balbo 43, I-00184 Rome
Branch Offs: Eighteen throughout Italy
Subjects: Local Government, Planning, Health
Founded: 1977

Baldini e Castoldi*, Viale Majno 23, I-20122 Milan Tel: (02) 782568
Dir: Dr Enrico Castoldi
Subjects: General Fiction, Juveniles, Memoirs
Founded: 1896

Giunti **Barbera** Editore, see Giunti Publishing Group

Editoriale **Bari**, see Editorialebari

Edizioni Oreste **Barjes**, see Giunti Publishing Group

Casa Editrice Giorgio **Baryes** Srl+, Via Dessiè 2, I-00199 Rome Tel: (06) 8393655/8380556
Chief Executive: Dr Giuseppe Salvemme; *Editorial:* Dr Giorgio Baryes

Subjects: Textbooks, Philosophy, Science
Founded: 1968

Casa Editrice Luigi **Battei**, Str Cavour 5/C, I-43100 Parma Tel: (0521) 33733/23077
Chief Executive: Antonio Battei; *Editorial:* Giacomo Battioni
Subjects: Local History, Art, Architecture, Urban Studies, Poetry, Essays
Founded: 1872

Edizioni d'Arte Carlo **Bestetti***, Via di San Giacomo 18, I-00187 Rome Tel: (06) 6790174
Man Dir: Carlo Bestetti
Subjects: Art, Architecture, Industry
Founded: 1947

Del **Bianco** Editore, Via S Daniele 11, CP 40, I-33100 Udine Tel: (0432) 22134 Cable Add: Del Bianco Udine
Subjects: Engineering, General Science, University & Secondary Textbooks, Art, History

Biblical Institute Press (Pontificio Istituto Biblico), Piazza della Pilotta 35, I-00187 Rome Tel: (06) 6781567
Man Dir: José A Esquivel
Subjects: Scientific Studies, Biblical Studies, Ancient languages, Archaeology
Founded: 1909

Bibliopolis—Edizioni di Filosofia e Scienze SpA, Via Arangio Ruiz 83, I-80122 Naples Tel: (081) 664606
Man Dir: Dr Francesco del Franco
Subjects: Science and Philosophy
1981: 15 titles *1982:* 22 titles *Founded:* 1976
ISBN Publisher's Prefix: 88-7088

Bietti SpA*, Via Crescenzio 58, I-00193 Rome Tel: (06) 6545501
Subjects: Fiction, Foreign Languages, Humanities, History, Hobbies, Juveniles, Literature Criticism, Education, Philosophy, Games, Sports, Theatre

B **Boggero** Editore, see Giunti Publishing Group

Bompiani, Via Mecenate 91, I-20138 Milan Tel: (02) 50951 Cable Add: Librifabbri Milano Telex: 311321 Fabbri I
Dir: Mario Andreose; *Rights & Permissions:* Rosaria Carpinelli
Subjects: Fiction, Non-fiction, Theatre, Science, Art, Juveniles, Dictionaries, Encyclopaedias
Miscellaneous: Member of Gruppo Editoriale Fabbri, Bompiani, Sonzogno, Etas SpA

Bonacci-Libreria Editrice, Via Paolo Mercuri 23, I-00193 Rome Tel: (06) 6565995
Man Dir: Giorgio Bonacci
Subjects: Belles Lettres, History, Secondary Textbooks
Bookshop: Bonacci — Libreria Editrice, Via Paolo Mercuri 23, I-00193 Rome
1981: 8 titles *1982:* 6 titles *Founded:* 1942

Giuseppe **Bonanno** Editore, Via Vittorio Emanuele 194, I-95024 Acireale Tel: (095) 601984
Chief Executive: Prof Puglisi Saverio; *Editorial:* Giuseppe Bonanno
Subjects: Il Risorgimento, Ancient History, Philosophy, Folklore, Modern Culture
Bookshop: Libreria Bonanno (at above address)
1981: 5 titles *1982:* 5 titles *Founded:* 1966

Casa Editrice **Bonechi**+, Via dei Cairoli 18b, I-50131 Florence Tel: (055) 576841/2 Telex: 571323 CEB
Man Dir: Giampaolo Bonechi; *Editorial:* Giovanna Magi
Subjects: Art, Travel, Reference

Edizioni **Bora** snc di E Brandani & C, Via Jacopo di Paolo 42, I-40128 Bologna Tel: (051) 356133/374394
Subject: Contemporary Art (Books and Periodicals)
1981: 7 titles *Founded:* 1971

Editore **Boringhieri** SpA, Corso Vittorio Emanuele 86, I-10121 Turin Tel: (011) 541371 Cable Add: Edibor
Man Dir: Paolo Boringhieri; *Editorial Manager:* Ernesto Ferrero
Subjects: Philosophy, Science, Psychology, Economics, Low- & High-priced Paperbacks, University Textbooks
Founded: 1957

SIL Srl Edizioni **Borla**, Via delle Fornaci 50, I-00165 Rome Tel: (06) 6381618
Man Dir: Dr Vincenzo D'Agostino
Subjects: Philosophy, Psychology, Sociology, Anthropology, Education, History, Religion, Politics, Juveniles, Periodicals

Bottega d'Erasmo, Via G Ferrari 9, I-10124 Turin Tel: (011) 830331/831264 Cable Add: Erasmus Turin
Subjects: Religion, Philosophy, Medieval, Art, Literature, Philology, History, Law

Ugo **Bozzi** Editore*, Via Polonia 2, I-00198 Rome Tel: (06) 862179 Cable Add: Uberart
Man Dir: Dr Ugo Bozzi
Subject: History of Art (in Italian and English)
Founded: 1965

Bracciodieta Editore, Corso Sonnino 8, I-70121 Bari Tel: (080) 540267
Man Dir: Dr Giuseppe Bracciodieta; *Editorial:* Domenico Bracciodieta; *Sales:* Rete Concessionari; *Publicity:* G S P Sas
Subsidiary Company: Editorialebari (qv)
Subjects: Fiction, Culture, Scholarly
Founded: 1979

Bramante Editrice SpA*, Via G Biancardi 1 bis, I-21052 Busto Arsizio Tel: (0331) 620324
Man Dir: Dr Guido Ceriotti
Subjects: History, Music, Art, General Science, Military, Architecture
Founded: 1958

Edizioni **Brenner***, Via Idria 6, I-87100 Cosenza Tel: (0984) 74537/74442
Man Dir, Editorial, Production: Walter Brenner; *Sales:* Franco De Buono; *Publicity:* Lucia D'Amato; *Rights & Permissions:* Iaconianni Enrico
Subjects: Ethnology, Local History, Medical Rehabilitation
Bookshop: Casa del Libro, Piazza dei Bruzi 18, I-87100 Cosenza
Founded: 1959

L'Erma di **Bretschneider** Srl, Via Cassiodoro 19, CP 6192, I-00199 Rome Tel: (06) 353259/350765
Chief Executive: Dr Roberto Marcucci; *Editorial:* Dr P Meneghelli
Subjects: Archaeology, Classical Philology, Ancient History
Bookshop: Libreria L'Erma (at above address)
Founded: 1946
ISBN Publisher's Prefix: 88-7062

Dr Giorgio **Bretschneider**, Via Crescenzio 43, I-00193 Rome Tel: (06) 659361 Cable Add: Giobrerom
Man Dir: Dr Giorgio Bretschneider
Subjects: Classical Antiquity, Archaeology, Philology, Ancient History
Bookshop: At above address

Edizioni **Bucalo***, CP 51, I-04100 Latina (Located at: Via Bixio 8, Latina) Tel: (0773) 40169
Chief Executive: Adriana Boccio; *All other offices:* Dr Salvatore Bucalo
Parent Company: C Sopra
Branch Off: Viale Regina Margherita 176, I-00198 Rome Tel: (06) 857837
Subjects: Law, Scholarly, Fiction, Encyclopaedias, Law Periodicals
Founded: 1965
ISBN Publisher's Prefix: 88-7456

Bulzoni Editore SRL, Via Dei Liburni 14, I-00185 Rome Tel: (06) 4955207
Man Dir, Editorial: Mario Bulzoni; *Sales:* Ivana Capitani; *Production:* Paola Bulzoni; *Publicity:* Anna Catarinozzi
Subjects: Medicine, Law, Sociology, Science, Fiction, Engineering, Arts, Literature, Philosophy, Linguistics, University Textbooks, Theatre, Cinema, Essays
Bookshop: Libreria Ricerche, Via Liburni 10/12, I-00185 Rome
Founded: 1969

C E D A M (Casa Editrice Dr A Milani), Via Jappelli 5, I-35100 Padua Tel: (049) 23234/23442
Dirs: Antonio Milani, Carlo Porta
Subjects: Belles Lettres, Philosophy, General & Social Science, Textbooks, Book Industry, Engineering, Arts, Literature, Languages, Fiction, Economics, Politics, Medicine

C E D I S Editrice Srl, Via Francesco Denza 52, I-00197 Rome Tel: (06) 878669
Chief Executive: Dr Massacesi Marco
Founded: 1973
ISBN Publisher's Prefix: 88-85018

C E L I (Edizioni)*, Via Gandino, I-40137 Bologna Tel: (051) 391755/309922
Subjects: Medicine, Civil Engineering, Electronics, Radio, Television

C E L U P Srl*, Via G Carducci 1/d, I-90141 Palermo Tel: (091) 586673
Chief Executive: Dr Lillo Buttige'
Bookshop: At above address
Founded: 1958

C E M, see Casa Editrice Marietti SpA

Edizioni **C E P I M***, Via Buonarroti 38, I-20145 Milan Tel: (02) 4982129/4694778
Man Dir: Sergio Bonelli; *Editorial:* Decio Canzio; *Sales:* Liliana Gentini; *Production:* Luigi Corteggi
Subsidiary Companies: Altamira; Araldo; Edizioni Daim Press; all in Milan
Subjects: Comic Strip Books, Far West Stories, Adventure Tales, Stories of Exploration and Travel
Founded: 1968

C L E U P — Cooperativa Libraria Editrice dell'Università di Padova, Via G Prati 19, I-35100 Padua Tel: (049) 650261
Chief Executives: Giorgio Raccis, Piero Gaffuri, Claudio Zoppini; *Editorial, Publicity:* Giorgio Raccis, Piero Gaffuri; *Sales:* Claudio Zoppini, Alfieri Lorenzon; *Rights & Permissions:* Giovanni Bernardi
Orders to: Libreria CLEUP, Via San Francesco 122, I-35100 Padua Tel: (049) 39557
Subjects: University Textbooks, Engineering, Agriculture, Architecture, Linguistics, Philosophy, Science, Local Culture, Mathematics, Statistics, Psychology, Psychoanalysis, Political Science, Sociology, Medicine, Surgery, Acupuncture, Cinema, Law, Economics
Bookshop: Libreria CLEUP, Via San Francesco 122, I-35100 Padua Tel: (049) 39557
1981: 40 titles *1982:* 40 titles *Founded:* 1962

Edizioni **Calderini**+, Emilia Lev 31, I-40139 Bologna Tel: (051) 492211 Cable Add: Calderini Telex: 214821 Calboz
Man Dir: S Perdisa; *Rights & Permissions:* Luisa Manzoni B; *Publicity:* Massimo Manzoni
Parent Company: Calderini SRL (at above address)
Associate Companies: Edagricole (qv); Gruppo Giornalistico Edagricole Srl (at above address); Officine Grafiche Calderini, 14 Emilia, I-40126 Ozzano
Branch Offs: Via Bronzino 14, Milan; Via Puglie 3, Rome
Subjects: Art, Sport, Electronics, Mechanics, Electrical Engineering, University & Secondary Textbooks, Nursing, Architecture, Natural Sciences, Travel Guides
Bookshops: Via Zamboni 18, Bologna; Via Roma 67, Padua; Via Boncompagni 73, Rome
1981: 46 titles *1982:* 98 titles *Founded:* 1952
ISBN Publisher's Prefix: 88-7019

Edizioni **Cantagalli***, CP 155, I-53100 Siena (Located at: Via Camporegio 33, Siena) Tel: (0577) 42102
Chief Executive: Pietro Cantagalli
Subjects: Patristics, Hagiography, Local History and Customs
Founded: 1927

Capitol Editrice Dischi CEB*, CP 441, I-40100 Bologna (Located at: Via Minghetti 17/19, I-40057 Cadriano di Granarolo Emilia (Bologna)) Tel: (051) 766612/766421/2 Cable Add: Edicapitol Bologna Telex: 511039 Edcapi I
Man Dir: Maurizio Malipiero; *Rights & Permissions:* Raffaele Malipiero; *Production Manager:* Guiseppe Parini
Subjects: General Fiction, Art, Biography, Reference, Medicine, Juveniles, Secondary & Primary Textbooks, Educational Materials, Audiovisual
Founded: 1956

Capone Editore Srl*, Via Caprarica 35, I-73020 Cavallino di Lecce Tel: (0832) 611877
Editorial: Lorenzo Capone
Subjects: Local History, Poetry, Essays, Contemporary Art, Ethnography
1981: 15 titles *Founded:* 1980

Nuova Casa Editrice Licinio **Cappelli** SpA, Via Marsili 9, I-40124 Bologna Tel: (051) 330411 Cable Add: Cappelli Editore Bologna Telex: 510198 pp bo i per cappelli
Man Dir: Mario Musso; *Editorial:* Dr Umberto Magrini
Subjects: General Fiction, Belles Lettres, Poetry, Biography, History, Art, Philosophy, Reference, Religion, Juveniles, Low-priced Paperbacks, Medicine, Psychology, General & Social Science, Primary, Secondary and University Textbooks, Filmscripts, Drama, Music, Politics
1981: 104 titles *1982:* 98 titles *Founded:* 1851

Casa Musicale Edizioni **Carrara** Srl, CP 158, I-24100 Bergamo (Located at: Via A da Calepio 4, Bergamo) Tel: (035) 243611 Cable Add: Carrara Musica Bergamo
Editorial, Production: Vinicio Carrara; *Sales, Publicity, Rights & Permissions:* Roberto Mazzoleni
Subjects: Musical Theory and Education, Sheet Music
Founded: 1912

Casa del Libro Editrice, Corso Garibaldi 168, I-89100 Reggio Calabria Tel: (0965) 94844
Chief Executive: Giuseppe Gangemi
Orders to: Licosa SpA (qv)
Branch Off: Via Giulia 95, Rome
Subjects: Architecture, Urban Studies, Ancient History, Local History
Bookshop: At above address
Founded: 1970

Casalini Libri+, Via B da Maiano 3, I-50014 Fiesole (Florence) Tel: (055) 599941 Cable Add: Casalini Fiesole
Man Dirs: Mario Casalini, Barbara Casalini
Subjects: History, Philosophy, Sociology, Musicology
Founded: 1968
Miscellaneous: Firm's main function is as a book exporter (see under Major Booksellers)

Edistudio di Brunetto **Casini**+, CP 213, I-56100 Pisa (Located at: Via Giordano Bruno 6/8, Pisa) Tel: (050) 48670 Cable Add: Edistudio CP 213 Pisa
Chief Executive: Brunetto Casini
Subsidiary Company: Composit (Fotocomposizione elaborazione grafica) (at above address)
Subjects: Esperanto (theory, history and teaching), Music, Local Culture and History
1981: 3 titles *1982:* 2 titles *Founded:* 1978
ISBN Publisher's Prefix: 88-7036

Il **Castello**-Collane Tecniche, Via Carlo Ravizza 16, I-20149 Milan Tel: (02) 462010
Chief Executive, Editorial: Mosé Menotti; *Sales:* Paola Alloni; *Production, Rights & Permissions:* Paolo Lazzarin
Subjects: Handbooks on Photography, Cinema, Leisure Activities, Sports, Cookery, Painting
1981: 11 titles *1982:* 14 titles *Founded:* 1955

Celuc Libri*, Via Santa Valeria 5, I-20123 Milan Tel: (02) 806976/800113
Man Dir: Giovanni Barbatiello
Subjects: History, Philosophy, Religion, Low-priced Paperbacks, Psychology, Engineering, General & Social Science, University Textbooks
Bookshop: At above address
Founded: 1969 (as CELUC), 1974 (as Celuc Libri Srl)

Centro Di*, Piazza de'Mozzi 1 r, CP 1500, I-50125 Florence Tel: (055) 23222/282729 Cable Add: Centrodi Florence
Man Dir: Dr F Marchi; *Sales Dir:* P Riccetti
Subjects: Art, Reference
Bookshop: Centro Di, Piazza d'Mozzi 1 r, I-50125, Florence; 18 via di San Giacomo, I-00187 Rome Tel: 6786963
Founded: 1968

Centro Documentazione Alpina, Corso Moncalieri 23/D, I-10131 Turin Tel: (011) 6509493
Editorial: Giorgio Daidola
Subject: Mountains
1982: 6 titles *Founded:* 1970

Centro Internazionale del Libro, see Giunti Publishing Group

Centro Studi Terzo Mondo+, Via GB Morgagni 39, I-20129 Milan Tel: (02) 2719041
Chief Executive: Prof Umberto Melotti; *Editorial, Rights & Permissions:* Elena Sala
Subjects: Problems of the Third World, Sociology, Anthropology, History, Economics, Geography, Political Science, Literature, Poetry
Founded: 1964

Cesco **Ciapanna** Editore SpA+, Via Lipari 8, I-00141 Rome Tel: (06) 897257/891576/893447 Telex: 613429 Fograf I
Chief Executive: Cesco Ciapanna; *Rights & Permissions:* Carla Alberti
Subjects: Photography, Hi-Fi, Solar Energy, Drugs, Science
Founded: 1967

Ciarrapico Editore+, Via Parioli 3, I-00197 Rome Tel: (06) 878676/803380
Publisher: Giuseppe Ciarrapico; *Editorial, Rights & Permissions:* Marcello Veneziani; *Dir:* Giovanni Pirrone; *Sales:* Renzo Rosci;

Publicity Manager: Rosella Giraldi
Associate Companies: Field Educational Italia, Piazza Montegrappa 4, Rome; La Fenice-Ciarrapico Editore (qv)
Subjects: Politics, History, Science, Law, Philology, Philosophy
1981-83: 37 titles
ISBN Publisher's Prefix: 88-7518

Edizioni **Cinque** Lune, Piazza Luigi Sturzo 24, I-00144 Rome Tel: (06) 5923248
Chief Executive: Dr Sergio Meconi; *Editorial:* Prof Carlo Materia
Subjects: History, Sociology, Economics
Bookshop: Libreria Internazionale Paesi Nuovi, Piazza Montecitorio 59/A, Rome
1981: 28 titles *1982:* 18 titles *Founded:* 1954

Editrice **Ciranna** — Roma, Via Gioberti 7, I-04100 Latina Tel: (0773) 481601
Chief Executive, Rights & Permissions: Dr Lidia Fabiano; *Editorial, Sales, Production, Publicity:* Dr Ferdinando Alfinito
Subjects: Textbooks on Language, Literature, History, Geography, Mathematics, Science, Philosophy, Education, Psychology, Art, Technology, Commerce, Law, Public Services
Founded: 1953

Città Armoniosa*, CP 243, I-42100 Reggio Emilia (Located at: Via Lungo Crostalo 1/A, I-42100 Reggio Emilia) Tel: (0522) 25973
Man Dir: Mario Ghinoi; *Editorial:* Giovanni Riva; *Sales:* Riccardo Mammi; *Production:* Massimo Rocchi; *Publicity:* Gino Ruozzi; *Rights & Permissions:* Paola Leoni
Parent Company: Novastampa di Masini Mauro SNC
Subsidiary Company: Novalito di Persona Francesco E C SNC, Via Cecati 15/A, I-42100 Reggio Emilia
Subjects: Fiction, Poetry, Theatre, Juveniles, Cartoons
Founded: 1976

Città Nuova Editrice, Via degli Scipioni 265, I-00192 Rome Tel: (06) 3595212/310955
Man Dirs: Ing Vittorio Fasciotti, Dr Giovanni Battista Dadda
Branch Off: Via Degli Scipioni 265, I-00192 Rome
Subsidiary Companies: Argentina: Ciudad Nueva, Rivadavia 4939 — 9° P "T", Buenos Aires 1424; Austria: Verlag Neue Stadt GmbH, Brucknergasse 13, A-2380 Perchtoldsdorf (Vienna); Belgium: Nieuwe Stad, Ramstraat 41, B-2000 Antwerp; Brazil: Cidade Nova Editora (qv); Colombia: Ciudad Nueva, Carrera 4a 58-90, Bogota, DD2; France: Nouvelle Cité (qv); Federal Republic of Germany: Verlag Neue Stadt GmbH (qv); Netherlands: Nieuwe Stad (qv); Philippines: New City (qv); Portugal: Cidade Nova, Rua Matola 19, 1800 Lisbon; Spain: Ciudad Nueva (qv); Switzerland: Verlag Neue Stadt (qv); UK: New City (qv); USA: New City Press, 206 Skillman Ave, Brooklyn, New York, NY 11211
Subjects: Religion, Philosophy, Psychology, Reference, Juveniles, Education, Patristics, Theology, Sociology
1981: 85 titles *1982:* 150 titles

Cittadèlla Editrice, Via Ancaiani 3, CP 46, I-06081 Assisi Tel: (075) 813595 Cable Add: Cittadella Editrice
All offices: Nello Giostra, Gabriella Persico, Giuseppina Pompei, Virginia Pagani
Subjects: Biography, Religion, Psychology, Social Science, Social Problems, Theology

Claudiana Editrice, Via Principe Tommaso 1, I-10125 Turin Tel: (011) 689804
President: Pastore Paolo Ribet; *Editorial:* Dr Carlo Papini; *Sales, Rights & Permissions:* Elena Vigliano

Subjects: History of Religion, Theology, Bible Studies, Ethics, Political Issues
Bookshops: Libreria Claudiana, Via Francesco Sforza 12A, I-20100 Milan; Libreria Claudiana, Piazza Libertà, I-10066 Torre Pellice (Turin); Via Pr Tommaso 1, I-10125 Turin; Libreria di Cultura Religiosa, Piazza Cavour 32, I-00193 Rome
Founded: 1855
ISBN Publisher's Prefix: 88-7016

La **Coccinella** Editrice Srl, Via Crispi 77/79, I-21100 Varese Tel: (0332) 224690 Telex: 380054 per La Coccinella
Chief Executive, Production, Publicity: Giorgio Vanetti; *Chief Executive, Sales, Rights & Permissions:* Giuliana Crespi
Subjects: Pre-school, Educational, Activity Books
1983: 32 titles *Founded:* 1977

Edizioni di **Comunità** SpA, Via Manzoni 12, I-20121 Milan Tel: 790957
Man Dir, Sales Dir: Dr Vittorio di Giuro; *Publicity Dir:* Dr Ezio Cagnola; *Advertising, Rights & Permissions:* R Cambiaghi
Subjects: Philosophy, Psychology, Social Science, Economics, Politics, Architecture, Town Planning
Founded: 1946

Fratelli **Conte** Editore Srl+, Via Andrea d'Isernia 59, I-80122 Naples Tel: (081) 683667/669771
Man Dirs: Ferdinando Conte, Mario Conte
Subjects: School Textbooks, Fiction
Founded: 1967

Cooperativa Libraria Editrice dell'Università di Padova, see CLEUP

Edizioni Libreria **Cortina** Verona Srl, Via Carlo Cattaneo 8, I-37121 Verona Tel: (045) 38821/594818 Telex: 431107 Cortin I
Chief Executive: Alfredo Sarcullo; *Publicity:* Elena Mauri
Associate Companies: Edizioni Libreria Cortina Milan, Largo Richini 1, I-20100 Milan; Edizioni Libreria Cortina Padua, Via Marzolo 2, I-35100 Padua; Libreria Scientifica Cortina (qv)
Subjects: Medicine, Science, Law, Engineering, Architecture, Mathematics
Bookshop: Libreria Cortina (at above address)
Founded: 1971
ISBN Publisher's Prefix: 88-85037

Edizioni **Cremonese** SpA+, Borgo Santa Croce 17, I-50122 Florence Tel: (055) 246371 Cable Add: Edizioni Cremonese
Man Dir: Alberto Stianti
Subjects: History, Reference, Engineering, General Science, University & Secondary Textbooks, Architecture, Mathematics, Aviation
1981: 45 titles *Founded:* 1930

La **Culturale**, Via GB Morgagni 39, I-20129 Milan Tel: (02) 2719041
Chief Executive: Prof Umberto Melotti; *Editorial, Rights & Permissions:* Elena Sala
Subjects: Sociology, Economics, Politics, History, Philosophy, Marxism
Founded: 1964

Edizioni **Curci** SRL, Galleria del Corso 4, I-20122 Milan Tel: (02) 794746 Cable Add: Curcimusic Telex: 332683 Curci I
President, General Manager: Giuseppe Gramitto Ricci
Subjects: Music, Arts, Textbooks
1981: 60 titles *1982:* 23 titles *Founded:* 1860

Armando **Curcio** Editore SpA, Via Arno 64, I-00198 Rome Tel: (06) 84871 Cable Add: Curcioroma Telex: 614666 Curcio I
Chairman: Dr Alfredo Curcio; *Man Dir:* Dr Silvio Rotunno
Subjects: Art, Reference, Geography,

History, Travel, Encyclopaedias
Founded: 1928

Edizioni **Dalla Parte** delle Bambine, Via Turati 38, I-20121 Milan Tel: (02) 6595406
Subject: Illustrated, feminist books for infants, children and women
1983: 41 titles *Founded:* 1975

Dall'Oglio Editore SpA, Via Santa Croce 20-2, I-20122 Milan Tel: (02) 8351575
President: Andrea dall'Oglio; *Man Dir:* Bruno Romano
Subjects: General Fiction, Belles Lettres, Poetry, Biography, History, Low-priced Paperbacks
Founded: 1925

Piero **Dami** Editore SRL*, Piazza Velasca 5, I-20122 Milan Tel: (02) 802731/866514 Cable Add: Eurostudio Milan Telex: 311499
Subjects: Fiction, Illustrated Children's Books, Animals

Giuseppe **De Bono** Editore*, Via Masaccio 220, I-50132 Florence Tel: (055) 576022
Chief Executive: Giuseppe De Bono; *Editorial:* Dr Franca Barbiera; *Sales:* Giovanni Saieva
Subjects: Textbooks, Education, Philosophy, Children's
Founded: 1958

De Donato Società Editrice Cooperativa, Lungomare Nazario Sauro 25, I-70121 Bari Tel: 331574/334159
Man Dir, Sales: Diego De Donato; *Editorial:* Isidoro Mortellaro; *Production:* Cesare Caleno
Subjects: Politics, Economics, Sociology, Literature, Ethnology, Psychology, Archaeology, Philosophy
1981: 39 titles *Founded:* 1970

Giovanni **De Vecchi** Editore SpA*, Via Vittor Pisani 16, I-20124 Milan Tel: 664851/2/3 Telex: 37081 devedit
Subjects: Archaeology, Astronomy, Psychology, Sports, Hunting and Fishing, Domestic Animals, Humour, Occult Sciences, Gardening and Agriculture, Medicinal Herbs, Medical, Yoga, Legal

Edizioni **Dedalo** SpA+, CP 362, I-70123 Bari (Located at: Traversa de Blasio, Zona Industriale, Bari) Tel: 371555/371025/371008
Man Dir: Raimondo Coga
Subjects: Politics, History, Art, Architecture, Urban Studies, Science
1981: 50 titles *Founded:* 1965
ISBN Publisher's Prefix: 88-220

Edizioni **Dehoniane**, Via Marechiaro 46, I-80123 Naples Tel: (081) 7694856 Cable Add: Edizioni Dehoniane Napoli
Chief Executive: Vitantonio Giampietro; *Editorial:* Luigi Cortese; *Sales, Publicity, Rights & Permissions:* Angelo Veneziani; *Production:* Pala Giusto, Rodi Masarati, Giuseppe Catani
Parent Company: Pro Mer It (at above address)
Subjects: Philosophy, Ethics, Education, Psychology, Religion, Sociology
Bookshop: Libreria Dehoniana, Via Depretis 60, I-80133 Naples
1981: 27 titles *Founded:* 1964

Edizioni **Dehoniane** Bologna (EDB), Via Nosadella 6, I-40123 Bologna Tel: (051) 330301/306812
Shipping Add: Via Dal Ferro 4, I-40138 Bologna
Man Dir: Andrea Tessarolo; *Sales Dir, Rights & Permissions:* Giuseppe Albiero; *Publicity Dir:* Sancini Vittorio
Subjects: Philosophy, Religion, Juveniles, Secondary & Primary Textbooks, Educational Materials

Bookshop: Libreria Presbyterium, Padua
Founded: 1965

Delta Editrice SpA*, Via Rizzoli 1, I-40125 Bologna Tel: (051) 234065 Telex: 51524
Subjects: History, Travel, Natural History, Astrology

Diki-Books Srl*, Via Della Spiga 1, I-20121 Milan Tel: 784129
Man Dir: Massimo Baletti
Subjects: Children's books, Foreign language texts for infants & primary schools
Founded: 1975

Edizioni **Dimensione** Umana, an imprint of Grupo Editoriale Le Stelle SpA (qv)

Dolphin Publishers SRL*, Via Volta 16, I-20093 Milan Tel: (02) 2532744 Telex: 321634 Qhitalia
Chief Executive: Fahd I Bacha; *Editorial:* Felizia Law; *Sales:* Shadi Soubra; *Production:* Eduardo Rosenfeld; *Publicity:* Flavio Guberti; *Rights & Permissions:* C J Clark
Parent Company: Dolphin Publishers, Panama 12
Associate Company: Altarib (Arabisation), Via Oldrado da Tresseno 5, Milan
Subjects: Children's, Educational, Medical and Scientific Textbooks in Arabic
Founded: 1978
ISBN Publisher's Prefix: 88-219

Domus Editoriale, Via Achille Grandi 5/7, I-20089 Rozzano (Milan) Tel: (02) 824721 Telex: 313589 Edidom I
Subjects: Art, Motorcars, Cooking, Tourism, Architecture, Periodicals

Edizioni **E B E**, Via dei Prefetti 17, I-00186 Rome Tel: (06) 6798448/6794144
Chief Executive: Giovanni Di Capua; *Sales:* Norma Merli
Orders to: Via FS Nitti 12, I-00191 Rome Tel: (06) 3272972
Subjects: Politics, Modern History, Children's
1982: 6 titles *1983:* 1 title *Founded:* 1973

E D B, see Edizioni Dehoniane Bologna

E D T/Musica+, Via Alfieri 19, I-10121 Turin Tel: (011) 515917/511496
Chief Executive: Enzo Peruccio
Subject: Musicology
1981: 6 titles *1982:* 5 titles *Founded:* 1976
ISBN Publisher's Prefix: 88-7063

E R G A (Edizioni Realizzazioni Grafiche — Artigiana), Via Francesco Montebruno 7N, I-16139 Genoa Tel: (010) 891833
Chief Executive: Marcello Merli; *Editorial:* Marco Merli
Subjects: Science, Literature, History, Religion, Sport, Folklore, Cookery, Local Interest
Founded: 1966

E R I — Edizioni R A I Radiotelevisione Italiana SpA+, Via Arsenale 41, I-10121 Turin Tel: (011) 57101 Cable Add: Edrad Turin
Man Dir: Dr Alberto Luna
Orders to: Via del Babuino 51, I-00187 Rome
Parent Company: RAI Radiotelevisione It, Viale Mazzini 14, Rome
Associate Companies: Sacis, Via del Babuino 9, Rome; Sipra, Via Bertola 34, Turin; Fonit Cetra, Via Meda 45, Milan; Telespazio, Corso d'Italia 42-43, Rome
Subjects: Art and Collector's editions, Literature and Civilization, Essays, General Culture, Sociology, Classics in Translation, Home and Garden, Children's books, Language courses, Communications, Cinema, Public opinion polls, Music
Bookshops: Via Arsenale 41, I-10121 Turin; Via del Babuino 51, I-00187 Rome
1982: 50 titles *Founded:* 1949

E S I, see Edizioni Scientifiche Italiane

Edagricole (Edizioni Agricole), Emilia Lev 31, CP 2202, I-40139 Bologna Tel: (051) 492211 Cable Add: Edagri Telex: 510336
Man Dir: Sergio Perdisa; *Editorial:* Luisa Manzoni; *Sales:* Luipi Perdisa Jr; *Publicity:* Massimo Manzoni
Associate Companies: Calderini Industrie Grafiche ed Editoriali; Edizioni Calderini (qv); Gruppo Giornalistico Edagricole
Branch Offs and Bookshops: Via Bronzino 14, Milan; Via Boncompagni 73, Rome; Via Zamboni 18, Bologna; Via Roma 67, Padua
Subjects: Agriculture, Veterinary Science, Gardening, Biology, Directories
1981: 101 titles *1982:* 186 titles *Founded:* 1936
ISBN Publisher's Prefix: 88-206

Edibimbi SRL, Via Speroni 14, I-21100 Varese Tel: (0332) 287766
Subject: Juveniles

Edipem SpA*, Via Giovanni da Verrazano 15, I-28100 Novara Tel: (0321) 471205
Subjects: Juridical, Medical, Scientific and Technical, Encyclopaedias, Classical Literature, School Books

Editalia (Edizioni d'Italia)*, Via di Pallacorda 7, I-00186 Rome Tel: (06) 6569537/6541592
Man Dir: Lidio Bozzini; *Rights & Permissions:* Arrigo Pecchioli
Subjects: History, Art, Customs
Founded: 1952

Editnemo*, Via Telesio 15, I-20145 Milan Tel: (02) 4983375
Man Dir: Sandro Nardini; *Sales Dir:* Alberto Nardini; *Rights & Permissions:* S A Nardini
Subject: Juveniles
Founded: 1972

Editorialebari, Corso Sonnino 8, I-70121 Bari Tel: (080) 540267
Parent Company: Bracciodieta Editore (qv)
Subjects: Fiction, Philosophy, Education
Founded: 1965

Editrice Bibliografica Srl, Viale Vittorio Veneto 24, I-20124 Milan Tel: (02) 6597950/6597246
Subjects: Bibliographies and Reference Publications for the Book Trade, Library Science
1982: 8 titles *1983:* 10 titles *Founded:* 1974
ISBN Publisher's Prefix: 88-7075

Editrice Cooperativa, Via Tagliamento 25, I-00198 Rome Tel: (06) 8444942/8441888
Chief Executive: Roberto Bigi
Founded: 1950

L'**Editrice Scientifica**, see Guadagni

Edizioni del Centro, I-25044 Capo di Ponte (BS) Tel: (0364) 42091 Cable Add: Centrostudi Capodiponte Telex: 301504 I Archeo
Chief Executive: Prof Emmanuel Anati; *Editorial:* Giovanna Filafusi; *Production:* Ariela Fradkin
Parent Company: Centro Camuno di Studi Preistorici (at above address)
Subjects: Archaeology, Anthropology, History of Religion, Art History, Prehistoric and Primitive Art
Founded: 1964

Giulio **Einaudi** Editore SpA*, Via Umberto Biancamano, CP 245, I-10121 Turin Tel: (011) 533653/545384 Telex: 220344
Subjects: General Fiction, Belles Lettres, Poetry, History, Music, Art, Philosophy, Juveniles, Low- & High-priced Paperbacks, Psychology, Social Science, University Textbooks
Founded: 1933

Electa Editrice, Via Trentacoste 7, I-20134 Milan Tel: (02) 23693 Telex: Tradex 313123
Dirs: Giorgio Fantoni, Massimo Vitta Zelman; *Editorial:* Carlo Pirovano; *Rights & Permissions:* Marisa Inzaghi
Subsidiary Companies: Alfieri Edizioni d'Arte (qv); Arcadia Electa, Milan; Electa Firenze, Florence; Electa Moniteur, Paris; Electa Promotion, Venice; Fantonigrafica, Venice
Subjects: Modern Art, Visual Art, Architecture, Photographic, Catalogues of major exhibitions
1981: 120 titles *Founded:* 1948

Edizioni dell'**Elefante**, Piazza dei Caprettari 70, I-00186 Rome Tel: (06) 6543710
Chief Executive: Dr Enzo Crea; *Editorial:* Benedetta Origo Crea
Subjects: History of Art, Classical and Rare Texts, Exhibition Catalogues, Essays, Miscellaneous
1981: 3 titles *1982:* 4 titles *Founded:* 1964

Emme Edizioni*, Via San Maurilio 13, I-20123 Milan Tel: (02) 865459/865951
Man Dir, Editorial: Rosellina Archinto Marconi; *Rights & Permissions:* Renata Discacciati
Subjects: How-to, Juveniles, High-priced Paperbacks, Educational Materials

L L Edizioni **Equestri** Srl*, Via Rosellini 5, I-20124 Milan Tel: (02) 6081990
Chief Executive: Lucio Lami; *Sales:* Paolo Brera
Orders to: Via Copernico 30, I-20125 Milan
Subjects: Horses, Equitation
Founded: 1974

L'**Erma** di Bretschneider, see Bretschneider

Edi **Ermes** Srl+, Via Timavo 12, I-20124 Milan Tel: (02) 6081097
Chief Executive: Dr Italo Grandi
Subjects: Medicine and Surgery, Veterinary Science, Biology, Psychiatry, Nutrition, Pharmacology, Economics
1981: 57 titles *1982:* 70 titles *Founded:* 1973
ISBN Publisher's Prefixes: 88-85019, 88-7051

Edizioni L'**Età** dell'Acquario, Via Vespucci 41, I-10129 Turin Tel: (011) 585214
Dir: Count Bernardino del Boca di Villaregia
Subjects: Alternative Movements, Theosophy, Anthropology, New Age
Founded: 1971

Etas Libri, Via Mecenate 91, I-20138 Milan Tel: (02) 50951 Cable Add: Librifabbri Milan Telex: 311321 Fabbri I
Dir: Filippo Ambrosini; *Rights & Permissions:* Rosaria Carpinelli
Subjects: Reference, Law, General & Social Science, Economics, Business Administration, Technical
Miscellaneous: Member of Gruppo Editoriale Fabbri, Bompiani, Sonzogno, Etas SpA

Eulama SA*, Via Torino 135, I-00184 Rome Tel: (06) 460636
Man Dir: Harald Kahnemann
Subjects: Fiction, Sociology, Law
Also Literary Agent (qv)

Edizioni **Europa***, Via G B Martini 6, I-00198 Rome Tel: (06) 8449124
Subjects: Art, Music, History, Politics, Economics

L'**Evento** Teatrale, an imprint of Edizioni Abete (qv)

Gruppo Editoriale **Fabbri, Bompiani,** Sonzogno, Etas Spa, see individual entries Bompiani, Etas Libri, Gruppo Editoriale Fabbri SpA, Sonzogno

Gruppo Editoriale **Fabbri** SpA+, Via Mecenate 91, I-20138 Milan Tel: (02) 50951 Cable Add: Librifabbri Milan Telex: 311321 Fabbri I
Man Dir: Mario Speranza; *International Department Dir:* Armando Peres
Subjects: Music, Art, Juveniles, Reference, Medicine, Secondary & Primary Textbooks, Leisure Books, General Encyclopaedias, Science, History, Nature
Founded: 1945
Miscellaneous: Other members of the group are Bompiani, Etas Libri and Sonzogno (qqv)

Faenza Editrice SpA*, Via Firenze 276, CP 68, I-48018 Faenza Tel: (0546) 43120
Cable Add: Editfaenza
Man Dir: Prof Goffredo Gaeta; *Editorial, Sales, Publicity:* Franco Rossi
Subjects: Architecture, Science, Technology, Industries, Crafts, Arts, Ceramics
Founded: 1965

Giangiacomo **Feltrinelli** SpA*, Via Andegari 6, I-20121 Milan Tel: (02) 808346/7 Cable Add: Fedit Milan
Subjects: General Fiction, Belles Lettres, Poetry, Art, Music, History, General Science, Reference, Paperbacks, University Textbooks, Philosophy, Juveniles
Founded: 1954

La **Fenice** — Ciarrapico Editore, Viale Parioli 3, I-00197 Rome Tel: (06) 803380/878676 Telex: 680285 Fielde I
Editorial: Dr Marcello Veneziani; *Sales:* Renzo Rosci; *Production:* Prof Gianni Pirrone
Parent Company: Gruppo Italfin '80, Via Pinciana 24, I-00197 Rome
Subsidiary Company: SPC (Stabilimenti Poligrafici Cassino), Villa Santa Lucia, Cassino
Associate Companies: Acta Medica (at above address); Ciarrapico Editore (qv); Field Educational Italia, Piazza Montegrappa 4, I-00195 Rome
Subjects: History, Military History, Philosophy
1981: 12 titles *1982:* 18 titles *Founded:* 1951
ISBN Publisher's Prefix: 88-7518

Edizioni **Ferro** SpA*, Via Cusani 5, I-20121 Milan Tel: (02) 866272
Man Dir: Pia Ferro
Subjects: Medicine, Pedagogy, Sociology
Founded: 1963

Libreria Editrice **Fiorentina** di Vittorio e Valerio Zani snc*, Via Giambologna 5, I-50132 Florence Tel: (055) 579921
Editorial: Vittorio Zani; *Sales:* Valerio Zani
Subjects: Religion, Social Problems, Education, Local Interest, Ecology, Alternative Culture
Bookshop: Via Ricasoli 105-107r, I-50122 Florence
1981: 36 titles *Founded:* 1902

S F **Flaccovio** Editore*, Via Ruggiero Settimo 37, I-90139 Palermo Tel: 589442/334249/584268
Subjects: General Science, History
Bookshops: Via R Settimo 37, Palermo; Piazza Orlando 15, Palermo; Via E Basile 136, Palermo; Piazza Don Bosco 3, Palermo; Libreria Dante, Quattro Canti Citta, Palermo

Fògola Editore in Torino*, Piazza Carlo Felice 19, I-10123 Turin Tel: (011) 535897/531570
Subjects: History, Fiction, Essays, Limited Editions of Classics
Bookshop: Libreria Dante Alighieri (at above address)
Founded: 1965

Il **Formichiere***, Via del Lauro 3, I-20121 Milan Tel: (02) 86693
Subjects: Theatre, Cinema, Music, Fiction, Psychology

Arnaldo **Forni** Editore SpA, Via Gramsci 164, I-40010 Sala Bolognese (Bologna) Tel: (051) 954142/954198
Man Dir: Arnaldo Forni
Subjects: Mainly reprints covering Masonry, Medicine, Middle Ages, Military, Minerology, Music, Theatre, Dance, Numismatology, Occultism, Ornithology, Renaissance, Science, History, Classics, Religion; Periodicals
1981: 65 titles *Founded:* 1973

Aldo **Francisci** Editore, Via Puccini 27, I-35031 Abano Terme (PD) Tel: (049) 810956
Chief Executive: Aldo Francisci
Subjects: Literature, Philosophy, Psychiatry, Sociology, Archaeology, Poetry, Local Guides, Politics, Economics, Education, Library Science, Art, Periodicals
1983: 80 titles *Founded:* 1977

Edizioni **Futuro***, Viale N Bixio 28, I-37124 Verona Tel: (45) 45955/49324 Telex: 480833
Chief Executive: Vinicio de Lorentiis; *Editorial:* Marco Marchesani; *Sales:* Gianna Bonuzzi; *Production:* Giorgio Bonuzzi; *Publicity:* Nicoletta Barbieri; *Rights & Permissions:* Alberto Bedendo
Subsidiary Company: Moderna International (at above address)
Associate Company: Composit (Photosetting) (at above address)
Subjects: Illustrated Biographies, Guides
Founded: 1979

Aulo **Gaggi** Editore, Via Andrea Costa 131-5, I-40134 Bologna Tel: (051) 410696
Man Dir, Rights & Permissions: Aulo Gaggi; *Editorial, Publicity:* Giovanna Galotti; *Sales:* Maurizio Bernardi; *Production:* Alessandra Zironi
Subject: Medicine
Founded: 1965

Giuseppe **Galzerano** Editore+, I-84040 Casalvelino Scalo (Salerno) Tel: (0974) 62028 Cable Add: Galzerano Casalvelino Scalo (sa)
Chief Executive and all other offices: Giuseppe Galzerano
Subjects: Politics, Anarchism, Popular and Local History, Memoirs, Poetry
1981: 6 titles *1982:* 13 titles *Founded:* 1975

Editrice **Gammalibri**+, Via Poma 4, I-20129 Milan Tel: (02) 718315
Man Dir: Domenico Nodari; *Publicity, Rights & Permissions:* Mauro Maggio
Subjects: Music, Sport, Politics, Cinema, Theatre, Literature
1981: 24 titles *1982:* 40 titles *Founded:* 1976

Editrice **Gargliano** SRL*, Via Benedetto Croce 9, I-03043 Cassino Tel: (0776) 21869
Cable Add: Editrice Gargliano Cassino
Chief Executives: Marisa Canzano, Santina Vitale; *Editorial:* Rodolfo Vitale; *Sales:* Antonella Rizza; *Production:* Antonio Violo; *Publicity:* Giovanni Violo; *Rights & Permissions:* Elena Vettese
Subjects: Philosophy, Education, Psychology, Italian, French and English Literature
Bookshop: Libreria Universitaria, Via Benedetto Croce 11, I-03043 Cassino
Founded: 1968

Garzanti Editore*, Via Senato 25, I-20121 Milan Tel: (02) 705721/705741 Cable Add: Garzantieditore Telex: Garzal 31461
Publisher: Dr Livio Garzanti; *Editorial:* Piero Gelli; *Sales Manager:* Francesco Rampini; *Rights & Permissions:* Paola Dala

Subsidiary Companies: Antonio Vallardi Editore (qv); Centri Garzanti, Via Senato 15; Enciclopedia Europea SaS, Via Senato 25 (all in Milan)
Subjects: General & Crime Fiction, Literature, Poetry, Art, Politics, Biography, History, Reference, Juveniles, Low- & High-priced Paperbacks, Secondary & Primary Textbooks, Encyclopaedias, Dictionaries
Bookshops: Libreria Garzanti, Galleria Vittorio Emanuele 66-68, I-20121 Milan; Libreria Garzanti, Palazzo Dell' Università, Pavia
Founded: 1861

Creazioni **Gensy**, see Giunti Publishing Group

Bruno **Ghigi** Editore+, Via Poletti 6, I-47037 Rimini Tel: (0541) 24269
All offices: Bruno Ghigi
Subject: History
Founded: 1955

Ghisetti e Corvi Editori SpA*, Corso Concordia 7, I-20129 Milan Tel: (02) 706232/706233/706234
Subjects: Primary and Secondary Textbooks
Founded: 1937
ISBN Publisher's Prefix: 88-85061

Editrice **Giannotta** di Sebastiano Pace Giannotta+, Viale Regina Margherita 2/e-2/f, I-95125 Catania Tel: (095) 447629
Cable Add: Editrice Giannotta
Man Dir, Editorial: Sebastiano Pace Giannotta
Subjects: Law, Literature, Philosophy, Sociology, Science, Sicilian Folklore and Dialect, University Textbooks, Cartography
Bookshop: Libreria Editrice Giannotta (at above address)
Founded: 1965

G **Giappichelli** Editore di Giorgio Giappichelli & C SAS, Via Po 21 ang Via Vasco 2, I-10124 Turin Tel: (011) 8397019/8397303
Subjects: University Publications, Humanities (Economics, Law, Philosophy, Politics, Sociology, Classical and Modern Philology)
Bookshops: Libreria Editrice Scientifica di G Giappichelli, Via Vasco 2, I-10124 Turin; Libreria della Facolta' Umanistiche, Via Verdi 39 bis, I-10124 Turin
Founded: 1921

Mario Lapucci — Edizioni del **Girasole***, Via Baccarini 80, I-48100 Ravenna Tel: (0544) 22830
Chief Executive: Mario Lapucci
Subjects: History, Language and Folklore of Romagna, Poetry, Miscellaneous
1981: 12 titles *Founded:* 1966

A **Giuffré** Editore SpA, Via Statuto 2, I-20121 Milan Tel: (02) 652341/2/3
Publicity Manager: Roberto Musicco
Branch Off: Via V Colonna 40, I-00193 Rome
Subjects: History, Law, Social & Political Science, Economics
Founded: 1931

Giunti Publishing Group*, Via V Gioberti 34, I-50121 Florence Tel: (055) 670451/5
Cable Add: Marzolib Florence
Telex: 571438 Giunti
Also: Via Scipione Ammirato 37, I-50136 Florence
Dirs: Dr Renato Giunti, Dr Sergio Giunti; *Rights & Permissions:* Roberto Borrani, Davide Mazzanti; *International Consultant:* Ljubivoje Stefanovic
Subjects: Art Books, Essays, Fiction, Psychology, Pedagogy, Mathematics, Chemistry, National Edition of Works of Leonardo da Vinci, Galileo Galilei, Italian publishers of National Geographic Society books, Linguistics, Dictionaries, School Textbooks, Juveniles, Popular Science, History, Guidebooks, Handbooks, Periodicals
Miscellaneous: Group comprises: Editrice Giunti Marzocco, Giunti Barbera Editore, Editrice Universitaria, Edizioni Ofiria, Nardini Editore — Centro Internazionale del Libro (qv), Giacomo Agnelli Editore, Giunti Martello Editore, Creazioni Gensy, Edizioni Oreste Barjes, ME/DI Sviluppo, OS Organizzazioni Speciali SRL (qv), B Boggero Editore, Lisciani e Giunti Editori

Società Editrice La **Goliardica** Pavese SRL+, Viale Taramelli 18, I-27100 Pavia Tel: (0382) 21101/29674
Chief Executive and all other offices: Dario De Bona
Subjects: Scientific Textbooks for Universities
1982: 85 titles *1983:* 120 titles *Founded:* 1977

Grafo Edizioni, Via Agostino Bassi 20, I-25124 Brescia Tel: (030) 393221/308957
Chief Executive: Roberto Montagnini; *Editorial:* Lucio Maninetti; *Sales:* Mauro Rota, Franco Agnelli; *Production:* Paola Pierattini
Subsidiary Companies: Cheiron; La Ricerca Folklorica (both at above address)
Subjects: History, Art, Popular Culture, Local Interest
1981: 23 titles *1982:* 17 titles *Founded:* 1974

Editoriale **Grasso***, Via San Vitale 53, I-40125 Bologna Tel: (051) 220440
Chief Executive, Production, Publicity: Domenico Grasso; *Editorial:* Serena Serafini; *Sales, Rights & Permissions:* Domenico Grasso Jr
Subjects: Medicine, Veterinary Science, Science
Bookshop: Libreria dello Studente, Via San Vitale 55/A, I-40125 Bologna
1981: 10 titles
ISBN Publisher's Prefix: 88-7055

Gregorian University Press (Università Gregoriana Editrice), Piazza della Pilotta 35, I-00187 Rome Tel: (06) 6781567
Man Dir: José A Esquivel
Subjects: Theology, Philosophy, Canon Law, Sociology, Psychology
1981: 13 titles *Founded:* 1914

Libreria Editrice **Gregoriana**, Via Roma 37, I-35100 Padua Tel: 36133/38869
Man Dir: Dr Gianfranco Zenatto
Subjects: Religion, Philosophy, Sociology, Psychology
Bookshop: Libreria Gregoriana (qv under Major Booksellers)
Founded: 1922

Ernesto **Gremese** Editore SRL*, Via Orazio 3, I-00192 Rome Tel: (06) 318136/386533
Chief Executive: Ernesto Gremese
Branch Off: Via Cola Di Rienzo 136, I-00192 Rome Tel: (06) 318136
Subjects: Literature, Textbooks
Bookshop: Libreria Editrice Ernesto Gremese, Via Cola di Rienzo 136, I-00192 Rome Tel: (06) 386533
Founded: 1974

Gremese Editore SRL+, Via Virginia Agnelli 88, I-00151 Rome Tel: (06) 532092/5377600
Chief Executive: Dr Gianni Gremese
Subjects: Illustrated Books on Cinema, Theatre, Music, Photography, Dance, Art, Sport, Technical, Literature
1981: 11 titles *1982:* 16 titles
ISBN Publisher's Prefix: 88-7605

Piero **Gribaudi** Editore, Corso Galileo Ferraris 67, I-10128 Turin Tel: (011) 500360
Publishers: Piero Gribaudi, Maria Luisa Gribaudi Monferrini
Subjects: Philosophy, Religion, Social Science

L'Editrice Scientifica SaS di L G **Guadagni**, Via Ariberto 20, I-20123 Milan Tel: (02) 8390274
Dir: Dr Leonarda Guadagni
Subjects: Pharmaceuticals, Chemistry, University Textbooks
Founded: 1940

Guanda Editore SRL*, Via Daniele Manin 13, I-20121 Milan Tel: (02) 654628, 650973
Man Dir: Dr Giancarlo Paolini; *Rights & Permissions:* Dr Carlo Alberto Corsi
Subjects: Poetry, General Fiction, Essays
Founded: 1933

Guida Editori SRL, Via Ventaglieri 83, I-80135 Naples Tel: (081) 341843
Publisher: Mario Guida
Subjects: History, Philosophy, Ideology, Sociology, Anthropology, Political Science, Environment, Urban Planning, Literature, Literary Criticism, Linguistics, Periodicals
1982: 400 titles

Guidicini e Rosa Editori Snc, Via Pasubio 74, I-40133 Bologna Tel: (0541) 416933
Chief Executives: Gabriele Guidicini, Rino Rosa
Subjects: Local Interest, History, Fiction, Poetry
1981: 7 titles *Founded:* 1976

Casa Editrice **Herbita***, Via Vincenzo Errante 44, I-90127 Palermo Tel: (091) 237716 Cable Add: Herbita Palermo
Chief Executive: Leonardo Palermo
Subjects: Politics, Law, Literature, Classics, Philosophy, Mathematics
Founded: 1973

Herder Editrice e Libreria, Piazza Montecitorio 117-120, I-00186 Rome Tel: (06) 6794628
Man Dir: Oriol Schaedel
Associate Companies: Verlag Herder & Co, Austria (qv); Verlag Herder GmbH & Co KG, Federal Republic of Germany (qv); Herder und Herder GmbH, Federal Republic of Germany (qv); A G Ploetz KG, Federal Republic of Germany (qv); Editorial Herder SA, Spain (qv); Herder AG, Switzerland (qv)
Subjects: Religion, History, Philosophy, Archaeology, Oriental Studies, Philology and Linguistics, Periodicals, Occasional titles
Founded: 1955

Hermes Edizioni SRL, Via Flaminia 158, I-00196 Rome Tel: (06) 3601656
General Manager: Giovanni Canonico; *Editorial:* Romualdo d'Alessandro; *Sales:* Graziella Torre; *Publicity:* Gigliola Porzi; *Rights & Permissions:* Luigi Coppe
Parent Company: Edizioni Mediterranee SRL (qv)
Subjects: Alternative Medicine, Astrology, Nature, Dietetics

Casa Editrice Libraria Ulrico **Hoepli** SpA+, Via Hoepli 5, I-20121 Milan Tel: (02) 865446 Cable Add: Hoepli Milan Telex: 313395 Hoepli I
Shipping Add: Via Mameli 13, I-20129 Milan
Man Dirs: Dr Ulrico Hoepli, Gianni Hoepli; *Sales Dir:* Dr Ulrico Carlo Hoepli; *Rights & Permissions:* Dr Susanna Schwarz Bellotti
Branch Off: Via Mameli 13, I-20129 Milan
Subjects: How-to, Art, Reference, Juveniles, Low- & High-priced Paperbacks, Engineering, General & Social Science, University & Secondary Textbooks, Handbooks, Technology
Bookshop: Ulrico Hoepli Libreria Internazionale (qv under Major Booksellers)
1981: 85 titles *1982:* 66 titles *Founded:* 1870

Idea Books, Via Cappuccio 21, I-20123 Milan Tel: (02) 807997 Cable Add: Ideabooks Milano Telex: 323352 Ideabk I
Dir: Filippo Passigli; *Editorial:* Andrea Cestelli-Guidi, Andrea Branzi, Alvise Passigli
Subjects: Visual Arts, Photography, Architecture, Design
Bookshops: Florence; Milan
Founded: 1976

Casa Editrice V **Idelson** di F Gnocchi+, Via Alcide De Gasperi 55, I-80133 Naples Tel: (081) 324733/324317 Cable Add: Idelson Naples
Chief Executive: Guido Gnocchi
Subjects: Medicine, Biology
Founded: 1911

Editrice **Innocenti** Snc+, Via Zara 36, I-38100 Trento Tel: (0461) 36521 Cable Add: Editrice Innocenti Trento
Chief Executive: Luciano Innocenti; *Publicity:* Silvia Nones
Associate Company: Casa Editrice Principato, Via Fauché 10, Milan
Subjects: Fiction, Scholarly, Languages
1982: 8 titles *Founded:* 1972

Editrice **Iskra**, Via Adige 3, I-20135 Milan Tel: (02) 576866
Chief Executive, Publicity: Renato de Pra
Subjects: History of the Workers' Movement, Politics, Economics, Philosophy
Founded: 1981

Isper Edizioni+, Corso Dante 124, I-10126 Turin Tel: (011) 633950
Chief Executive: Dr Carlo Actis Grosso
Branch Offs: Via Lambro 2, I-20129 Milan; Via G Paisiello 12, I-00198 Rome; Corso del Popolo 46, I-30172 Venice
Subjects: Business Studies, Management
Book Club: Isper Club (qv)
1981: 5 titles *1982:* 4 titles *Founded:* 1965

Istituto Centrale di Statistica*, Via C Balbo 16, I-00100 Rome Tel: (06) 4673 Cable Add: Istat Roma Telex: Istat 610338
President: Prof Guido M Rey; *Dir General, Information and Automation:* Prof Vicenzo Siesto; *Dir General, Technical Services:* Dr Luigi Pinto; *Dir General, Administrative Services:* Dr Carlo Viterbo
Branch Offs: Viale Liegi 13, I-00198 Rome; Via A Rava 150, I-00142 Rome
Subjects: Political Economy, Statistics, Demography
Bookshop: Via A Depretis 82, I-00184 Rome Tel: (06) 4751666
Founded: 1926

Istituto della Enciclopedia Italiana+, Piazza Paganica 4, CP 717, I-00186 Rome Tel: (06) 6544337 Cable Add: Enciclopedia
Subjects: Encyclopaedias, Dictionaries, Reference, Art, Audiovisual Materials

Casa Editrice **Istituto della Santa**, CP 139, I-28100 Novara (Located at: Via Negroni 4, Novara) Tel: (0321) 23079 Cable Add: Dellasanta Novara
Subjects: Textbooks for Secretarial, Commercial and Business Studies
Founded: 1956

Istituto di Studi Romani, Piazza dei Cavalieri di Malta 2, I-00153 Rome Tel: (06) 573442/573445
Dir: Dr Fernanda Roscetti
Subjects: History, Classical Literature, Bibliographies, Architecture, Art
Founded: 1925

Istituto Editoriale Italiano SpA*, Via Priv Passo Pordoi 21, I-20139 Milan
Subjects: Fine & Applied Arts, Illustrated Books, Encyclopaedias & Dictionaries

Istituto Geografico de Agostini SpA*, Via Giovanni da Verrazzano 15, I-28100 Novara Tel: (0321) 471201 Cable Add: Geografico Novara Telex: 20020 Igda No
Subjects: Belles Lettres, Art, Reference, History, Religion, Juveniles, Textbooks, Geography, Literature

Istituto Grafologico, see Girolamo Moretti

Istituto Italiano D'Arti Grafiche*, Via Zanica 92, I-24100 Bergamo Tel: (035) 246292/243645/249675 Cable Add: Grafiche Bergamo Telex: 30114
Man Dir: Comm Remo Montanari
Subjects: Art, Juveniles, Reference, Textbooks, Religion
Founded: 1873

Casa Editrice **Istituto Padano** di Arti Grafiche*, Viale delle Industrie 1, CP 201, I-45100 Rovigo Tel: (0425) 28164 Cable Add: Ipag Rovigo
Man Dir: Dr Amleto Brigo; *Sales:* Dr Carlo Brigo; *Production:* Dr Alberto Brigo
Subjects: Theology, Religion, Science
Founded: 1946

Istituto per l'Enciclopedia del Friuli Venezia Giulia*, Via dei Rizzani 17, I-33100 Udine Tel: (0432) 208055/297955
President: Romano Scarcia; *Chief Executive:* Cesare Russo; *Editorial:* Domenico Cerroni Cadoresi; *Sales:* Annamaria Toffolini
Subsidiary Company: Centro Diffusione, Via dei Torriani 5, I-33100 Udine
Associate Company: Esse Distribuzione Libraria Sas, Via dei Torriani 5, I-33100 Udine
Subjects: Encyclopaedias, Art, History, Guides, Linguistics, Essays, Fiction, Children's
Founded: 1969

Istituto Poligrafico e Zecca dello Stato*, Piazza Verdi 10, I-00100 Rome
Subjects: Law, Politics, Linguistics, Literature, Fiction, Arts, Stamps, Metal Coins
Founded: 1928
Miscellaneous: State Publishing House and Italian State Stationery Office, Mint and School of Medal's Art

Editrice **Italscambi**, CP 23, I-10100 Turin Tel: (011) 882483 Cable Add: Italscambi CP 23 Turin
Chief Executive: Lorenzo Masetta
Subsidiary Company: 'Controcampo' (current events periodical, at above address)
Subjects: Literature, Poetry, Fiction
Book Club: Centro Italscambi
1981: 16 titles *Founded:* 1972

Editoriale **Jaca** Book+, Via Aurelio Saffi 19, I-20123 Milan Tel: (02) 8052132/8057055 Telex: 331393
Man Dir: Dr Sante Bagnoli; *Editorial Dir:* Dr Maretta Campi; *Editors:* Dr Elio Guerriero (Theology), Dr Massimo Guidetti (History); *Production:* Dr Guido Orsi; *Rights & Permissions:* Laura Geronazzo; *Co-editions:* Daniela Bernabò
Subjects: History, Philosophy, Religion, Psychology, Social & Political Science, Economics, Juveniles, Fiction, Literature, Art, Co-editions
1982: 80 titles *Founded:* 1966

L U **Japadre** Editore*, CP 170, I-67100 L'Aquila (Located at: Corso Federico II 49, L'Aquila) Tel: 25587/26025/26488
Man Dir and other offices: Leandro Ugo Japadre
Branch Off: Via Catalani 50, Rome
Subjects: Art, Literature, History, Philosophy, Science, Technology, Economics, Religion, Psychology, Sociology, Folklore, Fiction, Poetry, Linguistics
Bookshops: 2 Corso Federico II 49, L'Aquila; Piazza dell'Annunziata 6, L'Aquila; Via Catalani 50/9, Rome
Founded: 1968
ISBN Publisher's Prefix: 88-7006

Casa Editrice Dr Eugenio **Jovene** SpA, Via Mezzocannone 109, I-80134 Naples Tel: 206518/206575 Cable Add: Jovene
Man Dir: Dr Alessandro Rossi
Subjects: Law, Economics
1981: 60 titles *Founded:* 1854

Kina Italia SpA*, Piazza Aspromonte 13, I-20131 Milan Tel: (02) 296263, 293284 Telex: 313130 Kina I
Subjects: Art, Tourist Publications

Edizioni **La Scala**, Monastero Padri Benedettini Madonna della Scala, I-70015 Noci/BA Tel: (080) 737400 Cable Add: Benedettini Noci
Chief Executive, Editorial: Padre Giuseppe Quirino Poggi
Subjects: Religion, Liturgy
1981: 6 titles *1982:* 9 titles *Founded:* 1947

La Tartaruga Edizioni, Via Turati 38, I-20121 Milan Tel: (02) 665036
Subjects: Literature, Essays, Theatre
Founded: 1975

Antonio **Lalli** Editore*, Via Fiume 60, I-53036 Poggibonsi (Siena) Tel: (0577) 939226/933305 Cable Add: Lalliedit Poggibonsi
Chief Executive: Antonio Lalli; *Editorial:* Fioranna Casamenti; *Publicity:* Mida Ciappi
Subjects: Fiction, Poetry, Drama, Biography, Memoirs, Local Interest and Dialect, Juveniles, Thrillers and Detective Novels, Humour, Sociology, Philosophy, Education, Politics, Customs, Religion, Cinema, Science, Bibliography, Rare Books, Art, Current Events, Comics
Founded: 1965

Editrice **Lanterna***, Via Robino 71 a/r, I-16142 Genoa Tel: 881441
Dirs: Lino De Benetti, Dino Galiazzo
Subjects: Religion, Theology, Sociology, Politics, Feminism, Non-violence
Founded: 1969

Mario **Lapucci**, see Edizioni del Girasole

Giuseppe **Laterza** e Figli SpA*, Via di Villa Sacchetti 17, I-00197 Rome Tel: (06) 803693/878053
Shipping Add: Via F Zippitelli 3, Zona Industriale, I-70123 Bari
Man Dir: Vito Laterza (Rome); *Editorial Dir:* Enrico Mistretta (Rome); *Sales Dir:* Domenico Scoppio (Bari); *Press, Publicity & Advertising:* Nico Perrone (Bari); *Rights & Permissions:* Eulama Agency, Via Torino 135, Rome
Branch Off: Via D Alighieri 51, I-70121 Bari Tel: (081) 213413/214024/219452
Subjects: Belles Lettres, Biography, Art, Reference, Religion, Architecture, Classics, History, Economics, Philosophy, Low- & High-priced Paperbacks, Psychology, Social Science, University & Secondary Textbooks
Bookshop: Via Sparano 134, I-70121 Bari
Founded: 1889

Edizioni **Laurus**, Via Benedetta 10/r, I-50123 Florence Tel: (055) 210960
Chief Executive: Mario Robuffo
Subject: Law
Founded: 1973

Le Edizioni del **Lavoro***, Via G B Martini 6, I-00198 Rome Tel: (06) 8449124
Subjects: History, Politics, Economics, Literature
Founded: 1945

Casa Editrice Felice **Le Monnier***, Via Scipione Ammirato 100, CP 202, I-50136 Florence Tel: (055) 676201
Subjects: Belles Lettres, Poetry, Biography, History, How-to, Music, Art, Philosophy, Religion, Juveniles, Multilingual Dictionaries, Languages

Casa Editrice Le **Lettere** SRL*, Viale Gramsci 18, I-50132 Florence Tel: (055) 571790
Chief Executive: Dr Giovanni Gentile; *Sales, Administration:* Carlo De Simone
Subjects: Facsimile Reprints of Rare Books, History, Language, Literature
Founded: 1956

Edizioni **Librex***, Via Bellezza 15, I-20136 Milan Tel: (02) 544407/584523 Cable Add: Librex Milan Telex: 34208
General Manager: Antonio Mancia; *Export Manager:* Anna Vanzo; *Production:* Fabiola Ferrario
Subjects: Reference, Juveniles, International Co-productions, Encyclopaedias

Licosa SpA*, Via Lamarmora 45, CP 552, I-50121 Florence Tel: 579751/3, 571809 Cable Add: Licosa Firenze Telex: 570466 Licosa I
Libreria Commissionaria Sansoni
Man Dirs: Dr Giovanni Gentile, Francesco Labardi
Branch Off: Via Bartolini 29, I-20155 Milan
Subjects: Philology, Linguistics, Archaeology, Art, Architecture
Bookshops: Via Lamarmora 45, Florence; Libreria Desi, Via Bartolini 29, Milan
Founded: 1954

Liguori Editore SRL+, Via Mezzocannone 19, I-80134 Naples Tel: (081) 206077 Cable Add: Liguori Napoli
Man Dir: Dr Rolando Liguori; *Editorial and Rights & Permissions:* Guido Liguori; *Sales:* Franco Liguori; *Publicity:* Maria Liguori
Orders to: Sales Department, Via Posilliro 394, I-80123 Naples Tel: (081) 669547
Subjects: Linguistics, Literary Criticism, Philosophy, History, Sociology, Anthropology, Law, Economics, Mathematics, Astronomy, Natural Sciences, Medicine, Technology, Periodical
Bookshop: Libreria Commissionaria Liguori SNC, Via Mezzocannone 21-23, I-80134 Naples Tel: (081) 206687
1982: 87 titles
ISBN Publisher's Prefix: 88-207

Casa Editrice **Liguria**, see Norberto Sabatelli

Lisciani e Giunti Editori, see Giunti Publishing Group

Linea Verde, an imprint of Gruppo Editoriale Le Stelle SpA (qv)

Vincenzo **Lo Faro** Editore*, Via San Giovanni in Laterano 276, I-00184 Rome Tel: (06) 734518/737336
Chief Executive: Vincenzo Lo Faro; *Editorial:* Letizia Carile
Subjects: Drama, Poetry, Philosophy, Education, Medicine, Religion, Ecology, Sociology, Encyclopaedias, Dictionaries, Art, Law, Fiction, Children's
Bookshop: Via San Giovanni in Laterano 260, I-00184 Rome
Founded: 1967

Editrice La **Locusta***, Via del Castello 20, I-36100 Vicenza Tel: (0444) 32604
Chief Executive: Rienzo Colla
Subjects: Essays, Religion, Poetry
Founded: 1954

Loescher Editore SpA, Via Vittorio Amedeo II 18, I-10121 Turin Tel: (011) 549333
Dir: Maurizio Pavia
Subjects: University & Secondary Textbooks
Founded: 1867

Luigi **Loffredo** Editrice*, Via Consalvo 99/H, Parco San Luigi, isol D, I-80126 Naples Tel: (081) 619073
Chief Executive: Mario Loffredo; *Editorial, Sales, Rights & Permissions:* Alfredo Loffredo; *Production:* Alfredo Loffredo Jr; *Publicity:* Enzo Loffredo
Subjects: Textbooks in Philosophy, Religion, Literary Criticism, Essays, Literature, Language, History, Mathematics, Science
Bookshop: Libreria Luigi Loffredo, Via Kerbaker 19/21, I-80129 Naples
Founded: 1880

Longanesi & C, Via Salvini 3, I-20122 Milan Tel: (02) 782551/5 Cable Add: Editlong Milan
President: Stefano Passigli; *Man Dir:* Mario Spagnol; *Editorial:* Lorenzo Pellizzari; *Sales:* Guglielmo Tognetti; *Production:* Pierangela Negri; *Publicity:* Mario Biondi; *Rights & Permissions:* Olivia Olivieri, Carla Tanzi
Subjects: General Fiction, Belles Lettres, Biography, History, How-to, Music, Art, Philosophy, Religion, Low-priced Paperbacks, Medicine, Psychology, General & Social Science
Founded: 1946

Longman Italia SRL, Via Giovanni Pascoli 55, I-20133 Milan
Associate company of Longman Group Ltd, UK (qv)

Angelo **Longo** Editore, Via Rocca ai Fossi 6, CP 431, I-48100 Ravenna Tel: (0544) 27026
Editorial, Production: Alfio Longo; *Sales:* Angelo Longo
Subjects: Art, Archaeology, Bibliography, Philology, Italian Classics, Philosophy, Linguistics, Pedagogy, Critical Literature, Sociology, History, History of Art, Poetry, Fiction, Theatre, History of Masonry
Bookshop: Libreria A Longo, Via A Diaz 39, I-48100 Ravenna (qv under Major Booksellers)
1981: 58 titles *Founded:* 1962

Lucarini Editore Srl, Viale Mazzini 146, I-00195 Rome Tel: (06) 334348/336217
Man Dir: Dr Luciano Lucarini
Orders to: Via Trionfale 8406, I-00135 Rome
Subjects: Contemporary Literature, Theatre, History, Philosophy, Fiction, Poetry, Literary Periodicals
1981: 15 titles *Founded:* 1976
ISBN Publisher's Prefix: 88-7033

Lusva Editrice*, CP 498, I-20122 Milan (Located at: Viale Caldara 20, Milan) Tel: (02) 544149
Chief Executive: Luca Maria Vizzotto
Subjects: Quality Books, Juveniles, Fiction, Poetry, Educational
Founded: 1977

Casa Editrice **M E B** SRL, Via Bonporti 36, I-35141 Padua Tel: (049) 661147/661873 Telex: 215669 Muzzio
Chief Executive: Dr Franco Muzzio; *Production:* Roberto Fardin
Subjects: Parapsychology, UFOs, Magic, Health, Sport, Manuals
Founded: 1956

M E/D I Sviluppo, see Giunti Publishing Group

Edizioni **Magistero**+, CP 306, I-40100 Bologna (Located at: Strada Maggiore 37, I-40125 Bologna) Tel: (051) 233980
Chief Executive: Giovanni Leonardi
Subjects: Education, Philosophy, Literature
Founded: 1976

Magnus Edizioni SpA+, Via Spilimbergo 180, I-33034 Fagagna UD Tel: (0432) 800081 Telex: 460656 Lema I
Chief Executive, Editorial, Rights & Permissions: René Leonarduzzi; *Sales, Publicity:* Antonio Stella; *Production:* Enrico Mazzoli
Subjects: Photography, Art, Illustrated Books, Travel
1981: 11 titles *1982:* 16 titles *Founded:* 1977
ISBN Publisher's Prefix: 88-7057

Organizzazione Editoriale David **Malato**, Via Volturno 7, I-00185 Rome Tel: (06) 461830
Chief Executive: Rosario Malato
Subjects: Law, Tourism, Culture
Founded: 1949
ISBN Publisher's Prefix: 88-7007

Malipiero SpA*, Viale Liguria 12-14, CP 788, I-40064 Ozzana Emilia (Bologna) Tel: (051) 799264 Cable Add: TLX 51260 Matex, Ozzanoemilia Telex: 51260
Dirs: Dr Pierpaolo Malipiero, Comm Giuseppe Malipiero; *Editorial Dir:* Donato Malipiero
Subjects: Juveniles, Hobbies, Education
Founded: 1969

Umberto **Manfredi***, Via Principe Paterno 100/102, I-90144 Palermo Tel: (091) 254053/453046
Chief Executive: Umberto Manfredi
Subjects: Italian Literature, Literary Criticism, Law, History
Founded: 1973

Manfrini Editori*, CP1, I-38060 Calliano (Trento) (Located at: Str Statale del Brennero) Tel: (0464) 84156 Cable Add: Grafiche Manfrini Telex: 400581 Manfri I
Man Dir: Edoardo Manfrini
Parent Company: R Manfrini SpA Vallagarina Arti Grafiche (at above address)
Branch Off: Via Virgilio 6, I-39100 Bolzano
Subjects: Tourist Guides & Books, Natural Science, Art, Literature, History, other Non-fiction
Founded: 1919
ISBN Publisher's Prefix: 88-7024

Casa Editrice **Marietti** SpA (CEM)+, Via Adam 15, I-15033 Casale Monferrato Tel: (0142) 76311 Telex: 212458 Edicem I
Man Dir: Dr Paolo Francalacci
Subjects: Religion, Secondary & Primary Textbooks, History, Philosophy, Essays, Fiction
1981: 45 titles *1982:* 30 titles *Founded:* 1820
ISBN Publisher's Prefix: 88-211

Aldo **Marino** Editore, Piazza Trento 3/D, I-95128 Catania Tel: 447971
Subjects: Literature, Literary Criticism, Science
Bookshop: Libreria Scientifica di Aldo Marino (at above address)
1981: 4 titles *1982:* 6 titles *Founded:* 1977

Alberto **Marotta** Editore SpA*, Via Francesco Giordani 21, I-80122 Naples Tel: (081) 685144 (PBX)
Man Dir: Alberto Marotta; *Editorial:* Dott Giuseppe Maggi; *Sales:* Pasquale Marotta
Branch Offs: Via Monte di Pieta 1/A, I-20121 Milan; Via Nizza 45, I-00198 Rome
Subjects: General Fiction, Belles Lettres, Poetry, Biography, Music, Art, Social Science, Dictionaries, Encyclopaedias, History, Neapolitan Studies, Medicine, Science
Bookshops: Via dei Mille 78-80-82; Via Francesco Giordani 46; Via Giuseppe Verdi 46 (all in Naples)
Founded: 1959

Marsilio Editori SpA, Fondamenta S Chiara, S Croce 518a, I-30125 Venice Tel: (041) 707188/707641
Man Dir: Dr Paolo Lenarda
Subjects: General Fiction, Architecture, Social & Political Science, Economics, Psychology, Literature, Arts

Editore **Martano**, Via Cesare Battisti 3, I-10123 Turin Tel: (011) 531758
Chief Executive: Liliana Dematteis
Subjects: Art, Cinema, Architecture, Music
Founded: 1968

Giunti **Martello** Editore, see Giunti Publishing Group

Editrice Giunti **Marzocco**, see Giunti Publishing Group

Marzorati Editore SRL+, Via Piero Martinetti 6, I-20147 Milan Tel: (02) 405050/4074613
Man Dir: Antonio Marzorati; *Editorial:* Romain Raineiro; *Sales:* Carlo Marzorati; *Production:* Franco Faglioni; *Publicity:* Patrizia Fatigati; *Rights & Permissions:* Francesca Marzorati
Subjects: Literature, History, Philosophy
Founded: 1942

Editrice **Massimo**, Corso di Porta Romana 122, I-20122 Milan Tel: (02) 5454104
Man Dir: Dr Cesare Crespi
Subjects: General Fiction, Biography, History, Religion, Juveniles, Low- & High-priced Paperbacks, Psychology, General & Social Science, Secondary Textbooks, Philosophy
Bookshops: Via dei Pellegrini 1, I-20122 Milan; Agenzia Mescat, Corso di Porta Romana 122, I-20122 Milan
1981: 29 titles *1982:* 28 titles *Founded:* 1951
ISBN Publisher's Prefix: 88-7030

Mastrogiacomo Editore, Via delle Piazze 13, I-35100 Padua Tel: (049) 22707
Man Dir: Dr Gaetano Mastrogiacomo
Subsidiary Company: Galleria d'Arte Moderna 'Images 70' (at above address)
Subjects: Cinema, Arts, Politics and Current Events, Poetry, Magic, Historical Research, Cookery, Fiction, Customs
Founded: 1977

Franca **May** Edizioni SRL*, Via Giacinta Pezzana 50, I-00197 Rome Tel: (06) 805738
Man Dir: Franca Fratini Gatto
Subject: Art
Founded: 1974

Nuove Edizioni Gabriele **Mazzotta** SRL*, Foro Buonaparte 52, I-20121 Milan Tel: (02) 8055803/8690050
Man Dir: Gabriele Mazzotta; *Sales Dir:* Alberto Bini; *Publicity Dir:* Nadine Bortolotti; *Rights & Permissions:* Maura Pizzorno
Subjects: History, Architecture, Art, Low- & High-priced Paperbacks, Psychology, Social Science, Photography
Founded: 1966

Edizioni **Medicea** Srl*, Via Por Santa Maria 8, I-50122 Florence Tel: (055) 212058
Subjects: Architecture, Radio and Television, Government, Urban Studies, Science
Founded: 1975

Organizzazione Editoriale **Medico Farmaceutica** SRL, Via Edolo 42, CP 10434, I-20125 Milan Tel: (02) 600376/6884386 Telex: 323598 Oemfmi I
Dir: Lucio Marini
Subjects: Medicine, Pharmacy
Founded: 1940
ISBN Publisher's Prefix: 88-7076

Edizioni **Mediterranee** SRL, Via Flaminia 158, I-00196 Rome Tel: (06) 3601656
General Manager: Giovanni Canonico; *Editorial:* Romualdo D'Alessandro; *Sales:* Graziella Torre; *Publicity:* Gigliola Porzi; *Rights & Permissions:* Luigi Coppe
Subsidiary Company: Hermes Edizioni SRL (qv)
Subjects: ESP, Parapsychology, Occult, Magic, Yoga, Zen, Meditation, UFOs, Astrology, Alternative Medicine, Philosophy, Psychology, Art, Archaeology, Sport
Founded: 1953

Il **Melograno**, an imprint of Edizioni Abete (qv)

Edizioni **Memorie** Domenicane, Piazza San Domenico 1, I-51100 Pistoia Tel: 28158
Editorial: Eugenio Marino, Emilio Panella
Parent Company: Provincia Romana dei Frati Predicatori, Piazza della Minerva 42, I-00186 Rome
Subjects: History, Theology
1981: 12 titles *1982:* 13 titles *Founded:* 1884

Casa Editrice **Menna** di Sinisgalli Menna Giuseppina*, CP 26, I-83100 Avellino (Located at: Via Vasto 15/19, Avellino)
Chief Executive: Nunzio Menna
Subjects: Poetry, Fiction, Theatre, History, Children's, Law
Bookshop: At above address
Founded: 1976

Messaggero di San Antonio+, CP 1100-1103, I-35123 Padua (Located at: Via Orto Botanico 11, Padua) Tel: (049) 664322 Cable Add: Messaggero Padova Telex: 430855 Msa I
Chief Executive: P Luciano Marini; *Editorial:* P Giacomo Panteghini; *Sales, Production, Publicity, Rights & Permissions:* P Salvatore Ruzza
Subjects: Religion, History, Biography, Current Events, Children's
Bookshop: Libreria Messaggero, Piazza del Santo 17, I-35123 Padua
1981: 44 titles *1982:* 44 titles

Nicola **Milano** Editore, Via Marsili 9, I-40124 Bologna Tel: (051) 330483
Chief Executive: Mario Musso
Parent Company: Nicola Milano Editore, Corso Ferrero 5, I-12060 Farigliano (Cuneo)
Subsidiary Company: Milano Stampa, Corso Ferrero 5, I-12060 Farigliano (Cuneo)
Subjects: Textbooks for Children, Scholarly
1981: 42 titles *1982:* 44 titles *Founded:* 1969

Milano Libri*, Via A Rizzoli 2, I-20132 Milan Tel: (02) 650518/651597
Subjects: Fiction, Juveniles, Essays, Manuals

Antonio **Milella***, CP 160, I-73100 Lecce Tel: (0832) 28885/28142
Subjects: Literary Essays, History, Philosophy, Education
Bookshops: Libreria Milella, Via Palmieri 30, I-73100 Lecce; Viale Taranto 1, I-73100 Lecce
1981: 30 titles
ISBN Publisher's Prefix: 88-7048

Minerva Italica SpA, CP 216, I-24100 Bergamo (Located at: Via Maglio del Rame 6, Bergamo) Tel: (035) 237331/232688
Man Dir: Arnoldi Gianni
Branch Offs: Via Alfani 68, I-50121 Florence; Via S Sebastiano is 247a, I-98100 Messina; Via Petrella 6, I-20124 Milan; Via A Emo 162-168, I-00136 Rome; via Lattanzio 90-94, I-70126 Bari
Subjects: General Fiction, Juveniles, University, Secondary & Primary Textbooks, Educational Materials
Founded: 1951

Lorenzo **Misuraca** Editore, CP 30, I-90015 Cefalù (PA) (Located at: Via Porpora 3, Cefalù) Tel: (0921) 22166/21255
Chief Executive: Lorenzo Misuraca; *Editorial:* Marianna Vizzini
Subjects: History, Literature, Philosophy, Poetry, Gastronomy, Occult, Theatre, Music, Essays, Fiction, Local Interest
Bookshop: Libreria Lorenzo Misuraca Editore, Via Porpora 5, I-90015 Cefalù
1981: 5 titles *Founded:* 1972

Edizioni **Moderne** Sas*, CP 218, I-35100 Padua (Located at: Via Magnasco 1, I-35100 Padua) Tel: (049) 611981 Cable Add: Edmod Padua
Chief Executive, Sales: Vincenzo Amicucci; *Editorial:* Prof Argeo Baccarin, Biancofiore Baccarin; *Production, Rights & Permissions:* Sonia Amicucci; *Publicity:* Laura Amicucci
Branch Off: Editorial Office, Via Europa 4, I-35012 Camposampiero (PD)
Subjects: Scholarly, Law, Economics
Founded: 1979

Moizzi*, Via Fiori Chiari 12, I-20121 Milan Tel: (02) 886169/873453
Subjects: Anthropology, Feminism

Monas Hierogliphica Editrice, Via Borghetto 5, I-20122 Milan Telex: 331837 Exeoua I
Editorial: Nicolas Monti; *Publicity:* Carla Manenti
Subjects: Art, Photography, Architecture
Founded: 1978

G B **Monauni***, Via Manci 141, I-38100 Trento Tel: (0461) 21445 Cable Add: Libreria Monauni Trento
Chief Executive: Dr Giambattista Monauni
Subjects: Art, Archaeology, Ethnology, Folklore, Fiction, Science, History
Bookshop: Libreria G B Monauni (at above address)
Founded: 1725

Arnoldo **Mondadori** Editore, CP 1772, I-20100 Milan (Located at: Via Mondadori 1, I-20090 Segrate) Tel: (02) 75412 Cable Add: Mondadori Segrate (MI) Telex: 320457 Mondmi I
Chairman, Chief Executive: Mario Formenton; *Vice-President, Man Dir:* Sergio Polillo; *Man Dir:* Massimo Colombo; *Editor-in-Chief:* Marco Polillo; *Sales:* Giovanni Ungarelli; *Advertising:* Silvana Biasutti; *Publicity:* Carlo Sartori; *Rights & Permissions:* Donatella Ciapessoni; *Special Projects:* Leone Buonanno; *General Managers:* Leonardo Mondadori (Books); Franco Migiarra (Educational), Fabio Formenton (Children's), Enzo Angelucci (International Publishing), Gianpaolo Grandi (Direct Marketing)
Associate Companies: Harlequin Mondadori; Il Saggiatore (qv); Sperling e Kupfer (qv)
Branch Offs: Mondadori EPEE, Paris, France; Arnoldo Mondadori Deutschland GmbH, Munich, Federal Republic of Germany; Arnoldo Mondadori Scandinavia, Stockholm, Sweden; Arnoldo Mondadori Co Ltd, UK; AME Publishing Ltd, New York, USA
Subjects: General Fiction, Classics, Romance, Detective Stories, Poetry, Biography, History, How-to, Music, Art, Philosophy, Reference, Religion, Juveniles, Low- & High-priced Paperbacks, Medicine, Psychology, General Science, Secondary Textbooks, Educational Materials
Book Club: CDE (Club degli Editori) - Gruppo Mondadori
Bookshops: Branches throughout Italy
Founded: 1907

Edizioni Scolastiche Bruno **Mondadori**+, Via Archimede 23, I-20129 Milan Tel: (02) 5456076
Man Dirs: Roberta Mondadori, Roberto Gulli; *General Manager:* Mario Candiani
Subject: Textbooks
1981: 20 titles *1982:* 28 titles

Mondadori Ragazzi, Via Belvedere 2, I-37100 Verona Tel: 934539 Telex: 34457 Mondedit

Edizioni del **Mondo** Giudiziario*, Viale Angelico 90, I-00195 Rome Tel: (06) 351071
Man Dir: Augusto Brusca; *Editorial, Sales, Production, Publicity:* Anna Tabili Brusca
Subject: Law
Founded: 1946

Mondoperaio edizioni Avanti SpA*, Via Tomacelli 146, I-00186 Rome
Editorial: Settimio Cavalli
Subjects: Political and Social Science, Philosophy, History of Labour and the Trade Unions, Workers' Movements in Italy and World-Wide, Periodicals

Monduzzi Editore Srl, Via Zamboni 7, I-40126 Bologna Tel: (051) 228286/7
Chief Executive: Dr Gianni Monduzzi; *Sales, Production:* Benedetti Claudio
Subjects: Medicine, Chemistry, Physics, Biological Sciences
1981: 15 titles *Founded:* 1979

Editrice **Morcelliana** SpA, Via Gabriele Rosa 71, I-25100 Brescia Tel: (030) 46451
Man Dir: Stephano Minelli
Associate Company: Editrice La Scuola SpA (qv)
Subjects: History, Philosophy, Religion, Social Science
1982: 32 titles *Founded:* 1925

Istituto Grafologico Girolamo **Moretti**, Scale San Francesco 8, I-60121 Ancona Tel: (071) 201759
Chief Executive: P Lamberto Torbidoni; *Editorial:* Francesco Merletti; *Sales:* P Floriano Ubaldi
Branch Off: Piazza San Francesco 7, I-61029 Urbino (Pesaro) Tel: (0722) 2639
Subject: Graphology
1981: 3 titles *1982:* 4 titles *Founded:* 1958

Verlag **Morra***, Via Calabritto 20, I-80121 Naples Tel: 402025
Man Dir: Giuseppe Morra; *Sales:* Giuseppe Orabona
Subject: Art
Founded: 1974

Federico **Motta** Editore SRL+, Via Branda Castiglioni 7, I-20156 Milan Tel: (02) 390404/390909/367708
Chief Executive, Rights & Permissions: J Federico Motta; *Editorial:* Ugo Lolli; *Sales:* Sergio Fino; *Production:* Italo di Giancamillo
Subjects: Encyclopaedias, Dictionaries, Classics, Art, Science
1982: 15 titles *1983:* 15 titles *Founded:* 1929

Società Editrice Il **Mulino***, Via Santo Stefano 6, I-40125 Bologna Tel: (051) 233415/6
Man Dir: Giovanni Evangelisti; *Sales Dir:* Marcello Bolognini; *Publicity Dir:* Edmondo Berselli; *Rights & Permissions:* Luisa Pece
Subjects: History, Philosophy, Linguistics & Literary Criticism, Political Science, Law, Economics, Reference, Low-priced Paperbacks, Psychology, Social Science, University Textbooks, Journals
Founded: 1954

Multigrafica Editrice Srl, Viale dei Quattro Venti 52/A, I-00152 Rome Tel: (06) 5892839/5891496
Chief Executive: Mario Bonsignori
Subjects: Art History, Architecture, History, Archaeology, Folklore, Law
1981: 16 titles *Founded:* 1970

Ugo **Mursia** Editore SpA, CP 10328, I-20124 Milan (Located at: Via Tadino 29, I-20124 Milan) Tel: (02) 209341 Cable Add: Umedizioni Milan
Subsidiary Companies: Nautilus SRL; Edizioni APE SpA (qv)
Man Dir: Dr Giancarla Mursia; *Editorial:* Dr Silvio Mursia; *Publicity:* Floriana De Martino; *Sales:* Fiorenza Mursia; *Production:* Dario Maggi; *Rights & Permissions:* Dr Flavio Fagnani
Subjects: General Fiction, Belles Lettres, Poetry, Biography, History, Art, Philosophy, Reference, Religion, Juveniles, General & Social Science
1981: 110 titles *1982:* 105 titles *Founded:* 1922

Franco **Muzzio** & C Editore Sas, Via Bonporti 36, I-35100 Padua Tel: (049) 661147/661873
Chief Executive: Franco Muzzio; *Editorial:* Odette Infanti, Ms M Boscarol; *Sales:* L Bogana; *Production:* R Fardin; *Publicity, Rights & Permissions:* Stelle Longato Muzzio
Associate Companies: Centro Grafico Editoriale, Via Bonporti 32, I-35100 Padua; Completo Software (at main company address)
Subjects: Electronics, Computers and Computer Science, Alternative Sources of Energy, Natural Sciences, Music
1981: 40 titles *Founded:* 1973
ISBN Publisher's Prefix: 88-7021

Casa Editrice Roberto **Napoleone**+, Via Antonio Chinotto 16, I-00195 Rome Tel: (06) 3612691/3612693
Chief Executive: Roberto Napoleone
1981: 40 titles *1982:* 35 titles *Founded:* 1974

Società Editrice **Napoletana** SRL*, Corso Umberto I 34, I-80138 Naples Tel: (02) 206602
Man Dir: Avv A De Dominicis
Subjects: Belles Lettres, Poetry, History, Art
Bookshop: Libreria Scientifica Editrice (at above address)

Nardini Editore — Centro Internazionale del Libro SpA*, Via Scipione Ammirato 37, I-50136 Florence Tel: (055) 670330
Subjects: Juveniles, Philosophy, Biography, Art, Essays, Classics, Science, Educational, Economics, Medical
Founded: 1956
Miscellaneous: Part of Giunti Publishing Group (qv)

New Interlitho SpA*, Via Curiel, I-20090 Trezzano S/N Tel: 4451926/4452753 Telex: 311140
Dir & Sales Manager: Renzo Aimini
Subjects: Juveniles, Encyclopaedias

Newton Compton Editori SRL*, Via Germanico 197, I-00192 Rome Tel: 3580205/3580201
Subjects: Paperbacks on General Fiction, Belles Lettres, Poetry, History, Philosophy, Social & General Science, Anthropology, Mathematics, Psychology, Political Science, Reference, How-to, Archaeology

Umberto **Nicoli** Editore*, Via Mistrali 7, I-43100 Parma Tel: (0521) 35959 Cable Add: Nicoli Editore Parma Telex: 530259 Cciaa Pr I
Chief Executive: Umberto Nicoli
Parent Company: Casa Editrice Nicoli, Via A Frank 4, I-43100 Parma
Subsidiary Company: Pubblitalia (at above address)
Subjects: Fiction, Essays, History, Poetry, Sport, Periodicals
Founded: 1976

Editrice **Nord** Sdf, Via Rubens 25, I-20148 Milan Tel: (02) 405708/4042207
Man Dir: Gianfranco Viviani; *Editorial:* Sandro Pergameno
Subjects: Fantasy and Science Fiction
1982: approx 300 titles

Edizioni di **Novissima***, Viale Castrense 9, I-00182 Rome Tel: (06) 774901
Subjects: General Fiction, Belles Lettres, Paperbacks

La **Nuova Foglio** SpA*, Piane di Chienti 12, I-62010 Pollenza (MC) Tel: (0733) 517145 Cable Add: La Nuova Foglio Pollenza
Subject: Art

Nuova Guaraldi Editrice di Ideal Pra SRL*, Via Masaccio 268, I-50100 Florence Tel: (055) 573968/575345
Man Dir: Marcello Mazzoni; *Production:* Alberto Dragone
Subjects: Sociology, Pedagogy, Anthropology, Public Health
Founded: 1970

La **Nuova Italia** Editrice*, Via Antonio Giacomini 8, I-50132 Florence Tel: (055) 2798
Man Dirs: Mario Casalini, Federico Codignola, Mario Ermini, Sergio Piccioni
Branch Offs: Via Dieta di Bari 38/c, I-70121 Bari; Via Brugnoli 7, I-40122 Bologna; Via D Cimarosa 14, I-09100 Cagliari; Via Etnea 688, I-95128 Catania; Corso Italia 158/D, I-87100 Cosenza; Via G Fattori 7-9, I-50132 Florence; Corso Europa 454/A, I-16132 Genoa; Via E Noe 11, I-20133 Milan; Via G Carducci 15, I-80121 Naples; Via Altichieri da Zevio 5, I-35100 Padua; Via F Cordova 95, I-90143 Palermo; Via G Galilei 8, I-65100 Pescara; Viale Carso 44-46, I-00195 Rome; Via Colli 24 (angolo Corso Montevecchio), I-10129 Turin; Via Adigetto 39, I-37100 Verona
Subjects: Biography, History, Art, Philosophy, Reference, Young Adult, Low- & High-priced Paperbacks, Psychology, Social Science, University & Secondary Textbooks
Founded: 1926

Nuova Vallecchi Editore SpA*, Via Gino Capponi 26, CP 409, I-50121 Florence Tel: (055) 587141/2/3 Cable Add: Nuova Vallecchi Editore, Firenze
Man Dir: Lodovico Bevilacqua
Subjects: Art, Fiction, Classics
Founded: 1975

Gruppo Editoriale **Nuova Vita** SpA, now Gruppo Editoriale Le Stelle SpA (qv)

Nuovi Sentieri Editore, CP 100, I-32100 Belluno (Located at: Via Ripa 2, Belluno) Tel: (0437) 20170/50308
Man Dir: Bepi Pellegrinon; *Editorial:* Loris Santomaso; *Sales:* Antonio Zullo
Subjects: Local History, Arts, Poetry, Literature, Photography
Founded: 1971

O E M F, see Medico Farmaceutica

O S (Organizzazioni Speciali SRL)*, Via Scipione Ammirato 37, I-50136 Florence Tel: 672997/675446
Subjects: Psychology, Economics, Education
Miscellaneous: Member of Giunti Publishing Group

Officina Edizioni di Aldo Quinti, see Quinti

Edizioni **Ofiria**, see Giunti Publishing Group

Casa Editrice Leo S **Olschki**, CP 66, I-50100 Florence Tel: (055) 687444/5
Shipping Add: Viuzzo del Pozzetto (Viale Europa), I-50126 Florence
Man Dir: Alessandro Olschki
Subjects: Biography, History, Music, Art, Reference, Bibliography, Religion, Paperbacks, Medicine, Social Science, University Textbooks, General Humanities
1982: 98 titles *Founded:* 1886

Olympia Press Italia*, Corso Concordia 9, I-20129 Milan Tel: (02) 780164
Man Dir: Mario Carrillo
Subjects: General Fiction, General Science, Erotica

ITALY

Nuove Edizioni Operaie SRL*, Via Crescenzio 58, I-00193 Rome Tel: (06) 6545506
Man Dirs: Angelo Ruggieri; Pietro Brugnoli
Subjects: Politics, Sociology, Religion, Culture
Founded: 1976

Organizzazioni Speciali SRL, see O S

Edizioni Orientalia Christiana, Piazza Santa Maria Maggiore 7, I-00185 Rome Tel: (06) 7312254/55
General Dir: Stanislas Swierkosz-Lenart
Subjects: Eastern Christianity (History, Theology, Liturgy, Canon Law etc), Periodicals
Founded: 1923

Edizioni Ottaviano*, Via Lanino 5, I-20144 Milan Tel: (02) 4227268
Subjects: Politics, Law
Founded: 1974

P E A — Produzioni Editoriale Aprile, see Aprile

Paideia Editrice, Via Corsica 58m, I-25123 Brescia Tel: (030) 222094
Man Dir: Prof Dr Giuseppe Scarpat; *Editorial:* Dr Marco Scarpat
Subjects: Belles Lettres, Poetry, Music, Art, Philosophy, Religion, University Textbooks
1981: 35 titles *1982:* 35 titles

Palatina Editrice, Borgo Giacomo Tommasini 9/A, I-43100 Parma
Chief Executives: Isabella Marchesi, Maria Casalinuovo; *Editorial:* Guglielmo Capacchi, Giancarlo Zarattini
Subjects: Local Interest, Art, History, Folklore
Bookshop: Libreria Palatina Editrice (at above address)
Founded: 1965

Fratelli Palombi SRL*, Via dei Gracchi 181-85, I-00195 Rome Tel: (01) 350606/354960
Man Dir: Dr Mario Palombi
Subsidiary Company: (Sales) Organizzazione Rab, Via del Crocifisso 51, I-00165 Rome
Subjects: Mainly concerning Rome (history, art)

G B Palumbo e C Editore SpA, Via B Ricasoli 59, I-90139 Palermo Tel: (091) 588850/334961
Manager: Giovan Battista Palumbo

Pan Editrice*, Via Solferino 32, I-20121 Milan Tel: (02) 667849-54
Man Dir: Isa Donelli
Subjects: Novels, Current Events, History, Art, Fiction
Founded: 1966

Panda Press SRL*, Viale Vaticano 44, I-00165 Rome Tel: 3581085 Telex: 311140
Man Dir: Renzo Aimini; *Rights & Permissions:* Louise Kissane
Subject: Juveniles, Encyclopaedias
Founded: 1971

Edizioni Panini SpA+, Viale Emilio Po 380, I-41100 Modena Tel: (059) 331133 Cable Add: Edipan Modena Italia Telex: 510650
Publisher: Franco Panini
Subjects: Educational, Sport, Card albums for children

Edizioni Paoline, Corso Regina Margherita 1, CP 1333, I-10100 Turin Tel: (011) 836744/5/6 Cable Add: Edipaoline
Man Dir, Sales: Gino Pizzeghello; *Editorial:* Valentino Gambi; *Production:* Francesco Chessa; *Publicity:* Lamberto Schiatti
Parent Company: Società San Paolo
Associate Companies: Edizioni Paoline Dischi — Audiovision; SAIE Editrice (qv); San Paolo Periodici, Milan
Subjects: General Fiction, Belles Lettres, Biography, History, How-to, Music, Art, Philosophy, Reference, Religion, Juveniles, Low- & High-priced Paperbacks, Medicine, Psychology
Bookshops: 98 bookshops throughout Italy
1981: 265 titles *1982:* 269 titles *Founded:* 1914

Edizioni Parallelo 38+, Via 3 Settembre 7, I-89100 Reggio Calabria Tel: (0965) 330300
Subjects: Art, Archaeology, Law, Economics, Poetry, History, Politics, Philosophy, Literature, Religion, Theatre, Fiction, Education, Psychology, Local Interest
1983: 215 titles *Founded:* 1970

Casa Editrice Pàtron SAS*, Quarto Inferiore, Via Badini 12-14, I-40127 Bologna Tel: 767003
Executive Dir: Bruno Pasquetto; *Production Dir:* Massimo Manzoni
Subjects: Literature, Linguistics, History, Philosophy, Psychology, Sociology, Art, Medicine, Engineering
Bookshops: Libreria Editrice Universitaria Pàtron, Via Marzolo 28, I-35100 Padua; Libreria Internazionale Pàtron, Via Zamboni 24, I-40126 Bologna

Luigi Pellegrini Editore+, CP 158, I-87100 Cosenza (Located at: Via Roma 80/b, Cosenza) Tel: (0984) 21472/25245/25066 Cable Add: Pellegrini Editore Cosenza
Chief Executive, Rights & Permissions: Luigi Pellegrini; *Editorial, Sales:* Walter Pellegrini; *Publicity:* Luciano Rossi
Subjects: History, Fiction, Essays, Poetry, Theatre
1981: 98 titles *1982:* 142 titles *Founded:* 1952

Il Pensiero Scientifico Società ARL*, Via Panama 48, I-00198 Rome Tel: 863633/859506
President: Annamaria De Feo; *General Manager:* Francesco De Fiore; *Publicity Manager:* Antonietta Bove; *Promotion Manager:* Luca De Fiore
Subject: Medicine

Pergamena Sas di G Giraldi*, Viale Ezio 7, I-20149 Milan Tel: (02) 495818
Chief Executive: Prof Giovanni Giraldi; *Sales:* Dr Giancarlo Giraldi
Subjects: Philosophy, Religion, Politics, Philology, Poetry
Founded: 1974

Piccin Editore sas*, Via Altinate 107, I-35100 Padua Tel: (049) 655566
Man Dir, Editorial, Production, Rights & Permissions: Dr Massimo Piccin; *Sales:* Dr Raffaello Steccanella
Subjects: Medicine, Chemistry, General Science
Bookshops: Via Festa del Perdono 14, Milan; Via Porciglia 10, Padua; Via Lancisi 37, Rome
Founded: 1954
ISBN Publisher's Prefix: 88-212

Editrice Piccoli SpA*, Via Rosellini 12, I-20124 Milan Tel: (02) 606341 Cable Add: Lapiccoli Milano
Man Dir, Editorial: Oliviero Dolci; *Sales:* Giuliano Barisone
Subject: Children's Books
1982: 69 titles *Founded:* 1943

La Pietra*, Via Fulvio Testi 75, I-20126 Milan Tel: (02) 6428440
Man Dir: Enzo Nizza
Subjects: Politics, Anti-Fascism and Resistance, History, Art
1981: 20 titles *1982:* 15 titles *Founded:* 1962

La Pilotta Editrice Coop RL*, Via Garibaldi 21, I-43100 Parma Tel: (0521) 206904
President: Dr Gian Paolo Anghinetti; *Editorial:* Prof Antonio Martinelli
Subjects: Poetry, Fiction, Essays
Founded: 1978

Pitagora Editrice*, Via del Legatore 3, I-40138 Bologna Tel: (051) 530003
Chief Executive: Franco Stignani; *Editorial:* Mauro Bovini; *Sales:* Adolfo Francuoni; *Publicity:* Angela Fabbri
Associate Company: Teconoprint Snc (at above address)
Subjects: Technology, Engineering, Mathematics, Geology, Linguistics
Bookshops: Via Saragozza 112, Bologna; Via Zamboni 57, I-40126 Bologna
Founded: 1958

Amilcare Pizzi SpA*, Via M de Vizzi 86, I-20092 Cinisello Balsamo Tel: (02) 6188821 Telex: 330006
Chairman: Rodolfo Pizzi; *Man Dir:* Fulvio G Nembrini; *Sales:* Adriano Gatti, Massimo Pizzi
Subsidiary Company: Silvana Editoriale SRL (qv)
Subjects: Art, Illustrated Books, Encyclopaedias, Paperbacks, Calendars, Catalogues
Founded: 1920

Studio Bibliografico Adelmo Polla, Via Prato 2, I-67044 Cerchio (Aq) Tel: (0863) 78522
Man Dir: Adelmo Polla; *Editorial:* Maria G Romanelli
Subjects: Literature, History (General & Local), Philology, Archaeology
1981: 21 titles *1982:* 23 titles *Founded:* 1974

Casa Editrice Neri Pozza, CP 513, I-36100 Vicenza (Located at: Via Gazzolle 6, I-36100 Vicenza) Tel: (0444) 27228/36585 Cable Add: Edipozza
Man Dir: Neri Pozza
Subjects: Ancient and Modern Art, Literary Criticism and History, Politics, Local Interest
Founded: 1946

Edizioni Luigi Pozzi Srl+, Via Panama 68, I-00198 Rome Tel: (06) 863548
Chief Executive: Luigi Pozzi; *Editorial:* Maurizio Pozzi
Subject: Medicine
1982: 10 titles *1983:* 27 titles *Founded:* 1893
ISBN Publisher's Prefix: 88-7025

Pratiche Editrice Scrl+, Via Ponchielli 4A, I-43100 Parma Tel: (0521) 25648
Chief Executive, Sales: Oreste Bergamaschi; *Editorial, Production:* Mario Lavagetto; *Publicity:* Enrico Chierici; *Rights & Permissions:* Susanna Boschi
Subjects: Literary Criticism, Linguistics, Psychoanalysis, Philosophy, Economics, Politics, Cinema
Founded: 1977

Priuli e Verlucca, Editori, Via Dora Baltea 12, I-10015 Ivrea Tel: (0125) 48364 Cable Add: Priuli Verlucca Ivrea Telex: 210619 Univra I (049 Priver)
Chairman: Cesare Verlucca; *Production Dir:* Gherardo Priuli
Subjects: Life and Traditions of the Alpine Region, Nature, Photographic Studies of Regional Costume and Culture, Graphic Arts
Founded: 1971

Lucio Pugliese Editore+, Via L Federico Menabrea 3/C, I-50136 Florence Tel: (055) 6902005
Subjects: Encyclopaedias, Literature, History, Children's
1981: 2 titles *1982:* 1 title *Founded:* 1968

Edizioni Il **Pungolo** Verde di G Massarelli*, CP 54, I-86100 Campobasso (Located at: Via A Depretis 18, Campobasso) Tel: (0874) 91018 Cable Add: Pungoloverde Campobasso
Chief Executive: Guido Massarelli; *Editorial:* Dr Gino Parente
Subjects: Poetry, Fiction, Art
Founded: 1947

Quadragono, Borgo Lozzo 5, I-31020 S Pietrodi Feletto (TV) Tel: (0438) 784011
Man Dir: Mario Vigiak
Subjects: Illustrated books for children and adults
Founded: 1974

Edizioni **Quasar**, Via IV Novembre 152, I-00187 Rome Tel: (06) 6789888
Subjects: Archaeology, Art, Photography
Founded: 1972
ISBN Publisher's Prefix: 88-85020

Editrice **Queriniana**, Via Piamarta 6, I-25100 Brescia Tel: (030) 294653
Man Dir: Gianfranco Ransenigo; *Sales:* Ettore Pelati; *Advertising:* Mario de Risio; *Rights & Permissions:* Rosino Gibellini
Branch Offs: Rome, Milan
Subjects: Philosophy, Religion, Theology
Founded: 1965

Officina Edizioni di Aldo **Quinti**, Via Passeggiata di Ripetta 25, I-00186 Rome Tel: (06) 6795349/5313460
Chief Executive: Aldo Quinti; *Publicity:* Jolanda Ridolfi
Subjects: Architecture, Urban Studies, Art, Sociology, Ethnology, Linguistics, Theatre, Cinema
Founded: 1964

Edizioni **R A I** Radiotelevisione Italiana (ERI) SpA, see ERI

Red/Studio Redazionale SRL+, Via Volta 43, I-22100 Como Tel: (031) 279146
Chief Executive: Maurizio Rosenberg Colorni; *Editorial:* Maurizio Rosenberg Colorni
Subjects: Alternative Medicine, Ecology, Soft Technologies, Natural Agriculture, Organic Nutrition, New Psychotherapies, Early Childhood
1981: 6 titles *1982:* 22 titles *Founded:* 1978
ISBN Publisher's Prefix: 88-7031

Franco Maria **Ricci** Editore, Via Cino Del Duca 4/8, I-20122 Milan Tel: (02) 798444/793117 Telex: 313514 Fmri
Man Dir: Franco Maria Ricci
Associate Companies: Leon Atayan, 6869 West Grand River Ave, Lansing, MI 48906, USA; Galerie 12, 12 rue des Beaux Arts, Paris 6, France
Subsidiary Company: Deco Press; Franco Maria Ricci, France (qv)
Subjects: Art, Graphic Design, Reference, Periodicals, Limited editions, including Bodoni editions and *Encyclopédie* of Diderot & D'Alembert
Bookshop: Franco Maria Ricci, 12 rue des Beaux-Arts, Paris 6, France
Book Clubs: Club dei Bibliofili; Collectors Club of Franco Maria Ricci
1981: 115 titles *1982:* 248 titles *Founded:* 1965

Riccardo **Ricciardi** Editore SpA, Via G Morone 3, I-20121 Milan Tel: (02) 875155/804248
Man Dir: Dr Maurizio Mattioli
Subjects: Italian Classics, History, Philology
1981: 5 titles *1982:* 2 titles

Edizioni del **Riccio** Sas di G Bernardi+, Via Ugo Foscolo 41, I-50124 Florence Tel: (055) 2298420
Chief Executive: Giuliano Bernardi
Subjects: Cookery, Linguistics, Psychoanalysis, Alternative Medicine
1981: 7 titles *1982:* 5 titles *Founded:* 1977

G e C **Ricordi** SpA*, Via Berchet 2, I-20121 Milan Tel: (02) 8881 Telex: 310177 Ricor I
President: N H Carlo Origoni; *Vice-President:* Eugenio Clausetti; *Man Dir:* Dr Guido Rignano
Subjects: Scholarly, Music, Art
Subsidiary Companies: Ricordi Dischi SpA (at above address); Arti Grafiche Ricordi SpA, Via Cortina d'Ampezzo 10, I-20139 Milan; Gruppo Editoriale Musica Leggera Ricordi (at above address)

Editori **Riuniti***, Via Serchio 9-11, I-00198 Rome Tel: (06) 866383
Man Dir: Roberto Bonchio; *Sales Dir, Publicity:* Giuseppe Paschetto; *Press Dir:* Giovanna Carlo; *Rights & Permissions:* Regina Stucchi
Subjects: General Fiction, Textbooks, Reference, Paperbacks, History, Art, General & Social Science, Politics, Religion, Juveniles
Founded: 1953

Rizzoli Editore SpA, Via Rizzoli 2, I-20132 Milan Tel: (02) 2588 Cable Add: Rizzoli Editore, Milan Telex: Rizzoli 312119
Chairman: Carlo Scognamiglio; *Man Dirs:* Giancarlo Mondavì, Michele Norsa; *Editorial:* Michele Norsa, Dr Sergio Pautasso; *Marketing:* Renato Mariano; *Rights & Permissions:* Vera Salvago
Associate Companies: G C Sansoni Editore Nuova SpA (qv), Milano Libri (qv)
Subsidiary Company: Sansoni SpA, Rizzoli International Publications, New York, NY, USA
Subjects: General Fiction, Belles Lettres, Poetry, Biography, History, Music, Hobbies, Medicine, Art, Religion, Juveniles, Low- & High-priced Paperbacks, Illustrated, Economics, Social Science, Reference, Textbooks
Bookshops: Libreria Rizzoli (qv under Major Booksellers)
1981: 292 titles *1982:* 275 titles *Founded:* 1909
Miscellaneous: Also Literary Agent (qv)

Libreria Editrice **Rogate**+, Via dei Rogazionisti 8, I-00182 Rome Tel: (06) 776430/7576115 Cable Add: Rogate Rogazionisti Rome
Editorial: Vito Magno; *Publicity:* Nunzio Spinelli
Subjects: Religion, Theology
1982: 150 titles *1983:* 180 titles *Founded:* 1976

Dott Prof Tommaso **Romano**, see Edizioni Thule

Rosenberg e Sellier Editori in Torino, Via Andrea Doria 14, I-10123 Turin Tel: (011) 532150 Cable Add: Rosenberg Sellier
Man Dir: Ugo Gianni Rosenberg; *Editorial, Rights & Permissions:* Katie Roggero, Cristina Savio; *Production, Publicity:* Katie Roggero
Subjects: Philology, Social Sciences, Philosophy, Literature
Bookshop: Rosenberg e Sellier SRL (qv under Major Booksellers)
Founded: 1883
Miscellaneous: Firm is International import-export bookseller and subscription agent

Rusconi Libri, Via Livraghi 1/B, I-20126 Milan Tel: (02) 2574141 Cable Add: Rusconi Editore Milan Telex: 312233
Publisher: Edilio Rusconi; *General Manager:* Ugo Braga; *Editorial:* Ferruccio Viviani (General Non-fiction), Roberto Giardina (Fiction), Paolo Buffa (Art and Illustrated); *Publicity:* Giuseppe Pederiali
Orders to: Eurolibri, Via Michelino 93, I-40127 Bologna; Bookservice, Via Casale Lumbroso 75, I-00166 Rome
Branch Off: Via Leonida Bissolati 76, I-00100 Rome
Subjects: General Fiction and Non-fiction, Belles Lettres, Poetry, History, Philosophy, Religion, Illustrated and Art, Science
Bookshops: Libreria Internazionale Rusconi, Via Vitruvio 43, I-20124 Milan
Founded: 1957

S A G E P*, Piazza Merani 1, I-16145 Genoa Tel: (010) 313453 Telex: 211343 SAGEP I
Publisher: Eugenio de Andreis; *Sales Manager:* Carla Bisacchi
Subjects: Architecture, Art, Economy, Ethnography, History, Natural Sciences, Travel and Tourism
Founded: 1965

S A I E Editrice*, Corso Regina Margherita 2, I-10153 Turin Tel: (011) 870887
Associate Company: Edizioni Paoline (qv)
Subjects: Reference, Encyclopaedias, Dictionaries, Literature Criticism, Multimedia, Philosophy, Linguistics, Languages, Economics, Religion, Medicine, History, Earth Sciences, Philosophy, Education, Art, Juveniles

S C O D E, Via Ampère 28/a, I-20131 Milan Tel: (02) 2360244/5 Cable Add: Scode Milano
President: Carlo Gandini
Subjects: Architecture, History, Hobbies, Arts, Maps, Literary Criticism, Religion, Encyclopaedias, Linguistics, Educational

S E I (Società Editrice Internazionale), Corso Regina Margherita 176, I-10152 Turin Tel: (011) 5211441/5 Cable Add: SEI Turin Telex: 221114 Csind I 114 Sei
Man Dir: Gian Nicola Pivano; *Editorial:* Francesco Meotto; *Sales:* Paolo Bottazzi; *Production:* Enrico Paolucci Delle Roncole
Branch Offs: Bari, Bologna, Cagliari, Florence, Genoa, Milan, Naples, Palermo, Padua, Rome, Turin, Pescara, Catania
Subjects: General Fiction, Belles Lettres, Biography, History, Art, Philosophy, Religion, Juveniles, Psychology, General & Social Science, Educational Materials, Textbooks, Paperbacks, Language Laboratories
1981: 63 titles *1982:* 55 titles *Founded:* 1908

S I A D Edizioni SRL+, Viale Cà Granda 2, I-20162 Milan Tel: (02) 6438768
Chief Executive: Dr Giovanni Armenia; *Rights & Permissions:* Patrizia Michellini
Associate Company: Armenia Editore Srl (qv)
Subjects: Paranormal, Astrology, Alternative Medicine
1981: 10 titles *1982:* 20 titles *Founded:* 1970

S I S A R Edizioni (Società italiana stampati affini reclame) SpA*, Via Marco d'Agrate 35, I-20139 Milan Tel: (02) 5393846/5397441/2
Man Dir: Occhipinti Mazio
Subjects: Art, Architecture
Founded: 1953

S T E M-Mucchi (Società Tipografica Editrice Modenese)*, Via Tabboni 4, I-41100 Modena Tel: (059) 222162/214152
Subjects: History, Philosophy, Science, Technical, Textbooks, Hobbies, Literature, Education, Law, Languages

Saar SRL*, Viale di Porta Vercellina 14, I-20123 Milan Tel: (02) 4696251 Cable Add: Saar Milan
Man Dir: Walter Gurtler; *Sales:* Sergio Balloni
Subject: Juveniles

Casa Editrice Liguria di Norberto **Sabatelli**, CP 181, I-17100 Savona (Located at: Via dei De Mari 4r, Savona) Tel: (019) 20917
Chief Executive: Norberto Sabatelli
Subjects: Fiction, Criticism, Theatre, Poetry, History, Art, Essays, Tourism, Gastronomy, Technical
1981: 18 titles *1982:* 15 titles *Founded:* 1934

Il **Saggiatore** SpA, Via San Senatore 10, I-20122 Milan Tel: (02) 875119/875892
President, Man Dir: Maria Laura Boselli; *Rights & Permissions:* Renata Castellina
Associate Company: Arnoldo Mondadori Editore (qv)
Subjects: History, Philosophy, Economics, Architecture, Mathematics, Social Sciences, Geography, Linguistics, Art, Music, Belles Lettres
Founded: 1958

La **Salamandra**, Via Fabio Filzi 27, I-20124 Milan Tel: (02) 667097
Man Dir, Editorial, all other offices: Giovanni Barbatiello
Subjects: Feminism, Critiques of society, Libertarian thought, Critical Marxism, Sexual freedom, Psychoanalysis, Biography, Autobiography
Founded: 1975

Salamon e Agustoni Editori, Via Montenapoleone 3, I-20121 Milan Tel: (02) 700832
Man Dir: H Salamon
Subject: Art, *Il Conoscitore di stampe — Print Collector*
Founded: 1970

Adriano **Salani** SpA*, Via Cittadella 7, I-50144 Florence Tel: (055) 472968/9 Cable Add: Salani Editore Florence
Man Dir: Mauro Finardi
Subjects: Art, Classics, History, Juveniles, Fiction
Founded: 1862

Salerno Editrice SRL+, Via di Donna Olimpia 186, I-00152 Rome Tel: (06) 5315688
Chief Executive: Prof Enrico Malato
Subjects: Literature, Essays, Fiction, Music, Biography, Sociology, Classics, Criticism
Founded: 1972
ISBN Publisher's Prefix: 88-85026

G C **Sansoni** Editore Nuova SpA*, Via Benedetto Varchi 47, I-50132 Florence Tel: (055) 243334/243641 Cable Add: Sansedi Telex: 57466 Sansint
Man Dir, General Manager: Vittorio Cosimini
Associate Company: Rizzoli Editore SpA (qv)
Subsidiary Companies: Licosa-Libreria Commissionaria Sansoni SpA, Via Lamarmora 45, I-50121 Florence; Industria Grafica L'Impronta SpA, Via di Scandicci Alto 28, I-50018 Scandicci (Florence)
Subjects: Belles Lettres, Poetry, Biography, History, How-to, Music, Art, Philosophy, Reference, Religion, Low- & High-priced Paperbacks, Medicine, Psychology, General & Social Science, Secondary & Primary Textbooks, Educational Materials, Juveniles, Law
Founded: 1873
Miscellaneous: Coproduction with Sansoni International

Fausto **Sardini** Editrice, Via Pace 37, I-25040 Bornato in Franciacorta (Brescia) Tel: (030) 725123 Cable Add: Fausto Sardini-Editore-Bornato
Chief Executive: Fausto Sardini; *Editorial:* Meris Apolone
Subjects: History, Art, Religion, Science, Poetry, Fiction, Local Interest
Bookshop: At above address
1981: 10 titles *Founded:* 1969

Scala Istituto Fotografico Editoriale*, Via Chiantigiana 56, I-50011 Antella-Florence Tel: (055) 641541 Cable Add: Scalafoto Telex: Scalapub 58428
Subjects: Textbooks, Multimedia, Illustrated Art Books, Photography, Audio-Visual Aids

Salvatore **Sciascia**, Corso Umberto 111, I-93100 Caltanissetta Tel: 21946 Cable Add: Sciascia Editore
Man Dir: Salvatore Sciascia
Subjects: History, Arts, Literature, Essays, Poetry, Literary Studies, Periodical *Galleria*
Bookshops: Corso Umberto 111, Caltanissetta; Via Liberta 96, Caltanissetta
Founded: 1946

Libreria **Scientifica Cortina**, Corso Marconi 34/A, I-10125 Turin Tel: (011) 6507074/6508665
Chief Executive: Walter Barp
Parent Company: Edizioni Libreria Cortina Torino (at above address)
Associate Companies: Edizioni Libreria Cortina Milan, Largo Richini 1, I-20100 Milan; Edizioni Libreria Cortina Padua, Via Marzolo 2, I-35100 Padua; Edizioni Libreria Cortina Verona (qv)
Subjects: University, School and Professional Textbooks on Medicine, Pharmacy, Veterinary Science, Nursing
Bookshop: At above address
1981: 12 titles *1982:* 8 titles

Edizioni **Scientifiche Italiane***, Via Chiatamone 7, I-80121 Naples Tel: (081) 393346/391921/230021
Subjects: General & Social Science, Architecture, History, Arts, Maps, Agriculture, Literature, Medicine, Music, Philosophy, Law, Religion, Languages
Bookshop: Corso Umberto 1, I-80138 Naples Tel: (081) 206247

Editrice La **Scuola** SpA+, Via Cadorna 11, Brescia Tel: (030) 47461 Cable Add: Scuola Brescia Telex: 300836 Scuola Brescia
President: Dr Ing Paolo Peroni; *Man Dir:* Dr Ing Adolfo Lombardi; *General Manager:* Dr Prof Giusto Marchese
Associate Companies: E Co S Didattica SpA, I-10799 Rome, Italy; Editrice Morcelliana SpA (qv); Studium (Edizioni Studium Vita Nova SpA) (qv)
Branch Offs: Bari, Bologna, Milan, Naples, Rome
Subjects: Philosophy, Religion, Juveniles, Psychology, Secondary & Primary Textbooks, Educational Materials
1981: 140 titles *1982:* 150 titles *Founded:* 1904
ISBN Publisher's Prefix: 88-350

Scuola Vita, an imprint of Gruppo Editoriale Le Stelle SpA (qv)

Sellerio Editore*, Via Siracusa 50, I-90141 Palermo Tel: (091) 250390/250587
Subjects: Literature, Popular Art, Anthropology, Archaeology, History, Photography, Semiotics, Sociology
Founded: 1969

Angelo **Signorelli** Editore, Via Paola Falconieri 84, I-00152 Rome Tel: (06) 539954/533827 Cable Add: Signorelli Editore Roma
Chief Executive: Oliviero Alpa; *Editorial:* Giorgia Signorelli, Gilberta Alpa
Subjects: Textbooks and Educational Materials
1981: 12 titles *1982:* 10 titles *Founded:* 1912

Silvana Editoriale Srl, Via M de Vizzi 86, I-20092 Cinisello Balsamo, Milan Tel: (02) 6172464
Chairman: Massimo Pizzi; *Foreign Rights:* Fulvio G Nembrini
Parent Company: Amilcare Pizzi SpA (qv)
Subjects: Art, Facsimile books, Photographs, Architecture, Illustrated books

Libraria Editoriale **Sodalitas** Sas*, Centro Internazionale Studi Rosminiani, Corso Umberto 15, I-28049 Stresa Tel: (0323) 31623/30091
Subjects: Philosophy, Theology

Sonzogno, Via Mecenate 91, I-20138 Milan Tel: (02) 50951 Cable Add: Librifabbri Milan Telex: 311321 Fabbri I
Dir: Mario Andreose; *Rights & Permissions:* Rosaria Carpinelli
Subjects: Adventure, Romance, Mystery, General Non-fiction
Miscellaneous: Member of Gruppo Editoriale Fabbri, Bompiani, Sonzogno, Etas SpA

La **Sorgente** Srl, Via Garofalo 44, I-20133 Milan Tel: (02) 230025/230720
Man Dir, Rights & Permissions: Dr Giorgio Vignati
Subject: Juveniles
Founded: 1936

So-Wen Srl*, Viale Regina Giovanna 24, I-20129 Milan Tel: (02) 202363/2046614
Chief Executive: Dr C Jack Brusini
Subjects: Acupuncture, Traditional Chinese Medicine, Homoeopathy
Founded: 1975

Sperling e Kupfer Editori SpA, Via Monte di Pietà 24, I-20121 Milan Tel: 876614 Cable Add: Kupferedit, Milan
General Manager: Tiziano M Barbieri; *Subsidiary Rights:* Ornella Robbiati; *Rights & Permissions:* Marica Fioroni
Associate Company: Arnoldo Mondadori Editore (qv)
Subjects: General Fiction & Non-fiction, Biography, Health, Travel, Sports, How-to
Founded: 1889

Spirali Edizioni*, Victor Hugo 1, I-20123 Milan Tel: (02) 871546/878574
Man Dir: Cristina Frua De Angeli; *Editorial:* Annalisa Scallo
Subjects: Psychoanalysis, Art, Law, Philosophy, Literature, Music, Poetry
1981: 29 titles *Founded:* 1978

Gruppo Editoriale Le **Stelle** SpA, Via G Vasari 15, I-20135 Milan Tel: (02) 5455641
Imprints: Edizioni Dimensione Umana, Linea Verde, Scuola Vita
Subjects: Fiction, Science, History, Geography, Religion, Music, Primary & Secondary Textbooks, Educational Materials, Pedagogy, Didactics, Picture Books

Edizioni di **Storia** e Letteratura*, Via Lancellotti 18, I-00186 Rome Tel: (06) 6540556
Chief Executive: Maddalena de Luca
Subjects: Scholarly, History, Philosophy, Economics, Politics, Social Studies, Literature
Founded: 1943

Studi Contemporanei, an imprint of Edizioni Abete (qv)

Studium (Edizioni Studium Vita Nova SpA)+, Via Crescenzio 63, I-00193 Rome Tel: (06) 6565846/655456 Cable Add: Studium Rome
Associate Company: Editrice La Scuola SpA (qv)
Subjects: Literature, History, Philosophy, Religion, General & Social Science, University Textbooks, Periodical—*Studium*
Founded: 1927
ISBN Publisher's Prefix: 88-382

Sugarco Edizioni SRL, Viale Tunisia 41, I-20124 Milan Tel: (02) 652192/6570569
Man Dir: Dr Massimo Pini; *Editorial:* Donatella Cerutti; *Sales:* Vincenzo Nagari; *Production:* Gianni Bagetto

Subjects: General Fiction, Belles Lettres, Biography, History, Philosophy, Guides
Founded: 1956

Tamburini Editore SpA*, Via Pascoli 55, I-20133 Milan Tel: (02) 292320/296662/235740 Cable Add: Tambeditor Milan
Man Dir: Gianni Tamburini; *Sales Dir:* Laura Piatti; *Publicity & Advertising, Rights & Permissions:* Sergio Guida
Subjects: Medicine, Psychology, Engineering, General Science, University & Secondary Textbooks
Bookshop: Via Pascole 55, I-20133 Milan
Founded: 1868

Edizioni del **Teresianum**, Piazza San Pancrazio 5/A, I-00152 Rome Tel: (06) 582362/5810140
Chief Executive: Ildefonso Moriones; *Sales, Publicity:* Makoto Wada
Parent Company: Edizioni dei Padri Carmelitani Scalzi, Corso d'Italia 38, I-00198 Rome
Subjects: Theology, Bibliography
1981: 6 titles *1982:* 12 titles *Founded:* 1966

Nicola **Teti** e C Editore SRL*, Via Enrico Nöe 23, I-20133 Milan Tel: (02) 2043597/2043539
Man Dir: Nicola Teti; *Editorial:* Piero Lavatelli; *Sales:* Vincenzo Fracchiolla; *Production:* Rita Vaccari, Vanna Guzzi; *Publicity:* Nino Oppo; *Rights & Permissions:* Rita Vaccari
Subjects: Textbooks, Encyclopaedias, Politics, Marxism, Social Science, Juveniles, Reprints of Socialist documents, Natural History, History, Pedagogy
Founded: 1971

Dott Prof Tommaso Romano — Edizioni **Thule**+, Via Ammiraglio Gravina 95, I-90139 Palermo Tel: (091) 323699
Chief Executive: Dr Tommaso Romano; *Publicity:* Studio Grafico FM-Arch Dely Anania; *Rights & Permissions:* Ignazio Romano
Subjects: Philosophy, Education, History, Theology, Fiction, Poetry, Sociology, Sport, Tourism, Criticism
Book Club: Edi Thule Club
1981: 30 titles *Founded:* 1971

Tilgher-Genova SAS*, Via Assarotti 52, I-16122 Genoa Tel: 870653/891140
Chief Executive: Lucio Bozzi
Subjects: Literary Criticism, Philosophy, Humanities
Founded: 1971

Todariana Editrice, Via Lazzaro Papi 15, I-20135 Milan Tel: (02) 5460353
Chief Executive, Editorial: Teodoro Giuttari
Subjects: Fiction, Poetry, Essays, Psychology, Sociology, Travel, Fantasy and Science Fiction, Dialect Studies
1981: 12 titles *Founded:* 1967
ISBN Publisher's Prefix: 88-7015

Edizioni della **Torre***, Via Toscana 70, I-09100 Cagliari Tel: (070) 490716/485770
Cable Add: Edizioni della Torre Cagliari
Chief Executive: Salvatore Fozzi
Subsidiary Company: Agenzia Libraria Fozzi, Via Toscana 72, I-09100 Cagliari
Subjects: History, Sociology, Literature, Linguistics, Local Interest
Founded: 1974

Trec Edizioni Pregiate*, Via Cassia Antica 132, I-00191 Rome Tel: 3288361
Sole Administrator: Antonino Pecora
Subjects: Old Artistic Treasures, Graphics, Reproduction of Antique Manuscripts, Illuminated Miniatures
Founded: 1971

Casa Editrice Luigi **Trevisini**, Via Tito Livio 10, I-20137 Milan Tel: (02) 5450704/5452647 Cable Add: Trevisini Milano
Chief Executive: Luigi Trevisini; *Editorial:* Dr Giusi Trevisini
Subject: School Textbooks
Founded: 1849

Edizioni Il **Tripode** SRL, Viale Gramsci 12, I-80122 Naples Tel: (081) 683086
Man Dir: Dr Giuseppe Martano

U T E T (Unione Tipografico-Editrice Torinese), Corso Raffaello 28, CP 1166 Ferrovia, I-10125 Turin Tel: (011) 6502184 Cable Add: UTET Turin
President: Dr Gianni Merlini
Subjects: Belles Lettres, History, Art, Architecture, Music, Religion, Philosophy, Reference, Psychology, Law, Veterinary Science, General & Social Science, Juveniles, University Textbooks
Founded: 1795

Umbria Editrice, I-06070 San Mariano (PG) Tel: (075) 798020
Chief Executive: Antonio Carlo Ponti
Subjects: Poetry, Fiction, Art, Essays
1981: 5 titles *Founded:* 1971

Edizioni **Unicopli** Scrl, Via Ruggero Bonghi 4, I-20141 Milan Tel: (02) 8466502
Chief Executive, Editorial, Production, Rights & Permissions: Angelo Guerini; *Sales, Publicity:* Gino La Rosa
Subjects: University Textbooks
1981: 60 titles *1982:* 80 titles *Founded:* 1980
ISBN Publisher's Prefix: 88-7061

Unites SRL, Annuario Politecnico Italiano*, Via Silvio Pellico 12, I-20121 Milan Tel: (02) 874566/874658 Telex: 334647 Techs I
Publicity: Gianola Carlo
Subjects: Year-books, Reference

Editrice **Universitaria**, see Giunti Publishing Group

Società Editrice **Universo***, Via G Battista Morgagni 1, I-00161 Rome Tel: (06) 859063/8445243
Subjects: Medicine, Physics, Chemistry, Engineering, Mathematics

Editrice **Uomini** Nuovi, I-21030 Marchirolo (Varese) Tel: (0332) 723007/723363
Chief Executive, Editorial: Giuseppe E Laiso; *Sales:* Ruth Laiso; *Publicity:* Anna Rossinelli; *Rights & Permissions:* Giuseppe Piccolo
Subjects: Christian Inspiration, the Church, Stories for Infants and Children
1981: 18 titles *Founded:* 1964

Vallardi Industrie Grafiche+, Via Trieste 20, I-20020 Lainate (Milan) Tel: (02) 9370284/5 Cable Add: Valgraf, Lainate Telex: 314523 Vallig I
Publisher: Giuseppe Vallardi; *Dir:* Victor Hayon; *Editorial:* Elisabetta Vallardi, Emanuela Vallardi
Subjects: Atlases, Juveniles

Società Editrice **Vannini**, Viale d'Italia 8b, CP 68, I-25100 Brescia Tel: (030) 56272/57089 Cable Add: Vannini Brescia
Subjects: Scholastic, Reference, Law
1982: 9 titles

Giovanni de **Vecchi** Editore SpA, see De Vecchi

Voce della Bibbia, CP 90, I-41043 Formigine (Modena) (Located at: Via Cavallotti 14, Formigine) Tel: (059) 556303
Chief Executive: David L Hansen
Parent Company: Back to the Bible Broadcast, Box 82808, Lincoln, Nebraska 68501, USA
Subject: Evangelism
Founded: 1961

G **Zanibon** Edizioni Musicali, Piazza dei Signori 44, I-35100 Padua Tel: (049) 30167 Cable Add: Zanibon Musica Padua
Chief Executive, Editorial: Dr Guglielmo Travaglia Zanibon; *Sales:* Ugo Armelin; *Rights & Permissions:* Tina Testa
Subsidiary Companies: Edizioni Drago; Edizioni Orfeo (both at above address)
Subjects: Instrumental and Chamber Music, Vocal Music, Educational, Musicology
Bookshop: At above address
Founded: 1908

Nicola **Zanichelli** SpA*, Via Irnerio 34, I-40126 Bologna Tel: (051) 293241/293236
Chairman: Giovanni Enriques; *Dir General:* Federico Enriques
Subjects: History, Philosophy, Reference, Mathematics, Chemistry, Biology, Engineering, General Science, University & Secondary Textbooks, Law, Psychology, Visual Design, Architecture, Juveniles, Physics, Electronics, Linguistics, Literature, Geography, Earth Sciences, Paperbacks
Bookshop: Libreria Zanichelli, Portici del Pavaglione, CP 227, I-40124 Bologna
Founded: 1859

Edizioni **Zara**, Via Toscana 80, I-43100 Parma Tel: (0521) 45945
Chief Executive: Isabella Marchesi; *Editorial:* Giancarlo Zarattini
Subject: University Textbooks
1981: 4 titles *1982:* 7 titles *Founded:* 1979

Literary Agents

Agenzia Letteraria Internazionale Srl, Via Manzoni 41, I-20121 Milan Tel: (02) 6572465/6572594/6572596

Agenzia Letteraria **Aval***, Via Fregene 16, I-00183 Rome Tel: (06) 7592856 Cable Add: Agaval
Contact: Ali Aval
Represents publishers for Italian translation rights and is also authors' agent

Ursula **Caputo***, Via Pisacane 25, I-20129 Milan

Dais Literary Agency, Via di Santa Maria in Monticelli 67, I-00186 Rome Tel: (06) 655356

Maria-Pia **D'Arborio***, Viale Tiziano 5, Rome

Eulama SA*, Via Torino 135, I-00184 Rome Tel: (06) 460636
President: Harald Kahnemann
Specializes in social sciences, politics, psychology, education, philosophy, religion, linguistics and literature, mass-media, architecture, urban studies, Latin-American literature and books for young readers

I L A (International Literary Agency), I-18010 Terzorio – IM Tel: San Remo (0184) 484048 Cable Add: Friedmann Terzorio (IM)
An American agency headquartered in Europe (with representatives in Britain, Spain, Holland and Scandinavia), specializing in handling of foreign language translation rights to multi-volume book and magazine projects, Children's books, Encyclopaedias, Best Sellers (in all European languages)

Living Literary Agency Elfriede Pexa, Via E Q Visconti 103, I-00193 Rome Tel: (06) 381720 Cable Add: I-00193 Living Roma
Also: Via Villoresi 13, I-20100 Milan Tel: (02) 838721 Telex: 335142 attn Living

William **Morris** Organization SpA*, Via Nomentana 60, I-00161 Rome

Natoli and Stefan Literary Agency, Galleria Buenos Aires 14, I-20124 Milan
Manager: G Natoli

Christa **Pucci***, Largo Generale Gonzaga del Vodice 2, I-00195 Rome Tel: (06) 3612471

Rizzoli Editore SpA, Via Rizzoli 2, I-20132 Milan
Also Publisher and Major Bookseller (qqv)

Mirella Vescovi **Tenderini**, Corso Venezia 46, I-20121 Milan Tel: (02) 796806/704622
Telex: 322298 Strain
Contact: Mirella V Tenderini

Book Clubs

C D E – Gruppo Mondadori, Via Durazzo 4, I-20134 Milan Telex: 320457 Mondmi I
Owned by: Arnoldo Mondadori Editore (qv)

Club dei **Bibliofili**, Via Cino del Duca 4-8, I-20122 Milan
Owned by: Franco Maria Ricci Editore (qv)
Also associated with Book Club, Les Amis de Franco Maria Ricci, France (qv)

Collectors Club of Franco Maria Ricci, Via Cino del Duca 4-8, I-20122 Milan
Owned by: Franco Maria Ricci Editore (qv)
Also associated with Book Club, Les Amis de Franco Maria Ricci, France (qv)

Edi Thule Club, Via Ammiraglio Gravina 95, I-90139 Palermo
Owned by: Edizioni Thule (qv)

Isper Club, Corso Dante 124, I-10126 Turin Tel: (011) 633950
Owned by: Isper Edizioni (qv)

Centro **Italscambi**, CP 23, Turin
Owned by: Editrice Italscambi (qv)

Major Booksellers

Casalini Libri, Via B da Maiano 3, I-50014 Fiesole (Florence) Tel: (055) 599941 Cable Add: Casalini Fiesole
Man Dirs: Mario Casalini, Gerda Casalini von Grebmer, Barbara Casalini
General Book Exporter

Libreria Internazionale Fratelli **Cocco**, Largo C Felice 76, I-09100 Cagliari, Sardinia Tel: 657785
Manager: Antonio Cocco
Also: Via Manno 9, I-09100 Cagliari, Sardinia Tel: 668207

Libreria **Feltrinelli***, Via del Babuino 41, Rome Tel: (06) 6793360
Also: Via Carlo Alberto 2 and Piazza Castello 9, Turin; Piazza Porta Ravegnana 1, Bologna; Via Cavour 12-20, I-50129 Florence Tel: (055) 292196

Libreria SF **Flaccovio**, Via Ruggiero Settimo 37, I-90139 Palermo Tel: 589442
Manager: Sergio Flaccovio

Libreria **Gregoriana**, Via Roma 37, I-35100 Padua
Also: Via Vescovado 33, I-35100 Padua
Owned by: Libreria Editrice Gregoriana (qv)

Ulrico **Hoepli** Libreria Internazionale, Via Hoepli 5, I-20121 Milan Tel: (02) 865446
Managers: Dr Ulrico Carlo Hoepli, Roberto Taneggi
Owned by: Casa Editrice Libraria Ulrico Hoepli SpA, Publishers (qv)

Libreria **Liberma***, CP 492 (San Silvestro) Rome (Located at: Via di Saponara 20A, I-00125 Acilia-Roma)
Manager: Adalina Vigiani

Libreria A **Longo**, Via A Diaz 39, I-48100 Ravenna Tel: (0544) 33500
Owned by: Angelo Longo Editore, Publisher (qv)

Libreria Internazionale Giuseppe **Luna***, Via Gramsci 41-43, I-06034 Foligno Tel: (0742) 52581

Libreria Editrice **Minerva***, Via Castiglione 13-15, Bologna

Libreria Commissionaria Internazionale di Raffaele **Pancaldi**, Via S Petronio Vecchio 3, I-40125 Bologna Tel: (051) 229466
Manager: Raffaele Pancaldi

Libreria Internazionale **Pàtron**, Via Zamboni 24, I-40126 Bologna Tel: (051) 275735

Libreria all' Accademia snc di **Randi** Pietro, Via S Lucia 1, I-35100 Padua
(The above is the head office address only)
Shops: Libreria Draghi-Randi, Via Cavour 17-19; Libreria Universitaria, Via 8 Febbraio 10; Libraria Accademia, Via Accademia 2-4; Libreria Nuova Moderna, Via Paolotti 5 (all CP 1003, I-35100 Padua) Tel: (049) 20425/35976/26676/24525/26648

Libreria Internazionale **Rizzoli** SRL, Galleria Colonna, Largo Chigi, Rome
Manager: Bruno Curti

Libreria **Rizzoli** della Rizzoli Editore SpA, Galleria Vittorio Emanuele II 79, I-20121 Milan
Manager: Aldo Allegri
Also: Largo Chigi, I-00187 Rome
Owned by: Rizzoli Editore SpA (qv)

Rosenberg e Sellier SRL, Via Andrea Doria 14, I-10123 Turin Tel: (11) 518388
Proprietors: Ugo Gianni Rosenberg, Elvi Rosenberg
Owned by: Rosenberg e Sellier Editori in Torino (qv)
International import-export booksellers and subscription agents

Libreria **Rosmini** di R Maly*, Corso Rosmini 30, I-38068 Rovereto

Libreria Internazionale **Seeber**, Via Tornabuoni 68 R, I-50123 Florence
Manager: Carla Rossi

Libreria **Sperling e Kupfer**, Piazza San Babila 1, I-20122 Milan Tel: 701495/790712/791912
Manager: Onorato Ciriotti

Major Libraries

Biblioteca **Ambrosiana**, Piazza Pio XI 2, I-20123 Milan Tel: (02) 800146
Librarian: Angelo Paredi

Biblioteca **Angelica**, Piazza S Agostino 8, I-00186 Rome Tel: (06) 655874/6568041
Dir: Dr Silvana Verdini

Biblioteca Comunale dell' **Archiginnasio**, Piazza Galvani 1, I-40124 Bologna
Tel: 225509/279731
Dir: Franco Bergonzoni
Publication: L'Archiginnasio Bollettino della Biblioteca Comunale di Bologna

Archivio Centrale dello Stato, Piazzale degli Archivi, EUR, I-00144 Rome Tel: (06) 5920371
General Dir: Dr Mario Serio
National Archives

Biblioteca dell' **Archivio Storico** Civico e Biblioteca Trivulziana, Castello Sforzesco, I-20121 Milan Tel: 6236, int 3946/3960/3967
Librarian: Prof Dr Giulia Bologna

Biblioteca Nazionale **Braidense***, Palazzo di Brera, Via Brera 28, I-20121 Milan Tel: (02) 872376/808345
Dir: Dr Letizia Pecorella Vergnano

Biblioteca Nazionale **Centrale**, Piazza Cavalleggeri 1, Florence Tel: (055) 244441/2/3
Dir: Dr Anna Lenzuni

Biblioteca Nazionale **Centrale**, Vittorio Emanuele II, Viale Castro Pretorio 105, I-00185 Rome Tel: (06) 4989
Dir: Dr Anna Maria Vichi Giorgetti
Publication: Bollettino delle opere moderne straniere acquistate delle Biblioteche Pubbliche Governative

Biblioteca Nazionale **Marciana**, Palazzi della Libreria Vecchia e della Zecca, San Marco 7, I-30124 Venice Tel: (041) 708788
Dir: Dr Gian Albino Ravalli Modoni

Biblioteca Nazionale **Vittorio Emanuele III***, I-80132 Naples (Palazzo Reale) Tel: (081) 407921/402842/425093
Dir: Dr Maria Cecaro

Biblioteca **Universitaria**, Largo Porta S Agostino 309, I-41100 Modena Tel: Central (059) 222248; Director 210530
Librarian: Dr Ernesto Milano

Biblioteca Musicale Governativa del **Conservatorio di Musica** S Cecilia, Via dei Greci 18, Rome Tel: (06) 6784552/12
Librarian: Dr Bianca Maria Antolini

Biblioteca **Estense**, Largo Porta San Agostino 309, I-41100 Modena Tel: Central (059) 222248; Director 230195
Dir: Dr Ernesto Milano

European University Institute Library, Badia Fiesolana, Via dei Roccettini 5, I-50016 San Domenico di Fiesole, Florence Tel: (055) 477931 Telex: 571528 Iue
Librarian: Michel Boisset

Biblioteca Medicea **Laurenziana**, Piazza S Lorenzo 9, I-50123 Florence Tel: (055) 210760/214443
Chief Librarian: Dr Antonietta Morandini

Biblioteca Comunale **Malatestiana**, Piazza Bufalini 1, I-47023 Cesena (Forlì) Tel: 21297
Librarian: Dr Antonio Brasini

Biblioteca **Palatina***, Palazzo della Pilotta, Parma Tel: (0521) 22217

Biblioteca **Riccardiana**, Via dei Ginori 10, I-50129 Florence Tel: (055) 212586, 211379
Dir: Dr Maria Jole Minicucci

Università degli Studi di Firenze, Biblioteca della Facolta di Lettere e Filosofia, Piazza Brunelleschi, I-50121 Florence Tel: (55) 264081
Dir: Dr Tomaso Urso

Library Associations

Associazione Italiana Biblioteche, c/o Istituto di Patologia del Libro, Via Milano 76, I-00184 Rome
Italian Library Association
Chairman: Dr Luigi Crocetti; *Secretary:* Prof Dr Attilio Mauro Caproni
Publications: Bollettino d'Informazioni; Quaderni del Bollettino d'Informazione

Associazione Nazionale Archivistica Italiana*, Viale Trastevere 215, I-00153 Rome
National Association of Italian Archivists
Secretary: Antonio Dentoni-Litta
Publication: Archivi e Cultúra (2 a year)

Ente Nazionale per le Biblioteche Popolari e Scolastiche*, Via Michele Mercati 4, I-00197 Rome
National Organization for Public and Academic Libraries
Publication: La Parola e il Libro (monthly)

Istituto Centrale per il Catalogo Unico delle Biblioteche Italiane e per le Informazioni Bibliografiche, Viale Castro Pretorio 105, Rome
Central Institute of the Union Catalogue of Italian Libraries and Bibliographical Information
Publications: Bibliografia Nazionale Italiana; Manuale di Catalogazione Musicale; Regole Italiane di Catalogazione per Autori; Soggettario per i Cataloghi delle Biblioteche Italiane

Istituto Centrale per la Patologia del Libro, Via Milano 76, I-00184 Rome
Central Institute of Book Pathology
Dir: Dr Maria Di Franco

Società Italiana di Documentazione e d'Informazione*, Via Vittoria Colunna 39, I-00139 Rome   Tel: (06) 3604841
Italian Association of Documentation and Information
Vice President: Carlo Cya
Publications: Documentazione e Informazione (yearly)

Library Reference Books and Journals

Books

Almanàcco dei Bibliotecari Italiani (Almanac of Italian Libraries), Fratelli Palombi Editori, Via del Gracchi 181-185, I-00192 Rome

Annuario Bibliografico per Le Biblioteche (Bibliographical Annual for Libraries), Federation of Italian Public Libraries, c/o La 'Società Umanitaria', Via Daverio 7, I-20122 Milan

Annuario delle Biblioteche Italiane (Italian Library Annual), Fratelli Palombi Editore, Via del Gracchi 181-185, I-00192 Rome

Guida delle Biblioteche Italiane (Guide to Italian Libraries), National Organization for Public and Academic Libraries, Via Michele Mercati 4, I-00197 Rome

Regole Italiane di Catalogazione per Autori (Italian Rules of Cataloguing by Author), Istituto Centrale per il Catalogo Unico delle Biblioteche Italiane e per le Informazioni Bibliografiche, Viale Castro Pretorio 105, Rome

Journals

Accademie e Biblioteche d'Italia (Academies and Libraries of Italy), Fratelli Palombi Editori, Via del Gracchi 181-185, I-00192 Rome

Archivi e Cultura (Archives and Culture), National Association of Italian Archivists, Viale Trastevere 215, I-00153 Rome

Bollettino d'Informazioni (Information Bulletin), Italian Library Association, c/o Istituto di Patologia del Libro, Via Milano 76, I-00184 Rome

La Parola e il Libro (The Word and the Book), National Organization for Public and Academic Libraries, Via Michele Mercati 4, I-00197 Rome

Soggettario per i Cataloghi delle Biblioteche Italiane (Subject Collections in Italian Libraries), Central Institute of the Union Catalogue of Italian Libraries and Bibliographical Information, Viale Castro Pretorio 105, Rome

Literary Associations and Societies

Accademia di Scienze, Lettere ed Arti, Piazza Indipendenza 17, Palermo
Secretary: Professor Romualdo Giuffrida

Accademia Ligure di Scienze e Lettere*, Via Balbi 10, I-16126 Genoa
Secretary-General: P Scotti

Accademia Nazionale di Scienze, Lettere ed Arti*, Palazzo Coccapani, Corso Vittorio Emanuele II 59, Modena
President: Professor Antonio Pignedoli
Publications: Atti e Memorie

Accademia Petrarca di Lettere, Arti e Scienze*, Via dell'Orto, Arezzo
Secretary: Dr Guido Goti
Publication: Atti e Memorie della Accademia, Studi Petrarcheschi

Accademia Toscana di Scienze e Lettere la Colombaria*, Via S Egidio 21-23, Florence

Accademia Virgiliana di Scienze, Lettere ed Arti di Mantova*, Via Accademia 47, I-46100 Mantua   Tel: (0376) 320314
President: Prof Eros Benedini
Librarian: Mons Luigi Bosio
Secretary: Comm G Amadei
Publications: Atti di Convegni tenuti presso l'Accademia Virgiliana; Atti e Memorie NS (annual)

Cenacolo di Studi Storico, Artistico, Letterari, Via Ammiraglio Gravina 95, I-90139 Palermo
President: Dr Tommaso Romano; *Secretary:* Prof Gaetano Arnò
Publication: Quaderni

Empire International Club, Via Ammiraglio Gravina 95, I-90139 Palermo   Tel: (091) 323699
President: Prof Dr Salvatore Barberi; *Secretary-General:* Prof Dr Tommaso Romano
Publication: Quaderni dell'Empire

Istituto Lombardo Accademia di Scienze e Lettere*, Via Brera 28, I-20121 Milan
President: Prof A Giordano

Keats-Shelley Memorial Association, Piazza di Spagna 26, Rome
Dir: Sir Joseph Cheyne
Publications: Bulletin, Journal, A Room in Rome

P E N International Centre, c/o Piazzo Belgiojoso 2, I-20123 Milan
Secretary: La Contessa Piovene

Società Dante Alighieri*, Palazzo di Firenze, Piazza Firenze 27, I-00186 Rome
Secretary-General: G Cota
Publication: Pagine della Dante (quarterly)
For the teaching and diffusion of Italian language and culture throughout the world

Società Dantesca Italiana, Via dell'Arte della Lana 1, I-50123 Florence
President: Prof Dr Francesco Mazzoni
Publications: Studi Danteschi, Quaderni degli Studi Danteschi, Edizione Nazionale delle Opere di Dante Alighieri
(Library open to public)

Società Letteraria*, Piazzetta Scalette Rubiani 1, Verona
Dir: Alfonso Balis Crema
Publication: Bollettino (annually)

Literary Periodicals

Belfagor, Leo S Olschki, CP 66, I-50100 Florence

Bibliofilia (Bibliophily) (text in English, French, German and Italian), Leo S Olschki, CP 66, I-50100 Florence

Il giornale storico della letteratura italiana (Historical Journal of Italian Literature), Loescher Editore, Via Vittorio Amedeo 18, I-10121 Turin

Italia Che Scrive (The Italy That Writes), Via dei Banchi Vecchi 61, Rome

Lettere Italiane (Italian Letters), Viuzzo del Pozzetto (Viale Europa), I-50126 Florence

Libri Paese Sera (*Paese Sera* book supplement), Società Editrice 'Il Rinnovamento', Via dei Taurini 19, I-00185 Rome

Nuòva Corrènte (New Current) (text in several languages), Via Lattuada 26, Milan

Paideia; literary review with bibliographical information (text in English, French, German and Italian), Via Corsica 58m, I-25100 Brescia

Penarete-Letture d'Italia (Readings from Italy), Via Beruto 7, I-20131 Milan

Pròve di Letteratura (Examinations of Literature), Nino Palumbo, Via Ai Castagneti 4, San Michele di Pagana, Rapallo

Rassegna della Letteratura Italiana (Review of Italian Literature), Casa Editrice G C Sansoni SpA, Via Varchi 47, I-50132 Florence

Revue des Etudes italiennes, Librairie Marcel Didier SA, 15 rue Cujas, F-75005 Paris

Rivista di Letteratura Moderne e Comparate (Review of Modern and Comparative Literature) (text in English, French and Italian), Casa Editrice G C Sansoni SpA, Via Varchi 47, I-50132 Florence

Uomini e libri (Men and Books), Emme Edizioni, Via San Maurilio 13, I-20123 Milan

Literary Prizes

Andersen Prize*
For a fairy tale for children. 300,000 lire. Awarded annually. Enquiries to Comune di Sestri Levante, CP 60, Genoa

Bagutta Prize
Founded in 1927 for the best book of the year, given for several literary forms including the novel and poetry. 2,100,000 lire, awarded annually. The 1983 winner was Giorgio Bassani for *In Rima e Senza* (Mondadori). Enquiries to Bagutta Restaurant, Via Bagutta 14, Milan

Bancarella Prize*
Founded in 1953 for books of high quality and great popular appeal. A golden album is awarded annually. Enquiries to Unione Librai Pontremolesi, Via Ricci Armani 8, Pontremoli, Massa Carrara

Bancarellino Prize*
Founded in 1958 for children's books of high quality and great popular appeal, preferably written by an Italian author. A golden album is awarded annually. Enquiries to Unione Librai Pontremolesi, Via Ricci Armani 8, Pontremoli, Massa Carrara

Campiello Prize
For the best Italian prose works. 16,000,000 lire. Awarded annually. Enquiries to Ca' Mocenigo Gambara, Secretariat of the Campiello Prize, Accademia 1056, Venice

Castello-Sanguinetto Prize*
For a novel for young readers between 11 and 14. 1,500,000 lire and 750,000 lire. Awarded annually. Enquiries to Castello-Sanguinetto Prize, Community of Sanguinetto, Verona

Golden Book Prize*
To the publisher who has most influenced the public culturally. Awarded annually. Enquiries to Italian Council of Ministers, Via Bancopagni 15, Rome

Golden Pen Prize*
To an author who has made an important contribution to Italian culture. 5,000,000 lire. Awarded annually. Enquiries to Italian Council of Ministers, Via Bancopagni 15, Rome

Laura Orvieto Prize*
For the manuscript of a book of fiction or poetry for children. 1,000,000 lire for a novel and 500,000 lire for poetry. Awarded every other year. Enquiries to Orvieto Prize, Piazza Indipendenza 23, Florence

Strega Prize*
Founded in 1947 by the Strega liquor producer Alberti for the best novel of the year. 1,000,000 lire. Awarded annually. Enquiries to Strega Prize, Via Fratelli Ruspoli 2, Rome

Tormargana Prize*
To outstanding writers, publishers, artists, architects, actors and film makers. Awarded every few months. Enquiries to Angelino Restaurant (Hosteria Angelino a Tormargana), Piazza Margana 37, I-00186 Rome

Viareggio Prizes*
Founded in 1929 for the best novel, poetry, essay, best first work, occasionally for drama and journalism. Sometimes given to foreign writers and poets. 3,000,000 lire. Awarded annually. The latest winner was Primo Levi for *Se Non Ora, Querido?* (Editore Einaudi). Enquiries to Viareggio Prize, Via Lima 28, Rome

Villa Benia Prize*
For the best storybook for young readers. Enquiries to International Institute for the Elimination of Speech Deficiencies, Villa Benia, Rapallo

Olga Visentini Prize*
For the best book for young people. 1,300,000 lire. Awarded biennially. Enquiries to Olga Visentini Foundation, Cerea, Verona

Translation Agencies and Associations

Associazione Italiana Traduttori e Interpreti (AITI)*, Via Arrigo Boito 126, I-00199 Rome Tel: 8393457
Italian Association of Translators and Interpreters
Secretary: Anna Bonanome-Via

Eulama*, Via Torino 135, I-00184 Rome Tel: (06) 460636 (also Publisher and Literary Agent)

Transafrica*, Via Trieste 34, I-25100 Brescia Tel: (030) 55080
Specialization: African texts

Ivory Coast

General Information

Language: French
Religion: 65% traditional, 23% Muslim, 12% Christian
Population: 7.6 million
Bank Hours: 0800-1130, 1430-1630 Monday-Friday
Shop Hours: 0800-1200, 1530-1830 or 1900 Monday-Friday; 0800-1200, 1430-1730 Saturday
Currency: CFA franc
Export/Import Information: Member of West African Economic Community. No tariff on books; single copies free but most advertising subject to customs duty, fiscal duty and VAT. No import licences required for imports from EEC or Franc Zone.
Copyright: Berne, Florence (see International section)

Book Trade Reference Journal

Bibliographie de la Côte-d'Ivoire, Bibliothèque nationale, BP V180, Abidjan (the national bibliography, published annually in two volumes since 1969)

Publishers

Centre d'Edition et de Diffusion africaines (CEDA), 04 BP 541, Abidjan 04 Plateau Tel: 222055/228137/326002 Telex: Ediceda 2451
Man Dir: Venance Kacou; *Editorial Dir:* Christian Lescure
Subjects: General Non-fiction, Biography, History, Africana, Philosophy, Reference, Religion, Juveniles, Law, Paperbacks, General & Social Science, Secondary & Primary Textbooks
Bookshop: At above address
Miscellaneous: Distributors on behalf of INADES, the National University of the Ivory Coast, and the bibliotheque nationale

Centre de Publications Evangeliques*, 08 BP 900, Abidjan 08 Tel: 444805
Dir: Marjorie Shelley; *Administrator, Sales:* Gary Lange; *Administrator, Publicity:* E T Emmett
Subjects: General Non-fiction, Religion, Christian Tracts, Paperbacks, Periodicals for adults and children
1981: 7 titles *Founded:* 1970

Government Printer*, Imprimerie nationale, BP V87, Abidjan

I N A D E S — Edition (Institut africain pour le developpement économique et social)*, 08 BP 8, Abidjan 08 Tel: 441594
Man Dir, Editorial: Raymond Deniel; *Sales:* Albert Hanrion
Subjects: African studies, Philosophy, Religion, Economics, Agriculture, Sociology, Essays
Founded: 1975

Les Nouvelles Editions Africaines+, 01 BP 3525, Abidjan 01 (Located at: 1 blvd de Marseille, Abidjan 01) Tel: 322812/326591
Parent Company: Les Nouvelles Editions Africaines, Senegal (qv)
Associate Company: Les Nouvelles Editions Africaines, Togo (qv)
Subjects: Bibliography, Fiction, Poetry, Theatre, Religion, Art, Juveniles, History, Textbooks

Université d'Abidjan, 01 BP V34, Abidjan 01 Tel: 439000 Cable Add: Rectuniv Abidjan Telex: 3469
Secretary-General in Charge of Publications: Mrs Dehail-Michèle
Subjects: General Non-fiction, History, Africana, Reference, Law, Medicine, General & Social Science, Economics, Geography, Linguistics, Sociology, Journals
Founded: 1964
ISBN Publisher's Prefix: 2-7166

Université Nationale de Côte d'Ivoire, see Université d'Abidjan

Major Booksellers

Librairie Carrefour, 08 BP 326, Abidjan 08 Tel: 442370
Manager: Monique Barnet

Centre d'Edition et de Diffusion africaines, 04 BP 541, Abidjan 04 Tel: 222055/228137/326002
Manager: Kacou Venance

Librairie de France*, ave Chardy, BP 228, Abidjan Tel: 322655 Cable Add: Lfcessci Telex: 2323

Maison des Livres*, 23 blvd de la République, BP 4645, Abidjan Tel: 322887

Librarie Villepastour, Rue de la Paix Marcory, 01 BP 2461, Abidjan 01 Tel: 353352/355117 Telex: 42454 Vil Ci
Manager: J Villepastour

Major Libraries

Archives nationales*, BP 1770, Abidjan

Bibliothèque centrale de la Côte d'Ivoire*, BP 6243, Abidjan-Treichville Tel: 227536
Librarian: Michel Amoikoy

Bibliothèque municipale*, BP 24, Plateau, Abidjan

Bibliothèque nationale*, BP V180, Abidjan Tel: 323872
Librarian: Seydou Gueye

Bibliothèque de l'Université nationale de Côte d'Ivoire, 08 BP 859, Abidjan 08 Tel: 439000 ext 3393 Telex: 469 Rectuniv
Librarian: Mme N'goran; *Publications enquiries:* Mme Dehail-Leoni
Publications include: Annales de l'Université d'Abidjan; Bibliographie de la Côte d'Ivoire

Centre culturel américain, Bibliothèque*, BP 1866, Abidjan

Centre culturel français, Bibliothèque, 01 BP 3995, Abidjan 01

I N A D E S (Institut africain pour le Développement économique et social) Documentation, 08 BP 8, Abidjan 08 Tel: 441594
Librarian: Marie Paule Coing
Publications: Le Fichier-Afrique (bi-monthly), Suggestions de Lectures (biannually); bibliographies

Library Associations

Association pour le Développement de la Documentation, des Bibliothèques et Archives de la Côte d'Ivoire (ADBACI)*, c/o Bibliothèque Nationale, BP V180, Abidjan
Secretary General: Cangah Guy

Literary Associations and Societies

P E N Centre de Côte d'Ivoire, BP 1718, Abidjan
Secretary: Jean Dodo

Literary Periodical

Revue de littérature de l'esthétique nègre-africaines, Les Nouvelles Editions Africaines, BP 20615, Abidjan

Literary Prize

Prix Littéraire Mobil*
First sponsored 1980. A prize of CFA 250,000 for an outstanding book by an author from the Ivory Coast (unpublished manuscripts also considered). The sponsors undertake the publication of the prize-winning book in English translation. Enquiries to Mobil Oil Cote d'Ivoire, 13 Impasse Paris-Village, 01 BP 1777, Abidjan 01

Jamaica

General Information

Language: English
Religion: Predominantly Protestant
Population: 2 million
Literacy Rate (1960): 80.5%
Bank Hours: 0900-1400 Monday-Thursday; 0900-1200, 1430-1700 Friday
Shop Hours: Downtown Kingston: 0900-1600 Monday and Tuesday, Thursday-Saturday; 0900-1200 Wednesday. Other areas: 0900-1700, with early closing Thursday
Currency: 100 cents = 1 Jamaican dollar
Export/Import Information: No tariff on books, but advertising matter dutied. No import licence required for books; no obscene literature permitted. Exchange restrictions
Copyright: No copyright conventions signed

Book Trade Organization

Booksellers' Association of Jamaica*, c/o Sangster's Book Stores Ltd, 101 Water Lane, Kingston Tel: 9223640
Secretary: Keith Shervington

Book Trade Reference Books and Journals

Book
Book Production in Jamaica: A Select List of Jamaican Publications, Jamaica Library Service, PO Box 58, Kingston 5

Journal
Jamaican National Bibliography, National Library of Jamaica, PO Box 823, 12-16 East St, Kingston

Publishers

Caribbean Universities Press Jamaica Ltd, PO Box 83, Kingston 7 (Located at: 18 Melmac Ave, Kingston 5) Tel: (92) 62628
Man Dir: Carmen Latty
Associate Company: Ginn & Co, UK (qv)
Subjects: Academic, Education (Spanish and English)

Government Printing Office*, 77 Duke St, Kingston
Subject: Law

Jamaica Publishing House Ltd, 97 Church St, Kingston Tel: (0922) 2038 Cable Add: Japub
Chairman: Fay E Saunders; *Acting Manager:* Leo A Oakley
Parent Company: Jamaica Teachers' Association
Subjects: Educational, Biography, Business, English language and literature, Geography, Geology, History, Home Economics, Languages, Mathematics, Music, Psychology, Social Sciences
1983: 2 titles *Founded:* 1969

Kingston Publishers Ltd*, 1A Norwood Ave, Kingston 5 Tel: 9265506/9260091 Cable Add: Kingbooks
Warehouse: 40 East St, Kingston Tel: 9225649
Chairman: L M J Henry
Founded: 1972

Longman Jamaica Ltd, PO Box 489, Kingston 10 (Located at: 95 Newport Blvd, Newport West, Kingston)
Associate Company: Longman Group Ltd, UK (qv)

Major Booksellers

Bolivar Bookshop, 1D Grove Rd, Kingston 10 Tel: 9268799
Owner: Hugh Dunphy

Henderson's Book Store*, 27 St James St, Montego Bay

Kingston Bookshop Ltd, 70b King St, Kingston Tel: (809) 9224056 Cable Add: Futurity Jamaica
Manager: S A R Fuller

Literary Supplies*, 38 Mandeville Plaza, Mandeville

Novelty Trading Co*, 53 Hanover St, Kingston

Readers' Book Shop*, Liguanea Plaza, 134 Old Hope Rd, Kingston 6

Sangster's Book Stores Ltd*, PO Box 366, 101 Water Lane, Kingston Tel: 9223640
Manager: B A Sangster

Shadeed's Educational & General Supplies Ltd*, 14 French St, Spanish Town
Manager: Leonora Newman

Stationery & Educational Book Centre Ltd*, Silver Slipper Plaza, Kingston 5

Teachers' Book Centre Ltd*, 95 Church St, Kingston Tel: (09) 24716/23843

Times Stores Ltd*, 8 King St, Kingston

Major Libraries

Jamaica Archives, Spanish Town

Jamaica Library Service*, PO Box 58, 2 Tom Redcam Dr, Kingston 5 Tel: 936 3310
Dir: Leila T Thomas
Publications include: Book production in Jamaica: a select list of Jamaican publications

National Library of Jamaica, PO Box 823, Kingston (Located at: 12 East St, Kingston) Tel: (92) 20620 Cable Add: Nalibjam
Dir: Stephney Ferguson
Publications: AIRS Index (quarterly index to the *Daily Gleaner of Jamaica*); *Jamaican National Bibliography*

University of the West Indies Library*, Mona, Kingston 7 Tel: Librarian 9276661 ext 294; Reference Desk 9276661 ext 296 or 9270923
Librarian: Mrs A Jefferson
Publication: Annual Report

Library Associations

Jamaica Library Association*, PO Box 58, Kingston 5
Honorary Secretary: Hermine C Salmon
Publications: Bulletin (annually), *JLA News* (quarterly)

Library Reference Journal

Bulletin, Jamaica Library Association, PO Box 58, Kingston 5

Literary Associations and Societies

P E N Club, 1 Norbrook Rd, Apt 4, Kingston 8
Secretary: George Clough

Japan

General Information

Language: Japanese
Religion: Buddhist and Shinto
Population: 115 million
Literacy Rate (1960): 96.6%
Bank Hours: 0900-1500 Monday-Friday; 0900-1200 Saturday
Shop Hours: No fixed weekly holiday; department stores usually close Wednesday or Thursday, others Sunday. Generally department store hours are 1000-1800
Currency: yen
Export/Import Information: No tariff on books and advertising matter. Only declaration by importer to a foreign exchange bank is required
Copyright: UCC, Berne, Florence (see International section)

Book Trade Organizations

Antiquarian Booksellers' Association of Japan*, 29 San-Ei-Cho, Shinjuku-ku, Tokyo 160 Tel: (03) 3595519 Cable Add: Yushodo Tokyo Telex: 0232-4136
President: Mitsuo Nitta

Copyright Research Institute, 2-12-8 Shimbashi, Minato-ku, Tokyo

Japan Book Importers Association, Room 603, Aizawa Bldg, 20-3 Nihonbashi 1-chome, Chuo-ku, Tokyo 103
Secretary: Mitsuo Shibata

Japan Book Publishers Association, 6 Fukuro-machi, Shinjuku-ku, Tokyo 162 Tel: (03) 2681301 Cable Add: Shosekiyo

Tokyo
Executive Dir: Sadaya Murayama;
Secretary: Masaaki Shigehisa
Publications: Japanese Books in Print, The Catalogue of Books in the Near Future, Bulletin of the Japanese Book Publishers Association

Japan I S B N Agency, c/o Japan Publishers Building, 6 Fukoro-machi, Shinjuku-ku, Tokyo 162 Tel: (03) 2684494
Secretary-General: Naotoshi Matsudaira

Nihon Shoten Kumiai Rengokai, 1-2 Kanda Surugadai, Chiyoda-ku, Tokyo 101
Tel: (03) 2940388
Japan Booksellers' Federation
Publications: Hitsubi Gakusansho Giten Mokuroku (Textbooks and Dictionaries: A List of Best Sellers); *Hitsubi Tosho Mokuroku 1000 ten* (General Books: A List of 1000 Best Sellers); *Kodomonohon Longseller-list* (Children's Books: A List of Best Sellers); *Zenkoku Shoten Meibo* (Address Book of Japan Booksellers); *Zenkoku Shoten Shinbun*

Publishers' Association for Cultural Exchange, 1-2-1, Sarugaku-cho, Chiyoda-ku, Tokyo 101 Tel: (03) 2915685 Cable Add: Publishersasso
President: Mr Shoichi Noma; *Man Dir:* Shoichi Nakajima
European Representation: c/o Euro-Japanische Gesellschaft eV, Bonifaciusplatz 3, D-6500 Mainz, Federal Republic of Germany
Publications: Guide to Publishers and Related Industries in Japan, Guide to Foreign Publishers, Annotated Catalogue of Books Published in Japan

Standard Book Numbering Agency, see Japan ISBN Agency

Textbook Publishers' Association of Japan (Kyokasho Kyokai), 20-2 Honshiocho Shinjuku-ku, Tokyo 160
Secretary: Masae Kusaka

Women Writers' Association*, 17 Yanaka-Shinizucho, Daito-ku, Tokyo

Book Trade Reference Books and Journals

Books

Annotated Catalogue of Books Published in Japan, Publishers' Association for Cultural Exchange, 1-2-1, Sarugaku-cho, Chiyoda-ku, Tokyo 101

Directory of Japanese Publishing and Bookselling, British Book and Educational Display Centre, Iwanami Jimbo-Cho Bldg, 1 Jimbo 2 2-chome, Kanda, Chiyoda-ku, Tokyo 101

Guide to Foreign Publishers, Publishers' Association for Cultural Exchange, 1-2-1, Sarugaku-cho, Chiyoda-ku, Tokyo 101

Journals

Biblia (text in Japanese), Tenri University Press, Tenri Central Library, Tenri City, Nara

Bulletin of the Japanese Book Publishers Association, 6 Fukuro-machi, Shinjuku-ku, Tokyo 162

The Catalogue of Books in the Near Future, Japan Book Publishers Association, 6 Fukuro-machi, Shinjuku-ku, Tokyo 162

A Comprehensive Bibliography of Japanese Periodicals, The Shuppan News Co Ltd, 2-4 Misaki-cho 3 chome, Chiyoda-ku, Tokyo 101

A Comprehensive Catalogue of Collected Works, Publishers in Japan, The Shuppan News Co Ltd, 2-4 Misaki-cho 3 chome, Chiyoda-ku, Tokyo 101

Guide to Publishers and Related Industries in Japan, Publishers' Association for Cultural Exchange, 1-2-1, Sarugaku-cho, Chiyoda-ku, Tokyo 101

Japan Book News, Publishing Research Associates, c/o Kyowa Book Co, Kanda, PO Box 173, Tokyo

Japanese Books in Print, Japan Book Publishers Association, 6 Fukuro-machi, Shinjuku-ku, Tokyo 162

Japanese Publications News and Reviews, 3-2-4 Misaki-cho, Chiyoda-ku, Tokyo

Newsletter, Tokyo Book Development Centre, 6 Fukuro-machi, Shinjuku-ku, Tokyo

Seihon Kai (text in Japanese), Tokyodo Co Ltd, 3-5 Kanda-Nishiki-cho, Chiyoda-ku, Tokyo

Shinkan Nyusu (News of New Books), Tokyo Shuppan Hanbai Co Ltd, 53 Higashigoken-cho, Shinjuku-ku, Tokyo

Shuppan Nenkan; information on publishing for the previous year, Shuppan Nyusu-sha, Tokyo (annual)

Suppan Nyusu (Publishers' News), Shuppan Nyusu-sha, 2-4 Misaki-cho 3-chome, Chiyoda-ku, Tokyo 101 (3 times a month)

Zen Nihon Shuppanbutsu Somokuroku (Japanese National Bibliography), National Diet Library, 10-1, 1-chome, Nagata-cho, Chiyoda-ku, Tokyo

Zenkoku Shoten Meibo (address book of Japanese booksellers), Japan Booksellers' Federation, 1-2 Kanda Surugadai, Chiyoda-ku, Tokyo 101

Publishers

A D A Edita Tokyo Co Ltd, 3-12-14 Sendagaya, Shibuya-ku, Tokyo 151
Tel: (03) 4031581
Director: Yukio Futagawa; *Sales Manager:* Takato Kawahara
Subject: Architecture
Founded: 1972

Akane Shobo Co Ltd*, 3-2-1 Nishikanda, Chiyoda-ku, Tokyo Tel: (03) 2630641
President: Mutsuto Okamoto; *Editor-in-Chief:* Yoshiaki Ushiro
Subjects: Juveniles, Science, Literature, Picture Books

Akita Shoten Publishing Co Ltd*, 2-10-8 Iidabashi, Chiyoda-ku, Tokyo 102 Tel: (03) 2647011
Man Dir: Sadami Akita; *Editorial:* Nobumichi Akutsu; *Sales:* Toshimichi Okubo
Subjects: General Subjects, Juveniles, History, Social Science, Literature, Magazines
Founded: 1948

Aoki Shoten Co Ltd*, 60 Kanda Jimbo-cho 1-chome, Chiyoda-ku, Tokyo 101 Tel: (03) 2920481
President: Noboru Yamane; *Foreign Trade:* Kiyoshi Furukawa; *Foreign Rights:* Toyoichi Eguchi
Subject: Social Science
Founded: 1947

Asakura Publishing Co Ltd*, 6-29 Shinogawama-chi, Shinjuku-ku, Tokyo 162 Tel: (03) 2600141
President: Kunizo Asakura; *Foreign Trade:* Nobuji Okada; *Foreign Rights:* Akira Hata
Subjects: Medicine, Natural Science, Engineering, Industry, History, Geography, Pedagogy, Sociology
Founded: 1929

Baifukan Co Ltd, 3-12 Kudan-Minami 4-chome, Chiyoda-ku, Tokyo 102 Tel: (03) 2625256
President: Kenji Yamamoto; *Editorial:* Masayuki Gotou, Tsuyoshi Nohara; *Sales, Publicity:* Itaru Yamamoto; *Production:* Fumio Shigematu; *Rights & Permissions:* Tsuyoshi Nohara
Subjects: Mathematics, Statistics, Computer Science, Physics, Chemistry, Biology, Engineering, Psychology, Sociology
1981: 24 titles *Founded:* 1924
ISBN Publisher's Prefix: 4-563

Baseball Magazine Sha, 3-3 Kanda-Nishiki-cho, Chiyoda-ku, Tokyo Tel: (03) 2917901/2917909
President: Tsuneo Ikeda; *Vice-President:* Ikuo Ikeda
Branch Off: Tokuma Building, 6-16 Nozaki-cho, Kita-ku, Osaka-shi, Osaka Tel: (06) 3156141/3156144
Subjects: Sports, Physical Education, Psychology, History, Fitness
Founded: 1946
ISBN Publisher's Prefix: 4-583

Bijutsu Shuppan-Sha, Inaoka Building, 2-36 Kanda, Jinbo-cho, Chiyoda-ku, Tokyo Tel: (03) 2342151 Cable Add: Fineart Book Tokyo
President: Atsushi Oshita; *Sales Manager:* Shonosuke Kaizu
Subsidiary Company: Bijutsu Shuppan Design Centre, Yamato Bldg, 1-7-4 Yaesu Chuo-ku, Tokyo 103
Subjects: Art, Architecture, Design
Founded: 1905

Bungeishunju Ltd*, 3 Kioi-cho, Chiyoda-ku, Tokyo Tel: (03) 2651211
President: Genzo Chiba; *Foreign Trade:* Yoneki Kobayashi; *Foreign Rights:* Itaro Abe
Subjects: General Fiction and Non-fiction, Philosophy, Religion, History, Geography, Social Science, Art, Economics, Politics, Natural Science, Industry, Language, Literature, High- and Low-priced Paperbacks
Founded: 1923

Centre for Academic Publications Japan, 4-16 Yayoi 2-chome, Bunkyo-ku, Tokyo 113 Tel: (03) 8150416
Man Dir: T Ohmi
Orders to: Business Centre for Academic Societies Japan (at above address)
Associate Company: Japan Scientific Societies Press, 2-10 Hongo, 6-chome, Bunkyo-ku, Tokyo 113
1982: 10 titles *Founded:* 1972

Chikuma Shobo Publishing Co Ltd, 8, 2-chome, Kanda Ogawamachi, Chiyoda-ku, Tokyo 101-91 Tel: (03) 2917651
Administrator: Kakuzaemon Nunokawa; *Editorial, Rights & Permissions:* Mineo Nakajima; *Sales, Publicity:* Akio Kikuchi; *Production:* Kazuyoshi Tsunoda
Subjects: General Fiction, Belles Lettres, Poetry, Biography, History, Religion, Music, Art, Philosophy, Juveniles, High-priced Paperbacks, Medicine, Psychology, General & Social Science, Secondary Textbooks
Founded: 1940

Child Honsha Co Ltd, 24-21 Koishikawa 5-chome, Bunkyo-ku, Tokyo 112 Tel: (03) 8133781
President: Shinko Miyata; *Editorial:* Yasuyuki Ouchi; *Sales, Publicity:* Hirosato Okada; *Production:* Fumio Moromachi;

Rights & Permissions: Ikuzo Shibasaki
Associate Company: Kyodo Printing Co Ltd
Subsidiary Companies: Basic Inc; Hisakata Child Co Ltd; Mikawa Child Co Ltd
Subjects: Juveniles, Education
Founded: 1930

Chuo-Tosho Co Ltd+, Motoseiganji-sagaru, Aburanokoji-dori, Kamigyo-ku, Kyoto 602 Tel: (075) 4412174
Chief Executive: Toshihiko Hirokou; *Editorial, Rights & Permissions:* Takanori Ikeda; *Sales:* Tetsuo Hattori; *Production:* Tsuneo Takeuchi; *Publicity:* Hiroshi Izumoji
Subjects: Secondary Textbooks, Japanese, English, Mathematics, History, Biography, Chemistry
Founded: 1950

Chuokoron-Sha Inc, 2-8-7 Kyobashi, Chuo-ku, Tokyo 104 Tel: (03) 5631261 Cable Add: Chuokoron Tokyo Telex: J32505 Chuokor
President: Hoji Shimanaka; *Man Dir:* Shigeru Takanashi; *International Section Manager:* Yukio Shimanaka
Subjects: General Fiction, Belles Lettres, History, Art, Philosophy, Low-priced Paperbacks, Politics, Economics, Natural Science, Social Science, Religion, Periodicals
1981: 330 titles *1982:* 351 titles *Founded:* 1886

Consolidated Labor Institute (Japan)*, 38 Yoyogi 1-chome, Shibuya-ku, Tokyo 151 Tel: (03) 3792281 Cable Add: Sogoroken Tokyo
President: Mrs Fujiko Hongo; *Foreign Trade Executive:* Kenji Hongo; *Foreign Rights Executive:* Chiyoshi Otuka
Subjects: Social Science, Law, Educational, History, Journals
Founded: 1950

Corona Publishing Co Ltd*, 4-46-10 Sengoku, Bunkyo-ku, Tokyo 112 Tel: (03) 9413131
Executive Director and Foreign Rights: Tatsuo Fujita; *Foreign Trade:* Tatsumi Gorai
Subjects: Natural Science, Technology
Founded: 1927

Daiichi Shuppan Co Ltd*, 1-39 Kanda Jimbo-cho, Chiyoda-ku, Tokyo 101 Tel: (03) 2914576
President: Gen Kurita; *Foreign Trade Executive:* Yoshiya Takamatsu; *Foreign Rights Executive:* Yoshiya Takamatsu
Subjects: Medicine, Natural Science, Nutrition, Magazines
Founded: 1945

Diamond Inc, 1-4-2 Kasumigaseki, Chiyoda-ku, Tokyo Tel: (03) 5046381 Cable Add: Keizaidia Tokyo
President: Yoshio Tsubouchi; *Editorial:* Mineo Iwamochi; *Sales:* Minami Takahashi; *Production:* Kiyoji Ogo; *Publicity:* Gunpei Sakai; *Rights & Permissions:* Katsuyoshi Saito
Associate Company: President KK
Subsidiary Companies: Diamond (weekly economics journal); Diamond Agency; Diamond Big; Diamond Fund; Diamond Graphics; Diamond Service
Branch Off: Osaka
Subjects: Non-fiction, Business, Economics, Management, Finance, Politics
Founded: 1913

Froebel-Kan Co Ltd*, 3-1 Kanda Ogawa-machi, Chiyoda-ku, Tokyo 101 Tel: (03) 2927781/9 Cable Add: Froebelkan Tokyo Telex: J24907
International Division: Harry H Idichi (General Manager); Tony S Endo (Manager)
Associate Company: Toppan Co (Singapore) Private Ltd, Singapore (qv)
Subjects: Juveniles, Educational Materials
Founded: 1907

Fukuinkan Shoten Publishers*, 1-9 Misakicho 1-chome, Chiyoda-ku, Tokyo 101 Tel: (03) 2923401/2303821 Cable Add: Fukuinkanshoten Tokyo
Man Dir: Tadashi Matsui; *Editorial:* Ken Minakuchi; *Sales:* Katsumi Sato, Kishiro Kikuma; *Publicity:* Hiroshi Ishikawa; *Rights & Permissions:* Minoru Tamura, Tamotsu Hozumi
Subjects: Children's books
Book Club: Fukuinkan Shoten Library
Founded: 1951

Fuzambo Publishing Co*, 1-3 Kanda Jimbo-cho, Chiyoda-ku, Tokyo 101 Tel: (03) 2912171
President: Kiichi Sakamoto
Subjects: General Works, Philosophy & Religion, History, Geography, Law, Literature, Language, Art, Juveniles, Dictionaries
Founded: 1886

Gakken Co Ltd+, 4-40-5 Kami-ikedai, Ohta-ku, Tokyo 145 Tel: (03) 7201111 Cable Add: Gakkencol Tokyo Telex: Gakkenco J26389
President: Hiroshi Furuoka; *Foreign Affairs Executive:* Ryu Tanaka; *Foreign Rights:* Kazuo Chuma
Subjects: General Fiction, Fine Arts, Encyclopaedias, Dictionaries, Juveniles, Children's Picture Books, Illustrated Books, History, Natural and Social Science, Japanese, Languages, Music, Textbooks, Reference, Education, Educational Materials, Audio-visual Aids, Magazines, Sports, Hobbies
1981: 363 titles *1982:* 350 titles *Founded:* 1946

Gakuseisha Publishing Co Ltd, 3-27-14 Shikahama, Adachi-ku, Tokyo 123 Tel: (03) 8573031
President: Masami Tsuruoka; *Foreign Rights Executive:* Tsuchiya Kozo
Subjects: Ancient History, Archaeology, Reference
Founded: 1952

Hakusui-Sha, 3-24 Kanda-Ogawamachi, Chiyoda-ku, Tokyo 101 Tel: (03) 2917811
President: Takashi Takahashi; *Foreign Trade Executive:* Souichi Kobayashi; *Foreign Rights Executive:* Kazuaki Fujiwara
Subjects: Dictionaries, Languages, Fiction, Non-fiction, Literature, Drama, Music, Art, Philosophy
Founded: 1915

Hakuyu-Sha*, 9 Ageba-cho, Shinjuku-ku, Tokyo 162 Tel: (03) 2688271
Man Dir: Eiji Takamori; *Foreign Trade Executive:* Montaro Ono; *Publicity & Advertising:* Kazuya Baba; *Foreign Rights:* Eiji Takamori
Subjects: Dictionaries, Natural Science, Industry
Founded: 1948

Hayakawa Publishing Inc, 2-2 Kanda-Tacho, Chiyoda-ku, Tokyo 101 Tel: (03) 2523111 Cable Add: Hayakawashobo Tokyo
Executive Vice-President, Foreign Trade & Rights Executive: Hiroshi Hayakawa
Subjects: Foreign Fiction, Non-fiction, History, Philosophy & Religion, Art, Juveniles, Natural, Social & Political Sciences, Literature, Magazines, Plays, Mysteries, Science Fiction, Fantasy

Heibonsha Ltd, Publishers, 5 Sanbancho, Chiyoda-ku, Tokyo 102 Tel: (03) 2650451 Cable Add: Booksheibonsha
President: Kunihiko Shimonaka; *Dirs:* Shoichiro Kobayashi, Motoo Imakire
Subjects: Encyclopaedias, Japanese & Chinese studies, General Non-fiction, Art, Reference, Education, History, Philosophy, Social Science, Periodical
Founded: 1914

Hikarinokuni Co Ltd*, 3-2 Uehon-machi, Tennoji-ku, Osaka 543 Tel: 7681151
Man Dir: Yotaro Matsumoto; *Editorial & Export Dir:* Masaaki Tsuchiya
Subjects: Juveniles, Education
Founded: 1945

Hirokawa Publishing Co*, PO Box 38 Hongo, Bunkyo-ku, Tokyo 113-91 (Located at: 27-14 Hongo 3-chome, Bunkyo-ku, Tokyo 113) Tel: (03) 8153651 Cable Add: Higesehi Tokyo
President: Genji Hirokawa; *Man Dir (Editor):* Setsuo Hirokawa; *Sales Dir:* Hideo Hirokawa
Subjects: Medicine, Pharmacy, Natural Sciences, Engineering
Founded: 1926

Hoikusha Publishing Co Ltd*, 17-13, 1-Chome Uemachi, Higashi-ku, Osaka 540 Tel: (06) 7621731 Cable Add: Hoikusha
President: Tatsuo Imai; *Man Dir:* Ryoji Nakanishi; *Editorial:* Hiroshi Murakami
Branch Off: 1-1 Minami-Otsuka, Toshima-ku, Tokyo 170
Subjects: Natural History, Poetry, Biography, History, How-to, Music, Art, High-priced Hard cover books, General Science, Illustrated Nature & Craft Books in English & Japanese
Founded: 1947
ISBN Publisher's Prefix: 4-586

Hokuryukan Co Ltd, 3-21 Kanda Nishiki-cho, Chiyoda-ku, Tokyo 101 Tel: (03) 2913855
President, Editorial: Motojiro Fukuda
Subjects: Juveniles, General Science, Reference, Engineering
Founded: 1891

The **Hokuseido** Press, 12 Nishikicho 3-chome, Kanda, Chiyoda-ku, Tokyo Tel: (03) 2943301 Cable Add: Hokusedpres Tokyo
Dir: Jumpei Nakatsuchi; *Sales, Advertising, Rights & Permissions:* Katsuo Wakiyama
Subjects: Belles Lettres, Poetry, Biography, Philosophy, Religion, University Textbooks
1981: 35 titles *1982:* 37 titles *Founded:* 1914

Holp Book Co Ltd, 19-13 Shinjuku 2-chome, Shinjuku-ku, Tokyo 160 Tel: (03) 3566211 Cable Add: Holpbook Tokyo Telex: 2322421
President: Makito Nakamori; *Editorial:* Shinya Ato; *Rights & Permissions, International Trade:* Minoru Shibuya
Branch Offs: 180 throughout Japan
Subsidiary Companies: Holp Shuppan, Publishers
Subjects: Art, Education, Geography, Juveniles, Literature, Mathematics, Reproductions, Science
1981: 80 titles *1982:* 100 titles *Founded:* 1964

Hyoronsha Publishing Co Ltd*, 2-16 Kanda Jimbo-cho, Chiyoda-ku, Tokyo 101 Tel: (03) 2651961
President: Mrs Mina Takeshita; *Chief Editor:* Saburo Tsuyama; *Sales Manager:* Zenzo Uchida
Subjects: Philosophy & Religion, Education, History, Social Science, Industry, Language, Juveniles, Reference
Founded: 1948

Ie-No-Hikari Association+, 11 Funagawara-cho, Ichigaya, Shinjuku-ku, Tokyo 162 Tel: (03) 2603151 Cable Add: Ienohikari Tokyo Telex: 2322367
Man Dir, Sales: Mareki Kuruba; *Editorial:*

Hachro Kanda; *Book Publication Department, Production:* Shiyozo Nitta; *Publicity:* Akira Suzuki
Subjects: General, Social Science, Agriculture, Industry, Periodicals
Founded: 1925

Igaku-Shoin Ltd, PO Box 5063, Tokyo International (Located at: 5-24-3 Hongo, Bunkyo-ku, Tokyo 11391) Tel: (03) 8111101 Cable Add: Igakushoin Telex: 2723334 (Head Office and Publishing Departments), 2722738 (Foreign Book Department)
President, Editor-in-Chief: Izumi Hasegawa; *Executive Vice-President:* Takao Tsubaki; *Vice-Presidents:* Naobumi Ando (Medical Publications), Noboru Nakajima (Nursing Publications), Osamu Nishikawa (Sales), Yu Kanehara (International); *Senior Editor* (International Publishing): Hideo Okada; *Managers:* Makoto Yamamoto (Foreign Books and Journals), Masayuki Nishizawa (Marketing and Book Imports)
Subsidiary Companies: Igaku-Shoin Medical Publishers Inc, 1140 Ave of the Americas, New York, NY 10036, USA; Medical Sciences International Ltd, Kida Bldg, 1-2-13 Yushima, Bunkyo-ku, Tokyo 113, Japan
Subjects: Medical and Dental Sciences, Nursing
Founded: 1944
ISBN Publisher's Prefixes: 4-260, 0-89640

The **International Nursing** Foundation of Japan+, 1-32 4-chome, Kudan-Kita, Chiyoda-ku, Tokyo 102 Tel: (03) 2646667 Cable Add: Infurse Tokyo
Man Dir: Dr Kazuharu Ogura; *Editorial:* Mrs Sada Nagano, Tetsuro Nishizaki; *Rights & Permissions:* Ichiro Takeuchi; *Publicity & Advertising:* Miss Fujiko Masame
Subjects: Nursing Science (National & International)
1982: 6 titles *Founded:* 1971

International Society for Educational Information Inc, Koryo Bldg, 2nd floor, Wakaba 1-18, Shinjuku-ku, Tokyo 160 Tel: (03) 3581138
Executive Director: Michiko Kaya
Subject: Japan

Ishiyaku Publishers Inc, 7-10 Honkomagome 1-chome, Bunkyo-ku, Tokyo 113 Tel: (03) 9443131 Cable Add: Mepharma Tokyo Telex: 2723298 Mdp J
President: Dr Takashi Imada; *Executive Dir:* Hiroshi Miura; *Editors-in-Chief:* Akio Fukushima, Takao Suda; *Marketing Dirs:* Yutaka Shimizu, Akira Iwase, Tai Watanabe
Orders to: Tokyo Mail Service Co Ltd, 23-5 Sugamo 4-chome, Toshima-ku, Tokyo 170
Branch Off: Kansai Branch, c/o Manden Bldg, 11-23 Nishi-Tenma 4-chome, Kita-ku, Osaka-shi 530
Bookshops: Shigaku Shoten Ltd, 2-5 Inohana 2-chome, Chiba-shi 280; Shiensha Ltd, c/o Yamashita Bldg, 9-5 Misakicho 2-chome, Chiyoda-ku, Tokyo 101
Subjects: Medicine, Dentistry, Pharmacology, Nutrition, Veterinary Medicine
Founded: 1921

Iwanami Shoten, Publishers, 2-5-5 Hitotsubashi, Chiyoda-ku, Tokyo Tel: (03) 2654111 Cable Add: Iwanamipress Tokyo Telex: J29495 Iwanami
Chairman: Yujiro Iwanami; *President:* Toru Midorikawa; *Executive Dir, Chief Editor, Publicity:* Yoshikatsu Nakajima; *Foreign Rights:* Takao Hori, Miyo Nakamura, Takeko Tomita
Subjects: Biography, Economics, History, Reference, Philosophy, Psychology, Art, Juveniles, Social & Natural Science, Paperbacks, University Textbooks, Dictionaries, Periodicals
1981: 427 titles *1982:* 475 titles *Founded:* 1913

Iwasaki Shoten Co Ltd*, 1-9-2 Suido, Bunkyo-ku, Tokyo 112 Tel: (03) 8129131
Man Dir: Koyu Moriyama; *Sales Manager:* Matsutoshi Ohkawa; *Editorial:* Masayasu Konishi
Subjects: Juveniles, Art
Founded: 1934

Japan Broadcast Publishing Co Ltd*, 41-1 Udagawa-cho, Shibuya-ku, Tokyo 150 Tel: (03) 4647311 Cable Add: Nhpublishco Tokyo
President: Kazuo Fujinei; *Foreign Trade Executive:* Michio Okubo; *Foreign Rights Executive:* Yoshio Nemoto
Subjects: Radio, Television, Philosophy, Religion, History, Geography, Social & Natural Sciences, Politics, Law, Economics, Engineering, Medicine, Technology, Industry, Art, Language, Juveniles, Literature, Reference, Textbooks
Founded: 1931

Japan Publications Inc, PO Box 5030 Tokyo International, Tokyo 101-31 (Located at: 1-2-1 Sarugaku-cho, Chiyoda-ku, Tokyo 101) Tel: (03) 2958411 Cable Add: Nichiboshuppan Tokyo: J 27161
President: Iwao Yoshizaki; *Executive Dir:* Soshichi Toyoshima; *Editor-in-Chief:* Richard L Gage; *Sales Dir:* Yukishige Takahashi; *Rights & Permissions:* Masatoshi Sato
Subsidiary Companies: Japan Publications Trading Co Ltd, PO Box 5030, Tokyo International, Tokyo 101-31
Subjects: History, How-to, Reference, Juveniles, Health, Hobbies, High-priced Paperbacks
1981: 60 titles *1982:* 72 titles *Founded:* 1942

Japan Times*, Publishing Department, 5-4, Shibaura 4-chome, Minato-ku, Tokyo 108
Man Dir: Toshio Tojo
Subjects: Non-fiction, Reference, Textbooks

Japan Travel Bureau Inc, Publishing Division, 8th Floor, OKI Bldg, 3 Kanda Kaji-Cho 3-chome, Chiyoda-ku, Tokyo 101 Tel: (03) 2578320 Cable Add: Jtbbook Tokyo J24418 Telex: 2228020
Man Dir: Shigeo Miyakoshi; *Editorial:* Yoshio Fukushima; *Foreign Trade, Foreign Rights:* Kunihiko Shibuya
Subsidiary Companies: Densan Process Co; Kotsu Print Co; Kotsu Seihon Co; Toyo Books Co
Branch Offs: The International Bldg, 45 Rockfeller Plaza, New York, NY 10020, USA; 624 South Grand Ave, Suite 1410, Los Angeles, Calif, 90014, USA; 402 Qantas Bldg, Union Sq, 360 Post St, San Francisco, Calif 94108, USA; The Royal Exchange Bldg, 56 Pitt St, Sydney, Australia; Waikiki Business Plaza, 2270 Kalakaua Ave, Honolulu, Hawaii 96815; 20 rue Quentin Bauchart, Paris 75008, France; Room 2123, Hotel Miramar, Nathan Rd, Kowloon, Hong Kong; 5 Rue Chantepoulet, Geneva, Switzerland; 50-51 Russell Square, London WC1B 4JQ, UK; c/o Guam Hilton Hotel, Ipao Beach, Guam; Via Emilia 47, Rome, Italy
Subjects: General, Travel Guides, Maps, History, Geography, Language
Founded: 1912
ISBN Publisher's Prefix: 0-87040

Kadokawa Shoten*, 2-13-3 Fujimi-cho, Chiyoda-ku, Tokyo 102 Tel: (03) 2657111
Man Dir: Haruki Kadokawa; *Editorial:* Sadaharu Mouri; *Sales:* Tsuguhiko Kadokawa; *Production:* Shigeo Nakai; *Publicity:* Akio Baba; *Rights & Permissions:* Hiroshi Tagami
Subjects: General Fiction, Fine Arts, History, Religion, Literature, Dictionaries
Founded: 1945

Kaibundo Publishing Co Ltd*, 2-5-4 Suido, Bunkyo-ku, Tokyo 112 Tel: Tokyo 815 3291
President: Yoshihiro Okada; *Editorial Dir:* Yuji Tamura; *Foreign Trade, Foreign Rights:* Shin-ichi Arihara
Subjects: Maritime Affairs, Ship-building, Safety Engineering, Insurance, Risk Management
Founded: 1914

Kairyudo Publishing Co Ltd, 3-18 Kanda Nishiki-cho Chiyoda-ku, Tokyo 101 Tel: (03) 2931811-9
Man Dir: Takahiro Nakamura; *Editorial, Foreign Trade, Foreign Rights:* Satoshi Kobayashi; *Sales:* Shoichi Akane; *Production:* Kazuo Kimura; *Publicity:* Mistunobu Okawa
Associate Company: Kairyukan Publishing Co Ltd
Branch Offs: Fukuoka, Nagoya, Osaka, Sapporo
Subjects: Textbooks, Natural Science, Art, Language, Reference, Teaching Aids
Founded: 1926

Kaisei-Sha, 3-5 Ichigaya, Sadohara-cho, Shinjuku-ku, Tokyo 162 Tel: (03) 2603221 Cable Add: Kaiseisha Telex: J32721 Kaiseico
President: Hiroshi Imamura; *Editorial Dir:* Mitsuo Takamori; *Sales Dir:* Rokuroh Isohata; *Editor, Foreign Rights:* Hiroshi Konno
Subject: Juveniles
1981: 120 titles *Founded:* 1936

Kaitaku-Sha, 2-5 Kanda Jinbo-cho, Chiyoda-ku, Tokyo 101 Tel: (03) 2657641
President: Kunio Naganuma; *Foreign Trade:* Takehito Yamaguchi; *Foreign Rights:* Yasuhiko Yamamoto
Subjects: Reference, Education, Language, Literature
Founded: 1927

Kajima Institute Publishing Co Ltd, 6-5-13 Akasaka, Minato-ku, Tokyo 107 Tel: (03) 5822251
President: Zenjiro Kawai; *Foreign Trade:* Kazuichi Kawamura; *Foreign Rights:* Sachie Furuta
Subjects: Architecture, Urban Engineering, Civil Engineering
Bookshops: Kasumigaseki Bookstore, 3-2-5 Kasumigaseki, Chiyoda-ku, Tokyo; Shinjuku Mitsui Building Bookstore, 2-1 Nishishinjuku, Shinjuku-ku, Tokyo; Shibuya Tohoseimei Building Bookstore, 2-15 Shibuya, Shibuya-ku, Tokyo
1982: 970 titles *Founded:* 1963

Kanehara & Co Ltd*, 31-14, 2-chome, Yushima, Bunkyo-ku, Tokyo 113 Tel: (03) 8117161 Cable Add: Kanekoraco Tokyo
President and General Manager: Hideo Kanehara; *Director (Foreign Business):* Hiroshi Kohno
Subjects: Medicine, Technology, Industry
Founded: 1875
Miscellaneous: Publish Ishihara's Tests for Colour-blindness

Kawade Shobo Shinsha*, 2-32-2, Sendagaya, Shibuya-ku, Tokyo 151 Tel: (03) 4783251
President: Masaru Shimizu
Subjects: General Fiction, Natural & Social Science, Art, History, Philosophy
Founded: 1957

Kenkyusha Ltd, 2 Kanda Surugadai 2-chome, Chiyoda-ku, Tokyo 101 Tel: (03) 2912301
President: Torao Uyeda; *Foreign Trade*

Executive: Shiro Nagai; *Foreign Rights Executive:* Yukio Kohno
Subjects: Reference, Languages, Dictionaries
1981: 3 titles *1982:* 3 titles *Founded:* 1907

Kinokuniya Co Ltd (Publishing Department), 17-7 Shinjuku 3-chome, Shinjuku-ku, Tokyo 160-91 Tel: (03) 3540131 Cable Add: Kinokuni
General Manager: Yoshibumi Araki; *Sales:* Takeo Sakuma
Associate Companies: Kinokuniya Book-Stores of America Co Ltd, 1581 Webster St, San Francisco, CA 94115, USA; 110 S Los Angeles St, Los Angeles, CA 90012, USA; Kinokuniya Publications Service of New York Co Ltd, 633 Third Ave, Suite 1925, New York, NY 10017, USA; Kinokuniya Publications Service of London Co, Radnor House, 93-97 Regent St, London W1, UK
Subjects: Biography, History, Music, Art, Philosophy, Politics, Medicine, Psychology, Engineering, General Science, Social Science, University Textbooks
Bookshops: 17-7 Shinjuku 3-chome, Shinjuku-ku, Tokyo 160 (54 branches throughout Japan)
Founded: 1926

Kodansha Ltd, 2-12-21 Otowa, Bunkyo-ku, Tokyo 112 Tel: (03) 9451111 Cable Add: Kodanshapublish Tokyo Telex: 2722570 Kodanc J
President: Koremichi Noma; *Editorial:* Akira Miki; *Sales:* Kanzo Yamaguchi; *Rights & Permissions:* Koki Mori
Subsidiary Companies: Kodansha International Ltd (qv); Kodansha Scientific Ltd (qv)
Branch Offs: Fukuoka, Hiroshima, Nagoya, Osaka, Sapporo, Sendai
Subjects: General Non-fiction, Religion, Philosophy, History, Geography, Art, Politics, Economics, Pedagogy, Sociology, Natural Science, Medicine, Social Science, Engineering, Language, Literature, Juveniles, Reference Books, Periodicals, Comics
Book Club: Kodansha Disney Children's Book Club
1981: 1,898 titles *1982:* 1,755 titles
Founded: 1909

Kodansha International Ltd, 2-12-21 Otowa, Bunkyo-ku, Tokyo Tel: (03) 9446491 Cable Add: Kodanshaint Tokyo
Man Dir: Saburo Nobuki; *Editorial:* R Jules Young; *Sales:* Keiji Suzuki; *Rights & Permissions:* Yukimori Akanoma; *Publicity:* Yoichi Masuda; *Production:* Kensuke Tada
Parent Company: Kodansha Ltd (qv)
Branch Offs: Kodansha International/USA Ltd, 10 East 53rd St, New York, NY 10022, USA; 44 Montgomery St, San Francisco, Calif 94104, USA
Subjects: Specializing in Japan and Asia: General Fiction, Belles Lettres, Art, How-to, History, Philosophy, Reference, Traditional Crafts, Martial Arts, Cooking
Founded: 1963
ISBN Publisher's Prefix: 0-87011

Kodansha Scientific Ltd, Nisho Bldg 4F, 9-25 Shin-Ogawa-Cho, Shinjuku-ku, Tokyo 162 Tel: (03) 2353761
Parent Company: Kodansha Ltd (qv)
Subjects: Scientific Texts, Reference
Founded: 1970

Komine Shoten Publishing Co Ltd, 6 Yotsuya Funa-machi, Shinjuku-ku, Tokyo
Man Dir: Hiroe Komine
Subjects: Education, Juveniles, Picture Books
Founded: 1946

Kosei Publishing Co Ltd, 2-7-1 Wada, Suginami-ku, Tokyo 166 Tel: (03) 3833151 Cable Add: Koseishuppansha Tokyo
President: Tadashi Furukawa; *Foreign Trade Executive:* Hiroshi Nomura
Subjects: Religion, Juveniles, English Translations, Literature, Magazines
1981: 48 titles *1982:* 61 titles *Founded:* 1950

Koseisha-Koseikaku Co Ltd*, 8 San-ei-cho, Shinjuku-ku, Tokyo 160 Tel: (03) 3597371
President: Hisao Satake; *Editorial:* Fukase Simao; *Publishing:* Hajime Torizuka
Subjects: Philosophy, Sociology, Natural Sciences, Technology, Industry, Astronomy
Founded: 1922

Kyo Bun Kwan Inc*, 4-5-1 Ginza, Chuo-ku, Tokyo 104 Tel: (03) 5618446 Cable Add: Kyobunkwan Tokyo
Subject: Religion
Bookshop: 4-5-1 Ginza, Chuo-ku, Tokyo 104
Founded: 1885

Kyoritsu Shuppan Co Ltd*, 6-19 Kobinata, 4-chome, Bunkyo-ku, Tokyo 112 Tel: (03) 9472511
Chief Man Dir: Masataka Takeuchi
Subjects: Natural Science & Technology, Medicine, Industry, Textbooks
Founded: 1926

McGraw-Hill Kabushiki Kaisha, Kyobashi PO Box 281, Tokyo 104 (Located at: 77 Bldg, 14-11 4-chome Ginza, Chuo-ku, Tokyo) Tel: (03) 5428821 Cable Add: McGrawHillinTokyo Telex: J28372
President: Riichi Inagaki
Parent Company: McGraw Hill Inc, 1221 Ave of the Americas, New York, NY 10020, USA
Associate Companies: See McGraw Hill Book Co (UK) Ltd, UK

Maruzen Co Ltd*, PO Box 5050, Tokyo International 10031 (Located at: 3-10 Nihonbashi 2-chome, Chuo-ku, Tokyo 103) Tel: (03) 2727211 Cable Add: Maruya Tokyo Telex: J26517
President: Shingo Iizumi; *Man Dir:* Kumao Ebihara; *Dir (Export and Import):* Yasuo Kanazawa; *General Manager (Publishing Division):* Junji Sekine; *Dir (Import):* Tadashi Fukuda
Subsidiary Companies: Maruzen Asia (Pte) Ltd, Singapore (qv); Maruzen International Co Ltd, New York, USA
Subjects: Linguistics, Medicine, Pure & Applied Chemistry, Technical, Architecture, Mathematics, Engineering, Economics, Management, Dictionaries
Bookshops: 3-10 Nihonbashi 2-chome, Chuo-ku, Tokyo 103; also at Fukuoka, Hiroshima, Kobe, Kyoto, Nagoya, Okayama, Osaka, Sapporo, Sendai, Tsukuba
Founded: 1869

Medical Friend Co Ltd, 1-32 4-chome Kudan Kita, Chiyoda-ku, Tokyo 102 Tel: (03) 264 6611
President: Kazuharu Ogura; *Editorial, Publicity, Advertising, Sales, Rights & Permissions:* Yoshihiro Ogura
Branch Off: 2-1207 1-chome Umeda, Kita-ku, Osaka 530
Subjects: Medical, Paramedical, Nursing Science & Arts, Expert Publications, Textbooks and Periodicals
1981: 90 titles *Founded:* 1947

Minerva Shobo Co Ltd, 1 Tsutsumidani-cho, Hinooka Yamashina, Yamashina-ku, Kyoto 607 Tel: Kyoto 5815191
President: Nobuo Sugita; *Editorial Dir:* Kiyoshi Igarashi; *Foreign Trade:* Keizo Sugita; *Foreign Rights:* Takeo Isozaki
Subjects: Philosophy & Religion, History, Social Welfare, Gerontology, Social Science, Literature, Reference
1981: 241 titles *Founded:* 1948

Misuzu Shobo Publishing Co Ltd, 17-15 Hongo 3-chome, Bunkyo-ku, Tokyo 113 Tel: (03) 8159181
Foreign Trade, Foreign Rights: Toshito Obi; *Sales Dir:* Yoshio Aida
Subjects: Art, Literature, Psychiatry, Mathematics, Natural Sciences, Human and Social Sciences
Founded: 1946

Morikita Shuppan Co Ltd*, 4-11 Fujimi 1-chome, Chiyoda-ku, Tokyo 102 Tel: (03) 2658341
President: Hajime Morikita; *Foreign Trade Executive:* Kazuo Mori; *Foreign Rights Executive:* Mohachi Yanagisawa
Subjects: Natural Science, Technology, College and University Textbooks
Founded: 1940 (as Morikita Shoten)

Nagai Shoten Co Ltd, 21-15, Fukushima 8-chome, Fukushima-ku, Osaka 553 Tel: (06) 4521881
President: Hideichi Nagai; *Man Dir, Editorial:* Tadao Nagai
Subject: Medicine
1981: 20 titles *1982:* 18 titles *Founded:* 1946

Nankodo Co Ltd+, PO Box 5272, Tokyo International, Tokyo 100-31 (Located at: 42-6, Hongo 3-chome, Bunkyo-ku, Tokyo 113) Tel: (03) 8117234 Cable Add: Booknankodo Telex: 2722203 Nankod J
President: Takehiko Kodachi; *Dirs:* Koji Arai (Publications), Masao Takahashi (Foreign Division); *Sales Dir:* Shoji Sano; *Managers:* Takayuki Izumi (Planning, Publicity), Iwao Tojo (Imports)
Branch Off: Oike-minami Teramachi dori, Nakakyo-ku, Kyoto 604
Subjects: Medicine, Language, Natural Science, Technology
1981: 65 titles *1982:* 65 titles *Founded:* 1879

Nanzando Co Ltd*, 4-1-11 Yushima, Bunkyo-ku, Tokyo 113 Tel: (03) 8143681
Man Dir: Kimio Suzuki
Subjects: Reference, High-priced Paperbacks, Medicine, University Textbooks, Pharmacology
Founded: 1901

Nihon Bunka Kagakusha Co Ltd, 15-17 Honkomagome 6-chome, Bunkyo-ku, Tokyo 113 Tel: (03) 9463131 Cable Add: Nihonbunkamm Tokyo
President: Mohachi Motegi; *Foreign Trade Executive:* Haruo Kurihara
Subjects: Education, Social Science, Medicine, Reference Books
Founded: 1948

Nihon Vogue (Publishing) Co Ltd, 34 Ichigaya-Honmuracho, Shinjuku-ku, Tokyo 162 Tel: (03) 2698711 Cable Add: Spinningwheel
Chief Executive: T Seto; *Editorial Manager:* S Noguchi; *Foreign Trade:* N Seto
Subjects: Knitting, Crocheting, Embroidery, Handicrafts (in Paperback)
Founded: 1954

Obunsha Co Ltd*, 55 Yokodera-cho, Shinjuku-ku, Tokyo 162 Tel: (03) 2666101 Cable Add: Obunsha Tokyo
President: Yoshio Akao; *Production Manager:* Masami Kobayashi; *Sales Manager:* Tomio Inayoshi; *Publicity Manager:* Tomomasa Nomura; *Books Department Manager:* Yoshio Amamiya; *Magazine Department Manager:* Seiichi Uchiyama
Affiliates: Asahi National Broadcasting Co Ltd, 6-4-10 Roppongi, Minato-ku, Tokyo 106; Bunsen Co Ltd, 5-2 Kojimachi, Chiyoda-ku, Tokyo 102; Japan Cultural Broadcasting Corporation, 1-5 Wakabacho, Shinjuku-ku, Tokyo 160; The Japan LL Education Center, 3-14-16 Shimo-ochiai, Shinjuku-ku, Tokyo

161; The Japan Society of English Study, 55 Yokodera-cho, Shinjuku-ku, Tokyo 162; The Nippon Students' Hall, 2-2-7 Hongo, Bunkyo-ku, Tokyo 113; Obunsha International Inc, 55 Yokodera-cho, Shinjuku-ku, Tokyo 162; The Society for Testing English Proficiency, 1 Yarai-cho, Shinjuku-ku, Tokyo 162
Branch Offs: Chubu, Chugoku, Hokkaido, Kansai, Kanto, Kyushu, Tohoku
Subjects: General Fiction, Biography, How-to, Reference, Encyclopaedias, Dictionaries, Magazines, Newspapers, General Science, Secondary Textbooks, Educational Materials
Founded: 1931

Ohmsha Ltd+, 1-3 Kanda Nishiki-cho, Chiyoda-ku, Tokyo 101 Tel: (03) 2330641 Cable Add: Ohmsha
President: S Mitsui; *Executive Dir:* Seiji Sato
Subjects: Science and Engineering, Periodicals
1981: 150 titles *1982:* 160 titles *Founded:* 1914

Ondori Sha Publishers Co Ltd*, 32 Nishi Goken-cho, Shinjuku-ku, Tokyo 162 Tel: (03) 2683101
President: Toshizo Takeuchi; *Editor:* Takeo Sanada; *Sales:* Shigeo Yamamoto
Subjects: Knitting, Lacework, Embroidery, Handicrafts
1981: 56 titles *Founded:* 1945

Ongaku No Tomo Sha Corporation, 6-30 Kagurazaka, Shinju-ku, Tokyo Tel: (03) 2352111 Cable Add: Ongakunotomo Tokyo Telex: J23718 Ontoa
President: Sunao Asaka; *Rights & Permissions:* Teruaki Kurata
Subsidiary Companies: Toa Music International Co, 6-32 Kagurazaka, Shinju-ku, Tokyo; Suiseisha Music Publishers, 3-3 Sanban-cho, Chiyoda-ku, Tokyo; Musica Nova, 6-30 Kagurazaka, Shinjuku-ku, Tokyo
Subjects: Educational, Periodicals, Folios
1981: 184 titles *1982:* 212 titles *Founded:* 1941

Oriental Economist Ltd (K K Toyo Keizai Shimposha)*, 4 Hongoku-cho 1-chome, Nihonbashi, Chuo-ku, Tokyo Tel: (03) 2704111
President: Yoshio Sano; *Man Dir:* Yasuji Tabuchi; *Foreign Trade:* Kazunari Ohgushi; *Foreign Rights:* Iko Furukawa
Subjects: Scholastic, Economics, General Non-fiction, Directories, Industry, Social Science
Founded: 1895

Otsuki Shoten Publishers*, 11-9 Hongo 2-chome, Bunkyo-ku, Tokyo 113 Tel: (03) 8134651 (Sales), (03) 8142931 (Editorial)
President, Production: Tomotaka Taira; *Editorial:* Isao Saho; *Sales:* Hiroshi Suzuki
Subjects: Economics, Philosophy, History, Socialism, General Arts
Founded: 1946

Pacifica Ltd*, Time-Life Books, PO Box 88, Tokyo 100-91 Tel: (03) 2706611 Cable Add: Publiftim Tokyo Telex: J 22276
Publisher: Mitsuo Honda; *Editor-in-chief:* Masatoshi Takeuchi; *Rights & Permissions:* Chiz Nakao
Parent Company: Time Inc
Subjects: General Fiction and Non-fiction
Founded: 1977

Poplar Publishing Co Ltd*, 5 Suga-cho, Shinjuku-ku, Tokyo 160 Tel: (03) 3572211 Cable Add: Poplarpub
President: Tadao Kubota; *Foreign Trade Executive:* Haruo Tanaka; *Foreign Rights Executive:* Hideo Tanaka; *Foreign Rights Editor:* Tetsuo Kubota
Subjects: Juveniles, Fiction, Biography, History, Geography, Natural Sciences, Picture Books
Founded: 1947

Prentice-Hall of Japan Inc, Akasaka Mansion Room 405, 12-23 Akasaka 2-chome, Minato-ku, Tokyo 107 Tel: 5832591
Manager (Books & Rights Sales): Tetsuo Fujiyama
Subjects: Engineering, Technology, Sciences, Social Sciences, Business, Economics, Humanities, Medicine, Nursing, ESL, Children's, Audio-visual materials
Miscellaneous: Firm is an affiliate of Prentice-Hall International, Englewood Cliffs NJ 07632, USA (see Prentice-Hall UK for Associated Companies)
Founded: 1961

The **Reader's Digest** of Japan Limited, 1-1 Hitotsubashi 1-chome, Chiyoda-ku, Tokyo 100 Tel: (03) 2844111 Cable Add: Readigest Tokyo Telex: J23941 Rdtyo
President: T D Wakefield; *Vice-President:* Shugi Fujimori; *Editor-in-Chief* (Magazine): Ko Shioya; *Editor* (Condensed Books): Yoshiko Tamura
Subjects: Geography, Education, Natural Science, Art, Language, Literature, Juveniles
Founded: 1946 (in Japan)

Risosha Ltd*, 46 Akagishita-machi, Shinjuku-ku, Tokyo 162 Tel: (03) 2681306
President: Tetsuo Shimomura; *Foreign Trade:* Tsugumoto Ishii; *Foreign Rights:* Kazumasa Doi
Subjects: Philosophy, Religion, Literature
Founded: 1927

Ryosho-Fukyu-Kai Co Ltd, 8-2 Kasuga 1-chome, Bunkyo-ku, Tokyo 112 Tel: (03) 8131251
President & Editor: Ichigaku Kawanaka; *Foreign Trade Executive:* Isao Hiramatsu; *Foreign Rights Executive:* Fumio Kimura; *Man Dir:* Kiyoshi Funakoshi
Subjects: Law, Social & Political Sciences, Public and Local Administration
Founded: 1914

Saera Shobo (Librairie Çà et Là), 1 Ichigaya-Sadoharacho, 3 chome, Shinjuku-ku, Tokyo 162 Tel: (03) 2684261
Chief Executive: Mitsusato Uraki
Imprint: Mitsusato Uraki
Subject: Children's
1981: 18 titles *1982:* 26 titles *Founded:* 1948
ISBN Publisher's Prefix: 378

Sangyo Tosho Publishing Co Ltd, 11-3 Iidabashi 2-chome, Chiyoda-ku, Tokyo 102 Tel: (03) 2537821
Man Dir: Katsuhisa Morita; *Editorial:* Takehiko Ezura; *Sales:* Eiji Horino
Subjects: Natural Science, Engineering, Technology, Industry, Philosophy, Religion
1982: 28 titles *Founded:* 1925

The **Sankei** Shimbun Shuppankyoku Co*, 3-15 Kanda Nishiki-cho, Chiyoda-ku, Tokyo 101 Tel: (03) 2950911 Telex: J2-2235
Man Dir: Masashi Onoda; *Editorial:* Katsumi Shirai; *Sales:* Hiroshi Ohsato; *Rights & Permissions:* Nobaru Enomoto
Parent Companies: The Sankei Shimbun (Newspaper), Fuji Television Co, Nippon Broadcasting Co
Subjects: History, Social & Political Sciences, Industry, Art, Literature, Juveniles, Journals
Founded: 1950

Sanseido Co Ltd, 2-22-14 Misaki-cho, Chiyoda-ku, Tokyo 101 Tel: (03) 2309411
President: Hisanori Ueno; *Man Dir:* Masaaki Moriya; *Editorial:* Takaaki Hisashi; *Sales:* Toshio Gomi; *Production:* Masaaki Moriya; *Publicity:* Yasuo Nomura; *Rights & Permissions:* Kohji Suzuki
Subjects: Law, History, Reference, High-priced Paperbacks, General & Social Science, Natural Science, University & Secondary Textbooks, Educational Materials, Dictionaries, Literature, Languages
Bookshop: Sanseido Bookstore Ltd, 1-1 Kanda-Jimbocho, Chiyoda-ku, Tokyo
Founded: 1881

Sansyusya Publishing Co Ltd*, 1-5-34 Shitaya, Taito-ku, Tokyo 110 Tel: (03) 8421711 Cable Add: Sansyusyapubl Tokyo
Man Dir: Kanji Maeda; *Sales, Publicity, Advertising, Rights & Permissions Dir:* Shohei Ohara
Subjects: Language Textbooks, Educational Materials, Scientific Linguistic Reprints
Founded: 1938

Sanyo Shuppan Boeki Co Inc, PO Box 5037, Tokyo International 100-31 Tel: (03) 6693761 Cable Add: Sanyobook Tokyo Telex: 2524435 Sanyob
President, Rights & Permissions: Toshiaki Ibe; *Editorial:* Makoto Ito; *Foreign Trade:* Masahiro Takeda
Associate Company: Shinryo Bunko K K (medical bookstore)
Branch Offs: Niihama, Osaka, Tsukuba
Subjects: Food and Cookery, Science, Chemistry
Founded: 1956
Miscellaneous: Also importers

Seibundo Shinkosha Publishing Co Ltd*, 5 Nishikicho 1-chome, Kanda, Chiyoda-ku, Tokyo 101 Tel: (03) 2921211 Cable Add: Varipubco Tokyo
Man Dir, Sales: Shigeo Ogawa; *Editorial:* Teruaki Shimada; *Publicity:* Kazuhiko Furuya
Subjects: Commerce, Agriculture, Horticulture & Landscaping, Natural Science, Technology, Industry, Audio Electronics, Hobbies, Games, Juvenile
Founded: 1912

Seiwa Shoten Co Ltd*, 2-5 Kamitakaido, 1-chome, Suginamiku, Tokyo 168 Tel: 3290031 Cable Add: Seiwapublishers
President: Youji Ishizawa; *Editor-in-Chief:* Yoshinori Asanuma; *Sales Manager:* Masaharu Fujiwara; *System Manager:* Yukio Shimura; *Foreign Books Manager:* Yumi Matsuzawa
Subjects: Medicine, Psychiatry, Psychology, Language
Book Club: Bookclub Psyche
Bookshops: 1-11 Kamitakaido, 1-chome, Suginamiku, Tokyo 168; 2-5 Kamitakaido, 1-chome, Suginamiku, Tokyo 168; 1-48 Sengawacho, Chofushi, Tokyo 182
Founded: 1976

Seizando-Shoten Publishing Co Ltd, 4-51 Minami-motomachi, Shinjuku-ku, Tokyo 160 Tel: (03) 3575861
President: Minoru Ogawa; *Editorial:* Yoshihiro Munekata; *Sales:* Teruo Kimura; *Production:* Yuhei Shibuya, Nobuyuki Tanaka; *Publicity:* Sakae Ogawa; *Rights & Permissions:* Kokichi Shioji
Subjects: Maritime, Technology, Transport
Founded: 1953
ISBN Publisher's Prefix: 4-7911

Sekai Bunka Publishing Inc*, 4-2-29 Kudan Kita, Chiyoda-ku, Tokyo 102 Tel: (03) 2625111 Cable Add: Sebunpub
President: Tsutomu Suzuki; *Foreign Trade & Rights:* Seihachiro Kawahata
Branch Off: 501 Fifth Ave, Suite 2102, New York, NY 10017, USA
Subjects: Art, History, Geography, Juveniles, Educational Materials, Audiovisual
Founded: 1946

Shakai Shiso-Sha*, 25-21 Hongo 1-chome, Bunkyo-ku, Tokyo 113 Tel: (03) 8138101
President: Kazuki Komorida; *Editorial:* Hitoshi Tanaka; *Sales:* Tadashi Kamatsuka
Subjects: General Fiction, Fine Arts, Architecture, Poetry, Music, History, Travel, Social Science, Theatre
Founded: 1947

Shiko-Sha Co Ltd, 10-12 Hiroo 2-chome, Shibuya-ku, Tokyo 150 Tel: (03) 4007151/4 Cable Add: Lmdecw Tokyo Telex: J24903
Man Dir: Yasoo Takeichi
Subject: Juveniles
Founded: 1950

Shinchosha Co*, 71 Yarai-cho, Shinjuku-ku, Tokyo 162 Tel: (03) 2665101 Cable Add: Shinchosha Telex: Shincho J27433
President: Ryoichi Sato; *Sales:* Shunichi Sato; *Publishing Department:* Hiroshi Nitta
Subjects: General Fiction, Fine Arts, History, Philosophy, Social Science, Reference, Literature, Periodicals
Founded: 1896

Shindan to Chiryo Co Ltd*, Room 406, Marunouchi Bldg, Marunouchi 2-4-1, Tokyo 100 Tel: (03) 2144957
President: Hiroshi Fujizane; *Editorial:* Takeshi Hisatsugi
Subject: Medicine
Founded: 1914

Shinkenchiku-Sha Co Ltd, 31-2 Yushima 2-chome, Bunkyo-ku, Tokyo 113 Tel: (03) 8117101 Cable Add: Japanarch Tokyo
President: Yoshio Yoshida; *General Manager:* Masao Nakamura; *Foreign Rights Executive:* Masao Nakamura
Subsidiary Company: The Japan Architect Co Ltd, 31-2, Yushima 2-chome, Bunkyo-ku, Tokyo 113
Subjects: Architecture, Periodicals
Founded: 1925

Shogakukan Publishing Co Ltd, 2-3-1 Hitotsubashi, Chiyoda-ku, Tokyo 101 Tel: (03) 2305655 Cable Add: Tokyo Shogakukan Telex: 2322192 (Shogak-J)
President: Tetsuo Ohga; *Man Dir:* Tokio Ueno; *Editorial:* Kanae Mishina; *Sales:* Kenichi Watanabe; *Production:* Mitsuo Kokubo
Associate Company: Shueisha Publishing Co Ltd (qv)
Subjects: Art, How-to, Juveniles, Dictionaries, Geography, History, Encyclopaedias, Travel, Literature, Non-fiction, Photography
Founded: 1922

Shokabo Publishing Co Ltd*, 8-1 Yonban-cho, Chiyoda-ku, Tokyo 102 Tel: (03) 2629166
Man Dir: Tatsuji Yoshino
Subjects: Mathematics, Natural Science, Technology
Founded: 1897

Shokoku-Sha Publishing Co Ltd*, 25 Saka-machi, Shinjuku-ku, J-160 Tokyo Tel: (03) 3593231
President: Genshichi Shimoide; *Sales Dir:* Hideo Shimizu; *Editorial Dir:* Taishiro Yamamoto
Subjects: Fine Arts, Technical, Architecture, Engineering, General Science, University Textbooks, Educational Materials
Founded: 1932

Shueisha Publishing Co Ltd*, 2-5-10 Hitotsubashi, Chiyoda-ku, Tokyo 101 Tel: (03) 2306111
President: Sueo Horiuchi; *Editorial:* Shusei Suzuki; *Sales:* Hisao Suzuki; *Foreign Trade:* Takeo Hasegawa; *Foreign Rights:* Hajime Kanazawa
Associate Company: Shogakukan Publishing Co Ltd (qv)
Subjects: General Fiction, Non-fiction, Art, Language, Literature, Juveniles, Periodicals
Founded: 1926

Shufu-to-Seikatsu Sha Ltd*, 5-7, 3-chome, Kyobashi, Chuo-ku, Tokyo 104 Tel: (03) 5625951
Man Dir: Tokumitsu Higuchi; *Editor-in-Chief:* Miss Miyako Kiyohara; *Publishing Department, Foreign Rights:* Shujiro Murakawa
Subjects: Philosophy & Religion, History, Medicine, Technology, Art, Literature, Juveniles
Founded: 1935

Shufunotomo Co Ltd*, 6, 1-chome Surugadai, Kanda, Chiyoda-ku, Tokyo 101 Tel: 2941111 Cable Add: Shufunotomo Tokyo Telex: 26925
President: Haruhiko Ishikawa; *Dir, International Department:* Atsushi Gohara; *Manager of International Department:* Kazuhiko Nagai
Subjects: Cookery, Flower Arrangement, Bonsai, Gardening, How-to, General Fiction
1981: 200 titles *Founded:* 1916

Shuppan News Co Ltd, 3-2-4, Misaki-cho, Chiyoda-ku, Tokyo Tel: (03) 2622077
Editorial: Takeo Yoshizawa; *Sales:* Keiji Kinoshita; *Rights & Permissions:* Tetsuzo Suzuki
Founded: 1949
ISBN Publisher's Prefix: 4-7852

The **Simul** Press Inc, Kowa Bldg No 9, 1-8-10, Akasaka, Minato-ku, Tokyo 107 Tel: (03) 5824221 Cable Add: Simulshuppan Tokyo
President and Editor-in-Chief: Katsuo Tamura; *Senior Man Dir:* Eiko Ikuta; *Dir (overseas affairs):* Masumi Muramatsu; *Senior Editor:* Daitaro Suwabe; *Marketing:* Motoo Miyashita; *Publicity:* Koichiro Watanabe
Associate Company: Simul International, Inc
Subjects: General, Philosophy and Religion, Social Sciences, History, Education, Business and Economics, Current Affairs, Language, Literature, English-language books on Japan and Asia
1981: 60 titles *1982:* 60 titles *Founded:* 1967

Sogensha Publishing Co Ltd*, 4-2 1-chome, Nishitenma, Kita-ku, Osaka 530 Tel: (06) 3632531
President: Bunji Yabe
Associate Company: Tokyo Sogensha Co Ltd (qv)
Subjects: Art, History, Philosophy, Religion, Low-priced Paperbacks, Medicine, Psychology, University Textbooks, Educational Materials
Founded: 1925

Syokabo Publishing Co Ltd*, 8-1 Yomban-cho, Chiyoda-ku, Tokyo 102 Tel: (03) 2629166
President: Tatsuji Yoshino; *Foreign Trade:* Tatsuji Yoshino; *Foreign Rights:* Kyohei Endo
Subjects: Natural Science and Engineering
Founded: 1895

Taishukan Publishing Co Ltd (Taishukan Shoten), 3-24 Kanda-Nishiki-cho, Chiyoda-ku, Tokyo 101 Tel: (03) 2942221
Man Dir: Toshio Suzuki; *Sales, Publicity & Advertising:* Shigeo Suzuki; *Rights & Permissions:* Toshio Saeki
Subjects: Reference, High-priced Paperbacks, Language & Linguistics, Sports, Social Science, University & Secondary Textbooks, Educational Materials, Dictionaries, Periodicals
1981: 63 titles *1982:* 67 titles *Founded:* 1918

Takahashi Shoten Co Ltd*, 22-13 Otowa 1-chome, Bunkyo-ku, Tokyo 112 Tel: (03) 9434525
President: Kyushiro Takahashi; *Foreign Trade Executive:* Yukihiko Takahashi
Subjects: Technology, Law Education, Medicine, Language, Juveniles
Founded: 1939 (as Kowado Co Ltd)

Tanko-Sha Publishing Co Ltd, Tanko Bldg, Horikawa Kuramaguchi-agaru, Kita-ku, Kyoto 603 Tel: Kyoto 4325151
Editorial Dir: Shiro Usui
Subjects: Philosophy & Religion, History, Art, Japanese Culture
Founded: 1945

Teikoku-Shoin Co Ltd*, 3-29 Kanda Jinbo-cho, Chiyoda-ku, Tokyo 101 Tel: (03) 2611584 Cable Add: Books Teikoku Telex: 2324921 Tekoku J
President: Takashi Goto; *Editorial, Foreign Rights:* Chozo Miyakawa; *Foreign Trade:* Yoshiaki Kai
Subjects: History, Geography, Maps, Atlases, Textbooks
Founded: 1926

Tokai University Press*, Shinjuku Tokai Bldg, 3-27-4 Shinjuku, Shinjuku-ku, Tokyo 160 Tel: (03) 3561541
Man Dir: Tatsuro Matsumae; *Editorial:* Yasunosuke Yamamoto; *Sales:* Eizaburo Okada; *Production:* Chimaju Kato; *Publicity:* Wataru Yamada
Orders to: Orion Books, Export Dept of Orion Service & Trading Co Inc, PO Box 5216, Tokyo International
Subjects: Philosophy, Religion, History, Social & Natural Science, Technology, Art, Language, Literature
Founded: 1962
Miscellaneous: Tokai University European Centre is at Strandvej 476, DK-2950, Vedbæk, Denmark

Tokuma-Shoten, 4-10-1 Shinbashi, Minato-ku, Tokyo Tel: 4336231
President: Yasuyoshi Tokuma; *Editor:* Minoru Hagiwara; *Foreign Trade:* Osamu Okamura
Subjects: General Fiction, Non-fiction, Belles Lettres, How-to, Social Science, Art, Games, Sports, Juveniles
Founded: 1954

Tokyo Kagaku Dozin Co Ltd*, 36-7 Sengoku 3-chome, Bunkyo-ku, Tokyo 112 Tel: (03) 9465311
President: Atsushi Ueki; *Editorial:* Minako Ozawa
Subjects: Natural Science, Medical Science, Chemistry
Founded: 1961

Tokyo News Service Ltd*, Tsukiji Hamarikyu Building, 10th Floor, 3-3, Tsukiji 5-chome, Chuo-ku, Tokyo 104 Tel: (03) 5428521 Cable Add: Tradenews Tokyo Telex: 2523285 Stnews J
President: T Okuyama
Branch Offs: Kobe Tel: (078) 3316658; Osaka Tel: (06) 2316051
Subjects: Social Science, Economics, Business, Nautical, Television, Tourism, General Non-fiction, Periodicals
Founded: 1947

Tokyo Sogensha Co Ltd*, 1-16 Shin Ogawa-machi, Shinjuku-ku, Tokyo 162 Tel: (03) 2688201
President: Takao Akiyama; *Editorial:* Jun Atsuki; *Sales:* Ichiro Hiramatsu; *Production:* Haruo Hashimoto; *Publicity:* Nobuko Okubo; *Rights & Permissions:* Yasunobu Togawa
Associate Company: Sogensha Publishing Co Ltd (qv)
Subjects: Detective Stories, Science Fiction,

Social Science, Literature
Founded: 1925

Tokyo Tosho Co Ltd*, 2-5 Suido, Bunkyo-ku, Tokyo 112 Tel: (03) 8147818
President: Susumu Otake; *Foreign Trade Executive:* Hiroyasu Katayama; *Foreign Rights:* Shigeaki Matsumoto
Subjects: Natural Science, Popular Science, Engineering, Biographies
Founded: 1955

Toppan Co Ltd, Shufunotomo Bldg, 1-6 Kanda Surugadai, Chiyoda-ku, Tokyo 101 Tel: 2953461 Cable Add: Toppan Book Tokyo Telex: J27317
Chief Executive: Kazuo Suzuki; *Man Dir:* Hiroyuki Watanabe; *Sales Dir:* Moto Sekino
Subsidiary Company: Toppan Co (Singapore) Private Ltd, Singapore (qv)
Subjects: Medicine, Psychology, Engineering, Social Science, Agriculture, Economics, Mathematics, Statistics, Zoology, Biology, Chemistry, Physics, Languages and Linguistics in authorized International Student Edition reprints for university students
1981: 7 titles *Founded:* 1963
ISBN Publisher's Prefix: 4-8101

Toyo Keizai Shimposha Ltd, see Oriental Economist Ltd (qv)

Tsuru-Shobo Co Ltd*, 12-2 Fujimi 2-chome, Chiyoda-ku, Tokyo 102 Tel: (03) 2654781 Cable Add: Bookstsuru Tokyo
Man Dir: Mitsusaburo Sadahira; *Foreign Rights & Permissions:* Hiro Nagano
Subjects: How-to, Juveniles, Art, Reference
Founded: 1926

Charles E **Tuttle** Co Inc, 2-6 Suido 1-chome, Bunkyo-ku, Tokyo 112 Tel: (03) 8117106/9 Cable Add: Tuttbooks Telex: 0272-3170
President, Editorial, Sales, Publicity: Keiko Iwamoto; *Production:* Satoru Iwamoto; *Rights & Permissions:* Keiko Iwamoto
Branch Offs: 402 Seki, Tama-ku, Kawasaki-shi 214; 2-7 Showa-cho, Suita-shi, Osaka 564; 1-3 1-chome, Tomari, Naha-shi, Okinawa 900
Subjects: Japanese & Asian Studies, Art, Domestic & Handicrafts, Fiction, Martial Arts, Poetry, Belles Lettres, Political & Social Science, Juveniles, Languages
Bookshops: Kanda Book Shop, 1-3 Jimbo-cho, Kanda, Chiyoda-ku, Tokyo 101; American Club Book Shop, 2-1-2, Azabudai, Minato-ku, Tokyo 106
1983: 52 titles *Founded:* 1948
ISBN Publisher's Prefix: 0-8048

U N A C Tokyo*, 1-4-7 Azabu-da, Minato-ku, Tokyo 106 Tel: (03) 5857069/5853069 Cable Add: Unacprod
Publisher: Masaomi Unagami

University of Tokyo Press+, 7-3-1 Hongo, Bunkyo-ku, Tokyo 113 Tel: (03) 8110964 Cable Add: Universitypress
Man Dir: Kazuo Ishii; *Associate Dirs:* Senzaburo Nakahira, Hitoshi Tada; *Editorial Dir:* Norihiro Saito; *Sales:* Kazuhiko Kurata; *International Trade, Publicity, Rights & Permissions:* Masami Yamaguchi; *Production Dir:* Hisakazu Bessho
Subjects: History, Philosophy, Reference, Religion, Medicine, Psychology, Engineering, Natural & Social Sciences, University Textbooks
Bookshop: Yurinsha Ltd, PO Box 63, Hongo Post Office, Tokyo
1981: 129 titles *1982:* 154 titles *Founded:* 1951
ISBN Publisher's Prefix: 0-86008

Mitsusato **Uraki**, an imprint of Saera Shobo (Librairie Çà et Là) (qv)

John **Weatherhill** Inc, 7-6-13 Roppongi, Minato-ku, Tokyo Tel: 4048871 Cable Add: Weatherhill Tokyo Telex: J26601
President: Yoshiharu Naya; *Vice President:* Takeshi Yamazaki; *Sales, Advertising:* Teruaki Ueno; *Rights & Permissions:* Miriam F Yamaguchi
Subjects: Belles Lettres, Poetry, Biography, History, How-to, Music, Art, Reference, Religion, Juveniles, High-priced Paperbacks — all on Asia
Founded: 1962

Yama-Kei (Publishers) Co Ltd, 1-1-33 Shiba-Daimon, Minato-ku, Tokyo 105 Tel: (03) 4364021
President: Yoshimitsu Kawasaki; *Foreign Trade:* Susumu Harada; *Foreign Rights:* Naotake Murakami
Branch Off: 1-12-12 Esaka-cho, Fukita-Shi, Osaka
Subjects: Mountaineering, Ski-ing, Geography, Natural Science
Founded: 1930

Yohan Publications Inc+, 14-9 Okubo 3-chome, Shinjuku-ku, Tokyo 160 Tel: (03) 2080181 Cable Add: Bookyohan
President: Masahiro Watanabe
Parent Company: Yohan (Western Publications Distribution Agency) (qv under Major Booksellers)
Subjects: Fiction, Non-fiction, Illustrated Books, English and other language teaching books
1981: 29 titles *1982:* 31 titles *Founded:* 1963
ISBN Publisher's Prefix: 4-89684

Yokendo Ltd, 5-30-15 Hongo, Bunkyo-ku, Tokyo 113 Tel: (03) 8140911
President: Toshio Oikawa
Subjects: Natural Science, Engineering, Industry
Founded: 1914

Yuhikaku Publishing Co Ltd*, 17 2-chome, Kanda Jinbo-cho, Chiyoda-ku, Tokyo 101 Tel: (03) 2641311 Cable Add: Yuhikakubook
Dirs: Shiro Egusa, Tadaatsu Egusa
Subjects: Law, Economics, Sociology, Psychology, History, Education
Founded: 1877

Yushodo Booksellers Ltd*, 29 San-ei-cho, Shinjuku-ku, Tokyo 160 Tel: (03) 3571411 Cable Add: Yushodo Tokyo Telex: 0232-4136
President: Mitsuo Nitta; *Editorial:* Yoshito Yamada
Subsidiary Companies: Publishers International Corp, Yushodo Film Publications Ltd
Branch Off: Kansai, Kyoto: Annex Building (Ohtsuka, Tokyo)
Subjects: Political Economics, Japanese Classical Literature
Miscellaneous: Company are also Booksellers

The **Zauho** Press*, Sogo Daiichi Bldg, 3-2 Kojimachi, Chiyoda-ku, Tokyo 102 Tel: (03) 2623661 Cable Add: Zauhopress
President: Shigeki Gotoh; *Foreign Trade Executive:* Yoshiki Gotoh; *Foreign Rights Executive:* Masao Nishida
Subjects: Art, History, Co-editions
Founded: 1925

Zoshindo Juken-Kenkyusha*, 19-15 2-chome Shinmachi, Nishi-ku Osaka 550
President: Shigetoshi Okamoto
Subjects: Education, Juveniles
1981: 502 titles *Founded:* 1890

Literary Agents

The **English Agency** (Japan), 305 Azabu Empire Mansion, 4-11-28 Nishi Azabu, Minato-ku, Tokyo Tel: (03) 4065385 Cable Add: Engagent
Dirs: Desmond Briggs, William Miller, Peter Thompson; *Manager:* Junzo Sawa
Specialization: English and American books

Japan Uni Agency Inc, Naigai Bldg, 1-1 Kanda Jimbocho, Chiyoda-ku, Tokyo 101 Tel: (03) 2950301 Cable Add: Uniliterary Telex: J27260
President: Noboru Miyata; *Dirs:* Yoshio Taketomi, Kozaburo Yano

Kern Associates, 1150-7 Irino, Hosokawa-cho, Miki-shi, Hyogo-Ken 673-07 Tel: (07948) 80323/82448
President: Lawrence E Kern
Specialization: Fiction, Non-fiction, Academic, Juvenile, Media book sales promotion, Dual language contracts (Japanese and English)

Kurita-Bando Literary Agency, 2-10-11 Gotenyama, Musashino-shi, Tokyo 180 Tel: (0422) 498745 Cable Add: Kblit Mitaka Telex: Unilit J27260
Dirs: Akiko Kurita, Yumiko Bando, Noboru Miyata

Orion Press, 55, 1-chome, Kanda-Jimbocho, Chiyoda-ku, Tokyo 101 Tel: (03) 2951405/2951406 Cable Add: Orionserv Tokyo Telex: J24447 Orionprs
Contact: T Sakai

Tuttle-Mori Agency Inc, Fuji Bldg 8F, 2-15 Kanda-Jimbocho, Chiyoda-ku, Tokyo Tel: (03) 230 4081 Cable Add: Tuttmori Tokyo Telex: 02324915 Tutmor J
President: Tom Mori; *Editorial Dir:* Kiyoshi Asano; *Editorial Manager:* Yoshikazu Iwasaki; *Business Department Dir:* Sakae Mino; *Business Department Manager:* Yuji Takeda
Also: Sandford J Greenburger Associates Inc, 825 Third Ave, New York, NY 10022, USA Tel: (212) 7538581 Cable Add: Inlitbur Telex: 420633
Contacts: Ms Nikki Smith, Ms Lucy Stille
61 Blenheim Terrace, London NW8 0EJ Tel: 624 9601 Telex: 28905 Monref G
Contact: Ms Anne Martyn
Dealing in Book Rights, Serial Rights, Co-Production, Motion Picture Rights, TV Rights, Radio Rights, Stage Rights, Merchandising Rights

Book Clubs

Books-on-Japan-in-English Club*, Shin Nichibo Bldg, 2-1 Sarugaku-cho 1-chome, Chiyoda-ku, Tokyo 101
President: Iwao Yoshizaki; *Secretary-General:* Akio Takeuchi
Founded: 1955
Miscellaneous: Club consists of 41 leading publishers, bookstores, exporters, and printers of English-language books and periodicals dealing with Japan and Orient

Fukuinkan Shoten Library*, 1-9 Misaki-cho 1-chome, Chiyoda-ku, Tokyo 101
Owned by: Fukuinkan Shoten Publishers (qv)
Subject: Children's Books

Kodansha Disney Children's Book Club, 2-12-21 Otowa, Bunkyo-ku, Tokyo 112
Owned by: Kodansha Ltd, Publisher (qv)
Subject: Children's Books

Bookclub **Psyche***, Seiwa Shoten Co Ltd, 2-5 Kamitakaido, 1-chome, Suginamiku, Tokyo 168

Owned by: Seiwa Shoten Co Ltd
Subject: Psychiatry

Major Booksellers

Asahiya Shoten Ltd (Booksellers), Osaka-Fukoku-Seimei Bldg 3F, 2-4 Komatsubara-cho Kita-ku, Osaka 530 Tel: (06) 3150971
Foreign Books Department: c/o Asahi Building, 17-9 Toyosaki 3-chome, Ohyodo-ku, Osaka 531 Tel: (06) 3727251
President: Takeshi Hayashima
16 bookstores throughout the country

Goethe Book Dealers Inc*, Room 560, Marunouchi Bldg, Chiyoda-ku, Tokyo 100 Tel: (03) 2117839

Ikubundo Publishers Co*, 30-21 Hongo 5-chome, Bunkyo-ku, Tokyo 113 Tel: (03) 8145571/5

Japan Publications Trading Co Ltd (Import and Export)*, 2-1, Sarugaku-cho 1-chome, Chiyoda-ku, Tokyo 101 Tel: (03) 2923751 Cable Add: Shutsubo Tokyo Telex: J27161 Jptco

Kinokuniya Co Ltd, 17-7 Shinjuku 3-chome, Shinjuku-ku, Tokyo 160-91 Tel: (03) 3540131 Telex: 02324759 (and 54 branches throughout Japan)

Kurita Shuppan Hanbai Co Ltd*, 3-1 Higashisakashita 1-chome, Itabashi-ku, Tokyo 174 Tel: (03) 9652111
Distributor

Maruzen Co Ltd*, 3-10 Nihonbashi 2-chome, Chuo-ku, Tokyo 103 Tel: (03) 2727211
Branches: Sapporo, Sendai, Tsukuba, Nagoya, Kyoto, Osaka, Kobe, Okayama, Hiroshima, Fukuoka
Importer/Exporter

Nippon Shuppan Hanbai KK*, 3 4-chome, Kanda Surugadai, Chiyoda-ku, Tokyo 101 Tel: (03) 2331111 Cable Add: Honnippan Tokyo Telex: J 25627 Nippan
Distributors

Tokyo Shuppan Hanbai Co Ltd (Distributors)*, 53 Higashigoken-cho, Shinjuku-ku, Tokyo 162 Tel: (03) 2696111 Cable Add: Hontohan Tokyo Telex: 2322141

Charles E **Tuttle** Co Inc, 2-6 Suido 1-chome, Bunkyo-ku, Tokyo 112 Tel: (03) 8117106
Manager: Satoru Iwamoto

United Publishers Services Ltd, Kenkyu-sha Bldg, 9 Kanda Surugadai 2-chome, Chiyoda-ku, Tokyo 101 Tel: (03) 2914541 Cable Add: Unitedbooks Tokyo
The largest stock holding agent of overseas publishers in the Japanese foreign book market

Yohan (Western Publications Distribution Agency), 14-9 Okubo 3-chome, Shinjuku-ku, Tokyo 160 Tel: (03) 2080181 Cable Add: Bookyohan Tokyo
President: Masahiro Watanabe

Major Libraries

Hokkaido University Library, Kita-8, Nishi-5, Sapporo 060 Tel: (011) 716-2111
Librarian: Yutaka Shioya
Publication: Yuin (The Hokkaido University Library Bulletin, only in Japanese, quarterly)

Kokuritsu Kobunshokan*, 3-2 Kitanomaru Park, Chiyoda-ku, Tokyo
National Archives

Kyoto Sangyo University Library*, Kamigamo, Kita-ku, Kyoto Tel: (075) 7012151

Kyushu University Library, 6-10-1 Hakozaki-machi, Fukuoka City, Fukuoka Prefecture

School of **Library** and Information Science, Keio University, Mita Minato-ku, Tokyo 108 Tel: (03) 4533920/4534511
Librarian: Junko Oka
Publication: Library and Information Science (annual)

Nagoya University Library*, Furo-cho, Chikusa-ku, Nagoya

National Diet Library, Nagata-cho, Chiyoda-ku, Tokyo 100 Tel: (03) 5812331
Librarian: Masahiro Arao

Osaka Gakuin University Library*, Kishibe, Suita City, Osaka

Osaka Prefectural Nakanoshima Library, 1-2-10 Nakanoshima, Kita-ku, Osaka Tel: (06) 2030474

Tenri Central Library, Tenri University, Somanouchi-cho 1050, Tenri City, Nara 632 Tel: (07436) 31511 ext 6750
Chief Librarian: Hidetsugu Ueda

Tohoku University Library, Kawauchi, Sendai City 980

Tokyo Metropolitan Central Library*, 5-7-13 Minami-Azabu, Minato-ku, Tokyo 106 Tel: (03) 4428451
Dir: Yoichi Maeda

The **Toyo** Bunko*, Honkomagome 2-chome, 28-21, Bunkyo-ku, Tokyo 113 Tel: (03) 9420121
Publications: Memoirs of the Research Department of the Toyo Bunko
Also Centre of East Asian Cultural Studies for UNESCO, for which publications include various directories, bibliographies, textbooks, etc

University Libraries, see under town names

University of Tokyo Library*, 3-1 Hongo 7-chome, Bunkyo-ku, Tokyo 113 Tel: (03) 8122111

Waseda University Library*, 6-1 Nishiwaseda 1-chome, Shinjuku-ku, Tokyo 160 Tel: (03) 2034141 ext 5132
Librarian: Harukaze Furukawa

Library Associations

Gakujutsu Bunken Fukyu-Kai*, c/o Tokyo Institute of Technology, 2-12-1 O-okayama, Meguro-ku, Tokyo
Association for Science Documents Information
President: Shu Kambara
Publications: Union Catalog of Books on Japan in Western Languages (English), *Reports on Progress in Polymer Physics in Japan* (English), *Directory of Japanese Scientific Periodicals* (English), *Aseismic Design and Testing of Nuclear Facilities* (English), *Union Index of Books in the Field of Documentation* (English)

Joho Shori Gakkai, Kikai Shinko-Kai Building No 3-5-8, Shiba-Koen, Minato-ku, Tokyo 105
Information Processing Society of Japan
President: Prof T Sakai
Publications: Journal of Information Processing (English, quarterly), *Joho-shori* (Journal of IPSJ, Japanese, monthly), *Transactions of IPSJ* (Japanese, bi-monthly)

Mita Society for Library and Information Science, School of Library and Information Science, Keio University, Mita, Minatoku, Tokyo 108 Tel: (03) 4533920
Secretary: Toshio Hamada
Publication: Library and Information Science (annual)

Nihon Toshokan Kyokai, 1-10, 1-chome, Taishido, Setagaya-ku, Tokyo 154 Tel: (03) 4106411
Japan Library Association
Secretary-General: Hitoshi Kurihara
Publications: Toshokan Zasshi (monthly), *Gendai no Toshokan* (quarterly), *Nippon no Sankotosho Shikiban* (quarterly), *Nippon no Tosho* (annually), *Sentei Tosho Somokuroku* (annually), *Toshokan nenkan* (annually)

Nippon Dokumentesyon Kyokai*, Sasaki Bldg, 5-7 Koisikawa 2, Bunkyo-ku, Tokyo 112 Tel: (03) 8133791
Japan Documentation Society
President: Y Nakamura
Publications: Documentation Study, Informant (microfiche, twice yearly)

Nippon Igaku Toshokan Kyokai, c/o Business Centre for Academic Societies, 4-16 Yayoi 2-chome, Bunkyo-ku, Tokyo 113
The Japan Medical Library Association
Publications: Igakuvtoshokan; List of current periodicals acquired by the Japanese Medical, Dental and Pharmaceutical Libraries; Union Catalogue of Foreign Books in the Libraries of Japan Medical Schools

Nippon Nogaku Toshokan Kyogikai (JAALD)*, Taiyo Seimei Building, 2-17-2, Shibuya, Shibuya-ku, Tokyo 150 Tel: (03) 4090722
Japan Association of Agricultural Librarians and Documentalists
Secretary: Mrs Shukuko Kamiya
Publications: Bulletin of JAALD (quarterly), *Japanese Agricultural Sciences Index* (monthly with semi-annual indexes), *JAALD Series* (occasional)

Nippon Toshokan Gakkai, c/o Japan Library Association, 1-10 Taishido 1-chome, Setagaya-ku, Tokyo
Japan Society of Library Science
Executive Secretary: Hidetoshi Hirano
Publications: Bibliography on Library Science (annual), *Toshokangakkai Nempo* (Annals) (quarterly)

Nippon Yakugaku Toshokan Kyogikai, c/o Library, Faculty of Pharmaceutical Sciences, University of Tokyo, Hongo 7-3-1, Bunkyo-ku, Tokyo 113
Japan Pharmaceutical Library Association
Publication: Yakugaku Toshokan (Pharmaceutical Library Bulletin)

Senmon Toshokan Kyogikai (SENTOKYO), c/o National Diet Library, 1-10-1, Nagata-cho, Chiyoda-ku, Tokyo 100 Tel: (03) 5811364
Japan Special Libraries Association
President: Shigeo Nagano; *Executive Dir:* Yoshitaro Tanabe
Publications: Bulletin (five times yearly), *Directory of Special Libraries*, 1982 (in Japanese); *Directory of Information Sources in Japan*, 1980 (in English)

Library Reference Books and Journals

Books

Directory of Information Sources in Japan (in English), Japan Special Libraries Association, c/o National Diet Library, 1-10-1 Nagata-cho, Chiyoda-ku, Tokyo 100

Directory of Special Libraries, Japan Special Libraries Association, c/o National Diet Library, 1-10-1 Nagata-cho, Chiyoda-ku, Tokyo 100

Nippon no Toshokan (Library of Japan), Japan Library Association, 1-10, 1-chome, Taishido Setagaya-ku, Tokyo

A Survey of Special Collections in Japan, The Shuppan News Co Ltd, 2-4 Misaki-cho 3-chome, Chiyoda-ku, Tokyo 101

Union Index of Books in the Field of Documentation, Association for Science Documents Information, c/o Tokyo Institute of Technology, 2-12-1 O-okayama, Meguro-ku, Tokyo

Journals

Biburosu Biblos, National Diet Library, 10-1, 1-chome, Nagata-cho, Chiyoda-ku, Tokyo

Bulletin, Japan Special Libraries Association, c/o National Diet Library, 1-10-1 Nagata-cho, Chiyoda-ku, Tokyo 100

Dokumentesyon Kenkyu (Documentation Study), Japan Documentation Society, Sasaki Bldg, 5-7 Koisikawa 2, Bunkyo-ku, Tokyo 112

Handbook, Special Libraries Association, c/o National Diet Library, 10-1, 1-chome, Nagata-cho, Chiyoda-ku, Tokyo

Library System (text in Japanese), Medical Library and Information Centre, Keio Unveristy, 35, Shinanomachi, Shinjuku-ku, Tokyo

Nippon no Sakotosho Shikiban (Reference Library Quarterly of Japan), Japan Library Association, 1-10, 1-chome, Taishido Setagaya-ku, Tokyo

Reference, National Diet Library, 10-1, 1-chome, Nagata-cho, Chiyoda-ku, Tokyo

Toshokan-Kai (Library World) (text in Japanese, table of contents in English), Japan Institution for Library Science, Tenri University, Tenri, Nara

Toshokan Zasshi (Library Journal), Japan Library Association, 1-10, 1-chome, Taishido Setagaya-ku, Tokyo

Sendai no Toshokan (Library of Today), Japan Library Association, 1-10, 1-chome, Taishido Setagaya-ku, Tokyo

Literary Associations and Societies

The **Dickens** Fellowship*, Bungei-Gakuba, Seijo University 6-1-20, Seijo Setagaya, Tokyo
Honorary Secretary: Prof Koichi Miyazaki

Japan Essayists' Club*, c/o Yujiro Chiba, 1-1-1 Shimbashi, Minato-ku, Tokyo

Japan Poet Club*, c/o Showa Joshi University, 1-7 Taishido, Setagaya-ku, Tokyo

Japan Poets' Association*, c/o Kazue Shinkawa, 5-9-3 Seta, Setagaya-ku, Tokyo

Nihon Dokubungakkai, c/o Ikubundo, Hongo 5-30-21, Bunkyo-ku, Tokyo 113
Japanese Society of German Literature
President: Prof Tozo Hayakawa
Publication: Doitsu Bungaku (German Literature) (twice yearly)

Nihon Eibungakkai, 601 Kenkyusha Bldg, 9 Surugadai 2-chome, Kanda, Chiyoda-ku, Tokyo 101
English Literary Society of Japan
President: Kei Koike
Publication: Studies in English Literature (three times yearly)

Nippon Bungaku Kyokai*, 2-17-10 Minami-otsuka, Toshima-ku, Tokyo Tel: (03) 9412740
Japanese Literature Association
President: Tamotsu Hirosue
Publication: Japanese Literature (monthly)

Nippon Furansu-go Furansu-bungaku Kai*, c/o La Maison franco-japonaise, 2-3, Kanda-Surugadai Chiyoda-ku, Tokyo
Japanese Society of French Language and Literature
President: Takeo Kuwabara
Publication: Etudes de Langue et Littérature françaises (half-yearly)

Nippon Hikaku Bungakukai*, Aoyamagakuim University, Shibuya-ku, Tokyo
Comparative Literature Society of Japan
General-Secretary: Saburo Ota
Publications: Journal (annually), *Bulletin* (quarterly)

Nippon Romazikai*, Yosida Honmati 27, Kyoto
Japanese Society of Roman Letters
President: Ogata-Zyun'iti
Publication: Romazi Sekai (The World of Roman Letters)

Nippon Rosiya Bungakkai*, Faculty of Literature Waseda University, Toyama-cho, Shinjuku-ku, Tokyo
Russian Literary Society of Japan
Secretary-General: General K Nakano
Publication: Bulletin

Japan P E N Club, Room 265, Syuwa Residential Hotel, 9-1-7 Akasaka, Minato-ku, Tokyo 107
Secretary: Yohji Akikawa
Publications include: Japanese Literature Today (1976-82) (annual), *Japan PEN News* (twice yearly)

Society for the Promotion of Japanese Literature*, c/o Bungei Shunju Publishing Co Ltd, 3-23 Kioi-cho, Chiyoda-ku, Tokyo 102

Literary Periodicals

Doitsu Bungaku (German Literature), Nihon Dokubungakkai, Hongo 5-30-21, Bunkyo-ku, Tokyo 113

Doshisha Literature; a journal of English literature and philology (text in English), Doshisha University, English Literature Society, Kyoto

Doshisha Studies in Foreign Literature (text in Japanese, English, French or German), Doshisha University, Foreign Literature Society, Kyoto

East-West Review; essays on literature and translations of literary works, Doshisha University, Department of English, Kyoto

Etudes de Langue et Littérature françaises (Studies in French Language and Literature), Nippon Furansu-go Furansu-bungaku Kai, c/o La Maison franco-japonaise, 2-3, Kanda-Surugadai Chiyoda-ku, Tokyo

Hon: a Book-bin for Scholars, Yushodo Booksellers Ltd, 29 Saneicho, Shinjuku-ku, Tokyo 160

Japan Quarterly, Asahi Shimbun-Sha, Tokyo

Japanese Literature, Nippon Bungaku Kyokai, 2-17-10 Minami-otsuka, Toshima-ku, Tokyo

Japanese Literature Today (1976-82) (annual), Japan P E N Club, Room 265, Syuwa Residential Hotel, 9-1-7 Akasaka, Minato-ku, Tokyo 107

Mototachi no Kagaribi (The Little Sister's Watchfire), Kodansha International Ltd, 2-12-21 Otowa, Bunkyo-ku, Tokyo

Outlook (Japan), Yoshidahon-machi, Sakyo-Ka, Kioto

The Sea, Chuokoron-Sha Inc, 2-8-7 Kyobashi, Chuo-ku, Tokyo 104

Studies in English Literature, Nihon Eibungakkai, 601 Kenkyusha Bldg, 9 Surugadai 2-chome, Kanda, Chiyoda-ku, Tokyo 101

Literary Prizes

Akutagawa Prize*
In memory of Ryunosuke Akutagawa for works written by previously unpublished authors. One of the most important literary prizes in Japan. 500,000 yen and a specially made watch. Awarded twice a year. Enquiries to The Society for the Promotion of Japanese Literature, c/o Bungei Shunju Publishing Co Ltd, 3-23 Kioi-cho, Chiyoda-ku, Tokyo 102

Culture Prize
For outstanding achievement in the following areas: illustrations, photographs, book designs, juvenile cartoons and picture books: 300,000 yen. Non-fiction: 500,000 yen. Awarded annually to publishers in Japan. Enquiries to Kodansha Ltd, 2-12-21 Otowa, Bunkyo-ku, Tokyo

Japan Essayists' Club Prize*
For the best essays and criticism including those in book form, especially the work of new authors. 100,000 yen. Awarded annually. Enquiries to Japan Essayists' Club, c/o Yujiro Chiba, 1-1-1 Shimbashi, Minato-ku, Tokyo

Japan Literary Prize*
Established 1969. For the best work published during the preceding year, including poetry and dramatic works. Jury of five critics and writers. 1,000,000 yen. Awarded annually, the latest winner was Nobuo Kojima for *Watashi no Sakka Henreki* (Ushio Publishing Co). Enquiries to Shincho-Sha, 71 Yarai-cho, Shinjuku-ku, Tokyo 162

Japan Poet Club Prize*
For an author who has contributed significantly to poetry. 50,000 yen. Awarded annually. Enquiries to Japan Poet Club, c/o Showa Joshi University, 1-7 Taishido, Setagaya-ku, Tokyo

Japan Translation Prize for Publisher*
For outstanding translations. Awarded annually. Enquiries to Japan Society of Translators, Rm 208, Shiba Mansion, 5-11-6 Toranomon, Minato-ku, Tokyo

Japan Woman Writer Prize*
For the best novel. 1,000,000 yen. Awarded annually. Enquiries to Chuokoron-Sha Inc, 2-8-7 Kyobashi, Chuo-ku, Tokyo 104

Japan Women Writers' Literary Prizes*
To encourage women novelists. Awarded annually. Enquiries to Women Writers' Association, 17 Yanaka-Shimizucho, Daito-ku, Tokyo

Kikuchi Prize*
In memory of Hiroshi Kan Kikuchi. 500,000 yen and a specially made clock. Awarded annually. This prize is given for significant achievement in Japanese literature, drama, cinema, newspaper, broadcasting, book or magazine publication. It can otherwise be given to the individual or group who showed the most creative achievement in the year in the introduction of Japanese literature to foreign countries. Enquiries to The Society for the Promotion of Japanese Literature, c/o Bungei Shunju Publishing Co Ltd, 3-23 Kioi-cho, Chiyoda-ku, Tokyo 102

Kishida Prize for Drama*
In commemoration of the playwright Kunio Kishida for an outstanding work by a new playwright. 200,000 yen. Awarded annually. Enquiries to Hakusui-Sha, 3-24 Ogawa-cho, Chiyoda-ku, Tokyo 101

Mainichi Publishing Culture Prize*
To the authors and publishers of works contributing to human culture. 100,000 yen. Awarded annually. Enquiries to Mainichi Newspapers Publishing Co, 1-1, 1-chome, Hitotsubashi, Chiyoda-ku, Tokyo

Mr H's Prize*
For works by a new poet. 100,000 yen and a table clock. Awarded annually. Enquiries to Japan Poets' Association, c/o Mrs Hideki Isomura, 5-9-3 Seta, Setagaya-ku, Tokyo

Naoki Prize*
In memory of Sanjugo Naoki, for the most promising writer of popular literature. 500,000 yen and a specially made watch. Awarded twice a year. Enquiries to The Society for the Promotion of Japanese Literature, c/o Bungei Shunju Publishing Co Ltd, 3-23 Kioi-cho, Chiyoda-ku, Tokyo 102

Noma Prize for Juvenile Novel
For the best juvenile novel. 1,000,000 yen. Awarded annually. Enquiries to Kodansha Ltd, 2-12-21 Otowa, Bunkyo-ku, Tokyo 112

Noma Prize for Literature
For the best Japanese novel of the year. 2,000,000 yen. Awarded annually. Enquiries to Kodansha Ltd, 2-12-21 Otowa, Bunkyo-ku, Tokyo 112

Oya Soichi Non-fiction Prize*
To encourage new non-fiction writers. 300,000 yen, plus round-the-world air ticket, contributed by JAL Co Ltd. Awarded annually. Enquiries to Bungei Shunju Co Ltd, 3-23 Kioi-cho, Chiyoda-ku, Tokyo 102

The Sankei Award for Children's Books and Publications*
For authors of outstanding works published for children, in Japanese (including translations). First prize of 500,000 yen, five prizes of 100,000 yen and an Artistic Design Prize of 100,000 yen. Publishers of the works are also recognized. Awarded annually. Enquiries to Sankei Newspaper Co, 1-7-2 Otemachi, Chiyoda-ku, Tokyo

Shogakukan Literary Prize
For the best novel, poem, drama and non-fiction children published during the preceding year. 500,000 yen. Awarded annually. Enquiries to Shogakukan Publishing Co Ltd, 2-3-1, Hitotsubashi, Chiyoda-ku, Tokyo 101

Tanizaki Junichiro Prize
To recall the works by Tanizaki and to celebrate the publisher's birthday. 1,000,000 yen. Enquiries to Chuokoron-Sha Inc, 2-8-7 Kyobashi, Chuo-ku, Tokyo 104

Yomiuri Literature Prize*
For the best work in six categories: novel, essay and travels, drama, literary study and translation, poetry and haiku, critique and biography. 500,000 yen each. Awarded annually. Enquiries to Yomiuri Newspapers Publishing Co, 1-7-1 Otemachi, Chiyoda-ku, Tokyo

Yoshikawa Prizes
For the most popular novel: 2,000,000 yen. For a new novelist: 500,000 yen. Awarded annually. Enquiries to Kodansha Ltd, 2-12-21 Otowa, Bunkyo-ku, Tokyo

Translation Agencies and Associations

Japan Society of Translators*, Room 208, Shiba Mansion, 5-11-6 Toranomon, Minato-ku, Tokyo

Jordan

General Information

Language: Arabic. English widely used by business people
Religion: Muslim (and large Christian minority)
Population: 3 million
Literacy Rate (1961): 39%
Bank Hours: 0830-1230 Saturday-Thursday
Shop Hours: 0900-1300, 1500-1900 Saturday-Thursday
Currency: 1000 fils = 1 dinar; 10 fils is known as a piastre
Export/Import Information: No tariffs on books and advertising matter, but tax applies. Import licences required but granted freely. Air freight must be by Jordanian national airline. Transportation insurance must be arranged in Jordan
Copyright: No copyright conventions signed

Book Trade Reference Books

Jordanian National Bibliography (annually), Jordan Library Association, PO Box 6289, Amman

Palestinian Bibliography: A List of Books Published by the Arabs in Palestine 1948-1980. Jordan Library Association, PO Box 6289, Amman

Palestinian-Jordanian Bibliography, Jordan Library Association, PO Box 6289, Amman

Publishers

Jordan Distribution Agency, PO Box 375, Amman Tel: 30191/2 Cable Add: Jodistag Amman Telex: 22083 Distag Jo
Chairman, General Manager: Raja Elissa; *Man Dir:* Nadia Elissa
Subjects: Jordanian Tourism and History
Founded: 1951

Jordan Press and Publishing Co Ltd*, Amman
Publishes daily newspaper, *al-Destour*
Founded: 1967
Miscellaneous: 25% of capital held by government

National Press Library*, Amman
Subjects: Education, Politics, Law, Textbooks

Major Booksellers

Gibralter Book Store*, Corner Faisal St, Amman

Al **Istiklal** Library*, PO Box 156, Amman

George Y **Koro***, Petra Library, PO Box 1061, Amman

Al **Ma'aref** Library*, PO Box 650, Amman

Yarmouk University Bookshop*, PO Box 566, Irbid Tel: 71100-15 Cable Add: Yarmouk Jordan Telex: 51533 Jo

Youth's Library Mohamad Ahmed Sharareh*, PO Box 180, Amman

Major Libraries

American Center Library, PO Box 676, Amman (Located at: 3rd Circle Jebel Amman) Tel: 41520/44371 ext 374
Librarian: Ms Jumana Esau

Amman Public Library, c/o City Librarian, PO Box 132, Amman Tel: 24174/36114 Telex: 21969 Amcity Jo
Librarian: Farouk Mo'az

British Council Library, Amman Centre, Jebel Amman, PO Box 925071, Amman Tel: 36147/36148 Telex: 21823 Bojor Jo

Public Library*, PO Box 348, Irbid

Public Library*, Nablus

University of Jordan Library*, University of Jordan, Amman Tel: 843555-74/843666-80 Telex: 21629 Unvj jo
Director: Dr Kamel Asali
Publications include: Al-Maktaba (monthly newsletter), *The Library Guide* (in English and Arabic), *Periodical Holdings* (in English and Arabic), *Arab References till 1980* (in Arabic), *Jordanian Publications in 1982*

Yarmouk University Library*, PO Box 566, Irbid Tel: 71100-71115 Cable Add: Yarmouk Jordan Telex: 51533 Yarmuk Jo
Director: Dr T Akasheh

Library Associations

Jordan Library Association*, PO Box 6289, Amman
President: Anwar Akroush; *Executive Secretary:* Medhat Mar'ei
Publications: Rissalat al-Maktaba (The Message of the Library) (quarterly); *Palestinian-Jordanian Bibliography 1900-1970, 1972; 1971-1975, 1976; Directory of Libraries in Jordan 1976, 1976; Jordanian National Bibliography* (annually); *Introduction to Librarianship* (in Arabic), 1981; *The Palestinian Bibliography: a List of Books Published by the Arabs in Palestine 1948-1980*

Library Reference Books and Journals

Book

Directory of Libraries in Jordan 1976, Jordan Library Association, PO Box 6289, Amman

Journal

Rissalat al-Maktaba (Message of the Library) (text in Arabic, summaries in English), Jordan Library Association, PO Box 6289, Amman

Kampuchea

General Information

It has not been possible to obtain information on publishing and bookselling in Kampuchea for several years. In view of the changed circumstances of the country, information obtained in the past has been omitted from this edition of *International Literary Market Place*
Language: Khmer, French
Religion: Theravada Buddhist
Population: 8.6 million
Literacy Rate (1962): 36.1%
Business Hours: 0700-1400 Monday-Saturday
Currency: riel
Export/Import Information: Little current information available; free foreign exchange market arrangements not operating
Copyright: UCC, Florence (see International section)

Kenya

General Information

Language: Swahili (also English)
Religion: About 30% Christian, 6% Muslim; rest follow traditional beliefs
Population: 14.9 million
Bank Hours: 0900-1400 Monday-Friday; 0900-1100 first and last Saturday of each month (except on coast, where banks open and close half an hour earlier)
Shop Hours: 0830-1230, 1400-1630 Monday-Friday; 0830-1200 or 1230 Saturday
Currency: 100 cents = 1 Kenya shilling
Export/Import Information: No tariff on books or advertising matter. Import licences and exchange controls
Copyright: UCC (see International section)

Book Trade Organizations

Kenya Booksellers' and Stationers' Association, PO Box 20373, Nairobi Tel: 01031
Secretary: Adrian P Louis

Kenya Publishers' Association, c/o PO Box 72532, Nairobi Tel: 336377
Secretary: G P Lewis

Book Trade Reference Books and Journals

Books

Catalogue of Government Publications, Government Printing Press, PO Box 30128, Nairobi

Kenya National Bibliography, Kenya National Library Service, Ngong Rd, PO Box 30573, Nairobi

Journal

Bookshop Bulletin, Kijabe St, PO Box 47540, Nairobi

Publishers

A F E R (African Ecclesial Review), an imprint of Gaba Publications (qv)

C P I, an imprint of Camerapix Publishers International Ltd (qv)

Camerapix Publishers International Ltd, PO Box 45048, Nairobi Tel: 23511/334398 Cable Add: Movietone Nairobi Telex: 22576
Man Dir: Mohamed Amin; *Editorial:* Brian Tetley; *Sales:* Mohamed Shaffi; *Production:* Duncan Willetts
Imprint: CPI
Subjects: Illustrated books, especially on Africa, Middle East and Asia
1982: 2 titles *1983:* 3 titles *Founded:* 1960

Comb Books+, PO Box 20019, Nairobi
Man Dir: David Maillu
Subjects: General Fiction, Social Anthropology, Sexual Problems, Educational
Founded: 1972

East African Directory Co*, PO Box 41237, Nairobi Tel: 24151
Man Dir: T A Bhatt
Parent Company: United Africa Press Ltd (qv)
Subject: Reference
Founded: 1947

East African Literature Bureau, see Kenya Literature Bureau

East African Publishing House*, Lusaka Close, PO Box 30571, Nairobi Tel: 557417 Cable Add: Afrobooks Nairobi
Man Dir: E N Wainaina; *Chief Editor, Rights & Permissions:* Richard C Ntiru; *Senior Editor:* D N Waiyaki; *Marketing, Publicity, Sales, Distribution:* J Kimani Kabue; *Production:* John Mwazo
Parent Company: E A Cultural Trust
Associate Company: Afropress Ltd, PO Box 30502, Nairobi
Branch Off: PO Box 3209, Dar es Salaam, Tanzania
Subjects: General Fiction & Non-fiction, Belles Lettres, Poetry, Biography, History, Africana, How-to, Study Guides, Reference, Religion, Juveniles, Books in Kiswahili and other East African languages, Paperbacks, General & Social Science, University, Secondary & Primary Textbooks
Founded: 1965

Evangel Publishing House, PO Box 28963, Nairobi Tel: 802033/802300/802331 Cable Add: Evangelit Nairobi
Man Dir, Editorial, Rights and Permissions: Rev B D Brand; *Sales, Publicity:* Rev Elkanah S Ayiga; *Production:* Martin Loyley
Subjects: General Non-fiction, Reference, Religion, Christian Tracts, Paperbacks, Children's Books
Bookshop: PO Box 28963, Nairobi

Foundation Books*, NCM House, Tom Mboya St, PO Box 73435, Nairobi Tel: 333118
Sub-regional co-ordinator, Regional Centre for Book Promotion in Africa; Co-publishing office Eastern Africa Region
Man Dir; Editorial: F O Okwanya; C R Ojienda; *Sales Manager:* J K Musyoki; *Production:* Sophia Wanjiku Ojienda
Subjects: Belles Lettres, Poetry, Biography, History, Africana, Juveniles, Books in Kiswahili, Paperbacks, Social Science, Secondary & Primary Textbooks, Adult Education Primers, Mathematics
Founded: 1974

Gaba Publications, AMECEA Pastoral Institute, PO Box 908, Eldoret
Dir: Roger Tessier; *Editor:* Brian Hearne
Imprints: AFER (African Ecclesial Review), Spearhead
Subjects: Religion, Anthropology, Scripture, Third World Theology, Religious Education
1981: 11 titles

Government Printer*, Government Printing Press, PO Box 30128, Nairobi

Heinemann Educational Books (East Africa) Ltd*, Kijabe St, PO Box 45314, Nairobi Tel: 22057/338642 Cable Add: Hebooks Nairobi
Man Dir, Rights and Permissions: Henry Chakava; *Editorial:* Paul N Njoroge, Ben Ole Mollel; *Sales:* Johnson K Mugweru
Parent Company: Heinemann Educational Books (International) Ltd, UK (qv)
Subjects: General Fiction & Non-fiction, Belles Lettres, Poetry, Biography, History, Africana, Study Guides, Juveniles, Swahili Language & Literature, Paperbacks, General & Social Science, University, Secondary & Primary Textbooks
1981: 26 titles *Founded:* 1967

Kenya Literature Bureau, Ngong' Rd, PO Box 30022, Nairobi Tel: 723450/722500 Cable Add: Literature Nairobi
Formerly East African Literature Bureau

The Jomo **Kenyatta** Foundation, PO Box 30533, Nairobi Tel: 20704/333714/333715 Cable Add: Foundation
Chief Executive: J K Arap Sang; *Publicity, Rights & Permissions:* Mrs A G O Ojany; *Editorial:* J Kariara; *Production Manager:* Ben Ole Mollei
Parent Organization: Ministry of Basic Education, PO Box 55980, Nairobi
Subjects: Secondary and Primary Textbooks
Founded: 1966

Longman Kenya Ltd, Funzi Rd, PO Box 18033, Nairobi Tel: 559479 Telex: 22724
Man Dir: T J Openda; *Publishing Manager:* A S Yahya; *Marketing and Distribution Manager:* T Kamuyu; *Rights & Permissions:* Longman Group Ltd, UK (qv)
Associate Company: Longman Group Ltd, UK (qv)
Subjects: General Fiction & Non-fiction, Belles Lettres, Poetry, Biography, History, Africana, Reference, Juveniles, Books in 14 Kenyan languages, Paperbacks, General & Social Science, Secondary & Primary Textbooks
Founded: 1965

New-Age Publishers*, PO Box 689, Nakuru Tel: 3309
Man Dir, Publicity: D S Bhawgu; *Editorial, Production:* M L Sharma
Subject: Textbooks
Founded: 1978

Newspread International, PO Box 46854, Nairobi Tel: 331402 Cable Add: Newspread Telex: 22143 Bureau
Man Dir: Kul Bhushan; *Publishing Manager:* Ashok Bharti; *Production Manager:* Benedict Mutisya Nzomo
Subjects: Reference
Founded: 1971

Njogu Gitene Publications*, PO Box 72989, Nairobi
Subjects: Belles Lettres, Poetry, Juveniles, Books in Kiswahili, Secondary & Primary Textbooks
Founded: 1970

Oxford University Press, East and Central Africa, PO Box 72532, Nairobi (Located at: First Floor, Science House, Monrovia St, Nairobi) Tel: 336377 Cable Add: Oxonian Nairobi

Regional Manager, Rights & Permissions: Giles Lewis; *Editor:* Esmé Gichuké; *Production:* Tibusi Lyimo; *Sales:* A K Ismaily
Branch Offs: Dar es Salaam, Tanzania (qv); Harare, Zimbabwe (qv)
Subjects: General Fiction & Non-fiction, Poetry, Biography, History, Africana, Reference, Books in East African languages, Paperbacks, General & Social Science, Secondary & Primary Textbooks
Founded: 1954
Miscellaneous: Firm is a branch of Oxford University Press, UK (qv)
ISBN Publisher's Prefix: 0-19

Salama Publications Ltd*, PO Box 48009, Nairobi
Subjects: How-to, Study Guides, Secondary Textbooks

Spearhead, an imprint of Gaba Publications (qv)

Success Publications*, PO Box 10893, Nairobi
Subjects: How-to, Study Guides

Text Book Centre Ltd, Kijabe St, PO Box 47540, Nairobi Tel: 330340/330341
Man Dir: M J Rughani; *General Manager:* C D Shah
Subjects: Belles Lettres, Poetry, Juveniles, Books in Kiswahili, Paperbacks, Secondary & Primary Textbooks
Bookshops: Kijabe St, PO Box 47540, Nairobi; Westlands Sarit Centre, Box 47540, Nairobi

Transafrica Books*, Kenwood House, Kimathi St, PO Box 49421, Nairobi Tel: 861253
Man Dir: John Nottingham
Subjects: General Fiction & Non-fiction, Belles Lettres, Poetry, Biography, History, Africana, How-to, Study Guides, Reference, Religion, Juveniles, Books in Kiswahili, Paperbacks, Social Science, Secondary & Primary Textbooks

United Africa Press Ltd*, Victoria House, Victoria St, PO Box 41237, Nairobi Tel: 24151
Man Dir: T A Bhatt
Subsidiary Company: East African Directory Co (qv)
Subjects: General, Educational, Reference, Animals
Founded: 1952

Uzima Press Ltd*, PO Box 48127, Nairobi (Located at: St John's Gate) Tel: 20239, 335699
Man Dir: Rev Horace Etemesi
Subjects: Religion, Fiction, Social Sciences, Books for new literates
Founded: 1974

Vipopremo Agencies*, Koinange St, PO Box 47717, Nairobi Tel: 27189
Subjects: How-to, Study Guides

Book Club

Academic Book Club*, PO Box 40144, Nairobi

Major Booksellers

The **Bookshop** Ltd*, Esso House, Kaunda St, PO Box 30247, Nairobi Tel: 23364

The **Catholic** Bookshop Ltd, Kaunda St, PO Box 30249, Nairobi Tel: 25172/338514
Manager: Sr Giovanna

Dhanani's Ltd*, Kimasi St, Corner House, PO Box 72399, Nairobi Tel: 27049

E S A Bookshop*, Church House, Government Rd, PO Box 30167, Nairobi Tel: 20158

Keswick Book Society, Portal House, Banda St, PO Box 10242, Nairobi Tel: 26047
Manageress: Miss M Håkanson

Macdonald's*, Kimathi St, PO Box 49240, Nairobi Tel: 21979

S J Moore Ltd*, Moi Ave, PO Box 30162, Nairobi Tel: 22213
Manager: Marjorie Oludhe Macgoye

Mount Kenya Bookshop Ltd*, PO Box 281, Nyeri Tel: 2513
Branches: PO Box 659, Nakuru Tel: 2806; PO Box 10, Kakamega Tel: 20163; PO Box 29, Meru Tel: 20036
Man Dir: David M Mwangi

Patwa (Embakasi) Ltd*, PO Box 19200, Nairobi Airport, Embakasi, Nairobi

Prestige Booksellers*, Prudential Assurance Bldg, PO Box 45425, Nairobi Tel: 23515

The **Textbook** Centre Ltd, Kijabe St, PO Box 47540, Nairobi Tel: 330340 Cable Add: Text books
Manager: C D Shah

University of Nairobi Bookshop*, PO Box 30197, Nairobi Tel: 334244 ext 2111 Cable Add: Varsity
Manager: Miss N N Kagondu

Wanyee Bookshop Ltd, Aga Khan Walk, PO Box 46815, Nairobi Tel: 331769

Major Libraries

Egerton College Library*, PO Njoro Tel: 27/44/47

Kabete Library*, University of Nairobi, PO Box 29053, Kabete

Kenya Agricultural Research Institute, PO Box 30148, Nairobi Tel: 2121 Cable Add: Agfororg
Librarian: Daniel Njoroge Kaiyare

Kenya National Archives, PO Box 49210, Nairobi Tel: 28959/26007/28020 Cable Add: Archives

Kenya National Library Service*, Ngong Rd, PO Box 30573, Nairobi Tel: 27871/29186
Librarian: Apollo R Oluoch
Publications: Annual Audit Report; Kenya National Bibliography; List of Adult Books, Quarterly Accession

Kenya Polytechnic Library, PO Box 52428, Nairobi Tel: 338231
Librarian: Cephas Dennis Odini

Kenya Technical Teachers' College Library, PO Box 44600, Nairobi Tel: 520211
Librarian: William G Kinyanjui
Publications include: Secondary School Library Facilities in Central Province, Kenya; The Problems of Providing Library Services to School Children in Developing Countries; Serials Literature, Exploitation and Use in Libraries

Kenyatta University College Library, PO Box 43844, Nairobi Tel: Kahawa 356-9; 247/421/459
Librarian: James Mwangi Nganga
Publications include: Directory of Research in the College; Annual Report; Directory of Libraries in Kenya: Occasional Bibliographies

McMillan Memorial Library, Banda St, PO Box 40791, Nairobi Tel: 21844
Chief Librarian: R G Opondo

Mines and Geological Department Library, Machakos Rd, PO Box 30009, Nairobi Tel: 541040 Cable Add: Mineralogy

Ministry of Agriculture Library*, Kilimo House, PO Box 30028, Nairobi Tel: 720609
Librarian: Mrs J N Kariuku

University of Nairobi Libraries*, PO Box 30197, Nairobi Tel: 334244 Cable Add: Varsity Nairobi
Branches: Chiromo, Kabete, Kikuyu

Library Association

Kenya Library Association*, PO Box 46031 Nairobi
Secretary: Miss I N Wanyaga
Publications: Maktaba; Kelias News (bi-monthly)

Library Reference Books and Journals

Book

Directory of Libraries in Kenya, Kenyatta University College Library, PO Box 43844, Nairobi

Journal

Maktaba, Kenya Literature Bureau, PO Box 30022, Nairobi (the official, biannual, journal of the Kenya Library Association)

Literary Periodicals

Busara, Kenya Literature Bureau, PO Box 30022, Nairobi (biannual literary magazine published under the auspices of the Department of Literature, University of Nairobi)

Dhana, Kenya Literature Bureau, PO Box 30022, Nairobi (The Makerere University, Department of Literature, journal of creative writing; twice yearly)

Joe; Africa's entertainment monthly, Joe Publications Ltd, PO Box 30362, Nairobi (a popular magazine with regular literary contributions, review of new books and plays, etc)

Joliso (East African Journal of Literature and Society), Kenya Literature Bureau, PO Box 30022, Nairobi (new literary and cultural magazine edited by Chris Wanjala and published twice yearly since 1973)

Umma, Kenya Literature Bureau, PO Box 30022, Nairobi (The University of Dar es Salaam, Department of Literature, journal of creative writing; twice yearly)

Democratic People's Republic of Korea

General Information

Language: Korean
Religion: Confucian, Buddhist
Population: 17 million

Currency: 100 jun = 1 won
Export/Import Information: No tariff information; all importation and exportation must go through Korea Publications Export & Import Corporation, Pyongyang

Book Trade Reference Journal

Catalogue of Korean Books, Korea Publications Export & Import Corporation, Pyongyang (English listing of books published in various languages)

Publishers

Academy of Sciences Publishing House*, Central District Nammundong, Pyongyang
Subjects: Science, Chemistry, Geology, Metallurgy, Physics, Biology, History, Maps, Mathematics, Meteorology, Education, Economics
Founded: 1953

Academy of Social Sciences Publishing House, Pyongyang
Subject: Social Sciences

Agricultural Books Publishing House, Pyongyang
President: Li Hyun U
Subjects: Agriculture, Industry

Educational Books Publishing House, Pyongyang
Subject: Education, Textbooks

Foreign Languages Publishing House, Pyongyang
President: L Ryang Hun
Subjects: Books on Korea, Foreign publications in translation, Periodicals (English language)

Higher Educational Books Publishing House, Pyongyang
Acting President: Shin Jong Sung
Subjects: Education, Academic, Mathematics, Physics

Industrial Publishing House, Pyongyang
Subjects: Trade, Industry

Kumsong Youth Publishing House, Pyongyang
Subjects: Children's, Juveniles

Literature and Art Publishing House, Pyongyang
Subjects: Fiction, Arts

Mass Culture Publishing House, Pyongyang

Railway Publishing House, Pyongyang
Subject: Railways

Science and Encyclopaedia Publishing House, Pyongyang
Subjects: Science, Dictionaries

Workers' Party of Korea Publishing House, Pyongyang
Subjects: Fiction, Politics

Major Booksellers

Korea Publications Export & Import Corporation, Chulpanmul, Pyongyang
Export Manager: Kim Myong Sob
The sole importing and exporting organization

Major Libraries

People's Grand Study Centre, Pyongyang

State Central Library*, Pyongyang

Library Associations

Library Association of the Democratic People's Republic of Korea*, State Central Library, Pyongyang Tel: 3-8741
Executive Secretary: Li Geug

Republic of Korea

General Information

Language: Korean (English also spoken in business)
Religion: Confucian, Buddhist
Population: 37 million
Literacy Rate (1970): 87.6% (94.3% Urban, 82.2% Rural)
Bank Hours: 0930-1600 Monday-Friday; 0930-1300 Saturday
Shop Hours: 0930-1200, 1300-1700 Monday-Friday; 0930-1300 Saturday
Currency: won
Export/Import Information: No tariffs on books and advertising matter. No import licences required. Exchange controls; prior deposits required at present
Copyright: No copyright conventions signed

Book Trade Organizations

Korean Publishers Association, 105-2 Sagan-dong, Chongno-ku, Seoul 110 Tel: (724) 0790, (723) 8402, (725) 2701 Cable Add: Bookhouse Seoul
Secretary: Doo-Young Lee
Publications: K P A Journal (monthly); *Korean Publication Yearbook* (annual); *Newsletter on New Books* (bi-weekly); *Books from Korea* (biennial)

Book Trade Reference Books and Journals

Books

Books from Korea, Korean Publishers Association, 105-2 Sagan-dong, Chongno-ku, Seoul 110

Catalogue of Government Publications (including University publications), National Assembly Library, Taepyong-ko, Chung-ku, Seoul

Korean Publication Yearbook, Korean Publishers Association, 105-2 Sagan-dong, Chongno-ku, Seoul 110

Journals

K P A Journal, Korean Publishers' Association, 105-2 Sagan-dong, Chongno-ku, Seoul 110

Han-gug Chulpanyungam (Korean Publication Yearbook) (text in Korean), Korean Publishers' Association, 105-2 Sagan-dong, Chongno-ku, Seoul 110

Korean National Bibliography (text in Korean), Central National Library, 6 Sokong-dong, Chung-ku, Seoul

Newsletter on New Books, Korean Publishers Association, 105-2 Sagan-dong, Chongno-ku, Seoul 110

Publishers

Baik Rog Publishing Co, 130-2 Insa-dong, Chongno-ku, Seoul 110 Tel: (724) 5240
President: Hi Kyung Kim
Subjects: Literature, Juvenile

Bak Yung Sa*, 184 Kwanchul-dong, Chongno-ku, Seoul 110
President: Won Ok Ahn
Subjects: Philosophy, Literature, Social Science
Founded: 1952

Beupmun Sa Publishing Co, 1-48 Cheung-dong, Chung-ku, Seoul 100 Tel: (725) 6317/6318/6319
President: Sung Soo Kim; *Man Dir:* Hyo Seon Bae; *Dirs:* Ki Byeong Yun, Ham Sung Yoo; *Editorial:* Bok Hyun Choe; *Publicity:* Chue Hwan Kim
Subsidiary Company: Minjungseorim Publishing Co (qv)
Subjects: Law, Accountancy, Economics, Management, Politics, Public Administration, Education, Psychology, Sociology
1981: 60 titles *1982:* 95 titles *Founded:* 1952

Changjak Kwa Pipyung Sa*, 3 Kongpyong-dong, Chongno-ku, Seoul 110
President: Yom Hong-gyong
Subjects: Literature and other subjects of general interest
Founded: 1974

Changjo Sa*, 92 Sinmun-ro 2-ka, Chongno-ku, Seoul 110
President: Deok Kyu Choi
Subjects: Literature, Linguistics, History
Founded: 1963

The **Christian Literature** Society of Korea*, 84-8 Chongno, 2-ka, Chongno-ku, Seoul 110 Tel: 74-3092, 1792, 5981 Cable Add: Chlisoofko
General Secretary: Rev Sun Chool Chough
Subjects: Religion, Theology, Sociology

Dan Kook University Press, 8 Hannam-dong, Yongsan-ku, Seoul 140 Tel: (793) 5034
President: Choong Shik Chang
Subjects: Literature, History, School Reference

Daihak Publishing Co, 125 4-ka, Myongryun-dong, Chongno-ku, Seoul 110 Tel: (764) 2745
President: Jin Young Yoon
Subjects: Juvenile, Technology

Dong Wha Publishing Co*, 130-4 Wonhyo-ro 1-ka, Yongsan-ku, Seoul 140 Tel: (713) 5412
President: In Kyu Lim; *Editorial Dir:* Kyoung-Sik Roh; *Sales Dir:* Byong-Don Ann; *Production Dir:* Chong-Choon Seo; *Publicity Dir:* Kun-Han Park
Subjects: Literature, Fine Arts, History, Philosophy, Children's Picture Books
Founded: 1968

Eulyoo Publishing Co Ltd*, PO Box 362 Gwanghwa-Mun, 46-1 Susong-dong, Chongno-ku, Seoul 110 Tel: (722) 4745 Cable Add: Eulyoo
President: Chin Sook Choung; *Man Dir:* Pil Young Choung; *Editorial, Production:* Il Joon Park; *Sales:* Byung Gi Choung
Subjects: General
Founded: 1945

Ewha Womans University Press*, 11-1 Daehyun-dong, Seodaemun-ku, Seoul 120 Tel: (362) 6076
President: Eui Sook Cheung
Subjects: Humanities, Social/Natural/Applied Sciences, Music, Fine Arts, Dance, Education, Sciences
1981: approx 20 titles *Founded:* 1954

Gimm-Young Press, 198-1 Kwanhun-dong, Chongno-ku, Seoul 110 Tel: (720) 5630
President: Chung Sub Kim
Subjects: Religion, Philosophy, Science

Han Jin Publishing Co, 65-15 3-ka Pil-dong, Chung-ku, Seoul 100 Tel: (261) 0184
President: Gab Jin Han
Subjects: Literature, Religion, Juvenile, Arts

Hak Won Sa*, 1-576 Yoeudo-dong, Yongdeungpo-ku, Seoul 150 Tel: (783) 7158
President: Ik Tal Kim
Subjects: Dictionaries, Medical, Philosophy
Founded: 1945

Hollym Corporation, Publishers, 14-5 Kwanchol-dong, Chongno-ku, Seoul 110 Tel: (725) 7551/5146
President: In Soo Rhimm; *Man Dir:* Shinwon Chu; *Sales Dir:* Yong Kwon Kim; *Publicity Dir:* Shin Won Chu; *Advertising Dir:* Tae Hong Jeong
Branch Off: Hollym International Corp, 18 Donald Place, Elizabeth, New Jersey 07208, USA
Subjects: English-language-only books on Korea comprising General Fiction, Belles Lettres, Poetry, Biography, History, Juveniles, High-priced Paperbacks
Book Club: Korea Book Club
Founded: 1963

Hwimoon Publishing Co*, 30 Kyunji-dong, Chongno-ku, Seoul 110 Tel: (72) 4897
Man Dir: Myong Hui Yi
Subjects: General Fiction, Belles Lettres, Poetry, Biography, History, Philosophy, Religion, Juveniles
Founded: 1961

Hyang Mun Sa, 39-16 Kyunji-dong, Chongno-ku, Seoul 110 Tel: 7224790/7250447
President: Joong Ryal Nah
Subjects: Agriculture, Science
Founded: 1957

Hyun Am Publishing Co*, 627-5 Ahyun-dong, Mapo-ku, Seoul 121 Tel: (362) 5022
Man Dir: Keun-Tae Cho
Subjects: Philosophy, Literature, Religion
Founded: 1951

Il Cho Kak, 9 Gongpyung-dong, Chongno-ku, Seoul 110 Tel: (73) 5430/1 Cable Add: Ichopublico Seoul
Man Dir: Man-Nyun Han; *Sales Dir:* L J Kim; *Publicity Dir:* J Y Choi
Subjects: History, High-priced Paperbacks, Medicine, Psychology, Engineering, General & Social Science, Secondary & University Textbooks, Educational Materials, Law, Philosophy
Founded: 1953

Il Ji Sa Publishing Co*, 46-1 Chunghak-dong, Chongno-ku, Seoul 110
Man Dir: Sung Jae Kim; *Publicity Dirs:* Byungki Yoo, Donhong Cho
Subjects: General Fiction, Belles Lettres, Criminology, Poetry, History, Reference, Low- & High-priced Paperbacks, University & Secondary Textbooks, Educational Materials
Founded: 1956

Jeongeumsa Publishing Co*, PO Box 7, 22-5 Chungmu-ro 5-ka, Chung-ku, Seoul 100 Tel: (27) 9580/3 & (25) 5681/2 Cable Add: Jeongeumsa
President: Yong Hae Choi; *Sales Dir:* Young-tek Yoon; *Publicity & Advertising:* Dae-hee Park
Subjects: General Fiction, Belles Lettres, Philosophy, Social Science
Bookshop: 22-5, 5-ka, Chungmu-Ro, Jung-gu, Seoul
Founded: 1928

Jisik Sanup Sa*, 18-8 Kwanchul-dong, Chongno-ku, Seoul 110
President: Kyung Hee Kim
Subjects: Fine Arts, Social Sciences, History, Literature, Technical and Scientific
Founded: 1969

Junpa Kwahak Sa*, 156-10 Dongkyo-dong, Mapo-ku, Seoul 121
President: Yung Soo Shon
Subjects: Sciences, Engineering
Founded: 1956

Jungwoo Sa, 432-12 Galhyun-dong, Eunpyung-ku, Seoul 122 Tel: (388) 6137
President: Je Sook Seo
Subjects: Literature, Religion

Kemongsa, 12-23 Kwanchul-dong, Chongro-ku, Seoul Tel: (74) 7818, (72) 2248 Telex: Kemsy K22642
President: Choon Sik Kim; *Publicity Manager:* In Chong Chung
Subjects: Juveniles, Education
Founded: 1950

Ko Mun Sa, 617-8 Ahyun-dong, Mapo-ku, Seoul 121 Tel: (392) 3831
President: Yun ki Baik
Subjects: Medicine, Pharmacy, Dictionaries

Korea Britannica Corporation, 162-1, 2-ka, Jangchung-dong, Chung-ku, Seoul Tel: 2612151/2617081/2664111 Cable Add: Britannica-Seoul Telex: Ebkorea K27286
Chief Executive: Changgi Hahn; *Sales Dir:* Kil Yong Kim; *Editorial, Publicity, Rights & Permissions:* Jay Sung Rhee; *Production:* Myong Sei Lee
Parent Company: Encyclopaedia Britannica Inc, Britannica Center, 310 South Michigan Ave, Chicago, Illinois 60604, USA
Subjects: General, Educational, Children's
Founded: 1968

Korea Directory Co*, 21-3 Mugyo-Dong, Chung-ku, Seoul 100 Tel: (776) 1140
President: Saeung Tae Kim
Subjects: Directories, Dictionaries, Periodicals

Korea Textbook Co Ltd, 62-7 1-ka Manri-dong, Chung-ku, Seoul 100 Tel: (392) 5855
President: Hak Soo Lee
Subjects: Arts, Education, Politics

Korea University Press*, 1 5-ka, Anam-dong, Sungbuk-ku, Seoul 132
President: Jun Yob Kim
Subjects: Philosophy, History, Literature, Sociology, Language, Education Psychology, Social Science, Natural Science, Engineering, Agriculture
Founded: 1956

The **Korean Culture** and Arts Foundation, 31 Dongsung-dong, Chongno-ku, Seoul 110 Tel: (762) 5231
President: Ji Young Song
Subject: Literature

Kwan Dong Publishing Co*, 195-11 Yeongun-dong, Chongno-ku, Seoul 110 Tel: (29) 6517, (99) 4638
President: Seung Woo Kim; *Editorial:* Hyo Ja Kim; *Sales:* Heung Jo Choi; *Production:* Ki Dong Park; *Publicity:* Ill Kyoun Oh; *Rights & Permissions:* Hyong Sook Park
Subjects: Literature, Textbooks, Monthly magazines
Founded: 1964

Kwang Jang Press, 80 Sagan-dong, Chongno-ku, Seoul 110 Tel: (722) 6704
President: Won Kim
Subjects: Arts, Engineering

Kwangmyong Printing & Publishing Co Ltd, CPO Box 3785, Seoul (Located at: 62 Manri-dong 1-ka, Chung-ku, Seoul) Tel: (753) 0671/9, 6584 Cable Add: Kwangmyong, Seoul Telex: K27229 Kortuna
President: Lee Hak-Soo; *Dir:* Yoon Yun-Bai
Subsidiary Companies: Korea Textbook Co; Kwangmyong Toppan Moore Printing Co
Subject: Korean Art (ancient and contemporary)
Founded: 1951

Kyobo Publishing Inc, 1-1 1-ka Chongno, Chongno-ku, Seoul 110 Tel: (722) 2455
President: Keun Soo Lee
Subjects: Literature, Politics, Law

Kyohak Sa*, 92 Sunhwa-dong, Seodaemun-ku, Seoul
Man Dir: Cheol U Yang
Subjects: Educational Materials, Industry, Non-fiction

Kyung Hee University Press, 1 Hoegi-dong, Dongdaemun-ku, Seoul 131 Tel: (966) 0061
President: Chi Yol An
Subjects: Language, History, Philosophy, Social Science

Kyung In Munwha Sa*, 86-2 Yunhee-dong, Seodaemun-ku, Seoul 120
President: Sang Ha Han
Subjects: General, History, Philosophy
Founded: 1969

Kyungnam University Press, 449 Weolyoung-dong, Masan, Kyungsang Namdo
President: Tae Lim Yoon
Subjects: Social Science, Philosophy

Min Eum Sa*, 44-1 Kwanchul-dong, Chongno-ku, Seoul 110
President: Maeng Ho Pak
Subjects: Literature, Philosophy, Engineering, Social Science
Founded: 1966

Minjungseorim Publishing Co*, 1-48 Cheung-dong, Chung-ku, Seoul 100 Tel: (725) 6317/9
President: Myong Hwan Kim; *Editorial:* Han Seong Yu
Parent Company: Beupmun Sa Publishing Co (qv)
Subjects: Dictionaries
Founded: 1979

Mun Woon Dang*, 45-3 Myongryun-dong, Chongno-ku, Seoul
President: Sung Bum Lee
Subjects: Engineering, Science
Founded: 1962

Omun Kak, 168-70 Samsung-dong, Kangnam-ku, Seoul 134
President: Yung Whan Kim; *Chief Executive:* Hyon Jai Park; *Editorial:* Jai Yung You; *Sales:* Jai Yong Kim; *Production:* In Soo Kim; *Publicity:* Jai Yung You; *Rights & Permissions:* Kae Choong Chang
Associate Company: Yueil Publishing and Marketing Cooperation, Room 509, Jungeun Bldg, 22-5 Chungmu-ro 5th Avenue, Chung-ku, Seoul 100
Subjects: Literature, Korean Language, Social Science, Children's Books, School Textbooks, Picture Books
Founded: 1959

Pan Korea Book Corporation, 134 1-ka Sinmunro, Chongno-ku, Seoul 110 Tel: (723) 1421
President: Yoon Sun Kim
Subjects: Language, Literature, Technology

252 REPUBLIC OF KOREA

Panmun Book Co Ltd*, CPO Box 1016, 40 Chongno 1-ka, Seoul 110 Tel: (723) 8688, (722) 5131/3 Cable Add: Panmuse Seoul
Man Dir: I H Liu; *Sales Dir:* H B Choi
Subjects: Medicine, General & Social Science, University Textbooks
Bookshops: 40 Chongro 1-ka, Seoul; 16 Kwangbok-dong 1-ka, Pusan
Founded: 1955

Pochinchai, 8 Dangsan-dong 5-ka, Yeungdeungpo-ku, Seoul 150 Tel: (633) 2123
President: Joon Ki Kim; *Chief Executive:* Dal-Hoon Lee; *Editorial:* Kang Hurh
Subjects: Technology, Arts

Sam Joong Dang Publishing Co*, 244-5 Huam-dong, Yongsan-ku, Seoul 140
President: Kun Suk Seo
Subjects: Literature, History, Philosophy, Social Science
Founded: 1946

Sam-sung Publishing Co*, 43-7 Kwanchul-dong, Chongno-ku, Seoul 110
President: Bong Kyu Kim
Subjects: Literature, Dictionaries, History, Children's Books
Founded: 1952

Samwha Publishing Co*, 15 Ulchiro 2-ka, Chung-ku, Seoul 100
President: Kon Su Yu
Subjects: Children's Books, Social Science, Linguistics, Fine Arts
Founded: 1962

Se Kwang Musical Publication Co*, 232-32 Seogye-dong, Yongsan-gu, Seoul Tel: (714) 0046/50
President: Pak Sin Jun; *Sales Dir:* Song Yeong Il; *Publicity Dir:* Ha Jung Hi
Subject: Music
Founded: 1953

Sejong Daewang Kinyom Saophoe*, 1-57 Chongryangli-dong, San, Dondaemun-ku, Seoul
President: Gwan Ku Yi
Subjects: Religion, Classical Literature, Modern History

Seomun Dang*, 94-97 Yongdeungpo, 3-dong, Yongdeungpo-ku, Seoul
President: Suk Ro Choi
Subjects: Philosophy, Ancient History, Literature, Fine Arts
Founded: 1973

Seoul Computer Press, CPO Box 8850, Seoul Tel: (261) 6566
President: Jin-Wang Kim
Subjects: Language, Literature, Social Science

Seoul International Tourist Publishing Co, 33-16 Nonhyun-dong, Gangnam-ku, Seoul 134 Tel: (542) 9308
President: Chung-Gil Shim
Subjects: Juvenile, Tourist Guides

Seoul National University Press, 56-1 Sinrim-dong, Kwanak-ku, Seoul 150 Tel: (877) 6141
President: E-Hyuk Kwon
Subjects: Language, Philosophy, Science

Shin Jin Gak, 1-67 Nogosan-dong, Mapo-ku, Seoul 121 Tel: (717) 6272
President: Jae-Gul Kim
Subjects: Arts, Literature

Si-sa-yong-o-sa Publishers Inc*, 5-3 Kwanchol-dong, Chongno-ku, Seoul 110 Tel: (269) 6621 Cable Add: English books, Seoul, Korea
President: Young Bin Min; *Vice-President:* Jae-shik Min; *Editorial Dir:* Chon-young Hwang; *Publicity Dir:* Chong-man Choi; *Sales Dir:* Kapchin Cho; *Production Dir:* Hyuk-hwan Kwon

Subjects: Linguistics, Language, Literature, Dictionary, Periodicals
1981: 59 titles *Founded:* 1961

Singu Munwha Sa*, 68-2 Susong-dong, Chongno-ku, Seoul
President: Yong Ik Yi
Subjects: Literature, History, Linguistics, Children's Books
Founded: 1952

Sogang University Press, 1 Sinsu-dong, Mapo-ku, Seoul 121 Tel: (715) 0149
President: Kwang-Lim Lee
Subjects: History, Literature, Language

Sung Eum Kak Seoul, 35-104 Samchung-dong, Chongno-ku, Seoul 110 Tel: (723) 0220
President: Dong-Min Ahn
Subjects: Philosophy, Religion

Tamgu Dang Book Centre*, 101-1 Kyungwun-dong, Chongno-ku, Seoul 110 Tel: (720) 8961
Shipping Add: PO Box 240, Kwang-hwa-mun, Seoul
President: Suk Woo Hong; *Sales Dir:* Jean Byong-hun; *Publicity Dir:* Kim Chang-su; *Advertising Dir:* Lee Chung-rim
Subjects: History, Classics, Art, Technology, Reference, Low- & High-priced Paperbacks, University & Secondary Textbooks
Founded: 1950

Universal Publications Agency Ltd*, UPA Building, 54 Kyonjindong, Chongno, Seoul
Manager: C Y Park
Miscellaneous: Also booksellers and distributors

Yonsei University Press*, 134 Shinchon-dong, Seodaemun-ku, Seoul 120 Tel: (392) 6201
President: Se Hee Ahn
Subjects: General, Philosophy, Religion, Social Science, Natural Science, Literature, Art, Technical Science
Founded: 1955

Book Club

Korea Book Club, 14-5 Kwanchol-dong, Chongno-ku, Seoul
Members: 10,000
Owned by: Hollym Corporation, Publishers (qv)
Founded: 1973

Major Booksellers

Airport Bookshop*, Civil International Airport, Seoul

Hyun Dae Mun Hak*, 136-46 Yunji-dong, Chongro-ku, Seoul Tel: (763) 7319
Wholesaler

Panmun Book Co Ltd*, CPO Box 1016, Seoul
Also: 16 Kwangbok-dong 1-ka, Pusan Tel: (73) 8688

Science Publications Centre*, 21 1-ka, Chongno, Chongno-ku, Seoul

Seung mun Book Co*, CPO Box 2485, 155-12 Kwanhun-dong, Chongno-gu, Seoul Tel: (723) 6148

Universal Publications Agency Ltd*, UPA Building, 54 Kyonjindong, Chongno, Seoul
Manager: C Y Park
Also distributors

Major Libraries

Dongguk University Library*, 263-ka, Pil-dong, Seoul

Ewha Womans University Library, 11-1 Daehyon-dong, Sudaemun-ku, Seoul 120 Tel: 362 6151 (ext 654)

International Communication Agency Library*, 63 1-ka, Ulchiro, Chung-ku, Seoul

Korea Institute of Science and Technology Library*, PO Box 131, Dong Dae Mun, Seoul Tel: 9678801/9678901 Telex: kistrok k 27380

Korea University Library*, 1 Anam-dong, Sungbuk-ku, Seoul

Kyungpook National University Central Library*, 1370 Sankyuck-dong, Pukku, Taegu Tel: 920268

National Assembly Library*, Yoi-dong 1, Yeongdeungpo-gu, Seoul
Publication: Review

Central **National Library***, 100-171 1-ka, Hoehyun-dong, Chung-ku, Seoul

Seoul National University Library*, San 56-1 Sinlim-dong, Gwanag-gu, Seoul 151

Transport Library*, Seoul

United Nations Depository Library, Korea University, 1 An-Am-dong, Sungbuk-ku, Seoul
Librarian: Park Hu-Yong

Yonsei University Library*, Yonsei University, 134 Sinchon-dong, Sudaemoon-ku, Seoul 120

Library Associations

Hanguk Seoji Hakhoe*, c/o National Assembly Library, 1-ka Taepyung, Chung-ku, Seoul
Korean Bibliographical Society

Hanguk Tosogwan Hakhoe*, c/o Department of Library Science, Sung Kyun Kwan University, 53, 3-ka, Myonglyun-dong, Chongno-ku, Seoul 110
Korean Library Science Society
Publication: Tosogwan Hak (Journal of the Korean Library Science Society, Korean with English abstracts)

Korean Library Association*, 100-177, 1-ka, Hoehyun-dong, Chung-ku, Seoul
Executive Director: Dae Kwon Park
Publications: KLA Bulletin (monthly); *Library Research* (bi-monthly); *Korean Decimal Classification; Korean Cataloging Rules; Statistics on Libraries in Korea; The Patterns of Book Cover Design in Korea (1392-1945)*

Korean Micro-Library Association*, Central National Library Bldg, 6 Sokong-dong, Chung-ku, Seoul
Publication: Micro-Library Bulletin

Library Reference Books and Journals

Books

Bibliography of Korean Bibliographies, Kyong'in Munwha Sa, 86-2 Yonhi-dong, Seodaemun-ku, Seoul

Korean Cataloging Rules, Korean Library Association, 100-177, 1-ka, Hoehyun-dong, Chung-ku, Seoul

REPUBLIC OF KOREA — LEBANON 253

Journals

KLA Bulletin, Korean Library Association, 100-177, 1-ka, Hoehyun-dong, Chung-ku, Seoul (monthly)

Library Research, Korean Library Association, 100-177, 1-ka, Hoehyun-dong, Chung-ku, Seoul (bi-monthly)

Micro-Library Bulletin, Korean Micro-Library Association, Central National Library Bldg, 6 Sokong-dong, Chung-ku, Seoul

National Assembly Library Review (test in Korean), National Assembly Library, Processing and Reference Bureau, Yoi-dong 1, Yeongdeungpo-gu, Seoul

Statistics on Libraries in Korea, Korean Library Association, 100-177, 1-ka, Hoehyun-dong, Chung-ku, Seoul

Tosogwan Hak (Journal of the Korean Library Science Society) (text in Korean with English abstracts), c/o Ewha Woman's University Library, 11-1 Daehyon-dong, Seodaemun-ku, Seoul 120

Literary Associations and Societies

Korean PEN Centre, 163 Ankuk-dong, Jongno-ku, Seoul 110
Secretary-General: Sang-Deuk Moon
Publications: The Korean PEN, Asian Literature

Literary Periodical

Korean Literary Magazine, Hyun Dae Mun Hak, 136-46 Yunji-dong, Chongro-ku, Seoul

Literary Prizes

Hyun Dae Mun Hak Prize*
Established 1955. Awarded annually in the categories of poetry, fiction, drama and literary criticism. Enquiries to Korean Literary Works, 136-46 Yunji-dong, Chongro-ku, Seoul

Literary Prize*
In recognition of an outstanding literary work. $US5,000. Awarded annually. Enquiries to Korean National Academy of Arts, 1 Seajong Ro, Chongro-ku, Seoul

Kuwait

General Information

Language: Arabic. English widely spoken
Religion: Muslim
Population: 1.2 million
Literacy Rate (1975): 59.6%
Bank Hours: 0800-1200 (0830-1230 during Ramadan) Saturday-Thursday
Shop Hours: 0800-1200 or 1230, 1530 or 1600-2030 Saturday-Thursday; 0800-1200 Friday (markets and shopping centres also open 1530-2030); during Ramadan: 0830 or 0900-1230, 1930-0130 or 0200 Saturday-Thursday
Currency: 1000 fils = 1 Kuwaiti dinar
Export/Import Information: No tariffs on books or advertising in reasonable quantity; all immoral and seditious publications prohibited. Import licence required. No exchange permit required
Copyright: No copyright conventions signed

Publishers

Kuwait Publishing House*, PO Box 5209
Tel: 510188

Ministry of Information*, PO Box 193, Kuwait Tel: 415301 Cable Add: Alirshad Telex: Mi 22030 Kt, Mi 46151 Kt
Subjects: Art, Geography, History, Physics, Sociology, Textbooks, Maps, Literature, Mathematics, Education, Linguistics

Press Agency*, PO Box 1019, Kuwait Tel: 432269/411495 Cable Add: Matboat Telex: Matboat 6046 Kt
Man Dir: Abdullah M N Harami; *Editorial:* K A Harami
Subjects: General (in Arabic and English)
Bookshops: in Kuwait and Salmiay
Founded: 1954

Wkallat Matbouat*, PO Box 1019
Subject: Travel, Maps

Major Booksellers

Gulf Union Co, Al-Othman Bldg, Al Soor St, Apt 14, PO Box 2911, Safat Tel: 411688/2440889 Cable Add: Florya Kuwait Telex: 23491 Florya Kt
Man Dir: Tahseen S Khaya

Major Libraries

Kuwait Central Library*, Kuwait City

Kuwait University Central Library*, Kuwait University, Libraries Department, PO Box 17140, Khaldiya, Kuwait Tel: 813182
Telex: Kuniver 2616 Kt

National Scientific and Technical Information Center (NSTIC) of the Kuwait Institute for Scientific Research, PO Box 24885, Safat Tel: 816988/816237 Cable Add: Science Telex: Kisr Kt 22299
Dir: Mrs Ferial Al-Freih

Library Association

Kuwait University Libraries Department*, Chief Librarian's Office, PO Box 17140, Khaldiya, Kuwait

Library Reference Journals

The Library Bulletin, Kuwait University Central Library, Kuwait City

The University Library, Kuwait University Libraries Department, PO Box 17140, Kuwait

Laos

General Information

Note: No replies were received to questionnaires sent to Laos for this edition of *International Literary Market Place*. The information given in the 1983-84 edition has been repeated here but should be treated with caution.

Language: Lao
Religion: Theravada Buddhist
Population: 3.5 million
Bank Hours: 0800-1200, 1400-1700 Monday-Friday
Shop Hours: 0800-2200 Monday-Friday
Currency: kip
Export/Import Information: No tariff on books (except children's picture books), none on most advertising matter. No import licences required for books. Exchange controls
Copyright: UCC (see International section)

Publishers

Lao-phanit*, Vientiane Ministère de l'Education nationale, Comité littéraire, Bureau des Manuels scolaires, Vientiane
Subjects: Education, Physics, Sociology, Economics, History, Cookery, Arts, Geography, Music, Fiction

Pakpassak Kanphin*, 9-11 quai Fa-Hguun, Vientiane

Major Libraries

Bibliothèque nationale*, BP 704, Vientiane

Centre national de Documentation*, Vientiane

Bibliothèque de l'**Ecole** royale de Médecine*, BP 131, Vientiane

Library Association

Association des Bibliothécaires Laotiens*, c/o Direction de la Bibliothèque nationale, Ministry of Education, BP 704, Vientiane
Association of Laos Librarians

Library Reference Journal

Journal officiel (Official Journal), Centre national de Documentation, Vientiane

Lebanon

General Information

Language: Arabic (French and English also used)
Religion: Half Christian, with Maronites predominant, half Muslim
Population: 3.1 million
Bank Hours: 0830-1230 Monday-Friday; 0830-1200 Saturday
Shop Hours: Vary. Generally 0900-1900 in winter, 0800-1500 in summer
Currency: 100 Lebanese piastres = 1 Lebanese pound
Copyright: UCC, Berne (see International section)

Publishers

Dar al **Adab***, Beirut
Subject: Fiction

Arab Institute for Research and Publishing*, Sakiat-Al Janzeer, PO Box 11-5460, Beirut Tel: 319586/312156 Cable Add: Moukayali
Subjects: Works in Arabic and English

Dar Assayad*, BP 1038, Beirut
Man Dir: Bassam Freiha
Subjects: Politics, Periodicals and Newspapers
Founded: 1943

Les Editions Arabes, part of Naufal Group SRL, Lebanon (qv)

Geoprojects Sàrl, PO Box 113, 5294 Beirut Tel: 344346 Telex: 22661 Eltoup le
Man Dir: Tahseen Khayat
Subjects: Tourist Maps & Guides Series, Arabic books
Founded: 1978

Dar el-Ilm Lilmalayin, PO Box 1085, Beirut (Located at: rue de Syrie, Beirut) Tel: 304445/816639/224502 Cable Add: Malayin Telex: 23166 Mlayin
Man Dir: Bahije Osman; *Editorial Dir:* Munir Balbaki; *Sales:* Saad Itani; *Production:* Taref Osman
Subsidiary Companies: Bardico Paper Co; Alulum Printers; Alharf Alelectroni Co; Dar Shehrazad Co
Subjects: Textbooks, Islamic Studies, Dictionaries, History, Mathematics, Physics, Law, Children, Health, Languages, Literature, Philosophy, Education, Psychology, Biographies
Founded: 1945

Institute for Palestine Studies, Publishing and Research Organization, Institute Bldg, Anis Nsouli St, PO Box 11-7164, Beirut Tel: 312512/814174 Cable Add: Dirasat Telex: Madaf 23317 le
Executive Secretary: Prof Walid Khalidi; *Editorial:* Taan Saab; *Sales:* Miss Afaf Minkara
Branch Off: 1322, 18th Street NW, PO Box 19449, Washington DC 20036, USA
Subjects: Palestine and the Arab-Israeli conflict
Founded: 1963

The **International Documentary** Centre of Arab Manuscripts*, Darwish Bldg, rue de Syrie, BP 2668, Beirut
Proprietor: Zouhair Baalbaki
Subjects: Reprints, Facsimiles
Founded: 1965

Dar al Kash'shaf, Assad Malhamee St, PO Box 112091, Beirut Tel: 815527/296805 Cable Add: Dakashaf Beirut
Proprietor: A M Fathallah
Subjects: Scouting, Atlases, Maps, Business
Founded: 1930

Khayat Book and Publishing Co SAL*, 90-94 rue Bliss, Beirut
Man Dir: Paul Khayat
Subjects: Fiction, History, Juveniles, Arts, Maps, Medicine, Education, Law, Religion, Social Sciences, Games, Sports, Economics, Books on the Middle East, Islam, Arabic, Reprints

Dar Al-Kitab Allubnani*, PO Box 3176, Beirut Tel: 237537/254054 Cable Add: Kitaliban Telex: 22865 Ktl
Man Dir: El-Zein Hassan
Subsidiary Company: Dar Al-Kitab Al-Masri, Egypt (qv)
Branch Offs: Paris, Geneva, Madrid, Casablanca
Subjects: Islamic, Turath, Textbooks (in Arabic, English, French)
Bookshop: Librairie de l'Ecole, PO Box 3176, Beirut
Founded: 1929

Librairie du Liban, Riad Al-Solh Sq, PO Box 945 Beirut Tel: 258259/295735 Cable Add: Librarie du Liban, Beirut Telex: 21037
Man Dirs: Khalil and George Sayegh; *Editorial:* Ahmad Khatib; *Sales:* Suhail Berjawi; *Production:* Albert Mutlag;

Publicity: George Sayegh; *Rights & Permissions:* Khalil Sayegh
Subjects: Textbooks, Fiction, Linguistics, Travel, Islam, Dictionaries, Children's Books
Bookshops: Lebanon Bookshop, Bliss St, Beirut; Librairie du Liban, Hamra St, Beirut; Librairie sayegh, Damascus, Syria; Sphinx Bookshop, Cairo, Egypt
Founded: 1944

Longman Arab World Centre*, PO Box 945, Beirut
Associate Company: Longman Group Ltd, UK (qv)

Dar Al-Maaref Liban SAL*, Esseily Bldg, sq Riad Al-Solh, PO Box 11-2320, Beirut Tel: 223574/294064/383621 Cable Add: Damaref Beirut
Man Dir: Dr Fouad Ibrahim; *General Manager:* Joseph Nachou; *Sales:* Joseph Ibrahim
Parent Company: Dar Al Maaref, Egypt (qv)
Subjects: Juveniles, Textbooks in Arabic
Founded: 1959

Mac Purcell*, PO Box 1135294, Beirut

Macdonald Middle East Sàrl, see Naufal Group SRL, Lebanon and BPCC PLC, UK

Darl el-Machreq Sàrl, c/o Librairie orientale, BP 946, Beirut Tel: 326469 Cable Add: Cathopress Telex: Impcat 22881
Man Dir, Rights & Permissions: Paul Brouwers; *Publicity:* Michel Mourad
Orders to: Librairie orientale, BP 1986, Beirut
Subjects: Archaeology, Geography, Educational, History, Dictionaries, Religion, Art, Literature, Languages, Science, Philosophy, Periodicals
Founded: 1853
ISBN Publisher's Prefix: 2-7214

Naufal Group SRL+, PO Box 11-2161, Naufal Bldg, Mamari St, Beirut Tel: 354394/354898 Telex: Naustn 22210 le
Man Dir, Rights & Permissions: Sami Naufal; *Editorial:* Kamal Khavli; *Sales, Production:* Ahmed Bahsoun; *Publicity:* Antoine Saadeh
Subsidiary Companies: Macdonald Middle East Sàrl; Les Editions Arabes
Imprints: Naufal, Macdonald, Editions Arabes
Subjects: Encyclopaedias and General Knowledge, Fiction, Children's Books, History, Law, Literature
Bookshops: Librairies Antoine (three shops), Hamra, BP 656, Beirut
1981: 20 titles *1982:* 35 titles *Founded:* 1970

Major Booksellers

Librairies Antoine*, Rue Patriarche Hoyek, Beirut Tel: 229745

Esquire*, Rue Sidani, Beirut Tel: 348074

Help Bookshop*, Rue Jeanne d'Arc, Im Saghiri, Beirut Tel: 341679

Tahseen S Khayat, Uncle Sam's Bookshop, PO Box 8375 Beirut Tel: 344346
See also United Arab Emirates

Lebanon Bookshop*, Bliss St, Beirut

Librairie du Liban*, Hamra St, Beirut

Librairie du Liban, Imm Esseily, pl Riad Solh, PO Box 11, 945 Beirut

Georges Murr*, Rue Ahmed Chawki, Beirut Tel: 233810

Major Libraries

Library of **American University** of Beirut, Beirut Tel: 340740 ext 28005 Telex: amunob 20801 le

Library of **Beirut Arab University***, PO Box 5020, Beirut

Bibliothèque nationale du Liban*, à la pl de l'Etoile, Imm du Parlement, Beirut Tel: 256160/256161

Bibliothèque orientale, rue de l'Université St Joseph, BP 293, Beirut
Dir: Martin J McDermott

Bibliothèque de l'**Ecole** supérieure des Lettres*, rue de Damas, Beirut

Library of the **Faculty of Engineering**, Université St Joseph, BP 1514, Beirut
Librarian: Henri Ketterer

Library of the **Faculty of Law***, Université St Joseph, BP 293, Beirut

Library of the **French Faculty of Medicine**, Pharmacy and Dentistry*, Université St Joseph, BP 5076, Beirut

Bibliothèque de l'**Institut** Français d'Archéologie du Proche Orient, rue Omar Daouk, BP 11-1424, Beirut
Dir: Georges Tate

Nami C **Jafet** Memorial Library, American University of Beirut, Beirut Tel: 340740 ext 28005

Library of the **Monastery of St-Saviour** (Basilian Missionary Order of St-Saviour)*, Saïda

Library of the **Near East School** of Theology, PO Box 13-5780, Chouran, Beirut

Library of the **Syrian Patriarchal Seminary***, Seminary of Charfet, Daroon-Harissa

Library Association

The **Lebanese Library** Association*, c/o National Library, pl de l'Etoile, Beirut Tel: 256160
Executive Secretary: Linda Sadaga
Publication: Newsletter

Library Reference Journals

Bulletin bibliographique (Bibliographic Bulletin), Bibliothèque nationale du Liban, à la pl de l'Etoile, Imm du Parlement, Beirut

Newsletter, The Lebanese Library Association, c/o National Library, pl de l'Etoile, Beirut

Literary Associations and Societies

Lebanese **P E N** Club, c/o M Camille Aboussouan, Délégation du Liban auprès de l'Unesco, 22 pl Général Catroux (ex Malsherbes), F-75017 Paris, France
President: M Camille Aboussouan

Lesotho

General Information

Language: English, Sesotho (a Bantu language)
Religion: Roman Catholic and Protestant
Population: 1.3 million
Literacy Rate (1966): 58.6%
Bank Hours: 0830-1300 Monday-Friday; 0830-1100 Saturday
Shop Hours: Winter: 0830-1630 Monday-Friday; 0830-1300 Saturday; Summer: 0800-1630 Monday-Friday; 0800-1300 Saturday. Usually closed weekdays 1300-1400
Currency: 100 lisente = 1 loti (plural: maloti). 1 loti = 1 rand. South African currency is also legal tender
Export/Import Information: No tariffs on books or advertising matter. No import licence required; no obscene literature permitted. Exchange controls being relaxed

Publishers

Government Printer*, Mazenod Printing Press, PO Mazenod, Maseru

Longman Lesotho (Pty) Ltd, PO Box 1174, Maseru 100
Associate Company: Longman Group Ltd, UK (qv)

Mazenod Institute, PO Box 18, Mazenod 160 (Railhead: Maseru Station) Tel: 05022224 Telex: 271 Bb
Manager: Father B Mohlalisi
Subjects: History, Africana, Religion, Sotho Language & Literature, Secondary & Primary Textbooks
Founded: 1933

Morija Sesuto Book Depot*, PO Box 4, Morija
Subjects: Belles Lettres, Poetry, History, Africana, Religion, Juveniles, Southern Sotho Language, Paperbacks, General Science, Secondary & Primary Textbooks
Founded: 1862

Saint Michael's Mission*, The Social Centre, PO Box 25, Roma
Man Dir: Rev Father M Ferrange;
Production: Peter Ntsaoana
Subjects: Biography, History, Africana, Religion, Social Science, Secondary & Primary Textbooks, Anthropology
Founded: 1968

Major Booksellers

Lesotho Book Centre*, PO Box MS 608, Maseru Tel: 3783

Mazenod Book Centre, PO Box 39, Mazenod (Located at: Mazenod. Railhead: Maseru Station) Tel: 05022224 Telex: 271 Bb
Manager: Rev Fr M Gareau

Morija Sesuto Book Depot*, PO Box MJ 4, Morija Tel: 204

Major Libraries

British Council Educational Resource Centre, PO Box 429, Maseru 100 Tel: 22609
Librarian: Rosina Mphethi

Lesotho National Library Service, PO Box 985, Maseru 100 Tel: 22592
Librarian: Ms Matseliso Moshoeshoe
Publication: Annual Report

National University of Lesotho Library*, PO Roma 180 Tel: 201 Cable Add: Uniter Telex: 303 BB
Librarian: Mrs M N Tau; *Acting Librarian:* Mrs M M Lebotsa

Library Association

Lesotho Library Association*, c/o The National Library, PO Box 985, Maseru 100
Secretary: Miss M Moshoeshoe

Liberia

General Information

No replies were received to questionnaires sent to Liberia for this edition of *International Literary Market Place*. The information given in the 1983-84 edition has been repeated here but should be treated with caution.

Language: English and a number of African languages
Religion: Muslim, Protestant; traditional beliefs followed by many
Population: 1.7 million
Literacy Rate (1962): 8.6%
Bank Hours: 0800-1200 Monday-Thursday; 0800-1400 Friday
Shop Hours: 0800-1300, 1500-1800 or longer
Currency: 100 cents = 1 Liberian dollar
Export/Import Information: No tariff on books and advertising matter. Public Fund Levy. No import licence or exchange control
Copyright: UCC (see International section)

Publishers

Cole & Yancy*, PO Box 286, Monrovia
Man Dir: Henry B Cole
Subjects: General, Reference, Annuals, Paperbacks
Bookshop: PO Box 286, Monrovia

Government Printer*, Government Printing Office, Department of State, Monrovia

Liberian Literary & Educational Publications*, PO Box 2387, Monrovia
Man Dir: S Henry Cordor
Subjects: General, Educational, Belles Lettres, Poetry

Major Booksellers

Wadih M Captan Bookstores*, Randall St, PO Box 414, Monrovia Tel: 21393

Cole and Yancy Bookshop Ltd*, PO Box 286, Monrovia

Liberian Educational Materials Supply Corporation*, New Port St, PO Box 2088, Monrovia Tel: 22356
Manager: N Chandru

National Bookstore*, Carey St, PO Box 590, Monrovia Tel: 222096

University Bookstore*, University of Liberia, Monrovia Tel: 22515 ext 225

Major Libraries

College of Our Lady of Fatima Library*, Harper

Cuttington College and Divinity School Library*, PO Box 277, Monrovia Tel: 21065

Government Public Library*, Ashmun St, Monrovia

International Communication Agency Library*, Broad St, Monrovia

University of Liberia Libraries*, PO Box 9020, Monrovia Tel: 22537
Dir: Dr C Wesley Armstrong
Publication: Newsletter

Libya

General Information

Language: Arabic
Religion: Muslim
Population: 2.7 million
Literacy Rate (1964): 21.7%
Bank Hours: Generally Winter: 0830-1230; Summer: 0800-1200 Saturday-Thursday
Shop Hours: Vary greatly. Friday is weekly holiday but some Christian shops closed Sunday. Many are open 0830-1230, 1500-1730 Saturday-Thursday (slightly earlier hours in summer months)
Currency: 1,000 dirhams = 1 Libyan dinar
Export/Import Information: No tariff on books; advertising dutied. Charity Tax and Municipal Tax levied on dutiable goods. Open General Licence for books. Exchange permit, liberally granted, required. Import and export of books is handled by the General Company for Publishing, Advertising and Distribution, Tripoli
Copyright: Berne (see International section)

Publishers

Aleatah University, General Administration of Libraries, Printing & Publications*, PO Box 13543, Tripoli Tel: 621988 Telex: 20629 TP Univ Ly
Subjects: Academic
Bookshop: University Bookshop, PO Box 13113, Tripoli
Founded: 1955

Dar Libya Publishing House*, PO Box 2487, Benghazi
Subject: Literature

General Press Corporation*, General Publication and Advertising Co, PO Box 959, Tripoli Tel: 45773/77/45537
Publicity: Moustafa A Elmasri
Subjects: General Books; Educational and Academic Books

Major Booksellers

General Company for Publishing, Advertising and Distribution*, Suf el Mahmudi, PO Box 959, Tripoli Tel: 457736777 Telex: 20235

Orient Bookshop*, PO Box 255, Tripoli

Major Libraries

American Cultural Center Library*, Al Qayrawaan St, Tripoli

Benghazi Public Library*, Shar'a 'Umar al-Mukhtar, Benghazi

Egyptian Cultural Center Library*, 310 'Umar al-Mukhtar St, Tripoli

al-Fateh University, The Central Library*, PO Box 13104, Tripoli Tel: 604000 ext 2466

Government Library*, 14 Shar'a al-Jazair, Tripoli

Institut Culturel Français Bibliothèque, 15-17 Sciara Karachi, PO Box 683, Tripoli Tel: 35567
Librarian: Mrs Girard Khadifa
Publication: Bulletin (monthly)

National Archives*, Castello, Tripoli

National Library, Secretariat of Information, PO Box 9127, Benghazi Tel: 96379/97073
Librarian: Mohammed O Fannoush

Qurinna Library*, Mukhtar St, Benghazi

Tripoli Public Library*, 14 Al-Jazair St, Tripoli

University of Garyounis Library*, Central Library Benghazi Tel: 87633
Librarian: Ahmed M Gallal

University of Libya*, Library, Benghazi Tel: 29713 Telex: 40175
Director: A M Gallal

Literary Associations and Societies

Intellectual Society of Libya*, 136 Shar'a Baladia, PO Box 1017, Tripoli

Liechtenstein

General Information

Language: German
Religion: Roman Catholic
Population: 25,000
Bank Hours: 0800-1230, 1330-1630 Monday-Friday
Shop Hours: 0800-1215, 1330-1830 Monday-Friday; 0800-1215, 1330-1600 or 1700 Saturday
Currency: Swiss
Export/Import Information: No tariff on books. Most books exempt from Turnover Tax. Advertising matter usually dutiable, some exempt from Turnover Tax. No import licences required. No exchange controls
Copyright: UCC, Berne, Florence (see International section)

Publishers

Buch und Verlagsdruckerei AG*, FL-9490 Vaduz, Im Städtle 32

Frank P van Eck, Egertastr 28, Postfach 816, FL-9490 Vaduz Tel: (075) 24257 Telex: 77030
Man Dir: Frank P van Eck
Subject: Art
Founded: 1982

A R Gantner Verlag KG*, FL-9490 Vaduz, Postfach 225 (Located at: Beckagässle 4)
Subjects: Art, Literature, Botany

Kraus-Thomson Organization Ltd, Bildgasse 64, FL-9494 Schaan Cable Add: Kraus Schaan Telex: 77800
President: Herbert W Gstalder; *Vice-president:* Günther W Sprunkel
Divisions: Kraus Reprint, Kraus International Publications, Kraus Periodicals, Kraus Microform
Branch Off: Route 100, Millwood, New York, NY 10546, USA
Subjects: Scholarly publications and reference works in all subjects and languages
Founded: 1956
ISBN Publisher's Prefix: 3-262

Liechtenstein Verlag AG, Schwefelstr 33, PO Box 133, FL-9490 Vaduz Tel: (075) 23925 Telex: 77826
Man Dir: Albart Piet Schiks
Subjects: Belles Lettres, Poetry, History, Educational Materials
Founded: 1945
Miscellaneous: Also a literary agent (qv)

Literarische Agentur und Verlagsgesellschaft*, Litag Etablissement, FL-9490 Vaduz, Beckägassle 4
Dir: Dr Anton Gantner

Park & Roche Establishment, 256 Kirchenstr, FL-9494 Schaan
Subjects: Music, Art, Architecture, History

Sändig Reprint Verlag, Postfach 74, FL-9494 Schaan (Located at: Fürst-Johannesstr 68)
Dir: Hans R Wohlwend
Subjects: Natural Sciences, Linguistics, Fiction, Folklore, Music
ISBN Publisher's Prefix: 3-253

Topos Verlag AG*, Aeulestr 74, Postfach 668, FL-9490 Vaduz Tel: (075) 21711 Cable Add: Topos Vaduz Telex: 77817
Man Dir: Graham A P Smith
Subjects: Law, Economics, Social Science, Periodicals
Founded: 1977
ISBN Publisher's Prefix: 3-289

Literary Agents

Liechtenstein Verlag AG, Schwefelstr 33, PO Box 133, FL-9490 Vaduz Tel: (075) 23925 Telex: 77826
Firm is also a publisher (qv)

Major Libraries

Liechtensteinische Landesbibliothek, Öffentliche Stiftung, Postfach 385, FL-9490 Vaduz Tel: (075) 66111
National Library
Director: Dr Alois Ospelt

Literary Associations and Societies

P E N Centre, Postfach 416, FL-9490 Vaduz Tel: (075) 27271
Secretary: Manfred Schlapp

Grand Duchy of Luxembourg

General Information

Language: French, German. Also Luxembourg dialect, Letzeburgesch
Religion: Roman Catholic
Population: 356,000
Bank Hours: 0900-1200, 1330-1630 Monday-Friday
Shop Hours: 0800-1200, 1400-1800 Monday-Saturday. Most close Monday morning
Currency: 100 centimes = 1 Luxembourg franc. Belgian currency also circulates. 1 Luxembourg franc = 1 Belgian franc
Export/Import Information: Member of the European Economic Community. In customs union with Belgium and Netherlands. No tariff on books except children's picture books from non-EEC; advertising other than single copies dutied. VAT on books and advertising. No import licence required. No exchange controls
Copyright: UCC, Berne, Florence (see International Section)

Book Trade Organizations

Fédération Luxembourgeoise des Editeurs de Livres, 23 allée Scheffer, 2520-Luxembourg Tel: 473125/24971
Luxembourg Federation of Book Publishers
General Secretary: Henri Grethen
Miscellaneous: A Department of the Fédération du Commerce Luxembourgeois

Fédération luxembourgeoise des Travailleurs du Livre, 38 rue Goethe, Luxembourg
Luxembourg Federation of Workers in the Book Trade
President: Mathias Warny
Secretary: Gusty Stefanetti

Book Trade Reference Journal

Bibliographie luxembourgeoise (Luxembourg Bibliography), National Library, 37 blvd F D Roosevelt, Luxembourg

Publishers

Editions Guy **Binsfeld**, 14 Place du Parc, 2313 Luxembourg Tel: 496868
Man Dir, Production, Publicity, Rights & Permissions: Guy Binsfeld; *Editorial:* Rolf Ketter; *Sales:* Constant Scholtes Jnr
Associate Company: Guy Binsfeld Idées et Actions (at above address)
Subjects: Belles Lettres, Law, Photography, Tourist Guides, Handicrafts, Art
1982: 12 titles *1983:* 18 titles *Founded:* 1980

Christian **Butterbach***, BP 516, Luxembourg Tel: 26926/26927/22022
Cable Add: Interferences
Owner and Manager: Christian Butterbach
Subjects: Literature, Periodical
Founded: 1959
ISBN Publisher's Prefix: 3-921400

Hasso **Ebeling** Verlag*, 4 rue Pierre de Coubertin, Luxembourg Tel: 488348 Telex: 1354

Man Dir: Hasso Ebeling
Subsidiary company: Ebeling Publishing Ltd, 63 Kings Rd, Windsor, Berkshire, UK Tel: 56 966 Telex: 848516
Subjects: Art, Architecture
Founded: 1974

Publisher **Krippler-Muller***, 52 blvd G-D Charlotte, Luxembourg Tel: 470339
Man Dir: J-P Krippler
Subjects: Belles Lettres, History, Maps, Regional Literature, Law, Languages
Bookshop: At above address
1981: 6 titles *Founded:* 1949

Edouard **Kutter***, 17 rue des Bains, Luxembourg
Subjects: Art, Photography, Facsimile editions on Luxembourg

Imprimerie **Saint-Paul** SA, 2 rue Christophe-Plantin, Luxembourg Tel: 49931 Telex: Wortlu 3471
Man Dir: André Heiderscheid; *Production:* Paul Thill; *Publicity:* Charles Jourdain
Subject: Literature
1981: 36 titles

Verlag-Buchhandlung Joseph **Thielen**, 222 route de Thionville, L-2610 Howald
Owner and Manager: Joseph Thielen
Founded: 1950

Literary Agents

Hasso **Ebeling***, 4 rue Pierre de Coubertin, Luxembourg Tel: 488348 Telex: 1354

Major Booksellers

Librairie De **Bourcy** Lucien***, 49 blvd Royal, Luxembourg

Librairie Paul **Bruck***, 22 Grand-rue, Luxembourg

Librairie du **Centre***, 49 blvd Royal, Luxembourg Tel: 26613/27999
Proprietor: L de Bourcy

Librairie R **Daman**, 4 rue de Brabant, Diekirch

Librairie **Diderich** Sàrl, 2 rue Victor-Hugo, PO Box 70, Esch-sur-Alzette Tel: 554083
Manager: J-Cl Diderich

Librarie **Ernster**, 27 rue du Fossé, Luxembourg
Manager: Pierre Ernster

Librairie **Française***, 1 pl d'Armes, Luxembourg

Messageries du Livre*, 18 rue Christophe Plantin, Luxembourg

Librairie **Muller-Groff***, 4a ave Pasteur, Luxembourg

Librairie Armand **Peiffer***, avc Monterey, Luxembourg

Librairie **Promoculture**, BP 1142, 14 rue Duchscher, 1011 Luxembourg Tel: 480691 Telex: 3112 Promo lu
Manager: Albert P Daming

Major Libraries

Archives de l'Etat, Plateau du St-Esprit, BP 6, L-2010 Luxembourg
National Archives

Bibliothèque de Gouvernement, 37 blvd F D Roosevelt, L-2450 Luxembourg

Bibliothèque de la Ville, 26 rue Emile Mayrisch, Esch-sur-Alzette
Librarian: Fernand Roeltgen

Bibliothèque nationale du Grand-Duché de Luxembourg, 37 blvd F D Roosevelt, 2450 Luxembourg Tel: 26255

Macau

General Information

Language: Portuguese, Cantonese (English used in business)
Religion: Chinese, the majority of population are Buddhist and Catholic is religion of Europeans
Population: 276,000
Literacy Rate (1970): 79.4%
Bank Hours: 0930-1700 Monday-Friday; 0930-1200 Saturday
Shop Hours: 0900-1730 Monday-Saturday
Currency: 100 avos = 1 pataca. Hong Kong currency is also widely used but there is no fixed exchange rate
Export/Import Information: Macau is a free port
Copyright: Berne, UCC (see International section)

Major Booksellers

The **World** Book Company, PO Box 201, 68 Rua Dos Mercadores Tel: 73591 Cable Add: Libiblioteca
Manager: V M Lam

Major Libraries

Biblioteca Nacional de Macau*, Edificio do Leal Senado, Macau

Biblioteca **Sir Robert Ho Tung***, Largo do Sto Agostinho, Macau

Democratic Republic of Madagascar

General Information

Language: French and Malagasy
Religion: About 40% Christian, 5% Muslim; rest follow traditional beliefs
Population: 8.3 million
Bank Hours: 0800-1100, 1400-1600 Monday-Friday. Closed afternoon preceding a holiday
Shop Hours: 0800-1200, 1400-1800 Monday-Saturday
Currency: Malagasy franc
Export/Import Information: For books and advertising matter, customs and import duties, also unique tax. Import licence required
Copyright: Berne, Florence (see International Section)

Book Trade Organization

Office du Livre Malagasy (OLM), BP 617, Tananarive Tel: 24449
Secretary-General: Juliette Ratsimandrava

Book Trade Reference Journal

Bibliographie annuelle de Madagascar, Bibliothèque universitaire de Madagascar, BP 908, Tananarive (The national bibliography, published annually since 1964)

Publishers

Editions **Ambozontany***, BP 40, 301 Fianarantsoa Tel: 50653
Man Dir: Justin Bethaz; *Editorial:* Nicola Giambrone; *Sales:* José Minien
Subjects: Scholarly, Cultural, Social, Historical, Religious
Bookshop: At above address
Founded: 1962

Maison d'Edition Protestante '**Antso**', 19 Lalana Venance Manifatra, BP 660, Tananarive Tel: 20886 Cable Add: Fijekrima Antso
Man Dir: Hans Andriamampianina; *Editor:* José Rambinintsoa
Subjects: Religion, Sociology, Politics, Economics, Children's, Juveniles, Practical, Journals
Bookshop: Bookshop Antso, Lot IIB 18, Totohabato Ranavalona 1, Tananarive
Founded: 1966

Government Printer*, Imprimerie nationale, BP 38, Tananarive

Madagascar Print & Press Co+, rue H Rabesahala, BP 953, Tananarive Tel: 22536 Telex: Madprint c/o Soam 22226 Mg
Man Dir: Editorial: Georges Ranaivosoa; *Sales:* Trano Mpampiely Vaovao; *Production:* Madprint, BP 953, Tananarive; *Publicity:* CEMOI, BP 46, Tananarive
Subsidiary Company: Communication et Media — Ocean Indien (CEMOI), BP 46, Tananarive
Associate Company: Nouvelle Société de Presse et d'Editions, 58 rue Tsiombikibo, Ambatovinaky, Tananarive
Subjects: General, Literature, History, Technical
Founded: 1969

Société de Presse et d'Edition de Madagascar*, BP 1570, Tananarive
Man Dir: Mrs Rajaofera-Andriambelo
Subjects: General Non-fiction, Reference, General Science, University Textbooks

Société **Malgache** d'Edition, BP 659, Ankorondrano, Tananarive Tel: 22635
Man Dir: Rahaga Ramaholimihaso; *Publicity:* Daniel Ramanandraibe
Subjects: University & Secondary Textbooks
Bookshop: At above address
Founded: 1959

Société Nouvelle de l'Imprimerie Centrale*, BP 1414, Tananarive
Man Dir: M Hantzberg
Subjects: Paperbacks, General Science, University, Secondary & Primary Textbooks
Founded: 1959

Imprimerie **Takariva***, 4 rue Radley, BP 1029, Antanimena, Tananarive Tel: 22128
Man Dir: Paul Rapatsalahy
Subjects: General Fiction, Malagasy Languages, Paperbacks, Secondary Textbooks
Founded: 1933

Trano Printy Loterana-Trano Printy Fiangonana Loterana Malagasy (TPFLM)- (Imprimerie Luthérienne), 9 ave Grandidier, BP 538, Antsahamanitra, Tananarive Tel: 24569/23340
Man Dir: Abel Arnesa; *Editorial:* Pastor Joseph Rasolofomanana; *Literary Editor:* Sabina Ralandinoro
Subjects: General Fiction, Religion, Paperbacks, Secondary & Primary Textbooks
Bookshop: At above address
Founded: 1875

Major Booksellers

Bibliomad, 11 rue de Nice, BP 602, Tananarive Tel: 23280
Manager: Ramaromandray Amédée

Librairie de Madagascar, 38 ave de l'Indépendance, BP 402, Tananarive Tel: 22454
Manager: Yves Blanche

Librairie lutherienne*, ave Grandidier, BP 538, Tananarive Tel: 23340

Librairie mixte Sàrl, 37 bis ave du 26 Juin 1960, Analakely, BP 3204, Tananarive Tel: 25130
Manager: Jean Razakasoa

Librairie universitaire*, 26 rue Amiral Pierre, Tananarive

Société Malgache d'Edition, BP 659, Ankorondrano, Tananarive Tel: 22635

Librairie **'Tout pour l'Ecole'**, Immeuble Vitasoa, rue de Nice, BP 1099, Tananarive Tel: 23521

Trano Printy Loterana*, 9 ave Grandidier, BP 538, Antsahamanitra, Tananarive Tel: 24569/23340

Major Libraries

Archives nationales de Madagascar*, BP 3384, Tananarive
Dir: Mrs Razoharinoro

Bibliotheque municipale*, ave 18 Juin, BP 729, Tananarive Tel: 21176

Bibliotheque nationale, BP 257, Anosy, Tananarive Tel: 25872
Librarian: Louis Ralaisaholimanana
Publications include: Bibliographie nationale de Madagascar

Bibliothèque universitaire*, Campus universitaire, BP 906, Tananarive Tel: 21103
Librarian: Miss de Nuce
Publication: Bibliographie annuelle

Bibliothèque du Centre culturel 'Albert **Camus'**, 14 ave de l'Indépendance, BP 488, Tananarive Tel: 21375/23647
Librarian: Dominique Seurin

Collège rural d'Ambatobe*, Bibliothèque, BP 1629, Tananarive

Institut national de la statistique et de la recherche economique, Publications and Documentation Section, BP 485 Tananarive Tel: 20081-83
Director: Raphael Ramanana Rahary; *Librarian:* Elisabeth Rakotomalala

United States Information Agency Library, 4 rue Dr Razafindratandra, Ambohidahy, 101 Tananarive

Library Reference Journal

Ny Boky loharanom-pandrosoana (Le Livre Source du Progrès) (The Book, Source of Progress) National Library, Antaninarenina, BP 257, Tananarive

Literary Periodical

Fanasina, BP 1574, Analakely-Tananarive (literary and current affairs weekly edited by Paul Rakotovololona)

Literary Prize

Literature Prize*
For an outstanding novel. 130,000 Malagasy francs. Awarded every two years. Enquiries to Malagasy Ministry of Cultural Affairs, Anosy-Tananarive

Malawi

General Information

Language: English, Cinyanja and Citumbuku (Bantu languages) are official languages
Religion: About 35% Christian (Roman Catholic and Presbyterian); 10% Muslim; rest follow traditional beliefs
Population: 5.7 million
Literacy Rate (1966; African Population): 22.1%
Bank Hours: 0800-1230 Monday, Tuesday, Thursday, Friday; 0800-1130 Wednesday; 0800-1030 Saturday
Shop Hours: 0730 or 0800-1600 or 1700 Monday-Friday (with some closing for lunch); until midday Saturday
Currency: 100 tambala = 1 Malawi kwacha
Export/Import Information: No tariff on books; some advertising matter subject to duty. No import licence required. Exchange controls
Copyright: UCC (see International section)

Book Trade Reference Journal

Malawi National Bibliography, c/o National Archives of Malawi, PO Box 62, Zomba

Publishers

Christian Literature Association in Malawi, PO Box 503, Blantyre Tel: 635046
Subjects: General Fiction, Poetry, Biography, History, Africana, Religion, Juveniles, Christian Tracts, Paperbacks
Bookshop: CLAIM, at above address
Founded: 1968

Government Printer (Imprimerie National), Government Printing Department, Office of the President and Cabinet, PO Box 37, Zomba

Major Booksellers

C L A I M Bookshop, PO Box 503, Blantyre Tel: 635046
Manager: J T Matenje

Central Bookshop Ltd*, PO Box 264, Blantyre Tel: 635447
Manager: A Hamid Sacranie
School suppliers

Malawi Book Service, PO Box 30044, Chichiri, Blantyre 3 (Located at: Ginnery Corner, Kamuzu Highway) Tel: 30044/5 Cable Add: Literature Blantyre Telex: 4537 Mbs Ml
General Manager: M U K Mlambala
Branch Offs: PO Box 344, Zomba (Tel: 745); PO Box 344, University Bookshop, Zomba (Tel: 568); PO Box 201, Lilongwe (Tel: 2068); PO Box 114, Mzuzu (Tel: 232)

Times Bookshop Ltd*, Victoria Ave, Private Bag 39, Blantyre Tel: 636355 Telex: 4112 Blantyre
Manager: Shaibu Itimu
Parent Company: Blantyre Printing and Publishing Co

Major Libraries

British Council Library, Press House, PO Box 30222, Capital City, Lilongwe 3 Tel: 730484/730266 Telex: 4476 Bricoun Ml
Also: Victoria Ave, PO Box 456, Blantyre Tel: 636500

Bunda College of Agriculture Library, University of Malawi, PO Box 219, Lilongwe Tel: 721455 Cable Add: Bundagric

Malawi National Library Service, PO Box 30314, Lilongwe 3 Tel: Lilongwe 730788
Dir: R S Mabomba
Regional Library for the North at PO Box 227, Mzuzu (Tel: Mzuzu 819); Regional Library for the South at PO Box 30074, Chichiri, Blantyre 3 (Tel: Blantyre 631388)

National Archives of Malawi, PO Box 62, Zomba Tel: 2478/9
Librarian: D D Najira
Publication: Malawi National Bibliography

Regional Library for the North, see Malawi National Library

Regional Library for the South, see Malawi National Library

University of Malawi, Chancellor College Library, PO Box 280, Zomba Tel: 2791
Librarian: B G Mphundi
Publications: Directory of Malawi Libraries, An Annotated Bibliography of Education in Malawi

University of Malawi, Polytechnic Library, PMB 303, Chichiri, Blantyre 3 Tel: Blantyre 32144 Telex: Polytechnic 632144 Blantyre
Librarian: Paul Kanthambi
Publication: Accessions List, Annual Report

Library Associations

The **Malawi Library Association**, PO Box 298, Zomba Tel: 2791
Secretary: J J Uta
Publication: MALA Bulletin

Library Reference Books and Journals

Book

Directory of Malawi Libraries, University of Malawi Library, PO Box 280, Zomba

Journals

Ecarbica Journal, National Archives of Malawi, PO Box 62, Zomba

Mala, University of Malawi Library, PO Box 280, Zomba

Literary Associations and Societies

The **Writers'** Group*, PO Box 280, Zomba
Secretary: Miss A M Lonje
Publications: Odi, The Muse

Literary Periodicals

Odi, The Writers' Group, PO Box 280, Zomba

The Muse, The Writers' Group, PO Box 280, Zomba

Malaysia

General Information

Language: Bahasa Malaysia (Malay) is official language; English widely used; Chinese, Tamil and several local languages
Religion: Predominantly Muslim (Islam is the official religion) and large Buddhist group
Population: 12.6 million
Literacy Rate (1970): Sabah 44.3% total (69.1% Urban, 38.9% Rural); Sarawak 38.3% (64.1% Urban, 32.6% Rural); West Malaysia 60.8% (68.2% Urban, 57.6% Rural)
Bank Hours: West Malaysia (some states observe Muslim weekly holiday): 1000-1500 Monday-Friday; 0930-1130 Saturday. Sabah: 0800-1200, 1400-1500 Monday-Friday; 0900-1100 Saturday. Sarawak: 1000-1500 Monday-Friday; 0930-1130 Saturday
Shop Hours: West Malaysia varies; average 0830-1830 Monday-Saturday. Sabah: 0800-1830 Monday-Saturday. Sarawak: 0900-1800 Monday-Friday; 0900-1300 Saturday
Currency: 100 cents = 1 Malaysian dollar (or ringgit)
Export/Import Information: No tariff on books. Advertising matter dutied per lb, subject to CIF surtax. No obscene literature allowed. Import licences required only in Sabah, for books not having on first or last printed page the name and address of printer and publisher. No exchange controls
Copyright: Florence (see International section)

Book Trade Organizations

Malaysian Book Publishers' Association, No 48B Jalan SS 2/67, Petaling Jaya, Selangor Tel: 762669/762614
Honorary Secretary: Johnny Ong

Standard Book Numbering Agency, c/o National Library of Malaysia, Bibliography and Indexing Division, 6th Floor, MABA Bldg, Jalan Hang Jebat, Kuala Lumpur 05-05 Tel: (03) 228472/228473 Cable Add: Natlib Kualalumpur Telex: Natlib Kuala Lumpur MA 30092
ISBN Administrator: Mrs Norpishah Mohd Noor

Book Trade Reference Journals

Berita Oxford (text in English and Malay), Oxford University Press, East Asian Branch, Bangunan Loke Yew, Jalan Belanda, Kuala Lumpur

Bibliografi Negara Malaysia (Malaysian National Bibliography), National Library of Malaysia, 1st Floor, Wisma Thakurdas, Jalan Raja Laut, Kuala Lumpur

Publishers

Academia Publications P Ltd*, 10 Jalan 217, Petaling Jaya, Selangor

Pustaka **Aman** Press Sdn Bhd*, 4200-A Simpang Tiga-Telipot, Jalan Pasir Puteh, Kota Bharu, Kelantan

Pustaka **Antara**, 399A Jalan Tuanku Abdul Rahman, Kuala Lumpur 02-01 Tel: 980044/980159/980237 Cable Add: Antara
Bookshop: 399A Jalan Tuanku Abdul Rahman, Kuala Lumpur 02-01

Anthonian Store Sdn Bhd, 235 Jalan Brickfields, Kuala Lumpur 09-08 Tel: 441711
Man Dir: Anthony B C Soh; *Editorial, Production, Rights & Permissions:* Francis C K Lee; *Sales:* Michael Julian
Associate Companies: Eastview Productions Sdn Bhd (qv); Anthonian (Pte) Ltd, Singapore; Pusat Bahan Sumber Sdn Bhd
Branch Offs: 70 Jalan Leech, Ipoh, Perak; 48, SS 2/67, Sungei Way, Subang, Selangor; Lot LG 02-07, Komplek Wilayah, Kuala Lumpur; 26 Lerong Taman Ipoh Satu, Ipoh Garden South, Ipoh, Perak
Subjects: Educational and General in English and Malay Languages
Bookshops: At above address and in 110 schools
1981: 10 titles *Founded:* 1949

Book Distributors Sdn Bhd*, 8-1/8-2 Jalan Batai, PO Box 944, Kuala Lumpur 01-02

The **Cultural Supplies** Co, see Syarikat Cultural Supplies Sdn Bhd

Dewan Bahasa dan Pustaka, PO Box 803, Kuala Lumpur 08-08 Tel: 481169 Cable Add: Bahasa
Director General: Datuk Hj Hassan Ahmad; *Editorial:* Baha Zain; *Sales:* Mokhtar Mohamad; *Production:* Rahmat Ramly; *Publicity:* A Rahim Esa; *Rights & Permissions:* Ghazali Ruslan
Branch Off: Kota Kinabalu, Sabah; Kuching, Sarawak
Subjects: Textbooks in Malay Language, Literature, General Books, Children's Books, Higher Education, Magazines and Journals
Bookshop: At above address
Founded: 1956

Eastern Universities Press, No 39 Jalan SS 20/11, Damansara Utama, Petaling Jaya, Selangor Tel: 783332/783669
Manager: Ng Tieh Chuan
Parent Companies: (Majority shareholder) Hodder & Stoughton, UK (qv); Eastern Universities Press Sdn Bhd, Singapore (qv)

Subjects: Primary and Secondary Schoolbooks, Art, Archaeology, Architecture, Biography, Botany, Customs and Usage, Economics and Politics, Languages, Sociology, Religion, Travel, Topography
1981: 340 titles

Eastview Production Sdn Bhd, 48A Jalan SS 2/67, Petaling Jaya, Selangor Tel: (03) 762614/762669
Man Dir: Johnny Ong
Associate Companies: Anthonian Store Sdn Bhd (qv); Pacific Book Centre, Singapore (qv under Major Booksellers); Pan Pacific Book Distributors (S) Pte Ltd, Singapore (qv); Manhattan Press (Singapore) Pte Ltd, Singapore (qv)
Imprints: Eastview Malaysiana Library, Eastview Visual Library
Subjects: General, Children's, Dictionaries, Textbooks
1981: 60 titles *Founded:* 1980

F E P International Sdn Bhd, 8246 Jalan 225, PO Box 1091, Petaling Jaya, Selangor Tel: 560877/560381 Cable Add: Bookmark
Man Dir: Lim Mok Hai
Subjects: Reference, Children's General Non-fiction, Secondary & Primary Textbooks, Dictionaries
1981: 155 titles

Penerbit **Fajar** Bakti Sdn Bhd*, 3 Jalan 13/3, PO Box 1050, Jalan Semangat, Petaling Jaya Tel: 563111 Cable Add: Oxonian Petaling Jaya Telex: 37578
Regional Manager: R E Brammah; *Regional Publisher:* J A Nicholson; *General Manager:* M Sockalingam; *Publishing Manager:* Mohd Yusoff Shamsuddin; *Sales:* Koh Seng Hwi; *Production:* Yap Kok Hoong; *Publicity:* Thor Gim Lock
Parent Company: Oxford University Press (qv)
Imprint: PFB
Subjects: Malay Language Teaching, Dictionaries, Reference, Secondary Textbooks, General (all in the Malay language)
Bookshop: At above address
1981: 95 titles *Founded:* 1969
ISBN Publisher's Prefix: 0-19

Federal Publications Sdn Bhd, Lot 8238, Jalan 222, Petaling Jaya, Selangor Tel: 561066/561119 Cable Add: Fedpubs Kuala Lumpur
General Manager: H H Chiam
Assistant Manager: Jesse W van den Driesen
Associate Companies: Federal Publications (S) Pte Ltd, Singapore (qv); Federal Publications (HK) Ltd, Hong Kong (qv)
Subjects: Education, General

Geetha Publishers Sdn Bhd*, 13A Jalan Kovil Hilir, Kuala Lumpur
Man Dir: Mr Sethu
Subjects: History, Education, How-to, Reference, Textbooks, Bibliography, Book Industry

Heinemann Educational Books (Asia) Ltd*, No 2, Jalan 20/16A, Paramount Garden, Petaling Jaya, Selangor Tel: 750033 Telex: Hebkl Ma 37504
Parent Company: Heinemann Educational Books (International) Ltd, UK (qv)

Penerbit **Jaya***, PO Box 6103, Pudu PO, Kuala Lumpur
Subjects: Dictionary (*English—Be hara hasaahara Malaysia Idiomatic Phrases*)

Longman Malaysia Sdn Bhd*, PO Box 63, Kuala Lumpur Tel: 941344/941461 Cable Add: Freegrove Kualalumpur
Man Dir: J E Ho
Parent Company: Longman Group Ltd, UK (qv)
Subjects: Educational Materials, Textbooks

Macmillan Malaysia, FL2 Wisma Fam, Jalan SS 5 A/9, Petaling Jaya, Selangor

Malaya Books Suppliers Co*, 183 Lebuh Carnarvon, Pulau Pinang

Malaya Educational Supplies Sdn Bhd*, 48 Jalan Raja Laut, Kuala Lumpur
Subject: Education

The **Malaya Press** Sdn Bhd*, 24B Jalan Bukit Bintang, Kuala Lumpur Tel: (03) 428831/425764
Man Dir: Yu Nan Shen; *Editorial:* Yiu Hong; *Sales:* Chong Tek Seng
Parent Company: Union Cultural Organization Sdn Bhd, 10 Jalan 217, Petaling Jaya, Malaysia
Associate Companies: Hong Kong Cultural Press Ltd, 9 College Rd, Kowloon, Hong Kong; Singapore Press (Pte) Ltd, 303 North Bridge Rd, Singapore 7
Subject: School Textbooks
Bookshops: Ipoh Book Co, 75 Market St, Ipoh, Perak; Malaya Book Co, 22-24 Jalan Bukit Bintang, Kuala Lumpur
Founded: 1958

Malaysian Law Publishers Sdn Bhd, PO Box 2549, Kuala Lumpur (Located at: no 18, First Floor, Lorong Bunus Enam, Off Jalan Masjid India, Kuala Lumpur) Tel: 932443/2 Cable Add: Law Pub Kl
Man Dir, Rights & Permissions: Hamid Ibrahim; *Editorial:* A Joseph; *Sales:* Kader Subahan; *Production:* Devan Menon; *Publicity:* Ahmad Daud
Parent Company: Rizal Holdings Sdn Bhd
Subsidiary Companies: Malaysian Current Law Journal Sdn Bhd; Metropolitan Law Tutors Sdn Bhd; Malaysian Law Press Distributors Sdn Bhd
Associate companies: Law Publishers (London) Ltd, 47 Brunswick Place, London N1 6EE, UK (Tel: (01) 2510077); Law Publishers (Australia) Pty Ltd, Anchor Hse, 234-242 George St, Sydney 2000, Australia; Legal Publication (S) Pte Ltd, 206 Colombo Court, Singapore 0617; Malaysian Library Services Sdn Bhd
Subjects: Legal Profession Books, Directories, Forms, Periodicals
Bookshop: At above address
1981: 40 titles *1982:* 50 titles *Founded:* 1979

Marican and Sons (M) Sdn Bhd, PO Box 958, Kuala Lumpur (Located at: 321 Jalan Tuanku Abdul Rahman, Kuala Lumpur 02-01 Tel: 981133/981218 Cable Add: Maricanews Telex: Ma 31697
Man Dir: Mr S Y Syed Muhammed; *Editorial, Rights & Permissions:* Dr Y Mansoor Marican; *Sales Manager:* Mr Dorai; *Publicity Manager:* Mr Rasul
Subsidiary Company: Marican and Sons (M) Sdn Bhd, 171 Middle Rd, Singapore 0718
Subjects: Children's, Politics, Statistics, Dictionaries
Bookshops: 321 Jalan Tuanku Abdul Rahman, Kuala Lumpur; 171 Middle Rd, Singapore 0718
1981: 1 title *1982:* 3 titles *Founded:* 1925
ISBN Publisher's Prefix: 0-9934

Pustaka Melayu Baru*, 1015 Selangor Mansion, Jalan Masjid India, Kuala Lumpur

Minerva Publications, PO Box 191, Seremban, Negeri Sembilan Tel: (06) 714436
Man Dir: Tajudin Muhammed
Parent Company: News and Periodicals Store, 96 Jalan Birch, Seremban, Negeri Sembilan
Subsidiary Companies: Bahagia Books Centre, 2115 Malayan Mansion, Kuala Lumpur; Best Book Agency, 40 Lapangan Merdeka, Petaling Jaya
Subject: English Literature
Bookshop: 96 Jalan Birch, Seremban, Negeri Sembilan
Founded: 1964

Oxford University Press*, 3 Jalan 13/3, PO Box 1050, Jalan Semangat, Petaling Jaya Tel: 563111 Cable Add: Oxonian Petaling Jaya Telex: 37578
Regional Manager: R E Brammah; *Regional Publisher:* J A Nicholson; *General Manager:* M Sockalingham; *Sales:* Koh Seng Hwi; *Production:* Yap Kok Hoong; *Publicity:* Thor Gim Lock
Parent Company: Oxford University Press, UK (qv)
Subsidiary Company: Penerbit Fajar Bakti Sdn Bhd (qv)
Branch Off: 4th Floor, Tong Lee Bldg, 35 Kallang Pudding Rd, Singapore 1334
Subjects: Educational, English Language Teaching, General, Dictionaries, Reference, Malaysiana, Asian subjects
Bookshop: 3 Jalan 13/3, Jalan Semangat, Petaling Jaya
Book Club: Triple Crown Club
1981: 68 titles *Founded:* 1957
ISBN Publisher's Prefix: 0-19

P F B, an imprint of Penerbit Fajar Bakti Sdn Bhd (qv)

Pan Malayan Publishing Co Sdn Bhd*, 211 Jalan Bandar, Kuala Lumpur 01-30

Penerbitan Buku Panther (Panther Books Malaysia)*, 135A Jalan Abdul Samad, Brickfields, Kuala Lumpur 09-02 Tel: 442364/442841
Chief Executive, Publicity: R Vijesurier; *Editorial, Production:* Bella Mary Peters; *Sales:* Irene Khoo
Branch Off: 8 Cambridge Rd, Singapore 10
Subjects: School Textbooks, Revision Guides, Travel Books, Street Guides
Founded: 1972

Preston Corporation Sdn Bhd, 18 Jalan 19/3, Petaling Jaya, Selangor Tel: 563734/5 Telex: Prest MA 37433
Associate Companies: Times Educational Co Sdn Bhd, Malaysia (qv); Vista Productions Ltd, A7/F Melbourne Industrial Bldg, 16 Westlands Rd, Quarry Bay, Hong Kong; Preston Corporation (Pte) Ltd, 9 Irving Place, Singapore 1336 (Telex: Presin rs 26690)
Subjects: School Books, General

Sino-Malay Publishing Co*, 183 Lebuh Carnarvon, Pulau Pinang

Pustaka Sistem Palajaran Sdn Bhd*, 77 & 79 Jalan Jejaka Dua, Batu 3, Cheras, Kuala Lumpur
Man Dir: Michael Ong
Subjects: School Textbooks, Children's Books

Pustaka Sri Jaya Sdn Bhd, 14 Jalan Kancil, off Jalan Pudu, Kuala Lumpur 06-13
Subjects: Juveniles, Textbooks

Syarikat Cultural Supplies Sdn Bhd*, 14 Lorong Brunei Dua, Off Jalan Pudu, Kuala Lumpur 06-18 Tel: (03) 427228/412791
Dir: Kow Ching Chuan

Syarikat Dian Sdn Bhd*, 97A Jalan Raja Abdullah, Kampung Baru, Kuala Lumpur

Syarikat United Book Sdn Bhd*, 187-189 Lebuh Carnarvon, Pulau Pinang

Text Books Malaysia Sdn Bhd*, Peti Surat 30, Segamat, Johore (Located at: 39 Jalan Buloh Kasap, Segamat, Johore)

Times Educational Co Sdn Bhd, 22 Jalan 19/3, Petaling Jaya, Selangor Tel: 571766 Cable Add: Timesbooks Telex: Prest MA 37433
Orders to: Preston Corporation Sdn Bhd, 18 Jalan 19/3, Petaling Jaya Selangor
Parent Company: Times Educational Co Ltd, A7/F Melbourne Industrial Bldg, 16 Westlands Rd, Quarry Bay, Hong Kong Telex: 63321 Timbk Hx
Associate Companies: Preston Corporation Sdn Bhd, Malaysia (qv); Preston-Times Printing & Publishing, Selangor, Malaysia; Preston Corporation (Private) Ltd, Singapore
Subjects: Textbooks (Primary & Secondary School), Children's Books, Cookery, General

Uni-Text Book Company, PO Box 1114, Jalan Semangat, Petaling Jaya, Selangor (Located at: 24 SS 24/13, Taman Megah, Petaling Jaya, Selangor) Tel: 753907/754005
Man Dir: Bob E S Lim; *Editorial:* E S Lim; *Production:* E H Lim; *Sales:* Theresa Chung
Associate Company: Uni-Text Distributors Private Ltd, at above address
Subjects: Malay History, Religion, Literature, Juvenile (Local and Regional Culture)
Bookshop: At above address

United Publishers Services (M) Sdn Bhd, 39 Jalan SS 20/11, Damansara Utama, Petaling Jaya
Man Dir, Editorial, Production, Rights & Permissions: Goh Kee Seah; *Sales, Publicity:* Ng Tieh Chuan
Associate Companies: United Publishers Service Hong Kong Ltd; United Publishers Services Tokyo Ltd, Japan (qv)
Branch Offs: No 8, 1st Floor, Leboh Naning, Penang; 106 Boon Keng Rd, 07-05 Singapore 1233
Subjects: Educational, General, Paperbacks
Founded: 1968

University of Malaya Press Ltd*, University of Malaya, Pantai Valley, Kuala Lumpur 22-11 Tel: (03) 574361 Cable Add: Vasitipres Kuala Lumpur
Man Dir, Publicity, Rights & Permissions: Omar Hj Mahmood; *Editorial:* Bahador Shah B Md Isa; *Sales:* Cooperatives Book Shop, University of Malaya; *Production:* Sudhrson R
Subjects: General Fiction, Belles Lettres, Poetry, History, Politics, Economics, General & Social Science, Medicine, Bahasa Malaysia
Founded: 1954

Utusan Publications and Distributors Sdn Bhd*, PO Box 2235, 46M Jalan Lima, off Jalan Chan Sow Lin, Kuala Lumpur
General Manager: Othman Karim

Book Club

Triple Crown Club*, 3 Jalan 13/3, PO Box 1050, Jalan Semangat, Petaling Jaya, Selangor Cable Add: Oxonian Petaling Jaya Telex: 37578
Members: 300
Owned by: Oxford University Press (Selangor) (qv)
Founded: 1963

Major Booksellers

Anthonian Store Sdn Bhd, 235 Jalan Brickfields, Kuala Lumpur 09-08 Tel: 441711
Branch Offs: 70 Jalan Leech, Ipoh, Perak; 48 SS 2/67, Sungei Way, Subang, Selangor; 26 Lorong Taman Ipoh Satu, Ipoh Garden South, Ipoh, Perak; Lot LG 02-07, Komplek Wilayah, Jalan Dang Wangi, Kuala Lumpur Also Publisher (qv)

Cosdel (Singapore) Pte Ltd*, PO Box 6073, Pudu, Kuala Lumpur 06-10 Tel: 489772/489224 (Located at: 23-25 Jalan Jejaka 7, Taman Maluri; Batu 3, Jalan Cheras, Kuala Lumpur)
Manager: Robert Foo
Distributors

Eastern Book Service Sdn Bhd (wholesalers)*, 10-A Jalan Telawi Empat, Bangsar Baru, Kuala Lumpur Tel: 941229
Cable Add: Eastbook
General Manager: Encik Abdul Malik
Publishers' agents and stockists

Johore Central Store Sdn Bhd*, 55-56 Jalan Ibrahim, Johor Bahru Tel: 23637

Kwang Hwa Bookstore Pte Ltd, 26 Carpenter St, PO Box 326, Kuching, Sarawak Tel: 22968
Manager: Francis Hsu Cheng Loo

M P H Distributors Sdn Bhd, PO Box 1076, 13 Jalan 13/6, Jalan Semangat, Petaling Jaya Tel: 567748/567719
Manager: Ho Foo Thiam

Marican & Sons (M) Sdn Bhd, 321 Jalan Tuanku Abdul Rahman, Kuala Lumpur 02-01 Tel: 981133/981218

Nabco Pendidekan Sdn Bhd, 24 Market St, Ipoh, Perak Tel: (05) 78456/518439
Man Dir: Walter Chong

Parry's Book Center (Sri Abdul Wahab Sdn Bhd), KL Hilton Hotel, PO Box 960, Kuala Lumpur Tel: 422631 (showroom), 922329, 924985 (office)
Dir: Abdul Wahab
University and Library suppliers. Also foreign publishers' representatives

Rex Book Store*, 40-2 K L Arcade, Jalan Masjid India, Kuala Lumpur

Times Distributors Sdn Bhd*, NZI Building, 2 Jalan 52/10, Petaling Jaya, Selangor
Also: 1 New Industrial Rd, Singapore 1953
General Manager: Rudolf Phua

University of Malaya Co-operative Bookshop Ltd*, PO Box 1127, Jalan Pantai Baru, Kuala Lumpur Tel: 565000/565425 Telex: MA 37453

Major Libraries

Arkib Negara Malaysia, Malay name of National Archives of Malaysia (qv)

British Council Library, PO Box 539, Jalan Bukit Aman, Kuala Lumpur 01-02 Tel: (03) 987555 Telex: MA 31052
Branches: Penang (PO Box 595); Kota Kinabalu (PO Box 746); Kuching (PO Box 615)

Kuala Lumpur Public Library*, Sam Mansion, Jalan Tuba, Kuala Lumpur

Lincoln Cultural Center*, 181 Jalan Ampang, Kuala Lumpur 04-07 Tel: 420291/425478/484865
Chief Librarian: Sophia Lim Enghwa

Ministry of Agriculture Library, Jalan Mahameru, Kuala Lumpur 10-02 Tel: 982011 Cable Add: Tani Kuala Lumpur
Librarian: Ms S Y Lai

National Archives of Malaysia, Jalan Duta, Kuala Lumpur Tel: 944669/943244/943627 Cable Add: Arkib Kualalumpur
Publications include: Annual Report of the National Archives; Bulletins

National Library of Malaysia*, 1st Floor, Wisma Thakurdas, Jalan Raja Laut, Kuala Lumpur 02-07
Deputy Director General: D E K Wijasuriya
Publications: Malaysian National Bibliography (quarterly, annually); *Malaysian Periodicals Index* (semi-annually); *Malaysian Newspaper Index* (semi-annually)

National University of Malaysia Library*, Bangi, Selangor Tel: 331500/331099
Chief Librarian: (acting) Zainal Azman Rajuddin

Perpustakaan Negeri Sabah, Malay name of Sabah State Library (qv)

Rubber Research Institute of Malaysia Library*, PO Box 150, Kuala Lumpur 16-03 Tel: 467033 Cable Add: Searching Telex: Rrim Ma 30369
Librarian: J S Soosai

Sabah State Library, Kota Kinabalu, Sabah Tel: Pengarah 54064/Pejabat Am 54333/54243/54493 Telex: Saslib ma 80236
Director: Mrs Adeline Leong

Sarawak State Library, Jalan Jawa, Kuching Tel: (082) 22911
State Librarian: Johnny Kueh

Selangor Public Library, 21 Jalan Raja, Kuala Lumpur 01-02 Tel: (03) 985777
Librarian: Mrs Shahaneem Mustafa
Publication: Annual Report; Accession List

Tun Razak Library, Jalan Club, Ipoh, Perak Tel: (05) 514979/514808
Librarian: Chang Sinn Nean
Publications: Malaysiana Collection (plus supplement); *Accession Lists* (in English, Malay, Chinese and Tamil)

Library **Tun Seri** Lanang, Universiti Kebangsaan Malaysia, Bangi, Selangor

Universiti Kebangsaan, see Library Tun Seri

University Library, Universiti Sains Malaysia, Minden, Penang Tel: 883822/881331 Cable Add: Unisains Telex: 40254 ma
Chief Librarian: Lim Huck Tee

University of Agriculture Malaysia Library, Serdang, Selangor Tel: 356101 Telex: Uniper ma 37454 Cable Add: Unipertama Sungaibesi
Chief Librarian: Tuan Syed Salim Agha

University of Malaya Library, Pantai Valley, Kuala Lumpur 22-11 Tel: 575887 Telex: Ma 37453
Acting Librarian: Mrs Khoo Siew Mun
Publications include: Kekal Abadi (quarterly newsletter)
Miscellaneous: Special Collections in Medicine, Law, Malay Languages/Culture, Chinese, Tamil

University of Technology Malaysia Library, Jalan Gurney, Kuala Lumpur Tel: 929033 Telex: 30090 Utm
Chief Librarian: Che Sham Hj Mohd Darus

Library Association

Persatuan Perpustakaan Malaysia, PO Box 2545, Kuala Lumpur
Library Association of Malaysia
Honorary Secretary: Mrs Laila Bte Hassan
Publications: Majallah Perpustakaan Malaysia (annually); *Berita PPM* (bi-monthly)

Library Reference Books and Journals

Book

Directory of Libraries in Malaysia, National Library of Malaysia, Jalan Raja Laut, Kuala Lumpur

Journals

Majallah Perpustakaan Malaysia (Official Journal) (text in English and Malay), Library Association of Malaysia, PO Box 2545, Kuala Lumpur

Sumber Pustaka, Library Association of Malaysia, PO Box 2545, Kuala Lumpur
Official Newsletter, text in English and Malay

Literary Associations and Societies

Dewan Bahasa dan Pustaka*, PO Box 803, Jalan Lapangan Terbang, Kuala Lumpur 08-08
Language and Literary Agency of the Ministry of Education
Dir General: Datuk Haji Hassan bin Ahmad
Publications: Dewan Bahasa, Dewan Masyarakat, Dewan Pelajar, Dewan Sastera (monthly); *Dewan Budaya, Dewan Siswa* (monthly); *Tenggara* (half-yearly)

Literary Periodical

Tenggara (half-yearly — text in English and Malay), Dewan Behasa dan Pustaka, PO Box 803, Jl Lapangan Terbang, Kuala Lumpur 08-08

Literary Prizes

Anugerah Sastera Negara Prize
National Literary Award. Founded 1980, the highest governmental award to an author writing in the national language, who has made a major contribution to the development of the country's literature. Award consists of M$30,000, publication and other benefits. Enquiries to Dewan Bahasa dan Pustaka, PO Box 803, Kuala Lumpur 08-08

Hadiah Sastera Malaysia Prize
Malaysian Literary Prize. Founded 1982, and awarded by the Malaysian Government biennially for creative writing in the national language, covering fiction, poetry, drama, criticism, translation, with the aim of encouraging new talent and enhancing the quality of the national literature. Enquiries to Dewan Bahasa dan Pustaka, PO Box 803, Kuala Lumpur 08-08

Mali

General Information

Language: French
Religion: Muslim
Population: 6 million
Literacy Rate (1960): 2.2%
Working Hours: 0730-1430 Monday-Thursday and Saturday; 0730-1230 Friday
Currency: Malian franc
Export/Import Information: Member of the West African Economic Community. No tariff on books but subject to VAT at varying rates. Advertising matter (more than single copy) subject to tariff, import tax and VAT. All goods subject to local tax of percentage of customs value. Import licence required. Importation is either by private importers or state enterprises. Exchange

controls for non-franc zone
Copyright: Berne (see International section)

Publishers

Government Printer (Imprimerie Nationale)*, ave Kassé Keita, BP 21, Bamako

Editions Imprimeries du Mali*, ave Kassé Keita, BP 21, Bamako Tel: 22041
Man Dir: Barthélémy Koné
Subsidiary Companies: Editions populaires; Imprimerie Kassé Keita; Imprimerie nationale
Subjects: General Fiction & Non-fiction, Belles Lettres, Poetry, Biography, History, Africana, Religion, Paperbacks, Social Science, University, Secondary & Primary Textbooks
Founded: 1972

Major Booksellers

Librairie **Deves et Chaumet***, BP 64, Bamako

Librairie populaire de Mali*, ave Kassé Keita, BP 28, Bamako Tel: 23403

Major Libraries

Bibliothèque municipale*, Bamako

Bibliothèque nationale*, ave Kassé Keita, BP 159, Bamako Tel: 224963
Director: Abdoul Aziz Diallo
Publication: Néant

Centre Djoliba recherche-formation pour le developpement, Bibliothèque*, BP 298, Bamako

Centre français de Documentation*, Ambassade de France, BP 1547, Bamako Tel: 24019

Ecole normale supérieure*, Bibliothèque, BP 241, Bamako

Library Association

Inspection des **Archives**, Musées et Bibliothèques du Mali*, BP 241, Bamako
Inspectorate of Archives, Museums and Libraries of Mali

Malta

General Information

Language: Maltese (English second language)
Religion: Roman Catholic
Population: 340,000
Literacy Rate (1948): 56%
Bank Hours: 0830-1230 Monday-Friday; 0830-1200 Saturday
Shop Hours: 0900-1300, 1530-1900 Monday-Saturday
Currency: 10 mils = 1 cent, 100 cents = 1 Maltese pound
Export/Import Information: No tariff on books or advertising. No import licence required. Exchange control by Central Bank
Copyright: Berne, UCC (see International section)

Publishers

A C **Aquilina** & Co, 58D Republic St, Valletta Tel: 624774 Cable Add: Aniliqua Vallettamalta
Publicity Manager: Josef Portelli
Subjects: Literature, History
Bookshop: At above address

Gulf Publishing Ltd*, 13 Valletta Bldgs, PO Box 576 Valletta Tel: 24186 Cable Add: Gulfpub Valletta Telex: MW950 Gulfpb
Man Dir, Editorial, Rights & Permissions: Emanuel Debattista; *Sales:* Victor Mifsud; *Production, Publicity:* Gaetan Cilia
Subjects: Leisure, Educational, Children's, Cookery, Technical, Tourism
1981: 42 titles *Founded:* 1978

Ideal, an imprint of A Vassallo and Sons Ltd (qv)

Lux Press*, St Joseph St, Hamrun
Subject: Literature

Mediterranean Publishing Co Ltd, PO Box 546, Valletta (Located at: 34E Archbishop St, Valletta) Tel: 25820/620300/607981 Cable Add: Mepuco Mw Telex: 532 Mepuco Mw
Man Dir: Leo Brincat
Founded: 1976

Progress Press*, PO Box 328, Valetta (Located at: Strickland House, 341 St Paul St, Valletta) Tel: 24031 Cable Add: Progress Telex: MW341
Man Dir: W B Asciak
Parent Company: The Allied Newspapers Ltd
Subjects: Literature, Malta
1981: 4 titles *Founded:* 1957

The **University of Malta** Press, Administration Bldg, The University of Malta, Msida Tel: 36451 Cable Add: University Malta
Subjects: Maltese Folklore & History, Maltese Legal History, Natural History, Linguistics
1981: 3 titles *Founded:* 1953

A **Vassallo** and Sons Ltd*, PO Box 6, Main Gate St, Victoria, Gozo Tel: 556609 Cable Add: Gocode
Imprint: Ideal
Subjects: School Textbooks, Maps, Guides
Bookshop: The Ideal Bookshop (qv under Major Booksellers)

Major Booksellers

A C **Aquilina** & Co*, 58D Republic St, Valletta Tel: 624774
Also Publisher (qv)

Hamrun Library*, The, 673 St Joseph Rd, Hamrun Tel: 28542

The **Ideal** Bookshop*, Vassallo Supermarket, Main Gate St, Victoria, Gozo Tel: 556609 Cable Add: Gocode
Owned by: A Vassallo and Sons Ltd (qv)

Merlin Library Ltd, Mountbatten St, Blata l-Bajda Tel: 625838 Telex: MW 558 Merlin
Dir: A J Gruppetta
Branch Off: 57 Old Bakery St, Valletta Tel: 603112
Also Wholesalers and Remainder Dealers

Giov **Muscat** & Co Ltd, PO Box 348, Valletta (Located at: 213 St Ursola St, Valletta, also 48 Merchants St, Valletta) Tel: 625729/27668 Cable Add: Herald Malta Telex: 727 Mw
Man Dir: J Muscat

Sapienza's Library, 26 Republic St, Valletta Tel: 625621
Manager: Louis Sapienza

Major Libraries

Gozo Public Library*, Vajringa St, Victoria, Gozo Tel: 556200

National Library of Malta*, 36 Old Treasury St, Valletta Tel: Central 26585
Librarian: Dr Vincent A Depasquale
Publication: Annual Report

University of Malta Library, Msida Tel: 514306
Librarian: Paul Xuereb
Publications include: Malta, Official Statistical Publications, 2nd ed, 1981; Il-Poezija bil-Malti 1964-74; Liberty to Print: Catalogue of an exhibition of Street Literature 1976; A Bibliography of Maltese Bibliographies 1978; Agriculture in the Maltese Islands: a Bibliography (1979)

Library Association

Ghaqda Bibljotekarji/Library Association (Valletta), c/o Din l-Art Helwa, 133 Melita St, Valletta
Secretary: Anthony F Sapienza
Publications: GhB/LA Newsletter; Bibliography of Children's Literature in Malta; Handlist of Writings on Art in Malta; Directory of Publishers, Printers, Book Designers and Book Dealers in Malta; Series of Occasional Papers

Library Reference Books and Journals

Book

A Bibliography of Maltese Bibliographies, University of Malta Library, Msida

Journal

GhB/LA Newsletter, Ghaqda Bibljotekarji/Library Association (Valletta), c/o Din l-Art Helwa, 133 Britannia St, Valletta

Martinique

General Information

Language: French
Population: 325,000
Literacy Rate (1967): 87.8%
Currency: French Guiana, Guadeloupe and Martinique franc
Export/Import Information: Tariff same as France. Overseas tax and reduced VAT on books. Small quantity of advertising free. No import licences required. Exchange restrictions as in France
Copyright: Berne, UCC (see International section)

Major Booksellers

A **Jean-Charles***, 32 et 47 rue Schoelcher, Fort de France Tel: 4155
Branches: 4

Major Libraries

Direction des Services d'**Archives** de la Martinique, Tartenson, Route de la Clairière, BP 649, 97262 Fort de France
Director: Miss Chauleau
Publication: Guide des Archives de la Martinique

Bibliothèque Victor **Schoelcher***, Rue de la Liberté, 97200 Fort de France, Martinique
Librarian: Jacqueline Leger

Mauritania

General Information

Language: Arabic and French
Religion: Muslim
Population: 1.5 million
Literacy Rate (1977): 17.4% of population aged 6 or over (36.9% of urban population, 11.5% rural)
Bank Hours: 0800-1115, 1430-1630 Monday-Friday
Shop Hours: Vary. Generally 0800-1200, 1430-1800 Monday-Saturday. Some closed Monday morning, some open Sunday morning
Currency: ouguiya
Export/Import Information: Member of the West African Economic Community. No tariff on books. Advertising matter (other than single copies) subject to fiscal, customs duty and added tax. Import licences and exchange controls apply to imports outside of EEC and franc zone
Copyright: Berne (see International section)

Publishers

Government Printer (Imprimerie Nationale)*, BP 618, Nouakchott

Imprimerie Commerciale et Administrative de Mauritanie*, BP 164, Nouakchott
Subjects: Education, Textbooks

Major Booksellers

Librairie-Papeterie **Mauritanie** Nouvelle*, BP 61, Nouakchott

Major Libraries

Arab Library*, Chinguetti

Direction des **Archives** nationales, Bibliothèque publique centrale, BP 77, Nouakchott
Director: Mohamed Ould Gaouad

Bibliothèque nationale*, BP 20, Nouakchott Tel: 24-35 or 278

Centre culturel **Saint-Exupery**, Bibliothèque*, BP 225, Nouakchott

Mauritius

General Information

Language: English and French
Population: 924,000
Bank Hours: 1000-1400 Monday-Friday, 0930-1130 Saturday
Shop Hours: 0800-1600 or later Monday-Saturday
Currency: 100 cents = 1 Mauritius rupee
Export/Import Information: No tariff on books and advertising but there is a special levy. No import licence required
Copyright: UCC (see International section)

Book Trade Reference Journal

Mauritius Archives, Memorandum of Books Printed in Mauritius, Mauritius Archives, Sunray Hotel, Coromandel

Publishers

De l'edition **Bukié** Banané, 5 rue Edwin Ythier, Rose Hill Tel: 41436
Man Dir: Dev Virahsawmy
Orders to: Librairie le Cygne, Route Royale, Rose Hill, Mauritius
Subjects: Creole Literature, Poetry, Drama
Founded: 1979

Government Printer (Imprimerie National)*, Government Printing Office, Elizabeth II Ave, Port Louis

Editions **Nassau***, rue Barclay, Rose Hill
Man Dir: R A Y Vilmont
Subjects: General Fiction, Paperbacks

Major Booksellers

Librairie **Allot***, Botanical Gardens St, Curepipe Tel: (230) 61253 Cable Add: Allot Mtius
Managers: M F Jean Allot, M A Charoux

Librairie **Bonanza***, Corner of Virgile Naz and Monsignor Gonin Sts, Port Louis Tel: 5179

Librairie **Bourbon***, 28 Bourbon St, Port Louis Tel: 21467
Manager: Mrs M Allagapen

Librairie Le **Colibri***, St Jean Rd, Quatre Bornes Tel: 2445; Arcades Atchia, Royal Rd, Rose Hill Tel: 1126

Librairie Le **Cygne***, Royal Rd, Rose Hill Tel: 2444

Librairie **Nationale***, 25 Bourbon St, Port Louis Tel: 0748

Librairie des **Mascareignes**, 5 Queen St, Rose Hill Tel: 42748 Cable Add: Manjoo Rose Hill

Nalanda Co Ltd, 30 Bourbon St, Port Louis Tel: 0160

Librairie du **Trèfle***, Royal St, Port Louis Tel: 1106; Les Arcades, Curepipe Tel: 25

Major Libraries

British Council Library, PO Box 111, Royal Rd, Rose Hill Tel: 42034/5

Carnegie Library, Queen Elizabeth II Terrace, Curepipe Tel: 86-4041/44
Librarian: I Dassyne

City Library, City Hall, Municipality of Port Louis, PO Box 422, Port Louis Tel: (2) 0831 Cable Add: Cerne/Port Louis
Librarian: Gaetan Benoit
Publications: Annual Report; Newspapers Index: Mauritius; Bibliography: Mauritiana in City Library

Junior Library*, Moka Rd, Rose Hill Tel: 42003
Librarian: Abdul Soogali

Mauritius Archives, Development Bank of Mauritius Complex, Coromandel
Dir: Dr P H Sooprayen
Publications: Annual Report of the Archives Department (including a bibliographical supplement), *Quarterly Memorandum of Books Printed in Mauritius and Registered in the Archives*

Mauritius Institute Public Library, PO Box 54, Port Louis Tel: 20639
Librarian: S Jean-Francois

University of Mauritius Library, Reduit Tel: 541041/45420
Librarian: B R Goordyal
Publications include: University of Mauritius Report (Annual); *University of Mauritius Calendar; Journal of the University of Mauritius*

Library Association

Mauritius Library Association, c/o School of Administration, University of Mauritius, Reduit
Secretary: R Dassayne
Publication: Mauritius Library Association Newsletter (quarterly)

Library Reference Journal

Mauritius Library Association Newsletter, Mauritius Library Association, c/o School of Administration, University of Mauritius, Reduit

Literary Associations and Societies

Académie mauricienne de Langue et de Littérature*, Curepipe
Secretary: C de Rauville
Publication: Oeuvres et Chroniques de l'Océan indien

Mexico

General Information

Language: Spanish
Religion: Roman Catholic
Population: 66.9 million
Literacy Rate (1970): 74.2%
Bank Hours: 0900-1330 Monday-Friday
Shop Hours: 1000-1900 Monday, Tuesday, Thursday, Friday; 1100-2000 Wednesday and Saturday
Currency: 100 centavos = 1 peso
Export/Import Information: Member of the Latin American Free Trade Association. Foreign language books and textbooks generally dutied per kg legal weight, children's picture books ad valorem or per kg, whichever greater, and require import

264 MEXICO

licence. Three copies of non-Spanish advertising catalogues free but all others require licence and dutied ad valorem. Customs request from Bank of Mexico all necessary information to decide cases of tariff
Copyright: UCC, Berne, Buenos Aires (see International section)

Book Trade Organizations

Cámara Nacional de Comercio, Sección de Librerías*, Paseo de la Reforma 42, México 1, DF Tel: 5922677 Telex: 1777262 Cn Come
National Trade Association, Booksellers' Section

Cámara Nacional de la Industria Editorial*, Holanda 13, Churubusco, México 21, DF Tel: 5449568/5492377
Mexican Publishers' Association
Secretary General: R Servin Arroyo

Centro Mexicano de Escritores AC, San Francisco No 12, Col del Valle, México 12, DF
Mexican Authors' Centre
Secretary of Executive Committee: Felipe García Beraza
Publication: Recent Books in Mexico

Agencia Nacional I S B N, Centro Nacional de Información de la Dirección General del Derecho de Autor, Nuevo Léon 91, Col Condesa Hipódromo, 06100 México, DF

Instituto Mexicano del Libro AC, Paseo de la Reforma 95, Depto 1024, 06030 México, DF Tel: 5352061
Mexican Book Institute
Secretary-General: Isabel Ruiz González

Standard Book Numbering Agency, see Agencia Nacional ISBN

Book Trade Reference Journals

Anuario Bibliográfico (Bibliographical Yearbook), National Library, República de El Salvador 70, México 1, DF

Bibliografía Mexicana (Mexican Bibliography), National Library, República de El Salvador 70, México 1, DF

Boletín Bibliográfico Mexicano (Mexican Bibliographical Bulletin), Editorial Porrúa SA, Argentina 15, 5° piso, México 1, DF

Fuente Editorial (a directory of the Mexican publishing industry), Deduce SA, Apdo 27-030, México 7, DF 06760

Recent Books in Mexico, Mexican Authors' Centre, San Francisco 12, Col Del Valle, México 12, DF

Publishers

Aconcagua Edic y Pub SA*, Blvd Adolfo López Mateos 235, Periferico, Col Mixcoac, México 19, DF Tel: 5635480
Man Dir: Julio Sanz Crespo; *Sales Dir:* Hector Delgado Narvaez
Subjects: Literature, History, How-to, Religion, Technology, Juveniles, Low-priced Paperbacks, University Textbooks, Educational Materials

M **Aguilar** Editor SA, Ave Universidad 757, 03100 México, DF Tel: 6886211 Cable Add: Guilarditor Telex: 1773621 Amedme
Man Dir: Antonio Ruano Fernández; *Editorial:* Francisco Carvajal Faro; *Sales:* Enrique Morales Buenromero; *Publicity:* Aurelio Reyes Gil
Parent Company: Aguilar SA de Ediciones, Spain (qv)
Subjects: Arts, Literature, History, Economy, Philosophy, Children's, Maps
1981: 2 titles *1982:* 3 titles *Founded:* 1965
ISBN Publisher's Prefix: 968-19

Alianza Editorial Mexicana*, José Morán 93-1A, México 18, DF Tel: 5159391/5167108
Man Dir: Alberto E Díaz
Associate Companies: See under Alianza Editorial SA, Spain

Arbol Editorial SA de CV, Presidente Carranza 52-4, Coyoacán, 04000 México, DF Tel: 5544613
Man Dir, Rights & Permissions: Gerardo Gally; *Production:* Margara Clavé
Subjects: Health, Naturism, Oriental Philosophy, Rural Technology
1981: 20 titles *Founded:* 1979
ISBN Publisher's Prefix: 968-461

Ariel-Seix Barral SA*, Morelos 98, 304 Mezanine, México 1, DF
President: Manuel Pijoan de Beristain; *Man Dir:* Fernando Valdes; *Sales:* Marco A Jimenez Higuera
Subjects: Novels, Poetry, University Textbooks
Parent Company: Ariel-Seix Barral Editoriales, Spain (qv)

Editorial **Avante** SA, Luis Gonzalez Obregon no 9-altos, Apdo 45796, 06020 Mexico, DF Tel: 5855400/5855298
Man Dir: Luis Quiros Presa; *Editorial, Production, Rights & Permissions:* Professor Noe Solchaga Zamudio; *Sales:* Mario Alberto Hinojosa; *Publicity:* Mauricio Esteban Luque
Imprints: Impressora Galve SA, Callejon de San Antonio Abad no 39, Col Transito, Mexico 8, DF
Subjects: Kindergarten Textbooks, Pre-School and Primary Teaching Aids, Poetry, Drama, Biography, Miscellaneous Educational, Social Sciences, Linguistics
1981: 4 titles *Founded:* 1950

Editorial **Azteca** SA*, Calle La Luna 225-227, México 3, DF Tel: 5261157 Cable Add: Edasa
Man Dir: Alfonso Alemón Jalomo; *Sales Dir:* Juan Alemón Jalomo
Subjects: General Literature, Technical, Popular Science
Founded: 1956

Editorial **Banca y Comercio** SA*, Reforma 202, México 6, DF Tel: 5353587
Man Dir: Luis Ruiz de Velasco; *Assistant Manager:* Martha C Gutiérrez
Subjects: Business & Administration, Mathematics, Law
Founded: 1934

Libreria y Ediciones **Botas** SA*, Justo Sierra 52, Apdo 941, México 1, DF Tel: 5223896/5224717
Man Dir: Andres Botas Arredondo; *Sales Dir:* Everado Jiménez Martínez
Subjects: Art, History, Economics, General Fiction, Philosophy, Law, General Science, Medicine, Reference
Founded: 1910

Editorial **Bruguera** Mexicana SA, CP 033 Ave Popacatapetl 421-3, México 13, DF
Parent Company: Editorial Bruguera SA, Spain (qv)

Ediciones el **Caballito** SA*, Isabel la Catolica 922, Col Postal, Delegacion Benito Juarez, 03410 México, DF Tel: 5903653/6963400
Man Dir, Editorial: Manuel Lopez Gallo; *Sales:* Alfonso Garcia Espino; *Production:* Teresa Dey; *Rights & Permissions:* Manuel Lopez Gallo, Teresa Dey
Subsidiary Company: Presencia Latinoamerica (at above address)
Associate Company: Impoli SA (at above address)
Subjects: Sociology, Mexican History and Economy, General Non-fiction
Bookshop: Libreria del Soltano SA, Ave Juarez 64, Sotano Centro, México 1, DF
1981: 20 titles *Founded:* 1967
ISBN Publisher's Prefix: 968-6011

Centro de Estudios Monetarios Latinoamericanos (CEMLA), Durango 54, México 7, DF Tel: 5330300 Cable Add: Cemla, Mexico Telex: 1771229 cemlme
Man Dir: Jorge González del Valle; *Editorial, Rights & Permissions:* Juan Manuel Rodriguez; *Sales:* Genoveva De Mária y Campos de Gil; *Production:* Cristina Conde
Subjects: Economics, Finance, Periodicals
Founded: 1952

El **Colegio** de México AC+, Depto de Publicaciones, Camino al Ajusco 20, 10740 México, DF Tel: 5682922/5686033 ext 364/5 Cable Add: Colmex Telex: 1777585 Colme
Man Dir: Jaime del Palacio; *Deputy Man Dir:* Antonio Valadez; *Promotion, Distribution:* Bertha Alavez; *Production:* Carlos Anaya
Subjects: Literature, Linguistics, Sociology, History, International Relations, Demography, Economy, Urbanistic Development, Asian and African Studies, Methodology, Political Science
Bookshop: Librería de El Colegio de México, Camino al Ajusco 20, 10740 México, DF
1983: 260 titles *Founded:* 1940

Compañia General de Ediciones SA de CV+, Mier y Pesado 128, 03100 México, DF Tel: 5437016/6874699 Cable Add: Sayrols Mexico Telex: 01771403 Dsayme
Man Dir: Gonzalo Araico; *Editorial, Production:* Eduardo Peña Alfaro; *Sales:* Jorge Vázquez
Subsidiary Company: Sayara Corporation, Vallarino Bldg, 11th Floor, Elvira Mendez and 52nd St, Panamá 4, Panama
Associate Companies: Libros y Revistas SA (qv); Publicaciones Sayrols SA de CV (qv)
Subjects: Literature, Popular, Science, General
Bookshops: Librería Mexico San Angel, Av Insurgentes Sur 2098, México, DF; Librería Mexico Monterrey, Galeana Sur 1032, Monterrey, Nvo Leon
1981: 31 titles *1982:* 9 titles *Founded:* 1949
ISBN Publisher's Prefix: 968-403

Editorial **Concepto** SA, Presidente Carranza 52-4, México 21, DF Tel: 5544613
Man Dir, Rights & Permissions: Gerardo Gally; *Production:* Margara Clavé
Subjects: Architecture, Psychology, Pedagogy, Children's books, Alternative Technology, How-to
1981: 92 titles *Founded:* 1977
ISBN Publisher's Prefix: 968-405

Ediciones **Contables y Administrativas**, SA*, Heriberto Frías 1451-101, Col del Valle, Delegacíon Benito Juárez, 03100 México, DF Tel: 5590443
Man Dir: Pedro Gasca Rocha; *Sales Dir:* Gustavo Gasca Bretón
Branch Off: Zaragoza 39-106, Guadalajara, Jalisco, Mexico
Subjects: Technical, Accounting & Management
Founded: 1967

Cía Editorial **Continental** SA (CESCA)*, Calzada de Tlalpan 4620, Apdo 22022, México 22, DF Tel: 5732300 Cable Add: Ediconti
Man Dir: Miguel León Garza; *Sales Manager:* Eduardo A Tappan
Subjects: Science & Technology, Textbooks
Founded: 1954

Ediciones **Cepilco** SA, an imprint of La Prensa Medica Mexicana SA (qv)

Editorial **Cosmos**, España 396, Col Granjas Estrella, 09880 México, DF Tel: 5829928
Man Dir: César Macazaga Ordoño; *Publicity:* Raul Macazaga
Subjects: Pre-Colombian History, Mexican Art and History
1981: 6 titles *Founded:* 1956

Publicaciones **Cosmos***, España 396, Col Granjas Estrella, 09880 México, DF Tel: 5829928
Man Dir: Catalina Ramirez de Arellano; *Editorial:* César Macazaga; *Sales, Publicity:* Raul Macazaga; *Production:* Carlos Macazaga
Subjects: Technical dictionaries (Spanish-English)
1981: 5 titles *Founded:* 1963
ISBN Publisher's Prefix: 968-7095

Publicaciones **Cultural** SA, see Publicaciones

Deduce SA*, Apdo 27-030, México 7, DF 06760 (Located at: Tuxpan 63 202A, Mexico 7) Tel: 5644398
Dir-General: Ramiro Lafuente López; *Sales:* Antonio López Ocampo; *Publicity:* Elia Torres Ortiz
Subjects: Bibliographies, Publishing, Teaching, Reference, Agriculture, Ecology (all in microfiche)

Editorial **Diana**, SA Roberto Gayol 1219, Apdo 44-986, 03100 México, DF Tel: 5750711 Cable Add: Edisa Telex: 1777618 Dime
Man Dir: José Luis Ramírez; *General Manager:* Homero Gayosso; *Sales:* Enrique Iván García; *Rights & Permissions:* Paulina Heredia
Subsidiary Companies: Editorial Universo SA (qv); Editorial Origen SA; Edivisión Cía Editorial
Subjects: Fiction, General Non-fiction, Technical, Juveniles
Bookshop: At above address
Founded: 1946

Editorial **Diogenes** SA, Apdo 82-016, Contadero Cuajimalpa, 05500 México, DF (Located at: Arteaga y Salazar 21, Contadero Cuajimalpa, México 18, DF) Tel: 9158120046
Subjects: Belles Lettres, History, Social & Political Science, Medicine
1981: 13 titles *1982:* 18 titles

Editorial **Don Bosco** SA, Apdo 920-Centro, Delegación Cuauhtémoc, 06000 México, DF Tel: 5121101
Dir: Acisclo Morett Parra; *Deputy Dir, Rights & Permissions:* Franz Erdmann; *Sales:* Milagros Magaña del Campo; *Production:* Francisco E Erdey
Parent Company: Moneda, 24-Centro, Delegación Cuauhtémoc, 06000 México, DF
Associate Companies: Don Bosco Verlag, Federal Republic of Germany (qv); Editorial y Librería Don Bosco, Ave 16 de Julio 1899, Casilla 4458, La Paz, Bolivia; Ediciones Don Bosco, Paseo S J Bosco 62, Barcelona 17, Spain
Subjects: Religious
Bookshop: Moneda, 24-Centro y 23 5 de Mayo, 06000 México, DF
1981: 2 titles *Founded:* 1958
ISBN Publisher's Prefix: 968-6662

E D A M E X, see Editores Asociados Mexicanos SA

Editorial **Edicol** SA*, Murcia 2, Col Mixcoac Ins, Apdo 19-376, México, DF Tel: 5637900/5981512 Telex: 01772885 Edime
Man Dir: Jorge Silva Escamilla; *Editorial:* Jorge Silva Ruiz; *Sales:* Gabriel Levy-Spira
Subjects: Design, Communication, Education, Sociology, Social Sciences, Languages and Literature, Reading Manuals
1981: 10 titles *Founded:* 1970
ISBN Publisher's Prefix: 968-408

Editora Nacional, Dr Erazo 42, PO Box 08720, México 7, DF Tel: 5782353
Subject: General Literature
Man Dir: Rubén Rendón Vargas

Editores Asociados Mexicanos SA (EDAMEX), Angel Urraza 1322, México 12, DF Tel: 5757035/5591499/5591566
Man Dir: Manuel Colmenares G; *Editorial, Rights & Permissions:* Mrs Ella de Gedovius; *Sales:* Hector Gonzalez; *Production:* Mauro Alvarado; *Publicity:* Elva Colmenares
Associate Company: Editorial Meridiano SA
Subjects: Social Sciences, Economics, Politics, Literature, Communications, Recreation, Humour
Founded: 1973
ISBN Publisher's Prefix: 968-409

Emecé Mexicana SA de CV, see Emecé Editores SA, Argentina

Empresas Editoriales SA, Praga 56, Apdo 6-791, México 6, DF Tel: 5110162
Subject: General Fiction
Founded: 1944

Ediciones **Era** SA, Apdo 74-092, 09080 México, DF (Located at: Ave 102, Col Granjas Esmeralda, Delegación Iztapalapa, 09810 México, DF) Tel: 5817744 Cable Add: Liberamex
Man Dir: Mrs Nieves Espresate Xirau
Subjects: General Fiction, Art, Belles Lettres, Social & Political Science, Economics, Quarterly Political Reviews
Founded: 1960

Editorial **Esfinge** SA, Colima 220-503, México 7, DF Tel: 5112771/5142823
Man Dir: Agustín Mateos Muñoz; *Sales Dir:* Eduardo Mateos Gay
Subjects: Literature, Law, Science, University, Secondary & Primary Textbooks
Founded: 1957

Espasa-Calpe Mexicana SA*, Pitagoras 1.139, México 12, DF
Head Office: Editorial Espasa-Calpe SA, Spain (qv)

Ediciones **Euroamericanas**, Apdo 24-434, 06700 Mexico, DF (Located at: Pomona 30, México) Tel: 5250266
Man Dir: Klaus Thiele; *Sales:* Alejandro Elías
Subjects: History and Anthropology of the Americas, Practical Technology, Languages
1981: 4 titles *1982:* 2 titles *Founded:* 1971
ISBN Publisher's Prefix: 968-414

Editorial **Extemporaneos** SA*, Poniente 126-A, No 400 Col Residencial Vallejo, Apdo 78-048, México 14, DF Tel: 5875424/5878785 Cable Add: Ediextempo México
Director General, Editorial: Lautaro Gondalez Porcel; *Sales, Publicity, Production:* Romeo Medina; *Rights & Permissions:* Eva Somlo
Subjects: Anthropology, Architecture, Art, Economics, Philosophy, Humour, Literature, Pedagogy, Politics, Sociology, Theatre

Book Club: Club de Lectores Extemporaneos
Bookshop: Librerias Extemporaneos SA, Hamburgo 260, México 6, DF
Founded: 1975
ISBN Publisher's Prefix: 968-415

Fernández Editores SA CV+, Eje 1 Pte México Coyoacán 321, Col General Anaya, México 13, DF Tel: 5244600/5342285
Man Dir: Luis Gerardo Fernández; *Production Manager:* Luis Ramón Fernández; *Sales Manager:* Luis Miguel Fernández
Subjects: Textbooks, Education, Technical Subjects, Children's Books
Founded: 1943

Fondo de Cultura Económica, Ave Universidad 975, Apdo 44975 México 12, DF Tel: 5244376 Cable Add: Doraca
Man Dir: Jaime García Terrés; *Senior Editor:* Felipe Garrido; *Business Manager:* Jorge Farías Negrete; *Production:* José C Vazquez; *Sales:* Cosme Olivares; *Publicity:* Alba Rojo; *Rights & Permissions:* Alicia Hammer
Subsidiary Company: Fondo de Cultura Económica, Spain (qv)
Branch Offs: Argentina: Suipacha 617, Buenos Aires; Chile: Tarapacá 1224, Santiago de Chile; Colombia: Carrera 18, No 33-46, Bogotá; Peru: Berlín 238, Miraflores, Lima; Venezuela: Edif Polar, planta baja, Plaza Venezuela, Caracas
Subjects: Economics, Sociology, History, Philosophy, Politics, Law, Scientific and Technical Studies, Mexican Studies and Archival Documents, Art, UNESCO Publications
Bookshop: Ave Universidad 975
Founded: 1934

Fondo Educativo Interamericano, Apdo 22-456, 1400 México, DF (Located at: San Marcos 102, Col Tlalpan, Delegación Tlalpan, CP 14060) Cable Add: Adiwes Telex: 01771410 Feime
President: Juan José Fernandez Gaos; *Editorial, Rights & Permissions:* Gilda Moreno; *Sales:* Ramon Romo; *Production:* Vicente Serradilla; *Publicity:* Barbara Fernandez
Parent Company: Addison-Wesley Publishing Co Inc, Reading, Mass 01867, USA
Associate Companies: Fondo Educativo Interamericano in Colombia, Panama, Puerto Rico, Venezuela (qqv); Addison-Wesley Publishers Ltd, UK (qv for other associate companies)
Subjects: All Educational
1981: 25 titles *1982:* 45 titles *Founded:* 1972
ISBN Publisher's Prefix: 968-50

Impresora **Galve** SA, an imprint of Editorial Avante SA (qv)

Editorial Gustavo **Gili** de Mexico SA*, Amores, 2027 Col del Valle Delegación B Juárez, 03100 México, DF Tel: 5240308l/5240135 Cable Add: Gusto México Telex: 1772918 Gilime
Above also address of Ediciones G Gili SA
Parent Company: Editorial Gustavo Gili SA, Spain (qv)

Editorial **Grijalbo** SA, Apdo 17-568, México 17, DF (Located at: Calz Sn Bartolo Navclpan 282, Col Argentina Poniente, Del Miguel Hidalgo, 11230 México, DF) Tel: 3584355 Cable Add: Grijalmex
Editorial: Aldo Falabella Tucci; *Sales:* Victor Lemus; *Editorial:* Rogelio Carvajal; *Publicity:* Enrique Aguilar
Parent Company: Ediciones Grijalbo SA, Spain (qv)
Associate Companies: Grijalbo SA, Argentina (qv); Grijalbo Bolivia Ltda,

MEXICO

Bolivia (qv); Editorial Grijalbo Ltda, Brazil (qv); Distribuidora exclusivo Grijalbo, Colombia; Grijalbo y Cía Ltda, Chile (qv); Distribuidora exclusiva Grijalbo SA, Perú (qv); Grijalbo SA, Venezuela (qv); Grijalbo Centroamerica y Panamá SA, Costa Rica; Editorial Grijalbo Ecuatoríana Ltda, Ecuador
Subjects: General Fiction & Non-fiction
Founded: 1954

Harla SA de CV, see Harper & Row Latinoamericana

Harper & Row Latinoamericana-Harla, SA de CV+, Antonio Caso 142, Apdo 30-546, México 4, DF Tel: 5924277 Cable Add: Harpemex Telex: 1777235
Dir General: Jaime Arvizu; *Sales:* Juan Granados (Home), Jorge Galuon (Export)
Parent Company: Harper & Row Publishers Inc, 10 East 53rd St, New York, NY 10022, USA
Associate Companies: Harper & Row (Australasia) Pty Ltd, Australia (qv); Editora Harper & Row do Brasil Ltda, Brazil (qv); Harper & Row Ltd (UK) (qv)
Subjects: University & Secondary Textbooks, Science & Technology, Medicine, Psychology, Engineering
1982: 92 titles *Founded:* 1970
ISBN Publisher's Prefix: 968-006

Editorial **Hermes** SA, Castilla 229-A, 03400 México 13, DF Tel: 5790468 Cable Add: Editermes
Man Dir: Sergio Sánchez Dávila
Associate Company: Editorial Sudamericana SA, Argentina (qv)
Subjects: General Fiction, Belles Lettres, History, Art
Founded: 1945

Editorial **Herrero** SA*, Río Amazonas 44, Apdo 2404, México 5, DF Tel: 5664900
General Dir: Donato Elías Herrero; *Manager:* Ricardo Arancón L
Subjects: Art, Technical, Textbooks
Founded: 1945

Impulso*, Tuxpan 63-205A, Apdo 27-718, México 7, DF Tel: 5647368 Cable Add: Ieelm, México Telex: 01776359
Director General: Rafael Giménez Navarro; *Sales:* Gerardo Sánchez; *Production:* Jose Antonio Lopez Ocampo
Parent Company: Ediapsa (Librerias de Cristal)
Subject: Children's Books
1981: 1 title *Founded:* 1976
ISBN Publisher's Prefix: 968-17

Editorial **Innovacion** SA*, España 396 Col Granjas Estrella, 09880 México, DF Tel: 6703485/5829928
Man Dir: Catalina Ramirez de Arellano; *Editorial:* César Macazaga; *Sales, Publicity:* Raul Macazaga; *Production:* Catalina Macazaga
Subjects: Camping, Touring, Pre-Hispanic and Mexican History, Novels
Founded: 1971

Instituto de Investigaciones Sociales — Universidad Nacional Autónoma de Mexico, Torre dos de Humanidades 7° piso, Ciudad Universitaria, México 20, DF Tel: 5505215 ext 2941-2949
A Department of the Universidad Nacional Autónoma (qv)
Man Dir: Julio Labastida Martín del Campo; *Sales Dir:* Armida Vázquez A
Subjects: Mexican and International Social Studies, Periodicals
Founded: 1939

Instituto Indigenista Interamericano, Ave Insurgentes Sur No 1690, Col Florida, 01030 México, DF Tel: 5240009/5241003 Cable Add: Indigeni

Man Dir, Rights & Permissions: Oscar Arze Quintanilla; *Sales:* Raquel Mendez de Hoyle
Subjects: Social Studies, Anthropology, Periodicals
Founded: 1940

Instituto Nacional de Antropologia e Historia*, Córdoba 45, México 7, DF Tel: 5144222
Subjects: Mexican Archaeology & Anthropology, History
Founded: 1822

Institute Nacional de Bellas Artes*, Dirección de Literatura, Lázaro Cárdenas 2 3°, Torre Latinoamericana, Centro de la Ciudad de México, México, DF
Subjects: Art, Biography, Literature, Philosophy, Reference, Educational Materials

Instituto Panamericano de Geografía e Historia, Ex-Arzobispado 29, 11860 México, DF Tel: 2775888/5151910 Cable Add: Ipaghis
Secretary General: Leopoldo Rodriguez; *Editorial Dir:* Lea Salinas
Subjects: Geography, Cartography, History, Anthropology, Geophysics, Folklore, Periodicals

Intersistemas SA de CV, 110 Fernando Alencastre, Delegación M Hidalgo, 11000 México, DF Tel: 5405600 Telex: 01772931 Isme
Man Dir: Pedro Vera Cervera; *Editorial:* Luis Félix López; *Sales:* Alfonso Juárez R; *Production:* Luis E Belatti; *Rights & Permissions:* Marco Antonio Chávez
Associate Companies: Sintagma SRL, Av Santa Fe no 5235, Piso 14, of 92, Buenos Aires 1425, Argentina (Agency); Editora de Publicaçoes Cientificas Ltda, Brazil (qv); Gráficas Enar SA, Pedro Muguruza 3-1°, Madrid 16, Spain; Patient Care Communications Inc, PO Box 1246, Darien, Connecticut 06820, USA
Subjects: Medical
1981: 5 titles *Founded:* 1970

Editorial **Iztaccihuatl** SA, Miguel Schultz No 21, Apdo 2343, México 4, DF Tel: 5352321 Cable Add: Eiztamexa
President: Orlando Vieyra Legorreta
Subject: General Literature
Founded: 1946

Editorial **Jus** SA*, Plaza de Abasolo 14, Col Guerrero, México 3, DF Tel: 5629959/5260616/5260540
Man Dir: Armando Avila Sotomayor; *Sales Manager:* Dalila Farias Godinez
Subjects: General Fiction, Law, Textbooks, History, Political & Social Sciences
Founded: 1941

Lasser Press Mexicana, SA, Praga 56, Col Juárez, Apdo 6-791, 06600 México, DF Tel: 5142215 Cable Add: Laspresa Telex: 1777529 Coseme
President: Guillermo Menéndez Castro; *Dir:* Guillermo Menéndez Valdés
Subjects: Non-fiction, Biographies, Contemporary International Literature (in Spanish)
1981: 30 titles *Founded:* 1972
ISBN Publisher's Prefix: 968-458

Libros y Revistas SA, Mier y Pesado 126-132, Colonia del Valle, 03100 México, DF Tel: 6874699 Telex: 01771403 dsayme
General Manager: Joaquin Roca Romero; *Editorial, Rights & Permissions:* Marcial Frigolet L; *Sales, Publicity:* Jesus Pernas; *Production:* Adriana Marti
Parent Company: Publicaciones Sayrols SA de CV (qv)
Associate Companies: Compania General de Ediciones SA de CV (qv); Metropolitana de Publicaciones SA

Subjects: Fiction, Educational, Dictionaries, Children's
1981: 8 titles *1982:* 10 titles *Founded:* 1925

Editorial **Limusa** SA, Balderas 95, 1° Piso, México 1, DF Tel: 5853500 Cable Add: Elimusa Telex: 01772581 Expo me
Man Dir: Carlos Noriega Milera; *Executive Vice-President:* Francisco Trilles Mercader; *General Manager:* Carlos Noriega Arias
Associate Company: John Wiley & Sons Ltd, UK (qv for other associates)
Subjects: Science & Technology, Social Science, History, Psychology, University & Secondary Textbooks
Founded: 1962

Logos Consorcio Editorial, SA+, General Molinos del Campo 64, Col San Miguel Chapultepec, 11850 México, DF Tel: 5151633
Man Dir: Enrico Garcia Alonso S
Subject: General

Libros **McGraw-Hill** de Mexico SA de CV, Apdo 5-237, México 5, DF (Located at: Atlacomulco 499-501, San Andrés Atoto, Naucalpan, 53500 Edo de México) Tel: 5769044 Cable Add: Lmchme Telex: 01774284
Man Dir: Raymundo Cruzado; *Publishers:* Guillermo Hernández, Moisés Pérez Zavala, Enrique Pereda; *Rights & Permissions:* Ernesto Bañuelos
Parent Company: McGraw-Hill Inc, 1221 Ave of the Americas, New York, NY 10020, USA
Associate Companies: See McGraw-Hill Book Co (UK) Ltd
Branch Offs: Monterrey, N L; Guadalajara, Jal
Subjects: Natural Sciences, Technology, Textbooks, Education, Business, General
Founded: 1967

Editorial El **Manual** Moderno SA de CV*, Ave Sonora 206, México 11, DF Tel: 5648979/5844065
Chairman & President: Dr Gustavo Setzer; *Editorial:* William Krützfeldt; *Marketing:* John Fischer; *Sales:* Juan Sánchez Villarreal; *Production:* Felipe Vázquez; *Rights & Permissions:* Angélica Sánchez
Associate Company: Elsevier-NDU nv, Netherlands (qv)
Subjects: Medicine, Psychology, Nursing, Veterinary Science, Chemistry
Founded: 1958
ISBN Publisher's Prefix: 968-426

Publicaciones **Marcombo** SA+, Apdo 61-197, México 6, DF (Located at: Roma 37 12-A Col Juárez, 06600 México) Tel: 5660067
Man Dir: Enrique Reyes Mofin; *Production, Publicity:* Gonzalo Ferreyra Cortés; *Rights & Permissions:* Baltazar Feregrino Paredes
Associate Company: Representaciones y Servicios de Ingeniería SA (qv)
Subjects: Engineering, Management, Electronics
1981: 8 titles *1982:* 10 titles *Founded:* 1980
ISBN Publisher's Prefix: 968-41

Masson Editores, Dakota 383, Colonia Napoles, 03810 México, DF Tel: 6870933 Telex: 77604
President: Pierre Lahaye; *Man Dir:* Bruno Vanneuville
Parent Company: Masson Editeur, France (qv)
Associate Companies: Editora Masson do Brasil Ltda, Brazil (qv); Masson italia editori — ETMI, via Pascoli 55, 20133 Milan, Italy; Toray-Masson, Spain (qv); Masson Publishing USA Inc, 111 West 57th St, New York, NY, USA
Founded: 1978

Editorial **Mexicana** SRL*, Orizaba 115 y 119, Apdo 7-852, México
Parent Company: Editorial Labor, Spain (qv)

Editores **Mexicanos** Unidos SA, L González Obregón 5-B, Apdo 45-671, 06020 México, DF Tel: 5128516/5218870
Man Dir, Editorial: Fidel Miro Solanes; *Dir:* Sonia Miro de Laclau; *Manager:* Roque Laclau Gaona
Subjects: General Fiction & Non-fiction
Bookshops: Libro-Mex Editores SRL, Argentina 23, México 1, DF
Founded: 1954
ISBN Publisher's Prefix: 968-15

Galeria de Arte **Misrachi** SA, Génova 20, 06600 México, DF Tel: 5334551
Manager: Enrique Beraha Misrachi; *Editorial, Sales, Production, Rights & Permissions:* Alberto J Misrachi; *Publicity:* Carlos Beraha Cohen
Subject: Art
Bookshops: Génova 20, 06600 México, DF; Central de Publicaciones SA, Ave Juárez 4, 06050 México, DF
Founded: 1933 (Central de Publicaciones); 1961 (Galeria de Arte)
ISBN Publisher's Prefix: 968-7047

Editorial Joaquín **Mortiz** SA, Tabasco 106, Apdo 7-832, México 7, DF Tel: 5331250
Cable Add: Morditor
Man Dir, Editorial: Joaquín Diez-Canedo; *Sales, Rights & Permissions:* Magdalena Blanco; *Production, Publicity:* Bernardo Giner de Los Ríos
Subjects: General Fiction & Non-fiction, History, Psychology, Social Science
Founded: 1962
ISBN Publisher's Prefix: 968-27

Organización Editorial **Novaro** SA+, Apdo 10500, México 1, DF Tel: 5760155 Cable Add: Novaromex Telex: 01774419 Novame
Director General: John S Wiseman
Subjects: Juveniles, Popular Paperbacks
Founded: 1950

Editorial **Nuestro** Tiempo SA, Ave Universidad no 771 desps 103, 104, Col del Valle, Delegación Benito Juárez, 03100 México, DF Tel: 6886564
Man Dir: Esperanza Nacif Barquet
Branch Off: Agencia Guadalajara, Alemania 1266, Col Vallarta, 44100 Guadalajara Jal Tel: 126037
Subjects: Social Sciences
1981: 26 titles *Founded:* 1966
ISBN Publisher's Prefix: 968-427

Nueva Editorial Interamericana SA de CV, Cedro 512, Apdo 26370, 06450 México, DF Tel: 5413155 Cable Add: Tusmexa
President: Luis Castañeda M; *Commercial Director:* Rafael Sáinz
Associate Company: CBS Publishing Group (see Holt-Saunders UK for other associates)
Subjects: Medicine and Health Sciences, General Science and Technology, Textbooks
1981: 94 titles *Founded:* 1944

Editorial **Nueva** Imagen SA, Apdo 600, México 1, DF (Located at: Escollo 316, México 20, DF) Tel: 6802988 Telex: 1771427 Eni Me
Administrative Dir: Enrique Sealtiel Alatriste L; *Editorial Dir:* Guillermo J Schavelzon
Subjects: General Fiction, History, Economics, Art, Science, Social Science, Anthropology, Sociology, Humour, Linguistics, Public Health, Latin American problems
1981: 80 titles *1982:* 80 titles *Founded:* 1976
ISBN Publisher's Prefix: 968-429

Ediciones **Oasis** SA*, Ave Oaxaca 28, Apdo 24-416, México 7, DF Tel: 5288807/5288293
Man Dir: Luis Mario Schneider; *Sales Dir:* Ricardo Rizzo Lavarino
Subjects: General Fiction, Belles Lettres, History, Education
Founded: 1954

Editorial **Orion***, Sierra Mojada 325, Lomas de Chapultepec, México 10, DF Tel: 5200224
Man Dir: Silvia Hernandez Vda de Cárdenas; *Sales Dir, Rights & Permissions:* Laura Hernandez Baltazar; *Publicity Dir:* Silvia Hernandez Baltazar; *Advertising:* Mariaelena Molina
Subsidary Companies: Edit Vila; Edit Cuzamil SA
Subjects: Literature, Philosophy, Religion, Mysticism, Yoga, Astrology, Theosophy, Psychology, & Parapsychology
Founded: 1942
ISBN Publisher's Prefix: 968-6053

Editorial **Patria** SA de CV, Uruguay 25, 2° piso, Apdo 784, 06000 México, DF Tel: 5127651/5184509/5486850
Man Dir: Isabel Lasa de la Mora; *Deputy Manager & Administrator:* Rafael Valdes; *Sales & Publicity Dir:* Santiago Hernandez; *Rights & Permissions:* Isabel Lasa
Subjects: Literature, Biography, History, Philosophy, How-to, Secondary & Primary Textbooks, Pre-School Teaching Aids, Children's Books
1981: 25 titles *1982:* 15 titles *Founded:* 1933
ISBN Publisher's Prefixes: 968-6054, 968-39

Libreria **Patria** SA*, 5 de Mayo No 43, Apdo 2055, México 1, DF Tel: 5852099
Man Dir: Francisco Majewski M
Orders to: Belisario Dominguez 53, México 1, DF
Subsidiary Company: Samara, Cia Papelera SA, Av 5 de Mayo 29-C, México 1, DF
Subjects: Textbooks, Literature, General
Bookshops: Av 5 de Mayo 43, Belisario Dominguez 53
Founded: 1940

Ediciones **Paulinas** SA*, Ave Taxqueña 1792, México 21, DF Tel: 5491454
General Manager: Ricardo Rojas Sarmiento
Subjects: Religion, Education
Bookshop: Librería San Pablo, Ave Madero 61-A, México 1, DF
Founded: 1948

Editorial **Pax** México*, Rep Argentina 9, Apdo 45-009, México 1, DF Tel: 5425890
Man Dir: Humberto Gally Grivé
Subjects: Technical, Psychology, Education
Bookshop: Librería Carlos Cesarman SA, Rep Argentina 9, México 1, DF
Founded: 1920

Editorial **Pomaire** SA*, Apdo 20-569, Manuel M Ponce 143, México 20, DF Tel: 6512853 Telex: 1771979 Pomame
Man Dir: Iván Mozó Lira
Head Off: Editorial Pomaire SA, Spain (qv for list of other branches)
Subjects: Fiction, Belles Lettres, Juveniles
Founded: 1962

Editorial **Porrúa** SA*, Argentina 15, 5° piso, México 1, DF Tel: 5224866 Cable Add: Porruas Mexico
Man Dir: José Antonio Pérez Porrúa; *Sales Dir:* Francisco Pérez Porrúa
Subject: General Literature
Bookshop: Librería de Porrúa Hnos y Cía, Argentina 15, México 1, DF
Founded: 1944

La **Prensa** Médica Mexicana*, Apdo 20-413, San Angel, Alvaro Obregón, México 01000, DF (Located at: Paseo de Las Facultades 26, Fraccionamiento Copilco-Universidad, Coyoacán, México 04360, DF) Tel: 5504500/5504690 Cable Add: Laprememex
Man Dir and Rights & Permissions: Carolina Amor de Fournier; *Administration:* Guadalupe Arias de Gutiérrez; *Production:* Dr Jorge Avendaño-Inestrillas; *Sales & Publicity Dir:* Juan de Dios Díaz-Salgado
Associate Company: Ediciones Copilco SA, Ezequiel Ordoñez 73, Copilco el Alto, Coyoacán, México 04360, DF
Subjects: Medicine, Social Science, Psychology, Biology, Veterinary
Bookshop: Librería de las Facultades, Paseo de las Facultades 26, Copilco-Universidad, Coyoácan, México 04360, DF
Founded: 1945
ISBN Publisher's Prefix: 968-435

Editorial **Progreso** SA*, Apdo 26-372, 02860 México, DF Tel: 5411189
Subjects: Secondary & Primary Textbooks

Publicaciones **Cultural** SA+, Lago Mayor 186, Colonia Anáhuac, México 17, DF Tel: 5456860/1/2
President: Gustavo González Lewis; *Man Dir:* Carlos Frigolet Lerma; *Assistant Manager:* Pedro de Andres Romero; *Sales:* Salvador Lopez Zavaleta; *Rights & Permissions:* Abelardo Fabrega Esteba
Subjects: University, Secondary and Primary Textbooks, Educational Materials
Founded: 1965
ISBN Publisher's Prefix: 968-6058

Publicaciones **Marcombo** SA, see Marcombo

Queromón Editores SA*, Bucareli 59-A, Apdo M-7914, México 6, DF Tel: 5356040
Cable Add: Queromón
Man Dir: Manuel Mallén Sangüesa
Subject: Juveniles
Founded: 1951

Representaciones y Servicios de Ingeniería SA+, Apdo 61-195, México 6, DF (Located at: Roma 37 12-A Col Juqrez, 06600 México) Tel: 5354143/5631925
Man Dir, Editorial: Enrique Reyes Morfín; *Production, Publicity:* Gonzalo Ferreyra Cortes; *Rights & Permissions:* Baltazar Feregrino Paredes
Associate Company: Publicaciones Marcombo SA (qv)
Subjects: Engineering, Management, Technology
1981: 8 titles *1982:* 8 titles *Founded:* 1965
ISBN Publisher's Prefix: 968-6062

Editorial **Reverté** Mexicana SA*, Río Pánuco 141-A, México 5, DF Tel: 5335658
Man Dir: Pedro Reverté Planells
Associate Companies: See under Editorial Reverté SA, Spain
Subjects: Science, Technical
Founded: 1955

Salvat Mexicana de Ediciones SA de CV, Mariano Escobedo 438, Col Nueva Anzures, 11590 México, DF Tel: 2507155 Telex: 017 74 268
Man Dir: José Luis R Rivero; *Editorial, Rights & Permissions:* Ramón Diez Suarez; *Sales:* Jorge M Vaca; *Production:* Jaime M Everart; *Publicity:* Felipe Ferreira y Rendon
Parent Company: Salvat Editores SA, Spain (qv)
Subsidiary Companies: Comercial Salvat de Mexico SA de CV, Distribuidora Codice SA de CV (both at Kelvin 10, 5° Piso, Col Nueva Anzures); Graficas Monte Alban SA de CV, Fracc Agroindustrial La Cruz, Queretaro, Qro
Branch Offs: Celaya 4, Col Roma Sur, México, DF; Domingo Diez 101 2° Piso, Col Lomas de la Selva, Cuernavaca, Mor;

Fco I Madero 331 Ote, Col Centro, Culiacán, Sin; Blvd Díaz Ordáz 1417-1 Altos, Chihuahua, Chih; Garmendia 83, Col Centro, Hermosillo, Son; Carlos A Madrazo 1301-B, Col Centro, Villahermosa, Tab; Madero 710, Col Centro, Mexicali BC; Priv 9-B, Sur 4116 L-A, Col G Pastor, Puebla, Pue; Octava Ote, 121 Sur, Col Centro, Tuxtla Ctz, Chis
Subjects: History, Geography, Art, Fiction, Medicine and Hospitals, Odontology, Veterinary, Psychology, Juveniles
Bookshops: Mariano Escobedo 438, Col Neuva Anzures; Odontología 69-9, Col Copilco Universidad; Calzada Tlalpan 4665, Col Tlalpan; Bucareli 38, Col Centro; Alvaro Obregón 273, Col Roma; Paris 7, Col Revolución (all México, DF); Plaza Satélite Local D-115, Ciudad, Edo de Méx; Galeana 300, San Luis Potosí; Condoplaza del Sol L-40, Guadalajara; Humboldt 107 Norte, Toluca; 2 Ote no 6 Desp 701, Puebla; Juan Ignacio Rayón 506 Ote, Monterrey NL
1981: 5 titles
ISBN Publisher's Prefix: 968-32

Publicaciones **Sayrols** SA de CV, Mier y Pesado 126-132, Col de Valle, 03100 México, DF Tel: 5437295/6874699 Cable Add: Sayrols Mexico Telex: 01771403 dsayme
Man Dir: Marcial Frigolet Lerma; *Editorial, Rights & Permissions:* Marcial Frigolet; *Sales, Publicity:* Jesus Pernas; *Production:* Adriana Marti
Subsidiary Companies: Libros y Revistas SA (qv); Metropolitana de Publicaciones SA
Associate Company: Compania General de Ediciones SA de CV (qv)
Subjects: Fiction, General Interest, Autobiographies, Dictionaries
1981: 20 titles *1982:* 10 titles *Founded:* 1925

Siglo XXI Editores SA de CV, Ave Cerro del Agua 248, Apdo 20626, México 20 DF Tel: 6587999 Cable Add: Sigloedit
Also: Col Romero de Terreros, 04310 Del Coyoacán
Man Dir, Editorial: Arnaldo Orfila R; *General Manager:* Concepción Zea; *Sales:* Juan Carlos Cena; *Production:* Martí Soler V; *Publicity:* Rosario Jiménez; *Rights & Permissions:* Guadalupe Ortiz
Branch Off: Apdo 32-140, Guadalajara, jal
Parent Company: Siglo XXI Editores de España SA, Spain (qv)
Associate Company: Siglo XXI de Colombia Ltda, Colombia (qv)
Subjects: General Fiction, History, Psychology, Economics, Arts, Literature, Health & Society & Technology, Education, Criminology & Law, Sociology, Anthropology, Architecture, Politics, Philosophy, Urban Studies, Linguistics, Latin-American Politics, Marxism
1981: 70 titles *Founded:* 1966
ISBN Publisher's Prefix: 968-23

Editorial **V Siglos**, SA*, Calle Oculistas 43, Col Sifón, México 13 DF Tel: 6700698/5811958/6703837
Man Dir: Guillermo Garavito Escobar; *Editorial, Production, Publicity, Rights & Permissions:* Amapola Garavito López; *Sales:* Daniel Márquez C
Subjects: General Fiction & Non-fiction, How-to
Bookshop: At above address
Founded: 1973

Editorial **Sopena** Mexicana SA*, Ave Chapultepec 153, Mexico City 6
Parent Company: Ramón Sopena SA, Spain (qv)

Time-Life International de México, SA, Apdo 5-592, Leibnitz 13, Mexico 5, DF (Located at: 8 piso, Reforma 195, Mexico 5, DF) Tel: 5469000 Cable Add: Tlimsa
Telex: (017) 71358
General Manager: Koos H Siewers
Subject: Non-fiction
Founded: 1962

Editorial **Tradicion** SA, Sur 22 Número 14 (entre Oriente 259 y Canal de San Juan), Col Agrícola Oriental, 08500 Iztacalco, México, DF Tel: 5582249
Man Dir: Jose Maria Abascal C; *Editorial:* Salvador Abascal; *Sales:* Juan Maldonado
Subjects: History, Mexican History, Political Science, Theology, Religion, Philosophy
1981: 17 titles *Founded:* 1972

Editorial **Trillas** SA*, Ave Río Churubusco 385 Pte, 03340 México, DF Tel: 5244480 Cable Add: Etrillasa
Man Dir: Francisco Trillas Mercador; *Editorial:* Gonzalo Godínez; *Sales:* Jesús Galera; *Production:* Alfonso Durán; *Publicity:* Jorge Mario Blostein; *Rights & Permissions:* Horacio Godoy Moore
Associate Companies: Cía Editorial Carmex SA, Argentina; Cía Editorial Comex SA, Colombia; Alamex SA, Spain; Limex Venezolana, Venezuela
Subjects: Psychology, Education, Mathematics, General & Social Science, Technical, University & Secondary Textbooks, Schoolbooks, Pre-school, Children's, Business
Bookshop: Librería Studio, Oscar Wilde 9, 11560 México, DF
1981: 120 titles *Founded:* 1954
ISBN Publisher's Prefix: 968-24

Universidad Nacional Autónoma de México*, Distribuidora de Libros de la Unam, Porto Alegre 260, 09440 México, DF Tel: 6742552/5395508
Subjects: General University Textbooks, Scholarly
Bookshops: Librería Insurgentes, Ave Insurgentes Sur 299, Col Hipódromo Condesa, 06170 México, DF Tel: 5845512/5842497; Librería de Zona Comercial, Corredor de Zona Comercial, Ciudad Universitaria, 04510 México, DF Tel: 5484118; Librería del Palacio de Minería, Tacuba 5, 06000 México, DF Tel: 5181315
Founded: 1935

Editorial **Universo** SA*, Trigo 153-B, Col Granjas Esmeralda, 09810 México, DF Tel: 6706038
Man Dir, Rights & Permissions: Eduardo Morfin Schad; *Editorial:* Fausto Rosales; *Sales:* Salvador Gorostieta; *Production:* Enrique Escamilla; *Publicity:* Maria del Refugio Salinas
Parent Company: Editorial Diana SA (qv)
Associate Companies: Editorial Origen SA; Edivision Cia Editorial SA
Branch Offs: Guadalajara, Monterrey; Buenos Aires, Argentina; Caracas, Venezuela
Subjects: General Interest, Fiction and Non-fiction
1981: 38 titles *Founded:* 1979
ISBN Publisher's Prefix: 968-35

Editorial **Varazen** SA*, Apdo 70-101, 06700 México, DF Tel: 5335274/5146573
Man Dir: Luis Maria Molachino Agostena
Parent Company: Editorial Teide SA, Spain (qv)
Subjects: Cultural, Educational
1981: 15 titles *Founded:* 1968
ISBN Publisher's Prefix: 968

Book Clubs

Bertelsmann de Mexico SA*, Div Circulo Mexicano de Lectores, Av la Paz No 26, México 20, DF, Col San Angel
Members: 200,000
Owned by: Verlagsgruppe Bertelsmann AG, Federal Republic of Germany (qv)

Círculo Mexicano de Lectores, see Bertelsmann de Mexico SA

Club de Lectores Extemporaneos*, Poniente 126-A, No 400 Col Residencial Vallejo, Apdo 78-048, México 14
Owned by: Editorial Extemporaneos SA (qv)

Major Booksellers

American Book Store SA*, Ave Madero No 25, Apdo 79 Bis, Col Centro Delegación Cuauhtemoc, 06000 México, DF Tel: 5127279/5127284/5120306
Branches: Circuito Médicos No 3, Ciudad Satélite, 53100 Edo de México Tel: 3930682/3930843; Ave Revolución No 1570-A, Delegación Alvaro Obregon, 01020 México, DF Tel: 5500162/5488901

Librería **Bellas Artes**, Ave Juárez No 18, México 1, DF Tel: 5182917
Manager: Miguel Noriega

Central de Publicaciones*, Ave Juárez 4, Apdo 2430, México 1, DF Tel: 5104331

Cia Internacional de Publicaciones SA de CV*, (Libreria Anglo Americana), Serapio Rendon 125, Apdo Postal 30-528, México 4, DF Tel: 5666400 Cable Add: Mexbri
Telex: Cxpme 01771743 Mex

Librería **Cosmos***, Ave Padre Mier 474 Oriente, Monterrey Tel: 431074

Librerías de Cristal*, Av Alvaro Obregón 85, México, DF Tel: 5116723
Many branches in Mexico City and other cities

Distribuidora Literaria SA, Apdo 24-448, 06700 México, DF (Located at: Pueble 182-D, Colonia Roma, México) Tel: 5287444
Man Dir: Klaus Thiele; *Sales:* Gerardo Juárez
Owned by: Ediciones Euroamericanas (qv)

Librería **Font***, López Cotilla 440, Guadalajara, Jalisco Tel: 140820

Librerías **Gonvill**, 8 de Julio No 825, Guadalajara, 44100 Jalisco
Manager: Jorge E González Villalobos

Librería **Hamburgo** Antonio Navarrete*, Insurgentes Sur No 58, México 6, DF Tel: 5287316/5145086
Also: Ribera de San Cosme 133, México 4, DF Tel: 5464736; Insurgentes Sur 317, México 11, DF Tel: 5744015; Tiber 87, México 5, DF Tel: 5285415

Librería **Letrán***, Ave San Juan de Letrán 5-C, México, DF Tel: 5123232

Librería Internacional SA de CV*, Ave Sonora 206, México 11, DF Tel: 5330905
Owned by: Elsevier-NDU nv, Netherlands (qv)

Librería **Tecnológico** SA, Ave E Garza Sada 2440, Col Tecnológico, Monterrey, Nuevo León Tel: 583812
Manager: Carlos Amero Diaz

Librería **Universitaria***, Insurgentes Sur No 299, México, DF Tel: 5646637 (and several branches)

Librolandia del Centro SA, Matamoros 83, Hermosillo, Sonora Tel: 20634/23193
Telex: Olsame 058878
Dir: Nicolás Estrada F
60 bookshops located in 33 cities throughout México

Librería Editorial Gerardo **Mayela**, Emiliano Zapata 60-B, 06060 México, DF Tel: 5225556
Manager: Manuel García Blanco

Editores **Mexicanos** Unidos*, Luis González Obregón 5-B, México, DF Tel: 5217596

Librería **Patria***, Ave 5 de Mayo 43, México 1, DF Tel: 5852099

Librería de **Porrúa** Hnos y Cía*, Apdo M-7990, Argentina 15, México 1, DF Tel: 5228800 Cable Add: Porruas

Librería **Studio** SA, Oscar Wilde 9, Local AB, 11560 México, DF Tel: 5167486

Major Libraries

Archivo General de la Nación*, Tacuba 8-20 Piso, Apdo 1999, México 1, DF Tel: 5851833
Librarian: Alejandra Moreno Toscano

Archivos Históricos y Bibliotecas*, Instituto Nacional de Antropologia e Historia, Calzada M Gandi y Paseo de la Reforma, México 5, DF Apdo Postal M20-29 Tel: 5536342/5536231

Biblioteca Central*, Ciudad Universitaria, Villa Obregón, AP 70-219 México 20, DF Tel: 5489780
Librarian: Q F B Margarita Almada de Ascencio
Publications: Informe de actividades; Directorio de Bibliotecas UNAM; Informes Técnicos, Catálogo de Públicaciones Periódicas

Biblioteca Central, Universidad Autónoma Chapingo, 56230 Chapingo, México
Incorporating previously named Escuela Nacional de Agricultura
Librarian: Rosa Maria Ojeda Trejo
Publications: Periodicals Chapingo, Agrociencia, Revista de Geografía Agrícola, Textual

Biblioteca de México, Plaza de la Ciudadela 6, 06040 México, DF Tel: 5104644/5104945
Librarian: Carmen E de García Moreno

Biblioteca Nacional de Agricultura, now at Biblioteca Central, Chapingo (qv)

Biblioteca Nacional de Antropología e Historia, Paseo de la Reforma y Gandhi, 11560 México, DF Tel: 5536231/5536342
Director: Yolanda Mercader Martinez

Biblioteca Nacional de México, República de El Salvador 70, Centro, 06000 México, DF Tel: 5129316/5103161/5121771
Also: Centro Cultural Universitario, Insurgentes Sur s/n, Delegación Coyoacán CP, 04510 México, DF

Biblioteca del **Congreso de la Unión***, Tacuba 29, México, DF

Biblioteca 'Benjamin **Franklin**' (USIS), Calle Londres 16, 06600 México, DF Tel: 5910244
Dir: Tom H Raymond
Publication: Boletín de Selección de Adquisiciones Recientes (quarterly)

Hermeroteca Nacional de México, Centro Cultural Universitario, Insurgentes Sur s/n, Delegación Coyoacán CP, 04510 México, DF
National Periodicals Library
Publication: Hemerografía literaria (annually)

Biblioteca del **Instituto Anglo-Mexicano de Cultura***, Calle M Antonio Caso 127, México 4, DF
British Council Library

Biblioteca del **Instituto Panamericano de Geografía** e Historia, Ex-Arzobispado 29, 11860 México, DF
Pan American Institute of Geography and History

Biblioteca del **Instituto Tecnológico** y de Estudios Superiores de Monterrey*, Sucursal de Correos 'J', 64849 Monterrey, Nuevo León

Biblioteca de la **Universidad Iberoamericana**, Centro de Informacion Academica, Ave Cerro de las Torres 395, Delegacion Coyoacán, 04200 México, DF Tel: 5448755 ext 34 Cable Add: Uniberomex
Director: Juan Anaya Duarte

Library Associations

Asociación de Bibliotecarios de Instituciones de Enseñanza Superior e Investigación (ABIESI)*, Apdo Postal 5-611, 06500 México, DF
Association of Librarians of Higher Education and Research Institutions
President: Nahúm Pérez Paz
Publications: Cuadernos de Abiesi; Archivos de Abiesi; Boletín de Abiesi

Asociación Mexicana de Bibliotecarios AC (AMBAC), Apdo 27-102, 06760 México, DF Tel: 5489780
Mexican Association of Librarians
Secretary: Guadalupe Carrión-Rodriguez
Publication: Noticiero (Bulletin); *Memorias de Jornadas*

Departamento de Bibliotecas y Publicaciones*, Dr Velasco 181, Col de los Doctores, México 7, DF Tel: 5788564/7614981

Escuela Nacional de Biblioteconomía y Archivonomía, Viaducto Miguel Alemán 155, 03400 México, DF
National School of Librarianship and Archives
Dir: Professor Eduardo Salas Estrada
Publication: Bibliotecas y Archivos

Instituto de Investigaciones Bibliográficas, c/o Biblioteca Nacional de México, República de El Salvador 70, Centro, 06000 México, DF
and Hemeroteca Nacional de México, New Building, Insurgentes Sur S/No Zona Cultural, Ciudad Universitaria, México 20, DF
Institute of Bibliographical Research
Dir: María del Carmen Ruiz Castañeda
Academic Secretary: Dr Tarsicio García Díaz
Publications: Boletín; Bibliografía Mexicana; Anuario Bibliográfico

Library Reference Books and Journals

Books

Anuario Bibliográfico, Instituto de Investigaciones Bibliograficas, c/o Biblioteca Nacional de Mexico, Republica de El Salvador 70, México 1, DF

Anuario de Bibliotecología Archivología Informática (Annual of Library Science, Archives, and Information Science), Universidad Nacional Autónoma de México, Ciudad Universitaria, Villa Obregón, México 20, DF

Bibliografía Mexicana, Instituto de Investigaciones Bibliograficas, c/o Biblioteca Nacional de Mexico, República de El Salvador 70, México 1, DF

Directorio de Bibliotecas de la Ciudad México (Directory of Libraries of the City of Mexico), Universidad de las Américas, Biblioteca, 16 Carretera Mexico-Toluca, México 10, DF

Journals

Bibliotecas y Archivos (Libraries and Archives), Escuela Nacional de Bibliotecomonía y Archivonomía, Viaducto Miguel Alemán 155, México 13, DF

Boletín (Bulletin), Institute of Bibliographical Researches, c/o National Library, República de El Salvador 70, México 1, DF

Boletín (Bulletin), National Archives, Palacio Nacional, México, DF

Boletín (Bulletin), National Library, República de El Salvador 70, México 1, DF

Noticiero (News), Mexican Association of Librarians, Apdo 27-132, México 7, DF

Literary Associations and Societies

Mexican **P E N** Centre, Apdo 21-997, México 21, DF
Secretary: Eduardo Lizalde

San Miguel **P E N** Centre, Apdo 288, San Miguel de Allende, Gto, México 37700
Secretary: Celia Wakefield

Sociedad Mexicana de Bibliografía*, Hemeroteca Nacional, Carmen 31, México 1, DF
Mexican Bibliographical Society
Dir: Dr Agustín Millares Carlo
Publication: Boletin (quarterly)

Literary Periodicals

Comunidad (Community), Universidad Iberoamericano, Cerro de las Torres 395, México 21, DF

Cuadernos Americanos (American Notebooks), Ave Coyocán 1035, Apdo Postal 965, México, DF

El Cuento (The Story); magazine of imagination, Ave División del Norte 521-101, México 12, DF

Lectura (Readings), Apdo 545, Bolivar 23-4, México, DF

Letras (Letters); literary and bibliographical publication, Libreria y Ediciones Botas SA, Justo Sierra 52, Apdo 941, Mexico 1, DF

Mexico Quarterly Review (text in English and Spanish), University of the Americas, 15 Sta Catavina Martir, via Puebla, Ruebla México

Plural, Cía Editorial Excelsior, SCL, Reforma 18, México, DF

Salamandra (Salamander), Editorial Alfonso Reyes, Adolfo Prieto 2407 Oriente, Monterrey, NL

Literary Prizes

National Prize for Literature*
For the best literary works in the fields of the novel, poetry, essay, biography, drama and motion picture scriptwriting. 100,000 Mexican pesos. Awarded annually. Enquiries to Mexican Ministry of Public Education, Brazil 21, México 1, DF

Xavier **Villaurrutia** Prize*
For poetry, prose, novel, short story, drama or essays by new or young authors. Prizes totalling 400,000 pesos are awarded annually. Most recent winners were Jésus Gardea (short story), Alí Chumacero (poetry), Sergio Fernández (novel), Fernando Curiel (essay). Enquiries to Sociedad Alfonsina Internacional, Ave Transmisiones 42, Lomas de San Angel Inn, México 20, DF

Monaco

General Information

Language: French
Religion: Roman Catholic
Population: 26,000
Bank Hours: 0830-1730 Monday-Friday
Shop Hours: 0830-1300, 1600-1930 Monday-Friday
Currency: French franc
Copyright: Berne, UCC (see International section)

Publishers

Académie Internationale de Tourisme, 4 rue des Iris, Monte-Carlo Tel: (93) 309768
President: Sami Rababy; *Editorial:* Paul Wagret
Subjects: Travel Literature, Dictionary of Tourism
Founded: 1951

Editions de l'**Oiseau-Lyre**, Les Remparts Tel: (93) 300944
Man Dir: Margarita M Hanson
Subject: Music

Editions **Regain***, Palais Miami, 10 blvd d'Italie, Monte-Carlo Tel: 506204
Subjects: Poetry, Literature
Founded: 1946

Les Editions du **Rocher**, 28 Rue du Comte Félix Gastaldi, Monaco Tel: 303341
Subject: General Literature

Editions du Livre André **Sauret** SA*, 8 quai Antoine 1er, BP 48, Monte-Carlo Tel: 306884
Subjects: Art, Fiction
ISBN Publisher's Prefix: 2-85051

Union Continentale d'Editions SA*, 17 rue de Millo, Monte-Carlo
Subject: Literature

Major Booksellers

Les **Beaux Livres***, 4 rue des Iris, Monte Carlo Tel: 307390
Manager: Claude Lepine

Quartier-Latin*, 26 blvd Princess-Charlotte, Monte Carlo Tel: 302621

Sainte-Devote*, 19 blvd Princess-Charlotte, Monte Carlo Tel: 302279

Major Library

Bibliothèque Louis Notari, 8 rue Louis Notari Tel: 309509
Director: Hervé Barral

Literary Associations and Societies

P E N Club, c/o Directeur du Musée d'Anthropologie Préhistorique, blvd du Jardin Exotique, Monte Carlo 98000
Secretary: Louis Barral

Mongolian People's Republic

General Information

Language: Mongolian
Religion: None (Tibetan Buddhist Lamaism suppressed in 1930's)
Population: 1.6 million
Bank Hours: Vary. 0800-1700 or 1800 with lunch closing
Shop Hours: Generally 0900-1500
Currency: 100 mongo = 1 tugrik

Publishers

Mongolgosknigotorg*, Ulan-Bator
Function: Distributor

State Press, Ulan-Bator
Subjects: Geography, Politics, Law

Major Booksellers

State Book Trading Office*, Leniny gudamch 41, Ulan-Bator Tel: 22312 Cable Add: Mongolbook

Major Libraries

State Archives*, Ulan-Bator State Public Library of the Mongolian People's Republic, Lenin Prospekt, Ulan-Bator Tel: 22396
Dir: M Bayaizul

Montserrat

General Information

Language: English
Religion: Anglican and other Protestant denominations and Catholic
Population: 11,000
Bank Hours: 0800-1200 Monday-Thursday; 0800-1200, 1500-1700 Friday

Shop Hours: 0800-1200, 1300-1600 Monday-Thursday; 0800-1200, 1300-1700 Friday; 0800-1300 Saturday
Currency: 100 cents = 1 East Caribbean dollar
Export/Import Information: No tariffs on books and advertising catalogues. Parcel Tax on each postal parcel. No import licences required
Copyright: Berne, UCC (see International section)

Major Booksellers

Empire Shop, George St, PO Box 210, Plymouth Tel: Montserrat 2400
Managers: Ernst and Edith Herman

Major Libraries

Montserrat Public Library*, Plymouth, Montserrat
Librarian: V J Grell

Morocco

General Information

Language: Arabic, French, Spanish
Religion: Muslim
Population: 18.9 million
Literacy Rate (1971): 21.4% (49.5% Urban, 11.5% Rural)
Bank Hours: Summer: 0830-1130; 1500-1700 Monday-Friday; rest of year: 0815-1130, 1415-1630 Monday-Friday
Shop Hours: Tangiers: 0900-1200, 1600-2000; rest: 0900-1200, 1500-1800 or 1900
Currency: 100 centimes = 1 dirham
Export/Import Information: No tariff on books; most advertising dutiable. Special Tax, and Stamp Duty of percentage of import duty. No import licences required. Exchange controls but permission liberally granted
Copyright: UCC, Berne (see International section)

Book Trade Organization

Syndicat des Librairies du Moroc, 10 ave Dar el Maghzen, Rabat
Moroccan Booksellers' Association

Book Trade Reference Journal

Bibliographie nationale marocaine, Bibliothèque générale et Archives du Maroc, ave Moulay Chérif, Rabat (national bibliography published monthly)

Publishers

Government Printer (Imprimerie Officielle)*, ave Jean Mermoz, Rabat-Chellah, Chellah

Dar El **Kitab***, pl de la Mosqueé, Quartier des Habous, BP 4018, Casablanca Tel: 63381 Telex: 26630 Darki
Foreign Department: 18 rue Marechal, Casablanca Tel: 241168/246326
President: Boutaleb Abdou Abdelhay;
Manager: Mrs Soad Kadiri; *Publicity*

Manager: Mounjedine Abdel-Ghani;
Production: Ferhat Mohamed
Subjects: History, Africana, Philosophy, General & Social Science
Founded: 1948

Editions **La Porte***, 281 ave Mohammed-V, Rabat Tel: 24977
Man Dir: Paul Souchon; *Sales:* Mohamed Rafii
Subsidiary Companies: Librairie aux Belles Images (Bookshop)
Subjects: Law — Constitutional, Social, Labour etc; Economics, Ministry of Justice Publications (in French and Arabic), Morocco Tourist Guides, Arab and French Language Teaching, Religion — the Koran, Islam
Bookshops: Librairie aux Belles Images (qv), address as above

Les Editions **Maghrebines***, 5-13 rue Soldat Roch, Casablanca Tel: 245148 Telex: Edima 22994 M
Subjects: General Non-fiction, History, Africana, Reference, Law, Science & Technology, General Science, Medicine
Founded: 1962

Major Booksellers

Librairie **'Aux Belles Images'***, 281 ave Mohammed V, Rabat Tel: 24977
Parent Company: Editions La Porte (Publisher — qv)

Librairie des **Colonnes**, 54 blvd Pasteur, BP 352, Tangier Tel: 36955
Director: Mrs R Muyal
Parent Company: Sté Atlantique d'Edition

Cultura-Maroc*, 10 rue Bendahan, Casablanca Tel: 275990

Librairie des **Ecoles***, 12 ave Hassan II, Casablanca Tel: 66741

Librairie **Farairre***, 43 rue de Foucauld, Casablanca Tel: 220388

Librairie de **France***, 4 rue Chenier, Casablanca Tel: 26534

Librairie **nationale***, 2 ave Mers Sultan, Casablanca Tel: 23678

Librairie **Livre-Service**, 40-46 ave Allal Ben Abdellah, Rabat Tel: (07) 24495 Telex: 32746 M Smer
Executive and General Manager: Alaoui Ismaïli Mustapha

Maghreb Livres*, 57 rue Oved Ziz, BP 725, Rabat Tel: 70340

S M E R Diffusion*, Service Commercial, 3 rue Ghazza, Rabat Tel: 23725

Major Libraries

Bibliothèque générale et Archives*, BP 41, Tetuan
Librarian: M M Dellero

Bibliothèque générale et Archives du Maroc*, ave Moulay Chérif, Rabat Tel: 71890/72152
Librarian: Fassi Abderrahmane
Publication: Bibliographie nationale marocaine

Bibliothèque municipale*, 142 ave de l'Armeé Royales, Casablanca Tel: 274170/223798
Dir: Haj Mohamed Bouzid

Bibliothèque municipale Meknes, Zankat Al-Wahda Al-Ifriquia, BP 47, Meknes Tel: 22881
Librarian: Mohammed Ajana

Centre Africain de Formation et de Recherche administrative pour le Développement, Centre de Documentation, BP 310, Tangier Cable Add: Cafrad Tangier Telex: 33664 M
Chief of Documentation Division: Edward S Asieou

Centre national de Documentation, Charii Maa El Ainaïn, Haut Agdal, BP 826, Rabat Tel: 74944 Telex: CND 31052 M Rabat
Director: Ahmed Fassi Fihri

Ecole Mohammedia d'Ingénieurs*, Bibliothèque, BP 765, Rabat Tel: 72647

Institut scientifique chérifien*, Bibliothèque, ave Moulay Chérif, Rabat
Publication: Travaux

Mission universitaire culturelle et de co-opération, Bibliothèque*, Ambassade de France, 121 blvd Zerktoutni, Casablanca

Bibliothèque de l'**Université Al Quarawiyin***, BP 790, Fès

Bibliothèque de l'**Université Ben Youssef***, Cité Universitaire, BP 314, Marrakech Tel: 25465
Librarian: Seddik Larbi

Bibliothèque de l'**Université Mohammed V***, ave Moulay Chérif, Rabat

Mozambique

General Information

Language: Portuguese in and near large towns; Bantu languages; English widely spoken in business circles
Religion: About 1 million Christian (mostly Roman Catholic), 800,000 Muslim (in north); rest follow traditional beliefs
Population: 9.9 million
Literacy Rate: Civilized Population, 1955, 87.5%; Noncivilized, 1950, 1.3%
Bank Hours: 0800-1100 Monday, Tuesday, Thursday, Friday; 0800-1000 Wednesday and Saturday
Shop Hours: 0800-1130, 1400-1700 Monday-Friday; 0800-1200 Saturday
Currency: 100 centavos = 1 Mozambique escudo
Export/Import Information: Children's picture books dutied per kg net weight, otherwise books and advertising matter duty-free. No additional taxes apply. Import licences and strict exchange controls; authorities have classified books and advertising as List 3 in priorities

Book Trade Organization

Instituto Nacional do Livro e do Disco, CP 4030, Avda 24 de Julho 1921, Maputo Tel: 20839/20870 Telex: 6-288 Inld Mo
INLD is a state organization responsible for the importation, exportation and distribution of books (and records), and all printing and publishing activities
Director: Arménio Correia

Publishers

Empresa Moderna Lda*, 13 Ave da Republica, CP 473, Maputo
Man Dir: Louis Galloti
Subjects: General Fiction & Non-fiction, History, Africana, University & Secondary Textbooks
Founded: 1937

Government Printer (Impressa Nacional de Moçambique)*, CP 275, Maputo

Editora **Minerva** Central*, CP 212, Maputo Telex: 6-561 Miner Mo
Man Dir: J F Carvalho
Subsidiary Company: J A Carvalho & Co Ltd
Subjects: Medicine, General Science, University & Secondary Textbooks
Founded: 1908

Major Booksellers

Academica Lda*, 47 rua Joaquim Lapa, Maputo Tel: 3576

Armazens Distribuidores Lta*, CP 1215, Maputo

A W **Bayly** & Co Lda*, CP 185, Maputo

Cooperative das Casas*, 32 rua Major Araujo, Maputo

Minerva Central*, J A Carvalho & Co Lda, CP 212, Maputo

Major Libraries

Arquivo Historico de Moçambique, CP 2033, Maputo
Librarian: Antonio Sopa

Biblioteca Municipal*, Maputo

Biblioteca Nacional de Moçambique*, CP 141, Maputo
Librarian: Joaquim Chigogoro Mussassa

Direção nacional de **Geologia**, (Centro de Documentação), CP 217, Maputo

Bibliotecas de **Universidade Eduardo Mondlane**, Divisão de Documentação, CP 1169, Maputo Tel: 741892/743017/741135
The University Eduardo Mondlane does not have a Central Library, but controls 15 departmental libraries. The Divisão de Documentação is the department responsible for all library and documentation services throughout the University.
Head of Services: M Maral

Namibia

General Information

Language: Afrikaans, German and English
Religion: About half of population Christian; rest follow traditional beliefs
Population: Estimates vary between 852,000 and 1.2 million (for 1974)
Literacy Rate: 35%
Currency: South African
Copyright: Berne (see International section)

Book Trade Reference Book

Namibische National Bibliographie 1971-75, contact Nordiska Afrikaininstitutets Bibliotek, BP 2126, S-750 02 Uppsala, Sweden

Publishers

Bureau for Indigenous Languages*, Department of Bantu Education, PMB 13236, Windhoek 9100 Tel: 24601 Cable Add: Imfundo Windhoek Telex: 3178
Head: W Zimmermann; *Rights & Permissions:* Department of Education and Training, Pretoria, South Africa
Subjects: Primary and Secondary School Textbooks in indigenous languages. Nama, Ndonga, Kwanyama, Kwangali, Mbukushu, Herero
Founded: 1964
ISBN Publisher's Prefix: 0-621

Gamsberg Publishers*, PO Box 22830, Windhoek 9000 (Located at: 8 Goethe St, Windhoek) Tel: 28714/35296
Man Dir, Editorial: Dr Hans Viljoen; *Sales:* Piet Grove; *Production:* Gerhard Swanepoel; *Publicity:* Annemarie Buys; *Rights & Permissions:* Petrus Amakali
Subjects: School Textbooks (in nine indigenous languages of Namibia, English, Afrikaans and German), Fiction, Poetry, Non-fiction
Bookshop: Edumeds Bookshop, PO Box 2961, Windhoek 9000 (Located at: 3 Goethe St, Windhoek)
Founded: 1977
ISBN Publisher's Prefix: 0-86848

Major Booksellers

Bible Society of South Africa*, 428 Kaiser St, Windhoek 9000
Regional office of Bible Society of South Africa, Republic of South Africa (qv)

Central News Agency*, PO Box 2104, Windhoek

Edumeds Pty Ltd, PO Box 2961, Windhoek 9000 (Located at: 3 Goethe St) Tel: 26371
Manager: P M Grové

Nasionale Boekhandel (SWA) (Pty) Ltd, PO Box 1099, Windhoek 9000 Tel: 37406
Manager: F Snyman
Owned by: Nasionale Boekhandel Ltd, South Africa (qv)

Major Libraries

Administration Library, Peter Muller St, PB 13186, Windhoek 9000 Tel: 29251
Librarian: Miss A M van Wyk

Government Archives, Department of National Education, PB 13250, Windhoek Tel: 38841

Technical High School Library*, PMB 12014, Windhoek 9111

Windhoek Public Library*, PO Box 3180, Windhoek 9000 Tel: 30295

Library Association

Cultural Promotion, PB 13186, 9000 Windhoek Tel: (061) 29251 Cable Add: Swasec Telex: 56665
Librarian: Mrs I Klüsener
The Cultural Promotion Department is responsible for public libraries in South West Africa and the Administration Library in Windhoek

Translation Agencies and Associations

Bureau for Indigenous Languages*, PMB 13236, Windhoek 9100

Nepal

General Information

Language: Nepali
Religion: Hindu, Tibetan Buddhist
Population: 13.4 million
Literacy Rate (1975): 19.2%
Bank Hours: 1000-1700 Sunday-Friday
Shop Hours: 1000-1700 Sunday-Friday
Currency: 100 paise = 1 Nepalese rupee
Export/Import Information: No tariff on books and advertising. Import licences required. Exchange controls

Publishers

Department of Publicity*, Ministry of Communications, Katmandu

Educational Enterprise*, Mahankalsthan, Katmandu Tel: 13749
Subject: Education

International Standards Books and Periodicals Organization*, Kamabakshee Tole, Katmandu City
Centre for Central General Selling, Distribution and Wholesale Supplies
Man Dir: Ganesh Lall Chhipa

Lakoul Press*, Palpa-Tanben
Subjects: Education, Physical Sciences

Mahabir Singh Chiniya Main*, Makhan Tola, Katmandu

Mandas Sugatdas, now International Standards Books and Periodicals Organization (qv)

Nepal Academy*, Ganabahal Dharhara, Katmandu
Subjects: Science, Literature, History, Art, Social Science

Ratna Pustak Bhandar*, Bhotahity, PO Box 98, Katmandu
Manager: G P Shrestha
Subjects: Textbooks, Nepalese Fiction
Founded: 1945

Sajha Prakashan, Co-operative Publishing Organization*, Pulchowk lalitpur, Katmandu Tel: 21023/21118 Cable Add: Sajha Prakashan Katmandu
Chairman: Shri Kshetra Pratap Adhikary; *General Manager:* Mr K C S Pradhan
Branch Offs: 40 branches and sub-offices throughout Nepal
Subjects: Literary, Educational Textbooks, General (published in English and Nepali)
Founded: 1966

Major Booksellers

Educational Enterprises (Pvt) Ltd*, Kingsway, Kantipath, Katmandu Tel: 12508/13749

International Progressive Books and Periodicals, 903 Ason Kamalakshee Tole, Pragatisheel Chowk Bitra, Katmandu City 30 (Katmandu GPO 7101) Tel: 11938 Cable Add: Anterpragatisheelsaphoopasa Katmandu Nepal
Man Dir: Ganesh Lall Ranjitkar; *Editorial:* Ganesh Dass Yamy, Aneeta Shobha Tuladhar; *Sales:* Padma L Tuladhar, Suneeta D Tuladhar, Parbatee S Ranjitkar; *Production:* Shanta S Ranjitkar; *Publicity:* Chandrawatee S Ranjitkar; *Rights & Permissions:* Renooka S Tuladhar
Orders to: Nayan Baneshowre Marg, PO Box 3000, Katmandu City 33 (Katmandu GPO 7101)
Branch Offs: Throughout Nepal
Subjects: Politics, Economics, Philosophy, History, Literature, Social Science, Science, Technology, Educational Textbooks, Engineering, Biology, Business, Mathematics, Medicine, Biography, Juveniles, Periodicals
Bookshops: Janapriya Pustak Shandar, Patan Dhoka, Lalitpur; Jagriti Books Centre, Itahary Sunsary, Koshee Zone; People's Books Centre, Chenpur Sakhuwa Sabha, Koshee Zone; People's Books and Periodicals Centre, Datraya Square, Bhaktapur; Banepa Books Depot, Banepa Nayan Bazar, Kabhrepalanchowk Dist
Founded: 1963

Januka Pustak Bhandar*, Budhhat Chowk, Biratnagar (Morang) Tel: 226 Cable Add: Januka Biratnagar

Nepal Booksellers*, 6/78 Dharmapath, Katmandu Tel: 14603
Manager: Pra Kash Shrestha

Ratna Pustak Bhandar*, Bhotahity, Katmandu

Sahayogi Prakashan*, Tripureshwar, Katmandu

Major Libraries

American Library*, Katmandu

Bir Library*, Ranipolhari, Katmandu

British Council Library, PO Box 640, Kanthi Path, Katmandu Tel: 11305/13796

National Library*, Katmandu

Nepal-Bharat Sanskritik Kendra Pustakalaya*, (Indian Embassy), Ganga Path, Katmandu

Tribhuvan University Library*, Kirtipur, Katmandu
Plays the leading role in library development

Library Association

Nepal Library Association*, PO Box 207 GPO, Asan Tole, Katmandu

Netherlands

General Information

Language: Dutch; Frisian in Friesland (though all speakers of Frisian also speak Dutch). English is common second language
Religion: Roman Catholic and Protestant
Population: 14 million
Bank Hours: 0900-1600 Monday-Friday
Shop Hours: 0900-1730 or 1800 Monday-Saturday. Many close Monday morning
Currency: 100 cents = 1 Netherlands gulden = 1 Dutch florin
Export/Import Information: Member of the

European Economic Community. No tariff on books except children's picture books from non-EEC; advertising other than single copies is dutied; VAT on books and advertising matter. Import licences required for certain countries (not US or UK)
Copyright: UCC, Berne, Florence (see International section)

Book Trade Organizations

Centraal Boekhuis BV, Erasmusweg 10, Postbus 125, 4100 AC Culemborg Tel: (03450) 14841

Collectieve Propaganda van het Nederlandse Boek (CPNB), Postbus 10576, 1001 EN Amsterdam (Located at: Langestr 61, 1015 AK Amsterdam) Tel: (020) 264971
Committee for the Collective Promotion of Dutch Books
Dir: Albert Voster
Publications: Boekenmolen (quarterly); *Premium Bookweek* (booklet); *Children's Bookweek* (booklet); *Books of the Month*

Bureau I S B N, Centraal Boekhuis, Postbus 125, 4100 AC Culemborg (Located at: Erasmusweg 10) Tel: 03450/14841 Telex: 40098 Cboek
ISBN Administrator: J van Leeuwen; *Secretary:* Mrs A D Aukema

Koninklijke Nederlandse Uitgeversbond, Keizersgracht 391, 1016 EJ Amsterdam Tel: (020) 267736
Royal Dutch Publishers' Association
Secretary-General: R M Uxij
Founded: 1880

Nederlandsche Vereeniging van Antiquaren, Kleine Houtstr 26, 2011 DP Haarlem Tel: (023) 323986
Netherlands Association of Antiquarian Booksellers

Nederlandsche Vereeniging voor Druk- en Boekkunst*, Bestevaerstr 10, Haarlem
Netherlands Society for the Art of Printing and Book Production
Secretary: F Mayer
Publications: Mededelingen (irregular) and books

Nederlandse Boekverkopersbond, Waalsdorperweg 119, 2597 HS The Hague Tel: (070) 244395
Dutch Booksellers' Association
President: J v d Plas; *Executive Secretary:* A Coyajee
Publication: De Boekverkoper (quarterly)

Standard Book Numbering Agency, see under ISBN

Stichting Speurwerk betreffende het Boek, Keizersgracht 257, 1016 EC Amsterdam Tel: (020) 264974
Book Research Foundation for the Netherlands
Secretary: A A Herpers
Publications: Speurwerk Boeken Omnibus (The Dutch Book Market — annual); *Boekenvakboek 1980* (Publishing Industry Statistics); *Structural Analysis of the Book Market in Netherlands*

Vereeniging ter bevordering van de belangen des Boekhandels, Lassusstr 9, Postbus 5475, 1007 AL Amsterdam
Association for the Promotion of the Interests of Booksellers and Publishers
Secretary: Mrs M van Vollenhoven
Publications: Boekblad (weekly); *Lijstenboek* (annual)

Vereniging van Uitgeversvertegenwoordigers*, Westerstr 62, Wormerveer
Association of Publishers' Representatives
Publication: Vertegenwoordiger

Book Trade Reference Books and Journals

Books

Bibliografie van in Nederland verschenen Officiële en Semi-officiële Uitgaven (Bibliography of Official and Semi-official Publications), Royal Library, Lange Voorhout 34, The Hague

Lystenboek (List of Dutch Booksellers), Nieuwsblad voor de Boekhandel, Postbus 5475, Amsterdam Z

Speurwerk Boeken Omnibus (The Dutch Book Market), Stichting Speurwerk betreffende het Boek, Keizersgracht 257, 1016 EC Amsterdam

Journals

Boekblad (News-sheet for the Book Trade), Vereniging ter Bevordering van de Belangen des Boekhandels, Lassusstr 9, Postbus 5475, Amsterdam Z

Boeken-kijkboek (Book Review), Commission for the Collective Promotion of the Netherlands Book, N Z Voorburgwal 44, Amsterdam C

Boekenband (The Bond of Books), Christelijke Blindenbibliotheek (Evangelical Library for the Blind), Putterweg 140, Ermelo

De Boekverkoper (The Bookseller), Dutch Booksellers' Association, Waalsdorperweg 119, NL-2019 The Hague

Book Mill, Netherlands Graphic Export Centre, Prinsengracht 668, Amsterdam Tel: (020) 234283

Brinkman's Cumulatieve Catalogus (Brinkman's Cumulative Book Catalogue), A W Sijthoff International Publishing Co BV, Schuttersveld 9, Postbus 9, Leiden

Buitenlandse Boek (The Foreign Book), Prinsengracht 1083, Amsterdam

Duitse Boek (The German Book), (text in Dutch and German), Editions Rodopi NV, Keizersgracht 302-304, Amsterdam

Gouden Uren (Golden Hours), Netherlands Book Club, Prinsevinkenpark 2, The Hague

Nieuwe Pockets en Paperbacks (New Pocketbooks and Paperbacks), Nederlandse Boek, Prinsengracht 1083, Amsterdam

Nijhoff Information; books and periodicals from the Netherlands in foreign languages, Martinus Nijhoff FB, Lange Voorhout 9-11, Postbus 269, The Hague

Prisma; book reviews for public libraries, Protestant Foundation for the Promotion of Librarianship and Reading Information in the Netherlands, Parkweg 20a, Voorburg

Spectrum Boekengids, Uitgeverij Het Spectrum BV, Park Voorn 4, De Meern

De Uitgever (The Publisher), Royal Dutch Publishers' Association, N Z Voorburgwal 44, Amsterdam C

Vertegenwoordiger (The Representative), Association of Publishers' Representatives, Westerstr 62, Wormer

Publishers

A P A (Academic Publishers Associated)*, Postbus 1850, NL-1000 BW Amsterdam
Man Dir: G van Heusden
Orders to: Postbus 122, NL-3600 AC Maarssen Tel: (030) 445700/436166
Subsidiary Companies: Fontes Pers (qv); Holland University Press BV (qv); Oriental Press BV (qv); Philo Press-Van Heusden-Hissink & Co CV (qv); University Press Amsterdam BV (qv)
Subjects: Academic Books in the Arts, Humanities and Sciences
1981: 30 titles *Founded:* 1967
Miscellaneous: Formerly Associated Publishers Amsterdam
ISBN Publisher's Prefixes: 90-302, 90-6022, 90-6023, 90-6024, 90-6025, 90-6037, 90-6039, 90-6042

Academic Publishers Associated, see APA

Addison-Wesley Publishing Group, Postbus 5598, 1007 AN Amsterdam (Located at: de Lairessestr 90, 1071 PJ Amsterdam) Tel: (020) 764044/45 Cable Add: Adiwes Amsterdam Telex: 14046 wss nl
General Manager and Dir: Frans Gianotten; *Rights & Permissions:* Irma Hojer, Addison-Wesley, USA; *Operations:* Jan Fleere
Parent Company: Addison-Wesley Publishing Co Inc, Reading, Mass 01867, USA
Subsidiary Companies: Addison-Wesley Publishers BV; Inter-European Editions
Associate Companies: Addison-Wesley Publishers Ltd, UK (qv for other associates)
Subjects: Humanities, Reference, Juveniles, General & Social Science, Technology, Economics, University, Secondary & Primary Textbooks, Educational Materials, General, EFL, Business, Management, Computer Science
Founded: 1942
ISBN Publisher's Prefixes: 0-201 (Addison-Wesley), 0-8053 (Benjamin), 0-8465 (Cummings)

Agathon, an imprint of Unieboek BV (qv)

Agon, an imprint of BV Uitgeversmaatschappij Elsevier (qv)

Uitgeverij **Ambo** BV, Amalialaan 23, PO Box 308, 3740 AH Baarn Tel: (02154) 18441 Telex: 43272
Publisher: H Pijfers
Imprints: Basis
Subjects: Religion, Philosophy, Psychiatry, Sociology, Psychology, History
Miscellaneous: Firm is a member of the Combo Group, Netherlands (qv)
1982: 50 titles
ISBN Publisher's Prefix: 90-263

Amsterdam Boek BV, now incorporated in Uitgeverij Het Spectrum BV (qv)

Ankh-Hermes BV*, Smyrnastr 5, Postbus 125, Deventer Tel: (05700) 33355
Man Dir, Rights & Permissions: Paul Kluwer
Subjects: Philosophy, Psychology, Astrology, Yoga, Alternative Medicine, Herbs, Eastern Religions
Founded: 1949
ISBN Publisher's Prefix: 90-202

BV Uitgeverij de **Arbeiderspers***, Singel 262, Postbus 3879, 1016 AC Amsterdam Tel: (020) 239326 Telex: 11556 Apqwu
Man Dir: Theo A Sontrop; *Editorial:* Martin Ros; *Publicity:* Gert Jan Hemmink
Associate Companies: Em Querido's Uitgeverij BV (qv); Wetenschappelijke Uitgeverij BV (qv)
Subjects: General Fiction & Non-fiction, Paperbacks
ISBN Publisher's Prefix: 90-295

Uitgeverij **Archipel**, an imprint of Succes BV (qv)

Argus, an imprint of BV Uitgeversmaatschappij Elsevier (qv)

Ark Boeken, an imprint of Vereeniging tot Verspreiding der H Schrift (qv)

A **Asher** & Co, BV*, Keizersgracht 526, 1017 EK Amsterdam Tel: (020) 222255 Cable Add: Asherbooks Telex: 14070 ashni-nl
Man Dir: Nico Israel; *Sales Dir:* Julius W Steiner
Associate Companies: Nico Israel (qv), Theatrum Orbis Terrarum (qv)
Subjects: General & Natural Science, Reference
Founded: 1830

Associated Publishers Amsterdam, renamed APA (Academic Publishers Associated) (qv)

Atrium, an imprint of Icob cv Uitgeverij (qv)

B R E S*, Madoerastr 10, 2585 VB The Hague Tel: (070) 656592
Editorial: A Gabrielli, J Klautz
Subjects: Comparative Religion, Parapsychology, Metaphysics, Philosophy, Alternative Medicine, Fantastic Art, Archaeology

Baedeker voor de Vrouw, an imprint of Succes BV (qv)

Bert **Bakker** BV, Herengracht 406, Amsterdam C Tel: (020) 241934
Man Dir: Bert Bakker; *Editorial:* Harko Keijzer, Caroline van Tuyll, Mai Spijkers; *Rights & Permissions:* Jenny de Vries
Subjects: Dutch and Foreign Literature, History, Psychology, Social Science, Family Interest
Founded: 1893
Miscellaneous: Firm is member of the Kluwer Group (qv)
ISBN Publisher's Prefix: 90-6019

A A **Balkema**, PO Box 1675, 3000 BR Rotterdam (Located at: Lisplein 11) Tel: (010) 666122 Telex: 41605 tkom nl
Man Dir: A T Balkema; *Rights & Permissions:* G Balkema-Pieterse
Branch Offs: Lisplein 11, 3037 AR Rotterdam; PO Box 3117, Cape Town, South Africa; 99 Main St, Salem, NH 03097, USA
Subjects: History (especially South African), Art, African Studies, Palaeontology, Biology, Ecology, Botany, Zoology, Soil and Rock Mechanics
1982: 40 titles *1983:* 40 titles *Founded:* 1932
ISBN Publisher's Prefix: 90-6191

Basis, an imprint of Uitgeverij Ambo BV (qv)

H J W **Becht's** Uitgeversmij bv/Uitgeverij J H de Bussy BV, Keizersgracht 810, PO Box 162, NL-1000 AD Amsterdam Tel: 242449 Telex: 18069 bebus nl
Dir: J Schilt; *Deputy Man Dir:* J B I M Kat
Associate Company: Wereldbibliotheek BV (qv)
Subjects: General Fiction and Non-fiction, Juveniles, Hobbies, Leisure Activities, History, Arts and Crafts, Health, General and Social Science, Textbooks
Book Club: (part-owner) Nederlandse Lezerskring Boek en Plaat BV

Uitgeverij **Bekadidact**, see Combo Uitgeversgroep

John **Benjamins** BV, Postbus 52519, 1007 HA Amsterdam (Located at: Amsteldijk 44, Amsterdam) Tel: (020) 738156 Cable Add: Benper, Amsterdam Telex: 15798 jbds
Man Dir: John L Benjamins
Branch Off: John Benjamins North America Inc, 1 Buttonwood Sq, Philadelphia, Pennsylvania 19130, USA Tel: (215) 5646379 Telex: 7106701085
Subjects: Linguistics, Literature, Philosophy, Reference, Social Science, Educational Materials, Reprints of Backfile-Periodicals
Founded: 1964
ISBN Publisher's Prefix: 90-272

De **Bezige** Bij, Van Miereveldstr 1, Postbus 5184, 1071 DW Amsterdam Tel: (020) 735731 Cable Add: Beebook
Man Dir: A J R Hamming
Subjects: General Fiction, Belles Lettres, Poetry, Children's Books
1982: 80 titles *Founded:* 1945
ISBN Publisher's Prefix: 90-234

Bigot en Van Rossum BV, Nassaulaan 10, Postbus 108, 3740 AC Baarn Tel: 17241 Telex: 73250 line nl ref 588
Dirs: J Verweij, J J van Willegen
Associate Company: BV Uitgeverij De Kern (qv)
Subjects: General Fiction, Paperbacks, Popular Non-fiction
1981: 20 titles *1982:* 26 titles *Founded:* 1934
ISBN Publisher's Prefix: 90-6134

Erven J **Bijleveld***, Janskerkhof 7, Utrecht Tel: (030) 317008
Man Dir: J B Bommeljé Jr
Subjects: Philosophy, Religion, Medicine, Psychology, Social Science, History
1981: approx 10 titles *Founded:* 1864

Andries **Blitz** BV*, Oud Blaricummerweg 31, Postbus 3, Laren Tel: (02153) 2401
Subjects: General Fiction, Belles Lettres, Poetry, Biography, History, Music, Art
Founded: 1929
ISBN Publisher's Prefix: 90-6081

H W **Blok** Uitgeverij BV, Schiedamsevest 59, 3012 BD Rotterdam Tel: (010) 122079
Subjects: Medical Year Books, Dutch for Spanish-speaking and Turkish-speaking, also Portuguese for Dutch-speaking persons, Gymnastics
ISBN Publisher's Prefix: 90-70008

Boek Promotions bv, Postbus 88, 1250 AB Laren NH (Located at: Neuhuijsweg 8, 1251 LW Laren NH) Tel: (02153) 10154
Owner: Peter J Houbolt
Act mainly as packagers for sponsored books

Boekencentrum BV+, Scheveningseweg 72, Postbus 84176, 2508 AD The Hague Tel: (070) 512111
Dirs: J Komen, G J Bothof
Subjects: Education, Theology, Religion

De **Boekerij**, an imprint of BV Uitgeversmaatschappij Elsevier (qv)

de **Boer** Maritiem, an imprint of Uniboek BV (qv)

Bohn, Scheltema en Holkema, Wetenschappelijke Uitgeverij, Emmalaan 27, Utrecht Tel: (030) 511274
Man Dir: Jan van Geelen
Subjects: University Textbooks (Medicine, Biology, Linguistics)
Founded: 1752
Miscellaneous: Firm is a member of the Kluwer Group (qv)
ISBN Publisher's Prefix: 90-313

Boom-Pers Boeken- en Tijdschriftenuitg BV, Kromme Elleboog 2, Postbus 58, 7940 AB Meppel Tel: (05220) 54306
Editorial & Directors' Off: Sarphatistr 9, 1017 WS Amsterdam Tel: (020) 226107 Cable Add: Boompers
Man Dirs: H L Bouman, J H Boom
Subjects: Philosophy, Philosophy of Science, Psychology, General, Social & Political Science, Periodicals
Bookshops: Kamper Boekhandel, Oude Str 82, Kampen; Elburger Boekhandel, Beekstr 26, Elburg; De Brunte, Snijderstr 11, Lelystad; Boekhandel Boom, Winkelcentrum Gordiaan, Lelystad; Boekhandel v/h G Taconis, Hoofdstraat West 10, Wolvega (all in Netherlands)
Founded: 1842
ISBN Publisher's Prefix: 90-6009

Born NV Uitgeversmaatschappij*, Esstr 10, Postbus 22, Assen
Man Dir: H Born
Subjects: General Fiction, How-to, Philosophy, Textbooks, Reference, Juveniles, Medicine, Engineering, Social Science, Low- & High-priced Paperbacks
Founded: 1885
Miscellaneous: Firm is a member of the Kluwer Group (qv)
ISBN Publisher's Prefix: 90-283

Bosch en Keuning NV*, Bremstr, Postbus 1, 3740 AA Baarn Tel: (02154) 8241 Telex: beka-43272
Man Dir: Aize de Visser
Subjects: Biography, History, Music, Art, Religion, Low- & High-priced Paperbacks, Medicine, Primary Textbooks, Educational Materials, Popular Science (Sesam Pocketbooks)
Book Club: (part-owner) Nederlandse Lezerskring Boek en Plaat BV
Founded: 1925
Miscellaneous: Firm is a member of the Combo Group (qv)
ISBN Publisher's Prefix: 90-246

Redactie **Bres***, Madoerastraat 10, 2585 VB The Hague Tel: 070-656592
Subjects: Fantastic Art, Metaphysics, Religion, Natural Medicine, Psychology

NV Boekhandel & Drukkerij voorheen E J **Brill**, Oude Rijn 33a, Leiden Tel: (071) 146646 Cable Add: Brill Leiden Telex: 39296
Manager: Dr W Backhuys
Branch Offs: Orient Buchhandlung am Friesenplatz, E J Brill GmbH, D-5000 Cologne 1, Antwerpener Str 6-12, Federal Republic of Germany; E J Brill London Ltd, 41 Museum St, London WC1A 1LX, UK
Subjects: Classical, Mediaeval and Renaissance Studies, Religion, Oriental & Islamic Studies, University Textbooks, Zoology, Botany, Geology, Palaeontology
1981: 155 titles *Founded:* 1683
ISBN Publisher's Prefix: 90-04

Educatieve Uitgeverij Ten **Brink** BV, Stationsweg 44, Postbus 56, 7940 AB Meppel Tel: (05220) 70622 Telex: c/o Drukkerij Ten Brink BV: 42469 Brink NL
Man Dir: B G ten Brink
Subject: Educational books for 6-18 year olds
Founded: 1848
ISBN Publisher's Prefix: 90-248

De **Brug**-Djambatan BV, Postbus 8411, 3503 RK Utrecht (Located at: Reactorweg 160, 3542 RK Utrecht) Tel: (030) 430254 Telex: 70245 Awbr nl Cable Add: Djambatan Utrecht
Man Dir: M C Hopman
Parent Company: NV Falkplan/CIB (qv)
Associate Companies: A W Bruna en Zoon's Uitgeversmaatschappij BV (qv); Bruna Pockethuis BV (qv)
Subjects: History, Reference, Geography, Cartography, Educational Materials (Atlases, Wall Maps)
Founded: 1949

A W **Bruna en Zoon's** Uitgeversmaatschappij BV+, Postbus 8411, 3503 RK Utrecht (Located at: Reactorweg 160, 3542 AD Utrecht) Tel: 430254 Cable Add: Brunazoon Telex: 70245 Awbru nl
Dir: Martin C Hopman; *Man Dir:* Joost C Bloemsma; *Rights & Permissions:* Ellen-C van der Ploeg
Parent Company: BV Friese Pers, Leeuwarden
Associate Companies: De Brug-Djambatan BV (qv); Bruna Pockethuis (qv); NV Falkplan/CIB, Utrecht
Branch Off: Antwerpsesteenweg 29A, B-2630

Aartselaar, Belgium
Subjects: General Fiction, Belles Lettres, History, Philosophy, High-priced Paperbacks, Psychology, General & Social Science
Book Club: E C I voor Boeken en Platen BV (part-owner)
Bookshop: Scholtens en Zoon BV (qv under Major Booksellers)
1981: 120 titles *Founded:* 1868
ISBN Publisher's Prefix: 90-229

Bruna Pockethuis BV+, Postbus 8411, 3503 RK Utrecht (Located at: Reactorweg 160, 3542 AD Utrecht) Tel: 430254 Cable Add: Brunazoon Telex: 70245 Awbru nl
Dir: Martin C Hopman; *Man Dir:* Joost C Bloemsma; *Rights & Permissions:* Ellen-C van der Ploeg
Parent Company: BV Friese Pers, Leeuwarden
Associate Companies: A W Bruna en Zoon's Uitgeversmaatschappij BV (qv); NV Falkplan/CIB (qv); De Brug-Djambatan bv (qv)
Imprints: Zwarte Beertjes, Pandora Pockets, Brunette
Branch Off: Antwerpsesteenweg 29A, B-2630 Aartselaar, Belgium
Subjects: Low-priced fiction and non-fiction paperbacks
1981: 120 titles *1982:* 120 titles *Founded:* 1955
ISBN Publisher's Prefix: 90-449

Brunette, an imprint of Bruna Pockethuis BV (qv)

Buijten en Schipperheijn BV Drukkerij en Uitg Mij v/h, Valkenburgerstr 106, NL-1001 Amsterdam Tel: (020) 236612
Subject: Philosophy, Religion, History, Literature
Founded: 1902
ISBN Publisher's Prefix: 90-6064

J H de **Bussy** BV, see H J W Becht's Uitgeversmij bv

Uitgeverij G F **Callenbach** BV*, Hoogstr 24, Postbus 86, Nijkerk Tel: (03494) 51241 Telex: beka-43722
Man Dir: G F Callenbach; *Rights & Permissions:* Mrs P van Elven-Scholtes
Subjects: General Fiction, Belles Lettres, Poetry, Religion, Juveniles, Low- & High-priced Paperbacks, Psychology, Psychiatry, Medicine, Sociology, Hobbies
Founded: 1854
Miscellaneous: Firm is a member of the Combo Group, Netherlands (qv)
ISBN Publisher's Prefix: 90-266

Uitgeverij **Cantecleer** BV, PO Box 24, 3730 AA De Bilt (Located at: Dorpsstraat 74, 3732 HK De Bilt) Tel: (030) 764014
Man Dir: J A J Jungerhans; *Editors:* L de Jonge, V de Vries, S Ruhe
Subjects: Art, Juveniles, Handicrafts, Travel Guides, Paperbacks
Founded: 1947
Miscellaneous: Firm is a member of the Combo Group (qv)
ISBN Publisher's Prefix: 90-213

Castrum Peregrini Presse, Herengracht 401, Postbus 645, 1000 AP Amsterdam Tel: (020) 235287
Man Dir: M R Goldschmidt
Subjects: History of Literature, History of Art, Belles Lettres, Poetry, Biography, History, Archaeology, Philology, History of Ideas, Reference
1981: 3 titles *1982:* 6 titles *Founded:* 1951
ISBN Publisher's Prefix: 90-6034

De **Centaur**, an imprint of Omega Boek BV (qv)

Cicero, an imprint of Uit-Mij 'West-Friesland' (qv)

Combo Uitgeversgroep*, Postbus 1, Bremstr 11, 3740 AA Baarn Tel: (02154) 18241
Members of the Combo Group in the Netherlands include: Uitgeverij Ambo BV (qv), Uitgeverij Bekadidact, Bosch en Keuning NV (qv), Uitgeverij Callenbach BV (qv), Uitgeverij Cantecleer BV (qv), Uitgeverij De Fontein BV (qv), Uitgeverij ten Have (qv), Uitgeverij Market Books BV, Uitgeverij 'In den Toren' (qv), Uitgeverij Van Walraven (qv)
ISBN Publishers' Prefixes: 90-263 (Ambo), 90-321 (Bekadidact), 90-246 (Bosch en Keuning), 90-266 (Callenbach), 90-213 (Cantecleer), 90-261 (De Fontein), 90-259 (ten Have), 90-6049 (Van Walraven)

Uitgeverij **Contact** BV, now fully integrated in Bert Bakker BV (qv)

Dick **Coutinho** BV+, Postbus 10, 1399 ZG Muiderberg (Located at: Badlaan 2, 1399 GN Muiderberg) Tel: (02942) 1888
Man Dir, Editorial: Dick Coutinho; *Sales:* Jeane Oosterbaan; *Production:* Marijke Faber; *Publicity, Rights & Permissions:* Marieke Tambach
Subjects: University textbooks
1981: 20 titles *1982:* 20 titles *Founded:* 1977
ISBN Publisher's Prefix: 90-6283

Federatie **D J O** (de jonge onderzoekers), Groesbeekseweg 70, 6524 DG Nijmegen Tel: (080) 229549
Publicity Manager: Drs L P v Loon

Dekker en Van de Vegt*, Fransestr 30, 6524 JC Nijmegen Tel: (080) 232765 Cable Add: Dekkervegt Nijmegen
Man Dir: K W J van Rossum
Parent Company: Van Gorcum BV (qv)
Subjects: High-priced Paperbacks, Medicine, Social Sciences, Psychology, Secondary Textbooks
1981: 19 titles *1982:* 21 titles *Founded:* 1856
ISBN Publisher's Prefix: 90-255

Delft University Press, Mijnbouwplein 11, 2628 RT Delft, PO Box 5 Tel: (015) 783254
Dir: Ir P A M Maas; *Editorial:* Lydia ter Horst-ten Wolde
1981: 45 titles *1982:* 43 titles *Founded:* 1972
ISBN Publisher's Prefix: 90-6275

Jacob **Dijkstra's Uitg Mij** BV*, Postbus 284, 9700 AG Groningen (Located at: Gotenburgweg 19, 9723 TK Groningen) Tel: (050) 184266

Dijkstra's Uitgeverij Zeist BV*, Dijnselburgerlaan 4, Postbus 48, 3700 AA Zeist Tel: (03404) 21021

Diligentia BV, NZ Voorburgwal 225, NL-1012-RL Amsterdam Tel: (020) 211911 Cable Add: Publipress Amsterdam Telex: 14407
Dir: R van den Bergh
Parent Company: VNU Business Press Group BV (qv)
Subjects: Trade Publications

van **Dishoeck**, an imprint of Unieboek BV (qv)

van **Ditmar**, see Nijgh en van Ditmar

De Brug-**Djambatan** BV, see De Brug

Uitgeversmaatschappij Ad **Donker** BV, Koningin Emmaplein 1, 3016 AA Rotterdam Tel: (010) 363009
Dir: Willem A Donker
Subjects: General Fiction, Biography, History, High-priced Paperbacks, Psychology, Sociology, Education
1982: 20 titles *Founded:* 1938
ISBN Publisher's Prefix: 90-6100

De **Driehoek** BV, Keizersgracht 756, 1017 EZ Amsterdam Tel: (020) 246426
Director: H J Heule
Subjects: Medicine, Health, Yoga, Herbs, Nutrition, Vegetarianism, Mysticism, Buddhism, Astrology

E C I voor Boeken en Grammofoonplaten BV+, Postbus 400, 4130 EK Vianen (ZH) (Located at: Laanakkerweg 14-16, 4124 PB Vianen (ZH)) Tel: 03473-79911 Telex: 47449
Man Dir: H Dijkstra; *Editorial:* G van Buuren, J T Schulten; *Rights & Permissions:* B Tromp
Parent Company: Verlagsgruppe Bertelsmann GmbH, Federal Republic of Germany (qv)
Book Club: ECI voor Boeken en Platen BV (part-owner)
Subjects: General Fiction and Non-fiction
1981: 120 titles *Founded:* 1967
ISBN Publisher's Prefix: 90-70038

East-West Publications Fonds BV, Anna Paulownastr 78, Postbus 85617, 2508 CH-The Hague Tel: (070) 461594
Subjects: Books on Sufism, Religions, Mysticism, Symbolism, Middle East Culture, Medieval Art & Iconography, Music, Children's

Educa International, a member of the Kluwer Group (qv)

Educaboek BV+, Industrieweg 1, Postbus 48, 4100 AA Culemborg Tel: (03450) 71911 Telex: 47306
Chairman: P D Zuiderveld; *Dirs:* B Balder; J Th Timmer
Subjects: Textbooks, Secondary, General and Vocational Education, Technical
Founded: 1970
Miscellaneous: Firm is a member of the Kluwer Group (qv for associate companies), and production and selling company for Stam Technische Boeken, Stam/Robijns, Tjeenk Willink-Noorduijn and Schoolpers (qqv)

Eindhoven Druk BV/Boekprodukties, Cederlaan 2, Postbus 382, 5600 AJ Eindhoven Tel: (040) 513620 Telex: 51476
Dir: Peter Smeets; *Product Manager:* W J Ambaum
Subjects: Children's Illustrated Paperbacks, Activity Books, Board Books

Elmar BV*, Delftweg 147, 2289 BD Rijswijk (2.H) Tel: (015) 123623
Man Dir: A C Roodnat
Subjects: Biography, History, How-to, Reference, Medicine & General Science, Sci-Fic, Sport
Founded: 1961

BV Uitgeversmaatschappij **Elsevier**+, Postbus 70707, 1007 KS Amsterdam (Located at: Rivierstaete, Amsteldijk 166, 1079 LH Amsterdam) Tel: (020) 5413413/5412333 Cable Add: Elsbook Telex: 14481
Man Dirs: F Snater (General), Drs N P van den Berg; *Deputy Man Dir, Finance and Administration:* A J F Schweitzer; *Deputy Man Dirs, Sales:* H Betzema (Fiction), J J C van der Wilk (Foreign Rights); *Publishers:* H J Schuurmans (Non-fiction), J Bogaerts (Literature, Children's Fiction), T Akveld (Fiction), P J Keyzer (Photography, Film), G van Kooten (Dictionaries), F G Szabó (Educational); *Sales:* J F Berkel (Non-fiction), S O Nieuwenhuis (Alternative Sales Channels); *Advertising, Publicity:* Ernest D P Benéder; *Rights:* J J C van der Wilk
Parent Company: Elsevier Boeken BV (qv)
Imprints: Agon, Argus, De Boekerij, Elsevier, Focus, Van Goor Jeugdboeken, Van Goor Zonen, W van Hoeve, Kramers, Manteau (Antwerpen en Amsterdam),

H Meulenhoff, Winkler Prins, Zuid-Hollandse Uitgeversmaatschappij
Subjects: Fiction, Non-fiction, Children's, Educational, Reference
Book Club: (part-owner) Nederlandse Lezerskring Boek en Plaat BV

Elsevier Biomedical Press, a division of Elsevier Science Publishers BV (qv)

Elsevier Boeken BV (Elsevier Books International), Postbus 70707, 1007 KS Amsterdam (Located at: Rivierstaete, Amsteldijk 166, 1079 LH Amsterdam) Tel: (020) 5413413/5412333 Cable Add: Elsbook Telex: 14481
This is the administrative company for BV Uitgeversmaatschappij Elsevier (qv)
Managers: F Snater, Drs N P van den Berg
Parent Company: Elsevier-NDU (qv)
Subsidiary Company: BV Uitgeversmaatschappij Elsevier (qv)

Elsevier-NDU nv, Jan van Galenstr 335, 1061 AZ Amsterdam Tel: (020) 5159111 (Internal and External Relations Tel: (020) 5152341/5152289) Cable Add: Elsevier Telex: 16479 epc nl
President: Prof P J Vinken; *Other members of Executive Board:* H N Appel, O ter Haar, D P van de Merwe, J H Verleur, L van Vollenhoven
Dutch Subsidiaries: Elsevier-NDU Nederland BV, Elsevier Services BV (both at above address), Elsevier Boeken BV (qv), BV Uitgeversmaatschappij Elsevier (qv), BV Uitgeverij W van Hoeve (all at Rivierstaete, Amsteldijk 166, 1079 LH Amsterdam; Nederlandse Dagbladunie BV, NRC BV (both at Westblaak 180, 3012 KN Rotterdam); Dagblad van Rijn en Gouwe BV, P Doelmanstr 8, 2405 CE Alphen a/d Rijn; BV De Dordtenaar, Johan de Wittstr 17-19, 3311 KG Dordrecht; Necomin BV, Uitgeversmaatschappij 'De Grondwet' BV, Koninklijke Van Poll BV (all at Molenstr 7, 4701 JK Roosendaal); Van Boekhoven-Bosch BV, Europalaan 12, 3526 KS Utrecht; Boom-Ruygrok BV, Hulswitweg 15, 2031 BG Haarlem; Henkes Senefelder BV, Van IJsendijkstr 150, 1442 LC Purmerend; Krips Repro BV, Kaapweg 6, 7944 HV Meppel; Misset Grafische Bedrijven BV, Uitgeversmaatschappij C Misset BV (both at IJsselkade 32, 7001 AP Doetinchem); Periodieken Service Holland BV, Keppelseweg 15, 7001 CE Doetinchem; Vlasveld & Co's Drukkerij BV, Parmentierplein 31, 3088 GN Rotterdam; Zetterij Holland BV, Welboom Bladen BV (both at Nw Zijds Voorburgwal 303, 1012 RM Amsterdam); BV Uitgevermaatschappij Bonaventura, Spuistr 110-112, 1012 VA Amsterdam; BV Uitgeversmaatschappij Annoventura, BV Uitgeversmaatschappij Interventura (both at Nw Zijds Voorburgwal 116-118, 1012 SH Amsterdam); Folio Groep BV, Naarderstr 35, 1211 AJ Hilversum; Koninklijke PBNA NV, Velperbuitensingel 6, 6828 CT Arnhem; Northprint BV, Industrieweg 1b, 7944 HS Meppel; Europe Data CV (50%), Bredestr 24, 6211 HC Maastricht; Het Vrije Volk BV (50%), W de Withstraat 25, 3012 BL Rotterdam
Foreign Subsidiaries: Elsevier US Holdings Inc, Congressional Information Service Inc, Greenwood Press Division, Elsevier Science Publishing Company Inc, Excerpta Medica Inc, Medical Examination Publishing Company Inc (all in USA); Elsevier SA, NDU Marketing SA, Elsevier Copyrights Management SA, Elsevier Sequoia SA (qv), Excerpta Medica SA (all in Switzerland); Elsevier Applied Science Publishers Ltd (qv); Elsevier International Bulletins; Elsevier-IRCS Ltd; Elsevier Publications (Cambridge) (all in UK); Elsevier Librico NV, Uitgeversmaatschappij A Manteau NV (qv), Elsevier Business Press NV, International Equipment News Europe NV (50%), Computer Product News Europe NV (50%) (all in Belgium); Selecciones Editoriales SA, Spain (qv); Vereinigte Fachverlage Krausskopf Ingenieur Digest GmbH, Elsevier Industrie Verlag GmbH (both in Federal Republic of Germany); Elsevier Scientific Publishers (Ireland) Ltd, Irish Elsevier Printers Ltd (both in Republic of Ireland); Librería Internacional SA de CV, Editorial El Manual Moderno SA de CV (qqv — both joint ventures in Mexico); Editora Campus Ltda, Brazil (qv); Excerpta Medica KK, Tokyo, Japan; Excerpta Medica Asia Ltd, Hong Kong
Subjects: Agricultural, Veterinary, Food and Environmental Sciences; Chemistry; Computer, Information and Communications Sciences; Earth and Planetary Sciences; Economics; Econometrics; History; Law; Life Sciences; Linguistics; Literature; Mathematics; Logic; Mechanics; Operations Research; Statistics; Management; Systems and Control; Physics; Psychology; Psychiatry; Social, Political and Instructional Sciences; Technology; Engineering; Clinical Medicine; Multilingual Dictionaries; Reference Works; Handbooks; Paperbacks; Juveniles; Textbooks; Illustrated Books; Atlases; Periodicals; Educational Materials; Electronic Databases; Printing Industry
Founded: 1979 (NV Uitgeversmaatschappij Elsevier 1880)
Miscellaneous: Elsevier-NDU nv is holding company which was formed in 1979 by a merger of NV Uitgeversmaatschappij Elsevier and Nederlandse Dagbladunie NV

Elsevier Science Publishers BV, Postbus 2400, 1000 CK Amsterdam (Located at: Molenwerf 1, 1014 AG Amsterdam) Tel: (020) 5803911 Cable Add: Elspubco Telex: 18582 espa nl
Man Dir: O ter Haar; *Dirs:* J J F Kels, Dr L J Mulder, Dr M F J Pijnenborg
Divisions: Biomedical; Excerpta Medica; Information & Business; North-Holland Physics Publishing; Science & Technology (all at above address); Excerpta Medica, Keizersgracht 305-311, 1016 ED Amsterdam; Elsevier Antiquariat, Lippijnstr 4, 1055 KJ Amsterdam
Orders to: ESP Services, PO Box 211, 1000 AE Amsterdam
Parent Company: Elsevier-NDU Nederland BV
Associate Company: Elsevier Science Publishing Co Inc, 52 Vanderbilt Ave, New York, NY 10017, USA
Imprints: Elsevier, North-Holland, Elsevier Applied Science, Excerpta Medica, Elsevier-IRCS, Elsevier International Bulletins, Elsevier Sequoia
Branch Offs: Editora Campus, Brazil (qv); Excerpta Medica Asia Ltd, Hong Kong; Elsevier Scientific Publishers (Ireland) Ltd, Irish Elsevier Printers Ltd (both in Republic of Ireland); 28-1, Yushima 3-chome, Bunkyo-ku, Tokyo 113, Japan; Excerpta Medica KK, Tokyo, Japan; Liaison Office South East Asia, CPO Box 1922, Seoul, Republic of Korea; Editorial El Manual Moderno SA de CV, Librería Internacional SA de CV (qqv, both in Mexico); Elsevier Sequoia SA, Excerpta Medica SA (both in Switzerland); Elsevier Applied Science Publishers Ltd (qv), Elsevier-IRCS Ltd, Elsevier International Bulletins, Elsevier Publications (Cambridge) (all UK); Excerpta Medica Inc, PO Box 3085, Princeton, NJ 08540, USA; Medical Examination Publishing Co Inc, New Hyde Park, NY, USA
Subjects: Agricultural, Veterinary, Food and Environmental Sciences; Chemistry; Computer, Information and Communications Sciences; Earth and Planetary Sciences; Economics; Econometrics; History; Law; Life Sciences; Linguistics; Literature; Mathematics; Logic; Mechanics; Operations Research; Statistics; Management; Systems and Control; Physics; Psychology; Psychiatry; Social, Political and Instructional Sciences; Technology; Engineering; Clinical Medicine; Multilingual Dictionaries
1981: 450 titles *Founded:* 1946
ISBN Publisher's Prefix: 0-444

Elsevier's Wetenschappelijke Uitgeverij, a division of Elsevier Science Publishers BV (qv)

Enschede en Zonen Grafische Inrichting BV, Klokhuisplein 5, Postbus 114, 2000 AC Haarlem Tel: (023) 319240 Telex: 41049

Eska*, Lijnmarkt 41-43, Utrecht Tel: (030) 328411 Telex: 47188
Publisher: Cees Smaling
Subjects: Periodicals, Hobbies
Miscellaneous: Firm is a member of the Kluwer Group (qv)

Excerpta Medica, an imprint of Elsevier Science Publishers BV (qv)

Uitgeverij **F E D** BV, subsidiary of Kluwer Fiscale en Juridische Boeken en Tijdschriften (qv)

Facsimile Uitgaven Nederland BV (FUN), subsidiary of Theatrum Orbis Terrarum (qv)

NV **Falkplan/CIB**, Postbus 8411, 3503 RK Utrecht (Located at: Reactorweg 60, 3542 AD Utrecht) Tel: (030) 430254 Cable Add: Falkplan, Utrecht Telex: 70245 Awbr nl
Man Dir: M C Hopman
Subsidiary Company: De Brug-Djambatan BV (qv)
Subject: Maps

Frank **Fehmers** Productions, Leidsegracht 2, 1016 CK Amsterdam Tel: (020) 238766 Cable Add: Intpubcon Telex: 16740 fepro nl
Man Dir: Frank Fehmers; *Rights & Permissions:* Edith Brinkers
Associate Companies: Frank Fehmers Productions Inc, 300 East 59th St, New York, NY 10022, USA; Frank Fehmers Productions Ltda, Brazil; Frank Fehmers Publishing BV, Curacao
Subjects: Juveniles, Television, Merchandising, Licensing, International Book and Film Co-productions
ISBN Publisher's Prefix: 90-6151

Fibula van Dishoek, an imprint of Unieboek BV (qv)

Focus, an imprint of BV Uitgeversmaatschappij Elsevier (qv)

Uitgeverij De **Fontein** BV, Amalialaan 23, Postbus 308, 3740 AH Baarn Tel: (02154) 18441 Telex: beka-43272
Man Dir: W Hazeu
Subjects: General Fiction & Non-fiction, Juveniles, High-priced Paperbacks
Founded: 1946
Miscellaneous: Firm is a member of the Combo Group (qv)
ISBN Publisher's Prefix: 90-261

Fontes Pers (APA)*, Postbus 1850, NL-1000 BW Amsterdam
Parent Company: APA (Academic Publishers Associated) (qv)
Subjects: Maritime History, History of Law
ISBN Publisher's Prefixes: 90-302, 90-6039

Foris Publications, Postbus 509, 3300 AM Dordrecht (Located at: Mijlweg 79, Dordrecht) Tel: (078) 510454 Cable Add:

Intergraph Dordrecht
Man Dir: Henk J La Porte; *Assistant Manager:* Mrs Bep Ijsselsijn-Oosterling
Parent Company: Intercontinental Graphics Holland BV
Subsidiary Company: ICG Printing BV
1981: 50 titles *Founded:* 1978
ISBN Publisher's Prefix: 90-701

W **Gaade** BV*, Postbus 10, 3958 ZT Amerongen Tel: (03434) 1044
Man Dir: Marinus Beck
Subjects: Art, Cultural History, Nature, Instructional Art and Craft Books, International Co-productions
1981: 30 titles *Founded:* 1954
ISBN Publisher's Prefix: 90-6017

Gaberbocchus Press, a subsidiary of Uitgeverij De Harmonie (qv)

Gamma, an imprint of Infopers (qv)

Van **Gennep** Ltd, Nes 128, 1012 KE Amsterdam Tel: (020) 247033
Man Dirs: R O van Gennep, J H Jansen; *Foreign Rights:* Ms Annelies de Korver
Bookshops: Van Gennep Nieuwezijds, Nieuwe Zijds Voorburgwal 330, Amsterdam C; Boekhandel Van Gennep, Nes 128, Amsterdam C; Boekhandel Van Gennep, Oude Binnenweg 131b, Rotterdam
Subjects: Belles Lettres, Poetry, History, Philosophy, Political Science, Economics, Marxist Publications, Architecture, Photography
1981: 37 titles *Founded:* 1969
ISBN Publisher's Prefix: 90-6012

BV Uitgeversbedryf Het **Goede Boek**, Koningin Wilhelminastr 8, Postbus 122, 1270 AC Huizen Tel: (02152) 53508
Dir: W E J Rikmans; *Advertising Dir:* F Rikmans
Subject: Children's Books
1981: 16 titles *1982:* 26 titles *Founded:* 1932
ISBN Publisher's Prefix: 90-240

de **Gooise**, an imprint of Uniboek BV (qv)

Van **Goor Jeugdboeken**, an imprint of BV Uitgeversmaatschappij Elsevier (qv)

Van **Goor Zonen**, an imprint of BV Uitgeversmaatschappij Elsevier (qv)

Van **Gorcum** BV+, Industrieweg 38, 9403 AB Assen Tel: (05920) 46846 Cable Add: Vangorcum
Man Dir: G Vlieghuis; *Dirs:* J W Meijer (General & Academic Books), K W J van Rossum (Dekker en Van de Vegt, Nijmegen); *Sales:* A W J Rousseau; *Rights & Permissions:* D Bakkes
Orders to: Van Gorcum, PO Box 43, 9400 AA Assen
Subsidiary Company: Dekker en Van de Vegt (qv)
Subjects: Social Science, Anthropology, Medicine, History, Language & Literature, Law, Philosophy, Psychology, Economics, Religion, Geography, Education, University Textbooks, Educational Materials
Founded: 1800
ISBN Publisher's Prefixes: 90-232 (Van Gorcum BV), 90-255 (Dekker en Van de Vegt)

J H **Gottmer** Publishers, Postbus 555, 2003 RN Haarlem (Located at: Prof van Vlotenweg 1a, Bloemendaal) Tel: (023) 257150 Telex: 41856
Dirs: Mrs H V M Gottmer, C van Wijk; *Publicity:* M P Gottmer
Subjects: General Fiction, Religion, Juveniles, Educational, General Non-fiction
Founded: 1937
ISBN Publisher's Prefix: 90-257

BV v/hB **Gottmer's** Uitgeversbedrijf, Sint Annastr 167, Postbus 103, 6500 AC Nijmegen Tel: (080) 231098
Man Dir: B Gottmer
Subjects: Religion, Humour, Cartoons, Scientific Works, Mysticism
Founded: 1950
ISBN Publisher's Prefix: 90-6075

Gouda Quint BV*, Postbus 1148, 6801 MK Arnhem (Located at: Willemsplein 2, Arnhem) Tel: (085) 454762
Man Dir: K H Mulder
Subjects: Textbooks, Law, Taxation, Periodicals
1981: 27 titles *Founded:* 1739
Miscellaneous: Firm is a member of the Kluwer Group (qv)
ISBN Publisher's Prefix: 90-6000

De **Graaf** Publishers, Zuideinde 40, Postbus 6, NL-2420 AA Nieuwkoop Tel: (01725) 1461 Cable Add: Degraaf Nieuwkoop
Man Dir: Bob de Graaf
Subsidiary Company: Miland Publishers (qv)
Subjects: Reference, Religion, University Textbooks
Founded: 1959
ISBN Publisher's Prefix: 90-6004

B R **Grüner** BV, Nieuwe Herengracht 31, 1011 RM Amsterdam Tel: (020) 264371 Cable Add: Veriditas
Publisher: Bruno Roland Grüner
Subjects: Philosophy, Religion, Social Science, Periodicals, Poetry, Politics, Classical Antiquity, Ancient History

de **Haan**, an imprint of Uniboek BV (qv)

Ten **Hagen** BV, Prinsessegr 21, Postbus 34, 2501 AG The Hague Tel: (070) 924311 Telex: 33079
Subjects: Publications for trade and industry
Miscellaneous: Firm is a member of the Kluwer Group, Netherlands (qv)

De **Harmonie**, Postbus 3547, 1001 AH Amsterdam (Located at: Singel 390, Amsterdam) Tel: (20) 245181
Man Dir: Jaco Groot; *Rights & Permissions:* Dieneke Corvers
Subsidiary Company: Gaberbocchus Press
Subjects: Modern Dutch and International Literature, Illustrated Books, Juveniles, Humour
1981: 18 titles *Founded:* 1972
ISBN Publisher's Prefix: 90-6169

Uitgeverij ten **Have** NV, Bremstr 11, Postbus 1, 3740 AA Barn Tel: (02154) 18241 Telex: beka-43272
Man Dir: Ton van der Worp
Subject: Religion
Founded: 1831
Miscellaneous: Firm is a member of the Combo Group, Netherlands (qv)
ISBN Publisher's Prefix: 90-259

Helmond, Zuiddijk 2a, Postbus 23, 5705 CS Helmond Tel: (04920) 39784 Telex: 51337
Man Dir: Dr M H J Hendriks
Subjects: How-to, Juveniles, Low- & High-priced Paperbacks, Primary Textbooks, Reference
Founded: 1913
ISBN Publisher's Prefix: 90-252

Uitgeverij **Heuff** Nieuwkoop,* Postbus 5347X, Weesp (Located at: Hoogstr 20, Weesp) Tel: (02940) 18900 Cable Add: Heuff/Nieuwkoop
Man Dir: H Heuff
Subjects: Music, Art, History, Illustrated Books, Juveniles, Fiction
Founded: 1970
ISBN Publisher's Prefix: 90-6141

Uitgeverij **Heureka***, Postbus 5347, 1380 GH Weesp (Located at: Hoogstr 20, 1381 VS Weesp) Tel: (02940) 17912
Man Dir: F H B Cladder
Subjects: History (Political, Social & Cultural)
1981: 35 titles *Founded:* 1976
ISBN Publisher's Prefix: 90-6262

Gérard Th Van **Heusden** (APA), see Philo Press-Van Heusden-Hissink & Co CV (APA)

Hippoboek/Studio de Zuid, see Zuidgroep BV

G W **Hissink** & Co (APA), see Philo Press-Van Heusden-Hissink & Co CV (APA)

W van **Hoeve**, a subsidiary of BV Uitgeversmaatschappij Elsevier (qv)

Van **Holkema** en Warendorf, an imprint of Uniboek BV (qv)

Holland, Spaarne 110, 2011 CM Haarlem Tel: (023) 323061
Man Dir: Rolf van Ulzen; *Sales Dirs, Permissions:* Ruurt van Ulzen, Ger Meesters
Subjects: General Fiction, Belles Lettres, Poetry, Reference, Juveniles, High-priced Paperbacks, General Science
Founded: 1921
ISBN Publisher's Prefix: 90-251

Holland University Press BV (APA)*, Postbus 1850, NL-1000 BW Amsterdam
Parent Company: APA (Academic Publishers Associated) (qv)
Subjects: Academic Books on the Humanities, European Studies
ISBN Publisher's Prefix: 90-302

Uitgeverij **Hollandia** BV, Postbus 70, 3740 AB Baarn (Located at: Beukenlaan 16-20, 3741 BP Baarn) Tel: (02154) 18941 Cable Add: Hollandia, Baarn Telex: 43776 incom attn Hollandia
Man Dir: J Muntinga
Subsidiary Company: Uitgeverij Kim Natuurboeken BV (qv)
Subjects: General Fiction, History, Nautical, Sports, Popular Medical, Gardening, Children's Books, Travel, *Hollandia* Pocket Books
Book Club: (part-owner) Nederlandse Lezerskring Boek en Plaat BV
1981: 75 titles *1982:* 60 titles *Founded:* 1899
ISBN Publisher's Prefix: 90-6045

NV **ICU** (Informatie en Communicatie Unie NV), now Wolters Samsom Groep (qv)

Stichting **I V I O**, Schans 18-02, Postbus 37, 8200 AA Lelystad Tel: (03200) 26514
Manager: C Meinhard
Subject: Educational

Icob cv Uitgeverij+, Postbus 392, 2400 AJ Alphen aan den Rijn (Located at: Ondernemingsweg 60, Alphen aan den Rijn) Tel: (01720) 37231 Telex: 39700 icob nl
Man Dir: Hans Meijer; *Editorial, Publicity:* Peter Albarda
Imprint: Atrium
Subjects: Art, Natural History, Reference, Illustrated
1981: 24 titles *1982:* 20 titles *Founded:* 1969
ISBN Publisher's Prefix: 90-6113

Ideeboek BV*, Koningslaan 19, 1075 AA Amsterdam
Parent Company: Meijer Pers BV (qv)
Subjects: General, Cookery

Uitgeverij **In den Toren***, Bremstr 11, Postbus 1, 3740 AA Baarn Tel: (02154) 18241 Telex: 43272
Man Dir: Aize de Visser
Subjects: History, Social Sciences, Politics
Miscellaneous: Firm is a member of the Combo Group (qv)

Infopers, PO Box 41, 7940 AA Mepel (Located at: Zuideinde 18, 7941 GH Meppel) Tel: (05220) 70559 Telex: 42685
Man Dir: J P Giehtoorn; *Editorial:* H G Andriese
Parent Company: Drukkerij Giethoorn bv (at above address)
Imprints: Gamma, Promoboek
Subjects: Psychology, Psychomedicine, Dancing, Business, Periodicals
1981: 6 titles *Founded:* 1978 (Gamma), 1982 (Infopers)
ISBN Publisher's Prefixes: 90-6380 (Gamma), 90-6639 (Infopers)

Inside Books BV, Prins Hendrikkade 175, 1011 TC Amsterdam Tel: (020) 229383
Man Dir: Jaap J Woudt; *Editorial:* Ms S Kalkman
Subjects: Cookery, Photography, Tourist Guides
1981: 8 titles *Founded:* 1976

Inter-European Editions, De Lairessestr 90, 1071 PJ Amsterdam Tel: 764044/45 Cable Add: Adiwes Amsterdam Telex: 1406 wssnl
Operations: Jan Fleere; *Man Dir:* Frans Gianotten
Parent Company: Addison-Wesley BV (qv)
Subsidiary Company: Inter-Editions, France (qv)
Subjects: General Science, University Textbooks, General Reading
ISBN Publisher's Prefix: 0-201

B M **Israel** BV, NZ Voorburgwal 264, 1012 RS Amsterdam Tel: (020) 247040 Cable Add: Isrealbook
General Manager: M Israel; *Publicity, Editorial:* H A Weidema
Subjects: Reference, History of Medicine, Sciences, Arts
Bookshop: Boekhandel en Antiquariaat B M Israel BV, at above address
ISBN Publisher's Prefix: 90-6078

Nico **Israel***, Keizersgracht 526, 1017 EK Amsterdam Tel: (020) 222255 Cable Add: Ennibook Telex: 14070 ashni nl
Man Dir: Nico Israel
Associate Companies: A Asher en Co BV (qv), Theatrum Orbis Terrarum (qv)
Subjects: History, Reference, University Textbooks, Geography, Cartography, Bibliography, Travel, Periodicals
Founded: 1950
ISBN Publisher's Prefix: 90-6072

Stichting De **Jonge** Onderzoekers, see Federatie DJO

Dr W **Junk**, Publishers, Lange Voorhout 9, Postbus 13713, 2501 ES-The Hague Tel: (070) 463256
Man Dir: Drs F W B van Eysinga
Publisher: Wil R Peters
Orders to: Kluwer Academic Publishers Group, Distribution Centre, Postbus 322, 3300 AH Dordrecht
Subjects: Biology, Ophthalmology
Founded: 1899
Miscellaneous: Firm is a member of the Kluwer Group (qv)
ISBN Publisher's Prefix: 90-6193

K B S, see Katholieke Bijbelstichting

Van **Kampen**, an imprint of Unieboek BV (qv)

Katholieke Bijbelstichting, Baroniestr 43, PB 27, 5280 AA Boxtel Tel: 04116 73537
Manager: A E van Wensen
Subjects: Religious literature on practical aspects of Catholic Bible work in Belgium and the Netherlands
1983: 6 titles

BV Uitgeverij De **Kern**, Nassaulaan 10, Postbus 108, 3740 AC Baarn Tel: 17241 Telex: 73250 line nl ref 588
Dirs: J Verweij, J J van Willegen
Associate Company: Bigot en Van Rossum BV (qv)
Subjects: General Fiction, Popular Non-fiction
1981: 32 titles *1982:* 30 titles *Founded:* 1977
ISBN Publisher's Prefix: 90-325

Uitgeverij **Kim** Natuurboeken BV*, Postbus 70, 3740 AB Baarn (Located at: Beukenlaan 16-20, 3741 BP Baarn) Tel: 18941 Cable Add: Hollandia Baarn Telex: 43776 incom attn Hollandia
Man Dirs: J Muntinga, M Muntinga
Parent Company: Hollandia BV (qv)
Subjects: Natural History, Nature Guides
1981: 4 titles

Uitgeverij **Kluitman** Alkmaar BV*, Postbus 231, 1700 AE Heerhugowaard (Located at: Kelvinstr 20, Heerhugowaard) Tel: (02207) 17326
Dirs: P Kluitman, W Gerla
Subject: Juveniles
Founded: 1864
ISBN Publisher's Prefix: 90-206

Kluwer Algemene Boeken BV, Postbus 235, 6710 BE Ede (Located at: Het Huis Kernhem, Kernhemseweg 7, 6718 ZB Ede) Tel: (08380) 19031 Cable Add: ZKede Telex: 37095 ZKede
Man Dir: J J Mons; *Sales:* J P H Delissen; *Chief Editor:* G L M Vlaskamp; *Permissions:* Mrs M van Minnen-Essink
Subjects: How-to, General Science, Atlases, Reference
Founded: 1970
Miscellaneous: Firm is a member of the Kluwer Group (qv)
ISBN Publisher's Prefix: 90-6117

Kluwer Group, Postbus 23, 7400 GA Deventer (Located at: Stromarkt 8, Deventer) Tel: (05700) 91911 Telex: 49660
Man Dirs: B Zevenbergen, J J C Alberdingk Thijm, A M W Resius, J Somerwil
Members of the Kluwer Group in the Netherlands: Publishing Houses: Bert Bakker (qv); Bohn, Scheltema en Holkema (qv); Uitgeversmij Born (qv); Born Periodieken; Binderij VD Sanden; van Dale Lexicografie; Educaboek (qv); Drukkerij De Lange van Leer; Drukkerij Salland; Drukkerij Tulp; Drukkerij Vada; Educa International; Eska Tijdschriften (qv); Gouda Quint (qv); Ten Hagen (qv); ID Tijdschriften; Institut voor Bedrijfswetenschappen; International Journals Group; Dr W Junk (qv); Kluwer Algemene Boeken (qv); Kluwer Algemene Informatieve Boeken; Kluwers Couranten Bedrijf (qv); Kluwer Law and Taxation Publishers (qv); Kluwer Publiekstijdschriften; Kluwer Sociaal-Wetenschappelijke Boeken en Tijdschriften (qv); Kluwer Technische Boeken (qv); Kluwer Technische Tijdschriften; Kluwerpers; Kon-Drukkerij VD Garde; Kosmos (qv); Libresso; Van Loghum Slaterus (qv); Luitingh (qv); NBD Product-Information Systems; Novapres; Martinus Nijhoff (qv); Noorduijn (qv); Oosthoek (qv); Reidel Publishing (qv); Rotapress; Ring van Rotterdamse Repetitozen; Scheltens & Giltay; Schoolpers (qv); Skarabee; van Soeren; Stam/Robijns (qv); Stam Technische Boeken (qv); Stam Tijdschriften (qv); Stenfert Kroese; W E J Tjeenk Willink (qv); Tjeenk Willink/Noorduijn (qv); L J Veen (qv); Zomer & Keuning Boeken (qv); Z & K Tijdschriften; Uitgeverij Kluwer
Members outside the Netherlands: Australasian Educa Press, Australia; Heideland-Orbis, Kosmos, NV M en I (all in Belgium); Educalivre, France; Hulton Educational Publications (qv); Kluwer Publishing Ltd (qv); Van Leer; MTP Press (qv); Stanley Thornes/Stam Press (qv) (all in UK); Information und Kontakt Kluwer Seminar; Kommentator Verlag (qv); Alfred Metzner Verlag (qv); Verlag Schubert; Verlag H Stam; Thalhammer Verlags GmbH (all in Federal Republic of Germany); Kluwer Caraçaó NV; De Curaçaosche Couran LNV (both in Netherlands Antilles); Ed Delta et Spès SA, Switzerland (qv); Kluwer Boston Inc, USA
Subjects: Law and Taxation, Academic Publications in various fields, Educational, Technical, Encyclopaedias, Trade Books and Magazines, Graphic Industries, Newspapers and Periodicals
Bookshops: Broese Kemink, Utrecht; Dekker Van de Vegt, Nijmegen; De Gelderse Boekhandel, Arnhem; Boekhandel Gianotten, Tilburg — Breda; International Journals Group, Amsterdam; Martinus Nijhoff, The Hague; Praamstra, Deventer; Scheltema Holkema Vermeulen, Amsterdam — Haarlem; Stamboekhandel, Eindhoven — Venlo; Studieboekencentrale, Ede/Zoetermeer Verwijs & Stam, The Hague; Wetenschappelijke Boekhandel Rotterdam, Rotterdam
Founded: 1889
ISBN Publisher's Prefixes: 90-6117 (Kluwer NV), 90-313 (Bohn, Scheltema & Holkema), 90-283 (Born), 90-11 (Educaboek), 90-267 (Kluwer Soc-Wet), 90-201 (Kluwer Tec), 90-6001 (Van Loghum Slaterus), 90-245 (Luitingh), 90-247 (Martinus Nijhoff), 90-6318 (Novapres), 90-207 (Stenfert-Kroese), 90-6117 (Kluwer Algemene Boeken), 90-200 (Kluwer Fiscale en Juridische Boeken), 90-6019 (Bert Bakker), 90-254 (Uitgeverij Contact), 90-6071 (Skarabee), 90-204 (Veen), 90-210 (Zomer & Keuning)

Kluwer Law and Taxation Publishers, Staverenstr 15, Postbus 23, 7400 GA Deventer Tel: (05700) 91911 Telex: 49295
International Publisher: Reinout J Kasteleijn
Subjects: Law, Taxation, Labour Law and Industrial Relations, Social Security; Periodicals
1982: 300 titles
Miscellaneous: Firm is a member of the Kluwer Group (qv)
ISBN Publisher's Prefixes: 90-268, 90-200, 90-312, 90-654

Kluwer Sociaal-Wetenschappelijke Boeken en Tijdschriften, Postbus 23, 7400 GA Deventer Tel: (05700) 20577 Telex: 49774
Publisher: Wouter van Zeytveld
Subjects: Business, Economics, Periodicals
Miscellaneous: Firm is a member of the Kluwer Group (qv)
ISBN Publisher's Prefix: 90-267

Kluwer Technische Boeken BV, Brink 25, Postbus 23, 7411 BS Deventer Tel: (05700) 91911 Telex: 49560 klutb nl
Man Dir: Noud H L van Herk; *Editorial:* Benno van Lochem; *Foreign Rights:* Oeble Hoekstra; *Sales:* Noud H L van Herk; *Production:* Dick Laus
Subsidiary Company: Kluwer Technische Boeken, Santvoortbeeklaan 21-23, Deurne, Belgium
Subjects: Electronics, Motor Engineering, Hobbies, Do-it-yourself, Engineering, Building, Dictionaries, Photography
1982: 65 titles
Miscellaneous: Firm is a member of the Kluwer Group (qv)
ISBN Publisher's Prefix: 90-2010

Kluwerpers, a member of the Kluwer Group (qv)

Kluwers Courantenbedrijf*, Zutphenseweg 51033, 7418 AH Deventer
Dir: A van Beck
Miscellaneous: Firm is a member of the Kluwer Group (qv)

F **Knuf** Publishers, Postbus 720, 4116 ZJ Buren Tel: (03447) 1691
Subjects: Musicology and Musical Theory, Biography and Musical History, Periodicals
ISBN Publisher's Prefix: 90-6027

Uitgeversmaatschappij J H **Kok** BV+, Gildestraat 5, 8263 AH Kampen Tel: (05202) 13545 Cable Add: Kok Kampen Telex: 42721 jh kok nl
Man Dir: W E Steunenberg; *Assistant Man Dir:* A C Van Dam; *Editorial:* B A Endedijk; *Rights & Permissions:* Gerrit Brinkman; *Educational:* Rien Jpenburg
Subsidiary Companies: De Groot Goudriaan, Kampen; Intermedium, Kampen; Uitgeverij Omniboek, The Hague; J N Voorhoeve, The Hague; La Rivière en Voorhoeve, Zwolle
Subjects: General Fiction, Belles Lettres, Poetry, Biography, History, How-to, Art Philosophy, Religion, Textbooks, Educational Materials, Reference, Juveniles, Psychology, General & Social Science, Low- & High-priced Paperbacks, Alternative Medicine
Book Club: VCL (series of novels)
Founded: 1894
ISBN Publisher's Prefix: 90-242

Kooyker Scientific Publications BV, PO Box 24 Nieuwe Rijn 15-16, 2300 AA Leiden Tel: (071) 144146 Telex: 39434 Kooy nl
Man Dir: Fj Arkenau
Subjects: Medicine, Psychology, Sociology, Education
1981: 1 title *Founded:* 1975
ISBN Publisher's Prefix: 90-6212

Kosmos BV, Maliebaan 45, Postbus 14095, 3508 SC Utrecht Tel: (030) 316694 Telex: 70684 Luve
Man Dir: Bert de Groot; *Editorial:* J Vonk, M ten Raa
Subjects: Natural History, Dogs, Travelling
Miscellaneous: Children's books now with Bert Bakker BV (qv). Kosmos BV is a member of the Kluwer Group (qv)

Kramers, an imprint of BV Uitgeversmaatschappij Elsevier (qv)

Kugler Publications BV, Postbus 516, 1180 AM Amstelveen (Located at: Prinsengracht 573, Amsterdam) Tel: (3120) 278070 Telex: 18180 Simon nl
Man Dir: Simon Kugler
Subjects: Medical, Criminology

Boekhandel en Uitgeverij **Laetitia**, Postbus 81078, 3009 GB Rotterdam (Located at: Tjonger 13, Rotterdam, Zevenkamp) Tel: (010) 216231
Man Dir: Nettie Essed; *Sales:* Dr W R W Donner
Parent Company: Essed Enterprises, 36A Schietbaanlaan, Rotterdam
Subsidiary Company: Steven Press, Zoetermeer
Subjects: Fiction, Children's, College Textbooks, Third World Literature especially Suriname and Netherlands Antilles
Bookshop: At above address
1981: 8 titles *Founded:* 1976
ISBN Publisher's Prefix: 90-6543

Allert de **Lange** BV*, Damrak 62, 1012 LM Amsterdam Tel: (020) 227363

Uitgeverij **Lannoo**, Nieuwe 's-Gravelandseweg 17, Postbus 17, 1400 AA Bussum Tel: (02159) 34241 Telex: 43064
Subjects: Travel, Children's, Religious, Poetry, Art, Paperbacks, Education, Psychology, Sports, Games
ISBN Publisher's Prefix: 90-209

Leiden University Press, NV Boekhandel en Drukkerij V/H E J Brill, Oude Rijn 33a, PO Box 9000, 2300 PA Leiden Tel: (071) 146646 Telex: 39296 Cable Add: Brill Leiden
Subjects: History, Languages, Law, Social Sciences, Biology, Medicine
ISBN Publisher's Prefix: 90-9004

Lemniscaat+, Vijverlaan 48, Postbus 4066, 3006 AB Rotterdam Tel: (010) 141744 Cable Add: Lemniscaat Rotterdam
President: J L Boele van Hensbroek; *Dirs:* Dr Marijke Boele van Hensbroek-Reesink, Bob Markus; *Rights & Permissions:* Suzanne Padberg
Subjects: Juveniles, Picture Books, Psychology, Social Science
1981: 22 titles *1982:* 26 titles *Founded:* 1963
ISBN Publisher's Prefix: 90-6069

Uitgeverij **Leopold** BV, Badhuisweg 232, The Hague Tel: (070) 549604
Man Dir: Liesbeth ten Houten; *Permissions:* Jacolien Kingmans
Parent Company: NV Uitgeverij Nijgh en Van Ditmar (qv)
Subjects: General Fiction, Juveniles, High-priced Paperbacks
Founded: 1923
ISBN Publisher's Prefix: 90-258

Littera Scripta Manet, Rijsseltweg 10, 7211 EP Eefde (Gorssel) Tel: (05759) 1950
Man Dir: A Rutgers; *Editorial:* Mrs R L Rutgers-Schiff; *Other Offices:* A Rutgers
Subjects: General Science, Ornithology
Bookshop: International Hobby-Bookshop, Gorssel
Founded: 1947
ISBN Publisher's Prefix: 90-6036

Van **Loghum** Slaterus*, Geert Grootestr 4, Postbus 23, NL-6600 Deventer Tel: (05700) 10811 Telex: 49295
Publisher: Fons Drabbe
Subjects: Humanities, Public Health, Education, Psychology, Social Science, Linguistics, Languages, Periodicals
Miscellaneous: Firm is a member of the Kluwer Group (qv)
1981: 60 titles
ISBN Publisher's Prefix: 90-6001

Luctor Publishing — Stadler & Sauerbier BV*, Weegbreestr 11, Postbus 33017, NL-3012 Rotterdam Tel: (010) 180081 Cable Add: Sensoffset Telex: 23411
Subjects: Juveniles, Educational

Uitgeverij **Luitingh** BV, Maliebaan 45, Postbus 14095, 3508 SC Utrecht Tel: (030) 316694 Telex: 70684 Luve
Man Dir: A de Groot
Subsidiary Companies: Novapres BV; Uitgeverij Skarabee BV
Subjects: General Fiction and Non-fiction, Games and Pastimes, How-to, Reference, Religion, Juveniles, Low- & High-priced Paperbacks, Homecrafts
Founded: 1946
Miscellaneous: Firm is a member of the Kluwer Group (qv)
ISBN Publisher's Prefix: 90-245

Otto **Maier** Benelux BV*, Heliumweg 16, Amersfoort Tel: (03490) 11445 Telex: 47991
Parent Company: Otto Maier Verlag, Federal Republic of Germany (qv)
Subjects: Architecture, Hobbies, Juveniles, Non-fiction

Malmberg BV, Leeghwaterlaan 16, Postbus 233, 's-Hertogenbosch Tel: (073) 215565 Cable Add: Malmberg 's-Hertogenbosch Telex: 50058
General Manager/Publisher: Dr M J van Dalen; *Marketing Dir:* Dr Th J M Huisman; *Production:* J Hillenaar

Associate Companies: Malmberg Boek bv, s'Hertogenbosch (educational reading programs); Uitgeverij Het Spectrum (qv); Uitgeverij J van In, Belgium (qv); International Visual Resource bv; Spectrum Boekhandel bv
Subjects: Pre-school, Primary & Secondary Textbooks, Educational Materials, Educational Juveniles, Teaching Equipment for Physics, Chemistry and Biology, Educational Software and Hardware
1981: 110 titles *1982:* 175 titles *Founded:* 1885
Miscellaneous: Firm is a member of VNU Book Group (qv)
ISBN Publisher's Prefix: 90-208

Manteau, an imprint of BV Uitgeversmaatschappij Elsevier (qv)

Meijer Pers BV*, PO Box 7897, 1008-AB Amsterdam (Located at: Koningslaan 19, 1075 AA-Amsterdam Tel: (020) 644131
Man Dir: G Michon
Parent Company: Meijer Wormerveer NV, Wormerveer
Subsidiary Company: Ideeboek BV (qv)
Subjects: General, Cookery
1982: 24 titles *Founded:* 1966

Meinema/Waltman*, Hippolytusbuurt 4, Postbus 3150, Delft Tel: (015) 125915
Subject: Textbooks

H **Meulenhoff**, an imprint of BV Uitgeversmaatschappij Elsevier (qv)

Meulenhoff Educatief BV*, Postbus 100, 1000 AC Amsterdam (Located at: Herengracht 507, 1017 BV Amsterdam) Tel: (020) 235707 Cable Add: Manuscript Telex: 16234
Man Dirs: D van Foeken, Cl W Suermondt, AC van Hoek, M A Nouwen; *Editorial:* T A vd Veen, W ten Oever, T Scheffer
Parent Company: Meulenhoff en Co BV (at above address)
Associate Companies: Meulenhoff Informatief BV, Meulenhoff International BV, Meulenhoff Nederland BV (qqv), European Book Service
Subjects: Educational Materials, Textbooks
ISBN Publisher's Prefix: 90-280

Meulenhoff Informatief BV*, Postbus 100, 1000 AC Amsterdam (Located at: Herengracht 507, 1017 BV Amsterdam) Tel: (020) 235707 Cable Add: Manuscript Telex: 16234
Editorial Dir: Mrs E van Unen
Parent Company: Meulenhoff en Co BV (at above address)
Associate Companies: Meulenhoff Educatief BV, Meulenhoff International BV, Meulenhoff Nederland BV (qqv)
Subjects: Informative Non-fiction, Reference
ISBN Publisher's Prefix: 90-290

Meulenhoff International*, Postbus 100, 1000 AC Amsterdam (Located at: Herengracht 507, 1017 BV Amsterdam) Tel: (020) 235707/241611 Cable Add: Intart Telex: 16234
Man Dir: W J van Hoorn
Parent Company: Meulenhoff en Co BV (at above address)
Associate Companies: Meulenhoff Educatief BV, Meulenhoff Informatief BV, Meulenhoff Nederland BV (qqv)
Subjects: Co-productions, General Non-fiction, Art
Miscellaneous: Firm's main activity is selling co-productions internationally

Meulenhoff Nederland BV*, Postbus 100, 1000 AC Amsterdam (Located at: Herengracht 507, 1017 BV Amsterdam) Tel: (020) 235707 Cable Add: Manuscript Telex: 16234
Man Dir: Laurens van Krevelen; *Financial*

Dir: Wim van der Wilk; *Editorial:* Wouter Donath Tieges; *Rights & Permissions:* Maarten Asscher
Parent Company: Meulenhoff en Co BV (at above address)
Associate Companies: Meulenhoff Educatief BV, Meulenhoff International, Meulenhoff Informatief BV (qqv), Meulenhoff/Landshoff
Subjects: Dutch and translated foreign literature, Science Fiction, Non-fiction
Founded: 1895
ISBN Publisher's Prefix: 90-290

Miland Publishers, Zuideinde 40, Postbus 6, NL-2420 AA Nieuwkoop
Parent Company: De Graaf Publishers (qv)
ISBN Publisher's Prefix: 90-6003

Mirananda Publishers BV+, Zijdeweg 5A, Wassenaar 2270 Tel: (01751) 78471
Man Dir: Carolus Vehulst; *Dir:* Manda Plettenburg
Orders to: Centraal Boekhuis, Erasmusweg 10, Culemborg
Subjects: Art (Western and Oriental), Religion, Mysticism, Yoga, Theosophy, Astrology, Popular Science, Psychology, Philosophy, Quality Paperbacks, Linguistics, Education, Literature, Outstanding Children's Books
1982: 23 titles *Founded:* 1976
ISBN Publisher's Prefix: 90-6271

Moussault, an imprint of Unieboek BV (qv)

Mouton Publishers, now in the Federal Republic of Germany (qv)

De **Muiderkring** BV, Nijverheidswerf 17-21, Postfach 10, NL 1400 AA Bussum Tel: (02159) 31851 Telex: 15171
Man Dir: R Bayards; *Sales Dept:* P Oosterlaak
Subjects: Specialist Literature connected with Electronics, Computers and Hobbies

Mulder en Co, subsidiary of Bigot & Van Rossum NV (qv)

Mulder Holland BV, Transformatorweg 35, 1014 AJ, Amsterdam Tel: (020) 824805 Cable Add: Emzet Amsterdam Telex: 14627
Subject: Juveniles
1983: 120 titles

Muusses, Van IJsendijkstr 154, Postbus 13, 1440 AA Purmerend Tel: (02990) 23746
Man Dir: A H van den Berg
Subjects: Infant, Primary, Secondary and Technical School Educational
Founded: 1872
ISBN Publisher's Prefix: 90-231

Uitgeverij **N I B**+, Postbus 144, 3700 AC Zeist (Located at: Wilhelminalaan 7, Zeist) Tel: (03404) 21624
Man Dir: Dr H C van Hummel; *Editorial:* A J W Boks
Subjects: Textbooks for Secondary Education on: Chemistry, Biology, Modern Languages, History, Physics, Mathematics, Science Education
ISBN Publisher's Prefix: 0075-4

Nederlandsche Zondagsschool Vereeniging*, Bloemgracht 65, NL-1016 KG Amsterdam Tel: (020) 239121
Subjects: Religion, Juveniles, Games
1981: 24 titles

Nederlandse Lezerskring Boek en Plaat BV, Postbus 2201, 1000 EK Amsterdam (Located at: Wildenborch 2, 1112 XB Diemen) Tel: (020) 906911 Telex: 16188
Man Dir: Hans van den Broek; *Operational Dir:* Henny Hornis; *Editorial Manager:* Hans van Hattum; *Marketing Manager:* Han Cohen

Uitgeverij H **Nelissen** BV+, Parkstr 47, 3743 ED Baarn Tel: (02154) 12386
Man Dir, Editorial, Permissions: R M M Nelissen; *Sales, Publicity, Production:* Dick Boer
Subjects: Religion, Sociology, Politics, Education, Philosophy, Social Sciences, Textbooks
1981: 20 titles *1982:* 21 titles *Founded:* 1922
ISBN Publisher's Prefix: 90-244

Nieuwe Stad, St Stephanusstr 11, Nijmegen
Parent Company: Città Nuova Editrice, Italy (qv for associate companies)

Nieuwe Wieken, an imprint of Omega Boek BV (qv)

NV Uitgeverij **Nijgh en Van Ditmar***, Badhuisweg 232, 2597 JS The Hague Tel: (070) 512711
Man Dir: A J J Siebelink; *Editorial:* N D Dekker, A E Blatter, J D M Mulder; *Permissions:* Ms L ten Houten
Subsidiary Companies: Uigeverij Leopold BV, Rotterdam University Press (qqv)
Subjects: General Fiction, Belles Lettres, Poetry, Biography, History, Juveniles, High-priced Paperbacks, Engineering, Secondary Textbooks, Home Economics
Founded: 1837
ISBN Publisher's Prefix: 90-236

Martinus **Nijhoff** Publishers, Postbus 566, 2501 CN The Hague (Located at: Lange Voorhout 9-11, The Hague) Tel: (070) 469460 Cable Add: Books Hague
Dir: F W B van Eysinga; *Production, Editorial:* G A M Aleven
Orders to: Kluwer Academic Publishers Group, Distribution Centre, Postbus 322, 3300 AH Dordrecht
Branch Off: Kluwer Academic Publishers, 190 Old Derby St, Massachusetts 02043, USA
Subjects: Biography, History, Music, Art, Philosophy, Religion, Textbooks, Reference, Psychology, Social Science, Medicine, Applied Sciences, Veterinary Sciences, Agriculture, International Law/Relations/Politics, Economics
Bookshop: Lange Voorhout 9-11, 2501 AX The Hague
Founded: 1853
Miscellaneous: Firm is a member of the Kluwer Group (qv)
ISBN Publisher's Prefix: 90-247

BV **Noord-Hollandsche** Uitgeversmaatschappij, a division of Elsevier Science Publishers BV (qv)

Noordhoff International Publishing, see Sijthoff en Noordhoff International Publishers

Noorduijn BV*, Postbus 1148, 6801 MK Arnhem (Located at: Willemsplein 2, Arnhem) Tel: (085) 454762
Man Dir: K H Mulder
Subjects: Law and Taxation
1981: 7 titles *Founded:* 1819
Miscellaneous: Firm is a member of the Kluwer Group (qv)
ISBN Publisher's Prefix: 90-203

North Holland, an imprint of Elsevier Science Publishers BV (qv)

Novapres BV, a subsidiary of Uitgeverij Luitingh (qv)

Omega Boek BV, Postbus 20072, 1000 HB Amsterdam (Located at: Sarphatistr 13, 1017 WS Amsterdam) Tel: (020) 231969/245284
Orders to: Centraal Boekhuis Culemborg
Imprints: De Centaur, Nieuwe Wieken, Triton Pers, Omega Jeugdboekerij
Subjects: General Fiction and Non-fiction, War Stories, Thrillers, Art, Children's Books, Gift Books
1981: 80 titles *Founded:* 1968
ISBN Publisher's Prefixes: 90-6057, 90-6142

Uitgeverij **Omniboek**, subsidiary of Uitgeversmaatschappij J H Kok BV (qv)

Oosthoek, Savannahweg 60, Utrecht Tel: (030) 434944
Man Dirs: H Smit, D Kok
Subject: Encyclopaedias
Miscellaneous: Firm is a member of the Kluwer Group (qv)
ISBN Publisher's Prefix: 90-6046

Orbit NV, a subsidiary of Theatrum Orbis Terrarum (qv)

Oriental Press BV (APA)*, Postbus 1850, NL-1000 BW Amsterdam
Parent Company: APA (Academic Publishers Associated) (qv)
Subjects: Oriental Studies, Text editions
ISBN Publisher's Prefix: 90-6023

Overseas Publishers Association Amsterdam BV*, Postbus 19720, 1000 CS Amsterdam (Located at: Leidseplein 29, 1017 PS Amsterdam)
Man Dir: W F C Stevens
Parent Company: Overseas Publishers Association Antilles NV
Associate Company: Central Data Services Ltd
Subjects: Scientific, Trade (also Licenses and Packages)
Founded: 1978

Pandora Pockets, an imprint of Bruna Pockethuis BV (qv)

Philo Press-Van Heusden-Hissink & Co CV (APA)*, Postbus 1850, NL-1000 BW Amsterdam
Parent Company: APA (Academic Publishers Associated) (qv)
Subjects: Academic (Arts and Humanities, History of Sciences, Oriental Studies)
ISBN Publisher's Prefixes: 90-6022, 90-6024, 90-6025

Uitgeverij **Ploegsma**, Postbus 19857, 1000 GW Amsterdam (Located at: Keizersgracht 616, 1017 ER Amsterdam) Tel: (020) 262907
Man Dir: Paul Brinkman
Subjects: Children's books, Juveniles, How-to, Natural Science, Handicraft, Leisure
ISBN Publisher's Prefix: 90-216

Polak en Van Gennep Uitg Mij BV*, Reguliersgracht 50, 1017 LT Amsterdam Tel: (020) 226288
Man Dir: B M Hosman
Subjects: Scientific Literature, General Literature
Founded: 1964
ISBN Publisher's Prefix: 90-253

Promoboek, an imprint of Infopers (qv)

Pudoc, Centre for Agricultural Publishing and Documentation, Gen Foulkesweg 19, Postbus 4, 6700 AA Wageningen Tel: (08370) 89222 Telex: 45015
Man Dir: A Rutgers; *Sales Dir:* J Vermeulen
Subjects: Natural Science, Agriculture
Founded: 1957
ISBN Publisher's Prefix: 90-220

Em **Querido's** Uitgeverij BV, Singel 262, 1016 AC Amsterdam Tel: (020) 237195
Man Dir: Ary T Langbroek
Associate Companies: Uitgeverij De Arbeiderspers BV, Wetenschappelijke Uitgeverij BV (qqv)
Imprint: Salamander Paperbacks
Subjects: General Fiction, Belles Lettres, Poetry, Biography, History, Music, Art, Juveniles, Low-priced Paperbacks
Founded: 1915
ISBN Publisher's Prefix: 90-214

van **Reemst**, an imprint of Unieboek BV (qv)

D **Reidel** Publishing Co, Postbus 17, Dordrecht (Located at: Voorstr 479-483, Dordrecht) Tel: (078) 135388 Cable Add: Reipubco Telex: 29245
Publisher: J F Hattink; *Promotion Managers:* L van der Zon (Sciences), P Debus (Humanities, Social Sciences), M Scrivener (Humanities) — North America), A Howard (Sciences — North America); *Production:* R Doornebal; *Permissions:* Ms E Zoeteman
Subsidiary Companies: D Reidel, 190 Old Derby St, Hingham, Mass 02034, USA
Subjects: Philosophy, Humanities, Linguistics, Mathematics, Astronomy, Chemistry, Environmental and Earth Sciences, Energy, Periodicals
1982: 130 titles *1983:* 165 titles
Miscellaneous: Firm is a member of the Kluwer Group (qv)
ISBN Publisher's Prefix: 90-277

Rekreaboek, an imprint of Zuidgroep BV (qv)

Peter de **Ridder** Press BV*, 8 Johan Vermeerstr, 2162 BJ Lisse Tel: 15239
Dir: Peter de Ridder
Subjects: Semiotics, Linguistics, Literary Theory, Anthropology
Founded: 1974
ISBN Publisher's Prefix: 90-316

Editions **Rodopi** bv, Keizersgracht 302-304, Amsterdam Tel: (020) 227507
Dir: Fred van der Zee
Subjects: History, Philosophy, Religion, University Textbooks, Languages and Literature, Classical Antiquity, Communications
Founded: 1966
ISBN Publisher's Prefix: 90-6203

Romen, an imprint of Unieboek BV (qv)

Rotterdam University Press, Badhuisweg 232, 2597 JS The Hague Tel: (070) 512711
Man Dir: N D Dekker
Parent Company: BV Uitgeverij Nijgh en Van Ditmar (qv)
Subjects: Economics, Development Planning, Social Science, University Textbooks
Founded: 1964
ISBN Publisher's Prefix: 0-90237

Uitgeverij **S M D** BV (Spruyt, Van Mantgem en De Does), Postbus 63, 2300 AB Leiden (Located at: Langebrug 87, 2311 TJ Leiden) Tel: (071) 146541
Subjects: Medical, Educational, Technical
1981: 43 titles *1982:* 72 titles *Founded:* 1907
ISBN Publisher's Prefix: 90-238

S U N socialistische Uitgeverij Nijmegen*, Bijleveldsingel 9, 6521 AM Nijmegen Tel: (080) 221700
Publicity, Permissions: Henk Hoeks
Subjects: Marxism, Culture, Philosophy, History of the Workers' Movements, Architecture, Periodicals
Founded: 1969
ISBN Publisher's Prefix: 90-6168

Salamander Paperbacks, an imprint of Em Querido's Uitgeverij BV (qv)

Samsom Uitgeverij BV, Postbus 4, Alphen aan den Rijn (Located at: Stadhoudersplein 1, 2404 BE Alphen aan den Rijn) Tel: (01720) 62324 Cable Add: Samsom Alphenrijn Telex: 39682
Man Dir: Drs W P N Schrijver; *Dirs:* P C Minderhout, H J Demoet, C J Steur, A S A Struik en M van Veen; *Publishing Dir:* C L Stafleu; *Rights & Permissions:* José van der Meer
Imprints: H D Tjeenk Willink BV, Stafleu, Stafleu en Tholen
Subjects: Business, Fiscal Law, Management, Textbooks, Social Science, Computer Science, Administration, Public Health, Medical, Nursing, Dental, Sports
Founded: 1882
Miscellaneous: Firm is a member of the Wolters Samsom Groep NV (qv)
ISBN Publisher's Prefixes: 90-14 (Samsom), 90-6092 (Tjeenk Willink)

Schoolpers*, PO Box 48, 4100 AA Culemborg Tel: (03450) 71911
Chairman: P D Zuiderveld; *Man Dir:* J Th Timmer; *Production & Sales:* Educaboek BV (qv)
Subject: Textbooks
Miscellaneous: Firm is a member of the Kluwer Group (qv)

Vereeniging tot Verspreiding der H **Schrift**, NZ Kolk 17-21, 1012 PV Amsterdam Tel: (020) 227978/254149
Man Dir, Rights & Permissions: J Ruijsink; *Sales, Publicity:* W Dronkers; *Production:* A Rietveld
Imprint: Ark Boeken
Subjects: Religious, Juveniles, Picture Books
Bookshop: NZ Kolk 21, Amsterdam
1981: 22 titles *1982:* 20 titles *Founded:* 1913
ISBN Publisher's Prefix: 90-338

Schuyt en Co CV*, Postbus 563, 2003 RN Haarlem (Located at: Gedempte Oude Gracht 35, 2011 GL Haarlem) Tel: (023) 325440 Telex: 41532 sco nl
General Manager: K C Schuyt; *Sales:* W G Kok
Subsidiary Company: Schuyt en Co nv, Hansahuis, Suikerrui 5, 2000 Antwerp, Belgium
Subjects: Juveniles, Art, History, Railways, Geography
Founded: 1953
ISBN Publisher's Prefix: 90-6097

Uitgeverij Gary **Schwartz**, Herengracht 22, Postbus 162, 3600 AD Maarssen Tel: (03465) 62778
Dir & Other Offices: Gary Schwartz
Subjects: Fine Art Books
1981: 3 titles *Founded:* 1972
ISBN Publisher's Prefix: 90-6179

Semic Press*, Brouwersgracht 97-99, Amsterdam Tel: 226341 Telex: 15558 semic nl
Man Dir: Hierro Guillermo
Subjects: Comic Magazines, Colouring Books, Albums, Pocket Books

Uitgeverij **Semper** Agendo BV*, Prins Willem Alexanderlaan 601, Postbus 327, Apeldoorn Tel: (055) 773232

Septuaginta BV Uitgeverij, now known as Icob cv (qv)

Servire BV Uitgevers*, Secr Varkevisserstr 52, 2225 LE Katwijk aan Zee Tel: (01718) 16741
Chief Executive: Felix Erkelens
Associate Companies: Momenta Publishing Ltd, UK (qv); Qalandar Verlag GmbH, Sauerbruchstr 8, D-708 Aalen 9, Federal Republic of Germany
Subsidiary Companies: Hunter House Inc, Publishers, 748 East Bonita Ave, Suite 105, Pomona, CA 91767, USA; Omnibus Book Service, UK (qv)
Subjects: Books in Dutch, German, English on Human Endeavour and Creativity, Mysticism, Alternative Living, Education, Psychology
Founded: 1932
ISBN Publisher's Prefixes: 90-6077, 90-6325

A W **Sijthoff's Uitg** Mij BV*, Postbus 4, 2400 MA Alphen aan den Rijn Tel: (01720) 62465 Cable Add: Sijthoff Alphen aan den Rijn Telex: 39682
Dir: Frans Pruyt; *Editorial:* Willemien Hoogendijk, Claartje E van den Beld
Subjects: How-to, Fiction (Detective), Non-fiction, History, Illustrated books
Founded: 1851
Miscellaneous: Firm is a member of the Wolters Samsom Groep NV (qv)
ISBN Publisher's Prefix: 90-218

Uitgeverij **Skarabee** BV, subsidiary of Uitgeverij Luitingh BV (qv)

Smeets Illustrated Projects, Molenveldstr 90, Postbus 17, 6001 HL Weert Tel: (04950) 38055 Telex: 37550
Manager: V Pokorny
Parent Company: Royal Smeets Offset
Subjects: Art, Illustrated Books

Uitgeverij Het **Spectrum** BV*, Park Voorn 4, 3454 JR De Meern Tel: (03406) 3737 Cable Add: Het Spectrum BV, De Meern Telex: 47677
Dir: R A J Huyzer
Orders to: Postbus 2073, 3500 GB Utrecht
Spectrum Amsterdam: Cronenburg 75, 1018 GM Amsterdam Tel: (020) 443226 Telex: 15033 (Orders to: Postbus 7801, 1008 AA, Amsterdam)
Subsidiary Company: Het Spectrum (IUM NV), Belgium (qv) (owned jointly with Internationale Uitgevers Maatschappij NV, Antwerp)
Associate Companies: L C G Malmberg bv (qv); Uitgeverij J van In, Belgium (qv); International Visual Resource bv; Spectrum Boekhandel bv
Subjects: General Fiction, Encyclopaedias, Science & Technical, Textbooks, Paperbacks, Juveniles, Partworks, Pocket Editions
Founded: 1935
Miscellaneous: Firm is a member of the VNU Book Group (qv)
ISBN Publisher's Prefix: 90-274

Spruyt, van Mantgem en de Does BV, see SMD

Staatsdrukkerij en Uitgeverijbedrijf*, Postbus 20014, 2500 EA The Hague (Located at: Chr Plantijnstr 1, The Hague) Tel: (070) 789911 Telex: 32486
Subjects: Government Publications
ISBN Publisher's Prefix: 90-9012

Stafleu, an imprint of Samsom Uitgeverij BV (qv)

Stafleu en Tholen, an imprint of Samsom Uitgeverij BV (qv)

Stafleu's Wetenschappelijke Uitgeversmaatschappij BV en Stafleu en Tholen BV, Postbus 4, 2400 MA Alphen aan den Rijn (Located at: Stadhoudersplein 1, 2404 MA Alphen aan den Rijn) Tel: (01720) 62054 Cable Add: Stafleu Publishers Alphen aan der Rijn Telex: 39682
Publisher: T Muntinga
Subjects: Medicine, Psychology, General Science, Nursing, Dental Science
Founded: 1947
Miscellaneous: Firm is a member of the Wolters Samsom Groep NV (qv)
ISBN Publisher's Prefixes: 90-6016, 90-6065

Stam/Robijns*, Industrieweg 1, Postbus 48, 4100 AA Culemborg Tel: (03450) 3143 Telex: 47306
Chairman: P D Zuiderveld; *Man Dir:* B Balder; *Production & Sales:* Educaboek BV (qv)
Subjects: Commercial and Business Education
Miscellaneous: Firm is a member of the Kluwer Group (qv)

Stam Technische Boeken*, Industrieweg 1, Postbus 48, 4100 AA Culemborg Tel: (03450) 3143 Telex: 47306
Chairman: P D Zuiderveld; *Man Dir:* B Balder; *Production & Sales:* Educaboek BV (qv)
Subjects: Architecture, Chemistry, Electrical Engineering, Electronics, Earth Sciences, Industries, Crafts, Civil & Mechanical Engineering, Agriculture, Aviation, Mathematics, Physics, Law, Linguistics, Languages, Transport, Economics
Miscellaneous: Firm is a member of the Kluwer Group (qv)

Stam Tijdschriften BV, PO Box 235, 2280 AE Ryswyk Tel: (070) 991516 Telex: 33702 Stam Nll
Subjects: Engineering, Building Construction, Electronics,, Chemistry, Economics, Computers, Periodicals
Miscellaneous: Firm is a member of the Kluwer Group (qv)
1983: 16 titles

Standaard Uitgeverij en Distributie BV, Postbus 204, 4900 A E Oosterhout (Located at: Beneluxweg 23, N-4904 SJ Oosterhout) Tel: (01620) 52673
Parent Company: Scriptoria NV, Antwerp, Belgium
Associate Company: Standaard Uitgeverij (Scriptoria NV), Belgium (qv)
Subjects: Juveniles, Religion, Paperbacks
ISBN Publisher's Prefix: 90-02

De Steenuil Uitgeverij, an imprint of Uit-Mij 'West-Friesland' (qv)

Uitgeverij M Stenvert en Zoon BV, Postbus 70, 7300 AB Apeldoorn (Located at: Sutton 10, Apeldoorn) Tel: (055) 414644

A J G Strengholt's Boeken, Anno 1928, BV+, Hofstede 'Oud Bussem', Flevolaan 41, Naarden Tel: (02159) 46266 Telex: 43191 hobu nl
Parent Company: Strengholt BV (at above address)
Orders to: Postbus 338, 1400 AH Bussum
Man Dirs: F E Breitenstein, G van Oorschot
Subjects: General Fiction, Belles Lettres, Biography, History, How-to, Music, Art, Textbooks, Reference, High-priced Paperbacks
1981-82: 80 titles *Founded:* 1928
ISBN Publisher's Prefix: 90-6010

Succes BV*, Uitgeversmaatschappij, Prinsevinkenpark 2, Postbus 16, The Hague Tel: 514351 Cable Add: Success Denhaag
Man Dir, Sales: P Schreuder; *Editorial, Permissions:* J Kasander; *Production:* J Verhoef; *Publicity:* R Wentholt
Parent Company: Buhrmann-Tetterode
Subsidiary Companies: Succes NV, Belgium, Success Verlag GmbH, Federal Republic of Germany
Imprints: Baedeker voor de Vrouw, Uitgeverij Archipel, Universiteit voor Zelfstudie
Subjects: General
Book Club: Nederlandse Boekenclub
Founded: 1928

Swets en Zeitlinger BV, Heereweg 347B, 2161 CA-Lisse Tel: (02521) 19113 Cable Add: Swezeit-Lisse Telex: 41325 slzis nl
Dirs: A Swets, C Schuurman; *Editorial, Permissions:* K J Plasterk; *Sales, Production, Publicity:* J Lammerts
Subsidiary Companies: Swets North America Inc, PO Box 517, Berwyn, Pa 19312, USA; Europeriodiques SA, 31 ave de Versailles, F-78170 La Celle St Cloud, France; Swets-Servicos para Bibliotecas Ltda, Rua Anfilófio de Carvalho 29, Grupo 410 Castelo, 20030 Rio de Janeiro, RJ, Brazil
Subjects: Music, Medicine, Child Psychology, Engineering, Life Sciences, Education, English Language, Psychological Tests
Founded: 1901
ISBN Publisher's Prefix: 90-265

Theatrum Orbis Terrarum*, Keizersgracht 526, 1017 EK Amsterdam Tel: (020) 222255 Cable Add: Toterra Telex: 14070 ashni nl
Publisher: Nico Israel
Subsidiary Companies: Orbit BV; Facsimile Uitgaven Nederland NV (FUN) (both at above address)
Associate Companies: A Asher & Co, Nico Israel (qqv)
Subjects: Biography, Bibliography, History, Cartography, Music, Art, Philosophy, Reference, Religion, High-priced Paperbacks, Medicine, General Science
Founded: 1963
ISBN Publisher's Prefix: 90-221

BV Uitgeverij en Boekhandel W J Thieme & Cie, Industrieweg 85, Postbus 7, 7200 AA Zutphen Tel: (05750) 10566 Cable Add: Thieme Zutphen Telex: 49789 thizu
Dirs: L Groenendijk, K Schillemans
Subjects: General Science, Biology, Schoolbooks
Founded: 1792
ISBN Publisher's Prefix: 90-03

Uitgeversmaatschappij de Tijdstroom BV, Postbus 14, Noorderwal 38, Lochem Tel: (05730) 3651 Telex: 49642
Man Dir: B Mathis
Subjects: Art, Antiques, Medicine, Nursing, Hospital Sciences, Physiotherapy
1981: 50 titles *Founded:* 1924
ISBN Publisher's Prefix: 90-6087

Time-Life Books BV, Ottho Heldringstr 5, NL-1066 AZ Amsterdam Tel: (020) 5104900 Cable Add: Time-Life Amsterdam Telex: 14288
Editorial: Kit van Tulleken (London); *Production:* T Maloney (London); *Rights & Permissions:* Christian Strasser (London, for Eastern Europe and Scandinavia), Richard Stollenwerck (Paris, for Southern Europe)
Subsidiary Company: Sceptre Books Ltd, UK (qv)
Branch Offs: Time & Life Bldg, New Bond St, London W1Y 0AA, UK; 21-23 rue d'Astorg, F-75008 Paris, France; Akademiestrasse 7, D-8000 Munich 40, Federal Republic of Germany
Subjects: Art, Cookery, Gardening, General, Social & Political Science, History, How-to, Photography
ISBN Publisher's Prefix: 90-6182

H D Tjeenk Willink BV, an imprint of Samsom Uitgeverij BV (qv)

W E J Tjeenk Willink BV, Koestr 8, Postbus 25, 8000 AA Zwolle
Man Dir: K E van der Linde; *Publicity:* W M de Wit
Subjects: Textbooks and Periodicals on Law
Miscellaneous: Firm is a member of the Kluwer Group (qv)
ISBN Publisher's Prefix: 90-271

Tjeenk Willink-Noorduijn BV*, Industrieweg 1, Postbus 48, 4100 AA Culemborg Tel: (03450) 71911 Telex: 47306
Chairman: P D Zuiderveld; *Man Dir:* J Th Timmer; *Production & Sales:* Educaboek BV (qv)
Subjects: Secondary Textbooks, Educational Materials
Miscellaneous: Firm is a member of the Kluwer Group (qv)

Uitgeverij De Toorts, Nijverheidsweg 1, Postbus 576, 2003 RN Haarlem Tel: (023) 319360 Cable Add: Gradus Haarlem Telex: 41494
Man Dir: J Hesseling; *Editorial:* Mrs M Klis, Mrs A de Vries, J de Vries; *Sales:* C Klemann; *Production:* Mrs A de Vries; *Publicity:* Mrs W Gaus; *Permissions:* D Grabijn
Subjects: Humanities, Labour, Medicine, Music, Psychology, Psychotherapy
Founded: 1936
ISBN Publisher's Prefix: 90-6020

Triton Pers, an imprint of Omega Boek BV (qv)

Unieboek BV*, Nieuwe 's-Gravenlandseweg 17-19, 1405 HK Bussum Tel: (02159) 34241 Cable Add: Unieboek Telex: 43064
Dirs: C A J van Dishoeck, J J Weggemans, N H Witteman, Drs I Gay; *Permissions:* Jane Baird
Branch Off: Kleine Houtstr 70-72, 2000 DR Haarlem Tel: (023) 319205
Subsidiary Company: Standaard Uitgeverij en Distributie BV (qv)
Imprints: Agathon, de Boer Maritiem, van Dishoeck, Fibula van Dishoeck, de Gooise, de Haan, van Holkema en Warendorf, van Kampen, Moussault, van Reemst, Romen, Villa, Wereldvenster
Subjects: General Fiction & Non-fiction (including multi-volume reference), Maritime, Music, Art, Archaeology, Cookery, Politics, Geography, Literature, Juveniles (all ages), History, Thrillers, Natural History
Founded: 1890
ISBN Publisher's Prefixes: 90-228, 90-269

Universitarie Pers Leiden, see Leiden University Press

Universiteit voor Zelfstudie, an imprint of Succes BV (qv)

University Press Amsterdam BV (APA)*, Postbus 1850, NL-1000 BW Amsterdam
Parent Company: APA (Academic Publishers Associated) (qv)
Subjects: History of Law, Political Studies
ISBN Publisher's Prefix: 90-6042

Stichting V A M, Papelaan 85, Voorschoten Tel: (01717) 4141
Foundation for training employers and employees in the motor trade
Subjects: Technical and educational books for the motor trade
1980-81: 15 titles *Founded:* 1940

V N U — Verenigde Nederlandse Uitgeversbedrijven BV, Postbus 4079, 2003 EB Haarlem (Located at: Ceylonpoort 5-25, 2037 AA Haarlem Schalkwijk) Tel: (023) 339000 Telex: 41549
Subsidiary Companies: V N U Magazine Group; V N U Book Group (qv); V N U Sales Group; V N U Industry Group; V N U Newspaper Group; V N U Business Press Group (qv)
Miscellaneous: Main activities are publication, printing, distribution and sales of books and periodicals covering especially business, scientific, technical, educational and children's interests

V N U Book Group, Park Voorn 4, 3454 JR De Meern Tel: (03406) 3737 Telex: 47677
Dir: R A J Huyzer
The Book Publishing Division of V N U — Verenigde Nederlandse Uitgeversbedrijven (qv)
Members of Group: Malmberg BV (qv); Uitgeverij Het Spectrum (qv); International Visual Resource, Verkoopkantoor Nederland bv, Amsterdam; Spectrum Boekhandel bv, De Meern; Uitgeverij Het Spectrum, Uitgeverij J van In (both in Belgium, qqv)

NETHERLANDS 283

V N U Business Press Group BV, NZ Voorburgwal 225, 1012 RL Amsterdam Tel: (020) 249465 Telex: 10366
Man Dir: F X I Koot
Parent Company: VNU — Verenigde Nederlandse Uitgeversbedrijven BV (qv)
Subsidiary Companies: Uitgeversmaatschappij Diligentia BV (qv), Uitgeverij Intermediair, New Media, VNU Data Publishing International BV (all in Amsterdam); Eurocentrafilm BV, The Hague; Business Press Group, Brussels, Belgium; VNU Business Publications BV, London, UK; VNU Amvest Inc, Washington DC, USA
Subjects: Information Sciences, Business and Marketing, Computer Usage, Data Management, Career Guidance
1981: 42 titles

Uitgeverij L J **Veen** BV, Postbus 14095, Maliebaan 45, 3508 SC Utrecht Tel: (030) 316694 Telex: 70684 Luve
Man Dir: Bert de Groot; *Editorial:* Marijke Bartels (Senior Editor), Marian van der Beek (Fiction), Christian van Gelderen (Non-fiction); *Sales Manager:* Chris de Graaf; *Publicity:* Nico Rietdijk; *Production:* Dick Gubbels
Subjects: General Fiction, Thrillers, Dutch and International Literature, General Non-fiction, History, Health, Astrology
Founded: 1887
Miscellaneous: Firm is a member of the Kluwer Group (qv)
ISBN Publisher's Prefix: 90-204

W **Versluys'** Uitg Mij BV, Postbus 4037, 1009 AA-Amsterdam (Located at: 2e Oosterparkstr 221-223, 1092 BL-Amsterdam) Tel: (020) 650817
Man Dir: H M A Bakker; *Sales Manager:* J H Goedheer; *Editor:* W L Miner
Subject: Textbooks
1981: 102 titles *1982:* 80 titles *Founded:* 1875
ISBN Publisher's Prefix: 90-249

Villa, an imprint of Unieboek BV (qv)

J N **Voorhoeve**, The Hague, subsidiary of Uitgeversmaatschappij J H Kok BV (qv)

De **Walburg** Pers, PO Box 222, Zaadmarkt 84a-86, Zutphen Tel: 05750/10522
Man Dir, Publicity, Rights & Permissions: Dr C F J Schriks; *Sales:* J Rietbergen; *Production:* J van 't Leven
Subjects: History, Culture, Monuments, Architecture, Theatre
1981: 40 titles *1982:* 40 titles *Founded:* 1961
ISBN Publisher's Prefix: 90-6011

Uitgeverij Van **Walraven** BV*, Emmalaan 1, Apeldoorn Tel: (055) 218959
Miscellaneous: Firm is a member of the Combo Group (qv)
ISBN Publisher's Prefix: 90-6049

Uitgeverij **Waltman**, see Meinema Waltman

Wereldbibliotheek BV, Keizersgracht 810, PO Box 162, 1000 AD Amsterdam Tel: 242449 Telex: 18069 bebus nl
Man Dir: J Schilt; *Deputy Man Dir:* J B I M Kat
Associate Company: H J W Becht's Uitgeversmij (qv)
Subjects: High quality Fiction and Non-fiction, Belles Lettres, Juveniles

Wereldvenster, an imprint of Unieboek BV (qv)

Uit-Mij **'West-Friesland'**, Kleine Noord 7-9, Postbox 45, 1620 AA- Hoorn Tel: (02290) 18941 Cable Add: Westfriesland
Man Dir: Mevr J C Jonkers-Butter; *Editorial, Rights & Permissions:* F H Jonkers; *Sales:* Mevr J Paulsen-Schönberger; *Publicity:* Th Nannings; *Production:* L J Sweerts
Imprints: Cicero, De Steenuil, Witte Raven
Subjects: General Fiction, Juveniles, General Science, Low- & High-priced Paperbacks
1981: 108 titles *Founded:* 1918
ISBN Publisher's Prefix: 90-205

Uitgeverij **Westers**, Hammarskjöldhof 7, 3527 HC Utrecht Tel: (030) 931043/932859 Cable Add: Westers Utrecht
Man Dir and other offices: R J N M Westers Sr
Subjects: Children's Books, Novels
Bookshop: At above address
1981: 20 titles *1982:* 17 titles *Founded:* 1967
ISBN Publisher's Prefix: 90-6107

Wetenschappelijke Uitgeverij*, Singel 262, 1016 AC Amsterdam Tel: (020) 247674 Cable Add: Scientpublish
Man Dir: Th A Sontrop; *Publicity:* Gert Jan Hemmink
Associate Companies: Uitgeverij De Arbeiderspers BV, Em Querido's Uitgeverij BV (qqv)
Subjects: Biography, History, Music, Art, Philosophy, Religion, High-priced Paperbacks, Medicine, Psychology, General & Social Science, Secondary & University Textbooks
Founded: 1948
ISBN Publisher's Prefix: 90-6287

Uitgeverij **Wever** BV, Zilverstr 4, Franeker Tel: (05170) 3147
Subjects: History, Philosophy, Politics, Theology

Winkler Prins, an imprint of BV Uitgeversmaatschappij Elsevier (qv)

Witte Raven, an imprint of Uit-Mij 'West-Friesland' (qv)

Wolters-Noordhoff BV, Bamsport 157, Postbus 58, 9700 MB Groningen Tel: (050) 226922 Telex: 53443
Man Dir: J de Groot, J Buiring; *Rights & Permissions:* P G A Geenen
Orders to: PO Box 567, 9700 A N Groningen
Associate Company: Wolters-Noordhoff-Longman BV (qv)
Subjects: Secondary, Primary & Tertiary Textbooks, Educational Materials, *Easy Readers*, Maps, Atlases
Founded: 1836, 1858
Miscellaneous: Firm is a member of the Wolters Samsom Groep NV (qv)
ISBN Publisher's Prefix: 90-01

Wolters-Noordhoff-Longman BV, Postbus 58, 9700 MB Groningen (Located at: Oude Boteringestr 22, 9700 MB Groningen) Tel: (050) 162236 Telex: 53443/53529
General Executive: Aloys Doodkorte
Associate Companies: Wolters-Noordhoff BV (qv); Longman Group Ltd, UK (qv)
Subjects: English Language Teaching

Wolters Samsom Groep NV, Meeuwenlaan 6, 8001 BC Zwolle Tel: (038) 215910 Telex: 42311
Members of Wolters Samsom Group: Samsom Uitgeverij BV (qv), A W Sijthoff's Uitg Mij BV (qv), Stafleu's Wetenschappelijke Uitgeverij (qv), H D Tjeenk Willink BV, Wolters Noordhoff BV (qv) (all Netherlands); NV Wolters Samsom, Belgium (qv); Croner Publications Ltd (qv), Eclipse Publications Ltd (both UK); Aspen Systems Corporation, Panel Publishers Inc (both USA)

Zomer en Keuning Boeken BV*, Postbus 235, 6710 BE Ede (Located at: Het Huis Kernhem, Kernhemseweg 7, 6718 ZB Ede) Tel: (08380) 19031 Cable Add: ZKede Telex: 37095 ZKede
Man Dir: J J Mons; *Sales:* J P H Delissen; *Chief Editor:* G L M Vlaskamp; *Permissions:* Mrs M van Minnen-Essink
Subjects: Nature, Gardening, Cookery, Handicrafts, Medicine, How-to, Reference, Religion (Protestant), Bibles
Book Club: Spiegelserie
Founded: 1919
Miscellaneous: Firm is a member of the Kluwer Group (qv)
ISBN Publisher's Prefix: 90-210

Zuid Boekprodukties BV, Postbus 335, 5680 AH Best
General Dir: D J Rog
Imprints: Zuidboek, Hippoboek, Rekreaboek
Subjects: Pets, Nature Study, Gardening, Plants and Flowers, Sports, Crafts, Hobbies, Cookery, Games, Photography, Film, Children's
1982: 350 titles *Founded:* 1975
ISBN Publisher's Prefix: 90-6248

Zuid-Hollandsche UM, an imprint of BV Uitgeversmaatschappij Elsevier (qv)

Zwarte Beertjes, an imprint of Bruna Pockethuis BV (qv)

Uitgeverij **Zwijsen** BV, Gasthuisring 58, Postbus 805, Tilburg Tel: (013) 353635
Man Dirs: J N A Verwielen, G M Janssen
Subjects: Juveniles, Primary Textbooks
Founded: 1846
ISBN Publisher's Prefix: 90-276

Remainder Dealers

Icob cv, Postbus 392, 2400 AJ Alphen aan den Rijn (Located at: Ondernemingsweg 60, Alphen aan den Rijn) Tel: (01720) 37231 Telex: 39700 icob nl
Man Dir: Hans Meijer

Literary Agents

Auteursbureau Greta **Baars-Jelgersma**, Den Heuvel 73, NL-6881 VD-Velp Tel: (85) 635017 Telex: Incom 43776/11000
Also: Bovensteweg 46, NL-6585 KD Mook Tel: (8896) 1470
Specialization: International co-printing of illustrated books; mediation of copyrights; translations from Scandinavian and German languages into Dutch

Gans en Rombach Auteursagenten, Postbus 144, 2060 AC Bloemendaal Tel: (023) 262907 Telex: 41737
Contact: Coen J Rombach

International Bureau voor Auteursrecht BV, Verdiweg 171, 3816 KD Amersfoort Tel: (033) 752778
Contact: Hans Keuls

International Literatuur Bureau BV*, Postbus 10014, 1201 DA Hilversum (Located at: Koninginneweg 2A, 1217 KW Hilversum) Tel: (035) 13500 Cable Add: ILB Telex: 73201 ILB
Contact: Menno Kohn

Amina **Marix Evans**, Amstel 272A, 1017 AM Amsterdam Tel: (020) 237668 Cable Add: Amina Amsterdam Telex: 26401 intx nl
Contact: Amina Marix Evans

Prins en Prins, De Lairessestr 6, Postbus 5400, 1007 AK Amsterdam Tel: (020) 761001 Cable Add: prinsrights
Chief Executive: Henk Prins

Servire BV Uitgevers*, Secr Varkerisserstr 52, Katwijk aan Zee Tel: (01718) 16741
Chief Executive: Felix Erkelens
Also Publishers (qv)

Book Clubs

E C I voor Boeken en Platen BV,
Laanakkerweg 14-16, Industrieterrein
Hagestein, 4124 PB Vianen ZH Tel: (03473)
79911 Telex: 47449
Owned by: ECI voor Boeken en
Grammofoonplaten BV (qv), A W Bruna en
Zoon's Uitgeversmaatschappij BV (qv)

English Book Club*, Leidsestr 52, 1017 PC,
Amsterdam
The above address is for Netherlands
enquiries. Head office is Book Club
Associates, UK (qv under UK Book Clubs)
Owned by: W H Smith & Son Ltd (London)
and Doubleday & Co Inc (New York)

Nederlandse Boekenclub,
Prinsevinkenpark 2, The Hague
Netherlands Book Club
Manager: C A M Schink
Branch Off: Nederlandse Boekenclub (Boek
en Platt), Belgium (qv)
Subjects: General
Members: 350,000
Owned by: Succes BV (qv)

Nederlandse Lezerskring Boek en Plaat BV,
Wildenborch 2, Diemen NH, Postbus 2201,
1000 EK Amsterdam
Members: 700,000
Owned by: H J W Becht
Uitgeversmaatschappij BV (qv), Bosch en
Keuning NV (qv), BV Uitgeversmaatschappij
Elsevier (qv), Uitgeverij Hollandia bv (qv),
NV Holdingmaatschappij De Telegraaf,
Verlagsgruppe Georg von Holtzbrinck
Founded: 1966

Spiegelserie Boekenclub*, Postbus 235, 6710
BE Ede (Located at: Het Huis Kernhem,
Kernhemseweg 7, 6718 ZB Ede)
Owned by: Zomer en Keuning Boeken BV
(qv)

V C L, Gildestraat 5, 8263 AH Kampen
Owned by: Uitgeversmaatschappij J H Kok
BV (qv)

Major Booksellers

Athenaeum Boekhandel, Spui 14-16,
Amsterdam Tel: (020) 233933
Manager: G Schut

Broese-Kemink BV, Stadhuisbrug 5,
Postbus 38, 3500 AA Utrecht Tel: (030)
313804
Managers: H F Tammen, J P Eenens, J H J
Schevers
Service centre: Zandweg 69C, 3454 J W de
Meern Tel: (03406) 4224 Telex: 40411 Boek

H **Coebergh**, Gedempte Oude Gracht 74,
Postbus 98, Haarlem Tel: (023) 319198
Manager: P van Andel

Dekker en Nordemann BV, now Faxon
Europe BV (qv)

Dekker v d Vegt, Plein 1944, No 129, 6500
GT Nijmegen Tel: (080) 221010 Telex: 9900-
48202 deveg
Owned by: Kluwer NV (qv)

Faxon Europe BV, Postbus 197, 1000 AD
Amsterdam (Located at: N Z
Vorburgwal 60, Amsterdam Tel: (020)
240885
Manager: D T van der Vat
International Bookseller and Subscription
Agency, with branch in Munich, Federal
Republic of Germany
Owned by: F W Faxon Company, USA

Boekhandel **Gianotten** BV, Heuvelpoort 359,
5038 DW Tilburg
Orders to: Jac Oppenheimstr 15, 5042 NM-
Tilburg Tel: (013) 682991 Telex: 52460
Two branches in Tilburg and one in Breda
Manager: Theo P M van Meijel
Owned by: Kluwer NV (qv)

Ginsberg Univ Boekhandel, Schuttersveld 9,
Postbus 9003, 2300 PA Leiden Tel: (071)
124642, 141773
Manager: Mrs C Bos-Vink

Kooyker BV, Nieuwe Rijn 15-16,
Postbus 24, 2300 AA Leiden Tel: (071)
144146 Telex: 39434 Kooynl
Man Dir: Fj Arkenau

Rudolf **Müller** International Booksellers
VoF, Overtoom 487, Postbus 9016, 1006 AA
Amsterdam Tel: (020) 165955 Telex: 12582
Rmbks nl
Managers: R Muller, Mrs C M Griffioen

Martinus **Nijhoff** BV, Postbus 269, Lange
Voorhout 9-11, 2501 AX The Hague Tel:
(070) 469460 Cable Add: Bookshague
Telex: 34164 nijbu nl
Manager: D T van der Vat
Owned by: Kluwer NV (qv)

Boekhandel **Scheltema**, Holkema Vermeulen
BV, Spui 10, 1012 WZ Amsterdam Tel:
(020) 267212 Telex: 17193
Manager: M Bakker

Scholtens en Zoon BV, Grote Markt 43-44,
Postbus 1, 9700 AA-Groningen Tel: (050)
139788
Manager: Peter Schaatsberg
Owned by: A W Bruna en Zoon's
Uitgeversmaatschappij BV (qv)

Universitaire Boekhandel Nederland,
Damsterdiep 1, 9711 SG Groningen Tel:
(31050) 136305 Telex: 77314 Ubnsb nl
Also: Haringvliet 100, 3011 TH Rotterdam
Tel: (31010) 143209 Telex: 24718 Ubnrt nl
Manager: F Renssen

Major Libraries

Bibliotheek van het **Centraal Bureau** voor de
Statistiek, Prinses Beatrixlaan 428, Postbus
959, 2270 AZ Voorburg
Library of the Netherlands Central Bureau
of Statistics

Hoofdafdeling **Documentaire Research** en
Informatieverstrekking van de
Exportbevorderings- en Voorlichtingsdienst,
Bezuidenhoutseweg 151, 2594 AG The
Hague Tel: (070) 798933 Telex: 31099 Ecza
nl Cable Add: Econinf
Documentary Research and Information
Department of the Netherlands Foreign
Trade Agency (formerly Economic
Information Service)
Head: J H Ypma

Bibliotheek- en Documentatie-centrum van
de **Economische Voorlichtingsdienst**, now
Hoofdafdeling Documentaire Research en
Informatieverstrekking van de
Exportbevorderings- en Voorlichtingsdienst
(qv)

Gemeentebibliotheek Rotterdam, Hoogstr
110, 3011 PV Rotterdam Tel: (010)
338911/338922
Rotterdam Municipal Library
Librarian: P J Th Schoots

Bibliotheek van het **Internationaal Instituut**
voor Sociale Geschiedenis, Kabelweg 51,
1014 BA Amsterdam Tel: (020) 843695
Library of the International Institute of
Social History
Librarian: W A Roose

Koninklijke Bibliotheek*, Lange Voorhout
34, The Hague Tel: (070) 644920 Telex:
31500
Royal (National) Library
Publications: (in co-operation with others)
Dutch Bibliography — Brinkman's
Cumulatieve Catalogus; Centrale Catalogus
voor Periodieken (Union Catalogue of
Periodicals, in book form); *Treasures of the
Royal Library* (illuminated medieval
manuscripts); *Bibliography of Translations*
(from the Dutch) *of North and South
Netherlandic Publications; Bibliography of
Cartographic Materials in the Netherlands;
Bibliography of Studies on Dutch Language
and Literature*

Bibliotheek der **Koninklijke Nederlandse
Akademie** van Wetenschappen,
Kloveniersburgwal 29, 1011 JV Amsterdam
Library of Royal Netherlands Academy of
Arts and Sciences
Dir: Dr J A W Brak

Bibliotheek der **Landbouwhogeschool**,
Postbus 9100, 6700 HA Wageningen Tel:
(08370) 82005 Telex: 45015
Library of the Agricultural University

Openbare Bibliotheek, Bilderdijkstr 1-3,
2513 CM The Hague Tel: (070) 469235
Public Library

Rijksmuseum Meermanno-
Westreenianum/Museum van het Boek,
Prinsessegracht 30, 2514 AP The Hague
Tel: (070) 462700
Book Museum
Keeper: R E O Ekkart

Bibliotheek der **Rijksuniversiteit***,
Wittevrouwenstr 9-11, Postbus 16007, 3500
DA Utrecht Tel: (030) 333116 Telex: NL
47103
Librarian: Dr J van Heijst

Bibliotheek der **Rijksuniversiteit te
Groningen**, Oude Kijk in't Jatstr 5, Postbus
559, 9700 AN Groningen

Bibliotheek der **Rijksuniversiteit te Leiden**,
Wille Singel 27, Leiden
And Postbus 9501, 2300 RA-Leiden Tel:
(071) 148333 ext 7501 Telex: 31513
Librarian: J R de Groot

Universiteitsbibliotheek, Universiteit van
Amsterdam, Singel 425, 1012 WP
Amsterdam Tel: (020) 5259111
Librarian: Dr E Braches

Library Associations

Algemene Nederlandse Bond van
Leesbibliotheekhouders*, Litslaan 14,
Santpoort-Zuid Tel: 7566
Netherlands Association of Reference
Librarians

Centrum voor Literatuuronderzoekers*,
Debijeweg 82, Rotterdam
Centre for Literary Research — a section of
the Dutch Librarians' Association

Convent van Universiteitsbibliothekarissen
in Nederland, Association of University
Librarians in the Netherlands — see UKB

Federatie van Organisaties van Bibliotheek-,
Informatie-, Dokumentatiewezen (FOBID)*,
Taco Scheltemastr 5, The Hague Tel:
(070) 264351
Federation of Library Information and
Documentation Organizations
Co-ordinating Officer: C J M Bruin

Nederlands Bibliotheek en Lektuurcentrum
(NBLC), Taco Scheltemastr 5, Postbus
93054, 2509 AB The Hague Tel: (070)
264351 Telex: 32102 nblc nl
Netherlands Centre for Public Libraries and
Literature
Executive Dir: D Reumer
*Publication: Bibliotheek en Samenleving;
Open* (published jointly with 2 other
associations: Nederlandse Vereniging van

Bedrijfsarchivarissen and Nederlandse Vereniging van Bibliothekarissen)

Nederlandse Vereniging van Bedrijfsarchivarissen, Aalsburg 2526, 6602 WD Wijchen
Netherlands Association of Business Archivists
Publication: Open (published jointly with 2 other associations: Nederlands Bibliotheek en Lektuurcentrum and Nederlandse Vereniging van Bibliothekarissen)

Nederlandse Vereniging van Bibliothecarissen, Documentalisten en literatuuronderzoekers (NVB), pa Mrs H J Krikke-Schoolten, Nolweg 13, 4209 AW Schelluinen
Netherlands Librarians' Society
Secretary: G Koers
Publication: Open (published jointly with 2 other associations: Nederlands Bibliotheek en Lektuurcentrum and Nederlandse Vereniging van Bedrijfsarchivarissen)

Protestantse Stichting tot Bevordering van het Bibliotheekwezen en de Lectuurvoorlichting in Nederland*, Parkweg 20a, Voorburg
Protestant Foundation for the Promotion of Librarianship and Reading Information in the Netherlands
Publication: Prisma

Stichting Bibliotheek en Documentatieacademies, Keizersgracht 225, Postbus 10895, 1001 EW Amsterdam Tel: (020) 265155
Foundation for Library and Documentation Academies
Secretary: J J M de Leuw

U K B (Samenwerkingsverband van de Universiteits- en Hogeschoolbibliotheken en de Koninklijke Bibliotheek), c/o J L M van Dijk, Librarian, Limburg University, Postbus 616, 6200 MD Maastricht Tel: (043) 888427 Telex: 56726
President: W R H Koops
Secretary: Dr J L M van Dijk

Vereniging van Archivarissen in Nederland*, Postbus 897, 8901 BR Leeuwarden
Association of Archivists in the Netherlands
Executive Secretary: Gonny Koolen
Publication: Nederlands Archievenblad

Vereniging voor het Theologisch Bibliothecariaat, Postbus 289, 6500 AG Nijmegen
Association for Theological Librarianship (the above is the address of the Secretariat)
Executive Secretary: R van Dijk
Publications: Mededelingen van de VTB; Bibliografie Doctorale Scripties Theologie

Library Reference Books and Journals

Books

Bibliotheek-en Documentatiegids (Library and Documentation Guide), NOBIN, Van Karnebeeklaan 19, The Hague

Brinkman's Cumulatieve Catalogus (Dutch Bibliography), Koninklijke Bibliotheek, Lange Voorhout 34, The Hague

Journals

Archievenblad (Archive News), Association of Archivists in the Netherlands, Ter Pelkwykpark 21, Zwolle

Bibliotheek en Samenleving (Library and Social Life), Netherlands Centre for Public Libraries and Literature, Central Bureau, Taco Schetemastr 5, Postbus 2054, The Hague

Mededelingen (Communications), Association for Theological Librarianship, Doddendaal 20, Nijmegen

Open, professional journal for librarians, researchers, archivists and documentalists, Netherlands Librarians' Society, Abel Tasmankade 9, Haarlem (published jointly with Netherlands Centre for Public Libraries and Literature, Netherlands Association of Business Archivists and Van Loghum Slaterus BV, Postbus 23, 7400 GA Deventer)

Literary Associations and Societies

The **Dickens** Fellowship*, Banstr 60, Amsterdam Z
Honorary Secretary: Frank H Keene

Foundation for the Promotion of the Translation of Dutch Literature, Singel 450, 1017 AV Amsterdam Tel: (020) 231056/257189
Dir: Joost de Wit
Publication: Writing in Holland and Flanders

Maatschappij der Nederlandse Letterkunde, R Breugelmans, c/o Cobetstr 47, 2313 KA Leiden
Society of Netherlands Literature (the above is the address of the Secretariat)
Publications: Tijdschrift voor Nederlandse Taal- en Letterkunde (quarterly), *Jaarboek der Maatschappij* (annually)

Friesian P E N Centre, Wormerveerstr 126, 1013 SL Amsterdam
Secretary: Pier Boorsma

Netherlands Centre of the International P E N, Operalaan 39, 2907 KA Capelle, a/d IJssel
Secretary: Martin Mooij

Literary Periodicals

Amsterdamer Publikationen zur Sprache und Literatur (Amsterdam Publication on Language and Literature), Editions Rodopi NV, Keizersgracht 302-304, Amsterdam

Boeken-Zoekblad (Hard-to-Find Books), 'Stabo/All-Round' BV, Oosterweg 68, Groningen

Castrum Peregrini; journal for literature and art (text in German), Castrum Peregrini Presse, Herengracht 401, Postbus 645, Amsterdam

Forum der Letteren (Forum of Letters), Smits NV, Westeinde 135, 15 The Hague

Gids (Guide), Meulenhoff Nederland NV, Prinsengracht 468, Amsterdam

Hemelspleet (Poles Apart), Bilderdijksstr 45a, Rotterdam

Hollands Maandblad (Holland Monthly), Drukkeij Trio, Nobelstr 27, The Hague

Kentering (The Turning-point) literary review, Nijgh & Van Ditmas, Badhuisweg 232, The Hague

Lezen om te Leven (Reading as a Life Style), 'Stabo/All-Round' BV, Oosterweg 68, Groningen

Quaerendo; a quarterly journal from the Low Countries devoted to manuscripts and printed books (text mainly in English, occasionally in French and German), Theatrum Orbis Terrarum, Keizersgracht 526, Amsterdam

Revisor (The Inspector), Keizersgracht 608, Amsterdam

Trotwaer (The Pavement), (text in Frisian), Miedema Pers, Nieuweburen 97-103, Postbus 45, Leeuwarden

Writing in Holland and Flanders (text in English), Foundation for the Promotion of Dutch Literary Works, Singel 450, Amsterdam C

Literary Prizes

Amsterdam Prizes*
For the best drama, novel, poetry, essay, novella and short story. Awarded annually. Enquiries to Amsterdam City Government, Town Hall, O Z Voorburgwal 197, Amsterdam

F Bordewijk Prize
For the best Dutch novel. 4,500 Dutch florins. Awarded annually. Enquiries to Jan Campertstichting, Burg de Monchyplein 9, The Hague

Jan Campert Prize
For outstanding Dutch poetry. 4,500 Dutch florins. Awarded annually. Enquiries to Jan Campertstichting, Burg De Monchyplein 9, The Hague

Dutch Literature Prize, see International Literary Prizes

Dutch Prize for the Best Children's Book*
For the best Dutch children's books – Golden Slate Pencils (maximum 3) and 3,000 Dutch florins. For foreign, translated books – Silver Slate Pencils (maximum 9, minimum 7). Also a Golden Brush for the best Dutch illustrated children's book and two Silver Brushes for foreign illustrated work. Awarded annually. Occasionally a Golden Key for a children's/young persons' book with new developments (technically or in subject matter) is awarded. Enquiries to the Commission for the Collective Promotion of the Dutch Book, Langestr 61, 1015 AK Amsterdam

The G H 's-**Gravesande** Prize
For special services to literature. 4,500 Dutch florins. Awarded irregularly. Enquiries to Jan Campertstichting, Burg De Monchyplein 9, The Hague

J Greshoff Prize
For the best Dutch essay. 4,500 Dutch florins. Awarded every two years. Enquiries to Jan Campertstichting, Burg de Monchyplein 9, The Hague

Nienke van **Hichtum** Prize
For the best Dutch children's book. 4,500 Dutch florins. Awarded every two years. Enquiries to Jan Campertstichting, Burg de Monchyplein 9, The Hague

Lucy B and C W van der **Hoogt** Prize
To an outstanding Dutch writer. 1,000 Dutch florins and a medal. Awarded annually. Enquiries to Maatschappij der Nederlandse Letterkunde (Society of Netherlands Literature), c/o Cobetstr 47, 2313 KA Leiden

Constantijn **Huygens** Prize
To a distinguished Dutch author for all his works. 9,000 Dutch florins. Awarded annually. Enquiries to Jan Campertstichting, Burg De Monchyplein 9, The Hague

Reina **Prinsen-Geerlings** Prize*
Established by the parents of Reina Prinsen-Geerlings to commemorate her execution by the Germans and awarded to a young Dutch author. 200 Dutch florins. Awarded annually. Enquiries to Reina Prinsen-Geerlings Foundation, Koninginneweg 141, Amsterdam

State Prize for Children's and Youth Literature
For the best author's work for children and young people. 6,500 Dutch florins. Awarded triennially. Enquiries to Netherlands Ministry of Welfare, Health and Culture, Postbus 5406, 2280 HK Rijswijk

State Prize for Literature, the P C Hooft Prize
For important and original literary works in Dutch. 10,000 Dutch florins. Awarded annually where possible: one year for poetry, the next year for prose, the next year for literary essay. Enquiries to Netherlands Ministry of Welfare, Health and Culture, Postbus 5406, 2280 HK Rijswijk

Vijverberg Prize, replaced by The G H 's-Gravesande Prize (qv)

Netherlands Antilles

General Information

Language: Dutch. English and Spanish widely spoken
Religion: Roman Catholic
Population: 246,000
Literacy rate (1971): 92.5%
Bank Hours: 0830-1130, 1400-1600 Monday-Friday. St Maarten: 0800-1300 Monday-Friday (also 1600-1700 on Friday)
Shop Hours: 0800-1200, 1400-1800 Monday-Saturday
Currency: 100 cents = 1 Netherlands Antilles gulden
Export/Import Information: No tariff on books or advertising. No import licences. No exchange controls
Copyright: Berne, UCC (see International section)

Publishers

Curaçaosche Drukkerij en Uitgevers Maatschappij*, Pietermaaiweg, Willemstad, Curaçao
Subjects: Geography, Travel

Van **Dorp Aruba** NV*, Nassaustr 77, PO Box 596, Oranjestad, Aruba

Drukkerij de Stad NV*, Compagniestr 41, Willemstad, Curaçao
Dir: Ronald Yrausquin
Subject: Law

Ediciones Populares*, Compagniestr 41, Willemstad, Curaçao
Dir: Ronald Yrausquin
Subjects: Popular Sciences, Literature
Founded: 1929

Tipografia Nacional*, Bitterstr 3, Curaçao
Subject: Law

De **Wit** Stores NV, VAD Bldg, L G Smith Blvd 110, Oranjestad, Aruba Tel: 23500 Cable Add: Dewitstores Telex: 5137 Vadws na
Man Dir: F Olmtak
Subjects: History of the Netherlands Antilles, Papiamentu Language Textbooks in English, Dutch and Spanish
Bookshop: Aruba Boekhandel (qv under Major Booksellers)

Major Booksellers

Aruba Boekhandel, Nassaustr 94, Oranjestad, Aruba Tel: 23648 Cable Add: Dewitstores Telex: 5137 Vadws na
Manager/Buyer: Mrs E Kock
Parent Company: De Wit Stores NV (qv)

Boekhandel **Augustinus**, Abraham de Veerstr 12, Curaçao Tel: 612782

Van **Dorp-Eddine** NV, PO Box 3001, Willemstad, Curaçao
Also: Schottegatweg Oost 185 Tel: 78966; Roodeweg 13 Tel: 26133/26139/26180; Breedestr Punda Tel: 611502/612177; Promenade Winkel Centrum Tel: 70544/70575

Kantoor Boekhandel Salinja NV KBS*, Schottegatweg Oost 106 Tel: 37288

Mensing's Caminada*, Schottegatweg Oost Tel: 70222
Manager: S Mensing

Novo Gift and Book Store*, Fokkerweg 74 Tel: 614118

Boekhandel **Salas***, Fokkerweg 50 Tel: 612303/612201/612564

Major Libraries

Openbare Leeszaal en Bibliotheek, Johan van Walbeeckplein 13, Willemstad, Curaçao Tel: 611582/612840
Public Reading Room and Library
Librarian: Rose Marie de Paula

Openbare Leeszaal en Boekerij*, Eilandgebied, Aruba
Public Reading Room and Library
Librarian: Alice van Romondt

Universiteits-Bibliotheek, Universiteit van de Nederlandse Antillen*, PO Box 682, Jan Noorduynweg z/n, Willemstad, Curaçao Tel: 84422 Telex: 110111
Librarian: Maritza F Eustatia

Library Associations

Asociation di Biblioteka i Archivo di Korsow (Carbido)*, Stoppelweg 4, Willemstad, Curaçao Tel: 23434
Association of Libraries and Archives
President: Maritza F Eustatia

New Caledonia

General Information

Language: French
Population: 138,000
Literacy Rate (1976): 91.3%
Business Hours: 0730-1100, 1400-1800 Monday-Friday; 0730-1100 Saturday
Currency: CFP franc
Export/Import Information: No tariff on books except luxury bindings and children's picture books. Advertising matter generally dutiable. Special Tax on all. No import licences required

Publishers

Modernix-Hachette Calédonie, 11 Ave du Maréchal-Foch, BP L1, Nouméa Tel: 272001 Telex: Cotrans 120 nm
Publisher and Distributor
Bookshop: At above address

Major Booksellers

Barrau*, 16 et 18 rue Anatole-France, Nouméa Tel: 3093

J-P Leyraud, 32 rue de la République, Nouméa Tel: 286032

Modernix, 11 ave du Maréchal-Foch, Nouméa Tel: 272001
Owned by: Modernix-Hachette Calédonie, Publisher (qv)

Montaigne*, 24 rue de Sébastopol, BP 267 Tel: 3488 Nouméa

Pentecost*, 24 rue de l'Alma, Nouméa Tel: 2114
Importer/Exporter

Major Libraries

Bibliothèque **Bernheim**, Bibliothèque territoriale de la Nouvelle-Caledonie, BP G1, Nouméa (Located at: no. 17, route 13, Nouméa) Tel: 272343
Librarian: Hélène Colombani
Publications include: Bulletin de liaison de la Bibliothèque Bernheim (quarterly)

South Pacific Commission Library*, South Pacific Commission, PO Box D5, Nouméa Cedex

New Zealand

General Information

Language: English
Religion: Predominantly Protestant
Population: 3.1 million
Bank Hours: 1000-1600 Monday-Friday
Shop Hours: 0900-1730 Monday-Friday (open until 2100 either Thursday or Friday). Some local shops open Saturday
Currency: 100 cents = 1 New Zealand dollar
Export/Import Information: No tariffs on books and advertising. No import licences, but literature 'indecent' or 'advocating violence, lawlessness, disorder or seditiousness' prohibited. No special exchange controls
Copyright: UCC, Berne, Florence (see International section)

Book Trade Organizations

Book Publishers Association of New Zealand, Box 78071, Grey Lynn, Auckland 2 (Located at: 180 Surrey Cres, Grey Lynn, Auckland 2) Tel: 767251
President: G Beattie; *Dir:* Gerard Reid
Publication: Publishing News (members only)

Booksellers Association of New Zealand (Inc), PO Box 11-377, Wellington Tel: (04) 728678
President: Ian Thomas; *Dir:* Kate R Fortune

Christian Booksellers' Association (NZ Chapter), 12 Rangiatea Rd, Epsom, Auckland 3
Secretary: M J Frith

The **New Zealand Authors** Fund, Department of Internal Affairs, Private Bag, Wellington Tel: 738699 Cable Add: Internal
Secretary: G Martell

New Zealand Book Trade Organization Inc, PO Box 11-377, Manners St, Wellington (Located at: Book House, 86 Boulcott St, Wellington) Tel: (04) 728678
Chairman: J Seymour; *Deputy Chairman:* R Goddard; *Secretary:* Kate Fortune

New Zealand Copyright Council, PO Box 78071, Auckland 2
Chairman: Gerard Reid; *Secretary:* Anne Rees

Standard Book Numbering Agency, National Library of New Zealand, Private Bag, Wellington 1 Tel: (04) 722101 Telex: NZ 30076
Librarian: D Williams (Bibliographic Unit of National Library)

Book Trade Reference Books and Journals

Books

New Zealand Books in Print, D W Thorpe Pty Ltd, 384 Spencer St, Melbourne, Victoria, Australia 3003

Journals

New Zealand Book World; journal of the New Zealand book trade, PO Box 9405, Courtenay Pl, Wellington

New Zealand Bookseller & Publisher, Stockton House (Publisher), PO Box 46, Albany, Auckland

New Zealand National Bibliography, National Library of New Zealand, PMB, Wellington 1

Spotlight; on the book, stationery, magazine, greeting cards, and toys trades in New Zealand, PO Box 3911, Auckland

Publishers

A B P (NZ) Ltd, see Associated Book Publishers (NZ) Ltd

Action Publications, PO Box 5160, Christchurch (Located at: 49 Hudson St, Christchurch) Tel: 516460
Man Dir: Desmond Sewell; *Sales:* Andrew Sewell
Subjects: Secondary Textbooks, Geography, Social Studies
1981: 3 titles *1982:* 5 titles *Founded:* 1971
ISBN Publisher's Prefix: 0-908586

Allied Press Ltd, 70 Lower High St, PO Box 517, Dunedin Tel: (024) 774760 Telex: Odt nz 5692
Man Dir: Werner Kornet
Parent Company: Otago Press and Produce Ltd, Lower Stuart St, Dunedin
Subjects: General Non-fiction, especially concerning New Zealand
Bookshop: Star Shop, Lower Stuart St, Dunedin
1981: 2 titles *1982:* 4 titles *Founded:* 1863
ISBN Publisher's Prefix: 0-86466

Ashton Scholastic Ltd, PO Box 12328, Auckland (Located at: 9-11 Fairfax Ave, Penrose, Auckland 6) Tel: (02) 596089 Cable Add: Ashco Telex: 21203
Man Dir: D H Nicol
Parent Company: Scholastic Inc, 730 Broadway, New York, NY 10003, USA
Branch Off: 290 Clyde Rd, PO Box 29031, Fendalton, Christchurch 5 Tel: 518614
Subjects: Educational, Children's, Periodicals, Teaching Aids
Book Clubs: Lucky Arrow, Teenage, Teachers' Book Shelf
1981-82: 2 titles *1982-83:* 2 titles *Founded:* 1962
ISBN Publisher's Prefix: 0-86896

Asia Pacific Research Unit Ltd*, PO Box 3978, Wellington Tel: (04) 736363 Cable Add: Haaspress
Man Dir: Anthony Haas; *Editorial:* Pam Brown
Associate Company: Asia Pacific Books (at above address)
Branch Offs: Auckland, New Zealand; Suva, Fiji; Sydney, Australia
Subjects: Economics, Geography, Politics, Social Change
Founded: 1970
ISBN Publisher's Prefix: 0-908583

Associated Book Publishers (NZ) Ltd, Private Bag, Auckland (Located at: 61 Beach Rd, Auckland) Tel: 796369 Telex: Abpub NZ 21944
General Manager: Kenneth W Shearman
Parent Company: Associated Book Publishers PLC, UK (qv for associate companies)
Subsidiary Companies: Methuen New Zealand, Sweet & Maxwell (NZ) Ltd (both at above address)
Subjects: General, Annuals
1981: 12 titles *1982:* 15 titles
ISBN Publisher's Prefixes: 0-456, 0-457

Auckland University Press, University of Auckland, PMB, Auckland Tel: (09) 737654/737656
Managing Editor: R D McEldowney
Orders to: (in New Zealand) Whitcoulls Ltd, PO Box 5844, Auckland; (outside New Zealand) nearest branch of Oxford University Press
Subjects: Demography, Ethnology, Geography, History, Biography, Language, Literature, Fiction, Poetry
1981: 8 titles *1982:* 5 titles *Founded:* 1966
Miscellaneous: Auckland University Press books are published jointly with the Oxford University Press (qv)
ISBN Publisher's Prefix: 0-19

Australia & New Zealand Book Co Pty Ltd, New Zealand Branch Office, PO Box 33-406, Auckland 9 (Located at: Unit 2, 10 Colway Pl, Glenfield, Auckland 10) Tel: (09) 4445346 Telex: 60184
Manager: John Seymour
Parent Company: Australia & New Zealand Book Co Pty Ltd, Australia (qv)
Founded: 1979

Thomas **Avery** & Sons Ltd, PO Box 442, New Plymouth, North Island Tel: (067) 78122 Cable Add: Avery New Plymouth
Man Dir: D V Avery
Subjects: History, Secondary & Primary Textbooks
Founded: 1882
Bookshop: Thomas Avery & Sons Ltd, 79 Devon St, New Plymouth, North Island

David **Bateman** Ltd, PO Box 65062, Mairangi Bay, Auckland 10 Tel: 4444680 Telex: NZ 60824 Hubpub
Shipping Add: Golden Heights, 30-34 View Rd, Glenfield, Auckland 10
Man Dir, Editorial: David L Bateman; *Sales:* David Presland Tack; *Publicity, Rights & Permissions:* Janet Bateman
Branch Offs: c/o Tony Tizzard, Fiesta Products, PO Box 4176, Christchurch; Sue Frewin, PO Box 678, Wellington
Subjects: Natural History, Art, Travel, Reference, General Non-fiction, Juveniles
1981: 3 titles *1982:* 8 titles *Founded:* 1979
ISBN Publisher's Prefix: 0-908610

Benton Ross Publishers Ltd, PO Box 33055, Takapuna, Auckland 9 (Located at: 9 Ewen Alison Ave, Devonport, Auckland 9) Tel: Auckland 451609
Man Dir, Editorial, Production: Robert M Ross; *Sales, Publicity:* Helen E Benton
Subjects: History, Politics, New Zealand
1981: 2 titles *1982:* 3 titles *Founded:* 1980
ISBN Publisher's Prefix: 0-908636

Brick Row Publishing Co Ltd, PO Box 190, Wellington 1 Tel: 897610 Cable Add: Brickrow Wellington
Editorial Office: 1 Cabot Place, Kingston Heights, Wellington 2 Tel: 897610
Man Dir, Editorial: Oswald L Kraus; *Sales, Publicity:* Ruth Kraus
Associate Company: Graphic and Allied Systems, PO Box 190, Wellington 1
Subjects: Poetry, Fiction, Crafts, General Non-fiction
1981: 3 titles *Founded:* 1978
ISBN Publisher's Prefix: 0-908595

Brookfield Press+, PO Box 1201 Auckland (Located at: 87 Edmund St, Auckland 5) Tel: 557637
Man Dir, Editorial, Production, Rights & Permissions: Richard Webster; *Sales, Publicity:* Don Wall
Parent Company: Brookings Bookshop (1971) Ltd (at above address)
Subsidiary Company: Brookings Agencies Ltd (at above address)
Subjects: General Fiction, New Zealand History, Poetry, Philosophy, Astrology, Psychic Phenomena, Esoteric
1981: 3 titles *1982:* 17 titles *Founded:* 1971
ISBN Publisher's Prefix: 0-86467

Bush Press Communications Ltd, PO Box 33-029, Takapuna, Auckland 9 (Located at: 141 Hurstmere Rd, Takapuna, Auckland 9) Tel: 495649
Man Dir: Gordon Ell
Subjects: Wildlife and Outdoor, Guide Books, Applied Arts, Hobbies, General New Zealand Non-fiction
1981: 3 titles *1982:* 8 titles *Founded:* 1979
ISBN Publisher's Prefix: 0-908608

Butterworths of New Zealand Ltd, PO Box 472, 33-35 Cumberland Pl, Wellington Tel: 851479 Cable Add: Butterwort Wellington Telex: 31306
Man Dir: D A Day; *Production:* P Kirk; *Sales:* W R Morrison
Parent Company: Butterworth & Co (Publishers) Ltd, UK (qv)
Subsidiary Company: IPC Business Press Ltd, PO Box 5002, Auckland
Subjects: Legal, Medical, Scientific, Technical
Bookshop: 14 Darby St, Auckland 1
1981: 7 titles *1982:* 9 titles *Founded:* 1914
ISBN Publisher's Prefix: 0-409

Cape Catley Ltd*, PO Box 199, Picton (Located at: Whatamongo Bay, Queen Charlotte Sounds) Tel: 1086 W, Picton
Man Dir: Christine C Catley
Orders to: A H & A W Reed, PO Box 14-029, Kilbirnie, Wellington 3
Subjects: Fiction, Memoirs, Local History
1981: 3 titles
ISBN Publisher's Prefix: 0-908561

Capper Press Ltd+, PO Box 1388, Christchurch Tel: 67170 Cable Add: Avonprint Christchurch
Publicity: Don Ellis
Associate Company: Avon Fine Prints Ltd
Subjects: Reprints of rare and out-of-print New Zealand, Australian and Pacific books

NEW ZEALAND

Bookshops: The Bookshop in Campbell Grant, 202 Hereford St, Christchurch

Caveman Publications Ltd, now Northcott Reeves, Publishers (qv)

The **Caxton** Press, 113 Victoria St, PO Box 25088, Christchurch Tel: 68516 Cable Add: Imprint
Man Dir: E B Bascand
Subjects: General Fiction, Belles Lettres, Poetry, Biography, History, Music, Art, High-priced Paperbacks, Juveniles, Education
ISBN Publisher's Prefix: 0-908563

Cicada Press, PO Box 64-009, Birkenhead South, Auckland 10 Tel: 480890
Man Dir: R K St Cartmail
Subjects: Poetry, Fiction, Fine Arts, Religion
1981: 1 title *1982:* 3 titles *Founded:* 1978
ISBN Publisher's Prefix: 0-908599

William **Collins** Publishers Ltd, PO Box 1, Auckland (Located at: 31 View Rd, Glenfield) Tel: 4443740 Cable Add: Folio Telex: 21685
Man Dir: B D Phillips
Branch Offs: PO Box 3737, Wellington; 234 Barbadoes St, PO Box 2162, Christchurch
Subjects: Fiction, History, Juveniles, Arts, Maps, Reference, Natural Science, Paperbacks, Educational, New Zealand titles
Founded: 1870
Miscellaneous: Firm is a branch of William Collins Sons & Co Ltd, UK (qv)

Doubleday New Zealand Ltd*, 8 Taylors Rd, Morningside, Auckland 3
Manager: Keith Paterson
Parent Company: Doubleday Australia Pty Ltd, Australia (qv)
Book Clubs: See Doubleday New Zealand Ltd, Book Club Division in Book Club section for individual clubs.

Dunmore Press Ltd, PO Box 5115, Palmerston North (Located at: 661 Main St, Palmerston North) Tel and Cable Add: 79242 Telex: Dunmore NZ 3960
Chairman: John Dunmore; *General Manager, Editorial:* Patricia Chapman; *Marketing:* Kevin Chapman; *Rights & Permissions:* Joanne Russ
Subjects: History, Fiction, General, Academic and University Textbooks
1981: 19 titles *1982:* 20 titles *Founded:* 1975
ISBN Publisher's Prefixes: 0-908564, 0-86469

Forum, an imprint of Sevenseas Publishing Pty Ltd (qv)

Fourth Estate Books Ltd, PO Box 9344, Wellington Tel: 859019 Cable Add: Natbus
Productions Manager: Caroline Mitchell
Parent Company: Fourth Estate Holdings
Subjects: Business, Law, Politics
Founded: 1976

Golden Press Pty Ltd, Private Bag, Rosebank, Auckland 7 (Located at: 717 Rosebank Rd, Avondale, Auckland) Tel: 884588/887763, also Christchurch 892179 Cable Add: Gold Press Auckland
General Manager: Alan Smith; *Marketing Services:* Marie Gerrard; *Sales:* Bruce Campbell
Parent Company: Western Publishing Co, USA
Imprints: Golden, Golden Press, Whitman
Branch Off: 35 Osborne St, Christchurch

Heinemann Publishers (New Zealand) Ltd+, PO Box 36064, Northcote Central, Auckland 9 Tel: 487193 Cable Add: Hebooks Telex: NZ 21902 Hebooks
Warehouse: Corner College Rd and Kilham Ave, Northcote, Auckland 9
Man Dir, Publicity, Rights & Permissions: D J Heap; *Sales:* Peter Redgrove; *Editorial,*
Production: David Ling
Parent Company: Heinemann Educational Books International Ltd, UK (qv for associate companies)
Subjects: University & School Textbooks, Fiction, Hobbies, Technical, Children's, General, Medical, Religious
1981: 19 titles *1982:* 20 titles *Founded:* 1969
ISBN Publisher's Prefix: 0-86863

Hodder & Stoughton Ltd, PO Box 3858, Auckland 1 (Located at: 44-46 View Rd, Glenfield, Auckland 10) Tel: 4443640 Cable Add: Expositor Auckland Telex: NZ 21422
Man Dir: M H Duffett
Parent Company: Hodder & Stoughton Ltd, UK (qv)
Subjects: Fiction, Non-fiction, Education, Children's books
1981: 18 titles *1982:* 21 titles

Holt-Saunders Pty Ltd, 10 Moa St, PO Box 22-245, Otahuhu, Auckland 6 Tel: 2762087 Cable Add: Aytcholt, Auckland
Manager: Ian C Swallow
Associate Company: Holt-Saunders Ltd, UK (qv for associate companies)

Hutchinson Group (NZ) Ltd, 32-34 View Rd, Glenfield, PO Box 40086, Auckland 10 Tel: 4447197/524 Telex: 60824 Hutpub
Man Dir: K C Pounder
Associate Company: Hutchinson Publishing Group Ltd, UK (qv)
Subjects: General & Academic
1982: 2 titles *Founded:* 1977
ISBN Publisher's Prefix: 0-09

Jacaranda Wiley Ltd, PO Box 2259, Auckland (Located at: 4 Kirk St, Grey Lynn, Auckland) Tel: 764620 Cable Add: Japress
Miscellaneous: Firm is a branch of Jacaranda Wiley, Australia (qv)

The **Joint Board** of Christian Education of Australia and New Zealand, PO Box 6133, Te Aro, Wellington 1
See entry under Australian head office for full details

Lindon Publishing, PO Box 39225, Auckland West Tel: 760647 Telex: Aknz 2553 CPO (Lindon)
Man Dir, Editorial, Publicity, Rights & Permissions: Michael Guy; *Sales:* Cathy Toohey; *Production:* Phillip Ridge
Subjects: Humour, Adventure, Cookery, General
1981: 5 titles *1982:* 13 titles *Founded:* 1981
ISBN Publisher's Prefix: 0-86470

Lodestar Press*, PO Box 6154, Wellesley St, Auckland
Man Dirs: D Lowe, K I Bullock; *Editorial, Sales, Production:* D Lowe
Subjects: Transport, Industrial Archaeology, Local History
1981: 7 titles *Founded:* 1975
ISBN Publisher's Prefix: 0-86465

Longman Paul Ltd+, CPO Box 4019, Auckland 1 (Located at: 182-190 Wairau Rd, Takapuna, Auckland 10) Tel: (09) 4444968 Cable Add: Freegrove Telex: NZ 21041
Publishing Dir: Rosemary Stagg; *Editors:* John Barnett, Jan Chilwell, Ken Harrop; *Sales Manager:* Elizabeth Nelson
Associate Company: Longman Group Ltd, UK (qv)
Subjects: General Fiction, Primary, Secondary & Tertiary Textbooks
1981: 22 titles *1982:* 17 titles *Founded:* 1968
ISBN Publisher's Prefix: 0-582

Thomas C **Lothian** Pty Ltd, 88 Nelson St, PO Box 68247, Auckland Tel: 733692 Cable Add: Lothwell Telex: NZ 60455
Manager: D M Forrester
Head Office: Thomas C Lothian Pty Ltd, 4-12 Tattersalls Lane, Melbourne, Victoria, Australia
Subjects: General Non-fiction, Educational, Children's
Founded: 1954
ISBN Publisher's Prefix: 0-85091

McGraw-Hill Book Co, New Zealand Ltd, 113 Vincent St, CPO Box 85, Auckland 1 Tel: 779368
Manager: Janet Powell
Associate Company: McGraw-Hill Book Co (UK) Ltd, UK (qv)
Subjects: Educational
Founded: 1974
ISBN Publisher's Prefix: 0-07

John **McIndoe** Ltd, PO Box 694, Dunedin Tel: 770355
Shipping Add: 51 Crawford St, Dunedin
Man Dir: J H McIndoe; *Advertising, Publicity, Rights & Permissions:* B L Turner
Subjects: General Fiction, Belles Lettres, Poetry, Biography, History, How-to, Music, Art, Reference, High-priced Paperbacks, Medicine, General Science, University Textbooks
Founded: 1893
ISBN Publisher's Prefixes: 0-908565, 0-86868

The **Macmillan Company** of New Zealand Ltd+, PO Box 33-570, Takapuna 9, Auckland 1332 (Located at: 48 Northcote Rd, Takapuna) Tel: (486) 090 Cable Add: Macpublish Telex: Coatink NZ 21971
General Manager, Sales, Production: David Joel; *Editorial, Rights & Permissions:* Mrs Raewyn Williams; *Publicity:* Mrs Carol Coffey
Parent Company: Macmillan Publishers Ltd, UK (qv)
1981: 6 titles *1982:* 6 titles *Founded:* 1977
ISBN Publisher's Prefix: 0-333

Mallinson Rendel Publishers Ltd, 5A Grass St, Oriental Bay, PO Box 9409, Wellington Tel: 857340
Joint Man Dirs: E A Mallinson, D Rendel; *Publicity:* Ann Mallinson
Associate Company: David Rendel Associates Ltd, PO Box 10058, Wellington
Subjects: Historical, Social, Philosophical, Poetry, Juveniles
1981: 8 titles *1982:* 6 titles *Founded:* 1980
ISBN Publisher's Prefix: 0-908606

Methuen New Zealand, a subsidiary of Associated Book Publishers (New Zealand) Ltd (qv)

Millwood Press Ltd, 291b Tinakori Rd, Wellington Cable Add: Siersprod
Dirs: Jim and Judy Siers
Subjects: New Zealand and Pacific
ISBN Publisher's Prefix: 0-908582

Moa Publications Ltd*, PO Box 26092, Auckland (Located at: 23A Pah Rd, Epsom, Auckland) Tel: 655306 Cable Add: Moabooks
Man Dir: John G Blackwell
Imprint: Orakau House
Subjects: Sport, General
1981: 7 titles *1982:* 10 titles *Founded:* 1971
ISBN Publisher's Prefix: 0-908570

G W **Moore** Ltd, PO Box 26-222, Epsom, Auckland (Located at: 69 Great South Rd, Remuera, Auckland) Tel: 548283
Man Dir: G W Moore; *Marketing Manager:* Graham O Walker
Bookshop: The Church Bookroom, 69 Great South Rd, Remuera, Auckland 1
Founded: 1963

New Zealand Council for Educational Research, PO Box 3237, Wellington Tel: 847939 Cable Add: Edsearch
Dir: John E Watson; *Sales Dir:* Lynette

Hardie Wills; *Publicity Dir, Rights & Permissions:* Alistair T A Campbell
Subject: Educational Materials
Founded: 1934
ISBN Publisher's Prefix: 0-908567

New Zealand Government Printing Office*, Private Bag, Wellington Tel: 737320 Telex: 31370 Govprnt
Bookshops: Hannaford Bldgs, Rutland St, Auckland; 159 Hereford St, Christchurch; Ward St, Hamilton; Princes St, Dunedin
ISBN Publisher's Prefix: 0-477

Newrick Associates Ltd*, PO Box 820, Wellington Tel: 728231/843676 Cable Add: Backgam Telex: 3353 AH Newrick
Man Dir: Henry P Newrick
Associate Companies: Medici Galleries Ltd, Professional Publications (qv)
Subjects: Art, Antiques, Reference
Founded: 1967

Nexus Books*, PO Box 67-008, Mount Eden, Auckland 3
Manager: A J C Begg
Subject: Mathematics
Founded: 1973
ISBN Publisher's Prefix: 0-85912

Northcott Reeves, Publishers, PO Box 1458, Dunedin (Located at: 2nd Floor, OSB Building, 106 George St, Dunedin) Tel: 772326
Publisher: Trevor Reeves; *Distribution:* Richard Layton
Subjects: Literature, Non-fiction, Health, Welfare, Medical, Social, Politics, Humour, Women's Books, Science Speculation, Law, Architecture
1982: 1 title *Founded:* 1962
ISBN Publisher's Prefix: 0-908562

Nova Pacifica Publishing Co Ltd+, PO Box 11-106 Wellington (Located at: 2-14 Allen St, Wellington Tel: 849126 Telex: NZ 3588 Attn Nova Pacifica
Man Dir, Editorial, Sales: Murray Humphries; *Production:* Raymond Labone
Subjects: Natural History, History of Science, New Zealand, General
1981: 1 title *1982:* 2 titles *Founded:* 1979
ISBN Publisher's Prefix: 0-908603

Orakau House, an imprint of Moa Publications Ltd (qv)

Otago Heritage Books, PO Box 5361, Dunedin Tel: 771500
Editorial: G J Griffiths; *Rights & Permissions:* J A Cox
Subjects: Local History, Educational
Bookshop: 356 Moray Place East, Dunedin
1982: 14 titles *Founded:* 1977

Outrigger Publishers, PO Box 13049, Hamilton
Man Dir, Editorial: Norman Simms; *Sales:* Peter Gibbons; *Publicity:* Martha Simms
USA Office: 814 Broadway, New York, NY 10003, USA
Subjects: Literature, Criticism, Folklore, Periodicals
ISBN Publisher's Prefix: 0-908571

Oxford University Press, PO Box 5294, 1st Floor, Trentham House, 28 Wakefield St, Auckland 1 Tel: (09) 799339/799514 Cable Add: Oxonian, Auckland Telex: NZ 60777
Regional Manager: David Cunningham (OUP Melbourne); *Managing Editor:* Anne French; *Sales Manager:* Noel Young
Subjects: History, Biography, Literature, Art, The Pacific, Children's Books
1982: 22 titles *1983:* 14 titles *Founded:* 1947
Miscellaneous: Branch of Oxford University Press, UK (qv)
ISBN Publisher's Prefix: 0-19

Pegasus Press Ltd, 14 Oxford Terrace, PO Box 2244, Christchurch 1 Tel: 64509
Chairman, Man Dir: Don Wallace; *Editor:* Robin Muir; *Rights & Permissions:* Pamela Rogers
Subjects: General Fiction, Poetry, Biography, History, Sports, Library and Paperback editions
Founded: 1948
ISBN Publisher's Prefix: 0-908568

Penguin Books (NZ) Ltd, PO Box 4019, Auckland 1 (Located at: 183-190 Wairau Rd, Auckland 10) Tel: 4444965 Cable Add: Penguinook Auckland Telex: 21041
Man Dir: Graham Beattie; *Sales & Publicity:* Colin Cox
Parent Company: Penguin Books Ltd, UK (qv)
Founded: 1973
ISBN Publisher's Prefix: 0-14

Pilgrims South Press Ltd*, PO Box 5101, Moray Pl, Dunedin (Located at: 371 York Pl, Dunedin) Tel: (024) 778275
Man Dir, Editorial, Production, Rights & Permissions: Stephen Higginson; *Sales, Publicity:* Niki Stewart
Branch Off: PO Box 9612, Newmarket, Auckland
Subjects: Art, Literature, Children's, History, Sociology, Anthropology
1981: 16 titles *Founded:* 1976

Pitman Publishing NZ Ltd*, PO Box 38688, Petone, Wellington
Associate Company: Pitman Publishing Ltd, UK (qv)
ISBN Publisher's Prefix: 0-85896

Port Nicholson Press Ltd+, PO Box 11-838 Wellington (Located at: 15 Mahina Rd, Eastbourne, Wellington
Man Dir, Editorial: Bridget Williams; *Sales:* Roy Parsons; *Production:* Lindsay Missen
Subjects: New Zealand Literature, History, Art, Natural History
1981: 1 title *1982:* 6 titles *Founded:* 1981
ISBN Publisher's Prefix: 0-908635

Price Milburn & Co Ltd, Private Bag, Petone (Located at: Corner Waione and Kirkcaldie Sts, Petone) Tel: (04) 687179 Cable Add: Mice Wellington
General Manager: Sidney Heppleston; *Sales Manager, Editor, Rights & Permissions:* Beverley Price
Parent Company: Education House Ltd
Subjects: Juveniles, Social Science, University, Secondary & Primary Textbooks, particularly Junior Readers
Founded: 1957
Miscellaneous: Publishes for New Zealand Institute of International Affairs, New Zealand University Press, Victoria University Press(qv), New Zealand Council for Civil Liberties, the Gondwanaland Press and Kea Press imprints
ISBN Publisher's Prefix: 0-7055

Professional Publications*, PO Box 820, Wellington Tel: 728231 Cable Add: Backgam Telex: 3353 AH Newrick
Man Dir: Henry P Newrick
Associate Companies: Medici Galleries Ltd, Newrick Associates Ltd (qv)
Subjects: Business, Economics, Taxation
Founded: 1979

A H & A W **Reed** Ltd Publishers, 68-74 Kingsford Smith St, Wellington Tel: (04) 873045 Cable Add: Reedkiwi Telex: NZ 31489
Executive Chairman: J M Reed; *Publisher:* P M Bradwell; *Managing Editor:* Geoff Walker
Branch Offs: 16 Beresford St, Auckland; 85 Thackeray St, Christchurch (both in New Zealand)
Subjects: General, Non-fiction, Biography, History, How-to, Art, Reference, Trade Paperbacks, Social Science, Politics, Horticulture, Natural History, Outdoor Pursuits, Sport, Cookery
1981-82: 69 titles *1982-83:* 72 titles
Founded: 1907
ISBN Publisher's Prefix: 0-589

Northcott **Reeves**, Publishers, see under Northcott

Ray **Richards** Publisher, PO Box 31240, Milford, Auckland 9 (Located at: 49 Aberdeen Rd, Castor Bay, Auckland 9) Tel: 469681
Man Dir: Ray Richards; *Editorial:* Barbara Richards; *Production:* Don Sinclair
Associate Company: Richards Literary Agency (qv)
Branch Off: 54 Ranui Terrace, Linden, Wellington
Subjects: New Zealand Biography, History, Agriculture
1982: 6 titles *1983:* 3 titles *Founded:* 1978
ISBN Publisher's Prefix: 0-908596

Benton **Ross**, Publishers Ltd, see Benton

Sevenseas Publishing Pty Ltd, 5-7 Tory St, PO Box 1431, Wellington 1 Tel: 859759 Cable Add: Vikseven
Man Dir, Editorial, Production, Rights & Permissions: Murdoch Riley; *Sales, Publicity Dir:* K Southern
Associate Companies: Viking Record Co Ltd, Delta Trading Co Ltd
Imprints: Forum, Viking Sevenseas Ltd
Branch Off: ANZ Bank Bldg, 68 Pitt St, Sydney, Australia
Subjects: How-to, Music, Art, South Pacific, Health, Nutrition, General
1982: 2 titles *1983:* 3 titles *Founded:* 1963
ISBN Publisher's Prefix: 0-85467

Shortland Educational Publications, PO Box 56133, Auckland Tel: 689959 Cable Add: Newspress
Managing Editor: Wendy Pye
Parent Company: NZ Newspapers Ltd, PO Box 1409, Auckland
Branch Offs: Newspaper House, Wellington; Christchurch Star, Christchurch
Subjects: Gardening, Cookery, Sports, Children's Activities, General
Founded: 1977
ISBN Publisher's Prefix: 0-86867

Southern Press Ltd, PO Box 50-134, Porirua, Wellington Tel: Wellington 331899
Man Dir, Editorial, Sales, Production, Rights & Permissions: R H Stott; *Publicity:* E Burgess
Subsidiary Company: Rails Publishing Ltd (at above address)
Subjects: Transport, Technology, New Zealand History
1981: 5 titles *1982:* 2 titles *Founded:* 1971
ISBN Publisher's Prefix: 0-908616

Stockton House, PO Box 46, Albany Tel: Auckland 4139528
Man Dir: R S Witter; *Publicity Manager:* Tani Witter
Subjects: Educational, General
Founded: 1974

Sweet & Maxwell (NZ) Ltd, a subsidiary of Associated Book Publishers (New Zealand) Ltd (qv)

Alister **Taylor** Publishers, The Mall, Russell, Bay of Islands Tel: Russell 633 Cable Add: Taylor, Russell Telex: NZ 60495 Taypub
Chief Executive: Alister Taylor; *Rights & Permissions:* Deborah Coddington; *Sales:* Randy Horwood
Subjects: Limited and Fine Editions, Fiction, Poetry, New Zealand, Art, Photography, Politics, General

1983: 16 titles *Founded:* 1971
ISBN Publisher's Prefix: 0-908578

University of Canterbury Publications, PB, Christchurch Tel: 482009 Cable Add: Canterbury University
Secretary: The Registrar
Subjects: Fine Art, History, Literature, Physics, Chemistry, Social Sciences, Natural Science, Political Science, Engineering
1981: 1 title *Founded:* 1960
ISBN Publisher's Prefix: 0-900392

University of Otago Press, PO Box 56, Dunedin Tel: 771640
Publicity Manager: B L Turner
Orders to: John McIndoe Ltd, PO Box 694, Dunedin
Subjects: Scholarly Monographs, Biography, Music, Poetry, Literature, History, Medicine
1981: 2 titles *Founded:* 1959
ISBN Publisher's Prefix: 0-908569

Victoria University Press, Victoria University of Wellington, Private Bag, Wellington Tel: 721000
Editorial, Production, Rights & Permissions: Pamela Tomlinson; *Sales:* John Seymour (ANZ)
Orders to: Australia and New Zealand Book Co Pty Ltd, PO Box 33-406, Auckland 9
Subjects: General Academic, New Zealand Drama, Short Stories, History, Politics, Sociology, Anthropology, Language and Communications, Law, Religion, Psychology, Zoology
1981: 7 titles *1982:* 7 titles
ISBN Publisher's Prefix: 0-86473

Viking Sevenseas Ltd, an imprint of Sevenseas Publishing Pty Ltd (qv)

Whitcoulls Publishers, Private Bag, Christchurch Tel: 794580 Telex: NZ 4205
Publishing Manager: Tony Izzard
Parent Company: Whitcoulls Ltd, Private Bag, Christchurch
Subjects: General, Fiction, Non-fiction, New Zealand, Educational
Bookshops: Throughout New Zealand (Whitcoulls Ltd — see Major Booksellers)
1981: 19 titles *1982:* 14 titles *Founded:* 1883
ISBN Publisher's Prefix: 0-7233

Whitman, an imprint of Golden Press Pty Ltd (qv)

Wilson & Horton Ltd, PO Box 32, Auckland Tel: 795050 Cable Add: Herald Telex: 2325
ISBN Publisher's Prefix: 0-86864

Literary Agents

Richards Literary Agency, PO Box 31240, Milford, Auckland (Located at: 49 Aberdeen Rd, Castor Bay, Auckland 9 and 54 Ranui Terrace, Linden, Wellington) Tel: 469681
Contacts: Ray Richards, Barbara Richards, Don Sinclair
Specializations: General, Educational, Academic, Juvenile, Film, Television, Stage, Radio

Book Clubs

Book New Zealand, see Doubleday New Zealand Ltd, Book Club Division

Book of the Month Club, see Doubleday New Zealand Ltd, Book Club Division

Doubleday Book Club, see Doubleday New Zealand Ltd, Book Club Division

Doubleday History Book Club, see Doubleday New Zealand Ltd, Book Club Division

Doubleday Military Book Club, see Doubleday New Zealand Ltd, Book Club Division

Doubleday New Zealand Ltd, Book Club Division, 8 Taylors Rd, Morningside, Auckland 3
Includes: Book of the Month Club, Book New Zealand, Doubleday Book Club, Doubleday History Book Club, Doubleday Military Book Club, The Literary Guild

The **Literary Guild**, see Doubleday New Zealand Ltd, Book Club Division

Lucky Arrow, PO Box 12328, Auckland
Owned by: Ashton Scholastic Ltd (qv)

Teachers' Book Shelf, PO Box 12328, Auckland
Owned by: Ashton Scholastic Ltd (qv)

Teenage, PO Box 12328, Auckland
Owned by: Ashton Scholastic Ltd (qv)

Major Booksellers

Jill Anderson's **A B C** Bookshop, 284 Trafalgar St, Nelson

Thomas **Avery** and Sons Ltd, 79 Devon St, New Plymouth
Manager: Kevin Avery

Beattie and Forbes, PO Box 186, Napier
Manager: Catherine Robins

G H **Bennett** & Co Ltd, 38-42 Broadway, PO Box 138, Palmerston North Tel: 83009 Cable Add: Bennibooks Telex: NZ 3649 Benbook
Man Dir: Bruce A McKenzie

Dorothy **Butler** Ltd, 170 Sunnybrae Rd, Auckland 9 Tel: 488359
Children's Book Specialists

Goddard's Bookshop Ltd, 21 Devonport Rd, PO Box 41, Tauranga
Man Dir: Ray Goddard

Hedley's Bookshop Ltd, PO Box 746, Masterton
Manager: David Hedley

Horizon Bookshop Ltd, PO Box 30-240, Wellington (Located at: Cnr High St and Waterloo Rd, Lower Hutt, Wellington) Tel: (04) 698406/663256
Manager: Steven Sedley

London Bookshops Ltd, 106 Cuba St, PO Box 6143, Wellington 1
Branches: St Luke's Shopping Centre, Mount Albert, Auckland; Shore City, Takapuna, Auckland; Downtown Mall, Queen St, Auckland; 99 Cashels St, Christchurch; 239 George St, Dunedin; 477 Victoria St, Hamilton; Hartham Pl, Porirua; Maidstone Mall, Upper Hutt; 326 Lambton Quay, Wellington; Kirkcaldies, Brandon St, Wellington
Dirs: D K Emanuel, P J Emanuel

Roy **Parsons**, Massey House, 126 Lambton Quay, Wellington 1

School Supplies Ltd, 9-11 Pollen St, Grey Lynn, PO Box 68443, Newton, Auckland
Branches: 5 Wall Pl, Linden, Wellington 1; PO Box 50-384 Porirua; Rathbone St, PO Box 224, Whangarei; PO Box 22-512, 363 Tuam St, Christchurch
Director: David Simpson

Unity Books Ltd, 42 Willis St, PO Box 3676, Wellington Tel: 738438
Manager: A H Preston

University Book Shop (Auckland) Ltd, Student Union Bldg, 34 Princes St, Auckland 1 Tel: 771869 Cable Add: Unibooks
Manager: Kitty Wishart

University Book Shop (Canterbury) Ltd*, University Drive, University of Canterbury, Christchurch Tel: 488579 Cable Add: Unibooks
Also: The Book Shop in the Arts Centre, Arts Centre, Christchurch Tel: 60568

University Book Shop (Otago) Ltd, 378 Great King St, PO Box 6060, Dunedin North Tel: 776976 Cable Add: Unibooks
Manager: Bill Noble

Whitcoulls Ltd, 111 Cashel St, PMB, Christchurch 1
52 branches throughout New Zealand
Man Dir: P E Bourne
Also Publisher (qv)

Major Libraries

Auckland Public Library, Lorne St, PO Box 4138, Auckland 1 Tel: 770209 Telex: NZ2750
Librarian: Mary A Ronnie

Canterbury Public Library*, PO Box 1466, 91 Gloucester St, Christchurch Tel: (03) 796914 Telex: NZ 4620
Librarian: J E D Stringleman
Publication: Canterbury Public Library Journal (monthly)

Canterbury University Library, Private Bag, Christchurch
Librarian: R W Hlavac

Dunedin Public Library*, PO Box 5542, Moray Place, Dunedin Tel: 743690
City Librarian: Michael Wooliscroft

General Assembly Library*, Parliament House, Wellington 1 Tel: 738288

National Archives, Air New Zealand Bldg, 129-141 Vivian St, Box 6148, Te Aro, Wellington Tel: 738699
Dir: R F Grover

National Library of New Zealand, Private Bag, Wellington 1 Tel: 722101 Telex: NZ 30076

Otago University Library, PO Box 56, Dunedin
Librarian: W J McEldowney
Publication: Annual Report

Palmerston North Public Library, PO Box 1948, Palmerston North Tel: 83076
Librarian: I W Malcolm

Alexander **Turnbull** Library, 44 The Terrace, PO Box 12349, Wellington Tel: 722107

University of Auckland Library, PB, Auckland Tel: Auckland 737999 Telex: NZ 21480
Librarian: P B Durey

Wellington Public Library, PO Box 1992, Wellington Tel: 729529
Librarian: B K McKeon

Library Associations

International Association of Music Libraries, New Zealand Branch, Alexander Palmer Library, PO Box 12-349, Wellington
Secretary: Jill Palmer
Publication: Continuo

New Zealand Library Association, 20 Brandon St, PO Box 12212, Wellington 1 Tel: 735834
Publications: A Way In: reading suggestions for adult new readers and their tutors; a book list; DISLIC (Directory of special libraries and information centres in New Zealand); Library Life (11 a year); *New Zealand Libraries* (4 a year); *Non-book Materials in Libraries; Guidelines for library*

practice; *Public Libraries in New Zealand* (1983); *Sing: a catalogue of choral scores in multiple copies held by New Zealand musical societies and libraries*; *Special Libraries and Collections: A New Zealand Directory*; *Standards for Special Libraries in New Zealand*; *Who's Who in New Zealand Libraries* (1980); *New Zealand Royal Commissions, Commissions and Committees of Enquiry* (checklist); *Surveying our reading habits*

Library Reference Books and Journals

Books

DISLIC (Directory of special libraries and information centres in New Zealand), New Zealand Library Association, 20 Brandon St, PO Box 12212, Wellington 1

Public Libraries in New Zealand, New Zealand Library Association, 20 Brandon St, PO Box 12212, Wellington 1

Special Libraries and Collections: A New Zealand Directory, New Zealand Library Association, 20 Brandon St, PO Box 12212, Wellington 1

Who's Who in New Zealand Libraries, New Zealand Library Association, 20 Brandon St, PO Box 12212, Wellington 1

Journals

Library Life (11 times yearly), New Zealand Library Association, 20 Brandon St, PO Box 12212, Wellington 1

New Zealand Libraries (quarterly), New Zealand Library Association, 20 Brandon St, PO Box 12212, Wellington 1

Literary Associations and Societies

Bibliographical Society of Australia and New Zealand, GPO Box 419, Adelaide, South Australia 5001, Australia
Secretary: Helen M Thomson
Publications: Bulletin (quarterly), *Broadsheet* (three times a year)

The **Dickens** Fellowship*, 18 Spencer St, Christchurch 2 Tel: 384308
Honorary Secretary: G J H Fox
Branches: Dunedin, Wellington

International Writers Workshop New Zealand Inc*, 13 Valkyria Pl, Auckland 10

New Zealand Book Council, PO Box 11377, Wellington
Secretary: Margaret McLeod
Publications: Writers in Schools; *Book Buyers in New Zealand*; *Books You Couldn't Buy* (censorship in New Zealand)

New Zealand Maori Artists & Writers Society Inc*, 8/87 Beresford St, Freemans Bay, Auckland 1

New Zealand Playwrights Association*, PO Box 3548, Wellington

New Zealand Women Writers' Society, 20 Downing St, Wellington 4
Secretary: Margaret Hayward

New Zealand Writers Guild*, PO Box 9116, Wellington

P E N International New Zealand Centre, PO Box 2283, Postal Centre, Wellington
Secretary: Jean Needham
Publication: PEN Gazette (quarterly)

Literary Periodicals

Arena; a literary magazine, Noel Farr Hoggard, PO Box 6188, Te Aro, Wellington

English in New Zealand; a teachers' quarterly, Stockton House (Publisher), PO Box 46, Albany

Islands; a New Zealand quarterly of arts and letters, Robin Dudding, 4 Scaly Rd, Torbay, Auckland 10

Landfall, Caxton Press, 113 Victoria St, PO Box 25088, Christchurch

Mate; a magazine of New Zealand writing, Wellesley St, PO Box 5670, Auckland

New Quarterly Cave; an international magazine of arts and ideas, Outrigger Publishers Ltd, 1 Von Tempsky St, Hamilton

Northland, Northland Magazine Inc, PO Box 694, Whangarei

Literary Prizes

Award for Achievement
Founded in 1958 for a contribution to literature. $500 (New Zealand). Awarded annually. 1982 winner, Bruce Mason. Enquiries to The Secretary, New Zealand Literary Fund. Department of Internal Affairs, Private Bag, Wellington

Bank of New Zealand Young Writers' Awards
For unpublished short stories written by young people in two age groups: Novice (any age); and Junior (school age). $250 and $150 (New Zealand). A grant of $150 is given to the library of the secondary school attended by the Junior awardee. Awarded every other year. Enquiries to New Zealand Women Writers' Society, 20 Downing St, Wellington 4

Best First Book of Poetry Award*
This prize incorporates the Jessie Mackay Award and is for the best first book of published poetry. $600 (New Zealand). Awarded annually. Enquiries to PEN International New Zealand Centre, PO Box 2283, Wellington

Best First Book of Prose Award*
This prize incorporates the Hubert Church Award and is for the best first book of prose. $600 (New Zealand). Awarded annually. Enquiries to PEN International New Zealand Centre, PO Box 2283, Wellington

Buckland Award
Founded in 1966 by the late Freda M Buckland for the work of the highest literary merit by a New Zealand writer. Awarded annually. Enquiries to Buckland Award, Trustees Executors and Agency Company of New Zealand Ltd, 24 Water St, PO Box 760, Dunedin

Choysa Bursary for Children's Writers
A bursary of $5,000 (New Zealand), established in 1979 to enable an author of imaginative work for children to work full-time for a period of up to one year on an approved project(s) which will reach book form. 1982 winner, Anne de Roo. Enquiries to The Secretary, New Zealand Literary Fund, Department of Internal Affairs, Private Bag, Wellington

Hubert **Church** Award, see Best First Book of Prose Award

Russell **Clark** Award
For the most distinguished illustrations for a children's book. Illustrator must be a citizen or resident of New Zealand. Bronze medal and $50 (New Zealand). Awarded annually. Enquiries to New Zealand Library Association, 20 Brandon St, PO Box 12212, Wellington 1

Esther **Glen** Award
For the best children's book by an author who is a citizen of, or resident in, New Zealand. Bronze medal and $50 (New Zealand). Awarded annually. Enquiries to New Zealand Library Association, 20 Brandon St, PO Box 12212, Wellington 1

I C I Writer's Bursary
Founded in 1978, this is an annual award of $6,000 (New Zealand), made to one or more writers (not necessarily of repute) with potential to work full-time for one year on an approved project. 1982 winner, Keri Hulme. Enquiries to The Secretary, New Zealand Literary Fund, Department of Internal Affairs, Private Bag, Wellington

Literary Fund Writing Bursary
Award of $4,000 (New Zealand) to enable writers of potential to work full-time on an approved programme for period of up to one year. Any type of original writing is eligible. 1983 award to Mary Logan. Enquiries to The Secretary, New Zealand Literary Fund, Department of Internal Affairs, Private Bag, Wellington

Jessie **Mackay** Award, see Best First Book of Poetry Award

Katherine **Mansfield** Memorial Award
For an unpublished short story. Sponsored by the Bank of New Zealand. $1,000 (New Zealand) in 1983. Awarded biennially. Enquiries to New Zealand Women Writers' Society, 20 Downing St, Wellington 4

New Zealand Book Awards
Annual awards of $2,000 (New Zealand) for the best book published each year in the categories of poetry, fiction, non-fiction and book production. 1982 winners: Fiction: *Meg* by Maurice Gee (Faber/Faber, Penguin); *Dandy Edison for Lunch* by Vincent O'Sullivan (McIndoe): Poetry: *Collected Poems* by Alistair Campbell (A Taylor): Non-fiction: *The South Island of New Zealand from the Road* by Robin Morrinson (A Taylor): Book Production (Major Award): *Portrait of Frances Hodgkins* by E H McCormick (Auckland UP). Enquiries to The Secretary, New Zealand Literary Fund, Department of Internal Affairs, Private Bag, Wellington

New Zealand Children's Books of the Year
Founded in 1982 by the New Zealand Government and designed to provide New Zealand children's books and their authors and illustrators with substantial recognition for literary and artistic excellence. The 1982 winners were: book of the year — the *Silent One* by Joy Cowley (Whitcoulls); picture story book of the year — *Kula and the Spider* by Patricia Grace, illustrated by Robin Kahukiwa (Longman Paul/Kidsarus 2). Enquiries to The Secretary, New Zealand Literary Fund, Department of Internal Affairs, Private Bag, Wellington

New Zealand Literary Fund
In addition to awards specifically mentioned, various grants are made from time to time by the above Fund to writers, publishers of creative literature and literary magazines. Enquiries to The Secretary, New Zealand Literary Fund, Department of Internal Affairs, Private Bag, Wellington

A W **Reed** Memorial Book Award
Annual award of $5,000 (New Zealand) for a work of non-fiction. Founded in 1979. The 1982 winner was Kerry Carman for *Portrait*

of a Garden. Enquiries to A H & A W Reed Ltd Publishers, 68-74 Kingsford Smith St, Wellington

Wattie Book of the Year Award
Established 1967. For the book of the year based on: (1) quality of writing and illustrations; (2) quality of editing, design and production; (3) impact on the community. Open only to members of the Publishers Association of New Zealand. First prize $6,000 (New Zealand), second $2,500 (New Zealand), third $1,500 (New Zealand). The joint 1982 winners were Sue McCauley for *Other Halves* (Hodder & Stoughton) and Doreen Blumhardt and Brian Blake for *Craft New Zealand* (A H & A W Reed). Enquiries to Book Publishers Association of New Zealand, PO Box 78071, Grey Lynn, Auckland 2

Young Writers' Incentive Awards*
For prose and poetry by New Zealanders under 20. $100 and $50 (New Zealand). Enquiries to PEN International New Zealand Centre, PO Box 2283, Wellington

Nicaragua

General Information

Language: Spanish
Religion: Roman Catholic
Population: 2.4 million
Literacy Rate (1971): 57.5% (80.5% of urban population, 34.6% rural)
Bank Hours: 0830-1500 Monday-Friday; 0830-1130 Saturday
Shop Hours: 0800-1200, 1430-1730 or longer Monday-Saturday
Currency: 100 centavos = 1 córdoba
Export/Import Information: Catalogues dutied per gross kilo. Compensatory Tax on advertising. No import licences or exchange controls
Copyright: UCC, Buenos Aires, Florence (see International section)

Publishers

Academia Nicaragüense de la Lengua*, Biblioteca Nacional, Managua
Subject: Languages

Editorial **San José***, Calle Central Este 607, Managua

Editorial **Unión***, Avda Central Norte, Managua
Subject: Travel

Universidad Nacional de Nicaragua, Librería y Editorial*, León
Subjects: Education, History, Mathematics, Law, Philology, Economics, Sciences, Politics, Literature

Major Booksellers

Librería **América***, Bosques de Altamira, Managua Tel: 80895

Librería **Blandon***, Apdo 2206, Managua

Centro Cultural Bautista*, Apdo 5776, Cuidad Jardin No E5, Managua Tel: 24714
Manager: Stanley D Stamps

Librería Recinto 'Ruben **Dario**'*, Universidad Nacional Autonoma de Nicaragua, Apdo 663, Managua

Librería Cultural **Nicaraguense***, Apdo 807, Managua Tel: 6663

Librería **Tecnológica Universitaria***, Universidad Centroamericana, Apdo 69, Managua Tel: 80351

Librería **Universitaria***, Universidad Nacional Autónoma de Nicaragua, León Tel: 2612

Librería **Recalde***, Apdo 666, Managua Tel: 81156/61239

Major Libraries

Archivo Nacional*, Casa de Gobierno, Managua
Publication: Boletin Tecnico Informativo del Archivo Nacional

Biblioteca Nacional*, Calle del Triunfo 302, Managua

Biblioteca Central del **Universidad Nacional** de Nicaragua*, León

Library Associations

Asociación de Bibliotecas Universitarias y Especializadas de Nicaragua*, Apdo 68, León
Association of University and Special Libraries of Nicaragua
Publication: Boletín

Asociación Nicaraguense de Bibliotecarios (ASNIBI)*, Biblioteca Nacional, Ministerio de Educacion Publica, Barrio 'La Fuente', Managua
Nicaraguan Association of Librarians
Executive Secretary: Susana Morales Hernández

Library Reference Journal

Boletín (Bulletin), Association of University and Special Libraries of Nicaragua, Apdo 68, León

Niger

General Information

Language: French
Religion: 85% Muslim; rest follow traditional beliefs
Population: 5 million
Bank Hours: 0800-1100, 1600-1700 (cool season 1530-1700) Monday-Friday
Business Hours: 0730-1230, 1600-1800 (cool season 1530-1730) Monday-Friday; 0730-1230 Saturday
Currency: CFA franc
Export/Import Information: Member of West African Economic Community. No tariff on books; advertising matter subject to Fiscal and Customs Duties (EEC members pay percentage of Customs Duty). Also Statistical Tax.
Copyright: Berne (see International section)

Publishers

Church World Service*, BP 624, Niamey Tel: 2449 Cable Add: Le Sahel Telex: 5232NI
Man Dir: Jon Otto
Subjects: Reference, Religion, Paperbacks

Government Printer (Imprimerie Générale du Niger)*, BP 61, Niamey

Major Booksellers

Librairie **Fellicelli et Poli***, BP 331, Niamey

Librairie **Mauclert** et Cie*, BP 10778, Niamey Tel: 722778

Major Libraries

Bibliothèque de l'**Ambassade** de France*, BP 154, Niamey

Archives nationales*, Présidence de la République, BP 550, Niamey

Centre d'Enseignement supérieur de Niamey*, Bibliothèque, BP 237, Niamey
University Education Centre

Centre de Documentation de l'Autorité du Bassin du Niger, BP 933, Niamey Tel: 723964 Telex: 5256 Augani
Documentation Centre of the Niger Basin Authority
Dir: Josué Ebolo Ebolo
Parent Organization: Niger Basin Authority (Autorité du Bassin du Niger), at above address
Publications: Concerning development of the natural resources of the River Niger Basin
Founded: 1971

Bibliothèqe l'**Ecole** nationale d'administration du Niger*, BP 542, Niamey Tel: 722853
Librarian: Elyane Maiga

Institut de recherche en Sciences humaines*, BP 318, Niamey Tel: 735141
Librarian: Sai'dou Harouna

Bibliothèque de l'**Université de Niamey***, BP 237, Niamey Tel: 732713

Nigeria

General Information

Language: English, Hausa
Religion: 45% Muslim (mainly in north), 35% Christian; rest follow traditional beliefs
Population: 72.2 million
Bank Hours: 0800-1500 Monday; 0800-1300 Tuesday-Friday
Shop Hours: Vary locally. 0800-1230, 1400-1630 Monday-Friday; 0800-1230 Saturday
Currency: 100 kobo = 1 naira
Export/Import Information: No tariffs on books or advertising matter. Open general licence. Obscene literature prohibited. Exchange controls
Copyright: UCC, Florence (see International section)

Book Trade Organizations

Nigerian Book Development Council*, 6 Obanta Rd, Apapa, Lagos State Tel: 874863
Secretary: Ms Eno Bassey

Nigerian Booksellers' Association*, PO Box 3168, Ibadan
President: 'Wunmi Adegbonmire; *Secretary:* Sam Olaniyan

Nigerian Publishers' Association*, c/o PMB 5164, Ibadan Tel: 417060 Telex: 31113
President: Akin Thomas
Publication: NPA Newsletter

Standard Book Numbering Agency*, The Director, National Library of Nigeria, 4 Wesley St, PMB 12626, Lagos Tel: 634704/656590/656591 Cable Add: Biblios Telex: 20117

University Booksellers Association of Nigeria*, c/o University of Ife Bookshop Ltd, Ile-Ife, Oyo State Tel: 2391
Secretary: R Agunbiade

Book Trade Reference Books and Journals

Books

Publishing in Nigeria, Ethiope Publishing Corporation, PMB 1192, Benin City (Contains several informative articles on the publishing scene in Nigeria)

Serials in Print in Nigeria, National Library of Nigeria, 4 Wesley St, PMB 12626, Lagos

Journals

National Bibliography of Nigeria, National Library of Nigeria, 4 Wesley St, PMB 12626, Lagos (Published annually since 1950. Cumulations before 1971 published by the Ibadan University Press. Also available as a weekly service)

New Nigeriana, University of Ife Bookshop Ltd, Ile-Ife (Bi-annual checklist, available free of charge from the Ife bookshop)

Nigerian Books in Print, National Library of Nigeria, 4 Wesley St, PMB 12626, Lagos

Northern Nigerian Publications, Ahmadu Bello University Library, Zaria (annual)

Publishers

A B I C (Publishers)*, PO Box 3120, Onitsha
President: C N C Asomugha; *Technical Manager:* T C Asomugha
Subjects: Reference, School Textbooks, Local History, Poetry, Trade Books, Children's
1981: 6 titles *1982:* 12 titles *Founded:* 1978
ISBN Publisher's Prefix: 978-2269

Academic, an imprint of Adebara Publishers Ltd (qv)

Academy Press Ltd, subsidiary of West African Book Publishers Ltd (qv)

Adebara Publishers Ltd*, PO Box 1970, Ibadan
Man Dir, Editorial: Dele Adebara; *Sales, Publicity:* Bisi Oke; *Production:* Layi Bankole; *Rights & Permissions:* Kayode Ayeni
Imprints: Academic, Bakolori, Eliri, Gangan, Golgotha, Ibaka, Okin
Branch Off: PO Box 173, Oshogbo
Subjects: Africana, Educational, Business, Professional, Children's, Reference, Novels, Radical Views, Scholarly, Research, Religion, Biography

Book Club: Lad-Bara Book Club
1981: 30 titles *Founded:* 1979
ISBN Publisher's Prefix: 978-147

African Universities Press*, Pilgrim Books Ltd, PMB 5617, Ibadan (Located at: New Oluyole Industrial Estate, Ibadan Expressway, Ibadan) Cable Add: Pilgrim Ibadan
Man Dir: John E Leigh; *Sales Manager:* N P Legg; *General Manager:* J A Kilanko
Parent Company: Pilgrim Books Ltd (at above address)
Subjects: Primary, Secondary and Tertiary Textbooks
Miscellaneous: Depots at 21 Ikorodu Rd, Obanikoro; PO Box 3560, Lagos; 74 Oguta Rd, PO Box 21, Onitsha; Old Jos Rd, PMB 1146, Zaria. Main warehouse at New Oluyole Industrial Estate (Phase 2), Ibadan Expressway, PMB 5617, Ibadan

Africana Publishers (Nig) Ltd*, PMB 1639, Onitsha (Located at: 79 Awka Rd, Onitsha)
Man Dir: P N C Omabu; *Editorial:* K B C Onwubiko; *Marketing:* Ralph O Ekpeh
Branch Off: 49 Zik's Ave, Uwani, Enugu
Subjects: How-to, Study Guides, General Science, Secondary & Primary Textbooks, *At a Glance* and *Made Easy* series; University & College books on Education, English, Management, Politics
Founded: 1971

Ahmadu Bello University Press Ltd*, PMB 1094, Zaria Tel: 2054 Cable Add: Unibello Press Zaria Telex: 75241 Zarabu Ng
Man Dir, Editorial, Rights & Permissions: Mrs Modupe Adeogun; *Editorial:* Anna Gourlay, Ben Anyaegbunam; *Production:* Mohamed Zongoma
Subjects: History, Africana, Reference, Social Sciences, Education, Veterinary Medicine
Founded: 1974
ISBN Publisher's Prefix: 978-125

Albah Publishers*, PO Box 6177, Bompai, Kano (Located at: 100 Kurawa, Kano City) Cable Add: Albah Kano
Chairman: Brig A S Wali; *Editorial & Production:* Bashari F Roukbah; *Sales & Publicity:* Duba Da Kyau (Holdings) Ltd
Associate Company: Brunswick Publishing Co, PO Box 555, Lawrenceville, Virginia 23868, USA
Subjects: Scholarly, Africana, Islam, Educational, Textbooks (in Hausa)
Bookshop: Baban Layi, Gyadi-Gyadi, Zariya Rd, Kano
Founded: 1978

Alliance West African Publishers & Co*, Orindingbin Estate, New Aketan Layout, PMB 1039, Oyo Tel: Oyo 124
Manager: Chief M O Ogunmola; *Editorial:* Poju Amori; *Sales:* L Oyeniji; *Publicity, Permissions:* Kehinde Ogunmola
Subjects: Biography, History, Africana, How-to, Study Guides, Nigerian Languages, General Science, Secondary & Primary School Textbooks
Founded: 1971

Aowa Press & Publications*, PO Box 3090, Ibadan
Subjects: How-to, Study Guides, Primary & Secondary Textbooks

Aromolaran Publishing Co Ltd*, PO Box 1800, Ibadan Tel: 410529 Telex: 31158 Arbook Nigeria
Man Dir: Adekunle Aromolaran; *Sales:* Mrs V M Aromolaran
Subjects: Belles Lettres, Poetry, Biography, How-to, Study Guides, Religion, Juveniles, Arts, Science and General Books for Primary and Secondary Schools and Universities
Founded: 1970

Bakolori, an imprint of Adebara Publishers Ltd (qv)

Black Academy Press, PO Box 255, Owerri, Imo State Tel: 230606/230273 Cable Add: Bapress
Man Dir: Dr S Okechukwu Mezu
Subjects: General Non-fiction, Belles Lettres, Poetry, Biography, History, Africana

C S S Bookshops, Agency and Publishing Division*, Bookshop House, 50-52 Broad St, PO Box 174, Lagos Tel: 633010/633081 Cable Add: Bookshops
Man Dir: Akin O Shenbanjo
Subsidiary Company: CSS Bookshops, PO Box 174, Lagos (and area offices at Aba, Abeokuta, Akure, Erungu, Ibadan, Ile-Ife, Jos, Port Harcourt, Zaria)
Subjects: General Non-fiction, Biography, History, Africana, Religion, General Science, Law, Medicine, Secondary & Primary Textbooks

Challenge Publications*, Publishing Division of ECWA Productions Ltd (qv)

Conch Magazine Ltd*, Publishers, 113 Douglas Rd, PO Box 573, Owerri
Man Dir: Sunday Anozie
Subsidiary Company: Conch Magazine Ltd, 65 Jenkenstown Rd, New Paltz, NY 12561, USA
Subjects: General Non-fiction, Belles Lettres, Poetry, History, Africana, Paperbacks, Social Science

Cross Continent Press Ltd*, 226 Murtala Muhammed Way, PO Box 282, Yaba, Lagos Tel: (01) 961894 Cable Add: Croconpres Lagos
Man Dir: T C Nwosu; *Editorial, Publicity:* O A Achonu; *Marketing:* N S Wokocha; *Financial:* L O Oshin
Subsidiary Companies: Editorial Consultancy & Agency Services (Authors' and Publishers' Agents and Consultants), GPO Box 4573, Lagos; Toscana Printers Ltd, PO Box 282, Yaba, Lagos
Subjects: General Fiction & Non-fiction, Belles Lettres, Poetry, Biography, How-to, Study Guides, Juveniles, Paperbacks, Primary, Secondary & Tertiary Textbooks
Founded: 1974
ISBN Publisher's Prefix: 978-134

Daily Times of Nigeria Ltd*, Book Sales Division, 3-7 Kakawa St, PO Box 139, Lagos Tel: 26611 Telex: 21333
Chief Executive: Dr P D Cole; *Editorial:* Peter Osugo; *Sales:* J Tan Olu; *Production:* E A Cole
Subsidiary Company: Times Press Ltd
Subjects: Reference, Nigerian *Who's Who*
Book Club: Times Book Club
Founded: 1925

Daystar Press (Publishers)*, Daystar House, PO Box 1261, Ibadan Tel: 23230
Man Dir, Editorial, Rights & Permissions: Modupe Oduyoye; *Production:* Gabriel Ojo; *Trade:* James Akimboye; *Publicity:* A Osuji
Subjects: Christian Religions, Health, Home & Family Life, Nigerian Culture
1981: 12 titles *Founded:* 1962
ISBN Publisher's Prefix: 978-122

E C W A Productions Ltd*, PMB 2010, Jos
Man Dir: Dr Philip S Usman
Subjects: General, Educational, Religion
Bookshops: Challenge Bookshops (qv)
Miscellaneous: Challenge Publications is Publishing Division of ECWA Productions Ltd

Educational Research Institute*, PO Box 277, Ibadan
Man Dir: Areoye Oyebola

Subjects: General Non-fiction, Biography, History, Africana, How-to, Study Guides, Religion, General & Social Science, Secondary & Primary Textbooks
Founded: 1970

Eliri, an imprint of Adebara Publishers Ltd

Elizabethan Publishing House, 41 Ogunlena Drive, Surulere, Lagos Tel: 835305
Chief Executive: Elizabeth Osisanya; *Dir:* Prof C A Kogbe
Subsidiary Company: Ogie Elegant-Twins, PO Box 3377, Surulere, Lagos Tel: 832113
Subjects: Academic, Geology, Nigerian Culture
Founded: 1976

Emotan Publishing Co (Nigeria) Ltd*, 152nd Ire St, Benin City
Man Dir: P O Onaghise
Subjects: General Fiction, Belles Lettres, Poetry, Paperbacks

Ethiope Publishing Corporation*, Ring Rd, PMB 1332, Benin City Tel: 243036 Cable Add: Ethiope Telex: 41110
Man Dir: Clement Okosun; *Publishing Manager, Rights & Permissions:* Sunday Olaye
Subjects: General Fiction, & Non-fiction, Belles Lettres, Poetry, Biography, History, Africana, How-to, Study Guides, Philosophy, Reference, Juveniles, Paperbacks, Science & Technology, General & Social Science, Law, University & Secondary Textbooks
Founded: 1970

Evans Brothers (Nigeria Publishers) Ltd*, Jericho Rd, PMB 5164, Ibadan Tel: 462970/71/72 Cable Add: Edbooks Ibadan Telex: 31104 Edbook
Man Dir: B O Bolodeoku; *Publishing Dir:* C T McGregor; *Trade Dir:* R A Oyewole; *Publishing Manager:* Valentine Olayemi; *Sales Dir:* S A Oke
Associate Company: Evans Brothers Ltd, UK (qv)
Branch Offs: Kaduna, Onitsha and Osogbo
Subjects: Educational generally: General Non-fiction, Belles Lettres, Poetry, Biography, History, Africana, Reference, Juveniles, Paperbacks, Science & Technology, General & Social Science, Secondary & Primary Textbooks
Founded: 1966
ISBN Publisher's Prefix: 978-167

Olaiya **Fagbamigbe** Ltd (Publishers)*, 11 Methodist Church Rd, PO Box 14, Akure Tel: 2075 Cable Add: Fagbamigbe Akure
Man Dir: O Fagbamigbe; *General Manager:* Oyewumi Oladeji; *Publicity:* Gbolagade Adesina; *Rights & Permissions:* E Fagbamigbe
Branch Offs: Old Ife Rd, PO Box 1176, Agodi, Ibadan
Subjects: Educational and General
Founded: 1976
ISBN Publisher's Prefix: 978-164

Gangan, an imprint of Adebara Publishers Ltd (qv)

Golgotha, an imprint of Adebara Publishers Ltd (qv)

Heinemann Educational Books (Nigeria) Ltd*, Ighodaro Rd, Jericho, PMB 5205, Ibadan Tel: 462060/462061/410267 Cable Add: Hebooks Ibadan Telex: 31113 Hebook NG
Deputy Chairman, Man Dir: Aigboje Higo; *Publishing Dir, Rights & Permissions:* Akin Thomas; *Sales & Publicity Dir:* Joe Osadolor
Parent Company: Heinemann Educational Books International Ltd, UK (qv for associate companies)
Branch Offs: 17 Sherikin Ruwa St, Gyelesu, Via Institute of Administration, PMB 1112, Zaria, Kaduna State; PO Box 2722, Jos, Plateau State; PMB 5648, Port Harcourt, Rivers State; PO Box 675, Benin City, Bendel State; PO Box 129, Kano, Kano State; PO Box 661, Ilorin, Kwara State; PO Box 1727, Enugu, Anambra State; PO Box 378, Gusau, Sokoto State; PO Box 46, Bida, Niger State; PO Box 95, Maiduguri, Borno State; PO Box 1165, Owerri, Imo State; PO Box 692, Yola, Gongola State; PO Box 197, Uyo, Cross River State
Subjects: Educational (Primary, Post-Primary and Tertiary), Law, Medicine and General
Founded: 1960
ISBN Publisher's Prefix: 978-129

Heritage Books*, 10-14 Calcutta Crescent, PO Box 610, Apapa, Lagos Tel: 871333
Man Dir: Naiwu Osahon; *Senior Editor, Rights & Permissions:* Bakin Kunama; *Advertising:* L Williams
Subsidiary Company: Obobo Books (qv)
Subjects: General Fiction and Non-fiction, Belles Lettres, Poetry, Black Power, Paperbacks, Periodical
Founded: 1971

I C I C (Directory Publishers) Ltd*, PMB 3204, Surulere, Lagos (Located at: Directory House, 28 Taoridi St, opp Census Office, Surulere, Lagos) Tel: 831909 Cable Add: ICIC
Man Dir: Olu Adeyemi
Subjects: General, Reference, Telephone and Business Directories
Founded: 1965

Ibadan University Press*, University of Ibadan, Ibadan Tel: 462550 ext 1244 Cable Add: Univpress Ibadan
Manager: Olatunji Akande
Subjects: Biography, History, Africana, Philosophy, Reference, Paperbacks, Medicine, Psychology, Science & Technology, General & Social Science, Law, University & Secondary Textbooks
Founded: 1952
ISBN Publisher's Prefix: 978-121

Ibaka, an imprint of Adebara Publishers Ltd (qv)

Ilesanmi Press & Sons (N) Ltd*, Akure Rd, PO Box 204, Ilesha Tel: 2062/2017 Cable Add: Ilesanmi Press Ilesha
Man Dir, Rights & Permissions: G E Ilesanmi; *Editorial, Sales, Publicity:* Bayo Olagunju; *Production:* Alhj Fabukoye
Branch Offs: Uyo, Kano, Ibadan, Lagos, Akure, Jos, Onitsha, Minna
Subjects: Educational Books generally; Biography, History, Africana, How-to, Study Guides, Books in Yoruba Language, Teacher Training Manuals, General & Social Science
Bookshop: Faji, Ilesha
Founded: 1956
ISBN Publisher's Prefix: 978-157

Institute of African Studies*, Publications Section, University of Ibadan, Ibadan Tel: 400550
Dir, Editorial, Rights & Permissions: Prof S O Biobaku; *Editorial:* Alex Iwara, R G Armstrong; *Sales, Production:* Chris W Purisch
Subject: Africana
Founded: 1964

Islamic Publications Bureau*, 136A Isolo Rd, Mushin, Lagos Tel: 876222 Cable Add: Alislam
Man Dir: Ahmad Patel; *Publicity:* Alhaji Sayyid A Abdulai
Branch Offs: 40 Sultan Bello Rd, PO Box 5106, Kaduna; 453 Airport Rd, New Commercial Layout, PO Box 420, Kano
Subjects: Islamic Literature and Arabic Books
Founded: 1969

Kolasanya Publishing Enterprise*, 2 Epe Rd, Oke-Owa, PMB 2099, Ijebu-Ode
Man Dir: Kola Osunsanya
Subjects: General Non-fiction, How-to, Study Guides, General Science, Secondary & Primary Textbooks

Lantern Books, an imprint of Literamed Publications Nigeria Ltd (qv)

Literamed Publications Nigeria Ltd*, PMB 21068, Ikeja, Lagos (Located at: Plot 45, Oregun Industrial Estate) Tel: 962512
Man Dir: O Lawal-Solarin; *Editorial Dir:* P U Nkwocha; *Marketing Manager:* S Lawal-Solarin; *Production;* C A Odeneye; *Advertising Manager:* Y Akinrinmade
Imprint: Lantern Books
Branch Off: 18 Langsmead, Blindley Heath, Lingsfield, Surrey, UK
Subjects: Educational, Political, Social, Children's Literature, Periodicals
Founded: 1969
ISBN Publisher's Prefix: 978-2281

Longman Nigeria Ltd*, 52 Oba Akran Ave, PMB 1036, Ikeja, Lagos Tel: 33007/33176 Cable Add: Longman Ikeja
Man Dir: Felix A Iwerebon; *Marketing Manager:* C O Ojiji; *Publishing Manager:* O Agboola; *Production:* A W Amaeshi
Associate Company: Longman Group Ltd, UK (qv)
Subjects: General Fiction & Non-fiction, Belles Lettres, Poetry, Biography, History, Africana, Reference, Religion, Juveniles, Books in Nigerian Languages (various), Paperbacks, Psychology, Science & Technology, General & Social Science, University, Secondary & Primary Textbooks
Founded: 1961

Macmillan Nigeria Publishers Ltd*, Lagos-Ibadan Expressway Link, PO Box 1463, Ibadan Tel: 413917 Cable Add: Macbooks Ibadan Telex: Mabook 31141
Man Dir: Olu Anulopo; *Publishing:* A Amori; *Marketing:* E Ohuka, I Ademokun; *Production:* A Adebusuvi; *Publicity:* D Obisesan
Orders to: PO Box 264, Yaba
Associate Company: Macmillan Education Ltd, UK (qv)
Branch Offs: PO Box 264, Yaba; PO Box 390, Onitsha; PMB 1286, Benin City; PO Box 434, Akure; PO Box 476, Owerri; PO Box 192, Uyo; PO Box 1395, Zaria
Subjects: Educational and General Fiction & Non-fiction: Biography, History, Africana, Religion, Juveniles, Books in various Nigerian Languages, Paperbacks, General & Social Science, University, Secondary, Primary and Nursery Textbooks
Founded: 1965
ISBN Publisher's Prefix: 978-132

Thomas **Nelson** (Nigeria) Ltd*, Nelson House, 8 Ilupeju By-Pass, PMB 21303, Ikeja, Lagos Tel: 961452 Cable Add: Thonelson Ikeja
Executive Chairman: Prof C O Taiwo; *Man Dir:* S O Daramola; *Marketing Dir:* E B Iyekolo; *Advisory Dir:* G E Muller; *Publishing Manager:* S Mabogunje
Parent Company: Thomas Nelson International, Toronto, Canada
Associate Companies: Thomas Nelson & Sons Ltd, UK (qv); University Publishing Co, Nigeria (qv)
Subjects: General Fiction and Non-fiction, Africana, Books in various Nigerian Languages, General & Social Science, Textbooks

New Horn Press Ltd*, PO Box 4138, Ibadan
Man Dir: Dr Abiola Irele; *Senior Editor, Rights & Permissions:* Kole Omotoso
Subjects: General Fiction & Non-fiction, Belles Lettres, Poetry, How-to, Study Guides, Paperbacks
Founded: 1974

Nigerian Institute of International Affairs*, PMB 1727, Lagos (Located at: Kofo Abayomi Rd, Victoria Island, Lagos) Tel: 615858/615606 Cable Add: Internations
Editorial, Production: Pat Abadom; *Sales:* Nsikak E Umoh; *Publicity:* Mr Balogun
Subjects: International Relations, Politics, Economics
Founded: 1963
ISBN Publisher's Prefix: 978-2276

Nigerian Publishers Services Ltd, BB2 Old Jos Rd, PO Box 722, Zaria
Dir, Chief Executive: T D Otesanya; *Marketing Manager:* Stephen Idowu-Kuola
Branch Off: 37A Omeagana St, Off Modebe Ave, PO Box 4073, Onitsha

Nigerian Trade Review*, PO Box 603, Lagos
Man Dir: Chief P A Dawodu
Subjects: General, Business Directories
Founded: 1958
Miscellaneous: Publish *General Trade Directory of Nigeria; Nigerian Insurance and Banking Directory*

Nok Publishers (Nigeria) Ltd*, PO Box 1005, Enugu, Anambra State (Located at: First Avenue, Independence Layout, Enugu) Tel: (042) 258168 (Enugu), (01) 632835 (Lagos) Telex: 21810 Gcwn Ng
Man Dir: B C Ude; *Editorial:* P O C Umeh; *Sales:* Leonard I Onyenso; *Production:* Louis Umerah
Parent Company: Nok Publishers International, 150 5th Avenue, New York, NY 10011, USA
Subjects: Africana (Art & Culture, History, Politics, Philosophy, Sociology, Religions, Literature, Folklore, Poetry, Education, Law, Economics), African Bibliographic Series
Founded: 1973
ISBN Publisher's Prefix: 0-88357

Northern Nigerian Publishing Co Ltd*, Gaskiya Bldg, PO Box 412, Zaria Tel: 2087 Cable Add: Gasmac Telex: 75243 Gasmac Nig
General Manager: Alhaji Husaini Hayat; *Assistant General Manager:* D G Shehu; *Managing Editor:* Gabriel Abu; *Marketing Manager:* Alhaji Mamman Maina; *Sales Manager:* Alhaji Abubakar Garba
Associate Company: Macmillan Education Ltd, UK (qv)
Subjects: General Non-fiction, Belles Lettres, Poetry, Biography, History, Africana, Religion, Juveniles, Books in Hausa and other Nigerian Languages, Paperbacks, Secondary & Primary Textbooks

Nwamife Publishers Ltd*, 10 Ibiam St, Uwani, PO Box 430, Enugu Tel: (042) 338254 CCable Add: Nwamife Enugu
Chairman: Dr Felix C Adi; *Sales, Production, Publicity:* Samuel Umesike; *Editorial, Rights & Permissions:* Dr Nina Mba
Subjects: General Fiction & Non-fiction; Belles Lettres, Poetry, Biography, History, Africana, How-to, Study Guides, Juveniles, Igbo Language & Literature, General Science, Law; University, Secondary & Primary Textbooks; Paperbacks
1981: 10 titles *Founded:* 1970
ISBN Publisher's Prefix: 978-124

Obobo Books*, PO Box 610, Apapa, Lagos (Located at: 10/14 Calcutta Crescent, Lagos) Tel: 871333
Chief Executive: Mrs Ivie Osahon; *Editorial:* Bakin Kunama; *Sales, Publicity:* P Obeng; *Production:* Maria Osibio
Parent Company: Heritage Books (qv)
Subjects: Children's, Short Stories, Colouring Series, Adventure Series, Biographies
Bookshop: Heritage (The Bookshop), PO Box 930, Apapa, Lagos
1981: 25 titles *Founded:* 1981
ISBN Publisher's Prefix: 978-186

Ogunsanya Press, Publishers and Bookstores Ltd*, Orita Challenge, PO Box 95, Ibadan Tel: Ibadan 23619 Cable Add: Pombapress
Man Dir, Editorial, Rights & Permissions: Lucas Justus Popo-Ola Ogunsanya; *Sales, Publicity:* J P F Adeyoju; *Production:* S B O Folayan
Branch Off: Popo-Ola Jubilee Lodge, Oke Imoru, PO Box 155, Ijebu Ode, Ogun State
Subjects: History, Geography, Mathematics, English, Science, Social Studies, Arabic
Bookshop: 64 Agbeni St (opp Foko Junction), Ibadan
Founded: 1970

Okin, an imprint of Adebara Publishers Ltd (qv)

Omoleye Publishing Co*, PO Box 1265, Ibadan, Oyo State Tel: (022) 413335
Man Dir: Mike Omoleye
Subjects: General, Fiction, Yoruba Culture
1982: 2 titles

Onibonoje Press & Book Industries (Nigeria) Ltd*, Felele Layout, PO Box 3109, Ibadan Tel: 413956
Chairman: Gabriel Onibonoje; *Man Dir:* J Olu Onibonoje; *Editorial Dir, Rights & Permissions:* E A Onibonoje
Branch Offs: Benin City, Jos, Kano, Lagos, Onitsha, Sokoto
Subjects: General Fiction & Non-fiction, Belles Lettres, Poetry, Biography, History, Africana, How-to, Study Guides, Religion, Juveniles, Yoruba Language & Literature, Paperbacks, General & Social Science, Primary, Secondary & Teacher Training College Textbooks
Book Club: Onibonoje Book Club
Bookshop and Showroom: SW8/77 Oke-Ado, Ibadan
Founded: 1958

Orisun Editions*, PO Box 3079, Ibadan
Man Dir: Bola Ige
Subjects: General, Belles Lettres, Poetry

Paico Ltd*, 46 Commercial Ave, PO Box 3944, Yaba, Lagos
Man Dir: A S Ette
Subjects: General Non-fiction, How-to, Study Guides, General Science, Secondary & Primary Textbooks
Founded: 1971

People's Publishing Co Ltd*, PO Box 3121, Lagos
Subjects: General Non-fiction, Socialism

Pilgrim Books Ltd, see African Universities Press

Publications International (Nigeria) Ltd*, PMB 5097, Ibadan
Man Dir: 'Bisi Talwo
Subjects: General, Secondary & Primary Textbooks
Founded: 1971

Scholar Publications International (Nigeria) Ltd*, PO Box 5097, Ibadan
Subjects: Government, Economics, English, Religion, Chemistry
Founded: 1972
ISBN Publisher's Prefix: 978-138

Sketch Publishing Co Ltd*, Sketch Bldgs, New Court Rd, PMB 5067, Ibadan Tel: 25191/93 Cable Add: Sketch
Man Dir: Felix A Adenaike; *Editorial:* 'Tola Adeniyi
Subjects: General Books, Reference Books
Founded: 1964

Spectrum Books Ltd*, Sunshine House, 2nd Commercial Rd, Oluyole Estate, PMB 5612, Ibadan Cable Add: Specta Telex: 31588
Chief Executive: Joop Berkhout; *Editorial:* John Asudo; *Sales, Publicity:* Peter Nelson
Associate Company: Safari Books (Export) Ltd, Portman House, 32 Hue St, St Helier, Jersey, Channel Islands, UK
Subjects: Educational, Fiction
1981: 30 titles *Founded:* 1978
ISBN Publisher's Prefix: 978-2265

Tana Press Ltd*, 2A Menkiti Lane Ogui, Enugu Tel: (042) 258305 Cable Add: Tana Telex: 51164 Lake NG
Man Dir: Flora Nwakuche; *Editorial:* Dr Nina Mba; *Sales, Publicity:* Nigerian Publishers Services Ltd
Subsidiary Company: Flora Nwapa & Co Publishers
Branch Off: PO Box 2, Oguta, Anambia State
Subjects: Children's, Short Studies, Novels
1981: 11 titles *Founded:* 1979
ISBN Publisher's Prefix: 978-2272

Third World First Publications, now Heritage Books (qv)

Town & Gown Press*, 4 Kajer St, Akoka, PMB 1073, Yaba, Lagos
Man Dir: J E Adetoro
Subjects: General Non-fiction, Belles Lettres, Poetry, Biography, History, Africana, Paperbacks, Secondary Textbooks

University of Ife Press, Ile-Ife, Oyo State Tel: 2291 ext 308 Cable Add: Press Ifevarsity
Acting Publishing Manager: Dr 'Sola Soile
Subjects: Biography, History, Africana, Philosophy, Reference, Religion, Law, Social Science, University Textbooks
Founded: 1968

University of Lagos Press*, PO Box 132, Yaba, Lagos
Chief Editor: Bodunde Bankole
Subjects: Biography, History, Africana, Law, Social Science, University Textbooks

University Press Ltd*, Three Crowns Building, Jericho, PMB 5095, Ibadan Tel: 411356/412056 Cable Add: Oxonian Ibadan Telex: Ibadan 31121 Oxonia Ng
Man Dir: Michael O Akinleye; *Publishing Services Manager:* B O Adeleke; *Editorial:* V Olayemi; *Production Manager:* C B Akinluyi; *Marketing Manager:* O Bankole
Warehouse: PMB 5142 Jericho, Ibadan Tel: 413117
Associate Company: Oxford University Press, UK (qv)
Subjects: General Fiction & Non-fiction, Poetry, Biography, History, Africana, Reference, Religion, Juveniles, Books in various Nigerian Languages, Paperbacks, Medicine, Science & Technology, General & Social Science, University, Secondary & Primary Textbooks
Founded: 1949

University Publishing Co*, 11 Central School Rd, PO Box 386, Onitsha Tel: 223 Onitsha Cable Add: Varsity Box 386 Onitsha
Dirs: F C Ogbalu, W C Ifezue; *Editorial:* J U Eburne; *Sales:* D O Orakwue; *Production:* I Nweke; *Publicity:* Christian Ogbalu; *Permissions:* Cecilia Ogbalu
Orders to: Varsity Bookshop, 64 New Market Rd, Onitsha

Associate Companies: Cynako International Press, Aba; Thomas Nelson (Nigeria) (qv); African Literature Bureau, Aba
Branch Offs: Azikiwe Rd, Aba; Eke-Amawbia, Awka; Varsity Bookshop/Press, Eke-Oyibo, Abagana, Njikoka LGA; 64 New Market Rd, Onitsha; Afor Igwe, Ogidi
Subjects: General Non-fiction, Belles Lettres, Poetry, Biography, History, Africana, Philosophy, Religion, Juveniles, Igbo Language & Literature, Quality Paperbacks, Primary & Secondary Textbooks, Periodicals, Books in Vernacular and Dialect
Bookshops: Varsity Bookshop/Press at: Oye-Agu, Abagana, Njikoka LGA; Eke-Amawbia, Amawbia, Awka LGA; Aba; Abiriba, Ohafia LGA
Founded: 1959
ISBN Publisher's Prefix: 978-160

Varsity Industrial Press*, 11 Central School Rd, PO Box 386, Onitsha
Man Dir: E O Ugwuegbulem
Subjects: Igbo Language & English, Primary & Secondary Textbooks
Book Club: Varsity Book Club

John West Publications Ltd*, John West House, Plot A Block 2, Acme Rd, Ogba, PMB 21001, Ikeja — Lagos Cable Add: Jakpress Telex: 26446 Wes Pal
Executive Dir: Bayo Fadoju
Subjects: General Non-fiction, Biography, How-to, Study Guides, Reference, Annuals, Paperbacks
Founded: 1962

West African Book Publishers Ltd*, PO Box 3445, Ilupeju Industrial Estate, Lagos Tel: 34555/6 Cable Add: Acadpress
Man Dir: B A Idris Animashaun; *Sales Manager:* J O A Onifade; *Editorial:* Laoye Egunjobi
Subsidiary Company: Academy Press Ltd, PO Box 3445, Lagos
Subjects: Reference, Guide Books, Paperbacks, Health, General Science
Founded: 1967

Literary Agents

Editorial Consultancy & Agency Services*, PO Box 4573, Lagos (Located at: 226 Murtala Muhammed Way) Tel: (01) 961894 Cable Add: Edicanses Lagos
Authors' & Publishers' Agents & Consultants
Editorial Director: T C Nwosu
Special Interests: Africana/Nigeriana, Fiction, Plays, Educational Books at all levels
Parent Company: Cross Continent Press Ltd (qv)

F C Ogbalu*, PO Box 386, 11 Central School Rd, Onitsha

Book Clubs

Academic Book Club*, PO Box 159, Ilaro, Ogun State Tel: (039) 440159
National Executive President/Coordinator: Ronald Ade Kolawole
Parent Company: Academic Book Club, PO Box 1507, Ontario, Canada

Lad-Bara Book Club*, PO Box 173, Oshogbo
Owned by: Adebara Publishers Ltd (qv)

Onibonoje Book Club*, PO Box 3109, Ibadan
Owned by: Onibonoje Press & Book Industries (Nigeria) Ltd (qv)
Subjects: Fiction, Drama

Times Book Club*, 3-7 Kakawa St, PO Box 139, Lagos
Owned by: Daily Times of Nigeria

Varsity Book Club*, PO Box 386, 11 Central School Rd, Onitsha
Organized by: Varsity Industrial Press (Publisher, qv)

Major Booksellers

Ahmadu Bello University Bookshop*, PMB 11, Zaria
Manager: Sam A Oyabambi

Benin University Bookshop*, University of Benin, PMB 1154, Benin City Tel: (052) 243780
Manager: S O Ehiede

Book Representation Co Ltd*, PMB 5349, E9/806B Ife Rd, Agodi Area, Ibadan

C S S (Nigeria) Bookshops Ltd*, Bookshop House, 50-52 Broad St, PO Box 174, Lagos Tel: 633010/633081 (branches throughout the country)

Challenge Bookshops*, Agege Motor Rd, PMB 12256, Lagos Tel: 847690
Man Dir: Dr Philip Usman, ECWA Productions Ltd (qv); *Trade Dir:* Sam Kolo; *General Manager (Sales):* Akuso Dogari
34 branches throughout the country, and several wholesale outlets
Owned by: ECWA Productions Ltd (Publisher, qv)

Edekes Bookshop Stores Ltd*, 2 Falolu Rd, PO Box 974, Surulere, Lagos

Hart Mossman & Co Ltd*, PMB 2283, Lagos

Kingsway Stores*, PO Box 652, Lagos
Major department store with book department — branches throughout the country

Kwaratech Bookshop*, Kwana State College of Technology, PMB 1375, Ilorin Tel: 2440 ext 14

Mabrochi International Co*, PO Box 1509, Surulere, Lagos
Manager: P I Igwe-Ofor
Also: Y11 Ibadan St, Kaduna, Kaduna State
Specializes in mail order services. Academic jobbers for overseas universities

Morison Arnold Ltd*, 63 Hadejia Rd, PO Box 251, Kano

Niger (Acada) Bookshop Ltd*, 90 Ojuelegba Rd, PMB 3151, Surulere, Lagos Tel: 834016

Nigerian Baptist Book Stores*, Baptist Building, PMB 5070, Oke Bola, Ibadan

Nigerian Book Suppliers Ltd*, PO Box 4440, 28 Akinremi St, Ikeja, Lagos State Tel: 932245 Telex: 20202 Tds Box 052 Ikeja
Man Dir: B Fatayi-Williams; *General Manager:* Mrs O Williams
Booksellers and library suppliers specializing in professional books (especially legal, management and accountancy), Africana, mass market paperback fiction, and library titles for tertiary level libraries
Associate Company: Universal Distributors Ltd (qv)

Odusote Bookstores Ltd*, 68 Lagos By-Pass, PO Box 244, Ibadan Tel: 414419 Cable Add: Odbook, Ibadan Telex: 31215 (Odbook NG)
Also: 177 Herbert Macaulay St, Yaba, Lagos State Tel: 861248
Man Dir: Ola Odusote

Rational Bookshops (Nigeria)*, Rational Bldgs, Oke-Bola, PO Box 3162, Ibadan

Universal Distributors Ltd*, PO Box 7036, Lagos Tel: 932245
Man Dir: B Fatayi-Williams; *General Manager:* Mrs O Williams; *Manager:* O Fatayi-Williams; *Bookshop Sales Manager:* Mrs V P Oseni
'Bestseller', three bookshops at Falomo Shopping Centre, Ikoyi, Lagos; Durbar Hotel, Kaduna; 18 Mission Rd, Benin City
Associate Company: Nigerian Book Suppliers Ltd (qv)

University Bookshop (Nigeria) Ltd*, University of Ibadan, Ibadan Tel: 62550 ext 1208 (branches in Ilorin, Port Harcourt, Calabar, and Maiduguri)
General Manager: Simon Walton

University of Ife Bookshop Ltd*, University of Ife, Ile-Ife Tel: Ife 2291 ext 2145 and 2146 Cable Add: Bookshop Ifevarsity
Branch at Ondo
Man Dir: Oyeniyi Osundina

University of Lagos Bookshop*, Yaba, Lagos Tel: 800501
Also: College of Medicine, University of Lagos, Idi-Araba, Surulere, Lagos

University of Nigeria Bookshop Ltd*, Nsukka Tel: 6251 ext 7
Manager: K K Oyeoku

Major Libraries

Agricultural Library*, PMB 1044, Samaru-Zaria Tel: 32571/4 ext 212
Librarian: Malam R Salami
Publications include: Library Accession List (monthly), *List of Current Serials in the Library* (annually), *KWIC Index to the Abstracting & Indexing Publications currently being received by the IAR Library*, 2nd edition 1976

Ahmadu Bello University Library*, Samaru-Zaria Tel: 06322553 Telex: 75241 Zarabu Ng

Anambra State Central Library*, PMB 1026, Enugu, Anambra State Tel: 254331, 254339 Cable Add: Libraries
Librarian: M Okoye

Bendel State Library*, PMB 1127, Benin City, Bendel State Tel: 243380 Cable Add: Library Benin
Dir: D O Oboro
Publication: Bendel Library Journal
Bendel Book Depot, a division of Bendel State Library, is also at the above address

Benin University Library, PMB 1191, Benin City Tel: 240115
University Librarian: O O Ogundipe;
Publications: Annual Report, Library News, List of Serials, Current Awareness Bulletin of the Medical Sub-library

Ibadan University Library, Ibadan Tel: 400550 ext 1424-26/1496 Telex: 31233 Iba Lib Ng
Librarian: T Olabisi Odeinde
Publications: Library Record (m); *Annual Report, 1980/81; Humanities: A Guide to Reference Sources in the Library* (1976) (Library Guide No 3); *Biological Sciences: A Guide to Reference Sources in the Library* (1976) (Library Guide No 4); *Education: A Guide to Reference Sources in the Library* (1978) (Library Guide No 5)

International Institute of Tropical Agriculture Library*, PMB 5320, Ibadan Tel: 413440 Cable Add: Tropfound Ikeja Telex: 31417 Tropic NG
Librarian: Dr S M Lawani

Library Board of **Kaduna** State*, PMB 2061, Bida Rd, Kaduna Tel: 242590/210322/214417
Dir: Shehu Ibrahim Shika
Publications: Annual Report, New Additions to Stock (monthly)

Kano State Library*, PMB 3094, Kano

Lagos City Council Libraries*, 48 Broad St, PMB 2025, Lagos Tel: 50246

National Archives of Nigeria Library*, PMB 4, University of Ibadan Post Office, Ibadan
Library Officer: O A Momoh
Publications: Catalogues; Bibliographies; Handlists; Guides

National Library of Nigeria*, 4 Wesley St, PMB 12626, Lagos Tel: 634704/656590/656591 Cable Add: Biblios Telex: 20117
Publications include: Libraries in Nigeria, A Directory; National Bibliography of Nigeria; Nigerian Books in Print; Nominal List of Practising Librarians in Nigeria; Serials in Print in Nigeria; Nigerbiblios (quarterly); *Afribiblios* (twice a year)
ISBN Publisher's Prefix: 978-128

Nnamdi Azikiwe Library*, University of Nigeria, Nsukka Tel: 6251 ext 59 Cable Add: Nigersity Library
Librarian: S C Nwoye
Publications: Nsukka Library Notes; UNLAN (University of Nigeria Library Accessions and News); Readers' Guide

University of Ife Library*, Ile-Ife Tel: 2290

University of Lagos Library*, Akoka, Yaba, Lagos Tel: 800502 ext 362/800504 ext 362

University of Nigeria Library, see Nnamdi Azikiwe

Library Associations

Anambra State School Libraries Association*, c/o Enugu Campus Library, University of Nigeria, Enugu Tel: 252080 Cable Add: Nigersity Enugu
Honorary Secretary: Dr Dorothy S Obi
Publications include: School Libraries Bulletin (3 times a year); *Manual for School Libraries on Small Budgets*

Nigerian Association of Agricultural Librarians and Documentalists (NAALD)*, c/o International Grain Legume Information Centre, IITA, PMB 5320, Ibadan Tel: 23741
Secretary: E N O Adimorah

Nigerian Library Association*, PMB 12655, Lagos Tel: 56590
Secretary: Inuwa Diko
Publications: Nigerian Libraries (3 a year), *NLA Newsletter*
(There are also regional associations in the various states under the umbrella of the Nigerian Library Association)

Library Reference Books and Journals

Books

Directory of Lagos Libraries, Oceana Publications Inc, Dobbs Ferry, NY 10522, USA

Libraries in Nigeria. A Directory, National Library of Nigeria, 4 Wesley St, PMB 12626, Lagos

Nominal List of Practising Librarians in Nigeria, National Library of Nigeria, 4 Wesley St, PMB 12626, Lagos (Useful listing providing names and addresses of practising librarians at 59 libraries in Nigeria. To be published annually in the future)

Journals

Afribiblios (twice a year), National Library of Nigeria, 4 Wesley St, PMB 12626, Lagos

Bendel Library Journal, Bendel State Library, PMB 1127, Benin City

ECS School Libraries Bulletin, East Central State School Libraries Association, c/o Enugu Campus Library, University of Nigeria, Enugu

Library Record, Ibadan University Library, Ibadan

NLA Newsletter, Nigerian Library Association, PMB 12655, Lagos

Nigerbiblios (quarterly), National Library of Nigeria, 4 Wesley St, PMB 12626, Lagos

Nigerian Libraries, Nigerian Library Association, PMB 12655, Lagos (the official publication of the Nigerian Library Association; the Association also publishes a mimeographed newsletter)

Nsukka Library Notes, University of Nigeria Library, Nsukka, Anambra State

Literary Associations and Societies

Nigerian Writers' Club*, 76 St Finbarrs College Rd, Akoka, Yaba, Lagos State
Publication: Visions at Dawn

In addition to the above, small literary societies and writers' circles, etc are attached to the English departments at the various universities

Literary Periodicals

Afriscope, Pan Afriscope (Nigeria) Ltd, 45 Saibu St, PMB 1119, Yaba, Lagos (Monthly — contains a regular 'Literary Scene' column which features book reviews and gives extensive coverage to cultural and literary events throughout Africa)

The Benin Review, Ethiope Publishing Corporation, PMB 1192, Benin City (The journal covers all the arts in Africa, both traditional and modern, and is also concerned with cultural life in the Black World generally)

The Muse; literary journal of the English Association at Nsukka, University of Nigeria, Nsukka (An irregularly published literary magazine. Another literary magazine, *Okike*, originally published from Nsukka, is now published in the USA)

Nigeria Magazine, Cultural Division, Federal Ministry of Information, PMB 12524, Lagos (Bi-monthly cultural and literary magazine published since 1932)

Oduma, Rivers State Council for Arts and Culture, 74-76 Bonny St, PMB 5049, Port Harcourt

Visions at Dawn, Nigerian Writers' Club, 76 St Finbarrs College Rd, Akoka, Yaba, Lagos State

Note: There are several more 'little magazines', largely in mimeographed form, published by English departments and writers' groups at the various universities

Literary Prizes

Ife Book Fair Prizes*
For children's books in the age groups up to 6, and 7 to 12. Awarded annually. Enquiries to Ife Book Fair Director, University of Ife Bookshop Ltd, Ile-Ife

Federal Radio Corporation of Nigeria*
Various literary and drama competitions are sponsored by the Federal Radio Corporation of Nigeria, Lagos, from time to time. Enquiries to Federal Radio Corporation of Nigeria, Broadcasting House, Ikoyi, Lagos

Nigerian Book Development Council Book Prize*
For the best book of social significance by a Nigerian author. 200 naira awarded annually. Enquiries to Nigerian Book Development Council Book Prize, c/o Ife Book Fair Director, University of Ife Bookshop Ltd, University of Ife, Ile-Ife

Nigerian Book Development Council Literary Prize*
For the best book written by a Nigerian and published in Nigeria (excluding children's books). 300 naira awarded annually. The most recent prizewinner was *Toward the Decolonization of African Literature* by Chinweizu, Onwuchekwa Jemie and Ikechukwu Madubuike (Fourth Dimension Publishers). Enquiries to Nigerian Book Development Council, 6 Obanta Rd, Apapa, Lagos State

Translation Agencies and Associations

Igbo Language Translation Agency*, c/o University Publishing Co Ltd, 11 Central School Rd, PO Box 386, Onitsha

The **Nigeria Educational Research** Council*, PO Box 8058, Lagos (Located at: 3 Jibowu St, Yaba, Lagos) Tel: 862272/862269 Cable Add: Edusearch, Lagos
The Research Council has a Translation Bureau attached to it

Norway

General Information

Language: Norwegian. There are two distinct forms: Bokmål (sometimes called Riksmål) and Nynorsk (formerly called Landsmål) whose relative importance has changed in recent years. About 90% of Norwegian books are now published in Bokmål and it is the medium of instruction in most schools. Danish and Swedish are usually intelligible to speakers of Norwegian
Religion: Lutheran
Population: 4.1 million
Bank Hours: 0845-1545 (1515 in summer) Monday-Wednesday and Friday; 0815-1800 (1700 in summer) Thursday
Shop Hours: 0830-1700 Monday-Friday; 0830-1400 Saturday
Currency: 100 øre = 1 Norwegian krone (plural: kroner)
Export/Import Information: Member of the European Free Trade Association. No tariff on books except children's picture books. Books exempt from VAT. No duty on advertising. No import licence required. Nominal exchange controls

NORWAY

Copyright: UCC, Berne, Florence (see International section)

Book Trade Organizations

Norsk Antikvarbokhandlerforening, Ullevålsveien 1, Oslo 1
Norwegian Antiquarian Booksellers' Association

Norsk Bokhandler Medhjelper Forening, Ovre Vollgate 15, Oslo 1
Norwegian Book Trade Employees' Association
Publications: Norsk Bokhandlermatrikkel, Norsk Boknøkkel

Norsk Bokhandlersamband, c/o Lunde Forlag, Grensen 19, Oslo 1
Norwegian Christians Booksellers' Union
Chairman: Birger Hoiset; *Secretary:* Paul Odland

Norsk Bokimport A/S*, Postboks 784, Ovre Vollgate 15, Oslo 1 Tel: (02) 417050 Telex: 72068 Nobok

Norsk Boknummerkontor, Universitetsbiblioteket i Oslo, Drammensvegen 42, Oslo 2 Tel: (02) 564980 Telex: 16078 Ub N
ISBN Agency
Administrator: Kari Grethe Randers-Pehrson

Norsk Forleggersamband, c/o Lunde Forlag, Grensen 19, Oslo 1
Norwegian Christian Publishers' Union
Chairman: Knut Ramboel; *Secretary:* Paul Odland

Norsk Musikkforleggerforening, PO Box 1499, Vika, Oslo 1
Norwegian Music Publishers' Association

Norske Bokhandlerforening, Ovre Vollgate 15, Oslo 1 Tel: (02) 410760
Norwegian Booksellers' Association
Publication: Bok og Samfunn

Den Norske Forfatterforening, Rådhusgata 7, Postboks 327 Sentrum, Oslo 1 Tel: (02) 424077
Norwegian Authors' Association
Secretary: Tordis Fjeldstad

Den Norske Forleggerforening, Ovre Vollgate 15, Oslo 1 Tel: (02) 421355/422285
Norwegian Publishers' Association
Dir: Paul Martens Røthe

Norwegian Association of Children's and Young People's Authors*, Rådhusgata 7, Oslo 1

Sentral Bokhandel A/S, Gml Drammensvei 48, Postboks 127, N-1321 Høvik Tel: (02) 532376
Dir: Cathrine Holst

Standard Book Numbering Agency, see Norsk Boknummerkontor

Book Trade Reference Books and Journals

Books

Bibliografi over Norges Offentlige Publikasjoner (Bibliography of Norwegian Government Publications), The Royal University Library, Drammeneseveien 42, N-1302, Oslo

Norsk Bokhandlermatrikkel (Norwegian Booksellers Membership List), Norwegian Book Trade Employees' Association, Ovre Vollgate 15, Oslo 1

Publishers

Ansgar Forlag A/S, Møllergate 26, Oslo 1 Tel: (02) 208518
Manager: Halvor Saebo
Subjects: Fiction, General, Religion
ISBN Publishers' Prefix: 82-503

H Aschehoug & Co (W Nygaard) A/S, Sehestedsgate 3, Oslo 1 Tel: (02) 429470 Cable Add: Aco Oslo
Man Dir: William Nygaard; *Assistant Man Dir:* Ole Sagfossen; *Dir, School Book Department:* Hallstein Laupsa; *Editorial:* Oivind Blom, Harald Horjen, Irja Thorenfeldt, Ivar Havnevik; *Marketing:* Erik Akre; *Rights & Permissions:* Harald Horjen
Subsidiary Companies: Kunnskapsforlaget I/S (qv) (jointly owned with Gyldendal Norsk Forlag — qv); Tanum-Norli Forlaget A/S (qv)
Book Club: Den Norske Bokklubben A/S (with three other Norwegian publishers)
Subjects: General Fiction and Non-fiction, Reference, Juveniles, Quality Paperbacks, General & Social Science, Secondary & Primary Textbooks
1981: 487 titles *Founded:* 1872
ISBN Publisher's Prefix: 82-03

Bergendal Forlag, Postboks 1894 Vika, Oslo 1 Tel: (02) 244861 Cable Add: Bergendalbok
Man Dir: Pål H Christiansen
ISBN Publisher's Prefix: 82-90382

Bladkompaniet A/S+, Stålfjæra 5, Oslo 9 Tel: (02) 257190
Man Dir, Rights & Permissions: Finn Arnesen; *Sales Dir:* Reidar Myhre; *Advertising:* Ole Wågenes
Subjects: General Fiction, Paperbacks, Magazines
1981: 110 titles *1982:* 110 titles *Founded:* 1915
ISBN Publisher's Prefix: 82-509

F Bruns Bokhandels Forlag A/S, Kongensgate 10, Postboks 476, N-7001 Trondheim Tel: (075) 20625
Dir: Fridthjov Brun
Subjects: Science, Technology
Bookshop: Kongensgate 10, Postboks 476, N-7000 Trondheim
Founded: 1873
ISBN Publisher's Prefix: 82-7028

J W Cappelens Forlag A/S+, Kirkegaten 15, Oslo 1 Tel: (02) 429440 Cable Add: Cappelen
Man Dirs: Sigmund Strømme, Jan Wiese; *Editorial:* Per Glad, Aase Gjerdrum, Egil A, Kristoffersen, Ola Haugen; *Sales:* Per Pedersen; *Production:* Erik Pettersen; *Rights & Permissions:* Eva Gröner
Subsidiary Company: Wennergren-Cappelen A/S, Nedre Vollgate 4, Oslo 1
Subjects: General Fiction, Non-fiction, Textbooks, Reference, Maps, Religion, Juveniles, Low- & High-priced Paperbacks, Encyclopaedias
Book Club: Den Norske Bokklubben A/S (with three other Norwegian publishers)
Antiquarian Booksellers: J W Cappelens Antikvariat, Kirkegaten 15, Oslo 1
1981: 298 titles *1982:* 301 titles *Founded:* 1829
ISBN Publisher's Prefix: 82-02

N W Damm og Søn A/S+, Tvetenveien 32, Postboks 6140 Etterstad, Oslo 6 Tel: (02) 649210 Cable Add: Damson
Dirs: Arne Damm, Per Støkken
Subjects: How-to, Children's Books, Textbooks, Dictionaries, Guidebooks
1982: 40 titles *Founded:* 1843
ISBN Publisher's Prefix: 82-517

Dreyers Forlag A/S, Arbiensgate 7, Oslo 2 Tel: (02) 443810 Cable Add: Dreyerbok
Man Dir: Hans B Butenschön; *Editorial:* Oistein Parmann; *Sales, Publicity:* Bodil Kruse; *Production:* Bjørn Pedersen
Subjects: General Fiction, Non-fiction, Belles Lettres, Music, Art, Low- & High-priced Paperbacks
Founded: 1942
ISBN Publisher's Prefix: 82-09

J W Eide Forlag A/S, Fosswinckelsgate 8, Postboks 146, N-5001 Bergen Tel: (05) 325801
Man Dir: Sigvald Flataker
Subjects: General Fiction, History, Music, Art, University, Secondary & Primary Textbooks, Educational Materials, Juveniles
ISBN Publisher's Prefix: 82-514

Elingaard Forlag A/S, now Nå Forlag (qv)

Fabritius Forlagshus, now part of Gyldendal Norsk Forlag (qv)

Fonna Forlag L/L*, St Olavs Plass 3, Postboks 6912 Oslo 1 Tel: (02) 201303/201201
Subjects: General Fiction, Poetry, Biography, Magazines, Juveniles
Founded: 1940
ISBN Publisher's Prefix: 82-513

E Greens Forlag*, Sverdrupsgaten 8, Oslo 5 Tel: (02) 376602
Subjects: General Fiction, Belles Lettres, Juveniles
ISBN Publisher's Prefix: 82-01

John Griegs Forlag, Vaskerelven 8, Postboks 248, N-5001 Bergen Tel: (05) 233900 Cable Add: Bokgrieg
Man Dir: Rolf Moe Nilssen
Subjects: Non-fiction, Fiction for Children, Co-editions
Founded: 1721
ISBN Publisher's Prefix: 82-533

Grøndahl og Søn Forlag A/S, Munkedamsveien 35, Oslo 2 Tel: (02) 419740 Cable Add: Bokgrøndahl
Man Dir: Finn P Nyquist; *Editor:* Tove Gulbrandsen
Subjects: General Non-fiction, Reference, Law, Textbooks, Illustrated Books, Fiction
Founded: 1812
ISBN Publisher's Prefix: 82-504

Gyldendal Norsk Forlag, Universitetsgaten 16, Postboks 6860 St Olavs Plass, Oslo 1 Tel: (02) 200710 Cable Add: Gyldendal Telex: 72880 Gyldn N
Man Dir: Andreas Skartveit
Subsidiary Company: Kunnskapsforlaget (jointly owned with H Aschehoug & Co A/S) (qqv)
Subjects: General Fiction, Science Fiction, Belles Lettres, Poetry, Art, Music, Biography, History, How-to, Politics, Philosophy, Psychology, Reference, Religion, Social Science, Secondary & Primary Textbooks, Children's books, *Easy Readers*, Encyclopaedias, Paperbacks, Periodicals
Book Club: Den Norske Bokklubben A/S (with three other Norwegian publishers)
Founded: 1925
ISBN Publisher's Prefix: 82-05

Henny's Forlag*, Postboks 1894 Vika, Oslo 1
Man Dir: M Andenäs; *Dirs:* P Christiansen, J Jansen
Subjects: General Fiction, Biography, History, How-to, Philosophy, Religion
Founded: 1962

Hjemmenes Forlag A/S*, Postboks 1739, Vika, Oslo 1 Tel: (02) 143151
Publisher: Yngve Woxholth
Subject: Cultural and Historical Books (mainly in colour)

Hjemmet A/S, Kristian den IVs gate 13, Oslo 1 Tel: (02) 429470 Telex: 76677
Man Dir: Torstein Bore
Parent Company: Gutenberghus Group, Denmark
Associate Companies: Ehapa Verlag GmbH, Federal Republic of Germany; Gutenberghus Publishing Service A/S, Denmark (qv); Hemmets Journal, Sweden (qv); Hjemmets Bokforlag A/S, Norway (qv)
Founded: 1911
ISBN Publisher's Prefix: 82-7315

Hjemmets Bokforlag A/S, Kristian Augusts gate 10, Oslo 1 Tel: (02) 429165 Telex: 17074 Novel
Man Dir: Kjell H Vestberg; *Assistant Man Dir:* June Heggenhougen
Parent Company: Gutenberghus Group, Denmark
Associate Companies: Ehapa Verlag GmbH, Federal Republic of Germany (qv); Gutenberghus Publishing Service A/S and Wangels Forlag A/S, Denmark (qqv); Hemmets Journal, Sweden (qv); Hjemmet A/S, Norway (qqv)
Subjects: General Fiction, Non-fiction, Reference, Juveniles, Quality Paperbacks
Book Clubs: Hjemmets Bokklubb, Hjemmets Kokebokklub, Donald Ducks Bokklub, Disney Junior Bokklub, Bokklubben Ny Krim
Founded: 1969
ISBN Publisher's Prefix: 82-7001

Kunnskapsforlaget I/S*, Postboks 6736, Sankt Olavs Plass, Sehestedsgt 4, Oslo 1 Tel: (02) 205215
Man Dir: Lars Bucher Johannessen; *Chief Editor:* Egil Tveterås; *Marketing Dir:* Reidar Bøe; *Production:* Rolf Andersson; *Sales Manager:* Tom Thorsteinsen
Parent Companies: H Aschehoug & Co A/S, Gyldendal Norsk Forlag (qqv)
Subjects: Encyclopaedias, Dictionaries
Founded: 1975
ISBN Publisher's Prefix: 82-573

Lunde Forlag og Bokhandel A/S+, Grensen 19, Oslo 1 Tel: (02) 429120 Cable Add: Norskluth
Editor: Torstein Lindhjem; *Production:* Paul Odland; *Rights & Permissions:* Jan Bøe
Subjects: General Fiction, Belles Lettres, Poetry, Biography, Music, Art, Religion, Juveniles, High-priced Paperbacks, Secondary & Primary Textbooks, Educational Materials
Bookshop: Lunde Forlag og Bokhandel A/S, C Sundtsgate 2, N-5000 Bergen, Norway
1981: 40 titles *Founded:* 1905
ISBN Publisher's Prefix: 82-520

Luther Forlag A/S, Kirkegaten 32, Oslo 1 Tel: (02) 422260
Man Dir: Nils Tore Andersen
Subjects: General Fiction, Biography, History, Religion, Juveniles, Low- & High-priced Paperbacks, Dictionaries
1982: approx 90 titles
ISBN Publisher's Prefix: 82-531

Harald **Lyche** & Co A/S, now incorporated in Erik Sandberg A/S (qv)

Ernst G **Mortensens** Forlag A/S, Sørkedalsveien 10A, Oslo 3 Tel: (02) 603090 Cable Add: Pressmort Telex: 17626
Man Dir: Carl L Mortensen; *Editorial:* Rigmor Foss, Solveig Høysaeten, Erling Waldal; *Sales:* O E Grønaker; *Information:* Knut-Jørgen Erichsen; *Advertising:* R Marthinsen; *Rights & Permissions:* Per R Mortensen, Jr
Subsidiary Companies: NPS/AssP (Norsk Presseservice/Associated Press A/S), Oslo; Forenede Trykkerier A/s, Oslo
Subjects: General, Periodicals
Founded: 1933
ISBN Publisher's Prefix: 82-527

N K I-forlaget, Løxavn 15, Postboks 113, N-1351 Rud Tel: (02) 135790
Publisher: Jan Lien; *Editorial:* Sverre Harald Amundsen, Solvar Hofsøy; *Sales, Publicity:* Anne L Fougli
Subsidiary Company: NKI Educational Services Ltd, UK (qv)
Subjects: Primary & Secondary Textbooks, Technical Textbooks, General Non-fiction
1981: 69 titles *1982:* 81 titles *Founded:* 1967
ISBN Publisher's Prefix: 82-562

Nå Forlag A/S (formerly Elingaard Forlag), Postboks 7058 H, Oslo 3 (Located at Oscarsgate 55, Oslo 2) Tel: (02) 565070
Parent Company: Libertas, Oscarsgate 55, Oslo 2
Subjects: Politics, Marketing, Economy
1981: 16 titles *1982:* 12 titles
ISBN Publisher's Prefix: 82-505

Noregs Boklag L/L*, Platous gate 9, Oslo 1 Tel: (02) 689424/193721
Manager: Per Roar Öian
Subjects: General Fiction, Plays, Poetry, Biography, Music, Juveniles
Founded: 1923
ISBN Publisher's Prefix: 82-522

Olaf **Norlis** Forlag A/S, see Tanum-Norli

Norsk Kunstforlag A/S+, Postboks 2559, Solli, Oslo 2 Tel: (02) 414603
Man Dir: Ivar Grimsmo
Subjects: General, Art, Atlases
ISBN Publisher's Prefix: 82-90069

Det **Norske** Samlaget, Postboks 4672 Sofienberg, Oslo 5 (Located at: Trondheimsvegen 15, Oslo 5) Tel: (02) 687600
Man Dirs: Audun Heskestad, Mads Liland; *Editorial:* Olav Hr Rue; *Sales:* Helga Kolstad
Subjects: General Fiction, Belles Lettres, Poetry, Biography, History, Philosophy, Religion, Textbooks, Reference, Juveniles, High-priced Paperbacks, Periodicals
1981: 117 titles *1982:* 139 titles *Founded:* 1868
ISBN Publisher's Prefix: 82-521

Novus Forlag A/S, Postboks 748, Sentrum, Oslo 1 Tel: (02) 353314
Publisher: Olav Røsset
Subjects: Education, General
1981: 10 titles *1982:* 4 titles *Founded:* 1972
ISBN Publisher's Prefix: 82-7099

Pax Forlag A/S, Gøteborggt 8, Oslo 5 Tel: (02) 379082
Man Dir, Rights & Permissions: Paul Hedlund; *Editorial:* Birgit Bjerck; *Administration:* Sissel Bugge; *Production:* Aage-H Hansen
Subjects: Fiction, Political and Social Science, Literature, Encyclopaedias, Quality Paperbacks
1981: 38 titles *1982:* 36 titles *Founded:* 1964
ISBN Publisher's Prefix: 82-530

Pedagogisk Forlag A/S*, Dronningensgaten 23, Oslo 1 Tel: (02) 414927
Subjects: Textbooks, Educational Materials

Rune Forlag*, Postboks 1202, N-7001 Trondheim Tel: (075) 32362
Publisher: Erling Skjølberg
Subject: General
ISBN Publisher's Prefix: 82-523

Erik **Sandberg** A/S, Nedre Vollgate 9, N-Oslo 1 Tel: (02) 110585 Telex: 17580
Chief Executive, Rights & Permissions: Trond Wikborg; *Editorial:* Tore Olsen, Bjørn Aarseth, Per Martinsen; *Sales:* Tor Nilsen; *Production:* Rolf Steinhaugen; *Publicity:* Solveig Thime
Subjects: Yearbooks (Pleasure Crafts, Prefab Housing, Cars, Hi-fi), Norwegian Farms Series, General Fiction, Non-fiction, Textbooks, Periodicals
Founded: 1973
ISBN Publisher's Prefix: 82-7316

Chr **Schibsteds** Forlag+, Kristian IV's Gate 1, Postboks 1178, Sentrum, Oslo 1 Tel: (02) 205060 Telex: 71230 aft n
General Manager: Ola Veigaard; *Editorial:* Per G Damsgaard; *Sales Dir:* Arne Andreassen; *Rights & Permissions:* Ola Veigaard
Orders to: Forlagsentralen, Postboks 6005, Etterstad, Oslo 6
Parent Company: Schibsted-gruppen, Postboks 1178, Sentrum, Oslo 1
Subjects: How-to, Reference, Juveniles, Nature
1981: 28 titles *1982:* 50 titles *Founded:* 1839
ISBN Publisher's Prefix: 82-516

Snøfugl Forlag, Postboks 95, N-7084 Melhus Tel: (07) 870473
Chief Executive, Editorial: Åsmund Snøfugl; *Sales:* Johan Snøfugl
Associate Company: A/s Bygdetrykk, 7084 Melhus
Subjects: General
Founded: 1972
ISBN Publisher's Prefix: 82-7083

Solum Forlag A/S*, Asveien 5, 1324 Lysaker Tel: 534692
Subject: General
ISBN Publisher's Prefix: 82-560

Stabenfeldt Forlag, Tanke Svilandsgate 55, Postboks 189, N-4001 Stavanger Tel: (04) 521553 Cable Add: Bokorm Telex: 40761
Publishing Dir: Tor Tjeldflåt
Subsidiary Companies: SE-bladene, Stabenfeldthus (Divisions)
Subjects: General Fiction & Non-fiction
1981: 4 titles *1982:* 3 titles *Founded:* 1920
ISBN Publisher's Prefix: 82-532

P F **Steensballes** Forlag, Postboks 130, N-2261 Kirkenaer Tel: (066) 47588
Publisher: Bjarne H Reenskaug
Subjects: Hunting, Fishing
ISBN Publisher's Prefix: 82-7004

Tanum-Norli Forlaget A/S, Kr Augustsgate 7A, Oslo 1 Tel: (02) 110260 Cable Add: Tanumlag
Publishing Dir: Steinar Gundersen; *Editorial:* Birger Huse
Parent Company: H Aschehoug & Co (W Nygaard) A/S (qv)
Subjects: General Non-fiction, Reference, Textbooks, Education
ISBN Publisher's Prefix: 82-518

Teknologisk Forlag, Tvetenveien 152, Oslo 6 Tel: (02) 261250
Man Dir, Rights & Permissions: Rudolf Jenssen; *Assistant Dir:* Tom Harald Jenssen; *Editorial Dir:* Tore Egeberg; *Sales Dir:* Karl H Ormen
Subjects: How-to, Philosophy, Textbooks, Reference, Engineering, General Science
Founded: 1958
ISBN Publisher's Prefix: 82-512

Tiden Norsk Forlag, Postboks 8326, Hammersborg (Located at: Storgt 23D, Oslo 1) Tel: (02) 335380 Cable Add: Tiden
Man Dir: Trygve Johansen; *Editorial and Rights & Permissions:* Miss Signe Bakken; *Production:* Karin Stok
Subsidiary Companies: Aktuell Kunst, Laeremiddelhuset
Subjects: General Fiction & Non-fiction, Textbooks, Reference, Paperbacks, Juveniles
Book Clubs: Den Norske Bokklubben A/S; Bokklubben Nye Bøker (with three other

Norwegian publishers)
Bookshop: Arbeidernes Bok- og Papirhandel, Youngstorget 4, Oslo 1
Founded: 1933
ISBN Publisher's Prefix: 82-10

Universitetsforlaget*, Postboks 2959, Tøyen, Oslo 6 Tel: (02) 276060 Cable Add: Universitypress, Oslo Telex: 11896 Ufor N
Man Dir: Tor Bjerkmann; *Editorial:* Fredrik Lund; *Sales Manager:* Magne Gaasemyr; *Rights & Permissions:* Vibeke Siegwarth
Orders to: Postboks 2977, Tøyen, Oslo 6
Subjects: Technical, Reference, Science, Paperbacks, Textbooks, Educational Materials
Founded: 1950
Miscellaneous: Publishers for the University of Oslo, The University of Bergen, the University of Tromsø, and other institutions of higher learning
ISBN Publisher's Prefix: 82-00

Literary Agents

E M B L A, see Pat Shaw Associates

Hanna-Kirsti **Koch***, Postboks 3043, Oslo 2
Contact: Eilif Koch

Ulla **Løhren** Literary Agency, Postboks 150, Tåsen, Oslo 8 (Located at: Gjennomfaret 7, Oslo) Tel: (02) 230207 Cable Add: Ullabooks
Dir: Ulla Løhren

Suzanne **Palme** Literary Agency, Postboks 7112, Homansbyen, Oslo 3 Tel: (02) 448174 Cable Add: Palmebook
Dir: Suzanne Palme

Pat **Shaw** Associates (formerly EMBLA)*, Fredbosvei 61, N-1370 Asker Tel: (02) 782829

Book Clubs

Bokklubbens **Barn**, see Den Norske Bokklubben A/S
Subject: Juveniles

Det **Beste** A/S*, Postboks 726-Sentrum, Oslo 1

Disney Junior Bokklub, Kristian Augusts gate 10, Oslo 1 Tel: (02) 429165 Telex: 17074
Owned by: Hjemmets Bokforlag A/S (qv)
Subject: Juvenile Fiction

Donald Ducks Bokklubb, Kristian Augusts gate 10, Oslo 1 Tel: (02) 429165 Telex: 17074
Owned by: Hjemmets Bokforlag A/S (qv)
Subject: Juvenile fiction

Bokklubbens **Ekstrabøker**, see Den Norske Bokklubben A/S

Hjemmets Bokklubb, Kristian Augusts gate 10, Oslo 1 Tel: (02) 429165 Telex: 17074
Owned by: Hjemmets Bokforlag A/S (qv)
Subjects: Fiction, Non-fiction

Hjemmets Kokebokklubb, Kristian Augusts gate 10, Oslo 1 Tel: (02) 429165 Telex: 17074
Owned by: Hjemmets Bokforlag A/S (qv)
Subject: Cookery

Bokklubbens **Kunstforlag**, see Den Norske Bokklubben A/S

Bokklubbens **Lyrikkvaennene***, see Den Norske Bokklubben
Subject: Poetry

Den **Norske Bokklubben** A/S, Postboks 150, Vollsveien 13, Lysaker, N-1321 Stabekk
Includes: Den Norske Bokklubben, Bokklubbens Barn, Bokklubbens Ekstrabøker, Bokklubbens Kunstforlag, Bokklubbens Lyrikkvenner, Bokklubben Nye Bøker
Members: 420,000
Owned by: H Aschehoug & Co (W Nygaard) A/S, J W Cappelens Forlag A/S, Gyldendal Norsk Forlag, Tiden Norsk Forlag (qqv)
Subjects: Fiction, Biography, Travel

Bokklubben **Ny Krim**, Kristian Augusts gate 10, Oslo 1 Tel: (02) 429165 Telex: 17074
Owned by: Hjemmets Bokforlag A/S (qv)
Subject: Crime Fiction

Bokklubben **Nye Bøker** (New Book Club), see Den Norske Bokklubben

Major Booksellers

F **Beyer** Bok-Og Papirhandel A/S, Strandgaten 4, N-5000 Bergen Tel: (05) 211185 Cable Add: Bokbeyer, Bergen
Manager: Birger Knudsen

F **Bruns** Bokhandel, Kongensgate 10, Postboks 476, N-7000 Trondheim

Gardum A/S, Søregate 22, Postboks 242, N-4001 Stavanger Tel: (04) 520200/520400
Manager: Reider Gardum

Ed B **Giertsen** A/S*, Småstrandgate, Postboks 217, N-5001 Bergen Tel: (05) 219680

Johan **Grundt** Tanum A/S, Postboks 1177, Sentrum, Oslo 1 Tel: (02) 801260 Cable Add: Tanumbok Telex: 72427 Tanum N
Manager: Leif Hammerlund
Import, export, wholesalers

Lyngs Bokhandel A/S, Postboks 328, N-7001 Trondheim (Located at: Olav Trygvasonsgate 26, N-7000 Trondheim) Tel: (07) 512544
Manager: Ragnvald C Knudsen

Olaf **Norlis** Bokhandel A/S*, Universitetsgaten 24, Oslo 1 Tel: (02) 336190
Shipping Add: 1850 Mysen
Specialists in school books, medical and maritime literature, antiquarian books. Also exporters.

Norsk Bokimport A/S*, Ovre Vollgate 15, Postboks 784, Oslo 1 Tel: (02) 417050 Telex: 72068 Nobok
Manager: Einar Bruvik
Importers

Erik **Qvist** Bokhandel A/S, Drammensveien 16, Oslo 2 Tel: (02) 445269
Manager: Erik Chr Qvist

Sellevolds Bokhandel A/S*, Nedre Slottsgate 8, Oslo 1 Tel: 425258/414150/421529
Manager: Arne Iversen

Sentral Bokhandel A/S, Gml Drammensvei 48, Postboks 127, N-1321 Høvik Tel: (02) 532376

H **Sundems** Bokhandel A/S*, Storgate 12, N-8000 Bodø Tel: (081) 20154
Manager: Carl August Veigård

Tapir, Universitet i Trondheim, N-7034 Trondheim NTH

Universitetsbokhandeln*, PO Box 307, Blindern, Oslo 3
Manager: Tom Vister

Major Libraries

Bergen offentlige Bibliotek Horda land Fylkesbibliotek*, Bergen
Municipal and County Library

Deichmanske Bibliotek, Henrik Ibsens gate 1, Oslo 1 Tel: (02) 204335 Telex: 18337 deich n
City Library of Oslo
Chief Librarian: Hans Fløgstad

Drammen Folkebibliotek*, Gamle Kirkeplass 7, Postboks 1136, N-3001 Drammen Tel: (03) 832890 Telex: 18483 Fbdra N
Public Library of Drammen

Fellesbiblioteket for det Kongelige Norske Videnskabers Selskab, Museet og Norges Laererhøgskole, Erling Skakkesgt 47C, N-7000 Trondheim Tel: (07) 592209 Telex: 55384 Bibl n

Styret for det **Industrielle Rettsvern** Bibliotek, Middelthunsgate 15b, Postboks 8160 Dep, Oslo 1 Tel: (02) 461900 Telex: 19152 nopat n
Library of the Norwegian Patent Office
Librarian: Ms Turi Stokke

Det **Kongelige Norske Videnskabers Selskab**, see Fellesbiblioteket

Kristiansand Folkebibliotek, Box 476, N-4601 Kristiansand Tel: (042) 29165 Telex: 21149 Kribi N
Municipal Library

Norges Landbrukshøgskoles Bibliotek, Postboks 12, N-1432 Ås-NLH Tel: (02) 949060 Telex: 17125 Nlhbi n
Library of the Agricultural University of Norway

Riksarkivet, Bankplass 3, N-Oslo 1
National Archives of Norway

Statistisk Sentralbyras Bibliotek, Postboks 8131 Dep, Oslo 1
Library of the Central Bureau of Statistics
Librarian: Randi Gran

Stavanger Bibliotek, Postboks 310-320, N-4001 Stavanger Tel: (04) 528020 Telex: 33181 fb sta n

Universitetsbiblioteket i Bergen*, Möhlenprisbakken 1, N-5000 Bergen Tel: (05) 210040 Telex: 42690 ubb n

Universitetsbiblioteket i Oslo, Drammensveien 42, N Oslo 2 Tel: (02) 564980 Telex: 76078 ubn
The Royal University Library (National Library)

Universitetsbiblioteket i Trondheim (Kongelige Norske Videnskabers Selskab Biblioteket)*, Erling Skakkes Gt 47C, N-7000 Trondheim Tel: (075) 92209
Library of the Royal Norwegian Society of Sciences and Letters

The **University of Trondheim**, Norwegian Institute of Technology*, The Library, Høgskoleringen 1, N-7034 Trondheim-NTH Tel: (075) 95110 Cable Add: NTHB Telex: 55186 nthhb n

Videnskabers Selskab Biblioteket, see Universitetsbibliotek i Trondheim

Library Associations

Arkivarforeningen*, Postboks 10, Kringsjå, Oslo 8
The Association of Archivists
Publication: Norsk arkivforum

Kommunale Bibliotekarbeideres Forening,
c/o Bjoern Bringsvaerd, Skien Bibliotek,
Postboks 349, N-3700 Skien
Municipal Librarians' Association
Publication: Kontakten (6 a year)

Norsk Biblioteklag*, Bogstadveien 8, Oslo 3
Norwegian Librarians' Association
Publications: Meldinger (6-8 a year)

Norsk Bibliotekforening*, Malerhaugveien
20, Oslo 6 Tel: (02) 688576
Norwegian Library Association
Secretary-Treasurer: Gro Langeland

Norsk Dokumentasjonsgruppe, Postboks
350, Blindern, Oslo 3 Tel: (02) 695880
Telex: 72042 Nsi N
Norwegian Documentation Society
President: Odd Brisner

Norsk Fagbibliotekforening, c/o Statoil,
Library, Postboks 1212, N-5001 Bergen Tel:
(05) 287400 ext 144
Norwegian Association of Special Libraries
Chairman: Cecilie Butenschøn

Norske Deitidsbibliotekarers Yrkeslag*,
N-7100 Rissa
Chairman: Solfrid Sjøli
Norwegian Association for Part-Time
Librarians

Norske Forskningsbibliotekarers Forening,
now Norsk Fagbibliotekforening (qv)

Riksbibliotektjenesten, Postboks 2439, Solli,
Oslo 2 (Located at: Drammensveien 42,
Oslo 2) Tel: (02) 550880 Telex: 16078 ub n
National Office for Research and Special
Libraries
Director: Gerhard Munthe
*Publications: Handbook of Research and
Special Libraries* (irregular), *Synopsis* (6 per
year), *Annual Report*

Library Reference Books and Journals

Books

Bibliothek og Forskning (Library and
Research), The University Library of Bergen,
Fastings Minde, N-5000 Bergen

Journals

Bok og Bibliotek (Book and Library),
Statens Bibliotektilsyn, Munkesdamsveien
62, N-1301 Oslo

Meldinger (Announcements), Norsk
Biblioteklag, Bogstadveien 8, Oslo 3

Literary Associations and Societies

Norske Akademi for Sprog og Litteratur*,
Oslo
Norwegian Academy for Language and
Literature
Secretary: L R Langslet

Det Norske Videnskaps-Akademi,
Drammensveien 78, Oslo 2 Tel: (02) 444296
Cable Add: Norakad
The Norwegian Academy of Science and
Letters
Secretary-General: Professor Dr A Semb-
Johansson; *Executive Secretary:* Kjell
Herlofsen
Publications: Skrifter, Avhandlinger, Årbok

Norwegian P E N Centre, Postboks 620 -
Sentrum, Oslo 1
Secretary: Kristin Brudevoll

Literary Periodicals

Edda (Scandinavian); literary research,
Universitetsforlaget, Postboks 307, Blindern,
Oslo 3

Norseman, Nordmanns-Forbundet,
Raadusgate 23b, Oslo

Samtiden (The Age); journal for politics,
literature and social questions, H Aschehoug
(W Nygaard), Sehestedsgate 3, Oslo 1

Syn og Segn (Vision and Tradition), Norske
Samlaget, Trondheimsveien 15, Oslo 5

Vinduet (The Window), Gyldendale Norsk
Forlag, Universitetsgate 16, Oslo 1

Literary Prizes

Bastian Prize
Awarded annually for an outstanding
translation by one of the members of the
Norwegian Association of Translators.
Enquiries to Norwegian Association of
Translators, Postboks 579 Sentrum, Oslo 1

Children's Book Prize
For the best books for children by
Norwegian authors, for illustrations by
Norwegian artists in books for children, for
picture-books, for translations and for comic
strips. Awarded annually. Enquiries to State
Directorate for Public and School Libraries,
Postboks 8145 Dep, Oslo 1

N W Damm Children's Book Prize
Founded in 1953, an award of 30,000
Norwegian kroner. 1982 winner: Aase Foss
Abrahamsen for *Videre like Vivinne*.
Enquiries to N W Damm og Søn A/S,
Tvetenveien 32, Postboks 6140, Etterstad,
Oslo 6

Translation Prize
Established 1968. For translations from
foreign literature. 25,000 Norwegian kroner.
Awarded annually. Enquiries to Norwegian
Cultural Council, Grev Wedels plass, Oslo 1

Tarjei **Vesaas** Debutant Prize
To a writer under 30 for the best first book
of prose or poetry. 8,000 Norwegian kroner.
Awarded annually. Enquiries to Norwegian
Authors' Association, Rådhusgata 7, Oslo 1

Translation Agencies and Associations

Norwegian Association of Translators,
Postboks 579 Sentrum, Oslo 1

Pakistan

General Information

Language: Urdu is national language but
English is used commercially
Religion: Muslim
Population: 76.8 million
Literacy Rate (1960): 21.8%
Bank Hours: 0900-1300 Saturday-
Wednesday; 0900-1100 Thursday
Shop Hours: 0930-1300, 1500-2000 Saturday-
Thursday
Currency: 100 paisa = 1 Pakistan rupee
Export/Import Information: No tariff on
books, magazines and advertising matter.
Import licence issued freely if required. Anti-
Islamic and obscene literature prohibited.
Exchange controls
Copyright: UCC, Berne, Buenos Aires,
Florence (see International section)

Book Trade Organizations

National Book Council of Pakistan,
National Education Council Building, Saria
Chowk, Sector G-8/4, Islamabad Tel:
51697/53581 Cable Add: Bookouncil
Also: Theosophical Hall, M A Jinnah Rd,
Karachi Tel: 71385/74148 Cable Add:
Bookcent; 126 Riwaz Garden, Lahore Tel:
68315 Cable Add: Bookouncil
Dir General: A Z Zafar Alam
Publications: Kitab (Urdu, monthly), trade
directories, manuals, bibliographies, survey
reports

Pakistan Publishers' and Booksellers'
Association*, YMCA Bldg, Shahra-e-Quaid-
e-Azami, Lahore
Also: 3 Fatima Jinnah Rd, Karachi 4

Book Trade Reference Books and Journals

Books

Books from Pakistan, National Book
Council of Pakistan, Theosophical Hall,
Bunder Rd, Karachi

Karachi Book Trade Directory, National
Book Council of Pakistan, Theosophical
Hall, Bunder Rd, Karachi

Journals

Kitab (text in Urdu), National Book Council
of Pakistan, National Education Council
Building, Saria Chowk, Sector G-8/4,
Islamabad

Pakistan National Bibliography, Directorate
of Libraries, National Bibliographical Unit,
c/o Liaquat Library, Stadium Rd, Karachi
(annual)

Publishers

Aane-Adab, Anarkali, Lahore Tel: 54069
Proprietor: Sh Abdul Salam

Ahsan Brothers*, Chowk Anarkali, Lahore
Proprietor: Mohammad Ahsan
Subjects: Literature, Education

Shaikh Muhammad **Ashraf**, 7 Aibak Rd,
New Anarkali, Lahore Tel: 53171/53489
Cable Add: Islamiclit Lahore
Publisher: Sh Muhammad Ashraf; *Man Dir:*
Shahzad Riaz; *Home Sales:* M D Khawaja;
Export Sales: Khurshid Hussain; *Literary
Adviser:* M Ashraf
Subjects: Books about Islam, Islamic
History, Biography in English
Bookshop: At above address
1981: 8 titles *1982:* 5 titles *Founded:* 1923

Azim Publishing House*, Khyber Bazar,
Peshawar Tel: 73313
Subjects: History, Literature, Islamiat,
Technical, Scientific

Barque & Co*, Barque Chambers, Barque
Sq, 87 Shahrah-e-Liaquat Ali Khan, PO Box
201, Lahore
Man Dir: A M Barque
Branch Off: Karachi
Subjects: Trade Directories, Journals,
Who's Who
Founded: 1930

The **Book** House*, PO Box 734, Lahore 2
(Located at: 8 Trust Building, Urdu Bazar,
Lahore 2) Tel: 61212 Cable Add:

Bookhouse
Proprietor: Muhammad Saeed; *General Manager:* Muhammad Hamid Saeed
Subjects: Religion, Library, Textbooks
Founded: 1951
Miscellaneous: Exporters of English and Urdu books and Textbooks

Carvan Book House*, Kutchery Rd, Lahore Tel: 52296
Proprietor: Ch Abdul Hameed
Subjects: General, Textbooks

Classic*, 42 Shahrah-e-Quaid-e-Azam, Lahore Tel: 61830 Cable Add: Classic 42 Mall Lahore
Man Dir, Editorial, Production, Permissions: Agha A Hussain; *Sales, Publicity:* S Akbar Zaidi
Orders to: Classic, 42 The Mall Lahore
Subsidiary Companies: Shish Mahal Kitab Ghar, Classic Bookshop (both in Lahore)
Associate Company: Menarva Publications, Lahore
Subjects: The Arts, National Topics, Fiction
Bookshop: 42 The Mall, Lahore
Founded: 1956

Crescent Publications*, Urdu Bazar, Lahore

East and West Publishing Co, 22 Corner Chambers, Chundrigar Rd, Karachi-0102 Tel: 212036 Cable Add: Goodbooks
Publisher: Rafique Akhtar
Subjects: Pakistan, Research Material, *Pakistan Year Book*
1982: 3 titles *Founded:* 1971

Economic and Industrial Publications*, Al-Masiha, 47 Abdullah Haroon Rd, PO Box 7843, Karachi 3
Subjects: Economics, Industrial Development, Finance; Periodical journals and reports on economics and investment
Founded: 1965

Ferozsons Ltd*, 60 Shahrah-e-Quaid-e-Azam, Lahore Tel: 301196 Cable Add: Ferozsons Telex: 44382 Feroz PK
Man Dir, Publicity: A Salam; *Editorial, Sales Dir:* Zaheer Salam
Branch Offs: 150 outlets throughout Pakistan
Subjects: Islamic, Regional, Juveniles, Dictionaries (native and foreign languages)
Bookshops: At above address, and 277 Peshawar Rd, Rawalpindi
Founded: 1894

Frontier Publishing Co*, Urdu Bazar, Lahore

Sh Ghulam Ali & Sons Ltd, Adbi Market, Chowk Anarkali, PO Box No 528, Lahore Tel: 52908/64065 Telex: 44422 Asia pk
Dirs: Sh Bashir Ahmad, Sh Niaz Ahmed, Arshad Niaz, Imran Ahmad
Branch Offs: M A Jinnah Rd, Karachi Tel: 217430/215322; Yadkar Line, Chotki Ghitti, Hyderabad Tel: 24431
Subjects: Islamic Studies, Holy Koran, Educational, Children's Books, General, Periodicals

Government Publications*, Manager of Publications, Central Publications Branch, Government of Pakistan, Stationery and Forms Building, University Rd, Karachi

Hamdard Foundation, Nazimabad, Karachi 18
President: Hakim Mohammed Said
Subjects: Health, History of Traditional Medicine, History of Science and Islam

Idara-e-Faroghe-Undu*, Aibak Rd, Lahore
Proprietor: Mohammad Tufail
Subjects: Literature, Education

Idara Siqafat-e-Islamia, Club Rd, Lahore

Ilmi Kitab Khana*, Urdu Bazar, Lahore Tel: 62833
Proprietor: Ch Sardar Mohammad
Subjects: Textbooks, Educational

Islami Kitab Khana*, Sadar Bazar, Mianwali, Punjab
Subject: Law

Islamic Book Centre*, 25B Masson Rd, PO Box 1625, Lahore 3 Tel: 66272 Cable Add: Islamibook
Man Dir: Rozina Saeed; *Sales Dir:* Muhammad Akram; *Publicity Dir:* Muhammad Sajid Saeed; *Advertising Dir:* Muhammad Hamid Saeed
Branch Off: J M Malik, 35 Cawdor Rd, Fallowsfields, Manchester M14 6LS, UK
Subjects: Religion, University, Secondary & Primary Textbooks, Reference

Institute of **Islamic Culture**, Club Rd, Lahore Tel: 53908 Cable Add: ICULT
Subject: Islamic ideology
Founded: 1950

Islamic Publications Ltd, 13-E Shahalam Market, Lahore 8 Tel: 325243 Cable Add: Alilm
Man Dir: Ashfaque Mirza; *General Manager:* Abdul W Khan
Subjects: Standard Islamic literature on current topics
Founded: 1960

Islamic Research Institute, PO Box 1035, Islamabad Tel: 27156/27295/21705 Cable Add: Islamserch
Dir: Dr Ahmad Hasan; *Sales:* Mumtaz Liaqat
Subjects: History, Law, Religion, Periodicals (in English, Arabic and Urdu)
Founded: 1960
Miscellaneous: The Institute is a Faculty of the Islamic University, Islamabad

Kazi Publications, PO Box 1845, Lahore (Located at: 121 Zalqarnain Chambers, Ganpat Rd, Lahore)
Man Dir, Editorial, Publicity, Rights & Permissions: Muhammad Iqbal Siddiqi; *Sales:* Zubair Ahmad; *Production:* Riaz Abid
Subjects: Islam, Religion, Holy Koran, Ahadith, Islamic History and Jurisprudence
Founded: 1978

Kitabi Dunya*, Mcleod Rd, Lahore
Proprietor: Ch Sultan Ahmed
Subject: Detective Fiction

Maktaba-i-Danial, an imprint of Pakistan Publishing House (qv)

Maktaba Jadeed*, PO Box 456, Lahore
Proprietor: Ch Rasheed Ahmed
Subject: Fiction

Maktaba Meri Library*, Chowk Urdu Bazar, Lahore 2
Proprietor: Basheer Ahmed
Subject: Paperbacks

Maktaba Shahkar*, Chowk Urdu Bazar, Lahore Tel: 354103
Proprietor: S Qasim Mahmud
Subjects: Encyclopaedias, Paperbacks

Malik Din Mohammad & Sons*, Bull Rd, Lahore Tel: 54315, 52621
Proprietor: Malik Mohammad Arif
Branch Off: Chundrigar Rd, Karachi
Subject: Islamic Studies

Malik Siraj-ud-Din & Sons, Kashmiri Bazar, Lahore 8 Tel: 52169/311498/65539 Cable Add: Serajsons Telex: 52169
Man Dir: A R Malik; *Editorial:* S A Malik; *Sales:* A A Malik; *Production, Publicity & Permissions:* S A Malik
Subsidiary Companies: Siraj Mohammadi Press, 73 Circular Rd, Outside Akbari Gate, Lahore; Ayaz Book Binding Works, Bazar Tezabian, Kashmiri Bazar, Lahore 8
Associate Companies: Gul I Khandan, Urdu Monthly; Islamic Juntrri, both at Kashmiri Bazar, Lahore 8
Branch Offs: Chowk Urdu Bazar, Lahore 2; 18-19 M J Hospital (WAQF), O/S Mori Gate, Circular Rd, Lahore
Subject: Religion
Book Club: Malik Siraj-ud-Din & Sons (Sales & Depot), Kashmiri Bazar, Lahore 8
1981: 6 titles *1982:* 8 titles *Founded:* 1934

Maqbool Academy*, Adabi Market, Chowk Anarkali, Lahore Tel: 64740
Proprietor: Maqbool Ahmed Malik
Subject: Fiction

Nafees Academy*, PO Box 91, Karachi (Located at: Stratchan Rd) Tel: 213303
Proprietor: Tariq Iqbal Gahandri
Subjects: History, Educational, General

The **Oriental & Religious** Publishing Corp Ltd*, Rabwah
Subjects: The Holy Koran in Arabic and English; Commentaries on the Koran; Books on Islam

Orientalia Publishers*, 6 Habib Bank Bldg, Chowk Urdu Bazar
Subjects: Islamic literature, Rare Oriental Books

Oxford University Press, PO Box 13033 Karachi 8 (Located at: 5 Bangalore Town, Main Sharae Faisal, Karachi
Manager: Zia Husan
Subjects: School & College Textbooks, Reference, General, Pakistan, Islamic Studies, *Oxford in Asia Historical Reprints*
1981: 10 titles

P P H, an imprint of Pakistan Publishing House (qv)

Pak Publishers*, Urdu Bazar, Lahore

Pakistan Law Times Publications*, Kabir St, Urdu Bazar, Lahore

Pakistan Publications*, Shahrah Iraq, PO Box 183, Karachi 1
Subjects: Books about Pakistan in Urdu, Arabic and English

Pakistan Publishing House*, Victoria Chambers 2 (1st floor), Abdullah Haroon Rd, Sadar, Karachi 3 Tel: 511457 Cable Add: Prilect
Dir: M Noorani; *Editorial Dir:* Kamran Noorani; *Sales Manager:* Matin M Khan; *Production Manager:* Mohammad Yusuf; *Rights & Permissions:* Mohammad Iqbal
Subsidiary Company: Maktaba-i-Danial, at above address
Associate Company: Pakistan Law House, Pakistan Chowk, PO Box 90, Karachi 1
Imprints: PPH, Maktaba-i-Danial
Subjects: History, Law, Literature
Founded: 1966

People's Publishing House*, PO Box 862, Lahore (Located at: 26 Shahrah-e-Quaid-e-Azam, Lahore) Tel: 54512
Man Dir, Publication: Abdur Rauf Malik; *Sales:* G Mustafa; *Publicity:* M Siddique
Subject: Social Science
Founded: 1947

Premier Book House, PO Box 1888, Lahore (Located at: Room 2, Shahin Market, Anarkali, Lahore) Tel: 64385
Proprietor: Mohammad Khalil
Subject: Islamic Literature
Bookshop: At above address
Founded: 1950

Publishers International*, Bandukwala Bldg 4, 1 1 Chundrigar Rd, Karachi
Man Dir: Kamaluddin Ahmad
Subjects: Advertising, Reference, Trade

Directories, Science, Technical
1981: 1 title *Founded:* 1948

Publishers United Ltd*, PO Box 1689, Lahore (Located at: 176 Anarkali, Lahore) Tel: 52238 Cable Add: Pubun (Warehouse: 9 Rattigan Rd, Lahore Tel: 53423)
Man Dir: Mohammad Amin
Subjects: Religion, Economics, Technical, Reference
Founded: 1942

Qaumi Kutab Khana*, Railway Rd, Lahore Tel: 53810
Proprietor: Mohammad Ahsan & Bros

Quaid-i-Azam University, Islamabad Tel: 29328 Cable Add: University
Manager: Maj M Arshad Javaid
Subjects: Social Sciences, Chemistry
Founded: 1973

'Rast Gufter' Press*, Bhawana Bazar, Lyallpur
Manager & Proprietor: Shamshar Ali Baskhshi
Founded: 1889

Royal Book Co*, PO Box 7737, Karachi 3 (Located at: 232 Saddar Cooperative Market, Abdullah Haroon Rd, Karachi 3) Tel: 514244
Proprietor: Jamshed Mirza
Branch Off: 402 Rehman Centre, Zaibunnisa St, Karachi
Subjects: Politics, Economics, Banking, General History, Asian Historical Reprints
Bookshop: At above address
1981: 7 titles *Founded:* 1963

H M Saeed Co*, Dr Ziauddin Ahmad Rd, Pakistan Chowk, Karachi
Proprietor: Mohammad Zaki
Subject: Islamic Studies, Literature (in Arabic, Urdu, Persian)

Sang-e-Meel Publications*, Chowk Urdu Bazar, Lahore
Proprietor: Niaz Ahmed
Subjects: History and Islamic Studies

Taj Co Ltd, Manghopir Rd, PO Box 530, Karachi Tel: Karachi 294221/292648 Cable Add: Kalampak
Man Dir: Amjad Hussain Khokhar
Branch Offs: Rawalpindi, Lahore
Subject: Religion
Bookshop: Agency Taj Co, M A Jinnah Rd, Karachi
Founded: 1929

Taxation*, 6 Liaquat Rd, Lahore 6

University Book Agency, Khyber Bazar, Peshawar Tel: 62534
Subjects: General, Textbooks

Urdu Academy Sind, Jinnah Rd, Karachi Tel: 614289 Cable Add: Literature
Proprietor: Ala-ud-Din Khalid
Branch Offs: Lahore, Hyderabad
Subjects: General, Textbooks
Founded: 1947

West-Pak Publishing Co Ltd*, PO Box 374, Lahore 2 Tel: 880409
Proprietor: Syed Mahmud Shah
Subject: Textbooks
Founded: 1932
Miscellaneous: Government Printers

Book Club

Malik Siraj-ud-Din & Sons, Kashmiri Bazar, Lahore 8
Owned by: Malik Siraj-ud-Din & Sons (Publisher, qv)

Major Booksellers

Bookcentre*, Lakshmi Mansion, Shahrah-e-Quiad-e-Azam, Lahore

Bookrama, 56 New Urdu Bazar, Karachi Importers and Library Suppliers, associated with S I Gillani, Bookseller (qv)
Manager: Shahzad Namjee

Ferozsons Ltd*, 60 Shahrah-e-Quaid-e-Azam, Lahore Tel: 301196 Cable Add: Ferozsons Telex: 44382 Feroz PK
Also: 277 Peshawar Rd, Rawalpindi
Managers: S M Khurshid, Aftab Awan

S I Gillani, Surriaya Mansion, PO Box 1463, 65 The Mall, Lahore Tel: 322970 Cable Add: Longman Lahore
Also: 1st Floor, London Book Co Bldg, 64/4 and 5 Bank Rd, Saddar, Rawalpindi
Contact: M Anwer Iqbal
See also Bookrama

Khyber Bookshop*, Peshawar University, Peshawar

Liberty Bookstall, International Division, PO Box 7427, Karachi 03 Tel: 513026/510798 Cable Add: Bookazine
Managing Partner: A Hussein
Branch Offs: Inter-Continental Hotel, Holiday Inn Hotel, Hotel Mehran, Karachi; Tapp St, Saddar, Karachi 03

S M Mir*, 40 Chartered Bank Chambers, Talpur Rd, Karachi 2 Tel: 237621
Also Publishers' Agent & Exporter

Mirza Book Agency, 65 Shahrah-e-Quaid-e-Azam, PO Box 729, Lahore 3 Tel: 66839 Cable Add: Knowledge
Managing Partner: M H Mirza

N G M Communication, PO Box 2614, Karachi 19
Export Booksellers, International Subscription Agents, Library Suppliers and Back Issue Dealers

Pak American Commercial Inc*, Zaibunnisa St, Karachi 3

Pak Book Corporation, Aziz Chambers, 21 Queen's Rd, Lahore Tel: 55972/56366 Cable Add: Magbookco
Man Dir: M A Khan Akter; *Dir:* M Iqbal Cheema
Branch Off: I & T Centre, G-6/1/1, Khayaban-e-suharwardy, Islamabad Tel: 22456 Cable Add: Pakbookco

Paradise Book Stall*, Shambhu Nath Rd, Saddar, Karachi 3 Tel: 512704 Cable Add: Magazines
Partner: Shaukat Ali

Paramount Book Stall*, Preedy St, Saddar, Karachi 3
Branches at Lahore, Peshawar
Also wholesaler

Petiwala Corporation*, Ismail Mansion, Strechen Rd, Pakistan Chowk, Karachi 1 Tel: 218643

Royal Book Co*, PO Box 7737, 232 Saddar Cooperative Market, Abdullah Haroon Rd, Karachi 3 Tel: 514244
Also: 402 Rehman Centre, Zaibunnisa St, Karachi

Major Libraries

Agriculture University Library, see under University

British Council Libraries*, 32 Mozang Rd, PO Box 88, Lahore Tel: 54278
Also: 14 Civic Centre, Ramna 6, PO Box 1135, Islamabad Tel: 22205 Telex: 5641; 20 Bleak House Rd, PO Box 10410, Karachi 0406 Tel: 51236/38 Telex: 25570; 35 The Mall, PO Box 49, Peshawar Tel: 73278

Central Secretariat Library*, Government of Pakistan, Islamabad

Ewing Memorial Library*, Forman Christian College, Lahore 11

Government College Library*, Lahore

Dr Mahmud Husain Library*, University of Karachi, Karachi 32 Tel: 418227
Librarian: Akhter Hanif
Publications include: Guide to Bibliographical Sources; Catalogue of rare books

Islamic Research Institute Library*, PO Box 1035, Islamabad

Khyber Medical College Library, Peshawar Tel: 40211/40226
Librarian: Sain Mohammad Malik

Liaquat Memorial Library*, Stadium Rd, Karachi 5

National Archives of Pakistan*, Commercial Area F/8, Nr Zafar Chowk, Islamabad
Branches: Quaid-e-Azam Papers Unit, Secretariat Block-D, Islamabad; SK Centre Bldg, 2nd Floor, Nr Frere Market Rd, AM2, Karachi

National Library*, Islamabad

Pakistan Forest Institute, Central Forest Library*, PO Forest Institute, Peshawar

Pakistan Institute of Nuclear Science & Technology Library*, PO Nilore, Rawalpindi

Pakistan Scientific and Technological Information Centre (PASTIC)*, 435 F-6/3 Islamabad

Planning Commission Library*, Government of Pakistan, 'P' Block, Pakistan Secretariat, Islamabad

Punjab Public Library, Lahore
Librarian: Mohammad Aslam

Punjab University Library, 1 Al-Biruni Rd, Lahore 2/12 Tel: 67962
Chief Librarian: M Anwar-ul-Haque
Publications include: Catalogues of manuscripts in various languages held by Library

Sind University Central Library*, University of Sind, New Campus, Jamshoro, Sind Tel: 71225
Librarian: Moinuddin Khan

University of Agriculture Library, Faisalabad Tel: 25911 ext 28 Cable Add: Agrivarsity
Librarian: Najaf Ali Khan

University of Baluchistan Library*, Quetta, Baluchistan

University of Engineering and Technology*, Lahore Tel: 339243 Cable Add: Univengtech
Acting Librarian: Mohammad Ramzan

University of Karachi Library, see Dr Mahmud Husain Library

University of Peshawar Library*, Peshawar
Librarian: I U Khan

Library Associations

Government of Pakistan Department of Libraries*, Liaquat Memorial Library Bldg, Stadium Rd, Karachi 5 Tel: 411435

Karachi University Library Science Alumni Association*, c/o Dept of Library Science, University of Karachi, Karachi 32

Secretary: S Zia Haider
Publication: Newsletter

Pakistan Library Association, Headquarters Office, Khyber Medical College, Peshawar
Secretary-General: Sain Mohammad Malik
Publications: PLA Newsletter; Proceedings of Annual Conference; Code of Ethics for Librarians; Standards of College Libraries; Standards of Special Libraries; Standards of University Libraries; P L A Constitution

Society for the Promotion and Improvement of Libraries, Hamdard Library, Al-Majeed Centre, Nazimabad, Karachi 18
President: Hakim Mohammed Said
Publications include: Plan for Development of Libraries in Pakistan

Library Reference Books and Journals

Book
Plan for Development of Libraries in Pakistan, Society for the Promotion and Improvement of Libraries, Hamdard Library, Al-Majeed Centre, Nazimabad, Karachi 18

Journals
Newsletter, Karachi University Library Science Alumni Association, Karachi 32

Newsletter, Pakistan Library Association, Khyber Medical College, Peshawar

Literary Associations and Societies

Anjuman Taraqqi-e-Urdu Pakistan, Baba-e-Urdu Rd, Karachi 1
For the promotion of the Urdu language and literature
President: Akhtar Husain; *Secretary:* Jamiluddin A'Ali
Publications: Urdu (quarterly), *Qaumi Zaban* (monthly)

Pakistan Board for Advancement of Literature*, Narsing Das Garden, Club Rd, Lahore

Pakistan Writers' Guild, Central Office, PO Box 697, Saddar Rd, Peshawar
Research Officer: Inamul Haq Javeid
Publication: Ham Qalam (monthly)

Punjab Text Board*, 21/E-11, Gulberg 111, Lahore
Similar Text Boards exist in Sind at Karachi, Baluchistan at Quetta, NWFP at Peshawar

Sindhi Adabi Board, Sind University Campus, Jamshoro, Hyderabad, Sind
To promote the language, literature and culture of the Sind region

Literary Periodicals

Ham Qalam, Pakistan Writers' Guild, Central Office, PO Box 697, Saddar Rd, Peshawar

Perspective, Pakistan Publications, Shahrah Iraq, PO Box 183, Karachi

Literary Prizes

Adamjee Prize*
Founded in 1960 for the best book of creative and progressive poetry, novel, short story, drama, travelogue or biography. 20,000 rupees. Awarded annually.
Administered by the Pakistan Writers' Guild in Karachi. Enquiries to Pakistan Writers' Guild, Central Office, PO Box 697, Saddar Rd, Peshawar

Dawood Prize for Literature*
Founded in 1963 for the best books on literary research, literary history, literary criticism; for research works on the Pakistan movement; and for the best translation. 25,000 rupees. Sponsored by the Dawood Foundation. Awarded annually. Enquiries to the Pakistan Writers' Guild, Central Office, PO Box 697, Saddar Rd, Peshawar

Habib Bank Prize for Literature*
Founded in 1968 for the best translation or adaptation of the year (into English or a Pakistani language) of a modern or classical work in any Pakistani language, 25,000 rupees. Awarded annually. Enquiries to Pakistan Writers' Guild, Central Office, PO Box 697, Saddar Rd, Peshawar

National Bank of Pakistan Prize for Literature*
Founded in 1964 for the best books on economics and scientific, technical and professional subjects. 25,000 rupees. Awarded annually. Enquiries to Pakistan Writers' Guild, Central Office, PO Box 697, Saddar Rd, Peshawar

Pakistan Board for Advancement of Literature Awards*
For academic works in Urdu, and for articles and poems published in Pakistan journals. Awarded annually. Enquiries to Pakistan Board for Advancement of Literature, Narsing Das Garden, Club Rd, Lahore

President's Award for Pride of Performance*
For notable achievements in literature. Awarded annually. Enquiries to Pakistan Ministry of Education, Islamabad

Prizes for Manuscripts for Juveniles*
Six prizes for creative writing in the field of children's literature in the Urdu language. Awarded annually. Enquiries to Pakistan Writers' Guild, Central Office, PO Box 697, Saddar Rd, Peshawar

Punjab Advisory Board for Books Prizes*
For books of high educational and literary value in the Urdu language. Awarded annually. Enquiries to the Secretary, Punjab Advisory Board for Books, Lahore

Regional Literature Awards*
For the best literary works, including the novel, short story, drama, poetry, biography, travel, literary criticism or research work, in each of the four regional languages of Punjabi, Pushto, Sindhi and Gujrati. Awarded annually. Enquiries to Pakistan Writers' Guild, c/o Regional Secretary, Princess Hotel, Montgomery Rd, Lahore

United Bank Prize for Literature*
Founded in 1967 for books in Urdu and Bengali in the following categories: for children up to 15 years of age; and poetry or prose, fiction or non-fiction, for young children. 20,000 rupees. Awarded annually. Enquiries to Pakistan Writers' Guild, Central Office, PO Box 697, Saddar Rd, Peshawar

Panama

General Information

Language: Spanish (English widely used)
Religion: Roman Catholic
Population: 1.8 million
Literacy Rate (1970): 78.3%
Bank Hours: 0800-1300 or 1330 Monday-Friday
Shop Hours: 0700 or 0800-1800 or 1900 Monday-Saturday, with 2-hour lunch closing
Currency: 100 centesimos = 1 balboa = $US1. US currency is used
Export/Import Information: No tariffs on books and advertising matter. No import licences or exchange controls
Copyright: UCC, Buenos Aires (see International section)

Publishers

Editorial **Bruguera** Centroamericana y Panamá SA, Apdo 358, Panamá 9A Tel: 692515 Cable Add: Brugcepa Telex: 2661 P Booth PG
Parent Company: Editorial Bruguera SA, Spain (qv)

Ediciones Librería **Cultural Panameña** SA, Apdo 2018, Panamá 1 Tel: 235628/236267 Cable Add: Culpasa
Man Dir, Editorial: A J Fraguela R; *Sales:* F M Fraguela Ruiz
Subjects: University, Secondary & Primary Textbooks, Antiquaria, Reference Works
Bookshop: Vía España 16, Apdo 2018, Panamá 1 (and two other branches)
Founded: 1955

Dirección de Estadística y Censo*, Contraloría General de la República, Apdo 5213, Panama 5 Tel: 643734 Cable Add: Estadicen-Contraloría Panama
Man Dir: D Castillo; *Editorial:* Amílcar Villarreal; *Sales, Production, Publicity:* R Tapia
Subject: Panamanian Statistics
1981: 18 titles *Founded:* 1941

Editorial Universitaria*, Estafeta Universitaria, Universidad de Panamá Tel: 642087 Cable Add: Cuidad Universitaria
Man Dir, Editorial: Dr Carlos M Gasteazoro; *Sales:* Eduvigis Vergara; *Production:* Prof Carlos N Ho; *Publicity:* Mary R de Natera
Subjects: History, Philosophy, Geography, Sciences, Law, Literature, Art, Architecture, Social Sciences, Technical, Education
Bookshops: University Bookshop
Founded: 1969

Fondo Educativo Interamericano*, Ave Federico Boyd y Calle 51, Edificio Eastern – 6° piso, Panamá
Editorial: Fondo Educativo Interamericano SA, Colombia (qv)
Parent Company: Addison-Wesley Publishing Co Inc, Reading, Mass 01867, USA
Associate Companies: See Fondo Educativo Interamericano, Mexico

Grijalbo Centroamericana y Panamá SA*, Apdo 362, del Costado Sur del ICE 50 Oeste 50 Sur, Los Yoses, San Pedro Montes de Oca
Parent Company: Ediciones Grijalbo SA, Spain (qv)

Ediciones **Instituto Nacional** de Cultura*, Apdo 662, Panamá 1 Tel: 220880/84 Cable Add: Inac
President: Aristides Martínez Ortega; *Editorial, Sales:* Arysteides Turpana; *Production:* Pedro Montañez; *Publicity:* Norma de la Espada
Subjects: Literature in general, History, Anthropology, Archaeology, Folklore, Sociology
Founded: 1976

Editorial **McGraw-Hill** Latinoamericana SA*, Apdo 6-1064 (El Dorado), Panamá Tel: 256822 Cable Add: Books-Panama

Telex: 3682331 Mhla
Man Dir, Editorial, Permissions: Hans Werner
Parent Company: McGraw-Hill de España, Spain (qv)
Subsidiary Company: Editorial McGraw-Hill Latinoamericana SA, Colombia (qv)
Associate Companies: see McGraw-Hill Book Co (UK) Ltd
Branch Off: Editorial McGraw-Hill Latinoamericana SA, Puerto Rico (qv)
Subjects: Scholarly, Reference, University, Secondary & Primary Textbooks
Founded: 1966

Major Booksellers

Librería **Argosy***, Vía Argentina y Vía España, Apdo 6620, Panamá 5 Tel: 235344
Proprietor: Gerasimos Kanelopulos

Librería **Cultural Panameña**, SA, Via España 16, Apdo 2018, Panamá 1 Tel: 235628 (and two other branches) Cable Add: Culpasa

Librería **Menéndez***, Galerías Obarrio, Via Brasil, Panamá
Branches: Ave Justo Arosemena y Calle 36, Panamá; Aeropuerto Tocumen, Panamá; Librería Santa Ana, Plaza Santa Ana, Panamá; Librería La Escolar SA, Plaza Cervantes, David

Servicio Continental de Publicaciones*, Calle 29 Este 5-70, Apdo 1379, Panamá Tel: 250614 (and 2 other branches)

Servicio de Lewis, Calle 26 y Ave Balboa, Apdo 1634, Panamá 1 Tel: 627000
Manager: Rodrigo A Burgos J

Major Libraries

Biblioteca Nacional, Calle 22 Este bis 1265, Apdo 2444, Zona 3, Panamá Tel: 624777/620393
Dir: Professor Algis Borrero E
Publications: Bibliografías nacionales

Biblioteca Bio-Médica del Laboratorio Conmemorativo **Gorgas***, Apdo 6991, Panamá 5 (Located at: Ave Justo Arosemena, No 35-30, Panamá 5) Tel: 274111/256550/620864 Cable Add: Gomela Telex: Gml pa 3480333
Also at Box 935, APO Miami, Florida 34002, USA
Gorgas Memorial Laboratory, Bio-medical Research Library
Dir: Dr Raymond H Watten
Medical Librarian: Professor Manuel Víctor De Las Casas

Universidad de Panamá, Biblioteca Interamericana Simón Bolívar, Estafeta Universitaría, Panamá
Librarian: Nuria F de González

Library Associations

Asociación de Bibliotecarios Graduados del Istmo de Panamá, c/o Director de la Biblioteca Bio-Médica del Laboratorio Cormemorativo Gorgas, Apdo 6991, Panamá 5 Tel: 274111
Association of Graduate Librarians of the Isthmus of Panama (AGLIP)
President: Professor Manuel Víctor De Las Casas
Secretary: Iris de Espinosa

Asociación Panameña de Bibliotecarios*, Calle 22 Este bis 1265, Apdo 2444, Zona 3, Panamá
Panama Library Association

President: Nuria F de González
Publication: Boletín

Universidad de Panama, Escuela de Bibliotecologia, Estafeta Universitaría, Panamá 3 Tel: 642837
University of Panama, School of Library Science
Dir: Margarita Jurado H
Publication: Boletín

Library Reference Journals

Boletín (Bulletin), Panama Library Association, c/o Inés Maria Herrera, President, Apdo 3435, Panamá

Boletín (Bulletin), University of Panama, School of Library Science, Apdo 3277, Panamá 3

Literary Prizes

Literary Prize*
Founded in 1946 by Ricardo Miró to pay tribute to those who furthered the cause of learning, arts and sciences. Awarded annually. A prize of $2,000 is given in each of five sections: poetry, short story, fiction, theatre, essay. Enquiries to 'Revista Nacional de Cultura', Instituto Nacional de Cultura, Apdo 662, Panamá 1

Papua New Guinea

General Information

Language: English is one of official languages, as is pidjin English or neo-Melanesian, and 700 distinct languages are in use
Religion: Majority follow traditional beliefs. Sizeable Anglican, Roman Catholic and Ecumenist congregations
Population: 3 million
Literacy Rate (1971): 32.1% of population aged 10 or over
Bank Hours: 0900-1400 Monday-Thursday; 0900-1700 Friday
Shop Hours: 0900-1700 Monday-Friday; 0900-1200 Saturday
Currency: 100 toea = 1 kina
Export/Import Information: No tariff on books and advertising but import tax on non-educational books. No import licence for books, but no obscene literature permitted

Book Trade Reference Books and Journals

Book

New Guinea Books (annual), University of Papua New Guinea Library, PO Box 319, University Post Office, Port Moresby

Journal

New Guinea Periodical Index (quarterly), University of Papua New Guinea Library, PO Box 319, University Post Office, Port Moresby

Publishers

The **Christian Book** Centre*, PO Box 222, Madang
Subjects: Literature, Religion

Gordon and Gotch (PNG) Pty Ltd, PO Box 1395, Port Moresby (Located at: Dogura Rd, 6 Mile, Saraga) Tel: 254551/254855 Cable Add: Gotchbooks Port Moresby
Telex: Pngotch NE 22263
General Manager: B J Stephensen
Parent Company: Gordon and Gotch (Australia) Pty Ltd
Subsidiary Companies: New Guinea Book Depot, Taurama Newsagency
Subjects: Travel, Natural History, Languages, Cookery, New Guinea History, Art and Folklore, Juveniles
Bookshop: Papua New Guinea Book Depot (at above address)
Founded: 1970
ISBN Publisher's Prefix: 0-909093

Isopang Publishing Pty Ltd*, Cnr Wards Rd and Mango St, Hohola, Port Moresby

Major Booksellers

Burns Philp (NG) Ltd*, Kieta, Bougainville (and other branches)

Papua New Guinea Book Depot, PO Box 1395, Port Moresby Tel: 254155 Cable Add: Gotchbooks Telex: Pngotch NE 22263
Manager: Don Smith
Owned by: Gordon and Gotch (PNG) Pty Ltd

Rabaul Newsagency*, c/o Bali Merchants Pty Ltd, PO Box 390, Rabaul

Steamships Trading Co*, PO Box 30, Goroka

University Book Shop Inc*, PO Box 114, University PO Tel: 245375 Cable Add: Unibooks Telex: NE 22366
Manager: R E Bakewell

Major Libraries

Administrative College of Papua New Guinea Library, PO Box 6177, Boroko Tel: Port Moresby 256133

University of Papua New Guinea Library, PO Box 319, University Post Office, Port Moresby Tel: Port Moresby 245280 Telex: 22366
Publications include: Guide to Manuscripts in the New Guinea Collection, by Nancy Lutton (1980); New Guinea Books (annual); New Guinea Periodical Index (quarterly)

Library Associations

National Library Service of Papua New Guinea, PO Box 5770, Boroko Tel: 256200

Papua New Guinea Library Association, PO Box 6177, Boroko Tel: 256200
Executive Secretary: Jenny Wal
Publications include: Directory of Libraries in Papua New Guinea; Library and Information Services for the Public; PNGLA Nius (newsletter of the PNGLA); The Best of Tok Tok; Tok tok bilong haus buk (journal of the PNGLA)

Library Reference Books

Directory of Libraries in Papua New Guinea, Papua New Guinea Library Association, PO Box 5368, Boroko

Guide to Manuscripts in the New Guinea Collection, by Nancy Lutton (1980), University of Papua New Guinea Library, PO Box 319, University Post Office, Port Moresby

Literary Periodicals

Kovave; journal of New Guinea liteature, Jacaranda Press Pty Ltd, 65 Park Rd, Milton, Queensland 40664, Australia

Papua New Guinea Writing, Literature Bureau, Office of Information, PO Box 2312, Konedobu

Paraguay

General Information

Language: Spanish (Guarani, an aboriginal Indian tongue, is universally spoken)
Religion: Roman Catholic
Population: 2.9 million
Literacy Rate (1972): 80.1% (88.6% of urban population, 74.1% rural)
Bank Hours: 0730-1100 Monday-Friday
Shop Hours: 0700 or 0730-1200, 1500-1800 Monday-Friday; open until noon Saturday
Currency: guarani
Export/Import Information: Member of Latin American Free Trade Association. Children's picture books and atlases are dutied, plus added tax and compensatory tax. Advertising catalogues subject to added tax and compensatory tax. Additional taxes on all goods; also Consular Fee. No import licences required. Exchange controls; foreign exchange surcharge
Copyright: UCC, Buenos Aires (see International section)

Book Trade Organization

Cámara Paraguaya del Libro*, Casilla de Correo 1705, Asunción
Paraguayan Publishers' Association
President: Lic don Rubén Lisboa; *Secretary:* Lic Nidia Vera Radice

Publishers

Editorial **Comuneros**, Presidente Cerro Corá 289, CC 980, Asunción Tel: 46176/44669
Proprietor: Ricardo Rolon
Subjects: Social History, Poetry
Bookshop: Librería Comuneros (qv)

Ediciones **Diálogo***, Calle Brasil 1391, Asunción
Manager: Miguel Angel Fernández
Subjects: Fine Arts, Literature, Poetry, Criticism, History, Science
Founded: 1957

Ediciones **Nizza***, Tacuari 144, Asunción Tel: 47160
President: Dr Jose Ferreira Martinez
Subject: Medicine
Bookshop: Agencia de Librerías Nizza (at above address)

Major Booksellers

Librería El **Ateneo***, General Diaz 347, Asunción Tel: 43668

El **Colegio** SA*, CC 1449, Asunción
Importer/Exporter, Wholesaler

Librería **Comuneros**, Presidente Cerro Corá 289, CC 980 Asunción Tel: 46176/44669
Owned by: Editorial Comuneros (qv)

Librería La **Cultura***, Palma esq Montevideo, Asunción Tel: 45093

Librería Internacional*, Estrella 721, Casilla de Correo 991, Asunción Tel: 41423
Manager: Adolfo N Buzó

Librería Universal, Palma 519, Casilla de Correo 432, Asunción Tel: 90633
Manager: Klaus Henning

Agencia de Librerías **Nizza***, Tacuari 144, Asunción Tel: 47160

Selecciones SA Comercial*, Iturbe 436, Asunción Tel: 41588

Major Libraries

Biblioteca y Archivo Nacionales*, Mariscal Estigarriba 95, Asunción
National Library and Archives

Biblioteca de la **Sociedad Científica** del Paraguay*, Ave España 505, Asunción
Library of the Paraguayan Scientific Society

Library Associations

Asociación de Bibliotecarios del Paraguay*, Calle Casilla de Correo 1505, Asunción
Association of Paraguayan Librarians
Secretary: Mafalda Cabrerar
Publication: Revista de Bibliotecologia y Documentación Paraguaya

Asociación de Bibliotecarios Universitarios del Paraguay*, c/o Professor Yoshiko M de Freundorfer, Head, Escuela de Bibliotecologia, Universidad Nacional de Asunción, Asunción
Paraguayan Association of University Librarians
President: Profesora Gloria Ondina Ortiz C;
Secretary: Celia Villamayor de Díaz

Comisión Paraguaya Documentación e Información*, c/o Instituto de Ciencias, Universidad Nacional, Ave España 1098, Asunción
Paraguayan Committee of Documentation and Information
Executive Secretary: Luis Fernando Meyer

Library Reference Journal

Revista de Bibliotecologia y Documentación Paraguaya (Review of Paraguay Library Science and Documentation), Association of Paraguay Librarians, Calle Casilla de Correo 1505, Asunción

Literary Associations and Societies

Paraguayan **P E N** Centre, San Rafael 658 (Esq Dr Migone), Asunción
Secretary: Lilian Stratta de Napout

Peru

General Information

Language: Spanish
Religion: Roman Catholic
Population: 16.8 million
Literacy Rate (1972): 72.5% (87.4% of urban population, 49.1% rural)
Bank Hours: January-March: 0830-1130 Monday-Friday; April-December: 0845-1245 Monday-Friday
Shop Hours: January-March: 0930-1245, 1615-1900 Monday-Saturday; April-December: 0900-1245, 1515-1900 Monday-Saturday (some close Saturday afternoon)
Currency: 100 centavos = 1 sol
Export/Import Information: Member of Andean Group within the Latin American Free Trade Association. Children's picture books and advertising matter dutied per kg + VAT, sales tax applies on advertising matter. No freight tax on books but there is wholesalers' tax. Import licences required. Exchange controls
Copyright: UCC, Buenos Aires (see International section)

Book Trade Organizations

Asociación Nacional de Escritores y Artistas (ANEA)*, Jirón de la Unión Belén 1054, Lima
National Association of Writers and Artists
President: Dr Pedro Ugarteche

Cámara Peruana del Libro*, Jirón Washington 1206, Of 507-08, Lima 1 Tel: 325694
Peruvian Publishers' Association
President: Andrés Carbone O

Book Trade Reference Journals

Anuario Bibliográfico Peruano (Peruvian National Bibliography), National Library, Ave Abancay, Apdo 2335, Lima 1

Biliografía Nacional (Peruvian monthly bibliographical information), National Library, Ave Abancay, Apdo 2335, Lima 1

Publishers

Librerías **A B C** SA, Apdo 5595, Lima (Located at: Las Magnolias 841, Of 201, San Isidro, Lima) Tel: 413712 Cable Add: Molagent
Man Dir: H H Moll; *Editorial:* Eduardo Nugent V
Associate Companies: Cordoba 685, Martinez, Argentina; Librerias Galax, Pl las Americas, Loc 59, Caracas, Venezuela
Subjects: History, Peruvian Art & Archaeology
Bookshops: At above company address, and Colmena 725, Lima; Centro Comercial Todos, San Isidro; Centro Comercial Galax, Chacarilla del Estanque; Edificio El Pacífico, Miraflores; Aeropuerto Jorge Chavez, Callao; Monasterio Santa Catalina, Arequipa
Founded: 1956

Editorial **Arica**, SA*, Casilla 3537, Lima 1 Tel: 401670
Man Dir: Boris Romero Accinelli; *Sales Manager:* Angélica Li; *Editorial Dir:* Benjamin Romero Accinelli
Subjects: Literature, Technical, Textbooks,

Educational Materials, Law, History
Founded: 1958

Asociación Editorial **Bruño**, Ave Arica 751, Breña, Apdo 1759, Lima Tel: 244134
Man Dir: Hno Francisco Alvarez Penelas
Subjects: University, Secondary & Primary Textbooks and Educational Materials
Founded: 1950

Editorial **Desarrollo**, SA, Ica 242, 1° piso, Apdo 3824, Lima Tel: 285380/286628
Cable Add: Edidesa
Man Dir: Lis Sosa Núñez; *Assistant Manager:* Bertha de Berrospi
Bookshop: Librería de Editorial Desarrollo (at above address)
Subjects: Business, Accounting, General Reference, Industrial Engineering
Founded: 1965

Editorial **Ecoma** SA*, Ave Arequipa 4168 'B', Miraflores 18, Lima Tel: 473017 Cable Add: Ecoma
Man Dir: Eduardo Congrains Martin; *Sales Dir:* Ramón Lalupu Lazaro
Subjects: Paperbacks, Literature, Biography, History, Philosophy, Juveniles
Founded: 1970

Distribuidora exclusivo **Grijalbo** SA*, Apdo 4978, Lima
Parent Company: Ediciones Grijalbo SA, Spain (qv)

Editorial **Horzonte***, Nicolás de Piérola 995, Lima 1 Tel: 279364
Man Dir: Humberto Damonte Larraín
Subjects: Literature, Social and Economic Sciences
Bookshop: At above address

Promotion Editorial **Inca** SA, now Ediciones Peisa (qv)

Instituto de Estudios Peruanos, Horacio Urteaga 694, Jesus Maria, Lima 11 Tel: 323070/244658 Cable Add: Ieperu
Man Dir: José Matos Mar; *Sales Manager:* Lucía Cano
Subjects: Peruvian studies in Agriculture, Archaeology, Economics, History, Anthropology
1981: 13 titles *1982:* 7 titles *Founded:* 1964

Iris SA, Jirón Junín 424, Lima 1
Parent Company: Editorial Bruguera SA, Spain (qv)

Librería-Editorial Juan **Mejía** Baca*, Jirón Azángaro 722, Lima Tel: 274067
Man Dir: Juan Mejía Baca
Subjects: Peruvian Literature and History
Founded: 1945

Mosca Azul Editores SRL*, PO Box 11020, Sta Beatriz, Lima 18 Tel: 470655
Dirs: Mirko Lauer, Abelardo Oquendo
Subjects: Fiction & Non-fiction, Social Science, University Textbooks
Founded: 1972

Ediciones **Peisa** (Promoción Editorial Inca SA)*, Emilio Althaus 460, Oficina 202, Lima 14 Tel: 718884
Man Dir: Martha Muñoz de Coronado; *Sales Dir:* Nora Muñoz de Degregori
Subjects: Peruvian Literature and History, Juvenile, Children's Books

Editorial **Plata** SA, Casilla 5595, Lima Tel: 413712
Man Dir: Herbert H Moll
Subjects: South America — History, Art, Guidebooks, Juveniles, Maps
Founded: 1971 (in Venezuela)

Librería **Studium** SA, Pl Francia 1164, Apdo 2139, Lima Tel: 326278 Cable Add: Studium
Man Dir: Andrés Carbone O; *Assistant Manager:* Andrés Carbone Montes;
Exports: José Córdova C
Subjects: Textbooks and General Culture
Bookshops: At above address and see under Major Booksellers
Founded: 1936

Fondo Editorial de la **Universidad Católica**, Apdo 1761, Lima 100 (Located at: Fundo Pando, Pueblo Libre, Lima 21) Tel: 622540 ext 220
Man Dir: Pedro Visconti C
Subjects: Anthropology, Archaeology, Economics, Ethnology, Law, Sciences, Education, Philosophy, History, Linguistics, Literature, Logic, Sociology, Theology, Psychology
1982: 8 titles

Universidad Nacional Mayor de San Marcos*, Apdo 454, Lima (Located at: Direccion Universitaria de Biblioteca y Publicaciones, Ave República de Chile 295, of 508, Lima) Tel: 319689
Man Dir: Juan de Dios Guevara, Rector de la Universidad
Subjects: Medicine, Law, Science, General Literature, Engineering, Textbooks
Founded: 1952

Editorial **Universo** SA*, Ave Nicolás Arriola 2285, La Victoria, Apdo 241, Lima 30 Tel: 241639/233190
Man Dir: Augusto Sandoval Valcárcel; *Executive Manager:* Paulino Advíncula Rios
Subjects: Social Science, Textbooks
Founded: 1967

Major Booksellers

Librarías **A B C** SA, Apdo 5595, Lima (Located at: Las Magnolias 841, Of 201, San Isidro, Lima)
Branches: Colmena 725, Lima; Centro Comercial Todos, San Isidro; Centro Comercial Galax, Chacarilla del Estanque; Edificio El Pacífico, Miraflores; Aeropuerto Jorge Chavez, Callao; Monasterio Santa Catalina, Arequipa
Company is also a Publisher (qv)

Librería **Arica***, Paseo de la República 3285, San Isidro, Lima 1 Tel: 401670

Editorial **Interamericana** SA*, Apdo 76, Lima 1 (Located at: Av 28 de Julio 787, Lima 1) Tel: 233471/241944/241845
General Manager: Dr José de la Riva-Agüero

Librería **Epoca***, Jirón Unión 1042, Apdo 4703, Lima Tel: 249545

Librería La **Familia** SA, Ave Nicolás de Piérola 346, Lima Tel: 243544/248031/325516 Telex: 20038 PE Dinsa
Manager: Armando B Ordoñez

Librería **Galería** Castro Soto*, Miguel Dasso 200, San Isidro, Lima Tel: 401343

Editorial **Horizonte***, Jirón Camaná 878, Lima Tel: 279364

Librería **Internacional** del Perú*, Casilla 1417, Boza 892, 2° piso, Lima Tel: 288611

Librería Juan **Mejía** Baca*, Jirón Azángaro 722, Lima Tel: 274067

Nicolas **Ojeda** Fierro e Hijos, see Librería 'La Universidad'

Librería **Studium** SA, Pl Francia 1164, Apdo 2139, Lima Tel: 326278
Branches: Jirón de la Unión 560, Lima; Colmena 626, Lima; Ave Larco 720, Miraflores; Saenz Peña 625, Callao; Francisco Pizarro 533, Trujillo; General Morán 123, Arequipa; Calle Moral 107A-107B, Arequipa; Elías Aguirre 251, Chiclayo; Calle Real 377, Huancayo; Calle Arequipa 110, Ayacucho; Tacna 216, Piura; Mesón de la Estrella 144, Cuzco (all in Peru)
Also Publisher (qv)

Librería de la **Universidad Nacional Mayor de San Marcos***, Jirón Unión (Belén) 1098, Lima 1 Tel: 2894255

Librería 'La **Universidad**', Nicolas Ojeda Fierro e Hijos SRL Ltda, Ave Nicolás de Piérola 639, Lima Tel: 282461/282036
Branch Off: Ave Nicolás de Piérola 677, Lima Tel: 282036

Major Libraries

Archivo General de la Nación*, Calle Manuel Cuadros s/n, Palacio de Justicia, Apdo 3124, Lima Tel: 275930

Biblioteca Nacional*, Ave Abancay, Apdo 2335, Lima 1 Tel: 277331/287690
Dir: José Tamayo Herrera
Publications: Anuario Bibliográfico Peruano (Bibliographical Annual of Peru); *Bibliografia Nacional* (Peruvian monthly bibliographical information); *Boletín de la Biblioteca Nacional* (Bulletin of the National Library); *Revista Fénix* (Phoenix Magazine); *Gaceta Bibliotecaria* (Library Gazette)

Biblioteca Central de la **Pontificia Universidad** Católica del Perú*, Final de la Ave Bolívar s/n, Pueblo Libre, Apdos 1761-5729, Lima

Biblioteca Central de la **Universidad Nacional de Cuzeco***, Apdo 167, Cuzco

Biblioteca Central de la **Universidad Nacional de San Agustín***, Apdo 23, Arequipa

Biblioteca Central de la **Universidad Nacional Mayor de San Marcos***, Apdo 454, Lima

Library Associations

Agrupación para la Integración de la Información Socio-Económica (ABIISE)*, Apdo 2874, Lima 100
Library Group for the Integration of Socio-economic Information
Dir: Isabel Olivera Rivarola
Publications: Directorio de Bibliotecas Especializadas del Perú

Asociación de Bibliotecas Agricolas*, c/o Library, Universidad Nacional Agraria, La Molina, Lima
Association of Agricultural Librarians

Asociación Peruana de Archiveros*, Jr Manuel Cuadros s/n, Palacio de Justicia, Apdo 3124, Lima Tel: 275930
Peruvian Association of Archivists

Asociación Peruana de Bibliotecarios*, General La Fuente 592, Lima 27
Peruvian Association of Librarians
Publication: Carta Informativa (Newsletter)
Executive Secretary: Amparo Geraldino de Orban

Library Reference Books and Journals

Book

Directorio de Bibliotecas Especializadas del Perú (Directory of Special Libraries of Peru), Library Group for the Integration of Socio-economic Information, Apdo 2874, Lima 100

Journals

Boletín (Bulletin), National Library, Ave Abancay, Apdo 2335, Lima 1

Boletín Bibliografico (Bibliographical Bulletin), Universidad Nacional Mayor de San Marcos, Ave República de Chile 295, Apdo 454, Lima

Fénix (Phoenix): review of Peruvian libraries, National Library, Ave Abancay, Apdo 2335, Lima 1

Gaceta Bibliotecaria del Peru (Peruvian Library Gazette), National Library, Ave Abancay, Apdo 2335, Lima 1

Literary Associations and Societies

Centro del P E N Internacional*, Santa Teresita 327, San Isidor, Lima
Secretary: Blanca Varela

Literary Periodicals

Después (Afterwards), Roca y Boloña 633, Lima 18

Revista Peruana de Cultura (Peruvian Review of Culture), Institute Nacional de Cultura, Ancash 390, Lima 1

Textual, Instituto Nacional de Cultura, Ancash 390, Lima 1

Literary Prizes

Premio José María **Arguedas***
For the best novel, under auspices of the Goodyear del Perú. Awarded every other year. Enquiries to Goodyear del Perú, Casio de la Republic 959, La Victoria, Apdo 1690, Lima

Premio **Universo***
For the best novel. Awarded every other year. Enquiries to Editorial Universo SA, Ave Nicolás Arriola 2285, San Luis, Apdo 241, Lima 30

Philippines

General Information

Language: Pilipino (also called Tagalog) is official language. English widely used. Nine other major languages of the Malayo-Polynesian group, and about 60 other languages, are also spoken
Religion: Predominantly Roman Catholic; Muslim on Mindanao and the Sulu Archipelago
Population: 46 million
Literacy Rate (1970): 83.3%
Bank Hours: 0900-1600 Monday-Friday
Shop Hours: Vary. Many open 0900-1200, 1400-1930 Monday-Saturday (some close 1730; some open Sunday)
Currency: 100 centavos =1 peso
Export/Import Information: Duty on books except those which are philosophical, historical, economic, scientific, technical or vocational, approved by Department of Education for use of certain institutions (not exceeding 10 copies for an institution, or 2 for an individual) or for encouragement of sciences or fine arts; no tariffs on Bibles and similar religious books. No duty on advertising matter. No import licences, but no obscene or immoral literature permitted. Release certificate issued on behalf of Central Bank required to clear goods. Imports subject to sales tax. No formal exchange controls but most imports need Letter of Credit (over $100 in any month, for example)
Copyright: Berne, UCC, Buenos Aires, Florence (see International section)

Book Trade Organizations

Book Development Association of the Philippines (BDAP), 40 Valencia St, New Manila, Quezon City 3008 Tel: 783976 Cable Add: Verareyes Manila Telex: Verareyes Manila c/o Etpimo PN
Secretary: Esther M Pacheco

Philippine Book Dealers' Association*, MCC PO Box 1103, Makati Commercial Centre, Makati, Metro Manila
President: Jose Benedicto

Philippine Educational Publishers' Association*, Phoenix Press Bldg, 927 Quezon Ave, Quezon City Tel: 991682/951026
President: Jesus Ernesto Sibal

Standard Book Numbering Agency, The National Library of the Philippines, T M Kalaw St, Manila
ISBN Administrator: Lily Orbase

Publishers

Abiva Publishing House Inc*, 851-881 G Araneta Blvd, Quezon City Tel: 615403/4
Man Dir: Luis Q Abiva Jr; *Sales Dir:* Alfredo de Guzman; *Publicity Dir:* Mila S Precioso; *Advertising Dir:* Felicito Q Abiva; *Rights & Permissions:* Milagros R Arceo
Subsidiary Company: Hiyas Press Inc
Subjects: History, Reference, Religion, General Science, Primary Textbooks, Educational Materials
Founded: 1963

Addison-Wesley Publishing Co Inc*, PO Box 1802, Manila Cable Add: Adiwes Manila
General Manager: Ricardo M Hizon
Miscellaneous: Firm is a branch of Addison-Wesley Publishing Co Inc, USA. See Addison-Wesley Publishers Ltd, UK for associated companies and ISBNs

Alemar-Phoenix Publishing House Inc*, 927 Quezon Ave, Quezon City 3008 Tel: 991682/951026
President: Jesus Ernesto R Sibal; *Vice-President, Sales:* José Emmanuel R Sibal; *Advertising Dir:* Pilar Fatima R Sibal; *Editor-in-Chief:* Avelina J Gil; *Production:* Elizabeth Pelipel; *Art Dir:* Dave Cruz
Orders to: Alemar's, 769 Rizal Ave, Manila
Parent Company: Alemar's (Sibal and Sons), 769 Rizal Ave, Manila
Subsidiary Company: Mabini Publishing House, 927 Quezon Ave, Quezon City
Associate Companies: Central Lawbook Publishing Co, Phoenix Press, 927 Quezon Ave, Quezon City; Educational Jobbers of the Philippines, Central Book Supply Inc, both at 769 Rizal Ave, Manila; Philippine Educational Systems Inc, Pacific Bank Bldg, Ayala Ave, Makati; Alemar's America Inc, 26 Broadway Suite 1210, New York, NY 10004, USA
Branch Offs: 519 Rizal Ave; Ateneo de Davaó Compound, Claro M Recto, Davao City
Subjects: Sciences, Social Studies, Religion, Languages, Literature, History, Sociology, Communication Arts, Accountancy
Bookshops: Alemar's, 769 Rizal Ave, Metro Manila; 526-8 United Nations Ave, Ermita, Metro Manila; 927 Quezon Ave, Quezon City; Makati Arcade, Makati; Commercial Center, Makati, Metro Manila; Corner General Roxas Ave, Times Sq St, Araneta Center, Cubao, Quezon City; Harrison Plaza Commercial Center, Malete, Metro Manila; Corner CM Recto and Nicanor Reyes Sts, Metro Manila; Taft Ave, Manila; Ateneo de Davao Compound, Davao City; 519 Rizal Ave, Cebu City
Book Club: Alemar's Best Sellers Club
Founded: 1958

Alip & Sons Publishing Inc*, 1306 Dos Castillas St, Manila
Man Dir: Dr E M Alip; *Sales Dir:* Ella B Ortega; *Publicity Dir:* Miss Bellen A Alip; *Advertising Dir:* Rita A Aramil
Subjects: Textbooks, Reference
Founded: 1946

Associated Publishers Inc*, 459 Quezon Ave, Quezon City, PO Box 449, Manila
President: Magdawgal B Elma
Subjects: Medicine, Education, Law
Founded: 1952

Bookman Publishing House, PO Box 709, Manila (Located at: 373 Quezon Ave, Quezon City) Tel: 614631/621706/62187 Cable Add: Bookman
President: Ceferino M Picache; *Sales Dir:* Soriano Seda; *Editorial Dir:* Mrs Patrocinio S Picache
Subsidiary Companies: Bookman Printing House, Mission Publishing Co (both at 373 Quezon Ave, Quezon City)
Subjects: Textbooks & Reference for Elementary, Secondary & Collegiate Schools, Educational Materials
1981: 9 titles *1982:* 3 titles *Founded:* 1945

Bustamente Press Inc*, 155 Panay Ave, Quezon City
President: Pablo N Bustamente Jr
Subjects: Textbooks on English, Sciences, Mathematics
Founded: 1949

Capitol Publishing House Inc*, 54 Don Alejandro A Roces Ave, Quezon City

Communication Foundation for Asia, PO Box SM-434, Manila 2806 Cable Add: Socomter Manila Telex: 27854 Cfa Ph
General Manager: Ramon Tagle Jr; *Editorial, Sales:* Belinda Tablante
Subjects: Religion, Textbooks, Development Communication, Social Philosophy
Founded: 1973

Erehwon Publishing House*, 569 Padre Faura, Ermita, Manila
Subjects: General Fiction, Belles Lettres, How-to
Bookshop: 569 Padre Faura, Ermita, Manila

Fotomatic Philippines Inc*, PO Box 295, Cebu City (Located at: F Ramos St, Cebu City) Tel: 92287/93702/71236
President, General Manager & Sales: Leonardo V Laconico; *Editorial:* Corsina L Sugarol; *Production:* Rosalinda A Laconico; *Rights & Permissions:* Andy Flores
Subjects: Primary, Secondary & University Textbooks
Founded: 1966

R M Garcia Publishing House, 903 Quezon Ave, Quezon City Tel: 999847/993286 Cable Add: Romgar
Orders to: PO Box 1860, Manila
Man Dir: Rolando M Garcia; *Editorial:* Ms J Cruz; *Sales, Publicity:* R G Garcia
Parent Company: R P Garcia Publishing & Printing Co

Subjects: College Textbooks for Philippine Schools; Elementary and Secondary Textbooks
Founded: 1951

Heritage Publishing House, PO Box 3667, Manila (Located at: 6 St William cor Lantana, Cubao, Quezon City)
President: Mario R Alcantara; *Man Dir:* Ricardo S Sanchez
Subjects: Art, Anthropology, History, Political Science
Bookshop: At above address
Miscellaneous: Previously MCS Enterprises Inc

Industry & Trade Publishers*, 5 Martelino St, Quezon City
Subjects: Business, Industry

Jonef Publications*, 1137 Looban, Paco, Manila Tel: 598910/502702/597647
Man Dir: J N Francisco
Subjects: Reference, Primary & Intermediate Textbooks
Founded: 1950

Lawyers' Co-operative Publishing Co (Philippines) Inc*, Quezon Blvd Extension 63, PO Box 449, Quezon City, Manila
President: Magdangal B Elma
Subjects: Law, Medicine, Dental, Nursing, Technical
Founded: 1913
Miscellaneous: Firm is an affiliate of Lawyers' Co-operative Publishing Co, New York, NY 14603

M C S Enterprises Inc, now Heritage Publishing House (qv)

Manor Press*, 715 Evangelista Sq, Quiapo, Manila

Modern Book Company Inc, 922 Rizal Ave, PO Box 632, Manila 2800 Tel: 274318
Cable Add: Moboco
Man Dir: Exequiel Villacorta
Subjects: History, Social Science, Secondary & Primary Textbooks
Bookshop: At above address
Founded: 1945

Mutual Books Inc*, 425 Shaw Blvd, Mandaluyong, Metro Manila Tel: 797538/796050/781545 Cable Add: Mubinc
Shipping Add: PO Box 245, Greenhills, San Juan, Metro Manila
President: Alfredo S Nicdao Jr
Associate Company: Alfredo S Nicdao Jr Inc
Subjects: Business, Economics, Management, Accounting, Mathematics, Secretarial
Founded: 1959

National Book Store, 701 Rizal Ave, Manila Tel: 494306/07/08 Cable Add: Nabost Manila Telex: 27890 NBS-PH
Man Dir: Benjamin C Ramos; *Sales Dir:* Mitto Licauco; *Publicity & Advertising:* Mrs Socorro C Ramos; *Rights & Permissions:* Alfredo C Ramos
Subjects: General Fiction & Non-fiction, How-to, Music, Art, Juveniles, Low-priced Paperbacks, University, Secondary & Primary Textbooks
Bookshops: At above address, and nine others in Manila, Metro Manila, Caloocan, and Quezon City
Founded: 1945
Miscellaneous: Firm reprints over 300 titles annually for foreign publishers

New City, PO Box 332, Manila (Located at: 1933 Donata St, Pasay City)
Parent Company: Città Nuova Editrice, Italy (qv for associate companies)

Philippine Arts and Architecture*, 1346 UN Ave, Ermita, Manila
Subjects: Art, Architecture

Philippine Book Co*, 851 Orouieta St, Sta Cruz, Manila Tel: 274337
Subjects: General Fiction, Belles Lettres, School texts
Bookshop: At above address

Philippine Education Co Inc*, PO Box 706, Makati Commercial Center, Manila (Located at: Banawe St, corner Quezon Ave, Quezon City) Tel: 604666, 603041/42 Cable Add: Pecoi Manila Telex: 7222321
General Manager: Antero L Soriano
Subjects: General Fiction, Belles Lettres, Art, Social Science, Textbooks, Educational Materials
Bookshops: Araneta Center, Cubao, Quezon City; Makati Commercial Center, West Drive Arcade, Makati; Broadway Centrum, Doña Juana Rodriguez and Aurora Blvd, Quezon City; Banawe St, corner Quezon Ave, Quezon City

Philippine International Publishing Co*, 1789 A Mabini St, Ermita, Manila

Regal Publishing Co*, 1729 J P Laurel St, San Miguel, Manila 2804 Tel: 7411181/2/3 Cable Add: Repress Manila
Man Dir, Editorial, Publicity: Corinna B Mojica; *Sales:* B Benipayo; *Production:* J B Benipayo; *Permissions:* A B Benipayo
Associate Companies: Benipayo Press Inc, 1131 Quezon Ave, Heroes Hills, Quezon City 3008
Subjects: Philippine Writings, Philippine and English Translations of German Books
1981: 2 titles *1982:* 1 title *Founded:* 1958

Sinag-Tala Publishers Inc, PO Box 536, Greenhills Post Office, Rizal 3113 (Located at: 2506 Taft Ave, Manila 2801) Tel: 582966/581524/505215 Cable Add: Sinapub Manila
Man Dir, Rights & Permissions: L A Uson; *Editorial:* B Brillantes, R Fajardo; *Sales:* D B Malabonga; *Production:* B S Perez
Subjects: Business, Economics, Educational Textbooks, Home and Family, Religion
1981: 14 titles *Founded:* 1969

Solidaridad Publishing House*, 531 Padre Faura, Ermita, Manila Tel: 586581/591241 Cable Add: Soldad
Man Dir: F Sionil Jose
Subjects: Biography, Fiction, History, Reference, Periodical
Bookshop: Solidaridad Bookshop, 531 Padre Faura, Ermita, Manila
Founded: 1965

Tamaraw Publishing Co*, Cebu Ave, Quezon City

University of the Philippines Press*, Gonzalez Hall, Diliman, Quezon City 3004
Acting Dir, Rights & Permissions: Luis D Beltran; *Editorial:* Renato Correa; *Sales, Publicity:* Pilar E Tongson; *Production:* Francisco Felix
Subjects: General Fiction, Belles Lettres, Art, Music, Religion, Philosophy, How-to, Medicine, Business, Law, Psychology, Political & Social Science, Science & Technology, Educational Materials

University Publishing Co*, Central Office, 1128 Washington, Sampaloc, Manila
Dirs: Dr José M Aruego and Constancia E Aruego
Subjects: Business, Law, Educational Materials
Founded: 1936

Vera-Reyes Inc+, 40 Valencia St, New Manila, Quezon City 3008 Tel: 783976 Cable Add: Verareyes Manila
Telex: Verareyes c/o 63199 Etpimo pn

Man Dir: L O Reyes
Subjects: Arts & Culture
Founded: 1964

Vision Publishing Corporation*, L & S Bldg, 1414 Roxas Blvd, Manila Tel: 571234/571225
Man Dir: Anacleto del Rosario; *Advertising Dir:* Betty B Tipon
Founded: 1962

Book Club

Alemar's Best Sellers Club*, 927 Quezon Ave, Quezon City
Members: 2,400
Owned by: Alemar's, 769 Rizal Ave, Manila
Founded: 1977

Major Booksellers

Alemar's, PO Box 2119, Manila (Located at: 769 Rizal Ave, Manila) Tel: 47552-4 Telex: 27634 ALE PH
Branches: see Alemar-Phoenix Publishing House (under Publishers)

Bookmark Inc, 357 T Pinpin, Escolta, Manila Tel: 497939; Ayala Arcade, Makati Commercial Center, Makati, Metro Manila Tel: 888245
Manager: Bienvenido A Tan Jr

Eastern Book Service Corp, No 3 Malamig, corner Matahimik St, UP Village, Quezon City 3004 Tel: 9222512 Cable Add: Eastbook Manila Telex: ITT 40199
Oprns pm
Manager: Linda F Sherman
Publishers' Agents and Stockists

Goodwill Trading Co Inc, (Goodwill Book Store), PO Box 2942, Manila Tel: 402427/402627/403368 Cable Add: Gotrade Manila Telex: 27302 Gtc Ph
President and General Manager: Manuel Cancio

G Miranda & Sons, 1887 C M Recto Ave, Manila Tel: 7311515/7310396/7414917

Modern Book Co Inc, 922 Rizal Ave, PO Box 632, Manila 2800
Manager: Exequiel Villacorta

National Book Store, 701 Rizal Ave, Manila Tel: 494306/07/08 Telex: 27890 Nbs-ph Cable Add: Nabost Manila
Branches: see entry under Publishers
General Manager: Ms Socorro C Ramos

Philippine Book Co*, 851 Oroquieta St, Sta Cruz, Manila Tel: 274337

Philippine Education Co Inc*, PO Box 620, Manila (Located at: 245 Banawe St, cnr Quezon Blvd, Quezon City) Tel: 604666, 603041/42 Cable Add: Pecoi Manila Telex: 7222321
General Manager: Antero L Soriano

Popular Book Store, MIT Bldg, Doroteo Jose, PO Box 2855, Manila Tel: 274762/274446 Cable Add: Pobost
General Manager: Joaquin Po; *Manager:* Katherine Ann P Palomera
Owned by: Popular Trading Corporation

Major Libraries

Ateneo de Manila University Libraries, PO Box 154, Manila

Ayala Museum Library & Iconographic Archives*, PO Box 259 MCC, Makati, Metro Manila 3116 Tel: 899925
Head Librarian: Estrella P Tobilla
Publications: Catalog of Filipiniana Books

and Bound Periodicals in the Ayala Museum Library and Iconographic Archives (1978); A Collection of Maps in the Ayala Museum Library and Iconographic Archives (1980); A Checklist of Rare and Contemporary Filipiniana Serials in the Ayala Museum Library and Iconographic Archives (1981)

Far Eastern University Library*, PO Box 609, Manila 2806

Manila City Library, Manila City Library, Room 372, Third Floor, Manila City Hall, Manila 2801

The **National Library** of the Philippines*, T M Kalaw St, PO Box 2926 Ermita, Manila Tel: (Filipiniana) 485519; (Reference) 485588; (Public Documents) 491114

Philippine Normal College Library & Library Science Departments*, Taft Ave, Manila 2801 Tel: 475314

Silliman University Library, Dumaguete City 6501
Librarian: Professor Eliseo P Bañas
Publications: Selected Philippine Periodical Index; Student's Library Manual (revised annually); *Stillman University Library Occasional Bulletin*

Ramona S **Tirona** Memorial Library, The Philippine Women's University, Taft Ave, Manila 2801 Tel: 503277
Librarian: Esperanza A Sta Cruz
Publications: Philippine Educational Forum, Administrative Bulletin, The Philwomenian, Research Abstracts, The Link

University of Manila Central Library*, 546 Dr M V de los Santos, Sampaloc, Manila

University of San Carlos Library System, P del Rosario St, Cebu City 6401
Dir: Mrs Marilou P Tadlip

University of Santo Tomas Library*, España, Manila 2806 Tel: 210081 (local 234)

University of the East Library, Claro M Recto Ave, Manila ZC 2806
Chief Librarian: Narcisa F Tioco

University of the Philippines Library*, Gonzalez Hall, Diliman, Quezon City 3004 Tel: 976061/8 (local 284)

Library Associations

Association of Special Libraries of the Philippines (ASLP)*, PO Box 4118, Manila
President: Potenciana D David
Publications: ASLP Bulletin (quarterly), *Directory of Special Library Resources in the Philippines*

Bibliographical Society of the Philippines*, c/o National Archives, National Library Bldg, T M Kalaw, Ermita, Manila
Secretary-Treasurer: Leticia R Maloles
Publication: Newsletter

National Institute of Science and Technology, Division of Documentation, see Scientific Library and Documentation Division

Philippine Library Association*, c/o National Library, T M Kalaw St, Manila 2801 Tel: 590177
Secretary: Ms H Ll Carpio
Publication: PLAI Bulletin (irregular); *PLAI Newsletter* (bi-monthly)

Scientific Library and Documentation Division*, National Science Development Board, Bicutan, Taguig, PO Box 3596, Manila
Chief: Dr Irene D Amores

University of the Philippines, Institute of Library Science, Diliman, Quezon City 3004 Tel: 976061 ext 249
Dir: Ursula Picache (Dean)
Publications: Journal of Philippine Librarianship, Newsletter

Library Reference Books and Journals

Books

Bibliography of Philippine Bibliographies, Ateneo de Manila University Press, PO Box 154, Manila

Directory of Special Library Resources in the Philippines Association of Special Libraries of the Philippines, PO Box 4118, Manila

Philippine Bibliography, University of the Philippines Library, Gonzalez Hall, Diliman, Quezon City 3004

Journals

Bulletin, Association of Special Libraries of the Philippines (ASLP), PO Box 4118, Manila

Bulletin, Philippine Library Association, c/o National Library, T M Kalaw, Ermita, Manila

Journal of Philippine Librarianship (text in English), University of the Philippines, Institute of Library Science, Diliman, Quezon City

Newsletter, Bibliographical Society of the Philippines, c/o National Archives, National Library Bldg, T M Kalaw, Ermita, Manila

Newsletter, University of the Philippines, Institute of Library Science, Diliman, Quezon City

Literary Associations and Societies

Kawika*, 1655 Soler, Santa Cruz
Society of Tagalog Writers
Secretary: Gemiliane Pinade
Publication: Liwayway (weekly)

International **P E N** Centre, Solidaridad Publishing House, 531 Padre Favra, Ermita, Manila
Secretary: F Sionil José

Literary Periodicals

Balthazar, Balthazar Publishing House, 1782 M Adriatico, Malate, Manila

Diliman Review, University of the Philippines, College of Arts and Sciences, Diliman, Quezon City D-505

Far Eastern University Journal, Far Eastern University, PO Box 609, Manila 2806

Manila Review (text in English); Philippines journal of literature and the arts, Bureau of National and Foreign Information, Department of Public Information, PO Box 3396, Manila

Philippine Studies, Ateneo de Manila University Press, PO Box 154, Manila

Literary Prizes

Cultural Centre of the Philippines Literary Awards
For the best volume of verse and best play written in English and in Pilipino languages, including fiction (novel), epic poetry, criticism and biography once every five years marking the special inaugurations of the Centre, with correspondingly bigger prizes. Open to Filipino citizens, resident or non-resident. Prizes 5,000 Philippine pesos for best verse volume, 7,000 Philippine pesos for best play. Prizes also for 2nd and 3rd places. Awarded annually and published in the series *Gantimpala*. Enquiries to Cultural Centre of the Philippines, Roxas Blvd, Manila

Carlos **Palanca** Memorial Awards for Literature
For novels, short stories, poetry, essays and plays written in English and in Pilipino languages. Annual awards are given in each of the language divisions for the best entries in the following six categories: novel — 25,000 Philippine pesos grand prize; short story, poetry, essay, one-act play — 7,000 Philippine pesos first prize; three-act play — 12,000 Philippine pesos first prize. Enquiries to Carlos Palanca Senior Memorial Foundation, 453 C Palanca St, Quiapo, Manila

Poland

General Information

Language: Polish (German and Russian used, English especially among young people)
Religion: Roman Catholic
Population: 36 million
Literacy Rate (1970): 97.8% (98.8% Urban, 96.5% Rural)
Bank Hours: 0900-1300 Monday-Friday; 0800-1300 Saturday
Shop Hours: 1100-1900 Monday-Saturday
Currency: 100 groszy = 1 zloty
Export/Import Information: Book importation done by the Foreign Trade Enterprise Ars Polona, ul Krakowskie Przedmieście 7, PO Box 1001, 00-068 Warsaw, which pays any duties applicable. Advertising may be placed through AGPOL Foreign Trade Advertising agency, ul Kierbedzia 4, PO Box 7, 00-957 Warsaw. No import licences as such required. All overseas trade is conducted in foreign currency. Small quantities of advertising materials duty free
Copyright: Berne, UCC (see International section)

Book Trade Organizations

A G P O L (Przedsiebiorstwo Reklamy i Wydawnictw Handlu Zagranicznego)*, ul Kierbedzia 4, PO Box 7, 00-957 Warsaw Tel: 416061 Telex: 813364 agpol pl Cable Add: Agpol Warszawa
Foreign Trade Publicity and Publishing Enterprise
Dir: Tadeusz Polanowski
Offers publicity services abroad for Polish foreign trade and in Poland for foreign

companies
Founded: 1956

Foreign Trade Enterprise **Ars Polona**, see RSW (below) and Major Booksellers

Bioru Międzynarodowego Numeru Ksiazki*, ul Jasna 26, 00-950 Warsaw
Editorial Office for **Polish Bibliography***, ul Jagiellońska 15, Cracow
Formerly Karol Estreicher Republication Centre of Polish 19th Century Bibliography
Dir: Professor Dr Karol Estreicher

Polskie Towarzystwo Wydawców Ksiazek*, ul Mazowiecka 2-4, 00-048 Warsaw
Tel: 260735
Polish Publishers' Association
Publication: Przegląd Księgarski i Wydawniczy (jointly with Zjednoczenie Księgarstwa, qv under Major Booksellers)

R S W (Robotnicza Spółdzielnia Wydawnicza) 'Prasa-Ksiazka-Ruch'*, ul Bagatela 14, 00-950 Warsaw Tel: 28851
Workers' Publishing Cooperative
Includes 'Ksiazka i Wiedza' (qv), Interpress (qv), Krajowa Agencja Wydawnicza (qv), Agencja Wydawnicza (qv) and Wydawnictwo Artystyczno-Graficzne; also the Foreign Trade Enterprise Ars Polona (qv under Major Booksellers)

Standard Book Numbering Agency, see Bioru Międzynarodowego Numeru Ksiazki

Stowarzyszenie Autorów Zaiks, 2 ul Hipoteczna, 00-092 Warsaw Tel: 277577
Telex: 812470 zaiks pl
Polish Society of Authors
President: Karol Malcużyński; *General Manager:* Witold Kolodziejski; *Foreign Dept Manager:* Wlodzimierz Lalak

Stowarzyszenie Księgarzy Polskich, ul Mokotowska 4-6, 00-641 Warsaw Tel: 252874
Association of Polish Booksellers (social organization for State book trade employees)
President: Tadeusz Hussak
Publication: Księgarz

Zjednoczenie Przedsiebiorstw Wydawniczych Naczelny Zarzad Wydawnictw*, ul Krakowskie Przedmieście 15-17, 00-071 Warsaw Tel: 268830
United Publishers — Central Publishing Board

Związek Literatów Polskich*, Krakowskie Przedmieście 87-89, 00-079 Warsaw Tel: 268421/260589
President: Jan Józef Szczepański
Union of Polish Writers

Book Trade Reference Books and Journals

Books

Bibliografia Bibliografii i Nauki o Książce. Bibliografia Poloniae Bibliographica (Bibliography of Bibliographies and Library Science), National Library, ul Hankiewicza 1, 00-973 Warsaw

Polish Publishers and Booksellers (text in English), Państwowy Instytut Wydawniczy, ul Foksal 17, 00-372 Warsaw

Journals

Biuletyn (Bulletin), Bibliographical Institute, National Library, ul Hankiewicza 1, 00-973 Warsaw

Books in Polish or Relating to Poland, The Polish Library, 238 King St, London W6, UK

Księgarz (The Bookseller), Association of Polish Booksellers, ul Mokotowska 4-6, 00-641 Warsaw

New Books (editions in English and Polish), Ossolineum, Rynek 9, PO Box 70, 50-106 Wroclaw

New Polish Publications; a monthly review of Polish books (editions in English, German and Russian), Ars Polona, ul Krakowskie Przedmieście 7, 00-068 Warsaw

Przegląd Księgarski i Wydawniczy (Publishing and Bookselling Review), Zjednoczenie Księgarstwa, ul Jasna 26, 00-950 Warsaw (published jointly with the Polish Publishers' Association)

Przewodnik Bibliograficzny. Urzędowy wykaz druków wydanych w Polskiej Rzeczypospolitej Ludowej (Bibliographical Guide. Official List of Publications Issued in Poland), National Library, ul Hankiewicza 1, 00-973 Warsaw

Rocznik Literacki (The Literary Yearbook), Państwowy Instytut Wydawniczy, ul Foksal 17, 00-372 Warsaw

Soon to Appear (French, German and Russian editions), Foreign Trade Publicity and Publishing Enterprise, ul Kierbedzia 4, PO Box 7, 00-957 Warsaw

Zapowiedzi Wydawnicze (Publishing Announcements), United Booksellers, ul Jasna 26, 00-950 Warsaw

Publishers

Agencja Autorska*, ul Hipoteczna 2, 00-092 Warsaw Tel: 278396
Authors' Agency
Associate Company: Polskie Wydawnictwo Muzyczne (qv)
Subjects: Contemporary Polish writers; Periodicals
Also Literary Agency (qv)

Wydawnictwo **Arkady**, ul Sienkiewicza 14, PO Box 169, 00-950 Warsaw Tel: 269316
Man Dir: Eugeniusz Piliszek
Orders to: Foreign Trade Enterprise Ars Polona, ul Krakowskie Przedmieście 7, 00-068 Warsaw
Subjects: Art, Architecture, Building
Founded: 1957
ISBN Publisher's Prefix: 83-213

Ars Christiana*, ul Ogrodowa 37, PO Box 471, 00-873 Warsaw Tel: 204738
Subjects: Religion Problems, Periodicals
Founded: 1951

Wydawnictwa **Artystyczne i Filmowe***, ul Pulawska 61, 02-595 Warsaw Tel: 455301/455584
Man Dir: Jerzy Wittlin; *Editorial:* Edward Rylukowski; *Editorial, Publicity:* Andrzej Dulewicz
Orders to: Ars Polona (see Major Booksellers)
Subjects: Art, Film, Theatre, Reprints of old books and engravings
Founded: 1959

Instytut Wydawniczy **Centralnej Rady Związków Zawodowych***, ul W Spasowskiego 1-3, 00-389 Warsaw Tel: 279011
Publishing House of Trade Unions
Dir: Tadeusz Lipski
Subjects: Health and Safety at Work, Workers' Education and Culture, Trade Union Movement, Living Conditions
Bookshop: Księgarnia Składowa, Marienstzat 8, 00-302 Warsaw
Founded: 1950
ISBN Publisher's Prefix: 83-202

Spółdzielnia Wydawnicza **'Czytelnik'***, ul Wiejska 12a, Warsaw Tel: 281441 Cable Add: Czytelnik Warsaw
Man Dir: Stanislaw Bebenek; *Publicity, Advertising:* Elżbieta Orzeszek
Subjects: General Fiction, Belles Lettres, Poetry, Juveniles, Low-priced Paperbacks, Social Science, Memoirs, Journalism
Founded: 1944

Drukarnia Narodowa, an imprint of Polskie Wydawnictwo Muzyczne (qv)

Państwowe Wydawnictwo **Ekonomiczne**, ul Niecala 4a, 00-098 Warsaw Tel: 278001
Cable Add: Pewue
State Economic Publishers
Man Dir: Zbigniew Gajczyk
Imprint: PWE
Subjects: Scholarly, Reference, Economics, Social Science, Business
Bookshop: At above address
1981: 83 titles *Founded:* 1949

Wydawnictwo **'Epoka'***, ul W Hibnera 11, PO Box 393, 00-018 Warsaw Tel: 278081
Cable Add: Wydawnictwo Epoka Warszawa
Subjects: Publications of the Central Committee of the Democratic Party, Periodicals
Founded: 1957

Wydawnictwa **Geologiczne**, ul Rakowiecka 4, PO Box 72, 00-975 Warsaw Tel: 495081
Dir: Franciszek Szejgis
Subjects: Academic and professional books on Geology, Surveying
1982: 63 titles *Founded:* 1953
ISBN Publisher's Prefix: 83-220

Wydawnictwo Harcerskie **'Horyzonty'**, incorporated in new organization Mlodziezowa Agencja Wydawnicza (qv)

Państwowy **Instytut** Wydawniczy, ul Foksal 17, PO Box 377, 00-950 Warsaw Tel: 260201 Cable Add: Piw
State Publishing Institute
Man Dir: Andrzej Wasilewski; *Deputy Editors-in-Chief:* Barbara Przybylowska, Michal Kabata; *Sales:* Honorat Wojtkowski; *Production:* Stefan Michalski; *Publicity:* Anna Zaluska; *Rights & Permissions:* Regina Malgorzata Greda
Subjects: General Fiction, Belles Lettres, Poetry, Biography, History, History of Culture, Essays, Memoirs
Founded: 1946
ISBN Publisher's Prefix: 83-06

Wydawnictwo **'Interpress'***, ul Bagatela 12, PO Box 388, 00-585 Warsaw Tel: 219325
Cable Add: Interpress Warszawa Telex: 814481/814775 pai pl
Editor-in-Chief: Lubomir Mackiewicz; *Editorial:* Janusz Podoski; *Production, Sales:* Witold Bójski; *Publicity, Rights & Permissions:* Jerzy Guz
Branch Offs: Dechant Heimbachstr 19, Bad Godesberg, D-5300 Bonn 2, Federal Republic of Germany (Tel: 353808); Hagalundsgatan 101, 151, S-171 50 Solna, Stockholm, Sweden (Tel: 821065); Atzgerdorferstr 48, A-1238 Vienna XXIII, Austria (Tel: 8833722)
Subjects: Contemporary and Historical Poland, Popular Science, Tourist Guides
Founded: 1967
Miscellaneous: Member of RSW (qv under Book Trade Organizations)
ISBN Publisher's Prefix: 83-223

Państwowe Wydawnictwo **'Iskry'***, ul Smolna 11-13, PO Box 897, 00-375 Warsaw Tel: 276001/3 (Central) 279415 (Director)
Cable Add: Iskry
Man Dir: Lukasz Szymański
Subjects: General Fiction, Belles Lettres, Poetry, Biography, Travel-Adventure books, How-to, Religion, Juveniles, Low- & High-

POLAND

priced Paperbacks, Social Science
Founded: 1952
ISBN Publisher's Prefix: 83-207

Państwowe Przedsiebiorstwo Wydawnictw **Kartograficznych***, ul Solec 18-20, 00-410 Warsaw Tel: 283251 Cable Add: Pepewuka, Warszawa
Dir: Jan Rzedowski (Tel: 280236)
Subjects: Geographical, Historical, Maps and Atlases; Geodetic, Cartographic books
1981: 120 titles *Founded:* 1951

Wydawnictwo **Katalogów i Cenników***, ul Wiejska 12a, 00-490 Warsaw Tel: 291396
Cable Add: Wukace Warszawa
Subject: Catalogues, Price Lists, Handbooks, Guidebooks
Founded: 1962

Wydawnictwa **Komunikacji i Lacznosci**, ul Kazimierzowska 52, PO Box 71, 02-546 Warsaw Tel: 492751 Telex: 812736 PL
Transport and Communications Publishers
Dir: Czesław Kulesza
Subjects: Mechanical Engineering, Aeronautics, Electronics, Radio, Communications, Transport
1981: 156 titles *1982:* 178 titles *Founded:* 1949
ISBN Publisher's Prefix: 83-206

Krajowa Agencja Wydawnicza (KAW), ul Wilcza 46, PO Box 179, 00-679 Warsaw Tel: 286481/286485 (5 lines) Telex: 813487 KAW PL
Man Dir, Editor-in-Chief: Dobrosław Kobielski
Subjects: Culture, Science, Educational material, Juveniles, Politics, Guides, Belles Lettres, Sport, Science and Detective Fiction
Founded: 1974
Miscellaneous: Member of RSW (qv under Book Trade Organizations)

Wydawnictwo **'Ksiazka i Wiedza'**, ul Smolna 13, PO Box 476, 00-950 Warsaw Tel: 275401 Cable Add: KiW Warszawa
Subjects: History, Politics, Sociology, Philosophy, Belles Lettres
Founded: 1948
Miscellaneous: Member of RSW (qv under Book Trade Organizations)

Państwowy Zakład Wydawnictw **Lekarskich**, Długa 38-40, PO Box 379, 00-238 Warsaw Tel: 314281 Cable Add: Wydlek Warszawa
Polish State Medical Publishers
Dir: Ignacy Nyka; *Editorial Secretary:* Bogdan Golebiowski; *Deputy Editor-in-Chief:* Maria Dziak
Subjects: Medicine, Biology, Biochemistry, Pharmacy, Psychology, Textbooks, Monographs, Dictionaries, Periodicals, Audio-Visual Materials
1981: approx 160 titles *Founded:* 1945

Wydawnictwo **Literackie**, ul Dluga 1, 31-147 Cracow Tel: 225423/224644/224761
Dir: Ireneusz Maślarz Tel: 225423;
Editorial: Katarzyna Krzemuska Tel: 228950
Subjects: Classical and Contemporary Belles Lettres, Memoirs, History, Literature, Theatre, Film, Art, Translations
1981: 200 titles *1982:* 213 titles *Founded:* 1953

Wydawnictwo **Lodzkie**+, ul Piotrkowska 171-173, PO Box 372, 90-447 Lodz Tel: 60331
Editorial Dir: Jacek Zaorski; *Sales & Publicity:* Janina Sobczak; *Production:* Grazyna Bis-Stepniak; *Rights & Permissions:* Alfreda Gorzkiewicz
Subjects: Polish Belles Lettres (mainly modern); Translations of literature from the Soviet Union and Yugoslavia, and from French, German and English; Socio-Scientific Literature; Humanities, Memoirs

1981: 60 titles *1982:* 64 titles *Founded:* 1957
ISBN Publisher's Prefix: 83-218

Wydawnictwo **Lubelskie**, ul Okopowa 7, 20-022 Lublin Tel: 27344
Dir, Editor-in-Chief: Ireneusz Caban
Subjects: Science, Social & Political Sciences, Humanities, Belles-Lettres, Juveniles, Poetry, Translations from Ukrainian
Founded: 1957

Ludowa Spóldzielnia Wydawnicza*, ul Grzybowska 4, 00-131 Warsaw Tel: 200251
Cable Add: LSW, Warszawa
People's Publishing Cooperative
Chairman, Editor-in-Chief: Leon Janczak
Subjects: Polish Literature, History, The Peasant Movement, Agricultural Problems
Founded: 1946

Wydawnictwo **Ministerstwa Obrony Narodowej**, ul Grzybowska 77, 00-844 Warsaw Tel: 201261/494705
Publishing House of the Ministry of National Defence
Dir: Lech Szymański
Subject: Military (History, Memoirs, Technical Literature)
Founded: 1947

Mlodziezowa Agencja Wydawnicza, ul Koszykowa 6A, PO Box 188, 01-564 Warsaw
Youth Publishing Agency and Publishing Co-operative
Agency Editor-in-Chief: Zygmunt Konopka (Tel: 280973); *Books Editor-in-Chief:* Wacław Zurek (Tel: 211757); *Publicity Manager:* Beata Wójcikiewicz (Tel: 289030); *Production Dir:* Zofia Kasińska (Tel: 219848)
Subjects: Literature for children and young people; Instructions and Programmes of Polish Socialist Youth Organizations; Belles Lettres, Sociology, Politics, Popular Science; Handbooks
Founded: 1974
Miscellaneous: This organization replaces the former Wydawnictwo Harcerskie 'Horyzonty'. It is also a Workers' Publishing Co-operative, allied to R S W (qv under Book Trade Organizations). Mlodziezowa acts as both Agency and Publisher for Polish youth

Wydawnictwo **Morskie***, ul Szeroka 38-40, 80-835 Gdansk Tel: 311031
Man Dir: Edward Mazurkiewicz; *Editorial:* Stanisław Ludwig; *Sales, Publicity:* Jerzy Szulczewski; *Production:* Wladysław Kawecki; *Rights & Permissions:* Magdalena Tomsio
Subjects: Maritime, Technical, Economics, Popular Science, Belles Lettres, History
Book Club: Publisher's Club
Bookshop: Publisher's Bookshop (qv under Major Booksellers)
Founded: 1951
ISBN Publisher's Prefix: 83-215

Polskie Wydawnictwo **Muzyczne**, al Krasińskiego 11a, PO Box 115, 31-111 Cracow Tel: 227044 Cable Add: PWM
Polish Music Publishers
Man Dir: Mieczysław Tomaszewski; *Editorial:* Stanisław Haraschin; *Sales:* Wladysław Duda; *Production:* Stanisław Blawacki; *Publicity:* Halina Czubińska; *Rights & Permissions:* Jan Paździora
Orders to: Ars Polona, ul Krakowskie Przedmieście 7, PO Box 1001, 00-068 Warsaw
Associate Company: Agencja Autorska (qv)
Subsidiary Company: Centralna Biblioteka Muzyczna-Nutowa, ul Senatorska 13-15, 00-075 Warsaw
Imprint: Drukarnia Narodowa
Branch Off: 'Synkopa', ul Senatorska 13-15, 00-075 Warsaw
Subject: Music
Book Club: Skladnica Ksiegarska
Bookshop: Skladnica Ksiegarska, ul Smoleńsk, Cracow
1981: 317 titles *Founded:* 1945

Instytut Wydawniczy **'Nasza Ksiegarnia'**, ul W Spasowskiego 4, PO Box 380, 00-389 Warsaw Tel: 262431 Cable Add: Nasza Ksiegarnia
Man Dir: Czeslaw Wiśniewski
Subjects: Juveniles, General Science, Education, Translations into Polish, Periodicals
1981: 167 titles *1982:* 218 titles *Founded:* 1921

Państwowe Wydawnictwo **Naukowe***, ul Miodowa 10, PO Box 391, 00-251 Warsaw Tel: 262291 Cable Add: Pewuen Warszawa
Polish State Academic and Scientific Publishing House. Publishes books in foreign languages and co-operates with foreign publishers
Man Dir: Stanislaw Puchala; *Sales Dir:* Jerzy Kozlowski; *Rights & Permissions:* Zygmunt Gebethner; *Editorial:* Work is divided among large number of teams which themselves are sub-divisions of four major groups dealing with the Humanities, Science & Technology, Popular Science and Language & Reference
Branch Offs: ul Wieckowskiego 13, 90-721 Lódź; ul Smoleńsk 14, 31-112 Cracow; ul Ratajczaka 35, 61-816 Poznań; ul Wierzbowa 15, 50-056 Wroclaw
Orders to: Ars Polona, Importers & Exporters, Krakowskie Przedmieście 7, PO Box 1001, 00-950 Warsaw Cable Add: Arspolona Warsaw; or to Orpan Export, Palac Kultury, 00-901 Warsaw
Subjects: History, Philosophy, Sociology, Psychology, Pedagogics, Economy, Law, Linguistics, Literary Studies, Geography, the Arts, Biology, Mathematics, Physics, Chemistry, Engineering, Agricultural Sciences, Political Science, Information on Warsaw, University Textbooks, Popular Scientific Works, Encyclopaedias, Polish Dictionaries, Scientific Periodicals (in Polish and foreign languages)
Founded: 1951

Wydawnictwa **Naukowo-Techniczne**, ul Mazowiecka 2-4, PO Box 359, 00-950 Warsaw Tel: 267271 Cable Add: Ente Warszawa
Man Dir: Czeslaw Kulesza
Subjects: Applied Mathematics & Physics, Computer Science, Electrical & Electronic Engineering, Chemistry, Automation, Machine Design and Technology, Foodstuffs Industry, Light Industry, Technical & Scientific Encyclopaedias, Dictionaries & Vocabularies at all levels
1982: 104 titles *Founded:* 1949

Wydawnictwa **Normalizacyjne***, ul Nowogrodzka 22, PO Box 206, 00-375 Warsaw Tel: 287261 Cable Add: Wuen Warszawa
Standardization Publishers
Subject: Standardization
Founded: 1956

Zaklad Narodowy im **Ossolińskich** Wydawnictwo Polskiej Akademii Nauk, Rynek 9, PO Box 911, 50-106 Wroclaw Tel: 38625 Cable Add: Ossolineum Wroclaw Telex: 0712771
Ossolineum-Publishing House of the Polish Academy of Sciences
Man Dir: Eugeniusz Adamczak; *Foreign Rights:* W Brodzki
Orders to: Foreign Trade Enterprise, Ars Polona, Krakowskie Przedmieście 7, PO Box 1001, 00-950 Warsaw

Branch Offs: ul Dluga 26, 00-238 Warsaw; Manifestu Lipcowego 19a, 31-110 Cracow; ul Lagiewniki 56, 80-855 Gdansk
Subjects: Bibliographies, History, Art, Philosophy, Psychology, Physical Sciences, Life Sciences, Earth Sciences, Law, Politics, Literature, Pedagogy/Education, Sociology, Technology, Geography, Economics, Languages, Ethnology; University Textbooks, Educational Materials
1981: 558 titles *1982:* 480 titles *Founded:* 1817
ISBN Publisher's Prefix: 83-04

P W E (Państwowe Wydawnictwo Ekonomiczne), see Ekonomiczne

P W N (Panstwowe Wydawnictwo Naukowe), see Naukowe

'**Pallottinum**' Wydawnictwo Stowarzyszenia Apostolstwa Katolickiego*, PO Box 1095, 60-959 Poznan (Located at: al S Przybyszewskiego 30, Poznan) Tel: (06) 47212
Publishers of the Catholic Apostolate Association
Manager: Stefan Dusza
Subjects: Catholic Philosophy and Theology
Founded: 1948

Instytut Wydawniczy **Pax**, ul Chocimska 8-10, 00-791 Warsaw Tel: 499517
Dir, Chief Editor: Janusz Stefanowicz
Subjects: Contemporary trends in Christian Theology, Philosophy and Literature
Founded: 1949

Wydawnictwo Stowarzyszenia Spoleczno-Kulturalnego '**Pojezierze**', ul Zwyciestwa 32, 10-578 Olsztyn Tel: 22352/22285
Publicity: Andrzej Wakar
Subjects: Belles Lettres, Popular Science, Art
ISBN Publisher's Prefix: 83-7002

Wydawnictwo **Poznańskie***, ul A Fredry 8, PO Box 63, 60-967 Poznań Tel: 58534
Man Dir: Dr Jerzy Ziolek; *Publicity Dir:* Mag Krystyna Woźniak
Subjects: History of Great Poland and Polish culture, Modern Polish and Foreign Fiction, Science Fiction
Founded: 1956
Miscellaneous: Specializes in translations from the literature of Scandinavian and German-speaking countries

Wydawnictwo **Prawnicze**, ul Wiśniowa 50, 02-520 Warsaw Tel: 496151-53
Man Dir: Dr Stanislaw Ziembinski (Tel: 494705)
Subjects: All aspects of Law and Criminology
Founded: 1952
ISBN Publisher's Prefix: 83-219

Wydawnictwo **Radia i Telewizji***, ul Chelmska 9, 00-724 Warsaw Tel: 412264
Subjects: Radio and Television
Founded: 1968

Państwowe Wydawnictwo **Rolnicze i Leśne**, al Jerozolimskie 28, PO Box 374, 00-024 Warsaw Cable Add: Pewril Warszawa Tel: 266451
State Agricultural and Forestry Publishers
Man Dir: Mr Marian Bajorek
Subjects: Textbooks, Reference, Agriculture, Forestry, Food Science, Veterinary Science
Founded: 1947

Zaklad Wydawnictw CRS '**Samopomoc Chlopska**'*, ul Jasna 1, PO Box 38, 00-013 Warsaw Tel: 271529 Cable Add: Zetwuceres Warszawa Telex: 81622
Publishing Institute of the 'Samopomoc Chlopska' — Peasant Cooperative
Subjects: Books and Periodicals for the Peasant Cooperative
Founded: 1957

Wydawnictwo '**Slask**', ul Armii Czerwonej 51, PO Box 36-67, 40-161 Katowice Tel: 583221
'Silesia' Publishing House
Dir and Editor-in-Chief: Jeremi Gliszczynski
Subjects: Mining and Metallurgy, Polish Literature for adults and youth, Translations from Czech and Slovak, Social and Political Literature, Popular Science
1982: 92 titles *Founded:* 1954

Wydawnictwo **Sport i Turystyka***, ul H Rutkowskiego 7-9, 00-021 Warsaw Tel: 262451
Sport and Tourism Publishers
Dir, Editor-in-Chief: Eugeniusz Skrzypek
Subjects: Sport, Travel, Tourism, Art
Founded: 1953

Zarzad Wydawnictwo **Statystycznich i Drukarni***, al Niepodleglosci 208, 00-925 Warsaw Tel: 259545/254886 Cable Add: GUS Telex: 814581
Statistical Publications and Printing Board of the Central Statistical Office
Man Dir: Jerzy Sufin-Suliga; *Editorial:* Christo Cwetkow
Subject: Statistics
Founded: 1966

Ksiegarnia **Świetego Wojciecha**, pl Wolności 1, PO Box 288, 60-967 Poznan Tel: 59186/7 Cable Add: Albertinum Poznan
St Adalbert's Bookshop
Man Dir: Dr Michal Maciolka
Branch Offs: ul Królewska 15, Lublin; ul Freta 48, Warsaw
Subjects: Biblical Texts, Theology, Periodicals
Bookshops: At above main and branch offices addresses
Founded: 1895

Wydawnictwa **Szkolne i Pedagogiczne***, pl H Dabrowskiego 8, 00-950 Warsaw, PO Box 480 Tel: 265451/55 Cable Add: Wuesipe Warszawa
Man Dir: Jerzy Loziński; *Rights & Permissions:* Andrzej Syta; *Advertising and Head of Foreign Department:* Marek Szopski
Orders to: Ars Polona, ul Krakowskie Przedmieście 7, PO Box 1001, 00-068 Warsaw (qv under Major Booksellers)
Branch Off: Delegatura WSiP, Basztowa 15, 31-143 Cracow
Subjects: Primary, Secondary and Vocational Textbooks, Education, Pedagogics, Psychology, Pedagogical Periodicals
Founded: 1945

Towarzystwo Przyjaciól Ksiazki (TPK)*, ul Hipoteczna 2 ZAIKS, 00-092 Warsaw Tel: 277304
Society of Friends of Books
Man Dir: Alexandre Bochenski
Branch Offs: Rynek Gl 35, 31-011 Kraków; Plac Wolnosci 12, 40-078 Katowice; uk św Jadwigi 3/4, 50-266 Wroclaw; ul Slowackiego 9, Rzeszów
Subject: Book Collecting
Founded: 1957

Wydawnictwa Kultura Zycia Codziennego '**Watra**'*, al Jerozolimskie 87, 02-001 Warsaw Tel: 212241-8
Subjects: Health, Domestic Science, Food, Family Life, Periodicals
Founded: 1954

Wydawnictwa Przemyslu Maszynowego '**Wema**'*, ul Danitowiczowska 18, PO Box 90, 00-950 Warsaw Tel: 275456
Chief Executive: Czeslaw Borski; *Editorial Dir:* Maria Hoffmann
Subject: Mechanical Engineering
1981: 1,253 titles *Founded:* 1967

'**Wiedza Powszechna**' Państwowe Wydawnictwo, ul Jasna 26, PO Box 162, 00-054 Warsaw Tel: 277651
Orders to: Ars Polona (see Major Booksellers)
Man Dir, Editor-in-Chief: Tadeusz Kosmala
Subjects: Encyclopaedias, Dictionaries, Language Handbooks, Popular Science
Founded: 1952

Wydawniczo Oświatowa Spóldzielnia Inwalidów '**Wspólna Sprawa**'*, ul Zelazna 40, 00-838 Warsaw Tel: 209071
Educational Publishing Co-operative of the Disabled
Subjects: Graphic art textbooks for primary and nursery schools; Periodicals for foreign language sessions; Games
Founded: 1956

Spoleczny Instytut Wydawniczy '**Znak**'*, ul Wiślna 12, 31-007 Cracow Tel: 24548
Man Dir: Jacek Wozniakowski
Subjects: Religious Subjects, Philosophy, History, Belles Lettres
Founded: 1959

Literary Agents

Agencja Autorska*, ul Hipoteczna 2, 00-950 Warsaw Tel: 278396
Contact: Wladyslaw Jakubowski, Andrzej Mierzejewski
Also Publisher (qv)

Mlodziezowa Agencja Wydawnicza, Polish Youth Publishing Agency – see main entry under Publishers

Book Clubs

Club of Twentieth Century Poetry*, Horizons of Technology Club of Popular Science Books, ul Nowolipie 4, 00-950 Warsaw

New Countryside Book Club*, ul Nowolipie 4, 00-950 Warsaw

Publisher's Club*, ul Szeroka 38-40, 80-835 Gdańsk
Owned by: Wydawnictwo Morskie (qv)

Skladnica Ksiegarska, ul Smoleńsk 33, Cracow
Owned by: Polskie Wydawnictwo Muzyczne (qv)

Major Booksellers

Ars Polona*, ul Krakowskie Przedmieście 7, PO Box 1001, 00-068 Warsaw Tel: 261201 Cable Add: Ars Polona Warszawa Telex: 813498
Foreign Trade Enterprise
Miscellaneous: Member of RSW (see under Book Trade Organizations)

Dom Ksiazki*, ul Smoleńsk 33, 31-112 Cracow Tel: 225472 Telex: Nr 0325418 Deka PL
Collective name for the State-owned Polish book-retailing enterprises. There are 18, each controlling 50-250 bookshops throughout Poland, subordinate to Zrzeszenie Ksiegarstwa (qv)

Orpan Export*, Palac Kultury, 00-901 Warsaw

Publisher's Bookshop*, ul Szeroka 38-40, 80-835 Gdańsk

Powszechna Ksiegarnia Wysylkowa*, ul Nowolipie 4, 00-950 Warsaw Tel: 310021
Organization for mail order, subordinate to Zrzeszenie Ksiegarstwa (qv)

Państwowe, Przedsiebiorstwo **'Skladnica Ksiegarska'***, ul Mazowiecka 9, 00-950 Warsaw
Organization for wholesale book trade, subordinate to Zrzeszenie Ksiegarstwa (qv)

Zrzeszenie Ksiegarstwa*, PO Box 48, 00-950 Warsaw (Located at: ul Jasna 26) Tel: (General) 277651; (Dir) 268393 Telex: 81-2448 deka pl
Dir: Kazimierz Majerowicz Tel: 268393 (Dir) or 277651
National organization for the sale of books; subordinate to the Minister of Culture and Art and controlling Skladnica Ksiegarska (wholesale), Dom Ksiazki (retail), and Powszechna Księgarnia Wysylkowa (mail order) (qqv under 'Major Booksellers')
Publication: Przeglad Ksiegarski i Wydawniczy (jointly with the Polish Publishers' Association)

Major Libraries

Naczelna Dyrekcja **Archiwów Państwowych**, ul Dluga 6, 00-950 Warsaw
Main Directorate of the Polish State Archives

Archiwum Akt Nowych, al Niepodleglości 162, 02-554 Warsaw

Archiwum Glówne Akt Dawnych, ul Dluga 7, 00-263 Warsaw Tel: 315491
Central Archives for Historical Documents
Dir: Dr Edward Potkowski

Biblioteka Jagiellońska*, Aleja Mickiewicza 22, 30-059 Cracow Tel: 333505/333500/336377; Secretary 330903; Director 331971 Telex: 0325682 bj pl
Dir: Dr Jan Pirozynski
Publication: Biuletyn Biblioteki Jagiellońskiej (Biannual)

Biblioteka Narodowa, ul Hankiewicza 1, 00-973 Warsaw Tel: Main Bldg 224621; Special Collections: 313241 Telex: 813702 bn pl
This is the National Library, Warsaw. See also Instytut Bibliograficzny
Dir: Dr Stanislaw Czajka
Publications: Rocznik Biblioteki Narodowej (The National Library Yearbook); *Katalog Rekopisów* (Catalogue of Manuscripts); *Katalog Mikrofilmów* (Catalogue of Microfilms); *Centralny Katalog Biezacych Czasopism Zagranicznych w Bibliotekach Polskich* (Union Catalogue of Current Foreign Periodicals in Polish Libraries)

Biblioteka Publiczna m st Warszawy, ul Koszykowa 26, 00-553 Warsaw Tel: 217852
Public Library of Warsaw
Librarian: Helena Zarachowicz
Publication: Prace Biblioteki Publicznej m st Warszawy

Centrum Informacji Naukowej, Technicznej i Ekonomicznej*, Skrytka pocztowa 355, al Neipodleglości 186, 00-950 Warsaw
National Centre for Scientific, Technical and Economic Information
Publications: Aktualne Problemy Informacji i Dokumentacji (bimonthly); *Informator Nauki Polskiej* (Polish Research Guide)

Glówna Biblioteka Lekarska*, Chocimska 22, 00-791 Warsaw Tel: 497851/497404 Telex: 814820
Central Medical Library
Dir: Prof Feliks Widy-Wirski

Biblioteka **Glówna Politchniki** Warszawskiej*, plac Jedności Robotniczej 1, 00-662 Warsaw Telex: 816467 bgpw pl
Library of the Technical University of Warsaw

Biblioteka **Glówna, Uniwersytet Mikolaja Kopernika**, ul Gagarina 13, 87-100 Toruń Tel: 13-408, 233-52 Telex: 055382 butor pl
Library of the University of Toruń
Librarian: Dr Bohdan Ryszewski

Biblioteka **Glówna Uniwersytetu im Adama Mickiewicza***, ul Fredry 10, 61-701 Poznan Tel: 50298 Telex: 0415260
Library of Adam Mickiewicz University

Instytut Bibliograficzny, Biblioteka Narodowa, ul Hankiewicza 1, 00-973 Warsaw
Bibliographical Institute (a Division of the National Library – see Biblioteka Narodowa)
Publications: Przewodnik Bibliograficzny; Bibliografia Zawartości Czasopism; Bibliografia Czasopism i Wydawnictw Zbiorowych; Polonica Zagraniczne

Zaklad Narodowy im **Ossolińskich** Biblioteka Polskiej Akademii Nauk, ul Szewska 37, 50-139 Wroclaw Tel: 444471/444472; Director 34304 Telex: 0342787 boss pl
Library of the National Ossoliński Institute of the Polish Academy of Sciences
Librarian: Dr Janusz Albin
Publication: Ze Skarbca Kultury (twice yearly)

Biblioteka **Śląska**, ul Francuska 12, 40-015 Katowice Tel: 516441/5 Telex: 0312534 bsk pl
Silesian Library
Dir: Dr Miroslaw Strzoda
Publication: Ksiaznica Śląska
Miscellaneous: A major Polish library. Specializes in scientific publications, but has many special collections covering Literature, History, Law and Religion and especially Silesian Interest

Biblioteka **Uniwersytecka w Warszawie***, Krakowskie Przedmieście 26-28 and 32, 00-927 Warsaw Tel: Chief Librarian 264155; Department of Scientific Information 264047 Telex: 817016 Buwar PL
Library of the University of Warsaw
Publications: Prace Biblioteki Uniwersyteckiej w Warszawie (irregularly); *Uniwersytet Warszawski Materialy bibliograficzne* (annually) in *Roczniki Uniwersytetu Warszawskiego*

Biblioteka **Uniwersytecka w Wroclawiu***, ul Karola Szajnochy 10, 50-076 Wroclaw Tel: 443432 Telex: 0712477 buw PL
Library of the University of Wroclaw
Librarian: Dr Bartlomiej Kuzak

Library Associations

Polish Academy of Sciences, Scientific Information Centre, ul Nowy Swiat 72, 00-330 Warsaw Tel: 268410 Telex: 815414 Oinpan
Publications: Katalog Mikrofilmów (Catalogue of imported microfilms) (annual); *Przeglad Informacji o Naukoznawstwie* (Review of information on the science of science); *Zagadnienia Informacji Naukowej* (Problems of scientific information)

Stowarzyszenie Bibliotekarzy Polskich*, ul Konopczyńskiego 5-7, 00-953 Warsaw Tel: 275296/270847
Polish Librarians' Association
Chairman: Stefan Kubów; *Secretary-General:* Wladyslawa Wasilewska
Publications: Przeglad Biblioteczny; Bibliotekarz; Poradnik Bibliotekarza; Informator Bibliotekarza i Ksiegarza

Library Reference Books and Journals

Books

Informator Bibliotekarza i Ksiegarza (Guide for the Librarian and Bookseller), Polish Librarians Association, ul Konopczyńskiego 5-7, 00-953 Warsaw

Rocznik Biblioteki Narodowej (National Library Yearbook), covers scientific library science (text in Polish with English summaries), National Library, ul Hankiewicza 1, 00-973 Warsaw

Journals

Aktualne Problemy Informacji i Dokumentacji (Current Problems in Information and Documentation) (summaries in English, French, Polish and Russian), National Centre for Scientific, Technical and Economic Information, ul Niepodleglości 186, 00-931 Warsaw

Bibliotekarz (The Librarian) (text in Polish, summaries in English and Russian), Polish Librarians Association, ul Konopczyńskiego 5-7, 00-953 Warsaw

Poradnik Bibliotekarza (The Librarian's Handbook), Polish Librarians Association, ul Konopczyńskiego 5-7, 00-953 Warsaw

Przeglad Biblioteczny (Library Review) (summaries in English), Polish Librarians Association, ul Konopczyńskiego 5-7, 00-953 Warsaw

Studia o Ksiazce (Studies on the Book), Ossolineum, Rynek 9, PO Box 70, 50-106 Wroclaw

Literary Associations and Societies

Instytut Badań Literackich, Nowy Świat 72, Palac Staszica, 00-330 Warsaw Tel: 265231/269945
Institute of Literary Research of the Polish Academy of Sciences
Acting Dirs: Prof Alina Witkowska, Dr Ryszard Górski
Publications: Pamietnik Literacki (Literary Journal quarterly); *Teksty* (Texts, fortnightly); *Biuletyn Polonistyczny* (Bulletin of Polish Literary Scholarship, quarterly); *Kwartalnik Historii Prasy Polskiej* (Quarterly of the History of the Polish Press); *Literary Studies in Poland* (semi-annual); and other Literary Study series
Founded: 1948

Polish **P E N** Centre, Palac Kultury i Nauki, 00-901 Warsaw Tel: 263948
Secretary: Wladyslaw Bartoszewski

Towarzystwo Literackie im Adama Mickiewicza, Nowy Świat 72, 00-330 Warsaw
Mickiewicz Literary Society
President: Prof Dr Mieczyslaw Klimowicz
Publication: Rocznik (Yearbook)

Towarzystwo Przyjaciól Ksiazki*, ul Hipoteczna 2, 00-092 Warsaw
Society of Friends of Books

Towarzystwo Przyjaciól Nauk w Przemyślu*, Plac Katedralny 2, 37-700 Przemyśl
Society of Science and Letters of Przemyśl
Chairman: Mieczyslaw Mazurek; *Secretary:* Tadeusz Burzyński
Publications include: Rocznik Przemyśki (23 vols); *Biblioteka Przemyska* (10 vols); *Rocznik Nauk Medycznych* (5 vols)

Literary Periodicals

Literatura (Literature), RSW, ul Bagatela 14, 00-950 Warsaw

Literatura na świecie (World Literature), Ars Polona, ul Krakowskie Przedmieście 7, PO Box 1001, 00-068 Warsaw

MKL (Miesiecznik Kulturalny Litery) (Monthly Journal of Literary Culture), Targ Drzewny 3-7, 80-886 Gdansk

Miesiecznik Literacki (Monthly Review of Literature), Ars Polona, ul Krakowskie Przedmieście 7, PO Box 1001, 00-068 Warsaw

Nowy Wyraz (New Expression), Ars Polona, ul Krakowskie Przedmieście 7, PO Box 1001, 00-068 Warsaw

Pamietnik Literacki (Literary Diary) (contents page in English, Polish and Russian), Institute of Literary Research of the Polish Academy of Sciences, Nowy Świat 72, Palac Staszica, 00-330 Warsaw

Poezja (Poetry), Ars Polona, ul Krakowskie Przedmieście 7, PO Box 1001, 00-068 Warsaw

Polish Literature (text in English and French), Agencja Autorska, ul Hipoteczna 2, 00-092 Warsaw

Ruch Literacki (The Literary Movement), Polish Academy of Sciences, Historico-Literary Commission, ul Slawkowska 17, Cracow

Teksty (Texts), RSW, ul Bagatela 14, 00-950 Warsaw

Twórczość (Literary monthly), Ars Polona, ul Krakowskie Przedmieście 7, PO Box 1001, 00-068 Warsaw

Zycie Literackie (Literary Life), ul Wislna 2, Cracow

Literary Prizes

Cracow City Literary Prize*
For the entire work of an author whose life and writings were connected with Cracow. Awarded annually. Enquiries to Cracow City Council and Cracow Section of the Union of Polish Writers, ul Krupnicza 22, Cracow

Polish Ministry of National Defence Prize
For the best book dealing with the history of the Polish Armed Forces and with the defence of the country. Awarded annually. Enquiries to Polish Ministry of National Defence Publishing House, ul Grzybowska 77, Warsaw

Polish Prime Minister Award for Literature for Children and Youth*
For the entire work of an author of books for children and young people. Awarded annually. Enquiries to Polish Prime Minister's Office, ul Ujazdowskie 113, Warsaw

Polish Union of Socialist Youth Prose Award*
For the best novel by an author under 30. Awarded annually. Enquiries to Polish Union of Socialist Youth and the Daily Paper 'Sztandar Mlodych', ul Wspolna 61, Warsaw

Warsaw City Prize*
For the entire work of a distinguished author writing for children and young people. Awarded annually. Enquiries to Warsaw Municipal Council, Department of Culture, pl Dzierzynskiego 3-5, Warsaw

Warsaw City Prize for Young Poets*
For best poetry written by a young author. Co-sponsored by the Warsaw Creative Youth Club of the Polish Union of Writers and the Students' Club 'Hybrydy'. Awarded annually. Enquiries to Warsaw Municipal Council, Department of Culture, pl Dzierzynskiego 3-5, Warsaw

Mariusz Zaruski Literary Prize*
For the authors of best books about the sea. Awarded annually. Enquiries to Marine Club of the League of the Friends of Soldiers, ul Chocimska 14, Warsaw

'Zycie Literackie' Prize*
For literary criticism, journalism and essays. Awarded annually. Enquiries to Zycie Literackie, ul Wislna 2, Cracow

Translation Agencies and Associations

Stowarsyszenie Tlumaczy Polskich*, ul Marszalkowska 2, 00-581 Warsaw
Polish Translators Association
President: Andrzej Kopczyński

Portugal

General Information

Language: Portuguese
Religion: Roman Catholic
Population: 9.8 million
Literacy rate (1970): 71%
Bank Hours: 0830-1200, 1300-1430 Monday-Friday
Shop Hours: 0900-1300, 1500-1900 Monday-Friday (some do not close midday); 0900-1300 Saturday. Generally closed Monday morning October-November
Currency: 100 centavos = 1 Portuguese escudo
Export/Import Information: Foreign language books from most countries dutied per kg (free from UK and reduced from EEC); atlases and children's picture books have higher tariff rate and children's picture books have an import surcharge. Small quantity of advertising duty-free. No import licence required for goods not exceeding a certain value, otherwise licence including permission to transfer foreign exchange required
Copyright: UCC, Berne (see International section)

Book Trade Organization

Associação Portuguesa dos Editores e Livreiros, Largo de Andaluz, 16-1° Esq°, 1000 Lisbon Tel: 546182 Cable Add: Apel
Portuguese Association of Publishers and Booksellers
President: Fernando Guedes; *Secretary-General:* Dr Jorge de Carvalho Sá Borges
Branch Offs: Rua D Diogo de Sousa 133, 4700 Braga; Rua Ferreira Borges 103, 3000 Coimbra; R da Fábrica 33-4° – Ap 42, 4000 Porto
Publication: Livros de Portugal, Boletim Bibliográfico (monthly)

Book Trade Reference Books and Journals

Book

O Mundo do Edição Luso-Brasileira (The World of Publishing, Portugal and Brazil), Publicações Europa-Americana, Apdo 8, Mem Martins

Journals

Boletim de Bibliografia Portuguesa (Portuguese Bibliographical Bulletin), National Library, Rua Ocidental do Campo Grande 83, Lisbon 5

Livros de Portugal (Portuguese Books), Portuguese Association of Publishers and Booksellers, Largo de Andaluz, 16-1°, Esq°, 1000 Lisbon

Publishers

Edições **70** Lda, Ave Duque d'Ávila 69 R/C Esq, 1000 Lisbon Tel: 556898/572001/578322
Man Dir: J J Soares da Costa; *Editorial, Rights & Permissions:* Carlos Araújo; *Production Dir:* Rui Oliveira; *Sales:* Alfredo Sarmento
Subjects: General Fiction, Literature, Biography, History, Philosophy, Psychology, Social Science, Politics, Economics, Educational, Occult, Leisure Pursuits, University Textbooks, Comics, Children's
1981: 126 titles *1982:* 85 titles *Founded:* 1970

A E I International*, Rua Conde Moser, Lote 1, 4° Dto, Monte Estoril, 2765 Estoril Tel: 2684400 Telex: 15494 Sertex P att AEI Portugal
Firm is also a Literary Agency

Edições **Afrontamento**, Rua Costa Cabral 859, Apdo 1309, Oporto Tel: 489271
Man Dir, Editorial, Production: José Sousa Ribeiro; *Sales, Publicity:* Marcela Figueiredo Torres; *Rights & Permissions:* Arnaldo Fleming
Subjects: General Literature, Social Sciences, Urbanism, Politics, Cinema
1981: 10 titles *1982:* 20 titles *Founded:* 1963

Arménio **Amado** Editora de Simões, Beirão & Ca Lda+, Ceira, 3000 Coimbra
Man Dir: Luis França
Subjects: Philosophy, Religion, Psychology, Social Science, Law, Architecture, History, Politics, Languages
Founded: 1929

Amigos do Livro, Rua Fernão Mendes Pinto 42, 1400 Lisbon Telex: 14295
Dirs: José Soares Marques Henriques, Carlos Henrique Silva Martins da Luz; *Sales Dir:* Fernando Rui da Costa Rodrigues; *Production Dir:* João José Quintas Poeiras; *Editorial & Publicity Dir:* Mário Correia
Subjects: Literature, Cartoon Strips, History, Science, Sport, Religion
1981: 4 titles
Founded: 1971

Livraria **Apostolado** da Imprensa, Rua da Boavista 591, Oporto Tel: 27875
Man Dir, Editorial: Manuel Morujão, Américo Nunes; *Publicity:* A Nunes da Rocha
Branch Off: Rua da Lapa 111, 1200 Lisbon Tel: 660214
Subjects: General Fiction, Belles Lettres, Poetry, Biography, Philosophy, Religion, Juveniles, Secondary Textbooks
Bookshop: At above address
Founded: 1922

Editora **Arcádia** Sarl*, Campo de Santa
Clara 160, Lisbon 2 Tel: 863151/3 Cable
Add: Arcádia
Shipping Add: Ave Camilo Castelo Branco,
9-A, Buraca-Damaia
Dirs: Ricardo F Martins, Dr João Rodrigues
Martins, Dr Alberto dos Santos Antonio;
Sales Dir: Alvaro A F Ferreira
Subjects: General Fiction, Belles Lettres,
Biography, History, How-to, Music, Art,
Philosophy, Religion, Juveniles, Paperbacks,
Medicine, Psychology, Engineering, General
& Social Science
Founded: 1957

Livraria **Arnado** Lda*, Rua Joao Machado
9-11, Coimbra Tel: 27573
Man Dir: José Fernandes de Almeida
Parent Company: Porto Editora Lda (qv)
Subsidiary Company: Empresa Literária
Fluminense Lda
Subjects: Scholarly, Scientific, Legal,
Literary
Founded: 1966

Editorial **Aster***, Largo D Estefânia 8-1°
Esq°, Lisbon 1 Tel: 534611/532973
*Man Dir, Sales, Publicity, Rights &
Permissions:* Fernando de Souza; *Editorial:*
Dr H Barrilaro Ruas; *Production:* João
Alves
Branch Offs: Praça Guilherme Gomes
Fernandes 24-2° Esq°, Oporto; Rua de
Santo André 7, 4700 Braga
Subjects: General Fiction, Belles Lettres,
Poetry, Biography, History, Music, Art,
Philosophy, Religion, Psychology, How-to,
Juveniles, Paperbacks, Secondary and
University Textbooks
Founded: 1954

Livraria Editora **Atlântida** Ltda*, Rua
Ferreira Borges 103, Coimbra
Dir: Afonso Queiró
Subject: Law

Editorial **'Avante!'**, Ave Santos Dumont
57-3°, 1000 Lisbon
Man Dir: Francisco Melo
Orders to: C D L (Central Distribuidora
Livreira) SARL, Ave Santos Dumont 57-4°,
1000 Lisbon
Subjects: Politics, Economics, Philosophy,
General Fiction
Founded: 1974

Livraria **Bertrand** SARL*, Apdo 37, 2701
Amadora codex Tel: 974571 Cable Add:
Libertran Telex: 12709
Man Dir: Amaro de Matos; *Editorial,
Rights & Permissions:* Piedade Ferreira;
Sales: Carlos Grade; *Production:* Pina
Mendes; *Publicity:* Ferreira da Cruz
Subjects: General Portuguese and Foreign
Literature, Social Sciences, Juveniles (all
ages), Dictionaries, School Books, Cartoon
Strips
Bookshops: (Lisbon) Rua Garrett 73/75,
Ave Roma 13-B, Rua Dr J Soares 4-A, Rua
D Estefânea 46-C/D; (Coimbra) Largo da
Portagem 9; (Oporto) Rua de Santo
António 43, 45, 65, Shopping Center,
Brasilia; (Aveiro) Ave Dr L Peixinho 87-B;
(Vian do Castelo) Rua Sacadura Cabral 32;
(Faro) Rua D Francisco Gomes 27
Founded: 1732

Brasília Editora (J Carvalho Branco & Cia
Lda)*, Rua José Falcão 173, CP 101, 4001
Oporto codex Tel: 315854 Cable Add:
Brasiliaeditora
Man Dir: J Carvalho Branco; *Editorial,
Rights & Permissions:* Dr Zulmira C
Branco; *Sales, Publicity:* Dr Isabel C
Branco; *Production:* J Silva Couto
Associate Company: Livraria Leitura —
Fernandes e Branco Lda, Rua de Ceuta 88,
Oporto
Subsidiary Company: Livraria Boa Leitura,
Av Almirante Reis 256, Lisbon
Subjects: Portuguese and Foreign Literature;
Belles Lettres, Fiction, Poetry, Biography,
How-to, Philosophy, Religion, Psychology,
Social Science, Politics, Yoga, Sex, Occult
Bookshops: Livraria Leitura, Ave Almirante
Reis 256B, Lisbon; Livraria Leitura, Rua de
Ceuta 88, Oporto
Founded: 1961

Editorial **Caminho** SARL, Alameda de
Santo António dos Capuchos 6B, 1100
Lisbon Tel: 542683/549381
Man Dir: Zeferino Antas de Sousa Coelho
Orders to: C D L — see 'Major Booksellers'
Subjects: General Fiction, Socio-Political,
Juveniles
Founded: 1977

Centro do Livro Brasileiro, Rua Almirante
Barroso 13-2°, Lisbon 1000 Tel:
560165/6/7 Cable Add: Celbrasil
Man Dir, Editorial: Alvaro Conçalves
Pereira
Subjects: Philosophy, Religion, Social
Science, Philology, Pure and Applied
Science, Art, History, Geography, General
Bookshop: Rua 31 de Janeiro 146, Oporto
1981: 42 titles *1982:* 50 titles *Founded:* 1963

Livraria **Civilização** (Américo Fraga
Lamares & Ca Lda)+, Rua Alberto Aires de
Gouveia 27, Oporto 1 Tel:
22286/22287/32382 Cable Add: Alamares
Man Dir: Arquitecto Moura Bessa; *Rights &
Permissions:* Maria Alice Moura Bessa
Branch Off: Ave Almirante Reis 102 r/c-
Dto, Lisbon 1 (Tel: 823389)
Subjects: Social and Political Science,
Economics, History, Art, Fiction, Juveniles
1981: 16 titles *Founded:* 1921

Edições **Cosmos**, Rua da Emenda 111-2°,
1200 Lisbon 2 Tel: 322050 Cable Add:
Cosmos-Lisboa
Man Dir: Manuel R de Oliveira
Subjects: Music, Sociology, History
Founded: 1938

Sá da **Costa** Editora*, Praça Luís de Camões
22 4, Lisbon 1294 codex Tel: 360721 Cable
Add: Livrosacosta Telex: 15574-P
Man Dir, Editorial: João Sá da Costa; *Sales,
Publicity:* João Nuno Camilo Alves;
Production: Idalina Sá da Costa
Subjects: Textbooks, History, Philosophy,
Literature, Classics, Essays
Bookshop: Rua Garrett 100-102,
Lisbon 1294 codex
Founded: 1913

Publicações **Dom Quixote** Lda, Rua
Luciano Cordeiro 119, 1098 Lisbon codex
Tel: 40250/538079/538088 Cable Add:
Quixote Telex: 14331 Quixot P
Man Dir: Nelson de Matos; *Editorial:*
Manuel Alberto Valente; *Production:*
Virgínia Caldeira; *Rights & Permissions:*
Marie Thérèse Newbery
Subjects: General Fiction, Belles Lettres,
Poetry, History, Education, Philosophy,
Social Science, Reference, Children's Books,
Cartoons, Humour
1981: 60 titles *Founded:* 1965

Editorial **Enciclopédia** Lda*, Rua António
Maria Cardoso 33, Lisbon 2 Tel:
326452/33330
Subjects: Encyclopaedias, Fiction, History,
Art, Technical
Founded: 1934

Livraria **Escolar** Infante*, Manuel Ferreira
& Gomes Lda, Rua de Santa Teresa 20-22,
Oporto Tel: 26281/317098
Publicity Manager: Manuel Gomes; *Sales
Manager:* Manuel Ferreira
Subjects: History, Religion, Juveniles,
Paperbacks, General & Social Science,
Secondary & Primary Textbooks,
Educational Materials, Law
Bookshop: Livraria Escolar Infante, Rua de
Santa Teresa 22, Oporto
Founded: 1962

Editorial **Estúdios** Cor Sarl*, Rua João
Pereira da Rosa 20-A, 1200 Lisbon Tel:
328889/362146 Telex: 15875 Lib P
Subjects: Belles Lettres, Biography, History,
Music, Art, Philosophy, Politics, Juveniles,
General Science, Translations, General
Fiction, Paperbacks
Founded: 1949

Publicações **Europa-America** Lda, Apdo 8,
Estrada Lisbon-Sintra Km 14, Mem
Martins Tel: 9211461/2/3 Cable Add:
Europamérica Telex: 42255 Pea P
Man Dir: Francisco Lyon de Castro; *Co-
Manager:* Tito Lyon de Castro; *Editorial
Dir:* José Moura Pimenta; *Sales Dir:*
Eduardo Lyon de Castro
Subsidiary Companies: Editorial Inquérito;
Grafica Europam Lda; Publicações Forum;
Publicações Trevo
Branch Offs: Delegação de Lisbon, Rua da
Flores, 45-1°, Lisbon; Delegação do Pôrto,
Rua 31 de Janeiro, 221 Porto
Subjects: General Fiction, Biography,
History, How-to, Music, Art, Philosophy,
Reference, Medicine, Psychology, General &
Social Science, Nursery books, Juveniles,
Low- & High-priced Paperbacks, University
Textbooks, Educational Materials, Belles
Lettres, Poetry, Engineering, Technical
Bookshops: Lojas Europa-America, Ave
Marquês de Tomar 1-B, Rua das Flores
45-1°, Lisbon; Ave António Enes 14-B, Ave
Elias Garcia 104-B, Queluz; Ave 1 de Maio
61, Castelo Branco; Pr Ferreira de Almeida
21-22, Faro; Av 25 de Abril 48, Almada;
Rua José Relvas, 15 B-C, Parede; Arcadas
do Parque, Estoril; (Centro Comercial Pão
de Açúcar, Lojas 6 e 7) Estrada Nacional
6-50, Cascais
Founded: 1945

Livraria Editora **Figueirinhas** Lda, Praça da
Liberdade 67, 4000 Oporto Tel:
24985/25751/317698
Man Dir, Publicity: João Pimenta; *Editorial,
Sales, Production, Rights & Permissions:*
Mario Figueirinhas
Subjects: General Literature
Founded: 1944

Forja Editora SARL*, Rua da Emenda 30
3° C, 1200 Lisbon Tel: 322334 Cable Add:
Ediforja
*Man Dir, Editorial, Production, Publicity,
Rights & Permissions:* Anibal Telo; *Sales:*
João Sá
Subjects: Fiction, Juveniles, Theatre,
Cinema
Founded: 1974

Editorial **Franciscana***, Montariol, Apdo 17,
4701 Braga codex Tel: 22490
Man Dir: António Pedro da Anunciação
Subjects: Biography, History, Music, Art,
Philosophy, Religion, Juveniles, Theology
Bookshops: Livraria Editorial Franciscana,
Rua de Cedofeita 350, Oporto; Montariol,
Braga
Founded: 1922

Editorial **Futura**, Ave 5 de Outubro 317-1°,
Lisbon 1600 Tel: 779114
Man Dir: José Chaves Ferreira
Subjects: General Literature
Founded: 1970

G E C T I (Gabinete de Especialização e
Cooperação Tecnica Internacional L), Ave
Republica 47-6D, PO Box 1918, 1004 Lisbon
codex Tel: 768877/771940/772154
Man Dir, Editorial: A Almeida Teixeira
Subjects: Business, Administration,
Marketing, Professional Training,

Programmed Learning
Founded: 1963

Gabinete de Especializacão e Cooperacão Tecnica Internacional, see GECTI

Livros **Horizonte** Lda, Rua das Chagas 17-1° Dt, Apdo 2818, 1200 Lisbon Tel: 366917/368505 Cable Add: Livroshorizonte
Man Dir, Rights & Permissions: Rog Mendes de Moura; *Sales:* Francisco Ramos Vasquez; *Production:* M Antónia Raposo; *Publicity:* M C Ribeiro da Silva
Subjects: Pedagogy, Philosophy, Sociology, Art, Dictionaries
Founded: 1953

Edições **I T A U** (Instituto Tecnico de Alimentação Humana) Lda, Ave da Républica 46-A r/c Esq, Lisbon 1 Tel: 733307/733482/733245
Man Dir: Júlio Roberto; *Editorial, Sales, Production, Publicity:* José Maria Paula
Orders to: Ave Elias Garcia 87-A, Lisbon 1
Parent Company: Instituto Tecnico de Alimentação Humana Lda
Subjects: Human Nutrition, Pedagogy, Poetry, Literature, Sociology, Juvenile Literature
1981: 15 titles *1982:* 5 titles *Founded:* 1969

Imprensa Nacional-Casa da Moeda*, Rua D Francisco Manuel de Melo No 5, Lisbon 1 Tel: 685684 Cable Add: INCM
Man Dir, Editorial, Sales & Publicity: Dr Américo Farinha de Carvalho
Branch Offs: 4 in Lisbon, 1 each in Oporto and Coimbra
Subjects: Political and Civil Administration, Archaeology, Arts, Economics, Ethnography, Ethnology, Pharmacy, Philology, Philosophy, History, Memoirs, Religion
Bookshops: Livraria Camões, Rua Bittencourt da Silva 12C, Rio de Janeiro, Brazil; Gabinete Portugues de Lectura, Rua do Imperador 290, Recife, Brazil
Founded: 1768

Editorial **Inquérito** Lda*, Travessa da Queimada 23, 1° D, 1200 Lisbon Tel: 328659
Subjects: General Fiction, Belles Lettres, History, Philosophy, Juveniles, Social Science, Law
Founded: 1938

Instituto Tecnico de Alimentação Humana, see I T A U

Américo Fraga **Lamares** & Ca Lda, see Livraria Civilização

Lello e Cia Lda*, Rua Conde de Vizela 12, Oporto 1 Tel: 23209
Dir: J Pinto Mesquita Lello
Subjects: Fine Arts, Education, Textbooks

Lello e Irmão, Rua das Carmelitas 144, Oporto 4000 Tel: 22037/318170 Cable Add: Jolello
Man Dir: Edgar Pinto Da Silva Lello
Subjects: General Literature, Juveniles, History, Dictionaries
Founded: 1881

Editora **Livros** do Brasil Sarl, Rua dos Caetanos 22, PO Box 2953, 1200 Lisbon Tel: 362621/323170/326113 Cable Add: Librasil
Man Dir, Rights & Permissions: Antonio de Souza-Pinto; *Editorial, Publicity:* Mascarenhas Barreto; *Sales:* José Manuel Lopes Filipe
Associate Company: Editores Associados Lda
Branch Off: Rua de Ceuta 80, Oporto
Subjects: General and Science Fiction, Politics, History, Biography, Philosophy, Scientific Research
Founded: 1944

Livraria **Lopes Da Silva**-Editora de M Moreira Soares Rocha Lda, Rua Chã 101-103, 4000 Oporto Tel: 21678/26017
Man Dir: Mário Moreira Soares Da Rocha
Subjects: Medicine, Science, Technical
1981: 142 titles *Founded:* 1870

Livraria **Luso-Espanhola** Lda, Rua Nova do Almada 86-90, 1294 Lisbon codex Tel: 324917/367667 Cable Add: Livraluso
Man Dir: Inocencio Casimiro Araujo
Branch Off: Livraria-Médica do Porto, Rua do Carmo 14, Oporto; Livraria Luso-Espahola, Rua da Sofia 121-1°, Coimbra
Subjects: Medicine, Technical, Textbooks, Economics
Bookshops: Livraria Luso-Espanhola e Brasileira Lda, Ave 13 Maio 23-4°, Rio de Janeiro, Brazil; Livraria Cientifico Médico do Porto, Rua do Carmo 14, Oporto
Founded: 1941

Editora **McGraw-Hill** do Portugal Ltda*, Rua Rosa Damasceno 11 A-B, 1900 Lisbon Tel: 577322 Telex: 14724 Mghill P
General Manager: Milton Assumpção
Parent Company: McGraw-Hill International Book Co, 1221 Ave of the Americas, New York, NY 10020, USA
Associate Company: McGraw-Hill Book Co (UK) Ltd (qv for other associate companies)

Fernando **Machado** e Co Ltd, Rua das Carmelitas 15, 4000 Oporto Tel: 25718
Man Dir: Manuel Correia Vieira
Branch Off: Rua dos Clérigos 23, 4000 Oporto
Bookshop: Livraria Fernando Machado (at above address)
Founded: 1922

Livraria Tavares **Martins***, Rua dos Clérigos 14, Oporto Tel: 23459
Man Dir: Américo Tavares Martins
Subjects: Drama, Poetry, Biography, History, Art, Philosophy, Religion, Juveniles
Founded: 1934

Meribérica — Editorial e Comercialização de Direitos Lda, Ave Alvares Cabral 84-1° Dto, 1296 Lisbon codex Tel: 688912/3/4
Man Dirs: Adriano Eliseu, Telmo Protásio; *Editorial:* Adriano Eliseu; *Production:* Branca Protásio
Subjects: Children's Books
Book Club: Clube Walt Disney

Editorial **Minerva**, Rua Luz Soriano 31-33, 1200 Lisbon Tel: 322535
Dir: Artur Augusto Campos
Subjects: General Fiction, Juveniles, Paperbacks, Reference
Founded: 1927

Moraes Editores SARL, Rua do Século 34-2°, 1200 Lisbon Tel: 325391/327717
Chairman: Dr Arlindo Carvalho; *Literary Dir:* Ivonne Cunha Rêgo; *Commercial Manager:* Marques Rosa
Subjects: General Fiction, Portuguese Literature, Politics, Sociology, Pedagogy, Human Sciences, Psychology, Law
Bookshop: Livraria Moraes, Largo do Picadeiro 11, 1200 Lisbon
Founded: 1955

Livraria Editora **Pax** Lda*, Rua do Souto 73-77, 4700 Braga Tel: 22604 Cable Add: Pax
Man Dir and other offices: José Moreira
Subjects: Fiction, Belles Lettres, Poetry, History, Ethnography, Travel, Spiritual Life, Theatre, Education

Parceria A M **Pereira** Lda*, Rua Augusta 44-54, Lisbon 2 Tel: 361730/361710 Cable Add: Parcepereira
Subjects: General Fiction, Belles Lettres, Biography, History, How-to, Juveniles, Social Science, Technical, Primary

Textbooks
Founded: 1848

Editorial **Perpétuo** Socorro*, Rua Dr Alves da Veiga 207, Oporto Tel: 564251
Subject: Religion, Education
Founded: 1946

Platano Editora SARL*, Ave de Berna, 31-2° Esq, Lisbon 1 Tel: 774250/779278 Telex: 13659 platan p
Editorial: Francisco Prata Ginja
Subsidiary Companies: Alicerce Editora Lda, Oporto; Paralelo Editora Lda, Lisbon
Associate Companies: Alicerce Editora SARL, Rio de Janeiro, Brazil
Subjects: Primary, Secondary and Technical School Books, Theatre, Poetry, Juveniles
Bookshop: Alicerce Editora Lda, Rua Guerra Junqueiro 456, Oporto

Editorial **Portico***, Rua Dr Julio Dantas 4, Lisbon 1

Porto Editora Lda+, Rua da Restauração 365, 4099 Porto codex Tel: 25813
Man Dirs: José A Teixeira, Vasco F Teixeira
Subsidiary Company: Livraria Arnado Lda (qv)
Associate Company: Empresa Literaria Fluminense Lda, Rua de S João Nepomuceno 8-A, Lisbon
Subjects: University, Secondary & Primary Textbooks, Educational Materials, Foreign Language Teaching and Dictionaries, Law, General Non-fiction
Bookshops: Rua da Fabrica 90, Oporto; Praça D Filipa de Lencastre 42, Oporto
Founded: 1944

Portugalia Editora Lda*, Rua Luciano Cordeiro 81-C, Lisbon 2 Tel: 535741
Man Dir: Diniz Gandon da Nazareth Fernandes
Branch Off: Rua da Condessa 74-78, Lisbon
Subjects: General Fiction, Belles Lettres, Poetry, Biography, History, Philosophy, Juveniles, Low- & High-priced Paperbacks, Psychology
Bookshop: Rua Luciano Cordeiro 81C, 1100 Lisbon
Founded: 1942

Editorial **Presença***, Rua Augusto Gil 35-A, 1000 Lisbon Tel: 766912/763060 Cable Add: Presença Lisboa
Man Dir, Editorial: Francisco Espadinha; *Sales:* Francisco Santos; *Production:* Manuel Aquino; *Publicity:* Elisabete Cardoso; *Rights & Permissions:* Carlos Grifo
Subjects: Sociology, Politics, Philosophy, History, Children's Books, Hobbies, School Textbooks
1981: 110 titles *Founded:* 1960

Edições António **Ramos**, Rua Padre Luis Aparício 9-1° F, 1100 Lisbon Tel: 577205
Man Dir, Editorial: António Ramos; *Sales:* Maria Júlia Rodrigues; *Production:* Paulo Ramos; *Publicity:* Nuno Vasco
Orders to: Diglivro, Rua das Chagas 2, 1200 Lisbon
Subjects: General Fiction and Non-fiction
Founded: 1977

Realizações Artis Lda, Rua das Taipas 12, r/c Esq, 1200 Lisbon Tel: 363796
Man Dirs: Rogério de Freitas, Leão Penedo
Subjects: Belles Lettres, Poetry, Biography, Music, Art
Founded: 1950

A **Regra** do Jogo, Rua Luz Soriano 19-S/L Esq, 1200 Lisbon Tel: 360113/373294
Man Dir, Rights & Permissions: José Leal de Loureiro; *Literary Dir:* Fernando Pereira Marques
Subjects: Fiction, Poetry, Music, History,

PORTUGAL

Juveniles, Anthropology, Philosophy, Economy
1982: 124 titles *Founded:* 1974

M Moreira Soares **Rocha** Lda, see Livraria Lopes Da Silva

Edições **Salesianas***, Rua Dr Alves da Veiga 128, Oporto Tel: 565750
Man Dir: João António Machado; *Editorial, Sales, Production, Publicity:* Elías de Jesus
Branch Off: Rua Saraiva de Carvalho 275, Lisbon
Subjects: Biography, Religion, Juveniles, Paperbacks, Psychology, Technical, Educational Materials
Bookshops: Livraria Salesiana, Largo Luis de Camões 6-9, Evora; Livraria Salesiana, Rua Sanaiva de Carvalho 275, Lisbon
Founded: 1947

Empresa de Publicidade **Seara** Nova SARL*, R Bernardo Lima 42-r/c, 1199 Lisbon codex Tel: 530869/571302
Man Dir, Editorial, Sales: Dr Ulpiano Nascimento; *Production, Publicity, Rights & Permissions:* Costa Marques
Subjects: Fiction, Sociology, Politics, Economics, History, Pedagogics, Juveniles, Belles Lettres
Bookshop: Livraria Seara Nova, R Conde Redondo 38-A, 1100 Lisbon
Founded: 1921

A M **Teixeira** e Cia (Filhos) Lda (Livraria Classica Editora)*, Praça dos Restauradores 17, 1298 Lisbon codex Tel: 321229/321391/321286 Cable Add: Classica
Editorial, Rights & Permissions: Antonio B Teixeira; *Production, Publicity:* Jose F Teixeira
Subjects: General Fiction, Belles Lettres, Poetry, History, Reference, Religion, Juveniles, General and Social Science, Psychology, University and Primary Textbooks, Agriculture, Philology, Electronics, Economics, Management
1981: 17 titles *Founded:* 1903

João Romano **Torres** & Cia Lda*, Livraria Romano Torres, Largo de Sao Mamede 3-A, 1200 Lisbon Tel: 601244
Man Dir: Amelia Lucas Torres Farinha; *Editorial, Publicity, Rights & Permissions:* Francisco de Noronha e Andrade; *Sales, Production:* Osorio Marques Martins
Subjects: Historical Works, World Classics, Romantic Fiction, Juvenile Adventure Stories
Founded: 1885

União Gráfica Sarl*, Rua de Santa Marta 48, Lisbon 2 Tel: 44191/46174 Cable Add: Novidades
Dir: Carlos M Castelo Gonçalves
Subjects: General Fiction, Belles Lettres, Poetry, Biography, History, Philosophy, Religion, Juveniles, Low- & High-priced Paperbacks, Psychology, Social Science
Founded: 1923

Editorial **Verbo** Sarl, Rua Carlos Testa 1, Lisbon Tel: 562131 Cable Add: Verbo
Man Dir: Fernando Guedes; *Sales Dirs:* David Duarte, Novais de Paula
Subjects: Encyclopaedias, History, Juveniles, General Science, Educational Materials
1981: 179 titles *1982:* 91 titles *Founded:* 1959
Miscellaneous: Door-to-door sales by EDC-Empresa de Divulgaçao Cultural SARL, Ar Duque de Avila 193, Lisbon; direct mail sales by Verbo Postal

Livraria **Verdade e Vida** Editora*, Cava da Tria, Fatima Tel: 97417
Subjects: Biography, History, Philosophy, Religion, Juveniles, Fiction, Education
Bookshop: At above address
Founded: 1945

Literary Agents

A E I International*, Rua Conde Moser, Lote 1, 4° Dto, Monte Estoril, 2765 Estoril Tel: 2684400 Telex: 15494 Sertex P att AEI Portugal
Firm is also a Publisher

Ilidio da Fonseca Matos, Rua de S Bernardo 68-3, 1200 Lisbon Tel: 669780 Cable Add: Ilphoto
Man Dir: Ilidio Matos

Book Clubs

Círculo de Leitores, Rua Eng Paulo de Barros 22, 1599 Lisbon codex Tel: 709215/709221/709224 Telex: 18343 cilecl p
Man Dir: Manfred Grebe; *Editorial Dir:* Manuel Dias de Carvalho
Subjects: Fiction, Biography, Juvenile, Encyclopaedias, Scientific, Historical, General Non-fiction, Special Editions
Owned by: Verlagsgruppe Bertelsmann GmbH, Federal Republic of Germany (qv)
Founded: 1971

Clube **Walt Disney**, Ave Alvares Cabral 84-1° Dto, 1296 Lisbon codex
Owned by: Meribérica-Editorial e Comercializaçao de Direitos Lda (qv)

Major Booksellers

Livraria **Bertrand***, Rua Garrett 73-75, Apdo 2078, Lisbon 2
Manager: Antero Braga

Biblarte Lda*, Rua de Sao Pedro de Alcantara 71, 1200 Lisbon
Manager: Ernesto Martins

Livraria **Buchholz***, Rua Duque de Palmela 4, 1296 Lisbon codex Tel: 547358
Manager: K Braun

C D L (Central Distribuidora Livreira) SARL*, Ave Santos Dumont 57-2°, 1000 Lisbon Tel: 731752, 769744, 779825
Dir: Mario Lino
Company has 17 other bookshops, 5 in Lisbon and 12 in other cities

Livraria **Castro e Silva***, Rua da Rosa 29-31, 1200 Lisbon Tel: 367380

Livraria **Sá da Costa***, Rua Garrett 100-102, 1294 Lisbon codex
Manager: Manuel F da Costa

D I G Ldá (Distribuidora de Informação Geral), Rua Vitor Cordon 45 (Páteo Bragança, porta B), 1200 Lisbon

Expresso SARL*, Apdo 21, Buraca/Damaia, Lisbon

Livraria **Nunes***, Rua de S Domingos de Benfica 5-A, Lisbon 4

Livraria **Portugal**, Dias e Andrade Lda*, Apdo 2681, Rua do Carmo 70-74, 1200 Lisbon codex

Regimprensa SARL*, Ave D José I, lote 12, Reboleira (Amadora), Lisbon

Editorial o **Século***, Rua do Século 73, Lisbon 2

Livraria **Sousa e Almeida***, Rua da Fabrica 42, Oporto

Major Libraries

Biblioteca da **Academia** das Ciências de Lisboa*, Rua da Academia das Ciências 19, Lisbon 2
Library of the Academy of Sciences

Biblioteca da **Ajuda**, Palacio da Ajuda, 1300 Lisbon Tel: 638592

Arquivo Nacional da Torre do Tombo, Palácio de S Bento, 1200 Lisbon Tel: 664415/667680
National Archives of Torre do Tombo
Dir: José Pereira da Costa

Biblioteca **Municipal** Central*, Palácio Galveias, Largo do Campo Pequeno, Lisbon

Biblioteca **Nacional***, Rua Ocidental do Campo Grande 83, 1751 Lisbon codex Tel: 767786/7/8

Biblioteca **Popular** de Lisboa, Rua Ivens 35 and Rua de Academia das Ciências 19, Lisbon
Librarian: Joaquim Daniel Ferreira das Neves

Biblioteca **Pública** de Braga*, Universidade do Minho, Praça do Municipio, 4700 Braga Tel: 27021/3
Librarian: Henrique Barreto Nunes

Biblioteca **Pública** de Ponta Delgada*, The Azores

Biblioteca **Pública** e Arquivo Distrital de Évora*, Largo do Conde de Vila Flor, Évora Tel: 22369
Public Library and District Archives
Librarian: António Leandro Alves

Biblioteca **Pública** Municipal do Porto, Passeio S Lázaro, 4099 Porto codex Tel: 565361
Municipal Library of Oporto
Dir: M F de Brito

Centro de Documentação Científica e Técnica*, Ave Prof Gama Pinto 2, 1699 Lisbon codex Tel: 731300/731350 Telex: 18428 educa p
Centre of Scientific and Technical Information, a branch of the Instituto Nacional de Investigação Científica (National Scientific Research Institute)
Dir: Carlos Pulido

Biblioteca do **Palácio** Nacional de Mafra*, Terreiro de João V, Mafra Tel: 52398

Biblioteca Geral da **Universidade de Coimbra**, 3049 Coimbra codex Tel: 25541
Dir: Prof Dr Luís de Albuquerque
Publications include: Acta Universitatis Conimbrigensis; Boletim; Sumários das Publicações Periódicas Portuguesas; also others on a variety of subjects

Library Association

Associação Portuguesa de Bibliotecários Arquivistas e Documentalistas, Edificio da Biblioteca Nacional, Campo Grande 83, 1751 Lisbon codex Tel: 767786
Portuguese Association of Librarians, Archivists and Documentalists
President: Maria José S Moura

Library Reference Books and Journals

Book

Lista das Bibliotecas Portuguesas (List of Portuguese Libraries), Centre of Scientific Documentation, Campo dos Mártires da Pátria 130, Lisbon

Journals

Boletim de Bibliografia Portuguesa (Portuguese Bibliographical Bulletin), National Library, Rua Ocidental do Campo Grande 83, Lisbon 5

Cadernos de Biblioteconomia, Arquivística e Documentacao (Library Management, Archives and Documentation) (summaries in English), Apdo 103, Coimbra

Sumários das Publicações Periódicas Portuguesas, Biblioteca Geral da Universidade de Coimbra, 3049 Coimbra codex

Literary Associations and Societies

Instituto Português da Sociedade Científica de Goerres*, Rua Visconde de Seabra 2-3, 1700 Lisbon
Researches into the language and literature of the 16th and 17th centuries
Portuguese Institute of the Goerres Research Society
Secretary: Dr Helga Bauer
Publication: Portugiesische Forschungen (Researches in Portuguese)

Portuguese **P E N** Centre*, Centro Nacional de Cultura, Rua António Maria Cardoso 68-1°, 1200 Lisbon
Secretary: Ana Hatherly

Literary Periodicals

Coloquio-Letras (Dialogue-Literature), Empresa Nacional de Publicidade, Ave da Liberdade 266, Lisbon 2

Jornal de Letras e Artes (Journal of Letters and Arts), Rua Vitor Bastos 14A, Lisbon 1

Ocidente (The West); Portuguese review of culture, Antonio H de Azevedo Pinto and Amelia de Azevedo Pinto, Rua de S Felix 41D

Peninsula, Agencia Internacional de Livraria e Publicações Lda, R S Pedro de Alcantara, 63-1 D, Lisbon

Seara Nova (New Harvest), Empresa de Publicidade 'Seara Nova' Sarl, R Bernardo Lima, 23-1 Esq, Lisbon

Literary Prizes

Children's and Juvenile Literature Prize*
For the best book written for readers between four and sixteen. 15,000 escudos. Awarded annually. Enquiries to Portugal State Secretariat for Information and Tourism, Palacio Foz, Lisbon 2

Ricardo **Malheiros** Prize*
6,000 escudos awarded annually to an author for a work of imaginative literature.
Enquiries to Academia das Ciências, rua Academia das Ciências 19, Lisbon 2

National Award for Poetry and the Novel*
Two prizes, one for the best book of poetry and the other for the best novel or book of short stories. 50,000 escudos each. Awarded annually. Enquiries to Portugal State Secretariat for Information and Tourism, Palacio Foz, Lisbon 2

National Essay Award*
For the best essay written by a Portuguese author and printed in Portuguese. 50,000 escudos. Awarded every other year.
Enquiries to Portugal State Secretariat for Information and Tourism, Palacio Foz, Lisbon 2

Revelation Awards (Poetry and Prose)*
Four prizes, two given for the best unpublished manuscript of poetry and two for prose. 5,000 escudos. Awarded annually. Enquiries to Portugal State Secretariat for Information and Tourism, Palacio Foz, Lisbon 2

Puerto Rico

General Information

Language: Spanish and English
Religion: Roman Catholic
Population: 3.3 million
Literacy Rate (1970): 89.2%
Bank Hours: 0900-1430 Monday-Friday
Shop Hours: 0900-1730 or 1800 Monday-Saturday
Currency: US currency
Export/Import Information: No tariff on books and advertising matter. No import licences required
Copyright: UCC (see International section)

Book Trade Organization

Sociedad Puertorriqueña de Escritores*, Apdo 4962, San Juan
Puerto Rican Society of Writers
President: Ernesto Juan Fonfrías

Book Trade Reference Journal

Anuario bibliográfico puertorriqueño (Puerto Rican Annual Bibliography), Estado Libre Asociado de Puerto Rico, Dept de Instrucción Pública, Río Piedras

Publishers

Editorial **Antillana**, an imprint of Editorial Cultural (qv)

Distribuidora **Cima** Inc, now incorporated with Editorial Cordillera Inc (qv)

Editorial **Club** de la Prensa*, Apdo 4692, San Juan, PR 00903
Subjects: Fiction, Maps, Folklore

Editorial **Cordillera** Inc, Calle O'Neill 157, Hato Rey, PR 00918 Tel: 7676188/7647635
Cable Add: Cordillera
Man Dir, Editorial, Production: Héctor E Serrano; *Sales, Publicity:* Isaac Serrano
Subjects: General Literature, Social Studies, Spanish
Founded: 1962
Miscellaneous: Incorporating Distribuidora Cima Inc
ISBN Publisher's Prefix: 0-88495

Editorial **Edil** Inc, Apdo 23088, Universidad de Puerto Rico, Río Piedras, PR 00931 (Located at: Calle Julian Blanco, Esquina Ramírez Pabón, Río Piedras, PR 00925) Tel: (809) 7632958/7643740 Cable Add: Edil
Man Dir: Norberto Lugo Ramírez; *Sales Dir:* Eunice Lugo Frank; *General Manager, Publicity Dir:* Consuelo Andino
Subjects: General Literature (especially major Puerto Rican and South American authors), Social & Political Sciences, Economics, Law, Education, Life Sciences, History, Language, Poetry, Drama, Belles Lettres
Founded: 1967

Editorial Cultural, Apdo 21056, Río Piedras Station, PR 00928 Tel: 7659767
Man Dir: Francisco Vázques; *Sales Dir:* Aida Vázquez; *Publicity Dir:* F V Alamo
Imprint: Editorial Antillana
Branch Off: Editorial Antillana, Roble 51, Río Piedras, PR 00925
Subjects: Literature, Biography, History, University and Secondary Textbooks
Bookshop: Librería Cultural (qv under Major Booksellers)
1981: 43 titles *1982:* 29 titles *Founded:* 1949

Fondo Educativo Interamericano*, Apdo 29853, 65th Infantry Station, Río Piedras
Parent Company: Addison-Wesley Publishing Co Inc, Reading, Mass 01867, USA
Associate Companies: See Fondo Educativo Interamericano, Mexico

Grijalbo Puerto Rico Inc, Apdo 23025 UPR, Río Piedras 00931
President: Norberto Lugo Ramírez; *Sales, Publicity:* Reinaldo Ocasio
Parent Company: Ediciones Grijalbo SA, Spain (qv)

Instituto de Cultura Puertorriqueña, Apdo 4184, San Juan, PR 00905 Tel: 7232115/7251988/7257515 Telex: 3453096
Dir: Dra Leticia del Rosario; *Editorial Dir:* Cristobal Vega Rosario; *Sales:* Ileana Colón de Barreto
Orders to: San Francisco 305, San Juan, PR 00901
Subjects: General Literature, History, Music, Poetry, Anthropology
Bookshop: Librería del Instituto de Cultura Puertorriqueña, San Francisco 305, San Juan, PR 00901
Founded: 1955

Editorial **McGraw-Hill** Latinoamericana SA, Apdo 20712, Río Piedras, PR 00928
Regional Manager Caribbean: Anibal Torres
Parent Company: McGraw-Hill International Book Co, 1221 Ave of the Americas, New York, NY 10020, USA
Subjects: Primary, Secondary & University Textbooks, Reference, Educational Materials
Miscellaneous: Branch office of Editorial McGraw-Hill Latinoamericana SA, Panama (qv)

Editorial y Librería La **Reforma**, Calle El Roble 54, Río Piedras, PR 00925 Tel: 7651635
Man Dir: Germán Stevenson
Parent Company: Fortress Church Supply Stores
Subject: Religion
Founded: 1954

University of Puerto Rico Press (EDUPR), Apdo X, Estacion UPR, Río Piedras, PR 00931 Tel: 7630812 Sales: 7518251
Cable Add: Edupr
Dir: Félix Rodríguez-García; *Chief Editor:* Brunhilda M Rexach; *Sales:* Rafael A Vales; *Publicity:* María Teresa Flórez
Subjects: General Fiction, Belles Lettres, Poetry, History, Art, Philosophy, Reference, Low- & High-priced Paperbacks, Medicine, Psychology, Engineering, General & Social Science, University Textbooks, Educational Materials
Founded: 1932
ISBN Publisher's Prefix: 0-8477

Puerto Rico

Major Booksellers

Librería **Alma Mater** Inc, 867 Cabrera St, Santa Rita, Río Piedras, PR 00925 Tel: 7646752/7646276
Manager: Elías Cruz

Distribuidora de Libros Inc*, Calle Norte 52, Apdo 1669, Río Piedras

Librería **Escorial***, Recinto Sur 313, San Juan, PR 00901 Tel: 7250972

Librería **Hispanoamericana***, Ave Ponce de León 1013, Apdo 20830, Río Piedras, PR 00928 Tel: 7633415

Librería **Contemporanea***, Ave González 1054, Río Piedras, PR 00925

Librería **Cultural**, Roble 51, Río Piedras, PR 00925 Tel: 7659767
Manager: Francisco Vazquez
Owned by: Editorial Cultural (qv)

Librería **Cultural Puertorriqueña** Inc*, Ave Fernandez Junco 1406 — Parada 20, Apdo 8863, Santurce, PR 00910

Librería **Universitaria** de Puerto Rico*, Apdo B J Estación UPR, Río Piedras

Librería La **Tertulia***, Amalia Marin esq Ave González, Río Piedras, PR 00925 Tel: 7651148

Librería **Thekes***, Plaza las Américas, San Juan Tel: 7651539

Major Libraries

Agricultural Experiment Station Library*, Box H, Río Piedras

Archivo General de Puerto Rico, Instituto de Cultura Puertorriqueña, Apdo 4184, San Juan, PR 00905 Tel: 7220331/7222113
National Archives of Puerto Rico
Dir: Miguel Angel Nieves

Biblioteca General de Puerto Rico (General Library), Instituto de Cultura Puertorriqueña, Apdo 4184, San Juan, PR 00905 Tel: 7242680/7230052
Dir: Esther Lugo Hill

Caribbean Regional Library, University Station, Apdo 21927, San Juan, PR 00931 Tel: 7640000 ext 3319
Librarian: Carmen M Costa de Ramos
Publications: Current Caribbean Bibliography (irregular)

Inter American University of Puerto Rico Library*, San Germán

University of Puerto Rico, General Library, Mayaguez Campus, Mayaguez

University of Puerto Rico, General Library, Río Piedras Campus, Box C, UPR Station 00931 Tel: (809) 7640000/7514080
Acting Dir: Ms Noris J Vázquez
Specialist collections in all fields of knowledge; book and newspaper library on Puerto Rican subjects

University of Puerto Rico, Medical Sciences Campus Library*, Apdo 5067, San Juan, PR 00936

Library Association

Sociedad de Bibliotecarios de Puerto Rico*, Apdo 22898, Universidad de Puerto Rico, Río Piedras, PR 00931 Tel: 8324040 ext 2108/2151
Society of Librarians of Puerto Rico
President: Luisa Vigo; *Executive Secretary:* Esther Hill
Publications: Boletín, Informa (News Letter), *Cuadernos Bibliotecologicos, Cuadernos Bibliograficos*

Library Reference Journals

Boletín (Bulletin) (text in English and Spanish), Society of Librarians of Puerto Rico, Apdo 22898, Universidad de Puerto Rico, Río Piedras, PR 00931

Informa (Newsletter), Society of Librarians of Puerto Rico, Apdo 22898, Universidad de Puerto Rico, Río Piedras, PR 00931

Literary Associations and Societies

Congreso de Poesia de Puerto Rico (Puerto Rican Congress of Poetry)*, c/o Colegio de Agricultura y Artes Mecánicas, Mayaguez
President: Francisco Lluch Mora

P E N Club de Puerto Rico, Ave Ponce de Léon 900, Miramar
Secretary: Dr Ivonne Ochart

Literary Periodicals

Asomante, Asociación de Graduadas de la Universidad de Puerto Rico, Apdo 1142, San Juan, PR 00902

Atenea (text in Spanish, English, French and Italian), University of Puerto Rico at Mayaguez, College of Arts and Sciences, Mayaguez, PR 00708

Sin Nombre (Nameless), Sin Nombre Inc, 55 Cordero St, Santurce, PR 00911

Zona Carga y Descarga (Loading and Unloading Area), Apdo 3871, San Juan, PR 00903

Qatar

General Information

Language: Arabic (English used commercially)
Religion: Wahabi Muslim, officially
Population: 201,000
Bank Hours: 0730-1130 Saturday-Thursday
Shop Hours: 0730-1200, 1430-1800 Saturday-Thursday (some open few hours Friday morning)
Currency: 100 dirhams = 1 Qatar riyal
Export/Import Information: No tariff on books or advertising matter. No import licence; no obscenity permitted

Major Booksellers

Abdulla **Abdulghani** & Sons Co*, PO Box 111, Doha

Codco Est*, PO Box 1990, Doha Tel: 26573/25867

Family Bookshop, PO Box 5769, Doha Tel: 424148 Cable Add: Fambook Doha
Manager: Abdallah Ghousseini
Owned by: Family Bookshop Group Co, PO Box 1020, Limassol, Cyprus

Major Libraries

National Library*, PO Box 205, Doha Tel: 22842/321390/321391 Telex: 4743
Dir: Mohammed Hamad Al-Nassr

Réunion

General Information

Language: French
Religion: Predominantly Roman Catholic
Population: 496,000
Literacy Rate (1967): 62.9%
Bank Hours: 0800-1500
Business Hours: Generally 0800-1200, 1400-1800
Currency: 100 centimes = 1 Réunion franc
Export/Import Information: No tariff on books and advertising. Books have reduced VAT. No import licence. Nominal exchange control over certain value
Copyright: Berne, UCC (see International section)

Major Booksellers

Librairie **Daude***, 97400 St-Denis

Firmin **Pause***, 2 rue Sadi-Carnot, Le Port

Librairie Universitaire de la Réunion*, 13 ave de la Victoire Tel: 210758
Manager: Apavou

Major Libraries

Archives départementales de la Réunion*, Le Chaudron, 97490 Sainte-Clotilde Tel: 280244
Librarian: Michel Chabin

Bibliothèque centrale de Prêt, pl Joffre, 97400 St-Denis Tel: 210324
Librarian: Marie-Colette Maujean

Bibliothèque départementale, 52 rue Roland Garros, 97400 St-Denis Tel: 211396/211586
Librarian: Alain-M Vauthier

Bibliothèque municipale*, blvd Hubert-Delisle, 97410 St-Pierre Tel: 250824
Librarian: Jules Volia

Bibliothèque universitaire*, Campus universitaire du Chaudron, 97400 Sainte-Clotilde Tel: 281873
Dir: Geneviève Boulbet

Literary Association

Association des écrivains réunionnais, BP 213, 97420 Le Port Tel: 280530
President: Alain Lorraine; *Secretary:* Alain Gili

Romania

General Information

Language: Romanian. German and Hungarian in some areas
Religion: Romanian Orthodox
Population: 21.9 million
Literacy Rate (1956): 85.8%
Bank Hours: 0900-1200, 1300-1500 Monday-Friday; 0900-1200 Saturday
Shop Hours: 0900-1900 Monday-Friday; early closing Saturday
Currency: 100 bani = 1 leu
Export/Import Information: Book import and export co-ordinated by the Publishing Centre, Piata Scînteii 1, R-71350 Bucharest, 1. The commercial operations are carried out by the Foreign Trade Company ILEXIM, Str 13 Decembrie 3, PO Box 1-136/1-137, R-70116 Bucharest. Import licences required. Exchange controls: terms of payment established in the sales contract made with the Romanian enterprise
Copyright: Berne (see International section)

Book Trade Organizations

Centrala Cartii*, Str Biserica Amzei 5-7, Bucharest

Centrala Editoriala*, Piata Scînteii 1, R-79715 Bucharest Tel: 183520
The state body which co-ordinates the whole book publishing and selling activity
General Dir: Gheorghe Trandafir

Uniunea Scriitorilor din Republica Socialista România, Calea Victoriei 115, R-71102 Bucharest
Writers' Union of the Socialist Republic of Romania
President: Dumitru Radu Popescu
Publications: România Litera, Luceafarul, Viata Românească, Secolul XX, Steaua, Orizont, Vatra, Convorbiri literare, Utunk, Igaz Szó, Neue Literatur, Knijevni Jivot

Book Trade Reference Journals

Bibliografia Republicii Populare Romîne (Romanian National Bibliography), Central State Library, Str Ion Ghica 4, Bucharest

Carti Noi (New Books), Book Centre, Str Biserica Amzei 5-7, Bucharest

Romanian Books; a quarterly bulletin (text in English or French), Publishing Centre, Foreign Relations Department, Piata Scînteii 1, R-71341 Bucharest

Romanian Books in Foreign Languages, Book Centre, Str Biserica Amzei 5-7, Bucharest

Publishers

Editura **Academiei** Republicii Socialiste România, Calea Victoriei 125, Bucharest R-79717 Tel: 507680 Cable Add: Edacad
Publishing House of the Academy of the Socialist Republic of Romania
Man Dir: C Busuioceanu; *Production:* F Stoenescu
Orders to: ILEXIM, PO Box 1-136/1-137, R-70116 Bucharest
Subjects: Scientific Works, Monographs, Documents, General Science, Social Science, Mathematics, Technical, Economics, Philology, Physics, Chemistry, Biology, Medicine, Periodicals (66 in Romanian and foreign languages)
1981: 121 titles *1982:* 97 titles *Founded:* 1948

Editura **Albatros**, Piata Scînteii 1, R-71341 Bucharest Tel: 180448
Man Dir: Mircea Sântimbreanu
Subject: Juveniles
Founded: 1969

Editura **'Cartea Românesca'***, Str Nuferilor 41, R-70749 Bucharest Tel: 149352
Publishing House of 'The Romanian Book'
Dir: Marin Preda
Subject: Romanian Contemporary Literature
Founded: 1969

Editura **Ceres***, Piata Scînteii 1, R-71341 Bucharest Tel: 180174
Man Dir: Gabriel Manoliu
Subjects: Agriculture, Veterinary Medicine, Textbooks
Founded: 1953

Editure Ion **Creanga**, Piata Scînteii 1, R-71341 Bucharest Tel: 182525
Man Dir: Tiberiu Utan; *Production, Publicity:* Jenica Panaitescu
Subjects: Poetry, Biography, History, Music, Art, Belles Lettres, Literature, Fiction — all for Juvenile appeal only
1982: 130 titles *Founded:* 1969

Editura **Dacia**, Str 1 Mai 23, R-3400, Cluj-Napoca Tel: (951) 145-48 and 116-65
Dir: Alexandru Caprariu; *Production Dir:* Vasile Vancea; *Publicity, Public Relations:* Mrs Dana Prelipceanu; *Rights & Permissions:* Aurel Câmpeanu, Mrs Miess Emma
Subjects: Literature, Art, Science (in Romanian, Hungarian, German)
1981: 129 titles *Founded:* 1969

Editura **Didactica si Pedagogica**, Str Spiru Haret 12, R-70738, Sectorul 1, Bucharest Tel: 152455
Man Dir: Dr C I Floricel; *Editorial:* Pop Avram; *Sales, Publicity, Rights & Permissions:* Stelian Galos
Subjects: History, Philosophy, Juveniles, Medicine, Psychology, Engineering, General & Social Science, University, Secondary & Primary Textbooks (in various languages), Educational Materials
Founded: 1951

Editura **Eminescu***, Piata Scînteii 1, R-71341 Bucharest Tel: 177380
Man Dir: Valeriu Rîpeanu
Subjects: Romanian Classical & Contemporary Literature, Poetry, History (all in various languages)

Editura **Facla**, Str Pestalozzi 14, R-1900 Timisoara Tel: 14212/18218
Dir: Ion Marin Almajan
Subjects: Socio-Political, Poetry, Fiction, Humour, Art and Music, Literary Criticism, Medicine, Scientific; Publications in Romanian, Hungarian, German, Serbo-Croat
Founded: 1972

Editura **Junimea***, 1 rue Gh Dimitroff, R-6600 Iassy Tel: 17290
Dir: Mircea Radu Iacoban
Subjects: Original and Translated Works in Literary and Technical fields, Literary Theory and Criticism
Founded: 1969

Editura **Kriterion***, Piata Scînteii 1, R-71341 Bucharest Tel: 176010/174060
Dir: Géza Domokos
Subjects: General Fiction, Classical & Contemporary Literature, How-to, Poetry, Music, Art, General Science, Education, Translations
Founded: 1969

Litera Publishing House*, Piata Scînteii 1, R-71341, Bucharest Tel: 182471
Subject: Literature

Editura **Medicala** (Medical Publishing House)*, Str Smîrdan 5, R-70006 Bucharest Tel: 142152
Man Dir: Dr Ghoerghe Panaitescu
Subjects: Medical & Pharmaceutical Literature, Textbooks
Founded: 1954
Miscellaneous: Specialize in reviews in Romanian and foreign languages

Editura **Meridiane***, Piata Scînteii 1, R-71341 Bucharest Tel: 181087
Man Dir: George Sorin Movileanu; *Editor-in-Chief:* Modest Morariu
Subjects: Fine Arts, Folk Art, Theatre, Cinema, Architecture, Economic, Social, Political and Cultural Information on Romania
1981: 115 titles *Founded:* 1952

Editura **Militara***, Str Izvor 137, R-79735 Bucharest Tel: 310852
Subjects: Belles Lettres, Poetry, Biography, History, Medicine, Psychology, Engineering, Social Science, Military, Fiction
Bookshop: Libraria Militara (Military Bookshop), Bd Gheorghe Gheorghiu-Dej 2, N2 Sector 5, Bucharest
1981: 70 titles *Founded:* 1950

Editura **Minerva**, Piata Scînteii 1, R-71341 Bucharest Tel: 176010/176020
Manager: Aurel Martin
Subjects: Literary (especially Classical and Foreign), Bilingual Editions, Poetry, Folklore, Various Series
Founded: 1969

Editura **Muzicala***, Str Poiana Narciselor 6 sector 7, R-70732 Bucharest Tel: 164099
Man Dir: Aurel Popa
Subjects: Scores, Musicology
Founded: 1958

Editura **Politica***, Piata Scînteii 1, R-71341 Bucharest Tel: 176010/172987
Man Dir: Valter Roman
Subjects: Biography, History, Philosophy, Reference, Political & Social Science, Economics, International Relations, University Textbooks
Founded: 1954

Editura **'Scrisul Românesc'***, Str Mihai Viteazul 1, R-1100 Craiova Tel: 30253
'Romanian Writing' Publishing House
Dir: Ilarie Hinoveanu
Subjects: Social & Political Science, Literature, Technical
Founded: 1972

Editura **Sport-Turism**, Str Vasile Conta 16, R-70139 Bucharest Tel: 121480
Sports and Tourism Publishing House
Editor: Gheorghe Constantinescu
Subjects: Sports, Travel Guides
Founded: 1975

Editura **Stiintifică si Enciclopedică**, Piata Scînteii 1, R-71341 Bucharest Tel: 175168
Man Dir: Dr Mircea Mâciu; *Production Manager, Sales Dir:* Alexandru Banciu
Subjects: Encyclopaedias, Dictionaries, Reference, Physical & Social Sciences, World Literature, Romanian Language Studies, Philology, Foreign Language Reference, Biography, History, How-to, Music, Art, Philosophy, High- & Low-priced Paperbacks, Medicine, Psychology, Engineering
1982: 155 titles *Founded:* 1975 (by amalgamation of Romanian Encyclopaedic Publishing House and Scientific Publishing House)
Miscellaneous: The Foreign Encyclopaedias Office supplies any encyclopaedic materials,

information, data, statistics, maps and illustrations concerning Romania required by foreign publishing houses

Editura **Tehnica**, Piata Scînteii 1, R-71341 Bucharest Tel: 180630
Man Dir: Mihai Condruc
Subjects: Engineering, General Science, Dictionaries, Reference
1981: 158 titles *Founded:* 1950

Editura **Univers***, Piata Scînteii 1, R-71341 Bucharest Tel: 181762
Man Dir: Professor Dr Romul Munteanu; *Sales Dir:* Emil Idriceanu; *Publicity, Advertising:* N Alexe
Subjects: Translations of Fiction, Poetry, Drama, Biography, Literary Criticism, Low-priced Paperbacks
Founded: 1961

Major Booksellers

I L E X I M — Foreign Trade Co, Str 13 Decembrie 3, PO Box 1-136/1-137, R-70116 Bucharest Tel: 157672 Telex: 11226
Carries out all the commercial operations connected with book import and export

Major Libraries

Academia de Studii Economice, Biblioteca Centrala, Piata Romana 6, sector 1, R-70167 Bucharest Tel: 110610 Telex: Asero 11863

Biblioteca **Academiei Republicii Socialiste România***, Calea Victoriei 125, Bucharest Tel: 503043

Biblioteca Filialei Cluj a **Academiei Republicii Socialiste România**, Str Kogalniceanu 12-17, Cluj
The Library of the Cluj Branch of the Academy of the RSR

Archivele Statului, Bul Gheorghe, Gheorghiu-Dej 29, Bucharest
National Archives

Biblioteca Centrala de Stat a Republicii Socialiste România*, Str Ion Ghica 4, R-70018 Bucharest Tel: 161260/507063/140746
Central State Library

Biblioteca Centrala Universitara, Str Onesti 1, Sectorul 1, Bucharest 1 Tel: 132557
Deputy Dir: Dr Ion Stoica
Publications include: Bibliografia semioticii românesti, 1960-1981; Literatura româna: Ghid bibliografic; Repertoriul periodicelor din principalele biblioteci din Bucuresti

Biblioteca Centrala Universitara*, Str Clinicilor 2, R-3400 Cluj-Napoca Tel: 21092

Biblioteca Centrala Universitara 'Mihail Eminescu'*, Str Pacurari 4, Jassy Tel: 40709

Biblioteca Judeteana Mures*, Str Enescu 2, Tîrgu-Mures

Biblioteca Judeteana Timis*, Piata Libertatii 3, Timisoara

Biblioteca **Facultatii** de Medicina din Bucuresti, renamed Institutul de medicinia si farmacie (qv)

Biblioteca Institutului Politehnic 'Gheorge **Gheorghiu-Dej**' Bucuresti*, Calea Grivitei 132, Bucharest

I N I D, see Institutul National de Informare si Documentare

Institutul de medicina si farmacie Biblioteca Centrala, Blvd Dr Petru Groza 8, R-76241 Bucharest
Central Library of the Institute of Medicine and Pharmacy (formerly Biblioteca Facultatii de Medicina)
Dir: Silvica Petre

Institutul National de Informare si Documentare (INID), Str Cosmonautilor 27-29, R-70141 Bucharest 1 Tel: 134010 Telex: 11247
National Institute for Information and Documentation
Dir: Gheorghe Anghel
Publications: Reviste de sumare ale periodicelor intrate in biblioteca INID (Current Contents Reviews of Periodicals in INID Library); *Abstracts of Romanian Scientific and Technical Literature* (in English, French, Russian and Romanian); *Information and Documentation Problems* (in English and Romanian)

Biblioteca Municipala 'Mihail **Sadoveanu'***, Str Nikos Beloiannis 4, Bucharest

University Libraries, see Biblioteca

Library Association

Asociatia Bibliotecarilor din RSR*, Biblioteca Centrala de Stat, Str Ion Ghica 4, R-70018 Bucharest Tel: 503765
Librarians' Association of Romania
Executive Secretary: St Gruia
Publication: Revista Bibliotecilor (Library Review) (monthly)

Library Reference Books and Journals

Book

Ghidul Bibliotecilor din România (Guide to Libraries in Romania), Editura Enciclopedică Româna, Calea Victoriei 126, Bucharest

Journals

Buletinul de Informare în Bibliologie (Librarianship Information Bulletin), Central State Library, Str Ion Ghica 4, Bucharest

Fise Signaletice ale Articolelor din Domeniul Bibliologiei (Indicative Cards for Articles in the Field of Librarianship), Central State Library, Str Ion Ghica 4, Bucharest

Information and Documentation Problems (text in English and Romanian), National Institute for Information and Documentation, Str Cosmonautilor 27-29, Bucharest 1

Revista Bibliotecilor (Library Review), Librarians' Association of Romania, Biblioteca Centrala de Stat, Str Ion Ghica 4, R-70018 Bucharest

Revista de Referate in Bibliologie (Librarianship Abstracts Review), Central State Library, Str Ion Ghica 4, Bucharest

Revista de Titluri: Informare Documentare (Review of Titles: Information and Documentation), National Institute for Information and Documentation, Str Cosmonautilor 27-29, Bucharest 1

Literary Associations and Societies

Institutul de Istorie si Teorie Literara 'George **Calinescu***, Blvd Republicii 73, Bucharest
Dir: Professor Dr Zoe Dumitrescu-Busulenga
Publication: Revista de Istorie si Teorie Literara (quarterly)

Centrul de Lingvistica Istorie Literara si Folclor*, Aleea Mihail Sadoveanu 12, Jassy
Dir: A Teodorescu
Publication: Anuar de Linguisticasi Istorie Literară

P E N Club, Casa Scriitorilor Mihail Sadoveanu, Calea Victoriei 115, Bucharest
Vice-Presidents: Eugen Jebeleanu, Horia Lovinescu; *Secretary:* Geo Dumitrescu

Literary Periodicals

Cahiers roumains d'Etudes Littéraires (Romanian Literary Studies) (text in French and English, occasionally German, Russian, Spanish, Italian), Editura Univers, Piata Scînteii 1, R-71341 Bucharest

Convorbiri Literare (Literary Conversations), Writers' Union of the Socialist Republic of Romania (Jassy branch), Palatul Culturii, Jassy

Manuscriptum (Manuscripts), Muzeul Literaturii Romane, Central State Library, Str Ion Ghica 4, Bucharest

Orizont (Horizon), Writers' Union of the Socialist Republic of Romania (Timisoara branch), Pta Vasile Roaita 3, Timisoara

Revista de Istorie si Teorie Literara (Review of Literary History and Theory) (summaries in French and Russian), Publishing House of the Academy of the Socialist Republic of Romania, Calea Victoriei 125, R-79717 Bucharest

Romania Literara (Literary Romania), Writers' Union of the Socialist Republic of Romania, Calea Victoriei 115, R-71102 Bucharest

Romanian Review (texts in English, French, German and Russian), Foreign Languages Press, Str Ion Ghica 5, Bucharest

Secolul XX (Twentieth Century), Writers' Union of the Socialist Republic of Romania, Calea Victoriei 115, R-71102 Bucharest

Steaua (The Star), Writers' Union of the Socialist Republic of Romania, Calea Victoriei 115, R-71102 Bucharest

Viata Romineasca (Romanian Life), Writers' Union of the Socialist Republic of Romania, Calea Victoriei 115, R-71102 Bucharest

Literary Prizes

Literary Award*
For literary works reflecting humanistic and democratic ideals. Awarded annually. Enquiries to Romanian Union of Communist Youth, Bucharest

Writers' Union Prize
For an outstanding contribution to Romanian literature in poetry, prose, drama, literary criticism, history of litterature, literary reportage, literature for children and youth, translations from world literature, and for a promising new literary work by a young writer. Awarded annually. Enquiries to Writers' Union of the Socialist Republic of Romania, Calea Victoriei 115, R-71102 Bucharest
(Separate prizes are awarded by Bucharest, Cluj, Jassy, Timisoara, Craiova, Sibiu, Brasov and Tirgu-Mures Writers' Associations. Awarded annually. For further information contact the appropriate Associations of the Writers' Union of the Socialist Republic of Romania)

Rwanda

General Information

Language: Kinyarwanda (a Bantu tongue) and French
Religion: About half of population follow traditional beliefs, most of the rest are Roman Catholic, some Muslim
Population: 4.5 million
Bank Hours: 0830-1130 Monday-Friday for cash transactions; other business 1400-1700 Monday-Friday
Shop Hours: Dawn to dusk
Currency: Rwanda franc
Export/Import Information: No tariff on books and advertising, but Statistical Tax. Import licence, for statistical purposes, and Foreign Exchange Licence required. Application to National Bank, through authorized bank

Publishers

Government Printer (Imprimerie de Kabgayi)*, BP 9, Gitarama

Government Printer (Imprimerie National du Rwanda)*, BP 351, Kigali

Editions **Rwandaises***, Caritas Rwanda, BP 1078, Kigali Tel: 6503
Man Dir: Abbé Cyriaque Munyansanga;
Editorial: Albert Nambaje
Subsidiary Company: Caritas Rwanda (at above address)
Subjects: Religion, Kinyarwanda language, General, Educational, Children's Paperbacks
Bookshop: At above address

Major Booksellers

Librairie **Caritas***, BP 1078, Kigali Tel: 6503

Librairie universitaire*, BP 125, Butare Tel: 325

Somec-Rwanda*, BP 628, Kigali Tel: 5378/5497

Major Libraries

Bibliothèque de l'**Institut national** de la recherche scientifique*, BP 218, Butare

Bibliothèque du **Service** geologique du Rwanda*, Ministère des Resources Naturelles, Mines et Carrières, BP 413, Kigali Tel: 6620

Bibliothèque de l'**Université Nationale du Rwanda***, BP 54, Butare Tel: 271
Librarian: Emmanuel Serugendo

Saudi Arabia

General Information

Language: Arabic (English widely understood)
Religion: Muslim (officially)
Population: 7.9 million
Bank Hours: 0830-1200, 1700-1900 Saturday-Wednesday; 0830-1130 Thursday. During Ramadan: 0930-1400 Saturday-Thursday
Shop Hours: Vary greatly. Generally (except during Ramadan): Jedda: 0900-1330, 1630-2000. Riyadh: 0830-1200, 1630-1930. Eastern Province: 0730-1200, 1430-1700 Saturday-Thursday
Currency: 5 halala = 1 qursh; 20 qursh = 1 Saudi riyal
Export/Import Information: No tariffs on books; advertising matter subject to ad valorem duty but if total duty on one consignment is less than 50 riyals, matter can enter free. Catalogues distributed gratis, usually admitted free. All printed matter except textbooks subject to censorship. No import licences required
Copyright: No copyright conventions signed

Publishers

Al **Jazirah** Organization for Press, Printing, Publishing*, PO Box 354, Riyadh (Located at: Al-Nassiriah St, Riyadh)
Dir-Gen: Saleh Al-Ajroush; *Editor-in-Chief:* Khalid el Malek
Subject: Politics, Law
Founded: 1964

Saudi Publishing and Distributing House*, PO Box 2043, Jeddah (Located at: Al-Jauhara Bldg, Flats 7 and 12, Baghdadia) Tel: 6424043/6432821 Telex: 402687 Fonoon SJ
Man Dir: Muhammed Salahuddin; *General Manager:* Mohammed Ali Al-Wazir
Subjects: Arabic and English publications

Major Booksellers

Al-**Adab** Bookshop*, Riyadh Tel: 27865

Dabbous Stores*, King St, Jeddah

Mohamed Noor Salah **Jamjoom & Bros***, PO Box 12, Jeddah

Al-**Maktaba***, King St, Jeddah

Riyadh Modern Bookshop*, Riyadh Tel: 27993

Ali **Wahbah** Bookshop*, Riyadh Tel: 67654

Major Libraries

Educational Library*, General Directorate of Broadcasting, Press and Publications, Jeddah

Institute of Public Administration Library, PO Box 205, Riyadh Tel: 4761600 Cable Add: Ipadmin Telex: 201160 SJ
Dir (Library and Documents Centre): Mostafa M Sadhan

Islamic University Library*, Medina Munawarah

King Abdulaziz University Library, Deanship of Library Affairs, King Abdulaziz University, PO Box 3711, Jeddah Tel: 6890256 Telex: 401141 Azizuni SJ
A Central Library with 10 branches in various faculties
Dean: Dr Ibrahim S Al-Alawi
Publications: Annual Index of Ummu'l-Qura; Catalogue of MSS in the Central Library

Dar al **Kutub** al-Wataniya*, King Faisal St, Riyadh

The **Library** and Documentation Centre, see Institute of Public Administration Library

National Library*, King Faisal St, Riyadh
Publication: Bulletin

Iman M Ben **Saud** University, Deanery Libraries*, PO Box 4124, Riyadh Tel: 30771/30661

Saudi Library*, Riyadh

University Libraries*, King Saud University, PO Box 2454, Riyadh Tel: 4766258 Cable Add: University Telex: 201010 Ksu SJ
Dean: Dr A S Al-Helabi

Library Reference Journal

Bulletin, National Library, King Faisal St, Riyadh

Senegal

General Information

Language: French
Religion: About 80% Muslim, 10% Christian (mostly Roman Catholic)
Population: 5 million
Literacy Rate (1961): 5.2%
Bank Hours: Generally 0800-1115, 1430-1630 Monday-Friday
Shop Hours: Vary, and some open Sunday morning, some close Monday morning. Generally are 0800-1200, 1430-1800 Monday-Saturday
Currency: CFA franc
Export/Import Information: Member of West African Economic Community. No tariff on books except atlases. Added taxes apply to atlases. Advertising matter (more than one copy) subject to fiscal and customs duty plus added taxes. Import licences and exchange controls apply for imports from outside EEC, Franc Zone, USA and Canada
Copyright: Berne, UCC (see International section)

Book Trade Reference Journal

Bibliographie du Sénégal, Archives du Sénégal, Immeuble administratif, ave Roume, Dakar

Publishers

Africa Editions, BP 1826, Dakar Tel: 210880
Man Dir: Joel Decuper
Subjects: General Literature, Reference Works, Annuals, Telephone Directory, Periodicals
Founded: 1958

Edition **Afrique-Levant***, 50 rue de Grammont, Dakar Tel: 36372
Man Dir: Mroueh Brahum
Subjects: General, Religion, Islam
Founded: 1974

Agence de Distribution de Presse*, BP 374, Dakar Tel: 23522
Man Dir: Michel Bedoux
Subjects: General, Reference
Miscellaneous: Affiliated to Librairie Hachette, Paris

Centre Sénégalaise d'Editions et de Diffusion*, 31 rue Wagane Diouf, BP 1745, Dakar Tel: 26994
Man Dir: Jacques Coudon Jaefus
Subjects: General Fiction, Law, Medicine,

Paperbacks, Secondary Textbooks
Founded: 1974

Codesria, Fann Residence, PO Box 3304, Dakar Tel: 230211 Telex: 3339 Codes SG
Chief Executive: Abdallah S Bujra;
Editorial: Abdallah S Bujra, Thandika Mkandawire, Cadman Atta-Mills
Subject: Socio-Economic Development in Africa

Government Printer (Imprimerie du Gouvernement)*, rue Fisque, BP 1, Dakar

Les **Nouvelles Editions** Africaines*, 10 rue A Assane Ndoye, BP 260, Dakar Tel: 211381, 221580
General Manager: Mamadou Seck;
Editorial: Roger Dorsinville; *Commercial Manager:* Ojibril Faye; *Publicity:* Anna Ba; *Production:* Dominique Zidonemba; *Dir, Finance and Administration:* Abdoulaye Fall
Subsidiary Companies: Les Nouvelles Editions Africaines, Ivory Coast (qv); Les Nouvelles Editions Africaines, Togo (qv)
Subjects: General Fiction & Non-fiction, Belles Lettres, Poetry, Biography, History, Africana, Philosophy, Religion, Juveniles, Paperbacks, Psychology, General & Social Science, University & Secondary Textbooks
Book Club: Club Afrique-Loisires
Founded: 1972
ISBN Publisher's Prefix: 2-7236

Société Africaine d'Edition*, 16 bis rue de Thiong, BP 1877, Dakar Tel: 217977, 220284
Man Dir: Pierre Biarnes
Branch Off: 32 rue de l'Echiquier F-75010 Paris, France Tel: 5230233
Subjects: African Political and Economic
Founded: 1961

Société d'Edition d'Afrique Nouvelle*, 9 rue Paul Holle, BP 283, Dakar Tel: 223825
Man Dir: Athanase Ndong; *Senior Editor, Rights & Permissions:* Alexis Gnonlonfoun
Subjects: African affairs, Religion, Magazines

Editions des **Trois Fleuves***, 57 ave du Pdt Lamine Gueye, BP 123, Dakar Tel: 222077
Man Dir: Roland de Boistel, Bertrand de Boistel
Subjects: General Non-fiction, Luxury Editions
Founded: 1972

Book Club

Club **Afrique-Loisires***, 10 rue A Assane Ndoye, BP 260, Dakar
Owned by: Les Nouvelles Editions Africaines (qv)

Major Booksellers

Afrique-Levant*, 60 rue de Grammont, Dakar Tel: 36372

Agence de Distribution de Presse*, 4 rue Carnot, BP 374, Dakar Tel: 220251

Librairie afrique*, 58 ave William Ponty, BP 1240, Dakar Tel: 23618

Librairie clairafrique*, pl de l'Indépendance, BP 2005, Dakar Tel: 222169

Librairie nouvelle de l'Ouest Africain (LINOA)*, Bldg Maginot, 43 ave Maginot, BP 2039, Dakar Tel: 26450

Librairie universitaire et technique*, BP 396, Dakar Tel: 210208

Mamadou Traoré Ray Autra*, BP 2380, Dakar

Librairie du **Point d'Interrogation***, BP 437, Dakar

Librairie Editions PFD **Sankore***, 25 ave William Ponty, BP 7040, Dakar Tel: 22105

Major Libraries

L'**Alliance** française, Bibliothèque*, 10 rue Colbert, BP 1777, Dakar Tel: 20105

Archives du Sénégal, Immeuble administratif, ave Roume, Dakar Tel: 215072
National Archives of Senegal
Dir: Saliou Mbaye
Publications include: Bibliographie du Sénégal

Centre culturel français Gaston **Berger**, Bibliothèque*, BP 368, St-Louis

Centre culturel américain, Bibliothèque*, pl de l'Indépendance, BP 49, Dakar Tel: 225928/220124

Centre culturel français, Bibliothèque*, 96 rue Blanchot, BP 4003, Dakar Tel: 211821/216427

Centre culturel français Gaston Berger, see Berger

Centre de Recherches et de Documentation du Sénégal (CRDS), rue Neuville, Pointe Sud, BP 382, St-Louis Tel: 611050
Librarian: Laurent Gomis

Bibliothèque de l'**Ecole** normale supérieure*, blvd Bourguiba, BP 5036, Dakar-Fann Tel: 212242
Librarian: Ayninc Niasse

Lycée de Jeunes Filles Ameth **Fall**, Bibliothèque*, BP 1, St-Louis Tel: 71000

I D E P, see Institut africain

Institut africain de Développement Economique et de Planification (IDEP), Bibliothèque, derrière Assemblée Nationale, BP 3186, Dakar Tel: 214831 Telex: 579 Dakar

Institut fondamental d'Afrique noire, Bibliothèque*, Université de Dakar, BP 206, Dakar-Fann Tel: 34002

Université de Dakar, Bibliothèque*, BP 2006, Dakar-Fann Tel: 216981

Library Associations

A N B A D S, see Association nationale des Bibliothécaires, Archivistes et Documentalistes sénégalais

Association nationale des Bibliothécaires, Archivistes et Documentalistes sénégalais (ANBADS)*, Ecole de Bibliothécaires, Archivistes et Documentalistes de Dakar (EBAD), PO Box 3252, Dakar Tel: 230739
Executive Secretary: Makane Fall

Commission des Bibliothèques de l'ASDBAM (Association Senegalaise pour le Développement de la Documentation, des Bibliothèques, des Archives et des Musées), BP 375, Dakar Tel: 34139
Commission of the Libraries of the Senegal Association for the Development of Documentation, Libraries, Archives and Museums

Library Reference Book

Répertoire des Bibliothèques et Organismes de Documentation au Sénégal (Catalogue of the Libraries and Documentation Centres of Senegal), Ecole de Bibliothécaires, Archivistes, et Documentalistes, BP 3252, Dakar-Fann (Information on 124 libraries, archives and documentation centres throughout Senegal)

Literary Associations and Societies

Senegal **P E N** Centre, 127 ave du Président Lamine Gueye, Dakar
Secretary: Mamadou Traoré Diop

Literary Periodical

L'Afrique littéraire et artistique, Société Africaine d'Edition, BP 1877, Dakar

Seychelles

General Information

Language: English and French
Religion: Roman Catholic
Population: 62,000
Literacy Rate (1971): 57.7%
Currency: 100 cents = 1 Seychelles rupee
Export/Import Information: No tariffs on books and advertising. Books on Open General Licence

Major Booksellers

Chez Nanon*, Royal St, Victoria

Newservice Ltd*, Seychelles News Service, PO Box 131, Kingsgate House, Mahe Tel: 22309 Cable Add: Legal Seychelles Telex: 231752 Legal
Man Dir: Jemy Wadia

Sierra Leone

General Information

Language: English
Religion: Majority follow traditional beliefs; significant numbers of Muslims and Christians
Population: 3.47 million
Literacy Rate (1963): 6.7%
Bank Hours: 0800-1330 Monday-Thursday; 0800-1400 Friday
Shop Hours: 0800-1200 or 1230, 1400-1630 or 1700 Monday-Friday; 0800-1230 Saturday
Currency: 100 cents = 1 leone
Export/Import Information: No tariff on books except children's picture books and advertising matter. Open general licence. Exchange controls

Book Trade Reference Journal

Sierra Leone Publications, Sierra Leone Library Board, PO Box 326, Freetown (the national bibliography, published annually since 1962)

Publishers

Njala Educational Services Centre*, Njala University, PMB, Freetown
Subjects: General, University and School Textbooks

Sierra Leone University Press*, Fourah Bay College, PO Box 87, Freetown Tel: 27300/23494/27399 Cable Add: Fourahbay
Chairman, Honorary Editor: Professor Eldred Jones; *Honorary Secretary, Rights & Permissions:* Professor W S Marcus Jones
Subjects: General Non-fiction, History, Africana, Religion, Social Science, University Textbooks
Founded: 1968

United Christian Council Literature Bureau*, Bunumbu Press, PO Box 28, Bo Tel: 462
Man Dir: Robert Sam-Kpakra
Subjects: Books in Mende, Temne, Susu

Major Booksellers

Fourah Bay College Bookshop Ltd*, University of Sierra Leone, Freetown Tel: 27351/25307

Njala University College Bookshop, PMB, Freetown Tel: Njala exchange: ext 26, 71 Cable Add: Njalunbooks
Manager: Prof D R G Gwynne-Jones

The **Sierra Leone** Diocesan Bookshops Ltd*, PO Box 104, Freetown Tel: 22302 Cable Add: Bookshop Freetown

Major Libraries

Public **Archives** of Sierra Leone*, c/o Institute of African Studies, PO Box 87, Freetown

British Council Library, Tower Hill, PO Box 124, Freetown Tel: 22223/7 Telex: 3453 Bricon SL

Fourah Bay College Library*, University of Sierra Leone, PO Box 87, Freetown Tel: 27337
Librarian: Gladys M Jusu-Sheriff
Publications include: Annual Report: List of New Accessions to the Sierra Leone Collection; Printed Catalogue of the Sierra Leone Collection; Report on Visit to Francophone University Libraries in West Africa

International Communication Agency Library*, American Embassy, Walpole St, Freetown

Milton **Margai** Teachers' College Library, Goderich, PMB, Freetown Tel: 024305
Librarian: Mrs Abator M Thomas

Njala University College Library (University of Sierra Leone)*, Private Mail Bag, Freetown Tel: 00412
Librarian: Mrs M O Akinsulure
Publications: Library Bulletin; Annual Report; Occasional papers

Sierra Leone Library Board, PO Box 326, Freetown Tel: 23848
Chief Librarian: Mrs G E Dillsworth
Publications: Annual Report; Sierra Leone Publications (annual)

University of Sierra Leone, see Njala

Library Association

Sierra Leone Library Association*, c/o Sierra Leone Library Board, PO Box 326, Freetown Tel: 23848
Secretary: Miss F Thorpe
Publications: Sierra Leone Library Journal (biannual), *Directory of Libraries and Information Services*

Library Reference Books and Journals

Book

Directory of Libraries and Information Services, Sierra Leone Library Association, PO Box 326, Freetown

Journal

Sierra Leone Library Journal, Sierra Leone Library Association, PO Box 326, Freetown

Republic of Singapore

General Information

Language: English
Religion: All major religions, especially Confucianism, Islam, Buddhism, Taoism
Population: 2.3 million
Literacy rate (1970): 68.9%
Bank Hours: 1000-1500 Monday-Friday; 0930-1130 Saturday
Shop Hours: 0900-1800 Monday-Saturday
Currency: 100 cents = 1 Singapore dollar
Export/Import Information: No tariffs on books and advertising. Import licences; no seditious publications permitted. Nominal exchange control
Copyright: Florence (see International section)

Book Trade Organizations

National Book Development Council of Singapore, Bukit Merah Branch Library, Bukit Merah Central, Singapore 0315 Tel: 2732730
Publication: Singapore Book World

Singapore Book Publishers' Association*, PO Box 846, Colombo Court Post Office, Singapore 0617
Honorary Secretary: Charles Cher (Tel: 2521255)

Singapore Booksellers' Association*, 428-429 Katong Shopping Centre, Singapore 15 Tel: 401495
President: N T S Chopra

Standard Book Numbering Agency, National Library, Stamford Rd, Singapore 0617 Tel: 3377355 Cable Add: Natlib Singapore Telex: rs 26620
ISBN Administrator: Mrs Lee-Khoo Guan Fong

Book Trade Reference Books and Journals

Books

Books in Singapore; a survey of publishing, printing, bookselling and library activity in the Republic of Singapore, Chopmen Enterprises, 428-429 Katong Shopping Centre (4th Floor), Singapore 15

Singapore Periodicals Index; published biennially by the National Library, Stamford Rd, Singapore 0617

Journals

The Memoranda of Books Registered in the 'Catalogue of Books Printed or Published in Singapore' under the Provisions of the Printers and Publishers Act, National Library, Stamford Rd, Singapore 0617

Singapore Book World, National Book Development Council of Singapore, Bukit Merah Branch Library, Bukit Merah Central, Singapore 0315

Singapore National Bibliography (SNB), National Library, Stamford Rd, Singapore 0617

Publishers

Addison-Wesley Singapore (Pte) Ltd*, Room 456 4th Floor, Peoples Park Centre, 101 Upper Cross St, Singapore 0105 Cable Add: Adiwes Singapore Telex: rs 20904 Adwes
Manager: Benjamin Kong Tan Ho
Associate Company: Addison-Wesley Publishers Ltd, UK (qv)

Angus & Robertson (South-East Asia) Ltd*, 159 Boon Keng Rd, Block 2, Ground Floor, Singapore 12 Tel: 2582663/2582889 Cable Add: Austbook Singapore Telex: rs 24297
Man Dir, Editorial, Rights & Permissions: Richard Walsh; *Sales:* Patrick Tan; *Publicity:* Bessie Tay, Ng Kheng Chuan
Associate Company: Angus & Robertson (UK) Ltd, UK (qv)
Branch Offs: Angus & Robertson (Publishers) Pty Ltd, Philippines; PO Box 1072, MCC Makati, Metro Manila, Philippines (Miss M Mariano)
Subjects: Educational, Business Management, Academic, Library Science, General, Medical, Children's Books
Founded: 1968

Apa Productions (Pte) Ltd+, 5 Lengkong Satu, Singapore 1441 Tel: 4450751 Cable Add: Apaproduct Telex: Apasin rs 36201
Publisher, Man Dir, Rights & Permissions: Hans Hoefer; *Editorial:* John Anderson; *Sales, Publicity:* Yvan Van Outrive; *Production:* Raymond Boey
Associate Company: Apa Productions (HK) Ltd, Hopewell Centre, 50th floor, Queen's Rd East, Hong Kong
Imprints: The Insight Chronicles; Insight Guides
Subjects: Travel Guides, Culture, History, Religion, Photography
1981: 5 titles *1982:* 3 titles *Founded:* 1971
ISBN Publisher's Prefix: 9971-925

Asia Pacific Press, an imprint of Times Books International (qv)

Graham **Brash** Pte Ltd, 36-C Prinsep St, Singapore 0718 Tel: 3382497/3383705 Cable Add: Bookscout Singapore Telex: rs 23718 Feenix GB
Man Dir: K C Campbell; *Sales Dir:* E L Tear
Subjects: General, Academic, Educational (in English, Chinese, Malay)

1983: 54 titles
ISBN Publisher's Prefix: 9971-947

Chopmen Enterprises*, 428-429 Katong Shopping Centre (4th Floor), Singapore 1543 Tel: 3441495 Cable Add: Nirmalji Singapore
Man Dir: N T S Chopra
Subjects: Reference, Social & General Science, Fiction, General, Religion, Poetry, Asiatic Studies, University & Secondary Textbooks, Paperbacks, Educational Materials
Founded: 1966
Miscellaneous: Also a Literary Agency (qv)
ISBN Publisher's Prefix: 9971-68

Eastern Universities Press Sdn Bhd, PO Box 1742, Singapore 1233 (Located at: 106 Boon Keng Rd 07-05, Singapore) Tel: 2982077 Cable Add: Eastup Telex: rs 36176
Man Dir: Goh Kee Seah; *Editorial, Production, Rights & Permissions:* Goh Eck Kheng
Orders to: United Publishers Services Pte Ltd (at above address)
Subsidiary Company: Eastern Universities Press (Malaysia) Sdn Bhd (qv)
Subjects: Biography, History, English Language, Cookery, Juvenile Fiction, Economics; Primary, Secondary and University Textbooks, General
Founded: 1958
ISBN Publisher's Prefix: 9971-71

F E P International Private Ltd, 348 Jalan Boon Lay, Singapore 2261 Tel: 2650311 Cable Add: bookmark Telex: fep rs 25601
Chairman: John Isaacs; *Man Dir:* David Chew; *Executive Dir:* Cho Jock Min; *International Marketing:* John Isaacs, David Chew, Teddy Lim; *Publishing:* Dr S Ramalingam (Science and Maths), Ms Goh Bee Choo (Language and Arts); *Rights & Permissions:* Teddy Lim
Branch Offs: Australia, Egypt, Ghana, Hong Kong, India, Jamaica, Kenya, Lesotho, Malaysia, Nigeria, Pakistan, Philippines, Swaziland, Thailand, Trinidad, UK, Zimbabwe
Subjects: Textbooks, Children's, Reference, Dictionaries, Encyclopaedias (in English, Chinese, Malay, Arabic)
Founded: 1960
Miscellaneous: Firm is also a large offset printer specializing in colour work
ISBN Publisher's Prefix: 9971-1

Federal Publications (S) (Pte) Ltd+, Times Jurong, 2 Jurong Port Rd, Singapore 2261 Tel: 2658855 Cable Add: Fedpubs, Singapore Telex: rs 35846
General Manager: H H Chiam; *Marketing Manager:* L H Teo; *Assistant General Manager:* Y H Mew
Parent Company: Times Publishing Berhad, 1 New Industrial Rd, Singapore 1953
Associate Companies: Federal Publications (HK) Ltd, Hong Kong (qv); Federal Publications Sdn Bhd, Malaysia (qv); STP Distributors Sdn Bhd, Singapore; Times Books International (qv); Times Distributors Sdn Bhd, Singapore; Times Periodicals Pte Ltd, 422 Thomson Rd, Singapore 1129
Subjects: Educational, Children's
1981: 112 titles *1982:* 100 titles *Founded:* 1957
ISBN Publisher's Prefix: 9971-4

Gunung Agung (S) Pte Ltd*, Suite 3808, OCBC Centre, Chulia St, Singapore 0104 Tel: 94450/93161 Cable Add: Gasing Singapore Telex: rs 34500
Chairman, Man Dir: Mr Masagung; *Manager, Books Division:* Ali Amran
Parent Company: Gunung Agung PT, Indonesia (qv)
Subjects: Indonesia, South East Asia, Asia
Founded: 1980

Heinemann Educational Books (Asia) Ltd*, 41 Jalan Pemimpin, Singapore 2057 Tel: 2521255 Telex: rs 24299
Head Off: Heinemann Educational Books (Asia) Ltd, Hong Kong (qv)

The **Insight Chronicles**, an imprint of Apa Productions (Pte) Ltd (qv)

Insight Guides, an imprint of Apa Productions (Pte) Ltd (qv)

Institute of Southeast Asian Studies, Heng Mui Keng Terrace, Pasir Panjang, Singapore 0511 Tel: 7780955 Cable Add: ISEAS
Man Dir: Kernial S Sandhu; *Editorial, Sales, Production, Publicity, Rights & Permissions:* Triena Ong; *Librarian:* Mrs Lim Pui Huen
Subjects: Modernization in Southeast Asia, Social and Political Change
1981: 31 titles *1982:* 32 titles *Founded:* 1968
ISBN Publisher's Prefix: 9971-902

Longman Malaysia Sdn Bhd*, 25 First Lok Yang Rd, Jurong Town, Singapore 2262 Tel: 2682666 Cable Add: Freegrove Singapore Telex: Lms rs 24268
Man Dir: James B Ho
Associate Company: Longman Group Ltd, UK (qv)
Subjects: Textbooks, Medical, Science and Technology

McGraw-Hill International Book Co+, 348 Jalan Boon Lay, Jurong, Singapore 2261 Tel: 2654633/2654156 Cable Add: McGrawbook Singapore Telex: rs 36791 McGraw
Man Dir: Ben D Johnston; *Marketing Manager (Asia):* R Radhakrishnan
Parent Company: McGraw-Hill Inc, 1221 Ave of the Americas, New York, NY 10020, USA
Subject: Educational Materials
Founded: 1969

Macmillan Southeast Asia Pte Ltd*, 41 Jalan Pemimpin, Singapore 2057 Tel: 2521337 Cable Add: Publish Singapore Telex: rs 23196
Executive Dir: Loh Mun Wai
Parent Company: Macmillan Publishers Ltd, UK (qv)

Malayan Law Journal (Pte) Ltd, 3 Shenton Way 14-03, Shenton House, Singapore 0106 Tel: 2203684 Cable Add: Malool Telex: rs 28904 Mljlaw
Chairman, Chief Executive, Man Dir, Publicity: Amir Mallal; *Man Dir, Editorial, Production, Rights & Permissions:* Al-Mansor Adabi; *Sales:* Y Jamalluddin
Branch Off: 4th Floor Bangunan Ming, Jalan Bukit Nanas, Kuala Lumpur 04-01, Malaysia (Tel: (03) 221218/9)
Subjects: Law, Accountancy, Tax
Bookshops: At above main and branch office addresses
1981-82: 18 titles *Founded:* 1932
ISBN Publisher's Prefix: 9971-70

Malaysia Press Sdn Bhd*, 745-747 North Bridge Rd, Singapore 0719 Tel: 2933454
Dir: Hassan Bin Omar; *Man Dir:* Abu Talib Bin Ally; *Publicity and Advertising:* Abdullah Bin Ally
Subsidiary Company: Pustaka Melayu (at above address)
Subjects: School Textbooks, Educational Books in the Malay language
Founded: 1950

Manhattan Press (Singapore) Pte Ltd+, 597 Havelock Rd, Singapore 0316 Tel: 7337522 Cable Add: Pacolmac Telex: rs 36496 Pacman
Man Dir: Seow Kui Lim; *Dir:* Loh Peng Yim; *Assistant General Manager:* Lawrence Tan; *Publishing Manager:* Tan Kok Eng; *Production Manager:* Miss Yeo Pheck Hoon
Parent Company: Pan Pacific Book Distributors (S) Pte Ltd (qv)
Associate Companies: Eastview Productions Sdn Bhd, Malaysia (qv) Tel: (03) 762669; Manhattan Press (HK) Ltd, Arcade Shop No D, Wei Chien Court, Wyler Gardens, Tokwawan, Kowloon, Hong Kong Tel: 3630272/3; Pan Pacific Pilipinas Book Centre, 54 Dr Lazcano, Kamuning, Quezon City, Philippines Tel: 998838
Subjects: Children's, General, Reference
Bookshops: As under Pan Pacific Book Distributors (S) Pte Ltd (qv)
1982: 75 titles *Founded:* 1979

Maruzen Asia (Pte) Ltd, Pasir Panjang PO Box 67, Singapore 0513 (Located at: 51 Ayer Rajah Crescent 07-05 to 07-17, Singapore 0513) Tel: 7759844-6 Telex: Mapore rs 26521 Cable Add: Maruzen Singapore
Man Dir: Yuki Hatori; *Editorial:* Tan Chee Teik; *Marketing:* Masaru Hirase; *Sales:* David Tan
Parent Company: Maruzen Co Ltd, Japan (qv)
Associate Company: Maruzen International Co Ltd, New York, USA
Subjects: Technical, Social and Medical Sciences, Asian Studies
1981: 21 titles *1982:* 22 titles *Founded:* 1978

Medical World Book Co Pte Ltd*, Newton PO Box 96, Singapore 11
Man Dir: Andrew Lee
Associate Company: University Education Press, Singapore (qv)
Subjects: Medical, Scientific and Technical books

Pustaka Nasional Pte Ltd*, Suite 1211, Shaw Towers Beach Rd, Singapore 0718 Tel: 2941917/8 Cable Add: Hudaya Telex: rs 25521 Smcc Pn
Subjects: Malay and Arabic books
Bookshop: At above address (also Distributors)
ISBN Publisher's Prefix: 9971-77

Oxford University Press, 10 New Industrial Rd, Singapore 1953 Tel: 7470566/7470567 Cable Add: Oxonian Singapore
Representative in Singapore: Goh Teow Huat
Subjects: Educational, General, Academic
Miscellaneous: Firm is a branch of Oxford University Press, UK (qv)

P G Medical Books*, 227 Tanglin Shopping Centre, 19 Tanglin Rd, Singapore 10 Tel: 2350006
Man Dir: Chan Poh Geok; *Editorial:* A S M Lim
Parent Company: P G Lim (Pte) Ltd
Subsidiary Company: P G Books (Pte) Ltd
Subjects: Medical
Founded: 1974

Pan Pacific Book Distributors (S) Pte Ltd+, 597 Havelock Rd (Teck Huat Chambers), Singapore 0316 Tel: 7337522 Cable Add: Pacolmac Telex: rs 36496 Pacman
Man Dir: Seow Kui Lim; *Publishing Consultant:* Loh Peng Yim; *Publishing Manager:* Tan Kok Eng; *Assistant General Manager:* Lawrence Tan; *Sales Manager:* Lim Eng Wee
Subsidiary Company: Manhattan Press (Singapore) Pte Ltd (qv)
Associate Companies: Eastview Productions Sdn Bhd, Malaysia (qv); Manhattan Press (HK) Ltd, Arcade Shop No D, Wei Chien Court, Wyler Gardens, Tokwawan, Kowloon, Hong Kong Tel: 3630272/3; Pan Pacific Pilipinas Book Centre, 54 Dr Lazcano, Kamuning, Quezon City, Philippines Tel: 998838
Subjects: Secondary and Primary Textbooks, Reference, General Literature

Bookshops: Anthonian Private Ltd, Apt Blk 231, 9 Bain St, Bras Basah Complex, Singapore 0718 Tel: 3373581/3363312; Pacific Book Centre (qv under Major Booksellers for all branches)
1981: 233 titles *1982:* 318 titles *Founded:* 1971
ISBN Publisher's Prefix: 9971-63

Prentice-Hall of Southeast Asia Pte Ltd*, 4 4B Block 1, Ayer Rajah Industrial Estate, Singapore 0513 Tel: 7759085 Cable Add: Prenhall Singapore
General Manager: K C Ang
Parent Company: Prentice-Hall International Inc, Englewood Cliffs, NJ 07632, USA
Associate Companies: See Prentice-Hall, UK
Subjects: Belles Lettres, Poetry, History, How-to, Music, Art, Philosophy, Reference, Religion, Medicine, Psychology, Engineering, Computer Textbooks, General and Social Science, University Textbooks, Educational and Audio-Visual Materials

Singapore University Press Pte Ltd, National University of Singapore, Kent Ridge, Singapore 0511 Tel: 7761148/775666 ext 323 Cable Add: Singpress
Manager, Editor: Rosalind Chan
Subjects: Scholarly studies relating to all aspects of life in South-east Asia, Sociology, Law, the Arts and Sciences, Medicine, Politics, Pedagogy, Bibliographies,
Periodical *Journal of SE Asian Studies*
Founded: 1971

Southeast Asian Ministers of Education Organization (SEAMEO), Regional Language Centre (RELC), see International section (International Organizations)

Stamford College Publishers, 218 Queen St, Singapore 0718 Tel: 3373144/8 Telex: rs 25596
Man Dir, Publicity: L P Nicol; *Editorial:* L Thomas; *Sales:* J Dennis; *Production:* Mr Arangasamy
Branch Off: Stamford Executive Bookshop, Petaling Jaya, Malaysia
Subjects: Educational Books
Bookshop: 218 Queen St, Singapore 0718
1981: 10 titles *1982:* 15 titles *Founded:* 1970
ISBN Publisher's Prefix: 9971-83

Times Books International+, Times Centre, 1 New Industrial Rd, Singapore 1953 Tel: 2848844 Cable Add: Times Telex: rs 25713
Man Dir: Lyndley J Holloway; *Group General Manager* (Books Division): Koh Hock Seng; *Editorial:* Mrs Shova Loh; *Publishing Manager, Sales, Rights & Permissions:* Shirley Hew
Parent Company: Times Publishing Bhd (at above address)
Subsidiary Companies: Straits Times Press Singapore (at above address); Times Distributors Bhd, 2 Jurong Port Rd, Singapore 2261
Associate Companies: Federal Publications (S) Pte Ltd, Singapore (qv); A H & A W Reed, Australia (qv); Federal Publications, Hong Kong; Times Publishing Bhd, Japan; Far East Publications, Thailand; Marshall Cavendish Ltd, UK (see Marshall Cavendish Books Ltd); Marshall Cavendish Corporation, 575 Lexington Ave, New York, NY 10022, USA
Imprint: Asia Pacific Press
Subjects: Asian Cookery, Asian Customs and Traditions, Politics, Social Commentary, Tropical Gardening, Literature & Creative Writing
Bookshops: Times The Bookshop (qv under Major Booksellers)
1981: 33 titles *1982:* 21 titles *Founded:* 1978
ISBN Publisher's Prefix: 9971-65

Toppan Co (Singapore) Private Ltd, PO Box 22, Jurong Town Post Office, Singapore 2262 (Located at: 38 Liu Fang Rd, Jurong, Singapore 2262) Tel: 2656666/2656105 Cable Add: Toppan Singapore Telex: rs 21596
Man Dir: Chu Bong; *Project Dir:* Y Kawada
Parent Company: Toppan Co Ltd, Japan (qv)
Associate Company: Froebel-Kan Co Ltd, Japan (qv)
Subjects: Agriculture, Biochemistry, Biology, Botany, Chemistry, Civil, Electrical and Industrial Engineering, Earth Sciences, Economics, Mathematics, Mechanics, Medicine, Physiology, Physics, Statistics, Zoology

University Education Press*, Newton, PO Box 96, Singapore 11
Manager: Yeo Teo Kong
Associate Company: Medical World Book Co, Singapore (qv)
Subjects: East and South-east Asia, Humanities, Social Sciences, History of Singapore

Wadsworth International — SE Asia*, 4-B 77 Ayer Rajah Industrial Estates, Ayer Rajah Rd, Singapore 5 Cable Add: Prenhall-Singapore Telex: rs 3727-0 Phsea
Head Off: 10 Davis Drive, Belmont, California 94002, USA

Literary Agents

Chopmen Enterprises*, 428-429 Katong Shopping Centre (4th Floor), Singapore 1543
Contact: N T S Chopra
Also a Publisher (qv)

Major Booksellers

Asia Book Co*, 71B, (2nd Floor) Block 52, Chin Swee Rd, Singapore 0316 Tel: 983186/983188/983420

Chopmen Bookshop*, B-72 Katong Shopping Centre (Lower Ground Floor), Singapore 15 Tel: 401606

East and West Centre Pte Ltd*, 124 First Floor, Bt Timah Plaza, Jalan Anak Bukit, Singapore 2158

Eastern Book Service Pte Ltd, 11 Irving Place, Singapore 1336 Tel: 2801077 Cable Add: Eastbook, Singapore Telex: rs 38962
Group Man Dir: Jack Sherman; *General Manager:* Deodato Reloj
Publishers' Agents and Stockists

Educational Aids Production Co Pte Ltd*, 33 Beo Crescent, Singapore 3

Educational Book Centre Pte Ltd, 69 Stamford Rd, Singapore 0617 Tel: 3377731

Far East Book Co, now known as East and West Centre Pte Ltd (qv)

Hashim bin Haji Abdullah, 134 Arab St, Singapore 0719 Tel: 2987196

M P H Bookstores (S) Pte Ltd, 71-77 Stamford Rd, Singapore 6 Tel: 3363633

Michael's Bookshop*, 22 Orchard Rd, Singapore 9 Tel: 361327

Modern Book Store*, 34 Bras Basah Rd, Singapore 7

Pustaka Nasional Pte Ltd*, Suite 1211 (12th Floor) Shaw Towers, Beach Rd, Singapore 0718 Tel: 2937791
Booksellers and Distributors
Miscellaneous: Firm has taken over the activities of the former Pustaka Nasional of 40 Kandahar St, Singapore 7

National Book Store*, 72 Bras Basah Rd, Singapore 7 Tel: 321165

Pacific Book Centre, 597 Havelock Rd (Teck Huat Chambers), Singapore 0316 Tel: 7336411/7337522 Cable Add: Pacolmac
Also: Alexandra Branch, Apt Blk 136, 155 Alexandra Rd, Singapore 0315 Tel: 4740577; Havelock Branch, Apt Blk 22, 675 Havelock Rd, Singapore 0316 Tel: 2724326; Queenstown Branch, Apt Blk 6C, 48 Margaret Drive, Singapore 0314 Tel: 4745701
Managing Partner: Low Tai Ee
Owned by: Pan Pacific Book Distributors (S) Pte Ltd (qv)

S T P Distributors Sdn Bhd, Times Centre, 1 New Industrial Rd, Singapore 1953 Tel: 2848844 Telex: rs 28068 STP
General Manager: Thomas Heng
Owned by: Times Publishing Berhad

Shanghai Book Co Pte Ltd, 81 Victoria St, Singapore 0718 Tel: 3360144 Cable Add: Shoobook
Manager: Wang Hung Jen

Singapore Book Store*, 66 Bras Basah Rd, Singapore 7

Times The Bookshop, 176 Orchard Rd 04-08/15, Centrepoint, Singapore 0923 Tel: 7343743
Also: 304 Orchard Rd 02-105, Lucky Plaza, Singapore 0923; 1 Colombo Court 01-02/05, Singapore 0617; Robinsons Specialist Centre (Level 3), Orchard Rd, Singapore 0923; Robinsons Clifford Centre (Basement 1), Collyer Quay, Singapore 0104; C K Tang (Level 3), Orchard Rd, Singapore 0923

University Bookstore*, 13 Orchard Rd, Singapore 9 Tel: 326311

The **World** Book Co (Pte) Ltd, 08-10 Tan Boon Liat Bldg, 315 Outram Rd, Singapore 0316 Tel: 2225755 Telex: rs 36020 Wbksin
Manager: Tommy Chung

Major Libraries

American Library Resource Center, American Embassy, 30 Hill St, Singapore 0617

Nanyang University Library*, Upper Jurong Rd, Singapore 2263
Since August 1980, the Nanyang University has been merged with the former University of Singapore to form the National University of Singapore Library (see below)

National Archives and Records Centre, Archives & Oral History Department, 17-18 Lewin Terrace, Singapore 0617

National Library*, Stamford Rd, Singapore 0617 Tel: 3377355/8 Cable Add: Natlib Singapore Telex: rs 26620
Dir: Mrs Hedwig Anuar
Major Publications: Annual Report; *Books about Singapore*, English plus Chinese editions, English edition (biennial); *Checklist of Current Serials*; *Singapore National Bibliography* (quarterly, with annual supplement); *Singapore Periodicals Index* (annual); *Union Catalogue of Scientific and Technical Serials*; Masterlist of Southeast Asian Microforms

National University of Singapore Library, Kent Ridge Rd, Singapore 0511 Tel: 7756666 Telex: rs 33943 Unispo
Chief Librarian: Peggy W C Hochstadt
Publications include: *Catalogue of Singapore/Malaysia Collection and Supplements*; *Accessions List* (monthly); *Annual Report*; handbooks and guides to the various libraries of the National University of Singapore Library System

Library Association

Library Association of Singapore*, c/o National Library, Stamford Rd, Singapore 0617
Honorary Secretary: Sylvia Yap
Publications include: Catalogue Manual for Small Libraries (1980); *LAS Newsletter* (quarterly); *Singapore Libraries* (annual); *Standards for Bibliographical Compilations* (1980); *Universal Bibliografical Control in Southeast Asia: Conference Papers and Proceedings* (1976); *Who's Who in Singapore Librarianship* (1976)

Library Reference Books and Journals

Books
Singapore Libraries (annual), Library Association of Singapore, c/o National Library, Stamford Rd, Singapore 0617

Journals
Checklist of Current Serials, National Library, Stamford Rd, Singapore 0617

LAS Newsletter (quarterly), Library Association of Singapore, Stamford Rd, Singapore 0617

Singapore Periodicals Index, National Library, Stamford Rd, Singapore 0617

Literary Associations and Societies

Chinese Language and Literary Society*, Jurong Rd, Singapore 22
Publication: Hsin Sheng

Literary Periodical

Hsin Sheng (New Life), Chinese Language and Literary Society, Jurong Rd, Singapore 22

Literary Prizes

National Book Development Council of Singapore Book Awards*
For outstanding works of creative and non-creative writing by local authors in any of the four official languages (Malay, English, Chinese, and Tamil). The awards are for fiction, poetry, drama, non-fiction, and children's and young people's books. Up to fifteen prizes of 500 to 1,000 Singapore dollars. Awarded every two years. Enquiries to National Book Development Council of Singapore, c/o National Library, Stamford Rd, Singapore 0617

Somalia

General Information

Note: No replies were received to questionnaires sent to Somalia for this edition of *International Literary Market Place*. The information given in the 1983-84 edition has been repeated here but should be treated with caution.

Language: Somali is the national language; Arabic, Italian and English are official languages and widely spoken. Swahili in southern coastal towns
Religion: Muslim
Population: 3.4 million
Bank Hours: 0800-1130 Saturday-Thursday
Shop Hours: 0800-1230, 1630-1900 Saturday-Thursday
Currency: 100 cents = 1 Somali or Samli shilling
Export/Import Information: No tariff on books; advertising matter distributed gratis is not dutied, otherwise Revenue and Customs Duty charged. Also Administration and Wharfage Taxes. Exchange controls

Publishers

Government Printer*, Ministry of Information, Mogadishu

Somalia d'Oggi*, Piazzale della Garesa, PO Box 315, Mogadishu
Subjects: Law, Economics

Major Booksellers

New Africa Booksellers*, PO Box 315, Mogadishu Tel: 30087

Samater's Bookshop*, PO Box 936, Mogadishu

Major Libraries

Local Government Council Library*, Hargeisa

National Library of Higher Education and Culture*, Ministry of Higher Education and Culture, Mogadishu

Biblioteca dell' **Universita Nazionale** della Somalia*, PO Box 15, Mogadishu
Tel: 2535

Republic of South Africa

General Information

Language: English and Afrikaans
Religion: Predominantly Protestant. Politically most important is the Dutch Reformed Church (about 3 million adherents). About 1.8 million Methodists, 1.5 million Anglicans, 1.2 million Roman Catholics. Most of the black population belongs to separatist churches, combining traditional and Christian beliefs
Population: 27.7 million
Literacy Rate (1960): 57% Total (50% Bantu, 98% White, 74% Asiatic, 69% Coloured)
Bank Hours: 0900-1530 Monday-Tuesday, Thursday, Friday; 0900-1300 Wednesday; 0830-1100 Saturday
Shop Hours: Vary province to province. Often 0830-1700 Monday-Friday; 0830-1230 Saturday
Currency: 100 cents = 1 rand
Export/Import Information: No tariffs on books or advertising matter. No import licence required. No obscene literature permitted. Exchange controls being relaxed
Copyright: Berne (see International section)

Book Trade Organizations

Associated Booksellers of Southern Africa Ltd, 1 Meerendal, Nightingale Way, Pinelands 7405 Tel: (021) 533952
Secretary: P G van Rooyen

Book Trade Association of South Africa, (President's Office) PO Box 105, Parow 7500 Tel: (021) 591131

Directorate of Publications, Private Bag 9069, Cape Town 8000 Tel: 456518 Telex: 5721667
Dir: Prof Dr A Coetzee
See also Publications Appeal Board below

Overseas Publishers' Representatives Association of Southern Africa, PO Box 61342, Marshalltown 2107 Tel: (011) 215247
Secretary: P Hardingham

Publications Appeal Board, Private Bag X114, Pretoria 001 Tel: 36353 Telex: 53668
Subsidiary to the Directorate of Publications (qv)

South African Publishers' Association, 1 Meerendal, Nightingale Way, Pinelands 7405 Tel: (021) 533952
Secretary: P G van Rooyen

Standard Book Numbering Agency, State Library, PO Box 397, Pretoria 0001 Tel: (012) 218931 Telex: SA 3778
ISBN Administrator: Dr H J Aschenborn

Book Trade Reference Books and Journals

Books
Books in Print South Africa, Cedarwood Text, PO Box 51254, Randburg 2125

Catalogue of Books (English) Published in Southern Africa, Still in Print (1970), C Struik, Corner Wale and Loop Sts, PO Box 1144, Cape Town

Journals
Central News, Central News Agency Ltd, PO Box 9, Cape Town 8000 (trade organ published by CNA, the large bookselling chain with branches throughout the country)

Index to South African Periodicals, Johannesburg Public Library, Market Sq, Johannesburg 2001

South African National Bibliography (text in Afrikaans, Bantu languages and English), The State Library, Vermeulen St, PO Box 397, Pretoria (published since 1933; annual volume and quarterly cumulations; also available as a weekly card service)

Publishers

Africana Book Society (Pty) Ltd*, PO Box 1071, Johannesburg
Man Dir: L W Bolze
Parent Company: Books of Zimbabwe Publishing Co (Pvt) Ltd, Zimbabwe (qv)
Subjects: General Academic, Biography, History, Africana, Hunting, Wildlife, Illustrated & Fine Editions, Reprints
Founded: 1975
ISBN Publisher's Prefix: 0-949973

B L A C Publishing House*, PO Box 17, Athlone, Cape Town
Man Dir: James Matthews
Subjects: General Fiction, Belles Lettres, Poetry, Paperbacks
Founded: 1974

REPUBLIC OF SOUTH AFRICA

A A Balkema Publishers, PO Box 3117, Cape Town (Located at: 93 Keerom St, Cape Town) Tel: (021) 229009/431935 Cable Add: Balkema Cape Town
Man Dir: A A Balkema
Head Office: A A Balkema, Netherlands (qv)
Subjects: Anthropology, African and Oriental Studies, Palaeontology, Archaeology, Botany, Zoology, Ecology, Agriculture, Soil Engineering
1981: 15 titles *Founded:* 1930
ISBN Publisher's Prefix: 0-86961

Jonathan **Ball** Publishers (Pty) Ltd*, PO Box 87045, Houghton 2041 Telex: 42-4235 SA
Man Dir, Rights & Permissions: Jonathan Augustus Ball; *Editorial:* Alison Lowry; *Sales:* Nicholas Britt
Orders to: Hodder & Stoughton Southern Africa, PO Box 32213, Braamfontein, Johannesburg 2017
Branch Off: PO Box 94, Cape Town (Located at: The Link, Cavendish Sq, Claremont)
Subjects: South African History & Politics, African Interest, Fiction
Founded: 1977
ISBN Publisher's Prefix: 0-86850

Bible Society of South Africa, PO Box 6215, Roggebaai, 8012 Cape Town Tel: 212040 Cable Add: Testaments Cape Town Telex: 5727964
Chief Executive, General Secretary, Rights & Permissions: Rev G E van der Merwe; *Editorial Dir:* Rev P L Olivier; *Sales, Production:* Rev A Stranex; *Publicity:* N Turley
Imprints: Bible Society, Bybelgenootskap
Branch Offs: Kempton Park, Bloemfontein, Durban, Port Elizabeth, Cape Town, Kwazulu, Windhoek
Subjects: Bibles, Scriptural Selections, Bible Society historical research material, Bible translation and research aids
Bookshops: 15 Anton Anreith Arcade, Roggebaai, CT 8001; 97 Russell St, Durban 4001; Brister House, 187 Main St, Port Elizabeth 6001; 65 Maitland St, Bloemfontein 9301; Bible House, 18 Central Ave, Kempton Park 1620
1981: 45 titles *1982:* 46 titles *Founded:* 1820 (as auxiliary of British & Foreign Bible Society), 1965 as autonomous body
ISBN Publisher's Prefix: 0-7982

Black Community Programmes Ltd*, 15 Leopold St, King Williams Town
Executive Dir: B A Khoapa; *Senior Editor:* Thoko Mbajwa
Subjects: General Non-fiction, Community Development, Reference, Annuals, Paperbacks
Founded: 1972

Books of Africa (Pty) Ltd, 1004 Cape of Good Hope Savings Bank Bldg, 117 St George's St, PO Box 1516, Cape Town 8000 Tel: 227921
Man Dir, Rights & Permissions: T V Bulpin; *Sales:* M Bulpin; *Production, Publicity:* H Rennie
Subsidiary Company: T V Bulpin Publications
Subjects: Biography, History, Africana, Art
1982: 6 titles *Founded:* 1962
ISBN Publisher's Prefix: 0-949956

The **Brenthurst** Press (Pty) Ltd, PO Box 87184, Houghton 2041 Tel: (011) 6466024
Chief Executive: N J Diemont; *Editorial and other Offices:* Mrs C Kemp
Subjects: Africana (fine editions of hitherto unpublished works from the private library of H F Oppenheimer of Johannesburg)
1982: 1 title *1983:* 1 title *Founded:* 1974
ISBN Publisher's Prefix: 0-909079

T V **Bulpin** Publications, a subsidiary of Books of Africa (Pty) Ltd (qv)

Butterworth Publishers (Pty) Ltd, PO Box 792, Durban 4000 (Located at: 8 Walter Place, Waterval Park, Mayville, Durban 4091) Tel: (031) 294247 Cable Add: Butterlaw Durban
Man Dir, Rights & Permissions: A McAdam; *Editorial, Production:* K Prinsloo, H Mellett; *Sales, Publicity:* A Vosloo
Parent Company: Butterworth & Co (Publishers) Ltd, UK (qv)
Branch Off: PO Box 27711, Sunnyside 0132
Subjects: Law, Medicine, Science & Technology, University Textbooks
1981: 200 titles *1982:* 200 titles *Founded:* 1935
ISBN Publisher's Prefix: 0-409

Bybelgenootskap, an imprint of Bible Society of South Africa (qv)

C M P Reprints, an imprint of Sasavona Publishers & Booksellers (qv)

C N A, see Central News Agency Ltd

C P S A, an imprint of The Ecumenical Literature Distribution Trust (qv)

C U M Books (Pty) Ltd, see Christian Publishing Co

Calvyn-Jubileumboekefonds, PO Box 20004, Noordbrug 2522 Tel: Potchefstroom 23986 (STD code 01481)
Associate Company: Interkerklike Uitgewerstrust (qv)

Killie **Campbell** Africana Library, see University of Natal Press

Centaur Publishers (Pty) Ltd, PO Box 1144, Cape Town 8000 Tel: (021) 216740 Cable Add: Dekena Telex: 5726713
Man Dir: G Struik; *Editorial Dir:* Peter Borchents; *Sales Dir:* Nick Pryke; *Production Dir:* Peter Struik; *Publicity:* Louise Sinclair; *Rights & Permissions:* W Reinders
Parent Company: Struik Holdings (Pty) Ltd (at above address)
Associate Companies: Drommedaris Uitgewers (Pty) Ltd; RSA Book Distributors (Pty) Ltd; SA Readers Choice (Pty) Ltd; Struik (Pty) Ltd (qv)
Subject: General
1982: 8 titles *Founded:* 1981

Central News Agency Ltd+, Laub St, New Centre, PO Box 10799, Johannesburg 2000 Tel: (011) 8361711
Subjects: General, Paperbacks
Bookshops: Retail outlets throughout the country (qv under Major Booksellers)

Christian Publishing Co — CUM Books (Pty) Ltd, PO Box 38, Roodepoort 1725 (Located at: Baanbreker Avenue 2, Helderkruin, Roodepoort 1725) Tel: (011) 7642466/7642734 Cable Add: Chrispub Telex: 84667
Chairman: Timo Crous; *General Manager, Production, Publicity, Rights & Permissions:* Sas Kloppers; *Editorial:* Coen Geldenhuys, Peet van Staden
Imprint: CUM Books (Pty) Ltd
Subjects: Religion, Juveniles, Paperbacks, Educational, General
Founded: 1939

Church Publishing Trust, see Interkerklike Uitgewerstrust

College of Careers (Pty) Ltd, PO Box 2081, Cape Town 8000 (Located at: Ambassador House, Wesley St, Cape Town 8001) Tel: 452041/452051 Cable Add: Colcareers
Man Dir: Richard S Pooler; *Editorial:* Amanda Snyman
Imprints: College of Careers Study Aids; College Tutorial Press; Faircape Books
Subjects: Educational, General
1981: 24 titles *Founded:* 1946
ISBN Publisher's Prefixes: 0-7985 (Study Aids), 0-949945 (College Tutorial Press)

College Tutorial Press, an imprint of College of Careers (Pty) Ltd (qv)

Collier-Macmillan South Africa (Pty) Ltd, taken over by Macmillan South Africa Publishers (Pty) Ltd (qv)

Collins Vaal (Pty) Ltd, PO Box 61342, Marshalltown 2107 (Located at: 1 Hardy St, City & Suburban, Johannesburg 2001) Tel: (011) 215247 Telex: 89298
Man Dir: Robert W Fisher; *Sales Dir:* Paul J Hardingham; *Publicity, Rights & Permissions:* Pamela S Wood
Parent Company: William Collins Sons & Co Ltd, UK (qv)
Branch Offs: Durban, Cape Town
Subjects: Southern Africa (wildlife, reference)
1982: 2 titles *Founded:* 1982
ISBN Publisher's Prefix: 0-0620

Delta Books (Pty) Ltd, PO Box 41021, Craighall 2024 (Located at: Hyde Park Corner, Jan Smuts Ave, Hyde Park, Johannesburg 2196) Tel: 7885030 Cable Add: Reppub
Man Dir, Rights & Permissions: Adriaan Donker; *Sales, Publicity:* Karin Donker; *Editorial:* Frances Perryer
Associate Company: Ad Donker (Pty) Ltd (qv)
Subjects: Botany, Gardening, Sports, Health, How-to
1982: 12 titles *Founded:* 1980

Ad **Donker** (Pty) Ltd, PO Box 41021, Craighall 2024 (Located at: Hyde Park Corner, Jan Smuts Ave, Hyde Park, Johannesburg 2196) Tel: 7885030 Cable Add: Reppub
Man Dir, Rights & Permissions: Adriaan Donker; *Sales, Publicity:* Karin Donker; *Editorial:* Frances Perryer
Subsidiary Company: Ad Donker Ltd, UK (qv)
Associate Companies: Delta Books (Pty) Ltd (qv); International Publishers' Representatives (SA) (Pty) Ltd
Subjects: General Fiction & Non-fiction, Poetry, Africana, Academic
1981: 20 titles *1982:* 20 titles *Founded:* 1973
ISBN Publisher's Prefixes: 0-949937, 0-86852

Dutch Reformed Church Publishers*, PO Box 4539, Cape Town 8000 Tel: 215540 Cable Add: D R C Publishers Telex: 76922
Man Dir: W J van Zijl; *Editorial, Rights & Permissions:* Mrs B Smit; *Sales:* A Peens; *Production:* W Theron; *Publicity:* Mrs M Volschenk
Parent Company: N G Kerk-Uitgewers, PO Box 2309, Kemptonpark 1620
Branch Off: PO Box 2309, Kempton Park, South Africa
Subjects: Christian Literature (educational and general)
Bookshops: 28 bookshops throughout South Africa
Founded: 1818
ISBN Publisher's Prefix: 0-86991

E L D Trust, an imprint of The Ecumenical Literature Distribution Trust (qv)

The **Ecumenical Literature** Distribution Trust, PO Box 2115, Johannesburg 2000 (Located at: 38 Melle St, Braamfontein, Johannesburg 2001) Tel: 396675
General Manager: W Westenborg; *Sales:* Ms K L Coupar
Imprints: CPSA, ELD Trust, Pula Press
Subjects: Religious, Liturgical
Bookshops: ELD Bookshops at 75 de Korte

St, Braamfontein, Johannesburg 2001; 11 Grace St, Port Elizabeth 6001; 18b Rissik St, Pietersburg 0700 (all in Republic of South Africa); The Moffat Bookshop, PO Box 34, Kuruman 8460; Botswana Book Centre, The Mall, Gaborone, Botswana (qv)
Founded: 1973 (as ELD Trust; 1970 CPSA, pre-1970 SPCK)
ISBN Publisher's Prefix: 0-86881

Educum Uitgewers Beperk*, PO Box 87, King Williams Town 5600

Erudita Publications (Pty) Ltd*, PO Box 25111, Ferrairas Town 2048, Transvaal
Subjects: Reference, Directories

Faircape Books, an imprint of College of Careers (Pty) Ltd (qv)

Femina, an imprint of Juventus/Femina (qv)

Flesch Financial Publications (Pty) Ltd, 58 Burg St, PO Box 3473, Cape Town Tel: (021) 436625 Cable Add: Fairlead Telex: 5727826
Man Dir: S Flesch; *Editorial:* C G Thompson; *Sales Manager:* Derek Wood
Branch Off: SARB House, 80 Commissioner St, PO Box 3473, Johannesburg
Subjects: Reference, Finance
1981: 2 titles *1982:* 2 titles *Founded:* 1966
ISBN Publisher's Prefix: 0-949989

Folio, an imprint of Juventus/Femina (qv)

Da **Gama** Publishers (Pty) Ltd*, 304 Locarno House, Loveday St, Johannesburg 2000
Man Dir: Daphne de Freitas
Subjects: General Non-fiction, Educational, Reference, Travel Books

Government Printer*, Bosman St, Pretoria

T W **Griggs** & Co (Pty) Ltd, PO Box 466, Durban 4000 (Located at: 341 West St, Durban 4001) Tel: 328571/2 Cable Add: Adamsco
Rights & Permissions: E G Rabjohn
Parent Company: Adams & Co Ltd (qv under Major Booksellers)
Subjects: Africana

H & R Academica (Pty) Ltd, PO Box 557, Pretoria 0001 (Located at: 607 Southern Life Bldg, 239 Pretorius St, Pretoria) Tel: (012) 218465 Cable Add: Hurou Pretoria
General Manager: J J Human; *Manager:* N Smith
Parent Company: Human & Rousseau Publishers (Pty) Ltd (qv)
Subjects: Secondary and University Textbooks
1981: 15 titles *1982:* 29 titles *Founded:* 1964
ISBN Publisher's Prefix: 0-86874

H A U M Academic Publishers, PO Box 460, Pretoria 0001
Associate Company: HAUM (Hollandsch Afrikaansche Uitgevers Maatschappij) (qv)
Subject: Tertiary Textbooks

H A U M (Hollandsch Afrikaansche Uitgevers Maatschappij), PO Box 1371, Cape Town 8000 (Located at: Monarch House, 58 Long St, Cape Town) Tel: (021) 435008 Cable Add: Haum Telex: 5721047 SA
Manager, Publisher: C J Hage
Associate Companies: HAUM Academic Publishers (qv); De Jager-HAUM (qv); Juventus/Femina Publishers (qv)
Subjects: General Fiction & Non-fiction, Belles Lettres, Poetry, Biography, History, Juveniles, Books in Afrikaans, Science and Technology, General Science, University Textbooks
Bookshops: HAUM Academic Bookshop; HAUM Booksellers (qqv under Major Booksellers)
1981: 31 titles *Founded:* 1894
ISBN Publisher's Prefix: 0-7986

Human & Rousseau Publishers (Pty) Ltd+, PO Box 5050, Cape Town 8000 (Located at: State House, 3-9 Rose St, Cape Town) Tel: (021) 251280 Cable Add: Persdiens Telex: 5720294
General Manager: J J Human; *Editor-in-Chief:* H D Büttner; *Publicity:* E Wolfaard
Parent Company: Nasionale Boekhandel Ltd (qv)
Subsidiary Company: H & R Academica (qv)
Branch Offs: Kelhof Building, 112 Pritchard St, Johannesburg Tel: (011) 237288; 607 Southern Life Building, 239 Pretorius St, Pretoria Tel: (012) 218465 Cable Add: Hurou Pretoria
Subjects: General Fiction & Non-fiction, Belles Lettres, Poetry, Biography, History, Africana, Philosophy, Reference, Religion, Juveniles, Books in Afrikaans, General Science, University and Secondary Textbooks
1981: 141 titles *1982:* 226 titles *Founded:* 1959
ISBN Publisher's Prefix: 0-7981

Hutchinson Group (SA) (Pty) Ltd, PO Box 337, Bergvlei 2012 Tel: (786) 2983 Cable Add: Hutchbooks Telex: 423981
Man Dir: E F Mason
Parent Company: Hutchinson Publishing Group Ltd, UK (qv for Associate Companies)
Subjects: General Fiction & Non-fiction, Belles Lettres, Poetry, University & Secondary Textbooks, Paperbacks, Juvenile
Founded: 1966

Institute for Reformational Studies, c/o Potchefstroom University for Christian Higher Education, Potchefstroom 2520 Tel: (01481) 23484 Cable Add: PUK Telex: 421363
Dir: Prof B J Van der Walt; *Editorial:* G L Kruger; *Sales:* Mrs G C Loots; *Publicity:* Mrs M C Swanepoel; *Rights & Permissions:* Mrs R E van Biljon
Parent Company: International Clearing House for Christian Higher Education
Subjects: Christianity, Christian Higher Education, Calvinism, The Reformation
1981-82: 36 titles *Founded:* 1966
ISBN Publisher's Prefix: 0-86990

Interkerklike Uitgewerstrust*, PO Box 2744, Pretoria 0001 Tel: (012) 215132 Inter-Church Publishing Trust
Chief Executive: B R Buys
Associate Companies: Calvyn-Jubileumboekefonds (qv); N G Kerkboekhandel Transvaal (qv); N G Kerk-Uitgewers
Subjects: Religious handbooks for Schools, Universities, Colleges and Churches; also Visual Aids
ISBN Publisher's Prefix: 0-620

De **Jager** — HAUM, PO Box 629, Pretoria 0001 (Located at: Forum Bldg, Bosman St, Pretoria) Tel: (012) 34092 Telex: 30435 RSA
Promotion: Vanessa du Plessis
Associate Company: HAUM (Hollandsch Afrikaansche Uitgevers Maatschappij) (qv)
Subject: School Textbooks

Juta & Co Ltd, PO Box 123, Kenwyn 7790 (Located at: Mercury Cres, Hillstar Industrial Township, Wetton, Cape Town) Tel: (021) 711181 Cable Add: Juta
Man Dir: J D Duncan; *Sales Manager:* L Massella; *Senior Editor, Rights & Permissions:* J Potgieter, J D Duncan
Branch Offs: Suite 5B Mangrove Beach Centre, Somtseu Rd, Durban 4001; PO Box 1010, Johannesburg 2000; PO Box 403, Umtata, Transkei
Subjects: Reference, Law, Medicine, Science and Technology; General School, University & Educational Textbooks
Bookshops: Church St, PO Box 30, Cape Town 8001; Cnr Pritchard & Loveday Sts, PO Box 1010, Johannesburg 2000; PO Box 123, Kenwyn 7790 (qqv under Major Booksellers)
1981: 119 titles *Founded:* 1853
ISBN Publisher's Prefix: 0-7021

Juventus/Femina Publishers, PO Box 1151, Pretoria 0001
Man Dir: Piet Scholtz; *Editorial:* Gert Basson; *Sales:* Gert Basson, Johan Steerkamp; *Production:* Marus Oberholtzer; *Publicity:* Vanessa du Plessis; *Rights & Permissions:* Hettie Scholtz
Associate Company: HAUM (Hollandsch Afrikaansche Uitgevers Maatschappij) (qv)
Imprints: Femina, Folio
Subjects: General, Juveniles, Family
Founded: 1980

Die **Kinderpers** Van SA*, PO Box 2652, Cape Town 8000
Subject: Children's Books

Longman Penguin Southern Africa (Pty) Ltd, now a subsidiary of Maskew Miller Longman (Pty) Ltd (qv)

Lovedale Press, Private Bag X1346, Alice Ciskei 5700, Cape Province Tel: Alice 167/278
Man Dir: R B Raven
Subjects: General Fiction and Non-fiction, Belles Lettres, Poetry, Biography, History, Africana, Books in various Southern African languages, Educational Books
Bookshops: 26 Fuller St, Butterworth, Transkei; Alice Bookshop, Main St, Alice Ciskei
Founded: 1841

Lux Verbi (Pty) Ltd, Posbus 1822, Cape Town 8000 (Located at: 33 Waterkant St, Cape Town) Tel: (021) 215540 Telex: 5726922
Executive Chairman: W J van Zijl
Subject: Christian Literature
Founded: 1956
ISBN Publisher's Prefix: 0-86997

M S A, an imprint of Macdonald Purnell (Pty) Ltd (qv)

Macdonald Purnell (Pty) Ltd, PO Box 51401, Randburg 2125 (Located at: 10 Burke St, Randburg) Tel: (011) 7875830/1 Cable Add: Purprint Johannesburg Telex: 4-24985 SA
Man Dir: J St Clair Whittall; *Sales Manager:* P B Will
Parent Company: BPCC PLC, UK (qv)
Associate Companies: Macdonald & Co (Publishers) Ltd, Purnell Books, both UK (qqv)
Imprint: MSA
Subjects: Educational, Co-editions, General
Founded: 1948
ISBN Publisher's Prefix: 0-86843

McGraw-Hill Book Co (South Africa) (Pty) Ltd, Hulley Rd, PO Box 371, Isando 1600 Tel: (011) 361181 Cable Add: McGraw-Hill Isando Telex: 89272
Man Dir, Editorial, Rights & Permissions: Alan Bricker; *Sales:* Owen Burgess; *Publicity:* Coral du Plessis
Parent Company: McGraw-Hill International Book Co, New York
Subjects: General Non-fiction, Medicine, Science and Technology, General Science, School and University Textbooks
1981: 29 titles *1982:* 50 titles *Founded:* 1966
ISBN Publisher's Prefix: 0-007

REPUBLIC OF SOUTH AFRICA 331

Macmillan South Africa Publishers (Pty) Ltd, Braamfontein Centre, PO Box 31487, Braamfontein 2017 Tel: 394841 Cable Add: Macbooks Telex: 425436 SA
Man Dir: David Mitchell
Parent Company: Macmillan Publishers Ltd, UK (qv)
Subjects: General Non-fiction, Biography, History, Africana, Reference, Social Science; University, Secondary and Primary Textbooks; Paperbacks
Founded: 1966
ISBN Publisher's Prefix: 0-86954

John **Malherbe** (Pty) Ltd*, Sanso Centre, 8 Adderley St, PO Box 1207, Cape Town 8001 Tel: (021) 431485 Telex: 570261
Man Dirs: John Malherbe, A Ashworth (Brit)
Subjects: General Fiction & Non-fiction, Belles Lettres, Poetry, Biography, History, Africana, Philosophy, Juveniles, Paperbacks
Book Club: Pluim Book Club
Founded: 1963
ISBN Publisher's Prefix: 0-86966

Maskew **Miller** Longman (Pty) Ltd+, PO Box 396, Cape Town 8000 (Located at: 81 Church St, Cape Town 8001) Tel: (021) 236300 Cable Add: Maskewmiller Capetown Telex: 576053
Man Dir: M A Peacock; *Publishing Manager, Rights & Permissions:* P Snyman; *Publishers:* N D van der Horst, I R Scott; *Sales:* G Visser; *Production:* A Visser; *Publicity:* M Markstein
Subsidiary Companies: Willem Gouws (Pty) Ltd; Longman Penguin Southern Africa (Pty) Ltd; Maskew Miller (Pty) Ltd; Maskew Miller (SWA) (Pty) Ltd, PO Box 9251, Eros, Namibia
Associate Company: Longman Group Ltd, UK (qv)
Branch Offs: Trust Bank Centre, George St, Kimberley; 17 Grace St, Port Elizabeth; Milpark Galleries, Auckland Park, Johannesburg; Morningside Centre, 197 Goble Rd, Morningside, Durban
Subjects: Juveniles, Books in Afrikaans, English and African languages, Paperbacks, Primary and Secondary Textbooks, Educational
Bookshops: At above main and branch offices addresses
ISBN Publisher's Prefix: 0-636

The **Methodist** Publishing House and Book Depot, 52 Burg St, PO Box 708, Cape Town 8000 Tel: (021) 220527 Cable Add: Methodist
Book Steward: M Fearns
Subjects: Religion, Books in Xhosa and Zulu
Bookshops: PO Box 1452, Benoni 1500; PO Box 708, Cape Town 8000; PO Box 108, Durban 4000; PO Box 8508, Johannesburg 2000; PO Box 1042, Kimberley 8300; PO Box 1233, Pietermaritzburg 3200; PO Box 666, Pinetown 3600
1981: 9 titles *Founded:* 1894
ISBN Publisher's Prefix: 0-949942

N G Kerk Jeugboekhandel, PO Box 396, Bloemfontein 9300
Formerly Sondagskool Boekhandel
Bookshop: At above address

N G Kerkboekhandel Transvaal (DRC Publishers), Schoemanstr 260, PO Box 245, Pretoria 0001 Tel: 218401
General Manager: J Olivier; *Editorial:* Miss M E S van den Berg
Associate Company: Interkerklike Uitgewerstrust (qv)
Branch Offs: 15 branches in Transvaal and Natal
Subjects: Religion, Theology
Bookshop: N G Kerkboekhandel Transvaal (qv under Major Booksellers)
1982: 38 titles *1983:* 54 titles

Nasionale Boekhandel Ltd, PO Box 122, Parow 7500 (Located at: 386 Voortrekker Rd, Parow) Tel: 591131 Cable Add: Nasboek
Group Man Dir: H G Jaekel
Subsidiary and Associate Companies: Cape Booksellers Ltd; Drakensberg Boekhandel; Human & Rousseau Publishers (Pty) Ltd (qv); Nasionale Boekwinkels Bpk (qv under Major Booksellers); Nasou Ltd (qv); Natal Booksellers Ltd, Durban; Oudiovista Productions (Pty) Ltd (qv); Tafelberg Publishers Ltd (qv); Via Afrika Ltd (qv); Via Afrika (Bophuthatswana) Ltd, Mafikeng; Via Afrika (Ciskei) Ltd, King Williamstown; Via Afrika (QwaQwa) Ltd, Phuthaditjhaba; Via Afrika (Transkei) Ltd, Umtata; Via Afrika (Lebowa) Ltd, Pietersburg; Rygill's Educational Suppliers, Pinetown; Heer Printers (Pty) Ltd, Pretoria (all in Republic of South Africa); Via Africa Botswana Ltd, Botswana (qv); Nasionale Boekhandel (SWA) (Pty) Ltd, Namibia (qv)
Subjects: General, Educational, Academic, Medicine
Founded: 1950

Nasou Ltd, 386 Voortrekker Rd, PO Box 105, Goodwood, Parow 7500 Tel: (021) 591131 Cable Add: Nasou Cape Town Telex: 5727751/5721125
Man Dir: H G Jaekel; *General Manager, Rights & Permissions:* W R van der Vyver; *Publicity & Advertising:* F D Maree
Parent Company: Nasionale Boekhandel Ltd (qv for Associate Companies)
Branch Offs: PO Box 361, Pietermaritzburg 3200; PO Box 9898, Johannesburg 2000; PO Box 1058, Bloemfontein 9300
Subjects: Reference, University, Secondary & Primary Textbooks
Founded: 1963
ISBN Publisher's Prefix: 0-625

Rebecca **Ostrowiak** School of Reading*, PO Box 4106, Germiston South 1411 Tel: 514262
Principals: Rebecca Ostrowiak, Edna Freinkel
Subjects: Remedial reading teaching for children and adults (Series *Teach Any Child to Read*)
Founded: 1965

Oudiovista Productions (Pty) Ltd, PO Box 122, Parow 7500 Tel: 591131 Cable Add: Oudiovista
Man Dir: H G Jaekel; *Manager:* G J Bezuidenhout
Parent Company: Nasionale Boekhandel Ltd (qv)
Subjects: Educational, Audio-Visual Aids
Founded: 1969

Oxford University Press Southern Africa, PO Box 1141, Cape Town 8000 (Located at: Top Floor, Harrington House, 37 Barrack St, Cape Town 8001) Tel: (021) 457266/7/8 Cable Add: Oxonian Capetown
General Manager: N C Gracie; *Editorial:* Ms G Gibson; *Sales Manager:* Peter Hyde
Parent Company: Oxford University Press, UK (qv)
Branch Offs: PO Box 41390 Craighall 2024; PO Box 37166, Overport 4067
Subjects: General Fiction and Non-fiction, Belles Lettres, Poetry, Biography, History, Africana, Juveniles; Books in Xhosa, Zulu, Sotho, Tswana, Shona and Afrikaans; General & Social Science, Educational, Textbooks, Music, Prayer Books; Paperbacks
1981: 16 titles *1982:* 19 titles *Founded:* 1915
ISBN Publisher's Prefix: 0-19

Perskor Books (Pty) Ltd, 28 Height St, Doornfontein, PO Box 845, Johannesburg 2000 Tel: 285460 Cable Add: Vaderland Telex: 83561, 87483/4
Man Dir: F Wessels; *Editorial, Rights & Permissions:* P V Heerden; *Sales:* S J Fourie; *Production:* A Bothma; *Publicity:* E Lotriet
Orders to: Perskor-Boekwinkel, 4 Banfield Rd, Industria North (Postal Add: PO Box, Maraisburg, 1700)
Subsidiary Company: Perskor Publishers (at above address)
Subjects: Education, Law, General
Book Clubs: Klub 707; Klub-Dagbreek; Klub Saffier
Bookshops: Perskor Bookshop; Johannesburgse Boekwinkel (qqv under Major Booksellers)
Founded: 1940
ISBN Publisher's Prefix: 0-628

David **Philip** Publisher (Pty) Ltd, PO Box 408, Claremont, Cape 7735 (Located at: 217 Werdmuller Centre, Claremont, Cape Province) Tel: Cape Town (021) 644136 Cable Add: Philipub, Cape Town Telex: 5727566 Philipub
Man Dir: David Philip; *Marketing Dir:* Murray Coombes; *Rights & Permissions Dir:* Marie Philip
Branch Off: 603 Geldenhuys, Jorissen St, Braamfontein 2001 Tel: (011) 397818
Subjects: General Fiction & Non-fiction, Belles Lettres, Poetry, Biography, History, Africana, Philosophy, Juveniles, Social Science, Politics, University Textbooks, Reference Books, Paperbacks
1981: 20 titles *1982:* 25 titles *Founded:* 1971
ISBN Publisher's Prefix: 0-908396

Pitman Publishing Co SA (Pty) Ltd, PO Box 41021, Craighall 2024 (Located at: Hyde Park Corner, Jan Smuts Ave, Hyde Park, Johannesburg 2196) Tel: 7885030 Cable Add: Reppub
Man Dir: Adriaan Donker
Associate Company: Pitman Books Ltd, UK (qv)
Subjects: Reference, Commercial and Business Studies, Secondary Textbooks, Shorthand
1981: 4 titles *1982:* 4 titles
ISBN Publisher's Prefix: 0-273

President Publishers*, PO Box 488, Krugersdorp 1740
Subjects: General Fiction, Books in Afrikaans

Pretoria Boekhandel (Pty) Ltd+, PO Box 23334, Innesdale 0031 Tel: (12) 761531
Man Dir: L S van der Walt
Subject: Children's fiction in Afrikaans
1981: 5 titles *1982:* 3 titles *Founded:* 1971
ISBN Publisher's Prefix: 0-86880

Pro Rege Press Ltd*, PO Box 343, Potchefstroom 2520
Associate Companies: N G Kerkboekhandel Transvaal (qv); Interkerklike Uitgewerstrust (qv); N G Kerk-Uitgewers
Subjects: General Fiction & Non-fiction, Religion, Secondary Textbooks
ISBN Publisher's Prefix: 0-949988

Publitoria (Pty) Ltd+, PO Box 23334, Innesdale 0031 Tel: (12) 761531
Man Dir: L S van der Walt
Subjects: Educational, Reference, School Textbooks
Founded: 1982
ISBN Publisher's Prefix: 0-86880

Pula Press, an imprint of The Ecumenical Literature Distribution Trust (qv)

Ravan Press (Pty) Ltd*, PO Box 31134, Braamfontein, Johannesburg 2017 (Located at: 23 O'Reilly Rd, Berea, Johannesburg) Tel: 6435552
Man Dir: Mike Kirkwood
Subjects: Specializes in Socio-Political

problems of Southern Africa; also General Fiction & Non-fiction, Poetry, Biography, History, Africana, Philosophy, Reference, Religion, Juveniles, Paperbacks, Periodicals
Founded: 1973
ISBN Publisher's Prefix: 0-86975

Daan **Retief** Publishers (Pty) Ltd+, PO Box 3570, Pretoria 0001 (Located at: DRU Building, 413 Hilda St, Hatfield, Pretoria) Tel: (012) 437731 Telex: 30851
Chairman: D J Retief; *Man Dir, Production:* M A C Jacklin; *Editorial, Sales, Publicity:* Eric Stander; *Rights & Permissions:* Dr H J M Retief
Parent Company: Erroll Marx Publishers (Pty) Ltd (at above address)
Imprints: D R U, E M U
Subjects: Children's, Romance, Textbooks, Educational, Popular Psychology, Spiritual
Book Clubs: Children's Book Club (Afrikaans), Young People's Book Club
1981: 110 titles *1982:* 115 titles *Founded:* 1974
ISBN Publisher's Prefix: 0-86814

S A Cultural Holdings (Pty) Ltd*, PO Box 9019, Johannesburg 2000 Tel: 219211 Telex: J83031 Cable Add: Knowingly
Man Dir: Jeffrey A Miller
Parent Company: Sage Holdings (Pty) Ltd
Subsidiary Companies: Encyclopaedia Britannica (SA) (Pty) Ltd; Ensiklopedie Afrikana (Edms) Bpk; Systems for Education (SA) (Pty) Ltd

S A Kultuurbeleggings, see S A Cultural Holdings (Pty) Ltd

Sasavona Publishers & Booksellers, Private Bag X8, Braamfontein 2017 (Located at: 9 De Beer St, Braamfontein, Johannesburg) Tel: 7255763
Manager: M A Chapatte
Parent Company: Swiss Mission in South Africa (at above address)
Imprint: CMP Reprints, Sasavona Books, Swiss Mission Publications
Subjects: Religion, Education, Literature, General
Bookshops: 9 De Beer St, Braamfontein; Masana Hospital, Bushbuckrige; Elim Hospital, North Transvaal; Shiluvane Via Letaba; and others
1981: 4 titles *1982:* 12 titles *Founded:* 1974 (1875 as Swiss Mission Publishing)
ISBN Publisher's Prefix: 0-907985

J L van **Schaik** (Pty) Ltd, Libri Bldg, Church St, PO Box 724, Pretoria Tel: (012) 212441 Cable Add: Bookschaik Pretoria Telex: 32340 SA
Man Dir: J J van Schaik
Subjects: General Fiction & Non-fiction, Belles Lettres, Poetry, Biography, History, Africana, How-to, Study Guides, Reference, Religion, Juveniles, Books in Afrikaans and Southern African languages, Psychology, General & Social Science, University & Secondary Textbooks
Bookshop: Church St, PO Box 724, Pretoria 0001 (qv under Major Booksellers)
1981: 37 titles *1982:* 54 titles *Founded:* 1914
ISBN Publisher's Prefix: 0-627

Shuter & Shooter (Pty) Ltd, 230 Church St, PO Box 109, Pietermaritzburg 3200, Natal Tel: (0331) 58151 Cable Add: Shushoo Telex: 643771 SA
Man Dir: M N Prozesky; *Editorial:* L van Heerden; *Sales:* D Ryder; *Publicity:* J A Wilken; *Production:* J Sharpe; *Rights & Permissions:* Mary Monteith
Parent Company: The Natal Witness (Pty) Ltd
Associate Company: Kwa-Zulu Booksellers (Pty) Ltd, PO Box 100, Imbali
Subsidiary Company: Shuter & Shooter (Transkei) (Pty) Ltd, PO Box 648, Umtata, Transkei
Branch Offs: 217 Werdmuller Centre, Newry St, Claremont 7700, Cape Town; E G Castle, 5th floor, Plein Centre, 100 Plein St, Johannesburg; Shop 18b, 18 Witklip St, Annadale, Pietersburg 0700
Subjects: General Non-fiction, Biography, History, Africana, Books in Zulu and Xhosa, Science and Technology, General and Social Sciences, Primary and Secondary Textbooks
Book Club: Indlouu Ubudlelwane Ngezincwadi (Zulu Book Club)
Bookshop: Church St, PO Box 109, Pietermaritzburg (qv under Major Booksellers)
1982: 170 titles *1983:* 181 titles *Founded:* 1925
ISBN Publisher's Prefix: 0-86985

Simondium Publishers (Pty) Ltd*, Old Mill Rd, PO Box 3737, Cape Town Tel: (021) 532011 Cable Add: Labels Capetown
Man Dir: W P Loubser
Subjects: General Fiction & Non-fiction

Sondagskool Boekhandel, now known as N G Kerk Jeugboekhandel (qv)

Ernest **Stanton** Publishers (Pty) Ltd*, PO Box 25803, Denver 2027, Transvaal (Located at: Keartland Press Bldg, Nicholson St, Denver 2094, Transvaal) Tel: (011) 6162100/16 Cable Add: Lithocraft Johannesburg Telex: 420048 Johannesburg
Man Dir, Editorial, Production: Ernest Stanton; *Sales, Marketing:* Richard Shurety; *Publicity, Rights & Permissions:* M V Stanton
Subsidiary Company: Professional Book Services (Pty) Ltd (at above address)
Subjects: South African interest, Biography, History, Politics, Reference, Flora and Fauna, Wild Life and Nature Conservation, Gardening, General Literature
Founded: 1964
ISBN Publisher's Prefix: 0-949997

Star Schools, 117 Everite House, 20 de Korte St, PO Box 31648, Braamfontein 2017 Tel: 396666
Man Dir: W M Smith
Subjects: Science & Maths, University & Secondary Textbooks
Founded: 1974
Miscellaneous: Affiliated with the Argus Group of Newspapers; Eastern Province Herald; SABC. Company previously known as Technitrain (Pty) Ltd

Struik (Pty) Ltd, Struik House, Oswald Pirow St, Foreshore, PO Box 1144, Cape Town 8000 Tel: (021) 216740 Cable Add: Dekena Capetown Telex: 57-26713
Man Dir, Sales, Publicity, Promotion and Advertising Manager: G Struik; *Production:* Pieter Struik
Parent Company: Struik Holdings (Pty) Ltd (at above address)
Associate Company: Centaur Publishers (Pty) Ltd (qv)
Subject: Southern Africa
Founded: 1957
ISBN Publisher's Prefix: 0-86977

Swiss Mission Publications, an imprint of Sasavona Publishers & Booksellers (qv)

Tafelberg Publishers Ltd+, 28 Wale St, PO Box 879, Cape Town 8000 Tel: (021) 410127 Cable Add: Boeknuus Cape Town Telex: 5721473 SA
Man Dir: H G Jaekel; *General Manager, Rights & Permissions:* D J van Niekerk; *Assistant General Manager, Marketing:* J Labuschagne
Parent Company: Nasionale Boekhandel Ltd (qv)
Subjects: General Fiction & Non-fiction, Belles Lettres, Poetry, Biography, History, Africana, How-to, Study Guides, Reference, Religion, Juveniles, Books in Afrikaans, Paperbacks
1981: 120 titles *1982:* 135 titles *Founded:* 1950
ISBN Publisher's Prefix: 0-624

Target Publishers (Edms) Bpk*, PO Box 910, Klerksdorp 2570

Taurus*, PO Box 85218, Emmarentia 2029 Tel: 7264059
Chief Executives: Ernst Lindenberg, John Miles, Ampie Coetzee
Parent Company: Licomil Co (Pty) Ltd (at above address)
Subject: South African Literature in English and Afrikaans
Founded: 1975

Technitrain (Pty) Ltd, now known as Star Schools (qv)

Thomson Publications South Africa (Pty) Ltd*, PO Box 8308, Johannesburg 2000 (Located at: Thomson House, Hendrick Verwoed, Will Scarlett, Randburg) Tel: 7892144
Man Dir: W Corry
Subjects: Reference, Daily/Monthly Bulletins and Journals, Annual/Biennial Buyers' Guides
Miscellaneous: Affiliated to Thomson Newspaper Group

Timmins Publishers (Pty) Ltd+, PO Box 94, Cape Town 8000 (Located at: Sanso Centre, 8 Adderley St, Cape Town 8001) Tel: (021) 252292/252294 Telex: 5720261
Chairman: A E Ashworth; *Man Dir:* R C Gaymer; *Dirs:* John Malherbe, H B Timmins
Subjects: General South African Non-fiction, Biography, History, Books in Afrikaans, Travel, Medicine, Gardening, Cookery
Bookshop: Booktrends (Pty) Ltd, PO Box 784805, Sandton 2146
1981: 20 titles *1982:* 20 titles *Founded:* 1937
ISBN Publisher's Prefix: 0-86978

Torpis Publishing Co, PO Box 1275, Bloemfontein Tel: (051) 71506
Man Dir: D Pistor

Treffer Uitgewers (Edms) Ltd*, Posbus 3599, Pretoria 0001

United Protestant Publishers (Pty) Ltd, see Lux Verbi (Pty) Ltd

University of Natal Press, PO Box 375, Pietermaritzburg 3200 Tel: (0331) 63320 Telex: 63719
Man Dir: Ms M P Moberly
Imprint: Killie Campbell Africana Library (Durban)
Subjects: South African History, Politics, Ornithology, Botany, Natal and Zulu Studies, Africana, General Literature, Reprints
1981: 4 titles *1982:* 3 titles *Founded:* 1947
ISBN Publisher's Prefix: 0-86980

University of South Africa*, Department of Publishing Services, PO Box 392, Pretoria 0001 Tel: (012) 4402202 Cable Add: Unisa Telex: 3777
Publications Management: by Publications Committee
Subjects: General Non-fiction, Belles Lettres, Anthropology, Accountancy, Botany, Chemistry, Communications, Criminology, Economics, Education, Fine Arts, Poetry, Biography, History, Africana, Philosophy, Reference, Religion, Theology, Psychology, Science & Technology, Social Science, Geography, Geology, Academic Journals,

Library Science, Linguistics, Literature, Law, Mathematics, Music, Physics, Politics, Statistics, University Textbooks
1981: 30 titles (also large number of textbooks, not for sale to booksellers)
Founded: 1873
ISBN Publisher's Prefix: 0-86981

University Publishers & Booksellers (Pty) Ltd, PO Box 29, Stellenbosch 7600 Tel: (02231) 70337/70397 Cable Add: Biblio Stellenbosch
Man Dir: B B Liebenberg
Subjects: General Non-fiction, Juveniles, University & Secondary Textbooks

Valiant Publishers (Pty) Ltd*, Sandton City, PO Box 78236, Sandton 2146 Tel: 7835012/5 Telex: 83023
Man Dir: F R Metrowich; *General Manager, Rights & Permissions:* A N Keevy
Subjects: General Non-fiction, History, Africana, Reference, Religion, TFH Pet Books
Founded: 1975

Via Afrika Ltd, PO Box 114, Parow 7500 Tel: (021) 591131 Cable Add: Via Afrika
Publisher: E R Arnold; *General Manager:* G J J Rousseau; *Production Manager:* W Struik; *Marketing Manager:* T Priem
Parent Company: Nasionale Boekhandel Ltd (qv)
Subjects: General Fiction, Belles Lettres, Poetry, Books in Zulu, Xhosa and other Southern African Languages, Science and Technology, General & Social Science, Secondary & Primary Textbooks
Bookshops: Via Afrika Bookstore (qv under Major Booksellers)
Founded: 1970
ISBN Publisher's Prefix: 0-7994

J P van der **Walt** en Seun (Pty) Ltd+, 380 Bosman St, PO Box 123, Pretoria 0001 Tel: (012) 3232341 Telex: 30691 SA
Man Dir: D H van der Walt; *Editorial:* R J J van Rensburg
Subjects: General Fiction & Non-fiction, Philosophy, Reference, Religion, Law, Juveniles, Books in Afrikaans, Paperbacks, University Textbooks
Book Clubs: Eike-Boekklub, Keurbiblioteek, Kinderkeur, Romankeur, Treffer-Boekklub
1981: 89 titles *1982:* 97 titles *Founded:* 1947
ISBN Publisher's Prefix: 0-7993

Waterkant-Uitgewers (Edms) Bpk*, PO Box 4539, Cape Town 8000 Tel: 215540
Man Dir: W J van Zijl; *Publicity:* Mrs E M Volschenk
Parent Company: N G Kerk-Uitgewers, PO Box 2309, Kemptonpark 1620
Associate Company: Waterkant Publishers
Subject: Christian Literature
Founded: 1980
ISBN Publisher's Prefix: 0-907992

Who's Who of Southern Africa, 47 Sauer St, PO Box 8620, Johannesburg Tel: 8363388
Managing Editor: D A Dalton
Parent Company: Argus Group, Johannesburg
Associate Companies: Argus South African Newspapers Ltd, 85 Fleet St, London EC4Y 1ED, UK and 1500 Broadway, New York, NY 10036, USA
Subjects: Reference, Annuals

Witwatersrand University Press, 1 Jan Smuts Ave, Johannesburg 2001 Tel: (011) 7162023
Chief Executive: Mrs N H Wilson
Subjects: General Non-fiction, Belles Lettres, Poetry, Biography, History, Philosophy, Reference, Religion, Medicine, Psychology, Science & Technology, Social Science, University and School Textbooks, Africana, Books in Zulu, Xhosa and other Southern African Languages
Bookshop: 36 Jorissen St, Johannesburg 2001
1981: 8 titles *1982:* 10 titles *Founded:* 1923
ISBN Publisher's Prefix: 0-85494

Literary Agents

The **International Press** Agency (Pty) Ltd, PO Box 67, Howard Place 7450 (Located at: 44 Howard Centre, Pinelands 7405, Cape Province) Tel: (021) 531926 Cable Add: Inpra Howard Place South Africa
Man Dir: Dr Ursula A Barnett

Book Clubs

Klub 707, PO Box 4892, Johannesburg 2000 Tel: 285460
Owned by: Perskor Books (Pty) Ltd (qv)
Subjects: Fiction: especially Suspense, Espionage, Whodunnits, Thrillers (in Afrikaans)

Africana Book Society Ltd*, PO Box 1071, Johannesburg
Owned by: Books of Zimbabwe Publishing Co (Pvt) Ltd, Zimbabwe (qv)
Subjects: Africana, Hunting, Wildlife, Historical Reprints

Associated Book Clubs, PO Box 9909, Johannesburg Tel: (011) 374300 Telex: 80312
Manager: R L Nathan
Subjects: General Books & Records
Members: 130,000

Children's Book Club, PO Box 3570, Pretoria 0001 Tel: (012) 437731 Telex: 30851
Specialization: Books in Afrikaans
Owned by: Daan Retief Publishers (Pty) Ltd (qv)

Klub-Dagbreek, PO Box 4892, Johannesburg 2000
Owned by: Perskor Books (Pty) Ltd (qv)
Subject: Fiction

Eike-Boekklub, 380 Bosman St, PO Box 123, Pretoria 0001
Owned by: J P van der Walt en Seun (Pty) Ltd (qv)
Subject: Children's Books

Indlouu Ubudlelwane Ngezincwadi, 230 Church St, PO Box 109, Pietermaritzburg 3200, Natal Tel: (0331) 58151 Cable Add: Shushoo Telex: 643771 SA
Zulu Book Club
Members: 103
Owned by: Shuter & Shooter (Pty) Ltd (qv)
Founded: 1981

Keurbiblioteek, 380 Bosman St, PO Box 123, Pretoria 0001
Owned by: J P van der Walt en Seun (Pty) Ltd (qv)
Subject: Fiction

Kinderkeur, 380 Bosman St, PO Box 123, Pretoria 0001
Owned by: J P van der Walt en Seun (Pty) Ltd (qv)

Pluim Book Club*, PO Box 1207, Cape Town 8000 (Located at: Sanso Centre, 8 Adderley St, Cape Town 8001)
Owned by: John Malherbe (Pty) Ltd (qv)
Subject: Adult Fiction

Romankeur, 380 Bosman St, PO Box 123, Pretoria 0001
Owned by: J P van der Walt en Seun (Pty) Ltd (qv)

Klub **Saffier**, PO Box 4892, Johannesburg 2000
Owned by: Perskor Books (Pty) Ltd (qv)
Subject: Fiction

Treffer-Boekklub, 380 Bosman St, PO Box 123, Pretoria 0001
Owned by: J P van der Walt en Seun (Pty) Ltd (qv)
Subject: Fiction

Young People's Book Club, PO Box 3570, Pretoria 0001 Tel: (012) 437731 Telex: 30851
Owned by: Daan Retief Publishers (Pty) Ltd (qv)

Major Booksellers

Adams & Co Ltd, 341 West St, PO Box 466, Durban 4000 Tel: (031) 328571/2
Manager: P D Adams

Bookwise (Pty) Ltd*, PO Box 260865, Shakespeare House, Commissioner St, Johannesburg 2000
Branches at Bedfordview, Braamfontein, Roggebaai

Central News Agency Ltd, PO Box 10799, Johannesburg 2000 Tel: (011) 8361711
Also: PO Box 9, Cape Town 8000 Tel: (021) 541261; PO Box 938, Durban 4000 Tel: (031) 451875 (and further 250 branches throughout the country)

Exclusive Books (Pty) Ltd, 48 Pretoria St, PO Box 17554, Hillbrow 2038, Transvaal Tel: (011) 6425068 (shop)/6438131 (office) Telex: 424094 SA
Also: PO Box 4628, Cape Town 8000 (Located at: Southern Life Arcade, 101 St Georges St, Cape Town 8000) Tel: (021) 226860 Telex: 5726078 SA
Man Dir: Benjamin Trisk
Owned by: Premier Group Ltd

Fogarty's Bookshop, PO Box 1881, Main St at Market Sq, Port Elizabeth 6000 Tel: (041) 21035/24655
Manager: Basil Fogarty

H A U M Academic Bookshop, PO Box 343, Stellenbosch 7600 (Located at: Trust Bank Centre, Andringa Street) Tel: 70385/70315
Manager: Mrs D C Mooi
Owned by: HAUM (Publisher, qv)

H A U M Booksellers, 480 Paul Kruger St, PO Box 460, Pretoria 0001 Tel: 36417, 34931 Telex: 30962 SA
Owned by: HAUM (Publisher, qv)

Johannesburgse Boekwinkel, RAU-Campus, PO Box 91119, Aucklandpark 2006 Tel: 7266034/5 Telex: 425557 SA
Owned by: Perskor Books (Pty) Ltd (qv)

Juta & Co Ltd, PO Box 30, Cape Town 8000 (Located at: Regis House, Church St, Cape Town 8001) Tel: (021) 224571; Cnr Pritchard/Loveday Sts, PO Box 1010, Johannesburg 2000 Tel: (011) 8336113; PO Box 123, Kenwyn 7790 Tel: 711181
Owned by: Juta & Co Ltd, Publishers (qv)

Literary Services (Pty) Ltd, PO Box 31361, Braamfontein 2017 Tel: 391711

Logans University Bookshop (Pty) Ltd, 227-229 Francois Rd, Durban
Office & Warehouse: 622 Umbilo Rd, Durban 4001 Tel: 253221
Also: Nedbank Plaza, Pietermaritzburg Tel: 41580; 660 Umbilo Rd, Durban (Medical Books); Moore Rd, Durban (General Books) Telex: 624583

Maskew Miller Longman (Pty) Ltd, 81 Church St, Cape Town 8001 Tel: (021) 236300
Branches: See under Publishers entry

N G Kerkboekhandel Transvaal, Schoemanstr 260, PO Box 245, Pretoria 0001 Tel: 218401
Owned by: N G Kerkboekhandel Transvaal (DRC Publishers) (qv)
Subjects: Religion, Theology, Books in Afrikaans and English

Nasionale Boekwinkels Bpk, PO Box 122, Parow 7500 Tel: 591131 Cable Add: Nasboek Cape Town
General Manager: G J Coetzee
Owned by: Nasionale Boekhandel Ltd (qv)
Branches: PO Box 119, Parow 7500 Tel: 591131; PO Box 912, Kimberley 8300; PO Box 2063, Cape Town 8000; PO Box 9898, Johannesburg 2000; PO Box 95, Port Elizabeth 6000; PO Box 1715, Port Elizabeth; PO Box 1058, Bloemfontein 9300; PO Box 1047, Bloemfontein 9300; 78 Maitland St, Bloemfontein 9301; PO Box 279, East London 5200; 46 Bok St, Welkom 9460; Griet se Akademiese Boekhandel, PO Box 2377, Stellenbosch 7600

Perskor Bookshop, PO Box 845, Johannesburg 2000
Owned by: Perskor Books (Pty) Ltd (qv)
Branches: PO Box 309, Kroonstad 9500; PO Box 133, Bellville 7530; PO Box 102, Maraisburg 1700; PO Box 15531, Lynn East 0039

Pilgrims Booksellers (Pty)*, PO Box 3559, Cape Town Telex: 57-24178
At Old Mutual Centre, Cavendish Sq and Main Rd, Sea Point (all Cape Town)
Manager: V Tarica

Van Schaik's Bookstore (Pty) Ltd, PO Box 724, Pretoria 0001 Tel: 212441 Cable Add: Bookschaik Telex: 32340 SA
Owned by: J L van Schaik (Pty) Ltd (qv)

Shuter & Shooter (Pty), Church St, PO Box 109, Pietermaritzburg Tel: (0331) 28121 Telex: 643771 SA
Owned by: Shuter & Shooter (Pty) Ltd (Publisher, qv)

United Book Distributors (Pty) Ltd*, PO Box 17294, Hillbrow 2038 (Located at: 1st Floor, Permad House, 28 Betty St, Jeppestown) Tel: (614) 6431/2/3 Cable Add: Unibooks Telex: 424094 SA
Manager: F J Van Zyn
Wholesalers and Distributors

Universitas Books (Pty) Ltd, PO Box 1557, 0001 Pretoria Tel: 212211 Cable Add: Africabook Telex: 30241 SA
Man Dir: E E Strauss
Owned by: Premier Group Ltd

Via Afrika Book Store, PO Box 9898, Johannesburg
Also: PO Box 248, Pietersburg; PO Box 380, Pietermaritzburg; PO Box 107, King William's Town; PO Box 259, Umtata
Owned by: Via Afrika Ltd (qv)

Major Libraries

Cape Provincial Library Service, Hospital & Chiappini Sts, PO Box 2108, Cape Town 8000 Tel: 214800
Dir: G R Morris

Cape Town City Libraries, PO Box 4728, Cape Town 8000 (Located at: Old Drill Hall, Parade St, Cape Town) Tel: 2102036
Librarian: C H Vermeulen

Centre for Scientific and Technical Information, PO Box 395, Pretoria 0001 Tel: (2712) 869211 Telex: 32087 SA Cable Add: Navorsinfo
Dir: Dr R van Houten
A department of the Council for Scientific and Industrial Research (CSIR), at the same address. Library stock covers Science and Technology

Department of National Education Library, Oranje-Nassau Bldg, Schoeman St, PB X122, Pretoria Tel: 269971
Senior Librarian: P J W Louw
Publication: Library News

Durban Municipal Library, PO Box 917, Durban 4000 Tel: (031) 320111
Librarian: M H Kennedy
Publications: Annual Report; Accessions Lists; Booklists; Bookworm (Staff Quarterly Magazine)

Government Archives, Cape Archives Depot, Library, 62 Queen Victoria St, PB X9025, Cape Town 8000 Tel: 411888 (Branch of Department of National Education)
Archivist: Miss M George

Government Archives, Natal Archives Depot, Library, 231 Pietermaritz St, PB X9012, Pietermaritzburg 3200 Tel: 24712
Chief Archivist: F Nel

Government Archives, Orange Free State Archives Depot, Library*, 8 Elizabeth St, PB X20504, Bloemfontein 9300 Tel: 72840
Archivist: J W Cronje

Government Archives, Transvaal Archives Depot, Library*, Union Bldgs, Church St, PB X236, Pretoria 0001 Tel: 24971
Archivist: Dr M H Buys

Johannesburg Public Library, Market Sq, Johannesburg 2001 Tel: 8363787
City Librarian: Miss L Kennedy
Publications: Municipal Reference Library Bulletin (monthly); Index to South African Periodicals (annual)

Library of Parliament, PO Box 18, Cape Town 8000 Tel: 458165
Chief Librarian: G Swanepoel

Orange Free State Provincial Library, PO Box X20606, Bloemfontein 9300 Tel: 70511 Telex: 267056
Librarian: G L Nordier

Pretoria Public Library*, Vermeulen St, Pretoria 0001 Tel: 216361
Librarian: F de Bruyn

Royal Society of South Africa Library*, University of Cape Town Libraries, Rondebosch 7700 Tel: (021) 698531
Librarian: Prof J H Day
Publications: Transactions of the Royal Society of South Africa (irregular)

South African Library, Queen Victoria St, Cape Town 8001
Tel: 431132/433829/432486
Dir: P E Westra
Publications: Quarterly Bulletin; Grey Bibliographies; Reprint series; Cape Almanac (Reprint) Series

State Library, Vermeulen St, PO Box 397, Pretoria 0001 Tel: (012) 218931 Telex: SA 3778
Librarian: Dr H J Aschenborn
Publications: South African National Bibliography; Reprint series; Micrographic series; Contributions to Library Science; Bibliographic series

Transvaal Provincial Library and Museum Service, PB X288, Pretoria 0001 Tel: 2802442 Cable Add: Transator Telex: 30302
Publications: Overvaal Musea, Book parade

University of Cape Town Libraries, Private Bag, Rondebosch 7700 Tel: (021) 698531 Telex: 5720327
Librarian: A S C Hooper
Publications: Bibliographical series (irregular); Jagger Journal (annually); Varia series (irregular)

University of Pretoria, Library Services*, Hillcrest, Pretoria Tel: (012) 436051
Dir: Prof E D Gerryts
Publication: Bibliotekdiens Verslagreeks (series of reports, published only in Afrikaans)

University of South Africa Library, PO Box 392, Pretoria 0001 Tel: (012) 4401904 Cable Add: Unisa Pretoria Telex: 3777
Dir: Prof J Willemse

University of the Witwatersrand Library, Private Bag 31550, Braamfontein 2017 Tel: (011) 7161111/7162366 (Publications) Cable Add: Uniwits Telex: SA 4-22460
Librarian: Prof R Musiker
Publications include: Witwatersrand Journal of Librarianship and Information Science; Historical and Literary Papers: Inventories of Collections, Bibliographical Series, Occasional Publications Series, Official Publications Series; Africana, Annual Report

Library Associations

African Library Association of South Africa*, c/o Library, University of the North, Private Bag X5090, Pietersburg 0700 Tel: Sovenga 33 Cable Add: Unikol Telex: 30808
Secretary-Treasurer: Mrs A N Kambule
Publication: Newsletter (quarterly)

South African Institute for Librarianship and Information Science, PO Box 28743, Sunnyside, Pretoria 0132
Publications: South African Journal for Librarianship and Information Science, Newsletter

Library Reference Books and Journals

Books

Handbook of South African Libraries, The State Library, Vermeulen St, PO Box 397, Pretoria

Journals

Bookworm, Durban Municipal Library, PO Box 917, Durban 4000

The Cape Librarian (text in Afrikaans and English), Cape Provincial Library Service, Hospital and Chiappini Sts, PO Box 2108, Cape Town

Free State Libraries, Orange Free State Provincial Library, PO Box X0606, Bloemfontein

Library News, Department of National Education Library, Oranje-Nassau Bldg, Schoeman St, PB X122, Pretoria 0001

Libri Natales, Natal Provincial Library, PB 9016, Pietermaritzburg 3200

Mousaion II, Department of Library Science, University of South Africa, PO Box 392, Pretoria

Municipal Reference Library Bulletin (monthly), Johannesburg Public Library, Market Sq, Johannesburg 2001

Newsletter, South African Institute for Librarianship and Information Science, PO Box 28743, Sunnyside, Pretoria 0132

Quarterly Bulletin of the South African Library, South African Library, Queen Victoria St, Cape Town 8001

Skoolbiblioteek/School Library, Transvaal Education Library Service, PB X290, Pretoria 0001

South African Journal for Librarianship and Information Science, South African Institute for Librarianship and Information Science, PO Box 28743, Sunnyside, Pretoria 0132 (the official publication of the South African Institute of Librarianship and Information Science, published quarterly)

Witwatersrand Journal of Librarianship and Information Science, University of the Witwatersrand Library, Private Bag 31550, Braamfontein 2017

Literary Associations and Societies

Artists' and Writers' Guild of South Africa*, 37-17th St, Parkhurst, Johannesburg 2001

South African **P E N** Centre (Cape), PO Box 15, Cape Town 8000
Chairman: Brian Bamford

Literary Periodicals

Contrast; South African literary journal (text in English and Afrikaans), South African Literary Journal Ltd, 3 Scott Rd, PO Box 3841, Claremont, Cape Town

Dialogue; a literary annual for young writers, PO Box 102, Wynberg 7824

English in Africa, Institute for the Study of English in Africa, Rhodes University, Grahamstown 6140. Critical articles on all aspects of African literature written in English

Kwanza Journal, PO Box 41, Pretoria 0001. Literary reviews; poetry, creative writing etc

New Classic, Ravan Press (Pty) Ltd, 508 Diakonia House, 80 Jorissen St, PO Box 31134, Braamfontein 2017 (important quarterly literary and cultural magazine, originally published as *The Classic*, edited by Sydney Sipho Sepamla)

New Coin, Institute for the Study of English in Africa, Rhodes University, Grahamstown 6140. Previously unpublished poems by South African poets

Ophir, Ravan Press (Pty) Ltd, 508 Diakonia House, 80 Jorissen St, PO Box 31134, Braamfontein (biannual poetry magazine)

South African Literary Journal, PO Box 3841, Cape Town 8000

Unisa English Studies, University of South Africa, PO Box 392, Pretoria 0001. Literary articles and reviews

Literary Prizes

Stephen **Black** Prize for Drama, see Department of National Education Literary Prizes

Jochem van **Bruggen** Prys vir Prosa, see Department of National Education Literary Prizes

C N A Literary Award
Established in 1961 for the best original works, one in English and one in Afrikaans, published for the first time during the calendar year of the competition. 3,500 rand each plus a bronze plaque. Awarded annually. Books must be in one of following categories: Novels, Short Stories, Poetry, Biography, Drama, History, Travel. Authors must be South African citizens or registered permanent residents of South Africa. The winners in 1982 were Andre Brink for the novel *A Chain of Voices* (Faber & Faber) and Elizabeth Eybers for a volume of poetry, *Bestand* (Human & Rousseau). Enquiries to The President, Book Trade Association of South Africa, PO Box 105, Parow 7500

Roy **Campbell** Prize for Poetry, see Department of National Education Literary Prizes

Department of National Education Literary Prizes
Established 1957 and awarded in 3-year cycles. In the English Section, the names of the prizes awarded are as follows: Stephen Black Prize for Drama; Roy Campbell Prize for Poetry; Pauline Smith Prize for Prose. In the Afrikaans Section, the names of the prizes are as follows: J W F Grosskopf Prys vir Drama; C Louis Leipoldt Prys vir Poesie; Jochem van Bruggen Prys vir Prosa. Prizes of 1250 rand are awarded in each of the two sections. The 1981 winner for prose in the English section was E W Maskew for *Fascadel Village*. Enquiries to Director-General for National Education, Private Bag X122, Pretoria 0001

English Association (South African Branch) Literary Prize
For an original unpublished manuscript by a South African citizen, permanent resident of South Africa or person who has lived in South Africa since 1 January 1982. Subject, literary form and amount of award vary from year to year. Usually awarded annually. Enquiries to English Association, PO Box 1180, Cape Town 8000

Percy **Fitzpatrick** Medal
For outstanding books for children written in English. Awarded biannually. Enquiries to South African Institute for Library and Information Science, c/o Prof Carl Lohann, Institute for Research into Children's Literature, Potchefstroom University, Potchefstroom 2520

J W F **Grosskopf** Prys vir Drama, see Department of National Education Literary Prizes

Katrine **Harris** Award
For outstanding illustrations in South African children's books, regardless of language. Awarded biannually. Enquiries to South African Institute for Library and Information Science, c/o Prof Carl Lohann, Institute for Research into Children's Literature, Potchefstroom University, Potchefstroom 2520

Hertzog Prize
A Prestige Prize for Afrikaans Literature. Prizes are awarded in rotation for Poetry, Drama and Prose. 1,500 rand. Awarded annually. Enquiries to South African Academy of Science and Arts, PO Box 538, Pretoria 0001

W A **Hofmeyr** Prize
Awarded annually for the best book of a belletristic nature published by Tafelberg, Human & Rousseau, Nasou and Via Afrika; 1000 rand and a Gold Medallion. Enquiries to Nasionale Boekhandel, Voortrekker Rd, PO Box 122, Parow 7500

Tienie **Holloway** Medal
Established in 1969 by Dr J E Holloway. A gold medal is awarded every three years to a writer who has produced the best work in Afrikaans literature for infants. Enquiries to South African Academy of Science and Arts, PO Box 538, Pretoria 0001

C P **Hoogenhout** Award
To encourage the production of outstanding Afrikaans children's books. Awarded biannually. Enquiries to South African Institute for Library and Information Science, c/o Prof Carl Lohann, Institute for Research into Children's Literature, Potchefstroom University, Potchefstroom 2520

C J **Langenhoven** Prize
For outstanding work in field of Afrikaans linguistics. 250 rand. Awarded every three years. Enquiries to South African Academy of Science and Arts, PO Box 538, Pretoria 0001

C Louis **Leipholdt** Prys vir Poesie, see Department of National Education Literary Prizes

H R **Malan** Prize
Awarded annually for the best non-fiction book published by Tafelberg, Human & Rousseau, Nasou and Via Afrika, 1000 rand and a Gold Medallion. Enquiries to Nasionale Boekhandel, Voortrekker Rd, PO Box 122, Parow 7500

Eugène **Marais** Prize
For a first, or early, work of belles lettres in Afrikaans by a young writer. 250 rand. Awarded annually. Enquiries to South African Academy of Science and Arts, PO Box 538, Pretoria 0001

Mofolo-Plomer Prize*
Initiated by Nadine Gordimer for a South African writer resident in Southern Africa or elsewhere. For a novel or a collection of short stories in English. Enquiries to Mofolo-Plomer Prize Committee, c/o Ravan Press (Pty) Ltd, PO Box 31134, Braamfontein 2017, Johannesburg

Perskor Prize for Literature
For the best literary work published in Afrikaans by Perskor Press. 5,000 rand awarded biennially. Enquiries to Perskor Publishers, PO Box 845, Johannesburg 2000

Perskor Prize for Youth Literature
For the best youth work published in Afrikaans by Perskor Press. 5,000 rand awarded biennially. Enquiries to Perskor Books (Pty) Ltd, PO Box 845, Johannesburg 2000

Gustav **Preller** Prize
For literary science and literary criticism in Afrikaans. Awarded every 3 years. Enquiries to South African Academy of Science and Arts, PO Box 538, Pretoria 0001

Scheepers Prize
For the best book written for children. 250 rand. Awarded every three years. Enquiries to South African Academy of Science and Arts, PO Box 538, Pretoria 0001

Olive **Schreiner** Prize for English Literature
For original literary work in English by a promising South African writer and published in South Africa. 500 rand. Awarded annually in one of the following categories: Prose, Poetry, Drama. Enquiries to English Academy of Southern Africa, Ballater House, 35 Melle Str, Braamfontein, Johannesburg 2001

Pauline **Smith** Prize for Prose, see Department of National Education Literary Prizes

336 REPUBLIC OF SOUTH AFRICA — SPAIN

South African Academy of Science and Arts Prizes
The Academy awards a number of prizes for works in Afrikaans; the following are noted in this section: Hertzog Prize; Tienie Holloway Medal; C J Langenhoven Prize; Eugène Marais Prize; Gustav Preller Prize; Scheepers Prize; Translation Prize. See individual entries for details. Enquiries to South African Academy of Science and Arts, PO Box 538, Pretoria 0001

Timmins Literary Award
A prize of 25,000 rand, awarded every three years. Awarded first in 1983 to Gordon Vorster for *The Textures of Silence*. Enquiries to Timmins Publishers (Pty) Ltd, PO Box 94, Cape Town 8000

Translation Prize
For translation of Belles Lettres from any language into Afrikaans. 250 rand awarded annually. Enquiries to South African Academy of Science and Arts, PO Box 538, Pretoria 0001

Spain

General Information

Language: Castilian (the most widely used) is what foreigners know as Spanish; Basque in the north, Catalan in the east, Galician in the north-west. Most speakers of Basque, Catalan and Galician also speak Castilian
Religion: Roman Catholic
Population: 37.1 million
Literacy Rate (1970): 90.1%
Bank Hours: Vary. Generally 0900-1300 or 0900-1600 Monday-Friday; half day Saturday
Shop Hours: Generally 0900-1300, 1700-2000 Monday-Saturday
Currency: 100 céntimos = 1 peseta
Export/Import Information: Varying tariffs on books, related to type, binding, language, etc; children's picture books dutied and taxed; compensatory tax on books in general. Most advertising matter is tariff-free but taxed. Import licence required; foreign books subject to censorship. Exchange controls
Copyright: UCC, Berne, Florence (see International section)

Book Trade Organizations

Agencia Española del ISBN*, Instituto Nacional del Libro Español, Calle Santiago Rusiñol 8, Madrid 3 Tel: (91) 2330802
ISBN Administrator: Gonzalo García Rubio

Asociación de Escritores y Artistas Españoles*, Calle de Leganitos 10, Madrid 13
Spanish Writers' and Artists' Association
Secretary: José G Manrique de Lara

Asociación Española de Editores de Musica (AEDEM)*, Carrera de San Jeronimo, No 29 1°C, Madrid 14
Spanish Association of Music Publishers

Federación de Asociaciones Nacionales de Distribuidores de Ediciones*, Reina Mercedes 18, Madrid 20
Federation of National Associations of Publications Distributors

Federación de Gremios de Editores de España, Calle Paseo de la Castellana 82 - 7° Izda, Madrid 6 Tel: 4115795/4115713
Federation of Spanish Publishers' Associations
Secretary: Jaime Brull

Gremi de Llibreters de Barcelona i Catalunya*, Calle Mallorca 272-276, 1a planta, Barcelona 37
Booksellers' Association of Barcelona and Catalonia
Publication: Librería

Instituto Nacional del Libro Español, Calle Santiago Rusiñol 8, Madrid 3 Tel: (01) 2330802/2330902/2334502
The National Institute of Spanish Books (which deals with the promotion of Spanish books)
Secretary: Eduardo Nolla López
Publications: El Libro Español (monthly); *Guía de Editores de España; Guía de Libreros y Distribuidores de España; Libros Españoles ISBN* (annual); *Libros Infantiles y Juveniles* (biannual)

Instituto Nacional del Libro Español, Delegación de Barcelona*, Calle Mallorca 272-276, Barcelona 37 Tel: (03) 2155650
Barcelona Section of The National Institute of Spanish Books
Executive Delegate: S Olives Canals
Publications: Catálogo ISBN, Catalogo de Libros de Ensenanze, Quién es quién

Publiexport, Paseo de la Castellana 166 - 7° A, Madrid 16 Tel: (91) 4586591/2505355 Telex: 49416 - Publ
United Publications Exporters — a group of more than 350 companies comprising publishers, printers, distributors and booksellers
President: D Raúl Rispa Márquez;
Secretary: Néstor García

Sociedad General Española de Librería*, Evaristo san Miguel 9, Madrid 8
Spanish Association for Bookshops

Spanish Book Center*, Milanesado 21-23, Barcelona 17 Tel: (93) 2039916 Telex: 54675 contb-e
Man Dir: Antonio Rodrigo
Export organization for all books published in Spain
Publication: New Books from Spain

Standard Book Numbering Agency, see Agencia Española del ISBN

Book Trade Reference Books and Journals

Books

Guía de Editores de España (Guide to the Publishers of Spain), Instituto Nacional del Libro Español, Calle Santiago Rusiñol 8, Madrid 3

Guía de Libreros y Distribuidores de España (Guide to the Booksellers and Distributors of Spain), Instituto Nacional del Libro Español, Calle Santiago Rusiñol 8, Madrid 3

Indice Cultural Español (Spanish Cultural Index), Dirección General de Relaciones Culturales, Ministerio de Asuntos Exteriores, Plaza de la Provincia 1, Madrid 12

Libros en Venta (Books for Sale); annual supplements including Spanish language book production of the year from all countries, Turner Ediciones SRL, Alsina 1535, 8° piso, of 803, 1088 Buenos Aires, Argentina

Libros Españoles ISBN (Spanish Books assigned ISBNs), Instituto Nacional del Libro Español, Calle Santiago Rusiñol 8, Madrid 3

Quién es Quién (Who's Who), Instituto Nacional del Libro Español, Delegación de Barcelona, Calle Mallorca 272-276, Barcelona 37

Journals

Bibliografía Española (Spanish Bibliography), Instituto Bibliográfico Hispánico, Calle de Atocha 106, Madrid 12

Bibliografía Española: Suplemento de Publicaciones Periódicas (Periodical Publications Supplement to Spanish Bibliography), Instituto Bibliográfico Hispánico, Calle de Atocha 106, Madrid 12

Cuadernos de Bibliografía Española (Notebook of Spanish Bibliography), Instituto Bibliográfico Hispánico, Calle de Atocha 106, Madrid 12

Librería (Bookselling), Gremi de Llibreters de Barcelona i Catalunya, Calle Mallorca 272-276, 1a planta, Barcelona 37

El Libro Español (The Spanish Book), Instituto Nacional del Libro Español, Calle Santiago Rusiñol 8, Madrid 3

New Books from Spain, Spanish Book Center, Milanesado 21-23, Barcelona 17

Publishers

Ediciones **29***, Mandri 41, Barcelona 22 Tel: (93) 2123836
Man Dir: Alfredo Lloreme Diez
Subjects: Fiction, Literature, Poetry, General Non-fiction
Founded: 1968
ISBN Publisher's Prefix: 84-7175

Edicions **62** SA, Provenza 278 - 1° 1a, Barcelona 8 Tel: (93) 2160062
Man Dir: Ramon Bastardes i Porcel;
Editorial Dir: Josep M Castellet; *Sales:* Joaquim Sabria
Associate Company: Ediciones Peninsula (qv)
Subsidiary Company: Distribuciones de Enlace SA (Distributors)
Subjects: General (in Catalan)
1981: 114 titles *1982:* 117 titles *Founded:* 1963
ISBN Publisher's Prefix: 84-297

Ediciones **99** SA*, Calle General Martínez Campos 42-Bajo, Madrid 10
Part of Grupo Editorial Guadiana (qv)

Editorial **A E D O S** SA+, Consejo de Ciento 391, Barcelona 9 Tel: (93) 3170141/3012845
Man Dir: Juan Badosa
Subjects: Agriculture, Veterinary Science, Sports, How-to, Biography
1981: 7 titles *1982:* 10 titles *Founded:* 1939
ISBN Publisher's Prefix: 84-7003

Publicacions de l'**Abadia** de Montserrat, Abadia de Montserrat, Barcelona Tel: 2450303
Shipping Add: Ausias March, 92-98, Barcelona 13
Man Dir: Josep Massot Muntaner; *Sales, Advertising & Publicity:* Jordi Ubeda;
Rights & Permissions: Bernabé Dalmau
Subjects: Religion, History, Geography, Biography, Literature, Juveniles, Travel (mostly in Catalán)
1981: 55 titles *1982:* 47 titles *Founded:* 1915
ISBN Publisher's Prefix: 84-7202

SPAIN 337

Ediciones **Acervo**, Julio Verne 5-7, Apdo 5319, Barcelona 6 Tel: (93) 212264/2474425
Man Dir: José A Llorens
Subsidiary Company: Ediciones Acervo de Argentina SRL, Argentina (qv)
Subject: General Literature
Founded: 1954
ISBN Publisher's Prefix: 84-70002

Editorial **Acribia**, Apdo 466, Saragossa (Located at: Calle Royo 23, Saragossa) Tel: 232089
Man Dir: Pascual López Lorenzo; *Sales, Publicity & Advertising:* Mercedes Marcen
Subjects: Veterinary Science, Agriculture, General Science, Medicine, Nutrition, Oceanography, Marine Biology
1981: 30 titles *Founded:* 1957
ISBN Publisher's Prefix: 84-200

Afha Internacional SA*, Aribau 200-210, Apdo 75, Barcelona 36 Tel: 2091800 Cable Add: Afhinter Telex: 52743
Man Dir: José Ma Llovet; *Editorial:* Diego de Herrera; *Sales:* Ramón Bertrand; *Production, Rights & Permissions:* Ulisses Farreras; *Publicity:* Pedro Richard
Parent Company: Ediciones Afha
Subsidiary Company: Editorial Columna
Imprint: Emograph
Subjects: Juveniles, Education
Founded: 1951
ISBN Publisher's Prefix: 84-201

Aguilar SA de Ediciones, Juan Bravo 38, Madrid 6 Tel: (91) 2763800 Cable Add: Guilarditor
Man Dir: Carlos Aguilar; *Sales Dir:* Enrique Montoya; *Rights & Permissions:* Tirso Echeandía
Branch Offs: Aguilar Argentina SA de Ediciones, Argentina (qv); Aguilar Chilena de Ediciones SA, Chile (qv); Aguilar Colombiana de Ediciones SA, Colombia (qv); Aguilar Mexicana de Ediciones SA, Mexico (qv); Aguilar Venezolana SA de Ediciones, Venezuela (qv)
Subjects: General Fiction, Belles Lettres, Poetry, Biography, History, Music, Art, Philosophy, Reference, Religion, Juveniles, Paperbacks, Medicine, Psychology, Engineering, General & Social Science, Law, Technical, Educational Materials, Maps and Cartographical Materials
ISBN Publisher's Prefix: 84-03

Editorial **'Alas'**, Valencia 234, Apdo 707, Barcelona 7 Tel: (93) 2537506
Subjects: Sports, How-to, Parapsychology, Crosswords, Martial Arts, Periodicals
ISBN Publisher's Prefix: 84-203

Ediciones **Alfaguara** SA*, Príncipe de Vergara 81 — 1° Madrid 7 Tel: (91) 2619700 Cable Add: Guara Madrid Telex: 43879 Edea E
Man Dir: Ignacio Cardenal; *Editor-in-Chief:* Jaime Salinas; *Rights & Permissions:* Rosa Aguilar
Subjects: General Fiction, Literature, Children's Books, Universal Classics
Founded: 1964
ISBN Publisher's Prefix: 84-204

Editorial **Alhambra** SA, Claudio Coello 76, Madrid 1 Tel: (91) 2764209/4316460 Cable Add: Edimbrasa
President: Erich Ruiz Albrecht; *Sales:* Angeles Zapatero Huerta, Miguel Angel Gimeno; *Production, Rights & Permissions:* Mercedes González de Amezúa; *Publicity:* María Teresa Esteban Fernández
Branch Offs: Enrique Granados 61, Barcelona 8; Doctor Albiñana 12, Bilbao 14; Plaza de las Descalsias 2, Granada; Pasadizo de Pernas 13, La Coruña 5; Saturnino Calleja 1, Madrid 2; Avda del Cristo 9, Oviedo; Reina Mercedes 35, Añadir, Sevilla 12; General Porlier 14, Santa Cruz de Tenerife; Cabillers 5, Valencia 3; Concepcion Arenal 25, Zaragoza 5; Editorial Alhambra Mexicana SA, Avenida División del Norte 2412, 03340 México DF, México
Subjects: Medicine, General Science, Literature, History, Philology, Philosophy, Psychology, Art, Nursing, Reference, University, Secondary and Primary Textbooks, Audiovisual Aids, Languages
1981: 80 titles *Founded:* 1952
ISBN Publisher's Prefix: 84-205

Alianza Editorial SA, Milán 38, Apdo 9107, Madrid 33 Tel: (91) 2000045 Telex: 45746
President: Diego Hidalgo; *Editorial:* Javier Pradera; *Sales & Marketing:* Faustino Linares; *Rights & Permissions:* Monica Acheroff
Associate Companies: Alianza Distribuidora de Colombia, Colombia; Alianza Editorial Mexicana, Mexico (qv); Distasa, Argentina (qv); Revista de Occidente SA (qv)
Subjects: General Fiction, Belles Lettres, Poetry, History, Music, Art, Philosophy, Political and Social Science, High-priced Paperbacks, Mathematics, General Science
1981: 141 titles *1982:* 169 titles *Founded:* 1965 (as publishers)
ISBN Publisher's Prefix: 84-206

Ediciones **Altea** SA, Príncipe de Vergara 84, Madrid 6 Tel: (91) 2625300 Cable Add: Edialtea Telex: 43879
Man Dir: Ignacio Cardenal; *Editorial Dir:* Miguel Azaola; *Sales:* Carlos Martínez; *Publicity:* Arturo Gonzalez; *Co-productions:* Juan Ramón Azaola
Subjects: Activity, Children's and Picture Books
Founded: 1973
ISBN Publisher's Prefix: 84-372

Editorial **Anagrama**, Calle La Cruz 44, Barcelona 34 Tel: (93) 2037652
Man Dir: Jorge de Herralde
Subjects: Literature, Philosophy, Psychology, Social Science, Anthropology
Founded: 1968
ISBN Publisher's Prefix: 84-339

Ediciones **Anaya** SA, Iriarte 4, Madrid 28 Tel: 2468606 Cable Add: Edinaya Telex: 22039 Anaya E
President: Germán Sánchez Ruiperez; *Man Dir:* Ambrosio María Ochoa Vázquez; *Editorial:* Ramiro Sánchez Sanz; *Rights & Permissions:* José M Delgado de Luque
Subjects: University, Secondary & Primary Textbooks, Educational Materials
Founded: 1959
ISBN Publisher's Prefix: 84-207

Editorial **Aranzadi***, Carlos III, 34, Pamplona Tel: 243112/249950
Man Dir: Estanislao de Aranzadi; *Sales Dir:* Javier de Epalza y Aranzadi
Subject: Law
Founded: 1929
ISBN Publisher's Prefix: 84-7018

Editorial **Argos** Vergara SA, Aragón 390, Barcelona 13 Tel: (03) 2457600 Cable Add: Leargos
President: Antonio Vilaplana
Subjects: Fiction, Non-fiction, Reference
ISBN Publisher's Prefix: 84-7178

Editorial **Ariel** SA+, Córcega 270 – 4°, Barcelona 8 Tel: (93) 2186400 Telex: 698255 Sxbl E
General Manager: Miguel García Piriz; *Publisher, Foreign Rights:* Marcelo Covian; *Advertising, Promotion:* Ricardo Muñoz Suay
Associate Company: Editorial Seix Barral SA (qv for subsidiary companies). The two Companies constitute the organization Ariel/Seix Barral Editoriales within the Planeta Group
Subjects: General and Social Sciences, Psychology, Philosophy, Religion, Economics, History, Literature, Texts in Catalan, Geography, Biography, University Textbooks
1981: 62 titles *Founded:* 1941
ISBN Publisher's Prefix: 84-344

Artesanal, an imprint of Ediciones de Arte y Bibliofilia (qv)

Ediciones de **Arte** y Bibliofilia+, Calle Ponzano 69, Madrid 3 Tel: (91) 4424339/4425178
Man Dir, Production, Rights & Permissions: Rafael Diaz-Casariego; *Editorial, Sales:* Ramon Diaz-Casariego
Subsidiary Company: Ediciones Velazquez, Calle Cristobal Bordiu 36, Madrid 3
Imprint: Artesanal
Subjects: Art, Bibliophily, Facsimiles
Bookshops: Librería Facsimilia, Calle Ponzano 52, Madrid 3; Librería Velazquez, Calle Cristobal Bordiu 36, Madrid 3
1981: 10 titles *Founded:* 1960
ISBN Publisher's Prefix: 84-85005

Asesoría Técnica de Ediciones SA, Ronda General Mitre 90, Barcelona 21 Tel: (93) 2479133/2477066
Man Dir, Editorial: José Dalmau Salvia; *Sales:* Antonio Dalmau Salvia; *Production:* José Luis Arribas; *Rights & Permissions:* Carmen de Eulate Echagüe
Subsidiary Company: Libroexpress
Subjects: Fiction, Anthropology, Computers, Communications, Science Fiction, Classics, Microbiology
1982: 400 titles
ISBN Publisher's Prefix: 84-7442

Asociación para el Progresso de la Dirección (APD)*, Montalban 3, Madrid 14 Tel: (91) 2325487
Dir of Publications: Vidal Pérez Herrero
Subject: Business Administration
ISBN Publisher's Prefix: 84-7019

Sociedad de Educación **Atenas** SA*, Mayor 81, Apdo 1096, Madrid 13 Tel: (91) 2480127
Subjects: Religion, Education, Psychology, Biography
ISBN Publisher's Prefix: 84-7020

Atika SA*, Fuencarral 160, Madrid 10 Tel: (91) 4459422
Man Dir: Mr Thermolle
Subjects: Technical, How-to, Automobile Manuals
Founded: 1964
ISBN Publisher's Prefix: 84-7022

Ayalga Ediciones SA, Apdo 1101, Salinas, Asturias (Located at: Calle Alcalde Luis Treillard 14 – 16, Salinas, Asturias) Tel: 511299/510599 Cable Add: Ayalga
Man Dir: José Antonio Mases; *Editorial:* Aquilino Escudero; *Sales:* Ricardo Revero; *Production:* Agustín Santarúa; *Publicity:* Astel
Subject: Asturian region
1981: 17 titles *1982:* 28 titles *Founded:* 1976
ISBN Publisher's Prefix: 84-7411

Editorial **Aymá** SA Editora, Travessera de Gracia 64, Barcelona 6 Tel: (93) 2000174 Cable Add: Aymol
President: Joan B Cendrós Carbonell
Subjects: General Fiction, Belles Lettres, Poetry, Biography, History, How-to, Music, Art, Philosophy, Religion, Low- and High-priced Paperbacks, Juveniles. In both Castilian and Catalan
Founded: 1952
ISBN Publisher's Prefix: 84-209

338 SPAIN

Editorial **Ayuso***, San Bernardo 34,
Madrid 8
Subject: Social Sciences
ISBN Publisher's Prefix: 84-336

Barral Editores SA*, Balmes 159,
Barcelona 8 Tel: (93) 2175773
Subjects: General Fiction, Belles Lettres,
Poetry, Art, Theatre, Paperbacks
Founded: 1964
ISBN Publisher's Prefix: 84-211

Ediciones **Bellaterra** SA*, Felipe de Paz 12,
Barcelona 28 Tel: (93) 3390511
Man Dir: Felio Riera Domenech; *Editorial:*
Jeannine Rochefort; *Sales:* Angeles Galán
Gallego
Subjects: Science & Technology, Social
Sciences
Founded: 1972
ISBN Publisher's Prefix: 84-7290

Ediciones **Betis***, Calle Bot 4 bis,
Barcelona 2 Tel: (93) 3175844
Man Dir, Editorial, Rights & Permissions:
Santiago Subirana; *Sales:* Eugenio Subirana
Subjects: Juveniles, Popular Science,
History, Philosophy, Infants
Founded: 1939
ISBN Publisher's Prefix: 84-7160

Biblioteca de Autores Cristianos de la
Editorial Católica SA, see Católica

Editorial **Biblioteca Nueva** SL, Almagro 38,
Madrid 4 Tel: (91) 4100436
Man Dir: José Ruiz-Castillo; *Sales Dir:* Paz
Casas Ruiz-Castillo
Subjects: Belles Lettres, Poetry, Biography,
History, Psychology
Founded: 1920
ISBN Publisher's Prefix: 84-7030

Editorial **Biblograf** SA, Calle Calabria 108,
Barcelona 15 Tel: (93)
2240000/2241907/2246606 Cable Add:
Biblograf
Man Dir: Ginés Sánchez Martínez
Subjects: Dictionaries, Philology
Founded: 1952
ISBN Publisher's Prefix: 84-7153

Editorial **Blume**, Calle Milanesado 21-23,
Barcelona 17 Tel: (93) 2042300/04/08
Cable Add: Ediblume Telex: 54675 Contbe
Man Dir, Editorial: Siegfried Blume; *Rights
& Permissions:* Rita Blume
Founded: 1965
Subjects: Architecture, Art, History, Politics,
Ecology, Nature Study, Gardening, Life
Sciences, books in Spanish, English and
Catalan
ISBN Publisher's Prefix: 84-7031

Hermann **Blume** Ediciones+, Calle Rosario
17, Madrid 5 Tel: (91)
2659200/2659209/2659208 Cable Add:
Blumediciones Telex: 27307 Att cod 781
Man Dir: Hermann Blume Plaza;
Production Dir: Juan Diego Pérez González;
Sales, Publicity, Promotion: Miguel Angel
San José; *Editions Coordinator and Rights:*
Louise Ciallella
Subjects: Architecture & Urbanism,
Alternative Technology, Natural Sciences,
Economics, Photography, Art (techniques &
materials), Nautical Handbooks, Sports,
Plants
Bookshop: At above address
1981: 31 titles *Founded:* 1975
ISBN Publisher's Prefix: 84-7214

Al-**Borak** SA*, Calle General Martínez
Campos, 42-Bajo, Madrid 10
Part of Grupo Editorial Guadiana (qv)

Bosch Casa Editorial SA, Calle Urgel 51 bis,
Barcelona 11 Tel: (93) 2548437
Man Dir: Agustín Bosch Domenech
Subjects: Law, Science & Technology,
Philology, General Literature
1981: 29 titles *1982:* 35 titles *Founded:* 1934
ISBN Publisher's Prefix: 84-7162

Editorial **Bruguera** SA, Camps y Fabrés 5,
Barcelona 6 Tel: (93) 2373640 Cable Add:
Brugueditor Telex: 52551
Man Dirs: Hugo Benítez, Consuelo
Bruguera; *Editorial:* Jorge Gubern, Félix
Arranz, Juan Carlos Martini, Ana Maria
Palé, Ricardo Juanco-Martí; *Sales:* Emilio
Martínez; *Production:* Guillermo Molinas
Carreño; *Rights & Permissions:* Ute Körner
de Moya
Subsidiary Companies: Editorial Bruguera
Argentina SAFIC, Argentina (qv); Editora
Bruguera do Brasil Ltda, Brazil (qv);
Distribuidora Rutas Ltda, Chile; Editorial
Bruguera Colombiana Ltda, Colombia (qv);
Editorial Bruguera Ecuatoriana SA,
Ecuador (qv); Editorial Bruguera Mexicana
SA, Mexico (qv); Editorial Bruguera
Centroamericana y Panamá SA, Panamá
(qv); Iris SA, Peru (qv); Editorial Bruguera
Venezolana SA, Venezuela (qv)
Branch Offs: Edificio Indobuilding local
1-8 y 1-13, Vía de los Poblados s/n (Barrio
Hortaleza), Madrid 33; Canarias 2-A, Bilbao
14; Puebla de Farnals 38, Valencia 11; Elda
44, Alicante; Juan M Rodríguez Correas 3-9,
Seville; Durán y Borrell 24-26, Barcelona 23
Subjects: General Fiction, Belles Lettres,
Reference, Biography, History, How-to,
Juveniles, Paperbacks
Bookshop: Librería Proa SA, Rambla de
Cataluña 72, Barcelona
Founded: 1954
ISBN Publisher's Prefix: 84-02

Editorial **Bruño**, Marqués de Mondéjar 32,
Madrid 28 Tel: (91) 2460607/06/05
Man Dir: Ermenter Ars Forner
Subjects: Secondary & Primary Textbooks,
Education, Communication
Founded: 1882
ISBN Publisher's Prefix: 84-216

Burulan, SA de Ediciones*, Avenida de
Francia 4, POB 754, San Sebastian
Tel: (93) 426220, (93) 416829 Cable Add:
Burulan Telex: 36228 Camino-E Ref
Burulan
Subjects: Encyclopaedias, Various
Publications for Children and Juveniles

C E D E L Ediciones+, Apdo 5326,
Barcelona 8 (Located at: Calle Mallorca 257,
Barcelona) Tel: (93) 2156039/2156088
Man Dir, Rights & Permissions: José-O
Avila; *Sales:* Francisco Ibañez
Subjects: Technical, Naturism
1981: 25 titles *1982:* 20 titles *Founded:* 1956
ISBN Publisher's Prefix: 84-352

Editorial **Cantabrica** SA*, Plaza Conde de
Aresti 5 - 1°, Bilbao Tel: (044) 217197
Man Dir: Rosario Fernandez Urcelay
Branch Offs: Calle Marqués de Sentemenat
55-57, Barcelona; Calle O'Connell, 43 bajo,
Madrid
Subject: Juveniles
Founded: 1960
ISBN Publisher's Prefix: 84-221

Luis de **Caralt** Editor SA+, Rosellón 246,
Barcelona 8 Tel: (93) 2156516 Cable Add:
Edinoguer Barcelona Telex: 52534
President: Emilio Ardevol; *Rights &
Permissions:* Maruchy Friart
Associate Company: Editorial Noguer SA
(qv)
Subjects: General Fiction and Non-fiction,
History, Art, Medicine, Geography,
Paperbacks
1982: 225 titles *Founded:* 1942
ISBN Publisher's Prefix: 84-217

Editorial **Castalia***, Zurbano 39, Madrid 10
Tel: (91) 4198940/4195857
Man Dir: Amparo Soler; *Sales Dir:* Federico
Ibáñez
Subjects: Literature, Criticism, Classics,
Philology
Founded: 1941
Miscellaneous: Specializes in editions of the
classics
ISBN Publisher's Prefix: 84-7039

Ediciones **Cátedra** SA+, Don Ramón de la
Cruz, Apdo 50512, Madrid Tel: (91)
4011200 Cable Add: Grupedi
Man Dir: Gustavo Domínguez; *Rights &
Permissions:* José Antonio Millán
Orders to: Grupo Editorial SA, Don Ramón
de la Cruz 67, Madrid 1
Subjects: Literature, Criticism, Humanities,
Linguistics, Art
Founded: 1974
ISBN Publisher's Prefix: 84-376

Biblioteca de Autores Cristianos de la
Editorial **Católica** SA+, Mateo Inurria 15,
Madrid 16 Tel: (91) 2592800 Cable Add:
Edica Telex: 27727
Dir: José Luis Gutiérrez García; *Sales:* Luis
Ortiz Pérez; *Publicity:* Bartolomé Parera
Galmés
Subjects: Philosophy, Religion, Theology,
Liturgy, History
Founded: 1912
ISBN Publisher's Prefixes: 84-720, 84-220

Ediciones **Ceac** SA+, Peru 164, Barcelona 20
Tel: (93) 3073004 Cable Add: Ediceac
Telex: 50564 Ceac
Man Dirs: Juan Martí, José Menal;
Advertising & Publicity Dir: J M Quesada;
Foreign Sales: M Busqué; *Foreign Rights:*
Albert Vidal
Subjects: Technical, Arts & Crafts,
Homecrafts & Domestic Science,
Psychology, Educational
1981-82: 80 titles *Founded:* 1954
ISBN Publisher's Prefix: 84-329

El **Cid** Editor SAE*, Cardenal Vives y Tutó
43 2° 3a, Barcelona 34 Tel: 2045067 Telex:
51130 Fonotx E clave 16-00591
Man Dir, Rights & Permissions: Dr
Eduardo Varela-Cid; *Editorial:* Osiris
Troiani; *Sales:* Adriana Buguña; *Production:*
José Luis Tolosa i Paredes; *Publicity:* Victor
Ramos
Parent Company: El Cid Editor SRL,
Argentina (qv)
Subsidiary Company: El Cid Editor CA,
Apdo 60010, Caracas 1060, Venezuela
Associate Companies (all in Argentina):
Ciudad Educativa SAIC, El Cid
Distribuidor SA (both at Alsina 500, 1087
Buenos Aires); La Casa de los Papeles,
Bolivar 218, 1066 Buenos Aires
Subjects: Fiction, Sociology and Social
Work, Juvenile, Economics, Geo-politics,
Research Technology, History
Bookshop: Librería del Colegio, Ciudad
Educativa SA, Buenos Aires, Argentina
Founded: 1970

Editorial **Científico Médica**, Vía
Layetana 53, Barcelona 3 Tel: (93) 3186832
Telex: 59347 E Cmb
Man Dir: Eugeniano Barrera San Martín;
Chief Editor: Dr Enrique Sierra Ruiz
Distributor: Científico Médica Dossat SA,
Plaza de Santa Ana 9, 1°, Madrid 12
Subjects: Medicine, Psychology, Veterinary
Science, Engineering, Architecture,
Technical Subjects
Founded: 1915
ISBN Publisher's Prefix: 84-224

Editorial **Cincel** SA+, Calle Alberto Aguilera
32, Madrid 15 Tel: (91) 4458862 Cable
Add: Cincel Telex: 46497 Kaci E
Man Dir: Carlos Rodriguez Alvarez;
Editorial, Rights & Permissions: José Rioja
Gomez; *Sales, Publicity:* Francisco Belloso

Cruzado; *Production:* José Martinez Alaminos
Parent Company: Editorial Kapelusz SA, Argentina (qv)
Subjects: Psychology, Textbooks, Education and educational materials
Bookshop: Libreria Cincel (at above address)
1981: 36 titles *1982:* 24 titles *Founded:* 1971
ISBN Publisher's Prefix: 84-7046

Ciudad Nueva, Andres Tamayo 4, Madrid 28
Parent Company: Citta Nuova Editrice, Italy (qv for associate companies)

Alberto **Corazón** Editor*, Roble 22, Madrid 15 Tel: (91) 2704378
Man Dir: Alberto Corazón; *Sales Dir:* José Miguel García
Subjects: Literature, History, Philosophy, Poetry, Social Sciences, University Textbooks
Founded: 1969
ISBN Publisher's Prefix: 84-7053

Ediciones **Cristiandad***, Huesca 30, Madrid 20 Tel: (91) 2701636
Subjects: Religion, History
ISBN Publisher's Prefix: 84-7057

Editorial **Critica** SA, Calle de la Cruz 58 - 1° 1a, Barcelona 34 Tel: 2049311
Man Dir: Gonzalo Pontón
Parent Company: Ediciones Grijalbo SA (qv)
Subjects: Social Sciences, Politics, Current Affairs, Marxism, Philosophy
Founded: 1976
ISBN Publisher's Prefix: 84-7423

Ediciones **Cultura** Hispánica, Ave de los Reyes Católicos 4, Madrid 3 Tel: (91) 2440600 (243, 283)
Publishing Dir: Cesar Olmos
Subjects: Literature, Poetry, Essays, Theatre, Biography, History, Art, Economics, Law, Philology, Social Science
ISBN Publisher's Prefix: 84-7232

Editorial **D O P E S A** (Documentacion Periodistica SA)*, Cardenal Reig s/n, Edificio Grupo Mundo, Barcelona 28 Tel: (93) 334200
Man Dir: Juan Agut; *Editorial:* Mauricio Waquez; *Sales, Publicity:* Pablo Bordona BA; *Production:* Manuel Gallego; *Rights & Permissions:* José Planas
Subjects: General
Bookshop: Libreria Grop, Ave Infanta Carlota 37, Barcelona 15
Founded: 1969
ISBN Publisher's Prefix: 84-7235

Ediciones **Daimon** — Manuel Tamayo*, Provenza 284, Barcelona 8 Cable Add: Edidaimón Telex: 97648 kyzt-6
Subjects: Art, History, How-to, Reference, Medicine, Cinematography, Photography, Sexology, Philosophy, Science, Psychology, Music
ISBN Publisher's Prefix: 84-231

Ediciones **Danae** SA, Paseo de Gracia 24-26, Barcelona 7 Tel: 3174508/3010182
Chairman: José Lluis Monreal; *General Manager:* José Maria Martí Costa; *Sales:* Luis López Cabañas; *Production, Rights & Permissions:* Carlos Gispert
Subjects: Belles Lettres, History, Geography, Social Science, Art, Religion, Technical, Encyclopaedias, Juveniles, General Culture
Founded: 1963
ISBN Publisher's Prefix: 84-7060

Editorial **De Vecchi** SA, Balmes 247, Barcelona 6 Tel: (93) 2171854/2171858
Cable Add: Deveditor Telex: 51042 Deve E
Man Dir: Giovanni de Vecchi
Subjects: How-to and Practical Books generally
Founded: 1967
ISBN Publisher's Prefix: 84-315

Debate SA, Alonso Cano 66, Madrid 3 Tel: 2341040 Telex: 45586
Man Dir: Angel Lucia Aguirre; *Editorial:* Francisco Pabon Torres
Subjects: Children's, Fiction, Feminism, Large-print books
1981: 25 titles *1982:* 30 titles *Founded:* 1977
ISBN Publisher's Prefix: 84-7444

Editorial de **Derecho Financiero**, an imprint of EDERSA (qv)

Editorial Revista de **Derecho Privado**, an imprint of EDERSA (qv)

Ediciones **Destino** SA, Consejo de Ciento 425, Barcelona 9 Tel: (93) 2462305
President: José Vergés; *Administration:* Andreu Teixidor
Subjects: General Fiction, Art Books, History, Children's
Bookshop: Libreria Ancora y Delfin (qv under Major Booksellers)
Founded: 1942
ISBN Publisher's Prefix: 84-233

Centro de **Difusión** del Libro, see CEDEL Ediciones

Dilagro SA*, Editorial-Libreria, General Britos 1, Lérida Tel: 233480
Man Dir: Jorge Marimón; *Sales Dir:* Antonio Miñano
Subjects: Agriculture, History and Customs of the region of Lérida
Bookshops: Libreria Ténica (at above address); Libreria Universitaria, Ave Cataluña 7, Lérida
ISBN Publisher's Prefix: 84-7234

Editorial **Dossat** SA, Plaza de Santa Ana 9, Madrid 12 Tel: (91) 4298568 Telex: 42572 Doat
Man Dir: Eugeniano Barrera San Martín
Branch Off: Via Layetana 53, Barcelona 3
Subjects: Medicine, Engineering, General Scientific, University Textbooks
ISBN Publisher's Prefix: 84-237

Ediciones **Doyma** SA, Travesera de Gracia 17-21, Barcelona 21 Tel: 2000711 Telex: 51964 Ink E
Man Dir: José Antonio Dotu Roteta; *Editorial, Rights & Permissions:* Esperanza Pous Arxe; *Sales:* Daniel Verges Renau; *Publicity:* Lorenzo Matas Muñoz
Subsidiary Companies: AP (Americana de Publicaciones), Cerrito 512, Buenos Aires, Argentina; Publicaciones Tecnicas Mediterraneo, Boldos 2369, Santiago, Chile; Publicaciones Americanas de México, Miguel A Laurent 630, México DF, Mexico
Subject: Medicine
1981: 4 titles *1982:* 11 titles *Founded:* 1971
ISBN Publisher's Prefix: 84-85285

Ediciones **Druida** SA+, Lluis Millet 59, Esplugues de Llobregat (Barcelona) Tel: 3721261
Man Dir: Miguel Pelucer Esteban; *Rights & Permissions:* Susana P Esteban
Subject: Children's
Founded: 1982
ISBN Publisher's Prefix: 84-860

Durvan SA de Ediciones, Colón de Larreátegui 13, Bilbao 1
President: Manuel Marín Correa; *Man Dir:* Lorenzo Portillo Sisniega
Subject: Encyclopaedias
Founded: 1960
ISBN Publisher's Prefix: 84-85001

E D E R S A (Editoriales de Derecho Reunidas SA)*, Caracas 21, Apdo 4032, Madrid 4 Tel: (91) 4101862/4199623 Cable Add: Revipriv
Man Dir: Antonio Alvarez de Morales
Imprints: Ediciones Pegaso, Editorial de Derecho Financiero, Editorial Revista de Derecho Privado
Subjects: Biography, History, Philosophy, Social Science, Law, Technical, University Textbooks
Founded: 1900
ISBN Publisher's Prefix: 84-7130

E D H A S A (Editora y Distribuidora Hispano-Americana SA), Diagonal 521 - 2°, Barcelona 29 Tel: (93) 2395104
Man Dir: Jaime Rodrigué
Associate Company: Editorial Sudamericana SA, Argentina (qv)
Subjects: Literature, History, Essays
ISBN Publisher's Prefix: 84-350

E U N S A (Ediciones Universidad de Navarra SA)+, POB 396, Pamplona (Located at: Plaza de los Sauces, 1 y 2 Barañain, Pamplona) Tel: (948) 256850 Cable Add: EUNSA Pamplona Telex: 37917 Unav E
Man Dir: Gerardo Izco; *Assistant Man Dir:* Pilar Otano; *Editorial:* Francisco Salvadó; *Sales:* Robert Kimball; *Production:* Luis María Echeverría; *Publicity:* Tomás C Lizarrondo; *Rights & Permissions:* Eugenia Puyales
Imprint: Biblioteca 'NT' (number of paperback series covering the Arts and Sciences, Current Affairs, Religion and Philosophy etc)
Subjects: Architecture, Business Administration, Economics, Education, History, Journalism, Law, Canon Law, Language and Literature, Medicine, Biology, Engineering, Nursing, Philosophy, Religion, Theology, Bibliography, Librarianship, Encyclopaedias, Periodicals
1981: 80 titles *1982:* 67 titles *Founded:* 1967
ISBN Publisher's Prefix: 84-313

Edaf Ediciones y Distribuciones SA, Jorge Juan 30, Madrid 1 Tel: (91) 4358260
President: Luciano Fossati; *Publicity:* Gerardo Fossati Demichelis
Branch Offs: Ediciones Antonio Fossati SACI, Calle Chile 2222, Buenos Aires, Argentina; Soriamex SA, Calle Rio Amazonas 44 2°, México 5, Mexico
Bookshop: Libreria Edaf, Jorge Juan 30, Madrid 1
Subjects: History, Philosophy, Juveniles, Reference, Textbooks, Natural Medicine, Sports
ISBN Publisher's Prefix: 84-7166

Edica SA, Calle Mateo Inurria 15, Apdo 466, Madrid 16 Tel: (91) 2592800 Cable Add: Edica Telex: 27727
Dir: Dr José Luis Gutierrez Garcia; *Sales:* Luis Ortiz Pérez; *Publicity:* Bartolomé Parera Galmés
Subjects: Theology, Asceticism, Mysticism, History, Philosophy, Hagiography, Pocket Editions
1981: 40 titles *1982:* 49 titles

Ediciones **Iberoamericanas** SA (EISA)*, Oñate 15, Madrid 20 Tel: (91) 2795804 Cable Add: Asepe
Dir: Rafael Ordoñez Miranda
Subjects: Social Sciences, Medicine, Biography, Religion, Psychology, Law, others
Founded: 1949
ISBN Publisher's Prefix: 84-7084

Edigraf, Editorial Vilcar y Gráficas Hamburg SA, Tamarit 130, Barcelona 15 Tel: (05) 3255550
Man Dir: Francisco Vilar
Subject: Juveniles
ISBN Publisher's Prefix: 84-7066

Editora Nacional+, Calle Torregalindo 10, Madrid 16 Tel: (91) 2508600
Dir: Alberto de la Puente O'Connor
Subjects: Poetry, History, Art, Essays, Literature, Law
Founded: 1937
ISBN Publisher's Prefix: 84-276

Ediciones **Elfos**, Milanesado 21-23 1a, Barcelona 17 Tel: 2042300/8/4 Telex: 54675 contb E
Man Dir: Rita Schnitzer
Subjects: Handicrafts, Nature Study, Ecology
Founded: 1980
ISBN Publisher's Prefix: 84-85791

Emograph, an imprint of Afha Internacional SA (qv)

Ediciones **Encuentro** SA+, Calle Alcalá 117 - 6° izda, Madrid 9 Tel: 4359500/4359039
Man Dir: José Miguel Oriol; *Editorial, Rights & Permissions:* Carmina Salgado; *Sales:* Miguel Rovira; *Production:* Norberto Moreno; *Publicity:* Fernando Sánchez
Subjects: Art, Philosophy, History, Economics, Politics, Theology, Education, Anthropology, Literature, Sociology, Facsimiles
1981: 17 titles *1982:* 20 titles *Founded:* 1979
ISBN Publisher's Prefix: 84-7490

Editorial **Espasa-Calpe** SA, Apdo 547, Madrid 34 (Located at: Carretera de Irún, km 12,200 (variante de Fuencarral))
Tel: (91) 7343800 Cable Add: Espacalpe
Man Dir: Fermín Vargas Lázaro
Branch Offs: Espasa-Calpe SA, Diputación 251, Barcelona 7; Espasa-Calpe SA, Alameda de Recalde 34, Bilbao 9 (both in Spain); Espasa-Calpe Argentina SA, Argentina (qv); Espasa-Calpe Mexicana SA, Mexico (qv); Espasa-Calpe Ecuatoriana CA, Roca, 830 y 9 de Octubre, Quito, Ecuador; Espasa-Calpe Colombiana Ltda, Carrera 7A núm 16-75, 5°, Apdo 8924, Bogota DE, Colombia
Subjects: General Fiction, Belles Lettres, Biography, History, How-to, Music, Art, Philosophy, Reference, Religion, Juveniles, Paperbacks, Medicine, Psychology, Law, Technical, University Textbooks
Bookshops: Casa del Libro Espasa-Calpe SA (qv under Major Booksellers)
Founded: 1925
ISBN Publisher's Prefix: 84-239

Editorial **Espaxs** SA*, Calle Rosellón 132, Barcelona 36 Tel: (93) 2530706 Cable Add: Editespaxs
Subject: Medicine
Bookshops: Librería Espaxs (at above address) and Calle Fernando el Católico 57, Zaragoza; Calle Zaragoza 5, Cadiz
ISBN Publisher's Prefix: 84-7179

Editorial **Everest** SA, Apdo 339, León (Located at: Carretera León-Coruña, Km 5 León) Tel: (987) 235904 Cable Add: Everest León Telex: 89916
Man Dir: José Antonio López Martínez; *Publications Dir:* Adrián Larrosa
Subsidiary Company: Everest Libros SA (at above address)
Subjects: Belles Lettres, History, How-to, Juveniles, Engineering, Technical, Secondary & Primary Textbooks, Tourist Guides, Paperbacks, Educational Materials
Founded: 1958
ISBN Publisher's Prefix: 84-241

Editorial **Fher** SA+, Apdo 362, Bilbao 2 (Located at: Villabaso 9, Bilbao) Tel: (044) 4318000 Cable Add: Gerfu Telex: 32195
Man Dir: Luis Irazabal; *Editorial:* Ignacio Aguirre Aguirre
Subject: Juveniles
Founded: 1941
ISBN Publisher's Prefix: 84-243

Fondo de Cultura Económica, Apdo 582, Madrid 33 (Located at: Vía de los Poblados s/n, Edificio Indubuilding 4-15, Madrid)
Tel: 7632800 Cable Add: Foraca
Man Dir: Ezequiel Mendez Vidal
Parent Company: Fondo de Cultura Económica, Mexico (qv)
Subjects: Economics, Sociology, History, Philosophy, Politics, Law, Anthropology, Psychology and Psychoanalysis, Science and Technology, Language, Literary Studies
Bookshop: Librería Mexico, Fernando el Católico 86, Madrid 15
1981: 9 titles *1982:* 4 titles *Founded:* 1934
ISBN Publisher's Prefix: 84-375

Editorial **Fontamara** SA, Calle Entenza 116 - 3° 3a, Barcelona 15 Tel: 3251683
Man Dir, Editorial: Emilio Olcina; *Sales:* Manuel Muñoz; *Production, Rights & Permissions:* Luisa Sañé
Subjects: Fiction, Social and Political Science, Humanities
1981: 48 titles *1982:* 64 titles *Founded:* 1973
ISBN Publisher's Prefix: 84-7367

Editorial **Fontanella** SA*, Escorial 50, Barcelona 24 Tel: (93) 2131731
Man Dir: F Fortuny Comaposada; *Permissions:* C Lopez
Subjects: Social and Political Science, Education, Psychology, Sexology, Religion, Philosophy, History, Economy, Biography
Founded: 1962
ISBN Publisher's Prefix: 84-244

Heraclio **Fournier** SA, Heraclio Fournier 19, POB 94, Vitoria Tel: 251100 Cable Add: Fournier Telex: 35510
Subjects: High-quality Illustrated Books (Art, History, Science, General Knowledge)

Fragua Editorial, Gaztambide 77 y Andres Mellado 64, Madrid 15 Tel: (91) 2442430/4497315/2431595
Man Dir: Mariano Muñoz Alonso
Subjects: Linguistics, Philosophy, Communications, Political Science
Bookshops: Librería Augustinus (qv under Major Booksellers), and at above address
Founded: 1971
ISBN Publisher's Prefix: 84-7074

Editorial **Fundamentos**+, Caracas 15, Madrid 4 Tel: (91) 4199619/4195584
Man Dir: Juan Serrarler Ibañez; *Permissions:* Cristina Vizcaino
Subjects: Social Sciences, Philosophy, Psychology, Psychiatry, Sexology, History, Theatre, Literature, Fiction, Cinema, Low-priced Paperbacks
1983: 365 titles *Founded:* 1970
ISBN Publisher's Prefix: 84-245

Ediciones **Gaisa** SL, now Mas Ivars Editores SL (qv)

La **Galera** SA Editorial+, Ronda del Guinardó 38, Barcelona 25 Tel: (93) 2557991/2360203
Man Dir: Romà Dòria Forcada
Subjects: Pre-School and Infant Teaching texts, Children's Books, Education
1981: 59 titles *1982:* 55 titles *Founded:* 1963
ISBN Publisher's Prefix: 84-246

Ediciones **Garriga** SA, París 143, Barcelona 36 Tel: (93) 2306825/2393547
Man Dir: Xavier Garriga Jové
Subjects: Art, Archaeology, Ancient History, Religion, Technical (Nautical)
Founded: 1957
ISBN Publisher's Prefix: 84-7079

Editorial **Gedisa** SA, Muntaner 460, entresuelo 1a, Barcelona 6 Tel: (93) 2016000 Telex: 51130 clave 16-00147
Man Dir, Sales: Antonio Escobar; *Production:* Elisa Rando; *Publicity:* Alfredo Landman; *Rights & Permissions:* Enrique Lynch
Subjects: Sexuality, Feminism, Psychoanalysis, Education, Contemporary Thought, Sociology, Linguistics
1981: 32 titles *1982:* 36 titles *Founded:* 1977
ISBN Publisher's Prefix: 84-7432

Geocolor SA*, Travesera de Gracia 15 3°-2°, Barcelona 21 Tel: 2009489
Man Dir, Editorial: Enric Gras P; *Sales:* Matt Areny; *Production:* Lidia Beltran; *Publicity:* Xavier Gras S
Subjects: Tourism, Art, Archaeology, Biography, Cookery, Magic
Founded: 1977
ISBN Publisher's Prefix: 84-7424

Editorial Gustavo **Gili** SA, Apdo 35149, Barcelona 29 (Located at: Rosellón 87-89, Barcelona) Tel: (93) 2591400 Cable Add: Gusto Barcelona Telex: 97196 Gili E
Man Dir: Gustavo Gili; *Sales:* Ramón Pascual; *Production:* Andres Martinez; *Foreign Rights:* Helma Hartmann
Associate Companies: Ediciones G Gili SA, Argentina (qv); Editorial Gustavo Gili Ltda, Chile (qv); Editora Gustavo Gili Ltda, Diagonal 45, 16B-11, Bogotá, Colombia; Editorial Gustavo Gili de México SA, Mexico (qv); Ediciones G Gili SA, Amores, 2027 Col del Valle Delegación B Juárez, 03100 México DF, Mexico
Branch Off: Alcántara 21, Madrid 6
Subjects: Architecture, Art, Design, Communication and Technology in general
Founded: 1902
ISBN Publisher's Prefix: 84-252

Editorial **Gredos** SA*, Sánchez Pacheco 81, Apdo 2076, Madrid 2 Tel: (91) 4157408/4156836
Man Dirs: Mr Calonge, Mr Escolar, Mr Yebra, Mr Oliveira
Subjects: Philology, Criticism, Classical Literature, Literary History, Dictionaries, Philosophy, Psychology, Economics, Fiction
Founded: 1944
ISBN Publisher's Prefix: 84-249

Ediciones **Grijalbo** SA, Calle Déu i Mata 98, Barcelona 29 Tel: 3223753 Cable Add: Edigrijalbo Telex: 53940 egri e
President: Juan Grijalbo; *General Manager:* José M Vives
Subsidiary Companies and Branch Offs: Ediciones Junior (at above address); Editorial Critica SA (qv); Grijalbo SA, Argentina (qv); Grijalbo Boliviana Ltda, Bolivia (qv); Grijalbo y Cía Ltda, Chile (qv); Distribuidora Exclusiva Grijalbo SA, Colombia; Grijalbo Ecuatoriana Ltda, Ecuador (qv); Editorial Grijalbo SA, Mexico (qv); Grijalbo Centroamericana y Panamá SA, Panama (qv); Distribuidora exclusivo Grijalbo SA, Peru (qv); Grijalbo Puerto Rico Inc, Puerto Rico (qv); Grijalbo Editor, Uruguay (qv); Grijalbo SA, Venezuela (qv)
Subjects: General Fiction & Non-fiction, Biography, Philosophy, History, Politics, Religion, Psychology, Technology, Art, Social Science, Reference Works
1981: 56 titles *Founded:* 1942
ISBN Publisher's Prefix: 84-253

Artes Gráficas **Grijelmo** SA, Uribitarte 4, Bilbao 1 Tel: (94) 4239628 Telex: 31209 aggc e
Man Dir, Rights & Permissions: Juan Carlos Grijelmo Mintegni; *Editorial:* Amancio Gerardo Grijelmo Ribechini; *Sales:* Juan Santiago Grijelmo Ribechini
Subsidiary Companies: Asuri de Edicions; Ediciones Deusto SA; IBC de Ediciones; Urmo SA de Ediciones (qv); Ediciones Moretón SA (qv)
Branch Offs: Barcelona, Madrid
Subject: Art

SPAIN 341

Grupo Editorial **Guadiana** SA*, Calle General Martínez Campos 42-Bajo, Madrid 10 Cable Add: Guadisa
Man Dir: Gabriel Camuñas
Subjects: Social Science, History, Business Administration
Founded: 1967
Miscellaneous: Firm is a holding company of Guadiana de Publicaciones SA, Al-Borak SA and Ediciones 99 SA
ISBN Publisher's Prefix: 84-251

Editorial **Herder** SA, Provenza 388, Barcelona 25 Tel: (93) 2577700 Cable Add: Herder Telex: 54120 Hegr E
Man Dir: Antonio Valtl Friedl
Associate Companies: Verlag Herder & Co, Austria (qv); Verlag Herder GmbH & Co KG, Federal Republic of Germany (qv); Herder und Herder GmbH, Federal Republic of Germany (qv); Verlag AG Ploetz GmbH & Co KG, Federal Republic of Germany (qv); Herder AG, Switzerland (qv)
Branch Offs: Hesperia SA Editorial y Librería, Ave Callao 565, Buenos Aires, Argentina; Herder Editorial y Librería, Calle 12, No 6/89, Apdo Aereo 6855, Bogotá, Colombia
Subjects: Philosophy, Theology, Religion, Medicine, Pedagogy, Psychology, Social Science, Reference Works, Economics, Languages, University & Secondary Textbooks, Atlases
Bookshop: Librería Herder (qv under Major Booksellers)
1982: 1,050 titles *Founded:* 1943
ISBN Publisher's Prefix: 84-254

Ediciones **Hiperión** SL+, Apdo 33010, Madrid 1 (Located at: Salustiano Olózaga 14, Madrid) Tel: 4010234/4013007
Man Dir, Editorial: Jesus Munárriz Peralta; *Sales:* Maite Merodio Benito
Subjects: Poetry, Novels, Essays, History, Philosophy
Bookshop: Librería Hiperion (at above address)
1981: 27 titles *1982:* 30 titles *Founded:* 1976
ISBN Publisher's Prefix: 84-7517

Editorial **Hispano Europea**+, Bori y Fontestá 6, Barcelona 21 Tel: (93) 2013709/2018500
Man Dir, Editorial, Publicity: J Prat Ballester; *Sales:* J Prat Rosal
Production: J Madueño Machado
Subjects: Business Management, Sports, Social Science, Industrial Processes, General Technology, Photography
Founded: 1956
ISBN Publisher's Prefix: 84-255

Hogar del Libro — Nova Terra, Calle Bergara 3-2°, Barcelona 2
Bookshop: Hogar del Libro (qv under Major Booksellers)
Founded: 1945
Miscellaneous: Group of companies comprising one publisher, one major distributor and eight bookshops
ISBN Publisher's Prefix: 84-7279

Hrvatska Revija, Apdo 14030, Barcelona 17 (Located at: San Juan Bosco 62, Barcelona) Tel: 2037408
Man Dir, Editorial: Vinko Nikolić
Subjects: Politics, History, Literature, Sociology, Memoirs; Periodical — *Hrvatska Revija* (in Croatian)
Founded: 1951
ISBN Publisher's Prefix: 84-399

Publicaciones **I C C E***, Calle Eraso 3, Madrid 28 Tel: (91) 2557200
Man Dir: F Cubells
Subjects: Education, Psychology Tests, History, Religion, Social Sciences
Founded: 1970
ISBN Publisher's Prefix: 84-7278

Ibérico Europea de Ediciones SA*, Serrano 44-3°, Madrid 1 Tel: (91) 2253527/2261578/2754492
Subjects: Biography, How-to, Music, Art, Social Science, Business Management
Founded: 1966
ISBN Publisher's Prefix: 84-256

Iberlibros — Unidad de Exportación*, Nuñez de Balboa 31, Madrid 1 Tel: (91) 2764391
Publisher: Alfonso Mangada Sans
Subjects: Human Sciences, Religion, Technical, School Texts, Dictionaries

Icaria Editorial SA, Apdo 9509, Barcelona 6 (Located at: Calle de la Torre 14, Barcelona) Tel: 2177686
Man Dir: Maria Rodriguez Bayraguet; *Editorial:* Rafael Argulloz; *Production:* Angela Ackermann
Subjects: Literature, Feminism
1981: 10 titles *1982:* 9 titles *Founded:* 1975
ISBN Publisher's Prefix: 84-7426

Editorial **Incafo** SA*, Castello 59, Apdo 202, Madrid 1 Tel: (226) 4313460 Telex: 42459 icf e
Man Dir, Editorial: Luis Blas Aritio; *Production:* Javier Echevarri; *Rights & Permissions:* Margarita Méndez de Vigo
Subjects: Natural History, Art, Ecology and Exploration in Spain and South America (including some books in English), Periodical
Book Club: Club del Libro de la Naturaleza
Founded: 1973
ISBN Publisher's Prefix: 84-85389

Editorial **Index** (Tormes, SL), Comandante Zorita 13-6°, Madrid 20 Tel: 2349150/2544980
Man Dir: R L Ortueta
Subjects: Science, Technology, Administration
1981: 300 titles *Founded:* 1965
ISBN Publisher's Prefix: 84-7087

Instituto de Estudios de Administración Local, Publicaciones*, Santa Engracia 7, Madrid 10
Dir: Gregorio Burgueño Alvarez
Subjects: Public Administration, Urbanism, City Planning, Periodicals
ISBN Publisher's Prefix: 84-7088

Instituto de Estudios Politicos*, Plaza Marina Española 8, Madrid 13 Tel: (91) 2415000, 2418300/09
Distributor: LESPO, Calle Arriza 16
Subjects: Law, Politics, History, Social Science, Philosophy
Founded: 1939
ISBN Publisher's Prefix: 84-259

Ediciones **Instituto Pontificio** San Pío X*, Ave Cardenal Herrera Oria 242, Apdo 54027, Madrid 35 Tel: (91) 7399151
Man Dir: Eduardo Malvido Miguel; *Editorial:* Serafin Tapia Nevado; *Sales:* José Luis Peralta García; *Production:* Rafael Pascual
Subjects: Theology, Pedagogy, Psychology, Religion
Bookshop: Librería La Salle, Bocángel 15, Madrid 28
Founded: 1964
ISBN Publisher's Prefix: 84-7221

Insula, Librería, Ediciones y Publicaciones SA*, Benito Gutiérrez 26, Madrid 8 Tel: (91) 2435415
Man Dir: Enrique Canito Barrera; *Publicity:* A Muñoz Canito
Subjects: Fiction, Poetry, Literary Studies, Criticism, Essays
Bookshop: At above address
1981: 40 titles *Founded:* 1944
ISBN Publisher's Prefix: 84-7185

Ediciones **Istmo**+, Colombia 18, Madrid 16 Tel: (91) 4574101/4582582
Man Dir: José Antonio Llardent Viciana; *Sales Dir:* Deogracias González; *Publicity Dir:* Leoncio Martín
Subjects: History, Reference, Social Science, Philosophy, Literature, University Texts
Founded: 1969
ISBN Publishers Prefix: 84-7090

Taller Ediciones **J B**, see Taller

Editorial **Jims** SA, Calle Regás 7-9, Barcelona 6 Tel: (93) 2188800 Cable Add: Editojims
Man Dir, Editorial, Publicity: Antonio Jimenez Sánchez; *Sales:* Teresa Jimenez Sayo; *Production:* Luis Jimenez Sayo
Subject: Medicine
1981: 18 titles *1982:* 13 titles *Founded:* 1956
ISBN Publisher's Prefix: 84-7092

Ediciones **Jover** SA, San Pedro Mártir 18, Barcelona 12 Tel: (93) 2185662/2185408/2185216 Cable Add: Edijover
Man Dir: Juan Jover Biosca; *Editorial:* Montserrat Jover López; *Production:* Antonio Pérez Sánchez
Subjects: Educational Materials
1981-82: 35 titles *Founded:* 1946
ISBN Publisher's Prefix: 84-7093

Editorial **Juventud** SA, Provenza 101, Apdo 3, Barcelona 29 Tel: (93) 2392000/3212100/2398383 Cable Add: Juventud
Man Dir: Pablo Zendrera
Subsidiary Companies: Editorial Juventud Argentina (qv); Editorial Juventud Ltda, Colombia (qv)
Subjects: General, Fiction, Biography, History, How-to, Music, Art, Nautical, Travel, Pocketbooks, Textbooks, Reference, Juveniles, Paperbacks
1981: 231 titles *1982:* 260 titles *Founded:* 1923
ISBN Publisher's Prefix: 84-261

Editorial **Kairos** SA, Numancia 110, Barcelona 29 Tel: (93) 2303746/2505166
Man Dir: Salvador Pániker; *Editorial, Rights & Permissions, Sales:* Agustín Pániker; *Production, Publicity:* Pilar Tomás
Subjects: Philosophy, Religion, Psychology, Reference, General and Social Science
1981: 10 titles *Founded:* 1966
ISBN Publisher's Prefix: 84-7245

L E D A (Las Ediciones de Arte)+, Riera San Miguel 37, Barcelona 6 Tel: (93) 2379389
Man Dir: Daniel Basilio Bonet
Subjects: Art and Craft techniques, Technical drawing
1981: 12 titles *1982:* 11 titles *Founded:* 1942
ISBN Publisher's Prefix: 84-7095

Editorial **Labor** SA, Calabria 235-239, Barcelona 29 Tel: (93) 3220551 Cable Add: Edilabor Telex: (51130) 1600091
Man Dir: Francisco Gracia Guillen
Branch Offs: Editorial Labor Argentina SA, Argentina (qv); Editorial Labor Colombiana Ltda, Colombia (qv); Editorial Labor del Ecuador SA, Ecuador (qv); Editorial Mexicana SRL, Mexico (qv); Editorial Labor de Venezuela SA, Venezuela (qv)
Subjects: Science and Technology, Medicine, Engineering, Encyclopaedias, Dictionaries, Humanities, History, Art, Business Management, Juveniles, University Textbooks
Founded: 1915
ISBN Publisher's Prefixes: 84-335 (Labor), 84-250 (Ediciones Guadarrama)

Editorial **Laia** SA, Calle Constitución 18-20, Barcelona 14 Tel: (93) 3328408
Man Dir: Benito Milla Navarro; *Executive*

Manager: Josep Verdura Tenas; *Editorial:* Ignasi Riera Gassiot; *Sales:* Frederic Pagès; *Production:* Montserrat Corral; *Publicity:* Mercè Guillén; *Rights & Permissions:* Pilar Esteve
Orders to: Itaca, SA Distribuciones Editoriales, Lopez de Hoyos 141 – 5°, Madrid 2
Subjects: General Non-fiction, Social Sciences, Politics, Literature, Essays, Psychology, Pedagogy
Founded: 1972
ISBN Publisher's Prefix: 84-7222

Editorial **Linosa-Linomonograph** SA*, Calle Riera de San Miguel 9, Barcelona 6 Tel: (93) 2285504/03/02
Man Dir: José Chimenos Reig; *Sales Dir:* José Antonio Chimenos Calderon; *Publicity Dir:* María Mercedes Chimenos Calderon; *Advertising Dir:* Elena Isabel Gil Fornas
Subjects: Fiction, Literature, History, How-to, Reference, Social Science, Juveniles
Founded: 1968
ISBN Publisher's Prefix: 84-7097

Editorial **Lumen** SA, Ramón Miquel y Planas 10, Barcelona 34 Tel: (93) 2043496/2042139
Man Dir: Esther Tusquets
Subjects: General Fiction, Belles Lettres, Biography, History, Art, Juveniles, Social Science, Paperbacks
Founded: 1939
ISBN Publisher's Prefix: 84-264

McGraw-Hill de España SA, Calle Santa Beatriz 4, Madrid 18 Tel: 4338777/78/79 Telex: 42710 Fonotx E clave (and key) 4200679
Man Dir: Eduardo Jimenez Ferry; *Editorial:* Antonio Garcia-Maroto; *Sales:* José Maria Garcia Acebes
Parent Company: McGraw-Hill International Book Co, 1221 Ave of the Americas, New York, NY 10020, USA
Associate Companies: Editora McGraw-Hill do Brasil Ltda, Brazil (qv); Editorial McGraw-Hill Latinoamericana SA, Colombia (qv); Libros McGraw-Hill de Mexico SA de CV, Mexico (qv); Editorial McGraw-Hill Latinoamericana SA, Panama (qv); Editora McGraw-Hill do Portugal Ltda, Portugal (qv); Editorial McGraw-Hill Latinoamericana SA, Puerto Rico (qv); McGraw-Hill Book Co (UK) Ltd, UK (qv)
Subjects: Scientific, Technical
Founded: 1973

Editorial **Magisterio** Español SA, Calle de Quevedo 1, Madrid 14 Tel: (91) 4292211 Cable Add: Magisterio Telex: 44259 em e
Man Dir: Manuel Méndez Encina; *Rights & Permissions:* María del Carmen Núñez Amador
Subjects: Education, Fiction, Essays, Philosophy, Pedagogy
Bookshop: Calle Cervantes 18, Madrid 14; Calle Ecuador 3, Barcelona 29
Founded: 1866
ISBN Publisher's Prefix: 84-265

Editorial **Marbán***, Joaquin Maria Lopez 72, Madrid 15 Tel: (91) 2433767/2444673
Man Dir, Editorial: José Marban Gonzalez; *Sales, Production, Publicity:* José M Marban Corral
Subjects: Medicine, Physiology
Founded: 1949
ISBN Publisher's Prefix: 84-7101

Marcombo SA de Boixareu Editores, Gran Via de les Corts Catalanes 594, Barcelona 7 Tel: (93) 3180079
Dir: Josep María Boixareu Vilaplana; *President:* José María Boixareu Ginesta; *Sales:* Juan Plans Comas; *Production:* José Costa Ardiaca; *Publicity:* José Romero González
Subsidiary Company: Boixareu Editores SA (at above address)
Branch Off: Marcombo-Boixareu Editores, Plaza de la Villa 1, Madrid 12
Subjects: Technology, Science, Automation, Economics, Accounting, How-to, University and Secondary Textbooks, Electronics, Mathematics
Bookshop: Librería Hispano Americana (qv under Major Booksellers)
1981: 25 titles *1982:* 36 titles *Founded:* 1949
ISBN Publisher's Prefix: 84-267

Editorial **Marfil** SA*, Plaza de Emilio Sala 3, Alcoy Tel: 541746/540233 Cable Add: Marfil
Sales: Rafael Ortiz Botí
Parent Company: Papeleras Reunidas SA
Subjects: Secondary & Primary Textbooks
Founded: 1947
ISBN Publisher's Prefix: 84-268

Editorial **Marin** SA, Calle Nicaragua 85-95, Barcelona 29 Tel: (93) 3216800 Cable Add: Marinedi Telex: 97065 Mlm E
Man Dirs: Manuel Marin Correa, Manuel Marin Bruna; *Editorial, Rights & Permissions:* Manuel Marin Correa; *Sales:* Manuel Marin Bruna
Subsidiary Companies: Artel SA; Eduvision SA
Branch Offs: Editorial Marin Argentina Srl, Ave Belgrano 3715, 1210 Buenos Aires, Argentina; Distribuidora Marin Colombiana Ltda, Carrera 15 no 32-41, Bogotá DE, Colombia; Editorial Marin SA, Anaxágoras 1400, Colonia Santa Cruz Atoyac, 03310 México DF, México; Marin Puerto Rico Inc, San Rafael 1400, Santurce, PR 00909, Puerto Rico
Subjects: Art Books, Reference, Medicine, Non-fiction, Encyclopaedias, Children's Books
Founded: 1900
ISBN Publisher's Prefix: 84-7102

Ediciones **Marova** SL+, Enrique Jardiel Poncela 4 – 4°, Madrid 16 Tel: (91) 2508762/2509653
Man Dir: Germán Alonso Fernández; *Manager:* Manuel Sobrado Royo; *Publicity & Advertising Manager:* Mariano Moreno
Subjects: Religion, Psychology, Education
Founded: 1956
ISBN Publisher's Prefix: 84-269

Marsiega Editorial SA, E Jardiel Poncela 4, Madrid 16 Tel: (91) 2505310
Parent Company: Promoción Popular Cristiana (qv under PPC)
Subject: Education
1981: 71 titles *1982:* 90 titles
ISBN Publisher's Prefix: 84-7103

Ediciones **Martínez** Roca SA+, Ave José Antonio 774, 7a planta, Barcelona 13 Tel: (93) 2251576 Telex: 97278 mrrm e
Man Dirs: Francisco Martínez Roca, Manuel Martínez Roca; *Sales:* Fernando Calvo; *Production:* Sergi Puyol; *Rights & Permissions:* Joaquim Guzmán
Branch Off: Ediciones Roca SA, General Francisco Murguía 7, Col Hipodromo de la Condesa, Mexico 06170 DF
Subjects: General Fiction & Non-fiction, Science & Technology, Human & Social Sciences, Chess, Occult Sciences, Science Fiction
1981: 73 titles *1982:* 70 titles *Founded:* 1965
ISBN Publisher's Prefix: 84-270

Mas Ivars Editores SL*, Gran Via Marques del Turia 64, Valencia Tel: (96) 3339321/3333976 Cable Add: Mas Ivars
Man Dir: Miguel Mas Ivars
Subjects: Juveniles, Encyclopaedias, Multi-volume Collections
Founded: 1960
ISBN Publisher's Prefix: 84-7077

Masson SA*, Balmes 151, Barcelona 8 Tel: (93) 2179954 Cable Add: Massonsa Telex: 54327 tmbn
Man Dir: Patrick Martin
Associate Companies: Editora Masson do Brasil Ltda, Brazil (qv); Masson Editeur, France (qv)
Subjects: Medicine, Science
ISBN Publisher's Prefix: 84-311

Editorial **Medica y Tecnica** SA, Ave Meridiana 328 planta 14, Barcelona 27 Tel: 3115361
Man Dir: Emílio Rotellar Lampre; *Production, Publicity:* José María Ripolles Segarra
Subjects: Medicine, Psychology, Behavioural Psychology, Language, Art
1981: 18 titles *1982:* 10 titles *Founded:* 1977
ISBN Publisher's Prefix: 84-85298

Ediciones **Mensajero**, Apdo 73, Bilbao 14 (Located at: Luis Gurrea 2, Bilbao) Tel: (94) 4457750 Cable Add: Mensajero Telex: 32182 Mensajero
Man Dir: Luis Manuel de la Encina; *Editorial, Production:* Jesús Leguina; *Sales:* Juan Aguirre; *Publicity:* Alvaro Sánchez
Branch Offs: Templarios 12, Barcelona 2; EAPSA, Velázquez 28, Madrid 1
Subjects: Social Science, Religion, Philosophy, Education, How-to, Psychology, Juveniles
1981: 78 titles *1982:* 84 titles *Founded:* 1915
ISBN Publisher's Prefix: 84-271

Editorial Luis **Miracle** SA*, Calle Sicilia 402, Barcelona 25 Tel: (93) 2581800/9 Cable Add: Micle
Editorial: Josefina Vera Vera
Subjects: Anthropology, Philosophy, Education, Economics, Social Science, Business, Psychology, History, Religion, Encyclopaedia
Founded: 1929
ISBN Publisher's Prefix: 84-7109

Editorial **Molino**, Calabria 166, Barcelona 15 Tel: (343) 2434769 Cable Add: Molino Barcelona
Man Dir: Luis del Molino Mateus; *Sales & Advertising Dir:* Pablo del Molino Sterna; *Permissions:* L A del Molino
Subjects: Juveniles, Popular Paperbacks, Cookery, Children's books, Education
Founded: 1933
ISBN Publisher's Prefix: 84-272

Editorial **Moll**+, Torre del Amor 4, Apdo 142, Palma de Mallorca 1 Tel: (071) 971224176/971224472
Man Dir: Francesc de B Moll
Subjects: Fiction, Literature, Biography, History, Art, Reference Works, Dictionaries, Linguistics, Social Sciences, Secondary & Primary Textbooks, Natural Science
Bookshop: Libros Mallorca, Fortuny 5, Palma de Mallorca
1981: 76 titles *1982:* 38 titles *Founded:* 1934
ISBN Publisher's Prefix: 84-273

Montaner y Simon SA*, Aragón 255, Apdo 322, Barcelona 7
Subjects: General Literature, History, Belles Lettres, Reference, Dictionaries, Encyclopaedias, Geography, Scientific and Technical
ISBN Publisher's Prefix: 84-274

José **Montesó** — Editor*, Vía Augusta 251-253, Barcelona 17 Tel: (93) 2301739
Man Dir: José M Montesó
Branch Off: Calle Paraná 480, Buenos Aires, Argentina
Subjects: How-to, Engineering, Technical, University Textbooks
Founded: 1928
ISBN Publisher's Prefix: 84-7186

Ediciones **Morata** SA+, Mejía Lequerica 12, Madrid 4 Tel: (91) 4480926 Cable Add: Moratedi
Man Dir: Flora Morata
Subjects: Psychology, Medicine, Pedagogy, Philosophy, Psychiatry, Sexology, Sociology, Politics, Mathematics, University Textbooks
Founded: 1920
ISBN Publisher's Prefix: 84-7112

Ediciones **Moretón** SA*, Espartero 10, Bilbao 9 Tel: (094) 4239169
Man Dir: C Moretón; *Sales:* Victoria Peña; *Publicity & Advertising:* Maria Saturnina Abón
Parent Company: Artes Gráficas Grijelmo SA (qv)
Subjects: Literature, Biography, History, Music, Art, Reference (in luxury and multi-volume editions)
Founded: 1964
ISBN Publisher's Prefix: 84-7113

Mundi-Prensa Libros SA, Castelló 37, Apdo 1223, Madrid 1 Tel: (91) 2754655/2760253 Cable Add: Mundipren Telex: 49370 Mpli E
Man Dir: Pedro Hernández; *Editorial, Publicity:* José Ma Hernández; *Sales:* Alfonso Hernández
Subjects: Agriculture, Technology, Ecology, Livestock, University & Secondary Textbooks
Bookshops: Librería Mundi-Prensa (qv under Major Booksellers); Librería Agrícola, Fernando VI, 2, Madrid 4
1981: 20 titles *1982:* 20 titles *Founded:* 1948
ISBN Publisher's Prefix: 84-7114

Editorial La **Muralla***, Constancia 33, Madrid 2 Tel: (91) 4161371/4153687/4159148
Man Dir: Lidio Nieto; *Sales Dir:* Miguel Lendínez; *Publicity, Rights & Permissions:* Pilar Jiménez; *Production:* Ana Riutort
Subjects: Art, Literature, Geography, History, Religion, Technology, Life and Culture, Biology, all in books with slides for visual education, Pre-school, Primary, Secondary and University Textbooks
Founded: 1968
ISBN Publisher's Prefix: 84-7133

Editorial **Musica** Moderna, Antonio Carmona Reverte, Calle Marqués de Cubas 6, Madrid 14 Tel: (91) 2215593
Editor, Dir: Andrés Carmona Reverte
Subject: Music
Founded: 1935

Biblioteca '**N T**', an imprint of EUNSA (qv)

Ediciones **Naranco** SA*, Asturias 27, Apdo 542, Oviedo Tel: 236537
President: Santiago Rubio Sáinido; *Man Dir:* Graciano García; *Production:* José Antxon F Lupiáñez; *Sales, Publicity:* Emilio García; *Rights & Permissions:* José Antonio A Rodríguez
Subjects: Photo-strip Editions of Don Quixote, Juveniles, Part-Works, weekly parts editions of major collections

Narcea SA de Ediciones+, Dr Federico Rubio 9, Madrid 20 Tel: (91) 2546484
Subjects: Education, Psychology, Pedagogy, Religion, Juveniles, Textbooks
ISBN Publisher's Prefix: 84-277

Ediciones **Nauta** SA, Loreto 16, Barcelona 29 Tel: (343) 2392204 Cable Add: Edinauta Telex: 54495 sele e
Man Dir: José Luis Ruiz de Villa Macho
Subjects: General Fiction and Non-fiction, Classics, Art Books, Reference
Founded: 1962
ISBN Publisher's Prefix: 84-278

Neguri Editorial SA, Juan de Ajuriaguerro 10, Bilbao 9 Tel: (94) 4245307 Telex: 31861 Ed E
President: José Angel Grijelmo; *Manager:* Elena Grijelmo
Subjects: Atlases, Plans of Spanish Cities, Road Maps
Bookshop: Librería Deusto, Calle O'Donnell 43, Madrid 9
1981: 4 titles *1982:* 7 titles *Founded:* 1960
ISBN Publisher's Prefix: 84-85085

Editorial **Noguer** SA+, Paseo de Gracia 96, Barcelona 8 Tel: (93) 2156516 Cable Add: Edinoguer Barcelona Telex: 52534
President: Emilio Ardevol; *Rights & Permissions:* Maruchy Friart
Associate Company: Luis de Caralt Editor SA (qv)
Subjects: General Fiction and Non-fiction, Belles Lettres, Biography, History, Encyclopaedias, Art, Juveniles, Paperbacks
1982: 250 titles *Founded:* 1949
ISBN Publisher's Prefix: 84-279

Ediciones **Norma** SA*, Sancho Davila 27, Madrid 28 Tel: 2565013
Man Dir, Editorial, Rights & Permissions: Florencio Valero
Subjects: Medicine, Health
1981: 10 titles *Founded:* 1978
ISBN Publisher's Prefix: 84-7487

Nova Terra, see Hogar del Libro

Oikos-Tau SA Ediciones, Montserrat 12-14, Vilassar de Mar, Apdo 5347, Barcelona Tel: (93) 7590791
Man Dir, Editorial: Jordi Garcia-Bosch; *Sales:* Climent Garcia-Bosch; *Production, Rights & Permissions:* Jordi Garcia-Jacas
Subjects: Scientific and Technical, Economics, Marketing and Management, Agriculture, Geography, Education, History, Politics, Psychology, Architecture, Town Planning
Bookshop: Il Racó del Llibre de Text, Gran Via 600, Barcelona
Founded: 1963
ISBN Publisher's Prefix: 84-281

Ediciones **Omega** SA, Platón 26, Barcelona 6 Tel: (93) 2013807/2010599 Telex: 98095 Omeg E
Man Dirs: Gabriel Paricio, Antonio Paricio
Subjects: Science & Technology, Photography, Cinema, Agriculture, University textbooks on Biology, Biochemistry, Geology
ISBN Publisher's Prefix: 84-282

Alfredo **Ortells** Ferriz, Sagunto 5, Valencia 9 Tel: (06) 3471000/3472112
Man Dir: Alfredo Ortells Ferriz
Subjects: Infants and Juvenile, Children's Classics, Popular Knowledge series, Dictionaries, Encyclopaedias
Founded: 1952
ISBN Publisher's Prefix: 84-7189

P P C (Promoción Popular Cristiana)*, E Jardiel Poncela 4, Apdo 19049, Madrid 16 Tel: (91) 2592300 Cable Add: Pepece Telex: 45051
Man Dir: José Ma Burgos; *General Manager:* Gonzalo Márquez; *Sales Dir:* Catalina Jaume; *Publicity & Advertising:* Pedro G Candanedo
Subsidiary Company: Marsiega Editorial SA (qv)
Subjects: Religion, Philosophy, Textbooks
Bookshops: Retail outlets throughout Spain (qv under Major Booksellers)
Founded: 1955
ISBN Publisher's Prefix: 84-288

Ediciones **Paidós** Ibérica SA+, Mariano Cubí 92, Barcelona 21 Tel: (93) 2000122 Telex: 97550 Edpi E
Man Dir: Enrique Folch; *Sales:* Juan León;
Production: Lluís Tarrasón
Parent Company: Editorial Paidós, Argentina (qv)
Associate Company: Editorial Paidós Mexicana, Ave Patriotismo 40, Colonia Escandón, 11800 México DF, Mexico
Subjects: Psychology, Psychoanalysis, Pedagogy, Communication, Sociology, Philosophy, Neurology, Physical Education, Linguistics, Religion, Parapsychology
1981: 33 titles *1982:* 15 titles *Founded:* 1979
ISBN Publisher's Prefix: 84-7509

Pala SA, now Sadko SA (qv)

Editorial **Paraninfo** SA, Magallanes 25, Madrid 15 Tel: (91) 4463350 Telex: 45890 Edpa E
Man Dir: Alfonso Mangada Sanz; *Sales Dirs:* Miguel Mangada Ferber, Manuel Montalbán Beltrán
Subjects: Science & Technology, Data Processing & Computation, Business Administration, How-to, Secondary & University Textbooks
Bookshops: Librería Paraninfo, Magallanes 25, Madrid 15; Meléndez Valdés 65, Madrid 15
1981: 112 titles *Founded:* 1948
ISBN Publisher's Prefix: 84-283

Parramon Ediciones SA, Calle Lepanto 264, Apdo 2001, Barcelona 13 Tel: (93) 2462482/3
Man Dir: José María Parramón; *Rights & Permissions:* Mercedes Ros
Subjects: Art, Photography, Drawing (Instruction), Languages, Botanical Interest, Reference, Music, Juveniles
1981: 190 titles *Founded:* 1958
ISBN Publisher's Prefix: 84-342

Ediciones **Partenon**, Paseo de la Habana 56, Madrid 16 Tel: (91) 2505498 Telex: 27307/22034/23261 Coime attn abonado 859
Man Dir: Rafael Torres Gorriz
Subjects: Literature, Language and Philology, Social Science, University Textbooks
Founded: 1969
ISBN Publisher's Prefix: 84-7119

Ediciones **Paulinas***, Protasio Gomez 15, Madrid 27 Tel: (91) 7425113
Subjects: Biography, Philosophy, Psychology, Education, Religion
ISBN Publisher's Prefix: 84-285

Editorial **Paz** Montalvo*, Jorge Juan 127, Madrid 9 Tel: (91) 4019722
Man Dir: José Fernando de Paz; *Advertising:* José Luis Fernández; *Publicity:* J L Fernández Boyano
Subjects: Medicine, Ophthalmology, Psychiatry, Paediatrics, Biochemistry and Associated Fields
Founded: 1947
ISBN Publisher's Prefix: 84-7121

Editorial **Pediátrica**, Mayor de Gracia 102, Barcelona 12 Tel: (93) 2174996
Man Dir: Anselmo Garrido
Subject: Medicine
1981: 7 titles *Founded:* 1969
ISBN Publisher's Prefix: 84-7193

Ediciones **Pegaso**, an imprint of EDERSA (qv)

Ediciones **Peninsula**, Provenza 278 - 1° 1a, Barcelona 8 Tel: (93) 2160062
Man Dir: Ramon Bastardes i Porcel; *Editorial Dir:* Josep M Castellet; *Sales:* Joaquim Sabria
Associate Company: Edicions 62 SA (qv)
Subsidiary Company: Distribuciones de Enlace SA
Subjects: General (in Castilian)
1982: 16 titles *Founded:* 1963
ISBN Publisher's Prefix: 84-297

Editorial Augusto E Pila Teleña, Paseo de Yeserias 35, Madrid 5 Tel: (91) 4743494
Man Dir: Augusto E Pila Teleña; *Editorial:* Augusto Pila; *Sales:* Raquel Laviste
Subjects: Physical Education, Sports
1982: 7 titles *Founded:* 1979
ISBN Publisher's Prefix: 84-85514

Ediciones Pirámide SA, Villafranca 22, Madrid 28 Tel: (91) 2458202/5 Telex: 43341 Gsri E
Chairman: Germán Sánchez Ruipérez; *Dir:* Guillermo de Toca; *Man Dir:* Jose María Esteban; *Rights & Permissions:* Esther Rincón Quemada, Guillermo de Toca
Subjects: Economics, Business, Science and Technology, Law, Psychology, Information Science, Medicine, Nursing
1981: 200 titles *Founded:* 1974
ISBN Publisher's Prefix: 84-368

Editorial Planeta SA+, Córcega 273, Barcelona 8 Tel: (93) 2175050 Cable Add: Ediplan Telex: 52632 Opib
Chairman: José Manuel Lara Hernández; *General Manager:* José Manuel Lara Bosch; *Sales Manager:* Javier Nieto Santa; *Production:* Jordi Brell; *Export Manager:* José Manuel Peidró; *Publicity:* Rafael Abella
Branch Offs: Editorial Planeta SAIC, Viamonte 1451, Buenos Aires, Argentina; Editorial Planeta Chilena SA, Olivares 1229 – 4° piso, Santiago, Chile; Planeta Colombiana Editorial SA, Calle 22, 6-27 Edificio Distral, Bogotá, Colombia; Editorial Planeta del Ecuador SA, Ave Francisco de Orellana 1811 y 10 de Agosto, Edificio El Cid planta baja, Quito, Ecuador; Difusion Editorial SA, Adolfo Prieto 1230, Colonia del Valle, México 03100 DF, Mexico; Ediciones Andinas SA, León Velarde 1263, Lince, Lima, Peru; Editorial Planeta Venezolana SA, Edificio Pigalle local B, Ave Leonardo Da Vinci, Colinas de Bello Monte, Caracas, Venezuela
Subjects: General Fiction & Non-fiction
Founded: 1952
ISBN Publisher's Prefix: 84-320

Editorial Playor, Santa Polonia 7, Madrid 14 Tel: (91) 4295125 Telex: 42252 IVSAE
Man Dir: Carlos A Montaner; *Sales:* Maria Angeles Remior; *Production:* Pio E Serrano
Subjects: Art, Linguistics, Literature, Spanish and Latin-American Studies, Cuban Studies, Illustrated Juvenile
ISBN Publisher's Prefix: 84-359

Plaza y Janés SA*, Editores, Virgen de Guadalupe 21-33, Esplugas de Llobregat, Barcelona Tel: (93) 3710200
Executive President: Carlos Plaza de Diego; *Man Dir:* Julio Jordán Seguí; *Editor-in-Chief:* José Moya
Subjects: General Fiction & Non-fiction, Classics, Paperbacks
ISBN Publisher's Prefix: 84-01

Ediciones Poligrafa SA, Balmes 54, Barcelona 7 Tel: (93) 3019100 Telex: 97041 Edpo E
President: Manuel de Muga; *Sales:* Juan de Muga
Subject: Art Books, with texts in several languages
ISBN Publisher's Prefix: 84-313

Editorial Pomaire SA*, Ave Infanta Carlota 114, Barcelona 29 Tel: (93) 2501363/2591336/2591340 Telex: 54220 Poes E
Man Dir: Sergio Tapia
Branch Offs: Argentina; Chile; Colombia; Costa Rica; Ecuador; Mexico; Uruguay; Venezuela (qqv)
Subjects: General Fiction & Non-fiction
Founded: 1957
ISBN Publisher's Prefix: 84-286

Editorial Popular SA, Apdo 14256, Madrid 13 (Located at: Calle Bola 3, Madrid) Tel: 2482788
Man Dir: Antonio Albarran Cano
Subjects: Adult and Popular Education
1981: 12 titles *1982:* 13 titles *Founded:* 1972
ISBN Publisher's Prefix: 84-85016

Ediciones José Porrúa Turanzas SA, Cea Bermúdez 10, Madrid 3 Tel: (91) 2542344/2541466
Man Dir, Editorial: José Porrúa Venero; *Sales:* Mauricio Maroto Maroto; *Production, Publicity:* Constantino García Garvía; *Rights & Permissions:* Enrique Porrúa Venero
Subsidiary Company: North American Division, 1383 Kersey Lane, Potomac, MD 20854, USA
Subjects: History of Mexico and Latin America, Humanistic Literature and Commentary
Bookshop: Librería José Porrúa Turanzas SA (qv under Major Booksellers)
Founded: 1958
ISBN Publisher's Prefixes: 84-7317, 0-935568

Editorial Pòrtic, Ave Marqués de Argentera 17, Barcelona 3 Tel: 3196684
Man Dir: Núria Fornas; *Administration and Sales:* Salvador Llimona
Subjects: Religion, Politics, Essays, Poetry & Prose-poetry, Novels, Memoirs (in Catalan)
Bookshop: Llibreria Claris, Calle Pau Claris 82, Barcelona 10
ISBN Publisher's Prefix: 84-7306

Pre-Textos, Calle Luis Santángel 10 – 1C, Valencia 5 Tel: 3333226
Man Dir: D Manuel Borrás Arana
Subjects: Literature, Essays, Philosophy, Poetry, Music
1981: 8 titles *1982:* 7 titles *Founded:* 1976
ISBN Publisher's Prefix: 84-85081

Editorial Prensa Española*, Padilla 6, Madrid 6 Tel: (91) 4462616
Dir: Rogelio González-Ubeda
Subjects: General Fiction & Non-fiction
Founded: 1905
ISBN Publisher's Prefix: 84-287

Editorial Prometeo, Pl Cánovas del Castillo 9-6a, Valencia 5 Tel: (96) 3344108
Man Dir: Juan de Dios Leal Castellote; *Sales Dir:* María Luisa Sagreras
Subjects: Fiction, Poetry, Literature, Geography & Travel, Philosophy
Founded: 1912
ISBN Publisher's Prefix: 84-7199

Ediciones de Promoción Cultural SA*, Rocafort 256-258, Barcelona 15 Tel: (93) 2590140 Cable Add: Edsprocusa
Man Dir: J Ma Mas Solench
Subjects: Social Sciences, Education, General Science & Technology, University Textbooks
Founded: 1972

Promoción Popular Cristiana, see PPC

Ediciones R O L SA, San Elias 31-33, Barcelona 6 Tel: (93) 2008033 Telex: 23261 sagalit 818
Man Dir: Nestor Bereciartu
Subjects: Nursing, Medicine, Sociology, Psychology, Periodicals
Founded: 1977
ISBN Publisher's Prefix: 84-85535

Selecciones del Reader's Digest (Iberia) SA, Calle Telémaco 3, Madrid 27 Tel: (91) 7420011 Cable Add: Readigest Telex: 27407
Director General: Richard Crosfield; *Editorial, Rights & Permissions:* Joaquín Amado; *Sales:* M Angel Senén; *Production:* John Servizio; *Publicity:* Xavier Muntañola
Parent Company: The Reader's Digest Association Inc, 200 Park Ave, New York, NY 10166, USA
Branch Off: Barcelona
Subjects: Education, Pocket editions, General Interest, Atlases
1981-82: 8 titles *Founded:* 1952
ISBN Publisher's Prefix: 84-7142

Editorial Reus SA, Preciados 23, Madrid Tel: (91) 2213619/2223054
Man Dir: Rafael Martinez Reus
Subjects: Law and General Culture
Bookshop: Librería Reus, Calle de Preciados 6, Madrid
Founded: 1852
ISBN Publisher's Prefix: 84-290

Editorial Reverté SA+, Calle Encarnación 86-88, Apdo 1237, Barcelona 24 Tel: (93) 2193452/2134058/2194353 Cable Add: Edirever Telex: 54996 Ervt E
Dir: Felipe Reverté Planells; *Editorial:* Juan Sala Inglabaga; *Sales:* Ernesto Granada Ribet; *Rights & Permissions:* Adriana Lorenzetti Mascó
Associate Companies: Editora Reverté Ltda, Brazil (qv); Editorial Reverté Colombiana SA, Calle 22, No 6-16, of 202 Bogotá, Colombia; Editorial Reverté Mexicana SA, Mexico (qv); Editorial Reverté Venezolana SA, Venezuela (qv)
Branch Off: Ave Angel Gallardo 613, Buenos Aires 5, Argentina
Subjects: Engineering, General Science, University & Secondary Textbooks
Founded: 1947
ISBN Publisher's Prefix: 84-291

Revista de Occidente SA, Milán 38, Madrid 33 Tel: (91) 2000045 Telex: 45746
Man Dir: Diego Hidalgo
Associate Company: Alianza Editorial SA (qv)
Subjects: History, Philosophy, Political & Social Science
Founded: 1923
ISBN Publisher's Prefix: 84-292

Ediciones Rialp SA*, Preciados 34, Madrid 13 Tel: (91) 2311004
Subjects: Belles Lettres, Poetry, History, Music, Art, Philosophy, Religion, Textbooks, Engineering, General & Social Science, High-priced Paperbacks
Founded: 1945
ISBN Publisher's Prefix: 84-321

Litografia A Romero SA*, Ave Angel Romero s/n, Apdo 324, Santa Cruz de Tenerife Tel: 221540-2 Cable Add: Larsa, Tenerife Telex: 92159 Larsa E
Dir: Edgardo Romero
Subjects: Textbooks, Juveniles

S A R P E, see Sociedad Anonima de Revistas Periodicos y Ediciones

Sadko SA, Paseo de los Olmos 5 (Parque Bidebieta), San Sebastian Tel: 398780/395345
President: Luis Gasca Burges; *Dir:* Miguel Arrieta Lasarte
Subjects: Juveniles, Reference Works, Cinema, Parapsychology, Astronautics
Miscellaneous: Formerly known as Pala SA (at same address)

Victor Sagi Servicios Editoriales*, Diagonal 614, Barcelona 21 Tel: (93) 2394300 Telex: 54254
Man Dir: C H Knapp; *Sales:* Eva Alsina
Parent Company: Victor Sagi Communications Group
Subjects: Cinema, Art, Photography, Health, General Interest
Founded: 1977
ISBN Publisher's Prefix: 84-85186

Editorial **Sal Terrae**+, Guevara 20, Apdo 77, Santander Tel: 212617
Man Dir: Manuel Gutiérrez
Subjects: Religion, Philosophy, Parapsychology, Essays, Biography, History, Juveniles, Textbooks
Founded: 1919
ISBN Publisher's Prefix: 84-293

Salvat Editores SA, Mallorca 41-49, Barcelona 29 Tel: (93) 2303607 Telex: 53132
Man Dir: Juan Salvat; *Dirs:* Enrique Barberá, Alfonso Elizalde, Luis Soler, Ramón Vilá
Branch Offs: Salvat Editores Argentina SA; Salvat Editores do Brasil Ltda; Salvat Editores Colombiana SA; Salvat Editores Chilena Ltda; Salvat Editores Ecuatoriana SA; Salvat Mexicana de Ediciones SA de CV, Mexico (qv); Salvat Editores de Puerto Rico Inc; Salvat Editores Venezolana SA, Edif Arauca, Gran Avenida, Apdo 51106-105, Caracas, Venezuela
Subjects: Reference, History, Art, Music, Literature, Medicine, Veterinary Science, Agriculture, Science, Technology, Geography, Paperbacks
Founded: 1869
ISBN Publisher's Prefix: 84-345

Salvat SA de Ediciones, Arrieta 25, Pamplona Tel: 248600 Telex: 37739 Saaae e
Subjects: Encyclopaedias, Dictionaries, Art, History
ISBN Publisher's Prefix: 84-7137

Editorial Miguel A **Salvatella**, Santo Domingo 5, Barcelona 12 Tel: (93) 2189026
Subjects: Primary Textbooks, Educational Materials
Founded: 1922
ISBN Publisher's Prefix: 84-7210

Editorial **San Martin***, Puerta de Sol 6, Apdo 97, Madrid 14 Tel: (91) 2214292/2216897
Man Dir: Jorge Tarazona
Subjects: History, Aviation, Military
Bookshop: Librería San Martin (at above address)
Founded: 1854
ISBN Publisher's Prefix: 84-7140

Santillana SA de Ediciones*, Calle Elfo 32, Madrid 27 Tel: (91) 4034000 Cable Add: Santillana Telex: 43879
President: Jesús de Polanco Gutérrez; *Vice-Presidents:* Francisco Pérez González, Ricardo Díez Hochleitner; *Man Dir:* Emiliano Martinez Rodriguez; *Editorial:* Antonio Ramos Perez; *Sales:* Jose Muñoz Juan; *Production:* Francisco Jerez Vazquez; *Publicity:* María Jesús de Polanco; *Rights & Permissions:* Gloria Roldan Perez
Associate Companies: Editorial Santillana, Argentina; Edyca SA, Dominican Republic; Nutesa, Mexico; Santillana del Pacifico SA, Chile; Santillana Publishing Co, USA; Teduca, Venezuela (qv); Tedupe, Peru
Branch Offs: Capitán Segarra 41, Alicante; Rambla de Cataluña 81, Barcelona 7; Ave del Ejército 3, Deusto (Vizcaya); Acera del Casino 15, Granada; Julián Romero Brionez 4, Las Palmas; Alonso Quintanilla 3, Oviedo; Placentines 2, Sevilla; Jacinto Benavente 19, Valencia 5; Polígono BENS parcela S-l-B, La Coruña; Avda José Luis Arrese 1, Local 5, Valladolid; Isabel la Católica 5, Zaragoza (all in Spain)
Subjects: Textbooks, Educational Materials for Kindergarten, Primary and Secondary, Teachers and Educational Specialists
Founded: 1960
ISBN Publisher's Prefix: 84-294

Secretariado Trinitario+, Filiberto Villalobos 82, Salamanca Tel: (923) 235602
Man Dir: Nereo Silanes; *Editorial:* José María de Miguel; *Rights & Permissions:* Laurentino Silanes
Subjects: Religion, Theology
1982: 12 titles *Founded:* 1967
ISBN Publisher's Prefix: 84-85376

Sedmay Ediciones SA*, Lopez de Hoyos 36, Madrid 6 Tel: 2624965 Telex: 43239
Man Dir: José Mayá Rius; *Export Manager:* Dr Sabine Kleinhaus
Subjects: Novels, Biography, Essays, Politics, Cinema, Juveniles

Editorial **Seix** Barral SA, Córcega 270 – 4°, Barcelona 8 Tel: 2186400/2186466 Cable Add: Seibarh Telex: 698255 Sxbl E
General Manager: Miguel García Piriz; *Editorial:* Pete Giunterrer; *Publicity, Rights & Permissions:* R Muñoz Suay
Associate Company: Editorial Ariel SA (qv). The two companies constitute the organization Ariel/Seix Barral Editoriales within the Planeta Group
Subsidiary Companies: Ediciones Formentor SRL, Argentina (qv); Formentor Ltda, Chile; Ariel Seix Barral Ltda, Ecuador; Ed Ariel-Seix Barral, Colombia; Ariel-Seix Barral SA, Mexico (qv); Ediciones Andinas SA, Peru; Ediciones Formentor SRL, Venezuela (qv); Ariel Seix Barral, Costa Rica
Subjects: Fiction from Spanish, Latin-American, German, French, English, Italian, Soviet Russian, North American, Oriental and other literatures; Poetry, Drama, the Classics, Literary Criticism, Linguistics, Economics, Philosophy, Science, Politics, History, Psychology, Sociology, the Arts, Memoirs, Travel
1981: 48 titles *Founded:* 1945
ISBN Publisher's Prefix: 84-332

Selecciones Editoriales SA*, Rita Bonnat 9, Barcelona 29 Tel: (93) 2303400 Telex: 54495 Sele e Barcelona 29
Parent Company: Elsevier-NDU nv, Netherlands (qv)
Subjects: General and Educational Reference Works

Ediciones del **Serbal** SA, Calle Witardo 45, Barcelona 14 Tel: 3223054
Man Dir, Editorial, Production: José María Riaño de Castro; *Sales, Publicity:* Isabel Baños Regel
1981: 12 titles *1982:* 28 titles *Founded:* 1980
ISBN Publisher's Prefix: 84-85800

Siglo XXI Editores de España SA+, Plaza 5, Apdo 48023, Madrid 33 Tel: (93) 7594809 Cable Add: Sigloedit
Man Dir, Production: Javier Abásolo; *Sales, Publicity:* Eduardo Rivas
Subsidiary Companies: Siglo XXI Editores de Colombia Ltda (qv); Siglo XXI Editores SA, Mexico (qv)
Subjects: Anthropology, Psychology, Sociology, History, Philosophy, Politics, Literature and Criticism
Bookshop: At above address
Founded: 1967
ISBN Publisher's Prefix: 84-323

Ediciones **Sigueme** SA, García Tejado 23-27, Apdo 332, Salamanca Tel: (923) 218203 Cable Add: Sigueme Salamanca
Man Dir, Editorial: Germán González; *Sales:* Primitivo Fernández; *Production:* Francisco Lansac; *Publicity:* Jorge Sans Vila
Subjects: Philosophy, Religion, Juveniles, Psychology, Social Science, University Textbooks, Cinema, Education
Bookshop: Librería Sigueme, García Tejado 23-27, Salamanca
1982: 35 titles *Founded:* 1958
ISBN Publisher's Prefix: 84-301

Ediciones **Sima***, Tercio Nuestra Señora del Camino 11, Bilbao 12 Tel: (044) 4312135
Man Dir: Victoria Inunciaga
Subject: Juveniles
Founded: 1975

Editorial **Sintes** SA, Apdo 1078, Barcelona Tel: (93) 3182838
Man Dirs, Editorial: Luis Sintes Pros, Jorge Sintes Pros
Orders to: Ronda Universidad 4, Barcelona 7
Subjects: Sports, Technical, Health
Bookshop: Librería Sintes, Ronda Universidad 4, Barcelona
Founded: 1968
ISBN Publisher's Prefix: 84-302

Sociedad Anonima de Revistas Periodicos y Ediciones (SARPE)+, Pedro Teixeira 8, Madrid 20 Tel: 4560048 Telex: 46148 Srpe
Man Dir: Alfredo Marron Gomez; *Editorial:* Marisa Perez Bodegas; *Sales:* José Aguilera Morena; *Production:* Andres Salcedo Peña; *Publicity:* Javier Jaen
Subjects: Cooking, Medicine, Homecraft, Plants and Flowers, Knitting and Sewing, History, Armament, Science, Zoology, Astronomy, Art, Music, Cars, Languages, Hobbies
1981: 3 titles *1982:* 6 titles *Founded:* 1952
ISBN Publisher's Prefix: 84-7291

Ramón **Sopena** SA*, Provenza 93-95, Barcelona 29 Tel: (93) 2303809 Cable Add: Sopenar Telex: 52195 Sopec E
Man Dir: Ramón Sopena Rimblas; *Rights & Permissions:* Domingo Castellar Andreu; *Production:* Antonio Bometon Garcés
Subsidiary Companies: Editorial Ramon Sopena del Río de la Plata SA y C, Argentina (qv); Editorial Sopena Colombiana SA, Colombia (qv); Editorial Sopena Mexicana SA, Mexico (qv); Editorial Ramón Sopena Venezolana SA, Venezuela (qv)
Subjects: History, Art, Reference, Juveniles, Paperbacks, General Science, Languages, Dictionaries, Atlases, Children's books
Founded: 1894
ISBN Publisher's Prefix: 84-303

Studium Ediciones*, Bailén 19, Madrid 13 Tel: (91) 2485921
Distribution: Difusora del Libro, Bailén 19, Apdo 5018, Madrid 13
Man Dir: José Guerrero Carrasco
Subjects: Religion, Philosophy, Psychology, Education, Juveniles
Founded: 1949
ISBN Publisher's Prefix: 84-304

Ediciones **Susaeta** SA*, Km 11 Carretera de Barcelona, Madrid 22 Tel: (91) 7472111 Telex: 22148 Ssta e
Sales Dir: Jose Ignacio Susaeta Erburu
Subjects: Juveniles, Children's
ISBN Publisher's Prefix: 84-305

T E A Ediciones SA, Apdo 19007, Madrid 16 (Located at: Calle Fray Bernardino de Sahagún 24, Madrid) Tel: 4588311 Cable Add: Teacegos Telex: 22135
Man Dir: Agustin Cordero Pando; *Sales:* Marina Gonzalez Criado; *Production:* Manuel Ruiz Claro
Parent Company: Tecnicos Especialistas Asociados SA (at above address)
Branch Offs: Muntaner 462, Barcelona 6; Hurtado de Amézaga 3, Bilbao 8; Monte Carmelo 6 – 2°, Seville 11
Subject: Psychology
Bookshop: TEA Libros (at above address)
1981: 15 titles *1982:* 18 titles *Founded:* 1957
ISBN Publisher's Prefix: 84-7174

Taller Ediciones JB*, Ambrós 8, Apdo 9129, Madrid 28 Tel: (91) 2551266
Man Dir: J Betancor; *Sales Dir:* I Izquierdo;

Publicity Dir: M Padorno; *Permissions:* J Betancor
Subjects: General Literature, Fiction, Philosophy, Psychology, Social Sciences, Art, Cinema
Founded: 1972

Taurus Ediciones SA*, Principe de Vergara 81, Madrid 6
Man Dir: José Ignacio C Abaitua; *Editorial:* José Maria F Guelbenzu
Subjects: Philosophy, Political Science, Linguistics and Philology, Literature, History, Biography, Aesthetics, Art History, Music, Cultural Anthropology
Founded: 1956
ISBN Publisher's Prefix: 84-306

Editores **Técnicos Asociados** SA, Maignón 26, Barcelona 24 Tel: (93) 2144178/2144266
Man Dir: Carlos Palomar; *Sales, Publicity & Advertising:* Juan Cuenca
Subjects: Engineering, Technical, Construction, Computers, Organization, How-to, University Textbooks
Founded: 1963
ISBN Publisher's Prefix: 84-7146

Editorial **Tecnos** SA, O'Donnell 27, Apdo 18, Madrid 9 Tel: (91) 4316400
Man Dir, Editorial: Alejandro Sierra Benayas; *Production:* Mariano Moreno; *Publicity, Rights & Permissions:* José María Castillo; *Sales:* Grupo Distribuidor Editorial SA, D Ramón de la Cruz 67, Madrid 1
Subjects: Social Sciences, History, Art, Philology, Science and Technology, Psychology, Philosophy, Literature, Law
1981: 48 titles *1982:* 32 titles *Founded:* 1947
ISBN Publisher's Prefix: 84-309

Editorial **Teide** SA, Calle Viladomat 291, Barcelona 15 Tel: (93) 2504507 Cable Add: Editeide
Man Dir, Rights & Permissions: Federico Rahola de Espona; *Editorial, Sales:* Federico Rahola Aguade; *Production:* Christian Rahola Aguade; *Publicity:* Francisco Queraltó
Subsidiary Companies: Editorial Varazen SA, Mexico (qv); Teide Ltda, Apdo 53694, Bogota 2, Colombia
Subjects: University, Secondary & Primary Textbooks, Pedagogy, Art, Educational Materials, Navigation, Dictionaries, Languages, Mathematics, Literature, Geography, History, Philosophy
Founded: 1940
ISBN Publisher's Prefix: 84-307

Editorial **Timun** Mas SA+, Via Layetana 17 Pral, Barcelona 1 Tel: (93) 3197400
Dirs: Juan Antonio Martí Castro, Guillermo Menal Alonso
Subjects: Children's, Juveniles, Teaching Manuals
1981: 108 titles

Ediciones **Toray** SA, Duero 6, Barcelona 31 Tel: (93) 3577550 Cable Add: Toray
Dirs: Mariano Torrecilla, Miguel Vilanova
Branch Offs: Príncipe de Vergara 11, Madrid 1; Junín 925, 1113 Buenos Aires, Argentina
Subjects: General Fiction, Art, Juveniles, Medicine, Psychology, University Textbooks
1982: 1,534 titles *Founded:* 1945
ISBN Publisher's Prefix: 84-310

Toray-Masson SA, now Masson SA (qv)

G del **Toro** Editor*, Hortaleza 81, Madrid 4 Tel: (91) 4190486/4199518/4190139
Subjects: Fiction & Non-fiction, Juveniles, Secondary Textbooks
ISBN Publisher's Prefix: 84-312

Instituto Eduardo **Torroja**, Apdo 19002, Madrid 33 (Located at: Serrano Galvache s/n, Madrid) Tel: (91) 2020440
Subjects: Construction, Engineering, Architecture
ISBN Publisher's Prefix: 84-7292

Tusquets Editores, Calle Iradier 24 bajos, Barcelona 17 Tel: (93) 2474170
Man Dirs: Beatriz de Moura, Antonio López Lamadrid; *Sales:* Josefa Valero; *Production, Rights & Permissions, Publicity:* Marta Ribalta
Subjects: Fiction, Literature in general, Biography, History, Philosophy, Art, Social Science, Eroticism, Gastronomy
1982: 33 titles *Founded:* 1969
ISBN Publisher's Prefix: 84-7223

Editorial **Txertoa***, Plaza de las Armerías 4, Apdo 767, San Sebastian 11 Tel: 459757/460941
Man Dir: Luis Aberasturi
Subjects: Literature, Biography, History and Art of the Basque Region
Founded: 1968
ISBN Publisher's Prefix: 84-7148

U N A L I SL, Fray Luis Amigó 8, Edificio Zafiro oficina A, Zaragoza 6 Tel: 373267
Man Dir: José María Saiz Navarro
Branch Off: Paseo Castellana 132, Madrid
Subjects: Regional Encyclopaedias, Literature, Religion, Occult, Hairdressing
1981: 13 titles *1982:* 9 titles *Founded:* 1972
ISBN Publisher's Prefix: 84-85656

Ultramar Editores SA, Mallorca 49, Barcelona 29 Tel: 3212400 Telex: 53132 Saedi E
Man Dirs: Jordi Pamies, Emilio Teixidor
Subjects: General Literature, Fiction, Science Fiction, Paperbacks, Juveniles
Founded: 1973
ISBN Publisher's Prefix: 84-7386

Unión Aragonesa del Libro SL, see UNALI SL

Universidad de Granada, Secretariados de Intercambio y Publicaciones, Hospital Real, Granada Tel: (958) 278400
Subjects: Literature, History, Law, Art, Sciences, Philosophy, Social Sciences, Philology, Biology, Geology, Botany, Anthropology, Archaeology, Medicine, Geography, Music, General Interest

Universidad de Malaga, Colonia Santa Inés, Malaga Tel: (952) 301212
Subjects: Sociology, Philosophy, History, Medicine

Ediciones **Universidad de Navarra** SA, see EUNSA

Urmo SA de Ediciones, Juan de Ajuriaguerra 10, Bilbao 9 Tel: (94) 4245307
Chairman: José Angel Grijelmo Ribechini
Parent Company: Artes Gráficas Grijelmo SA (qv)
Subjects: Engineering, General Science, University Textbooks
Founded: 1963
ISBN Publisher's Prefix: 84-314

Editorial **Vasco** Americana SA (EVA)*, Ave de Castilla 79, Apdo 731, Bilbao Tel: (044) 4333700
Subject: Juveniles and Children's books
ISBN Publisher's Prefix: 84-319

Editorial De **Vecchi**, see De Vecchi

Editorial **Verbo** Divino+, Carretera de Pamplona 41, Estella, Navarra Tel: 550449 Cable Add: Verbodivino
Man Dir: Father Fernando Villanueva; *Sales Dir:* Martín Esparza; *Advertising, Rights & Permissions:* Angel Beltran
Subjects: Religion, Bibles, Biography, Social Science, Educational Materials
Founded: 1957
ISBN Publisher's Prefix: 84-7151

Veron Editor, Ronda del General Mitre 163, Barcelona 22 Tel: (93) 2121599/2119300
Man Dir, Sales: Luis Veron Climent; *Editorial, Publicity:* Luis Veron Jane; *Production, Rights & Permissions:* Rafael Zendrera Pijoan
Subjects: Escapist Literature, Juvenile, Ancient & Modern Classics
Bookshop: Libreria Scriba, Ronda del General Mitre 100, Barcelona 21 Tel: (93) 2010096
1981: 6 titles *1982:* 3 titles *Founded:* 1965
ISBN Publisher's Prefix: 84-7255

Editorial **Vicens-Vives**, Ave de Sarriá 132-136, Barcelona 17 Tel: (93) 2034400
Man Dirs: Roser Rahola, Pere Vicens
Subjects: General Literature, Belles Lettres, Art, History, Biography, Geography, General Science, Mathematics, Secondary Textbooks, Education
ISBN Publisher's Prefix: 84-316

Editorial Luis **Vives** (Edelvives), Carretera de Madrid, Km 315 7, Apdo 387, Saragossa Tel: 344100 Cable Add: Edelvives
Man Dir: Ignacio Pérez; *Sales Dir:* Antonio Herrera
Branch Offs: Barcelona, Bilbao, Madrid, Málaga, Oviedo, Seville, Valencia, Valladolid, Vigo, Saragossa
Subjects: University, Secondary & Primary Textbooks, Educational Materials
1982: 65 titles *Founded:* 1932
ISBN Publisher's Prefix: 84-263

Xarait Ediciones, Juan Vigón 3, Madrid 3 Tel: 2341567
Proprietor, Dir: Miguel Ortiz Martinez
Subjects: Architecture, Art
Founded: 1978
ISBN Publisher's Prefix: 84-85434

Zero SA, now Zero-Zyx SA (qv)

Editorial **Zero-Zyx** SA*, Lérida 80, Madrid 20 Tel: (91) 2796591
Man Dir: Jesús Carrascosa; *Sales:* Jose Lozano; *Publicity & Advertising:* Manuel Irusta; *Rights & Permissions:* Teresa Garcia-Abad
Subjects: Belles Lettres, Poetry, Biography, History, Philosophy, Religion, Juveniles, Paperbacks, Psychology, Social Science
Founded: 1963

Literary Agents

A C E R, Calle Bolonia 5, Madrid 28 Tel: 2559943/2461776 Cable Add: Teleacer Telex: 47532 Leer E
Contacts: Marcel Laignoux, Gussie Laignoux, Anne Marie Vallat, Raquel de la Concha

Carmen **Balcells** Agencia Literaria*, Diagonal 580, Barcelona 21 Tel: (93) 2008565/2008933 Cable Add: Copyright Barcelona Telex: 50459 copy E (Barcelona)
Manager: Carmen Balcells
Branch Off: Rio de Janeiro, Brazil (qv)

Cecilio **Cardeñoso***, Juan Güell 74-76, Barcelona 28 Tel: (93) 3303416
Specializations: Philosophy, Psychology, Politics, Sociology, General Interest, Fiction

International Editors' Co SA, Rambla de Cataluña 39, Barcelona 7 Tel: (93) 3188980 Cable Add: Lifeplay
Manager: Isabel Monteagudo
Branch Off: Buenos Aires, Argentina (qv)

Andrés de **Kramer**, Castello 30, Madrid 1

José **Moya** y Ute Körner de Moya*, Ronda Guinardo 32 - 5° 5a, Barcelona 25

SPAIN

Saga Literaria SL, Calle Recoletos 11/3°-B, Madrid 1 Tel: 2756252 Telex: 23261 clave 818
Manager: Mrs Frédérique Porretta
Specializations: How-to, Juvenile, Fiction, Non-fiction, Part-works, Continuity series, Premium editions and sponsorship, Co-editions, Spanish and Latin American authors

J F **Yañez**, Agencia Literaria, Marco Aurelio 5 - 5° 3a, Barcelona 6 Tel: 2010714 Cable Add: Agenliter Telex: 97348 Gnlt E
Dirs: Julio F Yañez, Mrs Mayte Yañez
Specializations: Modern Literature, Documents and Memoirs; Educational: History, Art, Sociology; Topical Books on Modern Facts; Co-productions
Covering all Spanish- and Portuguese-speaking countries

Book Clubs

Círculo de Amigos de la Historia*, Valportillo Primera, Poligona Industrial 81, Madrid

Círculo de Lectores SA, Valencia 344, Barcelona 9 Tel: 2587600 Cable Add: Cilec Telex: 52532/52560
Members: 1,000,000
Owned by: Verlagsgruppe Bertelsmann GmbH, Federal Republic of Germany (qv)
Founded: 1962

Club del **Libro de la Naturaleza***, Castello 59, Madrid 1
Owned by: Editorial Incafo SA, Publisher (qv). The Club is open only to subscribers to the proprietors' periodical *Periplo*
Subjects: (Books published by Incafo at a 20% discount) Natural History, Geography, Ethnology, especially with regard to Spain and Spanish America

Major Booksellers

Librería **Ancora y Delfín**, Diagonal 564, Barcelona 21 Tel: (93) 2000746
Owned by: Ediciones Destino SA (qv)

Librería **Augustinus**, Gaztambide 75, Madrid 15 Tel: (91) 2442430
Owned by: Fragua Editorial (qv)
Manager: Mariano Muñoz Alonso

Librería **Bastinos**, see Librería Bosch

Librería **Bosch**, Ronda de la Universidad 11, Barcelona 7 Tel: (93) 3175308
Manager: José Bosch
Incorporating Librería Bastinos

Casa del Libro SA, Ronda de San Pedro 3, Barcelona 10 Tel: (93) 3182640

Cinc d'Oros — Jaime Farrás Solé*, Diagonal 462, Barcelona 6 Tel: 2170059

D E L S A, see SA de Distribución, Edición y Librerías

Librería **Díaz** de Santos, Científica y Técnica, Lagasca 95, Madrid 6 Tel: (91) 4013358 Telex: 45141 Dsan E
Also: Librería Díaz de Santos — Medicina, Maldonado 6, Madrid 6; Librería Díaz de Santos — Científica Técnica, Balmes 417/419, Barcelona 22; Díaz de Santos — Agropecuaria, Lagasca 38, Madrid 1

SA de **Distribución**, Edición y Librerías (DELSA), Serrano 80, Madrid 6 Tel: 4354780
13 branches throughout Spain
DELSA Importadora de Publicaciones SA is also at the above address

Casa del Libro **Espasa-Calpe** SA, Gran Via 29, Madrid 13 Tel: (91) 2216657
Also: Colón de Larreategui 41, Bilbao 9
Owned by: Editorial Espasa-Calpe SA (qv)

Librería **Francesa**, Paseo de Gracia 91, Barcelona 8 Tel: (93) 2151417
Manager: Josep María Blasi i Torrado

Librería **Herder**, Balmes 26, Barcelona 7 Tel: (93) 3170578 Telex: 54120 Hegr E
Manager: Hermann Nahm
Owned by: Editorial Herder SA (qv)

Librería **Hispano Americana**, Gran Via de las Cortes Catalanas 594, Barcelona 7 Tel: (93) 3175337/3180079
Manager: José M Boixareu Ginesta
Owned by: Marcombo SA de Boixareu Editores (qv)

Hogar del Libro SA, Calle Bergara 3, Barcelona 2 Tel: (343) 3182700 Telex: 50066 ogar
Manager: Sebastià Fàbregues
Branches: Calle Pau Clares 85, Barcelona 10; Via Augusta 64, Barcelona 6; Pg Sant Joan 106-108, Barcelona 37; Pg Plaça Major 12, Sabadell (Barcelona); Pg Plaça Major 34, Sabadell (Barcelona); Carretera Barcelona/Sabadell, Baricentro, Local 35, Sabadell (Barcelona); Ave Sarría 40, Barcelona 29
Also Publisher (qv), and Major Distributor, with seven other bookshops in Barcelona area

Insula, Librería, Ediciones y Publicaciones SA*, Benito Gutiérrez 26, Madrid 8 Tel: (91) 2435415
Owned by: Insula, Librería, Ediciones y Publicaciones SA (qv)

L I N E S A, see Librerías del Norte de España SA

H F **Martínez** de Murguía SA, Valverde 27, Madrid 13 Tel: (91) 2226634
Manager: Francisco Gugel
Universal supplier and distributor of books published in Spain

Miessner Libreros, José Ortega y Gasset 14, Madrid 6 Tel: (91) 4350978/4350998
Subjects: General Literature, Classical Studies, Language, Philosophy, Archaeology, Art, Hebraic and Islamic Studies

Librería **Mundi-Prensa**, Castelló 37, Apdo 1223, Madrid 1 Tel: (91) 2754655 Telex: 49370 Mpli E
Man Dir: Pedro Hernández
Owned by: Mundi-Prensa Libros SA (qv)
Subsidiary Company: Libreria Agricola, Fernando VI 2, Madrid 4
Specializations: Economics, Life Sciences, Agriculture, Engineering, Technology
Founded: 1948

Librerías del **Norte de España** SA (LINESA), Serrano 80, Madrid 6 Tel: (91) 2764810/2764826
Five branches in Spain

Librerías **P P C** (Promoción Popular Cristiana)*, San Mateo 30, Madrid Tel: (91) 4190034/4190906
Also: E Jardiel Poncela 4, Madrid 16 Tel: (91) 4582335; Librería PPC, Canuda 9, Barcelona Tel: (93) 3172939; Librería Remel, Carrer Badal 144, Barcelona Tel: (93) 2578652 (and 13 other branches of PPC throughout Spain)
Owned by: PPC (Publisher, qv)

Librería **Pássim**, Bailén 134, Barcelona 9 Tel: (93) 2574757 Cable Add: Pássim
Manager: Rosa Pujol
Publishes catalogues of new and out of print books about Spain and Latin America published in Spain. Specializes in export sales to foreign universities and libraries

Librería José **Porrúa** Turanzas SA, Cea Bermúdez 10, Madrid 3 Tel: (91) 2542344/2541466
Manager: José Porrúa Venero
Owned by: Ediciones José Porrúa Turanzas SA (qv)

Porter-Libros*, Ave Puerta del Angel 9, Barcelona 2 Tel: (93) 2226437

Librería Pedro **Pueyo***, Arenal 16, Madrid 13 Tel: (91) 2213344

Libreria **Rubiños**, Alcala 98, Madrid 9 Tel: (91) 2754227

Major Libraries

Archivo General de la **Administracion** Civil del Estado*, Ronda Fiscal 1, Alcalá de Henares, Madrid
General Archives of the Civil Administration of the State
Documents on administration no longer of current relevance

Archivo **General** de Indias*, Queipo de Llano 3, Seville
Archives of the Indies

Archivo **Historico Nacional**, Calle Serrano 115, Madrid Tel: 2617052
National Historical Archives
Director: Dr Sanchez Belda

Archivo y **Biblioteca** Capitulares*, Cathedral of Toledo, Toledo
Archives and Library of the Cathedral Chapter
Dir: Ramón Gonzálvez

Biblioteca del **Ateneo de Barcelona***, Calle Canude, Barcelona
Library of the Athenaeum of Barcelona

Biblioteca del **Ateneo de Madrid***, Prado 21, Madrid
Library of the Madrid Athenaeum
Librarian: María José Albo Alvarez

Biblioteca del **Ateneo Mercantil** Valenciano*, Plaza del Generalísimo, Valencia
Library of the Mercantile Athenaeum of Valencia

Biblioteca Nacional, Paseo de Recoletos 20, Madrid 1 Tel: (91) 2756800
Dir: D Hipolito Escolar Sobrino

Biblioteca General del **Consejo** Superior de Investigaciones Científicas, Medinaceli 4, Madrid
Library of the Council for Scientific Research
Librarian: Dolores Corróns

Archivo de la **Corona** de Aragon, Condes de Barcelona 2, Barcelona 2 Tel: 3150211
Royal Archives of Aragon
Dir: María-Mercedes Costa
Publications: Colección de Documentos Inéditos del Archivo de la Corona de Aragón (from 1847)

Biblioteca de **Catalunya** Diputación de Barcelona, Calle del Carmen 47, Apdo 1077, Barcelona 1 Tel: (Director) 3178990; (General) 3170778
Library of Cataluña

Hemeroteca Municipal de Madrid*, Plaza de la Villa 3, Madrid
Madrid Periodical Library

Biblioteca del **Instituto de Cooperacion** Iberoamericana, Ave Reyes Católicos 4, Madrid 3
Library of the Institute of Spanish-American Fellowship

348 SPAIN

Biblioteca del **Instituto de Cultura** Hispànica, now Biblioteca del Instituto de Cooperacion Iberoamericana (qv)

Biblioteca del **Instituto Nacional** del Libro Español*, Calle Mallorca 272-276, Barcelona 37
Library of the Spanish Publishers' and Booksellers' Association

Biblioteca de **Menéndez Pelayo**, Calle Rubio 6, Santander Tel: 234534/230663
Librarian: Manuel Revuelta Sañudo
Publication: Boletín de la Biblioteca de Menéndez Pelayo (annual)

Biblioteca del **Ministerio de Cultura**, Plaza de la Castellana 109 - 2a planta, Madrid 16
Library of the Ministry of Culture
Librarian: Araceli González Antón

Patrimonio Nacional, Biblioteca del **Palacio** Real, Calle Bailén s/n, Madrid 13 Tel: 2487404
Library of the Royal Palace
Librarian: Consolación Morales Borrero

Real Biblioteca de San Lorenzo de El Escorial, El Escorial, Madrid
Escorial Library

Universidad Autónoma de Barcelona, Biblioteca General, Campus Universitario, Bellaterra (Barcelona) Tel: 6920200, 6921166 Telex: 52040
Dir: M Mundó Marcet

Biblioteca de la **Universidad Complutense**, Noviciado 3, Madrid 8
Librarian: Fernando Huarte

Universidad Pontificia de Salamanca, Biblioteca Universitaria*, Calle de Libros, Salamanca Tel: 213964

Biblioteca **Universitaria de Barcelona***, Gran Via de las Cortes Catalanas 585, Barcelona 7 Tel: 3189947
Librarian: Mercedes Dexeus Mallol
Publications: Boletín de Noticias; Memorias

Library Associations

Associació de Bibliotecàris*, Via Augusta 120, Pl Baixa Local G, Barcelona 6 Tel: 2181997
Association of Librarians
Secretary: N Ventura

Asociación Española de Archiveros, Bibliotecarios, Museólogos y Documentalistas, Paseo de Recoletos 20, Madrid 1
National Association of Archivists, Librarians, Curators and Documentalists
President: David Torra Ferrer
Secretary: Antonio Magariños Compaired
Publications include: Boletín (with bibliography section)

Instituto Bibliográfico Hispánico, Calle de Atocha 106, Madrid 12 Tel: (91) 2283878
Dir: Vicente Sánchez Muñoz
Hispanic Bibliographical Institute
Publications: Bibliografía Española (monthly), *Bibliografía Española: Suplemento de Publicaciones Periódicas* (annual), *Indices de Revistas de Bibliotecología* (3 a year)

Servicio de Bibliotecas Populares de la Diputación Provincial de Barcelona*, Carmen 47, Barcelona 1 Tel: 3185996

Library Reference Books and Journals

Books

Bibliotheca Hispana (Spanish Library), Consejo Superior de Investigaciones Cientificas, Serrano 117, Madrid

Journals

Boletín (Bulletin), Asociación Español de Archiveros, Bibliotecarios, Museólogos y Documentalistas, Paseo de Recoletos 20, Madrid 1

Indices de Revistas de Bibliotecologia (Indexes to Library Science Periodicals), Instituto Bibliográfico Hispánico, Calle de Atocha 106, Madrid 12

Informacion Librera (Library Information), Javier Romani Sopena, Pelayo 11, 4, Barcelona

Revista de Archivos, Bibliotecas y Museos (Review of Archives, Libraries and Museums), Ministerio de Educación y Ciencia, Servicio de Publicaciónes, Ciudad Universitaria, Madrid 3

Literary Associations and Societies

Academia de Buenas Letras de Barcelona, Calle Obispo Cassador 3, Barcelona 22
Barcelona Academy of Belles Lettres
Secretary: José Alsina Clota
Publications: Boletín, Memorias

Ateneo Cientifico, Literario y Artistico, Calle del Prado 21, Madrid Tel: 4296251
Scientific, Literary and Artistic Athenaeum
President: Fernando Chueca Goitia; *General Secretary:* José Gerardo Manrique de Lara

Ateneo Cientifico, Literario y Artistico, Calle Cifuentes 25, Mahón, Minorca, Balearic Islands
Scientific, Literary and Artistic Athenaeum
Secretaries: Catalina Seguí de Vidal, Antonio Salas Cardona
Publication: Revista de Menorca (quarterly)

Mutualidad Laboral de Escritores de Libros*, General Mola 34, 2° izqda, Madrid 1 Tel: 2756192
Book Writers' Friendly Society

Spanish **P E N** Club (Cataluña), Rua Provenca 357, Barcelona 37
Secretary: Alex Broch

Real Academia de Córdoba, de Ciencias, Bellas Letras y Nobles Artes, Calle Ambrosio de Morales 9, Córdoba 3
Royal Cordobese Academy of Science, Literature and Fine Arts
Secretary: Manuel Nieto Cumplido
Publications: Boletín (half-yearly), scientific, historical and literary works

Real Academia Sevillana de Buenas Letras*, Plaza del Museo 8, Selville
Seville Royal Academy of Belles Lettres
Secretary: Dr Ildefonso Camacho Baños
Publication: Boletín de Buenas Letras (quarterly)

Sociedad de Ciencias, Letras y Artes, Dr Chil 33, Las Palmas, Canary Islands
Scientific, Literary and Art Society
Secretary: Nicolas Díaz-Saavedra de Morales
Publication: El Museo Canario (quarterly)

Sociedad General de Autores de España, Fernando VI 4, Apdo 484, Madrid 4
General Society of Spanish Authors
Secretary-General: José María Segovia Galindo

Literary Periodicals

Camp de l'Arpa, Valencia 72, Entlo 4a, Barcelona 15

Destino (Destiny), Ediciones Destino SL, Consejo de Ciento 425, 5, Barcelona 9

La Estafeta Literaria (The Literary Courier), Editora Nacional, Ave del Generalísimo 29, Madrid 16

Insula (Island); bibliographical review of sciences and letters, Ediciones y Publicaciones de Insula, Benito Gutiérrez 26, Madrid 8

Litoral; monthly poetry review, Visor-Libros, Calle del Roble 22, Madrid 20

Nuestro Tiempo (Our Time), Ediciones Universidad de Navarra SA, Plaza de los Sauces, 1 & 2 Barañain, Pamplona

Razon y Fe; Spanish-American review, Pablo Aranda 3, Madrid 6

Revista de Literatura (Review of Literature), Libreria Cientifico Medinaceli del CSIC, Madrid

Revista de Occidente (Review of the West), Revista de Occidente SA, General Mola 11, Madrid 1

Revista Literaria Azor (The Goshawk — a Literary Review), C Borell 128, 1 2A Barcelona 15

Serra d'Or, Publicaciones de l'Abadia de Montserrat, Abadia de Montserrat, Barcelona

El Urogallo (The Capercailzie), Matias Montero 24, Madrid 6

Literary Prizes

Adonais Prize*
For the best poetry in Castilian by a young poet. 10,000 pesetas awarded annually. Enquiries to Ediciones Rialp SA, Preciados 34, Madrid 13

Ateneo de Sevilla Prize
Established 1969. 2,000,000 pesetas awarded annually for a literary work. The most recent winner was Antonio Burgos for *Las Cabañuelas de Agosto*. Enquiries to Editorial Planeta SA, Córcega 273, Barcelona 8

Ateneo de Valladolid Prize*
Since 1950 the award has been for a short novel. Sponsored by the municipal government of Valladolid in collaboration with Ateneo de Valladolid. 500,000 pesetas is awarded annually. Enquiries to Ateneo de Valladolid, Plaza de España 10–12, Valladolid 1

Blasco Ibáñez Prize*
For an unpublished novel. A prize of 200,000 pesetas is awarded annually by Ediciones Prometeo, which publishes the winning work. Enquiries to Ediciones Prometeo, Plaza Cánovas de Castillo 9–6°, Valencia 5

Miguel de Cervantes Prize*
For the best novel published during the year. 200,000 pesetas. Awarded annually. Enquiries to Ministry of Information and Tourism, Ave Generalísimo 39, Madrid 16

Duke of Alba Prize
Established 1905 for original, unpublished works in Spanish. 48,000 pesetas. Awarded once every nine years. Enquiries to Royal Spanish Academy, Felipe IV 4, Madrid 14

Espejo de España Prize
Established 1975. 2,000,000 pesetas awarded annually for an essay. The most recent winner was Rafael García Serrano for *La Gran Esperanza*. Enquiries to Editorial Planeta SA, Córcega 273, Barcelona 8

Manuel **Espinosa** y Cortina Prize
Established 1891 for the best dramatic work performed for the first time. 4,000 pesetas. Awarded once every five years. Enquiries to Royal Spanish Academy, Felipe IV 4, Madrid 14

Fastenrath Prize
Established 1909 for works of excellence written in the Spanish language. 6,000 pesetas. Awarded annually in rotation for the following categories of writing: poetry; essays, criticism; novel or story; history, biography; drama. Enquiries to Royal Spanish Academy, Felipe IV 4, Madrid 14

Hucho de Oro Prize*
For an unpublished short story in Spanish. 300,000 pesetas and a chest of gold (hucha de oro) are presented annually. Enquiries to Confederación Española de Cajas de Ahorros (CECA), Calle de Alcala 27, Madrid 16

Ramon **Llull** Prize
Established 1981. 2,000,000 pesetas awarded annually for a literary work. The most recent winner was Pere Gimferrer for *Fortuny*. Enquiries to Editorial Planeta SA, Córcega 273, Barcelona 8

Marques of Cerralbo XVII Prize
Established 1922 for the best original, unpublished work related to Spanish language and literature. 40,000 pesetas. Awarded once every four years. Enquiries to Royal Spanish Academy, Felipe IV 4, Madrid 14

Eugenio **Nadal** Prize
For the best novel, preferably by a young writer. 1,000,000 pesetas. Awarded annually. Enquiries to Ediciones Destino SA, Consejo de Ciento 425, Barcelona 9

Alvarez **Quintero** Prize
Established 1949 for the best work in two categories alternately: novel or story collection and theatrical works. 5,000 pesetas. Awarded biennially. Enquiries to Royal Spanish Academy, Felipe IV 4, Madrid 14

Rivadeneyra Prizes
Established 1940 for the best work on Spanish literature and linguistics. Two prizes, of 30,000 pesetas and 20,000 pesetas. Awarded annually. Enquiries to Royal Spanish Academy, Felipe IV 4, Madrid 14

Sri Lanka

General Information

Language: Sinhalese and Tamil (also English)
Religion: Buddhist
Population: 14 million
Literacy Rate (1971): 77.6% (85.9% of urban population, 75% rural)
Bank Hours: 0900-1330 Monday-Friday
Shop Hours: 0800-1700 Monday-Friday
Currency: 100 cents = 1 Sri Lanka rupee
Export/Import Information: No tariff on books or advertising. Import licence required for most book importation. Exchange controls.
Copyright: Berne, Florence (see International section)

Book Trade Organizations

Booksellers' Association of Sri Lanka, PO Box 244, Colombo 2 Tel: 22675/7
Secretary: W L Mendis

Sri Lanka Publishers' Association*, 61 Sangaraja Mawatha, Colombo 10
Secretary-General: Eamon Kariyakarawana

Book Trade Reference Journal

Ceylon National Bibliography (text in English, Sinhalese and Tamail), Sri Lanka National Library Services Board, PO Box 1764, Colombo 7

Publishers

Architecture & Arts Publications Co*, 75 Ward Pl, Colombo 7
Subjects: Art, Architecture

W E **Bastian** & Co*, 23 Canal Row, Fort, PO Box 10, Colombo 1
Managing Proprietor: W D E Bastian
Subjects: Literary, Technical
Founded: 1904

H W **Cave** & Co, 81 Sir Baron Jayatilaka Mawatha, PO Box 25, Colombo 1 Tel: 22675/6/7 Cable Add: Cave Telex: 1241
Man Dir: B J L Fernando; *Dirs:* K Prabachandran, C J S Fernando; *Dir, General Manager:* J R W Rerera
Subjects: History, Archaeology, Juveniles, Literature, Law, Management, Medicine, Engineering, Economics, Education, Psychology, Environmental Studies
Founded: 1876

Ceylon Printers Ltd*, No 20 Sir Chittampalam Gardiner Mawatha, Colombo
Subject: Belles Lettres

Colombo Catholic Press*, 956 Gnanartha Pradipaya Mawatha, Colombo 8 Tel: 95984
Dir and Manager: Rev Father Benedict Joseph
Founded: 1865

M D **Gunasena** & Co Ltd*, 217 Olcott Mawatha, PO Box 246, Colombo 11 Tel: 23981/4 Cable Add: emdeegee Colombo Telex: 1306 a/b Davasa Colombo
Subjects: University & School Books on all subjects
Founded: 1915
Miscellaneous: Associated imprints include Ananda Books, Sirisara Vidyalaya

Hansa Publishers Ltd*, Hansa House, Clifford Ave, Colombo 3
Subjects: General and Children's Fiction, Biographical, Politics, Law, Economics, Children's Science

J K G **Jayawardena** & Co*, BTS Bldg, 203, 1/13 Olcott Mawatha, Colombo 11

Lake House Investments Ltd, 41 WAD Ramanayake Mawatha, PO Box 1453, Colombo 2 Tel: 33271/2/3
Chairman: R S Wijewardene; *Dir:* G B S Gomes; *Editorial, Production, Publicity, Rights & Permissions:* H Samaranayake (Tel: 35175); *Sales:* V L C Walatara (Tel: 27316)
Orders to and Bookshop: The Manager, Lake House Bookshop, 100 Sir Chittampalam Gardiner Mawatha, PO Box 244, Colombo 2
Subjects: Education, Law, General Fiction, Children's Books, Dictionaries, Medicine (in English and Sinhala)
Founded: 1965

Ministry of Cultural Affairs*, 212 Bauddhaloka Mawatha, Colombo 7 Tel: 85888 Cable Add: Sunlay
Dir, Publications: R L Wimaladharma; *Deputy Dir, Publications:* K G Amaradasa; *Editorial:* Prof D E Hettiaratchi, Prof J D Dheerasekera, D P Ponnamperuma
Subjects: Literature, Religion, Art, Culture
Bookshop: Jayanti Bookshop, 135 Dharmapala Mawatha, Colombo 7
Book Club: Book Club of the Ministry of Cultural Affairs of Sri Lanka (qv)
Founded: 1971

Department of **National Museums**, PO Box 854, Sir Marcus Fernando Mawata, Colombo 7 Tel: 94767
Subjects: Publications relating to Sri Lanka's Antiquities, Anthropology, Natural History, *Spolia Zeylanica* (Journal of the National Museums of Sri Lanka)
See also: National Museum Library (under Major Libraries)

K V G De **Silva** & Sons (Kandy)*, 86 D S Senanayake Veediya, Kandy Tel: 083254 Cable Add: Silco
Man Dir & Permissions: K V N De Silva; *Sales Dir:* Mrs D Dias; *Publicity & Advertising Dir:* Mrs K V N De Silva
Branch Off: 44/9 YMBA Building, Fort Colombo
Subjects: History, Religion, Local Interest
Bookshops: 86 D S Senanayake Veediya, Kandy; 44/9 YMBA Bldg, Fort, Colombo
Founded: 1898

The **Union** Press*, 169 Union Pl, PO Box 362, Colombo 2 Tel: 20485/35912 Cable Add: Unionpress
Managing Proprietor: A H Dhas
Founded: 1942

Book Club

Book Club of the **Ministry** of Cultural Affairs of Sri Lanka*, 135 Dharmabala Mawatha, Colombo 7
Owned by: Ministry of Cultural Affairs (qv)

Major Libraries

British Council Libraries, 47 Alfred House Gardens, Colombo 3 Tel: 81171/4 Telex: 21766 Bricon Ce
Branch Library: 170 Trincomalee St, Kandy

Ceylon Institute of Scientific and Industrial Research Library, 363 Bauddhaloka Mawatha, Colombo 7
Librarian: Clodagh Nethsingha
Publications: Current Technical Literature (quarterly); Bibliographical Series (irregular)

Colombo Public Library System, Sir Marcus Fernando Mawatha, Colombo 7 Tel: 595156/596530/91968
Chief Librarian: Mrs Ishvari Corea
Publications include: Libraries and People; A Manual for Public Libraries in Sri Lanka

National Archives, 7 Reid Ave, Colombo 7 Tel: 94523/96917 Cable Add: Archives

National Museum Library, Department of National Museums, PO Box 854, Sir Marcus Fernando Mawatha, Colombo 7 Tel: 93314
Librarian: Miss K V S F de Soysa
Publications: Sri Lanka Periodicals Index; Ceylon Periodicals Directory (Annual Supplements)
See also Department of National Museums (Publisher)

University of Peradeniya Library, University Park, Peradeniya Tel: (08) 88301 ext 240/242/381
Librarian: N T S A Senadeera
Publications (on exchange): *Modern Ceylon Studies: A Journal of the Social Sciences, Sri Lanka Journal of Humanities, Ceylon Journal of Science* (Biological Sciences)

Library Associations

Sri Lanka Library Association*, University of Sri Lanka, Colombo Campus, PO Box 1698, Colombo 3 (Located at: Reid Avenue, Colombo 7)
Secretary: Jayasiri Lankage
Publication: Sri Lanka Library Review (biannual)

Sri Lanka National Library Services Board, PO Box 1764, Colombo 7 (Located at: Independence Ave, Colombo) Tel: 598847
Director/Secretary: N Amarasinghe
Publications: Annual Report; Library News (quarterly); *Sri Lanka National Bibliography*

Library Reference Journals

Ceylon Periodicals Directory (annual supplements), National Museum Library, Department of National Museums, PO Box 854, Sir Marcus Fernando Mawatha, Colombo 7

Library News, Sri Lanka National Library Services Board, PO Box 1764, Colombo 7

Sri Lanka Library Review, Sri Lanka Library Association, University of Sri Lanka, Colombo Campus, PO Box 1698, Colombo 3

Sri Lanka Periodicals Index, National Museum Library, Department of National Museums, PO Box 854, Sir Marcus Fernando Mawatha, Colombo 7

Literary Associations and Societies

Afro-Asian Writers' Bureau*, 73 Castle St, Colombo 8
Publication: Call

The **Dickens** Fellowship*, University of Ceylon, Thurston Rd, Colombo
Honorary Secretary: M M Aryrtane

Literary Periodicals

Call (Editions in English and French), Afro-Asian Writers' Bureau, 73 Castle St, Colombo 8

New Ceylon Writing; creative and critical writing of Sri Lanka, Macquarie University, School of English and Linguistics, North Ryde, NSW 2113, Australia

Vidyodaya; journal of arts, science and letters (text in English, Sinhalese and Tamil), University of Sri Lanka, Vidyodaya Campus Library, Nugegoda

Literary Prizes

Literary Prizes for Sinhala Literature*
For the best books published in the previous year in the Sinhala language in the following categories: novels, short stories, poetry, translations, children's literature, scientific literature, drama; also three awards in miscellaneous literary areas and awards for original works in Pali, Sanskrit and Arabic.
5,000 Sri Lanka rupees each, excepting children's literature for which the prize is 2,000 rupees. Awarded annually. Enquiries to Ministry of Cultural Affairs, 212 Bauddhaloka Mawatha, Colombo 7

Don **Pedrick** Memorial Literary Award*
For the best original literary work in Sinhala. 1,000 Sri Lanka rupees. Awarded annually. Enquiries to Don Pedrick Memorial Literary Award Committee, 79 Dharmapala Mawata, Colombo 7

Sudan

General Information

Language: Arabic (English also used)
Religion: Muslim (Sunni sect) in north, traditional in south
Population: 17 million
Literacy Rate (1956): 9.6%
Bank Hours: 0830-1200 Saturday-Thursday
Shop Hours: 0800-1300, 1700-2000 Saturday-Thursday
Currency: 100 piastres (1,000 milliemes) = 1 Sudanese pound
Export/Import Information: No tariff on books; some advertising matter may be dutied. Import licences required. Exchange controls; annual foreign exchange budget

Publishers

Al-**Ayam** Press Co Ltd, Aboul Ela Bldgs, United Nations Sq, PO Box 363, Khartoum
Man Dir: Beshir Muhammad Said
Subjects: General Fiction & Non-fiction, Belles Lettres, Poetry, Reference, Magazines, Books in Arabic, Paperbacks
Founded: 1953

Government Printer*, Government Printing Press, PO Box 38, Khartoum

Khartoum University Press*, PO Box 321, Khartoum Tel: 80558/81806/81869
Man Dir, General Editor: Ali El-Mak; *Sales Manager:* Abdel Raham Ibrahim; *Editorial, Rights & Permissions:* Jamal Abdel Malik, Judy El-Nagar
Subjects: General Fiction and Non-fiction, Belles Lettres, Poetry, Biography, History, Africana, Philosophy, Reference, Religion, Books in Arabic, Paperbacks, Science & Technology, General & Social Science, University & Secondary Textbooks
Bookshop: PO Box 321, Khartoum
Founded: 1968

Major Booksellers

Apaya Bookshop, PO Box 110, Juba Tel: 2595 Cable Add: Sudchurch
Manager: Lole Kwaje Lole
The Bookshop of the Episcopal Church of Sudan (formerly The Church Bookshop)

Al **Bashir** Bookshop*, PO Box 1118, Khartoum

The **Church** Bookshop, now Apaya Bookshop (qv)

The **Khartoum** Bookshop*, PO Box 968, Khartoum Tel: 77594/74425 Cable Add: Newstand Khartoum
Manager: P N Flanginis
The **Sudan** Bookshop Ltd, PO Box 1610, Khartoum Tel: 74123/76781 Cable Add: Bookshop Khartoum Telex: 22480 sisco km
Man Dir: Joseph A Tadros

University of Khartoum Bookshop*, PO Box 321, Khartoum Tel: 72271

Major Libraries

Atbara Public Library*, Atbara

British Council Library, PO Box 1253, Khartoum (Located at: Hai Al Abbasia, Omdurman, Khartoum) Tel: 53568/53281 Telex: 22790 Bckht Sd
Librarian: Ali Hassan Salih

Central Records Office Library*, PO Box 1914, Khartoum Tel: 76082
Librarian: Beshir Osman Ahmed

College for Arab and Islamic Studies Library*, PO Box 328, Omdurman

Khartoum Polytechnic Library, PO Box 407, Khartoum Tel: 78922
Librarian: Hassan Mohammad-Ali

University of Cairo*, Khartoum Branch Library, PO Box 1055, Khartoum

University of Khartoum Library*, PO Box 321, Khartoum Tel: 72271

Library Association

Sudan Library Association*, PO Box 1361, Khartoum Tel: 75100 ext 235
Secretary: Mohd Omer Ahmed
Publication: Libraries Journal

Library Reference Journal

Libraries Journal (Text in Arabic and English), Sudan Library Association, PO Box 1361, Khartoum

Suriname

General Information

Language: Dutch. English is widely spoken
Religion: Hindu, Roman Catholic, Muslim, Protestant
Population: 374,000
Literacy Rate (1964): 83.6%
Bank Hours: 0800-1230 Monday-Friday; 0800-1100 or 1200 Saturday
Shop Hours: Generally 0700-1300, 1600-1800 Monday-Friday; 0700-1300, 1600-1900 Saturday
Currency: 100 cents = 1 Suriname gulden
Export/Import Information: No tariff on books except children's picture books; none on small quantities of advertising matter. Added taxes charged. Import licences liberally granted. Exchange controls
Copyright: Berne

Book Trade Organizations

Standard Book Numbering Agency, Publishers' Association Suriname, Domineestr 32, PO Box 1841, Paramaribo Tel: 72545
ISBN Administrator: Dr Ellen Kensmil

Publishers' Association **Suriname**, Domineestr 32, PO Box 1841, Paramaribo Tel: 72545

Publishers

Apollo's Reklame en Uitgeversburo, Torenlastr 3, PO Box 574, Paramaribo
ISBN Publisher's Prefix: 99914-908

NV Drukkerij **Eldorado**, Eldoradolaan 1, Paramaribo
ISBN Publisher's Prefix: 99914-51

Ideoplastos, Keizerstr 83, PO Box 1474, Paramaribo
ISBN Publisher's Prefix: 99914-902

C **Kersten & Co**, Steenbakkerijstr 27, Paramaribo Tel: 71133 Telex: 142
ISBN Publisher's Prefix: 99914-52

Mechtelli Tjin-A-Sie, Paramaribo Tel: 75861
ISBN Publisher's Prefix: 99914-909

Ministerie van Cultuur Jeugd en Sport, nk Dr S Redmondstr/Wanicastr, Paramaribo
ISBN Publisher's Prefix: 99914-1-0

Mavis A **Noordwijk**, Regentessestr 3, PO Box 2653, Paramaribo
ISBN Publisher's Prefix: 99914-907

C D **Ooft**, Dr H Benjaminstr 28, Paramaribo Tel: 99139
ISBN Publisher's Prefix: 99914-910

Orchid Press, PO Box 28, Paramaribo
ISBN Publisher's Prefix: 99914-904

Sint Kinderkrant Suriname, PO Box 3013, Paramaribo
ISBN Publisher's Prefix: 99914-53

Educatief Uitg **Sorava**, Vestastr 17, Ma Retraite
ISBN Publisher's Prefix: 99914-906

Vaco NV, PO Box 1841, Paramaribo Tel: 72545 Cable Add: Vaco Telex: 123 Inco sn (Located at: Domineestraat 26-32, Paramaribo)
Man Dir: E Hogenboom; *Publicity:* E Kennsmil
Subjects: History, Low-priced Paperbacks, Primary and Secondary Textbooks, Maps
Founded: 1952
Bookshop: Vaco NV, Domineestr 26-32, Paramaribo

F H R Oedayrajsingh **Varma**, PO Box 9192, Paramaribo
ISBN Publisher's Prefix: 99914-903

Leo **Victor***, Gemenlandsweg 4, Paramaribo

Stichting De **Volksboekwinkel**, Keizerstr 197, PO Box 3040, Paramaribo
ISBN Publisher's Prefix: 99914-901

Stichting **Volkslectuur**, Sapotillestr 25, Paramaribo
ISBN Publisher's Prefix: 99914-50

M **Waagmeester-Verkuyl**, Nickeriestr 22, PO Box 9166, Paramaribo
ISBN Publisher's Prefix: 99914-905

Stichting **Wetenschappelijke** Informatie, Verlengde Keizerstr 63, Paramaribo
ISBN Publisher's Prefix: 99914-900

Major Booksellers

Vaco NV, PO Box 1841, Domineestr 26-32, Paramaribo
Manager: F Terborg

Major Libraries

Bibliotheek CCS, see Cultural Centre

Library of the **Cultural Centre** Surinam (Bibliotheek CCS)*, Gravenstr 112-114, PO Box 1241, Paramaribo
Librarian: Mrs C Carrilho-Fazal Alikhan

Swaziland

General Information

Language: siSwari. English used in business
Religion: Tribal religions, some Christianity
Population: 544,000
Banks close 1100 Saturday
Currency: 100 cents = 1 lilangeni (plural: emalangeni). 1 lilangeni = 1 rand. South African currency is also legal tender
Export/Import Information: Same as South Africa

Publishers

Mabiya Publications (Pty) Ltd*, PO Box 601, Mbabane Tel: 2076

Macmillan Boleswa Publishers (Pty) Ltd, PO Box 1235, Manzini Tel: 84533
Man Dir: L A Balarin; *Editorial:* E Paren; *Sales, Publicity, Rights & Permissions:* M Neild
Parent Company: Macmillan Publishers Ltd, UK (qv for Associate Companies)
Subsidiary Companies: Macmillan Swazi National Publishing Co (at above address); Macmillan Botswana, PO Box 1155, Gaborone, Botswana
Subject: Educational
ISBN Publisher's Prefix: 0-333

Major Booksellers

Swaziland News Agency*, PO Box 157, Mbabane

Webster's (Pty) Ltd, PO Box 292, Mbabane Tel: 42560 Telex: 2174 Wd
Manager: Mrs M Armstrong

Major Libraries

William **Pitcher** Training College Library, PO Box 87, Manzini Tel: 52081/2

Swaziland College of Technology Library, PO Box 69, Mbabane Tel: 42681
Librarian: Miss N S Dlamini

Swaziland National Library Service, PO Box 1461, Mbabane Tel: Swaziland 42633 Telex: 2270 Wd
Dir: B J K Kingsley
Publication: Annual Report of the Director

University of Swaziland Library*, PB, Kwaluseni Tel: 52111 (Manzini) Telex: 2087 WD
Librarian: A W Z Kuzwayo

Library Reference Book

Directory of Swaziland Libraries, (1975, University of Botswana, Lesotho and Swaziland), PB, Kwaluseni

Sweden

General Information

Language: Swedish. Danish and Norwegian are usually intelligible to speakers of Swedish. German is common second language
Religion: Protestant
Population: 8.28 million
Bank Hours: 0930-1500 Monday-Friday
Shop Hours: 0900-1800 (later Friday) Monday-Friday; 0900-1400 or 1600 Saturday
Currency: 100 öre = 1 Swedish krona (plural: kronor)
Export/Import Information: Member of the European Free Trade Association. No tariff on books, Advertising Tax. VAT on most imported goods. No import licences. No exchange controls
Copyright: UCC, Berne, Florence (see International section)

Book Trade Organizations

Bok-, Pappers- och Kontorsvaruförbundet, Skeppargatan 27, S-114 52 Stockholm Tel: Växel (08) 630205
Swedish Federation of Book, Stationery and Office Supplies Dealers
Publications: Papper och Kontor; Svensk Bokhandel (jointly with Swedish Publishers' Association)

Bokbranschens Finansieringsinstitut AB, Sveavägen 52, S-111 34 Stockholm
Book Trade Finance Institute

Bokbranschens Marknadsinstitut AB, Sveavägen 52, S-111 34 Stockholm Tel: (08) 230225
Book Trade Marketing Institute
Man Dir: Kerstin Wachtmeister

Bokhandelsrådet, c/o Svenska Bokförläggareföreningen, Sveavägen 52, S-111 34, Stockholm
Book Trade Council

Föreningen Svenska Läromedelsproducenter, Klara Norra Kyrkogata 29, S-111 22 Stockholm Tel: (08) 242280
Swedish Association of Publishers and Manufacturers of Educational Material
Secretary: Siv Klässon

Kristna Bokförläggareföreningen, Skolgatan 11, Box 1623, S-701 16 Örebro Tel: (019) 119360
Christian Publishers' Association
Secretariat: Björn-Ingvar Olsson

Standard Book Numbering Agency, see Swedish National ISBN Centre

Svenska Antikvariatföreningen, Box 22549, S-104 22 Stockholm
Swedish Antiquarian Booksellers' Association

Svenska Bokförläggareföreningen, Sveavägen 52, S-111 34 Stockholm Tel: (08) 231800
Swedish Publishers' Association
Secretary: Lars Bergman
Publication: Svensk Bokhandel (jointly with the Swedish Booksellers' Association)

Svenska Bokhandels-Medhjälpare-Föreningen, Adolf Fredriks Kyrkogata 5-7, 1 tr, S-111 37 Stockholm Tel: (08) 210575
Swedish Booksellers' Assistants' Association

Svenska Bokhandlareföreningen, Division of Bok-, Pappers- och Kontorsvaruförbundet, Skeppargatan 27, S-114 52 Stockholm Tel:

352 SWEDEN

(08) 630205
Swedish Booksellers' Association, Division of the Swedish Federation of Book, Stationery and Office Supplies Dealers
Secretary: Per Nordenson

Svenska Musikförläggareföreningen UPA, c/o Svensk Musik, Birger Jarlsgatan 6B, Box 5091, S-102 42 Stockholm
Swedish Music Publishers' Association
General Manager: Christian Sylvan

Sveriges B-Bokhandlareförbund*, S-280 10 Sösdala Tel: (0451) 60096
Swedish Association of Smaller Booksellers

Sveriges Författarförbund, Grev Turegatan 29, Box 5087, S-102 42 Stockholm
Swedish Union of Writers
Secretary: Sonja Thunborg
Publication: Författaren

Swedish National ISBN Centre, Bibliographical Department, Royal Library, Box 5039, S-102 41 Stockholm Tel: (08) 241040 Telex: 1640 Kbs S
ISBN Administrator: Lars-Erik Sanner

Book Trade Reference Books and Journals

Books

Boksverige, Författare, Förlag, Bokhandel, Bibliotek (The Book in Sweden: Author, Publisher, Bookshop, Library), Albert Bonniers Förlag AB, Sveavägen 56, S-111 34 Stockholm

Svenska Bokförläggareföreningens. Matrikel över dess Medlemmar och Kommissionärer samt Bokhandelns Föreningar och Organisationer (Swedish Publishers' Association. List of Members and Agents, together with Book Trade Associates and Organizations), Swedish Publishers' Association, Sveavägen 52, S-111 34 Stockholm

Journals

Bokrevy (Book Review), Bibliotekstjänst AB, Tornvägen 9, Box, S-221 01 Lund

Bokvännen (The Bibliophile), Sällskapet Bokvännera, Ulvsatervagen 18, S-191 43 Sollentuna 3

Svensk Bokförteckning (Swedish National Bibliography), Kungliga Biblioteket (Royal Library, Bibliographical Institute), Box 5039, S-102 41 Stockholm 5. Cumulates into the Svensk Bokkatalog

Svensk Bokhandel (Swedish Book Trade), Svenska Bokförläggareföreningen, Sveavägen 52, S-111 34 Stockholm (jointly with Swedish Federation of Book, Stationery and Office Supplies Dealers)

Svensk Bokkatalog, see Svensk Bokförteckning

Text; Swedish bibliographical journal (text in English and Swedish), Centre for Bibliographical Studies, Uppsala

Publishers

Acta Universitatis Gothoburgensis, Box 5096, S-402 22 Gothenburg Tel: (031) 631000 Telex: 20896 (Ubgbg S)
Man Dir: Paul Hallberg
Parent Company: Göteborgs Universitetsbibliotek (qv under Major Libraries)
Subjects: Scholarly works in the humanities and the social sciences (monograph series)
1981: 11 titles 1982: 8 titles
ISBN Publisher's Prefix: 91-7346

Akademiförlaget, Box 3075, S-400 10 Gothenburg 3 Tel: (031) 179600
Manager: Gunnar Jedenius
Order Department: Esselte Studium AB, S-171 76 Solna Tel: (08) 7343000
Parent Company: Esselte Studium AB (qv)
Subjects: Languages, Medicine, Technical Economics, Textbooks
1981: 30 titles 1982: 30 titles Founded: 1835

Akademilitteratur Förlaget AB+, Box 50050, S-104 05 Stockholm Tel: (08) 155108 Cable Add: stockacademic Telex: 13115
Akademi S
Man Dir: Gunilla Widengren
Orders to: Förlagsdistribution AB, Box 505, S-175 20 Järfälla
Parent Company: Förlagsbokhandelsaktiebolaget Akademibokhandeln AB, Box 50016, S-104 05 Stockholm (a student-owned, non-profit-making chain of bookshops)
Subjects: Economics, Aesthetics, Philosophy, Law, Cultural History, Social Sciences, Linguistics, General
1981: 22 titles 1982: 26 titles Founded: 1976
ISBN Publisher's Prefix: 91-7410

Alba AB, Karlavägen 86, Box 10041, S-100 55 Stockholm Tel: (08) 600050
Telex: 11620 Bonbook
Man Dir & Editorial: Dr Daniel Hjorth; Rights & Permissions: Ann-Mari Torstensson
Parent Company: Albert Bonniers Förlag AB (qv)
Subjects: General Fiction and Non-fiction
1981: 35 titles Founded: 1977
ISBN Publisher's Prefix: 91-7458

Allhems Förlag AB, now part of Bokförlaget Atlantis AB (qv)

Allmänna Förlaget, Box 16427, S-103 27 Stockholm (Located at: Gustav Adolfs Torg 22-24, Stockholm) Tel: (08) 7399000
Cable Add: Libergraph Telex: 12801 S
Man Dir: Nils Zetterberg; Marketing: Lasse Stenberg
Parent Company: Liber Grafiska AB (qv)
Subjects: Publications for public authorities, including Swedish Government
1982: 800 titles
ISBN Publisher's Prefix: 91-38

Almqvist och Wiksell Förlag AB, Box 2052, S-103 12 Stockholm (Located at: Tryckerigatan 2, Stockholm) Tel: (08) 245290 Cable Add: Espub Telex: 16536
Man Dir: Göran Ahlberg; Publisher: Lasse Bergström
Subjects: General Fiction, Biography, Medicine, Reference, Juveniles, Low- and High-priced Paperbacks, Psychology, General and Social Science, University Textbooks
Founded: 1878
Miscellaneous: Firm is one of the companies comprising Esselte Förlag AB (qv)
ISBN Publisher's Prefix: 91-20

Almqvist och Wiksell International, Box 45150, S-140 30 Stockholm (Located at: Drottninggatan 108, Stockholm) Tel: (08) 237990 Cable Add: Almqvistbook Telex: 12430 Almqwik S
Dirs: Hans Molander, Lars-Erik Linder; Sales Manager: Bengt Sjöström
Subjects: Scientific & Technical books and periodicals
Miscellaneous: Publishers to the universities of Stockholm, Uppsala and Lund
ISBN Publisher's Prefix: 91-22

Almqvist och Wiksell Läromedel AB, Gamla Brogatan 26, Box 159, S-101 22 Stockholm 1 Tel: (08) 229180 Cable Add: Aweduc
Man Dir: Rolf Edfeldt; Marketing Dir: S-E Westerlund; International Sales: Claes Witthoff
Subjects: Schoolbooks and Educational Aids (all levels), Foreign Languages, Music
1981: 85 titles 1982: 98 titles

Apoteksbolaget AB*, Humlegårdsgatan 20, S-105 14 Stockholm Tel: (08) 240800
Telex: 11553 apobol s
Man Dir: Åke Nohrlander
Subject: Special Pharmaceutical Textbooks

Förlagsaktiebolaget Arbetarkultur*, Kungsgatan 84, S-112 27 Stockholm
Tel: (08) 543882
Man Dir: Claes-Göran Jönsson
Subjects: Fiction, Political Science, Social Sciences
ISBN Publisher's Prefix: 91-7014

AB Arcanum*, Box 14116, S-400 12 Gothenburg Tel: (031) 871516
Man Dir: Bo Ramme
Subjects: Homoeopathy, Natural Medicine, Osteopathy and other techniques (mainly as translations from other languages)

Askelin och Hägglund Förlag, Box 2008, S-103 11 Stockholm (Located at: Köpmangatan 6, Old Town, Stockholm)
Tel: (08) 246845/202089 Cable Add: Askhagpublish Stockholm Telex: 12442, 12443 Fotex S attn Askhagpublish
Man Dirs: Karl Hägglund, Christina Askelin; Junior Editor: Katarina Janouch; Rights & Permissions: Kerstin Öhrström
Subjects: General Fiction and Non-fiction, Journalism, Children's, Juveniles
1982: 16 titles 1983: 20 titles Founded: 1981
ISBN Publisher's Prefix: 91-7684

Askild och Kärnekull Förlag AB, Box 10148, S-100 55 Stockholm (Located at: Riddargatan 23B, Stockholm) Tel: (08) 140880 Cable Add: Timjan Telex: 12475
Man Dir, Publisher: Lars Grahn; Sales: Jerker Wennhag; Production: Stella Åkerstedt; Rights & Permissions, Publicity: Gunilla Canvert
Parent Company: Bokförlaget Natur och Kultur (qv)
Subjects: Fiction & Non-fiction, Science Fiction, Memoirs, Guidebooks, Cookery
1981: 75 titles Founded: 1969
ISBN Publisher's Prefixes: 91-582, 91-7008

Bokförlaget Atlantis AB+, Västra Trädgårdsgatan 11 B, S-111 53 Stockholm
Tel: (08) 240490 Cable Add: Atlantisbooks
Man Dir: Kjell Peterson; Dirs: Lars Falk, Ove Pihl; Production: Lennart Rolf; Rights & Permissions: Maj-Britt Jonsson
Subjects: Quality Non-fiction, Illustrated Books, Swedish and Foreign Fiction, including Classics, Art Books
1981: 35 titles Founded: 1977
ISBN Publisher's Prefix: 91-7486

Förlaget Barrikaden AB, Bjurholmsplan 22, S-116 63 Stockholm Tel: (08) 7149353
Man Dir, Editorial, Publicity, Rights & Permissions: Dag Hernried; Sales, Production: Eva Spångberg
Subjects: Fiction, Non-fiction, Children's
Founded: 1976
ISBN Publisher's Prefixes: 91-85328, 91-7712

Beckmans Bokförlag AB, now part of Liber Förlag (qv)

Berghs Förlag AB, Box 17049, S-200 10 Malmö 17 Tel: (040) 231333 Cable Add: Sebergh Malmö
Chairman: Sven-Erik Bergh; Man Dir, Production Manager: Ingrid Bergh; Executive Editor: Liselotte Weiss
Orders to: Seelig och Co, Stockholm (qv under Booksellers)
Associate Company: Edition Sven Erik Bergh im Europabuch AG, Switzerland (qv)

Subjects: General Fiction, Belles Lettres, Poetry, History, Music, Art, Juveniles, Religion, Low- and High-priced Paperbacks, Medicine, Psychology, General Science, Educational Materials, Mysteries, Thrillers, Books in German, Pocket book series
1981: 68 titles *Founded:* 1954

Bernces Förlag AB, Södergatan 20, S-211 34 Malmö Tel: (040) 77265 Cable Add: Bebolag
Man Dir: Arvid Bernce; *Editorial:* Margaret Bernce
Subjects: General Fiction and Non-fiction, Biography, Cookery, History, Reference, Art, Large Illustrated Books
ISBN Publisher's Prefix: 91-500

Biblioteksförlaget AB, Box 14143, S-104 41 Stockholm (Located at: Storgatan 25, Stockholm) Tel: (08) 143460 Telex: 11785 Unpress S
Man Dir: Per Ivarsson
Parent Company: Bokförlaget Natur och Kultur (qv)
Subjects: Reference, University and Secondary and Primary Textbooks, Atlases, Physics, Mathematics, Children's Books
1981: 40 titles *Founded:* 1923
ISBN Publisher's Prefix: 91-542

Bibliotekstjänst AB*, Tornavägen 9, Box 1706, S-221 01 Lund Tel: (046) 140480 Telex: 32200 btjlund s
Subjects: Library Science, Reference, Periodicals, Indexes
1981: 40 titles *Founded:* 1951
ISBN Publisher's Prefix: 91-7018

Bonnier Fakta Bokforlag AB*, Box 3159, S-103 63 Stockholm (Located at: Sveavägen 56, Stockholm) Tel: (08) 229120 Cable Add: Bonniers Telex: 11620 Bonbook S
Chief Executive: Bo Streiffert; *Sales:* Birger Åkerlund; *Production:* Arne Björkman; *Publicity:* Annika Lindholm; *Rights & Permissions:* Monica Norberg
Parent Company: Albert Bonniers Förlag AB (qv)
Subjects: General Non-fiction, Field Guides, Art, Handbooks, Cookery, University Textbooks, Dictionaries, Co-editions
1981: 60 titles *Founded:* 1981
ISBN Publisher's Prefix: 91-34

Albert **Bonniers** Förlag AB, Sveavägen 56, Box 3159, S-103 63 Stockholm Tel: (08) 229120 Cable Add: Bonniers Telex: 11620 Bonbook S
Chairman: Gerard Bonnier; *Man Dir:* Per-Olov Atle; *Editorial Dirs:* Karl O Bonnier, Åke Runnquist, Bo Streiffert; *Sales:* Lars Håkanson, Arne Berggren; *Rights & Permissions:* Monica Norberg
Subsidiary Companies: Alba AB (qv); Bokförlaget Forum AB (qv); Bonnier Fakta Bokforlag AB (qv); Bonniers Juniorförlag AB (qv); AB Wahlström och Widstrand (qv)
Associate Company: Åhlén & Åkerlund (Periodicals)
Subjects: General Fiction and Non-fiction, Medical and Technical, Reference Works, Juvenile, Young Adult, Paperbacks, Periodical
Book Clubs: Bokklubben Svalan, Bonniers Bokklubb, Bonniers Bokpaket, Underhållningsbokklubben, Stora Romanklubben, part-owner of Månadens Bok
1981: 350 titles *1982:* 350 titles *Founded:* 1837
ISBN Publisher's Prefix: 91-0

Bonniers Juniorförlag AB, Kammakargatan 9A, Box 3159, S-103 63 Stockholm Tel: (08) 229120 Telex: 11620 Bonbook S
Man Dir, Publisher: Karin Leijon; *Sales:* Bengt Nordin; *Co-Production:* Bonnier Juveniles International; *Production:* Ulla Persson; *Rights & Permissions:* Monica Norberg
Parent Company: Albert Bonniers Förlag AB (qv)
Subjects: Children's Books, Juveniles
1981: 70 titles *Founded:* 1979
ISBN Publisher's Prefix: 91-48

Bokförlaget **Bra Böcker** AB, Södra Vägen, S-263 00 Höganäs Tel: (042) 39000 Cable Add: BBBooks Telex: 72643 S Bbbooks
Publisher: Rolf G Janson; *President:* Bengt Revin; *Publishing Dir:* Sven Gunnar Särman; *Production:* Lars Danielsson; *Rights & Permissions:* Madeleine Ström
Subjects: General Fiction, History, Geography, Illustrated Books, Encyclopaedias
Book Clubs: Bra Böcker; Bra Deckare (detective novels); Bra Klassiker (classics); Bra Lyrik (poetry); Bra Spänning (thrillers)
Founded: 1965

Brombergs Bokförlag AB, Box 3158, S-103 63 Stockholm (Located at: Tegnérg 29, S-111 40 Stockholm) Tel: (08) 117730/117750
Man Dir, Editorial, Sales & Publicity: Dorotea Bromberg; *Production, Rights & Permissions:* Dr Adam Bromberg
Subjects: General Fiction and Non-fiction, Political Science, Popular Science, Medicine
1981: 40 titles *1982:* 36 titles *Founded:* 1975
ISBN Publisher's Prefix: 91-7608

Förlaget **By och Bygd**, Box 22087, S-104 22 Stockholm Tel: (08) 520955
Man Dir: Lars-Olof Johansson
Subjects: Politics, Social Questions

Carlsen/if AB*, Bredgrand 2, S-111 30 Stockholm Tel: (08) 246880
Man Dir: Arne Mossberg; *Sales:* Bengt Stagman
Parent Company: SEMIC (qv)
Associate Company: Carlsen Verlag GmbH, Federal Republic of Germany (qv)
Subjects: Children's Picture-books
Founded: 1968
ISBN Publisher's Prefix: 91-510

Bokförlaget **Carmina***, Norbyvägen 33, S-752 39 Uppsala Tel: (018) 110805
Man Dir: Jörn Johanson
Subjects: General Fiction, History, Art, Sciences, Classics, Textbooks

René **Coeckelberghs** Bokförlag AB*, Saltmätargatan 3B, Box 45059, S-104 30 Stockholm Tel: (08) 248245 Telex: 14277 reco S
Man Dir: René Coeckelberghs
Subjects: Fiction, Non-fiction, Poetry, Political Science, Social Sciences, High-priced Paperbacks
ISBN Publisher's Prefix: 91-7250

Combi International AB, now Förlagshuset Norden AB (qv)

Editions **Corniche**, a subsidiary of Bokförläggare Bengt Forsberg (qv)

Bokförlaget **Corona** AB, Nobelvägen 135, Box 5, S-201 20 Malmö Tel: (040) 189480
Publisher: Nils-Åke Janséus; *Dir:* Lars Welinder
Subjects: Juveniles, Textbooks, Education, Fiction, Non-fiction

Tidnings AB **Dagen**, S-105 36 Stockholm (Located at: Gammelgårdsvägen 38, Stora Essingen) Tel: (08) 130340 Cable Add: Dagen Telex: 10888 dagen
Man Dir, Production, Rights & Permissions: Sverre Larsson; *Editorial:* Olof Djurfeldt; *Sales:* David Edström; *Publicity Dir:* Rune Flygg; *Advertising Dir:* Gunnar Forsberg
Subsidiary Companies: Förlaget Filadelfia AB (qv), Normans Förlag AB (qv)

Subjects: Biography, History, Music, Art, Religion, Juveniles, Low-priced Paperbacks, Educational Materials
Bookshop: Gospel Center, Kungsgatan 62, S-111 22 Stockholm
Book Club: Den Kristna Bokringen, Dagenhuset, S-105 36 Stockholm
Founded: 1945

Dahlia Books, International Publishers and Booksellers, Box 1025, S-751 40 Uppsala Tel: (018) 100525 Cable Add: Dahlia, Uppsala
Man Dir: Gun-Britt Du Rietz
Subjects: Botany, Zoology, Australiana, Bibliography, Publications of the Royal Swedish Academy of Sciences
Founded: 1973
Miscellaneous: Major function of this company is bookselling (antiquarian and new) at above address

Delta Förlags AB*, Box 15123, S-161 15 Bromma Tel: (08) 254781
Man Dir: Sam J Lundwall
Subjects: General Fiction and Non-fiction, Science fiction, High-priced Paperbacks
Book Club: Delta Science Fiction Bok Klubb
Founded: 1973
ISBN Publisher's Prefix: 91-7228

Doxa University Books+, Kungsgatan 1, S-223 50 Lund Tel: (046) 127277 Cable Add: Doxabook Telex: 35546 Doxabok S
Man Dir: Bertil Belfrage; *Editorial:* Pavel Gabriel; *Sales:* Gun-Britt Grov
Orders to: Box 17, S-570 20 Bodafors
Subjects: Scholarly, Scientific, Textbooks; Paperbacks
1981: 40 titles *1982:* 40 titles *Founded:* 1974
ISBN Publisher's Prefix: 91-578

E C Print AB*, Kastellgatan 1, S-413 07 Gothenburg Tel: (031) 133099
Man Dir: Dr Carlos Ezeyza-Alvear; *Sales Manager:* Michael Törnros; *Production Manager:* Bengt Jacobsson
Subjects: Technical Manuals and Books, Dictionaries
1981: 15 titles *Founded:* 1978
ISBN Publisher's Prefix: 91-86236

E F S-förlaget, see Evangeliska Fosterlands-Stiftelsen Förlag

Ehrlingförlagen AB, Box 5268, S-102 45 Stockholm (Located at: Linnégatan 9-11, Stockholm) Tel: (08) 7830615 Cable Add: Ehrlingmusik
Man Dir: Staffan Ehrling
Associate Company: Belwin-Mills Nordiska AB
Subsidiary Companies: Thore Ehrling Musik AB, Nils-Georgs Musikförlags AB, Edition Sylvain AB; all at above address
Subject: Music
1981: 12 titles *Founded:* 1952

Elkan och Schildknecht, Emil Carelius AB, Västmannagatan 95, S-113 43 Stockholm Tel: (08) 338463/338464
Man Dir: Bengt Carelius
Subject: Music

Esselte Focus Uppslagsböcker AB+, Box 2120, S-103 13 Stockholm (Located at: Brunnsgränd 4, Stockholm) Tel: (08) 245290 Telex: 17924 Esvideo S
Focus International Book Production AB
Man Dir: Göran Ahlberg; *Publisher:* P Jonas Sjögren
Subject: Reference (Encyclopaedias)
Miscellaneous: Firm is one of the companies comprising Esselte Förlag AB (qv)

Esselte Förlag AB*, Tryckerigatan 2, S-103 12 Stockholm 2 Tel: (08) 228040 Telex: 17155 esprint s
Man Dir: Göran Ahlberg

Book Club: Vår Bok
1981: 350 titles
Miscellaneous: Esselte Förlag is the name of the Publishing Division within the Esselte Group. It consists of four independent houses, namely Almqvist och Wiksell Förlag AB (qv), Esselte Focus Uppslagsböcker AB (qv), P A Norstedt och Söners Förlag (qv), Esselte Video AB

Esselte Herzogs AB*, Box 155, S-131 06 Nacka Tel: (08) 7162680 Cable Add: Herzogs Telex: 12297
Man Dir: Rune Sirvell
Parent Company: Esselte AB, Sturegatan 11, Stockholm
Subjects: Bibles, Hymnals, Religion
Founded: 1862

Esselte Map Service, Garvargatan 9, Box 22069, S-104 22 Stockholm Tel: (08) 541920 Cable Add: Esseltemap Telex: 120 84 EMS S
General Manager: Lars Brenner;
Cartographic Manager: Siv Eklund;
Marketing Manager: Bo Gramfors
Subsidiary Companies: Esselte Kartor AB; Generalstabens Litografiska Anstalt (both at above address)
Subjects: Atlases, Maps
Founded: 1833

Esselte Studium AB, Sundbybergsvägen 1, S-171 76 Solna Tel: (08) 7343000 Cable Add: Esseltestudium Stockholm Telex: 11681 Studium S
Man Dir: Lars-G Ståhl
Subsidiary Company: Akademiförlaget (qv)
Subjects: Educational, Primary and Secondary Textbooks, Languages, Arts, Social Sciences, Natural Sciences, Mathematics, Technical and Scientific, Economics, Medical and Nursing, Dictionaries, Scandinavian University Books, Educational Aids
ISBN Publisher's Prefix: 91-24

Evangeliska Fosterlands-Stiftelsens Förlag (EFS-förlaget), Tegnérgatan 34, S-113 59 Stockholm Tel: (08) 340290 Cable Add: Stiftelsen Telex: 15112 Evan S
Man Dir: Matts Andersson
Subjects: Theology and Religion, General Fiction and Non-fiction, Poetry, Reference, Juveniles, Young Adult, High-priced Paperbacks
Founded: 1856
ISBN Publisher's Prefix: 91-7080

Fib's Lyrikklub, an imprint of Bokförlags AB Tiden (qv)

Förlaget Filadelfia AB*, Gammelgärdsvägen 38, S-105 36 Stockholm Tel: (08) 130340 Cable Add: Dagen Telex: 10888 dagen
Man Dir, Editorial, Production, Rights & Permissions: Sverre Larsson; *Sales:* David Edström; *Publicity:* Rune Flygg
Parent Company: Tidnings AB Dagen (qv)
Associate Companies: Den Kristna Bokringen (Book Club), Normans Förlag (qv)
Subjects: Christian religious
Founded: 1915
ISBN Publisher's Prefix: 91-536

Focus International Book Production AB, see Esselte Focus Uppslagsböcker AB

Författares Bokmaskin*, Svarvargatan 14, S-112 49 Stockholm Tel: (08) 535880
Associate Company: Bokmaskinen i Göteborg, Kungshojdsgatan 11, S-411 20 Göteborg Tel: (031) 133562
Subjects: General Fiction and Non-fiction, Poetry, Juvenile, Current Controversies

Bokförläggare Bengt **Forsberg**, Södra Tullgatan 4, S-211 40 Malmö Tel: (040) 76320 Cable Add: Godbok
Man Dir: Bengt Forsberg; *Sales Dirs:* Jörgen Forsberg, Claës Forsberg, Matts Forsberg
Subsidiary Company: Editions Corniche (qv)
Subjects: History, Medicine, Photography, Yearbooks
Founded: 1943
ISBN Publisher's Prefix: 91-7046

Bokförlaget **Forum** AB, Box 14115, S-104 41 Stockholm (Located at: Riddargatan 23A, Stockholm) Cable Add: Bokforum Telex: 16764 Forum S
Man Dir: Bertil Käll; *Marketing:* Jan-Olof Westrell; *Production:* Majbritt Hagdahl; *Rights & Permissions:* Monica Heyum
Shipping Address: Malmvägen 80-82, S-191 47 Sollentuna
Parent Company: Albert Bonniers Förlag AB (qv)
Subjects: General Fiction and Non-fiction, Popular History, How-to, Music, Art, High- & Low-priced Paperbacks
Book Club: Part-owner of Månadens Bok
1981: 90 titles *1982:* 90 titles *Founded:* 1944
ISBN Publisher's Prefix: 91-37

AB Carl **Gehrmans** Musikförlag, Apelbergsgatan 58, Box 505, S-101 26 Stockholm 1 Tel: (08) 103004 Cable Add: Musikgehrman
Man Dir: Kettil Skarby
Subject: Music
Founded: 1893

Generalstabens Litografiska Anstalt, a subsidiary of Esselte Map Service (qv)

Gidlunds Förlag, Box 12176, S-102 25 Stockholm (Located at: Karlsviksgatan 16, S-112 41 Stockholm) Tel: (08) 549985/540180
Man Dir: Krister Gidlund; *Sales Dir:* Gertrud Gidlund; *Editorial:* Karin Monié
Subjects: General Fiction, Belles Lettres, Poetry, Biography, History, Music, Art, Philosophy, Juveniles, High-priced Paperbacks, Psychology, Social Science
1981: 60 titles *1982:* 60 titles *Founded:* 1968
ISBN Publisher's Prefix: 91-7021

AB C W K **Gleerup** Bokförlag, now part of Liber Utbildning (qv)

Gullers Trading AB*, Kungsgatan 30xv, S-111 35 Stockholm Tel: (08) 230585 Telex: 13437 Cable Add: Gullersfoto
Publisher: Karl Werner Gullers; *Man Dir:* Per Schött
Subjects: Health, Industrial, Crafts, Nature

Gummessons Bokförlag, now merged with part of Skeab Förlag AB (qv) to form Verbum Förlag AB (qv)

Hälsaböcker/Allt om Hälsa AB*, Box 1, Torsvikssvängen 26, S-181 21 Lidingö Tel: (08) 7652760
Man Dir: Eskil Svensson
Subject: Health

Hamrelius och Stenvall Förlag AB*, Malmgatan 3, S-211 32 Tel: (040) 127703
Publishers: Gudmund Hamrelius, Frank Stenvall; *Sales:* Gudmund Hamrelius; *Production:* Frank Stenvall
Associate Company: Frank Stenvalls Förlag (qv)
Subjects: Popular Management, Travel
1982: 5 titles projected *Founded:* 1980
ISBN Publisher's Prefix: 91-7658

Hanse Production AB, Tranhusgatan 29, S-621 55 Visby Tel: (0498) 49318
Chief Executive: Thorbjörn Ödin
Subject: History, especially local history of the island of Gotland
Founded: 1978
ISBN Publisher's Prefix: 91-85716

Harriers Bokförlag AB*, Box 135, S-524 00 Herrljunga Tel: (0513) 11930
Man Dir, Publicity, Rights & Permissions: Per-Ove Lannerö; *Editorial, Production:* Nils-Erik Karlsson; *Sales:* Lennart Asberg, Göran Sjöström
Subjects: General Fiction and Non-fiction, Biography, Documentaries, Juvenile, Religious
Book Club: Önskeboken
1982: 40 titles *Founded:* 1932
ISBN Publisher's Prefix: 91-7068

Hemmets Journal AB*, Box, S-212 05 Malmö
Parent Company: Gutenberghus Group, Denmark
Associate Companies: Ehapa-Verlag GmbH, Federal Republic of Germany; Gutenberghus Publishing Service A/S, Denmark (qv), Hjemmet A/S, Hjemmets Bokforlag A/S (both Norway qqv)
Subjects: Juveniles, Fiction, Human Interest
Founded: 1927

Hermods, see Liber Utbildning

Hillelförlaget, Nybrogatan 19, S-114 39 Stockholm Tel: (08) 621078
Man Dir: Anna Rock
Subjects: Judaica, Jewish History, Hebrew Fiction

Lars **Hökerbergs** Bokförlag, Box 8071, S-104 20 Stockholm (Located at: Fleminggatan 21) Tel: (08) 244360
Man Dir: Rolf Hökerberg
Subsidiary Company: I T K Laromedel
Subjects: General Fiction and Non-fiction, Technical, Textbooks, Educational Materials, Vocational Training by Correspondence
1981: 43 titles *1982:* 57 titles *Founded:* 1882
ISBN Publisher's Prefix: 91-7084

I C A-Förlaget AB, Stora Gatan 41, S-721 85 Västerås Tel: (021) 194000 Telex: 40486 ica s Cable Add: Icaförlaget
Man Dir: Kjell Gustafsson; *Publisher:* Birgitta O'Nils; *Sales:* Ulf Åberg; *Production:* Stig Österlund
Branch Off: Grev Turegatan 19, S-114 38 Stockholm Telex: 19435 Ica-s
Subjects: Cookery, Handicrafts, Hobbies, Gardening, Health, Domestic Animals, Antiques, Periodicals
1982: 32 titles *Founded:* 1944
ISBN Publisher's Prefix: 91-534

Ingenjörsvetenskapsakademien (I V A), Grev Turegatan 14, Box 5073, S-102 42 Stockholm 5 Tel: (08) 220760 Cable Add: Ivacademi
Royal Swedish Academy of Engineering Sciences
Man Dir: Hans G Forsberg; *Editorial:* Per Stenson
Subjects: Science, Technology
ISBN Publisher's Prefix: 91-7082

Interpublishing AB Rahm and Stenström, Taptogatan 4, S-115 28 Stockholm Tel: (08) 637601/02 Cable Add: Interpublishing
Managers: Anders Rahm, Bengt Stenström
Subjects: Biography, History, Hobby, Engineering, General Science, Reference
Miscellaneous: Previously Interbook Publishing AB

Interskrift Publishing House*, Fabriksgatan 19, Box 135, S-524 00 Herrljunga Tel: (0513) 11930 Telex: Startex S 42109
Man Dir: Per-Ove Lannerö; *Editorial, Production:* Nils Erik Karlsson; *Rights & Permissions:* Rigmor Andersson
Parent Company: Tyndale House Publisher, 336 Gondersen Drive, Wheaton, Illinois 60187, USA
Associate Company: Living Bibles

International, Box 155, S-527 00 Herrljunga, Sweden
Subjects: Bibles, General Religious
Book Club: Info Book
Founded: 1974
ISBN Publisher's Prefix: 91-7336

Kursverksamhetens Förlag, Magle Lilla Kyrkogata 4, S-223 51 Lund Tel: (046) 148720/148710
Man Dir: Hjördis Lundgren; *Editorial, Production, Rights & Permissions:* Daqmar Hellstam; *Sales, Publicity, Assistant Editor:* Annalisa Mikaelsson
Subjects: Educational material for Adults, especially Swedish as a foreign language
1981-82: 9 titles *Founded:* 1971
ISBN Publisher's Prefix: 91-7434

L I C—Förlag, S-171 83 Solna Tel: (08) 981060 Cable Add: Licentral, Stockholm Telex: 10528 lic s
This is the Publishing Department of L I C, which deals with the supply of hospital and health care equipment
Chief Executive: Björn Bergman; *Publishing Manager:* Olle Sundling; *Editorial, Production:* Bernt Sahlberg; *Sales, Publicity, Rights & Permissions:* Olle Sundling
Parent Company: L I C (at above address)
Subjects: Educational books and pamphlets relating to health care
Founded: 1977
ISBN Publisher's Prefix: 91-7584

L Ts Förlag AB (Lantbrukarnas Riksförbund och Studieförbundet Vuxenskolan)+, Drottninggatan 104, S-105 33 Stockholm Tel: (08) 7875200 Cable Add: Lantförbundet Telex: 17830 Ltbok S
Man Dir, Editorial: Pär Frank; *Sales Dir:* Lars-Olaf Ericsson; *Production Manager:* Harry Krieg; *Permissions:* Elly Widell
Subjects: Fiction and Illustrated Books on Popular Science, Farming, Gardening, Handicraft, Pattern Books on Embroidery, Weaving and Wood-work, Economics, Social and Cultural History, Politics, Housekeeping, Children's Books, Study Material for Adult Education
1981: 153 titles *1982:* 115 titles *Founded:* 1935
ISBN Publisher's Prefix: 96-36

Bokförlaget Robert **Larson** AB, Box 3063, S-183 03 Täby Tel: (08) 7565640 Cable Add: Larsonbooks
Dirs: Birgitta and Robert Larson
Subsidiary Companies: Larson Norsk Förlag A/S, Fr Nansens pl 9, Oslo 1, Norway; Larson Publications Inc, 4936 Rte 414, Burdett, NY 14818, USA
Subjects: Astrology, Philosophy, Psychology, Self-help, Education, Vegetarianism
Founded: 1971
ISBN Publisher's Prefix: 91-514

Liber Förlag, S-162 89 Stockholm (Located at: Sorterargatan 23, Vällingby) Tel: (08) 7399000 Cable Add: Libergraph Telex: 12801 S
Also: S-205 10 Malmö (Located at Slottsgatan 24, Malmö) Tel: (040) 70650 Cable Add: Libergraph Telex: 12801 S
Vice-President: Ingemar Turnbo (Malmö); *Marketing:* Lasse Stenberg; *Rights & Permissions:* Alva Jansson (Malmö)
Orders to: Liber distribution, S-163 53 Spånga
Parent Company: Liber Grafiska AB (qv) of which Liber Förlag is General Publishing sector
Subjects: General Interest Non-fiction; Business Management, Economics, Computers, Law, Education, Psychology, Humanities, Social Sciences, University Textbooks
Book Clubs: Bättre Barnomsorg, Bättre Data, Bättre Ledarskap, Bättre Samhälle, Bättre Skola
1982: 250 titles
ISBN Publisher's Prefix: 91-38

Liber Grafiska AB, S-162 89 Stockholm (Located at: Sorterargatan 23, Vällingby) Tel: (08) 7399000 Cable Add: Libergraph Telex: 12801 S
Man Dir: Karl-Axel Swedérus; *Executive Vice-President:* Anders Jurell
There are three sectors of production: Publishing (see Liber Förlag), Media and Education (see Liber Utbildning) plus six subsidiaries including a bookshop (see below)
Subsidiary Companies: Allmänna Förlaget (qv), Skrivab Skol- och Kontorsmateriel AB (school and office materials), Liber Systems-Text and Image AB, IMTEC Image Technology AB (all in Sweden), Unicom (Norway)
Bookshop: AB C E Fritzes Kungl Hovbokhandel (qv under Major Booksellers)

Liber Hermods, Slottsgatan 24, S-205 10 Malmö Tel: (040) 70650 Cable Add: Libergraph
Subjects: Educational Courses for School and Adult Education
Miscellaneous: A division of Liber Utbildning (qv)

Liber Läromedel, Slottsgatan 24, S-205 10 Malmö Tel: (040) 70650 Cable Add: Libergraph
Vice-President: Gunnar Pilesjö
Subjects: Primary and Secondary School Educational Materials
Miscellaneous: A division of Liber Utbildning (qv)

Liber Utbildning, S-162 89 Stockholm (Located at: Sorterargatan 23, Vällingby) Tel: (08) 7399000 Cable Add: Libergraph Telex: 12801 S
Also: S-205 10, Malmö (Located at: Slottsgatan 24, Malmö) Tel: (040) 70650 Cable Add: Libergraph Telex: 12801 S
Marketing Manager: Christer Aldén (Stockholm); *Rights & Permissions:* Alva Jansson (Malmö)
Orders to: Liber Distribution, S 213 75 Malmö
Divisions: Liber Läromedel (qv); Liber Hermods (qv); Liber Yrkesutbildning (Stockholm, vocational training materials); Liber Yrkesutbildning-Teknik (qv); Liber UtbildningsFörlaget (qv)
1982: 500 titles (all divisions)
ISBN Publisher's Prefixes: 91-23, 91-40

Liber UtbildningsFörlaget, S-162 89 Stockholm (Located at: Sorterargatan 23, Vällingby) Tel: (08) 7399000 Cable Add: Libergraph Telex: 12801 S
Vice-President: Ulf Åkersten
Subjects: Teacher Further Education
Miscellaneous: A division of Liber Utbildning (qv)

Liber Yrkesutbildning, a division of Liber Utbildning (qv)

Liber Yrkesutbildning-Teknik, S-162 89 Stockholm (Located at: Sorterargatan 23, Vällingby) Tel: (08) 7399000 Cable Add: Libergraph Telex: 12801 S
Vice-President: Bengt Björnekärr
Subjects: Computer software, Electronics & Telecommunications Textbooks
Miscellaneous: A division of Liber Utbildning (qv)

Libris Publishing House+, Box 1623, Skolgatan 11, S-701 16 Örebro Tel: (019) 119360 Telex: 73155 Libris
Man Dir: Björn-Ingvar Olsson; *Editorial:* Gunnar Jonsson; *Production:* Arnold Segerlund; *Sales, Publicity:* Kenneth Pettersson; *Rights & Permissions:* Erik Österlund
Subjects: General Interest, Theological, Juveniles, Fiction
Bookshop: Libris Bookshop, Storgatan 23, Box 1623, S-701 16 Örebro
Book Club: Libris Bookclub
Founded: 1916
ISBN Publisher's Prefix: 91-7194

Lidman Production AB+, Karlavägen 71, Box 5098, S-102 42 Stockholm Tel: (08) 232805
Publisher: Sven Lidman
Subjects: Educational, Encyclopaedias

J A **Lindblads** Bokförlag AB, Warfvinges väg 30, S-112 51 Stockholm Tel: (08) 534640 Cable Add: Bookjal Telex: 17174 (Wahlströms)
Man Dir: Bertil Wahlstöm; *Production:* Gert Fransson; *Permissions:* Eva Melin
Shipping Add: c/o B Wahlströms Bokförlag AB, Lövåsvägen 24, S-791 00 Falun
Parent Company: B Wahlströms Bokförlag AB (qv)
Subjects: General Fiction and Non-fiction, Juveniles
Founded: 1894
ISBN Publisher's Prefix: 91-32

Abr **Lundqvists** Musikförlag AB, Katarina Bangatan 17, S-116 25 Stockholm Tel: (08) 436767
Editorial: Lars-Johan Rundquist, Anna Orvelius
Subject: Music
Founded: 1838

Bokförlaget **Medium** AB*, Box 511, S-162 15 Vällingby Tel: (08) 380340
Man Dir: Bo Pederby
Subject: School Textbooks
ISBN Publisher's Prefix: 91-512

Gustav **Melins** AB, Box 1376, S-171 27 Solna Tel: (08) 7343400 Cable Add: Grakoswe Telex: 11978
Man Dir: Göran Brämming
Subjects: Bibles, Hymn Books
Founded: 1898

Metodistkyrkans Förlag, see Sanctus

Bokförlaget **Natur och Kultur**, Box 27323, S-102 54 Stockholm (Located at: Banérgatan 37, Stockholm) Tel: (08) 232480 Cable Add: Naturkultur
Man Dir: Lars Almgren; *General Editors:* Lars Källquist (Textbooks), Lennart Wolff (General Books); *Publicity, Sales:* Lennart Röhr (Textbooks), Ini Ljung (General Books); *Rights & Permissions:* Britta Svensson
Subsidiary Companies: Askild och Kärnekull Förlag AB (qv); Biblioteksförlaget AB (qv)
Subjects: General Non-fiction: Biography, History, Psychology, General Science, Secondary & Primary Textbooks, Audiovisual Materials, Children's
1983: 150 titles *Founded:* 1922
ISBN Publisher's Prefix: 91-27

AB **Nautic***, Skeppsbron 3, S-411 21 Gothenburg Tel: (031) 111200/111500 Cable Add: Nautic Telex: 21785 nautic s
Man Dir: Björn Traung
Subjects: Nautical Literature, Sea Charts
Miscellaneous: Agent for International Hydrographic publications
Founded: 1953

Nautiska Förlaget Sjökortshallen AB*, Box 19059, S-104 32 Stockholm Tel: (08) 345493/345682 Cable Add: Namco
The Nautical Publishing Co Ltd
Manager: S Hiljding
Subjects: Shipping Publications, Sea Charts, Navigational Literature

SWEDEN

Bokforlaget Niloe AB, Box 45, S-451 15 Uddevalla (Located at: N Drottninggatan 15-17) Tel: (0522) 10708
Chairman: Olof Ericson; *Man Dir:* Sture Marcusson; *Editorial:* Harry Lundin
Subjects: Classical Literature, Reference
1981: 8 titles *1982:* 10 titles *Founded:* 1953
ISBN Publisher's Prefix: 91-7102

AB Nordbok, Box 7095, S-402 32 Gothenburg (Located at: Pusterviksgatan 13, Gothenburg) Tel: (031) 171085 Cable Add: Nordbokab Telex: 21782 Nordbok S
Publishers: Gunnar Stenmar, Turlough Johnston
Subjects: History, Reference, Educational Materials, How-to, Sports, Hobbies, Outdoor Interest, Cartography
1982: 3 titles *1983:* 6 titles *Founded:* 1974

Förlagshuset Norden AB+, Box 305, S-201 23 Malmö Tel: (040) 937250
General Manager: Sven-Erik Gunnerall
Subsidiary Company: Combi International AB
Subjects: Reference, Encyclopaedias, Technical
Founded: 1931

AB Nordiska Bokhandelns Förlag*, Box 1034, S-171 21 Solna Tel: (08) 980234 Cable Add: Nordbok
Man Dir: Hans Molander
Parent Company: Esselte Bokhandel Group
Subject: Medicine
Bookshop: Kungsgatan 4, Box 7, S-101 20 Stockholm
Founded: 1851
ISBN Publisher's Prefix: 91-516

AB Nordiska Musikförlaget (Edition Wilhelm Hansen Stockholm), Box 745, S-101 30 Stockholm (Located at: Drottninggatan 37, Stockholm) Tel: (08) 144240 Cable Add: Musicalia Telex: 11859
Manager: Barbro Rydefalk
Parent Company: Edition Wilhelm Hansen, Denmark (qv)
Associate Companies: J & W Chester Ltd, Eagle Court, London EC1M 5 QD, UK; Norsk Musikforlag, Postboks 1499, Vika, N-Oslo 1, Norway; Edition Wilhelm Hansen, Postfach 2684, D-6000 Frankfurt am Main, Federal Republic of Germany
Subject: Music
Bookshop: At above address

Normans Förlag AB, Dagenhuset, S-105 36 Stockholm Tel: (08) 130340 Cable Add: Normanbok
Man Dir: Sverre Larsson
Parent Company: Tidnings AB Dagen (qv)
Subject: Religion
ISBN Publisher's Prefix: 91-536

AB P A Norstedt och Söners Förlag, Tryckerigatan 2, Box 2052, S-103 12 Stockholm 2 Tel: (08) 228040 Cable Add: Espub Telex: 16536 esprint
Man Dir: Göran Ahlberg; *Editorial Dir:* Lasse Bergström; *Rights & Permissions:* Agneta Markas
Subjects: General Fiction, Belles Lettres, Poetry, Biography, History, How-to, Music, Art, Philosophy, Reference, Religion, High-priced Paperbacks, Medicine, Psychology, Engineering, General and Social Science, Law
Book Club: Part-owner of Månadens Bok
Founded: 1823
Miscellaneous: Firm is one of the companies comprising Esselte Förlag AB (qv)
ISBN Publisher's Prefix: 91-1

Nybloms Förlag*, Lästmakargatan 1E, Box 154, S-751 04 Uppsala 1 Tel: (018) 257350 Cable Add: Nybloms
Man Dir: Carl-G Swanström
Subjects: Archaeology, Popular Science, Hobbies, Technology, Biography, General Non-fiction
Founded: 1939
ISBN Publisher's Prefix: 91-85040

Bokförlaget Opal AB, Tegelbergsvägen 31, Box 20113, S-161 20 Bromma Tel: (08) 282179
Joint Publishers: Bengt Christell, Valborg Segerhjelm
Subject: Juveniles
Founded: 1973
ISBN Publisher's Prefix: 91-7270

Ordfront tryckeri & förlag AB+, Box 20133, S-104 60 Stockholm (Located at: Tjurbergsgatan 27, Stockholm) Tel: (08) 449390 Cable Add: Ordfront Stockholm
Man Dir: Leif Ericsson; *Editorial, Rights & Permissions:* Dan Israel
Subjects: Fiction, Home and International Politics, Social Science, History, Juveniles; Quality Paperbacks
1981: 22 titles *1982:* 17 titles *Founded:* 1969
ISBN Publisher's Prefix: 91-7324

Bokförlaget Plus AB*, Skt Eriksgatan 48, S-112 34 Stockholm Tel: (08) 547408
Man Dir: Bengt Svensson
Subjects: General Fiction and Non-fiction, Juvenile
Founded: 1976

Press' Förlag*, Box 78, S-651 03 Karlstad (Located at: Östra Kyrkogatan 4, Karlstad) Tel: (054) 185250
Man Dir, Rights: Barry Press; *Editorial:* Gotton Bagger-Jörgensen; *Permissions:* Lena Lagerkvist; *Publicity:* Madelaine Berggren
Subjects: Science, General Subjects
1981: 13 titles *Founded:* 1970
ISBN Publisher's Prefix: 91-7400

Bokförlaget Prisma AB, Kungsgatan 44, Box 3192, S-103 63 Stockholm Tel: (08) 237280 Cable Add: Prismabok
Man Dir: Stig Edling
Subjects: General Fiction, Quality Paperbacks, Politics, Social Science, Dictionaries, Handbooks, Reference, University Textbooks, General Science
1981: 90 titles *1982:* 75 titles *Founded:* 1963
ISBN Publisher's Prefix: 91-518

Proklama+, Box 6176, S-102 33 Stockholm (Located at: Hagagatan 3, Stockholm) Tel: (08) 345760
Man Dir: Jan Sundbom
Subject: Christian Books
Book Club: Proklama Pocketbokklubb
Bookshop: Proklama Bok-Café (at above address)
1981: 3 titles *1982:* 3 titles *Founded:* 1966
ISBN Publisher's Prefix: 91-7288

Psykologiförlaget AB, Störtloppsvägen 40, Box 461, S-126 04 Hägersten Tel: (08) 970395
Man Dir: Lars Lindquist
Subjects: Psychology, Education
1981: 2 titles *1982:* 6 titles *Founded:* 1957
ISBN Publisher's Prefix: 91-7418

AB Rabén och Sjögren Bokförlag+, Tegnérgatan 28, Box 45022, S-104 30 Stockholm 45 Tel: (08) 349960 Cable Add: Rosbook Stockholm
Man Dir: Kjell Bohlund; *Rights & Permissions:* Ulla Olsson, Madeleine Reinholdson
Subjects: Speciality: Juveniles; also General Fiction, Belles Lettres, Poetry, Biography, History, How-to, Music, Art, Philosophy, Reference, Paperbacks, Psychology, Social Science, University Textbooks; Book Club
Founded: 1942
ISBN Publisher's Prefix: 91-29

Bokförlaget Rediviva, Facsimileförlaget*, Box 19511, S-104 32 Stockholm Tel: (08) 157271
Man Dir: Greta Helms
Subjects: Speciality: Reprints generally; also Bibliography, Topography, Facsimile Reprints of old Swedish books of travel, Dictionary of Anonymous and Pseudonymous Swedish Literature
Founded: 1968
ISBN Publisher's Prefix: 91-7120

S A M-förlaget*, Box 615, S-551 18 Jönköping Tel: (46036) 119130 Cable Add: SAM
Man Dir and other offices: Torbjörn Wetterö
Subjects: Religious
ISBN Publisher's Prefix: 91-7484

S E M I C, Box 74, Landsvägen 57, S-172 22 Sundbyberg Tel: (46-8) 981140 Cable Add: semicpress, Stockholm Telex: 173 70 semic s
Man Dir: Kurt Björkman; *Editorial:* Agneta Hyllén (books), Ebbe Zetterstad (magazines); *Rights & Permissions:* Christer Nyberg (books), Jan-Olof Sohlén (magazines)
Parent Company: SEMIC International Publishing Co
Associate Company: A/S Interpresse, Denmark (qv)
Subsidiary Companies: Carlsen if International Publishers A/S, Denmark (qv); Carlsen Verlag GmbH, Federal Republic of Germany (qv); Carlsen/if AB (qv), Nordisk Bokdistribution, Malmö (both Sweden)
Subjects: Knitting, Crochet, Weaving, Cooking, Sports, Comic Magazines, Comic Albums, Comic Books, Children's Books, Christmas Publications
Book Club: Serie-pocket-klubben
Founded: 1950
ISBN Publisher's Prefix: 91-552

Förlaget Sanctus, (Metodistkyrkans Förlag), Box 5020, S-102 41 Stockholm (Located at: Sibyllegatan 18, S-114 42 Stockholm) Tel: (08) 670155
The Publishing House of the United Methodist Church in Sweden
Man Dir: Karin Hellberg
Orders to: Sibyllegatan 18, S-114 42 Stockholm
Subjects: Theology and Christian Devotional

Bokförlaget Settern HB, Drakabygget, S-286 00 Örkelljunga Tel: (0435) 80050/80070
Man Dir: Magdalena Rönneholm; *Sales, Publicity & Advertising Dir:* Jörgen Wahlén
Orders to: AB Seelig och Co (qv under Major Booksellers)
Subjects: General Fiction and Non-fiction, Paperbacks, Nature, Hunting & Fishing, Children's
Founded: 1974
ISBN Publisher's Prefix: 7586

Sjöstrands Förlag*, Hässelby Strandväg 22, S-162 39 Vällingby Tel: (08) 383856
Man Dir: Ulla-Britt Sjöstrand
Subjects: General Fiction and Non-fiction, Juveniles, Handbooks, History

Skeab Förlag AB, Älvsjö Ängsväg 6, Box 1504, S-125 25 Älvsjö Tel: (08) 860340 Cable Add: Skeab Publishing
Man Dir: Lars Kamlin; *Editorial:* Gösta Gahne
Orders to: Box 1501, S-125 25 Älvsjö
Associate Company: Verbum Förlag AB (qv)
Subjects: Textbooks and Educational Aids, Social Service, General Fiction, Handbooks
ISBN Publisher's Prefix: 91-526

Skolförlaget Gävle AB, Box 646, S-801 27 Gävle 1 (Located at: Rälsgatan 2, Gävle) Tel: (026) 115335 Cable Add: Skolförlaget Telex: 47152
Man Dir: Barbro Larsson; *Editorial:* Jan-Olov Molin, Eva Winkler, Margareta Molin; *Publicity:* Roland Börjesson
Subjects: School Textbooks (especially Languages & Mathematics), Educational Materials
Founded: 1922
ISBN Publisher's Prefix: 91-42

Smålänningens Forlag AB*, Sveavägen 98, S-113 50 Stockholm Tel: (08) 344296
Man Dir: Bengt-Ola Söder
Founded: 1964
Subjects: Hunting, Fishing, Hobbies
ISBN Publisher's Prefix: 91-7132

Sober Förlags AB, Bolidenvägen 14, S-121 63 Johanneshov Tel: (08) 810620
Man Dir: Torsten Friberg
Subjects: Alcohol, Narcotics and Tobacco addiction

Sparfrämjandet, Förlagsaktiebolag*, Box 16425, Drottninggatan 29, S-103 20 Stockholm Tel: (08) 141020 Telex: 11834 saveorg s
Man Dir: Torbjörn Hessling
Subjects: School Textbooks, Handbooks
Founded: 1925
ISBN Publisher's Prefix: 91-7208

Bokförlaget **Spektra** AB, Box 7024, S-300 07 Halmstad 7 Tel: (035) 36030 Cable Add: Comprint
Man Dirs: Åke Hallberg, Solveig Hallberg; *Literary Agent:* Lennart Sane Agency
Subjects: General Fiction, How-to, Music, Arts & Crafts, Reference, General Science
ISBN Publisher's Prefix: 91-7136

Språkförlaget Skriptor AB*, Södermalmstorg 8, Box 15055, S-104 65 Stockholm Tel: (08) 7430555 Telex: 10393 Kval S
Man Dir: Jan Olsson
Founded: 1960

Leif **Stegeland** Förlag AB*, Box 446, Södra Hamngatan 45, S-401 26 Gothenburg Tel: (031) 192540 Cable Add: Stegeland Telex: 27172 Stebook S
Man Dir: Leif Stegeland; *Sales Dir:* Gunnar Gärdhagen; *Rights & Permissions:* Agnita R-Börjesson
Subjects: Educational Materials, General Fiction and Non-fiction, Juveniles
Founded: 1967

Frank **Stenvalls** Förlag*, Malmgatan 3, S-211 32 Malmö Tel: (040) 127703
Man Dir: Frank Stenvall
Associate Company: Hamrelius och Stenvall Förlag AB (qv)
Subjects: Railway, Maritime, Motoring Interest
1981: 10 titles *1982:* 12 titles *Founded:* 1966
ISBN Publisher's Prefix: 91-7266

Stiftelsen Kursverksamhetens Förlag, see Kursverksamhetens

Studentlitteratur AB, Box 1719, S-221 01 Lund 1 Tel: (046) 307070 Cable Add: Studlitt Telex: 33345 educate s
Man Dir: Bertil Bratt; *Publishing Dir:* Margitta Edgren; *Rights & Permissions:* Inge Helander; *Production:* Johnny Månsson
Orders to: Box 1719, S-221 01 Lund 1
Subsidiary Companies: Bratt Institut für Neues Lernen GmbH, Federal Republic of Germany; Chartwell-Bratt (Publishing & Training) Ltd, UK (qqv)
Subjects: School and University Textbooks, covering Data Processing, Technology, Medicine, Social Sciences, Economics, Humanities
1981: 90 titles *Founded:* 1963
ISBN Publisher's Prefix: 91-44

Studieförlaget+, Box 386, S-751 06 Uppsala Tel: (018) 155390
Man Dir, Publicity, Rights & Permissions: Ella Fallgren; *Editorial:* Ella Fallgren, Karin Berger; *Sales:* Ingela Lindblom; *Production:* Karin Hallgren-Pettersson
Subjects: Educational, Languages (especially Swedish), Popular Science, Home Computers
1981: 15 titles *1982:* 18 titles *Founded:* 1973
ISBN Publisher's Prefix: 91-7382

Svenska Utbildningsförlaget Liber AB, now part of Liber Utbildnings (qv)

Sveriges Exportråd, Storgatan 19, Box 5513, S-114 85 Stockholm Tel: (08) 7838500 Cable Add: Export Stockholm Telex: 19620 export a
Publishing Department of the Swedish Trade Council
Subjects: International Marketing, Customs, Shipping & Export Regulations, Market Reports
Bookshop: At above address
1982: approx 100 titles (incl 65 Marketing Reports) *Founded:* 1887
ISBN Publisher's Prefix: 91-7548

Sveriges Radios Förlag*, S-105 10 Stockholm Tel: (08) 7840000 Cable Add: Broadcast Telex: 100 00 srcent s
Man Dir: Karl-Vilhelm Holne
Subjects: Juveniles, Paperbacks
Founded: 1947
ISBN Publisher's Prefix: 91-522

Teknografiska Institutet AB, Industrivägen 5, Box 1013, S-171 21 Solna Tel: (08) 834285
Man Dir: Rolf Ekelund
Subject: Technical books
Founded: 1946
ISBN Publisher's Prefix: 91-7172

Bokförlags AB **Tiden**, Torsgatan 2, Box 130, S-101 21 Stockholm 30 Tel: (08) 237640 Telex: 11934 Tidbook S
Man Dir: Ebbe Carlsson; *Managing Editor:* Hans-Erik Arleskar; *Editorial:* Kerstin Stålbrand, Ulla Freidh, Eva-Maria Westberg; *Sales:* Rod Bengtsson
Imprint: Fib's Lyrikklubb
Subjects: General Fiction and Non-fiction; Juveniles, Politics, History, Social Science, Psychology, Memoirs, Poetry, Illustrated Books, High-priced Paperbacks
Founded: 1912
ISBN Publisher's Prefix: 91-550

Tidnings AB Dagen, see Dagen

AB **Timbro**+, Birger Jarlsgatan 6B, S-114 34 Stockholm Tel: (08) 243775 Telex: 19996 Timbro
President: Kjell-Erik Sellin
Associate Company: Bokförlaget Ratio
Subjects: Non-fiction, Politics, Economics, Social Science
1983: 15 titles
ISBN Publisher's Prefixes: 91-7566 (Timbro), 91-7568 (Ratio)

Tomas Förlag KB, Mälarlunden 4, S-152 00 Strängnäs Tel: (0152) 10931
Man Dir: Alrik Hummel-Gumælius
Subject: Fiction
ISBN Publisher's Prefix: 91-85070

Bokförlaget **Trevi** AB, Barnhusgatan 3, S-111 23 Stockholm Tel: (08) 101850/101569
Owner: Solveig Nellinge
Subjects: General Fiction & Non-fiction, Biography, How-to, Illustrated Books
Founded: 1971
ISBN Publisher's Prefix: 91-7160

Unicart Kartografisk Produktion AB, Kungsgatan 24, S-111 35 Stockholm Tel: (08) 208838/118168 Cable Add: Universitypress Telex: 12442 or 12443 Fotex S attn Unicart
Man Dir: Wilhelm Tham
Subjects: Atlases, Wall Maps, Special Maps (for Encyclopaedias, Reference Works, Textbooks), Transparencies
Founded: 1973

Utbildningsbolaget M M AB, Box 145, S-139 00 Värmdö Tel: (0766) 22300
Man Dir: Mats Myrén
Subject: Teaching Aids

Vår Skola Förlag AB, Grev Magnigatan 11, S-114 55 Stockholm Tel: (08) 623351/623124
Man Dirs: Gunnel Rådahl, Stig Rådahl
Subjects: School Textbooks, Magazines for teachers and pupils, Non-fiction, Juveniles
ISBN Publisher's Prefix: 91-7396

Förlagsaktiebolaget **Västra** Sverige*, Box 10238, S-434 01 Kungsbacka Tel: (0300) 11570 Cable Add: Printer Telex: 21234 eba s
Man Dir: Per Elander; *Sales Dir, Permissions:* Otto Elander; *Advertising Dir:* Lars Henriksson
Subsidiary Company: Elanders Boktryckeri AB
Subjects: General Non-fiction, especially How-to, Hobbies, Hunting and Fishing, Paperbacks
Book Club: Jaktjournalens Bokklubb
Founded: 1912

Verbum Förlag AB, Box 1504, S-125 25 Älvsjö (Located at: Älvsjö Ängsväg 6, Älvsjö) Tel: (08) 860340
Man Dir: Lars Kamlin; *Editorial:* Tony Guldbrandzén; *Sales:* Ingemar Eriksson; *Marketing:* Ulf Heimdahl; *Rights & Permissions:* Elisabeth Jörgensen
Orders to: Box 1501, S-125 25 Älvsjö
Associate Company: Skeab Förlag AB (qv)
Subjects: Religion, Theology, Juveniles, Music, Audio-visuals
1982: approx 100 titles

AB **Wahlström och Widstrand***, Tysta Gatan 10, S-115 24 Stockholm Tel: (08) 679815 Cable Add: Wahlwid s Telex: 12757
Man Dir: Per I Gedin; *Sales Dir:* Sigvard Olsson; *Rights & Permissions:* Ulla Asplund
Parent Company: Albert Bonniers Förlag AB (qv)
Subjects: General Fiction & Non-fiction, Handbooks, University & Quality Paperbacks
Book Clubs: W e W Bookclub; part-owner of Månadens Bok
Founded: 1884
ISBN Publisher's Prefix: 91-46

B **Wahlströms** Bokförlag AB, Warfvinges väg 30, S-112 51 Stockholm Tel: (08) 244600 Cable Add: Wahlbook, Stockholm Telex: 17174
Man Dir: Bertil Wahlström; *Production:* Gert Fransson; *Permissions:* Eva Melin
Subsidiary Company: J A Lindblads Bokförlag AB (qv)
Subjects: General Fiction, Juveniles, Low-priced Paperbacks
1982: 400 titles *Founded:* 1911
ISBN Publisher's Prefix: 91-32

AB **Waldia** Förlag*, Brogatan 41, Box 35, S-571 00 Nässjö Tel: (038) 016200
Man Dir: Ernst Wallin

Ernst **Westerbergs** Förlags, Åkeshovsvägen 29, S-161 51 Bromma Tel: (08) 241650 Cable Add: Baptistförlaget
Man Dir: Bengt Sjöblom
Subjects: Education, Juveniles, Music, Religion
Founded: 1897

Wezäta Förlag*, Grafiska Vägen, Box 5057, S-402 22 Gothenburg Tel: (031) 400140 Cable Add: Wezätamelins Telex: 20872 Wemel S
Man Dir: Claes Lundgren; *Publishing Manager:* Göran Rusk
Parent Company: Esselte Wezäta AB (a member of the Printing Division of the Esselte Group)
Subject: How-to
Founded: 1886
ISBN Publisher's Prefix: 91-85074

Zindermans Förlag, Götgatan 13, Box 310, S-401 25 Gothenburg 1 Tel: (031) 136890/137832 Cable Add: Zindermans
Man Dir: Sune Stigsjöö
Subjects: General Fiction and Non-fiction, Biography, History, How-to, Psychology, Social & Political Science
Founded: 1960
ISBN Publisher's Prefix: 91-528

Literary Agents

Arlecchino Teaterförlag, Gränsvägen 14, S-131 41 Nacka Tel: (08) 7181717/8

D Richard **Bowen**, Box 30037, S-200 61 Malmö 30
Contact: D Richard Bowen Tel: (040) 161200/161230

Gösta **Dahl** och Son AB*, Aladdinsvägen 14, S-161 38 Bromma/Stockholm Tel: (08) 256235 Cable Add: Literarius

Teaterförlag Arvid **Englind** AB*, Karlavägen 56, Box 5124, S-102 43 Stockholm 5
Contact: Christèr Englind

Mrs Lena I **Gedin**, c/o Lennart Sane Agency, Holländareplan 9, S-292 00 Karlshamn Tel: (0454) 12356

Folmer **Hansen** Teaterförlag, Lundagatan 4, S-171 63 Solna Tel: (08) 279838 Cable Add: Folmerhansen Stockholm
Dir: Gerd Widestedt-Ericsson; *Dramaturgist:* Cecilia Önfelt; *Public Relations:* Marianne Krantz
Specialization: Foreign Plays in Scandinavia, Scandinavian Plays in Scandinavia and Abroad, Children's Plays

Monica **Heyum** Agency, Box 3300, Vendelsö, S-136 03 Handen Tel: (08) 7451934 Cable Add: Expression Stockholm
Dir: Monica Heyum

Lennart **Sane** Agency, Holländereplan 9, S-292 00 Karlshamn Tel: (0454) 12356 Cable Add: Saneagency Karlshamn
Dir: Lennart Sane; *Assistant Dirs:* Elisabeth Cederholm, Marie Helene Sane
Founded: 1968

Book Clubs

Bättre Barnomsorg, Slottsgatan 24, S-205 10 Malmö Tel: (040) 70650
Owned by: Liber Grafiska AB, run by Liber Förlag (qqv)
Subject: Education (book club for teachers)

Bättre Data, Slottsgatan 24, S-205 10 Malmö Tel: (040) 70650
Owned by: Liber Grafiska AB, run by Liber Förlag (qqv)
Subject: Computers

Bättre Ledarskap, Slottsgatan 24, S-205 10 Malmö Tel: (040) 70650
Contact: Ingemar Ternbo
Owned by: Liber Grafiska AB, run by Liber Förlag (qqv)
Subjects: Management, Business Administration, Economics
Founded: 1977

Bättre Samhälle, Slottsgatan 24, S-205 10 Malmö Tel: (040) 70650
Owned by: Liber Grafiska AB, run by Liber Förlag (qqv)
Subject: Social Science (book club for social workers)

Bättre Skola, Slottsgatan 24, S-205 10 Malmö Tel: (040) 70650
Contact: Ingemar Ternbo
Owned by: Liber Grafiska AB, run by Liber Förlag (qqv)
Subject: Education (book club for teachers)
Founded: 1975 (as Lärarbokklubben)

Bonniers Bokklubb, Sveavägen 56, S-103 63 Stockholm
Owned by: Albert Bonniers Förlag AB (qv)

Bonniers Bokpaket, Sveavägen 56, S-103 63 Stockholm
Owned by: Albert Bonniers Förlag AB (qv)

Bra Böcker, Södra Vägen, S-263 00 Höganäs Tel: (042) 39000
Owned by: Bokförlaget Bra Böcker AB (qv)

Bra Deckare, Södra Vägen, S-263 00 Höganäs Tel: (042) 39000
Specialization: Detective novels
Owned by: Bokförlaget Bra Böcker AB (qv)

Bra Klassiker, Södra Vägen, S-263 00 Höganäs Tel: (042) 39000
Specialization: Classics
Owned by: Bokförlaget Bra Böcker AB (qv)

Bra Lyrik, Södra Vägen, S-263 00 Höganäs Tel: (042) 39000
Specialization: Poetry
Owned by: Bokförlaget Bra Böcker AB (qv)

Bra Spänning, Södra Vägen, S-263 00 Höganäs Tel: (042) 39000
Specialization: Thrillers
Owned by: Bokförlaget Bra Böcker AB (qv)

Delta Science Fiction Bok Klubb*, Box 15123, S-161 15 Bromma
Owned by: Delta Förlags AB (qv)

Info Book*, Box 135, S-527 00 Herrljunga
Owned by: Interskrift Publishing House (qv)
Subject: Religion

Jaktjournalens Bokklubb*, Box 10238, S-434 01 Kungsbacka Tel: (0300) 19100 Cable Add: Printer, Kungsbacka Telex: 21234
Owned by: Elanders Boktryckeri AB, Box 10238, S-434 01 Kungsbacka (a printing company and a subsidiary of Förlagsaktiebolaget Västra Sverige, qv)

Den **Kristna Bokringen**, Dagenhuset, S-105 36 Stockholm
Members: 11,000
Owned by: Tidnings AB Dagen (qv)
Founded: 1970

Lärarbokklubben, now Bättre Skola (qv)

Libris Bookclub, Box 1623, S-701 16 Örebro
Owned by: Libris Publishing House (qv)

Månadens Bok, Box 2255, S-103 16 Stockholm (Located at: Skeppsbron 20) Tel: (08) 232310
Man Dir: Jonas Modig
Owned by: Albert Bonniers Förlag AB (qv), Bokförlaget Forum AB (qv), AB P A Nordstedt och Söners Förlag (qv), AB Wahlström och Widstrand (qv)

Önskeboken*, Box 135, S-524 00 Herrljunga
Owned by: Harriers Bokforlag AB (qv)

Proklama Pocketbokklubb, Trantorp, Hållsta, S-635 90 Eskilstuna
Owned by: Proklama (qv)

Readers' Digest AB, Box 6064, S-102 31 Stockholm 6 Tel: (08) 340780 Telex: 11689

Serie-pocket-klubben, Box 74, Landsvägen 57, S-172 22 Sundbyberg
Owned by: SEMIC (qv)

Stora Romanklubben, Sveavägen 56, S-103 63 Stockholm
Owned by: Albert Bonniers Förlag AB (qv)

Bokklubben **Svalan**, Sveavägen 56, S-103 63 Stockholm Tel: 229120 Telex: Bonbook 11620
Owned by: Albert Bonniers Förlag AB (qv)

Underhållningsbokklubben, Sveavägen 56, S-103 63 Stockholm
Owned by: Albert Bonniers Förlag AB (qv)

Vår Bok AB*, Tryckerigatan 2, Box 2052, S-103 12 Stockholm 2
Subjects: Classics, Current Affairs, Dictionaries, Encyclopaedias, Detective fiction, Periodicals
Owned by: Esselte Forlag AB (qv)

W e W Bookclub*, Tysta Gatan 10, S-115 24 Stockholm Tel: (08) 679815 Cable Add: Wahlwid S Telex: 12757
Owned by: AB Wahlström och Widstrand (qv)

Major Booksellers

Johan **Åkerbloms** Universitetsbokhandel, Östra Rådhusgatan 6, Box 83, S-901 03 Umeå Tel: (090) 125770
Manager: Bengt Gyllengahm
Also a subscription agency

Almqvist och Wiksell Bokhandel AB, Gamla Brogatan 26, Box 62, S-101 20 Stockholm Tel: (08) 237990

Esselte Bokhandel **Eckersteins**, Grönsakstorget, Box 3050, S-400 10 Gothenburg 3 Tel: (031) 171100
Manager: Erik Engström

AB C E **Fritzes** Kungl Hovbokhandel, Regeringsgatan 12, Box 16356, S-103 27 Stockholm Tel: (08) 238900 Cable Add: Bokfritze Telex: 123 87 S Fritzes
Man Dir: Eide Segerbäck
Parent Company: Liber Grafiska AB (qv)
Founded: 1837

AB **Gleerupska** Universitetsbokhandeln*, Box 1722, S-221 01 Lund Tel: (046) 117260

Gumperts Universitetsbokhandel AB, Norra Hamngatan 26, Box 3184, S-400 10 Gothenburg Tel: (031) 172080 Telex: 21178
Manager: Carl A Malmberg

Söderbokhandeln **Hansson och Bruce** AB, Götgatan 37, S-116 21 Stockholm Tel: (08) 405432
Manager: T Fredriksson

Esselte Bokhandel **Lundequistska**, Östra Ågatan 31, Box 610, S-751 25 Uppsala 1 Tel: (018) 139830
Manager: Hans Molander
Owned by: Esselte Bokhandel, Box 62, S-101 20 Stockholm Tel: (08) 237990

AB Edvin **Lundgrens** Bokhandel, Södergatan 3, S-211 34 Malmo Tel: (040) 76660

AB **Nordiska Bokhandeln***, Kungsgatan 4, Box 7, S-101 20 Stockholm Tel: (08) 227380
Forms part of Esselte Group of Booksellers

AB **Sandbergs** Bokhandel*, Humlegårdsgatan 12, Box 5518, S-114 85 Stockholm Tel: (08) 236480
Manager: Ann-Mari Ericson

AB Seelig och Co, Box 1308, S-171 25
Solna Tel: 08850300 Telex: 12081 Cable
Add: Seelig
Importers, Distributors and Wholesalers

Wettergrens Bokhandel AB, Västra
Hamngatan 22, S-411 17, Gothenburg
Tel: (031) 170090

Major Libraries

Göteborgs Stadsbibliotek*, Box 5404,
S-402 29 Gothenburg
City Library and County Library

Göteborgs Universitetsbibliotek,
Centralbiblioteket, Renströmsgatan 4, Box
5096, S-402 22 Gothenburg Tel: (031)
631000 Telex: 20896 Ubgbg s
Librarian: Paul Hallberg
Publications: Årsberättelse (Annual Report);
*Acta Bibliothecae Universitatis
Gothoburgensis* (irregular); *New Literature
on Women. A Bibliography* (quarterly)

Kungliga Biblioteket, Box 5039, S-102 41
Stockholm 5 Tel: (08) 241040 Telex: 19640
kbs s
The Royal Library — National Library of
Sweden
National Librarian: Lars Tynell
*Publications include: Kungliga Bibliotekets
Acta-serie; Kungliga bibliotekets
årsberättelse; Svensk Bokförteckning*

Kungliga Svenska Vetenskapsakademiens
Bibliotek, incorporated with Stockholm
Universitets Bibliotek (qv)

Lund Universitetsbibliotek, National
Lending Library, Box 1010, S-221 03 Lund
Tel: (46) 46107000 Telex: 32208 Lub Lund
Librarian: Björn Tell

Malmö Stadsbibliotek, Regementsgatan 3,
S-211 42 Malmö Tel: (040) 77810
City Library, County Library and Loan
Centre for Southern and Western Sweden
Librarian: Bengt Holmström
*Publications: Annual Report; Catalogue of
Annual Acquisition* (microfiche);
Bibliographies

Riksarkivet, Box 12541, S-102 29 Stockholm
(Located at: Fyrverkarbacken 13-17,
Stockholm)
National Record Office

Royal Institute of Technology Library,
S-100 44 Stockholm Tel: (08) 787 7000
Telex: 10389

Statistiska Centralbyråns Bibliotek, S-115 81
Stockholm Tel: (08) 140560 Telex: 15261
Swestat
Library of Statistics Sweden
Chief Librarian: Malkon Lindmark

Stiftelsen Svenska Barnboksinstitutet,
Tjärhovsgatan 36, S-116 21 Stockholm Tel:
446355
Swedish Institute for Children's Books
Librarian: Mary Orvig

Stockholm Universitets Bibliotek, S-106 91
Stockholm
Stockholm University Library
This Library incorporates the Library of the
Royal Swedish Academy of Sciences
(Kungliga Svenska Vetenskapsakademiens
Bibliotek) covering Humanities, Law, Social
Sciences, Mathematics and Science

Stockholms Stadsbibliotek, Box 6502,
S-113 83 Stockholm
City Library of Stockholm

Sveriges Lantbruksuniversitets Bibliotek,
Central Library Ultunabiblioteket, S-750 07
Uppsala Tel: (18) 171000 Telex: 76062
Ultbibl S

Libraries of the Swedish University of
Agricultural Sciences
Dir: Sten F Vedi

University Libraries, see under town names

Uppsala Universitetsbibliotek*, Box 510,
S-751 20 Uppsala Tel: (018) 139440 Telex:
76076 ubupps s
Librarian: Thomas Tottie
*Publication: Acta Bibliothecae R
Universitatis Upsalicusis*

Library Associations

Svenska Arkivsamfundet*, c/o Riksarkivet,
Box, S-100 26 Stockholm
Swedish Association of Archivists

Svenska Bibliotekariesamfundet*, Uppsala
Universitetsbibliotek, Box 510, S-751 20
Uppsala Tel: (018) 139440
Swedish Association of University and
Research Librarians
Executive Secretary: Birgit Antonsson
*Publication: Bibliotekariesamfundet
Meddelar*

Svenska Folkbibliotekarieförbundet, Box 36,
S-131 06 Nacka Tel: (08) 7162880
Union of Swedish Public Librarians
President: Irma Ridbäck, Jämtlands läns
bibliotek, S-831 80 Östersund

Sveriges Allmänna Biblioteksförening,
Winstrupsgatan 10, Box 1706, S-221 01
Lund
Swedish Library Association
Acting Secretary: Jan Nyberg
Publication: Biblioteksbladet

Tekniska Litteratursällskapet, Box 5073,
S-102 42 Stockholm
Swedish Society for Technical
Documentation
Secretary: Birgitta Levin
Publications: Tidskrift för Dokumentation
(4 a year)

Vetenskapliga Bibliotekens
Tjänstemannaförening VBT, c/o
D I K-förbundet, Box 36, S-131 06 Nacka
Tel: (08) 7162880
Association of Research Library Employees
President: Lillemor Lundström, Royal
Library, Box 5039, S-102 41 Stockholm Tel:
(08) 241040
Publication: Bibliofack

Library Reference Journals

Bibliofack, Vetenskapliga Bibliotekens
Tjänstemannaförening VBT, Box 36, S-131
06 Nacka

Bibliotekariesamfundet Meddelar (Reports
of the Librarians' Association), Svenska
Bibliotekariesamfundet, Uppsala
Universitetsbibliotek, Box 510, S-751 20
Uppsala

Biblioteket Presenterar Nya Boecker (The
Library Presents New Books),
Bibliotekstjänst AB, Tornavägen 9, Box
1706, S-221 01 Lund

Biblioteksbladet (Library Journal) (text in
Scandinavian languages, summaries in
English), Sveriges Allmänna
Biblioteksförening, Winstrupsgatan 10, Box
1706, S-221 01 Lund

Tidskrift för Dokumentation (Scandinavian
Documentation Journal) (text in Swedish,
occasionally in English, summaries in
English), Tekniska Litteratursällskapet, Box
5073, S-102 42 Stockholm

Literary Associations and Societies

Kungl Vitterhets Historie och Antikvitets
Akademien, Villagatan 3, S-114 32
Stockholm
Royal Academy of Letters, History and
Antiquities
Secretary: Nils Åke Nilsson
Publications: Fornvännen (journal),
Handlingar (memoirs), *Arkiv* (archives),
Årsbok (Yearbook), monographs, Library
and Archives

Litteraturfrämjandet, Bellmansgatan 30,
S-116 47 Stockholm Tel: (08) 449175
Foundation for Promotion of Literature

Svenska Pennklubben (Swedish Centre of
International P E N), AB P A Norstedt &
Söners Förlag, Tryckerigatan 2, Box 2052,
S-103 12 Stockholm 2
President: Thomas von Vegesack; *Secretary:*
Kerstin M Lundberg
International Secretary: Marianne Eyre

Samfundet de Nio, c/o Anders Öhman,
Smålandsgatan 14, S-111 46 Stockholm
Nine Swedish Authors' Society ('The Society
of Nine')
Secretary: Anders R Öhman (lawyer)
Publication: Svensk Litteraturtidskrift
(quarterly)

Svenska Österbottens Litteraturförening, c/o
Olof Haegerstrand, Fasanvaegen 4, S-775 00
Krylbo
Swedish Österbottens Literary Association
Publication: Horisont

Literary Periodicals

BLM (Bonniers Litteraera Magasin)
(Bonniers Literary Magazine), Albert
Bonniers Förlag AB, Sveavägen 56, S-111 34
Stockholm

Horisont (Horizon), Svenska Österbottens
Litteraturförening, c/o Harry Jarv,
Fyreerkarbacken 32, S-112 60 Stockholm

Ord och Bild (Word and Picture), Stiftelsen
Ord och Bild, Box 15116, S-104 65
Stockholm

Svensk Litteraturtidskrift (Swedish Journal
of Literature), Almqvist och Wiksell Förlag
AB, Gamla Brogatan 26, S-101 20
Stockholm

Swedish Books (The Translator's Review of
Work Produced in Swedish), Box 2387,
S-403 16 Gothenburg
Quarterly review, in English, of works
written in Swedish, originating from Sweden
or Swedish writers in Finland

Tulimuld (Scorched Earth); literary and
cultural magazine of Estonian exiles (text in
Estonian), Bernard Kangro, Skördevägen 1,
S-222 38 Lund

Literary Prizes

Aniarapriset
Aniara Prize, for adult literature in Sweden.
Awarded annually. Enquiries to Sveriges
Allmänna Biblioteksförening,
Winstrupsgatan 10, Box 1706, S-221 01
Lund

Ida **Bäckman** Prize, see Swedish Academy
Prizes

Bellmans Prize
For poetry. 50,000 Swedish crowns.
Awarded annually. Enquiries to Swedish
Academy, Börshuset, Källargränd 4,
S-111 29 Stockholm

SWEDEN — SWITZERLAND

Beskow Prize, see Swedish Academy Prizes

Blom Prize, see Swedish Academy Prizes

The Dalén-Engqvists Prize
Annual award for Swedish Literature and Cultural Journalism. 20,000 Swedish crowns. This prize cannot be applied for. Enquiries to Swedish Academy, Börshuset, Källargränd 4, S-111 29 Stockholm

Dobloug Prize, see Swedish Academy Prizes

Signe **Ekblad-Eldhs** Prize
To a famous Swedish writer. 30,000 Swedish crowns. Enquiries to Swedish Academy, Börshuset, Källargränd 4, S-111 29 Stockholm

The Lydia and Herman **Erikssons** Prize
Annual award to a Swedish writer for a work of prose or poetry. 20,000 Swedish crowns. This prize cannot be applied for. Enquiries to Swedish Academy, Börshuset, Källargränd 4, S-111 29 Stockholm

Karin **Gierows** Prizes, see Swedish Academy Prizes

Grand Prize
For outstanding literary work written in Swedish. 50,000 Swedish crowns. Awarded annually. Enquiries to The Foundation for Promotion of Literature, Bellmansgatan 30, S-116 47 Stockholm

Grand Prize for a Book of Poetry
For the best original collection of new poems written in Swedish by a single author. 25,000 Swedish crowns. Awarded annually. Enquiries to Litteraturfrämjandet, Bellmansgatan 30, S-116 47 Stockholm

Grand Prize for a Novel
For the best novel written in Swedish. 25,000 Swedish crowns. Awarded annually. Enquiries to Litteraturfrämjandet, Bellmansgatan 30, S-116 47 Stockholm

Kalleberger Foundation — The Tekla **Hanssons** and Gösta Ronnströms Prize
Annual award in memory of Tekla Hansson to a Swedish writer for a work of prose or poetry. 4,000 Swedish crowns. This prize cannot be applied for. Enquiries to Swedish Academy, Börshuset, Källargränd 4, S-111 29 Stockholm

Axel **Hirsch** Prize, see Swedish Academy Prizes

Nils **Holgersson** Plaque
The highest award for children's literature in Sweden. Awarded annually. Enquiries to Sveriges Allmänna Biblioteksförening, Winstrupsgatan 10, Box 1706, S-221 01 Lund

Kalleberger Foundation, see Hanssons

Ilona **Kohrtz** Prize, see Swedish Academy Prizes

The '**Nine**' Prize
For an author of outstanding literary merit, whether established or not. 25,000 Swedish crowns. Awarded annually. This prize cannot be applied for. Enquiries to Samfundet de Nio, Smålandsgatan 14, S-111 46 Stockholm

Royal Prize, see Swedish Academy Prizes

Birger **Schöldström** Prize, see Swedish Academy Prizes

Henrik **Schück** Prize, see Swedish Academy Prizes

Swedish Academy Prizes
In addition to those fully listed individually, the Swedish Academy awards the following prizes:
Royal Prize (Cultural/Literary: annual);
Beskow Prize (Literary: biennial); *Blom Prize* (Swedish Language: annual); *Ida Bäckman Prize* (Literature/Journalism: biennial); *Dobloug Prize* (Swedish Literature: annual); *Karin Gierows Prizes* (for (1) Cultural Information: annual; (2) Promotion of Knowledge: annual); *Axel Hirsch Prize* (Biographic/Historic: biennial); *Ilona Kohrtz Prize* (Prose/Poetry: annual); *Henrik Schück Prize* (Literary History: annual); *Birger Schöldström Prize* (Literary History/Biography: every 4 years); *Swedish Linguistics Prize* (annual); *Swedish into Foreign Language Translation Prize* (annual); *Translation into Swedish Prize* (annual); *Zibet Prize* (Literary/Historic referring to reign of Gustav III: irregular); miscellaneous prizes for work in literary or linguistic fields.
Enquiries to The Swedish Academy, Börshuset, Källargränd 4, S-111 29 Stockholm

Swedish into Foreign Language Translation Prize, see Swedish Academy Prizes

Swedish Linguistics Prize, see Swedish Academy Prizes

Translation into Swedish Prize, see Swedish Academy Prizes

Zibet Prize, see Swedish Academy Prizes

Zorn Prize
For outstanding literary work. 20,000 Swedish crowns. Awarded annually. Enquiries to Swedish Academy, Börshuset, Källargränd 4, S-111 29 Stockholm

Translation Agencies and Associations

E C Print AB, Kastellgatan 1, S-413 07 Gothenburg Tel: (031) 133099
Man Dir: Dr Carlos Ezeyza-Alvear
Technical Manuals and Books

Föreningen Auktoriserade Translatorer*, c/o Dr Solfrid Söderlind, Rörläggarvägen, S-161 46 Bromma Tel: (08) 268620
Swedish Association of Authorized Translators

Språktjänst, Box 5513, S-114 85 Stockholm (Located at: Styrmansgatan 6)
Translating and Interpreting Service of the Swedish Trade Council (See Sveriges Exportråd under Publishers)

Switzerland

General Information

Language: 65% German (dialect known as Swiss German or Schwyzerdütsch), 18% French (in southwest), 12% Italian (in Ticino), 1% Romansh (in Graubünden)
Religion: Protestant and Catholic
Population: 6.34 million
Bank Hours: 0800-1230, 1330-1630 Monday-Friday
Shop Hours: 0800-1200, 1330-1830 Monday-Friday; in most cities, closed Monday morning; 0800-1200, 1330-1600 or 1700 Saturday
Currency: 100 centimes = 1 Swiss franc
Export/Import Information: Member of the European Free Trade Association. No tariff on books. Most books exempt from Turnover Tax. Advertising matter usually dutiable, some exempt from Turnover Tax. No import licences required. No exchange controls
Copyright: UCC, Berne, Florence (see International Section)

Book Trade Organizations

A L S I, see Associazione dei Libraii della Svizzera Italiana

Association suisse des Editeurs de Langue française*, 2 ave Agassiz, CH-1001 Lausanne Tel: (021) 202811 Telex: 25730
Swiss Publishers' Association (French Language)
Secretary General: Robert Junod

Association suisse des Libraires de Langue française*, 2 ave Agassiz, CH-1001 Lausanne Tel: (021) 202811 Telex: 25730
Association of Swiss French-language Bookshops
Secretary: Robert Junod

Association suisse romande des Diffuseurs de Livres*, 2 ave Agassiz, CH-1001 Lausanne Tel: (021) 202811 Telex: 25730
Association of Book Distributors of French-speaking Switzerland
Secretary: Robert Junod

Associazione dei Libraii della Svizzera Italiana (ALSI)*, CH-6948 Porza Tel: (091) 519688
Association of Italian-speaking Swiss Booksellers
Secretary: Luigi Rusconi

S B I, see Schweizer Buchwerbung und Information

S E S I, see Societa Editori della Svizzera Italiana

S L E S R, see Societé des Libraires et Editeurs de la Suisse romande

Schweizer Buchwerbung und -Information (SBI)*, CH-8245 Feuerthalen Tel: (053) 44877
Swiss Book Publicity and Information Service
Dir: Edwin Nigg
Publications: Bücherkatalog des Schweizer Buchhandels, Schweizer Buchspiegel; also *Wir Lesen — Sie auch?* (an annual publication distributed to every household in German-speaking Switzerland)

Schweizer Buchzentrum*, Hägendorf, PO Box 522, CH-4600 Olten 1
Swiss Book Centre

Schweizer Verband der Musikalienhändler und Verleger, Lic iur B Thoma, Advokaturbüro Helmut F Groner, Zeughausgasse 9, PO Box, CH-6301 Zug Tel: (042) 219016
Swiss Association of Music Sellers and Publishers (a department of the Sekretariat des Musikhandels (Music Trade Secretariat) at above address)

Schweizerischer Adressbuchverleger-Verband, c/o Verlag for Wirtschaftsliteratur GmbH, Birmendorferstr 421, PO Box 271, CH-8055 Zurich Tel: (01) 4625030/4625036
Swiss Association of Directory Publishers
President: Chr Laemmel

Schweizerischer Buchhändler- und Verleger-Verband (SBVV)*, PO Box 408, CH-8034 Zurich (Located at: Bellerivestr 3, CH-8008 Zurich) Tel: (01) 2513345
Swiss Booksellers' and Publishers' Association (German language)
Secretary: Peter Oprecht
Publications: Der Schweizer Buchhandel (bi-monthly) (official organ of this association, also its French equivalent SLESR, and its Italian equivalents SESI and ALSI); *Das*

Schweizer Buch, Adressbuch des Schweizer Buchhandels, Schweizer Bücherverzeichnis; see also similar publications by the SBI (above)

Schweizerischer Bühnenverleger-Verband*, c/o Edition Eulenburg GmbH, Grütstr 28, CH-8134 Adliswil
Association of Swiss Publishers for the Stage
President: Albert Kunzelmann

Schweizerischer Schriftsteller-Verband, Kirchgasse 25, CH-8001 Zurich
Society of Swiss Writers
Secretary: Otto Böni

Societa Editori della Svizzera Italiana (SESI), Viale Portone 4, PO Box 282, CH-6501 Bellinzona Tel: (092) 258555/56 Telex: 846310 Aseg CH
Association of Publishers for Italian-speaking Switzerland
Dir: Romano Montalbetti

Société des Libraires et Editeurs de la Suisse romande (SLESR), 2 ave Agassiz, CH-1001 Lausanne Tel: (021) 202811 Telex: 25730
Booksellers' and Publishers' Association of French-speaking Switzerland
Secretary General: Robert Junod
Publications: La Librairie suisse (bi-monthly) (official organ of this association, also its German equivalent SBVV, and its Italian equivalents SESI and ALSI)

Standard Book Numbering Agency (French-language), see Agence francophone pour la Numérotation internationale du Livre, France

Standard Book Numbering Agency*, Schweizerischer Buchhändler und Verleger-Verband, Bellerivestr 3, CH-8008 Zurich
This is the agency for German-language ISBNs
ISBN Administrator: Peter Oprecht

Syndicat de la Librairie ancienne et du Commerce de l'Estampe en Suisse (Vereinigung der Buchantiquare und Kupferstichhändler in der Schweiz), Schloss Str 6, CH-9490 Vaduz
Association of Antiquarian Book and Print Sellers in Switzerland
President: Walter Alïcke

Verband evangelischer Buchhandlungen und Verlage der Schweiz, Badenerstr 69, CH-8026 Zurich Tel: (01) 2416630
Association of Swiss Protestant Booksellers and Publishers
Dir: Mr Voemel

Verband schweizerischer Antiquare und Kunsthändler*, Gerechtigkeitsgasse 30, CH-3011 Berne Tel: (031) 221104
Association of Swiss Antiquarian Booksellers and Art Dealers

Verband schweizerischer Zeitungsagenturen und Büchergrossisten (Union d'Agences suisses de Journaux et Livres en Gros)*, St Jakobsstr 25, CH-4002 Basle Tel: (061) 225500
Association of Swiss Newspaper Distributors and Book Wholesalers

Vereinigung der Schweizerischen Buchgemeinschaften, Hermetschloostr 77, CH-8048 Zurich Tel: 625100
Association of Swiss Book Clubs

Vereinigung katholischer Buchhändler und Verleger der Schweiz, c/o Anton Scherer, Bellerivestr 3, CH-8008 Zurich Tel: (01) 2527050
Association of Swiss Catholic Booksellers and Publishers

Book Trade Reference Books and Journals

Books

Adressbuch des schweizer Buchhandels, Schweizerischer Buchhändler- und Verleger-Verband, Bellerivestr 3, CH-8008 Zurich
Directory of the Swiss Book Trade, containing Lists of Publishers, Booksellers, Distributors, Trade Organizations and Cross-Reference Indices

Adressbuch für den deutschsprachigen Buchhandel. This 'Directory for the German-speaking Book Trade' lists all Swiss, Austrian and German publishers. See Book Trade Reference Books, Federal Republic of Germany

Bücherkatalog des Schweizer Buchhandels (Swiss Book Trade Book Catalogue), Schweizer Buchwerbung und -Information (SBI), CH-8245 Feuerthalen

Schweizer Buchspiegel (Swiss Book Mirror), Schweizer Buchwerbung und -Information (SBI), CH-8245 Feuerthalen

Wir Lesen — Sie Auch? (We are Readers — You, too?), Schweizer Buchwerbung und -Information (SBI), CH-8245 Feuerthalen

Journals

Bibliographie analytique des Bibliographies suisses courantes (Analytical Bibliography of Current Swiss bibliographies), Schweizerische Landesbibliothek (Bibliothèque nationale Suisse), Hallwylstr 15, CH-3003 Berne

Bibliographie des Publications officielles suisses (Bibliography of Swiss Official Publications), Schweizerische Landesbibliothek (Bibliothèque nationale suisse), Hallwylstr 15, CH-3003 Berne

Edition, Stauffacher Verlag AG, Birmensdorfer Str 318, CH-8055 Zürich 3 (book advertiser)

Guilde du Livre (Book Guild), 5 rue de l'Ecole Supérieure, CH-1005 Lausanne

La Librairie suisse (The Swiss Bookseller), Société des Libraires et Editeurs de la Suisse romande, 2 Ave Agassiz, CH-1001 Lausanne

Librarium (text in German and French), Schweizerische Bibliophilen-Gesellschaft, Zwingliplatz 3, CH-8001 Zurich

Das schweizer Buch (The Swiss Book); bibliographical bulletin, Schweizerischer Buchhändler- und Verleger-Verband (SBVV), Bellerivestr 3, CH-8008 Zurich

Schweizer Bücherverzeichnis (Index of Swiss Books), Schweizerischer Buchhändler- und Verleger-Verband (SBVV) Bellerivestr 3, CH-8008 Zurich

Der Schweizer Buchhandel (The Swiss Book Trade), Schweizerischer Buchhändler- und Verleger-Verband (SBVV), Bellerivestr 3, CH-8008 Zurich

Publishers

Editions **24 Heures**, 33 ave de la Gare, CH-1001 Lausanne Tel: (021) 203111 Telex: CH 24495
Man Dir: P Lamunière; *Advertising, Permissions:* L R Pisler
Subjects: Belles Lettres, History, Music, Art, Juveniles, Educational Materials
1981: 25 titles 1982: 26 titles *Founded:* 1969
Miscellaneous: Associated imprints include Imprimeries Réunies SA (qv)

A B C Verlag, Rüdigerstr 12, Postfach, CH-8021 Zurich Tel: (01) 2077291 Cable Add: ABC Verlag Zurich
Man & Sales Dir: Konrad Baumann
Subjects: Graphic Design, Art
1982: 6 titles 1983: 7 titles *Founded:* 1936
ISBN Publisher's Prefix: 3-85504

A L A Verlag, Klosbachstr 46, CH-8032 Zurich Tel: (01) 2510890
Man Dir and other offices: Berta Rahm
Subjects: Human Rights (and especially Women's Emancipation); Social Science, Biography, History
1981: 3 titles 1982: 2 titles *Founded:* 1968
ISBN Publisher's Prefix: 3-85509

A T Verlag AG+, Bahnhofstr 39-43, CH-5001 Aarau Tel: (064) 251133 Telex: 981146
Dir: A Haefeli
Subjects: Specialist, Reference, Non-fiction generally
Founded: 1847
Miscellaneous: This is the book publishing section of the Aargauer Tageblatt (newspaper)
ISBN Publisher's Prefix: 3-85502

Aare-Verlag, see Schweizer Jugend-Verlag

Aargauer Tageblatt, see AT Verlag

Editions **Adversaires**, now known as Editions François Grounauer (qv)

Aesopus Verlag GmbH, Grellingerstr 95, CH-4052 Basle Tel: (061) 423373 Telex: basel 63689
Man Dir: Nicolaus M Fisch
Branch Off: Greifstr 6, Wiesbaden, Federal Republic of Germany Tel: (06121) 467473 Telex: 04186895 Wgb
Subjects: Health, Sports, Medicine
Miscellaneous: Publish in nine languages

Editions L'**Age d'Homme** — La Cité, 10 Métropole, PO Box 263, CH-1003 Lausanne Tel: (021) 220095
Man Dir: Vladimir Dimitrijevic
Subjects: General Fiction, Belles Lettres, Poetry, Biography, Music, Art, Philosophy, Religion, Psychology, Social Science, Futurism and Esoterica, Slavica, Science Fiction, Cinema, Literary Criticism, Reprints
Bookshops: Librairie la Proue, Escaliers du Marché 17, CH-1000 Lausanne; Librairie Le Rameau d'Or, 19 blvd Georges Favon CH-1200 Geneva; Librairie Suisse et Européenne, L'Age d'Homme, 5 rue Férou, F-75006 Paris, France
Founded: 1966
ISBN Publisher's Prefix: 2-8251

Albanus Verlag*, J H Göhre, Hulfteggstr 10, Postfach, CH-8401 Winterthur 1 Tel: (052) 293503
ISBN Publisher's Prefix: 3-85510

Albatros Verlag AG*, Seestr 139, PO Box 140, CH-8706 Feldmeilen Tel: (01) 9232347
Subjects: Illustrated Reference Books, Animals and Plants, Technical, Culture
ISBN Publisher's Prefix: 3-7156

Ansata-Verlag, Paul A Zemp, Rosenstr 24, CH-3800 Interlaken Tel: (036) 221933
Subjects: Occultism, Esoteric Traditions, Astrology, Folklore, Psychology

Editions **Anthroposophiques Romandes***, 13 rue Verdaine, CH-1204 Geneva Tel: (022) 285150
Subjects: Anthroposophical/Rosicrucian Literature in French

Antonius-Verlag, Gärtnerstr 7, CH-4500 Solothurn Tel: (065) 223912
Subjects: Psychology, Therapeutics, Pedagogy
ISBN Publisher's Prefix: 3-85520

362 SWITZERLAND

Verlag der **Arche** Peter Schifferli AG*, Rosenbühlstr 37, CH-8044 Zurich Tel: (01) 2522154 Cable Add: Archeverlag
Owners: Christoph and Lorenz Schifferli
Orders to: Erikastr 11, CH-8003 Zurich
Branch Offs: Zurich (two), Konstanz (one), Vienna (two)
Associate Companies: Sanssouci Verlag AG, Zürich (qv); Dr Franz Hain, Austria (qv); E Pfister GmbH, Federal Republic of Germany (qv)
Subjects: General Fiction, Belles Lettres, Scholastic
Founded: 1944
ISBN Publisher's Prefix: 3-7160

Archimedes Verlag*, Rolf Christiani, Marktweg 7, PO Box 180, CH-8280 Kreuzlingen Tel: (072) 722672
Subjects: Mathematics, Electronics, Mechanical Engineering; Periodical *Technik heute*
ISBN Publisher's Prefix: 3-85525

Verlag für **Architektur**, Limmatquai 18, CH-8024 Zurich Tel: (00411) 2521100 Telex: 0045/59477
The Architectural Publishing Company
Man Dir: Dr Bruno Mariacher; *Rights & Permissions:* Rosemarie Roth
Parent Company: Artemis Verlags AG (qv for associate companies)

Editions **Ariston** Verlag, 39 rue Peillonnex, PO Box 82, CH-1225 Chêne-Bourg, Geneva Tel: (022) 481262/3 Cable Add: Ariston CH-1225 Chêne-Bourg
Man Dir, Editorial: Dr Heinz Bundschuh; *Sales, Rights & Permissions:* Mrs A Bundschuh; *Publicity:* C Chenevard
Subjects: How-to, Psychology, Nature Medicine, Parapsychology, Hypnosis, Yoga, Self-Help, General Fiction
1982: 130 titles *Founded:* 1964
Miscellaneous: Formerly Ramòn F Keller
ISBN Publisher's Prefix: 3-7205

Ars Edition*, PO Box 48, CH-6301 Zug
Head Office: Ars Edition GmbH, Federal Republic of Germany (qv)

Artemis Verlags AG, Limmatquai 18, CH-8001 Zurich Tel: (01) 2521100 (Administration), (01) 2522102 (Production, Editorial) Telex: 59477
Man Dir: Dr Bruno Mariacher; *Rights & Permissions:* Rosemarie Roth
Subsidiary Company: Verlag für Architektur (qv)
Associate Companies: Artemis und Winkler Verlag, Druckenmüller Verlag, Winkler-Verlag (qqv in Federal Republic of Germany)
Subjects: General Fiction, Philosophy, Art, Architecture, Encyclopaedias, Ancient/Medieval History, Literary History, Classics, Textbooks, Juvenile, Travel Guides
1981: 58 titles *Founded:* 1943
ISBN Publisher's Prefix: 3-7608

Athenaeum Verlag AG*, Via Miravalle 23, CH-6900 Lugano-Massagno Tel: (091) 571536 Cable Add: athenag
Man Dir: J-E Nussbaumer; *Administration:* J Wüst-Wolfensberger; *Editorial:* J Steiner
Branch Off: Buchauslieferung, Schweizer Buchzentrum, Olten
Subjects: General Non-fiction: Art, History, Science, Literature, Biography, Politics
Founded: 1972
ISBN Publisher's Prefix: 3-85532

Atlantis Verlag AG, Zinggentorstr 4, CH-6000 Lucerne Tel: (04141) 513721
Branch Off: Atlantis-Verlag GmbH & Co KG, Federal Republic of Germany (qv)
Subjects: Pictorial Geography and Travel, Art
Founded: 1930
ISBN Publisher's Prefix: 3-7611

Atrium Verlag AG*, Rütistr 4, CH-8030 Zürich Tel: (01) 473035
Subjects: Juveniles, Belles Lettres
Founded: 1936
ISBN Publisher's Prefix: 3-85535

Augustin-Verlag, Schlatterweg 11, CH-8240 Thayngen Tel: (053) 67131 Telex: 76657 Augu CH
Subjects: Geography, History, Textbooks (especially series of anatomical booklets for schoolchildren)
ISBN Publisher's Prefix: 3-85540

Editions de la **Baconnière** SA, PO Box 185, CH-2017 Boudry-Neuchâtel (Located at: 7 ave du Collège, Boudry-Neuchâtel) Tel: (038) 421004 Cable Add: Baconnière Boudry
Man Dir and all other offices: Marie-Christine Hauser
Orders to: Diffusion Payot (Booksellers), 30 rue des Côtes de Montbenon, CH-1002 Lausanne
Branch Off: 2 rue du Pré-Landry, CH-2017 Boudry
Subjects: Belles Lettres, Poetry, Biography, History, Music, Art, Philosophy, Reference, Psychology, Social Science, University Textbooks
1981: 11 titles *Founded:* 1927
ISBN Publisher's Prefix: 2-8252

H R **Balmer** AG Verlag, Neugasse 12, CH-6301 Zug Tel: (042) 214141 Telex: 868812
Man Dir: Christoph Balmer
Associate Company: Verlag Klett und Balmer & Co (qv)
Subjects: Local History, Literature, Psychology, Pedagogy
Bookshop: At above address
ISBN Publisher's Prefix: 3-85548

U **Bär** Verlag+, Tödistr 63, CH-8002 Zurich Tel: (01) 2022515
Man Dir: Dr Ulrich Bär; *Permissions:* Marianne Widmer
Subjects: How-to, Art, Reference

Librairie **Barblan et Saladin***, 10 rue de Romont, CH-1701 Fribourg Tel: (037) 226065
Bookshop: At above address
Founded: 1954

Bargezzi-Verlag AG+, Wasserwerkgasse 17-19, PO Box 1199, CH-3001 Berne Tel: (031) 221380 Cable Add: Bargezzi Berne
Man Dir, Editorial, Sales, Publicity, Rights & Permissions: Josef Grübel; *Production:* Hugo Tanner
Subjects: Novels, Religious Literature
Founded: 1948

Basileia Verlag, Missionsstr 21, CH-4003 Basle Tel: (061) 251766
Man Dir: Rudolf Kellenberger
Subject: Religion, Missionary Work, Third World
ISBN Publisher's Prefix: 3-85555

Basilius Presse AG*, PO Box 153, CH-4002 Basle (Located at: Güterstr 86, Basle) Tel: (061) 228000 Cable Add: Basiliuspresse Telex: 62553
Man Dir: R Degen
Subjects: General Fiction, Non-fiction, Juveniles, Music, Art (Paintings), High-priced Paperbacks, General Science
Founded: 1957
ISBN Publisher's Prefix: 3-85560

Baufachverlag AG, PO Box 6721, CH-8953 Dietikon (Located at: Schöneggstr 102, Dietikon) Tel: (01) 7407677 Telex: 52702 impagch
Dir: Wolfgang R Felzmann
Subject: Building Trade and Architecture (Technical and Specialist Books)
1982: 7 titles *Founded:* 1970
ISBN Publisher's Prefix: 3-85565

Beltz*, Rittergasse 20, PO Box 227, CH-4051 Basle Tel: (061) 239470
Owner: Dr Manfred Beltz Rübelmann
Subjects: Textbooks, Psychology, Juveniles, Social Science, Primary and University Textbooks
ISBN Publisher's Prefix: 3-407

Benteli Verlag, PO Box 102, CH-3000 Berne 8 (Located at: Gerechtigkeitsgasse 6, Berne) Tel: (031) 228866 Cable Add: Bag 3000 Berne 8
Man Dir: Ted Schaap (Scapa)
Subjects: General Fiction, Belles Lettres, Poetry, History, Art, Textbooks, Reference
Founded: 1899
ISBN Publisher's Prefix: 3-7165

Benziger AG, Bellerivestr 3, CH-8008 Zurich Tel: (01) 2527050 Cable Add: Benzigerverlag Zurich Telex: 004554545
Man Dir: Benno Bettschart; *Editorial:* Dr Renate Nagel, Dr Peter Moll, Anton Scherer; *Sales, Rights & Permissions Dir:* Robert F Oehler; *Production:* Walter Eberle; *Advertising Dir:* Heinrich Flüeler
Branch Off: Benziger Verlag, Federal Republic of Germany (qv)
Subjects: General Fiction, Poetry, Religion, Juveniles, Educational Materials
Bookshop: Carolus Buch und Kunst, Liebfrauenstr 4, D-6000 Frankfurt am Main
Founded: 1792
ISBN Publisher's Prefix: 3-545

Edition Sven Erik **Bergh** im Europabuch AG, Erlenweg 6, CH-6314 Unterägeri, Zug Tel: (042) 723077/721010 Cable Add: Sebergh CH-6314 Unterägeri Telex: 862553
Man Dir: Dr S E Bergh; *Editorial:* Liselotte Bergh; *Rights & Permissions:* Karin Bergh
Orders to: VVA — Vereinigte Verlagsauslieferung, Postfach 7777, D-4830 Gütersloh 1, Federal Republic of Germany
Associate Company: Berghs Förlag AB, Sweden (qv)
Subjects: General Fiction, Belles Lettres, Mystery Novels, Picture Books, Juveniles
1983: 18 titles *Founded:* 1970

Berichthaus Verlag, Dr Conrad Ulrich, Voltast 43, CH-8044 Zurich Tel: (01) 2526349
Orders to: Orell Füssli Verlag, Postfach, CH-8022 Zurich
Subject: History
ISBN Publisher's Prefix: 3-85572

Editions **Berlitz**, an imprint of Macmillan SA (qv)

Beyeler Editions Basle, Bäumleingasse 9, CH-4001 Basle Tel: (061) 235412
Owner: Ernst Beyeler
Subject: Art
Founded: 1967
ISBN Publisher's Prefix: 3-85575

Verlag **Bibellesebund**, Römerstr 151, CH-8404 Winterthur Tel: (052) 274801
Scripture Union of Switzerland
Secretary-General: Peter Hoppler; *Man Dir, Sales, Production, Publicity:* Martin Wassmer; *Editorial, Chief Reader, Rights & Permissions:* Wolfgang Steinseifer
Head Off: Scripture Union, UK (qv for other branches)
Subjects: Christian and Scriptural literature for all ages
1981: 10 titles *1982:* 10 titles *Founded:* 1930
ISBN Publisher's Prefix: 3-87982

Bibliographisches Institut AG, PO Box 130, CH-8021 Zurich (Located at: Hardturmstr 76, Zurich) Tel: (01) 446642 Telex: 823022 Bi CH
Man Dir: Rudolf Hans Fürrer; *Production:*

B Mannheim
Parent Company: Bibliographisches Institut AG, Federal Republic of Germany (qv)
Subjects: Philosophy, Linguistics, General Science, Reference Works
Founded: 1967
ISBN Publisher's Prefix: 3-411

Verlag **Bibliophile Drucke** von Josef Stocker AG, Hasenbergstr 7, CH-8953 Dietikon-Zurich Tel: (01) 7404444
Man Dir: Mr Stocker
Parent Company: Verlag Stocker-Schmid AG (qv)
Associate Company: Urs Graf-Verlag GmbH (qv)
Subjects: Belles Lettres, Poetry, Reference, Historical Manuscript facsimiles
Bookshop: Buchhandlung Stocker-Schmid (at above address)
ISBN Publisher's Prefix: 3-85577

Société **Biblique** de Genève, see La Maison de la Bible

Birkhäuser Verlag AG, PO Box 34, CH-4010 Basle (Located at: Elisabethenstr 19, Basle) Tel: (061) 231810 Cable Add: Edita Telex: 63475
Chairman: Carl Einsele; *Man Dir:* H Jo Pfeiffer; *Marketing Dir:* H P Thür; *Editorial Dir:* H Bender
Subsidiary Companies: Birkhäuser Verlag Federal Republic of Germany (qv); Birkhaeuser Boston Inc, 380 Green St, PO Box 2007, Cambridge, MA 02139, USA
Subjects: Art, Architecture, Engineering, Mathematics, Natural Science, Pharmacy, Railway Interest, General & Social Science, University Textbooks, Paperbacks, 25 scientific journals
1981: 92 titles *Founded:* 1879
ISBN Publisher's Prefix: 3-7643

Blaukreuz-Verlag Bern, PO Box 1196, Lindenrain 5a, CH-3001 Berne Tel: (031) 235866 Cable Add: Blaukreuzverlag
Man Dir: Eduard Müller
Parent Company: Blaues Kreuz der deutschen Schweiz
Subjects: Belles Lettres, Biography, Religion, Juveniles; Addiction Problems (Alcohol, Drugs, Tobacco), Periodicals
1981: 10 titles *1982:* 9 titles *Founded:* 1884
Miscellaneous: Publishes for the Blue Cross health and religious movement. See also Blaukreuz-Verlag Wuppertal, Federal Republic of Germany
ISBN Publisher's Prefix: 3-85580

Les Editions de la Fondation Martin **Bodmer**, PO Box 7, CH-1223 Cologny-Geneva Tel: (022) 362370
Subjects: Philology, Papyrus Editions
ISBN Publisher's Prefix: 3-85682

Boersig Verlag AG*, Drusbergstr 1, CH-8703 Erlenbach ZH
Subject: Art

Bohem Press Kinderbuchverlag*, Asylstr 67, CH-8007 Zürich Tel: (01) 2527714
Dir: O Bozejovsky v Rawennoff; *Art Dir:* S Zavrel
ISBN Publisher's Prefix: 3-85581

Brain Anatomy Institute, Untere Zollgasse 71, CH-3072 Ostermundigen/BE Tel: (031) 512411
Dir, Rights & Permissions: Prof G Pilleri
Subjects: Biology and Behaviour of Marine Animals, Comparative Anatomy, Investigations on Cetacea
Founded: 1969

Brunnen-Verlag, Wallstr 6, CH-4002 Basle Tel: (061) 234406 Telex: 64751 brb ch
Man Dir: Hans-Peter Züblin
Subjects: Religion, Evangelical Literature
Bookshops: Buchhandlung Pilgermission, Spalenberg 20, CH-4002 Basle; Untere Bahnhofstr 20, CH-9500 Wil/SG
1981: 23 titles *1982:* 30 titles *Founded:* 1921
Miscellaneous: Firm is a branch office of Brunnen-Verlag GmbH, Federal Republic of Germany (qv)
ISBN Publisher's Prefix: 3-7655

Bubenberg Verlag AG*, PO Box 2736, CH-3007 Berne (Located at: Monbijoustr 61) Tel: (031) 455941
Subjects: Belles Lettres, Poetry, How-to, Reference
Founded: 1951
ISBN Publisher's Prefix: 3-85585

Verlag Alfred **Bucheli***, Baarerstr 61, PO Box 281, CH-6301 Zug Tel: (004142) 211247 Telex: 78737
Subjects: Car and Motor Cycle Engineering, Flying

Verlag C J **Bücher**, formerly of Lucerne and Munich, now only in Federal Republic of Germany (qv)

Buchhaus AG, see Office du Livre SA

Büchler & Co AG, Seftigenstr 310, CH-3084 Wabern-Berne Tel: (031) 548111 Telex: 32697
Man Dir, Rights & Permissions: Dr Rudolf Gysi; *Marketing:* Erich Hirschel
Subjects: Reference, Guidebooks, Art, Educational Materials
1982: 9 titles *Founded:* 1886
ISBN Publisher's Prefix: 3-7170

Hugo **Buchser** SA, 4 Tour de l'Ile, CH-1211 Geneva 11 Tel: (022) 288155 Telex: 429469 hbsa ch
Man Dir: G M Maillard; *Editor-in-Chief:* Valentin Philibert; *Sales Dir:* Ph Maillard
Subjects: Watches, Jewellery, Technical Trades, Management, Directories, Periodicals
Founded: 1927

Bundesamt für Landestopographie, see Landestopographie

C E E L (Centre Expérimental pour l'Enseignement des Langues)*, Palais Wilson, 52 rue des Pâquis, CH-1211 Geneva 14 Tel: (022) 325893/325612
Centre for Experimentation and Evaluation of Language Learning Techniques
Man Dir: Nicolas Ferguson
Subject: Language Textbooks
Founded: 1972
ISBN Publisher's Prefix: 2-88047

Cahiers de la Renaissance Vaudoise, 18 rue du Petit-Chêne, CH-1003 Lausanne Tel: (021) 221914
President: Olivier Delacrétaz
Subjects: Belles Lettres, History, Secondary Textbooks, Politics, Militaria
ISBN Publisher's Prefix: 2-88017

Camera-Verlag*, Zürichstr 3-7, CH-6002 Lucerne Tel: (041) 391111 Cable Add: Cibag Telex: Innch 78122
Editor-in-Chief: Allan Porter
Subject: Photography (in separate editions in English, French, German)
ISBN Publisher's Prefix: 3-0008

Edizioni del Prof Mario Agliati **Cantonetto***, Via Greina 2, CH-6900 Lugano

Caritas-Verlag*, Löwenstr 3, PO Box 902, CH-6002 Lucerne Tel: (41) 501150 Telex: 78344
Subject: Religion
ISBN Publisher's Prefix: 3-85592

Carta, Lüthi und Ramseier, Haslerstr, CH-3000 Berne Tel: (031) 259548 Cable Add: Zeilerag Telex: 32391 (Zeiler AG)
Man Dir, Rights & Permissions: Lüthi Heinz; *Sales:* Volders Viktor; *Production:* Ramseier Ulrich
Orders to: Zeiler AG, Gartenstadtr 5, PO Box 32, Dept Geo-Carta, CH-3098 Köniz-Berne
Subjects: Maps of Europe and World in various scales and layouts, Atlases, Street Maps, Local Area Maps
Founded: 1964

Edizioni **Casagrande** SA, Via del Bramantino, PO Box 489, CH-6501 Bellinzona Tel: (092) 256622 Telex: 73131
Man Dir, Editorial: Libero Casagrande
Subsidiary Company: Istituto Grafico Casagrande
Associate Company: Istituto Editoriale Ticinese (IET) SA (qv)
Subjects: Literature, Art, Scholarship, History, Art History
Founded: 1950
ISBN Publisher's Prefix: 3-85897

Caux Verlag-, Theater- und Film-AG, PO Box 218, CH-6002 Lucerne Tel: (041) 422213
Subsidiary Company: Editions de Caux (qv)
Subjects: Social Science, Biography, Religion
ISBN Publisher's Prefix: 3-85601

Editions de **Caux**, CH-1824 Caux Tel: (021) 634821
Man Dir, Editorial, Production, Publicity: Chas Piguet; *Sales, Rights & Permissions:* B Utzinger
Parent Company: Caux Verlag-, Theater-und Film-AG (qv)
Subjects: Moral Rearmament, Social Sciences, Religion, Theatre, Biographies
Bookshop: Librairie de Caux, CH-1824 Caux
1981: 2 titles *1982:* 2 titles
ISBN Publisher's Prefix: 2-88037

Verlag Bo **Cavefors**, c/o Mandatropa AG, PO Box 5837, CH-8024 Zurich
Man Dir: Bo Cavefors
Subjects: Roman Catholic Theology, General Fiction, Poetry, University Textbooks
1983: 10 titles
ISBN Publisher's Prefix: 3-85593

Cedilivre SA, subsidiary of Editions Foma SA (qv)

Centre Expérimental pour l'Enseignement des Langues, see C E E L

VC Verlag **Chemie** AG, Elisabethenstr 19, PO Box 34, CH-4010 Basle
Parent Company: Verlag Chemie GmbH, Federal Republic of Germany (qv)

Christiana-Verlag, CH-8260 Stein am Rhein Tel: (054) 86820/86847 Telex: 76609
Man Dir: Arnold Guillet
Subject: Religion
Founded: 1948
ISBN Publisher's Prefix: 3-7171

Werner **Classen** Verlag, Splügenstr 10, PO Box 683, CH-8002 Zurich Tel: (01) 2015606 Cable Add: Classenverlag Zurich
Dir: Werner Classen
Subjects: Belles Lettres, Poetry, Music, Juveniles, Psychology, Humour, Technical Paperbacks
Founded: 1945
ISBN Publisher's Prefix: 3-7172

De **Clivo** Press*, Dr Walter Amstutz, Usterstr 126, PO Box, CH-8600 Duebendorf, Zurich Tel: (01) 8201224/8201212 Cable Add: declivopress Duebendorf Telex: CH 55256 Serco
Proprietor: Dr Walter Amstutz
ISBN Publisher's Prefix: 3-85634

SWITZERLAND

Imprimerie La Concorde, PO Box 330, CH-1010 Lausanne (Located at: 6 ch des Croisettes CH-1066 Épalinges) Tel: (021) 333141
Dir: Paul Perrin
Subjects: Religion, Science, Art
Founded: 1910
ISBN Publisher's Prefix: 2-88000

Cosmos-Verlag AG*, PO Box 2637, CH-3001 Berne (Located at: Oberer Wehrliweg 5, CH-3074 Muri bei Bern) Tel: (031) 526611 Telex: Cosmo 32556
Man Dir: H R Aeberli
Subjects: Tax and Finance Laws, Politics, High-priced Paperbacks, including publications on behalf of the Swiss Institute of Business Management (Schweizerisches Institut für Unternehmungs-führung im Gewerbe)
Founded: 1923
ISBN Publisher's Prefixes: 3-85621, 2-8296

Cratander AG*, Druckerei, Petersgasse 34, CH-4001 Basle Tel: (061) 258166
Subject: Civil Engineering
ISBN Publisher's Prefix: 3-85622

Edizioni Armando **Dadò**, Tipografia Stazione*, Via G A Orelli 29, CH-6600 Locarno (Located at: Via Bramantino 6) Tel: (093) 314802
Man Dir: Armando Dado
Subjects: Books in Italian on Art, History, Literature, Photography, Swiss Italian Costume

Daphnis-Verlag, J Fischlin, Rainweg 2, CH-8704 Herrliberg Tel: (01) 9153639
Man Dir: J Fischlin
Subjects: Belles Lettres, Poetry, Limited Editions
Founded: 1959
ISBN Publisher's Prefix: 3-85631

Editions **Delachaux et Niestlé** SA*, 79 route d'Oron, CH-1000 Lausanne 21 Tel: (021) 333041 Telex: 25822
Man Dir: David Perret; *Sales, Advertising Dir:* Jean-Jacques Lagane; *Permissions:* Yvette Perret
Subsidiary Company: Delachaux Niestlé, Spes, France (qv)
Subjects: Biography, How-to, Philosophy, Reference, Juveniles, Medicine, Pedagogy, Psychology, General & Social Science, Natural Sciences, Educational Materials
Founded: 1860
ISBN Publisher's Prefix: 2-603

Delphin Verlag*, PO Box 157, CH-8031 Zurich (Located at: Limmatstr 111) Tel: 440733/6 Cable Add: Delphinverlag Zürich Telex: 53815
Man Dir: Oswald Boxer
Parent Company: Delphin Verlag GmbH, Federal Republic of Germany (qv)
Subject: Juveniles, Non-fiction, Paperbacks
Founded: 1962
ISBN Publisher's Prefix: 3-7735

Editions **Delta et Spes** SA, 4 route de Préverenges, CH-1026 Denges (Lausanne) Tel: (021) 721294 Telex: 451165 dlta
Publisher, Man Dir: André Delcourt
Subjects: Textbooks and Teaching Aids in all subjects, Building and Architecture, Hotels and Catering
1981: 30 titles *1982:* 32 titles *Founded:* 1963/1917
Miscellaneous: Firm is part of Educa International, a member of the Kluwer Group, Netherlands (qv)

Desertina Verlag, CH-7180 Disentis Tel: (086) 7544142 Cable Add: Desertina Disentis
Man Dir, Rights & Permissions, Editorial, Production, Publicity: P Condrau; *Sales:* Ruedi Henny
Subjects: Belles Lettres of Romance Literature, Art Reproductions
Bookshop: Condrau, Disentis
Founded: 1953

Verlag Harri **Deutsch**, Riedstr 2, CH-3600 Thun Tel: (033) 223975
Man Dirs: Harri Deutsch, Dr Anton Reiter
Parent Company: Verlag Harri Deutsch, Federal Republic of Germany (qv)
Subjects: Maths, Physics, Chemistry, Other Natural Sciences, Technology, Economics
ISBN Publisher's Prefix: 3-87144

Diana-Verlag AG, Jupiterstr 1, CH-8032 Zurich Tel: (01) 534140 Cable Add: Dianaverlag
Dir: R V Siebenthal
Subject: Belles Lettres
Founded: 1946
ISBN Publisher's Prefix: 3-905414

Didax, an imprint of Editions Foma SA (qv)

Diogenes Verlag AG, Sprecherstr 8, CH-8032 Zurich Tel: (01) 2528111 Cable Add: Diogenesverlag Zurich Telex: 52810
Man Dirs & Owners: Daniel Keel (Publisher), Rudolf C Bettschart (Administration & Finance); *Editorial:* Beatrice Gyssler, Claudia Kühner, Dr Brigitta Neumeister-Taroni, Franz Sutter; *Sales:* Birgitt Nauman; *Production:* Christine Döring; *Rights & Permissions:* Marianne Liggenstorfer
Subjects: Fiction, Art, Paperbacks, Pocket Books, Children's Books
Founded: 1953
ISBN Publisher's Prefix: 3-257

Doulos Verlag*, Villa Meridiana, Titlisstr 14, CH-8032 Zurich (Located at: Kirchenweg 5, Zurich) Tel: (01) 2517560/475565 Cable Add: Doulosverlag Zurich
Proprietor, Man Dir: Dr Wolfgang M Metz
Associate Company: Leonis Verlag (qv)
Subjects: Christian Literature
Founded: 1981
ISBN Publisher's Prefix: 3-7158

Drei Eichen Verlag AG*, Mühlematt 11, CH-6390 Engelberg Tel: (041) 941129 Cable Add: Dreieichen Engelberg
Dirs: Hermann Kissener, Hans Rudi Marti, Peter Linder
Subjects: Comparative Religion, Popular Medicine, Education, Philosophy, Yoga Instruction
Founded: 1931
ISBN Publisher's Prefix: 3-7699

Drei Eidgenossen Verlag, Hüegelweg 15, CH-4102 Binningen Tel: (061) 475166
Man Dir: Mr Hosch
Subject: Juveniles
Founded: 1936
ISBN Publisher's Prefix: 3-85643

Droemersche Verlagsanstalt AG*, Stauffacherquai 46, PO Box 670, CH-8021 Zurich Tel: (00411) 394214
Subjects: Fiction, Non-fiction, Natural Sciences

Librairie **Droz** SA, PO Box 389, CH-1211 Geneva 12 (Located at: 11 rue Massot, Geneva) Tel: (022) 466666
Man Dir, Rights & Permissions: A Dufour; *Sales Dir:* Miss Gueguen
Subjects: French language publisher of Belles Lettres, Poetry, History, Literature, Reference, Religion, Social Science, University Textbooks
1981: 69 titles *Founded:* 1924
ISBN Publisher's Prefix: 2-600

Henry-Robert **Dufour**, 7 ave du Théâtre, CH-1005 Lausanne Tel: (021) 233062/233070 Telex: Hrd 26186
Subjects: French language publisher of General Non-fiction, Fine Arts, Technical, Industrial, Belles Lettres, Education

Gottlieb **Duttweiler** Institute for Economic & Social Studies, CH-8803 Rüschlikon-Zurich Tel: (01) 7240020 Cable Add: Green Meadow Telex: 55699
Subjects: Reference, Social Science, Economics
Bookshop: Verlagsbuchhandlung GDI, CH-8803 Rueschlikon-Zurich
Founded: 1963
Miscellaneous: Specialists in distributive trades, management education, economic growth and new forms of organization

Dynamis Verlag, PO Box 256, CH-8280 Kreuzlingen (Located at: Brückenstr 22, Kreuzlingen) Tel: (072) 727781 Cable Add: Dynamis
Man Dir: David Tschudi
Subject: Religion
Bookshop: Christliche Buchhandlung, Hauptstr 7, CH-8280 Kreuzlingen Tel: (072) 727781
Founded: 1973

Eagle Editions*, PO Box 85, CH-1211 Geneva 3
Branch Office of Eagle Editions, TPC Ltd, Box 1404, Terminal A, Vancouver, BC, Canada V6C ZP7
Subjects: Books in French and English

Ecart Publications*, 6 rue Plantamour, PO Box 253, CH-1211 Geneva 1 Tel: 457395/288803/313473
Man Dirs: John M Armleder, Patrick Lucchini; *Editorial:* John Armleder
Subsidiary Companies: Leathern Wing Scribble Press, The Geneva Pond Bubbles
Associate Companies: Centre d'Art Contemporain, 16 rue d'Italie, CH-1204 Geneva; Marika Malacorda Editions, Geneva (qv)
Subjects: Art (especially New Trends), Photography, Video, Cinema
Bookshop: Ecart Books, Librairie, 14 rue d'Italie, PO Box 253, CH-1211 Geneva 1
Founded: 1969

Eco-Verlags AG, Rotwandstr 62, Postfach, CH-8021 Zurich Tel: (01) 2428634
Man Dirs: Verena Stettler, Rolf Thut
Imprints: Neue Szene, Litheratheke
Subjects: Non-fiction, City Guides, Literature
1981: 10 titles *Founded:* 1976
ISBN Publisher's Prefix: 3-85647

Edita SA, 10 rue du Valentin, CH-1004 Lausanne Tel: (021) 205631 Telex: 26296 Cable Add: Editasa Lausanne
Man Dir: Ami Guichard; *Editorial:* Joseph Jobé, Constance Devantherey-Lewis, Jean-Rodolphe Piccard
Subjects: Art, Social and Military Popular Histories, Popular Histories of Transport (especially Automobiles), How-to, General Science
Founded: 1952
ISBN Publisher's Prefix: 2-88001

Editeurs Associés SA*, 5 rue César-Soulié, PO Box 84, CH-1260 Nyon Tel: (022) 612676 Telex: Buco 22886 Nyon
Man Dir: F Gendreau
Subjects: Fiction, History
Founded: 1966
ISBN Publisher's Prefix: 2-8291

Editions Universitaires SA (Universitätsverlag), Pérolles 42, CH-1700 Fribourg Tel: (037) 246812
Man Dir, Publicity: Dr Martin Nicoulin
Parent Company: Imprimerie et Librairies Saint-Paul SA (at above address)
Associate Companies: Editions Saint-Paul (qv), Editions de la Sarine (both at above address)

Subjects: Literature, History, Music, Art, Philosophy, Reference, Religions, Theology, Psychology, Economic and Political Sciences, Secondary and University Textbooks, Medicine, Ethnology, Law
Bookshop: Librairie et Edition de la Suisse Romande
ISBN Publisher's Prefixes: 3-7278 (German books), 2-8271 (French books)

Edito-Service SA, PO Box 307, CH-1211 Geneva 6 (Located at: 9 ter chemin de Roches, Geneva) Tel: (022) 357233 Cable Add: Editoservice Geneva
Man Dir: Gaston Burnand; *Publisher:* Jean-François Gonthier; *Literary Dept:* Pierrette Cuendet; *Rights & Permissions:* Anne Hauser
Subjects: General Fiction, Belles Lettres, Poetry, Biography, Nature, History, How-to, Music, Art, Religion, Juveniles, Medicine, Psychology, General Science, Educational Materials, Co-editions in all languages
1981: 360 titles

André **Eiselé***, Editeur, 17 route de Cossonay, PO Box 19, CH-1008 Prilly/Lausanne Tel: (021) 256324
Subjects: Arts, Education, Popular Science, Juveniles, Belles Lettres, Textbooks
ISBN Publisher's Prefix: 2-88002

Verlag **Eisenbahn**, R Jeanmaire & Co, Gut Vorhard, CH-5234 Villigen AG Tel: (056) 441595 Cable Add: Verlageisenbahn Villigen
Dirs: Rose Jeanmaire, Jeannine Claudine J dit-Quartier
Subjects: Railway, Tramcar and Model Rail Literature, Model Railways, Toys of the Past
Bookshops: Company acts as Distribution Centre for rail publications of every country, world-wide
Founded: 1961
ISBN Publisher's Prefix: 3-85649

Elsevier Sequoia SA, 50 ave de la Gare, PO Box 851, CH-1001 Lausanne 1 Tel: (021) 207381 Cable Add: Elsevier Lausanne Telex: 26620 elsa ch
Man Dir, Rights & Permissions: Louk Bergmans; *Editorial, Production:* Eef Vogelezang; *Sales, Publicity:* Peter van der Spek
Parent Company: Elsevier-NDU nv, Netherlands (qv for associate companies)
Subjects: Chemistry, Applied Physics, Technology, Energy, Environmental Sciences, Periodicals
1983: 6 titles *Founded:* 1967

Emmentaler Druck AG, PO Box 2502, Dorfstr 5, CH-3550 Langnau Tel: (035) 21911
Man Dir, Editorial, Sales: H R Bodenmann; *Production:* L Martin; *Publicity:* P Ebneter, H R Bodenmann
Subjects: Fiction, Photographic, Periodicals
1981: 4 titles *Founded:* 1845
ISBN Publisher's Prefix: 3-85654

Erker-Galerie AG*, Franz Larese und Jürg Janett, Gallustr 32, CH-9000 St Gallen Tel: (071) 227979/233607
Subject: Modern Art, Literature
Founded: 1964

Edition **Erpf** AG, PO Box 1383, CH-3001 Berne (Located at: Mottastr 6, Berne) Tel: (031) 446677 Cable Add: bucherpf
Man Dir: Hans Erpf
Subjects: Contemporary Literature, Caricature and Cartoons, Current Topics, Monographs, Bavarian and Bernese themes
1981: 11 titles *1982:* 16 titles *Founded:* 1979
ISBN Publisher's Prefix: 3-256

Eulenburg Edition GmbH*, Grütstr 28, CH-8134 Adliswil-Zürich Tel: (01) 7103681
Subjects: Instrumental Sheet Music; Books on Music and Musicians
Founded: 1945
ISBN Publisher's Prefix: 3-85662

Europa-Verlag AG, Rämistr 5, CH-8001 Zurich Tel: (01) 471629 Cable Add: Europaverlag Zurich Telex: 55210 feren ch
Man Dir: Emmie Oprecht
Associate Company: Verlag Oprecht, Zurich (Theatrical)
Subjects: History, Politics, Philosophy, Art, Belles Lettres
Founded: 1933
Miscellaneous: Distributor for UNESCO, Paris
ISBN Publisher's Prefix: 3-85665

Europabuch AG, see Edition Sven Erik Bergh im Europabuch AG

Evangelischer Schriften Verlag Schwengeler, see Schwengeler (Switzerland) and Telos (Federal Republic of Germany)

Ex Libris, Hermetschlossstr 77, CH-8023 Zurich
Subjects: Belles Lettres, Children's Books, Reference Books
Book Clubs: Ex Libris (qv), Edition Kunstkreis (qv)

Farb-Dia-Archiv Edmond Van Hoorick, see Verlag van Hoorick

Pierre Marcel **Favre***, rue de Bourg 29, PO Box 3569, CH-1002 Lausanne Tel: (021) 221717 Cable Add: Favrepublisa Lausanne
Man Dir: P M Favre
Subjects: Current Affairs, Politics, Sport, Ecology, Illustrated Editions, Fiction
1982: 100 titles *Founded:* 1975
ISBN Publisher's Prefix: 2-8289

Editions François **Feij**, pl de l'Eglise, CH-1166 Perroy Tel: (021) 752777

J **Fischlin**, see Daphnis-Verlag

Maurice et Pierre **Foetisch** SA, PO Box 2793, CH-1002 Lausanne (Located at: 6 rue de Bourg, CH-1002 Lausanne) Tel: (021) 239444/5 Telex: 24227
Man Dir and other offices: Jean-Claude Foetisch
Associate Company: Disco SA
Subjects: Music, Records, Pianos, TV, Educational, Textbooks (especially ASSIMIL Language Teaching Courses)
Founded: 1947

Editions **Foma** SA*, Ave de Longemalle 5, PO Box 226, CH-1020 Renens-Lausanne Tel: (021) 351361 Telex: CH-Cedil 25416
Man Dir, Editorial: J-L Peverelli; *Sales:* M Sculati; *Publicity:* Ann-Mari Mingard; *Rights & Permissions:* F Buhler
Subsidiary Companies: 5 Continents, Cedilivre SA
Imprints: Foma, Didax, Cedilivre
Subjects: Cinema, Photography, Psychology, Secondary and Primary Textbooks, Yoga, General Literature
Bookshop: Didax
Founded: 1948
ISBN Publisher's Prefix: 2-88003

Fortuna-Verlag W Heidelberger+, Postfach, CH-8172 Niederglatt/ZH Tel: (01) 8503586
Man Dir: W Heidelberger
Imprints: Fortuna Finanz Verlag, W Heidelberger AG
Subject: Financial Publications
1981: 4 titles *Founded:* 1953
ISBN Publisher's Prefix: 3-85684

Foto und Schmalfilm-Verlag (Gemsberg-Verlag), Garnmarkt 10, PO Box 778, CH-8401 Winterthur Tel: (052) 857171 Cable Add: Gemsberg-Verlag Telex: 896417

Production: Hans Ziegler
Parent Company: Ziegler Druck- und Verlags-AG (Proprietors)
Subjects: Amateur Photography and Filmmaking
Founded: 1950
ISBN Publisher's Prefix: 3-85701

Francke Verlag, PO Box 1445, CH-3001 Berne (Located at: Neuengasse 43, Berne) Tel: (031) 221715 Cable Add: Frankeverlag Bern
Man Dir: Dr Carl L Lang; *Production:* K Gschwend; *Publicity:* Mrs B Bieri
Parent Company: A Francke GmbH, Federal Republic of Germany (qv)
Subjects: Germanic, Romance and English Language Studies, History, Philology, Philosophy, Psychology, Reference; Periodicals
Bookshop: Buchhandlung A Francke AG (qv under Major Booksellers)
Founded: 1831
ISBN Publisher's Prefix: 3-7720

Fretz Verlag, Falkenstr 12, Postfach, CH-8021 Zurich Tel: (01) 2521449 Telex: 58897 frez
Publicity Manager: Walter Köpfli
Subjects: Fine and Applied Arts, Illustrated Books, Fiction
Founded: 1860
ISBN Publisher's Prefix: 3-85692

Fretz und Wasmuth Verlag AG*, Bellerivestr 5, CH-8008 Zurich Tel: (01) 323585
Subjects: Archaeology, Architecture, Civil Engineering, Fine & Applied Arts, Illustrated Books
Founded: 1927
ISBN Publisher's Prefix: 3-7180

Frobenius AG, Spalenring 31, CH-4012 Basle Tel: (061) 437610
Publicity: Edwin Reichle
Subjects: History, Law, Literature (especially local)
ISBN Publisher's Prefix: 3-85695

Orell **Füssli** Verlag, see Orell

G S Verlag Basle*, PO Box 55, CH-4003 Basle (Located at: Petersgraben 29, CH-4003 Basle) Tel: (061) 253514
Man Dir: Hugo Weibel
Branch Offs: Falkenplatz 22, CH-3012 Berne Tel: (031) 235651; Wiesenstr 48, PO Box 47, CH-8703 Erlenbach Tel: (01) 9105313
Subjects: General Fiction, Belles Lettres, Biography, History, Music, Art, Juveniles, Low-Priced Paperbacks
Founded: 1889
ISBN Publisher's Prefix: 3-7185

Editions Bertil **Galland***, 29 rue du Lac, CH-1800 Vevey Tel: (021) 511732
Proprietor: Bertil Galland
Subject: Modern Literature
Founded: 1972
ISBN Publisher's Prefix: 2-88015

Rudolf **Geering** Verlag, see Philosophisch-Anthroposophischer Verlag

Gemsberg-Verlag, see Foto und Schmalfilm-Verlag

Genfer Bibelgesellschaft, see Maison de la Bible

Pierre **Genuiard** Editeur, 9 ch de Primerose, CH-1007 Lausanne Tel: (021) 264632
Subjects: Religion, Philosophy, Psychology, Naturism, Esotericism, Rosicrucian Thought
Founded: 1949
ISBN Publisher's Prefix: 2-88005

Georg et Cie SA, Librairies-Editeurs, 21 rue de la Corraterie, CH-1211 Geneva 11 Tel: (022) 216633 Telex: 23985

Man Dir: Jacques Matile
Subjects: Medical Science, Administration, Law, Secondary & Primary Textbooks, Religion, Philosophy, Psychology, Economics, Statistics, Social & Natural Sciences, Politics, Military Subjects, Languages, Literature, Geography, Ethnology, Travel, History
Bookshop: 21 rue de la Corraterie, CH-1211 Geneva 11 (qv under Major Booksellers)
Founded: 1857
ISBN Publisher's Prefix: 2-8257

Georgi Publishing Company/Editions Georgi, CH-1813 Saint-Saphorin Tel: (021) 529508 Cable Add: Georgedi S Saphorin Lavaux
Owner/President: Heinz Georgi
Subjects: Scientific and technical books and journals in Architecture, Computer Science, Civil Engineering, Electrical Engineering and Electronics, Metallurgy, Human Ecology, Environment, Social and Political Sciences (publications may be in English, French or German, or a combination of two or three languages)
Founded: 1975
ISBN Publisher's Prefix: 2-604

Globi Verlag AG, Eichstr 23, CH-8045 Zurich Tel: (01) 4634135 Cable Add: Globiverlag Zurich Telex: 813282
Man Dir: Emil Herzog
Subjects: Juveniles (especially illustrated books), comics
Founded: 1934
ISBN Publisher's Prefix: 3-85703

Victor **Goldschmidt** Verlagsbuchhandlung, Mostackerstr 17, CH-4051 Basle Tel: (061) 236565
Subjects: German-Judaica, Hebraica
Founded: 1902
ISBN Publisher's Prefix: 3-85705

André et Pierre **Gonin***, Editions d'Art, 2 rue Etraz, CH-1003 Lausanne Tel: (021) 226492/229996
Subject: Art
Founded: 1902
ISBN Publisher's Prefix: 2-88016

Gotthelf-Verlag, Badenerstr 69, CH-8026 Zurich Tel: (01) 2428155 Telex: ch 812500
Man Dir: Max Hirt
Associate Company: CVB Buch und Druck (at above address)
Subjects: Religion, Juveniles
1981: 4 titles *1982:* 5 titles *Founded:* 1928
ISBN Publisher's Prefix: 3-85706

Editions du **Grand-Pont***, Jean-Pierre Laubscher, 2 pl Bel-Air, CH-1003 Lausanne Tel: (021) 223222

Editions du **Griffon**, PO Box 545, CH-2000 Neuchâtel (Located at: 17 Faubourg du Lac, Neuchâtel) Tel: (038) 252204
Chairman: Dr Marcel Joray
Subject: Modern Art (especially sculpture and the plastic arts generally)
Founded: 1944
ISBN Publisher's Prefix: 2-88006

Editions François **Grounauer***, 1 rue du Belvédère, CH-1203 Geneva 1 Tel: (022) 447948
Subjects: History, Politics, Social Sciences
Founded: 1972
Miscellaneous: Formerly known as Editions Adversaires
ISBN Publisher's Prefix: 2-88076

Th **Gut** & Co Verlag, Seestr, CH-8712 Stäfa Tel: (01) 9281101 Telex: 875668
Subjects: Politics, Swiss and Regional History and Culture
ISBN Publisher's Prefix: 3-85717

Gute Schriften Verein, see GS Verlag

Sumus Verlag Jutta **Gütermann**, see Sumus

Habegger AG Druck und Verlag*, Gutenbergstr 1, CH-4552 Derendingen-Solothurn Tel: (065) 411151 Telex: 34744
Dir: Gerda Raschendorfer; *Production Manager:* Josef Baumgartner; *Marketing:* Hanspeter Habegger
Subjects: Sports, Photography and Films, Texts in Dialect, Juvenile, Medical, Archaeology
1981: 16 titles *Founded:* 1900
ISBN Publisher's Prefix: 3-85723

F **Haeschel-Dufey**, Comptoir du Livre — now Editions Novos SA (qv)

Berchtold **Haller** Verlag, Nägeligasse 9, PO Box 15, CH-3000 Berne 7 Tel: (031) 222583 Cable Add: BEG Berne
Manager, Sales Dir: Peter Schranz
Branch Offs: Buchhandlung der Evangelischen Gesellschaft (at above address); Evangelische Buchhandlung, Schmiedengasse 26, CH-3400 Burgdorf; BEG-buechlade, Marktgasse 27, CH-4900 Langenthal
Subjects: Religion, Juveniles
1981: 3 titles *1982:* 3 titles *Founded:* 1848
ISBN Publisher's Prefix: 3-85570

Hallwag Verlag AG, Nordring 4, CH-3001 Berne Tel: (031) 423131 Cable Add: Hallwag Berne Telex: 32460 Halag CH
President: Otto Erich Wagner; *Editorial, Permissions:* Dr K Weibel; *Sales:* Jürg Burri
Branch Off: Hallwag Verlagsgesellschaft mbH, Federal Republic of Germany (qv)
Subjects: General Non-fiction, Travel, History, How-to, Music, Art, Culinary Arts, Horses, General Science, Maps
Founded: 1912
ISBN Publisher's Prefix: 3-444

Harwood Academic Publishers GmbH, Poststr 22, CH-7000 Chur
Editorial: Patricia Bardi; *Promotion, Marketing:* Jonathan Dahl; *Rights & Permissions:* Françoise Chantrel-Riols
Branch Offs: (USA Editorial) Harwood Academic Publishers, PO Box 786, Cooper Station, New York, NY 10276, USA; Harwood Academic Publishers, France (qv)
Subjects: Astronomy and Astrophysics, Chemical & Nuclear Engineering, Chemical & Chemical Technology, Earth & Extraterrestrial Sciences, Economics, Electronics & Electrical Engineering, Life Sciences & Medicine, Management Science & Business, Mathematics & Statistics, Mechanical Engineering, Metallurgy & Materials Science, Physics, Social Sciences, Learned Journals
Founded: 1978
ISBN Publisher's Prefix: 3-7186

Paul **Haupt** Bern, Falkenplatz 14, CH-3001 Berne Tel: (031) 232425 Cable Add: Hauptbern Telex: 33561 haupt ch
Man Dir: Dr Max Haupt; *Production:* Kurt Thönnes; *Sales, Publicity, Advertising:* Ulrich Dodel; *Permissions:* Annemarie Streit
Subjects: Business Economics, General and Social Science, University, Secondary and Primary Textbooks, Pedagogy, Handicrafts, How-to, Music, Art, Educational Materials
Bookshops: Falkenpl 14 and Triangel, Länggass Str 8 (both Berne); Höheweg 11, Interlaken
1981: 126 titles *1982:* 120 titles *Founded:* 1906
ISBN Publisher's Prefix: 3-258

Das **Haus** der Bibel, see Maison de la Bible

W **Heidelberger** AG, an imprint of Fortuna-Verlag (qv)

Helbing und Lichtenhahn Verlag AG, Steinenvorstadt 73, CH-4051 Basle Tel: (061) 231116
Dir: H Helbing; *Procuring Editor:* Hans Durrer
Associate Company: Sauerländer AG (qv)
Subjects: History, Law, Textbooks
Founded: 1822
ISBN Publisher's Prefix: 3-7190

Arts Graphiques **Héliographia** SA, PO Box 1060, CH-1001 Lausanne (Located at: 2 ave de Tivoli, Lausanne) Tel: (021) 204151 Telex: 24060
Man Dir: Philippe Luquiens

Verlag **Helvetica Chimica** Acta, Postfach, CH-4002 Basle Tel: (061) 376652
President: Dr K Heusler; *Editor:* Prof H-J Hansen; *Publicity:* Mrs R Stockbauer
Parent Company: Schweizerische Chemische Gesellschaft, Postfach, CH-4002 Basle
Subject: Chemistry
ISBN Publisher's Prefix: 3-85727

Herder AG*, Malzgasse 18, CH-4002 Basle 21 Tel: 230818 Telex: 64358
Associate Companies: Verlag Herder GmbH & Co KG, Verlag A G Ploetz GmbH & Co KG, Herder und Herder GmbH (all in Federal Republic of Germany, qqv); Verlag Herder & Co, Austria (qv); Editorial Herder SA, Spain (qv)

Rolf **Heyne** Verlag*, Bächerstr, CH-8832 Woolerau/SZ Tel: (01) 7841722 Telex: 75113
Man Dir: Rolf Heyne
Subjects: Reference, Pocket Books

Verlag für Psychologie Dr C J **Hogrefe***, Zeltweg 6, CH-8032 Zurich
Parent Company: Verlag für Psychologie, Göttingen, Federal Republic of Germany (qv)
Subjects: Psychology (handbooks, conference reports, directories)

Verlag Van **Hoorick**, Farb-Dia-Archiv Edmond Van Hoorick+, Postfach, CH-8805 Richterswil/ZH Tel: (01) 7844272
Manager: Edmond Van Hoorick
Subjects: Juvenile Picture Books, Meditation Practice, Picture Books of Switzerland, Germany, the Caribbean

Michael und Margret **Huber**, Badenerstr 39, CH-5452 Oberrohrdorf Tel: (056) 963100
Associate Company: Verlag Astrologisch-Psychologisches Institut, PO Box 87, CH-8134 Adliswil
Subjects: Astrology, Psychology, Children's, Occult, Eastern Religion

Hans **Huber** AG, Medical Publisher and Bookseller, Länggass-Str 76, Postfach, CH-3000 Berne 9 Tel: (031) 242533 Cable Add: Huberverlag Bern Telex: 32516
Board Delegate: Dr Walter Jäger; *Sales Dir:* Max Pauli; *Publicity & Advertising:* Peter Köhli
Branch Off: Verlag Hans Huber, Am Wallgraben 127-131, D-7000 Stuttgart-Vaihingen, Federal Republic of Germany
Subjects: Medicine, Psychology, Pedagogy
Bookshops: See under Major Booksellers
1982: 80 titles *Founded:* 1927
ISBN Publisher's Prefix: 3-456

Verlag **Huber** & Co AG, Promenadenstr 16, PO Box 83, CH-8500 Frauenfeld Tel: (054) 73739/73737 Telex: 76383
Man Dir, Publisher: Dr Peter Keckeis; *Sales, Publicity:* Peter Buff; *Production:* Peter Guarisco; *Rights & Permissions:* Silvia Fust
Subjects: Belles Lettres, Biography, History, Politics, Folklore, Linguistics, Art, Juveniles, Forestry, Agriculture, Thurgau Canton Interest, Educational Books and Materials

Bookshop: Buchhandlung Huber & Co AG, Freiestr 8, CH-8500 Frauenfeld
1981: 46 titles *Founded:* 1809
ISBN Publisher's Prefix: 3-7193

Humata Verlag Harold S Blume*, Dufourstr 7, CH-3000 Berne 6 Tel: (031) 444600
Man Dir: Harold S Blume
Shipping Add: PO Box 74, CH-3000 Berne
Subjects: How-to, Philosophy, Medicine, Psychology
Founded: 1951
ISBN Publisher's Prefix: 3-85120

Hüthig und Wepf Verlag, Eisengasse 5, CH-4001 Basle Tel: (061) 257574 Cable Add: Wepfco Telex: 0045-62027
Associate Companies: Verlag Wepf & Co (qv); Dr Alfred Hüthig Verlag GmbH, Federal Republic of Germany (qv)
Subsidiary Company: Hüthig & Wepf Verlag, Room 227, 661 Broadway, New York, NY 10012, USA
Branch Off: Hüthig und Wepf, im Weiher 10, D-6900 Heidelberg, Federal Republic of Germany
Subjects: Macromolecular Chemistry and Related Subjects, Periodicals
ISBN Publisher's Prefix: 3-85739

I N F E L (Informationsstelle für Elektrizitätsanwendung), PO Box 7340, CH-8023 Zurich (Located at: Bahnhofplatz 9, Zurich) Tel: (01) 2110355
Subject: Electrical Engineering
ISBN Publisher's Prefix: 3-85651

Editions **Ides et Calendes** SA, 19 Evole, CH-2001 Neuchâtel Tel: (038) 253861 Cable Add: Idecal
Man Dir: André Rosselet; *Administration Chief:* Alain Bouret
Subjects: Art, Belles Lettres, Law, University Textbooks
Founded: 1941
ISBN Publisher's Prefix: 2-8258

Imba Verlag, PO Box 1052, CH-1701 Fribourg (Located at: 4 ave de Beauregard, Fribourg) Tel: (037) 241341 Cable Add: Kanisiuswerk Fribourg
Man Dir: Martin Stieger; *Production Manager:* Rudolf Studer
Associate Company: Kanisius Verlag (qv)
Subjects: Social Science, Religion
ISBN Publisher's Prefix: 3-85740

Impressum Verlag AG*, Schöneggstr 102, CH-8953 Dietikon Tel: (01) 7407673
ISBN Publisher's Prefix: 3-7200

Imprimeries Réunies SA*, ave de la Gare, CH-1003 Lausanne Tel: (021) 203111 Telex: 24495
Subjects: Art, Belles Lettres, Natural Sciences, Geography, Travel
Miscellaneous: Associated imprints include Editions 24 Heures (qv)

Verlag **Industrielle Organisation**, Zürichbergstr 18, CH-8028 Zurich Tel: (01) 470802
Man & Publicity Dir: Dr Roland H Scheuchzer; *Sales, Advertising Dir:* Fritz Dedial
Subjects: Management and Organization, Personnel Studies, Problem-Solving Activities, Product Planning, Marketing, EDP, Periodicals
1981: 8 titles *1982:* 12 titles
ISBN Publisher's Prefix: 3-85743

Informationsstelle für Elektrizitätsanwendung, see INFEL

Institut für Heilpädagogik Verlag*, Löwenstr 5, D-6004 Lucerne Tel: (041) 225763
Therapeutic Pedagogy Institute Publishing House

Subjects: Education, Diagnostic Therapy Publications

Institut Universitaire de Hautes Etudes Internationales, 132 rue de Lausanne, CH-1211 Geneva 21 Tel: (022) 311730
The Graduate Institute of International Studies
Subjects: Politics, International Law, History, Economics

Inter Documentation Co AG, Poststr 14, Zug Tel: (42) 214974 Cable Add: Indoco ZUG Telex: 78819 Zugal
President: Dr L Vieli
Subsidiary Company: Inter Documentation Co BV, Hoge Woerd 151-153, 2311 HK Leiden, Netherlands
Subjects: Microfiche/microfilm editions of rare scholarly publications, especially in connection with Slavic and Oriental studies, African, Latin American, Middle Eastern and Jewish Studies, Development Plans, History, Musicology, Anthropology, Natural Sciences, Art, Social Sciences, Religion, Language, Political Science, Human Rights
Founded: 1957
ISBN Publisher's Prefix: 3-8575

'Interavia' SA (Société anonyme d'Editions aéronautiques internationales), 86 Ave Louis Casaï, CH-1216 Cointrin, Geneva Tel: (022) 980505 Telex: 22122 itav ch
Dirs: K Regelin, J Parvex, R H Gasser
Subjects: World Directory of Aviation and Astronautics (Interavia ABC-Annual); Periodicals
Founded: 1933
ISBN Publisher's Prefix: 3-85749

Edition **Interfrom**, PO Box 5005, CH-8022 Zurich (Located at: Scheideggstr 78) Tel: (01) 2020900
Publisher: Leo V Fromm; *Executive Vice-President:* Annette Harms-Hunold; *Sales Manager:* Annegret Busch; *Public Relations:* Ursula Malzahn
Associate Companies: Verlag A Fromm GmbH & Co, Federal Republic of Germany (qv); Fromm International Publishing Corp, 1212 Ave of the Americas, New York, NY 10036, USA (German into English Literary Translation)
Subjects: Authoritative Texts by German-speaking Authors on Politics, Economics, Culture and Education, Society, Nature and the Environment, also Periodicals, Newspapers
ISBN Publisher's Prefix: 3-7201

Iris Verlag AG, CH-3177 Laupen Tel: (031) 947744
ISBN Publisher's Prefix: 3-85751

Istituto Editoriale Ticinese (IET) SA, Via del Bramantino, PO Box 655, CH-6501 Bellinzona Tel: (092) 256624 Telex: 73131
Man Dir: Libero Casagrande
Subsidiary Company: Veladini — Grassi
Associate Company: Edizioni Casagrande SA (qv)
Subjects: Art, History, Educational, Miscellaneous
Founded: 1900

R **Jeanmaire** & Co, see Verlag Eisenbahn

J H Jeheber SA*, 3 chemin du Vallon, CH-1224 Chênes-Bougeries Tel: (022) 493543
Manager: Jean H Jeheber
Subjects: History, Religion, Juveniles, Sports and Games
Founded: 1797

Johannesverlag Einsiedeln, Arnold Böcklinstr 42, CH-4051 Basle
Chairman: Dr Hans Urs von Balthasar
Orders to: Bücherdienst, Kornhausstr 23, CH-8840 Einsiedeln

Subjects: Philosophy, Religion, Spirituality
1982: 13 titles *Founded:* 1947
ISBN Publisher's Prefix: 3-265

Juris Druck & Verlag AG, Basteiplatz 5, Talstrasse, CH-8001 Zurich Tel: (01) 2117727
Man Dir: Dr H Christen
Subjects: History, Music, Art, Philosophy, Religion, Medicine, Psychology, Engineering, General & Social Science
Bookshop: Juris Druck & Verlag AG, Buchhandlung, Postfach, CH-8039 Zurich
1981: 57 titles *Founded:* 1945
ISBN Publisher's Prefix: 3-260

Kanisius Verlag, 4 ave du Beauregard, CH-1701 Fribourg Tel: (037) 241341 Cable Add: Kanisiuswerk Fribourg
Man Dir, Publicity: Martin Stieger; *Production Manager:* Rudolf Studer
Associate Company: Imba Verlag (qv)
Subjects: Religion
Founded: 1898
ISBN Publisher's Prefix: 3-85764

S **Karger** AG, Medical and Scientific Publishers, Allschwilerstr 10, Postfach, CH-4009 Basle Tel: (061) 390880 Cable Add: Kargermed Basle Telex: CH 62652
Man Dir: Dr Thomas Karger; *Publicity:* H Blattner
Subsidiary Companies: Karger Libri AG (Bookshop and Subscriptions), Petersgraben 31, PO Box, CH-4009 Basle; S Karger GmbH, Federal Republic of Germany (qv); Katakura Libri Inc, Tokyo 113, Japan
Imprints: S Karger (Basle, Munich, Paris, London, New York, Tokyo, Sydney)
Subjects: Medical and Scientific Publications (Series and Journals); Reference Works, Medicine, Psychology, University Textbooks
Bookshop: Karger Libri AG, Petersgraben 31, Postfach, CH-4009 Basle
Founded: 1890
Miscellaneous: S Karger Literary Agency in North America: S Karger Publishers Inc, Suite 1105, 150 Fifth Ave, New York, NY 10011, USA
ISBN Publisher's Prefix: 3-8055

Verlag Ramòn F **Keller**, now known as Editions Ariston Verlag (qv)

Verlag Walter **Keller**, Lehmenweg 5, CH-4143 Dornach Tel: (061) 722755
Man Dir: Walter Keller
Subjects: Picture Books, Juvenile, Art, Geometry
Founded: 1969

Kinderbuchverlag Reich Luzern AG, see Reich

Kindler Verlag AG, Nelkenstr 20, CH-8006 Zurich Tel: (00411) 3633007 Cable Add: Kindlerverlag Zurich Telex: 045 57608
Publishers: Helmut Kindler, Nina Kindler
Subjects: Encyclopaedias, Psychology, Anthropology

Editions **Kister** SA*, 33 quai Wilson, CH-1211 Geneva 1 Tel: (022) 315000
Subjects: General Non-fiction, Mathematics, Physics, Music, Games and Sports, Reference Books
ISBN Publisher's Prefix: 3-463

Verlag **Klett und Balmer** & Co*, Chamerstr 12a, PO Box 347, CH-6301 Zug Tel: (042) 214131/32
Man Dir: Chr Balmer, Dr Thomas Klett; *Editorial, Sales, Publicity, Production, Rights & Permissions:* H Egli
Parent Company: Ernst Klett Verlag, Federal Republic of Germany (qv)
Associate Companies: H R Balmer AG Verlag (qv); Dialog Verlags AG, CH-3084 Wabern
Subjects: School Textbooks, Teachers'

Training, Educational Politics in Switzerland, Adult Education, fringe areas of Science, Philosophy
1981: 12 titles *Founded:* 1967
ISBN Publisher's Prefix: 3-264

Kobersche Verlagsbuchhandlung AG, PO Box 2481, CH-3001 Berne (Located at: Maulbeerstr 10, Berne) Tel: (031) 251648
Man Dir, Sales, Publicity: Harald F Blum
Subject: Religious/Philosophical, especially the teaching texts of Bô Yin Râ
1981: 10 titles *Founded:* 1926
ISBN Publisher's Prefix: 3-85767

Kolumbus-Verlag, Muhlebuhl 10, CH-5737 Menziken Tel: (064) 711370 Cable Add: Vdb Menziken
Man Dir: Dr G van den Bergh
Subjects: Schoolbooks (ref languages)

Galerie **Kornfeld** & Co, Laupenstr 41, CH-3008 Berne Tel: (031) 254673 Cable Add: Artus
Proprietor: Eberhard W Kornfeld
Subjects: Fine Arts (15th-20th centuries); 19th-20th Century Illustrated Books
Founded: 1864
ISBN Publisher's Prefix: 3-85773

Kossodo Verlag AG*, 27a chemin des Hutins, CH-1247 Anières/Geneva Tel: (022) 512247/511156
Dir: Martha Düssel
Subjects: Art Books, De Luxe Limited Editions
Founded: 1956
ISBN Publisher's Prefix: 3-7208

Verlag Karl **Krämer** & Co, Spiegelgasse 14, CH-8001 Zurich Tel: (01) 2510560
Man Dir: Florian F Adler
Associate Company: Karl Krämer Verlag GmbH und Co, Federal Republic of Germany (qv)
Subject: Architecture
ISBN Publisher's Prefix: 3-85774

Verlag René **Kramer** AG+, Strada di Gandria 48, PO Box 90, CH-6976 Lugano-Castagnola Tel: (091) 518941 Cable Add: Edikramer
Man Dir, Publicity: René Kramer
Subjects: Cookery, International Co-productions

Verlag und Druckerei G **Krebs** AG, St Alban-Vorstadt 56, Postfach, CH-4006 Basle Tel: (061) 239723
Dirs: Franz Käser, Willy Kohler; *Manager:* André Horisberger
Orders to: Gesellschaft für Volkskunde (at above address)
Imprint: Schweizerischen Gesellschaft für Volkskunde (Swiss Folklore Society)
Subjects: Folklore Studies, Swiss Handicrafts, Song Books; Periodicals
Founded: 1897
ISBN Publisher's Prefix: 3-85775

Kümmerly und Frey (Geographischer Verlag), Hallerstr 6-10, CH-3001 Berne Tel: (031) 235111 Cable Add: Kümmerlyfrey Telex: 32860
Man Dir: W Frey; *Dirs:* Dr B Peters-Kümmerly, Toni Kaufmann
Associate Companies: J Fink-Kümmerly und Frey Verlag GmbH, Federal Republic of Germany (qv); Kümmerly und Frey Verlags GmbH, Austria (qv)
Subjects: Geography, Maps, Topography, Photobooks
Founded: 1852
ISBN Publisher's Prefix: 3-259

Imprimerie Albert **Kündig** SA*, 10 rue Vieux-Collège, CH-1204 Geneva Tel: (022) 285188
Manager: André Kündig
Founded: 1828

Labor et Fides SA+, 1 rue Beauregard, CH-1204 Geneva Tel: (022) 291134/291133
Chairman: Pierre Gisel; *Man Dir, Sales, Production, Rights & Permissions, Editorial, Publicity:* Paulette Reymond
Subjects: Religion, Theology, Ethics, Poetry, General Subjects
1981-82: 28 titles *Founded:* 1924
ISBN Publisher's Prefix: 2-8259

Bundesamt für **Landestopographie**, Office Fédéral de Topographie, Seftigenstr 264, CH-3084 Wabern
Subject: Maps (Switzerland)

Herbert **Lang** & Cie AG*, PO Box 82, CH-3000 Berne 7 (Located at: Münzgraben 2, CH-3011 Berne) Tel: (031) 228871 Cable Add: Librilang Telex: 33173
President: Christoph H Lang
Subject: Science
Bookshop: At above address
Founded: 1813 (re-formed 1921)
Miscellaneous: Agents for libraries throughout the world
ISBN Publisher's Prefix: 3-261

Verlag Peter **Lang** AG, Jupiterstr 15, PO Box 277, CH-3000 Berne 15 Tel: (031) 321122 Telex: 32420 verl ch
Man Dir, Rights & Permissions: Peter Lang; *Editorial:* Gisela Quast; *Sales:* Reinold Brunner; *Production:* Françoise Santschy, Michel Droz, Andrea Keller; *Publicity:* René Knöpfel, Beatrice Ruckstuhl, Gertrud Leuenberger
Subsidiary Companies: Verlag Peter Lang GmbH, Federal Republic of Germany (qv); Peter Lang Inc, 34 East 39th St, New York, NY 10016, USA
Subjects: Art, Business, Economics, Education, Encyclopaedias, History, Language, Law, Literature, Philosophy, Psychology, Religion, Social Sciences, Reprints
1982: 648 titles *Founded:* 1977
ISBN Publisher's Prefixes: 3-261 (Switzerland), 3-8204 (Federal Republic of Germany)

Langenscheidt AG*, Hardturmstr 76, CH-8021 Zurich
Parent Company: Langenscheidt KG, Federal Republic of Germany (qv)
Subjects: Linguistics, Languages
ISBN Publisher's Prefix: 3-269

Franz **Larese** und Jürg Janett, see Erker-Galerie AG

Larousse (Suisse) SA, PO Box 502, CH-1211 Geneva 6 Tel: (022) 369140
Man Dir: Jean-Claude Viatte
Parent Company: Librairie Larousse, France (qv for Associate Companies)
Subjects: Reference Works, Dictionaries, School Books
ISBN Publisher's Prefix: 2-8276

Lector-Verlag GmbH*, Höhgaden, CH-8852 Altendorf Tel: (055) 633729 Cable Add: lectorverlag altendorfschwyz Telex: 875257 lecv ch
Man Dir: Walter E Krüttner
Subjects: Belles Lettres, Non-fiction, Art
Founded: 1978
ISBN Publisher's Prefix: 3-272

Lenos Verlag, Wallstr 9, CH-4051 Basle Tel: (061) 231333
Programme Dir, Reader, Publicity: Heidi Sommerer; *Sales:* Tom Forrer
Subjects: Belles Lettres, the Media, Pedagogy, Politics
1981: 12 titles *Founded:* 1970
ISBN Publisher's Prefix: 3-85787

Leobuchhandlung, Verlag der Quellen-Bändchen, Gallusstr 20, CH-9001 St Gallen Tel: (071) 222917 Telex: 77452 Leo ch
Man Dir: Eugen Hettinger
Bookshop: Leobuchhandlung (qv under Major Booksellers)
Founded: 1918
ISBN Publisher's Prefix: 3-85788

Leonis Verlag*, Villa Meridiana, Titlisstr 14, CH-8032 Zurich
Sales and distribution: PO Box 952, CH-8034 Zurich (Located at: Kirchenweg 5) Tel: (01) 2517560/475565 Cable Add: Leonisverlag Zurich
Owner & Man Dir: Dr Wolfgang M Metz
Associate Company: Doulos Verlag (qv)
Subjects: Biography, Politics, Social Science; Paperbacks, Travel Books
Founded: 1976
ISBN Publisher's Prefix: 3-721

Edition **Leu**, Kunst und Literatur, Asylstr 110a, CH-8032 Zurich Tel: (01) 692894
The above address is that of the Head Office. The Editorial Office is: Edition Leu-Redaktion, Hohlstr 281, CH-8004 Zurich Tel: (01) 4918560
Man Dir, Production, Publicity: Al' Leu; *Editorial:* Brigit Hotz, Daniel Bamert, Eveline Scherer, Manfred Ruppel, Erik Huber
Branch Off: Edition Leu, Spohrstr 55, D-6000 Frankfurt am Main, Federal Republic of Germany
Subjects: Non-commercial Art, Literature, including: Prose, Poetry, Mythology, Social Criticism, Experimental Literature, Graphics
Book Club: AGAV ev, Federal Republic of Germany (qv)
1983: 3 titles *Founded:* 1977
ISBN Publisher's Prefix: 3-85667

Lia Rumantscha (Ligia Romontscha), Via da la Plessur 47, CH-7000 Cuoira/Cuera Tel: (081) 224422/224448
Dir: Dr Bernard Cathomas
Subjects: Publishers of books in the Romansh language of Switzerland; dictionaries, grammar, linguistics, background and history of Romansh; Biography, Belles Lettres, Poetry, Music and Songs, Religion, Periodicals
Miscellaneous: Company also gives financial support to other publications in Romansh in the Romansh-speaking area

Limmat Verlag Genossenschaft, Wildbachstr 48, Postfach, CH-8034 Zurich Tel: (01) 556300
Publicity: Jürg Zimmerli
Subjects: Socialism, Socio-Political Studies, Feminist Juvenile, Fiction

Litheratheke, an imprint of Eco-Verlags AG (qv)

Logos-Verlag*, Witikonerstr 368, CH-8021 Zurich Tel: (01) 530340
Subject: Textbooks
Founded: 1932
ISBN Publisher's Prefix: 3-85790

E **Löpfe-Benz** AG Rorschach, Graphische Anstalt und Verlag, Pestalozzistr 5, CH-9400 Rorschach Tel: (071) 414341
Graphical Institute and Publisher
Dirs: Emil Enderle, Dieter Mildenberger; *Editorial:* Franz Mächler; *Sales:* Peter Kruijsen; *Advertising:* Theo Walser, Hans Schöbi, Peter Bick
Subsidiary Company: Nebelspalter Verlag (qv)
Subjects: Topical Works, Humour, Satire, Juvenile, Poetry, History, Periodical
Founded: 1875
ISBN Publisher's Prefix: 3-85819

The **Lutry** Press, an imprint of Marix Evans & Chilvers SA (qv)

Hans-Rudolf **Lutz**, Lessingstr 11, CH-8002 Zurich Tel: 2017672
Man Dir: H-R Lutz
Subjects: Biography, Art, Visual Communication, Revolutionary Art
1982: 2 titles *Founded:* 1966

McGraw-Hill Book Co*, Museggstr 7, CH-6004 Lucerne Tel: (041) 515060 Telex: 72386
Dir: Francine Peeters; *Production Manager:* Franz Gisler
Subjects: Illustrated General Literature, Reference Works, History, Pictorial Biographies
Miscellaneous: Firm is a co-publishing office of the McGraw-Hill Book Co, 1221 Ave of the Americas, New York, NY 10020, USA
See McGraw-Hill Book Co (UK) Ltd for associate companies

Macmillan SA, 1-3 ave des Jordils, CH-1000 Lausanne 6 Tel: (021) 277561 Cable Add: Berledit Lausanne Telex: 25492 CH
Man Dir: Marshall D Mascott; *Editorial:* Konrad Fuchs; *Marketing Dir:* J Nigel Cave; *Production Manager:* Jean-Paul Minder
Parent Company: Macmillan Inc, 866 Third Ave, New York, NY 10022, USA
Imprint: Editions Berlitz
Subjects: Travel, Tourism, Language Teaching, Dictionaries, Leisure
Founded: 1970

La **Maison** de la Bible, Société Biblique de Genève, PO Box 447, CH-1211 Geneva 3 Tel: (022) 285259 Cable Add: Bibles-Genève
Subjects: Scriptures, in many languages, Biblical Studies, Christian apologetics/testimony, Biography, Juvenile
Bookshop: La Maison de la Bible, 11 rue de Rive, CH-1211 Geneva 3
Founded: 1917
Miscellaneous: Also known by German name, Das Haus der Bibel (Genfer Bibelgesellschaft)
ISBN Publisher's Prefix: 2-8260

Marika **Malacorda** Editions, 1 rue de l'Évêché, CH-1204 Geneva
Dir: Marika Malacorda
Orders to: Ecart Publications (qv)

Manesse und Morgarten Verlag*, Morgartenstr 29, Postfach, CH-8004 Zurich Tel: (01) 2424455 Cable Add: Cozetthuber
Man Dir: Rolf Meyer; *Editorial, Rights & Permissions:* Dr F Hindemann; *Sales, Publicity:* Alex Aepli; *Production:* Kurt Oggier
Subjects: Literary Works (in German and in translation), Religion, Music, Presentation Editions
Founded: 1886
ISBN Publisher's Prefix: 3-7175

Manesse Verlag, Badergasse 9, CH-8001 Zurich Tel: (01) 2525551
Man Dir: Dr Federico Hindermann
Parent Company: Deutsche Verlags-Anstalt GmbH (DVA), Federal Republic of Germany (qv)
Subjects: World Classics translated from original languages into German, Literature of Antiquity, Far East, Folklore, Musical Biography
Founded: 1944
ISBN Publisher's Prefix: 3-7175

Librairie-Editions J **Marguerat**+, 2 pl St François, CH-1003 Lausanne 2 Tel: (021) 237717
Dir: Jean Marguerat
Subjects: Belles Lettres, History, Travel, Music, Geography, Ethnology
Founded: 1940
ISBN Publisher's Prefix: 2-88008

Marix Evans & Chilvers SA, CH-1099 Peney-le-Jorat, Vaud Tel: (021) 934535
President & Editorial: Timothy R Chilvers; *Sales Dir:* Martin F Marix Evans
Associate Company: Thames Head Ltd, UK (qv)
Imprint: The Lutry Press
Subjects: General, Music, Sport, Transport, Fiction, Biography, Co-editions
1982: 1 title *1983:* 2 titles *Founded:* 1981

Marva, PO Box 254, CH-1211 Geneva 26 (Located at: route des Acacias, Geneva) Tel: 925671 Cable Add: Marva Geneva 26
Publishers: Hennecke Kardel, Dietrich Bronder
Subject: Modern History (especially European and Nazi-related)

Editions la **Matze***, Guy Gessler, PO Box, CH-1951 Sion (Located at: rue du Mont 1, CH-1951 Sion) Tel: 2316521
Man Dir, Sales: Guy Gessler
Subjects: General Fiction, Military and General History, Archaeology, Swiss Painters series
Founded: 1975

Verlag A & G de **May***, 6 chemin des Sorbiers, PO Box 52, CH-1012 Lausanne Tel: (021) 289608
Subjects: History, Arts, Archaeology

Médecine et Hygiène, PO Box 229, CH-1211 Geneva 4 (Located at: 78 Ave de la Roseraie, Geneva) Tel: (022) 469355/56
Man Dir, Sales: J P Balavoine; *Publicity, Advertising Dir:* P Y Balavoine
Subjects: Medicine, Psychology, General Science, University Textbooks, Specialized Medical and other Periodicals
Founded: 1943

Peter **Meili** & Co, Fronwagpl 13, CH-8200 Schaffhausen Tel: (053) 54144/5 Telex: 7677 melbu ch
Subjects: History, Literature about the Schaffhausen area, Dialect Stories, Politics
Bookshop: Buchhandlung Meili & Co (qv under Major Booksellers)
Founded: 1838
ISBN Publisher's Prefix: 3-85805

Christoph **Merian** Verlag, St Alban-Vorstadt 5, CH-4052 Basle Tel: (061) 221288
Subjects: Basle and Area
ISBN Publisher's Prefix: 3-85616

Henri **Messeiller***, 11 rue St Nicolas, CH-2000 Neuchâtel Tel: (038) 251296
Subjects: Textbooks, Education, Art, Belles Lettres, Religion, Psychology, Law, Administration
Founded: 1887
ISBN Publisher's Prefix: 2-8261

Max S **Metz** Verlag AG*, Limmatquai 36, CH-8022 Zurich Tel: (01) 325357
Man Dir: Max S Metz
Subjects: Culture, Politics, Economics, Technical, History, Maps
Founded: 1946
ISBN Publisher's Prefix: 3-85807

Editions **Minkoff** Reprint, 46 chemin de la Mousse, CH-1225 Chêne-Bourg, Geneva Tel: (022) 485568
Dir: Youval Minkoff, Sylvie Minkoff
Subjects: Music and Musicology, Musical Iconography, Theatre, Art, Basic Reference Works
1981: 45 titles *1982:* 50 titles *Founded:* 1972
ISBN Publisher's Prefix: 2-8266

Moderne Industrie AG, Dörflistr 73, CH-8050 Zurich Tel: (01) 3118140 Telex: 57547
Subjects: Technical, Data Processing, Personnel, Marketing, Sales
ISBN Publisher's Prefix: 3-478

Alfred **Mohler** Verlag*, Seestr 1, CH-8800 Thalwil Tel: (01) 7207691
Founded: 1970
ISBN Publisher's Prefix: 3-85808

Editions **Mon Village** SA*, CH-1099 Vulliens, Vaud Tel: (021) 931363
Man Dir, Sales, Production, Publicity, Rights & Permissions: Albert-Louis Chappuis; *Editorial:* André Plomb
Subjects: Novels of rural life
Book Club: Club Mon Village SA
Founded: 1955

Mondo SA (Editions-Verlag-Edizioni), 20 ave de Corsier, CH-1800 Vevey Tel: (021) 528021 Telex: spnch 452100
Man Dir: P Mayor

Les Editions du **Mont-Blanc** SA*, 26 rue du Mont Blanc, CH-1201 Geneva Tel: (022) 315650
Man Dir: Chantal Buxo
Subjects: Philosophy, Religion, Medicine, Psychology, Social Science
Founded: 1942

Morgarten-Verlag, see Manesse und Morgarten Verlag

Verlag Rudolf **Mühlemann**, Haus Z Wolfau, CH-8570 Weinfelden Tel: (072) 225353/4
Founded: 1949
ISBN Publisher's Prefix: 3-85809

Jacques **Muhlethaler***, 49 ch de l'Etang, CH-1211 Châtelaine Tel: (022) 964452
Subjects: Fine & Applied Arts, Illustrated Books, Belles Lettres, Dietary, Handicrafts
Founded: 1945

Albert **Müller** Verlag AG, Bahnhofstr 69, PO Box 150, CH-8803 Rüschlikon/Zurich Tel: (01) 7241760 Cable Add: Müllerverlag Rüschlikon Telex: 56320 Amv ch
Man Dir: Adolf Recher-Vogel; *Editorial:* Dr Marta Jacober-Züllig; *Sales, Rights & Permissions:* Dr Bernhard Recher; *Publicity:* Dorothea von Walzel; *Production:* R Kleinschnittger
Subjects: Books on domestic and pet animals, especially horses, dogs, cats; also Juvenile animal and adventure Stories, How-to, Music, Reference, Sports, Recreation, Cookery, Wines, Self-Help, Health, Yoga, Homecrafts, Indian subjects
Founded: 1938
ISBN Publisher's Prefix: 3-275

N Z N-Buchverlag AG+, Zeltweg 71, PO Box A25, CH-8032 Zurich Tel: (01) 474951
President: Dr Jakob Weibel
Subjects: Art, Religion, Architecture, History
Founded: 1972
ISBN Publisher's Prefix: 3-85827

Les Editions **Nagel** SA, 5-5 bis rue de l'Orangerie, CH-1211 Geneva 7 Tel: (022) 341730/9 Cable Add: Nageledit Geneva
Man Dir: Louis Nagel
Subjects: Philosophy, Politics, Archaeology, Art, Travel Guides, *Who's Who in Switzerland*
Founded: 1952
ISBN Publisher's Prefix: 2-8263

Natura-Verlag*, Pfeffingerweg 1, CH-4144 Arlesheim Tel: (061) 721011
Subjects: Nature Cure, Philosophy, Therapeutic Pedagogy texts
ISBN Publisher's Prefix: 3-85817

Naville SA*, 5-7 rue Lévrier, CH-1201 Geneva Tel: (022) 322400 Telex: navico 28469
President: Hans Keller; *General Manager:* Gilles Martin
Founded: 1877

Nebelspalter Verlag, CH-9400 Rorschach Tel: (071) 414341
Parent Company: E Löpfe-Benz AG (qv)
Subjects: Humour, Satire, Cartoons, Periodical
ISBN Publisher's Prefix: 3-85819

Neptun-Verlag, Ing H Frei, PO Box 307, CH-8280 Kreuzlingen 1 Tel: (072) 727262 Telex: 882221 nept ch
Manager: H Frei-Gmür
Subjects: Contemporary History, Travel
Founded: 1946
ISBN Publisher's Prefix: 3-85820

Neue Diana Press AG*, Usteristr 9, CH-8001 Zurich Tel: (01) 2110830
Man Dirs: Dr Rolf Zollikofer, Dr Richard Bechtle
Subjects: General Fiction, Biography, History
Founded: 1973
ISBN Publisher's Prefix: 3-87158

Verlag **Neue Stadt***, PO Box 435, CH-8038 Zurich (Located at: Seestr 426, CH-8038 Zurich) Tel: (01) 4826011
Dir: Hans Jutz
Parent Company: Città Nuova Editrice, Italy (qv for associate companies)

Neue Szene, an imprint of Eco-Verlags AG (qv)

Neue Zürcher Zeitung AG, Buchverlag, Postfach, CH-8021 Zurich Tel: (01) 2581505 Telex: 52137 nzz ch
Publicity Manager: Walter Köpfli
Subject: Textbooks, Illustrated Books
Miscellaneous: Book publishing section of Zurich daily newspaper
ISBN Publisher's Prefix: 3-85823

Neufeld-Verlag und Galerie, PO Box, CH-9434 Au/SG Tel: (071) 712977 Cable Add: neufeld
Man Dir: K G Löpfe; *Editorial and other offices:* Ivo Löpfe
Orders to: Neufeld-Verlag und Galerie, Austria (qv)
Parent Company: Löpfe KG, A-6890 Lustenau, Austria
Associate Company: Neufeld-Verlag und Galerie, Austria (qv)
Branch Off: Levehus, Löwenstr, Zurich
Subject: Art
Founded: 1962

Verlag Arthur **Niggli** AG, CH-9052 Niederteufen AR Tel: (071) 331772 Cable Add: Niggliverlag, Niederteufen Appenzell
Man Dir: Arthur Niggli
Shipping Add: c/o Danzas und Co, St Gallen
Subsidiary Company: Gallery Ida Niggli Ltd, CH-9052 Niederteufen
Subjects: Visual Arts, Architecture, Fine Arts, Periodical
Bookshops: Buchhandlung Niggli, CH-9100 Herisan; Buchhandlung Niggli, CH-9032 Niederteufen
Founded: 1950
ISBN Publisher's Prefix: 3-7212

Nord-Süd Verlag, CH-8617 Mönchaltorf Tel: (01) 9351335 Cable Add: nordsued Telex: 875894 nsv ch
Dir, Editorial: Brigitte Sidjanski-Hanhart; *Sales, Production, Publicity, Rights & Permissions:* Davy Sidjanski
Orders to: Sauerländer AG, Postfach, CH-5001 Aarau Tel: (064) 221264 Telex: 68736 (for Switzerland)
Subjects: Children's Picture Books, Picture Calendars
1983: 14 titles *Founded:* 1961
ISBN Publisher's Prefix: 3-85825

Novalis Verlag AG*, Münsterplatz 34, CH-8201 Schaffhausen Tel: (053) 58719 Cable Add: Novalis Schaffhausen
Subjects: Arts, Social Sciences, Educational
ISBN Publisher's Prefix: 3-7214

Emil **Oesch** Verlag AG*, Seestr 3, CH-8800 Thalwil, Zurich Tel: 7201333 Cable Add: Oesch
Subjects: General Fiction, How-to, Philosophy, Religion, Psychology, General & Social Science, Educational Materials
Founded: 1935
ISBN Publisher's Prefix: 3-85833

L'**Oeuvre Gravée***, PO Box 205, CH-3000 Berne 8 (Located at: Münstergasse 36, CH-3011 Berne) Tel: (031) 225071 Cable Add: Schindlerart
Editorial, Publicity: Werner Schindler

Office du Livre SA (Buchhaus AG), PO Box 1061, CH-1701 Fribourg (Located at: 101 route de Villars, Fribourg) Tel: (037) 240744 Cable Add: Livreoffice Telex: 36227
Man Dir: Jean Hirschen; *Sales Manager:* Pierre Engel
Subjects: Art, Architecture, Asian Studies, Arts and Crafts, Golf
1981: 69 titles *1982:* 52 titles *Founded:* 1947
ISBN Publisher's Prefix: 37215

Edition **Olms** AG, PO Box 159, CH-8033 Zurich (Located at: Haldenbachstr 17) Tel: (01) 691160
Man Dir and Other Offices: Manfred Olms
Subjects: Art, Myth and Legend, Magic, Helvetica, Humour, Comics, Chess, Toy Catalogues, Rock Music
1981: 13 titles *1982:* 17 titles *Founded:* 1977
ISBN Publisher's Prefix: 3-283

Inigo von **Oppersdorff** Verlag, Klusweg 37, CH-8032 Zurich Tel: (01) 551140
Subjects: Belles Lettres, Poetry, History, Music, Art, Religion
Founded: 1966
ISBN Publisher's Prefix: 3-85834

Orell Füssli Verlag+, Postfach, CH-8022 Zurich (Located at Nüschelerstr 22, CH-8001 Zurich) Tel: (01) 2113630 Cable Add: Orellverlag Zurich Telex: 813021 orla ch
Man Dir: Gian Laube; *Editorial:* Ernst Halter, Armin Ochs, Jutta Radel; *Sales, Advertising, Rights & Permissions:* Harry Heusser
Parent Company: Orell Füssli Graphische Betriebe AG, Dietzingerstr 3, CH-8036 Zurich
Subjects: Belles Lettres, Biography, History, Geography, How-to, Music, Art, Juveniles, Educational Materials, Railways and Aircraft, Photographic Picture Books
Bookshop: Pelikanstr 10, CH-8022 Zurich (qv under Major Booksellers)
Founded: 1519
ISBN Publisher's Prefix: 3-280

Verlag **Organisator** AG, Löwenstr 16, CH-8021 Zurich Tel: (01) 2118155 Cable Add: orga/ch Telex: 813834
Man Dir, Editorial: Dr V Bataillard; *Sales, Publicity:* V A Bataillard; *Production:* K Raggenbach
Subjects: Swiss Law and Taxes, International Taxes, Industrial Management, Periodical
Bookshops: Basle, Lucerne, St Gallen, Schaffhausen, Winterthur, Zurich and many other Swiss towns
Founded: 1919
ISBN Publisher's Prefix: 3-7220

Origo-Verlag, Rathausgasse 30, CH-3011 Berne Tel: (031) 224480 Cable Add: Wildbuch
Man Dir: Alexander Wild (owner)
Associate Company: Verlag Alexander Wild (qv)
Subjects: Philosophy and Religion of East and West
Founded: 1947
ISBN Publisher's Prefix: 3-282

Orte-Verlag, PO Box 2028, CH-8006 Zurich (Located at: Ekkehardstr 14) Tel: (01) 3630234
Man Dir: Werner Bucher; *Publicity:* Barbara Giezendanner
Subjects: Poetry, Belles Lettres

Ostschweiz Druck und Verlag, Oberer Graben 8, CH-9001 Sankt Gallen Tel: (071) 208585 Telex: 77393
Man Dir, Sales: Dr Emil Dähler
Subjects: Belles Lettres, Poetry, History, Music, Art, Social Science
Bookshop: Thorbecke Verlag KG, Sigmaringen, Federal Republic of Germany
Founded: 1892
ISBN Publisher's Prefix: 3-85837

Ott Verlag AG Thun, Länggasse 57, CH-3600 Thun 7 Tel: (033) 221622 Cable Add: Ottpubl Thun Telex: 921299
Man Dir: Walter Knecht; *Publicity & Advertising:* Hans M Ott; *Sales Manager:* Ursula Seiler-Popp
Subsidiary Companies: Verlags und Versandbuchhandlung Thun AG, Thun; Translegal AG
Subjects: General Non-fiction, Lexicons, Earth Sciences, Military, Sports, Industry/Commerce
Founded: 1923
ISBN Publisher's Prefix: 3-7225

Editions du **Panorama**, PO Box 38, CH-2500 Bienne 3 Tel: (038) 252981
Man Dir: Paul Thierrin
Subjects: General Fiction, Commerce, Secondary Textbooks, Languages, Belles Lettres
1982: 5 titles *Founded:* 1951

Edizioni **Pantarei***, Via Sempione 2, CH-6900 Lugano
Subjects: Music, Belles Lettres

Park & Roche Establishment*, 11 rue Général Dufour, CH-1211 Geneva 11 Tel: 282744
Editorial, Permissions: Peter Bellew, Canto Lou Vent, Route de la Colle, 06570 St Paul de Vence, France Tel: (93) 329338
Subjects: Illustrated books on Art, Architecture, Cookery, Cultural History, Music, General Knowledge: published in international co-editions

Paulusverlag, see Editions Saint-Paul

Librairie **Payot** SA, PO Box 3212, CH-1002 Lausanne (Located at: 4 pl Pépinet, CH-1003 Lausanne) Tel: (021) 203331 Cable Add: Payotco Telex: 24961
Manager: Jean Hutter
Associate Company: Editions Payot, France (qv)
Subjects: Belles Lettres, Poetry, History, Music, Art, General and Natural Sciences, Philosophy, Psychology, Law, Commerce, Regional, University, Secondary & Primary Textbooks, Transport, Agriculture, Domestic, Sport
Bookshops: See under Major Booksellers
Founded: 1835
ISBN Publisher's Prefix: 2-601

Pedrazzini Tipografia, Via B Varenna 7, CH-6600 Locarno Tel: (093) 317734-35
Man Dir and other offices: Carlo Pedrazzini
Subjects: Scholastic, Historical, Church Historical, Literary, Printing and Book Production, Periodical
1983: 85 titles *Founded:* 1880

SWITZERLAND 371

Pendo-Verlag Wolfbachstr 9, CH-8032
Zurich   Tel: (01) 693737
Dirs: Gladys Weigner, Bernhard
Moosbrugger
Subjects: Travel, Religion, Literature and
Poetry, International Co-operation
ISBN Publisher's Prefix: 3-85842

Pharos-Verlag, Hansrudolf Schwabe AG,
PO Box 68, CH-4011 Basle (Located at:
Therwilerstr 5, CH-4011 Basle)   Tel: (061)
541021
Man Dir: Hansrudolf Schwabe; *Advertising
Dir:* Myrte Schwabe
Subjects: Juveniles, Railway Interest, Wines
Bookshop: Buchhandlung Münsterberg,
Münsterberg 13, CH-4011 Basle
Founded: 1958
ISBN Publisher's Prefix: 3-7230

Philosophisch-Anthroposophischer Verlag*,
Goetheanum, Hügelweg 63, Postfach,
CH-4143 Dornach   Tel: (061) 721116
Orders to: Koch, Neff und Oetinger & Co,
Schockenriedstr 37, Postfach 800620,
D-7000 Stuttgart 80, Federal Republic of
Germany
Subsidiary Company: Rudolf Geering-
Verlag (at above address)
Subjects: Philosophy, Anthroposophy,
Natural Sciences, Eurhythmics, Music,
Literature, Medicine (all especially in
connection with the thoughts of Rudolf
Steiner), Periodical
Bookshop: At above address
ISBN Publisher's Prefix: 3-7235

Phoebus-Verlag GmbH*, Malzgasse 7,
CH-4052 Basle
Subject: Arts
ISBN Publisher's Prefix: 3-85841

Phoenix Verlag AG, subsidiary of Scherz
Verlag AG (qv)

Editions **Pierrot** SA+, 51 ave de Rumine, CH-
1005 Lausanne   Tel: (021) 231447   Telex:
pclep 25404 ch
Dir: Ghislaine Vautier
Orders to: Éditions Pierrot, PO Box 3513,
CH-1002 Lausanne
Subjects: Literature, Juveniles, Periodical
(Children's)
Founded: 1966

R **Piper** & Co Verlag GmbH, Alte Landstr
67, CH-8700 Küsnacht   Tel: (01) 9104044
Parent Company: R Piper & Co Verlag,
Federal Republic of Germany (qv)
Subjects: Belles Lettres, Juveniles, Politics,
Social Science, Psychology, Education,
Natural Sciences
ISBN Publisher's Prefix: 3-7236

Polana AG*, PO Box 1173, CH-8036 Zürich
Man Dir: Dr Franz Braxator
Subjects: Belles Lettres, Poetry, Politics
1981: 3 titles   *Founded:* 1972

Populaires, Ave Tivoli 2, Lausanne   Tel:
(021) 204141
Man Dir, Publicity: Jean Studemann

Presses Centrales Lausanne SA*, 7 rue de
Genève, CH-1003 Lausanne   Tel: (021)
205901
Dir: Gilbert Rohrer
Subject: Art

Les **Presses de la Connaissance***, c/o Weber
SA d'Editions, 13 rue de Monthoux, PO
Box 385, CH-1211 Geneva 2   Tel: 326450
Cable Add: Livrart
Parent Company: Les Presses de la
Connaissance, Paris, France
Subjects: Mythology; Witnesses and
Testimonies

Verlag **Pro Juventute**, Seefeldstr 8, Postfach, CH-8008 Zurich   Tel: (01) 2517244
Orders to: Above address for German
editions; Pro Juventute, Secrétariat-romand,
Galeries St-François B, CH-1003 Lausanne,
for French, Italian editions
Subjects: Children's Books, Children's
Education and Welfare (family, playgroup,
playgrounds, pedagogy, teaching media):
texts in German, French, Italian and English

Editions **Pro Schola**, 29 rue des Terreaux,
CH-1000 Lausanne 9   Tel: (021) 236655
Cable Add: Dirbenedict   Telex: 24357
bbav ch
Man Dir: Dr Jean J Bénédict
Orders to: PO Box 300, CH-1000
Lausanne 9
Subjects: Language: Textbooks, Reference;
especially, language teaching by the
'Bénédict Direct Progressive Method'
Founded: 1928
ISBN Publisher's Prefix: 2-88009

Problem-Verlag*, Hirschmattstr 1, PO Box
834, CH-6000 Lucerne
Subject: Hobbies

Verlag für **Psychologie** Dr C J Hogrefe, see
Hogrefe

Psychosophische Gesellschaft, PO Box 204,
CH-8021 Zurich
Subjects: Psychology, Philosophy, Theology,
Pedagogy, Mysticism and Magic

R A Verlag, PO Box 120, CH-8640
Rapperswil
Subjects: Art, Education

Rabe Verlag Zurich, Oberdorfstr 23,
CH-8001 Zurich   Tel: (01) 478540   Cable
Add: rabeverlag Zurich
Depot at: CH-8608 Bubikon Zurich   Tel:
(055) 382383
Man Dir, Sales: Dr J Kanitz; *Editorial,
Rights & Permissions:* Dr Elsa Kanitz;
Production, Publicity: Dr P Portmann
Subjects: Art, Large-format graphics on
old/modern art
Founded: 1962
Miscellaneous: Firm is also a literary agent
ISBN Publisher's Prefix: 3-85852

Raeber AG Luzern*, Frankenstr 7-9,
CH-6002 Lucerne   Tel: (041) 235363
Telex: 72381
Man Dir: B L Raeber
Imprint: Edition Raeber
Subjects: General Fiction, Belles Lettres,
Poetry, History, Music, Art, Juveniles,
Secondary Textbooks, Religion
Bookshops: Raeber Buchhandlung,
Frankenstr 9, CH-6002 Lucerne;
Taschenbuchladen Kornmärt,
Kornmarktgasse 7, Lucerne
Founded: 1825
ISBN Publisher's Prefix: 3-7239

Verlag für **Recht und Gesellschaft** AG, PO
Box 646, CH-4010 Basle (Located at:
Wallstr 14, Basle)   Tel: (061) 231775   Cable
Add: Reges Verlag
Man Dir: Christian Fridli
Subject: Law, Taxation
Founded: 1933
ISBN Publisher's Prefix: 3-7242

Regenbogen-Verlag*, PO Box 240, CH-8025
Zurich   Tel: (01) 475860
General Manager: Theo Ruff
Orders to: Neue Bücher AG, Gotthardstr 49,
CH-8027 Zurich   Tel: (01) 2027474
Subjects: Travel Guides, Art Books, Swiss
Literature, Objets d'Art in the 'Edition
Regenbogen'
ISBN Publisher's Prefix: 3-85862

Kinderbuchverlag **Reich** Luzern AG,
Zinggentorstr 4, CH-6000 Lucerne 6   Tel:
(041) 516861   Telex: 72508 reic ch
Man Dir: Jürgen Braunschweiger; *Editorial:*
Heidrun Diltz; *Sales, Administration,
Publicity:* Sauerländer AG (qv)
Associate Company: Sauerländer AG (qv)
Subjects: Juvenile Fiction and Non-fiction
with photographic illustrations
Founded: 1979
ISBN Publisher's Prefix: 3-276

Reich Verlag AG+, Zinggentorstr 4, CH-6000
Lucerne 6   Tel: (041) 513721   Telex: 72508
reic ch
Man Dir: Jürgen Braunschweiger; *Sales &
Administration:* Alfons Wüest; *Editorial and
Publicity:* Heidrun Diltz
Imprints: Terra Hippologica, Terra Magica
Subjects: Photographic Picture Books,
Horses
Founded: 1974
ISBN Publisher's Prefix: 3-7243

Verlag Friedrich **Reinhardt** AG, Missionstr
36, CH-4012 Basle   Tel: (061) 253390   Cable
Add: Freinhardt Basel
Man Dir, Rights & Permissions: Dr Ernst
Reinhardt
Subjects: General Fiction, Belles Lettres,
Biography, History, How-to, Religion,
Juveniles, General Science, University
Textbooks, Educational Materials
1981: 19 titles *1982:* 16 titles   *Founded:* 1900
ISBN Publisher's Prefix: 3-7245

Editions **Rencontre** SA*, 29 chemin d'Entre-
Bois, CH-1018 Lausanne   Tel: (021) 373841
Cable Add: Rencontre Lausanne
Telex: 24876
General Manager: A Léglise; *Marketing,
Promotion:* R A Mast
Subjects: General Fiction, Belles Lettres,
Poetry, Biography, History, Music, Art,
Philosophy, Reference, Religion, Juveniles,
Medicine, General Science, Educational
Materials
Founded: 1950

Eugen **Rentsch** Verlag AG+, Nüschelerstr 22,
CH-8022 Zurich   Tel: (01) 2113630   Telex:
ch 813021 orla
Manager: Gian Laube
Subjects: Biography, History, Biology,
Psychology, Economy, Social Science,
Environmental, Political, Educational Books
and Materials, Children's Books
Founded: 1910
ISBN Publisher's Prefix: 3-7249

Rex-Verlag, PO Box 161, CH-6000
Lucerne 5 (Located at: St Karliquai 12,
Lucerne)   Tel: (041) 514914
Man Dir: Dr Zeno Inderbitzin
Subjects: Belles Lettres, Education, Guides
to Conduct, Juveniles, Religion
(Catholicism)
Bookshop: Rex Buchladen (at above
address)
Founded: 1931
ISBN Publisher's Prefix: 3-7252

Edizioni Raimondo **Rezzonico***, Via Luini,
CH-6600 Locarno

Ringier & Co AG*, Graphisches Institut und
Verlagsanstalt, Florastr, CH-4800 Zofingen
Tel: (062) 510101
President: Hans Ringier; *Executive
President:* Dr Hch Oswald
Subjects: Fashion, Directories
Founded: 1833
ISBN Publisher's Prefix: 3-85859

Editiones **Roche**, F Hoffman — La Roche &
Co AG, Postfach, CH-4002 Basle   Tel:
273611   Cable Add: Roche Basle   Telex:
62292a roch ch
Man Dir, Sales, Production, Publicity:
Martin Schneider
Orders to: Roche: Verlag Hans Huber,
Länggassstrasse 76, CH-3000 Berne 9;
Rocom: above Basle address
Imprint: Rocom
Subject: Medical
Founded: 1971

Rocom, imprint of Editiones Roche (qv)

Rodana Verlag, see Schweizer Spiegel Verlag AG

Hans **Rohr**, Buchhandlung und Antiquariat zum Oberdorf AG*, Oberdorfstr 5, CH-8024 Zurich 1 Tel: (01) 2513636 Telex: 56385
Man Dir: H Rohr
Subjects: Tourist Interest, Swiss History, Swiss Dialect, Classical Antiquity, Books on Films and the Cinema
Bookshops: Buchhandlung Hans Rohr, Oberdorfstr 5, CH-8024 Zurich (Antiquarian and General); Filmbuchhandlung Hans Rohr, Oberdorfstr 3, CH-8024 Zurich (Films and Cinema)
Founded: 1921
ISBN Publisher's Prefix: 3-85865

Rosepierre SA*, Chemin Château-l'Évêque 11, CH-1254 Jussy Tel: (022) 591452
Man Dir: Pierre Bouffard

Rotapfel-Verlag AG+, Frankengasse 6, CH-8024 Zurich Tel: (01) 470388
Dir: Dr Paul Toggenburger
Subjects: Textbooks, Juveniles, Beaux-arts, Belles Lettres, Biography
Founded: 1919
ISBN Publisher's Prefix: 3-85867

Roth et Sauter SA*, à l'Enseigne du Verseau, La Pâle, CH-1026 Denges/Lausanne Tel: (021) 717561 Telex: 458179 rsd ch
Man Dirs: Michel Logoz, Pierre Sauter
Imprints: include Editions du Verseau
Subjects: Art, Belles Lettres, General
Founded: 1890

Rotten-Verlags AG, Terbinerstr 2, CH-3930 Visp Tel: (028) 462252

Rütten und Loening Verlag GmbH, a subsidiary of Scherz Verlag AG (qv)

Verlag **S O I** (Schweizerisches Ost-Institut), Jubiläumsstr 41, CH-3000 Berne 6
Tel: (031) 431212 Cable Add: Schweizost Telex: 32728
Man Dir: Peter Sager; *Sales Manager:* Peter Burgunder; *Production Manager:* Peter Dolder
Subjects: History, Politics, Social Science, especially with respect to the Eastern Bloc countries
Bookshop: Buchhandlung SOI (at above address)
Founded: 1958
ISBN Publisher's Prefix: 3-85913

Société de l'Oeuvre **Saint-Augustin***, CH-1890 St-Maurice Tel: (025) 651022
Man Dir: R Donnet-Descartes

Editions **Saint-Paul**, Pérolles 42, CH-1700 Fribourg Tel: (037) 246812
Dir: Dr Martin Nicoulin
Parent Company: Imprimerie et Librairies Saint-Paul SA (at above address)
Associate Companies: Editions de la Sarine (at above address); Editions Universitaires SA (qv)
Subjects: Philosophy, Religion, Educational
Bookshops: Librairie Saint-Paul, Pérolles 38, CH-1700 Fribourg; Librairie du Vieux Comté, rue de Vevey, CH-1630 Bulle; Librairie de la Nef, 10 ave de la Gare, CH-1000 Lausanne
Miscellaneous: Company is also known as Paulusverlag
Founded: 1873

Salvioni & Co*, Via Franscini, CH-6500 Bellinzona

Sanssouci Verlag*, Rosenbühlstr 37, CH-8044 Zurich Tel: (01) 2522154 Cable Add: Archeverlag
Owners: Christoph and Lorenz Schifferli
Orders to: Erikastr 11, CH-8003 Zurich
Associate Companies: Verlag der Arche Peter Schifferli (qv); E Pfister GmbH, Federal Republic of Germany (qv); Dr Franz Hain, Austria (qv)
Subjects: General Fiction, Humour
ISBN Publisher's Prefix: 3-7254

Sauerländer AG, PO Box 570, CH-5001 Aarau (Located at: Laurenzenvorstadt 89, Aarau) Tel: (064) 221264 Telex: 981 195 sag ch
Publisher and Man Dir: Hans Christof Sauerländer; *Editorial:* Rolf Inhauser, Jitka Bodlakova, Dörthe Binkert, Martin Röthlisberger; *Sales:* Günter Reich; *Publicity:* Markus Zimmermann; *Rights & Permissions:* Ingrid Parge
Subsidiary Company: H R Sauerländer und Co, Federal Republic of Germany (qv)
Associate Companies: SABE-Verlagsinstitut für Lehrmittel, CH-8001 Zurich; Kinderbuchverlag Reich Luzern AG (qv); Helbing und Lichtenhahn Verlag AG (qv)
Subjects: Juvenile, Belles Lettres, Poetry, Biography, History, Medicine, Natural & Social Sciences, University, Secondary & Primary Textbooks, Educational Materials
Founded: 1807
ISBN Publisher's Prefix: 3-7941

Scherz Verlag AG, Marktgasse 25, CH-3000 Berne 7 Tel: (031) 226831 Cable Add: Scherzedit Telex: 32552 sherz ch
Chairman, Man Dir: Rudolf Streit-Scherz; *Sales Dirs:* Wolfgang Radaj, Alfred Vallotton; *Editorial Department:* Ursula Ibler, Jürgen Lütge, Gert Woerner; *Rights & Permissions:* Ursula Griessel
Subsidiary Companies: Otto Wilhelm Barth-Verlag KG, Federal Republic of Germany (qv); Phoenix Verlag AG, Rütten und Loening Verlag GmbH, Taschenbuch Verlag Spectrum (all Switzerland)
Branch Offs: Scherz Verlag GmbH, Federal Republic of Germany (qv); Scherz Verlag, c/o Lechner & Sohn, A-1232 Vienna, Heizwerkstr 5, Austria
Subjects: General Fiction & Non-fiction, Biography, History, Psychology, Parapsychology, Philosophy; Paperback series of Crime Thrillers
Bookshop: Buchhandlung Scherz AG (qv under Major Booksellers)
1981: 124 titles *1982:* 125 titles *Founded:* 1939
Miscellaneous: Company is also associated with the Litpress Literary Agency (qv)
ISBN Publisher's Prefix: 3-502

Verlag der Arche Peter **Schifferli** AG, see Arche

Otto **Schlaefli** Verlag*, Bahnhofstr 15, CH-3800 Interlaken Tel: (036) 221312/3
Subjects: Belles Lettres, Fiction
Founded: 1930
ISBN Publisher's Prefix: 3-85884

Schläpfer & Co AG, CH-9100 Herisau 1
Tel: (071) 513131 Telex: 77147
Man Dir: P Schläpfer
Branch Off: CH-9043 Trogen
Subjects: Domestic, Children's
Founded: 1974

Verlag fur **Schöne Wissenschaften** (Belles Lettres Publishing Co — Albert Steffen Foundation), Unterer Zielweg 36, CH-4143 Dornach
Subjects: Poetry, Art, Anthroposophy, Cultural History, Philosophy, Pedagogy, Therapeutics, Literary Criticism, the Works of Albert Steffen
Founded: 1928
ISBN Publisher's Prefix: 3-85889

Hermann **Schroedel** Verlag AG*, Hardstr 95, CH-4020 Basle Tel: (061) 423330
Associate Company: Hermann Schroedel Verlag KG, Federal Republic of Germany (qv)
Subjects: Artistic Picture Books for Nursery Children and Adults, Bibliophile Volumes, Facsimiles and Graphics
ISBN Publisher's Prefix: 3-285

Schubiger Verlag AG, Mattenbachstrasse 2, CH-8400 Winterthur Tel: (052) 297221
Man Dir: E R Benz; *Sales, Publicity:* G K Schäfer; *Production:* A Keller
Subject: Educational

Schulthess Polygraphischer Verlag AG, Zwingliplatz 2, CH-8022 Zurich Tel: (01) 2519336 Cable Add: Buchschulthess Telex: 56736
Man Dir, Advertising, Permissions: Dr Charlotte Mark-Hürlimann
Subjects: Law Commerce, Social Science, University Textbooks, Schoolbooks, Law, Periodical
1982: 81 titles *Founded:* 1791
Miscellaneous: Firm has incorporated the former Leemann AG Druckerei/Verlag since 1978
ISBN Publisher's Prefix: 3-7255

Hansrudolf **Schwabe** AG, see Pharos-Verlag

Schwabe & Co AG, Steinentorstr 13, CH-4000 Basle 10 Tel: (061) 235523 Cable Add: Schwabeco Basel
Man Dirs: Dr Christian Overstolz, Hans Reimann, Josef A Niederberger, Marc Götz
Subjects: Medicine, Pharmaceutics, History of Art and Civilization, Philosophy, Psychology, University and Secondary Textbooks
1981: 18 titles *1982:* 15 titles *Founded:* 1494
ISBN Publisher's Prefix: 3-7965

Aare-Verlag/**Schweizer Jugend**-Verlag*, Werkhofstr 23, CH-4502 Solothurn Tel: (065) 229458
Publishing Manager: Felix Furrer
Orders to: J F Schreiber Verlag, Postfach 285, D-7300 Esslingen, Federal Republic of Germany
Subjects: Reference, Juveniles, Primary Textbooks, Educational Materials
Miscellaneous: Aare-Verlag and Schweizer Jugend-Verlag are divisions of the one company, and are under the same management
ISBN Publisher's Prefix: 3-7260

Schweizer Spiegel Verlag AG & Rodana Verlag, Rämistr 18, PO Box 5837, CH-8024 Zurich 1 Tel: (01) 472195
Dir: Dr P Huggler
Subjects: Belles Lettres, Poetry, Music, Art, Philosophy, Juveniles, Psychology, Social Science
Founded: 1925
ISBN Publisher's Prefixes: 3-85900 (Schweizer Spiegel), 3-85863 (Rodana)

Schweizer Verlagshaus AG+, Klausstr 10, CH-8008 Zurich Tel: (01) 2519134 Cable Add: svzuerich Telex: 53514
Dirs: Dr Armin Meyer, Walter Meyer; *Editorial, Rights & Permissions:* Dr A Meyer; *Sales, Publicity:* Alfred Jurt
Subjects: General Fiction, Biography, Art, Music, How-to, History, Travel, General Science, Textbooks, Entertainment, Reference
Book Club: Affiliated with Neue Schweizer Bibliothek
Founded: 1907
ISBN Publisher's Prefix: 3-7263

Schweizerische Stiftung für Alpine Forschungen, Binzstr 17, CH-8045 Zurich
Tel: (01) 4610147
Swiss Foundation for Alpine Research
Subjects: Alpine Research Publications

Schweizerische Zentralstelle für Stahlbau, Seefeldstr 25, CH-8034 Zurich Tel: (01) 478980
Swiss Institute of Steel Construction
Man Dir: Urs Wyss

Schweizerischen Gesellschaft für Volkskunde, an imprint of Verlag und Druckerei G Krebs AG (qv)

Verlag der **Schweizerischen Schallplattenmission**, member of the Telos group (qv in Federal Republic of Germany), publishing evangelical paperbacks

Schweizerisches Jugendschriftenwerk*, Seehofstr 15, PO Box 8022, CH-8008 Zurich Tel: (01) 2517244
Subjects: Literature for Juveniles in the four Swiss languages — German, French, Italian and Romansh
Founded: 1931
ISBN Publisher's Prefix: 3-7269

Verlag **Schweizerisches katholisches Bibelwerk**, Université Miséricorde, CH-1700 Fribourg Tel: (037) 219385
Dir: Pierre Casetti
Subject: Roman Catholic Literature on biblical subjects
Miscellaneous: Company is a member of AMB (qv under Federal Republic of Germany)
ISBN Publisher's Prefix: 3-7203

Schweizerisches Ost-Institut, see Verlag SOI

Schwengeler-Verlag, Rosenberg, CH-9442 Berneck Tel: (071) 725666/525667
Man Dir: Bruno Schwengeler; *Managing Editor:* Walter Nitsche
Subjects: Christian Literature
Bookshop: Obere Graben 12, CH-8400 Winterthur
Founded: 1969
Miscellaneous: Member of the Telos group (qv in Federal Republic of Germany), publishing evangelical paperbacks
ISBN Publisher's Prefix: 3-85666

Schwitter Edition GmbH*, Allschwilerstr 90, PO Box 312, CH-4000 Basle 9
Tel: 061381230 Telex: 62934
Subjects: Art Books, Art Reproductions, Facsimiles

F P **Schwitter Holding** Inc+, PO Box 636, CH-8065 Zurich (Located at: Baarerstr 57, CH-6301 Zug) Tel: (057) 332555 Telex: 58178 swint
Man Dir: Fridolin Schwitter; *Editorial Dir:* Norma Schwitter
Subjects: Reference Works and Encyclopaedias, Science and Technology, Medicine, Countries and Peoples, Natural History, Art, Juveniles
Founded: 1972
ISBN Publisher's Prefix: 3-284

Editions **Scriptar** SA, 23 ave de la Gare, CH-1003 Lausanne Tel: (021) 202351 Cable Add: Orlog Telex: Green 25587
Publicity Manager: H Marquis
Subjects: Watches and Jewellery, Gemmology; Art productions connected with these interests
Founded: 1946
ISBN Publisher's Prefix: 2-88012

Edition **Seefeld**+, Minervastr 33, CH-8032 Zurich Tel: (01) 2524717 Telex: 58617 seef ch
Dirs: Claudio de Polo, Charles Whitehouse
Subjects: Facsimile reprints of old manuscripts, maps, drawings; Limited editions
Bookshop: Galerie Edition Seefeld (at above address)
Founded: 1976

Sinwel-Buchhandlung Verlag, Lorrainestr 10, CH-3000 Berne 11 Tel: (031) 425205
Subjects: Belles Lettres, Technical, Leisure Activities
ISBN Publisher's Prefix: 3-85911

Editions D'Art Albert **Skira** SA*, 89 route de Chêne, CH-1208 Geneva Tel: (022) 495533 Cable Add: Edart Geneva
Man Dir, Editorial: Mrs R Skira; *Sales, Production, Publicity:* Jean-Michel Skira
Parent Company: Flammarion et Cie, France (qv)
Subjects: Art, Art History, Art Reference, Low- & High-priced Paperbacks, Educational Materials
Founded: 1928
ISBN Publisher's Prefix: 2-605

Slatkine Reprints, PO Box 765, CH-1211 Geneva 3 (Located at: 5 rue des Chaudronniers, Geneva) Tel: (022) 204071/762551 Telex: 27078

Société Biblique de Genève, see La Maison de la Bible

Taschenbuch Verlag **Spectrum**, a subsidiary of Scherz Verlag AG (qv)

Speer-Verlag, R Römer, Hofstr 134, CH-8044 Zurich Tel: (01) 2511203 Cable Add: Sperverlag
Man Dir: R Römer
Subjects: General Fiction, Belles Lettres, Philosophy, Juveniles, Poetry
Founded: 1944
ISBN Publisher's Prefix: 3-85916

Spes SA, now incorporated in Editions Delta et Spes SA (qv)

Sphinx Verlag AG, Spalenberg 37, CH-4003 Basle Tel: (061) 258583 Telex: 65244
Dir: Dieter A Hagenbach
Subjects: Fantasy, Magic, Tarot, Gypsy Lore, Philosophy, Religion, Art, Shamanism, New Age, Alternative Lifestyles
Bookshops: Buchhandlung Sphinx, Nadelberg 47 and Spalenberg 38, CH-4003 Basle Tel: 259292
1982: 24 titles *1983:* 20 titles *Founded:* 1975
ISBN Publisher's Prefix: 3-85914

Verlag **Stämpfli** & Cie AG, Haller-Str 7-9, PO Box 2728, CH-3001 Berne Tel: (031) 232323 Cable Add: Buchstaempfli Bern Telex: 32950
Man Dir, Rights & Permissions: Dr Jakob Stämpfli; *Sales & Advertising Dir:* K Zeller
Subjects: Jurisprudence, Political Science, Economics, History, Social Science, University Textbooks, Swiss Law
1981: 35 titles *1982:* 40 titles *Founded:* 1799
ISBN Publisher's Prefix: 3-7272

Rudolf **Steiner** Verlag, Haus Duldeck, PO Box 135, CH-4143 Dornach Tel: (061) 722240/722511
Man Dir, Editorial, Sales: Benedikt Marzahn; *Publicity:* Richard Schneider; *Production:* B Marzahn, Carlo Frigeri; *Rights & Permissions:* Administrators of the Rudolf Steiner Literary Estate
Subjects: Anthroposophy: complete works of Rudolf Steiner
Bookshop: At above address
1982: 63 titles *Founded:* 1956
ISBN Publisher's Prefix: 3-7274

Stephanus Edition Verlags AG, PO Box 11, CH-7290 Seewis
Man Dir: Hans Braun
Subsidiary Company: Stephanus Edition Verlags GmbH, Federal Republic of Germany (qv)
Subjects: Juvenile Religious, Christian, Anti-Communist
Founded: 1978
ISBN Publisher's Prefix: 3-921213

Josef **Stocker** AG*, Kapellgasse 5, CH-6002 Lucerne Tel: (041) 224948
Subjects: Fiction, Law, Politics, Philosophy, Religion
Bookshop: As above
ISBN Publisher's Prefix: 3-85922

Verlag **Stocker-Schmid** AG, PO Box 66, CH-8953 Dietikon-Zurich (Located at: Hasenbergstr 7, Dietikon-Zurich) Tel: (01) 7404444
Man Dir: Mr Stocker
Subsidiary Companies: Verlag Bibliophile Drucke von Josef Stocker AG (qv); Urs Graf-Verlag GmbH (qv)
Bookshop: Buchhandlung Stocker-Schmid (at above address)
Subjects: Modern and Historical Weapons and Equipment of the Swiss Army, subjects of Swiss Interest, especially Bibliophile Editions, Facsimiles of Incunabula, Old Maps, Manuscripts
ISBN Publisher's Prefix: 3-7276

Stroemfeld Verlag AG, PO Box 79, CH-4007 Basle (Located at: Oetlingerstr 19, Basle)
Tel: (061) 324180
Man Dir: J Osolin
Associate Company: Verlag Roter Stern, Federal Republic of Germany (qv)
1981: 15 titles *Founded:* 1979
ISBN Publisher's Prefix: 3-87877

Strom-Verlag*, E Kobelt-Schultze, Staffelhof 21, CH-8055 Zurich 3 Tel: (01) 357415
Man Dir: Ernst Kobelt
Subjects: General Fiction, Art, Philosophy, High-priced Paperbacks, Psychology, Social Science, Poetry
ISBN Publisher's Prefix: 3-85921

Sumus Verlag Jutta Gütermann, Güstr 6, CH-8700 Küsnacht Tel: (01) 9106184/9230259 Cable Add: Sumus
Editorial: Jutta Gütermann
Subject: Belles Lettres in Large Print, Swiss Literature
Founded: 1976
ISBN Publisher's Prefix: 3-85926

Swedenborg Institut*, c/o Dr P Stamm, Lautengartenstr 12, CH-4052 Basle
President: Björn Holmström (resident at PO Box 99 MC, Principality of Monaco)
Subject: Religion
Founded: 1952
ISBN Publisher's Prefix: 3-85925

T V F, an imprint of Trachsel Verlag (qv)

Terra Hippologica, an imprint of Reich Verlag AG (qv)

Terra Magica, an imprint of Reich Verlag AG (qv)

Theologischer Verlag AG, Postfach, CH-8026 Zurich
Dir, Editorial: Werner Blum; *Rights & Permissions:* Werner Blum, R Jost; *Sales:* C Salden; *Publicity:* R Jost
Orders to: Auwiesenstr 1, Postfach, CH-8406 Winterthur
Subjects: Religion; Theology, emphasizing Scriptural Knowledge and Reformation History; Works of Barth, Brunner, Zwingli and Bullinger; Popular Religious Works
Bookshops: Nova Buchhandlung – Sihlstr 33, Zurich; Nansenstr 4, Zurich; Freiestr 5, Uster; Bahnhofstr 12, Wetzikon
Founded: 1934
ISBN Publisher's Prefix: 3-290

Theseus Verlag AG*, Freudwilerweg 7, CH-8044 Zurich
Subject: Eastern Religions

Thomas-Verlag*, Rennweg 14, CH-8000 Zurich
Subjects: Belles Lettres, Religion
ISBN Publisher's Prefix: 3-85938

Verlags und Versandbuchhandlung **Thun** AG, subsidiary of Ott Verlag AG Thun (qv)

Tipografia Stazionne, see Edizioni Armando Dado

Edizioni Giulio **Topi***, Cso Elvezia 9, CH-6900 Lugano

Trachsel Verlag, CH-3714 Frutigen Tel: (033) 711407
Man Dir: Ernst Trachsel-Pauli; *Editorial, Production, Rights & Permissions, Sales, Publicity:* Ernst Trachsel
Imprint: TVF
Subjects: Christian Religious
Bookshop: At above address
1981: 10 titles *1982:* 10 titles *Founded:* 1946
ISBN Publisher's Prefix: 3-7271

Trans Tech Publications SA*, Trans Tech House, CH-4711 Aedermannsdorf Tel: (062) 741379
Dir: Dr F H Wohlbier
Subjects: Materials Science, Technology for Heavy Industry, Mining Engineering, Geology, Energy Physics and Technology

Edizioni **Trelingue** SA, PO Box 8, CH-6948 Porza-Lugano
Subjects: Geography, Economics, Law

Tribune Editions*, PO Box 434, CH-1211 Geneva 11 Tel: (022) 212121 Telex: 23381 trib ch
Man Dir, Rights & Permissions: Brian Morris
Parent Company: La Tribune de Genève SA
Subjects: Current Affairs, History, Documentaries, Series on Health, also on Television, Illustrated Books, Juveniles
Founded: 1977

Editions du **Tricorne**, PO Box 229, CH-1211 Geneva 4 Tel: (022) 469355 Telex: 23246
Man Dir: Serge Kaplun
Subjects: Art, Psychology, Religion, Tapestry, Circus, Puppetry, Mathematics, Poetry, Local Interest
Founded: 1976
ISBN Publisher's Prefix: 2-8293

Editions des **Trois Collines***, 1 rue de la Cité, PO Box 470, CH-1211 Geneva Tel: (022) 561309
Dir: François Lachenal
Subjects: Art, Politics, Belles Lettres, Philosophy, Psychology
Founded: 1936

Editions des **Trois Continents**, 10 rue du Valentin, CH-1004 Lausanne 9 Tel: (021) 205631 Cable Add: editasa Telex: 26296 edita ch
Chairman: Ami Guichard
Subjects: History, Ethnology, Politics, Religion, Philosophy, General and Social Science, Art, Photography, Biography, Guide Books, Facsimile Editions; Co-Editions in all languages (including Mid- and Far-Eastern), especially books on Arab and Moslem world
Founded: 1976
ISBN Publisher's Prefix: 2-88042

U **Bär** Verlag, see Bär

Union Helvetia Fachbuchverlag, Adligenswilerstr 22, PO Box 1115, CH-6002 Lucerne Tel: (041) 515454
Subjects: Hotel-keeping and Catering (including Foreign Language Instruction), Gastronomy, Bar-tending
Bookshops: Adligenswilerstr 22, Lucerne; Freigutstr 10, Zurich; 16 ave des Acacias, Lausanne
Miscellaneous: Publishing branch of the Schweizerischer Zentralverband der Hotel- und Restaurant-Angestellten (Swiss Industrial Union of Hotel and Restaurant Employees)

Unionsverlag+, Zollikerstr 138, CH-8008 Zurich Tel: (01) 557282
Man Dir: Mechthild Wandeler; *Editorial:* Bernd Zocher; *Publicity:* Lucien Leitess
Subjects: Non-fiction, Swiss, Third World and International Literature
1981-82: 22 titles *Founded:* 1978
ISBN Publisher's Prefix: 3-293

Universitätsverlag, see Editions Universitaires SA

Uranium Verlag*, PO Box 42, CH-4104 Oberwil Tel: (042) 217744 Telex: Topaz 58280
Man Dir, Sales: L Young; *Editorial:* Mrs Young
Branch Off: Atzelbergstr 22, D-6000 Frankfurt am Main
Subjects: Children's Books (picture books and non-fiction)
Founded: 1976
ISBN Publisher's Prefix: 3-294

Urs Graf-Verlag GmbH, Hasenbergstr 7, CH-8953 Dietikon Tel: (01) 7404444
Man Dir: Mr Stocker
Parent Company: Verlag Stocker-Schmid AG (qv)
Associate Company: Verlag Bibliophile Drucke von Josef Stocker AG (qv)
Subjects: University Textbooks, Facsimile Editions of Maps and Manuscripts
ISBN Publisher's Prefix: 3-85951

V D A (Éditions de la Voie de l'Art SA)*, 8 Grand-rue, CH-1204 Geneva Tel: (022) 289655 Telex: 22409 equip ch
Man Dir: Stéphanie Hobeika
Subjects: Art, Literature, History, General Science, Philosophy, Religion, Instructional and Educational, Juvenile and Children's, Picture-books

Verlag **Verbandsdruckerei-Betadruck**, Maulbeerstr 10, PO Box 2741, CH-3001 Berne Tel: (031) 252911 Cable Add: verbandsdruck bern Telex: 32255
Man Dir: Markus Rubli
Subjects: Specialist Agricultural Texts, Swiss and Berne Regional Interest, General Non-fiction
Founded: 1919
Miscellaneous: Book publishing branch of the Verbandsdruckerei/Imprimerie Fédérative (Federal Press)
ISBN Publisher's Prefix: 3-7280

Verkehrshaus der Schweiz, Lidostr 3-7, CH-6006 Lucerne
Subjects: Transport, Traffic, Communications, Tourism, Planetarium, Cosmorama
ISBN Publisher's Prefix: 3-85954

Editions du **Verseau**, an imprint of Roth et Sauter SA (qv)

Verlag Alfred **Vetter**, Schifflaende 22, CH-8001 Zurich
ISBN Publisher's Prefix: 3-85956

Viktoria Verlag*, Obere Zollgasse 69e, CH-3072 Ostermundigen Tel: (031) 514283
Subjects: Belles Lettres, Books on Berne, Dialect Texts, Humour
ISBN Publisher's Prefix: 3-85958

Vogt-Schild AG Druck & Verlag*, CH-4501 Solothurn Tel: (065) 214131 Telex: 34646
Dirs: Dr Ulrich Luder, Dr Markus H Haferly; *Marketing:* Hans Rölli
Subjects: Road Transport, Chemistry, Pharmacy, Plastics, Environment, Hospital, Medical, Horology, Electronics
Founded: 1906
ISBN Publisher's Prefix: 3-85962

Editions de la **Voie de l'Art**, see VDA

Verlag Die **Waage**+, Dorfstr 90, CH-8802 Kilchberg, Zurich Tel: (01) 7155569
Publisher and all offices: Felix M Wiesner
Subjects: Old Chinese Fiction and Folktales in their original translations into German; also other Non-fiction and Belles Lettres, Poetry from other countries; Paperback series
Founded: 1951
ISBN Publisher's Prefix: 3-85966

Gebrüder **Wagner** & Co Verlag*, Meyer-str 14, CH-4024 Basle
Subject: Textbooks
ISBN Publisher's Prefix: 3-85969

Walter Verlag AG, Amthausquai 21, CH-4600 Olten Tel: (062) 341188 Cable Add: Walterverlag Olten Telex: 68226
Man Dir: Guido Elber; *Editorial:* Dr F J Metzinger, B Jentzsch, K Hetzar; *Sales:* C Götz; *Production:* T Frey; *Publicity:* K Wagner; *Rights & Permissions:* E Straumann
Subsidiary Company: Walter-Verlag GmbH, Federal Republic of Germany (qv)
Subjects: Literature, Cultural History, Travel Guides, Psychology, Religion, Picture Books
1981: 42 titles *Founded:* 1916
ISBN Publisher's Prefix: 3-530

Weber SA d'Editions*, 13 rue de Monthoux, PO Box 385, CH-1211 Geneva 2 Tel: (022) 326456/59 Cable Add: Livrart, Geneva
Man Dir: Marcel Weber; *All other offices:* Marcel and Hilde Weber
Subjects: Art, Architecture, Photography, Bibliophily, Practical Living
Founded: 1951
ISBN Publisher's Prefix: 3-295

Weltrundschau Verlag AG, Oberneuhofstr 1, PO Box 427, CH-6340 Baar Tel: (042) 315431 Cable Add: Worldreview Telex: 865309
Man Dir: G Braun; *Editorial:* E Gysling; *Rights & Permissions:* Jeunesse Verlagsanstalt, Kirchstr 1, FL-9490 Vaduz, Liechtenstein
Founded: 1959

Verlag **Wepf** & Co AG, Eisengasse 5, CH-4001 Basle Tel: (061) 257574 Cable Add: Wepfco Basle Telex: 62027
Dir: Robert Wepf
Associate Company: Hüthig und Wepf Verlag (qv)
Subjects: Geology, Mineralogy, Natural Sciences, Helvetica
Bookshops: Wepf & Co AG Buchhandlung und Antiquariat (qv under Major Booksellers); Marktgasse 42, CH-4310 Rheinfelden; Wepf GmbH, Obere Schanzstr 18, Postfach 1610, D-7858 Weil am Rhein, Federal Republic of Germany; Wepf & Co, Booksellers, Room 227, 611 Broadway, New York, NY 10012, USA
Founded: 1902
ISBN Publisher's Prefix: 3-85977

Werner Druck AG, Kanonengasse 32, CH-4001 Basle Tel: (061) 220690
President & Co-Dir: Dr H G Hinderling; *Co-Dir:* N Werner
Subjects: Fine & Applied Arts, Illustrated Books
Founded: 1862
ISBN Publisher's Prefix: 3-85979

Buchverlag der Druckerei **Wetzikon** AG*, CH-8620 Wetzikon
Subjects: Nature Protection, Belles Lettres
ISBN Publisher's Prefix: 3-85981

Verlag Alexander **Wild**, Rathausgasse 30, CH-3011 Berne Tel: (031) 224480 Cable Add: Wildbuch
Man Dir/Owner: Alexander Wild
Associate Company: Origo-Verlag (qv)

Subjects: Academic Publications
ISBN Publisher's Prefix: 3-7284

Verlag der **Wolfsbergdrucke**, J E
Wolfensberger AG, Bederstr 109, CH-8059
Zurich Tel: (01) 2012777 Telex: 58937
Dir: Ulla Wolfensberger
Subjects: Fine & Applied Arts, Illustrated Books, Juveniles
Founded: 1905
ISBN Publisher's Prefix: 3-85987

Wyss Verlag Bern (Wyss Druck und Verlag AG Bern), Effingerstr 17, CH-3001 Berne
Tel: (031) 253715
Dir: Christoph Wyss
Subjects: History, Jurisprudence, Art
Founded: 1849
ISBN Publisher's Prefix: 3-7285

Genossenschaft **Z-Verlag***, PO Box 6, CH-4020 Basle (Located at: Adlerstr 7, CH-4020 Basle) Tel: (061) 425765
Subjects: Problems connected with the Workers' Movement and Politics generally; Socio-political literature, Third World

Zbinden Druck und Verlag AG, St Albanvorstadt 16, CH-4006 Basle Tel: (061) 232105
Man Dir: Kurt Krause
Subjects: Belles Lettres, Poetry, Biography, Educational, Anthroposophical Literature
ISBN Publisher's Prefix: 3-85989

Paul A **Zemp**, see Ansata Verlag

Zodiaque, La Pierre-qui-Vire*, c/o Weber SA d'Éditions, 13 Rue de Monthoux, PO Box 385, CH-1211 Geneva 2 Tel: 326450
Cable Add: Livrart
Subjects: Collected Editions (various)

Buchverlag **Zollikofer** AG, Fürstenlandstr 122, PO Box 805, CH-9001 St Gallen Tel: (071) 292222 Telex: 77537
Parent Company: Zollikofer AG, Druckerei und Verlag, St Gallen
Subjects: Art, Educational, Popular Medicine, Travel Guides, Periodicals
Founded: 1789
ISBN Publisher's Prefix: 3-85993

Zumstein & Cie, Zeughausgasse 24, CH-3011 Berne
Parent Company: Hertsch & Co
Subject: Philately
1981: 3 titles *1982:* 4 titles
ISBN Publisher's Prefix: 3-85994

Adolf **Zwimpfer***, CH-8954 Geroldswil ZH
Associate Companies: Bayerische Verlagsanstalt Bamberg (BVB), Sankt Otto Verlag GmbH, both Federal Republic of Germany (qqv); Morawa & Co, Austria (qv)

Zytglogge Verlag, PO Box 13, CH-3073 Gümligen (Located at: Eigerweg 16, Gümligen) Tel: (031) 522030
Programme Dir: Beat Brechbühl; *Sales Dir:* Rolf Attenhofer; *Reader:* Willi Schmid; *Publicity:* Esther Neidhart
Associate Company: Verlag im Waldgut
Subjects: Belles Lettres, Pedagogy, Theatre, Art, Politics, History, Literature
Founded: 1964
ISBN Publisher's Prefix: 3-7296

Literary Agents

Ferenczy Verlag AG, Rämistr 5, CH-8024 Zurich Tel: (01) 2516054 Cable Add: Ferenczyverlag Zurich Telex: 55210 feren ch

Gesellschaft für Verlagswerte GmbH, Hafenstr 38, CH-8280 Kreuzlingen
Manager: Hans Baumgartner

Liepman AG, Maienburgweg 23, CH-8044 Zurich Tel: (01) 477660 Cable Add: Litagent Telex: Litag 56739

Dirs: Ruth Liepman, Eva Koralnik, Ruth Weibel

Linder AG Literary Agency, Postfach, CH-8032 Zurich (Located at: Jupiterstr 1, CH-8032 Zurich) Tel: (01) 534140 Cable Add: Linderag Zürich Telex: 55123 Linag ch
Man Dirs: Paul Fritz, Peter S Fritz
Founded: 1962
Specialization: Representation of American and English authors/agents/publishers in German-language areas

Litpress, Rudolf Streit & Co, Amtshausgässchen 3, CH-3011 Berne Tel: (031) 226831
Associated with Scherz Verlag AG (qv)
Dir: Ursula Griessel

N P A (Neue Presse Agentur), Haldenstr 5, Haus am Herterberg, CH-8500 Frauenfeld-Herten Tel: (054) 74374
Contact: René Marti
Specialization: Serialization in newspapers and magazines, especially women's and educational interest, fiction, exclusives

Niedieck Linder AG, Holzgasse 6, CH-8039 Zurich Tel: (01) 2021450 Telex: 56096 nck ch
General Manager: Gerda Niedieck
Founded: 1975
Specialization: Representation of German language authors on a world-wide basis and of Agenzia Letteraria Internazionale for German-speaking countries

Rabe Verlag Zurich, Oberdorfstr 23, CH-8001 Zurich Tel: (01) 478540

Book Clubs

Europaring der Buch- und Schallplattenfreunde*, Worblentalstr 33, CH-3063 Ittigen/Berne

Ex Libris, Hermetschlostr 77, CH-8048 Zurich
Owned by: Ex Libris, Publisher (qv)

Büchergilde Gutenberg*, Kanzleistr 126, CH-8021 Zurich
Owned by: Büchergilde Gutenberg Verlagsgesellschaft mbH, Federal Republic of Germany (qv)

Edition **Kunstkreis** im Ex Libris Verlag, Postfach, CH-8023 Zurich
Subject: Art
Owned by: Ex Libris, Publisher (qv)

Club **Mon Village** SA, CH-1099 Vulliens, Vaud Tel: (021) 931363
Owned by: Editions Mon Village SA (qv)
Subjects: Novels on rural life

Neue Schweizer Bibliothek, Schweizer Verlagshaus AG, Klaussstr 10, CH-8008 Zurich
Managers: Walter Meyer, Dr Armin Meyer
Affiliated with Schweizer Verlagshaus AG (qv)

Punktum, CH-8617 Mönchaltorf Tel: (01) 9352301
Owned by: Rada Matija AG, PO Box, CH-8625 Gossau
This club deals exclusively with children's books, intended as gifts

Schweizer Volksbuchgemeinde AG*, Habsburgerstr 44, CH-6003 Lucerne

Major Booksellers

Athena-Verlag AG*, Langmattweg 36, CH-4123 Allschwil 3 Tel: (061) 380343
Wholesaler

Librairie **Barblan et Saladin***, 10 Rue de Romont, CH-1701 Fribourg
See also entry under Publishers

Buchhandlung zum **Elsässer** AG, Postfach, CH-8022 Zurich (Located at: Limmatquai 18, CH-8001 Zurich) Tel: (01) 470847 Telex: 57268
Manager: Mrs Cornelia Schweizer

Fehr'sche Buchhandlung AG, Schmiedgasse 16, CH-9001 St Gallen Tel: (071) 221152
Manager: B Brun

Buchhandlung A **Francke** AG, Neuengasse 43, Von Werdt-Passage, CH-3001 Berne Tel: (031) 221715 Cable Add: Frankebuch Bern Telex: 32326
Manager: Christian Lang
Owned by: Francke Verlag (qv)

Georg et Cie SA, Librairie de l'Université, 21 rue de la Corraterie, CH-1211 Geneva 11 Tel: (022) 216633
Owned by: Georg et Cie SA (qv)
Manager: Jacques Matile

Gretener & Co, see Buchhandlung Stäheli

Hans **Huber**, Marktgasse 59, CH-3000 Berne 9 Tel: (031) 242532
General literature, medicine and psychology at above address
Also: Zeltweg 6, CH-8032 Zurich (Medicine, Psychology, Science)
Owned by: Hans Huber AG, Publisher (qv)

Buchhandlung **Jäggi** AG*, Freiestr 32, CH-4001 Basle Tel: (061) 255200 Telex: 63873

Leobuchhandlung, Gallusstr 20, CH-9001 St Gallen Tel: (071) 222917
Owned by: Leobuchhandlung, Verlag der Quellen-Bändchen (qv)

Buchhandlung **Meili** & Co, Fronwagpl 13, CH-8200 Schaffhausen Telex: 76777 meibu ch
Owned by: Peter Meili & Co, Publisher (qv)
Founded: 1838
International Bookseller and Publisher

Orell Füssli, Pelikanstr 10, CH-8022 Zurich 1 Tel: (01) 2118011
Owned by: Orell Füssli Verlag (qv)

Librairie **Payot** SA, 1 rue de Bourg, CH-1003 Lausanne Tel: (021) 203331 Telex: 24961
Also: 4 pl Pépinet, CH-1003 Lausanne; Tel: (021) 203331 Telex: 24961 for both shops; 107 Freiestr, CH-4051 Basle; 16 Bundegasse, CH-3011 Berne; 2 rue Vallin, PO Box 381, CH-1211 Geneva 11; 14 Grand-Rue, CH-1820 Montreux; 8a rue du Bassin, CH-2000 Neuchâtel; 51 rue d'Italie, CH-1800 Vevey; 9 Bahnhofstr, CH-8001 Zurich
Owned by: Librarie Payot SA, Publisher (qv)
Wholesale Supplier: Diffusion Payot SA, 30 rue des Côtes de Montbenon, CH-1003 Lausanne Tel: (021) 205221 Telex: 24953

Buchhandlung Hans **Rohr***, Oberdorfstr 5, CH-8024 Zurich
Antiquarian and General
Also: Filmbuchhandlung Hans Rohr, Oberdorfstr 3, CH-8024 Zurich (Film/Cinema)
Owned by: Hans Rohr AG (qv)

Dr A **Scheidegger***, Kaltackerstr 32, PO Box 4, CH-8908 Hedingen Tel: (01) 7615234 Telex: 59256
Wholesaler

Buchhandlung **Scherz** AG, Marktgasse 25, CH-3011 Berne Tel: (031) 226837
Owned by: Scherz Verlag AG (qv)

Buchhandlung **Stäheli**, Bahnhofstr 70, CH-8021 Zurich Tel: (01) 2117362 Telex: 813771 stae ch
Owned by: Gretener & Co (at above address)
Manager: Curt Gretener

Buchhandlung W **Vogel***, Marktgasse 41-43, CH-8400 Winterthur Tel: (052) 226588 Telex: 74622 vogel ch

Wepf & Co AG Buchhandlung und Antiquariat, Eisengasse 5, Postfach, CH-4001 Basle Tel: (061) 256377 Cable Add: Wepfco Basle Telex: 62027
Bookseller and Antiquarian Bookshop
Dir: H U Herrmann
Owned by: Verlag Wepf & Co AG (qv for other Wepf & Co bookshops)

Major Libraries

Archives fédérales, 24 rue des Archives, CH-3003 Berne Tel: (031) 618989
Swiss Federal Archives

Bibliothèque cantonale et universitaire (Kantons- und Universitätsbibliothek), 16 rue St-Michel, CH-1701 Fribourg

Bibliothèque cantonale et universitaire de Lausanne, 6 Pl de la Riponne, CH-1005 Lausanne Tel: (021) 228831
The above is the address of the cantonal collection. The University collection is at Doligny, CH-1015 Lausanne Tel: (021) 461111 Telex: 24014 Lauc Ch
Dir: Jean-Pierre Clavel

Bibliothèque de la Ville, 3 Place Numa-Droz, CH-2000 Neuchâtel Tel: (038) 251358
Librarian: Jacques Rychner
Publications: Ville de Neuchâtel: Bibliothèques et Musées (annual); *Bulletin de la Société neuchâteloise des sciences naturelles* (annual); *Memoires de la Société neuchâteloise des sciences naturelles* (irregular); *Bulletin de la Société neuchâteloise de géographie* (annual)

Bibliothèque Nationale Suisse, see Schweizerische Landesbibliothek

Bibliothèque publique et universitaire de Genève, Promenade des Bastions, CH-1211 Geneva 4 Tel: (022) 208266
Director: Gustave Möckli
Publication: Compte rendu (annual)

Fondation Martin **Bodmer**, Bibliotheca Bodmeriana, PO Box 7, CH-1223 Cologny/Geneva Tel: (022) 362370
Dir: Dr Hans E Braun

Bureau International du Travail, see International Labour Office Library

E T H Bibliothek (Eidgenössische Technische Hochschule Bibliothek), Rämistr 101, CH-8092 Zurich Tel: (01) 2562135 Telex: 53178 (ethbich)
Library of the Swiss Federal Institute of Technology
Director: Dr J-P Sydler

International Labour Office, Central Library and Documentation Branch, 4 rte des Morillons, CH-1211 Geneva 22 Tel: (022) 998676/996111 Cable Add: Interlab Genève Telex: 22271 bit ch
Manager: K Wild
Publications: International Labour Documentation (monthly), *Labordoc, ILO Thesaurus*; also ILO Publications and Documents, Library Catalogue, Register of Periodicals (all on microfiche); *Labordoc* (data base)

Schweizerische Landesbibliothek (Bibliothèque Nationale Suisse)*, Hallwylstr 15, CH-3003 Berne Tel: Secretary (031) 618921; Lending Department (031) 618931 Telex: 32526 slbbe ch
Swiss National Library

Schweizerisches Wirtschaftsarchiv (Archives Économiques Suisses), Postfach, CH-4003 Basle
Swiss Economic Archives
Librarian: Dr H U Sulser
Founded: 1910

Stadt- und Universitätsbibliothek, Münstergasse 61, CH-3000 Berne 7 Tel: (031) 225519

Stiftsbibliothek*, Klosterhof 6, CH-9000 St Gallen Tel: (071) 225719 (library of former Benedictine abbey of St Gall)

United Nations Library*, Palais des Nations, Geneva

Öffentliche Bibliothek der **Universität Basel**, Schönbeinstr 18-20, CH-4056 Basle Tel: (061) 252250
Public Library of Basle University
Dir: F Groebli

Zentralbibliothek Zürich, Kantons- Stadt- und Universitätsbibliothek, Zähringerpl 6, Postfach, CH-8025 Zurich Tel: (01) 477272 Telex: 54669 zbzh ch
Librarian: Dr Hermann Köstler

Library Associations

Association des Bibliothécaires Suisses (Vereinigung Schweizerischer Bibliothekare), Bibliothèque Nationale Suisse, Hallwylstr 15, CH-3003 Berne Tel: (031) 618911
Association of Swiss Librarians
Secretary: W Treichler
Publication: Nouvelles (jointly with Swiss Association for Documentation) (6 times a year)

Association suisse des Bibliothèques d'Hôpitaux*, c/o Mrs J Schmid-Schädelin, Executive Director, Hirschengraben 22, CH-8001 Zurich
Association of Swiss Hospital Libraries

Kantonale Kommission für Gemeinde- und Schulbibliotheken, Zurich, PO Box 474, CH-8610 Uster 1 Tel: (01) 9413725
Cantonal Commission for Municipal and School Libraries
President: Prof Dr Egon Wilhelm
Publications: Numerous handbooks, catalogues, relating to library procedures and practice

Schweizer Bibliotheksdienst, Zähringerstr 21, CH-3012 Berne Tel: (031) 238266
Swiss Library Service

Vereinigung Schweizerischer Archivare*, Bundesarchiv, Archivstr 24, CH-3003 Berne Tel: (031) 618988
Association of Swiss Archivists
Secretary: Dr Christoph Graf
Publication: Mitteilungen (News Sheet)
Founded: 1922

Vereinigung Schweizerischer Bibliothekare, see Association des Bibliothécaires Suisses

Library Reference Journals

Mitteilungen (News), Vereinigung Schweizerischer Archivare, Bundesarchiv, Archivstr 24, CH-3003 Berne

Nouvelles (News), Association des Bibliothécaires Suisses (Vereinigung Schweizerischer Bibliothekare), Bibliothèque Nationale Suisse, CH-3003 Berne (jointly with Swiss Association for Documentation)

Literary Associations and Societies

Gesellschaft für deutsche Sprache und Literatur in Zürich, Deutsches Seminar der Universität Zürich, Rämistr 74-76, CH-8001 Zurich
Society for German Language and Literature in Zurich
Secretary: J Etzensperger

Swiss-German **P E N Club Centre**, PO Box 1383, CH-3001 Berne
Secretary: Hans Erpf

P E N Club de Suisse romande, 4 rue Mont de Sion, CH-1206 Geneva Tel: (022) 462749
P E N Club for French-speaking Switzerland
Secretary: Juliette Monnin-Hornung
Publication: PEN Club romand Newsletter (twice yearly)

P E N Internazionale — Centro della Svizzera Italiana e Romancia, Via Signore in Croce 10, CH-6612 Ascona
Secretary: Maddalena Kerényi

Schweizerische Bibliophilen-Gesellschaft*, c/o Herrn Konrad Kahl, Wolfbachstr 17, CH-8032 Zurich
Swiss Society of Bibliophiles
President: Dr Conrad Ulrich
Publications include: Librarium, published 3 times a year since 1958

Literary Periodicals

Cenobio (text in French and Italian), Dr Pier-Riccardo Frigeri, PO Box 6655, CH-6901 Lugano

drehpunkt (Turning Point), PO Box 794, CH-4002 Basle

Ecriture (Writing), Editions Bertil Galland, 29 rue du Lac, CH-1800 Vevey

Etudes de Lettres (Literary Studies), Université de Lausanne, Faculté des Lettres, Lausanne

Niemo Press; topical press and literature references with commentary (text in German), Emil Rahm, CH-8215 Hallau

Revue de Belles-Lettres (Review of Belles Lettres) (text in French), Société de Belles-Lettres de Lausanne, 4 Plainpalais, PO Box 216, CH-1211 Geneva

Schweizer Monatshefte (Swiss Monthly Magazine), Gesellschaft Schweizer Monatshefte, PO Box 86, CH-8034 Zurich

Literary Prize

City of **Zurich** Literary Prize
Founded in 1930 by the City of Zurich to reward an author for his or her whole literary work. 20,000 francs now awarded at irregular intervals (originally prize awarded every three years). Enquiries to Präsidialabteilung, Postfach, CH-8022 Zurich

Translation Agencies and Associations

Association suisse des Traducteurs et Interprètes (ASTI), Therwilerstr 77, CH-4153 Reinach-Basle
Swiss Association of Translators and Interpreters

Syria

General Information

Language: Arabic. French and English are widely spoken in business and official circles
Religion: Sunni Muslim
Population: 8 million
Literacy Rate (1970): 40%
Bank Hours: 0800-1400 Saturday-Thursday
Shop Hours: Vary greatly. Closed Friday. Generally long lunch closing
Currency: 100 piastres = 1 Syrian pound
Export/Import Information: No tariffs on books except children's picture books, with additional taxes; most advertising matter is dutied. State organization for control and execution of publicity and advertising within Syria is Arab Advertising Organization, Damascus. The General Advertising Institute, PO Box 2842, must get samples of commercial advertising and promotional materials before distribution permitted. Import licence must be submitted to Commercial Bank of Syria in order to obtain exchange licence
Copyright: No copyright conventions signed

Publishers

Arab Advertising Organization*, 28 Moutanabbi St, PO Box 2842 & 3034, Damascus Tel: 225219/225220/1 Cable Add: Golan Damascus Telex: Golan 411923 SY
Dir-General: Haitham Basheer
Imprint: Golan
Branch Offs: Aleppo, Hama, Homs, Lattakia
Subject: Directories
Founded: 1963

Bureau des Documentations Syriennes et Arabes, an associated imprint of Office Arabe de Presse et de Documentation (qv)

Damascus University Press*, Damascus
Subjects: Education, History, Geography, Engineering, Medicine, Law, Sociology, School Textbooks

Golan, an imprint of Arab Advertising Organization (qv)

Office Arabe de Presse et de Documentation, 67 pl Chahbandar, PO Box 3550, Damascus Tel: 559166 Telex: 411613 Ofa Sy
President: Samir A Darwich
Subjects: Economics, Politics, Syria and the Arab World, Periodicals
Founded: 1964
Miscellaneous: Associated imprints include Bureau des Documentations Syriennes et Arabes, PO Box 3550, Damascus

Syrian Documentation Papers*, PO Box 2712, Damascus
Dir-General: Louis Farés
Subjects: Reference, Directories, Politics, Economics, Sociology, Law
Founded: 1968

al-**Tawjih** Press*, Palestine St, PO Box 3320, Damascus
Subject: Literature

Major Booksellers

Avicenne Librairie Internationale*, Tajhiz St, PO Box 2456 Tel: 112911 Telex: Omatel 11206 Sy for Avicenne
Manager: Jean-Pierre Dummar

Dar **Dimashk** (Adib Tunbakji) Bookshop*, Port Said St Tel: 111048

Dar **Al-Fikr** (Salem & Zu'bi) Bookshop*, Saadallah Al-Jabiri St, PO Box 962 Tel: 111041

Dakr Abdul **Wahab***, Port Said St Tel: 115486

Major Libraries

Damascus University Library*, Damascus
Publication: Bibliography of the Middle East

Dar al-Kutub al-Wataniah (National Library)*, Homs

Al **Maktabah** Al Wataniah (National Library)*, Bab El-Faradj, Aleppo

National Library of Latakia*, Latakia

Al **Zahiriah** (National Library)*, Bab el Barid, Damascus

Library Reference Journal

Damascus University Library Review, Damascus University Library, Damascus

Literary Periodical

Al-Mawqif Al-Adabi, Ittihad al-Kuttab al-Arab, Shari Murshid Khatir, Damascus

Taiwan

General Information

Language: Chinese: a single written language is used by speakers of several diverse spoken dialects. The most important spoken form is Mandarin, known in Taiwan as *Kuo-Yü* (= national tongue). Other important spoken forms in Taiwan are Amoy-Swatow (also called Taiwanese) and Fukienese
Religion: Confucian, Buddhist, Taoist, Christian
Population: 7.6 million
Literacy Rate (1956): 45.5%
Bank Hours: 0900-1200 Monday-Friday; 0900-1530 Saturday
Shop Hours: 0800-1700 Monday-Saturday
Currency: 100 cents = 1 new Taiwan dollar
Export/Import Information: No tariffs on books and advertising. Import licences required; exchange available when licence presented at authorized bank
Copyright: No copyright conventions signed

Book Trade Reference Books and Journals

Books

Books on China 1980: A Cumulative List with Descriptions of Original and Reprinted Western-Language Titles Available from Taiwan, Chinese Materials Center Inc, PO Box 22048, Taipei

Journals

Chinese National Bibliography (text in Chinese and English), National Central Library, 43 Nan Hai Rd, Taipei

Shu mo chi kan (Bibliography quarterly), (text in Chinese), Student Book Co Ltd, 298 Roosevelt Rd, 3rd Section, Taipei

Publishers

Business Publications Ltd*, PO Box 58432, Taipei (Located at: Hui Feng Bldg 3rd/4th Fl, No 20 Lane 14 Chi Lin Rd, Taipei) Tel: 5216457/5218784 Cable Add: Andypandy Telex: 21032 Andy
Man Dir: Michelle Yang; *Editorial:* Nigel White; *Sales, Publicity:* Hellen Tsai; *Production:* Dawn Chen; *Rights & Permissions:* Mark Van Roo
Associate Companies: Andy Pandy Ltd (Hui Feng Bldg 3rd Floor); Business English Center (4th Floor)
Subjects: International Business, Business English Textbooks, Business Dictionary (English/Chinese), Periodical: *Current Business Affairs in Taiwan and International Trade*
Bookshop: At above address
Founded: 1978

Cheng Chung Book Co*, 20 Hengyang Rd, Taipei
Subjects: Academic

Ch'eng Wen Publishing Company, c/o CMC Taipei Liaison Office, PO Box 22048, Taipei 100 Tel: (02) 3916416 Cable Add: Chewenpb Taipei
Chief Executive: Larry C Huang
Subjects: Scholarly, General Interest (in Chinese and English)
Founded: 1964

Chinese Materials Center, CMC Taipei Liaison Office, PO Box 22048, Taipei 100 Cable Add: Taient Taipei
President: Robert L Irick
Parent Company: Chinese Materials Center, Central PO Box 3075, Kowloon, Hong Kong
Subjects: China, Asia, Scholarly, General
Bookshop: At above Taipei address

Chung Hwa Book Co Ltd, 94 Chungking S Rd, Section 1, Taipei 100 Tel: 3117365/3117344/3113541 Cable Add: 2821 Taipei
Man Dir: D S Hsiung; *Sales Dir:* C C Ku; *Publicity Dir:* Mrs S M Sun
Subjects: General Fiction, Belles Lettres, Poetry, Biography, History, How-to, Music, Art, Philosophy, Reference, Religion, Juveniles, Low- & High-priced Paperbacks, Medicine, Psychology, Engineering, General & Social Science, University, Secondary & Primary Textbooks, Educational Materials
Founded: 1911

Far East Book Co, 66-1 (10th Floor) Chungking S Rd, Section 1, Taipei Tel: 3312022 Cable Add: 1418 Taipei
Manager: Pearl Y C Pu
Subjects: Art, Education, History, Physics, Dictionaries, Shakespeare in translation, Tang Poems

TAIWAN — TANZANIA

Fu-Hsing Book Co*, 44 Huai Ning St, Taipei
Subject: Textbooks

Great China Book Corporation*, 66 Chungking S Rd, Section 1, Taipei
Subject: Textbooks

Hua Kuo Publishing Co*, 218 King San St, Ho-Ping East Rd, Taipei
Publisher: T F Wang; *Publicity Manager:* Y M Yeh
Founded: 1950

San Min Book Co Ltd, 61 Chung Ching South Rd, Section 1, Taipei
Publicity Manager: Cheng-Chiang Liu
Subjects: History, Philosophy, Sociology, Literary

World Book Co, 99 Chungking South Rd, Section 1, Taipei Tel: 9110470
General Manager: Tsung Mou Shaw
Subjects: Chinese Classics, Novels, Reference & Textbooks for High School, College & University

Yee Wen Publishing Co Ltd+, PO Box 969, Taipei (Located at: 81 Kuang Min St, Pan Chiao) Tel: 9616321
Executive Manager: Tsu-Ken Yao
Branch Off: 21 Vista Court, South San Francisco, CA 94080, USA
Subjects: Chinese Art & History, Archaeology, Oracle Bone Studies, Ancient Chinese Language & Culture, Religion, Philosophy
Bookshop: At above address
1982: 23 titles *1983:* 20 titles
ISBN Publisher's Prefix: 0-88691

Major Booksellers

Chinese Materials Center, c/o CMC Taipei Liaison Office, PO Box 22048, Taipei 100
Cable Add: Taient Taipei
International distributor and publisher (qv)
President: Robert L Irick

J Cynthia Co Ltd*, PO Box 24-92, Taipei 106

H C Ling Book Store & Co Ltd*, PO Box 322, Taipei 100

Literature House Ltd, 6th Fl, 192 Ho-Ping East Rd, Section 1, Taipei Tel: 3923191
Manager: Julia Lee
Importer

Mei Ya Publications Inc (Sueling, Inc)*, PO Box 22555, Taipei Tel: 3923191
Manager: Julia Lee
Specialize in College and University textbook reprints (all copyrighted)

The **National** Book Co, 84-5 Section 3, Sing Sung South Rd, Taipei 107 Tel: 3210698
Cable Add: Natlbk Taipei
Manager: J K Chen

Southeast Book Co*, 105 Po Ali Rd, Taipei

Taipei Publications Trading Co+, PO Box 59326, Taipei
Manager: Y C Huang

Win Join Book Co Ltd*, PO Box 22, 32 Taipei (Located at: 105 Ho-Ping East Rd, Section 1, Taipei) Tel: 3934063/3419646/3914280 Telex: 26985 Jetwin
Manager: Mrs M C Tasy Lin

Major Libraries

Fu Ssu-Nien Library Institute of History and Philology, Academia Sinica, Taipei 115

Kuomintang Central Committee Library*, Taipei

National Central Library, 43 Nan Hai Rd, Taipei 107 Tel: 3147320/9 (Office of the Director); 3147322 (Reference Section); 3813215 (Resource and Information Centre for Chinese Studies)
Director: Chen-ku Wang

National War College Library*, Yangmingshan, Taipei

Taipei Municipal Library*, Hsin I Rd, Section 4, Taipei

Taiwan Branch Library, National Central Library*, 1 Hsinshen South Rd, Section 1, Taipei 106
Librarian: Henry H S Jeng

Library Associations

Library Association of China*, c/o National Central Library, 43 Nan Hai Rd, Taipei
Executive Dir: Karl M Ku
Publications: Library Association of China Newsletter (quarterly in Chinese); *Bulletin of the Library Association of China* (annually in Chinese)

Library Science Society*, c/o Department of Library Science, National Taiwan University, Roosevelt Rd, Section 4, Taipei
President: Prof Lawrence H Chen
Publication: T'u-Shü-Kuan Hsüeh-K'an (Bulletin of Department of Library Science, National Taiwan University); Chinese, partly in English

Library Reference Journals

Chung-kuo t'u-shu-kuan hsueh-hui hui-pao (Bulletin of the Library Association of China), National Central Library, 43 Nan Hai Rd, Taipei

Journal of Library and Information Science, National Taiwan Normal University, Department of Social Education, Taipei

Literary Associations and Societies

China National Association of Literature and the Arts*, No 4, Lane 22, Ningpo St West, Taipei

National Council of Ethnographic Arts and Literature of China*, 11 Terrace 5, Lane 5, Section 3, Jan-Ai Rd, Taipei

The Taipei Chinese Center, International **P E N**, 5th Floor — 33 Lane 180, Kwang Fu South Rd, Taipei 105 Cable Add: Taipenclub
Executive Secretary: Nancy C Ing
Publication: The Chinese PEN (quarterly, text in English)

Literary Periodicals

The Chinese PEN (quarterly, text in English), The Taipei Chinese Center, International PEN, 5th Floor — 33 Lane 180, Kwang Fu South Rd, Taipei 105

Counter Attack, National Institute for Compilation and Translation, 247 Chou-Shan Rd, Taipei

Tamkang Review, a journal mainly devoted to comparative studies between Chinese and foreign literatures (text in English), Tamkang College, Graduate Institute of Western Languages and Literature, King-Hua St, Taipei

Yeh ko (Evensongs) (text in Chinese or English), Tamkang College, English Department Evening School, Evensongs Association, No 5, Lane 199, King-hua St, Taipei

Translation Agencies and Associations

National Institute for Compilation and Translation, 247 Chou-Shan Rd, Taipei
Dir: Dr Hsien-Chu Hsiung
Publication: Counter Attack

Tanzania

General Information

Language: Swahili is official language. English is widely used
Religion: About 30% Muslim, 25% Christian (mostly Roman Catholic); rest follow traditional beliefs
Population: 16.6 million
Bank Hours: Mainland Tanzania: 0900-1200 Monday-Friday; 0900-1100 Saturday. Zanzibar: 0830-1130 Monday-Friday; 0830-1000 Saturday
Shop Hours: 0800-1200, 1400-1715 or 1800 Monday-Saturday
Currency: 100 cents = 1 Tanzania shilling
Export/Import Information: No tariff on books or advertising matter. Import licence and exchange controls
Copyright: Florence (see International section)

Book Trade Organization

Standard Book Numbering Agency, Tanzania Library Service, PO Box 9283, Dar es Salaam
ISBN Administrator: T E Mlaki

Book Trade Reference Journals

Government and Tanu Publications List, Government Publications Agency, PO Box 1801, Dar es Salaam

Tanzania National Bibliography, Tanzania Library Service, PO Box 9283, Dar es Salaam (the national bibliography, published annually since 1969)

Publishers

Africa Inland Church Literature Department, see Inland Publishers

Central Tanganyika Press, PO Box 15, Dodoma Tel: 22140
Manager: Frances M Weir
Subject: Religion
1981: 13 titles *1982:* 7 titles *Founded:* 1954
ISBN Publisher's Prefix: 9976-66

Dar es Salaam University Press, PO Box 35182, Dar es Salaam Tel: 49192 Cable Add: University Dar es Salaam
Director: D K Tungaraza
Subjects: History, Africana, Reference, Religion, Medicine, Psychology, Science & Technology, Social Science, University Textbooks, Academic Monographs

Eastern Africa Publications Ltd*, PO Box 1002, Arusha Tel: 3181 ext 1521 Cable Add: Eapl Arusha Telex: 42121 Concentre
General Manager: Cleveland Nkata; *Editorial:* Miss M S Teri; *Sales, Marketing, Publicity:* J J Mwijage; *Production:* S M S Poyowela
Orders to: Above address or PO Box 1408 Dar es Salaam
Parent Company: Tanzania Karatasi Associated Industries, PO Box 2418, Dar es Salaam
Branch Off: PO Box 1408, Dar es Salaam
Subjects: General Non-fiction, Poetry, Biography, History, Geography, Politics, Africana, Primary & Secondary Schools Reference Books in both Kiswahili and English
Founded: 1979

Government Printer*, Government Publications Agency, PO Box 2483, Dar es Salaam

Inland Publishers, PO Box 125, Mwanza Tel: 40064
Dir: Rev S M Magesa
Subjects: General Non-fiction, Religion, Books in Kiswahili and English, Paperbacks
Miscellaneous: A publishing division of Africa Inland Church Literature Department (at above address)

Longman Tanzania Ltd*, Independence Ave, PO Box 3164, Dar es Salaam Tel: 29748 Cable Add: Longman Dar es Salaam
Man Dir: A B Moshi
Associate Company: Longman Group Ltd, UK (qv)
Subjects: General Non-fiction, Belles Lettres, Poetry, Biography, History, Africana, Juveniles, Books in Kiswahili, General Science, Secondary & Primary Textbooks, Science & Technology
Founded: 1965

Ndanda Mission Press*, Ndanda PO Box 1004, Ndanda via Lindi
Subjects: Religion, Medical, Social
1980: 13 titles *1981:* 9 titles

Oxford University Press*, Maktaba Rd, PO Box 5299, Dar es Salaam Tel: 29209 Cable Add: Oxonian
Manager: Anthony Theobald
Subjects: General Non-fiction, Literature, Poetry, Biography, History, Africana, Reference, Books in Kiswahili, General & Social Science, Secondary & Primary Textbooks
Founded: 1969
Miscellaneous: Firm is a branch of Oxford University Press, East and Central Africa, Kenya (qv)

Pan-African Publishing Co Ltd, PO Box 4212, Dar es Salaam Tel: 22380
Man Dir: M W Kanyama Chiume
Subjects: Fiction, Science, Politics, History, General
Bookshop: Pan-African Bookshop, PO Box 5068, Tanga
1981: 2 titles *Founded:* 1977

T M P Book Department*, PO Box 550, Tabora
Subject: Religion

Tanzania Library Service, PO Box 9283, Dar es Salaam Tel: 26121 Cable Add: Tanlis

Parent Company: The Ministry of National Education, Dar es Salaam
Founded: 1963

Tanzania Mission Press, see T M P Book Department

Tanzania Publishing House*, 47 Independence Ave, PO Box 2138, Dar es Salaam Tel: 32164 Cable Add: Publish Dar es Salaam
General Manager: Walter Bgoya; *Sales Manager:* S Nkini
Subjects: General Fiction & Non-fiction, Belles Lettres, Poetry, Biography, History, Africana, Philosophy, Juveniles, Paperbacks, Social Science, University & Secondary Textbooks (in Kiswahili and English)
Founded: 1966

Major Booksellers

The **Cathedral** Bookshop*, Mansfield St, PO Box 2381, Dar es Salaam Tel: 22873

The **Dar es Salaam Bookshop**, Makunganya St, PO Box 9030, Dar es Salaam Tel: 23416
Manager: E Charokiwa

Dar es Salaam University Bookshop, PO Box 35090, Dar es Salaam Tel: 48300/49192 ext 2389
Manager: Miss C G Barabojik

Inland Bookshop*, PO Box 1402, Mwanza Tel: 2132
Branches in Bariadi, Geita, Magu, Masua, Musoma, Nansio, Sengerema, Shinyanga
Distribution Manager: Rev A Feisel
Owned by: Africa Inland Church Literature Department

International Bookshop, PO Box 21341, Dar es Salaam Tel: 21930/27458 Cable Add: Safina, Dar es Salaam
Dir: Murtaza Alidina
Wholesale, Distribution: International Publishers Agencies Ltd (at above address)
Retail Outlets: International Bookshop (at above address); Les Nouvelles, Kilimanjaro Hotel, Dar es Salaam

The **Standard** Bookshop*, Independence Ave, PO Box 1278, Dar es Salaam Tel: 23126

T M P Book Department*, PO Box 550, Tabora

Tanzania Elimu Supplies Ltd*, Textbook Division, Port Area, Kurasini, PO Box 20873, Dar es Salaam Tel: 25481 Cable Add: Elisup Telex: 41349

Tanzania Mission Press, see T M P Book Department

Major Libraries

American Center Library, US Information Service, PO Box 9170, Dar es Salaam Tel: 26611
Library Dir: G K Nagri

British Council Library, Independence Ave, Ohio St, PO Box 9100, Dar es Salaam Tel: 22726

Faculty of Agriculture, Forestry and Veterinary Science*, University of Dar es Salaam, c/o Sub Post Office, Morogoro Tel: 2511
Librarian: S S Mbwana
Publications include: Library Accessions List (quarterly)

Institute of Development Management Library, PO Box 4, Mzumbe, Morogoro Tel: 2401-4 ext 248 Telex: idm morogoro

Kibaha Public Library*, PO Box Kibaha, Kibaha Tel: 258

Kivukoni College Library*, PO Box 9193, Dar es Salaam Tel: 29215
Librarian: F Shechambo

Makumira Lutheran Theological College Library, PO Box 55, Usa River
Librarian: Christina Hedlund

Marangu College of National Education Library, PO Box 3080, Moshi Tel: 16 Marangu
Librarian: Joachim Mkumbara

Moshi Public Library, PO Box 863, Moshi Tel: 2432
Librarian: Alfred Zacharia Mwasha

Mwanza Regional Library*, PO Box 1363, Mwanza Tel: 2314
Librarian: Fabian M Kadamah

The **Medical** Library*, Faculty of Medicine, Muhimbili Medical Centre, PO Box 65012, Dar es Salaam Tel: 26211/27081 Cable Add: Muhimbili Dar es Salaam
Chief Librarian: D W K Mwapwele

National Archives of Tanzania*, India St, PO Box 2006, Dar es Salaam Tel: 23954

Tanzania Library Service, PO Box 9283, Dar es Salaam Tel: 26121 Telex: Tanlis
Publications: Tanzania National Bibliography; Directory of Libraries, Museums and Archives in Tanzania (1979)

University of Dar es Salaam Library, PO Box 35092, Dar es Salaam Tel: 48235
Chief Librarian: Ms E V Chiduo

Zanzibar Government Archives*, PO Box 116, Zanzibar

Library Association

Tanzania Library Association, PO Box 2645, Dar es Salaam Tel: 26121
Publications: Someni (journal); *Matukio* (TLA newsletter)

Library Reference Books and Journals

Book

Directory of Libraries, Museums and Archives in Tanzania (1979), Tanzania Library Service, PO Box 9283, Dar es Salaam

Journals

Matukio, Tanzania Library Association, PO Box 2645, Dar es Salaam

Someni (text in English), Tanzania Library Association, PO Box 2645, Dar es Salaam

Literary Periodical

Umma, Eastern Africa Publications Ltd, PO Box 1002, Arusha (a biannual literary magazine published under the auspices of the Department of Literature, University of Dar es Salaam)

Thailand

General Information

Language: Thai is official language. English is widely used in government and commercial circles. There are sizeable populations of Chinese, Malay and Khmer speakers
Religion: Theravada Buddhist
Population: 45 million
Literacy Rate (1970): 78.6% (87.7% Urban, 77.1% Rural)
Bank Hours: 0830-1530 Monday-Friday
Shop Hours: Vary. Those catering for tourists generally open 0830-1800 or later
Currency: 100 satangs = 1 baht
Export/Import Information: No tariff on books but Standard Profit Tax and Business Tax apply (also a Municipal Tax of percentage of Business Tax). Advertising subject to same taxes and ad val percentage of import duty. No import licences for books, but special permit required by importer for orders over a certain sum. Certificate of payment (from Exchange Control Authority) required
Copyright: Berne, Florence (see International section)

Book Trade Organizations

Publishers' and Booksellers' Association of Thailand*, 108 Sukhumvit Soi 53, Bangkok Tel: 3112447
President and Secretary: M L M Jumsai, Chalermnit Press, 1-2 Erawan Arcade, Bangkok Tel: 528759

Standard Book Numbering Agency, The National Library of Thailand, Samsen Rd, Bangkok 10300 Tel: 2815449 Telex: 84189 Natlib Th
ISBN Administrator: Mrs Suwakhon Phadung-Ath

Publishers

Aksorn Charerntat*, 142 Praengsanpasart, Tanao Rd, Bangkok Tel: 214587
Subjects: Textbooks, Industry, Arts, Maps, Literature, Mathematics, Education, Physics, Linguistics

Aksorn Charoen Tasna Ltd*, 195 Bamrung Muang Rd, Bangkok
Subject: Textbooks

Bandarnsarn*, 136-138 Nakorn Sawan Rd, Bangkok Tel: 82551
Subject: Thai books

Banmai*, 1 Soi Prasanmit, Sukhumvit, Bangkok

Barnakarn*, 236 Nakern Kashem, Bangkok Tel: 227796
Subject: Thai books

Barnakieh Trading*, 34 Nakorn Sawan Rd, Bangkok Tel: 825520
Subject: Thai books

Barnasilpa*, 1 Soi Praengsanpasart, Asdang Rd, Bangkok Tel: 220060
Subject: Thai books

Chalermnit Press*, 108 Sukhumvit Soi 53, Bangkok Tel: 2528759
Managers: M L M Jumsai, Mrs Jumsai
Subjects: Books on Thailand, Pocket books and Children's books in English, French & German, Magazines, Dictionaries
Bookshop: Chalermnit Bookshop (qv under Major Booksellers)
Founded: 1957

Chiangmai Book Centre*, 2 Kochasam Rd, Suriya Cinema, Chiangmai
Bookshop: At above address

Office of **Christian** Education and Literature, an imprint of Suriyaban Publishers (qv)

Dhammabucha*, 5/1-2 Asdang Rd, Bangkok Tel: 223549/850010
Subject: Thai books on Buddhism

Duang Kamol*, 244-246 Siam Sq Soi 2, Patumwan, Bangkok Tel: 2516335/6
Subjects: English, French and Thai books

Foreign Relations Publishing House*, 20 Rajprasong Trade Centre, Bangkok 10500 Tel: 2510630/3916456
President: M L Manich Jumsai, CBE
Subjects: Translation and publication of German Works (in collaboration with Publishers' and Booksellers' Association of Thailand (qv) and Deutscher Verein des Buchhandels)
Founded: 1980

Hor Samut Klang*, 5 Soi Praeng Sanpasart, Asdang Rd, Bangkok Tel: 219751
Subject: Thai books

Klang Vidhya*, 724 Wang Burapa, Bangkok 10200 Tel: 224546/2219331
Manager: Prachark Chaovanabutvilai
Subject: Thai books
Bookshop: At above address

Languages School*, Wat Phra Singha, Chiangmai

Narongsarn*, 647/14 Charernrat Rd, (Big Circle), Dhonburi, Bangkok

Nibondh*, 40-42 New Rd, Bangkok Tel: 212611
Subjects: English and Thai books
Bookshop: 40-42 New Rd, Bangkok; 975/4 Gaysorn Rd, Bangkok

Niyom Vidhya*, 192 Bamrungmuang Rd, Bangkok Tel: 217661
Subject: Thai Technical Textbooks

Norn*, 1/1 Boonsiri, Sukhumvit Rd, Paknam Tel: 90130
Subject: Thai books

Odeon Store LP*, 862 Wang Burapa, Bangkok Tel: 2210742/2216567 Cable Add: Odeonstore
Man Dir: Vichai Praepanich
Branch Off: Siain Sq soi 1, Bangkok
Subjects: Textbooks, Non-fiction, Paperbacks
Founded: 1947

Parnfah Pittaya*, 440-2 Nakornsawan Rd, Bangkok
Subjects: Thai books, Comics

Pikkhanet*, 99 Praeng Sanpasart, Tanao Rd, Bangkok Tel: 222850
Subject: Thai pocket books

Pittayakarn*, 226 Nakorn Kashem, Bangkok Tel: 221501
Subject: Thai books

Pra Cha Chang & Co Ltd*, 816/3 Talad Noi, New Rd, Bangkok
Subject: Academic

Prae Pittaya Ltd*, 716-718 Burapa Palace, PO Box 914, Bangkok Tel: 2214283/221286
Manager: Chitt Praepanich
Subjects: Fiction, Juveniles
Bookshop: as above

Pramuansarn Publishing House*, 703/15-16 Petchaburi Rd, Bangkok
Manager: Lime Taechatada
Subjects: Guidebooks, Popular Sciences, Juveniles
Founded: 1955

Praphansarn Book Centre*, 236/6-7 Beside Lido Theatre, Siam Square Soi 2, Rama I Rd, Bangkok Tel: 2512342/3
Man Dir: Suphol Taechatada

Prasarnmitr*, 3382 New Petchaburi Rd, Bangkok Tel: 915387/925230
Subject: Textbooks

Progress*, 882 Wang Burapa, Bangkok Tel: 226541
Subject: Thai books, English occasionally

Religious Revival Organization*, 176 Sukhumvit, Santikam Soi 1, T Samrong North, Samutprakarn

Ruamsarn (1977) Co Ltd*, Part, 864 Burapa Palace, Bangkok 2 Tel: 2216483
Man Dir: Bumrung Tawewatanasarn; *Sales Dir:* Nongyao Tawewatanasarn; *Publicity Dir:* Piya Tawewatanasarn; *Advertising Dir:* Piti Tawewatanasarn
Subsidiary Company: Bumrungsarn Ltd, Part, 864 Burapa Palace, Bangkok 2
Subjects: General Fiction, Belles Lettres, Poetry, Biography, History, How-to, Music, Art, Philosophy, Reference, Religion, Low-priced Paperbacks, General Science, University & Secondary Textbooks
Bookshops: Ruamsarn (1977) Co Ltd, 864 Burapa Palace, Bangkok 2; Dheerasarn Ltd, Part, 326-8 Siam Sq 4, Bangkok 10500; Tawesarn, 89/51 Near President Theatre, Bangkok 10500
Founded: 1951

Rungvit Sawarn-Apichon*, Chiengmai Book Centre, 2 Kochasarn Rd, opposite Suriya Cinema, Chiengmai

Sangna Vuddhichai Saranonda*, Prabhasarn, 130 Nakornsauran Rd, Bangkok

Sayam Paritat*, 14-6 Nakorn Lane, Taprachand, Maharat Rd, Bangkok Tel: 219108
Subject: Thai books

Sermwit Barnakarn*, 222 Nakorn Kashem, Bangkok Tel: 214541
Subject: Thai books

Siam Directory*, 2 Mansion, 96 Rajdamnern Ave, Bangkok
Subjects: History, Politics, Technical

Sinpattana*, 74 Pra Atit Rd, Bangkok Tel: 824357/816917
Subject: Thai books

Social Science Association Press*, 2 Chula Soi, Phya Thai Rd, Bangkok
Manager & Editor: Sulak Sivaraksa
Subject: Textbooks
Founded: 1961

Sommai Press*, 90-18 Ekkachai Rd, Bangkok Tel: 30037
Subject: Thai books

Suksapan Panit (Business Organization of Teachers Council of Thailand), Mansion 9, Rajadamnern Ave, Bangkok 10200 Tel: 816543/815044 Telex: 72031 Suksapa Th
Dir: Kamthon Sathirakul
Subjects: Juveniles, Textbooks, Dictionaries
Founded: 1950

Suksit Siam Co Ltd*, 1715 Rama IV Rd, Samyan, Bangkok 10500 Tel: 511630
Publicity: Mrs Nilchawee Sivaraksa
Subjects: Mainly Thai books on Social Science & Politics
Bookshop: At above address

Suriyaban Publishers, 14 Pramuan Rd, Bangkok Tel: 2347991 Cable Add: CCT Office
Man Dir, Editorial, Publicity, Rights & Permissions: Mrs Bampen Krishnakan; *Sales:* Philip Tsang; *Production:* Mrs

Bampen Krishnakan
Parent Company: Department of Christian Education and Literature, Church of Christ in Thailand, at above address
Imprint: Office of Christian Education and Literature
Subjects: Religion, Children's Books, Buddhism, Thai Culture
Bookshops: The Christian Bookstore, Suriyaban Bookstore (qqv under Major Booksellers)
Founded: 1953

Sutpaisarn*, 638 Somdet Chaopaya Rd, Bangkok Tel: 664392
Subject: Thai books on Law

Thai Commercial Printing Press*, Bangkok
Subjects: Law, Management

Thai Inc*, 96 Mansion, 2 Rajdamnern Ave, Bangkok
Subjects: Politics, History, Religion

Thai Watana Panich*, 599 Maitrijit Rd, Bangkok Tel: 210111
Subject: School books in Thai (occasionally English)

Tong-In Sunsawat*, Wat Prasing, Chiengmai
Subject: English books

Vadhana Panich*, 216-220 Bumrungmuang Rd, Bangkok
Subject: School Textbooks

Vajarindra*, 364 Sumeru Rd, Bangkok Tel: 816207

Viratham*, 141 St Louis Soi 2, Sathorn Tai Rd, Bangkok Tel: 866848
Subjects: English, French and English-Thai books

Wattana Panich*, 216-220 Bumrungmuang Rd, Bangkok
Subjects: Textbooks, Fiction, Maps

Major Booksellers

Asia Books Co Ltd, 6/1 Soi Chidlom, Ploenchit Rd, Bangkok 10500 Tel: 2526400/2520064/2516008 Cable Add: Asiabooks Telex: TH81043 TH87202 Asiabooks
Showroom: 221 Sukhumvit Rd, between Soi 15 and 17, Bangkok 10110 Tel: 2527277
Man Dir: Vinai Suttharoj; *General Manager:* Miss Somporn Suttharoj
Also publishers' agent, distributor and retailer of English books

Bangkok Central Book Depot*, Sikak Phya Sri, Bangkok

Central Department Store, 306 Silom Rd, Bangkok Tel: 2336930-9 Telex: Cetrac TH82768 Cable Add: Cetrac Bangkok
Manager: Mrs Ratana Norabhanlobh
Largest distributor, wholesaler and retailer of comics, magazines, paperbacks, all types of non-fiction books

Chalermnit Bookshop*, 1-2 Erawan Arcade, Bangkok Tel: 528759
Owned by: Chalermnit Press (qv)
Also importers

Christian Bookstore, 14 Pramuan Rd, Bangkok
Manager: Charu Panichkul
Owned by: Suriyaban Publishers (qv)

Dheerasarn Ltd*, Part, 326-8 Siam Sq, Bangkok 10500
Also at: Tawesarn 89/51 Near President Theatre, Bangkok 10500

International Book Distributors Co Ltd*, 1035-4 Pleonchit Shopping Centre, Pleonchit Rd, PO Box 5-59, Bangkok

Klang Vidhya*, 724 Wang Burapa, Bangkok
Also: 3931/26-29 Chumpol Rd, Nakorn Rajsima; 197/2 Srichan Rd, Tambon Wat Mai, Chantaburi

Nibondh (Gaysorn)*, 975/4 Gaysorn Rd, Bangkok
English books at the above address
English, Thai books and magazines at Nibondh (Sikak), 40-42 New Rd, Bangkok

Praepittaya Ltd*, 716-718 Burapa Palace, PO Box 914, Bangkok
Also importers and wholesaler

Pramual Sarn Book Centre Ltd*, Partnership, 678 Chalerm Khetr Bldg, Bangkok

Ruamsarn (1977) Co Ltd*, 864 Burapa Palace, Bangkok 2 Tel: 2216483
Manager: Nongyao Tawewatanasarn

Suksit Siam Co Ltd*, 1715 Rama IV Rd, Samyan, Bangkok 10500 Tel: 2511630
Also importers and library suppliers

Suriwongs Book Centre, Sri Don Chai Rd, Chiengmai 50000 Tel: 236299/235889
Manager: Miss J Jittidecharaks

Suriyaban Bookstore, 124/1 Silom Rd, Bangkok 10500 Tel: 2356200
Acting Manager: Philip Tsang
Owned by: Suriyaban Publishers (qv)

White Lotus Co Ltd, PO Box 1141, Bangkok Tel: 3927449 Cable Add: Andeco Telex: 82094 Ande Th

Major Libraries

British Council Library, 428 Rama I Rd, 2 Siam Sq, Bangkok 10500 Tel: 2526136

Chulalongkorn University, Academic Resource Center, Phya Thai Rd, Bangkok 10500
Director: Mrs Knid Tantavirat
Includes Central Library, Thailand Information Center and Audio-Visual Unit
Publications: Academic Resources Journal, Union Catalog of Chulalongkorn University Libraries

Department of Science Service Library, Rama VI St, Bangkok 10400 Tel: 2818881
Librarian: Miss Tweelak Boonkong

Main Library, **Kasetsart University**, Bangkok 10900 Tel: 5792539
Librarian: Mrs Piboonsin Watanapongse

National Archives Division*, Fine Arts Department, Samsen Rd, Bangkok 10300

The **National Library** of Thailand, Samsen Rd, Bangkok 10300 Tel: 2815449/2810263 Telex: 84189 Natlib Th
Director: Mrs Kullasap Gesmankit

Siriraj Medical Library, Library Division, Mahidol University, Siriraj Hospital, Bangkok 10700
Director: Miss Uthai Dhutiyabhodhi

Sri Nakharinwirot University Library*, Sukhumvit 23, Bangkok 10110

Thai National Documentation Centre (TNDC)*, 196 Phahonyothin Rd, Bang Khen, Bangkok 9

Thammasat University Libraries, Prachand Rd, Bangkok 10200 Tel: 2215886
Librarian: Mrs Phakaivan Chiamcharoen
Publications include: Dom Thad (journal); *Bibliography of the Ministry of Commerce's Publications in the University Libraries; Bibliography of Books in Thammasat University Libraries* (1980); *Thai Royal Gazette Index; Biography Index*

United Nations, Economic and Social Commission for Asia and the Pacific Library, United Nations Bldg, Rajadamnern Ave, Bangkok 10200
Librarian: Mr Allan F Windsor

Library Association

Thai Library Association*, 273-275 Viphavadee Rangsit Rd, Phayathai, Bangkok 10400 Tel: 2783439
Secretary: N Puakpong
Publication: Bulletin (6 a year)

Library Reference Books and Journals

Books

An Annotated Bibliography of Librarianship in Thailand, Department of Library Science, Chulalongkorn University, Faculty of Arts, Phya Thai Rd, Bangkok 10500

List of Scientific Libraries in Thailand, Thai National Documentation Centre, 196 Phahonyothin Rd, Bangkhen, Bangkok 9

Journal

Bulletin, Thai Library Association, 273-275 Viphavadee Rangsit Rd, Phayathai, Bangkok 10400

Literary Associations and Societies

P E N International — Thailand Centre, 56/21-22 Rama I Rd, Bangkok 10500 Cable Add: Asma Bangkok Telex: 87141 Chaiya Th
External Correspondent: K Direk

The **Siam** Society, PO Box 65, Bangkok (Located at: 131 Soi Asoke, Sukhumvit 21, Bangkok) Tel: 3914401
President: M R Patanachai Jayant; *Honorary Secretary:* Mrs Nongyao Narumit
Publications: Journal of the Siam Society (twice yearly), *Natural History Bulletin of the Siam Society* (annual)
Miscellaneous: Formerly The Thailand Society. Founded 1904. Under Royal Patronage. For promotion of Thai and South East Asian art, science and literature

Literary Prizes

Bangkok Bank Foundation Prize
For prose or poetry in Thai concerning history, art, culture, religion, social affairs, philosophy or new creative ideas. 50,000 baht each for prose and poetry. Awarded annually. Enquiries to Secretary, Bangkok Bank Foundation, Suapa Rd, PO Box 95, Bangkok

Kennedy Prize*
For promoting understanding of Thailand, the Thai people or Thai culture, using the Thai language. 30,000 baht each for prose and poetry. Awarded annually. Enquiries to John F Kennedy Foundation of Thailand, Ministry of Foreign Affairs, Bangkok 2

Togo

General Information

Language: French is official language
Religion: About 25% Christian (mostly Roman Catholic), 8% Muslim; rest follow traditional beliefs
Population: 2.4 million
Bank Hours: 0730-1130, 1430-1600 Monday-Friday
Shop Hours: 080-1200, 1430 or 1500-1730 or 1800 Monday-Friday; 0730-1230 Saturday
Currency: CFA franc
Export/Import Information: No tariff on books; advertising catalogues dutied. Additional taxes: Tax Forfaitaire, Statistical Tax, and Customs Stamp Tax of percentage of duties and added taxes. Small Wharfage Tax. Import licence required for goods from non-franc zones above a certain value; from franc zone, need authorization of Togolese Government Office. Exchange controls on non-franc zone.
Copyright: Berne (see International section)

Publishers

Ecole Professionelle de la Mission Catholique*, BP 341, Lomé
Subjects: Religion, Secondary & Primary Textbooks

Editogo*, BP 891, Lomé Tel: 213718/216106
Man Dir: Kokou Amedegnato
Subjects: General and Educational
Founded: 1962

Maison d'Edition de la Librairie-Imprimerie **Evangélique** du Togo, BP 378, Lomé Tel: 212967
Dir General: F K Agbobli; *Editorial:* W Y Aladji, J C van de Werk
Bookshop: Librairie Evangélique, 1 rue du Commerce, Lomé

Les **Nouvelles Editions** Africaines (NEA)*, BP 4862, Lomé (Located at: 239 blvd Circulaire, Lomé) Tel: 216761
Parent Company: Les Nouvelles Editions Africaines, Senegal (qv)
Associate Company: Les Nouvelles Editions Africaines, Ivory Coast (qv)

Book Club

Academic Book Club*, BP 3024, Lomé
Manager: R N Onuoha

Major Booksellers

Librarie du **Bon Pasteur***, rue du Commerce, BP 1164, Lomé Tel: 213279
Also at rue de l'Eglise Tel: 213628

Librairie **Evangélique**, 1 rue du Commerce, BP 378, Lomé Tel: 212967

Librairie/Editions Nouvelles Editions Africaines*, BP 4862, Lomé Tel: 6761

Nouvelle Librairie **Togolaise***, BP 2096, Lomé

Major Libraries

American Cultural Center Library*, BP 852, Lomé

Bibliothèque nationale*, BP 1002, Lomé Tel: 6367
Dir: Kanaoua Bekoutare

Centre culturel français, Bibliothèque*, BP 2090, Lomé Tel: 7232/3442
Librarian: Mme Lacrampe

Bibliothèque de l'**Ecole** normale supérieure*, Atakpamé

Bibliothèque de l'**Université du Benin***, BP 1515, Lomé Tel: 214843

Library Association

Association togolaise pour le Développement de la Documentation, des Bibliothèques, Archives et Musées*, c/o Bibliothèque de l'Université du Bénin, BP 1515, Lomé Tel: 214843
Secretary: E E Amah

Trinidad and Tobago

General Information

Language: English
Religion: Roman Catholic and Anglican
Population: 1 million
Literacy Rate (1970): 92.2%
Bank Hours: 0800-1230 Monday-Thursday; 0800-1200, 1500-1700 Friday
Shop Hours: 0800-1630 Monday-Friday; 0800-1200 Saturday
Currency: 100 cents = 1 Trinidad and Tobago dollar
Export/Import Information: No tariff on books; duty and postal fee on advertising matter. No import licence required for books; no obscene literature permitted. Exchange controls

Book Trade Organization

Booksellers' Association of Trinidad and Tobago, PO Box 531, 22 Abercromby St, Port of Spain
Secretary: Philip H Smith

Book Trade Reference Journals

Trinidad and Tobago and West Indian Bibliography, Central Library of Trinidad and Tobago, West Indian Reference Section, 20 Queens Park East, Port of Spain

Trinidad & Tobago National Bibliography, published jointly by Central Library of Trinidad and Tobago, PO Box 547, Port of Spain and the Library of the University of the West Indies, St Augustine

Publishers

Charran Educational Publishers*, 58 Western Main Rd, St James
Dirs: Reginald Charran, Betty Charran; *Sales:* David Deonarine
Subjects: Textbooks, Children's Books
Bookshop: Charran's Bookshop (1978) Ltd (qv under Major Booksellers)

Columbus Publishers Ltd, 64 Independence Sq, PO Box 140, Port of Spain Tel: 6253695

Dir: P A Hoadley
Subjects: General, Books for Students
1983: 20 titles *Founded:* 1969
ISBN Publisher's Prefix: 0-85643

Longman Caribbean (Trinidad) Ltd, 79 Belmont Circular Rd, Port of Spain
Dir: Percy Cezair
Associate Company: Longman Group Ltd, UK (qv)
Subject: General

Trinidad Publishing Co*, 22-26 St Vincent St, Port of Spain
Subjects: Law, Political Economy

Major Booksellers

Abercromby Bookshop, 22 Abercromby St, Port of Spain Tel: 6237752 Cable Add: Cassia, Port of Spain
Proprietor: Philip Smith

Asgar Ali Book Centre*, 90 Duke St, Port of Spain

Campus Corner Ltd, 72 Pembroke St, Port of Spain Tel: 6231678
Manager: Hilton S Young

Cassia House Bookshop, Corner Pembroke and Oxford Sts, Port of Spain Tel: 6235156 Cable Add: Cassia, Port of Spain
Manager: P Smith

Charran's Bookshop (1978) Ltd*, 58 Western Main Rd, St James
Manager: David Deonarine
Caribbean educational distributors, wholesale and retail

F W M Books Ltd, PO Box 6, Port of Spain Tel: 6226581
Manager: Teresa Daniel

Hobby Centre*, 86 Frederick St, Port of Spain

Jeffers Bookstore*, 28 Independence Square, Port of Spain

Victor **Manhin** Ltd, 49 High St, San Fernando

Muir **Marshall** Ltd*, 64a Independence Square, Port of Spain

Metropolitan Book Suppliers Ltd, 16 Plaza of Golden Doors, 6 Frederick St, Port of Spain
Manager: Terry Cassim

J C **Sealy**, The Book Shop, 22 Queen's Park West, Port of Spain

Stephens and Johnsons Book Department, PO Box 497, 8/10 Frederick St, Port of Spain Tel: 6234141/6232171 Cable Add: Stepjohn, Port of Spain Telex: 3485 Sterol Wg
Manager: Vishnu Maharaj
Owned by: Stephens & Ross Ltd (at above address)

Major Libraries

Carnegie Free Library*, 19-21 St James St, San Fernando Tel: 6523228
Librarian: Reynold Bassant

National Archives*, The Government Archivist, Whitehall, 29 Maraval Rd, Port of Spain

Central Library of **Trinidad and Tobago**, PO Box 547, Port of Spain Tel: 6234844/6236137 Cable Add: Centralib Trinidad
County-type Library Department of the Government
Dir: Mrs L C Hutchinson
Publication: Trinidad & Tobago National

Bibliography, published jointly with the library of the University of the West Indies, St Augustine

Trinidad Public Library*, Knox St, Port of Spain

University of the West Indies Library, St Augustine Tel: 6631364 Cable Add: Stomata, Port of Spain Telex: 303 Wg-Uwi
Librarian: Dr Alma Jordan
Publications: Bibliographic Series; Report on the Libraries (annual)

West Indian Reference Collection, Central Library of Trinidad and Tobago, 81 Belmont Circular Rd, Belmont Tel: 6241488/6243409

Library Association

Library Association of **Trinidad and Tobago***, c/o PO Box 1177, Port of Spain
Secretary: Lerlyn Marcelle
Publication: Blatt (Bulletin of the Library Association of Trinidad and Tobago) (annual)

Library Reference Journal

Blatt (Bulletin of the Library Association of Trinidad and Tobago), Library Association of Trinidad and Tobago, c/o PO Box 1177, Port of Spain

Tunisia

General Information

Language: Arabic. French is used in commerce
Religion: Muslim (Sunni)
Population: 6.08 million
Literacy Rate (1975): 38% (50.5% of urban population, 24.6% rural)
Bank Hours: Winter: 0800-1100, 1400-1600 Monday-Thursday; 0800-1100, 1300-1500 Friday; Summer: 0730-1100 Monday-Friday
Shop Hours: Generally 0800-1200, 1500-1800 Monday-Saturday
Currency: 1,000 millimes = 1 Tunisian dinar
Export/Import Information: Tunisia has preferential tariffs and EEC agreement but most books are dutied. Advertising matter free. Customs Formalities Tax per 1,000 kg or less gross weight, with minimum rate. Consumption Tax on duty and tax paid for books and for advertising matter. Advertising matter subject to Production Tax of percentage of duty and tax paid. Imports liberalized but in practice licences granted dependent on foreign exchange position
Copyright: UCC, Berne (see International section)

Book Trade Organization

Syndicat des Librairies de Tunisie*, 10 ave de France, Tunis
Tunisian Booksellers' Association

Book Trade Reference Books

Bibliographie nationale de la Tunisie (Tunisian National Bibliography), Bibliothèque nationale, 20 Souk-el-Attarine, Tunis

Répertoire des Unités de Documentation en Tunisia, Bibliothèque nationale, 20 Souk-el-Attarine, Tunis

Publishers

Editions **Bouslama***, 53 rue Nahas Pacha, Tunis 1 Tel: 243745243/100243323 Cable Add: Editions Bouslama
Man Dir, Rights & Permissions: Ali Bouslama; *Sales:* Hichem Bouslama; *Production:* Riadh Bouslama; *Publicity:* Hatem Bouslama
Branch Offs: 15 ave de France, 7 rue Amilkar, 15 bis rue Lamine El Abassi (all in Tunis)
Subject: History (French and Arabic languages)
Bookshops: 15 ave de France, 7 rue Amilkar (both in Tunis)
Founded: 1960

Ceres Productions, BP 56 Tunis Belvedere, Tunis Tel: 282033 LG Cable Add: Cerepro Telex: Ceresp 12363 TN
Man Dir: Mohamed Ben Smail; *Editorial:* Noureddine Ben Khader
Orders to: Demeter, 11A Montplaisir, Tunis Tel: 283579/893083
Subsidiary Company: Demeter (address as above)
Associate Company: Sud Editions (qv)

Dar Arabia Lil Kitab, 4 rue 7101 Al Manar II, BP 1104, Tunis Tel: 236600
Man Dir: Mohamed Ahmed En Neifer
Parent Company: Dar Arabia Lil Kitab, ave Ghouma Mahmoudi, BP 3185, Tripoli, Libya Tel: 47287
Subjects: General Literature, Biography, Bibliography, Linguistics, Pedagogy, Religion, History, Economics, Children's Books
1981-82: 84 titles *Founded:* 1975

Dar El Amal SA, d'Edition de Diffusion de Presse et de Publicité*, rue 2 Mars 1934, Tunis Tel: 264899 Telex: 12163 Tn
Man Dir: S Zoghlami; *Editorial, Production, Rights & Permissions:* N Tabka
Subjects: Economic and Social Politics
1981: 11 titles *1982:* 20 titles *Founded:* 1976

En-Najah*, Editions Hedi Ben Abdelgheni, 11 ave de France, Tunis Tel: 246886
Bookshops: At above address and 6 rue Ali Belhaouane, Sousse

Faculté des Lettres et Sciences Humaines de Tunis*, Service des Publications et Echanges, 94 blvd du 9 Avril 1938, BP 1128, Tunis Tel: 264417
Secretary: Ben Attia Taieb
Subjects: History, Africana, Philosophy, Paperbacks, Social Science, University Textbooks

Government Printer (Imprimerie Officielle de la République Tunisienne)*, Route de Rades Km2, Chouchet Rades, Tunis Tel: 295 124/014
Publication: Journal Officiel de la République Tunisienne

Maison Tunisienne d'Edition*, Rue de l'Oasis, El Menzah V, Tunis Tel: 235600/235873/235878 Cable Add: Matédition
Man Dir: Azouz Rebai
Subsidiary Company: Imprimerie de la MTE, Rue du 2 Mars 34, Tunis

Subjects: General Fiction & Non-fiction, Belles Lettres, Poetry, Biography, History, Africana, Philosophy, Reference, Religion, Juveniles, Paperbacks, Social Science, University & Secondary Textbooks, Law, Medicine, Literature, Sciences
Founded: 1966

Imprimerie/Librairie Al **Manar***, BP 121, Tunis Tel: 243224 Cable Add: Manar
Man Dir: T El M'Hamdi
Subsidiary Company: Librairie Al Manar, 60 ave Bab Djedid, Tunis
Subjects: History, Africana, Religion, Arabic Language, Islam

Société nationale d'Edition et de Diffusion*, 5 ave de Carthage, BP 440, Tunis Tel: 255000 Cable Add: Studiffusion
Bookshop: At above address

Sud Editions, 1 rue Clovis, Tunis Tel: 287718 Telex: 12363 TN
Man Dir: Ben Smaïl; *Sales:* Demeter (see below)
Orders to: Demeter, 11 ave Montplaisir, Tunis
Associate Company: Ceres Productions (qv)
Subjects: Art, Art History
Founded: 1976
ISBN Publisher's Prefix: 2-86444

Major Booksellers

La **Caravelle** Librairie*, 8 ave H Bourguiba, Sfex

Librairie **En-Najah***, Siège Social, 11 ave de France, Tunis Tel: 246886
Branch: 6 rue Ali Belhaouane, Sousse Tel: 0321282

Librairie Al **Manar***, 60 ave Bab Djedid, BP 121, Tunis Tel: 243224

Société Librairie nouvelle*, 15 ave de France, Bizerte

Société nationale d'Edition et de Diffusion*, 5 ave de Carthage, BP 440, Tunis Tel: 255000

Major Libraries

Archives nationales*, Présedence de la République, Pl du Gouvernment, Tunis

Bibliothèque nationale*, 20 Souk-el-Attarine, BP 42, Tunis Tel: 245338
Librarian: M H Ben Azzouna
Publications: Bibliographie nationale: Publications officielles et non officielles; Informations bibliographiques; Fahras al-Makhtūtât (le catalogue des manuscrits); Répertoire des Unités de Documentation en Tunisie; Bibliographie Nationale: Publications en série

British Council Library*, c/o British Embassy, 5 pl de la Victoire, Tunis Tel: 245100/259053

Ecole nationale d'Administration Bibliothèque*, 24 ave Docteur Calmette, Mutuelleville, Tunis 1060 Tel: 288300/288167/288435 Telex: Ena 13198
Librarian: Mansour Ghozzi
Publications: Servir (semi-annual)

Bibliothèque de la **Faculté de Droit** et des Sciences Politiques et Economiques de Tunis, Campus Universitaire, Belvédère, Tunis Tel: 262315
Chief Librarian: Néji Baccouche
Publications: Liste des Thèses et Mémoires déposés à la Faculté (half-yearly); *Liste des Nouvelles Acquisitions* (quarterly); *Liste des Publications du CERP de la Faculté*

Bibliothèque de la **Faculté des Lettres** et Sciences Humaines, 94 blvd du 9 Avril 1938, Tunis Tel: 260932
Chief Librarian: M Abdeljaoued

Bibliothèque de la **Faculté des Sciences** de Tunis*, Campus Universitaire El Menzeh, Tunis Tel: 264577

Bibliothèque de l'**Institut** supérieur d'Education et de Formation continue, 43 rue de la Liberté, Le Bardo Tel: 261092
Librarian: Mohamed Abdeljaoued

Direction de la **Lecture Publique**, 10 rue de Russie, Tunis Tel: 240079
Librarian: Béchir Elfani
Branches throughout the country

Library Association

Association tunisienne de Documentalistes, Bibliothécaires et Archivistes, 43 rue de la Liberté, Le Bardo
Tunisian Association of Record-Keepers, Librarians and Archivists
President: Mohamed Abdeljaoued
Publication: Bulletin ATD (4 a year)

Library Reference Journal

Bulletin, Association tunisienne des Documentalistes, Bibliothécaires et Archivistes, 43 rue de la Liberté, le Bardo

Literary Associations and Societies

Institut des Belles Lettres arabes, 12 rue Jamâa el Haoua, 1008 Tunis Bab Menara Tel: 260133
Institute of Arab Belles Lettres
Publication: Revue IBLA (biannual study of cultural problems in the Arab-Moslem world)

Union des Ecrivains tunisiens, 20 ave de Paris, Tunis Tel: 257591
Tunisian Writers' Union

Turkey

General Information

Language: Turkish (English spoken by many)
Religion: Predominantly Muslim
Population: 43.2 million
Literacy Rate (1975): 60.3%
Bank Hours: 0830-1200, 1330-1800 Monday-Friday
Shop Hours: 0900-1200, 1330-1900 Monday-Saturday
Currency: 100 kurus = 1 Turkish lira (or pound)
Export/Import Information: No tariffs on books and advertising matter. Advertising matter subject to Expenditure Tax. Books on liberalized list, so import licences are granted freely, but textbooks must be imported with permission of Ministry of Education. Exchange controls
Copyright: Berne, Florence (see International section)

Book Trade Organization

Türk Editörler Dernegi, Ankara Cad 60, Istanbul
Turkish Publishers' Association

Book Trade Reference Journal

Journal

Turkiye Bibliyografyasi (Turkish National Bibliography), National Library, Bibliographical Institute, Kumrular Sokak 3, Kizilay

Publishers

A B C Yayinevi*, PO Box 539, Karaköy, Istanbul (Located at: Tünel Meydanı, Seferoğlu Han, Beyoğlu, Istanbul) Tel: 444242/442581 Cable Add: Abckit, Istanbul
Man Dir: Artun Altıparmak; *Editorial:* Önder Renkliyıldırım; *Sales:* K Karakush; *Production:* Hasan Günaydın; *Publicity:* Ferit Gürsu; *Rights & Permissions:* Necip Inselel
Subjects: Foreign Language Courses, Dictionaries, Reference, Electronics
Bookshop: ABC Kitabevi (at above address)
1981: approx 5 titles *Founded:* 1977

Arkın Kitabevi, Ankara Cad 60, Istanbul Tel: 750734/750600/1 Cable Add: Birarkinlar Istanbul
Man Dir, Rights & Permissions: Ramazan Gökalp Arkın;
Branch Offs: Arkın Dagitim Ltd, Sti, Ankara Cad 60, Istanbul; Arkın Ofset Basimevi, Merter Sitesi Buberoğlu Sokak No 5, Bayrampasa, Istanbul
Subjects: Juveniles, Maps, Educational Materials, Reference, General Science, Secondary & Primary Textbooks
Bookshop: Arkın Kitabevi, Ankara Cad 60, Istanbul
Founded: 1957

Artel Publishing & Commercial Organization Co Ltd*, Halaskârgazi Cad 214/4, Osmanbey, Istanbul Tel: 486040
Man Dir: Engin Serozan
Subjects: Reference, High-priced Paperbacks, Educational Materials

Aydinlik Yayınları*, Nuruosmaniye Caddesi 34/204, Cagaloglu, Istanbul
Man Dir, Rights & Permissions: Mrs Leyla Yurdakul; *Editorial:* Dogan Yurdakul; *Sales:* Hüseyin Göçer; *Production:* Alp Hamuroglu; *Publicity:* Leyla and Dogan Yurdakul
Parent Company: Aydınlık Dergisi
Subjects: Marxism, Turkey and World Affairs
Founded: 1974

Dergâh Yayinlari AS, see Kara

Dogan Kardes Matbaacilik SAS*, Türbedar Sok 22, Istanbul
Subjects: Juveniles, Educational Materials, Weekly Magazines

Elif Kitabevi, Sahaflar Çarsisi 4, Beyazit, Istanbul Tel: 222096
Man Dir: Arslan Kaynardag; *Sales Dir:* Gani Yener
Subjects: Belles Lettres, Poetry, History, Music, Art, Philosophy, Social Science
Bookshop: Sahaflar Çarsisi 4, Beyazit, Istanbul
Founded: 1957
Miscellaneous: Firm distributes Turkish publications. Associated imprints include Elif Yayinlari

Gelisim Publishing, Levent, Istanbul Tel: 692420/682208 Cable Add: Gelbay Telex: 22270 Geby Tr
Chairman and Man Dir: Ercan Arikli
Associate Company: Süreli Yayınlar AS (Periodical Press Inc), Levent, Istanbul Tel: 692420
Subjects: Encyclopaedias, Reference, Non-fiction, Magazines

Hürriyet Yayinlari (Hür Yayin)*, Cemal Nadir Sokak 7-Cagaloglu, 1183 Istanbul Tel: 222038, 271502 Telex: 22276 HA Tr, 22277 HA Tr
Dir: Ali Z Oraloglu
Parent Company: Hürriyet Holding
Subjects: Fiction, History, Classics, Poetry, TV Series, Yearbooks, General Reference

Inkilâp Ve Aka Kitabevleri, Ankara Cad 95, Istanbul Tel: 222851
Man Dir: Nazar Fikri; *Sales Manager:* Aka Eren
Subjects: General Fiction & Non-fiction, Cartography, Politics, Religion, Literature, History, Juveniles, Technical, Domestic, Maps, Atlases

Ismail **Kara**/Dergâh Yayinlari AS Müessese Müdürü*, PO Box 1240, Sirkeci, Istanbul (Located at: Nuruosmaniye Cad 3/1 Cagaloglu, Istanbul) Tel: 265370
Man Dir: Ezel Erverdi; *Editorial:* Mustafa Kutlu; *Sales:* Fatih Gokdag; *Production:* Ahmet Debbagoglu; *Publicity:* Mustafa Modanlioglu
Subsidiary Companies: Dergâh kitapcilk AS, Ankara Cad 85 Cagaloglu, Istanbul; Emek matbaacilik ve ilancilik Ltd sti; Derya Dagitim AS, Babiali Cad 52 Cagaloglu, Istanbul
Subjects: Encyclopaedias, Islamic Classics, History, Books of 'Hareket', Modern Turkish Philosophy, Modern Turkish Policy, Culture, Islamic Thought, Western Thought, Education, Turkish Literature
Book Clubs: Dergâh kitabevi, Istanbul; Dergâh kitabevi, Erzurum
Bookshops: Dergâh kitabevi, Istanbul; Dergâh kitabevi, Erzurum
Founded: 1977

Karacan Yayınları AS*, Basın Sarayı, Cagaloglu, Istanbul Tel: 270034 Cable Add: Karacan Yayınları Cagaloglu
Man Dir: Ülkü Tamer; *Editorial:* Ulvi Okar; *Production:* Özhan Küçüktopuzlu; *Publicity:* Ali Alparslan
Parent Company: Karacan Holding AS
Affiliate Company: Filmel AS (TV rights for films)
Subjects: General Non-fiction, Fiction, History, Photography, Graphic Arts, Cinema
Bookshop: Basın Sarayi, Cagaloglu, Istanbul
Founded: 1970

Altin **Kitaplar** Publishing Co*, Altin Kitaplar, Cagaloglu, Istanbul Tel: 224045/268012
Publisher: Fethi Ul; *Man Dir:* Dr Turhan Bozkurt; *Editorial:* Mursit Ul; *Production:* Ugur Gergin; *Publicity:* Ferhan Filiztekin
Associate Companies: Ders Kitaplari SA, Babiali Cad 39, Istanbul; Bozkurt Publishing Co, Ticarethane Sokak Sultanahmet, Istanbul; Ulun Publishing Company, Babiali Cad 39, Istanbul
Subjects: Fiction, Non-fiction, Memoirs, Textbooks, Children's Books, Classics, History, Crime, Holy Koran
Bookshop: Altin Kitaplar, Cagaloglu, Istanbul
Founded: 1959

Redhouse Press*, PK 142, Istanbul
Dir: William Edmonds; *Editors:* Ann Edmonds, Richard Blakney, James Sowerwine

Subjects: Turkish-English Dictionaries, Guidebooks in English and French, Cookery (in English and Turkish), General, Children's
Bookshop: Redhouse Kitabevi, Rizapasa Yokusu 48, Sultanhaman, Istanbul
1981: 10 titles

Remzi Kitabevi*, Selvilimescit Sokak No 8, Cagaloglu, Istanbul Tel: 220583/227248
Cable Add: Remzi Kitabevi Istanbul
Man Dir: Erol Erduran
Subsidiary Company: Evrim Matbaacılık Ltd, Sirketi Cagaloglu, Istanbul
Subjects: General Fiction, Biography, History, Philosophy, Reference, Low-priced Paperbacks, Medicine, Psychology, General & Social Science, Secondary & Primary Textbooks, Educational Books, Children's Encyclopaedias
Bookshop: Ankara Cad 93, Istanbul
1981: 32 titles *Founded:* 1931

Sander Yayınları*, Kıragı Sok 78, Osmanbey, Istanbul Tel: 408475/483209
Man Dir, Production, Rights & Permissions: Necdet Sander; *Editorial:* Nuran Ücok; *Sales:* Fikret Sander; *Publicity:* Allegra Mitrani
Parent Company: Sander Kitabevi
Subjects: Literature, Fiction, Poetry, Essays, Political History, Sport, Education, Tourist Guides (of Turkey)
Bookshops: Sander Kitabevi, Halaskargazi Cad 275-277, Osmanbey, Istanbul; Istiklal Cad 178, Beyoğlu, Istanbul

Literary Agents

Hür Yayin ve Ticaret*, Cemai Nadir Sokak 7, Cagaloglu, Istanbul Tel: 222038/262000
Cable Add: PK 1183 Istanbul

Nurcihan **Kesim** Literary Agency, PO Box 868, Sirkeci, Istanbul Tel: 285800/285394
Telex: 22418 Nek Tr
Also: Nuruosmaniye Caddesi No 8, Cagaloglu, Istanbul
Man Dir: Nurcihan Kesim; *Sales:* Ertugrul Kesim; *Rights & Permissions:* Oya Alpar
Specialization: Fiction, Non-fiction, Art Works, Serials, Encyclopaedias

O N K Copyright Agency, Ankara Cad 40, PO Box 983, Istanbul Tel: 267074/275345
Cable Add: Copyright Istanbul Telex: 22627 Istg Tr box/8
Dir: Osman N Karaca
Specialization: Books, Serials, Plays, TV Programmes

Book Clubs

Dergâh kitabevi*, PO Box 1240, Sirkeci, Istanbul
Owned by: Ismail Kara (qv)

Dergâh kitabevi*, Erzurum
Owned by: Ismail Kara (qv)

Major Booksellers

A B C Kitabevi*, Tünel Meydanı 1, Beyoğlu, Istanbul
Owned by: ABC Yayinevi

Bilgi Yayinevi*, Tuna Cad, Kizilay, Ankara

Gençlik Kitabevi*, Muvakkithane Cad, 35 Kadiköy, Istanbul Tel: 363017

Hakki Biget*, Baskeny Yayinevi, Izmir Cad 55/22, Ankara

Haset Kitabevi AS, Istiklal cad 469, Beyoğlu, Istanbul Tel: 448460/449471
Telex: 24446 Hst Tr
Manager: Kenan Eren

Branches at Cumhuriyet Bulvari 143/G, Izmir; Ziya Gökalp cad 14/E, Yenisehir, Ankara
Formerly Hachette Kitabevi (Librairie Hachette-Succursale de la Turquie)

Nejat Yalki Kitabevi*, Valikonagi Cad, Nisantasi, Istanbul

Orhan Özsisman*, Datiç AS, 452 Sokak, No 5, Konak, Izmir

Redhouse Kitabevi*, Rizapasa Yokusu 48, Sultanhamam, Istanbul Tel: 223905

Sander Kitabevi, Necdet Sander, Halaskârgazi Cad 275-277, Osmanbey, Istanbul Tel: 483209/463075; Istiklal Cad 178, Beyoğlu, Istanbul Tel: 440134
Manager: Necdet Sander

Major Libraries

Ankara University Library*, Ankara

The **Beyazit** State Library, Imaret Sokak No 18, Beyazit, Istanbul Tel: 223167
Librarian: Hasan Duman

Bogaziçi University Library (formerly Robert College Library)*, Bebek, PK 2, Istanbul Tel: 653400
Acting Librarian: Nurten Gakir

Library of the **Grand National Assembly***, Palais de la Grande Assemblée Nationale, Ankara Tel: 251352
Librarian: Hilmi Celik

Il **Halk Kütüphanesi***, Balikesir
Provincial Public Library, formerly the Vatan Library

Istanbul Üniversitesi Merkez Kütüphanesi*, Besim Ömer Pasa Cad 15, Beyazit, Istanbul Tel: 222180
Istanbul University Central Library

Izmir General Library*, Millî Kütuphane Cad 39, Izmir

Middle East Technical University Library*, Ankara Tel: 237100/232780 Telex: 42761
Librarian: Dr O Tekia Aybas

Millet Library*, Fatih, Istanbul

Millî Kütüphane*, Kumrular Sokak 3, Kızılay, Ankara
National Library
Dir: Dr Müjgan Cunbur
Publications include: Turkiye Bibliyografyasi

Library of the **Mineral Research and Exploration Institute***, Ismet Inönü Bulvari, Ankara Tel: 234255
Librarian: Sevim Özertan;
Publication: Selected list of New Publications in *MTA News* (bi-annual)

Selimiye Library*, Edirne

Süleymaniye Kütüphanesi Müdürlüğü, Suleymaniye Mahallesi, Ayse Kadin Sokak 30; 35, Beyazit-Istanbul Tel: 206460
Library of the Süleymaniye
Librarian: Muammer Ülker
Publications: Istanbul Kütüphanelerine göre Birgili Mehmet Efendi Bibliyografyası; Istanbul Kütüphanelerine göre Ebussuud Bibliyografyası; Istanbul Kütüphanelerine göre Âli Bibliyografyası; Türkiye Yazmaları Toplu Kataloğu (TÜYATOK); Süleymaniye Kütüphanesi Farsça Yazmalar Indeks Kataloğu; Ibni Sina Kataloğu da yayımlanmak üzere hazırdır

Technical University Library*, Istanbul Teknik Üniversitesi, Merkez Kütüphane Mudürlöğü, Gümüssuyu Cad 87, Beyoğlu

Türdok (Turkish Scientific and Technical Documentation Centre), Atatürk Bulvari 221, Kavaklidere, Ankara Tel: 262770 Cable Add: Tübitak, Ankara Telex: 43186 Btak Tr
Parent Organization: The Scientific and Technical Research Council of Turkey (at above address)

Vatan Library, see Il Halk Kütüphanesi

Library Association

Türk Kütuphaneciler Dernegi, Elgün Sokağı 8/12, PK 175, Yenisehir, Ankara Tel: 301325
Turkish Librarians' Association
Secretary: Ms Benal Acır
Publication: Bülten (4 a year)

Library Reference Journal

Bülten (Bulletin), Turkish Librarians' Association, Elgün Sokağı 8/12, PK 175, Yenisehir, Ankara

Literary Associations and Societies

P E N Yazarlar Dernegi, Operatör Raifbey Sok 48/6, Sisli, Istanbul
PEN — Turkish Centre
President: Prof Tahsin Yücel

Turkish Language Society*, Ataturk Bulvari 221, Ankara

Literary Periodicals

Orta Dogu (Middle East), Celal Tevfik Karasapan, Tunali Hilmi Cad 121-5, Kavaklidere, Ankara

Varlik (Existence), Varlik Yayinevi, Cagaloglu Yokusu, Ankara Cad, Istanbul

Literary Prizes

Award for Literature and Scientific Publications*
To encourage the use of the Turkish language. Five prizes of 40,000 Turkish liras each for literature and one prize of 40,000 liras for scientific publication. Awarded annually. Enquiries to Turkish Language Society, Ataturk Bulvari 221, Ankara

Sait Faik Prize*
For the best short story. 5,000 Turkish liras. Awarded annually. Enquiries to Darussafaka Association, Halaskargazl Cad 231, Istanbul

Orhan Kemal Award*
To encourage publication of novels which reflect the views of Orhan Kemal. Awarded annually. Enquiries to Orhan Kemal Family and Associates, c/o Turkish Language Society, Ataturk Bulvari 221, Ankara

Fikret Madarali Prize*
For the best novel. Three prizes of 10,000, 5,000 and 3,000 Turkish liras. Awarded annually. Enquiries to Fikret Madarali Family and Associates, c/o Turkish Language Society, Ataturk Bulvari 221, Ankara

Uganda

General Information

Language: English is official language. Swahili is widely spoken in commercial centres
Religion: About 30% Christian, 5% Muslim; rest follow traditional beliefs
Population: 12.8 million
Literacy Rate (1959 African Population): 20%
Bank Hours: 0830-1230 Monday-Friday; 0800-1100 Saturday
Shop Hours: 0800-1230, 1400-1630 or longer Monday-Friday; 0800-1230 Saturday
Currency: 100 cents = 1 Uganda shilling
Export/Import Information: No tariff on books or advertising matter but subject to sales tax. Import licence and exchange controls (granted automatically with import license)

Book Trade Reference Journal

The Uganda Journal, PO Box 4980, Mapala (published by the Uganda Society and includes an annual bibliography of books published in or about Uganda)

Publishers

Centenary Publishing House Ltd+, PO Box 2776, Kampala Tel: 41599
Man Dir, Editorial, Production, Rights & Permissions: Rev Sam Kakiza; *Sales, Publicity:* V Kagga-Senyonga
Parent Organization: Church of Uganda, PO Box 14123, Kampala
Subjects: Religious, Educational, Children's, General
1981: 5 titles *1982:* 6 titles *Founded:* 1977

Government Printer, PO Box 33, Entebbe Cable Add: Printer Entebbe Telex: 61336 Print Uga

Longman Uganda Ltd*, PO Box 3409, Kampala Tel: 42940 Cable Add: Longman Kampala
Manager: M K L Mutyaba
Associate Company: Longman Group Ltd, UK (qv)
Subjects: Biography, History, Africana, Juveniles, Books in Luganda & other Ugandan Languages, General Science, Secondary & Primary Textbooks
Founded: 1965

Saint Paul Publications, PO Box 4392, Kampala Tel: 56346
Dir: Teresa Marcazzan; *Editor:* Joseph Bragotti
Subjects: Religious and Moral Formation
Bookshop: St Paul Book Centre (at above address)
1981-82: 11 titles *Founded:* 1979

Uganda Publishing House, MOF House, 37-39 Fifth St, Industrial Area, PO Box 2923, Kampala Tel: 59601/42362/34024
Man Dir: Laban O Erapu
Parent Company: Milton Obote Foundation, PO Box 4615, Kampala
Associate Company: Uganda School Supply Ltd, PO Box 20180, Kampala
Subjects: General Fiction & Non-fiction, Belles Lettres, Poetry, Biography, History, Africana, Reference, Juveniles, General & Social Science, Secondary & Primary Textbooks
Founded: 1966

Book Club

Academic Book Club*, PO Box 20171, Lugogo, Kampala
Manager: C G Ryumugabe

Major Booksellers

E S A Bookshop*, PO Box 2515, Kampala

Makerere University Bookshop*, PO Box 7062, Kampala

Saint Paul Book Centre, PO Box 4392, Kampala Tel: 56346

Uganda Bookshop*, Colville St, PO Box 7145, Kampala Tel: 43756-8 Cable Add: Bookshop

Major Libraries

Albert **Cook** Library, Makerere University, Makarere Medical School, PO Box 7072, Kampala Tel: 58731 Cable Add: Makunika Kampala
Medical Librarian: Leonard Ssennyonjo
Publications: East African Medical Bibliography (bi-monthly); *Bulletin and Accession List* (monthly) *Annual Report*

United States Information Service Library, PO Box 7186, Kampala Tel: 33231

Kabarole Public Library*, PO Box 28, Fort Portal Tel: 2255
Librarian: B N Bagenda

Makerere Institute of Social Research Library, PO Box 16022, Kampala Tel: 54582
Librarian: Mr Kawesa

Makerere University Library*, PO Box 16002, Kampala Tel: 31041/2
Librarian: T K Lwanga
Publication: Library Bulletin (quarterly)

National Institute of Education Library*, Makerere University, PO Box 7062, Kampala
Publication: Journal

Public Libraries Board, Buganda Rd, PO Box 4262, Kampala Tel: 54661 Cable Add: Library, Kampala
Dir: P K Birungi
Publications: Annual Report, Accessions List (quarterly), *Newsletter* (twice a year) and occasional publications

Uganda Technical College Library, PO Box 1991, Kampala Tel: 65211 ext 37 Cable Add: Technical
Chief Librarian: R Nganwa

Library Associations

Uganda Library Association*, PO Box 5894, Kampala Tel: 59581-3/33633
Executive Secretary: J N Kiyimba
Publication: Uganda Libraries

Uganda Schools Library Association*, PO Box 7014, Kampala
Executive Secretary: J W Nabembezi
Publication: Newsletter (quarterly)

Uganda Special Library Association*, c/o PO Box 9, Entebbe
Secretary: M D'Mello

Library Reference Journals

Journal of Ugandan Libraries (biannual), East African School of Librarianship, Makerere University, PO Box 7062, Kampala

Newsletter, Uganda Library Association, PO Box 7014, Kampala

Uganda Libraries, Uganda Library Association, PO Box 5894, Kampala

Literary Periodical

Dhana, East African Literature Bureau, PO Box 1317, Kampala (or PO Box 30022, Nairobi) (biannual literary magazine published on behalf of the Department of Literature at Makerere University)

Union of Soviet Socialist Republics

General Information

Language: Russian is the official language. Large number of other languages spoken including Ukrainian, Byelorussian, several Turkic languages, Armenian, Georgian, Lithuanian and Moldavian. English is the commonest foreign language known
Religion: About 25% Christian (mainly Russian Orthodox), 12% Muslim (in the southwest), 2 million Jewish, ½ million Buddhist; rest atheist
Population: 262 million
Literacy Rate (1970): 99.7% of population aged 9 to 49
Bank Hours: 0900-1600 Monday-Friday
Shop Hours: 0800-1900 Monday; 0800-2100 Tuesday-Saturday
Currency: 100 kopeks = 1 rouble
Export/Import Information: Foreign trade is state monopoly and duties and licences only the concern of the corporation Mezhdunarodnaya Kniga, Smolenskaya Sennaya 32-34, Moscow G-200. The State Bank of USSR or its subsidiary, USSR Bank for Foreign Trade, is only organization handling foreign currency matters
Copyright: UCC (see International section)

Book Trade Organizations

Gosudarstvenny komitet SSSR po delam izdatelstv, poligrafii i knizhnoi torgovli*, Petrovka ul 26, Moscow K-51
The USSR State Committee for Publishing, Printing and the Book Trade
Chairman: B I Stukalin

Publishing Council of the Academy of Sciences of the USSR*, Leninsky prospekt 13, Moscow

Standard Book Numbering Agency*, Bibliografičeskij Institut SSSR, Kremlevskaja nab 1-9, 119816 Moscow G-19
ISBN Administrator: Ju I Fartunin

UNION OF SOVIET SOCIALIST REPUBLICS 387

USSR Writers' Union*, Vorovskogo ul 52, Moscow
First Secretary of the Board: Georgy Markov
Publications: Voprosy Literatury (jointly with the Institute of World Literature of the USSR Academy of Sciences); *Novy Mir; Znamya; Druzhba Narodov; Voprosy Literatury; Yunost; Literaturnoye Obozreniye; Literaturnaya Utchyoba; Detskaya Literatura; Shagi* (anthology); *Sovetskaya Literatura* (in foreign languages); *Proizvedeniya i Mneniya* (in French); *Teatr; Sovetskaya Rodina; Zvezda; Kostyor; Literaturnaya Gazeta*

Vsesoyuznaya Knichnaya Palata*, Kremlevskaya naberezhnaya 1-9, Moscow
All-Soviet Book Chamber
Publications: Knizhnava Letopis'
All books and publications are registered and described

Book Trade Reference Books and Journals

Books

Knizhnaya Moskva: Putevoditel'-Spravochnik (Books in Mosco A Guide and Handbook), 'Reklama', Moscow

Spravochnik Normativnykh Materialov dlya Rabotnikov Knizhnoi Torgovli (Handbook of Rules and Precedents for Book Trade Workers), Izdatelstvo 'Kniga', Nezhdanovoi pereulok 8-10, Moscow K-9

Journals

Ezhegodnik Knigi SSSR (USSR National Bibliography), Izdatelstvo 'Kniga', Nezhdanovoi pereulok 8-10, Moscow K-9

Index to Forthcoming Russian Books; English translation of bibliographic entries from *Novye Knigi,* Scientific Information Consultants Ltd, 661 Finchley Rd, London W2 2HN, UK

Knizhnaya Letopis' (Book Chronicle) (weekly bulletin), All-Soviet Book Chamber, Kremlevskaya naberezhnaya 1-9, Moscow

Knizhnaya Letopis' — Dopolnitel'nyi Vypusk; monthly supplement to *Knizhnaya Letopis',* quoting 'restricted' publications, small imprints, 'not-for-sale' or institutional items etc, All-Soviet Book Chamber, Kremlevskaya naberezhnaya 1-9, Moscow

Knizhnaya Torgovlya (Book Trade), Mezhdunarodnaya Kniga, Smolenskaya Sennaya pl 32-34, Moscow G-200

Knizhnoe Obozrenie (Book Reviews), USSR Library Council, The Lenin State Library of the USSR, Prospect Kalinina 3, Moscow 101 000

Letopis' Pechati BSSR (Byelorussian National Bibliography), Godudarstvennaya Biblioteka BSSR im V I Lenina, Knizhnaya Palata BSSR, Minsk

Letopis' Periodicheskikh i Prodolzhaiushchikhsya Izdanii (Periodicals and Continuations), Mezhdunarodnaya Kniga, Smolenskaya Sennaya pl 32-34, Moscow G-200

Novye Knigi (New Books); announcements of forthcoming books, Mezhdunarodnaya Kniga, Smolenskaya Sennaya pl 32-34, Moscow G-200

Sakmatsvilo Literaturis Moambe (Bulletin of Children's Literature), Izdatelstvo Nakaduli, Mardzhanishvili ul 5, Tbilisi 380029

Sovetskaya Bibliografia (Soviet Bibliography), USSR Library Council, The Lenin State Library of the USSR, Prospect Kalinina 3, Moscow 101 000

Ukrainska Knyha (Ukrainian Book) (text in Ukrainian), Association of Book Lovers, Kyiv Publishing, 4800 North 12th St, Philadelphia, PA 19141, USA

Publishers

A P N, see Novosti

Atomizdat*, Zhdanoval 5, 103031 Moscow K-31 Tel: 2942228/2959993
Publishing House for Atomic Literature
Dir: V A Kulyamin
Subjects: Nuclear Science and Technology (peaceful use of nuclear energy)
Founded: 1963

Aurora Art Publishers*, Nevsky prospekt 7/9, 191065 Leningrad Tel: 2151924 Cable Add: Exportizdat Aurora Leningrad Telex: 121562
President, Rights & Permissions: Boris Pidemsky; *Editor-in-Chief:* Alla Slizhevskaya; *Production:* Faina Timofeyeva
Subject: Art
Founded: 1969
Miscellaneous: Publishes in foreign languages

Detskaya Entsiklopediya*, Bakuninskaja ul 55, Moscow 107042 Tel: 2695276
Children's Encyclopaedia
Subjects: Literature, Poetry, Historical & Biographical Novels, Science Fiction
Founded: 1933

Izdatelstvo **Detskaya Literatura***, Malyi Cherkaskii pereulok 1, Moscow
Children's Literature Publishing House
Dir: A A Vinogradov
Subject: Juveniles

Znak Pochyota Order **Dosaaf** Publishing House*, Novo-Ryazanskaya 26, Moscow 107066 Tel: 2676545
Voluntary Society for the Promotion of the Army, Air Force and Navy
Subject: Military
Founded: 1951

Izdatelstvo '**Ekonomika**'*, Berezhkovskaya naberezhnaya 6, Moscow 121864 Tel: 2404877
Economics Publishing House
Dir: I D Trotsenko
Subjects: Economics, Management, Commerce, Industry, Agriculture, Catering, Textbooks
Founded: 1963

Izdatelstvo **Energoizdat***, Shluzovaya naberezhnaya 10, Moscow 113114
Energy Publishing House
Dir: S P Rozanov; *Editor-in-Chief:* V Sidorov
Subjects: Scientific and technical literature on Power Engineering, Thermal, Hydro and Electrical Engineering, Automatic and Computer Science, Nuclear Power Engineering/Safety/Physics
Founded: 1931

Izdatelstvo **Finansy**, now Finansy i Statistika Publishing House USSR (qv)

Finansy i Statistika Publishing House USSR*, Chernyshevskogo ul 7, Moscow 101000 Tel: 2234822
Finance and Statistics Publishing House
Dir: V I Vinogradov
Subjects: Banking, Taxation, Accounts, Statistics, Computers, Demography
Founded: 1924

Izdatelstvo '**Fizkultura i Sport**'*, Kalyaevskaya ul 27, Moscow 101421 Tel: 2582690
Physical Culture & Sport Publishing House
Dir: Vasili A Zhiltsov
Subjects: Physical Culture, Sport
Founded: 1923

Gidrometeorizdat*, 2 Vasilyevsky Ostrov 23, Leningrad 199053 Tel: 2271531
Subjects: Meteorology, Hydrology, Atmosphere, Geology, Oceanology
Founded: 1936

Izdatelstvo **Iskusstvo***, Tsvetnov bul'var' 25, Moscow K-51 Tel: 2940775
Publishing House for Art Literature
Dir: E Y Savostianov
Branch Off: Leningrad
Subjects: Fine Arts, Music, Theatre
Founded: 1938 (as Izogiz & Iskusstvo)

Izvestiya Publishing House*, Pushkinskaya pl 5, Moscow K-6
Dir: Y I Balanenko
Subjects: Izvestiya, Official Publications of USSR and RSFSR Supreme Soviets

Izdatelstvo '**Khimiya**'*, Strominka ul 23, Block 4, Moscow B-76 Tel: 2682976
Publishing House for Chemistry
Dir: Ya S Mashkevich
Subject: Chemistry
Founded: 1963

Izdatelstvo '**Khudozhestvennaya Literatura**'*, Novo-Basmannaya ul 19, Moscow B-66 Tel: 2618865
Publishing House for Fiction & Poetry
Dir: V S Somov
Subjects: Fiction, Literature
Founded: 1930 (as The State Publishers of Fiction)

Izdatelstvo '**Kniga**'*, Nezhdanovoi ul 8-10, Moscow K-9 Tel: 2298269
Dir: V F Kravchenko
Subjects: Bibliography, Printing, Publishing, Graphic Arts, Book Trade, Bibliology, Bibliophilism, Librarianship, Miniature and Facsimile Editions
1981: 122 titles *Founded:* 1963

Izdatelstvo '**Kolos**'*, Sadovaya-Spasskaya ul 18, Moscow I-139 Tel: 2955824
Dir: I P Khramkov
Subjects: Agriculture, Veterinary Science
Founded: 1963

Izdatelstvo '**Legkaya i Pishchevaya Promyshlennost**'*, I Kadashevskii pereulok 12, Moscow 113035 Tel: 2330848
Food and Light Industry Publishing House
Dir: N N Zazin; *Editor-in-Chief:* T G Gromova
Subjects: Light Industries (textiles, leather, glass), Food Industry, Fishing Industry
Founded: 1932

Izdatelstvo '**Lenizdat**'*, Fontanka 59, Leningrad D-23 Tel: 2155821
Leningrad Publishing House
Subjects: Politics, Technical, Agriculture, Fiction, Juveniles, Art, Popular Science, Folklore
Founded: 1963

Izdatelstvo '**Lesnaya Promyshlennost**'*, Kirova ul 40a, Moscow 101000 Tel: 2287860
Forest Industry Publishing House
Dir: B S Oreshkin
Subjects: Forestry, Wood & Paper Products, Logging, Woodworking, Dendrochemistry, Nature Conservation
Founded: 1963

Izdatelstvo '**Malysh**'*, Butyrskii val 68, Moscow A-55 Tel: 2512242
Children's World Publishing House
Dir: I N Boronetsky
Subject: Pre-school Publications

UNION OF SOVIET SOCIALIST REPUBLICS

Izdatelstvo **'Mashinostroenie'***, Stromynsky pereulok 4, Moscow 1070768 Tel: 2683858
Publishing House for Mechanical Engineering
Dir: A V Astakhov
Subject: Mechanical Engineering
Founded: 1931

Izdatelstvo **'Meditsina'***, Petroverigskii pereulok 6-8, Moscow K-142 Tel: 2948785
Publishing House for Medicine
Dir: V I Maevsky
Subjects: Medicine, Health, Sciences
Founded: 1918

Izdatelstvo **'Metallurgiya'***, 2-oi Obydenskii pereulok 14, Moscow G-34, 119034 Tel: 2025532
Publishing House for Metallurgy
Dir: M A Kovalevskiy
Subject: Metallurgy
Founded: 1939

Izdatelstvo **'Mezhdunarodnye Otnosheniya'***, Kuznetskii most 24, 103031 Moscow K-31 Tel: 2945796
International Relations Publishing House
Dir: S P Emelyanikov
Subjects: International Information, Translations for UN Textbooks

Leidykla **'Mintis'***, Sierakausko 15, Vilnius Tel: 632943
Dir: Algimantas Garliauskas
Subjects: Politics, Law, Philosophy, Tourism, Sport Directories, Economics, History, Hobbies, Social Sciences, Textbooks, Juveniles, Periodicals, Calendars
Founded: 1949

Izdatelstvo **Mir***, 2 Pervy Rizhskii pereulok, Moscow I-110 Tel: 2861783 Telex: 411466 MIR SU
Dir: Dr V P Kartsev; *Editor-in-Chief:* Dr G B Kurganov
Orders to: Mezhdunarodnaya Kniga, Moscow
Subject: Translations from and into Russian of technical and scientific works
1981: 461 titles *Founded:* 1946

Izdatelstvo **Molodaya Gvardiya***, Sushchevskaya ul 21, Moscow K-30 Tel: 2511145
Young Guard Publishing House of All-Union Leninist Young Communist League
Dir: Vladimir Desyaterik
Subjects: Political Science, Social Science, History, Biography, Art, Science Fiction, Juveniles
Founded: 1922

Izdatelstvo **'Moskovskii Rabochiy'***, Christoprudny bul'var' 8, Moscow 103012 Tel: 2210735
Moscow Worker Publishing House
Dir: N H Eselyek
Subjects: General Fiction & Non-fiction
Founded: 1922

Izdatelstvo **Moskovskot niversiteta***, Hertzena ul 5-7, Moscow K-9 Tel: 2295091
Moscow University Press
Dir: Dr A K Avelitchev; *Rights & Permissions:* VAAP, Bolshaya Bronnaya 6a, Moscow
Subject: Sciences
Founded: 1926

Izdatelstvo **'Muzyka'**, Neglinnaja ul 14, Moscow 103045 Tel: 2230497
Music Publishing House
Publicity Manager: L Sidelnikov
Subjects: Music, Scores

Izdatelstvo **Mysl***, Leninsky prospekt 15, Moscow V-71 Tel: 2324248
Thought Publishing House
Dir: A P Porivaev
Subjects: Science, Economics, Geography, Philosophy, History
Founded: 1963

Izdatelstvo **'Nauka'***, Profsojuznaja ul 90, Moscow V-485 Tel: 3347151
Science Publishing House
Dir: G D Komkov
Subjects: Natural and Humanitarian Sciences, Physics and Mathematics Textbooks
Founded: 1727
Miscellaneous: There are six self-supporting branches of Nauka

Izdatelstvo **'Nedra'***, Tret'yakovskii pereulok 1-19, Moscow K-12 Tel: 2231735
Natural Resources Publishing House
Dir: M S Lvov
Subjects: Meteorology, Geology, Energy
Founded: 1963

Agentstvo Pechati **'Novosti'** (APN)+, Bolshaya Pochtovaya ul 7, Moscow 107082 Tel: 2655008/2692754 Telex: 411101
Novosti Press Agency Publishing House
Dir: A V Pushkov; *Editorial:* Yu S Fantalov; *Sales, Publicity:* S G Mishchenko; *Production:* V N Katkova
Subjects: History, Philosophy, Social Science, Politics, Economics, International Affairs, General Informative Books, Low- & High-priced Paperbacks
Founded: 1964

Pedagogika*, Lefortovsky pereulok 8, Moscow 107066 Tel: 2611282
Dir: Mr Razumny
Subjects: Science, Education, Reference, Pedagogics
Founded: 1969

Izdatelstvo **'Pishchevaya Promyshlennost'**, now incorporated in Izdatelsvo Legkaya i Pishchevaya Promyshlennost (qv)

Planeta Publishers*, Petrovka 8/11, Moscow 103031 Tel: 2230470
Subjects: Guidebooks, Illustrated books
Founded: 1969

Politizdat*, Myusskaya pl 7, Moscow D-47 Tel: 2531897
Publishing House for Political Literature
Dir: H B Tropkin
Subjects: Political Literature, History
Founded: 1931

Pravda Publishing House*, Pravdy ul 24, Moscow
Dir: B A Feldman

Profizdat*, Kirova ul 13, Moscow 101000 Tel: 2945740
Publishing House for All-Union Central Council of Trade Unions
Dir: Vladimir A Boldyrev
Subjects: Economics, Sociology, Psychology of Work, Trade Union Movement, Literature, Fiction, Prose
Founded: 1930

Progress Publishers*, Zubovsky bul'var' 17, Moscow 119021 Tel: 2469032
Dir: Volf Nikolayevich Sedykh; *Editor-in-Chief:* Viktor Ivanovich Neznanov; *Production:* Mikhail Pavlovich Kryakovkin
Subjects: Scientific Socialism, Marxism-Leninism, Philosophy, Political Economy, International Relations, International Communist and Workers Movement, History, Sociology, Law, Russian Classics and Modern Soviet Literature, Russian Translations of Fiction, Social and Political Literature, Art, Children's Books
Founded: 1931

Izdatelstvo **'Prosveshchenie'***, 3-ii proezd Marinoi Roshchi 41, Moscow 129110 Tel: 2891405
Dir: D D Zuev
Subjects: Education, Textbooks
Founded: 1963

Izdatelstvo **'Radio i Svyaz'***, Chistoprudnyi bul'var' 2, Moscow 101000 Tel: 2585351/2944807
Communications Publishing House
Dir: N Zabolotsky
Subjects: Communications (postal, telegraphic and wireless, television, Hi-Fi equipment), Philately, Radio Engineering, Electronics, Cybernetics, Computer Engineering, Radio Communications

Raduga Publishers, Zubovsky bul'var' 17, Moscow 119021
Dir: Victor Neznanov

Russky Yazyk*, Pushkinskaya ul 23, Moscow 103009 Tel: 2928166
Russian Language Publishers
Dir: V I Nasarov
Subjects: Textbooks, Reference, Dictionaries
Founded: 1974

Izdatelstvo **'Sovetskaya Entsiklopediya'***, Pokrovskii bul'var' 8, Moscow 109817 Tel: 2973562/2977483
Soviet Encyclopaedia Publishing House
Chairman of Editorial Council: A Prokhorov
Subjects: General, specialized and technical encyclopaedias and encyclopaedic reference
Founded: 1925

Izdatelstvo **'Sovetskaya Rossiya'***, Suapnova Proezd 13-15, Moscow K-12 Tel: 2213913
Soviet Russia Publishing House
Dir: E A Petrov
Subjects: Popular and Social Sciences, Children's, Political Propaganda, Art, Periodicals
Founded: 1957

Izdatelstvo **'Sovetskii Khudozhnik'***, Chernyahovskogo ul 4a, Moscow 125319 Tel: 1512502
Soviet Artist Publishing House
Dir: V Goryainov
Subject: Art, Reference
Founded: 1969

Izdatelstvo **'Sovetskii Kompozitor'***, 14-12 Sadovaya-Triumfalnaya St, Moscow 103006 Tel: 2092384
Soviet Composer Publishing House
Dir: M Y Kunin
Subject: Music (Reference, Bibliographies, Composers)
Bookshop: Magazin-Salon Sovetskaya Muzika (at above address)
Founded: 1967

Izdatelstvo **Sovietskii Pisatel***, ul Vorovskovo 11, 121069 Moscow 69 Tel: 2025051
USSR Writer's Union Publishing House
Dir: V N Eramenko
Subjects: Belles Lettres, Art History, Literary History, Poetry, Literary Criticism, Literary Translations
Founded: 1935
Miscellaneous: Publishes monthly magazine *Soviet Motherland* in Yiddish

Izdatelstvo **'Sovetskoe Radio'**, now Izdatelstvo Radio i Svyaz (qv)

Sovremennik Publishers*, Yartsevskaya 4, Moscow 121351 Tel: 1409205
Subjects: Fiction, Literary Criticism, Drama
Founded: 1970

Znak Pochyota Order Izdatelstvo **Standartov***, Novopresnensky pereulok 3, Moscow 123022 Tel: 2520348
Subject: Official Standards
Founded: 1926

Statistika, now Finansy i Statistika Publishing House USSR (qv)

Stroyizdat Publishing House*, Kalyayevskaya 23a, Moscow 102006 Tel: 2516967

Subjects: Building Sciences, Machinery, Urban Development, Architecture, Geology, Hydrogeology
Founded: 1932

Izdatelstvo **'Sudostroenie'***, Gogolya ul 8, Leningrad 191065 Tel: 2153048
Publishing House for Shipbuilding
Man Dir: V Iv Lapin; *Editor-in-Chief:* A L Mitrofanov; *Production:* V Iv Pashko; *Rights & Permissions:* A S Albov
Subjects: Shipbuilding, Ship Repairing, Ship Installations Equipment and Devices, Navigation, Underwater Exploration, University and Secondary Textbooks on these subjects
Bookshop: 'Sudostroenie', 40 Sadovuja St, Leningrad
Founded: 1940

Izdatelstvo **Svyaz**, now Izdatelstvo Radio i Svyaz (qv)

Izdatelstvo **'Transport'***, Basmannyi Tupik 6a, Moscow 107174 Tel: 2626773
Dir: V P Titov
Subjects: Railway, Automobile, Air, Sea and Naval Transport
Founded: 1923

Vsesoyuznoe Obyedineniye **'Vneshtorgizdat'***, Fadyeev ul 1, Moscow 107207 Tel: 411238 Telex: 7238 VTI SU
Foreign Trade Publishing House
President: Sergey P Emelyanikov; *Editorial:* Boris V Lensky; *Sales:* Leonid G Koftov; *Production:* Anatoly D Sorokin
Subject: Foreign Trade
Founded: 1925
Miscellaneous: Publish Catalogues, Prospectuses and Advertising Material in Russian and Foreign Languages on Soviet exports. Execute orders of foreign organizations for translation and publishing in Russian of maintenance and other documents

Voyenizdat*, Upravleniye Voyennogo Izdateltsva, Moscow K-160 Tel: 1950154
Chief: A I Kopytin
Subjects: Military aspects of politics, history; Military Fiction, memoirs

Izdatelstvo **'Vysshaya Shkola'***, Neglinnaya ul 29/14, Moscow Tel: 2210509
Higher School Publishing House
Dir: V G Panov
Subject: Textbooks (Secondary Education)
Founded: 1959

Izdatelstvo **'Yuridicheskaya Literatura'**, Kachalov ul 14, Moscow 121069 Tel: 2028384
Law Literature Publishing House
Dir: S A Chibiryaev
Subject: Law
Founded: 1917

Znanie*, Novaya ploshchad 3-4, Moscow K-12 Tel: 2271531
Knowledge Publishing House
Dir: V Belyakov
Subjects: General Science, Education, Culture, Politics
Founded: 1951

Literary Agents

V A A P, see entry below

Vsesoyuznoe agentstvo po avtorkskim pravam (VAAP)*, Bolshaya Bronnaya ul 6a, Moscow K-104 Tel: 2034599 Cable Add: Moscow Avtor Telex: 7627Avtor SU
Copyright Agency of the USSR
Contact: B Pankin, Chairman; or M Shisigin, Vice-Chairman

Major Booksellers

Mezhdunarodnaya Kniga*, Smolenskaya sennaya pl 32-34, Moscow G-200 Tel: 2441022 Cable Add: Mezhkniga Moscow Telex: 160
The sole organization in the USSR through which foreign purchasers can obtain books
The leading agent for distribution of USSR books and periodicals abroad is Les Livres Etrangers SA, 10 rue Armand-Moisant, F-75737 Paris cedex 15 Tel: (01) 7342727/5665680; retail bookshop Maison du Livre Etranger ('Dom Knigi'), 9 rue de l'Eperon, F-75006 Paris Tel: (01) 3261060

Major Libraries

Fundamental Library of the **Academy** of Medical Sciences*, Baltiyskaya ul 8, Moscow

Biblioteka **Akademii Nauk SSSR***, Birzhevaya liniya 1, Leningrad V-164 Tel: Director's Office 183592 and 184091; Information and Bibliographical Department 183991
Library of the Academy of Sciences of the USSR

Gosudarstvennaya publichnaya nauchno-tekhnicheskaya biblioteka Sibirskogo otdeleniya **Akademii Nauk SSSR***, Voskhod ul 15, 630200 Novosibirsk Tel: Director 661860; Reference and Bibliography Department 661991; Reader Registration 668071
State Public Scientific and Technical Library of the Siberian Department of the Academy of Sciences of the USSR

Institut nauchnoy informatsii po obschestvennym naukam **Akademii Nauk SSSR***, Krasikova ul 28/45, 117418 Moscow V-418 Tel: 1288930
Institute of Scientific Information in the Social Sciences of the Academy of Sciences of the USSR

Tsentral'nava nauchnaya biblioteka **Akademii Nauk USSR***, Vladimirskaya ul 62, 252601 Kiev 601 Tel: Director 243126; Reference/Bibliography Section 213231
Central Scientific Library of the Academy of Sciences of the Ukrainian SSR

All-Union Patent and Technical Library*, Berezhkovskaya naberezhnaya 24, Moscow

Central State **Archives of Early Russian** Historical Records*, Bolshaya Pirogovskaya ul 17, Moscow

Central State **Archives of the October Revolution** and Higher State Bodies*, Bolshaya Pirogovskaya ul 17, Moscow

Central State **Archives of the RSFSR***, Berezhkovskaya naberezhnaya 26, Moscow

Central State Historical **Archives of the USSR***, Naberezhnaya Krasnogo Flota 4, Leningrad

Central State Literature and Art **Archives of the USSR***, Leningradskoe chausee 50, Moscow
Dir: N B Volkova

Azerbaidzhanskaya gosudarstvennaya respublikanskaya biblioteka im M F Akhundova*, Tsentr ul Khagani 29, 37061 Baku Tel: 936801; Reference and Bibliography Department 936004
M F Akhundov State Republic Library of Azerbaizhan

Nauchnaya biblioteka im A M **Gor'kovo Leningradskovo** gosudarstvennovo universiteta im A A Zhdanova*, Universitetskaya naberezhnaya 7-9, Leningrad 199164 Tel: Director 2-182741; Reference and Information Department 2-189555
A M Gor'kii Scientific Library of the A A Zhdanov State University of Leningrad
Dir: Mrs K M Romanovskaya

Nauchnaya biblioteka im A M **Gor'kogo Moskovskogo** gos universiteta im M V Lomonosova*, Marx prospekt 20, Moscow K-9 Tel: Director's Office 2036525; Service Department 2033751
A M Gor'kii Scientific Library of The Lomonosov State University of Moscow

Vsesoyuznaya **Gosudarstvennaya ordena Trudovogo Krasnogo Znameni biblioteka** inostrannoi literatury*, Ulyanovskaya 1, Moscow 109240 Tel: 2972839
All-Union State Library of Foreign Literature

Gosudarstvennaya publichnaya istoricheskaya biblioteka RSFSR*, 101839 Moscow, Bogdana Khmel'nitskogo ul, Starosadskii per d 9 Tel: Director 2956514; Information 2280582
State Public Historical Library of the RSFSR

Gosudarstvennaya publichnaya nauchno-tekhnicheskaya biblioteka SSSR*, Kuznetskii most 12, Moscow K-31 Tel: Director K59288; Reference-Bibliography B87379
State Public Scientific and Technical Library of the USSR

Gosudarstvennaya ordena Lenina biblioteka SSSR imeni V I **Lenina***, Prospect Kalinina 3, Moscow 101000 Tel: 2024056 Telex: 7167 wgbibl su
V I Lenin State Library of the USSR
Secretary: G A Semenova

Gosudarstvennaya Respublikanskaya biblioteka Gruzinskoi SSR im K **Marksa***, Ketskhoveli ul 5, Tbilisi 380007 Tel: Director's Office 931233/999286
State Republican Karl Marx Library of the Georgian SSR

Gosudarstvennaya biblioteka UzSSR im Alishera **Navoi***, Alleya paradov 5, Tashkent 700000 Tel: 398658/394341/394440/394450
Alisher Navoi State Public Library of the Uzbek SSR

Gosudarstvennaya publichnaya biblioteka im M E **Saltykova-Schedrina***, Sadovaya ul 18, Leningrad D-69 Tel: 152856
M E Saltykov-Shchedrina State Public Library

Tartu Riikliku Ulikooli Teaduslik Raamatükogu*, Struve ul 1, 202400 Tartu, Estonian SSR Tel: Tartu 34121/286 Telex: 208010 Nauka
Scientific Library of Tartu State University
Librarian: Laine Peep
Publication: Publicationes bibliothecae universitatis litterarum Tartuensis; Raamataeg-restaureerimine; Teadusliku Raamatukogu töid (serials); *Eksliibris TRÜ Teaduslikus Raamatukogus*

The Scientific Library of the **Vilnius** Vincas Kapsukas State University*, Universiteto gatve 3, 232633 Vilnius Tel: 610616/611076 Telex: 261128 Vaiva
Librarian: J Tornau

Library Associations

Council on Libraries of the **Academy** of Sciences of the USSR*, Prospect Leninsky 14, Moscow
Academy Chairman: P N Fedoseev

U S S R Library Council*, The Lenin State Library of the USSR, Prospect Kalinina 3, Moscow 101000 Telex: 7167 wgbibl su Tel: 2024656/2228551
President: Professor N M Sikorsky;
Executive Secretary: G A Semenova
Publications: Bibliotekar (Librarian); *Sovetskoje bibliotekovedonie* (Formerly: *Biblioteki SSSR*) (Soviet Library Science); *Nauchnaya i tekhnicheskie biblioteki SSSR* (Scientific and Technical Libraries of the USSR); *Nauchnaya i tekhnicheskaya informatsiya* (Scientific and Technical Information) *Seriya I: Organizatsiya i metodika informatsionnoi raboty* (Organization and Methodology of Information Work) *Seriya 2: Informatsionnye processy i systemy* (Information Processes and Systems); *Sovetskaya Bibliografia* (Soviet Bibliography); *Bibliotekovedenie i bibliografiya za rubezhom* (Librarianship and Bibliography Abroad); Kniga *Issledovaniya i materialy* (Book Studies and Materials); *V mire knig* (In the World of Books); *Knizhnoe obozrenie* (Book Reviews); *Informatika* (Information Science) *Bibliotekovedenie i Bibliografovedenie Bibliograficheskaya informatsiya* (a) *Sovetskaya literatura* (b) *Inostrannaya literatura* (Library Science and Theory of Bibliography, Bibliographic Information (a) Soviet Literature (b) Foreign Literature); *Bibliotekovedenie i Bibliografovedenie* (Library Science and Theory of Bibliography) (a) *Nauchnyi Referativnyi Sbornik* (Abstracts Collection) (b) *Obzornaya informatsiya* (Survey Information) (c) *Express-informatsiya* (Express-Information)

Library Reference Books and Journals

Books

Bibliotekovedenie i bibliografiya za rubezhom (Librarianship and Bibliography Abroad), USSR Library Council, The Lenin State Library of the USSR, Prospect Kalinina 3, Moscow 101 000

Bibliotekovedenie i Bibliografovedenie, Bibliograficheskaya informatsiya (Library Science and Theory of Bibliography, Bibliographie Information), USSR Library Council, The Lenin State Library of the USSR, Prospect Kalinina 3, Moscow 101 000

Nauchnye i tekhnicheskie biblioteki SSSR (Scientific and Technical Libraries of the USSR), USSR Library Council, The Lenin State Library of the USSR, Prospect Kalinina 3, Moscow 101 000

Journals

Bibliotekar (The Librarian), USSR Library Council, The Lenin State Library of the USSR, Prospect Kalinina 3, Moscow 101 000

Sovetskoje bibliotekovedenie (Soviet Library Science), USSR Library Council, The Lenin State Library of the USSR, Prospect Kalinina 3, Moscow 101 000

Literary Periodicals

Culture and Life (text in English, French, German, Russian and Spanish), Union of Soviet Societies for Friendship and Cultural Relations with Foreign Countries, proezd Sapunova 13-15, Moscow-Centre

Litaratura i Mastatstva (Literature and Art), Ministerstva Kul'tury i Sayuz Pismennikaw BSSR, Zakharava ul 19, Minsk

Literaturnaya Gazeta (Literary Newspaper), USSR Union of Writers, Vorovskogo ul 52, Moscow

Literaturnaya Rossiya (Literary Russia), USSR Union of Writers, Vorovskogo ul 52, Moscow

Molodaya Gvardiya (The Young Guards), Vsesoyuznyi Leninskii Kommunisticheskii Soyuz Molodozhi, Tsentral'nyi Komitet, Sushchevskaya ul 21, Moscow A-55

Moskva; literary magazine, Arbart 20, Moscow

Neva, USSR Union of Writers, Vorovskogo ul 52, Moscow

Novyi Mir (New World); literary, artistic and socio-political journal, USSR Union of Writers, Vorovskogo ul 52, Moscow

Radyans'ke Literaturoznavstvo (Soviet Literary Studies), Akademiya Nauk Ukrayinskoyi SSR, Instytut Literatury im T H Shevchenka ta Spilka Pys'mennykiv Ukrayiny, Kirova 4, Kiev

Russian Literature, North-Holland Publishing Co, PO Box 211, Amsterdam, Netherlands

Russian Literature Triquarterly, Ardis Publishers, 2901 Heatherway, Ann Arbor, Mich 48104, USA

Russkaya Literatura (Russian Literature), Nauka (Science Publishing House), Podsosenskii pereulok 21, Moscow K-62 (journal of the Institute of Russian Literature of the USSR)

Soviet Literature (editions in English, German, Polish, Spanish, Japanese and Czech), USSR Union of Writers, Vorovskogo ul 52, Moscow

V Mire Knig (In the World of Books), USSR Library Council, The Lenin State Library of the USSR, Prospect Kalinina 3, Moscow 101 000

Voprosy Literatury (Questions of Literature), USSR Union of Writers, Vorovskogo ul 52, Moscow

United Arab Emirates

General Information

Language: Arabic (English used in business)
Religion: Muslim
Population: 711,000
Bank Hours: 0800-1200 Saturday-Thursday (1100 Thursday in Abu Dhabi)
Shop Hours: Abu Dhabi: Summer: 0800-1300, 1600-dusk Saturday-Thursday; Winter: 0800-1300, 1530-1900 Saturday-Thursday.
Northern Emirates: Summer: 0900-1300, 1630-2000 or 2100 Saturday-Thursday; Winter: 0900-1300, 1600-2000 or 2100 Saturday-Thursday
Currency: 100 fils = 1 UAE dirham
Export/Import Information: No tariff on books or advertising matter, except duty on imports in Dubai and ad valorem rates in Ras al Khaimah and Sharjah. No import licence required except for obscene publications in Dubai

Publishers

All Prints Distributors and Publishers, Hamdan St, PO Box 857, Abu Dhabi Telex: 22844 EM
Partners: Miss Bushra Khayat, Hassan S Khayat

Major Booksellers

Family Bookshop, PO Box 956 Abu Dhabi Tel: 368677 Cable Add: Fambooks
Manager: Mohamad Saffaf

Tahseen S **Khayat***, PO Box 857, Abu Dhabi Tel: 41853

Major Library

Centre for Documentation and Research*, Old Palace, PO Box 2380, Abu Dhabi
Dir: Mohammad Morsi Abdullah PhD
Publication: Arabian Gulf Research Review (quarterly)

United Kingdom

General Information

Language: English; Welsh in most of Wales (where it is used alongside English for official purposes). About 80,000 speak Scots Gaelic (in Highlands and Islands of Scotland). Irish is used in parts of Northern Ireland
Religion: Protestant officially. Numerous other religions have significant numbers of adherents
Population: 56 million
Bank Hours: 0930-1530 Monday-Friday
Shop Hours: Generally 0900-1730 Monday-Saturday. Early closing one day week usually.
Currency: 100 pence = 1 pound sterling
Export/Import Information: Member of the European Economic Community. No tariffs on books; advertising matter dutiable over a certain weight. No import licences required; nominal exchange controls. Advertising in UK is regulated by statutes and voluntary codes; for information contact Advertising Standards Authority Ltd, Brook House, Torrington Pl, London WC1
Copyright: UCC, Berne, Florence (see International section)

UNITED KINGDOM 391

Book Trade Organizations

Advisory Committee on the Selection of Low-Priced Books for Overseas, c/o The British Council, 11 Portland Pl, London W1N 4EJ Tel: (01) 636 6888
Secretary: G M Dickinson

Antiquarian Booksellers' Association, Book House, 45 East Hill, Wandsworth, London SW18 2QZ Tel: (01) 870 8259
Secretary: Bridget Cuming

Association of Authors' Agents, 2-3 Morwell St, London WC1B 3AR Tel: (01) 636 2901
Cable Add: Novelist London
President: Anthony Sheil
Secretary: Tessa Sayle

Association of British Directory Publishers, 154 High St, Beckenham, Kent BR3 1EA
Chairman: T M Hempenstall
Hon Secretary: C Henderson

Association of Learned & Professional Society Publishers, R J Millson, 30 Austenwood Close, Gerrards Cross, Bucks SL9 9DE Tel: Gerrards Cross 884357 (STD code 0753)

Association of Little Presses, 262 Randolph Ave, London W9 Tel: (01) 624 8565
Secretary: Clive Fencott

Association of Mail Order Publishers, 1 New Burlington St, London W1X 1FD Tel: (01) 437 0706
Dir: D R Vickers

Association of Publishers' Educational Representatives*
Secretary: Ron Wood, 23 Lynton Gardens, Harrogate, North Yorkshire HG1 4TE

Authors' Lending & Copyright Society, 430 Edgware Rd, London W2 1EH Tel: (01) 724 1386
Secretary-General: Elizabeth Thomas

B A S H, see Booksellers Association Service House Ltd

B O D, see Booksellers' Order Distribution

The **Book Development** Council, 19 Bedford Sq, London WC1B 3HJ Tel: (01) 580 6321
Chairman: Bryanennett
International Division of the Publishers Association

The **Book Marketing** Council, 19 Bedford Sq, London WC1B 3HJ Tel: (01) 580 6321/5
Chairman: Michael Turner
A home trade division of the Publishers Association, working to promote and expand sales of books in the home market
Publications include: Book Marketing News

Book Publishers' Representatives' Association
Honorary Secretary: Bob Davis, 3 Carolina Way, Tiptree, Essex CO5 0DW Tel: Tiptree 816710 (STD code 0621)

Book Tokens Ltd*, 152 Buckingham Palace Rd, London SW1W 9TZ Tel: (01) 730 9258
Secretary: J S Crowe

The **Book Trade** Benevolent Society, Dillon Lodge, The Booksellers Retreat, King's Langley, Herts WD4 8LT Tel: King's Langley 63128 (STD code 092 77)
Secretary: Ann Brown

Books in Progress, Literature Department, Arts Council of Great Britain*, 9 Long Acre, London WC2E 9LH Tel: (01) 379 6597
Register of Literary and Technical Research. Confidential (i.e. not open for inspection) register of works in progress. Writers planning to start work on a book or research project may contact the register to elicit whether subject already covered by another writer. There is no charge for writers registering work for inclusion or for enquiries

Booksellers Association of Great Britain and Ireland, 154 Buckingham Palace Rd, London SW1W 9TZ Tel: (01) 730 8214
Dir: Tim Godfray
Membership Secretary: M J Bedford
Publications: see Booksellers Association Service House Ltd

Booksellers Association Service House Ltd, 154 Buckingham Palace Rd, London SW1W 9TZ Tel: (01) 730 8214
Publications: List of Members, Lists of Specialist Booksellers, Directory of Book Publishers and Wholesalers, Trade Reference Book, Charter Group Economic Survey, Machine Readable Codes, and other publications relating to the bookselling trade

Booksellers Clearing House*, 152 Buckingham Palace Rd, London SW1W 9TZ Tel: (01) 730 9258
Man Dir: W A Barnes

Booksellers' Order Distribution Ltd (BOD), 4 Grosvenor Rd, Aldershot, Hants GU11 1DS Tel: Aldershot 20697 (STD Code 0252)
Man Dir and Secretary: Robin Young

British Copyright Council, 29-33 Berners St, London W1P 3DB Tel: (01) 580 5544

Children's Writers' Group, The Society of Authors, 84 Drayton Gardens, London SW10 9SB
Secretary: Diana Shine

Crime Writers' Association, c/o The Press Club Ltd, International Press Centre, 76 Shoe Lane, London EC4
Secretary: Marian Babson

Cyngor Llyfrau Cymraeg, see Welsh Books Council

Educational Publishers Council, 19 Bedford Sq, London WC1B 3HJ Tel: (01) 580 6321
Cable Add: Publasoc, London WC1 Telex: 21792 ref 2527
Dir: John R M Davies
Schools Division of The Publishers Association

Educational Writers' Group, 84 Drayton Gardens, London SW10 9SB Tel: (01) 373 6642
Secretary: Peta Sievwright

Guild of Travel Writers*, 20 Great Chapel St, London W1V 3AQ
Honorary Secretary: Gerry Brenes

I B I S, see International Book Information Services

Independent Publishers Guild
Secretary: Rosemary Pettit, 52 Chepstow Rd, London W2 Tel: (01) 727 0919

International Book Information Services, Waterside, Lowbell Lane, London Colney, St Albans, Herts AL2 1DX Tel: St Albans 25209 (STD code 0727) Cable Add: Bookinfo St Albans Telex: 261721
Operates a questionnaired computerized mailing list of academics, schools, libraries, booksellers, doctors worldwide. Also businesses and professionals

National Federation of Retail Newsagents, 2 Bridewell Pl, London EC4V 6AR Tel: (01) 353 6816
General Secretary: K E J Peters

Orders Clearing, Waterside, Lowbell Lane, London Colney, St Albans, Herts AL2 1DX Tel: St Albans 25209 (STD code 0727) Telex: 261721
Dir: M W Whitmarsh

P I C S, see Publishers' Information Card Services

Public Lending Right Office, Bayheath House, Prince Regent St, Stockton-on-Tees, Cleveland TS18 1DS Tel: Stockton-on-Tees 604699 (STD code 0642)
Registrar: John W Sumsion

Publishers Association, 19 Bedford Sq, London WC1B 3HJ Tel: (01) 580 6321
Cable Add: Publasoc London WC1 Telex: 21792
Chief Executive: C Bradley

Publishers' Information Card Services, IBIS Ltd, Waterside, Lowbell Lane, London Colney, St Albans, Herts AL2 1DX Tel: St Albans 25209 (STD code 0727) Telex: 261721
Man Dir: David Clark
Direct mail promotion for publishers

Publishers' Overseas Circle, c/o Helena Svojsikova, Collier Macmillan Ltd, Stockley Close, Stockley Rd, West Drayton, Middlesex UB7 9BE Tel: West Drayton 40651 ext 30 (STD code 08954)

Publishers Publicity Circle, c/o Rhoda Katz, 34 Wolseley Rd, London N8 8RP
Publications: Directory of members

Retail Book, Stationery and Allied Trades Employees' Association, 7 Grape St, London WC2 8DR Tel: (01) 836 4897
General Secretary: D A Williamson

School Bookshop Association, 1 Effingham Rd, Lee, London SE12 Tel: (01) 852 4953
Director: Richard Hill
Publications: Books for Keeps; How to Set up and Run a School Bookshop

Scottish Publishers' Association, 25a South West Thistle St Lane, Edinburgh EH2 1EW Tel: (031) 225 5795
Administrative Executive: Judy Moir;
Chairman: Stephanie Wolfe Murray;
Secretary: Colin Kirkwood
Publication: New Books from Scottish Publishers (twice a year)

Society of Authors, 84 Drayton Gardens, London SW10 9SD Tel: (01) 373 6642
General Secretary: Mark Le Fanu
Publication: The Author (quarterly)

The **Society of Indexers**
Secretary: Mrs C Robertson, 7A Parker St, Cambridge CB1 1JL Tel: Cambridge 311913 (STD code 0223)
Publication: The Indexer

Society of Young Publishers, c/o Ros Edwards, 10 Upper Grosvenor St, London W1X 9PA Tel: (01) 493 4141
Chairman: Ros Edwards (at above address)
Publication: Inprint (monthly)

Standard Book Numbering Agency Ltd, 12 Dyott St, London WC1A 1DF Tel: (01) 836 8911 ext 65
Parent Company: J Whitaker & Sons Ltd (qv)
Secretary: Miss E F Budworth
Publication: International Standard Book Numbering

U K National Serials Data Centre, British Library, Bibliographic Services Division, 2 Sheraton St, London W1V 4BH Tel: (01) 636 1544 ext 346 Telex: 21462 Blref G
Allocates International Standard Serial Numbers (ISSN) to serials published in UK

Welsh Books Council (Cyngor Llyfrau Cymraeg), Castell Brychan, Aberystwyth, Dyfed SY23 2JB Tel: Aberystwyth 4151 (STD code 0970)
Director: Alun Creunant Davies

Welsh Publishers' Union (Undeb Cyhoeddwyr Cymru), c/o Welsh Books Council, Castell Brychan, Aberystwyth, Dyfed SY23 2JB Tel: Aberystwyth 4151 (STD code 0970)

Writers' Guild of Great Britain, 430 Edgware Rd, London W2 1EH Tel: (01) 723 8074
General Secretary: Walter J Jeffrey

Book Trade Reference Books and Journals

Books

The Book Report; an annual appraisal of the UK book market, Euromonitor Publications Ltd, PO Box 26, London WC1N 2PN

Book Publishing, Jordan & Sons Ltd, PO Box 260, Bristol BS99 7DX

The British Book Trade, a Bibliographical Guide, André Deutsch Ltd, 105 Great Russell St, London WC1B 3LJ

The British Library General Catalogue of Printed Books to 1975 (first volumes of total estimated 360 published 1979, completion due 1985); K G Saur Ltd, Shropshire House, 2-20 Capper St, London WC1E 6JA

British Official Publications, Pergamon Press Ltd, Headington Hill Hall, Oxford OX3 0BW

Cassell & The Publishers Association Directory of Publishing in Great Britain, the Commonwealth, Ireland, Pakistan and South Africa, Cassell Ltd, 35 Red Lion Sq, London WC1R 4SG

Current British Directories; a guide to the directories published in Great Britain, Ireland, the British Commonwealth and South Africa, CBD Research Ltd, 154 High St, Beckenham BR3 1EA

Dealers in Books: a Directory of Dealers in Secondhand and Antiquarian Books in the British Isles, Sheppard Press Ltd, PO Box 42, Russell Chambers, London WC2E 8AX

Directory of Book Publishers and Wholesalers, Booksellers Association of Great Britain and Ireland, 154 Buckingham Palace Rd, London SW1W 9TZ

Picture Research Handbook, Samuel Smiles House, 11 Granville Park, London SE13 7DY

Printing Trades Directory, Benn Publications Ltd, Directories Division, Union House, Eridge Rd, Tunbridge Wells, Kent TN4 8HF

Publishing and Bookselling, Jonathan Cape Ltd, 30 Bedford Sq, London WC1B 3EL

Publishing and Bookselling Directory, Hamilton House Publishing, Grooms Lane, Creaton, Northampton NN6 8NS

Trade Reference Book, Booksellers Association of Great Britain and Ireland, 154 Buckingham Palace Rd, London SW1W 9TZ

Writer's and Artist's Yearbook, A & C Black Ltd, 35 Bedford Row, London WC1R 4JH

Journals

Antiquarian Book Monthly Review, 3 Brayfield House, Cold Brayfield, Nr Olney, Bucks

The Author, Society of Authors, 84 Drayton Gardens, London SW10 9SD

Book Exchange, Fudge & Co Ltd, 115 Old St, London EC1V 9JR

Book Market; for antiquarian and out-of-print books, Clique Ltd, 75 World's End Rd, Handsworth Wood, Birmingham B20 2NS

Book Marketing News, Book Marketing Council, 19 Bedford Sq, London WC1B 3HJ

Bookdealer, Fudge & Co Ltd, 115 Old St, London EC1V 9JR

Books for Keeps, School Bookshop Association, 1 Effingham Rd, London SE12 8NZ

Books from Scotland, Scottish Publishers' Association, 25a South West Thistle St Lane, Edinburgh EH2 1EW

Books of the Month and Books To Come, J Whitaker & Sons Ltd, 12 Dyott St, London WC1A 1DF

The Bookseller, J Whitaker & Sons Ltd, 12 Dyott St, London WC1A 1DF

Bookselling News, Booksellers' Association of Great Britain and Ireland, 154 Buckingham Palace Rd, London SW1W 9TZ

British Book News, British Council, 65 Davies St, London W1Y 2AA

British Book Production, National Book League, Book House, East Hill, Wandsworth, London SW18

British Books in Print, J Whitaker & Sons Ltd, 12 Dyott St, London WC1A 1DF (also monthly on microfiche)

British Paperbacks in Print, J Whitaker & Sons Ltd, 12 Dyott St, London WC1A 1DF

British National Bibliography, British Library, Bibliographic Services Division, Store St, London WC1E 7DG

Children's Books of the Year, National Book League, Book House, East Hill, London SW18

Clique; the antiquarian booksellers' medium, Clique Ltd, 75 World's End Rd, Handsworth Wood, Birmingham B20 2NS Tel: (021) 554 7308

Gee Report, 15 Hanover Sq, 3rd Floor, London W1

The Indexer, (Journal of British, Australian and American Societies of Indexers), c/o Hazel K Bell, 139 The Ryde, Hatfield, Herts AL9 5DP

List of Members, Booksellers Association of Great Britain and Ireland, 154 Buckingham Palace Rd, London SW1W 9TZ

Llais Llyfrau, Cyngor Llyfrau Cymraeg, Queen's Sq, Aberystwyth, Wales (list of all books published in Welsh during previous 6 months and list of books to be published)

National Newsagent, Bookseller, Stationer (weekly), National Newsagent Ltd, Lennox House, Norfolk St, London WC2

Publishers in the United Kingdom and their Addresses, J Whitaker & Sons Ltd, 12 Dyott St, London WC1A 1DF

Publishing News, 37-49 Brick St, London W1A 1AN

The Radical Bookseller, Unit 265, 27 Clerkenwell Close, London E1

School Book Review, (half-yearly) Europa Publications Ltd, 18 Bedford Sq, London WC1B 3JN

School Bookshop News, now *Books for Keeps* (qv)

Smith's Trade News, W H Smith & Son Ltd, Strand House, 10 New Fetter Lane, London EC4A 1AD

Standard Book Numbers Listing, J Whitaker & Sons Ltd, 12 Dyott St, London WC1A 1DF

Whitaker's Books of the Month and Books to Come, J Whitaker & Sons Ltd, 12 Dyott St, London WC1A 1DF

Whitaker's Classified Monthly Book List, J Whitaker & Sons Ltd, 12 Dyott St, London WC1A 1DF

Whitaker's Cumulative Book List, J Whitake & Sons Ltd, 12 Dyott St, London WC1A 1DF

Publishers

No 1 Publishing Co Ltd, 64 Pentonville Rd, London N1 Tel: (01) 278 3792 Cable Add: Dons Bar
Man Dir: D Murray; *Editorial:* R Hind; *Sales:* W Squires
Associate Company: Ramboro Enterprises Ltd (qv)
Branch Off: 20 Commercial Rd, London N18
Subjects: Children's, Dictionaries, Cookery, Reprints
1981: 10 titles *Founded:* 1960

A P Books/A P Financial Registers Ltd, 9 Courtleigh Gardens, London NW11 9JX Tel: (01) 458 1607
Chief Executive: Alan Philipp
Imprint: Oliver's Guides
Subjects: Trade Directories & Lists
1981: 9 titles *1982:* 10 titles *Founded:* 1969
ISBN Publisher's Prefixes: 0-906285, 0-906247

Abacus, an imprint of Sphere Books Ltd (qv)

Abacus Press, Abacus House, Speldhurst Rd, Tunbridge Wells, Kent TN4 0HU Tel: Tunbridge Wells 29783/27237 (STD code 0892) Cable Add: Abacus Tunbridgewells Telex: 877440 Pburns G ref Abacus
Man Dir, Publisher: N A Jaysekera; *Editorial, Publicity:* Mrs S Leech; *Marketing Dir, Sales:* Harry Robinson; *Rights & Permissions:* Mrs J M White
Associate Companies: Abacus-Kent Ltd; Abacus Distribution Services
Imprint: Computer Research Press
Subjects: Medicine, Science, Technology, Engineering, Mathematics, Computer Sciences, Architecture, Design, Agriculture, Environmental Sciences, Energy Conservation, Bioengineering
Founded: 1970
ISBN Publisher's Prefix: 0-85626

Abbeville Press, see André Deutsch Ltd

Abelard-Schuman Ltd, Furnival House, 14-18 High Holborn, London WC1 Tel: (01) 242 5832
Man Dir: R Michael Miller; *Publishing Dir, Production:* A D Mitchell; *Editorial, Rights:* Rosemary Lanning; *Publicity:* Clare Harrison
Parent Company: Blackie & Son Ltd (qv)
Imprints: include Grasshopper Books
Subjects: Children's Books
Founded: 1958
ISBN Publisher's Prefix: 0-200

Aberdeen University Press Ltd, see Pergamon Press Ltd

Abson Books, Abson, Wick, Bristol BS15 5TT Tel: Abson 2446 (STD code 027582)
Partners: Anthea Bickerton, Pat McCormack
Subjects: English Language Glossaries for American/Rhyming/Cockney slang and Scottish/Irish/Australian/CB idioms,

Cookery, Regional Eating Out Guides, Sports, Gardening, Local Bristol & Bath books
ISBN Publisher's Prefix: 0-902920

Academic and University Publishers Group, 1 Gower St, London WC1E 6HA Tel: (01) 580 3994 Cable Add: Amunpress Telex: 82445
General Manager: John Dawson; *Sales Representative:* Janet Clark; *Promotion:* J Browning
Orders to: International Book Distributors Ltd, 66 Wood Lane End, Hemel Hempstead, Hertfordshire Tel: Hemel Hempstead 58531 (STD code 0442)
Subjects: Belles Lettres, Poetry, Biography, History, Music, Art, Philosophy, Reference, Religion, Paperbacks, Medicine, Psychology, General & Social Science, Photography, Film
Founded: 1965
Miscellaneous: Group includes Duke University Press, University of Illinois Press, University of Kentucky Press, Louisiana State University Press, University of Missouri Press, University of Nebraska Press, University of North Carolina Press, University of Notre Dame Press, Ohio University Press, Pennsylvania State University Press, University of Texas Press, University of Washington Press, University of Wisconsin Press, State University of New York Press, British Film Institute

Academic Press Inc (London) Ltd, 24-28 Oval Rd, London NW1 7DX Tel: (01) 267 4466 Cable Add: Acadinc London NW1 Telex: 25775
Shipping Add: 35 Oval Rd, London NW1 7DX
Man Dir: P Jovanovich; *Editorial Dir:* P Brown; *Sales:* D Duff (General Manager), C C Perry (UK), A Lewellyn (Journals Marketing Manager); *Production Dir:* J M Fujimoto (Journals); *Advertising Manager, Rights & Permissions:* P A Spencer
Parent Company: Academic Press Inc, 111 Fifth Ave, New York, NY10003, USA. Ultimate parent company is Harcourt Brace Jovanovich Inc, 757 Third Ave, New York, NY 10017, USA
Subsidiary Companies: Grune and Stratton Ltd; Harcourt Brace Jovanovich Ltd (qv); Johnson Reprint Co Ltd; Seminar Press Ltd
Associate Companies: Hutchinson & Ross, Benefic Press (both at 24-28 Oval Rd, London NW1 7DX); Harcourt Brace Jovanovich Group (Australia) Pty Ltd, Australia (qv); Grune & Stratton Inc and Johnson Reprint Corporation (both at 111 Fifth Ave, New York, NY 10003); Academic Press Canada, 55 Barber Greene Rd, Don Mills, Ontario M3C 2A1, Canada; Academic Press do Brasil Editôra Ltda, Praça Jorge de Lima, São Paulo, Brazil; Academic Press Japan Inc, Iidabashi Hokoku Bldg, 3-11-3 Iidabashi, Chiyoda-ku, Tokyo, Japan
Subjects: Reference, Scientific, Technical, Medicine, Psychology, Social Science, University Textbooks, Educational Materials
1981: 251 titles *1982:* 232 titles
ISBN Publisher's Prefixes: 0-12 (Academic Press), 0-15 (Harcourt Brace Jovanovich), 0-8089 (Grune & Stratton), 0-384 (Johnson Reprint)

Academic Publications*, Highfield, Dane Hill, Haywards Heath, West Sussex RH17 7EX Tel: Dane Hill 790214 (STD code 0825) Cable Add: Copen Telex: 95246 (Copen-G)
Man Dir: F Frogley
Subjects: University Textbooks, Technical & Scientific, Medical, Philosophy, General Literature
Founded: 1974
ISBN Publisher's Prefix: 0-900307

Academy Editions, 42 Leinster Gardens, London W2 Tel: (01) 402 2141 Telex: 896928
Man Dir: Dr Andreas C Papadakis; *Rights & Permissions, Publicity:* Louisa Denman
Parent Company: Academy Art Books Ltd (at above address)
Subsidiary Companies: Academy Editions, France (qv); Architectural Design, 42 Leinster Gardens, London W2
Imprint: Alec Tiranti (firm also publishes *Architectural Design* and *Architectural Monographs*)
Subjects: Architecture, Fine and Applied Arts, Photography
Bookshops: Academy Bookshop & London Art Bookshop, 7/8 Holland St, London W8 Tel: (01) 937 6996
Founded: 1967
ISBN Publisher's Prefixes: 0-85670, 0-85458, 0-902620

Acorn Editions, an imprint of James Clarke & Co Ltd (qv)

Actinic Press Ltd, 129 St John's Hill, London SW11 1TD Tel: (01) 228 8091
Man Dir: J G F Miller
Orders to: Cressrelles Publishing Co Ltd, 311 Worcester Rd, Malvern, Worcestershire WR14 1AN
Subjects: Technical & Scientific, Medical
Founded: 1926
ISBN Publisher's Prefix: 0-900024

Addison-Wesley Publishers Ltd, 53 Bedford Sq, London WC1B 3DZ Tel: (01) 631 1636 Cable Add: Adiwes London WC1 Telex: 8811948
Dir, General Manager: Stanley B Malcolm; *Rights & Permissions:* Ann Nimmo
Parent Company: Addison-Wesley Publishing Co Inc, Reading, Mass 01867, USA
Associate Companies: Addison-Wesley Publishing Co, Australia (qv); Addison-Wesley (Canada) Ltd, 26 Prince Andrew Pl, Don Mills, Ontario, Canada; Addison-Wesley Publishing Group, Netherlands (qv); Addison-Wesley Publishing Co Inc, Philippines (qv); Addison-Wesley (Singapore) Private Ltd, Singapore (qv); Benjamin/Cummings Inc, UK (qv); Benjamin/Cummings Publishing Co Inc, 2727 Sand Hill Rd, Menlo Park, Calif 94025, USA; Fondo Educativo Interamericano, Colombia (qv); Fondo Educativo Interamericano CA, Mexico (qv); Fondo Educativo Interamericano: Panama, Puerto Rico, Venezuela (qqv)
Subjects: Reference, Business, Juveniles, Humanities, General & Social Sciences, Textbooks, Educational Materials, Medicine
Founded: 1942
ISBN Publisher's Prefixes: 0-201 (Addison-Wesley), 0-8053 (Benjamin/Cummings)

Adkinson Parrish Ltd, Maxwell House, 74 Worship St, London EC2A 2EN Tel: (01) 377 4600 Telex: 885233
Chairman: Robert Maxwell; *Man Dir:* T Hely Hutchinson; *Editorial Dir:* Clare Chatel
Parent Company: BPCC PLC (qv)
Subjects: General Non-fiction, Biography, History, How-to, Music, Art, Reference, Religion
Miscellaneous: Editorial and production organization producing books for international co-editions

Adlard Coles Ltd, see Granada Publishing

Alex **Aiken**, 48 Merrycrest Ave, Glasgow G46 6BJ Tel: (041) 637 2438
Principal: Alex Aiken
Subjects: Military and Naval History, Biography, Natural Sciences
Founded: 1971
ISBN Publisher's Prefix: 0-9502134

Airlife Publishing Ltd+, 7 St John's Hill, Shrewsbury, Salop SY1 1JE Tel: Shrewsbury 3651 (STD code 0743)
Man Dir, Rights & Permissions: A D R Simpson; *Editorial, Sales:* C A Nelson
Subject: Aviation
Founded: 1976
ISBN Publisher's Prefixes: 0-9504543, 0-906393

Akros Publications, 25 Johns Rd, Radcliffe-on-Trent, Nottingham NG12 2GW Tel: Radcliffe-on-Trent 4802 (STD code 06073)
Man Dir, Editorial, Production, Publicity, Rights & Permissions: Duncan Glen; *Sales:* Margaret Glen
Subjects: Scottish Poetry and Literary Criticism
Founded: 1965

Aladdin Books Ltd, 70 Old Compton St, London W1V 5PA Tel: (01) 734 5186 Telex: 21115
Man Dir: Charles Nicholas; *Art, Editorial Dir:* Charles Matheson; *Sales Dir:* Lynn Lockett
Subjects: Juveniles, Co-editions
Founded: 1980

Albyn Press Ltd, 2-4 Abbeymount, Edinburgh EH8 8JH Tel: (031) 661 9339
Man Dir: Charles Skilton
Parent Company: Charles Skilton Ltd (qv)
Subjects: Scottish, General
ISBN Publisher's Prefix: 0-284

Alden & Mowbray Ltd, see A R Mowbray & Co Ltd

Aldwych Press+, 3 Henrietta St, London WC2E 8LU Tel: (01) 240 0856
Man Dir, Rights & Permissions: Danny Maher; *Editorial, Sales, Publicity:* Jessica Kingsley
Subjects: Academic, Library Science, Sociology, Economics, Politics, European Studies, Reference, Philosophy, Military Studies, Law
1981: 15 titles *1982:* 8 titles *Founded:* 1979
ISBN Publisher's Prefix: 0-86172

Alison Press, an associate of Secker & Warburg Ltd (qv)

Ian **Allan** Ltd, Terminal House, Shepperton, Middlesex TW17 8AS Tel: Walton-on-Thames 28950 (STD code 09322) Cable Add: Ianallanshepp Telex: 929806
Chairman: I Allan; *Man Dir:* D I Allan; *Editorial:* M Harris (Magazines); *Sales:* J Nicol; *Production:* N Lerwill; *Publicity:* P Rix; *Rights & Permissions:* S Forty
Parent Company: Ian Allan (Group) Ltd
Associate Companies: A Lewis (Masonic Publishers) Ltd; Locomotive Publishing Co Ltd; Modern Transport Publishing Co Ltd; Railway Publications Ltd; Railway World Ltd; Town & County Books Ltd (qv)
Imprints: A Lewis, Modern Transport
Subjects: Railways, Road Transport, Aviation, Military, Naval, Photographic Landscape
1982: 103 titles *Founded:* 1945
ISBN Publisher's Prefix: 0-7110

Philip **Allan** Publishers Ltd+, Market Pl, Deddington, Oxford OX5 4SE Tel: Deddington 38652 (STD code 0869) Cable Add: Allanbooks Oxford
Man Dir, Editorial, Sales, Rights: Philip Allan; *Production:* Mary Middleton
Subjects: University & College Textbooks and Computer Software in Economics, Accounting and Business Studies
1982: 15 titles *1983:* 18 titles *Founded:* 1973
ISBN Publisher's Prefix: 0-86003

R L **Allan** & Son (Publishers) Ltd, see Pickering & Inglis Ltd

J A Allen & Co Ltd, 1 Lower Grosvenor Pl, London SW1W 0EL Tel: (01) 834 5606 Cable Add: Allenbooks London Telex: 28905/3810
Editorial: Derrick Parsons; *Sales Dir:* C Kendall; *Publicity & Advertising:* Mrs E Martyn; *Production:* W Ireson; *Rights & Permissions:* J A Allen
Subsidiary Companies: The Caduceus Press, Sporting Book Services (both at above address)
Branch Off: (Trade Counter) The Airfield, Norwich Rd, Mendlesham, Suffolk
Subject: Horsemanship, Horses & Horse Sports
Book Club: Horseman's Bookclub
Bookshop: The Horseman's Bookshop, 1 Lower Grosvenor Pl, London SW1
Founded: 1926
ISBN Publisher's Prefix: 0-85131

W H Allen & Co Ltd+, 44 Hill St, London W1X 8LB Tel: (01) 493 6777 Cable Add: Wyndhoward London Telex: 28117
Man Dir: Bob Tanner; *Sales Dir:* Ray Mudie; *Sales Managers:* Claire Watts (Export), Peter Williams (Home); *Editorial:* Mike Bailey, Amanda Girling, Hilary Muray; *Production Dir:* Mark Pickard; *Rights & Permissions:* Lesley Toll
Parent Company: Howard & Wyndham Ltd (at above address)
Imprints: W H Allen, Comet, Star, Tandem, Target, Allan Wingate (Publishers) Ltd
Subjects: Fiction, Non-fiction, Biography, History, Reference, Juveniles, Paperbacks, Social Science, Cookery
1981: 250 titles *1982:* 268 titles *Founded:* 1780
ISBN Publisher's Prefixes: 0-491 (W H Allen), 0-86379 (Comet), 0-352 (Star), 0-426 (Target), 0-85523 (Allan Wingate)

George Allen & Unwin (Publishers) Ltd, 40 Museum St, London WC1A 1LU Tel: (01) 405 8577 Cable Add: Deucalion London WC1 Telex: 826261
Chairman: Merlin S Unwin; *Editorial Dir:* David Fielder; *Promotions Manager:* Virginia Davidson Merritt; *Sales Manager:* Corydon Unwin; *Production:* Bob Heasman; *Foreign Rights Manager:* Alina Dadlez; *Paperbacks Manager:* David Fielder
Sales, Distribution, Accounts & Publicity Off: PO Box 18, Park Lane, Hemel Hempstead, Hertfordshire Tel: Hemel Hempstead 3244 (STD code 0442) Telex: 826261
Subsidiary Companies: George Allen & Unwin Australia Pty Ltd, Australia (qv); Allen & Unwin Inc, USA; Thomas Murby Ltd (qv)
Imprint: Unwin Paperbacks
Subjects: Biography, History, Outdoor and Indoor Sports, Animals, Music, Architecture, Railways, Carpets, Costume, Religions, Health, Nutrition, Child Care, Humour, Fantasy, Social Sciences, Humanities, Education, Life and Earth Sciences, Civil Engineering
Founded: 1914
ISBN Publisher's Prefix: 0-04

Allen Lane, 536 Kings Rd, London SW10 0UH Tel: (01) 351 2393 Cable Add: Penguinook London SW10 Telex: 263130 Penbok g
Chief Executive: Peter Mayer; *Editorial Dir:* Tony Lacey; *Editor-in-Chief:* Peter Carson; *Managing Editor:* Eleo Gordon; *Sales:* Alan Wherry (UK), Mike Hogben (Export); *Production:* Richard Keller; *Marketing:* David Brown; *Publicity:* Lorraine Cooper; *Rights & Permissions:* Carol Heaton
Orders to: Penguin Books, Bath Road, Harmondsworth, Middx
Parent Company: Penguin Books Ltd (qv) (Allen Lane is hardcover imprint)
Associate Company: Longman Group (qv)
Branch Off: See Penguin Books Ltd
Subjects: Fiction, General Non-fiction, Biography, Travel, Cookery, History, Art, Social Science
Founded: 1969
ISBN Publisher's Prefix: 0-7139

Allison & Busby Ltd+, 6a Noel St, London W1V 3RB Tel: (01) 734 1498
Dirs: Clive Allison, Margaret Busby; *Sales Dir:* Bill Swainson; *Publicity, Rights & Permissions:* Astrid Arnold, Sally Penrose; *Production:* Charmian Allwright
Imprint: Motive
Subjects: General Fiction, Belles Lettres, Music, Art, Poetry, Biography, History, Political & Social Science, Economics, Juveniles
1982: 37 titles *Founded:* 1968
ISBN Publisher's Prefix: 0-85031

Allman & Son (Publishers) Ltd, see Mills & Boon Ltd

Allyn & Bacon (London) Ltd+, 42 Colebrooke Row, London N1 8AF Tel: (01) 354 2096
International Sales Managers: Andrea Nettl (UK, Europe, Middle East), Michael Brightmore (South Africa, Australasia, Far East); *Publicity, Rights & Permissions:* Andrea Nettl
Orders to: International Book Distributors Ltd, 66 Wood Lane End, Hemel Hempstead, Hertfordshire Tel: Hemel Hempstead 58531 (STD code 0442)
Parent Company: Allyn & Bacon Inc, 7 Wells Ave, Newton, Massachusetts 02159, USA
Subjects: Tertiary/Reference: Biology, Chemistry, Computing, Business, Education, Engineering, Mathematics, Performing Arts, Physical Education, Psychology, Sociology
1982: approx 100 titles *1983:* approx 90 titles *Founded:* 1868 (USA)
ISBN Publisher's Prefix: 0-205

Alphabet & Image Ltd, see Alphabooks

Alphabooks+, Sherborne, Dorset Tel: Sherborne 814944 (STD Code 0935) Telex: 46534 Alphab G
Man Dir, Production: A E Birks-Hay; *Editorial:* M L Birks-Hay; *Sales:* C Morrison
Parent Company: Alphabet & Image Ltd (Packagers)
Subjects: Illustrated Books on Crafts, Fine Arts, Architecture, Horticulture, Archaeology, History, Bee-keeping
Founded: 1972
ISBN Publisher's Prefixes: 0-906670, 0-9506171

Althea's Nature Series, an imprint of Dinosaur Publications Ltd (qv)

Althea's Pet Series, an imprint of Dinosaur Publications Ltd (qv)

Althea's What to Expect Series, an imprint of Dinosaur Publications Ltd (qv)

Ambito Literario, an imprint of Johnston Green & Co (Publishers) Ltd (qv)

American Technical Publishers, an associate company of The Technical Press Ltd (qv)

American University Publishers Group Ltd, now Academic and University Publishers Group (qv)

Anchor, an imprint of Doubleday & Co Inc (qv)

Andersen Press Ltd+, 19-21 Conway St, London W1P 6JD Tel: (01) 387 2811, (01) 380 0438 Cable Add: Literarius London W1 Telex: 261212
Man Dir, Editorial: Klaus Flugge; *Sales:* (export) Clyde Hunter; *Publicity:* Sarah Gibson; *Rights & Permissions:* Audrey Adams
Associate Company: Hutchinson Publishing Group Ltd (qv)
Subjects: Children's Books
1981: 25 titles *1982:* 26 titles *Founded:* 1975
ISBN Publisher's Prefixes: 0-905478, 0-86264

Anderson Keenan Publishing Ltd*, 392 St John St, London EC1V 4NN Tel: (01) 278 3371
Man Dir: Denis Keenan; *Editorial:* Juliet Shepherd
Orders to: Croom Helm Ltd, 2-10 St John's Rd, London SW11
Subjects: Business Law, Accountancy, Auditing
1981: 6 titles *Founded:* 1978
ISBN Publisher's Prefix: 0-906501

Anglo-German Foundation, 17 Bloomsbury Sq, London WC1A 2LP Tel: (01) 404 3137
Secretary-General: Barbara Beck; *Administrator:* Ingrid Stringfellow
Subjects: Socio-economic, Educational
1981: 7 titles *Founded:* 1973
ISBN Publisher's Prefix: 0-905492

Angus & Robertson (UK) Ltd+, 16 Golden Sq, London W1R 4BN Tel: (01) 437 9602 Cable Add: Ausboko W1 Telex: 897284 Arpub G
Man Dir: Barry Winkleman; *Marketing Manager:* Murray Mahon; *Publicity:* Helen Priday; *Rights & Permissions:* Janet Rowe
Orders to: André Deutsch Ltd, 105 Great Russell St, London WC1
Parent Company: Angus & Robertson/Bay Books, Australia (qv)
Subjects: General Fiction & Non-fiction, Biography, Beauty & Health, Autobiography, Cookery, Craft, Natural History, Poetry, Sports & Outdoor Games, Children's Books
Founded: 1884
ISBN Publisher's Prefix: 0-207

Angus Hudson Ltd, Maxwell House, 74-90 Worship St, London EC2A 2EN Tel: (01) 377 4741 Telex: 885233 Macdon G
Man Dir: Angus Hudson; *Production:* Simonne Waud
Parent Co: Purnell Publishers Ltd, Paulton, Bristol BS18 5LQ (a wholly-owned subsidiary of BPCC PLC (qv))
Subjects: Religious and Quality Children's Books in international co-productions
1981: 27 titles *Founded:* 1976

Antique Collectors' Club, 5 Church St, Woodbridge, Suffolk Tel: Woodbridge 5501 (STD code 03943)
Man Dir, Editorial: John Steel; *Sales:* Brian Cotton; *Production:* Diana Steel
Imprints: Baron Publishing Ltd, Chancery House Publishing Ltd, Oriental Textile Press Ltd
Subjects: Fine Art Reference, Antiques, Gardening, Architecture
1981: 15 titles *Founded:* 1966
ISBN Publisher's Prefixes: 0-902028, 0-907462

Anvil Press Poetry Ltd, 69 King George St, London SE10 8PX Tel: (01) 858 2946
Editor: Peter Jay
Subject: Poetry
1981: 10 titles *1982:* 10 titles *Founded:* 1968
ISBN Publisher's Prefix: 0-85646

Appleford Publishing Group+, Appleford, Abingdon, Oxfordshire OX14 4PB Tel: Abingdon 82319 (STD code 0235)

Chief Executive, Editorial, Rights & Permissions: G E Duffield; *Production:* E Collie
Associate Companies: News Today Magazine, Marcham Books (both at above address); Sutton Courtenay Press (c/o above address)
Imprints: Marcham, Sutton Courtenay, G E Duffield
Subjects: Modern History, Religion, Social, Literary, Reference, Periodicals
Bookshop: Appleford Bookroom (at above address)
1981: 15 titles *1982:* 18 titles *Founded:* 1963

The **Appletree** Press Ltd, 7 James St South, Belfast BT2 8DL Tel: Belfast 243074/Belfast 246756 (STD code 0232)
Man Dir, Sales, Publicity: J D Murphy; *Editorial:* D Marshall, Peter Carr; *Rights & Permissions:* D Webster; *Production:* J Brown
Subjects: Social Studies, Literary Criticism, History, Music, Art, Juveniles, Low- & High-priced Paperbacks, Photography, Fishing, Guide Books, Reference, Folklore, Cookery, Books of Irish Interest
1982: 17 titles *1983:* 18 titles *Founded:* 1975
ISBN Publisher's Prefix: 0-904651

Applied Science Publishers Ltd, see Elsevier Applied Science Publishers

Aquarian Press Ltd+, Denington Estate, Wellingborough, Northamptonshire NN8 2RQ Tel: Wellingborough 76031 (STD code 0933) Cable Add: Thorgroup Wellingborough Telex: 311072 Thopub G
Chairman: J A Young; *Man Dir:* D J Young; *Rights & Permissions:* Marjorie Nelson; *Editorial Dir:* Michael Cox; *Production Dir:* D C J Palmer; *Sales Manager:* Tom Berry
Parent Company: Thorsons Publishers Ltd (qv)
Subjects: Astrology, Comparative Religion, Magic & Occultism, Occult History, Paranormal & Psychical Phenomena, Philosophy, Qabalah, Tarot
1982: 25 titles *1983:* 33 titles *Founded:* 1953
ISBN Publisher's Prefix: 0-85030

Aquila Essays, an imprint of Johnston Green & Co (Publishers) Ltd (qv)

Aquila Pamphlet Poets, an imprint of Johnston Green & Co (Publishers) Ltd (qv)

Aquila Poetry, an imprint of Johnston Green & Co (Publishers) Ltd (qv)

Aquila Publishing, an imprint of Johnston Green & Co (Publishers) Ltd (qv)

Aquila/The Phaethon Press, an imprint of Johnston Green & Co (Publishers) Ltd (qv)

Aquila The Wayzgoose Press, an imprint of Johnston Green & Co (Publishers) Ltd (qv)

Arcady Books Ltd+, 2 Woodlands Rd, Ashurst, Southampton SO4 2AD Tel: Ashurst 2601 (STD code 042 129)
Man Dir, Sales: Michael Edwards; *Editorial Dir, Production, Publicity, Rights & Permissions:* Anne-Marie Edwards
Subjects: Literature, Outdoor Activities, The New Forest, General Non-fiction
1981: 3 titles *1982:* 3 titles *Founded:* 1981
ISBN Publisher's Prefix: 0-907753

Architectural Press Ltd, 9 Queen Anne's Gate, London SW1H 9BY Tel: (01) 222 4333 Cable Add: Buildable London SW1 Telex: 8953505
Man Dir: Ron Norbury; *Managing Editor:* Maritz Vandenberg; *Sales Manager:* Rowan Crowley; *Publicity:* Sally Evans; *Production and Co-ordination Manager:* Keith Kneebone; *Rights & Permissions:* Cathy Miller
Subsidiary Companies and Imprints: Astragal Books, Telecommunications Press
Subject: Architecture
1981: 33 titles *Founded:* 1895
ISBN Publisher's Prefixes: 0-85139 (Architectural Press), 0-906525 (Astragal Books), 0-907401 (Telecommunications Press)

Arena, an imprint of Inter-Varsity Press (qv)

Arena Books, an imprint of Arrow Books Ltd (qv)

Argus Books Ltd, Wolsey House, Wolsey Rd, Hemel Hempstead, Hertfordshire HP2 4SS Tel: Hemel Hempstead 41221 (STD code 0442)
Man Dir: G D L R Home; *Publishing, Sales Manager:* M Blackman
Parent Company: Argus Press Ltd
Imprint: Model & Allied Publications (qv)
Subjects: Hobbies, Modelling
ISBN Publisher's Prefixes: 0-85242, 0-85344

Argus Communications (UK Division), DLM House, Edinburgh Way, Harlow, Essex CM20 2HL Tel: Harlow 39441 (STD code 0279) Telex: 817086
General Manager: Richard De Rosa
Parent Company: Argus Communications, One DLM Park, PO Box 5000, Allen, TX 75002, USA
Subjects: Religion, Popular Psychology, Education
Founded: (UK) 1975
ISBN Publisher's Prefixes: 0-913592, 0-89505

Aris & Phillips Ltd, Teddington House, Warminster, Wilts BA12 8PQ Tel: Warminster 213409 (STD code 0985) Telex: 449631 Warlib G attn Aris Phillips
Orders to: La Haule Books Ltd, West Lodge, La Haule, Saint Aubin, Jersey, Channel Islands
Man Dir: Adrian Phillips; *Editorial:* John Aris; *Sales, Publicity, Rights & Permissions:* Lucinda Phillips; *Production:* Philip Mudd
Associate Companies: La Haule Books Ltd, West Lodge, La Haule, Saint Aubin, Jersey, Channel Islands; Serindia Publications, 10 Parkfields, Putney, London SW15
Subjects: Ancient History, Oriental, Classical, Middle East, Archaeology, Egyptology
1981: 12 titles *1982:* 14 titles *Founded:* 1972
ISBN Publisher's Prefix: 0-85668

Arlington Books (Publishers) Ltd, 3 Clifford St, Mayfair, London W1X 1RA Tel: (01) 439 1688
Chairman, Man Dir: Desmond Elliott; *Rights & Permissions Dir:* Christine Lunness; *Sales Manager:* Ondine Upton; *Production and Editorial:* Angela Oram
Trade Dept: Biblios Ltd, Glenside Industrial Estate, Partridge Green, Horsham, West Sussex Tel: Horsham 710971 (STD code 0403)
Imprint: Columbine House
Subjects: General Fiction and Non-fiction, Health, Biography, Children's Books
Founded: 1960
ISBN Publisher's Prefix: 0-85140

Armada Books, see William Collins Sons & Co Ltd

Arms & Armour Press+, 2-6 Hampstead High St, London NW3 1QQ Tel: (01) 794 7868 Cable Add: Armsbooks London NW3 Telex: 8951899 Armsbk G
Man Dir: Lionel Leventhal; *Editorial Dir:* David Gibbons; *Production:* Beryl Gibbons
Parent Company: Lionel Leventhal Ltd (qv)
Associate Company: Ken Trotman Arms Books (at above address)
Subjects: Military
1981: 40 titles *Founded:* 1966
ISBN Publisher's Prefix: 0-85368

E J **Arnold** & Son Ltd, Parkside Lane, Dewsbury Rd, Leeds LS11 5TD Tel: Leeds 772112 (STD code 0532) Cable Add: Arnold Leeds Telex: 556347
This is the Educational Publishing Division of Pergamon Press Ltd (qv)
Man Dirs: C Bundy (E J Arnold), M E Wayte (Arnold-Wheaton)
Parent Company: Pergamon Press Ltd (qv)
Imprints: Arnold-Wheaton, Religious and Moral Education Press (qv)
Subjects: Primary and Secondary Educational, Religious Books for School and Trade, Educational Material, School Book Supply
1983: 150 titles *Founded:* 1863
Miscellaneous: E J Arnold & Son Ltd now incorporates E S A Creative Learning Ltd
ISBN Publisher's Prefixes: 0-560, 0-08

Edward **Arnold** (Publishers) Ltd, 41 Bedford Sq, London WC1B 3DQ Tel: (01) 637 7161 Cable Add: Scholarly London W1 Telex: 847918 Arnold G
Chairman & Man Dir: Anthony Hamilton; *Sales Dir:* George Davies; *Production:* Robin Smeeton; *Publicity:* Michael Soper (Education), John Russell (Tertiary); *Foreign Rights:* Arlene Seaton; *Permissions:* Angela Anderson
Subsidiary Company: Edward Arnold (Australia) Pty Ltd, Australia (qv)
Associate Company: Arnold-Heinemann Publishers (India) Pvt Ltd, India (qv)
Subjects: Humanities, Science, Engineering, Medicine, University, Secondary and Primary Textbooks, Technical, Education, English Language Teaching, Journals, Computer Software
1981: 224 titles *Founded:* 1890
ISBN Publisher's Prefix: 0-7131

Arnold-Wheaton, publishing imprint of merger of E J Arnold & Son Ltd (qv) and A Wheaton & Co Ltd

Arrow Books Ltd+, 17 Conway St, London W1P 6JD Tel: (01) 387 2811 Telex: 261212
Man Dir: Graham Lane; *Sales:* Richard Tucker; *Editorial:* Peter Lavery
Orders to: Tiptree Book Services, Church Rd, Tiptree, Colchester, Essex Tel: Tiptree 816362 (STD code 0621)
Parent Company: The Hutchinson Publishing Group Ltd (qv)
Associate Companies: Geographia Ltd (qv); Robert Nicholson Publications Ltd (qv)
Imprints: Arena Books, Beaver Books, Sparrow Books, Zenith
Subjects: Paperbacks: Adult, Children's, Fiction, Non-fiction
Founded: 1948
ISBN Publisher's Prefix: 0-09

Art Heritage, an imprint of Scorpion Publications Ltd (qv)

Artemis Press Ltd, an imprint of Vision Press Ltd (qv)

Artists House, an imprint of Mitchell Beazley London Ltd (qv)

Artus, an imprint of George Weidenfeld & Nicolson Ltd (qv)

Ascent Books Ltd*, 22 Chewter Lane, Windlesham, Surrey GU20 6JP Tel: 74741 (STD code 0276)
Man Dir, Editorial, Sales, Production, Rights & Permissions: Christopher Foster; *Publicity:* Ingela Claxton
Orders to: George Philip Services Ltd, PO Box 1, Littlehampton, West Sussex BN17 7EN Tel: Littlehampton 7453 (STD code 09064)
Subject: European History
ISBN Publisher's Prefix: 0-906407

Ash & Grant, 9 Henrietta St, London WC2E 8PS Tel: (01) 379 7169 Telex: 8954527 Deekay G
Publisher: Ian Grant; *Production:* Lorraine Baird
Orders to: WHS Distributors, St John's House, East St, Leicester LE1 6NE Tel: Leicester 551196 (STD code 0533)
Parent Company: Dorling Kindersley Ltd (qv)
Subjects: Current Affairs, Photography, Children's Books, Natural History, Art Books
1981: 7 titles *Founded:* 1973
ISBN Publisher's Prefix: 0-904069

Ashgrove Press Ltd+, 26 Gay St, Bath, Avon BA1 2PD Tel: Bath 25539 (STD code 0225)
Man Dir, Rights & Permissions: Robin Campbell; *Sales, Publicity:* Sue Graham-Brown
Subjects: Countryside, Current Affairs, Fiction, General, Health & Healing, Humour, Illustrated Editions, Philosophy, Psychology, Regional & Local, Religion
1981: 3 titles *1982:* 5 titles *Founded:* 1979
ISBN Publisher's Prefix: 0-906798

Ashmolean Museum Publications, Ashmolean Museum, Beaumont St, Oxford OX1 2PH Tel: Oxford 512651 (STD code 0865)
Publications Officer: R I H Charlton
Subjects: European & Oriental Art, Archaeology & History, Numismatics, Classical Studies, Egyptology
1981: 9 titles *1982:* 9 titles
ISBN Publisher's Prefixes: 0-900090, 0-907849

Associated Book Publishers PLC, 11 New Fetter Lane, London EC4P 4EE Tel: (01) 583 9855 Cable Add: Elegiacs London EC4P 4EE Telex: 263398
Chairman: P H B Allsop; *Marketing Dir:* C H Shirley
See subsidiary company individual entries for further details
Subsidiary Companies: Associated Book Publishers (Aust) Ltd (qv), Methuen Australia Pty Ltd (qv) (both in Australia); Associated Book Publishers (New Zealand) Ltd, New Zealand (qv); Associated Book Publishers (Services) Ltd; Sweet & Maxwell Spon (Booksellers) Ltd; Associated Book Publishers (UK) Ltd which incorporates the following: Chapman & Hall Ltd (qv); Current Law Publishers Ltd; Eyre & Spottiswood (Publishers) Ltd (qv); W Green & Son Ltd (qv); Methuen & Co Ltd (qv); Methuen Children's Books Ltd (qv); Methuen Educational Ltd; Methuen London Ltd (qv); Methuen Paperbacks Ltd (qv); Momentum Licensing Ltd; Police Review Publishing Co Ltd; E & F N Spon Ltd (qv); Stevens & Sons Ltd (qv); Sweet & Maxwell Ltd (qv); Tavistock Publications Ltd (qv)
Subjects: Legal, Periodicals, Academic & Scientific, Children's, General
Bookshops: Hammicks Wholesale and Hammicks Bookshops Ltd (qv under Major Booksellers)
Founded: 1958

Associated Business Press+, Ludgate House, 107-111 Fleet St, London EC4A 2AB Tel: (01) 583 8888 Cable Add: Busipress London EC4 Telex: 262251
Publishing Director: Peter Cooper
Parent Company: AGB Research PLC, 76 Shoe Lane, London EC4A 3JB
Subjects: Business, Management
Miscellaneous: Associated Business Press is the publishing imprint of Associated Business Programmes Ltd
ISBN Publisher's Prefix: 0-85227

Association for Science Education, College Lane, Hatfield, Hertfordshire AL10 9AA Tel: Hatfield 67411 (STD code 07072)
General Secretary: B G Atwood; *Publications Officer:* C B Hodge
Subjects: Science Education
ISBN Publisher's Prefix: 0-902786

Astragal Books, see Architectural Press Ltd

Athene Publishing Co, an imprint of Thorsons Publishers Ltd (qv)

The **Athlone** Press Ltd, 44 Bedford Row, London WC1R 4LY Tel: (01) 405 9836/7 Telex: 261507
Man Dir: Brian Southam; *Sales, Rights & Permissions:* Christine Owen; *Publicity Manager:* Sheila Traill
Warehouse: Marston Book Services Ltd, PO Box 87, Oxford OX4 1JB
Subjects: Architecture, Archaeology, Biological Sciences, Chemistry, Ecology, Physics, Astronomy, Computer Science, Economics, History, Music, Art, Philosophy, Medicine, Engineering, General & Social Science, University Textbooks, Law, Japanese and South East Asian Studies
1982: 25 titles *Founded:* 1949
ISBN Publisher's Prefix: 0-485

Atlantic, an imprint of Ramboro Enterprises Ltd (qv)

Atlantic Communications Ltd*, 19 Coalecroft Rd, London SW15 Tel: (01) 789 2740
Subjects: Contemporary History, Current Affairs, Ecology & the Environment

Augener, an imprint of Stainer & Bell Ltd (qv)

Aurum Press Ltd+, 33 Museum St, London WC1A 1LD Tel: (01) 631 4596 Telex: 299557 Aurum G
Joint Man Dirs: Timothy Chadwick, Michael Haggiag; *Publishing Dir:* Michael Haggiag; *Managing Editor:* Angela Dyer; *Sales Dir:* Neil Clitheroe; *Marketing Consultant:* Barrie Knight; *Special Projects:* Eugene Braun-Munk
Subjects: Large Format, Illustrated, General
1982: 7 titles *1983:* 13 titles *Founded:* 1977
ISBN Publisher's Prefix: 0-906053

Autobooks Ltd, Bradford Rd, East Ardsley, Wakefield, West Yorkshire WF3 2JN Tel: Wakefield 823971 (STD code 0924) Telex: 51458 Comhud G Autobooks
Man Dir: Brian Lewis; *Sales Manager:* David Clements
Parent Company: Siemssen Hunter Ltd
Subjects: Do-it-Yourself, Car Workshop Manuals
1983: 9 titles *Founded:* 1958
ISBN Publisher's Prefixes: 0-85146, 0-85147

Automobile Association, Fanum House, Basingstoke, Hampshire RG21 2EA Tel: Basingstoke 62929 (STD code 0256) Telex: 858538
Editorial: Ralph Robbins; *Sales:* Brian Stelling; *Publications General Manager:* Bill Halden
Subjects: Tourist Guides, Guidebooks, Maps, Atlases, Leisure, Travel
1981: 16 titles *1982:* 18 titles
ISBN Publisher's Prefix: 0-86145

Avebury Publishing Co Ltd, Olympic House, 63 Woodside Rd, Amersham, Bucks HP6 6AA Tel: Amersham 22121 (STD code 02403)
Man Dir: J M Dening
Orders to: The Distribution Centre, Blackhorse Rd, Letchworth, Herts SG6 1HN
Imprints: Avebury, Demand Reprints, Gregg International, International Dictionary Service
Subjects: Scholarly Monographs and Reprints in Humanities, Languages, Literature, Philosophy, Landscape Studies
Founded: 1977
ISBN Publisher's Prefixes: 0-86127 (Avebury), 0-576 (Gregg)

Avon-Anglia Publications & Services+, Annesley House, 21 Southside, Weston-super-Mare, Avon BS23 2QU Tel: Weston-super-Mare 31616 (STD code 0934)
Chief Executive: Geoffrey Body
Imprint: Kingsmead Press
Subjects: Transport, History, Countryside, Local Art & Architecture
1981: 7 titles *1982:* 5 titles *Founded:* 1976
ISBN Publisher's Prefixes: 0-905466 (Avon-Anglia), 0-906230, 0-901571 (both Kingsmead)

Award Publications Ltd, Spring House, Spring Place, London NW5 3BH Tel: (01) 485 7747 Telex: 296452 Award G
Man Dir: R Wilkinson
Subjects: Children's
1981: 10 titles *1982:* 16 titles *Founded:* 1955

B B C Publications, 35 Marylebone High St, London W1M 4AA Tel: (01) 580 5577 Cable Add: Broadcasts London Telex: 265781
General Manager: J G Holmes; *Head of Exports, Rights:* Ilinca Bossy; *Book Sales Manager:* R Chown; *Production Manager:* P Birch; *Publicity:* K J Bristow
Orders to: 144/152 Bermondsey St, London SE1 3TH
Subjects: General Fiction, History, How-to, Music, Art, Reference, Religion, Juveniles, Low- & High-priced Paperbacks, Medicine, Engineering, General & Social Science, Secondary Textbooks, Adult Education
Bookshops: 35 Marylebone High St, London W1M 4AA; Broadcasting House, Portland Pl, London W1A 1AA; BBC Television Centre, Wood Lane, London W12 7RJ
Founded: 1925
ISBN Publisher's Prefix: 0-563

B F I Publishing+, British Film Institute, 81 Dean St, London W1V 6AA Tel: (01) 437 4355 Cable Add: Brifilinst London W1 Telex: 27624
Head of Publishing: Geoffrey Nowell-Smith; *Editorial:* David Wilson; *Sales, Publicity:* Diana Watt; *Production:* John Smoker; *Rights & Permissions:* Roma Gibson
Warehouse: International Book Distributors Ltd, 66 Wood Lane End, Hemel Hempstead, Hertfordshire HP2 4RG
Subjects: Film, Television, Academic, General
Founded: 1980
ISBN Publisher's Prefix: 0-85170

B I M H Publications+, British Institute of Mental Handicap, Wolverhampton Rd, Kidderminster, Worcs DY10 3PP Tel: Kidderminster 850251 (STD code 0562)
Dir: Dr G B Simon; *Editorial Dir, and other offices:* Mrs S J Newbould
Subjects: Mental Handicap, Physical Handicap, Psychiatry, Psychology, Nursing, Education, Social Work, Periodicals
1981: 7 titles *1982:* 5 titles *Founded:* 1971
ISBN Publisher's Prefix: 0-906054

B P C C PLC+, Maxwell House, 74 Worship St, London EC2A 2EN Tel: (01) 377 4600 Telex: 886048
Formerly British Printing Corporation Ltd
Parent Company (77%): Pergamon Press Ltd (qv)
BPCC Divisions include:
BPCC Publishing Corporation Ltd, with the following members: Adkinson Parrish Ltd (qv), BPC Publishers Ltd, CEEPI Ltd (Caxton and English Educational Programmes International) (qv), Financial Weekly Ltd, Macdonald & Co (Publishers)

Ltd (qv), New Caxton Library Service Ltd (qv), Purnell Publishers Ltd (see Purnell Books), Waterlow Publishers Ltd (qv)
BPCC Communication & Information Corporation Ltd
The British Gravure Corporation Ltd
The Caxton Group
Overseas Subsidiaries include: Macdonald Purnell (Pty) Ltd, Republic of South Africa (qv); Marketing Services Ltd, New Zealand; IPA Distributusjon Als, Norway; KG Bertmarks Förlag AB, Sweden; Delphin Verlag GmbH, Federal Republic of Germany (qv); Macdonald Futura (Australia) Pty Ltd; Macdonald Middle East Sàrl, Lebanon; Cedibra Editora Brasileira Ltda, Brazil (qv); Macdonald Raintree Inc, USA (51% owned); Purnell Inc, USA
Associate Companies include: Rathbone Books Ltd, Usborne Publishing Ltd (qv), Victoria House Publishing Ltd
Subjects: General Fiction, Belles Lettres, Poetry, Biography, History, How-to, Music, Art, Philosophy, Reference, Low-priced Paperbacks & Part-works, Primary & Secondary Textbooks

B S C Books Ltd, 33 Maiden Lane, London WC2 Tel: (01) 836 3341
Man Dir: Bill Smith; *Sales:* Tim Finch
Imprint: The Booksmith
Bookshops: Booksmith chain
1980: 10 titles *1981:* 50 titles
Miscellaneous: Firm is also a wholesaler and remainder dealer
ISBN Publisher's Prefix: 0-900123

Bernard **Babani** (Publishing) Ltd+, The Grampians, Shepherds Bush Rd, London W6 7NF Tel: (01) 603 2581, (01) 603 7296 Cable Add: Radiobooks London W6
(Formerly Babani Press and Bernards (Publishers) Ltd)
Man Dir, Editorial: M H Babani; *Sales, Rights & Permissions:* S Babani; *Production, Publicity:* P Pragnell
Associate Companies: Babani Press; Bernards (Publishers) Ltd
Subjects: Low-priced Paperbacks, Radio Electronics, Computing
Founded: 1977 (Babani Press 1971, Bernards Publishers 1942)
ISBN Publisher's Prefixes: 0-85934, 0-900162

Bachman & Turner, 53 High St, Maidstone, Kent ME14 1SY Tel: Maidstone 681034 (STD code 0622)
Editorial: Marta Bachman; *Rights & Permissions:* Barbara Tomlinson
Parent Company: Londinium Press Ltd (qv)
Subjects: General Fiction, Biography, History, Music, Art, Philosophy
1982: 12 titles *Founded:* 1972
ISBN Publisher's Prefix: 0-85974

Backpacker's Guides Series, an imprint of Bradt Enterprises (qv)

Badger Books, an imprint of Studio Publications (Ipswich) Ltd (qv)

Samuel **Bagster** & Sons Ltd*, 1 Bath St, London EC1V 9LB Tel: (01) 251 2925
Subjects: Religious, Reference, Bibles, Prayer and Hymn Books
Founded: 1794
ISBN Publisher's Prefix: 0-85150

Bailey Bros & Swinfen Ltd, Warner House, Folkestone, Kent CT19 6PH Tel: Folkestone 56501 (STD code 0303) Cable Add: Forenbuks Telex: 96328
Man Dir: J R Bailey
Subsidiary Companies: Bailey Bros & Swinfen Exports Ltd; Bailey Subscription Agents Ltd
Imprints: Fantasy Library, Ghost Hunters' Library, Hour-Glass Press
Subjects: General Fiction, History, How-to, Reference, Engineering
Book Clubs: Bailey's German, French, Italian & Spanish Book Clubs
Founded: 1929
ISBN Publisher's Prefix: 0-561

Baillière Tindall, 1 St Anne's Rd, Eastbourne, East Sussex BN21 3UN Tel: Eastbourne 638221 (STD code 0323) Telex: 877503 Volmst
Man Dir: Robert Kiernan; *Publishing Dir:* David S B Inglis; *Publisher:* Aidan Reynolds; *Editorial Dir:* David Dickens; *Sales Dir:* Barend ter Haar
Parent Company: Holt-Saunders Ltd (qv)
Subjects: Medical, Veterinary, Nursing, Pharmaceutical
Founded: 1826
ISBN Publisher's Prefix: 0-7020

Howard **Baker Press** Ltd, 27A Arterberry Rd, London SW20 Tel: (01) 947 5482
Cable Add: Bakerbook London
Man Dir: W Howard Baker
Imprint: Greyfriars Press
Subjects: Fiction, Non-fiction, Political Science, Poetry, Autobiography, Biography, Reference, Specialist Facsimile Editions, Maps
Book Club: Greyfriars Book Club
1981: 22 titles
ISBN Publisher's Prefix: 0-7030

John **Baker (Publishers)** Ltd, 35 Bedford Row, London WC1R 4JH Tel: (01) 242 0946 Cable Add: Biblos, London WC1 Telex: 21792 ref 2546
Dirs: C A A Black, D E Gadsby
Parent Company: A & C Black Ltd (qv)
Subjects: Art, Archaeology, History
ISBN Publisher's Prefix: 0-212

The **Banner** of Truth Trust+, 3 Murrayfield Rd, Edinburgh EH12 6EL Tel: (031) 337 7310
Chief Executive: Mervyn T Barter; *Editorial:* Rev Iain H Murray; *Sales, Production:* Humphrey V Mildred
Branch Off: PO Box 621, Carlisle, Pennsylvania 17013, USA
Subject: Christian Faith
1981: 20 titles *1982:* 18 titles *Founded:* 1957
ISBN Publisher's Prefix: 0-85151

Barebone Books, a subsidiary of Picton Publishing (Chippenham) Ltd (qv)

Arthur **Barker** Ltd, 91 Clapham High St, London SW4 7TA Tel: (01) 622 9933 Cable Add: Nicobar London SW4 7TA Telex: 918066
Sales Dir: D Livermore; *Marketing Dir:* Rosalind Lewis; *Rights & Permissions:* Miss B J Maclennan
Parent Company: Weidenfeld (Publishers) Ltd (qv)
Subjects: Biography, How-to, Reference, Military History, Crime, Sport
Founded: 1931
ISBN Publisher's Prefix: 0-213

Barnes & Noble, see Harper & Row Ltd

Baron Publishing Ltd, an imprint of Antique Collectors' Club (qv)

Barracuda Books Ltd, Meadows House, Well St, Buckingham MK18 1EW Tel: Buckingham 814441 (STD code 0280)
Editorial Offices: Radclive Hall, Radclive, Buckingham
Chief Executive and Publisher: Clive Birch; *Sales Promotion:* Bernadette Halsall; *Sales:* Lorna Muckleston
Imprint: Sporting and Leisure Press
Subjects: Local History, Natural History
1981: 17 titles *1982:* 22 titles *Founded:* 1974
ISBN Publisher's Prefix: 0-86023

Barrie & Jenkins Ltd, an imprint of Hutchinson Books Ltd (qv)

John **Bartholomew & Son** Ltd, 12 Duncan St, Edinburgh EH9 1TA Tel: (031) 667 9341 Cable Add: Bartholomew Edinburgh Telex: 728134 Barts G
Man Dir: D A Ross Stewart; *Editorial:* J C Bartholomew; *Marketing:* M J Chittleburgh; *Production:* R G Bartholomew; *Rights & Permissions:* M J Chittleburgh; *Publishing:* C B Kirkwood; *Publicity:* Mrs C J Macefield
Subsidiary Companies: T & T Clark Ltd (qv), Map Marketing Ltd
Subjects: Maps, Atlases, Leisure Books
1983: 385 titles *Founded:* 1826
ISBN Publisher's Prefixes: 0-7028, 0-85152

Basic Books, see Harper & Row Ltd

The **Basilisk** Press Ltd, 32 England's Lane, London NW3 1YB Tel: (01) 722 2142
Man Dir: Charlene B Garry
Subjects: Literature, Botany, Architecture, Landscape Gardening
Bookshop: At above address
Founded: 1973

B T **Batsford** Ltd, 4 Fitzhardinge St, London W1H 0AH Tel: (01) 486 8484 Cable Add: Batsfordia London
Man Dir: Peter Kemmis Betty; *Editorial Dir:* William Waller; *Sales Dir:* Robert Beard; *Publicity Manager:* Margaret Berchowitz; *Production Dir:* Roger Huggins
Subjects: History, How-to, Music, Art & Craft, Juveniles, Psychology, Engineering, Social Science, Educational Materials, Topography, Needlecraft, Sports, Hobbies, Cookery, Costumes, Chess
Founded: 1843
ISBN Publisher's Prefix: 0-7134

Beacon Publishing, Jubilee House, Billing Brook Rd, Weston Favell, Northampton NN3 4NW Tel: Northampton 407288 (STD code 0604) Telex: 312242 Midtlx G
Joint Man Dirs: Alistair L Stewart, Richard J Thomas; *Editorial, Production:* Alistair L Stewart; *Sales, Publicity, Rights & Permissions:* Malcolm Orr-Ewing
Subjects: Business Reference, Leisure Reference
1981: 5 titles *1982:* 10 titles *Founded:* 1981
ISBN Publisher's Prefix: 0-906358

Beaumont Executive Press, an associate company of The Technical Press Ltd (qv)

Beaver Books, an imprint of Arrow Books Ltd (qv)

Becknell Books, PO Box 21, King's Lynn, Norfolk PE30 2QP Tel: King's Lynn 61328 (STD code 0553)
Editorial, Rights & Permissions: M D Beckett; *Sales:* P R Hemnell; *Production:* J Beckett; *Publicity:* S J Hemnell
Subject: Transport (Railways and Buses)
1981: 7 titles *1982:* 7 titles *Founded:* 1980
ISBN Publisher's Prefix: 0-907087

Bedford Square Press of the National Council for Voluntary Organizations*, 26 Bedford Sq, London WC1B 3HU Tel: (01) 636 4066
Subjects: Social Policy and Planning, Guides and Handbooks for Voluntary Organizations
1981: 10 titles
Miscellaneous: Bedford Square Press also publishes for or in association with other organizations
ISBN Publisher's Prefix: 0-7199

Bee In Bonnet, an imprint of Zomba Books (qv)

Bell & Hyman Ltd+, Denmark House, 37-39 Queen Elizabeth St, London SE1 2QB Tel: (01) 407 0709, (01) 407 5237 Cable Add: Bellhyman London SE1 Telex: 886245
Chairman, Man Dir: R P Hyman; *Marketing Dir:* N C Britten; *Production:*

Jim Pope; *Publicity:* Elizabeth Sich; *Publishing Manager, Rights:* Mary Butler
Subjects: Secondary and Further Education Textbooks, Collecting and Crafts, Chess, Pepys, Craft, How-to, Juveniles, English as a foreign language
Founded: 1838
ISBN Publisher's Prefix: 0-7135

Belton Books, an imprint of Stainer & Bell Ltd (qv)

Benjamin/Cummings Inc, 53 Bedford Sq, London WC1B 3DZ Tel: (01) 631 1636 Cable Add: Adiwes London WC1 Telex: 8811948
Manager: Stanley B Malcolm; *Rights & Permissions:* Irma Hoijer (USA)
Subjects: Reference, Science, Technology, University Textbooks
Founded: 1960
Miscellaneous: Firm is a member of the Addison-Wesley Publishing Group (qv)
ISBN Publisher's Prefix: 0-8053

Ernest **Benn** Ltd+, Sovereign House, Sovereign Way, Tonbridge, Kent TN9 1RW Tel: Tonbridge 362468 (STD code 0732) Telex: 95132 Benton G
Publisher: John Beer; *Editors:* Paul Langridge (Juveniles and Blue Guides), Tom Neville (Drama); *Publicity:* Frances Rae
Orders to: A & C Black Ltd, Howard Rd, Eaton Socon, Huntingdon, Cambridgeshire PE19 3EZ Tel: Huntingdon 212666 (STD code 0480)
Parent Company: Benn Brothers PLC, 12 Norwich St, London EC4A 1EJ
Associate Company: Benn Publications Ltd (at above Tonbridge address)
Imprints include: Benn Electronics Pubs Ltd, Benn Technical Books, Charles Knight Ltd, Tolley Publishing Co
Subjects: Guide Books, Fishing, Juvenile Picture Books, Drama
1983: 25 titles *Founded:* 1925
ISBN Publisher's Prefix: 0-510

Bernards (Publishers) Ltd, see Bernard Babani (Publishing) Ltd

Better Books, 15A Chelsea Rd, Lower Weston, Bath, Avon BA1 3DU Tel: Bath 28010 (STD code 0225)
Proprietor: H Welchman; *Publicity Manager:* Pip Mason
Subject: Remedial Education
1983: 10 titles *Founded:* 1974
ISBN Publisher's Prefix: 0-904700

Bibliagora+, PO Box 7, Hounslow TW3 2LA Tel: (01) 898 1234, (01) 894 6262 Telex: 935918 Bridge G
Man Dir: D Rex-Taylor; *Editorial:* Sev Hepton; *Sales:* Miss E Taylor; *Production:* C Webb; *Publicity:* A Cutting; *Rights & Permissions:* K Gee
Subsidiary Companies: Bridge Library, 1A Whitton Waye, Hounslow TW3 2LT; Lineage Research Unit, Out-of-Print Tracing Unit (both at PO Box 7, Hounslow TW3 2LX)
Imprint: St George & Dragon Press
Subjects: Indoor Games, Philosophy, Contract Bridge
Book Club: Bridge Book Club (qv)
1981: 24 titles *1982:* 29 titles *Founded:* 1973
Miscellaneous: Firm is also mail-order international bookseller: Bibliagora (Books old & new) (at main company address)
ISBN Publisher's Prefix: 0-906031

Clive **Bingley** Ltd, 16 Pembridge Rd, London W11 3HL Tel: (01) 229 1825 Telex: 21897 Laldn G
The above is the editorial and production office. Sales and publicity are at 7 Ridgmount St, London WC1E 7AE Tel: (01) 636 7543

Warehouse: Wentworth Book Co, Pindar Rd, Hoddesdon, Herts
Man Dir: Charles Ellis; *Editorial Consultant:* Clive Bingley; *Sales Manager:* Beverly Brentnall; *Publicity Manager:* Selina Bird
Parent Company: Library Association Publishing, 7 Ridgmount St, London WC1E 7AE
Subjects: Library Science, Textbooks, Reference, Directories, Bibliographies
1981: 20 titles *1982:* 18 titles *Founded:* 1965
ISBN Publisher's Prefix: 0-85157

Birmingham Museums and Art Gallery Publications Unit, Chamberlain Sq, Birmingham B3 3DH Tel: (021) 235 4051
Publications Manager: Trevor Jones
Subjects: Fine & Applied Arts, Archaeology, Natural History
ISBN Publisher's Prefix: 0-903504

Bison Books Ltd, Bolton House, 194 Old Brompton Rd, London SW5 0AS Tel: (01) 373 2549 Telex: 888014 Bison G
Director: Sydney L Mayer
Head Office: 17 Sherwood Pl, Greenwich, Connecticut 06830, USA
Subjects: Military and Modern History, Animals, Cookery, Transport, Sport, Modelling
Founded: 1975

A & C **Black** (Publishers) Ltd, 35 Bedford Row, London WC1R 4JH Tel: (01) 242 0946 Cable Add: Biblos London WC1 Telex: 21792 ref 2546
Man Dirs: Charles Black, David Gadsby; *Sales Dir:* Paul White
Orders to: Howard Rd, Eaton Socon, Huntingdon, Cambs PE19 3EZ Tel: Huntingdon 212666 (STD code 0480)
Subsidiary Companies: John Baker (Publishers) Ltd (qv); F Lewis (Publishers) Ltd (qv)
Subjects: History, Music, Art, Sports, Reference, Religion, Juveniles, Primary Textbooks, Chess, Crafts
Book Club: Fishing Book Club
Founded: 1807
ISBN Publisher's Prefix: 0-7136

Black Box Thrillers, an imprint of Zomba Books (qv)

Black Swan, an imprint of Corgi Books Ltd (qv)

The **Black Swan** Press, 28 Bosley's Orchard, Grove, Wantage, Oxon Tel: Wantage 4517 (STD code 02357)
Subjects: English classics in quality editions

Blacker Calmann Cooper Ltd, see John Calmann & Cooper Ltd

Blackie & Son Ltd, Bishopbriggs, Glasgow G64 2NZ Tel: (041) 772 2311 Cable Add: Blackie Glasgow
Man Dir: R Michael Miller; *Editorial:* A D Mitchell, Rosemary Lanning, Matthew Pryde (Children's); Dr A G MacKintosh (Academic); *Sales Managers:* Norman Clayton (Children's), John Drummond (Educational), Gerard Dummett (Academic); *Publicity:* John Drummond (Educational), Gerard Dummett (Academic), Clare Harrison (Children's)
Orders to: J M Dent (Distribution) Ltd, Dunhams Lane, Letchworth, Herts SG6 1LF Tel: Letchworth 6241 (STD code 04626)
Subsidiary Companies: Abelard-Schuman Ltd (qv); International Textbook Co Ltd (qv); Leonard Hill (qv); Surrey University Press (qv)
Branch Off: Furnival House, 14-18 High Holborn, London Tel: (01) 242 5832
Subjects: School Textbooks, Reference, Children's, Scientific & Engineering, General & Social Science, Quality Paperbacks
Founded: 1809
ISBN Publisher's Prefix: 0-216

Blackstaff Press Ltd, 3 Galway Park, Dundonald, Belfast BT16 0AN Tel: Dundonald 7161 (STD code 02318)
Man Dir: Anne Tannahill; *Chairman:* Michael Burns; *Publicity & Advertising Dir, Rights & Permissions:* Anne-Marie Conway; *Sales:* Sally Kelso; *Production:* Wendy Dunbar
Subjects: General Fiction, Poetry, Drama, Biography, History, Reference, Paperbacks, General & Social Science, Art, Music, Photography, Children's Books, Natural History, Folklore, Sport, Philosophy, Politics, Archaeology, Humour, Education
Founded: 1971
ISBN Publisher's Prefix: 0-85640

Basil **Blackwell** Publisher Ltd, 108 Cowley Rd, Oxford OX4 1JF Tel: Oxford 722146 (STD code 0865) Cable Add: Books Oxford Telex: 837022 Oxbook G
Man Dir: David Martin; *Editorial Dir:* John Davey; *Sales Dir:* Norman Drake; *Publicity:* Ludo Craddock; *Production:* Ray Addicott; *Rights & Permissions:* Stella Welford
Allied Company: Blackwell Scientific Publications Ltd (qv)
Subsidiary Companies: Blackwell Press Ltd; Blackwell Raintree Ltd; Marston Book Services Ltd, Oxford; Martin Robertson & Co Ltd (qv)
Imprints: Basil Blackwell, Blackwell Reference, Shakespeare Head Press
Subjects: Economics and Industrial Relations, History, Philosophy, Politics, Languages, Linguistics, History, Geography, Children's Books, Reference, Religion, Academic Paperbacks, Social Sciences, Primary and Secondary Textbooks, Journals
1982-83: 160 titles *Founded:* 1921
Miscellaneous: Member of the Blackwell Group (see B H Blackwell Ltd under Major Booksellers)
ISBN Publisher's Prefix: 0-631

Blackwell Scientific Publications Ltd, Osney Mead, Oxford OX2 0EL Tel: Oxford 240201 (STD code 0865) Cable Add: Research Oxford Telex: 837022
Man, Editorial Dir and Rights & Permissions: Per Saugman; *Sales Dir:* Keith Bowker; *Production:* John Robson; *Publicity:* Dominic Vaughan
Allied Company: Basil Blackwell Publisher Ltd (qv)
Subsidiary Company: Blackwell Scientific Publications (Australia) Pty Ltd, Australia (qv)
Branch Offs: 9 Forrest Rd, Edinburgh EH1 2QH; 8 John St, London WC1N 2ES; 52 Beacon St, Boston, Massachusetts 02108, USA
Subjects: Medicine, Dentistry, Nursing, Veterinary Medicine, Botany, Biology, Ecology, Earth Sciences, Zoology, University Textbooks
1981: 91 titles *Founded:* 1939
ISBN Publisher's Prefix: 0-632

William **Blackwood** & Sons Ltd, 162 Leith Walk, Edinburgh EH6 5DX Tel: (031) 554 2412
Man Dir, Publishing, Rights & Permissions: J M D Blackwood
Subjects: Scottish Subjects, General Non-fiction
Founded: 1804
ISBN Publisher's Prefix: 0-85158

Blaketon Hall Ltd, 11 North St, Ashburton, Devon Tel: Ashburton 53389 (STD code 0364) Cable Add: Blaketon-Hall Ashburton
Dir: John Shillingford; *Rights & Permissions:* Tina Randles

Subsidiary Company: South Group Publishers Ltd (at above address)
Subjects: Non-fiction, Practical, How-to, Pets, Hobbies, Handicrafts
Bookshop: Blaketon Hall Gallery (at above address)
1981: 6 titles *1982:* 6 titles *Founded:* 1976
ISBN Publisher's Prefix: 0-907

Blandford Books Ltd*, Link House, West St, Poole, Dorset BH15 1LL Tel: Poole 671171 (STD code 0202) Cable Add: Blandpress Poole Telex: 418304
Chairman: R G Dingwall; *Man Dir:* R B Erven; *Dir, Rights & Permissions:* T Goldsmith; *Publishing Manager:* Stuart Booth; *Sales Dir:* Christopher Lloyd; *Production Manager:* Alan Howell; *Publicity:* Sally Mayer
Parent Company: Link House Publications Ltd (at above address)
Subjects: History, Religion, Music, Art, Archaeology, Biology, Crafts, Education, Geography, Horticulture, Militaria, Natural History, Riding, Space, Astronomy, Transport, Educational, Academic
Founded: 1919
ISBN Publisher's Prefix: 0-7137

Geoffrey **Bles**, an imprint of Garnstone Press Ltd (qv)

Blond & Briggs Ltd, an imprint and subsidiary company of Frederick Muller Ltd (qv)

Blond Educational, an imprint and subsidiary company of Frederick Muller Ltd (qv)

Bloodaxe Books Ltd, PO Box 1SN, Newcastle upon Tyne NE99 1SN Tel: Newcastle upon Tyne 739703 (STD code 0632)
Dirs: Neil Astley (Editorial), Simon Thirsk
Orders to: Noonan Hurst Ltd, 131 Trafalgar Rd, London SE10 9TU Tel: (01) 692 1475
Subjects: Poetry (English language and in translation), Fiction, Drama, Literary Criticism
1981: 5 titles *1982:* 9 titles *Founded:* 1978
ISBN Publisher's Prefix: 0-906427

The **Bodley Head** Ltd, 9 Bow St, London WC2E 7AL Tel: (01) 379 6637 Cable Add: Bodleian London WC2 Telex: 299080
Chairman: Max Reinhardt; *Man Dir:* David Machin; *Editorial:* Maureen Rissik; *Home Sales:* Peter Sapieha; *Overseas Sales:* Quentin Hockliffe; *Publicity Dir:* Euan Cameron; *Production:* Sue Curnow; *Rights & Permissions:* Sarah Fulford (Adult), Jane Mettam (Children's), Guido Waldman
Subsidiary Companies: Max Reinhardt Ltd (qv); Hollis & Carter; T Werner Laurie; The Nonesuch Library; Putnam & Co Ltd (qv); (all at above address)
Subjects: General Fiction, Belles Lettres, Poetry, Biography, History, Juveniles
Founded: 1887
Miscellaneous: Firm is a member of the Chatto, Bodley Head & Jonathan Cape Ltd Group (qv)
ISBN Publisher's Prefix: 0-370

The **Book Guild** Ltd, Dial House, 221 High St, Lewes, Sussex BN7 2AE Tel: Lewes 890171 (STD code 0273)
Man Dir and Production: Gerald Konyn; *Editorial:* John Sangster; *Sales:* Aimee Konyn; *Publicity:* Terry Stone; *Rights & Permissions:* Catt Wilson Literary Agency
Orders to: Biblios PDS, Glenside Industrial Estate, Star Rd, Partridge Green, Horsham, Sussex Tel: Partridge Green 710971 (STD code 0403)
Subjects: Fiction, Biography, Travel, War, Adventure, Juvenile
1982: 8 titles *Founded:* 1981
ISBN Publisher's Prefix: 0-86332

Book Sales Ltd, 78 Newman St, London W1P 3LA Tel: (01) 636 7777 Telex: 21892 Musicsales
A division of Music Sales Ltd
Man Dir: Robert Wise; *Sales:* Ray Hellen
Subjects: Music (Learning and Biography), General Books
ISBN Publisher's Prefixes: 0-86001, 0-7119

The **Booksmith**, an imprint of BSC Books Ltd (qv)

Boosey & Hawkes Music Publishers Ltd, 295 Regent St, London W1R 8JH Tel: (01) 580 2060 Cable Add: Sonorous London W1 Telex: 8954613 Boosey G
Man Dir: R Antony Fell
Subjects: Music, Secondary & Primary Music Textbooks
ISBN Publisher's Prefix: 0-85162

David **Booth** (Publishing) Ltd, 6 Kings Ave, London SW4 8BD Tel: (01) 720 2309 Telex: 261507
Chief Executive, Editorial: David Booth; *Marketing Dir, Rights & Permissions:* Sonia Birch
Subject: Children's (Travel, Natural History, Leisure)
1983: 20 titles *Founded:* 1981

Bowker & Bertram Ltd (Marine Publishers)*, Whitewalls, Harbour Way, Old Bosham, Chichester, West Sussex PO18 8QH
Subjects: Marine (Literary and Technical)
1982: 7 titles

Bowker Publishing Co, PO Box 5, Epping, Essex CM16 4BU (Located at: Erasmus House, 58-62 High St, Epping) Tel: Epping 77333 (STD code 0378) Telex: 81410
Warehouse: H Kent Ltd, 135 South St, Bishop's Stortford, Hertfordshire
Chairman, Man Dir, Rights & Permissions: David Collischon; *Marketing Dir:* Patrick Wynne-Jones; *Publicity Manager:* Mrs Kasia Paveliev
Parent Company: The R R Bowker Co, 205 East 42nd St, New York, NY 10017, USA. Ultimate holding company Xerox Corporation
Subjects: Works of Bibliography, Reference, and Library Science handbooks for Libraries and the Book Trade
1981: 55 titles *1982:* 68 titles
ISBN Publisher's Prefixes: 0-8352, 0-85935

Marion **Boyars** Publishers Ltd, 18 Brewer St, London W1R 4AS Tel: (01) 439 7827 Cable Add: Bookdom
Man Dir, Editorial, Rights & Permissions: Marion Boyars; *Editorial:* Arthur Boyars, Ken Hollings; *Sales:* M Ellison; *Publicity:* Ken Hollings
Associate Company: Marion Boyars Inc, 457 Broome St, New York, NY 10013, USA
Subjects: General Fiction, Belles Lettres, Poetry, Literary Criticism, Plays, Music, Philosophy, Sociology, Psychology
Series: Open Forum, Ideas in Progress, Signature, Critical Appraisals
Founded: 1975
ISBN Publisher's Prefix: 0-7145

Boydell & Brewer Ltd, PO Box 9, Woodbridge, Suffolk IP12 3DF Tel: Shottisham 411320 (STD code 0394)
Chairman: R W Barber
Imprints: Boydell Press, D S Brewer
Distributors for: Suffolk Record Society, Royal Historical Society, Royal Society of Literature
Subjects: Mediaeval and Renaissance Literature and History, General Non-fiction, Sport
ISBN Publisher's Prefix: 0-85115 (Boydell), 0-85991 (Brewer)

Bracken Books, reprint imprint of Bestseller Publications Ltd (qv under Remainder Dealers)

Bradt Enterprises+, 41 Nortoft Rd, Chalfont St Peter, Bucks SL9 0LA Tel: Chalfont St Giles 3478 (STD code 02407)
Man Dir: Mrs Hilary Bradt; *Editorial:* Hilary Bradt; *Manager:* Janet Mears
Imprint: Backpacker's Guide Series
Branch Off: 95 Harvey St, Cambridge, Massachusetts 02140, USA
Subjects: Trekking, Backpacking, Travel
1981: 2 titles *1982:* 2 titles *Founded:* 1975
ISBN Publisher's Prefix: 0-9505797

Brassey's Publishers Ltd, Headington Hill Hall, Oxford OX3 0BW
Publisher: Robert Maxwell; *Publicity Manager:* Ian Maxwell
Subjects: Defence & Military Books
Founded: 1886
ISBN Publisher's Prefix: 0-08

Breslich & Foss+, 43 Museum St, London WC1A 1LY Tel: (01) 405 9701 Telex: 27950 (ref 2257)
Man Dir: Paula G Breslich; *Editorial:* Nicholas Robinson; *Publicity:* Camron Ltd; *Rights & Permissions:* Cathy Miller
Orders to: André Deutsch Ltd, 105 Great Russell St, London WC1B 3LJ
Subjects: Family reference, Leisure, Sports, Humour, Gift books, *Country Classics* series
1983: 8 titles *Founded:* 1983
ISBN Publisher's Prefix: 1-85004

D S **Brewer** Ltd, see Boydell & Brewer Ltd

Brilliance Books+, 14 Clerkenwell Green, London EC1 Tel: (01) 250 0730
Editorial: Jeanette Winterson, Tenebris Light, Roy Trevelion; *Sales, Rights & Permissions:* Tenebris Light; *Production:* Roy Trevelion; *Publicity:* Jeanette Winterson
Imprint: Plain Edition
Subjects: New fiction and reprints by homosexual authors (only)
1982-83: 12 titles *Founded:* 1982
ISBN Publisher's Prefix: 0-946189

Brimax Books Ltd, 4-5 Studlands Park Industrial Estate, Exning Rd, Newmarket, Suffolk CB8 7AU Tel: Newmarket 664611 (STD code 0638) Cable Add: Brimax Newmarket Telex: 817625 Brimax G
Man Dir: A G Rogers; *Editorial:* Marjorie Rogers; *Rights & Permissions:* Brimax Rights Ltd (at above address)
Subjects: General Children's Books, Activity Books, Cloth Books
ISBN Publisher's Prefixes: 0-900195, 0-904494, 0-86112

Bristol Classical Press, Department of Classics, University of Bristol, Bristol BS8 1RJ Tel: Bristol 214187 (STD code 0272)
Chief Executives: J H Betts, T A G Foss; *Editorial:* J H Betts; *Sales, Production, Publicity, Rights:* A Barrett
Subjects: Classics, Archaeology, English Literature, Scientific German Textbooks, Medical Etymology, Classical Studies
Founded: 1977
ISBN Publisher's Prefixes: 0-906515, 0-86292

The **British Academy**, 20-21 Cornwall Terrace, Regent's Park, London NW1 4QP Tel: (01) 487 5966 Cable Add: Britacademy, London NW1 Telex: 263194
Publications Officer: Hagan Powell; *Rights & Permissions:* Sian Evans
Subjects: Art & Archaeology, Classics, Dictionaries, History, Music, Natural Science & The Humanities, Numismatics, Philosophy, Literature, Economics, Jurisprudence, Social Anthropology, Shakespeare

1981: 17 titles *1982:* 17 titles *Founded:* 1902
ISBN Publisher's Prefix: 0-85672

British & Foreign Bible Society, Publishing Division, Stonehill Green, Westlea Down, Swindon SN5 7DG Telex: 44283
Executive Dir: T Houston; *Publishing Dir:* R Worthing-Davies; *Sales:* R Brock; *Customer Services:* N Crosbie; *Production:* J Ball
Subjects: Bibles, Testaments, Bible Books, Bible Study and Educational Materials (in English and many foreign languages)
Bookshop: Bible House Booklounge, 146 Queen Victoria St, London EC4
Founded: 1804
ISBN Publisher's Prefix: 0-564

The **British Design Council**, Production and Publishing Department, 65 Davies St, London W1Y 2AA Tel: (01) 499 8011
Headquarters: 10 Spring Gardens, London SW1A 2BN Tel: (01) 930 8466
Director: Piers Pendred; *Sales Manager:* Frances Nichols
Subjects: Those related to the promotion of a wider knowledge of Britain and the English language abroad and developing closer cultural relations with other countries. Among book and journal titles published or co-published are *British Book News, Media in Education and Development, English Language Teaching Journal, ELT Documents, Language Teaching, British Writers, Higher Education in the UK, How to Live in Britain*
1981: 33 titles
ISBN Publisher's Prefix: 0-901618

British Film Institute, see BFI Publishing

The **British Horse** Society, The British Equestrian Centre, Kenilworth, Warwickshire CV8 2LR Tel: Coventry 52241 (STD code 0203) Cable Add: Brithorse, Kenilworth
Subjects: Equestrian Reference Books
ISBN Publisher's Prefix: 0-900226

British Library, Bibliographic Services Division Publications, 2 Sheraton St, London W1V 4BH Tel: (01) 636 1544 Telex: 21462
Subjects: Bibliographies, Indexes, *British National Bibliography, British Education Index, British Catalogue of Music, Books in English, British Catalogue of Audiovisual Materials* (experimental), *Serials in the British Library, Cataloguing Aids*
Founded: 1973
ISBN Publisher's Prefixes: 0-7123 (previously 0-900220)

British Library, Lending Division Publications, Boston Spa, Wetherby, West Yorkshire LS23 7BQ Tel: Wetherby 843434 (STD code 0937) Telex: 557381
Dir-General: M B Line; *Head of Publications and External Relations:* Peter Haigh
Parent Body: The British Library, Sheraton St, London W1V 4BH
Subjects: Bibliographical
1981: 3 titles *1982:* 6 titles *Founded:* 1973
ISBN Publisher's Prefix: 0-7123

British Library, Reference Division Publications+, Great Russell St, London WC1B 3DG Tel: (01) 636 1544 Telex: 21462
Chief Executive: Hugh Cobbe; *Editorial:* David Way; *Sales, Publicity, Rights & Permissions:* Jane Carr
Parent Body: The British Library, Sheraton St, London W1V 4BH
Subjects: Arts (Western & Oriental), Bibliography, Reference
1981: 10 titles *1982:* 13 titles *Founded:* 1979
ISBN Publisher's Prefix: 0-7123

British Medical Association+, BMA House, Tavistock Sq, London WC1H 9JR Tel: (01) 387 4499 Cable Add: Aitiology Westcent London Telex: 265929
Publishing Dir: Anthony J Smith; *Editor:* Dr S P Lock; *Sales, Publicity:* M Long; *Production:* D Parrott; *Rights & Permissions:* Anthony J Smith, D Parrott
Subsidiary Company: Professional & Scientific Publications (at above address)
Imprint: British Medical Journal
Subject: Medical
1981: 5 titles *1982:* 7 titles *Founded:* 1857
ISBN Publisher's Prefix: 0-7279

British Museum (Natural History)+, Cromwell Rd, London SW7 5BD Tel: (01) 589 6323 Cable Add: Nathismus Southkens London
Head of Publications: Robert Cross; *Editorial:* Chris Owen, Myra Givans; *Sales, Publicity:* R Cowles; *Production:* Eric Dent; *Rights & Permissions:* S Daniels
Subjects: Natural History, Scientific, Popular, Periodicals
Bookshops: Museum Bookshop (address as above); Museum Bookshop at Zoological Museum, Tring, Herts
1981: 16 titles *1982:* 20 titles *Founded:* 1963
ISBN Publisher's Prefix: 0-0565

British Museum Publications Ltd+, 46 Bloomsbury St, London WC1B 3QQ Tel: (01) 323 1234
Man Dir, Rights & Permissions: M J Hoare; *Editorial:* Celia Clear; *Sales, Publicity:* Heather Dean; *Production:* Nicholas Russell
Orders to: Thames & Hudson Ltd, 44 Clockhouse Rd, Farnborough, Hampshire
Imprints: British Museum Publications, Colonnade
Subjects: Art, Archaeology, Oriental, Numismatics, Ethnography, General Guides to British Museum
Bookshop: British Museum, Great Russell St, London WC1
1981: 30 titles *1982:* 24 titles *Founded:* 1973
ISBN Publisher's Prefix: 0-7141

The **British Printing & Communication** Corporation PLC, see BPCC

British Tourist Authority, 64 St James's St, London SW1A 1NF Tel: (01) 629 9191 Cable Add: Tagbandi Ldn Telex: 21231 Btaadm G
Chief Executive: Leonard Lickorish; *Editorial:* Cyril Palmer; *Sales:* Stephen Mesquita; *Production:* Henry Kutner
Orders to: 4 Bromells Rd, London SW4 0BJ
Branch Off: 239 Old Marylebone Rd, London NW1 5QT
Subject: Travel to Britain
1981-82: approx 200 titles *Founded:* 1969
ISBN Publisher's Prefix: 0-7095

James **Brodie** Ltd*, 15 Queen Sq, Bath, Avon BA1 2HW Tel: Bath 22110 (STD code 0225)
Man Dir: Corinne Wimpress; *Sales Dir:* Jeremy D Wimpress
Subjects: Primary & Secondary Education, Classical Translations (*Brodie's* and *Kelly's Keys*), *Notes on Chosen Texts* series (produced by Brodie and generally published by Pan Books Ltd (qv))
1981: 6 titles *Founded:* 1906 (incorporated 1926)
ISBN Publisher's Prefix: 0-7142

Brodies Notes, an imprint of Pan Books Ltd (qv)

Broomsleigh Press, an imprint of Fudge & Co Ltd (qv)

Brown, Son & Ferguson, Ltd, 4/10 Darnley St, Glasgow G41 2SD Tel: (041) 429 1234 Cable Add: Skipper Glasgow
Chief Executive, Editorial, Production: T Nigel Brown; *Sales, Publicity:* J A Kyle; *Rights & Permissions:* L Ingram-Brown
Subsidiary Company: James Gowans Ltd (at above address)
Subjects: Nautical, Scottish Plays
1981: 15 titles *1982:* 10 titles *Founded:* 1858
ISBN Publisher's Prefix: 0-85174

Sinclair **Browne** Ltd, see Sinclair

Bunch Books, 14 Rathbone Place, London W1P 1DE Tel: (01) 631 1433 Cable Add: Bunch Books, London Telex: 8954139 ref Bunch G
Man Dir: Stephen England; *Production:* Stephen Rowe
Parent Company: H Bunch Associates Ltd
Subsidiary Companies: Sportscene Publishers Ltd, Sportscene Specialist Press Ltd
Subjects: Martial Arts, Film, TV, Biography, Leisure, General Interest, Motorcycles, Microcomputers, Hi-Fi
Founded: 1974

Burke Publishing Co Ltd, Pegasus House, 116-120 Golden Lane, London EC1Y 0TL Tel: (01) 253 2145 Cable Add: Burkebooks London EC1 Telex: c/o 27931
Chairman, Export Sales: H Starke; *Man Dir, Editorial, Rights & Permissions:* Miss N Galinski; *Production:* C Tuthill
Orders to: The Barn, Northgate, Beccles, Suffolk NR34 9AX
Subsidiary Company: Harold Starke Ltd (qv)
Imprint: Pre-School Publishing
Branch Offs: Burke Publishing (Canada) Ltd, 20 Queen St West, Suite 3000, Box 30, Toronto, Ontario, Canada M5H 1V5; Burke Publishing Co Inc, 540 Barnum Ave, Bridgeport, Connecticut 06608, USA
Subjects: Juveniles, Secondary & Primary Textbooks, Educational Materials
Founded: 1934
ISBN Publisher's Prefix: 0-222

Burke's Peerage Genealogical Books Ltd*, 1-2 Cambridge Gate, Regents Park, London NW1 Tel: (01) 629 4588
Publishers of *Burke's Peerage* and *Baronetage*

Burke's Peerage Ltd, 1 Hay Hill, London W1X 7LF Tel: (01) 409 1583 Telex: 916851
Dirs: Frederick Hogarth, Alec Trustram Eve
Subjects: Genealogy, Heraldry, Architectural, Biographical, Social History
Founded: 1826
ISBN Publisher's Prefix: 0-85011

Burnett Books, see André Deutsch Ltd

Burns & Oates Ltd+, Wellwood, North Farm Rd, Tunbridge Wells, Kent TN2 3DR Tel: Tunbridge Wells 44037 (STD code 0892) Telex: 957258
Man Dir, Sales: Charlotte de la Bedoyere; *Editorial, Rights & Permissions:* John Bright-Holmes; *Production:* Bobby Meyer
Associate Company: Search Press Ltd (qv)
Subjects: Philosophy, History, Religion, Moral Education
Founded: 1847
ISBN Publisher's Prefix: 0-86012

Business Books Ltd+, 17-21 Conway St, London W1P 6JD Tel: (01) 387 2811 Cable Add: Hutchbiz Telex: 261212
Man Dir: Mark Cohen; *Sales Dir:* John Fulford; *Editorial Dir, Rights & Permissions:* Vivien James; *Marketing Dir:* Janie Nicholas
Orders to (trade): Tiptree Book Services, Church Rd, Tiptree, Colchester, Essex
Parent Company: LWT (Holdings) PLC
Subjects: Management, Advertising, Marketing, Finance and Accounting, Personnel, Computers, Business Law, Small

Business
1981: 9 titles *1982:* 11 titles
Miscellaneous: Business Books Ltd is an imprint of Hutchinson Educational (qv)
ISBN Publisher's Prefixes: 0-220 (for pre-1979 publications), 0-09 (for 1979 onwards)

Butterworth & Co (Publishers) Ltd, Borough Green, Sevenoaks, Kent TN15 8PH Tel: Borough Green 884567 (STD code 0732) Cable Add: Butterwort Sevenoaks Kent TN15 8PH Telex: 95678
The above is the address of the Head Office and Scientific, Technical and Medical Book Publishing Divisions. The Journals Publishing Division is at Westbury House, Bury St, Guildford, Surrey GU2 5AW and the Legal Publishing Division at 88 Kingsway, London WC2 6AB Tel: (01) 405 6900 Cable Add: Butterwort London WC2
Chairman and Chief Executive: W Gordon Graham; *Dirs:* George Norton (Deputy Group Chairman), Neville Cusworth (Law), David Summers (Scientific, Technical and Medical), Don Saville (Financial), Peter Cheeseman (Services), Colin Whurr (Marketing); *International Sales Manager:* Phillip Woods; *Production:* Christopher Lake-Smith (Law), J Carruthers (Scientific, Technical and Medical); *Publicity:* Christopher Marshall, Graham Marshall; *Rights & Permissions:* R J Hedley-Jones (UK), Betty Cottrell (Foreign Rights)
Subsidiary Companies: Butterworths Pty Ltd, Australia (qv); Butterworth & Co (Canada) Ltd, 2265 Midland Ave, Scarborough, Ontario M1P 4S1, Canada; Butterworths of New Zealand Ltd, New Zealand (qv); Butterworth & Co (Asia) Pte Ltd, Crawford Post Office 770, Singapore 9119, Republic of Singapore; Butterworth Publishers (Pty) Ltd, Republic of South Africa (qv); Butterworth (Publishers), 10 Tower Office Park, Woburn, Mass 01801, USA; Butterworths (Legal Publishers), 160 Rov St, Suite 300, Seattle, Washington 98109, USA, 381 Elliot St, Newton, Upper Falls, Mass 02164, USA; 1104 Metric Blvd, Austin, Texas 78758, USA; D & S Publishers, PO Box 5105, Calumet, Clearwater, Florida 33518, USA; Mason Publishing Co, 366 Wacouta St, St Paul, Minnesota 55101, USA
Imprints: Focal Press, Newnes-Butterworths, Newnes-Technical
Bookshop: 9-12 Bell Yard, Temple Bar, London WC2
Subjects: Law, Medicine, Engineering, Technology, Science, Social Science, Business Studies, Photography
1983: approx 400 titles *Founded:* before 1905
ISBN Publisher's Prefixes: 0-406/7/8/9, 0-592, 0-861, 0-902, 0-6004, 0-240 (Focal)

Buzby Books Ltd, an imprint of Severn House Publishers Ltd (qv)

Bwrdd Croeso Cymru, see Wales Tourist Board

C B D Research Ltd, 154 High St, Beckenham, Kent BR3 1EA Tel: (01) 650 7745
Man Dir: G P Henderson
Subject: Reference
1982: 3 titles *Founded:* 1961
ISBN Publisher's Prefix: 0-900246

C C J Ltd, Ely House, 37 Dover St, London W1X 4HQ Tel: (01) 493 5061, (01) 499 4688 Cable Add: Unibooks London W1 Telex: 24224 ref 3545
Warehouse: International Book Distributors, 66 Wood End Lane, Hemel Hempstead, Hertfordshire Tel: Hemel Hempstead 58531 (STD code 0442)
Man Dir: J Trevor Brown; *Dirs:* James Clark, J E Goellner; *Sales:* Anna Simpson-Muellner (Export), J Trevor Brown (UK); *Promotion Manager:* Michael Richards
Miscellaneous: Firm is the London office of University of California Press (qv), Cornell University Press (qv), the Johns Hopkins University Press (qv), University Press of New England, Toronto University Press and McGill-Queen's University Press, National Academy Press
ISBN Publisher's Prefixes: 0-520 (California), 0-8014 (Cornell), 0-8018 (Johns Hopkins), 0-87451 (New England), 0-8020 (Toronto), 0-7735 (McGill-Queen's), 0-309 (NAP)

C E E P I Ltd (Caxton and English Educational Programmes International)+, Maxwell House, 74 Worship St, London EC2A 2EN Tel: (01) 377 4600 Cable Add: Interknow London EC2 Telex: 886048
Joint Man Dirs: John Emler, Edward Hornett
Subjects: Encyclopaedias, Education, Yearbooks, History, Reference, Dictionaries, *The New Caxton Encyclopedia, Chamber's Encyclopedia*
Miscellaneous: Firm is a member company of BPCC PLC (qv)
ISBN Publisher's Prefix: 0-907305

C E T, an imprint of Council for Educational Technology (qv)

C I O Publishing, Church House, Dean's Yard, London SW1P 3NZ Tel: (01) 222 9011
Editorial: Miss B England; *Production:* F W J Burford; *Publicity:* Helen Weeks
Trade Orders to: J M Dent & Sons (Distribution) Ltd, Dunham's Lane, Letchworth, Hertfordshire SG6 1LF
Parent Company: Central Board of Finance of the Church of England (at above London address)
Subjects: Publications for the Boards and Councils of the Church of England, Synod Reports, Christian Education
Bookshop: Church House Bookshop, Great Smith St, London SW1P 3BN
1981: 50 titles
ISBN Publisher's Prefix: 0-7151

C R E, an imprint of Commission for Racial Equality (qv)

C S E Books, 25 Horsell Rd, London N5 1XL Tel: (01) 607 9615
General Manager: Mayerlene Frow
Subject: Political Economy
Book Club: C S E Book Club
1981: 2 titles *Founded:* 1978
ISBN Publisher's Prefix: 0-906336

Cadogan Books Ltd+, 15 Pont St, London SW1X 9EH Tel: (01) 235 3851
Chairman: Lord Montagu of Beaulieu; *Man Dir:* C F Burness; *Editorial Dir:* Lorna Gentry; *Production, Marketing Manager:* Paula Levey
Subjects: Motoring, Travel, Business History
1982: 9 titles *Founded:* 1971
ISBN Publisher's Prefixes: 0-85614, 0-946313

John **Calder** (Publishers) Ltd, 18 Brewer St, London W1R 4AS Tel: (01) 734 3786 Cable Add: Bookdom London
Man, Publishing Dir: John Calder; *Sales:* Michael Hayes; *Production, Promotion, Rights & Permissions:* Susan Herbert
Subjects: Modern Literature, Classics, Belles Lettres, Poetry, Biography, History, Music, Opera, Philosophy, Reference, High-priced Paperbacks, Psychology, Social Science, Politics, Current Affairs
1982: 40 titles *Founded:* 1950
ISBN Publisher's Prefix: 0-7145

Caliban Books, 25 Nassington Rd, London NW3 Tel: (01) 380 0704
Man Dir: Peter Razzell
Orders to: Biblios Distribution Services Ltd, Glenside Industrial Estate, Star Rd, Partridge Green, Horsham, West Sussex RH13 8RA Tel: Partridge Green 710971 (STD code 0403)
Subjects: Social History, Historical Autobiography, History of Exploration, Psychotherapy
1983: 50 titles *Founded:* 1977
ISBN Publisher's Prefix: 0-904573

John **Calmann** & Cooper Ltd+, 71 Great Russell St, London WC1B 3BN Tel: (01) 831 6351 Telex: 298246 Owls G
Man Dir: Marianne Calmann; *Editorial:* Elisabeth Ingles; *Sales, Rights:* Laurence King; *Production:* Anne Massingham
Founded: 1976
Miscellaneous: Designers and producers of high quality illustrated books, and specialists in international co-editions

Cambridge Information and Research Services Ltd, School House, Heydon, Royston, Hertfordshire SG8 8PW Tel: Royston 838615 (STD code 0763)
Dir: Andrew R Buckley; *Managing Editor:* Peter Found
Subsidiary Company: Energy Publications (Cambridge), PO Box 147, Cambridge CB1 1NY
Subjects: Reference, Energy Management, Regional Locations, Social Science
1981: 8 titles *1982:* 10 titles *Founded:* 1975
ISBN Publisher's Prefix: 0-905332

Cambridge University Press, The Edinburgh Bldg, Shaftesbury Rd, Cambridge CB2 2RU Cable Add: Unipress, Cambridge Tel: Cambridge 312393 (STD code 0223) Telex: 817342
Chief Executive: G A Cass; *Acting Man Dir (Publishing Division):* A K Wilson; *Editorial Dirs:* R Davidson, A B du Plessis, S Mitton; *University Publisher:* M H Black; *Marketing:* D A Knight; *Sales Dirs:* John Adamson, Dennis Stanton; *Publicity:* Paul Clifford; *Production:* H McIlwrick; *Rights & Permissions:* Sarah Chapman, Irena Jeziorska
Branch Offs: Cambridge University Press, Australia (qv); Cambridge University Press (American Branch), 32 East 57th St, New York, NY 10022, USA, and 510 North Ave, New Rochelle, NY 10801, USA
Subjects: Agriculture, Anthropology, Archaeology, Architecture, Area Studies, Art, Astronomy, Bibliography, Biography, Biological Sciences, Chemistry, Classical Studies, Computer Science, Drama, Earth Sciences, Economics, Education (primary, secondary, tertiary and further education, trade, juvenile information books), Engineering, English Language Teaching, Environmental Sciences, Geography, History, Languages, Law, Linguistics, Literature, Materials Science, Mathematics, Medicine, Music, Philosophy, Physical Sciences, Politics, Psychology, Sociology, Theology, Bibles and Prayer Books, Examination Papers
1981: 540 titles *1982:* 560 titles *Founded:* 1534
ISBN Publisher's Prefix: 0-521

Cameron Books Ltd+, 2A Roman Way, London N7 8XG Tel: (01) 609 4019 Cable Add: Cameron London N7
Dirs: Ian A Cameron, Jill Hollis
Subjects: Non-fiction, Illustrated Reference Books, Encyclopaedias, Cinema, Cookery, Decorative Arts, Collecting, Children's Non-fiction
1981: 8 titles *1982:* 4 titles
ISBN Publisher's Prefix: 0-7153

Canongate Publishing Ltd+, 17 Jeffrey St, Edinburgh EH1 1DR Tel: (031) 556 0023/1954
Man Dir, Editorial, Production: Stephanie Wolfe Murray; *Dir:* Robin Hodge; *Sales Manager:* Dave Morgan; *Rights, Permissions & Publicity:* Sheila Webb
Subsidiary Companies: Southside (Publishers) Ltd, Q Press Ltd
Subjects: General Fiction, Poetry, Biography, History, Art, Current Affairs, Juveniles, Cookery
1981: 14 titles *1982:* 12 titles *Founded:* 1973
ISBN Publisher's Prefixes: 0-86241, 0-903937 (Canongate), 0-900025 (Southside), 0-905470 (Q Press)

Jonathan **Cape** Ltd, 30 Bedford Sq, London WC1B 3EL Tel: (01) 636 3344 Cable Add: Capajon London WC1 Telex: 299080
Orders to: Chatto, Bodley Head & Cape Services Ltd, 9 Bow St, London WC2 Tel: (01) 379 6831
Man Dir: Graham C Greene; *Editorial Dir:* Liz Calder; *Marketing Dir:* Roger Kirkpatrick; *Publicity Dir:* Rupert Lancaster; *Sales:* Quentin Hockliffe (Export), Peter Japieha (Home); *Production Dir:* Tim Chester; *Rights & Permissions:* Gaye Poulton; *Design Dir:* Ian Craig
Subsidiary Companies: Cape Goliard Press Ltd; Jackdaw Publications Ltd (both at 30 Bedford Sq, London WC1B 3EL)
Subjects: General Fiction, Belles Lettres, Literary Criticism, Drama, Humour, Poetry, Biography, History, Military History, Politics, International Affairs, Anthropology, Natural History, Science, Art, Philosophy, Juveniles, High-priced Paperbacks, Social Science, Educational Materials, Travel and Topography, Food and Drink
1981: 104 titles *Founded:* 1921
Miscellaneous: Firm is a member of the Chatto, Bodley Head & Cape Ltd Group (qv)
ISBN Publisher's Prefix: 0-224

Carcanet Press Ltd, 208-12 Corn Exchange Bldgs, Manchester M4 3BQ Tel: (061) 834 8730
Man Dir: Peter Jones; *Editorial Dir:* Michael Schmidt; *Sales Dir:* Helen Lefroy
Imprint: Fyfield Books
Subjects: Belles Lettres, Poetry, Low-priced Paperbacks
1982: approx 50 titles *Founded:* 1969
ISBN Publisher's Prefixes: 0-85635, 0-902145

Careers Research and Advisory Centre Ltd, distributed by Hobsons Press (Cambridge) Ltd (qv)

Carousel, an imprint of Corgi Books Ltd (qv)

Frank **Cass** & Co Ltd, Gainsborough House, 11 Gainsborough Rd, London E11 1RS Tel: (01) 530 4226 Cable Add: Simfay London Telex: 897719
Man Dir: Frank Cass; *Editorial:* Margaret Goodare; *Production:* John Smith; *Publicity:* Hayley Cass; *Trade Manager:* Richard Norris
Orders to: Macdonald & Evans Ltd, Estover Rd, Estover, Plymouth PL6 7PZ Tel: Plymouth 705251 (STD code 0752)
Associate Companies: The Woburn Press (qv); Vallentine Mitchell & Co Ltd (qv)
Subjects: Third World Studies, Economics, Economic History, Social History, Politics, History, Africana, Middle East Studies
Bookshop: Frank Cass (Books) Ltd, 10 Woburn Walk, London WC1
Founded: 1957
ISBN Publisher's Prefix: 0-7146

Cassell Ltd+, 1 Vincent Sq, London SW1P 2PN Tel: (01) 630 7881 Cable Add: Caspeg, London SW1 Telex: 28648 Caspeg
Also: 1 St Anne's Rd, Eastbourne, East Sussex BN21 3UN Tel: Eastbourne 638221 (STD code 0323) Cable Add: Volumists Eastbourne Telex: 877503 Volmst
Man Dir: Robert Kiernan; *Publishing Dir:* Stephen White (Eastbourne); *Publishers:* John Stockdale (ELT, Eastbourne); John Green (Schools, Eastbourne); *Export Sales:* John Mills; *Marketing Manager:* Barry Holmes; *Production:* Stanley Mitchell; *Publicity:* Piers Newton
Orders to: Above Eastbourne address
Parent Company: CBS Educational & Professional Publishing, 383 Madison Ave, New York, NY 10017, USA
Associate Company: Holt-Saunders Ltd (qv)
Imprints: Geoffrey Chapman (qv), Johnston & Bacon, Studio Vista
Subjects: (London): Reference, Religion, Educational, Travel; (Eastbourne): Educational (primary, secondary, tertiary), ELT
Founded: 1848
ISBN Publisher's Prefix: 0-304

Castle House Publications Ltd, Castle House, 27 London Rd, Tunbridge Wells, Kent TN1 1BX Tel: Tunbridge Wells 39606 (STD code 0892)
Man Dir: Donald Reinders; *Editorial:* Wendy Hunter; *Sales:* Andrew Durnell; *Publicity:* Amanda Harris; *Rights & Permissions:* Wendy Hunter
Associate Company: Weald Publishing Company (Europe) (at above address)
Subjects: Scientific, Academic, Medical
Founded: 1978
ISBN Publisher's Prefix: 0-7194

Cathay, an imprint of Octopus Books PLC (qv)

Catholic Truth Society, 38-40 Eccleston Sq, London SW1V 1PD Tel: (01) 834 4392 Cable Add: Apostolic London
General Secretary: David Murphy; *Editorial:* Brendan Walsh
Subject: Religion
Bookshop: 25 Ashley Pl, London SW1P 1LT
1981: 10 titles *1982:* 10 titles *Founded:* 1884
ISBN Publisher's Prefix: 0-85183

Paul **Cave** Publications Ltd, 74 Bedford Pl, Southampton SO1 2DF Tel: Southampton 333457 (STD code 0703), Southampton 23591
Man Dir: Paul Cave; *Sales:* Joan Cave
Subjects: Local History, Illustrated Guides, Magazines
Bookshop: At above address
1982: 10 titles *Founded:* 1960
ISBN Publisher's Prefix: 0-86146

Caxton and English Educational Programmes International, see CEEPI Ltd

Cedar Books, an imprint of World's Work Ltd (qv)

Celtic Revision Aids, an imprint of Sphere Books Ltd (qv)

Cement & Concrete Association, Wexham Springs, Slough SL3 6PL Tel: Fulmer 2727 (STD code 02816) Telex: 848352
Subjects: Engineering, Concrete, Cement
ISBN Publisher's Prefix: 0-7210

Centaur Press Ltd, Fontwell, Arundel, West Sussex BN18 0TA Tel: Eastergate 3302 (STD code 024368)
Man Dir: T J L Wynne-Tyson
Orders to: Fulham Wharf, Townmead Rd, London SW6 2SB
Subsidiary Company: The Linden Press (at above address)
Subjects: General, Biography, Philosophy, Social Science, Textbooks, Reference
Bookshop: Keele's, 9 St Pancras, Chichester, West Sussex
1981: 3 titles *Founded:* 1954
ISBN Publisher's Prefixes: 0-900000 (Centaur), 0-900001 (Linden Press)

Centre for Library and Information Management, Loughborough University, Loughborough, Leicestershire LE11 3TU Tel: Loughborough 213176 (STD code 0509) Cable Add: Technology Loughborough Telex: 34319
Director: Dr P Mann
Subject: Management of Library and Information Services
1981: 5 titles *1982:* 11 titles *Founded:* 1979
Miscellaneous: Previously Library Management Research Unit (1969-79)
ISBN Publisher's Prefix: 0-904924

Centurion Publications, an imprint of New Opportunity Press Ltd (qv)

Chadwyck-Healey Ltd, 20 Newmarket Rd, Cambridge CB5 8DT Tel: Cambridge 311479 (STD code 0223)
Dirs: Charles E Chadwyck-Healey, A M Chadwyck-Healey, H Fellner, P J Miller; *Publicity Manager:* Anna Dowson
Subjects: Reference, Non-fiction, Art, Economics, History, Literary History, Bibliography, Radio and TV

W & R **Chambers** Ltd+, 43-45 Annandale St, Edinburgh EH7 4AZ Tel: (031) 557 4571 Cable Add: Chambers Edinburgh Telex: 727967 G
Chairman: A S Chambers; *Marketing Dir:* Trevor Maher
Subjects: General, Textbooks, Reference, Juveniles, Educational Materials, Mathematical Tables, Low-priced Paperbacks
1981: 6 titles *1982:* 12 titles *Founded:* 1820
ISBN Publisher's Prefix: 0-550

Chancellor, an imprint of Octopus Books PLC (qv)

Chancerel Publishers Ltd, 40 Tavistock St, London WC2E 7PB Tel: (01) 240 2811
Man Dir: W D B Prowse
Associate Companies: Chancerel Editions SA, France (qv); Twinburn Ltd, London
Subjects: Leisure Activities (Sports, Hobbies), Co-editions, Educational (Geography, Modern Languages, English as a Foreign Language, Computers), Syndicated Strip Features
Founded: 1976
ISBN Publisher's Prefix: 0-905703

Chancery House Publishing Ltd, an imprint of Antique Collectors' Club (qv)

Geoffrey **Chapman**, 1 Vincent Sq, London SW1P 2PN Tel: (01) 630 7881 Cable Add: Caspeg London SW1 Telex: 28648 Caspeg
Man Dir: Robert Kiernan; *Publisher:* Stephen Butcher; *Editorial:* Anne Boyd; *Sales:* Elizabeth Hadshar; *Publicity:* Piers Newton
Parent Company: CBS Educational & Professional Publishing, 383 Madison Ave, New York, NY 10017, USA
Associate Company: Holt-Saunders Ltd (qv)
Subjects: Religion, Religious Educational, Liturgy, Specialized African Publishing
1981: 14 titles *Founded:* 1957
Miscellaneous: Geoffrey Chapman is an imprint of Cassell Ltd (qv)
ISBN Publisher's Prefix: 0-225

Chapman & Hall Ltd, 11 New Fetter Lane, London EC4P 4EE Tel: (01) 583 9855 Cable Add: Elegiacs London EC4P 4EE Telex: 263398

Man Dir: R Stileman; *Marketing:* Peter F Shepherd; *Production:* B West; *Publicity:* S Stacey; *Rights & Permissions:* G Thorniley
Orders to: Associated Book Publishers (Services) Ltd, North Way, Andover, Hants SP10 5BE Tel: Andover 62141 (STD code 0264)
Parent Company: Firm is incorporated in Associated Book Publishers (UK) Ltd (qv under Associated Book Publishers PLC)
Subjects: Science, Technology, Medicine
1982: 75 titles *Founded:* 1830
ISBN Publisher's Prefix: 0-412

Charnwood Library Series, see F A Thorpe (Publishing) Ltd

Chartwell-Bratt (Publishing & Training) Ltd+, Old Orchard, Bickley Rd, Bromley, Kent BR1 2NE Tel: (01) 467 1956 Telex: 8952171 Arena G
Man Dir: K J Munro; *Production:* R O'Gorman
Parent Company: Studentlitteratur AB, Sweden (qv)
Imprint: Studentlitteratur
Subjects: Computer Science, Management, Natural Sciences, Behavioural Science
Founded: 1980
ISBN Publisher's Prefix: 0-86238

Chatto & Windus (Educational) Ltd, an imprint of William Collins Sons & Co Ltd (qv)

Chatto & Windus Ltd/The Hogarth Press Ltd+, 40 William IV St, London WC2N 4DF Tel: (01) 379 6637 Cable Add: Bookstore London WC2 Telex: 299080
Chairman: Hugo Brunner; *Man Dir, Publishing Dir:* Carmen Callil; *Sales:* Roger Kirkpatrick (Marketing Dir), Peter Sapieha, Kate Griffin (Home), Quentin Hockliffe (Export); *Publicity & Advertising:* Juliet Nicolson; *Rights & Permissions:* Juliet Nicolson, Jill Rose
Orders to: 9 Bow St, London WC2E 7AL Tel: (01) 379 6637
Subjects: Fiction, Biography & Memoirs, Poetry, History, Literary Criticism, Cartoons, Philosophy, Illustrated Books, Travel, Psychology & Psychoanalysis, Social Sciences, Crime, Humour, Belles Lettres, Trade Paperbacks
Founded: 1855 (Chatto & Windus), 1917 (The Hogarth Press)
Miscellaneous: Firm is a member of Chatto, Bodley Head & Jonathan Cape Ltd Group (qv)
ISBN Publisher's Prefixes: 0-7011 (Chatto), 0-7012 (Hogarth)

Chatto, Bodley Head & Jonathan Cape Ltd, 35 Bow St, London WC2E 7AN Tel: (01) 379 6637 Cable Add: Chaboca London Telex: 299080
Group Members: Chatto & Windus Ltd/The Hogarth Press Ltd, Jonathan Cape Ltd, The Bodley Head Ltd, Virago Ltd (qqv)
Subsidiary Company: Triad Paperbacks (handled by Granada Publishing Ltd (qv))

The **Chemical Society**, see Royal Society of Chemistry

Child's Play (International) Ltd, Restrop Manor, Purton, Swindon, Wilts Tel: Swindon 770389 (STD code 0793), Swindon 850901 Telex: 449391
Man Dir: Michael Twinn; *Sales, Publicity:* Debra Stacey
Trade Orders to: 153 High St, Wootton Bassett, Swindon, Wilts
Subsidiary Company: Child's Play Inc, Chicago, USA
Associate Companies: D A Finnigan Ltd, Southport, UK; F X Schmid (UK) Ltd, Swindon
Subject: Juveniles (pre- and Primary School ages)
1981: 10 titles *1982:* 9 titles *Founded:* 1972
ISBN Publisher's Prefix: 0-85953

Chivers Press Publishers*, 93-100 Locksbrook Rd, Bath, Avon BA1 3HB Tel: Bath 331945 (STD code 0225)
Publisher: R H Lewis (to whom all correspondence)
Associate Companies: Chivers Book Sales Ltd; Firecrest Publishing Ltd (qv); Lythway Press (qv)
Imprints: New Portway Large Print, New Portway Facsimile Editions, Seymour Large Print Romances
Subjects: General Fiction and Non-fiction
ISBN Publisher's Prefixes: 0-85594 (Chivers), 0-85997 and 0-85119 (Portway), 0-86220 and 0-85119 (Seymour)

The **Christian Community** Press, see Floris Books

Christian Journals Ltd, PO Box 84, Belfast BT9 6TN Tel: Belfast 668268 (STD code 0232)
Man Dir: W G Forker; *Rights & Permissions:* Robert Brown
Subject: Religion
1981: 15 titles *Founded:* 1974
ISBN Publisher's Prefix: 0-904302

Church Book Room Press, an imprint of Church Society (qv)

Church Society, Whitefield House, 186 Kennington Park Rd, London SE11 4BT Tel: (01) 582 0132
Publishing Secretary: L J Bidewell
Imprints: Vine Books, Church Book Room Press
Subjects: Religious, Church History, Hymn Books
ISBN Publisher's Prefix: 0-85190

Churchill Livingstone+, Robert Stevenson House, 1-3 Baxter's Pl, Leith Walk, Edinburgh EH1 3AF Tel: (031) 556 2424 Cable Add: Churchliv Telex: 727511 Longman G (Edin)
Man Dir: R G B Duncan; *Editorial:* A T Stevenson; *Sales, Publicity & Advertising:* A J Smith; *Production:* C Cameron; *Rights & Permissions:* Irene Harper
Orders to: Longman Group Ltd, Trade Dept, Pinnacles, Harlow, Essex Tel: Harlow 29655 (STD code 0279)
Branch Offs: 5 Bentinck St, London W1M 5RN Tel: (01) 935 0121;
 Churchill Livingstone, 346 St Kilda Rd, Melbourne 3004 Australia Tel: (03) 699 1522; Churchill Livingstone Inc, 1560 Broadway, New York, NY 10036, USA Tel: (212) 819 5400
Subjects: Medicine, Dentistry, Nursing, Paramedical
1981: 143 titles *1982:* 167 titles *Founded:* 1863
Miscellaneous: Firm is a division of Longman Group Ltd (qv)
ISBN Publisher's Prefix: 0-443

City Arts, an imprint of John Offord (Publications) Ltd (qv)

Clarendon Press, see Oxford University Press

Robin **Clark** Ltd, 27-29 Goodge St, London W1P 1FD Tel: (01) 636 3992 Telex: 919034
Chairman: Naim Attallah; *Marketing Dir:* D Elliott; *Production Dir:* G Grant; *Editorial:* Rebecca Fraser; *Publicity Dir:* Juliette Foy
Associate Companies: Quartet Books Ltd (qv), The Women's Press Ltd (qv)
Subjects: Paperbacks: Reprints, Fiction, Biography, Social History, Humour
Founded: 1976
Miscellaneous: Firm is a member of the Namara Group, Namara House, 45-46 Poland St, London W1
ISBN Publisher's Prefix: 0-86072

T & T **Clark** Ltd*, 36 George St, Edinburgh EH2 2LQ Tel: (031) 225 4703 Cable Add: Dictionary Edinburgh
Man Dir: T G Ramsay D Clark; *Editorial, Sales, Production, Publicity, Rights & Permissions:* Geoffrey F Green
Parent Company: John Bartholomew & Son Ltd (qv)
Subjects: Philosophy, Theology, History, Law
Founded: 1821
ISBN Publisher's Prefix: 0-567

Anthony **Clarke** Books, 16 Garden Court, Wheathampstead, Hertfordshire AL4 8RF Tel: Wheathampstead 2460 (STD code 058283) Cable Add: Clarkbook St Albans
Proprietor: Anthony Clarke
Orders to: 27 Brewhouse Hill, Wheathampstead, Hertfordshire AL4 8RE
Subject: Religion
Bookshop: All Saints Bookshop, All Saints, London Colney, St Albans, Hertfordshire AL2 1AF
Founded: 1970
ISBN Publisher's Prefix: 0-85650

James **Clarke** & Co Ltd, 7 All Saints' Passage, Cambridge CB2 3LS Tel: Cambridge 350865 (STD code 0223) Telex: 817570
Man Dir: A C Brink
Imprint: Acorn Editions
Subjects: Librarianship, Religion, Textbooks, Reference, Technical
1981: 8 titles *Founded:* 1859
ISBN Publisher's Prefix: 0-227

E W **Classey**, PO Box 93, Faringdon, Oxfordshire SN7 7DR Tel: Uffington 399 (STD code 036782)
Publisher: E W Classey
Subject: Entomology
ISBN Publisher's Prefixes: 0-900848, 0-86096

Clematis Press Ltd, 18 Old Church St, London SW3 5DQ Tel: (01) 352 8755 Cable Add: Clematis London
Man Dir: Mrs Clara Waters
Trade Counter: Wentworth Book Co Ltd, Pindar Rd, Hoddesdon, Herts EN11 0HF
Subjects: Co-productions: Art, Architecture, Sport, Cookery
Founded: 1950
ISBN Publisher's Prefix: 0-568

Clio Press Ltd, 55 St Thomas' St, Oxford OX1 1JG Tel: Oxford 250333 (STD code 0865) Telex: 83130
Man Dir: John Durrant; *Editorial:* Veronica Babington Smith, Dr Robert Neville; *Sales:* Lesley Chaundy; *Publicity:* Jeremy Foreman, Robert Poulton
Parent Company: ABC-Clio Information Services, 2040 APS, Santa Barbara, California 93103, USA
Subjects: History, Politics, International Relations, Art, Bibliographies
1981: 20 titles *1982:* 14 titles *Founded:* 1971
ISBN Publisher's Prefix: 0-903450

William **Clowes** (Publishers) Ltd, now Hymns Ancient & Modern (qv)

Club Leabhar, an imprint of Johnston Green & Co (Publishers) Ltd (qv)

Cochuideachd Leabhneachean Gaidhlig, an imprint of Volturna Press (qv)

Collet's Holdings Ltd, Denington Estate, Wellingborough, Northants NN8 2QT Tel: Wellingborough 224351 (STD code 0933) Cable Add: Colholdin Wellingborough Telex: 311165 Chacom G

Colholdin
Man Dir: Eva Skelley; *Advertising:* Elisabeth Cook
Subjects: Music, Art (History), Textbooks, Reference (Modern Language, Audiovisual), General & Social Science, Low- & High-priced Paperbacks
Bookshops: Collet's London Bookshop, 64-66 Charing Cross Rd, London WC2; Collet's International Bookshop, 129-131 Charing Cross Rd, London WC2; Collet's Penguin Bookshop, 52 Charing Cross Rd, London WC2; Collet's Chinese Bookshop, 40 Great Russell St, London WC1
Founded: 1934
Miscellaneous: Specialists in Russian language teaching materials
ISBN Publisher's Prefix: 0-569

Collier Macmillan Ltd, Stockley Close, Stockley Rd, West Drayton, Middlesex UB7 9BE Tel: West Drayton 40651 (STD code 089 54) Cable Add: Pachamac West Drayton Telex: 897769 Casmac-G
Man Dir: Richard Bailey; *Sales & Marketing Manager, Publicity & Promotion:* Elaine Perkins
Parent Company: Crowell Collier Macmillan (Publishers) Ltd, London
Subjects: Academic, Primary and Secondary Textbooks, Trade, Medical, Professional Reference, English as a foreign Language, Dictionaries, Visual Learning Systems
1981: 202 titles *Founded:* 1964
ISBN Publisher's Prefix: 0-02

Collingridge, an imprint of Newnes Books (qv)

Rex **Collings** Ltd, 6 Paddington St, London W1M 3LA Tel: (01) 487 4201
Man Dir: Rex Collings
Orders to: Noonan Hurst Ltd, 131 Trafalgar Rd, London SE10 Tel: (01) 692 1475
Subjects: General, Poetry, Juveniles, Africana, Biography, Drama, Reference
1981: 17 titles *Founded:* 1969
ISBN Publisher's Prefixes: 0-86036, 0-901720

William **Collins** Sons & Co Ltd, 8 Grafton St, London W1X 3LA Tel: (01) 493 7070 Cable Add: Herakles London W1X Telex: 25611
Chairman: F I Chapman; *Man Dirs:* G Craig, C E Allen; *Divisional Dirs:* M Wotherspoon (General Trade Publishing), J Clement (Fontana), P Richardson (Educational, Reference, Bibles, Atlases), Alewyn Birch (Granada Publishing)
Orders to: PO Box, Glasgow G4 0NB Tel: (041) 772 3200 Telex: 778107
Subsidiary Companies: Chatto & Windus (Educational) Ltd; Granada Publishing Ltd (qv); Hart-Davis Educational Ltd; Harvill Press Ltd (qv); Pan Books Ltd (qv — one-third owned with William Heinemann Ltd and Macmillan Publishers Ltd, qqv)
Overseas Subsidiary Companies: Wm Collins Pty Ltd, Australia (qv); Wm Collins Sons & Co (Canada) Ltd, 100 Lesmill Rd, Don Mills, Ontario, Canada; Wm Collins Publishers Ltd, New Zealand (qv); Collins Vaal (Pty) Ltd, South Africa (qv)
Imprints include: Armada Books, Colour Cubs, The Crime Club, Dandelions, Flamingo, Fontana Books, Fount Paperbacks, Gem, Lions, Picture Lions
Subjects: General Fiction & Non-fiction, Belles Lettres, Biography, History, How-to, Art, Archaeology, Philosophy, Reference, Religion, Bibles, Low- & High-priced Paperbacks, General & Natural Sciences, University, Secondary & Primary Textbooks, Educational Materials, Juveniles, Military, Sports, Travel
Bookshops: Hatchards Ltd (qv under Major Booksellers); The Ancient House Bookshop, Ipswich, Suffolk
Founded: 1819
Miscellaneous: Collins-Longman Atlases, Westerhill Rd, Bishopbriggs, Glasgow G64 2QT distributes atlases for Wm Collins and the Longman Group
ISBN Publisher's Prefixes: 0-00 (Collins and Harvill), 0-069 (Armada), 0-061 (Fontana), 0-247 (Hart-Davis Educational)

Colonnade, an imprint of British Museum Publications (qv)

Colour Cubs, an imprint of William Collins Sons & Co Ltd (qv)

Colour Library International Ltd, 86 Epsom Rd, Guildford, Surrey GU1 2BX Tel: Guildford 579191 (STD code 0483) Telex: 859182
Man Dir: Barry Austin; *Editorial:* David Gibbon; *Sales:* Barry Austin, George Sprankling; *Production, Publicity:* Ted Smart; *Rights & Permissions:* Barry Austin, George Sprankling, Ted Smart
Subsidiary Company: Colour Library International (USA) Ltd, 163 East 64th St, New York, NY 10021, USA
Subjects: Travel, Nature, Art, Animals, Inspirational
Founded: 1959
ISBN Publisher's Prefixes: 0-906558, 0-86283

Columbia University Press, see University Presses of Columbia and Princeton

Columbine House, an imprint of Arlington Books (Publishers) Ltd (qv)

Colombus Books, 29 Elmfield Rd, Bromley, Kent BR1 1LT Tel: (01) 290 6611 Telex: 897948 Octabs G
Joint Man Dirs: Chris Holyfield, Medwyn Hughes; *Marketing:* Medwyn Hughes; *Promotion, Publicity Manager:* Dixie Nichols; *Sales Manager:* David Harris
Parent Company: Transatlantic Book Service Ltd (at above address)
Subjects: Popular
1982: 70 titles *1983:* 100 titles *Founded:* 1980
ISBN Publisher's Prefix: 0-86287

Comet, an imprint of W H Allen & Co Ltd (qv)

Commission for Racial Equality, Elliot House, 10-12 Allington St, London SW1 Tel: (01) 828 7022
Chief Executive: Peter Newson; *Editorial, Sales, Production, Publicity, Rights & Permissions:* Lionel Morrison
Imprint: C R E
Branch Offs: Manchester, Leeds, Birmingham, Leicester
Subject: Race & Community Relations
1981: 15 titles *1982:* 10 titles *Founded:* 1976
ISBN Publisher's Prefix: 0-907920

Common Ground, an imprint of Longman Group Ltd (qv)

Computer Research Press, an imprint of Abacus Press (qv)

Concertina Publications Ltd, 19 Broad Court, Covent Garden, London WC2B 5QN Tel: (01) 836 1758, (01) 836 2929
Subjects: Illustrated Non-fiction, Reference

Concorde Paperbacks, an imprint of Ward Lock Ltd (qv)

Condor Books, an imprint of Souvenir Press Ltd (qv)

Connoisseur Carbooks, see Motor Racing Publications Ltd

Conservative Political Centre, 32 Smith Sq, London SW1P 3HH Tel: (01) 222 9000 Cable Add: Constitute, London, SW1P 3HH
Director: David Knapp
Subjects: Reference Books, Politics, Political Economy, Sociology, Questions of the Day
ISBN Publisher's Prefix: 0-85070

Constable & Co Ltd, 10 Orange St, London WC2H 7EG Tel: (01) 930 0801 Cable Add: Dhagoba London WC2H 7EG
Man Dir: B K Glazebrook; *Editorial:* Elfreda Powell; *Sales:* Paul Marks; *Publicity & Editorial:* Miles Huddleston; *Rights & Permissions:* Christine Senior
Orders to: Tiptree Book Services Ltd, Tiptree, Colchester, Essex Tel: (0621) 816362 Cable Add: Literarius Tiptree Telex: 99487
Subjects: General Fiction, Literature, Antiques, Art, Biography, Memoirs, History, Politics, Current Affairs, Education, Food, Travel & Guidebooks, Gardening, Social Sciences, Natural History, General Science, Psychology & Psychiatry, Counselling, Social Work, Sociology, Philosophy, Religion, Mass Communications, Reference
Founded: 1896
ISBN Publisher's Prefix: 0-09

Construction Press, Longman House, Burnt Mill, Harlow, Essex CM20 2JE Tel: Harlow 26721 (STD code 0279) Telex: 81259
Editorial: Malcolm Hall; *Sales, Publicity:* Rosemary Parravani; *Production:* Terry Mann; *Rights & Permissions:* Lynette Owen
Orders to: Longman Group Ltd, Fourth Ave, Harlow, Essex CM19 5AA
Subjects: Architecture, Building, Civil Engineering
Founded: 1974
Miscellaneous: Firm is a division of Longman Group Ltd (qv)
ISBN Publisher's Prefixes: 0-904406, 0-86095

Conway Maritime Press Ltd, 24 Bride Lane, Fleet St, London EC4Y 8DR Tel: (01) 353 9665 Telex: 8814206 Popper G
Man Dir: W R Blackmore; *Editorial Dir:* Robert Gardiner; *Rights:* Jane Weeks
Orders to: Marston Book Services Ltd, PO Box 87, Marston St, Oxford OX4 1LB Telex: 837022
Associate Company: Paul Popper Ltd, 24 Bride Lane, Fleet St, London EC4Y 8DR
Subjects: Naval, Maritime
1982: 27 titles *Founded:* 1968
ISBN Publisher's Prefix: 0-85177

Leo **Cooper**, an associate of Secker & Warburg Ltd (qv)

Trewin **Copplestone** Books, now Sceptre Books Ltd (qv)

Corgi Books Ltd+, Century House, 61-63 Uxbridge Rd, Ealing, London W5 5SA Tel: (01) 579 2652 Cable Add: Transcable London W5 Telex: 267974
Man Dir, Chief Executive: Paul Scherer; *Publisher:* Patrick Janson-Smith; *Editorial Dirs:* Alan Earney, Andrew McKillop; *International Sales Dir:* John Blake; *Foreign, Subsidiary Rights:* Mary Bruton; *UK Marketing Dir:* Derek Searle; *Publicity, Promotion Dir:* Wendy Tury; *Production Dir:* Frank Gill; *Art Dir:* John Munday
Parent Company: Bantam Books Inc, 666 Fifth Ave, New York, NY 10103, USA
Associate Companies: Bantam Books of Canada Inc, 888 Dupont St, Toronto, Ontario, Canada; Transworld Publishers (Australia) Pty Ltd, Australia (qv); Transworld Publishers Pty Ltd, PO Box 27066, Benrose 2011, South Africa
Imprints include: Black Swan (trade paperbacks), Carousel (children's books)
Subjects: Mass-market and trade paperbacks in all general fiction and non-fiction areas
1982: 300 titles *Founded:* 1950
ISBN Publisher's Prefix: 0-552

Cornell University Press, Ely House, 37 Dover St, London W1X 4HQ Tel: (01) 493 5061, (01) 499 4688 Cable Add: Unibooks London W1 Telex: 24224 ref 3545
Warehouse: International Book Distributors, 66 Wood Lane End, Hemel Hempstead, Hertfordshire Tel: Hemel Hempstead 58531 (STD code 0442)
Man Dir: J Trevor Brown; *Promotion Manager:* Michael Richards; *Sales Manager:* Anna Simpson-Muellner
Parent Company: Cornell University Press, 124 Roberts Pl, Ithaca, NY 14850, USA
Subjects: Academic (all disciplines)
ISBN Publisher's Prefix: 0-8014

Coronet, an imprint of Hodder & Stoughton Ltd (qv)

D J **Costello** (Publishers) Ltd, 43 High St, Tunbridge Wells, Kent TN1 1XU Tel: Tunbridge Wells 45355 (STD code 0892) Telex: 95625 Derrick G
Man Dir, Editorial: David Costello; *Sales:* James Smith; *Production:* Martin Taylor; *Publicity:* Rosemary Costello; *Rights & Permissions:* Patrick Morrissey
Associate Companies: Weald UK Ltd (book marketing consultants, at above address)
Imprint: Costello Educational
Subjects: Special Education, Archaeology, Social Studies
1981: 5 titles *1982:* 5 titles *Founded:* 1979
ISBN Publisher's Prefix: 0-7104

Cotman House, an imprint of Jarrold Colour Publications (qv)

Cotmancolor, an imprint of Jarrold Colour Publications (qv)

Council for Educational Technology, 3 Devonshire St, London W1N 2BA Tel: (01) 636 4186
Dir: Geoffrey Hubbard; *Publications Officer:* Muriel Pashley
Imprint: C E T
Subjects: Educational Technology, Microelectronics & Computing, Teacher Education, Copyright, Librarianship of Newer Media, Open Learning
1981: 15 titles *1982:* 9 titles *Founded:* 1973
ISBN Publisher's Prefix: 0-86184

Country Life Books, an imprint of Newnes Books (qv)

Countryside Books, 3 Catherine Rd, Newbury, Berkshire RG14 7NA Tel: Newbury 43816 (STD code 0635)
Man Dir, Editorial, Sales, Production: Nicholas Battle; *Publicity, Rights & Permissions:* Suzanne Battle
Subsidiary Company: Local Heritage Books (at above address)
Subject: Local History
1981: 4 titles *1982:* 4 titles *Founded:* 1976
ISBN Publisher's Prefix: 0-905392

The **Crafts** Council, 12 Waterloo Pl, London SW1Y 4AU Tel: (01) 930 4811
Publications Officer: Marigold Coleman
Bookshop: Crafts Council Gallery, 12 Waterloo Pl, London SW1Y 4AU
Subject: Crafts
1981: 3 titles *1982:* 6 titles *Founded:* 1971
Miscellaneous: Government-financed body promoting Britain's artist craftsmen
ISBN Publisher's Prefix: 0-903798

Cressrelles Publishing Co Ltd, 311 Worcester Rd, Malvern, Worcestershire Tel: Malvern 65045 (STD code 06845)
Man Dir: Leslie Smith
Subjects: Juveniles, Pre-school Education, Fiction, General
1981: 6 titles *1982:* 4 titles *Founded:* 1972
ISBN Publisher's Prefix: 0-85956

The **Crime** Club, an imprint of William Collins Sons & Co Ltd (qv)

Paul H **Crompton** Ltd+, 638 Fulham Rd, London SW6 Tel: (01) 736 2551
Publicity & Sales: Paul Crompton; *Subscription Enquiries:* B Crompton; *Shop Enquiries:* C Hanson
Subjects: Oriental Martial Arts and Survival, Periodical *Karate & Oriental Arts*

Croner Publications Ltd, Croner House, 173 Kingston Rd, New Malden, Surrey KT3 3SS Tel: (01) 942 8966 Telex: 267778
Man Dir: A S Brode; *Marketing Dir:* D E Sleat
Subject: Business Reference Books
Miscellaneous: Firm is member of Wolters Samsom Groep BV, Netherlands (qv)
ISBN Publisher's Prefix: 0-900319

Croom Helm Ltd+, Provident House, Burrell Row, Beckenham, Kent BR3 1AT Tel: (01) 658 7813 Cable Add: Croomhelm Beckenham Telex: 912881 Cw UK Txg Attn CHP
Man Dirs: Christopher Helm, David Croom; *Editorial:* Peter Sowden (Social Sciences), Richard Stoneman (Humanities), Tim Hardwick (Medicine/Science), Jo Hemmings (Natural History); *Sales:* Graham Harris (Home), Amanda Halstead (Export); *Production:* Mike Conway; *Publicity:* Bernard Mercer; *Translation Rights:* Jean Eales
Branch Off: Croom Helm Australia, PO Box 391, Manuka, ACT 2603, Australia
Subjects: Academic and General Non-fiction in History, Politics, Sociology, Economics, Business, Development Studies, Geography, Law, Literature, Linguistics, Archaeology, Classical Studies, Education, Medical and Biological Sciences, the Middle East, Horticulture, Ornithology and Natural History, Guide Books
1982: 191 titles
ISBN Publisher's Prefixes: 0-85664, 0-7099

Crosby Lockwood Staples Ltd, see Granada Publishing Ltd

Curzon Press Ltd+, 42 Gray's Inn Rd, London WC1 Tel: (01) 242 8310
Man Dir: J F Standish
Subjects: Oriental and African Studies
1981: 18 titles *1982:* 18 titles *Founded:* 1970
ISBN Publisher's Prefix: 0-7007

D P Publications, 12 Romsey Rd, Eastleigh, Hants SO5 4AL Tel: Eastleigh 617353 (STD code 0703) or Watford 27569 (STD code 0923)
Subjects: Finance, Law, Accountancy, Quantitative Techniques, Management, Data Processing, Computer Science, Management Information Systems, Auditing, Costing, Programming, Computer Studies
1983: 19 titles
ISBN Publisher's Prefix: 0-905435

Dagon Books, an imprint of Studio Publications (Ipswich) Ltd (qv)

Dalesman Publishing Co Ltd, Clapham, Lancaster LA2 8EB Tel: Clapham 225 (STD code 04685)
Man Dir: D Bullock; *Editorial:* W R Mitchell; *Sales:* A N Jefferies; *Production:* D A W Joy
Subjects: Northern England
1981: 29 titles *1982:* 31 titles *Founded:* 1939
ISBN Publisher's Prefix: 0-85206

Terence **Dalton** Ltd, Water St, Lavenham, Sudbury, Suffolk Tel: Lavenham 247572 (STD code 0787)
Man Dir, Production, Rights & Permissions: T R Dalton; *Editorial:* R W Malster; *Sales, Publicity:* Mrs E H Whitehair
Associate Company: The Lavenham Press Ltd (at above address)
Imprints: Eastland Press, Galaxy Books, Mallard Reprints
Subjects: History, Topography, Maritime, Aviation
1981: 6 titles *1982:* 7 titles *Founded:* 1967
ISBN Publisher's Prefixes: 0-900963, 0-86138, 0-903214, 0-904623

Dance Books Ltd+, 9 Cecil Court, St Martin's Lane, London WC2N 4EZ Tel: (01) 836 2314
Man Dir, Production, Rights & Permissions: David Leonard; *Editorial, Publicity:* Richard Holland; *Sales:* John O'Brien
Subject: Dance and Human Movement
1981: 6 titles *1982:* 8 titles *Founded:* 1961
ISBN Publisher's Prefix: 0-903102

Dandelions, an imprint of William Collins Sons & Co Ltd (qv)

The C W **Daniel** Co Ltd, 1 Church Path, Saffron Walden, Essex CB10 1JP Tel: Saffron Walden 21909 (STD code 0799)
Man Dir: Ian Miller; *Editorial:* Jane Miller; *Sales:* Janice Jeffery; *Production:* Barnaby Miller; *Publicity:* Ida Honoroff; *Rights & Permissions:* Jane Miller
Subsidiary Company: Health Science Press (qv)
Subjects: Natural Healing, Homoeopathy
Founded: 1902
ISBN Publisher's Prefix: 0-85207

Darton, Longman & Todd Ltd, 89 Lillie Rd, London SW6 1UD Tel: (01) 385 2341
Cable Add: Librabook London SW6 1UD
Dirs: Adrian Brink, Leslie Kay, Miss Lesley Riddle, Miss E A C Russell; *Publishing Consultant:* J M Todd; *Publicity & Advertising:* Miss A Hornby
Subjects: History, Philosophy, Reference, Religion, Bibles, Quality Paperbacks, Medicine, Psychology, Secondary Textbooks, Travel Guides, Gardening
Founded: 1959
ISBN Publisher's Prefix: 0-232

Darwen Finlayson Ltd, Shopwyke Hall, Chichester, West Sussex Tel: Chichester 787636 (STD code 0243)
Chairman & Man Dir: Philip Harris; *Editorial Director:* Noel H Osborne
Parent Company: Phillimore & Co Ltd (qv)
Subjects: History, Historical Biography, Company Histories, Family Histories
ISBN Publisher's Prefix: 0-85208

Datapack Books, an imprint of E J Morten (Publishers) (qv)

David & Charles, Brunel House, Forde Rd, Newton Abbot, Devon TQ12 4PU Tel: Newton Abbot 61121 (STD code 0626) Cable Add: Books Nabbot Telex: 42904 Books G
Chairman: David St John Thomas; *Man Dir:* J Angell; *Marketing Dir:* Nigel Hollis; *Publishing Dir:* David Porteous; *Rights & Permissions:* Dieter L Klein
Parent Company: David & Charles (Holdings) Ltd
Subsidiary Company: David & Charles Inc, North Pomfret, Vermont 05053, USA
Subjects: History, How-to, Architecture, Archaeology, Reference, Engineering, General Science, Marine & Railway Transport, Countryside, Natural History, Cookery, Sport
Bookshop: St John Thomas, The Baker St Book & Record Shop, 33 Baker St, London W1M 1AE
Book Club: Readers Union Ltd; Nationwide Book Club
Founded: 1960
ISBN Publisher's Prefix: 0-7153

Peter **Davies** Ltd*, 10 Upper Grosvenor St, London W1X 9PA Tel: (01) 493 4141
Cable Add: Pedebooks London W1
Chairman: C S Pick; *Dir:* Nigel Hollis; *Rights:* Caroline Ball

Parent Company: William Heinemann International Ltd (qv)
Branch Offs: The Windmill Press, Kingswood, Tadworth, Surrey; 11a Gower Mews, London WC1
Subjects: General Fiction, Biography, History, Religion, Travel, Seafaring, Theatre, Countryside, Cookery
Founded: 1925
ISBN Publisher's Prefix: 0-432

Davis-Poynter Ltd*, 11 Bolt Court, Fleet St, London EC4A 3DQ Tel: (01) 583 6195
Orders to: George Philip & Son Ltd, PO Box 1, Arndale Rd, Lineside Industrial Estate, Littlehampton, West Sussex BN17 7EN Tel: Littlehampton 7453 (STD code 09064)
Man Dir Editorial, Publicity: R G Davis-Poynter; *Sales, Production, Rights & Permissions:* Susan Herbert
Subjects: Fiction, History, Politics, Naval & Military, Music, Poetry & Drama, Biography, Memoirs, Politics, Sociology, Travel, Gardening, Folklore, Popular Medicine, Nutrition
Founded: 1970
ISBN Publisher's Prefix: 0-7067

Davison Publishing Ltd*, 54 Elgin Ave, London W9 2HA Tel: (01) 289 7623
Dirs: Thomas Tessier, Phil Edwards
Imprint: Millington Books
Subjects: Science Fiction, Gothic/Romance Fiction, Biography, History, General Non-fiction, Quality Paperbacks
Founded: 1973
ISBN Publisher's Prefix: 0-86000

Dawson Publishing, Cannon House, Folkestone, Kent CT19 5EE
Tel: Folkestone 57421 (STD code 0303)
Cable Add: Dawbooks Folkestone
Telex: 96392
Man Dir: D A Brewer; *Publishing:* Gerald Dorman
Subjects: Music, Art, Geography, University Textbooks, Biography, History, Reference, Medicine, General & Social Science, Cartography
Bookshops: Dawson Book Service, 10-14 Macklin St, London WC2B 5NG; Cannon House, Folkestone, Kent CT19 5EE; Dawson-France SA, BP 40, F-91121 Palaiseau, France (all three general sales); Bow Windows Book Shop, 128 High St, Lewes, East Sussex BN7 1XL; Deighton, Bell & Co and Frank Hammond, both at 13 Trinity St, Cambridge CB2 1TD (all antiquarian sales); Stevens and Brown Ltd, Ardon House, Mill Lane, Godalming, Surrey GU7 1HA
Founded: 1809
ISBN Publisher's Prefix: 0-7129

Dean & Son, an imprint of The Hamlyn Publishing Group (qv)

Debrett's Peerage Ltd, 73-77 Britannia Rd, London SW6 Tel: (01) 736 6524 Telex: 24224 Monref G
Man Dir: Robert Jarman; *Editorial:* Suzanne Duke
Orders to: Webb & Bower (Publishers) Ltd, 9 Colleton Cres, Exeter, Devon EX2 4BY Tel: Exeter 35362/33733 (STD code 0392)
Subjects: Art, Design, History, Sport, Humour, Etiquette, British Royal Family and Peerage
1981: 6 titles *Founded:* 1769
ISBN Publisher's Prefix: 0-905649

Delightful Books, an imprint of Ramboro Enterprises Ltd (qv)

Demand Reprints, an imprint of Avebury Publishing Co Ltd (qv)

Denholm House Press, see National Christian Education Council

J M **Dent** & Sons Ltd, Aldine House, 33 Welbeck St, London W1M 8LX Tel: (01) 486 7233 Cable Add: Malaby London W1 Telex: 8954130
Chairman: V F Chamberlain; *Man Dir:* Peter Shellard; *Editorial:* Malcolm Gerratt, Peter Shellard (General), Vanessa Hamilton (Juvenile), Jocelyn Burton (Everyman); *Sales Dir:* Patrick Johnston; *Production:* David Rye; *Publicity Dir:* Elizabeth Newlands; *Contracts & Permissions:* John Sundell; *Rights:* Maggie Hemingway (General), Anne Rowell (Juvenile)
Orders to: J M Dent (Distribution) Ltd, Dunhams Lane, Letchworth, Herts SG6 1LF Tel: Letchworth 6241 (STD code 04626)
Parent Company: J M Dent & Sons (Holdings) Ltd
Subsidiary Companies: J M Dent Pty Ltd, Australia (qv); J M Dent & Sons (Canada) Ltd, Don Mills, Ontario
Associate Companies: J M Dent (Distribution) Ltd; J M Dent (Sales) Ltd; J M Dent & Sons (Letchworth) Ltd (Bookbinders)
Imprints: Everyman Fiction, Everyman's Library, Everyman's Reference Library, Everyman's University Library, Malaby Press
Subjects: Belles Lettres, Biography, History, Natural History, Music, Reference, Juveniles, Paperbacks, University Textbooks, Regional, Topography, Archaeology, Cookery, Gardening, Popular Science, Sport, Photography, Military History, Literary Fiction
Founded: 1888
Miscellaneous: Publishers of *Everyman's Encyclopaedia*
ISBN Publisher's Prefix: 0-460

Design Council Books, The Design Centre, 28 Haymarket, London SW1Y 4SU Tel: (01) 839 8000 Telex: 8812963
Publisher: Roy Dodd; *Editorial Dir, Rights:* Terry Bishop; *Sales, Publicity Manager:* Bill Garrett
Parent Company: The Design Council (at above address)
Imprints: Design Centre Books, The Design Council
Subjects: Design in the Home, Design for the General Public, Design Education and Design in General Education, Professional Design Practice and Theory, Engineering Design, Management, Educational Visual Aids, Design History
Bookshops: The Design Centre Bookshop and The Design Centre Bookshop Mail Order (at above address)
1981: 6 titles *1982:* 6 titles *Founded:* 1974
ISBN Publisher's Prefix: 0-85072

André **Deutsch** Ltd, 105 Great Russell St, London WC1B 3LJ Tel: (01) 580 2746 Cable Add: Adlib, London WC1 Telex: 261026 Adlib G
Chairman and Man Dir: André Deutsch; *Deputy Man Dirs:* Mike Beattie (Marketing), Dieter Pevsner (Editorial); *Editorial Dir:* Diana Athill; *Production Dir:* Jeff Sains; *Publicity & Advertising Manager:* Helen Ellis; *Rights & Permissions:* Caroline Owen
Associate Company: Private Eye Books
Imprint: The Language Library
Subjects: General Fiction, Belles Lettres, Poetry, Biography, History, Music, Art, Philosophy, Reference, Juveniles, Humour, Politics, Current Events, Travel, Cookery
1982: 88 titles *Founded:* 1951
ISBN Publisher's Prefix: 0-233

Diadem Books Ltd, 249 Knighton Church Rd, Leicester LE2 3JQ Tel: Leicester 709353 (STD code 0533)
Editorial: Ken Wilson; *Sales:* Ken Vickers
Subsidiary Company: Cordee (at above address)
Subjects: Walking, Backpacking, Trekking, Climbing, Skiing, Canoeing, Caving
1981: 4 titles *Founded:* 1972
ISBN Publisher's Prefixes: 0-904405, 0-906371

Diagram Visual Information Ltd, 11½ Adeline Pl, London WC1B 3JR Tel: (01) 637 4646 Telex: 21120 ref 2978
Dirs: Bruce Robertson, Wolfgang Foges
Subjects: Reference, Juveniles, Sport, Leisure Activities, Popular Health (creators of *Diagram Group* books)

Dial, an imprint of Doubleday & Co Inc (qv)

Keith **Dickson**, an imprint of Dickson Price Publishers Ltd (qv)

Dickson Price Publishers Ltd, PO Box 88, Gravesend, Kent DA13 9PR Tel: Gravesend 833732 (STD code 0474)
Man Dir, Editorial, Rights & Permissions: K E Dickson; *Production:* D S Wanstall
Imprints: Keith Dickson, Norman Price
Subjects: Electronics, Computing, Technical Modelling
1981: 6 titles *Founded:* 1980
ISBN Publisher's Prefixes: 0-907266, 0-85380

Dinosaur Publications Ltd+, Beechcroft House, Over, Cambridge CB4 5NE Tel: Swavesey 30324 (STD code 0954)
Joint Man Dirs: Mike Graham-Cameron, Edward Parker; *Managing Editor:* Althea Braithwaite; *Publicity Dir (Sponsored books):* Mike Graham-Cameron; *Home & Export Sales, Rights, Finance:* Edward Parker; *Production:* Jane Rose
Imprints: Althea, Althea's Nature Series, Althea's Pet Series, Althea's What to Expect Series, Dinosaur's Althea Books, Dinosaur's Action Series, National Trust Children's Series
Subjects: Juveniles, Educational Materials, Sponsored Books, Games
Founded: 1968
ISBN Publisher's Prefix: 0-85122

Dennis **Dobson** (Dobson Books Ltd)*, Brancepeth Castle, Durham DH7 8DF Tel: (0385) 780628
Man Dir: Margaret Dobson; *Sales, Publicity, Rights:* Oliver Dobson
Subjects: General Fiction, Belles Lettres, Poetry, Biography, History, Music, Art, Theatre, Juveniles, General & Social Science, Economics, Political Science
ISBN Publisher's Prefix: 0-234

Dolphin, an imprint of Doubleday & Co Inc (qv)

John **Donald** Publishers Ltd, 138 Stephen St, Edinburgh EH3 5AA
Editorial Dir: J B Tuckwell; *Sales Dir:* J G Angus
Subjects: Academic, Scottish
1982: 15 titles *Founded:* 1973
ISBN Publisher's Prefix: 0-85976

Ad **Donker** Ltd*, Gloucester Mansions, Cambridge Circus, London WC2
Orders to: Routledge-Harrap Storage Ltd, Broadway House, Newtown Rd, Henley-on-Thames, Oxfordshire RG9 1EN Tel: Henley-on-Thames 78321 (STD code 04912)
Parent Company: Ad Donker (Pty) Ltd, South Africa (qv)
Subjects: General Fiction & Non-fiction, Belles Lettres, Poetry, Biography, Reference
Founded: 1976

Dorling Kindersley Ltd+, 9 Henrietta St, Covent Garden, London WC2E 8PS Tel: (01) 240 5151 Telex: 8954527 Deekay G
Man Dirs: Christopher Dorling, Peter Kindersley; *Foreign Sales:* Caroline Oakes; *Editorial:* Christopher Davis; *Design:* Roger Bristow; *Production:* Lorraine Baird; *UK Publishing:* Ian Grant
Orders to: Victor Gollancz Ltd, 14 Henrietta St, Covent Garden, London WC2 Tel: (01) 836 2006
Subjects: Illustrated Reference Books for the International Market on Photography, Gardening, Cookery, Crafts, Family Health, Child Care, History, Sport, DIY, Leisure
1982: 11 titles *Founded:* 1974
ISBN Publisher's Prefix: 0-86318

Doubleday & Co Inc+, 100 Wigmore St, London W1H 9DR Tel: (01) 935 1269 Cable Add: Doubco Telex: 264676
Editorial, Rights & Permissions: Marianne Velmans
Orders to: Transatlantic Book Service Ltd, Devonshire House, 29 Elmfield Rd, Bromley, Kent BR1 1LT
Parent Company: Doubleday & Co, Inc, 245 Park Ave, New York, NY 10167, USA
Associate Companies: Doubleday Canada Ltd; Doubleday-France, Paris
Imprints: Anchor, Dial, Dolphin, Image
Subjects: General
Book Clubs: Book Club Associates (qv)
Founded: 1897
ISBN Publisher's Prefix: 0-385

Dragon Books, see Granada Publishing

Dragon's World Ltd, High St, Limpsfield, Surrey RH8 0DY Tel: Oxted 5044 (STD code 08833) Telex: 95631 Dragon G
Dir, Publisher, Sales, Rights & Permissions: H A Schaafsma; *Production:* 33 Portland Rd, London W11 4LH; *Publicity:* Irene Howells
Orders to: J M Dent & Son (Distribution) Ltd, Dunham Lane, Letchworth, Herts SG6 1LF
Imprint: Paper Tiger
Subjects: Illustrated Science Fiction, Fable, Fantasy, Art, Children's Books
Founded: 1976
ISBN Publisher's Prefix: 0-905895

Richard **Drew** Publishing Ltd, 20 Park Circus, Glasgow G3 6BE Tel: (041) 333 9341 Telex: 777308
Rights & Trade Enquiries: Richard Drew
Subjects: Leisure, General Interest, Fiction, Humour, Sport, Languages, Children's
1981: 35 titles *1982:* 45 titles

Gerald **Duckworth** & Co Ltd+, The Old Piano Factory, 43 Gloucester Crescent, London NW1 Tel: (01) 485 3484 Cable Add: Platypus
Man Dir: Colin Haycraft; *Sales Manager:* David Lines; *Publicity Advertising Manager, Rights & Permissions:* Juliet Dent
Subjects: Fiction, General, Academic
Founded: 1898
ISBN Publisher's Prefix: 0-7156

Duke University Press, see Academic and University Publishers Group

Dun & Bradstreet Ltd, PO Box 17, 26-32 Clifton St, London EC2P 2LY Tel: (01) 377 4377 Cable Add: Dunbrad London Telex: 886697
Man Dir: Richard Archer; *Editorial, Production:* H King; *Sales:* D Clark; *Publicity:* J Dawson
Orders to: 27 Paul St, London EC2A 4JU
Parent Company: Dun & Bradstreet Corporation, 299 Park Ave, New York, NY 10017, USA
Branch Offs: Bangor (Northern Ireland), Birmingham, Epsom, Glasgow, Leeds, Newcastle, Nottingham, Romford, Southampton
Subjects: Financial & Commercial Information, Buyers' Guides, Who Owns Whom
Founded: 1919
ISBN Publisher's Prefix: 0-900625

Martin **Dunitz** Ltd, 154 Camden High St, London NW1 0NE Tel: (01) 482 2202 Telex: 296307 Dunbks
Man Dir, Sales, Rights & Permissions: Martin Dunitz; *Editorial:* Piers Murray-Hill, Mary Banks; *Production:* Paul Valerio; *Publicity:* Tessa Robinson
Orders to: Mitchell Beazley London Ltd, Trade Dept, Mill House, 87-89 Shaftesbury Ave, London W1V 7AD
Subjects: Popular Health, Medical, Flying, General Illustrated
1982: 8 titles *1983:* 8 titles *Founded:* 1978
ISBN Publisher's Prefix: 0-906348

The **Dunrod** Press, 8 Brown's Rd, Newtownabbey, Co Antrim BT36 8RN Tel: Glengormley 2362 (STD code 02313)
General Manager: John Lindsay; *Editorial, Rights & Permissions:* Robert Witherspoon; *Sales:* Hugh Hall; *Production:* James Crawford; *Publicity:* John Graham
Associate Company: The Dunrod Press (Ireland), Dublin, Republic of Ireland
Branch Off: 28 North End Rd, Ballyclare, Co Antrim
Subjects: History, Current Affairs, General
1981: 4 titles *1982:* 3 titles *Founded:* 1979
ISBN Publisher's Prefix: 0-86202

E P Publishing Ltd, Bradford Rd, East Ardsley, Wakefield, West Yorkshire WF3 2JN Tel: Wakefield 823971 (STD code 0924) Cable Add: Edpro, Wakefield Telex: 451458 Comhud G
Man Dir, Sales, Rights & Permissions: Brian Lewis; *Editorial:* Frances Royle; *Production:* Paul Hicks; *Publicity:* Sharon Mitchell
Parent Company: Seymour Press Group Ltd, 334 Brixton Rd, London SW9 7AG
Subsidiary Company: British Trades Alphabet Ltd (at above Wakefield address)
Imprints: Lepus Books, SRP
Subjects: Sport, Leisure, History, Health, Reprints
1983: 34 titles *Founded:* 1946
ISBN Publisher's Prefixes: 0-7158 (E P Publishing), 0-86019 (Lepus Books), 0-85409 (SRP)

E S Training Services Ltd, Waverley Rd, Yate, Bristol BS17 5RB Tel: Chipping Sodbury 316774 (STD code 0454)
Man Dir: G H Wace; *Publications Manager:* T T Procter
Parent Company: Quandrol Investments Ltd
Subjects: Secondary & Primary Textbooks, Nautical, Management and Industrial Training Manuals, Audio-visual Aids
Founded: 1982

E S A Creative Learning Ltd, now part of E J Arnold & Son Ltd (qv)

E S C Publishing Ltd, 25 Beaumont St, Oxford OX1 2NP Tel: Oxford 512281 (STD code 0865) Telex: 83147
Dir: Nicholas Gingell
Associate Company: European Study Conferences Ltd, Kirby House, High St East, Uppingham, Oakham, Leicestershire
Subjects: Intellectual Property (Copyright, Patents and Trademarks) and Competition Law, Taxation, Industrial Relations, Periodicals
1981: 3 titles *1982:* 3 titles *Founded:* 1978
ISBN Publisher's Prefix: 0-906214

East-West Publications (UK) Ltd*, Jubilee House, Chapel Rd, Hounslow, Middlesex TW3 1XT Tel: (01) 572 6525
Man Dir: L W Carp
Associate Companies: Elron Press Ltd (qv); Maurice Temple Smith Ltd (qv); Wildwood House Ltd (qv); Words & Music Ltd; Words & Music (Wholesale) Ltd
Subjects: Far & Middle East Culture & Religion, Children's & Adults Reference Books, Children's Music, Music
ISBN Publisher's Prefix: 0-85692

Eastland Press, an imprint of Terence Dalton Ltd (qv)

Ebury Press, National Magazine House, 72 Broadwick St, London W1V 2BP Tel: (01) 439 7144 Cable Add: Shanmag London W1 Telex: 263879
Man Dir: Terry Mansfield; *Publisher:* Roger Barrett; *Editorial:* Robert Smith; *Marketing Dir:* Tim Whale; *Publicity, Rights:* Fiona Lindsay
Orders to: Michael Joseph Ltd, 44 Bedford Sq, London WC1 3DU
Parent Company: National Magazine Co Ltd, 72 Broadwick St, London W1V 2BP
Subjects: General Non-fiction, How-to, Reference
1981: 30 titles *1982:* 30 titles
ISBN Publisher's Prefix: 0-85223

The **Economist**, Publications Department, 25 St James's St, London SW1A 1HG Tel: (01) 839 7000 Cable Add: Mistecon Ldn Telex: 919555
Man Dir: David Gordon; *Rights & Permissions:* David McGill
Subsidiary Companies: Economist Intelligence Unit Ltd (UK); The Economist Newspaper Inc, 75 Rockefeller Plaza, NY 10019, USA
Branch Off: 75 Rockefeller Plaza, New York, NY 10019, USA
Subjects: Economic Reference Books, Diaries, Educational Materials
Founded: 1843
ISBN Publisher's Prefix: 0-85058

Eddison Press Ltd+, 7 Regal Lane, Soham, Ely, Cambridgeshire CB7 5BA Tel: Ely 721091 (STD code 0353) Telex: 81584
Dir: Roger W G Curtis
Imprints: Eddison Bluesbooks, Eddison Musicbooks
Subjects: Reference, Music
ISBN Publisher's Prefix: 0-85649

Eddison Sadd Editions Ltd+, 2 Julian Court, Julian Hill, Harrow-on-the-Hill, Middlesex HA1 3NF Tel: (01) 422 7087 Telex: 261234 (quote Eddison Sadd)
Editorial: Ian N Jackson; *Production:* Nicholas J Eddison; *Rights & Permissions:* Graham D Sadd
Parent Company: Eddison Sadd & Partners Ltd (at above address)
Subsidiary Company: The Communications Studio — Electronic Publishing (at above address)
Subjects: Illustrated reference for the international co-edition market
1982: 3 titles *Founded:* 1981

Edinburgh University Press+, 22 George Sq, Edinburgh EH8 9LF Tel: (031) 667 1011 Cable Add: Edinpress Telex: 727442
Man Dir, Rights & Permissions: A R Turnbull; *Assistant Secretary & Production Manager:* J McI Davidson; *Publicity:* Gillian Bates, 55 Linden Gardens, London W2 4HJ Tel: (01) 229 0384
Subjects: Belles Lettres, Poetry, Biography, History, Music, Art, Philosophy, Religion, Textbooks, Reference, Medicine, Psychology, General & Social Science
1981: 21 titles *1982:* 24 titles *Founded:* 1948
ISBN Publisher's Prefix: 0-85224

Edinburgh University Student Publications Board*, 1 Buccleuch Pl, Edinburgh EH8 9LW Tel: (031) 667 1011, (031) 667 5718, (031) 667 9278
Chief Executive: Margaret Roxton; *Sales, Publicity, Rights & Permissions:* Pamela Smith; *Production:* Neville Moir
Imprint: Polygon Books
Subjects: Politics, Sociology, Fiction, Poetry, History, all with special regard to Scotland

Educational Explorers Ltd, 11 Crown St, Reading, Berkshire RG1 2TQ Tel: Reading 873103 (STD code 0734)
Chairman: Dr Caleb Gattegno; *Man Dir:* M J Hollyfield
Parent Company: Educational Solutions (UK) Ltd of Reading
Associate Companies: Educational Solutions Inc, 80 Fifth Ave, New York, NY 10011; The Cuisenaire Co Ltd, and Educational Explorers Film Co Ltd, both of 11 Crown St, Reading, Berkshire RG1 2TQ
Subjects: Primary & Secondary Textbooks and Teachers Guides, Mathematics, Reading, Foreign Languages, Educational Psychology
ISBN Publisher's Prefix: 0-85225

Educational Productions Ltd, see E P Publishing Ltd

Educational Systems Ltd, now E S Training Services Ltd (qv)

Paul Elek Ltd, see Granada Publishing Ltd

Elliot Right Way Books+, Kingswood Bldgs, Lower Kingswood, Tadworth, Surrey KT20 6TD Tel: Mogador 832202 (STD code 0737)
Man Dir: Andrew G Elliot; *Sales Dir:* A Clive Elliot; *Production, Publicity Dir:* Malcolm G Elliot
Imprints: Paperfronts, Right Way Books
Subjects: How-to, Reference, Juveniles, Low-priced Paperbacks, Sport, Technical, Education
1981: 10 titles *1982:* 10 titles *Founded:* 1945
ISBN Publisher's Prefix: 0-7160

Aidan Ellis Publishing Ltd, Cobb House, Nuffield, Henley-on-Thames, Oxfordshire RG9 5RU Tel: Nettlebed 641496 (STD code 0491) Cable Add: Aidanellis Henley-on-Thames
Man Dir: Aidan Ellis
Orders to: J M Dent & Sons (Distribution) Ltd, Dunhams Lane, Letchworth SG6 1LF, Herts
Subjects: Fiction, General, Art, Belles Lettres
1982: 12 titles *Founded:* 1971
ISBN Publisher's Prefix: 0-85628

Elm Tree Books Ltd, see Hamish Hamilton Ltd

Elron Press Ltd, Jubilee House, Chapel Rd, Hounslow, Middlesex TW3 1TX Tel: (01) 572 6525
Dirs: Tim Jenns, L M Kershaw, L W Carp (Dutch); *Publicity:* Ms Kim Worts
Parent Company: East-West Holdings Ltd (at above address)
Associate Companies: East-West Publications (UK) Ltd, Maurice Temple Smith Ltd, Wildwood House Ltd (qqv)
Subjects: General Non-fiction, Illustrated Adult Reference, Children's Books
Miscellaneous: Provides editorial, design and production services for other publishers
ISBN Publisher's Prefix: 0-904499

Elsevier Applied Science Publishers, Rippleside Commercial Estate, Barking, Essex IG11 0SA Tel: (01) 595 2121 Cable Add: Elsbark Barking
Man Dir, Overseas Sales: Leslie E Rayner; *Production, Rights & Permissions:* Alan Chesterton; *UK Sales:* J Kumar Patel; *Promotions Manager:* Roger Barnett
Parent Company: Elsevier-NDU nv, Netherlands (qv)
Subjects: Agriculture, Architectural Science, Building, Civil Engineering, Bakery, Materials Science, Chemistry, Chemical Engineering, Mechanical Engineering, Environmental Science, Food Technology, Petroleum Technology, Plastics & Rubber, Dictionaries, Periodicals
1981: 68 titles *1982:* 58 titles *Founded:* 1971
ISBN Publisher's Prefix: 0-85334

Emblem, an imprint of Mitchell Beazley London Ltd (qv)

Embryo, an imprint of William Maclellan (qv)

Encyclopaedia Britannica International Ltd, Mappin House, 156-162 Oxford St, London W1N 0HJ Tel: (01) 637 3371 Cable Add: Knowingly London W1 Telex: 23866
Man Dir: Joe D Adams; *Sales Manager:* James Gray; *Advertising Manager:* M Cranch; *Production, Publicity, Rights & Permissions:* Robin Sales
Parent Company: Encyclopaedia Britannica Inc, Britannica Centre, 310 South Michigan Ave, Chicago, Ill 60604, USA
Associate Companies: Encyclopaedia Britannica (Australia) Inc, Australia (qv); Encyclopaedia Britannica Publications Ltd, 175 Holiday Dr, Cambridge, Ontario, Canada; Encyclopaedia Britannica, Federal Republic of Germany (qv); Korea Britannica Corporation, Republic of Korea (qv); Merriam-Webster Inc, 47 Federal St, Springfield, Mass 01101, USA
Subject: Reference
ISBN Publisher's Prefix: 0-85229

Energy Publications (Cambridge), see Cambridge Information and Research Services Ltd

Engineering Industry Training Board Publications+, PO Box 176, Watford, Hertfordshire WD1 1LB (Located at: 54 Clarendon Rd, Watford) Tel: Watford 38441 (STD code 0923)
Man Dir: R E Stevenson; *Editorial:* P Hodgkinson; *Sales, Publicity:* H Wilson; *Production, Rights & Permissions:* P Farrer
Branch Off: PO Box 75, Stockport, Cheshire SK4 1PH
Subject: Engineering training
1981: approx 20 titles *1982:* approx 25 titles *Founded:* 1967
ISBN Publisher's Prefix: 0-85083

Enigma Books+, 4 Brook St, London W1Y 1AA Tel: (01) 408 2112/(01) 499 3784 Telex: 295041 Enigma
Personnel: see Severn House Publishers Ltd
Orders to: Tiptree Books Services, Tiptree, Colchester, Essex CO5 0SR Tel: Tiptree 816362 (STD code 0621)
Parent Company: Severn House Publishers Ltd (qv)
Subjects: Fiction, Autobiography, Humour, General
1982: 6 titles *Founded:* 1981
ISBN Publisher's Prefix: 0-7278

Epworth Press, Room 195, 1 Central Bldgs, Westminster, London SW1H 9NR Tel: (01) 222 1455
Editorial, Rights & Permissions: Rev John Stacey; *Sales:* SCM Press Ltd (qv); *Publicity:* Richard Mulkern, SCM Press Ltd (qv)
Orders to: SCM Press Ltd, 26-30 Tottenham Rd, London N1 4BZ
Parent Body: The Methodist Conference
Subjects: Biblical, Theology
1981: 10 titles *1982:* 13 titles
ISBN Publisher's Prefix: 0-7162

Equinox (Oxford) Ltd, Mayfield House, 256 Banbury Rd, Oxford OX2 7DH Tel: Oxford 511151 (STD code 0865) Telex: 837484
Chairman: George Riches; *Man Dir:* Ben Lenthall; *Editorial Dir:* Michael Desebrock; *Marketing, Rights:* Ed Glover
Parent Company: Musterlin Ltd, Oxford
Associate Companies: Central Book Distribution; Phaidon Press (qv); Phaidon-Christie's UK
Subjects: Reference, Illustrated Non-fiction

Lawrence Erlbaum Associates Ltd, Chancery House, 319 City Rd, London EC1V 1LJ Tel: (01) 837 3500
Man Dir: M F Forster; *Dir:* L Erlbaum
Orders to: International Book Distributors, 66 Wood Lane End, Hemel Hempstead, Hertfordshire HP2 4RG
Parent Company: Lawrence Erlbaum Associates Inc, 365 Broadway, Hillsdale, NJ 07642, USA
Subjects: Behavioural Science and Related Disciplines
1981: 70 titles *1982:* 80 titles *Founded:* (UK) 1980
ISBN Publisher's Prefixes: 0-89859, 0-86377

Eurobook Ltd+, 49 Uxbridge Rd, London W5 5SA Tel: (01) 840 4411 Cable Add: Beurok London W5 Telex: 934610
Man Dir, Rights & Permissions: Peter S Lowe; *Editor:* Ruth Spriggs; *Sales, Publicity & Advertising:* Kim P Richardson; *Production:* Douglas Quiggan
Imprint: Peter Lowe
Subjects: Non-fiction and Children's Fiction for International Co-productions
Founded: 1968
ISBN Publisher's Prefix: 0-85654

Eurobooks, an imprint of Evangelical Press and Services Ltd (qv)

Euromonitor Publications Ltd+, PO Box 26, 18 Doughty St, London WC1N 2PN Tel: (01) 242 0042 Telex: 21120
Man Dir, Editorial: Robert Senior; *Marketing Dir:* Trevor Fenwick
Subjects: Business Information, Marketing, Statistical Reference
1982: 30 titles *1983:* 45 titles *Founded:* 1972
ISBN Publisher's Prefixes: 0-903706, 0-86338

Europa Publications Ltd, 18 Bedford Sq, London WC1B 3JN Tel: (01) 580 8236 Cable Add: Europub London
Chairman: C H Martin, OBE; *Man Dir:* P A McGinley; *Editorial:* Allan Oliver; *Business Manager:* J P Desmond; *Sales, Publicity & Advertising:* Peter Jackson
Subjects: Reference, History, International Affairs
1981: 11 titles *Founded:* 1928
ISBN Publisher's Prefix: 0-905118

European Law Centre Ltd, 4 Bloomsbury Sq, London WC1A 2RL Tel: (01) 404 4300 Telex: 21746
Man Dir: David Worlock; *Editorial, Rights & Permissions:* Neville March Hunnings; *Marketing Manager:* Charles Arthur
Parent Company: Thomson British Holdings Ltd, 4 Stratford Pl, London W1 (firm is a member of the International Thomson Organisation Ltd at same address)
Subject: European Law
Founded: 1978
ISBN Publisher's Prefix: 0-907451

European Schoolbooks Ltd*, Croft St, Cheltenham, Gloucestershire GL53 0HX Tel: Cheltenham 45252 (STD code 0242) Cable Add: Eurobooks, Cheltenham
Man Dir: F A Preiss; *Sales Manager:* D Young
Imprint: European Schoolbooks Hatier Ltd
Subjects: Educational, Modern Languages
ISBN Publisher's Prefix: 0-85048

Evangelical Press and Services Ltd, 16-18 High St, Welwyn, Herts AL6 9EQ Tel: Welwyn 7025 (STD code 043 871)
General Manager: J H Rubens
Subsidiary Company: Welwyn Books Ltd
Imprints: Ediciones Peregrino, Eurobooks
Subjects: Christian Books
Founded: 1967
ISBN Publisher's Prefix: 0-85234

Evans Brothers Ltd, 2A Portman Mansions, Chiltern St, London W1M 1LE Tel: (01) 935 7160 Cable Add: Byronitic London W1 Telex: 8811713 Evbook G
Chairman: L J Browning; *Man Dir:* S T Pawley; *Dirs:* F J Austin, P H Hughes; *Rights & Permissions:* Miss L Meintjes
Associate Company: Evans Brothers (Nigeria Publishers) Ltd, Nigeria (qv)
Subsidiary Company: Evans Brothers (Africa) Ltd (at above London address)
Subjects: English as a foreign language, Pre-school, Primary & Secondary Textbooks
1981: 80 titles *Founded:* 1905
ISBN Publisher's Prefix: 0-237

Evergreen Lives+, Glenside Industrial Estate, Partridge Green, Horsham, West Sussex RH13 8RA Tel: Partridge Green 710971 (STD code 0403)
Man Dir, Rights & Permissions: John Delieu; *Editors:* Michael and Mollie Hardwick; *Sales:* Jerry Stewart; *Production:* Bob Towell; *Publicity:* Jan Hopcraft
Orders to: Biblios Publishers' Distribution Services Ltd (at above address)
Branch Off: Evergreen Lives Marketing, 5 Conplan House, Nork Way, Banstead, Surrey SM7 1PB
Subjects: Illustrated Pocket Biographies
1983: 6 titles *Founded:* 1982
ISBN Publisher's Prefix: 0-7127

Everyman Fiction, an imprint of J M Dent & Sons Ltd (qv)

Everyman's Library, Reference Library and University Library, imprints of J M Dent & Sons Ltd (qv)

Excalibur, an imprint of Thorsons Publishers Ltd (qv)

Exley Publications Ltd+, 16 Chalk Hill, Watford, Hertfordshire WD1 4BN Tel: Watford 48328 (STD code 0923) Telex: 261234 Ref: H/5753L
Man Dir: Richard Exley; *Editorial Dir:* Helen Exley
Orders to: Noonan Hurst Ltd, 131 Trafalgar Rd, E Greenwich, London SE10 Tel: (01) 692 1475
Subjects: Anthologies, Humour, Gift Books, General Trade Books
1981: 10 titles *1982:* 9 titles *Founded:* 1976
ISBN Publisher's Prefix: 0-905521

Express Logic Ltd, PO Box 6, Hereford HR4 0UN Tel: Hereford 274516 (STD code 0432)
Man Dir: C B Tannatt Nash; *Sales, Production Manager:* Mrs M R Bishop
Parent Company: Business Management Promotions Ltd
Subjects: General Literature
Founded: 1970
ISBN Publisher's Prefix: 0-904464

Eyre & Spottiswoode (Publishers) Ltd, 11 New Fetter Lane, London EC4P 4EE Tel: (01) 583 9855 Cable Add: Exaltedly London EC4P 4EE Telex: 263398
Chairman: Charles Shirley; *Man Dir:* Austin Holder; *Promotion Dir:* David Ross
Parent Company: Firm is incorporated in Associated Book Publishers (UK) Ltd (qv under Associated Book Publishers PLC)
Subjects: Bibles, Book of Common Prayer, Summa Theologiae, Religion
Founded: 1769
ISBN Publisher's Prefix: 0-413

Eyre Methuen Ltd, now Methuen London Ltd (qv)

Faber & Faber Ltd, 3 Queen Sq, London WC1N 3AU Tel: (01) 278 6881 Cable Add: Fabbaf London WC1
Man Dir: Matthew Evans; *Sales & Marketing Dir:* Desmond Clarke; *Export Sales Manager:* Michael McLennan; *Publicity Manager:* Camilla Horne; *Rights & Permissions:* Judith Fiennes
Branch Off: Faber & Faber Inc, 39 Thompson St, Winchester, Massachusetts 01890, USA
Subjects: General Fiction, Belles Lettres, Poetry, Biography, History, How-to, Music, Art, Philosophy, Religion, Juveniles, Paperbacks, Medicine, Psychology, Social Science, University & Secondary Textbooks
Founded: 1929
ISBN Publisher's Prefix: 0-571

Falcon Books, an imprint of Kingsway Publications (qv)

Fantasy Library, an imprint of Bailey Brothers & Swinfen Ltd (qv)

The **Financial Times** Business Enterprises Ltd, Greystroke Pl, Fetter Lane, London EC4A 1ND Tel: (01) 405 6969 Telex: 883694 Icldn G
Man Dir: John McLachlan; *Sales Manager:* Patricia Morris; *Diary Dir:* John Suffolk; *Promotion and Development Manager:* Ken McAllister
Subjects: Investment and Financial Planning Guides, Directories, Specialized Banking Studies, Business Periodicals
ISBN Publisher's Prefix: 0-902101

Financial Training Publications Ltd, 131 Holland Park Ave, London W11 4UT Tel: (01) 603 4688 Telex: 8956468
Man Dir: John Gibbs; *Publisher:* Alistair MacQueen; *Managing Editor:* Heather Saward
Parent Company: Park Place Investments Ltd (at above address)
Associate Company: Wayland Publishers Ltd (qv)
Subjects: Accountancy, Finance, Law, Business and Management, also publishes professional examination study manuals for students
1982: 25 titles *1983:* 35 titles *Founded:* 1976
ISBN Publisher's Prefix: 0-906322

The **Findhorn** Press, The Park, Findhorn, Forres, Morayshire IV36 0TZ Tel: Findhorn 2582 (STD code 030 93)
Editorial, Rights & Permissions: Peter Königs; *Sales, Promotion:* Lucia Spowers; *Production:* John Boultbee
Parent Company: Findhorn Foundation (at above address)
Subjects: Spiritual, Biography, Fiction, Poetry, Conservation, Life styles, Personal Growth, Gardening, Cookery, Philosophy, New Age, Ecology
Bookshop: Phoenix Bookshop (at above address)
1981: 6 titles *1982:* 6 titles *Founded:* 1965
ISBN Publisher's Prefixes: 0-905249, 0-906191

Firecrest Publishing Ltd*, 93-100 Locksbrook Rd, Bath, Avon BA1 3HB Tel: Bath 331945 (STD code 0225)
Publisher: R H Lewis (to whom all correspondence)
Associate Companies: Chivers Book Sales Ltd; Lythway Press Ltd (qv); Chivers Press Publishers (qv)
Imprint: Firecrest Large Print
Subjects: Contemporary Fiction and Non-fiction
Founded: 1977
ISBN Publisher's Prefix: 0-85119

UNITED KINGDOM 409

Fishing News Books Ltd, 1 Long Garden Walk, Farnham, Surrey GU9 7HX Tel: Farnham 726868 (STD code 0252)
Editorial, Production: W E Redman; *Sales, Publicity, Rights & Permissions:* Vivien M Heighway
Subjects: Commercial Fisheries, Aquaculture, Marine Engineering, Scientific Angling
1981: 7 titles *1982:* 2 titles *Founded:* 1953
ISBN Publisher's Prefix: 0-85238

Flamingo, a paperback imprint of Fontana Books, see William Collins Sons & Co Ltd

Floris Books, 21 Napier Rd, Edinburgh EH10 5AZ Tel: (031) 337 2372
Editorial: Michael Jones; *Sales, Production, Publicity, Rights & Permissions:* Christian Maclean
Subsidiary Company: The Christian Community Press
Subjects: Religion, Children's Books, General
1981: 7 titles *1982:* 14 titles *Founded:* 1976
ISBN Publisher's Prefixes: 0-903540 and 0-86315 (Floris), 0-900285 (Christian Community Press)

Focal Press, an imprint of Butterworth & Co (Publishers) Ltd (qv)

The **Folio** Society Ltd, see Book Clubs

Fontana Books, see William Collins Sons & Co Ltd

Forbes Publications Ltd+, Redan House, Redan Pl, London W2 4SB Tel: (01) 229 9322
Man Dirs: Rosemary Crellin, Joan Forbes; *Marketing Manager:* Colin Forbes
Orders to: Holmes McDougall Ltd, Allander House, 137-41 Leith Walk, Edinburgh EH6 8NS
Subjects: Secondary, University, Commercial & Technical Education, Educational & Scientific, Reference Books, Home Economics, Nutrition, Health Education, Personal and Social Education, New Technology
ISBN Publisher's Prefix: 0-901762

Foreign Affairs Publishing Co Ltd, 139 Petersham Rd, Richmond, Surrey TW10 7AA Tel: (01) 948 4833
Director: Geoffrey Stewart-Smith
Subjects: Politics, Communist Affairs, Defence, East-West Relations
ISBN Publisher's Prefix: 0-900380

Fortune Press, see Charles Skilton Ltd

G T **Foulis** & Co Ltd+, Sparkford, Yeovil, Somerset BA22 7JJ Tel: North Cadbury 40635 (STD code 0963) Telex: 46212
Chairman: John H Haynes; *Man Dir:* Jim Scott; *Editorial Dirs:* Rod Grainger, Jeff Clew; *Sales Dir:* Andy Lynch; *Production Dir:* Roger Stagg
Parent Company: Haynes Publishing Group PLC (qv for associate companies)
Subjects: Motoring History, Biographies (car and motorcycle), Motor Sport, Touring, Speedway, Motorcycle Histories, Automobile Engineering
ISBN Publisher's Prefix: 0-85429

W **Foulsham** & Co Ltd+, Yeovil Rd, Slough SL1 4JH Tel: Slough 26769 (STD code 0753), Slough 30956; Trade Enquiries: Slough 38637 Cable Add: Bariebooks Slough Bucks Telex: 849041 Sharet g
Man Dir: R S Belasco; *Deputy Man Dir and Editorial:* B A R Belasco; *Dir Finance, Rights & Permissions:* Graham M Kitchen; *Sales Manager:* Brian Inns; *Production Manager:* Roy Mantel
Subjects: General Non-fiction, Technical, Educational
Founded: 1819
ISBN Publisher's Prefix: 0-572

The **Foundational** Book Co Ltd, 29 Pinfold Rd, Streatham, London SW16 2SL Tel: (01) 584 1053
Man Dir: Peggy M Brook
Subject: Religion
Founded: 1946
ISBN Publisher's Prefix: 0-85241

Fount Paperbacks, an imprint of William Collins Sons & Co Ltd (qv)

Fountain Press*, 65 Victoria St, Windsor, Berks SL4 1EH Tel: Windsor 56959 (STD code 07535)
Man Dir: H M Ricketts; *Sales Manager:* T Ackroyd
Subjects: Photography, Modelling, Model Engineering
Founded: 1923
ISBN Publisher's Prefix: 0-86343

L N **Fowler** & Co Ltd*, 1201-03 High Rd, Chadwell Heath, Romford, Essex RM6 4DH Tel: (01) 597 2491
Man Dir, Editorial, Production: W D Nagle; *Sales:* C J Nagle
Subjects: Astrology, Yoga, Alternative Healing
Bookshop: Fowler's New Age Bookshop (at above address)
1981: 8 titles *Founded:* 1880
ISBN Publisher's Prefix: 0-85243

W & G **Foyle** Ltd & John Gifford Ltd, 113-119 Charing Cross Rd, London WC2H 0EB Tel: (01) 437 0216 Cable Add: Foylibra London WC2
Chairman & Man Dir: Christina Foyle; *Man Dir:* (John Gifford Ltd): C Batty; *Editorial, Sales, Publicity, Rights & Permissions:* Jon Harris
Subjects: Crafts, Antiques, Reference, Gardening, Natural History
Bookshop: W & G Foyle (at above address)
Founded: 1904
Miscellaneous: Firm is owned by W & G Foyle Ltd
ISBN Publisher's Prefixes: 0-7071 (Foyle), 0-7072 (Gifford)

Gordon **Fraser** Gallery Ltd, Fitzroy Rd, London NW1 8TT Tel: (01) 722 0077 Cable Add: Frasercard London NW1 Telex: 25848
Dirs: Ian G Fraser, Margaret A F Moss; *General Manager:* Peter Guy; *Editorial:* Simon Kingston; *Marketing:* Alison Browne
Orders to: Eastcotts Rd, Bedford MK42 0JX
Subjects: Art, Photography, Graphic Arts, Quality Paperbacks
Founded: 1936
ISBN Publisher's Prefixes: 0-900406, 0-86092

Freeland Press Ltd, see The Technical Press Ltd

W H **Freeman** & Co Ltd, 20 Beaumont St, Oxford OX1 2NQ Tel: Oxford 726975 (STD code 0865)
Dirs: Sir Jonathan Backhouse, Julian Lynn-Evans, Neil Patterson, W Hayward Rogers
Parent Company: W H Freeman & Co, 660 Market St, San Francisco, Calif 94104, USA. Ultimate holding company Scientific American, 415 Madison Ave, New York, NY 10014, USA
Subjects: University Textbooks & Monographs in Pure & Applied Science
1981: 55 titles *1982:* 45 titles *Founded:* 1959
ISBN Publisher's Prefix: 0-7167

Samuel **French** Ltd, 52 Fitzroy St, London W1 Tel: (01) 387 9373
Chairman: Abbott van Nostrand; *Man Dir:* John Laurence Hughes; *Dirs:* John Bedding, George Ramsey
Associate Companies: Samuel French (Australia) Pty Ltd, Dominie Pty Ltd, 8 Cross St, Box 33 PO Brookvale, NSW 2100, Australia; Samuel French (Canada) Ltd, 80 Richmond St East, Toronto, Canada; Samuel French Inc, 25 West 45th St, New York, NY 10036 and 7623 Sunset Blvd, Hollywood, Calif 90046, USA
Subjects: Drama, Reference (Theatre)
Bookshop: French's Theatre Bookshop (at above London address)
Founded: 1830
ISBN Publisher's Prefix: 0-573

Fudge & Co Ltd+, 115 Old St, London EC1V 9JR Tel: (01) 251 4995-6
Man Dir: Charles Skilton
Associate Company: Charles Skilton (qv)
Imprints: Research Publishing Co, Broomsleigh Press, Skilton & Shaw
Subjects: Fiction, Biography, History, Spirituality, Juvenile, General
ISBN Publisher's Prefix: 0-7050

Futura, see Macdonald & Co (Publishers) Ltd

Fyfield Books, an imprint of Carcanet Press Ltd (qv)

Gaberbocchus Press Ltd, all correspondence to de Harmonie Publishers (Gaberbocchus Books), Singel 390, 1016 AJ Amsterdam, Netherlands

Galaxy Books, an imprint of Terence Dalton Ltd (qv)

Gall & **Inglis***, 62 Buckstone Terrace, Edinburgh EH10 6RQ Tel: (031) 445 1466
Man Dir: J Horsburgh
Subjects: Technical & Scientific, Commercial & Professional
ISBN Publisher's Prefix: 0-85248

Galliard, an imprint of Stainer & Bell Ltd (qv)

Garnstone Press Ltd*, Barlavington Farm House, Barlavington, Petworth, West Sussex Tel: Sutton, West Sussex 349 (STD code 07987)
Man & Sales Dir: Michael Balfour
Associated Imprint: Geoffrey Bles
Subjects: Non-fiction, Guides, Information, Hobbies, Prehistory, Ancient Science and Mysteries
Founded: 1966
ISBN Publisher's Prefixes: 0-900391, 0-85511 (Garnstone Press), 0-7138 (Geoffrey Bles)

The **Gavin** Press Ltd+, The Lodge, Limington, Yeovil, Somerset BA22 8EH Tel: Ilchester 840316 (STD code 0935)
Dir: Philip Snowden
Orders to: George Philip Services Ltd, Arndale Rd, Wick, Littlehampton, West Sussex BN17 7EN Tel: Littlehampton 7453 (STD code 09064)
Subjects: Countryside, History, Biography
1981: 2 titles *1982:* 5 titles *Founded:* 1980
ISBN Publisher's Prefix: 0-905868

Gee & Co, an imprint of Van Nostrand Reinhold (UK) Co Ltd (qv)

Gem, an imprint of William Collins Sons & Co Ltd (qv)

Genesis Publications Ltd, 45 Stoke Rd, Guildford, Surrey GU1 4HT Tel: Guildford 37431 (STD code 0483)
Man Dir: Brian Roylance
Subsidiary Company: Pageminster Press (at above address)
Subjects: Art, Autobiography, Botany, History, Poetry, Natural History, English Literature, Limited Editions
1981: 7 titles

Gentry Books Ltd, now part of Haynes Publishing Group PLC (qv)

Geographia Ltd+, 17-21 Conway St, London W1P 6JD Tel: (01) 387 2811 Telex: 261212
Man Dir: Graham Lane; *Marketing Dir:* Peter Smith
Parent Company: Hutchinson Publishing Group Ltd (qv)
Associate Companies: Arrow Books Ltd (qv); Robert Nicholson Publications Ltd (qv)
Subjects: Maps, Atlases, Guide Books
Bookshop: 63 Fleet St, London EC4Y 1PE Tel: (01) 353 2701
ISBN Publisher's Prefix: 0-09

The **Geographical** Association, 343 Fulwood Rd, Sheffield S10 3BP Tel: Sheffield 661666 (STD code 0742)
Honorary Secretary: Bryan Coates; *All other offices:* Noreen Pleavin
Subjects: Geography, Geography Teaching
1982: 10 titles *Founded:* 1901
ISBN Publisher's Prefix: 0-54000

Ghost Hunters' Library, an imprint of Bailey Brothers & Swinfen Ltd (qv)

Stanley **Gibbons** (Publications) Ltd, 399 Strand, London WC2R 0LX Tel: (01) 836 8444 Cable Add: Philatelic, London WC2R 0LX Telex: 28883
Orders to: Stangib House, Sarehole Rd, Birmingham B28 8EE Tel: (021) 777 7255
Subject: Philately
ISBN Publisher's Prefix: 0-85259

John **Gifford** Ltd, see W & G Foyle Ltd

Ginn & Co Ltd+, Prebendal House, Parson's Fee, Aylesbury, Buckinghamshire HP20 2QZ Tel: Aylesbury 88411 (STD code 0296) Cable Add: Ginnbooks Aylesbury Telex: 83535
Warehouse: Unit 1, Block H, Long Eaton Industrial Estate, Acton Grove, Long Eaton, Nottingham NG10 1GG
Man Dir: D Blunt; *Marketing Dir:* E F Keartland; *Editorial Dir:* W Shepherd; *Production Dir:* D Miller; *Publicity Manager:* R T Tadman; *International Manager:* A G Pittam
Parent Company: Heinemann Educational Books (International) Ltd (qv)
Associate Company: Caribbean Universities Press, Jamaica (qv)
Subjects: Primary & Secondary Textbooks
Founded: 1862 (USA), 1920 (London)
ISBN Publisher's Prefix: 0-602

Giraffe, an imprint of Scripture Union (qv)

Mary **Glasgow** Publications Ltd, 140 Kensington Church St, London W8 4BN Tel: (01) 229 9531 Telex: MGP KNT 31440
Man Dir: B J Clifton; *Editorial:* S Nugent, L K Upton, M J Calmann; *Marketing:* B J Clifton; *Sales & Distribution:* D J Raggett; *Production:* A E J Bedale; *Publicity:* Anne Scothern
Orders to: Brookhampton Lane, Kineton, Warwick CV35 0JB
Parent Company: Mary Glasgow (Holdings) Ltd (at above London address)
Subsidiary Companies: Sound Communication (Publishers) Ltd; The Kensington Bookshop Ltd
Subjects: Educational Magazines and Audiovisual Materials in EFL, Modern Languages, English, Geography
Founded: 1956
ISBN Publisher's Prefixes: 0-900400, 0-905999, 0-86158

Glaven, an imprint of Jarrold Colour Publications (qv)

Gleniffer Press, 11 Low Rd, Castlehead, Paisley, Renfrewshire PA2 6AQ Tel: (041) 889 9579
Man Dir: Ian Macdonald
Subjects: Poetry, History, Short Stories, Essays, Art, Specialists in Miniature Books, Limited Editions
1982: 3 titles *Founded:* 1968
ISBN Publisher's Prefixes: 0-9502177, 0-906005

Global Book Resources Ltd*, 109 Great Russell St, London WC1B 3NA Tel: (01) 580 2633 Cable Add: Globooks, London WC1
Man Dir: John Walter; *Publicity:* Jane Price
Subjects: Scientific, Technical, Medical, Scholarly
Miscellaneous: The firm is also an international agent and bookseller

David **Godine** Publisher — London, an imprint of Kudos Publications (qv)

George **Godwin** Ltd, an imprint of Longman Group Ltd (qv)

Golden Eagle Press Ltd, Montfort House, Frog Island, Leicester Tel: Leicester 50899 (STD code 0533)
Man Dir, Publicity: George Hart; *Editorial, Rights & Permissions:* Grace Hart; *Sales:* Mrs A Woodward; *Production:* Brian Blackwell
Subjects: Biography, Fiction
Founded: 1969
ISBN Publisher's Prefix: 0-901482

Golden Handshake, an imprint of Jay Landesman Ltd (qv)

Golden Pleasure Books, an imprint of The Hamlyn Publishing Group Ltd (qv)

Victor **Gollancz** Ltd, 14 Henrietta St, Covent Garden, London WC2E 8QJ Tel: (01) 836 2006 Cable Add: Vigollan London WC2 Telex: 261234 ref H5014A
Man Dirs: Livia Gollancz, Stephen Bray; *Sales Dir:* Nigel Sisson; *Publicity:* Nellie Flexner; *Rights & Permissions:* Jane Blackstock
Subjects: General Fiction, Belles Lettres, Biography, History, Music, Art, Architecture, Philosophy, Juveniles, Travel, Mountaineering, General & Social Science
Founded: 1928
ISBN Publisher's Prefix: 0-575

Gomer Press (J D Lewis & Sons Ltd), Llandysul, Dyfed SA44 4BQ Tel: Llandysul 2371 (STD code 055932) Cable Add: Gomerian Llandysul
Man Dir: J H Lewis; *Editorial, Rights & Permissions:* D Elis-Gruffydd; *Sales, Publicity:* John H Lewis; *Production:* J Huw Lewis
Parent Company: J D Lewis & Sons Ltd
Imprint: Gwasg Gomer
Subjects: Welsh Language Publications, Books on Wales
Bookshop: Gomerian Press, Llandysul, Dyfed
Founded: 1892
ISBN Publisher's Prefix: 0-85088

Gondola, an imprint of The Hamlyn Publishing Group Ltd (qv)

Gordon and Breach Science Publishers Ltd+, 42 William IV St, London WC2N 4DE Tel: (01) 836 5125 Cable Add: Sciencepub, London WC2 Telex: 23258
Dirs: Martin B Gordon (USA), J A Levene; *Editorial:* Grant McIntyre; *Marketing:* Charles Franklyn; *Production:* Fay Miller; *Rights:* Françoise Chantrel-Riols (58 rue Lhomond, Paris F-75005, France)
Orders to: (Books) Gordon and Breach Science Publishers Inc, 1 Park Ave, New York, NY 10016, USA; (Journals) STBS Ltd, 42 William IV St, London WC2N 4DE
Parent Company: Gordon and Breach Science Publishers Inc (at US address)
Subjects: Astronomy and Astrophysics, Chemistry & Nuclear Engineering, Chemistry & Chemical Technology, Civil Engineering, Computers, Systems & Control Engineering, Earth & Planetary Sciences, Economics, Electronics & Electrical Engineering, Languages & Dictionaries, Life Sciences & Medicine, Management Science & Business, Mathematics & Statistics, Mechanical Engineering, Metallurgy & Materials Science, Music, Dance, Physics, Social Sciences, Space Science & Technology, Learned Journals
ISBN Publisher's Prefix: 0-677

Gordon & Cremonesi*, New River House, 34 Seymour Rd, London N8 0BE Tel: (01) 348 7042 Cable Add: Cremones London N8
Man Dirs: Gilles Cremonesi, Heather Gordon
Orders to: Biblios, Glenside Industrial Estate, Partridge Green, Horsham, West Sussex RH13 8LD
Subjects: Biography, History, High-priced Paperbacks, Social Science
Founded: 1975
ISBN Publisher's Prefix: 0-86033

Henry **Goulden** Ltd, 22 High St, East Grinstead, West Sussex Tel: East Grinstead 22669 (STD code 0342)
Man Dir: L H Goulden
Subjects: Rudolf Steiner, Anthroposophy
ISBN Publisher's Prefix: 0-904822

Gower Press, a former imprint of Gower Publishing Co Ltd (qv)

Gower Publishing Co Ltd+, Gower House, Croft Rd, Aldershot, Hampshire GU11 3HR Tel: Aldershot 331551 (STD code 0252) Telex: 858001 Gower G
Man Dir, Sales, Rights & Permissions: N Farrow; *Marketing Dir:* C Simpson; *Customer Service Manager:* J Bennett; *Production Manager:* C Barber; *Editorial:* Malcolm Stern (Business), John Irwin (Social Science)
Imprints: Gower (also titles formerly published as Gower Press, Saxon House, Wilton Publications, Rotterdam University Press, Input Two-Nine, Grafton Books)
Subjects: Management and Business Information, Social Science, Computers, Library Science
1981: 120 titles *1982:* 130 titles *Founded:* 1967
ISBN Publisher's Prefixes: 0-566 (Gower Publishing), 0-7161 (Gower Press), 0-347 (Saxon House pre-1976), 0-904655 (Wilton), 0-905897 (Input Two-Nine)

Grafton Books, a former imprint of Gower Publishing Co Ltd (qv)

Frank **Graham**, 6 Queen's Terrace, Newcastle upon Tyne NE2 2PL Tel: Newcastle upon Tyne 813067 (STD code 0632)
Subject: Local History
Founded: 1960
ISBN Publisher's Prefix: 0-85983

Graham & Trotman Ltd+, Sterling House, 66 Wilton Rd, London SW1V 1DE Tel: (01) 821 1123 Cable Add: Infobooks London Telex: 298878 Gramco G
Man Dir, Rights & Permissions: A Graham; *Editorial:* G Bricault, J Carr, A Colborne, D Smith, R Wright; *Sales:* D Costello; *Marketing Dir:* I Pulley; *Production:* D Blakeley; *Marketing:* G Steddy, S Hennessey
Subjects: Business Reference, Business Management, Business Law, Earth Sciences, Pollution Control, Life Sciences, Electronics
1981: 34 titles *1982:* 50 titles *Founded:* 1974
ISBN Publisher's Prefix: 0-86010

Granada Publishing Ltd+, 8 Grafton St, London W1X 3LA Tel: (01) 493 7070 Cable Add: Herakles London W1X Telex: 25611
Chairman, Man Dir: A R H Birch; *Man Dirs:* Mark Barty-King (Hardback), T J Kitson (Paperback), D Fulton (Technical Division), Angela Sheehan (Editorial, Children's Division); *Sales Dirs:* T Palmer (Hardback), John Sexton (Paperback); *Production Dir:* Malcolm Lee; *Editorial:* John Booth, Nick Austin; *Rights & Permissions:* Ursula Mackenzie
Orders to: Westerhill Distribution Services Ltd, PO Box, Glasgow G4 0NB Tel: (041) 772 3200
Parent Company: William Collins Sons & Co Ltd (qv)
Subsidiary Companies: Granada Trade Books Ltd; Granada Technical Books Ltd; Adlard Coles Ltd; Crosby Lockwood Staples Ltd, Elek Books Ltd; Paul Elek Ltd; Rupert Hart-Davis Ltd; Mayflower Books Ltd; Panther Books Ltd; Dragon Books, Paladin Books (all UK)
Subjects: Agriculture, Aviation, Architecture, Computers, Building, Fiction, Leisure & Hobbies, Nautical and Sailing, Biography, History, Mathematics, Non-fiction, Physics, Science, Technology, Music, Art, Philosophy, Reference, Juveniles, Low- & High-priced Paperbacks, Engineering, General & Social Science, University, Primary & Secondary Textbooks
ISBN Publisher's Prefixes: 0-7053 (Granada), 0-229 (Adlard Coles), 0-246 (Granada Hardback Books), 0-586 (Panther Books), 0-583 (Mayflower Books)

Grant McIntyre Ltd, see under McIntyre

Granta Editions, 47 Norfolk St, Cambridge CB1 2LE Tel: Cambridge 352790 (STD code 0223) Telex: Omnift G 817135
Joint Man Dirs: Colin Walsh (Editorial), Tony Littlechild (Sales); *Production:* Sue Gardner; *Publicity:* Sue Fleming-Jones; *Rights & Permissions:* Sue Latham; *Book Orders:* Debra Hollamby
Parent Company: Book Production Consultants (at above address)
Subsidiary Company: Granta Technical Editions (at above address)
Subjects: General and Technical, Illustrated, Non-fiction, Sponsored Books
1981: 20 titles *Founded:* 1974
ISBN Publisher's Prefix: 0-906782

The **Graphic** Communications Centre Ltd, Bernard House, Granville Rd, Maidstone, Kent ME14 2BT Tel: Maidstone 675324 (STD code 0622)
Man Dir: J Tyman
Imprint: Graphics World
Subjects: Graphic Arts, Reference and Instructional
1981: 9 titles *Founded:* 1981
ISBN Publisher's Prefix: 0-86250

Grasshopper Books, an imprint of Abelard-Schuman Ltd (qv)

W **Green** & Son Ltd, St Giles St, Edinburgh EH1 1PU Tel: (031) 225 4879 Cable Add: Viridis Edinburgh
Subject: Scots Law
Parent Company: Firm is incorporated in Associated Book Publishers (UK) Ltd (qv under Associated Book Publishers PLC)
ISBN Publisher's Prefix: 0-414

J C R **Green** (Publishers) Ltd, now Johnston Green & Co (Publishers) Ltd (qv)

Gregg International, an imprint of Avebury Publishing Co Ltd (qv)

John **Gresham**, an imprint of Robert Hale Ltd (qv)

Gresham Books, The Gresham Press, PO Box 61, Henley-on-Thames, Oxfordshire RG9 3LQ Tel: Wargrave 53789 (STD code 073522)
Chief Executive: Mrs M V Green
Parent Company: Gift Book Promotions Ltd, 94 Wigmore St, London W1H 0BR
Subjects: Music, Hobbies, Leisure, Facsimile

Reproductions of Rare Books, Art, Crafts
Founded: 1979
ISBN Publisher's Prefix: 0-905418

Charles **Griffin** & Co Ltd, Charles Griffin House, Crendon St, High Wycombe, Buckinghamshire HP13 6LE Tel: High Wycombe 36341 (STD code 0494) Cable Add: Explanatus High Wycombe
Man Dir, Rights & Permissions: James R Griffin; *Sales, Publicity & Advertising Manager:* Kathleen Mansfield
Branch Off: Finance: 32-36 Dudley Rd, Tunbridge Wells, Kent TN1 1LF
Subjects: High-priced Paperbacks, Engineering, General & Social Science, University & Secondary Textbooks especially Statistics
1981: 3 titles *1982:* 6 titles *Founded:* 1820
ISBN Publisher's Prefix: 0-85264

Grisewood & Dempsey Ltd, Elsley Court, 20-22 Great Titchfield St, London W1P 7AD Tel: (01) 631 0878 Cable Add: Greatbooks, London Telex: 27725 Gridem
Chairman, Man Dir: D Grisewood; *Editorial:* J Olliver
Subjects: Children's Colour Information Books, Adult Reference
Founded: 1973
Miscellaneous: Firm is an editorial and production organization producing books for other publishers

Grosvenor Books+, 54 Lyford Rd, London SW18 3JJ Tel: (01) 870 2124
Man Dir, Rights & Permissions: J H V Nowell; *Sales Dir:* D A Hind; *Production Manager:* B Cummock; *General Manager:* D W Locke
Parent Company: The Good Road Ltd, 12 Palace St, London SW1E 5JF
Subjects: Contemporary Issues, Religion, Biography, Children's Books
1981: 7 titles *1982:* 6 titles
ISBN Publisher's Prefix: 0-901269

Guild Publishing*, 87 Newman St, London W1P 4EN Tel: (01) 637 0341 Cable Add: Booklub Telex: 24359 Bcalon
Parent Company: Book Club Associates (qv under Book Clubs)
Subjects: Archaeology, Juveniles, Cookery, History, Classic Reprints, Humour, Leisure, Natural History
1981: 7 titles

Guinness Superlatives Ltd, 2 Cecil Court, London Rd, Enfield, Middlesex EN2 6DJ Tel: (01) 367 4567 Cable Add: Mostest Telex: 23573 Enfield
Man Dir: D F Hoy; *Marketing Dir:* M J Hodge
Parent Company: Arthur Guinness Son & Co (Park Royal) Ltd, Park Royal, London NW10
Subject: Reference
Founded: 1954
ISBN Publisher's Prefixes: 0-900424, 0-85112

Gwasg Gomer, imprint of Gomer Press (qv)

Gwasg Prifysgol Cymru, an imprint of University of Wales Press (qv)

Gwasg y Dref Wen+, 28 Church Rd, Whitchurch, Cardiff CF4 2EA Tel: Cardiff 617860 (STD code 0222)
Man Dir, Production, Publicity, Rights & Permissions: Roger Boore; *Editorial:* Aled Islwyn; *Sales:* Anne Boore
Subjects: Welsh-language books for Children and Schools (Fiction & Non-fiction) including Welsh Children's Encyclopaedia, Picture Dictionary
1981: 29 titles *1982:* 29 titles *Founded:* 1970
ISBN Publisher's Prefix: 0-904910

H F L (Publishers) Ltd, 9 Bow St, London WC2E 7AL Tel: (01) 836 9081 Cable Add: Chaboca, London WC2E 7AL Telex: 299080
Man Dir: J R Hews; *Sales Dir:* Quentin Hockliffe
Subjects: Commercial & Technical Education, Legal & Parliamentary, Commercial & Professional
ISBN Publisher's Prefix: 0-372

H M & M Publishers Ltd, now part of John Wiley & Sons Ltd (qv)

H M S O, see Her Majesty's Stationery Office

Michael **Haag** Ltd/Travelaid Publishing, PO Box 369, London NW3 4ER Tel: (01) 794 2647
Man Dir: M Haag
Orders to: Biblios Pds Ltd, Glenside Industrial Estate, Partridge Green, Horsham, West Sussex Tel: Partridge Green 710971 (STD code 0403)
Subjects: General (Michael Haag Ltd), Travel (Travelaid Publishing)
1983: 3 titles (Michael Haag Ltd), 3 titles (Travelaid) *Founded:* 1976
ISBN Publisher's Prefix: 0-902743

Hacker Art Books, an imprint of Kudos & Godine Ltd (qv)

Peter **Haddock** Ltd*, Pinfold Lane, Bridlington, North Humberside YO16 5BT Tel: Bridlington 78121 (STD code 0262) Cable Add: Bridbooks Telex: 52180
Man Dir: Peter Haddock
Subjects: Low-priced Children's Painting, Activity and Story Books

Robert **Hale** Ltd, Clerkenwell House, 45-47 Clerkenwell Green, London EC1R 0HT Tel: (01) 251 2661 Cable Add: Barabbas London EC1
Warehouse: 4 Vestry Rd, Vestry Estate, Sevenoaks, Kent
Man Dir: John Hale; *Marketing Dir:* Martin Kendall; *Production Dir:* Eric Restall; *Publicity:* Lorna Macleod; *Rights & Permissions Dir:* Betty Weston
Subjects: General Fiction, Belles Lettres, Poetry, Biography, History, How-to, Topography, Music, Art, Sport, Philosophy, Reference, Religion, Low- & High-priced Paperbacks
1981: 791 titles *Founded:* 1936
ISBN Publisher's Prefix: 0-7090 (formerly 0-7091)

Hambleside Publishers Ltd, 12 Southgate St, Winchester, Hants SO23 9EF Tel: Winchester 60444 (STD code 0962) Cable Add: Hambleside Winchester Telex: 477357
Man Dir: D R Yellop; *General Manager:* Ms J A Hynard
Parent Company: Hambleside Group Ltd (at above address)
Associate Company: West African Book Publishers Ltd, Nigeria (qv)
Imprint: Terrapin
Subjects: Children's Fiction
1981: 5 titles *Founded:* 1977
ISBN Publisher's Prefix: 0-86042

Hamish **Hamilton** Ltd, Garden House, 57-59 Long Acre, London WC2E 9JL Tel: (01) 836 7733 Cable Add: Hamisham Westcent London Telex: 298265
President: Hamish Hamilton; *Chairman:* David Cole; *Man Dir, Editorial:* Christopher Sinclair-Stevenson; *Head of Children's Books:* David Grant; *Head of Elm Tree Books:* Roger Houghton; *Sales Dir:* Chris Weller; *Export Sales:* John Lyon; *Production Dir:* Peter Kilborn; *Publicity Manager:* Nella Bevan; *Rights & Permissions Dir:* Clare Alexander
Subsidiary Companies: Hamish Hamilton Children's Books Ltd; Elm Tree Books Ltd
Subjects: General Fiction, Biography, History, Music, Art, Juveniles
Founded: 1931
Miscellaneous: Company is a member of the Thomson Books Ltd group (qv), a part of International Thomson Organization Ltd (Canada)
ISBN Publisher's Prefix: 0-241

Hamlyn Paperbacks, the paperback division of The Hamlyn Publishing Group Ltd (qv)

The **Hamlyn Publishing** Group Ltd, Astronaut House, Hounslow Rd, Feltham, Middlesex TW14 9AR Tel: (01) 890 1480 Cable Add: Pleasbooks Feltham Telex: Pleasbks 25650
Trade Office: Sanders Lodge Industrial Estate, Rushden, Northamptonshire
Chief Executive: Hugh Campbell; *Sales:* David Foster (Export), David Burbage (Home), Terence Cross (Newnes); *Publicity:* Gillian Vincent; *Rights & Permissions:* Frances Oldham (Hamlyn), Jill Schmidt (Newnes)
Imprints: Dean & Son, Golden Pleasure Books, Gondola, Hamlyn, Newnes Books (qv), Odhams, Optimum, Pearson, Spring Books
Subjects: General Non-fiction, Fiction, History, How-to, Music, Arts, Crafts, Antiques, Cinema, Sports, Reference, Juveniles, Paperbacks, Travel, Cookery, Gardening, Natural History, Motoring
Book Club: Companion Book Club
Founded: 1947
Miscellaneous: Collingridge, Country Life and Temple Press are now incorporated in Newnes Books (qv)
ISBN Publisher's Prefixes: 0-600 (Beaver Books, Collingridge, Country Life, Hamlyn, Hamlyn Paperbacks, Newnes Books, Odhams, Optimum, Pearson, Spring, Temple Press), 0-601 (Golden Pleasure), 0-603 (Dean & Son)

Heinrich **Hanau** Publications Ltd*, PO Box 2JG, London W1A 2JG (Located at: 59 Old Compton St, London W1V 5PN) Tel: (01) 734 4353 Telex: 28604 Ref 909
Man Dir: John Hanau
Associate Company: H H Publications Ltd, Suite 460, 230 Park Ave, New York, NY 10017, USA
Subjects: International Co-publications
ISBN Publisher's Prefix: 0-902826

Handbag Books, an imprint of Kenneth Mason Publications Ltd (qv)

The **Handsel** Press+, 33 Montgomery St, Edinburgh EH7 5JX Tel: (031) 556 2796
Man Dir, Editorial, Rights & Permissions: Douglas Grant; *Publicity Manager:* Geraldine Raymond
Subject: Theology
1981: 24 titles *Founded:* 1976
Miscellaneous: Associated with Sussex University Press and The Scottish Academic Press (qqv)
ISBN Publisher's Prefix: 0-905312

J **Hannon** & Co (Publishers) Oxford, 2 Windrush Way, Radley Green, Abingdon, Oxon OX14 3SX Tel: Abingdon 29726 (STD code 0235)
Chief Executive, Editorial: Jim Hannon
Subsidiary Company: J Hannon & Co (Book Distributors) (at above address)
Branch Off: Tiuanagh, Boyle, Co Roscommon, Republic of Ireland
Subjects: Latin, Music, Poetry, Philosophy
Bookshop: J Hannon & Co, at above address
Founded: 1974
ISBN Publisher's Prefix: 0-904233

Hansen House (London) Ltd*, 1 Wythburn Pl, London W1H 5WL Tel: (01) 402 8497
Publisher: Charles Hansen
Subject: Music

Harcourt Brace Jovanovich Ltd, 24-28 Oval Rd, London NW1 7DX Tel: (01) 485 7074 Cable Add: Harbrex London NW1 Telex: 25775
Parent Companies: Harcourt Brace Jovanovich Inc, 757 Third Ave, New York, NY 10017, USA and Academic Press Inc (London) Ltd (qv)
Associate Company: Harcourt Brace Jovanovich Group (Australia) Pty Ltd, Australia (qv)
Subjects: Fiction, Educational, Religious, Technical & Scientific, Medical, Commercial & Professional, Music, Art & Architecture, Children's Books, Sports, Games & Pastimes, Poetry & Drama, History, Biography & Memoirs, Sociology, Philosophy, Psychology, Economics, School Books
ISBN Publisher's Prefix: 0-15

Harlequin, an imprint of Mills & Boon Ltd (qv)

Harper & Row Ltd, 28 Tavistock St, London WC2E 7PN Tel: (01) 836 4635 Cable Add: Harprow, London WC2E 7PN Telex: 267331
Man Dir: Paul Chapman; *Senior Editor:* Cathy Peck; *Marketing Manager:* Peter Gemmell; *Rights & Permissions:* New York Office
Parent Company: Harper & Row Inc, 10 East 53rd St, New York, NY 10022, USA
Subsidiary Companies: Ballinger Publishing Co; Barnes & Noble; Basic Books; Beacon Press; Russell Sage Foundation; Canfield Press; T Y Crowell; Industrial Press; J B Lippincott Co; Quadrangle/New York Times Book Co
Associate Companies: Editora Harper & Row do Brasil Ltda, Brazil (qv); Harper & Row Latinoamericana-Harla, SA de CV, Mexico (qv), Harper & Row (Australasia) Pty Ltd, Australia (qv)
Subjects: Academic, Medical, General
ISBN Publisher's Prefix: 0-06

Harrap Ltd+, 19-23 Ludgate Hill, London EC4M 7PD Tel: (01) 248 6444 Cable Add: Harrapbook London EC4 Telex: 28673 Consol G
Chairman, Man Dir: N W Berry; *Chief General Editor:* Simon Scott; *Publicity Dir:* C R Butterworth; *Educational & Dictionary Publisher:* Jean-Luc Barbanneau; *Educational Publicity Manager:* Doris Colley; *UK Sales Manager:* Brian Rice *Overseas Marketing Manager:* David Collins; *Rights & Permissions:* Martin Lee
Subjects: English as a foreign language, Dictionaries, General, Educational
1981: 55 titles *1982:* 65 titles *Founded:* 1901
ISBN Publisher's Prefix: 0-245

Paul **Harris** Publishing+, 40 York Pl, Edinburgh EH1 3HU Tel: (031) 556 9696 Cable Add: Publisher, Edinburgh Telex: 727891 Harris G
Man Dir, Publicity: Paul Harris; *Editorial:* Trevor Royle; *Production:* Robert Wishart
Orders to: George Philip Services Ltd, Arndale Rd, Wick, Littlehampton, West Sussex Tel: Littlehampton 7453 (STD code 09064)
Parent Company: Paul Harris Investments (Edinburgh) Ltd
Subjects: General Non-fiction, Maritime, Fine Arts, Limited Editions
1981: 21 titles *1982:* 20 titles *Founded:* 1974
ISBN Publisher's Prefixes: 0-904505, 0-86228

Harris & Baldwin, an imprint of Frederick Warne (Publishers) Ltd (qv)

Harrow House Editions, an imprint of Sceptre Books Ltd (qv)

Hart-Davis Educational Ltd, see William Collins Sons & Co Ltd

Harvard Business Review Library, an imprint of William Heinemann Ltd (qv)

Harvard University Press, 126 Buckingham Palace Rd, London SW1W 9SD Tel: (01) 730 9208 Cable Add: Chibooks Telex: 23933 Chibooks Ldn
Sales Manager: Warren Bertram; *Publicity Manager:* Sybil Richardson
Orders to: International Book Distributors Ltd, 66 Wood Lane End, Hemel Hempstead, Hertfordshire Tel: Hemel Hempstead 58531 (STD code 0442)
Associate Companies: The University of Chicago Press, The MIT Press (qqv)
Subjects: Biography, History, Music, Art, Philosophy, Reference, Paperbacks, Medicine, Psychology, Literature, General & Social Science, Education
1982: 160 titles *Founded:* 1913
Miscellaneous: Branch of Harvard University Press, Cambridge, Mass, USA
ISBN Publisher's Prefix: 0-674

The **Harvester** Press Ltd, 16 Ship St, Brighton, East Sussex Tel: Brighton 723031 (STD code 0273) Cable Add: Harvester Brighton
Chairman and Man Dir, Rights & Permissions: John Spiers; *Editorial Dir:* Edward Elgar; *Sales, Marketing:* Mark Holland; *Promotion, Advertising:* Bill Pidduck
Imprint: Wheatsheaf Books
Subjects: History, Politics, Economics, Philosophy, Psychology, Reference, Literature, Fiction, also Microform Publications
1982: 100 titles *Founded:* 1969
ISBN Publisher's Prefixes: 0-901759, 0-85527

Harvill Press Ltd, 8 Grafton St, London W1X 3LA Tel: (01) 493 7070 Cable Add: Herakles London SW1A Telex: Herakles London 25611
Parent Company: William Collins Sons & Co Ltd (qv)

J H **Haynes & Co** Ltd+, Sparkford, Yeovil, Somerset BA22 7JJ Tel: North Cadbury 40635 (STD code 0963) Telex: 46212
Chairman: John H Haynes; *Man Dir:* Jim Scott; *Executive Editorial Dir, Public Relations, Rights & Permissions:* Jeff Clew; *Editorial Dir:* Peter Ward; *Sales Dir:* Andy Lynch; *Production Dir:* Roger Stagg
Parent Company: Haynes Publishing Group PLC (qv for associate companies)
Imprints include: Gentry Books Ltd
Subjects: Car and Motorcycle owners workshop manuals/handbooks/servicing guides/paperbacks
ISBN Publisher's Prefixes: 0-85696, 0-900550, 0-85614 (Gentry)

Haynes Publishing Group PLC, Sparkford, Yeovil, Somerset BA22 7JJ Tel: North Cadbury 40635 (STD code 0963) Telex: 46212
Executive Chairman: John H Haynes; *Chief Executive:* Frank Day
Subsidiary Companies: J H Haynes & Co Ltd, G T Foulis & Co Ltd, Oxford Illustrated Press Ltd (qqv); Gentry Books Ltd; Haynes Publications Inc, California, USA
Founded: 1960

Health Science Press (C W Daniel) Ltd, 1 Church Path, Saffron Walden, Essex CB10 1JP Tel: Saffron Walden 21909 (STD code 0799)
Dirs: Ian Miller, Jane Miller
Parent Company: The C W Daniel Co Ltd (at above address)
Subjects: Homoeopathy, Acupuncture, Radionics, Radiesthesia, Nature Cure, Biochemistry, Diet and Health
ISBN Publisher's Prefix: 0-85032

Heatherbank Press, 163 Mugdock Rd, Milngavie, Glasgow G62 6BR Tel: (041) 956 2687, (041) 956 5923
Editorial: Sally Kuenssberg; *Sales, Marketing & Public Relations:* Rosemary Harvey
Subjects: Local History (Glasgow and Scotland), Biography, Community Publishing, History of Social Welfare
Founded: 1974
ISBN Publisher's Prefix: 0-905192

Heinemann Educational Books Ltd, 22 Bedford Sq, London WC1B 3HH Tel: (01) 637 3311 Cable Add: Hebooks London W1 Telex: 261888
Orders to: The Windmill Press, Kingswood, Tadworth, Surrey Tel: Mogador 3511 (STD code 073783)
Chairman: A R Beal; *Man Dir:* H MacGibbon; *Marketing Manager:* Robert Creffield
Parent Company: Heinemann Educational Books International Ltd (qv)
Associate Company: Arnold-Heinemann Publishers (India) Pvt Ltd, India (qv)
Subjects: Belles Lettres, History, Music, Engineering, General & Social Science, Economics, Political Science, University, Secondary & Primary Textbooks, Education
Founded: 1961
ISBN Publisher's Prefix: 0-435

Heinemann Educational Books International Ltd, 22 Bedford Sq, London WC1B 3HH Tel: (01) 637 3311 Cable Add: Hebooks London W1 Telex: 261888
Chairman: C S Pick; *Man Dir:* A R Beal; *Marketing Manager:* Robert Creffield
Parent Company: The Heinemann Group of Publishers Ltd (qv)
Subsidiary Companies: Ginn & Co Ltd (qv); Heinemann Educational Books Ltd (qv); William Heinemann Medical Books Ltd (qv) (all UK); Heinemann Publishers Australia Pty Ltd, Australia (qv); Heinemann Educational Books (Asia) Ltd, Hong Kong (qv); Heinemann Educational Books (Caribbean) Ltd, Jamaica; Heinemann Educational Books (East Africa) Ltd, Kenya (qv); Heinemann Publishers (New Zealand) Ltd, New Zealand (qv); Heinemann Educational Books (Nigeria) Ltd, Nigeria (qv); Heinemann Publishers Southern Africa (Pty) Ltd, Republic of South Africa; Heinemann Educational Books Inc, USA

The **Heinemann Group** of Publishers Ltd, 10 Upper Grosvenor St, London W1X 9PA Tel: (01) 493 4141 Cable Add: Sunlocks London W1 Telex: 8954961
This is the holding company of the Heinemann publishing companies
Chairman: Michael Kettle; *Man Dir:* Charles Pick
Parent Company: BTR PLC, Silvertown House, Vincent Sq, London SW1P 2PL
Subsidiary Companies: William Heinemann International Ltd (qv), Heinemann Educational Books International Ltd (qv), Heinemann Distribution Ltd

William **Heinemann International** Ltd, 10 Upper Grosvenor St, London W1X 9PA Tel: (01) 493 4141 Cable Add: Sunlocks London W1 Telex: 8954961
Shipping Add: The Windmill Press, Kingswood, Tadworth, Surrey Tel: Mogador 3511 (STD code 073783)
Chairman: Charles Pick; *Man Dir:* T G Rosenthal
Parent Company: The Heinemann Group of

414 UNITED KINGDOM

Publishers Ltd (qv)
Subsidiary Companies: William Heinemann Ltd (qv); Peter Davies Ltd (qv); Kaye & Ward Ltd (qv); Martin Secker & Warburg Ltd (qv); World's Work Ltd (qv) (all UK); Heinemann & Zsolnay Ltd (see Paul Zsolnay Verlag GmbH, Austria and Federal Republic of Germany); William Heinemann Inc, 229 South State St, Dover, Delaware 19901, USA
Founded: 1979

William **Heinemann** Ltd+, 10 Upper Grosvenor St, London W1X 9PA Tel: (01) 493 4141 Cable Add: Sunlocks London W1 Telex: 8954961
Chairman: T G Rosenthal; *Man Dir:* Brian Perman; *Marketing Dir:* Clyde Hunter; *Editorial:* David Godwin, Roger Smith; *Sales:* T R Manderson; *Production:* Peter Ireland; *Publicity:* Susan Boyd; *Rights & Permissions:* Jane Turnbull
Orders to: The Windmill Press, Kingswood, Tadworth, Surrey KT20 6TG Tel: Mogador 3511 (STD code 073783)
Parent Company: William Heinemann International Ltd (qv)
Subsidiary Companies: Pan Books Ltd (qv — one-third owned with William Collins Sons & Co Ltd and Macmillan Publishers Ltd, qqv)
Imprints: Harvard Business Review Library, Landmarks (with Martin Secker & Warburg Ltd), Loeb Classical Library, Made Simple Books, Heinemann/Octopus
Branch Off: William Heinemann Ltd, 100 Lesmill Rd, Don Mills, Ontario M3B 2T5, Canada
Subjects: General Fiction, Belles Lettres, Poetry, Biography, History, Music, Art, Philosophy, Juveniles, Psychology, Technical, Management, Finance
1981: approx 150 titles *Founded:* 1890
ISBN Publisher's Prefix: 0-434

William **Heinemann Medical Books** Ltd+, 23 Bedford Sq, London WC1B 3HH Tel: (01) 637 3311 Cable Add: Heinmed, London WC1B 3HH Telex: 261 888 (please quote 'medical') Answerback: Hebldn G
Editorial Dir: Dr Richard Barling; *Sales Manager:* Michael Pearman; *Production Managers:* Ninetta Martyn, Chris Jarvis; *Publicity Manager:* Hilary Large
Parent Company: Heinemann Educational Books International Ltd (qv)
Subjects: Medicine, Dentistry, Nursing, Veterinary Medicine, Medical Technology
1981: 22 titles *Founded:* 1913
ISBN Publisher's Prefix: 0-433

Heinemann/Octopus, an imprint of William Heinemann Ltd and Octopus Books PLC (qqv)

Helicon Press, Knight St, Sawbridgeworth, Hertfordshire CM21 9AX Tel: Bishop's Stortford 722318 (STD code 0279)
Man Dir, Editorial: Candida Tobin; *Sales, Production, Publicity, Rights & Permissions:* Christopher Dell
Imprint: Tobin Music Books
1981: 20 titles *Founded:* 1973
ISBN Publisher's Prefix: 0-905684

Ian **Henry** Publications Ltd+, 38 Parkstone Ave, Hornchurch, Essex RM11 3LW Tel: Hornchurch 42042 (STD code 04024)
Man Dir: Ian Wilkes; *Sales Dir:* William G S Oliver
Orders to: J M Dent & Sons Ltd, Dunhams Lane, Letchworth, Hertfordshire Tel: Letchworth 6241 (STD code 04626)
Associate Company: Emerson Book Supplies Ltd, 38 Parkstone Ave, Hornchurch, Essex RM11 3LW
Subjects: History, Fiction Reprints, Automobile Engineering, Medical, Costume, Local History
1981: 32 titles *1982:* 37 titles *Founded:* 1975
ISBN Publisher's Prefix: 0-86025

Her Majesty's Stationery Office, St Crispin's House, Duke St, Norwich NR3 1PD Tel: Norwich 22211 (STD code 0603) Telex: 97301 hemstonery
Director of Publishing: K Rhodes
Head Office: Sovereign House, Botolph St, Norwich NR3 1DN Tel: Norwich 22211 (STD code 0603)
London Office: Publications Centre, 51 Nine Elms Lane, London SW8 5DR Tel: (01) 211 3000 Cable Add: Hemstonery London Telex: 297138
Subjects: General Non-fiction, Government Publications
Bookshops: 49 High Holborn, London WC1V 6HB (counter sales); PO Box 276, London SW8 5DT (trade & mail orders); 13A Castle St, Edinburgh EH2 3AR; 258 Broad St, Birmingham B1 2HE; Southey House, Wine St, Bristol BS1 2BQ; 80 Chichester St, Belfast BT1 4JY; Brazennose St, Manchester M60 8AS
ISBN Publisher's Prefixes: 0-10, 0-11, 0-337

The **Herbert** Press Ltd+, 46 Northchurch Rd, London N1 4EJ Tel: (01) 254 4379
Man Dir: David Herbert
Orders to: A & C Black, Howard Rd, Eaton Socon, Huntingdon, Cambridgeshire PE19 3EZ Tel: Huntingdon 212666 (STD code 0480)
Subjects: Art, Design, Crafts, Music, Literature, Biography, Ballet, Theatre
1981: 4 titles *1982:* 4 titles *Founded:* 1975
ISBN Publisher's Prefix: 0-906969

Charles **Herridge** Ltd, Tower House, Abbotsham, Bideford, Devon EX39 5BH Tel: Bideford 3163 (STD code 02372) Telex: 42748 Roskem G
Dirs: Charles Herridge, Bridgid Herridge
Subjects: Natural History, Humour, Reference, Transport, How-to. Co-publishers and packagers
1981: 9 titles *Founded:* 1979

Heyden & Son Ltd, Spectrum House, Hillview Gardens, London NW4 2JQ Tel: (01) 203 5171 Cable Add: Heyspectra London Telex: 28303
Man Dir: K G Heyden
Subsidiary Companies: Heyden & Son GmbH, Devesburgstrasse 6, 4440 Rheine, Federal Republic of Germany; Heyden & Son Inc, 247 South 41st St, Philadelphia, Pa 19104, USA
Subjects: Technical & Scientific
ISBN Publisher's Prefix: 0-85501

Adam **Hilger** Ltd+, Techno House, Redcliffe Way, Bristol BS1 6NX Tel: Bristol 276693 (STD code 0272) Telex: 449149
Man Dir, Rights & Permissions: Cecil I Pedersen; *Editorial, Production:* Ken J Hall; *Sales, Publicity:* Charles J Withers; *Production:* Mrs J A McKernan; *Publicity:* Martin Beavis
Parent Body: Institute of Physics (qv)
Subjects: Mathematics, Computer Science, Electronics, Energy, Earth and Environmental Sciences, Astronomy, Physics, Technology, Optics/Colour Science, Analytical and Applied Chemistry, Plastics, Medical Physics, General Science, History of Science
1981: 16 titles *Founded:* 1967
ISBN Publisher's Prefix: 0-85274

Leonard **Hill**, see Leonard

Hilmarton Manor Press, Calne, Wiltshire SN11 8SB Tel: Calne 208 (STD code 0249 76)
Man Dir: C Baile de Laperriere
Subjects: Art reference, Photographic

1981: 4 titles *1982:* 11 titles *Founded:* 1969
ISBN Publisher's Prefix: 0-904722

Hippo Books, an imprint of Scholastic Book Services Inc (qv)

Hobsons Press (Cambridge) Ltd, Bateman St, Cambridge CB2 1LZ Tel: Cambridge 354551 (STD code 0223) Telex: 81546
Man Dir: Adrian Bridgewater; *Sales:* Alison Pearson
Subject: Education (Careers & Jobs)
Miscellaneous: Publishers under licence for the Careers Research and Advisory Centre Ltd
ISBN Publisher's Prefix: 0-86021

Hodder & Stoughton Children's Books, see Hodder & Stoughton Ltd

Hodder & Stoughton Ltd+, Mill Rd, PO Box 700, Dunton Green, Sevenoaks, Kent TN13 2YA Tel: Sevenoaks 450111 (STD code 0732) Cable Add: Expositor Sevenoaks Telex: 95122
London Off: 47 Bedford Sq, London WC1B 3DP Tel: (01) 636 9851 Telex: 885887
Chairman, Chief Executive: Philip Attenborough; *Sales (Hardback):* W J Bailey (Export), J B McEwen (Home); *Sales (Paperback):* E Bell, A Bourne (Export); *Publicity:* A Hammond, A Clark (Educational); *Production:* J A G Wilson (General/Paperback), C W Davies (Educational), G Cook (Children's); *Rights & Permissions:* Clare Bristow, Jennifer Luithlen (Children's)
Company is organized in divisions with the following divisional managing directors:
Hodder & Stoughton: Eric Major
Hodder & Stoughton Educational: Brian Steven
Hodder & Stoughton Paperbacks: Alan Gordon Walker
Hodder & Stoughton Children's Books: Colin Clark
Parent Company: Hodder & Stoughton Holdings Ltd
Subsidiary Companies (UK): Hodder & Stoughton Dunton Green Ltd, Hodder & Stoughton Storage Ltd, Hodder & Stoughton Overseas Ltd, The Lancet Ltd, The New English Library Ltd (qv)
Subsidiary Companies (outside UK): Hodder & Stoughton (Australia) Pty Ltd, Australia (qv); Hodder & Stoughton Ltd, New Zealand (qv); Hodder & Stoughton (Pty) Ltd, PO Box 548, Bergvlei, Sandton 2012, Republic of South Africa; Hodder & Stoughton Canada Ltd, 345 Nugget Ave, Unit 15, Agincourt, Ontario M1S 4J4, Canada
Associate Company: Hodder Dargaud Ltd
Imprints: include Coronet, Knight, Teach Yourself Books, Unibooks
Subjects: General Fiction, Religion and Theology, Educational, Children's (Fiction & Non-fiction), Medical, Dictionaries, Guidebooks, Travel, Sports & Games, Co-editors (Reader's Digest and Consumers' Association)
1981: 614 titles *1982:* 656 titles *Founded:* 1868
ISBN Publisher's Prefix: 0-340

Alison **Hodge**, Bosulval Farmhouse, Newmill, Penzance, Cornwall TR20 8XA Tel: Penzance 68093 (STD code 0736)
Man Dir: Alison Hodge
Subjects: Social and Economic History, Archaeology, Monographs, Art, Crafts, Photographic Studies
1981: 3 titles *1982:* 1 title *Founded:* 1979
ISBN Publisher's Prefix: 0-906720

Francis **Hodgson**, a division of the Longman Group Ltd (qv)

UNITED KINGDOM 415

The **Hogarth** Press Ltd, see Chatto & Windus Ltd/The Hogarth Press Ltd

The **Holland** Press, 37 Connaught St, London W2 2AZ Tel: (01) 262 6184, (01) 723 1623
Proprietor: R H Leech
Subjects: Reference, Music, Travel, Bibliography, Art, Cartography
Founded: 1956
ISBN Publisher's Prefixes: 0-900470, 0-946323

Hollis & Carter, see The Bodley Head Ltd

Holmes McDougall Ltd*, Allander House, 137-141 Leith Walk, Edinburgh EH6 8NS Tel: (031) 554 9444 Cable Add: Educational Telex: 727508
Man Dir: F J Baillie; *Editorial Dir:* E Ketley; *Export Manager, Rights & Permissions:* R B Shepherd
Subsidiary Companies: Holmes McDougall Bookselling; Pace/Minerva Posters; Scottish Field; Climber and Rambler; Business Scotland; Scottish Farmer; The Great Outdoors
Subjects: Secondary & Primary Textbooks, Scottish Interest
Founded: 1870
ISBN Publisher's Prefix: 0-7157

Holt-Blond Ltd, now Holt-Saunders Ltd (qv)

Holt, Rinehart & Winston, an imprint of Holt-Saunders Ltd (qv)

Holt-Saunders Ltd+, 1 St Anne's Rd, Eastbourne, East Sussex BN21 3UN Tel: Eastbourne 638221 (STD code 0323) Cable Add: Volumists Eastbourne Telex: 877503 Volmst
Warehouse: 23 Edison Rd, Eastbourne, East Sussex BN23 6PY
Man Dir: Robert Kiernan; *Professional Group Publishing Dir:* David S B Inglis; *Sales Dir:* Barend ter Haar; *Editorial Dir:* David Dickens; *Education Publishing Group Dir:* Stephen White; *Sales Manager:* Reg Wood; *Publishers:* John Stockdale (ELT), John Green (Schools), Stephen White (College); *Book Production Dir:* Mark Bide; *Publicity Manager:* Eoin MacGillivray; *Royalty Accountant:* Sandra Denham
Parent Company: CIP, (a division of Columbia Broadcasting System Inc), 383 Madison Ave, New York, NY 10017, USA
Associate Companies: Editorial Interamericana de Argentina SACeI, Argentina (qv); Holt-Saunders Pty Ltd, Australia (qv); Editora Interamericana do Brasil Ltda, Brazil (qv); Holt, Rinehart & Winston of Canada Ltd, 55 Horner Ave, Toronto, Ontario M8Z 4X6, Canada; Holt, Rinehart et Winston Ltée, 8035 rue Jarry est, Montreal H1J 1H6, Canada; W B Saunders Co Canada Ltd, 1 Goldthorne Ave, Toronto, Ontario M8Z 5T9, Canada; Editorial Interamericana SA, Apdo Aéreo 6131, Bogotá, Colombia; Editorial Interamericana del Ecuador SA, Ecuador (qv); Holt-Saunders Ltd, Ichibancho Central Bldg, 22-1 Ichibancho, Chiyodaku, Tokyo, Japan; Nueva Editorial Interamericana SA de CV, Mexico (qv); Holt-Saunders Pty Ltd, New Zealand (qv); Editorial Interamericana SA, Ave 28 de Julio 787, Lima 1, Peru; Distribuidora Interamericana SA, Hilarion Eslava 55, Madrid 15, Spain; Cassell Ltd, UK (qv); Geoffrey Chapman, UK (qv); Editorial Interamericana del Uruguay SA, Uruguay (qv); Holt, Rinehart & Winston Inc, 383 Madison Ave, New York, NY 10017, USA; W B Saunders Co, West Washington Sq, Philadelphia, Pa 19105, USA; Editorial Interamericana de Venezuela CA, Venezuela (qv)
Imprints: Baillière Tindall (qv), Holt, Rinehart & Winston, W B Saunders, Praeger Publishers, Praeger Scientific
Subjects: Medicine, Nursing, Veterinary, Dentistry, Biology, Mathematics, Physics, Chemistry, Primary, Secondary & University Textbooks, Business Studies, Education, ELT, Religion, Travel
Founded: 1900
ISBN Publisher's Prefixes: 0-03 (Holt, Rinehart & Winston), 0-7216 (Saunders)

Home Health Education Service*, Stanborough Press, Alma Park, Grantham, Lincs Tel: Grantham 4284 (STD code 0476)
Man Dir: Whitford A Shaw
Subjects: Secondary & Primary Education, Religion, Medical, Juveniles
ISBN Publisher's Prefix: 0-900703

Horseman's Handbooks, an imprint of Ward Lock Ltd (qv)

Ellis **Horwood** Ltd, Market Cross House, 1 Cooper St, Chichester, West Sussex PO19 1EB Tel: Chicester 789942 (STD code 0243) Cable Add: Horwood Chichester Telex: 86402 Horwood
Editorial: Ellis Horwood, Michael Horwood; *Sales, Production:* Clive Horwood; *Art & Design:* James Gillison; *Publicity:* Sue Gibson; *Marketing, Rights & Permissions:* Felicity Horwood
Orders to: John Wiley & Sons Ltd, Baffins Lane, Chichester, West Sussex
Subjects: Advanced Scientific Technology, Environmental Science, Engineering, Geology, Food Science, Water Science, Computer Science, Mathematics, Analytical Chemistry, Biological Chemistry, Medical Science, Sociology, Satellite Technology, School Level Computing
1983: 400 titles *Founded:* 1973
ISBN Publisher's Prefix: 0-85312

Hour-Glass Press, an imprint of Bailey Brothers & Swinfen Co Ltd (qv)

How & Why Books, imprint of Transworld Publishers Ltd (qv)

Angus **Hudson**, see Angus

Hugo's Language Books Ltd, 104 Judd St, London WC1H 9NF Tel: (01) 278 6136
Dirs: Mrs V Lock, Mrs J Lock, Mrs M Bolt, R J Batchelor-Smith; *Sales, Publicity, Rights & Permissions:* R J Batchelor-Smith
Subjects: How-to, Reference, Secondary Textbooks, Courses on disc, tape & cassette
1981: 4 titles (2 books, 2 cassettes) *1982:* 4 titles *Founded:* 1875
ISBN Publisher's Prefix: 0-85285

Hulton Educational Publications Ltd, Raans Rd, Amersham, Buckinghamshire HP6 6JJ Tel: Amersham 4196 (STD code 02403) Cable Add: Hulted Amersham Bucks Telex: 837916
Dirs: J van der Veen, L G Marsh
Subjects: History, Religion, Juveniles, General & Social Science, University, Secondary & Primary Textbooks, Educational Materials
1983: 85 titles *Founded:* 1954
Miscellaneous: Firm is a member of the Kluwer Group, Netherlands (qv)
ISBN Publisher's Prefix: 0-7175

C **Hurst** & Co (Publisher's) Ltd+, 38 King St, London WC2E 8JT Tel: (01) 240 2666
Shipping Add: J M Dent & Sons Ltd, Dunhams Lane, Letchworth, Hertfordshire SG6 1LF
Man Dir: Christopher Hurst; *Rights & Permissions:* Susanna Clarke
Subjects: Area Studies (Politics, International Relations, Economic Development)
Founded: 1968
ISBN Publisher's Prefixes: 0-905838, 0-903983

Hutchinson & Co (Publishers) Ltd, an imprint of Hutchinson Books Ltd (qv)

Hutchinson Books Ltd, Hutchinson House, 17-21 Conway St, London W1P 6JD Tel: (01) 387 2811 Cable Add: Literarius London W1 Telex: 261212
Man Dir: Roger Houghton; *Editorial:* James Cochrane; *Sales:* David Roy; *Export:* Gordon Bryant; *Marketing:* Jeremy Cox; *Rights:* Lavinia Trevor
Orders to: Tiptree Book Services, Church Rd, Tiptree, Colchester, Essex Tel: Tiptree 816362 (STD code 0621)
Imprints: Barrie & Jenkins Ltd, Hutchinson & Co (Publishers) Ltd, Hutchinson Children's Books Ltd, Popular Dogs Publishing Co Ltd, Rider & Co, Stanley Paul & Co Ltd, Vermilion
Subjects: General Fiction, Non-fiction, Crime, Biography, Memoirs, Travel, Reference, Children's, Dogs (care & breeding), Eastern Philosophy and Mysticism, Sports & Hobbies, Poetry, Humour, Graphics, Fashion
Miscellaneous: Hutchinson Books Ltd is a division of The Hutchinson Publishing Group Ltd (qv)

Hutchinson Children's Books Ltd, an imprint of Hutchinson Books Ltd (qv)

Hutchinson Educational+, 17-21 Conway St, London W1P 6JD Tel: (01) 387 2811
Man Dir: Mark Cohen; *Deputy Man Dir:* Bob Osborne; *Technical Dir:* Doug Fox; *Sales:* John Fulford; *Export:* Clyde Hunter
Orders to: Tiptree Book Services, Church Rd, Tiptree, Colchester, Essex Tel: Tiptree 816362 (STD code 0621)
Imprints: Hutchinson Technical Books, Hutchinson University Library, Business Books Ltd (qv)
Subjects: School Books, Technical, Academic, Vocational, Business
Miscellaneous: Hutchinson Educational is a division of The Hutchinson Publishing Group Ltd (qv)

The **Hutchinson Publishing Group** Ltd+, 17-21 Conway St, London W1P 5HL Tel: (01) 387 2811 Cable Add: Literatus London W1 Telex: 261212
Chief Executive: Charles Clark; *Man Dir:* Roger Houghton; *Editorial:* James Cochrane; *Sales:* David Roy; *Production:* Grahame Griffiths; *Marketing:* Jeremy Cox; *Rights & Permissions:* Lavinia Trevor
Orders to: Tiptree Book Services, Church Rd, Tiptree, Colchester, Essex CO5 0SR Tel: Tiptree 816362 (STD code 0621)
The Hutchinson Publishing Group operates three publishing divisions:
Hutchinson Books Ltd (qv), Hutchinson Educational Books (qv), Arrow Books Ltd (including Geographia Ltd and Robert Nicholson Publications Ltd — qqv)
Parent Company: LWT (Holdings) Ltd, South Bank Television Centre, Kent House, Upper Ground, London SE1 9LT
Associate Companies: Andersen Press Ltd (qv), Hutchinson Benham; Hutchinson Group (Australia) Ltd, Australia (qv); Hutchinson Group (NZ) Ltd, New Zealand (qv); Hutchinson Group (SA) (Pty) Ltd, South Africa (qv)
Subjects: General Fiction and Non-fiction, Antiques, Art, Biography, Children's, Hobbies, Humour, Maps, Memoirs, Music, Mysticism, Oriental Religion, Paperbacks, Reference, Science and Technical, Sport, Textbooks, Thrillers, Travel
Founded: 1887
ISBN Publisher's Prefix: 0-09

Hutchinson Technical Books, an imprint of Hutchinson Educational (qv)

Hutchinson University Library, an imprint of Hutchinson Educational (qv)

Hylton Lacy Publishers, an imprint of Profile Books Ltd (qv)

Hymns Ancient & Modern, St Mary's Works, St Mary's Plain, Norwich NR3 3BH Tel: Norwich 612914 (STD code 0603)
Publisher: Gordon Knights
Subjects: Hymn Books, Prayer Books, General Religion
ISBN Publisher's Prefix: 0-907547

Hyperion Books, an imprint of Ward Lock Ltd (qv)

I C Magazines Ltd, see International Communications

I C S A Publishing Ltd, an imprint of Woodhead-Faulkner (Publishers) Ltd (qv)

I P C, see International Publishing Corporation Ltd

I R L Press+, PO Box 1, Eynsham, Oxford OX8 1JJ Tel: Oxford 882283 (STD code 0865) Telex: 83147 Irl
Chief Executive: T R Otley; *Editorial, Production, Rights & Permissions:* E M Coast; *Sales, Publicity:* J C Bradley
Associate Company: Information Printing Ltd, Southfield Rd, Eynsham, Oxford OX8 1JJ
Branch Off: I R L Press Inc, Suite 907, 1911 Jefferson Davis Highway, Arlington, VA 22202, USA
Subjects: Biomedical Sciences, Technical
1981: 8 titles *1982:* 8 titles *Founded:* 1965
ISBN Publisher's Prefix: 0-904147

I T V Books, an imprint of Independent Television Books Ltd (qv)

Image, an imprint of Doubleday & Co Inc (qv)

Independent Television Books Ltd, 247 Tottenham Court Rd, London W1P 0AU Tel: (01) 636 3666 Telex: 27813
Chairman: Alwyn Wise; *Chief Executive:* John Doyle; *Publicity:* Jane Beaton; *Production:* Jerry Dixon
Parent Company: Independent Television Publications Ltd (at above address)
Imprints: ITV Books, TV Times Books, Look-In Books
Subjects: TV Tie-ins, Adult Education, Humour, Reference, Children's Paperbacks, Women's Interest, General

The **Initial Teaching** Alphabet Foundation, 9 Brindle Close, Bamber Bridge, Preston, Lancs PR5 6ZN Tel: Preston 36963 (STD code 0772)
Secretary: J Bromley
Subject: Primary Education
ISBN Publisher's Prefix: 0-254

Input Two-Nine, a former imprint of Gower Publishing Co Ltd (qv)

Institute of Personnel Management*, IPM House, Camp Rd, London SW19 4UW Tel: (01) 946 9100
Editorial, Rights & Permissions: Sally Herbert; *Marketing:* Veronica Lee; *Production:* Stephen West
Orders to: IPM Distribution Centre, The Technical Press Ltd, Freeland, Oxford OX7 2AP
Associate Company: The Technical Press Ltd (qv)
Subjects: Management, Personnel Management
ISBN Publisher's Prefix: 0-85292

The **Institute of Physics**+, Techno House, Redcliffe Way, Bristol BS1 6NX Tel: Bristol 297481 (STD code 0272) Telex: 449149
Publishing Dir: C I Pedersen; *Editorial:* Ken J Hall; *Sales, Publicity:* C J Withers
Orders to: (Books) Adam Hilger Ltd, Techno House, Redcliffe Way, Bristol BS1 6NX; (Journals/Magazines) Physics Trust Publications, 823-825 Bath Rd, Brislington, Bristol BS4 5NU
Subsidiary Company: Adam Hilger Ltd (qv)
Subjects: Physics, General Science, Journals
1981: 8 titles *Founded:* 1874
ISBN Publisher's Prefix: 0-85498

Institute of Pyramidology*, 31 Station Rd, Harpenden, Hertfordshire AL5 4XB Tel: Harpenden 64510 (STD code 05827) Telex: 826957 Institute of Pyramidology
Vice President: James Rutherford
Associate Company: Top Stone Books (qv)
Subject: Pyramidology
Founded: 1940
ISBN Publisher's Prefix: 0-903402

Institution of Chemical Engineers, George E Davis Bldg, 165-171 Railway Terrace, Rugby, Warwickshire CV21 3HQ Tel: Rugby 78214 (STD code 0788) Telex: 311780
General Secretary: Dr T J Evans; *Publications Manager:* A E Havard
Subject: Chemical Engineering
1981: approx 9 titles *1982:* approx 9 titles
Founded: 1922
ISBN Publisher's Prefix: 0-85295

The **Institution of Civil Engineers** (Publications Division), see Thomas Telford Ltd

Institution of Electrical Engineers*, Publishing Dept, PO Box 8, Southgate House, Stevenage, Herts SG1 1HQ Tel: Stevenage 3311 (STD code 0438) Cable Add: Voltampere Stevenage Telex: 261176
Publishing Dir: D S Hopper; *Books Publisher, Rights & Permissions:* Oliver Ball
Marketing Manager: Owen Byatt
Orders to: Publication Sales Dept, Institution of Electrical Engineers, PO Box 26, Hitchin, Herts SG5 1SA Tel: Hitchin 53331 (STD code 0462) Telex: 825962
Branch Off & Bookshop: Savoy Pl, London WC2R 0BL
Subjects: Electrical & Electronic Engineering, Power & Control & Science, Computer Technology, IEE Conference Publication, Colloquium Digests, Technical Regulations, Vacation Schools, Periodicals
1981: 17 titles *1982:* 21 titles *Founded:* 1871
ISBN Publisher's Prefix: 0-85296

Institution of Mechanical Engineers, see Mechanical Engineering Publications Ltd

Inter-Varsity Press, 38 De Montfort St, Leicester LE1 7GP Tel: Leicester 551700 (STD code 0533)
Man Dir: F R Entwistle; *Editorial:* D R W Wood; *Marketing, Publicity:* P S Rusted; *Production:* M R Sims; *Rights & Permissions:* Miss K M Gladstone
Orders to: IVP, Norton St, Nottingham NG7 3HR Tel: Nottingham 781054 (STD code 0602)
Parent Company: UCCF
Imprints: Arena; Tyndale Press
Subject: Religion
Bookshops: UCCF Bookcentre, Norton St, Nottingham
Founded: 1928
ISBN Publisher's Prefixes: 0-85110, 0-85111

Intercontinental Book Productions Ltd*, Berkshire House, Queen St, Maidenhead, Berkshire SL6 1NF Tel: Maidenhead 34433 (STD code 0628) Telex: 848036 Ibpmhdg
Man Dir: Michael J Morris; *Publishing Dir:* Desmond Marwood; *Production Dir:* David Wescott; *Foreign Rights Manager:* Elisabeth Marks
Subjects: Full colour co-edition packages, General Non-fiction, How-to, Juveniles, Paperbacks, Educational Aids and Toys
Founded: 1972
ISBN Publisher's Prefix: 0-85047

Intermediate Technology Publications Ltd, 9 King St, London WC2E 8HN Tel: (01) 836 9434 Telex: 268312 Wescom G Attn Intec
Editor & Publisher: N Burton; *Sales Dir:* J Elford
Parent Company: Intermediate Technology Development Group Ltd (at above address)
Subjects: Technology and Industries appropriate to Developing Countries (emphasis on low-cost, small-scale technology)
Bookshop: Intermediate Technology Bookshop (at above address)
1981: 6 titles *Founded:* 1974
ISBN Publisher's Prefix: 0-903031

International Bible Reading Association, see National Christian Education Council

International Biographical Centre, an imprint of Melrose Press, (qv)

International Communications*, PO Box 261, London WC2E 9LR (Located at: 63 Long Acre, London WC2E 9LR) Tel: (01) 404 4333 Cable Add: Machrak London WC2 Telex: 8811757 Araby G
Chairman & Man Dir: Ahmed Afif Ben Yedder; *Editorial, Rights & Permissions:* Emena Ben Yedder; *Sales:* Mike Cooper; *Production:* Hilda Igloi; *Publicity:* Helen Perry
Subsidiary Company: Ediafric — La Documentation Africaine, 57 ave d'Iena, F-75783 Paris Cedex 16, France
Associate Companies: IC Expo Ltd (at above London address); IC Publications Ltd, Suite 1121, 122 East 42nd St, New York, NY 10168, USA
Subjects: Economic monographs, yearbooks and travel guides on Africa and the Middle East
Founded: 1974
ISBN Publisher's Prefix: 0-905268

International Dictionary Service, an imprint of Avebury Publishing Co Ltd (qv)

International Textbook Co Ltd, Bishopbriggs, Glasgow G64 2NZ Tel: (041) 772 2311 Telex: 777283
London Off: Furnival House, 14-18 High Holborn, London Tel: (01) 242 5832
Dir: Dr Graeme MacKintosh; *Sales Manager:* Gerard Dummett
Parent Company: Blackie & Son Ltd (qv)
Associate Companies: Leonard Hill Ltd (qv); Surrey University Press (qv)
Subjects: Chemistry, Physics, Mathematics, Computing, Environmental Sciences, Business Studies, Hotel and Catering
Founded: 1902
ISBN Publisher's Prefix: 0-7002

The **Islamic Foundation**, 223 London Rd, Leicester LE2 1ZE Tel: Leicester 703555 (STD code 0533) Cable Add: Islamfound Leicester UK Telex: 341539 Islamf G
Director General, Editorial: K Murad; *Sales, Production, Publicity:* T A Dale
Subjects: Islamic Topics
1981: 24 titles *1982:* 10 titles *Founded:* 1973

J K Publishers, 23 Denne Rd, Horsham, West Sussex RH12 1JF Tel: Horsham 50726 (STD code 0403) Telex: 87315 Deltom
Man Dir: Mrs Z Rustom; *Editorial, Sales, Production, Publicity:* M Nanabhoy
Subjects: Social Sciences, Science, Technology, Medicine, Art, Yoga, Indian Philosophy, Astrology
Founded: 1977
ISBN Publisher's Prefix: 0-86249

Jackdaw Publications Ltd, see Jonathan Cape Ltd

Arthur **James** Ltd, The Drift, Greenhill Park Rd, Evesham, Worcs WR11 4NW Tel: Evesham 6566 (STD code 0386) Cable Add: James Evesham
Man Dir: F A Russell; *Editorial:* M Macqueen
Subjects: Religion, Psychology
Founded: 1935
ISBN Publisher's Prefix: 0-85305

Jane's Publishing Company Ltd, 238 City Rd, London EC1V 2PU Tel: (01) 251 9281 Telex: 23168
Man Dir: Sidney Jackson; *Commercial Dir:* John Stoddart; *Sales:* George Rainey (Europe), Jeremy Gambrill; *Production:* Ken Harris; *Publicity:* Richard Coltart
Parent Company: Thomson Books Ltd (qv for associate companies)
Subsidiary Company: Jane's Publishing Inc, 135 West 50th St, New York, NY 10020, USA
Subjects: Naval, Military, Aviation, Transport Reference
Founded: 1979
ISBN Publisher's Prefix: 0-7106

Jarrold Colour Publications, Barrack St, Norwich NR3 1TR Tel: Norwich 660211 (STD code 0603) Cable Add: Jarrolds Telex: 97497
Man Dir, Rights & Permissions: Antony Jarrold; *Sales Manager:* T A Thompson
Imprints: Cotman House, White Horse Books, Cotmancolor, Glaven, Walsingham
Subjects: Topography, Travel, Natural History, Gardening, Hobbies
Bookshop: Jarrold Colour Publications, Barrack St, Norwich NR3 1TR
1983: 500 titles *Founded:* 1770
ISBN Publisher's Prefixes: 0-85306, 0-7117

The **Johns Hopkins** University Press, Ely House, 37 Dover St, London W1X 4HQ Cable Add: Unibooks London W1 Telex: 24224 ref 3545
Warehouse: International Book Distributors Ltd, 66 Wood Lane End, Hemel Hempstead, Hertfordshire Tel: Hemel Hempstead 58531 (STD code 0442)
Man Dir: J Trevor Brown; *Publicity Manager:* Michael Richards; *Sales Managers:* Anna Simpson-Muellner (Export)
Parent Company: The Johns Hopkins University Press, Baltimore, Maryland 21218, USA
Subjects: Literature, Humanities, Social Sciences, Sciences
ISBN Publisher's Prefix: 0-8018

Johnson Publications Ltd*, 130 Wigmore St, London W1H 0AT Tel: (01) 486 6757
Subjects: Medicine, History, Archaeology, Biography, Memoirs, Politics, Political Economy, Sociology, Questions of the Day, Travel & Adventure, Directories & Guidebooks, General Literature
ISBN Publisher's Prefix: 0-85307

Johnson Reprint Co Ltd, see Academic Press Inc (London) Ltd

Johnston & Bacon, an imprint of Cassell Ltd (qv)

Johnston Green & Co (Publishers) Ltd+, PO Box 1, Portree, Isle of Skye IV51 9BT Tel: Sligachan 257 (STD code 047852)
President: C E Milne; *Chairman, Managing Editor:* J C R Green; *Production, Rights:* Anne Green; *Sales:* A B Simmons; *Publicity:* J B Thomson
Orders to: Johnston Green Distribution Ltd, Sedgwick Park, Horsham, Sussex RH13 8QH Tel: Lower Beeding 369 (STD code 040 376)
Subsidiary Companies: Aquila Publishing Co, Club Leabhar, Johnston Green Distribution Ltd (all at PO Box 1, Portree, Isle of Skye); Johnston Green Publishing (Ireland) Ltd, PO Box Drogheda, Co Louth, Republic of Ireland; Ambito Literario International, Corcega 269, Barcelona, Spain; Press Porcepic Ltd, 235 Market Sq, 560 Johnson St, Victoria, BC V8W 3C6, Canada
Associate Companies: Iolaire Marketing Services, APC Marketing Group (both at PO Box 1, Portree, Isle of Skye); Anne Johnston/The Moorlands Press (qv), Aquila/IBD (both at 11 Novi Lane, Leek, Staffordshire ST13 6NS)
Imprints: Ambito Literario, Aquila Essays, Aquila Pamphlet Poets, Aquila Poetry, Aquila Publishing, Aquila/The Phaethon Press, Aquila The Wayzgoose Press, Club Leabhar, Press Porcepic
Subjects: Poetry, Short Stories, Gaelic Language Books, Books by Highland Authors, Business, Literature, Criticism, Books on/by French, Irish, Welsh, Maltese, German, Spanish, South American, American, Portuguese, Low Countries, Italian writers, Translations, Children's, Philosophy, Cookery, Diet/Vegetarianism, Humour, Magazines
1981: 50 titles *1982:* approx 75 titles
Founded: 1968
ISBN Publisher's Prefixes: 0-903226 (Aquila), 0-7275 (Aquila), 0-907763 (Johnston Green), 0-86301 (Anne Johnston, The Moorlands Press), 0-902706 (Club Leabhar), 0-88878 (Press Porcepic)

Anne **Johnston/The Moorlands** Press, 11 Novi Lane, Leek, Staffordshire ST13 6NS Tel: Leek 373467 (STD code 0538)
Chief Executive, Publicity: Anne Johnston; *Editor, Rights & Permissions:* J C R Green; *Sales Manager:* Tony Simmons (Johnston Green Distribution Ltd); *Production:* Anne Green (Johnston Green & Co (Publishers) Ltd)
Orders to: Johnston Green Distribution Ltd, Sedgwick Park, Horsham, Sussex RH13 6QH Tel: Lower Beeding 369 (STD code 040 376)
Associate Company: Johnston Green & Co (Publishers) Ltd (qv)
Subjects: Poetry, Fiction, General Literature
1982: 6 titles *Founded:* 1977
ISBN Publisher's Prefix: 0-86301

Jordan & Sons Ltd, PO Box 260, 15 Pembroke Rd, Bristol BS99 7DX Tel: Bristol 732861 (STD code 0272) Telex: 449119
Man Dir: Philip Bates; *Editorial and Sales Dir:* Patrick Lockstone; *Publishing Executive:* Angela Gibbs; *Marketing Dir:* Andrew Kampe
Orders to: Kogan Page, 120 Pentonville Rd, London N1 9JN Tel: (01) 837 7851
Subsidiary Company: Oswalds of Edinburgh Ltd, 24 Castle St, Edinburgh EH2 3HT Tel: (031) 225 7308 Telex: 72428
Imprint: Rose-Jordan Ltd
London Off: Jordan House, 47 Brunswick Pl, London N1 6EE Tel: (01) 253 3030 Telex: 261010
Branch Offs: 3 Victoria St, Liverpool L2 5QF Tel: (051) 236 3631; 44 Whitchurch Rd, Cardiff CF4 3UQ Tel: Cardiff 371901 (STD code 0222)
Subjects: Secondary, University, Commercial & Technical Education, Legal & Parliamentary, Commercial, Business & Professional, Family and Company Law Journals
Founded: 1866
ISBN Publisher's Prefixes: 0-85308 (Jordan), 0-907313 (Rose-Jordan)

Michael **Joseph** Ltd+, 44 Bedford Sq, London WC1 3DP Tel: (01) 323 3200 Cable Add: Emjaybuks London WC1 Telex: 21322
Man Dir: Alan Brooke; *Editorial Dir:* Philippa Harrison; *Marketing Dir:* David Crane; *Export Sales Dir:* John Lyon; *Rights & Permissions:* Diana Mackay
Associate Companies: Pelham Books (qv); Pavilion Books
Subjects: General, Fiction, Biography, History, How-to, Reference, Young Adult, Quality Paperbacks, Music
Founded: 1936
Miscellaneous: Company is a member of the Thomson Books Ltd group (qv), a part of International Thomson Organization Ltd (Canada)
ISBN Publisher's Prefixes: 0-7181, 0-7207, 0-9075

The **Journeyman** Press Ltd+, 97 Ferme Park Rd, Crouch End, London N8 9SA Tel: (01) 348 9261 Cable Add: Journeyrad, London N8 Telex: 25247 Journeyrad
Man Dir: Peter Sinclair
Orders to: George Philip Services Ltd, Arndale Rd, Wick, Littlehampton, West Sussex BN17 7EN Tel: Littlehampton 7453 (STD code 09064)
Imprints: Journeyman Press, Radical Reprints
Branch Off: 17 Old Mill Rd, West Nyack, NY 10994, USA
Subjects: Politics, Social History, Fiction, Biography, Art, Poetry, Drama, Literary Criticism, Philosophy
1981: 10 titles *Founded:* 1975
ISBN Publisher's Prefix: 0-904526

Junction Books+, 15 St John's Hill, London SW11 1TN Tel: (01) 223 8209, (01) 223 8200
Man Dir, Rights & Permissions: Bill Garlick; *Editorial:* Michael Mason, Anne Beech, Victoria Barnsley; *Sales:* Peter Boyden; *Production:* Paul Saunders
Subjects: Politics, Sociology, Medicine, Cultural & Art History, Science, Technology, Literary Studies, Women's Studies, Reference, Business Studies
1981: 26 titles *1982:* 24 titles *Founded:* 1980
ISBN Publisher's Prefix: 0-86245

Jupiter Books (London) Ltd*, 167 Hermitage Rd, London N4 1LZ Tel: (01) 800 6601
Man Dir, Rights & Permissions: S H Austen; *Editorial Executive:* Martin Heard
Subjects: History, Music, Art, Juveniles
Founded: 1973
ISBN Publisher's Prefixes: 0-904041, 0-906379

Kahn & Averill, 9 Harrington Rd, London SW7 3ES Tel: (01) 743 3278
Man Dir: M Kahn
Orders to: 21 Pennard Mansions, Goldhawk Rd, London W12 8DL
Subjects: General Non-fiction (with emphasis on music)
Founded: 1947
ISBN Publisher's Prefix: 0-900707

Kaye & Ward Ltd+, The Windmill Press, Kingswood, Tadworth, Surrey Tel: Mogador 833511 (STD code 0737) Cable Add: Sunlocks Tadworth Telex: 947458 Press G
Man Dir: Christopher Forster; *Dir:* Austen Smith; *Editorial:* Rosemary Debham; *Sales:* Lionel Foot; *Promotion:* Miriam Maxim; *Trade Manager:* Janet Thompsett; *Exhibition Manager:* Peggy Lince; *Production Dir:* Robert Aspinall; *Rights & Permissions:* Jane Turnbull, Sally Riley, Elizabeth Wright, Miriam Maxim
Parent Company: William Heinemann International Ltd (qv)

Associate Company: World's Work Ltd (qv)
Subjects: Novels, Belles Lettres, Biography, History, How-to, Juveniles, Sport, Hobbies, Handicrafts
Founded: 1942
ISBN Publisher's Prefix: 0-7182

Kelly's Directories, Windsor Court, East Grinstead House, East Grinstead, West Sussex RH19 1XB Tel: East Grinstead 26972 (STD code 0342)
Publishing Dir: R J E Dangerfield
Parent Company: Information Services Ltd
Subject: Directories
Founded: 1799
ISBN Publisher's Prefix: 0-610

Kemps Group (Printers & Publishers) Ltd, 1-5 Bath St, London EC1V 9QA Tel: (01) 253 4761 Cable Add: Kemptory London EC1
Branch Off: Federation House, 2309 Coventry Rd, Sheldon, Birmingham B26 3PG Tel: (021) 742 6717
Subjects: Trade Directories and Yearbooks, Chamber of Commerce Publications (annual)
1981: 17 titles *Founded:* 1946
ISBN Publisher's Prefix: 0-86259

Kershaw Publishing Co Ltd, 109 Gt Russell St, London WC1B 3ND Tel: (01) 580 1862 Cable Add: Eurospan London WC2
Man Dir: Peter K Taylor; *Sales, Publicity, Advertising, Rights & Permissions:* Janet Buttery
Branch Off: Bolholt, Walshaw Rd, Bury, Lancs
Subjects: Mathematics, Business, Social Sciences, Scholarly Reprints
1981: 4 titles *1982:* 4 titles *Founded:* 1969
ISBN Publisher's Prefix: 0-901665

Kestrel Books, an imprint of Penguin Books Ltd (qv)

Keswick, an imprint of Marshall Morgan & Scott (Publications) Ltd (qv)

Key, an imprint of Scripture Union (qv)

William **Kimber** & Co Ltd, 100 Jermyn St, London SW1Y 6EE Tel: (01) 930 0446
Man Dir, Editor: William Kimber; *Rights & Permissions:* Amy Myers; *Production:* O J Colman; *Publicity Manager:* Betty Crockett
Orders to: 72-74 Paul St, London EC2A 4NA Tel: (01) 739 4755
Subjects: Biography, History, General, Fiction, Current Affairs, Travel, Memoirs, Naval, Military, Aviation
Founded: 1950
ISBN Publisher's Prefix: 0-7183

Kingfisher Books Ltd, Elsley Court, 20-22 Great Titchfield St, London W1P 7AD Tel: (01) 631 0878 Cable Add: Greatbooks London Telex: 27725 Gridem
Man Dir: D Grisewood
Subjects: Children's, General Non-fiction
Founded: 1977

Kingsmead Press, an imprint of Avon-Anglia Publications & Services (qv)

Kingsway Publications Ltd, Lottbridge Drove, Eastbourne, East Sussex BN23 6NT Tel: Eastbourne 27454 (STD code 0323)
Chairman: Gilbert W Kirby; *Man Dir:* Hugh D Fuller; *Sales Dir:* Geoff Booker
Imprints: Falcon Books, Kingsway Publications
Subjects: Religion, High- & Low-priced Paperbacks
1981: 35 titles *1982:* 38 titles *Founded:* 1977 (merger of Coverdale House Publishers Ltd and Victory Press)
ISBN Publisher's Prefixes: 0-86065 (Kingsway), 0-902088 and 0-85476 (titles formerly published as Coverdale and Victory respectively)

Kluwer Publishing Ltd, Harlequin Ave, Great West Rd, Brentford, Middx TW8 9EW Tel: (01) 568 6441
Man Dir: W E Porter; *Dir, Editorial, Rights & Permissions:* Colin Ancliffe; *Marketing:* Patrick Braybrooke; *Production:* Peter Phillips
Parent Company: Kluwer BV, Netherlands (qv)
Imprints: Kluwer Business Handbooks, Kluwer Medical, Kluwer-Harrap Handbooks
Subjects: Business, Management, Law, Taxation, Insurance, Finance, Health & Safety, Dentistry, Medicine, Farming Security, Video, Horticulture, Pensions
1982: 8 titles *1983:* 10 titles *Founded:* 1972
Miscellaneous: Firm was created by Kluwer BV, Netherlands (qv) and George G Harrap & Co (qv)

Knight, an imprint of Hodder & Stoughton Ltd (qv)

Charles **Knight** Ltd, an imprint of Ernest Benn Ltd

Kogan Page Ltd, 120 Pentonville Rd, London N1 9JN Tel: (01) 837 7851 Telex: 268048 Extldn G
Man Dir, Editorial, Rights & Permissions: Philip Kogan; *Publishing Dir:* Peter Newman; *Sales Dir:* Ralph Lobatto; *Production Dir:* Janson Woodall
Associate Company: Nichols Publishing Co, PO Box 96, New York, NY 10024, USA
Subjects: New Technology, Energy, Business & Management, Personnel, Training & Industrial Relations, Transport, Marketing, Commodities, Education & Educational Technology, Careers
1983: 80 titles *Founded:* 1967
ISBN Publisher's Prefix: 0-85038

Kudos & Godine Ltd, 45 Blackfriars Rd, London SE1 8NZ Tel: (01) 928 5796 Telex: 912881 Menbow
Chairman: George Bowen; *Man Dir:* Martin Bailey; *Marketing:* Darryl Richards
Orders to: Biblios Publishers' Distribution Services Ltd, Glenside Industrial Estate, Partridge Green, Horsham, Sussex Tel: Partridge Green 710971 (STD code 0403)
Parent Company: Mendham Bowen Ltd (at above address), 25% owned by David Godine Publisher Inc, 306 Dartmouth St, Boston, Mass 02116, USA
Imprints: Kudos, David Godine Publisher — London, Kudos & Godine, Hacker Art Books
Branch Off: c/o David Godine Publisher Inc (see above)
Founded: 1981 (re-founded)
ISBN Publisher's Prefixes: 0-906293 (Kudos), 0-87923 (Godine), 0-87817 (Hacker)

L D A (Learning Development Aids), an imprint of Living and Learning (Cambridge) Ltd (qv)

L S P Books Ltd, 8 Farncombe St, Farncombe, Surrey GU7 3AY Tel: Godalming 28622 (STD code 04868) Cable Add: Litserve, Godalming Telex: 919101 Vitiel G
Man Dir: C P de Laszlo
Imprint: Lorrimer Books
Subjects: Cinema, Reference, Popular Music
1982: 9 titles *Founded:* 1964
ISBN Publisher's Prefixes: 0-85321 (LSP), 0-8184 (Lorrimer)

Ladybird Books Ltd, PO Box 12, Beeches Rd, Loughborough, Leicestershire LE11 2NQ Tel: Loughborough 268021 (STD code 0509) Cable Add: Ladybird, Loughborough Telex: 341347
Man Dir: M P Kelley; *Editorial Dir:* V Mills; *Works Dir:* C W Hall; *Art Dir:* R Smith; *Sales Managers:* G Duncan (UK), R Webster (Export); *Publicity:* Mary Hagger
Associate Companies include: Longman Group Ltd, Penguin Books Ltd (qqv)
Subjects: Children's Books, Educational (Infants, Primary, Secondary), Educational Materials
Founded: 1924
Miscellaneous: Formerly Wills & Hepworth Ltd
ISBN Publisher's Prefix: 0-7214

Lakeland Paperbacks, an imprint of Marshall, Morgan & Scott (Publications) Ltd (qv)

Jay **Landesman** Ltd, 8 Duncan Terrace, London N1 8BZ Tel: (01) 837 7290 Telex: 935163
Man Dir, Publicity, Rights: Jay Landesman; *Editorial:* Cosmo Landesman; *Sales:* Stan Stunning; *Production:* Andrew Sanders
Orders to: Noonan-Hurst, 131 Trafalgar Rd, London SE10
Imprints: Golden Handshake, Polytantric Press
Subjects: Popular Culture, Social History, Satire, Bibliography, Biography, Poetry, Fiction
1981: 10 titles *Founded:* 1977
ISBN Publisher's Prefix: 0-905150

Landmarks, a joint imprint of William Heinemann Ltd and Martin Secker & Warburg Ltd (qqv)

Allen **Lane**, see Allen

The **Language** Library, an imprint of André Deutsch (qv)

Lansdowne International, see Rigby International

T Werner **Laurie**, see The Bodley Head Ltd

Lawrence & Wishart, 39 Museum St, London WC1 Tel: (01) 405 0103 Cable Add: Interbook London WC1
Man Dir: J Skelley
Subjects: Biography, History, Philosophy, Politics, Economics
Founded: 1936
ISBN Publisher's Prefix: 0-85315

Leicester University Press+, Fielding Johnson Bldg, University of Leicester, University Rd, Leicester LE1 7RH Tel: Leicester 551860/555510 (STD code 0533)
Secretary to the Press: P L Boulton
Subjects: Archaeology, History, Literature, International Relations, Politics
1981: 12 titles *Founded:* 1951
ISBN Publisher's Prefix: 0-7185

Leisure Arts Ltd*, 154-160 Upper Richmond Rd, London SW15 2SW Tel: (01) 789 6699 Cable Add: Cohallclub London Telex: 25881
Dirs: Leonard Joseph (USA), L Phillips, Lord Redesdale
Subsidiary Companies: International Art Club Editions, The Corsano Co (both at 18 St Ann's Crescent, London SW18 2LX)
Subjects: General Fiction, History, Art, Reference, Cooking, How-to, Philosophy, Poetry, Sport
Book Club: Heron Books
ISBN Publisher's Prefix: 0-900948

Leonard Hill, Wester Cleddens Rd, Bishopbriggs, Glasgow G64 2NZ Tel: (041) 772 2311 Cable Add: Blackie Glasgow Telex: 777283
London Off: Furnival House, 14-18 High Holborn, London Tel: (01) 242 5832
Dir: Dr Graeme MacKintosh; *Sales Manager:* Gerard Dummett
Orders to: J M Dent (Distribution) Ltd, Dunham's Lane, Letchworth, Herts SG16 1LF
Parent Co: Blackie & Son Ltd (qv)

UNITED KINGDOM 419

Associate Companies: International Textbook Co Ltd, Surrey University Press (qqv)
Subjects: Reference, Food Technology, Industrial Chemistry, Agriculture, Urban & Rural Planning
1981: 2 titles
ISBN Publisher's Prefix: 0-249

Leopard, an imprint of Scripture Union (qv)

Lepus Books, an imprint of E P Publishing Ltd (qv)

Charles **Letts** & Co Ltd, Diary House, Borough Rd, London SE1 1DW Tel: (01) 407 8891 Cable Add: Diarists London Telex: 884498
Chairman: A A Letts; *Sales Dir:* J A Kearns; *Marketing Dir:* T M Green
Subjects: Guide Books, Travel, Education, General Non-fiction
Founded: 1796
ISBN Publisher's Prefix: 0-85097

Lionel **Leventhal** Ltd, 2-6 Hampstead High St, London NW3 1QQ Tel: (01) 794 0246 Cable Add: Armsbooks Ldn NW3 Telex: 8951899
Chairman: Lionel Leventhal; *Man Dir:* Don Cook; *Editorial Dir:* David Gibbons
Subsidiary Company: Arms & Armour Press (qv)
Subjects: Illustrated Reference
Bookshop: Ken Trotman Arms Books, 2-6 Hampstead High St, London NW3 1QQ
Founded: 1966
ISBN Publisher's Prefix: 0-85368

A **Lewis**, an imprint of Ian Allan Ltd (qv)

F **Lewis** Publishers Ltd, 35 Bedford Row, London WC1R 4JH Tel: (01) 242 0946 Cable Add: Biblos London WC1 Telex: 21792 ref 2546
Dirs: Charles A A Black, David Gadsby, Leonard Brown
Parent Company: A & C Black (Publishers) Ltd (qv)
Subjects: Fine & Applied Art, Ceramics, Textiles
Founded: 1932
ISBN Publisher's Prefix: 0-85317

H K **Lewis** & Co Ltd, 136 Gower St, London WC1E 6BS Tel: (01) 387 4282 Cable Add: Publicavit, London WC1E 6BS
Subjects: Technical & Scientific, Medical, Foreign Languages, Dictionaries
ISBN Publisher's Prefix: 0-7186

J D **Lewis** & Sons Ltd, see Gomer Press

Library Association Publishing, 7 Ridgmount St, London WC1E 7AE Tel: (01) 636 7543 Telex: 21897 Laldn G
Man Dir: Charles Ellis; *Books Editor:* David Pratt; *Sales Office Manager:* Beverly Brentnall; *Publicity:* Selina Bird
Associate Company: Clive Bingley Ltd (qv)
Branch Off: 9 Station Rd, St Ives, Huntingdon, Cambridgeshire
Subjects: Bibliographies, Library Science, Directories, Catalogues, Indexes, Serials
1981: 22 titles *1982:* 14 titles *Founded:* 1981 (as Library Association Publishing)
ISBN Publisher's Prefix: 0-85365

Lifestyle Books, an imprint of Zomba Books (qv)

Frances **Lincoln** Ltd, Apollo Works, 5 Charlton King's Rd, London NW5 2SB Tel: (01) 482 3302 Telex: 21376
Man Dir: Frances Lincoln; *Sales:* Nicholas Kennedy
Associate Companies: Frances Lincoln Publishers Ltd, Weidenfeld (Publishers) Ltd (qv)
Subjects: High quality illustrated books for international co-editions: Art, Archaeology, Architecture, Design, DIY Crafts, Cookery, Gardening, Natural History, Health, Childcare, Photography, Computers
1981: 3 titles *1982:* 4 titles *Founded:* 1978
ISBN Publisher's Prefix: 0-906459

Linden Press, see Centaur Press Ltd

Lines, an imprint of Macdonald Publishers (Edinburgh) (qv)

Lion Publishing PLC, Icknield Way, Tring, Herts Tel: Tring 5151 (STD code 044 282) Telex: 825850 Lion G
Man Dir: David Vesey; *Editorial:* Pat Alexander; *Rights, International Sales:* Tony Wales, Paul Whitton, Margaret Hutchinson, Colin Nutt; *Marketing Manager:* Mark Beedell
Subsidiary Company: Lion Publishing Corporation (at above address and Michigan, USA)
Imprints: Albatross, Aslan
Subjects: Religion, Reference, Children, Educational Materials
1981: 60 titles *1982:* 60 titles *Founded:* 1972
ISBN Publisher's Prefix: 0-85648

Lions, an imprint of William Collins Sons & Co Ltd (qv)

Litor Publishers, 45 Grand Parade, Brighton, East Sussex BN2 2QA Tel: Brighton 603254 (STD code 0273) Telex: 87369
Dir: Bengt Christiansen
Subject: Children's Books
ISBN Publisher's Prefix: 0-85322

Little Stephen, an imprint of Mencap Publications (qv)

Liveright, an imprint of W W Norton & Co Ltd (qv)

Liverpool University Press, PO Box 147, Liverpool L69 3BX Tel: (051) 709 6022 ext 2429/2512 Cable Add: Cormorant
Chairman of the Board: R G Pearson; *Man Dir, Sales & Promotion:* Mrs R P Campbell
Orders to: The Stonebridge Press, 823-25 Bath Road, Brislington, Bristol BS4 5NU Tel: Bristol 778344 (STD code 0272)
Subjects: Architecture, Archaeology, Oriental Studies, Economics, Education, Philosophy, General & Social Science, Politics, History, Literature, Environmental Sciences, University Textbooks
Founded: 1899
ISBN Publisher's Prefix: 0-85323

Living & Learning (Cambridge) Ltd, Duke St, Wisbech, Cambridgeshire PE13 2AE Tel: Wisbech 63441 (STD code 0945)
Man Dir, Sales, Publicity, Rights & Permissions: Simon J Lyne; *Editorial:* Dennis B Blackmore; *Production:* Paul Beresford
Imprints: L D A (Learning Development Aids)
Subjects: Primary Education, Educational books and materials for children with learning difficulties
1981: 3 titles *1982:* 3 titles *Founded:* 1973
ISBN Publisher's Prefix: 0-905114

Lloyd-Luke (Medical Books) Ltd, 49 Newman St, London W1P 4BX Tel: (01) 580 4255
Man Dir, Editorial, Production, Rights & Permissions: Douglas Luke; *Sales, Publicity:* Susan H Luke
Subject: Medical
1981: 6 titles *1982:* 6 titles *Founded:* 1951
ISBN Publisher's Prefix: 0-85324

Local Heritage Books, a subsidiary company of Countryside Books (qv)

Locomotion Papers, an imprint of Oakwood Press (qv)

Locomotive Publishing Co Ltd, an associate company of Ian Allan Ltd (qv)

Lodenek Press Ltd*, 17 Duke St, Padstow, Cornwall Tel: Padstow 532282 (STD code 0841)
Man Dir, Production, Rights & Permissions: D R Rawe; *Editorial:* H J Ingrey; *Sales:* J E Fennell; *Publicity:* F Dann
Associate Company: Truran Publications, Trewolsta, Trewirgie Hill, Redruth, Cornwall
Subjects: Cornish, West Country and Celtic Books
Bookshop: 17 Duke St, Padstow
Founded: 1970
ISBN Publisher's Prefix: 0-902899

Loeb Classical Library, an imprint of William Heinemann Ltd (qv)

Londinium Press Ltd, 53 High St, Maidstone, Kent ME14 1SY Tel: Maidstone 681034 (STD code 0622)
Dir: C Thyer-Turner
Subsidiary Company: Bachman & Turner (qv)
Subjects: General Reference, Medicine, Tourism
Founded: 1980
ISBN Publisher's Prefix: 0-906264

London Magazine Editions, 30 Thurloe Pl, London SW7 Tel: (01) 589 0618
Man Dir: Alan Ross; *Sales Dir, Rights & Permissions:* Christopher Hawtree
Orders to: Biblios Publishers' Distribution Services Ltd, Glenside Industrial Estate, Star Rd, Partridge Green, Horsham, West Sussex RH13 8RA Tel: Partridge Green 710971 (STD code 0403)
Subsidiary: 'London Magazine' (a monthly review of the contemporary arts)
Subjects: General Fiction, Belles Lettres, Poetry, Biography, Memoirs
Founded: 1965

Longman Group Ltd+, Longman House, Burnt Mill, Harlow, Essex Tel: Harlow 26721 (STD code 0279) Cable Add: Longman Harlow Telex: 81259
Chairman: J Lee; *Chief Exec:* T J Rix; *Sales Dir:* M G P Wymer; *Publicity:* Chris Kirby; *Foreign Rights:* Lynette Owen; *Permissions:* David Lea
Branch Off: 5 Bentinck St, London W1M 5RN
Associate Companies: Longman Cheshire Pty Ltd, Penguin Books Australia Ltd (both Australia qqv); Longman Botswana Ltd, Botswana (qv); Armand Colin-Longman, France (qv); Langenscheidt-Longman GmbH, Federal Republic of Germany (qv); Longman Group (Far East) Ltd, Hong Kong (qv); Longman Italia Srl, Italy (qv); Longman Jamaica Ltd, Jamaica (qv); Longman Kenya Ltd, Kenya (qv); Longman Arab World Center, Lebanon (qv); Longman Lesotho Ltd, Lesotho (qv); Longman Malaysia Sdn Bhd, Malaysia (qv) and Singapore (qv); Longman Nigeria Ltd, Nigeria (qv); Wolters-Noordhoff-Longman BV, Netherlands (qv); Longman Paul Ltd, New Zealand (qv); Maskew Miller Longman (50% owned), Republic of South Africa (qv); Longman Tanzania Ltd, Tanzania (qv); Longman Caribbean (Trinidad) Ltd, Trinidad (qv); Longman Uganda Ltd, Uganda (qv); Allen Lane, UK (qv); Ladybird Books Ltd, UK (qv); Penguin Books Ltd, UK (qv); Longman Inc, 19 West 44th St, New York, NY 10036, USA; Longman Zimbabwe (Pvt) Ltd, Zimbabwe (qv)
Imprints: Churchill Livingstone (qv), Oliver & Boyd (qv), Oyez Longman Ltd (qv), Construction Press (qv), Common Ground, George Godwin Ltd, Francis Hodgson
Subjects: Biography, History, Children's Books, Dictionaries, Sociology, Education, Sciences, Geography, Travel, Educational Books, joint publishers of *York Notes*

1981: 850 titles *Founded:* 1724
ISBN Publisher's Prefixes: 0-582 (Longman), 0-7114 (George Godwin)

Look-In Books, an imprint of Independent Television Books Ltd (qv)

Lorrimer Books, an imprint of L S P Books Ltd (qv)

Louisiana State University Press, see American University Publishers Group Ltd

Peter **Lowe**, an imprint of Eurobook Limited (qv)

Robson **Lowe** Ltd, 10 King St, St James's, London SW1Y 6QX Tel: (01) 839 4034 Cable Add: Stamps London SW1 Telex: 916429
Group Man Dir: Charles Leonard; *Publicity & Advertising:* Peter Collins, Louise Burman
Parent Company: Christies International Group
Branch Offs: The Auction House, 39 Poole Hill, Bournemouth, Dorset BH2 5PX; Robson Lowe International, Via Dell'Orso 7a, 20121 Milan, Italy; Robson Lowe (Bermuda) Ltd, Harrington Sound, PO Box 88, Bermuda
Subjects: Philately, Postal History
1981: 8 titles *Founded:* 1920
ISBN Publisher's Prefix: 0-85397

Lucis Press Ltd, Suite 54, 3 Whitehall Court, London SW1A 2EF Tel: (01) 839 4512
Dirs: Mary Bailey (USA), J J G Bourne, Winifred H Brewin, S I W Nation
Associate Company: The Lucis Publishing Co, 866 United Nations Plaza, Suite 566-7, New York NY 10017, USA
Subjects: Educational, Religious, Sociology, Questions of the Day, Philosophy, Esoteric, Astrology
ISBN Publisher's Prefix: 0-85330

Lund Humphries Publishers Ltd, 26 Litchfield St, London WC2H 9NJ Tel: (01) 836 4243 Cable Add: Lundhumpub London WC2
Parent Company: A Zwemmer Ltd (qv) who also distribute for Lund Humphries
Subjects: Art, Architecture, Graphic Arts, Languages
1981: 9 titles
ISBN Publisher's Prefix: 0-85331

Lutterworth Press, Luke House, Farnham Rd, Guildford, Surrey Tel: Guildford 77536 (STD code 0483) Cable Add: Lutteric Guildford Telex: 858623 Telburg
Man Dir: M E Foxell; *Sales, Publicity Manager:* L J Folkes; *Rights & Permissions:* J Bunn
Subjects: Biography, History, How-to, Music, Reference, Religion, Juveniles, Paperbacks, Antiques, Architecture, Astronomy, General Science, Gardening, Leisure and Craft, Chess, Sport, Travel, Arts
1981: 30 titles *Founded:* 1932
ISBN Publisher's Prefix: 0-7188

Luxor Press Ltd, see Charles Skilton Ltd

Lyle Publications Ltd, Glenmayne, Galashiels, Selkirkshire TD1 3NR Tel: Galashiels 2005 (STD code 0896)
Dirs: T Curtis, Annette Curtis
Subjects: Antiques, Price Guides, Art Reference
ISBN Publisher's Prefix: 0-86248

Lythway Press Ltd*, 93-100 Locksbrook Rd, Bath, Avon BA1 3HB Tel: Bath 331945 (STD code 0225)
Publisher: R H Lewis (to whom all correspondence)
Associate Companies: Chivers Book Sales Ltd; Chivers Press Publishers (qv); Firecrest Publishing Ltd (qv)
Imprint: Lythway Large Print
Subjects: General Fiction, Mystery, Crime, Romance
Founded: 1972
ISBN Publisher's Prefixes: 0-85046, 0-85119

M C B University Press Ltd, 198-200 Keighley Rd, Bradford, West Yorkshire BD9 4JQ Tel: Bradford 499821 (STD code 0274) Telex: 51317
Man Dir: Professor Gordon Wills; *Sales:* Christine Hudson; *Production, Rights & Permissions:* Anne Bennett; *Publicity:* Kathryn Toledano
Branch Off: PO Box 10812, Birmingham, Alabama 35201, USA
Subjects: Professional, Management
Founded: 1969
ISBN Publisher's Prefixes: 0-86176, 0-95440

M E P, an imprint of Mechanical Engineering Publications Ltd (qv)

M I N D (National Association for Mental Health), 22 Harley St, London W1N 2ED Tel: (01) 637 0741
Dir: Christopher Heginbotham; *Editorial:* Janet Manning; *Publicity:* Simon Hebditch
Orders to: MIND Bookshop, 155-57 Woodhouse Lane, Leeds LS2 3EF
Subjects: Mental Health/Illness/Handicap
1981: 7 titles *1982:* 5 titles *Founded:* 1946
ISBN Publisher's Prefix: 0-900557

The **M I T** Press, 126 Buckingham Palace Rd, London SW1W 9SD Tel: (01) 730 9208 Cable Add: Chibooks Telex: 23933 Chibooks Ldn
Sales Manager: Warren Bertram; *Publicity Manager:* Sybil Richardson
Orders to: IBD Ltd, 66 Wood Lane End, Hemel Hempstead, Hertfordshire Tel: Hemel Hempstead 58531 (STD code 0442)
Associate Companies: University of Chicago Press, Harvard University Press (both at above address)
Subjects: Biography, History, Music, Art, Philosophy, Reference, Paperbacks, Architecture, Medicine, Psychology, Engineering, General & Social Science, Education, Linguistics
1982: 140 titles *Founded:* 1932
Miscellaneous: Branch of MIT Press, Cambridge, Mass, USA
ISBN Publisher's Prefix: 0-262

M R P, see Motor Racing Publications Ltd

M T P Press Ltd, Falcon House, Cable St, Lancaster LA1 1PE Tel: Lancaster 68765 (STD code 0524) Telex: 65212
Man Dir: D G T Bloomer; *Sales Dir, Rights & Permissions:* C K Tims; *Managing Editor:* P M Lister; *Production Manager:* M Clark; *Publicity:* M Shaw
Parent Company: Kluwer Group, Netherlands (qv)
Subjects: Medicine, Psychology
1981: 90 titles *1982:* 85 titles *Founded:* 1969
ISBN Publisher's Prefix: 0-85200

M W H London Publishers, 233 Seven Sisters Rd, London N4 2DA Tel: (01) 272 5170 Cable Add: Muslimdar London N4 Telex: 8812176 Muslim G
Man Dir: Ashur A Shamis
Associate Company: Muslim Information Services, UK
Subjects: Islamic and Arabic Studies
Bookshop: At above address
Founded: 1970
Miscellaneous: Formerly Muslim Welfare House
ISBN Publisher's Prefix: 0-906194

Macdonald 3/4/5, an imprint of Macdonald & Co (Publishers) Ltd (qv)

Macdonald & Co (Publishers) Ltd, Maxwell House, 74 Worship St, London EC2A 2EN Tel: (01) 377 4600 Cable Add: Macdon Telex: 885233
Chairman: Robert Maxwell; *Vice-Chairman:* R A Hobbs; *Man Dir:* Timothy Hely-Hutchinson; *Deputy Man Dir:* Ken Pickett, *Marketing & Sales Dir:* Terry Melia; *Editorial:* Clare Chatel (Non-fiction), Susan Fletcher (Fiction & Paperback), Geoffrey Peters (Queen Anne Press), Mary Tapissier (Children's Division); *Production:* Ken Pickett; *Publicity:* Sian Thomas; *Rights & Permissions:* Pat James (UK Rights), Roberta Bailey (Overseas Rights)
Orders to: Purnell Book Centre, Paulton, Bristol BS18 5LQ Tel: Midsomer Norton 413301 (STD code 0761)
Parent Company: BPCC PLC (qv)
Associate Companies: Purnell Books (qv); Macdonald Futura Australia (Pty) Ltd, Australia; Macdonald Purnell (Pty) Ltd, Republic of South Africa (qv)
Imprints: Macdonald Educational, Macdonald Futura, Macdonald Queen Anne Press, Orbit, Parrot Books, Phoebus Publishing Co, Playfair, Troubadour
Subjects: General Fiction and Non-fiction, Children's, Sport, Educational, Adult Illustrated
1981: approx 350 titles *1982:* approx 450 titles *Founded:* 1981 (previously Macdonald & Jane's and Futura Publications (both founded 1973), and Macdonald/Futura (founded 1980))
ISBN Publisher's Prefixes: 0-356 (Macdonald, Macdonald Educational, Queen Anne Press), 0-7088, 0-86007 (Futura), 0-7107 (Troubadour)

Macdonald & Evans Ltd+, Estover Rd, Plymouth, Devon PL6 7PZ Tel: Plymouth 705251 (STD code 0752) Cable Add: MacEvans, Plymouth Telex: 45635
Chairman, Man Dir: R B North; *Editorial:* D A F Sutherland; *Sales:* R F Bayliss (UK), B R W Hulme (Export); *Publicity:* Tessa Chancellor; *Production:* W J Antrobus; *Rights & Permissions:* B R W Hulme
Subsidiary Companies: Macdonald & Evans (Publications) Ltd; Macdonald & Evans Distribution Services Ltd (all at Estover, Plymouth)
Subjects: Commercial, Professional & Business Studies, Dance & Movement, Geography, Language & Literature, Law, Science & Technology, Social Studies
1981: 51 titles *1982:* 52 titles *Founded:* 1907
ISBN Publisher's Prefix: 0-7121

Macdonald Edinburgh, an imprint of Macdonald Publishers (Edinburgh) (qv)

Macdonald Educational, an imprint of Macdonald & Co (Publishers) Ltd (qv)

Macdonald Futura, an imprint of Macdonald & Co (Publishers) Ltd (qv)

Macdonald Guidelines, an imprint of Macdonald & Co (Publishers) Ltd (qv)

Macdonald Publishers (Edinburgh), Edgefield Rd, Loanhead, Midlothian EH20 9SY Tel: (031) 440 0246
Man Dir: Ian McNee; *Publishing Manager, Rights & Permissions:* Sally Morris; *Publicity:* Fiona Morrison; *Sales:* Sarah Stott
Imprints: Lines, Macdonald Edinburgh
Subjects: Biography, Criticism, Fiction, General Non-fiction, Children's Books, Poetry
ISBN Publisher's Prefix: 0-904265

Macdonald Queen Anne Press, an imprint of Macdonald & Co (Publishers) Ltd (qv)

Macdonald Starters, an imprint of Macdonald & Co (Publishers) Ltd (qv)

McGraw-Hill Book Co (UK) Ltd, Shoppenhangers Rd, Maidenhead, Berkshire SL6 2QL Tel: Maidenhead 23431 (STD code 0628) Cable Add: McGrawHill Telex: 848484
Group Vice-President: George F Wallace; *Rights & Permissions:* Lena Armstrong; *Marketing Dir:* Ian Savage
Parent Company: McGraw-Hill Inc, 1221 Ave of the Americas, New York, NY 10020, USA
Associate Companies: McGraw-Hill Book Co Australia Pty Ltd, Australia (qv); McGraw-Hill Ryerson Ltd, Canada; Editora McGraw-Hill do Brasil Ltda, Brazil (qv); Editorial McGraw-Hill Latinoamericana SA, Colombia (qv); McGraw-Hill Book Co GmbH, Federal Republic of Germany (qv); Tata McGraw-Hill Publishing Co Ltd, India (qv); McGraw-Hill Kogakusha Ltd, Japan (qv); Libros McGraw-Hill de Mexico SA de CV, Mexico (qv); McGraw-Hill Book Co, New Zealand, Ltd, New Zealand (qv); Editorial McGraw-Hill Latinoamericana SA, Panama (qv); Editora McGraw-Hill, Portugal (qv); Editorial McGraw-Hill Latinoamericana SA, Puerto Rico (qv); McGraw-Hill International Book Co, Singapore (qv); McGraw-Hill Book Co (SA) (Pty) Ltd, Republic of South Africa (qv); McGraw-Hill Book Co, Switzerland; McGraw-Hill de España SA, Spain (qv)
Subjects: Reference, Medicine, Psychology, Engineering, Computing, General & Social Science, University, Secondary Textbooks, Educational Materials, Gregg Shorthand, Further Education
Founded: 1899
ISBN Publisher's Prefix: 0-07

Grant **McIntyre** Ltd, now incorporated in Basil Blackwell Publisher Ltd (qv)

William **Maclellan** (Embryo) Ltd, 268 Bath St, Glasgow G2 4JR Tel: (041) 332 8507
Imprint: Embryo
Subjects: Art, Folklore, Poetry, Music, Travel, Philosophy, Fiction, Current Affairs
ISBN Publisher's Prefix: 0-85335

Macmillan Children's Books, 4 Little Essex St, London WC2R 3LF Tel: (01) 836 6633 Cable Add: Publish London WC2 Telex: 262024
Publishing Dir: Michael Wace; *Rights:* Sharon Alpe
Subjects: Picture books, Fiction, Non-fiction, Pop-up, Novelty
1983: 60 titles
Miscellaneous: A Division of Macmillan Publishers Ltd (qv)

Macmillan Education Ltd, Houndmills, Basingstoke, Hampshire RG21 2XS Tel: Basingstoke 29242 (STD code 0256) Cable Add: Publish Basingstoke Telex: 858493
Chairman: A Soar; *Man Dir:* J E Jackman; *Publishing Dir:* R S Balkwill (Primary & Secondary Schools Educational Media); *Marketing Dirs:* P Bruce-Gardyne (UK), D Fothergill (Export)
Parent Company: Macmillan Publishers Ltd (qv)
Subjects: Reference, Juveniles, Secondary & Primary Textbooks, Educational Materials
ISBN Publisher's Prefix: 0-333

Macmillan London Ltd, 4 Little Essex St, London WC2R 3LF Tel: (01) 836 6633 Cable Add: Publish London WC2 Telex: 262024
Chairman: N Byam Shaw; *Publisher:* Julian Ashby; *Publishing Dirs:* Lord Hardinge (Crime & Suspense), Nicholas Chapman (Papermac), Michael Alcock, James Hale (Fiction), Michael Wace; *Rights & Permissions:* Mary Pachnos; *Sales Dir:* David Rivers; *Publicity Manager:* Marion Milne; *Production Manager:* Geoffrey Barlow
Parent Company: Macmillan Publishers Ltd (qv)
Imprints: Nautical Books, Papermac
Subjects: General Fiction, Poetry, Biography, History, Natural History, Nautical, Suspense, Art, Reference, Juveniles, High-priced Paperbacks
ISBN Publisher's Prefix: 0-333

The **Macmillan Press** Ltd+, 4 Little Essex St, London WC2R 3LF Tel: (01) 836 6633 Cable Add: Publish London WC2 Telex: 262024
Chairman: A Soar; *Man Dir:* S A Josephs; *Sales:* D Knight (Manager), D Menzies-Kitchin (UK), R Machesney (Export); *Marketing Manager:* P Lewis; *Publishing Dirs:* T M Farmiloe, S Selzer; *Rights Manager:* N Piggot
Parent Company: Macmillan Publishers Ltd (qv)
Subjects: College and University Textbooks, Monographs and Reference Books in Science, Technology, Medicine, Humanities, Social Sciences
ISBN Publisher's Prefix: 0-333

Macmillan Publishers Ltd, 4 Little Essex St, London WC2R 3LF Tel: (01) 836 6633 Cable Add: Publish London WC2 Telex: 262024
Firm is a holding company
Chairman: Alexander D A Macmillan; *Man Dir:* N G Byam Shaw
Orders to: Macmillan Distribution Ltd, Houndmills, Basingstoke, Hants Tel: Basingstoke 29242 (STD code 0256)
Parent Company: Macmillan Ltd
Subsidiaries in the UK: Grove's Dictionaries of Music Ltd; Hospital and Social Service Publications Ltd; Macmillan Education Ltd (qv); Macmillan Journals Ltd; Macmillan London Ltd (qv); The Macmillan Press Ltd (qv); Macmillan Children's Books Ltd (qv); Macmillan Publishers (UK) Ltd; Macmillan Publishers (Overseas) Ltd; Macmillan Publishers Group Administration Ltd; Macmillan Accounts and Administration Ltd; Macmillan Distribution Ltd; Macmillan Information Systems Ltd; The Macmillan Company of Europe Ltd; Globe Book Services Ltd; Macmillan Reference Publications Ltd; Macmillan Schools Ltd; Macmillan Production Ltd; Macaus (UK) Ltd; Macmillan Film Productions Ltd; Pan Books Ltd (qv — one-third owned with William Collins Sons & Co Ltd and William Heinemann Ltd, qqv).
Subsidiaries outside the UK: Artists of Australia, The Macmillan Co of Australia Pty Ltd (qv), Mary Martin Bookshop Pty Ltd (all Australia); Petersen and Macmillan GmbH, Federal Republic of Germany; Macmillan Publishers (HK) Ltd (qv), Peninsula Publishers Ltd (both Hong Kong); Macmillan Shuppan KK, Japan; Macmillan Kenya (Publishers) Ltd, Kenya; Editorial Macmillan de México SA de CV, Mexico; The Macmillan Co of New Zealand Ltd, Mary Martin Bookshop (NZ) Ltd (both New Zealand); Macmillan South East Asia Private Ltd, Singapore (qv); Macmillan Mail (Pty) Ltd, Macmillan South Africa (Publishers) (Pty) Ltd (qv) (both Republic of South Africa); Macmillan Boleswa Publishers (Pty) Ltd (qv), Macmillan Swaziland National Publishing Company Ltd (both Swaziland); Grove's Dictionaries of Music Inc, Melton Peninsula Inc, Nature Publishing Co Inc, St Martin's Press Inc (all USA); Macmillan (Publishers) Zimbabwe (Private) Ltd, Zimbabwe
Associate Companies: Macmillan India Ltd, India (qv); Gill & Macmillan Ltd, Republic of Ireland (qv); Macmillan Nigeria Publishers Ltd, Nigeria (qv); The Northern Nigerian Publishing Co Ltd, Nigeria (qv); The College Press (Pvt) Ltd, Zimbabwe (qv)
Branch Office outside the UK: PO Box 10722, Off Link Rd, Accra, Ghana

Julia **MacRae** Books+, 12a Golden Sq, London W1R 4BA Tel: (01) 437 0713 Telex: 262655 Groluk
Man Dir: Julia MacRae; *Sales Dir:* George Taylor; *Rights & Permissions:* Linda Summers; *Publicity:* Victoria Sackville-West
Associate Company: Franklin Watts Ltd (qv)
Subjects: Juveniles, Picture Books, Music, General
1981: 32 titles *Founded:* 1979
ISBN Publisher's Prefix: 0-86203

Made Simple Books, an imprint of William Heinemann Ltd (qv)

Magna Print Books, Magna House, Long Preston, Skipton, North Yorkshire Tel: Long Preston 225 (STD code 07294)
Man Dir, Production: Derek Cressey; *Sales:* Margaret Cressey
Parent Company: Library Magna Books Ltd
Imprint: Magna Large Print Series
Subjects: Fiction, Non-fiction, Handicrafts & Pastimes in Large Print
1981: 87 titles *1982:* 96 titles *Founded:* 1973
ISBN Publisher's Prefix: 0-86009

Magnet, an imprint of Methuen Paperbacks (qv)

Magnum Books, now incorporated in Methuen Paperbacks (qv)

Mainstream Publishing Co (Edinburgh) Ltd, 25A South Thistle St Lane, Edinburgh EH2 1EN Tel: (031) 225 2804
Dirs: Bill Campbell, Peter Mackenzie, Gordon Brown; *Publicity:* Bill Campbell; *Sales:* Eric Flannigan; *Rights & Permissions:* Peter Mackenzie
Subjects: Literature, History, Current Affairs, Politics, General
1981: 6 titles *Founded:* 1978
ISBN Publisher's Prefix: 0-906391

Malaby Press, an imprint of J M Dent & Sons Ltd (qv)

Mallard Reprints, an imprint of Terence Dalton Ltd (qv)

Manchester University Press+, Oxford Rd, Manchester M13 9PL Tel: (061) 273 5539
Publisher: J M N Spencer; *Editorial:* Ray Offord; *Marketing, Publicity:* Lloyd Spencer; *Production:* Max Nettleton; *Rights & Permissions:* Ms P Williams
Associate Company: Longwood Press, 51 Washington St, Dover, New Hampshire 03820, USA
Subjects: English Language and Literature, Modern Languages, History, Philosophy, Religion, Medicine, Psychology, Engineering, General & Social Science, Economics, Geography, University Textbooks
Founded: 1912
ISBN Publisher's Prefix: 0-7190

Mansell Publishing Ltd, 6 All Saints St, London N1 9RL Tel: (01) 837 6676 Telex: 28604 ref 1647
Man Dir: John E Duncan; *Editorial:* Veronica Higgs, Peter Harrison; *Marketing Dir:* June S Eaton; *Promotion:* Catherine Johnston; *Production:* Grant Shipcott
Parent Company: The H W Wilson Co, 950 University Ave, Bronx, New York, NY 10452, USA
Subjects: Bibliographic Reference
Founded: 1966
ISBN Publisher's Prefix: 0-7201

Manxman Publications, an imprint of Shearwater Press Ltd, Isle of Man (qv)

Map Productions Ltd, see George Philip & Son Ltd

Marcham Books, Appleford, Abingdon, Oxfordshire OX14 4PB Tel: Abingdon 82319 (STD code 0235)
Chief Executive, Editorial, Rights & Permissions: G E Duffield; *Sales, Publicity:* G Elwes; *Production:* E Collie
Associate Companies: Appleford Printers, Appleford Bookroom, E Collie Associates
Branch Off: Isle of Man
Subjects: Religion, History, Sociology, Children
1982: 6 titles *Founded:* 1963

Market House Books Ltd+, Market House, Market Sq, Aylesbury, Bucks HP20 1TN Tel: Aylesbury 84911 (STD code 0296) Telex: 83635
Chairman: A Isaacs; *Dir and Production:* J Daintith
Associate Company: Laurence Urdang Associates Ltd (at above address)
Founded: 1969
Miscellaneous: Firm compiles reference books (dictionaries, encyclopaedias, etc) and provides editorial and computerised typesetting services for publishers

Marshall, an imprint of Frederick Warne (Publishers) Ltd (qv)

G H **Marshall**, Waterside, The Green, Long Itchington, Rugby, Warwickshire CV23 8PH Tel: Southam 4080 (STD code 092681)
Man Dir: G H Marshall
Subjects: Paramedical, Educational
1983: 78 titles *Founded:* 1975
ISBN Publisher's Prefix: 0-86240

Marshall Cavendish Books Ltd, 58 Old Compton St, London W1V 5PA Tel: (01) 734 6710 Cable Add: Marcav London W1 Telex: 23880
Dirs: W D Warburton, P L Edwards, E C P Glaze; *Editorial:* Nicholas Wright; *Sales:* Philip Costick, Nicholas Wright; *Production:* Barry Roberts; *Rights & Permissions:* Philip Costick
Parent Company: Marshall Cavendish Ltd (at above address)
Associate Companies: Marshall Cavendish Partworks Ltd, Marshall Cavendish Children's Books Ltd (both at above address); Marshall Cavendish Schools & Library Division, 142 West Merrick Rd, Freeport, NY 11520, USA
Subjects: Partworks, Reference, General Mass Market
1981: 19 titles *1982:* 11 titles *Founded:* 1968
ISBN Publisher's Prefixes: 0-462, 0-85080, 0-85685

Marshall Editions Ltd+, 71 Eccleston Sq, London SW1V 1PJ Tel: (01) 834 0785 Cable Add: Marsheds Telex: 22847 Marsh G
Man Dir & Editorial: Bruce Marshall; *Dirs:* John Bigg, Candy Lee; *Sales:* Barbara Anderson; *Production:* Barry Baker
Subjects: Highly-illustrated Non-fiction including Cookery, Wine, Sailing, Travel, Wild Life, Photography, Interior Design, Home-making, Medicine, Science, Technology
1981: 6 titles *1982:* 6 titles *Founded:* 1977

Marshall, Morgan & Scott Publications Ltd+, 3 Beggarwood Lane, Basingstoke, Hampshire Tel: Basingstoke 59211 (STD code 0256)
Chairman: William Fitch; *Man Dir:* John Hunt; *Sales, Publicity & Advertising:* Chris Mungeam
Imprints: include Keswick, Lakeland Paperbacks, Oliphants
Subjects: Christian
1982: 80 titles *Founded:* 1859
ISBN Publisher's Prefix: 0-551

Marsland Press, an imprint of Volturna Press (qv)

Martin Books, an imprint of Woodhead-Faulkner (Publishers) Ltd (qv)

Martin Robertson & Co Ltd+, 108 Cowley Rd, Oxford OX4 1JF Tel: Oxford 724041 (STD code 0865) Cable Add: Marcobooks Oxford Telex: 837022
Chief Executive: Michael Hay; *Sales:* Norman Drake; *Production:* Ray Addicott; *Promotion:* Joss Marsh; *Rights & Permissions:* Stella Welford
Orders to: Marston Book Services, PO Box 87, Oxford OX4 1LB Telex: 837022
Parent Company: Basil Blackwell Publishers Ltd (qv)
Subjects: Social Sciences at Degree Level, Sociology, Politics, Public Administration, Economics, Social Policy, Criminology, International Affairs, Women's Studies
1981: 30 titles *1982:* 45 titles *Founded:* 1969
ISBN Publisher's Prefix: 0-85520

Kenneth **Mason** Publications Ltd, The Old Harbourmaster's, 8 North St, Emsworth, Hampshire PO10 7DD Tel: Emsworth 77977 (STD code 02434)
Man Dir: Kenneth Mason
Orders to: J M Dent (Distribution) Ltd, Dunhams Lane, Letchworth, Herts SG6 1LF
Imprint: Handbag Books
Subjects: Nautical, Leisure Activities, Licensing, Slimming Paperbacks
1981: 12 titles *1982:* 14 titles *Founded:* 1958
ISBN Publisher's Prefixes: 0-85937, 0-900534

Mayflower Books Ltd, see Granada Publishing Ltd

Kevin **Mayhew** Ltd, 55 Leigh Rd, Leigh-on-Sea, Essex SS9 1JP Tel: Southend-on-Sea 76425 (STD code 0702)
Man Dir, Editorial, Production: Kevin Mayhew; *Rights & Permissions:* Robert Kelly; *Sales, Publicity:* Anthony P Castle
Subjects: Popular Religious Liturgy, Music, Theology, Educational
1981: 25 titles *1982:* 16 titles *Founded:* 1976
ISBN Publisher's Prefix: 0-905725

Mayhew-McCrimmon Ltd+, 10-12 High St, Great Wakering, Southend-on-Sea, Essex Tel: Southend-on-Sea 218956 (STD code 0702)
Dirs: Donald McCrimmon, Joan McCrimmon, Sylvia McDonald
Associate Companies: Celebration Records; Rainbow Books; House of McCrimmon
Subjects: Religion, Primary & Secondary Textbooks, Educational Materials, Music, Prayer Books, Liturgy, Hymn Books
1982: 150 titles *Founded:* 1968
ISBN Publisher's Prefix: 0-85597

Meadowfield Press Ltd, ISA Bldg, Dale Rd Industrial Estate, Shildon, Co Durham DL4 2QZ Tel: Morpeth 55860 (STD code 0670), Bishop Auckland 773065 (STD code 0388)
Man Dir: J Gordon Cook
Associate Company: Merrow Publishing Co Ltd (qv)
Subjects: Technical, Scientific, Academic

Mechanical Engineering Publications Ltd+, PO Box 24, Northgate Ave, Bury St Edmunds, Suffolk IP32 6BW Tel: Bury St Edmunds 63277 (STD code 0284) Telex: 817376
Publications Dir: Patrick Daley; *Editorial, Rights & Permissions:* Fred Whiteley; *Sales, Publicity:* Peter Williams; *Production:* Peter Batchelor
Imprint: MEP
Subjects: Mechanical Engineering and allied subjects
1981-82: 35 titles *Founded:* 1974
Miscellaneous: Publishers to the Institution of Mechanical Engineers
ISBN Publisher's Prefix: 0-85298

The **Medici** Society Ltd, 34-42 Pentonville Rd, London N1 9HG Tel: (01) 837 7099 Cable Add: Medici N1
Man Dir: J Gurney; *Rights & Permissions, Art Dir:* H B Jane
Subjects: Art, Juveniles
Bookshops: The Medici Galleries, 7 Grafton St, London W1X 3LA; 26 Thurloe St, London SW7 2LT; 63 Bold St, Liverpool L1 4HP
1983: 5 titles *Founded:* 1908
ISBN Publisher's Prefix: 0-85503

Melbourne House (Publishers) Ltd, Glebe Cottage, Glebe House, Station Rd, Cheddington, Leighton Buzzard, Beds LU7 7NA Tel: (01) 405 6347 Telex: 28257 Octabs
Dir & Publisher: Alfred Milgrom; *Marketing Dir, Rights & Permissions:* Naomi Besen; *Sales Dir:* Christine Laugharne; *Publicity Dir:* Linden Loader
Orders to: Noonan Hurst Ltd, 131 Trafalgar Rd, Greenwich, London SE10 9TU
Subjects: General Fiction and Non-fiction, Computers
Founded: 1978
ISBN Publisher's Prefix: 0-86161

Melrose Press Ltd+, 7 Regal Lane, Soham, Ely, Cambs CB7 5BA Tel: Ely 721091 (STD code 0353) Cable Add: Melrospres Ely Telex: 81584
Chief Executive: Dr Ernest Kay; *Editorial:* Joan Doran; *Sales, Publicity, Rights:* Roger W G Curtis; *Production:* Nicholas S Law
Imprint: International Biographical Centre
Subject: Reference
1981: 5 titles *1982:* 7 titles *Founded:* 1969
ISBN Publisher's Prefix: 0-900332

Mencap Publications, Mencap National Centre, 123 Golden Lane, London EC1Y 0RT Tel: (01) 253 9433
Man Dir: Brian Rix CBE; *Editorial, Production, Rights & Permissions:* Mary Bromwich; *Sales:* Peter Pascoe; *Publicity:* Alan Leighton
Parent Company: Royal Society for Mentally Handicapped Children and Adults (at above address)
Imprint: Little Stephen
Subject: Mental Handicap
Bookshop: The Bookshop (at above address)
1981: 8 titles *1982:* 6 titles *Founded:* 1971
ISBN Publisher's Prefix: 0-855

Mercat Press, 53-59 South Bridge, Edinburgh EH1 1YS Tel: (031) 556 6743 Cable Add: Bookman Edinburgh
Joint Man Dirs: James Thin, Ainslie Thin
Parent Company: James Thin Ltd (at above address)
Subsidiary Company: Melven Press (at above address)
Associate Company: Melven Bookshop Ltd, 60 Fountainhall Rd, Edinburgh EH9 2LP
Subjects: Scottish
Bookshops: James Thin Ltd, 53-59 South Bridge, Edinburgh; The Edinburgh Bookshop, 57 George St, Edinburgh; Melven, 29 Union St, Inverness; Melven, 176 High St, Perth; Melven, The Centre, Aviemore
1981: 8 titles *1982:* 4 titles *Founded:* 1970
ISBN Publisher's Prefix: 0-901824

Meresborough Books, 7 Station Rd, Rainham, Gillingham, Kent ME8 7RS Tel: Medway 371591 (STD code 0634)

UNITED KINGDOM 423

Proprietors: Hamish and Barbara Mackay-Miller
Subsidiary Company: Bygone Kent, 5 Meresborough Cotts, Meresborough, Gillingham, Kent ME8 8PP
Imprints: Bygone Kent, Meresborough Books
Subjects: Kent Local History
Bookshop: Rainham Bookshop, 7 Station Rd, Rainham, Gillingham, Kent ME8 7RS
1981: 22 titles *1982:* 12 titles *Founded:* 1977
ISBN Publisher's Prefix: 0-905270

The **Merlin** Press Ltd*, 3 Manchester Rd, London E14 Tel: (01) 987 7959
Man Dir: Martin Eve
Imprint: Seafarer Books
Subjects: History, Economics, Philosophy, Political & Social Science
Founded: 1956
ISBN Publisher's Prefix: 0-85036

Charles E **Merrill** Publishing International, 84 Easton St, High Wycombe, Buckinghamshire HP11 1LT Tel: High Wycombe 22794 (STD code 0494) Telex: 261378
Sales, Advertising, Publicity, Rights & Permissions: Stephen M Smith
Parent Company: Charles E Merrill Publishing Co, 1300 Alum Creek Drive, Columbus, Ohio, USA
Subjects: Education, Educational Psychology, Special Education, Technology, Social Sciences, Business & Economics, Science, Communication & Speech, Mathematics, Multi-media Programmes
1981: 80 titles *Founded:* 1842
ISBN Publisher's Prefix: 0-675

The **Merrion** Press*, 16 Groveway, London SW9 0AR Tel: (01) 735 7791, (01) 733 5173
Dir: Susan Shaw
Subjects: Finely produced books on English Literature, Printing, Calligraphy, Fine Arts
ISBN Publisher's Prefix: 0-903560

Merrow Publishing Co Ltd, ISA Bldg, Dale Rd Industrial Estate, Shildon, Co Durham DL4 2QZ Tel: Morpeth 55860 (STD code 0670), Bishop Auckland 773065 (STD code 0388)
Man Dir: J Gordon Cook
Associate Company: Meadowfield Press Ltd (qv)
Subjects: Technical, Scientific, Academic
ISBN Publisher's Prefixes: 0-900541, 0-904095

Metal Bulletin Books Ltd, Park House, Park Terrace, Worcester Park, Surrey KT4 7HY Tel: (01) 330 4311 Cable Add: Metalbul Worcester Park Telex: 21383 Metbul-G
Man Dir: T J Tarring; *Sales & Advertising Dir:* B R Orbell; *Editorial Dir:* R P Cordero
Branch Offs: 45/46 Lower Marsh, London SE1 7RG; 708 Third Ave, New York, NY 10017, USA
Subjects: Steel and Metal Industries, Industrial Minerals
Founded: 1937

Methodist Publishing House, Wellington Rd, Wimbledon, London SW19 8EU Tel: (01) 947 5256/9 Cable Add: Metodico, London SW19 8EU
General Manager: Albert M Jakeway
Subjects: Methodist Hymn Books and Service Books
Founded: 1733
ISBN Publisher's Prefixes: 0-7150, 0-7162, 0-7192, 0-901027, 0-946550

Methuen & Co Ltd+, 11 New Fetter Lane, London EC4P 4EE Tel: (01) 583 9855 Cable Add: Elegiacs London EC4 Telex: 263398
Man Dir: John Naylor; *Editorial:* Janice Price; *Sales:* Peter Shepherd; *Production:* Carol Somerset; *Promotion:* Linda Casbolt; *Rights & Permissions:* Glenys Thorniley
Orders to: Associated Book Publishers (Services) Ltd, North Way, Andover, Hampshire SP10 5BE Tel: Andover 62141 (STD code 0264)
Parent Company: Firm is incorporated in Associated Book Publishers (UK) Ltd (qv under Associated Book Publishers PLC)
Subjects: Academic
ISBN Publisher's Prefix: 0-416

Methuen Children's Books Ltd, 11 New Fetter Lane, London EC4P 4EE Tel: (01) 583 9855 Cable Add: Elegiacs, London EC4P 4EE Telex: 263398
Chairman: Charles Shirley; *Man Dir:* Marilyn Malin; *Sales, Publicity:* David Ross; *Production:* Christopher Holgate; *Rights & Permissions:* Diane Spivey
Orders to: Associated Book Publishers (Services) Ltd, North Way, Andover, Hampshire SP10 5BE Tel: Andover 62141 (STD code 0264) Cable Add: APT Andover Telex: 47214
Parent Company: Firm is incorporated in Associated Book Publishers (UK) Ltd (qv under Associated Book Publishers PLC)
Imprints: Methuen/Walker Books, Pocket Bears (with Moonlight Publishing Ltd)
Subjects: Juveniles, Fiction & Non-fiction
ISBN Publisher's Prefix: 0-416

Methuen London Ltd, 11 New Fetter Lane, London EC4P 4EE Tel: (01) 583 9855 Cable Add: Elegiacs London EC4 Telex: 263398
Chairman: Christopher Falkus; *Man Dir:* Geoffrey Strachan; *Editorial:* Ann Mansbridge, Nicholas Hern, Elsbeth Lindner; *Marketing Dir:* Charles Shirley; *Promotion Dir:* David Ross; *Rights & Permissions:* Diane Spivey
Parent Company: Firm is incorporated in Associated Book Publishers (UK) Ltd (qv under Associated Book Publishers PLC)
Subjects: General Fiction, Belles Lettres, Poetry, Biography, History, Low- & High-priced Paperbacks, Current & Social Affairs, Plays, Humour, Film
ISBN Publisher's Prefix: 0-413

Methuen Paperbacks, 11 New Fetter Lane, London EC4P 4EE Tel: (01) 583 9855 Cable Add: Elegiacs London EC4 Telex: 263398
Chairman: (Trade Division): Christopher Falkus; *Editorial Dir:* Geoffrey Strachan; *Marketing Dir:* David Ross; *Production Dir:* Chris Holgate; *Art Dir:* Peter Bennet; *Publicity:* David Ross; *Rights & Permissions:* Diane Spivey
Parent Company: Associated Book Publishers PLC (qv)
Imprints: Magnet, Magnum
ISBN Publisher's Prefix: 0-417

Methuen/Walker Books, an imprint of Methuen Children's Books Ltd

Maurice **Michael***, Partridge Green, Horsham, West Sussex Tel: Horsham 710412 (STD code 0403) Cable Add: Bartolo Horsham Telex: 912881 Bartolo
Publisher: Maurice Michael
Subjects: Co-editions, Illustrated Histories: Military, Gardening, Sport, Cookery

Michelin Tyre Co Ltd Maps & Guides Dept, 81 Fulham Rd, London SW3 6RD Tel: (01) 589 1460 Cable Add: Pneumicilin London Telex: 919071
Sales Manager: E G Whiston
Associate Company: Michelin et Cie (Services de Tourisme), France (qv)
Subjects: Guides (Tourist, Hotel & Restaurant), Maps
ISBN Publisher's Prefixes: 0-206, 0-392

Midas Books (Planned Action Ltd), 12 Dene Way, Speldhurst, Tunbridge Wells, Kent TN3 0NX Tel: Langton 2860 (STD code 089286)
Man Dir: Ian Morley-Clarke; *Editorial:* Kathleen Morley-Clarke, William Eden, Robert Hardcastle, Candida Hunt; *Production:* Raymond Green, Eric Hardisty
Subjects: Militaria, Transport, Sport, Biography, Art, Craft Library Series
Founded: 1968
ISBN Publisher's Prefix: 0-85936

J Garnet **Miller** Ltd, 129 St John's Hill, London SW11 1TD Tel: (01) 228 8091
Man Dir: J G F Miller
Orders to: Cressrelles Publishing Co Ltd, 311 Worcester Rd, Malvern, Worcestershire WR14 1AN
Subsidiary Company: Steele's Play Bureau
Subjects: Music, Drama, Juveniles, General Science
Founded: 1951
ISBN Publisher's Prefix: 0-85343

Harvey **Miller** Publishers+, 20 Marryat Rd, London SW19 5BD Tel: (01) 946 4426
Publishers: Mrs Elly Miller, Harvey Miller
Orders to: Oxford University Press Distribution Services, Saxon Way West, Corby, Northamptonshire NN18 9ES Tel: Corby 741519 (STD code 0536)
Subjects: History of Art, Medical Atlases
1981: 3 titles *1982:* 3 titles
Miscellaneous: Publishers of *Courtauld Institute Illustration Archives*
ISBN Publisher's Prefix: 0-19

Millington Books, an imprint of Davison Publishing Ltd (qv)

Mills & Boon Ltd, 15-16 Brook's Mews, London W1A 1DR Tel: (01) 493 8131 Cable Add: Millsator London W1 Telex: 24420
Chairman: John Boon; *Man Dir:* Mark Abbott; *Editorial:* Alan Boon, Horst Bausch, Jacqui Bianchi; *Sales, Marketing:* Ron Hedley (Hardbacks, UK), Ken Kemp (International), Geoff Britton (UK Retail), Susan Boustead (Mail Order); *Production:* Michael Saraceno; *Rights & Permissions:* Deborah Burgess
Orders to: Distribution & Management Services, Sheldon Way, Larkfield, Kent
Subsidiary Company: Mills & Boon Pty Ltd, Suite 404, 282 Victoria Ave, Chatswood, NSW 2067, Australia
Imprints: Mills & Boon (Romantic Fiction), Harlequin (Romantic Fiction)
Subjects: Romantic Fiction
Founded: 1908
Miscellaneous: Firm incorporates Allman & Son (Publishers) Ltd
ISBN Publisher's Prefix: 0-263

The **Minerva** Press Ltd*, 44 Great Russell St, London WC1B 3PA Tel: (01) 580 7200
Subjects: Natural History, Art & Architecture, General Children's Books, Oriental, Travel & Adventure, General Literature
ISBN Publisher's Prefix: 0-85636

Minimax Books Ltd, Broadgate Lane, Deeping St James, Peterborough PE6 8EG Tel: Market Deeping 346709 (STD code 0778) Telex: 32376 Angtel
Man Dir, Editorial: Lynn Green; *Production:* Bob Lavender; *Publicity, Rights & Permissions:* Lynn Green, Bob Lavender
Subjects: Local Interest, Children's, General
1981: 12 titles *1982:* 29 titles *Founded:* 1979
ISBN Publisher's Prefix: 0-906

Mirror Books Ltd, Athene House, 66-73 Shoe Lane, London EC4P 4AB Tel: (01) 353 0246 Cable Add: Mirror London EC1 Telex: 27286

Man Dir: Peter K Robins; *Editorial, Rights & Permissions:* Michael Glover, Anthony Finn; *Production:* Bernard Smith; *Press Officer:* James Hole
Parent Company: Mirror Group Newspapers Ltd
Subjects: General Non-fiction, Specialist Horse Racing
1981: 52 titles *1982:* 55 titles
ISBN Publisher's Prefix: 0-85939

Mitchell Beazley London Ltd, 87-89 Shaftesbury Ave, London W1V 7AD Tel: (01) 439 7211 Telex: 261401
Dir: David Hight; *Publicity:* Helen Hibbert
Parent Company: Mitchell Beazley Ltd
Imprints: Emblem, Artists House
Subjects: General Books, Encyclopaedias, Dictionaries, Atlases, Practical Books, Quality Paperbacks, Pocket Books
1983: approx 50 titles *Founded:* 1969
ISBN Publisher's Prefixes: 0-85533 (Mitchell Beazley), 0-86134 (Artists House)

Model & Allied Publications Ltd, Wolsey House, Wolsey Rd, Hemel Hempstead, Hertfordshire HP2 4SS Tel: Hemel Hempstead 41221 (STD code 0442)
Man Dir: G D L R Home
Subjects: Modelling, Hobbies, Leisure Interests
Miscellaneous: An imprint of Argus Books Ltd (qv)
ISBN Publisher's Prefixes: 0-85076, 0-85242, 0-85344

Modern English Publications Ltd+, PO Box 129, Oxford OX2 8JU Tel: Stow-on-the-Wold 31592 (STD code 0451) Telex: 83147 Via Or
Managing Editor: Susan Holden
Orders to: Marston Book Services, PO Box 87, Oxford OX4 1LB Telex: 837022
Imprint: Roundabout
Subject: Language Teaching
1981: 8 titles *1982:* 3 titles *Founded:* 1976
ISBN Publisher's Prefix: 0-906149

Modern Transport, an imprint of Ian Allan Ltd (qv)

The **Molendinar** Press, now Richard Drew Publishing Ltd (qv)

Monthly Review Press*, 47 The Cut, London SE1 8LL Tel: (01) 261 1354
Publisher: Jules Geller
Subjects: University, Commercial & Technical Education, Politics, Social Science
ISBN Publisher's Prefix: 0-85345

Moonlight Publishing Ltd, 131c Kensington Church St, London W8 7LP Tel: (01) 229 9275
Dirs: Christine Baker, Robin Baker
Orders to: Methuen Books Ltd, ABP (UK) Ltd, North Way, Andover, Hampshire SP10 5BE Tel: Andover 62141 (STD code 0264)
Imprint: Pocket Bears (with Methuen Children's Books Ltd)

Moonraker Press*, 26 St Margarets St, Bradford-on-Avon, Wiltshire Tel: Bradford-on-Avon 3469 (STD code 02216)
Man Dir, Sales, Publicity & Advertising, Rights & Permissions: Anthony Adams
Subjects: Biography, History, Reference
Founded: 1975
ISBN Publisher's Prefix: 0-239

Moorland Publishing Company Ltd, 9-11 Station St, Ashbourne, Derbyshire DE6 1DE Tel: Ashbourne 44486 (STD code 0335)
Editorial Dir, Production: Dr J A Robey; *Sales, Publicity, Rights & Permissions:* J Stepanova
Subjects: History, Geography, General Non-fiction, Railways, Natural History, Architecture, Archaeology, Collecting, Sport
1981: 17 titles *Founded:* 1972
ISBN Publisher's Prefixes: 0-903485, 0-086190

The **Moorlands** Press, see Anne Johnston

Morgan-Grampian Book Publishing Co Ltd, 30 Calderwood St, Woolwich, London SE18 6QH Tel: (01) 855 7777 Cable Add: Industpress London Telex: 896238
Subjects: Reference, Directories
Founded: 1975
ISBN Publisher's Prefix: 0-86213

E J Morten (Publishers), 6 Warburton St, Didsbury, Manchester 20 Tel: (061) 445 7629
Man Dir, Rights & Permissions: Eric Morten; *Sales:* A Blunden; *Publicity:* Jos Pryce
Parent Company: E J Morten (Booksellers) Ltd, 2-10 Warburton St, Didsbury, Manchester 20
Imprints: Datapack Books, Pride Publications
Subjects: Local History
Bookshops: Morten's Bookshops Ltd, Chestergate, Macclesfield
Founded: 1969
ISBN Publisher's Prefix: 0-85972

Motive, an imprint of Allison & Busby Ltd (qv)

Motor Racing Publications Ltd, 28 Devonshire Rd, Chiswick, London W4 2HD Tel: (01) 994 6783
Man Dir, Editorial, Publicity, Rights & Permissions: John Blunsden; *Sales:* Bryan Kennedy; *Production:* Jim Starr
Associate Company: Connoisseur Carbooks (address as above)
Imprint: MRP
Branch Offs: (Editorial and Promotion) 56 Fitzjames Ave, Croydon, Surrey CR0 5DD; (Production) 1530 London Rd, Norbury, London SW16 4EU Tel: (01) 679 7358
Subjects: Motor Racing and Rallying, Racing Car Design, Motoring History including Cars, Trucks and Motorcycles
1982: 10 titles *Founded:* 1948
ISBN Publisher's Prefix: 0-900549

A R Mowbray & Co Ltd, St Thomas House, Becket St, Oxford OX1 1SJ Tel: Oxford 242507 (STD code 0865)
Man Dir: K B Baker; *Sales Dir:* Eva Jesse; *Rights & Permissions:* Rosemary Bourne
Subjects: Christian Religion
Bookshops: 28 Margaret St, Oxford Circus, London W1N 7LB; 14 King's Parade, Cambridge CB2 1SR; St Martins, The Bull Ring, Birmingham B5 5BB
1981: 50 titles *1982:* 60 titles *Founded:* 1858
ISBN Publisher's Prefix: 0-264

Frederick Muller Ltd, Dataday House, 8 Alexandra Rd, London SW19 7JZ Tel: (01) 946 9188 Cable Add: Efmull London SW19 Telex: 928536 Muller Datday G
Joint Man Dirs: Antony White, Anthony Blond; *Publicity:* Susie Guggenheim; *Rights & Permissions:* Hilary Whyte; *Sales:* Century Publishing Co Ltd, 76 Old Compton St, London W1V 5PA Tel: (01) 439 9416
Subsidiary Companies and Imprints: Blond & Briggs Ltd, Blond Educational
Subjects: General, Biography, History, Sport, Reference, Children's, Science & Technology, Fiction, Art, Natural History, Music, Horticulture, Humour
1981: 60 titles *Founded:* 1933
ISBN Publisher's Prefixes: 0-584 (Muller), 0-85634 (Blond & Briggs)

Munch Bunch Books, an imprint of Studio Publications (Ipswich) Ltd (qv)

Thomas **Murby** & Co*, 40 Museum St, London WC1A 1LU Tel: (01) 405 8577 Cable Add: Deucalion, London WC1A 1LU
Orders to: Park Lane, Hemel Hempstead, Hertfordshire HP2 4TE Tel: Hemel Hempstead 3244 (STD code 0442)
Parent Company: George Allen & Unwin (Publishers) Ltd (qv)
Subjects: Technical & Scientific, Geology
ISBN Publisher's Prefix: 0-04

Donald **Murray** (Ramboro Books), 64 Pentonville Rd, London N1 9HD Tel: (01) 837 6301
Subjects: Children's Books, Dictionaries, Art, Cookery
Miscellaneous: Also Remainder Dealers

John **Murray** (Publishers) Ltd, 50 Albemarle St, London W1X 4BD Tel: (01) 493 4361 Cable Add: Guidebook London W1 Telex: 21312 Murray G
Man Dir, Sales Dir: John R Murray; *Editorial:* John G Murray, John R Murray, Duncan McAra, Roger Hudson, Osyth Leeston, Maggie Pringle; *Educational Marketing Dir:* Nick Perren; *Sales Manager:* John Harbour; *Publicity & Advertising:* John Gammons; *Rights & Permissions:* Valerie Ripley
Subjects: General Fiction, Travel, Aviation, Nautical, Poetry, Biography, History, Architecture, Music, Art, Craft, Philosophy, Religion, Reference, Juveniles, Low- & High-priced Paperbacks, General Science, Textbooks, *Easy Readers*, *Success Study Books* series
Founded: 1768
ISBN Publisher's Prefix: 0-7195

Music Sales Ltd, see Book Sales Ltd

Musical Box, an imprint of Zomba Books (qv)

Muslim Welfare House, see M W H London Publishers

N C C Publications+, The National Computing Centre Ltd, Oxford Rd, Manchester M1 7ED Tel: (061) 228 6333 Telex: 668962
Manager: G E Hall; *Publicity:* L Cupitt
Orders to: John Wiley & Sons Ltd, Distribution Centre, Shripney Rd, Bognor Regis, West Sussex PO22 9SA Tel: Bognor Regis 829121 (STD code 0243)
Subjects: Computing and allied subjects
1983: 125 titles *Founded:* 1971
ISBN Publisher's Prefix: 0-85012

N E L, an imprint of New English Library (qv)

The **N F E R-Nelson** Publishing Co Ltd, Darville House, 2 Oxford Rd East, Windsor, Berkshire SL4 1DF Tel: Windsor 58961 (STD code 07535)
Man Dir: Michael Thompson; *Publishing Dir:* Timothy Cornford; *Marketing Dir:* Paul Gardner
Associate Company: Thomas Nelson & Sons Ltd (qv)
Subjects: Education, Special Education, Social Sciences, Psychology, Educational Materials
Founded: 1981
Miscellaneous: A joint venture of the National Foundation for Education Research in England and Wales and Thomas Nelson & Sons Ltd, educational publishers
ISBN Publisher's Prefixes: 0-85633, 0-901225

N K I Educational Services Ltd*, 33 Market Place, Dereham, Norfolk NR19 2AP Tel: Dereham 5710 (STD code 0362)
Man Dir: Alan N Kershaw
Parent Company: NKI Foundation, Norway (qv)
Subjects: Engineering, Technology

Founded: 1980
ISBN Publisher's Prefix: 0-907244

National Christian Education Council, Robert Denholm House, Nutfield, Redhill, Surrey RH1 4HW Tel: Nutfield Ridge 2411 (STD code 073 782)
General Secretary: Rev G R Chapman; *Publicity:* Eric A Thorn
Subjects: Primary, Secondary, Education, Religion, Maps & Atlases, Music, Bible Reading Guides, Pictures, Drama
Subsidiary Companies: Denholm House Press, International Bible Reading Association
1981: 22 titles *1982:* 18 titles
ISBN Publisher's Prefixes: 0-7197 (National Christian Council), 0-85213 (Denholm House)

National Computing Centre, see NCC

National Council for Civil Liberties, 21 Tabard St, London SE1 4LA Tel: (01) 403 3888
Publications Officer: Charles Foster
Subjects: Rights and Civil Liberties, Guides to the Law
1983: 10 titles *Founded:* 1934
ISBN Publisher's Prefixes: 0-901108, 0-946088

National Council for Voluntary Organizations, see Bedford Square Press

National Extension College+, 18 Brooklands Ave, Cambridge CB2 2HN Tel: Cambridge 316644 (STD code 0223)
Executive Dir: Richard Freeman; *Senior Editor:* John Meed; *Assistant Dir, Production, Publicity, Rights & Permissions:* Tim Wheatley
Subject: Educational courses for self-instruction
1981: 25 titles *1982:* 30 titles *Founded:* 1963
ISBN Publisher's Prefix: 0-86082

National Foundation for Educational Research in England & Wales, see NFER

National Magazine Co Ltd, see Ebury Press

National Portrait Gallery (Publications Dept), 2 St Martin's Place, London WC2H 0HE Tel: (01) 930 1552
Head of Publications: Jacob Simon; *Editorial, Production:* Paula Lley; *Publications Manager:* Roger Sheppard; *Rights & Permissions:* Judith Prendergast
Subjects: Art (particularly portraits in the Gallery), Reference
Founded: 1976 (book publishing division)
ISBN Publisher's Prefix: 0-904017

National Trust Children's Series, an imprint of Dinosaur Publications Ltd (qv)

Natural History Museum, see British Museum (National History)

Nautical Books, an imprint of Macmillan London Ltd (qv)

Thomas **Nelson** & Sons Ltd, Nelson House, Mayfield Rd, Walton-on-Thames, Surrey KT12 5PL Tel: Walton-on-Thames 46133 (STD code 09322) Cable Add: Thonelson Walton-on-Thames Telex: 929365 Nelson G
Man Dir: Timothy Sherwen; *Marketing Dir:* G Wright; *Production Dir:* Malcolm Givans; *Rights & Permissions:* Allan Ramsay
Parent Company: Thomas Nelson International, a division of International Thomson Organization Ltd (Canada)
Subsidiary Company: Nelson Filmscan Ltd (video English-language teaching)
Associate Companies: The NFER/Nelson Publishing Co Ltd (qv); Van Nostrand Reinhold (UK) Co Ltd (qv); Thomas Nelson (Nigeria) Ltd, Nigeria (qv)
Subjects: Secondary/Primary/Further Education Textbooks, Educational Materials, English Language Teaching, Books for Caribbean/Africa/South East Asia
1981: 230 titles *Founded:* 1798
ISBN Publisher's Prefix: 0-17

New Cavendish Books, 23 Craven Hill, London W2 Tel: (01) 262 7905
Publisher: Allan Levy
Subjects: Toys (history & collection), Mechanical Antiquities, Models, 19th and 20th Century Art and Technology
Founded: 1973

New Caxton Library Service Ltd, Maxwell House, 74 Worship St, London EC2A 2EN Tel: (01) 377 4600
Parent Company: BPCC PLC (qv)
Subjects: University, Secondary & Primary Textbooks, English Dictionaries, Reference Books, Maps & Atlases, Juveniles, History, Archaeology, Biography & Memoirs, Encyclopaedias
ISBN Publisher's Prefix: 0-903322

New City, London, 57 Twyford Ave, London W3 9PZ Tel: (01) 992 7666
Chairman, Editorial: D Bregant; *Sales, Production, Publicity, Rights & Permissions:* R van Geffen
Parent Company: Città Nuova Editrice, Italy (qv for associate companies)
Subjects: Christian Concerns, Spirituality, Witness, Ecumenism
1981: 2 titles *1982:* 3 titles *Founded:* 1958
ISBN Publisher's Prefix: 0-904287

New Educational Press, an imprint of Riband Books Ltd (qv)

The **New English Library** Ltd, 47 Bedford Sq, London WC1B 3DP Tel: (01) 323 4881 Cable Add: Nelpublish
Editorial Dir: Nick Webb; *Sales Dirs:* J McEwen (Hardcover), Ed Bell (Paperback); *Publicity Manager:* Brian Levy; *Rights & Permissions:* Jane Sinclair
Orders to: Hodder & Stoughton Ltd, Mill Rd, Dunton Green, Sevenoaks, Kent TN13 2YA Tel: Sevenoaks 450111 (STD code 0732)
Parent Company: Hodder & Stoughton Holdings Ltd
Imprint: NEL
Subjects: General Fiction & Non-fiction, Science Fiction, Biography, Paperbacks
Founded: 1957
ISBN Publisher's Prefix: 0-450

New Leaf Publishing Ltd+, BCM – New Leaf, London WC1N 3XX Tel: (01) 435 3056 Telex: 261507 Ref 3228
Man Dir: Michael Wright
Orders to: Patrick Stephens Ltd, Bar Hill, Cambridge CB3 8EL Tel: Crafts Hill 80010 (STD code 0954)
Associate Company: New Leaf Books Ltd (packager, at above address)
Subjects: Photography, Design
Founded: 1982
ISBN Publisher's Prefix: 0-907916

New Left Books, now Verso Editions/NLB (qv)

New Opportunity Press Ltd, 76 St James' Lane, London N10 3RD Tel: (01) 444 7281 Telex: 28604 ref 607
Chairman: R H Begley; *Publishing Dirs:* S L Pullan (New Opportunity Press and Centurion), A N Felix (Nova Communications)
Imprints: Centurion Publications, Nova Communications
Subjects: Careers, Employment, Personnel, Industrial Relations
1982: approx 21 titles *Founded:* 1971
ISBN Publisher's Prefix: 0-86263

New Park Publications Ltd*, 21b Old Town, Clapham, London SW4 0JT Tel: (01) 622 7029
Editorial: Judith White; *Sales:* Waveney Grant
Subjects: Politics, History, Marxism, Biography
Bookshops: Paperbacks Centre, 28 Charlotte St, London W1P 1HP; 10-12 Atlantic Rd, London SW9; 389 Green St, London E13; 96 Magdalen St, Anglia Sq, Norwich; Hope St Book Centre, 321 Hope St, Glasgow G2 3PT; Merseybooks, 34-36 Manchester St, Liverpool L1 6ER
Founded: 1951
ISBN Publisher's Prefixes: 0-902030, 0-86151

New Portway, an imprint of Chivers Press Publishers (qv)

New University Education, an imprint of Clive Bingley Ltd (qv)

Newnes Books, 84-88 The Centre, Feltham, Middlesex TW13 4BH Tel: (01) 844 1177 Telex: 918327 Newnes
Trade Office: Sanders Lodge Industrial Estate, Rushden, Northamptonshire
Chief Executive: Hugh Campbell; *Sales:* Terence Cross; *Publicity:* John Warsany; *Rights & Permissions:* Jill Schmidt
Imprints: Country Life, Collingridge, Temple Press
Subjects: Architecture, Fine and Applied Arts, Natural History, Ornithology and Sport (Country Life), Gardening (Collingridge), Motoring (Temple Press)
ISBN Publisher's Prefix: 0-600

Newnes-Butterworths, an imprint of Butterworth & Co (qv)

Newnes-Technical, an imprint of Butterworth & Co (qv)

Robert **Nicholson** Publications Ltd, 17-21 Conway St, London W1P 5HL Tel: (01) 387 2811
Man Dir: Graham Lane; *Editorial Dir:* Jacqueline Krendel
Parent Company: The Hutchinson Publishing Group Ltd (qv)
Associate Companies: Arrow Books Ltd (qv); Geographia Ltd (qv)
Subjects: Maps, Guides, Atlases
ISBN Publisher's Prefix: 0-905522

Nile & Mackenzie Ltd, 43 Dover St, London W1 Tel: (01) 493 0351 Cable Add: Nilemac Telex: 8954665 Gits G (Nilemac)
Man Dir: D S Sehbai; *Rights & Permissions:* Angela Monfries
Subjects: Reference, Juveniles, Educational Materials
Founded: 1974

James **Nisbet** & Co Ltd, Digswell Pl, Welwyn, Hertfordshire AL8 7SX Tel: Welwyn Garden 25491 (STD code 070 73) Cable Add: Stebsin, Welwyn Garden City
Chairman: G H B McLean
Subjects: Economics, University, Secondary & Primary Textbooks, Education
Founded: 1810
ISBN Publisher's Prefix: 0-7202

The **Nonesuch** Library, see The Bodley Head Ltd

Norfolk Press*, 82 Hurlingham Court, Ranelagh Gdns, London SW6 3UR Tel: (01) 736 0189
Man Dir: Raymond Holdsworth
Orders to: G L Publications, 27 Camden Rd, London NW1 9NL Tel: (01) 267 2346
Subjects: Religion, Philosophy, History, Literature, Outdoor Life
Founded: 1969
ISBN Publisher's Prefix: 0-85211

Northwood Books, 93-99 Goswell Rd, London EC1V 7QA Tel: (01) 253 9355 Telex: 894461 Itp Ln G
Man Dir: Malcolm Gill (International Thomson Publishing Ltd); *Publisher:* Diana Briscoe; *Production:* Desmond Dear
Parent Company: International Thomson Publishing Ltd, Elm House, Elm St, London WC1X 0BP
Subjects: Horology, Gemmology, Precious Metals, Porcelain, Catering and Hotel Management, Building and Construction, Communications, Medicine, Printing, Meat Trades, Agriculture
1981: 14 titles *1982:* 12 titles *Founded:* 1954
ISBN Publisher's Prefix: 0-7198

W W Norton & Co Ltd, 37 Great Russell St, London WC1B 3NU Tel: (01) 323 1579 Cable Add: Gavia London WC1 Telex: 21879 attn Gavia
Man Dir: R A Cameron; *Sales:* Harvey Kesselman; *Publicity:* Julia Wellard
Orders to: John Wiley & Sons Ltd, Distribution Centre, 1 Oldlands Way, Bognor Regis, Sussex PO22 9SA
Associate Company: New Directions (at above address)
Imprint: Liveright
Subjects: History, Biography, Politics, Nautical, Economics, Music, Psychology, English & American Literature, Life Sciences
1981: 100 titles *1982:* 95 titles *Founded:* 1980
ISBN Publisher's Prefix: 0-393

Nova Communications, an imprint of New Opportunity Press Ltd (qv)

Nova Hrvatska Ltd, 30 Fleet St, London EC4Y 1AJ Tel: (01) 947 0498 Telex: 8811204 Nova G
Man Dir: J Kusan; *Sales Dir:* G Saganic
Subjects: Joint publishers with Hrvatska Revija of Munich and Barcelona of: Secondary Textbooks, Educational Materials, Memoirs. Also *Hrvatska Revija* (quarterly literary review), *Nova Hrvatska* (Fortnightly current affairs magazine)
Founded: 1959
Miscellaneous: Publishers of reprinted *Croatian Orthography* and *Croatian Grammar* (Zagreb editions), of original documents from political trials in Yugoslavia (of Croatian historian Dr Franjo Tudjman, economist Dr Marko Veselica and poet Vlado Gotovac) — all sentenced in 1982

Novello & Co Ltd, Borough Green, Sevenoaks, Kent TN15 8DT Tel: Borough Green 883261 (STD code 0732) Cable Add: Novellos Sevenoaks
Man Dir: G Rizza; *Commercial Manager:* C R Flogdell; *Publicity & Advertising Manager:* R H Pritchard; *Rights & Permissions:* B Axcell
Subject: Music

Nutshell Press, a subsidiary of Picton Publishing (Chippenham) Ltd (qv)

Oakwood Press, Tarrant Cottage, Great Hinton, Trowbridge, Wilts BA14 6BY Tel: Keevil 870621 (STD code 0380)
Man Dir: R W Kidner
Orders to: Element Books, The Old Brewery, Tisbury, Salisbury, Wilts
Imprints: Oakwood Library of Railway History, Locomotion Papers
Subjects: Transport History
1981: 11 titles *Founded:* 1934
ISBN Publisher's Prefix: 0-85361

Oasis Books*, 12 Stevenage Rd, London SW6 6ES Tel: (01) 736 5059
Man Dir: Ian Robinson
Subjects: General Fiction, Poetry, Literature, Translations, Periodical *Telegram*
1981: 10 titles *Founded:* 1969
ISBN Publisher's Prefix: 0-903375

The **Octagon** Press Ltd+, 14 Baker St, London W1M 1DA Tel: (089 286) 2045 Cable Add: Octapress London W1
Man Dir: Sally Mallam; *Editorial, Production Manager:* Sonia May; *Sales, Rights & Permissions:* George Schrager; *Publicity:* Robert Gates
Subjects: Philosophy, Religion, Psychology, Sociology, Anthropology
ISBN Publisher's Prefixes: 0-900860, 0-86304

Octopus Books PLC, 59 Grosvenor St, London W1X 9DA Tel: (01) 493 5841 Cable Add: Octobooks Telex: 27278
Chairman: Paul Hamlyn; *Man Dir:* Timothy Clode; *Marketing Dir:* Peggy Singleton; *Rights & Permissions:* Sue Thomson
Imprints: Cathay, Sundial, Heinemann/Octopus, Playtime Press, Robin Books, Treasure, Chancellor, Peerage
Branch Offs: Octopus Pty Ltd, 21st Floor, National Mutual Bldg, 44 Market St, NSW 2000, Australia; Octopus Books Inc, 747 Third Ave, New York, NY 10017, USA
Subjects: Children's Classics, Cookery, Handicrafts, Gardening, Natural History, Militaria, Transport, Entertainment, Art, Antiques, Adult and Children's Fiction
Founded: 1971
ISBN Publisher's Prefixes: 0-7064, 0-86178, 0-915712, 0-904644, 0-906320, 0-904230, 1-85001, 0-86273, 1-85002, 0-907407, 0-907812, 0-907486, 0-907408

Odhams Books, an imprint of Hamlyn Publishing Group Ltd (qv)

John **Offord** (Publications) Ltd, PO Box 64, Eastbourne, East Sussex BN21 3LW Tel: Eastbourne 37841 (STD code 0323)
Man Dir: John Offord; *Editorial:* Nicholas Wood; *Publicity:* Sandy Rowe; *Rights & Permissions:* John Offord, Nicholas Wood
Associate Company: Cooper Harvey Ltd (at above address)
Imprint: City Arts
Subjects: Entertainment and Arts Administration, Reference
1981: 4 titles *Founded:* 1972
ISBN Publisher's Prefix: 0-903931

Ohio University Press, see American University Publishers Group Ltd

The **Oleander** Press, 17 Stansgate Ave, Cambridge CB2 2QZ Tel: Cambridge 244688 (STD code 0223)
Office for USA & Canada: 210 Fifth Ave, New York, NY 10010, USA
Subjects: Middle East & Far East, Cambridge and Cambridgeshire, Arabia, Language & Literature, Libya, Poetry, Drama, Travel, Reference
Founded: 1960
ISBN Publisher's Prefixes: 0-900891, 0-902675, 0-906672

Oliphants, an imprint of Marshall, Morgan & Scott Publications Ltd (qv)

Oliver & Boyd, Robert Stevenson House, 1/3 Baxter's Pl, Edinburgh EH1 3ZB Tel: (031) 556 2424 Cable Add: Almanac Edinburgh Telex: 727511
Man Dir: Roger Watson; *General Manager:* A A Dunnett; *Man Editor:* A Paulin; *Sales Manager & Publicity:* Rhys Edwards
Subjects: Secondary & Primary Textbooks, Educational Materials
Miscellaneous: Firm is a division of Longman Group Ltd (qv)
ISBN Publisher's Prefix: 0-05

Oliver's Guides, an imprint of A P Books/A P Financial Registers Ltd (qv)

Online Publications Ltd, Argyle House, Joel St, Northwood Hills, Middlesex HA6 1TS Tel: Northwood 28211 (STD code 09274) Cable Add: Online Northwood Telex: 923498
Man Dir: Richard Elliot-Green; *Publications Manager:* Rollo Turner
Associate Company: Online Conferences Ltd (at above address)
Subjects: Communications and Computers, Information Technology
1981: 7 titles *Founded:* 1970
ISBN Publisher's Prefix: 0-903796

Open Books Publishing Ltd, West Compton House, Shepton Mallet, Somerset Tel: Pilton 548 (STD code 074 989)
Man Dir: Patrick Taylor
Subjects: Social Sciences, General Non-fiction
Founded: 1974
ISBN Publisher's Prefix: 0-7291

Open University Educational Enterprises Ltd+, 12 Cofferidge Close, Stony Stratford, Milton Keynes MK11 1BY Tel: Milton Keynes 566744 (STD code 0908) Telex: 826147
Man Dir: P S Wright; *Publisher* (Open University Press): John Skelton; *Production Controller:* Bill Pickup; *Marketing Coordinator, Publicity:* Sue Gedney; *Rights Manager:* Joyce Anlezark
Subjects: Arts, Education, Mathematics, Science, Social Science, Technology, Adult Education
1981: 114 titles *1982:* 222 titles *Founded:* 1977
ISBN Publisher's Prefix: 0-335

Optimum, an imprint of The Hamlyn Publishing Group Ltd (qv)

Orbis Publishing Ltd, 20-22 Bedfordbury, London WC2N 4BT Tel: (01) 379 6711 Cable Add: Orbooks London WC2 Telex: 22725
Man Dir: Martin Heller; *Editorial:* John Mason; *Sales:* Geoffrey Howard; *Production:* Jan Williams; *Publicity:* Rosanna Bortoli; *Rights & Permissions:* Charles Merullo
Subjects: Ancient History and Archaeology, Architecture, Aviation, Cookery, Educational, English Literature, Fine Arts, Gardening, General Non-fiction, Military History, Motoring, Nautical, Ornithology, Practical Crafts, Sociology, How-to, Music, Reference, Juveniles, Medicine, General Science, Natural History
1981: 42 titles
ISBN Publisher's Prefix: 0-85613

Orbit, an imprint of Macdonald & Co (Publishers) Ltd (qv)

Ordnance Survey, British Government Map Publishers, Romsey Rd, Maybush, Southampton SO9 4DH Tel: Southampton 775555 (STD code 0703) ext 305 Cable Add: Ordsurvey, Southampton
Deputy Dir: Allan Marles; *Publishing Manager:* Mrs S J Page
Subject: Maps

Oriel Press Ltd, Stocksfield Studio, Branch End, Stocksfield, Northumberland NE43 7NA Tel: Stocksfield 3065 (STD code 06615)
Man Dir: Bruce Allsopp; *Sales Manager:* David O'Connor
Orders to: Routledge & Kegan Paul PLC (qv)
Parent Company: Routledge & Kegan Paul PLC (qv)
Subjects: Religious, Technical & Scientific, Reference Books, Art & Architecture, History, Archaeology, Biography & Memoirs, Politics, Political Economy,

Sociology, Questions of the Day, Philosophy, Oriental, Directories & Guidebooks
ISBN Publisher's Prefix: 0-85362

Oriental Textile Press Ltd, an imprint of Antique Collectors' Club (qv)

Osprey Publishing Ltd+, 12-14 Long Acre, London WC2E 9LP Tel: (01) 836 7863 Cable Add: Philip London WC2 Telex: 21667
Man Dir: M A Bovill; *Export Sales Manager:* Marilyn Wheeler; *Editorial Dir, Rights & Permissions:* Tim Parker; *Marketing Manager:* Alan Greene
Associate Company: George Philip & Son Ltd (qv)
Subjects: History, Militaria, Motoring, Aviation, Reference
ISBN Publisher's Prefix: 0-85045

Overseas Publications Interchange Ltd*, 40 Elsham Rd, London W14 8HB Tel: (01) 994 4723
Subjects: Publish and distribute books in Russian and East European languages — especially Soviet and Polish dissident literature

Peter **Owen** Ltd, 73 Kenway Rd, London SW5 0RE Tel: (01) 373 5628, (01) 370 6093
Man Dir, Sales & Advertising, Publicity, Rights & Permissions: Peter Owen
Subjects: General Fiction, Belles Lettres, Biography, Music, Art, Sociology
Founded: 1950
ISBN Publisher's Prefix: 0-7206

Oxfam, 274 Banbury Rd, Oxford OX2 7DZ Tel: Oxford 56777 (STD code 0865) Cable Add: Oxfam Oxford Telex: 83610
Director-General: Brian W Walker; *Publications Officer:* Suzanne Blumhardt
Imprint: Oxfam Public Affairs Unit
Subjects: Poverty, Third World Development and Appropriate Technology
1981: 5 titles *1982:* 4 titles *Founded:* 1942
ISBN Publisher's Prefix: 0-85598

Oxfam Public Affairs Unit, an imprint of Oxfam (qv)

Oxford Illustrated Press Ltd+, Sparkford, Yeovil, Somerset BA22 7JJ Tel: North Cadbury 40635 (STD code 0963) Telex: 46212
Editorial Office: Little Holcombe, Stag Lane, Newington, Oxford OX9 8AJ Tel: Oxford 890026 (STD code 0865)
Chairman: John H Haynes; *Man Dir:* Jim Scott; *Editorial Dir:* Jane Marshall; *Sales Dir:* Andy Lynch; *Production Dir:* Roger Stagg
Parent Company: Haynes Publishing Group PLC (qv for associate companies)
Subjects: Illustrated Leisure, Travel Guides, Sport, Transport, Art, Gardening, Cookery
ISBN Publisher's Prefix: 0-902280

Oxford Microform Publications Ltd, 19A Paradise St, Oxford OX1 1LD Tel: Oxford 246252 (STD code 0865) Telex: 83649
Chairman: Peter Ashby; *Publisher:* Tony Sloggett; *Production:* Henry Mumford-Smith
Subsidiary Company: Oxford Microform & Publishing Services Ltd
Subjects: Scholarly & Scientific Journals, Research, Collections, Serial Publications in Economics, Colour Microfiche in Art, Science, Humanities, Bibliography
ISBN Publisher's Prefix: 0-904735

Oxford Polytechnic Press, Oxford Polytechnic, Gipsy Lane, Headington, Oxford OX3 0BP Tel: Oxford 64777 (STD code 0865) Cable Add: Polypress Oxford
Chief Executive: Keith Vaughan; *Editorial,*

Rights & Permissions: Laura Cohn
Subjects: General
1982: 2 titles *Founded:* 1972
ISBN Publisher's Prefix: 0-902692

Oxford Railway Publishing Co Ltd, Link House, West St, Poole, Dorset BH15 1LL Tel: Poole 671171 (STD code 0202) Cable Add: Blandpress Poole Telex: 418304
Chairman, Chief Executive: R B Erven; *Sales Dir:* C P Lloyd; *Production Manager:* G L Charters; *Rights & Permissions:* A J Kearley
Parent Company: Link House Publications Ltd (at above address)
Subjects: Railways and Transport
Bookshops: The Railway Book Centre, 8 The Roundway, Headington, Oxford; The Railway Book & Model Centre, 302 Holdenhurst Rd, Bournemouth
ISBN Publisher's Prefixes: 0-902888, 0-86093

Oxford University Press, Walton St, Oxford OX2 6DP Tel: Oxford 56767 (STD code 0865) Cable Add: Clarendon Press Oxford Telex: (Clarpress) 837330
Secretary to the Delegates and Chief Executive: G B Richardson; *Academic and General Publisher:* R A Denniston; *Educational Publisher:* M A Morrow; *Sales and Marketing:* S W H Wratten; *Rights & Permissions:* Anthony Mulgan
Orders to: OUP Distribution Services, Saxon Way West, Corby, Northamptonshire NN18 9ES Tel: Corby 741519 (STD code 0536)
London Off and Music Departments: Ely House, 37 Dover St, London W1X 4AH Tel: (01) 629 8494
Associate Companies: Cornelsen und Oxford University Press GmbH, Federal Republic of Germany (qv); University Press Ltd, Nigeria (qv)
Branch Offs: Oxford University Press, Australia (qv); Oxford University Press, 70 Wynford Dr, Don Mills 403, Toronto, Ontario, Canada; Oxford University Press, Hong Kong (qv); Oxford University Press, India (qv); Oxford University Press, P T Pustaka Ilmu, Jalan Kebong Kacang XII/23, Jakarta Pusat, Indonesia; Oxford University Press KK, Enshu Bldg, 3-3 Otsuka, 3-chome, Bunkyo-ku, Tokyo, Japan; Oxford University Press East and Central Africa, Kenya (qv); Oxford University Press, Malaysia (qv); Oxford University Press, New Zealand (qv); Oxford University Press, Pakistan (qv); Oxford University Press, Singapore (qv); Oxford University Press Southern Africa, Republic of South Africa (qv); Oxford University Press, Tanzania (qv); Oxford University Press, c/o Intersaf Co Ltd, 140 Wireless Rd, 12th Floor, Shell House, Bangkok, Thailand; Oxford University Press, 2-3 Stafford St, Glasgow G4 0HA, UK; Oxford University Press, 200 Madison Ave, New York, NY 10016, USA; Oxford University Press East Africa, Zimbabwe (qv)
Subjects: Belles Lettres, Poetry, Biography, History, English Language Teaching, Music, Art, Classics, Language, Law, Philosophy, Reference, Bibles, Religion, Juveniles, Paperbacks, Medicine, Psychology, Engineering, General & Social Science, Atlases, University, Secondary & Primary Textbooks, Educational Materials, Journals
1982: 1,273 titles *Founded:* 1478
ISBN Publisher's Prefix: 0-19

Oyez Longman Publishing Ltd, 21-27 Lamb's Conduit St, London WC1N 3NJ Tel: (01) 242 2548
Man Dir: Julian Platt; *Sales, Publicity Manager:* Mike Deasy
Orders to: Longman Group, Pinnacles, Fourth Ave, Harlow, Essex CM19 5AA

Subjects: Law, Tax, Commercial & Professional
1981: 250 titles *1982:* 226 titles
Miscellaneous: Firm is a division of Longman Group Ltd (qv)
ISBN Publisher's Prefixes: 0-85120, 0-85121

P S G, an imprint of John Wright & Sons Ltd (qv)

Packard Publishing Ltd+, 16 Lynch Down, Funtington, Chichester, West Sussex PO18 9LR Tel: West Ashling 621 (STD code 024 358)
Man Dir: Michael Packard
Subjects: Biology, Conservation, Landscape Architecture, Planning, Applicable Mathematics, Education
1981: 2 titles *Founded:* 1977
ISBN Publisher's Prefix: 0-906527

Paintaway, an imprint of Ramboro Enterprises Ltd (qv)

Paladin Books, see Granada Publishing Ltd

Pan Books Ltd, 18/21 Cavaye Pl, London SW10 9PG Tel: (01) 373 6070 Cable Add: Pandition London Telex: 917466
Warehouse: Houndmills, Basingstoke, Hampshire
Man Dir: S H Master; *Deputy Man Dir:* T W V McMullan; *Sales Dirs:* R J Williams (Home), N S Potts (Export); *Publicity Dir:* M Cheyne; *Editorial Dir:* A S Mehta
Parent Companies: William Collins Sons & Co Ltd, William Heinemann Ltd, Macmillan Publishers Ltd (qqv — each one-third owners)
Subsidiary Company: Pan Books (Australia) Pty Ltd, Australia (qv)
Imprints: Brodies Notes, Pan, Pavanne, Picador, Piccolo, Study Aids
Subjects: Low-priced Paperbacks, General Fiction & Non-fiction
Founded: 1947
ISBN Publisher's Prefix: 0-330 (Pan)

Panther Books Ltd, see Granada Publishing Ltd

Paper Tiger, an imprint of Dragon's World Ltd (qv)

Paperfronts, an imprint of Elliot Right Way Books (qv)

Papermac, an imprint of Macmillan London Ltd (qv)

Walter **Parrish** Ltd, see Adkinson Parrish Ltd

Parrot Books, a Futura imprint of Macdonald & Co (Publishers) Ltd (qv)

The **Paternoster** Press Ltd, Paternoster House, 3 Mount Radford Crescent, Exeter, Devon EX2 4JW Tel: Exeter 50631 (STD Code 0392)
Chairman and Man Dir: Jeremy H L Mudditt; *Editorial, Rights and Permissions:* P E Cousins; *Sales, Publicity, Advertising:* Jeremy H L Mudditt
Subjects: History, Philosophy, Religion, Paperbacks
Founded: 1934
ISBN Publisher's Prefix: 0-85364

Stanley **Paul** & Co Ltd, an imprint of Hutchinson Books Ltd (qv)

Pavanne, an imprint of Pan Books Ltd (qv)

Pavilion Books, see Michael Joseph Ltd

Pearson, an imprint of The Hamlyn Publishing Group Ltd (qv)

Peerage, an imprint of Octopus Books PLC (qv)

Pelham Books Ltd, 44 Bedford Sq, London WC1B 3DU Tel: (01) 323 3200 Cable Add: Emjaybuks London WC1 Telex: 21322

Publisher and Sales Dir: R Douglas-Boyd; *Publicity & Advertising:* Sally Partington; *Rights & Permissions:* Sarah Fulford
Associate Company: Michael Joseph Ltd (qv)
Subjects: Sports, Crafts, Biography, How-to, Reference, Juveniles
1981: 78 titles
Miscellaneous: Company is a member of the Thomson Books Ltd group (qv), a part of International Thomson Organization Ltd (Canada)
ISBN Publisher's Prefix: 0-7207

Pelican, an imprint of Penguin Books Ltd (qv)

Pemberton Publishing Co Ltd*, 88 Islington High St, London N1 8EN Tel: (01) 226 7251 Cable Add: Ratiopres London N1 4EN
Managing Editor, Rights & Permissions: Nicolas Walter
Parent Company: Rationalist Press Association (at above address)
Subjects: Philosophy, Religion, Low-priced Paperbacks, Psychology, General & Social Science, University Textbooks
Founded: 1960
ISBN Publisher's Prefix: 0-301

Penguin Books Ltd, 536 King's Rd, London SW10 0UH Tel: (01) 351 2393 Cable Add: Penguinook SW10 Telex: 263130 Penbok G
Warehouse & Accounts: Bath Rd, Harmondsworth, West Drayton, Middlesex UB7 0DA Tel: (01) 759 1984 Cable Add: Penguinook West Drayton Telex: 263130
Chairman: James Lee; *Vice-Chairman:* R J E Blass; *Chief Executive:* P Mayer; *Editorial Dir:* Peter Carson; *Development Dir:* John Hitchin; *Sales, Marketing:* Patrick Wright; *Publicity:* Dotti Irving; *Rights & Permissions:* Carol Heaton; *Press Officer:* Jenny Wilford
Parent Company: Pearson Longman Ltd, Millbank Tower, Millbank, London SW1P 4QZ
Associate Companies: Longman Group Ltd (qv); Ladybird Books Ltd (qv); Viking Penguin Inc, 40 West 23 St, New York, NY 10010, USA
Subsidiary Companies: Penguin Books Australia Ltd, Australia (qv); Penguin Books Canada Ltd, 2801 John St, Markham, Ontario L3R 1B4, Canada; Penguin Books New Zealand Ltd, New Zealand (qv); Frederick Warne (Publishers) Ltd, UK (qv)
Imprints: Allen Lane (qv), Kestrel Books (qv) (both hardcover); others include Pelican Books, Peregrine Books, Puffin Books
Book Clubs: Puffin Book Club; Junior Puffin Club
Subjects: Low- & High-priced Paperbacks (General Fiction, General Non-fiction, Juveniles, Technical, Educational)
Bookshops: Penguin Bookshops at: Covent Garden, London WC2; Liberty's, Regent St, London WC1; 10 King St, Richmond, Surrey
1981: 400 titles *Founded:* 1935
ISBN Publisher's Prefixes: 0-14 (Penguin), 0-7139 (Allen Lane), 0-7226 (Kestrel)

Pennsylvania State University Press, see American University Publishers Group Ltd

Pentos PLC, New Bond Street House, 1-5 New Bond St, London W1Y 0SB Tel: (01) 499 3484 Telex: 24544 Pentos G
Firm is (non-publishing) ultimate holding company of group of subsidiaries owned by (non-publishing) Pentos Publishing Group Ltd and Pentos Bookselling Group Ltd
Publishing members: Ward Lock Ltd (qv); Athena Reproductions Ltd

The company owns Dillon's University Bookshop, UK and Hodges Figgis & Co Ltd, Republic of Ireland (qqv under Major Booksellers), also Sisson & Parker Ltd (UK)

Peregrine Books, an imprint of Penguin Books Ltd (qv)

Ediciones **Peregrino**, an imprint of Evangelical Press and Services Ltd (qv)

Peter **Peregrinus**, see Peter

Pergamon Press Ltd, Headington Hill Hall, Oxford OX3 0BW Tel: Oxford 64881 (STD code 0865) Cable Add: Pergapress Telex: 83177
Chairman & Publisher: I R Maxwell; *Joint Man Dirs:* G F Richards, R Hobbs; *Sales, Manager:* J G Ennals; *Marketing Dir:* W Snyder; *Rights & Permissions:* Anna Moon
Associate and Subsidiary Companies: The Aberdeen University Press Ltd, UK; E J Arnold & Son Ltd, UK (qv); BPCC PLC, UK (qv); Pergamon Infotech Ltd, UK; Pergamon Press (Australia) Pty Ltd, Australia (qv); Pergamon Press Canada Ltd, Toronto, Canada; Pergamon Press Sàrl, Paris, France; Pergamon Press GmbH, Kronberg, Federal Republic of Germany; Bumpus, Haldane & Maxwell, UK; Pergamon Press Inc, Elmsford, New York, USA
Imprints include: Brasseys Publishers Ltd
Subjects: Philosophy, Religion, Music, Art, Biography, History, General Science, Life Sciences & Medicine, Veterinary Sciences, Physical Sciences, Engineering, Psychology, Social & Behavioural Sciences and Liberal Arts, Business Management, Secondary & University Textbooks, Educational Materials
Founded: 1949
ISBN Publisher's Prefix: 0-08

Permanent Press, 52 Cascade Ave, London N10 Tel: (01) 444 8591
Man Dir: Robert Vas Dias
Branch Off: 1040 Park Ave, New York, NY 10028, USA
Subject: Poetry
Founded: 1972
ISBN Publisher's Prefix: 0-905258

Peter **Peregrinus** Ltd, an imprint of The Institution of Electrical Engineers (qv)

The **Phaethon** Press, Aquila/The Phaethon Press – an imprint of Johnston Green & Co (Publishers) Ltd (qv)

Phaidon Press Ltd+, Littlegate House, St Ebbe's St, Oxford OX1 1SQ Tel: Oxford 246681 (STD code 0865) Cable Add: Phaidon Oxford Telex: 83308
Chairman: George Riches; *Man Dir:* Derek Philips; *Editorial Dirs:* Simon Haviland, Jean-Claude Peissel; *Production Dir:* Alan Peebles; *Marketing Dir:* Geoff Cowen; *Rights & Permissions:* Ed Glover, Betty Lin
Orders to: Unit B, Ridgeway Trading Estate, Iver, Buckinghamshire
Associate Companies: Equinox (Oxford) Ltd (qv), Phaidon & Christie's Ltd
Subjects: Art, Art History, Applied and Performing Arts
1982: 32 titles *Founded:* 1923
ISBN Publisher's Prefix: 0-7148

George **Philip & Son** Ltd, 12-14 Long Acre, London WC2E 9LP Tel: (01) 836 7863 Telex: 21667
Orders to: Lineside Industrial Estate, Littlehampton, West Sussex
Man Dir, Rights & Permissions: M A Bovill; *Export Sales Manager:* Marilyn Wheeler; *Marketing Manager:* Alan Greene
Associate Companies: George Philip Printers; E Stanford Ltd; Stanford Maritime Ltd (qv); Map Productions Ltd; Osprey Publishing Ltd (qv)
Subjects: Atlases and Maps, Textbooks,

Educational Materials, Maritime, Militaria, Motoring, General
Founded: 1834
ISBN Publisher's Prefix: 0-540

Philip & Tacey Ltd, see Philograph Publications Ltd

Phillimore & Co Ltd, Shopwyke Hall, Chichester, West Sussex PO20 6BQ Tel: Chichester 787636 (STD code 0243) Cable Add: Phillimore Chichester
Honorary President: Lord Darwen; *Chairman & Man Dir:* Philip Harris; *Editorial Dir:* Noel H Osborne
Subsidiary Company: Darwen Finlayson Ltd (qv)
Subjects: History, Historical Biography, Architectural History, Archaeology, Genealogy, Heraldry
Bookshop: The Phillimore Bookshop, Shopwyke Hall, Chichester
Founded: 1875 (incorporated: 1897)
ISBN Publisher's Prefixes: 0-900592, 0-85033

Philograph Publications Ltd*, North Way, Andover, Hampshire SP10 5BA Tel: Andover 61171 (STD code 0264) Telex: 47496
Man Dir: Jon Tacey
Associate Company: Philip & Tacey Ltd, Andover
Subjects: Primary Education, Teaching Aids
ISBN Publisher's Prefix: 0-85370

Phoebus Publishing Co, an imprint of Macdonald & Co (Publishers) Ltd (qv)

Piatkus Books, 17 Brook Rd, Loughton, Essex Tel: (01) 508 7362 Telex: 21667
Man Dir: Judy Piatkus; *Editorial Dir:* Gill Cormode; *Sales & Publicity Dir:* Philip Cotterell
Orders to: George Philip Services Ltd, PO Box 1, Littlehampton, West Sussex BN17 7EN Tel: Littlehampton 7453 (STD code 09064)
Parent Company: Judy Piatkus (Publishers) Ltd (address as above)
Subjects: Fiction, Cookery, Leisure, Arts, History, Biography, Humour
1981: 53 titles *1982:* 63 titles *Founded:* 1979
ISBN Publisher's Prefix: 0-86188

Picador, an imprint of Pan Books Ltd (qv)

Piccolo, an imprint of Pan Books Ltd (qv)

Pickering & Inglis Ltd, 3 Beggarwood Lane, Basingstoke, Hampshire RG23 7LP Tel: Basingstoke 59211 (STD code 0256) Telex: 858066
Man Dir: Nicholas Gray; *Production Dir:* Jim Girling
Orders to: Unit 3, Kempshott Industrial Estate, Basingstoke, Hampshire RG23 7LP Tel: Basingstoke 59211 (STD code 0256)
Subsidiary Companies: R L Allan & Son (Publishers) Ltd; A McLay & Co Ltd, St Fagans Rd, Fairwater, Cardiff CF5 3XB (Printers)
Subjects: Religion, Juveniles
Bookshop: 26 Bothwell St, Glasgow G2 6PA
1981: 30 titles *1982:* 40 titles *Founded:* 1870
ISBN Publisher's Prefix: 0-7208

Picton Publishing (Chippenham) Ltd+, Citadel Works, Bath Rd, Chippenham, Wiltshire SN15 2AB Tel: Chippenham 650391 (STD code 0249) Cable Add: Pictonchip
Chief Executive, Sales, Publicity, Rights & Permissions: D B Picton-Phillips; *Editorial:* M Wicks; *Production:* A P Hayter
Subsidiary Companies: Barebones Books (basic scholastic), The Military Chest (magazine), Nutshell Press (RAF series)
Subjects: Philately, Thematic, Theatre, Military
Bookshop: The Military Chest, Goose St,

UNITED KINGDOM 429

Beckington, Nr Bath, Somerset
1981: 10 titles *1982:* 10 titles *Founded:* 1972
ISBN Publisher's Prefix: 0-902633

Picture Lions, an imprint of William Collins Sons & Co Ltd (qv)

Frances **Pinter** Ltd+, 5 Dryden St, Covent Garden, London WC2E 9NW Tel: (01) 240 2430 Telex: 299533
Chief Executive, Editorial: Frances Pinter; *Sales Dir:* Pamela Fulton
Orders to: Marston Book Services, PO Box 87, Oxford OX4 1LB Tel: Oxford 724041 (STD code 0865)
Subjects: International Relations, Political Economy, Social Policy, Socio-legal Studies, Technology
1982: 51 titles
ISBN Publisher's Prefixes: 0-903804, 0-86187

Pitkin Pictorials Ltd*, 11 Wyfold Rd, London SW6 6SG Tel: (01) 385 4351 Cable Add: Pitkins London SW6
Subjects: Architectural History, and Guides for the Tourist Industry
ISBN Publisher's Prefix: 0-85372

Pitman Publishing Ltd+, 128 Long Acre, London WC2E 9AN Tel: (01) 379 7383 Cable Add: Ipandsons London WC2 Telex: 261367
Chairman: Nicolas Thompson; *Man Dir:* Stephen Neal; *Editorial Dir:* Navin Sullivan; *Sales Dir:* Neill Ross; *Distribution Dir:* Jim Johnson; *Export Dir:* Ian Pringle; *Home Sales Dir:* Kenneth Welhan; *Production Dir:* Alan Smith; *Promotion:* Alick Kitchin; *Rights & Permissions:* Veronica Sahiby
Orders to: Pitman Books, Slaidburn Crescent, Fylde Rd, Southport, Merseyside PR9 9YF
Parent Company: Pitman PLC, 6 Southampton Pl, London WC1A 2DQ Tel: (01) 405 2177
Associate Companies & Branch Offs: Pitman Publishing Pty Ltd, Australia (qv); Copp Clark Pitman Publishing Co, 517 Wellington St West, Toronto M5V 1G1, Ontario, Canada; Pitman Publishing New Zealand Ltd, New Zealand (qv); Pitman Pte Ltd, Tannery Block, Ruby Industrial Complex, 35 Tannery Rd 04-03, Singapore 1334, Republic of Singapore; Pitman Publishing Co SA (Pty) Ltd, Republic of South Africa (qv); Pitman Learning Inc, 6 Davis Dr, Belmont, California 94002, USA; Pitman Publishing Inc, 1020 Plain St, Marshfield, Massachusetts 02050, USA
Subjects: Scientific & Technical Textbooks and Professional/Reference, Medical, Business/Management, Secretarial/Commercial Studies
ISBN Publisher's Prefixes: 0-272, 0-273

Plain Edition, an imprint of Brilliance Books (qv)

Playfair, an imprint of Macdonald & Co (Publishers) Ltd (qv)

Playtime Press, an imprint of Octopus Books PLC (qv)

Plexus Publishing Ltd, 30 Craven St, London WC2N 5NT Tel: (01) 839 1315 Telex: 261234 Ref H599IC
Sales, Production: Terence Porter; *Editorial, Publicity, Rights & Permissions:* Sandra Wake, Nicola Hayden
Orders to: J M Dent & Sons (Distribution) Ltd, Dunhams Lane, Letchworth, Hertfordshire SG6 1LF Tel: Letchworth 6241 (STD code 04626)
Subjects: Illustrated Books on Film, Rock, Folk, Biography, Popular Culture and Art
Founded: 1973
ISBN Publisher's Prefix: 0-85965

Plough Publishing House, Darvell, Robertsbridge, East Sussex TN32 5DR Tel: Robertsbridge 880626 (STD code 0580) Telex: 957493 Coplay G
Man Dir, Rights & Permissions: Peter P Cavanna; *Sales, Publicity & Advertising Dir:* Mrs Cavanna
Subjects: Biography, Reference, Religion, Juveniles
Founded: 1937
Miscellaneous: Firm is the publishing house of the Hutterian Society of Brothers
ISBN Publisher's Prefix: 0-87486

Pluto Press, The Works, 105A Torriano Ave, London NW5 2RX Tel: (01) 482 1973 Cable Add: Plutonic Telex: Pluto 21879/25247
Man Dir: Nina Kidron; *Editorial:* Richard Kuper; *Sales:* Ric Sissons; *Production:* David Williams; *Rights & Permissions:* Jane Gregory
Subjects: Current Affairs, Politics, Social Sciences, Low- & High-priced Paperbacks, Popular Culture, Biography, History, Workers' Handbooks, Plays, Literature
1981: 32 titles *1982:* 35 titles *Founded:* 1971
ISBN Publisher's Prefixes: 0-902818, 0-904383, 0-86104

Pocket Bears, a joint imprint of Methuen Children's Books Ltd and Moonlight Publishing Ltd (qqv)

Policy Studies Institute, 1/2 Castle Lane, London SW1E 6DR Tel: (01) 828 7055
Dir: John Pinder; *Editor:* Eileen Reid
Subjects: Politics, Economics, Education, Social Policy, Public Administration
1981: 11 titles *1982:* 12 titles
ISBN Publisher's Prefix: 0-85374

Polybooks Ltd, see Charles Skilton Ltd

Polygon Books, an imprint of Edinburgh University Student Publications Board (qv)

Polytantric Press, an imprint of Jay Landesman Ltd (qv)

Polytech Publishers Ltd, 36 Hayburn Rd, Stockport SK2 5DB Tel: (061) 427 6606
Man Dir: Frank Wood
Subjects: Technical, Business Studies, Economics
1983: 41 titles *Founded:* 1969
ISBN Publisher's Prefix: 0-85505

Pond Press, 7 Beasleys Ait, Sunbury-on-Thames, Middlesex Tel: Sunbury-on-Thames 80091 (STD code 09327)
Subjects: Reference Books, Directories & Guidebooks, Sports, Games & Pastimes
ISBN Publisher's Prefix: 0-85375

Popular Dogs Publishing Co Ltd, an imprint of Hutchinson Books Ltd (qv)

H **Pordes**, 529b Finchley Rd, London NW3 7BH Tel: (01) 435 9878/9
Subjects: History, Reference
Founded: 1947
Book Club: The Jewish Book Club (R Pordes)
Miscellaneous: See also under Remainder Dealers
ISBN Publisher's Prefix: 0-85376

T & A D **Poyser** Ltd, Town Head House, Calton, Waterhouses, Stoke-on-Trent, Staffordshire ST10 3JQ Tel: Waterhouses 366 (STD code 053 86)
Man Dir: Trevor Poyser; *Sales, Foreign Rights:* Dorothy Poyser
Subjects: Ornithology, Aviation
Founded: 1972
ISBN Publisher's Prefix: 0-85661

Praeger Publishers, an imprint of Holt-Saunders Ltd (qv)

Praeger Scientific, an imprint of Holt-Saunders Ltd (qv)

Pre-School Publishing Co, an imprint of Burke Publishing Co Ltd (qv)

Prentice-Hall International+, 66 Wood Lane End, Hemel Hempstead, Hertfordshire HP2 4RG Tel: Hemel Hempstead 58531 (STD code 0442) Cable Add: Prenhall Hemel Telex: 82445
Sales Managers: Gary Utterson (Western Europe, Middle East, Africa excl south), Tony Murray (Eastern Europe), Roy Jones (UK Trade); *Rights & Permissions:* Tony Murray
Associate Companies: Prentice-Hall Inc, Englewood Cliffs, NJ 07632, USA; Prentice-Hall of Australia Pty Ltd, Australia (qv); Prentice-Hall of Canada Ltd, 1870 Birchmount Rd, Scarborough, Ontario, Canada; Prentice-Hall of India Pvt Ltd, India (qv); Prentice-Hall of Japan Inc, Japan (qv); Arco Publishing Inc, 219 Park Ave South, New York, NY 10003, USA; Institute for Business Planning Inc, IBP Plaza, 320 Hudson Terrace, Englewood Cliffs, NJ 07632, USA; Parker Publishing Co, West Nyack, NY 10994, USA; Reston Publishing Co, Box 547, Reston, Va 22090, USA; International Book Distributors Ltd, UK *Division:* Appleton-Century-Crofts (US)
Subjects: History, Music, Art, Philosophy, Religion, Medicine, Psychology, University Textbooks and Postgraduate Material in Science and Technology, Sociology, Education, Business, Economics, English, English as a Second language, Political Science, Speech, Drama, Trade Books
Founded: 1913
Miscellaneous: Firm is a branch of Prentice-Hall International Inc, Englewood Cliffs, NJ 07632, USA
ISBN Publisher's Prefixes: 0-13 (Prentice-Hall and Parker), 0-668 (Arco), 0-87624 (Institute for Business Planning), 0-87909 (Reston), 0-8385 (Appleton-Century-Crofts)

Press Porcepic, an imprint of Johnston Green & Co (Publishers) Ltd (qv)

Norman **Price**, an imprint of Dickson Price Publishers Ltd (qv)

Pride Publications, an imprint of E J Morten (Publishers) (qv)

Primary Communications Research Centre, University of Leicester, Leicester LE1 7RH Tel: Leicester 556223 (STD code 0533) Telex: 341198
Publications Officer: Joyce Collins
Subjects: Scholarly Communication, Publishing, New Information Technology
1981: 3 titles *1982:* 4 titles *Founded:* 1976
ISBN Publisher's Prefix: 0-906083

Princeton University Press, see University Presses of Columbia and Princeton

George **Prior** Associated Publishers Ltd*, Lower Ground Floor, High Holborn House, 52 High Holborn, London WC1V 6RL Tel: (01) 405 6603, (01) 405 6626
Warehouse: Biblios, Glenside Industrial Estate, Partridge Green, Horsham, West Sussex RH13 8RA Tel: Horsham 710971 (STD code 0403)
Man Dir, Publicity, Rights & Permissions: George Prior; *Editorial:* F Laner
Subsidiary Companies: George Prior Publishers; Book Mail International; George Prior Co, PO Box 68363, Portland, Oregon 97268, USA
Subjects: General Fiction (some titles in large print), History, Music, Art, Philosophy, Reference, High-priced Paperbacks, Social Science
Founded: 1972
ISBN Publisher's Prefixes: 0-904000, 0-86043

Priory Press Ltd, see Wayland Publishers Ltd

Prism Press, Stable Court, Chalmington, Dorchester, Dorset DT2 0HB Tel: Maiden Newton 20524 (STD code 0300)
Dirs: Julian King, Colin Spooner
Subjects: Alternative Technology, Self-Sufficiency, Philosophy, Politics, Literature, Cookery, Wine and Beermaking, Computing
1983: 65 titles *Founded:* 1974
Miscellaneous: Distributed by George Philip & Co, PO Box 1, Littlehampton, West Sussex
ISBN Publisher's Prefixes: 0-904727, 0-907061

Profile Books Ltd, Dial House, 65 Victoria St, Windsor, Berks SL4 1EH Tel: Windsor 69777 (STD code 07535)
Dirs: P E Butler; *Mail Order:* Miss S Weare
Imprints: Profile Publications, Hylton Lacy Publishers
Subjects: Aircraft, Cars, AFVs, Warships, Small Arms, Locomotives, Textbooks (*Writers and their Work* series)

Projecta (UK) Ltd, PO Box 15, Royston, Hertfordshire SG8 5NQ Tel: Royston 47003 (STD code 0763) Telex: 8812703 Lonsec G
Man Dir: C J Gravatt
Subject: English as a Foreign Language (for schools/home study)
1981: 4 titles *1982:* 3 titles *Founded:* 1980

Prospice, an imprint of Aquila Publishing (qv)

Proteus Books Ltd, Bremar House, Sale Pl, London W2 1PT Tel: (01) 402 7360 Telex: 21969
Man Dir, Marketing, Sales: Michael Brecher; *Managing Editor:* Kay Rowley; *Production:* Bob Christie; *Publicity:* Debra Ritterband; *Rights & Permissions:* Elisabeth Wilson
Subsidiary Company: Proteus Publishing Co Inc, 9 West 57th St, Suite 4504, New York, NY 10019, USA (Tel: 212 7514558)
Subjects: General Non-fiction, Fiction, Travel and Professional Guides, Leisure, Photographic, Biography, Film, Rock
1981: 30 titles *1982:* 60 titles *Founded:* 1977
ISBN Publisher's Prefixes: 0-906071, 0-86276

Psychic Press Ltd, 20 Earlham St, London WC2H 9LW Tel: (01) 240 3032 Cable Add: Psychic London WC2
Man Dir: Tony Ortzen; *Advertising Dir:* Ronald Baker; *Rights & Permissions:* Gordon Adams
Subjects: Philosophy, Reference
Bookshop: Psychic News Bookshop, 20 Earlham St, London WC2H 9LW
Founded: 1932
ISBN Publisher's Prefix: 0-85384

Puffin Books, an imprint of Penguin Books Ltd (qv)

Purnell Books, Paulton, Bristol BS18 5LQ Tel: Midsomer Norton 413301 (STD code 0761) Cable Add: Purbook Bristol Telex: 44713
Man Dir: David Bailey; *Publishing Dir:* Michael Gabb; *Managing Editor:* Sue Hook; *Sales Dir:* A Badger; *Production:* Martyn Lewis; *Publicity:* Heather Burns; *Rights & Permissions:* Clarissa Cridland
Parent Company: Purnell Publishers Ltd, Paulton, Bristol BS18 5LQ, a wholly-owned subsidiary of BPCC PLC (qv)
Associate Companies: Macdonald & Co (Publishers) Ltd (qv); Macdonald Purnell (Pty) Ltd, Republic of South Africa (qv)
Imprint: Sampson Low
Subjects: Reference, Juveniles, Leisure (under Sampson Low imprint)
ISBN Publisher's Prefixes: 0-361, 0-430, 0-562 (Sampson Low)

Putnam & Co Ltd, 9 Bow St, London WC2E 7AL Tel: (01) 836 9081 Cable Add: Bodleian London WC2 Telex: 299080
Parent Company: The Bodley Head (qv for further details)

Q Press Ltd, see Canongate Publishing Ltd

Q E D Publishing Ltd, 32 Kingly Court, London W1 Tel: (01) 734 4611 Telex: 298844
Man Dir: Laurence F Orbach; *Art Dirs:* Alastair Campbell, Edward Kinsey; *Editorial Dir:* Jeremy Harwood; *Rights & Co-editions:* Fabian Russell-Cobb
Parent Company: Quarto Publishing Ltd (qv)
Subjects: International Co-editions, Illustration Techniques, Wine, Animals, Performing Arts

Quaker Home Service, Friends House, Euston Rd, London NW1 2BJ Tel: (01) 387 3601
General Secretary: Jo Farrow; *Assistant General Secretary:* Clifford E Barnard
Orders to: Friends Book Centre (at above address)
Subjects: Religious, Social and Historical Topics with a Quaker content
Bookshop: Friends Book Centre (at above address)
Founded: 1882
ISBN Publisher's Prefix: 0-85245

Quartet Books Ltd, 27-29 Goodge St, London W1P 1FD Tel: (01) 636 3992, (01) 636 0968 Telex: 919034
Chairman: Naim Attallah; *Editorial:* Zelfa Hourani, Nigella Lawson, Deborah Right; *Sales Dir:* Penny Grant; *Marketing Dir:* David Elliott; *Production Dir:* Gary Grant; *Publicity Dir:* Juliette Foy
Subsidiary Companies: Quartet Crime (at above address), Namara Publications, Namara House, 45-46 Poland St, London W1; Quartet Books Australia Pty Ltd, Australia (qv); Quartet Books Inc, Suite 1300, 360 Park Ave South, New York, NY 10011, USA
Associate Company: Robin Clark Ltd (qv)
Imprint: Quartet Or Books
Subjects: Fiction, Biography, Memoirs, Music, History, Philosophy, Politics, Social Science, Trade Paperbacks, Psychology, The Arab World, Sexual Politics, Photography, Crime, Children's Books
Bookshop: The Quartet Bookshop, Namara House, 45-46 Poland St, London W1 Tel: (01) 437 1019
Founded: 1972
Miscellaneous: Firm is a member of the Namara Group, Namara House, 45-46 Poland St, London W1
ISBN Publisher's Prefix: 0-7043

Quarto Publishing Ltd, 32 Kingly Court, London W1 Tel: (01) 734 4611 Telex: 298844
Man Dir: Laurence F Orbach; *Editorial Dir:* Jeremy Harwood; *Art Dir:* Robert J Morley; *Rights & Co-editions:* Fabian Russell-Cobb
Parent Company: Quarto Ltd, 212 Fifth Ave, New York, NY 10010, USA
Subsidiary Companies: QED Publishing Ltd (qv); Quill Publishing Ltd (qv)
Subjects: International Co-editions, Illustrated books on Wine & Food, Transport, Travel, Photography, Music
1981: 12 titles

Queen Anne Press Ltd, see Macdonald & Co (Publishers) Ltd (qv)

Quentin Press Ltd, 10 Brook St, Wivenhoe, nr Colchester, Essex CO7 9DS Tel: Wivenhoe 5433 (STD code 0206 22) Cable Add: Paterson, Colchester Telex: 896616MP Sendit G, Markit 987562 Cochac
Man Dir: Mark Paterson
Subjects: High-class Illustrated Books
Founded: 1978
Miscellaneous: Packagers of books for other publishers

Quill Publishing Ltd, 32 Kingly Court, London W1 Tel: (01) 734 4611 Cable Add: Quartopub Telex: 298844 Quarto
Man Dir: Laurence F Orbach; *Art Dir:* Nigel Osborne; *Publicity:* Robert Morley; *Rights & Permissions:* Fabian Russell-Cobb
Parent Company: Quarto Publishing Ltd (qv)
Subjects: International Co-editions, Horse Racing, Popular Medicine
Founded: 1980

Quiller Press Ltd, 50 Albemarle St, London W1X 3HE Tel: (01) 499 6529 Telex: 21120
Man Dir, Editorial: J J Greenwood; *Rights & Permissions:* Ms A E Carlile
Orders to: Tiptree Book Services, Church Rd, Tiptree, Colchester, Essex Tel: Tiptree 816362 (STD code 0621)
Subjects: General Non-fiction, Sponsored books
1982: 12 titles *1983:* approx 12 titles
Founded: 1981
ISBN Publisher's Prefix: 0-907621

Quintet Publishing Ltd+, 76 Old Compton St, London W1V 5PA Tel: (01) 439 7086 Telex: 8952387 Answer G
Man Dir: Robert Adkinson; *Editorial:* Clare Howell
Subjects: Art, Reference, Leisure, Travel, How-to
Founded: 1982

R I B A Publications Ltd, Finsbury Mission, Moreland St, London EC1V 8VB Tel: (01) 251 0791 Cable Add: Ribazo London
Man Dir: R H McKie; *Production:* M Stribbling
Parent Company: Royal Institute of British Architects
Associate Company: RIBA Services Ltd
Subjects: Architecture and Design
Bookshop: RIBA Bookshop, 66 Portland Place, London W1N 4AD
Founded: 1967
ISBN Publisher's Prefix: 0-900630

Radical Reprints, an imprint of The Journeyman Press (qv)

Railway Publications Ltd, an associate company of Ian Allen Ltd (qv)

The **Rainbird** Publishing Group, 40 Park St, London W1Y 4DE Tel: (01) 491 4777 Cable Add: Rainmac London Telex: 261472
Editorial: David Roberts, Karen Goldie Morrison (Natural History); *Production:* David Bann; *Rights & Permissions:* Valerie Reuben
Subsidiary Companies: George Rainbird Ltd; Rainbird Reference Books Ltd
Subjects: Art, Archaeology, Architecture, History, Travel, Hobbies, Leisure, Sport, Natural History, Crafts, Medical
Founded: 1951
Miscellaneous: Company is a member of the Thomson Books Ltd group (qv), a part of International Thomson Organization Ltd (Canada)
ISBN Publisher's Prefix: 0-902935

Rainbow Books, an imprint of Brown Watson Ltd (qv)

Ramboro Enterprises Ltd, 64 Pentonville Rd, London N1 9HD Tel: (01) 837 6301 Cable Add: Dons Bar Telex: 24224 ref 1297
Man Dir, Sales: Donald Murray; *Rights & Permissions:* W Squires
Associate Company: Number One Publishing Co Ltd

Imprints: Atlantic, Delightful Books, Paintaway, Ramboro, University, Varsity
Subjects: Children's Books, Art, Cookery, Dictionaries
Founded: 1960
Miscellaneous: Also Remainder Dealers

The **Ramsay** Head Press, 36 North Castle St, Edinburgh EH2 3BN Tel: (031) 225 5646
Editorial Dir: Norman Wilson
Subjects: Biography, Literature, Poetry, Art, Architecture, History, Fiction, Reference, New Assessments series (critical studies of outstanding figures in literature and arts)
1981: 6 titles *1982:* 8 titles *Founded:* 1971
ISBN Publisher's Prefix: 0-902859

Rationalist Press Association, see Pemberton Publishing Co Ltd

The **Reader's Digest** Association Ltd, 25 Berkeley Sq, London W1X 6AB Tel: (01) 629 8144 Cable Add: Readigest London W1X 6AB Telex: 264631
Subjects: Fiction, English Dictionaries, Reference, Maps & Atlases, Travel, Encyclopaedias, Guidebooks
ISBN Publisher's Prefix: 0-276

Redcliffe Press Ltd, 14 Dowry Sq, Hotwells, Bristol BS8 4SH Tel: Bristol 290158 (STD code 0272)
Chairman, Editorial, Production: John Sansom; *Sales:* Rosemary Clinch; *Publicity:* Sarah Helyar; *Rights & Permissions:* Merilyn Chambers
Subjects: Local Interest, Architecture, Conservation, Cricket, Literature, Poetry
1982: 6 titles *Founded:* 1976
ISBN Publisher's Prefix: 0-905459

Thomas **Reed** Publications Ltd, 36-37 Cock Lane, London EC1A 9BY Tel: (01) 248 7881 Telex: 883526
Man Dir, Rights & Permissions: K Allan Brunton-Reed; *Editorial Dir:* Jean Fowler; *Sales Manager:* Steve Lemon
Parent Company: Thomas Reed Ltd, Double Century House, High Street West, Sunderland, Tyne & Wear
Associate Companies: Thomas Reed Industrial Press Ltd (London address); Thomas Reed Printers Ltd (Sunderland address)
Imprint: Reed's
Subjects: Marine Engineering, Naval Architecture, Navigation, Seamanship, Yachting
1981: 3 titles *1982:* 4 titles *Founded:* 1782
ISBN Publisher's Prefix: 0-900335

Max **Reinhardt** Ltd, 9 Bow St, London WC2E 7AL Tel: (01) 836 9081 Cable Add: Bodleian London WC2 Telex: 299080
Parent Company: The Bodley Head (qv for further details)

Religious and Moral Education Press, Hennock Rd, Exeter, Devon EX2 8RP Tel: Exeter 74121 (STD code 0392) Telex: 42749
Publisher: Simon Goodenough
Subjects: Religious titles for schools and trade
Founded: 1921
Miscellaneous: Religious and Moral Education Press is an imprint of E J Arnold & Son Ltd (qv)
ISBN Publisher's Prefix: 0-08

Research Publishing Co, an imprint of Fudge & Co Ltd (qv)

Riband Books Ltd*, Sedgwick Park, Horsham, West Sussex Tel: Lower Beeding 369 (STD code 040376) Cable Add: Riband Horsham
Man Dir: M T Bizony; *Sales Manager:* A B Simmons

Imprint: New Educational Press
Subjects: General Fiction, Belles Lettres, Poetry, History, Music, Art, Philosophy, Reference, High-priced Paperbacks, General Science, Technical, University, Primary & Secondary Textbooks, Educational Materials, Large-type Reprints
Founded: 1955
ISBN Publisher's Prefix: 0-85141

The **Richmond** Publishing Co Ltd+, Orchard Rd, Richmond, Surrey Tel: (01) 876 1091
Subjects: Botany, History, Social Sciences, Limited & De Luxe Editions
ISBN Publisher's Prefix: 0-85546

Rider & Co, an imprint of Hutchinson Books Ltd (qv)

Rigby International & Lansdowne International Pty Ltd, 5 Great James St, London WC1
London office of Rigby Publishers, Australia (qv for Group details)

Right Way Books, an imprint of Elliot Right Way Books (qv)

Rivers Press, an imprint of Writers and Readers Publishing Co-operative (qv)

Martin **Robertson**, see Martin

Robin Books, an imprint of Octopus Books PLC (qv)

Robinson & Watkins Books Ltd, 21 Cecil Court, Charing Cross Rd, London WC2N 4HB Tel: (01) 836 2182/3778
Man Dir: Hannah Robinson
Subjects: Oriental Philosophy, Western Mysticism, Esoteric, Inner Development, Evolution, Meditation
Bookshops: At above address and Bridge St, Dulverton, Somerset TA22 9HY Tel: Dulverton 23395 (STD code 0398)
ISBN Publisher's Prefix: 0-7724

Robson Books Ltd, Bolsover House, 5-6 Clipstone St, London W1P 7EB Tel: (01) 637 5937 Cable Add: Robsobook London W1
Man Dir: Jeremy Robson; *Sales Manager:* Martin Hanks; *Editor:* Susan Rea; *Publicity Manager:* Cheryll Roberts
Subjects: General, Biography, Music, Humour
1981: 52 titles *Founded:* 1973
ISBN Publisher's Prefixes: 0-903895, 0-86051

Rochester Press, 38 High St, Chatham, Kent Tel: Medway 43884 (STD code 0634)
Man Dir, Rights & Permissions: Malcolm John; *Sales, Publicity:* Janice Wain; *Editorial:* Geoffrey Hopkins
Subject: Transport
Bookshop: Transport Bookshop (at above address)
1981: 27 titles *Founded:* 1976
ISBN Publisher's Prefixes: 0-905540, 0-946379

Rodale Press Ltd*, Chiltern House, Oxford Rd, Aylesbury, Bucks HP19 3AS Tel: Aylesbury 25952 (STD code 0296) Telex: 837520
Man Dir: Dick Weston; *Editorial, Rights & Permissions:* Ned Halley; *Sales:* Keith Wallace
Parent Company: Rodale Press Inc, 33 East Minor St, Emmaus, Pa 18049, USA
Subjects: Gardening, Cookery, Health, Reference
Founded: 1954
ISBN Publisher's Prefix: 0-87857

George **Ronald**, 46 High St, Kidlington, Oxford OX5 2DN Tel: Oxford 5273 (STD code 08675) Cable Add: Talisman Oxford
General Manager: Russell Busey
Subjects: Religion, The Bahá'í Faith, High-

priced Paperbacks
1982: 10 titles *Founded:* 1947
ISBN Publisher's Prefix: 0-85398

Barry **Rose** (Publishers) Ltd, Little London, Chichester, West Sussex PO19 1PG Tel: Chichester 783637 (STD code 0243)
Chairman and Man Dir: Barry Rose
Associate Companies: Professional Training Consultants Ltd; Countrywise Press Ltd; Justice of the Peace Ltd
Founded: 1971
ISBN Publisher's Prefixes: 0-85992, 0-900500

Rose-Jordan Ltd, an imprint of Jordan & Sons Ltd (qv)

Roundabout, an imprint of Modern English Publications Ltd (qv)

Routledge & Kegan Paul PLC, 39 Store St, London WC1E 7DD Tel: (01) 637 7651 Cable Add: Columnae London WC1
Orders to: Broadway House, Newtown Rd, Henley-on-Thames, Oxfordshire RG9 1EN Tel: Henley-on-Thames 78321 (STD code 04912)
Chairman: Norman Franklin; *Group Man Dir:* Philip Sturrock; *Sales Dir:* Malcolm Campbell; *Publicity Dir:* Terence Lucas; *Foreign Rights:* Gela Jacobson
Subsidiary Companies: Kegan Paul International (at above company address); Oriel Press Ltd (qv)
Branch Offs: 296 Beaconsfield Parade, Middle Park, Melbourne, Victoria 3206, Australia; Routledge & Kegan Paul of America, 9 Park St, Boston, Mass 02108, USA
Subjects: General Fiction, Belles Lettres, Biography, History, Education, Occult, Art, Philosophy, Reference, Religion, High-priced Paperbacks, Psychology, Social Science, University & Secondary Textbooks
Bookshop: Kegan Paul, Trench, Trubner & Co, 39 Store St, London WC1E 7DD
Founded: 1834
ISBN Publisher's Prefix: 0-7100

Roxby & Lindsey Holdings Ltd, 98 Clapham Common North Side, London SW4 9SG Tel: (01) 228 2558 Telex: 261234 ref H5654D
Man Dir: Hugh Elwes; *Rights & Permissions:* Barbara Fuller
Subjects: Illustrated Reference Books, Encyclopaedias
1981: 10 titles *Founded:* 1973

The **Royal Society** of Chemistry, Burlington House, London W1V 0BN Tel: (01) 734 9864 Telex: 268001
Chief Executive: Dr R D Guthrie; *Editorial:* Dr Phil Gardam; *Sales, Publicity:* Dr Ash Kabi; *Production:* Don Grimmer; *Rights & Permissions:* Dr Ivor Williams
Orders to: Distribution Centre, Blackhorse Rd, Letchworth, Hertfordshire SG6 1HN
Associate Company: Turpin Transactions Ltd, Blackhorse Rd, Letchworth, Hertfordshire SG6 1HN
Branch Offs: Russell Sq, London WC1; The University, Nottingham NG7 2RD
Subjects: Chemistry, Chemical Technology
1981: 31 titles *Founded:* 1851
ISBN Publisher's Prefixes: 0-85186, 0-85404, 0-901886

S A G E Publications Ltd, 28 Banner St, London EC1Y 8QE Tel: (01) 253 1516 Cable Add: Sagepub London
Man Dir: David Brooks; *Editorial Manager:* Penelope Head; *Marketing Manager:* Philip Glover
Associate Companies: SAGE Publications Inc, 275 South Beverly Dr, Beverly Hills, California 90212, USA; SAGE Publications India Private Ltd, PO Box 3605, New Delhi 110024, India

Subjects: Social Sciences (Sociology, Political Science, Methodology, International Relations, Human Services, Evaluation, Psychology, Communication)
Founded: 1971
ISBN Publisher's Prefix: 0-8039

S C M Press Ltd, 26-30 Tottenham Rd, London N1 4BZ Tel: (01) 249 7262 Cable Add: Torchpres London N1
Man Dir: The Rev John Bowden; *Sales, Publicity:* Richard Mulkern; *Production:* Mark Hammer; *Rights & Permissions:* Margaret Lydamore
Subjects: Religion, Theology, Religious Education, Ethics
Bookshop: SCM Bookroom (at above address)
1981: 52 titles *1982:* 48 titles *Founded:* 1929
ISBN Publisher's Prefix: 0-334

S P C K (The Society for Promoting Christian Knowledge)+, Holy Trinity Church, Marylebone Rd, London NW1 4DU Tel: (01) 387 5282 Cable Add: Futurity London NW1
General Secretary: Patrick Gilbert; *Editorial:* Robin Brookes; *Sales Manager:* Alan Goodworth; *Promotion:* Alice Watson
Subsidiary Company: Indian Society for Promoting Christian Knowledge (ISPCK), India (qv)
Subjects: Bible Reference Works & Commentaries, Theology, Church History, Worship, Education, Biography & Autobiography
Bookshops: At above address and throughout the UK (37 outlets)
1982: 55 titles *Founded:* 1698
Miscellaneous: Divisions of this Society are Sheldon Press (qv) and Triangle (qv)
ISBN Publisher's Prefix: 0-281

S R P, an imprint of E P Publishing Ltd (qv)

S T L Books, PO Box 48, 9 London Rd, Bromley, Kent BR1 1BY Tel: (01) 290 1090 Cable Add: Mobiliser Bromley Telex: 896706 EBE G
Dir: G M Davey; *General Manager:* Dave Brown
Orders to: S T L Distributors, 1 Sherman Rd, Bromley, Kent BR1 3JH
Parent Company: Send the Light (at above address)
Subjects: Religion, Juveniles, Bibles
Bookshops: Bromley Christian Supply Centre, 9 London Rd, Bromley, Kent; Christian Bookshop, 17 Lordship Lane, London SE22; Bolton Christian Bookshop, 204 St Georges Rd, Bolton, Lancs; Coventry Christian Bookshop, 21 City Arcade, Coventry CV1 3HX
1981: 8 titles *1982:* 8 titles *Founded:* 1963
ISBN Publisher's Prefix: 0-903843

Saint Andrew Press, 121 George St, Edinburgh EH2 4YN Tel: (031) 225 5722 Cable Add: Free, Edinburgh
Secretary to Publications Committee: T B Honeyman; *Editorial:* Mary Kerr; *Production Manager:* John Leslie; *Publicity, Marketing:* Bill Morrison
Subjects: Religion, Theology, Current Issues, History
1981: 22 titles *1982:* 20 titles
Miscellaneous: Parent body is The Church of Scotland Committee on Publications
ISBN Publisher's Prefix: 0-7152

Saint George & Dragon Press, an imprint of Bibliagora (qv)

Saint James Press*, 3 Percy St, London W1P 9FA Tel: (01) 580 4155
Man Dir: George Walsh
Subject: Reference
Founded: 1968
ISBN Publisher's Prefixes: 0-900997, 0-86066

Saint Paul Publications, St Paul's House, Middlegreen, Slough SL3 6BT Tel: Slough 20621 (STD code 0753)
Associate Company: Saint Paul Publications, Ballykeeran, Athlone, Republic of Ireland
Subject: Christian Religion
Related Bookshops: Saint Paul Book Centres at 199 Kensington High St, London W8 6BA; 133 Corporation St, Birmingham B4 6PH; 82 Bold St, Liverpool L1 4HR; 5A-7 Royal Exchange Sq, Glasgow G1 3AH
1981: 15 titles *1982:* 14 titles *Founded:* 1967
ISBN Publisher's Prefix: 0-85439

Saint Paul's Bibliographies, West End House, West End Terrace, Winchester SO22 5EN Tel: Winchester 64037 (STD code 0962)
Dirs: R S Cross, Mrs M C E Cross
Parent Company: Foxbury Enterprises Ltd (at above address)
Subject: Bibliographies
1982: 5 titles *1983:* 14 titles
ISBN Publisher's Prefix: 0-906795

Salamander Books Ltd+, 27 Old Gloucester St, London WC1N 3AF Tel: (01) 242 6693 Cable Add: Salamander London WC1 Telex: 261113
Chairman: J Proost; *Man Dir, Production:* Malcolm Little; *Editorial:* Ray Bonds; *Sales, Rights & Permissions:* Janet Pilch
Orders to: Hodder & Stoughton Services, Mill Rd, Dunton Green, Sevenoaks, Kent TN13 2XX
Parent Company: Henri Proost & Cie, Belgium (qv)
Subjects: Illustrated Reference Books: Military, Natural History, Music
1981: 14 titles *1982:* 17 titles *Founded:* 1974
ISBN Publisher's Prefix: 0-86101

The **Salamander Press** Edinburgh Ltd+, 34 Shandwick Pl, Edinburgh EH2 4RT Tel: (031) 226 4721
Publishers: Tom Fenton, Jennifer Law; *Sales:* Tom Fenton; *Production:* Jennifer Law
Subjects: Fiction, Poetry, Drama, Memoirs, Cookery, General, Children's Books
1981: 4 titles *1982:* 11 titles *Founded:* 1981
ISBN Publisher's Prefix: 0-907540

Salesian Publications & Don Bosco Film Strips, Blaisdon Hall, Longhope, Gloucestershire GL17 0AQ Tel: Longhope 830247 (STD code 0452)
Subject: Religion

The **Saltire** Society, Saltire House, Atholl Crescent, Edinburgh EH3 8HA Tel: (031) 228 6621
Imprint: Saltire Classics
Subjects: Scottish Art, Literature, Music
Founded: 1936
Miscellaneous: Associated with The Scottish Civic Trust, 24 George Sq, Glasgow, in publishing *The Scottish Review*
ISBN Publisher's Prefix: 0-85411

Salvationist Publishing & Supplies Ltd, 117-121 Judd St, King's Cross, London WC1H 9NN Tel: (01) 387 1656 Cable Add: Savingly, London WC1H 9NN
Rights & Permissions: Col David W Ramsay
Associate Company: Campfield Press, St Albans
Subjects: Religion, Music, Juveniles
ISBN Publisher's Prefix: 0-85412

Sampson Low, a division of Purnell Books (qv)

Sandles, an imprint of World International Publishing Ltd (qv)

Sangam Books Ltd, 36 Molyneux St, London W1H 4DS Tel: (01) 402 1522 Cable Add: San Book
Chief Executive, Sales, Publicity: A A de Souza; *Editorial:* E Raghavan
Parent Company: Orient Longman Ltd, India (qv)
Subjects: Social Sciences, Scientific Technical, Medical, Children's Books
1981: 48 titles *1982:* 56 titles *Founded:* 1981
ISBN Publisher's Prefixes: 0-86125, 0-86131, 0-86132

W B Saunders, an imprint of Holt-Saunders Ltd (qv)

K G Saur Ltd, Shropshire House, 2-10 Capper St, London WC1E 6JA Tel: (01) 637 1571 Telex: 24902 Saur G
Man Dir and Production: J M A Aretz; *Editorial:* Judi Vernau, Laureen Bailey
Parent Company: K G Saur Verlag KG, Federal Republic of Germany (qv)
Subjects: Library/Academic Reference, Literary, Music
Founded: 1978
ISBN Publisher's Prefixes: 0-085157, 0-086291

Saxon House, a former imprint of Gower Publishing Co Ltd (qv)

Scala/Philip Wilson, an imprint of Philip Wilson Publishers (qv)

Sceptre Books Ltd, Time & Life Bldg, New Bond St, London W1Y 0AA Tel: (01) 499 4080
Man Dir: David Owen; *Rights & Permissions:* Ruth Sandys; *Production:* Terry Maloney
Parent Company: Time-Life Books BV, Netherlands (qv)
Associate Company: Harrow House Editions Ltd (at above address)
Subjects: Illustrated Reference Books and Series for the International Co-edition Market
Founded: 1980
ISBN Publisher's Prefix: 0-905663

Schofield & Sims Ltd+, Dogley Mill, Fenay Bridge, Huddersfield, West Yorkshire HD8 0NQ Tel: Huddersfield 607080 (STD code 0484) Cable Add: Schosims Huddersfield
Chairman: John S Nesbitt; *Man Dir:* J Stephen Platts; *Sales Dir:* Jack Brierley
Subjects: Secondary & Primary Textbooks, Educational Materials, Computer Software
1981: 73 titles *1982:* 53 titles *Founded:* 1901
ISBN Publisher's Prefix: 0-7217

Scholastic Book Services Inc+, 10 Earlham St, London WC2H 9LN Tel: (01) 240 5753 Telex: 264604 Sbs Lon G
Editors: Dorothy Wood, Mia Macrossan
Parent Company: Scholastic Inc, 730 Broadway, New York, NY 10003, USA
Associate Company: Scholastic Publications Ltd (qv)
Subjects: Children's Fiction and Non-fiction
1983: 45 titles *Founded:* 1964
ISBN Publisher's Prefix: 0-590

Scholastic Publications Ltd, 9 Parade, Leamington Spa, Warwickshire CV32 4DG Tel: Southam 3910 (STD code 092681) Telex: 312138 Splf G
Man Dir: John Cox; *Educational Publisher:* Annie Smith; *Marketing:* Philip Hodson; *Editor Book Clubs:* Jackie Andrews; *Production:* Douglas Brown; *Advertising:* Bob Challinor
Parent Company: Scholastic Inc, 730 Broadway, New York, NY 10003, USA
Associate Company: Scholastic Book Services Inc (qv)
Subjects: Primary Education, Juvenile Fiction and Non-fiction, Educational Magazines, Computer Software
Book Clubs: Lucky, See-Saw, Chip, Scene, Criterion

1983: 45 titles *Founded:* 1964
ISBN Publisher's Prefix: 0-590

School of Oriental & African Studies, Malet St, London WC1E 7HP Tel: (01) 637 2388 Cable Add: Soasul London WC1
Publications Officer: M J Daly
Subjects: Oriental and African Language, Literature, History, Religion, Bibliography, Art
1981: 6 titles *1982:* 11 titles *Founded:* 1917
ISBN Publisher's Prefix: 0-901877, 0-7286

Science Research Associates Ltd, Newtown Rd, Henley-on-Thames, Oxfordshire RG9 1EW Tel: Henley-on-Thames 5959 (STD code 04912) Cable Add: Sciresuk, Henley-on-Thames RG9 1EW Telex: 848454
Man Dir, Editorial, Sales: Brian Preston; *Production, Advertising, Publicity:* B H Sheldrake; *Rights & Permissions:* K L Turner
Parent Company: Science Research Associates Inc, 155 North Wacker Dr, Chicago, Illinois 60606 (Science Research Associates Inc is a subsidiary of IBM)
Associate Companies: Science Research Associates Pty Ltd, Australia (qv); Science Research Associates (Canada) Ltd, 707 Gordon Baker Rd, Willowdale, Ontario, Canada
Subjects: University, Secondary & Primary Textbooks, Commercial & Technical Education, Academic & Vocational Guidance Publications, Educational & Industrial Tests, Micro-computer courseware
ISBN Publisher's Prefix: 0-574

Scientechnica (Publishers) Ltd, an imprint of John Wright & Sons Ltd (qv)

Scolar Press+, 13 Brunswick Centre, London WC1N 1AF Tel: (01) 278 6381 Cable Add: Catchword London WC1 Telex: 262284 Ref 3747
Man Dir: James Price; *Editorial:* Sean Magee; *Sales, Publicity:* Cecelia Nickson
Subjects: English Literature, History, Music, Art, Horticulture, Photographic, Social Sciences, Facsimile and Limited Editions
1982: 20 titles *Founded:* 1966
ISBN Publisher's Prefixes: 0-85417, 0-85967

Scorpion Communications & Publications Ltd, 377 High St, Stratford, London E15 4QZ Tel: (01) 555 3339 Telex: 896988 Scoops G
Editorial: L Harrow; *Sales:* W Saville; *Production, Publicity, Rights & Permissions:* Colin Larkin
Associate Company: Scorpion Pica, 400A Hale End Rd, Chingford, London E4
Imprints: Scorpion International, Art Heritage
Subjects: Specialist Islamic Publishers: Art, Architecture, Photography, Music, Oriental Carpets, General Non-fiction, Business Reference
1982: approx 7 titles *Founded:* 1976
ISBN Publisher's Prefix: 0-905906

Scottish Academic Press Ltd+, 33 Montgomery St, Edinburgh EH7 5JX Tel: (031) 556 2796
Dirs: J Steven Watson, Douglas Grant, David Dorward, Alan Rodwell, Robert Walker, Harry Whittaker
Subjects: Scholarly, Scottish interest
1981: 16 titles *1982:* 18 titles *Founded:* 1969
Miscellaneous: Associated with Sussex University Press and The Handsel Press (qqv)
ISBN Publisher's Prefix: 0-7073

Scripture Union+, 130 City Rd, London EC1V 2NJ Tel: (01) 250 1966
Publishing Dir: David Rosser; *Production Manager:* Andrew Lee; *Sales, Marketing Manager:* John Lane; *Managing Editor:* John Grayston; *Rights & Permissions:* Jill Harris; *Overseas Rights Adminstrator:* Diana Dusart
Mail Order: 9-11 Clothier Rd, Bristol BS4 5RL Tel: Bristol 719709 (STD code 0272)
Subsidiary Companies: Frontier Youth Trust; Inter School Christian Fellowship; Scripture Union Publishing
Imprints: Giraffe, Key, Leopard, Swift, Tiger
Subjects: Music, Religion, Juveniles, Educational Materials
Bookshops: 5 Wigmore St, London W1H 0AD; 77 Bridge St, Manchester M3 2RH; 16 Park St, Croydon CR0 1YE; 3 King Edward St, Leeds LS1 6AX; 3 Suffolk Rd, Cheltenham, Gloucestershire; 280 St Vincent St, Glasgow G2; 30 Cow Wynd, Falkirk, Stirlingshire; 21 Rutland Sq, Edinburgh; 8 Kings Rd, Brighton, East Sussex BN1 1NE; 22 Fisher St, Carlisle, Cumbria CA3 8RH; 14 North Bridge St, Sunderland, Tyne and Wear SR5 1LD; 14 Eton St, Richmond, Surrey TW9 1EE; 13 Lower Hillgate, Stockport, Cheshire SK1 1JQ; 12 Wellington Pl, Belfast BT1 6JB; 38 Ardconnel, Inverness; 68-70 Princes St, Perth; 4 Peterborough Rd, Harrow, Middx HA1 2BQ; Good News Centre, 165 St George's Way, St John's Centre, Liverpool L1 1NE; The Bible and Book Shop, 34 Iron Gate, Derby DE1 3GN; 66 Queens Rd, Watford, Hertfordshire; 41 Telford St, Wick
Founded: 1867
ISBN Publisher's Prefixes: 0-85421, 0-86201

Seafarer Books, an imprint of The Merlin Press Ltd (qv)

Search Press Ltd+, Wellwood, North Farm Rd, Tunbridge Wells, Kent TN2 3DR Tel: Tunbridge Wells 44037 (STD code 0892) Telex: 957258
Man Dir, Sales: Charlotte de la Bedoyere; *Editorial, Rights & Permissions:* John Bright-Holmes; *Production:* Bobby Meyer
Associate Company: Burns & Oates Ltd (qv)
Subjects: Philosophy, Theology, Literature and Literary Criticism, Poetry, History, Biography, Religion, General, Moral Education, Mysticism, Third World, Children's, Arts and Crafts
Founded: 1962
ISBN Publisher's Prefix: 0-85532

Martin **Secker & Warburg** Ltd, 54 Poland St, London W1V 3DF Tel: (01) 437 2075 Cable Add: Psophidian London W1
Chairman: T G Rosenthal; *Publishing Dir:* Peter Grose; *Editorial Dir:* A J Blackwell; *Sales Dir:* T R Manderson; *Production Dir:* P Ireland; *Publicity Dir:* Beth Macdougall; *Rights & Permissions:* Gillian Vale
Orders to: The Windmill Press, Kingswood, Tadworth, Surrey KT20 6TG Tel: Mogador 3511 (STD code 073783)
Parent Company: William Heinemann International Ltd (qv)
Associate Companies: Alison Press, 5 Harley Gardens, London SW10 9SW; Leo Cooper, 190 Shaftesbury Ave, London WC2 8JZ
Imprints include: Landmarks (with William Heinemann Ltd)
Subjects: General Fiction, Belles Lettres, Poetry, Biography, History, Military History, Music, Cinema, Art, Philosophy, Reference, Psychology, Social Science, Sport, High-priced Paperbacks, Criticism, Photography, Judaica, Political Science
1981: 80 titles *1982:* 97 titles *Founded:* 1910
ISBN Publisher's Prefix: 0-436

Seeley, Service, an imprint of Frederick Warne (Publishers) Ltd (qv)

Serindia Publications, 10 Parkfields, Putney, London SW15 6NH Tel: (01) 788 1966 Telex: 923421
Proprietor: Anthony Aris
Orders to: La Haule Books Ltd, West Lodge, La Haule, Jersey, Channel Islands
Associate Company: Aris & Philips Ltd (qv)
Subject: Oriental Art
Founded: 1976
ISBN Publisher's Prefix: 0-906026

Settle & Bendall (Wigmore) Ltd, 32 Savile Row, London W1X 1AG Tel: (01) 734 0171
Man Dir, Editorial, Rights & Permissions: D Settle; *Sales, Publicity:* M McCarthy; *Production:* P Morris
Parent Company: Wigmore House Publishing Ltd (at above address)
Associate Company: Wigmore Professional (at above address)
Imprints: Settle & Bendall (Wigmore), Wigmore House Publishing
Subjects: Medical, Travel, General, Guidebooks
1981: 3 titles *1982:* 8 titles *Founded:* 1980
ISBN Publisher's Prefix: 0-907070

Severn House Publishers Ltd, 4 Brook St, London W1Y 1AA Tel: (01) 499 3784/(01) 408 2112
Chairman: Edwin Buckhalter; *Publishing Dir:* Delia Cooke; *Sales Dir:* David Roy (Hutchinson Publishing Group)
Orders to: Tiptree Book Services Ltd, St Luke's Chase, Tiptree, Colchester, Essex CO5 0SR Tel: Tiptree 816362 (STD code 0621)
Parent Company: Severn House Books (Holdings) Ltd, 4 Brook St, London W1Y 1AA
Subsidiary Companies: Enigma Books (qv); Severn House Paperbacks Ltd (at above address)
Subjects: Fiction, Thrillers, Romance, War, Historical, Science Fiction, Westerns, Film and TV tie-ins, Juveniles, Natural History, Cookery, Biography, Humour
1983: 140 titles *Founded:* 1974
ISBN Publisher's Prefix: 0-7278

Seymour Large Print Romances, an imprint of Chivers Press Publishers (qv)

Shakespeare Head Press, an imprint of Basil Blackwell Publisher Ltd (qv)

Shaw & Sons Ltd, Shaway House, Lower Sydenham, London SE26 5AE Tel: (01) 778 5131
Man Dir: A Garnish; *Editorial Consultant:* G Morris; *Editorial:* D Hubber; *Sales, Publicity:* W Ponter; *Rights & Permissions:* Miss P Brown
Subjects: Legal, Local Government, General
1981: 9 titles *1982:* 10 titles *Founded:* 1750
ISBN Publisher's Prefix: 0-7219

Sheba Feminist Publishers, 488 Kingsland Rd, London E8 4AE Tel: (01) 254 1590
Orders to: Central Books, 14 The Leathermarket, London SE1 3ER Tel: (01) 407 5447
Subjects: Women's Studies, Children's Books
1981: 6 titles *1982:* 6 titles *Founded:* 1980
ISBN Publisher's Prefix: 0-907179

Sheed & Ward Ltd, 2 Creechurch Lane, London EC3A 5AQ Tel: (01) 283 6330
Dirs: M T Redfern, K G Darke
Subjects: History, Philosophy, Reference, Religion
Founded: 1926
ISBN Publisher's Prefix: 0-7220

Sheldon Press, SPCK Bldg, Marylebone Rd, London NW1 4DU Tel: (01) 387 5282 Cable Add: Futurity London NW1
General Secretary: P N G Gilbert; *Senior Editor:* Darley Anderson; *Sales Manager:*

Alan Goodworth; *Publicity Manager:* Alice Watson
Subjects: Biography, Health & Self Help, Humour, Philosophy, Religion, Psychology, Animals
1982: 25 titles
Miscellaneous: A division of SPCK (qv)
ISBN Publisher's Prefix: 0-85969

Shepheard-Walwyn (Publishers) Ltd+, Suite 34, 26 Charing Cross Rd, London WC2H 0DH Tel: (01) 240 5992 Cable Add: Shepwyn, London WC2 Telex: 261234 H5680D
Man Dir: A R A Werner; *Production Dir:* B K Shaw
Subjects: General Non-fiction
1981: 5 titles *1982:* 4 titles *Founded:* 1971
ISBN Publisher's Prefix: 0-85683

Sheppard Press Ltd, PO Box 42, Russell Chambers, Covent Garden, London WC2E 8AX Tel: (01) 240 0406 Cable Add: Iffcass London WC2
Man Dir: T Rendall Davies
Subjects: Book Trade Reference
1982: 4 titles *Founded:* 1944
ISBN Publisher's Prefix: 0-900661

Shire Publications Ltd, Cromwell House, Church St, Princes Risborough, Aylesbury, Buckinghamshire HP17 9AJ Tel: Princes Risborough 4301 (STD code 08444)
Man Dir: John W Rotheroe
Subjects: Paperbacks on Antiques, Collecting, Architecture, Social History, Military History, Transport, Archaeology, Hand Craft Industries
Founded: 1966
ISBN Publisher's Prefix: 0-85263

Shiva Publishing Ltd+, 4 Church Lane, Nantwich, Cheshire CW5 5RQ Tel: (0270) 628272 Telex: 367258 Gaseqp
Man Dir: Miss Biga Weghofer
Subjects: Educational Software, Personal Computing, Geology, Physics, Mathematics
1981: 7 titles *Founded:* 1979
ISBN Publisher's Prefix: 0-906812

Shuckburgh Reynolds Ltd, 8 Northumberland Pl, London W2 5BS Tel: (01) 727 9636 Telex: 267009
Editorial Dirs: David Reynolds, Julian Shuckburgh; *Production Dir:* Robert Christie; *Design Dir:* Roger Pring; *Rights & Permissions:* Paul Marsh, c/o Anthony Sheil Associates Ltd (qv)
Subjects: Illustrated Non-fiction: History, Biography, Art, Music, Literature, Cinema, Countryside, Astrology, Puzzle Books, Humour
1981: 5 titles *1982:* 6 titles *Founded:* 1979

Sidgwick & Jackson Ltd, 1 Tavistock Chambers, Bloomsbury Way, London WC1A 2SG Tel: (01) 242 6081 Cable Add: Watergate Westcent London Telex: 8952953
Man Dir: William Armstrong; *Sales:* Nigel Newton; *Editorial:* Margaret Willes; *Publicity:* Victoria Stace; *Foreign Rights:* Jane Gregory
Subjects: General Fiction, Belles Lettres, Biography, History, Music, Art, Philosophy, Religion, General & Social Science, Large Format Soft Cover Books, Science Fiction
Founded: 1908
ISBN Publisher's Prefix: 0-283

Sigma Technical Press, 5 Alton Rd, Wilmslow, Cheshire SK9 5DY Tel: Wilmslow 531035 (STD code 0625)
Man Dir, Production: Graham Beech; *Editorial:* Graham Beech, V Kinsella; *Sales, Publicity, Rights & Permissions:* through John Wiley & Sons Ltd (qv) Tel: Chichester 784531 (STD code 0243)
Orders to: John Wiley & Sons Ltd, Distribution Centre, Shripney Rd, Bognor Regis, West Sussex PO22 9SA Tel: Bognor Regis 829121 (STD code 0243)
Subjects: Computing, New Technology
1982: 8 books, 3 software titles *1983:* 16 books, 5 software titles
Founded: 1978
ISBN Publisher's Prefix: 0-905104

Sinclair Browne Ltd, 10 Archway Close, London N19 3TD Tel: (01) 263 3438
Man Dir, Editorial: Patrick Browne; *Publicity:* Vicky Carne; *Rights & Permissions:* Martin Bailey
Imprint: Sinclair Browne
Subjects: Topical Non-fiction, Literature, Fiction, Computer Books
Book Club: Translation Book Club
Founded: 1981
ISBN Publisher's Prefixes: 0-86300, 0-946195

Charles **Skilton** Ltd, 2-4 Abbeymount, Edinburgh EH8 8JH Tel: (031) 661 9339
Man Dir: Charles Skilton
Associate Company and Branch Off: Fudge & Co Ltd (qv)
Subsidiary Companies: Albyn Press Ltd (qv), Luxor Press Ltd, Tallis Press Ltd, Fortune Press, Polybooks (all at 2-4 Abbeymount, Edinburgh 8)
Subjects: Art, Graphic Arts, Reference, Biography, Antiquarian, Cookery, Sexology, Scottish
Founded: 1943
ISBN Publisher's Prefixes: 0-284 (Skilton, Albyn, Luxor, Tallis), 0-85240 (Fortune), 0-7050 (Fudge)

Skilton & Shaw, an imprint of Fudge & Co Ltd (qv)

Thomas **Skinner** Directories, Windsor Court, East Grinstead House, East Grinstead, West Sussex RH1G 1XE Tel: East Grinstead 26972 (STD code 0342)
Publishing Dir: D W Lee; *Publisher:* W J Irlam
Parent Company: Information Services Ltd
Subject: Directories
ISBN Publisher's Prefixes: 0-611, 0-900808

Colin **Smythe** Ltd, PO Box 6, Gerrards Cross, Buckinghamshire SL9 8XA Tel: Gerrards Cross 886000 (STD code 0753) Cable Add: Smythebooks Gerrardscross
Man Dir: Colin Smythe
Subjects: Belles Lettres, Poetry, Biography, History, Music, Art, Philosophy, Reference, Religion, Parapsychology, High-priced Paperbacks, English and Anglo-Irish Literature & Criticism, Drama, Folklore
1981: 12 titles *1982:* 14 titles *Founded:* 1966
ISBN Publisher's Prefixes: 0-900675, 0-901072, 0-86140

The **Society for Promoting** Christian Knowledge, see SPCK

Society for Research into Higher Education*, University of Surrey, Guildford, Surrey GU2 5XH Tel: Guildford 39003 (STD code 0483)
Publications Officer: Sally Kington
Subjects: Higher and Further Education
Founded: 1964
Miscellaneous: The Society is a registered charity
ISBN Publisher's Prefix: 0-900868

Soncino Press Ltd+, 459 Finchley Rd, London NW3 Tel: (01) 431 2998 Cable Add: Soncino London NW3
Man Dir: P Bloch
Subsidiary Company: J Saville & Co Ltd (at above address)
Branch Off: 5 Essex St, New York, NY 10002, USA
Subject: Religion (Jewish)
Founded: 1929
ISBN Publisher's Prefix: 0-900689

Sotheby Publications, an imprint of Philip Wilson Publishers (qv)

Southside, see Canongate Publishing Ltd

Souvenir Press Ltd+, 43 Great Russell St, London WC1B 3PA Tel: (01) 580 9307, (01) 637 5711 Cable Add: Publisher London WC1 Telex: 24710
Man Dir, Rights & Permissions: Ernest Hecht; *Editorial:* Tessa Harrow; *Marketing Dir:* Kenneth Kemp; *Production:* Rodney King; *Publicity & Advertising Manager:* Sue Palmer
Associate Company: Souvenir Press (Australia) Pty Ltd
Subsidiary Companies: Souvenir Press (Educational & Academic) Ltd; Euro-Features Ltd; Pictorial Presentations Ltd; Pop-Universal Ltd; Condor Books
Imprints: Condor Books, Souvenir Press
Branch Off: 311 Singel, Amsterdam, Netherlands
Subjects: General Fiction, Belles Lettres, Poetry, Biography, History, How-to, Music, Art, Philosophy, Religion, Juveniles, Large-format Paperbacks, Medicine, Psychology, Social Science, Sport
Bookshop: Souvenir Press Bookshop (at above London address)
1982: 53 titles *Founded:* 1954
ISBN Publisher's Prefix: 0-285

Sparrow Books, an imprint of Arrow Books Ltd (qv)

Sphere Books Ltd, 30-32 Gray's Inn Rd, London WC1X 8JL Tel: (01) 405 2087 Cable Add: Spherbooks London Telex: 299342
Man Dir: Michael Goldsmith; *Editorial Dirs:* Ms Chris Holifield (Fiction), Rob Shreeve (Non-fiction); *Sales Dir:* Dag Smith; *Production Dir:* Susan Beavan; *Marketing Dir:* Stuart MacDonald; *Rights Manager:* Nann du Sautoy
Orders to: Sphere Order Dept, TBL Book Service Ltd, 17-23 Nelson Way, Tuscam Trading Estate, Camberley, Surrey GU15 3EU Tel: Camberley 62144 (STD code 0276)
Warehouse: High St, Sandhurst, Camberley, Surrey
Imprints: include Abacus, Celtic Revision Aids, Sphere
Subjects: General Fiction and Non-fiction, Biography, History, How-to, Travel, Music, Art, Philosophy, Reference, Low- & High-priced Paperbacks, Medicine, Psychology, General & Social Science
Founded: 1967
Miscellaneous: Company is a member of the the Thomson Books Ltd group (qv), a part of International Thomson Organization Ltd (Canada)
ISBN Publisher's Prefixes: 0-7221 (Sphere), 0-349 (Abacus)

Spokesman Books*, Bertrand Russell House, Gamble St, Nottingham NG7 4ET Tel: Nottingham 708318 (STD code 0602) Cable Add: Russfound
Editorial: Ken Coates; *Sales, Publicity:* Ann Kestenbaum; *Production, Rights & Permissions:* Ken Fleet
Parent Company: Bertrand Russell Peace Foundation Ltd (at above address)
Associate Company: Russell Press Ltd (at above address)
Subjects: International Affairs, Disarmament, Economics, Politics, Industrial Relations, Labour History, Trade Unionism
Founded: 1970
ISBN Publisher's Prefix: 0-85124

E & F N **Spon** Ltd, 11 New Fetter Lane, London EC4P 4EE Tel: (01) 583 9855 Cable Add: Fenspon London EC4 Telex:

263398
Editorial: Phillip Read; *Marketing:* Peter F Shepherd; *Production:* Brian West; *Rights:* Glenys Thorniley; *Permissions:* Jean Richardson
Parent Company: Firm is incorporated in Associated Book Publishers (UK) Ltd (qv under Associated Book Publishers PLC)
Subjects: Reference, Engineering, Building, Applied Sciences
Founded: 1834
ISBN Publisher's Prefix: 0-419

Sporting and Leisure Press, an imprint of Barracuda Books Ltd (qv)

Spring Books, an imprint of The Hamlyn Publishing Group (qv)

Springwood Books Ltd*, 22 Chewter Lane, Windlesham, Surrey GU20 6JP Tel: 74741 (STD code 0276)
Man Dir, Editorial, Sales, Production, Rights & Permissions: Christopher Foster; *Publicity:* Ingela Claxton
Orders to: George Philip Services Ltd, PO Box 1, Littlehampton, Sussex BN17 7EN Tel: Littlehampton 7453 (STD code 09064)
Subjects: Fiction, Poetry, Biography, Children's Books, History, Finance, Music, Archaeology, Art, Cookery, Sport
Founded: 1976
ISBN Publisher's Prefixes: 0-905947, 0-86254

Spurbooks, an imprint of Frederick Warne (Publishers) Ltd (qv)

Stacey International, 128 Kensington Church St, London W8 4BH Tel: (01) 221 7166 Cable Add: Staceybook London W8 Telex: 298768
Man Dir: Tom Stacey
Subjects: Illustrated Non-fiction, Encyclopaedic, Geography, Islamic and Arab Subjects, World Affairs
1981: 12 titles *Founded:* 1974
ISBN Publisher's Prefix: 0-905743

Stage 1*, 47 The Cut, London SE1 8LL Tel: (01) 261 1354
Publisher: Richard Handyside
Subjects: University & Secondary Education, Politics, Economics, Social Sciences
ISBN Publisher's Prefix: 0-85035

Stainer & Bell Ltd, 82 High Rd, London N2 9PW Tel: (01) 444 9135
Man Dir: Bernard A Braley; *Executive Chairman & Editorial Dir:* Allen Percival; *Sales, Marketing Manager:* Glynis Richards
Imprints: include Augener, Belton Books, Galliard, A Weekes, Joseph Williams
Subjects: Music, Education, Drama, History, Religion, Biography, Sociology
Founded: 1907
ISBN Publisher's Prefix: 0-85249

Stam Press Ltd, Raans Rd, Amersham, Buckinghamshire HP6 6JJ Tel: Amersham 4196 (STD code 02403) Telex: 837916
Man Dir: C Breedt Bruijn
Parent Company: The Kluwer Group, Netherlands (qv)
Subjects: Engineering, Shipbuilding, Space Dynamics

Stanford Maritime Ltd, 12-14 Long Acre, London WC2E 9LP Tel: (01) 836 7863 Cable Add: Philip London WC2 Telex: 21667
Man Dir: M A Bovill; *Export Sales Manager:* Marilyn Wheeler; *Editorial Dir, Rights & Permissions:* Tim Parker; *Marketing Manager:* Alan Greene
Orders to: George Philip Services Ltd, Arndale Rd, Lineside Industrial Estate, Littlehampton, West Sussex BN17 7EN Tel: Littlehampton 7453 (STD code 09064)
Associate Company: George Philip & Son Ltd (qv)

Subjects: Nautical books and charts for yachtsmen and professional seamen
Bookshop: At above address
ISBN Publisher's Prefix: 0-540

Star, an imprint of W H Allen & Co Ltd (qv)

Harold **Starke** Ltd, Pegasus House, 116-120 Golden Lane, London EC1Y 0TL Tel: (01) 253 2145
Editorial, Rights & Permissions: Miss N Galinski; *Sales:* H Starke; *Production:* C Tuthill
Orders to: The Barn, Northgate, Beccles, Suffolk NR34 9AX
Parent Company: Burke Publishing Co Ltd (qv)
Subjects: General Non-fiction, Reference, Medical
Founded: 1960
ISBN Publisher's Prefix: 0-287

State University of New York Press, see American University Publishers Group Ltd

Rudolf **Steiner** Press, 38 Museum St, London WC1A 1LP Tel: (01) 242 4249
Manager: E Lloyd
Subjects: Art & Architecture, Philosophy, Education, Religion, Social Sciences, Natural Sciences, Agriculture
Bookshop: At above address
Founded: 1920
ISBN Publisher's Prefix: 0-85440

Patrick **Stephens** Ltd, Bar Hill, Cambridge CB3 8EL Tel: Crafts Hill 80010 (STD code 0954) Cable Add: Peeselpubs, Cambridge Telex: 817677
Chairman: Patrick Stephens; *Man Dir, Editorial:* Darryl Reach; *Sales Manager:* Peter Townsend; *Production Dir:* Ian Heath; *Publicity:* Bruce Quarrie; *Rights & Permissions:* Robert Allen
Subjects: How-to, Maritime, Military, Model Making, Motoring, Motorcycling, Aviation, Photography, Wargaming, Railways, Angling, Boating & Sailing, Commercial Vehicles, Collecting, Countryside, Films & Filming, History, Music, Biographies
1981: 117 titles *Founded:* 1961
ISBN Publisher's Prefix: 0-85059

Stevens & Sons Ltd, 11 New Fetter Lane, London EC4P 4EE Tel: (01) 583 9855 Cable Add: Subjicio London EC4
Man Dir: C D O Evans
Parent Company: Firm is incorporated in Associated Book Publishers (UK) Ltd (qv under Associated Book Publishers PLC)
Subjects: Reference books for lawyers and solicitors, Textbooks for law students and law teachers
Founded: 1888
ISBN Publisher's Prefix: 0-420

Stillitron, 72 New Bond St, London W1Y 0QY Tel: (01) 493 1177 Cable Add: Stillitron, Ldn Telex: 23475
President: Gerald B Stillit
Subject: Modern Languages
Founded: 1964
ISBN Publisher's Prefix: 0-288

Stobart & Son Ltd+, 67-73 Worship St, London EC2A 2EL Tel: (01) 247 0501
Publicity: S Byfield; *Rights & Permissions:* B J Davies
Subjects: Woodwork, Timber, Forestry, Handicrafts
1981: 3 titles *1982:* 3 titles
ISBN Publisher's Prefix: 0-85442

Arthur H **Stockwell** Ltd, Elms Court, Torrs Park, Ilfracombe, Devon EX34 8BA Tel: Ilfracombe 62557 (STD code 0271)
Man Dir, Production, Rights & Permissions: D P Stockwell; *Editorial:* S Jones; *Sales,*

UNITED KINGDOM 435

Publicity: S Hammond
Subjects: Fiction, Non-fiction, Travel, Biography, Religious, War, Humour, Juvenile, Poetry
1982: approx 95 titles *Founded:* 1898
ISBN Publisher's Prefix: 0-7223

Student Christian Movement Press, see S C M Press Ltd

Studentlitteratur, an imprint of Chartwell-Bratt (Publishing & Training) Ltd (qv)

Studio Publications (Ipswich) Ltd+, 32 Princes St, Ipswich, Suffolk IP1 1RJ Tel: Ipswich 217127/218872 (STD code 0473)
Man Dir, Rights & Permissions: Barrie John Henderson; *Publicity, Editorial Manager:* Trevor Weston
Imprints: Badger Books, Dagon Books, Munch Bunch Books
Subject: Children's Books
1981: 26 titles *1982:* 24 titles *Founded:* 1975
ISBN Publisher's Prefixes: 0-904584, 0-86215

Studio Vista, an imprint of Cassell Ltd (qv)

Study Aids, an imprint of Pan Books Ltd (qv)

Sundial, an imprint of Octopus Books PLC (qv)

Surrey University Press, Bishopbriggs, Glasgow G64 2NZ Tel: (041) 772 2311 Telex: 777283
London Off: Furnival House, 14-18 High Holborn, London Tel: (01) 242 5832
Dir: Dr Graeme MacKintosh; *Sales Manager:* Gerard Dummett
Parent Company: Blackie & Son Ltd (qv)
Associate Companies: International Textbook Co Ltd, Leonard Hill (qqv)
Subjects: Engineering, Microbiology, Biomedicine, Chemistry, Physics, Hotel & Catering Studies
Founded: 1972
ISBN Publisher's Prefix: 0-903384

Surveyors Publications, 12 Great George St, Parliament Sq, London SW1P 3AD Tel: (01) 222 7000 ext 272 Cable Add: Surveyable London SW1 Telex: 915443 Rics G
Man Dir: Robert Steel CBE; *Dir:* T H Hooper
Orders to: Norden House, Basing View, Basingstoke, Hants RG21 2HN
Parent Company: Surveyors Holdings Ltd, 12 Great George St, London SW1P 3AD
Associate Company: RICS Journals Ltd, PO Box 87, 1 Pemberton Row, London EC4P 4HL
Subjects: Surveying and related subjects for the Royal Institution of Chartered Surveyors
Bookshop: The Royal Institution of Chartered Surveyors Bookshop, 12 Great George St, Parliament Sq, London SW1P 3AD
Founded: 1981

Sussex University Press*, Sussex House, Falmer, Brighton, East Sussex BN1 9RH Tel: Brighton 606755 (STD code 0273)
Publications Committee: Professors G F A Best, R J Blin-Styole, D F Pocock, A K Thorlby
Subjects: Scholarly
Founded: 1971
Miscellaneous: Associated with The Scottish Academic Press and The Handsel Press (qqv)
ISBN Publisher's Prefix: 0-85621

Sussex Video Ltd, associate company of World Microfilms Publications Ltd (qv) producing educational videotapes

Sweet & Maxwell Ltd, 11 New Fetter Lane, London EC4P 4EE Tel: (01) 583 9855 Cable Add: Subjicio London EC4
Man Dir: C D O Evans
Parent Company: Firm is incorporated in Associated Book Publishers (UK) Ltd (qv under Associated Book Publishers PLC)
Subjects: Law (Reference & University Textbooks), Business
Founded: 1799
ISBN Publisher's Prefix: 0-421

Swift, an imprint of Scripture Union (qv)

Systems Publications Ltd, now Caxton Publications Ltd (qv)

T V Times Books, an imprint of Independent Television Books Ltd (qv)

Talbot House Press, an inprint of The Technical Press Ltd (qv)

Tallis Press Ltd, see Charles Skilton Ltd

Tandem, an imprint of W H Allen & Co Ltd (qv)

The **Tantivy** Press Ltd, Magdalen House, 136-148 Tooley St, London SE1 2TT Tel: (01) 407 7566 Cable Add: Tantivy London SE1
Man Dir, Rights & Permissions: Peter Cowie; *Publicity:* Cecily Hatchitt
Subject: General Non-fiction
1982: 12 titles
ISBN Publisher's Prefix: 0-900730

Target, an imprint of W H Allen & Co Ltd (qv)

Tarquin Publications, Stradbroke, Diss, Norfolk IP21 5JP Tel: Diss 84218 (STD code 0379)
Chief Executive, Editorial, Rights & Permissions: Gerald Jenkins; *Sales:* Margaret Jenkins
Subject: Children's Mathematical & Art/Craft cut-out books
1981: 6 titles *1982:* 6 titles *Founded:* 1970
ISBN Publisher's Prefix: 0-906212

Tate Gallery Publications, Millbank, London SW1P 4RG Tel: (01) 834 5651/2 Cable Add: Tategal London
Publications Manager: Iain Bain; *Sales Manager:* Brian Lawler; *Rights & Permissions:* Graham Langton; *Shop Manager:* Stanley Bennett
Retail Shop: Tate Gallery, Millbank, London SW1P 4RG
Subjects: Art books and catalogues
1982: 16 titles *Founded:* 1931
ISBN Publisher's Prefixes: 0-900874, 0-905005

Tavistock Publications Ltd, 11 New Fetter Lane, London EC4P 4EE Tel: (01) 583 9855 Cable Add: Subjicio London
Orders to: Associated Book Publishers (Services), North Way, Andover, Hampshire Tel: Andover 62141 (STD code 0264)
Editorial Dir: Gill Davies; *Marketing Dir:* Peter Shepherd; *Promotion:* Andrew Welham; *Rights & Permissions:* Glenys Thorniley
Parent Company: Firm is incorporated in Associated Book Publishers (UK) Ltd (qv under Associated Book Publishers PLC)
Subjects: Sociology, Social Work, Anthropology, Psychiatry, Psychology, Philosophy, Social Medicine, Paperbacks, Reference
Bookshop: Sweet & Maxwell Spon Booksellers, North Way, Andover, Hampshire
Founded: 1947
ISBN Publisher's Prefix: 0-422

Taylor & Francis Ltd, 4 John St, London WC1N 2ET Tel: (01) 405 2237 Telex: 858540
Man Dir: A R Selvey; *Publishing Dir:* M I Dawes; *Sales & Marketing Manager:* K R Courtney
Orders to: Taylor & Francis Ltd, Rankine Rd, Basingstoke, Hampshire RG24 0PR
Subsidiary Companies: Falmer Press Ltd (at above London address); Taylor & Francis (Printers) Ltd; International Publications Service, Taylor & Francis Inc, New York, USA
Imprints include: Wykeham
Subjects: Physics, Medicine, Psychology, Engineering, Education, General Science, International Affairs
Founded: 1798
ISBN Publisher's Prefixes: 0-85066 (Taylor & Francis), 0-85109 (Wykeham), 0-905273 (Falmer)

Teach Yourself Books, an imprint of Hodder & Stoughton Ltd (qv)

Teacher Publishing Co Ltd*, Derbyshire House, Lower St, Kettering, Northamptonshire NN16 8BB Tel: Kettering 518407 (STD code 0536)
ISBN Publisher's Prefix: 0-900642

Teakfield Ltd, now Gower Publishing Co Ltd

The **Technical** Press Ltd, Freeland, Oxford OX7 2AP Tel: Freeland 881788 (STD code 0993) Cable Add: Tecpreslon Oxford Telex: 23152 Tecpreslon
Chairman: Paul Stobart; *Publications Manager:* David Wilson
Associate Companies: American Technical Publishers; Beaumont Executive Press; Freeland Press Ltd (details as for The Technical Press); Institute of Personnel Management (qv)
Imprint: Talbot House Press
Subjects: How-to, Reference, Engineering, General Science, College, University & Secondary Textbooks, Business
1981: 7 titles *Founded:* 1933
ISBN Publisher's Prefixes: 0-8269 (American Technical Publishers), 0-946065 (Beaumont Executive Press), 0-900363 (Freeland), 0-85292 (IPM), 0-291 (Technical Press)

Telecommunications Press, see Architectural Press Ltd

Thomas **Telford** Ltd, 1-7 Great George St, London SW1P 3AA Tel: (01) 222 7722 Telex: 946185 Iceas G
Marketing Manager: John Fisher
Subjects: Civil and Nuclear Engineering and related fields
Bookshop: Telford International Bookshop (at above address) (largely a mail order operation)
1982: 124 titles *Founded:* 1972
Miscellaneous: Thomas Telford Ltd is the publishing company of the Institution of Civil Engineers and the British Nuclear Energy Society
ISBN Publisher's Prefixes: 0-901948, 0-7277

Temple Press, an imprint of Newnes Books (qv)

Maurice **Temple Smith** Ltd, Jubilee House, Chapel Rd, Hounslow, Middlesex TW3 1XT Tel: (01) 572 6525
Man Dir: Maurice Temple Smith
Associate Companies: East-West Publications (UK) Ltd; Elron Press Ltd; Wildwood House Ltd (qqv)
Subjects: History, Social Studies, Psychology, Politics, High-priced Paperbacks
Founded: 1970
ISBN Publisher's Prefix: 0-85117

Terrapin, an imprint of Hambleside Publishers Ltd (qv)

Thames & Hudson Ltd+, 30-34 Bloomsbury St, London WC1B 3QP Tel: (01) 636 5488 Cable Add: Thameshuds London WC1 Telex: 25992/3
Man Dir: Thomas Neurath; *Editorial:* Jamie Camplin; *Sales:* Simon Huntley; *Production:* Werner Guttmann; *Publicity:* Kate Fletcher; *Rights & Permissions:* Ian Middleton
Orders to: Thames & Hudson (Distributors) Ltd, 44 Clockhouse Rd, Farnborough, Hampshire GU14 7RA Tel: Farnborough 41602 (STD code 0252)
Associate Companies: Thames & Hudson (Australia) Pty Ltd, 86 Stanley St, West Melbourne, Victoria 3003, Australia; Thames & Hudson Inc, 500 Fifth Ave, New York, NY 10036, USA
Subjects: Art, Architecture, History, Archaeology, Biography, Photography, Topography, Music, Theatre
1981: approx 150 titles *Founded:* 1949
ISBN Publisher's Prefix: 0-500

Thames Head Ltd+, Avening, Tetbury, Gloucestershire GL8 8NB Tel: Nailsworth 2136 (STD code 045383) Cable Add: Thameshead Tetbury Telex: 437128 RDS Ltd
Sales, Rights & Permissions: Martin F Marix Evans; *Production:* David Playne
Orders to: Blakes, Much Hadham, Hertfordshire SG10 6BT Tel: Much Hadham 2167 (STD code 027984) Cable Add: Marixbook Muchhadham
Associate Company: Marix Evans & Chilvers SA, Switzerland (qv)
Subjects: Sport, How-to, Social and Military History, Music, General Non-fiction (in co-editions)
1983: 2 titles *1984:* approx 10 titles
Founded: 1981
ISBN Publisher's Prefix: 0-907733

A **Thomas**, an imprint of Thorsons Publishers Ltd (qv)

Thomson Books Ltd, Garden House, 57-59 Long Acre, London WC2E 9JL Tel: (01) 836 7733 Telex: 298265
Man Dir: R F M Bennett
Parent Company: International Thomson Organization Ltd (Canada)
Group Companies' Imprints:
Paperback: Abacus; Sphere Books (qv)
General Trade: Elm Tree; Hamish Hamilton (qv); Hamish Hamilton Children's Books; Michael Joseph (qv); Pelham (qv); Rainbird (qv)
Naval, Military, Aviation: Jane's Publishing Co Ltd (qv)
Founded: 1977
Miscellaneous: See separate group company entries where marked (qv) for further information. T B L Book Service Ltd, 17-23 Nelson Way, Tuscam Trading Estate, Camberley, Surrey GU15 3EU, is the warehousing and distribution subsidiary of the company

Stanley **Thornes** (Publishers) Ltd, Old Station Rd, off Liddington Estate, Leckhampton Rd, Cheltenham, Glos GL53 0DN Tel: Cheltenham 584429 (STD code 0242), Cheltenham 42127/42451 Telex: 43592
Man Dir: Stanley Thornes; *Production Dir:* Roy Kendall; *Trade Sales Manager:* Margot van de Weijer
Parent Company: The Kluwer Group, Netherlands (qv)
Subjects: Mathematics, Engineering, Business Studies, Modern Languages, English Language, Sciences, Education, Catering, Beauty Therapy
1982: 180 titles
ISBN Publisher's Prefix: 0-85950

UNITED KINGDOM 437

Thornhill Press Ltd, 24 Moorend Rd, Cheltenham, Glos GL53 0AU Tel: Cheltenham 519137 (STD code 0242)
Man Dir: D Badham-Thornhill
Subjects: Topographical Guides, Sport and some general titles
1981: 6 titles *1982:* 6 titles *Founded:* 1972
ISBN Publisher's Prefixes: 0-904110, 0-946328

Thornton Cox Ltd, c/o 84-86 Baker St, London W1N 1DL
Man Dir: Richard Cox
Orders to: Geographia Ltd, 17-21 Conway St, London W1P 5HL
Subjects: Travel Guides
Founded: 1966
ISBN Publisher's Prefix: 0-902726

F A Thorpe (Publishing) Ltd, The Green, Bradgate Rd, Anstey, Leicester LE7 7FU Tel: Leicester 364325 (STD code 0533)
Man Dir: Dr F A Thorpe, OBE
Subjects: Fiction, Travel & Adventure, Non-fiction
Miscellaneous: Publishers of Ulverscroft Large Print Books and Charnwood Library Series
ISBN Publisher's Prefixes: 0-85456, 0-7089

Thorsons Publishers Ltd+, Denington Estate, Wellingborough, Northamptonshire NN8 2RQ Tel: Wellingborough 76031 (STD code 0933) Cable Add: Thorgroup Wellingborough Telex: 311072 Thopub G
Chairman: J A Young; *Man Dir:* D J Young; *Rights & Permissions:* Marjorie Nelson; *Editorial Dir:* J R Hardaker; *Production Dir:* D C J Palmer; *Sales Manager:* Tom Berry
Subsidiary Companies: Aquarian Press Ltd (qv); Turnstone Press Ltd (qv)
Associate Company: Laser Cassettes Ltd
Imprints: Athene Publishing Co, Excalibur, A Thomas
Subjects: Natural Health & Healing, Special Diets Cookery, Alternative Medicine, Hypnotism and Hypnotherapy, Practical Psychology, Self-Help, Books for Women, Animal Rights, Yoga and related disciplines
1983: 106 titles *Founded:* 1930
ISBN Publisher's Prefixes: 0-7225, 0-85454, 0-907783

The **Thule** Press, incorporated in The Findhorn Press (qv)

Thurman Publishing Ltd, 28 The Mill Trading Estate, Acton Lane, Harlesden, London NW10 7NP Tel: (01) 961 4477 Telex: 24339
Dirs: S J T Marshall, R C Williams, D Z Williams; *Sales:* S J T Marshall; *Production, Publicity:* Mrs C Piper; *Rights & Permissions:* Mrs C Piper, S J T Marshall
Subjects: Children's Books
Founded: 1974
ISBN Publisher's Prefix: 0-85985

Tiger, an imprint of Scripture Union (qv)

Time-Life Books, Time-Life International, 153 New Bond St, London W1Y 0AA Tel: (01) 499 4080 Cable Add: Timeinc London W1 Telex: 22557
Orders to: (UK) WHS Distributors, St John's House, East St, Leicester LE1 6NE Tel: Leicester 551196 (STD code 0533) (Export) Above London address
European Head Off: Time-Life Books BV, Netherlands (qv)

Times Books Ltd, 16 Golden Sq, London W1R 4BN Tel: (01) 434 3767 Telex: 897284
Man Dir: B Winkleman; *Senior Editor:* P Middleton; *Editors:* A Hudson, A Freegard, P Batchelor; *Production Manager:* D Osler
Subjects: Atlases, General Non-fiction, Reference
ISBN Publisher's Prefix: 0-7230

Alec **Tiranti** Ltd, an imprint of Academy Editions (qv)

Tobin Music Books, an imprint of Helicon Press (qv)

Tolley Publishing Co, an imprint of Ernest Benn Ltd (qv)

Topaz Publishing Ltd, 67 High St, Great Missenden, Bucks Tel: Great Missenden 4161 (STD code 02406) Cable Add: Rosco Gt Missenden Telex: 837663 Datres G Attn Topaz
Man Dir, Editorial & Sales: Colin Rose; *Rights & Permissions:* Diana Rose
Subjects: Non-fiction, Popular Science, Psychology, Humour, Gambling
Founded: 1975
ISBN Publisher's Prefix: 0-905553

Tops'l Books+, 13 Wise's Firs, Sulhamstead, Berkshire RG7 4EH Tel: Burghfield Common 2851 (STD code 073529)
Chief Executive: Colin Elliott
Subject: Maritime History
1982: 2 titles *Founded:* 1978
ISBN Publisher's Prefix: 0-906397

Town & County Books Ltd, Terminal House, Shepperton, Middlesex TW17 8AS Tel: Walton-on-Thames 228950 (STD code 0932) Telex: 929806
Chief Executive: Ian Allan; *Editorial, Production:* Alan Hollingsworth; *Sales, Publicity, Rights & Permissions:* Roderick Dymont
Parent Company: Ian Allan Group (at above address)
Associate Companies: Ian Allan Ltd (qv), Lewis Masonic (at above address)
Subjects: British Landscape, History & Architecture, Fashion, Photography
1983: 10 titles *Founded:* 1982
ISBN Publisher's Prefix: 0-86364

Transport Publishing Company, 128 Pikes Lane, Glossop, Derbyshire SK13 8EH Tel: Glossop 61508 (STD code 04574)
Man Dir: John A Senior
Subsidiary Company: Senior Publications (at above address)
Subject: Transport
1981: 8 titles *1982:* 10 titles *Founded:* 1973
ISBN Publisher's Prefixes: 0-903839, 0-86317

Transworld Publishers Ltd, see Corgi Books Ltd

Travelaid Publishing, see Michael Haag Ltd/Travelaid Publishing

Treasure, an imprint of Octopus Books PLC (qv)

Trefoil Books Ltd+, 15 St John's Hill, London SW11 Tel: (01) 223 7037
Man Dir: Conway Lloyd Morgan; *Editorial Dir:* Melissa Denny; *Marketing Dir, Publicity:* Christiane Logan; *Production, Rights & Permissions:* Melissa Denny, Conway Lloyd Morgan
Subjects: Art, Fine Arts, Decorative Arts, Architecture, Exhibition Catalogues
1981: 2 titles *1982:* 8 titles *Founded:* 1981
ISBN Publisher's Prefix: 0-86294

Triad Paperbacks, a subsidiary company of the Chatto, Bodley Head & Jonathan Cape Ltd group (qv), but handled by Granada Publishing Ltd (qv)

Triangle Books+, Holy Trinity Church, Marylebone Rd, London NW1 4DU Tel: (01) 387 5282 Cable Add: Futurity London NW1
General Secretary: Patrick Gilbert; *Editorial:* Myrtle Powley; *Sales Manager:* Alan Goodworth; *Promotion:* Alice Watson
Subject: Popular Religious Paperbacks
1981: 6 titles *1982:* 12 titles
Miscellaneous: A division of SPCK (qv)
ISBN Publisher's Prefix: 0-281

Trigon Press, 117 Kent House Road, Beckenham, Kent BR3 1JJ Tel: (01) 778 0534
Man Dir, Sales: Roger Sheppard; *Editorial, Production:* Judith Sheppard; *Publicity:* Angela Roberts; *Rights & Permissions:* Pat Palmer
Subsidiary Company: Museum and Gallery Publishing (at above address)
Subjects: Bibliography, Business, Typography, Book Collecting, Publishing, Bookselling
Founded: 1974
ISBN Publisher's Prefix: 0-904929

Troubadour, an imprint of Macdonald & Co (Publishers) Ltd (qv)

Turnstone Press Ltd+, Denington Estate, Wellingborough, Northamptonshire NN8 2RQ Tel: Wellingborough 76031 (STD code 0933) Cable Add: Thorgroup Wellingborough Telex: 311072 Thopub G
Man Dir: D J Young; *Production Dir:* D C J Palmer; *Sales Manager:* Tom Berry; *Editorial:* Michael Cox, John Hardaker; *Rights & Permissions:* Marjorie Nelson
Parent Company: Thorsons Publishers Ltd (qv)
Subjects: Pre-history, Archaeology (alternative), Psychology, Health and Healing, Ecology, Social Issues
1983: 14 titles *Founded:* 1971
ISBN Publisher's Prefix: 0-85500

Tyndale Press, an imprint of Inter-Varsity Press

Uffici, an imprint of Clematis Press Ltd (qv)

Ulverscroft Large Print Books Ltd, see F A Thorpe (Publishing) Ltd

Uni Books, an imprint of Volturna Press (qv)

Unibooks, an imprint of Hodder & Stoughton Ltd (qv)

United Writers Publications Ltd+, Trevail Mill, Zennor, St Ives, Cornwall TR26 3BW Tel: Penzance 796038 (STD code 0736)
Man Dir, Editorial: Sydney Sheppard; *Sales:* Malcolm Sheppard; *Production:* Richard J Sheppard; *Publicity:* Giles Harmon; *Rights & Permissions:* Julian Tremayne
Subjects: Biography, Travel, General Fiction, Writers' & Poets' Yearbook
1982: 7 titles *Founded:* 1962
ISBN Publisher's Prefix: 0-901976

University, an imprint of Ramboro Enterprises Ltd (qv)

University College Cardiff Press+, University College, PO Box 78, Cardiff CF1 1XL Tel: Cardiff 44211 (STD code 0222)
Chairman of Editorial Board: Dr C W L Bevan CBE; *Editorial:* D P M Michael CBE (Secretary); *Sales, Production, Publicity, Rights & Permissions:* Bryan Turnbull
Subjects: Teaching Physics, Communist Studies, Astronomy, Music, Law and Society, Bee-keeping, Philosophy
Founded: 1978

University Microfilms International, (Xerox Information Resources Group), 30-32 Mortimer St, London W1N 7RA Tel: (01) 631 5030 Telex: 8811363 Exel G
Man Dir: Tim Smartt; *Sales Manager:* Kim Deshayes; *Publicity Manager:* Avril Pizer; *Area Sales Managers:* Steven Hall, Susan Orchard
Parent Company: Ultimate holding company Xerox Corporation
Subjects: Multi-disciplinary information products in paper & micro-formats, including dissertations, journals, newspapers, books and research collections

UNITED KINGDOM

1981-82: 60,000 dissertations, 8,000 serials in microform, 6,700 on-demand reprints of o/p books *Founded:* 1938 (USA); 1952 (UK)

University of California Press, Ely House, 37 Dover St, London W1X 4HQ Tel: (01) 499 4688, (01) 493 5061 Cable Add: Unibooks London W1 Telex: 24224 Ref 3545
Warehouse: International Book Distributors Ltd, 66 Wood Lane End, Hemel Hempstead, Hertfordshire Tel: Hemel Hempstead 58531 (STD code 0442)
Man Dir: Trevor Brown; *Publicity Manager:* Michael Richards; *Sales Manager:* Anna Simpson-Muellner (Export)
Parent Company: University of California Press, 2223 Fulton St, Berkeley, California 94720, USA
Subjects: Academic (all disciplines)
ISBN Publisher's Prefix: 0-520

The **University of Chicago** Press, 126 Buckingham Palace Rd, London SW1W 9SD Tel: (01) 730 9208 Cable Add: Chibooks Telex: 23933 Chibooks Ldn
Sales Manager: Warren Bertram; *Publicity Manager:* Sybil Richardson
Orders to: International Book Distributors Ltd, 66 Wood Lane End, Hemel Hempstead, Hertfordshire Tel: Hemel Hempstead 58531 (STD code 0442)
Associate Companies: Harvard University Press, The MIT Press (both at above address)
Subjects: Biography, History, Music, Art, Philosophy, Reference, Paperbacks, Medicine, Psychology, General & Social Science, Literature, Education
1982: 200 titles *Founded:* 1891
Miscellaneous: Branch of The University of Chicago Press, Chicago, Illinois, USA
ISBN Publisher's Prefix: 0-226

University of Illinois Press, see American University Publishers Group Ltd

University of Kentucky Press, see American University Publishers Group Ltd

University of London Press Ltd (now Hodder & Stoughton Educational), see Hodder & Stoughton Ltd

University of Missouri Press, see American University Publishers Group Ltd

University of Nebraska Press, see American University Publishers Group Ltd

University of North Carolina Press, see American University Publishers Group Ltd

University of Notre Dame Press, see American University Publishers Group Ltd

University of Texas Press, see American University Publishers Group Ltd

University of Wales Press+, 6 Gwennyth St, Cathays, Cardiff CF2 4YD Tel: Cardiff 31919 (STD code 0222)
Dir: John Rhys; *Sales:* Richard Houdmont
Imprint: Gwasg Prifysgol Cymru
Subjects: History, Music, Art, Reference, Religion, Science, Humanities, Social Sciences, University, Secondary Textbooks (Welsh & English), Journals, Microfiche
1981: 40 titles *1982:* 30 titles *Founded:* 1922
ISBN Publisher's Prefixes: 0-7083, 0-900768

University of Washington Press, see American University Publishers Group Ltd

University of Wisconsin Press, see American University Publishers Group Ltd

University Presses of Columbia and Princeton, 15A Epsom Rd, Guildford, Surrey GU1 3JT Tel: Guildford 68364 (STD code 0483)
Manager: Wolfgang Wingerter
Parent Companies: Columbia University Press, New York, USA and Princeton University Press, Princeton, New Jersey, USA
Subjects: Academic Books and Paperbacks in the Humanities, Social and Natural Sciences
1982: 200 titles *1983:* approx 190 titles
ISBN Publisher's Prefixes: 0-231 (Columbia), 0-691 (Princeton)

University Tutorial Press Ltd, 2 Hills Rd, Cambridge CB2 1NG Tel: Cambridge 350949/59550 (STD code 0223) Telex: 817343 Blucam G
Man Dir, Production Manager: J B Briggs; *Editorial Manager:* S J Boyd; *Trade Dir:* R E Everard
Orders to: 842 Yeovil Rd, Slough SL1 4JQ
Subjects: University & Secondary Textbooks
1981: 12 titles *1982:* 4 titles *Founded:* 1901
ISBN Publisher's Prefix: 0-7231

Unwin Paperbacks, an imprint of George Allen & Unwin (Publishers) Ltd

Update Books Ltd, 33-34 Alfred Pl, London WC1E 7DP Tel: (01) 637 4544 Cable Add: Updatepub London WC1
Executive Chairman: Dr Abraham Marcus; *Man Dir:* Stephen Townsend; *Editorial, Rights & Permissions:* Ms G Evans; *Advertisement Manager:* Frank Middleton; *Production Dir:* John Snow
Parent Company: Update Group Management Ltd
Associate Companies: The Update Group Ltd; Update Publications Ltd
Subjects: Medical, Dental, Hospital
1982: 13 titles
ISBN Publisher's Prefix: 0-906141

Laurence **Urdang** Associates Ltd, see Market House Books Ltd

Usborne Publishing Ltd, 20 Garrick St, London WC2E 9BJ Tel: (01) 379 3535 Cable Add: Uspub, London WC2 Telex: 8953598 Uspub G
Man Dir: Peter Usborne; *Production, Rights & Permissions:* David Lowe
Associate Company: BPCC PLC (qv)
Subjects: Children's Books (Non-fiction)
Founded: 1973
ISBN Publisher's Prefix: 0-86020

Vallentine, Mitchell & Co Ltd, Gainsborough House, 11 Gainsborough Rd, Leytonstone, London E11 1RS Tel: (01) 530 4226 Cable Add: Valmico London Telex: 897719
Warehouse: Macdonald & Evans Ltd, Estover Rd, Estover, Plymouth PL6 7PZ
Man Dir: Frank Cass; *Editorial:* Margaret Goodare; *Trade:* Richard Norris; *Production:* John Smith; *Publicity:* Hayley Cass
Associate Companies: Frank Cass & Co Ltd (qv); The Woburn Press (qv)
Subjects: Jewish Studies, Literature, History, Politics
Founded: 1950
ISBN Publisher's Prefix: 0-85303

Van Duren Publishers Ltd, PO Box 1, Gerrards Cross, Buckinghamshire SL9 7AE Tel: Gerrards Cross 886575 (STD code 0753)
Man Dir, Rights & Permissions: Peter Bander van Duren; *Production Dir:* Leslie C Hayward
Subjects: Matters concerning Holy See or Catholic Church, Heraldry (Ecclesiastical & Secular), Non-fiction
1983: 5 titles *Founded:* 1973
ISBN Publisher's Prefix: 0-905715

Van Nostrand Reinhold (UK) Co Ltd+, Molly Millar's Lane, Wokingham, Berkshire RG11 2PY Tel: Wokingham 789456 (STD code 0734) Telex: 847798 BORDS-G
Man Dir: J G Paul; *Dir and General Manager:* D J Smith; *Publisher:* Dominic Recaldin; *Marketing Manager:* Michael McWhinnie; *Sales Manager:* Peter Daniels; *Sales Promotion Manager:* Roger Horton
Parent Company: Thomson International, Royal Bank Plaza, PO Box 20, Suite 3515, Toronto, Canada
Associate Company: Thomas Nelson & Sons Ltd (qv)
Imprint: Gee & Co
Subjects: Art, Reference, Professional, General & Social Science, University and College Textbooks, High-priced Paperbacks, Psychology, Engineering, Technical Handbooks, Practical, Crafts
ISBN Publisher's Prefix: 0-442

Variorum, 20 Pembridge Mews, London W11 3EQ Tel: (01) 727 5492
Proprietor: Mrs E Turner
Subjects: History, Architecture, Arts, Reference, Religion, University Textbooks, Archaeology, Economics, Mediaeval and Canon Law
1981: 21 titles *1982:* 21 titles *Founded:* 1969
ISBN Publisher's Prefixes: 0-902089, 0-86078

Varsity, an imprint of Ramboro Enterprises Ltd (qv)

Venton Educational Ltd, The Uffington Press, High St, Melksham, Wiltshire SN12 6LA Tel: Melksham 703424 (STD code 0225)
Man Dir, Editorial, Publicity, Rights & Permissions: Colin Venton; *Sales:* Stuart Murray; *Production:* Sally Cuff
Subsidiary Company: Colin Venton Ltd (at above address)
Associate Company: Melksham Typesetting Service Ltd, High St, Melksham, Wiltshire
Imprint: White Horse Library
Subjects: Careers, Maritime, Motoring, Travel, West Country, 'Vet' Books
Founded: 1954
ISBN Publisher's Prefixes: 0-85993 (Venton Educational), 0-85475 (Colin Venton)

Ventura Publishing Ltd, 44 Uxbridge St, London W8 7TG Tel: (01) 221 6395 Telex: 8953658 Venpub G
Man Dir, Rights & Permissions: Robin Ellis
Subjects: Children's Novelty, Adult Reference
Founded: 1977
Miscellaneous: Firm is mainly an editorial and production organization producing books for other publishers
ISBN Publisher's Prefix: 0-906284

Verbatim+, PO Box 199, Aylesbury, Buckinghamshire HP20 1TQ Tel: Aylesbury 27314 (STD code 0296)
Man Dir, Editorial, Rights & Permissions: Laurence Urdang; *Sales:* Hazel Hall; *Production:* Frank R Abate; *Publicity:* Martha Martin
Parent Company: Laurence Urdang Inc (at above address)
Associate Companies: Laurence Urdang Inc, PO Box 668, Essex, Connecticut 06426, USA; Laurence Urdang Associates Ltd, Market House, Market Square, Aylesbury, Buckinghamshire HP20 1TN
Subject: Language
Book Club: Verbatim Book Club
1981: 5 titles *1982:* 6 titles *Founded:* 1974
ISBN Publisher's Prefix: 0-930454

Veritas Foundation Publication Centre, 4-12 Praed Mews, London W2 1QZ Tel: (01) 262 6879
Man Dir: W Dluzewski; *Sales:* T Wachowiak
Associate Company: Veritas Foundation Press
Subjects: Poland, Polish Culture
Bookshop: 4-8 Praed Mews, London W2 1QZ Tel: (01) 723 1364
Founded: 1948

Vermilion, an imprint of Hutchinson Books Ltd (qv)

Verso Editions/NLB, 15 Greek St, London W1 Tel: (01) 437 3546
Orders to: International Book Distributors, 66 Wood Lane End, Hemel Hempstead, Hertfordshire HP2 4RG Tel: Hemel Hempstead 58531 (STD code 0442)
Subjects: Philosophy, History, Economics, Aesthetics, Psychology, Sociology, Political Theory, Contemporary Politics
1981: 12 titles
ISBN Publisher's Prefixes: 0-902308, 0-86091

Vine Books, an imprint of Church Society (qv)

Virago Ltd+, 41 William IV St, London WC2N 4DB Tel: (01) 379 6977 Cable: Caterwaul London WC2
Chairman: Carmen Callil; *Joint Man Dirs:* Ursula Owen, Harriet Spicer; *Dir:* Kate Griffin; *Publicity Dir:* Lennie Goodings; *Rights & Permissions:* Lynn Knight
Orders to: Chatto, Bodley Head & Cape Services Ltd, 9 Bow St, London WC2E 7AL Tel: (01) 379 6637 Telex: 299080
Subjects: Fiction, Biography, History, Philosophy, Education, Politics, Social Science & History, Women's Studies, Education, Health, Reference, Feminist Books, Illustrated Large-format Paperbacks
1982: 53 titles *1983:* 60 titles *Founded:* 1976
Miscellaneous: Firm is a member of Chatto, Bodley Head & Jonathan Cape Ltd Group (qv)
ISBN Publisher's Prefix: 0-86068

Virgin Books, 61-63 Portobello Rd, London W11 3DD Tel: (01) 221 7535 Telex: 262195 Virgin G
Chief Executive, Rights & Permissions: John Brown; *Editorial, Production:* Cat Ledger; *Sales, Publicity:* Norman Dinesen
Orders to: Tiptree Book Services, Tiptree, Essex CO5 0SR Tel: Tiptree 816362 (STD code 0621)
Subjects: Popular Music, Entertainment, General Non-fiction, Computer Software
1981: 19 titles *1982:* 25 titles *Founded:* 1979
ISBN Publisher's Prefix: 0-907080

Virtue & Co Ltd, 25 Breakfield, Coulsdon, Surrey CR3 2UE Tel: (01) 668 4632 Cable Add: Virtutis Croydon Telex: 261507 Ref 3393
Man Dir: Michael Virtue; *Sales Dir:* R S Cook
Branch Offs: London, Dublin
Subjects: Hotel and Catering, Reference, Religion, Educational Materials
Founded: 1819
ISBN Publisher's Prefix: 0-900778

Vision Press Ltd, Fulham Wharf, Townmead Rd, London SW6 2SB Tel: (01) 589 9773
Man Dir: Alan Moore
Imprint: Artemis Press
Subjects: Belles Lettres, Biography, History, Music, Art, Philosophy, Religion, Psychology, Educational
Founded: 1947
ISBN Publisher's Prefix: 0-85478

Voltaire Foundation, Taylor Institution, St Giles, Oxford OX1 3NA Tel: Oxford 512931 (STD code 0865) Telex: 83295 Nuclox G (mark for Voltaire Foundation)
Publications Manager: Andrew Brown
Subjects: Modern Languages, History, Philosophy
1982: 15 titles *Founded:* 1971
ISBN Publisher's Prefix: 0-7294

Volturna Press, 52 Ormonde Rd, Hythe, Kent Tel: Hythe (Kent) 69465 (STD code 0303)

Sole Partner: Dr D M C MacEwan
Imprints: Cochuideachd Leabhrachean Gàidhlig, Marsland Press, Uni Books
Branch Off: Peterhead, Aberdeenshire
Subjects: Religion, Conservation, Biographies, Family Memoirs, Academic; All types of books in minor languages including Scottish Gaelic
1982: 5 titles *Founded:* 1968
ISBN Publisher's Prefix: 0-85606

W I Books Ltd, 39 Eccleston St, London SW1W 9NT Tel: (01) 730 7212
Chief Executive: Anne Ballard; *General Manager:* Sue Jacquemier
Parent Company: National Federation of Women's Institutes (at above address)
Subjects: Crafts, Home Economics, Cookery, Women's Interests
1981: 18 titles *1982:* 15 titles *Founded:* 1979
ISBN Publisher's Prefix: 0-9005566

Wadsworth International Group, 44 Bedford Row, London WC1R 4LE Tel: (01) 405 1982 Telex: 262284 ref 617
Head Office: 10 Davis Drive, Belmont, California 94002, USA Tel: 348383

Wales Tourist Board, Sales and Distribution Centre, Davis St, Cardiff CF1 2FU Tel: Cardiff 487387 (STD code 0222) Telex: 497269
Sales & Distribution Manager: Rhys Jones
Subjects: Maps, History, Archaeology, Holiday Accommodation & Travel Guides, Angling, Guides & Posters
ISBN Publisher's Prefix: 0-900784

Walker Books Ltd, 17-19 Hanway House, 7-12 Hanway Pl, London W1P 9DL Tel: (01) 636 0374 Telex: 8955572
Man Dir: Sebastian Walker; *Editorial:* Wendy Boase; *Production:* Judy Burdsall; *UK Publishing:* Ted Collins
Imprint: Zebra Books
Subjects: Children's Books: Full-colour Non-fiction, Picture Books, Novelty, Pop-up Books, Board Books
1981: 46 titles *Founded:* 1978
ISBN Publisher's Prefix: 0-7445

Walsingham, an imprint of Jarrold Colour Publications (qv)

Henry E **Walter** Ltd, 26 Grafton Rd, Worthing, West Sussex Tel: Worthing 204567 (STD code 0903)
Subjects: Religious, Children's Books (Rewards and Activity)
ISBN Publisher's Prefix: 0-85479

The **Warburg** Institute (University of London), Woburn Sq, London WC1H 0AB Tel: (01) 580 9663
Assistant Secretary: Angela Barlow (to whom all enquiries about publications)
Subject: Cultural History
1982: 2 titles *Founded:* (The Institute) 1921
Miscellaneous: The Institute is a non-commercial organization
ISBN Publisher's Prefix: 0-85481

Ward Lock Educational Ltd, 47 Marylebone Lane, London W1M 6AX Tel: (01) 486 3271 Cable Add: Warlock London W1 Telex: 266231 Wleco G
Warehouse: Bookpoint Ltd, 39 Milton Trading Estate, Abingdon, Oxfordshire OX14 4TD Tel: Abingdon 835001 (STD code 0235)
Man Dir, Marketing Dir, Sales, Rights & Permissions: Judith Reinhold; *Production:* Deborah Anderson; *Publicity:* Sandy Buchschacher
Subjects: Educational
1981: 60 titles *1982:* 50 titles
Miscellaneous: Firm is a member of the Ling Kee Group, Hong Kong (qv)
ISBN Publisher's Prefix: 0-7062

Ward Lock Ltd+, 82 Gower St, London WC1E 6EQ Tel: (01) 637 9472 Telex: 262364 Warlok G
Warehouse: Ward Lock Ltd (Distribution), Great Ducie St, PO Box 111, Manchester M60 3BL
Chairman: G A Hazard; *Man Dir:* Peter Lock; *Special Projects Editor:* David Holmes; *Marketing:* John Harris; *Sales:* David Williams (Home & Export); *Publicity:* Stella Mayo; *Production:* David Sheldrake; *Rights & Co-editions:* Katherine Davies
Imprints: Concorde Paperbacks, Horseman's Handbooks, Hyperion Books
Subjects: Cookery, Gardening, Equestrian, Sailing, Crafts, Yoga, Sports, Hobbies, Pets, Specialist Colour Illustrated International Co-editions, How-to, Children's Information Books, Paperbacks, Reference, Guide Books
1981: 50 titles *1982:* 42 titles *Founded:* 1854
Miscellaneous: Holding company is Pentos PLC (qv for associated publishing companies)
ISBN Publisher's Prefix: 0-7063

Frederick **Warne** (Publishers) Ltd, 40 Bedford Sq, London WC1B 3HE Tel: (01) 580 9622 Cable Add: Warne London WC1 Telex: 25963
Chairman, Man Dir: D W Bisacre; *Marketing Dir:* R D Traube; *Production, Publishing Programme Dir:* Susan Coley; *Rights:* Karen Garner; *Licensing & Permissions:* Anne Irvin
Orders to: Warne House, Vincent Lane, Dorking, Surrey RH4 3FW Tel: Dorking 885081 (STD code 0306) Telex: 859635
Parent Company: Penguin Books Ltd (qv)
Associate Company: Frederick Warne & Co Inc, 2 Park Ave, New York NY 10016, USA
Imprints: Harris & Baldwin, Marshall, Seeley Service, Spurbooks, Warne Gerrard
Subjects: How-to, Music, Art, Reference, Religion, Juveniles, Natural History, Primary Textbooks, Educational Wall Charts, Military, Transport, Recreation, Outdoor Activities
1981: 70 titles *Founded:* 1865
ISBN Publisher's Prefix: 0-7232

Waterlow Publishers Ltd, Maxwell House, 74 Worship St, London EC2A 2EN Tel: (01) 377 4600 Telex: 888804
Man Dir: V Williamson
Parent Company: BPCC PLC (qv)
Subjects: Banking, Legal, General Business
ISBN Publisher's Prefix: 0-900791

Watkins Publishing, now Robinson & Watkins Books Ltd (qv)

W **Watson** & Co*, St Ann's Hill, Carlisle, Cumbria
Subject: Religion

Franklin **Watts** Ltd, 12a Golden Sq, London W1R 4BA Tel: (01) 437 0713 Cable Add: Frawatts London W1 Telex: 262655 Groluk
Man Dir: David Howgrave-Graham; *Marketing Dir:* Rosemary Lister; *Editorial Dir:* Chester Fisher; *Sales Dir:* George Taylor; *Rights & Permissions:* Elizabeth Hamilton
Associate Companies: Julia MacRae Books (qv); The Grolier Society of Australia Pty Ltd, Australia (qv)
Subjects: Reference, Juveniles
Founded: 1969
ISBN Publisher's Prefixes: 0-85166, 0-531, 0-86313

Wayland Publishers Ltd+, 49 Lansdowne Pl, Hove, East Sussex BN3 1HS Tel: Brighton 722561 (STD code 0273) Cable Add: Bookwright Hove Telex: 23961
Orders to: PO Box 8, Bridge St, Hemel Hempstead, Hertfordshire HP1 1EE
Man Dir: John Lewis; *Managing Editor:*

Roger Cleeve; *Production Manager:* Neville Buxton; *Sales Manager:* Peter Hyem
Associate Company: Financial Training Publications Ltd (qv)
Subsidiary Company: Priory Press Ltd
Subjects: Illustrated School Library Books, Biography, Geography, History, Natural History, Science, Arts and Crafts, Transport, Careers
1982: 90 titles *Founded:* 1969
ISBN Publisher's Prefixes: 0-85340 (Wayland), 0-85078 (Priory Press)

The **Wayzgoose** Press, now Aquila/The Wayzgoose Press, an imprint of Johnston Green & Co (Publishers) Ltd (qv)

Webb & Bower (Publishers) Ltd, 9 Colleton Crescent, Exeter, Devon EX2 4BY Tel: 35362 (STD code 0392) Cable Add: Webbower Exeter Telex: 42544 Webbow G
Man Dir: Richard Webb; *Editorial Dir:* Delian Bower; *Publishing Dir:* Nicholas Facer; *Publicity:* Carole Pengelly and Tony Mulliken, 14 St Albans St, The Haymarket, London SW1 (Tel: (01) 839 6594)
Subjects: General Non-fiction, Illustrated Books
1982: 25 titles *1983:* 24 titles *Founded:* 1978

A **Weekes**, an imprint of Stainer & Bell Ltd (qv)

Weidenfeld (Publishers) Ltd, 91 Clapham High St, London SW4 7TA Tel: (01) 622 9933 Cable Add: Nicobar SW4 7TA Telex: 918066
Chairman, Chief Executive: Lord Weidenfeld; *Deputy Chairman, Publishing Dir:* Michael O'Mara; *Man Dir:* Ray Compton; *Deputy Man Dir, Production Dir:* Richard Hussey; *Sales Dir:* David Livermore; *Marketing Dir:* Rosalind Lewis; *Rights & Permissions:* Miss B J MacLennan
Subsidiary Company: Arthur Barker Ltd (qv)
Associate Company: Frances Lincoln Ltd (qv)
Imprints: Include Artus, World University Library
Subjects: General Fiction, Belles Lettres, Poetry, Biography, History, Music, Art, Philosophy, Reference, Religion, High-priced Paperbacks, Psychology, General & Social Science, University Textbooks
ISBN Publisher's Prefix: 0-297

A **Wheaton** & Co Ltd, see Arnold-Wheaton

Wheatsheaf Books, an imprint of the Harvester Press Ltd (qv)

J **Whitaker** & Sons Ltd, 12 Dyott St, London WC1A 1DF Tel: (01) 836 8911 Cable Add: Whitmanack London WC1
Subsidiary Companies: The Standard Book Numbering Agency Ltd; Whitaker's Book Listing Services Ltd (both at 12 Dyott St, London)
Subjects: Reference, Bibliography
Founded: 1841
ISBN Publisher's Prefixes: 0-85021 (Whitaker), 0-949999 (Standard Book Numbering Agency)

White Eagle Publishing Trust+, New Lands, Brewells Lane, Liss, Hampshire GU33 7HY Tel: Liss 3300 (STD code 073082)
Man Dir: Mrs Y G Hayward; *Sales, Rights & Permissions:* G R H Dent; *Publicity & Advertising:* Colum Hayward
Subjects: Religion, Astrology
1981: 1 title *1982:* 5 titles *Founded:* 1953
Miscellaneous: Publishing house of the White Eagle Lodge, an undenominational Christian church
ISBN Publisher's Prefix: 0-85487

White Horse Books, an imprint of Jarrold Colour Publications (qv)

White Horse Library, an imprint of Venton Educational Ltd (qv)

Whittet Books Ltd, The Oil Mills, Weybridge, Surrey KT13 8LD Tel: Weybridge 42274 (STD code 0932) Telex: 929823 Vinins G
Chief Executive: Annabel Whittet
Parent Company: A Whittet & Co Ltd, at above address
Subjects: Non-fiction, History, Illustrated, Practical
1981: 3 titles *Founded:* 1976
ISBN Publisher's Prefix: 0-905483

Wigmore House Publishing, an imprint of Settle & Bendall (Wigmore) Ltd (qv)

Wildwood House Ltd, Jubilee House, Chapel Rd, Hounslow, Middlesex TW3 1XT Tel: (01) 572 6526 Cable Add: Wildwood London
Orders to: J M Dent & Sons (Distribution) Ltd, Dunhams Lane, Letchworth, Hertfordshire SG6 1LF Tel: Letchworth 6241 (STD code 04626)
Chairman: L W Carp; *Dir:* L Kershaw; *Managing Editor:* Maurice Temple Smith; *Rights & Permissions:* Kim Worts; *Sales Manager:* Rathan Sippy
Parent Company: East-West Holdings Ltd (at above address)
Associate Companies: East-West Publications (UK) Ltd; Elron Press Ltd; Maurice Temple Smith Ltd (qqv)
Subjects: General Non-fiction, Biography, History, How-to, Music, Art, Philosophy, Reference, Religion, Medicine, Psychology, General & Social Science, Occasional Fiction, Feminism, Ecology
Founded: 1972
Miscellaneous: Firm is a member of the East-West Group
ISBN Publisher's Prefix: 0-7045

John **Wiley** & Sons Ltd, Baffins Lane, Chichester, West Sussex PO19 1UD Tel: Chichester 784531 (STD code 0243) Cable Add: Wilebook Chichester Telex: 86290
Warehouse: John Wiley & Sons Ltd, Distribution Centre, Southern Cross Trading Estate, Shripney Rd, Bognor Regis, West Sussex PO22 9SA Tel: Bognor Regis 829121 (STD code 0243)
Man Dir: M B Foyle; *Editorial Dir:* J D Cameron; *Marketing Dir:* J Wilde; *Sales Dir:* S Usansky; *Publicity:* J D E Lea
Parent Company: John Wiley & Sons Inc, 605 Third Ave, New York, NY 10158, USA
Associate Companies: Heyden & Son Ltd, Jacaranda Wiley Ltd, Australia (qv); John Wiley & Sons Canada Ltd, 22 Worcester Rd, Rexdale, Ontario, Canada; Wiley Eastern Ltd, India (qv); Editorial Limusa SA, Mexico (qv)
Subjects: Chemistry, Physics, Life Sciences, Earth Sciences, Mathematics, Medicine, Psychology, Engineering, Reference, Social Science, Business Science, University Textbooks, Educational Material
Miscellaneous: Firm incorporates HM & M Publishing and publishing activities of Heydon & Son Ltd, UK (qv)
ISBN Publisher's Prefixes: 0-471 (Wiley), 0-470 (Halsted), 0-85602 (HM & M)

Wilfion Books Publishers+, 12 Townhead Terrace, Paisley, Renfrewshire PA1 2AX Tel: (041) 887 1241 Ext 299
Dirs: Konrad Hopkins, Ronald van Roekel
Subjects: Poetry, Psychic/Spiritual Phenomena, Translations, Fiction, Biography
1983: 23 titles *Founded:* 1975

Joseph **Williams**, an imprint of Stainer & Bell Ltd (qv)

Philip **Wilson** Publishers Ltd, Russell Chambers, Covent Garden, London WC2E 8AA Tel: (01) 379 7886 Telex: 22158
Man Dir: Philip Wilson; *Editorial Dir:* Anne Jackson; *Sales, Publicity Manager:* Juliana Powney; *Production Dir:* Peter Ling
Imprints: Scala/Philip Wilson, Sotheby Publications (USA office: 81 Adams Drive, Totowa, NJ 07512, USA)
Subjects: Art, Antiques, Reference
Founded: 1975
ISBN Publisher's Prefix: 0-85667

Wilton Publications, a former imprint of Gower Publishing Co Ltd (qv)

Wine & Spirit Publications Ltd, Harling House, 47-51 Gt Suffolk St, London SE1 0BS Tel: (01) 261 1604
Man Dir: P V Straker
Subjects: General Non-fiction, Wine, Spirits, Food, Entertaining
Founded: 1958

Allan **Wingate** (Publishers) Ltd, an imprint of W H Allen & Co Ltd (qv)

Wisdom Publications, Conishead Priory, Ulverston, Cumbria LA12 9QQ Tel: Ulverston 54029 (STD code 0229)
Editorial: Dr Nicholas Ribush; *Production:* Robina Courtin; *Publicity, Sales, Rights & Permissions:* Marie Obst
Associate Company: Mahayana Publications, 5/5 Shantiniketan, New Delhi 110021, India
Subject: Buddhism
1981: 6 titles *1982:* 2 titles *Founded:* 1976
ISBN Publisher's Prefix: 0-86171

H F & G **Witherby** Ltd and Witherby & Co Ltd, 32 Aylesbury St, London EC1R 0ET Tel: (01) 407 6771
Man Dirs: Antony Witherby (H F & G Witherby), Alan Witherby (Witherby & Co Ltd)
Subjects: Biography, History, How-to, Secondary & University Textbooks, Reference, Natural Science, Insurance & Banking, Oil & Shipping
ISBN Publisher's Prefixes: 0-85493 (H F & G Witherby), 0-900886 (Witherby & Co)

The **Woburn** Press, Gainsborough House, 11 Gainsborough Rd, Leytonstone, London E11 1RS Tel: (01) 530 4226 Cable Add: Simfay London Telex: 897719
Warehouse: Macdonald & Evans Ltd, Estover Rd, Estover, Plymouth PL6 7PZ
Man Dir: Frank Cass; *Editorial:* Margaret Goodare; *Trade:* Richard Norris; *Production:* John Smith; *Publicity:* Hayley Cass
Associate Companies: Frank Cass & Co Ltd (qv); Vallentine, Mitchell & Co Ltd (qv)
Subjects: Literature Criticism, Educational Studies, Social Science, General Literature
Founded: 1969
ISBN Publisher's Prefix: 0-7130

Wolfe Medical Publications Ltd, Wolfe House, 3 Conway St, London W1P 6HE Tel: (01) 636 4622 Cable Add: Wolfebooks London Telex: Wmpltd G 8814230
Chairman & Man Dir: Peter Wolfe; *Deputy Man Dir:* Peter Heilbrunn; *Editorial:* Patrick Daly; *Sales Dir:* Michael Manson; *Marketing:* Stuart Binns; *Production:* Colin MacPherson; *Publicity:* Evanna Morris; *Rights & Permissions:* Fiona Aretz
Subjects: Medical, Dental, Veterinary, Scientific
1981: 12 titles *1982:* 11 titles *Founded:* 1969
ISBN Publisher's Prefix: 0-7234

Wolfe Publishing Ltd, see Wolfe Medical Publications Ltd

UNITED KINGDOM 441

Oswald Wolff (Publishers) Ltd, 9 Park Lorne, Park Rd, London NW8 7JL Tel: (01) 258 0401 Cable Add: Bookwolff
Man & Sales Dir, Rights & Permissions: Mrs I R Wolff; *Editorial Dir:* R W Last
Subjects: German Studies: Biography, History, Music, Art, Literary Criticism, High-priced Paperbacks
Founded: 1958
ISBN Publisher's Prefix: 0-85496

The **Women's** Press Ltd+, 124 Shoreditch High St, London E1 6JE Tel: (01) 729 5257 Cable Add: Namara London SW1 Telex: 919034
Man Dir, Editorial: Ros de Lanerolle; *Rights & Permissions:* Sarah Lefanu; *Design:* Suzanne Perkins; *Publicity:* Katy Nicholson; *Sales:* Mary Hemming
Orders to: Quartet Books Ltd, 27 Goodge St, London W1 Tel: (01) 636 3992
Parent Company: Namara Ltd, 18b Wellington Court, Knightsbridge, London SW1
Associate Company: Robin Clark Ltd (qv)
Subjects: Fiction, Literature and Criticism, Art History, Politics, Physical and Mental Health (all women writers)
Book Club: The Women's Press Book Club
1981: 20 titles *Founded:* 1977
ISBN Publisher's Prefix: 0-7043

Woodhead-Faulkner (Publishers) Ltd+, Fitzwilliam House, 32 Trumpington St, Cambridge CB2 1QY Tel: Cambridge 66733 (STD code 0223) Cable Add: Woodfaulk Cambridge Telex: 817343 Blucam G
Man Dir: Martin J Woodhead; *Editorial:* Ian C Faulkner; *Sales:* Gilmour Drummond
Imprints: ICSA Publishing Ltd, Martin Books
Subjects: Business Investment and Finance, Social Welfare and Rehabilitation, Careers, Popular Non-fiction
1981: 35 titles *1982:* 40 titles *Founded:* 1972
ISBN Publisher's Prefixes: 0-85941 (Woodhead-Faulkner, Martin Books), 0-902197 (ICSA)

Workshop Press Ltd*, 2 Culham Court, Granville Rd, London N4 4JB Tel: (01) 348 4054
Subjects: Poetry
1981: 2 titles
ISBN Publisher's Prefix: 0-902705

World Book—Childcraft International, Canterbury House, Sydenham Rd, Croydon, Surrey CR9 2LR Tel: (01) 686 6421 Cable Add: World Book Int, Croydon Telex: 946314
Man Dir: J R Threlfall; *Editorial, Publicity:* Howard Timms
Parent Company: World Book Inc, Merchandise Mart Plaza, Chicago, Illinois, USA
Subjects: Primary & Secondary Education, English Dictionaries, Reference Books, Juveniles, Encyclopaedias
1981: 4 titles *1982:* 4 titles
ISBN Publisher's Prefix: 0-7166

World International Publishing Ltd+, PO Box 111, Manchester M60 3BL (Located at: Great Ducie St, Manchester M60 3BL) Tel: (061) 834 3110 Cable Add: World Manchester Telex: 668609
Man Dir: Robin Wood; *Editorial, Rights & Permissions:* Mae Broadley; *Sales Dir:* Bernie Wroe; *Production Manager:* David Sheldrake
Parent Company: Egmont Ltd, a UK subsidiary of the Gutenberghus Group, Copenhagen, Denmark
Imprints: Cliveden Press, Sandles, World
Subjects: Children's Books and Annuals
1983: 149 titles
ISBN Publisher's Prefix: 0-7235

World Microfilms Publications Ltd, 62 Queen's Grove, London NW8 6ER Tel: (01) 586 3092 Cable Add: Microworld
Man Dir: Stephen Albert
Associate Companies: Pidgeon Audio Visual, Sussex Tapes Exports, Sussex Video Ltd (all at above address)
Subjects: Research Collections in Microform, Periodical Reprints in Microform
1982: 30 titles *Founded:* 1969

World of Information, 21 Gold St, Saffron Walden, Essex CB10 1EJ Tel: Saffron Walden 21150 (STD code 0799) Cable Add: Jaxpress Telex: 817197 Jaxprs G
Publishers: David J C Jamieson, Anthony Axon; *Sales:* Michael G Morris; *Publicity:* Sue Hewitt
Parent Company: Middle East Review Co Ltd (at above address)
Subject: Third World Countries (Commerce, Economics, Politics, Development)
1983: 7 titles *Founded:* 1972
ISBN Publisher's Prefix: 0-904439

World of Islam Festival Trust, 33 Thurloe Pl, London SW7 2HQ Tel: (01) 581 3522 Cable Add: Islamtrust London SW7
Dir: Alistair Duncan
Orders to: Scorpion Publications Ltd, 377 High St, London E15 4QZ Telex: 896988 Scoops G
Subjects: Islamic Art, Culture and Civilisation
Founded: 1974
ISBN Publisher's Prefix: 0-905035

World University Library, an imprint of Weidenfeld & Nicolson Ltd (qv)

World's Work Ltd+, The Windmill Press, Kingswood, Tadworth, Surrey Tel: Mogador 833511 (STD code 0737) Cable Add: Sunlocks Tadworth Telex: 947458 Press G
Man Dir: C Forster; *Editorial:* Josephine Shepherd; *Production Dir:* Robert Aspinall; *Trade Manager:* Daphne Mallard; *Exhibition Manager:* Peggy Lince; *Promotion Manager:* Miriam Maxim; *Sales:* Lionel Foot; *Rights & Permissions:* Jane Turnbull, Sally Riley, Elizabeth Wright, Miriam Maxim
Parent Company: William Heinemann International Ltd (qv)
Associate Company: Kaye & Ward Ltd (qv)
Imprint: Cedar Books
Subjects: Business, How-to, Religion, Juveniles, Sport, Archaeology
ISBN Publisher's Prefix: 0-437

Gordon **Wright Publishing**, 25 Mayfield Rd, Edinburgh EH9 2NQ Tel: (031) 667 1300
Proprietor: Gordon Wright
Subjects: General, Scottish Literature, Non-fiction and Fiction
Founded: 1969
ISBN Publisher's Prefix: 0-903065

John **Wright & Sons** Ltd, 823-825 Bath Rd, Bristol BS4 5NU Tel: Bristol 778344 (STD code 0272) Cable Add: Wright Publishers Bristol Telex: 449752
Chairman: H A Harrison; *Publishing Dir:* David Kingham; *Editorial:* Dr John Gillman; *Marketing Dir, Rights & Permissions:* Anthony Gresford; *Production:* R Lamb; *Publicity:* Anne Davenport; *Translations:* Jean M Eales
Parent Company: John Wright & Sons (Holdings) Ltd (at above address)
Associate Company: John Wright PSG Inc, 545 Great Rd, Littleton, MA 01460, USA
Subsidiary Company: Henry Ling Ltd, Dorchester, Dorset
Imprints: Wright/PSG, PSG, Scientechnica
Subjects: Medicine, Veterinary Medicine, Dentistry, Psychology, Science, University Textbooks
Bookshop: John Wright & Sons (Bookselling) Ltd, 44 Triangle West, Bristol BS8 1EX
1981: 42 titles *1982:* 60 titles *Founded:* 1825
ISBN Publisher's Prefixes: 0-7236 (Wright/PSG), 0-88416 (PSG), 0-85608 (Scientechnica)

Writers and Readers Publishing Co-operative+, 144 Camden High St, London NW1 0NE Tel: (01) 485 3883, (01) 267 0511
Man Dir and Editorial Dir: Glenn Thompson; *Sales Dir and Rights & Permissions:* Siân Williams; *Publicity & Advertising Dir:* Gary Pulsifer
Subsidiary Company: Rivers Press
Subjects: Education, Primary, Secondary & University Textbooks, Feminism, General Literature, Fiction, Poetry, Juveniles, Politics, Sociology, Humour, Biography, Art
Founded: 1974
ISBN Publisher's Prefixes: 0-904613, 0-906386, 0-906495, 0-86316

Wykeham, an imprint of Taylor & Francis Ltd (qv)

Xerox Publishing Group Ltd, see Bowker Publishing Co and University Microfilms International

Yale University Press Ltd, 13 Bedford Sq, London WC1B 3JF Tel: (01) 580 2693 Cable Add: Yalepress London WC1 Telex: 896075 Yupldn G
Marketing Dir: Stephanie Sutton; *Editorial, Production Dir:* John Nicoll; *Publicity, Rights & Permissions:* Kathleen Yorke
Orders to: International Book Distributors, 66 Wood Lane End, Hemel Hempstead, Hertfordshire HP2 4RG Tel: Hemel Hempstead 58531 (STD code 0442) Telex: 82445
Subject: Scholarly Books
Miscellaneous: Firm is the British office of Yale University Press, 302 Temple St, New Haven, Conn 06511, USA
ISBN Publisher's Prefix: 0-300

York Notes, jointly published by Longman/York Press

Zebra Books, an imprint of Walker Books Ltd (qv)

Zed Press+, 57 Caledonian Rd, London N1 9DN Tel: (01) 837 4014 Telex: 912881 Zed
Man Dir, Sales, Publicity, Rights & Permissions: Roger van Zwanenberg; *Editorial Dir:* Robert Molteno
Branch Off: Biblio Inc, 81 Adams Drive, Totowa, NJ 07512, USA
Subjects: Third World Social Science, Africa, Middle East, Asia, Imperialism
1982: 40 titles *1983:* 50 titles *Founded:* 1976
ISBN Publisher's Prefixes: 0-905762, 0-862320

Hans **Zell** Publishers, PO Box 56, 14 St Giles, Oxford OX1 3EL Tel: Oxford 512934 (STD code 0865) Telex: 837184 Bemsco G
Chief Executive: Klaus G Saur; *Editorial, Sales, Rights & Permissions:* Hans M Zell
Orders to: (Books) K G Saur Verlag KG, Postfach 711009, D-8000 Munich 71, Federal Republic of Germany; (Journals) Hans Zell Publishers, PO Box 56, Oxford OX1 3EL
Parent Company: K G Saur Verlag KG, Federal Republic of Germany (qv)
Subjects: Reference, Africana, Periodicals
1983: 7 titles *Founded:* 1975
ISBN Publisher's Prefixes: 0-86070, 0-905450

Zenith, an imprint of Arrow Books Ltd (qv)

Zeno Booksellers & Publishers, 6 Denmark St, London WC2H 8LP Tel: (01) 836 2522 Cable Add: Zengreek London WC2
Man Dir: M P Zographos
Subjects: Belles Lettres, Poetry, History, Art, Travel
Bookshop: 6 Denmark St, London WC2H 8LP (specializing in Greek books, Greece, The Balkans, Middle East, Antiquarian and Modern)
Founded: 1944
ISBN Publisher's Prefixes: 0-900834, 0-7228

Zomba Books, Zomba House, 165-67 Willesden High Rd, London NW10 2SG Tel: (01) 459 8899 Telex: 237316 Zomba
Man Dir: Maxim Jakubowski; *Managing Editor:* Emily White; *Marketing, Publicity Manager:* Cathy O'Bryan-Tear
Orders to: W H Smith Distributors, St John's House, East St, Leicester LE1 6NE Tel: Leicester 551196 (STD code 0533)
Parent Company: Marlowlynn Ltd (at above London address)
Imprints: Black Box Thrillers, Bee In Bonnet, Lifestyle Books, Musical Box
Branch Off: Zomba House, 1348 Lexington Ave, New York, NY 10028, USA
Subjects: Fashion, Fiction, Fitness, Film Biographies, Humour, Leisure, Music, Social Polemic
1983: 16 titles *Founded:* 1982
ISBN Publisher's Prefix: 0-946391

A **Zwemmer** Ltd, 26 Litchfield St, London WC2H 9NJ Tel: (01) 836 1749 Cable Add: Zwemmera Lesquare London WC2H 9NJ
Warehouse: Unit 27, Bermondsey Trading Estate, Rotherhithe New Rd, London SE16
Man Dir: D Zwemmer
Subsidiary Company: Lund Humphries Publishers Ltd (qv), for whom Zwemmer Ltd is also distributor
Subjects: Art, Architecture
Bookshops: Zwemmers Bookshop, 24 Litchfield St, London WC2H 9NJ; Zwemmers OUP Bookshop, 72 Charing Cross Rd, London WC2H 0BE

Remainder Dealers

Atlas Book Sales Ltd*, Atlas House, 61-71 Collier St, London N1 9BE Tel: (01) 837 9601 Telex: 261396 Atlas G
Sales: Grahame Parish

B S C Books Ltd, 33 Maiden Lane, London WC2 Tel: (01) 836 3341 (Owners of the Booksmith chain of bookshops; also publishers)
Sales: Tim Finch

Bestseller Publications Ltd, 24 Friern Park, Finchley, London N12 9DA Tel: (01) 446 4461 Telex: 22303
Also issue reprints under imprint Bracken Books

Roy **Bloom** Ltd, 81 Goswell Rd, London EC1 Tel: (01) 251 4345 Telex: 24224 Ref 2121
Sales: Paul White

Bridge Book Co Ltd, Unit 4, Goldsworth Park Trading Estate, Woking, Surrey GU21 3BA Tel: Woking 20505 (STD code 04862) Cable Add: Pembridge Woking Remainder paperback book merchants, importers and exporters in bulk

Godfrey Cave Books Ltd, 42 Bloomsbury St, London WC1B 3QJ Tel: (01) 636 9177
Man Dir: John Maxwell

Harvey Sales, 39 Chartwell Dr, Wigston, Leicester LE8 2FL Tel: Leicester 881334 (STD code 0533) Telex: 34694 Chamco G
Sales: Vance Harvey

HighText Ltd, 68 Salusbury Rd, London NW6 6NU Tel: (01) 328 5022/4859 Telex: 261507 Ref 2439
International remainder wholesaler

Donald **Murray** (Ramboro Books), 64 Pentonville Rd, London N1 9HD Tel: (01) 837 6301
See also under Publishers

H **Pordes** Ltd, 529b Finchley Rd, London NW3 7BH Tel: (01) 435 9878/9
See also under Publishers

Ramboro Enterprises Ltd, 64 Pentonville Rd, London N1 9HD Tel: (01) 837 6301 Telex: 24224
See also under Publishers

W J **Williams** & Son (Books) Ltd, Barton under Needwood, Burton-on-Trent, Staffordshire DE13 8BA Tel: Barton under Needwood 2948 (STD code 028 371)

Literary Agents

Michael **Bakewell** & Associates Ltd, see MBA Literary Agents Ltd

Blake Friedmann Literary Agency, 42 Bloomsbury St, London WC1B 3QJ Tel: (01) 580 1678/9, (01) 636 0366, (01) 323 4938 Telex: 27950 ref 3820
Contacts: Carole Blake, Julian Friedmann
Specialization: Thrillers, Film and TV Development, Syndication for journalists, and broad range of Fiction and Non-fiction

Carew Hunt Associates*, 5 Ridgmount Gdns, London WC1 Tel: (01) 323 2831
Contact: Victoria Carew Hunt
Specialization: Antiques, Crime fiction

E J **Carnell** Literary Agency, Rowneybury Bungalow, nr Old Harlow, Essex CM20 2EX Tel: Harlow 29408 (STD code 0279)
Contacts: Leslie Flood, Pamela Buckmaster
Specialization: Science Fiction, Fantasy

Curtis Brown, 1 Craven Hill, London W2 3EP Tel: (01) 262 1011 Cable Add: Browncurt Telex: 261536
Chairman: Richard Odgers

John **Farquharson** Ltd, 162-168 Regent St, London W1R 5TB Tel: (01) 437 9700 Cable Add: Jofachad London W1 Telex: 8954665 Gits Farson
Contact: George Greenfield, Vanessa Holt or Vivienne Schuster
Also: 250 West 57th St, New York, NY 10107, USA Tel: (212) 245 1993 Cable Add: Jofachad New York
Contact: Jane Gelfman

Blake **Friedmann** Literary Agency, see Blake

Peter **Galliner** Associates Ltd, 27 Walsingham, St John's Wood Park, London NW8 6RH Tel: (01) 722 5502 Telex: 21792 Ref 728
Chairman: Peter Galliner
Represent foreign publishers, scouts; specialists in international co-productions

David **Grossman** Literary Agency Ltd, 12-13 Henrietta St, London WC2 Telex: 21879 G Attn Onandup

June **Hall** Literary Agency, 19 College Cross, London N1 Tel: (01) 609 5991

A M **Heath** & Co Ltd, 40-42 William IV St, London WC2N 4DD Tel: (01) 836 4271 Cable Add: Script London WC2 Telex: 27370
Dirs: Mark Hamilton, Michael Thomas, Hester Green

David **Higham** Associates Ltd*, 5-8 Lower John St, Golden Sq, London W1R 4HA Tel: (01) 437 7888 Cable Add: Highlit London W1 Telex: 28910 Highqs Ldn
Contacts: Bruce Hunter, Jacqueline Korn, Anthony Crouch, John Rush

Hughes Massie Ltd, 31 Southampton Row, London WC1B 5HL Tel: (01) 405 8137 Cable Add: Litaribus London Telex: 298391
Dirs: Edmund Cork, Patricia Cork, J E Lunn, Brian Stone, Herta Ryder

Inpra International Press Agency, PO Box 149a, Surbiton, Surrey KT6 5JH Tel: (01) 398 7723/8723 Cable Add: Barpress, Surbiton
Contacts: Shelley Power, Pamela Hickey

Intercontinental Literary Agency, foreign rights company of A D Peters & Co Ltd (qv)

Philip & Pamela **Joseph** Associates Ltd*, 12 Eresby House, Rutland Gate, London SW7 1BG Tel: (01) 589 7669
Specialization: Fiction, Juvenile, Non-fiction

London Independent Books Ltd, 1a Montagu Mews North, London W1H 1AJ Tel: (01) 935 8090 Cable Add: Trifem London W1
Dirs: Carolyn Whitaker, Patrick Whitaker

London Syndication, 42 Bloomsbury St, London WC1B 3QJ Tel: (01) 580 1678 Telex: 27950 ref 3820
Contact: Carole Blake
Represents feature writers and mass market short stories for newspapers and magazines; handles all book rights for its journalist clients

M B A Literary Agents Ltd, 118 Tottenham Court Rd, London W1P 9HL Tel: (01) 387 2076, (01) 387 4785
Dirs: Diana Tyler, John Richard Parker

Andrew **Nurnberg** Associates Ltd, Clerkenwell House, 45-47 Clerkenwell Green, London EC1R 0HT Tel: (01) 251 0321 Cable Add: Nurnbooks London Telex: 23353
Specialization: Translation Rights

Mark **Paterson** & Associates, 10 Brook St, Wivenhoe, nr Colchester, Essex CO7 9DS Tel: Wivenhoe 5433 (STD code 0206 22) Cable Add: Paterson Colchester Telex: 896616MP Sendit G or markit 987562 Cochac
Specialization: Psychoanalysis, Psychiatry, Sigmund Freud copyrights, but other subjects also handled

Peterborough Literary Agency, The Daily Telegraph, 135 Fleet St, London EC4P 4BL Tel: (01) 353 4242 ext 3681 Cable Add: Telenews London EC4 Telex: 22874 Telesyndic
Executive Managers: Ewan MacNaughton, Andrea Whittaker

A D **Peters** & Co Ltd*, 10 Buckingham St, London WC2N 6BU Tel: (01) 839 2556
Man Dir: Michael Sissons

Laurence **Pollinger** Ltd, 18 Maddox St, London W1R 0EU Tel: (01) 629 9761 Cable Add: Laupoll London W1
Man Dir: Gerald J Pollinger; *Foreign Rights:* Margaret Pepper

Deborah **Rogers** Ltd, 49 Blenheim Crescent, London W11 2EF Tel: (01) 221 3717 Cable Add: Deborgers London W11
Dirs: Deborah Rogers, Patricia White (USA), Ann Warnford-Davis

Sheri **Safran** Associates (UK) Ltd, 37 Sutherland Pl, London W2 Tel: (01) 229 7819
Also: Sheri Safran Associates, 866 United Nations Plaza, Suite 4030, New York, NY

10017, USA Tel: (212) 355 3362
Representing British and American authors of general fiction and non-fiction and children's books. UK representative for several American publishers and literary agents

Tessa **Sayle**, Literary and Dramatic Agency, 11 Jubilee Pl, London SW3 3TE Tel: (01) 352 4311 Cable Add: Bookishly London

Patrick **Seale** Books Ltd, 2 Motcomb St, Belgrave Sq, London SW1X 8JU Tel: (01) 235 0934 Cable Add: Obseale London SW1

Anthony **Sheil** Associates Ltd, 2-3 Morwell St, London WC1B 3AR Tel: (01) 636 2901 Cable Add: Novelist
Man Dir: Anthony Sheil; *Foreign Rights Dir:* Paul Marsh
Also: Wallace & Sheil Agency Inc, 177 East 70th St, New York, NY 10021, USA Tel: (212) 5709090

Peter **Tauber** Press Agency, 94 East End Rd, London N3 2SX Tel: (01) 346 4165 Cable Add: Tauberpres London N3
Dirs: Peter Tauber, Robert Tauber
Specialization: Fiction, Non-fiction

Watson, Little Ltd, Suite 8, 26 Charing Cross Rd, London WC2 0DG Tel: (01) 836 5880
Dirs: Sheila Watson, Amanda Little

A P **Watt** Ltd, 26-28 Bedford Row, London WC1R 4HL Tel: (01) 405 1057 Cable Add: Longevity London
Contact: Hilary Rubinstein, Caradoc King or Linda Shaughnessy

Book Clubs

20th Century Classics, see Book Club Associates

Ancient History Book Club, see Book Club Associates

Arts Book Society, see Readers Union Ltd

Arts Guild, see Book Club Associates

Aviation Book Club, see Book Club Associates

Biography Book Club, see Book Club Associates

Birds and Natural History Book Society, see Readers Union Ltd

Book Club Associates, 87-91 Newman St, London W1P 4EN Tel: (01) 637 0341 Cable Add: Booklub Telex: 24359
Chief Executive: S T Remington; *General Manager (Editorial and Creative):* J Goehr
Monthly Book Clubs: Ancient History Book Club; Biography Book Club; Book of the Month Club; Family Book Club; History Guild; Literary Guild; Master Storytellers; Military Book Society; Mystery Guild; World Books
Bi-monthly Book Club: Book Lovers; Home Reference Library
Quarterly Book Clubs: Arts Guild; Aviation Book Club; British Heritage; Encounters; English Book Club (Netherlands and Federal Republic of Germany); Home & Garden Guild; On the Road; Military Guild; The Railway Book Club; Readers Choice; World of Nature
Book Series: 20th Century Classics, Kings & Queens of England, Great English Classics, Great Mysteries
Subsidiary Company: Guild Publishing (qv under Publishers)
Owned by: W H Smith & Son Ltd (London) and Doubleday & Co Inc (New York)

Book Lovers, see Book Club Associates

Book of the Month Club, see Book Club Associates

Books for Children, Park House, Dollar St, Cirencester, Gloucestershire GL7 2AN Tel: Cirencester 67081 (STD code 0285)

The **Bookworm** Club, 20 Trinity St, Cambridge CB2 3NG Tel: Cambridge 358351 (STD code 0223) exts 210, 211
Owned by: W Heffer & Sons Ltd (at above address)
Subject: Paperbacks for 5-12-year-olds

Bridge Book Club, PO Box 7, Hounslow TW3 2LA Tel: (01) 898 7700
Owned by: Bibliagora (qv)

British Heritage, see Book Club Associates

C S E Book Club, 25 Horsell Rd, London N5 1XL
Owned by: C S E Books (qv)

Chip Book Club, Scholastic Publications, 9 Parade, Leamington Spa, Warwickshire CV32 4DG Tel: Leamington Spa 831101 (STD code 0926)
Subjects: Books for junior and secondary levels
Owned by: Scholastic Publications (qv)

Collectors' Editions Book Club, see Heron Books

Companion Book Club, Hamlyn Group, Mail Order Division, Sanders Lodge Estate, Rushden, Northants Tel: Rushden 58621 (STD code 0933)
Members: 12,500
Owned by: The Hamlyn Group (Feltham)
Subjects: Fiction, Biographies, True Adventure

Country Book Society, see Readers Union Ltd

Craft Book Society, see Readers Union Ltd

Cricket Book Society, see Readers Union Ltd

Criterion: Teachers' Bookshelf Book Club, Scholastic Publications, 9 Parade, Leamington Spa, Warwickshire CV32 4DG Tel: Leamington Spa 831101 (STD code 0926)
Owned by: Scholastic Publications (qv)

Encounters, see Book Club Associates

Family Book Club, see Book Club Associates

Fishing Book Club, Howard Rd, Eaton Socon, Huntingdon, Cambridgeshire PE19 3EZ Tel: Huntingdon 212666 (STD code 0480)
Owned by: A & C Black (Publishers) Ltd (qv)

The **Folio** Society Ltd, 202 Great Suffolk St, London SE1 1PR Tel: (01) 407 7411 Cable Add: Folios
Man Dir: H Lynner; *Sales, Publicity, Advertising, Rights & Permissions:* J Letts
Subsidiary Companies: Folio Press, Folio Fine Editions (both UK); Folio Books Ltd New York, c/o Expediters of the Printed Word Ltd, 527 Madison Ave, Suite 1217, New York, NY 10022, USA
Subjects: General Fiction, Belles Lettres, Poetry, Biography, History
Bookshop: Folio Gallery, 5 Royal Arcade, 28 Old Bond St, London W1
Founded: 1947
Miscellaneous: Publications, except for some by Folio Press, are for sale to members only

French Book Club, Warner House, Folkestone, Kent CT19 6PH
Owned by: Bailey Bros & Swinfen Ltd (qv)

Gardeners Book Society, see Readers Union Ltd

German Book Club, Warner House, Folkestone, Kent CT19 6PH
Owned by: Bailey Bros & Swinfen Ltd (qv)

Great English Classics, see Book Club Associates

Great Mysteries, see Book Club Associates

Greyfriars Book Club, 27A Arterberry Rd, London SW20
Owned by: Howard Baker Press Ltd (qv)

Heron Books, 2nd Floor, Lawrence House, St Andrew's Hill, Norwich, Norfolk Tel: (0603) 60111
Includes: Collectors' Editions Book Club, The Nobel Prize Library
Owned by: Leisure Arts Ltd (qv)
Miscellaneous: Also publishes finely bound, illustrated reprints, including Literary Heritage (English classics), Russian Classics, Books That Have Changed Man's Thinking, Immortal Moderns; and collected works of individual authors

History Guild, see Book Club Associates

Home and Garden Guild, see Book Club Associates

Home Reference Library, see Book Club Associates

Horseman's Bookclub, 1 Lower Grosvenor Pl, London SW1
Owned by: J A Allen & Co Ltd (London)

Italian Book Club, Warner House, Folkestone, Kent CT19 6PH
Owned by: Bailey Bros & Swinfen Ltd (qv)

The **Jewish Book Club**, 529b Finchley Rd, London NW3 7BH
Owned by: R Pordes

Junior Puffin Club, Penguin Books Ltd, Bath Rd, Harmondsworth, Middlesex UB7 0DA Tel: (01) 759 1984
Members: 10,000
Owned by: Penguin Books Ltd (qv)
Founded: 1978

Kings & Queens of England, see Book Club Associates

The **Leisure Circle** Ltd, York House, Empire Way, Wembley, Middlesex HA9 0PF Tel: (01) 902 8888 Telex: 8951315
Man Dir: Dr M Herriger; *Publishing:* C Goulden; *Sales:* D Lory; *Marketing:* F Elpert; *Member Service:* L Grothues
Owned by: Verlagsgruppe Bertelsmann GmbH (Federal Republic of Germany) (qv)
Subjects: General Fiction, Non-fiction, Biography, History, Children's Books

Lifestyle Book Society, see Readers Union Ltd

Literary Guild, see Book Club Associates

Lucky Book Club, Scholastic Publications, 9 Parade, Leamington Spa, Warwickshire CV32 4DG Tel: Leamington Spa 831101 (STD code 0926)
Subjects: Books for infants and juniors
Owned by: Scholastic Publications (qv)

Mainstream Book Club, 23-25 Broad St, Oxford Tel: Oxford 248870 (STD code 0865)
Owned by (majority share): B H Blackwell Ltd (qv under Major Booksellers)
Subject: Middle-of-the-road political books

Maritime Book Society, see Readers Union

Master Storytellers, see Book Club Associates

Military Book Society, see Book Club Associates

Military Guild, see Book Club Associates

Mystery Guild, see Book Club Associates

Nationwide Book Service, see Readers Union Ltd

The **Nobel Prize** Library, see Heron Books

On the Road, see Book Club Associates

Phoenix Book Society, see Readers Union Ltd

Photographic Book Society, see Readers Union Ltd

Poetry Book Society, 105 Piccadilly, London W1V 0AU Tel: (01) 629 9495
Publications: Bulletin (quarterly); *Poetry Supplement* (annual)
Members: 1,000
Founded: 1954

The **Puffin** Club, Penguin Books Ltd, Bath Rd, Harmondsworth, Middlesex UB7 0DA Tel: (01) 759 1984
Members: 30,000
Owned by: Penguin Books Ltd (qv)
Founded: 1967

The **Railway** Book Club, see Book Club Associates

Read On! Club, 20 Trinity St, Cambridge CB2 3NG Tel: Cambridge 358351 (STD code 0223) exts 210, 211
Owned by: W Heffer & Sons Ltd (at above address)
Paperbacks for 12+ year-olds

Readers Choice, see Book Club Associates

Readers Union Book Society, see Readers Union Ltd

Readers Union Ltd, PO Box 6, Newton Abbot, Devon TQ12 2DW Tel: Newton Abbot 69881 (STD code 0626) Cable Add: Books Nabbot Telex: 42904
Chief Executive: J Angell; *Marketing Dir:* A Jacques
Includes: Arts Book Society, Birds and Natural History Book Society, Country Book Society, Craft Book Society, Cricket Book Society, Gardeners Book Society, Lifestyle Book Society, Maritime Book Society, Nationwide Book Service, Phoenix Book Society, Photographic Book Society, Readers Union Book Society
Owned by: David & Charles (Holdings) Ltd (Devon)
Founded: 1937

The **Red House Post**, The Red House, Witney, Oxon OX8 6YQ
Owned by: Red House Books Ltd
Subjects: Children's

Scene Book Club, Scholastic Publications, 9 Parade, Leamington Spa, Warwickshire CV32 4DG Tel: Leamington Spa 831101 (STD code 0926)
Owned by: Scholastic Publications (qv)
Subjects: Books for secondary school

See-Saw Book Club, Scholastic Publications, 9 Parade, Leamington Spa, Warwickshire CV32 4DG Tel: Leamington Spa 831101 (STD code 0926)
Owned by: Scholastic Publications (qv)
Subjects: Books for nursery and infants

Spanish Book Club, Warner House, Folkestone, Kent CT19 6PH
Owned by: Bailey Bros & Swinfen Ltd (qv)

Translation Book Club, 10 Archway Close, London N19 3TD Tel: (01) 263 3438
Owned by: Sinclair Browne Ltd (qv)

Verbatim Book Club, PO Box 199, Aylesbury, Buckinghamshire HP20 1TQ Tel: Aylesbury 27314 (STD code 0296)

The **Women's** Press Book Club, 124 Shoreditch High St, London E1 6JE Tel: (01) 729 4751
Owned by: The Women's Press Ltd (qv)

Founded: 1980
Subjects: Books by and about women, with emphasis on fiction, art, politics, health

World Books, see Book Club Associates

World of Nature, see Book Club Associates

Major Booksellers

Austick's Headrow Bookshop, 64 The Headrow, Leeds LS1 8EH Tel: Leeds 439607 (STD code 0532)
Manager: J M Blanchfield

B H **Blackwell** Ltd*, 48-51 Broad St, Oxford Tel: Oxford 49111 (STD code 0865)
Book Club: Mainstream Book Club

Bookwise Service Ltd*, Trade Division, Unit 1, Langham Trading Estate, Catteshall Lane, Godalming, Surrey Tel: Godalming 4152 (STD code 04868) Telex: 859601
Manager: H G E Tompkins
Major wholesalers

Bowes & Bowes Books, 1 Trinity St, Cambridge CB2 1SX Tel: Cambridge 355488 (STD code 0223)
Manager: J M Atkins

Burchell & Martin Library Suppliers, 34 Granville St, Birmingham B1 2LJ Tel: (021) 643 8888 Telex: 337001
Owned by: Berowne Ltd

Dillon's University Bookshop, 1 Malet St, London WC1E 7JB Tel: (01) 636 1577
Owned by: Pentos Ltd (qv)

W & G **Foyle** Ltd, 113-119 Charing Cross Rd, London WC2H 0EB Tel: (01) 437 5660

William **George's** Sons Ltd*, 89 Park St, Bristol BS1 5PW Tel: Bristol 276602 (STD code 0272)

Grant Educational Co Ltd*, 91 Union St, Glasgow (Home and Export)

Haigh & Hochland Ltd*, 11 Whitworth St, Manchester 1 Tel: (061) 236 9950; The Precinct Centre, Oxford Rd, Manchester M13 9QZ Tel: (061) 273 4156

Hammicks Wholesale, 16 Newman Lane, Alton, Hants GU34 2PJ Tel: Alton 85822 (STD code 0420) (wholesalers)
There are Hammicks Bookshops Ltd at Alton, Chichester, Farnham, Basingstoke, Horsham, London, Southampton, Windsor

Harrods Ltd, Knightsbridge, London SW1 Tel: (01) 730 1234 Cable Add: Harrods London Telex: 24319

Hatchards Ltd, 187 Piccadilly, London W1V 9DA Tel: (01) 439 9921 Telex: 8953970
Also: Hatchards within Harvey Nichols, Knightsbridge, London SW1; Hatchards at Hanningtons, 53 Market St, Brighton, East Sussex
Owned by: William Collins Sons & Co Ltd (qv)

Heffers Booksellers, 20 Trinity St, Cambridge CB2 3NG Tel: Cambridge 358351 (bookshop), 350098 (customer accounts) (STD code 0223) Telex: 81298
Also: (all Cambridge) 30 Trinity St (children's books); 13 Trinity St and The Shop, Norwich Union Bldg, Downing St (both paperbacks); 51 Trumpington St (Penguins); Grafton Centre
Owned by: W Heffer & Sons Ltd

Hudsons Bookshops, now incorporated in Burchell & Martin Library Suppliers (qv)

John **Menzies** (Holdings) Ltd*, Villiers House, 40 Strand, London WC2 Tel: (01) 930 0033
Manager: J McNair
Branches throughout the United Kingdom. Also major library supplier

Parker & Son Ltd*, 27 Broad St, Oxford OX2 7LP Tel: Oxford 54156 (STD code 0865)

Sherratt & Hughes (Bowes & Bowes), 17 St Ann's Sq, Manchester M2 7PD Tel: (061) 834 7055
Manager: I G Allan

John **Smith** & Son (Glasgow) Ltd, 57-61 St Vincent St, Glasgow G2 5TB Tel: (041) 221 7472 Cable Add: Books: Glasgow Telex: 777967 Chacomb G-362

W H **Smith** & Son Ltd, 11 Kingsway, London WC2B 6YA Tel: (01) 836 5951;
W H Smith & Son Ltd (Wholesale), Strand House, 10 New Fetter Lane, London EC4A 1AD Tel: (01) 353 0277 (many branches throughout the United Kingdom)

James **Thin**, Bookseller, 53-59 South Bridge, Edinburgh Tel: (031) 556 6743

Major Libraries

Belfast Public Library, Central Library, Royal Ave, Belfast, Northern Ireland Tel: Belfast 43233 (STD code 0232) Telex: 747359
Chief Librarian: I A Crawley

Birmingham Public Libraries, Central Library, Chamberlain Sq, Birmingham B3 3HQ Tel: (021) 235 4511 Telex: 337655
Librarian: B H Baumfield
Publication: Bibliography of National Socialist Literature

Bodleian Library, Oxford OX1 3BG Tel: Oxford 244675 (STD code 0865) Telex: 83656
Librarian: J W Jolliffe

British Library Bibliographic Services Division, 2 Sheraton St, London W1V 4BH Tel: (01) 636 1544
Publications: British National Bibliography; British Education Index; British Catalogue of Music; Books in English (microfiche); *Serials in the British Library; British Catalogue of Audio Visual Materials*
See also entry under Publishers

British Library Lending Division, Boston Spa, Wetherby, West Yorkshire LS23 7BQ Tel: Boston Spa 843434 (STD code 0937) Telex: 557381
Publications: Keyword Index to Serial Titles (on microfiche); Current Serials Received; Index of Conference Proceedings Received; Interlending and Document Supply (formerly Interlending Review); British Reports, Translations and Theses; *Research in British Universities, Polytechnics and Colleges*
The Lending Division lends only to libraries and organizations, not to individual members of the public
See also entry under Publishers

British Library of Political and Economic Science*, 10 Portugal St, London WC2A 2HD Tel: (01) 405 7686 Telex: 24655 Blpes G
Librarian: D A Clarke
Publication: A London Bibliography of the Social Sciences

British Library Reference Division, Great Russell St, London WC1B 3DG Tel: (01) 636 1544
Publications include: British Library Journal

(twice yearly); Catalogue of Additions to the Manuscripts in the British Museum; General Catalogue of Printed Books, microfiche supplement 1976-82; Catalogue of the Newspaper Collections in the British Library; Subject Index of Modern Books, supplements to 1961-70; Guide to the Department of Oriental Manuscripts and Printed Books
See also entry under Publishers

British Library, Science Reference Library*, 25 Southampton Bldgs, Chancery Lane, London WC2A 1AW Tel: (01) 405 8721 Telex: via 266959
and Aldwych Reading Room, 9 Kean St, Drury Lane, London WC2B 4AT Tel: (01) 636 1544 ext 229 Telex: 22717
Librarian: M W Hill
List of publications available on request

Cambridge University Library, West Rd, Cambridge CB3 9DR Tel: Cambridge 61441 (STD code 0223) Telex: 81395
Librarian: Dr F W Ratcliffe
List of publications available on request

The **Dean and Chapter** Library, The College, Durham DH1 3EH Tel: Durham 62489 (STD code 0385)
Deputy Librarian: R C Norris

Durham University Library, Stockton Rd, Durham DH1 3LY Tel: Durham 64971 (STD code 0385) Telex: 537351 Durlib
Librarian: Agnes M McAulay

Edinburgh University Library, George Sq, Edinburgh EH8 9LJ Tel: (031) 667 1011 Telex: 727442 Unived G

Guildhall Library, Aldermanbury, London EC2P 2EJ Tel: (01) 606 3030
Librarian: Godfrey Thompson

India Office Library and Records, Orbit House, 197 Blackfriars Rd, London SE1 8NG Tel: (01) 928 9531
Director: B C Bloomfield
Publications include: *Catalogue of Persian Manuscripts in the Library of India Office*, 1980 (reprint of 1903 edition); *Gandhi and the Civil Disobedience: documents in the India Office Records, 1922-1946*, 1980; *A List and Index of Parliamentary Papers relating to India 1908-1947*, 1981; *Catalogue of the Sinhalese Manuscripts in the India Office Library*, 1981; *Catalogue of Urdu books in the India Office Library 1800-1920* (supplementary to James Fuller Blumhardt's catalogue of 1900), 1982; *Guide to the Records of the India Office Military Department*, 1982

Leeds University Library, Leeds LS2 9JT Tel: Leeds 431751 (STD code 0532)
Librarian: D Cox
Publications include: *Catalogue of German Literature Printed in the 17th and 18th Centuries*

Liverpool City Libraries, William Brown St, Liverpool L3 8EW Tel: (051) 207 2147 Telex: 629500
Librarian: R Malbon

Llyfrgell Genedlaethol Cymru (National Library of Wales), Aberystwyth, Dyfed SY23 3BU Tel: Aberystwyth 3816 (STD code 0970) Telex: 35165
Librarian: R Geraint Gruffydd
Publications: The National Library of Wales Journal (semi-annual); *Handlist of Manuscripts in the National Library of Wales* (annual); *Bibliotheca Celtica* (annual)

The **Mitchell** Library (Glasgow District Libraries)*, North St, Glasgow G3 7DN Tel: (041) 248 7121 Telex: 778732
Librarian: R A Gillespie

National Library of Scotland, George IV Bridge, Edinburgh EH1 1EW Tel: (031) 226 4531 Telex: 72638 Nlsedi G
Map Room: NLS Annexe, 137 Causewayside, Edinburgh EH9 1PH Tel: (031) 667 7848

National Library of Wales, see Llyfrgell Genedlaethol Cymru

Oxford University Taylor Institution Library, St Giles, Oxford OX1 3NA Tel: Oxford 53152 ext 404 (STD code 0865)

P R O N I (Public Record Office of Northern Ireland), 66 Balmoral Ave, Belfast BT9 6NY

Public Record Office, Ruskin Ave, Kew, Richmond, Surrey TW9 4DU Tel: (01) 876 3444
and Chancery Lane, London WC2A 1LR Tel: (01) 405 0741
National archive for the records of the British courts of law and central departments of state

John Rylands University Library of Manchester, Oxford Rd, Manchester M13 9PP Tel: Main Library Bldg (061) 273 3333; Deansgate Bldg (061) 834 5343
Librarian: M A Pegg
Publication: The Bulletin of the John Rylands University Library of Manchester

School of Oriental and African Studies Library, Malet St, London WC1E 7HP Tel: (01) 637 2388
Librarian: V T H Parry
Publications include: *Library Guide*, 1980

Scottish Record Office, PO Box 36, HM General Register House, Edinburgh EH1 3YY Tel: (031) 556 6585

Trinity College Library, Cambridge CB2 1TQ Tel: Cambridge 358201 (STD code 0223)
Librarian: Dr J P W Gaskell

University Libraries, see also under names of towns

University of London Library, Senate House, Malet St, London WC1E 7HU Tel: (01) 636 4514 Telex: 269400 Shul G
Director: V T H Parry

Wellcome Institute for the History of Medicine Library, 183 Euston Rd, London NW1 2BP Tel: (01) 387 4477

Westminster City Libraries*, Central Administration, Marylebone Rd, London NW1 5PS Tel: (01) 828 8070 Telex: 263305
City Librarian: Melvyn Barnes

Library Associations

A R L I S (The Art Libraries Society), c/o Learning Resources, Brighton Polytechnic, Faculty of Art and Design, Grand Parade, Brighton BN2 2JY Tel: Brighton 604141 ext 228/229 (STD code 0273)
Secretary: Lyn Turpin
Publications: Art Libraries Journal (quarterly), *ARLIS News-sheet* (six a year), *Directory* (annually)

Aslib, 3 Belgrave Sq, London SW1X 8PL Tel: (01) 235 5050 Telex: 23667
Formerly the Association of Special Libraries and Information Bureaux
Dir: Dennis A Lewis
Publications: Index to Theses accepted for Higher Degrees in the Universities of Great Britain and Ireland (half-yearly), *Journal of Documentation* (quarterly), *Aslib Proceedings* (monthly), *Aslib Information* (monthly), *Aslib Book List* (monthly), *Program* (quarterly), *Forthcoming International Scientific and Technical Conferences* (quarterly), handbooks, reports, directories and membership list

Association of Assistant Librarians
Honorary Secretary: Mrs R Aldrich, Clwyd Library Service, Rhuddlan Area Library, Church St, Rhyl, Clwyd Tel: Rhyl 53814 (STD code 0745)
Publications include: *Fiction Index; Song Index; Junior Fiction Index; Which Library School*

Association of British Library and Information Studies Schools (ABLISS), c/o K J McGarry, School of Librarianship, Polytechnic of North London, 207-225 Essex Rd, London N1 3PN
Chairman: K J McGarry

Association of British Theological and Philosophical Libraries, King's College Library, Strand, London WC2R 2LS
Honorary Secretary: Miss E M Elliott
Publication: Bulletin

Association of London Chief Librarians, *Honorary Secretary:* D F Parker, Wandsworth Public Library, Town Hall, Wandsworth, London SW18 2PU Tel: (01) 874 6464 ext 563
Publications: Directory of London Public Libraries

Association of Scottish Health Sciences Librarians*, Miss D Lindsay, Librarian, Medical Library, Royal Infirmary, Castle St, Glasgow G4 0SF

Bibliographical Society, British Library (Reference Division), Great Russell St, London WC1B 3DG
Honorary Secretary: Mrs Mirjam Foot
Publications: The Library (quarterly), various books on bibliographical subjects

British and Irish Association of Law Librarians, c/o Harding Law Library, University of Birmingham, PO Box 363, Birmingham B15 2TT
Honorary Secretary: Miss D M Blake
Publication: The Law Librarian

Circle of State Librarians*,
Honorary Secretary: Mrs D C Scott, c/o Royal Botanic Gardens, Kew, Richmond, Surrey TW9 3AE Tel: (01) 940 1171 Ext 222
Publication: State Librarian (3 a year)

Classification Research Group,
Honorary Secretary: Mrs I C McIlwaine, School of Library, Archive and Information Studies, University College, London WC1

Committee for Postgraduate Awards in Librarianship and Information Work, c/o Office of Arts and Libraries, Department of Education and Science, Elizabeth House, 39 York Rd, London SE1 7PH Tel: (01) 928 9222
Secretary: Ms S Scales

Friends of the National Libraries*, c/o The British Library, Great Russell St, London WC1B 3DG Tel: (01) 636 1544 ext 207
Honorary Secretary: J F Fuggles
Publication: Annual Report

Institute of Information Scientists, Harvest House, 62 London Rd, Reading, Berks RG1 5AS Tel: Reading 861345 (STD code 0734)
Honorary Secretary: Dr J M Pope
Publications: Journal of Information Science; Inform

Institute of Reprographic Technology, PO Box 101, Witham, Essex CM8 1QS Tel: Witham 516297 (STD code 0376)
Secretary: Mrs J C Odell

446 UNITED KINGDOM

International Association of Music Libraries, Archives and Documentation Centres, (UK Branch), c/o Miss A E Smart, The Library, Royal Northern College of Music, 124 Oxford Rd, Manchester M13 9RD
General Secretary: Miss A E Smart
Publication: Brio (twice yearly)

Library and Information Council for England, c/o Department of Education and Science, Office of Arts and Libraries, Elizabeth House, York Rd, London SE1 7PH Tel: (01) 928 9222 Telex: 23171
Secretary: Ms S E Boorman
Publications include: Library Information series

Library Advisory Council for Wales*, Education Services Division, Welsh Office, Cathays Park, Cardiff Tel: Cardiff 825111 (STD code 0222) ext 4670
Secretary: Peter G Smith

The **Library Association**, 7 Ridgmount St, London WC1E 7AE Tel: (01) 636 7543 Telex: 21897
Secretary-General: K Lawrey
Publications include: Library Association Record, Current Technology Index (both monthly), *British Humanities Index, Journal of Librarianship, Current Research* (all quarterly), *Library and Information Science Abstracts* (bi-monthly), *Year Book* (annually), books and pamphlets on librarianship and bibliography, including *Guide to Reference Material; Libraries in the United Kingdom and the Republic of Ireland: a complete list of public library services and a select list of academic and other library addresses; A Librarian's Handbook; British Library and Information Work*

School Library Association, Victoria House, 29-31 George St, Oxford OX1 2AY Tel: Oxford 722746 (STD code 0865)
Secretary: Miriam Curtis
Publications: The School Librarian (quarterly); also books on school library management, and annotated book lists

School Library Association in Scotland, 35 Bloomfield Place, Arbroath, Angus DD11 3LP Tel: Arbroath 74060 (STD code 0241)

Scottish Library Association, c/o Secretary, R Craig, Department of Librarianship, University of Strathclyde, Livingstone Tower, Richmond St, Glasgow G1 1XH Tel: (041) 552 4400 ext 3706
Publications: SLA News (every two months); Scottish Library Studies Series

Society of Archivists, South Yorkshire County Record Office, Ellin St, Sheffield, South Yorkshire S1 4PL Tel: Sheffield 29191 ext 33 (STD code 0742)
Secretary: Mrs C M Short
Publication: Journal of the Society of Archivists

Society of County Librarians, County Library Headquarters, County Hall, Hertford SG13 8EJ Tel: Hertford 54242 ext 5481 (STD code 0992) Telex: 81272
Secretary: E M Broome

Society of Metropolitan & County Chief Librarians, c/o Central Library and Arts Centre, Walker Pl, Rotherham, South Yorkshire S65 1JH

Standing Conference of National and University Libraries (SCONUL), 102 Euston St, London NW1 2HA Tel: (01) 387 0317
Executive Secretary: A J Loveday

Welsh Library Association, Clwyd Library Service, County Library Headquarters, County Civic Centre, Mold, Clwyd CH7 6NW Tel: Mold 2121 ext 481 (STD code 0352) Telex: 61454
Honorary Secretary: Dwynwen Roberts
Publications include: A Bibliography of Anglo-Welsh Literature 1900-65; Bibliographies, Reference books and indexes to periodicals relating to Wales

Library Reference Books and Journals

Books

Address List of Public Library Authorities in the United Kingdom and the Republic of Ireland, The Library Association, 7 Ridgmount St, London WC1E 7AE

Aslib Directory, Association of Special Libraries and Information Bureaux, 3 Belgrave Sq, London SW1X 8PL

Aslib Membership List, Association of Special Libraries and Information Bureaux, 3 Belgrave Sq, London SW1X 8PL

British Library and Information Work, The Library Association, 7 Ridgmount St, London WC1E 7AE

British Library General Catalogue of Printed Books (to 1975, part-published; 1976-82, published), K G Saur Ltd, 2-10 Capper St, London WC1E 6JA

Guide to Reference Material, The Library Association, 7 Ridgmount St, London WC1E 7AE

A Librarians's Handbook; documentary and statistical material, The Library Association, 7 Ridgmount St, London WC1E 7AE

Libraries in the United Kingdom and the Republic of Ireland: a complete list of public library services and a select list of academic and other library addresses, The Library Association, 7 Ridgmount St, London WC1E 7AE

Libraries Yearbook, James Clarke & Co Ltd, 7 All Saints' Passage, Cambridge CB2 3LS

Library Association Year Book, The Library Association, 7 Ridgmount St, London WC1E 7AE

Who's Who in Librarianship and Information Science, Abelard-Schuman Ltd, Furnival House, 14-18 High Holborn, London W2 1EG

Journals

Archives, British Records Association, Indian Office Records, 197 Blackfriars Rd, London WC1

Art Libraries Journal, ARLIS (The Art Libraries Society), c/o Secretary, Ms Lyn Turpin, Learning Resources, Brighton Polytechnic, Faculty of Art and Design, Grand Parade, Brighton BN2 2JY

Aslib Information, Aslib Journal of Documentation, Aslib Proceedings, Aslib Book List, Association of Special Libraries and Information Bureaux, 3 Belgrave Sq, London SW1X 8PL

Assistant Librarian, Association of Assistant Librarians, c/o Editor, Brian Arnold, Central Library, Southgate, Stevenage Hertfordshire SG1 1HD

BLL Review, British Library, Lending Division, Boston Spa, Wetherby, West Yorkshire LS23 7BQ

Bibliotheck; a Scottish journal of bibliography and allied topics, Library Association, Scottish Group, University College & Research Section, c/o Editor, Douglas S Mack, University Library, Stirling FK9 4LA

Brio, International Association of Music Libraries (UK Branch), Music Department, Town Hall, Green Lanes, Palmers Green, London N13 4XD

British Library Journal, British Library, Reference Division, Great Russell St, London WC1B 3DG

Information Scientist, Institute of Information Scientists, 657 High Rd, Tottenham, London N17

Journal of Documentation, Association of Special Libraries and Information Bureaux, 3 Belgrave Sq, London SW1X 8PL

Journal of Librarianship, The Library Association, 7 Ridgmount St, London WC1E 7AE

Journal of the Society of Archivists, Society of Archivists, c/o Editor, Mrs F Strong, South Cloister, Eton College, Windsor, Berkshire SL4 6DB

The Law Librarian, British and Irish Association of Law Librarians, c/o Harding Law Library, University of Birmingham, PO Box 363, Edgbaston, Birmingham B15 2TT

The Library, Bibliographical Society, British Academy, Burlington House, London W1V 0NS

Library and Information Science Abstracts, The Library Association, 7 Ridgmount St, London WC1E 7AE

Library Association Record, The Library Association, 7 Ridgmount St, London WC1E 7AE

Library Review, W & R Holmes (Book), 30 Clydeholm Rd, Glasgow G14 0BJ

New Library World, Clive Bingley (Journals) Ltd, 16 Pembridge Rd, London W11 3HL

Private Library, Private Libraries Association, Ravelston, South View Rd, Pinner, Middlesex

SLA News, Scottish Library Association, c/o M C Head, Department of Librarianship, Robert Gordon's Institute of Technology, St Andrew's St, Aberdeen AB1 1HG

State Librarian, c/o Editor, Mrs B Howard, Civil Service Department Library, Whitehall, London SW1A 2AZ

Literary Associations and Societies

Yr **Academi** Gymreig (The Welsh Academy), Swyddfa'r Academi Gymreig, 4 Llawr, Adeilad Cory, Heol Bute, Caerdydd/Cardiff CF1 6AJ
Secretaries: Mrs Sue Harries (English Language Section), Mrs Marion Arthur Jones (Welsh Language Section), 4th Floor, Cory Bldg, Bute St, Cardiff CF1 6AJ

Association for Scottish Literary Studies, Department of English, University of Aberdeen, Aberdeen AB9 2UB Tel: Aberdeen 40241 ext 219 (STD code 0224)
Secretary: Dr D S Robb
Publications: Scottish Literary Journal

(twice yearly plus review supplements); *Scottish Language* (annually); an edited work of Scottish literature (annually)

Association of British Science Writers, c/o 21 Albemarle St, London W1X 4BS
Chairman: Anthony Michaelis
Secretary: Peter Cooper

Authors' Club, 40 Dover St, London W1X 3RB
Secretary: Mrs Huldine Ridgway

Francis **Bacon** Society Inc, Canonbury Tower, Islington, London N1
Chairman: Noel Fermar
Publication: Baconiana (periodically), *Jottings* (periodically)

Books across the Sea, The English-Speaking Union, Dartmouth House, 37 Charles St, London W1X 8AB Tel: (01) 408 0013
Librarian: Jean Huse
Publication: Ambassador Booklist (quarterly)

The **British Science Fiction** Association Ltd, 18 Gordon Terrace, Blantyre, Lanarkshire G72 9NA
Membership Secretary: Sandy Brown
Publications: Vector (bi-monthly critical journal); *Focus* (semi-annual SF writers' magazine); *Matrix* (bi-monthly newsletter); *Paperback Inferno* (bi-monthly reviews)

The Incorporated **Brontë** Society, The Brontë Parsonage, Haworth, Keighley, West Yorkshire BD22 8DR Tel: Haworth 42323 (STD code 0535)
Honorary Secretary: A H Preston
Publication: Brontë Society Transactions (annually)

Bulwer-Lytton Circle, 125 Markyate Rd, Dagenham, Essex RM8 2LB
Founder: E Ford
Publication: Bulwer-Lytton Chronicle

Cambridge Bibliographical Society, University Library, Cambridge CB3 9DR Tel: Cambridge 61441 (STD code 0223)
Honorary Secretary: F R Collieson
Publications: Transactions (annually); *Monographs* (irregular)

The **Dickens** Fellowship, Dickens House, 48 Doughty St, London WC1N 2LF Tel: (01) 405 2127
Honorary Secretary: Alan Watts
Publication: The Dickensian (four-monthly)

Early English Text Society, Exeter College, Oxford
Honorary Dir: Professor John Burrow;
Executive Secretary: Dr Malcolm Godden
Publications: Texts (annually)

East Anglian Writers*, Wood Cottage, Wattisfield, Suffolk
Honorary Secretary: P Somerset Fry

Edinburgh Bibliographical Society, c/o National Library of Scotland, George IV Bridge, Edinburgh EH1 1EW Tel: (031) 226 4531 ext 248
Honorary Secretary: I C Cunningham
Publication: Transactions (irregular — for members only)

Edwardian Studies Association, 125 Markyate Rd, Dagenham, Essex
Publication: Edwardian Studies

English Association, 1 Priory Gardens, London W4 1TT Tel: (01) 995 4236
Secretary: Lt-Col R T Brain
Publications: English (3 times yearly), *Essays and Studies, The Year's Work in English Studies, Guide to Degree Courses in English*

Federation of Children's Book Groups, 3 Cotswold Rd, Preston Grange, North Shields, Tyne and Wear NE29 9QJ Tel: North Shields 595689 (STD code 0632)
Chairman: Marjorie Taylor

Thomas **Hardy** Society Ltd, 18 Tristram Dr, Creech St. Michael, Taunton, Somerset TA3 5QU Tel: Henlade 443344 (STD code 0823)
Secretary: John C Pentney
Publications: Thomas Hardy and the Modern World, 1974; *Budmouth Essays on Thomas Hardy*, 1976; *Thomas Hardy's Sister Kate*, 1982

The Sherlock **Holmes** Society of London, The Old Crown Inn, Lopen, nr South Petherton, Somerset TA13 5JX Tel: South Petherton 40717 (STD code 0460)
Honorary Secretary: Captain W R Michell

The **Hopkins** Society*, 162 Turkey St, Enfield, Middx EN1 4NW
Chief Executive: Dr A Thomas
Publications: Hopkins Research Bulletin, Annual lecture, Annual sermon

Johnson Society of London, Round Chimney, Playden, Rye, East Sussex TN31 7UR Tel: Iden 252 (STD code 07978)
Honorary Secretary: Miss S B S Pigrome
Publication: The New Rambler (annually; enquiries to the Editor, Albany, Shoreham Rd, Otford, Kent TN14 5RL)

Kipling Society, 18 Northumberland Ave, London WC2N 5BJ
Honorary Secretary: John Shearman Tel: (01) 930 6733
Publication: The Kipling Journal (quarterly)

Charles **Lamb** Society, 1A Royston Rd, Richmond, Surrey TW10 6LT Tel: (01) 940 3837
Honorary Secretary: Mrs M R Huxstep
Publication: The Charles Lamb Bulletin (quarterly)

Lancashire Authors' Association, Kings Fold, Pope Lane, Penwortham, Preston, Lancashire PR1 9JN Tel: Preston 742236 (STD code 0772)
Honorary General Secretary: J D Cameron
Publication: The Record (quarterly)

London Writer Circle, 37 Manor Farm Rd, Bitterne Park, Southampton SO9 3FQ
Honorary Secretary: Miss M E Harris

The **National Book League**, Book House, 45 East Hill, Wandsworth, London SW18 2QZ Tel: (01) 870 9055
Dir: Martyn Goff, OBE
Branch: 15A Lynedoch St, Glasgow G3 6EF Tel: (041) 332 0391
Libraries: Reference library of current British children's books; The Mark Longman Library on books and the book trade, with a book information service
Publications: Booknews, British Book Design and Production, Children's Books of the Year, annotated book lists on specialist topics

Oxford Bibliographical Society, Bodleian Library, Oxford
Secretary: Dr P Bulloch
Publications: First Series, Vols I-VII, 1923-46; *New Series*, Vol I, 1948- ; *Occasional Publications*, No 1, 1967-

P E N English Centre, 7 Dilke St, Chelsea, London SW3 4JE Tel: (01) 352 6303
Secretary: Miss Josephine Pullein-Thompson
Publications: Broadsheet (biannually); *New Poetry, New Stories* (annually, in conjunction with Arts Council)

P E N Scottish Centre, 18 Moray Pl, Edinburgh EH3 6DT Tel: (031) 225 6218
Hon Secretary: Mrs Jo Currie

The **Poetry** Society, 21 Earls Court Sq, London SW5 9DE Tel: (01) 373 7861
General Secretary: Brian G Mitchell
Publications: The Poetry Review; Newsletter (quarterly)

Romantic Novelists' Association, Flat 6, 61 Langley Park Rd, Sutton, Surrey SM2 5MA
Secretary: Tilly Armstrong

Royal Literary Fund, 144 Temple Chambers, London EC4Y 0DT Tel: (01) 353 7150

Royal Society of Literature of the United Kingdom, 1 Hyde Park Gardens, London W2 2LT Tel: (01) 723 5104
Secretary: Mrs P M Schute
Publications: Transactions, Report, Special Editions

Shakespearean Authorship Trust*, 11 Old Square, Lincoln's Inn, London WC2A 3TS
Honorary Secretary: Dr D W Thomson Vessey
Publication: The Bard (semi-annual)

Bernard **Shaw** Centre, 125 Markyate Rd, Dagenham, Essex RM8 2LB
Director: E Ford
Publications: Shaw Centre Series

Bernard **Shaw** Society, 125 Markyate Rd, Dagenham, Essex RM8 2LB
Secretary: E Ford
Publications: The Shavian, etc

Society for the Study of Mediaeval Languages and Literature,
Treasurer: Dr D G Pattison, Magdalen College, Oxford OX1 4AU
Publications: Medium Aevum, Medium Aevum Monographs (new series)

Society of Australian Writers*, Australia House, Strand, London WC2
Secretary: Alessandra Miach

The **Tolkien** Society*, 9 Bossard Court, Leighton Buzzard, Bedfordshire LU7 7DF
Secretary: Mrs Helen Armstrong
Distribution/Publications: 11 Regal Way, Harrow, Middlesex HA3 0RZ
Publications: Amon Hen (bulletin, approx 6 issues a year), *Mallorn* (journal, approx twice a year)

Jules **Verne** Circle, 125 Markyate Rd, Dagenham, Essex RM8 2LB
Founder: E Ford
Publication: Jules Verne Voyages

H G **Wells** Society, Department of Language and Literature, Polytechnic of North London, Prince of Wales Rd, London NW5 3LB
Secretary: C Rolfe
Publications: Newsletter (tri-annual), *The Wellsian* (annual)

Wellsiana—The World of H G Wells, 125 Markyate Rd, Dagenham, Essex RM8 2LB
Publication: Wellsiana

The **Welsh** Academy, see Academi Gymreig

Literary Periodicals

Bananas (quarterly), 60 Elgin Crescent, London W11

Book Collector, Collector Ltd, 58 Frith St, London W1V 6BY

Books, National Book League, Book House, East Hill, London SW18 2QZ

Books and Bookmen, 43 Museum St, London WC1A 1LY

Books & Issues, Stephen Trombley, 40 Mildmay Grove, London N1

Critical Quarterly, Manchester University Press, Oxford Rd, Manchester M13 9PL

Encounter, Encounter Ltd, 59 St Martins Lane, London WC2

The Fiction Magazine, 5 Jeffreys St, London NW1 9PS

Good Book Guide, Braithwaite & Taylor Ltd, PO Box 400, Havelock Terrace, London SW8 4AU Tel: (01) 622 1262. Independent book-review magazine published in conjunction with an international mail-order bookselling service

The Literary Review, 51 Beak St, London W1R 3DH

The London Review of Books, 6a Bedford Sq, London WC1

PN Review (bi-monthly), 330 Corn Exchange Bldgs, Manchester M4 3BG

Notes and Queries; for readers and writers, collectors and librarians, Oxford University Press, Press Rd, Neasden, London NW10 0DD

Phoenix; a magazine for writers, Phoenix Publications, 60 Abbey House, 2 Victoria St, London SW1

Poetry London, 24 Old Gloucester St, London W1

Poetry Review, Poetry Society, 21 Earls Court Sq, London SW5

Quarto, merged with *The Literary Review* (qv) 1982

Review of English Studies; a quarterly journal of English literature and the English language, The Clarendon Press, Walton St, Oxford OX2 6DP

Scottish Language, Association for Scottish Literary Studies, Department of English, University of Aberdeen, Aberdeen AB9 1FX

Scottish Literary Journal, Association for Scottish Literary Studies, Department of English, University of Aberdeen, Aberdeen AB9 1FX

Taliesin; the Welsh literary journal, Garth Martin, Ffordd Llysonnen, Carmarthen

Telegram, 12 Stevenage Rd, London SW6 6ES, 3 times a year

Times Literary Supplement, Priory House, St Johns Lane, London EC1M 4BX

Transatlantic Review, 33 Ennismore Gardens, London SW7

Literary Prizes

Angel Literary Prize
Established in 1982 by the Angel Hotel, Bury St Edmunds, for writers living and working in East Anglia. There are two annual awards — £1,000 for a work of non-fiction and £500 for a work of the imagination. Enquiries to Mrs V A Donovan, Angel Hotel, Bury St Edmunds, Suffolk

Authors' Club First Novel Award*
For the most promising first novel published in English in the UK in the preceding year. Award consists of a silver-plated quill presented to the author at a dinner. Awarded annually. Enquiries to the Honorary Secretary, Authors' Club, 40 Dover St, London W1X 3RB

Authors' Club Sir Banister Fletcher Prize Trust*
For the most deserving book on architecture or the arts. Awarded annually. Enquiries to the Honorary Secretary, Authors' Club, 40 Dover St, London W1X 3RB

Besterman Medal
The Library Association awards this medal annually for an outstanding bibliography or guide to the literature first published in the United Kingdom during the preceding year. Recommendations for the award are invited from members of The Library Association. Among criteria for the award are the authority of the work, quality of articles and entries, accessibility of information, scope and coverage, up-to-dateness, and originality. Enquiries to The Library Association, 7 Ridgmount St, London WC1E 7AE

James Tait **Black** Memorial Prizes
These literary prizes were founded by the late Mrs Janet Coats Black in memory of her husband, a partner in the publishing house of A & C Black Ltd, London. Mrs Black set aside £11,000 to be used for two prizes of whatever income the fund would produce after paying expenses. The prizes, supplemented by the Scottish Arts Council, now amount annually to approximately £1,000 each. One prize is given to the author of the best biography in the English language first published in the United Kingdom during the year and the other to the author of the best novel. The choice is made in the spring for books of the preceding year by the Regius Professor of Rhetoric and English Literature at the University of Edinburgh, preferably, or the Professor of English at the University of Glasgow. For books published during 1982, the awards were made to Richard Ellmann for his biography *James Joyce* (Oxford University Press), and to Bruce Chatwin for his novel *On The Black Hill* (Cape). Enquiries to Department of English Literature, David Hume Tower, George Sq, Edinburgh EH8 9JX

Arnold Vincent **Bowen** Competition
Awarded annually for the best single lyric poem in English of up to thirty lines. Prize of £30. Enquiries to the General Secretary, The Poetry Society, 21 Earls Court Sq, London SW5

British Science Fiction Award*
Awarded annually for the best science fiction book published in Britain for the first time in the previous year. Enquiries to Alan Dorey (BSFA Chairman), 20 Hermitage Woods Crescent, St John's, Woking, Surrey GU21 1UE

Carnegie Medal
First awarded 1936. Instituted by The Library Association to commemorate the centenary of Andrew Carnegie's birth in 1835. Annual award for an outstanding book for children written in English and first published during the preceding year in the UK. Recommendations for the award are made by members of The Library Association. The 1982 Medal was awarded to Margaret Mahy for *The Haunting* (Dent). Enquiries to The Library Association, 7 Ridgmount St, London WC1E 7AE

Sid **Chaplin** Literary Award*
Established in 1977 to encourage the writing of short stories. £100 and a scroll to be awarded annually. The 1981 award was won by Norman Kirtlan. A separate prize of £25 for the best story by a writer aged eighteen or under was awarded to Miss Sally Anne Stonely. Enquiries to Public Relations Department, Aycliffe and Peterlee Development Corporations, Newton Aycliffe, Co Durham

John **Creasey** Memorial Award
Founded 1973. Magnifying glass with onyx handle and inscribed plate for best first crime-fiction novel. Awarded annually by a panel of reviewers. Enquiries to Crime Writers' Association, c/o The Press Club Ltd, 76 Shoe Lane, London EC4

Eleanor **Farjeon** Award
The Eleanor Farjeon Award was established in 1965 to commemorate the work of the late children's author. The Children's Book Circle makes an annual award of £500 (minimum) which may be given to a librarian, teacher, author, artist, publisher, reviewer, bookseller or television producer who, in the judgment of the Awards Committee, is considered to have done outstanding work for children's books. Awarded in 1983, with financial assistance from the Arts Council of Great Britain, to Jean Russell. Enquiries to Janetta Otter-Barry, Blackie & Son Ltd, Furnival House, 14-18 High Holborn, London WC1

Prudence **Farmer** Poetry Prize
Founded 1974. Awarded annually for the best poem printed in the *New Statesman* during the previous year. In 1982 the prize was awarded to John Levett. Enquiries to Literary Editor, 14-16 Farringdon Lane, London EC1R 3AU

Kathleen **Fidler** Award
First awarded in 1982. Annual award of £500 and a trophy for an unpublished novel written for 8-12 year-olds. The author may have had previous books published, but this must be the first for this age range. The award is sponsored by Blackie & Son Ltd, who have first option on the winning entry. Enquiries to The National Book League, 15A Lynedoch St, Glasgow G3

Authors' Club Sir Bannister **Fletcher** Prize Trust, see under Authors' Club

John **Florio** Prize
Established in 1963 under the auspices of the Italian Institute and the British-Italian Society, and named after John Florio. For the best translation into English of a twentieth-century Italian work of literary merit and general interest, published by a British publisher during the preceding year. £500. Enquiries to Secretary, Translators Association, 84 Drayton Gardens, London SW10 9SD

Gold Dagger Award
Inaugurated 1956, revised 1970. A gilded dagger for the best crime-fiction novel of the year awarded annually by a panel of reviewers. Enquiries to Crime Writers' Association, c/o The Press Club Ltd, 76 Shoe Lane, London EC4

Kate **Greenaway** Medal
First awarded 1955. Offered annually by The Library Association for the most distinguished work in the illustration of children's books first published in the UK during the preceding year. Recommendations for the award are made by members of The Library Association. The 1982 medal was awarded to Michael Foreman for illustrating *Long Neck and Thunder Foot* (Kestrel) written by Helen Piers, and *Sleeping Beauty and Other Favourite Fairy Tales* (Gollancz) translated by Angela Carter. Enquiries to The Library Association, 7 Ridgmount St, London WC1E 7AE

Eric **Gregory** Trust Fund Awards
A number of awards are made each year to encourage young poets. Candidates for awards must be British subjects by birth, ordinarily resident in the UK and under the age of 30 on 31 March in the year of the award. Candidates must submit a published or unpublished volume of belles lettres, poetry or drama-poems. In 1983 the £3,000 award was made to Martin Stokes, and awards of £1,250 to Hilary Davis, Deirdre

Shanahan, Lisa St Aubin de Teran, Michael O'Neill. Enquiries to Society of Authors, 84 Drayton Gardens, London SW10 9SB

Garavi Gujarat Annual Book Award for Racial Harmony
Two awards — major prize of £1,000 and a children's book prize of £100 — for any book, fiction or non-fiction, which best promotes racial harmony, published in the UK in year ending 30 June of year of presentation. Enquiries to Homi Framroze, Garavi Gujarat Publications, Garavi Gujarat House, 1-2 Silex St, London SE1

Hawthornden Prize
Founded in 1919 by Miss Alice Warrender and administered now by the Society of Authors. It is awarded annually in June to a British subject under 41 for the best work of imaginative literature. In 1981 it was increased to £750 through the generosity of the Arts Council of Great Britain. It is especially designed to encourage young authors, and the word 'imaginative' is given a broad interpretation. Biographies are not excluded. Books do not have to be submitted for the prize; it is awarded without competition. A panel of judges chooses the winner. In 1983 the prize was awarded to Timothy Mo for *Sour Sweet* (Jonathan Cape). Enquiries to Society of Authors, 84 Drayton Gardens, London SW10 9SB

Heinemann Award for Literature
A foundation was established in 1944 through a bequest in the will of the late William Heinemann, eminent British publisher. The Royal Society of Literature administers the annual foundation award which is 'primarily to reward those classes of literature which are less remunerative, namely, poetry, criticism, biography, history, etc' and 'to encourage the production of works of real merit'. The amount of the award is not definitely specified. Submitted works must have been written originally in English and published during the calendar year previous to the year in which the prize is presented. A reading committee decides on the winner, whose name is announced in April or May; the prize is presented at a meeting of the Royal Society of Literature in June or July. The award for 1982 was to Derek Walcott for *The Fortunate Traveller* (Faber & Faber). Enquiries to Royal Society of Literature, 1 Hyde Park Gardens, London W2 2LT

Felicia **Hemans** Prize for Lyrical Poetry
For a lyrical poem by past and present members and students of the University of Liverpool. Books or cash awarded annually. Enquiries to Registrar, University of Liverpool, PO Box 147, Liverpool L69 3BX

Winifred **Holtby** Memorial Prize
Founded in 1966 by Vera Brittain in memory of Winifred Holtby. An annual award for the best regional novel of its year. Submissions by publishers, not by individual authors. The award for 1982 was to Kazuo Ishiguro for *A Pale View of Hills* (Faber & Faber). Enquiries to Secretary, Royal Society of Literature, 1 Hyde Park Gardens, London W2 2LT

Literary Contest Prize for Spastics Society
Annual monetary prize for literary achievement by a UK resident who is handicapped. Enquiries to Nina Heycock, Chenil House, 181-183 King's Rd, Chelsea, London SW3 5EB

Martin Luther **King** Memorial Prize*
Inaugurated 1968. For a literary work reflecting the ideals to which Dr King devoted his life. It may be given for a novel, work of non-fiction, poetry collection, play, television, radio or film script first published or performed in the UK during the preceding year. Prize of £100 awarded annually. Enquiries to National Westminster Bank, 7 Fore St, Chard, Somerset TA20 1PJ. No enquiries answered without stamped and addressed envelope

MIND Book of the Year Award
Inaugurated in 1981 by MIND and the National Book League in memory of Allen Lane. Awarded annually to the author(s) of the book (fiction or non-fiction) which outstandingly furthers public understanding of the prevention, causes, treatment or experience of mental illness and/or mental handicap. Award is £1,000. The 1982 award was made to Rosemary Crossley and Anne McDonald for *Annie's Coming Out* (Pelican). Enquiries to The National Book League, Book House, 45 East Hill, Wandsworth, London SW18 2QZ

McColvin Medal
This annual award is given for an outstanding reference book first published in the United Kingdom during the preceding year. Encyclopaedias, dictionaries, biographical dictionaries, annuals, yearbooks and directories, handbooks and compendia of data, and atlases are eligible. Recommendations are invited from members of The Library Association who are asked to submit a preliminary list of not more than three titles. Enquiries to The Library Association, 7 Ridgmount St, London WC1E 7AE

Arthur **Markham** Memorial Prize
Instituted 1927. For a poem, short story, first chapter of a novel or a one-act play by a manual worker in coal-mining. There are specified themes and strict limits on length. Prizes totalling £125 annually. Enquiries to Registrar and Secretary, The University, Sheffield S10 2TN

Kurt **Maschler** Award
An annual award in memory of Erich Kästner and Walter Trier for 'a work of imagination in the children's field in which text and illustration are of excellence and so presented that each enhances, yet balances, the other'. The prize is £1,000, the author and illustrator each receiving in addition a sculpted 'Emil'. Books published in the current year in the UK by a British author and/or artist or someone resident for ten years are eligible. The 1983 award was for *The Sleeping Beauty* (Victor Gollancz) by Angela Carter, illustrated by Michael Foreman. Enquiries to The National Book League, Book House, 45 East Hill, Wandsworth, London SW18 2QZ

Somerset **Maugham** Award
Founded 1946 by Somerset Maugham to encourage young writers to travel abroad. Given to a promising author of a published work of poetry, fiction, criticism, biography, history, philosophy, belles lettres or travel. Candidates must be British subjects by birth and ordinarily resident in the UK and under 30. Awards of £1,000 must be used for foreign travel. The 1983 award was to Lisa St Aubin de Teran for *Keepers of the House* (André Deutsch). Enquiries to Society of Authors, 84 Drayton Gardens, London SW10 9SB

Netta **Muskett** Award
Established 1960. For an unpublished romantic novel by an author who has not previously had a romantic novel published. A trophy is awarded annually and the winning novel is guaranteed publication. If a manuscript is not accepted for publication, the award is not made. Enquiries to Tilly Armstrong, Romantic Novelists' Association, Flat 6, 61 Langley Park Rd, Sutton, Surrey SM2 5MA

National Poetry Competition
Founded in 1978. Awarded annually for a poem written in English by a resident of the United Kingdom or the Republic of Ireland. £2,000 first prize, £1,000 second, £500 third and fifteen other smaller prizes. The 1982 winner was Philip Grass. Enquiries to The Poetry Society, 21 Earls Court Sq, London SW5 9DE

Sir Roger **Newdigate** Prize for English Verse
The Newdigate Prize Foundation was established in 1806 by Sir Roger Newdigate who had been a member of Parliament for Oxford University from 1750 to 1780. This foundation was the first one founded solely to award a literary prize. The sum of £1,000 was bequeathed by Sir Roger with the stipulation that £21 of the income should be awarded each year to a member of Oxford University for 'a copy of English verse of fifty lines and no more, in recommendation of the study of the ancient Greek and Roman remains of architecture, sculpture, and painting'. Later, with the consent of the Newdigate heirs, these restrictions were modified. The award, increased to about £150, is now open to undergraduate members of the University of Oxford who have not exceeded four years from their matriculation. It is given for a poem of no more than 300 lines on a given subject. Three judges award the prize. Announcement is made by Oxford University annually in May or early June; the winner recites part of the poem at commemoration in June. Enquiries to Head Clerk, University of Oxford, University Offices, Wellington Sq, Oxford OX1 2JD

Frederick **Niven** Literary Award
Founded in 1950 by Pauline, widow of the Scottish novelist Frederick Niven. For the best novel by a Scotsman or Scotswoman published during the preceding three years. £500 awarded every three years. Enquiries to Honorary Secretary, PEN Scottish Centre, 18 Moray Pl, Edinburgh EH3 6DT

George **Orwell** Memorial Fund Prize
Established in 1982 and given alternately for a project of imaginative or non-fiction writing on Orwell or in the Orwellian spirit. Applicants must be registered as occasional students at Birkbeck College or University College, London. £2,000 is awarded annually. The 1982 (fiction) prize went to David Alan and the 1983 (non-fiction) prize to Bill Wallis. Enquiries to Secretary & Clerk to the Governors, Birkbeck College, University of London, Malet Street, London WC1E 7HX

George **Orwell** Memorial Prize, now known as the Penguin/George Orwell Memorial Prize (qv)

The **Other** Award
Commendation of a number of books a year as 'progressive books of literary merit for children'. In 1982 the chosen books were Keith Ajegbo's *Black Lives White Worlds* (Cambridge University Press), Susan Hemmings' *Girls Are Powerful* (Sheba), Marlene Fanta Shyer's *Welcome Home, Jellybean* (Granada), Raymond Briggs' *When the Wind Blows* (Hamish Hamilton) and Sallie Purkis & Elizabeth Merson's *Into the Past* series (Longman). Enquiries to 4 Aldebert Terrace, London SW8 1BH

Penguin/George Orwell Memorial Prize
For a social or political novel. Further details not yet formulated.

Provincial Booksellers Fairs Association Annual Book Awards*
Two awards of £250 each are made annually covering different types of books. Enquiries to Mrs Edna Whiteson Ltd, 343 Bowes Rd, London N11

The **Queen's** Gold Medal for Poetry
Instituted in 1933 by King George V, at the suggestion of the Poet Laureate, John Masefield, this Medal is given for a book of verse, on the recommendation of a committee of eminent men and women of letters headed by the Poet Laureate. The Medal is usually given for a book by a British subject writing in the English language, but an exceptional translation may also be considered. The Medal is not necessarily awarded every year. Last awarded in 1981 to Dennis Joseph Enwright. Enquiries to the Press Secretary to the Queen, Buckingham Palace, London SW1

R N A Major Award
Established 1960. For the best romantic novel (modern or historical) published during the year. Trophy awarded annually, open to non-members. The award in 1983 was to Eva Ibbotson for *Magic Flutes* (Century). Enquiries to Tilly Armstrong, Romantic Novelists' Association, Flat 6, 61 Langley Park Rd, Sutton, Surrey SM2 5MA

Schlegel-Tieck Prize
Established in 1964 under the auspices of the Translators Association, a subsidiary organization of the Society of Authors, to be awarded annually for the best translation published by a British publisher during the previous year. Only translations of German twentieth-century works of literary merit and general interest will be considered. The work should be entered by the publisher and not the individual translator. The 1982 prize was awarded to Paul Salla and A J Ryder for their translation of *A History of European Integration 1945-47* by Walter Lipgens (Oxford University Press). Enquiries to Secretary, The Translators Association, 84 Drayton Gardens, London SW10 9SD

Scott-Moncrieff Prize
Established in 1964 under the auspices of the Translators Association of the Society of Authors to be awarded annually for the best translation published by a British publisher during the previous year. Only translations of French twentieth-century works of literary merit and general interest will be considered. The work should be entered by the publisher and not the individual translator. The £1,000 prize for a book published in 1982 was won by Sian Reynolds for her translation of *Wheels of Commerce* by Fernand Braudel (Collins). Enquiries to Secretary, Translators Association, 84 Drayton Gardens, London SW10 9SD

Scottish Arts Council Book Awards
A limited number of Awards, value £600 each, are made twice yearly by the Scottish Arts Council to published books of literary merit written by Scots or writers resident in Scotland. All types of books are eligible for consideration. Books are submitted by the author's publisher. Enquiries to Literature Department, The Scottish Arts Council, 19 Charlotte Sq, Edinburgh EH2 4DF

Scottish Book of the Year
Founded 1981 by The Saltire Society and The Royal Bank of Scotland. For a book of a literary nature written by an author of Scottish descent or living in Scotland, or a book which deals with the work or life of a Scot or with a Scottish problem, event or situation. The Royal Bank contributes £1,000 to be awarded annually. Smaller prizes might be given for one or two additional books which were felt deserving of commendation. Enquiries to The Saltire Society, Saltire House, Atholl Crescent, Edinburgh EH3 8HA

Silver Dagger Award
Inaugurated 1956, revised 1970. A silvered dagger for the runner-up crime-fiction novel of the year (see Gold Dagger Award). Awarded annually by a panel of reviewers. Enquiries to Crime Writers' Association, c/o The Press Club Ltd, 76 Shoe Lane, London EC4

W H Smith & Son Literary Award
Established 1959 to encourage and bring international esteem to authors of the Commonwealth. Given to an author whose book, written in English and published in the UK, makes the most significant contribution to Literature. Award of £4,000 annually. The award for 1983 was made to A N Wilson for *Wise Virgin* (Secker & Warburg). Enquiries to W H Smith & Son Ltd, Strand House, 10 New Fetter Lane, London EC4A 1AD

W H Smith Young Writers' Competition
Established in 1958 as the Children's Literary Competition, and previously run by the Daily Mirror, the competition aims to encourage creativity in written English. Open to all children in the UK and of British nationality abroad, up to the age of 16 years. Ninety-three awards including cash prizes to schools and children totalling £4,025 are made and the award-winning work is published in book form. Enquiries to Public Relations Department, W H Smith & Son Ltd, Strand House, 10 New Fetter Lane, London EC4A 1AD

Reginald **Taylor** Prize
Instituted 1932. For the best unpublished essay, not exceeding 7,500 words, on any subject of archaeological, art historical, or antiquarian interest within the period from the Roman era to AD 1830. Prize of £100 awarded annually. Enquiries to Paul Everson, Honorary Editor, British Archaeological Association, c/o County Offices, Newland, Lincoln

Dylan **Thomas** Award
Instituted in 1983 in honour of the contribution made to English letters by Dylan Thomas and to encourage writers working in two literary genres in which Dylan Thomas's work is celebrated. £1,000 awarded to a poet or short-story writer. The winner of the 1983 award was Peter Reading for *Diplopic* (Secker & Warburg). Enquiries to The Poetry Society, 21 Earls Court Sq, London SW5 9DE

Tom-Gallon Trust Award
Founded 1943. Given to short-story writers of limited means. Entrants must submit a list of already published fiction, one published or unpublished short story, and a brief statement of their financial position and willingness to devote substantial time to writing fiction as soon as they are financially able. It is awarded every other year. The award has been increased to £500 through the generosity of the Arts Council of Great Britain. Enquiries to Society of Authors, 84 Drayton Gardens, London SW10 9SB

The **Universe** (The Catholic Newspaper) Literary Prize
An annual prize, worth £250, for the book which best supports and defends Christian values. Any book written in English and published in Britain and Ireland in the relevant year is eligible. Enquiries to The National Book League, Book House, 45 East Hill, Wandsworth, London SW18 2QZ

Welsh Arts Council Awards to Writers
Since 1968, the Welsh Arts Council has given awards to authors whose books are of exceptional literary merit or which make an important contribution to the literature of Wales. The books must be written in English or Welsh. The prizes are awarded to recognize achievement, to draw attention to writers of promise and to encourage the writing of creative literature in English and Welsh. Cash prizes of £1,000 awarded annually. Bursaries of up to £12,500 each are awarded to enable writers to devote themselves, for periods of up to one year, to their writing. Enquiries to Welsh Arts Council, Museum Pl, Cardiff CF1 3NX

Wheatley Medal
Instituted 1961. Presented by The Library Association, after consultation with The Society of Indexers, for a book published in the UK during the preceding three years which sets an outstandingly high standard in the quality of its index. The 1982 medal was awarded to Peter W M Blaney for *The Texts of King Lear and their Origins, Vol 1: Nicholas Okes and the First Quarto* (Cambridge University Press). Enquiries to The Library Association, 7 Ridgmount St, London WC1E 7AE

Whitbread Literary Awards
Instituted 1971. Annual awards of £3,000 each to acknowledge outstanding published books in each of three categories of literature: best novel; best biography or autobiography; best children's novel. An additional award of £1,000 is given for the best novel by a new author, chosen by a poll of leading literary editors. Authors must be domiciled in the UK or the Republic of Ireland. 1982 awards were made to John Wain for *Young Shoulders* (Macmillan); Edward Crankshaw for *Bismarck* (Macmillan); W J Corbett for *The Song of Pentecost* (Methuen); and Bruce Chatwin for *On the Black Hill* (Jonathan Cape). Enquiries to the Booksellers Association of Great Britain and Ireland, 154 Buckingham Palace Rd, London SW1W 9TZ

Francis **Williams** Book Illustration Award*
This award is a bequest enabling monetary prizes to be given every five years to practising book illustrators, professional or student, for books published or originating in Great Britain in which illustration is a major element. Books privately printed or in limited editions are excluded. Illustrations of a purely technical nature and photographs are excluded. The first Exhibition and prizegiving was held at the Victoria and Albert Museum in 1972. In 1982 a prize of £300 was given in each of the following categories: (1) best children's book — Raymond Briggs for *The Snowman* (Hamish Hamilton, 1978), (2) best descriptive illustration — Sara Milda for *In and Out of the Garden* (Sidgwick & Jackson, 1982), (3) best literary illustration — Paul Hogarth for *Poems* by Robert Graves (Limited Editions Club, 1980), (4) best art director — Tom Phillips for *Dante's Inferno* (Tom Phillips, 1981-83), (5) best illustrator — Edward Bawden, CBE for the sum of his work. Enquiries to The Victoria and Albert Museum Library, South Kensington, London SW7 2RL or The National Book League, Book House, East Hill, Wandsworth, London SW18 2QZ

Griffith John **Williams** Memorial Prize (Gwobr Goffa Griffith John Williams)
Awarded to non-members of the Welsh Academy for the best literary work in Welsh produced in the previous year. About £60 awarded annually. Enquiries to Yr Academi Gymreig, 4 Llawr, Adeilad Cory, Heol Bute, Cardiff CF1 6AJ

Wolfson History Awards
Founded 1972. Two awards are made annually to authors of published works on history. One (of £8,000) is given for an author's published body of work; in 1982 this was awarded to Sir Stevan Runciman. The other award (of £5,000), given to encourage the writing of scholarly history for the general public, was made to Professor McManners for *Death and the Enlightenment*. Enquiries to The Wolfson Foundation, c/o Paisner & Co (Solicitors), Bouverie House, 154 Fleet St, London EC4A 2DQ

Yorkshire Arts Association Literary Awards
The Association offers a number of biennial awards, together worth up to £4,000 for published books of poetry, drama, novels or works of non-fiction, having strong literary connections with Yorkshire. Some of the awards are usually made to new writers (ie with only one work in print) whilst the others are for more established authors (with two or more books published). Enquiries to The Literature Officer, Yorkshire Arts Association, Glyde House, Glydegate, Bradford, West Yorkshire BD5 0BQ

Translation Agencies and Associations

Tek Translation & International Print Ltd, 11 Uxbridge Rd, London W12 8LH Tel: (01) 749 3211 Telex: 265658 Tek G
Technical specialists in over 100 languages, including Chinese, Arabic, Japanese, Russian

Traducta Ltd, 21a Harold Rd, London SE19 Tel: (01) 771 4582
Contact: Denise Baldry

Translators Association, 84 Drayton Gardens, London SW10 9SD Tel: (01) 373 6642

Translators' Guild Ltd, Mangold House, 24a Highbury Grove, London N5 2EA Tel: (01) 359 7445/6386
Secretary: A Bell
Publication: Newsletter of the Translators' Guild (quarterly)

Upper Volta

General Information

Language: French, officially
Religion: About 1 million Muslim, ¼ million Roman Catholic; rest follow traditional beliefs
Population: 6.6 million
Bank Hours: 0800-1200 Monday-Friday
Shop Hours: 0800-1200, 1500-1800 Monday-Saturday
Currency: CFA franc
Export/Import Information: Member of West African Economic Community. No tariff on books except children's picture books and atlases; single advertising catalogues sent as printed matter free but otherwise dutied. Statistical Tax and Customs Stamp Tax. No import licences required for imports from EEC or Franc Zone
Copyright: Berne (see International section)

Publishers

Government Printer, Imprimerie Nationale*, BP 7040, Ouagadougou

Les **Presses** Africaines*, BP 90, Ouagadougou
Man Dir: M Armand
Subjects: General Fiction, Religion, Secondary & Primary Textbooks
Bookshop: Librairie Jeunesse d'Afrique, BP 90, Ouagadougou
Book Club: Librairie 'Jeunesse et Afrique'

Book Club

Librairie **'Jeunesse et Afrique'***, BP 90, Ouagadougou
Owned by: Les Presses Africaines (Ouagadougou)

Major Booksellers

Librairie **Attié***, BP 64, Ouagadougou

Librairie **Evangélique***, BP 29, Ouagadougou

Librairie de **France***, BP 73, Ouagadougou

Librairie **Jeunesse d'Afrique***, BP 90, Ouagadougou

Major Libraries

American Cultural Center Library, BP 539, Ouagadougou

Archives nationales*, Ouagadougou

Bibliothèque universitaire*, Université de Ouagadougou, BP 7021, Ouagadougou Tel: 32944 Telex: 5270 UV
Librarian: Boureima Zorome

Bibliothèque du **Grand** Seminaire de Koumi*, BP 149, Bobo Dioulasso Tel: 99753
Librarian: C Jouneau

Library Association

Association voltaique pour le Développement des Bibliothèques, des Archives et de la Documentation (AVDBAD)*, BP 1140, Ouagadougou
Voltan Association for the Development of Libraries, Archives and Documentation
Executive Secretary: Louis Aristide Rouamba

Uruguay

General Information

Language: Spanish
Religion: Roman Catholic
Population: 2.9 million
Literacy Rate (1975): 93.9%
Bank Hours: 1300-1700 Monday-Friday
Shop Hours: 0900-1200, 1400-1900 Monday-Friday; 0900-1230 Saturday
Currency: peso
Export/Import Information: Member of the Latin American Free Trade Association. No tariffs on books or single copies catalogues but surcharge on advertising matter. Additional surcharge on all imports, plus VAT CIF, plus Stamp Tax of percentage of total invoice value. No import licences. No exchange controls
Copyright: Berne, Buenos Aires (see International section)

Book Trade Organizations

Asociación de Libreros del Uruguay*, Ave Uruguay 1325, Montevideo
Uruguayan Booksellers' Association

Asociación Uruguaya de Escritores*, Bartolomé Mitre 1260, Montevideo
Uruguayan Writers' Association

Cámara Uruguaya del Libro*, Carlos Roxlo 1446 piso 1°, Apdo 2, Montevideo Tel: 411860
Uruguayan Publishers' Association
Secretary: Arnaldo Medone

Book Trade Reference Journals

Anuario bibliográfico uruguayo (Uruguayan Bibliographical Annual), National Library, Calle Guayabo 1793, Montevideo

Bibliografía uruguaya (Uruguayan Bibliography), Biblioteca de Poder Legislativo, Palacio Legislativo, Ave Agradiada, Montevideo

Publishers

Editorial **Arca** SRL, Andes 1118, Montevideo
Man Dir: Alberto Oreggioni
Subjects: General Literature, History, Social Science

Barreiro y Ramos SA, Juan Carlos Gómez 1436, Casilla de Correo 15, Montevideo Tel: 919202 Cable Add: Bareiramos
Man Dir: Gaston Barreiro Zorrilla; *Sales Dir:* Raúl Catelli
Subjects: General Literature, Textbooks Reference
Bookshops: Juan Carlos Gómez 1436 (For branches see under Major Booksellers)
Founded: 1871

Editorial y Librería Juridica Amalio M **Fernández**, 25 de Mayo 477, planta baja, Of 11, Montevideo Tel: 952684
Man Dir: Amalio M Fernández; *Editorial:* Carlos W Deamestoy Perez; *Sales:* Andrés Paz López
Subjects: Law, Sociology
Founded: 1951

Fundación de Cultura Universitaria, 25 de Mayo 568, 1155 Montevideo Tel: 913385
Man Dir: Luis Carlos Benvenuto; *Editorial Dir:* Carlos Fuques
Branch Off: Guayabo 1860, Montevideo
Subjects: Social Science, Law
Founded: 1968

Grijalbo Editor, Buenos Aires 280, Montevideo
Parent Company: Ediciones Grijalbo, Spain (qv)

Editorial **Interamericana** SA, Casilla de Correos 357, Montevideo
Manager: Mirta Gaidos
Associate Company: Holt-Saunders Ltd (qv for other associates)

Editorial **Medina** SRL*, Gaboto 1521, Montevideo Tel: 44100/45800
Man Dir: Marcos Medina Vidal
Subject: Low-priced Paperbacks
Founded: 1933

URUGUAY — VATICAN CITY STATE

A **Monteverde** y Cia SA*, 25 de Mayo 577, Casilla de Correo 371, Montevideo Tel: 902473
Man Dir: Héctor Mussini; *Sales Dir:* Néstor Barón; *Production:* Leandro Mendaro
Subjects: Literature, Primary & Secondary Textbooks, Educational Materials
Bookshop: Palacio del Libro, 25 de Mayo 577, Montevideo
Founded: 1879

Mosca Hnos SA, Ave 18 de Julio 1578, Montevideo Tel: 404131 Cable Add: Moscaher
Man Dir: Miguel Angel Mosca; *Sales Dir:* Raúl Mosca
Subjects: General Literature, Religion, Textbooks
Bookshop: Ave 18 de Julio 1578, Montevideo
Founded: 1888

Editorial **Nuestra Tierra***, Cerrito 566, Montevideo Tel: 916217
Man Dir: Daniel Aljanati; *Editorial Dir:* Jaime D Aljanati
Subject: General Literature
Founded: 1968

Ediciones **Papacito***, Andes 1340, Montevideo Tel: 902872
Publicity: Carmelo Porcelli
Bookshop: Librerías Papacito, 18 de Julio 1409, Montevideo Tel: 987250
Subject: Essays

Editorial **Pomaire** Ltda*, Pablo de Maria 1588, Piso 2, Apdo 6, Montevideo Tel: 46121
Man Dir: Luis A Artigas G
Parent Company: Editorial Pomaire SA, Spain (qv for other branches)

Major Booksellers

Albe Soc Com*, Cerrito 566, Montevideo Tel: 85692

America Latina, 18 de Julio 2089, Montevideo Tel: 415127
Manager: Ismael Muñoz

Librería Los **Apuntes***, Eduardo Acevedo 1490, Montevideo Tel: 43651

Barreiro y Ramos SA, Juan Carlos Gómez 1430, Montevideo Tel: 986621
Branches at: Ave 18 de Julio 941 and 1777; Ave General Flores 2426; Ave 8 de Octubre 3728; Ave Agraciada 3945; Ave Rivera 2684; Calle 21 de Setiembre 2753; Arocena 1599 (all in Montevideo); Ave General Artigas 714, Las Piedras

Feria del Libro, Ave 18 de Julio 1308, Montevideo Tel: 902070
Manager: Domingo A Maestro

Librería Amalio M **Fernández**, 25 de Mayo 477 planta baja ofic 11, Montevideo Tel: 952684

Ibana, SA, Julio Herrera y Obes 1626, Montevideo Tel: 914738
Manager: Tomás J Raphael

Librería **Inglesa***, Sarandi 580, Montevideo Tel: 901955

Librería Adolfo **Linardi**, Linardi y Risso, Juan Carlos Gomez 1435, Montevideo Tel: 912749/901506 Cable Add: Linbooks

Mosca Hnos, Ave 18 de Julio 1578, Montevideo Tel: 404131

Palacio del Libro*, 25 de Mayo 577, Casilla de Correo 371, Montevideo Tel: 902473
Man Dir: Hector Mussini

Librerías **Papacito***, 18 de Julio 1409, Montevideo Tel: 902872
Manager: Carmelo Porcelli

Major Libraries

Archivo General de la Nación*, Calle Convención 1474, Montevideo

Biblioteca **Artigas-Washington** (USIS), Calle Paraguay 1217, Montevideo Tel: 917423

Biblioteca Central de Educación básica, secundaria y superior*, Eduardo Acevedo 1419, Montevideo
Central Library of Primary, Secondary and Higher Education
Dir: David Yudchak

Biblioteca Nacional del Uruguay*, 18 de Julio 1790, Casilla de Correo 452, Montevideo Tel: 45030/496011

Centro Nacional de Información y Documentación*, Avda Libertador Brig General Lavalleja No 2025, Montevideo
Dir: Professor Juan José Solari
Publications: Anales, Enciclopedia de educación, Legislación escolar

Departamento de Documentación y Biblioteca, Faculted de Humanidades y Ciencias, Universidad de la República, Tristán Narvaja 1674, Montevideo Tel: 491104
Dir: Matilde Jaureguiberry Barbagelata

Biblioteca del **Instituto Cultural** Anglo-Uruguayo, San José 1426, Montevideo Tel: 910570/908468/904201/903708
Librarian: Cristina Scaron

Biblioteca del **Museo** Histórico Nacional*, Casa Lavalleja, Zaballa 1469, Montevideo

Biblioteca del **Poder** Legislativo, Palacio Legislativo, Ave Agraciada, Montevideo Tel: 409111
Library of the Legislative Power
Dir: Luis Hector Boions Pombo
Publications include: Anales Parlamentarios (semestrial); *Boletin Bibliografico* (monthly); *Fichas Analiticas de Articulos de Publicaciones Periodicas* (monthly); *Bibliografía uruguaya* (irregular)

Biblioteca Municipal 'Dr Joaquín de **Salterain'***, Palacio Municipal, Ave 18 de Julio, Santiago de Chile

Library Associations

Agrupación Bibliotecológica del Uruguay, Cerro Largo 1666, Montevideo Tel: 405740
Uruguayan Library and Archive Science Association
President: Luis Alberto Musso
Publications: Bibliografía uruguaya sobre Brasil, Aportes para la historia de la bibliotecología en el Uruguay, Bibliografía y documentación en el Uruguay, La estrella del sur-Indice, Bibliografía bibliográfica y bibliotecologica, Uruguay-Brasil y sus medallas, Bibliografía de numismática uruguaya, Anales del Senado del Uruguay, El Río de la Plata en el Archivo General de Indias de Sevilla, Legislación uruguaya sobre Brasil, Bibliografía de historia de la República O del Uruguay; Bibliografía del Poder Legislativo

Asociación de Bibliotecólogos y Afines del Uruguay, Entre Ríos 1118, Casilla de Correo 1315, Montevideo
Uruguayan Library Association
President: Estela Peluffo de Chapt
Secretary: Amelia Uran de Repetto

Library Reference Books

Bibliografía bibliográfica y bibliotecologica del Uruguay (Bibliography of Bibliography and Library Science in Uruguay), Uruguayan Library and Archive Science Association, Cerro Largo 1666, Montevideo

Bibliografía y documentación en el Uruguay (Bibliography and Documentation in Uruguay), Uruguayan Library and Archive Science Association, Cerro Largo 1666, Montevideo

Literary Associations and Societies

Academia Nacional de Letras, Calle 1° de Mayo 1445 (Palacio Taranco), Montevideo
Secretary: Luis Bausero
Publications: Boletín de la Academia Nacional de Letras

Literary Periodical

Revista de la Biblioteca Nacional (National Library Review), National Library, Calle Guayabo 1793, Montevideo

Literary Prizes

Concurso Literario Municipal (Municipal Literary Competition)*
Three prizes are awarded in each of the following four groups: prose, fiction, essay, and biography and history. Enquiries to Intendencia Municipal de Montevideo (Palacio Municipal), 18 de Julio 1360, Montevideo

Gran Premio Nacional de Literatura*
For the total work of an author, Awarded every three years. Enquiries to Ministerio de Educación y Cultura, Sarandi 444, Montevideo

Premio de Remuneraciones Literarias*
Four prizes: poetry; fiction, juveniles or biography; essays; science and technology, sociology, history, education or philosophy. Awarded annually. Enquiries to Ministerio de Educación de Cultura, Sarandi 444, Montevideo

Premio Nacional de Literatura*
For a book in the field of culture. Awarded every two years. Enquiries to Ministerio de Educación y Cultura, Sarandi 444, Montevideo

Vatican City State

General Information

Language: Italian
Religion: Roman Catholic
Population: 728
Currency: Vatican lira = Italian lira. Italian currency is used
Copyright: Berne, UCC (see International section)

VATICAN CITY STATE — VENEZUELA 453

Publishers

Biblioteca Apostolica Vaticana*, I-00120 Vatican City   Tel: 6983302
Man Dir: Don Alphons M Stickler
Subjects: Philology, Classics, Mediaeval History, Manuscript Facsimiles, Exhibition Catalogues

Tipografia Poliglotta Vaticana*, Vatican City
Dir: Very Rev Angelo Vedani
Subjects: Juveniles, Education, Natural & Social Science

Libreria Editrice Vaticana, I-00120 Vatican City   Tel: 6983345/6984834
Dir: Rag Brenno Bucciarelli
Subjects: Religion, Philosophy, Literature, Art, Latin Philology, Theology, History, Works of Karol Wojtyla
Bookshop: I-00120 Vatican City
1981: 35 titles   *Founded:* 1926

Major Library

Biblioteca Apostolica Vaticana*, I-00120 Vatican City   Tel: (06) 6983302
Vatican Apostolic Library

Venezuela

General Information

Language: Spanish
Religion: Roman Catholic
Population: 13.1 million
Literacy Rate (1971): 82.4%
Bank Hours: 0830-1130, 1400-1630 Monday-Friday
Shop Hours: 0900-1300, 1500-1900 Monday-Saturday
Currency: 100 centimos = 1 bolívar
Export/Import Information: Member of the Latin American Free Trade Association. No import licences or exchange controls
Copyright: UCC (see International section)

Book Trade Organizations

Asociación Nacional de Escritores Venezolanos*, Velázquez a Miseria 22, Apdo 429, Caracas
National Association of Venezuelan Writers
General Secretary: Angel Mancera Galetti
Publication: Cuadernos

Cámara de Editores*, Puente Yanes a Tracabordo 80-82, Edificio Belvel, Of 4-3, Apdo 14234, Caracas 101
Publishers' Association

Cámara Venezolana del Libro*, Torre Lincoln piso 10, Ave Lincoln con Ave las Acacias, Sabana Grande, Apdo 51858, Caracas 1050   Tel: 7812809
Venezuelan Publishers' Association
Secretary: M Morales C

Book Trade Reference Book

Bibliografía Venezolana (Venezuelan Bibliography), Instituto Autónomo Biblioteca Nacional y de Servicios de Bibliotecas, Apdo 6525, Caracas 1010-A

Publishers

Aguilar Venezolana SA de Ediciones*, Calle Capitolio, Edificio Indelco, Sótano 1, Bolita Sur, Caracas   Tel: 333505/391832
Man Dir: Juan-Ramón Igual
Parent Company: Aguilar SA de Ediciones, Spain (qv)

Ernesto **Armitano**, Editor, Cuarto Transversal de la Ave Principal de Boleita, Edificio Centro Industrial 2° piso, Apdo 50853, Sabana Grande, Caracas
Tel: 342565/68   Cable Add: Armitpress Caracas Venezuela   Telex: 23115 Paneco
Man Dir: E Armitano; *Sales Dir:* P Salazar
Subjects: Venezuelan Painters, Venezuelan Studies (some titles also in English, German, French and Italian)

Editorial **Ateneo** de Caracas, Apdo 662, Caracas (Located at: Edificio Ateneo de Caracas piso 3, Plaza Morelos, Los Caobos)   Tel: 5734622 (orders 7819497)
President: María Teresa Castillo; *Editorial Dir:* Carmen Ramia; *Sales:* Victor García; *Production:* Enrique Revecco
Subjects: Psychology, Arts, Sciences, Politics, History, Literature, Poetry, Children
Bookshops: Librería Ateneo de Caracas (at above address); Librería El Foro, Pasaje Humboldt, Gradillas a Sociedad, Caracas
1981-82: 25 titles   *Founded:* 1978
ISBN Publisher's Prefix: 84-8350

Biblioteca **Ayacucho**, Apdo 14413, Caracas 1010 (Located at: Edificio JA p/1° Ave Universidad, de Corazón de Jesús a Coliseo, Caracas)   Tel: 5454411/5454507   Cable Add: Biayacucho   Telex: 24689 Taica VC
President of Editorial Commission: Dr José Ramón Medina; *Editorial, Rights & Permissions:* Prof Ángel Rama; *Sales, Publicity:* Dr Daniel Divinsky; *Production:* Prof José Antonio Escalona
Subjects: Latin-America, Classic and Contemporary Literature, Belles Lettres, Politics, History, Art
1981: 20 titles   *1982:* 30 titles   *Founded:* 1975
ISBN Publisher's Prefix: 84-660

Editorial **Bruguera** Venezolana SA*, Apdo 68306, Sector 106, Ave Avila Sur, Residencias Sta, Clara, Caracas 1062
Parent Company: Editorial Bruguera SA, Spain (qv)

Colegial Bolivariana CA*, Ave Diego Cisneros (Principal de Los Ruices), Edificio Co-Bo, Apdo del Corres 70324, Caracas 107
Tel: 2391433   Cable Add: Colegial
Man Dir: José Juzgado C
Subjects: Primary & Secondary Textbooks, Juveniles
Founded: 1961

Distribuciones **E D I M E**, Apdo 51666, Caracas 105 (Located at: Centro Comercial San Bernardino, loc C-5 y C-6, Plaza La Estrella, San Bernardino, Caracas 1011)
Tel: 523709/522776   Cable Add: Agedime
Man Dir: Nils Koehler; *Sales Dir, Publicity & Advertising:* E Mascaraque; *Permissions:* Juan Agero
Subjects: Literature, Biography, History & Art of Venezuela, Low-priced Paperbacks
1982: 8 titles   *Founded:* 1948

Ediciones de la Biblioteca (EBUC), Departamento de Distribución de Publicaciones, Biblioteca, Apdo 47004 Caracas (Located at: 1 er piso, Universidad Central de Venezuela, Caracas)   Tel: 6626242
Editorial Dir: Marcio S Meléndez
Subjects: Belles Lettres, History, Philosophy, Paperbacks, Medicine, Psychology, Engineering, General & Social Science, Law, University Textbooks
Founded: 1961

Fondo Editorial Común SC, Final de la Ave El Bosque, Edificio Royal Palace, Oficina 401, Plaza Brión-Chacaito, Caracas 1050
Tel: 723714   Cable Add: Editcomun   Telex: 21753 Comun VC, 28462 Dirfc VC
President: Alba Illaramendi; *Vice-President:* Carlos Suarez; *Man Dir:* Raul Alvarez; *Director:* Peter Neumann
Subjects: Social Science, Communication, Urban Planning, Law

Fondo Educativo Interamericano CA, Apdo del Este 62361, Caracas (Located at Calle Madariaga, Qta El Lago, Los Chaguaramos, Caracas)   Tel: 6612356/6618407   Cable Add: Adiwes Caracas   Telex: 21901 Fondo VC
President: Jorge José Giannetto; *Editorial:* in Bogotá, Colombia (qv)
Parent Company: Addison-Wesley Publishing Co Inc, Reading, Mass 01867, USA
Associate Companies: See Fondo Educativo Interamericano, Mexico
Subjects: Mathematics, Biology, Engineering, Business, Textbooks

Ediciones **Formentor** SRL*, 3a Transversal de Los Palos Grandes, Quinta Horizonte, entre 1a Ave y Luis Roche, Caracas 106
Parent Company: Ariel/Seix Barral Editoriales, Spain (qv)

Editorial **Grijalbo** SA+, Ave Los Laboratorios Edificio Ofinca 3a, PB, Los Ruices, Caracas   Tel: 316746/316721
Man Dir: Manuel Morales
Parent Company: Ediciones Grijalbo SA, Spain (qv)

Grolier de Venezuela*, Apdo 50930, Caracas (Located at: Edificio Continental, Esq Jabillos, S Grande)   Tel: 762659/7828609
Man Dir: Gilberto Livay
Associate Companies: See under the Grolier Society of Australia

Editorial **Interamericana de Venezuela** CA*, Apdo 50785, Caracas   Tel: 729492/723720
General Manager: Pedro Alvarez
Associate Company: Holt-Saunders Ltd, UK (qv for other associates)

Editorial **Kapelusz** Venezolana SA, Apdo 14234, Caracas 1011-A (Located at: Ave Urdaneta, Animas a Platanal, Edificio Camoruco, Caracas 1011-A)   Tel: 5629177/5629188   Cable Add: Kapelusz   Telex: 24039 Ekave VC
Man Dir: Horacio Perotti Beraldo
Parent Company: Editorial Kapelusz Colombiana SA (qv)
Subject: Secondary & Primary Textbooks
Founded: 1963

Editorial **Labor** de Venezuela SA*, Apdo 14054, Caracas (Located at: Ave Andrés Bello, Edificio Garten, Caracas)   Tel: 7811398/7815819
Man Dir: Jaime Salgado Palacio
Parent Company: Editorial Labor, Spain (qv)

Editorial **Libertador**, Apdo 1331, 4001-A Maracaibo   Tel: 227970
Sales Dir, Rights & Permissions, Production: John Cornell
Subjects: History, Religion, How-to, Juveniles, Bible Textbooks
1982: 140 titles   *Founded:* 1966

Monte Avila Editores CA*, Apdo 70712, (zona 1070), Caracas (Located at: Ave Principal de la Castellana con 1a, Transversal-Qta Cristina, (zona 2003), Caracas)   Tel: 326020/330760/332137
Man Dir: Juan Liscano; *Editorial, Rights & Permissions:* Oscar Rodriguez Ortiz; *Sales:* Servando Alvarez; *Production:* Hugo García

454 VENEZUELA

Robles
Subjects: Fiction, Literature, Biography, History, How-to, Art, Philosophy, Medicine, Psychology, General Science, Social Science, University Textbooks
Founded: 1968

Editorial **Natura** SRL*, Ave Boyaca (Cota Mil), Edificio Fundación La Salle, PB 3, Apdo 8150, Caracas 101
Tel: 727145/747467
Man Dir: Serafín Mazparrote
Orders to: Distribuciones Maytex SRL, Ave Norte-Sur 4, No 154 (Pilita a Mamey), Caracas
Subjects: Primary & Secondary Textbooks, Science

Editorial **Plata** SA, now in Peru (qv)

Editorial **Pomaire** Venezuela SA, Apdo 51960 Caracas 1050-A (Located at: Edificio Santa Clara-Avda, Avila, Altamira, Caracas) Tel: 2839755/2835766
Man Dir: José Cayuela
Parent Company: Editorial Pomaire SA, Spain (qv for other branches)

Editorial **Reverté** Venezolana SA*, Apdo 68685, Caracas (Located at: Peligro a Pele el Ojo, Edif Torre Carabobo, PB, Caracas 106) Tel: 5726670
Associate Companies: See Editorial Reverté SA, Spain

Editorial Ramón **Sopena** Venezolana SA*, Apdo 14267, Caracas (Located at: Alcabala a Puente Anauco, Edificio AN-VI, 1er piso, Caracas) Tel: 5729709/5728368
Man Dir: A García Sánchez
Parent Company: Ramón Sopena SA, Spain (qv)

Teduca, Técnicas Educativas, CA*, 4a Ave No 15, Qta Mari-Ana, Altamira, Caracas
Tel: 338078/339185
Chairman: Hugo Manzanilla; *General Manager:* Carlos García Ortubia
Parent Company: Santillana SA de Ediciones, Spain (qv)
Subject: Education

Editorial **Tiempo** Nuevo SA*, Apdo 50304, Caracas (Located at: Calle San Antonio, Edificio Hotel Royal, Sabana Grande, Caracas) Tel: 729073
Man Dir: Benito Milla Navarro; *Sales Dir:* Ricardo Lozano
Subject: General Literature
Founded: 1970

Ediciones **Vega** SRL, Apdo 51662, Caracas 1050 (Located at: Plaza Las Tres Gracias, Edificio Odeón, Los Chaguaramos, Caracas) Cable Add: Edivega
Man Dir: Fernando Vega Alonso
Subjects: University Textbooks, Technical
Bookshop: Librería Técnica Vega, Plaza Las Tres Gracias, Los Chaguaramos, Caracas
Founded: 1965

Major Booksellers

El **Amigo** de Todos*, Madrices a Ibarras, Loc 7, Edificio Bergantín, Caracas
Tel: 815580

Librería del **Este**, Ave Miranda 52, Edificio Galipán, Apdo 60-337, Caracas 1060-A Tel: 332604/322301/315838
Manager: Juan Pericás

Librerías **Kuai-Mare***, Final Ave Abraham Lincoln, Edificio Fundacomun PB, Chacaito, Caracas 105 Tel: 716657
This is the distribution side of the Instituto Autónomo Bibioteca Nacional y de Servicios de Bibliotecas, specializing in publications by Venezuelan official, cultural and university organizations. There are five other branches

Librería **Lectura***, Centro Comercial Chacaito, local 129, Caracas Tel: 717861

Librería **Cultural** SA*, Apdo 15156, Ave 5 de Julio 17-31, Maracaibo Tel: 525724/525531/524382 Cable Add: Licultura
Man Dir: Angel Vela González

Librería **Cultural** Venezolana*, Santa Capilla a Mijares 26, Caracas Tel: 813306

Librería **Medica** Paris, Gran Ave, Edif Medica Paris, Apdo 60681, Caracas 1060-A Tel: 7812709 Telex: 21420
Manager: Pierre Paneyko

Librería **Mundial***, Véroes a Jesuitas 16, Caracas Tel: 820337

Organización de Bienestar Estudiantil (OBE)*, Universidad Central de Venezuela, Ciudad Universitaria, Caracas

El **Palacio** del Libro*, Bloque 3, loc 4, El Silencio, Caracas Tel: 452854

Librería **Politécnica** Moulines*, Calle Villaflor, Apdo 50738, Sabana Grande, Caracas 105 Tel: 710692/729370

Publicaciones Españolas SA, Pele el Ojo a Puente Brion, Ave Mexico, Caracas Tel: 5715943/5727302/5725224 Telex: 26286 Pesa Vc

Librería **Selecta***, Ave 3, 231-23, Apdo 111, Mérida Tel: 23609

Librería **Suma***, Real Sabana Grande 90, Apdo del Este 5346, Caracas Tel: 724449

Tecni Ciencia Libros*, Torre Phelps, Mezz, Central, Plaza Venezuela, Caracas
Tel: 552091

Librería Técnica **Vega**, Plaza Tres Gracias, Edificio Odeón, Apdo 3093, Caracas 1010
Tel: 6622848/6622702
Manager: Lucia Ribas
Owned by: Fernando Vega, Ediciones Vega SRL (qv)

Major Libraries

Archivo General de la Nación*, Santa Capilla a Carmelitas 5, Caracas

Biblioteca de la Universidad Catolica 'Andres **Bello**', Apdo 29068, Caracas 1021
Librarian: Dr Carmelo Salvatierra

Biblioteca del Congreso*, Plaza del Capitolio, Caracas

Biblioteca Nacional, Ave Universidad, Frente al Congreso Nacional, Caracas 1010
Tel: 4832705
See also Instituto Autónomo Biblioteca Nacional y de Servicios de Bibliotecas

Servicios Bibliotecarios Generales 'Tulio **Febres Cordero**', Edificio Administrativo de la ULA 2° piso, Ave Tulio Febres Cordero, 5101 Mérida Tel: (074) 526244/527244/528244 ext 463/553 Telex: 74173 Cdchula
Director: Lic Beatriz Martínez de Cartay

Instituto Autónomo Biblioteca Nacional y de Servicios de Bibliotecas, Apdo 6525, Caracas 1010-A (Located at: Calle París con Caroní, Edificio Macanao, Las Mercedes, Caracas 1060) Tel: 911444
National Library, Public Library Services, Audiovisual Archive of Venezuela
Publications include: Anuarios Bibliograficos (to 1977); *Bibliografía Venezolana* (from 1978); *Catalogo de Publicaciones Oficiales*; *Boletín Bibliotécnico*
See also Librerías Kuia-Mare (Major Booksellers)

Biblioteca del **Instituto Venezolano** de Investigaciones Científicas, Altos de Pipe, Km 11 Carretera Panamericana, Apdo 1827, Caracas 1010-A
Library of the Venezuelan Institute for Scientific Research

Biblioteca Central de la **Universidad Central** de Venezuela*, Ciudad Universitaria, Caracas Tel: 619811

Biblioteca Central de la **Universidad de Zulia***, Grano de Oro Apdo 526, Maracaibo
Tel: 515390
Librarian: Margarita Alvárez
Publication: Boletín (biennial)

Library Associations

Colegio de Bibliotecólogos y Archivólogos de Venezuela (Colbav), Apdo 6282, Caracas 1010 Tel: 7813245
Venezuelan College of Librarians and Archivists
Executive Secretary: Lic Bernarda Lozada

Colegio de Bibliotecólogos, Archivólogos y Afines del Estado Zulia*, Apdo 1295, Maracaibo
College of Librarians and Archivists of Zulia State
Secretary: Lic Lourdes Crespo
Publications include: Boletín CBAEZ; Directorio de Bibliotecólogos y Archivólogos, Región Zulia

Library Reference Journals

Codex, Boletin de la Escuela de Bibliotéconomia y Archivos (Bulletin of the School of Librarianship and Archives), Universidad Central de Venezuela, Facultad de Humanidades y Educación, Escuela de Bibliotéconomia y Archivos, Ciudad Universitaria, Caracas

Directorio de Bibliotecólogos y Archivólogos, Region Zulia (Directory of Librarians and Archivists of Zulia State), CBAEZ, Apdo 1295, Maracaibo

Literary Associations and Societies

Galaxia*, Canje al Apdo 4023, Carmelitas 101, Caracas
Venezuelan Writers' Group
Director-Editor: Modesto Vargas Lopez
Publications: Galaxia 71;
Books by Venezuelan Authors

Venezuelan P E N Centre, Apdo 29023, Caracas 101 Tel: 454507/4412538
President: José Ramón Medina
Publications: Con Textos; Colección Plural

Literary Periodicals

Analítica para una Problemática del Sujeto, Editorial Ateneo de Caracas, Plaza Morelos, Apdo 662, Caracas

Con Textos, Venezuelan PEN Centre, Apdo 29023, Caracas 101

Colección Plural, Venezuelan PEN Centre, Apdo 29023, Caracas 101

Cuadernos (Notebooks), National Association of Venezuelan Writers, Velázquez a Miseria 22, Apdo 429, Caracas

Galaxia 71, Venezuelan Writers' Group, Canje al Apdo 4023, Carmelitas 101, Caracas

Literary Prizes

Municipal Prize for Prose and Poetry*
For the best prose or poetry work published in the Federal District or an unpublished work from any part of Venezuela. 5,000 bolivares. Awarded annually. Enquiries to Caracas Municipal Council of Federal District, Caracas

El Nacional Annual Story Award*
For the best story by a Venezuelan or foreign resident in Venezuela. Awarded annually. Enquiries to Edificio El Nacional, Puente Nuevo a Puerto Escondido, Apdo 209, Caracas

National Prize for Literature*
Awarded annually to the best Venezuelan author. 30,000 bolivares. Also includes contestants in narrative prose and essays. Enquiries to Concejo Nacional de la Cultura (CONAC), Apdo 50995, Caracas 105

Socialist Republic of Viet Nam

General Information

Language: French and English as well as Vietnamese
Religion: Taoist predominantly
Population: 49.9 million
Currency: 10 xu = 1 hào; 10 hào = 1 dông
Export/Import Information: None available at present
Copyright: Florence (see International section)

Book Trade Organization

Syndicat des Libraires*, 185 rue Catinat, Hô Chí Minh City
Union of Booksellers

Book Trade Reference Book

Thu-tich Quôc-gia Viet Nam (National Bibliography of Viet Nam), The Archives Service of the Prime Minister's Office of the Socialist Republic of Viet Nam, 72 Nguyên-Du, PO Box 15, Hô Chí Minh City

Publishers

Foreign Languages Publishing House*, Hanoi
Chief Editor: Nguyen Huu Ngoc
Subjects: Books and Periodicals from Viet Nam (English language)

Giao Duc Publishing House*, 81 Tran Hung Dao, Hanoi
Dir: Nguyen Si Ty
Subjects: Education, School Books
Founded: 1957

Khoa Hoc (Social Sciences) Publishing House*, Hanoi
Subject: Social Science

Lao Dong (Labour) Publishing House*, Hanoi

Nha Xuat Ban Van Hoc (Literature Publishing House)*, 49 Tran Hung Dao, Hanoi
Dir: Nhu Phong
Subject: Literature

Pho Thong (Popularization) Publishing House*, Hanoi

Popular Army Publishing House*, Hanoi
Subject: Military

Sa Tu-Thu Dich-Thuat Va An-loat*, Le Ván Duyèt, Hô Chí Minh City
Subjects: All Academic, Textbooks
Miscellaneous: Also translation agency

Scientific Publishing House*, Hanoi
Subject: Scientific

Su Hoc (Historical) Publishing House*, Hanoi
Subjects: Politics, Philosophy, Marxist Classics

Su That (Truth) Publishing House, 24 Quang Trung St, Hanoi Tel: 52008 (Controlled by the Central Committee of the Communist Party of Viet Nam)
Subjects: Marxist-Leninist Classics, Politics, Philosophy, Social Science
Founded: 1945

Trung-Tam San Xuat Hoc-Lieu, Tran-binh-Trong 240, Hô Chí Minh City 5
Subjects: Textbooks, Audiovisual, Instruction Materials

Vietnamese Publishing House*, Hanoi
Subjects: Politics, Law

Y Hoc Publishing House*, Hanoi
Subject: Medical

Major Booksellers

Xunhasoba*, 32 Hai Ba Trung, Hanoi
Distributor for foreign orders

Major Libraries

The **Archives Service** of the Prime Minister's Office of the Socialist Republic of Viet Nam*, South Viet Nam Branch, 72 Nguyên-Du, Hô Chí Minh City

Municipal Library*, 22 Yersin St, Dalat

National Institute of Administration Library*, 10 Tran Quoc Toan, Hô Chí Minh City

Bibliothèque des **Sciences Générales***, 69 Ly tu Trong, Hô Chí Minh City
Dir: Thanh Nghi

Social Sciences Library*, 34 Ly tu Trong, Hô Chí Minh City

Thu Viên Quóc Gia Viet Nam, 31 Tràng Thi, Hanoi Tel: 52643
National Library of the Socialist Republic of Viet Nam

Library Association

Hôi Thu-Viên Viet Nam*, 8 Le Qui Don, Hô Chí Minh City
Vietnamese Library Association
Secretary: Nguyen Van Thu
Publication: Thu'-Viên Tâp-san (Library Bulletin)

Library Reference Journal

Thu'-Viên Tâp-san (Library Bulletin), Vietnamese Library Association, 8 Le Qui Don, Hô Chí Minh City

Literary Periodical

Van Hoc, c/o Phan Kim Thinh, 449 Bhai Ba Trung, Q3 Hô Chí Minh City

Translation Agencies and Associations

Sa Tu-Thu Dich-Thuat Va An-loat*, Le Ván Duyèt, Hô Chí Minh City
Main function is as Publisher (qv)

Western Samoa

General Information

Note: No replies were received to questionnaires sent to Western Samoa for this edition of *International Literary Market Place*. The information given in the 1983-84 edition has been repeated here but should be treated with caution.

Language: Samoan, English
Population: 154,000
Literacy Rate (1971): 97.8%
Bank Hours: 0930-1500 Monday-Friday
Shop Hours: 0800-1200, 1330-1630 Monday-Friday; 0800-1230 Saturday
Currency: 100 sene = 1 tala
Export/Import Information: No tariff on most books, printed advertising generally free but some subject to duty. No import licence or exchange controls

Major Libraries

Avele College Library*, Avele

Nelson Memorial Public Library*, PO Box 598, Apia

People's Democratic Republic of Yemen

General Information

Language: Arabic, English is common second language
Religion: Muslim
Population: 1.9 million
Literacy rate (1973): 27.1% of population aged 10 or over (40.9% of urban population, 22.6% rural, 5.8% nomads)
Bank Hours: 0800-1200 Saturday-Thursday
Shop Hours: 0800-1230, 1500-2100 Saturday-Thursday
Currency: 1,000 fils = 1 South Yemen dinar
Export/Import Information: 14th October

Corporation, PO Box 4227, Crater has sole right to import and distribute books. Import licences required. Exchange controls

Major Booksellers

14th October Corporation*, PO Box 4227, Crater, Aden
Sole importer and distributor of books

Major Libraries

Miswat Library*, Aden
(Previously called Lake Library. Administration by Aden Municipality)

Teachers' Club Library*, Aden

Yemen Arab Republic

General Information

Language: Arabic (English and Russian common foreign languages)
Religion: Muslim
Population: 5.6 million
Bank Hours: 0800-1200 (1130 Thursday) Saturday-Thursday
Shop Hours: 0800-1200, 1600-2100 Saturday-Thursday
Currency: 100 fils = 1 Yemeni riyal
Export/Import Information: No tariff on books except on children's picture books. Advertising matter dutied. Defence and Statistical Taxes; Cooperation Tax is percentage of CIF. Small Welfare Tax, Import licence required; no pornography permitted. Exchange control approval readily available, generally

Major Libraries

British Council Library, PO Box 2157, Sana'a (Located at: Beit 41, Mottahar, Harat Handhal, Sana'a) Tel: 73179

Library of the **Great Mosque of Sana'a***, Sana'a

Yugoslavia

General Information

Language: Serbo-Croatian in most of the country; Slovene in Slovenia, Macedonian in Macedonia. In some communities, Albanian, Bulgarian, Hungarian, Italian, Romanian, Turkish. English is commonest foreign language known
Religion: About 40% Eastern Orthodox, 30% Roman Catholic, 10% Muslim
Population: 21.9 million
Literacy Rate (1971): 83.5% (92.3% Urban, 77.7% Rural)
Bank Hours: 0730-1200 Monday-Friday
Shop Hours: 0800-1200, 1700-2000 Monday-Friday; 0800-1500 Saturday. Some open weekdays continuously and early Sunday morning
Currency: 100 para = 1 new dinar
Export/Import Information: No tariffs on books except on publications of Yugoslav publishers printed abroad. Advertising catalogues for such books dutied, otherwise free; non-Yugoslavian language advertising materials dutied. Special equalization tax, Customs clearance charge and import surcharge when goods are subject to duty. No import licences required. Exchange controls. The basic commercial unit is known as an enterprise but there are no state monopolies
Copyright: Berne, UCC (see International section)

Book Trade Organization

Association of Yugoslav Publishers and Booksellers, YU-11000 Belgrade, Kneza Milosa 25/I, Poštanski fah 883 Tel: (011) 642533/642248
Dir: Ognjen Lakićević
Publications: Knjiga i svet (The Book and the World); *Catalogue of Book Fair in Belgrade; Directory of Members of the Association of Yugoslav Publishers and Booksellers; Publishing Plans of the Publishing Houses in Yugoslavia* (annual); *Books Published by Yugoslav Publishers* (annual)

Book Trade Reference Journals

Bibliografija domace i strane literature (Bibliography of Native and Foreign Literature) (text in Serbo-Croatian), Centralna Biblioteka JNA, Belgrade, Balkanska 53a

Bibliografija Jugoslavije (Yugoslavia Bibliography), Yugoslav Bibliographic Institute, YU-11000 Belgrade, Terazije 26

Books Published by Yugoslav Publishers. Association of Yugoslav Publishers and Booksellers, YU-11000 Belgrade, Kneza Milóša 25/I, Póstanski fah 883

Directory of Members, Association of Yugoslav Publishers and Booksellers, YU-11000 Belgrade, Kneza Milósa 25/I, Poštanski fah 883

Katalog Medunarodnog Sajma Knjige u Beogradu (Catalogue of the International Book Fair at Belgrade), Association of Yugoslav Publishers and Booksellers, YU-11000 Belgrade, Kneza Milósa, Póstanski fah 883

Knjiga i svet (The Book and the World), Association of Yugoslav Publishers and Booksellers, YU-11000 Belgrade, Kneza Milóša 25/I, Poštanski fah 883

Publishing Plans of the Publishing Houses in Yugoslavia, Association of Yugoslav Publishers and Booksellers, YU-11000 Belgrade, Kneza Milósa 25/I, Póstanski fah 883

Slovenska Bibliografija (Slovene Bibliography), Državna Založba Slovenije, YU-61000 Ljubljana, Mestni trg 26, Poštanski fah 50-1

Publishers

A L F A — Radna organizacija za izdavačku djelatnost*, YU-41000 Zagreb, Čerinina 9a, Poštanski fah 32 Tel: (041) 217614
Manager: Stjepan Martinović
Subjects: War, History, Popular Science, Fiction

August Cesarec*, YU-41000 Zagreb, Braće Oreški 18 Tel: (041) 576615/576651
Dir: Mirko Andrić
Subjects: Belles Lettres, Politics, Science, Fiction

B I G Z, an imprint of Beogradski Izdavačko-Grafički Zavod (qv)

Beogradski Izdavačko-Grafički Zavod, YU-11000 Belgrade, blvd vojode Mišića 17, Poštanski fah 340 Tel: 651666 Cable Add: BEOGRAF Telex: 11855 yu bigz
Man Dir: Gojko Zečar; *Editorial Dir, Permissions:* Vidosav Stevanović
Imprint: BIGZ
Subjects: Belles Lettres, Poetry, Philosophy, Juveniles, Social Science, University Textbooks, Encyclopaedias, Periodicals
Book Club: Book Lovers' Club
Founded: 1831

Birografika*, YU-24000 Subotica, Put Moše Pjade 72 Tel: (024) 26215 Cable Add: YU BIGRAF 15111
Dir: Andrija inž Bukvić

Borba*, YU-11000 Belgrade, trg Marksa i Engelsa 7, Poštanski fah 629 Tel: (011) 334531/344201
Dir: Novica Dukić

Bratsvo-Jedinstvo*, YU-21000 Novi Sad, Arse Teodorovića 11, Poštanski fah 274 Tel: 28032/28036
Dir: Srboslav Bojović
Subjects: Textbooks in Serbo-Croatian, Belles Lettres

C D D (Centar društvenih djelatnosti Saveza socijalističke omladine Hrvatske)*, YU-41001 Zagreb, Opaticka 10, Poštanski fah 99 Tel: (041) 419026/443809/447055/415659/449817
General Manager: Josip Čondić; *Publishing Manager:* Petar Strpić; *Art Manager:* Ivan Dorogi
Subjects: Fiction, Marxism, Philosophy, Social Sciences, Political Journalism, Science Journalism; *Pitanja* (Scientific and Cultural Review); *Polet* (Youth Weekly)

Cankarjeva Založba, YU-61001 Ljubljana, Kopitarjeva 2, Poštni predal 201/IV Tel: 323841
Man Dir: Martin Žnideršič
Subjects: Belles Lettres, Poetry, General Fiction, Biography, History, How-to, Philosophy, Reference, Social Science, Psychology
Bookshops: See under Major Booksellers
Founded: 1945

Dečje Novine*, YU-32300 Gornji Milanovac, Takovska 6 Tel: (032) 81527/81073/81195 Telex: 13731 YU DNGRM
Subjects: Juveniles, Picture-books, Albums

Delta Press*, YU-11000 Belgrade, Draže Pavlovića 14, Poštanski fah 467 Tel: (011) 333969
Dir: Jovan Janićijević
Subjects: Reference Material, Juveniles and Young People, Social Sciences
Founded: 1969

Državna Založba Slovenije, YU-61000 Ljubljana, Mestni trg 26, Poštanski fah 50-1 Tel: (061) 214733 Cable Add: DZS Ljubljana
Man Dir: Dragana Kraigher-Senk
Subjects: General Fiction, Belles Lettres,

Poetry, Biography, History, Music, Art, Philosophy, Reference, General & Social Science, University, Secondary & Primary Textbooks, Educational Materials
Bookshops: See under Major Booksellers
Founded: 1945

NiP Edit*, YU-51000 Rijeka, bulevar Marxa i Engelsa 20, Poštanski fah 137-138 Tel: 22516/22443/22646 Telex: 24247
Director: Ennio Machia
Subjects: Books, Papers, Periodicals in Italian
Bookshop: YU-51000 Rijeka, Korzo Narodne Revolucije 37

Forum*, YU-21000 Novi Sad, vojvode Mišića 1, Poštanski fah 200 Tel: 57207 Telex: 14199
Director: Kálmán Petkovics
Subjects: Periodicals, Fiction, Politics in Hungarian and Serbo-Croatian
Bookshop: See under Major Booksellers

Glas*, YU-11000 Belgrade, Vlajkovićeva 8 Tel: (011) 335380
Director: Radojko Mrlješ
Provides complete printing services to other publishers

Globus*, YU-41000 Zagreb, Ilica 12, Poštanski pretinac 232 Tel: (041) 447300/447500 Cable Add: Globus Zagreb
Editors: V Ogrizović, I Sor, B Zadro, I Županov, A Buljan
Parent Company: ČGP Delo, YU-61000 Ljubljana, Titova Cesta 35
Subjects: Politics, History, Sociology, Philosophy, General Fiction, Handbooks
Founded: 1948

Izdavačka ustanova **Gradina***, YU-18000 Niš, ul Pobede br 38/I, Poštanski fah 242 Pobede 38/I Tel: 25864
Dir: Dobrivoje Jevtić
Subjects: Belles Lettres, Science, Art, Periodicals
Bookshops: (all at Niš) ul Pobede br 38; Pobede 113; Voždova 74; 12 februar 56a; Obilićev venac 50

Gradjevinska Knjiga*, YU-11000 Belgrade, trg Marksa i Engelsa 8, Poštanski fah 798 Tel: (011) 333565
Man Dir: Ljubica Jurela; *Sales Dir:* Radovan Vuković
Subjects: Technical, Engineering & University Textbooks
Bookshops: Gradjevinska Knjiga, Narodnog fronta 14 & bulevar Revolucije 84; Student, 27 marta 78 (all in Belgrade)

Grafički zavod Hrvatske, YU-41000 Zagreb, Frankopanska 26, Poštanski fah 227 Tel: (041) 418600/419005 Cable Add: GZH Zagreb Telex: 21606 Yugzh
Man Dir: Vladimir Štokalo; *Editors:* Vjeran Zuppa, Albert Goldstein, Nenad Popović; *Sales:* Vilma Lopuh; *Publicity:* Zvezdana Milovanović; *Rights & Permissions:* Maja Kotur
Subjects: Belles Lettres, Art, Tourism, Dictionaries
1981: 60 titles *1982:* 60 titles *Founded:* 1874

Grafos*, YU-11000 Belgrade, Simina 9A, Poštanski fah 459 Tel: 623980 Cable Add: Grafos Belgrade
Dir: Vito Marković
Subjects: Lexicography, Rare Publications, Fiction, Science, Juveniles, Periodicals

I C S Izdavačko Informativni Centar Studenata*, YU-11000 Belgrade, Balkanska 4/III Tel: 325854
Dir: Aleksandar Urdarević
Bookshops: Novi Belgrade: Studentski grad, II Blok & Dom kultur Studenski grad, bulevar Avnoja 152a; Belgrade: Fakultet političkih nauka, Jove Ilića 165 &
Arhitektonski fakultet, bulevar Revolucije 73

Informator*, Izdavački i Birotehnički Zavod, YU-41001 Zagreb, Masarykova ul 1, Poštanski fah 794 Tel: 442222 Cable Add: YU INF Telex: 21264
General Dir: Nikola Šaranović
Subjects: Dictionaries, Law

Jedinstvo*, YU-38000 Priština, Dom Štampe bb, Poštansk: pregradak 81 Tel: (038) 27549/29090 Cable Add: Jedinstvo Pristina
Director: Milan Šešlija
Subjects: Belles Lettres, Social & Political Science, History, Philosophy, Medicine

Jugoreklam*, YU-61000 Ljubljana, Moše Pijade 5, Poštanski fah 142 Tel: 316075
Dir: Hinko Urbanc
Branch Offs: YU-11000 Belgrade: Nebojšina 2 & Dure Dakovića 88; YU-41000 Zagreb, Petretičev trg 4; YU-63320 Velenje, Celjska 27
Subjects: Juveniles, Economics

Jugoslovenska Revija, YU-11000 Belgrade, Terazije 31 Tel: 332625 Telex: 12954 Yurew
Dir: Rajko Bobot
Subjects: Art, Tourism, Periodicals

Izdavački Zavod **Jugoslavenske Academije** Znanosti i Umjetnosti*, YU-41000 Zagreb, Gundulićeva 24, Poštanski fah 1017 Tel: 449099
Publishing House of the Yugoslav Academy of Sciences and Arts
Man Dir: Josip Hanževački
Subjects: History, Philosophy, Medicine, Technical, General & Political Science, Education
Founded: 1918

Jugoslavenski Leksikografski Zavod, YU-41000 Zagreb, Strossmayerov trg 4, Poštanski fah 410 Tel: 434177/434227
Director: Dr Ivo Cecić
Subjects: Encyclopaedias, Bibliographies, Dictionaries
Bookshop: Poslovnica, Zagreb, Masarykova 26
Founded: 1951

Jugoslavija*, Izdavački Zavod, YU-11000 Belgrade, Nemanjina 34, Poštanski fah 52 Tel: 643870/643852 Cable Add: Pubzavod Belgrade Telex: 11265
Shipping Add: c/o Transjug-Split, YU-11000 Belgrade, Pop Lukina 12
Dir, Editor-in-Chief: Živislav-Žika Bogdanović
Subjects: Art, Travel Guides, Reference, How-to, General Non-fiction, Juveniles, Science Fiction & Epic Fantasy
Founded: 1948

Izdavački Centar **Komunist***, Belgrade, trg Marksa i Engelsa 11, Poštanski fah 233 Tel: 335061/334189
Dir: David Atlagić
Subjects: Communism, Marxism, Literary Criticism
Bookshop: Klub Citalaca 70, Belgrade, trg Marksa i Engelsa 9

Kršćanska sadašnjost*, YU-41000 Zagreb, Marulićev trg 14, Postf 02748 Tel: 444102
Subjects: Bible, Liturgy, Theology, Art History, Church History, Fine Arts, Periodicals
Miscellaneous: Company also acts as a press agency

Kultura (Izdavačko Pretprijatie)*, YU-91000 Skopje, bulevar JNA 68A, Poštanski fah 298 Tel: 35361/23437 Cable Add: Kultura
Man Dir: Dušan Crvenkovski
Subjects: Art, Philosophy, Political Science, Economics, Juveniles
Bookshops: See under Major Booksellers
Founded: 1945

Sveučilišna Naklada Liber*, YU-41000 Zagreb, Savska cesta 16, Poštanski fah 493 Tel: (041) 415602
Dir: Slavko Goldstein
Subjects: Croatian culture and scientific heritage, Literature, *Povijesti*, *Temelji*, *Znanstven Radovi* and *Razlog* collections
Miscellaneous: Publishing service of Zagreb University

Libertatea*, YU-26000 Pančevo, Žarka Zrenjanina br 7, Poštanski fah 27 Tel: 3401/3351 Cable Add: Libertatea Pančevo
Dir: Todor Gilezan
Subjects: Textbooks, Periodicals, Rare Publications, Reprints, Romanian Language publications

Makedonska Knjiga (Knigoizdatelstvo), YU-91000 Skopje, 11 Oktomvri bb, Poštanski fah 349 Tel: (091) 235524 Cable Add: Makedonska Kniga
Man Dir: Nikola Todorov
Subjects: General Fiction, Belles Lettres, Art, Juveniles
Bookshops: See under Major Booksellers

Medicinska Knjiga, YU-11000 Belgrade, Mata Vidakovića 24, Poštanski fah 681 Tel: (011) 458135/458165
Dir: Petar Janković; *Editor-in-Chief:* Mile Medić; *Sales Dir:* Dobrica Mitrović; *Publicity Manager:* Ivan M Stanković
Branch Offs: YU-41000 Zagreb, Belostenčeva 3-5 Tel: (041) 272320; YU-91000 Skopje, Naroden Front 33 Tel: (091) 228930; YU-71000 Sarajevo, Rave Janković 99A Tel: (071) 618370
Subjects: Medicine, Pharmacy, Stomatology, Textbooks, Popular literature
Bookshops: Belgrade, Niš, Zagreb
Book Club: Klub Čitalaca MK
Founded: 1946

Medicinska Naklada*, YU-41000 Zagreb, Šalata bb, Poštanski fah 517 Tel: (041) 33630
Dir: Mirko Madjor

'Minerva'*, YU-24000 Subotica, trg 29 novembra br 3, Poštanski fah 116 Tel: (024) 25701 Cable Add: Minerva Subotica
Dir: Josip Prčić
Subjects: Textbooks, Dictionaries, Scientific and Children's Literature
Bookshops: YU-24000 Subotica: ul oktobra 4; Maksima Gorkog 20; Put M Pijade 25

Misla*, YU-91000 Skopje, Gradski zid, Blok 2, Poštanski fah 460 Tel: 23336 Cable Add: Misla Skopje
Dir: Božin Pavlovski; *Head of Sales:* Vančo Spasovski

Mladinska Knjiga*, YU-61000 Ljubljana, Titova 3, Poštanski fah 36/I Tel: (060) 24851 Telex: 31345 yu emka
Director General: Karel Trplan; *Publishing Dir:* Ivan Bizjak; *Editor-in-Chief:* Borut Ingolič; *Sales:* Joze Wagner; *Production:* Marjan Černe; *Co-production:* Ciril Treek; *Publicity:* Nace Borštnar
Branch Off: YU-11000 Belgrade, 27 Merte; YU-41000 Zagreb, Ilica 30
Subjects: Children's books, General Fiction, Art, Popular Science, Geography, How-to
Book Club: Svet Knjige
Bookshops: See under Major Booksellers
Founded: 1945

Mladost*, YU-11000 Belgrade, Maršala Tita 2, Poštanski fah 252 Tel: (011) 323390
Dir: Borisav Džuverović
Subjects: Marxist literature, Philosophy, Fiction, Periodical *Mladost*
Founded: 1956

Mladost, Izdavačko knjižarska radna organizacija, YU-41000 Zagreb, Ilica 30, Poštanski fah 1028 Tel: (041) 440211 Cable Add: Ikape Zagreb Telex: 21263
Man Dir: Branko Juričević; *Import-Export Dir:* Branko Vuković; *Publisher:* Josip Fruk; *Production Manager:* Stipan Medak; *Marketing Manager:* Eduard Osredečki
Subjects: Picture Books, Juveniles, General Fiction, Belles Lettres, Poetry, History, How-to, Music, Art, Philosophy, Reference, General & Social Science, Sports, Hobby Books, Dictionaries
Book Club: Mladost's Book Fans Club
Bookshops: See under Major Booksellers
Founded: 1948

Muzička Naklada*, Zagreb, Nikole Tesle 10/I, Poštanski fah 543
Dir: Albert Trinki
Subject: Music
Founded: 1952

Nakladni Zavod Matice Hrvatske*, YU-41000 Zagreb, ul Matice Hrvatske 2, Poštanski fah 515 Tel: (041) 271616/271379/274935
Man Dir, Rights & Permissions: Tomislav Previšić; *Editorial:* Zane Tvrtko; *Sales, Publicity:* Milovan Radošević; *Production:* Anto Galic; *Publicity:* Luka Roić
Branch Offs: YU-71000 Sarajevo, M Djudje 10; YU-11000 Belgrade, Trščanska 5
Subjects: General Fiction, Reference, Art, Literature, Political & General Science, Biography, History, Dictionaries
Bookshops: 41000 Zagreb, Ilica 62, Dure Salaja 3; YU-50000 Dubrovnik, Poljana Paska Miličevića bb; YU-54400 Djakovo, ul Jna 15; YU-47000 Karlovac, Pavleka Miškine 4; YU-54500 Našice, Radičeva 23; YU-51270 Senj, Trg Oslobodjenja 1; YU-79000 Mostar, Braće Brkića 8; YU-51000 Rijeka, Djure Djakovića 20
1981: 67 titles *Founded:* 1960

Naprijed, YU-41000 Zagreb, Palmotićeva 30, Poštanski fah 1029 Tel: 442001/442400/442283 Cable Add: Izdavacko Naprijed Telex: 21449 yu ikpnzg
Man Dir: Autun Žvan
Subjects: Philosophy, General Fiction, History, Art, General Science, Psychology, Political & Social Science, Economics

Narodna Biblioteka Srbije*, YU-11000 Belgrade, Skerlićeva 1 Tel: 451242/9
Dir: Svetislav Durić
Subjects: Bibliography, Reference, History

Narodna Knjiga*, YU-11000 Belgrade, Safarikova 11, Poštanski fah 241 Tel: (011) 328610
Dir: Vidak Perić
Subjects: Politics, Encyclopaedias, Dictionaries, Textbooks, Science, Juveniles, Belles Lettres

Narodne Novine*, YU-41000 Zagreb, Ratkajev prolaz 4, Poštanski fah 557 Tel: 411611/411666
Dir: Ilija Dautović
Subjects: Science, Textbooks, Careers
Bookshops: 21 throughout Yugoslavia

Naša Djeca*, YU-41000 Zagreb, Gajeva 25, Poštanski fah 563 Tel: (041) 447077 Cable Add: Násadjeca
Dir: Petar Butković
Subject: Juveniles

Naša Kniga*, YU-91000 Skopje, Partizanski odred 17, Poštanski fah 132 Tel: (091) 228066/237014
Dir: Vlado Popovski
Subjects: Textbooks, Sociology, Politics, Agriculture, Literature

Naučna Knjiga*, YU-11000 Belgrade, Uzun Mirkova 5, Poštanski fah 690 Tel: 637230 Cable Add: Naučna Knjiga
Man Dir: Dragoslav Joković
Subjects: Reference, Medicine, Engineering, Science, University Textbooks, Educational Materials, Maps, Atlases
Bookshops: 'Znanje', Belgrade, Gračanička br 16; 'Naučna knjiga', Belgrade, Knez Mihailova br 19
Founded: 1947

Nio Pobjeda — Oour Izdavačko-Publicistička Djelatnost, YU-81000 Titograd, ul Petra Matovića 206 Tel: (081) 34254
Dir: Ljubo Burić; *Publishing Dir:* Mileta Radovanović; *Editors:* Branko Banjević, Djerdj Djokaj, Ratko Vujošević, Vojislav Minić; *Sales, Trade Dir:* Miodrag Raonić
Branch Offs: YU-11080 Zemun, Karadordev trg 7 Tel: (011) 600652; YU-21000 Novi Sad, Šafarikova 15 Tel: (021) 51086; YU-38000 Priština, Miladin Popovića bb Tel: (038) 24062
Subjects: Belles Lettres, Popular and Scientific Literature and Lexicography
Founded: 1962

Nolit Publishing House, YU-11000 Belgrade, Terazije 27/II, Poštanski fah 369 Tel: (011) 333353 Cable Add: Nolit BGD Telex: 11603 nolit bgd
Man Dir: Dragoljub Gavaric; *Editorial:* Miloš Stambolić; *Sales:* Branko Nikezić; *Production:* Srboljub Milošević
Subjects: General Fiction, Philosophy, Psychology, Sociology, Agriculture, History, Art, Juveniles
Bookshops: See under Major Booksellers
Founded: 1928

Mip Nota*, YU-19350 Knjaževac, Karadordeva 15/I, Poštanski fah 63 Tel: 84375/84516 Cable Add: Nota-Knjaževac
Dir: Nenad Živković; *Editorial:* Stojanović Ljubomir; *Sales:* Jovanovic Negica; *Production:* Nikolić Alexsandar; *Rights & Permissions:* Simić Dura
Branch Off: YU-11000 Belgrade, Balkanska 9
Subject: Music
Founded: 1970

Nova Knjiga*, Obrenovac, Maršala Tita

Obod*, YU-81250 Cetinje, Njegoševa 3, Poštanski fah 59 Tel: 22020 Cable Add: Obod Cetinje
Dir: Slobodan Koljević
Branch Off: Belgrade, Dobračina 32
Subjects: Belles Lettres, Fiction, Textbooks, Dictionaries
Bookshop: Belgrade, Njegoševa 11

Obzor*, YU-21000 Novi Sad, bulevar 23, Oktobra 31/V, Poštanski fah 267 Tel: 21555 Cable Add: Obzor, Novi Sad
Dir: Anna Makanová
Bookshop: Bački Petrovac Bodviš Jan

NIP Oslobodjenje*, YU-71000 Sarajevo, Maršala Tita 13, Poštanski fah 663 Tel: 35177/34233 Telex: 41148/41136
Dir: Ivica Lovrić

Otokar Keršovani-Rijeka*, YU-51410 Opatija, Maršala Tita 65, Poštanski fah 13 Tel: 711099/711922 Cable Add: Otakar Keršovani
Man Dir: Vladimir Bakotić; *Editorial:* Drago Crnčević
Branch Offs: Zagreb, Biankinijeva 11; Belgrade, Zrmanjska 2/a; Sarajevo, Kralja Tomislava 19
Subjects: Fiction, Horticulture, Picture Books
Founded: 1954

Pomurska založba*, YU-69000 Murska Sobota, Lendavska c1, Poštni p.136 Tel: 6923491 Telex: 35-229 Yu Zgp Msb
Dir: Jože Ternar; *Editor-in-Chief:* Jože Hradil
Subjects: Literature, Fiction, Poetry, Essays (Original and Translations)
Bookshops: Dobra knjiga, 69000 Murska Sobota, Titova c; Knjigarna Ljutomer, YU-69240; Knjigarna Lendava, YU-69220; Knjigarna Gornja Radgona, YU-69250; Knjigarna Lenart, YU-62230

Izdavačko **Preduzeće Matice Srpske***, YU-21000 Novi Sad, trg Svetozara Markovića 2 Tel: (021) 29777/43040 (director)
Dir: Sava Josić
Subjects: Belles Lettres, Science, Politics, Juveniles, Textbooks, Encyclopaedias, Dictionaries
Bookshops: Belgrade, Studentski trg 5; Backa Palanka, Maršala Tita 40 and others

Izdavačko **Preduzeće Sloboda***, YU-11000 Belgrade, Vojvode Stepe 315 Tel: 462131/461721/462341 Cable Add: Sloboda Belgrade
Dir: Streten Hrkalović
Subjects: Belles Lettres, Juveniles, Reference

Primorski Tisk*, YU-66000 Koper, Muzejski trg 7, Poštanski fah 132 Tel: 23291
Dir: Črtomir Kolenc
Branch Off: Studenski servis, Ljubljana, Borstnikov trg 25
Subject: Fiction
Bookshops: 9 throughout Yugoslavia

Privredni Pregled*, YU-11000 Belgrade, Maršala Birjuzova 3, Poštanski fah 903 Tel: 623399/625662 Cable Add: Privredni Pregled Bgd Telex: 11509 yu pp
Dir: Toma Marković
Branch Offs: Zagreb, Moše Pijade 21; Ljubljana, Hala 'Tivoli'; Skopje, Orce Nikolova 79; Sarajevo, Maršala Tita 86
Subject: Production Reference Books

Prosveta, YU-11001 Belgrade, Terazije 16 Tel: 687441 Telex: 11609 YU
General Dir: Mirko Miloradović; *Editor-in-Chief:* Milisav Savić; *Export Manager:* Ivanka Djaja; *Rights & Permissions:* Branka Simić
Subjects: Lexicography, Humanities
Book Club: Prosveta
Bookshops: See under Major Booksellers
1982: approx 200 titles *Founded:* 1945

Prosvetno Delo*, YU-91000 Skopje, Ulica Ivo Lola Ribar, bb, Gradski zid, Blok IV, Poštanski fah 6 Tel: 33675/31398
Man Dir: Mihajlo Korveziroski
Subjects: Reference, Textbooks, Educational Materials, Juveniles
Bookshop: Br 1 Skopje, bulevar Kočo Racin, kula B-20

Prosvjeta*, YU-41000 Zagreb, Berislavićeva 10, Poštanski fah 634 Tel: 445450/444664 Cable Add: Prosvjeta Zagreb
Dir: Branislav Ćelap
Subjects: Journalism, Business Books
Bookshop: Zagreb, trg Bratstva i Jedinstva 5

Prosvjeta (Novinsko-izdavačko i Štamparsko)*, Bjelovar, Vladimira Nazora 25 Tel: 3150 Cable Add: Nišp Prosvjeta Bjelovar
Dir: Branimir Premužić; *Production:* Ivan Ninić
Branch Off: Zagreb, Moše Pijade 31

Prva Književna Komuna*, YU-79000 Mostar, trg 14 februar 3/III Tel: 25798 Cable Add: PKK Mostar
Man Dir: Ico Mutevelić
Subjects: Bibliophile Editions, Tourist Publications
Bookshop: Mostar, ul Stari most 3

Izdavačka Organizacija **Rad***, YU-11000 Belgrade, Moše Pijade 12, Poštanski fah 881 Tel: (011) 330923/339758/338994
Man Dir: Milenko Kovačević; *Sales Dir:* Milovan Vlahović
Subjects: Belles Lettres, Poetry, Biography, Philosophy, Low-priced Paperbacks, Engineering, Social Science, Politics, Economics, University Textbooks
Bookshops: Papirus, Belgrade, Terazije 26; Zagreb, Frankopanska 5, and 20 other bookshops throughout Yugoslavia

Radnička Štampa, YU-11000 Belgrade, trg Marksa i Engelsa 5, Poštanski fah 995 Tel: (011) 330927 Cable Add: Radnička štampa Belgrade
Dir: Stanislav Marinković; *Sales Manager:* Čedo Maleš
Subjects: Social, Political and Economic Sciences, Textbooks, Encyclopedias, *Rad* newspaper

Republički Zavod za Unapredivanje Školstva*, YU-81000 Titograd, Novaka Miloševa 36 Tel: (081) 24168, 24126 (Director)
Republic Bureau for the Advancement of Education
Subjects: Primary and Secondary Textbooks, Education

Rilindja*, YU-38000 Priština, Dom Štampe, Poštanski fah 27 Tel: (038) 23868/28611/28411
Dir: Rexhep Zogaj
Subjects: Textbooks, Belles Lettres (in Albanian), Periodicals, *Rilindja* newspaper

Savez Inženjera i Tehničara Jugoslavije, 11000 Belgrade, Kneza Mološa 9, Poštanski fah 187 Tel: 343653/335816/332924
Union of Engineers and Technicians of Yugoslavia
Secretary: Dr Petar Radičević
Founded: 1945

Savremena Administracija*, YU-11001 Belgrade, Knez Mihajlova 6/V, Poštanski fah 479 Tel: 648567/647436/687913
Dir: Živorad Jevtić
Subjects: Literature, Law, Work Study, Economics, Reference
Founded: 1954

Škola za Strane Jezike, YU-41000 Zagreb, Varšavska 14 Tel: (041) 419895
Subjects: Language textbooks and teaching materials

'Školska knjiga', YU-41000 Zagreb, Masarykova 28, Poštanski fah 1039 Tel: 449505/448111 Cable Add: Školska knjiga Zagreb
Man Dir: Professor Josip Malić; *Sales Manager:* Marko Šiša
Subjects: University, Secondary & Primary Textbooks, Educational Materials, History, Music, Art, Philosophy, Reference, Juveniles, Low- & High-priced Paperbacks, Medicine, Psychology, Engineering, General & Social Science, Belles Lettres, Poetry, Biography, How-to
Bookshops: Knjižara 'Školske knjige', YU-41000 Zagreb, Bogovićeva 1/a; knjižara 'Školska knjiga', YU-41000 Zagreb, Masarykova 28; knjižara 'Studentski trg', YU-11000 Belgrade, Studentski trg 6
1981: 120 titles *1982:* 129 titles *Founded:* 1950

Sloboda*, YU-11040 Belgrade, Vojvode Stepe 315 Tel: (011) 462131/461721/462341 Cable Add: Sloboda Beograd
Dir: Miroslav Marković
Subjects: Historical Literature, Belles Lettres, Juveniles, Encyclopaedias

Slovo ljubve*, YU-11000 Belgrade, Mutapova 12 Tel: (011) 436360/454987
Dir: Ljubiša Pantić; *Editorial, Production:* Rade Vojvodić; *Sales:* Voja Petrović; *Publicity:* Snežana Dabić
Bookshop: Belgrade, Save Kovačevića 26
Book Club: Klub Čitalaca
1981: 27 titles *Founded:* 1971

Službeni List*, YU-11000 Belgrade, Jovana Ristića 1, Poštanski fah 226 Tel: 650155 Telex: 11756 yu slist
Dir: Dušan Mašović
Subjects: Službeni List (Official Register) in languages of peoples and nationalities of Yugoslavia, Legal, University Textbooks, Federation Regulations, Periodicals
Bookshops: Belgrade: Prodavnica 1, Brankova 16; Prodavnica 2, 29 Novembra 1a

Sportska Knjiga*, YU-11000 Belgrade, Makedonska 19, Poštanski fah 720 Tel: 325361 Cable Add: Sportska Knjiga
Dir: Dragoslav Bajić; *Editor:* Sava Bjelajac
Subject: Sport
Bookshop: Belgrade, Makedonska 19
Founded: 1949

Srpska Književna Zadruga*, YU-11000 Belgrade, Maršala Tita 19 Tel: 330305/334977
President: Risto Tošović
Subjects: History, Belles Lettres
Bookshop: At above address
Founded: 1892

Stvarnost+, YU-41000 Zagreb, Frankopanska 11, Poštanski fah 734 Tel: 413808
Man Dir: Mirko Mador; *Editorial:* Marijan Sinković; *Sales:* Vlado Polić
Subjects: General Fiction, Biography, History, How-to, Music, Art, Philosophy, Reference, Juveniles, High-priced Paperbacks, Medicine, General & Social Science
Book Club: Klub 42
Bookshop: Zagreb: Knjizara Stvarnost, Savska 1; Jlica 163b; Roosevveltov trg 4
Founded: 1952

Svjetlost*, YU-71000 Sarajevo, Petra Preradovića 3, Poštanski fah 129 Tel: (071) 512144/31100 Cable Add: Svjetlost Sarajevo Telex: 41326 yu Ikpres
Man Dir: Abdulah Jesenković; *Sales Dir:* Rizvanbegović Enver; *Editorial:* Miodrag Bogićvić
Branch Offs: Belgrade, Obilićev venac 10; Zagreb, Šubičeva 65
Subjects: Belles Lettres, Reference, Science, Juveniles, Business, Textbooks, Business Directories, Encyclopaedias, Periodicals
Bookshops: See under Major Booksellers

Tehnička Knjiga*, YU-11000 Belgrade, ul 7 jula br 26/I, Poštanski fah 307 Tel: (011) 626046
Man Dir: Prvoslav Trajković
Subjects: General Science, Engineering, Secondary & Primary Textbooks

Tehnička Knjiga, YU-41000 Zagreb, Jurišićeva 10, Poštanski fah 816 Tel: (041) 278172 Cable Add: Tehnoknjiga
Man Dir: Kuzman Ražnjević; *Dir, Chief Editor:* Zvonko Vistrička
Subjects: Science, Technical Engineering, Periodicals
Bookshops: See under Major Booksellers, also Knjizara Tehnička Knjiga, Zagreb, Masarykova 19; Antikvarijat, Zagreb, Masarykova 17
Founded: 1947

Tehnika, formerly publishing house of Savez Inženjera i Tehničara Jugoslavije (qv)

Tiskarna Ljudske Pravice*, Kopitarjeva 2, YU-61000 Ljubljana Tel: 323841 Telex: 31177 ljudne
Subjects: Children's and Juvenile Books; Periodicals and Newspapers

Turistička Štampa*, YU-11000 Belgrade, Knez Mihajlova 21/II, Poštanski fah 606 Tel: (011) 621080/632322
Man Dir: Nikola Korbutovski; *Editorial:* Misha Radulović
Subjects: Art, Tourist Guides, Maps, Periodicals
Bookshop: Belgrade, Obilićev venac 26

Veselin Masleša*, YU-71000 Sarajevo, Sime Milutinovića 4, Poštanski fah 237 Tel: (071) 34633/24634 Cable Add: Vesmas Masleša Telex: 41154 ju vesmas
Man Dir, Editorial, Rights and Permissions: Ahmed Hromadžić
Branch Offs: Zagreb, Belgrade, Skopje
Subjects: General Fiction, General & Political Science, Reference, Philosophy, Juveniles
Bookshops: See under Major Booksellers
Founded: 1950

Vesti*, YU-31000 Titovo Užice, 4 jula br 14 Tel: 21262
Dir: Mihajlo Rebić

Vojnoizdavački Zavod*, YU-11002 Belgrade, Balkanska 53 Tel: (011) 641586
Subject: Military

Vuk Karadžic*, YU-11000 Belgrade, Kraljevića Marka 9, Poštanski fah 762 Tel: (011) 628066/628043/620024 (Director) Cable Add: Vuk Karadžić Belgrade
Man Dir: Slobodan Durić; *Editorial:* Vojin Ančić
Branch Offs: Zagreb, Nikole Tesle 14/III; Sarajevo, Sime Milutinovića 10; Novi Sad, Laze Kostića 22; Svetozarevo, Slavke Durdević bb zgr B-3
Subjects: Encyclopaedias and Reference, Art, Popular Science, History, Criticism, Psychology, Sociology, Philosophy, Children's books, Education, Periodicals
Bookshop: See under Major Booksellers
Founded: 1956

Založba Obzorja*, YU-62000 Maribor, Partizanska 5, Poštanski fah 135 Tel: 25681/21086
Dir: Drago Simončič
Subjects: Professional, Science, Journalism

Zavod za Izdavanje Udžbenika*, YU-71000 Sarajevo, Otokara Keršovanija 3, Poštanski fah 262 Tel: 33728
Man Dir: Dr Ljubomir Berberović
Subjects: Education, Textbooks

Zavod za Obrazovanje Kadrova za Administrativne Poslove SR Srbije*, Izdavačko-Stamparska OOUR Stručna Knjiga, YU-11000 Belgrade, ul Lole Ribara 48 Tel: 341332/342512/342514 Cable Add: Stručna knjiga
Dir: Mrs V Brgulan
Subjects: Textbooks, Business, Management

Zavod za Udžbenike i Nastavna Sredstva, YU-11000 Belgrade, Obilićev Venac 5, Poštanski fah 312 Tel: 335337
Dir: Dr Tomislav Bogavac
Subjects: Textbooks, Educational Materials
Bookshop: YU-11000 Belgrade, Kosovska 45

Zavod za Udžbenike i Nastavna Sredstva Sap Kosovo*, YU-38000 Priština, Beogradska 29, Poštanski fah 112 Tel: (038) 24752
Dir: Ramuš Rama
Subjects: Textbooks, Educational Materials
Bookshop: Priština, Lenjinova 66
Founded: 1958

Nakladni Zavod **'Znanje'***, YU-41000 Zagreb, Socijalističke revolucije 17, Pretinac 955 Tel: (041) 411500/411483/411474 Cable Add: Znanje Zagreb
Man Dir: Dragutin Brenčun
Branch Offs: Sarajevo, A Šenoe 14; Belgrade, Bulevar Lenjina 119
Subjects: General Fiction, Popular Science, Agriculture
Bookshops: August Šenoa, Socijalističke revolucije 17; Trg Republike 17; 'Ivan Goran Kovačić', Martićeva 12; Antikvarijat, Tin Ujević, Zrinjevac 17 (all in Zagreb)
Founded: 1946

Literary Agents

Jugoslovenska Autorska Agencija, Belgrade, Majke Jevrosime 38 Tel: (011) 325902/323155 Cable Add: Autoragencija
General Manager: Mrs Ljiljana Mladenović
Main activities: Protection of the copyrights of Yugoslav authors in Yugoslavia and abroad and of foreign authors in Yugoslavia; marketing of foreign authors' works in Yugoslavia and acquiring options and authorization for the works of Yugoslav authors

V P A (Vjesnikova Press Agencija), YU-41000 Zagreb, Ave bratstva i jedinstva 4 Tel: (041) 515555 Telex: 21121

Book Clubs

Book Lovers' Club, YU-11000 Belgrade, Kosovska 37
Owned by: Beogradski Izdavačko-Grafički Zavod (qv)

Klub 42, Zagreb, Rooseveltov trg 4
Owned by: Stvarnost (qv)

Klub Čitalaca*, Belgrade, Save Kovačevića 26
Owned by: Slovo Ljubve (qv)

Klub Čitalaca MK, YU-11000 Belgrade, Mata Vidakovića 24 Tel: (011) 458165
Members: 3000
Owned by: Medicinska Knjiga (qv)
Founded: 1981

Mladost's Book Fans Club, Zagreb, Radićeva 37
Owned by: Mladost (qv under Publishers)

Prosveta, YU-11000 Belgrade, Andricev venac
Owned by: Prosveta (qv under Publishers)

Svet Knjige, Ljubljana, Nazorjeva 6
Members: 165,000
Owned by: Mladinska Knjiga (qv)
Founded: 1971

Major Booksellers

Cankarjeva Zalozba, YU-61001 Ljubljana, Kopitarjeva 2, Poštni predal 201-IV Tel: (061) 214250
Branches: Kopitarjeva 2, Trg osvoboditve 7, Titova 15, Miklošičeva 16, Tržaška 59, Zaloska 35 (all in Ljubljana); Trbovlje, 1 junija 27; Vrhnika, Usnjarska stolpič S 15
Importer/Exporter, Antiquarian bookseller, also Publisher (qv)

Državna Založba Slovenije, YU-61000 Ljubljana, Mestni trg 26, Postanski fah 50/1 Tel: 310736
Also: DZS at Bled, C Svobode 15; Brežice, C Prvih borcev 37; Celje, trg V Kongresa 3; Ljubljana, Mestni trg 26; Ljubljana, Šubičeva 1a; Ljubljana, Titova 25; Ljubljana, Čopova 3; Export-Import, Ljubljana, Kotnikova 12
Importer/Exporter, also Publisher (qv)

Export-Press*, YU-11000 Belgrade, Francuska 27, Poštanski fah 358 Tel: (011) 625363
Importer/Exporter (the latter particularly as supplier to various US libraries, and UK and US Slavic departments)

Forum*, YU-21000 Novi Sad, Vojvode Mišića 1, Poštanski fah 200 Tel: (021) 57207
Importer/Exporter, also Publisher (qv)

Jugoslovenska Knjiga*, Trg Republike 5/VIII, Poštanski fah 36, YU-11000 Belgrade Tel: 621992 Cable Add: Jugoknjiga Beograd Telex: 12466 yu jkbdg
Import and Export of Books, Periodicals and Newspapers

Kultura*, YU-91000 Skopje, JNA 68a, Postanski fah 298 Tel: 35361
32 bookshops throughout Yugoslavia
Also Publisher (qv)

Makedonska Knjiga, YU-91000 Skopje, 11 Oktomvri bb, Poštanski fah 349 Tel: (091) 231610
Man Dir: Nikola Todorov
28 bookshops in Skopje and in all major towns in Macedonia
Owned by: Makedonska Knjiga (Knigoizdatelstvo) (qv)

Mladinska Knjiga*, YU-61000 Ljubljana, Titova 3, Poštanski fah 36/1 Tel: (061) 221233 Telex: 31695 Yu Emka Ex
23 bookshops throughout Yugoslavia
Importer/Exporter, also Publisher (qv)

Mladost, YU-41000 Zagreb, Ilica 30, Poštanski fah 1028 Tel: (041) 440211 Telex: 21263 YU MLADZG
Branches: 20 in Zagreb, 2 in Rijeka, 1 in Osijek, 1 in Belgrade, 1 in Zadar, 2 in Split, 1 in Pula, 1 in Banja Luka, 1 in Sarajevo, 1 in Dubrovnik
Importer/Exporter, also Publisher (qv)

Nolit, YU-11000 Belgrade, Terazije 27/II, Poštanski fah 369 Tel: (011) 333353
50 bookshops throughout Yugoslavia
Importer/Exporter
Owned by: Nolit Publishing House (qv)

Prosveta, YU-11000 Belgrade, Terazije 16/I Tel: (011) 687441 (import)/686624 (export)
Over 50 bookshops throughout Yugoslavia
Importer/Exporter, also Publisher (qv)

Svjetlost*, YU-71000 Sarajevo, Radojke Lakić 3 Tel: (071) 38678
42 bookshops throughout Yugoslavia
Importer/Exporter, also Publisher (qv)

Tehnička Knjiga, YU-41000 Zagreb, Jurišićeva 10, Poštanski fah 816 Tel: (041) 271608
General Manager: Kuzman Raznjević
Importer/Exporter (Technical Books)
Owned by: Tehnička Knjiga, Zagreb (qv under Publishers)

Veselin Masleša*, YU-71000 Sarajevo, Sime Milutinovića 4 i 2 Tel: (071) 24634
Also: Sarajevo, Maksima Gorkog 2 & Pavla Goranina 2; Belgrade, Terazije 38. Over 30 group bookshops throughout Yugoslavia
Importer/Exporter, also Publisher (qv)

Vuk Karadžic*, YU-11000 Belgrade, Kraljevića Marka 9, Poštanski fah 762 Tel: (011) 628066/628043
Manager: Slobodan Durić
Importer/Exporter, also Publisher (qv)

Major Libraries

Arhiv Hrvatske, YU-41000 Zagreb, Marulićev trg 21
Archives of Croatia
Publications: Archival Review (annual); *Acts of Croatian Parliament*

Arhiv na SR Makedonija*, Skopje, Kej Dimitar Vlahov bb, Poštanski fah 496
Archives of Macedonia

Arhiv SR Slovenije, YU-61000 Ljubljana, Zvezdarska 1 Tel: 216551
Dir: Marija Oblak-Čarni

Arhiv Srbije*, YU-11000 Belgrade, Karnedžijeva 2
Librarian: Mrs L Mirković
Archives of Serbia

Institute for Scientific and Technical Documentation and Information*, Belgrade, Katanićeva 15
Publication: Yugoslav Research Guide

Jugoslovenski centar za tehničku i naučnu dokumentaciju*, Belgrade, S Penezića-Krcuna 29, Poštanski fah 724
Dir: Aleksić Miodrag
Yugoslav Centre for Technical and Scientific Documentation
Publications: Bulletin of Documentation (24 series abstracts from technical literature), *Informatika* (periodical for theory and practice of documentation and information), *Bibliography on Automatic Data Processing, Scientific and Professional Meetings in Yugoslavia and Foreign Countries, MF-Technique* (journal on applying microfilm)

Univerzitetska biblioteka 'Svetozar Marković', YU-11000 Belgrade, Bulevar revolucije 71 Tel: (011) 342116/341446
University Library 'Svetozar Markovič'

Nacionalna i Sveučilišna Biblioteka, YU-41001 Zagreb, Marulićev trg 21, Poštanski fah 550 Tel: Director 445440; Secretariat, Information Office, other departments 446322
National and University Library
Director: Veseljko Velčić
Publications: Bibliografija knjiga tiskanih u SR Hrvatskoj; Bibliografija rasprava, članaka i književnih radova u časopisima SR Hrvatske

Centralna **narodna biblioteka** SR Crne Gore*, Cetinje, Njegoševa 100
Central National Library of Montenegro

Narodna biblioteka SR Srbije*, YU-11000 Belgrade, Skerlićeva 1 Tel: 451242/9
National Library of Serbia

Narodna i univerzitetska biblioteka Bosne i Hercegovine*, YU-71000 Sarajevo, Obala 42
National and University Library of Bosnia and Herzegovina

Narodna in univerzitetna knjižnica (Ljubljana), YU-61001 Ljubljana pp 259, Turjaška 1 Tel: Central (061) 217744; Information (061) 214930
National and University Library

Naučna biblioteka, Rijeka, Dolac 1
Research Library

Narodna i univerzitetska biblioteka **'Kliment Ohridski'***, YU-91000 Skopje, bulevar 'Goce Delčev' br 6, Poštanski fah 566 Tel: 226848
'Kliment Ohridski' National and University Library

Biblioteka **Srpske** Akademije Nauka i Umetnosti, YU-11001 Belgrade, Knez Mihailova 35
Library of the Serbian Academy of Sciences and Arts
Librarian: Mile Žegarac

Library Associations

Društvo bibliotekara Bosne i Hercegovine*, YU-71000 Sarajevo, Obala 42 Tel: (071) 537202
Library Association of Bosnia and Herzegovina
Executive Secretary: Žuljević Emir
Publication: Bibliotekarstvo (yearly)

Društvo bibliotekarjev Slovenije, YU-61000 Ljubljana, Turjaška 1 Tel: 217744
Library Association of Slovenia
Executive Secretary: Ana Martelanc
Publications: Knjižnica (quarterly)

Društvo na arhivskite rabotnici i arhivite na SRM*, YU-91000 Skopje
Society of Archivists of Macedonia
Secretary: Krasimira Ilievska
Publication: Makedonski arhivist

Hrvatsko bibliotekarsko društvo*, YU-41000 Zagreb Marulićev trg 21
Croatian Library Association
Secretary: Nada Gomerčić
Publications: Vjesnik bibliotekara Hrvatske (quarterly), *Knjiga i čitaoci* (six per year)

Jugoslovenski bibliografski institut, YU-11000 Belgrade, Terazije 26 Tel: 687760
Yugoslav Bibliographic Institute
Dir: Dr Venceslav Glišić
Publishes the *Yugoslavia Bibliography*, which includes books, pamphlets, music scores and articles of literary, scientific interest, philology, art and sport

Savez bibliotečkih radnika Srbije*, YU-11000 Belgrade, Skerlićeva 1 Tel: 451242/455488
Union of Library Workers of Serbia
Executive Secretary: Dušica Ristić
Publication: Bibliotekar (bimonthly)

Savez društava bibliotekara Jugoslavije*, YU-38000 Priština, Poštanski fah 136 Tel: 20273
League of the Librarians' Associations of Yugoslavia
Official titles: Savez društava bibliotekara Jugoslavije (Serbo-Croatian), Sojuz na društvata na bibliotekarite na Jugoslavija (Macedonian), Zveza društev bibliotekarjev Jugoslavije (Slovene)
The headquarters of the League is situated in each of the six republics and two provinces of Yugoslavia in turn and changes every two years
Secretary: Ms B Zdravković

Sojuz na društvata na bibliotekarite na Jugoslavija (Macedonian), see Savez društava bibliotekara Jugoslavije

Sojuz na društvata na bibliotekarite na SR Makedonija*, 'Kliment Ohridski' National and University Library, YU-91000 Skopje, bulevar 'Goce Delčev' br 6, Poštanski fah 566 Tel: 226846
Librarians' Society of Macedonia
President: Slave Risteski; *Secretary:* Dimitar Dimitrov
Publication: Bibliotekarska iskra

Zveza društev bibliotekarjev Jugoslavije (Slovene), see Savez društava bibliotekara Jugoslavije

Library Reference Books and Journals

Books

Biblioteke u Jugoslaviji (Libraries in Yugoslavia), Yugoslav Bibliographic Institute, YU-11000 Belgrade, Terazije 26

Biblioteke u SR Srbiji (Libraries in Serbia), National Library of Serbia, YU-11000 Belgrade, Skerlićeva 1

Journals

Bibliotekar (The Librarian), Union of Library Workers of Serbia, YU-11000 Belgrade, Skerlićeva 1

Bibliotekarska iskra (The Librarian's Spark), Librarians' Society of Macedonia, 'Kliment Ohridski' National and University Library, YU-91000 Skopje, ul 'Goce Delčev' bb

Bibliotekarstvo (Librarianship), Library Association of Bosnia and Herzegovina, YU-71000 Sarajevo, Obala 42

Knjiga i čitaoci (Book and Readers), Croatian Library Association, YU-41000 Zagreb, Marulićev trg 21

Knjižnica (The Library) (text in Slovenian, summaries in English) Library Association of Slovenia, YU-61000 Ljubljana, Turjaška 1

Makedonski arhivist (Macedonian Archivist) (text in Macedonian, summaries in French), Society of Archivists of Macedonia, YU-91000 Skopje

Viesnik bibliotekara hrvatske (Croatian Librarians' Bulletin), Croatian Library Association, YU-41000 Zagreb, Marulićev trg 21

Literary Associations and Societies

Društvo na pisatelite na SRM*, YU-91000 Skopje, Maksim Gorki 18
Society of Writers of Macedonia
Secretaries: Adem Gajtani, Eftim Manev

Društvo za srpski jezik i književnost*, Belgrade University, Belgrade
Society of Serbian Language and Literature
Secretary: D Pavlović
Publication: Pritozi za knjizevnost, jezik, istorija i folklor

Literary Club **'Oktobar'***, Kraljevo, Mire Cukulica 2
Publication: Oktobar

Yugoslav P E N Club, Serbian Centre, YU-11000 Belgrade, 7 Francuska br
Secretary: David Albahari

Pedagoško-književni zbor, pedagoško društvo SR Hrvatske*, Zagreb
Pedagogical and Literary Union of Croatia

Sojuz na društvata za makedonski jazik i literatura*, Institute for the Macedonian Language 'Krste Misirkov', YU-91000 Skopje, Grigor Prlicev 5
Federation of Societies for Macedonian Language and Literature
Secretary: Olga Ivanova
Publication: Literaturen zbor (Literary Door)

Literary Periodicals

Bagdala; literature, art and culture (text in Serbo-Croatian), Knjizevni Klub, Krusevac, Obilićeva 20

Brazde (Furrows); journal for literature and culture, Narodni Univerzitet, Bijeljina, Vase Pelagica 1

Bridge; literary review, Zagreb, trg Republike 7

Delo (The Literary Work) (text in Serbo-Croatian), Nolit Publishing House, YU-11000 Belgrade, Terazije 27/II, Poštanski fah 369

Forum; journal of the Section for Contemporary Literature of the Yugoslav Academy of Sciences and Arts (Text in Serbo-Croatian), Zagreb 1, Zrinski trg 11

Izraz (Expression); journal of literary and artistic criticism, Sarajevo, Radojke Lakio Broj 3-1, Poštanski fah 322

Književna kritika (Literary Criticism), Izdavačka Organizacija Rad, YU-11000 Belgrade, Moše Pijade 12

Književne novine (Literary News) (text in Serbo-Croatian), Novinsko Izdavačko Preduzeće 'Knjizevne Novine', Belgrade, Francuska 7

Literaturen zbor (Literary Door) (text in Macedonian); journal of the Federation of Societies for Macedonian Language and Literature, Institute for the Macedonian Language, 'Krste Misirkov', YU-91000 Skopje, Grigor Prličev 5

Lumina (Light); literary and cultural review, Panciova, Zarka Zrenjanina 7

Macedonian Review; history, culture, literature, arts, Cultural Life, Skopje, Poštanski fah 85

Oktobar (October); review of literature, art and culture, Literary Club 'Oktobar', Kraljevo, Mire Cukulica 2

Pregled naših i stranih knjiga i članaka (Review of Domestic and Foreign Books and Articles), Centralna biblioteka JNA, Belgrade, Balkanska 53a

Razgledi (Perspectives), review of literature, art and culture (text in Macedonian), Maršala Tita Iv Baraka, Skopje, Maršala Tita 4, Poštanski fah 345

Savremenik (Contemporary); literary monthly (text in Serbo-Croatian), Beogradski Izdavačko-Grafički Zavod, YU-11000 Belgrade, bulevar vojode Mišića 17, Poštanski fah 340

Stremez (Aspiration); journal for literature and culture (text in Macedonian), Prilep, Joska Jordanovski 2

Stremliena; literary review published every two months, Jedinstvo, YU-38000 Priština, Dom Štampe bb, Postanski, pregradak 81

Stvaranje (Creation); journal for literature and culture, Cedo Vukovic, Titograd, Marka Miljanova 11A

Translation Agencies and Associations

Društvo na literaturnite preveduvači na SRM*, YU-91000 Skopje
Society of Literary Translators of Macedonia
Secretary: Taško Širilov

Zaire

General Information

Language: Officially French; Swahili common in east, Lingala in west
Religion: About 25% Roman Catholic; rest follow traditional beliefs
Population: 27.7 million
Bank Hours: 0800-1130 Monday-Friday
Shop Hours: 0800-1200, 1500-1800 Monday-

ZAIRE

Friday; 0800-1200 Saturday
Currency: 100 makuta (singular likuta) = 1 zaïre; 100 sengi = 1 likuta
Export/Import Information: No tariff but for books not of educational, scientific or cultural use there is a revenue tax; children's picture books and atlases are also taxed. Small quantities of advertising matter free. Statistical Tax on all imports. Goods subject to duty also subject to Turnover Tax of percentage of CIF value + customs + statistical tax. No import licences for books. Exchange controls
Copyright: Berne, Florence (see International section)

Book Trade Reference Journal

Bibliographie nationale (National Bibliography), Bibliothèque nationale, 10 blvd Col Rshatshi, BP 3090, Kinshasa-Gombe

Publishers

Bureau d'Etudes et de Recherches pour la Promotion de la Santé, BP 1977, Kangu-Mayombe
Man Dir, Rights & Permissions: Dr J Courtejoie
Subject: Health Education

C E E B A Publications, BP 246, Bandundu Cable Add: CEEBA Bandundu
Man Dir, Editorial: Dr Hermann Hochegger; *Sales:* Cit Mbambi
Orders to: Steyler Verlag, D-5205 St Augustin, Federal Republic of Germany
Parent Company: Anthropos Institut
Subjects: Social Anthropology, Ethnology, Myths, Rituals, Sociology, Linguistics, Arts, Agriculture, History, Religion, Development, Dietetics, Development
1981: 10 titles *1982:* 11 titles *Founded:* 1965

C E L T A (Centre de Linguistique Théorique et Appliquée), BP 1607, Lubumbashi
Dirs: Ff Rossé René, Matumele Maliya; *General Manager:* Max Pierre
Parent Organization: Faculté des Lettres, BP 1825, Lubumbashi
Subsidiary Company: Antenne de Kinshasa, BP 3093, Kinshasa-Gombe
Subjects: Local Languages, French
Bookshop: BP 1607, Lubumbashi
1981: 4 titles *1982:* 2 titles *Founded:* 1971

Centre International de Sémiologie*, 109 Ave Pruniers, Zone de Kampemba, BP 1825, Campus de Lubumbashi
Secretary: Dr V Y Mudimbe
Publications: Bulletins on Medical Anthropology, Religious Syncretisms, Culture-contact, Africanisms

Centre Protestant d'Editions et de Diffusion (CEDI)*, 209 ave Kalemie, BP 11398, Kinshasa I Tel: 22202
Man Dir: Makela Lutantu
Subjects: General Fiction, Belles Lettres, Poetry, Biography, Religion, Juveniles, Christian Tracts, Books in Kikongo, Lingala and other Zaïre languages, Paperbacks
Bookshops: CEDI Bookshop, 209 ave Kalemie, BP 11398, Kinshasa I
Founded: 1935

Commission de l'Education chrétienne*, BP 3258, Kinshasa-Gombe Tel: 30087 Telex: 203 DIA
Man Dir: Abbé Dibalu-Didi
Subjects: Educational, Academic, Religion

Faculté de Theologie Catholique de Kinshasa, BP 1534, Kinshasa-Limete Tel: 78476
Dir: Prof Atal Sa Angang; *Editorial:* Prof Atal, Prof Mulago, Prof Tshiamalenga
Subjects: Theology, Philosophy, African Religions
1981-82: 9 titles *Founded:* 1957

Government Printer (Imprimerie du Gouvernement Central)*, BP 3021, Kinshasa-Kalina

Editions **Impala**, BP 1607, Lubumbashi
Chief Executive, Rights & Permissions: Ruhama Mukandoli; *Editorial, Sales, Production, Publicity:* Max Pierre
Parent Company: Pelta (at above address)
Associate Company: Maison des Langues Vivantes, rue des Pierres 9, B-1000 Brussels, Belgium
Subjects: Language, Linguistics
Bookshops: Librairie St Paul, Lubumbashi; Librairie Les Volcans, Goma Libreza, Bukavu; Maison des Langues Vivantes, Brussels, Belgium
1981: 1 title *1982:* 1 title *Founded:* 1981

Editions **Lokole***, BP 5085 Kinshasa X (Located at: ave Colonel Ebeya no 1082, Kinshasa-Gombe) Tel: 22559
Dir: Nzengo Popo
Miscellaneous: State organization charged with the promotion of literature in Zaïre

Editions du **Mont Noir***, BP 1944, Lubumbashi
Man Dir: V Y Mudimbe; *Sales:* Pierre Detienne; *Secretary and Publicity:* Mukala Kadima Nzuji
Subjects: General Fiction, Belles Lettres, Poetry, Reference
Founded: 1971

P U Z, an imprint of Presses universitaires du Zaïre et l'Office du Livre (qv)

Les **Presses Africaines***, pl du 27 Octobre, BP 12924, Kinshasa I
Man Dir: Mwamba-di-Mbuyi
Subjects: General Non-fiction, Belles Lettres, Poetry, Paperbacks

Presses universitaires du Zaïre et l'Office du Livre (PUZ), Boul du 30 Juin 4113, BP 1682 Kinshasa I Tel: 30652 Cable Add: PUZ Enseignement Telex: 21394 Bce Es
Man Dir, Rights & Permissions: Ngalamu Lume Karku; *Editorial:* Kalala Ntumba; *Sales:* Kabukala Mulowayi; *Production:* Kawumbu Kabemba; *Publicity:* Bampangidi Shambuyi
Parent Company: Unaza/Rectorat, BP 13-399, Kinshasa-Gombe
Imprint: PUZ
Branch Off: Lubumbashi
Subjects: Belles Lettres, Poetry, Biography, History, Africana, Philosophy, Reference, Religion, Paperbacks, Psychology, Medicine, Science & Technology, Agronomy, Social Science, University Textbooks, Economics, Law, Literature, Education
Bookshops: Librairie des Presses universitaires (qv under Major Booksellers); Librairie Universitaire de l'ISP/Kawanga; Librairie du 'Groupe du Mukuba', Lubumbashi
Founded: 1972

Editions **Saint Paul**, 76 ave du Commerce, BP 8505, Kinshasa Tel: 25544
Dir: Sister Lucia d'Agosto
Subjects: General Fiction & Non-fiction, Belles Lettres, Poetry, Religion, Juveniles, Christian Tracts, Paperbacks
Bookshops: See under Major Booksellers

Librairie Les **Volcans***, 22 ave Président Mobuto, BP 400, Goma (Kivu) Tel: 366
Man Dir: Ruhama Mukandoli; *Sales Manager:* Pierre Mangez
Subjects: Reference, Social Science
Bookshop: 22 ave President Mobuto, BP 400, Goma (Kivu)

Literary Agents

Le **Gai Savoir***, BP 12924, Kinshasa I

Major Booksellers

C E D I Bookshop*, 209 ave Kalemie, BP 11398, Kinshasa I Tel: 22202
Man Dir: Makela Lutantu

Diffusion de la Presse*, BP 505, Kisangani

La **Générale des Carrières et des Mines** (GECAMINES)*, BP 450, Lubumbashi Telex: 234
Also: BP 8714, Kinshasa Telex: 21207

Librairie de l'**Institut national** d'Etudes politiques*, BP 2307, Kinshasa Tel: 31649

Okapi Centre de Diffusion*, BP 908, Kinshasa

Librairie des **Presses** universitaires, BP 1682, Kinshasa I Tel: 24786
Owned by: Presses universitaires du Zaïre et l'Office du Livre (PUZ) (qv)

Procure scolaire, BP 70, Kananga
Manager: Wilfried Meulemeester

Librairie **Saint Paul**, 76 ave du Commerce, BP 8505, Kinshasa
Also: BP 2447, Lubumbashi
Owned by: Editions Saint Paul (qv)

Librairie **Salutiste***, 249 ave du Plateau, BP 8905, Kinshasa

Librairie **Sarma***, BP 7098, Kinshasa

Librairies **Sodimca***, BP 2700, Kinshasa

Librairie Les **Volcans***, 22 ave Président Mobutu, BP 400, Goma
Owned by: Librairie Les Volcans, Publisher (qv)

Librairie du **Zaïre***, 12 ave des Aviateurs, BP 2100, Kinshasa I Tel: 26748

Major Libraries

Archives nationales du Zaïre*, 42 ave Valcke, BP 3428, Kinshasa

Bibliothèque nationale*, 10 blvd Col Rshatshi, BP 3090, Kinshasa-Gombe Tel: 30834
Publication: Bibliographie nationale

Bibliothèque publique de Kinshasa*, BP 410, Kinshasa Tel: 3070
Librarian: M Mongu

Bibliothèque publique de Kisangani*, 2 ave Bawaboli, BP 1741, Kisangani Tel: 2617

Bibliothèque publique de Lubumbashi*, 827 ave Delvaux, Lubumbashi
Supplies 25 branch libraries

Centre culturel français, Bibliothèques*, BP 5236, Kinshasa

Institut pédagogique national*, Bibliothèque, BP 8815, Kinshasa I Tel: 80573

Institut pour la recherche scientifique en Afrique centrale, Bibliothèque*, Dépêche Spéciale, Bukavu, Kivu Tel: 3080
Chief Librarian: Ruhima Kibuka

Bibliothèque centrale de l'**Université nationale du Zaïre***, Campus de Kinshasa, BP 125, Kinshasa XI Tel: 30123 ext 161
Librarian: Tubomeshi Milambo
Publication: Chronique des Bibliothèques

Bibliothèque centrale de l'**Université de Kisangani**, BP 2012, Kisangani Tel: 2153
Chief Librarian: Label Kakes Muzila

Bibliothèque centrale de l'**Université nationale, Campus de Lubumbashi***, BP 2896, Lubumbashi Tel: 4479

Library Association

Association Zaïroise des Archivistes, Bibliothècaires et Documentalistes*, BP 805, Kinshasa XI Tel: 30123/4
Zaire Association of Archivists, Librarians and Documentalists
Executive Secretary: E Kabeba-Bangasa
Publication: Mukanda

Library Reference Books and Journals

Book

Liste des bibliothèques publiques (List of Public Libraries), Ministère de la culture et des arts, Bibliothèque centrale, Kinshasa-Kalina

Journal

Mukanda: archives, libraries and documentation bulletin, Association Zaïroise des Archivistes, Bibliothècaires et Documentalistes, BP 805, Kinshasa XI

Literary Periodicals

Cahiers de Littérature et de Linguistique appliqué (Journal of Literature and Applied Linguistics), Université nationale du Zaïre, Faculté des Lettres, BP 1825, Campus de Lubumbashi

Dombi; Congolese review of letters and the arts, BP 3498, Kinshasa-Kalina (bi-monthly 'little magazine' edited by Philippe Masegabio)

Zambia

General Information

Language: English is official language
Religion: About 50% Christian (25% Roman Catholic, 25% Protestant); rest follow traditional beliefs
Population: 5.5 million
Literacy Rate (1969): 47.3%
Bank Hours: 0815-1245 Monday, Tuesday, Wednesday, Friday; 0815-1200 Thursday; 0815-1100 Saturday
Shop Hours: Generally 0800-1700 Monday-Friday; 0800-1300 Saturday
Currency: 100 ngwee = 1 Zambia kwacha
Export/Import Information: No tariffs on books but all imports subject to sales tax. Single copies of advertising free. Import licence required. Exchange controls
Copyright: UCC (see International section)

Book Trade Organization

Booksellers' and Publishers' Association of Zambia, c/o PO Box 8199, Lusaka
Secretary: P M Wele

Publishers

Africa Literature Centre*, PO Box 1319, Kitwe Tel: 84712/3 Cable Add: Mincen
Man Dir: E C Makunike
Subjects: General, Educational, Religion, Books in Zambian Languages
Bookshop: At above address

Directory Publishers of Zambia Ltd*, PO Box 71659, Ndola (Located at: Rooms 101-103 First Floor, Security House, Buteko Ave, Ndola) Tel: 4882
Man Dir, Rights & Permissions: D E Smith; *Editorial & Publicity:* Mrs D E Bell; *Sales:* Mrs J M Maxwell
Subjects: Reference, Directories
Founded: 1958

Government Printer*, PO Box 30136, Lusaka

Institute of African Studies, PO Box 30900, Lusaka Tel: 252539/252544 Cable Add: Insas Telex: 44370
Editorial: Prof Robert Serpell, Prof L P Tembo, Dr J Milimo, Dr C Ng'andwe, Dr C J J Mphaisha; *Other Offices:* Miss M A Sifuniso, University Publications Office of University of Zambia, PO Box 32379, Lusaka
Parent Organization: University of Zambia, PO Box 32379, Lusaka
Branch Off: Ndola Campus of University of Zambia, PO Box 21692, Kitwe
Subjects: Social Research in Africa
Bookshops: University of Zambia Bookshops at PO Box 32379, Lusaka and PO Box 21692, Kitwe
Founded: 1938

Multimedia Zambia+, PO Box 8199, Woodlands, Lusaka Tel: 253864/215950 Telex: 40630 Za
Executive Dir: Gabriel S Chifwambwa
Parent Company: Christian Council of Zambia/Zambia Episcopal Conference
Subjects: Political Biographies, Cookery, Comparative Religion, Educational Textbooks for Juveniles, Fiction, Social Sciences, Historical Communications
Founded: 1971

N E C Z A M Library, an imprint of National Educational Company of Zambia Ltd (qv)

National Educational Company of Zambia Ltd, Chishango Rd, PO Box 32664, Lusaka Tel: 218259/218419/215612 Cable Add: Neczam Lusaka
General Manager: M C Kendolo; *Editorial:* H Lombe; *Production:* G K Simanwe; *Rights & Permissions:* Paulsen Himwiinga
Parent Company: Kenneth Kaunda Foundation, PO Box 32708, Lusaka
Associate Company: National Educational Distribution Company of Zambia Ltd, PO Box 32666, Lusaka
Imprint: NECZAM Library
Subjects: General, Poetry, Biography, History, Agriculture, Children's Books, Educational, Language, Literature, Fiction, Folklore, Drama, Politics, Sociology, Zambia Primary Course
Book Club: Read-a-Book Club
Bookshop: Chishango Rd, PO Box 32664, Lusaka
Founded: 1967

Prometheus Publishing Co*, PO Box 1850, Lusaka
Subjects: General Non-fiction, Biography, History, Africana, Social Science

Temco Publishing Ltd*, No 10 Kabelenga Rd, PO Box 30886, Lusaka Tel: 211883 Cable Add: Longman Telex: ZA 45250
Man Dir, Editorial, Production, Publicity, Rights & Permissions: S V Tembo; *Sales:* K T Msumba
Subjects: Educational, General
Founded: 1977

Book Club

Read-a-Book Club, PO Box 32664, Lusaka Tel: 218259/218419/218612
Owned by: National Educational Company of Zambia Ltd (qv)

Major Booksellers

The **Bookshelf***, Caravelle House, Buteko Ave, PO Box 977, Ndola Tel: 3438

Christian Bookshop*, PO Box 1206, Kitwe

Christian Council of Zambia*, Farmers House, PO Box 315, Lusaka Tel: 73287

Kingstons (Zambia) Ltd*, PO Box 70139, Ndola
Department store with book department (12 other branches)

Malsa Book Service Ltd*, Cairo Rd, PO Box 1700, Lusaka Tel: 81155

Standard Books Ltd*, PO Box 94, Lusaka

University Bookshop, PO Box 32379, Lusaka Tel: 252576 Cable Add: UNZA Bookshop, Lusaka Telex: 44370 Za
Manager: E M Kalenga
Owned by: University of Zambia

Zambia Catholic Bookshop*, PO Box 71581, Ndola

Major Libraries

Evelyn **Hone** College Library, PO Box 30029, Lusaka Tel: 211557

Helen **Kaunda** Memorial Library, Cha Cha Cha Rd, PO Box 90140, Luanshya Tel: 510315
Librarian: Charles Sambondu

Kitwe Public Library, PO Box 20070, Kitwe Tel: 213685

Lusaka District Libraries*, PO Box 31304, Katondo Rd, Lusaka Tel: 217282
City Librarian: P G Lilanda
Publications: Annual Report; New Additions List (quarterly)

Mindolo Ecumenical Foundation, Hammarskjold Memorial Library, PO Box 21493, Kitwe Tel: 215198/214572 Cable Add: Mincen Kitwe Telex: 50250 Za
Librarian: Nyambe Namushi
Publications: Annual Report; Mindolo Newsletter (occasional); various reports of conferences and research programme

National Archives of Zambia*, PO Box RW 10, Ridgeway, Lusaka Tel: 51677

National Institute of Public Administration Library*, PO Box 31990, Lusaka Tel: 72128

Natural Resources Development College Library, PO Box CH 99, Lusaka Tel: 214620

Ndola Public Library*, PO Box 70388, Ndola Tel: 4225/2637
Librarian: K Mumba Chisaka

464 ZAMBIA — ZIMBABWE

Nkrumah Teachers' College Library*, PO Box 80404, Kabwe Tel: 3221
Librarian: Francesca K Ng'Ambi

Northern Technical College Library, PO Box KJ 93, Ndola Tel: 86211-5 ext 18
Librarian: Lemmy Virgilio Luswili

University of Zambia Library, PO Box 32379, Lusaka Tel: 213221 Cable Add: UNZA-Library Telex: 44370 Za
Chief Librarian: D O Bampoe; *Librarians:* H Mwacalimba (Lusaka Campus); M C Lundu (Ndola Campus)
Publications include: Zambiana Gazette; Bulletin

Zambia Institute of Technology Library, PO Box 21993, Kitwe Tel: 212066
Librarian: M C Banda
Publications: Annual Report; ZIT Prospectus (annual)

Zambia Library Service, Educational Services Centre, PO Box 30802, Lusaka Tel: 254655 Cable Add: Zamlibs
Chief Librarian: M Walubita
Publications include: Bulletin (quarterly); *Directory of Library Centres* (annually); *Buyer's Guide to Library Equipment* (twice a year)

Library Association

Zambia Library Association, PO Box 32839, Lusaka
Secretary: Zilole M K Phiri
Publications: Zambia Library Association Journal; Zambia Library Association Newsletter

Library Reference Books and Journals

Books

Directory of Libraries in Zambia, Zambia Library Association, PO Box 32839, Lusaka (provides details on all the major libraries in the country)

Directory of Library Centres, Zambia Library Service, PO Box 30802, Lusaka

Journal

Zambia Library Association Journal, PO Box 32839, Lusaka

Literary Associations and Societies

Mphala Creative Society*, c/o International House 5-13, University of Zambia, PO Box 2379, Lusaka
Publication: The Jewel of Africa

Literary Periodical

The Jewel of Africa, Mphala Creative Society, c/o International House 5-13, University of Zambia, PO Box 2379, Lusaka (literary and cultural quarterly edited by Steven May and published since 1968)

Zimbabwe

General Information

Language: English and native dialects
Population: 6.9 million
Bank Hours: 0830-1400 Monday, Tuesday, Thursday, Friday; 0830-1200 Wednesday; 0830-1100 Saturday
Shop Hours: 0800 or 0830-1700 Monday-Friday; 0800 or 0830-1200 or 1230 Saturday
Currency: 100 cents = 1 Zimbabwe dollar
Export/Import Information: No tariff on books. Advertising matter in bulk has duty and VAT charged. No import licence required for books or advertising matter

Book Trade Organizations

Booksellers' Association of Zimbabwe*, PO Box 1934, Harare (Located at: Equity House, Rezende St, Harare) Tel: 708611
Secretary: A Muchaziwepi

Standard Book Numbering Agency, National Archives, Private Bag 7729, Causeway, Harare Tel: 792741
ISBN Administrator: Miss R Molam

Book Trade Reference Journal

Zimbabwe National Bibliography, National Archives, Causeway, Private Bag 7729, Harare

Publishers

B & T Directories (Pvt) Ltd*, PO Box 2119, Bulawayo Tel: 68131/68145 Cable Add: Publishers Telex: 3333 ZW
Subject: Directories

Books of Zimbabwe Publishing Co (Pvt) Ltd*, 137A Rhodes St, PO Box 1994, Bulawayo Tel: 61135
Man Dir & Editor: L W Bolze; *Rights & Permissions:* Joan Hopcroft
Orders to: Books of Zimbabwe Publishing Co, PO Box 1994, Bulawayo
Subsidiary Company: Africana Book Society (Pty) Ltd, PO Box 1071, Johannesburg 2000 Republic of South Africa (qv)
Subjects: Rhodesiana Reprints & New Works, Fine Prints, Antique Maps of Africa, General Fiction and Non-fiction, Biography, History, Colour-plate Fine editions, Education, Visual Aids
Book Clubs: Books of Zimbabwe Book Club, Africana Book Society, Republic of South Africa (qv)
Founded: 1968
ISBN Publisher's Prefix: 0-86920

A C Braby (Zimbabwe) (Pvt) Ltd*, PO Box 1027, Bulawayo Tel: 68131/68145 Cable Add: Publishers Telex: 3333 ZW
Subjects: Reference, Directories, Telephone Books, Diaries

The **College** Press (Pvt) Ltd+, PO Box 3041, Harare (Located at: 15 Douglas Rd, Harare) Tel: 704141 Cable Add: Libris Telex: 3758 ZW
Man Dir: Christopher Paterson; *Dep Man Dir & Sales:* Ben Mugabe; *Sales Manager:* Engelbert Luphahla; *Managing Editor:* Margo Bedingfield; *Production:* Hilda Smith; *Publicity:* Trisha Mbanga
Subsidiary Companies: Galaxie Press (1974) (Pvt) Ltd (qv); Scholastic Books (Pvt) Ltd
Associate Companies: Macmillan Publishers Ltd, UK (qv); Teachers Forum (Pvt) Ltd, Harare
Imprints: Scholastic Books, Ventures
Branch Offs: PO Box 298, Bulawayo; PO Box 963, Mutare; PO Box 1239, Gweru; PO Box 355, Masvingo
Subjects: Educational titles for Zimbabwe and Africa generally, General Interest titles for Zimbabwe
1981: 8 titles *1982:* 44 titles *Founded:* 1968
ISBN Publisher's Prefix: 0-86925

M O Collins (Pvt) Ltd, PO Box 3094, Dublin House, Victoria St/Albion Rd, Harare Tel: 704719
Man Dir: Brig M O Collins
Subjects: Atlases
Founded: 1965
ISBN Publisher's Prefix: 0-86919

Peter Dearlove Publishers*, PO Box UA 106, Harare
Man Dir: Peter Dearlove
Subjects: General Non-fiction, Biography, History, Africana, Paperbacks, Social Science

Flame Lily, an imprint of The Literature Bureau (qv)

Galaxie Press (Pvt) Ltd*, PO Box 3041, Harare
Parent Company: The College Press (Pvt) Ltd (qv)

Gemini Publishers, PO Box 49, Mount Pleasant, Harare Tel: 701515
Secretary: C Grill
Subjects: Science Fiction, Poetry
1982: 2 titles

Government Printerature, PO Box 8062, Causeway, Harare

The **Literature Bureau**, Ministry of Education and Culture, PO Box 8137, Causeway, Harare Tel: 26929 Cable Add: Litburo
Acting Chief Publications Officer: D B Hlazo; *Senior Editorial Officer:* O Chiromo (Shona); P Mpofu (Ndebele)
Imprint: Flame Lily
Branch Off: PO Box 555, Bulawayo
Subjects: General Fiction & Non-fiction, Belles Lettres, Poetry, Biography, History, Africana, How-to, Study Guides, Books in Shona, Ndebele and English
Book Clubs: Shona Readers' Book Club, Ndebele Readers' Book Club
Bookshop: See under Major Booksellers
Founded: 1954
Miscellaneous: Formerly Rhodesia Literature Bureau
ISBN Publisher's Prefix: 0-86926

Longman Zimbabwe (Pvt) Ltd, PO Box ST125, Southerton, Harare Tel: 62711/2/3/4 Cable Add: Longman Harare Zimbabwe
Man Dir, Marketing Manager: S G Mpofu; *General Manager:* D R Mackenzie; *Publishing Manager, Rights & Permissions:* Marilyn Poole; *Publicity:* Sue McMillan
Associate Company: Longman Group Ltd, UK (qv)
Subjects: General Fiction & Non-fiction, Belles Lettres, Poetry, Biography, History, Africana, Juveniles, Books in Shona and Ndebele, Paperbacks, General & Social Science, Secondary & Primary Textbooks
1981-82: 37 titles *Founded:* 1964
ISBN Publisher's Prefix: 0-582

Mambo Press, PO Box 779, Gweru Tel: 4016/3806
Man Dir: Albert Plangger; *Sales Manager:* James Amrein
Branch Offs: Speke Ave/First St, PB 66002 Kopje, Harare Tel: 705899; Masvingo,

PB 9213, Gokomere Tel: 2519-12
Subjects: General Fiction & Non-fiction, Poetry, Religion, Books in Shona, Ndebele and English, Secondary & Primary Textbooks
Bookshops: See under Major Booksellers
Founded: 1958
ISBN Publisher's Prefix: 0-86922

Mimosa Publishers*, PO Box GD 135, Greendale, Harare Tel: 2068119
Man Dir: Anthony S Coetsee; *Editorial:* Gillian Coetsee; *Sales:* Penny Coetsee; *Production:* Patrick S Coetsee; *Publicity:* Rosemary Anne Coetsee
Subject: Fiction
Founded: 1975

Oxford University Press East Africa, Rooms 317-20, Roslin House, Baker Ave, PO Box 3892, Harare Tel: 27848 Cable Add: Oxonian
Publicity: Mrs A W Harvey
Subjects: General Non-fiction, Belles Lettres, Poetry, Biography, History, Africana, Books in Shona & other Zimbabwean Languages, Secondary Textbooks, Music, Prayer Books
Founded: 1915
ISBN Publisher's Prefix: 0-19

Publications Central Africa*, PO Box 1027, Bulawayo Tel: 68131/68145 Cable Add: Publishers Telex: 3333 ZW
Subjects: Reference, Annuals, Directories

Scholastic Books, an imprint of The College Press (Pvt) Ltd (qv)

University of Zimbabwe*, Publications Officer, PO Box MP45, Mount Pleasant, Harare Tel: 303211 ext 236 Cable Add: University Telex: 4152 ZW
Subjects: Biography, History, Africana, Philosophy, Reference, Religion, Medicine, Science & Technology, General & Social Science, University Textbooks, Journal *Zambezia*

Ventures, an imprint of The College Press (Pvt) Ltd (qv)

Book Clubs

Books of Zimbabwe Book Club*, 137A Rhodes St (14th, 15th Aves), PO Box 1994, Bulawayo
Owned by: Books of Zimbabwe Publishing Co (Pvt) Ltd, Bulawayo (qv)
Subjects: Reproduction of scarce early Rhodesiana/Africana, New Zimbabwean Writing
Founded: 1968

Ndebele Readers' Book Club, Box 8137, Causeway, Harare Tel: 26929 Cable Add: Litburo
Sponsored by: The Literature Bureau (qv)
Subject: Ndebele Literature
Members: 375
Founded: 1978

Shona Readers' Book Club, Box 8137, Causeway, Harare Tel: 26929 Cable Add: Litburo
Sponsored by: The Literature Bureau (qv)
Subject: Shona literature
Members: 331
Founded: 1978

Major Booksellers

Adventist Book Centre*, 114 Jameson St, PO Box 573, Bulawayo Tel: 61845

Alpha Books*, PO Box 1056, Harare Tel: 22553
Manager: L Craven

Baptist Book Centre, PO Box 831, Gweru (Located at: 5th Street, Mandis Bldg, Gweru) Tel: (154) 4242
Manager: Shayne T Masimira

Belmont Press, PO Box 31, Masvingo Tel: 2633
Managers: D G Hill, D Pender
Also printers, stationers, office suppliers

Book Centre, PO Box 3799, Harare (Located at: Gordon Ave and Angwa St, Harare) Tel: 704621 Cable Add: textbook
Miscellaneous: This bookshop is associated with Books of Africa (qv under Publishers, Republic of South Africa)

The **Book Exchange***, 57 Stanley Ave, Harare Tel: 22468

Evans Shepherd*, PO Box 36, Harare Tel: 702531

Kingstons Ltd*, PO Box 2374, Harare Tel: 700526
Wholesaler, also retailer with 7 branches

The **Literature Bureau**, PO Box 8137, Causeway, Harare (Located at: Electra House, Jameson Ave, Harare) Tel: 26929 Cable Add: Litburo
Wholesale and retail distributors, also Publisher (qv)

Mambo Press Bookshop*, Speke Ave/First St, PB 66002, Kopje, Harare Tel: 705899
Also: PO Box 779 Gweru
Owned by: Mambo Press (qv)

Matopo Book Centre, PO Box 554, Bulawayo Tel: (19) 71152
Manager: Agrippa V Masiye

National Books of Zimbabwe, PO Box 2020, Bulawayo (Located at: Africa House, Fife St/10th Ave, Bulawayo) Tel: (19) 74921/67507
Manager: P T O Trumper

National Books of Zimbabwe, PO Box 4828, Harare Tel: 703257
(Apex Holdings (Pvt) Ltd trade under the above name)
General Manager: J H Felgate
Owned by: Apex Corporation of Zimbabwe

Townsend & Co (Pvt) Ltd*, PO Box 3281, Harare Tel: 24611/26679
Manager: D Evans

Major Libraries

Roger **Bone** Library, Hillside Teachers' College, Cecil Ave, PB 2, Hillside, Bulawayo Tel: 42283

Bulawayo Municipal Libraries, PO Box 2292, Bulawayo Tel: 70111

Bulawayo Public Library, PO Box 586, Bulawayo Tel: Bulawayo 60966
Librarian: R W Doust
Publications: Triennial Report; Spectrum: Quarterly Guide to new books

Harare City Library, PO Box 1087, Harare Tel: 704921
Librarian: Mrs M Ross-Smith

Harare Polytechnic Library*, Causeway, PO Box 8074, Harare Tel: 705951
Librarian: Mrs D M Thorpe

Library of Parliament, PO Box 8055, Causeway, Harare Tel: 700181 ext 230/231
Librarian: W H C Gurure

National Archives, Pvt Bag 7729, Causeway, Harare Tel: 792741
Dir: Mrs A S Kamba
Publications include: Zimbabwe National Bibliography; Directory of Zimbabwean Libraries

National Free Library of Zimbabwe, Twelfth Ave, PO Box 1773, Bulawayo Tel: 62359/69827 Telex: 3128
Librarian: N Johnson
Publication: Shelfmark

Queen Victoria Memorial Library, now Harare City Library (qv)

Turner Memorial Library*, Queen's Way Civic Complex, PO Box 48, Mutare Tel: 63412
Librarian: B M Jarvis

University of Zimbabwe Library, PO Box MP45, Mount Pleasant, Harare Tel: 303211 Cable Add: University Telex: 4152 Univ Z Zw
Librarian: S Made

Library Association

Zimbabwe Library Association*, PO Box 3133, Harare
Honorary Secretary: Miss R Molam
Publication: The Zimbabwean Librarian

Library Reference Books and Journals

Book

Directory of Zimbabwean Libraries, National Archives, Pvt Bag 7729, Causeway, Harare

Journal

The Zimbabwean Librarian, Zimbabwe Library Association, PO Box 3133, Harare

Literary Associations and Societies

P E N Centre of Zimbabwe, PO Box 1900, Harare
Secretary: Nora S Kane, 4 Avonfriars, Oxford Rd, Avondale, Harare

Poetry Society of Zimbabwe*, PO Box A70, Avondale, Harare
Secretary: Miss J Glendinning

Writer's Club, PO Box 768, Harare
Secretaries: Patricia Coulton, Dot Korni

Shona/Ndebele Writers' Association*, PO Box 7009, Mzilikazi
Secretary: Mrs J G Sibanda

Literary Periodicals

Moto, PO Box 779, Gweru (A political, cultural and religious weekly originally published by Mambo Press in 1958, with contributions in English and Shona. It was banned for some years, but publication recommenced in January 1980.)

Two Tone, PO Box MP79, Mount Pleasant, Harare. Poems published in English, Ndebele and Shona (with English translations)

Literary Prizes

The **Literature Bureau** Annual Literary Award
500 Zimbabwe dollars for the best works in Shona and Ndebele. Most genres, including translations, qualify for entry. Enquiries to The Literature Bureau, PO Box 8137, Causeway, Harare

Longman Zimbabwe Literary Awards*
The awards are for outstanding published works in English, Shona or Sindebele by residents of Zimbabwe. Three awards each of 200 Zimbabwe dollars, one in respect of each language. Enquiries to P E N Centre of Zimbabwe, PO Box 1900, Harare

International Section

Copyright Conventions

The Universal Copyright Convention was sponsored by UNESCO in 1952. It states that 'Each signatory country extends to foreign works covered by UCC the same protection which such country extends to works of its own nationals published within its own borders'.

The Berne Convention is a system of international copyright which is maintained among countries which have become signatories to the International Copyright Union for the Protection of Literary and Artistic Works. This Union plan, which was first agreed upon at Berne, Switzerland, in 1888, has been subject to revisions every 20 years. The basic principle of the agreement is that any work properly copyrighted in its country of origin has protection in every Union country. Any work originating in a non-Union country, if it is simultaneously published in a Union country has the same standing as it would if it had originated in a Union country. Since different countries have different relationships under one or more of the revisions (Paris, 1896; Berlin, 1908; Rome, 1928; Brussels, 1948; and Stockholm, 1968), persons interested in obtaining information, including application of the various provisions to territorial areas, should consult the Bureau de l'union internationale pour la protection des oeuvres littéraires et artistiques, 32 chemin des Colombettes, Geneva, Switzerland.

The Florence Agreement, also known as the 'free flow of books', is a UNESCO-sponsored international agreement aimed at easing the flow of books and other scientific, educational and cultural materials, through the elimination or reduction of tariffs and other barriers.

The Buenos Aires Convention: In most Latin-American countries, compliance with the copyright law of the country of first publication protects the work in other countries of the Buenos Aires Convention, 1910. To secure copyright, each work must carry a notice to the effect that any use of the book or article will not be permitted without the consent of the copyright owner, and that copyright is reserved in English or any other language; for complete safety it is advised to add 'All rights reserved'. A later revision of the Buenos Aires Convention was made at the Washington Conference (Pan-American Copyright Convention) of 1946 which goes into greater detail than the Buenos Aires Convention. This Convention has been ratified by Argentina, Bolivia, Brazil, Chile, Costa Rica, Cuba, Dominican Republic, Ecuador, Guatemala, Haiti, Honduras, Mexico, Nicaragua and Paraguay

International Organizations

International Book Trade, Literary and Library Organizations

ACURIL*, Box S, University Station, San Juan, Puerto Rico 00931 Tel: (809) 7640000 ext 3319
Association of Caribbean University, Research and Institutional Libraries
General Secretary: Oneida R Ortiz;
President: (1982-83) Ivonne Stephenson (Librarian, University of Guyana, Turkeyen, Georgetown, Guyana)
Publications: ACURIL Newsletter; Proceedings of Annual Conference; CARINDEX (Indexing Committee — English)

AIBDA, c/o IICA-CIDIA, 7170 Turrialba, Costa Rica
Inter-American Association of Agricultural Librarians and Documentalists
Secretary-Treasurer: Ana María Paz de Erickson
Publications: AIBDA Actualidades (irregular, free to members); *Bibliografía Agrícola Latinoamericana* (up to 1975); *Boletín Informativo, Boletín Técnico* (up to 1979); *Boletín Especial* (these three bulletins sent free to members); *Informe RIBDA; Revista Aibda* (twice yearly); *Páginas de Contenido: Ciencias de la Información* (quarterly, free to members)

Arab Regional Branch of the International Council on Archives*, Dr Salah Abdel-Sabour, President, c/o The National Library, Midan Ahmed Maher (Post Office), Bab El-Khalq, Cairo, Egypt
Secretary General: M J Abdusalim (Sudan)

Asociación Interamericana de Bibliotecarios y Documentalistas Agrícolas, see AIBDA

Asociación Latinoamericana de Escuelas de Bibliotecología y Ciencias de la Información (ALEBCI), Universidad Javeriana, Dep de Ciencia de la Info, Carrera 7a 40-62, Bogotá, Colombia Tel: 2854912
Latin American Association of Schools of Library and Information Science
Secretary: Ms O Rogas
Publications: ALEBCI; Boletín Informativo

Association des Bibliothèques Internationales*, c/o Library, United Nations, Palais des Nations, CH-1211 Geneva 10, Switzerland
Association of International Libraries
President: Th Dimitrov
Publication: Newsletter

Association for the Promotion of the International Circulation of the Press, Beethovenstr 20, CH-8002 Zürich, Switzerland
Association pour la Promotion de la Diffusion Internationale de la Presse
Vereinigung zur Förderung des internationalen Pressevertriebes
President: Josette Boveri (Milan); *Man Dir:* Arnold Kaulich

Association internationale de Bibliophilie, c/o Bibliothèque nationale, 58 rue de Richelieu, F-75084 Paris cedex 02, France
This is a book collectors' association
Secretary-General: Antoine Coron
Publication: Le Bulletin du Bibliophile (quarterly)

Association internationale des Critiques littéraires, see International Association of Literary Critics

Association internationale des Documentalistes et Techniciens de l'Information AID*, 74 rue des Saints-Pères, F-75007 Paris, France
International Association of Documentalists and Information Officers
General Secretary: Dr Jacques Samain
Publication: Bulletin

Association of International Libraries (AIL)*, c/o United Nations Library, CH-1211 Geneva 10, Switzerland Tel: 366011/310211 Telex: 289696
Secretary: O Cerny

Association of Libraries of Judaica and Hebraica in Europe*, Bibliothèque de l'Alliance Israelite Universelle, 45 rue La Bruyère, F-75425 Paris, France
Chairman: Georges Weill
Publication: Annual newsletter

Bibliographical Society of Australia and New Zealand (BSANZ), GPO Box 419, Adelaide, SA 5001, Australia
Secretary: Helen M Thomson
Publications: Bibliographical Society of Australia and New Zealand Bulletin; Broadsheet; occasional publications

Centre régional de Promotion du Livre en Afrique (CREPLA)*, BP 1646, Yaoundé, Cameroun Tel: 224782/222936
Regional Centre for Book Promotion in Africa (co-sponsored by UNESCO)
Secretary: William Moutchia
Publication: Bulletin

Centro Regional para el Fomento del Libro en América Latina y el Caribe (CERLAL), Calle 70 No 9-52, Apdo Aereo 17438, Bogotá, Colombia Tel: 2495141/2554574 Cable Add: Cerlal

Regional Centre for Encouragement of Books in Latin America and Caribbean
Director: Jaime Jaramillo Uribe; *Secretary-General:* Lucila de Jiménez
Publications: CERLAL: noticias sobre el Libro y Bibliografía (news on books and bibliographies); *Boletín Bibliográfico del CERLAL* (current Latin-American bibliography)

The **Commonwealth** Library Association, c/o Church Teachers' College, PO Box 41, Mandeville, Manchester, Jamaica
Secretary: Joan E Swaby
Publication: COMLA Newsletter (quarterly), published from Marine Parade Library, Marine Parade Rd, Singapore 1544, Republic of Singapore

Congress of South-East Asian Librarians IV (CONSAL IV)*, Thai Library Association, 273-275 Viphavadee Rangsit Rd, Phayathai, Bangkok 10400, Thailand Tel: 2783439/2790773
Chairman: Mrs Maenmas Chavalit
Publications include: Proceedings of Congresses on Regional Co-operation for the Development of National Information Services

Conseil international des Associations de Bibliothèques de Théologie, Kardinal-Fringsstr 1-3, Postfach 100690, Cologne 1, Federal Republic of Germany
International Council of Theological Library Associations
Secretary: J A Cervelló-Margalef

East and Central Africa Regional Branch of the International Council of Archives (ECARBICA)*, c/o Kenya National Archives, PO Box 49210, Nairobi, Kenya Tel: 26007/28020/28959 Cable Add: Archives
Publication: ECARBICA Journal

European Association for the Promotion of Poetry, Boskantstr 30, B-3200 Leuven, Belgium Tel: (016) 235351/254788
General Secretary: E Van Itterbeek
Publications: TT (trimestrial poetry review); *Leuvende cahiers* (European series)

European Association of Directory Publishers*, rue Antoine Dansaert 42, B-1000 Brussels, Belgium Tel: 5124499
Association Européene des Editeurs d'Annuaires
Europäischer Adressbuchverleger-Verband
President: Dr Marini; *Secretary-General:* Jean Lerat

F I D, see International Federation for Documentation

Fédération internationale des Libraires (FIL), see International Booksellers Federation

Fédération internationale des Traducteurs (FIT), Heiveldstr 245, B-9110 Gent/Sint-Amandsberg, Belgium
International Federation of Translators
Secretary-General: Dr Rene Haeseryn

Groupe des Editeurs de Livres de la CEE, 111 ave du Parc, B-1060 Brussels, Belgium Tel: (02) 5382167
EEC Book Publishers Group

I B B Y, see International Board on Books for Young People

I S B N, see International ISBN Agency

I S S N, see International Serial Data System

Intergovernmental Copyright Committee, see United Nations Educational, Scientific and Cultural Organization

International Association for Mass Communication Research, c/o Professor J D Halloran, Centre for Mass Communication Research, University of Leicester, 104 Regent Road, Leicester LE1 7LT, UK Tel: (0533) 555557
Association internationale des études et recherches sur l'information
Administrative Secretary: Peggy Gray
Publications include: Mass Media and Socialization; Mass Media and Man's View of Society; Mass Media and National Cultures; New Structures of International Communication: The Role of Research

International Association of Agricultural Librarians and Documentalists — IAALD*, 3 Burlescoombe Leas, Southend-on-Sea, Essex SS1 3QF, UK Tel: (01) 937 8191 ext 276 Telex: 262318
Association Internationale des Bibliothécaires et Documentalistes Agricoles
Secretary-Treasurer: Miss P J Wortley
Publications: Quarterly Bulletin; Current Agricultural Serials; Primer for Agricultural Libraries

International Association of Law Libraries (IALL)*, c/o Vanderbilt Law Library, Nashville, Tennessee 37203, USA
Association internationale des bibliothèques de droit
Treasurer: Professor Arno Liivak; *President:* Professor Igor I Kavass; *Secretary:* Adolf Sprudzs
Publications: International Journal of Legal Information; Directory (every three years)

International Association of Literary Critics, 38 rue du Faubourg St Jacques, F-75014 Paris, France
Association internationale des Critiques littéraires (NGO)
President: Robert André
Publication: Revue

International Association of Metropolitan City Libraries (INTAMEL), Gemeentebibliotheek Rotterdam, Hoogstr 110, 3011 PV Rotterdam, Netherlands

International Association of Music Libraries, Archives and Documentation Centres (IAML), c/o Music Library/Hornbake Library, University of Maryland, College Park, Maryland 20742, USA
Association internationale des bibliothèques, archives et centres de documentation musicaux (AIBM)
Internationale Vereinigung der Musikbibliotheken, Musikarchive und Musikdokumentations zentren (IVMB)
President: Anders Lönn (Musikaliska akademiens bibliotek, Stockholm); *Secretary-General:* Neil Ratliff
Publication: Fontes artis musicae

International Association of Orientalist Librarians*
Secretary-Treasurer: John E Leide, c/o Asian Studies Program, University of Hawaii at Manoa, 315 Moore Hall, 1890 East-West Road, Honolulu, Hawaii 96822, USA
Publication: International Association of Orientalist Librarians Bulletin (half-yearly)

International Association of School Librarianship, School of Librarianship, Western Michigan University, Kalamazoo, Michigan 49008, USA Tel: (616) 3831849
Executive Secretary: Ms J Lowrie
Publications: Newsletter of the International Association of School Librarianship (quarterly to members); *Annual Conference Proceedings; Directory of National School Library Associations; People to Contact for Visiting School Libraries/Media Centers*

International Association of Scholarly Publishers (IASP), c/o Universitetsforlaget, Postboks 2959, Tøyen, Oslo 6, Norway Tel: (472) 276060
President: Edvard Aslaksen
Publication: Newsletter
Founded: 1972

International Association of Technological University Libraries (IATUL), c/o Dr Sven Westberg, Chief Librarian, Chalmers Tekniska Høgskolas Bibliotek, S-41296 Gothenburg, Sweden Tel: (31) 810100 Telex: 2369 Chalbib
Secretary: Dr Sven Westberg
Publications: IATUL Proceedings; IATUL Conference Proceedings

International Board on Books for Young People (IBBY), Leonhardsgraben 38a, CH-4051 Basle, Switzerland Tel: (061) 253404
Secretary: Mrs Leena Maissen
Publications: Bookbird (quarterly); *20 Years of IBBY; IBBY's International Guide to Sources of Information about Children's Literature; Congress Reports;* Book lists

International Booksellers Federation (IBF), A-1010 Vienna, Grünangergasse 4, Austria Tel: (0222) 521535 Cable Add: Buchverein Wien Att IBF
Fédération internationale des Librairies (FIL)
Internationale Buchhändler-Vereinigung (IBV)
General Secretary: Dr Gerhard Prosser; *President:* Michael G Zifcak
Publications include: The Maintained Price of Books; The Image of the Bookseller; Books and their Prices; Book, Book Trade and Society; What is IBF?

International Center for the Registration of Serials, see International Serial Data System

International Comparative Literature Association, Institut de littérature comparée, Université de la Sorbonne-Nouvelle (Paris-III), 17 rue de la Sorbonne, F-75005 Paris, France
Association internationale de littérature comparée
Secretaries-General: Prof Yves Chevrel, Université de Paris-Sorbonne, 1 rue Victor-Cousin, F-75230 Paris cedex 05, France; Prof Gerald Gillespie, Stanford University, Stanford, California 94305, USA
Publications: ICLA Bulletin, AILC Information
Founded: 1954

International Confederation of Societies of Authors and Composers*, 11 rue Keppler, F-75116 Paris, France
Confédération internationale des sociétés d'auteurs et compositeurs
Secretary-General: Jean-Alexis Ziegler
Publication: Interauteurs

International Copyright Union for the Protection of Literary and Artistic Works, now World Intellectual Property Organization (WIPO) (qv)

International Council of Theological Library Associations, see Conseil international des Associations de Bibliothèques de Théologie

International Council on Archives, 60 rue des Francs-Bourgeois, F-75003 Paris, France Tel: (1) 2771130
Conseil international des archives
Executive Secretary: Dr Charles Kecskemeti
Publications: Archivum; ADPA/Archives and Automation; Bulletin of the Microfilm Committee; Bulletin of the ICA; Bulletin of the Business Archives Committee; CAD Information, Bulletin of the Commission for Archival Development

International Federation for Documentation (FID), PO Box 90402, 2509 LK, The Hague, Netherlands Tel: (070) 140671
Fédération internationale de documentation
Publications: FID News Bulletin; International Forum on Information and Documentation; R & D Projects in Documentation and Librarianship; FID Directory; Annual Report; Extensions and Corrections to the UDC (annual); Proceedings of Congresses and Seminars, UDC editions in several languages, Studies on Information Science, Manuals, Bibliographies and Directories

International Federation of Film Archives, Coudenberg 70, B-1000 Brussels, Belgium Tel: (02) 5111390
Fédération internationale des archives du film (FIAF)
Executive Secretary: Brigitte van der Elst
Publications include: International Index to Film and TV Periodicals (annual); *A Handbook for Film Archives; International Directory to Film and TV Documentation Sources; Cinema 1900-1906, an analytical study*

International Federation of Library Associations and Institutions (IFLA), c/o The Royal Library, Postbus 95312, 2509 CH, The Hague, Netherlands Tel: (70) 140884 Telex: 34402
Fédération internationale des associations de bibliothécaires et des bibliothèques
Secretary-General: Miss M Wijnstroom
Publications: IFLA Journal including *IFLA News, IFLA Annual, IFLA Directory, IFLA Publications* (series of monographs, published by K G Saur KG, Federal Republic of Germany (qv))

International Federation for Modern Languages and Literatures, The Queen's University of Belfast, Belfast BT7 1NN, UK Tel: (0232) 245133
Secretary-General: Prof D A Wells
Publication: Proceedings of the Triennial Congresses
Founded: 1928

International Fiction Association*, Department of German and Russian, University of New Brunswick, Fredericton, New Brunswick, Canada
Publication: The International Fiction Review (bi-annual)

International Group of Scientific, Technical and Medical Publishers (STM), Keizersgracht 462, 1016 GE Amsterdam, Netherlands Tel: (020) 225214
Secretary-General: P Nijhoff Asser

International Institute for Children's Literature and Reading Research (UNESCO category C), A-1040 Vienna, Mayerhofgasse 6, Austria Tel: 650359
Institut International de Littérature pour Enfants et de Recherches sur la Lecture
Director: Dr Lucia Binder
Publications include: Bookbird; Jugend und Buch; PA-Kontakte

International Institute of Iberoamerican Literature, 1312 CL, University of Pittsburgh, Pa 15260, USA
Secretary-Treasurer: Keith A McDuffie
Publications: Revista Iberoamericana; Memorias

International ISBN Agency, Staatsbibliothek Preussischer Kulturbesitz, Potsdamerstr 33, Postfach 1407, D-1000 Berlin 30, Federal Republic of Germany
This is the international ISBN office. For national offices and further details please see the ISBN System section of this book
Publications: User's Manual, ISBN Review, International ISBN Publishers' Directory

International League of Antiquarian Booksellers (ILAB), c/o Antiquarian Booksellers Association, Book House, East Hill, Wandsworth, London SW18 2QZ, UK Tel: (01) 870 8259
President: John Lawson; *Secretary:* Dr Leona Rosenberg, 40 East 88th St, PO Box 188, Gracie Station, New York, NY 10028, USA

International Publishers Association, 3 ave de Miremont, CH-1206 Geneva, Switzerland Tel: (022) 463018 Cable Add: Inpublass
Secretary-General: J Alexis Koutchoumow
Publications: IPA Publishing News; Freedom to Publish (La Liberté de Publication) by Peter Calvocoressi; *Roadmap for the Electronic Publisher* by Dr J Kist
Founded: 1896

International Reading Association, 800 Barksdale Rd, PO Box 8139, Newark, Delaware 19714, USA Tel: (302) 7311600 Cable Add: Reading Newark Delaware

International Scientific Film Library (ISFL)*, 31 rue Vautier, B-1040 Brussels, Belgium
Cinémathèque scientifique internationale
Director-Curator: P Bormans
Publications: Catalogue of Films Deposited; The Pioneers of the Scientific Cinema (series)
Founded: 1961

International Serial Data System*, 20 rue Bachaumont, F-75002 Paris, France Tel: (01) 2367381/5089837 Telex: 680047
The International Center for the Registration of Serials, which administers the International Standard Serial Number (ISSN) system, is at the above address

International Study Group of Restorers of Archives, Libraries and Graphic Reproductions, Geschäftsstelle der IADA, Postfach 540, 3550 Marburg, Federal Republic of Germany Tel: (06421) 25078
Internationale Arbeitsgemeinschaft der Archiv-, Bibliotheks-und Grafikrestauratoren
General Secretary: Ludwig Ritterpusch
Publications: IADA-Mitteilungen, in: Maltechnik

International Translations Centre, Doelenstr 101, 2611 NS Delft, Netherlands
The object of the Centre is to encourage, improve and facilitate the use of literature published in less accessible languages and of interest to science and industry, and also to promote international co-operation in this field
Director of Centre: D van Bergeijk
Publications: World Transindex; Journals in Translation; Database WTI

International Youth Library*, D-8000 Munich 22, Kaulbachstr 11a, Federal Republic of Germany
Internationale Jugendbibliothek
Publications: Catalogues of various exhibitions; *Prize Book Catalogue; The Best of the Best; Bewältigung der Gegenwart? Das Porträt der Frau in der zeitgenössischen Jugendliteratur*

Internationale Buchhändler-Vereinigung (IBV), see International Booksellers Federation

Ligue des Bibliothèques Européennes de Recherche (LIBER), c/o Dr Roland Mathys, Zentralbibliothek Zürich, Zahringerplatz 6, Postfach 8025, Zurich, Switzerland
League of European Research Libraries
President: Gerhard Munthe
Publication: LIBER Bulletin

Library Luxembourg, Commission of the European Communities, Bâtiment Jean Monnet, BP 1907, Luxembourg, Grand Duchy of Luxembourg Tel: 43011 Telex: 3423/3446 Comeur Lux

Middle East Librarians Association*, Room 310, Main Library, Ohio State University, 1858 Neil Avenue Mall, Columbus, Ohio 43210, USA Tel: (614) 4223362
Publication: MELA Notes (three times a year)

Nordisk Musikforleggerunion*, Gothersgade 9-11, DK-1123, Copenhagen, Denmark
Also: Postboks 1499, Vika, Oslo, Norway
Nordic Music Publishers Union

Nordisk Vitenskapelig Bibliotekarforbund*, c/o The Royal Swedish Academy of Sciences, S-10505 Stockholm, Sweden Tel: (08) 155534
Scandinavian Association of Research Librarians
President: P M Bryhn, Universitetsbiblioteket i Oslo, Drammensveien 42, Oslo 2, Norway
Publications: Monographs, Guides (available from Bibliotekcentralen, Telegrafvej 5, DK-2750 Ballerup, Denmark)

Organization of American States*, Office of Publications, 17th Street and Constitution Ave, NW Washington, DC 20006, USA
There are OAS offices/bookstores in 31 countries outside the USA
Subjects: Development of American Nations (Regional, Social, Historical), Bibliography, Cultural Affairs, Economics, Education, Human Rights, Law, Sciences, Statistics, Periodicals
ISBN Publisher's Prefix: 0-8270

International P E N, 38 King St, London WC2E 8JT, UK Tel: (01) 379 7939
A World Association of Writers
General-Secretary: Alexandre Blokh
Publications: International PEN Bulletin (in English and French, with the assistance of UNESCO); various regional bulletins

Bibliothèque du **Parlement** Européen, Centre Européen, Luxembourg, Grand Duchy of Luxembourg Tel: 43001 Telex: 3494/2894 Euparl Lu

The **Penman** Club, 175 Pall Mall, Leigh-on-Sea, Essex SS9 1RE, UK Tel: Southend-on-Sea 74438 (STD Code 0702)
Secretary: Leonard G Stubbs
Literary advice, criticism

INTERNATIONAL ORGANIZATIONS 469

Private Libraries Association (PLA), Ravelston, South View Rd, Pinner, Middlesex, UK
An international society of book collectors
Executive Secretary: Frank Broomhead
Publications include: The Private Library (official journal); *Newsletter*

S E L T A, see Swedish-English Literary Translators' Association

S T M, see International Group of Scientific, Technical and Medical Publishers

Scandinavian Association of Directory Publishers (SADP), Tordenskioldsgt 4, Oslo 1, Norway Tel: (02) 412335
President: K Bryde

Seminar on the Acquisition of Latin American Library Materials (SALALM), SALALM Secretariat, Memorial Library, University of Wisconsin-Madison, Madison, Wisconsin 53706, USA Tel: (608) 2623240
Executive Secretary: Suzanne Hodgman
Publications: Newsletter; Papers; Microfilming Projects Newsletter; Bibliography Series

Société internationale de Bibliographie classique, 11 ave René Coty, F-75014 Paris, France
General Secretary: Juliette Ernst Tel: 3276790
Publication: L'Année philologique (Bibliographie de l'antiquité gréco-latine 1924 ss)

Société internationale des Bibliothèques-Musées des Arts du Spectacle (SIBMAS)*, 1 rue de Sully, 75004 Paris, France Tel: 2774421
International Society of Libraries and Museums for the Performing Arts
Publications: L'Information du Spectacle; Bibliothèques et Musées des Arts du Spectacle dans le Monde (both France)

Southeast Asian Regional Branch of the International Council on Archives (SARBICA), c/o National Archives of Malaysia, Jalan Duta, Kuala Lumpur, Malaysia Tel: 943244
Chairman: Luis Cordero (Philippines)
Publications: Southeast Asian Archives; Southeast Asian Microfilms Newsletter; Masterlist of Southeast Asian Microforms

Standing Conference of African University Libraries (SCAUL)*, c/o E Bejide Bankole, University Librarian, University of Lagos, PO Box 46, Yaba, Lagos, Nigeria
Publication: SCAUL Newsletter

Standing Conference on Library Materials on Africa (SCOLMA), c/o Institute of Commonwealth Studies, 27 Russell Sq, London WC1B 5DS, UK Tel: (01) 580 5876
Publication: African Research and Documentation (Subscriptions to Subscriptions Manager, University Library, University of Birmingham, Birmingham B15 2TT, UK)

Swedish-English Literary Translators' Association (SELTA), 7 Lyndhurst Gardens, London N3 1TA, UK Tel: (01) 349 0140
Hon Secretary: Tom Geddes
SELTA aims to promote the publication of Swedish literature in English and to represent the interests of those involved in its translation
Publication: Swedish Book Review (bi-annual)

Union des Editeurs de Langue française*, 35 rue Grégoire de Tours, F-75279 Paris cedex 06, France
Union of French-language Publishers

Union of Writers of the African Peoples*, c/o National Association of Writers, PO Box 2738, Accra, Ghana
Union des Ecrivains Negro Africains
Secretary-General: Wole Soyinka, Dept of Literature, University of Ife, Ife-Ife, Nigeria
Objectives include the operation of a writers' publishing co-operative and the encouragement of the use of Swahili as the common language of all black African peoples.
Publication: African World Alternatives

United Nations Economic Commission for Africa Library, PO Box 3001, Addis Ababa, Ethiopia Tel: 447200 Cable Add: Eca Telex: 21029
Librarian: Abdel-Rahman M Tahir

West African University Booksellers Association, c/o The General Secretary's Office, University Bookshop, PO Box 1, University of Ghana, Legon, Ghana Tel: 75381 ext 8827
Secretary: S O Cofie

World Intellectual Property Organization (WIPO), 34 chemin des Colombettes, CH-1211 Geneva 20, Switzerland Tel: (022) 999111 Cable Add: Ompi Telex: 22376 Ompi
Organisation Mondiale de la Propriété Intellectuelle
Director General: Dr Arpad Bogsc
Administers, among other conventions, the Berne Convention for the Protection of Literary and Artistic Works. Its library, specializing in intellectual property, is open to the public
Publications: Le Droit d'Auteur; La Propriété industrielle; Les Marques internationales

United Nations Agencies with Publishing Activities

Asian Cultural Centre for Unesco, 6 Fukuromachi, Shinjuku-ku, Tokyo 162, Japan Tel: (269) 4435 Cable Add: Asculcentre Tokyo
Executive Dir: Taichi Sasaoka
Founded: 1971

Food and Agriculture Organization of the United Nations (FAO), Via delle Terme di Caracalla, I-00100 Rome, Italy Tel: (06) 5797 Cable Add: Foodagri Rome
Director-General: E Saouma; *Chief Editor:* K H Richmond; *Sales, Advertising & Publicity Dir:* C Beauchamp
Subjects: Agriculture, World Food Situation, Economics & Statistics, Fisheries, Forestry & Forest Products, Nutrition, Legislation, Educational Materials
Founded: 1945
A specialized agency of the United Nations, the Food and Agriculture Organization was created in 1945. Since the purpose of FAO is to increase world agricultural production and raise the standard of living, all its publications are directed toward that goal. The FAO titles consist of monographs, periodicals, official records of the work of FAO, yearbooks and annuals — in sum, what the FAO describes as a 'world intelligence service on production, price and trade that covers almost every commodity used to feed, clothe and house people throughout the world'. Unsolicited manuscripts are automatically rejected. Technical articles of no more than 2,500 words on international aspects of the animal industry, forestry, and food and nutrition are occasionally accepted; no payment is made
ISBN Publisher's Prefixes: 92-5 (publications by Headquarters), 92-851 (African Regional Office), 92-852 (Regional Office for Asia and Far East), 92-853 (European Regional Office), 92-854 (Latin American Regional Office), 92-855 (Near East Regional Office)

International Atomic Energy Agency (IAEA), Vienna International Centre, A-1400 Vienna, Wagramerstr 5, Postfach 100, Austria Tel: 2360 Cable Add: Inatom Vienna
Publications Dir: A K Brown; *Editorial:* R F Kellerher; *Sales, Publicity:* K Fiala; *Production, Rights & Permissions:* W Dietl
Subjects: Life Sciences, Nuclear Safety and Environmental Protection, Physics, Chemistry, Geology and Raw Materials, Reactors and Nuclear Power, Industrial Applications, Miscellaneous
1981: 58 titles *1982:* 50 titles *Founded:* 1957
The International Atomic Energy Agency is an international organization within the United Nations family, having the general purpose of seeking 'to accelerate and enlarge the contribution of atomic energy to peace, health and prosperity throughout the world'. The Agency's publications result, almost exclusively, from its own activities; published material is of intense interest only to a relatively small group of scientists and technicians and, therefore, unlikely to be published commercially.
ISBN Publisher's Prefix: 92-0

International Bureau of Education (IBE), Palais Wilson, CH-1211 Geneva 14, Switzerland Tel: 313735 Cable Add: Intereduc Geneve Telex: 22644
Dir: James B Chandler; *Chief, Publications Unit:* Rodney Stock; *Editorial, Sales, Production, Publicity, Rights & Permissions:* See United Nations Educational, Scientific and Cultural Organization
Orders to: National distributors of Unesco publications, or Unesco, 7 pl de Fontenoy, F-75700 Paris, France
Subject: Comparative Education
Founded: 1925
Founded in 1925 as a private organization, the IBE was given new status in 1929 whereby it became the first inter-governmental organization in the field of education. It became an integral part of UNESCO in 1969, and today serves all 159 Member States of the Organization as a centre of comparative education.

International Institute for Educational Planning (IIEP)*, 7-9 rue Eugène-Delacroix, F-75016 Paris, France Tel: (01) 5042822 Cable Add: Eduplan Paris Telex: 620074
Dir: Sylvain Lourié; *Publications Officer:* John Hall
Subjects: Economics of education, costs and financing; administration and management of education (including statistics, methodologies, techniques and models); curriculum development and evaluation (including the qualitative aspects of education); manpower and employment; educational technology; etc
1981: 20 titles *Founded:* 1963
Established by UNESCO, IIEP is an international centre for advanced training and research in educational planning. The

Institute's aim is to contribute to the development of education by expanding both knowledge and the supply of competent professionals in the field of educational planning. In this endeavour the Institute cooperates with interested training and research institutions throughout the world. IIEP is financed by UNESCO and by voluntary contributions from individual member states. The programme and budget of the Institute is approved by its own Governing Board.
ISBN Publisher's Prefix: 92-803

International Labour Organisation (ILO), International Labour Office, ILO Publications, 4 route des Morillons, CH-1211 Geneva 22, Switzerland Tel: (022) 996111 Cable Add: Interlab Geneva Telex: 22271
Director-General: Francis Blanchard; *Chief, Editorial Services:* R P Payró; *Chief, Marketing & Rights Services:* I M C S Elsmark
Branch Offs: 96-98 Marsham St, London SW1P 4LY, UK; 1750 New York Ave NW, Washington, DC 20006, USA; 75 Albert St, Fuller Bldg, Suite 202, Ottawa, Ontario K1P 5E7, Canada; Hohenzollernstr 21, D-5300 Bonn 2, Federal Republic of Germany
Subjects: Conditions of Work and Welfare, Cooperatives, Developing Countries & Technical Cooperation, Economics, Income Distribution, Intermediate Technology, Employment and Employment Creation, Holidays & Weekly Rest, Human Rights, Labour Standards & Administration, Migration of Workers & Popular Questions, Productivity & Management Development & Training, Occupational Safety & Health, Statistics, Social Security, Trade Unions, Unemployment, Vocational Guidance & Training, Wages & Hours of Work, Worker's Education, Women's questions, Audiovisual material, Microfiches, Periodicals
From the creation of the ILO in 1919, publishing has formed an important part of its activities. The publishing work falls into six main categories: international exchange of factual information; analysis of trends in social affairs; issuing the results of ILO research, including comparative studies as a basis for international cooperation in solving economic and social problems; issuing the required reports for the discussions of international labour conferences leading to the adoption of international labour standards; providing government officials, employers and workers with practical information and guidance; and issuing official records.
This substantial publishing programme has over 1,300 titles in print which cover not only studies, monographs, handbooks, training material and periodicals, but also reports on conditions and practices in different countries prepared for the General Conference, regional conferences and meetings for special industries and subjects.
ISBN Publisher's Prefix: 92-2

International Maritime Organization (IMO), 4 Albert Embankment, London SE1 7SR, UK Tel: (01) 735 7611 Cable Add: Intermar Telex: 04423588
Subjects: Texts of International Maritime Treaties concluded under its auspices, Maritime Technical Publications
1981: 41 titles *1982:* 40 titles
ISBN Publisher's Prefix: 92-801

International Telecommunication Union (ITU), pl des Nations, CH-1211 Geneva 20, Switzerland Tel: 995111 Telex: 421000 Uit Ch
Secretary-General: Richard E Butler
The ITU was founded in 1865 as the International Telegraphic Union. It became the International Telecommunication Union in 1934 and a specialized agency of the UN in 1947. Structure: 4 permanent organs – General Secretariat, International Telegraph and Telephone Consultative Committee (CCITT), International Radio Consultative Committee (CCIR) and the International Frequency Registration Board (IFRB). It encourages world cooperation for the improvement and rational use of telecommunications.
ISBN Publisher's Prefixes: 92-61, 92-71

U N C T A D, see United Nations Conference on Trade and Development

U N E S C O, see United Nations Educational, Scientific and Cultural Organization

U N E S C O Institute for Education (UIE), Feldbrunnenstr 58, D-2000 Hamburg 13, Federal Republic of Germany Tel: (040) 447843 Cable Add: Edinst
Dir: Dr Ravindra H Dave
The UIE was created in 1951 with the financial support of UNESCO and a number of member states. It is funded by the Federal Republic of Germany, UNESCO and other donors, and housed in premises provided by the City of Hamburg. It is a research and dissemination centre which has enabled more than 2,000 scholars to participate in international cooperative research projects and has developed a particular interest in lifelong education. Major areas of the current research programme include the relation of lifelong education to national systems of education, to the curriculum, to learning strategies for neo-literates, teacher training and evaluation. Publications include over 120 titles and the quarterly *International Review of Education*, for which there is a concessionary subscription rate for developing countries. In the field of lifelong education and related aspects, it has published over 20 books under the series of UIE Monographs, Case Studies, Advances in Lifelong Education and UIE Studies on Post-literacy and Continuing Education, based on both theoretical and operational research.
ISBN Publisher's Prefix: 92-820

United Nations, Sales Section, Publishing Division, New York, NY 10017, USA
Chief of Section: Thomas S Hinds
European Office: Palais des Nations, Geneva, Switzerland
Chief of Unit: Roland Furstenberg
Subjects: Reference, Economics, International Trade, International Law, Social Science
Founded: 1945
Since 1946, United Nations has published more than 2,000 reports, studies, annual surveys, yearbooks, and monthly and quarterly periodicals in addition to the United Nations official records. Reflecting the varied work of the Organization, the subjects include international trade, world and regional economic questions, international law, social questions, atomic energy, public administration, and literature concerning the role and activities of the United Nations.
ISBN Publisher's Prefix: 92-1

United Nations Conference on Trade and Development (UNCTAD)*, Palais des Nations, CH-1211 Geneva 10, Switzerland Tel: (022) 346011 Cable Add: Unations Geneve Telex: 289696
Secretary-General: Gamani Corea
Subjects: Trade & Development
Founded: 1964

United Nations Educational, Scientific and Cultural Organization (UNESCO), 7 pl de Fontenoy, F-75700 Paris, France Tel: (01) 5771610 Cable Add: Unesco Paris Telex: 204461 Paris
Director-General: Amadou-Mahtar M'Bow; *Director, The Unesco Press:* Henri Lopes; *Executive Assistants:* Bruce Clark (English), Eduardo Sainz (Spanish), Jean-Luc Joannon (French); *Production:* Rolf Ibach; *Rights & Permissions:* Suzanne Adlung *Director, Copyright Division:* Marie-Claude Dock
Orders to: The Unesco Press, Commercial Services (at above address)
Subjects: Education, Science, Social Science, Culture, Communications
Bookshop: Unesco (at above address)
1981: 118 titles *Founded:* 1946
UNESCO now has more than 1,000 titles in print, intended for specialists in the fields of education, science and technology, social sciences, human rights, libraries, documentation and archives, copyright, culture, art, museums and monuments, and communications. Books are also produced for a broad public with a view to fostering international artistic, intellectual and cultural exchange.
UNESCO acts as Standard Book Numbering Agency, administering ISBNs, for UN publications.
UNESCO maintains responsibility, within its Copyright Division, for the Intergovernmental Copyright Committee.
UNESCO publishes ten periodicals (mostly quarterlies), including the illustrated monthly review *The Unesco Courier* (25 languages) and *Copyright Bulletin* (quarterly, in English, French and Spanish).
Miscellaneous: Co-publish with commercial publishers under joint imprint. Titles issued in English, French and Spanish; sometimes also in Arabic and Russian.
ISBN Publisher's Prefix: 92-3

United Nations Research Institute for Social Development (UNRISD), Palais des Nations, CH-1211 Geneva 10, Switzerland Tel: 988400 Cable Add: Unations Geneve Telex: 289696
Dir: Solon L Barraclough
Orders to: Reference Center (at above address)
Subjects: Social Development, Food systems, Participation
Founded: 1963

United Nations University, Toho Seimei Bldg, 15-1 Shibuya 2-chome, Shibuya-ku, Tokyo 150, Japan Tel: (03) 4992811 Cable Add: Unatuniv Tokyo Telex: J25442
Rector: Mr Soedjatmoko; *Editor:* James E Ricketson; *Sales Manager:* Satish Tandon; *Chief of Academic Services:* Shigeo Minowa
Branch Offs: Liaison Office, Room 1180, UNDC Bldg, UN Plaza, New York, NY 10017, USA; Information Office, c/o UNIC, 14-15 Stratford Pl, London W1, UK
Subjects: Food & Nutrition, Human & Social Development, Traditional Technology, Natural Resources, Energy & Environment
1981: 105 titles *1982:* 55 titles *Founded:* 1975
ISBN Publisher's Prefix: 92-808

Universal Postal Union (UPU)*, CP, CH-3000 Berne 15, Switzerland Tel: (031) 432211 Cable Add: Upu Berne Telex: 32842 Upu Ch
Director-General: Mohamed Ibrahim Sobhi
Founded: 1874
ISBN Publisher's Prefix: 92-62

World Health Organization (WHO), 20 ave Appia, CH-1211 Geneva 27, Switzerland Tel: (022) 912111 Cable Add: Unisante Geneva Telex: 27821
Chief, Distribution & Sales Section: M J Harriague
Subjects: Reference, Medicine, Psychology, Social Science, Textbooks
The WHO is a specialized agency of the United Nations with primary responsibility for international health matters and public health. Through this organization the health professions of some 160 countries exchange their knowledge and experience with the aim of making possible the attainment by all citizens of the world by the year 2000 of a level of health that will permit them to lead a socially and economically productive life.
Founded: 1948
ISBN Publisher's Prefix: 92-4

World Meteorological Organization (WMO), CP 5, CH-1211 Geneva 20, Switzerland
In early 1951, the WMO took over the work of the 78-year-old International Meteorological Organization; later that year, it became a specialized agency of the United Nations. It promotes world-wide cooperation in meteorology and hydrology by establishing a network of observation stations, helps to bring about the development of service centres, sets up systems of rapid exchange of information, standardizes statistics and observations, furthers the application of meteorology to aviation, shipping, water problems, agriculture and other human activities, promotes activities in operational hydrology, furthers close cooperation between meteorological and hydrological services, and encourages research and training in meteorology and hydrology.
The publications of WMO include the records and reports of the WMO constituent bodies; cloud atlases; manuals on nomenclature; weather reporting; and guides to regulations and instrumentation.
ISBN Publisher's Prefix: 92-63

Other International Organizations with Publishing Activities

American-Scandinavian Foundation, 127 East 73rd St, New York, NY 10021, USA Telex: 661553 Amscan
President/Administrator: Patricia McFate
Publications: Scandinavian Review (quarterly cultural/literary magazine); *Scan* (monthly membership newsletter)

Association of African Universities*, PO Box 5744, Accra-North, Ghana Tel: 65461 ext 623 Cable Add: Afuniv Accra
Secretary-General: Prof Levy Makary
Subject: Higher Education in Africa
Founded: 1967

Centre international de documentation parlementaire (CIDP), Union interparlementaire, pl du Petit-Saconnex, CP 99, CH-1211 Geneva 19, Switzerland Tel: 344150

Commonwealth Agricultural Bureaux, Farnham House, Farnham Royal, Slough SL2 3BN, UK Tel: Farnham Common 2281 (Editorial), 2662 (Sales) (STD code 02814) Cable Add: Comag Slough Telex: 847964 Comagg G
Executive Director: N G Jones; *Editorial:* J R Metcalfe; *Sales, Publicity, Rights & Permissions:* G P Rimington; *Production:* P Healey
Subjects: Agriculture, Applied Biology, Forestry, Economics, Rural Sociology, Nutrition, Environmental Medicine
1981: 16 titles *1982:* 10 titles *Founded:* 1929
ISBN Publisher's Prefix: 0-85198

Conference of European Churches, 150 route de Ferney, PO Box 66, CH-1211 Geneva 20, Switzerland Tel: (022) 989400 Cable Add: Oikoumene Telex: 23423 Oik Ch
General Secretary: Dr Glen Garfield Williams
Orders to: (English) The Saint Andrew Press, 121 George St, Edinburgh EH2 4YN, UK; (French) Editions Labor et Fides, 1 rue Beauregard, CH-1204 Geneva, Switzerland; (German) Conference of European Churches, 150 route de Ferney, PO Box 66, CH-1211 Geneva 20, Switzerland
Subjects: Ecumenical Theology, International Relationships
1981: 2 titles *1982:* 3 titles *Founded:* 1959
ISBN Publisher's Prefix: 2-88070

Council of Europe, Publications Section*, Palais de l'Europe, F-67006 Strasbourg cedex, France Tel: (88) 614961 Cable Add: Europa Strasbourg Telex: 870943
Head of Publications: J A Tsimaratos
Subjects: Human Rights, Law, Criminology, Public Health, Sociology, Nature, Consumer Protection, Education, Sport
Founded: 1949

Institut Panafricain pour le Developpement (IPD), Secretariat-General, BP 4056, Douala, United Republic of Cameroun Tel: 421061/424335 Telex: 23627 Uipe Ch
Editor: J B Adotevi; *Editorial, Sales, Production, Publicity:* A J B Adotevi; *Rights & Permissions:* Pr Yaney Ewussie
Orders (for Europe) to: IPD Bureau de Genève, rue de Varembe 3, Postfach 38, CH-1211 Geneva 20, Switzerland
Subject: Development (in particular rural development)
Founded: 1964

International African Institute, 38 King Street, London WC2E 8JR, UK Tel: (01) 379 7636 Cable Add: Afrilac London WC2
Branch Offs: Paris, Nigeria

Subjects: Academic books on Africa, including History, Ethnography, Environmental Studies, Bibliography
1983: 2 titles *Founded:* 1926
Miscellaneous: 1,500 institutions and individuals are subscribing members and the governing body includes representatives from 50 countries, 30 in Africa
ISBN Publisher's Prefix: 0-85302

International Association of Sound Archives, Open University, Media Library, Walton Hall, Milton Keynes, Bucks MK7 6AA, UK

International Union for Conservation of Nature and Natural Resources (IUCN), ave du Mont Blanc, CH-1196 Gland, Switzerland Tel: (022) 647181 Cable Add: Iucnature Gland Telex: 22618 Iucn Ch
Dir General: Dr Kenton R Miller
Orders to: Unipub, Box 433, Murray Hill Station, New York, NY 10016, USA (for North America); IUCN at above Swiss address (for rest of world)
Subjects: Conservation and development, Land and freshwater animals, Marine and coastal ecology and management, National parks and other protected areas, regional conservation, Environmental policy and law papers
Founded: 1948
ISBN Publisher's Prefix: 2-88032

International Union of Geological Sciences (IUGS), 'Episodes' Secretariat, Room 177, 601 Booth St, Ottawa, Canada K1A 0E8 Tel: (613) 9954927 Telex: 0533117 Emar Ott
Union internationale des Sciences Géologiques
Rights & Permissions: Dr A R Berger
Subjects: Earth Sciences, Quarterly *Episodes* (since 1978)
Founded: 1961

League of Arab States, Department of Documentation and Information*, Tahrir Square, Cairo, Egypt Tel: 811960 exts 236, 270, 274 Telex: 92111 Alsun

Southeast Asian Ministers of Education Organization (SEAMEO), Regional Language Centre (RELC), 30 Orange Grove Rd, Singapore 1025, Republic of Singapore Tel: 7379044 Cable Add: Relcentre
Dir: Mrs Tai Yu-lin
Subjects: Language Teaching and Research, Linguistics, English in multilingual, multicultural situations
1981: 40 titles *Founded:* 1968

World Council of Churches (WCC), 150 route de Ferney, CP 66, CH-1211 Geneva 20, Switzerland Tel: (022) 989400 Cable Add: Oikoumene Geneva Telex: 23423 Oik Ch
General Secretary: Dr Philip A Potter; *Director, Publications:* Jan H Kok
Subjects: Ecumenism, Church Unity, Mission and Evangelism, Dialogue with people of other faiths and ideologies, Social Justice, Human Rights, Development, Racism
Founded: 1948
ISBN Publisher's Prefix: 2-8254

International Bibliography

Books

The ABC of Copyright, The UNESCO Press, 7 pl de Fontenoy, F-75700 Paris, France. Published in Arabic, English, French, Russian, Spanish

Adressbuch für den deutschsprachigen Buchhandel (Directory of the German-language Book Trade), Buchhändler-Vereinigung GmbH, Adressbuch-Redaktion, Postfach 2404, D-6000 Frankfurt 1, Federal Republic of Germany

ALA World Encyclopedia of Library & Information Services, American Library Association, 50 East Huron St, Chicago, Illinois 60611, USA

The African Book World and Press: A Directory, Hans Zell Publishers, PO Box 56, Oxford OX1 3EL, UK. Information in English and French

African Books in Print, Mansell Publishing Ltd, 6 All Saints St, London N1 9RL, UK

Author's and Writer's Who's Who, see *International Authors and Writers Who's Who*

Bibliographie nationale courante de l'Année ... des pays d'Afrique d'expression française (National Bibliography for the Year ... of Francophone African Countries), annual bibliography covering books and other materials, published in Francophone Africa since 1967, Ecole de Bibliothécaires, Archivistes, et Documentalistes, Université de Dakar, BP 3252, Dakar, Senegal

Bibliography of the Middle East; a complete and classified list of all the books published in about ten Middle Eastern countries, Damascus University Library, Damascus, Syria

Bibliothèques et Musées des Arts du Spectacle dans le Monde (Performing Arts Libraries and Museums of the World), Société internationale des Bibliothèques et Musées des arts du Spectacle, c/o President, 1 rue de Sully, F-75004 Paris, France

Book-Auction records, Wm Dawson & Sons Ltd, Cannon House, Park Farm Rd, Folkestone, Kent CT19 5EE, UK

Book Markets in Western Europe (1978), Euromonitor Publications Ltd, PO Box 26, 18 Doughty St, London WC1N 2PN, UK

Book Publishers Directory (USA & Canada), Gale Research Co, Book Tower, Detroit, Michigan 48226, USA

The Book Trade of the World, Verlag für Buchmarktforschung, Beim Strohhause 34, D-2000 Hamburg 1, Federal Republic of Germany. André Deutsch Ltd, 105 Great Russell St, London WC1B 3LJ, UK; R R Bowker Co, 205 East 42nd St, New York, NY 10017, USA

Book World Directory of the Arab Countries, Turkey and Iran, Mansell Publishing, 6 All Saints St, London N1 9RL, UK

Bookdealers in India, Pakistan and Sri Lanka, Sheppard Press, PO Box 42, Russell Chambers, Covent Garden, London WC2E 8AX, UK

Bookman's Price Index, Gale Research Co, Book Tower, Detroit, Michigan 48226, USA

The Bowker Annual of Library and Book Trade Information, Bowker Publishing Co, Erasmus House, High St, Epping, Essex CM16 4BU, UK

British Library General Catalogue of Printed Books to 1975 (360 Vols: Vols 1-213 published); *British Library General Catalogue of Printed Books 1976-82* (published). K G Saur Ltd, Shropshire House, 2-10 Capper St, London WC1E 6JA, UK

Cassell & The Publishers Association Directory of Publishing, Cassell Ltd, 1 Vincent Sq, London SW1P 2PN, UK

Catalogue général des ouvrages parus en langue française (Catalogue of Books Published in the French Language), Cercle de la Librairie, 35 rue Grégoire de Tours, F-75279 Paris cedex 06, France

Contemporary Authors, Gale Research Co, Book Tower, Detroit, Michigan 48226, USA

Copyright Laws and Treaties of the World, The Unesco Press, 7 pl de Fontenoy, F-75700 Paris, France. Published in English, French and Spanish

Cumulative Book Index, H W Wilson Co, 950 University Ave, New York, NY 10452, USA (world index of English language books)

Current African Directories; incorporating *African Companies*, a guide to directories published in or concerned with Africa, and to sources of information on business enterprises in Africa. CBD Research Ltd, 154 High St, Beckenham, Kent BR3 1EA, UK

Current European Directories; annotated guide to international, national, city and specialized directories and similar reference works for all countries of Europe, CBD Research Ltd, 154 High St, Beckenham, Kent BR3 1EA, UK

Dictionarium bibliothecarii praticum (ad usum internationalem in XXII linguis) (The Librarian's practical dictionary in 22 languages), Akadémiai Kiadó, H-1054 Budapest V, Alkotmány u 21, Hungary; and K G Saur Verlag KG, Postfach 711009, D-8000 Munich 71, Federal Republic of Germany

Directory of Documentation, Libraries and Archives Services in Africa, UNESCO, pl de Fontenoy, F-75700 Paris, France

Directory of Government Printers and Prominent Bookshops in the African Region, UN Economic Commission for Africa, Africa Hall, PO Box 3001, Addis Ababa, Ethiopia

Directory of Libraries and Documentation Centres in the United Nations System, United Nations, Sales Section, Publishing Service, 801 United Nations Plaza, New York, NY 10017, USA

Directory of Special Libraries and Information Centers (USA & Canada), Gale Research Co, Book Tower, Detroit, Michigan 48226, USA

Le Droit d'Auteur (Author's Right), WIPO, 34 Chemin des Colombettes, CH-1211 Geneva 20, Switzerland

Ensemble; international literary yearbook (text in English, French, German), Deutscher Taschenbuch Verlag, Postfach 400422, D-8000 Munich 40, Federal Republic of Germany

European Bookdealers: A Directory of Dealers in Secondhand and Antiquarian Books on the Continent of Europe, Sheppard Press Ltd, PO Box 42, Russell Chambers, Covent Garden, London WC2E 8AX, UK

European Law Libraries Guide (Guide européen des bibliothèques de droit), Morgan-Grampian Book Publishing Co Ltd, 30 Calderwood St, Woolwich, London SE18 6QH, UK

Guia de Bibliografia Especializada (Guide to Specialist Libraries), Brazilian Library Association, Rua Martins Torres 99, Santa Rosa, Niterói, 24000 Rio de Janeiro, Brazil (covers all Latin America)

Guide du Livre Ancien et du Livre d'occasion (Guide to Antiquarian and Second-Hand Books), Syndicat du Livre ancien et des Metiers annexes, 14 ave de Friedland, F-75008 Paris, France

IFLA Directory (biennial), International Federation of Library Associations, The Royal Library, Postbus 95312, 2509 CH The Hague, Netherlands

IFLA Standards for Public Libraries, K G Saur Verlag KG, Postfach 711009, D-8000 Munich 71, Federal Republic of Germany

Index translationum, International bibliography of translations, UNESCO, 7 pl de Fontenoy, F-75700 Paris, France

International Academic and Specialist Publishers' Directory, Bowker Publishing Co, Erasmus House, High St, Epping, Essex CM16 4BU, UK

International Authors and Writers Who's Who, information on 10,000 of world's leading writers, including index of pseudonyms and literary agents. Melrose Press Ltd, 7 Regal Lane, Soham, Ely, Cambridgeshire CB7 5BA, UK; Gale Research Co, Book Tower, Detroit, Michigan 48226, USA

International Bibliography of Reprints/Internationales Verzeichnis der Reprints, K G Saur Verlag KG, Postfach 711009, D-8000 Munich 71, Federal Republic of Germany

International Bibliography of the Book Trade and Librarianship, 1976-79, K G Saur Verlag KG, Postfach 711009, D-8000 Munich 71, Federal Republic of Germany

International Book Trade Directory, Bowker Publishing Co, Erasmus House, High St, Epping, Essex CM16 4BU, UK Listing details of booksellers world-wide

International Books in Print, K G Saur Verlag KG, Postfach 711009, D-8000 Munich 71, Federal Republic of Germany; Bowker Publishing Co, Erasmus House, High St, Epping, Essex CM16 4BU, UK Listing titles published in the English language outside the UK and USA

International Directory of Antiquarian Booksellers, International League of Antiquarian Booksellers, Hans Bagger, Rosenkilde & Bagger Ltd, PO Box 2184, DK-1017 Copenhagen, Denmark

International Directory of Booksellers, K G Saur Verlag KG, Postfach 711009, D-8000 Munich 71, Federal Republic of Germany

International Directory of Children's Literature, George Kurian Reference Books, PO Box 519, Baldwin Place, NY 10505, USA

International ISBN Publishers' Directory, Bowker Publishing Co, Erasmus House, High St, Epping, Essex CM16 4BU, UK

International Literary Market Place, Bowker Publishing Co, Erasmus House, High St, Epping, Essex CM16 4BU, UK (covers the world apart from the North American continent, which is covered by *Literary Market Place*)

International Maps and Atlases in Print, Bowker Publishing Co, Erasmus House, High St, Epping, Essex CM16 4BU, UK

International Who's Who in Poetry, Melrose Press Ltd, 7 Regal Lane, Cambridge CB7 5BA, UK; Gale Research Co, Book Tower, Detroit, Michigan 48226, USA

Irregular Serials and Annuals: An International Directory, Bowker Publishing Co, Erasmus House, High St, Epping, Essex CM16 4BU, UK

Jahrbuch der Auktionspreise (Yearbook of Auction Prices), Hauswedell & Co, Postfach 723, D-7000 Stuttgart 1, Federal Republic of Germany (book auction prices in Germany, Austria, Switzerland and the Netherlands)

Large Type Books in Print, Bowker Publishing Co, Erasmus House, High St, Epping, Essex CM16 4BU, UK

Libros en Venta en Hispanoamérica y España, Melcher Ediciones, Apdo 6000, San Juan, PR 00906, Puerto Rico; K G Saur Verlag KG, Postfach 711009, D-8000 Munich 71, Federal Republic of Germany

Literary and Library Prizes, Bowker Publishing Co, Erasmus House, High St, Epping, Essex CM16 4BU, UK

Literary Market Place, R R Bowker Co, 205 East 42nd St, New York, NY 10017, USA (covers North American continent — rest of world covered by *International Literary Market Place*)

A Manual of European Languages for Librarians, Bowker Publishing Co, Erasmus House, High St, Epping, Essex CM16 4BU, UK

Private Press Books; an annual bibliography of the work of private presses throughout the world, Private Libraries Association, Ravelston, South View Rd, Pinner, Middlesex, UK

Publishers' International Directory/ Internationales Verlagsadressbuch, K G Saur Verlag KG, Postfach 711009, D-8000 Munich 71, Federal Republic of Germany

Publishing in Africa in the Seventies, University of Ife Press, Ile-Ife, Nigeria

Répertoire international des Editeurs et Diffuseurs de Langue française (International List of French-Language Publishers and Distributors), Syndicat national de l'Edition, 35 rue Grégoire de Tours, F-75279 Paris cedex 06, France

Répertoire international des Libraires de Langue française (International List of French Language Bookshops), Cercle de la Librairie, 35 rue Grégoire de Tours, F-75279 Paris cedex 06, France

Sources of Serials: International Serials Publishers and their Titles with Copyright and Copy Availability Information, Bowker Publishing Co, Erasmus House, High St, Epping, Essex CM16 4BU, UK

South Asian Bibliography: A Handbook and Guide, Harvester Press, 16 Ship St, Brighton, East Sussex, UK

Subject Collections in European Libraries, Bowker Publishing Co, Erasmus House, High St, Epping, Essex CM16 4BU, UK

Subject Guide to International Books in Print, K G Saur Verlag KG, Postfach 711009, D-8000 Munich 71, Federal Republic of Germany; Bowker Publishing Co, Erasmus House, High St, Epping, Essex CM16 4BU, UK

Ulrich's International Periodicals Directory, Bowker Publishing Co, Erasmus House, High St, Epping, Essex CM16 4BU, UK

Who Distributes What and Where: An International Directory of Publishers, Imprints, Agents and Distributors, R R Bowker Co, 205 East 42nd St, New York, NY 10017, USA; Bowker Publishing Co, Erasmus House, High St, Epping, Essex CM16 4BU, UK

Who's Who at the Frankfurt Book Fair: An International Publishers' Guide, K G Saur Verlag KG, Postfach 711009, D-8000 Munich 71, Federal Republic of Germany

Willings Press Guide, Thomas Skinner Directories, Windsor Court, East Grinstead House, East Grinstead, West Sussex RH19 1XE, UK

World Guide to Libraries, K G Saur Verlag KG, Postfach 711009, D-8000 Munich 71, Federal Republic of Germany

World Guide to Library Schools and Training Courses in Documentation (Guide mondial des écoles de bibliothecaires et documentalists), Clive Bingley Ltd, 7 Ridgmount St, London WC1A 7AE, UK

World Guide to Special Libraries, K G Saur Verlag KG, Postfach 711009, D-8000 Munich 71, Federal Republic of Germany

World Photography Sources, Directories, 436 East 88th St, New York, NY 10028, USA

The Writers' & Artists' Yearbook, Adam & Charles Black Ltd, 35 Bedford Row, London WC1R 4JH, UK

The Writers Directory, Macmillan Publishers Ltd (Journals Division), Canada Rd, Byfleet, Surrey KT14 7BR, UK

Journals

African Book Publishing Record (text occasionally in French), Hans Zell Publishers, PO Box 56, Oxford OX1 3EL, UK; K G Saur Verlag KG, Postfach 711009, D-8000 Munich 71, Federal Republic of Germany

African Books Newsletter; a checklist of recent books published in English, arranged according to subject, K K Roy (Private) Ltd, 55 Gariahat Rd, PO Box 10210, Calcutta 700019, India

African Research and Documentation, Standing Conference on Library Materials on Africa, c/o Institute of Commonwealth Studies, 27 Russell Sq, London WC1B 5DS, UK

L'Afrique littéraire, 2 rue Cretet, F-75009 Paris, France

Asian Book Development, Asian Cultural Centre for Unesco, 6 Fukuro-machi, Shinjuku-ku, Tokyo, Japan

Asian Books Newsletter; a checklist of recent books published in English, arranged according to subject, K K Roy (Private) Ltd, 55 Gariahat Rd, PO Box 10210, Calcutta 700019, India

Babel (International Journal of Translation), Kultura, H-1389 Budapest 62, Postafiók 149, Hungary

Bibliografía actual de Caribe (Current Caribbean Bibliography) Caribbean Regional Library, Ponce de León 452, Hato Rey, Puerto Rico 00919

Bibliographie Documentation, Terminologie (Bibliography, Documentation, Terminology) (Editions in English, French, Russian and Spanish), UNESCO, Département de la Documentation des Bibliothèques et des Archives, 7 pl de Fontenoy, F-75700 Paris, France

Bibliotheca Orientalis; international bibliographical and reviewing bi-monthly for Near Eastern and Mediterranean Studies (text in English, French and German), Nederlands Instituut voor Het Nabije Oosten, Postbus 9515, 2300 RA Leiden, Netherlands

Boletín Bibliográfico del CERLAL (current Latin-American bibliography), CERLAL, Calle 70 No 9-52, Apdo Aereo 17438, Bogotá, Colombia

Bookbird, literature for children and young people, news from all over the world, recommendations for translation, International Institute for Children's Literature and Reading Research, Karl Werner, A-1040 Vienna, Mayerhofgasse 6, Austria

'The Bookseller' Frankfurt Rights Guide, 12 Dyott St, London WC1A 1DF, UK

Bulletin, Bibliographical Society of Australia and New Zealand, 117 St George's Road, North Fitzroy, Victoria 3068, Australia

Le Bulletin de Bibliophile (text in English, French and German), Association Internationale de Bibliophilie, 58 rue de Richelieu, F-75084, Paris cedex 02, France

Bulletin de l'Association internationale des Documentalistes et Techniciens de l'Information (Bulletin of the International Association of Documentalists and Information Officers), 74 rue des Saints-Pères, F-75007 Paris, France

CERLAL; noticias sobre el Libro y Bibliografia (news on books and bibliographies), CERLAL, Calle 70 No 9-52, Apdo Aereo 17438, Bogotá, Colombia

CREPLA Information Bulletin, Centre Régional de Promotion du Livre en Afrique, BP 1646, Yaoundé, United Republic of Cameroun

Caribbean Quarterly, Department of Extra-Mural Studies, University of the West Indies, Mona, Kingston 7, Jamaica

Copyright (monthly), World Intellectual Property Organization, 34 chemin des Colombettes, CH-1211 Geneva 20, Switzerland

Copyright Bulletin (quarterly), UNESCO, The Unesco Press, 7 pl de Fontenoy, F-75700 Paris, France. Published in English, French, Spanish

Fichero Bibliográfico Hispanoamericano; monthly review of librarians, booksellers, distributors and publishers, Melcher Ediciones, Apdo 6000, San Juan, PR 00906, Puerto Rico

Frankfurt Rights Guide, see *Bookseller*

Germanistik, Internationales Referatenorgan mit bibliographischen Hinweisen (German Language and Literature: International Review Journal with Bibliographical References), Max Niemeyer Verlag, Postfach 2140, D-7400 Tübingen, Federal Republic of Germany

Helikon Vilagirodalmi Figyelo. (Helikon Review of World Literature) (summaries in French and Russian), Akademiai Kiadó, H-1054 Budapest V, Alkotmány u 21, Hungary

Heritage (African quarterly of arts and letters), PO Box 610, Apapa, Lagos, Nigeria

Inter-American Review of Bibliography (Revista Interamericana de Bibliografia), Organization of American States, 17th Street and Constitution Ave, NW Washington, DC 20006, USA

International Association of Orientalist Librarians Bulletin (half-yearly), International Association of Oriental Librarians, c/o Asian Studies Program, University of Hawaii at Manoa, 315 Moore Hall, 1890 East-West Rd, Honolulu, Hawaii 96822, USA

International Cataloguing, IFLA Committee on Cataloguing, Longman Group Ltd, Journals Dept, Fourth Ave, Harlow, Essex CM19 5AA, UK

International Fiction Review, (bi-annually) Dr S Elkhadem, Dept of German and Russian, University of New Brunswick, Federicton, NB, Canada

International Library Review (quarterly), Academic Press Inc (London) Ltd, 24-28 Oval Rd, London NW1 7DX, UK

International PEN Bulletin of Selected Books (issued with the assistance of UNESCO) (text and title in English and French), International PEN, 38 King St, London WC2E 8JT, UK

Journal, East and Central Africa Regional Branch of the International Council on Archives, c/o Kenya National Archives, Jogoo House 'A', PO Box 30520, Nairobi, Kenya

The Journal of Commonwealth Literature, Hans Zell Publishers, PO Box 56, Oxford OX1 3EL, UK; K G Saur Verlag KG, Postfach 711009, D-8000 Munich 71, Federal Republic of Germany

Jugend und Buch (Youth and Books), International Institute for Children's Literature and Reading Research, Karl Werner, A-1040 Vienna, Mayerhofgasse 6, Austria (Co-Sponsor: Österreichischer Buchklub der Jugend)

LIBER Bulletin (text in English and French), Ligue des Bibliothèques européenes de Recherche, c/o The Library, European University Institute, Badia Fiesolana, Florence, Italy

Latin American Books Newsletter, K K Roy (Pvt) Ltd, PO Box 10210, Calcutta 700019, India

Library & Information Science Abstracts (LISA) (bi-monthly), The Library Association, 7 Ridgmount St, London WC1E 7AE, UK

Pacific Islands Books News Letter, K K Roy (Pvt) Ltd, PO Box 10210, Calcutta 700019, India

Publishers Weekly, R R Bowker Co, PO Box 1428, Riverton, NJ 08077, USA; Bowker Publishing Co, Erasmus House, High St, Epping, Essex CM16 4BU, UK

Review; journal on contemporary Latin American literature in English translation, Center for Inter-American Relations, 680 Park Ave, New York, NY 10021, USA

Revista Interamericana de Bibliografia, see Inter-American Review of Bibliography

SCALS Newsletter, c/o School of Librarians, Archivists and Documentalists, University of Dakar, BP 2006, Dakar, Senegal (official publication of the Standing Conference of African Library Schools)

SCAUL Newsletter, c/o E Bejide Bankole, University Librarian, University of Lagos, Yaba, Lagos, Nigeria (official publication of the Standing Conference of African University Libraries)

Scandinavian Public Library Quarterly, A/L Biblioteksentralen, Malerhaugveien 20, N-Oslo 6, Norway

Scandinavian Review (quarterly cultural/literary magazine), American-Scandinavian Foundation, 127 East 73 St, New York, NY 10021, USA

South Asia Library Notes and Queries, University of Chicago Library, 5801 Ellis Ave, Chicago, Illinois 60637, USA

Southeast Asian Archives, Southeast Regional Branch of the International Council on Archives, c/o National Archives and Library of Malaysia, Jalan Duta, Kuala Lumpur, Malaysia

UNESCO Journal of Documentation Science, Librarianship and Archives Administration, UNESCO, The Unesco Press, 7 pl de Fontenoy, F-75700 Paris, France

Ulrich's Quarterly, Bowker Publishing Co, Erasmus House, High St, Epping, Essex CM16 4BU, UK

World Book News, Euromonitor Publications Ltd, PO Box 26, 18 Doughty St, London WC1N 2PN, UK

International Literary Prizes

Jane **Addams** Children's Book Award
Established 1979. To the author of the book for children that is most outstanding in literary merit and contains themes on brotherhood and peace. Awarded triennially. Enquiries to Women's International League for Peace and Freedom, 1 rue de Varembé, CH-1211 Geneva 20, Switzerland

Alexander Prize
For an essay in English on a historical subject; must be a genuine work of original research, not hitherto published, and not awarded any other prize. Silver medal, awarded annually. Enquiries to Secretary, Royal Historical Society, University College London, Gower St, London WC1E 6BT, UK

American-Scandinavian Foundation/PEN Translation Prizes*
Initiated in 1980 by 'Scandinavian Review' (quarterly magazine of ASF) to bring best of contemporary Scandinavian literature to American readers. There are two prizes of US $1,000, one each for poetry and fiction, in addition to publication. To be awarded annually, in May, to the best translations of work by a Danish, Finnish, Icelandic, Norwegian or Swedish author born within the last 100 years. Enquiries to American-Scandinavian Foundation, 127 East 73rd St, New York, NY 10021, USA

Hans Christian **Andersen** Medals
The International Board on Books for Young People (IBBY) makes these awards every two years to a living author and a living illustrator who, through their live's works, have made distinguished contributions to international children's and young adult literature. (Until 1966 a prize was awarded for a specific book and to an author only.) A jury of ten members, appointed by the Executive Committee of IBBY, makes the decision from selections submitted from member countries all over

the world. Awarded in 1982 to Lygia Bojunga Nunes, Brazil (author) and Zbigniew Rychlicki, Poland (illustrator). Enquiries to IBBY Secretariat, Leonhardsgraben 38a, CH-4051 Basle, Switzerland

Arts Council Awards and Bursaries
Full details of the help given to playwrights is available on request. Enquiries to Drama Director, Arts Council of Great Britain, 105 Piccadilly, London W1V 0AU, UK

Austrian State Prize for European Literature
A prize of 200,000 Austrian schillings and testimonial, established in 1965, are presented by the Austrian Minister of Education to a renowned European author for the sum of his work. Awarded annually. Enquiries to Bundesministerium für Unterricht und Kunst, A-1014 Vienna, Postfach 65, Sektion IV/Abteilung 3A, Austria

Bennett Award
For a writer of substantial achievement whose work has not received full recognition, or who is at a critical stage. US$12,500, biennially. No applications or nominations accepted. Enquiries to The Hudson Review, 684 Park Ave, New York, NY 10021, USA

Benson Medal
Founded 1916 by Dr A C Benson. For a body of meritorious work in poetry, fiction, history, biography or belles lettres. A silver medal given at the discretion of the Council of the Royal Society of Literature. Applications are not invited. Last awarded in 1982 to Dr A L Rowse (UK). Enquiries to Royal Society of Literature of the United Kingdom, 1 Hyde Park Gardens, London W2 2LT, UK

Anton **Bergmann** Prize
For the author of a historical account or monograph, written in Dutch and relating to a Flemish town or community in Belgium. 50,000 Belgian francs. Awarded every five years for a work appearing in print or (provisionally) in manuscript form, during the period. Foreign authors may also compete, provided work is in Dutch and is published in Belgium or the Netherlands. Winner for 17th period (1975-1980), P Van Nieuwenhuysen. Enquiries to Académie Royale de Belgique, Palais des Académies, 1 rue Ducale, B-1000 Brussels, Belgium

David **Berry** Prize
For an essay in English on any subject dealing with Scottish history within the reigns of James I to James VI inclusive. Monetary prize awarded every three years. Enquiries to Secretary, Royal Historical Society, University College London, Gower St, London WC1E 6BT, UK

Best Book of the Sea Award
Established 1971. Sponsored by King George's Fund for Sailors. For a non-fiction book about the sea, published during the calendar year, judged to have made the most valuable contribution to the knowledge and enjoyment of those who love the sea. £500 and a medal. Enquiries to John Coote, King George's Fund for Sailors, 1 Chesham St, London SW1, UK

Biennial International Art Book Prize
To promote the publication of fine illustrated books on archaeology, fine arts, architecture and applied arts, including photography. Prize consists of silver and bronze medals, free flight and hotel accommodation in Jerusalem during the Jerusalem International Book Fair for the publisher and designer of the winning entry. Prizes are awarded in three categories with the overall winner selected from these three. All entries to be exhibited as a special exhibit of the International Book Fair and to remain in the Israel Museum Library. Next award in 1985 for books published in 1983-84. Enquiries to Sheila Boofty, The Public Affairs Department, The Israel Museum, Jerusalem, Israel

James **Blish** Award*
Awarded biennially for excellence in science fiction criticism which has been published in the English language. The prize is a bronze plaque and a small sum of money. First awarded in 1977. Enquiries to Science Fiction Foundation, North East London Polytechnic, Longbridge Road, Dagenham, Essex RM8 2AS, UK

Boardman Tasker Prize for Mountain Literature
Established in 1983 to commemorate the lives of distinguished mountaineers Peter Boardman and Joe Tasker who died in 1982 on Mount Everest. An annual prize of £1,000 will go to an author of a published work of non-fiction or fiction which makes an outstanding contribution to mountain literature. Enquiries to Mrs D Boardman, 56 St Michael's Ave, Bramhall, Cheshire

Bologna Book Fair 'Critici in erba' Prize
Award by a jury of nine children, between 6 and 9 years of age, for the best illustrated book among those sent by the publishers exhibiting at the Bologna Children's Book Fair. 1983 award went to *Our Changing World* by Ingrid Selberg, illustrated by Andrew Miller (William Collins, UK). Enquiries to Fiera del Libro per Ragazzi — Ente Autonomo per le Fiere di Bologna, Piazza della Costituzione 6, I-40128 Bologna, Italy

Bologna Book Fair Graphic Prize for Children and Youth
Awarded for typographical, artistic and technical merit or innovation at the Bologna Children's Book Fair, by an international committee of graphic designers appointed by the Fair authorities. The prizes, consisting of golden plates, are awarded to the publishers of the winning works. The graphic prize for the book for children was awarded in 1983 to *The Favershams* by Roy Gerrard (Victor Gollancz, UK). The graphic prize for the book for young people was awarded in 1983 to *Il était une fois, les mots . . .* by Yves Pinguilly and André Belleguie (La Farandole/Messidor, France). Enquiries to Fiera del Libro per Ragazzi — Ente Autonomo per le Fiere di Bologna, Piazza della Costituzione 6, I-40128 Bologna, Italy

Booker McConnell Prize
Instituted in 1969. £10,000 donated by Booker McConnell Ltd and administered by The National Book League, for any full-length novel, written in English by a citizen of The Commonwealth, the Republic of Ireland, Pakistan or the Republic of South Africa. Any United Kingdom publisher who publishes works of fiction may enter not more than four full-length novels, with scheduled publication dates between 1 January and 30 November. Awarded in 1983 to John Coetzee for *Life & Times of Michael K* (Secker & Warburg, UK). Enquiries to The National Book League, Book House, East Hill, Wandsworth, London SW18 2QZ, UK

Books Abroad/English-Speaking Union of the United States Best Book of Belles Lettres
Instituted 1973, to foster creative writing by African and Asian writers in the English language. US$2,000. Awarded annually. Enquiries to Professor Charles R Larson, 3600 Underwood St, Chevy Chase, Maryland 20815, USA

Bremen Literature Encouragement Prize
Given by Rudolf-Alexander-Schröder Foundation to young German-speaking poets and writers in order to encourage literature. 5,000 DM awarded annually. Enquiries to Senator für Wissenschaft und Kunst, Freie Hansestadt Bremen, D-2800 Bremen 1, Federal Republic of Germany

Bremen Literature Prize
Given by Rudolf-Alexander-Schröder Foundation to German-speaking poets and writers in order to encourage literature. 10,000 DM awarded annually. Enquiries to Senator für Wissenschaft und Kunst, Freie Hansestadt Bremen, D-2800 Bremen 1, Federal Republic of Germany

John W **Campbell** Memorial Award
Founded 1973 for the best science-fiction novel in any language. First prize according to funding of sponsoring institution. Enquiries to The Secretary, Prof T A Shippey, School of English, Leeds University, Leeds LS2 9JT, UK

Carducci Prize*
Established 1950. For poetry, monographs and essays on poetry and poets. 1,000,000 lire. Awarded annually. Enquiries to Bologna University, Bologna, Italy

Casa de las Américas Literary Award*
An annual prize of US$3,000 (or equivalent in national currency) is awarded to an author for unpublished work in one or other of the following groups (alternately, each year): (1) novels, plays, 'testimonial' books, essays on artistic and literary themes — Brazilian and French Caribbean (or national language) works. (2) short stories, poetry, essays on historical and social themes, books for children and young people and Anglo-Caribbean (or national language) works. In 1984 works in group (2) can be entered and the following may participate: (a) Latin-American and Caribbean authors (born or naturalized); (b) essayists from any other country, dealing with Latin-American and Caribbean themes. The winning work will be published. Enquiries to Casa de las Américas, G y Tercera, Vedado 3, Havana, Cuba
or CP 2, CH-3000 Berne 16, Switzerland

Pierre **Chauveau** Medal
Established 1952. In recognition of an outstanding contribution to literature. Medal and C$1,500. Awarded biennially. Enquiries to Royal Society of Canada, 344 Wellington St, Ottawa, Ontario K1A 0N4, Canada

Children's Book Award
Established 1974. For a new author who shows unusual promise. Awarded annually for a first or second book. Enquiries to International Reading Association, 800 Barksdale Rd, PO Box 8139, Newark, Delaware 19714, USA

Cholmondeley Award for Poets
Established by the Marchioness of Cholmondeley in 1965 for 'the benefit and encouragement of poets of any age, sex or nationality'. The non-competitive award is for work generally, *not* for a specific book

and submissions are not required. Approximately £3,000 awarded annually. 1983 award was shared by Craig Raine, John Fuller and Anthony Thwaite. Enquiries to Society of Authors, 84 Drayton Gardens, London SW10 9SD, UK

Collins Religious Book Award
Founded 1969 to commemorate the 150th anniversary of the publisher William Collins Sons & Co Ltd. For the book which has made the most distinguished contribution to the relevance of Christianity in the modern world. Open to living citizens of The Commonwealth, the Republic of Ireland and the Republic of South Africa. Prize of £2,000 awarded every two years. Enquiries to William Collins Sons & Co Ltd, 8 Grafton St, London W1X 3LA, UK

The **Commonwealth** Poetry Prize
Instituted 1972. For a first published book of poetry (in English) by an author from a Commonwealth country other than Britain (nationals of other countries living in Britain are eligible). £500 awarded annually. Awarded in 1983 to Grace Nichols (Guyana) for *I is a Long-Memoried Woman* (Karnak House). Enquiries to Promotions Assistant, Library & Resources Centre, The Commonwealth Institute, Kensington High Street, London W8 6NQ, UK

Thomas **Cook** Travel Book Awards
Two awards: one of £1,500 for the best travel book and one of £500 for the best guide book of the year. Books must have been published in the twelve months ending 31 October. Enquiries to The National Book League, Book House, East Hill, Wandsworth, London SW18 2QZ, UK

Albert **Counson** Prize*
For a scholarly work on romance languages, in relation to or connected with Belgium. Monetary prize. Awarded every five years. Enquiries to Royal Academy of French Language and Literature, Palais de Académies, 1 rue Ducale, B-1000 Brussels, Belgium

Count of Cartagena Prizes
Established 1929. For unpublished works by Spaniards or Latin-Americans written in Spanish on a theme to be decided for each competition. 90,000 pesetas. Awarded annually. Enquiries to Royal Spanish Academy, Felipe IV 4, Madrid, Spain

The Rose Mary **Crawshay** Prizes
Founded 1888. Awarded by the Council of the British Academy to women writers of any nationality for an historical or critical work of value on any subject concerning English literature. Preference is given to works on Byron, Shelley or Keats. One or more prizes awarded annually. Applications are not sought. Enquiries to The Secretary, British Academy, 20-21 Cornwall Terrace, London NW1 4QP, UK

Franz **Cumont** Prize
For a work by a Belgian or foreign author dealing with the history of religion or science in antiquity, i.e. in the Mediterranean area prior to the time of Mohammed. No application necessary. The prize cannot be divided, except where one or more authors have acted in collaboration. 100,000 Belgian francs. Awarded every three years. Winner for fourth period (1979-1981) R Schilling. Enquiries to Académie Royale de Belgique, Palais des Académies, 1 rue Ducale, B-1000 Brussels, Belgium

Cyril and Methodius Prize*
For original research in the field of old Bulgarian literature, linguistics and art. 2,000 leva. Awarded annually. Enquiries to Bulgarian Academy of Sciences, Institute of Literature, blvd Vitosha 39, Sofia C, Bulgaria

Isaac **Deutscher** Memorial Prize
Instituted 1968. For a work published or in typescript in any of the main European languages which contributes to the development of Marxist thought. £100 awarded annually. Enquiries to Isaac Deutscher Memorial Prize, c/o Lloyds Bank Ltd, 68 Warwick Sq, London SW1, UK

Ernest **Discailles** Prize
Alternates between the best work on the history of French literature and on contemporary history. Open to (1) Belgians, (2) foreigners who are studying or have studied at the University of Ghent. 50,000 Belgian francs. Awarded every five years. Winner for 15th period (1977-1981) José Lambert. Enquiries to Académie Royale de Belgique, Palais des Académies, 1 rue Ducale, B-1000 Brussels, Belgium

Dobloug Prize
For outstanding literary work by one Norwegian and one Swedish writer. 40,000 Swedish crowns awarded annually. Enquiries to Swedish Academy, Börshuset, Källargränd 4, S-111 29 Stockholm, Sweden

Duff **Cooper** Memorial Prize
First awarded 1956. For a non-fictional literary work published in English or French. The Prize is the interest from a Trust Fund. Awarded annually. The 1982 winner was Richard Ellmann for *James Joyce* (2nd edition) (Oxford University Press, UK). Enquiries to Lord Norwich, 24 Blomfield Rd, London W9, UK

Dutch Literature Prize
Established 1956. To the most outstanding prose writer, essay writer or poet in the Netherlands and in Belgium writing in Dutch. 18,000 Dutch florins. Awarded triennially. Enquiries to Netherlands Government, c/o Ministry of Welfare, Health and Culture, Postbus 5406, 2280 HK Rijswijk Z-H, Netherlands or Belgian Government, Ministry of Culture, Brussels, Belgium

Mary **Elgin** Prize
Established in 1969 for the encouragement of gifted new writers of fiction published by Hodder & Stoughton. £50 awarded annually. Awarded in 1983 to Dawn Lowe-Watson for *A Sound of Water*. Enquiries to Hodder & Stoughton, 47 Bedford Square, London WC1, UK

Camille **Engelman** Prize*
For the outstanding literary work of the year (published or unpublished) written in French. Monetary prize. Awarded annually. Enquiries to Royal Academy of French Language and Literature, Palais des Académies, 1 rue Ducale, B-1000 Brussels, Belgium

English-Speaking Union Book Award
For the best non-technical work published in the English language by an author whose native language is not English. US$2,000 annually (plus travel to the US for presentation). Enquiries to the English-Speaking Union, 16 East 69 St, New York, NY 10021, USA

Etna-Taormina International Poetry Prize*
Established 1951. To one or more poets. Awarded irregularly. Enquiries to Ente Provinciale Turismo, Largo Paisiello 5, Catania, Italy

Christopher **Ewart-Biggs** Memorial Prize
Established in 1977 to commemorate Christopher Ewart-Biggs, the British Ambassador to Ireland, who was assassinated in Dublin in 1976. This award is to be made annually to writings from any nationality where the published work contributes most to peace and understanding in Ireland, closer ties between the peoples of Britain and Ireland, or to cooperation between the partners of the European Community. Entries should be in English or French and the prize is £1,500. In 1982 the award was made to the magazine *Fortnight: an Independent Review for Northern Ireland*. Enquiries to The National Book League, Book House, East Hill, Wandsworth, London SW18 2QZ, UK

The Geoffrey **Faber** Memorial Prize
Established in 1963 by Faber & Faber Ltd as a memorial to the founder and first Chairman of the firm, this prize of £500 is awarded annually, with the assistance of The Arts Council of Great Britain. It is given, in alternate years, for a volume of verse and for a volume of prose fiction. It is given to that volume of verse or prose fiction first published originally in the UK during the two years preceding the year in which the Award is given which is, in the opinion of the judges, of the greatest literary merit. To be eligible for the prize the volume of verse or prose fiction in question must be by a writer who is: (a) not more than forty years old at the date of publication, (b) a citizen of the United Kingdom and Colonies, of any other Commonwealth state, of the Republic of Ireland or of the Republic of South Africa. There are three judges, who are reviewers of poetry or fiction as the case may be, and they are nominated each year by the editors or literary editors of newspapers and magazines which regularly publish such reviews. Faber & Faber invite nominations from such editors and literary editors. No submissions for the prize are to be made. The 1983 prize was awarded to Graham Swift for his novel *Shuttlecock* (Allen Lane/Penguin, UK). Enquiries to Faber & Faber Ltd, 3 Queen Sq, London WC1N 3AU, UK

Antonio **Feltrinelli** Prize*
Each year the Lincei Academy (the National Italian Academy of Sciences) awards Antonio Feltrinelli prizes for accomplishment in the various branches of sciences, humanities, and literature. These prizes were instituted by an Italian businessman who died in 1942 and bequeathed his fortune to the Academy for the purpose of 'rewarding toil, study, intelligence...those men who with greater success distinguished themselves with high achievements in art and science, since they are the true benefactors of their own country as well as of all humanity'. The literature award is granted every five years and the amount varies. Enquiries to Accademia Nazionale dei Lincei, Via della Lungara 10, I-00165 Rome, Italy

French Language Prize
Established 1914. For work done abroad in the best interests of the French language. 50 francs; two prizes of 20 francs and medals. Awarded annually. Enquiries to French Academy, Institut de France, 23 quai de Conti, F-75006 Paris, France

Rómulo Gallegos International Novel Prize
The prize was established in 1965 by the National Institute of Culture and Fine Arts of the Republic of Venezuela. Originally instituted to mark the 80th anniversary of the birth of the illustrious author Rómulo Gallegos, which was celebrated in August 1964, the first award was made in 1967, the 400th anniversary of the founding of Caracas — birthplace of the novelist. Competition is open to any writer from Latin America, Spain or the Philippines whose novel is written in Spanish and has been published originally in one of the countries of the above designated areas. The amount of the prize is approximately $22,223 and will be granted every five years — the next award to be in 1987. Enquiries to Consejo Nacional de la Cultura, Premio Internacional de Novela 'Rómulo Gallegos', Apdo 50995, Caracas 105, Venezuela or from Centro de Estudios Latinoamericanos 'Rómulo Gallegos', Apdo 75667, Caracas 1070A, Venezuela

German Peace Prize
The Peace Prize of the German Book Trade (Friedenspreis des Deutschen Buchhandels) is awarded annually during the Frankfurt Book Fair. The prize is supported by the Börsenverein des deutschen Buchhandels (organization of the German Book Trade) and is awarded without regard to nationality, race or creed. Prize of 25,000 DM since 1979. Enquiries to Börsenverein des deutschen Buchhandels eV, Friedenspreisarchiv, Grosser Hirschgraben 17-21, Postfach 2404, D-6000 Frankfurt am Main 1, Federal Republic of Germany

The **German Youth** Book Award
The German Youth Book Award is given by the Federal Ministry for Youth, Family and Health. The selection of the books and the arrangements for granting the award are in the hands of the Arbeitskreis für Jugendliteratur eV, a body in which the organizations concerned with promoting good books for the young in Germany are represented. The selection is restricted to books published in the German language, primarily books from the Federal Republic of Germany, Austria and Switzerland (translations included). The rules for the award have been altered periodically. The award consists of a total of four prizes, each 7,500 DM, which can be awarded for picture books, fiction, non-fiction and for appreciation of outstanding achievement. 1982 prizes were to Susi Bohdal for *Selina, Pumpernickel und di Katze Flora* (Nord-Süd Verlag), Guus Kuijer (translated by Hans-Georg Lenzen) for *Erzähl mir von Oma* (Verlag Friedrich Oetinger), Myron Levoy (translated by Fred Schmitz) for *Der gelbe Vogel* (Benziger Verlag), Cornelia Julius for *Von feinen und von kleinen Leuten* (Beltz Verlag). Enquiries to Arbeitskreis für Jugendliteratur eV, Elisabethstr 15, D-8000 Munich 40, Federal Republic of Germany

Grand Prix des Biennales Internationales de Poésie, see International Grand Prize for Poetry

Grand Prize for the Dissemination of the French Language
For work contributing to the dissemination of the French language. Monetary prize. Enquiries to French Academy, Institut de France, 23 Quai de Conti, F-75006 Paris, France

The **Guardian Award** for Children's Fiction
Instituted in 1967 and awarded annually. The prize of £250 (subject to revision) is given for an outstanding work of fiction for children by a citizen of The Commonwealth. The 1983 winner was Anita Desai for *A Village by the Sea* (Heinemann, UK). Enquiries to Literary Editor, The Guardian, 119 Farringdon Rd, London EC1R 3ER, UK

The **Guardian Fiction** Prize
Instituted in 1965 and awarded annually. The prize of £500 is given for a novel published by a citizen of The Commonwealth and is intended to encourage ambitious and original work. The 1982 winner was John Banville for *Kepler* (Secker & Warburg, UK). The judges are the Literary Editor and fiction reviewers of *The Guardian*. Enquiries to Literary Editor, The Guardian, 119 Farringdon Rd, London EC1R 3ER, UK

Wilhelm **Heinse** Medal for Literature in Essay Form*
Founded 1978. 1981 winner was Prof Dr Dolf Sternberger. Enquiries to Akademie der Wissenschaften und der Literatur, Geschwister-Schollstr 2, D-6500 Mainz, Federal Republic of Germany

Rafael **Heliodoro Valle** Prize
Founded in 1976 to reward an especially notable living writer aged over 50. 250,000 pesos is awarded in odd-numbered years (the prize is awarded in even-numbered years to a historian for research work and synthesis). The writer must have been born in Latin America and the work written in Spanish or Portuguese. Enquiries to Instituto de Investigaciones Bibliograficas, Apdo 29-124, México 1, DF, Mexico

Hérédia Prize
Given in alternate years to (1) a Latin American writer for a piece of prose or poetry written in French; (2) the author of a collection of sonnets (printed or typed). Monetary award. Awarded annually. Enquiries to French Academy, Institut de France, 23 Quai de Conti, F-75006 Paris, France

The Georgette **Heyer** Historical Novel Prize
Established in 1977 for previously unpublished outstanding historical novel written in English. The novel should be set pre-1939 and have a minimum length of 40,000 words. Annual award of £2,000 and the guarantee of hardback and paperback publication. Awarded for 1983 to Kathleen Herbert for *The Queen of the Lightning* (The Bodley Head). Enquiries to The Bodley Head, 9 Bow St, Covent Garden, London WC2E 7AL, UK
or Transworld Publishers Ltd, Century House, 61-63 Uxbridge Rd, Ealing W5 5SA, UK

David **Higham** Prize for Fiction
Founded 1975. For the best first novel or book of short stories, in the opinion of the judges, written in English by a citizen of The Commonwealth, Republic of Ireland, Pakistan or Republic of South Africa. Prize of £500 awarded annually. Awarded in 1982 to Glyn Hughes for *Where I Used to Play on the Green* (Victor Gollancz, UK). Enquiries to The National Book League, Book House, East Hill, Wandsworth, London SW18 2QZ, UK

Clarence L **Holte** Prize
Founded in 1977. Awarded for published writings of excellence in literature and the humanities making important contributions to the cultural heritage of Africa and the African Diaspora. The prize is biennial. Enquiries to Roberta J Yancy and Mary Walker, Twenty-First Century Foundation, 112 West 120 St, New York, NY 10027, USA

The **Hugo** Awards*
Established 1953 as Science Fiction Achievement Awards for the best science fiction writing in several categories. Chrome-plated rocket ship. Awarded annually. Enquiries to c/o Howard DeVore, 4705 Weddel St, Dearborn Heights, Michigan 48125, USA

Alice **Hunt Bartlett** Prize
To the poet the Society most wishes to honour. In the case of poems translated into English, the prize of £500 will be divided equally between the poet and translator. The original poet must be living. Awarded annually. Closing date for entries each year is 31 January. The 1983 award was to Medbh McGuckian for *The Flower Master*. Enquiries to The Secretary, The Poetry Society, 21 Earls Court Sq, London SW5 9DE, UK

International Grand Prize for Poetry
For poetry by a living author. 100,000 Belgian francs awarded biennially. Entries are judged by an international jury of 15 and submissions are not invited. Enquiries to La Maison Internationale de Poésie, 147 chaussée de Maecht, Brussels, Belgium

International Literary Braille Competition Awards
Established 1940. To an individual who is legally blind. Cash prizes in the categories of fiction, non-fiction and poetry. Awarded every five years. Enquiries to Jewish Braille Institute of America Inc, 110 East 30 St, New York, NY 10016, USA

International Prize of French Friendship*
For poetry written in French by a foreigner. Awarded biennially. Enquiries to Société des Poètes français, Hôtel de Massa, 38 rue du Faubourg St Jacques, F-75014 Paris, France

International Publications Cultural Award
Established in 1966. Awarded to books or periodical publications published in a European language in Japan which contribute to raising the level of world culture or to increasing understanding of Japan. The 'Grand Prix' is awarded by the Foreign Minister and special prizes are awarded by the Japan Foundation, the Mainichi Newspaper, the Japan Broadcasting Corporation and the Publishers Association for Cultural Exchange. Enquiries to Secretary, Publishers Association for Cultural Exchange, 1-2-1 Sarugaku-cho, Chiyoda-ku, Tokyo 101, Japan

Irish-American Cultural Institute Literary Awards
Established 1966. For writers in the Irish or English language. Awards total US$10,000, for each language in alternate years. $10,000 awarded to Peadar O'Donnell (Dublin) in 1982. $5,000 awarded to poet John Hewitt (Belfast) in 1983; further $5,000 to be awarded for that year. Enquiries to Irish-American Cultural Institute, 683 Osceola Ave, St Paul, Minnesota 55105, USA

Irish Poetry Award, see Prize for Poetry in Irish

The Jerusalem Prize
This international prize of $3,000 was established in 1963 and is awarded during the Jerusalem International Book Fair which is held every two years. The award is made to an author or philosopher whose life's work has been devoted to the idea of 'The Freedom of the Individual in Society'. In 1983 the winner was V S Naipaul. Enquiries to Zev Birger, Chairman and Managing Director, Jerusalem International Book Fair, 12 Sarei Israel, PO Box 1241, Jerusalem 91012, Israel

Jewish Chronicle — Harold H Wingate Book Awards, see H H Wingate Prize

Stanislas Julien Prize
For the best work related to China. Monetary prize. Awarded annually. Enquiries to Academy of Inscriptions and Belles-Lettres, 23 quai de Conti, F-75006 Paris, France

Kalinga Prize
This prize, awarded annually by UNESCO, was established in 1951 by the Kalinga Foundation Trust, for the dual purpose of recognizing outstanding interpretation of science to the general public and of strengthening scientific and cultural links between India and other nations. The recipient of the prize is selected by an international jury and may be anyone who has contributed to the promotion of the public understanding of science and technology. The winner receives a cash prize of £1,000 sterling. The award takes its name from an ancient empire of the Indian subcontinent, which was conquered in the third century BC by the Emperor Asoka, who was so appalled by the cost of his conquest in terms of human life and suffering that he swore never to wage war again. The 1981 prize was awarded jointly to David Attenborough (UK) and Dennis Flanagan (USA). Enquiries to UNESCO SC/SER/SCW, 7 pl de Fontenoy, F-75700 Paris, France

Gottfried Keller Prize
Founded in 1921 by Martin Bodmer for Swiss and other writers who have honoured the Swiss spirit. Now biennial prize of 15,000 Swiss francs. Enquiries to Martin-Bodmer-Stiftung, 19-21 chemin du Guignard, CH-1223 Cologny-Geneva, Switzerland

Mandat des Poètes Prize*
Founded in 1950 by Pierre Béarn, to aid a French-language poet of talent, young or old, in time of need. Awarded annually. Enquiries to Pierre Béarn, 60 rue Monsieur-le-Prince, F-75006 Paris, France

Katherine Mansfield Menton Memorial Prize*
Instituted 1959. Two prizes awarded for published short stories, one English and one French. Just over £100 each. Awarded triennially. Enquiries to The Secretary, PEN English Centre, 7 Dilke St, London SW3 4JE, UK (Enquiries regarding the French short story to Mrs Danielle Dordet, General Secretary, PEN Club français, 6 rue François Miron, F-75004 Paris, France — marked Prix Menton)

Medicis Foreign Prize*
Established 1970. For the best foreign novel appearing in French during the preceding year. Monetary prize. Awarded annually. Enquiries to Medicis Prize, c/o Francine Mallet, 25 rue Dombasle, Paris 15, France

Ramón Menéndez Pidal Prize
For an outstanding work in the fields of Spanish linguistics or Spanish literature. 30,000 pesetas. Awarded biennially. Enquiries to Royal Spanish Academy, Felipe IV No 4, Madrid, Spain

Neustadt International Prize for Literature
'World Literature Today', an international literary quarterly, established in 1969 an award for distinguished and continuing artistic achievement in the fields of poetry, drama or fiction. A new international jury of twelve is appointed for each successive award by the editor in consultation with the editorial board. Each juror presents one candidate for the prize. A majority (7) of the jury must be present for the deliberations and the final voting. Representative selections of a candidate's work must be available to the jury in either French or English translation. Announcement of the winner is made in February, and the award is officially presented at The University of Oklahoma, Norman, Oklahoma, every other year. The prize is an award certificate, a replica of an eagle's feather in silver, and US$25,000. 'World Literature Today' dedicates one issue to the recipient. The University of Oklahoma Press will seriously consider the publication of a book by or on the winner. Prize not open to application. Enquiries to 'World Literature Today', 630 Parrington Oval, Room 110, Norman, Oklahoma 73019, USA

Martinus Nijhoff Prize
Established 1953. For translation of literary work into and from Dutch. 7,500 Dutch florins. Awarded annually. Enquiries to Prince Bernhard Fund, Postbus 19750, 1000 GT, Amsterdam, Netherlands

Nobel Prize for Literature*
Of all the literary prizes, the Nobel Prize for literature is the highest in value and in honour bestowed. It is one of the five prizes founded by Alfred Bernhard Nobel (1833-1896); the other four awards are for physics, chemistry, physiology or medicine, and peace. By the terms of Nobel's will, the prize for literature is to be given to the person 'who shall have produced in the field of literature the most distinguished work of an idealistic tendency'. It consists of a gold medal, a diploma and a sum of money; the amount in 1983 was over US$150,000. The award is administered by the Swedish Academy in Stockholm and official presentation is made on December 10, the anniversary of Nobel's death. No one may apply for the Nobel Prize; there is no competition. It is awarded to an author usually for his total literary output and not for any single work. Awarded in 1983 to William Golding (UK). Enquiries to Swedish Academy, Källargränd 4, Börshuset, S-111 29 Stockholm, Sweden

The Noma Award for Publishing in Africa
Established in 1979 by Shoichi Noma, Honorary Chairman of the Japanese publishing company Kodansha Ltd, for African writers whose work in its original form has been published in Africa. The annual award of US$3,000 is given for an outstanding work in any of the following categories (i) scholarly or academic, (ii) children's books, (iii) literature and creative writing (including fiction, drama or poetry). Awarded in 1983 to Dr A N E Amissah (Ghana) for *Criminal Procedure in Ghana* (Sedco Publishers, Ghana). Enquiries to The African Book Publishing Record, PO Box 56, Oxford OX1 3EL, UK

The Noma Literary Prize
Established by the Japanese publishing company Kodansha Ltd in cooperation with UNESCO, Paris. Annual award of US$5,000. Enquiries to Kodansha Ltd, 212-21 Otowa, Bunkyo-ku, Tokyo 112, Japan

Nordic Council Literary Prize
Established 1962. To an individual author for a current work of literature in one of the Scandinavian languages. 75,000 Danish crowns. Awarded annually. Enquiries to Nordic Council, Box 7765, S-103 96 Stockholm, Sweden

Odd Fellows (Manchester Unity) Social Concern Book Awards
Established 1977. Two prizes (usually worth a total of £1,000) are awarded annually for the book, or pamphlet of not less than 10,000 words, in an area of social concern (to be specified each year). Entries must first have appeared in English and been written by citizens of The Commonwealth, Republic of Ireland, Pakistan or Republic of South Africa. Enquiries to The National Book League, Book House, East Hill, Wandsworth, London SW18 2QZ, UK

Pavol Országh-Hviezdoslav Prize
Awarded annually by the Union of Slovak Writers to outstanding translators of Slovak literature abroad during the preceding year. Awarded in 1983 to Gustav Just (German Democratic Republic). Enquiries to Zväz slovenských spisovateľov, 81508 Bratislava, ul Obrancov mieru 14, Czechoslovakia

Yugoslav P E N Club Award
For the translation of a book from and into languages spoken or used in Yugoslavia. Monetary prize. Enquiries to Yugoslav PEN Club, Serbian Centre, YU-11000 Belgrade, 7 Francuska St, Yugoslavia

Hungarian P E N Club Medal
For translation of Hungarian literary work into foreign languages. Awarded when merited. Enquiries to Hungarian PEN Club, H-1051 Budapest V, Vörösmarty tér 1, Hungary

Polish P E N Club Prizes
Founded by Robert Graves for best translations of foreign poetry and prose into Polish, and of Polish literature into foreign languages. Three awards 20,000 zlotys each. Awarded annually. Enquiries to Polish PEN Club, Palac Kultury i Nauki, 00-901 Warsaw, Poland

Leopoldo Panero Prize*
For poetry. 100,000 pesetas. Awarded annually. Enquiries to Madrid Institute of Hispanic Culture, Ave Reyes Catolicos, Ciudad Universitaria, Madrid, Spain

Lorne Pierce Medal
Established 1926. For achievement and conspicuous merit in the field of imaginative or critical literature, in English or French. Medal and C$1,500. Awarded biennially. Enquiries to Royal Society of Canada, 344 Wellington St, Ottawa, Ontario K1A 0N4, Canada

Pilgrim Award
Established 1970 and awarded annually by a committee of the Science Fiction Research Association for outstanding contributions made over a period of time to scholarship relating to the study of science fiction and modern fantasy. Enquiries to Science Fiction Research Association Inc, Box 3186, The College of Wooster, Wooster, Ohio 44691, USA

Planeta Prize
Established 1952. For the best unpublished novel. Open to writers of Spanish speaking countries. 8,000,000 pesetas, and publication by Planeta. Awarded annually. Latest winner is Jesús Fernández Santos for *Jaque a la Dama*. Enquiries to Editorial Planeta SA, Córcega 273, Barcelona 8, Spain

Edgar Poe Prize*
To the best foreign poet writing in the French language. 100 French francs. Awarded annually. Enquiries to Maison de Poésie, 11 bis rue Ballu, F-75009 Paris, France

Polish Authors' Society (Zaiks) Prizes
For best translations of Polish literature into foreign languages. Three prizes, 20,000 zlotys each. Awarded annually. Enquiries to Stowarzyszenie Autorów Zaiks, ul Hipoteczna 2, 00-092 Warsaw, Poland

Poetry in Irish, see Prize for Poetry in Irish

Prince Pierre de Monaco Prize for Literature
Restricted to French-speaking writers. For the entirety of the literary work of one author. 30,000 French francs awarded annually. 1983 winner was Jacques Laurent. Enquiries to Fondation Prince Pierre de Monaco, Ministère d'Etat, Monaco

Prize for Poetry in Irish*
Established 1962. To the author of best book of poetry in the Irish language (Gaelic). IR£1,000. Enquiries to Arts Council, 70 Merrion Sq, Dublin 2, Republic of Ireland

Putnam Awards*
Established 1960. For outstanding manuscripts in the English language already under contract to the house, fiction or non-fiction, not previously published by Putnam's. Advance of US$7,500 against royalties and US$7,500 for advertising and promotion. Not more than three awarded annually. Enquiries to G P Putnam's Sons, 200 Madison Ave, New York, NY 10016, USA

Regina Medal
Established 1959. For recognition of continued distinguished contributions to children's literature. Silver Medal. Awarded annually. Won in 1983 by Tomie de Paola. Enquiries to Catholic Library Association, 461 West Lancaster Ave, Haverford, Pennsylvania 19041, USA

Alfonso Reyes Prize*
Founded 1973. Awarded by the Federal Government of Mexico to an author of any nationality for his or her literary output on the study of the works of Alfonso Reyes or on Mexico. 200,000 Mexican pesos annually. Enquiries to Ministry of Public Education, Brazil 21, México 1, DF, Mexico.

John Llewelyn **Rhys** Memorial Prize
Established in 1941 by the widow of an airman killed on active service who was awarded the Hawthornden Prize posthumously. For a 'memorable work' by a Commonwealth citizen who was under 30 at the time of its publication. Prize of £500 awarded annually for a book published in English in the year of the award. Entries should be received by 1 July of the year of the award. 1982 prize awarded to William Boyd for *An Icecream War* (Hamish Hamilton, UK). Enquiries to The National Book League, Book House, East Hill, Wandsworth, London SW18 2QZ, UK

Rose of French Poets Prize
Established 1949. For a foreign poet who has celebrated France in his verse. Medal awarded every two years. Awarded in 1983 to Karl Wydler (Switzerland). Enquiries to Société des Poètes Français, Hôtel de Massa, 38 rue du Faubourg St Jacques, F-75014 Paris, France

Salon de l'Enfance et de la Jeunesse Grand Literary Prize
Founded in 1953 with the object of encouraging authors towards the betterment of children's literature. 4,000 French francs is awarded for an original work in French which has been published in the preceding year and which is intended for children in the 10-12 years age group; the entries are judged mainly by a jury of 10 French children in this group. A further 2,000 French francs may be given for an outstanding work of science fiction. Enquiries to Grand Prix de Littérature du Salon de l'Enfance et de la Jeunesse, 11 rue St-Florentin, F-75008 Paris, France

Science Fiction Achievement Awards, see The Hugo Awards

Sinclair Prize for Fiction
Founded in 1982. For a previously unpublished novel which originally must have been written in the English language and which is not only of great literary merit but also of social and political significance. Annual award of £5,000, plus possible publication. Enquiries to The National Book League, Book House, East Hill, Wandsworth, London SW18 2QZ, UK

'La Sonrisa Vertical' Prize
Founded in 1978 in homage to Lopez Barbadillo. Awarded annually for the best erotic novel written in Spanish or another language of the Spanish State. The prize is 500,000 pesetas advance on the work prior to publication, together with an artistic object designed by Francis Closas. The 1982 jury considered that no manuscript deserved to receive the prize. Enquiries to La Sonrisa Vertical, Tusquets Editores, Calle Iradier 24 bajos, Barcelona 17, Spain

The **'Times Educational Supplement'** Information Book Awards
Instituted 1972. For outstandingly good information books originating in any Commonwealth country. Two awards are offered for a book for children up to the age of 9 and for a book for those aged between 10 and 16, both awards for £150. The judges may award a further £150 to the illustrator of either or both books. In 1982 the junior category award was won by Phillippa Aston for *A Day With a Miner* (Wayland, UK), the senior category award was won by John Kilbracken for *The Easy Way to Bird Recognition* (Kingfisher, UK). Enquiries to Literary Editor, Times Educational Supplement, Priory House, St John's Lane, London EC1M 4BX, UK

Triennial Prize for Bibliography
The International League of Antiquarian Booksellers (ILAB) awards a prize, every three years, of $1,000 to the author of the best work, published or unpublished, of learned bibliography, of research into the history of the book or typography, or a book of general interest on the subject. The competition is open, without restriction, but entries must be submitted in a language which is universally read. An already published work is eligible only if it has an imprint bearing a date within the three years preceding the closing date for submission. Enquiries to Dr Frieder Kocher-Benzing, Rathenaustr 21, D-7000 Stuttgart 1, Federal Republic of Germany

Triple First Award
Founded 1981. For a previously unpublished first novel by an author who must be a citizen of The Commonwealth, Republic of Ireland, United States of America, Republic of South Africa or Pakistan. To be awarded annually. An advance of £5,000 for world rights and guaranteed hardback, book club and paperback publication by The Bodley Head, Book Club Associates and Penguin Books Ltd. Enquiries to The Bodley Head, 9 Bow St, Covent Garden, London WC2E 7AL, UK

The **Universe** — The Catholic Newspaper — Literary Prize
For the book, written in English and published in Britain or Ireland, which best supports and defends Christian values. £250 awarded annually. Enquiries to The National Book League, Book House, East Hill, Wandsworth, London SW18 2QZ, UK

Welsh Arts Council International Writer's Prize
Awarded every two years to encourage international literary and cultural exchanges. The prize of £1,000 is given to an author for excellence of writing and his/her contribution to literature generally. The prizewinner's works, if not in English or Welsh, are usually translated into Welsh. In 1982 the award went to Margaret Attwood (Canada). Enquiries to Welsh Arts Council, Museum Pl, Cardiff CF1 3NX, UK

H H Wingate Prize
Originally instituted in 1977 by the 'Jewish Chronicle' and the Wingate Foundation. Awarded to the book which best stimulates an interest in and awareness of Jewish concern among a wider reading public. Books must be published in English and authors normally resident in the UK, Israel, The Commonwealth, Republic of South Africa, Pakistan or the Republic of Ireland are eligible. £3,000 is awarded annually. Enquiries to The National Book League, Book House, East Hill, Wandsworth, London SW18 2QZ, UK

Abraham Woursell Prize (University of Vienna)
Instituted 1965. For young creative writers. 300,000 Austrian schillings annually for five years. Enquiries to Selection Committee Chairman, Faculty of Philosophy, University of Vienna, Austria

'Yorkshire Post' Book of the Year Award Instituted 1964. First prize of £600 and runner-up prize of £450 for the best books published each year. Translations, reissues and works of a strictly scientific or technical nature are excluded. If the first prize is awarded to a non-fiction work, the runner-up prize goes to a fiction work and vice versa. First prize in 1982 to John Mortimer for *Clinging to the Wreckage* (Weidenfeld & Nicolson, UK) and the Novel of the Year Prize to Elizabeth Jane Howard for *Getting It Right* (Hamish Hamilton, UK). In addition there were Best First Work Awards to new authors in 1982. £450 first prize to David Fraser for *Alanbrooke* (William Collins, UK) and the runner-up prize of £300 to Dan van der Vat for *The Grand Scuttle* (Hodder & Stoughton, UK). (There are also special annual awards of £500 each for the books selected to advance the popular appreciation of art and of music.) Enquiries to Ford Longman, Secretary, Book of the Year Awards, Yorkshire Post Newspapers Ltd, PO Box 168, Wellington St, Leeds LS1 1RF, UK

'Young Observer'/Rank Organisation Fiction Prize
Founded 1981 for the best fiction work for teenage readers written by a citizen of The Commonwealth, Republic of Ireland, Pakistan or Republic of South Africa. £600 awarded annually. The joint winners in 1982 were Jan Mark for *Aquarius* (Kestrel, UK) and Mary Melwood for *The Watcher Bee* (André Deutsch, UK). Enquiries to Janet Crumbie, 'Young Observer', 8 St Andrew's Hill, London EC4V 5JA, UK

Young People's Book Prize
For an outstanding book or the collected works of a writer or illustrator in the field of juvenile literature. 3,000 Swiss francs or more. Awarded annually. 1983 award to Katharina Zimmermann for *Damek*. Enquiries to Swiss Teachers Association, Ringstr 54, CH-8057 Zurich, Switzerland

The ISBN System

Background

The question of the need and feasibility of an international numbering system for books was first discussed at the third international Conference on Book Market Research and Rationalization in the Book Trade held in November 1966 in Berlin. At that time a number of publishers and book distributors in Europe were considering the use of computers in order processing and inventory control and it was evident that a pre-requisite of an efficient machine system was a unique and simple identification number for a published item.
The system which fulfilled this requirement and which became known as the International Standard Book Number (ISBN) System developed out of the book numbering system introduced into the United Kingdom in 1967.
In a report to the British Publishers Association, Professor F G Foster of the London School of Economics stated that there was '...a clear need for the introduction into the book trade of standard numbering... and substantial benefits would accrue to all parties therefrom'. After further study and deliberation, a detailed plan for standard numbering was produced. At the same time, the Technical Committee Documentation of the International Organization for Standardization (ISO/TC 46) set up a working party (with the British Standards Institution acting as secretariat) to investigate the possibility of adapting the British system for international use.
A meeting was held in London in 1968 with representatives from Denmark, France, Federal Republic of Germany, Eire, the Netherlands, Norway, the United Kingdom, the United States of America and an observer from UNESCO. Other countries contributed written suggestions and expressions of interest. A report of the meeting was circulated to all countries belonging to the ISO. Comments on this report and subsequent proposals were considered at meetings held in Berlin and Stockholm in 1969.
As a result of these meetings there emerged ISO Recommendation 2108 which sets out the principles and procedure for international standard book numbering. The purpose of the ISO Recommendation is to coordinate and standardize internationally the use of book numbers so that an International Standard Book Number (ISBN) identifies one title or edition of a title from one specific publisher and is unique to that edition.
The ISBN applies in the main to books — for which the system was originally created — but, by extension, it may be used for any item produced by publishers or collected by libraries.

How the International Standard Book Number (ISBN) is Built Up

Every International Standard Book Number (ISBN) consists of ten digits and whenever it is printed it is preceded by the letters ISBN. (Note: In those countries where the Latin alphabet is not used, an abbreviation in the characters of the local alphabet may be used in addition to the Latin letters ISBN.)
The ten-digit number is divided into four parts of variable length, each part when printed being separated by a hyphen or space. (Note: Experience suggests that the hyphen is preferable to the space.)
The four parts are as follows:

Part 1. Group Identifier
This part identifies the national, geographic or other similar grouping of publishers.

Part 2. Publisher's Prefix
This part identifies a particular publisher within a group.

Part 3. Title Identifier
This part identifies a particular title or edition of a title published by a particular publisher.

Part 4. Check Digit
This is a single digit at the end of the ISBN which provides an automatic check on the correctness of the ISBN.

Group identifier
Group identifiers are allocated by the International ISBN Agency and a publisher wishing to participate in the ISBN system must belong to a recognized ISBN group. Groups are determined by national, geographic, language or other pertinent considerations. Experience has shown that groups based on national or geographic considerations are the most satisfactory. The following group identifiers are in use at present:

0 and 1	Australia, English-speaking Canada, New Zealand, Republic of South Africa, UK, USA, Zimbabwe
2	France, French-speaking Belgium, French-speaking Canada, French-speaking Switzerland
3	Austria, Federal Republic of Germany, German-speaking Switzerland
4	Japan
5	Union of Soviet Socialist Republics
81	India
82	Norway
83	Poland
84	Spain, Spanish-speaking South America (partly)
85	Brazil
87	Denmark
88	Italy
90	Netherlands, Dutch-speaking Belgium
91	Sweden
92	United Nations
950	Argentina
951	Finland
958	Colombia
962	Hong Kong
963	Hungary
965	Israel
967	Malaysia
968	Mexico
971	Philippines
974	Thailand
977	Egypt
978	Nigeria
9963	Cyprus
9964	Ghana
9971	Singapore
9976	Tanzania
99914	Suriname

Publisher's Prefix
The publisher's prefix designates the publisher of a given book. Publishers with a large output of books are assigned a short publisher's prefix; publishers with a small output of books are assigned a longer publisher's prefix.

Title identifier
The title identifier is assigned to a particular title or edition of a title by the publisher from within the range of numbers assigned to him and which will depend upon the length of his publisher's prefix. Title identifiers are normally assigned by the publisher himself. Publishers who assign their own title identifiers may use them to identify titles in the publishing house throughout the planning stages.

Check digit
The 'check digit' is the last digit in an ISBN and is computed as the result of an elaborate calculation on the other nine digits.
This calculation is performed almost instantaneously by an electronic computing device, and is a means of detecting incorrectly transcribed numbers. The check digit is calculated on a modulus 11 with weights 10-2, using X in lieu of 10 where ten would occur as a check digit.
This means that each of the first nine digits of the ISBN — ie excluding the check digit itself — is multiplied by a number ranging from 10 to 2 and the sum of the products thus obtained, plus the check digit, must be divisible, without remainder, by 11. For example:

	Group Identifier		Publisher's Prefix		
ISBN ..	0	8	4	3	6
Weight ..	10	9	8	7	6
Products ..	0 +	72 +	32 +	21 +	36 +

	Title Number			Check Digit
ISBN ..	1	0	7	2	7
Weight ..	5	4	3	2	
Products ..	5 +	0 +	21 +	4 +	7

Total: 198

As 198 can be divided by 11 without remainder 0 8436 1072 7 is a valid International Standard Book Number.

The number of digits in each part; and how to recognize them in an ISBN
The number of digits in each of the identifying parts 1, 2 and 3 is variable, though the total number of digits contained in these parts is always 9. These nine digits together with the check digit bring the total number of digits in an ISBN to ten.
The number of digits in the group identifier will vary according to the likely output of books in a group. Thus groups with an expected large output will get numbers of one or two digits and publishers with an expected large output will get numbers of two or three digits.
Exceptionally, a one-digit number may be assigned to a publisher but it will be appreciated that the assignment of one-digit publisher identifiers greatly reduces the range of possible identifiers in the group. For ease of reading, the four parts of the ISBN are divided by spaces or hyphens. These spaces or hyphens, however, are not retained in a computer which depends upon the special distribution of ranges of numbers for the recognition of the parts.

Scope of the ISBN

For the purposes of the ISBN system books and other items to be numbered include:

Printed books and pamphlets

Microform publications

Braille publications

Mixed media publications

Machine-readable tapes designed to produce readable printout

Other similar media

Except:
Ephemeral printed materials such as diaries, calendars, advertising matter and the like

Art prints and art folders without title page and text

Sound recordings

Serial publications

Application of ISBN

General
A separate ISBN must be assigned to every different edition of a book, but NOT to an unchanged impression or unchanged reprint of the same book in the same format and by the same publisher. Price changes do not need new ISBN.

Facsimile reprints
A separate ISBN must be assigned to a facsimile reprint produced by a different publisher.

Books in different formats
A separate ISBN must be assigned to the different formats in which a particular title is published. For example: a hardback edition and a paperback edition each receives a separate ISBN. On the same principle, a microform edition receives a separate ISBN.

Multi-volume works
An ISBN must be assigned to the whole set of volumes of a multi-volume work as well as to each individual volume in the set.

Back stock
A publisher is required to number his back stock and publish the ISBN in his catalogues.
He must also print the ISBN in the first available reprint of an item from his back stock.

Collaborative publications
A publication issued as a coedition or joint imprint with other publishers is assigned an ISBN by the publisher in charge of distribution.

Books sold or distributed by agents
According to the principles of the ISBN system, a particular edition, published by a particular publisher receives only one ISBN and this ISBN must be retained no matter where or by whom the book is distributed or sold.
A book imported by an exclusive distributor or sole agent from an area not yet in the ISBN system and for which therefore no ISBN has been assigned, may be assigned an ISBN by the exclusive distributor.
A book imported by an exclusive distributor or sole agent to which a new title-page, bearing the imprint of the exclusive distributor, has been added in place of the title page of the original publisher, is to be given a new ISBN by the exclusive distributor or sole agent. The ISBN of the original publisher is also to be given as a related ISBN.
A book imported by several distributors from an area not yet in the ISBN system and for which, therefore, no ISBN has been assigned, may be assigned an ISBN by the group agency responsible for those distributors.

Publishers with more than one place of publication
A publisher operating in a number of places which are listed together in the imprint of a book will assign only one ISBN to the book. A publisher operating separate and distinct offices or branches in different places may have a publisher identifier for each office or branch. Nevertheless, each book published is to be assigned only one ISBN, the assignment being made by the office or branch responsible for publication.

Register of ISBNs
Every publisher must keep a register of ISBNs that have been assigned to published and forthcoming books. The register is to be kept in numerical sequence giving ISBN, author, title and edition (where appropriate).

ISBN not to be re-used under any circumstances
An ISBN once allocated must not under any circumstances be re-used. This is of the utmost importance to avoid confusion. It is recognized that, owing to clerical errors, numbers will be incorrectly assigned. If this happens, the number must be deleted from the list of usable numbers and must not be assigned to another title. Every publisher will have sufficient numbers in his range for the loss of these numbers to be insignificant. Publishers should advise the group agency of the numbers thus deleted and of the titles to which they were erroneously assigned.

Printing of the ISBN

General
The ISBN must appear on the item itself. This is essential for the efficient running of the system.

Printing of ISBN on books
In the case of books, the ISBN must appear whenever possible: On the reverse of the title-page, or, if this is not possible, on the base of the title-page, or, if this too is not possible, at some other conspicuous location in the book. On the base of the spine.
On the back of the cover in 9-point type or larger.
On the back of the dust-jacket, and on the back of any other protective case or wrapper.
The ISBN should always be printed in type large enough to be easily legible (eg not smaller than 9 point).

Administration of the ISBN System

General
The administration of the ISBN system is carried on at three levels. These are the international, group and publisher levels.

International administration
The international administration of the system is in the hands of the International Standard Book Number Agency which has an Advisory Panel representing the ISO and the publishing and library world. The address of the International Agency is:

The International Standard Book
Number Agency,
Staatsbibliothek Preussischer
Kulturbesitz,
Potsdamer Str 33, Postfach 1407,
D-1000 Berlin 30,
Federal Republic of Germany

The principal functions of the International Agency are:

To supervise the use of the system

To approve the definition and structure of groups

To allocate identifiers to groups

To advise groups on the setting up and functioning of group agencies

To advise group agencies on the allocation of publisher identifiers

To promote the world-wide use of the system

In addition, the International Agency also offers the following services. It will:

Provide a group agency with lists of ISBNs (with computer-generated check digits) for the use of publishers in the group.

Provide international registers of publishers, prefixes and publishers' names.

Provide from information supplied by group agencies a computer printout of lists of publishers' prefixes, names and locations.

Provide from information supplied by group agencies a computer printout of invalid or duplicate ISBNs.

Group administration
Groups are administered by Group Agencies. Within the group there may be several national agencies, eg group 0/1 has separate agencies in USA, United Kingdom, Canada, Australia etc, with the main agency for the whole group in the UK.

The functions of a group agency are:

To manage and administer the affairs of the group.

To handle relations with the International ISBN Agency on behalf of all the publishers in the group.

To decide, in consultation with trade organizations and publishers, the publisher identifier ranges required.

To allocate publishers' prefixes to publishers eligible to join the group and to maintain a register of publishers and their prefixes.

To decide, in consultation with trade organizations and publishers, which publishers shall assign numbers to their own titles and which publishers shall have numbers assigned to their titles by the group agency.

To provide technical advice and assistance to the publishers and to ensure that standards and approved procedures are observed in the group.

To make available a manual of instruction for publishers.

To make available computer printouts of ISBNs to publishers numbering their own books with check digits already calculated. (Such printouts may be obtained from the International Agency on request.)

To validate all ISBNs assigned by publishers numbering their own books and keep a register of them.

To inform publishers of any invalid or duplicate ISBNs assigned by them.

To assign numbers to all publications from those publishers who do not assign their own ISBNs and advise the publishers concerned of ISBNs assigned upon request.

To achieve, thereby, total numbering in the group.

To arrange with book listing and bibliographic agencies for the publication of ISBNs with the titles to which they refer.

To arrange with publishers for the numbering of their back lists and for the publication of these in appropriate trade lists and bibliographies.

To maintain liaison with all elements of the book trade and introduce new publishers to the system.

To assist the trade in the use of the ISBN in computer systems.

The national agencies are:

Argentina
Isay Klasse, Cámara Argentina del Libro, Ave Belgrano 1580 6° piso, 1093 Buenos Aires

Australia
Mrs Cornell Platzer, National Library of Australia, Parkes Pl, Canberra, ACT 2600

Austria
H Walter Ess, Hauptverband des Österreichischen Buchhandels, A-1010 Vienna 1, Grünangergasse 4

Belgium (Dutch-speaking)
Netherlands agency

Belgium (French-speaking)
French agency

Brazil
Agência Brasileira do ISBN, Biblioteca Nacional, Ave Rio Branco 219/39 – 3° andar, 20042 Rio de Janeiro, RJ

Canada (English-speaking)
Paul McCormick, National Library of Canada, 395 Wellington St, Ottawa, Ontario K1A ON4

Canada (French-speaking)
Louise Tessier, ISBN/BNQ, Bureau du dépôt légal, Bibliothèque nationale du Québec, 1700 rue St-Denis, Montreal, Québec H2X 3K6

Colombia
Centro Regional para el Fomento del Libro en América Latina y el Caribe, Apdo Aéreo 17438, Calle 70 No 9-52, Bogotá

Cyprus
Savvas L Petrides, c/o Cyprus Centre for Registration of Books & Serials, Ministry of Education Cultural Service, Office of the Inspector of Libraries, Nicosia

Denmark
Morten Garde, Dansk Bogfortegnelse, Bibliotekscentralen, Telegrafvej 5, DK-2750 Ballerup

Egypt
Dr Ezz El Dine Ismail, General Egyptian Book Organization, Corniche el Nil, Boulac, Cairo

Finland
Dr Thea Aulo, Finnish ISBN Numbering Agency, Bibliographic Department, Helsinki University Library, PL 312, SF-00170 Helsinki 17

France
Agence francophone pour la Numérotation internationale du Livre (AFNIL-ISBN), 35 rue Grégoire de Tours, F-75279 Paris 6e

Federal Republic of Germany
Wilfried H Schinzel, Buchhändler-Vereinigung GmbH, Postfach 2404, D-6000 Frankfurt am Main 1

Ghana
Mr A N de Heer, Ghana Library Board, Research Library on African Affairs, PO Box 2970, Accra

Hong Kong
Y C Lo, Books Registration Unit, Room 2201-2, Park-in Commercial Centre, Dundas St, Mongkok, Kowloon

Hungary
Dr Susánszky Zoltánné, Országos Széchényi Könyvtár Magyar ISBN Iroda, Pollack Mihálytér 10, H-1827 Budapest

India
Mrs S Narasimhan, Ministry of Education & Social Welfare (Department of Education), Raja Rammohun Roy National Educational Resources Centre, 1W-3, CR Barracks, Kasturba Gandhi Marg, New Delhi 1-110001

Israel
Israel ISBN Group Agency, c/o Centre for Public Libraries, PO Box 242, Jerusalem 91002

Italy
Gianni Merlini, Assoziacione Italiana Editori, Agenzia per l'Area di Lingua Italiana ISBN, Via delle Erbe 2, I-20121 Milan

Japan
Mr Naotoshi Matsudaira, Japan Book Publishers Association, 6 Fukuro-machi, Shinjuku-ku, Tokyo

Malaysia
Mrs Norpishah Mohd Noor, National Library of Malaysia, Bibliography and Indexing Division, 2526 Jalan Perdana, Kuala Lumpur

Mexico
Agencia Nacional ISBN, Centro Nacional de Información de la Direccion General del Derecho de Autor, Nuevo León 91, Col Condesa Hipódromo, 06100 Mexico DF

Netherlands
J van Leeuwan, Bureau ISBN, Centraal Boekhuis, Postbus 125, 4100 AC Culemborg

New Zealand
D C McIntosh, National Library of New Zealand, Private Bag, Wellington 1

Nigeria
The Director, National Library of Nigeria, 4 Wesley St, PMB 12626, Lagos

Norway
Mrs Kari Grethe Randers-Pehrson, Norsk Boknummerkontor, Universitetsbiblioteket i Oslo, Drammensvegen 42, Oslo 2

Philippines
Lily Orbase, The National Library of the Philippines, TM Kalaw St, Manila

Poland
Bioru Miedzynarodowego Numeru Ksiazki, ul Jasna 26, 00-950 Warsaw

Singapore
Mrs Lee-Khoo Guan Fong, National Library, Stamford Rd, Singapore 0617

Republic of South Africa
Dr H J Aschenborn, State Library, PO Box 397, Pretoria 0001

Spain
Gonzalo García Rubio, Instituto Nacional del Libro Español, Santiago Rusiñol 8, Madrid 3

Suriname
Dr Ellen Kensmil, Suriname Publishers' Association, Domineestr 26, Paramaribo

Sweden
Lars Erik Sanner, Swedish National ISBN-Centre, Bibliographical Department, Royal Library, Box 5039, S-10241 Stockholm 5

Switzerland (French-speaking)
French agency

Switzerland (German-speaking)
Peter Oprecht, Schweizerischer Buchhandler- und Verleger-Verband, Bellerivestr 3, CH-8008 Zurich

Tanzania
T E Mlaki, Tanzania Library Service, PO Box 9283, Dar es Salaam

Thailand
Mrs Suwakhon Phadung-Ath, National Library, Samsen Rd, Bangkok 10300

Union of Soviet Socialist Republics
Ju I Fartunin, Bibliograficeskij Institut SSSR, Kremlevskaja nab 1/9, 119816 Moscow G-19

UK
Miss E F Budworth, Standard Book Numbering Agency Ltd, 12 Dyott St, London WC1A 1DF

United Nations
Mr Naidenov, Book & International Cultural Exchange Promotions Division, UNESCO, 7 pl de Fontenoy, F-75700 Paris

USA
Emery Koltay, Standard Book Numbering Agency, 1180 Ave of the Americas, New York, NY 10036

Zimbabwe
Goodwell Motsi, National Archives of Zimbabwe, Private Bag 7729, Causeway, Harare

ISBN and ISSN

In addition to the International Standard Book Number System, a complementary numbering system for serial publications has also been established.
A serial is defined as any publication issued in successive parts, usually bearing numerical or chronological designations and intended to be continued indefinitely. Serials include periodicals, yearbooks and monographic series.
The International Standard Serial Number System (ISSN) is administered by the International Centre for the Registration of Serials (ISDS), whose address is:

International Serial Data System,
20 rue Bachaumont, F-75002 Paris,
France

Publishers of serials should apply to the International Serials Data System or to their National Serials Data Centre, if there is one, for ISSNs for their serial publications. Certain publications, such as yearbooks, annuals, monographic series, etc, should be assigned an ISSN for the serial title (which will remain the same for all the parts or individual volumes of the serial) and an ISBN for each individual volume.
Both ISSN and ISBN where they are assigned must be given on the publication and clearly identified.

(The above information is from the ISBN *Users' Manual*, compiled by the International ISBN Agency, Staatsbibliothek Preussischer Kulturbesitz, Berlin, Federal Republic of Germany.)

Book Trade Calendar

DATE	EVENT	CONTACT
1984		
January 7–13	American Library Association: Midwinter Conference. Washington DC, USA	American Library Association, 50 East Huron St, Chicago, Illinois 60611, USA Tel: (312) 944 6780
January 26–February 6	16th Cairo International Book Fair. Cairo, Egypt	General Egyptian Book Organization, Corniche El Nil, Boulac, Cairo, Egypt Tel: 775649
February 4–14	6th World Book Fair. New Delhi, India	National Book Trust, A-5 Green Park, New Delhi 110016, India Tel: 664020
March 4–10	1984 Writers' Week. Adelaide Festival of Arts, Adelaide, Australia	Writers' Week Committee, Adelaide Festival, Adelaide Festival Centre, King William Rd, Adelaide, South Australia 5000, Australia Tel: (08) 510121
March 7–8	Book Print Fair. London, UK	Book Print Fair, The PAMS Group, Faringdon Ave, Harold Hill, Romford, Essex RM3 8XL, UK Tel: (04023) 40059
March 10–18	Brussels International Book Fair. Brussels, Belgium	International Book Fair, 111 Ave du Parc, B-1060 Brussels, Belgium Tel: (02) 5382167
March 11–16	22nd International Publishers Association Congress. Mexico City, Mexico	The Publishers Association, 19 Bedford Sq, London WC1, UK Tel: (01) 580 6321 or Cámara Nacional de la Industrial Editorial, Holanda 13, Churubusco, México 21, DF, Mexico Tel: 5449568
March 11–17	Leipzig International Book Fair (at Leipzig Spring Fair). Leipzig, German Democratic Republic	Leipziger Messeamt, Markt 11-15, Postfach 720, DDR-7010, Leipzig, German Democratic Republic Tel: (71810) 8830
March 20–24	20th Didacta. Basle, Switzerland	Eurodidac, Jägerstr 5, CH-4058 Basle, Switzerland Tel: (061) 265052/53
March 29–April 1	3rd International Scientific & Technical Book Fair (at Milan Trade Fair). Milan, Italy	METIS, Provincia di Milano, Via Guicciardini 6, I-20129 Milan, Italy Tel: (02) 77402902
April 2	International Children's Book Day. (1984 Sponsor: Brazil)	IBBY Secretariat, Leonhardsgraben 38a, CH-4051 Basle, Switzerland Tel: (061) 253404
April 5–8	21st Children's Book Fair and 18th Exhibition for Illustrators. Bologna, Italy	Managing Director, Ente Autonomo per le Fiere di Bologna, Piazza della Costituzione 6, I-40128, Bologna, Italy Tel: (051) 503050
April 6–23	10th Buenos Aires International Book Fair. Buenos Aires, Argentina	Executive Committee, International Book Fair, Ave Cordoba 875 – 8vo piso, Buenos Aires 1054, Argentina Tel: 3116761/3115610

BOOK TRADE CALENDAR 485

DATE	EVENT	CONTACT
1984 (Cont'd)		
April 8–14	National Library Week. USA	American Library Association, 50 East Huron St, Chicago, Illinois 60611, USA *Tel:* (312) 944 6780
April 10–13	The London Book Fair (incorporating Academic Book Fair). London, UK	The London Book Fair, 16 Pembridge Rd, London W11 3HL, UK *Tel:* (01) 229 1825
April 19	The Publishers Association: Annual General Meeting. London, UK	The Publishers Association, 19 Bedford Sq, London WC1B 3HJ, UK *Tel:* (01) 580 6321
May	Children's Book Fortnight. New Zealand	Book Publishers Association of New Zealand, PO Box 78-071, Grey Lynn, Auckland 2, New Zealand *Tel:* Auckland 767 251
May	International Association of Literary Critics: Congress. Alghero, Sardinia	Association internationale des critiques littéraires, 38 rue du Faubourg St-Jacques, F-75014 Paris, France *Tel:* (1) 3220647
May 1–6	Quebec International Book Fair. Quebec, Canada	Quebec International Book Fair, 2590 blvd Laurier, Chambre 860, Sainte-Foy, Quebec, Canada G1V 4M6 *Tel:* (418) 6581974
May 2–6	New Zealand Booksellers 63rd Annual Conference. Rotorua, New Zealand	Booksellers Association of New Zealand (Inc), PO Box 11-377, Wellington, New Zealand *Tel:* Wellington 728 678
May 3–5	Book Publishers Association of New Zealand: Annual Conference. Rotorua, New Zealand	Book Publishers Association of New Zealand, PO Box 78-071, Grey Lynn, Auckland 2, New Zealand *Tel:* Auckland 767 251
May 6–10	International Reading Association: 29th Annual Convention. Atlanta, Georgia	Director of Conferences, International Reading Association, 800 Barksdale Rd, PO Box 8139, Newark, Delaware 19711, USA *Tel:* (302) 731 1600
May 9–13	The Booksellers Association of Great Britain & Ireland: Annual Conference and Trade Exhibition. Blackpool, Lancashire, UK	Administration Secretary, The Booksellers Association of Great Britain & Ireland, 154 Buckingham Palace Rd, London SW1W 9TZ, UK *Tel:* (01) 730 8214
May 11–14	Union internationale des industries graphiques de reproduction: 38th International Congress. Interlaken, Switzerland	Union Internationale des Industries graphiques de reproduction, 142 blvd St-Germain, F-75006 Paris, France *Tel:* (1) 3257707
May 11–19	P E N 47th International Congress. Tokyo, Japan	International PEN, 38 King St, London WC2E 8JT, UK *Tel:* (01) 379 7939 (Japanese PEN *Tel:* (402) 1171/72)
May 14–17	International Booksellers Federation: General Assembly. Vienna, Austria	International Booksellers Federation, Grünangergasse 4, A-1010 Vienna, Austria *Tel:* (222) 521535

DATE	EVENT	CONTACT
1984 (Cont'd)		
May 23–28	29th International Book Fair. Warsaw, Poland	Ars Polona, Secretariat of International Book Fair, Krakowskie Przedmiescie 7, 00-068 Warsaw, Poland *Tel:* 178641
May 23–31	16th International Technical and Scientific Book Exhibition. Budapest, Hungary	Managing Director, Müszaki Könyvkiadó, H-1014 Budapest, Szentháromság ter 1, Hungary *Tel:* 160273
May 26–29	American Booksellers Association: Annual Convention. Washington, DC, USA	Executive Director, American Booksellers Association, 122 East 42nd St, New York, NY 10168, USA *Tel:* (212) 867 9060
June 6–11	16th Sofia International Book Fair. Sofia, Bulgaria	International Book Fair, Department for Exhibitions & Fairs, 11 Slaveikov Sq, Sofia, Bulgaria *Tel:* 87 9111
June 7–12	Canadian Library Association: Annual Conference. Toronto, Ontario, Canada	Canadian Library Association, 151 Sparks St, Ottawa, Ontario K1P 5E3, Canada *Tel:* (613) 232 9625
June 23–29	American Library Association: Annual Conference. Dallas, Texas, USA	American Library Association, 50 East Huron St, Chicago, Illinois 60611, USA *Tel:* (312) 944 6780
July 30– August 2	International Reading Association: 10th World Congress. Hong Kong	Director of Conferences, International Reading Association, 800 Barksdale Rd, PO Box 8139, Newark, Delaware 19711, USA *Tel:* (302) 731 1600
August 5–8	The International Association of Printing House Craftsmen, Inc: Annual Convention. McAfee, New Jersey, USA	The International Association of Printing House Craftsmen, Inc, 7599 Kenwood Rd, Cincinnati, Ohio 45236, USA *Tel:* (513) 891 0611
August 11–17	36th Writers' Summer School. Swanwick, Derbyshire, UK	The Secretary, Writers' Summer School, The Red House, Mardens Hill, Crowborough, Sussex TN6 1XN, UK *Tel:* (08926) 3943
August 16–26	São Paulo VIII Biennial Book Fair. São Paulo, Brazil	São Paulo VIII Bienal Internacional do Livro, Av Ipiranga 1267–10° andar, 01039 São Paulo 2 Sp, Brazil *Tel:* 229 7855
August 19–24	IFLA Annual Conference. Nairobi, Kenya	IFLA, c/o The Royal Library, Postbus 95312, 2509 CH The Hague, Netherlands *Tel:* (070) 140884
August 22–27	International Federation for Modern Languages and Literatures: XVI International Congress. Budapest, Hungary	FILLM XVIth Congress Secretariat, H-1014 Budapest, Orszaghaz ul 30.1.48, Hungary
August 28– September 1	2nd Zimbabwe International Book Fair and Exhibition. Harare, Zimbabwe	African Book Publishing Record, Hans Zell Publishers, PO Box 56, Oxford OX1 3EL, UK *Tel:* (0865) 512934

DATE	EVENT	CONTACT
1984 (Cont'd)		
August (end)	Annual General Meetings of: South African Publishers Association Associated Booksellers of Southern Africa Overseas Publishers Representatives Book Trade Association. Cape Town, Republic of South Africa	Associated Booksellers of Southern Africa Ltd, 1 Meerendal, Nightingale Way, Pinelands, Republic of South Africa *Tel:* Pinelands 7405
September 1–9	16th Singapore Festival of Books and Book Fair. Singapore, Republic of Singapore	Book Fair Director, Festival of Books Singapore Pte Ltd, 865 Mountbatten Rd 05-28, Katong Shopping Centre, Singapore 1543, Republic of Singapore *Tel:* 3441495
September 2–7	Distripress Annual Congress. San Francisco, USA	Distripress, Beethovenstr 20, CH-8002 Zurich, Switzerland *Tel:* (01) 202 4121
September 10–13	UK Library Association Annual Conference and Exhibition. Brighton, Sussex, UK	Conferences Officer, The Library Association, 7 Ridgmount St, London WC1E 7AE, UK *Tel:* (01) 636 7543
September 15–18	The International League of Antiquarian Booksellers: International Congress. London, UK	The International League of Antiquarian Booksellers, Book House, 45 East Hill, London SW18 2QZ, UK *Tel:* (01) 870 8259
September 17–27	Federation Internationale de Documentation (FID): 42nd Conference and Congress. The Hague, Netherlands	Federation Internationale de Documentation, PO Box 90402, 2509 LK The Hague, Netherlands
September 18–21	Aslib 57th Annual Conference. University of East Anglia, Norwich. Norfolk, UK	Conference Organizer, Aslib, 3 Belgrave Sq, London SW1X 8PL, UK *Tel:* (01) 235 5050
September 19–22	International Antiquarian Book Fair. London, UK	The International League of Antiquarian Booksellers, Book House, 45 East Hill, London SW18 2QZ, UK *Tel:* (01) 870 8259
October 3–8	36th Frankfurt Book Fair. Frankfurt am Main, Federal Republic of Germany	Ausstellungs- und Messe-GmbH des Börsenvereins des deutschen Buchhandels, Postfach 2404, D-6000 Frankfurt am Main 1, Federal Republic of Germany *Tel:* (0611) 13061
October 6–13	Children's Book Week. UK	Administrator, Children's Book Week, National Book League, Book House, 45 East Hill, Wandsworth, London SW18 2QZ, UK *Tel:* (01) 874 6361
October 9–13	International Board on Books for Young People: 19th Biennial Congress. Nicosia, Cyprus	IBBY Secretariat, Leonhardsgraben 38a, CH-4051 Basle, Switzerland *Tel:* (061) 253404
October 23–27	Books USA 1984. Milan, Italy	Trade Promotion Officer, US International Marketing Center, Via Gattemelata 5, I-20149 Milan, Italy
October 25–31	29th Belgrade International Book Fair. Belgrade, Yugoslavia	Association of Yugoslav Publishers and Booksellers, YU-11000 Belgrade, Kneza Miloša 25/I *Tel:* (011) 642248
October 26–30	International Book Fair – Liber '84. Barcelona, Spain	Jaime Brull, Salon Internacional del Libro, IFEMA, Ave de Portugal s/n, Apdo 11.0.11, Madrid 11, Spain *Tel:* (91) 4115795/4115713

DATE	EVENT	CONTACT
1984 (Cont'd)		
November	New Zealand Book Week. New Zealand	Book Publishers Association of New Zealand, PO Box 78-071, Grey Lynn, Auckland 2, New Zealand *Tel:* Auckland 767 251
November 1–4	Book Manufacturers' Institute: Annual Conference. Southampton, Bermuda	Book Manufacturers' Institute Inc, 111 Prospect St, Stamford, Connecticut 06901, USA *Tel:* (203) 324 9670
November 4–5	Socialist Book Fair. London, UK	Bookmark (SBF), 264 Seven Sisters Rd, London N4 2DE, UK *Tel:* (01) 802 6145
November 7–11	9th Ife Book Fair. Ile-Ife, Nigeria	The Fair Director, Ife Book Fair, University of Ife Bookshop Ltd, University of Ife, Ile-Ife, Oyo State, Nigeria
November 7–14	Ghana 8th National Book Week (including Book Exhibition). Accra, Ghana	Executive Director, Ghana Book Development Council (Ministry of Education), PO Box M 430, Ministry Branch Post Office, Accra, Ghana *Tel:* 29178
November 12–17	German Youth Book Week. Federal Republic of Germany	Börsenverein des deutschen Buchhandels eV, Grosser Hirschgraben 17-21, D-6000 Frankfurt am Main 1, Federal Republic of Germany *Tel:* (0611) 1306332
November 12–18	National Children's Book Week. USA	The Children's Book Council, 67 Irving Pl, New York, NY 10003, USA *Tel:* (212) 254 2666
November 14–15	Expo Printec (international book and magazine print fair). Brussels, Belgium	Expo Printec, Fairway Marketing, Faringdon Ave, Harold Hill, Romford, Essex RM3 8XL, UK *Tel:* (04023) 40059
November 18–December 18	Jewish Book Month. USA	The Jewish Book Council of the National Jewish Welfare Board, 15 East 26th St, New York, NY 10010, USA *Tel:* (212) 532 4949
December 3–6	3rd Middle East Book Fair. Bahrain	Middle East Book Fair, Overseas Exhibition Services Ltd, 11 Manchester Sq, London W1M 5AB, UK *Tel:* (01) 486 1951
December 10–24	Colombo Children's Book Fair. Colombo, Sri Lanka	Colombo Children's Book Fair, 415 Galle Rd, Colombo 4, Sri Lanka *Tel:* Colombo 84146
December 27–30	Modern Language Association of America: Annual Convention. Washington, DC, USA	Modern Language Association of America, 62 Fifth Ave, New York, NY 10011, USA *Tel:* (212) 741 5588
1985		
February 2–8	American Library Association: Midwinter Conference. Washington, DC, USA	American Library Association, 50 East Huron St, Chicago, Illinois 60611, USA *Tel:* (312) 944 6780
March (early)	Scottish Antiquarian Book Fair. Edinburgh, Scotland	Mrs Grant, 13c Dundas St, Edinburgh, Scotland *Tel:* (031) 556 9698

DATE	EVENT	CONTACT
1985 (Cont'd)		
March 10–16	Leipzig International Book Fair (at Leipzig Spring Fair). Leipzig, German Democratic Republic	Leipziger Messeamt, Markt 11-15, Postfach 720, DDR-7010 Leipzig, German Democratic Republic *Tel:* (71810) 8830
April 2	International Children's Book Day	IBBY Secretariat, Leonhardsgraben 38a, CH-4051 Basle, Switzerland *Tel:* (061) 253404
April 10–13	The London Book Fair (incorporating Academic Book Fair). London, UK	The London Book Fair, 16 Pembridge Rd, London W11 3HL, UK *Tel:* (01) 229 1825
April 23–28	Quebec International Book Fair Quebec, Canada	Quebec International Book Fair, 2590 blvd Laurier, Chambre 860, Sainte-Foy, Quebec G1V 4M3, Canada *Tel:* (418) 658 1974
April 24–28	New Zealand Booksellers 64th Annual Conference. Christchurch, New Zealand	Booksellers Association of New Zealand (Inc), PO Box 11-377, Wellington, New Zealand *Tel:* Wellington 728 678
April 28– May 3	12th Jerusalem International Book Fair. Jerusalem, Israel	The Jerusalem International Book Fair, 12 Sarei Israel St, PO Box 1241, Jerusalem 91012, Israel *Tel:* (02) 524545/524896
May	Children's Book Fortnight. New Zealand	Book Publishers Association of New Zealand, PO Box 78-071, Grey Lynn, Auckland 2, New Zealand *Tel:* Auckland 767 251
May 1–5	The Booksellers Association of Great Britain & Ireland: Annual Conference and Trade Exhibition. Brighton, Sussex, UK	Administration Secretary, The Booksellers Association of Great Britain & Ireland, 154 Buckingham Palace Rd, London SW1W 9TZ, UK *Tel:* (01) 730 8214
May 5–9	International Reading Association: 30th Annual Convention. New Orleans, Louisiana, USA	Director of Conferences, International Reading Association, 800 Barksdale Rd, PO Box 8139 Newark, Delaware 19711, USA *Tel:* (302) 731 1600
May 20– June 2	Didacta Interamericana. Bogotá, Colombia	Eurodidac, Jägerstr 5, CH-4058 Basle, Switzerland *Tel:* (061) 265052/53
May 22–27	30th International Book Fair. Warsaw, Poland	Ars Polona, Secretariat of International Book Fair, Krakowskie Przedmiescie 7, 00-068 Warsaw, Poland *Tel:* 178641
May 25–28	American Booksellers Association: Annual Convention. San Francisco, California, USA	Executive Director, American Booksellers Association, 122 East 42nd St, New York, NY 10168, USA *Tel:* (212) 867 9060
June 1–5	International Booksellers Congress and IBF General Assembly. Toronto, Canada	International Booksellers Federation, Grünangergasse 4, A-1010 Vienna, Austria *Tel:* (222) 521535

490 BOOK TRADE CALENDAR

DATE	EVENT	CONTACT
1985 (Cont'd)		
June 13–18	Canadian Library Association: Annual Conference. Calgary, Alberta, Canada	Canadian Library Association, 151 Sparks St, Ottawa, Ontario K1P 5E3, Canada *Tel:* (613) 232 9625
July 6–8	American Library Association: Annual Conference. Chicago, Illinois, USA	American Library Association, 50 East Huron St, Chicago, Illinois 60611, USA *Tel:* (312) 944 6780
August 17–23	37th Writers' Summer School. Swanwick, Derbyshire, UK	The Secretary, Writers' Summer School, The Red House, Mardens Hill, Crowborough, Sussex TN6 1XN, UK *Tel:* (08926) 3943
August 18–24	IFLA Annual Conference. Chicago, Illinois, USA	IFLA, c/o The Royal Library, Postbus 95312, 2509 CH The Hague, Netherlands *Tel:* (070) 140884
August (end)	Edinburgh Book Festival. Edinburgh, Scotland	Valerie Bierman, 25A South West Thistle Street Lane, Edinburgh EH2, Scotland *Tel:* (031) 225 1915
September	5th Moscow International Book Fair. Moscow, USSR	General Directorate of International Book Exhibitions & Fairs, USSR Godkomizdat, 16 ul Chekhova, Moscow 103006, Union of Soviet Socialist Republics *Tel:* 299 4034
September	Aslib Joint Conference. Bournemouth, Dorset, UK	Conference Organizer, Aslib, 3 Belgrave Sq, London SW1X 8PL, UK *Tel:* (01) 235 5050
October 9–14	37th Frankfurt Book Fair. Frankfurt am Main, Federal Republic of Germany	Ausstellungs- und Messe-GmbH des Börsenvereins des deutschen Buchhandels, Postfach 2404, D-6000 Frankfurt am Main 1, Federal Republic of Germany *Tel:* (0611) 13061
November	New Zealand Book Week. New Zealand	Book Publishers Association of New Zealand, PO Box 78-071, Grey Lynn, Auckland 2, New Zealand *Tel:* Auckland 767 251
November 3–6	Book Manufacturers' Institute: Annual Conference. Arizona, USA	Book Manufacturers' Institute Inc, 111 Prospect St, Stamford, Connecticut 06901, USA *Tel:* (203) 324 9670
November 7–December 7	Jewish Book Month. USA	The Jewish Book Council of the National Jewish Welfare Board, 15 East 26th St, New York, NY 10010, USA *Tel:* (212) 532 4949
November 17–23	National Children's Book Week. USA	The Children's Book Council, 67 Irving Pl, New York, NY 10003, USA *Tel:* (212) 254 2666
December	UNESCO Intergovernmental Copyright Committee: 6th Session. Paris, France	Copyright Division, UNESCO, 7 Pl de Fontenoy, F-75700 Paris, France *Tel:* (1) 577 1610
December 10–24	Colombo Children's Book Fair. Colombo, Sri Lanka	Colombo Children's Book Fair, 415 Galle Rd, Colombo 4, Sri Lanka *Tel:* Colombo 84146

DATE	EVENT	CONTACT
1985 (Cont'd)		
December 27–30	Modern Language Association of America: Annual Convention. Chicago, USA	Modern Language Association of America, 62 Fifth Ave, New York, NY 10011, USA *Tel:* (212) 741 5588
Date unknown at time of going to press	V Malta International Book Fair. Valletta, Malta	Malta International Book Fair, Ministry of Education, Lascaris, Valletta, Malta *Tel:* 605983/21401
Date unknown at time of going to press	International Association of Literary Critics: Conference. Belem, Brazil	Association international des critiques littéraires, 38 rue du Faubourg St-Jacques, F-75014 Paris, France *Tel:* (1) 3220647
1986		
April 2	International Children's Book Day	IBBY Secretariat, Leonhardsgraben 38a, CH-4051 Basle, Switzerland *Tel:* (061) 253404
April 8–11	The London Book Fair (incorporating Academic Book Fair). London, UK	The London Book Fair, 16 Pembridge Rd, London W11 3HL, UK *Tel:* (01) 229 1825
April 22–27	Quebec International Book Fair. Quebec, Canada	Quebec International Book Fair, 2590 blvd Laurier, Chambre 860, Sainte-Foy, Quebec G1V 4M6, Canada *Tel:* (418) 6581974
May	Children's Book Fortnight. New Zealand	Book Publishers Association of New Zealand, PO Box 78-071, Grey Lynn, Auckland 2, New Zealand *Tel:* Auckland 767 251
May 4–8	International Reading Association: 31st Annual Convention. Atlantic City, New Jersey, USA	Director of Conferences, International Reading Association, 800 Barksdale Rd, PO Box 8139, Newark, Delaware 19711, USA *Tel:* (302) 731 1600
May 24–27	American Booksellers Association: Annual Convention. New Orleans, Louisiana, USA	Executive Director, American Booksellers Association, 122 East 42nd St, New York, NY 10168, USA *Tel:* (212) 867 9060
June	P E N International Congress. Hamburg, Federal Republic of Germany	International PEN, 38 King St, London WC2E 8JT, UK *Tel:* (01) 379 7939 (German PEN *Tel:* Darmstadt 23120)
June 4–9	17th Sofia International Book Fair. Sofia, Bulgaria	International Book Fair, Department for Exhibitions & Fairs, 11 Slaveikov Sq, Sofia, Bulgaria *Tel:* 87 9111
June 27– July 3	American Library Association: Annual Conference. New York, USA	American Library Association, 50 East Huron St, Chicago, Illinois 60611, USA *Tel:* (312) 944 6780
August	International Board on Books for Young People: 20th Biennial Congress. Japan, Tokyo	IBBY Secretariat, Leonhardsgraben 38a, CH-4051 Basle, Switzerland *Tel:* (061) 253404
August 16–22	38th Writers' Summer School. Swanwick, Derbyshire, UK	The Secretary, Writers' Summer School, The Red House, Mardens Hill, Crowborough, Sussex TN6 1XN, UK *Tel:* (08926) 3943

492 BOOK TRADE CALENDAR

DATE	EVENT	CONTACT

1986 (Cont'd)

August 25–30	IFLA Annual Conference. Tokyo, Japan	IFLA, c/o The Royal Library, Postbus 95312, 2509 CH The Hague, Netherlands *Tel:* (070) 140884
October	38th Frankfurt Book Fair. Frankfurt am Main, Federal Republic of Germany	Ausstellungs- und Messe-GmbH des Börsenvereins des deutschen Buchhandels, Postfach 2404, D-6000 Frankfurt am Main 1, Federal Republic of Germany *Tel:* (0611) 13061
November	New Zealand Book Week. New Zealand	Book Publishers Association of New Zealand, PO Box 78-071, Grey Lynn, Auckland 2, New Zealand *Tel:* Auckland 767 251
November	National Children's Book Week. USA	The Children's Book Council, 67 Irving Pl, New York, NY 10003, USA *Tel:* (212) 254 2666
December 10–24	Colombo Children's Book Fair. Colombo, Sri Lanka	Colombo Children's Book Fair, 415 Galle Rd, Colombo 4, Sri Lanka *Tel:* Colombo 84146
December 27–30	Modern Language Association of America: Annual Convention.	Modern Language Association of America, 62 Fifth Ave, New York, NY 10011, USA *Tel:* (212) 741 5588

Index

The order of the index is word by word so that, for example, Alpha Literatur comes before Alphabet & Image.

Some words at the beginning of names are ignored when indexing. These include initials and forenames of personal names (so Jonathan Cape Ltd is listed under C) and words which simply mean 'publisher', 'bookseller' or 'company' (so Verlag Peter Lang is listed under L). In the text the first word of a name that is counted when indexing is printed in bold type.

Names which start with numbers written as numerals are put before A in the index (so Edition No 1 is the first entry in the index, while Les Editions des Deux Coqs d'Or is listed under D).

1, Edition No (France) 91
1, No, Publishing Co Ltd (United Kingdom) 392
3 Arches (Belgium) 34
4 Fevereiro, Livraria (Angola) 2
'8' Nentori Publishing House (Albania) 1
'13 Calle, Librería, El Tecolote' (Guatemala) 177
14th October Corporation (People's Democratic Republic of Yemen) 456
20th Century Classics (United Kingdom) 443
24 Heures, Editions (Switzerland) 361
29, Ediciones (Spain) 336
62, Edicions, SA (Spain) 336
70, Edições, Lda (Portugal) 315
99, Ediciones, SA (Spain) 336
707, Klub (Republic of South Africa) 333

'A' Publishing Institute (Israel) 213
A B C, Editions, Jeunesse SARL (Belgium) 34
A B C, Jill Anderson's, Bookshop (New Zealand) 290
A B C Kitabevi (Turkey) 385
A B C, Librarías, SA (Peru) 307
A B C, Librerías, SA (Argentina) 8
A B C, Librerías, SA (Peru) 306
A B C Verlag (Switzerland) 361
A B C Yayinevi (Turkey) 384
A B E F (France) 110
A B G R A (Asociación de Bibliotecarios Graduados de la República Argentina) (Argentina) 9
A B I C (Publishers) (Nigeria) 293
A B M, Librairie-Papeterie (Benin) 45
A B M, Maison d'Edition (Benin) 45
A B P (NZ) Ltd (New Zealand) 287
A B, The, Book Club (BAB) (Iceland) 184
A C E R (Spain) 346
A C P O (Colombia) 65
A C U R I L (International Organizations) 466
A D A C Verlag GmbH (Federal Republic of Germany) 122
A D A Edita Tokyo Co Ltd (Japan) 238
A D I S Health Science Press (Australia) 10
A D I S Press Australasia Pty Ltd (Australia) 10
A D I S Press Publications Ltd (Hong Kong) 178
A D L A F (Federal Republic of Germany) 122
A E D O S, Editorial, SA (Spain) 336
A E I International (Portugal) 315
A E I International (Portugal) 318
A F E R (African Ecclesial Review) (Kenya) 248
A G A V ev (Federal Republic of Germany) 167
A G I R (Artes Graficas Industrias Reunidas SA) (Brazil) 48
A G P O L (Przedsiebiorstwo Reklamy i Wydawnictw Handlu Zagranicznego) (Poland) 310
A I B D A (International Organizations) 466
A L A Verlag (Switzerland) 361
A L F A — Radna organizacija za izdavačku djelatnost (Yugoslavia) 456
A L S I (Switzerland) 360

A M B (Arbeitsgemeinschaft mitteleuropäischer Bibelwerke) (Federal Republic of Germany) 122
A M P (France) 110
A M Z Editrice SpA (Italy) 219
A N B A D S (Senegal) 324
A N Z (Australia) 10
A P A (Academic Publishers Associated) (Netherlands) 273
A P Books/A P Financial Registers Ltd (United Kingdom) 392
A P C K (Republic of Ireland) 209
A P C O L (Australia) 10
A P E, Bologna (Italy) 219
A P E, Edizioni, SpA (Italy) 219
A P N (Union of Soviet Socialist Republics) 387
A R E D I P (Agence de Recherches Droits Internationaux et Promotion) (France) 91
A R E S, Edizioni (Italy) 219
A R L I S (The Art Libraries Society) (United Kingdom) 445
A Sp B (Federal Republic of Germany) 168
A T Verlag AG (Switzerland) 361
A U Press & Publications (India) 186
A Z Editora SA (Argentina) 3
Aadab, Al-, Bookshop (Bahrain) 32
Aadiesh Book Depot (India) 186
Aane-Adab (Pakistan) 301
Aar-Verlag (Federal Republic of Germany) 122
Aare-Verlag (Switzerland) 361
Aarestrup, Emil, Prize (Denmark) 81
Aargauer Tageblatt (Switzerland) 361
Abacacia, Editorial, SRL (Argentina) 3
Abaco, Editorial, de Rodolfo Depalma SRL (Argentina) 3
Abacus (United Kingdom) 392
Abacus Press (United Kingdom) 392
Abadia, Publicacions de l', de Montserrat (Spain) 336
Abakon Verlagsgesellschaft mbH (Federal Republic of Germany) 122
Abakus Schallplatten Barbara Fietz (Federal Republic of Germany) 122
Abbeville Press (United Kingdom) 392
Abbey's Bookshop (Australia) 20
Abdulghani, Abdulla, & Sons Co (Qatar) 320
Abelard-Schuman Ltd (United Kingdom) 392
Abeledo, Editorial, Perrot SAE e I (Argentina) 3
Abercromby Bookshop (Trinidad and Tobago) 382
Aberdeen University Press (United Kingdom) 392
Abete, Edizioni (Italy) 219
Abhinav Publications (India) 186
Abhishek Publications (India) 186
Abiva Publishing House Inc (Philippines) 308
Abril, Editorial, SA (Argentina) 3
Abril SA Cultural e Industrial (Brazil) 48
Abson Books (United Kingdom) 392
Abtour, Georges, SA, Librairie-Papeterie (Chad) 62
Academi, Yr, Gymreig (The Welsh Academy) (United Kingdom) 446
Academia (Czechoslovakia) 71
Academia Amazonense de Letras (Brazil) 57
Academia Argentina de Letras (Argentina) 9
Academia, Biblioteca da, das Ciências de Lisboa (Portugal) 318
Academia Cachoeirense de Letras (Brazil) 57
Academia Catarinense de Letras (Brazil) 57
Academia Cearense de Letras (Brazil) 57
Academia de Buenas Letras de Barcelona (Spain) 348
Academia de Ciencias de la República de Cuba (Cuba) 69
Academia de Letras (Brazil) 57
Academia de Letras da Bahia (Brazil) 57
Academia de Letras de Piauí (Brazil) 57
Academia de Studii Economice, Biblioteca Centrala (Romania) 322
Academia Feminina Espírito Santense de Letras (Brazil) 57
Academia Matogrossense de Letras (Brazil) 57
Academia Mineira de Letras (Brazil) 57
Academia Nacional de Letras (Uruguay) 452
Academia Nicaragüense de la Lengua (Nicaragua) 292
Academia Paranaense de Letras (Brazil) 57

Academia Paulista de Letras (Brazil) 57
Academia Pernambucana de Letras (Brazil) 57
Academia Publications P Ltd (Malaysia) 259
Academia Riograndense de Letras (Brazil) 57
Academic (Nigeria) 293
Academic and University Publishers Group (United Kingdom) 393
Academic Book Club (United Republic of Cameroun) 61
Academic Book Club (Kenya) 249
Academic Book Club (Nigeria) 296
Academic Book Club (Togo) 382
Academic Book Club (Uganda) 386
Academic Press Inc (London) Ltd (United Kingdom) 393
Academic Press, The (India) 186
Academic Publications (United Kingdom) 393
Academic Publishers (India) 186
Academic Publishers Associated (Netherlands) 273
Academica Lda (Mozambique) 271
Académie des Lettres et des Arts (France) 111
Académie Goncourt (France) 111
Académie Internationale de Tourisme (Monaco) 270
Académie mauricienne de Langue et de Littérature (Mauritius) 263
Académie royale de Langue et de Littérature françaises (Belgium) 43
Académie royale des Sciences, des Lettres et des Beaux-Arts de Belgique (Belgium) 43
Academiei, Editura, Republicii Socialiste România (Romania) 321
Academiei Republicii Socialiste România, Biblioteca (Romania) 322
Academiei Republicii Socialiste România, Biblioteca Filialei Cluj a (Romania) 322
Academon (The Hebrew University Students' Printing and Publishing House) (Israel) 213
Academy, Council on Libraries of the, of Sciences of the USSR (Union of Soviet Socialist Republics) 390
Academy Editions (France) 91
Academy Editions (United Kingdom) 393
Academy, Fundamental Library of the, of Medical Sciences (Union of Soviet Socialist Republics) 389
Academy Microfilms (Dublin) (Republic of Ireland) 209
Academy of Comparative Philosophy & Religion (India) 186
Academy of Islamic Research and Publications (India) 186
Academy of Sciences Publishing House (Democratic People's Republic of Korea) 250
Academy of Social Sciences Publishing House (Democratic People's Republic of Korea) 250
Academy of the Hebrew Language (Israel) 213
Academy of Thirteen Prize (France) 111
Academy Press Ltd (Nigeria) 293
Academy, The, Press (Republic of Ireland) 209
Accademia di Scienze, Lettere ed Arti (Italy) 235
Accademia Ligure di Scienze e Lettere (Italy) 235
Accademia Nazionale di Scienze, Lettere ed Arti (Italy) 235
Accademia Petrarca di Lettere, Arti e Scienze (Italy) 235
Accademia Toscana di Scienze e Lettere la Colombaria (Italy) 235
Accademia Virgiliana di Scienze, Lettere ed Arti di Mantova (Italy) 235
Accidentia und Zester Druck- und Verlagsgesellschaft mbH (Federal Republic of Germany) 123
Accion Cultural Popular ACPO - Editorial Andes (Colombia) 65
Acco SV (Belgium) 34
Accordo, Edizioni (Italy) 219
Acervo, Ediciones (Spain) 337
Acervo, Ediciones, de Argentina SRL (Argentina) 3
Achiasaf Publishing House Ltd (Israel) 213
Achiever (Israel) 213
Ackermanns, F A, Kunstverlag (Federal Republic of Germany) 123
Acme, Editorial, SA (Argentina) 3
Aconcagua Edic y Pub SA (Mexico) 264
Acorn Books (Republic of Ireland) 209
Acorn Editions (United Kingdom) 393
Acribia, Editorial (Spain) 337

494 INDEX

Acropole, Editions (France) 91
Acrópolis, Librería (Guatemala) 177
Acta Medica Belgica ASBL (Belgium) 34
Acta Universitatis Gothoburgensis (Sweden) 352
Actinic Press Ltd (United Kingdom) 393
Action Publications (New Zealand) 287
Actuaquarto (Belgium) 34
Acum Ltd (Society of Authors, Composers and Music Publishers in Israel) (Israel) 212
Adab, Al-, Bookshop (Saudi Arabia) 323
Adab, Dar al (Lebanon) 253
Adam Publishers (Israel) 213
Adamjee Prize (Pakistan) 304
Adams & Co Ltd (Republic of South Africa) 333
Addams, Jane, Children's Book Award (International Literary Prizes) 474
Addis Ababa University Library (Ethiopia) 86
Addis Ababa University Press (Ethiopia) 86
Addison-Wesley Publishers Ltd (United Kingdom) 393
Addison-Wesley Publishing Co (Australia) 10
Addison-Wesley Publishing Co Inc (Philippines) 308
Addison-Wesley Publishing Group (Netherlands) 273
Addison-Wesley Singapore (Pte) Ltd (Republic of Singapore) 325
Adebara Publishers Ltd (Nigeria) 293
Adelphi Edizioni SpA (Italy) 219
Adeyle Brothers (Bangladesh) 32
Adeylebros & Co (Bangladesh) 32
Adkinson Parrish Ltd (United Kingdom) 393
Adlard Coles Ltd (United Kingdom) 393
Administracion, Archivo General de la, Civil del Estado (Spain) 347
Administration Library (Namibia) 272
Administrative College of Papua New Guinea Library (Papua New Guinea) 305
Adonais Prize (Spain) 348
Adressbuchausschuss der Deutschen Wirtschaft (Federal Republic of Germany) 120
Adult, Directorate of, Education (India) 186
Advaita Ashrama (India) 186
Advance Publishing Co Ltd (Ghana) 171
Adventist Book Centre (Zimbabwe) 465
Adversaires, Editions (Switzerland) 361
Advisory Committee on the Selection of Low-Priced Books for Overseas (United Kingdom) 391
Adwinsa Publications (Ghana) Ltd (Ghana) 171
Adyar-Verlag (Austria) 24
Æskunnar, Bókaútgáfa (Iceland) 183
Aesopus Verlag GmbH (Switzerland) 361
Affiliated East-West Press Pvt Ltd (India) 186
Afghan Kitab (Afghanistan) 1
Afha Internacional SA (Spain) 337
Afram Publications (Ghana) Ltd (Ghana) 171
Africa Christian Press (Ghana) 172
Africa Editions (Senegal) 323
Africa Inland Church Literature Department (Tanzania) 378
Africa Literature Centre (Zambia) 463
African Library Association of South Africa (Republic of South Africa) 334
African Universities Press (Nigeria) 293
Africana Book Society Ltd (Republic of South Africa) 333
Africana Book Society (Pty) Ltd (Republic of South Africa) 328
Africana Publishers (Nig) Ltd (Nigeria) 293
Afrique-Levant (Senegal) 324
Afrique-Levant, Edition (Senegal) 323
Afrique-Loisires, Club (Senegal) 324
Afro-Asian Writers' Bureau (Sri Lanka) 350
Afro-Asian Writers, Permanent Bureau of (Egypt) 83
Afrontamento, Ediçoes (Portugal) 315
Agam Kala Prakashan (India) 186
Agathon (Netherlands) 273
Age d'Homme, Editions L', — La Cité (Switzerland) 361
Age d'Homme-Karolinger Verlag GmbH & Co KG (Austria) 24
Age', 'The, Book of the Year (Australia) 22
Agence belge des grandes Editions SA (Belgium) 34
Agence belge des grandes Editions SA (Belgium) 42
Agence de Distribution de Presse (Senegal) 323
Agence de Distribution de Presse (Senegal) 324
Agence francophone pour la Numération internationale du Livre (AFNIL-ISBN) (France) 90
Agência Brasileira do ISBN (Brazil) 47
Agencia Española del ISBN (Spain) 336
Agencja Autorska (Poland) 311
Agencja Autorska (Poland) 313
Agents Editores Ltda (Brazil) 48
Agenzia Letteraria Internazionale Srl (Italy) 233
Agenzia per l'Area di Lingua Italiana ISBN (Italy) 219
Agir, Livraria (Brazil) 55
Agis Verlag GmbH (Federal Republic of Germany) 123
Agnelli, Giacomo, Editore (Italy) 219
Agon (Netherlands) 273
Agora-Verlag (Federal Republic of Germany) 123
Agricole Publishing Academy (India) 186

Agricultural Books Publishing House (Democratic People's Republic of Korea) 250
Agricultural Experiment Station Library (Puerto Rico) 320
Agricultural Institute Library (Ethiopia) 86
Agricultural Library (Nigeria) 296
Agricultural Science, Central Library of (Israel) 218
Agriculture University Library (Pakistan) 303
Agrupación Bibliotecológica del Uruguay (Uruguay) 452
Agrupación para la Integración de la Información Socio-Económica (ABIISE) (Peru) 307
Aguilar Argentina SA de Ediciones (Argentina) 3
Aguilar Chilena de Ediciones SA (Chile) 63
Aguilar Colombiana de Ediciones (Colombia) 65
Aguilar, Editora Nova, SA (Brazil) 48
Aguilar, M, Editor SA (Mexico) 264
Aguilar SA de Ediciones (Spain) 337
Aguilar Venezolana SA de Ediciones (Venezuela) 453
Aguirre, Librería (Colombia) 67
Ahd, Al, Al Gadeed Bookstore (Egypt) 84
Ahlwalia Book Depot (India) 186
Ahmadu Bello University Bookshop (Nigeria) 296
Ahmadu Bello University Library (Nigeria) 296
Ahmadu Bello University Press Ltd (Nigeria) 293
Ahmedabad Publishers' & Booksellers' Association (India) 185
Ahnert, L B, -Verlag (Federal Republic of Germany) 123
Ahora, Publicaciones, C por A (Dominican Republic) 81
Ahram, Al (Egypt) 85
Ahram, Al, Book Club (Egypt) 84
Ahram, Al, Bookshops (Egypt) 84
Ahram, Al, Establishment (Egypt) 83
Ahsan Brothers (Pakistan) 301
Aiken, Alex (United Kingdom) 393
Ain Shams University Library (Egypt) 84
Airlife Publishing Ltd (United Kingdom) 393
Airport Bookshop (Republic of Korea) 252
Ajanta Books International (India) 186
Ajanta Books International (India) 201
Ajanta Publications (India) (India) 187
Ajuda, Biblioteca da (Portugal) 318
Akademie-Verlag (German Democratic Republic) 116
Akademiförlaget (Sweden) 352
Akademii Nauk SSSR, Biblioteka (Union of Soviet Socialist Republics) 389
Akademii Nauk SSSR, Gosudarstvennaya publichnaya nauchno-tekhnicheskaya biblioteka Sibirskogo otdeleniya (Union of Soviet Socialist Republics) 389
Akademii Nauk SSSR, Institut nauchnoy informatsii po obschestvennym naukam (Union of Soviet Socialist Republics) 389
Akademii Nauk USSR, Tsentral'naya nauchnaya biblioteka (Union of Soviet Socialist Republics) 389
Akademilitteratur Förlaget AB (Sweden) 352
Akademische Druck- und Verlagsanstalt (Austria) 24
Akademische Verlagsgesellschaft (Federal Republic of Germany) 123
Akademische Verlagsgesellschaft Athenaion (Federal Republic of Germany) 123
Akademisk Boghandel (Denmark) 79
Akademisk Forlag (Denmark) 75
Akadia, Librería, Editorial (Argentina) 3
Akadoma (Indonesia) 205
Akane Shobo Co Ltd (Japan) 238
Akateeminen Kirjakauppa (Finland) 88
Akateeminen Kustannusliike Oy (Finland) 87
Åkerbloms, Johan, Universitetsbokhandel (Sweden) 358
Akhil Bhartiya Hindi Prakashak Sangh (India) 185
Akhila Bharaliya Sanskrit Parishad (India) 187
Akita Shoten Publishing Co Ltd (Japan) 238
Akros Publications (United Kingdom) 393
Aksorn Charerntat (Thailand) 380
Aksorn Charoen Tasna Ltd (Thailand) 380
Akutagawa Prize (Japan) 246
Al Book Co (Pvt) Ltd (India) 201
Aladdin Books Ltd (United Kingdom) 393
'Alas', Editorial, Valencia 234 (Spain) 337
Alba Buchverlag GmbH und Co KG (Federal Republic of Germany) 123
Alba Publikation Alf Teloeken GmbH und Co KG (Federal Republic of Germany) 123
Albah Publishers (Nigeria) 293
Albanus Verlag (Switzerland) 361
Albatros (Czechoslovakia) 71
Albatros, Editions (France) 91
Albatros, Editorial, SRL (Argentina) 3
Albatros, Editura (Romania) 321
Albatros Verlag AG (Switzerland) 361
Albatross Books (Australia) 10
Albe Soc Com (Uruguay) 452
Albér, Verlag Karl, GmbH (Federal Republic of Germany) 123
Albert I, Koninklijke Bibliotheek (Belgium) 43
Albertelli, Ermanno, Editore (Italy) 219
Albin, Editions, Michel (France) 91

Albyn Press Ltd (United Kingdom) 393
Alcheh, Librairie Française (Israel) 217
Alda, B P (Indonesia) 205
Alden & Mowbray Ltd (United Kingdom) 393
Aldwych Press (United Kingdom) 393
Aleatah University, General Administration of Libraries, Printing & Publications (Libya) 255
Alef Publishers Ltd (Israel) 213
Alekh Prakashan (India) 187
Alemany, Juan Max (Dominican Republic) 81
Alemar-Phoenix Publishing House Inc (Philippines) 308
Alemar's (Philippines) 309
Alemar's Best Sellers Club (Philippines) 309
Alexander Prize (International Literary Prizes) 474
Alexandria Municipal Library (Egypt) 84
Alfa, Editorial, Argentina SA (Argentina) 3
Alfa Edizioni e Rappresentanze Editoriali (Italy) 219
Alfa — Vydavateľstvo technickej a ekonomickej literatúry (Czechoslovakia) 71
Alfa y Omega, Editora (Dominican Republic) 81
Alfaguara, Ediciones, SA (Spain) 337
Alfani, Libreria, Editrice Srl (Italy) 219
Alfieri Edizioni d'Arte (Italy) 219
Algamiia Almasriia Lilmaktabat Almadrasiia (Egypt) 84
Algemene Nederlandse Bond van Leesbibliotheekhouders (Netherlands) 284
Algemene Vlaamse Boekverkopersbond (Belgium) 33
Algona Publications Pty Ltd (Australia) 10
Alhambra, Editorial, SA (Spain) 337
Ali Publications (Bangladesh) 32
Alianza Editorial Mexicana (Mexico) 264
Alianza Editorial SA (Spain) 337
Alice, The, Literary Award (Australia) 22
Alinari Fratelli SpA Istituto di Edizioni Artistiche (Italy) 219
Alip & Sons Publishing Inc (Philippines) 308
Alison Press (United Kingdom) 393
Alkaios-Tropaiatis (Greece) 174
All India Booksellers' & Publishers' Association (India) 185
All Prints Distributors and Publishers (United Arab Emirates) 390
All-Union Patent and Technical Library (Union of Soviet Socialist Republics) 389
Állami könyvterjesztő vállalat (Hungary) 182
Állami könyvterjesztő vállalat országos antikvár (Hungary) 182
Allan, Ian, Ltd (United Kingdom) 393
Allan, Philip, Publishers Ltd (United Kingdom) 393
Allan, R L, & Son (Publishers) Ltd (United Kingdom) 393
Allara Publishing (Australia) 10
Allen & Co, W H, Ltd (United Kingdom) 394
Allen & Unwin, George, Australia Pty Ltd (Australia) 11
Allen & Unwin, George, (Publishers) Ltd (United Kingdom) 394
Allen, J A, & Co Ltd (United Kingdom) 394
Allen Lane (United Kingdom) 394
Allhems Förlag AB (Sweden) 352
Alliance, L', française, Bibliothèque (Senegal) 324
Alliance West African Publishers & Co (Nigeria) 293
Allied Irish Banks' Awards for Literature (Republic of Ireland) 212
Allied Press Ltd (New Zealand) 287
Allied Publishers Private Ltd (India) 187
All'Insegna, Edizioni, del Veltro (Italy) 219
Allison & Busby Ltd (United Kingdom) 394
Allman & Son (Publishers) Ltd (United Kingdom) 394
Allmänna Förlaget (Sweden) 352
Allot, Librairie (Mauritius) 263
Allyn & Bacon (London) Ltd (United Kingdom) 394
Alma Mater, Librería, Inc (Puerto Rico) 320
Alma'Arif (Indonesia) 205
Almenna Bókafélagid (Iceland) 183
Almqvist och Wiksell Bokhandel AB (Sweden) 358
Almqvist och Wiksell Förlag AB (Sweden) 352
Almqvist och Wiksell International (Sweden) 352
Almqvist och Wiksell Läromedel AB (Sweden) 352
Alonso, Editorial Rodolfo, SRL (Argentina) 3
Alpha 9 GmbH (Federal Republic of Germany) 123
Alpha-Beta Publications Ltd (India) 187
Alpha Books (Australia) 11
Alpha Books (Zimbabwe) 465
Alpha Literatur Verlag (Federal Republic of Germany) 123
Alphabet & Image Ltd (United Kingdom) 394
Alphabooks (United Kingdom) 394
Alphonsiana, Bibliotheca, VZW (Belgium) 34
Alpina, Editions (France) 91
Alsatia SA (France) 91
Altberliner Verlag (German Democratic Republic) 116
Altea, Ediciones, SA (Spain) 337
Alternative Publishing Co-operative Ltd (Australia) 11
Alternative Verlag GmbH (Federal Republic of Germany) 123
Althea's Nature Series (United Kingdom) 394
Althea's Pet Series (United Kingdom) 394
Althea's What to Expect Series (United Kingdom) 394

Althoff, Anneliese (Federal Republic of Germany) 123
Altiora NV (Belgium) 34
Alumni Press (Indonesia) 205
Alves, Livraria Francisco, Editora SA (Brazil) 48
Alviella, Goblet d', Prize (Belgium) 44
Am Hasefer (Israel) 213
Am Oved Publishers Ltd (Israel) 213
Amado, Arménio, Editora de Simões, Beirão & Ca Lda (Portugal) 315
Amalthea-Verlag (Austria) 25
Aman, Pustaka, Press Sdn Bhd (Malaysia) 259
Amar Prakashan (India) 187
Amarko Book Agency (India) 187
Amazonen Frauenverlag GmbH (Federal Republic of Germany) 123
Ambassade, Bibliothèque de l', de France (Niger) 292
Ambika Publications (India) 187
Ambito Literario (United Kingdom) 394
Ambo, Uitgeverij, BV (Netherlands) 273
Ambozontany, Editions (Democratic Republic of Madagascar) 257
Ambro Lacus, Buch- und Bildverlag W Kremnitz (Federal Republic of Germany) 123
Ambrosiana, Biblioteca (Italy) 234
America Latina (Uruguay) 452
América, Librería (Colombia) 67
América, Librería (Nicaragua) 292
Américalee, Editorial, SRL (Argentina) 3
American Book Store SA (Mexico) 268
American Books (Argentina) 8
American Bookstore (Greece) 176
American Center Library (India) 202
American Center Library (Jordan) 247
American Center Library, US Information Service (Tanzania) 379
American Cultural Center Library (Libya) 256
American Cultural Center Library (Togo) 382
American Cultural Center Library (Upper Volta) 451
American Library (Nepal) 272
American Library Resource Center (Republic of Singapore) 327
American-Scandinavian Foundation (International Organizations) 471
American-Scandinavian Foundation/PEN Translation Prizes (International Literary Prizes) 474
American Technical Publishers (United Kingdom) 394
American University in Cairo Library (Egypt) 84
American University in Cairo Press (Egypt) 83
American University, Library of, of Beirut (Lebanon) 254
American University Publishers Group Ltd (United Kingdom) 394
Americana, Editorial (Argentina) 3
Americas, Editora Das, SA Edameris (Brazil) 48
Amerind Publishing Co (P) Ltd (India) 187
Amerind Publishing Co (P) Ltd (India) 204
Amérique et d'Orient, Editions d' (France) 91
Amichai Publishing House Ltd (Israel) 213
Amigo, El, de Todos (Venezuela) 454
Amigos del Libro, Ediciones los (Bolivia) 46
Amigos del Libro, Editorial los (Bolivia) 46
Amigos del Libro, Librería los (Bolivia) 46
Amigos do Livro (Portugal) 315
Amikam (Israel) 213
Amina Book Stall (India) 187
Amir Kabir Publishing & Distributing Corporation (Iran) 207
Amir Publishing Co Ltd (Israel) 213
Amis de Milosz, Les (France) 91
Amis, Les, de Franco Maria Ricci (France) 109
Amitié, Editions de l' (France) 91
Amitié par le Livre, L' (France) 91
Amitié par le Livre, L' (France) 109
Amitié par le Livre, L', Prize (France) 111
Amman Public Library (Jordan) 247
Amorrortu Editores SA (Argentina) 3
Amphora, Editions, SA (France) 91
Amsterdam Boek BV (Netherlands) 273
Amsterdam Prizes (Netherlands) 285
Amudha Nilayam Ltd (India) 187
Anabas-Verlag Günter Kämpf KG (Federal Republic of Germany) 123
Anagrama, Editorial (Spain) 337
Anambra State Central Library (Nigeria) 296
Anambra State School Libraries Association (Nigeria) 297
Anand Book Club (India) 201
Anand Paperbacks (India) 187
Ananda Ashram (India) 187
Anaya, Ediciones, SA (Spain) 337
Anchor (United Kingdom) 394
Ancient History Book Club (United Kingdom) 443
Ancora, Editrice, Milano (Italy) 219
Ancora y Delfin, Libreria (Spain) 347
And/or (Australia) 11
Andersen, Hans Christian, Medals (International Literary Prizes) 474
Andersen, Hans Christian, Prize (Denmark) 81
Andersen Press Ltd (United Kingdom) 394
Andersen Prize (Italy) 235

Anderson Keenan Publishing Ltd (United Kingdom) 394
Andes, Editorial (Colombia) 65
Andhra Pradesh Sahitya Akademi Awards (India) 203
Andreas, Jörn, Verlag (Austria) 25
Andreas und Andreas Verlagsbuchhandel (Austria) 25
Andrei, Organização, Editora Ltda (Brazil) 48
Andromeda, Ediciones (Argentina) 3
Angel Literary Prize (United Kingdom) 448
Angelet (Belgium) 34
Angeli, Franco, Editore (Italy) 219
Angelica, Biblioteca (Italy) 234
Angkasa (Indonesia) 205
Anglo American, The, Bookshop (Egypt) 84
Anglo-Chinese Textbook Publishers Organization Ltd (Hong Kong) 178
Anglo Egyptian, The, Bookshop (Egypt) 84
Anglo-German Foundation (United Kingdom) 394
Anglo-Hellenic Agency (Greece) 175
Anglohellenic (Greece) 174
Angolana, Nova Editorial, SARL (Angola) 2
Angst, Verlag Roland (Federal Republic of Germany) 123
Angus & Robertson/Bay Books (Australia) 11
Angus & Robertson Bookshops (Australia) 20
Angus & Robertson (South-East Asia) Ltd (Republic of Singapore) 325
Angus & Robertson (UK) Ltd (United Kingdom) 394
Angus & Robertson Writers' Fellowship (Australia) 22
Angus Hudson Ltd (United Kingdom) 394
Angyra Publishing House, D A Papadimitriou SA (Greece) 174
Aniarapriset (Sweden) 359
Anjuman Kitab-Khana-I-Afghanistan (Afghanistan) 1
Anjuman Taraqqi-e-Urdu Pakistan (Pakistan) 304
Ankara University Library (Turkey) 385
Ankh-Hermes BV (Netherlands) 273
Ankur Publishing House (India) 187
Anowuo Educational Publications (Ghana) 172
Anrich Verlag GmbH (Federal Republic of Germany) 123
Ansata-Verlag (Switzerland) 361
Ansay Pty Ltd (Australia) 11
Ansgar Forlag A/S (Norway) 298
Antara, Pustaka (Indonesia) 205
Antara, Pustaka (Malaysia) 259
Antenna Edições Técnicas Ltda (Brazil) 48
Anthonian Store Sdn Bhd (Malaysia) 259
Anthonian Store Sdn Bhd (Malaysia) 260
Anthropos, Editions, SA (France) 91
Anthroposophiques Romandes, Editions (Switzerland) 361
Antillana, Editorial (Puerto Rico) 319
Antiquarian Book House (India) 187
Antiquarian Booksellers' Association (United Kingdom) 391
Antiquarian Booksellers' Association of Japan (Japan) 237
Antique Collectors' Club (United Kingdom) 394
Antoine, Editions Jacques, SPRL (Belgium) 34
Antoine, Librairies (Lebanon) 254
Antonius-Verlag (Switzerland) 361
'Antso', Maison d'Edition Protestante (Democratic Republic of Madagascar) 257
Antwerp Bibliophile Society (Belgium) 44
Antwerpse Lloyd NV (Belgium) 34
Anugerah Sastera Negara Prize (Malaysia) 261
Anvil Books Ltd (Republic of Ireland) 209
Anvil Press Poetry Ltd (United Kingdom) 394
Anwari Publications (Bangladesh) 32
Ao Livro Técnico (Brazil) 55
Ao Livro Técnico SA Industria a Comércio (Brazil) 48
Aoki Shoten Co Ltd (Japan) 238
Aowa Press & Publications (Nigeria) 293
Apa Productions (Pte) Ltd (Republic of Singapore) 325
Apaya Bookshop (Sudan) 350
Ape, Milan (Italy) 219
Ape, Organizzazione Didattica Editoriale (Italy) 220
Apollo's Reklame en Uitgeversburo (Suriname) 351
Apostolado, Livraria, da Imprensa (Portugal) 315
Apostolica, Biblioteca, Vaticana (Vatican City State) 453
Apostolica Vaticana, Biblioteca (Vatican City State) 453
Apoteksbolaget AB (Sweden) 352
Appleford Publishing Group (United Kingdom) 394
Appletree, The, Press Ltd (United Kingdom) 395
Applied Science Publishers Ltd (United Kingdom) 395
Aprile, Ruggero (Italy) 220
Apuntes, Librería Los (Uruguay) 452
Aquarian Press Ltd (United Kingdom) 395
Aquarius Editora e Distribuidora de Livros Ltda (Brazil) 48
Aquila Essays (United Kingdom) 395
Aquila Pamphlet Poets (United Kingdom) 395
Aquila Poetry (United Kingdom) 395
Aquila Publishing (United Kingdom) 395
Aquila/The Phaethon Press (United Kingdom) 395
Aquila The Wayzgoose Press (United Kingdom) 395
Aquilina, A C, & Co (Malta) 262
Aquilina, A C, & Co (Malta) 262
Arab Advertising Organization (Syria) 377
Arab, Al, Bookshop (Egypt) 84

Arab Archivists Institute (Iraq) 208
Arab Institute for Research and Publishing (Lebanon) 253
Arab Library (Mauritania) 263
Arab Publishing, Al, House (Egypt) 83
Arab Regional Branch of the International Council on Archives (International Organizations) 466
Arango, Biblioteca Luis-Angel (Colombia) 67
Aranha, Graca, Prize (Brazil) 57
Arani-Verlag GmbH (Federal Republic of Germany) 123
Aranzadi, Editorial (Spain) 337
Ararat Verlag GmbH (Federal Republic of Germany) 123
Arbalète, L' (France) 92
Arbeiderspers, BV Uitgeverij de (Netherlands) 273
Arbeiterbewegung und Gesellschaftswissenschaft, Verlag (Federal Republic of Germany) 123
Arbeitsgemeinschaft Buchgemeinschaften und verwandte Unternehmen im Börsenverein des Deutschen Buchhandels eV (Federal Republic of Germany) 120
Arbeitsgemeinschaft der Archive und Bibliotheken in der evangelischen Kirche (Federal Republic of Germany) 168
Arbeitsgemeinschaft der kirchlichen Büchereiverbände Deutschlands (Federal Republic of Germany) 168
Arbeitsgemeinschaft der Kunstbibliotheken (Federal Republic of Germany) 168
Arbeitsgemeinschaft der Parlaments- und Behördenbibliotheken (Federal Republic of Germany) 168
Arbeitsgemeinschaft der Regionalbibliotheken (Federal Republic of Germany) 168
Arbeitsgemeinschaft der Spezialbibliotheken eV (ASpB) (Federal Republic of Germany) 169
Arbeitsgemeinschaft der Vertriebsfachverbände (Federal Republic of Germany) 120
Arbeitsgemeinschaft Deutsche Lateinamerika-Forschung (ADLAF) (Federal Republic of Germany) 123
Arbeitsgemeinschaft für juristisches Bibliotheks- und Dokumentationswesen (Federal Republic of Germany) 169
Arbeitsgemeinschaft für medizinisches Bibliothekswesen (Federal Republic of Germany) 169
Arbeitsgemeinschaft katholisch theologischer Bibliotheken (Federal Republic of Germany) 169
Arbeitsgemeinschaft literarische und Sachbuchverlage (Federal Republic of Germany) 120
Arbeitsgemeinschaft mitteleuropäischer Bibelwerke (Federal Republic of Germany) 123
Arbeitsgemeinschaft rechts- und staatswissenschaftlicher Verleger (Federal Republic of Germany) 120
Arbeitsgemeinschaft sozialistischer und demokratischer Verleger und Buchhändler (Federal Republic of Germany) 123
Arbeitsgemeinschaft von Jugendbuchverlegern in der Bundesrepublik Deutschland eV (Federal Republic of Germany) 120
Arbeitsgemeinschaft wissenschaftliche Literatur eV (Federal Republic of Germany) 120
Arbeitskreis für Jugendliteratur eV (Federal Republic of Germany) 121
Arbeitskreis für Jugendliteratur eV (Federal Republic of Germany) 170
Arbeitswelt, Verlag Die, GmbH (Federal Republic of Germany) 123
Arbetarkultur, Förlagsaktiebolaget (Sweden) 352
Arbó SAC e I (Argentina) 3
Arbol Editorial SA de CV (Mexico) 264
Arca, Editorial, SRL (Uruguay) 451
Arcade-Fonds, Editions, Mercator (Belgium) 34
Arcádia, Editora, Sarl (Portugal) 316
Arcady Books Ltd (United Kingdom) 395
Arcana Editrice Srl (Italy) 220
Arcane Bookshop (Cyprus) 70
Arcanum, AB (Sweden) 352
Archaeological Survey of India (India) 187
Archbishopric, Library of the (Cyprus) 70
Arche, Verlag der, Peter Schifferli AG (Switzerland) 362
Archer-Burton, The Kitty, Award (Australia) 22
Archief- en Bibliotheekwezen in België (Belgium) 43
Archiginnasio, Biblioteca Comunale dell' (Italy) 234
Archimedes Verlag (Switzerland) 362
Archipel, Uitgeverij (Netherlands) 273
Architectural Press Ltd (United Kingdom) 395
Architecture & Arts Publications Co (Sri Lanka) 349
Architektur, Verlag für (Federal Republic of Germany) 123
Architektur, Verlag für (Switzerland) 362
Archiv der Universität Wien (Austria) 30
Archivele Statului (Romania) 322
Archives, Central Historical (Bulgaria) 59
Archives, Central, of the People's Republic of Bulgaria (Bulgaria) 59
Archives de l'Etat (Grand Duchy of Luxembourg) 257
Archives départementales de la Réunion (Réunion) 320
Archives, Department of (Bahamas) 31
Archives, Direction des Services d', de la Martinique (Martinique) 263
Archives du Sénégal (Senegal) 324
Archives et bibliothèque nationale (Gabon) 115

496 INDEX

Archives fédérales (Switzerland) 376
Archives générales du Royaume (Belgium) 43
Archives, Inspection des, Musées et Bibliothèques du Mali (Mali) 262
Archives nationales (Algeria) 2
Archives nationales (France) 109
Archives nationales (Ivory Coast) 236
Archives nationales (Niger) 292
Archives nationales (Tunisia) 383
Archives nationales (Upper Volta) 451
Archives nationales de la République Populaire du Benin (Benin) 45
Archives nationales de Madagascar (Democratic Republic of Madagascar) 258
Archives nationales, Direction des, Bibliothèque publique centrale (Mauritania) 263
Archives nationales du Cameroun (United Republic of Cameroun) 61
Archives nationales du Zaïre (Zaire) 462
Archives of Early Russian, Central State, Historical Records (Union of Soviet Socialist Republics) 389
Archives of the October Revolution, Central State, and Higher State Bodies (Union of Soviet Socialist Republics) 389
Archives of the RSFSR, Central State (Union of Soviet Socialist Republics) 389
Archives of the USSR, Central State Historical (Union of Soviet Socialist Republics) 389
Archives of the USSR, Central State Literature and Art (Union of Soviet Socialist Republics) 389
Archives, Public, of Sierra Leone (Sierra Leone) 325
Archives Service, The, of the Prime Minister's Office of the Socialist Republic of Viet Nam (Socialist Republic of Viet Nam) 455
Archives, The Central, for the History of the Jewish People (formerly Jewish Historical General Archives) (Israel) 218
Archivio Centrale dello Stato (Italy) 234
Archivio Storico, Biblioteca dell', Civico e Biblioteca Trivulziana (Italy) 234
Archivo General de Centro (Guatemala) 177
Archivo General de Indias (Spain) 347
Archivo General de la Nación (Dominican Republic) 82
Archivo General de la Nación (Mexico) 269
Archivo General de la Nación (Peru) 307
Archivo General de la Nación (Uruguay) 452
Archivo General de la Nación (Venezuela) 454
Archivo General de Puerto Rico (Puerto Rico) 320
Archivo Histórico Municipal de la Habana (Cuba) 69
Archivo Historico Nacional (Spain) 347
Archivo Nacional (Nicaragua) 292
Archivo Nacional de Colombia, Biblioteca Nacional (Colombia) 67
Archivo Nacional de Historia (Ecuador) 83
Archivo y Biblioteca Capitulares (Spain) 347
Archivos Históricos y Bibliotecas (Mexico) 269
Archiwów Państwowych, Naczelna Dyrekcja (Poland) 314
Archiwum Akt Nowych (Poland) 314
Archiwum Główne Akt Dawnych (Poland) 314
Arciere, Edizioni L', Srl (Italy) 220
Aredit, Publications (France) 92
Arena (United Kingdom) 395
Arena Books (United Kingdom) 395
Arena-Verlag Georg Popp GmbH & Co (Federal Republic of Germany) 124
Argalia Editore delle Arti Grafiche Editoriali Srl (Italy) 220
Argente, Sentos & Cia Lda (Angola) 2
Argentine National Prize for Literature (Argentina) 9
Argos, Editorial, Vergara SA (Spain) 337
Argos Press (Federal Republic of Germany) 124
Argosy, Librería (Panama) 305
Arguedas, Premio José María (Peru) 308
Argus (Netherlands) 273
Argus Books Ltd (United Kingdom) 395
Argus Communications (UK Division) (United Kingdom) 395
Arhiv Hrvatske (Yugoslavia) 460
Arhiv na SR Makedonija (Yugoslavia) 460
Arhiv SR Slovenije (Yugoslavia) 460
Arhiv Srbije (Yugoslavia) 460
Århus Kommunes Biblioteker (Denmark) 80
Arica, Editorial, SA (Peru) 306
Arica, Librería (Peru) 307
Ariel, Editorial, SA (Spain) 337
Ariel Publishing House (Israel) 213
Ariel-Seix Barral SA (Mexico) 264
Aries Lima (Indonesia) 205
Arinos, Afonso, Prize (Brazil) 57
Aris & Phillips Ltd (United Kingdom) 395
Ariston, Editions, SA (Switzerland) 362
Ark Boeken (Netherlands) 273
Arkady, Wydawnictwo (Poland) 311
Arkana-Verlag (Federal Republic of Germany) 124
Arkib Negara Malaysia (Malaysia) 261
Arkın Kitabevi (Turkey) 384
Arkistoyhdistys ry (Finland) 89
Arkivarforeningen (Norway) 300

Arkivforeningen (Denmark) 80
Arlecchino Teaterförlag (Sweden) 358
Arlen House Ltd (Republic of Ireland) 209
Arlington Books (Publishers) Ltd (United Kingdom) 395
Armada Books (United Kingdom) 395
Armando, Editore Armando (Italy) 220
Amazens Distribuidores Lta (Mozambique) 271
Armed Forces Library Service (Ghana) 173
Armenia Editore Srl (Italy) 220
Armitano, Ernesto (Venezuela) 453
Armon Publishing House Ltd (Israel) 213
Arms & Armour Press (United Kingdom) 395
Arnado, Livraria, Lda (Portugal) 316
Arnar og Örlygs, Bókaklúbbur (Iceland) 184
Arnaud, Casa Editrice (Italy) 220
Arndt, Ernst-Moritz-, Universität Universitätsbibliothek (German Democratic Republic) 119
Arnkrone Forlaget A/S (Denmark) 75
Arnold, E J, & Son Ltd (United Kingdom) 395
Arnold, Edward, (Australia) Pty Ltd (Australia) 11
Arnold-Heinemann Publishers (India) Pvt Ltd (India) 187
Arnold (Publishers), Edward, Ltd (United Kingdom) 395
Arnold-Wheaton (United Kingdom) 395
Aromolaran Publishing Co Ltd (Nigeria) 293
Arquivo Historico de Moçambique (Mozambique) 271
Arquivo Nacional (Brazil) 56
Arquivo Nacional da Torre do Tombo (Portugal) 318
Arrow (Australia) 19
Arrow Books Ltd (United Kingdom) 395
Arrow Co (Israel) 213
Ars Christiana (Poland) 311
Ars Edition (Switzerland) 362
Ars Edition GmbH (Federal Republic of Germany) 124
Ars Polona (Poland) 313
Ars Polona, Foreign Trade Enterprise (Poland) 311
Arsan Publishing House Ltd (Israel) 213
Arscia, Editions, SA (Belgium) 34
Arsenal, Bibliothèque de l' (France) 109
Arsenal, Das, Verlag für Kultur und Politik GmbH (Federal Republic of Germany) 124
Arsenides, John, Ekdotis (Greece) 174
Arsip Nasional Republik Indonesia (Indonesia) 206
Art Address Verlag Müller GmbH und Co KG (Federal Republic of Germany) 124
Art, Bibliothèque d', et d'Archéologie (Fondation Jacques Doucet) (France) 109
Art Heritage (United Kingdom) 395
Art, The, Publisher (Hong Kong) 179
Artbook International (Federal Republic of Germany) 124
Arte, Ediciones de, y Bibliofilia (Spain) 337
Arte, Editorial, y Literatura (Cuba) 69
Arte, Editrice, e Pensiero SRL (Italy) 220
Arted (Editions d'Art) (France) 92
Artel Publishing & Commercial Organization Co Ltd (Turkey) 384
Artemis Press Ltd (United Kingdom) 395
Artemis und Winkler Verlag (Federal Republic of Germany) 124
Artemis Verlags AG (Switzerland) 362
Artenova, Editora, Ltda (Brazil) 48
Artes, Livraria Editora, Medicas Ltda (Brazil) 48
Artesanal (Spain) 337
Arthaud, Editions, SA (France) 92
Artia (Czechoslovakia) 71
Artia (Czechoslovakia) 73
Artibus et Literis (Federal Republic of Germany) 167
Artigas-Washington, Biblioteca, (USIS) (Uruguay) 452
Artis-Historia, SC (Belgium) 34
Artisjus (Hungary) 182
Artists' and Writers' Guild of South Africa (Republic of South Africa) 335
Artists House (United Kingdom) 395
Artrey, Editions d' (France) 92
Arts & Science University Library (Burma) 60
Arts Book Society (United Kingdom) 443
Arts Council Awards and Bursaries (International Literary Prizes) 475
Arts et Métiers Graphiques (France) 92
Arts et Voyages, Editions (Belgium) 34
Arts Graphiques, Compagnie Française des, SA (France) 92
Arts Guild (United Kingdom) 443
Artus (United Kingdom) 395
Artystyczne i Filmowe, Wydawnictwa (Poland) 311
Aruba Boekhandel (Netherlands Antilles) 286
Asahiya Shoten Ltd (Booksellers) (Japan) 245
Asakura Publishing Co Ltd (Japan) 238
Ascent Books Ltd (United Kingdom) 395
Aschehoug Dansk Forlag A/S (Denmark) 75
Aschehoug, H, & Co (W Nygaard) A/S (Norway) 298
Aschendorffsche Verlagsbuchhandlung (Federal Republic of Germany) 124
Asempa Publishers (Ghana) 172
Asesoría Técnica de Ediciones SA (Spain) 337
Asgar Ali Book Centre (Trinidad and Tobago) 382
Ash & Grant (United Kingdom) 396
Asher, A, & Co, BV (Netherlands) 274
Ashgrove Press Ltd (United Kingdom) 396

Ashish Publishing House (India) 187
Ashmolean Museum Publications (United Kingdom) 396
Ashraf, Shaikh Muhammad (Pakistan) 301
Ashton & Denton Publishing Co (CI) Ltd (Channel Islands) 62
Ashton Scholastic (Australia) 11
Ashton Scholastic Ltd (New Zealand) 287
Asia Afrika (Indonesia) 205
Asia Book Co (Republic of Singapore) 327
Asia Books Co Ltd (Thailand) 381
Asia Pacific Press (Republic of Singapore) 325
Asia Pacific Research Unit Ltd (New Zealand) 287
Asia Press Bookstore Ltd (Hong Kong) 180
Asia Press Ltd (Hong Kong) 179
Asia Publishing Co (India) 187
Asia Publishing House (P) Ltd (India) 187
Asian Cultural Centre for Unesco (International Organizations) 469
Asian Educational Services (India) 187
Asian Literary Market Review (India) 187
Asian Publishers (India) 187
Asian Publishers (India) 187
Asian Trading Corporation (India) 187
Asiathèque, L' (France) 92
Asiatic Society Library (India) 202
Askelin och Hägglund Förlag (Sweden) 352
Askild och Kärnekull Förlag AB (Sweden) 352
Aslib (United Kingdom) 445
Asmara Bookshop (Ethiopia) 86
Asmara Public Library (Ethiopia) 86
Asmara University Library (Ethiopia) 86
Asociación Argentina de Bibliotecas y Centros de Información Cientificos y Tecnicos (Argentina) 9
Asociación Bautista Argentina de Publicaciones (Argentina) 3
Asociación Bibliotecologica Guatemalteca (Guatemala) 177
Asociación Boliviana de Bibliotecarios (ABB) (Bolivia) 47
Asociación Colombiana de Bibliotecarios (Colombia) 67
Asociación Costarricense de Bibliotecarios (Costa Rica) 69
Asociación de Bibliotecarios de El Salvador (El Salvador) 85
Asociación de Bibliotecarios de Instituciones de Enseñanza Superior e Investigación (ABIESI) (Mexico) 269
Asociación de Bibliotecarios del Paraguay (Paraguay) 306
Asociación de Bibliotecarios Graduados del Istmo de Panamá (Panama) 305
Asociación de Bibliotecarios Universitarios del Paraguay (Paraguay) 306
Asociación de Bibliotecarios y Archiveros de Honduras (Honduras) 178
Asociación de Bibliotecas Agricolas (Peru) 307
Asociación de Bibliotecas Universitarias y Especializadas de Nicaragua (Nicaragua) 292
Asociación de Bibliotecólogos y Afines del Uruguay (Uruguay) 452
Asociación de Escritores y Artistas Españoles (Spain) 336
Asociación de Ex-Alumnos de la Escuela Nacional de Bibliotecarios (Argentina) 9
Asociación de Libreros del Uruguay (Uruguay) 451
Asociación Dominicana de Bibliotecarios (ASODOBI) (Dominican Republic) 82
Asociación Ecuatoriana de Bibliotecarios (AEB) (Ecuador) 83
Asociación Educacionista Argentina (Argentina) 3
Asociación Española de Archiveros, Bibliotecarios, Museólogos y Documentalistas (Spain) 348
Asociación Española de Editores de Musica (AEDEM) (Spain) 336
Asociación General de Archivistas de El Salvador (El Salvador) 85
Asociación Interamericana de Bibliotecarios y Documentalistas Agrícolas (International Organizations) 466
Asociación Latinoamericana de Escuelas de Bibliotecología y Ciencias de la Información (ALEBCI) (International Organizations) 466
Asociación Mexicana de Bibliotecarios AC (AMBAC) (Mexico) 269
Asociación Nacional de Autores de Obras Didacticas (AUCOLDI) (Colombia) 65
Asociación Nacional de Escritores Venezolanos (Venezuela) 453
Asociación Nacional de Escritores y Artistas (ANEA) (Peru) 306
Asociación Nicaraguense de Bibliotecarios (ASNIBI) (Nicaragua) 292
Asociación Panameña de Bibliotecarios (Panama) 305
Asociación para el Progresso de la Dirección (APD) (Spain) 337
Asociación Peruana de Archiveros (Peru) 307
Asociación Peruana de Bibliotecarios (Peru) 307
Asociación Uruguaya de Escritores (Uruguay) 451
Asociatia Bibliotecarilor din RSR (Romania) 322
Asociation di Biblioteka i Archivo di Korsow (Carbido) (Netherlands Antilles) 286
Aspioti-Elka SA (Greece) 174

INDEX 497

Assam Publishers' & Booksellers' Association (India) 185
Assayad, Dar (Lebanon) 254
Assimakopouli (Greece) 174
Assimil, Editions, SA (France) 92
Assimil, Uitgaven Nelis PVBA (Belgium) 34
Assimil-Verlag KG (Federal Republic of Germany) 124
Asso Verlag Anneliese Althoff (Federal Republic of Germany) 124
Associação Brasileira de Bibliotecários (Brazil) 56
Associação Brasileira de Livreiros Antiquarios (Brazil) 47
Associação Brasileira do Livro (Brazil) 47
Associação dos Arquivistas Brasileiros (Brazil) 56
Associação Paulista de Bibliotecários (Brazil) 56
Associação Portuguesa de Bibliotecários Arquivistas e Documentalistas (Portugal) 318
Associação Portuguesa dos Editores e Livreiros (Portugal) 315
Associação Profissional de Bibliotecários do Estado do Rio de Janeiro (APBERJ) (Brazil) 56
Associação Rio-Grandense de Bibliotecários (Brazil) 56
Associació de Bibliotecaris (Spain) 348
Associated Book Clubs (Republic of South Africa) 333
Associated Book Publishers (Aust) Ltd (Australia) 11
Associated Book Publishers (NZ) Ltd (New Zealand) 287
Associated Book Publishers PLC (United Kingdom) 396
Associated Booksellers of Southern Africa Ltd (Republic of South Africa) 328
Associated Business Press (United Kingdom) 396
Associated Publishers Amsterdam (Netherlands) 274
Associated Publishers Inc (Philippines) 308
Associated Publishing House (India) 188
Association belge de Documentation (Belgium) 43
Association de l'Ecole nationale supérieure de Bibliothécaires (France) 110
Association des Amis du Livre (French Guiana) 114
Association des Archivistes français (France) 110
Association des Bibliothécaires, Archivistes, Documentalistes et Muséographes du Cameroun (ABADCAM) (United Republic of Cameroun) 61
Association des Bibliothécaires-Documentalistes de l'Institut d'Etudes sociales de l'Etat (Belgium) 43
Association des Bibliothécaires et du Personnel des Bibliothèques des Ministères de Belgique (Belgium) 43
Association des Bibliothécaires français (France) 110
Association des Bibliothécaires Laotiens (Laos) 253
Association des Bibliothécaires Suisses (Vereinigung Schweizerischer Bibliothekare) (Switzerland) 376
Association des Bibliothèques ecclésiastiques de France (ABEF) (France) 110
Association des Bibliothèques Internationales (International Organizations) 466
Association des Diplômés de l'Ecole de Bibliothécaires-Documentalistes (France) 110
Association des Ecrivains belges de langue française (Belgium) 44
Association des Ecrivains combattants (France) 111
Association des écrivains réunionnais (Réunion) 320
Association des Editeurs belges (Belgium) 33
Association des Editeurs et des Libraires d'Athènes (Greece) 173
Association des Sociétés scientifiques médicales belges (ASBL) (Belgium) 34
Association for Science Education (United Kingdom) 396
Association for Scottish Literary Studies (United Kingdom) 446
Association for the Promotion of the International Circulation of the Press (International Organizations) 466
Association for the Study of Australian Literature (Australia) 21
Association française des Documentalistes et Bibliothécaires spécialisés (France) 110
Association internationale de Bibliophilie (International Organizations) 466
Association internationale des Critiques littéraires (International Organizations) 466
Association internationale des Documentalistes et Techniciens de l'Information AID (International Organizations) 466
Association nationale des Bibliothécaires, Archivistes et Documentalistes sénégalais (ANBADS) (Senegal) 324
Association nationale des Bibliothécaires d'Expression française (Belgium) 43
Association nationale des Bibliothécaires Municipaux (France) 110
Association nationale des Poètes et Ecrivains camerounais (APEC) (United Republic of Cameroun) 61
Association of African Universities (International Organizations) 471
Association of Arts and Letters (Greece) 176
Association of Assistant Librarians (United Kingdom) 445
Association of Australian University Presses (Australia) 9
Association of Authors' Agents (United Kingdom) 391
Association of British Directory Publishers (United Kingdom) 391
Association of British Library and Information Studies Schools (ABLISS) (United Kingdom) 445

Association of British Science Writers (United Kingdom) 447
Association of British Theological and Philosophical Libraries (United Kingdom) 445
Association of Hebrew Writers (Israel) 212
Association of International Libraries (AIL) (International Organizations) 466
Association of Learned & Professional Society Publishers (United Kingdom) 391
Association of Libraries of Judaica and Hebraica in Europe (International Organizations) 466
Association of Little Presses (United Kingdom) 391
Association of London Chief Librarians (United Kingdom) 445
Association of Mail Order Publishers (United Kingdom) 391
Association of Publishers' Educational Representatives (United Kingdom) 391
Association of Registered Archivists of Iran Secretariat (Iran) 208
Association of Scottish Health Sciences Librarians (United Kingdom) 445
Association of Special Libraries of the Philippines (ASLP) (Philippines) 310
Association of Translators (Denmark) 81
Association of Yugoslav Publishers and Booksellers (Yugoslavia) 456
Association pour la Médiathèque Publique (AMP) (France) 110
Association pour le Développement de la Documentation, des Bibliothèques et Archives de la Côte d'Ivoire (ADBACI) (Ivory Coast) 236
Association professionnelle des Bibliothécaires et Documentalistes (Belgium) 43
Association suisse des Bibliothèques d'Hôpitaux (Switzerland) 376
Association suisse des Editeurs de Langue française (Switzerland) 360
Association suisse des Libraires de Langue française (Switzerland) 360
Association suisse des Traducteurs et Interprètes (ASTI) (Switzerland) 377
Association suisse romande des Diffuseurs de Livres (Switzerland) 360
Association togolaise pour le Développement de la Documentation, des Bibliothèques, Archives et Musées (Togo) 382
Association tunisienne de Documentalistes, Bibliothécaires et Archivistes (Tunisia) 384
Association voltaique pour le Développement des Bibliothèques, des Archives et de la Documentation (AVDBAD) (Upper Volta) 451
Association Zaïroise des Archivistes, Bibliothècaires et Documentalistes (Zaire) 463
Associazione dei Libraii della Svizzera Italiana (ALSI) (Switzerland) 360
Associazione Italiana Biblioteche (Italy) 234
Associazione Italiana Editori (Italy) 219
Associazione Italiana Traduttori e Interpreti (AITI) (Italy) 236
Associazione Librai Antiquari d'Italia (Italy) 219
Associazione Librai Italiani (Italy) 219
Associazione Nazionale Archivistica Italiana (Italy) 234
Astab Books Ltd (Ghana) 172
Astan Qods Central Library (Iran) 207
Aster, Editorial (Portugal) 316
Ästhetik und Kommunikation Verlags-GmbH (Federal Republic of Germany) 124
Astir (Greece) 174
Astragal Books (United Kingdom) 396
Astrea, Editorial, de Alfredo y Ricardo Depalma SRL (Argentina) 3
Astrolabe, L' (France) 92
Astrolabio-Ubaldini, Casa Editrice, Editore (Italy) 220
Atbara Public Library (Sudan) 350
Atelier (Egypt) 85
Atelier im Bauernhaus, Verlag (Federal Republic of Germany) 124
Atelier Verlag Andernach (AVA) (Federal Republic of Germany) 124
Atenas, Sociedad de Educación, SA (Spain) 337
Ateneo Científico, Literario y Artistico (Spain) 348
Ateneo Científico, Literario y Artistico (Spain) 348
Ateneo de Barcelona, Biblioteca del (Spain) 347
Ateneo de Madrid, Biblioteca del (Spain) 347
Ateneo de Manila University Libraries (Philippines) 309
Ateneo de Sevilla Prize (Spain) 348
Ateneo de Valladolid Prize (Spain) 348
Ateneo, Editorial, de Caracas (Venezuela) 453
Ateneo, Editorial El (Argentina) 3
Ateneo, Edizioni Dell', SpA (Italy) 220
Ateneo, El (Argentina) 8
Ateneo, Librería El (Paraguay) 306
Ateneo Mercantil, Biblioteca del, Valenciano (Spain) 347
Athena-Verlag AG (Switzerland) 375
Athenaeum Boekhandel (Netherlands) 284
Athenaeum Verlag AG (Switzerland) 362
Athenaion (Federal Republic of Germany) 124

Athenäum Verlag GmbH (Federal Republic of Germany) 124
Athene Publishing Co (United Kingdom) 396
Atheneu, Livraria, Ltda (Brazil) 49
Athenon, Ekdotike, SA (Greece) 174
Athens Academy Library (Greece) 176
Athens College Library (Greece) 176
Athens Union (Greece) 176
Athesia, Verlagsanstalt (Italy) 220
Athlone, The, Press Ltd (United Kingdom) 396
Atica, Editora, SA (Brazil) 49
Atika SA (Spain) 337
Atlantic (United Kingdom) 396
Atlantic Communications Ltd (United Kingdom) 396
Atlantica Editrice SRL (Italy) 220
Atlántida, Editorial, SA (Argentina) 4
Atlântida, Livraria Editora, Ltda (Portugal) 316
Atlantis, Bokförlaget, AB (Sweden) 352
Atlantis M Pechlivanides & Co SA (Greece) 174
Atlantis Verlag AG (Switzerland) 362
Atlantis-Verlag GmbH & Co Kg (Federal Republic of Germany) 124
Atlas Book Sales Ltd (United Kingdom) 442
Atlas-Diagoras (Greece) 174
Atlas, Editora, SA (Brazil) 49
Atlas, The, Bookshop (Ghana) 172
Atma Ram & Sons (India) 188
Atma Ram & Sons (India) 201
Atomizdat (Union of Soviet Socialist Republics) 387
Atrium (Netherlands) 274
Atrium Verlag AG (Switzerland) 362
Attié, Librairie (Upper Volta) 451
Attila, Jozsef, Prize (Hungary) 183
Atual Editora Ltda (Brazil) 49
Au Messager (Central African Republic) 62
Au Ping-Pong, Librairie (French Polynesia) 115
Aubanel SA (France) 92
Aubier-Montaigne, Editions, SA (France) 92
Auckland Public Library (New Zealand) 290
Auckland University Press (New Zealand) 287
Audiffred, François-Joseph, Prize (France) 111
Audivox (Belgium) 34
Audivox (Belgium) 42
Auer, Verlag Ludwig (Federal Republic of Germany) 124
Aufbau-Verlag Berlin und Weimar (German Democratic Republic) 116
Augener (United Kingdom) 396
August Cesarec (Yugoslavia) 456
Augustin-Verlag (Switzerland) 362
Augustiniennes, Etudes (France) 92
Augustinus, Boekhandel (Netherlands Antilles) 286
Augustinus, Librería (Spain) 347
Aujourd'hui, Editions d' (France) 92
Aujourd'hui Prize (France) 111
Aulis Verlag Deubner & Co KG (Federal Republic of Germany) 124
Aurelia Books PVBA (Belgium) 34
Auria, M d', Editore della 'EST — Editoriale Studi e Testi — SNC' (Italy) 220
Aurobindo, Sri, Books Distribution Agency (SABDA) (India) 188
Aurora Art Publishers (Union of Soviet Socialist Republics) 387
Aurora, Asociación Ediciones La (Argentina) 4
Aurora, Gráfica Editora, Ltda (Brazil) 49
Aurora Press (Australia) 11
Aurum Press Ltd (United Kingdom) 396
Aurum Verlag GmbH & Co KG (Federal Republic of Germany) 124
Aussaat-und-Schriftenmissions-Verlag GmbH (Federal Republic of Germany) 124
Aussenhandels-Ausschuss (Federal Republic of Germany) 124
Austick's Headrow Bookshop (United Kingdom) 444
Australasian Publishing Co Pty Ltd (Australia) 11
Australia & New Zealand Book Co Pty Ltd (Australia) 11
Australia & New Zealand Book Co Pty Ltd, New Zealand Branch Office (New Zealand) 287
Australian Academy of Science (Australia) 11
Australian Advisory Council on Bibliographical Services (AACOBS) (Australia) 20
Australian Archives, NSW Regional Office (Australia) 20
Australian Awards for Young Writers (Australia) 22
Australian Book Publishers Association (Australia) 11
Australian Booksellers Association (Australia) 10
Australian Copyright Council (Australia) 10
Australian Council, The, for Educational Research Ltd (Australia) 11
Australian Encyclopaedia Pty Ltd (Australia) 11
Australian Government Publications (Australia) 20
Australian Government Publishing Service (Australia) 11
Australian Institute of Aboriginal Studies (Australia) 11
Australian Institute of Criminology (Australia) 11
Australian Library Promotion Council (Australia) 21
Australian Literature Society (Australia) 21
Australian Literature Society Gold Medal (Australia) 22
Australian National Gallery (Australia) 12
Australian National University Library (Australia) 20

498 INDEX

Australian National University Press (Australia) 12
Australian Natives' Association Literature Award (Australia) 22
Australian School Library Association (Australia) 21
Australian Society of Archivists Inc (Australia) 21
Australian Society of Authors Ltd (Australia) 21
Australian Society of Indexers (Australia) 10
Australian Standard Book Numbering Agency (Australia) 12
Australian Universities Press Pty Ltd (Australia) 12
Australian Writers' Guild Ltd (Australia) 21
Austrian Children's and Young People's Book Prizes (Austria) 31
Austrian State Prize for European Literature (International Literary Prizes) 475
Austrian State Prize for Literature for Children and Young People (Austria) 31
Authors' Club (United Kingdom) 447
Authors' Club First Novel Award (United Kingdom) 448
Authors' Club Sir Banister Fletcher Prize Trust (United Kingdom) 448
Authors' Guild of India (India) 185
Authors' Lending & Copyright Society (United Kingdom) 391
Autobooks Ltd (United Kingdom) 396
Automobile Association (United Kingdom) 396
Autonomie, Edizioni delle, Srl (Italy) 220
Autoren-und Verlagsgesellschaft, Syndikat (Federal Republic of Germany) 124
Autoren, Verlag der, GmbH & Co KG (Federal Republic of Germany) 124
Autran, Joseph, Prize (France) 111
'Aux Belles Images', Librairie (Morocco) 271
'Aux Frères Réunis', Librairie (United Republic of Cameroun) 61
Auzou, Editions Philippe (France) 92
Aval, Agenzia Letteraria (Italy) 233
Avant-Scène, Editions l' (France) 92
'Avante!', Editorial (Portugal) 316
Avante, Editorial, SA (Mexico) 264
Avebury Publishing Co Ltd (United Kingdom) 396
Avele College Library (Western Samoa) 455
Avery, Thomas, & Sons Ltd (New Zealand) 287
Avery, Thomas, and Sons Ltd (New Zealand) 290
Aviation Book Club (United Kingdom) 443
Avicenne Librairie Internationale (Syria) 377
Avicenum, zdravotnické nakladatelství (Czechoslovakia) 71
Avinash Reference Publications (India) 188
Avon-Anglia Publications & Services (United Kingdom) 396
Award for Achievement (New Zealand) 291
Award for Literature and Scientific Publications (Turkey) 385
Award Publications Ltd (United Kingdom) 396
Awqaf, Al- (Iraq) 208
Axel-Juncker Verlag Jacobi KG (Federal Republic of Germany) 125
Ayacucho, Biblioteca (Venezuela) 453
Ayala Museum Library & Iconographic Archives (Philippines) 309
Ayalga Ediciones SA (Spain) 337
Ayam, Al-, Press Co Ltd (Sudan) 350
Aydinlik Yayinlari (Turkey) 384
Aymá, Editorial, SA Editora (Spain) 337
Ayuso, Editorial, San Bernardo (Spain) 338
Azerbaidzhanskaya gosudarstvennaya respublikanskaya biblioteka im M F Akhundova (Union of Soviet Socialist Republics) 389
Azhar, Al-, University Library (Egypt) 84
Azim Publishing House (Pakistan) 301
Azteca, Editorial, SA (Mexico) 264

B A B (Iceland) 184
B A E S A (Buenos Aires Edita SA) (Argentina) 4
B A G Buchhändler-Abrechnungs-Gesellschaft mbH (Federal Republic of Germany) 121
B A S H (United Kingdom) 391
B & T Directories (Pvt) Ltd (Zimbabwe) 464
B B C Publications (United Kingdom) 396
B F I Publishing (United Kingdom) 396
B I G Z (Yugoslavia) 456
B I M H Publications (United Kingdom) 396
B K V-Brasilienkunde Verlag GmbH (Federal Republic of Germany) 125
B L A C Publishing House (Republic of South Africa) 328
B L V Verlagsgesellschaft mbH (Federal Republic of Germany) 125
b m p (Federal Republic of Germany) 125
B O D (United Kingdom) 391
B P C C PLC (United Kingdom) 396
B P I, Editions, (Bureau de Presse et d'Informations) (France) 92

B R E S (Netherlands) 274
B R G M, Editions (France) 92
B R Publishing Corporation (India) 188
B S C Books Ltd (United Kingdom) 397
B S C Books Ltd (United Kingdom) 442
B S-Verlag Manfred Kerler (Federal Republic of Germany) 125
B V B (Federal Republic of Germany) 125
Baars-Jelgersma, Auteursbureau Greta (Netherlands) 283
Babani, Bernard, (Publishing) Ltd (United Kingdom) 397
Babylon Übersetzungen (Federal Republic of Germany) 167
Babylon Übersetzungen (Federal Republic of Germany) 171
Bachem, J P, Verlag GmbH (Federal Republic of Germany) 125
Bachman & Turner (United Kingdom) 397
Backer, De, Publishers PVBA (Belgium) 34
Backpacker's Guides Series (United Kingdom) 397
Bacon, Francis, Society Inc (United Kingdom) 447
Bacon, S John, Pty Ltd (Australia) 12
Baconnière, Editions de la, SA (Switzerland) 362
Badger Books (United Kingdom) 397
Baedeker, Buchhandlung G D (Federal Republic of Germany) 167
Baedeker, Karl, GmbH (Federal Republic of Germany) 125
Baedeker voor de Vrouw (Netherlands) 274
Baedekers Autoführer-Verlag GmbH (Federal Republic of Germany) 125
Baekelmans, Lode, Prize (Belgium) 44
Baensch, Hans A (Federal Republic of Germany) 125
Bagchi, K P, & Co (India) 188
Bagster, Samuel, & Sons Ltd (United Kingdom) 397
Bagutta Prize (Italy) 235
Baha'i Publishing Trust (India) 188
Baha'i Verlag GmbH (Federal Republic of Germany) 125
Baha'ies, Maison d'Editions, ASBL (Belgium) 34
Bahamas Anglo American Book Store (Bahamas) 31
Bahamas Book & Bible House (Bahamas) 31
Bahn, Friedrich, Verlag GmbH (Federal Republic of Germany) 125
Bahrain Bookshop (Bahrain) 32
Bahrain Writers and Literators Association (Bahrain) 32
Baifukan Co Ltd (Japan) 238
Baik Rog Publishing Co (Republic of Korea) 250
Bailey Bros & Swinfen Ltd (United Kingdom) 397
Baillière, Editions J-B (France) 92
Baillière Tindall (United Kingdom) 397
Bak Yung Sa (Republic of Korea) 250
Bakalov', Knigoizdatelstvo 'Georgi (Bulgaria) 58
Baker Press, Howard, Ltd (United Kingdom) 397
Baker (Publishers), John, Ltd (United Kingdom) 397
Bakewell, Michael, & Associates Ltd (United Kingdom) 442
Bakker, Bert, BV (Netherlands) 274
Bakolori (Nigeria) 293
Balai, PN, Pustaka (Indonesia) 205
Balcells, Carmen, Agencia Literaria (Brazil) 55
Balcells, Carmen, Agencia Literaria (Spain) 346
Baldini e Castoldi (Italy) 220
Bale Bandung — Sumur Bandung (Indonesia) 205
Balkan-Press (Federal Republic of Germany) 167
Balkema, A A (Netherlands) 274
Balkema, A A, Publishers (Republic of South Africa) 329
Ball, Jonathan, Publishers (Pty) Ltd (Republic of South Africa) 329
Balland, André (France) 92
Balme Library (Ghana) 173
Balmer, H R, AG Verlag (Switzerland) 362
Banca y Comercio, Editorial, SA (Mexico) 264
Bancarella Prize (Italy) 235
Bancarellino Prize (Italy) 235
Banco, Biblioteca del, Central de la República Argentina (Argentina) 8
Bandarnsarn (Thailand) 380
Banga Sahitya Bhavan (Bangladesh) 32
Bangalore Book Bureau (India) 201
Bangalore, The, Printing & Publishing Co Ltd (India) 188
Bangkok Bank Foundation Prize (Thailand) 381
Bangkok Central Book Depot (Thailand) 381
Bangladesh Books International Ltd (Bangladesh) 32
Bangladesh Books International Ltd (Bangladesh) 32
Bangladesh Granthagar Samity (Bangladesh) 32
Bangladesh Institute of Development Studies Library (Bangladesh) 32
Bangladesh Pustak Prokashak o Bikreta Samity (Bangladesh) 32
Bani Mandir (India) 188
Bani Publications (India) 188
Bank of New Zealand Young Writers' Awards (New Zealand) 291
Banmai (Thailand) 380
Banner, The, of Truth Trust (United Kingdom) 397
Bansal & Co (India) 188
Bantam (Australia) 12
Baptist Book Centre (Zimbabwe) 465

Bar-David Literary Agency (Israel) 217
Bar Ilan University, Book Publishing Committee (Israel) 213
Bar Ilan University Library (Israel) 218
Bär, U, Verlag (Switzerland) 362
Bar Urian Publishing House (Israel) 213
Barbera, Giunti, Editore (Italy) 220
Barbiaux (Drukkerij G — Uitgeverij de Garve) PVBA (Belgium) 34
Barblan et Saladin, Librairie (Switzerland) 362
Barblan et Saladin, Librairie (Switzerland) 375
Bardet, René, Prize (France) 111
Barebone Books (United Kingdom) 397
Bärenreiter-Verlag (Federal Republic of Germany) 125
Bargezzi-Verlag AG (Switzerland) 362
Bari, Editoriale (Italy) 220
Barjes, Edizioni Oreste (Italy) 220
Barker, Arthur, Ltd (United Kingdom) 397
Barlevi (Israel) 213
Barn, Bokklubbens (Norway) 300
Barnakarn (Thailand) 380
Barnakieh (Thailand) 380
Barnasilpa (Thailand) 380
Barnes & Noble (United Kingdom) 397
Baron Publishing Ltd (United Kingdom) 397
Barque & Co (Pakistan) 301
Barr Smith, The, Library (Australia) 20
Barracuda Books Ltd (United Kingdom) 397
Barral Editores SA (Spain) 338
Barrau (New Caledonia) 286
Barre, André, Prize (France) 111
Barreiro y Ramos SA (Uruguay) 451
Barreiro y Ramos SA (Uruguay) 452
Barrie & Jenkins Ltd (United Kingdom) 397
Barrikaden, Förlaget, AB (Sweden) 352
Barry Editorial Com Ind SRL (Argentina) 4
Bartels und Wernitz, Verlag, KG (Federal Republic of Germany) 125
Barth, Johann Ambrosius, Verlagsbuchhandlung (German Democratic Republic) 116
Barth, Otto Wilhelm, -Verlag KG (Federal Republic of Germany) 125
Bartholomew & Son, John, Ltd (United Kingdom) 397
Barthou, Alice Louis, Prize (France) 111
Barthou, Louis, Prize (France) 111
Barthou, Max, Prize (France) 111
Barudio und Hess Verlag (Federal Republic of Germany) 125
Baryes, Casa Editrice Giorgio, Srl (Italy) 220
Baschet et Cie, Editeurs (France) 92
Baseball Magazine Sha (Japan) 238
Bashir, Al, Bookshop (Sudan) 350
Basic Books (United Kingdom) 397
Basileia Verlag (Switzerland) 362
Basilisk, The, Press Ltd (United Kingdom) 397
Basilius Presse AG (Switzerland) 362
Basis (Netherlands) 274
Basis-Verlag (Federal Republic of Germany) 125
Bassermann'sche, Friedrich, Verlagsbuchhandlung im Falken-Verlag GmbH (Federal Republic of Germany) 125
Bastei-Verlag Gustav H Lübbe (Federal Republic of Germany) 125
Bastian Prize (Norway) 301
Bastian, W E, & Co (Sri Lanka) 349
Bastilla, Ediciones la (Argentina) 4
Bastinos, Librería (Spain) 347
Bateman, David, Ltd (New Zealand) 287
Batsford, B T, Ltd (United Kingdom) 397
Battei, Casa Editrice Luigi (Italy) 220
Battenberg, Ernst, Verlag (Federal Republic of Germany) 125
Bättre Barnomsorg (Sweden) 358
Bättre Data (Sweden) 358
Bättre Ledarskap (Sweden) 358
Bättre Samhälle (Sweden) 358
Bättre Skola (Sweden) 358
Bauer, Hermann, Verlag KG (Federal Republic of Germany) 125
Baufachverlag AG (Switzerland) 362
Bauverlag GmbH (Federal Republic of Germany) 125
Bauwesen, VEB Verlag für (German Democratic Republic) 116
Baxters Ltd (Bermuda) 46
Bay Books (Australia) 12
Bayard-Presse SA, Editions du Centurion (France) 92
Bayerische Staatsbibliothek (Federal Republic of Germany) 168
Bayerische Verlagsanstalt Bamberg (B V B) (Federal Republic of Germany) 125
Bayerischer Schulbuch-Verlag (Federal Republic of Germany) 125
Bayly, A W, & Co Lda (Mozambique) 271
Beacon Publishing (United Kingdom) 397
Beattie and Forbes (New Zealand) 290
Beatty, The Chester, Library and Gallery of Oriental Art (Republic of Ireland) 211
Beauchesne, Editions (France) 92

Beaufort, Mme (French Guiana) 114
Beaumont Executive Press (United Kingdom) 397
Beaux Livres, Les (Monaco) 270
Beaver Books (United Kingdom) 397
Becher, Institut für Literatur Johannes R (German Democratic Republic) 120
Becher, Johannes R, Prize (German Democratic Republic) 120
Bechtle (Federal Republic of Germany) 126
Becht's, H J W, Uitgeversmij bv/Uitgeverij J H de Bussy BV (Netherlands) 274
Beck, Edition Monika (Federal Republic of Germany) 126
Beck, Verlag C H (Federal Republic of Germany) 126
Beckers SA Editions (Belgium) 34
Beckmans Bokförlag AB (Sweden) 352
Becknell Books (United Kingdom) 397
Bedford Square Press of the National Council for Voluntary Organizations (United Kingdom) 397
Bedout, Editorial, SA (Colombia) 65
Bee In Bonnet (United Kingdom) 397
Beernaert Prize (Belgium) 44
Beginners' Prize (German Democratic Republic) 120
Behzad Bookshop (Afghanistan) 1
Behzad Bookstore (Afghanistan) 1
Beijing daxue tushuguan (People's Republic of China) 64
Beijing tushuguan (People's Republic of China) 64
Beirut Arab University, Library of (Lebanon) 254
Beit Lochamei Hagetha'ot (Israel) 213
Bekadidact, Uitgeverij (Netherlands) 274
Belaieff, M P (Federal Republic of Germany) 126
Belfast Public Library (United Kingdom) 444
Belfond, Editions Pierre (France) 92
Belgian Government Prizes for Literature (Ministry of Flemish Culture) (Belgium) 44
Belgian Government Prizes for Literature (Ministry of French Culture) (Belgium) 44
Belgisch Instituut voor Voorlichting en Documentatie (INBEL) (Belgium) 34
Belin, Editions (France) 92
Belis-Vinck, Boekhandel (Belgium) 42
Belize Book Shop (Anglican Diocese) (Belize) 45
Belize Library Association (Belize) 45
Bell & Hyman Ltd (United Kingdom) 397
Bell, SA Editorial (Argentina) 4
Bellas Artes, Librería (Mexico) 268
Bellaterra, Ediciones, SA (Spain) 338
Belle, Uitgeverij van, PVBA (Belgium) 34
Bellens, Librairie (Belgium) 42
Belles Lettres', Société d'Edition 'Les (France) 92
Bellmans Prize (Sweden) 359
Bello, Andrés, Prize (Chile) 64
Bello', Biblioteca de la Universidad Catolica 'Andres (Venezuela) 454
Bello', Clubs de Lectores 'Andrés (Chile) 63
Bello, Editorial Andrés, / Editorial Juridica de Chile (Chile) 63
Bello, Librería Andrés (Chile) 63
Belmont Press (Zimbabwe) 465
Belser, Chr, AG für Verlagsgeschäfte und Co KG (Federal Republic of Germany) 126
Belton Books (United Kingdom) 398
Beltz (Switzerland) 362
Beltz Verlag (Federal Republic of Germany) 126
Ben-Gurion University of the Negev Library (Israel) 218
Ben-Zvi Institute (Israel) 213
Bendel State Library (Nigeria) 296
Benediktinerklosters, Bibliothek des, Melk in Niederösterreich (Austria) 30
Bengali Academy Literary Awards (Bangladesh) 33
Benghazi Public Library (Libya) 256
Benibengor Book Agency (Ghana) 172
Benin University Bookshop (Nigeria) 296
Benin University Library (Nigeria) 296
Benjamin/Cummings Inc (United Kingdom) 398
Benjamins, John, BV (Netherlands) 274
Benn, Ernest, Ltd (United Kingdom) 398
Bennett Award (International Literary Prizes) 475
Bennett, G H, & Co Ltd (New Zealand) 290
Benson Medal (International Literary Prizes) 475
Benteli Verlag (Switzerland) 362
Benton Ross Publishers Ltd (New Zealand) 287
Benziger AG (Switzerland) 362
Benziger Verlag (Federal Republic of Germany) 126
Beogradski Izdavačko-Grafički Zavod (Yugoslavia) 456
Berchmans, Johannes, Verlag GmbH (Federal Republic of Germany) 126
Berg/Bodman, Verlag Schumann KG (Federal Republic of Germany) 126
Berg International Editeurs (France) 92
Bergadi Editions (Greece) 174
Bergen offentlige Bibliotek Horda land Fylkesbibliotek (Norway) 300
Bergendal Forlag (Norway) 298
Berger, Centre culturel français Gaston, Bibliothèque (Senegal) 324
Berger, Ferdinand, und Söhne (Austria) 25
Berger-Levrault SA (France) 92

Bergh, Edition Sven Erik (Federal Republic of Germany) 126
Bergh, Edition Sven Erik, im Europabuch AG (Switzerland) 362
Berghaus Verlag (Federal Republic of Germany) 126
Berghs Förlag AB (Sweden) 352
Bergland-Buch', Verlag 'Das, (R Kiesel GmbH) (Austria) 25
Bergland Verlag (Austria) 25
Bergmann, Anton, Prize (International Literary Prizes) 475
Bergmann, J F (Federal Republic of Germany) 126
Bergs, H M, Forlag ApS (Denmark) 75
Bergverlag Rudolf Rother GmbH (Federal Republic of Germany) 126
Berhan Bookshop and Stationery (Ethiopia) 86
Berichthaus Verlag, Dr Conrad Ulrich (Switzerland) 362
Berlin Verlag Arno Spitz (Federal Republic of Germany) 126
Berliner Handpresse Wolfgang Joerg und Erich Schoenig (Federal Republic of Germany) 126
Berliner Stadtbibliothek (German Democratic Republic) 119
Berliner Union GmbH (Federal Republic of Germany) 126
Berliner Verleger- und Buchhändlervereinigung eV (Federal Republic of Germany) 121
Berlingske Forlag A/S (Denmark) 75
Berlitz, Editions (Switzerland) 362
Berlitz, Société Internationale des Ecoles, SA (France) 92
Bermuda Archives (Bermuda) 46
Bermuda Book Store Ltd (Bermuda) 46
Bermuda Library (Bermuda) 46
Bermuda Press Ltd (Bermuda) 46
Bermudian Publishing Co (Bermuda) 46
Bernard, Librería Claudio (El Salvador) 85
Bernard und Graefe Verlag (Federal Republic of Germany) 126
Bernards (Publishers) Ltd (United Kingdom) 398
Bernces Förlag AB (Sweden) 353
Bernhardt, Verlag Alexander (Austria) 25
Bernheim, Bibliothèque, Bibliothèque territoriale de la Nouvelle-Caledonie (New Caledonia) 286
Berry, David, Prize (International Literary Prizes) 475
Bertelsmann, C, Verlag GmbH (Federal Republic of Germany) 126
Bertelsmann de Mexico SA (Mexico) 268
Bertelsmann GmbH, Verlagsgruppe (Federal Republic of Germany) 126
Bertelsmann International, Verlagsgruppe, GmbH (Federal Republic of Germany) 126
Bertelsmann Lesering (Federal Republic of Germany) 167
Bertrand, Livraria (Portugal) 318
Bertrand, Livraria, SARL (Portugal) 316
Beskow Press (Sweden) 360
Besondere, Verlag Das (Federal Republic of Germany) 126
Best Book of the Sea Award (International Literary Prizes) 475
Best First Book of Poetry Award (New Zealand) 291
Best First Book of Prose Award (New Zealand) 291
Beste, Det, A/S (Norway) 300
Beste, Verlag Das, GmbH (Federal Republic of Germany) 126
Besterman Medal (United Kingdom) 448
Bestetti, Edizioni d'Arte Carlo (Italy) 220
Bestseller Publications Ltd (United Kingdom) 442
Beta, Editora, Ltda (Brazil) 49
Beta, Editorial, SRL (Argentina) 4
Betis, Ediciones (Spain) 338
Beton-Verlag GmbH (Federal Republic of Germany) 127
Better Books (United Kingdom) 398
Better Yourself Books (India) 188
Betz, Annette, Verlag (Austria) 25
Betz, Annette, Verlag (Federal Republic of Germany) 127
Betzel, Elke, Verlag (Federal Republic of Germany) 127
Beuhler's Shoppe (Belize) 45
Beupmun Sa Publishing Co (Republic of Korea) 250
Beuroner Kunstverlag GmbH (Federal Republic of Germany) 127
Beuth Verlag GmbH (Federal Republic of Germany) 127
Beyazit, The, State Library (Turkey) 385
Beyeler Editions Basle (Switzerland) 362
Beyer, F, Bok-Og Papirhandel A/S (Norway) 300
Bezige, De, Bij (Netherlands) 274
Bhai Santokh Singh Prize (India) 203
Bhaimi Prakashan (India) 188
Bhakti, P T, Centra Baru (Indonesia) 205
Bhaktivedanta Book Trust (India) 188
Bharat-Bharati (India) 188
Bharat Law House (India) 188
Bharati Sahitya Sadan Sales (India) 188
Bharatiya Jnanpith (India) 188
Bharatiya Publishing House (India) 188
Bharatiya Vidya Bhavan (India) 188
Bhratara Karya Aksara (Indonesia) 205
Bialik Prize for Literature (Israel) 218
Bialik, The, Institute (Israel) 213

Bianchi, Alfredo A, Essay Prize (Argentina) 9
Bianco, Del, Editore (Italy) 220
Bias Editora (Argentina) 4
Bias Editora (Libros Jurídicos) (Argentina) 8
Bias (Société Nouvelle des Editions) SA (France) 93
Bibellesebund eV (Federal Republic of Germany) 127
Bibellesebund, Verlag (Switzerland) 362
Bible Society of South Africa (Namibia) 272
Bible Society of South Africa (Republic of South Africa) 329
Bible, The, Churchmen's Missionary Society (Ethiopia) 86
Bibliagora (United Kingdom) 398
Biblical Institute Press (Pontificio Istituto Biblico) (Italy) 220
Bibliofiilien Seura (Finland) 89
Bibliographical Society (United Kingdom) 445
Bibliographical Society of Australia and New Zealand (Australia) 21
Bibliographical Society of Australia and New Zealand (New Zealand) 291
Bibliographical Society of Australia and New Zealand (BSANZ) (International Organizations) 466
Bibliographical Society of the Philippines (Philippines) 310
Bibliographisches Institut AG (Federal Republic of Germany) 127
Bibliographisches Institut AG (Switzerland) 362
Bibliographisches Institut GmbH (Austria) 25
Bibliographisches Institut, VEB, Leipzig (German Democratic Republic) 116
Bibliomad (Democratic Republic of Madagascar) 258
Bibliomed — Medizinische Verlagsgesellschaft mbH (Federal Republic of Germany) 127
Bibliophile Drucke, Verlag, von Josef Stocker AG (Switzerland) 363
Bibliophile, Le, (The Book Lover) (Haiti) 178
Bibliopolis—Edizioni di Filosofia e Scienze SpA (Italy) 220
Biblioteca Central (Mexico) 269
Biblioteca Central (Mexico) 269
Biblioteca Central de Educación básica, secundaria y superior (Uruguay) 452
Biblioteca Centrala de Stat a Republicii Socialiste România (Romania) 322
Biblioteca Centrala Universitara (Romania) 322
Biblioteca Centrala Universitara (Romania) 322
Biblioteca Centrala Universitara 'Mihail Eminescu' (Romania) 322
Biblioteca de Autores Cristianos de la Editorial Católica SA (Spain) 338
Biblioteca de México (Mexico) 269
Biblioteca del Congreso (Venezuela) 454
Biblioteca Dominicana (Dominican Republic) 82
Biblioteca Ecuatoriana 'Aurelio Espinosa Pólit' (Ecuador) 83
Biblioteca Estadual (Brazil) 56
Biblioteca General de Puerto Rico (General Library) (Puerto Rico) 320
Biblioteca Histórica Cubana y Americana (Cuba) 69
Biblioteca Judeteana Mures (Romania) 322
Biblioteca Judeteana Timis (Romania) 322
Biblioteca Municipal (Angola) 2
Biblioteca Municipal (Mozambique) 271
Biblioteca Municipal Central (Portugal) 318
Biblioteca Múnicipal Mário de Andrade (Brazil) 56
Biblioteca Nacional (Argentina) 8
Biblioteca Nacional (Brazil) 56
Biblioteca Nacional (Costa Rica) 68
Biblioteca Nacional (Dominican Republic) 82
Biblioteca Nacional (El Salvador) 85
Biblioteca Nacional (Nicaragua) 292
Biblioteca Nacional (Panama) 305
Biblioteca Nacional (Peru) 307
Biblioteca Nacional (Portugal) 318
Biblioteca Nacional (Spain) 347
Biblioteca Nacional (Venezuela) 454
Biblioteca Nacional de Agricultura (Mexico) 269
Biblioteca Nacional de Antropología e Historia (Mexico) 269
Biblioteca Nacional de Chile de la Dirección de Bibliotecas, Archivos y Museos (Chile) 63
Biblioteca Nacional de Colombia (Colombia) 67
Biblioteca Nacional de Guatemala (National Library) (Guatemala) 177
Biblioteca Nacional de Honduras (Honduras) 178
Biblioteca Nacional de Macau (Macau) 257
Biblioteca Nacional de Maestros (Argentina) 8
Biblioteca Nacional de México (Mexico) 269
Biblioteca Nacional de Moçambique (Mozambique) 271
Biblioteca Nacional del Ecuador (Ecuador) 83
Biblioteca Nacional del Uruguay (Uruguay) 452
Biblioteca Nacional Doutor Antonio Agustinho Neto (Angola) 2
Biblioteca Nacional José Martí (Cuba) 69
Biblioteca Nazionale Braidense (Italy) 234
Biblioteca Nazionale Centrale (Italy) 234

Biblioteca Nazionale Centrale, Vittorio Emanuele II (Italy) 234
Biblioteca Nazionale Marciana (Italy) 234
Biblioteca Nazionale Vittorio Emanuele III (Italy) 234
Biblioteca Nueva, Editorial, SL (Spain) 338
Biblioteca Popular de Lisboa (Portugal) 318
Biblioteca Pública de Braga (Portugal) 318
Biblioteca Pública de Ponta Delgada (Portugal) 318
Biblioteca Publica do Estado do Rio de Janeiro (Brazil) 56
Biblioteca Pública e Arquivo Distrital de Évora (Portugal) 318
Biblioteca Pública Municipal do Porto (Portugal) 318
Biblioteca Publico Central (Argentina) 8
Biblioteca Universitaria (Italy) 234
Biblioteca y Archivo Nacional de Bolivia (Bolivia) 47
Biblioteca y Archivo Nacionales (Paraguay) 306
Biblioteca y Centro Nacional de Documentación Pedagógica, Sección de Servicios Bibliotecarios (Colombia) 67
Bibliotecarios Agricolas Colombianos (Colombia) 67
Bibliotecas Públicas, Dirección de, Municipales (Argentina) 9
Biblioteka Jagiellońska (Poland) 314
Biblioteka Kombëtare (Albania) 1
Biblioteka Narodowa (Poland) 314
Biblioteka Publiczna m st Warszawy (Poland) 314
Bibliotekarforbundet (Denmark) 80
Bibliotekernes Oplysningskontor (Denmark) 80
Biblioteksboghandelen ApS (Denmark) 79
Bibliotekscentralen (Denmark) 80
Bibliotekscentralens Forlag (Denmark) 75
Biblioteksförlaget AB (Sweden) 353
Bibliotekstjänst AB (Sweden) 353
Bibliotheca, Verlag, Christiana (Federal Republic of Germany) 167
Bibliotheek CCS (Suriname) 351
Bibliothek für Zeitgeschichte (Federal Republic of Germany) 168
Bibliotheksverband der Deutschen Demokratischen Republik (German Democratic Republic) 119
Bibliothèque cantonale et universitaire de Lausanne (Switzerland) 376
Bibliothèque cantonale et universitaire (Kantons- und Universitätsbibliothek) (Switzerland) 376
Bibliothèque centrale de la Côte d'Ivoire (Ivory Coast) 236
Bibliothèque centrale de la Ville de Bruxelles (Belgium) 43
Bibliothèque centrale de Prêt (Réunion) 320
Bibliothèque centrale municipale (Algeria) 2
Bibliothèque de Gouvernement (Grand Duchy of Luxembourg) 257
Bibliothèque de la Ville (Grand Duchy of Luxembourg) 257
Bibliothèque de la Ville (Switzerland) 376
Bibliothèque de l'Université nationale de Côte d'Ivoire (Ivory Coast) 236
Bibliothèque départementale (Réunion) 320
Bibliothèque du petit Séminaire (Haiti) 178
Bibliothèque Franconie (French Guiana) 114
Bibliothèque générale et Archives (Morocco) 271
Bibliothèque générale et Archives du Maroc (Morocco) 271
Bibliothèque Louis Notari (Monaco) 270
Bibliothèque mazarine (France) 109
Bibliothèque municipale (Ivory Coast) 236
Bibliothèque municipale (Democratic Republic of Madagascar) 258
Bibliothèque municipale (Mali) 262
Bibliothèque municipale (Morocco) 271
Bibliothèque municipale (Réunion) 320
Bibliothèque municipale de Besançon (France) 109
Bibliothèque municipale de Constantine (Algeria) 2
Bibliothèque municipale de Grenoble (France) 110
Bibliothèque municipale de la Ville de Lyon (France) 110
Bibliothèque municipale d'Oran (Algeria) 2
Bibliothèque municipale Meknes (Morocco) 271
Bibliothèque nationale (Algeria) 2
Bibliothèque nationale (France) 110
Bibliothèque nationale (Guinea) 177
Bibliothèque nationale (Ivory Coast) 236
Bibliothèque nationale (Laos) 253
Bibliotheque nationale (Democratic Republic of Madagascar) 258
Bibliothèque nationale (Mali) 262
Bibliothèque nationale (Mauritania) 263
Bibliothèque nationale (Togo) 382
Bibliothèque nationale (Tunisia) 383
Bibliothèque nationale (Zaire) 462
Bibliothèque nationale d'Haïti (National Library) (Haiti) 178
Bibliothèque nationale du Benin (Benin) 45
Bibliothèque nationale du Cameroun (United Republic of Cameroun) 61
Bibliothèque nationale du Grand-Duché de Luxembourg (Grand Duchy of Luxembourg) 257
Bibliothèque nationale du Liban (Lebanon) 254
Bibliothèque nationale et universitaire de Strasbourg (France) 110
Bibliothèque nationale populaire (Popular Republic of Congo) 68
Bibliothèque Nationale Suisse (Switzerland) 376
Bibliothèque orientale (Lebanon) 254
Bibliothèque paroissiale (Chad) 62
Bibliothèque publique (Burundi) 60
Bibliothèque publique de Kinshasa (Zaire) 462
Bibliothèque publique de Kisangani (Zaire) 462
Bibliothèque publique de Kitega (Burundi) 60
Bibliothèque publique de Lubumbashi (Zaire) 462
Bibliothèque publique et universitaire de Genève (Switzerland) 376
Bibliothèque universitaire (Democratic Republic of Madagascar) 258
Bibliothèque universitaire (Réunion) 320
Bibliothèque universitaire (Upper Volta) 451
Biblique de Genève, Société (Switzerland) 363
Biblique, Société, Française (France) 93
Biblograf, Editorial, SA (Spain) 338
Biblos (Israel) 213
Bidang Bibliografi dan Deposit, Pusat Pembinaan Perpustakaan (Indonesia) 206
Biederstein Verlag (Federal Republic of Germany) 127
Bielmas Librairie-Papeterie (Chad) 62
Biennial International Art Book Prize (International Literary Prizes) 475
Bierman og Fothergill – Bierman og Bierman ApS (Denmark) 75
Bierman og Fothergill – Bierman og Bierman ApS (Denmark) 79
Bietti SpA (Italy) 220
Bigot en Van Rossum BV (Netherlands) 274
Bihar Hindi Granth Akademi (India) 188
Bihar Pustak Vyayasayi Sangh (India) 185
Bihar State, The, Textbook Publishing Corporation Ltd (India) 188
Bijleveld, Erven J (Netherlands) 274
Bijutsu Shuppan-Sha (Japan) 238
Bilac, Olavo, Prize (Brazil) 57
Bilgi Yayinevi (Turkey) 385
Billeret, Librairie (Chad) 62
Bina Ilmu (Indonesia) 205
Binacipta (Indonesia) 205
Bingley, Clive, Ltd (United Kingdom) 398
Binsfeld, Editions Guy (Grand Duchy of Luxembourg) 256
Biography Book Club (United Kingdom) 443
Bioru Miedzynarodowego Numeru Ksiazki (Poland) 311
Bir Library (Nepal) 272
Birchalls (Australia) 20
Birds and Natural History Book Society (United Kingdom) 443
Birkhäuser Verlag (Federal Republic of Germany) 127
Birkhäuser Verlag AG (Switzerland) 363
Birmingham Museums and Art Gallery Publications Unit (United Kingdom) 398
Birmingham Public Libraries (United Kingdom) 444
Biro, Perpustakaan, Pusat Statistik (Indonesia) 206
Birografika (Yugoslavia) 456
Bison Books Ltd (United Kingdom) 398
Biswakosh (Bangladesh) 32
Bitan (Israel) 213
Bitter, Georg, Verlag (Federal Republic of Germany) 127
Bjarnarsonar, Bókaútgáfa Thórhalls (Iceland) 183
Björk, Bókaútgáfan (Iceland) 183
Björnssonar, Bokaforlag Odds (Iceland) 183
Black, A & C, (Publishers) Ltd (United Kingdom) 398
Black Academy Press (Nigeria) 293
Black Box Thrillers (United Kingdom) 398
Black Community Programmes Ltd (Republic of South Africa) 329
Black, James Tait, Memorial Prizes (United Kingdom) 448
Black Mask Ltd (Ghana) 172
Black, Stephen, Prize for Drama (Republic of South Africa) 335
Black Swan (United Kingdom) 398
Black Swan Press, The (United Kingdom) 398
Blacker Calmann Cooper Ltd (United Kingdom) 398
Blackie & Son Ltd (United Kingdom) 398
Blackstaff Press Ltd (United Kingdom) 398
Blackwater, The, Press (Republic of Ireland) 209
Blackwell, B H, Ltd (United Kingdom) 444
Blackwell Publisher, Basil, Ltd (United Kingdom) 398
Blackwell Scientific Publications (Australia) Pty Ltd (Australia) 12
Blackwell Scientific Publications Ltd (United Kingdom) 398
Blackwood, William, & Sons Ltd (United Kingdom) 398
Bladkompaniet A/S (Norway) 298
Blake Friedmann Literary Agency (United Kingdom) 442
Blaketon Hall Ltd (United Kingdom) 398
Blanc, Charles, Prize (France) 111
Blanchart, Editions Gérard, & Cie SA (Belgium) 34
Blandford Books Ltd (United Kingdom) 399
Blandon, Libreria (Nicaragua) 292
Blanvalet Verlag (Federal Republic of Germany) 127
Blas de la Rosa (Dominican Republic) 81
Bläschke, Josef Gotthard, -Verlag (Austria) 25
Blasco Ibáñez Prize (Spain) 348
Blaukreuz-Verlag Bern (Switzerland) 363
Blaukreuz-Verlag Wuppertal (Federal Republic of Germany) 127
Blazek und Bergmann (Federal Republic of Germany) 167
Bleicher Verlag (Federal Republic of Germany) 127
Bles, Geoffrey (United Kingdom) 399
Blindenstudienanstalt, Deutsche, eV (Federal Republic of Germany) 127
Blish, James, Award (International Literary Prizes) 475
Blitz, Andries, BV (Netherlands) 274
Bloch Editores SA (Brazil) 49
Blok, H W, Uitgeverij BV (Netherlands) 274
Blok, Nakladatelství (Czechoslovakia) 71
Blom Prize (Sweden) 360
Blond & Briggs Ltd (United Kingdom) 399
Blond Educational (United Kingdom) 399
Blondel La Rougery SA (France) 93
Bloodaxe Books Ltd (United Kingdom) 399
Bloom, Roy, Ltd (United Kingdom) 442
Blücher, Editora Edgard, Ltda (Brazil) 49
Bluett & Co Ltd (Republic of Ireland) 209
Blume Ediciones, Hermann (Spain) 338
Blume, Editorial (Spain) 338
Boardman Tasker Prize for Mountain Literature (International Literary Prizes) 475
Boccard, Editions E de (France) 93
Bock und Herchen Verlag (Federal Republic of Germany) 127
Bodleian Library (United Kingdom) 444
Bodley Head, The, Ltd (United Kingdom) 399
Bodmer, Fondation Martin, Bibliotheca Bodmeriana (Switzerland) 376
Bodmer, Les Editions de la Fondation Martin (Switzerland) 363
Boeck, Maison d'Edition A de, SA (Belgium) 34
Boek Promotions bv (Netherlands) 274
Boekencentrum BV (Netherlands) 274
Boekerij, De (Netherlands) 274
Boer, de, Maritiem (Netherlands) 274
Boersig Verlag AG (Switzerland) 363
Bog- og Papirbranchens Kreditor-Udvalg (Denmark) 75
Bogans Forlag A/S (Denmark) 75
Bogaziçi University Library (formerly Robert College Library) (Turkey) 385
Bøger, Clemens, og Papir I/S (Denmark) 79
Boggero, B, Editore (Italy) 220
Boghallen (Denmark) 79
Bogvennerne (Denmark) 81
Bohem Press Kinderbuchverlag (Switzerland) 363
Böhlau-Verlag GmbH & Cie (Federal Republic of Germany) 127
Böhlau, Verlag Hermann, Nachf GmbH (Austria) 25
Böhlaus, Hermann, Nachfolger (German Democratic Republic) 116
Bohmann Druck und Verlag AG (Austria) 25
Bohn, Scheltema en Holkema (Netherlands) 274
Boighar (Bangladesh) 32
Boje-Verlag (Federal Republic of Germany) 127
Bok-, Pappers- och Kontorsvaruförbundet (Sweden) 351
Bokas hf (Iceland) 183
Bókavardafélag Islands (Iceland) 185
Bokbranschens Finansieringsinstitut AB (Sweden) 351
Bokbranschens Marknadsinstitut AB (Sweden) 351
Bokhandelsrådet (Sweden) 351
Boldt, Harald, Verlag GmbH (Federal Republic of Germany) 127
Bolivar Bookshop (Jamaica) 237
Bolivian Grand Prize for Literature (Bolivia) 47
Bollmann-Bildkarten-Verlag GmbH & Co KG (Federal Republic of Germany) 127
Bologna Book Fair 'Critici in erba' Prize (International Literary Prizes) 475
Bologna Book Fair Graphic Prize for Children and Youth (International Literary Prizes) 475
Bolte, Dr, KG (Federal Republic of Germany) 127
Bombay Booksellers' and Publishers' Association (India) 185
Bombay University Library (India) 202
Bompiani (Italy) 220
Bon Pasteur, Librarie du (Togo) 382
Bonacci-Libreria Editrice (Italy) 220
Bonanno, Giuseppe, Editore (Italy) 220
Bonanza, Librairie (Mauritius) 263
Bond Alleenverkopers van Nederlandstalige Boeken (BANB) (Belgium) 33
Bone, Roger, Library (Zimbabwe) 465
Bonechi, Casa Editrice (Italy) 220
Bonetti, Pascal, Grand Prize (France) 111
Bongers, Verlag Aurel, KG (Federal Republic of Germany) 127
Bonn Aktuell GmbH (Federal Republic of Germany) 127
Bonner Buchgemeinde (BBG) (Federal Republic of Germany) 167
Bonnier Fakta Bokforlag AB (Sweden) 353
Bonniers, Albert, Förlag AB (Sweden) 353
Bonniers Bokklubb (Sweden) 358

Bonniers Bokpaket (Sweden) 358
Bonniers Juniorförlag AB (Sweden) 353
Bonum, Librería, SACI (Argentina) 4
Book and Printing Center — Israel Export Institute (Israel) 212
Book Association of Ireland (Republic of Ireland) 208
Book Australia (Australia) 19
Book Centre (Zimbabwe) 465
Book Centre, The (Gibraltar) 173
Book Club Associates (United Kingdom) 443
Book Collectors' Society of Australia (Australia) 21
Book Development Association of the Philippines (BDAP) (Philippines) 308
Book Development, The, Council (United Kingdom) 391
Book Distributors Sdn Bhd (Malaysia) 259
Book Exchange, The (Zimbabwe) 465
Book Field Centre (India) 189
Book Guild, The, Ltd (United Kingdom) 399
Book Lovers (United Kingdom) 443
Book Lovers' Club (Yugoslavia) 460
Book Mark (India) 189
Book Marketing Ltd (Hong Kong) 179
Book Marketing, The, Council (United Kingdom) 391
Book New Zealand (New Zealand) 290
Book-of-the-Month Club (Australia) 19
Book of the Month Club (New Zealand) 290
Book of the Month Club (United Kingdom) 443
Book Publishers' Association of Israel (Israel) 212
Book Publishers Association of New Zealand (New Zealand) 286
Book Publishers' Representatives' Association (United Kingdom) 391
Book Publishers', The, Association of Israel, International Promotion and Literary Rights Department (Israel) 217
Book Publishing Institute (Afghanistan) 1
Book Representation Co (Nigeria) 296
Book Sales Ltd (United Kingdom) 399
Book Society of Islamic Republic of Iran (Iran) 208
Book, The, House (Pakistan) 301
Book Tokens Ltd (United Kingdom) 391
Book Trade Association of South Africa (Republic of South Africa) 328
Book Trade Group (Queensland) (Australia) 10
Book Trade, The, Benevolent Society (United Kingdom) 391
Bookcentre (Pakistan) 303
Booker McConnell Prize (International Literary Prizes) 475
Booklinks Corporation (India) 189
Bookman, A/S (Denmark) 79
Bookman, A/S (Iceland) 184
Bookman of the Year Award (Australia) 22
Bookman Publishing House (Philippines) 308
Bookmark Inc (Philippines) 309
Bookmart, The (Bermuda) 46
Bookrama (Pakistan) 303
Books Abroad/English-Speaking Union of the United States Best Book of Belles Lettres (International Literary Prizes) 475
Books across the Sea (United Kingdom) 447
Books Bargain (India) 201
Books for Asia (Hong Kong) 179
Books for Children (United Kingdom) 443
Books for Neoliterates Prizes (India) 203
Books in Progress, Literature Department, Arts Council of Great Britain (United Kingdom) 391
Books of Africa (Pty) Ltd (Republic of South Africa) 329
Books of Zimbabwe Book Club (Zimbabwe) 465
Books of Zimbabwe Publishing Co (Pvt) Ltd (Zimbabwe) 464
Books-on-Japan-in-English Club (Japan) 244
Books Registration Unit (Hong Kong) 178
Booksellers' and Publishers' Association of South India (India) 185
Booksellers Association of Great Britain and Ireland (Republic of Ireland) 208
Booksellers Association of Great Britain and Ireland (United Kingdom) 391
Booksellers' Association of Jamaica (Jamaica) 237
Booksellers Association of New Zealand (Inc) (New Zealand) 286
Booksellers' Association of Sri Lanka (Sri Lanka) 349
Booksellers' Association of Trinidad and Tobago (Trinidad and Tobago) 382
Booksellers' Association of Zimbabwe (Zimbabwe) 464
Booksellers Association Service House Ltd (United Kingdom) 391
Booksellers Clearing House (United Kingdom) 391
Booksellers' Order Distribution Ltd (BOD) (United Kingdom) 391
Bookshelf, The (Zambia) 463
Bookshop, The, Ltd (Kenya) 249
Booksmith, The (United Kingdom) 399
Bookventure (India) 189
Bookwise (Australia) Pty Ltd (Australia) 12
Bookwise (Pty) Ltd (Republic of South Africa) 333
Bookwise Service Ltd (United Kingdom) 444
Bookworm, The, Club (United Kingdom) 443

Boolarong Publications (Australia) 12
Boole Press Ltd (Republic of Ireland) 209
Boom-Pers Boeken- en Tijdschriftenuitg BV (Netherlands) 274
Boosey & Hawkes Music Publishers Ltd (United Kingdom) 399
Boosey & Hawkes Sagem (France) 93
Boostan Publishing House (Israel) 213
Booth, David, (Publishing) Ltd (United Kingdom) 399
Bora, Edizioni, snc di E Brandani & C (Italy) 221
Borak, Al-, SA (Spain) 338
Borba (Yugoslavia) 456
Bordas-Dunod, Société, Bruxelles SA (Belgium) 34
Bordas, Editions (France) 93
Bordas et Fils, Pierre (France) 93
Bordewijk, F, Prize (Netherlands) 285
Bordin Prize (France) 111
Borgarbókasafn (Iceland) 185
Borgens Forlag A/S (Denmark) 75
Boringhieri, Editore, SpA (Italy) 221
Borla, SIL Srl Edizioni (Italy) 221
Born NV Uitgeversmaatschappij (Netherlands) 274
Bornemann, Editions (France) 93
Borntraeger, Gebrüder, Verlagsbuchhandlung (Federal Republic of Germany) 127
Borotha-Schoeler, Verlag Dr Gerda (Austria) 25
Børsen Forlaget A/S (Denmark) 75
Börsenverein der Deutschen Buchhändler zu Leipzig (German Democratic Republic) 115
Börsenverein des deutschen Buchhandels eV (Federal Republic of Germany) 121
Bosch Casa Editorial SA (Spain) 338
Bosch en Keuning NV (Netherlands) 274
Bosch, Librería (Spain) 347
Boscq, Jean-Pierre (France) 109
Bösendahl, C (Federal Republic of Germany) 128
Bosse, Gustav, Verlag GmbH & Co KG (Federal Republic of Germany) 128
Botas, Libreria y Ediciones, SA (Mexico) 264
Botella, Ediciones, al Mar (Argentina) 4
Botswana Book Centre (Botswana) 47
Botswana Library Association (Botswana) 47
Botswana National Archives (Botswana) 47
Botswana National Library Service (Botswana) 47
Bottega d'Erasmo (Italy) 221
Boubée, Société Nouvelle Editions N (France) 93
Boukoumanis' Editions (Greece) 174
Bourbon, Librairie (Mauritius) 263
Bourcy, Librairie De, Lucien (Grand Duchy of Luxembourg) 257
Bourdeaux-Capelle SA (Belgium) 34
Bouret, Editorial (France) 93
Bourgois, Christian (France) 93
Bourrelier, Editions Colin (France) 93
Bouscatel, Jean, Foundation Prize (France) 112
Bouslama, Editions (Tunisia) 383
Boutique, La, Bleue (French Guiana) 114
Bouvier-Parviliez, Ernest, Prize (Belgium) 44
Bouvier, Universitätsbuchhandlung, GmbH (Federal Republic of Germany) 167
Bowen, Arnold Vincent, Competition (United Kingdom) 448
Bowen, D Richard (Sweden) 358
Bowes & Bowes Books (United Kingdom) 444
Bowker & Bertram Ltd (Marine Publishers) (United Kingdom) 399
Bowker Publishing Co (United Kingdom) 399
Boyars, Marion, Publishers Ltd (United Kingdom) 399
Boyce, David, Publishing & Associates (Australia) 12
Boydell & Brewer Ltd (United Kingdom) 399
Bozzi, Ugo, Editore (Italy) 221
Bra Böcker (Sweden) 358
Bra Böcker, Bokförlaget, AB (Sweden) 353
Bra Deckare (Sweden) 358
Bra Klassiker (Sweden) 358
Bra Lyrik (Sweden) 358
Bra Spänning (Sweden) 358
Braby, A C, (Zimbabwe) (Pvt) Ltd (Zimbabwe) 464
Bracciodieta Editore (Italy) 221
Bracken Books (United Kingdom) 399
Bradley, Mrs W A (France) 109
Bradt Enterprises (United Kingdom) 399
Bragi, Bókaútgáfan (Iceland) 183
Brain Anatomy Institute (Switzerland) 363
Bramante Editrice SpA (Italy) 221
Branding, De, NV (Belgium) 34
Brandstetter, Oscar, Verlag GmbH & Co KG (Federal Republic of Germany) 128
Branner og Korch's Forlag A/S (Denmark) 75
Brash, Graham, Pte Ltd (Republic of Singapore) 325
Brasil-América, Editora, (EBAL) SA (Brazil) 49
Brasil, Editora do, SA (Brazil) 49
Brasília Editora (J Carvalho Branco & Cia Lda) (Portugal) 316
Brasília Editora Ltda (Brazil) 49
Brasilienkunde Verlag GmbH (Federal Republic of Germany) 128
Brasiliense, Editora, SA (Brazil) 49

Brasiliense, Livraria, Editora SA (Brazil) 56
Brassey's Publishers Ltd (United Kingdom) 399
Bratislava Town Prize (Czechoslovakia) 74
Bratsvo-Jedinstvo (Yugoslavia) 456
Bratt Institut für Neues Lernen GmbH (Federal Republic of Germany) 128
Braumüller, Wilhelm, Universitätsverlag GmbH (Austria) 25
Braun und Schneider, Verlag (Federal Republic of Germany) 128
Braun, Verlag G, GmbH (Federal Republic of Germany) 128
Braunkohle, Verlag die (Federal Republic of Germany) 128
Bréa Éditions (France) 93
Bread and Cheese Club (Australia) 21
Breidenstein, Umschau Verlag, GmbH (Federal Republic of Germany) 128
Breitkopf und Härtel (Federal Republic of Germany) 128
Breitkopf und Härtel, VEB, Musikverlag (German Democratic Republic) 116
Breitschopf, Julius, KG (Federal Republic of Germany) 128
Breitschopf, Verlagsbuchhandlung Julius (Austria) 25
Breklumer Verlag (Federal Republic of Germany) 128
Bremen Literature Encouragement Prize (International Literary Prizes) 475
Bremen Literature Prize (International Literary Prizes) 475
Brendow-Verlag (Federal Republic of Germany) 128
Brennan, Christopher, Award (Australia) 22
Brenner, Edizioni (Italy) 221
Brenner Prize (Israel) 218
Brentano's (France) 109
Brenthurst, The, Press (Pty) Ltd (Republic of South Africa) 329
Brepols, Editions, SA (France) 93
Brepols IGP Publishers (Belgium) 34
Bres, Redactie (Netherlands) 274
Breslich & Foss (United Kingdom) 399
Bretschneider, Dr Giorgio (Italy) 221
Bretschneider, L'Erma di, Srl (Italy) 221
Brewer, D S, Ltd (United Kingdom) 399
Brice Advertising and Publishing Ltd (Bahamas) 31
Brick Row Publishing Co Ltd (New Zealand) 287
Bridge Book Club (United Kingdom) 443
Bridge Book Co Ltd (United Kingdom) 442
Bridge Bookshop Ltd (Isle of Man) 212
Brigg Verlag GmbH (formerly Verlag die Brigg) (Federal Republic of Germany) 128
Bright Careers Institute (India) 189
Brill, NV Boekhandel & Drukkerij voorheen E J (Netherlands) 274
Brilliance Books (United Kingdom) 399
Brimax Books Ltd (United Kingdom) 399
Brink, Educatieve Uitgeverij Ten, BV (Netherlands) 274
Bristol Classical Press (United Kingdom) 399
British Academy, The (United Kingdom) 399
British & Foreign Bible Society (United Kingdom) 400
British and Irish Association of Law Librarians (United Kingdom) 445
British Copyright Council (United Kingdom) 391
British Council Educational Resource Centre (Lesotho) 255
British Council Libraries (Pakistan) 303
British Council Libraries (Sri Lanka) 349
British Council Library (Bangladesh) 32
British Council Library (United Republic of Cameroon) 61
British Council Library (Colombia) 67
British Council Library (Cyprus) 70
British Council Library (Ethiopia) 86
British Council Library (Ghana) 173
British Council Library (Greece) 176
British Council Library (Hong Kong) 180
British Council Library (India) 202
British Council Library (Jordan) 247
British Council Library (Malawi) 258
British Council Library (Malaysia) 261
British Council Library (Mauritius) 263
British Council Library (Nepal) 272
British Council Library (Sierra Leone) 325
British Council Library (Sudan) 350
British Council Library (Tanzania) 379
British Council Library (Thailand) 381
British Council Library (Tunisia) 383
British Council Library (Yemen Arab Republic) 456
British Design Council, The, Production and Publishing Department (United Kingdom) 400
British Film Institute (United Kingdom) 400
British Heritage (United Kingdom) 443
British Horse, The, Society (United Kingdom) 400
British Library Bibliographic Services Division (United Kingdom) 444
British Library, Bibliographic Services Division Publications (United Kingdom) 400
British Library Lending Division (United Kingdom) 444

502 INDEX

British Library, Lending Division Publications (United Kingdom) 400
British Library of Political and Economic Science (United Kingdom) 444
British Library Reference Division (United Kingdom) 444
British Library, Reference Division Publications (United Kingdom) 400
British Library, Science Reference Library (United Kingdom) 445
British Library, The (India) 202
British Medical Association (United Kingdom) 400
British Museum (Natural History) (United Kingdom) 400
British Museum Publications Ltd (United Kingdom) 400
British Printing & Communication, The, Corporation PLC (United Kingdom) 400
British Science Fiction Award (United Kingdom) 448
British Science Fiction, The, Association Ltd (United Kingdom) 447
British Tourist Authority (United Kingdom) 400
Brno Literary Prize (Czechoslovakia) 74
Brockhaus, F A (Federal Republic of Germany) 128
Brockhaus, R, Verlag (Federal Republic of Germany) 128
Brockhaus, VEB F A, Verlag, Leipzig (German Democratic Republic) 116
Brodie, James, Ltd (United Kingdom) 400
Brodies Notes (United Kingdom) 400
Broele, Vanden, PVBA (Belgium) 35
Broese-Kemink BV (Netherlands) 284
Brombergs Bokförlag AB (Sweden) 353
Bronfman's Agency Ltd (Israel) 214
Bronfman's Agency Ltd (Israel) 217
Brönner Verlag Breidenstein GmbH (Federal Republic of Germany) 128
Brontë, The Incorporated, Society (United Kingdom) 447
Bronze Swagman Award (Australia) 22
Brookfield Press (New Zealand) 287
Broomsleigh Press (United Kingdom) 400
Broquette-Gonin Grand Prize (France) 112
Broschek Druck GmbH & Co KG (Federal Republic of Germany) 128
Broschek Verlag (Federal Republic of Germany) 128
Broutta, Michèle, Oeuvres Graphiques Contemporaines (France) 93
Brown, Emanuel (Israel) 217
Brown, Son & Ferguson, Ltd (United Kingdom) 400
Browne, Sinclair, Ltd (United Kingdom) 400
Bruck, Librairie Paul (Grand Duchy of Luxembourg) 257
Brücken-Verlag GmbH Literaturvertrieb Import-Export (Federal Republic of Germany) 128
Bruckmann Kunst, Studio, im Druck Fine Art GmbH (Federal Republic of Germany) 128
Bruckmann, Verlag F, KG (Federal Republic of Germany) 128
Brug, De, -Djambatan BV (Netherlands) 274
Bruggen, Jochem van, Prys vir Prosa (Republic of South Africa) 335
Bruguera, Editora, do Brasil Ltda (Brazil) 49
Bruguera, Editorial, Argentina SAFIC (Argentina) 4
Bruguera, Editorial, Centroamericana y Panamá SA (Pañama) 304
Bruguera, Editorial, Colombiana Ltda (Colombia) 65
Bruguera, Editorial, Mexicana SA (Mexico) 264
Bruguera, Editorial, SA (Spain) 338
Bruguera, Editorial, Venezolana SA (Venezuela) 453
Bruna, A W, & Zoon NV (Belgium) 35
Bruna en Zoon's, A W, Uitgeversmaatschappij BV (Netherlands) 274
Bruna Pockethuis BV (Netherlands) 275
Brunei, The, Press (Brunei) 58
Brunette (Netherlands) 275
Brunnen-Verlag (Switzerland) 363
Brunnen-Verlag GmbH (Federal Republic of Germany) 128
Brunner Verlagsgellschaft (Federal Republic of Germany) 128
Brunnquell-Verlag der Bibel-und Missions-Stiftung Metzingen (Federal Republic of Germany) 128
Bruño, Asociación Editorial (Peru) 307
Bruño, Editorial (Spain) 338
Bruns, F, Bokhandel (Norway) 300
Bruns, F, Bokhandels Forlag A/S (Norway) 298
Bruylant, Etablissements Emile, SA (Belgium) 35
Bubenberg Verlag AG (Switzerland) 363
Bucalo, Edizioni (Italy) 221
Buch und Verlagsdruckerei AG (Liechtenstein) 256
Buch und Werbung — Helmut Krüger GmbH (Federal Republic of Germany) 128
Buchclub 65 (German Democratic Republic) 119
Buchclub 69 GmbH (Federal Republic of Germany) 167
Bucheli, Verlag Alfred (Switzerland) 363
Bücher, Verlag C J (Switzerland) 363
Bucher, Verlag C J, GmbH (Federal Republic of Germany) 128
Buchet/Chastel, Editions (France) 93
Buchexport — Volkseigener Aussenhandelsbetrieb der Deutschen Demokratischen Republik (German Democratic Republic) 115

Buchhändler-Abrechnungs — Gesellschaft mbH (Federal Republic of Germany) 121
Buchhändler-Vereinigung GmbH (Federal Republic of Germany) 121
Buchhaus AG (Switzerland) 363
Buchholz, Librería (Colombia) 67
Buchholz, Livraria (Portugal) 318
Buchholz Verlag für Spiele und Freizeit (Federal Republic of Germany) 129
Buchklub der Schüler (German Democratic Republic) 119
Büchler & Co AG (Switzerland) 363
Buchmarkt- und Medien-Forschung, Verlag für (Federal Republic of Germany) 129
Büchner, Georg, Prize (Federal Republic of Germany) 170
Büchse, Verlag, der Pandora GmbH (Federal Republic of Germany) 129
Buchser, Hugo, SA (Switzerland) 363
Buckland Award (New Zealand) 291
Budapesti Müszaki Egyetem Központi Könyvtára (Hungary) 182
Buenos Aires Literary Prizes (Argentina) 9
Buijten en Schipperheijn BV Drukkerij en Uitg Mij v/h (Netherlands) 275
Bukié, De l'edition, Banané (Mauritius) 263
Bulan Bintang, Penerbit & Pustake NV (Indonesia) 205
Bulawayo Municipal Libraries (Zimbabwe) 465
Bulawayo Public Library (Zimbabwe) 465
Bulgarian Academy of Sciences, Central Library, (Bulgaria) 59
Bulgarian Academy of Sciences, Institute of Literature (Bulgaria) 59
Bulgarian Publishing Award (Bulgaria) 59
Bulgarian Union of Public Libraries (Bulgaria) 59
Bulgarian Writers' Union (Bulgaria) 59
'Bulgarska Kniga', Obedinenie (Bulgaria) 58
Bulgarskata Akademia, Izdatelstvo na, na Naukite (Bulgaria) 58
Bulgarskata Komunisticheska Partiya, Izdatelstvo na (Bulgaria) 58
Bulgarski Houdozhnik (Bulgaria) 58
Bulgarski Pissatel (Bulgaria) 58
Bulgarskiya Zemedelski Naroden Suyuz, Izdatelstvo na (Bulgaria) 58
Bulpin, T V, Publications (Republic of South Africa) 329
Bulwer-Lytton Circle (United Kingdom) 447
Bulzoni Editore SRL (Italy) 221
Buma Kor, Editions (United Republic of Cameroun) 61
Bumi Restu (Indonesia) 205
Bunch Books (United Kingdom) 400
Bund-Verlag GmbH (Federal Republic of Germany) 129
Bunda College of Agriculture Library (Malawi) 258
Bundes-Verlag eG (Federal Republic of Germany) 129
Bundesamt für Landestopographie (Switzerland) 363
Bundesarbeitsgemeinschaft der katholisch-kirchlichen Büchereiarbeit (Federal Republic of Germany) 169
Bundesarchiv (Federal Republic of Germany) 168
Bundesgremium des Handels mit Büchern, Kunstblättern und Musikalien, Zeitungen und Zeitschriften (Austria) 24
Bundeskanzeramt, Administrative Bibliothek und Österreichische Rechtsdokumentation in (Austria) 30
Bundesverband der deutschen Versandbuchhändler eV (Federal Republic of Germany) 121
Bundesverband der Dolmetscher und Übersetzer eV (BDÜ) (Federal Republic of Germany) 171
Bundesverband des werbenden Buch- und Zeitschriftenhandels eV (Federal Republic of Germany) 121
Bungeishunju Ltd (Japan) 238
Burchell & Martin Library Suppliers (United Kingdom) 444
Burckhardthaus-Laetare Verlag GmbH (Federal Republic of Germany) 129
Burda, Verlag Aenne (Federal Republic of Germany) 129
Bureau de Presse et d'Informations (France) 93
Bureau de Recherches Géologiques et Minières (BRGM) (France) 93
Bureau des Documentations Syriennes et Arabes (Syria) 377
Bureau d'Etudes et de Recherches pour la Promotion de la Santé (Zaire) 462
Bureau for Indigenous Languages (Namibia) 272
Bureau for Indigenous Languages (Namibia) 272
Bureau International du Travail (Switzerland) 376
Bureau of Ghana Languages (Ghana) 172
Bureau of Ghana Languages (Ghana) 173
Burke Publishing Co Ltd (United Kingdom) 400
Burke's Peerage Genealogical Books Ltd (United Kingdom) 400
Burke's Peerage Ltd (United Kingdom) 400
Burma Library Association (Burma) 60
Burmese Publishers' Union (Burma) 59
Burnett Books (United Kingdom) 400
Burns & Oates Ltd (United Kingdom) 400
Burns Philp (NG) Ltd (Papua New Guinea) 305
Büro für Urheberrechte (German Democratic Republic) 119
Burulan, SA de Ediciones (Spain) 338

Burundi Literature Center (Burundi) 60
Busche, Kartographischer Verlag, GmbH (Federal Republic of Germany) 129
Buschmann, J E, PVBA (Belgium) 35
Busck, Arnold, International Boghandel A/S (Denmark) 79
Busck, Nyt Nordisk Forlag Arnold, A/S (Denmark) 75
Bush Press Communications Ltd (New Zealand) 287
Bushatsky, Livraria e Editora Juridica José, Ltda (Brazil) 49
Business Books Ltd (United Kingdom) 400
Business Promotion Bureau (India) 189
Business Publications Ltd (Taiwan) 377
Buske, Helmut, Verlag (Federal Republic of Germany) 129
Busse Kunstdokumentation GmbH (Federal Republic of Germany) 129
Bussesche Verlagshandlung GmbH (Federal Republic of Germany) 129
Bussy, J H de, BV (Netherlands) 275
Bustamente Press Inc (Philippines) 308
Butler, Dorothy, Ltd (New Zealand) 290
Butterbach, Christian (Grand Duchy of Luxembourg) 256
Butterworth & Co (Publishers) Ltd (United Kingdom) 401
Butterworth Publishers (Pty) Ltd (Republic of South Africa) 329
Butterworths of New Zealand Ltd (New Zealand) 287
Butterworths Pty Ltd (Australia) 12
Butzon und Bercker, Verlag, GmbH (Federal Republic of Germany) 129
Buzby Books Ltd (United Kingdom) 401
Bwrdd Croeso Cymru (United Kingdom) 401
By och Bygd, Förlaget (Sweden) 353
Bybelgenootskap (Republic of South Africa) 329
Byleveld, Erven J (Belgium) 35

C B D Research Ltd (United Kingdom) 401
C C J Ltd (United Kingdom) 401
C D D (Centar društvenih djelatnosti Saveza socijalističke omladine Hrvatske) (Yugoslavia) 456
C D E – Gruppo Mondadori (Italy) 234
C D L (Central Distribuidora Livreira) SARL (Portugal) 318
C D U (France) 93
C E D A M (Casa Editrice Dr A Milani) (Italy) 221
C E D A R, The, Press (Barbados) 33
C E D E (Centro de Estudios sobre Desarollo Economico) (Colombia) 65
C E D E L Ediciones (Spain) 338
C E D I Bookshop (Zaire) 462
C E D I S Editrice Srl (Italy) 221
C E D S (France) 93
C E D-Samsom (Belgium) 35
C E E B A Publications (Zaire) 462
C E E L (Centre Expérimental pour l'Enseignement des Langues) (Switzerland) 363
C E E P I Ltd (Caxton and English Educational Programmes International) (United Kingdom) 401
C E E S, Librería (Guatemala) 177
C E F A, Editions, (Centre d'Education à la Famille et à l'Amour) (Belgium) 35
C E F A G (France) 93
C E L (France) 93
C E L I (Edizioni) (Italy) 221
C E L S E (Compagnie d'Editions Libres, Sociales et Economiques SA) (France) 93
C E L T A (Centre de Linguistique Théorique et Appliquée) (Zaire) 462
C E L U P Srl (Italy) 221
C E M (Italy) 221
C E P A – Centro Editor de Psicologia Aplicada Ltda (Brazil) 49
C E P A D (France) 93
C E P Edition (France) 93
C E P I M, Edizioni (Italy) 221
C E P L (Centre d'Etude et de Promotion de la Lecture) (France) 93
C E T (United Kingdom) 401
C F E Belgique (Belgium) 35
C F W Publications Ltd (Hong Kong) 179
C I E S P A L, Fondo Editorial de, (Centro Internacional de Estudios Superiores de Comunicación para América Latina) (Ecuador) 82
C I L F (France) 93
C I O Publishing (United Kingdom) 401
Č K P (Členská knižnica Pravdy) (Czechoslovakia) 73
C L A I M Bookshop (Malawi) 258
C L D (France) 93
C L E, Editions (United Republic of Cameroun) 61
C L E U P — Cooperativa Libraria Editrice dell'Università di Padova (Italy) 221
C M P Reprints (Republic of South Africa) 329
C N A (Republic of South Africa) 329
C N A Literary Award (Republic of South Africa) 335

C N R S, Editions du, (Centre national de la recherche scientifique) (France) 93
C N R S, Laboratoire Intergeo (France) 93
C O R, Ediciones (Cuba) 69
C P I (Kenya) 248
C P S A (Republic of South Africa) 329
C R E (United Kingdom) 401
C R E R (France) 93
C S E Book Club (United Kingdom) 443
C S E Books (United Kingdom) 401
C S I R Central Reference and Research Library (Ghana) 173
C S I R O (Commonwealth Scientific and Industrial Research Organization) (Australia) 12
C S I R O (Commonwealth Scientific and Industrial Research Organization) (Australia) 20
C S S Bookshops, Agency and Publishing Division (Nigeria) 293
C S S (Nigeria) Bookshops Ltd (Nigeria) 296
C U M Books (Pty) Ltd (Republic of South Africa) 329
C V K und Schroedel GmbH & Co Geographische Verlagsgesellschaft KG (Federal Republic of Germany) 129
Caann Verlag GmbH (Federal Republic of Germany) 129
Caballito, Ediciones el, SA (Mexico) 264
Cabay (Belgium) 35
Cacoulides, Librairie, (T Cacoulides & Co) (Greece) 176
Cadogan Books Ltd (United Kingdom) 401
Cahiers d'Art, Editions (France) 94
Cahiers de la Renaissance Vaudoise (Switzerland) 363
Cahiers Fiscaux, Les, Européens Sàrl (France) 94
Cairo University Press (Egypt) 83
Calder, John, (Publishers) Ltd (United Kingdom) 401
Calderini, Edizioni (Italy) 221
Caliban Books (United Kingdom) 401
Calicanto, Editorial (Argentina) 4
Calinescu', Institutul de Istorie si Teorie Literara 'George (Romania) 322
Callenbach, Uitgeverij G F, BV (Netherlands) 275
Callwey, Verlag Georg D W (Federal Republic of Germany) 129
Calmann & Cooper, John, Ltd (United Kingdom) 401
Calmann-Lévy, Editions, Sàrl (France) 94
Calozet, Editions, SPRL (Belgium) 35
Calvyn-Jubileumboekefonds (Republic of South Africa) 329
Calwer Verlag (Federal Republic of Germany) 129
Calypso Distributors Ltd (Bahamas) 31
Cámara Argentina de Editores de Libros (Argentina) 3
Cámara Argentina de Editoriales Tecnicas (Argentina) 3
Cámara Argentina de Publicaciones (Argentina) 3
Cámara Argentina del Libro (Argentina) 3
Cámara, Biblioteca de la, Oficial de Comercio, Agricultura e Industria del Distrito Nacional (Dominican Republic) 82
Cámara Boliviana del Libro (Bolivia) 46
Câmara Brasileira do Livro (Brazil) 48
Cámara Chilena del Libro AG (Chile) 62
Cámara Colombiana de la Industria Editorial (Colombia) 65
Cámara Colombiana del Libro (Colombia) 65
Cámara de Editores (Venezuela) 453
Cámara Nacional de Comercio, Sección de Librerías (Mexico) 264
Cámara Nacional de la Industria Editorial (Mexico) 264
Cámara Paraguaya del Libro (Paraguay) 306
Cámara Peruana del Libro (Peru) 306
Cámara Uruguaya del Libro (Uruguay) 451
Cámara Venezolana del Libro (Venezuela) 453
Cambridge Bibliographical Society (United Kingdom) 447
Cambridge Information and Research Services Ltd (United Kingdom) 401
Cambridge University Library (United Kingdom) 445
Cambridge University Press (Australia) 12
Cambridge University Press (United Kingdom) 401
Camera-Verlag (Switzerland) 363
Camerapix Publishers International Ltd (Kenya) 248
Cameron Books Ltd (United Kingdom) 401
Cameroun Book Centre (United Republic of Cameroun) 61
Caminho, Editorial, SARL (Portugal) 316
Campbell, John W, Memorial Award (International Literary Prizes) 475
Campbell, Killie, Africana Library (Republic of South Africa) 329
Campbell, Roy, Prize for Poetry (Republic of South Africa) 335
Campert, Jan, Prize (Netherlands) 285
Campiello Prize (Italy) 236
Campus Corner Ltd (Trinidad and Tobago) 382
Campus, Editora, Ltda (Brazil) 49
Campus Verlag GmbH (Federal Republic of Germany) 129
Camus', Bibliothèque du Centre culturel 'Albert (Democratic Republic of Madagascar) 258
'Canberra Times', The, National Short Story of the Year Competition (Australia) 22
Cangallo, Editorial, SACI (Argentina) 4

Cankarjeva Založba (Yugoslavia) 456
Cankarjeva Zalozba (Yugoslavia) 460
Canongate Publishing Ltd (United Kingdom) 402
Cantabrica, Editorial, SA (Spain) 338
Cantagalli, Edizioni (Italy) 221
Cantecleer, Uitgeverij, BV (Netherlands) 275
Canterbury Public Library (New Zealand) 290
Canterbury University Library (New Zealand) 290
Cantonetto, Edizioni del Prof Mario Agliati (Switzerland) 363
Cantor, Editio (Federal Republic of Germany) 129
Canuto, Livraria, Ltda (Brazil) 56
Cape Catley Ltd (New Zealand) 287
Cape Coast University Bookshop (Ghana) 172
Cape, Jonathan, Ltd (United Kingdom) 402
Cape Provincial Library Service (Republic of South Africa) 334
Capel (Republic of Ireland) 209
Capendu, Editions (France) 94
Capital Book House (India) 189
Capitol Editrice Dischi CEB (Italy) 221
Capitol Publishing House Inc (Philippines) 308
Cappelens, J W, Forlag A/S (Norway) 298
Cappelli, Nuova Casa Editrice Licinio, SpA (Italy) 221
Capper Press Ltd (New Zealand) 287
Captan, Wadih M, Bookstores (Liberia) 255
Caputo, Ursula (Italy) 233
Caraïbes, Editions (Haiti) 178
Caralt, Luis de, Editor SA (Spain) 338
Caravelle, La, Librairie (Tunisia) 383
Carcanet Press Ltd (United Kingdom) 402
Cardeñoso, Cecilio (Spain) 346
Carducci Prize (International Literary Prizes) 475
Careers Research and Advisory Centre Ltd (United Kingdom) 402
Carew Hunt Associates (United Kingdom) 442
Caribbean Regional Library (Puerto Rico) 320
Caribbean Universities Press Jamaica Ltd (Jamaica) 237
Caribe, Editora El (Dominican Republic) 81
Caribe Grolier Inc (Dominican Republic) 82
Carinthia, Verlag (Austria) 25
Carit Andersens Forlag A/S (Denmark) 76
Caritas, Librairie (Rwanda) 323
Caritas-Verlag (Switzerland) 363
Carl, Verlag Hans, GmbH & Co KG (Federal Republic of Germany) 129
Carlsen/if AB (Sweden) 353
Carlsen if International Publishers A/S (Denmark) 76
Carlsen Verlag GmbH (Federal Republic of Germany) 129
Carmelitana VZW ('De Karmelieten') (Belgium) 35
Carmina, Bokförlaget (Sweden) 353
Carnegie Free Library (Trinidad and Tobago) 382
Carnegie Library (Mauritius) 263
Carnegie Medal (United Kingdom) 448
Carnell, E J, Literary Agency (United Kingdom) 442
Caro y Cuervo, Instituto (Colombia) 65
Carousel (United Kingdom) 402
Carrara, Casa Musicale Edizioni, Srl (Italy) 221
Carré-Chapron (France) 94
Carrefour, Librairie (Ivory Coast) 236
Carroll's Horwitz Publications (Australia) 12
Carson-Gold, Ronald, Memorial Short Story Competition (Australia) 22
Carta, Lüthi und Ramseier (Switzerland) 363
Carta, The Israel Map and Publishing Co Ltd (Israel) 214
'Cartea Românesca', Editura (Romania) 321
Carto PVBA (Belgium) 35
Cartographia (Hungary) 181
Caruana, Francis (Gibraltar) 173
Carvajal SA (Colombia) 65
Carvan Book House (Pakistan) 302
Casa de la Cultura Ecuatoriana, Biblioteca de la (Ecuador) 83
Casa de las Américas (Cuba) 69
Casa de las Américas Literary Award (International Literary Prizes) 475
Casa del Libro Editrice (Italy) 221
Casa del Libro, Librería (Colombia) 67
Casa del Libro SA (Spain) 347
Casagrande, Edizioni, SA (Switzerland) 363
Casalini Libri (Italy) 222
Casalini Libri (Italy) 234
Casavalle, Carlos, Prize (Argentina) 9
Casini, Edistudio di Brunetto (Italy) 222
Cass, Frank, & Co Ltd (United Kingdom) 402
Cassell Ltd (United Kingdom) 402
Cassia House Bookshop (Trinidad and Tobago) 382
Castaigne, Librairie, SPRL (Belgium) 42
Castalia, Editorial (Spain) 338
Casteilla, Editions André (France) 94
Castello-Collane, Il, Tecniche (Italy) 222
Castello-Sanguinetto Prize (Italy) 236
Casterman, Editions (Belgium) 35
Casterman, Editions (France) 94
Castex, Louis, Prize (France) 112
Castle House Publications Ltd (United Kingdom) 402
Castro e Silva, Livraria (Portugal) 318

Castrum Peregrini Presse (Netherlands) 275
Catalogue de l'Edition Française (France) 94
Catalunya, Biblioteca de, Diputación de Barcelona (Spain) 347
Cátedra, Ediciones, SA (Spain) 338
Cátedra, Livraria Editora, Ltda (Brazil) 49
Catenacci, Hercule, Prize (France) 112
Cathasia (France) 94
Cathay (United Kingdom) 402
Cathedral Book Centre (Belize) 45
Cathedral, The, Bookshop (Tanzania) 379
Catholic, Central, Library (Republic of Ireland) 211
Catholic, Central, Library Association Inc (Republic of Ireland) 211
Catholic, The, Bookshop Ltd (Kenya) 249
Catholic Truth Society (United Kingdom) 402
Católica, Biblioteca de Autores Cristianos de la Editorial, SA (Spain) 338
Caux, Editions de (Switzerland) 363
Caux Verlag-, Theater- und Film-AG (Switzerland) 363
Cavalier Press Pty Ltd (Australia) 12
Cave, H W, & Co (Sri Lanka) 349
Cave, Paul, Publications Ltd (United Kingdom) 402
Cavefors, Verlag Bo (Switzerland) 363
Caveman Publications Ltd (New Zealand) 288
Caxton and English Educational Programmes International (United Kingdom) 402
Caxton, The, Press (New Zealand) 288
Caymi, Editorial (Argentina) 4
Ceac, Ediciones, SA (Spain) 338
Cedar Books (United Kingdom) 402
Cedibra Editora Brasileira Ltda (Brazil) 49
Cedic, Editions (France) 94
Cedilivre SA (Switzerland) 363
Celcius — J J Vallory (Argentina) 4
Celtic Revision Aids (United Kingdom) 402
Celuc Libri (Italy) 222
Cement & Concrete Association (United Kingdom) 402
Cemerlang (Indonesia) 205
Cenacolo di Studi Storico, Artistico, Letterari (Italy) 235
Centaur, De (Netherlands) 275
Centaur Press Ltd (United Kingdom) 402
Centaur Publishers (Pty) Ltd (Republic of South Africa) 329
Centenary Publishing House Ltd (Uganda) 386
Centraal Boekhuis BV (Netherlands) 273
Centraal Bureau, Bibliotheek van het, voor de Statistiek (Netherlands) 284
Central Book Depot (Publishers) (India) 189
Central Bookshop Ltd (Malawi) 258
Central Bureau of Statistics, Economic Library (Ghana) 173
Central de Publicaciones (Mexico) 268
Central Department Store (Thailand) 381
Central Hindi Directorate (India) 189
Central Hindi Directorate Awards (India) 203
Central Institute for Scientific and Technical Information (of the State Committee for Science, Technical Progress and Higher Education) (Bulgaria) 59
Central Institute of Indian Languages (India) 189
Central Library (India) 202
Central Library (India) 202
Central Medical Library (Bulgaria) 59
Central News Agency (Namibia) 272
Central News Agency Ltd (Republic of South Africa) 329
Central News Agency Ltd (Republic of South Africa) 333
Central Records Office Library (Sudan) 350
Central Scientific Technical Library (Bulgaria) 59
Central Secretariat Library (India) 202
Central Secretariat Library (Pakistan) 303
Central Statistical, Library of the, Office of Finland (Finland) 89
Central Tanganyika Press (Tanzania) 378
Centrala Cartii (Romania) 321
Centrala Editoriala (Romania) 321
Centralnej Rady Zwiazków Zawodowych, Instytut Wydawniczy (Poland) 311
Centre Africain de Formation et de Recherche administrative pour le Développement (Morocco) 271
Centre belge de Traduction (Belgium) 45
Centre Bibliothèque d'Information (Gabon) 115
Centre culturel américain, Bibliothèque (Chad) 62
Centre culturel américain, Bibliothèque (Gabon) 115
Centre culturel américain, Bibliothèque (Ivory Coast) 236
Centre culturel américain, Bibliothèque (Senegal) 324
Centre culturel américain, Bibliothèque de Prêt (United Republic of Cameroun) 61
Centre culturel du Burundi (Burundi) 61
Centre culturel français, Bibliothèque (United Republic of Cameroun) 61
Centre culturel français, Bibliothèque (Chad) 62
Centre culturel français, Bibliothèque (Popular Republic of Congo) 68
Centre culturel français, Bibliothèque (Ivory Coast) 236
Centre culturel français, Bibliothèque (Senegal) 324
Centre culturel français, Bibliothèque (Togo) 382
Centre culturel français, Bibliothèqueque (Central African Republic) 62

504 INDEX

Centre culturel français, Bibliothèques (Zaire) 462
Centre culturel français de Constantine, Bibliothèque (Algeria) 2
Centre culturel français d'Oran, Bibliothèque (Algeria) 2
Centre culturel français Gaston Berger (Senegal) 324
Centre culturel français St-Exupéry Bibliothèque (Gabon) 115
Centre d'Archives et de Documentation politiques et sociales (France) 110
Centre de Diffusion du Livre Camerounais (United Republic of Cameroun) 61
Centre de Documentation (Haiti) 178
Centre de Documentation de l'Autorité du Bassin du Niger (Niger) 292
Centre de Documentation Pédagogique, Bibliothèque (Chad) 62
Centre de Documentation Universitaire et Société d'Edition d'Enseignement Supérieur Réunis (CDU & SEDES) (France) 94
Centre de Littérature Chrétienne (Benin) 45
Centre de Littérature Evangélique (Gabon) 115
Centre de Publications Evangeliques (Ivory Coast) 236
Centre de Recherches et de Documentation du Sénégal (CRDS) (Senegal) 324
Centre d'Edition et de Diffusion africaines (Ivory Coast) 236
Centre d'Edition et de Diffusion africaines (CEDA) (Ivory Coast) 236
Centre d'Edition et de Production de Manuels scolaires de l'UNESCO (United Republic of Cameroun) 61
Centre d'Edition et de Production pour l'Enseignement et la Recherche (CEPER) (United Republic of Cameroun) 61
Centre d'Education à la Famille et à l'Amour (Belgium) 35
Centre d'Enseignement supérieur de Niamey (Niger) 292
Centre d'Etude et de Promotion de la Lecture (France) 94
Centre d'Etudes et de Documentation, Editions du, Scientifiques (CEDS Editions) (France) 94
Centre Djoliba recherche-formation pour le developpement, Bibliothèque (Mali) 262
Centre Expérimental pour l'Enseignement des Langues (Switzerland) 363
Centre for Academic Publications Japan (Japan) 238
Centre for Documentation and Research (United Arab Emirates) 390
Centre for Library and Information Management (United Kingdom) 402
Centre for Pedagogical Information and Documentation (Bulgaria) 59
Centre for Public Libraries (Israel) 218
Centre for Scientific and Technical Information (Republic of South Africa) 334
Centre français de Documentation (Mali) 262
Centre international de documentation parlementaire (CIDP) (International Organizations) 471
Centre International de Sémiologie (Zaire) 462
Centre international d'Etudes de la Formation religieuse Lumen Vitae ASBL (Belgium) 35
Centre, Librairie du (Grand Duchy of Luxembourg) 257
Centre National, Bibliothèque du, de la recherche scientifique et technique (Benin) 45
Centre national d'Art et de Culture Georges Pompidou (France) 94
Centre national de Documentation (Laos) 253
Centre national de Documentation (Morocco) 271
Centre national de Documentation scientifique et technique (Belgium) 43
Centre National de la Recherche Scientifique (France) 94
Centre national de Recherches 'Primitifs Flamands' ASBL (Belgium) 35
Centre national des Lettres (France) 111
Centre national d'Etudes et de Recherches socio-économiques (CERSE) ASBL (Belgium) 35
Centre Orstom de Brazzaville, Bibliothèque (Popular Republic of Congo) 68
Centre Protestant d'Editions et de Diffusion (CEDI) (Zaire) 462
Centre Publications (Australia) 12
Centre régional de Promotion du Livre en Afrique (CREPLA) (International Organizations) 466
Centre Sénégalaise d'Editions et de Diffusion (Senegal) 323
Centro, Biblioteca del, Cultural Costarricense-Norteamericano (Costa Rica) 68
Centro Cultural Bautista (Nicaragua) 292
Centro de Documentacão Científica e Técnica (Portugal) 318
Centro de Documentação e Informaçao da Camara dos Deputados (Brazil) 56
Centro De Documentación Bibliotecológica (Argentina) 9
Centro de Estudios Monetarios Latinoamericanos (CEMLA) (Mexico) 264
Centro de Investigação e Documentação (Brazil) 56
Centro Di (Italy) 222
Centro do Livro Brasileiro (Portugal) 316
Centro Documentazione Alpina (Italy) 222
Centro Editor de America Latina SA (Argentina) 4
Centro Editor de Psicologia Aplicada Ltda (Brazil) 49
Centro Editorial Latino Americano Ltda (Brazil) 49

Centro Filosófico-Literario (Colombia) 67
Centro, Fundación, de Investigación y Educación Popular (CINEP) (Colombia) 65
Centro Internazionale del Libro (Italy) 222
Centro Latinoamericano de Demografía (CELADE) (Chile) 63
Centro Mexicano de Escritores AC (Mexico) 264
Centro Nacional de Documentación Científica y Tecnológica (Bolivia) 47
Centro Nacional de Documentación e Información Educativa (Bolivia) 47
Centro Nacional de Información y Documentación (Uruguay) 452
Centro Nacional de Información y Documentación (CENID) (Chile) 64
Centro Regional para el Fomento del Libro en América Latina y el Caribe (CERLAL) (International Organizations) 466
Centro Studi Terzo Mondo (Italy) 222
Centrul de Lingvistica Istorie Literara si Folclor (Romania) 322
Centrum Informacji Naukowej, Technicznej i Ekonomicznej (Poland) 314
Centrum voor Literatuuronderzoekers (Netherlands) 284
Centurion, Editions du (France) 94
Centurion Publications (United Kingdom) 402
Cepadues Éditions (CEPAD) SA (France) 94
Cepilco, Ediciones, SA (Mexico) 265
Cercle Belge de la Librairie (Belgium) 33
Cercle d'Art, Editions, SA (France) 94
Cercle de la Librairie (Syndicat des Industries et Commerces du Livre) (France) 90
Cerdas (Indonesia) 205
Ceres (Belgium) 35
Ceres, Editura (Romania) 321
Ceres Productions (Tunisia) 383
Ceres-Verlag Rudolf-August Oetker KG (Federal Republic of Germany) 130
Cerf, Editions du (France) 94
Certificate of Honour (India) 203
Cervantes, Librería (Ecuador) 83
Cervantes, Librería, — Libroclub de Guatemala (Guatemala) 177
Cervantes, Miguel de, Prize (Spain) 348
České socialistické republiky, Státní knihovna (Czechoslovakia) 73
Českého fondu, Výtvarná služba, výtvarných umělcu, sekce krásné knihy a grafiky (Czechoslovakia) 70
Československý spisovatel (Czechoslovakia) 71
Ceylon Institute of Scientific and Industrial Research Library (Sri Lanka) 349
Ceylon Printers Ltd (Sri Lanka) 349
Chacko, I C, Award (India) 203
Chadwyck-Healey Ltd (United Kingdom) 402
Chaix, Editions R (France) 94
Chalantika (Bangladesh) 32
Chalermnit Bookshop (Thailand) 381
Chalermnit Press (Thailand) 380
Chalet, Editions du (France) 94
Challenge (Australia) 12
Challenge Bookshops (Nigeria) 296
Challenge Publications (Nigeria) 293
Chambers, W & R, Ltd (United Kingdom) 402
Chambre syndicale des Editeurs d'Annuaires et de Publications similaires (France) 90
Champ Libre, Editions (France) 94
Champs-Elysées, Librairie des, SA (France) 94
Chanakya Publications (India) 189
Chancellor (United Kingdom) 402
Chancerel Editions SA (France) 94
Chancerel Publishers Ltd (United Kingdom) 402
Chancery House Publishing Ltd (United Kingdom) 402
Chand, S, & Co Ltd (India) 189
Chandigarh Booksellers' Association (India) 185
Changjak Kwa Pipyung Sa (Republic of Korea) 250
Changjo Sa (Republic of Korea) 250
Chanlis (Belgium) 35
Chantecler, Editions (Belgium) 35
Chaplin, Sid, Literary Award (United Kingdom) 448
Chapman & Hall Ltd (United Kingdom) 402
Chapman, Geoffrey (United Kingdom) 402
Charles-Lavauzelle, Editions, SA (France) 94
Charnwood Library Series (United Kingdom) 403
Charotar Publishing House (India) 189
Charran Educational Publishers (Trinidad and Tobago) 382
Charran's Bookshop (1978) Ltd (Trinidad and Tobago) 382
Charte, La, NV (Belgium) 35
Chartwell-Bratt (Publishing & Training) Ltd (United Kingdom) 403
Chat, Editions du, Perché (France) 94
Chatam Sofer Institute (Israel) 214
Chateauneuf-du-Pape Grand Prize (France) 112
Chatto & Windus (Educational) Ltd (United Kingdom) 403
Chatto & Windus Ltd/The Hogarth Press Ltd (United Kingdom) 403

Chatto, Bodley Head & Jonathan Cape Australia Pty Ltd (Australia) 12
Chatto, Bodley Head & Jonathan Cape Ltd (United Kingdom) 403
Chaukhambha Orientalia (India) 189
Chauveau, Pierre, Medal (International Literary Prizes) 475
Chavée, Honoré, Prize (France) 112
Chemical Society, The (United Kingdom) 403
Chemie, VC Verlag, AG (Switzerland) 363
Chemie, Verlag, GmbH (Federal Republic of Germany) 130
Chemin Facile (United Republic of Cameroun) 61
Chêne, Editions du (France) 94
Cheng Chung Book Co (Taiwan) 377
Ch'eng Wen Publishing Company (Taiwan) 377
Cherche-Midi, Le, Éditeur (France) 94
Cheshire (Australia) 12
Chetana Pvt Ltd (India) 189
Chevalier Press (Australia) 12
Chez Nanon (Seychelles) 324
Chi Rho (Australia) 12
Chiangmai Book Centre (Thailand) 380
Chiendent, Editions du, Sàrl (France) 95
Chikuma Shobo Publishing Co Ltd (Japan) 238
Child Honsha Co Ltd (Japan) 238
Childerset Pty Ltd (Australia) 12
Children Book House (India) 189
Children's and Juvenile Literature Prize (Portugal) 319
Children's Book Award (International Literary Prizes) 475
Children's Book Club (Republic of South Africa) 333
Children's Book Council of Australia (Australia) 10
Children's Book of the Year Awards (Australia) 22
Children's Book Prize (Norway) 301
Children's Book Trust (India) 189
Children's, The, Press Ltd (Republic of Ireland) 209
Children's Writers' Group (United Kingdom) 391
Child's Play (International) Ltd (United Kingdom) 403
China Cultural Corporation (Hong Kong) 179
China National Association of Literature and the Arts (Taiwan) 378
China National Publishing Industry Trading Corp (People's Republic of China) 64
China Publications Centre (Guoji Shudian) (People's Republic of China) 64
China Studien- und Verlagsgesellschaft mbH (Federal Republic of Germany) 130
China Youth Publishing House (People's Republic of China) 64
Chindwin Book Distributors (Burma) 60
Chinese Language and Literary Society (Republic of Singapore) 328
Chinese Language and Literature Association (Hong Kong) 180
Chinese Materials Center (Taiwan) 377
Chinese Materials Center (Taiwan) 378
Chinese Philatelic Magazine Press (People's Republic of China) 64
Chinese University of Hong Kong Library System (Hong Kong) 180
Chinese University Press, The (Hong Kong) 179
Chinmaya Mission (India) 189
Chip Book Club (United Kingdom) 443
Chiré, Editions de (France) 95
Chiron, Editions (France) 95
Chispa, Editorial La, Ltda (Colombia) 65
Chivers Press Publishers (United Kingdom) 403
Cholmondeley Award for Poets (International Literary Prizes) 475
Chomhairle, An, Leabharlanna (Republic of Ireland) 211
Chongqing Library (People's Republic of China) 64
Chopmen Bookshop (Republic of Singapore) 327
Chopmen Enterprises (Republic of Singapore) 326
Chopmen Enterprises (Republic of Singapore) 327
Chopsticks Publications Ltd (Hong Kong) 179
Chotard et Associés, Editeurs (France) 95
Chowkhamba Sanskrit Series Office (India) 189
Choysa Bursary for Children's Writers (New Zealand) 291
Chrissi Penna — Les Editions de la Plume d'Or (Greece) 174
Christian Book Shop (Bahamas) 31
Christian Book, The, Centre (Papua New Guinea) 305
Christian Booksellers' Association (NZ Chapter) (New Zealand) 287
Christian Bookselling Association of Australia (Australia) 10
Christian Bookshop (Zambia) 463
Christian Bookstore (Thailand) 381
Christian Community, The, Press (United Kingdom) 403
Christian Council of Zambia (Zambia) 463
Christian Journals Ltd (United Kingdom) 403
Christian Literature (Belize) 45
Christian Literature Association in Malawi (Malawi) 258
Christian Literature Crusade (Barbados) 33
Christian Literature, The, Society of Korea (Republic of Korea) 250
Christian, Office of, Education and Literature (Thailand) 380

INDEX 505

Christian Publishing Co — CUM Books (Pty) Ltd (Republic of South Africa) 329
Christian, The, Literature Society (India) 189
Christian-Verlag GmbH (Federal Republic of Germany) 130
Christiana-Verlag (Switzerland) 363
Christians, Hans, Druckerei und Verlag (Federal Republic of Germany) 130
Christliche Verlagsanstalt GmbH (Federal Republic of Germany) 130
Christliche Verlagsgessellschaft mbH (Federal Republic of Germany) 130
Christlicher Bildungskreis Verlags GmbH (Federal Republic of Germany) 167
Christliches Verlagshaus GmbH (Federal Republic of Germany) 130
Christophorus-Verlag GmbH (Federal Republic of Germany) 130
Chronique, Editions de la, des Lettres Françaises (France) 95
Chryssos Typos (Greece) 174
Chugh Publications (India) 189
Chulalongkorn University, Academic Resource Center (Thailand) 381
Chung Hwa Book Co Ltd (Taiwan) 377
Chuo-Tosho Co Ltd (Japan) 239
Chuokoron-Sha Inc (Japan) 239
Chur, Verlag Ernst (Federal Republic of Germany) 130
Church Book Room Press (United Kingdom) 403
Church, Hubert, Award (New Zealand) 291
Church Publishing Trust (Republic of South Africa) 329
Church Society (United Kingdom) 403
Church, The, Bookshop (Sudan) 350
Church World Service (Niger) 292
Churchill Livingstone (Australia) 12
Churchill Livingstone (United Kingdom) 403
Cia Internacional de Publicaciones SA de CV (Mexico) 268
Ciapanna, Cesco, Editore SpA (Italy) 222
Ciarrapico Editore (Italy) 222
Cicada Press (New Zealand) 288
Cicero (Netherlands) 275
Cicero International Art GmbH (Federal Republic of Germany) 130
Cid, El, Editor SAE (Spain) 338
Cid, El, Editor SRL (Argentina) 4
Cidade Nova Editora (Brazil) 49
Ciencias Sociales, Editorial de (Cuba) 69
Científica Argentina, Editorial (Argentina) 4
Científica Técnica, Livraria (Brazil) 56
Científico, Editorial, Técnica (Cuba) 69
Científico Médica, Editorial (Spain) 338
Cima, Distribuidora, Inc (Puerto Rico) 319
Cima, Librería, Cia Ltda (Ecuador) 83
Cinc d'Oros — Jaime Farrás Solé (Spain) 347
Cincel, Editorial, SA (Spain) 338
Cinque, Edizioni, Lune (Italy) 222
Ciordia, Editorial, SRL (Argentina) 4
Ciranna, Editrice, — Roma (Italy) 222
Circle of State Librarians (United Kingdom) 445
Circle of the Greek Children's Book IBBY (Greek Section) Prizes (Greece) 176
Circle, The, of Greek Children's Books (Greece) 174
Círculo de Amigos de la Historia (Spain) 347
Círculo de Lectores SA (Argentina) 8
Círculo de Lectores SA (Colombia) 67
Círculo de Lectores SA (Colombia) 67
Círculo de Lectores SA (Spain) 347
Círculo de Leitores (Portugal) 318
Círculo do Livro SA (Brazil) 55
Círculo Mexicano de Lectores (Mexico) 268
Circus Books (Australia) 12
Città Armoniosa (Italy) 222
Città Nuova Editrice (Italy) 222
Cittadella Editrice (Italy) 222
City Arts (United Kingdom) 403
City Library (Mauritius) 263
City, The, Bookshop (Ethiopia) 86
Ciudad Educativa, Librería, SA (Antigua Librería del Colegio) (Argentina) 8
Ciudad Nueva (Spain) 339
Civilização, Editora, Brasileira SA (Brazil) 49
Civilização, Livraria, (Américo Fraga Lamares & Ca Lda) (Portugal) 316
Claassen-Verlag GmbH (Federal Republic of Germany) 130
Clarendon Press (United Kingdom) 403
Claretiana, Editorial (Argentina) 4
Claridad, Editorial, SA (Argentina) 4
Clarion Book Club (India) 201
Clark, Robin, Ltd (United Kingdom) 403
Clark, Russell, Award (New Zealand) 291
Clark, T & T, Ltd (United Kingdom) 403
Clarke, Anthony, Books (United Kingdom) 403
Clarke, James, & Co Ltd (United Kingdom) 403
Clasicos Roxsil (El Salvador) 85
Classen, Werner, Verlag (Switzerland) 363
Classey, E W (United Kingdom) 403

Classic (Pakistan) 302
Classics Club (India) 201
Classification Research Group (United Kingdom) 445
Classroom Magazine (Australia) 12
Claudiana Editrice (Italy) 222
Claudius Verlag GmbH (Federal Republic of Germany) 130
Clausens, J Fr, Forlag (Denmark) 76
Clauwaert, Boekengilde de (Belgium) 42
Clauwaert, De (Belgium) 35
Clé International (France) 95
Clearway (Australia) 12
Cleary, R J (Australia) 12
Clematis Press Ltd (United Kingdom) 403
Clifford, The, Press (Australia) 12
Clio Press Ltd (United Kingdom) 403
Clivo, De, Press (Switzerland) 363
Clócomhar, An, TTA (Republic of Ireland) 209
Clódhanna Teo (Republic of Ireland) 209
Cloister Book Store Ltd (Barbados) 33
Close Up, Editora, SA (Argentina) 4
Clowes, William, (Publishers) Ltd (United Kingdom) 403
Club de Lectores (Argentina) 4
Club de Lectores Extemporaneos (Mexico) 268
Club de Poetas (Argentina) 9
Club dei Bibliofili (Italy) 234
Club des Masques (France) 95
Club du Livre d'Art (France) 109
Club du Livre SA (France) 109
Club, Editorial, de la Prensa (Puerto Rico) 319
Club 'El Libro del Mes' (Argentina) 8
Club for Bibliophiles (Hungary) 182
Club Français du Livre (France) 109
Club Leabhar (United Kingdom) 403
Club of Twentieth Century Poetry (Poland) 313
Club of Young Readers (Czechoslovakia) 73
Co-op Books (Publishing) Ltd (Republic of Ireland) 209
Coccinella, La, Editrice Srl (Italy) 222
Cocco, Libreria Internazionale Fratelli (Italy) 234
Cochuideachd Leabhneachean Gaidhlig (United Kingdom) 403
Codco Est (Qatar) 320
Codecri, Editora, Ltda (Brazil) 50
Codesria (Senegal) 324
Codices Selecti (Austria) 25
Coebergh, H (Netherlands) 284
Coeckelberghs, René, Bokförlag AB (Sweden) 353
Cogedi SA (Belgium) 35
Cohen, Mo (Federal Republic of Germany) 167
Cole & Yancy (Liberia) 255
Cole and Yancy Bookshop Ltd (Liberia) 255
Cole Publications (Australia) 13
Colediciones, Colombiana de Ediciones SA (Colombia) 65
Colegial Bolivariana CA (Venezuela) 453
Colegio de Belén, Biblioteca del (Cuba) 69
Colegio de Bibliotecarios de Chile (Chile) 64
Colegio de Bibliotecarios de Costa Rica (Costa Rica) 69
Colegio de Bibliotecarios de la Provincia de Buenos Aires (Argentina) 4
Colegio de Bibliotecólogos, Archivólogos y Afines del Estado Zulia (Venezuela) 454
Colegio de Bibliotecólogos y Archivólogos de Venezuela (Colbav) (Venezuela) 454
Colegio, El, de México AC (Mexico) 264
Colegio, El, SA (Paraguay) 306
Colegio, Librería del, SA (Argentina) 4
Colibrant (Belgium) 35
Colibri, Librairie Le (Mauritius) 263
Colin, Armand, Editeur (France) 95
Collectieve Propaganda van het Nederlandse Boek (CPNB) (Netherlands) 273
Collectors Club of Franco Maria Ricci (Italy) 234
Collectors' Editions Book Club (United Kingdom) 443
College Book House (India) 189
Collège camerounais des Arts, des Sciences et de la Technologie, Bibliothèque (United Republic of Cameroun) 61
College for Arab and Islamic Studies Library (Sudan) 350
Collège Jésus Marie Bibliothèque (Gabon) 115
College of Agriculture Library (Ethiopia) 86
College of Agriculture Library, University of Baghdad (Iraq) 208
College of Careers (Pty) Ltd (Republic of South Africa) 329
College of Our Lady of Fatima Library (Liberia) 255
College of the Bahamas Library (Bahamas) 31
Collège rural d'Ambatobe (Democratic Republic of Madagascar) 258
College, The, Press (Pvt) Ltd (Zimbabwe) 464
College Tutorial Press (Republic of South Africa) 329
Collet's Holdings Ltd (United Kingdom) 403
Collier Macmillan Ltd (United Kingdom) 404
Collier-Macmillan South Africa (Pty) Ltd (Republic of South Africa) 329
Collingridge (United Kingdom) 404
Collings, Rex, Ltd (United Kingdom) 404
Collins Booksellers Pty Ltd (Australia) 20
Collins, M O, (Pvt) Ltd (Zimbabwe) 464

Collins Religious Book Award (International Literary Prizes) 476
Collins, Tom, Poetry Prize (Australia) 22
Collins Vaal (Pty) Ltd (Republic of South Africa) 329
Collins, William, Pty Ltd (Australia) 13
Collins, William, Publishers Ltd (New Zealand) 288
Collins, William, Sons & Co Ltd (United Kingdom) 404
Colloquium Verlag Otto H Hess (Federal Republic of Germany) 130
Colmegna SA (Argentina) 4
Colombian Novel Contest Awards (Colombia) 67
Colombo Catholic Press (Sri Lanka) 349
Colombo Public Library System (Sri Lanka) 349
Colombus Books (United Kingdom) 404
Colonial, Editora (Dominican Republic) 81
Colonnade (United Kingdom) 404
Colonnes, Librairie des (Morocco) 271
Colour Cubs (United Kingdom) 404
Colour Library International Ltd (United Kingdom) 404
Columba, Editorial, SA (Argentina) 4
Columbia University Press (United Kingdom) 404
Columbine House (United Kingdom) 404
Columbus Publishers Ltd (Trinidad and Tobago) 382
Columbus Verlag Paul Oestergaard GmbH (Federal Republic of Germany) 130
Comb Books (Kenya) 248
Combi International AB (Sweden) 353
Combo Uitgeversgroep (Netherlands) 275
Comet (United Kingdom) 404
Comindus, Editions (France) 95
Comisión Paraguaya Documentación e Información (Paraguay) 306
Comissão Brasileira de Documentação Agricola (CBDA) (Brazil) 56
Commemorative Editions Pty Ltd (Australia) 13
Commercial Press (People's Republic of China) 64
Commission belge de Bibliographie (Belgium) 44
Commission de l'Education chrétienne (Zaire) 462
Commission des Bibliothèques de l'ASDBAM (Association Sénégalaise pour le Développement de la Documentation, des Bibliothèques, des Archives et des Musées) (Senegal) 324
Commission for Racial Equality (United Kingdom) 404
Committee for Postgraduate Awards in Librarianship and Information Work (United Kingdom) 445
Common Ground (United Kingdom) 404
Commonwealth Agricultural Bureaux (International Organizations) 471
Commonwealth, The, Library Association (International Organizations) 467
Commonwealth, The, Poetry Prize (International Literary Prizes) 476
Communication Foundation for Asia (Philippines) 308
Compagnie d'Editions Libres, Sociales et Economiques (France) 95
Compagnie Européenne de Fournitures et de Services Informatiques (France) 95
Compañia General de Ediciones SA de CV (Mexico) 264
Compañia Impresora Argentina SA (Argentina) 4
Companion Book Club (United Kingdom) 443
Compass Verlagsgesellschaft Rudolf Hanel und Sohn (Austria) 25
Complexe, Editions, SPRL (Belgium) 35
Computer Research Press (United Kingdom) 404
Comuneros, Editorial (Paraguay) 306
Comuneros, Librería (Paraguay) 306
Comunità, Edizioni di, SpA (Italy) 222
Concept Publishing Co (India) 189
Concepto, Editorial, SA (Mexico) 264
Concert Verlag G Kowalski (Federal Republic of Germany) 130
Concertina Publications Ltd (United Kingdom) 404
Conch Magazine Ltd (Nigeria) 293
Concorde, Imprimerie La (Switzerland) 364
Concorde Paperbacks (United Kingdom) 404
Concordia Editora Ltda (Brazil) 50
Concours, Le, Médical (France) 95
Concurso Literario Municipal (Municipal Literary Competition) (Uruguay) 452
Condor Books (United Kingdom) 404
Conference of European Churches (International Organizations) 471
Confraria dos Amigos do Livro Ltda (Brazil) 50
Congreso, Biblioteca del, de la Nacion (Argentina) 8
Congreso, Biblioteca del, Nacional (Bolivia) 47
Congreso, Biblioteca del, Nacional (Chile) 63
Congreso de Poesia de Puerto Rico (Puerto Rican Congress of Poetry) (Puerto Rico) 320
Congress of South-East Asian Librarians IV (CONSAL IV) (International Organizations) 467
Congresso de la Unión, Biblioteca del (Mexico) 269
Conjunta, Editorial, SRL (Argentina) 4
Connemara (State Central) Public Library (India) 202
Connoisseur Carbooks (United Kingdom) 404
Conquista, Empresa de Publicações Ltda (Brazil) 50
Conseil international des Associations de Bibliothèques de Théologie (International Organizations) 467

506 INDEX

Consejo, Biblioteca General del, Superior de Investigaciones Científicas (Spain) 347
Conselho Federal de Biblioteconomia (CFB) (Brazil) 56
Conservative Political Centre (United Kingdom) 404
Conservatorio di Musica, Biblioteca Musicale Governativa del, S Cecilia (Italy) 234
Consolidated Labor Institute (Japan) (Japan) 239
Constable & Co Ltd (United Kingdom) 404
Construction Press (United Kingdom) 404
Contabilidad, Ediciones, Moderna SACIC (Argentina) 4
Contables y Administrativas, Ediciones, SA (Mexico) 264
Contact NV (Belgium) 35
Contact, Uitgeverij, BV (Netherlands) 275
Conte, Fratelli, Editore Srl (Italy) 222
Contempora, Editorial, SRL (Argentina) 4
Continental, Cía Editorial, SA (CESCA) (Mexico) 265
Convent van Universiteitsbibliothekarissen in Nederland (Netherlands) 284
Conway Maritime Press Ltd (United Kingdom) 404
Cook, Albert, Library (Uganda) 386
Cook, James, Australian Literary Studies Award (Australia) 22
Cook, Thomas, Travel Book Awards (International Literary Prizes) 476
Cooper, Leo (United Kingdom) 404
Cooperativa Libraria Editrice dell'Università di Padova (Italy) 222
Cooperative das Casas (Mozambique) 271
Coopérative de l'Enseignement Laïc (CEL) SA (France) 95
Coopérative Regionale de l'Enseignement Religieux (CRER) (France) 95
Copernic (France) 95
Coppée, François, Prize (France) 112
Coppenrath, Verlag F (Federal Republic of Germany) 130
Copplestone, Trewin, Books (United Kingdom) 404
Copress-Verlag (Federal Republic of Germany) 130
Copyright Agency Ltd (Australia) 10
Copyright Research Institute (Japan) 237
Coquito, Ediciones (Dominican Republic) 82
Corazón, Alberto, Editor (Spain) 339
Cordillera, Editorial, Inc (Puerto Rico) 319
Cordoba Stories Prizes (Colombia) 67
Corgi (Australia) 13
Corgi Books Ltd (United Kingdom) 404
Cork University Press (Republic of Ireland) 209
Cornell University Press (United Kingdom) 405
Cornelsen und Oxford University Press GmbH (Federal Republic of Germany) 130
Cornelsen-Velhagen und Klasing GmbH & Co Verlag für Lehrmedien KG (Federal Republic of Germany) 131
Cornelsen-Velhagen und Klasing Verlagsgesellschaft mbH & Co KG (Federal Republic of Germany) 131
Cornfeld, Gaalyah (Israel) 214
Corniche, Editions (Sweden) 353
Corona, Archivo de la, de Aragon (Spain) 347
Corona, Bokförlaget, AB (Sweden) 353
Corona Publishing Co Ltd (Japan) 239
Corona Verlag KG (Federal Republic of Germany) 131
Coronet (United Kingdom) 405
Corporan, Rafael, de los Santos (Dominican Republic) 81
Correa, Viriato, Prize (Brazil) 57
Corregidor, Ediciones, SAICI y E (Argentina) 4
Corsica, Verlagshaus (France) 95
Cortina, Edizioni Libreria, Verona Srl (Italy) 222
Corvina Press (Hungary) 181
Corvus Verlag (Federal Republic of Germany) 131
Cosdel (Singapore) Pte Ltd (Malaysia) 261
Cosmopolita SRL (Argentina) 4
Cosmos, Edições (Portugal) 316
Cosmos, Editora (Dominican Republic) 81
Cosmos, Editorial (Mexico) 265
Cosmos, Librería (Mexico) 268
Cosmos, Publicaciones (Mexico) 265
Cosmos-Verlag AG (Switzerland) 364
Costa, Livraria Sá da (Portugal) 318
Costa Rica, Editorial (Costa Rica) 68
Costa, Sá da, Editora (Portugal) 316
Costello, D J, (Publishers) Ltd (United Kingdom) 405
Cotman House (United Kingdom) 405
Cotmancolor (United Kingdom) 405
Cotta'sche Buchhandlung, Verlag J G (Federal Republic of Germany) 131
Council for Educational Technology (United Kingdom) 405
Council of Europe, Publications Section (International Organizations) 471
Council of Libraries (Albania) 1
Counson, Albert, Prize (International Literary Prizes) 476
Count of Cartagena Prizes (International Literary Prizes) 476
Country Book Society (United Kingdom) 443
Country Life Books (United Kingdom) 405
Countryside Books (United Kingdom) 405
Courrier du Livre Sàrl (France) 95
Coutinho, Dick, BV (Netherlands) 275
Couto, Editora e Gráfica Miguel, SA (Brazil) 50
Cracow City Literary Prize (Poland) 315

Craft Book Society (United Kingdom) 443
Crafts, The, Council (United Kingdom) 405
Cramer, J (Federal Republic of Germany) 131
Cratander AG (Switzerland) 364
Crawshay, The Rose Mary, Prizes (International Literary Prizes) 476
Crea, Editorial, SA (Argentina) 4
Creadif (Belgium) 35
Creanga, Editure Ion (Romania) 321
Creasey, John, Memorial Award (United Kingdom) 448
Crédit Communal de Belgique - Service Culturel (Belgium) 35
Cremers (Schoollandkaarten) PVBA (Belgium) 35
Cremonese, Edizioni, SpA (Italy) 222
Crépin-Leblond, Editeurs, et Cie SA (France) 95
Crescent Publications (Pakistan) 302
Crescent Publishers (Bangladesh) 32
Crescent Publishing Co (India) 190
Crespillo, Editorial, SA (Argentina) 4
Cressrelles Publishing Co Ltd (United Kingdom) 405
Cricket Book Society (United Kingdom) 443
Crime, The, Club (United Kingdom) 405
Crime Writers' Association (United Kingdom) 391
Crisp (Belgium) 35
Cristal, Librerías de (Mexico) 268
Cristiandad, Ediciones (Spain) 339
Criterion: Teachers' Bookshelf Book Club (United Kingdom) 443
Critica, Editorial, SA (Spain) 339
Croft Press (Australia) 13
Cromograf SA (Ecuador) 82
Crompton, Paul H, Ltd (United Kingdom) 405
Croner Publications Ltd (United Kingdom) 405
Croom Helm Ltd (United Kingdom) 405
Crosby Lockwood Staples Ltd (United Kingdom) 405
Cross Continent Press Ltd (Nigeria) 293
Cuala Press (Republic of Ireland) 209
Cubanas, Ediciones (Cuba) 69
Cuello, Casa (Dominican Republic) 82
Cujas, Editions (France) 95
Cultrix, Editora (Brazil) 50
Cultura, Casa de la, Ecuatoriana (Ecuador) 82
Cultura, Ediciones, Hispánica (Spain) 339
Cultura, Librería La (Paraguay) 306
Cultura, Librería y Editorial (Chile) 63
Cultura-Maroc (Morocco) 271
Cultura Médica, Editora, Ltda (Brazil) 50
Cultura, Premio Nacional de (Bolivia) 47
Cultural Centre, Library of the, Surinam (Bibliotheek CCS) (Suriname) 351
Cultural Centre of the Philippines Literary Awards (Philippines) 310
Cultural Colombiana Ltda (Colombia) 65
Cultural, Librería, Colombiana (Colombia) 67
Cultural, Librería, Salvadoreña SA de CV (El Salvador) 85
Cultural Panameña, Ediciones Librería, SA (Panama) 304
Cultural Promotion (Namibia) 272
Cultural, Publicaciones, SA (Mexico) 265
Cultural Supplies, The, Co (Malaysia) 259
Culturale, La (Italy) 222
Culture et Civilisation, Editions (Belgium) 36
Culture Prize (Japan) 246
Cumann Leabharfhoilsitheoirí Éireann (CLÉ) (Republic of Ireland) 208
Cumann Leabharlann na h-Éireann (Republic of Ireland) 211
Cumann Leabharlannaithe Scoile (CLS) (Republic of Ireland) 211
Cumont, Franz, Prize (International Literary Prizes) 476
Cura Verlag GmbH (Austria) 25
Curaçaosche Drukkerij en Uitgevers Maatschappij (Netherlands Antilles) 286
Curci, Edizioni, SRL (Italy) 222
Curcio, Armando, Editore SpA (Italy) 222
Currawong Press Pty Ltd (Australia) 13
Currency Press Pty Ltd (Australia) 13
Current Books (India) 190
Current Technical Literature Co (Pvt) Ltd (India) 201
Currey O'Neil Ross Pty Ltd (Australia) 13
Curriculum Development Centre (Australia) 13
Curtis Brown (United Kingdom) 442
Curzon Press Ltd (United Kingdom) 405
Cuspide, Distribuidora (Argentina) 8
Cuttington College and Divinity School Library (Liberia) 255
Cygne, Librairie Le (Mauritius) 263
Cygnet Books (Australia) 13
Cyngor Llyfrau Cymraeg (United Kingdom) 391
Cynthia, J, Co Ltd (Taiwan) 378
Cyprus Booksellers Association (Cyprus) 70
Cyprus Library Association (Cyprus) 70
Cyprus Museum, Library of the (Cyprus) 70
Cyril and Methodius National Library (Bulgaria) 59
Cyril and Methodius Prize (International Literary Prizes) 476
'Czytelnik', Spóldzielnia Wydawnicza (Poland) 311

D A F S A (Société de Documentation et d'Analyses Financières) (France) 95
D C Book Club (India) 201
D C Books (India) 190
D E B Verlag (das europäische Buch Literaturvertrieb GmbH) (Federal Republic of Germany) 131
D E L S A (Spain) 347
D I F E L (Brazil) 50
D I G Ldá (Distribuidora de Informação Geral) (Portugal) 318
D I L I A (Czechoslovakia) 73
D J I (Federal Republic of Germany) 131
D J O, Federatie, (de jonge onderzoekers) (Netherlands) 275
D K Agencies (India) 201
D K F Trust (India) 190
D K Publications (India) 190
D K Publishers' Distributors (India) 201
D M F D (France) 109
D O P E S A, Editorial, (Documentacion Periodistica SA) (Spain) 339
D P Publications (United Kingdom) 405
D R W-Verlag Weinbrenner-KG (Federal Republic of Germany) 131
D T V (Federal Republic of Germany) 131
D V A (Federal Republic of Germany) 131
Dabbous Stores (Saudi Arabia) 323
Dacca Book Mart (Bangladesh) 32
Dacca University Library (Bangladesh) 32
Dacia, Editura (Romania) 321
Dacosta, Les Editions Roger (France) 95
Dadò, Edizioni Armando, Tipografia Stazione (Switzerland) 364
Dagbreek, Klub- (Republic of South Africa) 333
Dagen, Tidnings AB (Sweden) 353
Dageraad, De, PVBA (Belgium) 36
Dagon Books (United Kingdom) 405
Dahl, Gösta, och Son AB (Sweden) 358
Dahlia Books (Sweden) 353
Daihak Publishing Co (Republic of Korea) 250
Daiichi Shuppan Co Ltd (Japan) 239
Daily-Bul, Le (Belgium) 36
Daily Times of Nigeria Ltd (Nigeria) 293
Daimon, Ediciones, — Manuel Tamayo (Spain) 339
Dais Literary Agency (Italy) 233
Dalén-Engqvists Prize, The (Sweden) 360
Dalesman Publishing Co Ltd (United Kingdom) 405
Dalla Parte, Edizioni, delle Bambine (Italy) 223
Dall'Oglio Editore SpA (Italy) 223
Dalloz, Jurisprudence Générale (France) 95
Dalton, Gilbert, Ltd (Republic of Ireland) 209
Dalton, Terence, Ltd (United Kingdom) 405
Daman, Librairie R (Grand Duchy of Luxembourg) 257
Damascus University Library (Syria) 377
Damascus University Press (Syria) 377
Dami, Piero, Editore SRL (Italy) 223
Damm, N W, Children's Book Prize (Norway) 301
Damm, N W, og Søn A/S (Norway) 298
Damnitz Verlag GmbH (Federal Republic of Germany) 131
Dan Kook University Press (Republic of Korea) 250
Danae, Ediciones, SA (Spain) 339
Dance Books Ltd (United Kingdom) 405
Dandelions (United Kingdom) 405
Daneshdjou Bookstore (Iran) 207
Dangles, Editions, SA (France) 95
Daniel, The C W, Co Ltd (United Kingdom) 405
Danish Academy Prize for Literature (Denmark) 81
Danish Authors' Colleagues Prize (Denmark) 81
Danish Authors' Lyric Prize (Denmark) 81
Danish Critics Literary Prize (Denmark) 81
Danish Prize for Children's Literature (Denmark) 81
Danish Translations Centre (DTC) (Denmark) 81
Danmark Book Club (Denmark) 79
Danmark, Forlaget, A/S (Denmark) 76
Danmarks Biblioteksforening (Denmark) 80
Danmarks Forskningsbiblioteksforening (Denmark) 80
Danmarks Skolebibliotekarforening (Denmark) 80
Danmarks Skolebiblioteksforening (Denmark) 80
Danmarks Tekniske Bibliotek (Denmark) 80
Danov', Darzhavno Izdatelstov 'Christo G (Bulgaria) 58
Dansk Boghandlermedhjaelperforening (Denmark) 75
Dansk Bogtjeneste (Denmark) 75
Dansk Central-Boghandel (Denmark) 79
Dansk Exlibris Selskab (Denmark) 81
Dansk Forfatterforening (Denmark) 75
Dansk Historisk Haandbogsforlag Ltd (Denmark) 76
Dansk Litteraturselskab, Nyt (Denmark) 81
Dansk Musikbiblioteksforening (Denmark) 80
Dansk Teknisk Litteraturselskab — DTL (Denmark) 80
Danske Antikvarboghandlerforening (Denmark) 75
Danske Boghandleres Importørforening (DANBIF) (Denmark) 75
Danske Boghandleres Kommissionsanstalt (DBK) (Denmark) 75
Danske Boghandlerforening, Den (Denmark) 75
Danske Bogsamleres Klub (Denmark) 79
Danske Forlaeggerforening, Den (Denmark) 75

INDEX 507

Danske Sprog-og Litteraturselskab (Denmark) 81
Dap-Reinart Uitgeven (Belgium) 42
Dap-Reinart, Uitgeverij, SV (Belgium) 36
Daphins-Verlag (Switzerland) 364
Daphne Diffusion SPRL (Belgium) 36
Daphne, Editions (Belgium) 36
Dar al-Kutub al-Wataniah (National Library) (Syria) 377
Dar Arabia Lil Kitab (Tunisia) 383
Dar El Amal SA, d'Edition de Diffusion de Presse et de Publicité (Tunisia) 383
Dar es Salaam Bookshop, The (Tanzania) 379
Dar es Salaam University Bookshop (Tanzania) 379
Dar es Salaam University Press (Tanzania) 379
Dar Libya Publishing House (Libya) 255
Dar-ul-Kutub (Egypt) 84
D'Arborio, Maria-Pia (Italy) 233
Dardanos, G, — H Karakatsanis & Co Ltd — Gutenberg (Greece) 174
Dardelet, Editions, SA (France) 95
Dargaud Editeur (France) 95
Dario', Librería Recinto 'Ruben (Nicaragua) 292
Darling Downs Institute Press (Australia) 13
Darmstädter Blätter, Verlag, Schwarz und Co (Federal Republic of Germany) 131
Darton, Longman & Todd Ltd (United Kingdom) 405
Darwen Finlayson Ltd (United Kingdom) 405
Das Beste, Verlag (Federal Republic of Germany) 131
Dastane Ramchandra & Co (India) 190
Datapack Books (United Kingdom) 405
Daude, Librairie (Réunion) 320
Dauphin, Editions du (France) 95
Dausien, Werner (Federal Republic of Germany) 131
Dauzat, Albert, Prize (France) 112
Davar (Israel) 214
David & Charles (United Kingdom) 405
David Prize (Cuba) 70
Davidsfonds VZW (Belgium) 36
Davies, Peter, Ltd (United Kingdom) 405
Davis-Poynter Ltd (United Kingdom) 406
Davison Publishing Ltd (United Kingdom) 406
Dawood Prize for Literature (Pakistan) 304
Dawson Publishing (United Kingdom) 406
Daystar Press (Publishers) (Nigeria) 293
Daystar Publications (India) 190
Daystar Publications (India) 201
De Bono, Giuseppe, Editore (Italy) 223
De Donato Società Editrice Cooperativa (Italy) 223
De Vecchi, Editions, SA (France) 95
De Vecchi, Editorial, SA (Spain) 339
De Vecchi, Giovanni, Editore SpA (Italy) 223
Dean and Chapter, The, Library (United Kingdom) 445
Dean & Son (United Kingdom) 406
Dearlove, Peter, Publishers (Zimbabwe) 464
Debate SA (Spain) 339
Debooks (India) 190
Debresse, Nouvelles Editions (France) 96
Debrett's Peerage Ltd (United Kingdom) 406
Debutantenpreis (German Democratic Republic) 120
Dečje Novine (Yugoslavia) 456
Decker's, R v, Verlag G Schenck GmbH (Federal Republic of Germany) 131
Decomble, Librairie Générale de l'Enseignement Mme (France) 96
Découverte/Maspero, La (France) 96
Dedalo, Edizioni, SpA (Italy) 223
Deduce SA (Mexico) 265
Deep & Deep Publications (India) 190
Dehoniane, Edizioni (Italy) 223
Dehoniane, Edizioni, Bologna (EDB) (Italy) 223
Deichmanske Bibliotek (Norway) 300
Dejaie, Maison d'Editions Cl (Belgium) 36
Dekker en Nordemann BV (Netherlands) 284
Dekker en Van de Vegt (Netherlands) 275
Dekker v d Vegt (Netherlands) 284
Delachaux et Niestlé, Editions, SA (Switzerland) 364
Delachaux et Niestlé Spes, Editions (France) 96
Delacroix, Eve, Prize (France) 112
Delagrave, Librairie, Sàrl (France) 96
Delarge, Jean-Pierre, SA (France) 96
Delarue, Editions (France) 96
Deldebat de Gonzalva Foundation Prize (France) 112
Delft University Press (Netherlands) 275
Delhi Library Association (India) 202
Delhi Public Library (India) 202
Delhi State Booksellers' and Publishers' Association (India) 185
Delhi University Library System (India) 202
Delightful Books (United Kingdom) 406
Delius, Klasing und Co (Federal Republic of Germany) 131
Delmas, Editions J, et Cie (France) 96
Delphin Verlag (Switzerland) 364
Delphin Verlag GmbH (Federal Republic of Germany) 131
Delp'sche Verlagsbuchhandlung (Federal Republic of Germany) 131
Delta Books (Pty) Ltd (Republic of South Africa) 329
Delta, Editions (Belgium) 36

Delta Editrice SpA (Italy) 223
Delta et Spes, Editions, SA (Switzerland) 364
Delta Förlags AB (Sweden) 353
Delta Press (Yugoslavia) 456
Delta Science Fiction Bok Klubb (Sweden) 358
Deltas (Belgium) 36
Demand Reprints (United Kingdom) 406
Démuth, Dr rer pol Dr Julius (Federal Republic of Germany) 167
Denayer, Felix, Prize (Belgium) 44
Denholm House Press (United Kingdom) 406
Denis & Co PVBA (Belgium) 36
Denis, Firma, & Co PVBA (Belgium) 42
Dennis, C J, Award (Australia) 22
Denoël, Editions, SA (France) 96
Dent, J M, & Sons Ltd (United Kingdom) 406
Dent, J M, Pty Ltd (Australia) 13
Denzel Verlag Auto-und Wander Führer (Austria) 25
Depalma SRL (Argentina) 4
Departamento de Bibliotecas (Colombia) 67
Departamento de Bibliotecas y Publicaciones (Mexico) 269
Departamento de Documentación y Biblioteca (Uruguay) 452
Department of National Education Library (Republic of South Africa) 334
Department of National Education Literary Prizes (Republic of South Africa) 335
Department of Publicity (Nepal) 272
Department of Science Service Library (Thailand) 381
Derecho Financiero, Editorial de (Spain) 339
Derecho Privado, Editorial Revista de (Spain) 339
Dergâh kitabevi (Turkey) 385
Dergâh kitabevi (Turkey) 385
Dergâh Yayinlari AS (Turkey) 384
Desai Bookshops (Fiji) 86
Desarrollo, Editorial, SA (Peru) 307
Desbordes-Valmore, Marceline, Prize (France) 112
Deschamps (Haiti) 178
Desclée de Brouwer SA (France) 96
Desclée, Editeurs (Belgium) 36
Desclée et Cie, Editions (France) 96
Desertina Verlag (Switzerland) 364
Desforges, Librairie (France) 96
Design Council Books (United Kingdom) 406
Desire und Gegenrealismus (Federal Republic of Germany) 131
Desmet-Huysmans PVBA (Belgium) 36
Dessain et Tolra SA (France) 96
Dessain NV, H (Belgium) 36
Dessain SPRL, F (Belgium) 36
Dessart, Engelbert, Verlag KG (Federal Republic of Germany) 131
Destino, Ediciones, SA (Spain) 339
Desvigne, Librairie André (France) 96
Detskaya Entsiklopediya (Union of Soviet Socialist Republics) 387
Detskaya Literatura, Izdatelstvo (Union of Soviet Socialist Republics) 387
Deubner, Dr Peter, Verlag GmbH (Federal Republic of Germany) 131
Deuticke, Franz, Verlagsges mbH (Austria) 25
Deutsch, André, Ltd (United Kingdom) 406
Deutsch, Verlag für (Federal Republic of Germany) 131
Deutsch, Verlag Harri (Federal Republic of Germany) 131
Deutsch, Verlag Harri (Switzerland) 364
Deutsche Akademie für Sprache und Dichtung (Federal Republic of Germany) 170
Deutsche Bibelgesellschaft (Federal Republic of Germany) 131
Deutsche Bibliothek (National Library) (Federal Republic of Germany) 168
Deutsche Blindenstudienanstalt eV (Federal Republic of Germany) 132
Deutsche Buch-Gemeinschaft C A Koch's Verlag Nachfolger (Austria) 29
Deutsche Buch-Gemeinschaft C A Koch's Verlag Nachfolger (Federal Republic of Germany) 132
Deutsche Buch-Gemeinschaft C A Koch's Verlag Nachfolger (Federal Republic of Germany) 167
Deutsche Bücherei (German Democratic Republic) 119
Deutsche Gesellschaft für Dokumentation eV (Federal Republic of Germany) 169
Deutsche Jugend-Presse-Agentur KG (Federal Republic of Germany) 132
Deutsche Philips GmbH (Federal Republic of Germany) 132
Deutsche Shakespeare-Gesellschaft West eV (Federal Republic of Germany) 170
Deutsche Staatsbibliothek (German Democratic Republic) 119
Deutsche Verlags-Anstalt GmbH (DVA) (Federal Republic of Germany) 132
Deutscher Adressbuch-Verlag für Wirtschaft und Verkehr GmbH (Federal Republic of Germany) 132
Deutscher Apotheker Verlag Dr Roland Schmiedel GmbH und Co (Federal Republic of Germany) 132

Deutscher Betriebswirte-Verlag GmbH (Federal Republic of Germany) 132
Deutscher Bücherbund GmbH & Co (Federal Republic of Germany) 167
Deutscher Buchkreis (Federal Republic of Germany) 167
Deutscher Eichverlag (Federal Republic of Germany) 132
Deutscher Fachschriften-Verlag Braun GmbH & Co KG (Federal Republic of Germany) 132
Deutscher Gemeindeverlag GmbH (Federal Republic of Germany) 132
Deutscher Instituts-Verlag GmbH (Federal Republic of Germany) 132
Deutscher, Isaac, Memorial Prize (International Literary Prizes) 476
Deutscher Jugendbuchpreis (Federal Republic of Germany) 170
Deutscher Kunstverlag GmbH (Federal Republic of Germany) 132
Deutscher Landwirtschaftsverlag, VEB (German Democratic Republic) 116
Deutscher Leihbuchhändler-Verband eV (Federal Republic of Germany) 169
Deutscher Literatur-Verlag (Federal Republic of Germany) 132
Deutscher Taschenbuch, D T V-, Verlag GmbH & Co KG (Federal Republic of Germany) 132
Deutscher Verband evangelischer Büchereien eV (Federal Republic of Germany) 169
Deutscher Verlag der Wissenschaften, VEB (German Democratic Republic) 116
Deutscher Verlag für Grundstoffindustrie, VEB (German Democratic Republic) 116
Deutscher Verlag für Kunstwissenschaft GmbH (Federal Republic of Germany) 132
Deutscher Verlag für Musik, VEB (German Democratic Republic) 116
Deutscher Wirtschaftsdienst John von Freyend GmbH (Federal Republic of Germany) 132
Deutsches Bibliotheksinstitut (Federal Republic of Germany) 169
Deutsches Jugendinstitut (DJI) (Federal Republic of Germany) 132
Deutsches Jugendschriftenwerk eV (Federal Republic of Germany) 121
Deux Coqs d'Or, Les Editions des (France) 96
Deux Magots Prize (France) 112
Deves et Chaumet, Librairie (Mali) 262
Devlin, Denis, Memorial Award for Poetry (Republic of Ireland) 212
Dewallens, A (Belgium) 36
Dewan Bahasa dan Pustaka (Malaysia) 259
Dewan Bahasa dan Pustaka (Malaysia) 261
Dewan, Perpustakaan, Perwakilan Rakjat Gotong Rojong (Indonesia) 206
Dey Sahitya Kutir (P) Ltd (India) 190
Dezsery Ethnic Publications (Australia) 13
Dhammabucha (Thailand) 380
Dhanani's Ltd (Kenya) 249
Dhanpat Rai & Sons (India) 190
Dheerasarn Ltd (Thailand) 381
Diadem Books Ltd (United Kingdom) 406
Diagram Visual Information Ltd (United Kingdom) 406
Dial (United Kingdom) 406
Diálogo, Ediciones (Paraguay) 306
Diamond Comics (P) Ltd (India) 190
Diamond Inc (Japan) 239
Dian Rakyat (Indonesia) 205
Diana, Editorial (Mexico) 265
Diana-Verlag AG (Switzerland) 364
Dianus-Trikont Buchverlag GmbH (Federal Republic of Germany) 132
Díaz, Librería, de Santos, Cientifica y Técnica (Spain) 347
Dickens, The, Fellowship (Argentina) 9
Dickens, The, Fellowship (Australia) 21
Dickens, The, Fellowship (France) 111
Dickens, The, Fellowship (Japan) 246
Dickens, The, Fellowship (Netherlands) 285
Dickens, The, Fellowship (New Zealand) 291
Dickens, The, Fellowship (Sri Lanka) 350
Dickens, The, Fellowship (United Kingdom) 447
Dickson, Keith (United Kingdom) 406
Dickson Price Publishers Ltd (United Kingdom) 406
Dictionnaire, La Maison du (France) 96
Didactica si Pedagogica, Editura (Romania) 321
Didax (Switzerland) 364
Diderich, Librairie, Sàrl (Grand Duchy of Luxembourg) 257
Diderot, Livre Club (France) 109
Didier Editions, John (France) 96
Didot-Bottin, Société, SA (France) 96
Diederichs, Eugen, Verlag GmbH & Co KG (Federal Republic of Germany) 132
Diesterweg, Verlag Moritz, /Otto Salle Verlag (Federal Republic of Germany) 133
Dieterich'sche Verlagsbuchhandlung (German Democratic Republic) 117
Dietz Verlag (German Democratic Republic) 117

508 INDEX

Dietz, Verlag J H W, Nachf GmbH (Federal Republic of Germany) 133
Diffusion de la Presse (Zaire) 462
Difros (Greece) 174
Difusão Editorial SA (DIFEL) (Brazil) 50
Difusión, Centro de, del Libro (Spain) 339
Difusión, Editorial (Bolivia) 46
Difusión, Editorial, SA (Argentina) 4
Difusión, Librería (Bolivia) 46
Dijkstra's Uitg Mij, Jacob, BV (Netherlands) 275
Dijkstra's Uitgeverij Zeist BV (Netherlands) 275
Diki-Books Srl (Italy) 223
Dilagro SA (Spain) 339
Diligentia BV (Netherlands) 275
Diligentia-Uitgeverij (Belgium) 36
Dillon's University Bookshop (United Kingdom) 444
Dimashk, Dar, (Adib Tunbakji) Bookshop (Syria) 377
Dimensione, Edizioni, Umana (Italy) 223
Dimitrov' Academy, Central Agricultural Library of the 'G, of Agricultural Sciences (Bulgaria) 59
Dini Book Depot (India) 190
Dinosaur Publications Ltd (United Kingdom) 406
Diogenes, Editorial, SA (Mexico) 265
Diogenes Verlag AG (Switzerland) 364
Dipa-Verlag und Druck GmbH & Co (Federal Republic of Germany) 133
Diponegoro, C V (Indonesia) 205
Direcção dos Serviços de Geologia e Minas de Angola Biblioteca (Angola) 2
Dirección de Cultura, Biblioteca de la (Bolivia) 47
Dirección de Estadística y Censo (Panama) 304
Dirección de Publicaciones (Costa Rica) 68
Direction des Bibliothèques des Musées et de l'Information Scientifique et Technique (France) 110
Directorate of Archives and Libraries (Bangladesh) 32
Directorate of Publications (Republic of South Africa) 328
Directory Publishers of Zambia Ltd (Zambia) 463
Discailles, Ernest, Prize (International Literary Prizes) 476
Disesa (Dominican Republic) 82
Dishoeck, van (Netherlands) 275
Disney Junior Bokklub (Norway) 300
Dissal SA Le CU (El Salvador) 85
Distasa (Argentina) 4
Distribución, SA de, Edición y Librerías (DELSA) (Spain) 347
Distribuidora de Libros (Guatemala) 177
Distribuidora de Libros Inc (Puerto Rico) 320
Distribuidora Escolar SA (DISESA) (Dominican Republic) 82
Distribuidora Literaria SA (Mexico) 268
Distributors' Centre for Israeli Books Ltd (Israel) 217
Ditmar, van (Netherlands) 275
Diwan, The, Library, Ministry of Education (Iraq) 208
Djambatan, De Brug-, BV (Netherlands) 275
Djambatan, P T, Penerbit NV (Indonesia) 205
Doaba House (India) 190
Döblin, Alfred-, Institution Prize (Federal Republic of Germany) 170
Doblinger, Ludwig, (Bernard Herzmansky) Musikverlag (Austria) 25
Dobloug Prize (Sweden) 360
Dobloug Prize (International Literary Prizes) 476
Dobson, Dennis, (Dobson Books Ltd) (United Kingdom) 406
Doctrine and Life Book Club (Republic of Ireland) 211
Documentaire Research, Hoofdafdeling, en Informatieverstrekking van de Exportbevorderings- en Voorlichtingsdienst (Netherlands) 284
Documentation et d'Analyses, Société de, Financières (France) 96
Documentation Française, La (France) 96
Documentation Internationale, Bibliothèque de, Contemporaine (France) 110
Documentation Research and Training Centre (India) 202
Dodoni (Greece) 174
Doepgen, Edition, Verlag (Belgium) 36
Dogan Kardes Matbaacilik SAS (Turkey) 384
Doin Editeurs (France) 96
Dokumentasi Ilmiah Nasional, Pusat (Indonesia) 206
Dokumentation Saur, Verlag, KG (Federal Republic of Germany) 133
Dokumentationsstelle für neuere österreichische Literatur (Austria) 30
Dollar Books (Australia) 13
Dolmen, The, Press Ltd (Republic of Ireland) 209
Dolphin (United Kingdom) 406
Dolphin Publishers SRL (Italy) 223
Dom Ksiazki (Poland) 313
Dom Quixote, Publicações, Lda (Portugal) 316
Domi, Ekdoseis, AE (Greece) 174
Domini sumus Verlag GmbH (Federal Republic of Germany) 133
Dominican Books — Distribution Inc (Dominican Republic) 81
Dominican Publications (Republic of Ireland) 209
Domowina, VEB, Verlag (German Democratic Republic) 117

Domus Editoriale (Italy) 223
Don Bosco, Editorial, SA (Mexico) 265
Don Bosco Verlag der Gesellschaft der Salesianer (Federal Republic of Germany) 133
Donald Ducks Bokklubb (Norway) 300
Donald, John, Publishers Ltd (United Kingdom) 406
Donauland, Buchgemeinschaft (Austria) 29
Dong Wha Publishing Co (Republic of Korea) 250
Dongguk University Library (Republic of Korea) 252
Donker, Ad, Ltd (United Kingdom) 406
Donker, Ad, (Pty) Ltd (Republic of South Africa) 329
Donker, Uitgeversmaatschappij Ad, BV (Netherlands) 275
Dopravy, Nakladatelství, a spoju (Czechoslovakia) 71
Dorikos Makridis (Greece) 174
Dorling Kindersley Ltd (United Kingdom) 407
Dorp Aruba, Van, NV (Netherlands Antilles) 286
Dorp-Eddine, Van, NV (Netherlands Antilles) 286
Dosaaf, Znak Pochyota Order, Publishing House (Union of Soviet Socialist Republics) 387
Dossat, Editorial, SA (Spain) 339
Doubleday & Co Inc (United Kingdom) 407
Doubleday Australia Pty Ltd (Australia) 13
Doubleday Australia Pty Ltd, Book Club Division (Australia) 19
Doubleday Book Club (Australia) 19
Doubleday Book Club (New Zealand) 290
Doubleday-France (France) 96
Doubleday History Book Club (Australia) 19
Doubleday History Book Club (New Zealand) 290
Doubleday Military Book Club (New Zealand) 290
Doubleday New Zealand Ltd (New Zealand) 288
Doubleday New Zealand Ltd, Book Club Division (New Zealand) 290
Doucet, Bibliothèque littéraire Jacques (France) 110
Douglas, The, Public Library (Isle of Man) 212
Doulos Verlag (Switzerland) 364
Dove Communications Pty Ltd (Australia) 13
Doxa University Books (Sweden) 353
Doyma, Ediciones, SA (Spain) 339
Draeger Editeur (France) 96
Dragon Books (United Kingdom) 407
Dragon's World Ltd (United Kingdom) 407
Drammen Folkebibliotek (Norway) 300
Drei Eichen Verlag AG (Switzerland) 364
Drei Eidgenossen Verlag (Switzerland) 364
Dreisam-Verlag (Federal Republic of Germany) 133
Dreiseitel, Galerie (Federal Republic of Germany) 133
Drejtoria Quëndrore e Përhapjes dhe e Propagandimit të Librit (Albania) 1
Dressler, Cecilie, Verlag (Federal Republic of Germany) 133
Drew, Richard, Publishing Ltd (United Kingdom) 407
Dreyers Forlag A/S (Norway) 298
Driehoek, De, BV (Netherlands) 275
Droemersche Verlagsanstalt AG (Switzerland) 364
Droemersche Verlagsanstalt Th Knaur Nachf (Federal Republic of Germany) 133
Droguet et Ardant (France) 96
Droit et de Jurisprudence, Librairie Générale de (France) 97
Droste Verlag GmbH (Federal Republic of Germany) 133
Drouot, Librairie, (Ets Robert Drouot) (Benin) 45
Droz, Librairie, SA (Switzerland) 364
Druckenmüller Verlag (Federal Republic of Germany) 133
Druffel-Verlag (Federal Republic of Germany) 133
Druida, Ediciones, SA (Spain) 339
Drukarnia Narodowa (Poland) 311
Drukkerij de Stad NV (Netherlands Antilles) 286
Drummond (Australia) 13
Društvo bibliotekara Bosne i Hercegovine (Yugoslavia) 461
Društvo bibliotekarjev Slovenije (Yugoslavia) 461
Društvo na arhivskite rabotnici i arhivite na SRM (Yugoslavia) 461
Društvo na literaturnite prevoduvači na SRM (Yugoslavia) 461
Društvo na pisatelite na SRM (Yugoslavia) 461
Društvo za srpski jezik i književnost (Yugoslavia) 461
Državna Založba Slovenije (Yugoslavia) 456
Državna Založba Slovenije (Yugoslavia) 460
Duang Kamol (Thailand) 380
Duas Cidades, Livraria (Brazil) 56
Duas Cidades, Livraria, Ltda (Brazil) 50
Dublin Institute for Advanced Studies (Republic of Ireland) 209
Dublin Public Libraries (Republic of Ireland) 211
Duckworth, Gerald, & Co Ltd (United Kingdom) 407
Duculot, Editions et Imprimerie J, SA (Belgium) 36
Duculot, Jules, Prize (Belgium) 44
Duden, Konrad, Prize (Federal Republic of Germany) 170
Duff Cooper Memorial Prize (International Literary Prizes) 476
Dufour, Henry-Robert (Switzerland) 364
Duke of Alba Prize (Spain) 348
Duke University Press (United Kingdom) 407
Dülk, Monika, Verlag (Federal Republic of Germany) 133
Dumas-Millier Prize (France) 112

Dumjahn, Horst-Werner, Verlag (Federal Republic of Germany) 133
Dummer, Wolfgang, und Co (Federal Republic of Germany) 133
Dümmlers, Ferd, Verlag (Federal Republic of Germany) 133
DuMont Buchverlag GmbH & Co KG (Federal Republic of Germany) 133
Dun & Bradstreet Ltd (United Kingdom) 407
Duncker und Humblot (Federal Republic of Germany) 133
Dunedin Public Library (New Zealand) 290
Dunia, P T, Pustaka Jaya (Indonesia) 205
Dunitz, Martin, Ltd (United Kingdom) 407
Dunmore Press Ltd (New Zealand) 288
Dunod (France) 97
Dunrod, The, Press (United Kingdom) 407
Dupuch, Etienne, Jr Publications Ltd (Bahamas) 31
Dupuis, Editions Jean, SA (Belgium) 36
Dupuis, Maison d'Editions J, Fils et Cie SA (France) 97
Durban Municipal Library (Republic of South Africa) 334
Durham University Library (United Kingdom) 445
Durvan SA de Ediciones (Spain) 339
Dustri-Verlag Dr Karl Feistle (Federal Republic of Germany) 133
Dutch Literature Prize (Netherlands) 285
Dutch Literature Prize (International Literary Prizes) 476
Dutch Prize for the Best Children's Book (Netherlands) 285
Dutch Reformed Church Publishers (Republic of South Africa) 329
Dutens, Alfred, Prize (France) 112
Duttweiler, Gottlieb, Institute for Economic & Social Studies (Switzerland) 364
Duvivier, Charles, Prize (Belgium) 44
'Dvir Bialik' Municipal Central Public Library (Israel) 218
Dvir, The, Publishing Co Ltd (Israel) 214
Dymock's Pty Ltd (Australia) 20
Dynamis Verlag (Switzerland) 364

E A Books (Australia) 13
E A C (France) 97
E B A L (Brazil) 50
E B E, Edizioni (Italy) 223
E C A Bookshop Co-op Society (Ethiopia) 86
E C A (Ediciones Culturales Argentinas) (Argentina) 4
E C I voor Boeken en Grammofoonplaten BV (Netherlands) 275
E C I voor Boeken en Platen BV (Netherlands) 284
E C Print AB (Sweden) 353
E C Print AB (Sweden) 360
E C W A Productions Ltd (Nigeria) 293
E D A M E X (Mexico) 265
E D B (Italy) 223
E D E R S A (Editoriales de Derecho Reunidas SA) (Spain) 339
E D H A S A (Editora y Distribuidora Hispano-Americana SA) (Spain) 339
E D H I S (France) 97
E D I M E, Distribuciones (Venezuela) 453
E D T/Musica (Italy) 223
E D U I D A, Ediciones, SA (Spain) 339
E F S-förlaget (Sweden) 353
E L D Trust (Republic of South Africa) 329
E M B L A (Norway) 300
E M E S C O Book Club (India) 201
E O S Verlag, Erzabtei Sankt Ottilien (Federal Republic of Germany) 133
E P A SA (France) 97
E P Book Depot (Ghana) 172
E P O (Belgium) 36
E P Publishing Ltd (United Kingdom) 407
E P U (Brazil) 50
E R B (Czechoslovakia) 73
E R G A (Edizioni Realizzazioni Grafiche — Artigiana) (Italy) 223
E R I — Edizioni R A I Radiotelevisione Italiana SpA (Italy) 223
E S A Bookshop (Kenya) 249
E S A Bookshop (Uganda) 386
E S A Creative Learning Ltd (United Kingdom) 407
E S C Publishing Ltd (United Kingdom) 407
E S D U C K (Egypt) 83
E S F, Editions, (Editions Sociales Françaises) (France) 97
E S H (English for Speakers of Hebrew) (Israel) 214
E S I (Italy) 223
E S Training Services Ltd (United Kingdom) 407
E T A (Editora Técnica de Aviação Ltda) (Brazil) 50
E T H Bibliothek (Eidgenössische Technische Hochschule Bibliothek) (Switzerland) 376
E T S F (France) 97
E U D E B A (Editorial Universitaria de Buenos Aires) (Argentina) 5

E U N S A (Ediciones Universidad de Navarra SA) (Spain) 339
Eagle Editions (Switzerland) 364
Early English Text Society (United Kingdom) 447
Eason & Son Ltd (Republic of Ireland) 209
Eason & Son Ltd (Republic of Ireland) 211
East African Directory Co (Kenya) 248
East African Literature Bureau (Kenya) 248
East African Publishing House (Kenya) 248
East and Central Africa Regional Branch of the International Council of Archives (ECARBICA) (International Organizations) 467
East and West Centre Pte Ltd (Republic of Singapore) 327
East and West Publishing Co (Pakistan) 302
East Anglian Writers (United Kingdom) 447
East Asia Book Co (Hong Kong) 180
East-West Publications Fonds BV (Netherlands) 275
East-West Publications (UK) Ltd (United Kingdom) 407
Eastern Africa Publications Ltd (Tanzania) 379
Eastern Book Co (India) 190
Eastern Book Service Corp (Philippines) 309
Eastern Book Service Ltd (Hong Kong) 180
Eastern Book Service Pte Ltd (Republic of Singapore) 327
Eastern Book Service Sdn Bhd (wholesalers) (Malaysia) 261
Eastern Law House Pvt Ltd (India) 190
Eastern Universities Press (Malaysia) 259
Eastern Universities Press Sdn Bhd (Republic of Singapore) 326
Eastland Press (United Kingdom) 407
Eastview Production Sdn Bhd (Malaysia) 259
Ebeling, Hasso (Grand Duchy of Luxembourg) 257
Ebeling, Hasso, Verlag (Grand Duchy of Luxembourg) 256
Ebeling Verlag GmbH (Federal Republic of Germany) 133
Ebibi Book Centre (United Republic of Cameroon) 61
Eblana, The, Bookshop (Republic of Ireland) 211
Ebraesp Editorial Ltda (Brazil) 50
Ebury Press (United Kingdom) 407
Ecart Publications (Switzerland) 364
Ecclesia Press (Republic of Ireland) 209
Echevarría', Biblioteca 'José Antonio (Cuba) 69
Echeverría, Aquileo T, Prize (Costa Rica) 69
Echter Würzburg Fränkische Gesellschafts-Druckerei (Federal Republic of Germany) 133
Eck, Frank P van (Liechtenstein) 256
Eckersteins, Esselte Bokhandel (Sweden) 358
Eco-Verlags AG (Switzerland) 364
Ecole, Bibliothèque l', nationale d'administration du Niger (Niger) 292
Ecole, Bibliothèque de l', des Langues orientales (France) 110
Ecole, Bibliothèque de l', normale supérieure (Senegal) 324
Ecole, Bibliothèque de l', normale supérieure (Togo) 382
Ecole, Bibliothèque de l', royale de Médecine (Laos) 253
Ecole, Bibliothèque de l', supérieure des Lettres (Lebanon) 254
Ecole, L', /L'Ecole des Loisirs Sàrl (France) 97
Ecole Mohammedia d'Ingénieurs (Morocco) 271
Ecole nationale d'Administration Bibliothèque (Tunisia) 383
Ecole nationale polytechnique, Bibliothèque (Algeria) 2
Ecole normale primaire et supérieure, Bibliothèque (Central African Republic) 62
Ecole normale supérieure (Mali) 262
Ecole normale supérieure, Bibliothèque (Burundi) 60
Ecole normale supérieure, Bibliothèque (United Republic of Cameroun) 61
Ecole normale supérieure Bibliothèque (Gabon) 115
Ecole normale supérieure de l'Afrique centrale, Bibliothèque (Popular Republic of Congo) 68
Ecole Professionelle de la Mission Catholique (Togo) 382
Ecoles, Librairie des (Morocco) 271
Ecoma, Editorial, SA (Peru) 307
Econ-Verlag GmbH (Federal Republic of Germany) 133
Econ Verlagsgruppe (Federal Republic of Germany) 134
Economic and Industrial Publications (Pakistan) 302
Economische Voorlichtingsdienst, Bibliotheek- en Documentatie-centrum van de (Netherlands) 284
Economist, The, Publications Department (United Kingdom) 407
Ecumenical Literature, The, Distribution Trust (Republic of South Africa) 329
Edaf Ediciones y Distribuciones SA (Spain) 339
Edagricole (Edizioni Agricole) (Italy) 223
Edameris (Brazil) 50
Edanim Publishers (Israel) 214
Edart São Paulo Livraria Editora Ltda (Brazil) 50
Eddison Press Ltd (United Kingdom) 407
Eddison Sadd Editions Ltd (United Kingdom) 407
Edekes Bookshop Stores Ltd (Nigeria) 296
Edelcid Libros Científicos (Guatemala) 177
Edi-Art (Belgium) 36
Edi Thule Club (Italy) 234
Edibimbi SRL (Italy) 223
Edica SA (Spain) 339

Edicient SAIC (Argentina) 5
Ediciones de la Biblioteca (EBUC) (Venezuela) 453
Ediciones Iberoamericanas SA (EISA) (Spain) 339
Ediciones Pedagógicas Dominicanas C por A (Dominican Republic) 81
Ediciones Populares (Netherlands Antilles) 286
Edicol, Editorial, SA (Mexico) 265
Edigraf, Editorial Vilcar y Gráficas Hamburg SA (Spain) 339
Edil, Editorial, Inc (Puerto Rico) 319
Edinburgh Bibliographical Society (United Kingdom) 447
Edinburgh University Library (United Kingdom) 445
Edinburgh University Press (United Kingdom) 407
Edinburgh University Student Publications Board (United Kingdom) 408
Edinorma Ltda y Cia SCA (Colombia) 66
Edipem SpA (Italy) 223
Ediscience (France) 97
Edisud (France) 97
Edit, NiP (Yugoslavia) 457
Edita SA (Switzerland) 364
Editalia (Edizioni d'Italia) (Italy) 223
Editart, Société, Quatre Chemins (France) 97
Editeurs Associés SA (Switzerland) 364
Editeurs de Litterature Biblique (Belgium) 36
Editeurs Réunis, Les (France) 97
Edition No I (France) 97
Editions Arabes, Les (Lebanon) 254
Editions des Archives Contemporaines (France) 97
Editions interuniversitaires (Belgium) 36
Editions Juridiques et Techniques (France) 97
Editions Maritimes et d'Outre-Mer SA (France) 97
Editions Modernes Média (France) 97
Editions Sociales Françaises (France) 97
Editions Sociales-Messidor, Les (France) 97
Editions Techniques et Scientifiques Françaises (France) 97
Editions techniques et scientifiques SPRL (Belgium) 36
Editions Techniques SA (France) 97
Editions Universitaires-Editions du Jour SA (France) 97
Editions universitaires, Les, d'Egypte (Egypt) 83
Editions universitaires SA (Belgium) 36
Editions Universitaires SA (Universitätsverlag) (Switzerland) 364
Editnemo (Italy) 223
Edito-Service SA (Switzerland) 365
Editogo (Togo) 382
Editora Cultural Dominicana (Dominican Republic) 82
Editora Educativa Dominicana (Dominican Republic) 82
Editora Interamericana Ltda (Brazil) 50
Editora Internacional (Dominican Republic) 82
Editora Moderna Ltda (Brazil) 50
Editora Nacional (Mexico) 265
Editora Nacional (Spain) 340
Editora Nacional, Cía (Brazil) 50
Editora Pedagogica e Universitaria Ltda (EPU) (Brazil) 50
Editorama SA (Dominican Republic) 82
Editores Asociados Mexicanos SA (EDAMEX) (Mexico) 265
Editori, Associazione Italiana degli, di Musica (AIDEM) (Italy) 219
Editorial and Publishing Services (Ghana) 172
Editorial Consultancy & Agency Services (Nigeria) 296
Editorial Cultural (Puerto Rico) 319
Editorial Interamericana del Ecuador CA (Ecuador) 82
Editorial Interamericana SA (Peru) 307
Editorial Librería Dominicana (Dominican Republic) 82
Editorial Sudamericana SA (Argentina) 5
Editorial Universidad SRL (Argentina) 5
Editorial Universitaria (Honduras) 178
Editorial Universitaria (Panama) 304
Editorial Universitaria Centroamericana (EDUCA) (Costa Rica) 68
Editorial Universitaria de Buenos Aires (Argentina) 5
Editorial Universitaria de la Universidad de El Salvador (El Salvador) 85
Editorialebari (Italy) 223
Editrice Bibliografica Srl (Italy) 223
Editrice Cooperativa (Italy) 223
Editrice Scientifica, L' (Italy) 223
Edizioni del Centro (Italy) 223
Educa International (Netherlands) 275
Educaboek BV (Netherlands) 275
Education et Culture (France) 109
Educational Aids Production Co Pte Ltd (Republic of Singapore) 327
Educational Book Centre (Israel) 217
Educational Book Centre Pte Ltd (Republic of Singapore) 327
Educational Books Publishing House (Democratic People's Republic of Korea) 250
Educational Company, The, of Ireland Ltd (Republic of Ireland) 209
Educational Enterprise (Nepal) 272
Educational Enterprises (India) 190
Educational Enterprises (Pvt) Ltd (Nepal) 272
Educational Explorers Ltd (United Kingdom) 408
Educational Library (Saudi Arabia) 323

INDEX 509

Educational Material Aid (Australia) 13
Educational Productions Ltd (United Kingdom) 408
Educational Publishers' Association (India) 185
Educational Publishers Council (United Kingdom) 391
Educational Research Institute (Nigeria) 293
Educational Systems Ltd (United Kingdom) 408
Educational, The, Publishing House Ltd (Hong Kong) 179
Educational Writers' Group (United Kingdom) 391
Educum Uitgewers Beperk (Republic of South Africa) 330
Edumeds Pty Ltd (Namibia) 272
Eduskunnan Kirjasto (Finland) 89
Edutec International Ltd (Hong Kong) 179
Edwardian Studies Association (United Kingdom) 447
Edwards & Shaw Pty Ltd (Australia) 13
Effendi Harahap Bookstore (Indonesia) 206
Efstathiadis, P, & Sons SA (Greece) 174
Efstathiadis, P, & Sons SA (Greece) 176
Egan, Wm, & Sons (Republic of Ireland) 211
Egerton College Library (Kenya) 249
Eghbal Co (Iran) 207
Egyptian Association for Archives and Librarianship (Egypt) 84
Egyptian Cultural Center Library (Libya) 256
Egyptian Society, The, for the Dissemination of Universal Culture and Knowledge (ESDUCK) (Egypt) 83
Egyptian Society, The, for the Dissemination of Universal Culture and Knowledge (ESDUCK) (Egypt) 84
Egyptian Society, The, for the Dissemination of Universal Culture and Knowledge (ESDUCK) (Egypt) 85
Ehrenwirth Verlag GmbH (Federal Republic of Germany) 134
Ehrlingförlagen AB (Sweden) 353
Eibungakkai, Nihon (Japan) 246
Eichborn Verlag (Federal Republic of Germany) 134
Eide, J W, Forlag A/S (Norway) 298
Eike-Boekklub (Republic of South Africa) 333
Einaudi, Giulio, Editore SpA (Italy) 223
Eindhoven Druk BV/Boekprodukties (Netherlands) 275
Eiselé, André (Switzerland) 365
Eisenbahn-Kurier Verlag (Federal Republic of Germany) 134
Eisenbahn, Verlag, R Jeanmaire & Co (Switzerland) 365
Ejlers', Christian, Forlag A/S (Denmark) 76
Ekblad-Eldhs, Signe, Prize (Sweden) 360
Eked Publishing House (Israel) 214
Ekenäs Tryckeri AB (Finland) 87
Ekonomiczne, Państwowe Wydawnictwo (Poland) 311
'Ekonomika', Izdatelstvo (Union of Soviet Socialist Republics) 387
Ekstrabøker, Bokklubbens (Norway) 300
El-Am Publishing (Israel) Ltd (Israel) 214
El Dorado Ltda (Colombia) 67
Elder, Anne, Poetry Award (Australia) 22
Eldorado, A Casa do Livro, Ltda (Brazil) 56
Eldorado, NV Drukkerij (Suriname) 351
Electa Editrice (Italy) 224
Elefante, Edizioni dell' (Italy) 224
Eleftheroudakis, G C, Co Ltd (Greece) 176
Eleftheroudakis, G C, SA (Greece) 174
Elek, Paul, Ltd (United Kingdom) 408
Eletrônicas Editora, Seleções, Ltda (Brazil) 50
Elfos, Ediciones (Spain) 340
Elgin, Mary, Prize (International Literary Prizes) 476
Elif Kitabevi (Turkey) 384
Elingaard Forlag A/S (Norway) 298
Eliri (Nigeria) 294
Elisas Sourasky Central Library, Tel Aviv University (Israel) 218
Elizabethan Publishing House (Nigeria) 294
Elkan och Schildknecht (Sweden) 353
Ell, David, Press Pty Ltd (Australia) 13
Ellenberg Verlag GmbH (Federal Republic of Germany) 134
Ellermann, Verlag Heinrich, GmbH & Co KG (Federal Republic of Germany) 134
Elliot Right Way Books (United Kingdom) 408
Ellis, Aidan, Publishing Ltd (United Kingdom) 408
Elm Tree Books Ltd (United Kingdom) 408
Elmar BV (Netherlands) 275
Elpis Verlag GmbH (Federal Republic of Germany) 134
Elron Press Ltd (United Kingdom) 408
Elsässer, Buchhandlung zum, AG (Switzerland) 375
Elsevier Applied Science Publishers (United Kingdom) 408
Elsevier Biomedical Press (Netherlands) 276
Elsevier Boeken BV (Elsevier Books International) (Netherlands) 276
Elsevier, BV Uitgeversmaatschappij (Netherlands) 275
Elsevier, Editions, Séquoia Sàrl (France) 97
Elsevier Librico NV (Belgium) 36
Elsevier-NDU nv (Netherlands) 276
Elsevier Science Publishers BV (Netherlands) 276
Elsevier Sequoia SA (Switzerland) 365
Elsevier's Wetenschappelijke Uitgeverij (Netherlands) 276
Elwert, N G, Verlag (Federal Republic of Germany) 134
Elwert und Meurer GmbH (Federal Republic of Germany) 134

Elwert und Meurer GmbH, Buchhandlung (Federal Republic of Germany) 167
Emblem (United Kingdom) 408
Embryo (United Kingdom) 408
Emecé Editores SA (Argentina) 5
Emecé Mexicana SA de CV (Mexico) 265
Emecé, Premio, Annual Prize (Argentina) 9
Eminescu, Editura (Romania) 321
Emmanuel Publishing Services (Ghana) 172
Emmaus (Belgium) 36
Emme Edizioni (Italy) 224
Emmentaler Druck AG (Switzerland) 365
Emograph (Spain) 340
Emotan Publishing Co (Nigeria) Ltd (Nigeria) 294
Empire International Club (Italy) 235
Empire Shop (Montserrat) 270
Emporium, The (Belize) 45
Empresa Moderna Lda (Mozambique) 271
Empresas Editoriales SA (Mexico) 265
En-Najah (Tunisia) 383
En-Najah, Librairie (Tunisia) 383
Enciclopédia, Editorial, Lda (Portugal) 316
Encounters (United Kingdom) 443
'Encouragement Prize' (Austria) 31
Encre, Editions (France) 97
Encuentro, Ediciones, SA (Spain) 340
Encyclopaedia Africana Project (Ghana) 172
Encyclopaedia Britannica (Federal Republic of Germany) 134
Encyclopaedia Britannica (Australia) Inc (Australia) 13
Encyclopaedia Britannica de Venezuela SA (Dominican Republic) 82
Encyclopaedia Britannica International Ltd (United Kingdom) 408
Encyclopaedia Judaica (Israel) 214
Encyclopaedia Universalis France SA (France) 97
Energoizdat, Izdatelstvo (Union of Soviet Socialist Republics) 387
Energy Publications (Cambridge) (United Kingdom) 408
Engel, Friedemann von, Verlag (Federal Republic of Germany) 134
Engelbert-Verlag GmbH (Federal Republic of Germany) 134
Engelman, Camille, Prize (International Literary Prizes) 476
Engels, Carl, Musikverlag (Federal Republic of Germany) 134
Engineering Industry Training Board Publications (United Kingdom) 408
Englind, Teaterförlag Arvid, AB (Sweden) 358
Englisch, F, Verlag GmbH (Federal Republic of Germany) 134
English Agency, The, (Japan) (Japan) 244
English Association (United Kingdom) 447
English Association (South African Branch) Literary Prize (Republic of South Africa) 335
English Book Club (Netherlands) 284
English Book Store (India) 201
English Bookshop, The (Iceland) 184
English-Speaking Union Book Award (International Literary Prizes) 476
Enigma Books (United Kingdom) 408
Enke, Ferdinand, Verlag (Federal Republic of Germany) 134
Ennsthaler, Wilhelm (Austria) 25
Enossis Ellenon Bibliothakarion (Greece) 176
Enriquillo, Editora (Dominican Republic) 82
Enschede en Zonen Grafische Inrichting BV (Netherlands) 276
Enseignement laïc, Coopérative de l' (France) 97
Enseignement Sàrl, Librairie Générale de l' (France) 97
Ensslin Jugendbuchverlag (Federal Republic of Germany) 134
Ensslin und Laiblin Verlag GmbH & Co KG (Federal Republic of Germany) 134
Ente Nazionale per le Biblioteche Popolari e Scolastiche (Italy) 235
Entente, Editions (France) 97
Enterprise nationale du Livre (ENAL) (Algeria) 2
Entreprise Moderne d'Edition (France) 97
Enzyklopädie, VEB Verlag, Leipzig (German Democratic Republic) 117
Eötvös Loránd Tudományegyetem Egyetemi Könyvtár (Hungary) 182
Epargne, Les Editions de l' (France) 97
Epi SA Editeurs (France) 97
Epoca, Librería (Peru) 307
'Epoka', Wydawnictwo (Poland) 311
Eppinger, Hans P (Federal Republic of Germany) 134
Epworth Press (United Kingdom) 408
Equestri, L L Edizioni, Srl (Italy) 224
Equinox (Oxford) Ltd (United Kingdom) 408
Era Book Enterprises (India) 190
Era, Ediciones, SA (Mexico) 265
Era Publications (Australia) 13
Erasme, Editions, (Scriptoria NV) (Belgium) 36
Erdmann, Edition (Federal Republic of Germany) 134

Erdmann Verlag, Horst, für Internationalen Kulturaustausch (Federal Republic of Germany) 134
Erehwon Publishing House (Philippines) 308
Erel PVBA (Belgium) 37
Eremiten-Presse und Verlag GmbH (Federal Republic of Germany) 134
Eres, Edition, Horst Schubert Musikverlag (Federal Republic of Germany) 134
Eresco PT (Indonesia) 205
Erhvervsarkivet-Statens Erhvervshistoriske Arkiv (Denmark) 80
Erichsens, Chr, Forlag A/S (Denmark) 76
Erikssons, The Lydia and Herman, Prize (Sweden) 360
Erker-Galerie AG (Switzerland) 365
Erlanger Foundation Prize (France) 112
Erlangga (Indonesia) 205
Erlbaum, Lawrence, Associates Ltd (United Kingdom) 408
Erma, L', di Bretschneider (Italy) 224
Ermes, Edi, Srl (Italy) 224
Ernst, Wilhelm, und Sohn (Federal Republic of Germany) 134
Ernster, Librairie (Grand Duchy of Luxembourg) 257
Erota-Press (Federal Republic of Germany) 135
Erpf, Edition, AG (Switzerland) 365
Erudita Publications (Pty) Ltd (Republic of South Africa) 330
Escobo (Dominican Republic) 82
Escolar, Livraria, Infante (Portugal) 316
Escorial, Librería (Puerto Rico) 320
Escorts Book Award (India) 203
Escuela Nacional de Biblioteconomía y Archivonomía (Mexico) 269
Esfinge, Editorial, SA (Mexico) 265
Eshkol-Jerusalem (Israel) 214
Eska (Netherlands) 276
Espacio Editora SA (Argentina) 5
Española, Librería, SCA (Argentina) 8
Espasa-Calpe Argentina SA (Argentina) 5
Espasa-Calpe, Casa del Libro, SA (Spain) 347
Espasa-Calpe, Editorial, SA (Spain) 340
Espasa-Calpe Mexicana SA (Mexico) 265
Espaxs, Editorial, SA (Spain) 340
Espejo de España Prize (Spain) 349
Espinosa, Manuel, y Cortina Prize (Spain) 349
Espiritualista, Editora (Brazil) 50
Esquire (Lebanon) 254
Ess Ess Publications (India) 190
Esselte Focus Uppslagsböcker AB (Sweden) 353
Esselte Förlag AB (Sweden) 353
Esselte Herzogs AB (Sweden) 354
Esselte Map Service (Sweden) 354
Esselte Studium AB (Sweden) 354
Est-Ouest, Editions (Belgium) 37
Este, Librería del (Venezuela) 454
Estense, Biblioteca (Italy) 234
Estoup et Roy, Publications, Sàrl (France) 98
Estrada, Angel, y Cia SA (Argentina) 5
Estúdios, Editorial, Cor Sarl (Portugal) 316
Età, Edizioni L', dell'Acquario (Italy) 224
Etablissements Généraux d'Imprimerie SA (Belgium) 37
Etairia Ellinon Logotechnon (Greece) 174
Etas Libri (Italy) 224
Etelä-Suomen Kustannus Oy (Finland) 87
Eteria Ellinikon Ekdoseon (Greece) 174
Ethiope Publishing Corporation (Nigeria) 294
Ethiopian Library Association (Ethiopia) 86
Ethiopian Manuscript Microfilm Library (Ethiopia) 86
Etna-Taormina International Poetry Prize (International Literary Prizes) 476
Etudes Augustiniennes (France) 98
Eugenides Foundation Technical Library (Greece) 176
Eulama (Italy) 236
Eulama SA (Italy) 224
Eulama SA (Italy) 233
Eulenburg Edition GmbH (Switzerland) 365
Eulenhof-Verlag Ehrhardt Heinold (Federal Republic of Germany) 135
Eulenspiegel Verlag für Satir und Humor (German Democratic Republic) 117
Eulyoo Publishing Co Ltd (Republic of Korea) 250
Euphorion, Freundeskreis des, Verlags (Federal Republic of Germany) 167
Euphorion Verlag Hans Imhoff (Federal Republic of Germany) 135
Eurasia Publishing House Pvt Ltd (India) 190
Eurédif (Société Européenne d'Edition et de Diffusion) (France) 98
Euroamericanas, Ediciones (Mexico) 265
Eurobook Ltd (United Kingdom) 408
Eurobooks (United Kingdom) 408
Euromonitor Publications Ltd (United Kingdom) 408
Europa (Belgium) 37
Europa-America, Publicações, Lda (Portugal) 316
Europa, Edizioni (Italy) 224
Europa, Forlaget (Denmark) 76
Európa Könyvkiadó (Hungary) 181

Europa-Lehrmittel, Verlag, Nourney, Vollmer GmbH & Co (Federal Republic of Germany) 135
Europa Publications Ltd (United Kingdom) 408
Europa-Verlag AG (Switzerland) 365
Europa Verlags-GmbH (Austria) 25
Europabuch AG (Switzerland) 365
Europäische Bildungsgemeinschaft Verlags GmbH (Federal Republic of Germany) 167
Europäische Buch, Das (Federal Republic of Germany) 135
Europäische Gemeinschaften (European Communities) (Federal Republic of Germany) 135
Europäische Verlagsanstalt GmbH (Federal Republic of Germany) 135
Europaring der Buch- und Schallplattenfreunde (Federal Republic of Germany) 167
Europaring der Buch- und Schallplattenfreunde (Switzerland) 375
European Association for the Promotion of Poetry (International Organizations) 467
European Association of Directory Publishers (International Organizations) 467
European Law Centre Ltd (United Kingdom) 408
European Press Scientific Publisher (Belgium) 37
European Schoolbooks Ltd (United Kingdom) 408
European University Institute Library (Italy) 234
Europrisma-Verlag (Federal Republic of Germany) 135
Evangel Publishing House (Kenya) 248
Evangelical Press and Services Ltd (United Kingdom) 409
Evangélique, Librairie (Togo) 382
Evangélique, Librairie (Upper Volta) 451
Evangélique, Maison d'Edition de la Librairie-Imprimerie, du Togo (Togo) 382
Evangelisch Lutherischen Mission, Verlag der (Federal Republic of Germany) 135
Evangelische Verlagsanstalt GmbH (German Democratic Republic) 117
Evangelischen Gesellschaft, Verlag und Schriftenmission der, für Deutschland GmbH (Federal Republic of Germany) 135
Evangelischer Missionsverlag (Federal Republic of Germany) 135
Evangelischer Presseverband für Bayern eV (Federal Republic of Germany) 135
Evangelischer Pressverband in Österreich (Austria) 25
Evangelischer Schriften Verlag Schwengeler (Switzerland) 365
Evangelisches Verlagswerk GmbH (Federal Republic of Germany) 135
Evangeliska Fosterlands-Stiftelsens Förlag (EFS-förlaget) (Sweden) 354
Evans Brothers Ltd (United Kingdom) 409
Evans Brothers (Nigeria Publishers) Ltd (Nigeria) 294
Evans Shepherd (Zimbabwe) 465
Evento, L', Teatrale (Italy) 224
Everest, Editorial, SA (Spain) 340
Evergreen Lives (United Kingdom) 409
Everyman Fiction (United Kingdom) 409
Everyman's Library, Reference Library and University Library (United Kingdom) 409
Ewald, Johannes, Prize (Denmark) 81
Ewart-Biggs, Christopher, Memorial Prize (International Literary Prizes) 476
Ewha Womans University Library (Republic of Korea) 252
Ewha Womans University Press (Republic of Korea) 251
Ewing Memorial Library (Pakistan) 303
Ex Libris (Switzerland) 365
Ex Libris (Switzerland) 375
Excalibur (United Kingdom) 409
Excerpta Medica (Netherlands) 276
Exclusive Books (Pty) Ltd (Republic of South Africa) 333
Exley Publications Ltd (United Kingdom) 409
Expansion, L', Scientifique Française (France) 98
Exped-Expansaõ Editorial Ltda (Brazil) 50
Expert Verlag GmbH (Federal Republic of Germany) 135
Export-Press (Yugoslavia) 460
Express Edition GmbH (Federal Republic of Germany) 135
Express Logic Ltd (United Kingdom) 409
Expresso SARL (Portugal) 318
Extemporaneos, Editorial, SA (Mexico) 265
Extrabuch Verlag in der pädex-Verlags-GmbH (Federal Republic of Germany) 135
Eymundssonar, Bókaverslun Sigfusar (Iceland) 183
Eyre & Spottiswoode (Publishers) Ltd (United Kingdom) 409
Eyre Methuen Ltd (United Kingdom) 409
Eyrolles, Éditions (France) 98

F A D L's Forlag A/S (Foreningen af danske Laegestuderendes Forlag) (Denmark) 76
F A W Barbara Ramsden Award (Australia) 22
F A W Christopher Brennan Award (Australia) 23

INDEX 511

F A W John Shaw Neilson Poetry Award (Australia) 23
F A W Local History Award (Australia) 23
F A W Regional Branch Awards (Australia) 23
F B V Frauenbuchvertrieb GmbH (Federal Republic of Germany) 167
F E D, Uitgeverij, BV (Netherlands) 276
F E N A M E — Fundação Nacional de Material Escolar (Brazil) 50
F E P International (HK) Ltd (Hong Kong) 179
F E P International Private Ltd (Republic of Singapore) 326
F E P International Sdn Bhd (Malaysia) 259
F I D (International Organizations) 467
F N A C (France) 109
F T D, Editora, SA (Brazil) 51
F W M Books Ltd (Trinidad and Tobago) 382
Fabbri, Bompiani, Gruppo Editoriale, Sonzogno, Etas Spa (Italy) 224
Fabbri, Gruppo Editoriale, SpA (Italy) 224
Faber & Faber Ltd (United Kingdom) 409
Faber, The Geoffrey, Memorial Prize (International Literary Prizes) 476
Fabien Prize (France) 112
Fabril Editora SA (Argentina) 5
Fabritius Forlagshus (Norway) 298
Fachbuchverlag, VEB (German Democratic Republic) 117
Fackel-Buchklub, Verlags- und Vertriebs GmbH (Federal Republic of Germany) 167
Fackelträger-Verlag GmbH (Federal Republic of Germany) 135
Fackelverlag G Bowitz GmbH (Federal Republic of Germany) 135
Facla, Editura (Romania) 321
Facsimile Uitgaven Nederland BV (FUN) (Netherlands) 276
Facultas Verlag (Austria) 25
Facultatii, Biblioteca, de Medicina din Bucuresti (Romania) 322
Faculté de Droit, Bibliothèque de la, et des Sciences Politiques et Economiques de Tunis (Tunisia) 383
Faculté de Theologie Catholique de Kinshasa (Zaire) 462
Faculté des Lettres, Bibliothèque de la, et Sciences Humaines (Tunisia) 384
Faculté des Lettres et Sciences Humaines de Tunis (Tunisia) 383
Faculté des Sciences, Bibliothèque de la, de Tunis (Tunisia) 384
Faculty of Agriculture, Forestry and Veterinary Science (Tanzania) 379
Faculty of Engineering, Library of the (Lebanon) 254
Faculty of Law, Library of the (Lebanon) 254
Fællesekspeditionen (Denmark) 75
Faenza Editrice SpA (Italy) 224
Fagbamigbe, Olaiya, Ltd (Publishers) (Nigeria) 294
Fagbibliotekforening, Norsk (Norway) 301
Faglitteratur, Forlaget for, A/S (Denmark) 76
Faik, Sait, Prize (Turkey) 385
Faircape Books (Republic of South Africa) 330
Fajar, Penerbit, Bakti Sdn Bhd (Malaysia) 259
Falcon Books (United Kingdom) 409
Falk-Verlag für Landkarten und Stadtpläne Gerhard Falk GmbH (Federal Republic of Germany) 135
Falken-Verlag GmbH (Federal Republic of Germany) 135
Falkplan/CIB, NV (Netherlands) 276
Fall, Lycée de Jeunes Filles Ameth, Bibliothèque (Senegal) 324
Fallon, C J, Ltd (Republic of Ireland) 209
Faltermaier, Dr Martin (Federal Republic of Germany) 135
Familia et Patria PVBA (Belgium) 37
Familia, Librería La, SA (Peru) 307
Family Book Club (United Kingdom) 443
Family Bookshop (Qatar) 320
Family Bookshop (United Arab Emirates) 390
Family Bookshop (Bahrain) WLL (Bahrain) 32
Fantasia Prize (France) 112
Fantasy Library (United Kingdom) 409
Far East Book Co (Republic of Singapore) 327
Far East Book Co (Taiwan) 377
Far East Publications Ltd (Hong Kong) 180
Far Eastern University Library (Philippines) 310
Farairre, Librairie (Morocco) 271
Farandole/Messidor, Editions La (France) 98
Farb-Dia-Archiv Edmond Van Hoorick (Switzerland) 365
Farjeon, Eleanor, Award (United Kingdom) 448
Farmer, Prudence, Poetry Prize (United Kingdom) 448
Farquharson, John, Ltd (United Kingdom) 442
Fastenrath Prize (Spain) 349
Fateh, al-, University, The Central Library (Libya) 256
Fausto, Ediciones Librerías (Argentina) 5
Fausto, Librerías (Argentina) 8
Favorit-Verlag Huntemann & Co (Federal Republic of Germany) 135
Favre, Jules, Prize (France) 112
Favre, Pierre Marcel (Switzerland) 365
Faxon Europe BV (Netherlands) 284
Fayard, Librairie Arthème (France) 98
Fazer, Edition (Finland) 87

Febres Cordero', Servicios Bibliotecarios Generales 'Tulio (Venezuela) 454
Federação Brasileira de Associações de Bibliotecários — Comissão Brasileira de Documentação Jurídica (FEBAB/CBDJ) (Brazil) 56
Federação Brasileira de Associações de Bibliotecários (FEBAB) (Brazil) 56
Federación Argentina de Librerías, Papelerías y Actividades Afines (Argentina) 3
Federación de Asociaciones Nacionales de Distribuidores de Ediciones (Spain) 336
Federación de Gremios de Editores de España (Spain) 336
Federal Publications (HK) Ltd (Hong Kong) 179
Federal Publications (S) (Pte) Ltd (Republic of Singapore) 326
Federal Publications Sdn Bhd (Malaysia) 259
Federal Radio Corporation of Nigeria (Nigeria) 297
Federatie van Organisaties van Bibliotheek-, Informatie-, Dokumentatiewezen (FOBID) (Netherlands) 284
Fédération des Amicales de Documentalistes et Bibliothécaires de l'Education nationale (France) 110
Fédération française des Syndicats de Libraires (France) 90
Fédération internationale des Libraires (FIL) (International Organizations) 467
Fédération internationale des Traducteurs (FIT) (International Organizations) 467
Fédération Luxembourgeoise des Editeurs de Livres (Grand Duchy of Luxembourg) 256
Fédération luxembourgeoise des Travailleurs du Livre (Grand Duchy of Luxembourg) 256
Fédération panhellénique des Editeurs et Libraires (Greece) 174
Federspiel, Librería Universal Carlos (Costa Rica) 68
Fehling, Willy F P, GmbH (Federal Republic of Germany) 135
Fehmers, Frank, Productions (Netherlands) 276
Fehr'sche Buchhandlung AG (Switzerland) 375
Feij, Editions François (Switzerland) 365
Feistle, Dr Karl (Federal Republic of Germany) 135
Felag bokavarda i islenskum rannsoknarbokasofnum (Iceland) 185
Félag Islenzkra Bókaútgefenda (Iceland) 183
Félag Islenzkra Bókaverzlana (Iceland) 183
Feldheim Publishers Ltd (Israel) 214
Fellesbiblioteket for det Kongelige Norske Videnskabers Selskab (Norway) 300
Fellicelli et Poli, Librairie (Niger) 292
Fellowship of Australian Writers (NSW) (Australia) 21
Fellowship of Australian Writers, Victorian (Australia) 21
Fellowship of Australian Writers (WA) (Australia) 21
Feltrinelli, Antonio, Prize (International Literary Prizes) 476
Feltrinelli, Giangiacomo, SpA (Italy) 224
Feltrinelli, Libreria (Italy) 234
Femina (Republic of South Africa) 330
Fémina Prize (France) 112
Femmes d'aujourd'hui, Groupe (France) 98
Femmes, Des (France) 98
Fenice, La, — Ciarrapico Editore (Italy) 224
Ferenczy Verlag AG (Switzerland) 375
Ferguson, John, Pty Ltd (Australia) 14
Feria Chilena del Libro (Chile) 63
Feria del Libro (Uruguay) 452
Fernández Editores SA CV (Mexico) 265
Fernández, Editorial y Librería Juridica Amalio M (Uruguay) 451
Fernández, Librería Amalio M (Uruguay) 452
Ferozsons (Pakistan) 302
Ferozsons Ltd (Pakistan) 303
Ferro, Edizioni, SpA (Italy) 224
Fersobe, Papeleria, Hnos (Dominican Republic) 82
Feu, Editions du, Nouveau (France) 98
Feuervogel-Verlag GmbH (Federal Republic of Germany) 135
'Feuilles Familiales', Les, ASBL (Belgium) 37
Fher, Editorial, SA (Spain) 340
Fib's Lyrikklub (Sweden) 354
Fidler, Kathleen, Award (United Kingdom) 448
Fierro', Librería 'Martín (Argentina) 8
Fietkau, Wolfgang, Verlag (Federal Republic of Germany) 135
Fietz, Barbara (Federal Republic of Germany) 135
Figgis, Allen, & Co Ltd (Republic of Ireland) 209
Figueirinhas, Livraria Editora, Lda (Portugal) 316
Fiji Library Association (FLA) (Fiji) 86
Fikentscher und Co (Federal Republic of Germany) 135
Fikr, Dar Al-, (Salem & Zu'bi) Bookshop (Syria) 377
Filadelfia AB, Förlaget (Sweden) 354

Filipacchi, Editions (France) 98
Filon, Ekdoseis (Greece) 174
Financial Times, The, Business Enterprises Ltd (United Kingdom) 409
Financial Training Publications Ltd (United Kingdom) 409
Finansy i Statistika Publishing House USSR (Union of Soviet Socialist Republics) 387
Finansy, Izdatelstvo (Union of Soviet Socialist Republics) 387
Findhorn, The, Press (United Kingdom) 409
Fine Arts Press Pty Ltd (Australia) 14
Fink GmbH, Wilhelm, & Co Verlags KG (Federal Republic of Germany) 136
Fink — Kümmerly und Frey, J, Verlag GmbH (Federal Republic of Germany) 136
Fink Verlag, Emil (Federal Republic of Germany) 136
Finken-Verlag (Federal Republic of Germany) 136
Finlands Svenska Författareförening (Finland) 89
Finot, Jean, Prize (France) 112
Fiorentina, Libreria Editrice, di Vittorio e Valerio Zani snc (Italy) 224
Firecrest Publishing Ltd (United Kingdom) 409
Firma KLM Private Ltd (Incorporating Firma KL Mukhopadhyay) (India) 190
First Book Prize (Argentina) 9
Fischbacher, Librairie, International Art Book Distribution (import-export) (France) 98
Fischer Taschenbuch Verlag GmbH (Federal Republic of Germany) 136
Fischer, VEB Gustav, Verlag, Jena (German Democratic Republic) 117
Fischer, Verlag für Medizin Dr Ewald (Federal Republic of Germany) 136
Fischer Verlag, Gustav, GmbH & Co KG (Federal Republic of Germany) 136
Fischer Verlag, Rita G (Federal Republic of Germany) 136
Fischer Verlag, S, GmbH (Federal Republic of Germany) 136
Fischer Verlag, W (Federal Republic of Germany) 136
Fischlin, J (Switzerland) 365
Fisher, H (Israel) 214
Fishing Book Club (United Kingdom) 443
Fishing News Books Ltd (United Kingdom) 409
Fitzpatrick, Percy, Medal (Republic of South Africa) 335
Five Lamps, The, Press (Republic of Ireland) 209
Fix, Verlag Johannes (Federal Republic of Germany) 136
'Fizkultura i Sport', Izdatelstvo (Union of Soviet Socialist Republics) 387
Flaccovio, Libreria SF (Italy) 234
Flaccovio, S F, Editore (Italy) 224
Flambeau, Editions Le (United Republic of Cameroun) 61
Flame Lily (Zimbabwe) 464
Flamingo (United Kingdom) 409
Flammarion (France) 109
Flammarion et Cie (France) 98
Flat, Paul, Prize (France) 112
Fleischhauer und Spohn Verlag (Federal Republic of Germany) 136
Flesch Financial Publications (Pty) Ltd (Republic of South Africa) 330
Fletcher, Authors' Club Sir Bannister, Prize Trust (United Kingdom) 448
Fleurs, Editions, SA (France) 98
Fleury, Ernest, Prize (France) 112
Fleuve, Editions, Noir (France) 98
Flor, Ediciones de la, SRL (Argentina) 5
Florio, John, Prize (United Kingdom) 448
Floris Books (United Kingdom) 409
Főapátsági Könyvtár (Hungary) 182
Focal Press (United Kingdom) 409
Foch, Marshal, Prize (France) 112
Focus (Netherlands) 276
Focus International Book Production AB (Sweden) 354
Focus Ireland (Republic of Ireland) 209
Focus-Verlag (Federal Republic of Germany) 136
Foetisch, Maurice et Pierre, SA (Switzerland) 365
Fogarty's Bookshop (Republic of South Africa) 333
Fògola Editore in Torino (Italy) 224
Fogtdals Blade A/S (Denmark) 76
Foilseacháin Náisiúnta Tta (Republic of Ireland) 209
Folens and Co Ltd (Republic of Ireland) 209
Folio (Republic of South Africa) 330
Folio, The, Society Ltd (United Kingdom) 409
Folio, The, Society Ltd (United Kingdom) 443
Foma, Editions, SA (Switzerland) 365
Fondo de Cultura Económica (Mexico) 265
Fondo de Cultura Económica (Spain) 340
Fondo Editorial Común SC (Venezuela) 453
Fondo Educativo Interamericano (Mexico) 265
Fondo Educativo Interamericano (Panama) 304
Fondo Educativo Interamericano (Puerto Rico) 319
Fondo Educativo Interamericano CA (Venezuela) 453
Fondo Educativo Interamericano SA (Colombia) 66
Fonds, Bibliothèque, Quetelet (Belgium) 43
Fonds Mercator SA (Belgium) 37
Fonna Forlag L/L (Norway) 298

512 INDEX

Font, Librería (Mexico) 268
Fontamara, Editorial, SA (Spain) 340
Fontana Books (United Kingdom) 409
Fontane, Theodor, Prize (Federal Republic of Germany) 170
Fontanella, Editorial, SA (Spain) 340
Fontein, Uitgeverij De, BV (Netherlands) 276
Fontes Pers (APA) (Netherlands) 276
Fonteyn, S A , Medical Books NV (Belgium) 37
Food and Agriculture Organization of the United Nations (FAO) (International Organizations) 469
Foras, An, Forbartha (Republic of Ireland) 209
Forbes Publications Ltd (United Kingdom) 409
Foreign Affairs Publishing Co Ltd (United Kingdom) 409
Foreign Language Bookshop (Australia) 20
Foreign Languages Press (People's Republic of China) 64
Foreign Languages Publishing House (Democratic People's Republic of Korea) 250
Foreign Languages Publishing House (Socialist Republic of Viet Nam) 455
Foreign Relations Publishing House (Thailand) 380
Forening for Boghaandvaerk (Denmark) 75
Forening for Forlagsfolk (Denmark) 75
Foreningen af Medarbejdere ved Danmarks Forskningsbiblioteker (Denmark) 80
Föreningen Auktoriserade Translatorer (Sweden) 360
Föreningen Svenska Läromedelsproducenter (Sweden) 351
Forense, Editora, —Universitaria Ltda (Brazil) 51
Författares Bokmaskin (Sweden) 354
Förg, Alfred, GmbH & Co KG (Federal Republic of Germany) 136
Foris Publications (Netherlands) 276
Forja Editora SARL (Portugal) 316
Forkel-Verlag GmbH (Federal Republic of Germany) 136
Formar, Editora e Encadernadora, Ltda (Brazil) 51
Formentor, Ediciones, SRL (Argentina) 5
Formentor, Ediciones, SRL (Venezuela) 453
Formgebung, Rat für (Federal Republic of Germany) 136
Formichiere, Il (Italy) 224
Forni, Arnaldo, Editore SpA (Italy) 224
Forsamlingsforbundets Forlags AB (Finland) 87
Forsberg, Bokförläggare Bengt (Sweden) 354
Fortschritt für alle-Verlag (Federal Republic of Germany) 136
Fortuna-Verlag W Heidelberger (Switzerland) 365
Fortune Press (United Kingdom) 409
Fortuny, Pascal, Prize (France) 112
Forum (New Zealand) 288
Forum (Yugoslavia) 457
Forum (Yugoslavia) 460
Forum, Bokförlaget, AB (Sweden) 354
Forum, Forlaget, A/S (Denmark) 76
Forum littéraire camerounais (United Republic of Cameroun) 61
Forum Verlag GmbH (Austria) 25
Főszékesegyházi Könyvtár (Hungary) 182
Foto und Schmalfilm-Verlag (Gemsberg-Verlag) (Switzerland) 365
Fotokinoverlag, VEB (German Democratic Republic) 117
Fotomatic Philippines Inc (Philippines) 308
Foucher, Les Editions (France) 98
Foulis, G T, & Co Ltd (United Kingdom) 409
Foulsham, W, & Co Ltd (United Kingdom) 409
Foundation Books (Kenya) 248
Foundation for the Promotion of the Translation of Dutch Literature (Netherlands) 285
Foundational, The, Book Co Ltd (United Kingdom) 410
Fount Paperbacks (United Kingdom) 410
Fountain Press (United Kingdom) 410
Four Courts Press Ltd (Republic of Ireland) 210
Four Winds Press (Australia) 14
Fourah Bay College Bookshop Ltd (Sierra Leone) 325
Fourah Bay College Library (Sierra Leone) 325
Fouraignan Foundation Prize (France) 112
Fournier, Heraclio, SA (Spain) 340
Fourth Estate Books Ltd (New Zealand) 288
Fowler, L N, & Co Ltd (United Kingdom) 410
Foyle, W & G, Ltd (United Kingdom) 444
Foyle, W & G, Ltd & John Gifford Ltd (United Kingdom) 410
Fragua Editorial (Spain) 340
Fralit-F K Albrecht (Federal Republic of Germany) 167
Française, Librairie (Grand Duchy of Luxembourg) 257
France-Caraïbes (France) 98
France Empire, Editions (France) 98
France Expansion (France) 98
France, Librairie de (Ivory Coast) 236
France, Librairie de (Morocco) 271
France, Librairie de (Upper Volta) 451
France-Loisirs (France) 98
Francesa, Librería (Spain) 347
Franciscaines, Les Editions, SA (France) 99
Franciscan Printing Press (Israel) 214
Franciscana, Editorial (Portugal) 316
Francisci, Aldo, Editore (Italy) 224
Francité, Editions de la, (Imprimeries Havaux) (Belgium) 37

Francke, A, GmbH (Federal Republic of Germany) 136
Francke, Buchhandlung A, AG (Switzerland) 375
Francke Buchhandlung, Verlag der, GmbH (Federal Republic of Germany) 136
Francke Verlag (Switzerland) 365
Franckh'sche Verlagshandlung W Keller & Co (Federal Republic of Germany) 136
Frank Bros & Co (Publishers) Pvt Ltd (India) 190
Frank Publishing Ltd (Ghana) 172
Frankfurter Bücher, Verlag (Federal Republic of Germany) 136
Frankfurter Fachverlag Michael Kohl GmbH & Co KG (Federal Republic of Germany) 136
Frankfurter Kinderbücher, Verlag, GmbH (Federal Republic of Germany) 136
Fränkische Gesellschafts-Druckerei Würzburg/Echter Verlag (Federal Republic of Germany) 136
Franklin', Biblioteca 'Benjamin, (USIS) (Mexico) 269
Franklin Book Programs Inc (Afghanistan) 1
Franklin, Miles, Award (Australia) 23
Frankonius Verlag GmbH (Federal Republic of Germany) 136
Franz, Ernst, und Sternberg-Verlag (Federal Republic of Germany) 137
Franzis-Verlag GmbH (Federal Republic of Germany) 137
Fraser, Gordon, Gallery Ltd (United Kingdom) 410
Frau, Verlag für die (German Democratic Republic) 117
Frauenbuchverlag (Federal Republic of Germany) 137
Frauenoffensive, Verlag (Federal Republic of Germany) 137
Frauenpresse (Federal Republic of Germany) 137
Frech-Verlag GmbH und Co Druck KG (Federal Republic of Germany) 137
Free German Authors' Association (Federal Republic of Germany) 170
Freeland Press Ltd (United Kingdom) 410
Freeman, W H, & Co Ltd (United Kingdom) 410
freies Geistesleben, Verlag (Federal Republic of Germany) 137
Freitas, Livraria, Bastos (Brazil) 56
Freitas, Livraria, Bastos SA (Brazil) 51
Fremad (Denmark) 76
Fremdsprachen, Verlag für (Federal Republic of Germany) 137
French Book Club (United Kingdom) 443
French Faculty of Medicine, Library of the, Pharmacy and Dentistry (Lebanon) 254
French Language Prize (International Literary Prizes) 476
French, Samuel, Ltd (United Kingdom) 410
Fretz und Wasmuth Verlag AG (Switzerland) 365
Fretz Verlag (Switzerland) 365
Freud, Sigmund, Prize (Federal Republic of Germany) 170
Freund Publishing House Ltd (Israel) 214
Freytag-Berndt und Artaria, Kartographische Anstalt (Austria) 25
Frias, Universidad Boliviana Tomás, Div de Extensión Universitaria (Bolivia) 46
Fricke, Verlag Dieter, GmbH (Federal Republic of Germany) 137
Friedman, S (Israel) 214
Friedmann, Blake, Literary Agency (United Kingdom) 442
Friedrich, Erhard, Verlag (Federal Republic of Germany) 137
Friends of Antiquity (Czechoslovakia) 73
Friends of the National Libraries (United Kingdom) 445
Frimodts, J, Forlag (Denmark) 76
Frisia-Verlag GmbH (Federal Republic of Germany) 137
Fritzes, A B C E, Kungl Hovbokhandel (Sweden) 358
Frobenius AG (Switzerland) 365
Froebel-Kan Co Ltd (Japan) 239
Fromm, Verlag A, GmbH & Co (Federal Republic of Germany) 137
Frommann, Friedrich, Verlag, Günther Holzboog GmbH & Co (Federal Republic of Germany) 137
Fromme, Georg, und Co (Austria) 26
Frontier Publishing Co (Pakistan) 302
Frossard, Henri (France) 99
Frost, Robert, Award (Australia) 23
Fu-Hsing Book Co (Taiwan) 378
Fu Ssu-Nien Library Institute of History and Philology (Taiwan) 378
Fuchs, Dr Heinrich (Austria) 26
Fudge & Co Ltd (United Kingdom) 410
Fukuinkan Shoten Library (Japan) 244
Fukuinkan Shoten Publishers (Japan) 239
Fundação Instituto Brasileiro de Geografia e Estatística (Brazil) 51
Fundação Nacional de Material Escolar (Brazil) 51
Fundación de Cultura Universitaria (Uruguay) 451
Fundamentos, Editorial (Spain) 340
Fürstelberger, Hans (Austria) 29
Füssli, Orell, Verlag (Switzerland) 365
Futura (United Kingdom) 410
Futura, Editorial (Portugal) 316
Futuro, Edizioni (Italy) 224
Fuzambo Publishing Co (Japan) 239

Fyfield Books (United Kingdom) 410

G 3, La Societé, (Groupement d'Intérêt Economique) (France) 99
G D Bücherei (Federal Republic of Germany) 137
G D K Publications (India) 191
G E C T I (Gabinete de Especializacão e Cooperacão Tecnica Internacional L) (Portugal) 316
G I A SA (Belgium) 37
G M T, Forlaget (Denmark) 76
G S Verlag Basle (Switzerland) 365
Gaade, W, BV (Netherlands) 277
Gaba Publications (Kenya) 248
Gabalda, J, et Cie (Librairie Lecoffre) SA (France) 99
Gaber, Franz-J (Federal Republic of Germany) 137
Gaberbocchus Press (Netherlands) 277
Gaberbocchus Press Ltd (United Kingdom) 410
Gabinete de Especializacão e Cooperacão Tecnica Internacional (Portugal) 317
Gabler, Betriebswirtschaftlicher Verlag Dr Theodor, GmbH (Federal Republic of Germany) 137
Gad, G E C, Dansk og Udenlandsk Boghandel A/S (Denmark) 79
Gades, Hans, Harbour Pilots Succ A/S (Denmark) 76
Gads, G E C, Forlag (Denmark) 76
Gaggi, Aulo, Editore (Italy) 224
Gai Savoir, Le (Zaire) 462
Gaisa, Ediciones, SL (Spain) 340
Gakken Co Ltd (Japan) 239
Gakujutsu Bunken Fukyu-Kai (Japan) 245
Gakuseisha Publishers Co Ltd (Japan) 239
Galaxia (Venezuela) 454
Galaxie Press (Pvt) Ltd (Zimbabwe) 464
Galaxy Books (United Kingdom) 410
Galera, La, SA Editorial (Spain) 340
Galería, Librería, Castro Soto (Peru) 307
Galerna, Editorial, SA (Argentina) 5
Galgotia Booksource (India) 191
Galgotia, E D, & Sons (India) 201
Galgotia Publications (India) 191
Galilée, Editions (France) 99
Gall & Inglis (United Kingdom) 410
Galland, Editions Bertil (Switzerland) 365
Gallegos, Rómulo, International Novel Prize (International Literary Prizes) 477
Gallery, The, Press (Republic of Ireland) 210
Galliard (United Kingdom) 410
Gallimard, Editions (France) 99
Galliner, Peter, Associates Ltd (United Kingdom) 442
Galve, Impresora, SA (Mexico) 265
Galzerano, Giuseppe, Editore (Italy) 224
Gama, Da, Publishers (Pty) Ltd (Republic of South Africa) 330
Gambia College Library (The Gambia) 115
Gambia National Library (The Gambia) 115
Gambia, The, Methodist Bookshop Ltd (The Gambia) 115
Gamma (Netherlands) 277
Gamma, Editions (Belgium) 37
Gamma, Editions (France) 99
Gammalibri, Editrice (Italy) 224
Gamsberg Publishers (Namibia) 272
Ganesh & Co (India) 191
Gangan (Nigeria) 294
Gangarams Book Bureau (India) 201
Gans en Rombach Auteursagenten (Netherlands) 283
Gantner, A R, Verlag KG (Liechtenstein) 256
Gantrelle, Joseph, Prize (Belgium) 44
García Cambeiro, Fernando (Argentina) 5
Garcia, R M, Publishing House (Philippines) 308
García SA, Librería y Papelería Casa (Argentina) 5
Gardeners Book Society (United Kingdom) 443
Gardet, Imprimerie Librairie (France) 99
Gardum A/S (Norway) 300
Garigliano, Editrice, SRL (Italy) 224
Garnier, Editions, Frères (France) 99
Garnier-Flammarion (France) 99
Garnstone Press Ltd (United Kingdom) 410
Garriga, Ediciones, Argentinas SA (Argentina) 8
Garriga, Ediciones, SA (Spain) 340
Garve, De, PVBA (Belgium) 37
Garzanti Editore (Italy) 224
Gauthier-Villars, Société (France) 99
Gautier-Languereau, Les Editions, Sàrl (France) 99
Gavin, The, Press Ltd (United Kingdom) 410
Gaya, P T, Favorit Press, Book Division (Indonesia) 205
Gazit (Israel) 214
Gedin, Mrs Lena I (Sweden) 358
Gedisa, Editorial, SA (Spain) 340
Gedit SA (Belgium) 37
Gee & Co (United Kingdom) 410
Geering, Rudolf, Verlag (Switzerland) 365
Geest und Portig, Akademische Verlagsgesellschaft, KG (German Democratic Republic) 117
Geeta Prize (India) 203

INDEX 513

Geetha Book House (India) 191
Geetha Publishers Sdn Bhd (Malaysia) 259
Gegenrealismus, Verlag für (Federal Republic of Germany) 137
Gegner Prize (France) 112
Gehrmans, AB Carl, Musikförlag (Sweden) 354
Geisenheyner und Crone (Federal Republic of Germany) 167
Gelisim Publishing (Turkey) 384
Gem (United Kingdom) 410
Gemeentebibliotheek Rotterdam (Netherlands) 284
Gemini Publishers (Zimbabwe) 464
Géminis, Editorial, SRL (Argentina) 5
Gemsberg-Verlag (Switzerland) 365
Gençlik Kitabevi (Turkey) 385
General Assembly Library (New Zealand) 290
General Company for Publishing, Advertising and Distribution (Libya) 255
General Egyptian Book Organization (Egypt) 83
General Egyptian Book Organization (Egypt) 83
General Organization, The, for Government Press Affairs (Egypt) 84
General Press Corporation (Libya) 255
Générale des Carrières et des Mines, La, (GECAMINES) (Zaire) 462
Generalstabens Litografiska Anstalt (Sweden) 354
Genesis Publications Ltd (United Kingdom) 410
Genfer Bibelgesellschaft (Switzerland) 365
Genillard, Pierre, Editeur (Switzerland) 365
Genin, Editions M H (France) 99
Gennadius Library (Greece) 176
Gennep, Van, Ltd (Netherlands) 277
Gensy, Creazioni (Italy) 225
Gente Nueva, Editorial (Cuba) 69
Gentofte Kommunebibliotek (Denmark) 80
Gentry Books Ltd (United Kingdom) 410
GeoCenter Verlagsvertrieb GmbH (Federal Republic of Germany) 137
Geocolor SA (Spain) 340
Geodetický a kartografický podnik v Praze NP (Czechoslovakia) 71
Geographia Ltd (United Kingdom) 410
Geographical, The, Association (United Kingdom) 410
Géographie, Bibliothèque de (France) 110
Geologia, Direção nacional de, (Centro de Documentação) (Mozambique) 271
Geological Survey Department Library (Botswana) 47
Geological Survey Department Reference Library (Ghana) 173
Geological Survey of India (India) 191
Geologiczne, Wydawnictwa (Poland) 311
Geoprojects Sàrl (Lebanon) 254
Georg et Cie SA (Switzerland) 365
Georg et Cie SA (Switzerland) 375
George's, William, Sons Ltd (United Kingdom) 444
Georgi, Kunstverlag Dr Rudolf, Woldemar Klein (Federal Republic of Germany) 137
Georgi Publishing Company/Editions Georgi (Switzerland) 366
Georgian House Pty Ltd (Australia) 14
Geraldine, The, Press (Republic of Ireland) 210
Gérard, Editions, et Cie SPRL (Belgium) 37
Gerber, Carl, Verlag (Federal Republic of Germany) 137
Gerhardt Verlag (Federal Republic of Germany) 137
Germain, Françoise (France) 109
German Book Club (United Kingdom) 443
German Peace Prize (International Literary Prizes) 477
German Youth Book Award (Federal Republic of Germany) 170
German Youth, The, Book Award (International Literary Prizes) 477
Gerold & Co (Austria) 26
Gerold & Co (Austria) 29
Gerstenberg Verlag (Federal Republic of Germany) 137
Gerth, Musikverlag Klaus (Federal Republic of Germany) 137
Geschichte und Politik, Verlag für (Austria) 26
Gesellschaft für Bibliothekswesen und Dokumentation des Landbaues (GBDL) (Federal Republic of Germany) 169
Gesellschaft für deutsche Sprache und Literatur in Zürich (Switzerland) 376
Gesellschaft für Information und Dokumentation mbH (GID) (Federal Republic of Germany) 169
Gesellschaft für Verlagswerte GmbH (Switzerland) 375
Geuthner, Librairie Orientaliste Paul, SA (France) 99
Ghana Association of Writers (Ghana) 171
Ghana Book Development Council (Ghana) 171
Ghana Book Publishers' Association (Ghana) 171
Ghana Booksellers' Association (Ghana) 171
Ghana Institute of Management and Public Administration, Library and Documentation Centre (Ghana) 173
Ghana Library Association (Ghana) 173
Ghana Library Board (Ghana) ·173
Ghana Publishing Corporation (Ghana) 172
Ghana Publishing Corporation, Distribution and Sales Division (Ghana) 172
Ghana Universities Press (Ghana) 172

Ghaqda Bibljotekarji/Library Association (Valletta) (Malta) 262
Gharelu Library Yojna (India) 201
Gheorghiu-Dej, Biblioteca Institutului Politehnic 'Gheorge,' Bucuresti (Romania) 322
Ghetto Fighters' House Publishers (Israel) 214
Ghigi, Bruno, Editore (Italy) 225
Ghisetti e Corvi Editori SpA (Italy) 225
Ghost Hunters' Library (United Kingdom) 410
Ghulam, Sh, Ali & Sons Ltd (Pakistan) 302
Giannotta, Editrice, di Sebastiano Pace Giannotta (Italy) 225
Gianotten, Boekhandel, BV (Netherlands) 284
Giao Duc Publishing House (Socialist Republic of Viet Nam) 455
Giappichelli, G, Editore di Giorgio Giappichelli & C SAS (Italy) 225
Gibbons, Stanley, (Publications) Ltd (United Kingdom) 410
Gibert Jeune SNC (France) 99
Gibert, Librairie Joseph (France) 109
Gibraltar Bookshop (Gibraltar) 173
Gibraltar Garrison Library (Gibraltar) 173
Gibraltar Junior Bookshop (Gibraltar) 173
Gibraltar Library Service (Gibraltar) 173
Gibralter Book Store (Jordan) 247
Gidlunds Förlag (Sweden) 354
Gidrometeorizdat (Union of Soviet Socialist Republics) 387
Gierows, Karin, Prizes (Sweden) 360
Giertsen, Ed B, A/S (Norway) 300
Gieseking, Verlag Ernst und Werner (Federal Republic of Germany) 137
Gieseking Wirtschaftsverlag GmbH (Federal Republic of Germany) 137
Gifford & Craven (Republic of Ireland) 210
Gifford, John, Ltd (United Kingdom) 410
Gigord, Editions De (France) 99
Gilbert, Girault, SPRL (Belgium) 37
Giles Prize (France) 112
Gili, Ediciones G, SA (Argentina) 5
Gili, Editora Gustavo, do Brasil SA (Brazil) 51
Gili, Editorial Gustavo, de Mexico SA (Mexico) 265
Gili, Editorial Gustavo, Ltda (Chile) 63
Gili, Editorial Gustavo, SA (Spain) 340
Gill & Macmillan Ltd (Republic of Ireland) 210
Gillani, S I (Pakistan) 303
Gilles und Francke Verlag (Federal Republic of Germany) 137
Gimm-Young Press (Republic of Korea) 251
Ginn & Co Ltd (United Kingdom) 410
Ginsberg Univ Boekhandel (Netherlands) 284
Giovanis (Greece) 174
Giraffe (United Kingdom) 410
Girardet, Verlag W (Federal Republic of Germany) 137
Girasole, Mario Lapucci — Edizioni del (Italy) 225
Gisbert y Cia SA (Bolivia) 46
Gisbert y Cia SA (Bolivia) 46
Gitanjali Prakashan (India) 191
Giuffrè, A, Editore SpA (Italy) 225
Giunti Publishing Group (Italy) 225
Gjellerup, Jul, Forlagsaktieselskab (Denmark) 76
Gjellerups, Jul, Boghandel ApS (Denmark) 79
Glas (Yugoslavia) 457
Glasgow, Mary, Publications Ltd (United Kingdom) 410
Glashuetten/Taunus (Federal Republic of Germany) 137
Glaven (United Kingdom) 410
Gleerup, AB C W K, Bokförlag (Sweden) 354
Gleerupska, AB, Universitetsbokhandeln (Sweden) 358
Glem, Editorial, SACIF (Argentina) 5
Glen, Esther, Award (New Zealand) 291
Glenat, Editions J, SA (France) 99
Gleniffer Press (United Kingdom) 410
Global Book Resources Ltd (United Kingdom) 411
Global Editora e Distribuidora Ltda (Brazil) 51
Globetrotter-Verlag (Federal Republic of Germany) 137
Globi Verlag AG (Switzerland) 366
Globo, Editora, SA (Brazil) 51
Globo, Livraria do (Brazil) 56
Globus (Yugoslavia) 457
'Globus' Zeitungs-, Druck- und Verlagsanstalt GmbH (Austria) 26
Glock und Lutz Verlag Heroldsberg (Federal Republic of Germany) 137
Glogau Verlag (Federal Republic of Germany) 138
Glombig, PR Verlag Kurt (Federal Republic of Germany) 138
Glöss, Verlagsgesellschaft R, und Co (Federal Republic of Germany) 138
Glówna Biblioteka Lekarska (Poland) 314
Glówna Politechniki, Biblioteka, Warszawskiej (Poland) 314
Glówna, Uniwersytet Mikolaja Kopernika, Biblioteka (Poland) 314
Glówna Uniwersytetu im Adama Mickiewicza, Biblioteka (Poland) 314
Glückauf, Verlag, GmbH (Federal Republic of Germany) 138

Goddard's Bookshop Ltd (New Zealand) 290
Godfrey Cave Books Ltd (United Kingdom) 442
Godine, David, Publisher — London (United Kingdom) 411
Godwin, George, Ltd (United Kingdom) 411
Goede Boek, BV Uitgeversbedrijf Het (Netherlands) 277
Goel Publishing House (India) 191
Goethe Book Dealers Inc (Japan) 245
Goethe-Institut – Deutsche Bibliothek (Belgium) 43
Goethe Prize (Federal Republic of Germany) 170
Golan (Syria) 377
Gold Dagger Award (United Kingdom) 448
Golden Book House (Bangladesh) 32
Golden Book Prize (Italy) 236
Golden Eagle Books Ltd (Republic of Ireland) 210
Golden Eagle Press Ltd (United Kingdom) 411
Golden Handshake (United Kingdom) 411
Golden Pen Prize (Italy) 236
Golden Pleasure Books (United Kingdom) 411
Golden Press Pty Ltd (Australia) 14
Golden Press Ltd (New Zealand) 288
Goldmann, Wilhelm, Verlag GmbH (Federal Republic of Germany) 138
Goldschmidt, Victor, Verlagsbuchhandlung (Switzerland) 366
Goldsmith, The, Press Ltd (Republic of Ireland) 210
Goldstadtverlag (Federal Republic of Germany) 138
Golgotha (Nigeria) 294
Goliardica, Società Editrice La, Pavese SRL (Italy) 225
Gollancz, Victor, Ltd (United Kingdom) 411
Gomer Press (J D Lewis & Sons Ltd) (United Kingdom) 411
Gómez, P A (Dominican Republic) 82
Goncourt, Editorial y Librería (Argentina) 5
Goncourt Prize (France) 112
Gondola (United Kingdom) 411
Gondolat Könyvkiadó (Hungary) 181
Gondrom Verlag GmbH & Co Kg (Federal Republic of Germany) 138
Gondu (Burma) 60
Gonin, André et Pierre (Switzerland) 366
Gonski, Buchhandlung Heinrich (Federal Republic of Germany) 167
Gonthier, Société Nouvelle des Editions, Sàrl (France) 99
Gonvill, Librerías (Mexico) 268
Good Companions (India) 191
Good Earth Publishing Co (Hong Kong) 179
Goodwill Trading Co Inc (Philippines) 309
Gooise, de (Netherlands) 277
Goor Jeugdboeken, Van (Netherlands) 277
Goor Zonen, Van (Netherlands) 277
Gorachek, V, KG (Federal Republic of Germany) 171
Gorachek, V, KG (Federal Republic of Germany) 138
Gorcum, Van, BV (Netherlands) 277
Gordon and Breach Science Publishers Ltd (United Kingdom) 411
Gordon & Cremonesi (United Kingdom) 411
Gordon and Gotch (PNG) Pty Ltd (Papua New Guinea) 305
Gorgas, Biblioteca Bio-Médica del Laboratorio Conmemorativo (Panama) 305
Gor'kogo Moskovskogo, Nauchnaya biblioteka im A M, gos universiteta im M V Lomonosova (Union of Soviet Socialist Republics) 389
Gor'kovo Leningradskovo, Nauchnaya biblioteka im A M, gosudarstvennovo universiteta im A A Zhdanova (Union of Soviet Socialist Republics) 389
Göschl, Alois, & Co (Austria) 26
Gosudarstvennaya ordena Trudovogo Krasnogo Znameni biblioteka, Vsesoyuznaya, inostrannoi literatury (Union of Soviet Socialist Republics) 389
Gosudarstvennaya publichnaya istoricheskaya biblioteka RSFSR (Union of Soviet Socialist Republics) 389
Gosudarstvennaya publichnaya nauchno-tekhnicheskaya biblioteka SSSR (Union of Soviet Socialist Republics) 389
Gosudarstvenny komitet SSSR po delam izdatelstv, poligrafii i knizhnoi torgovli (Union of Soviet Socialist Republics) 386
Göteborgs Stadsbibliotek (Sweden) 359
Göteborgs Universitetsbibliotek (Sweden) 359
Gotthelf-Verlag (Switzerland) 366
Gottlob, Adam, Oehlenschläger Prize (Denmark) 81
Gottmer, J H, Publishers (Netherlands) 277
Gottmer's, BV v/hB, Uitgeversbedrijf (Netherlands) 277
Gouda Quint BV (Netherlands) 277
Gouden, Uitgeverij het, Spoor (Belgium) 37
Goulden, Henry, Ltd (United Kingdom) 411
Government Archives (Namibia) 272
Government Archives, Cape Archives Depot, Library (Republic of South Africa) 334
Government Archives, Natal Archives Depot, Library (Republic of South Africa) 334
Government Archives, Orange Free State Archives Depot, Library (Republic of South Africa) 334
Government Archives, Transvaal Archives Depot, Library (Republic of South Africa) 334
Government College Library (Pakistan) 303

514 INDEX

Government, Directorate of, Publications (India) 191
Government Library (Libya) 256
Government of India Librarians Association (India) 202
Government of Pakistan Department of Libraries (Pakistan) 303
Government Press (Afghanistan) 1
Government Press, The (The Gambia) 115
Government Printer (Botswana) 47
Government Printer (Burundi) 60
Government Printer (United Republic of Cameroun) 61
Government Printer (Chad) 62
Government Printer (Popular Republic of Congo) 68
Government Printer (Egypt) 84
Government Printer (Ethiopia) 86
Government Printer (Ivory Coast) 236
Government Printer (Kenya) 248
Government Printer (Liberia) 255
Government Printer (Lesotho) 255
Government Printer (Democratic Republic of Madagascar) 257
Government Printer (Somalia) 328
Government Printer (Republic of South Africa) 330
Government Printer (Sudan) 350
Government Printer (Tanzania) 379
Government Printer (Uganda) 386
Government Printer (Zambia) 463
Government Printer (Zimbabwe) 464
Government Printer (Impressa Nacional de Moçambique) (Mozambique) 271
Government Printer (Imprimerie Centrale d'Afrique) (Central African Republic) 62
Government Printer (Imprimerie Centrale d'Afrique) (Gabon) 115
Government Printer (Imprimerie de Kabgayi) (Rwanda) 323
Government Printer (Imprimerie du Gouvernement) (Senegal) 324
Government Printer (Imprimerie du Gouvernement Central) (Zaire) 462
Government Printer (Imprimerie Générale du Niger) (Niger) 292
Government Printer (Imprimerie National) (Malawi) 258
Government Printer (Imprimerie National) (Mauritius) 263
Government Printer (Imprimerie National du Rwanda) (Rwanda) 323
Government Printer (Imprimerie Nationale) (Mali) 262
Government Printer (Imprimerie Nationale) (Mauritania) 263
Government Printer, Imprimerie Nationale (Upper Volta) 451
Government Printer (Imprimerie Officielle) (Morocco) 270
Government Printer (Imprimerie Officielle de la République Tunisienne) (Tunisia) 383
Government Printer (Office nationale d'edition de presse et d'imprimerie) (Benin) 45
Government Printer, The, (Ghana Publishing Corporation, Printing Division) (Ghana) 172
Government Printing Centre (Finland) 87
Government Printing Office (Jamaica) 237
Government Public Library (Liberia) 255
Government Publications (Pakistan) 302
Government Teacher Training College Library (Botswana) 47
Gower Press (United Kingdom) 411
Gower Publishing Co Ltd (United Kingdom) 411
Goyanarte Editor SA (Argentina) 5
Gozo Public Library (Malta) 262
Graaf, De, Publishers (Netherlands) 277
Graal, Edições, Ltda (Brazil) 51
Graal, Ordem do, na Terra (Brazil) 51
Grabert-Verlag (Federal Republic of Germany) 138
Gracklauer, O, Verlag und Bibliographische Agentur (Federal Republic of Germany) 121
Gradina, Izdavačka ustanova (Yugoslavia) 457
Gradjevinska Knjiga (Yugoslavia) 457
Gräfe und Unzer GmbH (Federal Republic of Germany) 138
Grafički zavod Hrvatske (Yugoslavia) 457
Grafisk Forlag (Denmark) 76
Grafo Edizioni (Italy) 225
Grafos (Yugoslavia) 457
Grafton Books (United Kingdom) 411
Graham & Trotman Ltd (United Kingdom) 411
Graham, Frank (United Kingdom) 411
Grahames Bookshop (Australia) 20
Gralsbotschaft, Verlag der Stiftung, GmbH (Federal Republic of Germany) 138
Gram Editora (Argentina) 5
Gramedia Bookshop (Indonesia) 206
Gramedia, PT (Indonesia) 205
Gran Colombia, Librería La (Colombia) 67
Gran Premio Nacional de Literatura (Uruguay) 452
Granada Publishing Australia Pty Ltd (Australia) 14
Granada Publishing Ltd (United Kingdom) 411
Grancher, Jacques, Editeur (France) 99

Grand, Bibliothèque du, Seminaire de Koumi (Upper Volta) 451
Grand Franco-Belgian Literary Prize (Belgium) 44
Grand Franco-Belgian Literary Prize (France) 112
Grand National Assembly, Library of the (Turkey) 385
Grand-Pont, Editions du (Switzerland) 366
Grand Prix des Biennales Internationales de Poësie (International Literary Prizes) 477
Grand Prize (Sweden) 360
Grand Prize for a Book of Poetry (Sweden) 360
Grand Prize for a Novel (Sweden) 360
Grand Prize for Literature (France) 112
Grand Prize for Poetry Criticism (France) 112
Grand Prize for the Dissemination of the French Language (International Literary Prizes) 477
Grand Prize of French Poets (France) 112
Granda, Editorial Juan Carlos (Argentina) 5
Grant Educational Co Ltd (United Kingdom) 444
Grant McIntyre Ltd (United Kingdom) 411
Granta Editions (United Kingdom) 411
Graphic, The, Communications Centre Ltd (United Kingdom) 411
Grass Roots (Australia) 14
Grasset et Fasquelle, Société des Editions (France) 99
Grasshopper Books (United Kingdom) 411
Grassin, Jean, Editeur (France) 99
Grasso, Editoriale (Italy) 225
Gratien, Emilio (French Guiana) 114
Gravesande, The G H 's-, Prize (Netherlands) 285
Graziano, Librería Alfa (Argentina) 8
Graziano, Librería y Editorial Alfa, SACI (Argentina) 5
Great Austrian State Prize (Austria) 31
Great China Book Corporation (Taiwan) 378
Great English Classics (United Kingdom) 443
Great Mosque of Sana'a, Library of the (Yemen Arab Republic) 456
Great Mysteries (United Kingdom) 443
Gredos, Editorial, SA (Spain) 340
Green & Son, W, Ltd (United Kingdom) 411
Green Book House Limited (Bangladesh) 32
Green, J C R, (Publishers) Ltd (United Kingdom) 411
Greenaway, Kate, Medal (United Kingdom) 448
Greene & Co (Republic of Ireland) 211
Greenhouse Publications (Australia) 14
Greens, E, Forlag (Norway) 298
Greenwood Press (Hong Kong) 179
Gregg International (United Kingdom) 411
Gregorian University Press (Università Gregoriana Editrice) (Italy) 225
Gregoriana, Libreria (Italy) 234
Gregoriana, Libreria Editrice (Italy) 225
Gregory, Eric, Trust Fund Awards (United Kingdom) 448
Gregory Medal (Republic of Ireland) 212
Gremese Editore SRL (Italy) 225
Gremese, Ernesto, Editore SRL (Italy) 225
Gremi de Llibreters de Barcelona i Catalunya (Spain) 336
Gremial de Libreros de Guatemala (Guatemala) 176
Grenfell 'Henry Lawson' Festival Prizes (Australia) 23
Grente, Cardinal, Foundation Prize (France) 112
Gresham Books (United Kingdom) 411
Gresham, John (United Kingdom) 411
Greshoff, J, Prize (Netherlands) 285
Gretener & Co (Switzerland) 375
Grevas Forlag (Denmark) 76
Greven Verlag Köln GmbH (Federal Republic of Germany) 138
Greyfriars Book Club (United Kingdom) 443
Gribaudi, Piero, Editore (Italy) 225
Griegs, John, Forlag (Norway) 298
Griffin, Charles, & Co Ltd (United Kingdom) 412
Griffon, Editions du (Switzerland) 366
Griggs, T W, & Co (Pty) Ltd (Republic of South Africa) 330
Grigori, Librairie Kassandra M (Greece) 176
Grigoris Publications (Greece) 174
Grijalbo Boliviana Ltda (Bolivia) 46
Grijalbo Centroamericana y Panamá SA (Panama) 304
Grijalbo, Distribuidora exclusivo, SA (Peru) 307
Grijalbo Ecuatoriana Ltda (Ecuador) 83
Grijalbo, Ediciones, SA (Spain) 340
Grijalbo Editor (Uruguay) 451
Grijalbo, Editorial, Ltda (Brazil) 51
Grijalbo, Editorial, SA (Mexico) 265
Grijalbo, Editorial, SA (Venezuela) 453
Grijalbo Puerto Rico Inc (Puerto Rico) 319
Grijalbo SA (Argentina) 5
Grijalbo y Cía Ltda (Chile) 63
Grijelmo, Artes Gráficas, SA (Spain) 340
Grip, PT (Indonesia) 205
Grisewood & Dempsey Ltd (United Kingdom) 412
Grolier de Venezuela (Venezuela) 453
Grolier, The, Society of Australia Pty Ltd (Australia) 14
Grøndahl og Søn Forlag A/S (Norway) 298
Grønlandske Forlag, Det (Denmark) 76
Groos, Julius, Verlag KG (Federal Republic of Germany) 138
Grosskopf, J W F, Prys vir Drama (Republic of South Africa) 335

Grossman, David, Literary Agency Ltd (United Kingdom) 442
Grossohaus Wegner und Co (Federal Republic of Germany) 167
Grosvenor Books (United Kingdom) 412
Grote'sche Verlagsbuch-handlung KG (Federal Republic of Germany) 138
Grounauer, Editions François (Switzerland) 366
Ground, Editora, Ltda (Brazil) 51
Groupe des Editeurs de Livres de la CEE (International Organizations) 467
Groupe Expansion (France) 99
Gründ, Librairie (France) 99
Grundlagen, Verlag, und Praxis GmbH & Co (Federal Republic of Germany) 138
Grundt, Johan, Tanum A/S (Norway) 300
Grüner, B R, BV (Netherlands) 277
Grünewald, Matthias-, -Verlag (Federal Republic of Germany) 138
Grupo Bibliografico Nacional de la Republica Dominicana (Dominican Republic) 82
Gruyter, Walter de, & Co, Mouton Publishers (Federal Republic of Germany) 138
Gryphon Books Pty Ltd (Australia) 14
Guadagni, L'Editrice Scientifica SaS di L G (Italy) 225
Guadalupe, Editorial (Argentina) 5
Guadiana, Grupo Editorial, SA (Spain) 341
Guanabara, Editora, Koogan SA (Brazil) 51
Guanda Editore SRL (Italy) 225
Guardian Award, The, for Children's Fiction (International Literary Prizes) 477
Guardian Fiction, The, Prize (International Literary Prizes) 477
Guazzelli, Livraria Pioneira Editora/Enio Matheus, e Cia Ltd (Brazil) 51
Gudjónssonar, Bókaútgáfa Gudjóns Ó (Iceland) 184
Guénégaud, Librairie, Sàrl (France) 99
Guhl, Verlag Klaus (Federal Republic of Germany) 138
Guida Editori SRL (Italy) 225
Guidicini e Rosa Editori Snc (Italy) 225
Guild of Travel Writers (United Kingdom) 391
Guild Publishing (United Kingdom) 412
Guildhall Library (United Kingdom) 445
Guillot, Editions d'Art Albert (France) 99
Guinness (Denmark) 76
Guinness Superlatives Ltd (United Kingdom) 412
Guitarra Facil (Colombia) 67
Gujarat, Garavi, Annual Book Award for Racial Harmony (United Kingdom) 449
Gujarat State English Language Booksellers' Association, Academic Book Centre (India) 185
Gujarat Textbook, The, Publishers' Association (India) 185
Gujarat Vidyapith Granthalaya (India) 202
Gulf Publishing Ltd (Malta) 262
Gulf Union Co (Kuwait) 253
Gullers Trading AB (Sweden) 354
Gummeruksen Kirjakauppa (Finland) 88
Gummerus, K J, Oy (Finland) 87
Gummessons Bokförlag (Sweden) 354
Gumperts Universitetsbokhandel AB (Sweden) 358
Gunasena, M D, & Co Ltd (Sri Lanka) 349
Gundert, D, Verlag (Federal Republic of Germany) 138
Gundolf, Friedrich, Prize for Germanistics abroad (Federal Republic of Germany) 170
Gunung Agung, PT (Indonesia) 205
Gunung Agung, PT (Indonesia) 206
Gunung Agung (S) Pte Ltd (Republic of Singapore) 326
Gunung Mulia, BPK (Indonesia) 205
Gunung Mulia, Toko Buku BPK (Indonesia) 206
Guoji Shudian (People's Republic of China) 64
Güse, Verlag August, GmbH (Federal Republic of Germany) 138
Gut, Th, & Co Verlag (Switzerland) 366
Gute Schriften Verein (Switzerland) 366
Gutenberg, Büchergilde (Federal Republic of Germany) 167
Gutenberg, Büchergilde (Switzerland) 375
Gutenberg, Dardanos (Greece) 174
Gutenberg-Gesellschaft (Federal Republic of Germany) 138
Gutenberg-Gesellschaft (Federal Republic of Germany) 170
Gutenberg Verlagsgesellschaft mbH, Büchergilde (Federal Republic of Germany) 138
Gutenberghus Publishing Service A/S (Denmark) 76
Gütermann, Sumus Verlag Jutta (Switzerland) 366
Gütersloher Verlagshaus Gerd Mohn (Federal Republic of Germany) 138
Guttentag', Premio de Novela 'Erich (Bolivia) 47
Guyana Library Association (Guyana) 177
Guyana Medical Science Library (Guyana) 177
Guyana National Printers Ltd (Guyana) 177
Guyana National Trading Corporation (GNTC) (Guyana) 177
Gwasg Gomer (United Kingdom) 412
Gwasg Prifysgol Cymru (United Kingdom) 412
Gwasg y Dref Wen (United Kingdom) 412

Gyan Bharati (India) 191
Gyldendal Norsk Forlag (Norway) 298
Gyldendal, Søren, Prize (Denmark) 81
Gyldendals Bogklub (Denmark) 79
Gyldendals Børnebogklub (Denmark) 79
Gyldendalske Boghandel — Nordisk Forlag A/S (Denmark) 76

H A D U - Hagemann Lehrmittel- und Verlagsgesellschaft mbH (Federal Republic of Germany) 138
H A U M Academic Bookshop (Republic of South Africa) 333
H A U M Academic Publishers (Republic of South Africa) 330
H A U M Booksellers (Republic of South Africa) 333
H A U M (Hollandsch Afrikaansche Uitgevers Maatschappij) (Republic of South Africa) 330
H & R Academica (Pty) Ltd (Republic of South Africa) 330
H F L (Publishers) Ltd (United Kingdom) 412
H K Health Knowledge Publication (Hong Kong) 179
H M & M Publishers Ltd (United Kingdom) 412
H M S O (United Kingdom) 412
H U C I T E C Ltda — Editora de Humanismo, Ciência e Tecnologia (Brazil) 51
Haack, VEB Hermann (German Democratic Republic) 117
Haag, Michael, Ltd/Travelaid Publishing (United Kingdom) 412
Haag und Herchen Verlag (Federal Republic of Germany) 139
Haan, de (Netherlands) 277
Haase, P, & Søns Forlag A/S (Denmark) 76
Habegger AG Druck und Verlag (Switzerland) 366
Habelt, Dr Rudolf, GmbH (Federal Republic of Germany) 139
Habib Bank Prize for Literature (Pakistan) 304
Hablitzel, Chris (Federal Republic of Germany) 139
Hachette/Enseignement (Hachette Educational) (France) 99
Hachette Guides Bleus (France) 100
Hachette International (Belgium) 37
Hachette International (France) 100
Hachette-Jeunesse (France) 100
Hachette, Librairie (Popular Republic of Congo) 68
Hachette, Librairie (Egypt) 84
Hachette, Librairie (France) 99
Hachette, Librairie (Gabon) 115
Hachette, Librería (Argentina) 8
Hachette, Libreria, SA (Argentina) 5
Hachette-Littérature Générale (France) 100
Hachette Pacifique, Librairie, SA (French Polynesia) 115
Hachette Pratique (France) 100
Hachette-Réalités (France) 100
Hachette, Société congolaise (Popular Republic of Congo) 68
Hacker Art Books (United Kingdom) 412
Hadar (Israel) 214
Haddock, Peter, Ltd (United Kingdom) 412
Hädecke, Walter, Verlag (Federal Republic of Germany) 139
Hadiah Sastera Malaysia Prize (Malaysia) 261
Hadow, Lyndal, Short Story Award (Australia) 23
Hadwiger, Anna, GmbH (Austria) 29
Haeschel-Dufey, F (Switzerland) 366
Hagedorn, Hans Hermann (Federal Republic of Germany) 167
Hageland, A van (Belgium) 42
Hagemann, Lehrmittelverlag Wilhelm (Federal Republic of Germany) 139
Hagen, Ten, BV (Netherlands) 277
Hager, Buchvertrieb, GmbH (Federal Republic of Germany) 139
Hagerups, H, Forlag (Denmark) 77
Hahn's, Mary, Kochbuchverlag (Federal Republic of Germany) 139
Haigh & Hochland Ltd (United Kingdom) 444
Hain, Verlag Anton (Federal Republic of Germany) 139
Hak Won Sa (Republic of Korea) 251
Hakibbutz Hameuchad Publishing House Ltd (Israel) 214
Hakki Bigeç (Turkey) 385
Hakkim's Bookshop (Bangladesh) 32
Hakusui-Sha (Japan) 239
Hakuyu-Sha (Japan) 239
Halban, Peter, Literary Agency (Israel) 217
Hale, Robert, Ltd (United Kingdom) 412
Hali Prize (India) 203
Halk Kütüphanesi, Il (Turkey) 385
Hall, June, Literary Agency (United Kingdom) 442
Haller, Berchtold, Verlag (Switzerland) 366
Hallwag Verlag AG (Switzerland) 366
Hallwag Verlagsgesellschaft mbH (Federal Republic of Germany) 139
Hälsaböcker/Allt om Hälsa AB (Sweden) 354

Hambleside Publishers Ltd (United Kingdom) 412
Hamburger Lesehefte Verlag Iselt & Co Nfl mbH (Federal Republic of Germany) 139
Hamburgische Geschichte, Verein für (Federal Republic of Germany) 170
Hamburgo, Librería, Antonio Navarrete (Mexico) 268
Hamdard Foundation (Pakistan) 302
Hameau, Le, Editeur (France) 100
Hamidia Library (Bangladesh) 32
Hamilton, Hamish, Ltd (United Kingdom) 412
Hamlet, Forlaget (Denmark) 77
Hamlyn Paperbacks (United Kingdom) 412
Hamlyn Publishing, The, Group Ltd (United Kingdom) 412
Hammer, Peter, Verlag GmbH (Federal Republic of Germany) 139
Hammicks Wholesale (United Kingdom) 444
Hamrelius och Stenvall Förlag AB (Sweden) 354
Hamrun Library (Malta) 262
Han Jin Publishing Co (Republic of Korea) 251
Hanau, Heinrich, Publications Ltd (United Kingdom) 412
Handbag Books (United Kingdom) 412
Handsel, The, Press (United Kingdom) 412
Hanguk Seoji Hakhoe (Republic of Korea) 252
Hanguk Tosogwan Hakhoe (Republic of Korea) 252
Hanna, Fred, Ltd (Republic of Ireland) 211
Hannon, J, & Co (Publishers) Oxford (United Kingdom) 412
Hans Prakashan (India) 191
Hans Publishers (India) 191
Hansa Publishers Ltd (Sri Lanka) 349
Hansa Verlag Ingwert Paulsen Jr (Federal Republic of Germany) 139
Hanse Production AB (Sweden) 354
Hansen, Edition Wilhelm (Denmark) 77
Hansen, Folmer, Teaterförlag (Sweden) 358
Hansen House (London) Ltd (United Kingdom) 413
Hanser, Carl, Verlag (Federal Republic of Germany) 139
Hänssler-Verlag (Federal Republic of Germany) 139
Hansson och Bruce, Söderbokhandeln, AB (Sweden) 358
Hanssons, Kalleberger Foundation — The Tekla, and Gösta Ronnströms Prize (Sweden) 360
Hanstein, Peter, Verlag GmbH (Federal Republic of Germany) 139
Hanthawaddy Book House (Burma) 59
Hanthawaddy Bookshop (Burma) 60
Harare City Library (Zimbabwe) 465
Harare Polytechnic Library (Zimbabwe) 465
Haraucourt, Edmond, Prize (France) 112
Harbra (Brazil) 51
Harcourt Brace Jovanovich Group (Australia) Pty Ltd (Australia) 14
Harcourt Brace Jovanovich Ltd (United Kingdom) 413
Hardiman, James, Library (Republic of Ireland) 211
Hardy, Thomas, Society Ltd (United Kingdom) 447
Hargreen Publishing Co (Australia) 14
Harjeet & Co (India) 191
Harla SA de CV (Mexico) 266
Harlekin-Presse (Federal Republic of Germany) 139
Harlequin (United Kingdom) 413
Harmi-Press Publications, Haroula Papadimitriou (Greece) 174
Harmonie, De (Netherlands) 277
Harper & Row (Australasia) Pty Ltd (Australia) 14
Harper & Row, Editora, do Brasil Ltda (Brazil) 51
Harper & Row Latinoamericana-Harla, SA de CV (Mexico) 266
Harper & Row Ltd (United Kingdom) 413
Harrach und Sabrow (Federal Republic of Germany) 139
Harrap Ltd (United Kingdom) 413
Harrassowitz, Otto (Federal Republic of Germany) 167
Harrassowitz, Verlag Otto (Federal Republic of Germany) 139
Harriers Bokförlag AB (Sweden) 354
Harris & Baldwin (United Kingdom) 413
Harris, Firma (Indonesia) 205
Harris, Katrine, Award (Republic of South Africa) 335
Harris, Paul, Publishing (United Kingdom) 413
Harrods Ltd (United Kingdom) 444
Harrow House Editions (United Kingdom) 413
Hart-Davis Educational Ltd (United Kingdom) 413
Hart Mossman & Co Ltd (Nigeria) 296
Hartmann, Verlag Karlheinz (Federal Republic of Germany) 139
Harvard Business Review Library (United Kingdom) 413
Harvard, John, Lending Library (Bahamas) 31
Harvard University Press (United Kingdom) 413
Harvester, The, Press Ltd (United Kingdom) 413
Harvey, Denise, & Company (Greece) 174
Harvey Sales (United Kingdom) 442
Harvill Press Ltd (United Kingdom) 413
Harwood Academic Publishers (France) 100
Harwood Academic Publishers GmbH (Switzerland) 366
Haryana Sahitya Prize (India) 203
Hasanuddin, Library of, University (Indonesia) 206
Hasbach, A L (Austria) 29
Haset Kitabevi AS (Turkey) 385
Hashichpul Mifal (Israel) 217

Hashim bin Haji Abdullah (Republic of Singapore) 327
Háskólabókasafn (Iceland) 185
Hatchards Ltd (United Kingdom) 444
Hatier, Librairie, SA (France) 100
Hatje, Verlag Gerd (Federal Republic of Germany) 139
Hatta, Perpustakaan Jajasan (Indonesia) 206
Haude und Spener Verlag (Federal Republic of Germany) 139
Haufe, Rudolf, Verlag GmbH & Co KG (Federal Republic of Germany) 139
Haug, Karl F, Verlag GmbH & Co KG (Federal Republic of Germany) 139
Haupt, Paul, Bern (Switzerland) 366
Hauptverband der graphischen Unternehmungen Österreichs (Austria) 24
Hauptverband des österreichischen Buchhandels (Austria) 24
Haus, Das, der Bibel (Switzerland) 366
Haus, Volksbuchhandlung, des Buches (German Democratic Republic) 119
Hauschild, Verlag H M, GmbH (Federal Republic of Germany) 140
Hauswedell, Dr Ernst, und Co Verlag (Federal Republic of Germany) 140
Hautot, Pierre, SA (France) 100
Havaux, Imprimeries (Belgium) 37
Have, Uitgeverij ten, NV (Netherlands) 277
Havez-Planque, Marie, Prize (France) 112
Hawthorn, The, Press Pty Ltd (Australia) 14
Hawthornden Prize (United Kingdom) 449
Hayakawa Publishing Inc (Japan) 239
Hayez, Imprimerie, SPRL (Belgium) 37
Haynes & Co, J H, Ltd (United Kingdom) 413
Haynes Publishing Group PLC (United Kingdom) 413
Hazan, Fernand, Editeur SA (France) 100
Health Science Press (C W Daniel) Ltd (United Kingdom) 413
Heath, A M, & Co Ltd (United Kingdom) 442
Heatherbank Press (United Kingdom) 413
Heckners Verlag (Federal Republic of Germany) 140
Hedley's Bookshop Ltd (New Zealand) 290
Heenemann, H, Verlagsgesellschaft mbH (Federal Republic of Germany) 140
Heering-Verlag GmbH (Federal Republic of Germany) 140
Heffers Booksellers (United Kingdom) 444
Heibonsha Ltd, Publishers (Japan) 239
Heibrand (Belgium) 37
Heideland, Boekhandel (Belgium) 42
Heideland NV (Heideland PVBA) (Belgium) 37
Heideland-Orbis (M & I NV) (Belgium) 37
Heidelberger, W, AG (Switzerland) 366
Heidmük-Verlag Günther U Müller (Federal Republic of Germany) 140
Heidrich, Leopold (Austria) 29
Heiliger & Co Ltd (Israel) 217
Heima er Bezt Book Club (Iceland) 184
Heimskringla (Iceland) 184
Heinemann Australia, William (Australia) 14
Heinemann Award for Literature (United Kingdom) 449
Heinemann Educational Australia (Australia) 14
Heinemann Educational Books (Asia) Ltd (Hong Kong) 179
Heinemann Educational Books (Asia) Ltd (Malaysia) 259
Heinemann Educational Books (Asia) Ltd (Republic of Singapore) 326
Heinemann Educational Books (East Africa) Ltd (Kenya) 248
Heinemann Educational Books International Ltd (United Kingdom) 413
Heinemann Educational Books Ltd (United Kingdom) 413
Heinemann Educational Books (Nigeria) Ltd (Nigeria) 294
Heinemann/Ginn (Australia) 14
Heinemann Group, The, of Publishers Ltd (United Kingdom) 413
Heinemann International Ltd, William (United Kingdom) 413
Heinemann Ltd, William (United Kingdom) 414
Heinemann Medical Books, William, Ltd (United Kingdom) 414
Heinemann/Octopus (United Kingdom) 414
Heinemann Publishers Australia Pty Ltd (Australia) 14
Heinemann Publishers (New Zealand) Ltd (New Zealand) 288
Heinemann, Verlag Egon (Federal Republic of Germany) 140
Heinold, Ehrhardt (Federal Republic of Germany) 140
Heinrichshofen's Verlag (Federal Republic of Germany) 140
Heinse, Wilhelm, Medal for Literature in Essay Form (International Literary Prizes) 477
Heintz, Verlag Georg (Federal Republic of Germany) 140
Heinzle's, Gebhard, Erben (Austria) 29
Hekla Forlag ApS (Denmark) 77
Helbing und Lichtenhahn Verlag AG (Switzerland) 366
Helgafell, Bókábudin (Iceland) 184

Helgafell, Bókaútgáfan (Iceland) 184
Helicon Press (United Kingdom) 414
Helikon Kiadó (Hungary) 181
Heliodoro Valle, Rafael, Prize (International Literary Prizes) 477
Héliographia, Arts Graphiques, SA (Switzerland) 366
Helios, Uitgeverij (Belgium) 37
Hellenic Distribution Agency (Cyprus) Ltd (Cyprus) 70
Helmond (Netherlands) 277
Help Bookshop (Lebanon) 254
Helsingin Kaupunginkirjasto - Valtakunnallinen yleisten kirjastojen keskuskirjasto (Finland) 89
Helsingin Yliopiston Kirjasto (Finland) 89
Helsinki Prize (Finland) 90
Helvetica Chimica, Verlag, Acta (Switzerland) 366
Hemans, Felicia, Prize for Lyrical Poetry (United Kingdom) 449
Hemeroteca Municipal de Madrid (Spain) 347
Hemisferio, Editorial, Sur SA (Argentina) 5
Hemkunt Publishers Pvt Ltd (India) 191
Hemma, Editions (Belgium) 37
Hemmets Journal AB (Sweden) 354
Hemus Editora Ltda (Brazil) 51
'Hemus' Foreign Trade Organization (Bulgaria) 58
Henderson's Book Store (Jamaica) 237
Henle, G, Verlag (Federal Republic of Germany) 140
Henny's Forlag (Norway) 298
Henry, Ian, Publications Ltd (United Kingdom) 414
Henschelverlag Kunst und Gesellschaft (German Democratic Republic) 117
Henssel Verlag (Federal Republic of Germany) 140
Her Majesty's Stationery Office (United Kingdom) 414
Herbert, The, Press Ltd (United Kingdom) 414
Herbig, F A, Verlagsbuchhandlung (Federal Republic of Germany) 140
Herbita, Casa Editrice (Italy) 225
Herchen (Federal Republic of Germany) 140
Herder AG (Switzerland) 366
Herder & Co (Austria) 29
Herder-Buchgemeinde (Federal Republic of Germany) 167
Herder, Editorial, SA (Spain) 341
Herder Editrice e Libreria (Italy) 225
Herder, Libreria (Spain) 347
Herder und Herder GmbH (Federal Republic of Germany) 140
Herder, Verlag, & Co (Austria) 26
Herder, Verlag, GmbH & Co, KG (Federal Republic of Germany) 140
Hérédia Prize (International Literary Prizes) 477
Heritage (Australia) 14
Heritage (Israel) 214
Heritage Books (Nigeria) 294
Heritage Publishers (India) 191
Heritage Publishing House (Philippines) 309
Hermann (Editeurs des Sciences et des Arts) SA (France) 100
Hermeroteca Nacional de México (Mexico) 269
Hermes, Editorial, SA (Mexico) 266
Hermes Edizioni SRL (Italy) 225
Hermods (Sweden) 354
Herne, Editions de l' (France) 100
Hernieuwen-Uitgaven PVBA (Belgium) 37
Hernovs Book Club (Denmark) 79
Hernovs Forlag (Denmark) 77
Herold Druck- und Verlagsgesellschaft mbH (Austria) 26
Herold Verlag Brück KG (Federal Republic of Germany) 140
Heron Books (United Kingdom) 443
Herrera, Casa (Dominican Republic) 82
Herrera, Febio (Dominican Republic) 82
Herrero, Editorial, SA (Mexico) 266
Herridge, Charles, Ltd (United Kingdom) 414
Hertenstein-Presse (Federal Republic of Germany) 140
Hertoghs, Drukkerij-Uitgeverij (Belgium) 37
Hertzog Prize (Republic of South Africa) 335
Herzmansky, Bernhard (Austria) 26
Herzog August Bibliothek (Federal Republic of Germany) 168
Hessische Landes- und Hoch-schulbibliothek Darmstadt (Federal Republic of Germany) 168
Hessischer Verleger- und Buchhändler-Verband eV (Federal Republic of Germany) 121
Hestia Bookstore (Greece) 176
Hestia-Verlag GmbH (Federal Republic of Germany) 140
Heuff, Uitgeverij, Nieuwkoop (Netherlands) 277
Heureka, Uitgeverij (Netherlands) 277
Heures Claires, Editions d'Art Les, SA (France) 100
Heusden, Gérard Th Van, (APA) (Netherlands) 277
Heyden & Son Ltd (United Kingdom) 414
Heyer, The Georgette, Historical Novel Prize (International Literary Prizes) 477
Heymanns, Carl, Verlag KG (Federal Republic of Germany) 140
Heyn, Buchhandlung Johannes (Austria) 29
Heyn, Johannes (Austria) 26
Heyne, Rolf, Verlag (Switzerland) 366
Heyne, Wilhelm, Verlag (Federal Republic of Germany) 140

Heyum, Monica, Agency (Sweden) 358
Hichtum, Nienke van, Prize (Netherlands) 285
Hicks Smith & Sons Pty Ltd (Australia) 14
Hidakarya Agung (Indonesia) 205
Hiersemann, Anton, Verlag (Federal Republic of Germany) 141
Higginbothams Ltd (India) 201
High Council of Arts & Literature (Egypt) 85
High Court of Australia Library (Australia) 20
Higham, David, Associates Ltd (United Kingdom) 442
Higham, David, Prize for Fiction (International Literary Prizes) 477
Higher Educational Books Publishing House (Democratic People's Republic of Korea) 250
HighText Ltd (United Kingdom) 442
Hikarinokuni Co Ltd (Japan) 239
Hilal, Dar Al, Publishing Institution (Egypt) 84
Hildur, Bókaútgáfan (Iceland) 184
Hilger, Adam, Ltd (United Kingdom) 414
Hilger, Edition E (Austria) 26
Hill, Leonard (United Kingdom) 414
Hill of Content Publishing Co Ltd (Australia) 14
Hillelförlaget (Sweden) 354
Hilmarton Manor Press (United Kingdom) 414
Himachal Publishers' & Booksellers' Association (India) 185
Himalaya Prakashan (India) 191
Himalaya Publishing House (India) 191
Himalayan Books (India) 191
Himpunan Masyarakat Pencinta Buku (Indonesia) 206
Hind Pocket Books Private Ltd (India) 191
Hinder und Deelmann, Verlag (Federal Republic of Germany) 141
Hindi Book Centre (India) 201
Hindi Pracharak Sansthan (India) 191
Hindustan Publishing Corporation (India) (India) 191
Hinstorff, VEB, Verlag (German Democratic Republic) 117
Hinzelin, Emile, Foundation Prize (France) 112
Hiperión, Ediciones, SL (Spain) 341
Hippo Books (United Kingdom) 414
Hippoboek/Studio de Zuid (Netherlands) 277
Hippokrates-Verlag GmbH (Federal Republic of Germany) 141
Hirmer Verlag (Federal Republic of Germany) 141
Hirokawa Publishing Co (Japan) 239
Hirsch, Axel, Prize (Sweden) 360
Hirsch, Carlos, SRL (Argentina) 8
Hirschsprungs, H, Forlag (Denmark) 77
Hirt, Ferdinand (Federal Republic of Germany) 141
Hirt, Ferdinand, mbH & Co KG (Austria) 26
Hirzel, S, Verlag GmbH und Co (Federal Republic of Germany) 141
Hispanas, Ediciones (Guatemala) 177
Hispano Americana, Libreria (Spain) 347
Hispano Europea, Editorial (Spain) 341
Hispanoamericana, Libreria (Puerto Rico) 320
Hissink, G W, & Co (APA) (Netherlands) 277
Histoire Sociale, Editions d', (EDHIS) (France) 100
Historical Society of Afghanistan (Afghanistan) 1
History Guild (United Kingdom) 443
Hjemmens Forlag A/S (Norway) 298
Hjemmet A/S (Norway) 299
Hjemmets Bokforlag A/S (Norway) 299
Hjemmets Bokklubb (Norway) 300
Hjemmets Kokebokklubb (Norway) 300
Hladbúd hf (Iceland) 184
Hliðskjálf, Bókaútgáfan (Iceland) 184
Hna Lon Hla (Burma) 60
Hobbit Presse (Federal Republic of Germany) 141
Hobby Centre (Trinidad and Tobago) 382
Hobby, Editorial (Argentina) 5
Hobsons Press (Cambridge) Ltd (United Kingdom) 414
Hoch (Federal Republic of Germany) 141
Hodder & Stoughton (Australia) Pty Ltd (Australia) 14
Hodder & Stoughton Children's Books (United Kingdom) 414
Hodder & Stoughton Ltd (New Zealand) 288
Hodder & Stoughton Ltd (United Kingdom) 414
Hodemacher, Münchner Verlagsbüro Horst, — Axel Poldner GmbH & Co KG (Federal Republic of Germany) 167
Hodge, Alison (United Kingdom) 414
Hodges Figgis & Co Ltd (Republic of Ireland) 211
Hodgson, Francis (United Kingdom) 414
Hoepli, Casa Editrice Libraria Ulrico, SpA (Italy) 225
Hoepli, Ulrico, Libreria Internazionale (Italy) 234
Hoernle, Volksbuchhandlung Edwin (German Democratic Republic) 119
Hoeve, W van (Netherlands) 277
Hofacker, Ing W, GmbH Verlag (Federal Republic of Germany) 141
Hofbauer, Buchhandlung Karl (Austria) 29
Hoffman, Agence (France) 109
Hoffmann (Federal Republic of Germany) 167
Hoffmann, Dieter, Verlag (Federal Republic of Germany) 141

Hoffmann, Julius, Verlag (Federal Republic of Germany) 141
Hoffmann und Campe Verlag (Federal Republic of Germany) 141
Hofmann, Verlag Karl (Federal Republic of Germany) 141
Hofmeister, VEB Friedrich, Musikverlag (German Democratic Republic) 117
Hofmeyr, W A, Prize (Republic of South Africa) 335
Hogar del Libro — Nova Terra (Spain) 341
Hogar del Libro SA (Spain) 347
Hogarth, The, Press Ltd (United Kingdom) 415
Hogrefe, Verlag für Psychologie Dr C J (Switzerland) 366
Hohenloher Druck- und Verlagshaus (Federal Republic of Germany) 141
Hohenstaufen Verlag Schumann KG Berg/Bodman (Federal Republic of Germany) 141
Hôi Thu-Viên Viet Nam (Socialist Republic of Viet Nam) 455
Hoikusha Publishing Co Ltd (Japan) 239
Hökerbergs, Lars, Bokförlag (Sweden) 354
Hokkaido University Library (Japan) 245
Hokuryukan Co Ltd (Japan) 239
Hokuseido, The, Press (Japan) 239
Holberg Medal (Denmark) 81
Holgersson, Nils, Plaque (Sweden) 360
Holkema, Van, en Warendorf (Netherlands) 277
Hölker, Verlag Wolfgang (Federal Republic of Germany) 141
Holland (Netherlands) 277
Holland, The, Press (United Kingdom) 415
Holland University Press BV (APA) (Netherlands) 277
Hollandia, Uitgeverij, BV (Netherlands) 277
Holle Verlag GmbH (Federal Republic of Germany) 141
Hollinek, Brüder, & Co GmbH (Austria) 26
Hollis & Carter (United Kingdom) 415
Holloway, Tienie, Medal (Republic of South Africa) 335
Höllrigl, Eduard (Austria) 29
Holly, Jan, Prize (Czechoslovakia) 74
Hollym Corporation, Publishers (Republic of Korea) 251
Holmes McDougall Ltd (United Kingdom) 415
Holmes, The Sherlock, Society of London (United Kingdom) 447
Holon Literary Prize (Israel) 218
Holp Book Co Ltd (Japan) 239
Holsten Verlag Wolf Schenke KG (Federal Republic of Germany) 141
Holt-Blond Ltd (United Kingdom) 415
Holt, Rinehart & Winston (United Kingdom) 415
Holt-Saunders Ltd (United Kingdom) 415
Holt-Saunders Pty Ltd (Australia) 14
Holt-Saunders Pty Ltd (New Zealand) 288
Holtby, Winifred, Memorial Prize (United Kingdom) 449
Holte, Clarence L, Prize (International Literary Prizes) 477
Holy Land Map Co Ltd (Israel) 214
Holzapfel, Verlag Gebr (Federal Republic of Germany) 141
Holzboog, Gunther, GmbH & Co (Federal Republic of Germany) 141
Holzmann, Hans, Verlag GmbH und Co KG (Federal Republic of Germany) 141
Home and Garden Guild (United Kingdom) 443
Home Health Education Service (United Kingdom) 415
Home Library Plan (India) 201
Home Reference Library (United Kingdom) 443
Hommes et Techniques, Editions (France) 100
Hone, Evelyn, College Library (Zambia) 463
Hong Kong Book Centre Ltd (Hong Kong) 180
Hong Kong Booksellers' & Stationers' Association (Hong Kong) 178
Hong Kong Cultural Press Ltd (Hong Kong) 179
Hong Kong Educational Publishers Association Ltd (Hong Kong) 178
Hong Kong Junior Chamber of Commerce Libraries (Hong Kong) 180
Hong Kong Library Association (Hong Kong) 180
Hong Kong Polytechnic Library (Hong Kong) 180
Hong Kong Publishers' & Distributors' Association (Hong Kong) 178
Hong Kong Publishing Co Ltd (Hong Kong) 179
Hong Kong University Press (Hong Kong) 179
Hong Kong Witman Publishing Co (Hong Kong) 179
Hönsetryk, Forlaget (Denmark) 77
Hoogenhout, C P, Award (Republic of South Africa) 335
Hoogt, Lucy B and C W van der, Prize (Netherlands) 285
Hoorick, Verlag Van, Farb-Dia-Archiv Edmond Van Hoorick (Switzerland) 366
Hopkins, The, Society (United Kingdom) 447
Hor Samut Klang (Thailand) 380
Horatio-verlag und Agentur (Federal Republic of Germany) 141
Horay, Pierre, Editeur (France) 100
Horizon Bookshop Ltd (New Zealand) 290
Horizonte, Editorial (Peru) 307
Horizonte, Livros, Lda (Portugal) 317
Horizontes, Editora, de América (Dominican Republic) 82

INDEX 517

Hörnemann, Werner, Verlag (Federal Republic of Germany) 141
Horseman's Bookclub (United Kingdom) 443
Horseman's Handbooks (United Kingdom) 415
Horst-Werner Dumjahn Verlag (Federal Republic of Germany) 141
Horwitz Grahame Books Pty Ltd (Australia) 15
Horwood, Ellis, Ltd (United Kingdom) 415
'Horyzonty', Wydawnictwo Harcerskie (Poland) 311
Horzonte, Editorial (Peru) 307
Høst og Søns Forlag (Denmark) 77
Hour-Glass Press (United Kingdom) 415
Hove, M van, DPN (Belgium) 37
Høvring's, Birgitte, Icelandic World Literature (Denmark) 77
How & Why Books (United Kingdom) 415
Howard Book Co (Hong Kong) 180
Hraundragni Book Club (Iceland) 184
Hrvatska Revija (Spain) 341
Hrvatsko bibliotekarsko društvo (Yugoslavia) 461
Hua Kuo Publishing Co (Taiwan) 378
Huber AG, Hans (Switzerland) 366
Huber & Co AG, Verlag (Switzerland) 366
Huber, Hans (Switzerland) 375
Huber, Michael und Margret (Switzerland) 366
Hucho de Oro Prize (Spain) 349
Hudson, Angus (United Kingdom) 415
Hudsons Bookshops (United Kingdom) 444
Hueber-Holzmann Pädagogischer Verlag (Federal Republic of Germany) 142
Hueber, Max, Verlag (Federal Republic of Germany) 141
Huemul, Editorial, SA (Argentina) 6
Huemul, Librería, SA (Argentina) 6
Huemul, Librería, SA (Argentina) 8
Hugendubel, Heinrich (Federal Republic of Germany) 168
Hughes Massie Ltd (United Kingdom) 442
Hugo, The, Awards (International Literary Prizes) 477
Hugo's Language Books Ltd (United Kingdom) 415
Hugues, Clovis, Prize (France) 113
Hulton Educational Publications Ltd (United Kingdom) 415
Human & Rousseau Publishers (Pty) Ltd (Republic of South Africa) 330
Humanismo, Editora de, Ciência e Tecnologia (Brazil) 51
Humanitas, Editorial (Argentina) 6
Humanoïdes, Les, Associés (France) 100
Humata Verlag Harold S Blume (Switzerland) 367
Humboldt-Buchhandlung (German Democratic Republic) 119
Humboldt-Taschenbuchverlag Jacobi KG (Federal Republic of Germany) 142
Humboldt Universität zu Berlin (German Democratic Republic) 119
Humboldt, Volksbuchhandlung Alexander von (German Democratic Republic) 119
Hundertmark, Edition (Federal Republic of Germany) 142
Hune, Librairie La (France) 109
Hung Fung Book Co (Hong Kong) 179
Hungarian Foreign Trade Organization (Hungary) 182
Hunt Bartlett, Alice, Prize (International Literary Prizes) 477
Hür Yayin ve Ticaret (Turkey) 385
Hürriyet Yayinlari (Hür Yayin) (Turkey) 384
Hurst, C, & Co (Publisher's) Ltd (United Kingdom) 415
Husain, Dr Mahmud, Library (Pakistan) 303
Husum Druck- und Verlagsgesellschaft mbH & Co KG (Federal Republic of Germany) 142
Hutchinson & Co (Publishers) Ltd (United Kingdom) 415
Hutchinson Books (United Kingdom) 415
Hutchinson Children's Books Ltd (United Kingdom) 415
Hutchinson Educational (United Kingdom) 415
Hutchinson Group (Australia) Ltd (Australia) 15
Hutchinson Group (NZ) Ltd (New Zealand) 288
Hutchinson Group (SA) (Pty) Ltd (Republic of South Africa) 330
Hutchinson Publishing Group, The, Ltd (United Kingdom) 415
Hutchinson Technical Books (United Kingdom) 415
Hutchinson University Library (United Kingdom) 416
Hüthig, Dr Alfred, Verlag GmbH (Federal Republic of Germany) 142
Hüthig und Pflaum Verlag GmbH & Co KG (Federal Republic of Germany) 142
Hüthig und Wepf Verlag (Switzerland) 367
Hutten, Ulrich v, Volksbuchhandlung (German Democratic Republic) 119
Huygens, Constantijn, Prize (Netherlands) 285
Hviezdoslavova knižnica (Czechoslovakia) 73
Hwimoon Publishing Co (Republic of Korea) 251
Hyang Mun Sa (Republic of Korea) 251
Hyderabad, The, & Secunderabad Publishers' & Booksellers' Association (India) 185
Hyfte, Van, -De Coninck (Belgium) 37
Hyland House Publishing Pty Ltd (Australia) 15
Hylton Lacy Publishers (United Kingdom) 416
Hymns Ancient & Modern (United Kingdom) 416
Hyoronsha Publishing Co Ltd (Japan) 239

Hyperion Books (United Kingdom) 416
Hyun Am Publishing Co (Republic of Korea) 251
Hyun Dae Mun Hak (Republic of Korea) 252
Hyun Dae Mun Hak Prize (Republic of Korea) 253

I B A M (Brazil) 51
I B B Y (International Organizations) 467
I B E P (Brazil) 51
I B H Publishing Co (India) 191
I B I (India) 191
I B I C T (Brazil) 51
I B I S (United Kingdom) 391
I B I S Information Services Ltd (Australia) 10
I B R A (Ghana) 172
I B R A S A (Instituição Brasileira de Difusão Cultural SA) (Brazil) 51
I B R E X — Distribuidora de Livros e Material de Escritório Ltda (Brazil) 56
I C A-Förlaget AB (Sweden) 354
I C C E, Publicaciones (Spain) 341
I C I C (Directory Publishers) Ltd (Nigeria) 294
I C I Writer's Bursary (New Zealand) 291
I C Magazines Ltd (United Kingdom) 416
I C S A Publishing Ltd (United Kingdom) 416
I C S Izdavačko Informativni Centar Studenata (Yugoslavia) 457
I C U, (Informatie en Communicatie Unie NV) (Netherlands) 277
I D E P (Senegal) 324
I d W-Verlag GmbH (Federal Republic of Germany) 142
I E Aust Publications (Australia) 15
I G A, Distribuidora Cultural (Guatemala) 177
I G N (Institut Géographique National) (France) 100
I L A (International Literary Agency) (Italy) 233
I L E X I M — Foreign Trade Co (Romania) 322
I L S (Institut für Lernsysteme) GmbH (Federal Republic of Germany) 142
I M H V (Federal Republic of Germany) 121
I M S F (Federal Republic of Germany) 142
I N A D E S — Edition (Institut africain pour le developpement économique et social) (Ivory Coast) 236
I N A D E S (Institut africain pour le Développement économique et social) Documentation (Ivory Coast) 236
I N B E L (Belgium) 37
I N F E L (Informationsstelle für Elektrizitätsanwendung) (Switzerland) 367
I N I D (Romania) 322
I P C (United Kingdom) 416
I P E A (Instituto de Planejamento Econômico e Social) Servicio Editorial (Brazil) 51
I P L (Istituto Propaganda Libraria) (Italy) 219
I R L Press (United Kingdom) 416
I S B N (International Organizations) 467
I S B N, Agencia Nacional de (Mexico) 264
I S B N, Bureau (Netherlands) 273
I S P C K (India) 191
I S P-Verlag (Internationale Sozialistische Publikationen) (Federal Republic of Germany) 142
I S S N (International Organizations) 467
I T A U, Edições, (Instituto Tecnico de Alimentaçao Humana) Lda (Portugal) 317
I T V Books (United Kingdom) 416
I V I O, Stichting (Netherlands) 277
Ibadan University Library (Nigeria) 296
Ibadan University Press (Nigeria) 294
Ibaka (Nigeria) 294
Ibana, SA (Uruguay) 452
Ibérico Europea de Ediciones SA (Spain) 341
Iberlibros — Unidad de Exportación (Spain) 341
Ibero-Americano, Livro, Ltda (Brazil) 51
Ibero-Americano, Livro, Ltda (Brazil) 56
Ibero-Amerikanisches Institut (Federal Republic of Germany) 168
Ibis (Denmark) 77
Icaria Editorial SA (Spain) 341
Iceland Review (Iceland) 184
Iceland Travel Books (Iceland) 184
Icelandic Cultural Fund, Publishing Department (Iceland) 184
Icelandic Libertarians', The, Book Club (Iceland) 184
Icelandic Libertarians', The, Bookshop (Iceland) 184
Ichtiar Baru (Indonesia) 205
Icob cv (Netherlands) 283
Icob cv Uitgeverij (Netherlands) 277
Icon (Belgium) 44
Icthus, Librería (Bolivia) 46
Idara-e-Faroghe-Undu (Pakistan) 302
Idara Siqafat-e-Islamia (Pakistan) 302
Idarah-I-Adabiyat-I-Delli (India) 191
Idea Books (Italy) 226
Idea Verlag GmbH (Federal Republic of Germany) 142
Ideal (Malta) 262
Ideal, The, Bookshop (Malta) 262
Ideeboek BV (Netherlands) 277

Idelson, Casa Editrice V, di F Gnocchi (Italy) 226
Ideoplastos (Suriname) 351
Ides et Calendes, Editions, SA (Switzerland) 367
Idunn (Iceland) 184
Ie-No-Hikari Association (Japan) 239
Ife Book Fair Prizes (Nigeria) 297
Igaku-Shoin Ltd (Japan) 240
Igbo Language Translation Agency (Nigeria) 297
Ikaros Ekdotiki (Greece) 174
Ikatan Penerbit Indonesia (IKAPI) (Indonesia) 205
Ikatan Pustakawan Indonesia (Indonesia) 207
Ikhwan, PD & I (Indonesia) 205
Ikubundo Publishers Co (Japan) 245
Il Cho Kak (Republic of Korea) 251
Il Ji Sa Publishing Co (Republic of Korea) 251
Ilesanmi Press & Sons (N) Ltd (Nigeria) 294
Ilidio da Fonseca Matos (Portugal) 318
Illustration, Editions de l' (France) 100
Ilm, Dar el-, Lilmalayin (Lebanon) 254
Ilmi Kitab Khana (Pakistan) 302
Image (United Kingdom) 416
Imba Verlag (Switzerland) 367
Imha (Greece) 175
Imhoff, Hans (Federal Republic of Germany) 142
Impala, Editions (Zaire) 462
Imparudi (Imprimerie et Papeterie du Burundi) (Burundi) 60
Imperial News Agency and Bookshop (Gibraltar) 173
Imprensa Nacional-Casa da Moeda (Portugal) 317
Impressum Verlag AG (Switzerland) 367
Imprimerie Commerciale et Administrative de Mauritanie (Mauritania) 263
Imprimeries Réunies SA (Switzerland) 367
Impulso (Mexico) 266
In den Toren, Uitgeverij (Netherlands) 277
In, Uitgeverij J van (Belgium) 37
Inba Nilayam (India) 192
Inca, Promotion Editorial, SA (Peru) 307
Incafo, Editorial, SA (Spain) 341
Independent Publishers Guild (United Kingdom) 391
Independent Television Books Ltd (United Kingdom) 416
Index, Editorial, (Tormes, SL) (Spain) 341
Index eV (Federal Republic of Germany) 142
India Book House (India) 192
India Book House (India) 201
India Office Library and Records (United Kingdom) 445
Indian Association of Academic Librarians (India) 202
Indian Association of Special Libraries and Information Centres (India) 202
Indian College Library Association (India) 202
Indian Council for Cultural Relations (India) 192
Indian Council of Agricultural Research (India) 192
Indian Council of Medical Research (India) 192
Indian Council of Social Science Research (ICSSR) (India) 192
Indian Council of World Affairs Library (India) 202
Indian Documentation Service (India) 192
Indian Folklore Society (India) 192
Indian Folklore Society (India) 203
Indian Institute of Advanced Study (India) 192
Indian Institute of Technology Central Library (India) 202
Indian Institute of World Culture (India) 192
Indian Library Association (India) 202
Indian Museum (India) 192
Indian National Academy of Letters Awards (India) 203
Indian National Scientific Documentation Centre (India) 204
Indian Press (Publications) Pvt Ltd (India) 192
Indian Printing and Publishing Co (Fiji) 86
Indian Publications (India) 192
Indian Publishing House (India) 192
Indian Society for Promoting Christian Knowledge (ISPCK) (India) 192
Indira, P T (Indonesia) 205
Indira, P T (Indonesia) 206
Indlouu Ubudlelwane Ngezincwadi (Republic of South Africa) 333
Indrajaya (Indonesia) 205
Industrial Publishing House (Democratic People's Republic of Korea) 250
Industrias ABC (Angola) 2
Industrielle Organisation, Verlag (Switzerland) 367
Industrielle Rettsvern, Styret for det, Bibliotek (Norway) 300
Industry & Trade Publishers (Philippines) 309
Info Book (Sweden) 358
Infoboek (Belgium) 38
Infopers (Netherlands) 278
Información, La (Dominican Republic) 82
Information Processing Association of Israel (Israel) 218
Informations Forlag ApS (Denmark) 77
Informations-Zentrum Buch (Federal Republic of Germany) 121
Informationsstelle für Elektrizitätsanwendung (Switzerland) 367
Informator (Yugoslavia) 457
Ingeniero, Librería del (Colombia) 67
Ingenjörsvetenskapsakademien (I V A) (Sweden) 354

Initial Teaching, The, Alphabet Foundation (United Kingdom) 416
Inkata Press Pty Ltd (Australia) 15
Inkilâp Ve Aka Kitabevleri (Turkey) 384
Inland Bookshop (Tanzania) 379
Inland Publishers (Tanzania) 379
Inn-Verlag (Austria) 26
Innkaupasamband Bóksala HF (Iceland) 183
Innocenti, Editrice, Snc (Italy) 226
Innovacion, Editorial, SA (Mexico) 266
Inpra International Press Agency (United Kingdom) 442
Input Two-Nine (United Kingdom) 416
Inquérito, Editorial, Lda (Portugal) 317
Insel Verlag (Federal Republic of Germany) 142
Insel-Verlag Anton Kippenberg (German Democratic Republic) 117
Inside Books BV (Netherlands) 278
Insight Chronicles, The (Republic of Singapore) 326
Insight Guides (Republic of Singapore) 326
Instituição Brasileira de Difusão Cultural SA (Brazil) 51
Institut africain de Développement Economique et de Planification (IDEP), Bibliothèque (Senegal) 324
Institut belge d'Information et de Documentation (INBEL) (Belgium) 38
Institut belge d'Information et de Documentation (INBEL) (Belgium) 43
Institut, Bibliothèque de l', Français d'Archéologie du Proche Orient (Lebanon) 254
Institut, Bibliothèque de l', supérieur d'Education et de Formation continue (Tunisia) 384
Institut Culturel Français Bibliothèque (Libya) 256
Institut Dagang Muchtar (Indonesia) 205
Institut de Bibliothéconomie et des Sciences documentaires (Algeria) 2
Institut de France, Bibliotheque de l' (France) 110
Institut de recherche en Sciences humaines (Niger) 292
Institut des Belles Lettres arabes (Tunisia) 384
Institut d'etudes politiques et de l'information, Bibliothèque (Algeria) 2
Institut fondamental d'Afrique noire, Bibliothèque (Senegal) 324
Institut für Heilpädagogik Verlag (Switzerland) 367
Institut für Jugendbuchforschung der J W Goethe-Universität (Federal Republic of Germany) 169
Institut für Lernsysteme (ILS) (Federal Republic of Germany) 142
Institut für Marxistische Studien und Forschungen eV (IMSF) (Federal Republic of Germany) 142
Institut Geógraphique National (France) 100
Institut Murundi d'Information et de Documentation (IMIDOC) (Burundi) 60
Institut national agronomique, Bibliothèque (Algeria) 2
Institut national, Bibliothèque de l', de la recherche scientifique (Rwanda) 323
Institut national de la statistique et de la recherche economique (Democratic Republic of Madagascar) 258
Institut national de recherches et documentation, Bibliothèque (Guinea) 177
Institut national de Recherches et Documentation (National Research and Documentation Institute) (Guinea) 177
Institut national de Sténodactylographie (Belgium) 38
Institut national, Librairie de l', d'Etudes politiques (Zaire) 462
Institut national pour la formation et la recherche en éducation (Centre de documentation et d'information pédagogique) (Benin) 46
Institut of Slovak Literature (Czechoslovakia) 74
Institut Panafricain pour le Developpement (IPD) (International Organizations) 471
Institut Pasteur d'Algérie, Bibliothèque (Algeria) 2
Institut pédagogique national (Zaire) 462
Institut, Perpustakaan Pusat, Teknologi Bandung (Indonesia) 207
Institut polytechnique de Conakry Bibliothèque (Guinea) 177
Institut polytechnique de l'Afrique centrale Bibliothèque (Gabon) 115
Institut pour la recherche scientifique en Afrique centrale, Bibliothèque (Zaire) 462
Institut royal des Relations internationales (Belgium) 38
Institut royal des Sciences naturelles de Belgique, Bibliothèque (Belgium) 43
Institut scientifique chérifien (Morocco) 271
Institut supérieure des sciences de l'éducation, Bibliothèque (Popular Republic of Congo) 68
Institut Universitaire de Hautes Etudes Internationales (Switzerland) 367
Institute for Christian Publishing & Communications Research (India) 192
Institute for Palestine Studies, Publishing and Research Organization (Lebanon) 254
Institute for Publishing Hebrew Books (Israel) 214
Institute for Reformational Studies (Republic of South Africa) 330
Institute for Scientific and Technical Documentation and Information (Yugoslavia) 460
Institute for the Talmudic Encyclopaedia and Complete Israeli Talmud (Israel) 214
Institute for the Translation, The, of Hebrew Literature Ltd (Israel) 214
Institute Nacional de Bellas Artes (Mexico) 266
Institute of African Studies (Nigeria) 294
Institute of African Studies (Zambia) 463
Institute of African Studies Library (Ghana) 173
Institute of Arab Research & Studies Library (Egypt) 84
Institute of Development Management Library (Tanzania) 379
Institute of Economics Library (Burma) 60
Institute of Education Library (Burma) 60
Institute of Education Library, Kabul University (Afghanistan) 1
Institute of Ethiopian Studies Library (Ethiopia) 86
Institute of Information Scientists (United Kingdom) 445
Institute of Personnel Management (United Kingdom) 416
Institute of Physics, The (United Kingdom) 416
Institute of Public Administration (Republic of Ireland) 210
Institute of Public Administration Library (Saudi Arabia) 323
Institute of Pyramidology (United Kingdom) 416
Institute of Reprographic Technology (United Kingdom) 445
Institute of Southeast Asian Studies (Republic of Singapore) 326
Institute of Technology, Rangoon, Library (Burma) 60
Institute, The, for the Translation of Hebrew Literature Ltd (Israel) 213
Institute, The, for the Translation of Hebrew Literature Ltd (Israel) 218
Institution of Chemical Engineers (United Kingdom) 416
Institution of Civil Engineers, The, (Publications Division) (United Kingdom) 416
Institution of Electrical Engineers (United Kingdom) 416
Institution of Mechanical Engineers (United Kingdom) 416
Instituto Anglo-Mexicano de Cultura, Biblioteca del (Mexico) 269
Instituto Autónomo Biblioteca Nacional y de Servicios de Bibliotecas (Venezuela) 454
Instituto Bibliográfico Hispánico (Spain) 348
Instituto, Biblioteca del, Chileno-Británico de Cultura (Chile) 63
Instituto Brasileiro de Administraçao Municipal (IBAM) (Brazil) 51
Instituto Brasileiro de Edições Pedagógicas (IBEP) (Brazil) 52
Instituto Brasileiro de Geografia, Fundação, e Estatística (Brazil) 52
Instituto Brasileiro de Informação em Ciência e Tecnologia (IBICT) (Brazil) 52
Instituto Brasileiro de Informação em Ciência e Tecnologia (IBICT) (Brazil) 57
Instituto Campineiro de Ensino Agrícola (Brazil) 52
Instituto Centro Americano de Administración Pública (ICAP) (Costa Rica) 68
Instituto Cubano del Libro (Cuba) 69
Instituto Cultural, Biblioteca del, Anglo-Uruguayo (Uruguay) 452
Instituto de Bibliográfia del Ministerio de Educación de la Provincia de Buenos Aires (Argentina) 9
Instituto de Cooperacion, Biblioteca del, Iberoamericana (Spain) 347
Instituto de Cultura, Biblioteca del, Hispànica (Spain) 348
Instituto de Cultura Puertorriqueña (Puerto Rico) 319
Instituto de Estudios de Administración Local, Publicaciones (Spain) 341
Instituto de Estudios Peruanos (Peru) 307
Instituto de Estudios Politicos (Spain) 341
Instituto de Investigaciones Bibliográficas (Mexico) 269
Instituto de Investigaciones Sociales — Universidad Nacional Autónoma de Mexico (Mexico) 266
Instituto de Literatura (Argentina) 9
Instituto de Literatura, Biblioteca del, y Linguistica (Cuba) 69
Instituto de Planejamento Econômico e Social (Brazil) 52
Instituto de Publicaciones Navales (Argentina) 6
Instituto Indigenista Interamericano (Mexico) 266
Instituto Interamericano de Cooperación para la Agricultura (IICA) (Costa Rica) 68
Instituto Mexicano del Libro AC (Mexico) 264
Instituto Nacional, Biblioteca del, del Libro Español (Spain) 348
Instituto Nacional de Antropologia e Historia (Mexico) 266
Instituto Nacional del Libro Español (Spain) 336
Instituto Nacional del Libro Español, Delegación de Barcelona (Spain) 336
Instituto Nacional do Livro (Brazil) 48
Instituto Nacional do Livro e do Disco (Mozambique) 271
Instituto Nacional, Ediciones, de Cultura (Panama) 304
Instituto Panamericano de Geografía, Biblioteca del, e Historia (Mexico) 269
Instituto Panamericano de Geografía e Historia (Mexico) 266
Instituto Pontificio, Ediciones, San Pío X (Spain) 341
Instituto Português da Sociedade Cientifica de Goerres (Portugal) 319
Instituto Pre-universitario, Biblioteca del, de la Habana (Cuba) 69
Instituto Tecnico de Alimentaçao Humana (Portugal) 317
Instituto Tecnológico, Biblioteca del, y de Estudios Superiores de Monterrey (Mexico) 269
Instituto Venezolano, Biblioteca del, de Investigaciones Científicas (Venezuela) 454
Instituts für Weltwirtschaft, Bibliothek des, — Zentralbibliothek der Wirtschaftswissenschaften (Federal Republic of Germany) 168
Institutul de medicina si farmacie Biblioteca Centrala (Romania) 322
Institutul National de Informare si Documentare (INID) (Romania) 322
Instytut Badań Literackich (Poland) 314
Instytut Bibliograficzny (Poland) 314
Instytut, Państwowy, Wydawniczy (Poland) 311
Insula, Librería, Ediciones y Publicaciones SA (Spain) 341
Insula, Librería, Ediciones y Publicaciones SA (Spain) 347
Intellectual Publishing House (India) 192
Intellectual Society of Libya (Libya) 256
Inter American University of Puerto Rico Library (Puerto Rico) 320
Inter Documentation Co AG (Switzerland) 367
Inter-European Editions (Netherlands) 278
Inter-India Publications (India) 192
Inter-Kunst und Buch GmbH (Federal Republic of Germany) 142
Inter-Médica, Editorial, SAICI (Argentina) 6
Inter-Varsity Press (United Kingdom) 416
Interallié Prize (France) 113
Interamericana de Venezuela, Editorial, CA (Venezuela) 453
Interamericana, Editorial, SA (Uruguay) 451
'Interavia' SA (Société anonyme d'Editions aéronautiques internationales) (Switzerland) 367
Interbankendienst, Uitgaven van, NV (Belgium) 38
Interbooks (Belgium) 38
Interciencia, Livraria, Ltda (Brazil) 52
Intercontinental Book Productions Ltd (United Kingdom) 416
Intercontinental Literary Agency (United Kingdom) 442
InterEditions Paris (France) 100
Interessengemeinschaft Musikwissenschaftlicher Herausgeber und Verleger (IMHV) (Federal Republic of Germany) 121
Interfrom, Edition (Switzerland) 367
Intergéo, CNRS Laboratoire (France) 100
Intergovernmental Copyright Committee (International Organizations) 467
Interkerklike Uitgewerstrust (Republic of South Africa) 330
Intermediate Technology Publications Ltd (United Kingdom) 416
Internationaal Instituut, Bibliotheek van het, voor Sociale Geschiedenis (Netherlands) 284
International African Institute (International Organizations) 471
International Association for Mass Communication Research (International Organizations) 467
International Association of Agricultural Librarians and Documentalists — IAALD (International Organizations) 467
International Association of Law Libraries (IALL) (International Organizations) 467
International Association of Literary Critics (International Organizations) 467
International Association of Metropolitan City Libraries (INTAMEL) (International Organizations) 467
International Association of Music Libraries, Archives and Documentation Centres (IAML) (International Organizations) 467
International Association of Music Libraries, Archives and Documentation Centres, (UK Branch) (United Kingdom) 446
International Association of Music Libraries, Australian Branch (IAMLANZ) (Australia) 21
International Association of Music Libraries, New Zealand Branch (New Zealand) 290
International Association of Orientalist Librarians (International Organizations) 467
International Association of Scholarly Publishers (IASP) (International Organizations) 467
International Association of School Librarianship (International Organizations) 467
International Association of Sound Archives (International Organizations) 471
International Association of Technological University Libraries (IATUL) (International Organizations) 467
International Atomic Energy Agency (IAEA) (International Organizations) 469
International Bible Reading Association (United Kingdom) 416
International Biographical Centre (United Kingdom) 416

INDEX 519

International Board on Books for Young People (IBBY) (International Organizations) 467
International Book Distributors Co Ltd (Thailand) 381
International Book House (Pvt) Ltd (India) 201
International Book Information Services (United Kingdom) 391
International Book Promotion (France) 100
International Book Traders (India) 201
International Booksellers Federation (IBF) (International Organizations) 467
International Bookshop (Tanzania) 379
International Bookshop, The (Iceland) 184
International Bureau of Education (IBE) (International Organizations) 469
International Bureau voor Auteursrecht BV (Netherlands) 283
International Center for the Registration of Serials (International Organizations) 467
International Children's Book Service (Denmark) 79
International Communication Agency Library (Guinea) 177
International Communication Agency Library (Republic of Korea) 252
International Communication Agency Library (Liberia) 255
International Communication Agency Library (Sierra Leone) 325
International Communications (United Kingdom) 416
International Comparative Literature Association (International Organizations) 467
International Confederation of Societies of Authors and Composers (International Organizations) 467
International Copyright Union for the Protection of Literary and Artistic Works (International Organizations) 467
International Council of Theological Library Associations (International Organizations) 467
International Council on Archives (International Organizations) 467
International Dictionary Service (United Kingdom) 416
International Documentary, The, Centre of Arab Manuscripts (Lebanon) 254
International Editors' Co (Argentina) 8
International Editors' Co SA (Spain) 346
International Federation for Documentation (FID) (International Organizations) 467
International Federation for Modern Languages and Literatures (International Organizations) 468
International Federation of Film Archives (International Organizations) 467
International Federation of Library Associations and Institutions (IFLA) (International Organizations) 467
International Fiction Association (International Organizations) 468
International Grand Prize for Poetry (International Literary Prizes) 477
International Group of Scientific, Technical and Medical Publishers (STM) (International Organizations) 468
International Institute for Children's Literature and Reading Research (UNESCO category C) (International Organizations) 468
International Institute for Educational Planning (IIEP) (International Organizations) 469
International Institute of Advanced Buddhistic Studies Library (Burma) 60
International Institute of Iberoamerican Literature (International Organizations) 468
International Institute of Tropical Agriculture Library (Nigeria) 296
International ISBN Agency (International Organizations) 468
International Labour Office, Central Library and Documentation Branch (Switzerland) 376
International Labour Organisation (ILO) (International Organizations) 470
International League of Antiquarian Booksellers (ILAB) (International Organizations) 468
International Literary Braille Competition Awards (International Literary Prizes) 477
International Literatuur Bureau BV (Netherlands) 283
International Maritime Organization (IMO) (International Organizations) 470
International Nursing, The, Foundation of Japan (Japan) 240
International Press, The, Agency (Pty) Ltd (Republic of South Africa) 333
International Prize of French Friendship (International Literary Prizes) 477
International Progressive Books and Periodicals (Nepal) 272
International Publications Cultural Award (International Literary Prizes) 477
International Publishers Association (International Organizations) 468
International Reading Association (International Organizations) 468
International Science Services (Israel) 214
International Scientific Film Library (ISFL) (International Organizations) 468
International Serial Data System (International Organizations) 468
International Society for Educational Information Inc (Japan) 240
International Standards Books and Periodicals Organization (Nepal) 272
International Study Group of Restorers of Archives, Libraries and Graphic Reproductions (International Organizations) 468
International Telecommunication Union (ITU) (International Organizations) 470
International Textbook Co Ltd (United Kingdom) 416
International Translations Centre (International Organizations) 468
International Union for Conservation of Nature and Natural Resources (IUCN) (International Organizations) 471
International Union of Geological Sciences (IUGS) (International Organizations) 471
International Writers Workshop New Zealand Inc (New Zealand) 291
International Youth Library (International Organizations) 468
Internationale Buchhändler-Vereinigung (IBV) (International Organizations) 468
Internationale Pers, De (Belgium) 38
Internationale Presse, Import- und Export GmbH (Federal Republic of Germany) 168
Internationale Solidarität, Verlag, Verlagsgesellschaft mbH (Federal Republic of Germany) 142
Internationale Vereinigung der Musikbibliotheken (Federal Republic of Germany) 169
Internationales Landkartenhaus GmbH (Federal Republic of Germany) 142
'Interpress', Wydawnictwo (Poland) 311
Interpresse, A/S (Denmark) 77
Interprint (India) 192
Interpublishing AB Rahm and Stenström (Sweden) 354
Intersea (Argentina) 6
Intersistemas SA de CV (Mexico) 266
Interskrift Publishing House (Sweden) 354
Intertrade Publications (India) Pvt Ltd (India) 192
Inversiones Editoriales La Carreta (Colombia) 66
Ipler, Editorial, Ltda (Colombia) 66
Iranian Documentation Centre (IRANDOC) (Iran) 207
Iraq Library Association (Iraq) 208
Iraq Museum, Library of the (Iraq) 208
Iraq Natural History, Library of the, Research Centre and Museum (Iraq) 208
Iris SA (Peru) 307
Iris Verlag AG (Switzerland) 367
Irish Academic Press (Republic of Ireland) 210
Irish Academy of Letters (Republic of Ireland) 212
Irish-American Cultural Institute Literary Awards (International Literary Prizes) 477
Irish Book Publishers' Association (Republic of Ireland) 208
Irish Educational Publishers' Association (Republic of Ireland) 208
Irish Heritage Series (Republic of Ireland) 210
Irish Humanities Centre (Publishing) (Republic of Ireland) 210
Irish Management Institute (Republic of Ireland) 210
Irish Poetry Award (International Literary Prizes) 477
Irish Society for Archives (Republic of Ireland) 211
Irish Times, The, Ltd (Republic of Ireland) 210
Irish University Press (Republic of Ireland) 210
Irisiana Druck und Verlag (Federal Republic of Germany) 142
Ísafoldar, Bókaverzlun (Iceland) 184
Ísafoldarprentsmidja hf (Iceland) 184
Iselt und Co Nfl mbH (Federal Republic of Germany) 142
Ishiyaku Publishers Inc (Japan) 240
Iskra, Editrice (Italy) 226
'Iskry', Państwowe Wydawnictwo (Poland) 311
Iskusstvo, Izdatelstvo (Union of Soviet Socialist Republics) 387
Islam, Perpustakaan (Indonesia) 207
Islami Kitab Khana (Pakistan) 302
Islamia Library (Bangladesh) 32
Islamic Book Centre (Pakistan) 302
Islamic Cultural Bookshop (Bahrain) 32
Islamic Culture, Institute of (Pakistan) 302
Islamic Foundation, The (United Kingdom) 416
Islamic Publications Bureau (Nigeria) 294
Islamic Publications Ltd (Pakistan) 302
Islamic Research Institute (Pakistan) 302
Islamic Research Institute Library (Pakistan) 303
Islamic University Library (Saudi Arabia) 323
Islamiyah (Indonesia) 206
Island Press (Australia) 15
Island, The, Shop (Bahamas) 31
Íslenzka bókmenntafélag (Iceland) 185
Íslenzka Bókmenntafélag, Hid (Iceland) 184
Isopang Publishing Pty Ltd (Papua New Guinea) 305
Isper Club (Italy) 234
Isper Edizioni (Italy) 226
Israbook (Israel) 217
Israel Academy, The, of Sciences & Humanities (Israel) 214
Israel, B M, BV (Netherlands) 278
Israel Book Importers' Association (Israel) 213
Israel Exploration Society (Israel) 214
Israel ISBN Group Agency (Israel) 213
Israel Library Association (Israel) 218
Israel, Nico (Netherlands) 278
Israel Program for Scientific Translations (Israel) 214
Israel Society of Special Libraries and Information Centres (ISLIC) (Israel) 218
Israel State Archives (Israel) 218
Israel Universities Press (Israel) 214
Israel Yearbook Publications (Israel) 214
Israeli Music Publications Ltd (Israel) 214
Israeli Prize in Humanities and Social Sciences (Israel) 218
Israeli Prize in Jewish Studies, Hebrew Literature and Education (Israel) 218
Israeli Prize in the Arts (Israel) 218
Istanbul Üniversitesi Merkez Kütüphanesi (Turkey) 385
Istiklal, Al, Library (Jordan) 247
Istituto Centrale di Statistica (Italy) 226
Istituto Centrale per il Catalogo Unico delle Biblioteche Italiane e per le Informazioni Bibliografiche (Italy) 235
Istituto Centrale per la Patologia del Libro (Italy) 235
Istituto della Enciclopedia Italiana (Italy) 226
Istituto della Santa, Casa Editrice (Italy) 226
Istituto di Studi Romani (Italy) 226
Istituto Editoriale Italiano SpA (Italy) 226
Istituto Editoriale Ticinese (IET) SA (Switzerland) 367
Istituto Geografico de Agostini SpA (Italy) 226
Istituto Grafologico (Italy) 226
Istituto Italiano D'Arti Grafiche (Italy) 226
Istituto Lombardo Accademia di Scienze e Lettere (Italy) 235
Istituto Padano, Casa Editrice, di Arti Grafiche (Italy) 226
Istituto per l'Enciclopedia del Friuli Venezia Giulia (Italy) 226
Istituto Poligrafico e Zecca dello Stato (Italy) 226
Istmo, Ediciones (Spain) 341
Italian Book Club (United Kingdom) 443
Italscambi, Centro (Italy) 234
Italscambi, Editrice (Italy) 226
Ittihad, Al, Bookstore (Egypt) 84
Iwanami Shoten (Japan) 240
Iwasaki Shoten Co Ltd (Japan) 240
Izmir General Library (Turkey) 385
Izrael Publishing House Ltd (Israel) 214
Iztaccihuatl, Editorial, SA (Mexico) 266
Izvestiya Publishing House (Union of Soviet Socialist Republics) 387

J B, Taller Ediciones (Spain) 341
J K Export House (India) 202
J K Publishers (United Kingdom) 416
J R O-Kartografische Verlagsgesellschaft mbH (Federal Republic of Germany) 142
J U R I F Belgique (Belgium) 38
Jaca, Editoriale, Book (Italy) 226
Jacaranda Wiley Ltd (Australia) 15
Jacaranda Wiley Ltd (New Zealand) 288
Jackdaw Publications Ltd (United Kingdom) 417
Jacobi, Verlag, KG (Federal Republic of Germany) 142
Jaeger und Waldmann (Federal Republic of Germany) 142
Jafet, Nami C, Memorial Library (Lebanon) 254
Jaffe Books (India) 201
Jager, De, — HAUM (Republic of South Africa) 330
Jäggi, Buchhandlung, AG (Switzerland) 375
Jahreszeitenverlag (Federal Republic of Germany) 142
J'ai Lu, Editions (France) 100
Jaico Book Shop (India) 202
Jaico Publishing House (India) 192
Jain Publishers, B (India) 192
Jain Publishing Co (India) 192
Jaipur Publishing House (India) 192
Jaisingh & Mehta Publishers Pvt Ltd (India) 192
Jakobsohn, Verlag Eduard (Federal Republic of Germany) 142
Jaktjournalens Bokklubb (Sweden) 358
Jamaica Archives (Jamaica) 237
Jamaica Library Association (Jamaica) 237
Jamaica Library Service (Jamaica) 237
Jamaica Publishing House Ltd (Jamaica) 237
James, Arthur, Ltd (United Kingdom) 417
Jamjoom & Bros, Mohamed Noor Salah (Saudi Arabia) 323
Jane's Publishing Company Ltd (United Kingdom) 417
Janin, Jules, Prize (France) 113
Janssen, Stern-Verlag, und Co (Federal Republic of Germany) 142

Janssens, J, PVBA (Belgium) 38
Januka Pustak Bhandar (Nepal) 272
Japadre, L U, Editore (Italy) 226
Japan Book Importers Association (Japan) 237
Japan Book Publishers Association (Japan) 237
Japan Broadcast Publishing Co Ltd (Japan) 240
Japan Essayists' Club (Japan) 246
Japan Essayists' Club Prize (Japan) 246
Japan I S B N Agency (Japan) 238
Japan Literary Prize (Japan) 246
Japan Poet Club (Japan) 246
Japan Poet Club Prize (Japan) 246
Japan Poets' Association (Japan) 246
Japan Publications Inc (Japan) 240
Japan Publications Trading Co Ltd (Import and Export) (Japan) 245
Japan Society of Translators (Japan) 247
Japan Times (Japan) 240
Japan Translation Prize for Publisher (Japan) 246
Japan Travel Bureau Inc (Japan) 240
Japan Uni Agency Inc (Japan) 244
Japan Woman Writer Prize (Japan) 246
Japan Women Writers' Literary Prizes (Japan) 246
Jarrold Colour Publications (United Kingdom) 417
Jasomirgott-Verlag (Austria) 26
Jaya Baya, Yayasan (Indonesia) 206
Jaya, Penerbit (Malaysia) 259
Jayawardena, J K G, & Co (Sri Lanka) 349
Jaypee Brothers (India) 193
Jazirah, Al, Organization for Press, Printing, Publishing (Saudi Arabia) 323
Jean-Charles, A (Martinique) 262
Jean-Christophe Prizes (France) 113
Jeanmaire, R, & Co (Switzerland) 367
Jedinstvo (Yugoslavia) 457
Jeffers Bookstore (Trinidad and Tobago) 382
Jeheber, J H, SA (Switzerland) 367
Jeng's Bookshop (The Gambia) 115
Jeongeumsa Publishing Co (Republic of Korea) 251
Jerusalem City (Public) Library (Israel) 218
Jerusalem Publishing House Ltd (Israel) 214
Jerusalem, The, Prize (International Literary Prizes) 478
Jespersen og Pios Forlag (Denmark) 77
Jeune Afrique, Editions (France) 100
Jeune France Prize (France) 113
Jeunesse d'Afrique, Librairie (Upper Volta) 451
'Jeunesse et Afrique', Libraire (Upper Volta) 451
Jeunesse et Poésie Prize (France) 113
Jewish Agency, The (Israel) 215
Jewish Book Club, The (United Kingdom) 443
Jewish Chronicle — Harold H Wingate Book Awards (International Literary Prizes) 478
Jewish National and University Library (Israel) 218
Jims, Editorial, SA (Spain) 341
Jing Kung Book Store (Hong Kong) 180
Jing Kung Educational Press (Hong Kong) 179
Jisik Sanup Sa (Republic of Korea) 251
Jnanada Prakashan (India) 193
Jnanpith Literary Award (India) 203
Joannides, A, & Co (Cyprus) 70
Joerg, Wolfgang, und Erich Schoenig (Federal Republic of Germany) 142
Johannesburg Public Library (Republic of South Africa) 334
Johannesburgse Boekwinkel (Republic of South Africa) 333
Johannesverlag Einsiedeln (Switzerland) 367
Johns Hopkins, The, University Press (United Kingdom) 417
Johnson Publications Ltd (United Kingdom) 417
Johnson Reprint Co Ltd (United Kingdom) 417
Johnson Society of London (United Kingdom) 447
Johnston & Bacon (United Kingdom) 417
Johnston Green & Co (Publishers) Ltd (United Kingdom) 417
Johnston/The Moorlands, Anne, Press (United Kingdom) 417
Joho Shori Gakkai (Japan) 245
Johore Central Store Sdn Bhd (Malaysia) 261
Joie, La, par les Livres (France) 111
Joint Board, The, of Christian Education of Australia and New Zealand (Australia) 15
Joint Board, The, of Christian Education of Australia and New Zealand (New Zealand) 288
Jonckheere, Tobie, Prize (Belgium) 44
Jonef Publications (Philippines) 309
Jonge, Stichting De, Onderzoekers (Netherlands) 278
Jonsson, Snaebjörn, & Co hf (The English Bookshop) (Iceland) 184
Jonsson, Sveinbjörn (Iceland) 184
Jónssonar, Bókaútgáfa Thorsteins M (Iceland) 184
Jordan & Sons Ltd (United Kingdom) 417
Jordan Distribution Agency (Jordan) 247
Jordan Library Association (Jordan) 247
Jordan Press and Publishing Co Ltd (Jordan) 247
Joseph, Michael, Ltd (United Kingdom) 417
Joseph, Philip & Pamela, Associates Ltd (United Kingdom) 442

Joshi, Sumnesh, Award (India) 204
Journal des Notaires et des Avocats SA (France) 100
Journeyman, The, Press Ltd (United Kingdom) 417
Jouy Prize (France) 113
Jovene, Casa Editrice Dr Eugenio, SpA (Italy) 226
Jover, Ediciones, SA (Spain) 341
József Attila Tudományegyetem Központi Könyvtára (Hungary) 182
Jubilee Library Association (Burma) 60
Judía, Biblioteca Popular (Argentina) 6
Jüdischer Verlag (Federal Republic of Germany) 142
Jugend und Volk Verlag GmbH (Federal Republic of Germany) 142
Jugend und Volk Verlagsgesellschaft mbH (Austria) 26
Jugenddienst-Verlag (Federal Republic of Germany) 142
Jugoreklam (Yugoslavia) 457
Jugoslavenska Academije, Izdavački Zavod, Znanosti i Umjetnosti (Yugoslavia) 457
Jugoslavenski Leksikografski Zavod (Yugoslavia) 457
Jugoslavija (Yugoslavia) 457
Jugoslovenska Autorska Agencija (Yugoslavia) 460
Jugoslovenska Knjiga (Yugoslavia) 460
Jugoslovenska Revija (Yugoslavia) 457
Jugoslovenski bibliografski institut (Yugoslavia) 461
Jugoslovenski centar za tehničku i naučnu dokumentaciju (Yugoslavia) 460
Julien, Stanislas, Prize (International Literary Prizes) 478
Julliard, Editions René (France) 100
Juncker, Axel, -Verlag Jacobi KG (Federal Republic of Germany) 142
Junction Books (United Kingdom) 417
Jungbrunnen, Verlag (Austria) 26
Junge Welt, Verlag (German Democratic Republic) 117
Jungjohann, Verlag (Federal Republic of Germany) 143
Jungwoo Sa (Republic of Korea) 251
Junimea, Editura (Romania) 321
Junior International (Federal Republic of Germany) 142
Junior Library (Mauritius) 263
Junior Puffin Club (United Kingdom) 443
Junius Verlag GmbH (Federal Republic of Germany) 143
Junk, Dr W (Netherlands) 278
Junpa Kwahak Sa (Republic of Korea) 251
Junta de Educação Religiosa e Publicações da Convenção Batista Brasileira (JUERP) (Brazil) 52
Jupiter Books (London) Ltd (United Kingdom) 417
Jupiter, Editions, Sàrl (France) 101
Jurídica, Ediciones y Librería (Argentina) 6
Jurídica, Editorial, de Chile (Chile) 63
Juridica-Verlag GmbH (Austria) 26
Juridiques et Techniques, Editions (France) 101
Jurif (Société d'Etudes Juridiques Internationales et Fiscales) (France) 101
Juris Druck & Verlag AG (Switzerland) 367
Jus, Editorial, SA (Mexico) 266
Jusautor (Bulgaria) 58
Juta & Co Ltd (Republic of South Africa) 330
Juta & Co Ltd (Republic of South Africa) 333
Juventa Verlag, Dr Martin Faltermaier (Federal Republic of Germany) 143
Juventud, Editorial, Argentina (Argentina) 6
Juventud, Editorial, Ltda (Colombia) 66
Juventud, Editorial, SA (Spain) 341
Juventud, Librería (Bolivia) 46
Juventud, Librería y Editorial (Bolivia) 46
Juventus/Femina Publishers (Republic of South Africa) 330
Jyväskylän Yliopiston Kirjasto (Finland) 89

K B S (Netherlands) 278
K M C (Czechoslovakia) 73
K M P (Kruh milovníkov poèzie) (Czechoslovakia) 73
Kabarole Public Library (Uganda) 386
Kabel, Ernst, Verlag GmbH (Federal Republic of Germany) 143
Kabete Library (Kenya) 249
Kabul University, Institute of Geography (Afghanistan) 1
Kadokawa Shoten (Japan) 240
Kaduna, Library Board of, State (Nigeria) 297
Kaffke, Verlag Gerhard, GmbH & Co KG (Federal Republic of Germany) 143
Kahn & Averill (United Kingdom) 417
Kahn, Lonnie, and Co Ltd (Israel) 217
Kaibundo Publishing Co Ltd (Japan) 240
Kairali Mudralayam (India) 193
Kairos, Editorial, SA (Spain) 341
Kairyudo Publishing Co Ltd (Japan) 240
Kaisei-Sha (Japan) 240
Kaiser, Buchhandlung Chr (Federal Republic of Germany) 168
Kaiser, Chr, Verlag (Federal Republic of Germany) 143
Kaitaku-Sha (Japan) 240
Kajima Institute Publishing Co Ltd (Japan) 240
Kakoulides, C (Greece) 176
Kalinga Prize (International Literary Prizes) 478

Kalleberger Foundation (Sweden) 360
Kaloudis, Gr (Greece) 176
Kalyani Publishers (India) 193
Kamp, Verlag Ferdinand, GmbH & Co KG (Federal Republic of Germany) 143
Kampen, Van (Netherlands) 278
Kanehara & Co Ltd (Japan) 240
Kangaroo Press (Australia) 15
Kanisius Verlag (Switzerland) 367
Kanisius, Yayasan (Indonesia) 206
Kano State Library (Nigeria) 297
Kansan Kirjarengas (Finland) 88
Kantonale Kommission für Gemeinde- und Schulbibliotheken, Zurich (Switzerland) 376
Kantoor Boekhandel Salinja NV KBS (Netherlands Antilles) 286
Kapelusz, Editorial, Colombiana SA (Colombia) 66
Kapelusz, Editorial, SA (Argentina) 6
Kapelusz, Editorial, Venezolana SA (Venezuela) 453
Kara, Ismail, /Dergâh Yayinlari AS Müessese Müdürü (Turkey) 384
Karacan Yayınları AS (Turkey) 384
Karachi University Library Science Alumni Association (Pakistan) 303
Karas-Sana Oy (Finland) 87
Karavias, Athanassios (Greece) 175
Karavias, Nikolaos (Greece) 175
Karger, S, AG, Medical and Scientific Publishers (Switzerland) 367
Karger, S, GmbH Verlag für Medizin und Naturwissenschaften (Federal Republic of Germany) 143
Karilas, Tauno, Prize (Finland) 90
Karisto, Arvi A, Oy (Finland) 87
Karl-Marx-Universität (German Democratic Republic) 119
Karl-May-Verlag, Joachim Schmid & Co (Federal Republic of Germany) 143
Karnataka Cooperative Publishing House Ltd (India) 193
Karnataka Publishers' and Booksellers' Association (India) 185
Karni Publishers Ltd (Israel) 215
Karo-Bücher (Federal Republic of Germany) 143
Kartograficznych, Państwowe Przedsiebiorstwo Wydawnictw (Poland) 312
Kartographisches Institut Bertelsmann (Federal Republic of Germany) 143
Kartograpischer Verlag Wagner & Co KG (Federal Republic of Germany) 143
Karunia (Indonesia) 206
Kasetsart University, Main Library, (Thailand) 381
Kash'shaf, Dar al (Lebanon) 254
Kastaniotis Editions (Greece) 175
Katalogów i Cenników, Wydawnictwo (Poland) 312
Kataria, B D, & Sons (India) 193
Katholieke Bijbelstichting (Netherlands) 278
Katholieke Universiteit Leuven (Belgium) 43
Katholisches Bibelwerk, Verlag, GmbH (Federal Republic of Germany) 143
Katzmann-Verlag KG (Federal Republic of Germany) 143
Kaufmann (Greece) 176
Kaufmann, Verlag Ernst (Federal Republic of Germany) 143
Kaunda, Helen, Memorial Library (Zambia) 463
Kavanagh, Patrick, Award (Republic of Ireland) 212
Kawade Shobo Shinsha (Japan) 240
Kawanku, Yayasan (Indonesia) 206
Kawika (Philippines) 310
Kaye & Ward Ltd (United Kingdom) 417
Kaynar Buchhandlung (Federal Republic of Germany) 143
Kazi Publications (Pakistan) 302
Keats-Shelley Memorial Association (Italy) 235
Kedros (Greece) 175
Keesing — Internationale Drukkerij en Uitgeverij NV (Belgium) 38
Keip KG Antiquariat (Federal Republic of Germany) 143
Keller, Franckh'sche Verlagshandlung, W, & Co (Federal Republic of Germany) 143
Keller, Gottfried, Prize (International Literary Prizes) 478
Keller, Verlag Ramòn F (Switzerland) 367
Keller, Verlag Walter (Switzerland) 367
Kelly Books (Australia) 15
Kelly's Directories (United Kingdom) 418
Kemal, Orhan, Award (Turkey) 385
Kemongsa (Republic of Korea) 251
Kemps Group (Printers & Publishers) Ltd (United Kingdom) 418
Kendriya Hindi Sansthan (India) 193
Kenkyusha Ltd (Japan) 240
Kennedy, Albertine, Publishing (Republic of Ireland) 210
Kennedy Prize (Thailand) 381
Kentron Ekdoseos Ellinon Syngrafeon (Greece) 176
Kenya Agricultural Research Institute (Kenya) 249
Kenya Booksellers' and Stationers' Association (Kenya) 248
Kenya Library Association (Kenya) 249
Kenya Literature Bureau (Kenya) 248

INDEX 521

Kenya National Archives (Kenya) 249
Kenya National Library Service (Kenya) 249
Kenya Polytechnic Library (Kenya) 249
Kenya Publishers' Association (Kenya) 248
Kenya Technical Teachers' College Library (Kenya) 249
Kenyatta, The Jomo, Foundation (Kenya) 248
Kenyatta University College Library (Kenya) 249
Képzömüvészeti Alap Kiadóvállalata (Hungary) 181
Kerala Publishers & Booksellers Association (India) 185
Kerala Sahitya Akademi (India) 193
Kerala Sahitya Akademi Awards (India) 204
Kerala University, Department of Publications (India) 193
Kerle, Verlag F H (Federal Republic of Germany) 143
Kern Associates (Japan) 244
Kern, BV Uitgeverij De (Netherlands) 278
Kernerman Publishing (Israel) 215
Kerr, The Alfred, Prize for Literary Criticism (Federal Republic of Germany) 171
Kershaw Publishing Co Ltd (United Kingdom) 418
Kersten & Co, C (Suriname) 351
Kesari Award (India) 204
Kesim, Nurcihan, Literary Agency (Turkey) 385
Kestrel (Australia) 15
Kestrel Books (United Kingdom) 418
Keswick (United Kingdom) 418
Keswick Book Society (Kenya) 249
Keter Publishing House Jerusalem Ltd (Israel) 215
Keurbibliotheek (Republic of South Africa) 333
Keure, Die, NV (Belgium) 38
Key (United Kingdom) 418
Keysersche Buchhandlung (German Democratic Republic) 119
Keysersche Verlagsbuchhandlung GmbH (Federal Republic of Germany) 143
Keystone Picture Books (Australia) 15
Khanna Publishers (India) 193
Khartoum Polytechnic Library (Sudan) 350
Khartoum, The, Bookshop (Sudan) 350
Khartoum University Press (Sudan) 350
Khayat Book and Publishing Co SAL (Lebanon) 254
Khayat, Tahseen S (Lebanon) 254
Khayat, Tahseen S (United Arab Emirates) 390
'Khimiya', Izdatelstvo (Union of Soviet Socialist Republics) 387
Khoa Hoc (Social Sciences) Publishing House (Socialist Republic of Viet Nam) 455
'Khudozhestvennaya Literatura', Izdatelstvo (Union of Soviet Socialist Republics) 387
Khyber Bookshop (Pakistan) 303
Khyber Medical College Library (Pakistan) 303
Kibaha Public Library (Tanzania) 379
Kibu-Verlag GmbH (Federal Republic of Germany) 143
Kiefel, Johannes, Verlag (Federal Republic of Germany) 143
Kiehl, Friedrich, Verlag GmbH (Federal Republic of Germany) 143
Kienreich, Jos A (Austria) 29
Kienreich, Jos A (Austria) 29
Kiepenheuer, Gustav, Verlag (German Democratic Republic) 117
Kiepenheuer und Witsch, Verlag (Federal Republic of Germany) 143
Kier, Editorial, SACIFI (Argentina) 6
Kier, Librería (Argentina) 8
Kikuchi Prize (Japan) 247
Kilda Verlag (Federal Republic of Germany) 143
Kilkenny, The, Bookshop Ltd (Republic of Ireland) 211
Kim, Uitgeverij , Natuurboeken BV (Netherlands) 278
Kimber, William, & Co Ltd (United Kingdom) 418
Kina Italia SpA (Italy) 226
Kinderbuchverlag, Der, Berlin (German Democratic Republic) 117
Kinderbuchverlag Reich Luzern AG (Switzerland) 367
Kinderkeur (Republic of South Africa) 333
Kinderpers, Die, Van SA (Republic of South Africa) 330
Kindler Verlag AG (Switzerland) 367
Kindler Verlag GmbH (Federal Republic of Germany) 144
King Abdulaziz University Library (Saudi Arabia) 323
King, Martin Luther, Memorial Prize (United Kingdom) 449
King Paul National Foundation Prize (Greece) 176
King Shing Publishing Co (Hong Kong) 179
Kingfisher Books Ltd (United Kingdom) 418
Kings & Queens of England (United Kingdom) 443
Kingsmead Press (United Kingdom) 418
Kingston Bookshop Ltd (Jamaica) 237
Kingston Publishers Ltd (Jamaica) 237
Kingstons Ltd (Zimbabwe) 465
Kingstons (Zambia) Ltd (Zambia) 463
Kingsway International Publications Ltd (Hong Kong) 179
Kingsway Publications Ltd (United Kingdom) 418
Kingsway Stores (Nigeria) 296
Kingsway Stores, Books and Periodicals Department (Ghana) 172
Kinokuniya Co Ltd (Japan) 245
Kinokuniya Co Ltd (Publishing Department) (Japan) 241
Kinta (Indonesia) 206

Kipling Society (United Kingdom) 447
Kirja-ja Paperikauppiasliitto (Finland) 87
Kirja-Otava, Kuopion (Finland) 88
Kirjallisuudentutkijain Seura (Finland) 89
Kirjaneliö, Kustannusliike (Finland) 87
Kirjastonhoitajaliitto — Bibliotekarieförbundet ry (Finland) 89
Kirjastonhoitajien Keskusliitto-Bibliotekariernas Centralforbund ry (Finland) 89
Kirjastovirkailijat-Biblioteksanstallda ry (Finland) 89
Kirjayhtymä Oy (Finland) 87
Kiryat Sefer Ltd (Israel) 215
Kishida Prize for Drama (Japan) 247
Kister, Editions, SA (Switzerland) 367
Kitab, Dar Al-, Allubnani (Lebanon) 254
Kitab, Dar El (Morocco) 270
Kitab Ghar (India) 193
Kitab Mahal (W D) Pvt Ltd (India) 193
Kitabastan (India) 193
Kitaplar, Altin, Publishing Co (Turkey) 384
Kitwe Public Library (Zambia) 463
Kivukoni College Library (Tanzania) 379
Kivunim — Arsan Publishing House Ltd (Israel) 215
Klang Vidhya (Thailand) 380
Klang Vidhya (Thailand) 381
Klasing und Co GmbH (Federal Republic of Germany) 144
Klein, Kunstverlag Dr Rudolf Georgi, Waldemar (Federal Republic of Germany) 144
Klein, Preben (Denmark) 79
Klens-Verlag GmbH (Federal Republic of Germany) 144
Klett-Cotta Verlag (Federal Republic of Germany) 144
Klett, Ernst, Verlag (Federal Republic of Germany) 144
Klett und Balmer, Verlag, & Co (Switzerland) 367
Klima, Librairie R (French Polynesia) 115
Klincksieck, Editions (France) 101
Klinkhardt und Biermann Verlagsbuchhandlung GmbH (Federal Republic of Germany) 144
Klopp, Erika, Verlag GmbH (Federal Republic of Germany) 144
Klostermann, Vittorio, GmbH (Federal Republic of Germany) 144
Klotz, Ehrenfried, Verlag (Federal Republic of Germany) 144
Klub 42 (Yugoslavia) 460
Klub Čitalaca (Yugoslavia) 460
Klub Čitalaca MK (Yugoslavia) 460
Klub čtenár technické literatury (Czechoslovakia) 73
Klub přátel poezie (Czechoslovakia) 73
Kluitman, Uitgeverij, Alkmaar BV (Netherlands) 278
Kluwer Algemene Boeken BV (Netherlands) 278
Kluwer Group (Netherlands) 278
Kluwer Law and Taxation Publishers (Netherlands) 278
Kluwer, NV Uitgeverij (Belgium) 38
Kluwer Publishing Ltd (United Kingdom) 418
Kluwer Sociaal-Wetenschappelijke Boeken en Tijdschriften (Netherlands) 278
Kluwer Technische Boeken BV (Netherlands) 278
Kluwerpers (Netherlands) 278
Kluwers Courantenbedrijf (Netherlands) 278
Kluwer's, Maarten, Internationale Uitgeversonderneming NV (Belgium) 38
Knapp, Fritz, Verlag GmbH (Federal Republic of Germany) 144
Knapp, Wilhelm, Verlag (Federal Republic of Germany) 144
Knaur, Droemer, Verlag (Federal Republic of Germany) 144
Knaus, Albrecht, Verlag (Federal Republic of Germany) 144
Knecht, Verlag Josef, -Carolusdruckerei GmbH (Federal Republic of Germany) 144
Knesset Library (Israel) 218
'Kniga', Izdatelstvo (Union of Soviet Socialist Republics) 387
Knight (United Kingdom) 418
Knight, Charles, Ltd (United Kingdom) 418
Knihovna Národniho muzea (Czechoslovakia) 73
Kniha (The Book) (Czechoslovakia) 73
Knorr und Hirth Verlag GmbH (Federal Republic of Germany) 144
Knowledge Book House (Burma) 60
Knowledge Printing & Publishing House (Burma) 59
Knuf, F, Publishers (Netherlands) 279
Ko Mun Sa (Republic of Korea) 251
Københavns Kommunes Biblioteker (Denmark) 80
Københavns Stadsarkiv (Denmark) 80
Kobersche Verlagsbuchhandlung AG (Switzerland) 368
Koch, Hanna-Kirsti (Norway) 300
Koch, Neff und Oetinger & Co (Federal Republic of Germany) 168
Koch, Verlagsanstalt Alexander, GmbH (Federal Republic of Germany) 144
Koch, Volksbuchhandlung Robert (German Democratic Republic) 119
Koch's, C A, Verlag Nachfolger (Federal Republic of Germany) 144

Kodansha Disney Children's Book Club (Japan) 244
Kodansha International Ltd (Japan) 241
Kodansha Ltd (Japan) 241
Kodansha Scientific Ltd (Japan) 241
Koehler, K F, Verlag (Federal Republic of Germany) 144
Koehler und Amelang (VOB) (German Democratic Republic) 117
Koehlers Verlagsgesellschaft (Federal Republic of Germany) 144
Koerner, Verlag Valentin, GmbH (Federal Republic of Germany) 144
Kogan Page Ltd (United Kingdom) 418
Kohlhammer, Unternehmensgruppe Verlag W, GmbH (Federal Republic of Germany) 144
Kohl's Technischer Verlag Erwin Kohl GmbH & Co KG (Federal Republic of Germany) 145
Kohrtz, Ilona, Prize (Sweden) 360
Koivu, Rudolf, Prize (Finland) 90
Kok, Uitgeversmaatschappij J H, BV (Netherlands) 279
Koko Kansan Kirjakerho Oy (Finland) 88
Kokuritsu Kobunshokan (Japan) 245
Kolasanya Publishing Enterprise (Nigeria) 294
Kolibri-Verlag (Federal Republic of Germany) 145
Kollaros, I D, & Co Corporation (Greece) 175
'Kolos', Izdatelstvo (Union of Soviet Socialist Republics) 387
Kolumbus-Verlag (Switzerland) 368
Komar (Federal Republic of Germany) 145
Komine Shoten Publishing Co Ltd (Japan) 241
Komitet za Izkoustvo i Koultoura (Bulgaria) 59
Komma, Forlaget, A/S (Denmark) 77
Kommentator, Verlag (Federal Republic of Germany) 145
Kommunale Kulturarbeideres Forening (Norway) 301
Komunikacji i Laczności, Wydawnictwa (Poland) 312
Komunist, Izdavački Centar (Yugoslavia) 457
Kongelige Bibliotek, Det (Denmark) 80
Kongelige Danske Videnskabernes Selskab (Denmark) 81
Kongelige Norske Videnskabers Selskab, Det (Norway) 300
Königshausen und Neumann, Verlag (Federal Republic of Germany) 145
Koninklijk Instituut voor Internationale Betrekkingen (Belgium) 38
Koninklijke Academie voor Nederlandse Taal- en Letterkunde (Belgium) 44
Koninklijke Academie voor Wetenschappen, Letteren en Schone Kunsten van België (Belgium) 44
Koninklijke Bibliotheek (Netherlands) 283
Koninklijke Nederlandse Akademie, Bibliotheek der, van Wetenschappen (Netherlands) 284
Koninklijke Nederlandse Uitgeversbond (Netherlands) 273
Konkani Bhasha Mandal (India) 193
Konkordia GmbH für Druck und Verlag (Federal Republic of Germany) 145
Konrad, Anton H, Verlag (Federal Republic of Germany) 145
Konsalik Novel Prize (Federal Republic of Germany) 171
Könyvértékesítő vállalat (Hungary) 182
Könyvtártudományi és módszertani központ (Hungary) 182
Konzepte der Humanwissenschaften (Federal Republic of Germany) 145
Konzert (Federal Republic of Germany) 145
Kookaburra Technical Publications Pty Ltd (Australia) 15
Kooyker BV (Netherlands) 284
Kooyker Scientific Publications BV (Netherlands) 279
Korea Book Club (Republic of Korea) 252
Korea Britannica Corporation (Republic of Korea) 251
Korea Directory Co (Republic of Korea) 251
Korea Institute of Science and Technology Library (Republic of Korea) 252
Korea Publications Export & Import Corporation (Democratic People's Republic of Korea) 250
Korea Textbook Co Ltd (Republic of Korea) 251
Korea University Library (Republic of Korea) 252
Korea University Press (Republic of Korea) 251
Korean Culture, The, and Arts Foundation (Republic of Korea) 251
Korean Library Association (Republic of Korea) 252
Korean Micro-Library Association (Republic of Korea) 252
Korean Publishers Association (Republic of Korea) 250
Koren Publishers (Israel) 215
Kornfeld, Galerie, & Co (Switzerland) 368
Koro, George Y (Jordan) 247
Kosei Publishing Co Ltd (Japan) 241
Koseisha-Koseikaku Co Ltd (Japan) 241
Kösel-Verlag GmbH & Co (Federal Republic of Germany) 145
Koshal Book Depot (India) 201
Kosi Books (India) 193
Koska, Verlag A F (Austria) 26
Kosmos BV (Netherlands) 279
Kosmos Gesellschaft (Federal Republic of Germany) 167
Kosmos, Livraria (Brazil) 56
Kosmos, Livraria, Editora (Brazil) 52
Kossodo Verlag AG (Switzerland) 368
Kossuth Könyvkiadó (Hungary) 181

522 INDEX

Kossuth Lajos Tudományegyetem Egyetemi Könyvtár (Hungary) 182
Kothari Publications (India) 193
Kowalski, G, Konzert Verlag (Federal Republic of Germany) 145
Kowalski, Gerhard (Federal Republic of Germany) 167
Koymantereas (Greece) 175
Közgazdasági és Jogi Könyvkiadó (Hungary) 181
Központi statisztikai hivatal könyvtár és dokumentációs szolgálat (Hungary) 182
Kraft Prize (Argentina) 9
Krains, Hubert, Prize (Belgium) 44
Krajowa Agencja Wydawnicza (KAW) (Poland) 312
Kraks Legat (Denmark) 77
Kráľ, Fraňo, Prize (Czechoslovakia) 74
Kramer, Andrés de (Spain) 346
Krämer Verlag GmbH, Karl, und Co (Federal Republic of Germany) 145
Kramer Verlag, Karin (Federal Republic of Germany) 145
Krämer, Verlag Karl, & Co (Switzerland) 368
Kramer, Verlag René, AG (Switzerland) 368
Kramer Verlagsbuchhandlung, Dr Waldemar (Federal Republic of Germany) 145
Kramers (Netherlands) 279
Kraus-Thomson Organization Ltd (Liechtenstein) 256
Krausskopf, Vereinigte Fachverlage, Ingenieur Digest GmbH (Federal Republic of Germany) 145
Krebs, Verlag und Druckerei G, AG (Switzerland) 368
Kremayr und Scheriau, Verlag (Austria) 26
Kremnitz, Buch- und Bildverlag W (Federal Republic of Germany) 145
Kreuz Verlag (Federal Republic of Germany) 145
Krieg, Walter (Austria) 29
Kriegsarchivs Wien, Bibliothek des (Austria) 30
Kriminalistik Verlag GmbH (Federal Republic of Germany) 145
Krippler-Muller, Publisher (Grand Duchy of Luxembourg) 257
Krishna Brothers (India) 193
Krishna Prakashan Mandir (India) 193
Kristiansand Folkebibliotek (Norway) 300
Kristillinen Kirjarengas (Finland) 88
Kristna Bokförläggareföreningen (Sweden) 351
Kristna Bokringen, Den (Sweden) 358
Kristne Bogklub, Den (Denmark) 79
Kritak uitgeverij (Belgium) 38
Kriterion, Editura (Romania) 321
Kröner, Alfred, Verlag (Federal Republic of Germany) 145
Krščanska sadašnjost (Yugoslavia) 457
Krüger, Buch und Werbung-Helmut, GmbH (Federal Republic of Germany) 145
Kruger, Wolfgang, Verlag (Federal Republic of Germany) 145
Kruh (Czechoslovakia) 71
Kruh priateľov detskej knihy (Czechoslovakia) 74
'Ksiazka i Wiedza', Wydawnictwo (Poland) 312
Kuai-Mare, Librerías (Venezuela) 454
Kuala Lumpur Public Library (Malaysia) 261
Kübler Verlag Michael Akselrad (Federal Republic of Germany) 145
Kubon und Sagner (Federal Republic of Germany) 145
Kudos & Godine Ltd (United Kingdom) 418
Kugler Publications BV (Netherlands) 279
Kultura (Hungary) 182
Kultura (Yugoslavia) 460
Kultura (Izdavačko Pretprijatie) (Yugoslavia) 457
Kumar, C B, Award (India) 204
Kumm, Wilhelm, Verlag (Federal Republic of Germany) 145
Kümmerley und Frey (Federal Republic of Germany) 145
Kümmerly und Frey (Geographischer Verlag) (Switzerland) 368
Kümmerly und Frey Verlags GmbH (Austria) 26
Kumsong Youth Publishing House (Democratic People's Republic of Korea) 250
Kundalini Research and Publication Trust (India) 193
Kündig, Imprimerie Albert, SA (Switzerland) 368
Kungl Vitterhets Historie och Antikvitets Akademien (Sweden) 359
Kungliga Biblioteket (Sweden) 359
Kungliga Svenska Vetenskapsakadamiens Bibliotek (Sweden) 359
Kunkumam Award (India) 204
Kunnskapsforlaget I/S (Norway) 299
Kunnuparampil Books (India) 193
Kunst und Wissen Erich Bieber OHG (Federal Republic of Germany) 145
Kunst und Wohnen Verlag (Federal Republic of Germany) 145
Kunst, VEB Verlag der (German Democratic Republic) 117
Kunstforlag, Bokklubbens (Norway) 300
Kunstkreis, Edition, im Ex Libris Verlag (Switzerland) 375
Kunstkreis für Bibliophile Mappen (Federal Republic of Germany) 167

Kunstwissenschaft, Deutscher Verlag für (Federal Republic of Germany) 145
Kuomintang Central Committee Library (Taiwan) 378
Kupferberg, Florian, Verlag (Federal Republic of Germany) 145
Küpper, Verlag Helmut (Federal Republic of Germany) 145
Kurita-Bando Literary Agency (Japan) 244
Kurita Shuppan Hanbai Co Ltd (Japan) 245
Kurnia Esa (Indonesia) 206
Kursverksamhetens Förlag (Sweden) 355
Kutter, Edouard (Grand Duchy of Luxembourg) 257
Kuttippuzha Award (India) 204
Kutub, Dar Al, Al Hadeetha (Egypt) 84
Kutub, Dar al, al-Wataniya (Saudi Arabia) 323
Kutub Khana Ishayat-ul-Islam (India) 193
Kuwait Central Library (Kuwait) 253
Kuwait Publishing House (Kuwait) 253
Kuwait University Central Library (Kuwait) 253
Kuwait University Libraries Department (Kuwait) 253
Kwan Dong Publishing Co (Republic of Korea) 251
Kwang Hwa Bookstore Pte Ltd (Malaysia) 261
Kwang Hwa, Sharikat Toko Buku (Brunei) 58
Kwang Jang Press (Republic of Korea) 251
Kwangmyong Printing & Publishing Co Ltd (Republic of Korea) 251
Kwaratech Bookshop (Nigeria) 296
Kwong Hin Bookstore (Hong Kong) 180
Kyi-Pwar-Ye Book House (Burma) 59
Kynning Ltd (Iceland) 184
Kyo Bun Kwan Inc (Japan) 241
Kyobo Publishing Inc (Republic of Korea) 251
Kyohak Sa (Republic of Korea) 251
Kyoritsu Shuppan Co Ltd (Japan) 241
Kyoto Sangyo University Library (Japan) 245
Kyriakou, K P, (Books — Stationery) Ltd (Cyprus) 70
Kyrios-Verlag GmbH (Federal Republic of Germany) 146
Kyung Hee University Press (Republic of Korea) 251
Kyung In Munwha Sa (Republic of Korea) 251
Kyungnam University Press (Republic of Korea) 251
Kyungpook National University Central Library (Republic of Korea) 252
Kyushu University Library (Japan) 245

L & S Publishing Co (Australia) 15
L D A (Learning Development Aids) (United Kingdom) 418
L E D A (Las Ediciones de Arte) (Spain) 341
L E R, Livraria (Brazil) 56
L I C E T (France) 101
L I C —Förlag (Sweden) 355
L I N E S A (Spain) 347
L I S A (Livros Irradiantes SA) (Brazil) 52
L I T A (Czechoslovakia) 73
L I T E C (Brazil) 52
L I T E C, Libraries Techniques SA (France) 101
L I T E C — Livraria Editora Técnica Ltda (Brazil) 56
L K G (German Democratic Republic) 119
L N-Verlag Lübeck, Lübecker Nachrichten GmbH (Federal Republic of Germany) 146
L P 3 E S (Lembaga Penelitian, Pendidikan Dan Penerangan Ekonomi Dan Social) (Indonesia) 206
L S P Books Ltd (United Kingdom) 418
L T C-Livros Técnicos e Científicos Editora SA (Brazil) 52
L T Editions (France) 101
L T r Editora Ltda (Brazil) 52
L Ts Förlag AB (Lantbrukarnas Riksförbund och Studieförbundet Vuxenskolan) (Sweden) 355
La Paz, Librería (Bolivia) 46
La Porte, Editions (Morocco) 271
La Scala, Edizioni (Italy) 226
La Tartaruga Edizioni (Italy) 226
Lääketieteellinen Keskuskirjasto (Finland) 89
Labbé-Vauquelin Foundation Prize (France) 113
Labor, Editions (Belgium) 38
Labor, Editorial, Argentina SA (Argentina) 6
Labor, Editorial, Colombiana Ltda (Colombia) 66
Labor, Editorial, de Venezuela SA (Venezuela) 453
Labor, Editorial, del Ecuador SA (Ecuador) 83
Labor, Editorial, do Brasil SA (Brazil) 52
Labor, Editorial, SA (Spain) 341
Labor et Fides SA (Switzerland) 368
Lachispa (Colombia) 66
Lacus, Ambro, Buch- und Bildverlag W Kremnitz (Federal Republic of Germany) 146
Lad-Bara Book Club (Nigeria) 296
Lademann Ltd, Publishers (Denmark) 77
Ladybird (Australia) 15
Ladybird Books Ltd (United Kingdom) 418
Laetare (Federal Republic of Germany) 146
Laetitia, Boekhandel en Uitgeverij (Netherlands) 279
Lafenestre, Georges, Foundation Prize (France) 113
Laffont, Les Editions Robert (France) 101
Lafite, Elisabeth (Austria) 26

Lafontaine Prize (France) 113
Laget, Librairie Léonce (France) 101
Lagos City Council Libraries (Nigeria) 297
Lahn-Verlag (Federal Republic of Germany) 146
Lahumière, Editions (France) 101
Laia, Editorial, SA (Spain) 341
Lake House Investments Ltd (Sri Lanka) 349
Lakeland Paperbacks (United Kingdom) 418
Lakoul Press (Nepal) 272
Lakshmi Narain Agarwal (India) 193
Lalit Kala Akademi (National Academy of Art) (India) 193
Lalli, Antonio, Editore (Italy) 226
Lalvani Brothers (India) 193
Lamares, Américo Fraga, & Ca Lda (Portugal) 317
Lamarre-Poinat, Editions, SA (France) 101
Lamb, Charles, Society (United Kingdom) 447
Lambert Prize (France) 113
Lambertus Verlag GmbH (Federal Republic of Germany) 146
Lampe, Editions, d'Or ASBL (Belgium) 38
Lamuv Verlag GmbH (Federal Republic of Germany) 146
Lamy SA, Editions Juridiques et Techniques (France) 101
Lancashire Authors' Association (United Kingdom) 447
Landbouwhogeschool, Bibliotheek der (Netherlands) 284
Landbuch-Verlag GmbH (Federal Republic of Germany) 146
Landesgremium Kärnten des Handels mit Büchern, Kunstblättern, Musikalien, Zeitungen und Zeitschriften (Austria) 24
Landesgremium Niederösterreich des Handels mit Büchern, Kunstblättern, Musikalien, Zeitungen und Zeitschriften (Austria) 24
Landesgremium Oberösterreich des Handels mit Büchern, Kunstblättern, Musikalien, Zeitungen und Zeitschriften (Austria) 24
Landesgremium Salzburg des Handels mit Büchern, Kunstblättern, Musikalien, Zeitungen und Zeitschriften (Austria) 24
Landesgremium Steiermark des Handels mit Büchern, Kunstblättern, Musikalien, Zeitungen und Zeitschriften (Austria) 24
Landesgremium Tirol des Handels mit Büchern, Kunstblättern, Musikalien, Zeitungen und Zeitschriften (Austria) 24
Landesgremium Vorarlberg des Handels mit Büchern und Musikalien (Austria) 24
Landesgremium Wien des Handels mit Büchern, Kunstblättern, Musikalien, Zeitungen und Zeitschriften (Austria) 24
Landesman, Jay, Ltd (United Kingdom) 418
Landestopographie, Bundesamt für (Switzerland) 368
Landesverband der Buchhändler und Verleger in Niedersachsen eV (Federal Republic of Germany) 121
Landesverband der Verleger und Buchhändler Bremen-Unterweser eV (Federal Republic of Germany) 121
Landesverband der Verleger und Buchhändler Rheinland-Pfalz eV (Federal Republic of Germany) 121
Landesverband der Verleger und Buchhändler Saar eV (LVBS) (Federal Republic of Germany) 121
Landesverband des werbenden Buch- und Zeitschriftenhandels von Südwestdeutschland eV (Federal Republic of Germany) 121
Landmarks (United Kingdom) 418
Landsberger Verlagsanstalt Martin Neumeyer (Federal Republic of Germany) 146
Landsbókasafn Islands (Iceland) 185
Landwirtschaftliche Zentralbibliothek (German Democratic Republic) 119
Landwirtschaftlicher Staatsverlag (Agricultural Publishing House) (Czechoslovakia) 71
Landy, Livraria D (Brazil) 56
Lane, Allen (Australia) 15
Lane, Allen (United Kingdom) 418
Lang, Herbert, & Cie AG (Switzerland) 368
Lang, Verlag Peter, AG (Switzerland) 368
Lang, Verlag Peter, GmbH (Federal Republic of Germany) 146
Lange, Allert de, BV (Netherlands) 279
Langen, Albert, -Georg Müller Verlag (Federal Republic of Germany) 146
Langen-Müller, Verlagsgruppe, /Herbig (Federal Republic of Germany) 146
Langenhoven, C J, Prize (Republic of South Africa) 335
Langenscheidt AG (Switzerland) 368
Langenscheidt Group, The (Federal Republic of Germany) 146
Langenscheidt-Hachette GmbH (Federal Republic of Germany) 146
Langenscheidt KG (Federal Republic of Germany) 146
Langenscheidt-Longman GmbH (Federal Republic of Germany) 146
Langenscheidt-Verlag GmbH (Austria) 26
Langewiesche-Brandt, Verlag, KG (Federal Republic of Germany) 146
Langewiesche, Karl Robert, Nachfolger Hans Koester KG (Federal Republic of Germany) 146
Langlois Prize (France) 113

INDEX 523

Language and Literature Bureau Library (Brunei) 58
Language Book Centre (Australia) 20
Language, The, Library (United Kingdom) 418
Languages School (Thailand) 380
Lanka Booksellers' Association (India) 185
Lannoo (Belgium) 38
Lannoo, Uitgeverij (Netherlands) 279
Lanore, Librairie Fernand, Sàrl (France) 101
Lanore, LT Editions-J, -H Laurens (France) 101
Lansdowne Editions (Australia) 15
Lansdowne International (United Kingdom) 418
Lansdowne Press (Australia) 15
Lantern Books (Nigeria) 294
Lanterna, Editrice (Italy) 226
Lao Dong (Labour) Publishing House (Socialist Republic of Viet Nam) 455
Lao-phanit (Laos) 253
Lapautre, Michelle (France) 109
Lappeenrannan Kirjakauppa Oy (Finland) 88
Lapucci, Mario (Italy) 226
Lärarbokklubben (Sweden) 358
Larcier, Maison Ferdinand, SA (Belgium) 38
Larese, Franz, und Jürg Janett (Switzerland) 368
Larousse, Ediciones, Argentina SA (Argentina) 6
Larousse, Librairie (France) 101
Larousse (Suisse) SA (Switzerland) 368
Larson, Bokförlaget Robert, AB (Sweden) 355
Lasie Australia Co Ltd (Australia) 21
Lasser Press Mexicana, SA (Mexico) 266
Lasserre, Luis, y Cía, SACIFI (Argentina) 6
Lasten Keskus Oy (Finland) 87
Laterna Magica, Verlag, Joachim F Richter (Federal Republic of Germany) 146
Laterza, Giuseppe, e Figli SpA (Italy) 226
Latina SA (Argentina) 6
Latomus ASBL (Belgium) 38
Lattès, Editions Jean-Claude (France) 101
Laudes, Editora, SA (Brazil) 52
Laurens, Editions Henri, Successeurs Sàrl (France) 101
Laurenziana, Biblioteca Medicea (Italy) 234
Laurie, T Werner (United Kingdom) 418
Laurus, Edizioni (Italy) 226
Lavauzelle, Editions Charles-, SA (France) 101
Lavigerie, Les Presses (Burundi) 60
Lavoro, Le Edizioni del (Italy) 226
Law Books in Hindi Prize (India) 204
Law Books in Hindi Publishers (India) 193
Law Publishers (India) 193
Law, The, Book Co Ltd (Australia) 15
Lawrence & Wishart (United Kingdom) 418
Lawyers' Co-operative Publishing Co (Philippines) Inc (Philippines) 309
Lax, August (Federal Republic of Germany) 146
Le Cri, Edition (Belgium) 38
Le Monnier, Casa Editrice Felice (Italy) 227
Le Mouël, Eugène, Foundation Prize (France) 113
Le Prat, Editions Guy (France) 101
League of Arab States, Department of Documentation and Information (International Organizations) 471
Lebanese Library, The, Association (Lebanon) 254
Lebanon Bookshop (Lebanon) 254
Lechevalier, Editions, Sàrl (France) 101
Lecoffre, Librairie (France) 101
Leconte, Sébastien-Charles, Foundation Prize (France) 113
Lector-Verlag GmbH (Switzerland) 368
Lectura, Librería (Venezuela) 454
Lecture Publique, Direction de la (Tunisia) 384
Ledori (Israel) 215
Lee, T H, & Co Ltd (Hong Kong) 179
Leeds University Library (United Kingdom) 445
Lee's Book Centre (Bahamas) 31
Lefebvre, Francis (France) 101
Legislación Económica Ltda (Colombia) 66
'Legkaya i Pishchevaya', Izdatelstvo, Promyshlennost' (Union of Soviet Socialist Republics) 387
Legrand, Editions (Belgium) 38
Lehmann, Librería Imprenta y Litografía, SA (Costa Rica) 68
Lehmann, Librería Imprenta y Litografía, SA (Costa Rica) 68
Lehnert & Landrock (Egypt) 84
Leibniz-Volksbuchhandlung (German Democratic Republic) 119
Leicester University Press (United Kingdom) 418
Leiden University Press (Netherlands) 279
Leiftur hf (Iceland) 184
Leins, Verlag Hermann (Federal Republic of Germany) 146
Leipholdt, C Louis, Prys vir Poesie (Republic of South Africa) 335
Leipzig, VEB Edition (German Democratic Republic) 117
Leipziger Kommissions- und Grossbuchhandel (LKG) (German Democratic Republic) 119
Leisure Arts Ltd (United Kingdom) 418
Leisure Circle, The, Ltd (United Kingdom) 443
Leitfadenverlag Dieter Sudholt (Federal Republic of Germany) 146

Lekarskich, Państwowy Zakład Wydawnictw (Poland) 312
Lekha Prokashani (Bangladesh) 32
Lello & Cia Lda (Angola) 2
Lello & Cia Lda (Angola) 2
Lello e Cia Lda (Portugal) 317
Lello e Irmão (Portugal) 317
Lembeck, Verlag Otto (Federal Republic of Germany) 146
Lemniscaat (Netherlands) 279
Lenclud, Anne, Pierre Lenclud (France) 109
Lenina, Gosudarstvennaya ordena Lenina biblioteka SSSR imeni V I (Union of Soviet Socialist Republics) 389
'Lenizdat', Izdatelstvo (Union of Soviet Socialist Republics) 387
Lenos Verlag (Switzerland) 368
Lensing, Verlag Lambert, GmbH (Federal Republic of Germany) 147
Lentz, Georg, Verlag (Federal Republic of Germany) 147
Leo, Franz, & Co KG (Austria) 29
Leobuchhandlung (Switzerland) 375
Leobuchhandlung, Verlag der Quellen-Bändchen (Switzerland) 368
Leon Editions (Greece) 175
Leonard Hill (United Kingdom) 418
Leonardo da Vinci, Nova Livraria, Ltda (Brazil) 56
Leong Brothers (Brunei) 58
Leonhardt, Karl Ludwig (Federal Republic of Germany) 167
Leonhardt Literary Agency ApS (Denmark) 79
Leonis Verlag (Switzerland) 368
Leopard (United Kingdom) 419
Leopold, Uitgeverij, BV (Netherlands) 279
Lepus Books (United Kingdom) 419
Lerner, Ediciones, Ltda (Colombia) 66
Lerner, Librería (Colombia) 67
Leroy, Editions Dominique (France) 101
Lerú, Editorial Victor, SA (Argentina) 6
Leske Verlag und Budrich GmbH (Federal Republic of Germany) 147
'Lesnaya Promyshlennost', Izdatelstvo (Union of Soviet Socialist Republics) 387
Lesoil, Uitgeverij Leon, VZW (Belgium) 38
Lesotho Book Centre (Lesotho) 255
Lesotho Library Association (Lesotho) 255
Lesotho National Library Service (Lesotho) 255
Lessing Prize der Freien und Hansestadt Hamburg (Federal Republic of Germany) 171
Lethielleux (France) 101
Letouzey, Société Nouvelle des Editions, et Ané Sàrl (France) 101
Letrán, Librería (Mexico) 268
Letras Cubanas, Editorial (Cuba) 69
Lettere, Casa Editrice Le, SRL (Italy) 227
Lettres Modernes Minard (France) 101
Letts, Charles, & Co Ltd (United Kingdom) 419
Leu, Edition, Kunst und Literatur (Switzerland) 368
Leuchter-Verlag EG (Federal Republic of Germany) 147
Leuven University Press (Belgium) 38
Levéltári Osztály, Művelődési Minisztérium (Hungary) 183
Leven, The Grace, Prize for Poetry (Australia) 23
Leventhal, Lionel, Ltd (United Kingdom) 419
Lewin-Epstein Ltd (Israel) 215
Lewin-Epstein-Modan, A, Ltd (Israel) 215
Lewis, A (United Kingdom) 419
Lewis, F, Publishers Ltd (United Kingdom) 419
Lewis, H K, & Co Ltd (United Kingdom) 419
Lewis, J D, & Sons Ltd (United Kingdom) 419
Lex Editora SA (Brazil) 52
Lexicon, The, Bookshop (Isle of Man) 212
Lexika-Verlag (Federal Republic of Germany) 147
Lexikothek Verlag GmbH (Federal Republic of Germany) 147
Ley, La, SA Editora e Impresora (Argentina) 6
Leykam Buchverlagsges mbH (Austria) 26
Leyraud, J-P (New Caledonia) 286
Lia Rumantscha (Ligia Romontscha) (Switzerland) 368
Liaoning Library (People's Republic of China) 64
Liaquat Memorial Library (Pakistan) 303
Liban, Librairie du (Lebanon) 254
Liban, Librairie du (Lebanon) 254
Liber Förlag (Sweden) 355
Liber Grafiska AB (Sweden) 355
Liber Hermods (Sweden) 355
Liber Juris, Editora, Ltda (Brazil) 52
Liber Läromedel (Sweden) 355
Liber, Sveučilišna Naklada (Yugoslavia) 457
Liber Utbildning (Sweden) 355
Liber UtbildningsFörlaget (Sweden) 355
Liber Verlag GmbH (Federal Republic of Germany) 147
Liber Yrkesutbildning (Sweden) 355
Liber Yrkesutbildning-Teknik (Sweden) 355
Liberian Educational Materials Supply Corporation (Liberia) 255
Liberian Literary & Educational Publications (Liberia) 255
Liberma, Libreria (Italy) 234
Libertador, Editorial (Venezuela) 453

Libertatea (Yugoslavia) 457
Liberty Bookstall (Pakistan) 303
Libra Books Pty Ltd (Australia) 15
Librairie afrique (Senegal) 324
Librairie Bilingue/The Bilingual Bookshop (United Republic of Cameroon) 61
Librairie centrafricaine (Central African Republic) 62
Librairie clairafrique (Senegal) 324
Librairie Commerciale et Technique (Licet) Sàrl (France) 101
Librairie de Madagascar (Democratic Republic of Madagascar) 258
Librairie du Liban (Lebanon) 254
Librairie/Editions Nouvelles Editions Africaines (Togo) 382
Librairie encyclopédique, Editions de la (Belgium) 38
Librairie évangélique (Central African Republic) 62
Librairie évangélique (Chad) 62
Librairie Evangélique du Burundi (Burundi) 60
Librairie Générale de Droit et de Jurisprudence (France) 101
Librairie Générale Française SA (France) 101
Librairie lutherienne (Democratic Republic of Madagascar) 258
Librairie mixte Sàrl (Democratic Republic of Madagascar) 258
Librairie Nationale (Mauritius) 263
Librairie nationale (Morocco) 271
Librairie nouvelle de l'Ouest Africain (LINOA) (Senegal) 324
Librairie-Papeterie Moderne (United Republic of Cameroon) 61
Librairie-Papeterie Protestante CEBEC (United Republic of Cameroon) 61
Librairie-Papeterie Universelle (French Guiana) 114
Librairie Populaire (United Republic of Cameroon) 61
Librairie Populaire (Popular Republic of Congo) 68
Librairie populaire de Mali (Mali) 262
Librairie universitaire (Democratic Republic of Madagascar) 258
Librairie universitaire (Rwanda) 323
Librairie Universitaire de la Réunion (Réunion) 320
Librairie universitaire et technique (Senegal) 324
Librairies Techniques SA (France) 101
Libraport (Guinea) 177
Library Advisory Council for Wales (United Kingdom) 446
Library and Information Council for England (United Kingdom) 446
Library Association of Australia (Australia) 21
Library Association of Barbados (Barbados) 33
Library Association of China (Taiwan) 378
Library Association of Singapore (Republic of Singapore) 328
Library Association of the Democratic People's Republic of Korea (Democratic People's Republic of Korea) 250
Library Association Publishing (United Kingdom) 419
Library Association, The (United Kingdom) 446
Library Automated Systems, The, Information Exchange (Australia) 21
Library Board of Western Australia, The (Australia) 20
Library of Parliament (Republic of South Africa) 334
Library of Parliament (Zimbabwe) 465
Library, School of, and Information Science (Japan) 245
Library Science Society (Taiwan) 378
Library Service of Fiji (Fiji) 86
Library, The, and Documentation Centre (Saudi Arabia) 323
Library, The, Shop (Republic of Ireland) 211
Librería Central (Colombia) 67
Librería Científica SA (Ecuador) 83
Librería Contemporanea (Puerto Rico) 320
Librería Continental (Colombia) 67
Librería Cultural (Puerto Rico) 320
Librería Cultural Nicaraguense (Nicaragua) 292
Librería Cultural Panameña, SA (Panama) 305
Librería Cultural Puertorriqueña Inc (Puerto Rico) 320
Librería Cultural SA (Venezuela) 454
Librería Cultural Venezolana (Venezuela) 454
Librería Española (Ecuador) 83
Librería Inglesa (Uruguay) 452
Librería Internacional (Paraguay) 306
Librería Internacional del Perú (Peru) 307
Librería Internacional SA de CV (Mexico) 268
Librería Nacional (Colombia) 67
Librería Tecnológica Universitaria (Nicaragua) 292
Librería Tecnológico SA (Mexico) 268
Librería Universal (Guatemala) 177
Librería Universal (Paraguay) 306
Librería Universitaria (Chile) 63
Librería Universitaria (Ecuador) 83
Librería Universitaria (Mexico) 268
Librería Universitaria (Nicaragua) 292
Librería Universitaria de Puerto Rico (Puerto Rico) 320
Librex, Edizioni (Italy) 227
Libris Bookclub (Sweden) 358
Libris Publishing House (Sweden) 355
Libro de la Naturaleza, Club del (Spain) 347

Libroclub de Guatemala (Guatemala) 177
Librolandia del Centro SA (Mexico) 269
Libros y Revistas SA (Mexico) 266
Licet (France) 101
Lichtenberg Verlag GmbH (Federal Republic of Germany) 147
Lichterfelde, Edition (Federal Republic of Germany) 147
Licosa SpA (Italy) 227
Lidador, Editora, Ltda (Brazil) 52
Lidis, Editions, SA (France) 101
Lidman Production AB (Sweden) 355
Lidové nakladatelství (Czechoslovakia) 71
Liebenzeller Mission, Verlag der (Federal Republic of Germany) 147
Liebing, Rudolf (Federal Republic of Germany) 147
Liechtenstein Verlag AG (Liechtenstein) 256
Liechtenstein Verlag AG (Liechtenstein) 256
Liechtensteinische Landesbibliothek (Liechtenstein) 256
Lied, VEB, der Zeit Musikverlag (German Democratic Republic) 117
Liepman AG (Switzerland) 375
Lietzow, Edition/Galerie (Federal Republic of Germany) 147
Life Sciences Research Reports (Federal Republic of Germany) 147
Lifestyle Book Society (United Kingdom) 443
Lifestyle Books (United Kingdom) 419
Ligel, Editions (France) 101
Light & Life Publishers (India) 193
Ligue des Bibliothèques Européennes de Recherche (LIBER) (International Organizations) 468
Liguori Editore SRL (Italy) 227
Liguria, Casa Editrice (Italy) 227
Lile, Editions Michel de, et Philippe Auzou (France) 101
Lilja, Bókagerdin (Iceland) 184
Lima, Waldyr, Editora (Brazil) 52
Limes Verlag (Federal Republic of Germany) 147
Limmat Verlag Genossenschaft (Switzerland) 368
Limonado, Editora Max, Ltda (Brazil) 52
Limpert Verlag (Federal Republic of Germany) 147
Limusa, Editorial, SA (Mexico) 266
Linardi, Librería Adolfo (Uruguay) 452
Lincoln, Biblioteca (Argentina) 8
Lincoln Cultural Center (Malaysia) 261
Lincoln, Frances, Ltd (United Kingdom) 419
Lindblads, J A, Bokförlag AB (Sweden) 355
Linden Press (United Kingdom) 419
Linder AG Literary Agency (Switzerland) 375
Lindhardt og Ringhof (Denmark) 77
Lindon Publishing (New Zealand) 288
Linea Verde (Italy) 227
Lines (United Kingdom) 419
Ling, H C, Book Store & Co Ltd (Taiwan) 378
Ling Kee Group, The (Hong Kong) 179
Ling Kee Publishing Co Ltd (Hong Kong) 179
Lingen Verlag (Federal Republic of Germany) 147
Lingenbrink, Barsortiment Georg, (Wholesale Bookseller) (Federal Republic of Germany) 168
Linosa-Linomonograph, Editorial, SA (Spain) 342
Lion Publishing PLC (United Kingdom) 419
Lions (United Kingdom) 419
Lipi Prakashan (India) 193
Lisciani e Giunti Editori (Italy) 227
Lisieux, Office Central de, SA (France) 102
List, Paul, Verlag (German Democratic Republic) 117
List, Paul, Verlag KG (Federal Republic of Germany) 147
Listín, Editora, Diario (Dominican Republic) 82
Litchfield, Jessie, Memorial Award (Australia) 23
Litera Publishing House (Romania) 321
Literackie, Wydawnictwo (Poland) 312
Literamed Publications Nigeria Ltd (Nigeria) 294
Literar-Mechana, Wahrnehmungsgesellschaft für Urheberrechte GmbH (Austria) 24
Literarische Agentur und Verlagsgesellschaft (Liechtenstein) 256
Literarischer Verein in Stuttgart eV (Federal Republic of Germany) 170
Literary Award (Romania) 322
Literary Contest Prize for Spastics Society (United Kingdom) 449
Literary Critics' Grand Prize (France) 113
Literary Fund Writing Bursary (New Zealand) 291
Literary Guild (United Kingdom) 443
Literary Guild, The (Australia) 19
Literary Guild, The (New Zealand) 290
Literary Prize (Republic of Korea) 253
Literary Prize (Panama) 305
Literary Prize of the Resistance (France) 113
Literary Prizes for Sinhala Literature (Sri Lanka) 350
Literary Services (Pty) Ltd (Republic of South Africa) 333
Literary Supplies (Jamaica) 237
Literas-Verlag GmbH (Austria) 26
Literature and Art Publishing House (Democratic People's Republic of Korea) 250
Literature Board of the Australia Council (Australia) 10
Literature Board of the Australia Council (Australia) 23
Literature Bureau, The (Zimbabwe) 464
Literature Bureau, The (Zimbabwe) 465

Literature Bureau, The, Annual Literary Award (Zimbabwe) 465
Literature House Ltd (Taiwan) 378
Literature Prize (Federal Republic of Germany) 171
Literature Prize (Democratic Republic of Madagascar) 258
Literature Prize of the Province of Steiermark (Austria) 31
Literaturkritikernes Laug (Critics Literary Prize) (Denmark) 81
Litheratheke (Switzerland) 368
Lito, Editions (France) 102
Litolff's, Henry, Verlag (Federal Republic of Germany) 147
Litor Publishers (United Kingdom) 419
Litpress (Switzerland) 375
Littera Scripta Manet (Netherlands) 279
Littérature, Editeurs de, biblique (Belgium) 38
Litteraturfrämjandet (Sweden) 359
Little Flower, The, Co (India) 193
Little Hills Press (Australia) 16
Little Stephen (United Kingdom) 419
Little Swan (India) 193
Liveright (United Kingdom) 419
Liverpool City Libraries (United Kingdom) 445
Liverpool University Press (United Kingdom) 419
Living & Learning (Cambridge) Ltd (United Kingdom) 419
Living Literary Agency Elfriede Pexa (Italy) 233
Livraria Editora Técnica Ltda (LITEC) (Brazil) 52
Livre de Paris, Le, Hachette (France) 102
Livre de Poche, Le (France) 102
Livre-Service, Librairie (Morocco) 271
Livres de France (Egypt) 84
Livro Cientifíco, Estante do (Brazil) 55
Livros, Editora, do Brasil Sarl (Portugal) 317
Livros Irradiantes SA (Brazil) 52
Lloyd Anversois SA (Antwerpse Lloyd NV) (Belgium) 38
Lloyd-Luke (Medical Books) Ltd (United Kingdom) 419
Llull, Ramon, Prize (Spain) 349
Llyfrgell Genedlaethol Cymru (National Library of Wales) (United Kingdom) 445
Lo Faro, Vincenzo, Editore (Italy) 227
Lobato, Monteiro, Prize (Brazil) 57
Local Government Council Library (Somalia) 328
Local Heritage Books (United Kingdom) 419
Local History Award (Australia) 23
Löcker Verlag (Austria) 26
Locomotion Papers (United Kingdom) 419
Locomotive Publishing Co Ltd (United Kingdom) 419
Locusta, Editrice La (Italy) 227
Lodenek Press Ltd (United Kingdom) 419
Lodestar Press (New Zealand) 288
Lodzkie, Wydawnictwo (Poland) 312
Loeb Classical Library (United Kingdom) 419
Loeper, von, Verlag GmbH (Federal Republic of Germany) 147
Loescher Editore SpA (Italy) 227
Loewes Verlag KG (Federal Republic of Germany) 147
Loffredo, Luigi, Editrice (Italy) 227
Lofler, Paul, Foundation Prize (France) 113
Logans University Bookshop (Pty) Ltd (Republic of South Africa) 333
Loghum, Van, Slaterus (Netherlands) 279
Logos Consorcio Editorial, SA (Mexico) 266
Logos-Verlag (Switzerland) 368
Logosófica, Editora (Brazil) 52
Lohlé, Carlos, SA (Argentina) 6
Løhren, Ulla, Literary Agency (Norway) 300
Lohses Forlag (Denmark) 77
Lok Vangmaya Griha (Pvt) Ltd (India) 193
Lokole, Editions (Zaire) 462
Lombard SA (Belgium) 38
Londinium Press Ltd (United Kingdom) 419
London Bookshops Ltd (New Zealand) 290
London Independent Books Ltd (United Kingdom) 442
London Magazine Editions (United Kingdom) 419
London Syndication (United Kingdom) 442
London Writer Circle (United Kingdom) 447
Lonely Planet Publications Pty Ltd (Australia) 16
Longanesi & C (Italy) 227
Longman Arab World Centre (Lebanon) 254
Longman Botswana (Pty) Ltd (Botswana) 47
Longman Caribbean (Trinidad) Ltd (Trinidad and Tobago) 382
Longman Cheshire Pty Ltd (Australia) 16
Longman Group (Far East) Ltd (Hong Kong) 179
Longman Group Ltd (United Kingdom) 419
Longman Italia SRL (Italy) 227
Longman Jamaica Ltd (Jamaica) 237
Longman Kenya Ltd (Kenya) 248
Longman Lesotho (Pty) Ltd (Lesotho) 255
Longman Malaysia Sdn Bhd (Malaysia) 259
Longman Malaysia Sdn Bhd (Republic of Singapore) 326
Longman Nigeria Ltd (Nigeria) 294
Longman Paul Ltd (New Zealand) 288
Longman Penguin Southern Africa (Pty) Ltd (Republic of South Africa) 330

Longman Tanzania Ltd (Tanzania) 379
Longman Uganda Ltd (Uganda) 386
Longman Zimbabwe Literary Awards (Zimbabwe) 465
Longman Zimbabwe (Pvt) Ltd (Zimbabwe) 464
Longo, Angelo, Editore (Italy) 227
Longo, Libreria A (Italy) 234
Look-In Books (United Kingdom) 420
Lope de Vega, Librería y Papelería (Dominican Republic) 82
Lopes Da Silva, Livraria, -Editora de M Moreira Soares Rocha Lda (Portugal) 317
Lopes, Julia, de Ameida Prize (Brazil) 57
López Libreros Editores (Argentina) 6
Löpfe-Benz, E, AG Rorschacht, Graphische Anstalt und Verlag (Switzerland) 368
Lorber-Verlag (Federal Republic of Germany) 147
Lorch-Verlag GmbH (Federal Republic of Germany) 147
Lord International (India) 194
Lorrimer Books (United Kingdom) 420
Losada, Editorial, SA (Argentina) 6
Lothian Publishing Co Pty Ltd (Australia) 16
Lothian, Thomas C, Pty Ltd (New Zealand) 288
Lotu Pasifika Productions (Fiji) 86
Lotus, Uitgeverij, /Editions Lotus (Belgium) 38
Louisiana State University Press (United Kingdom) 420
Lovedale Press (Republic of South Africa) 330
Lowden Publishing Co (Australia) 16
Lowe, Peter (United Kingdom) 420
Lowe, Robson, Ltd (United Kingdom) 420
Löwit, R, GmbH (Federal Republic of Germany) 147
Loyola, Edições, SA (Brazil) 52
Lübbe, Gustav, Verlag GmbH (Federal Republic of Germany) 147
Lubelskie, Wydawnictwo (Poland) 312
Lucarini Editore Srl (Italy) 227
Luchterhand, Hermann, Verlag GmbH & Co KG, Neuwied und Darmstadt (Federal Republic of Germany) 147
Lucis Press Ltd (United Kingdom) 420
Lucky (Australia) 19
Lucky Arrow (New Zealand) 290
Lucky Book Club (United Kingdom) 443
Luctor Publishing — Stadler & Sauerbier BV (Netherlands) 279
Ludowa Spółdzielnia Wydawnicza (Poland) 312
Ludwig, W, Verlag (Federal Republic of Germany) 147
Luitingh, Uitgeverij, BV (Netherlands) 279
'Lumen Christi', Edições (Brazil) 52
Lumen, Editions, Vitae ASBL (Belgium) 39
Lumen, Editorial, SA (Spain) 342
Lumiere Biblique (France) 102
Luna, Libreria Internazionale Giuseppe (Italy) 234
Lund Humphries Publishers Ltd (United Kingdom) 420
Lund Universitetsbibliotek (Sweden) 359
Lunde Forlag og Bokhandel A/S (Norway) 299
Lundequistska, Esselte Bokhandel (Sweden) 358
Lundgrens, AB Edvin, Bokhandel (Sweden) 358
Lundqvists, Abr, Musikförlag AB (Sweden) 355
l'Université, Editions de, de Bruxelles (Belgium) 41
Lusaka District Libraries (Zambia) 463
Luso-Espanhola, Livraria, Lda (Portugal) 317
Lusva Editrice (Italy) 227
Luther Forlag A/S (Norway) 299
Luther-Verlag GmbH (Federal Republic of Germany) 147
Lutheran Publishing House (Australia) 16
Lutherisches Verlagshaus GmbH (Federal Republic of Germany) 148
Lutry, The, Press (Switzerland) 368
Lutterworth Press (United Kingdom) 420
Lutz, Hans-Rudolf (Switzerland) 369
Lutz, Verlag Waldemar (Federal Republic of Germany) 148
Lux Press (Malta) 262
Lux Verbi (Pty) Ltd (Republic of South Africa) 330
Luxembourg, Library, Commission of the European Communities (International Organizations) 468
Luxor Press Ltd (United Kingdom) 420
Lyche, Harald, & Co A/S (Norway) 299
Lydecken, Arvid, Prize (Finland) 90
Lyle Publications Ltd (United Kingdom) 420
Lyngs Bokhandel A/S (Norway) 300
Lypsa, Industria Editorial (Honduras) 178
Lypsa, Librería (Honduras) 178
Lyrikbogklubben Borgen-Gyldendal (Denmark) 79
Lyrikkvaennene, Bokklubbens (Norway) 300
Lythway Press Ltd (United Kingdom) 420

M A M (The House of the Cyprus Book) (Cyprus) 70
M A M (The House of the Cyprus Book) (Cyprus) 70
M B A Literary Agents Ltd (United Kingdom) 442
M C B University Press Ltd (United Kingdom) 420
M C S Enterprises Inc (Philippines) 309
M D I, Editions, (La Maison des Instituteurs) (France) 102
M E B, Casa Editrice, SRL (Italy) 227

INDEX 525

M E/D I Sviluppo (Italy) 227
M E D S I (Médecine et Sciences Internationales) (France) 102
M E P (United Kingdom) 420
M F B (Phono- und Schriftenmission des Missionstrupps Frohe Botschaft eV) (Federal Republic of Germany) 148
M I M (Belgium) 39
M I N D Book of the Year Award (United Kingdom) 449
M I N D (National Association for Mental Health) (United Kingdom) 420
M I T International (Hong Kong) 180
M I T, The, Press (United Kingdom) 420
M P H Bookstores (S) Pte Ltd (Republic of Singapore) 327
M P H Distributors Sdn Bhd (Malaysia) 261
M P Text Book Corporation (India) 194
M R P (United Kingdom) 420
M S A (Republic of South Africa) 330
M T P Press Ltd (United Kingdom) 420
M V G (Federal Republic of Germany) 148
M W H London Publishers (United Kingdom) 420
Ma'alot (Israel) 215
Mäander Verlag GmbH (Federal Republic of Germany) 148
Ma'arachot (Israel) 215
Ma'aref, Al, Library (Jordan) 247
Maaref, Dar Al (Egypt) 84
Maaref, Dar Al-, Liban SAL (Lebanon) 254
Ma'arif, Al, Ltd (Iraq) 208
Ma'ariv Book Club (Israel) 217
Ma'ariv Book Guild (Sifriat Ma'ariv) (Israel) 215
Maatschappij der Nederlandse Letterkunde (Netherlands) 285
Mabiya Publications (Pty) Ltd (Swaziland) 351
Mabrochi International Co (Nigeria) 296
Mac Purcell (Lebanon) 254
Macaulay Fellowship (Republic of Ireland) 212
Macchi, Ediciones (Argentina) 6
McColvin Medal (United Kingdom) 449
Macdonald 3/4/5 (United Kingdom) 420
Macdonald & Co (Publishers) Ltd (United Kingdom) 420
Macdonald & Evans Ltd (United Kingdom) 420
Macdonald Edinburgh (United Kingdom) 420
Macdonald Educational (United Kingdom) 420
Macdonald Futura (United Kingdom) 420
Macdonald Guidelines (United Kingdom) 420
Macdonald Middle East Sàrl (Lebanon) 254
Macdonald Publishers (Edinburgh) (United Kingdom) 420
Macdonald Purnell (Pty) Ltd (Republic of South Africa) 330
Macdonald Queen Anne Press (United Kingdom) 420
Macdonald Starters (United Kingdom) 420
Macdonald's (Kenya) 249
Mace, Jean, Prize (France) 113
McGraw-Hill Book Co (Switzerland) 369
McGraw-Hill Book Co Australia Pty Ltd (Australia) 16
McGraw-Hill Book Co GmbH (Federal Republic of Germany) 148
McGraw-Hill Book Co, New Zealand Ltd (New Zealand) 288
McGraw-Hill Book Co (South Africa) (Pty) Ltd (Republic of South Africa) 330
McGraw-Hill Book Co (UK) Ltd (United Kingdom) 421
McGraw-Hill de España SA (Spain) 342
McGraw-Hill, Editora, do Brasil Ltda (Brazil) 52
McGraw-Hill, Editora, do Portugal Ltda (Portugal) 317
McGraw-Hill, Editorial, Latinoamericana SA (Colombia) 66
McGraw-Hill, Editorial, Latinoamericana SA (Panama) 304
McGraw-Hill, Editorial, Latinoamericana SA (Puerto Rico) 319
McGraw-Hill Inc (France) 102
McGraw-Hill International Book Co (Republic of Singapore) 326
McGraw-Hill Kabushiki Kaisha (Japan) 241
McGraw-Hill, Libros, de Mexico SA de CV (Mexico) 266
Machado de Assis Prize (Brazil) 57
Machado, Fernando, e Co Ltd (Portugal) 317
Machbarot Lesifrut (Israel) 215
Machreq, Darl el-, Sàrl (Lebanon) 254
McIndoe, John, Ltd (New Zealand) 288
McIntyre, Grant, Ltd (United Kingdom) 421
Mackay, Jessie, Award (New Zealand) 291
McKee et Mouche (France) 109
MacKern, Librerías, SA (Argentina) 8
Mackintosh Hall, John, Library (Gibraltar) 173
Maclellan, William, (Embryo) Ltd (United Kingdom) 421
Macmillan Boleswa Publishers (Pty) Ltd (Swaziland) 351
Macmillan Children's Books (United Kingdom) 421
Macmillan Co, The, of Australia Pty Ltd (Australia) 16
Macmillan Company, The, of New Zealand Ltd (New Zealand) 288
Macmillan Education Ltd (United Kingdom) 421
Macmillan India Ltd (India) 194
Macmillan London Ltd (United Kingdom) 421
Macmillan Malaysia (Malaysia) 260

McMillan Memorial Library (Kenya) 249
Macmillan Nigeria Publishers Ltd (Nigeria) 294
Macmillan Press, The, Ltd (United Kingdom) 421
Macmillan Publishers (HK) Ltd (Hong Kong) 179
Macmillan Publishers Ltd (United Kingdom) 421
Macmillan SA (Switzerland) 369
Macmillan South Africa Publishers (Pty) Ltd (Republic of South Africa) 331
Macmillan Southeast Asia Pte Ltd (Republic of Singapore) 326
McNamara's Books (Australia) 16
Macondo Ediciones SRL (Argentina) 6
McPhee Gribble Publishers Pty Ltd (Australia) 16
MacRae, Julia, Books (United Kingdom) 421
McRae Russell, The Walter, Award (Australia) 23
Madagascar Print & Press Co (Democratic Republic of Madagascar) 257
Madáh (Czechoslovakia) 71
Madarali, Fikret, Prize (Turkey) 385
Made Simple Books (United Kingdom) 421
Madhyo Pradesh Hindi Granth Academy (India) 194
Madju (Indonesia) 206
Madras Literary Society and Auxiliary of the Royal Asiatic Society (India) 203
Madras Literary Society Library (India) 202
Maeght Editeur (France) 102
Magalhães, Livraria, Sarl (Angola) 2
Magasin du Nord A/S (Denmark) 79
Maghreb Livres (Morocco) 271
Maghrebines, Les Editions (Morocco) 271
Magic-Strip SPRL (Belgium) 39
Magisterio, Editorial, Español SA (Spain) 342
Magistero, Edizioni (Italy) 227
Magna Print Books (United Kingdom) 421
Magnard, Les Editions, Sàrl (France) 102
Magnes, The, Press (Israel) 215
Magnet (United Kingdom) 421
Magnum Books (United Kingdom) 421
Magnus Edizioni SpA (Italy) 227
Magnus Verlag (Federal Republic of Germany) 148
Magvető Könyvkiadó (Hungary) 181
Magwe College Library (Burma) 60
Magyar Bibliofil társaság (Hungary) 183
Magyar Irodalomtörténeti Társaság (Hungary) 183
Magyar Írók Szövetsége (Hungary) 181
Magyar Írok Szövetsége (Hungary) 183
Magyar Könyvkiadók és Könyvterjesztők Egyesülése (Hungary) 181
Magyar Könyvtárosok Egyesülete (Hungary) 183
Magyar Központi Levéltár, Uj (Hungary) 182
Magyar Országos Levéltár (Hungary) 182
Magyar Tudományos Akadémia Irodalomtudományi Intézete (Hungary) 183
Magyar Tudományos Akadémia Könyvtára (Hungary) 182
Magyar Tudományos Akadémiai Kiadó (Hungary) 181
Mahabir Singh Chiniya Main (Nepal) 272
Mahajan Brothers (India) 194
Maier, Otto, Benelux BV (Netherlands) 279
Maier, Otto, Verlag (Federal Republic of Germany) 148
Maille-Latour-Landry Prize (France) 113
Mainichi Publishing Culture Prize (Japan) 247
Mainstream Book Club (United Kingdom) 443
Mainstream Publishing Co (Edinburgh) Ltd (United Kingdom) 421
Mairs Geographischer Verlag (Federal Republic of Germany) 148
Mai's Reiseführer Verlag (Federal Republic of Germany) 148
Maison de la Presse, Société congolaise Hachette (Popular Republic of Congo) 68
Maison des Instituteurs, La (France) 102
Maison des Livres (Ivory Coast) 236
'Maison des Livres', Librairie (Algeria) 2
Maison du Dictionnaire, La (France) 102
Maison, La, de la Bible (Switzerland) 369
Maison, La, du Livre (Benin) 45
Maison, La, Rustique SA (France) 102
Maison Tunisienne d'Edition (Tunisia) 383
Maisondieu Prize (France) 113
Maisonneuve-Editions d'Amérique, Adrien, et d'Orient (France) 102
Maisonneuve et Larose, Editions G P (France) 102
Maisonneuve SA, Editeur (France) 102
Máj (Czechoslovakia) 73
Majerive, Marie, Prize (Czechoslovakia) 74
Majlis Press (Iran) 207
Makedonska Knjiga (Yugoslavia) 460
Makedonska Knjiga (Knigoizdatelstvo) (Yugoslavia) 457
Makerere Institute of Social Research Library (Uganda) 386
Makerere University Bookshop (Uganda) 386
Makerere University Library (Uganda) 386
Makor Publishing Ltd (Israel) 215
Maktaba, Al- (Saudi Arabia) 323
Maktaba-i-Danial (Pakistan) 302
Maktaba Jadeed (Pakistan) 302
Maktaba Meri Library (Pakistan) 302

Maktaba Shahkar (Pakistan) 302
Maktabah, Al, Al Wataniah (National Library) (Syria) 377
Makumira Lutheran Theological College Library (Tanzania) 379
Mál og menning (Iceland) 184
Mal og menning (Iceland) 184
Malabar, Toko Buku (Indonesia) 206
Malaby Press (United Kingdom) 421
Malacorda, Marika, Editions (Switzerland) 369
Malan, H R, Prize (Republic of South Africa) 335
Malatestiana, Biblioteca Comunale (Italy) 234
Malato, Organizzazione Editoriale David (Italy) 227
Malawi Book Service (Malawi) 258
Malawi Library Association, The (Malawi) 258
Malawi National Library Service (Malawi) 258
Malaya Books Suppliers Co (Malaysia) 260
Malaya Educational Supplies Sdn Bhd (Malaysia) 260
Malaya Press, The, Sdn Bhd (Malaysia) 260
Malayan Law Journal (Pte) Ltd (Republic of Singapore) 326
Malaysia Press Sdn Bhd (Republic of Singapore) 326
Malaysian Book Publishers' Association (Malaysia) 259
Malaysian Law Publishers Sdn Bhd (Malaysia) 260
Malheiros, Ricardo, Prize (Portugal) 319
Malherbe, John, (Pty) Ltd (Republic of South Africa) 331
Mali, Editions Imprimeries du (Mali) 262
Malik Din Mohammad & Sons (Pakistan) 302
Malik Siraj-ud-Din & Sons (Pakistan) 302
Malik Siraj-ud-Din & Sons (Pakistan) 303
Malipiero Editore (Italy) 227
Mallard Reprints (United Kingdom) 421
Mallings ApS (Denmark) 77
Mallinson Rendel Publishers Ltd (New Zealand) 288
Malmberg BV (Netherlands) 279
Malmö Stadsbibliotek (Sweden) 359
Maloine, Librairie (France) 102
Malpertuis Prize (Belgium) 45
Máls og menningar, Bókabúd (Iceland) 184
Malsa Book Service Ltd (Zambia) 463
'Malysh', Izdatelstvo (Union of Soviet Socialist Republics) 387
Mamadou Traoré Ray Autra (Senegal) 324
Mambo Press (Zimbabwe) 464
Mambo Press Bookshop (Zimbabwe) 465
Mame, Nouvelles Editions (France) 102
Månadens Bok (Sweden) 358
Manar, Imprimerie/Librairie Al (Tunisia) 383
Manar, Librairie Al (Tunisia) 383
Manchester University Press (United Kingdom) 421
Mandarino, Editora, Ltda (Brazil) 53
Mandas Sugatdas (Nepal) 272
Mandat des Poètes Prize (International Literary Prizes) 478
Manese and Morgarten Verlag (Switzerland) 369
Manesse Verlag (Switzerland) 369
Manfredi, Umberto (Italy) 227
Manfrini Editori (Italy) 227
Mangold, Paul, Verlag (Austria) 26
Manhattan Press (Singapore) Pte Ltd (Republic of Singapore) 326
Manhin, Victor, Ltd (Trinidad and Tobago) 382
Manila City Library (Philippines) 310
Mann, Gebr, Verlag GmbH & Co (Federal Republic of Germany) 148
Mann, Thomas, Prize (Federal Republic of Germany) 171
Mann, Volksbuchhandlung Thomas (German Democratic Republic) 119
Mannin Dealer Agencies (Isle of Man) 212
Manohar Publications (India) 194
Manoharlal, Munshiram, Publishers Pvt Ltd (India) 194
Manole, Editora, Ltda (Brazil) 53
Manor Press (Philippines) 309
Manosabdam Books (India) 194
Mansell Publishing Ltd (United Kingdom) 421
Mansfield, Katherine, Memorial Award (New Zealand) 291
Mansfield, Katherine, Menton Memorial Prize (International Literary Prizes) 478
Mansk, The, Svenska Publishing Co Ltd (Isle of Man) 212
Mansour, S J (Israel) 215
Manteau (Netherlands) 279
Manteau, Uitgeversmaatschappij A, NV (Belgium) 39
Manual, Editorial El, Moderno SA de CV (Mexico) 266
Manxman Publications (United Kingdom) 422
Manz Verlag (Federal Republic of Germany) 148
Manz'sche Verlags- und Universitätsbuchhandlung (Austria) 27
Manz'sche Verlags- und Universitätsbuchhandlung (Austria) 29
Map Productions Ltd (United Kingdom) 422
Mapa Fiscal Editora Ltda (Brazil) 53
Maqbool Academy (Pakistan) 302
Marabout, Les Nouvelles Editions, SA (Belgium) 39
Marais, Eugène, Prize (Republic of South Africa) 335

Marangu College of National Education Library (Tanzania) 379
Marbán, Editorial (Spain) 342
Marca, Editorial, Ltda (Colombia) 66
Marchal, Joseph-Edmond, Prize (Belgium) 45
Marcham Books (United Kingdom) 422
Marcombo, Publicaciones, SA (Mexico) 266
Marcombo SA de Boixareu Editores (Spain) 342
Marcus, Y, & Co Ltd (Israel) 215
Marczell, Tibor (Federal Republic of Germany) 148
Mardaga, Pierre, SA (Belgium) 39
Maredsous ASBL (Belgium) 39
Marfiah (Indonesia) 206
Marfil, Editorial, SA (Spain) 342
Marg Publications (India) 194
Margai, Milton, Teachers' College Library (Sierra Leone) 325
Marguerat, Librairie-Editions J (Switzerland) 369
Marhold, Carl, Verlagsbuchhandlung (Federal Republic of Germany) 148
Marican and Sons (M) Sdn Bhd (Malaysia) 260
Marican & Sons (M) Sdn Bhd (Malaysia) 261
Marie-Médiatrice, Editions, ASBL (Belgium) 39
Marietti, Casa Editrice, SpA (CEM) (Italy) 227
Marin, Editorial, SA (Spain) 342
Marino, Aldo, Editore (Italy) 227
Maritim, Edition (Federal Republic of Germany) 148
Maritime Book Society (United Kingdom) 443
Maritimes et d'Outre-Mer, Editions, SA (France) 102
Marix Evans, Amina (Netherlands) 283
Marix Evans & Chilvers SA (Switzerland) 369
Markazi Maktaba Islami (India) 194
Market House Books Ltd (United Kingdom) 422
Markham, Arthur, Memorial Prize (United Kingdom) 449
Marković', Univerzitetska biblioteka 'Svetozar (Yugoslavia) 460
Marksa, Gosudarstvennaya Respublikanskaya biblioteka Gruzinskoi SSR im K (Union of Soviet Socialist Republics) 389
Maro Verlag (Federal Republic of Germany) 148
Marotta, Alberto, Editore SpA (Italy) 227
Marova, Ediciones, SL (Spain) 342
Marques of Cerralbo XVII Prize (Spain) 349
Marshall (United Kingdom) 422
Marshall, Alan, Award (Australia) 23
Marshall Cavendish Books Ltd (United Kingdom) 422
Marshall Editions Ltd (United Kingdom) 422
Marshall, G H (United Kingdom) 422
Marshall, Morgan & Scott Publications Ltd (United Kingdom) 422
Marshall, Muir, Ltd (Trinidad and Tobago) 382
Marsiega Editorial SA (Spain) 342
Marsilio Editori SpA (Italy) 227
Marsland Press (United Kingdom) 422
Martano, Editore (Italy) 228
Martello, Giunti, Editore (Italy) 228
Martin Books (United Kingdom) 422
Martin Educational (Australia) 16
Martin Robertson & Co Ltd (United Kingdom) 422
Martindale Press Pty Ltd (Australia) 16
Martínez, Ediciones, Roca SA (Spain) 342
Martínez, H F, de Murguía SA (Spain) 347
Martínez, H F, de Murguía SAC y E (Argentina) 8
Martins Forlag (Denmark) 77
Martins, Livraria, Editora SA (Brazil) 53
Martins, Livraria Tavares (Portugal) 317
Maruzen Asia (Pte) Ltd (Republic of Singapore) 326
Maruzen Co Ltd (Japan) 241
Maruzen Co Ltd (Japan) 245
Marva (Switzerland) 369
Marwah Publications (India) 194
Marxistische Blätter, Verlag, GmbH (Federal Republic of Germany) 148
Marymar Ediciones SA (Argentina) 6
Marzocco, Editrice Giunti (Italy) 228
Marzorati Editore SRL (Italy) 228
Mas Ivars Editores SL (Spain) 342
Masa Baru (Indonesia) 206
Mascareignes, Librairie des (Mauritius) 263
Maschler, Kurt, Award (United Kingdom) 449
'Mashinostroenie', Izdatelstvo (Union of Soviet Socialist Republics) 388
Mason, Kenneth, Publications Ltd (United Kingdom) 422
Maspero, François, Editeur (France) 102
Masque, Le (France) 102
Masri, Dar Al-Kitab Al- (Egypt) 84
Mass Culture Publishing House (Democratic People's Republic of Korea) 250
Mass, Rubin, Ltd (Israel) 215
Massada Press Ltd (Israel) 215
Massada Press Ltd (Israel) 217
Massada Publishers Ltd (Israel) 215
Massimo, Editrice (Italy) 228
Massin, Editions Charles, et Cie (France) 102
Masson Editeur (France) 102
Masson, Editora, do Brasil Ltda (Brazil) 53
Masson Editores (Mexico) 266
Masson SA (Spain) 342

Master Storytellers (United Kingdom) 443
Mastrogiacomo Editore (Italy) 228
Matica slovenská (Czechoslovakia) 71
Matica slovenská (Czechoslovakia) 73
Matice moravská (Czechoslovakia) 74
Matopo Book Centre (Zimbabwe) 465
Matthaes, Hugo, Druckerei und Verlag GmbH & Co KG (Federal Republic of Germany) 148
Matthes und Seitz Verlag GmbH (Federal Republic of Germany) 148
Matthias-Estienne (France) 109
Matthias-Grünewald-Verlag (Federal Republic of Germany) 148
Matthiesen Verlag Ingwert Paulsen Jr (Federal Republic of Germany) 148
Matze, Editions la (Switzerland) 369
Mauclert, Librairie, et Cie (Niger) 292
Maudrich, Verlag Wilhelm (Austria) 27
Maudrich, Wilhelm (Austria) 29
Maugham, Somerset, Award (United Kingdom) 449
Mauritanie, Librairie-Papeterie, Nouvelle (Mauritania) 263
Mauritius Archives (Mauritius) 263
Mauritius Institute Public Library (Mauritius) 263
Mauritius Library Association (Mauritius) 263
Maximilian-Verlag (Federal Republic of Germany) 148
Maximilian-Verlagsgruppe (Federal Republic of Germany) 148
May, Franca, Edizioni SRL (Italy) 228
May, Karl-, -Verlag (Federal Republic of Germany) 148
May, Verlag A & G de (Switzerland) 369
Mayela, Librería Editorial Gerardo (Mexico) 269
Mayer, Edition Hansjörg (Federal Republic of Germany) 148
Mayer, Editions (France) 102
Mayer, Ludwig, Ltd (Israel) 217
Mayersche Buchhandlung, J A (Federal Republic of Germany) 168
Mayer'sche, J A, Buchhandlung (Federal Republic of Germany) 148
Mayfair Paperbacks (India) 194
Mayflower Books Ltd (United Kingdom) 422
Mayhew, Kevin, Ltd (United Kingdom) 422
Mayhew-McCrimmon Ltd (United Kingdom) 422
Mayoor Paperbacks (India) 194
Mazarine, Editions (France) 102
Mazenod Book Centre (Lesotho) 255
Mazenod, Editions d'Art Lucien (France) 102
Mazenod Institute (Lesotho) 255
Mazzotta, Nuove Edizioni Gabriele, SRL (Italy) 228
Mead & Beckett Publishing (Australia) 16
Meadowfield Press Ltd (United Kingdom) 422
Mebso Bookshop (Iran) 207
Meca, Editora, Ltda (Brazil) 53
Mechanical Engineering Publications Ltd (United Kingdom) 422
Mechtelli Tjin-A-Sie (Suriname) 351
Meddens, Les Ateliers d'Art graphique, SA (Belgium) 39
Medea Frauenverlag (Federal Republic of Germany) 149
Médecine, Bibliothèque Interuniversitaire de (France) 110
Médecine et Hygiène (Switzerland) 369
Médecines et Sciences Internationales (France) 102
Médica, Editorial, Panamericana SA (Argentina) 6
Medica, Libreria, Paris (Venezuela) 454
Médica, Libreria y Editorial La (Argentina) 6
Medica y Tecnica, Editorial, SA (Spain) 342
Medical Friend Co Ltd (Japan) 241
Medical Librarians' Group (Australia) 21
Medical, The, Library (Tanzania) 379
Medical World Book Co Pte Ltd (Republic of Singapore) 326
Medicala, Editura, (Medical Publishing House) (Romania) 321
Medicea, Edizioni, Srl (Italy) 228
Medici, The, Society Ltd (United Kingdom) 422
Medicina Könyvkiadó (Hungary) 181
Medicinsk Forlag ApS (Denmark) 77
Medicinska Knjiga (Yugoslavia) 457
Medicinska Naklada (Yugoslavia) 457
Medicis Foreign Prize (International Literary Prizes) 478
Médicis Prize (France) 113
Medico Farmaceutica, Organizzazione Editoriale, SRL (Italy) 228
Medina, Editorial, SRL (Uruguay) 451
Mediterranean Publishing Co Ltd (Malta) 262
Mediterranee, Edizioni, (Italy) 228
Meditsina i Fizkultura (Bulgaria) 58
'Meditsina', Izdatelstvo (Union of Soviet Socialist Republics) 388
Medium, Bokförlaget, AB (Sweden) 355
Medizin, Buchhandlung für (German Democratic Republic) 119
Medizin, Verlag für, Dr Ewald Fischer GmbH (Federal Republic of Germany) 149
Medizinisch-Literarische Verlagsgesellschaft mbH (Federal Republic of Germany) 149
Meeking, The Charles, Award (Australia) 23
Meenakshi Prakashan (India) 194

Meera Memorial Award (India) 204
Meerut Publishers' Association (India) 185
Meerwein, Rose M (Federal Republic of Germany) 167
Megalong Books (Australia) 16
Megapress, Verlagsbuchhandlung, Franz-J Gaber und W Poth GbR (Federal Republic of Germany) 149
Megiddo Publishing Co (Israel) 215
Mei Ya Publications Inc (Sueling, Inc) (Taiwan) 378
Meijer Pers BV (Netherlands) 279
Meili, Buchhandlung, & Co (Switzerland) 375
Meili, Peter, & Co (Switzerland) 369
Meinema/Waltman (Netherlands) 279
Meiner, Felix, Verlag GmbH (Federal Republic of Germany) 149
Meisenheim, Verlag Anton Hain, GmbH (Federal Republic of Germany) 149
Meissner, Otto, Verlag (Federal Republic of Germany) 149
Mejía, Librería-Editorial Juan, Baca (Peru) 307
Mejía, Librería Juan, Baca (Peru) 307
Mekise Nirdamin Society (Israel) 218
Melantrich (Czechoslovakia) 71
Melawai, Toko Buku (Indonesia) 206
Melayu, Pustaka, Baru (Malaysia) 260
Melbourne House (Publishers) Ltd (United Kingdom) 422
Melbourne University Press (Australia) 16
Melhoramentos, Companhia, de São Paulo (Brazil) 53
Melins, Gustav, AB (Sweden) 355
Melissa Publishing House (Greece) 175
Mella (Dominican Republic) 82
Mellinger, J Ch, Verlag GmbH, Wolfgang Militz und Co KG (Federal Republic of Germany) 149
Melograno, Il (Italy) 228
Melrose Press Ltd (United Kingdom) 422
Melzer GmbH, Verlag Abi (Federal Republic of Germany) 149
Melzer Verlag KG (Federal Republic of Germany) 149
Memorie, Edizioni, Domenicane (Italy) 228
Mencap Publications (United Kingdom) 422
Mendes, Odorico, Prize (Brazil) 57
Menéndez, Librería (Panama) 305
Menéndez Pelayo, Biblioteca de (Spain) 348
Menéndez, Ramón, Pidal Prize (International Literary Prizes) 478
Mengès, Editions (France) 102
Menna, Casa Editrice, di Sinisgalli Menna Giuseppina (Italy) 228
Menningarsjóds og Pjódvinafélagsins, Bókaútgáfa (Iceland) 184
Mensajero, Ediciones (Spain) 342
Mensch und Arbeit, Verlag, Robert Pfützner GmbH (Federal Republic of Germany) 149
Mensing's Caminada (Netherlands Antilles) 286
Mentor-Verlag Dr Ramdohr KG (Federal Republic of Germany) 149
Menzies, John, (Holdings) Ltd (United Kingdom) 444
Merabbu, Toko Buku (Indonesia) 206
Mercat Press (United Kingdom) 422
Mercatorfonds Arcade (Belgium) 39
Mercatorfonds SA (Belgium) 39
Mercier, The, Bookshop Ltd (Republic of Ireland) 211
Mercier, The, Press Ltd (Republic of Ireland) 210
Merck, Johann Heinrich, Prize (Federal Republic of Germany) 171
Merckx, Editeur Paul F (Belgium) 39
Mercure de France SA (France) 103
Mercurius PVBA (Belgium) 39
Meresborough Books (United Kingdom) 422
Mergus Verlag Hans A Baensch (Federal Republic of Germany) 149
Merian, Christoph, Verlag (Switzerland) 369
Meribérica — Editorial e Comercialização de Direitos Lda (Portugal) 317
Meridiane, Editura (Romania) 321
Merkaz Le-Chinuch Torani (Israel) 215
Merlin Library Ltd (Malta) 262
Merlin, The, Press Ltd (United Kingdom) 423
Merlin Verlag Andreas Meyer Verlags GmbH und Co KG (Federal Republic of Germany) 149
Merrill, Charles E, Publishing International (United Kingdom) 423
Merrion, The, Press (United Kingdom) 423
Merrow Publishing Co Ltd (United Kingdom) 423
Merve Verlag (Federal Republic of Germany) 149
Messageries Centrales du Livre (France) 103
Messageries du Livre (Grand Duchy of Luxembourg) 257
Messaggero di San Antonio (Italy) 228
Messeiller, Henri (Switzerland) 369
Messepublikationen, Verlag für (Federal Republic of Germany) 149
Messidor (France) 103
Messinger, Sylvie, Editrice (France) 103
Mestre Jou SA (Brazil) 53
Mestre Jou SA (Brazil) 56
Městská knihovna v Praze (Czechoslovakia) 73
Metal Bulletin Books Ltd (United Kingdom) 423
'Metallurgiya', Izdatelstvo (Union of Soviet Socialist Republics) 388

INDEX 527

Methodist Book Depot Ltd (Ghana) 172
Methodist Publishing House (United Kingdom) 423
Methodist, The, Publishing House and Book Depot (Republic of South Africa) 331
Methuen & Co Ltd (United Kingdom) 423
Methuen Australia Pty Ltd (Australia) 16
Methuen Children's Books Ltd (United Kingdom) 423
Methuen London Ltd (United Kingdom) 423
Methuen New Zealand (New Zealand) 288
Methuen Paperbacks (United Kingdom) 423
Methuen/Walker Books (United Kingdom) 423
Metodistkyrkans Förlag (Sweden) 355
Metropolitan Book Suppliers Ltd (Trinidad and Tobago) 382
Metz, Max S, Verlag AG (Switzerland) 369
Metzlersche Verlagsbuchhandlung, J B (Federal Republic of Germany) 149
Metzner, Alfred, Verlag (Federal Republic of Germany) 149
Meulenhoff Educatief BV (Netherlands) 279
Meulenhoff, H (Netherlands) 279
Meulenhoff Informatief BV (Netherlands) 279
Meulenhoff International (Netherlands) 279
Meulenhoff Nederland BV (Netherlands) 279
Mexicana, Editorial, SRL (Mexico) 267
Mexicanos, Editores, Unidos (Mexico) 269
Mexicanos Unidos, Editores, SA (Mexico) 267
Meyer, Editions d'Art Lucien de, ASBL (Belgium) 39
Meysmans (Belgium) 39
Meyster Verlag (Federal Republic of Germany) 149
Mezhdunarodnaya Kniga (Union of Soviet Socialist Republics) 389
'Mezhdunarodnye Otnosheniya', Izdatelstvo (Union of Soviet Socialist Republics) 388
Mezőgazdasági Könyvkiadó Vállalat (Hungary) 181
Michael, Maurice (United Kingdom) 423
Michaelmark Books Ltd (Israel) 215
Michael's Bookshop (Republic of Singapore) 327
Michaels og Licht (Denmark) 79
Michaut, Narcisse, Prize (France) 113
Michel, Editions Albin (France) 103
Michelin (Département Cartes & Guides) SA (Belgium) 39
Michelin et Cie (Services de Tourisme) (France) 103
Michelin Tyre Co Ltd Maps & Guides Dept (United Kingdom) 423
Micolini's, Progress-Verlag Dr, Wtw (Austria) 27
Microshur Ltd (Israel) 215
Microzine (Australia) 16
Midas Books (Planned Action Ltd) (United Kingdom) 423
Middelhauve, Gertraud, Verlag (Federal Republic of Germany) 149
Middle East Book Centre (Egypt) 84
Middle East Librarians Association (International Organizations) 468
Middle East Technical University Library (Turkey) 385
Miessner Libreros (Spain) 347
Mifalei Tarbut Vehinuch (Israel) 215
Mihalopoulos, John, & Son SA (Greece) 176
Miland Publishers (Netherlands) 280
Milano Editore, Nicola (Italy) 228
Milano Libri (Italy) 228
Milella, Antonio (Italy) 228
Milind Publications Pvt Ltd (India) 194
Militara, Editura (Romania) 321
Militärverlag der DDR (VEB) (German Democratic Republic) 117
Military Book Club (Australia) 19
Military Book Society (United Kingdom) 443
Military Guild (United Kingdom) 443
Militz, Wolfgang, und Co KG (Federal Republic of Germany) 149
Miller, Harvey, Publishers (United Kingdom) 423
Miller, J Garnet, Ltd (United Kingdom) 423
Miller, Louis P, Prize (France) 113
Miller, Maskew, Longman (Pty) Ltd (Republic of South Africa) 331
Miller, Maskew, Longman (Pty) Ltd (Republic of South Africa) 334
Millet Library (Turkey) 385
Millî Kütüphane (Turkey) 385
Millier, Marcelle, Prize (France) 113
Millington Books (United Kingdom) 423
Mills & Boon Ltd (United Kingdom) 423
Millwood Press Ltd (New Zealand) 288
Mimbar, Toko Buku Pustaka (Indonesia) 206
Mimosa Publishers (Zimbabwe) 465
Min Eum Sa (Republic of Korea) 251
Minard, Lettres Modernes (France) 103
Minard, Librairie (France) 103
Mindolo Ecumenical Foundation, Hammarskjold Memorial Library (Zambia) 463
Mineral Research and Exploration Institute, Library of the (Turkey) 385
'Minerva' (Yugoslavia) 457
Minerva Associates (Publications) Pvt Ltd (India) 194
Minerva Central (Mozambique) 271
Minerva, Editor (Hungary) 181
Minerva, Editora, Central (Mozambique) 271

Minerva, Editorial (Portugal) 317
Minerva, Editura (Romania) 321
Minerva Italica SpA (Italy) 228
Minerva, Libreria Editrice (Italy) 234
Minerva Publications (Malaysia) 260
Minerva Publikation (Federal Republic of Germany) 149
Minerva Publishing, The, House (India) 194
Minerva Shobo Co Ltd (Japan) 241
Minerva, The, Press Ltd (United Kingdom) 423
Minerva's Express (Australia) 16
Mines and Geological Department Library (Kenya) 249
Minimax Books Ltd (United Kingdom) 423
Ministère de l'Education, Bibliothèque centrale du, nationale (Belgium) 43
Ministère de l'Education, Editions du, Nationale (Guinea) 177
Ministerie van Cultuur Jeugd en Sport (Suriname) 351
Ministerio das Relações Exteriores, Biblioteca do (Brazil) 56
Ministerio de Cultura, Biblioteca del (Spain) 348
Ministerio de Educación del Gobierno de El Salvador (El Salvador) 85
Ministerio de Educacion, Editorial del, 'Jose de Pineda Ibarra' (Guatemala) 176
Ministerrat der Deutschen Demokratischen Republik, Ministerium für Kultur, Hauptverwaltung Verlage und Buchhandel (German Democratic Republic) 116
Ministerstvo kultury ČSR, Odbor knižní kultury (Czechoslovakia) 70
Ministerstwa Obrony Narodowej, Wydawnictwo (Poland) 312
Ministry, Book Club of the, of Cultural Affairs of Sri Lanka (Sri Lanka) 349
Ministry of Agriculture Library (Kenya) 249
Ministry of Agriculture Library (Malaysia) 261
Ministry of Cultural Affairs (Sri Lanka) 349
Ministry of Culture and Information, Book Publishing Department (Afghanistan) 1
Ministry of Culture, Department of Ancient Literature and Culture, (Burma) 60
Ministry of Defence Publishing House (Israel) 215
Ministry of Education, Department of Educational Publications (Afghanistan) 1
Ministry of Education Library (Afghanistan) 1
Ministry of Education Library (Cyprus) 70
Ministry of Education Library (Egypt) 84
Ministry of Information (Kuwait) 253
Ministry of Information & Broadcasting (India) 194
Ministry of Justice Library (Egypt) 84
Minjungseorim Publishing Co (Republic of Korea) 251
Minkoff, Editions, Reprint (Switzerland) 369
Minoas (Greece) 175
Minoas (Greece) 176
'Mintis', Leidykla (Union of Soviet Socialist Republics) 388
Minuit, Les Editions de, SA (France) 103
Mir, Izdatelstvo (Union of Soviet Socialist Republics) 388
Mir, S M (Pakistan) 303
Miracle, Editorial Luis, SA (Spain) 342
Mirananda Publishers BV (Netherlands) 280
Miranda, G, & Sons (Philippines) 309
Miroir Sprint Publications (France) 103
Mirror Books Ltd (United Kingdom) 423
Mirza Book Agency (Pakistan) 303
Misla (Yugoslavia) 457
Misr Bookshop (Egypt) 84
Misr Import & Export Co (Egypt) 84
Misr, Maktabet (Egypt) 84
Misrachi, Galeria de Arte, SA (Mexico) 267
Missio aktuell Verlag GmbH (Federal Republic of Germany) 149
Mission universitaire culturelle et de co-operation, Bibliothèque (Morocco) 271
Missionstrupp Frohe Botschaft (Federal Republic of Germany) 149
Mistral, Editora Nacional Gabriela, Ltda (Chile) 63
Misuraca, Lorenzo, Editore (Italy) 228
Misuzu Shobo Publishing Co Ltd (Japan) 241
Miswat Library (People's Democratic Republic of Yemen) 456
Mita Society for Library and Information Science (Japan) 245
Mitchell Beazley London Ltd (United Kingdom) 424
Mitchell, The, Library (Glasgow District Libraries) (United Kingdom) 445
Mitra & Ghosh Publishers Pvt Ltd (India) 194
Mitre, Editorial Librería, SRL (Argentina) 6
Mitteldeutscher Verlag Halle-Leipzig (German Democratic Republic) 117
Mittler, E S, und Sohn GmbH (Federal Republic of Germany) 149
Mizrachi, M, Publishers (Israel) 215
Mladá fronta (Czechoslovakia) 71
Mladá fronta Award (Czechoslovakia) 74
Mladé letá (Czechoslovakia) 71
Mladé letá Prize (Czechoslovakia) 74
Mladinska Knjiga (Yugoslavia) 457
Mladinska Knjiga (Yugoslavia) 460

Mladost (Yugoslavia) 457
Mladost (Yugoslavia) 458
Mladost (Yugoslavia) 460
Mladost's Book Fans Club (Yugoslavia) 460
Mlodziezowa Agencja Wydawnicza (Poland) 312
Mlodziezowa Agencja Wydawnicza (Poland) 313
Moa Publications Ltd (New Zealand) 288
Moadim (Israel) 217
Mockel, Albert, Grand Prize for Poetry (Belgium) 45
Model & Allied Publications Ltd (United Kingdom) 424
Modern Book Agency Private Ltd (India) 194
Modern Book Co Inc (Philippines) 309
Modern Book Company Inc (Philippines) 309
Modern Book Store (Republic of Singapore) 327
Modern Cairo Bookshop (Egypt) 84
Modern English Publications Ltd (United Kingdom) 424
Modern Teaching Aids Pty Ltd (Australia) 16
Modern Transport (United Kingdom) 424
Moderne, Edizioni, Sas (Italy) 228
Moderne Industrie AG (Switzerland) 369
Moderne Industrie, Verlag, Wolfgang Dummer & Co (Federal Republic of Germany) 150
Moderne Instructie Methoden (MIM) PVBA (Belgium) 39
Moderne Jugend Heute GmbH (Austria) 27
Moderne Verlags GmbH (MVG), Wolfgang Dummer & Co (Federal Republic of Germany) 150
Modernix (New Caledonia) 286
Modernix-Hachette Calédonie (New Caledonia) 286
Modtryk, Forlaget, AMBA (Denmark) 77
Modulverlag GmbH (Austria) 27
Mofolo-Plomer Prize (Republic of South Africa) 335
Mohammadi Library (Bangladesh) 32
Mohler, Alfred, Verlag (Switzerland) 369
Mohn, Gütersloher Verlagshaus Gerd (Federal Republic of Germany) 150
Mohn, Vereinigte Verlagsauslieferung R, HG (Federal Republic of Germany) 168
Mohr, J C B, (Paul Siebeck) (Federal Republic of Germany) 150
Mohr, Robert (Austria) 29
Moizzi (Italy) 228
Molden, Verlag Fritz (Austria) 27
Molden, Verlag, — S Seewald GmbH (Federal Republic of Germany) 150
Molendinar, The, Press (United Kingdom) 424
Molho's International Bookshop (Greece) 176
Molino, Editorial (Spain) 342
Moll, Editorial (Spain) 342
Mollat, Librairie (France) 109
Molodaya Gvardiya, Izdatelstvo (Union of Soviet Socialist Republics) 388
Mon Village, Club, SA (Switzerland) 375
Mon Village, Editions, SA (Switzerland) 369
Monas Hieroglihica Editrice (Italy) 228
Monastery of St-Saviour, Library of the, (Basilian Missionary Order of St-Saviour) (Lebanon) 254
Monauni, G B (Italy) 228
Mönch-Verlag GmbH & Co (Federal Republic of Germany) 150
Mondadori, Arnoldo, Editore (Italy) 228
Mondadori, Edizioni Scolastiche Bruno (Italy) 228
Mondadori Ragazzi (Italy) 228
Mondo, Edizioni del, Giudiziario (Italy) 229
Mondo SA (Editions-Verlag-Edizioni) (Switzerland) 369
Mondoperaio edizioni Avanti SpA (Italy) 229
Mondrup, Svend, International Literary Agency (Denmark) 79
Monduzzi Editore Srl (Italy) 229
Monfort, Gérard (France) 103
Mongolgosknigotorg (Mongolian People's Republic) 270
Moniteur, Editions du, et Editions de l'Usine Nouvelle (France) 103
Monitor Verlag (Federal Republic of Germany) 150
Monserrate, Ediciones, Ltda (Colombia) 66
Mont-Blanc, Les Editions du, SA (Switzerland) 369
Mont Noir, Editions du (Zaire) 462
Montaigne (New Caledonia) 286
Montaner y Simon SA (Spain) 342
Montchrestien, Editions, Sàrl (France) 103
Monte Avila Editores CA (Venezuela) 453
Montel, Publications Photo-Cinema Paul (France) 103
Monterrey, Editora, Ltda (Brazil) 53
Montesó, José, — Editor (Spain) 342
Monteverde, A, y Cia SA (Uruguay) 452
Monthly Review Press (United Kingdom) 424
Montserrat Public Library (Montserrat) 270
Montsouris, Editions de, SA (France) 103
Montyon Prize (France) 113
Moonlight Publishing Ltd (United Kingdom) 424
Moonraker Press (United Kingdom) 424
Moore, G W, Ltd (New Zealand) 288
Moore, S J, Ltd (Kenya) 249
Moorland Publishing Company Ltd (United Kingdom) 424
Moorlands, The, Press (United Kingdom) 424
Moos, Heinz, Verlag GmbH & Co KG (Federal Republic of Germany) 150
Mor-Carmi, M C, Ltd (Israel) 215

Móra Ferenc Ifjúsági Könyvkiadó (Hungary) 181
Moraes, Editora, Ltda (Brazil) 53
Moraes Editores SARL (Portugal) 317
Morancé, Editions Albert (France) 103
Morata, Ediciones, SA (Spain) 343
Morawa & Co (Austria) 27
Morcelliana, Editrice, SpA (Italy) 229
Moreau, Editions Alain (France) 103
Morel Editeurs (France) 103
Moreno, Fernando, Poetry Prize (Argentina) 9
Moreshet (Israel) 216
Moressopoulos, Editions (Greece) 175
Moretón, Ediciones, SA (Spain) 343
Moretti, Istituto Grafologico Girolamo (Italy) 229
Moretus Plantin, Bibliothèque Universitaire (Belgium) 43
Morgan-Grampian Book Publishing Co Ltd (United Kingdom) 424
Morgarten-Verlag (Switzerland) 369
Morgen, Buchverlag Der (German Democratic Republic) 117
Morija Sesuto Book Depot (Lesotho) 255
Morija Sesuto Book Depot (Lesotho) 255
Morikita Shuppan Co Ltd (Japan) 241
Morison Arnold Ltd (Nigeria) 296
Morra, Verlag (Italy) 229
Morris, William, Organization SpA (Italy) 233
Morsak Verlag (Federal Republic of Germany) 150
Morskie, Wydawnictwo (Poland) 312
Morten, E J, (Publishers) (United Kingdom) 424
Mortensens, Ernst G, Forlag A/S (Norway) 299
Mortiz, Editorial Joaquín, SA (Mexico) 267
Morus-Verlag (Federal Republic of Germany) 150
Mosaik Verlag (Federal Republic of Germany) 150
Mosca Azul Editores SRL (Peru) 307
Mosca Hnos (Uruguay) 452
Mosca Hnos SA (Uruguay) 452
Moshi Public Library (Tanzania) 379
'Moskovskii Rabochiy', Izdatelstvo (Union of Soviet Socialist Republics) 388
Moskovskogo Universiteta, Izdatelstvo (Union of Soviet Socialist Republics) 388
Mossad Harav Kook (Israel) 216
Mosul Museum, Library of the (Iraq) 208
Mosul Public Library (Iraq) 208
Motilal Banarsidass (India) 194
Motilal Banarsidass (India) 202
Motive (United Kingdom) 424
Motor Racing Publications Ltd (United Kingdom) 424
Motorbuch-Verlag (Federal Republic of Germany) 150
Motta, Federico, Editore SRL (Italy) 229
Mouj Prakashan Griha (India) 194
Mount Kenya Bookshop Ltd (Kenya) 249
Moussault (Netherlands) 280
Mouton Publishers (Federal Republic of Germany) 150
Mouton Publishers (Netherlands) 280
Mouvement pour le Couple et la Famille (Belgium) 39
Moving Into Maths Pty Ltd (Australia) 16
Mowbray, A R, & Co Ltd (United Kingdom) 424
Moxon Paperbacks (Ghana) 172
Moya, José, y Ute Körner de Moya (Spain) 346
Mphala Creative Society (Zambia) 464
Mr H's Prize (Japan) 247
Mühlemann, Verlag Rudolf (Switzerland) 369
Muhlethaler, Jacques (Switzerland) 369
Muiderkring, De, BV (Netherlands) 280
Mukherjee, A, & Co Pvt Ltd (India) 194
Mukherji Book House (India) 194
Mulder en Co (Netherlands) 280
Mulder Holland BV (Netherlands) 280
Mulino, Società Editrice Il (Italy) 229
Müller, Albert, Verlag AG (Switzerland) 369
Müller, Emil (Federal Republic of Germany) 150
Muller, Frederick, Ltd (United Kingdom) 424
Muller-Groff, Librairie (Grand Duchy of Luxembourg) 257
Müller/Herbig, Verlagsgruppe Langen- (Federal Republic of Germany) 150
Müller Jüristischer, C F, Verlag GmbH (Federal Republic of Germany) 150
Müller, Otto, Verlag KG (Austria) 27
Müller, Rudolf, International Booksellers VoF (Netherlands) 284
Müller und Kiepenheuer, Verlag (Federal Republic of Germany) 150
Müller und Steinicke Verlag (Federal Republic of Germany) 150
Müller Verlag, Albert Langen-Georg (Federal Republic of Germany) 150
Müller, Verlag Ars Sacra Josef (Federal Republic of Germany) 150
Müller, Verlag C F (Federal Republic of Germany) 150
Müller, Verlagsgesellschaft Rudolf, GmbH (Federal Republic of Germany) 150
Mullick Bros (Bangladesh) 32
Mullick Bros (Bangladesh) 32
Multieditions Ltd (Greece) 175
Multigrafica Editrice Srl (Italy) 229
Multimedia Zambia (Zambia) 463

Mun Woon Dang (Republic of Korea) 251
Munch Bunch Books (United Kingdom) 424
Munchner Arbeitsgemeinschaft der Verlagshersteller (Federal Republic of Germany) 121
Münchner Verlagsbüro, Horst Hodemacher-Axel Poldner (Federal Republic of Germany) 167
Mundi, Editorial, SAIC y F (Argentina) 6
Mundi-Prensa, Librería (Spain) 347
Mundi-Prensa Libros SA (Spain) 343
Mundial, Librería (Venezuela) 454
Mundo, Editorial, Técnico SRL (Argentina) 6
Mundus, Österreichische Verlagsgesellschaft mbH (Austria) 27
Municipal Library (Bulgaria) 59
Municipal Library (Cyprus) 70
Municipal Library (Cyprus) 70
Municipal Library (Israel) 218
Municipal Library (Socialist Republic of Viet Nam) 455
Municipal Prize for Prose and Poetry (Venezuela) 455
Munin Verlag GmbH (Federal Republic of Germany) 150
Munksgaard Export & Subscription Service (Denmark) 77
Munksgaard, International Booksellers & Publishers Ltd (Denmark) 77
Münster Verlag (Federal Republic of Germany) 150
Muralla, Editorial La (Spain) 343
Murby, Thomas, & Co (United Kingdom) 424
Murr, Georges (Lebanon) 254
Murray, Donald, (Ramboro Books) (United Kingdom) 424
Murray, Donald, (Ramboro Books) (United Kingdom) 442
Murray, John, (Publishers) Ltd (United Kingdom) 424
Mursia, Ugo, Editore SpA (Italy) 229
Muscat, Giov, & Co Ltd (Malta) 262
Musée de l'Homme, Bibliothèque du (France) 110
Musée royal de Mariemont, Bibliothèque du (Belgium) 43
Musées Nationaux, Editions de la Réunion des (France) 103
Museo, Biblioteca del, Histórico Nacional (Uruguay) 452
Museo de Zoologia, Biblioteca del (Cuba) 69
Museo y Biblioteca Municipal (Ecuador) 83
Muséum national, Bibliothèque centrale du, d'Histoire naturelle (France) 110
Muséum National, Editions du, d'Histoire naturelle (France) 103
Museum, Perpustakaan, Nasional, Departemen Pendidikan dan Kebudayaan (Indonesia) 207
Music Sales Ltd (United Kingdom) 424
Musica Budapest, Editio (Hungary) 181
Musica, Editorial, Moderna (Spain) 343
Musical Box (United Kingdom) 424
Musikverleger Union Österreich (Austria) 24
Musin, Louis, Editeur (Belgium) 39
Muskett, Netta, Award (United Kingdom) 449
Muslim Welfare House (United Kingdom) 424
Muster-Schmidt Verlag (Federal Republic of Germany) 150
Müszaki Könyvkiadó (Hungary) 181
Müszaki Könyvklub (Hungary) 182
Mutiara (Indonesia) 206
Mutual Books Inc (Philippines) 309
Mutualidad Laboral de Escritores de Libros (Spain) 348
Muusses (Netherlands) 280
Müvelt Nép Könyvterjesztö Vállalat (Hungary) 182
'Muzica', Darzhavno Izdatelstvo (Bulgaria) 58
Muzicala, Editura (Romania) 321
Muzička Naklada (Yugoslavia) 458
Muzyczne, Polskie Wydawnictwo (Poland) 312
'Muzyka', Izdatelstvo (Union of Soviet Socialist Republics) 388
Muzzio, Franco, & C Editore Sas (Italy) 229
Mwanza Regional Library (Tanzania) 379
Myna Press (India) 195
Mysl, Izdatelstvo (Union of Soviet Socialist Republics) 388
Mystery Guild (United Kingdom) 443

N C C Publications (United Kingdom) 424
N D V (Neue Darmstädter Verlagsanstalt) (Federal Republic of Germany) 150
N E C Z A M Library (Zambia) 463
N E L (United Kingdom) 424
N F E R-Nelson, The, Publishing Co Ltd (United Kingdom) 424
N F F (Nouvelles Feuilles Familiales) (Belgium) 39
N G Kerk Jeugboekhandel (Republic of South Africa) 331
N G Kerkboekhandel Transvaal (Republic of South Africa) 331
N G Kerkboekhandel Transvaal (DRC Publishers) (Republic of South Africa) 331
N G M Communication (Pakistan) 303
N I B, Uitgeverij (Netherlands) 280
N I S H Shtypshkronjave 'Mihal Duri' (Albania) 1

N K I-forlaget (Norway) 299
N K I Educational Services Ltd (United Kingdom) 424
N O E (France) 103
N P A (Neue Presse Agentur) (Switzerland) 375
N S T (Nová sovietska tvorba) (Czechoslovakia) 73
'N T', Biblioteca (Spain) 343
N Z N-Buchverlag AG (Switzerland) 369
Nå Forlag A/S (formerly Elingaard Forlag) (Norway) 299
Nabco Pendidekan Sdn Bhd (Malaysia) 261
Nachrichten-Verlags-GmbH (Federal Republic of Germany) 150
Nación', Premio de 'La, Prize (Argentina) 9
Nacional, El, Annual Story Award (Venezuela) 455
Nacionalna i Sveučilišna Biblioteka (Yugoslavia) 460
Nadal, Eugenio, Prize (Spain) 349
Nafees Academy (Pakistan) 302
Nagai Shoten Co Ltd (Japan) 241
Nagel, Edition (Federal Republic of Germany) 151
Nagel, Les Editions, SA (Switzerland) 369
Nagoya University Library (Japan) 245
Nah Shperndarjes Të Librit (NST) (Albania) 1
Nahda, Dar al-, al Arabia (Egypt) 84
Naim Frasheri (Albania) 1
Nakladni Zavod Matice Hrvatske (Yugoslavia) 458
Nalanda Books (India) 195
Nalanda Co Ltd (Mauritius) 263
Namboodiri, K R, Award (India) 204
Námsgagnastofnun (Iceland) 184
Nanjing tushuguan (People's Republic of China) 64
Nankodo Co Ltd (Japan) 241
Nanyang University Library (Republic of Singapore) 327
Nanzando Co Ltd (Japan) 241
Naoki Prize (Japan) 247
Napoleone, Casa Editrice Roberto (Italy) 229
Napoletana, Società Editrice, SRL (Italy) 229
Naprijed (Yugoslavia) 458
Naranco, Ediciones, SA (Spain) 343
Narcea SA de Ediciones (Spain) 343
Nardini Editore — Centro Internazionale del Libro SpA (Italy) 229
narodna biblioteka, Centralna, SR Crne Gore (Yugoslavia) 460
Narodna biblioteka SR Srbije (Yugoslavia) 460
Narodna Biblioteka Srbije (Yugoslavia) 458
Narodna i univerzitetska biblioteka Bosne i Hercegovine (Yugoslavia) 460
Narodna in univerzitetna knjižnica (Ljubljana) (Yugoslavia) 460
Narodna Knjiga (Yugoslavia) 458
Narodna Kultura (Bulgaria) 58
Narodna Mladezh (Bulgaria) 58
'Narodna Prosveta', Darzhavno Izdatelstvo (Bulgaria) 58
Narodne Novine (Yugoslavia) 458
Narongsarn (Thailand) 380
Narosa Publishing House (India) 195
Narr, Gunter, Verlag (Federal Republic of Germany) 151
Naša Djeca (Yugoslavia) 458
Naša Kniga (Yugoslavia) 458
Naše Vojsko, Nakladatelství a distribuce knih (Czechoslovakia) 71
Naše vojsko Prizes (Czechoslovakia) 74
Nasional, Pustaka, Pte Ltd (Republic of Singapore) 326
Nasional, Pustaka, Pte Ltd (Republic of Singapore) 327
Nasionale Boekhandel Ltd (Republic of South Africa) 331
Nasionale Boekhandel (SWA) (Pty) Ltd (Namibia) 272
Nasionale Boekwinkels Bpk (Republic of South Africa) 334
Nasou Ltd (Republic of South Africa) 331
Nassau, Editions (Mauritius) 263
Nassau Public Library (Bahamas) 32
'Nasza Ksiegarnia', Instytut Wydawniczy (Poland) 312
Nateev-Printing and Publishing Enterprises Ltd (Israel) 216
Nathan, Fernand, Editeur (France) 103
Nation, Verlag der (German Democratic Republic) 117
National Academy of Letters (India) 203
National Archives (Egypt) 84
National Archives (Libya) 256
National Archives (New Zealand) 290
National Archives (Sri Lanka) 349
National Archives (Trinidad and Tobago) 382
National Archives (Zimbabwe) 465
National Archives and Records Centre (Republic of Singapore) 327
National Archives Division (Thailand) 381
National Archives of Fiji (Fiji) 86
National Archives of India (India) 202
National Archives of Malawi (Malawi) 258
National Archives of Malaysia (Malaysia) 261
National Archives of Nigeria (Nigeria) 297
National Archives of Pakistan (Pakistan) 303
National Archives of Tanzania (Tanzania) 379
National Archives of Zambia (Zambia) 463
National Assembly Library (Egypt) 84
National Assembly Library (Republic of Korea) 252
National Award for Poetry and the Novel (Portugal) 319
National Bank, Library of the (Afghanistan) 1

INDEX 529

National Bank of Pakistan Prize for Literature (Pakistan) 304
National Book Agency (P) Ltd (India) 195
National Book Centre of Bangladesh (Bangladesh) 32
National Book Council (Australia) 10
National Book Council Awards (Australia) 23
National Book Council of Pakistan (Pakistan) 301
National Book Development Council of Singapore (Republic of Singapore) 325
National Book Development Council of Singapore Book Awards (Republic of Singapore) 328
National Book Institute Prizes (Brazil) 57
National Book League, The (United Kingdom) 447
National Book Store (Philippines) 309
National Book Store (Philippines) 309
National Book Store (Republic of Singapore) 327
National Book, The, Co (Taiwan) 378
National Book Trust India (India) 195
National Books of Zimbabwe (Zimbabwe) 465
National Books of Zimbabwe (Zimbabwe) 465
National Bookshop and Branches (Bahrain) 32
National Bookstore (Liberia) 255
National Central Library (Taiwan) 378
National Centre of Archives (Iraq) 208
National Christian Education Council (United Kingdom) 425
National Computing Centre (United Kingdom) 425
National Council for Civil Liberties (United Kingdom) 425
National Council for Voluntary Organizations (United Kingdom) 425
National Council of Applied Economic Research, Publications Division (India) 195
National Council of Educational Research & Training, Publication Department (India) 195
National Council of Ethnographic Arts and Literature of China (Taiwan) 378
National Diet Library (Japan) 245
National Educational Company of Zambia Ltd (Zambia) 463
National Essay Award (Portugal) 319
National Extension College (United Kingdom) 425
National Federation of Retail Newsagents (Republic of Ireland) 209
National Federation of Retail Newsagents (United Kingdom) 391
National Foundation for Educational Research in England & Wales (United Kingdom) 425
National Free Library of Zimbabwe (Zimbabwe) 465
National Grand Prize for Literature (France) 113
National Grand Prize for Poetry (France) 113
National House for Publishing, Distributing and Advertising (Iraq) 208
National Information and Documentation Centre (Egypt) 84
National Information and Documentation Centre (Egypt) 84
National Institute for Compilation and Translation (Taiwan) 378
National Institute of Administration Library (Socialist Republic of Viet Nam) 455
National Institute of Education Library (Uganda) 386
National Institute of Public Administration Library (Zambia) 463
National Institute of Science and Technology, Division of Documentation (Philippines) 310
National Institute, The, of Research Library (Botswana) 47
National Library (Burma) 60
National Library (Guyana) 177
National Library (Iran) 207
National Library (Iraq) 208
National Library (Libya) 256
National Library (Nepal) 272
National Library (Pakistan) 303
National Library (Qatar) 320
National Library (Saudi Arabia) 323
National Library (Republic of Singapore) 327
National Library and Archives of Ethiopia (Ethiopia) 86
National Library, Central (Republic of Korea) 252
National Library for Agricultural Sciences (Indonesia) 207
National Library 'Ivan Vazov' (Bulgaria) 59
National Library of Australia (Australia) 16
National Library of Australia (Australia) 20
National Library of Greece (Greece) 176
National Library of Higher Education and Culture (Somalia) 328
National Library of Ireland (Republic of Ireland) 211
National Library of Ireland Society (Republic of Ireland) 211
National Library of Jamaica (Jamaica) 237
National Library of Latakia (Syria) 377
National Library of Malaysia (Malaysia) 261
National Library of Malta (Malta) 262
National Library of New Zealand (New Zealand) 290
National Library of Nigeria (Nigeria) 297
National Library of Scotland (United Kingdom) 445
National Library of Wales (United Kingdom) 445

National Library Service (Belize) 45
National Library Service of Papua New Guinea (Papua New Guinea) 305
National Library, The, Government of India (India) 202
National Library, The, of Thailand (Thailand) 381
National Library, The, of the Philippines (Philippines) 310
National Literary Awards (Burma) 60
National Magazine Co Ltd (United Kingdom) 425
National Minorities Publishing House (People's Republic of China) 66
National Museum (India) 195
National Museum Library (India) 202
National Museum Library (Sri Lanka) 349
National Museums, Department of (Sri Lanka) 349
National Poetry Competition (Republic of Ireland) 212
National Poetry Competition (United Kingdom) 449
National Portrait Gallery (Publications Dept) (United Kingdom) 425
National Press Library (Jordan) 247
National Prize for Literature (Chile) 64
National Prize for Literature (Mexico) 270
National Prize for Literature (Venezuela) 455
National Publishing House (India) 195
National Scientific and Technical Information Center (NSTIC) of the Kuwait Institute for Scientific Research (Kuwait) 253
National Technological University, Library of the, of Athens (Greece) 176
National Trust Children's Series (United Kingdom) 425
National University of Lesotho Library (Lesotho) 255
National University of Malaysia Library (Malaysia) 261
National University of Singapore Library (Republic of Singapore) 327
National War College Library (Taiwan) 378
Nationale Forschungs- und Gedenkstätten der klassischen deutschen Literatur — Zentralbibliothek der deutschen Klassik (German Democratic Republic) 119
Nationale, Librairie, (Ministère Education National) (Benin) 45
Nationwide Book Service (United Kingdom) 444
Natoli and Stefan Literary Agency (Italy) 234
Natsionalniya Savet, Izdatelstvo na, na Otetchestveniya Front (Bulgaria) 58
Natur och Kultur, Bokförlaget (Sweden) 355
Natura, Editorial, SRL (Venezuela) 454
Natura-Verlag (Switzerland) 369
Natural History Museum (United Kingdom) 425
Natural Resources Development College Library (Zambia) 463
Naučna biblioteka (Yugoslavia) 460
Naučna Knjiga (Yugoslavia) 458
Naufal Group SRL (Lebanon) 254
'Nauka, Darzhavno Izdatelstvo, i Izkustvo' (Bulgaria) 58
'Nauka', Izdatelstvo (Union of Soviet Socialist Republics) 388
Naukowe, Państwowe Wydawnictwo (Poland) 312
Naukowo-Techniczne, Wydawnictwa (Poland) 312
Nauta, Ediciones, SA (Spain) 343
Nautic, AB (Sweden) 355
Nautical Books (United Kingdom) 425
Nautiska Förlaget Sjökortshallen AB (Sweden) 355
Nauwelaerts, NV Uitgeverij, Edition SA (Belgium) 39
Navajivan Trust (India) 195
Navers, Rasmus, Forlag (Denmark) 78
Naville SA (Switzerland) 369
Navoi, Gosudarstvennaya biblioteka UzSSR im Alishera (Union of Soviet Socialist Republics) 389
Navyug Publishers (India) 195
Naya Prokash (India) 195
Ndanda Mission Press (Tanzania) 379
Ndebele Readers' Book Club (Zimbabwe) 465
Ndërmarrja e Botimeve Ushtarake (Albania) 1
Ndërmarrja e Librit (Albania) 1
Ndola Public Library (Zambia) 463
Near East School, Library of the, of Theology (Lebanon) 254
Nebelspalter Verlag (Switzerland) 370
Nederlands Bibliotheek en Lektuurcentrum (NBLC) (Netherlands) 284
Nederlandsche Boekhandel, Uitgeverij De (Belgium) 39
Nederlandsche Vereeniging van Antiquaren (Netherlands) 273
Nederlandsche Vereeniging voor Druk- en Boekkunst (Netherlands) 273
Nederlandsche Zondagsschool Vereeniging (Netherlands) 280
Nederlandse Boekenclub (Netherlands) 284
Nederlandse Boekenclub (Boek en Plaat) (Belgium) 42
Nederlandse Boekverkopersbond (Netherlands) 273
Nederlandse Lezerskring Boek en Plaat BV (Netherlands) 280
Nederlandse Lezerskring Boek en Plaat BV (Netherlands) 284
Nederlandse Vereniging van Bedrijfsarchivarissen (Netherlands) 285
Nederlandse Vereniging van Bibliothecarissen, Documentalisten en literatuuronderzoekers (NVB) (Netherlands) 285

'Nedra', Izdatelstvo (Union of Soviet Socialist Republics) 388
Née, Alfred, Prize (France) 113
Neeraj Publishing House (India) 195
Neff, Paul, Verlag KG (Austria) 27
Neff, Paul, Verlag KG (Federal Republic of Germany) 151
Negara, Perpustakaan (Indonesia) 207
Nègre, Librairie SA Gaston (Benin) 45
Neguri Editorial SA (Spain) 343
Nehru Memorial Museum and Library (India) 202
Neilson, John Shaw, Poetry Award (Australia) 23
Nejat Yalki Kitabevi (Turkey) 385
Nelissen, Uitgeverij H, BV (Netherlands) 280
Nelson Memorial Public Library (Western Samoa) 455
Nelson, Thomas, & Sons Ltd (United Kingdom) 425
Nelson, Thomas, Australia (Australia) 17
Nelson, Thomas, (Nigeria) Ltd (Nigeria) 294
Nem Chand & Brothers (India) 195
Nepal Academy (Nepal) 272
Nepal-Bharat Sanskritik Kendra Pustakalaya (Nepal) 272
Nepal Booksellers (Nepal) 272
Nepal Library Association (Nepal) 272
Neptun-Verlag (Switzerland) 370
Neruda, Librería e Importadora (El Salvador) 85
Neske, Verlag Günther (Federal Republic of Germany) 151
Netzach (Israel) 216
Neue Berlin, Verlag das (German Democratic Republic) 118
Neue Brehm-Bücherei, Die (German Democratic Republic) 119
Neue Darmstädter Verlagsanstalt (Federal Republic of Germany) 151
Neue Diana Press AG (Switzerland) 370
Neue Gesellschaft, Verlag, GmbH (Federal Republic of Germany) 151
Neue Kommentare (Federal Republic of Germany) 151
Neue Kritik, Verlag, KG (Federal Republic of Germany) 151
Neue Mitte, Edition (Austria) 27
Neue Schulmann, Verlag der (Federal Republic of Germany) 151
Neue Schweizer Bibliothek (Switzerland) 375
Neue Stadt, Verlag (Switzerland) 370
Neue Stadt, Verlag, GmbH (Federal Republic of Germany) 151
Neue Szene (Switzerland) 370
Neue Wirtschafts-Briefe, Verlag, GmbH (Federal Republic of Germany) 151
Neue Zürcher Zeitung AG (Switzerland) 370
Neuer Jugendschriften-Verlag (Federal Republic of Germany) 151
Neuer Weg, Verlag, GmbH (Federal Republic of Germany) 151
Neues Leben, Verlag (German Democratic Republic) 118
Neufeld-Verlag und Galerie (Austria) 27
Neufeld-Verlag und Galerie (Switzerland) 370
Neugebauer, Buchhandlung W, GmbH und Co KG (Austria) 30
Neugebauer, Wolfgang (Austria) 27
Neukirchener Verlag des Erziehungvereins GmbH (Federal Republic of Germany) 151
Neumann-Neudamm, Verlag J, KG (Federal Republic of Germany) 151
Neumann, Verlag Dr Thomas (Federal Republic of Germany) 151
Neumeyer, Martin (Federal Republic of Germany) 151
Neureuter, Verlag für Messepublikationen Thomas, KG (Federal Republic of Germany) 151
Neustadt International Prize for Literature (International Literary Prizes) 478
New Africa Booksellers (Somalia) 328
New-Age Publishers (Kenya) 248
New Aqua, P T, Press/Aries Lima (Indonesia) 206
New Book Centre (India) 195
New Cavendish Books (United Kingdom) 425
New Caxton Library Service Ltd (United Kingdom) 425
New City (Philippines) 309
New City, London (United Kingdom) 425
New Countryside Book Club (Poland) 313
New Directions (Australia) 17
New Educational Press (United Kingdom) 425
New English Library, The, Ltd (United Kingdom) 425
New Era Publications ApS (Denmark) 78
New Horn Press Ltd (Nigeria) 295
New Interlitho SpA (Italy) 229
New Leaf Publishing Ltd (United Kingdom) 425
New Left Books (United Kingdom) 425
New Light Publishers (India) 195
New Opportunity Press Ltd (United Kingdom) 425
New Order, The, Book Co (India) 195
New Park Publications Ltd (United Kingdom) 425
New Portway (United Kingdom) 425
New South Wales Booksellers' Association (Australia) 10
New South Wales University Press Ltd (Australia) 17
New University Education (United Kingdom) 425
New Writers' Press (Republic of Ireland) 210
New Writers Stipendium for Literature (Austria) 31

New Zealand Authors, The, Fund (New Zealand) 287
New Zealand Book Awards (New Zealand) 291
New Zealand Book Council (New Zealand) 291
New Zealand Book Trade Organization Inc (New Zealand) 287
New Zealand Children's Books of the Year (New Zealand) 291
New Zealand Copyright Council (New Zealand) 287
New Zealand Council for Educational Research (New Zealand) 288
New Zealand Government Printing Office (New Zealand) 289
New Zealand Library Association (New Zealand) 290
New Zealand Literary Fund (New Zealand) 291
New Zealand Maori Artists & Writers Society Inc (New Zealand) 291
New Zealand Playwrights Association (New Zealand) 291
New Zealand Women Writers' Society (New Zealand) 291
New Zealand Writers Guild (New Zealand) 291
Newdigate, Sir Roger, Prize for English Verse (United Kingdom) 449
Newman, M (Israel) 216
Newnes Books (United Kingdom) 425
Newnes-Butterworths (United Kingdom) 425
Newnes-Technical (United Kingdom) 425
Newrick Associates Ltd (New Zealand) 289
Newservice Ltd (Seychelles) 324
Newspread International (Kenya) 248
Newton Compton Editori SRL (Italy) 229
Nexus Books (New Zealand) 289
Ney's Libros and Revistas (Honduras) 178
Nha Xuat Ban Van Hoc (Literature Publishing House) (Socialist Republic of Viet Nam) 455
Nibondh (Thailand) 380
Nibondh (Gaysorn) (Thailand) 381
Nicholson, Robert, Publications Ltd (United Kingdom) 425
Nici (Belgium) 39
Nicolaische Verlagsbuchhandlung Beuermann GmbH (Federal Republic of Germany) 151
Nicoli, Umberto, Editore (Italy) 229
Niederösterreichisches Pressehaus, Verlag, mbH (Austria) 27
Niedersächsische Staats- und Universitätsbibliothek (Federal Republic of Germany) 168
Niedieck Linder AG (Switzerland) 375
Niedlich, Buchhandlung Wendelin, KG (Federal Republic of Germany) 168
Niemeyer, Max, Verlag (Federal Republic of Germany) 151
Niemeyer, VEB Max, Verlag (German Democratic Republic) 118
Niemeyer, Verlag C W (Federal Republic of Germany) 151
Nieuwe Stad (Netherlands) 280
Nieuwe Wieken (Netherlands) 280
Nigar, Librería y Editorial, SRL (Argentina) 6
Niger (Acada) Bookshop Ltd (Nigeria) 296
Nigeria Educational Research, The, Council (Nigeria) 297
Nigerian Association of Agricultural Librarians and Documentalists (NAALD) (Nigeria) 297
Nigerian Baptist Book Stores (Nigeria) 296
Nigerian Book Development Council (Nigeria) 293
Nigerian Book Development Council Book Prize (Nigeria) 297
Nigerian Book Development Council Literary Prize (Nigeria) 297
Nigerian Book Suppliers Ltd (Nigeria) 296
Nigerian Booksellers' Association (Nigeria) 293
Nigerian Institute of International Affairs (Nigeria) 295
Nigerian Library Association (Nigeria) 297
Nigerian Publishers' Association (Nigeria) 293
Nigerian Publishers Services Ltd (Nigeria) 295
Nigerian Trade Review (Nigeria) 295
Nigerian Writers' Club (Nigeria) 297
Niggli, Verlag Arthur, AG (Switzerland) 370
Night Owl Publishers Pty Ltd (Australia) 17
Nihon Bunka Kagakusha Co Ltd (Japan) 241
Nihon Dokubungakkai (Japan) 246
Nihon Shoten Kumiai Rengokai (Japan) 238
Nihon Toshokan Kyokai (Japan) 245
Nihon Vogue (Publishing) Co Ltd (Japan) 241
Nijgh en Van Ditmar, NV Uitgeverij (Netherlands) 280
Nijhoff, Martinus, BV (Netherlands) 284
Nijhoff, Martinus, Prize (International Literary Prizes) 478
Nijhoff, Martinus, Publishers (Netherlands) 280
Nikas (Greece) 175
Nile & Mackenzie Ltd (United Kingdom) 425
Niloe, Bokforlaget, AB (Sweden) 356
Nimaroo Publishers (Australia) 17
'Nine', The, Prize (Sweden) 360
Nio Pobjeda — Oour Izdavačko-Publicistička Djelatnost (Yugoslavia) 458
Niove (Dominican Republic) 82
Nippon Bungaku Kyokai (Japan) 246
Nippon Dokumentesyon Kyokai (Japan) 245
Nippon Furansu-go Furansu-bungaku Kai (Japan) 246

Nippon Hikaku Bungakukai (Japan) 246
Nippon Igaku Toshokan Kyokai (Japan) 245
Nippon Nogaku Toshokan Kyogikai (JAALD) (Japan) 245
Nippon Romazikai (Japan) 246
Nippon Rosiya Bungakkai (Japan) 246
Nippon Shuppan Hanbai KK (Japan) 245
Nippon Toshokan Gakkai (Japan) 245
Nippon Yakugaku Toshokan Kyogikai (Japan) 245
Nirmal Book Agency (India) 195
Nisbet, James, & Co Ltd (United Kingdom) 425
Nitzanim (Israel) 216
Niugini Press (Australia) 17
Niven, Frederick, Literary Award (United Kingdom) 449
Niyom Vidhya (Thailand) 380
Nizet, Librairie A-G, Sàrl (France) 103
Nizza, Agencia de Librerías (Paraguay) 306
Nizza, Ediciones (Paraguay) 306
Njala Educational Services Centre (Sierra Leone) 325
Njala University College Bookshop (Sierra Leone) 325
Njala University College Library (University of Sierra Leone) (Sierra Leone) 325
Njogu Gitene Publications (Kenya) 248
Nkrumah Teachers' College Library (Zambia) 464
Nnamdi Azikiwe Library (Nigeria) 297
Nobel, Livraria (Brazil) 56
Nobel, Livraria, SA Editora (Brazil) 53
Nobel Prize for Literature (International Literary Prizes) 478
Nobel Prize, The, Library (United Kingdom) 444
Nobèle, F De (France) 103
Noblet Indústria Gráfica e Editora Ltda (Brazil) 53
Noguer, Editorial, SA (Spain) 343
Nok Publishers (Nigeria) Ltd (Nigeria) 295
Nolit (Yugoslavia) 460
Nolit Publishing House (Yugoslavia) 458
Noma Award, The, for Publishing in Africa (International Literary Prizes) 478
Noma Literary, The, Prize (International Literary Prizes) 478
Noma Prize for Juvenile Novel (Japan) 247
Noma Prize for Literature (Japan) 247
Nomos Verlagsgesellschaft mbH und Co KG (Federal Republic of Germany) 151
Nonesuch, The, Library (United Kingdom) 425
Noord-Hollandsche, BV, Uitgeversmaatschappij (Netherlands) 280
Noordhoff International Publishing (Netherlands) 280
Noordnederlands Boekbedrijf, Het, NV (Belgium) 39
Noorduijn BV (Netherlands) 280
Noordwijk, Mavis A (Suriname) 351
Nord, Editrice, Sdf (Italy) 229
Nord-Süd (Switzerland) 370
Nordbok, AB (Sweden) 356
Norddeutscher Verleger- und Buchhändler-Verband eV (Federal Republic of Germany) 121
Norden, Förlagshuset, AB (Sweden) 356
Nordic Council Literary Prize (International Literary Prizes) 478
Nórdica, Editorial, Ltda (Brazil) 53
Nordisk Boghandel (Denmark) 79
Nordisk Musikforleggerunion (International Organizations) 468
Nordisk Vitenskapelig Bibliotekarforbund (International Organizations) 468
Nordiska Bokhandeln, AB (Sweden) 358
Nordiska Bokhandelns, AB, Förlag (Sweden) 356
Nordiska Musikförlaget, AB, (Edition Wilhelm Hansen Stockholm) (Sweden) 356
Nordiska Teaterforlaget Edition Wilhelm Hansen (Denmark) 79
Nordjyske Landsbibliotek, Det (Denmark) 80
Noregs Boklag L/L (Norway) 299
Norfolk Press (United Kingdom) 425
Norges Landbrukshøgskoles Bibliotek (Norway) 300
Norlis, Olaf, Bokhandel A/S (Norway) 300
Norlis, Olaf, Forlag A/S (Norway) 299
Norma, Ediciones, SA (Spain) 343
Norma, Editorial, y Cia SCA (Colombia) 66
Norma PVBA (Belgium) 39
Normalizacyjne, Wydawnictwa (Poland) 312
Normans Förlag AB (Sweden) 356
Norn (Thailand) 380
Norris Press (Isle of Man) 212
Norsk Antikvarbokhandlerforening (Norway) 298
Norsk Bibliotekforening (Norway) 301
Norsk Biblioteklag (Norway) 301
Norsk Bokhandler Medhjelper Forening (Norway) 298
Norsk Bokhandlersamband (Norway) 298
Norsk Bokimport A/S (Norway) 298
Norsk Bokimport A/S (Norway) 300
Norsk Boknummerkontor (Norway) 298
Norsk Dokumentasjonsgruppe (Norway) 301
Norsk Forleggersamband (Norway) 298
Norsk Kunstforlag A/S (Norway) 299
Norsk Musikkforleggerforening (Norway) 298
Norske Akademi for Sprog og Litteratur (Norway) 301
Norske Bokhandlerforening (Norway) 298

Norske Bokklubben, Den, A/S (Norway) 300
Norske Deitidsbibliotekarers Yrkeslag (Norway) 301
Norske Forfatterforening, Den (Norway) 298
Norske Forleggerforening, Den (Norway) 298
Norske Forskningsbibliotekarers Forening (Norway) 301
Norske Samlaget, Det (Norway) 299
Norske Videnskaps-Akademi, Det (Norway) 301
Norstedt, AB P A, och Söners Förlag (Sweden) 356
Norte de España, Librerías del, SA (LINESA) (Spain) 347
Norte, Editorial, SAIC (Argentina) 6
Norte, Librería (Argentina) 8
North Holland (Netherlands) 280
Northcott Reeves, Publishers (New Zealand) 289
Northern Nigerian Publishing Co Ltd (Nigeria) 295
Northern Technical College Library (Zambia) 464
Northwood Books (United Kingdom) 426
Norton, W W, & Co Ltd (United Kingdom) 426
Norwegian Association of Children's and Young People's Authors (Norway) 298
Norwegian Association of Translators (Norway) 301
Nota, Mip (Yugoslavia) 458
Notre Dame, Librairie (Benin) 45
Notre Dame, Librairie (Chad) 62
Nottbeck, Verlag Wissenschaft und Politik, Berend von (Federal Republic of Germany) 151
Nouveau Cercle Parisien du Livre (France) 109
Nouveautés de l'Enseignement-éditions andré casteilla (France) 103
Nouvel Office d'Edition (France) 103
Nouvelle Agence, La (France) 109
Nouvelle Cité (France) 103
Nouvelle Diffusion (Belgium) 39
Nouvelle, Librairie (Gabon) 115
Nouvelles Editions Françaises (France) 103
Nouvelles Editions Latines (France) 103
Nouvelles Editions, Les, Africaines (Ivory Coast) 236
Nouvelles Editions, Les, Africaines (Senegal) 324
Nouvelles Editions, Les, Africaines (NEA) (Togo) 382
Nouvelles Editions Marabout, Les, SA (Belgium) 39
Nouvelles Editions Rationalistes SA (France) 103
Nouvelles Editions Vokaer SA (Belgium) 39
Nouvelles Feuilles Familiales (Belgium) 39
Nova Aguilar, Editora, SA (Brazil) 53
Nova Communications (United Kingdom) 426
Nova, Editorial, SACI (Argentina) 6
Nova Epoca Editorial Ltda (Brazil) 53
Nova Fronteira, Editora, SA (Brazil) 53
Nova Hrvatska Ltd (United Kingdom) 426
Nova Knjiga (Yugoslavia) 458
Nova Pacifica Publishing Co Ltd (New Zealand) 289
Nova Terra (Spain) 343
Novalis Verlag AG (Switzerland) 370
Novapres BV (Netherlands) 280
Novaro, Organización Editorial, SA (Mexico) 267
Novel Prize (France) 113
Novel Prize (Republic of Ireland) 212
Novello & Co Ltd (United Kingdom) 426
Novelty Trading Co (Jamaica) 237
Novissima, Edizioni di (Italy) 229
Novo Gift and Book Store (Netherlands Antilles) 286
'Novosti', Agentstvo Pechati, (APN) (Union of Soviet Socialist Republics) 388
Novus Forlag A/S (Norway) 299
Nüchtern, Verlag Monika (Federal Republic of Germany) 151
Nuestra Tierra, Editorial (Uruguay) 452
Nuestro Tiempo, Editorial, SA (Mexico) 267
Nueva Editorial Interamericana SA de CV (Mexico) 267
Nueva Imagen, Editorial, SA (Mexico) 267
Nueva Visión (Argentina) 8
Nueva Visión, Ediciones, SAIC (Argentina) 6
Nuevo, Editorial, Continente (Honduras) 178
Numismatischer Verlag P N Schulten (Federal Republic of Germany) 151
Nunes, Livraria (Portugal) 318
Nuorten Kirjakerho (Finland) 88
Nuova Foglio, La, SpA (Italy) 229
Nuova Guaraldi Editrice di Ideal Pra SRL (Italy) 229
Nuova Italia, La, Editrice (Italy) 229
Nuova Vallecchi Editore SpA (Italy) 229
Nuova Vita, Gruppo Editoriale, SpA (Italy) 229
Nuovi Sentieri Editore (Italy) 229
Nurnberg, Andrew, Associates Ltd (United Kingdom) 442
Nusa Indah (Indonesia) 206
Nusser Verlag (Federal Republic of Germany) 151
Nutshell Press (United Kingdom) 426
Nwamife Publishers Ltd (Nigeria) 295
Ny Krim, Bokklubben (Norway) 300
Nybloms Förlag (Sweden) 356
Nye Boker, Bokklubben, (New Book Club) (Norway) 300
Nymphenburger Verlagshandlung GmbH (Federal Republic of Germany) 151

INDEX 531

O E M F (Italy) 229
O N K Copyright Agency (Turkey) 385
O R S T O M (France) 103
O S (Organizzazioni Speciali SRL) (Italy) 229
Oakwood Press (United Kingdom) 426
Oasis Books (United Kingdom) 426
Oasis, Ediciones, SA (Mexico) 267
Obelisk, Nakladatelství (Czechoslovakia) 71
Obelisk-Verlag (Austria) 27
Oberbaumverlag (Federal Republic of Germany) 152
Oberösterreichischer Landesverlag (Austria) 27
Obobo Books (Nigeria) 295
Obod (Yugoslavia) 458
Obra, La (Argentina) 7
O'Brien Educational (Republic of Ireland) 210
O'Brien, The, Press (Republic of Ireland) 210
Obunsha Co Ltd (Japan) 241
Obzor (Yugoslavia) 458
Obzor, vydavateľstvo kníh a časopisov NP (Czechoslovakia) 71
Oceania Printers Ltd (Fiji) 86
Octagon, The, Press Ltd (United Kingdom) 426
Octopus Books PLC (United Kingdom) 426
Octopus Verlag (Austria) 27
Odana Editions Pty Ltd (Australia) 17
Odd Fellows (Manchester Unity) Social Concern Book Awards (International Literary Prizes) 478
Odense Centralbibliotek (Denmark) 80
Odense Universitetsbibliotek (Denmark) 80
Odense University Press (Denmark) 78
Odeon Book Club (Klub čtenář) (Czechoslovakia) 73
Odeon, nakladatelství krásné literatury a umění (Czechoslovakia) 71
Odeon Store LP (Thailand) 380
Odhams Books (United Kingdom) 426
O'Donovan, Anne, Pty Ltd (Australia) 17
Odörfer-Verlags GmbH (Federal Republic of Germany) 152
Odusote Bookstores Ltd (Nigeria) 296
Oeil, L', Ouvert (France) 109
Oekumenischer Verlag Dr R-F Edel (Federal Republic of Germany) 152
Oesch, Emil, Verlag AG (Switzerland) 370
Oestergaard, Paul, GmbH (Federal Republic of Germany) 152
Oetinger, Verlag Friedrich (Federal Republic of Germany) 152
Oetker, August (Federal Republic of Germany) 152
Oeuvre Gravée, L' (Switzerland) 370
Ofer Publishing House (Israel) 216
Offene Worte, Verlag (Federal Republic of Germany) 152
Office Arabe de Presse et de Documentation (Syria) 377
Office Central de Lisieux SA (France) 103
Office de Documentation Bibliographique et de Diffusion (France) 104
Office de la Recherche Scientifique et Technique Outre-Mer (French Guiana) 114
Office de la Recherche Scientifique et Technique Outre Mer (ORSTOM) (France) 104
Office de Promotion de L'Edition Française (France) 90
Office du Livre Malagasy (OLM) (Democratic Republic of Madagascar) 257
Office du Livre SA (Buchhaus AG) (Switzerland) 370
Office international de Librairie (Belgium) 42
Office national des Librairies Populaires (ONLP) (Popular Republic of Congo) 68
Officina Edizioni di Aldo Quinti (Italy) 229
Offord, John, (Publications) Ltd (United Kingdom) 426
Ofiria, Edizioni (Italy) 229
Ogbalu, F C (Nigeria) 296
Ogunsanya Press, Publishers and Bookstores Ltd (Nigeria) 295
Ohio University Press (United Kingdom) 426
Ohm, Karl, Verlag (Federal Republic of Germany) 152
Ohmsha Ltd (Japan) 242
Ohridski, Narodna i univerzitetska biblioteka 'Kliment, ' (Yugoslavia) 460
Oikos-Tau SA Ediciones (Spain) 343
Oireachtas Library (Republic of Ireland) 211
Oiseau-Lyre, Editions de l' (Monaco) 270
Ojeda Fierro, Nicolas, e Hijos (Peru) 307
Okapi Centre de Diffusion (Zaire) 462
Okin (Nigeria) 295
'Oktobar', Literary Club (Yugoslavia) 461
Olamenu (Israel) 216
Oldenbourg, R, Verlag GmbH (Federal Republic of Germany) 152
Oldenbourg, Verlag (Austria) 27
Oleander, The, Press (United Kingdom) 426
Oliphants (United Kingdom) 426
Olive Books of Israel (Israel) 216
Oliver & Boyd (Australia) 17
Oliver & Boyd (United Kingdom) 426
Oliver's Guides (United Kingdom) 426
Olle und Wolter, Verlag (Federal Republic of Germany) 152
Olms, Edition, AG (Switzerland) 370
Olms, Georg, Verlag (Federal Republic of Germany) 152

Olschki, Casa Editrice Leo S (Italy) 229
Ölschläger, Verlag für Wirtschaftsskripten, Dipl Kfm C, GmbH (Federal Republic of Germany) 152
Ölschläger, Verlag, GmbH (Federal Republic of Germany) 152
Olympia, Nakladatelství (Czechoslovakia) 72
Olympia Press Italia (Italy) 229
Olympio, Livraria José, Editora SA (Brazil) 53
Olzog, Günter, Verlag GmbH (Federal Republic of Germany) 152
O'Mahony & Co Ltd (Republic of Ireland) 211
Omega Boek BV (Netherlands) 280
Omega, Ediciones, SA (Spain) 343
Omniboek, Uitgeverij (Netherlands) 280
Omnibus Books (Australia) 17
Omoleye Publishing Co (Nigeria) 295
Omun Kak (Republic of Korea) 251
On the Road (United Kingdom) 444
Oncken Verlag KG (Federal Republic of Germany) 152
Ondori Sha Publishers Co Ltd (Japan) 242
O'Neil, Lloyd, Pty Ltd (Australia) 17
Ongaku No Tomo Sha Corporation (Japan) 242
Onibonoje Book Club (Nigeria) 296
Onibonoje Press & Book Industries (Nigeria) Ltd (Nigeria) 295
Online Publications Ltd (United Kingdom) 426
Önskeboken (Sweden) 358
Ontwikkeling, Uitgeverij S V (Belgium) 39
Ooft, C D (Suriname) 351
Oosthoek (Netherlands) 280
Opal, Bokförlaget, AB (Sweden) 356
Opdebeek, Uitgeverij (Belgium) 39
Open Books Publishing Ltd (United Kingdom) 426
Open University Educational Enterprises Ltd (United Kingdom) 426
Openbare Bibliotheek (Netherlands) 284
Openbare Leeszaal en Bibliotheek (Netherlands Antilles) 286
Openbare Leeszaal en Boekerij (Netherlands Antilles) 286
Operaie, Nuove Edizioni, SRL (Italy) 230
Ophrys, Editions (France) 104
Oppersdorff, Inigo von, Verlag (Switzerland) 370
Optimum (United Kingdom) 426
Opus Records and Publishing House (Czechoslovakia) 72
Orac, Verlag (Austria) 27
Orakau House (New Zealand) 289
Orange Free State Provincial Library (Republic of South Africa) 334
Orangerie Galerie und Verlag, Gerhard F Reinz (Federal Republic of Germany) 152
Orante, Editions de l' (France) 104
Orban, Editions Olivier (France) 104
Orbe, Editorial (Cuba) 69
Orbis en Orion Uitgevers NV (Belgium) 39
Orbis, Nakladatelství (Czechoslovakia) 72
Orbis Publishing Ltd (United Kingdom) 426
Orbit (United Kingdom) 426
Orbit NV (Netherlands) 280
Orchid Press (Suriname) 351
Orders Clearing (United Kingdom) 391
Ordfront tryckeri & förlag AB (Sweden) 356
Ordina Editions (Belgium) 39
Ordnance Survey (United Kingdom) 426
Orell Füssli (Switzerland) 375
Orell Füssli Verlag (Switzerland) 370
Orellana, Librería (Chile) 63
Organisation, Les Editions d' (France) 104
Organisator, Verlag, AG (Switzerland) 370
Organización de Bienestar Estudiantil (OBE) (Venezuela) 454
Organization for African Unity Library (Ethiopia) 86
Organization of American States (International Organizations) 468
Organizzazioni Speciali SRL (Italy) 230
Orhan Özsisman (Turkey) 385
Oriel Press Ltd (United Kingdom) 426
Orient Book Club (India) 201
Orient Bookshop (Libya) 255
Orient Longman Ltd (India) 195
Orient Paperbacks (India) 195
Oriental & Religious, The, Publishing Corp Ltd (Pakistan) 302
Oriental Economist Ltd (K K Toyo Keizai Shimposha) (Japan) 242
Oriental Press BV (APA) (Netherlands) 280
Oriental Textile Press Ltd (United Kingdom) 427
Orientalia Christiana, Edizioni (Italy) 230
Orientalia Publishers (Pakistan) 302
Orientaliste, Librairie (France) 104
Orientaliste, Uitgeverij, PVBA (Belgium) 39
Oriente, Editorial (Cuba) 69
Origo-Verlag (Switzerland) 370
Orion (Belgium) 39
Orion, Ediciones (Argentina) 7
Orion, Editorial (Mexico) 267
Orion-Heimreiter Verlag GmbH (Federal Republic of Germany) 152
Orion Press (Japan) 244

Orissa Sahitya Akademi Award (India) 204
Orisun Editions (Nigeria) 295
Ormeraie, Michel de l' (France) 104
Örn og Örlygur, Bókaútgafan, hf (Iceland) 184
Orpan Export (Poland) 313
Országh-Hviezdoslav, Pavol, Prize (International Literary Prizes) 478
Országos Müszaki, Információs Központ és Könyvtár (Hungary) 182
Országos Széchényi Könyvtár (Hungary) 182
Országos Széchényi Könyvtár Magyar ISBN Iroda (Hungary) 181
Orte-Verlag (Switzerland) 370
Ortells, Alfredo, Ferriz (Spain) 343
Orvieto, Laura, Prize (Italy) 236
Orwell Memorial Fund Prize, George (United Kingdom) 449
Orwell Memorial Prize, George (United Kingdom) 449
Osaka Gakuin University Library (Japan) 245
Osaka Prefectural Nakanoshima Library (Japan) 245
Oscar Press (Greece) 175
Oslobodenje, NIP (Yugoslavia) 458
Osprey Publishing Ltd (United Kingdom) 427
Ossolińskich Biblioteka, Zaklad Narodowy im, Polskiej Akademii Nauk (Poland) 314
Ossolińskich, Zaklad Narodowy im, Wydawnictwo Polskiej Akademii Nauk (Poland) 312
Österreichische Exlibris-Gesellschaft (Austria) 30
Österreichische Gesellschaft für Dokumentation und Information (Austria) 30
Österreichische Gesellschaft für Literatur (Austria) 30
Österreichische Nationalbibliothek (Austria) 30
Österreichische Verlagsanstalt GmbH (Austria) 27
Österreichischen Akademie der Wissenschaften, Bibliothek der (Austria) 30
österreichischen Akademie der Wissenschaften, Verlag der (Austria) 27
österreichischen Gewerkschaftsbundes, Verlag des, GmbH (Austria) 27
Österreichischen Patentamtes, Bibliothek des (Austria) 30
Österreichischer Agrarverlag, Druck- und Verlags- GmbH (Austria) 27
Österreichischer Buchhändlerverband (Austria) 24
Österreichischer Buchklub der Jugend (Austria) 29
Österreichischer Bundesverlag GmbH (Austria) 27
Österreichischer Schriftstellerverband (Austria) 30
Österreichischer Verlegerverband (Austria) 24
Österreichisches Institut für Bibliotheksforschung, Dokumentations- und Informationswesen (Austria) 30
Österreichisches Katholisches Bibelwerk (Austria) 27
Österreichisches Staatsarchiv (Austria) 30
Osterrieth, Verlag (Federal Republic of Germany) 152
Ostrowiak, Rebecca, School of Reading (Republic of South Africa) 331
Ostschweiz Druck und Verlag (Switzerland) 370
Osveta (Czechoslovakia) 72
Oswald, Editions Pierre Jean (France) 104
Otago Heritage Books (New Zealand) 289
Otago University Library (New Zealand) 290
Otava Kustannusosakeyhtiö (Finland) 87
Other, The, Award (United Kingdom) 449
Otokar Keršovani-Rijeka (Yugoslavia) 458
Otpaz (Israel) 216
Otsuki Shoten Publishers (Japan) 242
Ott Verlag AG Thun (Switzerland) 370
Ottaviano, Edizioni (Italy) 230
Otzar Hamoreh (Israel) 216
Oude, De, Linden NV (Belgium) 39
Oudiovista Productions (Pty) Ltd (Republic of South Africa) 331
Oulun Yliopiston Kirjasto (Finland) 89
Outback Press Pty Ltd (Australia) 17
Outrigger Publishers (New Zealand) 289
Ouvrières, Les Editions, SA (France) 104
Oveja, Editorial La, Negra Ltda (Colombia) 66
Overseas Publications Interchange Ltd (United Kingdom) 427
Overseas Publishers Association Amsterdam BV (Netherlands) 280
Overseas Publishers' Representatives Association of Southern Africa (Republic of South Africa) 328
Owen, Peter, Ltd (United Kingdom) 427
Oxfam (United Kingdom) 427
Oxfam Public Affairs Unit (United Kingdom) 427
Oxford & I B H Publishing Co (India) 195
Oxford Bibliographical Society (United Kingdom) 447
Oxford Book and Stationery Co (India) 202
Oxford Illustrated Press Ltd (United Kingdom) 427
Oxford Microform Publications Ltd (United Kingdom) 427
Oxford Polytechnic Press (United Kingdom) 427
Oxford Railway Publishing Co Ltd (United Kingdom) 427
Oxford University Press (Australia) 17
Oxford University Press (Hong Kong) 180
Oxford University Press (India) 195
Oxford University Press (Kenya) 248
Oxford University Press (Malaysia) 260
Oxford University Press (New Zealand) 289

532 INDEX

Oxford University Press (Pakistan) 302
Oxford University Press (Republic of Singapore) 326
Oxford University Press (Tanzania) 379
Oxford University Press (United Kingdom) 427
Oxford University Press East Africa (Zimbabwe) 465
Oxford University Press Southern Africa (Republic of South Africa) 331
Oxford University Taylor Institution Library (United Kingdom) 445
Oxonian Press (P) Ltd (India) 196
Oya Soichi Non-fiction Prize (Japan) 247
Oyez Longman Publishing Ltd (United Kingdom) 427

P A C, Editions, (Presse-Auto-Conseil) (France) 104
P A T C O (Indonesia) 206
P C A-Halbart SA (Belgium) 42
P E A — Produzioni Editoriale Aprile (Italy) 230
P E N All-India Centre (India) 203
P E N, Bulgarian, Centre (Bulgaria) 59
P E N Centre (Greece) 176
P E N Centre (Indonesia) 207
P E N Centre (Liechtenstein) 256
P E N Centre de Côte d'Ivoire (Ivory Coast) 237
P E N Centre of Zimbabwe (Zimbabwe) 465
P E N, Centro del, Internacional (Peru) 308
P E N, Chilean, Centre (Chile) 64
P E N, China, Centre (People's Republic of China) 65
P E N Club (Jamaica) 237
P E N Club (Monaco) 270
P E N Club (Romania) 322
P E N Club Award, Yugoslav (International Literary Prizes) 478
P E N Club, Belgian French Centre, International (Belgium) 44
P E N Club Centre, Swiss-German (Switzerland) 376
P E N Club de Bolivia (Centro Internacional de Escritores) (Bolivia) 47
P E N Club de Puerto Rico (Puerto Rico) 320
P E N Club de Suisse romande (Switzerland) 376
P E N Club, Flemish Centre, International (Belgium) 44
P E N Club français (France) 111
P E N Club International de Argentina (Argentina) 9
P E N Club Medal, Hungarian (International Literary Prizes) 478
P E N-Club, Österreichischer (Austria) 30
P E N Club Prizes, Polish (International Literary Prizes) 478
P E N Club, Yugoslav, Serbian Centre (Yugoslavia) 461
P E N Clube do Brasil (Associação Universal de Escritores) (Brazil) 57
P E N, Cyprus (Cyprus) 70
P E N, Czechoslovakian, Centre (Czechoslovakia) 74
P E N, Dacca Centre for International, Madhura (Bangladesh) 33
P E N, Danish, Centre (Denmark) 81
P E N, Egyptian, Centre (Egypt) 85
P E N English Centre (United Kingdom) 447
P E N, Finnish, Club (Finland) 89
P E N, Friesian, Centre (Netherlands) 285
P E N, Guangzhou Chinese, Centre (People's Republic of China) 65
P E N, Hong Kong Chinese, Centre (Hong Kong) 180
P E N, Hong Kong English, Centre (Hong Kong) 180
P E N Internacional de Escritores de Colombia (Colombia) 67
P E N, International (International Organizations) 468
P E N, International, Centre (Iceland) 185
P E N International Centre (Italy) 235
P E N, International, Centre (Philippines) 310
P E N, International, (Melbourne Centre) (Australia) 21
P E N International New Zealand Centre (New Zealand) 291
P E N, International, (Sydney Centre) (Australia) 21
P E N International — Thailand Centre (Thailand) 381
P E N Internazionale — Centro della Svizzera Italiana e Romancia (Switzerland) 376
P E N, Irish (Republic of Ireland) 212
P E N, Israeli, Centre (Israel) 218
P E N, Japan, Club (Japan) 246
P E N, Korean, Centre (Republic of Korea) 253
P E N, Lebanese, Club (Lebanon) 254
P E N, Magyar, Club (Hungary) 183
P E N, Mexican, Centre (Mexico) 269
P E N, Netherlands Centre of the International (Netherlands) 285
P E N, Norwegian, Centre (Norway) 301
P E N, Paraguayan, Centre (Paraguay) 306
P E N, Polish, Centre (Poland) 314
P E N, Portuguese, Centre (Portugal) 319
P E N, San Miguel, Centre (Mexico) 269
P E N Scottish Centre (United Kingdom) 447
P E N, Senegal, Centre (Senegal) 324
P E N, South African, Centre (Cape) (Republic of South Africa) 335

P E N, Spanish, Club (Cataluña) (Spain) 348
P E N, Svenska Pennklubben (Swedish Centre of International,) (Sweden) 359
P E N, The Taipei Chinese Center, International (Taiwan) 378
P E N, Venezuelan, Centre (Venezuela) 454
P E N Yazarlar Dernegi (Turkey) 385
P E N Zentrum Bundesrepublik Deutschland (Federal Republic of Germany) 170
P E N Zentrum Deutsche Demokratische Republik (German Democratic Republic) 120
P F B (Malaysia) 260
P G Medical Books (Republic of Singapore) 326
P I A G (Federal Republic of Germany) 152
P I C S (United Kingdom) 391
P O F (France) 104
P P C, Librerías, (Promoción Popular Cristiana) (Spain) 347
P P C Ltd (Barbados) 33
P P C (Promoción Popular Cristiana) (Spain) 343
P P H (Pakistan) 302
P R O N I (Public Record Office of Northern Ireland) (United Kingdom) 445
P R Verlag Wiesbaden, H G Schwieger (Federal Republic of Germany) 152
P S G (United Kingdom) 427
P U F (France) 104
P U F, Librairie générale des (France) 109
P U L (France) 104
P U Z (Zaire) 462
P W E (Państwowe Wydawnictwo Ekonomiczne) (Poland) 313
P W N (Panstwowe Wydawnictwo Naukowe) (Poland) 313
P Y C Edition (France) 104
Pacific Book Centre (Republic of Singapore) 327
Pacific Publications (Australia) Pty Ltd (Australia) 17
Pacifica Ltd (Japan) 242
Pacifico, Editorial del, SA (Chile) 63
Pacifique, Les Editions du (France) 104
Pacifique, Société Nouvelle des Editions du (French Polynesia) 115
Packard Publishing Ltd (United Kingdom) 427
Päd extra buchverlag in der pädex Verlags GmbH (Federal Republic of Germany) 152
Pädagogischer Verlag Schwann/Bagel GmbH (Federal Republic of Germany) 152
Padilla, Editorial (Dominican Republic) 82
Padilla, Editorial (Dominican Republic) 82
Paedagogiki Academia, Library of the (Cyprus) 70
Paes Barreto, Rômulo (Brazil) 55
Pagan Publishing House (Burma) 60
Pahl-Rugenstein Verlag (Federal Republic of Germany) 152
Paico Ltd (Nigeria) 295
Paico Publishing House (India) 196
Paideia Editrice (Italy) 230
Paidós, Ediciones, Ibérica SA (Spain) 343
Paidós, Editorial (Argentina) 7
Paintaway (United Kingdom) 427
Pak American Commercial Inc (Pakistan) 303
Pak Book Corporation (Pakistan) 303
Pak Kitab Ghar (Bangladesh) 32
Pak Publishers (Pakistan) 302
Pakistan Board for Advancement of Literature (Pakistan) 304
Pakistan Board for Advancement of Literature Awards (Pakistan) 304
Pakistan Forest Institute, Central Forest Library (Pakistan) 303
Pakistan Institute of Nuclear Science & Technology Library (Pakistan) 303
Pakistan Law Times Publications (Pakistan) 302
Pakistan Library Association (Pakistan) 304
Pakistan Publications (Pakistan) 302
Pakistan Publishers' and Booksellers' Association (Pakistan) 301
Pakistan Publishing House (Pakistan) 302
Pakistan Scientific and Technological Information Centre (PASTIC) (Pakistan) 303
Pakistan Writers' Guild (Pakistan) 304
Pakpassak Kanphin (Laos) 253
Pala SA (Spain) 343
Palácio, Biblioteca do, Nacional de Mafra (Portugal) 318
Palacio del Libro (Uruguay) 452
Palacio, El, del Libro (Venezuela) 454
Palacio, Patrimonio Nacional, Biblioteca del, Real (Spain) 348
Paladin Books (United Kingdom) 427
Palanca, Carlos, Memorial Awards for Literature (Philippines) 310
Palatina, Biblioteca (Italy) 234
Palatina Editrice (Italy) 230
Pallas SA (Brazil) 55
Pallas, Vydavatel'stvo SFVU (Czechoslovakia) 72
'Pallottinum' Wydawnictwo Stowarzyszenia Apostolstwa Katolickiego (Poland) 313
Palme, Suzanne, Literary Agency (Norway) 300

Palmerston North Public Library (New Zealand) 290
Palombi, Fratelli, SRL (Italy) 230
Paludans, Erik, Boghandel (Denmark) 80
Paludans, Jörgen, Forlag A/S (Denmark) 78
Palumbo, G B, e C Editore SpA (Italy) 230
Památník národního písemnictví, Strahovská knihovna (Czechoslovakia) 73
Pamplona and its Culture Prize (Colombia) 68
Pan African Institute for Development (United Republic of Cameroun) 61
Pan-African Publishing Co Ltd (Tanzania) 379
Pan Books (Australia) Pty Ltd (Australia) 17
Pan Books Ltd (United Kingdom) 427
Pan Editrice (Italy) 230
Pan Korea Book Corporation (Republic of Korea) 251
Pan Library ('Circle of the Friends of Progress') (Greece) 176
Pan Malayan Publishing Co Sdn Bhd (Malaysia) 260
Pan Pacific Book Distributors (S) Pte Ltd (Republic of Singapore) 326
Pancaldi, Libreria Commissionaria Internazionale di Raffaele (Italy) 234
Panchasheel Prakashan (India) 196
Panda Press SRL (Italy) 230
Pandora Pockets (Netherlands) 280
Panero, Leopoldo, Prize (International Literary Prizes) 478
Panhellenic Federation of Publishers and Booksellers (PFPB) (Greece) 174
Panini, Edizioni, SpA (Italy) 230
Panjab University Publication Bureau (India) 196
Panmun Book Co Ltd (Republic of Korea) 252
Panmun Book Co Ltd (Republic of Korea) 252
Pannedille, Ediciones (Argentina) 7
Panorama, Editions du (Switzerland) 370
Panorama, Nakladatelství a vydavatelství (Czechoslovakia) 72
Pansegrau, Wilhelm, Verlag (Federal Republic of Germany) 152
Pantarei, Edizioni (Switzerland) 370
Pantelides (Greece) 176
Panther Books Ltd (United Kingdom) 427
Panther, Penerbitan Buku, (Panther Books Malaysia) (Malaysia) 260
Panton (Czechoslovakia) 72
Paoline, Edizioni (Italy) 230
Papachrysanthou Chryss SA (Greece) 175
Papacito, Ediciones (Uruguay) 452
Papacito, Librerías (Uruguay) 452
Papadimitriou, D A (Greece) 175
Papadimitriou, Haroula (Greece) 175
Papadopoulos, Kyr I, E E (Greece) 175
Papaioannou (Greece) 175
Papazissis Publishers SA (Greece) 175
Paper Tiger (United Kingdom) 427
Paperback Centre (Republic of Ireland) 211
Paperfronts (United Kingdom) 427
Papermac (United Kingdom) 427
Papeterie Centrale (Central African Republic) 62
Papua New Guinea Book Depot (Papua New Guinea) 305
Papua New Guinea Library Association (Papua New Guinea) 305
Papusa Ltda (Colombia) 66
Papyros Press (Greece) 175
'Papyrus' (Central African Republic) 62
Parabel Verlag GmbH und Co KG (Federal Republic of Germany) 152
Paracelsus Verlag GmbH (Federal Republic of Germany) 152
Paradise Book Stall (Pakistan) 303
Parag Prakashan (India) 196
Parallelo 38, Edizioni (Italy) 230
Paramount Book Corporation (Bangladesh) 32
Paramount Book Stall (Pakistan) 303
Paraninfo, Editorial, SA (Spain) 343
Pardo, Casa, SAC (Argentina) 7
Pardo, Librería General de Tomas (Argentina) 8
Parera, Librería (Chile) 63
Parey, Verlag Paul (Federal Republic of Germany) 152
Parimal Prakashan (India) 196
Paris-Caraïbes (France) 104
Paris Grand Prize for Literature (France) 113
Paris Prize (France) 113
Parissianos, Grigorios, 'Epistemonikai Ekdoseis' (Greece) 175
Park & Roche Establishment (Liechtenstein) 256
Park & Roche Establishment (Switzerland) 370
Parkash Brothers (India) 196
Parker & Son Ltd (United Kingdom) 444
Parkland Verlag GmbH (Federal Republic of Germany) 153
Parlement, Bibliothèque du (Belgium) 43
Parlement, Bibliothèque du, Européen (International Organizations) 468
Parliament Library (Greece) 176
Parliament Library (Ketab-khaneh Majles-e Shoraye Melli) (Iran) 207

INDEX 533

Parliament Library, No 2 (Ketab-khaneh Majles-e Shoraye Eslami, no 2) (Iran) 208
Parma (Brazil) 53
Parnfah Pittaya (Thailand) 380
Parramon Ediciones SA (Spain) 343
Parrish, Walter, Ltd (United Kingdom) 427
Parrot Books (United Kingdom) 427
Parry's Book Center (Sri Abdul Wahab Sdn Bhd) (Malaysia) 261
Parsifal Publishing Co (Belgium) 39
Parsons, Roy (New Zealand) 290
Partenon, Ediciones (Spain) 343
Parthenón, Livraria (Brazil) 56
Passavia Universitätsverlag und -Druck GmbH (Federal Republic of Germany) 153
Passavia, Verlag (Federal Republic of Germany) 153
Pássim, Librería (Spain) 347
Patent, Trade Marks and Designs Office Library (Australia) 20
Paternoster, The, Press Ltd (United Kingdom) 427
Paterson, Mark, & Associates (United Kingdom) 442
Path Publishers (India) 196
Patio, Galerie, Verlag (Federal Republic of Germany) 153
Patmos, Uitgeverij (Belgium) 40
Patmos Verlag GmbH (Federal Republic of Germany) 153
Patria, Editorial, SA de CV (Mexico) 267
Patria Grande, Editora (Argentina) 7
Patria, Librería (Mexico) 269
Patria, Libreria, SA (Mexico) 267
Pàtron, Casa Editrice, SAS (Italy) 230
Pàtron, Libreria Internazionale (Italy) 234
Pattloch, Paul, Verlag GmbH & Co KG (Federal Republic of Germany) 153
Patwa (Embakasi) Ltd (Kenya) 249
Paul, M P, Award (India) 204
Paul, M P, Prize (India) 204
Paul, Stanley, & Co Ltd (United Kingdom) 427
Paulinas, Ediciones (Argentina) 7
Paulinas, Ediciones (Chile) 63
Paulinas, Ediciones (Spain) 343
Paulinas, Ediciones (Mexico) 267
Paulinas, Edições (Brazil) 53
Paulinus Verlag (Federal Republic of Germany) 153
Paulsen, Ingwert, Jr (Federal Republic of Germany) 153
Paulusverlag (Switzerland) 370
Pause, Firmin (Réunion) 320
Pauvert, Jean-Jacques, Editeur (France) 104
Pavanne (United Kingdom) 427
Pavilion Books (United Kingdom) 427
Pawel Pan Presse (Federal Republic of Germany) 153
Pawlak, Manfred, Grossantiquariat und Verlagsgesellschaft mbH (Federal Republic of Germany) 153
Pax-Chile, Librería y Editorial, Ltda (Chile) 63
Pax, Editorial, México (Mexico) 267
Pax Forlag A/S (Norway) 299
Pax, Instytut Wydawniczy (Poland) 313
Pax, Livraria Editora, Lda (Portugal) 317
Payot, Editions (France) 104
Payot, Librairie, SA (Switzerland) 370
Payot, Librairie, SA (Switzerland) 375
Paz e Terra, Editora (Brazil) 54
Paz, Editorial, Montalvo (Spain) 343
Peace and Socialism International Publishers (Czechoslovakia) 72
Pearl Publishers (India) 196
Pearson (United Kingdom) 427
Pédagogie Moderne (France) 104
Pedagogika (Union of Soviet Socialist Republics) 388
Pedagogisk Forlag A/S (Norway) 299
Pedagoško-književni zbor, pedagoško društvo SR Hrvatske (Yugoslavia) 461
Pedersen, Agentur für wissenschaftliche Literatur Ulf, GmbH (Federal Republic of Germany) 153
Pediátrica, Editorial (Spain) 343
Pédone, Editions (France) 104
Pedrazzini Tipografia (Switzerland) 370
Pedrick, Don, Memorial Literary Award (Sri Lanka) 350
Peerage (United Kingdom) 427
Peeters, Editions, SPRL (Belgium) 40
Pegaso, Ediciones (Spain) 343
Pegasus Books (Australia) 17
Pegasus Press Ltd (New Zealand) 289
Peiffer, Librairie Armand (Grand Duchy of Luxembourg) 257
Peisa, Ediciones, (Promoción Editorial Inca SA) (Peru) 307
Pelajar (Indonesia) 206
Pelham Books Ltd (United Kingdom) 427
Peli, Alexander, Ltd (Israel) 216
Pelican (Australia) 17
Pelican (United Kingdom) 428
Pelita Masa (Indonesia) 206
Pellegrini, Luigi, Editore (Italy) 230
Pembangunan (Indonesia) 206
Pemberton Publishing Co Ltd (United Kingdom) 428
Pembimbing Masa (Indonesia) 206
Pembimbing, P T, Masa (Indonesia) 206

Pembinaan, Pusat, Perpustakaan, Departemen P dan K Bidang. Bibliografi dan Deposit (Indonesia) 207
Peña, A, Lillo SA (Argentina) 7
Pendo-Verlag (Switzerland) 371
Penguin Books Australia Ltd (Australia) 17
Penguin Books Ltd (United Kingdom) 428
Penguin Books (NZ) Ltd (New Zealand) 289
Penguin/George Orwell Memorial Prize (United Kingdom) 449
Peninsula, Ediciones (Spain) 343
Penman, The, Club (International Organizations) 468
Pennsylvania State University Press (United Kingdom) 428
Pensamento, Editora (Brazil) 54
Pensée Moderne Jacques Grancher (France) 104
Pensiero, Il, Scientifico Società ARL (Italy) 230
Pentecost (New Caledonia) 286
Pentos PLC (United Kingdom) 428
People's Grand Study Centre (Democratic People's Republic of Korea) 250
People's Literature Publishing House (People's Republic of China) 64
People's Publishing Co Ltd (Nigeria) 295
People's Publishing House (Pakistan) 302
People's Publishing House (P) Ltd (India) 196
People's Sports Publishing House (People's Republic of China) 64
Pequeña, Una, Librería (Ecuador) 83
Père Castor (France) 104
Peregrine Books (United Kingdom) 428
Peregrino, Ediciones (United Kingdom) 428
Peregrinus, Peter (United Kingdom) 428
Pereira, Parceria A M, Lda (Portugal) 317
Perfecting Press (Hong Kong) 180
Pergamena Sas di G Giraldi (Italy) 230
Pergamini Editions (Greece) 175
Pergamon Press (Australia) Pty Ltd (Australia) 17
Pergamon Press Ltd (United Kingdom) 428
Periféria, Ediciones, SRL (Argentina) 7
Perimed Fachbuch-Verlagsgesellschaft mbH (Federal Republic of Germany) 153
Perlinger Verlag (Austria) 28
Permanent Press (United Kingdom) 428
Perpétuo, Editorial, Socorro (Portugal) 317
Perpustakaan Negeri Sabah (Malaysia) 261
Perrin, Librairie Académique (France) 104
Persatuan Perpustakaan Malaysia (Malaysia) 261
Perskor Books (Pty) Ltd (Republic of South Africa) 331
Perskor Bookshop (Republic of South Africa) 334
Perskor Prize for Literature (Republic of South Africa) 335
Perskor Prize for Youth Literature (Republic of South Africa) 335
Perspectiva, Editora (Brazil) 54
Pestalozzi-Verlag graphische Gesellschaft mbH (Federal Republic of Germany) 153
Peter Peregrinus Ltd (United Kingdom) 428
Peter, Verlag J P, Gebr Holstein (Federal Republic of Germany) 153
Peterborough Literary Agency (United Kingdom) 442
Peters, A D, & Co Ltd (United Kingdom) 442
Peters Musikverlag, C F, GmbH & Co KG (Federal Republic of Germany) 153
Peters Verlag, Dr Hans (Federal Republic of Germany) 153
Petersen, Hans Heinrich, Buchimport GmbH (Federal Republic of Germany) 168
Petiwala Corporation (Pakistan) 303
Pevsner Public Library (Israel) 218
Pfanneberg, Fachbuchverlag Dr, & Co (Federal Republic of Germany) 153
Pfeiffer, Verlag J, GmbH & Co (Federal Republic of Germany) 153
Pfister, E, GmbH (Federal Republic of Germany) 153
Pflaum, Richard, Verlag KG (Federal Republic of Germany) 153
Pfriemer, Udo, Verlag GmbH (Federal Republic of Germany) 153
Pfützner, Robert, GmbH (Federal Republic of Germany) 153
Phaethon, The, Press (United Kingdom) 428
Phaidon Press Ltd (United Kingdom) 428
Phaneromeni, Library of (Cyprus) 70
Pharmacie, Bibliothèque Interuniversitaire de (France) 110
Pharos-Verlag, Hansrudolf Schwabe AG (Switzerland) 371
Phébus, Editions (France) 104
Philip & Son, George, Ltd (United Kingdom) 428
Philip & Tacey Ltd (United Kingdom) 428
Philip, David, Publisher (Pty) Ltd (Republic of South Africa) 331
Philippine Arts and Architecture (Philippines) 309
Philippine Book Co (Philippines) 309
Philippine Book Co (Philippines) 309
Philippine Book Dealers' Association (Philippines) 308
Philippine Education Co Inc (Philippines) 309

Philippine Education Co Inc (Philippines) 309
Philippine Educational Publishers' Association (Philippines) 308
Philippine International Publishing Co (Philippines) 309
Philippine Library Association (Philippines) 310
Philippine Normal College Library & Library Science Departments (Philippines) 310
Philips GmbH, Fachbuch-Verlag (Federal Republic of Germany) 153
Phillimore & Co Ltd (United Kingdom) 428
Philo Press-Van Heusden-Hissink & Co CV (APA) (Netherlands) 280
Philograph Publications Ltd (United Kingdom) 428
Philosophia Verlag GmbH (Federal Republic of Germany) 153
Philosophisch-Anthroposophischer Verlag (Switzerland) 371
Pho Thong (Popularization) Publishing House (Socialist Republic of Viet Nam) 455
Phoebus Publishing Co (United Kingdom) 428
Phoebus-Verlag GmbH (Switzerland) 371
Phoenix Book Society (United Kingdom) 444
Phoenix Verlag AG (Switzerland) 371
Photographic Book Society (United Kingdom) 444
Physica-Verlag Rudolf Liebing GmbH und Co (Federal Republic of Germany) 154
Physik-Verlag GmbH (Federal Republic of Germany) 154
Piatkus Books (United Kingdom) 428
Picador (Australia) 17
Picador (United Kingdom) 428
Picard, Editions A et J, SA (France) 104
Piccin Editore sas (Italy) 230
Piccoli, Editrice, SpA (Italy) 230
Piccolo (Australia) 17
Piccolo (United Kingdom) 428
Piccolo-Bøger (Denmark) 78
Pickering & Inglis Ltd (United Kingdom) 428
Picton Publishing (Chippenham) Ltd (United Kingdom) 428
Picture Lions (United Kingdom) 429
Piedra Santa (Guatemala) 176
Piedra Santa (Guatemala) 177
Pierce, Lorne, Medal (International Literary Prizes) 478
Pierron, Editions (France) 104
Pierrot, Editions, SA (France) 371
Pietra, La (Italy) 230
Pigmalión (Argentina) 8
Pikkhanet (Thailand) 380
Pila, Editorial Augusto E, Teleña (Spain) 344
Pilgrim Award (International Literary Prizes) 479
Pilgrim Books Ltd (Nigeria) 295
Pilgrim Publishers (India) 196
Pilgrims Booksellers (Pty) (Republic of South Africa) 334
Pilgrims South Press Ltd (New Zealand) 289
Pilotta, La, Editrice Coop RL (Italy) 230
Pimodan, De, Foundation Prize (France) 113
Pinchgut Press (Australia) 17
Pineda Libros (Chile) 63
Pinguin-Verlag, Pawlowski KG (Austria) 28
Pink and Blue Editora Ltda (Brazil) 54
Pinter, Frances, Ltd (United Kingdom) 429
Pinx-Verlag Kurt Glombig (Federal Republic of Germany) 154
Pioneer Design Studio Pty Ltd (Australia) 17
Piper, R, & Co Verlag (Federal Republic of Germany) 154
Piper, R, & Co Verlag GmbH (Switzerland) 371
Pirámide, Ediciones, SA (Spain) 344
'Pishchevaya Promyshlennost', Izdatelstvo (Union of Soviet Socialist Republics) 388
Pitagora Editrice (Italy) 230
Pitambar Publishing Co (India) 196
Pitcher, William, Training College Library (Swaziland) 351
Pitkin Pictorials Ltd (United Kingdom) 429
Pitman Publishing Co SA (Pty) Ltd (Republic of South Africa) 331
Pitman Publishing Ltd (United Kingdom) 429
Pitman Publishing NZ Ltd (New Zealand) 289
Pitman Publishing Pty Ltd (Australia) 17
Pitou, Charles, Foundation Prize (France) 113
Pittayakarn (Thailand) 380
Pizzi, Amilcare, SpA (Italy) 230
Place, Editions Jean-Michel (France) 104
Plain Edition (United Kingdom) 429
Plambeck & Co, Druck und Verlag GmbH (Federal Republic of Germany) 154
Planeta, Editorial, SA (Spain) 344
Planeta Prize (International Literary Prizes) 479
Planeta Publishers (Union of Soviet Socialist Republics) 388
Planning Commission Library (Pakistan) 303
Plantin-Moretus, Museum (Belgium) 43
Plantyn, Uitgeverij, SA NV (Belgium) 40
Plata (Peru) 307
Plata, Editorial, SA (Venezuela) 454
Platano Editora SARL (Portugal) 317
Play to Learn (Australia) 17
Playfair (United Kingdom) 429

534 INDEX

Playor, Editorial (Spain) 344
Playtime Press (United Kingdom) 429
Plaza y Janés, Editorial Argentina, SA (Argentina) 7
Plaza y Janés SA (Spain) 344
Pleamar, Editorial (Argentina) 7
Plessl, Gerd, Agency (Federal Republic of Germany) 167
Plexus Publishing Ltd (United Kingdom) 429
Ploegsma, Uitgeverij (Netherlands) 280
Ploetz, Verlag A G , GmbH & Co KG (Federal Republic of Germany) 154
Plon, Librairie, SA (France) 104
Plough Publishing House (United Kingdom) 429
Pluim Book Club (Republic of South Africa) 333
Pluma, Editorial, Ltda (Colombia) 66
Plus, Bokförlaget, AB (Sweden) 356
Plus Ultra, Editorial, SAI & C (Argentina) 7
Pluto (Australia) 17
Pluto Press (United Kingdom) 429
Pochinchai (Republic of Korea) 252
Pock, Max, Universitätsbuchhandlung (Austria) 30
Pocket Bears (United Kingdom) 429
Pocket, Presses (France) 104
Poder, Biblioteca del, Legislativo (Uruguay) 452
Podzun-Pallas Verlag GmbH (Federal Republic of Germany) 154
Poe, Edgar, Prize (International Literary Prizes) 479
Poeschel, C E, Verlag (Federal Republic of Germany) 154
Poètes Présents (France) 109
Poetry Book Society (United Kingdom) 444
Poetry in Irish (International Literary Prizes) 479
Poetry Society of Australia (Australia) 21
Poetry Society of Zimbabwe (Zimbabwe) 465
Poetry, The, Society (United Kingdom) 447
Pohjalainen Kirjakauppa Oy (Finland) 88
Pohl Druckerei und Verlagsanstalt Otto Pohl (Federal Republic of Germany) 154
Poincaré, Raymond, Prize (France) 113
Point d'Interrogation, Librairie du (Senegal) 324
'Pojezierze', Wydawnictwo Stowarzyszenia Spoleczno-Kulturalnego (Poland) 313
Polak, Emil, Prize (Belgium) 45
Polak en Van Gennep Uitg Mij BV (Netherlands) 280
Polana AG (Switzerland) 371
Polding, The, Press (Australia) 17
Poldner, Axel (Federal Republic of Germany) 167
Policy Studies Institute (United Kingdom) 429
Poligrafa, Ediciones, SA (Spain) 344
Poligraficheskata Promishlenost i Kulturnite Instituti, Sekciya na Bibliotechnite Rabotnitsi pri Centralniya Komitet na Profesionalniya Sŭyuz na Rabotnitsite ot (Bulgaria) 59
Polish Academy of Sciences, Scientific Information Centre (Poland) 314
Polish Authors' Society (Zaiks) Prizes (International Literary Prizes) 479
Polish Bibliography, Editorial Office for (Poland) 311
Polish Ministry of National Defence Prize (Poland) 315
Polish Prime Minister Award for Literature for Children and Youth (Poland) 315
Polish Union of Socialist Youth Prose Award (Poland) 315
Politécnica Moulines, Librería (Venezuela) 454
Politica, Editura (Romania) 321
Political and Social History, Library of (Indonesia) 207
Politikens Forlag A/S (Denmark) 78
Politizdat (Union of Soviet Socialist Republics) 388
polizeiliches Fachschrifttum, Verlag für (Federal Republic of Germany) 154
Polla, Studio Bibliografico Adelmo (Italy) 230
Pollinger, Laurence, Ltd (United Kingdom) 442
Polskie Towarzystwo Wydawców Ksiazek (Poland) 311
Polybooks Ltd (United Kingdom) 429
Polyglott-Verlag Dr Bolte KG (Federal Republic of Germany) 154
Polyglotte Buch- und Schallplatten-Verlag und Vertrieb (Federal Republic of Germany) 154
Polygon Books (United Kingdom) 429
Polygraph Verlag GmbH (Federal Republic of Germany) 154
Polytantric Press (United Kingdom) 429
Polytech Publishers Ltd (United Kingdom) 429
Polyteknisk Boghandel og Forlag (Denmark) 80
Pomaire, Editorial, Ltda (Chile) 63
Pomaire, Editorial, Ltda (Uruguay) 452
Pomaire, Editorial, SA (Argentina) 7
Pomaire, Editorial, SA (Colombia) 66
Pomaire, Editorial, SA (Costa Rica) 68
Pomaire, Editorial, SA (Ecuador) 83
Pomaire, Editorial, SA (Mexico) 267
Pomaire, Editorial, SA (Spain) 344
Pomaire, Editorial, Venezuela SA (Venezuela) 454
Pompidou, Centre Georges, Edition (France) 104
Pomurska založba (Yugoslavia) 458
Pond Press (United Kingdom) 429
Pontificia Universidad, Biblioteca Central de la, Católica del Perú (Peru) 307
Pool Editorial Ltda (Brazil) 54
Poolbeg Press Ltd (Republic of Ireland) 210

Poona Booksellers' & Publishers' Association (India) 185
Poplar Publishing Co Ltd (Japan) 242
Popp, Edition Georg, GmbH & Co (Federal Republic of Germany) 154
Populaires (Switzerland) 371
Popular Army Publishing House (Socialist Republic of Viet Nam) 455
Popular Book Depot (India) 202
Popular Book Store (Philippines) 309
Popular Dogs Publishing Co Ltd (United Kingdom) 429
Popular, Editorial, SA (Spain) 344
Popular Prakashan Pvt Ltd (India) 196
Pordes, H (United Kingdom) 429
Pordes, H, Ltd (United Kingdom) 442
Porgès, Hélène, Prize (France) 113
Porrúa, Ediciones José, Turanzas SA (Spain) 344
Porrúa, Editorial, SA (Mexico) 267
Porrúa, Librería de, Hnos y Cía (Mexico) 269
Porrúa, Librería José, Turanzas SA (Spain) 347
Port Nicholson Press Ltd (New Zealand) 289
Porter-Libros (Spain) 347
Pòrtic, Editorial (Spain) 344
Portico, Editorial (Portugal) 317
Porto Editora Lda (Portugal) 317
Portugal, Livraria, Dias e Andrade Lda (Portugal) 318
Portugalia Editora Lda (Portugal) 317
Possev-Verlag V Gorachek KG (Federal Republic of Germany) 154
Postmarket (Australia) 20
Poth, W, GbR (Federal Republic of Germany) 154
Powszechna Ksiegarnia Wysylkowa (Poland) 313
Poyser, T & A D, Ltd (United Kingdom) 429
Poznańskie, Wydawnictwo (Poland) 313
Pozza, Casa Editrice Neri (Italy) 230
Pozzi, Edizioni Luigi, Srl (Italy) 230
Pra Cha Chang & Co Ltd (Thailand) 380
Prabhat Prakashan (India) 196
'Práca', Vydavateľstvo ROH (Czechoslovakia) 72
Práce (Czechoslovakia) 72
Pracharak Book Club (India) 201
Prachi Prakashan (India) 196
Prachner, Georg (Austria) 28
Prachner, Georg, KG (Austria) 30
Pradnya Paramita (Indonesia) 206
Pradnya Paramita (Indonesia) 206
Prae Pittaya Ltd (Thailand) 380
Praeger Publishers (United Kingdom) 429
Praeger Scientific (United Kingdom) 429
Praepittaya Ltd (Thailand) 381
Praesentverlag Heinz Peter (Federal Republic of Germany) 154
Pragati Prakashan (India) 196
Pragopress (Czechoslovakia) 72
Prague Literary Prize (Czechoslovakia) 74
Prakash Prakashan (India) 196
Prakasham Publications (India) 196
Pramual Sarn Book Centre Ltd (Thailand) 381
Pramuansarn Publishing House (Thailand) 380
Praphansarn Book Centre (Thailand) 380
Prasarnmitr (Thailand) 380
Präsenz-Verlag der Jesus-Bruderschaft (Federal Republic of Germany) 154
Pratiche Editrice Scrl (Italy) 230
Pravda, Nakladatelstvo (Czechoslovakia) 72
Pravda Publishing House (Union of Soviet Socialist Republics) 388
Prawnicze, Wydawnictwo (Poland) 313
Prayer Books (India) 196
Pre-Ecole (Belgium) 40
Pre-School Publishing Co (United Kingdom) 429
Pre-Textos (Spain) 344
Preduzeće Matice Srpske, Izdavačko (Yugoslavia) 458
Preduzeće Sloboda, Izdavačko (Yugoslavia) 458
Prélat, Julien, Sàrl (France) 104
Preller, Gustav, Prize (Republic of South Africa) 335
Premier Book House (Pakistan) 302
Premier, Librerías (Argentina) 8
Premio de Remuneraciones Literarias (Uruguay) 452
Premio Nacional de Literatura (Uruguay) 452
'Prensa', Biblioteca Pública Gratuita de 'La (Argentina) 8
Prensa, Editorial, Española (Spain) 344
Prensa Médica, La, Mexicana (Mexico) 267
Prentice-Hall International (United Kingdom) 429
Prentice-Hall of Australia Pty Ltd (Australia) 18
Prentice-Hall of India Pvt Ltd (India) 196
Prentice-Hall of Japan Inc (Japan) 242
Prentice-Hall of Southeast Asia Pte Ltd (Republic of Singapore) 327
Presbiteriana, Casa Editora (Brazil) 54
Presbyterian Book Depot and Printing Press Ltd (PRESBOOK) (United Republic of Cameroun) 61
Presbyterian Book Depot Ltd (Ghana) 172
Presbyterian Book Depot Ltd (Ghana) 172
Preschool (Belgium) 40
Presença, Editorial (Portugal) 317
Présence Africaine, Société Nouvelle (France) 104
Presencia, Editorial, Ltda (Colombia) 66
President Publishers (Republic of South Africa) 331

President's Award for Pride of Performance (Pakistan) 304
Press Agency (Kuwait) 253
Press Department, Library of the (Afghanistan) 1
Press' Förlag (Sweden) 356
Press Porcepic (United Kingdom) 429
Presse-Auto-Conseil (France) 105
Presse-Grosso (Federal Republic of Germany) 121
Presse, La, Internationale (Belgium) 40
Presse, Verlag, Informations Agentur GmbH (PIAG) (Federal Republic of Germany) 154
Presses Africaines, Les (Zaire) 462
Presses agronomiques de Gembloux ASBL (Belgium) 40
Presses Centrales Lausanne SA (Switzerland) 371
Presses de la Cité, Les (France) 105
Presses de la Connaissance, Les (Switzerland) 371
Presses de la Fondation Nationale des Sciences Politiques (France) 105
Presses de la Renaissance (France) 105
Presses d'Ile-de-France, Les, Sàrl (France) 105
Presses d'Or (France) 109
Presses, Les, Africaines (Upper Volta) 451
Presses, Librairie des, universitaires (Zaire) 462
Presses Monastiques, Les (France) 105
Presses universitaires de Bruxelles ASBL (Belgium) 40
Presses universitaires de Bruxelles, Librairie des (Belgium) 42
Presses Universitaires de France (PUF) (France) 105
Presses Universitaires de Grenoble (France) 105
Presses universitaires de Liège ASBL (Belgium) 40
Presses Universitaires de Lille (PUL) (France) 105
Presses Universitaires de Louvain-la-Neuve (Belgium) 40
Presses Universitaires de Lyon (France) 105
Presses Universitaires de Namur (Belgium) 40
Presses Universitaires de Nancy (France) 105
Presses Universitaires du Zaïre et l'Office du Livre (PUZ) (Zaire) 462
Pressler, Guido, Verlag (Federal Republic of Germany) 154
Prestel Verlag (Federal Republic of Germany) 154
Prestige Booksellers (Kenya) 249
Preston Corporation Sdn Bhd (Malaysia) 260
Pretoria Boekhandel (Pty) Ltd (Republic of South Africa) 331
Pretoria Public Library (Republic of South Africa) 334
Preussler, Helmut, Verlag (Federal Republic of Germany) 154
Price Milburn & Co Ltd (New Zealand) 289
Price, Norman (United Kingdom) 429
Pride Publications (United Kingdom) 429
Primary Communications Research Centre (United Kingdom) 429
Primary Education (Australia) 18
Primor, Editora, Ltda (Brazil) 54
Primor, Gráfica Editora, Ltda (Brazil) 54
Primorski Tisk (Yugoslavia) 458
Prince Pierre de Monaco Prize for Literature (International Literary Prizes) 479
Princeton University Press (United Kingdom) 429
Prins en Prins (Netherlands) 283
Prinsen-Geerlings, Reina, Prize (Netherlands) 285
Printox (India) 196
Prior, George, Associated Publishers Ltd (United Kingdom) 429
Priory Press Ltd (United Kingdom) 430
Príroda, vydavateľstvo kníh a časopisov (Czechoslovakia) 72
Prism Books (Poetry Society of Australia) (Australia) 18
Prism Press (United Kingdom) 430
Prisma, Bokförlaget, AB (Sweden) 356
Prisma, Het, NV (Belgium) 40
Prisma Verlag GmbH (Federal Republic of Germany) 154
Prisma-Verlag Zenner und Gürchott (German Democratic Republic) 118
Prithviraj Memorial Award (India) 204
Priuli e Verlucca, Editori (Italy) 230
Privat, Editions Edouard, SA (France) 105
Private Libraries Association (PLA) (International Organizations) 469
Privredni Pregled (Yugoslavia) 458
Prix Littéraire Mobil (Ivory Coast) 237
Prizes for Manuscripts for Juveniles (Pakistan) 304
Pro Civitate (Belgium) 40
Pro Juventute, Verlag (Switzerland) 371
Pro Media Literaturvertrieb GmbH (Federal Republic of Germany) 168
Pro Rege Press Ltd (Republic of South Africa) 331
Pro Schola, Editions (Switzerland) 371
Problem-Verlag (Switzerland) 371
Procure, La (Belgium) 40
Procure scolaire (Zaire) 462
Prodim SPRL (Belgium) 40
Production et Diffusion medico-techniques SPRL (Belgium) 40
Professional Publications (New Zealand) 289
Profil, Nakladatelství (Czechoslovakia) 72

Profile Books Ltd (United Kingdom) 430
Profizdat (Union of Soviet Socialist Republics) 388
Profizdat, Izdatelstvo (Bulgaria) 58
Progrès, Editions le (Egypt) 84
Progreso, Editorial, SA (Mexico) 267
Progress (Thailand) 380
Progress Press (Malta) 262
Progress Publishers (Union of Soviet Socialist Republics) 388
Progressive Corporation Pvt Ltd (India) 196
Projecta (UK) Ltd (United Kingdom) 430
Proklama (Sweden) 356
Proklama Pocketbokklubb (Sweden) 358
Prolam SRL (Ediciones Economia y Empresa) (Argentina) 7
Prometeo, Editorial (Spain) 344
Prometheus Publishing Co (Zambia) 463
Promoboek (Netherlands) 280
Promoción Cultural, Ediciones de, SA (Spain) 344
Promoción Popular Cristiana (Spain) 344
Promoculture, Librairie (Grand Duchy of Luxembourg) 257
Promotion Littéraire (France) 109
Proost, Henri, & Cie (Belgium) 40
Pröpster, Albert (Federal Republic of Germany) 154
Propyläen Verlag (Federal Republic of Germany) 154
Prose Poétique Prize (France) 113
Prospice (United Kingdom) 430
'Prosveshchenie', Izdatelstvo (Union of Soviet Socialist Republics) 388
Prosveta (Yugoslavia) 458
Prosveta (Yugoslavia) 460
Prosveta (Yugoslavia) 460
Prosvetno Delo (Yugoslavia) 458
Prosvjeta (Yugoslavia) 458
Prosvjeta (Novinsko-izdavačko i Štamparsko) (Yugoslavia) 458
Protestante, Librairie (Benin) 45
Protestantse Stichting tot Bevordering van het Bibliotheekwezen en de Lectuurvoorlichting in Nederland (Netherlands) 285
Proteus Books Ltd (United Kingdom) 430
Proton Editora Ltda (Brazil) 54
Provence, Librairie de (France) 109
Provincial Book Depot (Bangladesh) 32
Provincial Booksellers Fairs Association Annual Book Awards (United Kingdom) 450
Provincial Library (Bangladesh) 32
Proyección, Editorial, SRL (Argentina) 7
Prugg Verlag (Austria) 28
Prva Književna Komuna (Yugoslavia) 458
Psyche, Bookclub (Japan) 244
Psychic Press Ltd (United Kingdom) 430
Psychologie, Verlag für, Dr C J Hogrefe (Federal Republic of Germany) 154
Psychologie, Verlag für, Dr C J Hogrefe (Switzerland) 371
Psychosophische Gesellschaft (Switzerland) 371
Psykologiförlaget AB (Sweden) 356
Publi-Union (France) 105
Public Lending Right Office (United Kingdom) 391
Public Lending Right Scheme (Australia) 10
Public Lending Right Scheme (Australia) 21
Public Libraries Board (Uganda) 386
Public Library (Afghanistan) 1
Public Library (Barbados) 33
Public Library (Jordan) 247
Public Library (Jordan) 247
Public Library, Central, Dacca (Bangladesh) 32
Public Organization, The, for Books and Scientific Appliances (Egypt) 83
Public Organization, The, for Books and Scientific Appliances (Egypt) 84
Public Record Office (United Kingdom) 445
Public Record Office of Ireland (Republic of Ireland) 211
Publicaciones Cultural SA (Mexico) 267
Publicaciones Españolas SA (Venezuela) 454
Publicaciones Marcombo SA (Mexico) 267
Publicações Cientificas, Editora de, Ltda (Brazil) 54
Publication Board (India) 196
Publications & Information Directorate (India) 196
Publications Appeal Board (Republic of South Africa) 328
Publications Central Africa (Zimbabwe) 465
Publications de L'Ecole Moderne Française (PEMF) (France) 109
Publications Filmées d'Art et d'Histoire (France) 105
Publications International (Nigeria) Ltd (Nigeria) 295
Publications Orientalistes de France (POF) (France) 105
Publiexport (Spain) 336
Publishers' & Booksellers' Association of Andhra Pradesh (India) 185
Publishers' and Booksellers' Association of Bengal (India) 185
Publishers' and Booksellers' Association of Thailand (Thailand) 380
Publishers' and Booksellers' Guild (India) 185
Publishers Association (United Kingdom) 391

Publishers' Association for Cultural Exchange (Japan) 238
Publishers' Association of South India (India) 185
Publisher's Bookshop (Poland) 313
Publisher's Club (Poland) 313
Publishers' Information Card Services (United Kingdom) 391
Publishers International (Pakistan) 302
Publishers' Overseas Circle (United Kingdom) 391
Publishers Publicity Circle (United Kingdom) 391
Publishers United Ltd (Pakistan) 303
Publishing Council of the Academy of Sciences of the USSR (Union of Soviet Socialist Republics) 386
Publishing Department (People's Republic of China) 64
Publitoria (Pty) Ltd (Republic of South Africa) 331
Pucci, Christa (Italy) 234
Pudoc, Centre for Agricultural Publishing and Documentation (Netherlands) 280
Pueblo, Editorial, y Educación (Cuba) 69
Pueyo, Librería Pedro (Spain) 347
Puffin (Australia) 18
Puffin Books (United Kingdom) 430
Puffin, The, Club (United Kingdom) 444
Pugliese, Lucio, Editore (Italy) 230
Pula Press (Republic of South Africa) 331
Pungolo, Edizioni Il, Verde di G Massarelli (Italy) 231
Punjab Advisory Board for Books Prizes (Pakistan) 304
Punjab Public Library (Pakistan) 303
Punjab State University Textbook Board (India) 196
Punjab Text Board (Pakistan) 304
Punjab University Library (Pakistan) 303
Punjabi Publishers' Association (India) 185
Punjabi Pustak Bhandar (India) 197
Punktum (Switzerland) 375
Punnoose, K P, Communications Co (India) 201
Purnell Books (United Kingdom) 430
Pushtu Toulana, Afghan Academy (Afghanistan) 1
Pustet, Anton (Federal Republic of Germany) 155
Pustet, Universitätsverlag Anton (Austria) 28
Pustet, Verlag Friedrich (Federal Republic of Germany) 155
Puthigar Limited (Bangladesh) 32
Putnam & Co Ltd (United Kingdom) 430
Putnam Awards (International Literary Prizes) 479
Pygmalion, Editions, — Gérard Watelet (France) 105

Q E D Publishing Ltd (United Kingdom) 430
Q Press Ltd (United Kingdom) 430
Qaumi Kutab Khana (Pakistan) 303
Qinghua daxue tushuguan (People's Republic of China) 64
Quadragono (Italy) 231
Quaid-i-Azam University (Pakistan) 303
Quaker Home Service (United Kingdom) 430
Quartet Books Australia Pty Ltd (Australia) 18
Quartet Books Ltd (United Kingdom) 430
Quartier-Latin (Monaco) 270
Quartier-Latin, Librairie (French Polynesia) 115
Quarto Publishing Ltd (United Kingdom) 430
Quasar, Edizioni (Italy) 231
Quatre Chemins, Société (France) 105
Queen Anne Press Ltd (United Kingdom) 430
Queen Victoria Memorial Library (Zimbabwe) 465
Queen's, The, Gold Medal for Poetry (United Kingdom) 450
Queensland Book Depot (Australia) 20
Queensway Bookshop and Stores Ltd (Ghana) 172
Quell-Verlag (Federal Republic of Germany) 155
Quelle Press (Federal Republic of Germany) 167
Quelle und Meyer Verlag GmbH & Co (Federal Republic of Germany) 155
Quentin Press Ltd (United Kingdom) 430
Querido's, Em, Uitgeverij BV (Netherlands) 280
Queriniana, Editrice (Italy) 231
Queromón Editores SA (Mexico) 267
Quevedo, Ediciones, Sacif (Argentina) 7
Quill Publishing Ltd (United Kingdom) 430
Quiller Press Ltd (United Kingdom) 430
Quillet, Librairie Aristide, SA (France) 105
Quintero, Alvarez, Prize (Spain) 349
Quintet Publishing Ltd (United Kingdom) 430
Quinti, Officina Edizioni di Aldo (Italy) 231
Quisqueyana, Editora Colegial, SA (Dominican Republic) 82
Quisqueyana, Editora Colegial, SA (Dominican Republic) 82
Qurinna Library (Libya) 256
Qvist, Erik, Bokhandel A/S (Norway) 300

'R', Editions, Société Civile Typo, Graphique et Littéraire (France) 105
R A I, Edizioni, Radiotelevisione Italiana (ERI) SpA (Italy) 231
R A Verlag (Switzerland) 371
R E C T A Foldex (France) 105
R E M I (France) 105
R I B A Publications Ltd (United Kingdom) 430
R K W (Federal Republic of Germany) 155
R N A Major Award (United Kingdom) 450
R O L, Ediciones, SA (Spain) 344
R S W (Robotnicza Spóldzielnia Wydawnicza) 'Prasa-Ksiazka-Ruch' (Poland) 311
R T L (Radio Télé Luxembourg)/Poésie 1 Prize (France) 114
R V (Federal Republic of Germany) 155
Rabaul Newsagency (Papua New Guinea) 305
Rabe Verlag Zurich (Switzerland) 371
Rabe Verlag Zurich (Switzerland) 375
Rabén och Sjögren, AB, Bokförlag (Sweden) 356
Rache, André De (Belgium) 40
Rad, Izdavačka Organizacija (Yugoslavia) 459
Radha Krishna Prakashan (India) 197
Radha Soami Satsang Beas (India) 197
Radia i Telewizji, Wydawnictwo (Poland) 313
Radiant Publishers (India) 197
Radical Book Club (India) 201
Radical Reprints (United Kingdom) 430
'Radio i Svyaz', Izdatelstvo (Union of Soviet Socialist Republics) 388
Radio, Société des Editions (France) 105
Radius-Verlag GmbH (Federal Republic of Germany) 155
Radnička Štampa (Yugoslavia) 459
Raduga Publishers (Union of Soviet Socialist Republics) 388
Raeber AG Luzern (Switzerland) 371
Raghav, Ranghey, Award (India) 204
Rahman Brothers (Bangladesh) 32
Railway Publications Ltd (United Kingdom) 430
Railway Publishing House (Democratic People's Republic of Korea) 250
Railway, The, Book Club (United Kingdom) 444
Rainbird, The, Publishing Group (United Kingdom) 430
Rainbow Books (United Kingdom) 430
Rainer Verlag GmbH (Federal Republic of Germany) 155
Rajasthan Hindi Granth Academy (India) 197
Rajasthan Pustak Vyavasayee Sangh (India) 186
Rajasthan Sahitya Akademi Awards (India) 204
Rajesh Publications (India) 197
Rajhans Prakashan Mandir (India) 197
Rajkamal Prakashan Pvt Ltd (India) 197
Rajneesh Foundation (India) 197
Rajpal & Sons (India) 197
Rakennuskirja Oy (Finland) 88
Ram Prasad & Sons (India) 197
Ramakrishna, Sri, Math (India) 197
Ramboro Enterprises Ltd (United Kingdom) 430
Ramboro Enterprises Ltd (United Kingdom) 442
Ramdohr, Dr, KG (Federal Republic of Germany) 155
Ramdor Publishing Co Ltd (Israel) 216
Ramos, Edições António (Portugal) 317
Ramsay, Editions (France) 105
Ramsay, The, Head Press (United Kingdom) 431
Ramsden, Barbara, Award (Australia) 23
Ramsey Library (Isle of Man) 212
Randi, Libreria all' Accademia snc di, Pietro (Italy) 234
Randow, Dokument und Analyse Verlag Bogislaw von (Federal Republic of Germany) 155
Ranner, Verlag Dr Herta (Austria) 28
'Rast Gufter' Press (Pakistan) 303
Rastogi Publications (India) 197
Rational Bookshops (Nigeria) 296
Rationalisierungs-Kuratorium der Deutschen Wirtschaft eV (RKW) (Federal Republic of Germany) 155
Rationalist Press Association (United Kingdom) 431
Ratna Pustak Bhandar (Nepal) 272
Ratna Pustak Bhandar (Nepal) 272
Ratnabharati (India) 197
Rau, Walter, Verlag (Federal Republic of Germany) 155
Rauch, Karl, Verlag KG (Federal Republic of Germany) 155
Rauhen Hauses, Agentur des, Verlag GmbH (Federal Republic of Germany) 155
Rauriser Encouragement Award (Austria) 31
Rauriser Literature Prize (Austria) 31
Rautenberg, Gerhard, Druckerei und Verlag GmbH & Co KG (Federal Republic of Germany) 155
Rav Kook Institute (Israel) 216
Ravan Press (Pty) Ltd (Republic of South Africa) 331
Ravensburger Graphische Betriebe Otto Maier GmbH (Federal Republic of Germany) 155
Ravensburger Verlag GmbH (Federal Republic of Germany) 155
Ravenstein Verlag GmbH (Federal Republic of Germany) 155
Rayas, G (Greece) 175
Razon, Editora La (Dominican Republic) 82

Read-a-Book Club (Zambia) 463
Read On! Club (United Kingdom) 444
Readers' Book Shop (Jamaica) 237
Readers Choice (United Kingdom) 444
Readers Club (Czechoslovakia) 73
Readers' Digest AB (Sweden) 358
Reader's Digest Condensed Book Services Pty Ltd (Australia) 20
Reader's Digest SA (Belgium) 40
Reader's Digest, Selecciones del, (Iberia) SA (Spain) 344
Reader's Digest, Sélection du, SA (France) 105
Reader's Digest Services Pty Ltd (Australia) 18
Reader's Digest, The, Association Ltd (United Kingdom) 431
Reader's Digest, The, of Japan Limited (Japan) 242
Readers Union Book Society (United Kingdom) 444
Readers Union Ltd (United Kingdom) 444
Real Academia de Córdoba, de Ciencias, Bellas Letras y Nobles Artes (Spain) 348
Real Academia Sevillana de Buenas Letras (Spain) 348
Real Biblioteca de San Lorenzo de El Escorial, Madrid (Spain) 348
Réalisations pour l'Enseignement Multilingue International (REMI) (France) 106
Realizações Artis Lda (Portugal) 317
Recalde, Librería (Nicaragua) 292
Recht und Gesellschaft, Verlag für, AG (Switzerland) 371
Recht und Wirtschaft, Verlagsgesellschaft, mbH (Federal Republic of Germany) 155
Reclam, Philipp, Jun Verlag GmbH (Federal Republic of Germany) 155
Reclam, Verlag Philipp, jun (German Democratic Republic) 118
'Recognition Prize' (Austria) 31
Record, Distribuidora, de Serviços de Imprensa SA (Brazil) 54
Red House Post, The (United Kingdom) 444
Red/Studio Redazionale SRL (Italy) 231
Redcliffe Press Ltd (United Kingdom) 431
Redhouse Kitabevi (Turkey) 385
Redhouse Press (Turkey) 384
Rediviva, Bokförlaget, Facsimileförlaget (Sweden) 356
Reed, A H & A W, Ltd Publishers (New Zealand) 289
Reed, A H & A W, Pty Ltd (Australia) 18
Reed, A W, Memorial Book Award (New Zealand) 291
Reed, Thomas, Publications Ltd (United Kingdom) 431
Reemst, van (Netherlands) 281
Reeves, Northcott, Publishers (New Zealand) 289
Reforma, Editorial y Librería La (Puerto Rico) 319
Regain, Editions (Monaco) 270
Regal Publishing Co (Philippines) 309
Regenbogen-Verlag (Switzerland) 371
Regimprensa SARL (Portugal) 318
Regina Medal (International Literary Prizes) 479
Regional Library for the North (Malawi) 258
Regional Library for the South (Malawi) 258
Regional Literature Awards (Pakistan) 304
Regra, A, do Jogo (Portugal) 317
Reich Luzern, Kinderbuchverlag, AG (Switzerland) 371
Reich Verlag AG (Switzerland) 371
Reichert, Dr Ludwig, Verlag (Federal Republic of Germany) 155
Reichl, Otto, Verlag (Federal Republic of Germany) 155
Reichmann, Livraria Científica Ernesto, Ltda (Brazil) 56
Reidel, D, Publishing Co (Netherlands) 281
Reim, Verlag Knut (Federal Republic of Germany) 155
Reinart Uitgaven (Belgium) 40
Reinhardt, Ernst, GmbH & Co Verlag (Federal Republic of Germany) 155
Reinhardt, Max, Ltd (United Kingdom) 431
Reinhardt, Verlag Friedrich, AG (Switzerland) 371
Reinheimer, Verlag Wilhelm G (Federal Republic of Germany) 155
Reise- und Verkehrsverlag GmbH (RV) (Federal Republic of Germany) 155
Reiter, Elisabeth (Austria) 29
Reitzel, C A, A/S (Denmark) 78
Reitzel, C A, A/S (Denmark) 80
Reitzels, Hans, Forlag A/S (Denmark) 78
Reka-Or Production and Publishing Ltd (Israel) 216
Rekha Prakashan (India) 197
Rekreaboek (Netherlands) 281
Religious and Moral Education Press (United Kingdom) 431
Religious Life Review Book Club (Republic of Ireland) 211
Religious Revival Organization (Thailand) 380
Remaja Karya (Indonesia) 206
Rembrandt Verlag GmbH (Federal Republic of Germany) 155
Remzi Kitabevi (Turkey) 385
Renacimiento, Librería, SA de CV (El Salvador) 85
Renaissance, La, du Livre SA (Belgium) 40
Renaitour, J-M, Prize (France) 114
Renard, Fondation André (Belgium) 40
Rencontre, Editions, SA (Switzerland) 371
Renner, Verlag Klaus G (Federal Republic of Germany) 155

Rentrop, Verlag Norman (Federal Republic of Germany) 156
Rentsch, Eugen, Verlag AG (Switzerland) 371
Representaciones y Servicios de Ingeniería SA (Mexico) 267
Representative Church Body Library (Republic of Ireland) 211
Republički Zavod za Unapredivanje Školstva (Yugoslavia) 459
Research Library on African Affairs (Ghana) 173
Research Publishing Co (United Kingdom) 431
Researchco (India) 197
Resenha, Editora, Tributaria Ltda (Brazil) 54
Residenz Verlag (Austria) 28
Retail Book, Stationery and Allied Trades Employees Association (United Kingdom) 391
Retief, Daan, Publishers (Pty) Ltd (Republic of South Africa) 332
Reus, Editorial, SA (Spain) 344
Revelation Awards (Poetry and Prose) (Portugal) 319
Reverté, Editora, Ltda (Brazil) 54
Reverté, Editorial, Mexicana SA (Mexico) 267
Reverté, Editorial, SA (Spain) 344
Reverté, Editorial, Venezolana SA (Venezuela) 454
Review Publications Pty Ltd (Australia) 18
Revista de Occidente SA (Spain) 344
Revista, Editora, dos Tribunais Ltda (Brazil) 54
Revue, La, nouvelle ASBL (Belgium) 40
Rex Book Store (Malaysia) 261
Rex Bookstore (Brunei) 58
Rex-Verlag (Switzerland) 371
Reyes, Alfonso, Prize (International Literary Prizes) 479
Reyes, Librería Universitaria Jose T (Honduras) 178
Reynaud, Jean, Prize (France) 114
Rezzonico, Edizioni Raimondo (Switzerland) 371
Rheingauer Verlagsgesellschaft mbH (Federal Republic of Germany) 156
Rheinland-Palatinate Prize (Federal Republic of Germany) 171
Rheinland-Verlag GmbH (Federal Republic of Germany) 156
Rhodos, International Science and Art Publishers (Denmark) 78
Rhys, John Llewelyn, Memorial Prize (International Literary Prizes) 479
Rialp, Ediciones, SA (Spain) 344
Riband Books Ltd (United Kingdom) 431
Riccardiana, Biblioteca (Italy) 234
Ricci, Franco Maria (France) 106
Ricci, Franco Maria, Editore (Italy) 231
Ricciardi, Riccardo, Editore SpA (Italy) 231
Riccio, Edizioni del, Sas di G Bernardi (Italy) 231
Richards Literary Agency (New Zealand) 290
Richards, Ray, Publisher (New Zealand) 289
Richmond, The, Publishing Co Ltd (United Kingdom) 431
Ricordi Americana SAEC (Argentina) 7
Ricordi, G e C, SpA (Italy) 231
Ridder, Peter de, Press BV (Netherlands) 281
Rideel, Editora, Ltda (Brazil) 54
Rider & Co (United Kingdom) 431
Riederer, Dr, Verlag GmbH (Federal Republic of Germany) 156
Riemaecker, De, Uitgeverij (Belgium) 40
Rigby Bookshop (Australia) 20
Rigby International & Lansdowne International Pty Ltd (United Kingdom) 431
Rigby Publishers Ltd (Australia) 18
Right Way Books (United Kingdom) 431
Rigsarkivet (Denmark) 80
Rijksmuseum Meermanno-Westreenianum/Museum van het Boek (Netherlands) 284
Rijksuniversiteit, Bibliotheek der (Netherlands) 284
Rijksuniversiteit te Gent, Bibliotheek van de (Belgium) 43
Rijksuniversiteit te Groningen, Bibliotheek der (Netherlands) 284
Rijksuniversiteit te Leiden, Bibliotheek der (Netherlands) 284
Ríkisútgáfa Námsbóka (Iceland) 184
Riksarkivet (Norway) 300
Riksarkivet (Sweden) 359
Riksbibliotektjenesten (Norway) 301
Rilindja (Yugoslavia) 459
Ringier & Co AG (Switzerland) 371
Ringier/Heering-Verlag GmbH (Federal Republic of Germany) 156
Rio Grafica e Editora SA (Brazil) 54
Risosha Ltd (Japan) 242
Ristin Voitto ry (Finland) 88
Rithöfundasamband Islands (Iceland) 183
Ritzau KG Verlag Zeit und Eisenbahn (Federal Republic of Germany) 156
Riuniti, Editori (Italy) 231
Rivadeneyra Prizes (Spain) 349
Rivers Press (United Kingdom) 431
Rivière, Yves (France) 106
Riyadh Modern Bookshop (Saudi Arabia) 323
Rizzoli Editore SpA (Italy) 231

Rizzoli Editore SpA (Italy) 234
Rizzoli, Libreria, della Rizzoli Editore SpA (Italy) 234
Rizzoli, Libreria Internazionale, SRL (Italy) 234
Roberge Prizes (France) 114
Robert, Dictionnaire Le (France) 106
Robert, Editions E, L'Ecole et la Famille (France) 106
Roberts Stationery Ltd (Barbados) 33
Robertson, Martin (United Kingdom) 431
Robin Books (Australia) 18
Robin Books (United Kingdom) 431
Robinson & Watkins Books Ltd (United Kingdom) 431
Robinson, J, & Co (Israel) 217
Robson Books Ltd (United Kingdom) 431
Rocha, M Moreira Soares, Lda (Portugal) 318
Roche, Editiones (Switzerland) 371
Rocher, Les Editions du (Monaco) 270
Rocheron, Albéric, Foundation Prize (France) 114
Rochester Press (United Kingdom) 431
Rochus-Verlag (Federal Republic of Germany) 156
Rocom (Switzerland) 372
Rodale Press Ltd (United Kingdom) 431
Rodana Verlag (Switzerland) 372
Röderberg-Verlag GmbH (Federal Republic of Germany) 156
Rodopi, Editions, bv (Netherlands) 281
Rodríguez, Librería (Argentina) 7
Rodríguez, Librería (Argentina) 8
Roebuck Books (Australia) 18
Roeland Kamer Fonds VZW (Belgium) 40
Roerdomp, De (Belgium) 40
Rogan, Barbara, Literary Agency (Israel) 217
Rogate, Libreria Editrice (Italy) 231
Rogers, Deborah, Ltd (United Kingdom) 442
Rogner und Bernhard GmbH & Co Verlags KG (Federal Republic of Germany) 156
Rohan, Duchess of, Foundation Prize (France) 114
Rohr, Buchhandlung Hans (Switzerland) 375
Rohr, Hans, Buchhandlung und Antiquariat zum Oberdorf AG (Switzerland) 372
Roitman, Lev, Verlag (Federal Republic of Germany) 156
Rojas, Pablo, Paz Prize (Argentina) 9
Rojas, Ricardo, Prize (Argentina) 9
Rökkur, bókaútgáfan (Iceland) 184
Roli Books International (India) 197
Rolnicze i Leśne, Państwowe Wydawnictwo (Poland) 313
Romankeur (Republic of South Africa) 333
Romano, Dott Prof Tommaso (Italy) 231
Romantic Novelists' Association (United Kingdom) 447
Rombach und Co GmbH, Verlag & Druckhaus (Federal Republic of Germany) 156
Rombaldi, Editions, SA (France) 106
Romen (Netherlands) 281
Romero, Litografía A, SA (Spain) 344
Ronald, George (United Kingdom) 431
Rooney Prize (Republic of Ireland) 212
Roorkee Press (India) 197
Rosa, Editora Ana (Brazil) 54
Rosda (Indonesia) 206
Rose, Barry, (Publishers) Ltd (United Kingdom) 431
Rose-Jordan Ltd (United Kingdom) 431
Rose of French Poets Prize (International Literary Prizes) 479
Rose-Verlag und Edition Rose-Verlag (Federal Republic of Germany) 156
Rosenberg e Sellier Editori in Torino (Italy) 231
Rosenberg e Sellier SRL (Italy) 234
Rosenheimer Verlagshaus Alfred Förg GmbH & Co KG (Federal Republic of Germany) 156
Rosenkilde og Bagger (Denmark) 78
Rosenwald, Guide (France) 106
Rosepierre SA (Switzerland) 372
Rosmini, Libreria, di R Maly (Italy) 234
Ross, Benton, Publishers Ltd (New Zealand) 289
Ross, Libreria (Argentina) 8
Rossel Edition SA (Belgium) 40
Rossel, Victor, Prize (Belgium) 45
Rostock, Wilhelm-Pieck-Universität, Universitätsbibliothek (German Democratic Republic) 119
Rotapfel-Verlag AG (Switzerland) 372
Rotbuch Verlag GmbH (Federal Republic of Germany) 156
Roter Morgen, Verlag (Federal Republic of Germany) 156
Roter Stern, Verlag (Federal Republic of Germany) 156
Röth, Erich, -Verlag, Kassel (Federal Republic of Germany) 156
Roth et Sauter SA (Switzerland) 372
Rother, Bergverlag Rudolf (Federal Republic of Germany) 156
Rotten-Verlags AG (Switzerland) 372
Rotterdam University Press (Netherlands) 281
Rötzer, E, Verlag (Austria) 29
Roucoules Foundation Grand Prize for Poetry (France) 114
Roudil, Editions (France) 106
Rouff, Editions, SA (France) 106
Rouge et Or, G P (France) 106
Rougery, La (France) 106
Roundabout (United Kingdom) 431

Routledge & Kegan Paul PLC (United Kingdom) 431
Rowohlt Taschenbuch Verlag GmbH (Federal Republic of Germany) 156
Roxby & Lindsey Holdings Ltd (United Kingdom) 431
Roy, K K, (Pvt) Ltd (India) 197
Roy, Publications (France) 106
Royal Afghanistan Press Department (Afghanistan) 1
Royal Book Co (Pakistan) 303
Royal Book Co (Pakistan) 303
Royal College of Surgeons in Ireland Library (Republic of Ireland) 211
Royal Dublin Society Library (Republic of Ireland) 211
Royal Gazette Ltd (Bermuda) 46
Royal Institute of Technology Library (Sweden) 359
Royal Literary Fund (United Kingdom) 447
Royal Palace, Library of the (Afghanistan) 1
Royal Prize (Sweden) 360
Royal Society of Literature of the United Kingdom (United Kingdom) 447
Royal Society of South Africa Library (Republic of South Africa) 334
Royal Society, The, of Chemistry (United Kingdom) 431
Ruamsarn (1977) Co Ltd (Thailand) 380
Ruamsarn (1977) Co Ltd (Thailand) 381
Rubber Research Institute of Malaysia Library (Malaysia) 261
Rubiños, Libreria (Spain) 347
Rubinstein, E (Israel) 216
Rübsamen, Verlag Wilhelm C (Federal Republic of Germany) 156
Ruedo Ibérico (France) 106
Ruhland Verlag (Federal Republic of Germany) 156
Runa Press (Republic of Ireland) 210
Rune Forlag (Norway) 299
Runge, W, Verlag (Federal Republic of Germany) 156
Rungvit Sawarn-Apichon (Thailand) 380
Rupa & Co (India) 197
Rupa & Co (India) 202
Rural, The, Library (Isle of Man) 212
Rusconi Libri (Italy) 231
Russell, George, (AE) Memorial Awards (Republic of Ireland) 212
Russky Yazyk (Union of Soviet Socialist Republics) 388
Rustem, K, & Bro (Cyprus) 70
Rütten und Loening, Verlag, Berlin (German Democratic Republic) 118
Rütten und Loening Verlag GmbH (Switzerland) 372
Ruy Diaz SAEIC (Argentina) 7
ruže, Nakladatelství (Czechoslovakia) 72
Rwandaises, Editions (Rwanda) 323
Ryborsch, VWK, GmbH (Federal Republic of Germany) 156
Rylands, John, University Library of Manchester (United Kingdom) 445
Ryosho-Fukyu-Kai Co Ltd (Japan) 242

S A Cultural Holdings (Pty) Ltd (Republic of South Africa) 332
S A D E, Medalla de Oro de la, (Sociedad Argentina de Escritores) (Argentina) 9
S A D E (Sociedad Argentina de Escritores) (Argentina) 3
S A G E P (Italy) 231
S A G E Publications Ltd (United Kingdom) 431
S A I E Editrice (Italy) 231
S A Kultuurbeleggings (Republic of South Africa) 332
S A M-förlaget (Sweden) 356
S A R P E (Spain) 344
S A S S-Verlagsgesellschaft mbH und Co KG (Federal Republic of Germany) 156
S B I (Switzerland) 360
S C M Press Ltd (United Kingdom) 432
S C O D E (Italy) 231
S E C A Codes Rousseau (France) 106
S E C F — Editions Radio (France) 106
S E D E S (France) 106
S E I (Società Editrice Internationale) (Italy) 231
S E L T A (International Organizations) 469
S E M I C (Sweden) 356
S E N H A, Société d'Exploitation des Nouveaux Humanoïdes Associés (France) 106
S E S I (Switzerland) 360
S I A D Edizioni SRL (Italy) 231
S I M E P SA (France) 106
S I S A R Edizioni (Società italiana stampati affini reclame) SpA (Italy) 231
S L A M (France) 90
S L E S R (Switzerland) 360
S M D, Uitgeverij, BV (Spruyt, Van Mantgem en De Does) (Netherlands) 281
S M E R Diffusion (Morocco) 271
S N-Verlag, Salzburger Nachrichten Verlags GmbH & Co KG (Austria) 28
S N E D, Librairie, (Société nationale d'Edition et de Diffusion) (Algeria) 2

S N L (France) 106
S N T L-Nakladatelství technické literatury (Czechoslovakia) 72
S O I, Verlag, (Schweizerisches Ost-Institut) (Switzerland) 372
S O S, Editions, (Editions du Secours Catholique) (France) 106
S P C K (The Society for Promoting Christian Knowledge) (United Kingdom) 432
S P E L D (France) 106
S P K K (Spoločnosť priateľov' krásnych kníh) (Czechoslovakia) 73
S R P (United Kingdom) 432
S T E M-Mucchi (Società Tipografica Editrice Modenese) (Italy) 231
S T L Books (United Kingdom) 432
S T M (International Organizations) 469
S T P Distributors Sdn Bhd (Republic of Singapore) 327
S U D E L (Société Universitaire d'Editions et de Librairie) (France) 106
S U N socialistische Uitgeverij Nijmegen (Netherlands) 281
S Z O T Prizes (Hungary) 183
Sa Tu-Thu Dich-Thuat Va An-Loat (Socialist Republic of Viet Nam) 455
Sa Tu-Thu Dich-Thuat Va An-loat (Socialist Republic of Viet Nam) 455
Saar SRL (Italy) 231
Saarbrücker Druckerei, S D V, und Verlag GmbH (Federal Republic of Germany) 156
Sabah State Library (Malaysia) 261
Sabatelli, Casa Editrice Liguria di Norberto (Italy) 232
Sabe U (Burma) 60
Sabzerou, Shahrokh (Iran) 207
Sachs, Nelly, Prize (Federal Republic of Germany) 171
Sächsische Landesbibliothek (German Democratic Republic) 119
Sadan Publishing House Ltd (Israel) 216
Sadko SA (Spain) 344
Sadoveanu', Biblioteca Municipala 'Mihail (Romania) 322
Saeed, H M, Co (Pakistan) 303
Saera Shobo (Librairie Çà et Là) (Japan) 242
Saffier, Klub (Republic of South Africa) 333
Safran, Sheri, Associates (UK) Ltd (United Kingdom) 442
Saga Literaria SL (Spain) 347
Saga Publishing Co (Iceland) 184
Saggiatore, Il, SpA (Italy) 232
Sagi, Victor, Servicios Editoriales (Spain) 344
Sagittaire, Les Editions du (France) 106
Sagner, Verlag Otto (Federal Republic of Germany) 156
Sahal, Kanhaiyalal, Award (India) 204
Sahayogi Prakashan (Nepal) 272
Sahitya Akademi (India) 203
Sahitya Akademi Awards (India) 204
Sahitya Akademi Library (India) 202
Sahitya Bhawan Pvt Ltd (India) 197
Sahitya Pravarthaka Benefit Fund Awards (India) 204
Sahitya Pravarthaka Co-operative Society Ltd (India) 197
Sahitya Samsad (India) 197
Saint-André, Publications de (Belgium) 40
Saint Andrew Press (United Kingdom) 432
Saint-Augustin, Société de l'Oeuvre (Switzerland) 372
Saint-Cricq-Theis Prize (France) 114
Saint-Exupery, Centre culturel, Bibliothèque (Mauritania) 263
Saint-Genois Prize (Belgium) 45
Saint George & Dragon Press (United Kingdom) 432
Saint-Germain-des-Près, Editions, SA (France) 106
Saint James Press (United Kingdom) 432
Saint-Joseph (Gabon) 115
Saint Louis de Gonzague, Bibliothèque (Haiti) 178
Saint Louis, Publications des Facultés universitaires (Belgium) 40
Saint Michael's Mission (Lesotho) 255
Saint Paul Book Centre (Uganda) 386
Saint-Paul, Département des Classiques Africains, Editions (France) 106
Saint-Paul, Editions (Switzerland) 372
Saint Paul, Editions (Zaire) 462
Saint-Paul, Editions, SA (France) 106
Saint-Paul, Imprimerie, SA (Grand Duchy of Luxembourg) 257
Saint Paul, Librairie (Burundi) 60
Saint Paul, Librairie (United Republic of Cameroun) 61
Saint Paul, Librairie (Zaire) 462
Saint Paul, Librairie/Imprimerie (United Republic of Cameroun) 61
Saint Paul Publications (India) 197
Saint Paul Publications (Uganda) 386
Saint Paul Publications (United Kingdom) 432
Saint Paul's Bibliographies (United Kingdom) 432
Sainte-Devote (Monaco) 270
Sainte-Geneviève, Bibliothèque (France) 110
Saintour Prize (France) 114
Sajha Prakashan, Co-operative Publishing Organization (Nepal) 272
Sal Terrae, Editorial (Spain) 345
Saladdine Publications & Distributors Inc (Egypt) 84

Salama Publications Ltd (Kenya) 249
Salamander Books Ltd (United Kingdom) 432
Salamander Paperbacks (Netherlands) 281
Salamander Press, The, Edinburgh Ltd (United Kingdom) 432
Salamandra, La (Italy) 232
Salamon e Agustoni Editori (Italy) 232
Salani, Adriano, SpA (Italy) 232
Salas, Boekhandel (Netherlands Antilles) 286
Salerno Editrice SRL (Italy) 232
Salesian Publications & Don Bosco Film Strips (United Kingdom) 432
Salesianas, Edicões (Portugal) 318
Salle, Otto, Verlag (Federal Republic of Germany) 156
Salon de l'Enfance et de la Jeunesse Grand Literary Prize (International Literary Prizes) 479
Salterain', Biblioteca Municipal 'Dr Joaquín de (Uruguay) 452
Saltire, The, Society (United Kingdom) 432
Saltykova-Schedrina, Gosudarstvennaya publichnaya biblioteka im M E (Union of Soviet Socialist Republics) 389
Salutiste, Librairie (Zaire) 462
Salvadoreña, Distribuidora (El Salvador) 85
Salvat Editores SA (Spain) 345
Salvat Mexicana de Ediciones SA de CV (Mexico) 267
Salvat SA de Ediciones (Spain) 345
Salvatella, Editorial Miguel A (Spain) 345
Salvationist Publishing & Supplies Ltd (United Kingdom) 432
Salvator, Editions, Sàrl (France) 106
Salvator Verlag GmbH (Federal Republic of Germany) 157
Salvioni & Co (Switzerland) 372
Salzburger Druckerei, Verlag der (Austria) 28
Salzer, Eugen, Verlag (Federal Republic of Germany) 157
Sam Joong Dang Publishing Co (Republic of Korea) 252
Sam-sung Publishing Co (Republic of Korea) 252
Samater's Bookshop (Somalia) 328
Sambucco, Auberge du (France) 106
Samfund til Udgivelse af Gammel Nordisk Litteratur (Denmark) 81
Samfundet de Nio (Sweden) 359
Samlerens Bogklub (Denmark) 79
Samlerens Forlag A/S (Denmark) 78
Sammenslutningem af Danmarks Forskningsbiblioteker (Denmark) 80
Sammler, Verlag für (Austria) 28
Sammlung Luchterhand (Federal Republic of Germany) 157
'Samopomoc Chlopska', Zaklad Wydawnictw CRS (Poland) 313
Samouhos, A, Bookstore (Greece) 176
Sampson Low (United Kingdom) 432
Samsom (CED) (Belgium) 40
Samsom Uitgeverij BV (Netherlands) 281
Samwha Publishing Co (Republic of Korea) 252
San José, Editorial (Nicaragua) 292
San Martin, Editorial (Spain) 345
San Min Book Co Ltd (Taiwan) 378
San Pablo, Librería (Chile) 63
San Pablo, Librería (Colombia) 67
Sanchi Prakashan (India) 198
Sanctus, Förlaget (Sweden) 356
Sand et Tchou, Editions, Sàrl (France) 106
Sandberg, Erik, A/S (Norway) 299
Sandbergs, AB, Bokhandel (Sweden) 358
Sander Kitabevi, Necdet Sander (Turkey) 385
Sander Yayınları (Turkey) 385
Sanderus PVBA (Belgium) 40
Sändig, Dr Martin, GmbH (Federal Republic of Germany) 157
Sändig Reprint Verlag (Liechtenstein) 256
Sandkühler, Martin (Federal Republic of Germany) 168
Sandles (United Kingdom) 432
Sandy Beach Book Store (Barbados) 33
Sane, Lennart, Agency (Sweden) 358
Sang-e-Meel Publications (Pakistan) 303
Sangam Books (India) 198
Sangam Books Ltd (United Kingdom) 432
Sangam Sarada Printing Press (Fiji) 86
Sangna Vuddhichai Saranonda (Thailand) 380
Sangster's Book Stores Ltd (Jamaica) 237
Sanguily', Biblioteca 'Manuel (Cuba) 69
Sangyo Tosho Publishing Co Ltd (Japan) 242
Sankei, The, Award for Children's Books and Publications (Japan) 247
Sankei, The, Shimbun Shuppankyoku Co (Japan) 242
Sanket Library Yojna (India) 201
Sankore, Librairie Editions PFD (Senegal) 324
Sankt-Benno Verlag GmbH (German Democratic Republic) 118
Sankt Gabriel, Verlag (Austria) 28
Sankt-Johannis-Druckerei, Verlag der, C Schweickhardt (Federal Republic of Germany) 157
Sankt Otto Verlag GmbH (Federal Republic of Germany) 157
Sankt Peter, Verlag (Austria) 28

'Sanlian Shudian' Publishing House (People's Republic of China) 64
Sanseido Co Ltd (Japan) 242
Sanskrit Pustak Bhandar (India) 198
Sanskriti (India) 198
Sansoni, G C, Editore Nuova SpA (Italy) 232
Sanssouci Verlag (Switzerland) 372
Sansthan, Rashtriya Sanskrit (India) 198
Sansyusya Publishing Co Ltd (Japan) 242
Santa Fe, Librería (Argentina) 8
Santiago, Editorial, Rueda SRL (Argentina) 7
Santillana SA de Ediciones (Spain) 345
Santo Domingo, Biblioteca Municipal de (Dominican Republic) 82
Sanyo Shuppan Boeki Co Inc (Japan) 242
Sapienza's Library (Malta) 262
Sapphire Books Pty Ltd (Australia) 18
Sappl, Paul, Schulbuch- und Lehrmittelverlag (Austria) 28
Saraiva SA, Livreiros Editores (Brazil) 54
Saraswat Library (India) 198
Sarawak State Library (Malaysia) 261
Sardini, Fausto, Editrice (Italy) 232
Sari Agung, Toko Buku (Indonesia) 206
Sarita Prakashan (India) 198
Sarkar, M C, & Sons (P) Ltd (India) 198
Sarma, Librairie (Zaire) 462
Sarment, Editions Le (France) 106
Sarmiento, Librería (Argentina) 8
Sarmiento Prize (Argentina) 9
Sarpay Beikman Best Manuscripts Awards (Burma) 60
Sarpay Beikman Board (Burma) 59
Sarpay Beikman Book Club (Burma) 60
Sarpay Beikman Bookshop (Burma) 60
Sarpay Lawka (Burma) 60
Sarvier — Editora de Livros Medicos Ltda (Brazil) 54
Sasavona Publishers & Booksellers (Republic of South Africa) 332
Sassafras Verlag (Federal Republic of Germany) 157
Sasta Sahitya Mandal (India) 198
Sastra Hudaya (Indonesia) 206
Satire Verlag GmbH (Federal Republic of Germany) 157
Satya Press (India) 198
Saud, Iman M Ben, University, Deanery Libraries (Saudi Arabia) 323
Saudi Library (Saudi Arabia) 323
Saudi Publishing and Distributing House (Saudi Arabia) 323
Sauer, I H, Verlag GmbH (Federal Republic of Germany) 157
Sauerländer AG (Switzerland) 372
Sauerländer, Verlag (Federal Republic of Germany) 157
Sauerländer's, J D, Verlag (Federal Republic of Germany) 157
Saunders, W B (United Kingdom) 432
Saur, K G, Editeur Sarl (France) 106
Saur, K G, Ltd (United Kingdom) 432
Saur, K G, Verlag KG (Federal Republic of Germany) 157
Sauramps, Librairie 109
Sauret, Editions du Livre André, SA (Monaco) 270
Savez bibliotečkih radnika Srbije (Yugoslavia) 461
Savez društava bibliotekara Jugoslavije (Yugoslavia) 461
Savez Inženjera i Tehničara Jugoslavije (Yugoslavia) 459
Savremena Administracija (Yugoslavia) 459
Sawan Kirpal Publications (India) 198
Saxon House (United Kingdom) 432
Sayam Paritat (Thailand) 380
Sayle, Tessa, Literary and Dramatic Agency (United Kingdom) 443
Sayrols, Publicaciones, SA de CV (Mexico) 268
Scala Istituto Fotografico Editoriale (Italy) 232
Scala/Philip Wilson (United Kingdom) 432
Scandinavia Publishing House (Denmark) 78
Scandinavian Association of Directory Publishers (SADP) (International Organizations) 469
Scarabée & Co, éditeurs (France) 106
Scarabée d'Or (France) 106
Scene Book Club (United Kingdom) 444
Sceptre Books Ltd (United Kingdom) 432
Schäfer, Karl A, Buch-und Offsetdruckerei-Goldstadtverlag (Federal Republic of Germany) 157
Schaffstein, Hermann, Verlag (Federal Republic of Germany) 157
Schaik, J L van, (Pty) Ltd (Republic of South Africa) 332
Schaik's, Van, Bookstore (Pty) Ltd (Republic of South Africa) 334
Schapire Editor SRL (Argentina) 7
Schattauer, F K, Verlag GmbH (Federal Republic of Germany) 157
Schaubroeck PVBA (Belgium) 40
Schauenburg, Moritz, Verlag GmbH und Co KG (Federal Republic of Germany) 157
Schaum (Federal Republic of Germany) 157
Scheepers Prize (Republic of South Africa) 335
Scheffler, Verlag Heinrich (Federal Republic of Germany) 157
Scheidegger, Dr A (Switzerland) 375

Scheltema, Boekhandel, Holkema Vermeulen BV (Netherlands) 284
Schenck, G (Federal Republic of Germany) 157
Schendl, Dr A, GmbH und Co KG (Austria) 28
Scherpe Verlag (Federal Republic of Germany) 157
Scherz, Buchhandlung, AG (Switzerland) 376
Scherz Verlag AG (Switzerland) 372
Scherz Verlag GmbH (Federal Republic of Germany) 157
Scheuerer, Gertrud E, Verlag (Federal Republic of Germany) 157
Schibsteds, Chr, Forlag (Norway) 299
Schiele und Schön, Fachverlag, GmbH (Federal Republic of Germany) 157
Schifferli, Verlag der Arche Peter, AG (Switzerland) 372
Schildts, Holger, Förlagsaktiebolag (Finland) 88
Schiller Prize (Federal Republic of Germany) 171
Schilling, Kurt (Federal Republic of Germany) 157
Schillinger, Verlag Karl, KG (Federal Republic of Germany) 157
Schindele, G, Verlag GmbH (Federal Republic of Germany) 157
Schindler, Mrs Karin, — Dr J E Bloch Literary Agency (Brazil) 55
Schirmer/Mosel Verlag GmbH (Federal Republic of Germany) 157
Schlaefli, Otto, Verlag (Switzerland) 372
Schläpfer & Co AG (Switzerland) 372
Schlegel-Tieck Prize (United Kingdom) 450
Schlender, Verlag Bert (Federal Republic of Germany) 157
Schlueck, Thomas (Federal Republic of Germany) 167
Schmid, Joachim, & Co (Federal Republic of Germany) 158
Schmidt, Erich, Verlag GmbH (Federal Republic of Germany) 158
Schmidt-Römhild, Max, Verlag (Federal Republic of Germany) 158
Schmidt-Römhild, Verlag für polizeiliches Fachschrifttum Georg (Federal Republic of Germany) 158
Schmidt, Verlag Dr Otto, KG (Federal Republic of Germany) 158
Schmiedel, Dr Roland (Federal Republic of Germany) 158
Schmitz, Wilhelm, Verlag (Federal Republic of Germany) 158
Schmücking, Galerie, Verlag (Federal Republic of Germany) 158
Schneekluth, Franz, Verlag (Federal Republic of Germany) 158
Schneider Verlag GmbH, Franz, & Co KG (Federal Republic of Germany) 158
Schneider, Verlag Lambert, GmbH (Federal Republic of Germany) 158
Schneider Verlag, Rudolf (Federal Republic of Germany) 158
Schnell und Steiner, Verlag, GmbH und Co (Federal Republic of Germany) 158
Schocken Publishing House Ltd (Israel) 216
Schoelcher, Bibliothèque Victor (Martinique) 263
Schoenbergske Forlag, Det, A/S (Nyt Nordisk Forlag Arnold Busck A/S) (Denmark) 78
Schofield & Sims Ltd (United Kingdom) 432
Scholar Publications International (Nigeria) Ltd (Nigeria) 295
Scholastic (Australia) 18
Scholastic Book Services Inc (United Kingdom) 432
Scholastic Books (Zimbabwe) 465
Scholastic Publications Ltd (United Kingdom) 432
Schöldström, Birger, Prize (Sweden) 360
Scholtens en Zoon BV (Netherlands) 284
Schönbrunn-Verlag GmbH (Austria) 28
Schöne Wissenschaften, Verlag fur, (Belles Lettres Publishing Co — Albert Steffen Foundation) (Switzerland) 372
Schönen Bücher, Verlag die (Federal Republic of Germany) 158
Schöningh, Ferdinand, Verlag (Federal Republic of Germany) 158
School Bookshop Association (United Kingdom) 391
School Library Association (United Kingdom) 446
School Library Association in Scotland (United Kingdom) 446
School of Administration Library (Ghana) 173
School of Oriental & African Studies (United Kingdom) 433
School of Oriental and African Studies Library (United Kingdom) 445
School Supplies Ltd (New Zealand) 290
Schoolpers (Netherlands) 281
Schott Frères Sàrl (France) 106
Schott Frères SPRL (Éditeurs de Musique) (Belgium) 40
Schottentor (Austria) 30
Schott's, B, Söhne, Musikverlag (Federal Republic of Germany) 158
Schreiber, Verlag J F, GmbH (Federal Republic of Germany) 158
Schreiner, Olive, Prize for English Literature (Republic of South Africa) 335

Schrift, Vereeniging tot Verspreiding der H (Netherlands) 281
Schriftenmission, Verlag und, der Ev Ges für Deutschland GmbH (Federal Republic of Germany) 158
Schroedel, Hermann, Verlag AG (Switzerland) 372
Schroedel Schulbuchverlag GmbH (Federal Republic of Germany) 158
Schroeder, Kurt, Verlag (Federal Republic of Germany) 158
Schroeder, Marion von, Verlag GmbH (Federal Republic of Germany) 158
Schroll, Anton, & Co (Austria) 28
Schroll, Anton, & Co GmbH (Federal Republic of Germany) 158
Schroll, Ferdinand (Federal Republic of Germany) 158
Schubiger Verlag AG (Switzerland) 372
Schück, Henrik, Prize (Sweden) 360
Schule und Elternhaus, Verlag (Federal Republic of Germany) 159
Schuler Verlagsgesellschaft mbH (Federal Republic of Germany) 159
Schulfernsehen, v g s — Verlagsgesellschaft, mbH & Co KG (Federal Republic of Germany) 159
Schulte, Verlag, und Gerth GmbH & Co KG (Federal Republic of Germany) 159
Schulten, P N (Federal Republic of Germany) 159
Schulthess Polygraphischer Verlag AG (Switzerland) 372
Schultz, A/S J H, Forlag (Denmark) 78
Schultz Medical Information (Denmark) 78
Schulverlag Vieweg GmbH (Federal Republic of Germany) 159
Schulz, Verlag R S (Federal Republic of Germany) 159
Schumann, Hohenstaufen Verlag, KG (Federal Republic of Germany) 159
Schünemann, Carl Ed, KG (Federal Republic of Germany) 159
Schütz, Verlag K W, KG (Federal Republic of Germany) 159
Schuyt en Co CV (Netherlands) 281
Schwabe AG, Hansrudolf (Switzerland) 372
Schwabe & Co AG (Switzerland) 372
Schwabenverlag AG (Federal Republic of Germany) 159
Schwalbach, Verlag Haus (Federal Republic of Germany) 159
Schwaneberger Verlag GmbH (Federal Republic of Germany) 159
Schwann/Bagel, Pädagogischer Verlag, GmbH (Federal Republic of Germany) 159
Schwann, Edition (Federal Republic of Germany) 159
Schwartz, Otto, & Co (Federal Republic of Germany) 159
Schwartz Publishing Group (Victoria) Pty Ltd (Australia) 18
Schwartz, Uitgeverij Gary (Netherlands) 281
Schwarz Bildbücher (Federal Republic of Germany) 159
Schwarz, Verlag GmbH (Federal Republic of Germany) 159
Schwarze, Dr Wolfgang, Verlag (Federal Republic of Germany) 159
Schweickhardt, Verlag der Sankt-Johannis-Druckerei C (Federal Republic of Germany) 159
Schweitzer, J, Verlag (Federal Republic of Germany) 159
Schweizer Bibliotheksdienst (Switzerland) 376
Schweizer Buchwerbung und -Information (SBI) (Switzerland) 360
Schweizer Buchzentrum (Switzerland) 360
Schweizer Jugend, Aare-Verlag/, -Verlag (Switzerland) 372
Schweizer Spiegel Verlag AG & Rodana Verlag (Switzerland) 372
Schweizer Verband der Musikalienhändler und Verleger (Switzerland) 360
Schweizer Verlagshaus AG (Switzerland) 372
Schweizer Volksbuchgemeinde AG (Switzerland) 375
Schweizerbart'sche Verlagsbuchhandlung, E (Federal Republic of Germany) 159
Schweizerische Bibliophilen-Gesellschaft (Switzerland) 376
Schweizerische Landesbibliothek (Bibliothèque Nationale Suisse) (Switzerland) 376
Schweizerische Stiftung für Alpine Forschungen (Switzerland) 372
Schweizerische Zentralstelle für Stahlbau (Switzerland) 372
Schweizerischen Gesellschaft für Volkskunde (Switzerland) 373
Schweizerischen Schallplattenmission, Verlag der (Switzerland) 373
Schweizerischer Adressbuchverleger-Verband (Switzerland) 360
Schweizerischer Buchhändler- und Verleger-Verband (SBVV) (Switzerland) 360
Schweizerischer Bühnenverleger-Verband (Switzerland) 361
Schweizerischer Schriftsteller-Verband (Switzerland) 361
Schweizerisches Jugendschriftenwerk (Switzerland) 373
Schweizerisches katholisches Bibelwerk, Verlag (Switzerland) 373
Schweizerisches Ost-Institut (Switzerland) 373

INDEX 539

Schweizerisches Wirtschaftsarchiv (Archives Économiques Suisses) (Switzerland) 376
Schwengeler-Verlag (Switzerland) 373
Schwieger, H G (Federal Republic of Germany) 159
Schwinghammer, Verlag Junge Gemeinde E, KG (Federal Republic of Germany) 159
Schwitter Edition GmbH (Switzerland) 373
Schwitter Holding, F P, Inc (Switzerland) 373
Scialtiel, Bureau littéraire international Marguerite (France) 109
Sciascia, Salvatore (Italy) 232
Science and Encyclopaedia Publishing House (Democratic People's Republic of Korea) 250
Science and Engineering Library (Ethiopia) 86
Science Fiction Achievement Awards (International Literary Prizes) 479
Science Publications Centre (Republic of Korea) 252
Science Research Associates Ltd (United Kingdom) 433
Science Research Associates Pty Ltd (Australia) 18
Sciences et Lettres, Editions (Belgium) 40
Sciences Générales, Bibliothèque des (Socialist Republic of Viet Nam) 455
Scientechnica (Publishers) Ltd (United Kingdom) 433
Scientia Verlag und Antiquariat Kurt Schilling (Federal Republic of Germany) 159
Scientific and Cultural Publications Center (Iran) 207
Scientific Book Agency (India) 198
Scientific Documentation Centre (Iraq) 208
Scientific Library and Documentation Division (Philippines) 310
Scientific Publishing House (Socialist Republic of Viet Nam) 455
Scientific Translations International Ltd (Israel) 218
Scientifica Cortina, Libreria (Italy) 232
Scientifiche Italiane, Edizioni (Italy) 232
Scientology Publications Organization ApS (Denmark) 78
Scipione Autores Editores Ltda (Brazil) 54
Scolar Press (United Kingdom) 433
Scolavox (France) 106
Scorpion Communications & Publications Ltd (United Kingdom) 433
Scott-Moncrieff Prize (United Kingdom) 450
Scottish Academic Press Ltd (United Kingdom) 433
Scottish Arts Council Book Awards (United Kingdom) 450
Scottish Book of the Year (United Kingdom) 450
Scottish Library Association (United Kingdom) 446
Scottish Publishers' Association (United Kingdom) 391
Scottish Record Office (United Kingdom) 445
Scribae-Uitgevers VZW (Belgium) 40
Scriptar, Editions, SA (Switzerland) 373
Scriptor Verlag (Federal Republic of Germany) 159
Scripts Publications (Australia) 18
Scripture in Church Book Club (Republic of Ireland) 211
Scripture Union (United Kingdom) 433
'Scrisul Românesc', Editura (Romania) 321
Scuola, Editrice La, SpA (Italy) 232
Scuola Vita (Italy) 232
Se Kwang Musical Publication Co (Republic of Korea) 252
Seafarer Books (United Kingdom) 433
Seale, Patrick, Books Ltd (United Kingdom) 443
Sealy, J C (Trinidad and Tobago) 382
Seara, Empresa de Publicidade, Nova SARL (Portugal) 318
Search Press Ltd (United Kingdom) 433
Secker & Warburg, Martin, Ltd (United Kingdom) 433
Second Back Row Press Pty Ltd (Australia) 18
Secours, Editions du, Catholique (France) 107
Secretaría de Estado de Relaciones Exteriores, Biblioteca de la (Dominican Republic) 82
Secretariado Trinitario (Spain) 345
Século, Editorial o (Portugal) 318
Sécuritas, La Société, SA (France) 107
Sedco Publishing Ltd (Ghana) 172
Seditas (Société d'Editions et de Diffusion Tambourinaire-Sofradel) (France) 107
Sedmay Ediciones SA (Spain) 345
See-Saw Book Club (United Kingdom) 444
Seeber, Libreria Internazionale (Italy) 234
Seefeld, Edition (Switzerland) 373
Seeley, Service (United Kingdom) 433
Seelig, AB, och Co (Sweden) 359
Seemann, E A, Verlag (Federal Republic of Germany) 159
Seemann, VEB E A, Buch- und Kunstverlag (German Democratic Republic) 118
Seemant Prakashan (India) 198
Seewald, S (Federal Republic of Germany) 159
Seewald Verlag GmbH & Co (Federal Republic of Germany) 159
Seghers, Les Editions, SA (France) 107
Seibt Verlag GmbH (Federal Republic of Germany) 159
Seibundo Shinkosha Publishing Co Ltd (Japan) 242
Seiwa Shoten Co Ltd (Japan) 242
Seix, Editorial, Barral SA (Spain) 345
Seizando-Shoten Publishing Co Ltd (Japan) 242
Seizoenen, De, PVBA (Belgium) 40

Sejong Daewang Kinyom Saophoe (Republic of Korea) 252
Sekai Bunka Publishing Inc (Japan) 242
Selangor Public Library (Malaysia) 261
Selcon SAEC & I (Selección Contable) (Argentina) 7
Selecciones Editoriales SA (Spain) 345
Selecciones, Librería (Ecuador) 83
Selecciones, Librería, SRL (Bolivia) 46
Selecciones SA Comercial (Paraguay) 306
Seleções Eletrônicas Editora Ltda (Brazil) 54
Selecta, Librería (Venezuela) 454
Sélection, Editions, J Jacobs SA (France) 107
Selimiye Library (Turkey) 385
Selina Publishers (India) 198
Sella, Shalom (Israel) 217
Sellerio Editore (Italy) 232
Sellevolds Bokhandel A/S (Norway) 300
Sellier Verlag GmbH (Federal Republic of Germany) 159
Sembrador, Editorial El (Chile) 63
Sembrador, Librería El (Chile) 63
Semences, Editions, Africaines (United Republic of Cameroun) 61
Semic Press (Netherlands) 281
Seminar on the Acquisition of Latin American Library Materials (SALALM) (International Organizations) 469
Seminario de Integración Social Guatemalteca (Guatemala) 177
Seminario, Librería del (Colombia) 67
Semper, Uitgeverij, Agendo BV (Netherlands) 281
Sénevé, Les Editions du (France) 107
Senmon Toshokan Kyogikai (SENTOKYO) (Japan) 245
Senouhy Publishers (Egypt) 84
Sentis, Santiago, Melendo (Argentina) 7
Sentral Bokhandel A/S (Norway) 298
Sentral Bokhandel A/S (Norway) 300
Seomun Dang (Republic of Korea) 252
Seoul Computer Press (Republic of Korea) 252
Seoul International Tourist Publishing Co (Republic of Korea) 252
Seoul National University Library (Republic of Korea) 252
Seoul National University Press (Republic of Korea) 252
Septieme Rayon (France) 107
Septimus Editions (France) 107
Septuaginta BV Uitgeverij (Netherlands) 281
Serbal, Ediciones del, SA (Spain) 345
Serie-pocket-klubben (Sweden) 358
Serindia Publications (United Kingdom) 433
Sermwit Barnakarn (Thailand) 380
Service, Bibliothèque du, geologique du Rwanda (Rwanda) 323
Service SPRL (Belgium) 40
Service Technique pour l'Education (France) 107
Services, Direction générale des, de Bibliothèques, Archives et Documentation (Popular Republic of Congo) 68
Services interbancaires SA (Belgium) 40
Servicio Continental de Publicaciones (Panama) 305
Servicio de Bibliotecas Populares de la Diputación Provincial de Barcelona (Spain) 345
Servicio de Documentación y Biblioteca (Dominican Republic) 82
Servicio de Lewis (Panama) 305
Servire BV Uitgevers (Netherlands) 281
Servire BV Uitgevers (Netherlands) 283
Setberg (Iceland) 184
Settern, Bokförlaget, HB (Sweden) 356
Settle & Bendall (Wigmore) Ltd (United Kingdom) 433
Seuil, Editions du (France) 107
Seung mun Book Co (Republic of Korea) 252
Seven Seas Publishers (German Democratic Republic) 118
Sevenseas Publishing Pty Ltd (New Zealand) 289
Severin Presse (Austria) 28
Severn House Publishers Ltd (United Kingdom) 433
Severočeské nakladatelství (Czechoslovakia) 72
Seymour Large Print Romances (United Kingdom) 433
Shadeed's Educational & General Supplies Ltd (Jamaica) 237
Shakai Shiso-Sha (Japan) 243
Shaker, Ahmed, Al Ansary (Egypt) 84
Shakespeare Head Press (Australia) 18
Shakespeare Head Press (United Kingdom) 433
Shakespearean Authorship Trust (United Kingdom) 447
Shanghai Book Co Ltd (Hong Kong) 180
Shanghai Book Co Pte Ltd (Republic of Singapore) 327
Shanghai tushuguan (People's Republic of China) 64
Sharbain's Bookshop (Israel) 217
Sharda Prakashan (India) 198
Shaw & Sons Ltd (United Kingdom) 433
Shaw Centre, Bernard (United Kingdom) 447
Shaw, Pat, Associates (formerly EMBLA) (Norway) 300
Shaw Society, Bernard (United Kingdom) 447
Shazar Prize (Israel) 218
Shearwater Press Ltd (Isle of Man) 212
Sheba Feminist Publishers (United Kingdom) 433
Sheed & Ward Ltd (United Kingdom) 433
Sheil, Anthony, Associates Ltd (United Kingdom) 443
Sheldon Press (United Kingdom) 433
Shell Book of the Year (Australia) 23

Shepheard-Walwyn (Publishers) Ltd (United Kingdom) 434
Sheppard Press Ltd (United Kingdom) 434
Sherratt & Hughes (Bowes & Bowes) (United Kingdom) 444
Sheth, R R, & Co (India) 198
Sheth, R R, & Co (India) 202
Shikmona Publishing Co Ltd (Israel) 216
Shiko-Sha Co Ltd (Japan) 243
Shiksha Bharati (India) 198
Shimoni, Joseph (Israel) 216
Shin Jin Gak (Republic of Korea) 252
Shinchosha Co (Japan) 243
Shindan to Chiryo Co Ltd (Japan) 243
Shinkenchiku-Sha Co Ltd (Japan) 243
Shire Publications Ltd (United Kingdom) 434
Shishu Sahitya Samsad Pvt Ltd (India) 198
Shiva Publishing Ltd (United Kingdom) 434
Shkencore e Universitetit Shtetëror të Tiranës, Biblioteka (Albania) 1
Shkodër Public Library (Albania) 1
Shmulik (Israel) 216
Shogakukan Literary Prize (Japan) 247
Shogakukan Publishing Co Ltd (Japan) 243
Shokabo Publishing Co Ltd (Japan) 243
Shokoku-Sha Publishing Co Ltd (Japan) 243
Shona/Ndebele Writers' Association (Zimbabwe) 465
Shona Readers' Book Club (Zimbabwe) 465
Short Story Prize (France) 114
Shortland Educational Publications (New Zealand) 289
Shree Mahavir Book Depot (Publishers) (India) 198
Shree Saraswati Sadan (India) 198
Shri Ram Centre for Industrial Relations and Human Resources (India) 198
Shuckburgh Reynolds Ltd (United Kingdom) 434
Shueisha Publishing Co Ltd (Japan) 243
Shufu-to-Seikatsu Sha Ltd (Japan) 243
Shufunotomo Co Ltd (Japan) 243
Shumawa Book House (Burma) 60
Shumawa Publishing House (Burma) 60
Shuppan News Co Ltd (Japan) 243
Shuter & Shooter (Pty) (Republic of South Africa) 334
Shuter & Shooter (Pty) Ltd (Republic of South Africa) 332
Shwepyidan Printing & Publishing House (Burma) 60
Si-sa-yong-o-sa Publishers Inc (Republic of Korea) 252
Siam Directory (Thailand) 380
Siam, The, Society (Thailand) 381
Siamandas (Greece) 175
Sibelius-Akatemian Kirjasto (Finland) 89
Sideris, J, OE Ekdoseis (Greece) 175
Sidgwick & Jackson Ltd (United Kingdom) 434
Sidhawat Award (India) 204
Siebeck, Paul (Federal Republic of Germany) 160
Siebert und Engelbert Dessart Verlag GmbH (Federal Republic of Germany) 160
Siebert Verlag GmbH (Federal Republic of Germany) 160
Siegler, J (Federal Republic of Germany) 160
Siemens AG — ZVW 5 Verlag (Federal Republic of Germany) 160
Sierra Leone Library Association (Sierra Leone) 325
Sierra Leone Library Board (Sierra Leone) 325
Sierra Leone, The, Diocesan Bookshops Ltd (Sierra Leone) 325
Sierra Leone University Press (Sierra Leone) 325
Sifriat Poalim Ltd (Israel) 216
Sifriat Poalim Ltd (Israel) 217
Siglo XX, Ediciones, SAC & I (Argentina) 7
Siglo XXI Editores de Colombia Ltda (Colombia) 66
Siglo XXI Editores de España SA (Spain) 345
Siglo XXI Editores SA de CV (Mexico) 268
Siglos, Editorial V, SA (Mexico) 268
Sigma Technical Press (United Kingdom) 434
Sigmar, Editorial, SACI (Argentina) 7
Signal-Verlag Hans Frevert (Federal Republic of Germany) 160
Signorelli, Angelo, Editore (Italy) 232
Sigueme, Ediciones, SA (Spain) 345
Sijthoff en Noordhoff International Publishers (Netherlands) 281
Sijthoff's Uitg, A W, Mij BV (Netherlands) 281
Sikkel, Uitgeverij De, NV (Belgium) 40
Silliman University Library (Philippines) 310
Sillon, Editions Le, d'Or (Belgium) 41
Siloé, Editions, Sàrl (France) 107
Silva, K V G De, & Sons (Kandy) (Sri Lanka) 349
Silvaire, Editions André, SA (France) 107
Silvana Editoriale Srl (Italy) 232
Silver Dagger Award (United Kingdom) 450
Silvio Romero Prize (Brazil) 57
Sima, Ediciones (Spain) 345
Siman Krai (Israel) 216
Símbolo, Edições (Brazil) 54
Simon Stevin NV (Belgium) 41
Simon, Verlag Ludwig (Federal Republic of Germany) 160
Simondium Publishers (Pty) Ltd (Republic of South Africa) 332

Simson, Samuel, Ltd (Israel) 216
Simul, The, Press Inc (Japan) 243
Sinag-Tala Publishers Inc (Philippines) 309
Sinai Publishing Co (Israel) 216
Sinclair Browne Ltd (United Kingdom) 434
Sinclair Prize for Fiction (International Literary Prizes) 479
Sind University Central Library (Pakistan) 303
Sindbad (France) 107
Sindhi Adabi Board (Pakistan) 304
Sindicato Nacional dos Editores de Livros (Brazil) 48
Singapore Book Publishers' Association (Republic of Singapore) 325
Singapore Book Store (Republic of Singapore) 327
Singapore Booksellers' Association (Republic of Singapore) 325
Singapore University Press Pte Ltd (Republic of Singapore) 327
Singer, SCI, Communications Inc (Federal Republic of Germany) 167
Singu Munwha Sa (Republic of Korea) 252
Sinite Parvulos VBVB (Belgium) 41
Sino-Malay Publishing Co (Malaysia) 260
Sinodalno Izdatelstvo (Bulgaria) 58
Sinpattana (Thailand) 380
Sint-Ignatius, Bibliotheek der Universitaire Faculteiten (Belgium) 43
Sint Kinderkrant Suriname (Suriname) 351
Sintal (Belgium) 41
Sintes, Editorial, SA (Spain) 345
Sinwel-Buchhandlung Verlag (Switzerland) 373
Sir Robert Ho Tung, Biblioteca (Macau) 257
Sirey, Editions (France) 107
Siriraj Medical Library, Library Division (Thailand) 381
Sistem, Pustaka, Palajaran Sdn Bhd (Malaysia) 260
Sistema Bibliotecario (Honduras) 178
Sitti, A B, Syamsiyah (Indonesia) 206
Sjöstrands Förlag (Sweden) 356
Skandinavia Verlag (Federal Republic of Germany) 167
Skarabee, Uitgeverij, BV (Netherlands) 281
Skarv - Nature Publications ApS (Denmark) 78
Skattekartoteket, A/S (Denmark) 78
Skeab Förlag AB (Sweden) 356
Sketch Publishing Co Ltd (Nigeria) 295
Skilton & Shaw (United Kingdom) 434
Skilton, Charles, Ltd (United Kingdom) 434
Skinner, Thomas, Directories (United Kingdom) 434
Skira, Editions D'Art Albert, SA (Switzerland) 373
Skjaldborg, Bókaútgáfan, sf (Iceland) 184
Skladnica Ksiegarska (Poland) 313
'Składnica Ksiegarska', Państwowe, Przedsiebiorstwo (Poland) 314
Škola za Strane Jezike (Yugoslavia) 459
Skolförlaget Gävle AB (Sweden) 357
'Školska knjiga' (Yugoslavia) 459
Skuggsja bókaforlag (Iceland) 184
Skyline Publishing House (India) 198
Skypress International (Federal Republic of Germany) 160
'Slask', Wydawnictwo (Poland) 313
Ślaska, Biblioteka (Poland) 314
Slatkine Reprints (Switzerland) 373
Slezak, Verlag Josef Otto (Austria) 28
Sloboda (Yugoslavia) 459
Slovart Co Ltd (Czechoslovakia) 73
Slovenská kartografia NP (Czechoslovakia) 72
Slovenská knižničná RADA (Czechoslovakia) 74
Slovenská technická knižnica (Czechoslovakia) 73
Slovenské pedagogické nakladateľstvo (Czechoslovakia) 72
Slovenské ústredie knižnej kultúry (Czechoslovakia) 70
Slovenskej akadémie, Ustredná knižnica, vied (Czechoslovakia) 73
Slovenskej akadémie vied, Vydavateľstvo (Czechoslovakia) 72
Slovenský spisovateľ (Czechoslovakia) 72
Slovenský spisovateľ Prize (Czechoslovakia) 74
Slovo ljubve (Yugoslavia) 459
Služebni List (Yugoslavia) 459
Smålänningens Forlag AB (Sweden) 357
Smart & Mookerdum (Burma) 60
Smeets Illustrated Projects (Netherlands) 281
Smena (Czechoslovakia) 72
Smena Prize (Czechoslovakia) 74
Smith & Son, W H, Literary Award (United Kingdom) 450
Smith, John, & Son (Glasgow) Ltd (United Kingdom) 444
Smith, Lawrence (Argentina) 8
Smith, Pauline, Prize for Prose (Republic of South Africa) 335
Smith, W H, & Son Ltd (United Kingdom) 444
Smith Young Writers', W H, Competition (United Kingdom) 450
Smriti Prakashan (India) 198
Smythe, Colin, Ltd (United Kingdom) 434
Snaefell, Bókaútgáfan (Iceland) 184
Snoeck-Ducaju en Zoon NV (Belgium) 41
Snøfugl Forlag (Norway) 299

So-Wen Srl (Italy) 232
Sober Förlags AB (Sweden) 357
Sobrier-Arnould Prize (France) 114
Social Science Association Press (Thailand) 380
Social Science Documentation Centre (India) 204
Social Sciences Library (Socialist Republic of Viet Nam) 455
Socialistisk Bogklub ApS (Denmark) 79
Sociedad Anonima de Revistas Periodicos y Ediciones (SARPE) (Spain) 345
Sociedad Científica, Biblioteca de la, del Paraguay (Paraguay) 306
Sociedad de Bibliófilos Chilenos (Chile) 64
Sociedad de Bibliotecarios de Puerto Rico (Puerto Rico) 320
Sociedad de Ciencias, Letras y Artes (Spain) 348
Sociedad de Libreros del Ecuador (Ecuador) 82
Sociedad General de Autores de España (Spain) 348
Sociedad General de Autores de la Argentina (Argentina) 3
Sociedad General Española de Librería (Spain) 336
Sociedad Mexicana de Bibliografía (Mexico) 269
Sociedad Puertorriqueña de Escritores (Puerto Rico) 319
Sociedade Brasileira, Biblioteca da, de Cultura Inglesa (Brazil) 56
Società Dante Alighieri (Italy) 235
Società Dantesca Italiana (Italy) 235
Societa Editori della Svizzera Italiana (SESI) (Switzerland) 361
Società Italiana di Documentazione e d'Informazione (Italy) 235
Società Letteraria (Italy) 235
Societäts-Verlag (Federal Republic of Germany) 160
Société Africaine d'Edition (Senegal) 324
Société belge des Auteurs, Compositeurs et Editeurs (SABAM) (Belgium) 44
Société Biblique belge ASBL (Belgium) 41
Société Biblique de Genève (Switzerland) 373
Société de Langue et de Littérature wallonnes ASBL (Belgium) 44
Société de Presse et d'Edition de Madagascar (Democratic Republic of Madagascar) 257
Société de Recherche appliquée à l'Education (France) 107
Société d'Edition d'Afrique Nouvelle (Senegal) 324
Société d'Edition d'Enseignement Supérieur (France) 107
Société d'Editions Scientifiques, Dimedia (France) 107
Société des anciens Textes français (France) 111
Société des Bibliophiles (France) 109
Société des Gens de Lettres (France) 111
Société des Libraires et Editeurs de la Suisse romande (SLESR) (Switzerland) 361
Société des Poètes Français (France) 111
Société d'Etudes dantesques (France) 111
Société d'Etudes Juridiques Internationales et Fiscales (France) 107
Société d'Exploitation des Nouveaux Humanoïdes Associés (France) 107
Société d'Exploitation et de Diffusion des Codes Rousseau (France) 107
Société d'Histoire littéraire de la France (France) 111
Société d'Information médicale et d'enseignement post-universitaire (France) 107
Société du Nouveau Littré (SNL) Dictionnaire 'Le Robert' (France) 107
Société du Vieux Montmartre (France) 111
Société Française des Imprimeries Administratives Centrales (France) 107
Société française des Traducteurs (France) 114
Société internationale de Bibliographie classique (International Organizations) 469
Société internationale des Bibliothèques-Musées des Arts du Spectacle (SIBMAS) (International Organizations) 469
Société Kenkoson d'Etudes Africaines (United Republic of Cameroun) 61
Société Librairie nouvelle (Tunisia) 383
Société Malgache d'Edition (Democratic Republic of Madagascar) 257
Société Malgache d'Edition (Democratic Republic of Madagascar) 258
Société nationale d'Edition et de Diffusion (Tunisia) 383
Société nationale d'Edition et de Diffusion (Tunisia) 383
Société nationale d'Edition et de Diffusion (SNED) (Algeria) 2
Société Nouvelle de l'Imprimerie Centrale (Democratic Republic of Madagascar) 257
Société royale des Bibliophiles et Iconophiles de Belgique (Belgium) 44
Société Universitaire d'Editions et de Librairie (France) 107
Society for Promoting, The, Christian Knowledge (United Kingdom) 434
Society for Research into Higher Education (United Kingdom) 434
Society for the Promotion and Improvement of Libraries (Pakistan) 304
Society for the Promotion of Japanese Literature (Japan) 246

Society for the Study of Mediaeval Languages and Literature (United Kingdom) 447
Society of Aesthetes, Art and Literary Critics (Bulgaria) 59
Society of Archivists (United Kingdom) 446
Society of Arts, Literature and Welfare (Bangladesh) 33
Society of Australian Writers (Australia) 21
Society of Australian Writers (United Kingdom) 447
Society of Authors (United Kingdom) 391
Society of County Librarians (United Kingdom) 446
Society of Editors (Australia) 10
Society of Indexers, The (United Kingdom) 391
Society of Metropolitan & County Chief Librarians (United Kingdom) 446
Society of Women Writers (Australia) 10
Society of Young Publishers (United Kingdom) 391
Sodalitas, Libraria Editoriale, Sas (Italy) 232
Sodel (Editeur) SA (France) 107
Söderström et Co Förlagsaktiebolag (Finland) 88
Sodexport (France) 109
Sodimca, Librairies (Zaire) 462
Soeroengan (Indonesia) 206
Soethoudt, Walter (Belgium) 41
Sofia City and District State Archives (Bulgaria) 59
Sofia Press Agency (Bulgaria) 58
Sofiac (Sociéte Française des Imprimeries Administratives Centrales) (France) 107
Sofiiski Universitet 'Kliment Ohridsky' Biblioteka (Bulgaria) 59
Sofradel-Seditas (France) 107
Sofradif Editions Philippe Auzou (France) 107
Sogalivre, Librairie (Gabon) 115
Sogang University Press (Republic of Korea) 252
Sogensha Publishing Co Ltd (Japan) 243
Sojuz na društvata na bibliotekarite na Jugoslavija (Macedonian) (Yugoslavia) 461
Sojuz na društvata na bibliotekarite na SR Makedonija (Yugoslavia) 461
Sojuz na društvata za makedonski jazik i literatura (Yugoslavia) 461
Sol, Ediciones del, SA (Argentina) 7
Solar (France) 107
Soledi (Imprimeur-Editeur) SA (Belgium) 41
Soleil Noir, Editions (France) 107
Solidaridad Publishing House (Philippines) 309
Solum Forlag A/S (Norway) 299
Somaiya Publications Pvt Ltd (India) 198
Somalia d'Oggi (Somalia) 328
Somec-Rwanda (Rwanda) 323
Sommai Press (Thailand) 380
Sommer og Sörensen Forlag ApS (Denmark) 78
Somogy, Editions d'Art Aimery (France) 107
Sonapal (Benin) 45
Soncino Press Ltd (United Kingdom) 434
Sondagskool Boekhandel (Republic of South Africa) 332
Sonnenweg-Verlag (Federal Republic of Germany) 160
Sonneville Press (Uitgeversmij) PVBA (Belgium) 41
Sonrisa, 'La, Vertical' Prize (International Literary Prizes) 479
Sonzogno (Italy) 232
Sopena, Editorial, Argentina SACI e I (Argentina) 7
Sopena, Editorial, Mexicana SA (Mexico) 268
Sopena, Ramón, SA (Spain) 345
Sopena Venezolana, Editorial Ramón, SA (Venezuela) 454
Soprep (Editions de l'Instant Durable) (France) 107
Sorava, Educatief Uitg (Suriname) 351
Sorbonne, Bibliothèque de la (France) 110
Sorgente, La, Srl (Italy) 232
Sorrett (Australia) 18
Sotheby Publications (United Kingdom) 434
Soulanges, Editions Louis, 'Le Livre Ouvert' (France) 107
Source, Les Editions de la, Sàrl (France) 107
Sousa e Almeida, Livraria (Portugal) 318
Sousa, Luisa Claudio de, Prize (Brazil) 57
South African Academy of Science and Arts Prizes (Republic of South Africa) 336
South African Institute for Librarianship and Information Science (Republic of South Africa) 334
South African Library (Republic of South Africa) 334
South African Publishers' Association (Republic of South Africa) 328
South Asian Publishers Pvt Ltd (India) 198
South Australian Government Biennial Literature Prize (Australia) 23
South China Morning Post Ltd (Hong Kong) 180
South End Press (Australia) 18
South Head Press (Poetry Australia) (Australia) 18
South Pacific Commission Library (New Caledonia) 286
Southeast Asian Ministers of Education Organization (SEAMEO) (International Organizations) 471
Southeast Asian Ministers of Education Organization (SEAMEO), Regional Language Centre (RELC) (Republic of Singapore) 327
Southeast Asian Regional Branch of the International Council on Archives (SARBICA) (International Organizations) 469
Southeast Book Co (Taiwan) 378

Southern Press Ltd (New Zealand) 289
Southside (United Kingdom) 434
Souvenir Press Ltd (United Kingdom) 434
'Sovetskaya Entsiklopediya', Izdatelstvo (Union of Soviet Socialist Republics) 388
'Sovetskaya Rossiya', Izdatelstvo (Union of Soviet Socialist Republics) 388
'Sovetskii Khudozhnik', Izdatelstvo (Union of Soviet Socialist Republics) 388
'Sovetskii Kompozitor', Izdatelstvo (Union of Soviet Socialist Republics) 388
'Sovetskoe Radio', Izdatelstvo (Union of Soviet Socialist Republics) 388
Soviet Land Nehru Awards (India) 204
Sovietskii Pisatel, Izdatelstvo (Union of Soviet Socialist Republics) 388
Sovremennik Publishers (Union of Soviet Socialist Republics) 388
Spaendende, Bogklubben, Bøger (Denmark) 79
Spangenberg (Federal Republic of Germany) 160
Spanish Book Center (Spain) 336
Spanish Book Club (United Kingdom) 444
Spanos, Costas (Greece) 175
Sparevirke, A/S (Denmark) 78
Sparfrämjandet, Förlagsaktiebolag (Sweden) 357
Sparrow Books (United Kingdom) 434
Spearhead (Kenya) 249
Spearman, Neville, (Jersey) Ltd (Channel Islands) 62
Spectrum Books Ltd (Nigeria) 295
Spectrum, Het, (IUM NV) (Belgium) 41
Spectrum Publications (India) 199
Spectrum Publications Pty Ltd (Australia) 18
Spectrum, Taschenbuch Verlag (Switzerland) 373
Spectrum, Uitgeverij Het, BV (Netherlands) 281
Spectrum Verlag Stuttgart GmbH (Federal Republic of Germany) 160
Spee Buchverlag GmbH (Federal Republic of Germany) 160
Speer-Verlag (Switzerland) 373
Spektra, Bokförlaget, AB (Sweden) 357
Spemann, W, Verlag (Federal Republic of Germany) 160
Sperling e Kupfer Editori SpA (Italy) 232
Sperling e Kupfer, Libreria (Italy) 234
Spes SA (Switzerland) 373
Sphere Books Ltd (United Kingdom) 434
Sphinx, Le, SA (Belgium) 41
Sphinx, The (Egypt) 84
Sphinx Verlag AG (Switzerland) 373
Spiegel-Bucher (Federal Republic of Germany) 160
Spiegelserie Boekenclub (Netherlands) 284
Spiess, Verlag Volker (Federal Republic of Germany) 160
Spirali Edizioni (Italy) 232
Spitz, Arno (Federal Republic of Germany) 160
Splichal SA (Belgium) 41
Spokesman Books (United Kingdom) 434
Společnost přátel knihy pro mládež (Czechoslovakia) 74
Společnost pro Československou literaturu, Index-, v zahraničí (Czechoslovakia) 74
Společnost pro krásné písmo a typografii (Czechoslovakia) 70
Spolek Českých bibliofilu (Czechoslovakia) 74
Spon, E & F N, Ltd (United Kingdom) 434
Sponholtz, Adolf, Verlag (Federal Republic of Germany) 160
Sport (Czechoslovakia) 72
Sport i Turystyka, Wydawnictwo (Poland) 313
Sport-Turism, Editura (Romania) 321
Sporting and Leisure Press (United Kingdom) 435
Sportska Knjiga (Yugoslavia) 459
Sportverlag (German Democratic Republic) 118
Sprachmethodik, Verlag für (Federal Republic of Germany) 160
Språkförlaget Skriptor AB (Sweden) 357
Språktjänst (Sweden) 360
Spring Books (United Kingdom) 435
Springer Books (India) Pvt Ltd (India) 199
Springer-Verlag Berlin — Heidelberg — New York — Tokyo GmbH & Co KG (Federal Republic of Germany) 160
Springer-Verlag KG (Austria) 28
Springwood Books Ltd (United Kingdom) 435
Spruyt, van Mantgem en de Does BV (Netherlands) 281
Spurbooks (United Kingdom) 435
Sreberk, J (Israel) 216
Sree Rama Publishers (India) 199
Sri Jaya, Pustaka, Sdn Bhd (Malaysia) 260
Sri Lanka Library Association (Sri Lanka) 350
Sri Lanka National Library Services Board (Sri Lanka) 350
Sri Lanka Publishers' Association (Sri Lanka) 349
Sri Nakharinwirot University Library (Thailand) 381
Srpska Književna Zadruga (Yugoslavia) 459
Srpske, Biblioteka, Akademije Nauka i Umetnosti (Yugoslavia) 459
St Paul's Bookshop (Isle of Man) 212
Staackmann, L, Verlag KG (Federal Republic of Germany) 160

Staatlich genehmigte Literarische Verwertungsgesellschaft (LVG) Gen mbH (Austria) 24
Staats- und Universitätsbibliothek (Federal Republic of Germany) 168
Staatsarchiv, Zentrales (German Democratic Republic) 119
Staatsbibliothek Bamberg (Federal Republic of Germany) 168
Staatsbibliothek Preussischer Kulturbesitz (Federal Republic of Germany) 168
Staatsdrukkerij en Uitgeverijbedrijf (Netherlands) 281
Staatsverlag der Deutschen Demokratischen Republik (German Democratic Republic) 118
Stabenfeldt Forlag (Norway) 299
Stacey International (United Kingdom) 435
Stadsbibliotheek (Belgium) 43
Stadt- und Bezirksbibliothek Leipzig (German Democratic Republic) 119
Stadt- und Universitätsbibliothek (Federal Republic of Germany) 168
Stadt- und Universitätsbibliothek (Switzerland) 376
Städte-Verlag, E v Wagner und J Mitterhuber (Federal Republic of Germany) 160
Stafleu (Netherlands) 281
Stafleu en Tholen (Netherlands) 281
Stafleu's Wetenschappelijke Uitgeversmaatschappij BV en Stafleu en Tholen BV (Netherlands) 281
Stage 1 (United Kingdom) 435
Stäheli, Buchhandlung (Switzerland) 376
Stähle und Friedel Verlagsgesellschaft mbH und Co (Federal Republic of Germany) 160
Stahleisen, Verlag, mbH (Federal Republic of Germany) 160
Stainer & Bell Ltd (United Kingdom) 435
Stalling Verlag GmbH, Druck und Verlagshaus (Federal Republic of Germany) 160
Stam Press Ltd (United Kingdom) 435
Stam/Robijns (Netherlands) 281
Stam Technische Boeken (Netherlands) 282
Stam Tijdschriften BV (Netherlands) 282
Stamford College Publishers (Republic of Singapore) 327
Stämpfli, Verlag, & Cie AG (Switzerland) 373
Standaard Hoofdstadboekhandel (Belgium) 42
Standaard Uitgeverij en Distributie BV (Netherlands) 282
Standaard Uitgeverij (Scriptoria NV) (Belgium) 41
Standard Book Numbering Agency (Argentina) 3
Standard Book Numbering Agency (Australia) 10
Standard Book Numbering Agency (Austria) 24
Standard Book Numbering Agency (Belgium) 33
Standard Book Numbering Agency (Brazil) 48
Standard Book Numbering Agency (Colombia) 65
Standard Book Numbering Agency (Cyprus) 70
Standard Book Numbering Agency (Denmark) 75
Standard Book Numbering Agency (Egypt) 83
Standard Book Numbering Agency (Finland) 87
Standard Book Numbering Agency (France) 90
Standard Book Numbering Agency (Federal Republic of Germany) 121
Standard Book Numbering Agency (Ghana) 171
Standard Book Numbering Agency (Hong Kong) 178
Standard Book Numbering Agency (Hungary) 181
Standard Book Numbering Agency (India) 186
Standard Book Numbering Agency (Israel) 213
Standard Book Numbering Agency (Italy) 219
Standard Book Numbering Agency (Japan) 238
Standard Book Numbering Agency (Malaysia) 259
Standard Book Numbering Agency (Mexico) 264
Standard Book Numbering Agency (Netherlands) 273
Standard Book Numbering Agency (New Zealand) 287
Standard Book Numbering Agency (Nigeria) 293
Standard Book Numbering Agency (Norway) 298
Standard Book Numbering Agency (Philippines) 308
Standard Book Numbering Agency (Poland) 311
Standard Book Numbering Agency (Republic of Singapore) 325
Standard Book Numbering Agency (Republic of South Africa) 328
Standard Book Numbering Agency (Spain) 336
Standard Book Numbering Agency (Suriname) 350
Standard Book Numbering Agency (Sweden) 351
Standard Book Numbering Agency (Switzerland) 361
Standard Book Numbering Agency (Switzerland) 361
Standard Book Numbering Agency (Tanzania) 378
Standard Book Numbering Agency (Thailand) 380
Standard Book Numbering Agency (Union of Soviet Socialist Republics) 386
Standard Book Numbering Agency (Zimbabwe) 464
Standard Book Numbering Agency Ltd (United Kingdom) 391
Standard Books Ltd (Zambia) 463
Standard, The, Book Depot (India) 199
Standard, The, Bookshop (Tanzania) 379
Standartov, Znak Pochyota Order Izdatelstvo (Union of Soviet Socialist Republics) 388
Standing Conference of African University Libraries (SCAUL) (International Organizations) 469
Standing Conference of National and University Libraries (SCONUL) (United Kingdom) 446

Standing Conference on Library Materials on Africa (SCOLMA) (International Organizations) 469
Stanford Maritime Ltd (United Kingdom) 435
Stanké, Les Editions Internationales Alain (France) 107
Stanton, Ernest, Publishers (Pty) Ltd (Republic of South Africa) 332
Stapp Verlag Wolfgang Stapp (Federal Republic of Germany) 160
Stappaerts, NV Uitgeverij (Belgium) 41
Star (Australia) 20
Star (United Kingdom) 435
Star Book Bank (India) 201
Star Publications (P) Ltd (India) 202
Star Publications (Pvt) Ltd (India) 199
Star, Pustaka (Indonesia) 206
Star Schools (Republic of South Africa) 332
Star, The, Press (Brunei) 58
Starczewski, Hanns-Joachim, Verlag/Künstlerhof-Galerie (Federal Republic of Germany) 161
Starke, Harold, Ltd (United Kingdom) 435
State Archives (Mongolian People's Republic) 270
State Book Trading Office (Mongolian People's Republic) 270
State Central Library (India) 202
State Central Library (Democratic People's Republic of Korea) 250
State Institute of Languages (India) 199
State Librarians' Council (Australia) 21
State Library (Burma) 60
State Library (Republic of South Africa) 334
State Library of New South Wales, The (Australia) 20
State Library of Queensland (Australia) 20
State Library of South Australia (Australia) 20
State Library of Tasmania (Australia) 20
State Library of Victoria (Australia) 20
State of Victoria Short Story Awards (Australia) 23
State Press (Mongolian People's Republic) 270
State Prize for Children's and Youth Literature (Netherlands) 286
State Prize for Literature, the P C Hooft Prize (Netherlands) 286
State Prizes for Literature (Finland) 90
State Stipendium for Literature (Austria) 31
State University of New York Press (United Kingdom) 435
Stationery & Educational Book Centre Ltd (Jamaica) 237
Stationery Office (Oifig an tSolathair) (Republic of Ireland) 210
Statisticke a evidencni vydavatelství tiskopisu (Czechoslovakia) 72
Statistics Library (Finland) 89
Statistika (Union of Soviet Socialist Republics) 388
Statistisk Sentralbyras Bibliotek (Norway) 300
Statistiska Centralbyråns Bibliotek (Sweden) 359
Statisztikai Kiadó Vállalat (Hungary) 182
Státní pedagogické nakladatelství (Czechoslovakia) 72
Státní technická knihovna (Czechoslovakia) 73
Státní vědecká knihovna (Czechoslovakia) 73
Státní vědecká knihovna (Czechoslovakia) 73
Státní vědecká knihovna odbor technické literatury (Czechoslovakia) 73
Státní zemědělské nakladatelství (Czechoslovakia) 72
Statsbiblioteket (Denmark) 80
Statystycznich i Drukarni, Zarzad Wydawnictwo (Poland) 313
Stauda, Johannes, Verlag (Federal Republic of Germany) 161
Stavanger Bibliotek (Norway) 300
Steamships Trading Co (Papua New Guinea) 305
Steensballes, P F, Forlag (Norway) 299
Steenuil, De (Netherlands) 282
Stegeland, Leif, Förlag AB (Sweden) 357
Steimatzky Ltd (Israel) 216
Steimatzky Ltd (Israel) 217
Steiner, Franz, Verlag GmbH (Federal Republic of Germany) 161
Steiner, Rudolf, Press (United Kingdom) 435
Steiner, Rudolf, Verlag (Switzerland) 373
Steinkopf, J F, Verlag GmbH (Federal Republic of Germany) 161
Steinkopff, Dr Dietrich, Verlag (Federal Republic of Germany) 161
Steintor Verlag, Rudolf Jüdes (Federal Republic of Germany) 161
Stella, Editorial (Argentina) 7
Stella, Editorial (Dominican Republic) 82
Stelle, Gruppo Editoriale Le, SpA (Italy) 232
Stenvalls, Frank, Förlag (Sweden) 357
Stenvert, Uitgeverij M, en Zoon BV (Netherlands) 282
Stephanus Edition Verlags AG (Switzerland) 373
Stephanus Edition Verlags GmbH (Federal Republic of Germany) 161
Stephens and Johnsons Book Department (Trinidad and Tobago) 382
Stephens, Patrick, Ltd (United Kingdom) 435
Stephenson, Carl, Verlag GmbH & Co (Federal Republic of Germany) 161
Steppe (Belgium) 41

Ster, De, PVBA (Belgium) 41
Sterling Book Club (India) 201
Sterling Publishers Pvt Ltd (India) 199
Stern-Verlag Janssen und Co (Federal Republic of Germany) 161
Stern-Verlag Janssen und Co (Federal Republic of Germany) 168
Sternberg-Verlag (Federal Republic of Germany) 161
Stevens & Sons Ltd (United Kingdom) 435
Steyler Verlag (Federal Republic of Germany) 161
Stichting Bibliotheek en Documentatieacademies (Netherlands) 285
Stichting Speurwerk betreffende het Boek (Netherlands) 273
Stiehm, Lothar, Verlag GmbH (Federal Republic of Germany) 161
Stiftelsen Kursverksamhetens Förlag (Sweden) 357
Stiftelsen Svenska Barnboksinstitutet (Sweden) 359
Stiftsbibliothek (Switzerland) 376
Stiintifică si Enciclopedică, Editura (Romania) 321
Stillitron (United Kingdom) 435
Stimme-Verlag GmbH (Federal Republic of Germany) 161
Stobart & Son Ltd (United Kingdom) 435
Stock, Editions (France) 107
Stocker, Josef, AG (Switzerland) 373
Stocker, Leopold, Verlag (Austria) 28
Stocker-Schmid, Verlag, AG (Switzerland) 373
Stockholm Universitets Bibliotek (Sweden) 359
Stockholms Stadsbibliotek (Sweden) 359
Stockton House (New Zealand) 289
Stockwell, Arthur H, Ltd (United Kingdom) 435
Stollfuss Verlag Bonn GmbH & Co KG (Federal Republic of Germany) 161
Stone, Walter, Memorial Award (Australia) 23
Stora Romanklubben (Sweden) 358
Storia, Edizioni di, e Letteratura (Italy) 232
Story-Scientia, E, NV M & I (Belgium) 41
Story-Scientia, J, PVBA (Belgium) 42
Stowarzyszenie Tlumaczy Polskich (Poland) 315
Stowarzyszenie Autorów Zaiks (Poland) 311
Stowarzyszenie Bibliotekarzy Polskich (Poland) 314
Stowarzyszenie Ksiegarzy Polskich (Poland) 311
Strache, Verlag Dr Wolf, GmbH & Co KG (Federal Republic of Germany) 161
Strakosch, Carl, og Olaf Nordgreen (Denmark) 79
Strandbergs Forlag (Denmark) 78
Strassova, Greta (France) 109
Středočeské nakladatelství knihkupectví (Czechoslovakia) 72
Strega Prize (Italy) 236
Strengholt's, A J G, Boeken, Anno 1928, BV (Netherlands) 282
Stroemfeld Verlag AG (Switzerland) 373
Strom-Verlag (Switzerland) 373
Stroyizdat Publishing House (Union of Soviet Socialist Republics) 388
Strubes Forlag og Boghandel A/S (Denmark) 78
Struik (Pty) Ltd (Republic of South Africa) 332
Student Christian Movement Press (United Kingdom) 435
Studentlitteratur (United Kingdom) 435
Studentlitteratur AB (Sweden) 357
Students', The, Book Co (India) 199
Studi Contemporanei (Italy) 232
Studia Croatica (Argentina) 7
Studia, Editions, SA (France) 108
Studieförlaget (Sweden) 357
Studio Book Club (Sweden) 63
Studio, Libreria (Chile) 63
Studio, Librería, SA (Mexico) 269
Studio Publications (Ipswich) Ltd (United Kingdom) 435
Studio Vista (United Kingdom) 435
Studium Ediciones (Spain) 345
Studium (Edizioni Studium Vita Nova SpA) (Italy) 232
Studium, Librería, SA (Peru) 307
Studium, Librería, SA (Peru) 307
Studium, Verlag für das, der Arbeiterbewegung GmbH (Federal Republic of Germany) 161
Study Aids (United Kingdom) 435
Stürtz Verlag (Federal Republic of Germany) 161
Stvarnost (Yugoslavia) 459
Styria, Buchhandlung (Austria) 30
Styria, Verlag (Austria) 28
Su Hoc (Historical) Publishing House (Socialist Republic of Viet Nam) 455
Su Librería (Ecuador) 83
Su That (Truth) Publishing House (Socialist Republic of Viet Nam) 455
Sub Rosa Frauenverlag (Federal Republic of Germany) 161
Subodh Pocket Books (India) 199
Succes BV (Netherlands) 282
Success Publications (Kenya) 249
Sud Editions (Tunisia) 383
Sudan Library Association (Sudan) 350
Sudan, The, Bookshop Ltd (Sudan) 350
Südbuch Vertriebsgesellschaft mbH (Federal Republic of Germany) 161

Süddeutsche Verlagsgesellschaft Ulm (Federal Republic of Germany) 161
Süddeutscher Verlag Buchverlag (Federal Republic of Germany) 161
Sudha Publications Pvt Ltd (India) 199
Sudhindra Award (India) 204
'Sudostroenie', Izdatelstvo (Union of Soviet Socialist Republics) 389
Sudri, Bókaútgáfan (Iceland) 184
Südwest Verlag GmbH und Co KG (Federal Republic of Germany) 161
Suenson, Finn, Forlag (Denmark) 78
Sugar and Snails Books (Australia) 18
Sugarco Edizioni SRL (Italy) 232
Suhrkamp Verlag KG (Federal Republic of Germany) 161
Suksapan Panit (Business Organization of Teachers Council of Thailand) (Thailand) 380
Suksit Siam Co Ltd (Thailand) 380
Suksit Siam Co Ltd (Thailand) 381
Süleymaniye Kütüphanesi Müdürlügü (Turkey) 385
Sulina, Livraria (Brazil) 56
Sulina, Livraria, Editora (Brazil) 55
Sultan Chand and Sons (India) 199
Sultan's Library (Cyprus) 70
Suma, Librería (Venezuela) 454
Suman Prakashan (P) Ltd (India) 199
Sumatera (Indonesia) 206
Summit Books (Australia) 18
Sumur Bandung (Indonesia) 206
Sumus Verlag Jutta Gütermann (Switzerland) 373
Sun Books Pty Ltd (Australia) 18
Sun Papermac (Australia) 18
Sun Yat-Sen Library (Hong Kong) 180
Sundems, H, Bokhandel A/S (Norway) 300
Sundial (United Kingdom) 435
Sung Eum Kak Seoul (Republic of Korea) 252
Suomalainen Kirjakauppa Oy (Finland) 88
Suomalainen Tiedeakatemia (Finland) 89
Suomalaisen Kirjallisuuden Seura (Finland) 88
Suomalaisen Kirjallisuuden Seura (Finland) 89
Suomen Antikvariaattiyhdistys-Finska Antikvariatforeningen (Finland) 87
Suomen Arvostelijain Liitto (Finland) 89
Suomen Kääntäjäin Yhdists (Finland) 90
Suomen Kirjailijaliitto (Finland) 87
Suomen Kirjallisuuspalvelun Seura (Finland) 89
Suomen Kirjastoseura (Finland) 89
Suomen Kustannusyhdistys (Finland) 87
Suomen Nuortenkirjaneuvosto ry (Finland) 87
Suomen Tieteellinen Kirjastoseura (Finland) 89
Supraphon (Czechoslovakia) 73
Sur, Editorial, SA (Argentina) 7
Sur Prize (India) 204
Suriname, Publishers' Association (Suriname) 351
Suriwongs Book Centre (Thailand) 381
Suriyaban Bookstore (Thailand) 381
Suriyaban Publishers (Thailand) 380
Surjeet Book Depot (India) 201
Surjeet Book Depot (Regd) (India) 199
Surrey University Press (United Kingdom) 435
Surveyors Publications (United Kingdom) 435
Susaeta, Ediciones, SA (Spain) 345
Sussex University Press (United Kingdom) 435
Sussex Video Ltd (United Kingdom) 435
Sutpaisarn (Thailand) 381
Suuri Suomalainen Kirjakerho Oy (Finland) 88
Suva Book Shop (Fiji) 86
Suva City Library (Fiji) 86
Suyuz Knigoizdatelite i Knizharite (Bulgaria) 58
Svalan, Bokklubben (Sweden) 358
Svenska Antikvariatföreningen (Sweden) 351
Svenska Arkivsamfundet (Sweden) 359
Svenska Bibliotekariesamfundet (Sweden) 359
Svenska Bokförläggareföreningen (Sweden) 351
Svenska Bokhandels-Medhjälpare-Föreningen (Sweden) 351
Svenska Bokhandlareföreningen (Sweden) 351
Svenska Folkbibliotekarieförbundet (Sweden) 359
Svenska Litteratursällskapet i Finland (Finland) 89
Svenska Musikförläggareföreningen UPA (Sweden) 352
Svenska Österbottens Litteraturförening (Finland) 90
Svenska Österbottens Litteraturförening (Sweden) 359
Svenska Utbildningsförlaget Liber AB (Sweden) 357
Svepomoc (Czechoslovakia) 73
Sveriges Allmänna Biblioteksförening (Sweden) 359
Sveriges B-Bokhandlareförbund (Sweden) 352
Sveriges Exportråd (Sweden) 357
Sveriges Författarförbund (Sweden) 352
Sveriges Lantbruksuniversitets Bibliotek (Sweden) 359
Sveriges Radios Förlag (Sweden) 357
Svet Knjige (Yugoslavia) 460
Svjetlost (Yugoslavia) 459
Svjetlost (Yugoslavia) 460
Svoboda (Czechoslovakia) 73
Svoboda Book Club (Czechoslovakia) 73
Svyaz, Izdatelstvo (Union of Soviet Socialist Republics) 389
Swami, Sree Padmanabha, Prize (India) 204

Swan (India) 199
Swan, Anni, Prize (Finland) 90
Swaziland College of Technology Library (Swaziland) 351
Swaziland National Library Service (Swaziland) 351
Swaziland News Agency (Swaziland) 351
Swedenborg Institut (Switzerland) 373
Swedish Academy Prizes (Sweden) 360
Swedish-English Literary Translators' Association (SELTA) (International Organizations) 469
Swedish into Foreign Language Translation Prize (Sweden) 360
Swedish Linguistics Prize (Sweden) 360
Swedish National ISBN Centre (Sweden) 352
Sweet & Maxwell Ltd (United Kingdom) 436
Sweet & Maxwell (NZ) Ltd (New Zealand) 289
Swets en Zeitlinger BV (Netherlands) 282
Świetego Wojciecha, Ksiegarnia (Poland) 313
Swift (United Kingdom) 436
Swindon Book Co (Hong Kong) 180
Swiss Mission Publications (Republic of South Africa) 332
Syarikat Cultural Supplies Sdn Bhd (Malaysia) 260
Syarikat Dian Sdn Bhd (Malaysia) 260
Syarikat United Book Sdn Bhd (Malaysia) 260
Sybex Verlag GmbH (Federal Republic of Germany) 161
Sydney University Press (Australia) 18
Syllogos Ekdoton Bibliopolon (Greece) 174
Symposion-Verlag, J Siegler (Federal Republic of Germany) 161
Syndicat belge de la Librairie ancienne et moderne (Belgium) 33
Syndicat de la Librairie ancienne et du Commerce de l'Estampe en Suisse (Vereinigung der Buchantiquare und Kupferstichhändler in der Schweiz) (Switzerland) 361
Syndicat des Critiques littéraires (France) 111
Syndicat des Libraires (Socialist Republic of Viet Nam) 455
Syndicat des Libraries de Tunisie (Tunisia) 383
Syndicat des Répresentants littéraires français (France) 90
Syndicat national de la Librairie Ancienne et Moderne (SLAM) (France) 90
Syndicat national de l'Edition (France) 90
Syndicat national des Annuaires et Supports divers de Publicité (France) 90
Syndicat national des Importateurs et Exportateurs de Livres (France) 90
Syndikat Autoren- und Verlagsgesellschaft (Federal Republic of Germany) 162
Syokabo Publishing Co Ltd (Japan) 243
Syrian Documentation Papers (Syria) 377
Syrian Patriarchal Seminary, Library of the (Lebanon) 254
Systems Publications Ltd (United Kingdom) 436
Szabó, Fövárosi, Ervin Könyvtár (Hungary) 182
Szépirodalmi Kiadó (Hungary) 182
Szkolne i Pedagogiczne, Wydawnictwa (Poland) 313

T B L (Tübinger Beiträge zur Linguistik) Verlag (Federal Republic of Germany) 162
T E A Ediciones SA (Spain) 345
T E A (Tipográfica Editora Argentina) (Argentina) 7
T E B R O C (Tehran Book Processing Centre) (Iran) 208
T M P Book Department (Tanzania) 379
T M P Book Department (Tanzania) 379
T R- Verlagsunion GmbH (Federal Republic of Germany) 162
T Ü V, Verlag, Rheinland GmbH, Sicherheitstechnik, Energie und Umweltschutz (Federal Republic of Germany) 162
T V F (Switzerland) 373
T V Times Books (United Kingdom) 436
Tabajara, Edições (Brazil) 55
Table, Les Editions de la, Ronde (France) 108
Tafe Educational Books (Australia) 18
Tafelberg Publishers Ltd (Republic of South Africa) 332
Tagore Award (India) 204
Tai Kuen Book Co (Hong Kong) 180
Taipei Municipal Library (Taiwan) 378
Taipei Publications Trading Co (Taiwan) 378
Taishukan Publishing Co Ltd (Taishukan Shoten) (Japan) 243
Taiwan Branch Library, National Central Library (Taiwan) 378
Taizé, Les Presses de (France) 108
Taj Co Ltd (Pakistan) 303
Tájekoztatási tudományos társaság (Hungary) 183
Takahashi Shoten Co Ltd (Japan) 243
Takariva, Imprimerie (Democratic Republic of Madagascar) 257
Talbot House Press (United Kingdom) 436
Talbot Press Ltd (Republic of Ireland) 210
Tallandier, Librairie Jules (France) 108
Taller Ediciones JB (Spain) 345
Tallis Press Ltd (United Kingdom) 436

Talmudic Encyclopaedia Publications (Israel) 216
Tamaraw Publishing Co (Philippines) 309
Tamayo, Franz, Prize (Bolivia) 47
Tamburini Editore SpA (Italy) 233
Tamgu Dang Book Centre (Republic of Korea) 252
Tamil Puthakalayam (India) 199
Tammi Kustannusosakeyhtiö (Finland) 88
Tampere Prize (Finland) 90
Tampereen Kirjakauppa Oy (Finland) 88
Tampereen Yliopiston Kirjasto (Finland) 89
Tana Press Ltd (Nigeria) 295
Táncsics Szakszervezeti Kiadó (Hungary) 182
Tandem (United Kingdom) 436
Tanizaki Junichiro Prize (Japan) 247
Tanko-Sha Publishing Co Ltd (Japan) 243
Tankönyvkiadó Vállalat (Hungary) 182
Tansy Books (Republic of Ireland) 210
Tantivy, The, Press Ltd (United Kingdom) 436
Tanum-Norli Forlaget A/S (Norway) 299
Tanzania Elimu Supplies Ltd (Tanzania) 379
Tanzania Library Association (Tanzania) 379
Tanzania Library Service (Tanzania) 379
Tanzania Library Service (Tanzania) 379
Tanzania Mission Press (Tanzania) 379
Tanzania Mission Press (Tanzania) 379
Tanzania Publishing House (Tanzania) 379
Tapir (Norway) 300
Tara Press (Fiji) 86
Taraporevala (DB) Sons & Co Pvt Ltd (India) 199
Taraporevala Publishing Industries Pvt Ltd (India) 199
Tarate (Indonesia) 206
Tarbut Vehinuch (Israel) 216
Tardy, Editions, SA (France) 108
Target (United Kingdom) 436
Target Publishers (Edms) Bpk (Republic of South Africa) 332
Taride, Editions, Sàrl (France) 108
Tarquin Publications (United Kingdom) 436
Tartu Riikliku Ulikooli Teaduslik Raamatükogu (Union of Soviet Socialist Republics) 389
Tasmanian Booksellers' Association (Australia) 10
Tassier, Suzanne, Prize (Belgium) 45
Tata McGraw-Hill Publishing Co Ltd (India) 199
Tate Gallery Publications (United Kingdom) 436
Tatran (Czechoslovakia) 73
Tauber, Peter, Press Agency (United Kingdom) 443
Taurus (Republic of South Africa) 332
Taurus Ediciones SA (Spain) 346
Tavistock Publications Ltd (United Kingdom) 436
Tawjih, al-, Press (Syria) 377
Taxation (Pakistan) 303
Taylor, Alister, Publishers (New Zealand) 289
Taylor & Francis Ltd (United Kingdom) 436
Taylor, Reginald, Prize (United Kingdom) 450
Taylorix Fachverlag Stiegler und Co (Federal Republic of Germany) 162
Tcherikover Publishers Ltd (Israel) 216
Tchernichowsky Prize (Israel) 218
Tchou, Société d'Exploitation de, Editeur Sàrl (France) 108
Teach Yourself Books (United Kingdom) 436
Teacher Publishing Co Ltd (United Kingdom) 436
Teachers' Book Centre Ltd (Jamaica) 237
Teachers' Book Shelf (New Zealand) 290
Teachers Bookshelf (Australia) 20
Teachers' Club Library (People's Democratic Republic of Yemen) 456
Teachers' Union (Israel) 216
Teakfield Ltd (United Kingdom) 436
Technica (Bulgaria) 58
Technical Chamber, Library of the, of Greece (Greece) 176
Technical Chamber of Greece (Greece) 175
Technical High School Library (Namibia) 272
Technical Institutes, Central Library of the Higher (Bulgaria) 59
Technical, The, Press Ltd (United Kingdom) 436
Technical University Library (Turkey) 385
Techniek, De (Belgium) 41
Technik Tabellen Verlag Fikentscher und Co (Federal Republic of Germany) 162
Technik, VEB Verlag (German Democratic Republic) 118
Technip, Société des Éditions (France) 108
Technique et Documentation (Librairie Lavoisier) (France) 108
Technique et Vulgarisation SA (France) 108
Techniques de l'Ingénieur Sàrl (France) 108
Techniques Professionels, Editions (France) 108
Technitrain (Pty) Ltd (Republic of South Africa) 332
Tecni Ciencia Libros (Venezuela) 454
Técnicos Asociados, Editores, SA (Spain) 346
Técnicos e Científicos, Livros, Editora SA (Brazil) 55
Tecnoprint, Editora, Ltda (Brazil) 55
Tecnos, Editorial, SA (Spain) 346
Tecolote, El (Guatemala) 177
Teduca, Técnicas Educativas, CA (Venezuela) 454
Teenage (Australia) 20
Teenage (New Zealand) 290

Tegopoulos (Greece) 175
Tehnica, Editura (Romania) 322
Tehnička Knjiga (Yugoslavia) 459
Tehnička Knjiga (Yugoslavia) 459
Tehnička Knjiga (Yugoslavia) 460
Tehnika (Yugoslavia) 459
Tehran Book Processing Centre (TEBROC) (Iran) 207
Tehran, Central Library and Documentation Centre of, University (Iran) 208
Tehran University Press (Iran) 207
Teide, Editorial, SA (Spain) 346
Teikoku-Shoin Co Ltd (Japan) 243
Teirlinck, Auguste, Prize (Belgium) 45
Teissonnière, Paul, Prize (France) 114
Teixeira, A M, e Cia (Filhos) Lda (Livraria Classica Editora) (Portugal) 318
Tejerina, Alfonso, Ltda (Bolivia) 46
Tek Translation & International Print Ltd (United Kingdom) 451
Teknillisen Korkeakoulun Kirjasto (Finland) 89
Teknisk Forlag A/S (Denmark) 78
Tekniska Litteratursällskapet (Sweden) 359
Teknografiska Institutet AB (Sweden) 357
Teknologisk Forlag (Norway) 299
Teknologisk Instituts Forlag (Denmark) 78
Tel Aviv University Library (Israel) 218
Tel Aviv University, Publications Sales Division (Israel) 216
Telecommunications Press (United Kingdom) 436
Téléscope, Le (France) 109
Telex-Verlag Jaeger und Waldmann (Federal Republic of Germany) 162
Telford, Thomas, Ltd (United Kingdom) 436
Teloeken, Alf, Verlag KG (Federal Republic of Germany) 162
Telos series of Paperbacks (Federal Republic of Germany) 162
Temco Publishing Ltd (Zambia) 463
Temis, Editorial, Ltda (Colombia) 66
Temis, Librería, Ltda (Colombia) 67
Tempel, Uitgeverij De (Belgium) 41
Temple Press (United Kingdom) 436
Temple Smith, Maurice, Ltd (United Kingdom) 436
Tende Verlag GmbH (Federal Republic of Germany) 162
Tenderini, Mirella Vescovi (Italy) 234
Tenri Central Library (Japan) 245
Tequi, Librairie Pierre, et Editions Tequi (France) 108
Tercer, Ediciones, Mundo Ltda (Colombia) 66
Tercer, Librería, Mundo (Colombia) 67
Teresianum, Edizioni del (Italy) 233
Terra Hippologica (Switzerland) 373
Terra Magica (Switzerland) 373
Terra Sancta Arts (Israel) 216
Terrapin (United Kingdom) 436
Tertulia, Librería La (Puerto Rico) 320
Tests, Editions (France) 108
Teti, Nicola, e C Editore SRL (Italy) 233
Teubner, B G, GmbH (Federal Republic of Germany) 162
Teubner, BSB B G, Verlagsgesellschaft (German Democratic Republic) 118
Text Book Centre Ltd (Kenya) 249
Text Books Malaysia Sdn Bhd (Malaysia) 260
Text und Kritik, Edition, GmbH (Federal Republic of Germany) 162
Textbook Publishers' Association of Japan (Kyokasho Kyokai) (Japan) 238
Textbook, The, Centre Ltd (Kenya) 249
Thacker & Co Ltd (India) 199
Thai Commercial Printing Press (Thailand) 381
Thai Inc (Thailand) 381
Thai Library Association (Thailand) 381
Thai National Documentation Centre (TNDC) (Thailand) 381
Thai Watana Panich (Thailand) 381
Thames & Hudson Ltd (United Kingdom) 436
Thames Head Ltd (United Kingdom) 436
Thammasat University Libraries (Thailand) 381
Than Myit Baho Publishing House (Burma) 60
Thaning og Appels Forlag (Denmark) 78
Theatrum Orbis Terrarum (Netherlands) 282
Theiss, Konrad, Verlag GmbH (Federal Republic of Germany) 162
Thekes, Librería (Puerto Rico) 320
Theodor (Haiti) 178
Theologischer Verlag AG (Switzerland) 373
Theoria, Ediciones, SRL (Argentina) 7
Theosophical Publishing, The, House (India) 199
Thesen Verlag Vowinckel und Co (Federal Republic of Germany) 162
Theseus Verlag AG (Switzerland) 373
Thiele und Schwarz, Druck- und Verlagshaus (Federal Republic of Germany) 162
Thielen, Verlag-Buchhandlung Joseph (Grand Duchy of Luxembourg) 257
Thieme, BV Uitgeverij en Boekhandel W J, & Cie (Netherlands) 282

Thieme, Georg, Verlag (Federal Republic of Germany) 162
Thieme, VEB Georg, Leipzig (German Democratic Republic) 118
Thiemig, Karl, AG München (Federal Republic of Germany) 162
Thienemanns, K, Verlag (Federal Republic of Germany) 162
Thiers Prize (France) 114
Thin, James, Bookseller (United Kingdom) 444
Third World First Publications (Nigeria) 295
Thjódsaga, Bókaútgáfan (Iceland) 184
Thjodskjalasafn (National Archives) (Iceland) 185
Tholenaar, Jan, Verlag GmbH, G D Bücherei (Federal Republic of Germany) 162
Thomas, A (United Kingdom) 436
Thomas, Dylan, Award (United Kingdom) 450
Thomas-Verlag (Switzerland) 373
Thomasons, Joseph, & Co (India) 200
Thomson Books Ltd (United Kingdom) 436
Thomson Press (India) Ltd (India) 200
Thomson Publications South Africa (Pty) Ltd (Republic of South Africa) 332
Thone, Imprimerie Georges, SA (Belgium) 41
Thorbecke, Jan, Verlag GmbH & Co (Federal Republic of Germany) 162
Thornes, Stanley, (Publishers) Ltd (United Kingdom) 436
Thornhill Press Ltd (United Kingdom) 437
Thornton Cox Ltd (United Kingdom) 437
Thorpe, D W, Pty Ltd (Australia) 18
Thorpe, F A, (Publishing) Ltd (United Kingdom) 437
Thorsons Publishers Ltd (United Kingdom) 437
Three Hierarchs, Library of the (Greece) 176
Thu Viên Quốc Gia Viet Nam (Socialist Republic of Viet Nam) 455
Thudhammawaddy Press (Burma) 60
Thule, Dott Prof Tommaso Romano — Edizioni (Italy) 233
Thule, The, Press (United Kingdom) 437
Thun, Verlags und Versandbuchhandlung, AG (Switzerland) 374
Thurman Publishing Ltd (United Kingdom) 437
Thwe Thauk (Burma) 60
Tibetan, Central, Secretariat (India) 200
Tiden, Bokförlags AB (Sweden) 357
Tiden Norsk Forlag (Norway) 299
Tiderne Skifter (Denmark) 78
Tidnings AB Dagen (Sweden) 357
Tiempo Contemporaneo, Editorial (Argentina) 8
Tiempo, Editorial, Nuevo SA (Venezuela) 454
Tiers Monde, Librairie du (Algeria) 2
Tieteellisen Informoinnin Neuvosto (Finland) 89
Tieteellisten Kirjastojen Virkailijat — Vetenskapliga Bibliotekens Tjänstemannaförening ry (Finland) 89
Tietoteos Publishing Co (Finland) 88
Tiger (United Kingdom) 437
Tijdstroom, Uitgeversmaatschappij de, BV (Netherlands) 282
Tilgher-Genova SAS (Italy) 233
Timbro, AB (Sweden) 357
Time-Life Books (United Kingdom) 437
Time-Life Books BV (Netherlands) 282
Time-Life International de México, SA (Mexico) 268
Times Book Centre (Hong Kong) 180
Times Book Club (Nigeria) 296
Times Books International (Republic of Singapore) 327
Times Books Ltd (United Kingdom) 437
Times Bookshop Ltd (Malawi) 258
Times Distributors Sdn Bhd (Malaysia) 261
Times Educational Co Ltd (Hong Kong) 180
Times Educational Co Sdn Bhd (Malaysia) 260
'Times Educational Supplement', The, Information Book Awards (International Literary Prizes) 479
Times Stores Ltd (Jamaica) 237
Times The Bookshop (Republic of Singapore) 327
Timmins Literary Award (Republic of South Africa) 336
Timmins Publishers (Pty) Ltd (Republic of South Africa) 332
Timun, Editorial, Mas SA (Spain) 346
Tintamas Indonesia PT (Indonesia) 206
Tipografia Nacional (Netherlands Antilles) 286
Tipografia Poliglotta Vaticana (Vatican City State) 453
Tipografia Stazionem (Switzerland) 373
Tips für Trips (Federal Republic of Germany) 162
Tiranti, Alec, Ltd (United Kingdom) 437
Tirona, Ramona S, Memorial Library (Philippines) 310
Tiskarna Ljudske Pravice (Yugoslavia) 459
Tisserand, Lucien, Prize (France) 114
Tiszáninneni Református Egyházkerület Nagykönyvtára (Hungary) 182
Titania-Verlag Ferdinand Schroll (Federal Republic of Germany) 162
Tjeenk Willink, H D, BV (Netherlands) 282
Tjeenk Willink-Noorduijn BV (Netherlands) 282
Tjeenk Willink, W E J, BV (Netherlands) 282
Tobin Music Books (United Kingdom) 437
Todariana Editrice (Italy) 233
Today & Tomorrow's Printers & Publishers (India) 200

Toeche-Mittler, S, Verlag (Federal Republic of Germany) 162
Togolaise, Nouvelle Librairie (Togo) 382
Tohoku University Library (Japan) 245
Toison, Libris, d'Or SA (Belgium) 42
Tokai University Press (Japan) 243
Toko Messir (Indonesia) 206
Tokuma-Shoten (Japan) 243
Tokyo Kagaku Dozin Co Ltd (Japan) 243
Tokyo Metropolitan Central Library (Japan) 245
Tokyo News Service Ltd (Japan) 243
Tokyo Shuppan Hanbai Co Ltd (Distributors) (Japan) 245
Tokyo Sogensha Co Ltd (Japan) 243
Tokyo Tosho Co Ltd (Japan) 244
Tolkien, The, Society (United Kingdom) 447
Tolley Publishing Co (United Kingdom) 437
Tom-Gallon Trust Award (United Kingdom) 450
Tomas Förlag KB (Sweden) 357
Tomus Verlag GmbH (Federal Republic of Germany) 163
Tong-In Sunsawat (Thailand) 381
Tonger, P J, Musikverlag GmbH & Co (Federal Republic of Germany) 163
Toonder, Marten, Award (Republic of Ireland) 212
Toorts, Uitgeverij De (Netherlands) 282
Topaz Publishing Ltd (United Kingdom) 437
Topelius Prize (Finland) 90
Topi, Edizioni Giulio (Switzerland) 374
Topos Verlag AG (Liechtenstein) 256
Toppan Co Ltd (Japan) 244
Toppan Co (Singapore) Private Ltd (Republic of Singapore) 327
Tops'l Books (United Kingdom) 437
Tor (Israel) 216
Toray, Ediciones, SA (Spain) 346
Toray-Masson SA (Spain) 346
Tormargana Prize (Italy) 236
Toro, G del, Editor (Spain) 346
Torpis Publishing Co (Republic of South Africa) 332
Torre, Edizioni della (Italy) 233
Torres, João Romano, & Cia Lda (Portugal) 318
Torroja, Instituto Eduardo (Spain) 346
Toucan Press (Channel Islands) 62
Toulon (Belgium) 41
Tourist, VEB, Verlag (German Democratic Republic) 118
Touropa-Urlaubsberater (Federal Republic of Germany) 163
'Tout pour l'Ecole', Librairie (Democratic Republic of Madagascar) 258
Towarzystwo Literackie im Adama Mickiewicza (Poland) 314
Towarzystwo Przyjaciół Ksiazki (Poland) 314
Towarzystwo Przyjaciół Ksiazki (TPK) (Poland) 313
Towarzystwo Przyjaciół Nauk w Przemyślu (Poland) 314
Town & County Books Ltd (United Kingdom) 437
Town & Gown Press (Nigeria) 295
Townsend & Co (Pvt) Ltd (Zimbabwe) 465
Townsville Foundation for Australian Literary Studies Award (Australia) 23
Toyo Keizai Shimposha Ltd (Japan) 244
Toyo, The, Bunko (Japan) 245
Trachsel Verlag (Switzerland) 374
Tradicion, Editorial, SA (Mexico) 268
Traducta Ltd (United Kingdom) 451
Trakl, Georg, Prize (Austria) 31
Trano Printy Loterana (Democratic Republic of Madagascar) 258
Trano Printy Loterana-Trano Printy Fiangonana Loterana Malagasy (TPFLM)-(Imprimerie Luthérienne) (Democratic Republic of Madagascar) 258
Trans-Pacific Publishers (Fiji) 86
Trans Tech Publications SA (Switzerland) 374
Transafrica (Italy) 236
Transafrica Books (Kenya) 249
Translation Book Club (United Kingdom) 444
Translation into Swedish Prize (Sweden) 360
Translation Prize (Norway) 301
Translation Prize (Republic of South Africa) 336
Translatørforeningen (Denmark) 81
Translators Association (United Kingdom) 451
Translators' Guild Ltd (United Kingdom) 451
'Transport', Izdatelstvo (Union of Soviet Socialist Republics) 389
Transport Library (Republic of Korea) 252
Transport Publishing Company (United Kingdom) 437
Transpress, VEB Verlag für Verkehrswesen (German Democratic Republic) 118
Transvaal Provincial Library and Museum Service (Republic of South Africa) 334
Transworld Publishers (Australia) Pty Ltd (Australia) 19
Transworld Publishers Ltd (United Kingdom) 437
Trauner, Rudolf, Verlag (Austria) 28
Trautvetter und Fischer Nachf (Federal Republic of Germany) 163
Travancore Law House (India) 200
Travelaid Publishing (United Kingdom) 437
Travintal Ltd (Greece) 175
Tre Böcker, Bokklubben (Finland) 88

Treasure (United Kingdom) 437
Trec Edizioni Pregiate (Italy) 233
Treffer-Boekklub (Republic of South Africa) 333
Treffer Uitgewers (Edms) Ltd (Republic of South Africa) 332
Trèfle, Librairie du (Mauritius) 263
Trefoil Books Ltd (United Kingdom) 437
Trejos, Librería (Costa Rica) 68
Trelingue, Edizioni, SA (Switzerland) 374
Tres Américas Libros (Argentina) 8
Tres Tiempos, Ediciones, SRL (Argentina) 8
Trèves, Editions (Federal Republic of Germany) 163
Trevi, Bokförlaget, AB (Sweden) 357
Trévise, Editions de (France) 108
Trevisini, Casa Editrice Luigi (Italy) 233
Triad Paperbacks (United Kingdom) 437
Triangle Books (United Kingdom) 437
Triangulo, Livraria, SA (Brazil) 56
Tribhuvan University Library (Nepal) 272
Tribune Editions (Switzerland) 374
Tribüne Verlag und Druckereien des FDGB (German Democratic Republic) 118
Tricorne, Editions du (Switzerland) 374
Triennial Prize for Bibliography (International Literary Prizes) 479
Trigon Press (United Kingdom) 437
Trikont-Dianus (Federal Republic of Germany) 163
Trillas, Editorial, SA (Mexico) 268
Trimurti Publications Pvt Ltd (India) 200
Trinidad and Tobago, Central Library of (Trinidad and Tobago) 382
Trinidad and Tobago, Library Association of (Trinidad and Tobago) 383
Trinidad Public Library (Trinidad and Tobago) 383
Trinidad Publishing Co (Trinidad and Tobago) 382
Trinity College Library (Republic of Ireland) 211
Trinity College Library (United Kingdom) 445
Tripathi, N M, Pvt Ltd (India) 200
Tripathi, N M, Pvt Ltd (India) 202
Triple Crown Club (Malaysia) 260
Triple First Award (International Literary Prizes) 479
Tripode, Edizioni Il, SRL (Italy) 233
Tripoli Public Library (Libya) 256
Triton Pers (Netherlands) 282
Trobisch, Editions, GmbH (Federal Republic of Germany) 163
Trois Arches (Belgium) 41
Trois Collines, Editions des (Switzerland) 374
Trois Continents, Editions des (Switzerland) 374
Trois Fleuves, Editions des (Senegal) 324
Tropen, CV Toko Buku (Indonesia) 206
Troquel, Editorial, SA (Argentina) 8
Troubadour (United Kingdom) 437
Trubert, Maurice, Prize (France) 114
Trung-Tam San Xuat Hoc-Lieu (Socialist Republic of Viet Nam) 455
Tryma Book Shop (Bahamas) 31
Tsakalos Prize (Greece) 176
Tsuru-Shobo Co Ltd (Japan) 244
Tübinger Vereinigung für Volkskunde eV (Federal Republic of Germany) 163
Tuduv Verlagsgesellschaft mbH (Federal Republic of Germany) 163
Tun Razak Library (Malaysia) 261
Tun Seri, Library, Lanang, Universiti Kebangsaan Malaysia (Malaysia) 261
Tuncho, Librería, Granados G (Guatemala) 177
Türdok (Turkish Scientific and Technical Documentation Centre) (Turkey) 385
Turismo Editorial (Argentina) 8
Turistička Štampa (Yugoslavia) 459
Türk Editörler Dernegi (Turkey) 384
Türk Kütuphaneciler Dernegi (Turkey) 385
Turkish Language Society (Turkey) 385
Turkish Public Library (Cyprus) 70
Turm-Verlag (Federal Republic of Germany) 163
Turmberg-Verlag (Musikverlag Klaus Gerth) (Federal Republic of Germany) 163
Turnbull, Alexander, Library (New Zealand) 290
Turner Ediciones SRL (Argentina) 8
Turner Memorial Library (Zimbabwe) 465
Turnstone Press Ltd (United Kingdom) 437
Turoe Press Ltd (Republic of Ireland) 210
Turtledove Publishing Ltd (Israel) 216
Turton & Armstrong (Australia) 19
Tusch, Edition (Austria) 28
Tusquets Editores (Spain) 346
Tuttle, Charles E, Co Inc (Japan) 244
Tuttle, Charles E, Co Inc (Japan) 245
Tuttle-Mori Agency Inc (Japan) 244
Tüv Rheinland, Verlag, GmbH (Federal Republic of Germany) 163
Twistaplot (Australia) 19
Txertoa, Editorial (Spain) 346
Tycooly International Publishing Ltd (Republic of Ireland) 210

Tyndale Press (United Kingdom) 437
Typos (Greece) 175
Tyrolia (Austria) 30
Tyrolia, Verlagsanstalt (Austria) 28

U B S Publishers' Distributors Ltd (India) 202
U Bär Verlag (Switzerland) 374
U C A Editores (El Salvador) 85
U D E F Export (France) 90
U F R G S, Editora da, (Universidade Federal do Rio Grande do Sul) (Brazil) 55
U G A, Editions, (Uitgeverij) (Belgium) 41
U G E 10/18 (France) 108
U K B (Samenwerkingsverband van de Universiteits- en Hogeschoolbibliotheken en de Koninklijke Bibliotheek) (Netherlands) 285
U K National Serials Data Centre (United Kingdom) 391
U N A C Tokyo (Japan) 244
U N A L I SL (Spain) 346
U N C T A D (International Organizations) 470
U N E A C Prize (Cuba) 70
U N E S C O (International Organizations) 470
U N E S C O Institute for Education (UIE) (International Organizations) 470
U O P C (Belgium) 41
U O P C (Belgium) 43
U P Indonesia (Indonesia) 206
U S S R Library Council (Union of Soviet Socialist Republics) 390
U S S R Writers' Union (Union of Soviet Socialist Republics) 387
U T B (Federal Republic of Germany) 163
U T E T (Unione Tipografico-Editrice Torinese) (Italy) 233
Ueberreuter, Verlag Carl (Austria) 28
Uffici (United Kingdom) 437
Uganda Bookshop (Uganda) 386
Uganda Library Association (Uganda) 386
Uganda Publishing House (Uganda) 386
Uganda Schools Library Association (Uganda) 386
Uganda Special Library Association (Uganda) 386
Uganda Technical College Library (Uganda) 386
Uhl, Verlag Dr Alfons (Federal Republic of Germany) 163
Ullstein, Verlag, GmbH (Federal Republic of Germany) 163
Ulmer, Verlag Eugen, GmbH & Co (Federal Republic of Germany) 163
Ultima Hora (Dominican Republic) 82
Ultramar Editores SA (Spain) 346
Ulverscroft Large Print Books Ltd (United Kingdom) 437
Umbria Editrice (Italy) 233
Umschau Verlag Breidenstein GmbH (Federal Republic of Germany) 163
Underhållningsbokklubben (Sweden) 358
Ungarischer Kultureller und Sozialer Fonds eV in der BRD (Federal Republic of Germany) 163
Ungdommens Forlag og Aamodts Forlag A/S (Denmark) 78
Unges, De, Forlag, Unitas Forlag (Denmark) 79
Uni Books (United Kingdom) 437
Uni-Taschenbücher (UTB) GmbH (Federal Republic of Germany) 163
Uni-Text Book Company (Malaysia) 260
União dos Escritores Angolanos (Angola) 2
União Gráfica Sarl (Portugal) 318
Unibooks (United Kingdom) 437
Unicart Kartografisk Produktion AB (Sweden) 357
Unicopli, Edizioni, Scrl (Italy) 233
Unicorn Books (Australia) 19
Unieboek BV (Netherlands) 282
Unilit Publishing Co (Ghana) 172
Unión Aragonesa del Libro SL (Spain) 346
Union Book Club (Denmark) 79
Union Classics Library (Denmark) 79
Union Continentale d'Editions SA (Monaco) 270
Union Crime Club (Denmark) 79
Unión de Escritores y Artistas de Cuba (Cuba) 69
Union d'Editeurs Français (France) 91
Union des Ecrivains algériens (Algeria) 2
Union des Ecrivains algériens (Algeria) 2
Union des Ecrivains tunisiens (Tunisia) 384
Union des Editeurs de Langue française (International Organizations) 469
Union des Editeurs de Langue française (UELF) (Belgium) 33
Union des Industries graphiques et du Livre (UNIGRA) (Belgium) 33
Unión, Ediciones (Cuba) 69
Unión, Editorial (Nicaragua) 292
Union et Orientation de Presse et de Culture (UOPC) SA (Belgium) 41
Union Helvetia Fachbuchverlag (Switzerland) 374
Union Novel Library (Denmark) 79
Union of Writers and Artists of Albania (Albania) 1

INDEX 545

Union of Writers of the African Peoples (International Organizations) 469
Union Press Ltd (Hong Kong) 180
Union, The, Press (Sri Lanka) 349
Union Verlag Berlin VOB (German Democratic Republic) 118
Union Verlag Stuttgart (Federal Republic of Germany) 163
Unione Editori di Musica Italiani (UNEMI) (Italy) 219
Unionsverlag (Switzerland) 374
United Africa Press Ltd (Kenya) 249
United Bank Prize for Literature (Pakistan) 304
United Book Distributors (Pty) Ltd (Republic of South Africa) 334
United Bookshop & Stationers Ltd (Bahamas) 31
United Christian Council Literature Bureau (Sierra Leone) 325
United Nations (International Organizations) 470
United Nations Conference on Trade and Development (UNCTAD) (International Organizations) 470
United Nations Depository Library (Republic of Korea) 252
United Nations, Economic and Social Commission for Asia and the Pacific Library (Thailand) 381
United Nations Economic Commission for Africa Library (Ethiopia) 86
United Nations Economic Commission for Africa Library (International Organizations) 469
United Nations Educational, Scientific and Cultural Organization (UNESCO) (International Organizations) 470
United Nations Library (Switzerland) 376
United Nations Research Institute for Social Development (UNRISD) (International Organizations) 470
United Nations University (International Organizations) 470
United Protestant Publishers (Pty) Ltd (Republic of South Africa) 332
United Publishers (India) 202
United Publishers Services Ltd (Japan) 245
United Publishers Services (M) Sdn Bhd (Malaysia) 260
United States Book Association (Australia) 10
United States Information Agency Library (Democratic Republic of Madagascar) 258
United States Information Service Library (Uganda) 386
United Writers Publications Ltd (United Kingdom) 437
Unites SRL, Annuario Politecnico Italiano (Italy) 233
Uniting Church Press (Australia) 19
Unity Books Ltd (New Zealand) 290
Uniunea Scriitorilor din Republica Socialistă România (Romania) 321
Univers, Editura (Romania) 322
Universa PVBA (Belgium) 41
Universal Book Distributors (India) 202
Universal Book Shop (India) 202
Universal Books (Australia) 19
Universal Books (Australia) 19
Universal Business Directories Pty Ltd (Australia) 19
Universal Distributors Ltd (Nigeria) 296
Universal Edition AG (Austria) 29
Universal Library (Israel) 218
Universal Librería, Imprenta y Fotolitografía (Carlos Federspiel & Co) SA (Costa Rica) 68
Universal Postal Union (UPU) (International Organizations) 471
Universal Publications Agency Ltd (Republic of Korea) 252
Universal Publications Agency Ltd (Republic of Korea) 252
Universe, The, (The Catholic Newspaper) Literary Prize (United Kingdom) 450
Universe, The, — The Catholic Newspaper — Literary Prize (International Literary Prizes) 479
Universidad Autónoma, Biblioteca de la, de Santo Domingo (Dominican Republic) 82
Universidad Autónoma de Barcelona, Biblioteca General (Spain) 348
Universidad Autónoma de Santo Domingo, Ciudad Universitaria (Dominican Republic) 82
Universidad Boliviana, Biblioteca Universitaria, Departamento de Bibliotecas, Tomás Frías (Bolivia) 47
Universidad Católica de Chile, Biblioteca Central de la Pontificia (Chile) 63
Universidad Católica de Valparaíso, Biblioteca de la (Chile) 64
Universidad Católica, Fondo Editorial de la (Peru) 307
Universidad Católica Madre y Maestra (Dominican Republic) 82
Universidad Católica, Pontificia, de Ecuador (Ecuador) 83
Universidad Central, Biblioteca Central de la, de Venezuela (Venezuela) 454
Universidad Central, Biblioteca General de la, de las Villas (Cuba) 69
Universidad Central de Ecuador, Biblioteca de la (Ecuador) 83
Universidad Central de la Villas, Carretera de Camajuani (Cuba) 69

Universidad Central del Ecuador, Dpto de Publicaciones (Ecuador) 83
Universidad Centroamericana, Biblioteca de la, José Simeón Cañas (El Salvador) 85
Universidad Complutense, Biblioteca de la (Spain) 348
Universidad de Buenos Aires, Instituto Bibliotecológico, (Argentina) 8
Universidad de Chile, Biblioteca Central de la (Chile) 64
Universidad de Concepción, Biblioteca Central de la (Chile) 64
Universidad de Costa Rica, Biblioteca de la (Costa Rica) 68
Universidad de El Salvador, Biblioteca Central de la (El Salvador) 85
Universidad de Granada (Spain) 346
Universidad de Guayaquil, Biblioteca General, (Ecuador) 83
Universidad de Guayaquil, Dpto de Publicaciones (Ecuador) 83
Universidad de la Habana (Cuba) 69
Universidad de la Habana, Biblioteca Central 'Rubén Martínez Villena' de la (Cuba) 69
Universidad de los Andes, Centro de Estudios sobre Desarollo Economico (CEDE) (Colombia) 67
Universidad de Malaga (Spain) 346
Universidad de Navarra, Ediciones, SA (Spain) 346
Universidad de Oriente, Biblioteca Central de la (Cuba) 69
Universidad de Panama, Biblioteca Interamericana Simón Bolívar (Panama) 305
Universidad de Panama, Escuela de Bibliotecología (Panama) 305
Universidad de San Carlos, Biblioteca Central de la (Guatemala) 177
Universidad de San Carlos de Guatemala, Editorial Universitaria (Guatemala) 177
Universidad de Zulia, Biblioteca Central de la (Venezuela) 454
Universidad del Salvador, Biblioteca de la (Argentina) 8
Universidad, Editorial, de Costa Rica (Costa Rica) 68
Universidad Iberoamericana, Biblioteca de la (Mexico) 269
Universidad', Librería 'La, Nicolas Ojeda Fierro e Hijos SRL Ltda (Peru) 307
Universidad Mayor de San Andres (Bolivia) 46
Universidad Mayor de San Andrés, Biblioteca Central de la (Bolivia) 47
Universidad Mayor de San Francisco Xavier, Biblioteca Central de la (Bolivia) 47
Universidad Mayor de San Simón, Biblioteca Central de la (Bolivia) 47
Universidad Nacional Autónoma de México (Mexico) 268
Universidad Nacional, Biblioteca Central del, de Nicaragua (Nicaragua) 292
Universidad Nacional de Colombia, Biblioteca Central (Colombia) 67
Universidad Nacional de Córdoba, Biblioteca Mayor de la (Argentina) 8
Universidad Nacional de Cuzeco, Biblioteca Central de la (Peru) 307
Universidad Nacional de La Plata, Biblioteca Pública de la (Argentina) 8
Universidad Nacional de Nicaragua, Librería y Editorial (Nicaragua) 292
Universidad Nacional de San Agustín, Biblioteca Central de la (Peru) 307
Universidad Nacional Mayor de San Marcos (Peru) 307
Universidad Nacional Mayor de San Marcos, Biblioteca Central de la (Peru) 307
Universidad Nacional Mayor de San Marcos, Librería de la (Peru) 307
Universidad Pontificia de Salamanca, Biblioteca Universitaria (Spain) 348
Universidade de Brasilia, Biblioteca Central (Brazil) 56
Universidade de Brasilia, Clube do Livro da (Brazil) 55
Universidade de Brasilia, Editora (Brazil) 55
Universidade de Coimbra, Biblioteca Geral da (Portugal) 318
Universidade de Luanda Biblioteca (Angola) 2
Universidade de São Paulo, Editora da (Brazil) 55
Universidade de São Paulo, Sistema de Bibliotecas da, (SIBI) (Brazil) 56
Universidade Eduardo Mondlane, Bibliotecas de (Mozambique) 271
Universidade Federal do Rio de Janeiro, Centro de Ciências da Saude da (Brazil) 56
Universidade Federal do Rio Grande do Sul (Brazil) 55
Universidade Federal do Rio Grande do Sul, Biblioteca Central (Brazil) 56
Università degli Studi di Firenze, Biblioteca della Facolta di Lettere e Filosofia (Italy) 234
Universita Nazionale, Biblioteca dell', della Somalia (Somalia) 328
Universitaire Boekhandel Nederland (Netherlands) 284
Universitaire Pers Leuven (Belgium) 41
universitaires, Editions, SA (Belgium) 41
universitaires, Presses, de Bruxelles, de Liège, de Namur (Belgium) 41

Universitaires, Presses, de France, de Grenoble, de Lille, de Lyon, de Nancy (France) 108
universitaires, Publications des Facultés, Saint Louis (Belgium) 41
Universitaria de Barcelona, Biblioteca (Spain) 348
Universitária de Direito, Livraria e Editora, Ltda (Brazil) 55
Universitaria, Editorial (Chile) 63
Universitaria, Editrice (Italy) 233
Universitaria, Librería, de la Universidad de El Salvador (El Salvador) 85
Universitaria, Librería, UCA (El Salvador) 85
Universitarias, Ediciones, de la Universidad Católica de Valparaíso (Chile) 63
Universitarie Pers Leiden (Netherlands) 282
Universitas Books (Pty) Ltd (Republic of South Africa) 334
Universitas Verlag (Federal Republic of Germany) 163
Universität Basel, Öffentliche Bibliothek der (Switzerland) 376
Universitäts- und Landesbibliothek Sachsen-Anhalt (German Democratic Republic) 119
Universitäts- und Stadtbibliothek (Federal Republic of Germany) 168
Universitätsbibliothek (German Democratic Republic) 119
Universitätsbibliothek (Federal Republic of Germany) 168
Universitätsbibliothek der Eberhard-Karls-Universität (Federal Republic of Germany) 168
Universitätsbibliothek der Technischen Universität (German Democratic Republic) 119
Universitätsbibliothek Erlangen-Nürnberg (Federal Republic of Germany) 168
Universitätsbibliothek Graz (Austria) 30
Universitätsbibliothek Heidelberg (Federal Republic of Germany) 168
Universitätsbibliothek Innsbruck (Austria) 30
Universitätsbibliothek Wien (Austria) 30
Universitätsbuchhandlung (German Democratic Republic) 119
Universitätsbuchhandlung (German Democratic Republic) 119
Universitätsbuchhandlung (German Democratic Republic) 119
Universitätsverlag (Switzerland) 374
Université Al Quarawiyin, Bibliothèque de l' (Morocco) 271
Université Ben Youssef, Bibliothèque de l' (Morocco) 271
Université Catholique de Leuven, Bibliothèque centrale de l' (Belgium) 43
Université d'Abidjan (Ivory Coast) 236
Université d'Alger, Bibliothèque universitaire, (Algeria) 2
Université de Constantine, Bibliothèque de l' (Algeria) 2
Université de Dakar, Bibliothèque (Senegal) 324
Université de Kisangani, Bibliothèque centrale de l' (Zaire) 463
Université de Liège, Bibliothèque générale de l' (Belgium) 43
Université de Niamey, Bibliothèque de l' (Niger) 292
Université de Strasbourg, Bibliothèque de l' (France) 110
Université de Yaoundé, Bibliothèque (United Republic of Cameroun) 61
Université d'Oran, Bibliothèque (Algeria) 2
Université du Benin, Bibliothèque de l' (Benin) 46
Université du Benin, Bibliothèque de l' (Togo) 382
Université du Burundi, Bibliothèque de l' (Burundi) 60
Université du Tchad, Bibliothèque de l' (Chad) 62
Université Jean-Bédel Bokassa, Bibliothèque de l' (Central African Republic) 62
Université, Librairie de l' (France) 109
Université libre de Bruxelles, Bibliothèques de l' (Belgium) 43
Université Marien Ngouabi, Bibliothèque universitaire, (Popular Republic of Congo) 68
Université Mohammed V, Bibliothèque de l' (Morocco) 271
Université nationale, Bibliothèque de l', du Gabon (Gabon) 115
Université nationale, Campus de Lubumbashi, Bibliothèque centrale de l' (Zaire) 463
Université Nationale de Côte d'Ivoire (Ivory Coast) 236
Université Nationale du Rwanda, Bibliothèque de l' (Rwanda) 323
Université nationale du Zaïre, Bibliothèque centrale de l' (Zaire) 463
Université Omar Bongo, Bibliothèque Centrale de l' (Gabon) 115
Universiteit voor Zelfstudie (Netherlands) 282
Universiteits-Bibliotheek, Universiteit van de Nederlandse Antillen (Netherlands Antilles) 286
Universiteitsbibliotheek (Netherlands) 284
Universitetsbibliotek, Odense (Denmark) 80
Universitetsbiblioteket, 1 afd (Denmark) 80
Universitetsbiblioteket, 2 afd (Denmark) 80
Universitetsbiblioteket i Bergen (Norway) 300
Universitetsbiblioteket i Oslo (Norway) 300
Universitetsbiblioteket i Trondheim (Kongelige Norske Videnskabers Selskab Bibliotek) (Norway) 300

Universitetsbogladen (Panumbogladen/Naturfagsbogladen) (Denmark) 80
Universitetsbokhandeln (Norway) 300
Universitetsforlaget (Norway) 300
Universiti Kebangsaan (Malaysia) 261
Universities Administration Office (Burma) 60
Universities' Central Library (Burma) 60
Universitná knižnica (Czechoslovakia) 73
University (United Kingdom) 437
University Book Agency (Pakistan) 303
University Book Shop (Auckland) Ltd (New Zealand) 290
University Book Shop (Canterbury) Ltd (New Zealand) 290
University Book Shop Inc (Papua New Guinea) 305
University Book Shop (Otago) Ltd (New Zealand) 290
University Book Store (Hong Kong) 180
University Booksellers Association of Nigeria (Nigeria) 293
University Bookshop (Ghana) 173
University Bookshop (Ghana) 173
University Bookshop (Zambia) 463
University Bookshop (Nigeria) Ltd (Nigeria) 296
University Bookstore (Liberia) 255
University Bookstore (Republic of Singapore) 327
University Co-operative Bookshop Ltd (Australia) 20
University College Cardiff Press (United Kingdom) 437
University College Cork Library (Republic of Ireland) 211
University College Dublin Library (Republic of Ireland) 211
University College Galway, James Hardiman Library (Republic of Ireland) 211
University Education Press (Republic of Singapore) 327
University Karlovy, Knihovny fakult a ústavu (Czechoslovakia) 73
University Libraries (Finland) 89
University Libraries (Japan) 245
University Libraries (Romania) 322
University Libraries (Saudi Arabia) 323
University Libraries (Sweden) 359
University Libraries (United Kingdom) 445
University Library (Afghanistan) 1
University Library (Honduras) 178
University Library (Iceland) 185
University Library, Universiti Sains Malaysia (Malaysia) 261
University Microfilms International (United Kingdom) 437
University of Agriculture Library (Pakistan) 303
University of Agriculture Malaysia Library (Malaysia) 261
University of Ain Shams Library (Egypt) 84
University of Alexandria Library (Egypt) 84
University of Auckland Library (New Zealand) 290
University of Baghdad, Central Library of the (Iraq) 208
University of Baluchistan Library (Pakistan) 303
University of Botswana Library (Botswana) 47
University of Cairo (Sudan) 350
University of Cairo Library (Egypt) 84
University of California Press (United Kingdom) 438
University of Canterbury Publications (New Zealand) 290
University of Cape Coast Library (Ghana) 173
University of Cape Town Libraries (Republic of South Africa) 334
University of Chicago, The, Press (United Kingdom) 438
University of Dar es Salaam Library (Tanzania) 379
University of Engineering and Technology (Pakistan) 303
University of Ferdowsi Library (Iran) 208
Universiti Garyounis Library (Libya) 256
University of Ghana Library (Ghana) 173
University of Haifa Library (Israel) 218
University of Hong Kong Libraries (Hong Kong) 180
University of Ife Bookshop Ltd (Nigeria) 296
University of Ife Library (Nigeria) 297
University of Ife Press (Nigeria) 295
University of Illinois Press (United Kingdom) 438
University of Isfahan Library (Iran) 208
University of Jordan Library (Jordan) 247
University of Kabul Bookstores (Afghanistan) 1
University of Karachi Library (Pakistan) 303
University of Kentucky Press (United Kingdom) 438
University of Khartoum Bookshop (Sudan) 350
University of Khartoum Library (Sudan) 350
University of Lagos Bookshop (Nigeria) 296
University of Lagos Library (Nigeria) 297
University of Lagos Press (Nigeria) 295
University of Liberia Libraries (Liberia) 255
University of Libya (Libya) 256
University of London Library (United Kingdom) 445
University of London Press Ltd (United Kingdom) 438
University of Loránd Eötvös Central Library (Hungary) 182
University of Malawi, Chancellor College Library (Malawi) 258
University of Malawi, Polytechnic Library (Malawi) 258
University of Malaya Co-operative Bookshop Ltd (Malaysia) 261
University of Malaya Library (Malaysia) 261
University of Malaya Press Ltd (Malaysia) 260
University of Malta Library (Malta) 262

University of Malta, The, Press (Malta) 262
University of Manila Central Library (Philippines) 310
University of Mauritius Library (Mauritius) 263
University of Melbourne Library (Australia) 20
University of Missouri Press (United Kingdom) 438
University of Nairobi Bookshop (Kenya) 249
University of Nairobi Library (Kenya) 249
University of Natal Press (Republic of South Africa) 332
University of Nebraska Press (United Kingdom) 438
University of New South Wales (Australia) 19
University of New South Wales Library (Australia) 20
University of Nigeria Bookshop Ltd (Nigeria) 296
University of Nigeria Library (Nigeria) 297
University of North Carolina Press (United Kingdom) 438
University of Notre Dame Press (United Kingdom) 438
University of Otago Press (New Zealand) 290
University of Papua New Guinea Library (Papua New Guinea) 305
University of Peradeniya Library (Sri Lanka) 350
University of Peshawar Library (Pakistan) 303
University of Pretoria, Library Services (Republic of South Africa) 334
University of Puerto Rico, General Library, Mayaguez Campus (Puerto Rico) 320
University of Puerto Rico, General Library, Río Piedras Campus (Puerto Rico) 320
University of Puerto Rico, Medical Sciences Campus Library (Puerto Rico) 320
University of Puerto Rico Press (EDUPR) (Puerto Rico) 319
University of Queensland Library (Australia) 20
University of Queensland Press (Australia) 19
University of Rajshahi Library (Bangladesh) 32
University of Salonika, Library of the (Greece) 176
University of San Carlos Library System (Philippines) 310
University of Santo Tomas Library (Philippines) 310
University of Science and Technology Library (Ghana) 173
University of Sierra Leone (Sierra Leone) 325
University of Sofia Library (Bulgaria) 59
University of South Africa (Republic of South Africa) 332
University of South Africa Library (Republic of South Africa) 334
University of Swaziland Library (Swaziland) 351
University of Sydney Library (Australia) 20
University of Tabriz, Central Library, (Iran) 208
University of Technology Malaysia Library (Malaysia) 261
University of Texas Press (United Kingdom) 438
University of the East Library (Philippines) 310
University of the Philippines, Institute of Library Science (Philippines) 310
University of the Philippines Library (Philippines) 310
University of the Philippines Press (Philippines) 309
University of the West Indies (Barbados) 33
University of the West Indies Library (Jamaica) 237
University of the West Indies Library (Trinidad and Tobago) 383
University of the Witwatersrand Library (Republic of South Africa) 334
University of Tokyo Library (Japan) 245
University of Tokyo Press (Japan) 244
University of Trondheim, The, Norwegian Institute of Technology (Norway) 300
University of Wales Press (United Kingdom) 438
University of Washington Press (United Kingdom) 438
University of Western Australia Library (Australia) 20
University of Western Australia Press (Australia) 19
University of Wisconsin Press (United Kingdom) 438
University of Zambia Library (Zambia) 464
University of Zimbabwe (Zimbabwe) 465
University of Zimbabwe Library (Zimbabwe) 465
University Press Amsterdam BV (APA) (Netherlands) 282
University Press Ltd (Bangladesh) 32
University Press Ltd (Nigeria) 295
University Press, The, of Ireland (Republic of Ireland) 210
University Presses of Columbia and Princeton (United Kingdom) 438
University Publishers (India) 200
University Publishers & Booksellers (Pty) Ltd (Republic of South Africa) 333
University Publishing Co (Israel) 216
University Publishing Co (Nigeria) 295
University Publishing Co (Philippines) 309
University Tutorial Press Ltd (United Kingdom) 438
Universo, Editorial, SA (Mexico) 268
Universo, Editorial, SA (Peru) 307
Universo, Premio (Peru) 308
Universo, Società Editrice (Italy) 233
Uniwersytecka w Warszawie, Biblioteka (Poland) 314
Uniwersytecka w Wrocławiu, Biblioteka (Poland) 314
Unwin Paperbacks (United Kingdom) 438
Uomini, Editrice, Nuovi (Italy) 233
Update Books Ltd (United Kingdom) 438
Upkar Prakashan (India) 200
Upper India, The, Publishing House Pvt Ltd (India) 200
Uppsala Universitetsbibliotek (Sweden) 359

Urachhaus, Verlag, Johannes M Mayer GmbH und Co KG (Federal Republic of Germany) 163
Uraki, Mitsusato (Japan) 244
Urania-Verlag (für populärwissenschaftliche Literatur) (German Democratic Republic) 118
Uranium Verlag (Switzerland) 374
Urban Council Public Libraries (Hong Kong) 180
Urban und Schwarzenberg (Austria) 29
Urban und Schwarzenberg GmbH (Austria) 30
Urban und Schwarzenberg, Verlag, (Medical Publishers) (Federal Republic of Germany) 163
Urdang, Laurence, Associates Ltd (United Kingdom) 438
Urdu Academy Sind (Pakistan) 303
Urdu Akademy Awards (India) 204
Ure Smith (Australia) 19
Urmo SA de Ediciones (Spain) 346
Urs Graf-Verlag GmbH (Switzerland) 374
Usborne Publishing Ltd (United Kingdom) 438
Usine Nouvelle, Editions de l' (France) 108
Ústřední knihovnická rada ČSSR (Czechoslovakia) 74
Utbildningsbolaget M M AB (Sweden) 357
Utusan Publications and Distributors Sdn Bhd (Malaysia) 260
Uudet Kirjat (Finland) 88
Uusi Kirjakerho Oy (Finland) 88
Uusi Tie, Kustannus Oy (Finland) 88
Uzima Press Ltd (Kenya) 249

V A A P (Union of Soviet Socialist Republics) 389
V A M, Stichting (Netherlands) 282
V C L (Netherlands) 284
V C T A Publishing Pty Ltd (Australia) 19
V D A (Éditions de la Voie de l'Art SA) (Switzerland) 374
V D D (Federal Republic of Germany) 169
V D E-Verlag GmbH (Verband Deutscher Elektrotechniker) (Federal Republic of Germany) 164
V D I-Verlag GmbH (Verlag des Vereins Deutscher Ingenieure) (Federal Republic of Germany) 164
V-Dia-Verlag GmbH (Federal Republic of Germany) 164
V E D A, vydavateľstvo Slovenskej akadémie vied (Czechoslovakia) 73
V F M (Federal Republic of Germany) 164
V G S (Federal Republic of Germany) 164
V M B (Federal Republic of Germany) 164
V N U Book Group (Netherlands) 282
V N U Business Press Group BV (Netherlands) 283
V N U — Verenigde Nederlandse Uitgeversbedrijven BV (Netherlands) 282
V P A (Vjesnikova Press Agencija) (Yugoslavia) 460
V S A (Verlag für das Studium der Arbeiterbewegung GmbH) (Federal Republic of Germany) 164
V V A (Vereinigte Verlagsauslieferung GmbH) (Federal Republic of Germany) 168
V W G Ö (Austria) 29
V W K (Verlag für Wirtschafts-und-Kartographie Publikationen) Ryborsch GmbH (Federal Republic of Germany) 164
Vaad Hayeshivot Be'eretz Israel (Israel) 217
Vaco NV (Suriname) 351
Vaco NV (Suriname) 351
Vademecum de Pharmacie (Belgium) 41
Vadhana Panich (Thailand) 381
Vagabond (Australia) 19
Vahlen, Franz, GmbH (Federal Republic of Germany) 164
Vaillant Carmanne, Imprimerie H, SA (Belgium) 41
Vaillant, Les Editions, /Miroir Sprint Publications (France) 108
Vajarindra (Thailand) 381
Vakils Feffer & Simons Ltd (India) 200
Valabrègue, Antony, Prize (France) 114
Valafell, Bókaútgáfan (Iceland) 184
Vale, The Helen, Foundation (Australia) 19
Valencia, Carlos, Editores SA (Colombia) 67
Valiant Publishers (Pty) Ltd (Republic of South Africa) 333
Vallancey International Ltd (Channel Islands) 62
Vallardi Industrie Grafiche (Italy) 233
Vallentine, Mitchell & Co Ltd (United Kingdom) 438
Valtionarkisto (Finland) 89
Van de Velde, Editions (France) 108
Van de Velde, Editions Francis (France) 108
Van Duren Publishers Ltd (United Kingdom) 438
Van Leer, The, Jerusalem Foundation (Israel) 217
Van Nostrand Reinhold (UK) Co Ltd (United Kingdom) 438
Vandenhoeck und Ruprecht (Federal Republic of Germany) 164
Vander Publishing (Belgium) 41
Vanderlinden, Librairie (Belgium) 41
Vanderlinden, Librairie, SA (Belgium) 41
Vani Prakashan (India) 200
Vanmelle, L, (Drukkerij) NV (Belgium) 42
Vannini, Società Editrice (Italy) 233

INDEX 547

Vantage House (Australia) 19
Vår Bok AB (Sweden) 358
Vår Skola Förlag AB (Sweden) 357
Varazen, Editorial, SA (Mexico) 268
Vardikos, D & J (Greece) 175
Vargas, Fundação Getúlio (Brazil) 55
Variorum (United Kingdom) 438
Varma, F H R Oedayrajsingh (Suriname) 351
Varsity (United Kingdom) 438
Varsity Book Club (Nigeria) 296
Varsity Industrial Press (Nigeria) 296
Vasco, Editorial, Americana SA (EVA) (Spain) 346
Vasiliou, J, Bibliopoleion (Greece) 175
Vassallo, A, and Sons Ltd (Malta) 262
Västra, Förlagsaktiebolaget, Sverige (Sweden) 357
Vatan Library (Turkey) 385
Vaticana, Libreria Editrice (Vatican City State) 453
Vavrín (Czechoslovakia) 73
Vecchi, Editions de (France) 108
Vecchi, Editora, SA (Brazil) 55
Vecchi, Editorial De (Spain) 346
Vecchi, Giovanni de, Editore SpA (Italy) 233
Veen, Uitgeverij L J, BV (Netherlands) 283
Vega, Ediciones, SRL (Venezuela) 454
Vega, Librería Técnica (Venezuela) 454
Velhagen und Klasing GmbH & Co (Federal Republic of Germany) 164
Venceremos, Edition (Federal Republic of Germany) 164
Venton Educational Ltd (United Kingdom) 438
Ventura Publishing Ltd (United Kingdom) 438
Ventures (Zimbabwe) 465
Venus Press & Book Depot (India) 200
Vera-Reyes Inc (Philippines) 309
Verband bayerischer Buch- und Zeitschriftenhändler eV (Federal Republic of Germany) 121
Verband bayerischer Verlage und Buchhandlungen eV (Federal Republic of Germany) 121
Verband der Antiquare Österreichs (Austria) 24
Verband der Bibliothe des Landes Nordrhein-Westfalen eV (Federal Republic of Germany) 169
Verband der Schulbuchverlage eV (Federal Republic of Germany) 121
Verband der Verlage und Buchhandlungen in Baden-Württemberg eV (Federal Republic of Germany) 121
Verband der Verlage und Buchhandlungen in Nordrhein-Westfalen eV (Federal Republic of Germany) 121
Verband der wissenschaftlichen Gesellschaften Österreichs (VWGÖ) (Austria) 29
Verband des werbenden Buch- und Zeitschriftenhandels Gross-Berlin eV (Federal Republic of Germany) 121
Verband deutscher Adressbuchverleger eV (Federal Republic of Germany) 121
Verband deutscher Antiquare eV (Federal Republic of Germany) 121
Verband deutscher Bahnhofsbuchhändler (Federal Republic of Germany) 121
Verband deutscher Buch- Zeitungs- und Zeitschriften-Grossisten eV (Federal Republic of Germany) 121
Verband deutscher Bühnenverleger eV (Federal Republic of Germany) 121
Verband deutscher Schriftsteller (Federal Republic of Germany) 121
Verband deutscher Schulbuchhändler eV (Federal Republic of Germany) 121
Verband deutscher Werkbibliotheken eV (Federal Republic of Germany) 169
Verband deutschsprachiger Übersetzer literarischer und wissenschaftlicher Werke eV (VDU) (Federal Republic of Germany) 171
Verband evangelischer Buchhandlungen und Verlage der Schweiz (Switzerland) 361
Verband katholischer Verleger und Buchhändler eV (Federal Republic of Germany) 121
Verband norddeutscher Buch- und Zeitschriftenhändler eV (Federal Republic of Germany) 122
Verband österreichischer Archivare (Austria) 30
Verband österreichischer Kommissionäre, Grossbuchhändler und Auslieferer (Austria) 24
Verband österreichischer Volksbüchereien und Volksbibliothekare (Austria) 30
Verband schweizerischer Antiquare und Kunsthändler (Switzerland) 361
Verband schweizerischer Zeitungsagenturen und Büchergrossisten (Union d'Agences suisses de Journaux et Livres en Gros) (Switzerland) 361
Verbandsdruckerei-Betadruck, Verlag (Switzerland) 374
Verbatim (United Kingdom) 438
Verbatim Book Club (United Kingdom) 444
Verbo, Editora, Ltda (Brazil) 55
Verbo, Editorial, Divino (Spain) 346
Verbo, Editorial, Sarl (Portugal) 318
Verbum Förlag AB (Sweden) 357
Verdade e Vida, Livraria, Editora (Portugal) 318
Vereeniging der Antwerpsche Bibliophielen (Belgium) 44
Vereeniging ter bevordering van de belangen des Boekhandels (Netherlands) 273

Verein Angehörige des mittleren und nichtdiplomierten Bibliotheksdienstes eV (Federal Republic of Germany) 169
Verein der Bibliothekare an öffentlichen Bibliotheken eV (Federal Republic of Germany) 169
Verein der Diplom-Bibliothekare an wissenschaftlichen Bibliotheken eV (Federal Republic of Germany) 169
Verein Deutscher Archivare (VdA) (Federal Republic of Germany) 169
Verein Deutscher Bibliothekare eV (Federal Republic of Germany) 169
Verein Deutscher Dokumentare eV (VDD) (Federal Republic of Germany) 169
Verein für Verkehrsordnung im Buchhandel eV (Federal Republic of Germany) 122
Vereinigung der Schweizerischen Buchgemeinschaften (Switzerland) 361
Vereinigung evangelischer Buchhändler (Federal Republic of Germany) 122
Vereinigung katholischer Buchhändler und Verleger der Schweiz (Switzerland) 361
Vereinigung österreichischer Bibliothekare (Austria) 30
Vereinigung Schweizerischer Archivare (Switzerland) 376
Vereinigung Schweizerischer Bibliothekare (Switzerland) 376
Vereinigung selbständiger Verlagsvertreter (Federal Republic of Germany) 122
Vereniging ter Bevordering van het Vlaamse Boekwezen (Belgium) 33
Vereniging van Archivarissen in Nederland (Netherlands) 285
Vereniging van de belgische medische Wetenschappelijke Genootschappen VZW (Belgium) 42
Vereniging van Religieus-Wetenschappelijke Bibliothecarissen (Belgium) 43
Vereniging van Uitgevers van Nederlandstalige Boeken (Belgium) 33
Vereniging van Uitgeversvertegenwoordigers (Netherlands) 273
Vereniging voor het Theologisch Bibliothecariaat (Netherlands) 285
Vergara, Javier, Editor SA (Argentina) 8
Vergara, José Ma, y Vergara Prize (Colombia) 68
Vergeures, Editions de (France) 108
Veríssimo, José, Prize (Brazil) 57
Veritas Foundation Publication Centre (United Kingdom) 438
Veritas Publications (Republic of Ireland) 210
Veritas-Verlag (Austria) 29
Verkehrshaus der Schweiz (Switzerland) 374
Verlag für Deutsch (Federal Republic of Germany) 164
Verlag für Fremdsprachen (Federal Republic of Germany) 164
Verlain, Valentine Abraham, Prize (France) 114
Verlaine Prize (France) 114
Verlegervereinigung Rechtsinformatik eV (Federal Republic of Germany) 122
Vermilion (United Kingdom) 439
Verne, Jules, Circle (United Kingdom) 447
Veron Editor (Spain) 346
Verrycken, Editions (Belgium) 42
Verseau, Editions du (Switzerland) 374
Versluys', W, Uitg Mij BV (Netherlands) 283
Verso Editions/NLB (United Kingdom) 439
Vertente Editora Ltda (Brazil) 55
Vértice Ltda (Colombia) 67
Vertige (France) 108
Vervuert, Klaus Dieter, Buchhandel und Verlag (Federal Republic of Germany) 164
Vesaas, Tarjei, Debutant Prize (Norway) 301
Veselin Masleša (Yugoslavia) 459
Veselin Masleša (Yugoslavia) 460
Vesti (Yugoslavia) 459
Vetenskapliga Bibliotekens Tjänstemannaförening VBT (Sweden) 359
Vetter, Verlag Alfred (Switzerland) 374
Veyrier (France) 108
Via Afrika Book Store (Republic of South Africa) 334
Via Afrika Botswana Ltd (Botswana) 47
Via Afrika Ltd (Republic of South Africa) 333
Viareggio Prizes (Italy) 236
Vicens-Vives, Editorial (Spain) 346
Victor, Leo (Suriname) 351
Victoria Public Library (United Republic of Cameroun) 61
Victoria University Press (New Zealand) 290
Victorian Fellowship of Australian Writers (Australia) 21
Videnskabers Selskab Biblioteket (Norway) 300
Vidhi Sahitva Prakashan (India) 200
Vidyapuri (India) 200
Vidyarthi Mithram Book Depot (India) 202
Vidyarthi Mithram Novel Club (India) 201
Vidyarthi Mithram Press & Book Depot (India) 200
Vie, Les Editions, ouvrière ASBL (Belgium) 42
Vienna Prize, City of (Austria) 31
Vienna Prize for Books, City of, for Children and Young People (Austria) 31

Vietnamese Publishing House (Socialist Republic of Viet Nam) 455
Vieweg & Sohn, Friedr, Verlagsgesellschaft mbH (Federal Republic of Germany) 164
Vieweg, Schulverlag (Federal Republic of Germany) 164
Vigília, Editora, Ltda (Brazil) 55
Vigot, Editions, Frères (France) 108
Vijverberg Prize (Netherlands) 286
Vikas Publishing House Pvt Ltd (India) 200
Viking Sevenseas Ltd (New Zealand) 290
Viktoria Verlag (Switzerland) 374
Villa (Netherlands) 283
Villa Benia Prize (Italy) 236
Villa Books Ltd (Republic of Ireland) 211
Villaurrutia, Xavier, Prize (Mexico) 270
Ville de Paris, Service des Travaux Historiques de la, et Bibliothèque historique de la Ville de Paris (France) 110
Villepastour, Librairie (Ivory Coast) 236
Vilnius, The Scientific Library of the, Vincas Kapsukas State University (Union of Soviet Socialist Republics) 389
Vilo, Editions, SA (France) 108
Vincentz, Curt R, Verlag (Federal Republic of Germany) 164
Vindrose, Forlaget, ApS (Denmark) 79
Vine Books (United Kingdom) 439
Vintens Forlag Ltd (Denmark) 79
Vipopremo Agencies (Kenya) 249
Virago Ltd (United Kingdom) 439
Viratham (Thailand) 381
Virdi, Major Tek Singh, Literary Prizes (India) 204
Virenque, Claire, Prize (France) 114
Virgin Books (United Kingdom) 439
Virtue & Co Ltd (United Kingdom) 439
Visa Books (Australia) 19
Visão, Editora, Ltda (Brazil) 55
Visentini, Olga, Prize (Italy) 236
Vishal Publications (India) 200
Vision Books Pvt Ltd (India) 200
Vision Press Ltd (United Kingdom) 439
Vision Publishing Corporation (Philippines) 309
Visscher, Albert de, Editeur (Belgium) 42
Vitamine, Editions (France) 108
Vives, Editorial Luis, (Edelvives) (Spain) 346
Vivliofilia (Greece) 176
Vivliografiki Etaireia tis Ellados (Greece) 176
Vlaams Ekonomisch Verbond VZW (Belgium) 42
Vlaamse Bijbelstichting (Belgium) 42
Vlaamse Toeristenbond VZW (Belgium) 42
Vlaamse Vereniging van Bibliotheek-, Archief en Documentatie-Personeel (Belgium) 43
Vlasis, Frères (Greece) 175
Vlijt, De, NV (Belgium) 42
'Vneshtorgizdat', Vsesoyuznoe Obyedineniye (Union of Soviet Socialist Republics) 389
Voce della Bibbia (Italy) 233
Voenno Izdatelstvo (Bulgaria) 58
Vogel, Buchhandlung W (Switzerland) 376
Vogel-Verlag KG (Federal Republic of Germany) 164
Vogt-Schild AG Druck & Verlag (Switzerland) 374
Voie de l'Art, Editions de la (Switzerland) 374
Vojnoizdavački Zavod (Yugoslavia) 459
Vokaer, Nouvelles Editions, SA (Belgium) 42
Volcans, Librairie Les (Zaire) 462
Volcans, Librairie Les (Zaire) 462
Volk, Boekhandel Het (Belgium) 43
Volk, Drukkerij Het, NV (Belgium) 42
Volk und Gesundheit, VEB Verlag (German Democratic Republic) 118
Volk und Welt, Verlag, (Verlag für internationale Literatur) (German Democratic Republic) 118
Volk und Wissen Volkseigener Verlag Berlin (German Democratic Republic) 118
Volksboekwinkel, Stichting De (Suriname) 351
Volkslectuur, Stichting (Suriname) 351
Volksverband der Bücherfreunde Verlag GmbH & Co (Federal Republic of Germany) 167
Vollmer, Emil, Verlag (Federal Republic of Germany) 164
Vollmer/Löwit Verlagsgruppe (Federal Republic of Germany) 164
Volney Prize (France) 114
Voltaire Foundation (United Kingdom) 439
Volturna Press (United Kingdom) 439
Voluntad Editores Ltda y Cia SCA (Colombia) 67
Voluntary Health Association of India (India) 200
Voorhoeve, J N (Netherlands) 283
Vora & Co Publishers Pvt Ltd (India) 200
Vorarlberger Verlagsanstalt GmbH (Austria) 29
Voss, Johann Heinrich, Translation Prize (Federal Republic of Germany) 171
Vowinckel, Kurt, Verlag (Federal Republic of Germany) 164
Vowinckel, Thesen Verlag, und Co (Federal Republic of Germany) 164
Voyenizdat (Union of Soviet Socialist Republics) 389
Vozes Editora Ltda (Brazil) 55
Vries, C De, Brouwers PVBA (Belgium) 42
Vrin, Librairie Philosophique J (France) 108

Vroente, De (Belgium) 42
Vsesoyuznaya Knichnaya Palata (Union of Soviet Socialist Republics) 387
Vsesoyuznoe agenstvo po avtorkskim pravam (VAAP) (Union of Soviet Socialist Republics) 389
Vuibert, Librairie, SA (France) 108
Vuk Karadžic (Yugoslavia) 459
Vuk Karadžic (Yugoslavia) 460
Vulkan (Denmark) 79
Východoslovenské vydavatel'stvo NP (Czechoslovakia) 73
Vyncke, PVBA Imprimerie-Editions (Belgium) 42
Vyšehrad (Czechoslovakia) 73
'Vysshaya Shkola', Izdatelstvo (Union of Soviet Socialist Republics) 389

W e W Bookclub (Sweden) 358
W I Books Ltd (United Kingdom) 439
W R S-Verlag (Wirtschaft, Recht und Steuern) (Federal Republic of Germany) 164
Waage, Verlag Die (Switzerland) 374
Waagmeester-Verkuyl, M (Suriname) 351
Wachholtz, Karl, Verlag (Federal Republic of Germany) 164
Wadsworth International Group (Australia) 19
Wadsworth International Group (United Kingdom) 439
Wadsworth International — SE Asia (Republic of Singapore) 327
Wagenbach, Verlag Klaus (Federal Republic of Germany) 164
Wagner, Gebrüder, & Co Verlag (Switzerland) 374
Wagner, Kartographischer Verlag, & Co KG (Federal Republic of Germany) 164
Wagner, Universitätsverlag, GmbH (Austria) 29
Wagner'sche Universitätsbuchhandlung (Austria) 30
Wahab, Dakr Abdul (Syria) 377
Wahbah, Ali, Bookshop (Saudi Arabia) 323
Wahle, Eugène (Belgium) 42
Wahlström och Widstrand, AB (Sweden) 357
Wahlströms, B, Bokförlag AB (Sweden) 357
Waiwen Shudian (People's Republic of China) 64
Walburg, De, Pers (Netherlands) 283
Waldia, AB, Förlag (Sweden) 357
Wales Tourist Board (United Kingdom) 439
Walker Books Ltd (United Kingdom) 439
Walraven, Uitgeverij Van, BV (Netherlands) 283
Walsingham (United Kingdom) 439
Walt Disney, Clube (Portugal) 318
Walt Disney Wonderful World of Reading (Denmark) 79
Walt, J P van der, en Seun (Pty) Ltd (Republic of South Africa) 333
Walter, Henry E, Ltd (United Kingdom) 439
Walter Verlag AG (Switzerland) 374
Walter-Verlag GmbH Freiburg (Federal Republic of Germany) 164
Waltman, Uitgeverij (Netherlands) 283
Wangels Forlag A/S (Denmark) 79
Wanyee Bookshop Ltd (Kenya) 249
Warana Writers' Awards (Australia) 23
Warburg, The, Institute (United Kingdom) 439
Ward Lock Educational Ltd (United Kingdom) 439
Ward Lock Ltd (United Kingdom) 439
Ward River Press (Republic of Ireland) 211
Warga (Indonesia) 206
Warne, Frederick, (Publishers) Ltd (United Kingdom) 439
Warsaw City Prize (Poland) 315
Warsaw City Prize for Young Poets (Poland) 315
Was Is Press (Australia) 19
Waseda University Library (Japan) 245
Wasmuth, Ernst, Verlagsbuchhandlung KG (Federal Republic of Germany) 165
Watelet, Gerard (France) 108
Waterkant-Uitgewers (Edms) Bpk (Republic of South Africa) 333
Waterlow Publishers Ltd (United Kingdom) 439
Waterville Publishing House (Ghana) 172
Watkins Publishing (United Kingdom) 439
'Watra', Wydawnictwa Kultura Zycia Codziennego (Poland) 313
Watson, Little Ltd (United Kingdom) 443
Watson, W, & Co (United Kingdom) 439
Watt, A P, Ltd (United Kingdom) 443
Wattana Panich (Thailand) 381
Wattie Book of the Year Award (New Zealand) 292
Watts, Franklin, Ltd (United Kingdom) 439
Wayfarer Book Store Ltd (Barbados) 33
Wayland Publishers Ltd (United Kingdom) 439
Wayzgoose, The, Press (United Kingdom) 440
Weatherhill, John, Inc (Japan) 244
Webb & Bower (Publishers) Ltd (United Kingdom) 440
Weber (France) 108
Weber SA d'Editions (Switzerland) 374
Weber-Stumfohl, Herta (Federal Republic of Germany) 167
Webster's (Pty) Ltd (Swaziland) 351

Weekes, A (United Kingdom) 440
Wehr und Wissen Verlagsgesellschaft mbH (Federal Republic of Germany) 165
Weichert, A, Verlag (Federal Republic of Germany) 165
Weickhardt, Con, Award (Australia) 23
Weickhardt, Patricia, Award (Australia) 23
Weidenfeld (Publishers) Ltd (United Kingdom) 440
Weidlich, Wolfgang, Verlag (Federal Republic of Germany) 165
Weilburg-Verlag (Austria) 29
Weilin ja Göös, Amer-yhtymä Oy (Finland) 88
Weill, Galerie Lucie (France) 109
Weill Publishers Ltd (Israel) 217
Weinert, Erich-, -Buchhandlung (German Democratic Republic) 119
Weinmann, Verlag (Federal Republic of Germany) 165
Weis, Rupertusbuchhandlung Augustin, und Söhne KG (Austria) 30
Weismann Verlag-Frauenbuchverlag GmbH (Federal Republic of Germany) 165
Weiss, Gebrüder, Verlag (Federal Republic of Germany) 165
Weiss, J J, Prize (France) 114
Weitbrecht Edition (Federal Republic of Germany) 165
Weizmann Institute of Science Libraries (Israel) 218
Weizmann, The, Science Press of Israel (Israel) 217
Weka, Editions (France) 109
Wellcome Institute for the History of Medicine Library (United Kingdom) 445
Wellington Public Library (New Zealand) 290
Wells, H G, Society (United Kingdom) 447
Wellsiana—The World of H G Wells (United Kingdom) 447
Welsermühl, Verlag (Federal Republic of Germany) 165
Welsh Arts Council Awards to Writers (United Kingdom) 450
Welsh Arts Council International Writer's Prize (International Literary Prizes) 479
Welsh Books Council (Cyngor Llyfrau Cymraeg) (United Kingdom) 391
Welsh Library Association (United Kingdom) 446
Welsh Publishers' Union (Undeb Cyhoeddwyr Cymru) (United Kingdom) 392
Welsh, The, Academy (United Kingdom) 447
Welt im Heim Morawa & Co (Austria) 29
Weltforum Verlag GmbH (Federal Republic of Germany) 165
Weltkreis-Verlags-GmbH (Federal Republic of Germany) 165
Weltrundschau Verlag AG (Switzerland) 374
Welz, Verlag Galerie, Salzburg (Austria) 29
'Wema', Wydawnictwa Przemyslu Maszynowego (Poland) 313
Wenschow, Karl, GmbH (Federal Republic of Germany) 165
Wentworth Books Pty Ltd (Australia) 19
Wepf & Co AG Buchhandlung und Antiquariat (Switzerland) 376
Wepf, Verlag, & Co AG (Switzerland) 374
Wereldbibliotheek BV (Netherlands) 283
Wereldbibliotheek NV (Belgium) 42
Wereldvenster (Netherlands) 283
Werner Druck AG (Switzerland) 374
Werner Söderström Osakeyhtiö (WSOY) (Finland) 88
Werner Söderström Osakeyhtiö (WSOY) (Finland) 88
Werner Verlag GmbH (Federal Republic of Germany) 165
Wesmael-Charlier, Maison d'Editions Ad, SA (Belgium) 42
West African Book Publishers Ltd (Nigeria) 296
West African University Booksellers Association (International Organizations) 469
'West-Friesland', Uit-Mij (Netherlands) 283
West Indian Reference Collection (Trinidad and Tobago) 383
West, John, Publications Ltd (Nigeria) 296
West-Pak Publishing Co Ltd (Pakistan) 303
Westbooks Pty Ltd (Australia) 19
Westdeutscher Verlag GmbH (Federal Republic of Germany) 165
Westerbergs, Ernst, Förlags (Sweden) 357
Westermann Verlag GmbH (Federal Republic of Germany) 165
Western Australian Booksellers' Association (Australia) 10
Westers, Uitgeverij (Netherlands) 283
Westminster City Libraries (United Kingdom) 445
Wetenschappelijke, Stichting, Informatie (Suriname) 351
Wetenschappelijke Uitgeverij (Netherlands) 283
Wettergrens Bokhandel AB (Sweden) 359
Wetzikon, Buchverlag der Druckerei, AG (Switzerland) 374
Wever, Uitgeverij, BV (Netherlands) 283
Wewel, Erich, Verlag (Federal Republic of Germany) 165
Wezäta Förlag (Sweden) 358
Wheatley Medal (United Kingdom) 450
Wheaton, A, & Co Ltd (United Kingdom) 440
Wheatsheaf Books (United Kingdom) 440
Wheeler, A H, & Co (P) Ltd (India) 200

Whitaker, J, & Sons Ltd (United Kingdom) 440
Whitbread Literary Awards (United Kingdom) 450
Whitcoulls Ltd (New Zealand) 290
Whitcoulls Publishers (New Zealand) 290
White Eagle Publishing Trust (United Kingdom) 440
White Horse Books (United Kingdom) 440
White Horse Library (United Kingdom) 440
White Lotus Co Ltd (Thailand) 381
White, Patrick, Award (Australia) 23
Whitman (New Zealand) 290
Whitman, Australia Pty Ltd (Australia) 19
Whittet Books Ltd (United Kingdom) 440
Who's Who of Southern Africa (Republic of South Africa) 333
Who's Who — the International Red Series Verlag GmbH (Federal Republic of Germany) 165
Wiart, Carton de, Prize (Belgium) 45
Wichmann, Herbert, Verlag GmbH (Federal Republic of Germany) 165
Widjaja (Indonesia) 206
'Wiedza Powszechna' Państwowe Wydawnictwo (Poland) 313
Wiener Dom-Verlag (Austria) 29
Wiener Goethe-Verein (Austria) 30
Wiener Stadt- und Landesarchiv (Austria) 30
Wiener Stadt- und Landesbibliothek (Austria) 30
Wiener Urtext Edition-Musikverlag GmbH & Co KG (Austria) 29
Wigmore House Publishing (United Kingdom) 440
Wilco Publishing House (India) 200
Wild & Woolley Pty Ltd (Australia) 19
Wild, Verlag Alexander (Switzerland) 374
Wildfire (Australia) 19
Wildgans, Anton, Prize of Austrian Industry (Austria) 31
Wildwood House Ltd (United Kingdom) 440
Wiley Eastern Ltd (India) 200
Wiley, John (Australia) 19
Wiley, John, & Sons Ltd (United Kingdom) 440
Wilfion Books Publishers (United Kingdom) 440
Wilke Literary Award (Australia) 23
Wilkenschildts Forlag (Denmark) 79
Williams Book Illustration Award, Francis (United Kingdom) 450
Williams, Joseph (United Kingdom) 440
Williams Memorial Prize, Griffith John, (Gwobr Goffa Griffith John Williams) (United Kingdom) 450
Williams, W J, & Son (Books) Ltd (United Kingdom) 442
Willis Bookshops (Republic of Ireland) 211
Wilson & Horton Ltd (New Zealand) 290
Wilson, Philip, Publishers Ltd (United Kingdom) 440
Wilton Publications (United Kingdom) 440
Win Join Book Co Ltd (Taiwan) 378
Windhoek Public Library (Namibia) 272
Windswept (Australia) 19
Wine & Spirit Publications Ltd (United Kingdom) 440
Wingate, Allan, (Publishers) Ltd (United Kingdom) 440
Wingate, H H, Prize (International Literary Prizes) 479
Winkler Prins (Netherlands) 283
Winkler-Verlag (Federal Republic of Germany) 165
Winter, Carl, Universitätsverlag GmbH (Federal Republic of Germany) 166
Winthers Forlag ApS (Denmark) 79
Wirtschaft, Recht, Steuern (Federal Republic of Germany) 166
Wirtschaft und Recht, Fachbuchhandlung für (Austria) 30
Wirtschaft, Verlag Die (German Democratic Republic) 118
Wirtschafts- und Kartographie, Verlag für, -Publikationen, Ryborsch (Federal Republic of Germany) 166
Wirtschaftsskripten, Verlag für (Federal Republic of Germany) 166
Wirtschaftsverlag (Federal Republic of Germany) 166
Wisdom Publications (United Kingdom) 440
Wison Verlag GmbH (Federal Republic of Germany) 166
Wissen Verlag GmbH (Federal Republic of Germany) 166
Wissenschaft und Politik, Verlag (Federal Republic of Germany) 166
Wissenschaft, Wirtschaft und Technik, Verlag für, GmbH und Co KG (Federal Republic of Germany) 166
Wissenschaftliche Buchgesellschaft (Federal Republic of Germany) 166
Wissenschaftliche Buchgesellschaft (Federal Republic of Germany) 166
Wissenschaftliche Verlagsgesellschaft mbH (Federal Republic of Germany) 166
Wissenschaftlicher Autoren Verlag (Federal Republic of Germany) 166
Wit, De, Stores NV (Netherlands Antilles) 286
Witherby, H F & G, Ltd and Witherby & Co Ltd (United Kingdom) 440
Witte Raven (Netherlands) 283
Wittig, Friedrich, Verlag (Federal Republic of Germany) 166
Wittwer, Buchhandlung Konrad, KG (Federal Republic of Germany) 166
Wittwer, Verlag Konrad, KG (Federal Republic of Germany) 166

Witwatersrand University Press (Republic of South Africa) 333
Witzstrock, Gerhard, GmbH (Federal Republic of Germany) 166
Wizware (Australia) 19
Wkallat Matbouat (Kuwait) 253
Wobbledagger (Australia) 19
Woburn, The, Press (United Kingdom) 440
Wøldike, Forlaget, K/S (Denmark) 79
Wolfe Medical Publications Ltd (United Kingdom) 440
Wolfe Publishing Ltd (United Kingdom) 440
Wolff, Oswald, (Publishers) Ltd (United Kingdom) 441
Wolfhound Press (Republic of Ireland) 211
Wolfrum, Kunstverlag (Austria) 29
Wolfrum, Kunstverlag (Austria) 30
Wolfsbergdrucke, Verlag der (Switzerland) 375
Wolfson History Awards (United Kingdom) 451
Wolmar, Valentine de, Prize (France) 114
Wolters Leuven, J B, NV (Belgium) 42
Wolters-Noordhoff BV (Netherlands) 283
Wolters-Noordhoff-Longman BV (Netherlands) 283
Wolters Samsom België NV (Belgium) 42
Wolters Samsom Groep NV (Netherlands) 283
Women Writers' Association (Japan) 238
Women's Literary Society (Greece) 176
Women's Literary Society Prizes (Greece) 176
Women's Movement Children's Literature Co-op Ltd (Australia) 19
Women's, The, Press (Republic of Ireland) 211
Women's, The, Press Book Club (United Kingdom) 444
Women's, The, Press Ltd (United Kingdom) 441
Woodhead-Faulkner (Publishers) Ltd (United Kingdom) 441
Word and Vision Ltd (Greece) 175
Workers' Party of Korea Publishing House (Democratic People's Republic of Korea) 250
Workers' Press (People's Republic of China) 64
Workshop Press Ltd (United Kingdom) 441
World Book—Childcraft International (United Kingdom) 441
World Book Co (Taiwan) 378
World Books (United Kingdom) 444
World Council of Churches (WCC) (International Organizations) 471
World Health Organization (WHO) (International Organizations) 471
World Homoeopathic Links (India) 201
World Intellectual Property Organization (WIPO) (International Organizations) 469
World International Publishing Ltd (United Kingdom) 441
World Meteorological Organization (WMO) (International Organizations) 471
World Microfilms Publications Ltd (United Kingdom) 441
World of Books, The, Ltd (Federal Republic of Germany) 166
World of Information (United Kingdom) 441
World of Islam Festival Trust (United Kingdom) 441
World of Nature (United Kingdom) 444
World Press, The, Pvt Ltd (India) 201
World, The, Book Co (Pte) Ltd (Republic of Singapore) 327
World, The, Book Company (Macau) 257
World University Library (United Kingdom) 441
World's Work Ltd (United Kingdom) 441
Wort und Welt Verlag (Austria) 29
Woursell, Abraham, Prize (University of Vienna) (International Literary Prizes) 479
Wright & Sons, John, Ltd (United Kingdom) 441
Wright, Ellen (France) 109
Wright Publishing, Gordon (United Kingdom) 441
Writers & Readers (Australia) 19
Writers and Readers Publishing Co-operative (United Kingdom) 441
Writer's Club (Zimbabwe) 465
Writers' Guild of Great Britain (United Kingdom) 392
Writers' Publishing House (People's Republic of China) 64
Writers', The, Group (Malawi) 259
Writers' Union Prize (Romania) 322
Writers Workshop (India) 201
'Wspólna Sprawa', Wydawniczo Oświatowa Spółdzielnia Inwalidów (Poland) 313
Wunderlich, Rainer, Verlag Hermann Leins (Federal Republic of Germany) 166
Württembergische Bibliotheksgesellschaft (Federal Republic of Germany) 169
Württembergische Landesbibliothek (Federal Republic of Germany) 168
Würzburg, Echter, Fränkische Gesellschaftsdruckerei und Verlag GmbH (Federal Republic of Germany) 166
Wykeham (United Kingdom) 441
Wyss Verlag Bern (Wyss Druck und Verlag AG Bern) (Switzerland) 375

Xarait Ediciones (Spain) 346
Xenos Verlagsgesellschaft mbH (Federal Republic of Germany) 166
Xerox Publishing Group Ltd (United Kingdom) 441
Xunhasoba (Socialist Republic of Viet Nam) 455

Y Hoc Publishing House (Socialist Republic of Viet Nam) 455
Y M C A-Press (France) 109
Yachdav, United Publishers Co Ltd (Israel) 217
Yad Eliahu Chitov (Israel) 217
Yad Vashem — Martyrs' and Heroes' Remembrance Authority (Israel) 217
Yale University Press Ltd (United Kingdom) 441
Yama-Kei (Publishers) Co Ltd (Japan) 244
Yañez, J F, Agencia Literaria (Spain) 347
Yarmouk University Bookshop (Jordan) 247
Yarmouk University Library (Jordan) 247
Yasaguna, C V (Indonesia) 206
Yavneh Ltd (Israel) 217
Yedioth Ahronoth Enterprises (Book Dept) (Israel) 217
Yee Wen Publishing Co Ltd (Taiwan) 378
Yeshurun (Israel) 217
Yesod (Israel) 217
Yiannakis, Iakovou (Cyprus) 70
Yliopistokirjakauppa Oy (Finland) 89
Yoga Life (India) 201
Yohan Publications Inc (Japan) 244
Yohan (Western Publications Distribution Agency) (Japan) 245
Yokendo Ltd (Japan) 244
Yomiuri Literature Prize (Japan) 247
Yonsei University Library (Republic of Korea) 252
Yonsei University Press (Republic of Korea) 252
York Notes (United Kingdom) 441
Yorkshire Arts Association Literary Awards (United Kingdom) 451
'Yorkshire Post' Book of the Year Award (International Literary Prizes) 480
Yoruba (Barbados) 33
Yoshikawa Prizes (Japan) 247
'Young Observer'/Rank Organisation Fiction Prize (International Literary Prizes) 480
Young People's Book Club (Republic of South Africa) 333
Young Writers' Incentive Awards (New Zealand) 292
Youth Publishing House (People's Republic of China) 64
Youth's Library Mohamad Ahmed Sharareh (Jordan) 247
Yritystieto Oy — Foretagsdata AB (Finland) 88
Yuhikaku Publishing Co Ltd (Japan) 244
Yundum College Library (The Gambia) 115
Yunnan Provincial Library (People's Republic of China) 64
'Yuridicheskaya Literatura', Izdatelstvo (Union of Soviet Socialist Republics) 389
Yushodo Booksellers Ltd (Japan) 244
Yuval (Israel) 217
Yvert et Tellier, Editions Philateliques (France) 109

Z A Reprints (German Democratic Republic) 118
Z O E (Greece) 175
Z V W 5 (Federal Republic of Germany) 166
Z-Verlag, Genossenschaft (Switzerland) 375
Zabern, Verlag Philipp von (Federal Republic of Germany) 166
Zahar Editores (Brazil) 55
Zahiriah, Al, (National Library) (Syria) 377
Zaïre, Librairie du (Zaire) 462
Zak, S, & Co (Israel) 217
Založba Obzorja (Yugoslavia) 459
Zambia Catholic Bookshop (Zambia) 463
Zambia Institute of Technology Library (Zambia) 464
Zambia Library Association (Zambia) 464
Zambia Library Service (Zambia) 464
Zambon, Dr (Federal Republic of Germany) 166
Zanibon, G, Edizioni Musicali (Italy) 233
Zanichelli, Nicola, SpA (Italy) 233
Zanzibar Government Archives (Tanzania) 379
Západočeské nakladatelství (Czechoslovakia) 73
Zara, Edizioni (Italy) 233
Zaruski, Mariusz, Literary Prize (Poland) 315
Zauho, The, Press (Japan) 244
Zavalia, Victor P de, Editor (Argentina) 8
Zavod za Izdavanje Udžbenika (Yugoslavia) 459
Zavod za Obrazovanje Kadrova za Administrativne Poslove SR Srbije (Yugoslavia) 459
Zavod za Udžbenike i Nastavna Sredstva (Yugoslavia) 459
Zavod za Udžbenike i Nastavna Sredstva Sap Kosovo (Yugoslavia) 459
Zbinden Druck und Verlag AG (Switzerland) 375
Zebra Books (United Kingdom) 441

Zebra Books for Children (India) 201
Zechner und Hüthig Verlag GmbH (Federal Republic of Germany) 166
Zed Press (United Kingdom) 441
Zeit, Verlag, im Bild (German Democratic Republic) 118
Zelkowitz (Israel) 217
Zell, Hans, Publishers (United Kingdom) 441
Zemizdat, Darzhavno Izdatelstvo (Bulgaria) 58
Zemp, Paul A (Switzerland) 375
Zenith (United Kingdom) 441
Zeno Booksellers & Publishers (United Kingdom) 442
Zentralantiquariat der DDR — Reprintabteilung (ZA Reprints) (German Democratic Republic) 118
Zentralbibliothek der deutschen Klassik (German Democratic Republic) 119
Zentralbibliothek Zürich (Switzerland) 376
Zentralgesellschaft für buchgewerbliche und graphische Betriebe (Austria) 30
Zentralinstitut für Bibliothekswesen (German Democratic Republic) 120
Zentralinstitut für Information und Dokumentation der Deutschen Demokratischen Republik (German Democratic Republic) 120
Zentralstelle für maschinelle Dokumentation (Federal Republic of Germany) 169
Zero SA (Spain) 346
Zero Verlag und Vertrieb (Federal Republic of Germany) 166
Zero-Zyx, Editorial, SA (Spain) 346
Zester Druck- und Verlagsgesellschaft mbH (Federal Republic of Germany) 166
Zettner, Verlag Andreas, KG (Federal Republic of Germany) 166
Zeunert, Verlag Wolfgang, GmbH & Co KG (Federal Republic of Germany) 166
Zhejiang tushuguan (People's Republic of China) 65
Zhong-guo guo jia tushuguan (People's Republic of China) 65
Zhong-guo ke xue yuan tushuguan (People's Republic of China) 65
Zhong Hua Book Co (People's Republic of China) 64
Zhongshan Library of Guangdong Province (People's Republic of China) 65
Zibet Prize (Sweden) 360
Ziemsen, A, Verlag (German Democratic Republic) 119
Zig-Zag, Empressa Editora, SA (Chile) 63
Zimbabwe Library Association (Zimbabwe) 465
Zimmer, Verlag Wolfgang (Federal Republic of Germany) 166
Zindermans Förlag (Sweden) 358
Zip Editora Ltda (Brazil) 55
Zjednoczenie Przedsiebiorstw Wydawniczych Naczelny Zarzad Wydawnictw (Poland) 311
Zmora, **Bitan**-Publishers (Israel) 217
'Znak', Społeczny Instytut Wydawniczy (Poland) 313
Znanie (Union of Soviet Socialist Republics) 389
'Znanje', Nakladni Zavod (Yugoslavia) 460
Zodiaque (France) 109
Zodiaque, La Pierre-qui-Vire (Switzerland) 375
Zolindakis, Har (Greece) 175
Zollikofer, Buchverlag, AG (Switzerland) 375
Zomba Books (United Kingdom) 442
Zomer en Keuning Boeken BV (Netherlands) 283
Zorn Prize (Sweden) 360
Zoshindo Juken-Kenkyusha (Japan) 244
Zrinyi Katonai Kiadó (Hungary) 182
Zrzeszenie Ksiegarstwa (Poland) 314
Zsolnay, Paul, Verlag GmbH (Austria) 29
Zsolnay, Paul, Verlag GmbH (Federal Republic of Germany) 166
Zuckmayer, Carl, Medal (Federal Republic of Germany) 171
Zuid Boekprodukties BV (Netherlands) 283
Zuid-Hollandsche UM (Netherlands) 283
Zuidnederlandse Uitgeverij NV (Belgium) 42
Zumstein & Cie (Switzerland) 375
Zur & Zur Ltd (Israel) 217
Zuri Book Shop (Afghanistan) 1
Zurich, City of, Literary Prize (Switzerland) 376
Zväz československých spisovatelů (Czechoslovakia) 70
Zväz českých spisovatelu (Czechoslovakia) 70
Zväz slovenských knihovníkov a informatikov (Czechoslovakia) 74
Zväz slovenských spisovateľov (Czechoslovakia) 70
Zväz slovenských spisovateľov Prize (Czechoslovakia) 74
Zveza društev bibliotekarjev Jugoslavije (Slovene) (Yugoslavia) 461
Zwarte Beertjes (Netherlands) 283
Zweipunkt Verlag KG (Federal Republic of Germany) 167
Zwemmer, A, Ltd (United Kingdom) 442
Związek Literatów Polskich (Poland) 311
Zwijsen, Uitgeverij, BV (Netherlands) 283
Zwimpfer, Adolf (Switzerland) 375
'Zycie Literackie' Prize (Poland) 315

APR 2 7 1984

Ref

Z
291.5
I 5
1984-85

DATE DUE

BOOKS ARE SUBJECT
RECALL AFTER